W9-CAS-563

1980

BRITANNICA
BOOK OF THE YEAR

1980

BRITANNICA BOOK OF THE YEAR

ENCYCLOPÆDIA BRITANNICA, INC.

CHICAGO, TORONTO, LONDON, GENEVA, SYDNEY, TOKYO, MANILA, SEOUL

Library of Congress Catalog Card Number: 38–12082
International Standard Book Number: 0–85229–372–0
International Standard Serial Number: 0068–1156

BRITANNICA BOOK OF THE YEAR

(Trademark Reg. U.S. Pat. Off.)
Printed in U.S.A.

THE UNIVERSITY OF CHICAGO

The Britannica Book of the Year is published with the editorial advice of the faculties of the University of Chicago.

CONTENTS

SPECIAL REPORTS

QUEUILLE—SYGMA

CHINA'S FUTURE

by Deng Xiaoping

The Party Vice-Chairman and Vice-Premier of the People's Republic of China explains the background and reasons behind the Four Modernizations

We are standing at another turning point in Chinese history. Last year, we launched a vast program that we have called the Four Modernizations: the modernization of China's industry, agriculture, science and technology, and national defense. This program has aroused worldwide interest. And I should like to stress that it is related to the interests of all the world's peoples.

For us in China this is in a real sense a new revolution—a socialist revolution. The purpose of revolution, after all, is to liberate and develop the productive forces of a country. If a revolution is divorced from the development and modernization of production—on which the prosperity of any people depends—then the aim and goals of this revolution are mere empty words. We opposed China's old society because it oppressed people and held them back from developing the forces of production. The people of China chose socialism because they believed it would provide better conditions for developing China's productive energies. They felt that socialism could revitalize China, eliminate its poverty, and provide its people with a better and happier life.

Our view is very clear but it has not always been shared by everyone. For fully ten years the "gang of four" tried to edge China off its true course. They even had a slogan: "We would prefer a poor society under socialism to a rich society under capitalism." That is absurd!

We do not want capitalism, but we do want a prosperous socialist society. We believe that the socialist system is superior to capitalism. Its superiority, however, must be demonstrated.

The gang of four and Lin Biao put false choices before the Chinese people. They did incalculable harm to the social fabric and the economic system of China. The huge program of modernization that Chairman Mao Zedong and Premier Zhou Enlai had initiated was delayed for fully ten years by that kind of ultraleft politics.

Of course we had brief setbacks even before this. But in the early 1960s the gap between China's economic level and that of the rest of the world was not that great. Beginning in the late '60s, however, the gap began to widen. Over the next 11 or 12 years it became even wider.

Besides this economic gap, we also had a critical political factor to contend with. For some years after the founding of the People's Republic of China in 1949, China was cut off from the rest of the world. We here were not responsible for this isolation. It was imposed on us from the outside by anti-Chinese feeling and, in particular, by forces opposed to Chinese socialism. Nonetheless, China was forcibly isolated from the rest of the world. Through the early '50s, we still received some support from the Soviet Union. But by the end of the decade, even that aid was terminated.

Toward the end of the '60s, world conditions began to change. Possibilities for opening up contacts between China and the rest of the world appeared. But then, for our own reasons, we isolated ourselves!

Today, however, we have learned to use this favourable international climate to accelerate our advance toward the Four Modernizations. Whether or not we can attain the goals we have set for ourselves is a large question in the minds of many. There are even skeptics among the Chinese people themselves, despite the confidence of the great majority. Foreign observers, in particular, question the grounds on which we base our confidence. Let me state, therefore, the four basic reasons for thinking we can achieve our goals.

First: China's vast area is rich in natural resources. Whether we speak of energy resources, minerals, ferrous or nonferrous metals, or rare earths, there are few natural resources that are not found in China. Once these resources are tapped, they will represent immense material power.

Second: During the past 30 years we did some stupid things. Despite such mistakes, we were able to lay the groundwork for China's agricultural, industrial, and technical development. In all these areas, we reached a jumping-off point for advancing to the Four Modernizations. The proliferation of ma-

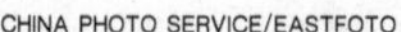

CHINA PHOTO SERVICE/EASTFOTO

An American technical expert (right) advising workers at a Chinese fertilizer plant.

chine tools is a good example. In the early '50s, Japan had 800,000 lathes. Now China has two million lathes of its own. If Japan could develop so swiftly over the past 20 years from a base of 800,000, why cannot China develop similarly from our base of two million?

Over the past 30 years we invested more than 600 billion yuan in capital construction. We built up an independent and fairly broad-based economy. Today we produce over 100 million tons of petroleum a year and 600 million tons of coal. In steel, our annual production exceeds 30 million tons—admittedly not as much as we had hoped. In any case, we are justified in saying that a material base exists for our Four Modernizations.

Third: The Chinese people are not stupid. Our great problem is to determine how to bring their inventive genius into full play. That is why we are calling for the emancipation of people's minds. For more than a decade Lin Biao and the gang of four put the Chinese people in mental straitjackets, stifling their native wisdom and creative talent. We are now restating the policy first set forth by Chairman Mao: "Let a hundred flowers bloom! Let a hundred schools of thought contend!" This is why we wish to strengthen democracy in our country.

In ancient times we Chinese made extraordinary contributions to human progress. In modern times we have made all too few. Visitors to China can view all sorts of fascinating archaeological discoveries and admire great examples of ancient art. They see too few modern things. This is quite incompatible with China's position in the world. We must not only use our talents for China's modernization, but also contribute to the betterment of mankind.

Fourth: China has now adopted a policy of opening its doors to the world in a spirit of international cooperation. Of course we must rely primarily on our own resources and efforts, but modernization would be impeded if we rejected international cooperation. In no country has the process of modernization occurred in isolation. To accelerate China's modernization we must not only make use of the experience of other countries, we must also avail ourselves of foreign funding.

Thus, we have ample grounds for confidence in the Four Modernizations program. Our principles, our goals, our policies are clear. After smashing the gang of four in 1976, we had to devote considerable energy to dealing with the problems they left, but since 1978 we have at last been able to focus intently on the task of modernization.

We still have difficulties to meet and many complex questions to solve. There is, for example, the

A Visit with Vice-Chairman Deng

by Frank Gibney

Deng Xiaoping is the driving force behind China's unprecedented program of modernization. Though he holds the posts of senior vice-premier, vice-chairman of the Communist Party, and not least of all chief of staff of the People's Liberation Army, he is, strictly speaking, outranked by 55-year-old Premier Hua Guofeng, who is also chairman of the Chinese Communist Party, and by 80-year-old Chief of State Ye Jianying. Nonetheless, it is 76-year-old Deng who has formulated China's policies for the next 20 years, and it is on him that China's nearly 1,000,000,000 people are relying for a better life.

For a man with such awesome responsibilities, Deng talks about his plans with an easy authority. He knows where he wants to go and has both the brain and the wit to explain the route well. Like many other good politicians, he also has the nice faculty of sailing into an objection or criticism almost before it is raised. He speaks quickly, smoking almost incessantly. His vitality even lends a certain warmth to the vast formal reception room in Beijing's Great Hall of the People, ornamented with large classical Chinese landscapes that have new hydroelectric projects peeking out from among the trees.

A resolute pragmatist, Deng is no respecter of precedents. To implement his plans, he has sought out the help of successful capitalist nations, notably the U.S. and Japan, because he is willing to play down ideology when it stands in the way of efficiency. Years ago Deng shocked party dogmatists with his now famous comment: "What does it matter if the cat is white or black, so long as it catches rats."

Volatile Career. Deng's return to power in his mid-70s is itself extraordinary. He was taken into custody at the start of the Cultural Revolution (1966–69) and confined for nine years. It was a decade of mass arrests, forced-labour deportations, and vicious mob violence carried out by Chairman Mao's Red Guards. Education was totally disrupted for an entire generation. Deng was finally rehabilitated and made first vice-premier and a party vice-chairman, only to be denounced again and dismissed by ultraleftists for his "right deviationist policies." After the death of Mao Zedong and the imprisonment in October 1976 of the "gang of four" (one of whom was Mao's widow, Jiang Qing), Deng once again returned to power.

For a man who has had so many ups and downs, Deng exudes extraordinary confidence, and not without reason. Now that Mao and Zhou Enlai are gone, there is probably no one in China who can match Deng's experience and proven abilities. He made the Long March (1934–35) with Mao from southeast China to the northwest, and for years he was one of Mao's closest supporters. In 1956 he became general secretary of the Chinese Communist Party, a post previously held only by Mao himself, and in that capacity trained a whole generation of cadres. He also sometimes alludes to the fact that he is the only person around who commanded all of China's regional armies.

It is Deng's mission to repair the damage done by the Cultural Revolution and restore the productive energies of a country that went into a kind of trance in the early '60s with its personality cult of Chairman Mao. As early as 1956, after Nikita Khrushchev detailed Stalin's crimes to the Soviet 20th party congress, Deng warned China's 8th party congress of the inherent dangers in "deification of the individual."

The new China envisioned by Deng must rely on persuasion, technology, and concrete incentives rather than on sheer power, sacred party texts, and rote repetition of Mao's "thoughts." But relaxation of controls has already sparked demands for complete democracy, the so-called Fifth Modernization. Deng, consequently, has the delicate task of leading the new revolution of modernization without permitting the new freedom to degenerate into bickering and factionalism.

The Future. Deng admits worries about the future as readily as he acknowledges China's past failures and blunders. To hear the leader of a great nation admit "we did many stupid things" is quite refreshing. He worries most about the succession of power and the lost generation that was almost destroyed by the Cultural Revolution. Unlike some of China's other recent party leaders, Deng's tastes are frugal. "I have the highest salary in the country and there are no more than ten like me," he told us, "and how much do you think that is—400 yuan a month [about $250]—not enough to buy a car, only a bicycle."

XIAHUA NEWS AGENCY

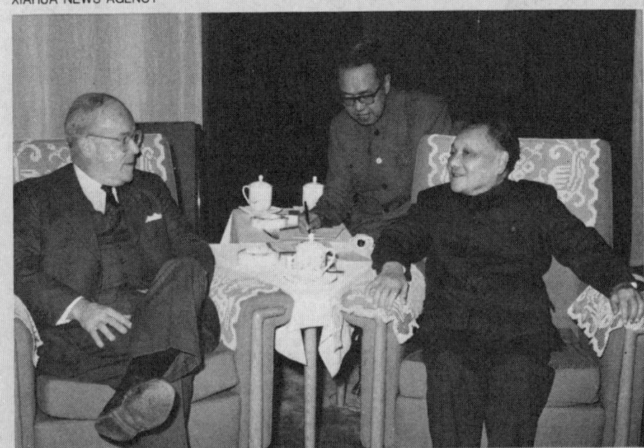

Britannica's Frank Gibney conferring with Deng Xiaoping. An interpreter stands between them.

One of Deng's greatest challenges is to provide sufficient incentives to motivate Chinese workers without disrupting the wage and price scales that have been virtually frozen for two decades. Another is to initiate orderly procedures to retire China's gerontocratic officials while training young successors. No one realizes better than Deng himself that he is racing against time. "If this thing up there," he says, pointing to his head, "if it just keeps functioning, I can go on for six more years. Then I will become a consultant or adviser. Vitality is bound to decrease. A man should know himself."

Frank Gibney, Vice-Chairman of the Britannica Board of Editors, was the founding president of TBS-Britannica, Tokyo.

basic matter of administration. Many of our government agencies are overstaffed, often with far more people than are needed. Restructuring these organs is not an easy job because the more modernized the economy becomes, the fewer people one needs. Yet we have so many people. Where will they go? What will they do? We also need a great deal of talent to master modern science and technology. Unfortunately a whole generation of youth was inadequately educated. Some lost an entire decade of schooling, thanks to the work of the gang of four. Many were influenced by the gang of four, but the great majority of them have come to realize the errors of the past. In fact, the whole April 5 movement, which opposed the gang of four, was launched by young people. Still these young people have been impeded from acquiring the technical and specialized skills that they need.

These factors make it necessary for us to follow, for quite some time, a policy that permits automation, mechanization, semimechanization, and manual operations to exist side by side. Gradually we will shift to full mechanization and automation. Even when we attain the goals we have now set, our per capita national income and level of consumption may still be much lower than those of the highly developed countries. The Chinese people will certainly not stop at that point, however. They will continue to take great strides forward, and eventually they will catch up to and surpass the highly developed countries.

Some of our managerial systems are in part a legacy of Soviet models. We did not travel the Soviet road to socialism in every respect. In China, for example, we allowed the existence of many political parties; and in our transformation of the national bourgeoisie, we bought their property rather than confiscating it. In China, therefore, this transformation was achieved smoothly. Chairman Mao advocated a lively political atmosphere in which there are "both democracy and centralism, discipline and freedom, unified will and personal ease of mind." This is quite different from the situation in the Soviet Union. On the other hand, I would say that in our economic system—especially regarding the management and organization of our enterprises—we were influenced a great deal by the Soviet Union.

In point of fact, the managerial skills of the capitalist countries, particularly various methods of developing science and technology, are part of mankind's common heritage. There is no reason why these managerial skills cannot be put to good use in a socialist China. But restructuring the national economy to accommodate such skills and techniques will not be easy.

We should like to expand the role of the market economy as we develop further. This has led some to question whether China is moving in the direction of capitalism. We are not. It is incorrect to assume that a market economy can exist only under capitalism. Under socialism, a market economy can exist side by side with a planned production economy and they can be coordinated. If there are similarities between a market economy under socialism and under capitalism, there are also crucial differences. Under socialism, the market economy operates in the context of a two-sector system. Some means of production are owned by the nation as a whole, others are owned by collectives. Relations between the two sectors can be regulated by the market, but the common basis is still socialist ownership. By nature a socialist society is designed to enrich the whole population; an exploiting class will never arise.

Of course, if an enterprise in China is established with foreign capital, a new element is injected. Naturally the owners will be capitalists. But in other sectors of the economy, public ownership will predominate. Let me give you a vivid example of this. At the present time, former Chinese capitalists are still living in China. They still have their money and personal property. These capitalists have organized investment corporations to serve the state, but all the profits will go to the state.

Investments will be made in China also by overseas Chinese, and these will be structured on capitalist lines. But the great majority of these overseas Chinese are investing their money out of a desire to help the socialist motherland. In any case, no matter how much foreign capital is invested in China, the overall amount will still be relatively limited. In no way will it change our country's socialist system.

While we wish to emancipate people's minds, we must also restore the fine social traditions and socialist morality that existed for quite some time in the past. Indeed, if a visitor had come to China in 1964, he would have seen that the socialist morality of this country was very high. During some very difficult years before that, the Chinese people were still highly disciplined and took to heart the interests of the whole country.

After 1964, Lin Biao and the gang of four disrupted this high social morality. They almost destroyed it. In that period their supporters often cited the slogan: "To rebel is justified." This was used as an excuse for mass violence. "To rebel is justified," they said, means that you can beat people up, smash their houses and loot their possessions. What the gang of four preached was literally anarchy.

Even now some of our youth still bear traces of that poisonous influence. When we now call for developing and encouraging democracy, they inter-

HENRI BUREAU—SYGMA

Following the death of Mao Zedong, the Cultural Revolution came to an end and its leaders were overthrown. Above, a demonstration against the "gang of four" in Guangzhou (Canton).

pret this to mean anarchy. This happened in the case of the so-called Democracy Wall in Beijing. We may have made a mistake in allowing it to last for so long. For despite the good intentions of some of those dissidents, the wall had been used to manipulate public opinion with distorted rumours and outright falsehoods, even to the point of endangering national security. The wall came to be controlled by people who preferred troublemaking to working at their jobs. Foreigners who regarded the activities at Democracy Wall as a barometer of the political climate in China were quite deceived.

It is imperative, therefore, that while emphasizing socialist democracy we strengthen the application of socialist law. Nor will we tolerate any deterioration of the high standards we set in social relationships. For the Four Modernizations to succeed, we must maintain a political atmosphere of unity and tranquillity. After years of social turmoil, the Chinese people are determined not to let any kind of social disorder interfere with their efforts to achieve rapid material and social progress.

The problems China faces in its modernization program are indeed complex. As we move into the 1980s, it is hard to envisage the results of improvements two or three years hence. The prospects for the future depend in large part on how well we train our successors. I have passed my 75th birthday. People of my age should really be concerned about the future. By that I mean, we must find good and reliable successors, so that once a succession takes place, new turmoil will not break out again. Our leadership is now of one mind. We are convinced that China will continue on its present course. This confidence is based on the feeling that our policies are in the greatest interest of the Chinese people and will contribute to humanity as a whole.

As for myself, I have already declared that by 1985 I shall become only an adviser or consultant. We are going to introduce a retirement system for our officials in China. If its application covers me personally, I will be happy to accept it.

As I see the shape of the future, an economically and militarily stronger China will play a vital role in restraining hegemonism and defending world peace. Moreover, the modernization of China will be an important factor in the whole world's prosperity. At present, the developed countries comprise only 1,000,000,000 people out of a world population of 3,600,000,000. Our own population is not far from 1,000,000,000. Thus, we can certainly expect the world economy to undergo a fundamental change when China modernizes. We hope the people in the developed countries will come to enjoy a still better life. We hope the people in the developing countries will become better off as soon as possible. China's modernization will certainly brighten both these prospects.

THE INTERNATIONAL YEAR OF THE CHILD

by Paul Harrison

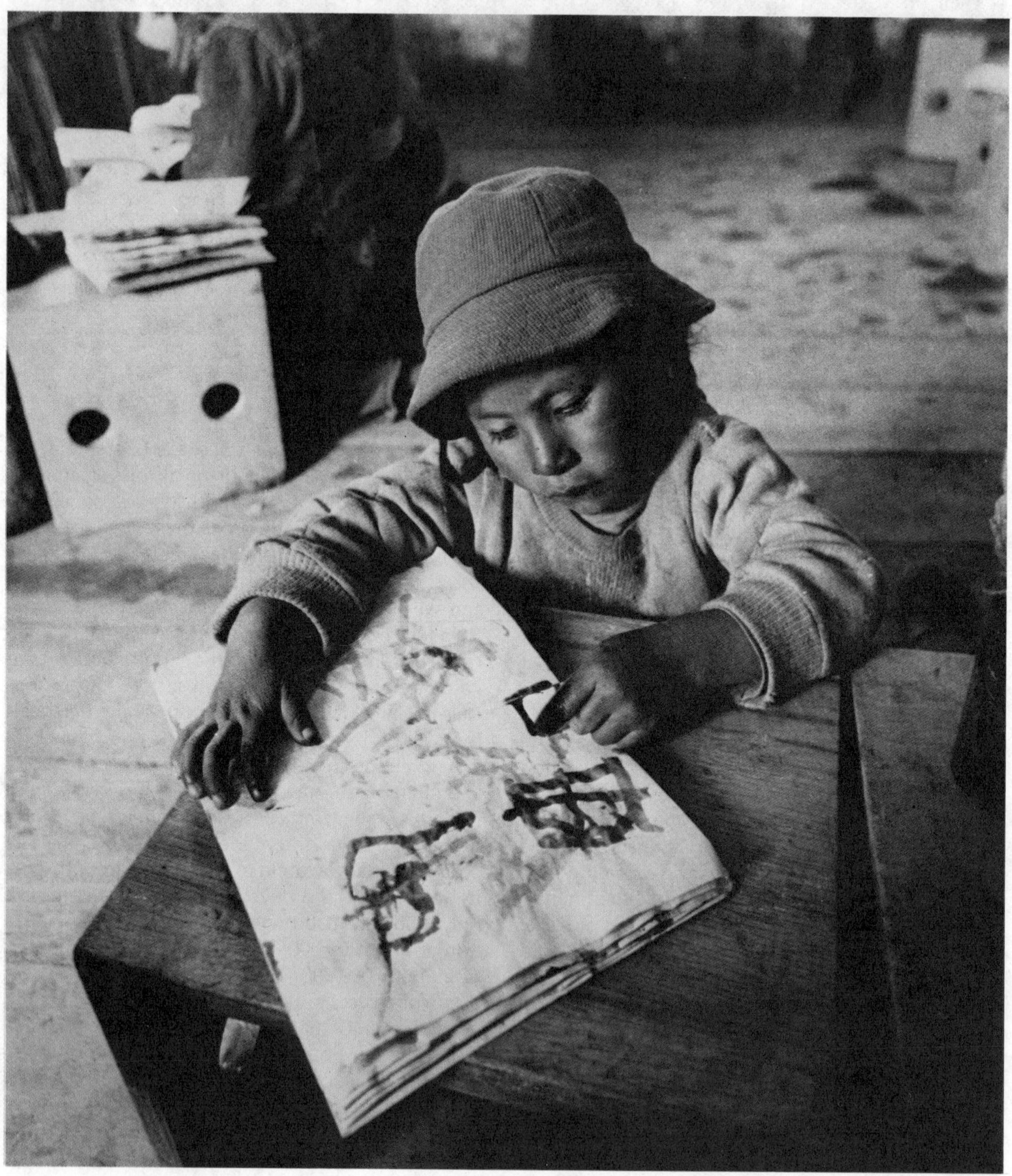

PAUL HARRISON

On Dec. 21, 1976, the United Nations General Assembly passed a resolution designating 1979 as the International Year of the Child (IYC). The major aims were to raise awareness of children's needs and their importance for national progress and to stimulate short- and long-term measures to improve the lot of children. It was decided to avoid the expense of a massive international conference and to devote resources and energies instead into direct action to benefit children everywhere, especially in the less developed countries. To coordinate, inform, and encourage national efforts and international cooperation, a small international secretariat was set up in 1977. Its modest budget was around $6 million through December 1980.

National and International Programs. The strategy brought results. The IYC gave rise to a greater volume of publicity than any of the recent world conferences on environment, population, food, women, and so on. An IYC plaque was taken into orbit by a Polish cosmonaut and circled the globe in the Soviet space station Salyut 6. Queen Elizabeth II attended the biggest children's party ever held in Britain, with 160,000 participants. Events of this kind took place in almost every country and were accompanied by massive media coverage, which did not neglect the serious aspects. More than 2,000 new initiatives were launched by governments, voluntary organizations, and international agencies.

UNICEF financed a series of studies in less developed countries on the situation of children, to provide the factual foundations for new programs. UNESCO launched programs to provide textbooks for the children of migrant workers. The International Labour Organization (ILO) intensified its campaign against child labour, while the World Health Organization (WHO) focused on mother and child health at its 32nd assembly. Nongovernmental organizations (NGO's) and voluntary agencies launched their own programs. The idea for the year originated with Canon Joseph Moerman, secretary-general of the International Catholic Child Welfare Bureau, an NGO. Some 200 international groupings joined together in an NGO Committee for IYC. NGO's were also active at the national level. In Britain, for example, the U.K. Association for the IYC grouped more than 400 voluntary agencies, while in France NGO's submitted a white paper on children's needs to the government. Hundreds of schools in developed nations adopted projects and collected funds to help children in poor countries.

Paul Harrison, a free-lance writer on development, has worked for several UN agencies including the International Year of the Child Secretariat. He is author of Inside the Third World *and* The Third World Tomorrow.

In October a plenary session of the UN General Assembly discussed national and international actions that might follow up the IYC. It was likely that UNICEF would continue to coordinate international action to help children. Individual countries reported on their own national efforts and long-term plans. IYC commissions were set up in all but a handful of UN member states. Many countries created permanent children's boards to check on progress in child welfare, to review existing legislation, or to recommend new measures. Some set specific targets: India aimed to lower its infant mortality by 5% in 1979 through immunization and drinking water programs; Liberia declared 1979–89 the Decade of the African Child, by the end of which it hoped to provide free education for all up to university level and free medical care for all mothers and children.

An important reason for choosing 1979 was that it marked the 20th anniversary of the UN General Assembly's adoption, on Nov. 20, 1959, of the Declaration of the Rights of the Child. The declaration's ten principles affirmed, among others, the right of children to enjoy the benefits of social security, adequate nutrition, housing, recreation, medical services, and free and compulsory primary education on the basis of equal opportunity; their right to be protected against all forms of neglect, cruelty, and exploitation, including child labour; and their right to grow up in an atmosphere of affection and security, wherever possible with their own parents.

In 1979 the UN Commission on Human Rights considered a proposed draft convention on children's rights, for submission to the UN General Assembly. This would strengthen such rights by making provision for their enforcement in countries that ratified the convention. In other forums, new rights were proposed to broaden the 1959 list, including the right to adequate parenting, the right of illegitimate children to equal status, and the right to a national agency or ministry protecting and promoting children's rights.

The Legacy of Poverty. If the year brought forth action to improve the situation in the future, it also underlined the fact that most children, at the end of the 1970s, were being deprived of their rights on a massive scale, mainly in less developed countries but also, to an unacceptable degree, in the developed countries. Third world children suffered because of their countries' lack of resources for development, as well as pronounced inequalities in the way available resources were distributed. These children faced a situation of absolute material deprivation. In developed countries the majority of children were at greater risk of relative deprivation of a moral, social, or emotional kind, although absolute deprivation still affected substantial minorities.

In 1979, out of a total world population of some 4,375,000,000, there were about 1,557,000,000 children under 15. Of these, 284 million lived in the industrialized regions, where they made up only 25% of the population. The other 1,273,000,000 lived in less developed countries and constituted 40% of their population. Inevitably, the Year of the Child focused more on the plight of this poor majority. Four out of every five children in the third world live in rural areas or in the squalid shantytowns fringing the cities. For most, the poverty and lack of education of their parents, combined with little or no access to essential services of health, sanitation, and education, prevent the realization of their full human potential, making them more likely to grow up uneducated, unskilled, and unproductive. Thus a legacy of poverty is passed on from generation to generation, while the human resources that are essential for economic development are blighted.

Disease and Malnutrition. The extent to which the right to health is denied the poor child is tragically delineated in the statistics for infant mortality. Among countries with per capita incomes below $280 in 1976, 129 children in every 1,000 born alive would die in their first 12 months. In the poorest rural areas, the rate might rise to 250 per 1,000. Of the 122 million children born in the Year of the Child, 12 million will die before their first birthday and another 5 million before they reach the age of five. Less than 400,000 of these deaths will be in the developed countries.

Some will die soon after birth, often because of lack of trained attendants or gross malnutrition of the mother. Maternal mortality associated with childbirth is also high, leaving an estimated one million motherless children a year in Africa and Asia. Among children who survive their first month, the most common cause of death is a combination of malnutrition and some form of diarrheal disease. A cross-national survey in Latin America, the best nourished of the poor continents, found that malnutrition was the underlying or associated cause of 57% of infant deaths. It is often an attack of diarrhea that precipitates the onset of serious malnutrition. A host of illnesses await the survivors. In Sri Lanka, Bangladesh, and Venezuela, over 90% of six-year-olds were found to harbour parasitic worms. Ten- to 14-year-olds in Bangkok, Thailand, had an average of three diseases, defects, or parasitic conditions each. The six major killer diseases of childhood—diphtheria, whooping cough, tetanus, poliomyelitis, measles, and tuberculosis—claim around five million young victims a year.

WHO believes that 80% of infant illness may be linked directly or indirectly to lack of clean water and poor sanitation. Bias in government investment channeled four-fifths of investment in this sector in the first half of the 1970s into the urban areas, where about three-quarters of households had access to safe water and sanitation in 1975. In the rural areas, where more than two-thirds of the population still lives, only 22% had safe water and only 15% had adequate sanitation.

Health services are equally thin and uneven. Less than 10% of third world children are immunized against the six killer diseases, though vaccination protection costs less than $1 per child. Doctor-patient ratios, which average about 1 to 600 in the West, typically range from 1 to 4,000 up to 1 to 60,000 in the poorer countries. Rural doctors may have to serve six times as many patients as their urban colleagues.

Malnutrition is widespread among rural and poor urban children. The median value for incidence of severe and moderate child malnutrition in surveys in Latin America was 19%, in Africa 26%, and in Asia 31%. On this basis, more than an estimated 130 million children under five may be affected. Lack of vitamin A blinds an estimated 100,000 children each year. One child in four may be anemic. The incidence of malnutrition is worse among mothers and children than among adult men, and considerably worse among the urban poor and the landless in rural areas than among higher income groups. Child malnutrition is not the result of inadequate overall food production. Rather, it occurs because the poor lack money to buy or land to grow food and because of inequality in food distribution among nations, among social classes, and sometimes even among members of the same family.

Educational Deprivation. In the field of education, most less developed countries made substantial progress in the first decades of independence. The percentage of third world children aged 6 to 11 attending school rose from 45 in 1960 to 62 in 1975; for 12- to 17-year-olds the percentage in school rose from 21 to 35. However, this was still far short of the developed countries' enrollment ratios of 93 and 84%, respectively, for the two age groups. In Africa and Asia, the level of enrollment remained substantially lower for girls than for boys. In recent years, lack of resources has slowed down progress, so there may actually be more children out of school in 1985 than there were in 1975.

Discouraging as they are, the enrollment figures reflect attendance, not successful completion of schooling. UNESCO has estimated that less than half the children who started primary school in 1965 finished the course. One in three dropped out after only one year. This massive toll of educational failure is concentrated among children of the poor.

Their mental development may be seriously retarded even before they reach school age, as a result of malnutrition and lack of stimulation—both conditions aggravated in larger families with closely spaced children. But they are also handicapped by unequal access to education. Shanty areas, and especially rural areas, are underprovided with schools both quantitatively and qualitatively. Poor families are less able to bear the costs of fees, books, and clothing. Instruction is often in a language other than that used in the home.

Child Labour. Where access to education is inadequate, and where poor families need to supplement their incomes, children tend to be precipitated prematurely into the world of work. The ILO estimates that there were at least 52 million children at work in 1979. Some 1.3 million of these were in developed countries, mainly in southern Europe. Child labour may stunt physical development through bad lighting and ventilation, heavy loads, or long hours. It disrupts family life. Rarely does it involve vocational training, which might compensate for lack of schooling.

Action Needed. Ending the absolute deprivation of hundreds of millions of children in the third world will require a considerable increase in the flow of financial resources from developed and oil-rich countries. Third world governments, too, must reorder their priorities, investing far more in rural areas, helping small farmers and small entrepreneurs, and creating jobs on a massive scale.

More limited actions, such as reaching the international targets of clean water, adequate sanitation, and immunization for all by 1990, would have a considerable effect. UNICEF and WHO recommend that health services be restructured to provide a basic level of service to everyone—by using modestly trained village personnel and low-cost equipment, by involving the community in decision making, and through contributions of labour and money. Techniques exist to single out mothers and children at greatest risk for special attention.

Rapid improvements could be made at little cost by disseminating information on family planning and promoting breast feeding, which is declining in urban areas. Infant mortality can be cut further by teaching mothers how to make nutritious weaning foods and a simple rehydration fluid for children with diarrhea.

In education, the school system can be made more efficient by introducing such measures as automatic promotion from one class to the next, double shifts, or courses reduced in length but improved in relevance. Community resources can be harnessed here as well. Better provision of schools in rural areas, instruction in indigenous languages, and scheduling classes with the farming calendar in mind can increase access.

PAUL HARRISON

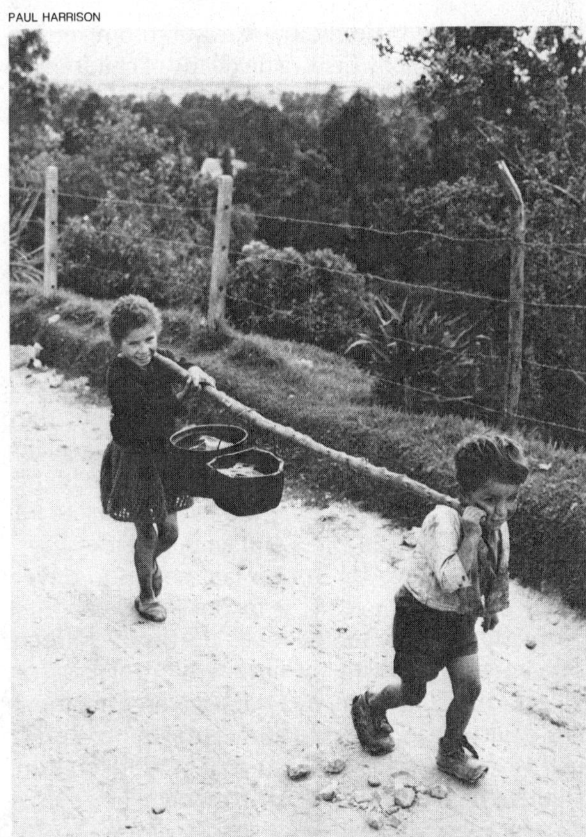

Dirty water and poor sanitation are blamed for 80% of child illnesses in less developed countries.

Child labour cannot be eliminated by legislation, which exists in many countries but is widely flouted. The only remedy is to remove the causes, chiefly family poverty and poor access to education. Until child labour can be abolished completely, the ILO recommends that children be protected from long hours, night work, and heavy or dangerous tasks.

Deprivation amid Plenty. The material affluence of the majority of families in developed countries should not be a cause for complacency about the conditions of children. Sectors of absolute deprivation, preventing children from reaching their physical and mental potential, still exist in the West among low-income groups, in depressed regions, and in inner cities where housing, health, educational, and recreational facilities deteriorated as the better-off families migrated to the suburbs. A recent report to the U.S. National Academy of Sciences suggested that as many as 30% of the nation's youngest children lived in families whose ability to rear them was severely crippled by lack of money. Children of racial minorities, children of migrant workers (thought to number 3.5 million in Europe alone), and the one child in ten who is handicapped in some way face additional disadvantages.

Even for the majority, there is still room for improvement in many fields. The needs of children are not adequately considered in planning or policy-making. Inside cities, parking lots are far more common than play areas, while most new housing developments provide few amenities for the young.

Inadequate Health Care. There are important advances to be made in child health. Indeed, in recent years there has been an alarming drop in child vaccination in some countries, including the U.S. and the U.K., with an attendant threat of future epidemics. Infant mortality rates have dropped to 10 or less per 1,000 live births in the Nordic countries, but they remain 40 to 60% higher in the English-speaking nations. Among low-income groups they are higher still; in 1975 the rate among U.S. whites was 14 per 1,000, but it was 24 per 1,000 among blacks.

As many as two-thirds of infant deaths in developed countries now occur in the first week after birth. Most are accounted for by deaths of children, often premature, with low birth weights of less than 3 kg (6½ lb). If they survive, such children are much more likely than others to grow up with physical or mental handicaps. Low-birth-weight children constitute a high proportion of births in English-speaking countries: 26% in Britain and the U.S. in the early 1970s and 31% in Canada, against only 16% in Sweden. A great deal of infant mortality and child handicap could be prevented by campaigns to reduce the incidence of low birth weight: extending coverage of prenatal care and advice on nutrition, giving special attention to women at risk of pregnancy complications, and encouraging the wider spacing of children.

This entire family lives in one room eight feet square in a slum in Calcutta.

PAUL HARRISON

More education in safety and in nutrition for pupils and parents could contribute to the health of older children. Accidents, chiefly in the home and on the road, cause between 25 and 44% of deaths among girls aged 1 to 14 in industrialized countries, and between 37 and 62% among boys. Prevention of obesity could lower the incidence of arterial disease in later life.

Unequal Opportunities. The achievement of near-universal primary and secondary enrollment in developed countries has not remedied all educational deficiencies. Educational attainments are highly unequal between social classes, suggesting that the goal of equal opportunity still has not been reached and that society is losing the contributions of low-income-group children who do not attain their potential. Here an important field for action is the extension of education downward. Properly conceived, preschool education can help to compensate for poor home background, especially if the parents are actively involved so they have a chance to improve their own child-rearing practices.

Experience suggests that compensatory education, if it is to have lasting effects, should be sustained for a year or more and followed up with further remedial work at the primary level. Preschool education is spreading everywhere, but English-speaking countries still lag behind some European countries. In 1970 a survey for the Organization for Economic Cooperation and Development found that English-speaking countries had between 54 and 58% of their three- to six-year-olds enrolled, a long way behind France's 84% or Belgium's 96%.

At the higher stages, education needs to be made more relevant to adult life. An increase in vocational content would help combat youth unemployment, and courses designed to prepare students for parenthood could raise the standard for parenting. Involvement of schoolchildren in community work could help overcome the alienation caused by the enforced uselessness of Western teenagers.

Children and Social Change. There have been deeper changes in Western societies that have adversely affected the position of children. The excessive emphasis on violence by the mass media is both a result and a cause of increasing juvenile delinquency. Violence against children persists. There

State of the World's Children: Regional Breakdown, 1975

	Total children under 15	% of population under 15	Life expectancy at birth (years)	Infant mortality rate[1]	School enrollments % Aged 6–11 Total	Aged 6–11 Female[2]	Aged 12–17 Total
World	1,439,000,000	36	60	99	70	64	50
More developed	281,000,000	25	71	22	93	94	84
Less developed	1,158,000,000	40	56	113	62	53	35
North America	60,000,000	25	73	15	99	99	95
Europe	112,000,000	24	71	20	95	96	80
U.S.S.R.	66,000,000	26	69	28	99	99	80
Oceania	7,000,000	32	68	41	88	87	73
Africa	178,000,000	44	46	147	51	43	31
Asia	883,000,000	38	58	105	63	54	35
Latin America	134,000,000	42	62	84	78	78	56

[1]0–12 months; per 1,000 live births.
[2]Percent of females in total population enrolled in school.
Sources: Population Reference Bureau, Inc., *World's Children Data Sheet* (1979); *UNESCO Statistical Yearbook, 1977* (for school enrollments).

may be 400,000 or more incidents of child abuse a year in the U.S. and at least four to six injuries per 1,000 children in the U.K. In 1979 Sweden took two unprecedented steps toward reducing the level of violence in society. From July, it became illegal for parents to use corporal punishment against their children (although penalties for smacking were not envisaged), and at the end of the year the sale of war toys was banned.

Accelerating changes in family patterns are taking their toll on children. In less developed countries the supportive extended family is breaking into nuclear units under the pressure of urbanization and migration, but in industrialized countries even the bonds of the nuclear family are weakening. Divorce rates have risen rapidly. The number of single-parent families, with their attendant risks of emotional and material deprivation for children, have grown alarmingly—from 570,000 in the U.K. in 1971 to 750,000 only five years later. In the U.S. female-headed households rose from 4.5 million in 1960 to 7.5 million in 1976.

Even within two-parent families, social trends have tended to reduce the amount of parent-child contact, essential for social and mental development. Television is one factor. In an Institute of Community Studies survey in southern England, 97% of fathers said they had watched TV more than a dozen times in the previous year, but only 62% had played with their children as often. Shift work, disrupting family social life, now affects more than 20% of workers in most countries.

But the biggest change is the great increase, in most developed countries, in the proportion of mothers going out to work. For example, in 1960, 28% of U.S. mothers of children under 18 worked, compared with 46% in 1976. Yet there are few countries where day-care facilities have expanded fast enough to compensate. As a result, two central social values are coming into conflict: equality for women and adequate care for children. One of the major challenges for Western societies will be to reconcile these goals.

More places need to be provided in day care and preschool education facilities. Maternity (or paternity) leave should be extended, with jobs protected, to allow parents more time with very young children. In France, the Soviet Union, and Hungary mothers receive substantial allowances to stay at home and look after young children. More part-time jobs and more flexible working hours would make contact with older children easier.

Looking to the Future. This article has dealt separately with the problems of children in less developed and developed countries. In reality, they form a continuum, with absolute deprivation shading gradually into relative and social deprivation as economic growth proceeds. Many newly learned lessons apply equally to both: the importance of prenatal care and nutrition of the mother-to-be, the contribution that preschool education can make to equalizing educational opportunities, the benefits of involving parents in programs for children, and, finally, the fact that none of these forms of intervention can have a great effect unless the worst inequalities in the distribution of income and services for children are evened out.

The IYC did much to focus our consciences on the needs of the world's children. As UNICEF's director, Henry Labouisse, has remarked, we already possess the resources and the know-how required to meet them. It remains to be seen whether the political will can be mustered to do the job and to divert the necessary resources from wasteful or destructive uses, especially military spending. On that depends our children's welfare and the world's future.

CALENDAR OF EVENTS

JANUARY

1 *New Year's Day*
8 *Battle of New Orleans (1815)*
14 *Birth of Albert Schweitzer (1875)*
15 *Birth of Martin Luther King, Jr. (1929)*
16 *U.S. Prohibition Amendment enacted (1920)*
20 *Super Bowl XIV in Pasadena, Calif.*
21 *Death of Lenin (1924)*
31 *Birth of Franz Peter Schubert (1797)*

1 **New Year's Day.** There is nothing new about New Year's. It has been celebrated one way or another for thousands of years, usually in connection with some seasonal or agricultural event. Spring was a popular time; the Romans celebrated the beginning of the year in March, which coincided roughly with the vernal equinox. In those days, the months of September, October, November, and December really were—as their names indicate—the seventh, eighth, ninth, and tenth months of the year. But in 153 BC the Romans changed New Year's to January 1 to mark the beginning of the terms of office for newly elected consuls. Emperors Julius Caesar and Augustus made further changes in the calendar; for their trouble they got the months of July and August named for them. In the 16th century Pope Gregory XIII made more than 1,500 additional changes and is generally regarded as the father of the modern calendar.

15 **Birth of Martin Luther King, Jr.** A major figure in the U.S. civil rights movement of the 1960s, King first came to national attention in 1956 when he led an antidiscrimination boycott of the public buses in Montgomery, Ala. After a year, the U.S. Supreme Court ruled that racial segregation in intrastate, as well as interstate, commerce is unlawful. In subsequent years King, a Baptist minister, organized the Southern Christian Leadership Conference, played a major role in the 1963 civil rights march on Washington, D.C., and lent powerful support to antidiscrimination and voter registration drives in the South. Such activities helped spur passage of the federal Civil Rights Act of 1964. That same year King won the Nobel Prize for Peace. He was also largely responsible for the passage of the Voting Rights Act the following year. King died on April 4, 1968, the victim of an assassin's bullet.

16 **Prohibition.** The temperance movement promoting moderation in the use of intoxicating liquors had been gathering strength in the U.S. since the 1820s, but it was not until Jan. 16, 1919, that the Prohibition Amendment—the 18th Amendment to the U.S. Constitution—was ratified by the necessary 36 states. The amendment forbade the manufacture, sale, or transportation of intoxicating liquors within the United States and all its territories and also outlawed their importation or exportation. The Prohibition Amendment took effect on Jan. 16, 1920, and was enforced according to guidelines provided by the National Prohibition Act (the Volstead Act) passed on Oct. 28, 1919. Both the observance and the enforcement of the law left much to be desired, however, particularly in cities, and the Age of Prohibition was soon characterized by bootleggers, gangsters, and speakeasies. Prohibition became a national political issue in 1932 when the Democratic Party came out against it; Franklin D. Roosevelt's election that year was considered a mandate for repeal. On Dec. 5, 1933, to almost no one's surprise, the 18th Amendment was repealed by the 21st Amendment.

FEBRUARY

6 *New Zealand Day*
11 *Birth of Thomas Edison (1847)*
12 *Birth of Abraham Lincoln (1809)*
14 *St. Valentine's Day*
16 *Chinese New Year (Year of the Monkey)*
20 *Ash Wednesday*
26 *Birth of William "Buffalo Bill" Cody (1846)*
29 *Leap Year Day*

14 **St. Valentine's Day.** There were at least two St. Valentines—both Christian martyrs of the 3rd century and both with feast days on February 14. How this saint, or these saints, became associated with hearts and flowers and other symbols of romantic love is a subject of much speculation. The most plausible theory holds that St. Valentine's Day, as it is now celebrated, derives from the Roman feast of Lupercalia. Lupercus was roughly equivalent to the Greek god Pan and was honoured by the Romans at the same time as Juno. During Lupercalia the names of young women were put into a container and drawn out by an equal number of young men; the matched pairs were considered to be sweethearts for the ensuing year, which at that time began in March. In 1415 Charles, duc d'Orléans, sent valentines to his wife while imprisoned in the Tower of London. And valentines are mentioned in the writings of Chaucer, Shakespeare, and Pepys. Valentines began to be fashionable in the U.S. about 1723 and became commercial items around 1800.

29 **Leap Year.** In most years there are 365 days; in Leap Year there are 366. The extra day is added every fourth year by stretching February from 28 days to 29. The necessity for the extra day stems from a slight dissimilarity between our calendar year of 365 days and the solar year of 365.242 days. Because of this fractional difference, roughly a fourth of a day, the quadrennial extra day neatly brings the calendar into agreement with the Sun. Leap Year in this decade will occur in 1980, 1984, and 1988. Tradition holds that a woman may propose marriage to a man during Leap Year, but the tradition is not taken seriously today, if indeed it ever was. As late as the last century, however, it was an unwritten law in Great Britain that a man who rejected a woman's proposal had to give her a silk dress.

MARCH

1 *Birth of Frédéric Chopin (1810)*
3 *Doll Festival in Japan*
6 *Birth of Michelangelo (1475)*
15 *Ides of March; assassination of Julius Caesar in 44 BC*
17 *St. Patrick's Day*
20 *Vernal equinox in the Northern Hemisphere; autumnal equinox in the Southern Hemisphere*
21 *Birth of Benito Juárez (1806)*
22 *King George III signs the Stamp Act (1765)*

17 **St. Patrick's Day.** The saying that "everybody's Irish on St. Patrick's Day" is more appropriate than most people know: St. Patrick himself was not even Irish. He was a Britannic Celt, but he was born in a place called Bannavem Taberniae. Scholarly research has so far failed to discover where this place was, but it was definitely not in Ireland. St. Patrick arrived on the Emerald Isle sometime during the last quarter of the 4th century and quickly set about civilizing and Christianizing the Irish. Patrick founded churches and schools, and legend says he performed miracles, one of the best known of which was the elimination of snakes from the island. Patrick may have also made the shamrock famous because, according to another legend, he used the tiny, three-leafed plant to instruct the Irish in the doctrine of the Trinity. Patrick's missionary activities earned him the title of Patron Saint of Ireland.

20 **Vernal equinox.** The first day of spring in the Northern Hemisphere is determined by the vernal equinox. It is the exact moment when the centre of the Sun appears to pass directly over the celestial equator on its apparent journey northward. This apparent movement of the Sun results from the changing declination of the Earth's axis as it orbits the Sun. The vernal equinox always occurs on or about March 21. In 1980 it will occur at precisely 6:10 AM, Eastern Standard Time, on March 20. In the Southern Hemisphere it will be the first day of fall.

22 **The Stamp Act.** Among the grievances the American colonies had against England in prerevolutionary days was the enactment of the Stamp Act on

March 22, 1765. Its author was George Grenville, first lord of the Treasury as well as chancellor of the Exchequer. The Stamp Act was one of a series of measures designed by Grenville to bolster imperial defenses, regulate colonial trade, and obtain American revenue. Under the act, revenue stamps had to be affixed to such things as legal documents, newspapers, and licenses. The proceeds from the stamps went back to England. The colonists objected strenuously to the Stamp Act, which they considered both burdensome and unconstitutional. It was, of course, a form of "taxation without representation." Vigorous opposition to the act led to its repeal after one year, but not before it had helped stir up sentiments that eventually culminated in the American Revolution.

APRIL

- **1** *April Fool's Day*
- **1** *First day of Passover*
- **4** *Good Friday*
- **6** *Easter Sunday*
- **10** *Bataan Day in the Philippines*
- **14** *Pan American Day*
- **15** *Deadline for filing U.S. personal income tax report*
- **15** *Birth of Leonardo da Vinci (1452)*
- **21** *Boston Marathon*

6 Easter. Of all the Christian feast days, Easter is the most important, commemorating as it does the resurrection of Jesus Christ and the reconciliation of all mankind with God. Christians believe that just as Christ rose from the dead, so will they. The Apostle Paul wrote: "Now if Christ is preached as raised from the dead, how can some of you say that there is no resurrection of the dead? But if there is no resurrection of the dead, then Christ has not been raised; if Christ has not been raised, then our preaching is in vain and your faith is in vain" (I Corinthians 15:12–14). A movable feast, Easter in the Western Church is always celebrated on a Sunday between March 22 and April 25, on the Sunday following the first full moon after the vernal equinox. This formula came out of the Council of Nicaea called by Emperor Constantine in the year 325. Owing to their talent for astronomy, the Alexandrians were put in charge of determining the exact date that Easter would fall each year. According to the Venerable Bede, the famous historian of the 7th and 8th centuries, the word Easter is derived from Eostre, the name of the Anglo-Saxon goddess of spring. Legend says it was Eostre who opened the gates of Valhalla to the murdered Sun God who had enlightened mankind.

15 U.S. Federal income tax deadline. The 16th Amendment to the U.S. Constitution, better known as the income tax amendment, was proposed to the state legislatures in 1909 and ratified on February 14, 1913. It was the first amendment enacted in the 20th century and stated that "the Congress shall have power to lay and collect taxes on incomes, from whatever source derived. . . ." It was not the first time that a federal income tax had been collected in the U.S.; incomes were taxed between 1862 and 1872 to finance the cost of the Civil War. With the ratification of the 16th Amendment, however, the federal income tax was here to stay, though it affected a far smaller proportion of the population than it does today. It was, in essence, a tax on the rich, albeit not a very harsh one. Not many people earned $20,000 a year in 1913. Those who did paid a mere $200, one percent of their income. A married couple with an income of $4,000 or less paid no taxes at all.

MAY

- **1** *International Labour Day*
- **3** *Kentucky Derby*
- **7** *Sinking of the Lusitania (1915)*
- **11** *Mother's Day in the U.S.*
- **19** *Victoria Day in Canada*
- **21** *Lindbergh lands in Paris (1927)*
- **25** *Pentecost (Whitsunday)*
- **26** *Memorial Day in the U.S.*
- **30** *Death of Joan of Arc (1431)*

3 The Kentucky Derby. Run every year since 1875, the Kentucky Derby has become the classic U.S. horse race for three-year-olds. The race takes place the first Saturday in May at historic Churchill Downs in Louisville, Ky. It is the first part of the coveted Triple Crown of horse racing, followed by the Preakness and the Belmont Stakes. (The last horse to win the Triple Crown, and only the 11th in history ever to win it, was Affirmed in 1978.) The fastest time for the Derby was posted in 1973 by Secretariat: 1 minute 59 and 2/5 seconds over the mile and a quarter.

25 Pentecost. This religious festival commemorates the descent of the Holy Spirit upon the apostles and is also considered the birthday of the Christian church. It always occurs 50 days after Easter and ten days after the ascension of Jesus Christ into heaven. The name comes from the Greek *pentekoste,* meaning fiftieth. In the Anglican Church, Pentecost is also known as Whitsunday, that is, White Sunday. It was common practice to conduct baptisms on this day; those to be baptised were customarily attired in white robes.

26 Memorial Day. Formerly known in the U.S. as Decoration Day, Memorial Day was originally designated as a day to honour those who had died in the Civil War. Now all the dead are remembered on this day, including civilians and casualties of later wars. Credit for conceiving the first observance of a memorial day is usually accorded to Henry G. Welles, a druggist from the town of Waterloo, N.Y. Ceremonies took place there on May 5, 1865. Other communities claiming to be the first to observe Memorial Day are Columbus, Miss., and Boalsburg, Pa. In 1868 the Grand Army of the Republic, an organization of Union war veterans, launched a campaign to make Memorial Day a national holiday. Beginning with an order to their own posts around the country, they later brought pressure to bear on state legislatures. The campaign first bore fruit in 1873 when the state of New York made Memorial Day a legal holiday. Other states soon followed suit. Until passage of the Monday Holiday Law in 1971, the day was celebrated on May 30 in most states. Now the official observance is the last Monday in May.

JUNE

- **2** *Coronation of Queen Elizabeth II (1953)*
- **6** *D-Day (1944)*
- **11** *Kamehameha Day*
- **15** *Father's Day in the U.S.*
- **17** *Chinese Dragon Boat Festival*
- **21** *Summer solstice in the Northern Hemisphere; winter solstice in the Southern Hemisphere*
- **23** *Wimbledon tennis tournament begins*
- **27** *Birth of Helen Keller (1880)*

23 Wimbledon. The annual grass court championships at Wimbledon, England, constitute the most prestigious event in the world of tennis. Yet, had it not been for a decline in the popularity of croquet, the venerable tournament might not exist today. It all began in 1875 when the All-England Croquet Club found itself in financial difficulties. In an attempt to remedy the problem, the members decided to add the sport of lawn tennis to their schedule of activities. Tennis caught on immediately and the name of the organization was changed to the All-England Croquet and Lawn Tennis Club. The financial problems, however, remained. Meeting again in 1877, the members voted to seek a way out of their financial straits by holding an open tennis tournament. The contest attracted 22 entrants and there was only one event, men's singles. The winner was Spencer W. Gore, a young man of 27 and a terrible prophet. He predicted that tennis would never rank among the great sports because it was much too boring.

27 Birthday of Helen Keller. Born healthy and normal on June 27, 1880, in Tuscumbia, Ala., Helen Keller was stricken with a disease at age 19 months that rendered her blind, deaf, and mute. When she was about six years old her parents hired a 20-year-old tutor by the name of Anne Sullivan who had been blind herself but had partially recovered. Thanks to Sullivan and later to special schools, Keller learned to speak, read, and write. In 1904 she graduated with honours from Radcliffe College and went on to become a prolific writer of books and magazine articles. Her writings and other activities made her one of the most inspirational figures of her time. On June 1, 1968, she died at her home in Easton, Conn., just short of her 88th birthday.

JULY

1 *Dominion Day in Canada*
4 *U.S. Independence Day*
10 *Birth of John Calvin (1509)*
14 *Bastille Day in France (1789)*
15 *Birth of Rembrandt (1606)*
23 *National Day in Egypt*
24 *Birth of Simón Bolívar (1783)*
27 *Completion of first Atlantic cable (1866)*

1 **Dominion Day.** The national holiday of Canada, Dominion Day marks the anniversary of the day in 1867 when the Dominion of Canada came into being under the British North America Act. The Dominion consisted originally of just four provinces: Nova Scotia, New Brunswick, Canada East (now Quebec), and Canada West (now Ontario). Prince Edward Island and Newfoundland declined to join; the western provinces had not yet been established.

4 **U.S. Independence Day.** American independence from Great Britain has always been celebrated on July 4, the day in 1776 when the Continental Congress voted to approve the Declaration of Independence. Yet, like many historic events, the break with Great Britain did not take place in a single day. Of equal importance, perhaps, is July 2, when the Lee Resolution, one of the Declaration's three principal sections, was passed. It states in part: "That these United Colonies are, and of Right ought to be, Free and Independent States." In a letter to his wife, John Adams wrote: "The Second of July, 1776, will be the most memorable epoch in the history of America. I am apt to believe that it will be celebrated by succeeding generations as the great anniversary festival." Adams went on to describe the various forms the celebration might take. A good case could also be made for July 8, the day that the Declaration was read to the public for the first time, or August 2, when most of the members of the Continental Congress signed it.

14 **Bastille Day.** Known also in France as La Fête Nationale, or National Day, Bastille Day commemorates the day in 1789 when a revolutionary mob stormed the Bastille in Paris. The Bastille was both prison and royal arms depot and, as such, it was also a symbol of despotism. When the crowd attacked, it was not seeking to free the prisoners, who numbered only seven, but to seize and distribute the arms and munitions stored inside. The attack succeeded and two days later the assembly of electors in Paris decided to tear the Bastille down. Because it was so large and sturdy, the demolition job took several years to complete. But the French Revolution was well under way.

AUGUST

4 *Acquittal of John Peter Zenger (1735)*
6 *Hiroshima Peace Day*
7 *PGA golf championship begins*
12 *Ponce de Leon Day in Puerto Rico*
15 *Independence Day in India*
26 *U.S. women granted suffrage (1920)*
29 *Birth of Oliver Wendell Holmes (1809)*

4 **Acquittal of Zenger.** When the governor of New York, William Cosby, dismissed Chief Justice Lewis Morris for opposing Cosby's attempts to enrich himself at the colony's expense, Morris and his backers offered printer John Peter Zenger the financial support to establish the *New York Weekly Journal*, an antiadministration newspaper. After Zenger printed several satirical attacks on the governor's actions, in November 1734, Cosby had Zenger arrested and charged with libel. But the following year a jury found Zenger innocent. At the trial, Zenger's lawyer, the prominent Andrew Hamilton of Philadelphia, reiterated the right of the press to "liberty both of exposing and opposing arbitrary power by speaking and writing the truth."

6 **Hiroshima Peace Day.** On August 6, 1945, the U.S. Air Force bomber "Enola Gay" dropped an atomic bomb on the Japanese industrial city of Hiroshima. It was the first such bomb to be used in warfare. The blast killed an estimated 75,000 people and many thousands more were left with permanent injuries. Over four square miles in the heart of the city suffered complete devastation. On August 9 the U.S. dropped another atomic bomb on the Japanese city of Nagasaki with nearly as great damage. World War II in the Pacific ended a few days later on August 14; the Japanese formally surrendered on September 2. In memory of the victims, and as a reminder of the horror of atomic warfare, since 1947 a peace observance has been held in Hiroshima every August 6.

26 **U.S. women granted suffrage.** "The right of citizens of the United States to vote shall not be denied or abridged by the United States or any State on account of sex." So reads the 19th Amendment to the U.S. Constitution. It took effect on August 26, 1920, and for the first time in history gave American women the right to vote in all national elections. It could not, however, provide for equal treatment of women in other important areas. In the early '70s, therefore, a campaign was launched to pass the Equal Rights Amendment (ERA). Supporters of the proposed amendment consider it the logical sequel to the 19th Amendment and have even adopted the same wording. Section One of the ERA reads: "Equal rights under the law shall not be denied or abridged by the United States or by any state on account of sex." As 1980 began, the ERA was still short of the 38 states necessary for ratification.

SEPTEMBER

1 *Labor Day in the U.S.*
11 *Rosh Hashana*
20 *Yom Kippur*
22 *Autumnal equinox in the Northern Hemisphere; vernal equinox in the Southern Hemisphere*
22 *Hanging of Nathan Hale (1776)*
25 *Balboa discovers the Pacific (1513)*
28 *Birth of Confucius (551 BC)*
29 *Birth of Enrico Fermi (1901)*

1 **Labor Day in the U.S.** The last U.S. holiday of the summer never needed a Monday Holiday Law to make it part of a three-day weekend. It has been celebrated on the first Monday of September ever since its inception in 1882. On September 5 of that year, some 10,000 members of New York City's Central Labor Union got together and paraded around Union Square. Later on they enjoyed themselves with picnics, fireworks, dancing, and oratory. Credit for inspiring that first Labor Day celebration belongs to Peter J. McGuire, a leader of the Knights of Labor and president and founder of the United Brotherhood of Carpenters and Joiners of America. Soon afterward the Knights of Labor passed a resolution designating the first Monday of September as a day to honour Labor. The first state to make Labor Day a legal holiday was Oregon in 1887. New Jersey and New York followed suit the same year. Today Labor Day is a legal holiday in all 50 states and the District of Columbia.

20 **Yom Kippur.** The most solemn of all Jewish holidays, Yom Kippur, or Day of Atonement, concludes the ten-day observance of the Jewish New Year. Rosh Hashana is the first day of the month of Tishri; Yom Kippur is the tenth. As with all Jewish holidays, the observance of Yom Kippur begins at sundown the previous day. It is a time of prayer, fasting, and repentance for all Jews. The origin of the present rite goes back to AD 70 following the destruction of the Second Temple of Jerusalem. The earliest origins of the day may go back as far as the 2nd millennium BC.

OCTOBER

2 *Birth of Mahatma Gandhi (1869)*
5 *Day of the Republic in Portugal*
9 *Leif Eriksson Day*
10 *National Day in the Republic of China*
12 *Columbus Day (traditional)*
18 *Alaska Day*
20 *National Heroes Day in Jamaica*
24 *United Nations Day*
26 *Reformation Day (1517)*
31 *Halloween*

12 **Columbus Day.** On October 12, 1492, Christopher Columbus walked ashore on the Bahama island of San Salvador (Watling Island) and claimed it for Ferdinand and Isabella of Spain. On this and subsequent voyages—there were four in all—the famed explorer made additional discoveries in the Caribbean and along the coasts of South and Central America. But, contrary to popular belief, he never set foot on the continent of North America. He didn't even know there was a North America. What Columbus set out to find was a new western route to the Indies. When he landed in the Bahamas he thought he had succeeded. Consequently, he called the islands the Indies and the people who inhabited them Indians, names that persist even today. The first celebration of Columbus Day in the U.S. is believed to have been held on Oct. 12, 1792, in New York by the Columbian Order or Society of St. Tammany. But the greatest boost to the day's popularity occurred in 1893 at Chicago's Columbian Exposition, planned to coincide with the 400th anniversary of Columbus's discovery. (It was supposed to open in 1892 but was delayed several months.) Various U.S. states had already begun holding observances when Pres. Franklin Roosevelt urged a national observance in 1934 and proclaimed one in 1937. With the passage of the Monday Holiday Law in 1971, Columbus Day in the U.S. was changed from October 12 to the second Monday in October. In 1980 that day occurs on October 13.

24 **United Nations Day.** The United Nations was born over a period of several years. The Declaration of the United Nations was signed in Washington in 1942; many details of the international peace organization were worked out at the Dumbarton Oaks Conference in 1944. But it wasn't until Oct. 24, 1945, that all the necessary signatures were affixed to the Charter and the UN became a reality. The UN directly succeeded the League of Nations, which was born in 1919 as a result of World War I and died in the '40s (for all practical purposes) as a result of World War II. The aim of the UN, essentially the same as that of its predecessor, is contained in the opening lines of the Charter: "We the peoples of the United Nations determined to save succeeding generations from the scourge of war. . . . " Though primarily a peacekeeping organization, the UN also addresses itself to economic and social problems, including those of poverty, hunger, disease, illiteracy, and human rights.

NOVEMBER

3 *National Day in Panama*
4 *U.S. presidential election*
5 *Guy Fawkes Day*
7 *Bolshevik Revolution (1917)*
20 *Mexican Revolution (1910)*
22 *Assassination of John F. Kennedy (1963)*
27 *Thanksgiving Day in the U.S.*
30 *First Sunday of Advent*

4 **U.S. Election Day.** Until 1845 there was no single election day in the U.S. In that year, however, an act of Congress established election day as the first Tuesday after the first Monday in November. National elections are always held on this date, and always during even-numbered years. Every fourth year is a presidential election year. In this decade, presidential elections will be held in 1980, 1984, and 1988. U.S. representatives are elected every two years, U.S. senators every six. (Approximately one-third of the 100 U.S. senators are elected every two years.) State and local governments may also elect their officials on election day if they wish, and many do. But they may also hold elections at any other time.

7 **The Bolshevik Revolution.** Sometimes known as the Russian Revolution, the Bolshevik Revolution of 1917 brought Lenin to power and has been traditionally considered the beginning of the Soviet Communist dictatorship as we know it today. In the U.S.S.R. the revolution is known as the Great October Socialist Revolution. Owing to the change from the old to the new calendar, the date is now celebrated on November 7. There were two revolutions in Russia in 1917. This was the second. The first or February Revolution (March, according to the new calendar) resulted in the overthrow of the tsarist regime and the installation of a Provisional Government. The second or Bolshevik Revolution overthrew the Provisional Government. The new government, the Council of People's Commissars, abolished without compensation all private ownership of large landed estates. These, together with the possessions of the imperial family, the churches, and the monasteries, were taken over by the state. The eight-hour workday, workers' committees for the management of factories, and nationalization of banks and industries soon followed.

27 **U.S. Thanksgiving Day.** The first Thanksgiving in the U.S. was celebrated at Plymouth, Mass., in 1621 by the Pilgrims. Their guests were approximately 90 Indians under the leadership of Massasoit. The Pilgrim leader at the time was William Bradford. The menu was extensive and included venison, duck, and wine, but it is uncertain that there was any turkey, cranberry sauce, or pumpkin pie. In 1789 and again in 1795 days of thanksgiving were proclaimed by Pres. George Washington. Another day of thanksgiving was proclaimed by Pres. James Madison in remembrance of the War of 1812. But credit for causing Thanksgiving to become a national holiday belongs to Sarah Josepha Hale, a prominent magazine editor who campaigned for better than a third of a century. Her efforts were finally rewarded in 1863 when a national day of thanksgiving was proclaimed by Pres. Abraham Lincoln. In 1939 and 1940 Pres. Franklin Roosevelt set the next-to-last Thursday of November as the official day of observance in order to provide an extra week of shopping between Thanksgiving and Christmas. Many Americans ignored Roosevelt, however, and continued celebrating Thanksgiving on the fourth Thursday. Congress ended the confusion in 1941 by passing a joint resolution that set Thanksgiving as the fourth Thursday of November.

DECEMBER

2 *Proclamation of the Monroe Doctrine (1823)*
3 *Hanukka*
16 *Boston Tea Party (1773)*
20 *Louisiana Purchase (1803)*
21 *Winter solstice in the Northern Hemisphere; summer solstice in the Southern Hemisphere*
25 *Christmas Day*
26 *Boxing Day*
27 *Birth of Louis Pasteur (1822)*
31 *New Year's Eve*

20 **Louisiana Purchase.** One of the great real estate bargains in history, the Louisiana Purchase of 1803 transferred roughly the western half of the Mississippi River Basin from France to the U.S. for the total sum of $27,267,622. But even at many times this amount, the purchase would have been a bargain. Included were all or parts of the present states of Louisiana, Arkansas, Missouri, Iowa, North Dakota, South Dakota, Nebraska, Oklahoma, Kansas, Colorado, Wyoming, Montana, and Minnesota. Thomas Jefferson was president at the time. Acting on his behalf in Paris were James Monroe and Robert R. Livingston, the U.S. minister to France. The agreement was dated April 30. The U.S. took formal possession of the area on December 20.

25 **Christmas Day.** Also known as the Feast of the Nativity, Christmas has been celebrated on December 25 since the 4th century. As everyone knows, it commemorates the birth of Christ. The biblical account (Luke 2:1-7) is familiar even to non-Christians: "In those days a decree went out from Caesar Augustus that all the world should be enrolled. This was the first enrollment, when Quirinius was governor of Syria. And all went to be enrolled, each to his own city. And Joseph also went up from Galilee, from the city of Nazareth, to Judea, to the city of David, which is called Bethlehem, because he was of the house and lineage of David, to be enrolled with Mary, his betrothed, who was with child. And while they were there, the time came for her to be delivered. And she gave birth to her first-born son and wrapped him in swaddling cloths, and laid him in a manger, because there was no place for them in the inn." No one really knows whether Jesus was born on December 25 or even whether the year of his birth was correctly ascertained. It is possible that the date of Christ's birth might have been arbitrarily fixed on December 25 to coincide with the feast of the Persian Sun god Mithra. Some of the customs associated with Christmas might have come from the Roman Saturnalia, a period of merrymaking that ran from December 17 to 23. It was, of course, common in those times to incorporate elements of the pagan feasts into those of the Christian holy days. Christmas is the only annual religious holiday that is also a U.S. legal holiday.

CHRONOLOGY OF EVENTS

JANUARY

1 *China and the U.S. establish full diplomatic relations*

The People's Republic of China and the U.S. formally established full diplomatic relations as promised in a surprise announcement made in both Beijing (Peking) and Washington, D.C., on Dec. 15, 1978. The U.S. simultaneously severed diplomatic relations with the Chinese Nationalist government in Taiwan. In his December televised address, Pres. Jimmy Carter said the U.S. would recognize the government in Beijing "as the sole legal government of China. Within this context the people of the United States will maintain cultural, commercial and other unofficial relations with the people of Taiwan." He also said he had "paid special attention to ensuring that normalization of relations between the United States and the People's Republic will not jeopardize the well-being of the people of Taiwan." It was later learned that the Chinese government had given no assurances to the U.S. that it was willing to renounce military force as a means of reuniting Taiwan with the rest of China.

3 *Cambodian rebels step up offensive*

Cambodian rebels fighting as the Kampuchean United Front for National Salvation continued to move rapidly toward the national capital of Phnom Penh and the vital port of Kompong Som. Officials of the besieged government of Premier Pol Pot conceded that the United Front, which was heavily supported by troops and matériel from Vietnam, had already gained control of a fourth of the country.

Spain and Vatican void concordat by new agreements

Representatives of Spain and Vatican City State signed four agreements that abrogated the concordat of 1953, which was entered into during the rule of Francisco Franco, and redefined the status of the Roman Catholic Church in Spain. The changes were prompted by provisions of the recently approved Spanish constitution which, among other things, guarantees freedom of religion and no longer forbids divorce.

6 *Bakhtiar new Iranian prime minister*

In an effort to restore order to strife-torn Iran, Shah Mohammad Reza Pahlavi replaced the two-month-old military government of Gen. Gholam Reza Azhari with a civilian government headed by Shahpur Bakhtiar as prime minister. From his exile in France, Ayatollah Ruhollah Khomeini denounced the new regime as satanic and ordered his followers in Iran to refuse to support it.

7 *Cambodian capital falls to rebels*

The insurgent Kampuchean United Front for National Salvation announced the fall of Phnom Penh, the capital of Cambodia, and the end of Premier Pol Pot's regime. The following day Heng Samrin was named president of the People's Revolutionary Council, which would govern the country. Heng and other members of the council were believed to have had roles in Pol Pot's government before defecting. Though it was widely reported that some 100,000 Vietnamese troops were chiefly responsible for the overthrow of the Cambodian government, official radio announcements made no mention of their presence.

Cambodian peasants in Svay Rieng Province gathered to read news of the formation of a new government after the overthrow of the Pol Pot regime in January.

INTERFOTO MTI/PICTORIAL PARADE

8 *Chinese plead for more democracy*

Several thousand persons who gathered in Beijing's (Peking's) famed Tian An Men (T'ien An Men) Square to commemorate the anniversary of the death of longtime premier Zhou Enlai (Chou Enlai) created a stir when they produced banners demanding an end to hunger and suffering and a new respect for democracy and human rights. On January 14–15 a similar rally was held by more than a hundred peasants who identified themselves as "persecuted people from all parts of China." They likewise pleaded for the elimination of hunger and oppression.

11 *UN debates Cambodian conflict*

Over the objections of the Soviet Union and Czechoslovakia, the UN Security Council agreed to let Cambodia, in the person of former head of state Prince Norodom Sihanouk, present a demand for the withdrawal of Vietnamese forces from Cambodia. Sihanouk made it clear that his denunciation of Vietnam was not an implied defense of Premier Pol Pot, whose brutal regime was widely accused of genocide after it came to power in Cambodia in 1975.

13 *Formation of Iranian regency council precedes shah's departure into exile*

A nine-member regency council, with constitutional powers equal to those of the shah, was constituted in Iran, but Prime Minister Shahpur Bakhtiar made it clear that during Shah Mohammad Reza Pahlavi's forthcoming "extended vacation" outside the country the council would be granted only limited authority and would be subservient to his Cabinet. On January 16 the shah flew to Egypt for a brief visit with Pres. Anwar as-Sadat without announcing where he would take up permanent residence. Most observers believed his 37-year rule had come to an end. Two days later Sayed Jalaleddin Tehrani, head of the regency council, flew from Iran to France where, on January 22, he met with Ayatollah Khomeini, declared the council illegal, and resigned his post.

15 *Vietnamese pullout from Cambodia vetoed in Security Council*

The U.S.S.R. and Czechoslovakia both voted against a UN Security Council resolution calling for the withdrawal of "all foreign forces" from Cambodia. The other 13 members of the Security Council voted for the pullout. The seven third world nations that sponsored the resolution chose not to mention Vietnam by name, hoping thereby to avoid a Soviet veto.

19 *North and South Korea agree to discuss reunification*

Pres. Park Chung Hee of South Korea proposed talks with North Korea on the subjects of reunification and prevention of war. So far as South Korea was concerned, the talks could be held at any time, in any place, and at any level without preconditions. On January 25 North Korea responded by suggesting both sides hold a congress. The following day South Korea accepted the idea, but indicated that the congress should have an official governmental status.

Somoza rejects plebiscite plan

Anastasio Somoza Debayle rejected a plan calling for a plebiscite on his future as president of Nicaragua. A three-man team from the Dominican Republic, Guatemala, and the U.S. submitted a compromise proposal that would permit members of the Somoza government to join representatives of the Organization of American States in supervising the voting. Somoza, however, would have to leave the country if voters expressed disapproval of his regime. The president's refusal to go into exile under any circumstances doomed the plan and discouraged moderates who hoped a plebiscite would prevent further bloodshed. It also generated new support for the Sandinista National Liberation Front, which insisted that peace would come only with total victory over Somoza and his supporters.

21 *Pittsburgh Steelers win Super Bowl*

The Pittsburgh Steelers professional football team defeated the Dallas Cowboys 35–31 in Super Bowl XIII, played in the Orange Bowl in Miami, Fla. A TV audience estimated at 95 million saw what was widely regarded as the finest Super Bowl contest to date. Steeler quarterback Terry Bradshaw, voted the game's most valuable player, threw for a record 318 yd and a record four touchdown passes as Pittsburgh won an unprecedented third Super Bowl championship.

22 *Canadian governor-general installed*

Edward R. Schreyer, a 43-year-old former premier of Manitoba, was installed as Canada's 22nd governor-general. In the largely ceremonial post, Schreyer would represent Queen Elizabeth II, Canada's head of state.

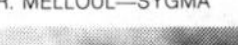

R. MELLOUL—SYGMA

Chinese Vice-Premier Deng Xiaoping was greeted by U.S. Pres. Jimmy Carter when Deng arrived in Washington for an official visit on January 28.

24 *Japan announces 1978 trade figures*

The Japanese Finance Ministry announced that the nation had registered a record trade surplus of U.S. $19.7 billion during 1978. Exports totaled $105,-630,000,000, an increase of 17.1% over the previous year; imports amounted to $85,960,000,000, a 7.8% increase over 1977. Though the huge trade surplus caused serious concern abroad, the statistics were somewhat distorted. Because of the decline of the U.S. dollar against the Japanese yen, Japanese exports, in terms of yen, declined 5% during 1978, while imports were down 12.6%.

25 *John Paul II visits Latin America*

Pope John Paul II, on his first trip overseas as head of the Roman Catholic Church, was greeted by hundreds of thousands on his arrival in Santo Domingo, capital of the Dominican Republic. During an open-air mass, the pope made a broad appeal for social justice and respect for human rights. The next day he flew to Mexico City, where he was welcomed by an estimated one million cheering people. On January 27, after celebrating mass at the shrine of the Virgin of Guadalupe, he opened the long-awaited third Latin-American Bishops' Conference. The pontiff praised the spirit of the previous conference, held in Colombia in 1968, but expressed disapproval of the "theology of liberation." His exhortation to "educate individuals and collectivities, form public opinion, and offer orientations to the leaders of the peoples" as part of the church's mission to evangelize was interpreted as an indirect but clear admonition to priests who had become actively involved in leftist political activities. On January 31 the pope returned to Rome.

28 *Chinese vice-premier visits U.S.*

Chinese First Vice-Premier Deng Xiaoping (Teng Hsiao-p'ing) was warmly received in Washington, D.C., at the start of an official nine-day visit to the U.S. Deng and President Carter held a series of talks on January 29–30 and on January 31 signed agreements for cultural and scientific exchanges to solidify the bonds recently forged between their two countries. Carter remarked that Sino-American relations were now on "a new and irreversible course"; Deng noted that "there are many more areas of bilateral cooperation and more channels waiting for us to develop."

30 *Iran to permit Ayatollah Khomeini to return from exile*

Four days after an estimated 100,000 demonstrators rallied in Teheran for the return from exile of Ayatollah Ruhollah Khomeini, the government of Prime Minister Shahpur Bakhtiar reopened the airport, which had been closed on January 24, and agreed to permit the 77-year-old Islamic leader to reenter the country.

U.S. has record trade deficit in 1978

The U.S. Department of Commerce announced that the U.S. merchandise trade deficit for 1978 reached a record $28,450,-000,000. At the end of that year the U.S. had registered 31 consecutive monthly trade deficits. With the cost of insurance and freight added to the cost of imports, the trade deficit amounted to $39,-560,000,000; in 1977 the figure was $36,-410,000,000. The 1978 trade deficit with Japan rose to $11,570,000,000 from $8,020,000,000 the previous year, and with West Germany to $3 billion from $1,250,000,000 in 1977.

31 *New president is named in Algeria*

A congress of the National Liberation Front (FLN), Algeria's only political party, named Col. Chadli Bendjedid to the presidency. He would succeed Houari Boumédienne, who died on Dec. 27, 1978, after 13 years in office. In a national referendum on February 7, voters overwhelmingly approved the appointment.

FEBRUARY

1 *Peru gets new prime minister*

Gen. Pedro Richter Prada was sworn in as Peruvian prime minister, minister of war, and commander of the Army. He replaced Gen. Oscar Molina Pallochia, who retired after one year in office and 35 years in the military. Richter announced that the Army supported the plan to return the country to civilian rule.

Ayatollah Khomeini returns to Iran

An estimated three million people lined the motorcade route of Ayatollah Ruhollah Khomeini when he returned to Iran from France after nearly 15 years in exile. The Islamic religious leader denounced Parliament and the government of Prime Minister Shahpur Bakhtiar as illegal and promised to replace them with his own supporters. Khomeini also condemned the former regime of Shah Mohammad Reza Pahlavi and prayed, he said, that God would "cut off the hands" of foreigners living in Iran. That same day Bakhtiar, who still had the support of the Army, gave notice that he would use strong action to prevent any attempt by Khomeini to take over the country and turn it into an Islamic state.

2 *Ecuador delays national elections*

The military government of Ecuador announced that the presidential runoff election and elections for congress would be transferred from April 8 to April 29 to allow more candidates to register. All government employees, including those in teaching positions, were excluded from public office, according to provisions of the new constitution.

4 *Chinese vice-premier leaves U.S.*

Deng Xiaoping (Teng Hsiao-p'ing), first vice-premier of China, concluded his nine-day tour of the U.S. after having visited Washington, D.C.; Atlanta, Ga.; Houston, Texas; and Seattle, Wash. During his stay Deng repeatedly denounced the Soviet Union as a dangerous threat to world stability and peace and on several occasions expressed hope that China would learn much from U.S. advances in technology. On February 5 Deng flew to Tokyo, for talks with Prime Minister Masayoshi Ohira and other Japanese officials. Before returning to Beijing (Peking) on February 8, Deng reportedly told his hosts that Vietnam would have to be punished for its invasion of Cambodia.

5 *Khomeini defies Bakhtiar by naming Bazargan prime minister*

Ayatollah Khomeini, refusing to compromise with the government of Prime Minister Shahpur Bakhtiar, named Mehdi Bazargan prime minister and head of a provisional government in Iran. The following day Bakhtiar told Parliament that he would remain in office until the next election, even if every member of Parliament resigned.

6 *Congo president resigns*

Gen. Joachim Yhombi-Opango, president of the Congo since April 1977, resigned his position as chief of state but agreed to serve on the Central Committee of the ruling Congolese Labour Party. On February 8 Col. Denis Sassou-Nguesso assumed the presidency.

7 *Bendjedid elected Algerian president*

Col. Chadli Bendjedid, the 49-year-old acting minister of defense, was elected president of Algeria and successor to the late Houari Boumédienne. Bendjedid, who ran unopposed, was assured the presidency at the end of January when the National Liberation Front, the country's only political party, chose him as a compromise candidate.

Ayatollah Ruhollah Khomeini arriving in Teheran after the ouster of the shah.

A.F.P./PICTORIAL PARADE

8 *U.S. withdraws support for Somoza*

The Carter administration announced that it was severing military ties with Nicaragua, cutting back its economic aid to the country, and drastically reducing its personnel in the capital city of Managua. The U.S. hoped that such moves would induce Pres. Anastasio Somoza Debayle to negotiate peace with the Sandinista rebels and thus put an end to bloodshed.

11 *Khomeini supporters oust Bakhtiar and seize control of Iran*

After several days of intense violence that involved civilian guerrillas as well as military units fighting against one another, supporters of Ayatollah Ruhollah Khomeini were assured of victory when the Army declared its neutrality and Prime Minister Shahpur Bakhtiar resigned. Khomeini's exuberant followers created near anarchy in many cities, including Teheran, where they invaded the imperial palace and other important centres and summarily executed some of the high-ranking military officers taken into custody. Flushed with victory, many refused to heed the ayatollah's plea to turn in their weapons. Mehdi Bazargan, named by Khomeini to head a provisional government, sought to restore a semblance of authority by announcing appointments to his Cabinet.

13 *Latin-American bishops end meeting*

The third Latin-American Bishops' Conference ended in Puebla, Mexico, with a plea for an end to poverty, repression, and injustice, all of which were said to be worsening. Priests, teachers, scientists, doctors, and public servants were called upon to help ameliorate the condition of peasants and urban workers whose lives for the most part are "an abomination." The official conference document, following directives laid down by Pope John Paul II when he opened the conference, did not support any specific political party or ideology.

14 *U.S. and Mexican presidents discuss bilateral issues*

President Carter arrived in Mexico to discuss several sensitive issues with Mexican Pres. José López Portillo. López Portillo openly criticized past U.S. policies toward Mexico and the sudden interest it had shown in Mexico following the discovery of huge reserves of oil and natural gas. The Mexican president urged that the search for lasting solutions to fundamental problems avoid anything "that would make us lose the respect of our children." On February 16 it was announced that

WIDE WORLD

Graffito reading "Carter is coming to exchange peanuts for oil" greeted Pres. Jimmy Carter when he arrived in Mexico for talks with Mexican Pres. José López Portillo.

negotiations for the U.S. purchase of natural gas would begin in March. No conclusion was reached on the sale of Mexican oil nor on the delicate question of illegal immigration of Mexicans into the U.S. Agreements, however, were signed on scientific and technological cooperation.

U.S. ambassador assassinated in Afghanistan

The U.S. ambassador to Afghanistan, Adolph Dubs, was shot and killed after being kidnapped in Kabul by Muslim extremists. The four terrorists reportedly demanded the release of several Muslims in government custody. Though it was not clear who fired the shots that killed Dubs, the U.S. condemned Afghanistan for attacking, rather than negotiating with, the kidnappers. The U.S. also expressed shock over the role of Soviet officials who were reported to have provided the Afghans with weapons and allegedly directed the attack itself. On February 22 the U.S. announced that its aid to Afghanistan would be drastically cut through fiscal year 1980.

17 *Chinese troops invade Vietnam*

Several hundred thousand Chinese troops, supported by planes and artillery that had been moved into position over a period of weeks, invaded Vietnam along most of the border separating the two countries. China justified the attack as "punishment" for Vietnam's intrusion into Cambodia and for its alleged violations of Chinese territory. The invasion, China said, would be limited in scope because it did not covet a single inch of Vietnamese territory. Although initial reports indicated that Vietnamese forces were offering much stronger resistance than expected, Chinese troops penetrated 15 mi (24 km) into Vietnam by February 22, the same day a Thai source reported the U.S.S.R. had begun airlifting military supplies to its Vietnamese allies. On February 26 Vietnam acknowledged that Chinese troops were 25 mi (40 km) inside its border; other sources said the Chinese had advanced up to 40 mi (64 km). Although the Soviet Union and most of its supporters condemned only China, Romania said Vietnam shared the blame for having helped to overthrow the Cambodian government. The U.S. urged China to withdraw from Vietnam and Vietnam to withdraw from Cambodia. On February 23 the UN Security Council convened to discuss the matter, but no action was taken because China and the U.S.S.R. held opposite views and each had the power to veto any resolution.

21 *French employment plan proposed*

Robert Fabre, special adviser to the French government on employment, offered a plan that he hoped would ease unemployment by opening up several hundred thousand jobs. The plan included such things as reduction of the workweek, retirement after 37.5 years of work, new work projects, temporary subsidies to companies having difficulties, and a prohibition against pensioners holding jobs. Finances to support the plan would come in part from new taxes on the rich and a crackdown on tax evaders.

23 *Greece imposes limit on prices*

Pres. Konstantinos Tsatsos of Greece, hoping to curtail the nation's inflation, signed a decree authorizing the imposition of heavy fines on anyone found exceeding price levels reached at the end of 1978. Limits were also expected to be placed on wage increases, on certain profits, on some incomes, and on a variety of other things that influence the rate of inflation.

24 *Fighting erupts along Yemen border*

Yemen (San'a'; North Yemen) and Yemen (Aden; South Yemen) exchanged accusations when fighting erupted along their common border. The next day in Cairo the foreign minister of North Yemen requested the president of the Arab League to call a meeting so that a fact-finding mission could verify the "flagrant invasion" of North Yemen's territory by pro-Soviet South Yemen troops. On February 26 South Yemen reported the capture of Harib, the only major border settlement in North Yemen not already occupied by South Yemen forces. On February 28 Saudi Arabia, which shares a border with North Yemen, placed its troops on alert. Fearful that the fighting might spread to other parts of the Arabian Peninsula, Saudi Arabia also recalled its troops serving with an Arab League contingent in Lebanon and requested the Arab League to take steps to end the conflict. Both Yemens finally agreed to settle their dispute through mediation.

25 *Turkey extends martial law*

The Turkish Parliament voted 337–225 to extend martial law for an additional two months. The motion was supported by all but the Justice Party, which constituted the main opposition to the government of Prime Minister Bulent Ecevit. Most members of Parliament agreed that even though political and religious violence had not ceased, it had decreased since martial law was first declared in December 1978.

28 *Era ends for Rhodesian Parliament*

Rhodesia's Parliament adjourned after its final session as the legislative body of a government controlled by the country's white minority. A new Parliament having a majority of black members would be selected in April in a general election.

Bazargan assails Khomeini Council

Iranian Prime Minister Mehdi Bazargan threatened to resign unless the Revolutionary Council of Ayatollah Khomeini ceased usurping powers belonging to the provisional government. Bazargan vented his frustrations during a broadcast when he noted that people acting in Khomeini's name were not only operating independently of the established government but in some cases were actively interfering in government affairs.

MARCH

1 *Sadat warns local Muslim extremists*

During a speech at Alexandria University, a stronghold of fundamentalist Islam, Egyptian Pres. Anwar as-Sadat warned that he would not permit religion to be injected into Egyptian politics. He was especially critical of the outlawed but still active Muslim Brotherhood. Sadat said the Brotherhood had "changed from a religious organization to an underground terrorist organization."

Spain votes for parliament

The Unión Centro Democrático (UCD), headed by Premier Adolfo Suárez González, was victorious in the first parliamentary elections held since the adoption of a new constitution in December 1978. In the Congress of Deputies, the 350-seat lower house, the UCD won 168 seats, while the Partido Socialista Ohrero Español (PSOE) was second with 121. Though eight seats short of an absolute majority, the UCD was assured of four more years in office as head of a coalition government. In the Senate it held 120 of 208 seats, compared with 68 secured by the PSOE.

Wales and Scotland reject devolution

In a national referendum, Welsh voters overwhelmingly rejected devolution (home rule); in Scotland 52% of those who voted approved the measure, but the total represented less than one-third of the total electorate, far less than the 40% needed for passage. Some negative votes were cast by those advocating total independence. The results were a significant political setback for British Prime Minister James Callaghan, who had strongly backed the proposal.

5 *Iran resumes oil exports*

After an interruption of 69 days, Iran resumed exportation of crude oil. The chairman of the National Iranian Oil Company used the occasion to announce that Iran would henceforth limit its exports to between one-half and one-third of the level before the revolution.

Voyager 1 relays data on Jupiter

The U.S. Voyager 1 spacecraft relayed a wealth of information after it came within some 276,000 km (172,500 mi) of Jupiter, the largest planet in our solar system. The data included sharp photographs of Jupiter's four largest moons: Io, Europa, Ganymede, and Callisto.

Chinese troops to leave Vietnam

China announced that it had "attained the goals" it set for itself when it invaded Vietnam on February 17 and would immediately begin to withdraw its troops. On March 15 China reported it had completed the pullout.

J. C. CRITON—SYGMA

After a peace agreement was worked out in Chad, warring factions agreed to end hostilities and to establish a coalition government.

7 *Full details of South African scandal to remain secret*

Eschel Rhoodie, the former head of South Africa's disbanded Department of Information, met with former secret police chief Gen. Hendrik van den Bergh in Paris and reportedly agreed to withhold further details of an influence-buying scheme allegedly involving Pres. B. J. Vorster and other high government officials. In exchange for his silence, Rhoodie would receive a large sum of money and guaranteed employment overseas. Rhoodie had accused government officials of sanctioning efforts to bribe, if necessary, foreign legislators, businessmen, and journalists to induce them to promote South African interests. Rhoodie also accused government officials of illegally funding a pro-apartheid South African newspaper and of backing efforts to buy the U.S. newspaper the *Washington* (D.C.) *Star*. Vorster denied any part in the schemes and said Cornelius Mulder, the former information minister and Rhoodie's superior, was responsible for whatever had happened.

12 *Venezuela's new president sworn in*

Luis Herrera Campins of the Social Christian Party (COPEI) was inaugurated as president of Venezuela. In a national election held in December 1978 he had defeated Luis Piñerúa Ordaz, candidate of the ruling Acción Democrática.

13 *Common Market inaugurates new monetary system*

The new European Monetary System (EMS) was officially inaugurated by nations belonging to the European Economic Community. Greater monetary stability was expected once all the Common Market currencies, except that of Great Britain, were linked together to prevent any one currency from rising or falling in value beyond certain limits in respect to the other currencies.

Gairy ousted in Grenada coup

Sir Eric Gairy, who had left for New York on March 12, was ousted as prime minister of Grenada in a predawn coup carried out by members of the New Jewel Movement. Maurice Bishop, leader of the New Jewel Movement, promised to restore all democratic freedoms and to respect personal property. Bishop also requested Gairy's extradition so he could stand trial for murder, fraud, and violations of the democratic rights of the people.

14 *Korean talks remain deadlocked*

Delegates from North and South Korea met in Panmunjom in their third attempt since January to initiate talks on reunification and other issues. Progress was again impeded by a dispute over the makeup of the official delegations. South Korea refused to accept the Democratic

Front for Reunification of the Fatherland as a legitimate representative of North Korea; for its part, North Korea would not permit a resumption of talks by the South-North Coordinating Committee (SNCC), although it had been authorized by both sides in November 1972. Three plenary meetings, followed by ten meetings conducted by vice chairmen, had taken place under the auspices of the SNCC from 1972 to 1975. North Korea insisted that the SNCC had gone out of existence when talks broke off four years earlier.

15 *Brazilian president assumes office*

Gen. João Baptista da Figueiredo assumed the office of president of Brazil and promised freedom of expression within "a process free from influences that may distort it and jeopardize its representativeness." Among problems confronting Figueiredo were inflation, a huge foreign debt, underproductive agriculture, and an unequal distribution of wealth.

Pact ends civil war in Chad

Pres. Félix Malloum, Premier Hissen Habré, and the leaders of two factions of Frolinat, a group of Muslim guerrillas, signed an agreement in Kano, Nigeria, that called for an end to hostilities and the formation of a coalition government representing all parties in the civil war. On March 20 France announced it was withdrawing the 2,500 troops that had been supporting the president.

16 *Khomeini calls halt to executions*

Ayatollah Ruhollah Khomeini ordered a halt to the secret trials and summary executions that were being carried out by his Revolutionary Council over the strong protests of Prime Minister Mehdi Bazargan. Bazargan, who described the executions as irreligious, inhuman, disgraceful, and an embarrassment to his government, had tendered his resignation on March 8, but Khomeini had refused to accept it.

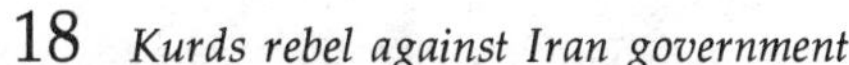

18 *Kurds rebel against Iran government*

Kurdish tribesmen in Iran's northwestern city of Sanandaj attacked the army barracks after one of their members was killed during a demonstration protesting a lack of arms with which to patrol the area. The Kurds also charged that as members of the Sunni sect of Islam they were discriminated against by the majority Shi'ites. On March 25 the government sought to defuse the long smouldering resentment by naming a Kurd governor-general of Kurdistan and by granting limited autonomy to the region. This included the right to operate Kurdish-language schools and maintain security forces.

22 *U.K. envoy slain in The Netherlands*

The British ambassador to The Netherlands, Sir Richard Sykes, was shot and killed by two unknown assassins as he left his residence in The Hague. There was no obvious motive for the killing, but the Provisional Irish Republican Army (IRA) was suspected of involvement. Before assuming his post in The Netherlands, Sykes had been sent to Ireland to investigate the slaying there of Great Britain's ambassador. The Provisional IRA had claimed responsibility for that death.

23 *Paris demonstration ends in riot*

After tens of thousands of demonstrators completed a peaceful march in Paris protesting growing unemployment and impending layoffs in steel plants, a group of more than 100 radicals wearing protective helmets and apparently unconnected with the march began smashing up stores and cafes. They also challenged the police with gasoline bombs and stones. The Independent Fighting Brigades for Popular Autonomy, a little-known radical group, later claimed credit for the violence.

26 *Egypt and Israel sign peace treaty*

Egyptian Pres. Anwar as-Sadat and Israeli Prime Minister Menahem Begin signed a formal peace treaty during a ceremony on the lawn of the White House in Washington, D.C. President Carter, who was extravagantly praised by both leaders for helping to work out the historic agreement, also signed the Arabic, Hebrew, and English versions of the treaty as a witness. Sadat's speech included a plea for an end to war and bloodshed, an end to suffering and denial of rights, and an end to despair and loss of faith. Begin called the signing of the treaty "a great day in the annals of two ancient nations." Among other things, the treaty called for the gradual withdrawal of Israeli troops from the Sinai Peninsula and the abandonment of Israel's civilian settlements there, the deployment of UN forces along border areas, the establishment of diplomatic relations between the two countries, freedom of passage through the Suez Canal, the purchase of Sinai oil by Israel, and negotiations to settle the delicate issue of Palestinian self-rule in the Israeli-occupied West Bank and Gaza Strip areas.

Canadian Parliament dissolved

Canadian Prime Minister Pierre Elliott Trudeau asked the governor-general to dissolve Parliament and set May 22 as the date for national elections. His five-year term was due to expire in less than four months. Trudeau, a Liberal, was under fire because of Canada's economic difficulties and the separatist movement in Quebec. A strong challenge was expected to come from the Progressive Conservatives, led by Joe Clark.

27 *OPEC again raises oil prices*

During a meeting in Geneva, the 13 member nations of the Organization of Petroleum Exporting Countries (OPEC) agreed to increase the basic price of oil by what they termed a "moderate and modest" 9% to $14.55 per barrel. According to a price-rise schedule worked out by OPEC in December 1978, the increase on April 1 was to have been 3.8%. OPEC nations would also be permitted to add any surcharges that seemed "justifiable in the light of their own circumstances." After the meeting concluded, Algeria, Libya, and Nigeria announced they would impose a surcharge of $4 per barrel. The OPEC ministers accused oil companies of reaping unjustified windfall profits and urged all countries that imported oil to control the prices charged by such oil companies. Western Europe concurred with the U.S. that the OPEC price increase was "untimely and unjustified."

28 *Accident occurs at U.S. nuclear plant*

A major nuclear accident occurred near Harrisburg, Pa., when the cooling system of the No. 2 reactor at the Three Mile Island nuclear power plant malfunctioned. On March 30 the Nuclear Regulatory Commission (NRC) warned that a meltdown of the reactor core was still a

WIDE WORLD

Egyptian Pres. Anwar as-Sadat, U.S. Pres. Jimmy Carter, and Israeli Prime Minister Menahem Begin stood at attention to listen to the anthems of their three countries at a peace treaty signing ceremony in Washington on March 26.

possibility. If it had happened, the results would have been catastrophic. As a precautionary measure, the governor of Pennsylvania advised two days later that pregnant women and preschool children be moved five miles from the plant to avoid the escaping radioactive gases. Meanwhile, nuclear safety experts, unsure of what had happened, worked to cool down the nuclear fuel and reduce the size of a potentially dangerous hydrogen bubble that had formed inside the reactor. By April 2 the situation had stabilized and the hydrogen bubble had shrunk dramatically. On April 9 Harold Denton, NRC director of nuclear reactor regulation, announced that the crisis was over. The accident intensified the debate on the safety of all 72 U.S. nuclear reactors, which at the time provided 13% of the nation's electrical power. The problem of safety was crucial, because in some areas of the country nuclear power accounted for more than half of all electricity generated. A definitive explanation of the accident and recommendations for the future would not be forthcoming until a thorough study of the reactor and plant procedures was completed.

British Labour government falls

For the first time in 55 years, the British House of Commons voted "no confidence in Her Majesty's government." Since neither the ruling Labour Party nor the Conservatives had an absolute majority in the Commons, minority parties played a crucial role in the final 311–310 vote. The next day Prime Minister James Callaghan announced that Parliament would be dissolved on April 7 and that national elections would take place on May 3.

30 *Verdet replaces Manescu in Romania*

Ilie Verdet, first deputy premier and chairman of Romania's state planning commission, replaced Manea Manescu as chairman of the Council of Ministers, the equivalent of premier. The change was reportedly part of Pres. Nicolae Ceausescu's continuing effort to improve the nation's economic health.

31 *Arab League denounces Egypt*

Representatives from 18 Arab League nations and the Palestine Liberation Organization (PLO) agreed at a meeting in Baghdad, Iraq, to impose sanctions on Egypt for concluding a peace treaty with Israel. On March 28 Syria, Libya, and the PLO walked out of the conference when it appeared that other nations were unwilling to take drastic measures against Egypt. Among other things, all finally agreed to a complete economic boycott of Egypt and the severance of diplomatic relations. Anticipating such actions, Egypt suspended relations with the Arab League on March 27.

APRIL

1 *Chinese activists decry government restrictions on criticism*

A mimeographed document circulated in Beijing (Peking) denounced China's rulers for repressing criticism of government policies. It also proclaimed "to the whole world that the Chinese government does not want any true democratic freedoms." On March 18 an editorial in the *Renmin Ribao* (*Jen-min jih-pao*) reported that First Vice-Premier Deng Xiaoping (Teng Hsiao-p'ing), during an address to Communist Party officials on March 16, had denounced those who through posters or through letters to President Carter and the U.S. ambassador accused China of violating human rights. The editorial warned that such persons would not be treated gently. On March 29 the Beijing Revolutionary Committee ordered the removal of posters from the centre of the city and served notice that antigovernment or anti-Communist rallies and publications would not be tolerated. Though wall posters would still be permitted at designated spots, the protestors wanted wider dissemination of their grievances. On April 4 police arrested four members of the Human Rights Alliance as they attempted to put up posters. The posters that appeared in Shanghai on April 15 were reportedly left untouched by local authorities.

2 *Vorster cleared in South African influence-buying scandal*

A committee headed by Judge Rudolf Erasmus completed its investigation and issued a report exonerating South African Pres. B. J. Vorster of charges first leveled against him by Eschel Rhoodie, former head of the government's Department of Information. Vorster was accused of involvement in an illegal scheme to bribe, if necessary, foreigners who were in a position to promote South African interests. The report also concluded that no current member of the Cabinet was involved in a cover-up. The report did not deny that the Department of Information had given money to the *Citizen*, a pro-apartheid newspaper, or that it had offered to help purchase the *Washington* (D.C.) *Star*. On April 6 Cornelius Mulder, the former minister of information, was expelled from the ruling National Party when he refused to endorse the Erasmus report and accept full responsibility for the affair.

3 *Belgian political crisis ends*

A government crisis that had lasted nearly six months was ended when King Baudouin I of Belgium announced that Wilfried Martens, chairman of the Flemish Social Christian Party, would become prime minister and the head of a five-party coalition government. Paul Vanden Boeynants, whose government resigned after an inconclusive election on Dec. 17, 1978, remained in the government as deputy prime minister. Other members of the coalition were the French-speaking Social Christian party, both the Flemish- and French speaking Belgian Socialist parties, and the Front Démocratique des Francophones.

4 *Bhutto hanged in Pakistan*

Former Pakistani prime minister Zulfikar Ali Bhutto was hanged in a Rawalpindi prison on charges of having conspired to murder a political opponent in 1974. Immediately after the predawn execution, Bhutto's body was spirited out of the prison and flown to his home province of Sind for burial. Pres. Mohammad Zia-ul-Haq rejected local and international pleas for clemency after Bhutto's lawyers failed to persuade the Supreme Court to review its February decision upholding the death sentence. On April 5 violence erupted in various cities throughout Pakistan as pro-Bhutto demonstrators set vehicles afire and fought police. Hundreds of persons were reported arrested.

5 *Carter decontrols U.S. oil prices*

In a nationwide television address, President Carter announced that he would decontrol prices for domestic oil in two stages. On June 1 controls on the price of oil from 80% of the nation's marginally productive wells would be removed; controls on the other 20% would be lifted one year later. Carter then called on Congress to tax "the unearned billions of dollars" that oil companies would reap as windfall profits. He urged that the money be used to help poor families meet rising fuel bills, to finance public transportation projects, and to underwrite the cost of research for alternative sources of energy.

11 *Capital of Uganda captured*

Kampala, the capital of Uganda, was captured by troops consisting of some 5,000 Tanzanians and 3,000 Ugandans. Other exiled Ugandans living in Tanzania immediately announced the formation of a provisional government with 67-year-old Yusufu Lule heading a 14-member Cabinet. In a radiobroadcast, deposed president Idi Amin, who had ruled the country for eight years, said his troops still controlled 90% of Uganda's territory. Many observers were skeptical of the claim and believed that Amin's army was in total disarray following the withdrawal of Libyan forces a few days earlier. Libyan

YVES-GUY BERGES—SYGMA

A slashed and mutilated portrait of former president Idi Amin lies amid the rubble after the Ugandan dictator was overthrown.

leader Muammar al-Qaddafi denied that any of his troops were present in Uganda, but on March 27 he threatened to invade Tanzania unless its soldiers pulled out of Uganda. On April 13 Lule was sworn in as the new president of Uganda.

12 *Trade accord initialed in Geneva*

A comprehensive international trade agreement was initialed in Geneva after five and one-half years of negotiations. The trade conference was another in a series that began in 1947 when the initial General Agreement on Tariffs and Trade (GATT) was formulated in Geneva. A total of 99 nations took part in the latest discussions, but most less developed nations boycotted the signing ceremony because, they charged, the special concessions promised to them in the 1973 Japan Declaration had failed to materialize. Olivier Long, director general of GATT, expressed hope that the new bilateral agreements would "lead to more optimism in business circles about the prospects for continued growth in world trade." On the average, tariffs would be reduced about one-third, but the actual percentage rate of decrease would vary from country to country and from item to item. Most provisions of the agreement would go into effect in January 1980 if the U.S. Congress and other national legislatures approved the pact before that date.

14 *Liberians riot over food prices*

In Monrovia, the capital of Liberia, a demonstration to protest a substantial increase in the price of rice turned into a violent confrontation with the military. As the riot developed, rampaging youths ransacked stores and caused millions of dollars in property damage. Hundreds were reported injured and more than 40 killed. On April 24 the Liberian congress granted Pres. William R. Tolbert, Jr., emergency powers for one year so that persons suspected "of undermining the security of the state" could be detained without trial for 30 days. Tolbert also closed the University of Liberia, which he characterized as a "breeding ground of revolutionary ideas"; he also expelled three members of the Soviet embassy.

18 *China and Vietnam meet in Hanoi*

Chinese and Vietnamese representatives met in Hanoi in an attempt to reconcile differences aggravated by Vietnam's intrusion into Cambodia and China's subsequent invasion of Vietnam. Though Vietnam's deputy foreign minister offered a three-point peace plan, nothing was settled. At a second meeting on April 26 China's deputy foreign minister rejected Vietnam's plan and suggested a ten-point plan of his own. After the two delegations had exchanged recriminations, the parley ended in a deadlock with no immediate prospects that relations between the two Communist nations would soon be normalized.

20 *Palace of Senators bombed in Rome*

A large bomb containing an estimated 4 kg (8.8 lb) of high explosives went off outside Rome's Palace of the Senators on Capitoline Hill. Two groups claimed responsibility for the blast: a neo-Fascist organization that went by the name Armed Revolutionary Cells and a previously unknown group that called itself the Italian Popular Movement. Damage to the historic palace, which had been rebuilt centuries ago according to plans drawn up by Michelangelo, together with damage inflicted on two adjacent structures—the Capitoline Museum and the Palace of the Conservators—was estimated to be in excess of $1 million.

21 *Muzorewa wins Rhodesia election*

In the first universal suffrage elections since Rhodesia proclaimed its independence from Britain in 1965, Methodist Bishop Abel Muzorewa's United African National Council won 51 of the 100 parliamentary seats. According to official reports, 63.9% of the electorate cast ballots during the five-day election. The Rev. Ndabaningi Sithole, whose Zimbabwe African National Union finished second with 12 seats, first acknowledged that the election was "free and fair" but later charged that the voting was replete with "gross irregularities." The United National Federal Party won nine seats; the remaining 28 seats were reserved for whites. After the results were officially announced on April 24, Muzorewa made an impassioned appeal for international recognition of the new government.

23 *Argentina arrests labour leaders*

Argentina's military junta averted a major strike scheduled for April 27 by arresting 20 of the country's most influential labour leaders. The men were first called by the Ministry of Labour to a meeting, during which they admitted violating the government ban on union activities. At the end of the meeting all were taken into police custody. The strike had been called, among other reasons, to protest the government's ban on labour unions and the inadequacy of the 4% monthly increase in wages. The 1978 inflation rate

The blacks of Rhodesia lined up to vote, many of them for the first time in their lives, in elections held April 17–21.

MAGGIE STEBER—SIPA PRESS/BLACK STAR

was 170%, and the rate for the current year was expected to top 100%. Nine of the 20 arrested leaders were released by April 27 after it became clear that the call for a strike would go unheeded.

24 *Cambodians pour into Thailand*

An estimated 50,000 to 80,000 Cambodian civilian refugees and soldiers were reported to have crossed the border into Thailand between April 21 and April 24 to escape a Vietnamese-led assault. Thai officials, who had ordered the forceful repatriation of some 6,000 Cambodians on April 19, reported April 29 that most of the newly arrived Cambodians had already left Thailand in accordance with government policy that denied permanent sanctuary to the neighbouring Cambodians. Officials, who denied that the granting of temporary asylum compromised Thai neutrality, said there was no effective way to prevent the influx and noted that Cambodians were not allowed to use their weapons while in Thailand.

27 *U.S. exchanges two Soviet spies for five dissidents in U.S.S.R.*

Five leading dissidents from the U.S.S.R. were exchanged at Kennedy International Airport in New York City for two Soviet citizens convicted in October 1978 of espionage in the U.S. The dissidents were Aleksandr Ginzburg, Valentin Moroz, Georgy Vins, Mark Dymshits, and Eduard Kuznetsov. Only the latter two were Jewish activists. The two Soviet spies, Valdik Enger and Rudolf Chernyaev, were employed at the United Nations at the time of their arrest.

Indonesia releases more prisoners

The Indonesian government released 1,259 political prisoners, the first of 9,562 such persons scheduled to be set free before the end of the year. According to some observers, this would leave about 2,500 behind bars. About 10,000 reportedly had been released in 1978 and an equal number during the previous year. Following an abortive coup in 1965, nearly 575,000 alleged Communists and Communist sympathizers had been rounded up and herded into camps, but of that number only about 800 were eventually charged with specific offenses and put on trial. Most were simply detained for years without being charged or sentenced.

29 *Ecuador elects new president*

Jaime Roldós Aguilera, the 38-year-old candidate of the Concentración de Fuerzas Populares party, was elected president of Ecuador. He defeated Sixto Durán Ballén Cordovez of the Frente Nacional Constitucionalista, who was unofficially supported by the ruling military junta. To allay any fears about the future, the minister of government announced that Roldós would be inaugurated in August because the armed forces were "absolutely determined" to see democracy reestablished in Ecuador. Osvaldo Hurtado Larrea, the newly elected vice-president, would have responsibility for implementing a new economic policy aimed at helping the large number of poor who had benefited very little from Ecuador's booming oil profits.

30 *UN repudiates Rhodesian election*

The UN Security Council voted 12–0 for a resolution condemning the recent election in Rhodesia. It then called upon member nations to continue their economic boycott of Rhodesia. France, the U.K., and the U.S. did not vote. The U.S. had not yet decided on the fairness of the election and still had hopes that the new government in Rhodesia, headed by Bishop Abel Muzorewa, could be persuaded to negotiate with the Patriotic Front guerrilla forces under the leadership of Joshua Nkomo and Robert Mugabe.

MAY

1 *Bombings continue to rock France*

A series of night explosions caused extensive damage but no casualties in the metropolitan area of Paris. The targets included police stations, a Rothschild bank, the headquarters of the French Employers' Federation, and an office of the Union pour la Démocratie Française, the political party of Pres. Valéry Giscard d'Estaing. Several obscure organizations claimed credit for the bombings. A few days earlier similar violence reportedly occurred in southwest France and on the French island of Corsica. About the same time, the office of the Paris newspaper *Le Monde* was also bombed. On May 6, the third anniversary of the Corsican National Liberation Front (CNLF), Corsica was rocked by 27 bombings. The CNLF, an outlawed organization, claimed responsibility for 22 other explosions that were set off in Paris on May 31.

2 *Ohira and Carter issue communiqué*

Japanese Prime Minister Masayoshi Ohira and President Carter issued a joint communiqué in Washington, D.C., that included a pledge to strive for a "more harmonious pattern of international trade and payments" during the next several years. To help reduce its huge trade surplus, Japan promised to increase its U.S. imports, especially of manufactured goods. The U.S. reiterated its determination to control domestic inflation in order to strengthen its position in international trade. The two leaders also concurred that the U.S. military presence in South Korea was an important factor in preserving stability in the region. Carter and Ohira also agreed in writing that their nations would cooperate during the next decade in research on new energy technology that would give priority to magnetic fusion and the liquefaction of coal.

3 *Thatcher wins British election*

Margaret Thatcher became the first female prime minister in Great Britain's history when the Conservative Party (Tories) that she headed soundly defeated the ruling Labour Party in the parliamentary elections. The Conservatives captured 339 seats (an increase of 55) in the 635-seat House of Commons; Labour Party candidates won 268 seats (a decrease of 40). The election gave the Conservatives an absolute majority in Parliament and brought to an end the Labour government of James Callaghan. Other parties represented in the new Parliament included the Liberals (11), Northern Ireland Catholics (2), Scottish nationalists (2), and Welsh nationalists (2). A nonpartisan speaker of the House holds the other seat. On May 4 Queen Elizabeth II accepted Callaghan's resignation at Buckingham Palace and requested 53-year-old Thatcher to form a new government. During the campaign, Callaghan pleaded for a continuation of his policies which, he claimed, had reduced inflation. Thatcher promised voters greater control over trade unions, major tax cuts, and less government involvement in business and in the lives of individuals.

Headquarters of Christian Democrats bombed in Rome

One policeman was killed and two others were seriously injured when two floors of the Rome headquarters of the ruling Christian Democrats were destroyed by bombs. After handcuffing two police guards, the terrorists entered the building about 9:30 AM and spray-painted the walls with the initials and the five-pointed star of the Red Brigades. Office workers were handcuffed, but they were led outside before the explosions occurred. The terrorists, who numbered between 10 and 15, alluded to the early June parliamentary elections in a painted warning that read: "We will transform the fraudulent elections into a real class war." Former president Giuseppe Saragat declared: "Political terrorism is turning into a full-scale civil war and must be confronted not only by the police but also by the armed forces of the republic." When the revolutionaries withdrew from the building, they were covered by other terrorists who fired automatic weapons as all made their escape.

CENTRAL PRESS/PICTORIAL PARADE

Margaret Thatcher became the first woman to be Britain's prime minister when her Conservative Party was swept into power in the May 3 election.

6 *Socialists retain power in Austria*

Austrian Chancellor Bruno Kreisky was assured of an unprecedented fourth term when the Socialist Party gained two seats in the parliamentary elections for a new total of 95. The People's Party, led by Josef Taus, won 77 seats, 3 less than they held before the voting. The remaining 11 seats in the 183-seat National Council were won by the Freedom Party. Many observers felt that the 68-year-old chancellor's victory was mainly attributable to Austria's economic prosperity. Inflation stood at 3.5% and unemployment at 2.2%.

8 *Violence grips El Salvador*

A reported 23 persons were killed and 70 wounded outside the municipal cathedral of San Salvador, the capital of El Salvador, when police opened fire on supporters of the Popular Revolutionary Bloc (BPR)—a coalition of antigovernment students, teachers, peasants, and workers. Four days earlier the BPR occupied the cathedral and seized the French and Costa Rican embassies; both ambassadors and members of their staffs were taken hostage. The rebels then demanded that police release five ranking members of the BPR. They also reiterated long standing demands for fundamental social reforms. On May 8, as 100 or so supporters of the BPR apparently sought refuge inside the cathedral, 23 were shot and killed by the police. On May 11 the government released two members of the BPR but disclaimed any knowledge of the other three. The BPR reacted angrily by taking over the Venezuelan embassy. Despite a wave of peaceful sympathy strikes and a plea from the Roman Catholic archbishop to free the three other BPR leaders, Pres. Carlos Humberto Romero refused. On May 18 Romero called for a national forum to discuss ways to end the violence, but most antigovernment factions ignored the invitation. On May 21, after BPR leftists inside the Venezuelan embassy refused to leave or accept safe passage out of the country, the government cut off their food, water, and electricity. The next day 14 pro-BPR demonstrators were shot to death as they attempted to bring food and water to the beleaguered rebels. The Popular Liberation Forces, a guerrilla organization, responded to these killings by assassinating the minister of education. On May 24 the president declared a 30-day state of siege, suspended the constitution, and convoked a peace forum that was boycotted by major opposition groups, including church leaders and most labour unions. On May 25, under threat of being forcefully removed by police, the BPR peacefully left the cathedral.

9 *U.S. and U.S.S.R. complete SALT II*

The U.S. announced that, after seven years of negotiations, a new draft treaty limiting strategic arms had finally been completed by representatives of the U.S. and the Soviet Union. Though the exact wording of the accord would still have to be worked out by negotiating teams in Geneva, the SALT II treaty went beyond the SALT I agreement, which was signed in 1972 and expired in 1977. If and when SALT II was formally signed by the U.S. and the U.S.S.R. and ratified by the U.S. Senate , negotiations for a SALT III agreement would get under way. Though Carter declared that SALT II would "lessen the danger of nuclear destruction, while safeguarding our military security in a more stable, predictable and peaceful world," it was certain that the U.S. Congress would debate the provisions of the treaty with great intensity before the Senate vote on ratification.

11 *Students sentenced in South Africa*

Four of 11 black students on trial in South Africa were sentenced to serve prison terms for their reputed roles in the 1976 riots in Soweto, the main black township outside Johannesburg. On April 30 a judge of the Transvaal Supreme Court had found the students guilty of sedition because they "knew that to organize a gathering in [Soweto] would provoke a confrontation with the police and therefore it is seditious." Daniel Sechaba Montsitsi, leader of the Soweto Students Representative Council, received the heaviest sentence: four years in prison and an additional four years that were suspended. The seven who were released from custody were given suspended five-year sentences.

16 *ASEAN confronts refugee problem*

A two-day international conference on Indochinese refugees concluded in Jakarta, Indonesia, with only modest steps being taken to resolve the growing crisis. The meeting was sponsored by Indonesia, Malaysia, the Philippines, Singapore, and Thailand—the five countries comprising the Association of Southeast Asian Nations (ASEAN)—but the UN High Commissioner for Refugees and delegates from 19 other countries also participated. The refugee problem in Southeast Asia had reached staggering proportions because tens of thousands of refugees were seeking asylum in countries that could not permanently support them. During the two-week period preceding the conference, some 9,000 Vietnamese refugees arrived in Malaysia, some 7,000 in Indonesia, and another 7,000 in Hong Kong. Thailand reportedly continued to receive about 7,000 Laotian refugees each month in addition to 1,000 boat people from Vietnam. More than 25,000 refugees had already been granted permanent residence in Hong Kong and Macau, but Hong Kong authorities reported that more than 35,000 refugees actually landed in the crown colony during the first three months of 1979. On April 25 the General Accounting Office of the U.S. Congress reported that 219,000 Vietnamese, Cambodians, and Laotians were living in Asian refugee camps. Of this number about 147,000 were in Thailand and 51,000 in Malaysia. Thousands upon thousands of others had drowned at sea. A Vietnamese official said during the conference that between 400,000 and 600,000 people in southern Vietnam wanted to leave the country and would be permitted to go when other nations signified a willingness to accept them. Most were ethnic Chinese. While acknowledging the magnitude and complexity of the problem, the conference delegates agreed to accept refugees destined for resettlement elsewhere. Indonesia and the Philippines each designated a small island for this purpose.

22 *Joe Clark replaces Pierre Trudeau as prime minister of Canada*

The Progressive Conservatives (PC), led by 39-year-old Joe Clark, won a plurality, but not an absolute majority, in Canada's

282-seat Parliament, thereby ending the 11-year rule of Prime Minister Pierre Trudeau and the Liberals. The PC gained 38 seats for a new total of 136; the Liberals' loss of 19 seats reduced their total to 114. The New Democratic Party increased its representation from 17 to 26 seats, while the Social Credit Party won 6 seats, 3 less than it held in the previous Parliament. The Liberals captured 40% of the popular vote, compared with 36% by the PC. Joe Clark, the youngest prime minister in Canadian history and the first PC head of government since 1963, campaigned mostly on the need for change. His promises included a reduction in taxes for corporations and individuals, and close cooperation with provincial premiers on constitutional reforms.

25 *Chicago air crash kills 274*

All 272 persons aboard an American Airlines DC-10 jetliner were instantly killed when the plane lost an engine during takeoff and crashed moments later at Chicago's O'Hare International Airport. Two persons on the ground also lost their lives. On May 29 the Federal Aviation Administration grounded all DC-10s operated by U.S. carriers until the engine-mounting bolts could be inspected. DC-10s operated by foreign nations would not be granted landing rights in the U.S. until inspections were satisfactorily completed. The crash was the worst air disaster in U.S. history.

26 *Talks between Common Market and less developed nations falter*

Talks between the European Economic Community (EEC) and 57 less developed nations from Africa, the Caribbean, and the Pacific area (ACP nations) ended in Lomé, the capital of Togo, without agreement on a new five-year assistance program. The original Lomé Convention, which covered the years 1975–80, permitted many ACP goods free entry into EEC markets and guaranteed purchase of a minimum quantity of ACP sugar at fixed prices. The ACP nations wanted guaranteed earnings on more export items and special concessions on mineral exports. They also insisted that anything less than $9,750,000,000 in aid was unacceptable. The EEC had offered $6.7 billion in addition to $1.6 billion for price supports and food programs.

New government named in Finland

Finnish Pres. Urho K. Kekkonen named Social Democrat Mauno Koivisto prime minister to replace Kalevi Sorsa, who had headed a five-party coalition government since May 1977. After the March 18–19 elections, Sorsa had remained on as caretaker until Kekkonen named a successor. The new four-party coalition controlled 133 seats in the 200-seat unicameral Parliament and, except for the Liberals, included the same parties as the previous government: Social Democrats, the Centre Party, the Swedish People's Party, and the Communist-dominated Finnish People's Democratic League. Koivisto, indicated that employment, tax relief, and constitutional reforms to facilitate the passage of economic legislation would be given high priority in his planning.

28 *Andean Group marks anniversary*

Bolivia, Colombia, Ecuador, Peru, and Venezuela—the five nations comprising the Andean Group—marked the tenth anniversary of their alliance during a meeting in Cartagena, Colombia. The five nations created a court of justice, agreed that Venezuela would be the area's major producer of steel, planned to strengthen both the Andean Development Corporation and the Latin American Free Trade Association, and appointed Colombian Pres. Julio César Turbay Ayala to represent them in negotiations with the European Economic Community.

Greece admitted to Common Market

Greek Prime Minister Konstantinos Karamanlis and representatives of the European Economic Community (EEC) signed documents in Athens that formally admitted Greece to membership in the Common Market. When Greece's participation became active on Jan. 1, 1981, it would have five years to readjust its tariffs and meet other EEC requirements.

31 *Muzorewa heads new government of Zimbabwe Rhodesia*

A black-dominated government, with Bishop Abel Muzorewa as prime minister, officially assumed power at midnight in Rhodesia, which at the same hour changed its name to Zimbabwe Rhodesia. The newly adopted constitution gave blacks a majority in the Cabinet for the first time. Muzorewa, who was sworn in on May 29, urged everyone to work tirelessly for a national unity that would be "the envy of the whole world." As expected, former prime minister Ian Smith was one of the five whites named to the 17-member Cabinet. However, as minister without portfolio his influence was greatly diminished. Two Cabinet posts were given to members of the Zimbabwe African National Union even though its leader, the Rev. Ndabaningi Sithole, refused to accept a Cabinet appointment or serve in Parliament. Shortly after losing the April election to Muzorewa, Sithole had reversed his original stand and denounced the election as fraudulent.

NATO approves SALT II agreement

All 15 member nations of the North Atlantic Treaty Organization (NATO) endorsed the draft version of SALT II, the strategic arms limitation treaty recently completed by U.S. and U.S.S.R. negotiators. The NATO defense ministers had earlier warned that a rejection of the treaty by the U.S. Senate would be disastrous. During their annual meeting in The Hague, the NATO foreign ministers were especially concerned about future SALT negotiations, which they hoped would result in new limits on intermediate-range nuclear missiles.

JUNE

3 *President of Mauritania resigns*

The government of Mauritania announced the resignation of Lieut. Col. Mustafa Ould Salek as head of the Military Committee for National Recovery. Ould Salek, who assumed power following a coup in July 1978, stepped down for "personal reasons." He had been severely criticized for not ending Mauritania's military involvement in the Western Sahara.

4 *Vorster resigns over role in scandal*

South African Pres. B. J. Vorster was forced to resign when a government commission reversed its decision of April 2 and declared that Vorster "knew everything" about the financial irregularities that had occurred in the government's Department of Information. The commission, headed by Judge Rudolf Erasmus, concluded that Vorster was not only consulted about secret funds that were to be used illegally to bolster South Africa's image overseas but that he deliberately concealed the affair from members of the Cabinet. Vorster had held the post of prime minister from 1966 until his resignation in September 1978, when he became president. On June 19 Vorster was succeeded as state president by Marais Viljoen.

6 *Portuguese premier resigns*

After the Socialist and Communist parties introduced censure motions in Parliament, Portuguese Premier Carlos Mota Pinto resigned after little more than six months in office. The main issue was the nation's budget. An earlier offer to resign had been refused by the president. Mota Pinto's centre-right nonpartisan Cabinet was expected to act as caretaker until a new government was formed.

7 *Carter retains Rhodesia sanctions*

President Carter announced that the U.S. trade sanctions against Zimbabwe

KEYSTONE

Pope John Paul II knelt to pray at the "death wall" on a visit to the former Nazi concentration camp at Auschwitz.

Rhodesia would continue in force because changes in the country's governmental structure were not substantial enough to warrant a change in U.S. policy. Among other things, Carter stated that the majority black population "never had a chance to consider or to vote for or against the constitution" under which elections were held that gave Bishop Abel Muzorewa's United African National Council 51 of 100 seats in the new Parliament. Carter also criticized the constitution on the grounds that it gave whites power disproportionate to their numbers.

European Assembly holds elections

In the first direct elections for the European Parliamentary Assembly, voters in Denmark, Great Britain, Ireland, and The Netherlands chose their representatives. Three days later similar elections were held in Belgium, France, Italy, Luxembourg, and West Germany. With the changeover from appointments by national legislatures to elections by national suffrage, the number of parliamentary seats was increased from 198 to 410. Though the Assembly currently lacked substantive legislative powers, it would oversee the Commission of the European Economic Community and serve as a forum for discussing important issues facing the EEC.

10 *Pope John Paul II visits Poland*

Pope John Paul II ended a nine-day, emotion-packed visit to his native Poland after celebrating mass in Krakow in the presence of more than one million people. The pontiff characterized his visit as "an event without precedent, an act of courage on both sides." Though Poland is ruled by a Communist government, its 35 million citizens are predominantly Roman Catholic. The day before his departure, the pope visited Nowa Huta, an industrial section of Krakow. While serving as archbishop of the city before his election as pope, John Paul had succeeded in overcoming 20 years of government opposition to the building of a new church and then personally dedicated the edifice in 1977. Authorities, however, refused to allow the pope to visit the church during his papal visit, so he preached his sermon at a nearby monastery.

11 *Luxembourg prime minister resigns*

Gaston Thorn, the Liberal Party prime minister of Luxembourg, resigned from office following the defeat of his coalition government in elections the previous day. Though Liberals were elected to fill 15 seats (a gain of one) in the 59-seat Chamber of Deputies, the Workers' Socialist Party, the partner in the coalition, lost three seats for a new total of 14. The opposition Christian Social Party won 24 seats with 34.5% of the popular vote but needed support from outside the party to form a coalition government.

16 *Ghana executes former leaders*

Gen. Ignatius Kutu Acheampong, former Ghanaian head of state, and Lieut. Gen. Edward K. Utuka, former commander of the border guards, were executed after being convicted by a military tribunal of "using their positions to amass wealth while in office and recklessly dissipating state funds to the detriment of the country." The executions were part of an anti-corruption campaign launched by Flight Lieut. Jerry Rawlings, who took over control of the government on June 4. On June 26 Lieut. Gen. Fred W. K. Akuffo and Lieut. Gen. Akwasi Afrifa, both former heads of state, were executed on similar charges of corruption. On June 30 Rawlings, responding to widespread criticism from African as well as Western nations, promised that future sentences would not exceed life imprisonment.

18 *SALT II signed in Vienna*

U.S. President Carter and Soviet Pres. Leonid I. Brezhnev formally signed the Strategic Arms Limitation Treaty II at a ceremony in Vienna. The treaty, however, was still subject to ratification by the U.S. Senate. The two presidents, who held their first formal meeting on June 16, reportedly discussed numerous issues of international importance during a series of meetings that preceded the signing of the treaty.

Chinese premier scales down goals

In a speech before the National People's Congress in Beijing (Peking), Chinese Premier Hua Guofeng (Hua Kuo-feng) acknowledged that China had been unduly optimistic when it adopted its 1978 program of rapid modernization. Hua announced that China could not initiate its program of high-speed economic development for three more years; meanwhile, the nation would expand its light industries, produce more consumer goods, increase salaries, and expand exports. Vice-Premier Li Xiannian (Li Hsien-nien) was reported to have given a speech in May during which he acknowledged that 20 million people were unemployed and some 100 million undernourished. He

U.S. Pres. Jimmy Carter and Soviet Pres. Leonid Brezhnev signed the SALT II accord in Vienna on June 18. The pact faced tough sledding in the U.S. Senate.

BOCCON-GIBOD—SIPA PRESS/BLACK STAR

blamed the discredited "gang of four" for China's "poor economic base," which, he said, could not be improved in a short time.

20 *Lule ousted as Ugandan president*

Ugandan Pres. Yusufu Lule was forced from office when the 30-member National Consultative Council appointed Godfrey Binaisa, a 59-year-old lawyer, head of state in his place. Lule, who challenged the legitimacy of the council's authority, had made Cabinet and local government appointments without consulting the council. Lule left Uganda on June 22, one day after violence erupted during demonstrations on his behalf.

21 *Quebecers to vote on separation*

René Lévesque, premier of the Canadian province of Quebec, announced that a referendum on Quebec sovereignty would be held in the spring of 1980. Lévesque said the referendum would be "a mandate to repatriate all our taxes and our legislative powers while maintaining economic links with Canada."

27 *Syria and Israel clash in air battle*

Syrian and Israeli jets clashed in an air battle over southern Lebanon when Syrian jet fighters intercepted Israeli aircraft that were bombing Palestinian targets near Damur and Sayda. It was the first such aerial combat since 1974. Syria claimed that two Israeli planes had been shot down and said four of its own planes had been hit. Israel claimed five Syrian MiG–21s had been downed and denied that any of its own planes had been lost to enemy fire.

Lomé Convention extended for five years

The European Economic Community (EEC) and 57 less developed countries from Africa, the Caribbean, and the Pacific (ACP nations) concluded three days of talks in Brussels that resulted in a five-year extension of the Lomé Convention, due to expire on March 1, 1980. Despite objections from some of the ACP nations, the EEC stood firm in offering $7,660,000,000 in aid, an additional $410 million in food, and $34 million to support nongovernmental organizations. The EEC also agreed to support exports from the less developed nations and assist development projects. The terms of the agreement did not differ substantially from those offered by the EEC a month earlier.

28 *U.S. to accept more refugees*

President Carter announced in Tokyo that the U.S. would accept 14,000 Indochinese refugees per month for a period of 12 months. The current quota was just half that number. The UN reported that 215,000 Indochinese refugees had entered the U.S. since 1975; France had accepted 52,000 and Australia 20,800. On June 25 Malaysia, already overburdened with a huge refugee population, had announced that 13,000 refugees in 60 boats had been forced back to sea during the previous week. On June 26 the Malaysian home affairs minister proposed that Washington establish centres in the U.S. for some 200,000 refugees because "the problem of the boat people is the hangover of the United States involvement in South Vietnam and because the United States is the loudest proponent of human rights and humanitarian principles."

Syria executes 15 terrorists

Syria executed 15 members of the Muslim Brotherhood who had been convicted of murder and subversion. Three others were sentenced to life imprisonment. The executions were part of an intensified campaign to put an end to a wave of wanton killings that had allegedly been carried out by members of the Muslim Brotherhood.

29 *Japan and West limit oil imports*

On the second day of their fifth annual economic summit, the leaders of Japan and six major Western nations reached agreement in Tokyo on basic policies regarding their importation of foreign oil. The conference got under way as the Organization of Petroleum Exporting Countries (OPEC) increased the price of crude oil to between $18 and $23.50 a barrel. Japanese Prime Minister Masayoshi Ohira, British Prime Minister Margaret Thatcher, Canadian Prime Minister Joe Clark, French Pres. Valéry Giscard d'Estaing, Italian Premier Giulio Andreotti, U.S. President Carter, and West German Chancellor Helmut Schmidt all agreed to specific country-by-country limits on oil imports through 1985. The U.S. goal would be a limit of 8.5 million bbl daily during the next five years. Japan, which has no domestic supplies, would be permitted to increase its daily imports to 6.9 million bbl by 1985, approximately 1.5 million bbl more than its current daily level. Canada's 1985 limit was set at 600,000 bbl per day, roughly twice its current level. The other nations said they would announce specific limits after a meeting of the European Economic Community later in the year.

JULY

1 *China concludes People's Congress*

China's National People's Congress ended a two-week session after endorsing policies that were sure to have far-reaching consequences. For the first time since the Communists came to power in 1949, the government adopted a formal code of criminal law. Among other things, the code guaranteed defendants the right to legal counsel and stipulated that the accused must be brought to trial within five and a half months of his arrest. The Congress also approved the appointments of three economic specialists to the rank of vice- premier. One of the new appointees, Chen Yun (Ch'en Yün), was named head of the newly created State Finance and Economic Commission. In addition, the Congress sanctioned popular elections that would determine the makeup of local people's congresses. In another unprecedented move, China revealed that in 1979 its military budget would total $12,640,000,000.

Mexico elects new Parliament

Mexico's Institutional Revolutionary Party won an overwhelming majority of the seats in elections for the Chamber of Deputies. Pres. José López Portillo, in an effort to revitalize democratic participation in government, had in 1978 given opposition parties the right to register. The Communist Party, one of three parties that gained enough of the popular vote to qualify as a permanent political party, would have significant representation in the government because the 100 additional seats being added to Parliament were reserved for minority parties.

3 *Germany to continue prosecution of Nazi war criminals*

West Germany's Bundestag (lower house of Parliament), after a bitter debate, voted 255 to 222 to remove the statute of limitations on murder, allowing for the further prosecution of Nazi war crimes. The bill was expected to pass with relative ease in the upper house. Without new legislation, no new prosecutions could have been initiated after December 31. Those supporting the bill argued that West Germany had a responsibility to history to continue the prosecutions. Opponents claimed that a change in West Germany's judicial tradition would be a capitulation to foreign pressures. The statute of limitations affecting the prosecution of Nazi crimes had been extended for four years in 1965 and for ten in 1969.

4 *Ben Bella released in Algeria*

Algerian Pres. Chadli Bendjedid ordered the release of 63-year-old Ahmed Ben Bella, a former president (1963–65), who 14 years earlier had been ousted in a bloodless coup and placed under house arrest by his successor, the late Houari Boumédienne. Many considered Ben Bella a national hero for his role in Algeria's struggle for independence.

UPI

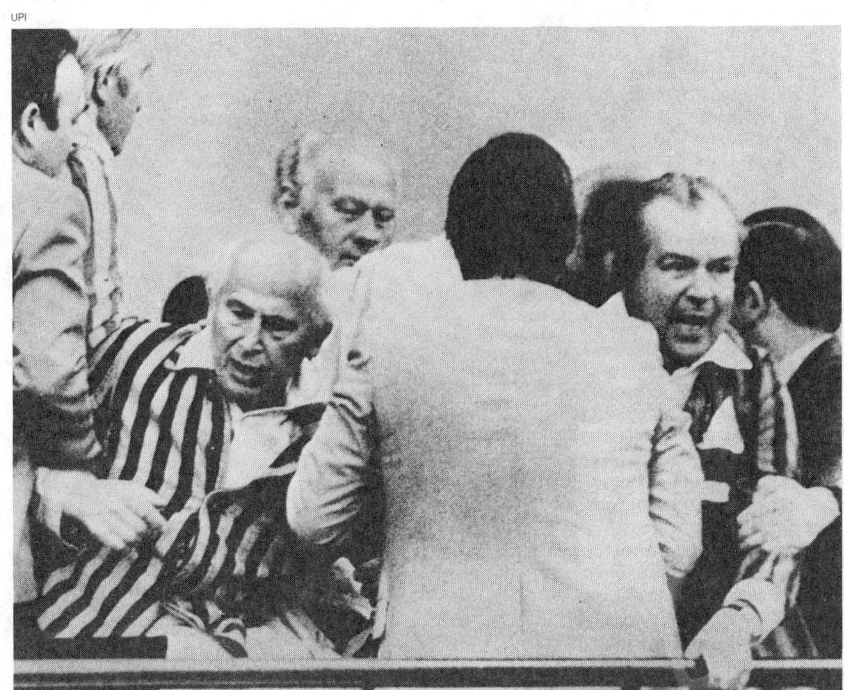

Former inmates of Nazi concentration camps dressed in their old prison uniforms demonstrated before the West German Parliament against a statute of limitations on Nazi war crimes.

7 *Nigerian civilian government begins to take shape*

As a step toward establishing the first civilian government since 1966 in oil-rich Nigeria, Africa's most populous country, voters elected five senators from each of the nation's 19 states. A president, governors, and members of the national House of Representatives and state legislatures would be chosen in subsequent elections. Five parties won seats in the Senate: National Party of Nigeria 36; Unity Party of Nigeria 28; Nigeria People's Party 16; Great Nigeria People's Party 8; and People's Redemption Party 7.

10 *Ghana elects president after coup*

Hilla Limann was chosen president of Ghana in a runoff election that became necessary when none of the six candidates received a majority of the popular vote on June 18. Limann's People's National Party, won a majority of seats in the 140-seat Parliament. The runner-up candidate was Victor Owusu of the Popular Front Party. Limann announced that after he took office in October he would continue the anti- corruption fight initiated by Flight Lieut. Jerry Rawlings, who had led a coup on June 4 that overthrew Gen. Fred Akuffo. In the weeks following the coup, three former heads of state were among those tried and executed on charges of flagrant corruption.

North Korea rejects three-way talks

North Korea formally rejected a proposal that the U.S. join North and South Korea in talks to lessen tensions in the peninsula and eventually reunite the country. Carter first discussed the matter with South Korean officials in Seoul after attending an economic summit meeting in Tokyo.

11 *Skylab returns to Earth*

The U.S. space station Skylab, while orbiting the Earth for the 34,981st time since its launching in 1973, entered the atmosphere and disintegrated over Australia and the Indian Ocean. There were no reports of injuries or property damage. Though NASA scientists were unable to control Skylab's descent, they were able to delay its entry long enough to spare heavily populated areas from potential harm. The space agency had estimated that 20–25 tons of material from the 77-ton station would strike the Earth and that the largest single piece would weigh about 2,270 kg (5,000 lb).

Whaling banned in three areas

During its annual meeting in London, the International Whaling Commission banned for at least ten years all whale hunting in the Red Sea, Arabian Sea, and most of the Indian Ocean. Among the species protected by the sanctuary was the sperm whale, which was classified as endangered because of overhunting. The ban would most seriously affect the Japanese and Soviet whaling industries.

13 *FAA lifts ban on DC-10 flights*

The U.S. Federal Aviation Administration ended its grounding of DC-10 aircraft operated by U.S. carriers. It also announced that foreign-operated DC-10s would be permitted to land at U.S. airports. Some foreign nations had put their DC-10s back into service several weeks earlier after they had passed inspection. The FAA ban was imposed on June 6 after a DC-10 lost an engine during takeoff from Chicago's O'Hare International Airport and crashed, killing 274 persons.

15 *Carter outlines new energy program*

In a nationally televised speech, President Carter outlined a new ten-year national energy program that would reduce U.S. dependence on foreign oil. The cost would be about $140 billion. The speech followed ten days of closed talks at Camp David, Md., where Carter sought advice from a large number of government and nongovernment people. Carter's program included strict limits on oil imports, the development of alternative and synthetic fuels, greater use of coal, a more efficient use of solar energy, a "bold conservation program," improvements in mass transportation systems, and financial aid to poor people who were already overburdened with high energy costs.

Indian Prime Minister Desai resigns

Indian Prime Minister Morarji Desai resigned when more than 100 members of his Janata Party deserted him in the lower house of Parliament. Without their support Desai had no hope of surviving a vote of no confidence the next day. Desai was beset by serious factionalism within his own party, economic problems, labour unrest, outbursts of violence, and resignations from his Cabinet and from the Janata Party. On July 28, 77-year-old Charan Singh, leader of a breakaway faction of the Janata Party, was sworn in as prime minister.

16 *Hussein named president of Iraq*

Iraqi Pres. Ahmad Hassan al-Bakr resigned from office because of poor health and appointed Saddam Hussein as his successor. Hussein became head of state, head of government, chairman of the Revolutionary Command Council, commander of the armed forces, and secretary-general of the Ba'ath Party. According to later reports, five high-ranking members of the Revolutionary Council were among 36 persons arrested a few days later on charges of plotting a coup. Some were said to have been executed.

17 *Somoza resigns and leaves Nicaragua*

The Congress of Nicaragua accepted the resignation of Pres. Anastasio Somoza Debayle, who then left for exile with 45 of his top aides. On June 23 the Organization of American States had called for the "immediate and definitive replacement" of Somoza, whose family had amassed immense wealth during the 46 years they ruled the country. On July 18 Francisco Urcuyo Malianos, Somoza's successor, fled to Guatemala. Early the following day the Sandinistas took control of Managua, the capital, thus ending years of turmoil and seven weeks of civil war that had left more than 10,000 dead and half a million homeless.

20 *U.S. troops to remain in Korea*

President Carter called a halt to the withdrawal of U.S. combat troops stationed in South Korea. The remaining 32,000 troops would stay for at least two more years to counterbalance the "steady growth" of Soviet military power and give the U.S. a favourable "strategic posture in East Asia." In 1977 Carter had said he would recall all U.S. troops from South Korea within four or five years.

21 *UN holds conference on refugees*

The UN concluded a two-day conference in Geneva on the urgent problem of Indochinese refugees. France, one of the 65 nations in attendance, called for "an immediate moratorium on the further expulsion of people from Vietnam." UN Secretary-General Kurt Waldheim later told the delegates that Vietnam had authorized him to announce that it would "make every effort to stop illegal departures." Before the conference ended, various nations pledged a total of $190 million to aid the refugees and agreed to resettle at least 266,000 in their countries. At one point, China's vice-foreign minister accused Vietnam of genocide, military dictatorship, and aggression. Waldheim had to interrupt the speaker to prevent the angry Vietnamese delegation from disrupting the conference.

OAU parley ends in discord

During the 16th annual meeting of the Organization of African Unity (OAU) in Monrovia, Liberia, regional differences became a major issue for the first time. Open discord prevailed when Sudan and Nigeria denounced Tanzania for its invasion of Uganda and the overthrow of Idi Amin. The speeches prompted the president of Uganda to walk out in protest. Liberian Pres. William Tolbert criticized fellow African leaders for ignoring violations of human rights, notably in Uganda, on the pretext that members of the OAU had endorsed a principle of noninterference in the internal affairs of other nations. Before adjourning, the conference delegates urged the outside world not to recognize the government of Zimbabwe Rhodesia. It also condemned Israel but supported Egyptian Pres. Anwar as-Sadat's peace negotiations, despite protests from Libya, Algeria, and other North African Arab states.

WIDE WORLD

Lee A. Iacocca, president of Chrysler Corp., turned aside as Chrysler chairman John J. Riccardo read a statement announcing a $207 million deficit in the automaker in the second quarter.

23 *Khomeini bans music in Iran*

Ayatollah Ruhollah Khomeini issued a prohibition against the broadcasting of music over radio and television. He declared that music "corrupted Iranian youth." The religious leader also stated that music "stupefies persons listening to it and makes their brains inactive and frivolous." He then linked independence of the country with the suppression of music. The following day the director of National Radio and Television announced that the ban would apply to the holy month of Ramadan, which was soon to begin; after that time "an appropriate decision" would be made. Khomeini, who also reaffirmed his ban against men and women swimming at the same beaches or in the same pools, had previously banned most Western movies, alcoholic drink, and singing by women.

30 *UN delays debate on Palestinians*

The UN Security Council agreed to postpone until August 23 a debate on Palestinian rights that could have been acrimonious. The U.S. urged the delay because it opposed the wording of a resolution submitted by Kuwait. The resolution referred to the Palestinian right "to self-determination and national independence." The U.S. preferred "the legitimate rights" of the Palestinians and their right "to participate in the determination of their own future." The latter expressions left room for negotiations, and for that reason had been adopted by Egypt and Israel when they signed the 1978 Camp David accords.

31 *Chrysler faces financial crisis*

John J. Riccardo, chairman of Chrysler Corp., announced that the automobile manufacturing company that he headed had lost a record $207 million in the second quarter of 1979 and needed $1 billion in cash from the federal government to continue in business. Riccardo sought the funds as cash advances against future tax credits. Chrysler, the third largest U.S. automaker, employed some 250,000 workers and had sales of $16,340,700,000 in 1978. Its suppliers and numerous other segments of the economy would also be seriously affected if Chrysler were forced to declare bankruptcy.

ZANU rejoins National Assembly

The Rev. Ndabaningi Sithole announced that the Zimbabwe African National Union (ZANU) which he heads would rejoin the Zimbabwe Rhodesia National Assembly and also assume the two Cabinet posts to which it was entitled under the constitution. His declared purpose was to bolster the government of Prime Minister Abel Muzorewa at a time when it was seeking international recognition and an end to the economic boycott that was adversely affecting the country.

AUGUST

1 *Dominicans protest gasoline prices*

Hundreds of persons, many of them transit drivers, piled trash and garbage cans on the main streets of Santo Domingo to protest a 50% increase in the price of gasoline. The scene became violent when police and troops tried to control protesters who were hurling rocks at automobiles. Four persons were reported killed, 30 injured, and more than 700 arrested.

3 *Head of Equatorial Guinea ousted*

Pres. Francisco Macías Nguema of Equatorial Guinea was overthrown in a military coup. The junta that took over control of the government was headed by Lieut. Col. Teodoro Obiang Nguema Mbasogo. In mid-August the former president was captured near his native village and, according to reports, was to be put on trial for committing serious crimes during his 11 years in office.

5 *New Italian government sworn in*

Francesco Cossiga, a Christian Democrat, was sworn in as premier of a three-party coalition government in Italy. The 24-member Cabinet included 16 Christian Democrats, 4 Social Democrats, 2 Liberals, and 2 nonpartisan economists. The coalition represented only 291 votes in the 630-seat Chamber of Deputies, but the 62 Socialists promised to be neutral. In the first two votes of confidence on August 11 and 12, the Socialists kept their promise and abstained.

Reward offered for capture of Amin

Ugandan Pres. Godfrey L. Binaisa offered a "huge award" for the capture of deposed president Idi Amin. Binaisa, who made his offer during a conference of Commonwealth nations in Zambia, said he believed Amin was moving back and forth between Libya and Sudan.

6 *Bokassa implicated in massacre*

Emperor Bokassa I of the Central African Empire was involved in the murder of about 100 schoolchildren, according to a report published in Paris. The story detailed the findings of a panel of judges from the five African nations of Ivory Coast, Liberia, Rwanda, Senegal, and Togo. After interviewing more than 150 witnesses, the jurists concluded that Bokassa not only visited the prison in Bangui on April 18, the day government troops killed the children, but in some capacity was probably personally responsible for the murders. On August 9 the U.S. State Department announced it was terminating foreign aid to the country and reconsidering international loans because of human rights violations. On August 17 France cut off all but humanitarian and educational aid to its former colony.

Bolivia gets temporary president

The Bolivian Congress, anxious to end 12 years of military rule, resolved a presidential election deadlock by declaring Walter Guevara Arze provisional president until August 1980. At that time new elections would be held, but Guevara would not be permitted to seek the presidency. Three former presidents were deadlocked in the July 1 election, when Hernán Siles Zuazo won 37% of the popular vote, Víctor Paz Estenssoro 29%, and Hugo Banzer Suárez less than 18%. Five other candidates also ran. Since none of the candidates received 50% of the popular vote, the 27 senators and 117 members of the Chamber of Deputies were free to elect either Siles, or Paz, or Banzer. None of the three, however, was able to muster an absolute majority of congressional votes. Congress then turned to a compromise candidate and gave the office to Guevara, the Senate president.

8 *Iraq executes 21 officials*

Iraq executed 21 officials by firing squad for taking part in an alleged plot against the government. On the previous day they were declared guilty after a closed trial. One other defendant was convicted in absentia. Among the executed were five former members of the ruling Revolutionary Command Council. The special court also sentenced 33 persons to prison and declared 13 others innocent of conspiracy.

10 *Ecuador gets new president*

Jaime Roldós Aguilera, a 38-year-old member of the Concentración de Fuerzas Populares party, was sworn in as president of Ecuador during a ceremony attended by high-ranking Latin-American officials and by U.S. Secretary of State Cyrus R. Vance and Rosalynn Carter. In a runoff election on April 29, Roldós easily defeated Sixto Durán Ballén Cordovez to become the third democratically elected president currently holding office in a major South American country. The others were in Venezuela and Colombia.

Tribal leaders of the Western Sahara gathered to celebrate at the royal palace at Rabat, Morocco, after Morocco annexed Tiris el-Gharbia.

D'OIRON—SIPA PRESS/BLACK STAR

11 *South Korean police raid party headquarters of opposition*

South Korean police raided the headquarters of the New Democratic Party in Seoul to eject women textile workers who were staging a sit-in to protest loss of their jobs. About 100 persons were injured and 198 arrested. One woman committed suicide. The women had earlier been expelled from the dormitory of a textile company that went bankrupt when the owner reportedly fled the country with $3 million in goods. Kim Young Sam, leader of the New Democratic Party, charged that the attack was another example of the "systematic campaign" being conducted against political opponents.

Morocco takes over Western Sahara

Morocco formally annexed Tiris el-Gharbia, an area of the Western Sahara that had been occupied by Mauritania. The entire Western Sahara was an overseas province of Spain until early in 1976 when Spain ceded the territory to Morocco and Mauritania. At that time, the original name, Spanish Sahara, was changed. Morocco, which laid claim to the entire region, fought both Mauritania and the Polisario Front, a native guerrilla organization seeking independence. When Mauritania agreed on August 5 to withdraw from the conflict, the territory it intended to turn over to the Polisario was occupied by Moroccan troops.

13 *China to slow population growth*

Chinese Vice-Premier Chen Muhua (Ch'en Mu-hua) set forth the government's plans for population control in an article published in the *Renmin Ribao* ("People's Daily"). The nation's goal, she wrote, would be to reduce the birthrate to 5 per 1,000 persons by 1985. The rate was 23.4 in 1971 and 12.05 in 1978. When new laws were enacted, couples having more than two children would be subject to additional taxes and other economic penalties. Chen acknowledged the 1985 goal would be difficult to reach because 80% of China's people live in rural areas and half of the population is not yet 21. Chen further noted that because of economic problems only 41% of China's youth graduate from high school.

14 *Geneva disarmament conference ends*

The Committee on Disarmament concluded its 1979 session without formulating any new resolutions. Basic differences could not be resolved because delegates held different views on which issues should have priority. The committee, founded in 1962 as the Conference of the Eighteen-Nation Committee on Disarmament, is not an agency of the UN, though it meets under UN auspices and presents its recommendations to that body.

15 *Young resigns as UN ambassador*

Andrew Young resigned his post as U.S. ambassador to the United Nations after it was revealed he had violated his government's established Middle East policy by secretly meeting in July with Zehdi Labib Terzi, a UN observer for the Palestine Liberation Organization. The ambassador expressed no regret for his action and said he could give no assurances that, given the same situation, he "wouldn't do it again, almost exactly the same way." Though President Carter did not request Young's resignation, he accepted it. On several other occasions Young had become the centre of heated controversy because of the intemperate criticism he leveled at other nations.

16 *Nigeria elects civilian president*

Nigeria's Federal Electoral Commission ruled that Alhaji Shehu Shagari, the 54-year-old leader of the National Party of Nigeria, had won the presidential election of August 11, even though the votes he received fell somewhat short of constitutional requirements. He received at least 25% of the popular vote in two-thirds (13) of the states. Shagari, scheduled to assume office in October, would be Nigeria's first civilian president in 13 years.

Park Tong Sun case dismissed

A U.S. district court judge dismissed a 36-count indictment against Park Tong Sun, a South Korean businessman. Park had been indicted by the U.S. Department of Justice in August 1978 on charges of conspiracy, bribery, mail fraud, racketeering, failure to register as a foreign agent, and of making illegal contributions to U.S. politicians. During the government's investigation of South Korean influence buying on Capitol Hill, Park testified that he gave about $850,000 to 31 present and former members of Congress to further his business interests, but he denied that he ever acted as an agent of the South Korean government. Only one congressman was convicted and sent to prison. Though Park no longer had to face criminal charges, the Internal Revenue Service claimed he still owed $4.5 million in unpaid taxes and penalties.

18 *Muslims establish rebel government in Afghanistan*

Muslim rebels announced the establishment of an insurgent government in Paktia, a province in central eastern Afghanistan bordering Pakistan. The Islamic Front, one of the rebel organizations, claimed 300 government troops had been killed in the takeover and 34 leaders of the ruling Khalq Party executed. The pro-Marxist Afghan government, which seized power in April 1978, was heavily backed by Soviet military personnel and armaments.

WIDE WORLD

A Soviet plane containing the wife of Bolshoi Ballet defector Aleksandr Godunov was detained for three days at New York's Kennedy International Airport while officials argued whether her departure for the Soviet Union was voluntary.

20 *Indian Prime Minister Singh resigns*

Indian Prime Minister Charan Singh resigned when it became apparent he could not survive a vote of no confidence. His fate was sealed when Indira Gandhi announced that the 79 members of her Congress (I) Party in the lower house of Parliament would not support him. Singh had been in office less than a month. Pres. N. Sanjiva Reddy dissolved Parliament and requested Singh to head a caretaker government until general elections could be held in three months.

21 *Nicaragua issues bill of rights*

Nicaragua's Sandinista junta issued a provisional bill of rights guaranteeing basic rights and promising new social programs, especially in the areas of health care and education. In 52 articles, the bill sets forth a wide range of liberties that may not be curtailed except in extraordinary circumstances. Torture, slavery, and the forceful control of religious and political freedoms are among the things explicitly forbidden. Citizens are also given the right to form political parties and to determine their future economic, social, and cultural development. A spokesman for the junta indicated that the country would be ready for elections in about three years. In an effort to bolster the country's financial structure, the government announced on August 24 that all large-denomination currencies would have to be exchanged for six-month bank certificates by August 26. The move was intended to render worthless the estimated 200 million córdobas ($20 million) reportedly taken out of the country just before the government of Anastasio Somoza Debayle collapsed.

23 *Soviet dancer defects to U.S.*

Aleksandr Godunov, a 30-year-old principal dancer with the Bolshoi Ballet, was granted political asylum in the U.S. after defecting during the Bolshoi's New York engagement. His wife, Ludmila Vlasova, was then spirited aboard a Soviet plane at Kennedy International Airport and kept incommunicado by Soviet officials. The plane remained on the ground for three days before U.S. officials were allowed to talk with Vlasova in a "noncoercive environment." Only after Vlasova assured U.S. authorities that she was voluntarily leaving her husband and returning to Moscow of her own free will was the plane cleared for takeoff.

27 *Lord Mountbatten killed by IRA*

Earl Mountbatten of Burma, a British hero during World War II, was killed when a bomb planted by members of the Provisional Irish Republican Army (IRA) destroyed his fishing boat off the coast of Ireland. Two young boys and the dowager Lady Brabourne also lost their lives; three others were injured. A spokesman for the Irish government said all of Ireland condemned "this cowardly and heartless outrage." The same day 18 British soldiers and one civilian were killed in an IRA ambush in Northern Ireland. On August 30 Irish police charged two suspected members of the IRA with murder. Both had been arrested during a routine police check a few hours before the explosion occurred and, while they were in police custody, traces of explosives and seawater were detected on their clothing.

SEPTEMBER

1 *Pioneer 11 returns data on Saturn*

The U.S. unmanned spacecraft Pioneer 11 transmitted important data to Earth after coming within 20,200 km (12,560 mi) of Saturn's clouds. The information included data about Saturn's atmosphere and photos of the planet's rings and moons. Pioneer 11 was launched in 1973 and surveyed Jupiter in 1974; it then headed for Saturn.

3 *Nonaligned nations meet in Cuba*

Fidel Castro, president of Cuba's Council of State, opened the sixth summit conference of nonaligned nations in Havana with a violent attack on the U.S. He also denounced China for its new political ties to the U.S. Yugoslav President Tito, who was among the founders of the organization in 1961, attempted to counter the pro-Soviet stance taken by Castro, who would head the nonaligned movement for the next three years. Tito urged the delegates to resist bloc politics and called for the total withdrawal of all foreign troops from the territories of other countries. His indirect reference to Cambodia was a repudiation of Castro's open support of Vietnam, which had helped overthrow the government of Pol Pot and installed the regime of Heng Samrin. Because Yugoslavia, Malaysia, Singapore, and other Southeast Asian nations refused to recognize Heng Samrin's government, neither of the rival Cambodian representatives was seated during the conference.

7 *U.S. warns Soviet Union on combat troops in Cuba*

President Carter warned the Soviet Union that "relations between our two countries will inevitably be adversely affected" unless the Soviet combat brigade in Cuba was disbanded. The president acknowledged that the force posed no direct military threat to the U.S., but its presence in Cuba was "a very serious matter" inasmuch as it was stationed "in a country which acts as a Soviet proxy in military adventures in other areas of the world." On September 10 *Pravda*, the Soviet Communist Party newspaper, denied that the Soviet military personnel in Cuba were combat troops.

New archbishop of Canterbury named

The Right Rev. Robert Runcie, bishop of the diocese of St. Albans, was named the 102nd archbishop of Canterbury. He would become "primate of all England," the senior bishop of the Anglican Communion, and the spiritual leader of 65 million Anglicans on Jan. 26, 1980, when the Most Rev. Donald Coggan planned to retire.

GAMMA/LIAISON

Yugoslavian Pres. Tito (at podium) spoke in opposition to Cuba's Fidel Castro at the sixth summit conference of nonaligned nations in Havana.

8 *Second plane lands in Cambodia with food and medicines*

A second plane, loaded with desperately needed food and medical supplies, landed in Cambodia as part of an international effort to stave off starvation and disease. According to an agreement reached in August, emergency supplies would be transshipped in Bangkok, Thailand, to the capital city of Phnom Penh. The situation was desperate because local agriculture had been severely disrupted by fighting still going on between guerrilla forces loyal to Premier Pol Pot and Cambodian forces that had taken control of the country with the support of Vietnamese troops. The rescue mission was headed by the International Red Cross and UNICEF.

10 *Parley on Rhodesia begins in London*

Lord Carrington, the British foreign secretary, opened a meeting in London to discuss with all concerned parties the future of Zimbabwe Rhodesia. The current government of the strife-torn country was represented by Prime Minister Abel Muzorewa and 11 other officials. One of those was former prime minister Ian Smith, who had unilaterally broken Rhodesia's colonial ties to Britain in 1965 and proclaimed a republic in 1970. Joshua Nkomo and Robert Mugabe, co-leaders of the Patriotic Front, the guerrilla organization fighting the central government, also attended. Carrington cautioned that no settlement "can fully satisfy the requirements of either side." The negotiations were expected to be long and difficult.

11 *Chilean junta to remain in power*

Chilean Pres. Augusto Pinochet Ugarte, rejecting demands that he set a timetable for restoration of democratic government, declared: "The political process remains in total force, particularly in the face of the resentful demands of those who want to drag us toward Marxist totalitarianism." Pinochet extolled his government's economic record since the overthrow of Salvador Allende in September 1973. Pinochet also announced a new plan to reduce extreme poverty through programs financed by public and private capital.

12 *Amnesty International claims many murdered in Guatemala*

Amnesty International, a London-based human rights organization, charged that 2,000 persons had been murdered, many of them for political reasons, in Guatemala since May 1978. The list of victims included politicians, students, journalists, labour leaders, and Indians. Those responsible for the killings were said to be operating with the full approval of the government.

U.S. lawmakers reject registration for military draft

The U.S. House of Representatives voted 252–163 against a resolution that would have required all 18-year-old males to register for possible induction into the armed forces at some future date. Advocates of the measure contended that the current all-volunteer program had been a failure and that the need for conscription was much greater than Pentagon officials had been willing to admit publicly.

13 *Beijing demonstrations continue*

Some 1,000 persons attended a rally in Tian An Men (T'ien An Men) Square in

SVENSKT—SIPA PRESS/BLACK STAR

Liberal Minister of Finance Ingemar Mundebo and Conservative leader Gosta Bohman handed out ballots on September 16 for Sweden's parliamentary elections. The centre and right parties came up with a one-vote edge in the Parliament to seize power from the ruling Social Democrats.

Beijing (Peking) to demand an end to the special privileges enjoyed by Chinese Communist Party officials and to support greater respect for human rights. One speaker declared: "We have wiped out capitalists, landlords, and rich peasants, but now we have a new rich class." On September 9 about 300 writers held a public gathering to discuss the state of literature in China. The following day high school graduates marched to government offices in Beijing to protest their exclusion from universities even though they had passed the entrance examinations. On September 15 the *Renmin Ribao* ("People's Daily") reported the establishment of a special commission of 1,000 persons that would investigate complaints.

16 *Taraki ousted in Afghanistan*

Nur Mohammad Taraki, president of the Revolutionary Council in Afghanistan, was replaced by Hafizullah Amin, who had succeeded Taraki as prime minister in March. Incomplete and contradictory reports from Afghanistan suggested that Taraki was killed during a violent takeover. On September 17 Amin announced that his rule marked the beginning of a "better Socialist order." He also declared that Afghanistan would continue to have good relations with all nations, especially with the Soviet Union.

Sweden elects new Parliament

In an extremely close election, the non-Socialist political bloc, made up of the Conservative, Centre, and Liberal parties, won 175 of the 349 seats in the Swedish Parliament. It was not until mailed-in ballots were counted that the three parties were assured of the final seat needed for an absolute majority. The vote count gave the Conservative Party 73 seats, the Centre Party 64, and the Liberal Party 38. The opposition Social Democrat and Communist parties won 154 and 20 seats, respectively. Ola Ullsten, prime minister of the current Liberal Party minority government, resigned September 20 to negotiate on forming a new coalition government with the other two non-Socialist parties.

19 *UN backs Pol Pot representative*

The nine-member Credentials Committee of the United Nations refused to replace the Cambodian delegate representing the overthrown government of Pol Pot with one representing the current government of Heng Samrin. The change was urged by Vietnam, which had reinforced Heng Samrin's forces during their takeover of the country. Belgium, China, Ecuador, Pakistan, Senegal, and the U.S. voted against the resolution for the removal of the Pol Pot delegate. The three votes supporting Heng Samrin came from the Congo, Panama, and the U.S.S.R. On September 21 the UN General Assembly endorsed the decision of the Credentials Committee. The vote was 71–35 with 34 abstentions and 12 absentees.

20 *Emperor Bokassa ousted in coup*

Central African Emperor Bokassa I was deposed in a bloodless coup by former president David Dacko, who restored the country to the status of a republic. Dacko publicly thanked France and the African countries that had helped him assume power. Dacko promised a return to democracy and an end to oppression.

21 *Production of Concorde terminated*

British and French officials announced in London that their governments would not undertake the development of a second-generation Concorde aircraft. A total of 16 Concordes had been built at an estimated total cost of $2.5 billion. Neither Air France, which had four of the aircraft in service, nor British Airways, which had five, had been able to make a profit on the planes. Of the seven unsold Concordes, three went to Air France, two to British Airways, and two remained with the manufacturers.

26 *Coup foiled in Dominican Republic*

The armed forces announced that a plot to overthrow the government of Pres. Antonio Guzmán Fernández had been foiled with the arrest the previous day of eight of the ten conspirators. Seven were present or former high-ranking military officers, the other three civilians. All were said to be closely associated with former president Joaquín Balaguer.

27 *President of Mexico visits U.S.*

Mexican Pres. José López Portillo arrived in the U.S. on an official state visit. On September 21 Mexico and the U.S. had reached agreement on the sale of Mexican natural gas to the U.S. Both leaders expressed satisfaction with the outcome of their discussions. During his visit López Portillo also addressed the UN General

A constitutional conference held in London to discuss the future of Zimbabwe Rhodesia involved all concerned parties in the long-standing Rhodesian conflict.

ASHLEY ASHWOOD—CAMERA PRESS/PHOTO TRENDS

Assembly on the worldwide problem of energy. After presenting his nine-point program, he reminded the delegates that energy sources "are the shared responsibility of all mankind" and "must not be the privilege of the powerful."

29 *China condemns Cultural Revolution*

In a speech commemorating the 30th anniversary (October 1) of the People's Republic of China, Vice-Chairman Ye Jianying (Yeh Chien-ying) described the Cultural Revolution of 1966–69 as "an appalling catastrophe suffered by all our people." The late Chairman Mao Zedong (Mao Tse-tung), who inspired and directed the Cultural Revolution, was characterized as a great revolutionary but not a god. Ye noted that Mao's thought was not his alone; it was "also the product of the wisdom of his comrades in arms." Ye's emphasis on seeking "truth from facts" was seen as another indication that China would continue to give greater emphasis to material progress than to ideology.

Equatorial Guinea executes deposed president Macías Nguema

Francisco Macías Nguema, overthrown as president of Equatorial Guinea on August 3, was executed after a trial attended by international observers. He was convicted of mass murders, treason, and misuses of government funds.

OCTOBER

1 *U.S. to step up Cuban surveillance*

In a nationally televised address, President Carter said the U.S. would intensify its surveillance of Cuba to make sure that the Soviet combat brigade there, the presence of which was recently made public, was neither enlarged nor given additional capabilities. Carter said he had received assurances "from the highest levels of the Soviet government" that the troops (described by the U.S.S.R. as merely training personnel) "are not and will not be a threat to the United States or to any other nation."

3 *U.S.S.R. permitted to buy U.S. grain in record quantities*

The U.S. Department of Agriculture announced that the Soviet Union would be permitted to buy a record 25 million metric tons of U.S. wheat and corn during the next 12 months. The U.S. held substantial reserves from its 1978 crops and in 1979 produced 57.8 million metric tons of wheat and 185 million tons of corn. In late November Soviet Pres. Leonid Brezhnev confirmed earlier U.S. predictions when he said the 1979 Soviet harvest was only 179 million metric tons, the lowest figure since 1972.

4 *Opposition leader expelled from South Korean Assembly*

Kim Young Sam, leader of the opposition New Democratic Party, was expelled from the South Korean National Assembly by the unanimous vote of 159 members of the Assembly belonging to the ruling Democratic Republican Party or appointed by Pres. Park Chung Hee. Nine charges were leveled at Kim, including that of attempting to disrupt the constitutional order. On October 13 all 70 members of the opposition resigned in protest; 66 of that number represented the New Democratic Party. On October 17 martial law was imposed in Pusan following anti-government demonstrations.

7 *Pope John Paul II concludes visits to Ireland and the U.S.*

Pope John Paul II ended historic visits to Ireland and the U.S. after drawing huge and enthusiastic crowds everywhere he went. The pontiff arrived in Dublin on September 29 and later celebrated a mass attended by one-third of Ireland's entire population. The following day he had planned to visit Northern Ireland. The trip, however, was canceled because of recent violence there. Instead, John Paul visited the Irish town of Drogheda. After arriving in the U.S. on October 1, the pope visited Boston, New York, Philadelphia, Des Moines and Cumming in Iowa, Chicago, and Washington, D.C. He also addressed the UN General Assembly and became the first pope ever to visit a U.S. president in the White House. In his numerous speeches, Pope John Paul touched on such topics as human rights, world peace, social justice, and the "frightful disparities" between the rich and poor. He also reaffirmed the traditional teachings of the Roman Catholic Church on such matters as divorce, birth control, abortion, human sexuality, priestly celibacy, and the all-male priesthood. On October 7 Pope John Paul II left the U.S. to return to Rome.

Japan's Liberal-Democratic Party wins national election

Japanese Prime Minister Masayoshi Ohira's Liberal-Democratic Party (LDP) won only 248 of the 511 seats in the (lower) House of Representatives but gained a workable majority when 10 of the 19 independents pledged their support. Encouraged by optimistic polls, Ohira had dissolved Parliament on September 7 and called for national elections. He had high hopes the LDP would capture 271 seats in the House of Representatives. The LDP's unexpectedly poor showing was attributed in part to Ohira's plan to impose new taxes to offset a substantial budget deficit. On November 6 Ohira was reelected prime minister, narrowly defeating former prime minister Takeo Fukuda in a runoff election in the House. Ohira won by a vote of 138 to 121. The prime minister then received a majority in a largely token vote in the (upper) House of Councillors.

NATO remains firm on new missiles

NATO issued a statement reaffirming its determination to deploy Pershing II and cruise missiles in Europe to help rectify a military imbalance that strongly favoured the Soviet Union and its allies. The U.S.S.R. had offered to withdraw up to 20,000 Soviet troops from East Germany and called for a freeze on missile deployment in Europe. West German Chancellor Helmut Schmidt, however, noted that the U.S.S.R. was replacing obsolete missiles with "modern rockets that are not

Sticky crude oil blankets a beach on Mustang Island, Texas; the oil spill from a Mexican well in the Gulf of Mexico was the worst in history.

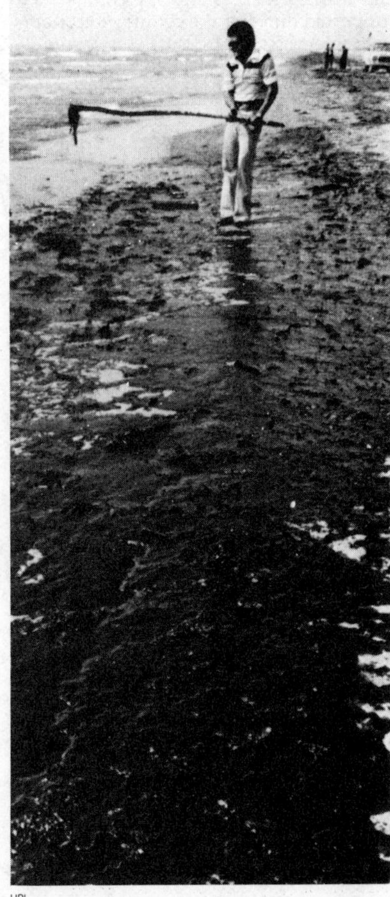

UPI

only more mobile but that also carry three warheads instead of one as before."

8 *Rhoodie sentenced in South Africa*

Eschel Rhoodie, former head of South Africa's Department of Information, was given a six-year prison sentence for his role in a scandal involving the illegal use of funds to gain foreign support for South Africa's policies.

9 *Fälldin heads Swedish government*

Former prime minister Thorbjörn Fälldin, leader of the Centre Party, was selected to head a three-party non-Socialist coalition government in Sweden. He replaced Ola Ullsten, whose Liberal Party also formed part of the ruling coalition. Gosta Bohman, leader of the Conservative Party, was passed over as too conservative, even though his party won nine more seats than the Centrists in the September 16 parliamentary election.

10 *Manila police arrest more students*

Police arrested 24 students in Manila and were reported to be searching for 50 others. All were said to be political activists opposed to the martial law regime of Pres. Ferdinand Marcos. During several recent demonstrations at the University of the Philippines in Manila, student groups had blamed Marcos and the U.S., which supported him, for the country's economic problems.

12 *Castro addresses United Nations*

Fidel Castro, president of Cuba's Council of State, addressed the UN General Assembly as chairman of the nonaligned movement, which had recently met in Havana. During a speech that lasted more than two hours, Castro castigated the U.S. as the chief cause of many of the world's most serious problems. A major portion of his speech was devoted to the economic inequities between nations. Among other things, Castro called on the U.S. and other rich "imperialists" to provide $300 billion in grants and low-interest loans to less developed countries over the next ten years. The Cuban leader said that sum was equal to the world's annual military budgets and "the United States alone will in the 1980s spend six times this much on military activities." Castro's four-day visit to New York marked the first time in 19 years that he had been to the U.S.

Israeli Foreign Minister Moshe Dayan waved a greeting to reporters after announcing his resignation from the government post.

WIDE WORLD

15 *Runaway offshore Mexican oil well partially controlled*

Pemex, Mexico's state-controlled oil company, successfully installed a specially designed metal cone over the Ixtoc 1 oil well. The well had spewed an estimated 2.4 million bbl of oil into the Bay of Campeche since it blew out on June 3. The cone was expected to control about 85% of the well's flow.

El Salvador government toppled

The military government of Gen. Carlos Humberto Romero was overthrown by relatively unknown army officers who, after taking control of army garrisons, ordered Romero to leave the country. The following day the "revolutionary government junta" declared that Romero had gained power through "scandalous election fraud" and was responsible for the nation's disastrous social and economic conditions. It also proclaimed a state of siege and a 30-day suspension of constitutional guarantees.

Chinese premier visits Europe

Chinese Premier Hua Guofeng (Hua Kuofeng) arrived in Paris to start a three-week visit to France, West Germany, Britain, and Italy. Hua said he was making the trip to gain personal inspiration for China's program of modernization. The premier reportedly stopped first in Paris because France was the first Western nation to open diplomatic relations with the People's Republic of China.

16 *China sentences leading dissident*

Wei Jingsheng (Wei Ching-sheng), a 29-year-old Chinese dissident who worked as an electrician and edited the publicly sold journal *Exploration*, was sentenced to 15 years in prison by a Beijing (Peking) court for counterrevolutionary activities and for having passed military secrets to a foreigner. During the one-day trial, Wei refused the assistance of a state-appointed lawyer. Speaking in his own defense, Wei insisted that all the information he possessed was available to ordinary citizens because he had no access to government documents. He also noted: "The Constitution gives the people the right to criticize leaders because they are human beings and not deities." He also claimed that the prosecutor's case was based on the false notion that a true revolutionary supports those in power and a counterrevolutionary opposes them. Wei declared that such reasoning was characteristic of the now-discredited "gang of four."

Turkish prime minister resigns

Turkish Prime Minister Bulent Ecevit resigned after an analysis of the October 14 elections gave the opposition Justice Party all 5 of the contested seats in the National Assembly and 33 of the 50 seats contested in the Senate. Turkey was currently faced with serious economic problems and persistent political and sectarian violence.

17 *Pirates capture World Series*

The Pittsburgh Pirates of the National League won the professional baseball championship by defeating the Baltimore Orioles of the American League four games to three in the World Series. The Pirates made a spectacular comeback by winning the last three games. Willie Stargell, the Pirates' 38-year-old first baseman, batted .400 (12 for 30), set a record with seven extra-base hits, hit all three Pirate home runs, and was named most valuable player of the Series.

21 *Moshe Dayan resigns Cabinet post*

Israeli Foreign Minister Moshe Dayan announced his resignation, effective on October 23. On October 2 he had informed Prime Minister Menahem Begin by letter that he felt it necessary to quit his post because he could not properly perform his duties. Dayan noted, among other things, that he had been given no active role in determining Israel's policy on the complicated issue of Palestinian autonomy in the West Bank and Gaza Strip.

22 *Deposed shah arrives in U.S.*

Iran's deposed shah, Mohammad Reza Pahlavi, arrived secretly in the U.S. Two days later physicians at the New York Hospital-Cornell Medical Center removed his gallbladder and several gallstones that were blocking the bile duct. The former Iranian leader was temporarily admitted into the U.S. after doctors in Mexico decided that medical treatments available in the U.S. were needed to prevent further deterioration of the shah's condition.

23 *Denmark elects new Parliament*

Danish Prime Minister Anker Jørgensen's Social Democratic Party gained 4 seats in the 179-seat unicameral Folketing (parliament) for a total of 69, but was still 21 seats short of a majority. Jørgensen had called for an election on September 28 after the Liberal Democrats, who formed the other part of the coalition govern-

WIDE WORLD

Park Keun Hae, eldest daughter of Korean president Park Chung Hee, bowed before her father's casket at his funeral in Seoul.

ment, withdrew their support because of differences on economic matters. Ten parties were represented in the new Parliament. On October 26 Jørgensen presented his Cabinet to Queen Margrethe II.

25 *U.S.S.R. and South Yemen sign pact*

The People's Democratic Republic of Yemen (Aden; South Yemen) signed a 20-year treaty of friendship with the Soviet Union. The treaty stipulated that the two countries would "continue to develop cooperation in the military field in the interest of strengthening their defense capacity." The increase of Soviet military and economic influence in the southwest corner of the Arabian Peninsula was especially worrisome to Saudi Arabia and the Yemen Arab Republic (San'a'; North Yemen), both of which share borders with South Yemen.

26 *Pres. Park Chung Hee assassinated*

South Korean Pres. Park Chung Hee was assassinated by Kim Jae Kyu, head of the Korean Central Intelligence Agency (KCIA). The premeditated attack occurred during a private dinner at a restaurant maintained by the KCIA near the president's residence. Kim also shot and killed Cha Chi Chol, head of the Presidential Security Service. Other KCIA agents shot and killed five other presidential bodyguards in adjoining rooms. Initial reports said that Kim feared he was about to be replaced and considered his archrival Cha responsible. Shortly after the killings Kim and his five accomplices were arrested. The Cabinet, which convened in an emergency session, named Prime Minister Choi Kyu Hah as acting president. On October 27 most of the country was placed under martial law. The martial law commander, Chung Sung Hwa, immediately imposed emergency restrictions. The U.S., fearful that North Korea might try to exploit the situation, put the troops it had stationed in South Korea on alert and dispatched naval forces to the area. On October 28 Kim Young Sam, leader of the opposition New Democratic Party and a severe critic of the president, termed the assassination "a national calamity."

NOVEMBER

1 *Military seizes power in Bolivia*

Bolivia returned to military rule after less than three months of civilian government under Pres. Walter Guevara Arze, who had been named provisional president by the Congress on August 6. Col. Alberto Natusch Busch, leader of the Army coup, assumed the presidency. During the following days Natusch used troops, tanks, and aircraft in an attempt to stamp out resistance and force an end to a general strike called to protest his rule. On November 16 a compromise was enacted that ended the immediate threat of civil war. Natusch stepped down, Guevara was bypassed, and Lydia Gueiler Tejada, the president of the Senate, was appointed interim president by the Congress pending elections in 1980.

3 *Grenada arrests 12 persons in plot*

The government of Grenada arrested 12 persons it said were involved in a plot to overthrow the government of Prime Minister Maurice Bishop, who gained power in March in a coup that toppled Sir Eric Gairy. The government reported that three separate landings were to have been made on the island and that security forces were searching the beaches for accomplices and hidden arms.

4 *Iranians seize U.S. embassy and take diplomats hostage*

Several hundred Iranian militants seized the U.S. embassy in Teheran and took some 90 persons hostage. About 60 were U.S. citizens who had diplomatic immunity as members of the embassy staff. The militants announced that the Americans would be held until the deposed shah, undergoing medical treatment in a New York City hospital, was returned to Iran to stand trial for crimes allegedly committed during the years he ruled the country. President Carter declared he would not extradite the shah and demanded the release of all U.S. hostages. On November 6 Iranian Prime Minister Mehdi Bazargan resigned his post when it became clear that Ayatollah Ruhollah Khomeini and the Revolutionary Council sanctioned detention of the U.S. personnel, even though it was a clear violation of international law.

8 *Kenya holds national elections*

Daniel arap Moi, president of Kenya, was confirmed in office in a national election but one-third of the Cabinet was defeated. Most of the 158 members of Parliament had faced challenges, even though the country has only one political party. More

Staff members of the U.S. embassy in Teheran were bound and blindfolded after militants seized the embassy on November 4.

than half of those who sought reelection were voted out of office.

Irish prime minister visits U.S.

Irish Prime Minister John Lynch arrived in Washington, D.C., to seek U.S. help in halting the terrorist violence that had brought intense suffering to Northern Ireland. Carter promised that the U.S. government would do everything possible "to prevent American citizens' assistance to the terrorists in Ireland, who do so much to obstruct the realization of the hopes and dreams of all the Irish people, no matter what their religious background or convictions." When speaking to U.S. congressmen, Lynch condemned the Irish Republican Army and urged the U.S. to deny its members "guns, money, or moral support."

10 *South Korea to choose president*

Choi Kyu Hah, acting president of South Korea, announced that a new president would be chosen to replace the late Park Chung Hee. The 1972 constitution stipulated that a successor be chosen by the National Conference for Unification within 90 days of the death of the incumbent president. Choi suggested that the new chief executive revise the much-criticized constitution as soon as possible after assuming office. On November 12 Kim Jong Pil, a former prime minister and head of the Korean Central Intelligence Agency, was elected to head the ruling Democratic Republican Party.

11 *Israel arrests West Bank mayor*

Bassam Shaka, the Arab mayor of the West Bank city of Nablus, was arrested by Israeli military authorities for allegedly supporting terrorism. When certain remarks attributed to Shaka that were allegedly sympathetic to Palestinian terrorism were published in an Israeli newspaper, members of the Knesset (parliament) demanded that Shaka be deported to Jordan. Twenty-five Arab mayors in the West Bank and Gaza Strip resigned to protest Shaka's arrest. After a series of meetings, a military committee accepted recommendations from Defense Minister Ezer Weizman and other Cabinet members that Shaka be set free. He was released on December 5 and returned to his post in Nablus.

14 *UN demands that Vietnam remove its troops from Cambodia*

The UN General Assembly adopted a resolution calling for the immediate withdrawal of all foreign troops from Cambodia in an indirect reference to Vietnamese troops occupying the country. The vote was 91–21 with 29 abstentions. The resolution was sponsored by the Association of Southeast Asian Nations, whose members are Indonesia, Malaysia, the Philippines, Singapore, and Thailand.

15 *Identity of British spy revealed*

British Prime Minister Margaret Thatcher revealed to the House of Commons that Sir Anthony Blunt, the highly respected art historian who had served as art adviser to Queen Elizabeth II, had been a spy for the Soviet Union. Blunt, who was knighted in 1956, privately confessed his guilt in 1964 after receiving immunity from prosecution for promising to help Britain uncover Soviet espionage. During World War II Blunt was able to pass classified information to the Soviets while a member of the British Security Service. He belonged to a spy ring that included Kim Philby, Guy Burgess, and Donald Maclean and in 1951 helped the latter two escape to Moscow. Blunt was stripped of his knighthood after the revelation.

20 *Grand Mosque in Mecca attacked by Muslim extremists*

Several hundred armed Muslim extremists, some apparently from Arab nations outside Saudi Arabia, seized control of the Grand Mosque in Mecca while thousands were worshipping inside the huge compound. Because the terrorists barricaded themselves inside Islam's most sacred shrine, Saudi military units were delayed in their counterattack until religious authorities had ruled that such action was justified. It took almost two weeks of bloody fighting to subdue the last invaders holed up in the lower levels of the mosque. More than 150 persons were said to have died during the fighting. The leader, identified by some sources as Muhammad Abdullah al-Kahtani, reportedly claimed to be the promised Islamic messiah who had come to establish Allah's kingdom on Earth. To his followers, this meant an end to Western influences in Saudi Arabia and adherence to strict Islamic precepts.

23 *Mountbatten assassin convicted*

The Special Criminal Court in Dublin convicted Thomas McMahon of murdering Earl Mountbatten of Burma on August 27 and sentenced him to life imprisonment with no right of appeal. A second defendant, arrested with McMahon shortly before the bomb had exploded, was acquitted.

26 *Peru prepays some foreign loans*

Peru reached an agreement with representatives of nearly 300 international banks on prepayment of debts that saved the country more than $182.5 million in interest and commissions. Manuel Moreyra Loredo, president of Peru's central bank, attributed Peru's improved financial condition to new petroleum exports, better prices for exported commodities, and close adherence to an austere financial program approved by the International Monetary Fund. He also remarked that it was more difficult to persuade the bankers to accept prepayment than it had been to secure the loans in the first place.

Joyful constituents raised Bassam Shaka, mayor of the West Bank city of Nablus, after he was released by Israeli authorities. He had been arrested for making remarks considered sympathetic to Palestinian terrorists.

WIDE WORLD

KEYSTONE

Sir Anthony Blunt, a highly respected art historian and former art adviser to Queen Elizabeth II, was revealed to have been a spy for the Soviet Union during World War II.

300,000 Afghans flee into Pakistan

More than 300,000 Afghan refugees were reported to have fled into Pakistan to avoid the ravages of a civil war that had been raging for months between Muslim rebels and government troops. On December 14 an Afghan government official admitted that "a large number of Soviet experts" were helping the government, but he denied they were engaged in actual combat. According to some reports, however, Soviet military personnel were in charge of several military airfields in Afghanistan and were flying bombing missions against rebel positions.

27 *Tikhonov promoted in Politburo*

Nikolay Tikhonov, the 74-year-old first vice-chairman of the Soviet Council of Ministers and a longtime supporter of Pres. Leonid Brezhnev, was promoted to full membership in the Politburo, the executive committee of the Communist Party Central Committee which sets national policy. The appointment was seen as a confirmation of Brezhnev's power both as president and as head of the Communist Party.

28 *U.S.S.R. buys more Australian wheat*

Australia's Wheat Board announced that the U.S.S.R. had placed an order for two million tons of wheat to be delivered during the first half of 1980. Nearly one million tons had already been purchased by the Soviet Union earlier in the year. Soviet Pres. Leonid Brezhnev had acknowledged that his nation's 1979 harvest had fallen some 50 million tons short of projected goals.

29 *Entire Cabinet resigns in Ecuador*

Ecuadorian Pres. Jaime Roldós Aguilera lost his entire Cabinet when all 11 members resigned because of bitter feuding within the Concentración de Fuerzas Populares (CFP). Roldós had been elected president on April 29 as the candidate of the CFP but reportedly refused to follow the lead of Assad Bucaram, his wife's uncle, who was president of the unicameral legislature and head of the CFP. Bucaram had wanted to run for the presidency himself but was barred by the military junta from doing so. After assuming office on August 10, Roldós acted independently and refused to play the role of a stand-in for Bucaram. On December 9 a new Cabinet was announced. It introduced new faces but did not alter the previous political balance.

7,000 Somoza supporters face trial

Sergio Ramírez Mercado, a member of the junta that replaced Nicaraguan Pres. Anastasio Somoza Debayle, announced the formation of nine tribunals that would begin trying some of the 7,000 persons accused of collaborating with the Somoza regime. The prisoners, none of whom faced a death penalty, would be permitted to choose their own lawyers and appeal their verdicts to special courts. Somoza himself would be tried in absentia on the charge of genocide.

30 *EEC rejects U.K. demands*

The European Council ended a two-day meeting in Dublin without agreeing to British Prime Minister Margaret Thatcher's request that her nation's contributions to the European Economic Community (EEC) budget be drastically reduced. Though Britain is considered the third poorest of the nine member nations, its net contribution is the largest. Thatcher objected that more than 70% of the EEC budget was earmarked for agricultural price supports, which benefit Britain only marginally. Thatcher argued that nearly all of Britain's estimated $2.2 billion contribution should be eliminated. A reduction of $700 million was offered by other EEC members, but Thatcher considered this totally inadequate. All parties finally agreed to discuss the issue again at the next meeting in early 1980.

Abrogation of Taiwan treaty upheld by federal court

President Carter's abrogation of the U.S. mutual defense treaty with the Republic of China (Taiwan) was upheld 6–1 by the U.S. Court of Appeals for the District of Columbia. The ruling overturned the decision of a lower court, which had ruled the president needed the consent of Congress. In explaining its decision, the court made it clear that it was ruling only on the Taiwan treaty, which was based on the "novel and somewhat indefinite relationship" between the two countries. The court said that in such circumstances, the president must have the power to pursue the nation's foreign policy "in a rational and effective manner."

DECEMBER

3 *Violence follows Iran's adoption of Islamic constitution*

In a nationwide two-day plebiscite that began on December 2, Iranians overwhelmingly approved a new constitution that established Shi'ite Islam as the state religion and made Ayatollah Ruhollah Khomeini the country's political and religious leader for life. On December 5 several supporters of Ayatollah Kazem Shariat-Madari, a rival and critic of Khomeini, were killed in Qom, where Khomeini resided. The next day Shariat-Madari's followers in Azerbaijan Province expressed their dissatisfaction with the constitution by seizing the government radio and television stations in the provincial capital of Tabriz. When they invaded government buildings they were joined by members of the armed forces and local police. In Kurdistan, six helicopters reportedly dropped bombs on three villages to quell a rebellion there. Elsewhere in the country, several other ethnic minorities vented their anger by boycotting the plebiscite.

U.S. sailors killed in Puerto Rico

Puerto Rican terrorists, armed with automatic rifles, ambushed a U.S. Navy bus that was carrying 18 passengers to the Navy communications centre at Sabana Seca, near San Juan. Two persons were killed and ten injured. Three radical Puerto Rican nationalist groups claimed credit for the murders. A second attack by two unidentified gunmen occurred on December 9 at the Roosevelt Roads naval base in eastern Puerto Rico. No casualties were reported.

4 *UN demands release of hostages*

All 15 members of the UN Security Council approved a resolution demanding the immediate release of all American hos-

CRISIS IN IRAN

JANUARY

6 Shah installed Bakhtiar as prime minister.
16 Shah went into exile; his first stop was Egypt.

FEBRUARY

1 Khomeini arrived in Teheran, where he was welcomed by three million people.
5 Khomeini named Bazargan prime minister; Bakhtiar refused to step aside.
11 Bakhtiar resigned and slipped out of the country.
14 U.S. embassy attacked but Khomeini supporters quickly freed the hostages.
28 Bazargan threatened to resign because the Revolutionary Council was usurping governmental powers.

MARCH

9 Kurdish tribesmen attacked government army barracks in Sanandaj.
30 Shah left Morocco for The Bahamas.

APRIL

1 Iran became an Islamic Republic.

JUNE

10 Shah moved to Mexico.

AUGUST

10 Iran canceled $9 billion in contracts for U.S. arms.

OCTOBER

22 Shah arrived in New York for medical treatment.

NOVEMBER

4 Militants seized U.S. embassy in Teheran and took some 90 persons hostage; about 60 were U.S. citizens. Militants demanded return of the shah.
5 Carter rejected militants' demand and insisted hostages be released immediately. Other militants seized U.S. consulates in Tabriz and Shiraz and invaded U.K. embassy in Teheran.
6 Bazargan resigned; Revolutionary Council took over the government.
10 Carter announced that Iranian students with invalid visas would be deported.
11 Iranians in Lebanon invaded U.S. embassy.
12 Carter suspended Iranian oil imports.
14 Iran announced it would withdraw billions of dollars from U.S. banks. Carter ordered all Iranian government funds frozen.
16 Iran said it would no longer accept oil payments in U.S. dollars.
18 Khomeini said hostages would be put on trial as spies if shah was not returned.
19 Khomeini ordered the release of two black Marines and a woman.
20 Ten more U.S. hostages were released: six black men and four women. The Grand Mosque in Mecca, Saudi Arabia, was seized by armed Muslim extremists.
21 After Khomeini accused the U.S of involvement in the attack on the Grand Mosque, a mob in Pakistan destroyed the U.S. embassy; two Americans were killed. Anti-American demonstrations soon followed in Bangladesh, India, the Philippines, and several countries in the Middle East.
22 The last non-American hostages were released from the U.S. embassy in Teheran. Khomeini warned that the hostages would be killed if the U.S. attempted a rescue.
25 Waldheim called for a UN Security Council meeting on Iran.
28 Iran filed suit in New York to recover money allegedly stolen by the shah and his family.
29 Mexico withdrew shah's reentry visa. U.S. filed suit against Iran before the International Court of Justice.

DECEMBER

1 UN debate on Iran began.
2 Shah left New York hospital for U.S. Air Force base in Texas.
4 UN Security Council unanimously approved a resolution calling for the immediate release of all the hostages.
7 Shah's nephew was shot and killed in Paris.
9 Followers of Shariat-Madari fought government troops for control of the radio and television station in Tabriz.
9 Ghotbzadeh said an international "grand jury" would be convened to investigate past U.S. involvement in Iran.
10 U.S. presented its legal case against Iran before the International Court of Justice.
11 Iran was ordered to reduce its diplomatic personnel in the U.S.
15 Shah left the U.S. and took up residence on Panama's Contadora Island. The International Court of Justice ordered the immediate release of the hostages.
21 U.S. announced it would request the UN Security Council to impose economic sanctions against Iran.
25 Four clergymen were permitted to hold Christmas services for 43 hostages separated into small groups. Seven others were unaccounted for. Militants said the missing hostages did not want, or were not permitted, to attend the Christmas services.
27 U.S. Court of Appeals ruled that the president had the right to order that visas of only Iranian students be checked.
28 Followers of Shariat-Madari took some ten Khomeini supporters hostage in Tabriz.
29 U.S. presented its case for economic sanctions against Iran before the UN. U.S. agreed to delay UN vote until Waldheim had returned from a trip to Teheran.
31 UN Security Council voted 11–0 to meet on January 7 to discuss economic sanctions if Waldheim's trip were to fail.

tages being held by Iranian militants in the U.S. embassy in Teheran. Before the voting, Donald F. McHenry, the U.S. ambassador to the UN, reminded the delegates that the illegal detention of diplomatic personnel had implications for all nations, no matter what their other differences might be. The U.S.S.R. voted for the resolution but otherwise gave the U.S. only minimal support in its dispute with Iran over the hostages.

6 *Choi Kyu Hah elected in South Korea*

Choi Kyu Hah, acting president of South Korea, received 2,465 of 2,549 votes cast by the National Conference for Unification and became the nation's chief executive. Choi then announced that one of his top priorities would be a revision of the constitution so that elections for a new president could be held relatively soon. (Five years still remained from the unexpired term of the late president Park Chung Hee.) The following day Choi rescinded Emergency Decree No. 9, which forbade criticism of the constitution. The order was termed an act of "national reconciliation" and was in accordance with the unanimous vote of the National Assembly on December 1. On December 8 opposition leader Kim Dae Jung was freed from house arrest and 68 violators of the decree were released from prison. Choi's swearing-in ceremony was held on December 21.

7 *Ireland gets new prime minister*

Charles J. Haughey, Ireland's 54-year-old health minister, was elected prime minister in place of John Lynch, who unexpectedly resigned on December 5. Members of Parliament belonging to the ruling Fianna Fail party chose Haughey over Finance Minister George Colley by a vote of 44–38.

12 *Gen. Chung arrested in South Korea*

Gen. Chung Sung Hwa, chief of staff of the South Korean Army and martial law administrator, was arrested in Seoul for alleged involvement in the assassination of Pres. Park Chung Hee. Other high-ranking military personnel were arrested at the Ministry of National Defense. A number of persons were killed before members of the Army Security Command under Gen. Chon Too Hwan could make the arrests. Chon apparently acted without the prior approval of Pres. Choi Kyu Hah. On December 13 the government announced a reorganization of the army command, with Gen. Chon's associates filling vacancies. Some foreign observers believed the events weakened the position of those favouring a return to democratic government.

13 *Court rules that Quebec language bill must be changed*

The Canadian Supreme Court ruled unanimously that sections of Quebec's 1977 language bill (Bill 101) were unconstitutional and must be changed. The ruling meant that French could no longer be considered the only official language of the provincial assembly and courts.

14 *Canadian Parliament dissolved*

Canadian Prime Minister Joe Clark's Progressive Conservative government was toppled on December 13 when a budget motion was defeated in the House of Commons by a vote of 139–133. Clark viewed the defeat as equivalent to a vote of no confidence. The next day he asked the governor-general to dissolve Parliament and call for new elections in February 1980. On December 18 former prime minister Pierre Trudeau, who had been defeated by Clark in May and who had announced his retirement from politics on November 21, agreed to resume leadership of the Liberal Party for the general election.

15 *World Court condemns Iran*

The International Court of Justice, after five days of deliberations, ruled 15–0 that Iran must immediately release all U.S. hostages being held in the U.S. embassy in Teheran. In their written decision the judges noted: "There is no more fundamental prerequisite for the conduct of relations between states than the inviolability of diplomatic envoys and embassies. . . ." U.S. Attorney General

Benjamin Civiletti had presented his nation's case to the court on December 10; Iran refused to send a representative.

Deposed shah leaves U.S. for Panama

The deposed shah of Iran left Lackland Air Force Base in Texas and flew to Panama, where he took up residence on the Pacific coast island of Contadora. He accepted Panama's long-standing invitation after Mexico had suddenly announced on November 29 that the shah's visitor's visa would not be renewed.

17 *Margaret Thatcher visits the U.S.*

British Prime Minister Margaret Thatcher and President Carter met in the White House to exchange views on a broad range of topics. Carter later expressed appreciation for Britain's "unequivocal support on the Iranian issue." The SALT II treaty and the Zimbabwe Rhodesia situation were also discussed. Carter told Thatcher that no decision had been reached on Britain's request for arms and equipment to be used against terrorists by Northern Ireland police.

London talks on Zimbabwe Rhodesia finally succeed

After nearly four months of difficult negotiations in London, a settlement was finally reached on the future of Zimbabwe Rhodesia. On December 12 Lord Soames had arrived in Salisbury, the nation's capital, as temporary governor—thereby ending nearly 15 years of unilateral Rhodesian independence. That same day Britain lifted its trade sanctions against the country. The UN, the U.S., and many African states soon followed suit. Before Soames departed London, Joshua Nkomo and Robert Mugabe, co-leaders of the Patriotic Front guerrilla organization, had accepted the basic plan for a cease-fire. On December 11 Bishop Abel T. Muzorewa's government, which had ruled the country for six months, voted itself out of power. On December 21 a peace agreement was formally signed in London by all the parties involved. On December 23 a Commonwealth peacekeeping force of 1,300 men took up positions to monitor assembly areas for government and guerrilla troops. Some fighting continued after the truce took effect on December 27, but the overall picture was optimistic. The Patriotic Front had already been granted permission to engage in political activity, bans against several newspapers had been lifted, martial law courts had been dissolved, and many political prisoners had been set free. On December 28 Soames announced that elections would be held in February 1980.

20 *OPEC meeting ends in discord*

Ministers of the 13 OPEC nations ended a four-day meeting in Caracas, Venezuela, without agreeing on a new price structure. As a consequence, each nation would set its own prices for crude oil until the next meeting in six months.

M. PHILIPPOT—SYGMA

Heavy Soviet tanks and armoured personnel carriers prowled the streets of Kabul, Afghanistan, after the Soviet Union invaded that country in December.

Killers of Park Chung Hee to die

Kim Jae Kyu, former head of the Korean Central Intelligence Agency, and five of his aides were sentenced to death by a South Korean military court for the October 26 assassination of Pres. Park Chung Hee and five of his bodyguards. Kim Kae Won, who had been Park's chief of staff, was also sentenced to die for his complicity in the plot. An eighth defendant was sentenced to prison for obstructing justice by hiding guns and other items belonging to the accused.

27 *Soviet Union invades Afghanistan; president is executed*

Hafizullah Amin, the man who assumed the presidency of Afghanistan in mid-September after directing a coup that led to the overthrow and death of Nur Mohammad Taraki, was ousted in a coup engineered by the Soviet Union. He was then executed. Though Amin had been supported by the U.S.S.R., he was unable to put down a Muslim rebellion that threatened to arouse Muslim areas of the Soviet Union. Babrak Karmal, a former deputy prime minister residing in exile in Czechoslovakia, was brought back to Afghanistan and installed as president. In one of his first speeches, he denounced Amin as an agent of U.S. imperialism. The role of the Soviet Union in Afghanistan shocked the world because tens of thousands of fully equipped Soviet soldiers carried out the coup and because the Soviet Union continued to airlift additional military contingents and supplies into the country after Amin had been deposed. The Soviets took control of many strategic points in the capital city of Kabul and elsewhere. On December 31 President Carter declared it was imperative that world leaders immediately make it clear to the Soviet Union that its actions would have "severe political consequences."

Pol Pot replaced by Khieu Samphan

The ousted Cambodian regime's ambassador to China confirmed in Beijing (Peking) that Khieu Samphan had replaced Pol Pot as premier while retaining his position as head of state. Pol Pot was named commander of the guerrilla forces fighting the Vietnamese-supported government of Heng Samrin. The changes were reportedly made around mid-December during a secret party congress of 167 representatives who met somewhere in Cambodia.

31 *UN conditionally approves economic sanctions against Iran*

The UN Security Council approved a resolution calling for economic sanctions against Iran if it failed to free all American hostages within a week. The vote was 11–0, with 4 abstentions: Bangladesh, Czechoslovakia, Kuwait, and the Soviet Union. On January 7 UN Secretary-General Kurt Waldheim would report to the Security Council the results of his personal efforts in Iran to have the hostages released.

Gold prices set all-time records

The price of gold bullion on the London exchange finished the year at $524 an ounce, far more than double the $226 price that had prevailed at the end of 1978. Similar increases were posted in Hong Kong, Zürich, New York, and Chicago. Gold prices reached $300 an ounce on July 18, $400 on October 10, and $500 on December 26. Analysts said the increases were attributable mainly to political and economic uncertainties.

— UNUSUAL BUT NOTEWORTHY EVENTS OF 1979 —

Not all the news events of 1979 made prominent headlines. Among items reported less breathlessly in the worldwide press were the following:

The Blue Dolphin Restaurant in San Leandro, Calif., has been the scene of numerous memorable gatherings, but none perhaps quite so unforgettable as the wedding reception that took place in mid-June. As the 300 guests chatted happily among themselves, they suddenly grew silent when the newlyweds began arguing in loud voices. Dismay turned to disbelief when the groom grabbed the wedding cake and threw it in his bride's face. By the time a police squad pulled up, guests were breaking chairs and smashing mirrors. It took half an hour for more than 30 police to get the crowd under control. By that time the newlyweds had disappeared, possibly laughing on their way to a blissful honeymoon.

The credit manager of a Maryland carpet company was told by doctors that he had a rare, incurable intestinal disease. A lawyer later testified that when his client heard the news he "went off the deep end" by embezzling $29,000 for a series of wild parties. Later the doctors arrived at a new diagnosis: the patient was merely allergic to the surgical gloves used during exploratory surgery.

John Naylor, a 45-year-old former British Army boxing champion, wanted about $190,000 for his eight-bedroom, 17th-century house in Whatlington, England, but 30-year-old Kevin Reardon was willing to pay only $153,000. When no compromise could be reached, both agreed to resolve their differences in a makeshift ring. Naylor quickly dropped the price to $163,000 after being floored 16 times during the first two rounds.

Canadian mortician Ken Timlick of Vancouver has been accused of unethical conduct for offering clients the option of buying $6 coffins. His innovation has also made the British Columbia Funeral Service Association unhappy. Long bothered by the high cost of funerals, Timlick finally hit upon a novel solution. He suggests that clients save money by renting an expensive looking catafalque during the period of visitation and for the funeral service. The catafalque is removed at the cemetery and the deceased is buried in the simple enclosed coffin. Its interior is lined with satinlike fabric sewn by Timlick's wife. MacMillan Bloedel Ltd., a wood products company, manufactures the coffins out of cardboard.

High-fibre foods can possibly prevent some serious diseases. What bothered the U.S. Federal Trade Commission about Fresh Horizons bread was not the high level of its fibre content but the fact that consumers were not given sufficient information about the product. The bakers were warned that future advertisements must clearly state either that "the source of this fiber is wood" or that the bread "contains fiber derived from pulp of trees."

WIDE WORLD

The French call it noblesse oblige. Prince Charles of Great Britain put it more colourfully when he exclaimed during an early spring trip to the Orient, "Boy, the things I do for England!" The future king then gallantly accepted and downed a dish of curried snake.

During the summer it was suggested that all those who find marathon running a bore get together and express their feelings by standing still for 26 miles.

Safecracker Imre Kiss boasted to police in Budapest, Hung., that he had a perfect record of 85 burglaries and no arrests until an optometrist insisted he wear glasses because of an unusual eye condition. On his 86th job, Kiss gave the police all the evidence they needed. He left his glasses inside the safe when he departed.

A parish magazine in Normanton, England, reported that a clergyman was annoyed when a parishioner failed to open the door when he dropped by for a visit. He left his card with a quotation from Revelation 3:20: "Behold, I stand at the door and knock; if any man hear my voice, and open the door, I will come in to him." The following Sunday the woman parishioner handed the clergyman her card with a quotation from Genesis 3:10. It read, "I heard thy voice in the garden and I was afraid, because I was naked; and I hid myself."

Reader's Digest, which has already condensed some of the best-known best-sellers of modern times, is planning to condense the best-seller of all time. Editors expect to reduce the Revised Standard Version of the Bible by 40%, mainly by omitting genealogies and repetitions.

Frugality has its rewards, sometimes in unexpected ways for unexpecting beneficiaries. When a Cleveland, Ohio, demolition team moved in with heavy equipment to level an abandoned building on Ellen Avenue, 50-year-old U.S. Treasury bills began floating through the air. Neighbours and passersby quickly took advantage of the windfall profits. Halvor Holbeck was not surprised that his uncle had used the walls of the house as a safe deposit vault. When the man died in 1964, some $200,000 in bonds, cash, gold coins, and bank accounts had been found in one of the six other houses he owned. As far as Holbeck is concerned, the estimated $80,000 picked up in the wreckage belongs to those who retrieved it.

Racetrack touts say one sure way to beat the odds is to stick with a top jockey and double your bet on each successive race until he wins. In time, they say, you're bound to break even or come out ahead. When Steve Cauthen, the 1977 jockey of the year, had 110 consecutive losses in 1978, a series of bets—beginning with $2 and doubled each time he lost—finally would have paid off in the 111th race a bet of about $2,596,100,000,000,000,000,000,000,000,000,000.

Biographers name Waxhaw as the birthplace of Andrew Jackson, seventh president of the U.S. And that's precisely why Carolinians from both North and South claim him as a native son. Everyone seems to agree that Jackson was born in the Waxhaw area in the house of a maternal aunt. The unanswered question is the house of which of two aunts? One lived just south of the present state borders, the other two miles north. In August the matter was settled, at least in a practical way, to the satisfaction of a good number of football fans. Until next summer the 17-inch stoneware bust of Jackson will rest in the Union County courthouse in North Carolina because three northern high school football teams scored a total of 36 points to the 6 points scored by three opposing teams from the south. The contest was billed as the first annual Old Hickory Football Classic.

When John Howard eloped in 1926, he was only 17. The romance was quickly ended by the 16-year-old girl's mother, who persuaded a judge to grant an annulment. Years passed, and John and Ruth both married twice. Then, 53 years after their elopement, John visited his boyhood sweetheart in a French Lick, Ind., rest home. When Ruth confessed that her love for John had never died, the two were married. John had no idea when he left Phoenix, Ariz., that things would develop so quickly. Otherwise, he said, he would have brought along his teeth.

Very careful planning, attention to details, the finest of materials, and first-class workmanship are all essential in the building of a dream house. Then you move in expensive belongings and live in the house four years before ordering the place torn down. Finally, you call in an architect and draw up plans for another house that has none of the defects that went undetected the first time around. That, more or less, was the scenario followed by 36-year-old Edgar Kaiser, Jr., whose $300,000 mansion didn't suit his needs. The chairman and chief executive officer of Kaiser Resources plans to use $600,000 from his coal and oil profits to replace the original mansion built on a site that offers a view of Locarno Beach, English Bay, and the North Shore Mountains in British Columbia.

U.S. Trust used a computer model to figure out that almost 520,000 Americans are now millionaires. During the past decade the annual average increase has been 14%, which means that approximately one of every 424 U.S. citizens now has assets valued in seven figures. The Manhattan firm pointed out that millionaires aren't what they used to be, partly because U.S. dollars aren't either.

Supermarkets that used to offer customers vegetables, bread, and meat now stock ladies' nylons, spray paint, and hardware. This gave Dr. Louis Gonzales an idea. While looking for back-to-school clothes or a chain-link fence, maybe visitors to a shopping mall would like to have their teeth checked. During his first two months in a San Bruno, Calif., Sears store, Gonzales attracted some 200 patients. That reportedly is many times more than a dentist might expect in the first two years of a new practice. Gonzales apparently is filling a genuine need while he fills genuine cavities.

The California gasoline shortage in May frustrated drivers, inflamed tempers, sparked latent creativity, and set off a seemingly endless round of controversy. One irate driver in southern California informed the government and those who saw his lettered van: "I'm not going to take it any more. No gas, no taxes." Professional football player Johnny Rodgers bought a service station in San Diego so he and his friends could spend their time doing something more satisfying than waiting in line to have their tanks filled. Dr. Myles Lippe counted himself lucky one morning in San Francisco when he found only one car in front of his at a gas station scheduled to open in only an hour. When the doctor's beeper sounded, the paging service said a patient needed help. Lippe phoned the patient, determined the ailment was not serious, explained his plight, and asked the man if he could drop by the gas station for "an office visit." After examining the man in his car, the doctor confirmed his earlier diagnosis and wrote a prescription. Two attorneys from Pacific Palisades seemed to enjoy having an excuse to ride their horses through traffic to their law offices in Beverly Hills. The controversy also found its way into print when a reader suggested going back to the horse and buggy. Another reader countered by suggesting that a few senior citizens be asked how the streets smelled in the good old days. That brought an antinuclear-energy reader into the act, who reminded persons with sensitive noses that the half-life of most radioactive materials is considerably longer than the half-life of horse manure.

Horserace fans in the Detroit area who paid $60 each for tickets to the Kentucky Derby didn't have to go to the track to lose their money. The 5,000 seats in section 32 were clearly counterfeits because Churchill Downs has no section 32.

A Soviet newspaper reported the case of V. I. Matveyev, who entered a hospital to have an artificial joint implanted in a left toe. When Matveyev awoke from surgery, his right foot was bandaged but not his left. He also had a bandage on his right hand. When Matveyev demanded an explanation, the surgeon became irate and wanted to know if Matveyev thought he was smarter than the doctor. As to the hand, it had an unpleasant scar that was removed. The doctor told Matveyev to stop complaining and go back to work after buying a pair of shoes three sizes larger than usual. The matter was taken to local authorities who suspended the doctor's license for three months and warned him to lay off the vodka on the eve of operations.

Publish or perish, that old bugaboo of the academic world, haunts even the high and mighty. Archer J. P. Martin, a Nobel laureate in 1952, was informed by the University of Houston's department of chemistry that his services were no longer needed. The principal complaint was that Martin had not published enough scientific papers during his five years on the faculty. Martin was surprised by the news because, he said, he joined the university with the understanding that "essentially, I could do any work I pleased here" and "I certainly got the impression that I had this chair for as long as I was able to stagger into the laboratory."

Speeding motorists in Florida had their trials postponed in February after judges viewed films showing a tree clocked at 86 mph. The fact that the radarlike devices commonly used by police to check the speed of passing cars can indeed malfunction was further confirmed when a house was recorded doing 28 mph. And it wasn't even a mobile home.

An anonymous letter writer informed the New York State Department of Taxation and Finance that a certain Jody Gerard was not paying quarterly sales taxes on his fishing worm business. When two tax agents showed up at Gerard's home in upstate Eddyville, he was scared half to death. He had not kept a ledger, had filed no quarterly reports, and had remitted no taxes. The agents assigned Gerard a tax number, registered him as the operator of a small business, and explained the procedures to be followed in keeping financial records and filing reports. Gerard listened attentively and seemed satisfied, even though it cost him 50 cents to purchase the 64-cent bank check he needed to pay back taxes. For a 12-year-old, that seemed like a lot of money.

Two pit bulldogs in Sunnyvale, Calif., don't seem to like the uniforms worn by the police. Bill Manley, a Santa Clara County animal control officer, says the dogs are normally very friendly, but after taking a look at uniformed officer Ruben Grijalva they moved in to attack. Grijalva got to his patrol car safely and started to drive away slowly when he felt a thud, then another, followed by two more. The dogs had chewed through all four tires.

Illinois state senators bowed their heads devoutly as the Rev. Tony Ahlstrom offered a prayer to open the floor session in May. Those same heads suddenly became rigid with attention when the clergyman prayed

WIDE WORLD

Penthouse International took a gamble when it decided to build a casino in Atlantic City, N.J., on property that included the home belonging to Mrs. Anthony Bongiovanni. When the owner steadfastly spurned a Penthouse offer that reportedly exceeded $100,000, casino architects returned to their drawing boards and revised the blueprints. The Bongiovanni house is now flanked on three sides by the casino. Some of the trouble might have been avoided if casino officials had listened more carefully when Mrs. Bongiovanni took a firm stand against roulette wheels, blackjack tables, slot machines, keno cards, and poker. She clearly meant "no dice."

for fewer laws, especially laws containing loopholes.

For people who have everything, Carleton Nash of Granby, Mass., offers antiques estimated to be 180 million years old. For as little as $60 or as much as $1,000, visitors to Nash-ional Dino Land can take home petrified dinosaur footprints dug up in Nash's quarry. Members of the academic community have expressed disapproval, but Nash thinks it's nice to provide the general public with high-class conversation pieces. He is also aware that the 5,000 or so dinosaur tracks he has removed during the past 40 years have made an unmistakable imprint on his bankbook.

Minnesota state representatives, who apparently love a well-turned phrase, agreed to rate each other's oratorical performances on the floor. During May one legislator received a near-perfect 9.8 from colleagues who then proceeded to defeat the man's proposed legislation by an eloquent vote of 63–59.

Alert Chicago police spotted a stolen car behind the house occupied by Walter Gniadek, on parole for auto theft. After braving bitterly cold weather for two days, auto theft investigators agreed to abandon the stakeout but not the case. Instead, they talked a snow crew into ringing doorbells and telling residents they had to move their cars so the snowplow could get through. Gniadek went straight to the 1979 Ford Bronco, got into the driver's seat, and was promptly arrested.

Unemployment compensation depends on many factors. When Judith King took her daughter to the California Employment Development Department in Hollywood to file for benefits, the claim was rejected. The two-year-old had appeared in only three toy commercials on television—not enough, said the application processor, to establish a genuine "attachment to the labor market."

Saudi Arabian football teams can generate loyalties as undying as those in any other country in the world. When Ittihad and Ahli lined up in June to do battle for the Saudi Cup, Abdul Rahman al- ʿUtaibi was cheering for Ittihad while his wife was rooting for Ahli. After each of Ahli's four unanswered goals, ʿUtaibi was so angry he swore the traditional Islamic oath of divorce. Since Islamic law requires only that the oath be uttered three times to become effective, ʿUtaibi wife left the stadium a divorced woman. A few days after a local newspaper carried the story, Mecca's summary court ruled that "it is the consensus of scholars that divorce is invalid if it results from extreme anger." The court did not define extreme anger, nor did it indicate whether a 10–0 loss justified greater anger than a 1–0 loss.

Airline passengers expecting to debark at General Mitchell Field in Milwaukee, Wis., will get a start when they look out the window and see the huge sign that fun-loving Mark Gubin painted on the roof of his photographic studio. It reads, "Welcome to Cleveland."

Social Security benefits, according to U.S. government projections, will amount to about $64,000 annually by the time today's young adults reach retirement age in 2025. At that time the average worker's wage is expected to be $162,000, with Social Security taxes levied on earnings up to $378,000 a year. By comparison, the average worker's 1979 earned income was about $11,500, with a maximum of $22,900 subject to a 6.13% Social Security tax. By 1986 the tax would not only increase to 7.15% but would be assessed on a substantially higher level of income than is now permitted by law.

Pigeons have such keen eyesight that the U.S. Navy in Hawaii is training them for rescue missions. Riding in special compartments beneath helicopters, the pigeons are trained to peck a food lever whenever they spot an orange-coloured life jacket. Their reaction time is about 30 seconds faster than that of the crew. On a simulated rescue mission early in the year, the birds signaled a find. The pilot then zeroed in on an orange-coloured surfboard.

The U.S. Justice Department, according to a report given to Congress in March, estimates that as much as 10% of every tax dollar is wasted or stolen. As if to prove the point, the U.S. Treasury notified the town clerk of Cloud Lake, Fla., that the town had been designated a major disaster area by the president of the U.S. If disaster had indeed struck Cloud Lake, none of the seven businesses in town was aware of it. Dorothy Gravelin, the town clerk, was even more perplexed when she learned that none of the neighbouring towns had received a similar notice. She contacted the state capital, but no one could offer an explanation. Finally, an employee of the U.S. Office of Revenue Sharing in Washington, D.C., solved the mystery: Cloud Lake had suffered a major disaster when its crops froze in January 1977. Gravelin pointed out that Cloud Lake has no crops; the closest fields are located 20 miles west of town. To which the bureaucrat replied, "There's probably some indirect effect, like farmers who wouldn't be spending as much money in town." She then went on to say that the federal government's request was really very simple. As soon as the forms acknowledging the existence of a disaster were filled out and returned, the money would be on its way. All $22.61.

UPI

Judge Vernon Foster of the Los Angeles Superior Court ruled in August that Clayton Moore, who for some 30 years appeared in public and on television as the "Lone Ranger," could no longer wear his distinctive black mask. The court decision was in response to a lawsuit brought against Moore by Lone Ranger Television and the Wrather Corp., which now owns the rights to the Lone Ranger character and plans to use a different actor in a future Lone Ranger movie. Thanks to reruns of old Lone Ranger television shows, millions of today's youngsters (not to mention their mothers and fathers) are unimpressed by the court ruling. They still claim there is only one authentic "masked man." He's the one now wearing the court-approved sunglasses.

It's a politician's dream: once elected, you automatically stay in office until someone challenges you at the polls and wins. For Jack Cossey that dream became a nightmare. After two terms as mayor of Magnum, Okla., he wanted to retire but he couldn't persuade anyone else to run for the office. James Travis found himself in the same predicament. No one wanted to be police and fire commissioner.

When Col. Richard Eckhardt was informed by the Pentagon that he was being replaced as chief of staff of the Army National Guard in Kansas, he took the matter to federal court. Eckhardt told the judge he had been promised the position for three more years, when he would reach 60 years of age and qualify for retirement. The situation was complicated because the job is classified as civil service, and Eckhardt has to be a member of the National Guard to keep it. But Army Reserve regulations stipulate that Eckhardt can't remain in the National Guard unless he is promoted every five years. A promotion, however, would give him the rank of general, and generals are not allowed to hold the position. Presumably even combat veterans sometimes find it harrowing to get caught in the cross fire of conflicting regulations.

Michigan police ran a summer contest to select the most creative excuse given by motorists for speeding. Wayne Coleman of the state's Department of Natural Resources was named a winner when he reported that a driver claimed 20 stuttering youths forced him to exceed the speed limit. It seems the driver's wife was the guest of honour at a farewell party given by the youngsters at the conclusion of their summer camp. By the time all had expressed their appreciation, speeding was the only way the couple could get back on schedule.

U.S. Sen. Henry Jackson, co-sponsor of an amendment to the 1974 Trade Act, reminded Chinese Vice-Premier Deng Xiaoping (Teng Hsiao-p'ing) during his visit to the U.S. that the amendment prohibits the granting of credits or "most favoured na-

UPI

Homemade water skis and a little encouragement from Chuck Best of Sanford, Fla., were all Twiggy needed to get started. Now she zips along at 12 mph behind a remote-controlled motorboat feeling pity for other squirrels who have nothing more exciting to do during the summer than run up trees. It took Best about a month to train Twiggy, who was bribed with generous gobs of peanut butter.

tion" status to a socialist country that denies or prohibits the right or opportunity of its citizens to migrate. Deng reportedly replied, "I'll have a million Chinese in Seattle on Monday morning."

Death has always been considered the only sure way to avoid taxes. But that may no longer be true in Bandung, Indonesia, where municipal authorities began considering a special tax to be levied on luxury goods. One of the items on the list was elaborate tombstones.

George Lewis, a loyal denizen of the Big Apple, has organized the Society for the Prevention of Disparaging Remarks About New York City. He has suffered long enough, he says, from such cheap shots as, "The only way to get crosstown in New York City traffic is to be born there." Besides boycotting detractors and trying to persuade them to mend their ways, Lewis wants to promote more positive remarks, such as "New York is so fast paced it's the only city where you can be coming and going at the same time."

Keith Augustine was about to be sentenced in a Durban, South Africa, court for culpable homicide in the stabbing death of a young black two years earlier. The hospital had confirmed that the victim died of stab wounds after arriving in an ambulance. As Petrus van Loggerenberg sat listening to the case, he realized the scene of the murder was a tearoom he frequently visited. He spoke with the owner, who assured him that Amos Ngeme, the victim of the stabbing, was very much alive. In fact, Ngeme had gone to the tearoom the day after the stabbing to thank the owner for calling an ambulance. Further checking revealed that the person who died in the hospital had never been identified.

A reader complained to advice columnist Ann Landers that a neighbour had humiliated her by naming her dog Marvin "knowing perfectly well that is my husband's name." Landers didn't think the woman stood much of a chance in court because the writer's husband leans out the window and barks like a dog whenever the neighbour calls her animal.

The psychiatrist who allegedly encouraged 25-year-old Tom Hansen to sue his mother and father for "parental malpractice" may be having second thoughts. Two months after the son's $350,000 suit was dismissed in court, Mrs. Hansen's lawyer filed suit in Boulder, Colo., against the psychiatrist. Mrs. Hansen contends that her son's action not only caused her great grief, humiliation, shock, and anger, but made her the object of "ridicule and embarrassment throughout the United States and the rest of the world."

Jon B. Minnoch was, as he later said, being slowly crushed to death by his own weight when a fire department rescue unit rushed him to Seattle's University Hospital in March 1978. He could neither move nor speak because his circulatory and respiratory systems were failing. There was no convenient way to find out how heavy Minnoch was, but doctors estimated his weight at more than 1,400 lb—the heaviest human being in medical history. Since that time Minnoch has lost over 900 lb under the watchful eye of Robert Schwartz, an endocrinologist. And he hopes to be down to 300 lb by the end of 1979. When he slims down to about 210 lb, he plans to have his picture taken. Minnoch, who was adhering to a rigorous crash diet at the time of his rescue, hopes that his example will inspire those with similar but less serious problems to "give it one more shot."

Mistaken identities are common enough, but police in Maywood, Ill., could not remember any instance to rival the mistake made in April. A murder victim was identified as William Allen by his father, mother, brother, and stepfather. A few hours later Allen returned home from a party. Police then used fingerprints to identify the corpse as that of a parolee from Joliet State Prison.

Ground-breaking ceremonies reached new heights in February thanks to elaborate procedures worked out by NASA scientists. The Jet Propulsion Laboratory in Pasadena, Calif., set things in motion by transmitting a signal to Voyager 1 as it sped through outer space some 400 million mi from Earth. The spacecraft then sent the signal to a tracking station in Australia, where it was relayed by a satellite and telephone lines to central Kansas. There it activated a laser beam device that detonated a small explosive charge, which left a six-inch hole in a parking lot at Hutchinson Junior College. The elaborate stunt was appropriate enough because the lot had been designated as the site of a $2 million space museum.

Hollywood now has Superman, but Craig Field in Jacksonville, Fla., has Superbird. Not content to perch atop the control tower, Superbird—many think it's a male ring-neck pheasant—escorts each plane as it roars down the runway on takeoff. Robbie Rose, a traffic watch pilot, says the bird plays around the sand hills until he hears a plane rev up its motors. Then Superbird lines up beside the plane and "when you start your roll, he starts his roll." Once the plane takes to the air, Superbird just relaxes until another plane moves to the runway.

Nondiscrimination took another step forward when Caesar's Boardwalk Regency casino in Atlantic City, N.J., installed 23 slot machines that could be easily operated by persons in wheelchairs. The nickel and quarter one-armed bandits also carry instructions in Braille for those who are blind. Nowadays true democracy seems to demand that all citizens be given an equal opportunity to lose money honestly.

A switchboard operator in Los Angeles answered a call with her usual "Good morning, this is the Pacific Telephone Co." After a period of silence, an embarrassed female asked if the number she had reached was really that of the telephone company. Before hanging up she confessed that she found the number in her husband's coat pocket and simply had to find out whose phone it was.

Carol Boatner thought it would be an interesting experience for 14 Seabreeze High School students to attend a real court session. Indeed it was. As they sat in rapt attention, the Florida students were amazed to see an enraged defendant suddenly charge the bench. They were even more amazed when Volusia County Judge Darrel Carnell reached under his black robe and pulled out a pistol. Later the judge would not say whether the gun was loaded or not. In this case, it was enough that the defendant thought it was.

DISASTERS OF 1979

The loss of life and property from disasters in 1979 included the following:

AVIATION

February 12, Near Kariba, Rhodesia. An Air Rhodesia four-engine turboprop plane crashed and burned some 47 km (29 mi) east of Kariba after it was shot down by heat-seeking missiles fired by black guerrilla forces; all 50 persons aboard were killed.

March 14, Doha, Qatar. A Jordanian Boeing 727 crashed and burned when it attempted to make a landing during a thunderstorm; 45 persons were killed and 19 others were rescued.

March 14, Beijing (Peking), China. A Trident jet transport plane on a military training flight crashed shortly after takeoff and ripped through a factory on the outskirts of Beijing; 44 persons were known dead.

March 17, Moscow, U.S.S.R. A Soviet Tupolev-104 airliner crashed near Moscow's Vnukovo Airport shortly after takeoff when one of the engines caught fire; 90 persons were killed.

March 29, Near Ancienne-Lorette Airport, Que. A turboprop F-27 crashed into an orchard moments after takeoff; 17 of the 24 persons aboard were killed when the plane exploded.

April 23, Ecuador. A commercial airplane carrying 57 persons disappeared on a 400-km (250-mi) flight between Quito and Cuenca; all aboard were presumed dead.

May 7, Near San Francisco, Arg. An Argentine Air Force helicopter crashed some 480 km (300 mi) northwest of Buenos Aires; 10 of the 16 persons aboard lost their lives.

May 25, Chicago, Ill. An American Airlines DC-10 jumbo jet crashed and exploded moments after takeoff from O'Hare International Airport when the jetliner lost an engine because of an array of structural weaknesses; there were no survivors among the 272 persons aboard flight 191 bound for Los Angeles. Two others on the ground also lost their lives in the worst U.S. aviation disaster in history to date.

May 27, Off the coast of Dakar, Senegal. A military transport plane, carrying the prime minister of Mauritania and 11 other persons, plunged into the Atlantic Ocean during a sandstorm; there were no survivors.

May 30, Owls Head, Maine. A twin-engine commuter airplane went down about a mile and a half short of the runway at Owls Head Airport, slammed into a rock ledge, and flipped over; 17 of the 18 persons aboard were killed.

June 11, Idaho. A U.S. Forest Service DC-3 airplane crashed after losing one of its engines; only 2 of the 12 persons aboard survived.

CHICAGO TRIBUNE/SYGMA

A total of 274 persons (272 in the plane and 2 on the ground) were killed in the May 25 crash of American Airlines flight 191 from Chicago to Los Angeles. The DC-10 jetliner had just taken off when it lost an engine and crashed less than a mile from O'Hare International Airport.

July 11, North Sumatra, Indon. A domestic Indonesian airliner flying at an altitude of 1,800 m (6,000 ft) crashed into a 2,100-m (7,000-ft) mountain; all 61 persons aboard were killed.

August 4, Western India. An Indian Airlines turboprop airplane en route from Poona to Bombay slammed into a hill; all 39 passengers and 4 crew members were presumed dead.

August 11, Soviet Union. Two Soviet Tupolev-134 jetliners collided over the Ukraine in a crash that was believed to be the second worst air collision in aviation history; a reliable Soviet source reported that there were no survivors and 173 fatalities.

September 13, Near Cagliari, Sardinia. An Italian airliner on a flight from Milan to Cagliari crashed into the mountains before making its landing approach; all 31 persons aboard were killed.

September 14, Near Klamath Falls, Ore. A DC-7 airplane used to fight forest fires went down and crashed on Surveyor Peak; 12 persons aboard, all employees of Butler Aircraft Co., were killed.

October 7, Athens, Greece. A DC-8 jetliner carrying 154 persons caught fire shortly after landing at Athens airport; 14 persons were killed and 10 others were injured.

October 28, Near San Diego, Calif. A Mexican twin-engine turboprop airplane, carrying four U.S. prisoners to a border exchange in Tijuana, slammed into a telephone pole on top of Spring Canyon and burst into flames after the pilot became disoriented in dense fog; all ten persons aboard the craft were killed.

October 31, Mexico City, Mexico. A Western Airlines DC-10 airplane crashed into a truck and then hit an airport building after landing on a closed runway at Mexico City Airport; 73 persons including 2 on the ground were killed.

November 26, Near Taif, Saudi Arabia. A Pakistan International Airlines Boeing 707 jetliner carrying 156 persons, mostly pilgrims returning from Mecca, crashed shortly after takeoff from Jidda airport; all 156 persons aboard were killed.

November 28, Near McMurdo Station, Antarctica. A New Zealand DC-10 airplane on a sight-seeing flight over Antarctica plowed into Mt. Erebus, a 3,780-m (12,400-ft) active volcano; all 257 persons aboard were dead.

December 22, Amazon jungle, Peru. A twin-engine Buffalo air force plane crashed in the jungle while flying from Pucallpa to Puerto Esperanza; all 27 persons aboard died.

December 23, Near Port Moresby, Papua New Guinea. A passenger plane making a scheduled domestic flight crashed into a mountain in the Owen Stanley Range after leaving Port Moresby; all 15 persons aboard were killed.

December 23, Near Ankara, Turkey. A Turkish Airlines Fokker F-28 slammed into a hill at Cubuktepe during dense fog while making its approach to Ankara's Esenboga Airport; 39 of the 43 persons aboard were trapped in the burning plane.

FIRES AND EXPLOSIONS

January 20, Hoboken, N.J. A blaze in a five-story tenement building reduced the structure to rubble and killed at least 19 persons; officials believed arson was the cause of the fire.

February 15, Warsaw, Poland. A mysterious explosion ripped through a crowded Warsaw bank; 44 persons were known dead and 110 others were injured in the blast.

February 21, Lahore, Pak. A powerful explosion in a fireworks factory demolished the three-story building and three adjacent homes; 13 persons were killed and 75 others were injured, 15 of them seriously.

March 16, Northern Norway. A fast-burning fire swept through a nursing home and killed 11 elderly persons who were overcome with the fumes of burning plastic furniture.

April 2, Farmington, Mo. An early-morning fire swept through a retirement home that boarded elderly persons and some mental patients from the state hospital; 25 of the building's 38 residents were killed when the roof collapsed and trapped them.

April 17, Shogi, India. A hut that was used for storing rock blasting materials exploded when it was struck by a bolt of lightning; 14 persons were killed in the blaze and 7 others were injured.

May 8, Manchester, England. A fire that started on the third floor of an F. W. Woolworth's store forced 350 people to fight for a means of escape from the fiery inferno; at least 10 persons were killed and 48 others were treated for smoke inhalation and burns.

July 12, Saragossa, Spain. A fire swept through the ten-story Hotel Corona de Aragón after a pastry machine exploded; the blaze claimed the lives of 80 persons and injured 70 others in the worst hotel fire in Spain's history.

July 13, Taipei, Taiwan. An explosion in a four-story building occurred when chemicals stored in the basement exploded; the blast ripped through the roof, claiming the lives of 18 persons and injuring 61 others.

July 29, Tuticorin, India. A fire erupted in a tent movie theatre when an electrical spark set the screen on fire during a matinee;

92 persons, mostly women and children, were killed and 80 others were injured.

July 31, Cambridge, Ohio. A fast-burning fire in a Holiday Inn set by an arsonist trapped hundreds of guests; 10 persons were killed and 78 others were injured, some critically, when they smashed windows and jumped from the second story.

August 7, Lloret de Mar, Spain. A roaring fire believed to have been set by arsonists trapped campers in a valley behind the resort town of Lloret de Mar; at least 20 persons were known dead.

September 28, Vienna, Austria. An intense fire that swept through the four-story Am Augarten Hotel claimed the lives of 25 persons.

November 11, Pioneer, Ohio. A fire in a home for elderly and mentally retarded persons was apparently started by a four-year-old boy who set fire to a couch; 14 persons were killed in the blaze.

November 30, Tachia, Taiwan. A series of explosions in a firecracker factory leveled 14 cement-and-brick buildings and damaged 9 others; 12 persons lost their lives and more than 70 others were listed in critical condition.

December 6, Antonio Escobedo, Mexico. A predawn fire in a hotel perched in the Sierra Madre range caused $50,000 in damages and the deaths of all 24 guests.

December 6, Rosario, Arg. A blazing fire trapped patrons of a nightclub in central Rosario; 16 persons died in restrooms where they fled to escape the smoke and flames and 10 others were injured.

December 27, Lancaster County, S.C. A fire in a 150-year-old jail claimed the lives of 10 of 11 inmates; the blaze was apparently caused by one or more of the prisoners who set fire to mattresses.

MARINE

January 1, Caribbean Sea. The "Master Michael," a Cypriot tanker carrying 1.8 million gal of diesel fuel, caught fire in a storm and later sank; 30 of the vessel's 35 crewmen were missing and presumed dead; one other was known dead.

January 4, Off the coast of Salerno, Italy. The 790-ton Italian freighter "Stabia Prima" sank south of Salerno; one person was rescued but 12 others were missing and believed dead.

January 8, Bantry Bay, Ireland. The French oil tanker "Betelgeuse" broke in two after two powerful explosions threw crewmen into a sea of flaming oil; at least 50 persons were believed dead.

June 26, Off the coast of Italy. The 12,000-ton French freighter "Emmanuel Delmas" burst into flames when it collided and locked bows with the 5,000-ton Italian tanker "Vera Berlingieri" in dense fog; 18 seamen were known dead and 14 others were still missing and believed dead.

July 20, East of Tobago. Two Liberian-registered but Greek-owned supertankers, the "Atlantic Empress" and the "Aegean Captain," collided during heavy rains off the east coast of Tobago; 34 of the 75 crewmen were missing and presumed dead.

August 14, English Channel and Irish Sea. Monstrous gale force winds accompanied by huge waves endangered the lives of sailors participating in the prestigious Fastnet yacht race, a 975-km (605-mi) event that is part of the Admiral's Cup competition; 18 persons lost their lives in the world's worst yachting disaster to date, and 23 yachts sank.

August 15, Southern Bangladesh. A cyclone that struck southern Bangladesh sank about 40 boats; some 50 fishermen were killed and 100 others were reported missing at sea.

October 20, Off the coast of northern Japan. The fate of the 91-ton "Ildong No. 15," a South Korean fishing boat carrying 23 crew members, remained unknown after a typhoon.

November 1, Gulf of Mexico. The Liberian freighter "Mimosa" rammed into the Liberian tanker "Burmah Agate," which was carrying 16.8 million gal of crude oil; the fiery collision occurred in choppy seas off the coast of Galveston, Texas, and 31 of the 35 Taiwanese crewmen aboard the tanker were presumed dead.

Early November, Near Khulna, Bangladesh. A cargo ship slammed into a crowded river launch near Khulna, 130 km (80 mi) southwest of Dacca; at least 200 Muslims en route to a celebration were feared drowned.

November 6, English Channel. A British freighter, the 1,028-ton "Pool Fisher," capsized and sank in the English Channel in winds of about 45 mph; it was believed that 13 persons aboard the ship drowned.

December 26, Off British Columbia. An ore freighter, the "Lee Wang Zin," capsized during a violent storm with waves up to 7.6 m (25 ft) high and ran aground off the coast of Alaska; the 30 Taiwanese crewmen aboard were feared dead.

MINING

February 24, Glace Bay, Nova Scotia. A powerful explosion at a colliery took the lives of 12 miners and critically injured 4 others; the cause of the blast was unknown.

April 14, Chungsun, South Korea. An explosion in a mine shaft killed at least 26 miners and injured 40 others.

May 15, Hokkaido, Japan. An explosion following a toxic methane gas leak in a coal mine claimed the lives of nine miners and injured nine others; seven miners were reported missing and feared dead.

SYGMA

A luxury hotel fire in Saragossa, Spain, on July 12 took 80 lives and left 70 injured.

June 16, Northern Colombia. A landslide at an unregistered emerald mine claimed the lives of 17 persons.

October, Poland. Three separate coal-mine explosions in Poland claimed the lives of 43 miners and trapped 20 others underground; the first blast (October 5), at the Nowa Ruda mine near Walbrzych, killed 7 persons; the second (October 10), in Bytom, killed 34 miners; and the third (October 31), in Czechowice-Dziedzice, claimed the lives of 2 others.

October 27, Mungyong, South Korea. An underground fire in Unsong Mine trapped 126 coal miners when smoke and gas made rescue attempts all but impossible; after the smoke-filled shafts began to clear, 400 rescue workers entered the mine and recovered the bodies of 42 miners who apparently succumbed to smoke inhalation and rescued 84 others.

MISCELLANEOUS

February, Naples, Italy. A "mysterious disease" that killed more than 60 children under age four from June 1978 through February 1979 was in fact traceable to a type of brain damage and to respiratory infections and other contagious diseases, all known disorders.

Early June, Eastern India. A severe heat wave and drought left 238 people dead in India in a two-week period.

Late June, Pakistan. Intensive heat with temperatures soaring to 48° C (118° F) in the provinces of Sind and Punjab killed at least 70 persons.

Early July, Rajasthan State, India. Cholera and blistering temperatures killed nearly 100 persons in two weeks.

July 18, French Alps. Ten of 12 mountain climbers were feared dead when their ropes became tangled and the climbers plunged, one by one, into a deep crevasse on La Tour Ronde in the French Alps.

Early August, Bihar, India. A week-long cholera epidemic reportedly claimed the lives of 215 persons.

Early September, Lucknow, India. Illicitly distilled liquor killed 16 persons who drank it.

November, Dominican Republic. Gastroenteritis and other ills claimed the lives of 22 children who had been living in refugee camps since Hurricane David devastated the country in August.

Early December, West Java, Indon. At least 11 persons died of malnutrition as a result of contracting cholera; 45 others were afflicted with the disease and hospitalized.

December 3, Cincinnati, Ohio. Eleven persons waiting outside Riverfront Coliseum to attend a rock concert by The Who were trampled and crushed to death when thousands of rock fans surged against the doors; the calamity involved dozens of other injuries.

NATURAL

January 16, Northeast Iran. An earthquake measuring between 6.7 and 7.5 on the Richter scale completely devastated the villages of Boznabad, Khorramabad, and Ebrahimabad; at least 199 persons were known dead but the casualty list was expected to increase substantially.

Early February, Southeast Brazil. Torrential rains in the states of Minas Gerais, Espírito Santo, and Rio de Janeiro left thousands of people homeless and more than 200 persons dead.

February 19, New York and New Jersey. A crippling snowstorm dumped 13 in of snow on New York, nearly 20 in New Jersey, and left hundreds of people stranded in the snow; 13 storm-related deaths were reported.

February 21, Central Java, Indon. Mt. Sinila, which was considered a dormant volcano, erupted and spewed lava that in some places was 7 m (24 ft) deep; at least 175 persons were killed and 1,000 others were injured.

Early March, Flores Island, Indon. Landslides and floods resulting from heavy rains partially submerged 20 villages with mud and boulders; 97 people were reported killed, 8,000 were homeless, and 150 others were injured.

March 21, Himachal Pradesh State, India. Thundering avalanches trapped some 2,000 people in Pin Valley; at least 230 others were feared dead.

March 27, Fiji. Cyclone Meli blasted the eastern and southern Fiji islands, left some 1,000 families homeless, and killed at least 50 persons.

April 10, Red River Valley, Texas and Oklahoma border. A raging tornado packing winds of up to 225 mph left a path of death and destruction when it ripped through a corridor on the border of Oklahoma and Texas known as Tornado Alley; the city of Wichita Falls in Texas was hardest hit; more than 59 persons were killed and some 800 others were injured, some critically.

April 15, Yugoslavia and Albania. The most powerful earthquake in the history of Yugoslavia struck the southern coast of that country and northern Albania; the quake, measuring 7.2 on the Richter scale, obliterated streets, leveled schools, factories, hospitals, and hotels, and claimed more than 100 lives.

April 16–17, Philippines. A violent typhoon, the first of the season, left hundreds homeless, caused property damage of $3.5 million, and killed at least 12 persons; 55 others were missing.

April 21–22, Northeastern Dominican Republic. Battering torrential rains severely damaged the country's rice and banana crops, forced thousands to evacuate their homes, left 40 persons missing, and killed 12 others.

April 29, West Sumatra, Indon. Severe flooding following the eruption of the Merapi volcano destroyed several natural dams and swept away seven mountain villages on the slopes of the volcano; some 80 persons were killed.

May 12–13, India. A devastating cyclone that affected some 1,500 villages swept the southeast Indian state of Andhra Pradesh and neighbouring Tamil Nadu; more than 350 persons were killed.

May 29, Central Java, Indon. Torrential rains destroyed some 3,000 ha (7,400 ac) of rice paddy fields and leveled 600 dwellings; 15 persons lost their lives in the storm.

May 30, Lombok Island, Indon. A powerful earthquake measuring 7.6 on the Richter scale killed 34 persons and injured 48 others.

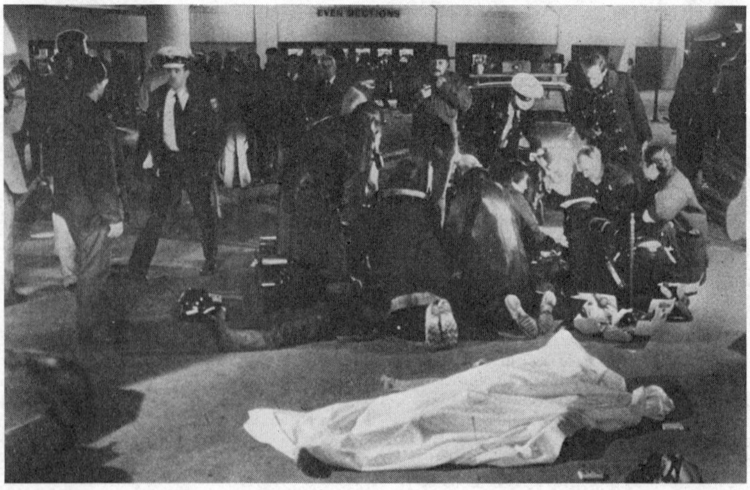

Firemen work to try to revive one of the dozens of people trampled by an out-of-control crowd rushing to get the best seats at a rock concert in Cincinnati, Ohio, in December. Eleven persons were suffocated to death in the crush.

UPI

June 13, Balikpapan, Borneo, Indon. Severe flooding following heavy rains crippled the town of Balikpapan; at least 13 persons lost their lives in the floodwaters and some 6,000 others were evacuated.

June 26–30, Southwestern Japan. Torrential rains killed at least 23 persons and left 28,000 people homeless; hardest hit was Yukuhashi on the island of Kyushu.

Late June, Montego Bay, Jamaica. Two days of torrential rainfall caused 14 ft of floodwater that drowned 32 persons; 25 others were reported missing.

July 2, Valdepeñas, Spain. A flash flood that hit the wine-growing town of Valdepeñas killed at least 22 persons.

July 9, Jiangsu (Kiangsu) Province, China. An earthquake measuring 6 on the Richter scale struck Jiangsu Province; 41 persons were killed and dozens of others were injured.

July 18, Lomblem Island, Indon. A 1.8-m (6-ft) tidal wave believed to have been caused by the collapse of Gunung Werung volcano ravaged the remote island of Lomblem; 539 persons were killed.

August 11, Morvi, India. An earthen dam completed in 1978 collapsed in the industrial town of Morvi when it could no longer contain the waters of the swollen Machhu River; a 6-m (20-ft) wall of water inundated the town, flattened homes, and was reported to have killed as many as 5,000 people.

August 25–26, Southern South Korea. Severe flooding and landslides following torrential rainfall caused by Typhoon Judy swept away bridges and flooded villages; nearly 60 persons were feared dead and some 20,000 others were left homeless.

Late August and early September, Caribbean and east coast of U.S. Hurricane David, one of the deadliest storms of its kind in this century, rampaged through the Caribbean with winds of up to 150 mph and blasted the Dominican Republic, Dominica, Puerto Rico, Haiti, Cuba, and The Bahamas; the storm also hit the eastern coast of the U.S. in Florida, Georgia, and New York. The death toll in all of the affected areas was estimated at more than 1,000 persons, and the damage estimate was in the billions of dollars.

Early September, Florida, Alabama, and Mississippi. Hurricane Frederic, the worst Gulf storm in a decade, caused 160 km (100 mi) of coastal destruction, ruining property valued at hundreds of millions of dollars; Pascagoula, Miss., and Mobile, Ala., were hardest hit. Although eight persons were killed, the prompt evacuation of nearly half a million people was credited with preventing more widespread loss of life.

September 12, Sicily, Italy. The eruption of Mt. Etna left dozens of people buried under gigantic volcanic rocks; at least nine persons were found dead and rescue workers believed that other victims were "literally blown to pieces."

October 13, Assam State, India. The swollen Brahmaputra River overflowed its banks and swept away thousands of homes in the northeastern state of Assam; at least 13 persons drowned in the floodwaters.

October 16, French Riviera. Two large tidal waves, cresting up to 3 m (10 ft), hit a 95-km (60-mi) stretch of the French Riviera, including Nice's main thoroughfare; the freak waves were attributed to an underwater landslide. Eleven construction workers in Nice were swept to sea and presumed dead, as was a businessman in Antibes.

October 17, Near Groblersdal, South Africa. A hailstorm accompanied by flash floods caused a large dam to burst and the Elands River to overflow; at least 20 persons were swept away.

October 19, Japan. Typhoon Tip caused extensive damage throughout Japan as it whipped through the country packing 55-mph winds; the storm caused at least 36 deaths, including 12 U.S. Marines who were killed by an explosion at the Mt. Fuji Marine training base.

October 23, Near Puerto Montt, Chile. Heavy rains triggered a giant mudflow that buried a village near Puerto Montt and claimed at least 30 lives.

November 14, Northeastern Iran. A powerful earthquake struck near Mashhad, the capital of Khorasan Province in northeastern Iran, ripping through 14 mud-brick villages; the village of Bohnabad near the epicentre was hardest hit with 148 casualties.

November 21, Colorado, Nebraska, and Wyoming. A deadly blizzard pelted parts of three states with 70-mph winds and record snowfalls (60.5 cm [24 in] in Cheyenne, Wyoming, and 43 cm [17 in] in Denver, Colorado, during a 24-hour period); hundreds of motorists were stranded and there were at least ten storm-related deaths.

November 23, Colombia. A powerful earthquake, Colombia's worst in 20 years, rocked the capital city of Bogotá and caused extensive damage in the areas of Risaralda, Quindío, Caldas, the Cauca Valley, and Antioquia. The city of Pereira, some 160 km (100 mi) west of Bogotá, was hardest hit with 20 persons killed and 100 others injured. The quake, which claimed at least 41 lives, also injured 600 others and destroyed 1,000 buildings.

November 25, El Playón and Lebrija, Colombia. After the Playonero River burst its banks, floodwaters and mud descended on the small towns of El Playón and Lebrija, in northeastern Colombia; 62 bodies were recovered from the wreckage.

November 27, Northeastern Iran. A severe earthquake measuring between 6 and 6.5 on the Richter scale destroyed five villages in northeastern Iran; 16 persons were killed and 23 others were injured.

December 12, Colombia-Ecuador border. An earthquake measuring between 7.7 and 8.1 on the Richter scale leveled buildings, touched off tidal waves, and killed at least 200 persons in the border zone of Colombia and Ecuador; hardest hit was the Colombian fishing village of La Charca where nearly all the homes toppled into a lake, at least 62 persons were killed and more than 350 others were injured.

December 19, Bali, Indon. An earthquake measuring over 6 on the Richter scale shook the island of Bali and destroyed 22,000 homes; 27 persons were killed and 160 others were injured.

RAILROADS

January 4, Near Ankara, Turkey. Two crowded express trains collided head-on during a blizzard when the automatic switches designed to keep them separated apparently froze; of the estimated 1,300 passengers aboard the two trains, 190 were hospitalized and 56 others were believed dead in Turkey's worst rail disaster to date.

January 9, Near Ankara, Turkey. A commuter train rammed into a stationary passenger train in heavy fog in Turkey's second rail disaster in one week; 30 persons were killed and nearly 100 others were injured.

January 19, Mexico City, Mexico. A freight train crashed into the rear of a suburban bus when the bus driver attempted to beat the train at a crossing; of the 80 passengers aboard the bus, 17 were killed and at least 35 were injured.

January 26, Western Bangladesh. An express train traveling to Parbatipur derailed and its locomotive and several passenger cars crashed into a ditch; at least 70 persons were killed and 182 others injured, making it the country's worst rail disaster to date.

April 3, Sara Buri Province, Thailand. A passenger train and a loaded oil tanker truck collided in central Thailand; at least 20 persons lost their lives in the ensuing blaze.

April 22, Pakistan. A locomotive was reported to have rammed into the rear of a stationary passenger train some 80 km (50 mi) northeast of Karachi; 44 persons were killed and 37 others were seriously injured.

June 17, Near Abidjan, Ivory Coast. An express train traveling to Ouagadougou, the capital of Upper Volta, derailed north of Abidjan; 15 persons were killed and 60 others were injured.

July 10, Mt. Vesuvius, near Naples, Italy. Two crowded six-car trains traveling on the same track in opposite directions collided on the Circumvesuviana line, which circles the slopes of the volcano; at least 13 persons were killed and 60 others were injured.

August 21, Near Bangkok, Thailand. A freight train that was switching tracks slammed into the second car of a six-coach passenger train in Taling Chan station; 51 persons were found dead and 200 others were injured in Thailand's worst rail crash.

September 13, Stalac, Yugos. A freight train that went through a red signal plowed into a crowded express train and crushed some cars to a quarter of their original size; the crash killed 60 persons and 100 others were injured.

October 20, Near Tarbes, France. A bus carrying a group of Spaniards from the shrine at Lourdes, France, drove through a railroad crossing, became stuck on the tracks, and was hit by a train; 21 persons were reported dead and 32 were injured.

October 20, Cairo, Egypt. A passenger train and a bus carrying people to work collided at a grade crossing in Cairo; 30 persons were killed and 25 others were injured.

October 30, Djibouti. A train derailed and crashed just north of the border post of Ali Sabieh; the accident claimed the lives of 50 persons and injured 30 others.

December 3, Near Londa, Karnataka State, India. An express train derailed en route to Bangalore; 25 persons were killed and more than a dozen others were injured.

December 6, Near Las Franquesas del Valles, Spain. A crewless train rolled out of a station, careened down a steep incline, and crashed into a stationary passenger train at a speed close to 70 mph; at least 14 persons were killed and 60 others injured.

December 23, Near Sarupeta, India. An express train rammed the rear of a stationary passenger train in Assam State; 25 persons were injured and 18 others were killed.

TRAFFIC

January 11, Panama Canal. A U.S. Army truck returning from a firing range on the west bank of the Panama Canal smashed through a bridge guardrail and careened down a bank bordering the canal; 16 soldiers were killed.

March 14, Greece. A Greek bus collided with a Yugoslav gasoline tanker-truck near the border of the two countries; 30 persons burned to death and 22 others were seriously injured.

March 27, Kiambu, Kenya. A minibus taxi and a truck crashed in central Kenya; police reported 11 persons were killed.

March 30, Southern India. A bus accident in the Quilon district of southern India claimed the lives of 34 persons and injured 100 others.

WIDE WORLD

More than 59 persons were killed and over 800 injured when a tornado ripped through Wichita Falls, Texas, on April 10.

April 10, Near Benavente, Spain. A school bus filled with teenagers returning from an Easter-week trip went out of control on a dangerously sharp curve and plunged into a rain-swollen river; 50 of the 60 passengers were killed as the bus swiftly sank.

April 13, Thailand. A head-on collision between a rice truck and a bus claimed the lives of 22 persons.

April 17, Rio de Janeiro State, Brazil. A bus carrying sugar-refinery workers plummeted into the Paraíba do Sul River and sank; reports indicated that some 25 or 30 men lost their lives.

June 2, Near Samchok, South Korea. A bus plunged over a cliff in eastern South Korea after colliding with a truck; at least 20 persons were known dead and 20 others were injured.

June 2, Phangnga Province, Thailand. A chartered bus carrying 68 persons collided with a loaded gasoline truck; 52 persons were killed and 13 others were seriously injured.

June 9, Near Saint-Hyacinthe, Que. A chartered bus carrying 49 senior citizens slid off a slippery curve during a rainstorm, slammed into a series of concrete pillars, and split in two; 11 persons were killed.

June 20, Brazil. A truck rammed into several vehicles, including a bus that was stopped on a highway under repair; 40 persons were killed in the accident.

Early July, Buriram Province, Thailand. When two buses carrying children to a school picnic crashed into a parked truck, 22 children and 5 adults were killed and 53 others were injured; the drivers of all three vehicles fled the scene of the accident.

July 8, Near Bogotá, Colombia. A bus that swerved to avoid hitting a pedestrian overturned and caught fire; 44 persons died and 7 were injured.

July 14, Lugezi, Tanzania. An overcrowded bus plunged into Lake Victoria; 60 persons lost their lives.

July 18, Sicily, Italy. A truck collided head-on with three cars after it crashed through the centre rail dividing the highway; 14 persons were killed and 2 others were critically injured.

August 10, Near Mahad, India. A tourist bus skidded in heavy rain and fell off a bridge into the Savitri River; 35 persons were believed drowned.

August 15, Near Novi Sad, Yugos. A bus collided with a truck and then plunged headlong into a deep ravine; 14 persons were known dead and 48 others sustained injuries.

August 18, Great Rift Valley, Kenya. A multivehicle pileup resulted when a bus carrying a wedding party collided head-on with a coffee bean truck; a trailer-truck slammed into the coffee truck and another trailer-truck crashed into the pileup; 44 persons were killed and dozens of persons were injured.

August 24, Northern Thailand. A truck and a tour bus collided head-on, resulting in the deaths of 17 persons.

August 31, Benoni, South Africa. A mobile crane plunged down an embankment and rammed into a crowded commuter train entering Northmead station; 10 persons were killed and 40 others were injured.

September 27, Venezuela. A passenger bus that swerved out of control crashed into a truck and two other vehicles; all four vehicles burst into flames and 40 persons lost their lives.

October 26, Near Burhanpur, India. A bus apparently out of control plunged into a canal near Burhanpur; 12 persons were killed and 13 others were injured.

October 29, Near Ahmadabad, India. A truck slammed into a closed gate of a railroad crossing in western India; 12 persons lost their lives in the crash and 39 others were injured.

December 21, Ilagan, Philippines. A bus carrying Filipinos home for Christmas fell into the Marana River when the bus driver drove onto a concrete bridge that had been partially washed away by a typhoon in November; 43 persons were known dead.

ISLAM RESURGENT

by Elie Kedourie

FRANCOIS LOCHON—GAMMA/LIAISON

The world has looked on with amazement at the events in Iran in 1978–79, which led to the downfall of Shah Mohammad Reza Pahlavi and his virtual replacement by a hitherto obscure Muslim divine, Ayatollah Ruhollah Khomeini (*see* BIOGRAPHIES). Not the least surprising aspect of the Iranian revolution is the part played by Islam. The fact that the shah's supplanter seems to have succeeded purely by appealing to religious sentiment has astonished Western onlookers, who take it as an article of faith that religion and politics have nothing to do with one another. But a moment's reflection will persuade us that this belief is very recent. Over most of recorded history in all parts of the world, religion and politics have been intimately connected.

These general remarks, however, are not enough to explain why Islam has suddenly come into special prominence, not only in Iran but in Pakistan, Libya, and elsewhere. Nor will they serve to indicate the peculiar characteristics of a religious movement that has suddenly captured the world's attention. Islam is now entering its 15th century. It has been, and will remain, a world religion. It has retained the loyalty of its followers in the Middle East, North Africa, central Asia, the Indian subcontinent, Malaysia, and Indonesia. In sub-Saharan Africa it is expanding rapidly, vying successfully with Christianity in the conversion of pagans.

Early Moves to Westernization. From the end of the 18th century onward, Muslim civilization, in common with other non-Western civilizations, found itself at a disadvantage in its relations with the West. As it emerged from the Industrial Revolution, the West gradually came to enjoy economic predominance over preindustrial societies, and its advantage was reinforced by superior military power, itself made possible in large part by the scientific and technological progress that underlay Western economic strength. With this economic and military superiority, the Western powers were able to establish overseas empires and, in general, to extend their political influence over the non-Western world, Islam included.

These developments, naturally enough, were seen by Muslim rulers as posing a dangerous threat to their own power and to Islam in general. From about the end of the 18th century, they were preoccupied with finding ways to protect themselves and, by and large, the solution that they came to favour was westernization. In the beginning, westernization meant simply importing Western weapons and military techniques, reforming Muslim armies and giving them modern weapons.

It soon became clear, however, that westernization could not be confined to the purely military sphere. For one thing, Western military organization entailed profound changes in bureaucratic organization and in the relations between government and the governed. The introduction of European-style conscript armies required the minute organization of supply services and an accurate population census. It necessitated a direct relationship between the government and each individual subject. As the 19th century advanced it became apparent that, despite the military measures that had been taken, the Muslim states were becoming, if anything, weaker vis-à-vis the West than they had been before. It now began to be thought that, if Islam was to stand on its own, it would have to adopt certain features of Western civilization that, in the eyes of the westernizers, held the real secret of Western superiority: education, freedom of thought, representative government. From being a fairly crude and simple means of obtaining or regaining military power, westernization now became an ideal.

This ideal attracted increasing numbers of educated and patriotic Muslims who looked with despair on the weakness and corruption of their backward homelands. It reached a culmination in the movements for constitutional and parliamentary governments that gathered force in various Muslim countries beginning with the second half of the 19th century—in the proclamation of an Ottoman constitution in 1876, in the Persian Revolution of 1905–06, in the Young Turk Revolution of 1908–09, in the Kemalist movement which laid the foundation of a parliamentary republic in Turkey and separated religion and the state.

Traditionalist Resistance. Westernizing arguments were not the only ones to be heard in the Muslim world, however. From the start, there were some who condemned westernization as an insidious device of the hereditary Christian enemy. Resistance to westernization was manifest among the Muslim masses, who remained attached to traditional values. Westernizing reforms meant greater centralization and more meticulous control by authority over all kinds of economic activities and social arrangements. They increased the burden of government, whether through taxation, conscription, or vexatious bureaucratic regulations. Eventually, westernization also meant the introduction of new codes of law under which all subjects, regardless of creed, were to be treated equally. This was

Professor of politics at the London School of Economics and Political Science and fellow of the British Academy, Elie Kedourie has held visiting professorships at the universities of Princeton, Harvard, Monash (Melbourne), and Tel Aviv. His publications include Nationalism, Nationalism in Asia and Africa, The Chatham House Version, Arabic Political Memoirs, *and* In the Anglo-Arab Labyrinth.

seen as a threat to the privileged position of Muslims in the traditional Islamic polity.

The direct military threat posed by the West elicited not only the westernizing response but also a traditionalistic one. The French conquest of Algeria in the 1830s provoked a resistance movement led by Abdelkader, who aspired to set up a Muslim polity on the model of that established by the Prophet Muhammad and his immediate successors. The Russian conquest of the Caucasus in the mid-19th century gave rise to a resistance movement under Shaykh Shamil, the head of a mystical brotherhood, which took the Russians many years and great effort to subdue.

Later in the century, the Mahdi successfully established a Muslim polity after defeating Egyptian forces in the Sudan. Egypt, which had occupied the Sudan in the 1820s, had a Muslim government, but in the eyes of the Mahdi and his followers it was irremediably tainted by Western corruption and infidelity. Similar Mahdist movements appeared elsewhere in the Muslim world: in Morocco in the late 19th century; in Somaliland during World War I, where the leader was known to the British authorities by the expressive nickname of the "Mad Mullah"; on the Northwest Frontier in India during the 1930s, where the elusive Fakir of Ipi led the British a dance for years.

In some cases westernizing Muslim governments aroused opposition among their own subjects. The Muslim masses had been imbued for centuries with the belief that obedience to the ruler was a religious duty, and they were accustomed to utter passivity in the face of misgovernment, exactions, and tyranny. But in the Ottoman Empire, in Egypt, and in Tunis subjects were moved to protest and occasional resistance in the face of reforms that their rulers believed to be enlightened, beneficent, indeed necessary.

At the end of World War I the westernizers seemed securely in power, but as time went on their position was undermined by developments both inside and outside Islam. One of these concerned the manifest weakness of the Islamic countries, which decades of westernization had clearly failed to remedy. Egypt, which had undergone a radical modernization, was unable to prevent British occupation in 1882. The Ottoman Empire, another modernizing state, had begun the 19th century as a power to be reckoned with and ended it as the "Sick Man of Europe." World War I saw its final destruction, as well as the extension of Western rule over almost the whole Islamic world.

Western Prestige Wanes. The westernizers, then, did not seem able to deliver the goods, and this was true economically as well as militarily. Their reforms had not brought any great prosperity; indeed, the gap between the industrialized world and the Islamic lands seemed to be widening. Modern means of communication brought this home to increasing numbers of people in the Muslim world, and the same means opened up wider horizons of political action, making the people less disposed to continue in the traditional passive acquiescence of their forefathers.

CULVER PICTURES

The Young Turk Revolution of 1908–09 represented a large step toward westernization in the Ottoman Empire.

The prestige the westernizers had attained in the Muslim world was by and large a reflection of the prestige that the West itself enjoyed. They represented within Islam what seemed to be the thrust of history. But the two World Wars destroyed that prestige, perhaps irrevocably. This process had begun even before 1914, when Japan defeated Russia in 1905. The victory had powerful echoes throughout the whole East, the Muslim world included. If Japan could do this, then Europeans were not as invincible as had been thought. In World War II, again, Japan defeated the British, the French, the Dutch, and the Americans and occupied areas where Western rule had seemed solid and unshakable. Even though Japan was defeated in the end, the blow to the prestige of the West and of the westernizers was tremendous.

The prestige of Western liberalism was also badly damaged during the 20th century. The ideals of constitutional government and the supremacy of an impersonal rule of law were challenged, mocked, and vilified by Nazism and Bolshevism. People could now argue that Western ideals of government were not demonstrably superior; other systems of political thought and political organization were just as legitimate and successful, if not more so.

Islam and Nationalism. Another element that served to renew the prestige of Islam particularly concerned the Arab world. Among Western-derived political ideas, nationalism was the easiest to transplant in the East and the most powerful in its appeal. This was certainly the case in the Arab world after World War I. Arab nationalism claimed that the Arabs formed a single nation and thus were entitled to unite to form one state. But who are the Arabs, and how did they come to acquire self-identity? The answer has to be that the Arabs are defined by Islam.

The theory of Arab nationalism meant very little to the traditional Islamic masses as long as it was the affair of westernized leaders. Arab nationalism became acceptable to them only when Arabism and Islam were amalgamated. Thus, until the late 1930s Egyptians had little interest in Arab nationalism, and even the outbreak of war with Israel in 1948 did not elicit the popular enthusiasm to be found, for example, in Iraq or Syria. Political leaders and intellectuals in Cairo may have thought a pan-Arab policy had advantages for Egypt. King Farouk, in particular, believed that such a policy would gain him preeminence in the Middle East. But the population at large paid little heed until a genuinely Islamic movement, the Muslim Brotherhood, took up the cause.

The Muslim Brotherhood. The phenomenon of the Muslim Brotherhood deserves further consideration. The movement had very small beginnings. In 1928 a schoolteacher in the Suez Canal town of Ismailia, Hassan al-Banna, decided that the situation of the poor Egyptian workers, or fellahin, drifting into urban areas to look for work was unbearable. Economic deprivation and spiritual disorientation were transforming them into a dust of lost souls. If they were to be restored to a sense of identity and of self-respect, they had to be instilled with the virtues of Islamic piety, imbued with Islamic solidarity, and encouraged to practice self-help.

The movement's rapid success suggests that the westernizing elites had failed their followers in yet another respect: what they were offering could not satisfy the spiritual needs of the multitude. What is particularly striking about the Muslim Brotherhood is that it was established and flourished not only without official help but—for the greater part of its history—in the teeth of official opposition. When Farouk fell in 1952, the Brotherhood numbered about 1.5 million and constituted the most important autonomous, indigenous movement in Egypt.

In its teaching, conforming to the genius and tradition of Islam, the religious and the political were inextricably mixed. It taught that existing society in Egypt—and elsewhere in the world of Islam—was being eaten away by Western godlessness and paganism. The only remedy was to overthrow the westernized political and social institutions and replace them with an Islamic polity such as had existed at the time of the Prophet and his immediate successors. When the Free Officers replaced Farouk, the leaders of the Brotherhood believed that a true Muslim regime would be inaugurated, but they were soon undeceived. They clashed with the new ruler, Gamal Abd-al Nasser, were suppressed, and went underground. But when Nasser died in 1970, the Brotherhood was still very influential. And in succeeding years it has become apparent that Islam as a rule of life and a system of thought is more popular than ever.

THE BETTMANN ARCHIVE

The Battle of Tall al-Kabir (Sept. 13, 1882), in which the British were victorious, ended for a time dreams of Egyptian nationalism.

Concepts of Islamic Criminal Law

As revolution swept over Iran in the spring of 1979 reports began to emerge from Teheran concerning "trials" of "traitors," sometimes leading to immediate execution. If the reports could be credited, these revolutionary trials seemed highly suspect to observers accustomed to Western procedures of criminal law.

The circumstances of the trials were reminiscent of the familiar practices of revolutionary "justice." The accused were brought before their accusers—often a crowd—and given only a perfunctory opportunity to respond to the accusations, which could come from anyone in the assembly and need not be supported by testimony of others. A decision of guilt or innocence was made on the spot or very soon after the accusation. If the accused was found guilty a punishment was also proclaimed; if the punishment was death, the victim was often shot within a matter of hours.

The threat, late in the year, to put the personnel of the U.S. embassy in Teheran on trial aroused even greater concern in the West about the true nature of Islamic justice, especially as it was exercised in Iran.

A meeting of scholars in Siracusa, Italy, late in May 1979, attempted to discover answers to this question, among others. Held under the auspices of the International Institute of Higher Studies in Criminal Sciences and chaired by the dean of that institute, M. Cherif Bassiouni (who is also a professor of law at De Paul University in Chicago), the assembly heard papers and comments by a distinguished international panel of legal experts.

This First International Conference on the Protection of Human Rights in the Islamic Criminal Justice System arrived at some conclusions that are likely to be somewhat comforting to Western observers of revolutions in Islamic countries.

The concept of human rights, they said, is an old one in Islamic law, and the letter and spirit of Islamic law on the subject of the protection of the rights of the criminally accused are in harmony with the fundamental principles of human rights under international law. Specifically, the spirit and principles of Islamic law include the following rights of the criminally accused:

- The right to be free from arbitrary arrest and detention.
- The right to be presumed innocent until proven guilty by an impartial tribunal in accordance with the rule of law.
- The application of the Principle of Legality which calls for the right of the accused to be tried for crimes specified in the Qur'an (Koran) or whose clear and well-established meaning is determined by law.
- The right to a fair and public trial.
- The right to present evidence and call witnesses in one's own defense.
- The right to counsel of one's own choosing.
- The right to a decision on the merits based on legally admissible evidence.
- The right to have the decision rendered in public.
- The right of appeal.

Of these rights none was considered more important than the Principle of Legality, first stated 2,000 years ago in the ancient Latin formula: *Nullum crimen nulla poena sine lege* (there is no crime and no punishment where there is no law [that states it is a crime]).

There may be justifications for the actions of the Iranian revolutionary tribunals as reported to the West. Many or even all of the accused may have been as guilty as their accusers said they were; the guilty may have therefore deserved to be punished. It is not possible to render judgment on that question. It is evident, however, on the basis of the high authority of the Siracusa conference, that the actions of the Iranian revolutionary tribunals were illegal—by Islamic law as well as by other standards. (CHARLES VAN DOREN)

The Crescent Waxes. This renewed prestige of Islam was reinforced by developments elsewhere in the Arab world. The 1969 coup in Libya brought to power officers who had been inspired by Nasser's example but who turned out to be much more Islamic than their mentor. Under the leadership of Muammar al-Qaddafi, the government became increasingly Islamic in its tendencies, using its burgeoning oil profits to propagate its ideology both within and outside Libya.

The rise in oil prices has meant even greater riches for Saudi Arabia, the stronghold of Wahhabism. This fundamentalist and puritan version of Islam is by no means acceptable to the rest of the Muslim world, but Saudi Arabia now enjoys all the prestige that great riches bring, and this in turn has enhanced the prestige of its kind of Islam. The Saudi rulers, of course, are not radical in the sense that Qaddafi is radical, but they share with him a fundamentalist, puritan outlook. Under certain circumstances, this can lead to political and economic radicalism, far as such ideas might be from the views of the present Saudi government.

Fundamentalist puritanism is also the hallmark of the revolution in Iran. Shiʿism, the dominant form of Islam in Iran, differs greatly from Wahhabism and from the Sunni Islam that is Qaddafi's starting point. Yet all three share the same vision of a return to pure, pristine Islam and the same desire that all aspects of life be ruled by Islamic norms. Khomeini's teaching is akin to that of the Muslim Brotherhood in its denunciation of godlessness and its emphasis on the vanity of westernization. That it proved to have such a resonance among the urban masses of Iran shows that there, too, there has been a reaction against the discomforts and disruptions that accompany westernization.

A New Activism. Khomeini's teaching also has points in common with that of Qaddafi. The Libyan ruler has put forward a doctrine that he calls the "third theory" (*i.e.*, one distinct from both capitalism and Communism). What this "third theory" promotes is in fact a kind of collectivism, a kind of socialism that is claimed to be the essence of Islam. The argument is that since all Muslims are brethren, they are entitled to share equally in the wealth that Islamic society produces. An Islamic government sees to it that this equality obtains.

Clearly, this theory includes a large admixture of European collectivist ideas. In its last months, the shah's regime denounced its opponents as "Islamic Marxists"—a polemical and tendentious label that, nevertheless, contained some grains of truth. The collectivism and egalitarianism associated with the new Islamic activism have obvious points of contact with Soviet and Eastern European political doctrines. At the same time, the collectivism and egalitarianism of these new doctrines find echoes in Islamic tradition, making them acceptable to the Islamic masses. It is this affinity that might cause Wahhabi Islam to take a radical turn.

This new activism has another point of similarity with Bolshevism. Both are hostile to Western constitutional government, which both denounce as a sham and a deception. Bolshevism does so on the Marxist grounds that the only political reality is the class struggle and that constitutionalism is only a disguise for domination by the bourgeoisie. Muslim radicalism does so because constitutional government is at best irrelevant to Islamic ideals and at worst incompatible with the maintenance of Islamic cohesion, which requires uniformity of belief.

Also like the Marxists, Khomeini and Qaddafi denounce the West as exploitative and imperialist. The Christian West, of course, has long been regarded with enmity in Islam, although this hostility diminished somewhat during the period of westernization. But the Marxist notion that Western imperialism is the inevitable outcome of capitalist processes is now extremely widespread, and this idea is being used to articulate and rationalize the ancient Islamic hostility.

Islamic Vision and Reality. Two guesses may be hazarded about future developments related to these trends, which are likely to persist and perhaps become stronger. In the first place, the vision that the leaders of these movements offer to their followers is that of society modeled on what is thought to have existed in the first century of Islam. This vision is contrasted with present discontents: injustice, oppression, poverty. Conceivably, it is these discontents that provide an audience for the doctrines. What is questionable, however, is whether the substance of the vision can be realized under modern conditions and whether, if realized, it would long satisfy the masses. However traditional their inclinations, they have glimpsed a rival vision: that of the plenty and comfort that modern industrial society offers. One may wonder whether, in the end, there will not prove to be a profound misunderstanding between the visionaries and their followers that may have far-reaching and incalculable consequences.

CHARLES SPENGLER—SYGMA

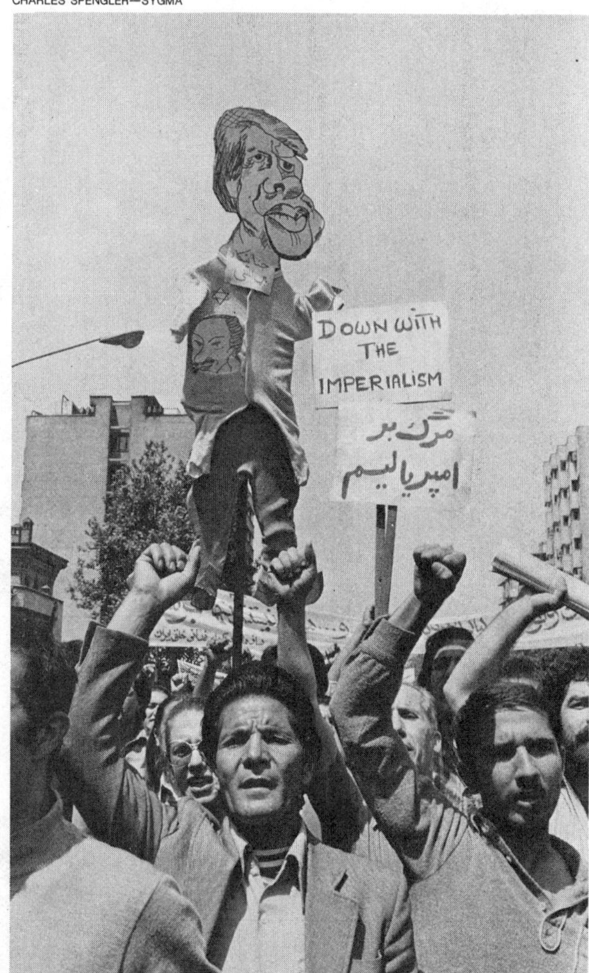

In 1979 Iranians, spurred by religious leaders, protested in the streets against the "imperialism" of the West.

In the second place, these doctrines are now backed by great financial resources, and their propagators take advantage of Western techniques of communication. These techniques, which can easily be subjected to government control, make it possible to conduct vast and unremitting campaigns of indoctrination, unheard of in the days of the Mahdi, the Mad Mullah, or even the Fakir of Ipi. As a result, a kind of iron curtain might gradually come to separate the universe of Western political discourse and that of Muslim discourse. A state of affairs might arise in which Westerners and Muslims have little to say to one another. This could mark the end of an era in which westernizers hoped that the Muslim world would become as open and prosperous as the West and the West hoped that it would live in amity and concord with the Muslim world.

LOUIS GOLDMAN—PHOTO RESEARCHERS

TWO PEOPLES—ONE LAND

by Patrick Seale

A century ago a handful of Jews from the ghettos of eastern Europe began to trickle into Palestine, then a run-down province of the Ottoman Empire. Most were young, poor, and ill equipped by experience for a pioneering life in this thinly populated land of arid mountain, malarial swamp, and marginal agriculture. A hundred years later, the movement they inaugurated had produced a dynamic, thrusting state, with Western standards of intellectual achievement, productive efficiency, and social welfare. The state of Israel is a phenomenon, an unprecedented experiment in nation building. But like many experiments, it has had its cost.

Zionist and Palestinian. Part of the problem created by the existence of Israel concerns the local Arab inhabitants and their descendants, most of them now exiles without citizenship rights anywhere. Zionists and Palestinians (whether in Israeli-occupied territory or elsewhere) constitute two national movements disputing a single stretch of land. This dispute lies at the heart of the Middle East conflict. Another part is Israel's effect on the region of which it is physically, but not culturally, a part. Simply by existing, Israel has challenged and continues to challenge the Arab nation-states around it. Most importantly, it challenges the aspirations of pan-Arabism to primacy in western Asia.

The Arabs have so far failed to find an institutional framework to express their kinship, but the fact remains that from Oman to Mauritania and from Sudan to Syria they form a sort of family. They share a language and a culture and (for the most part) a religion. Even in the present, disunited state of affairs, they believe that all Arab lands are the concern of all Arabs. That Israel, a nation of alien language, culture, and religion, should commandeer part of this Arab heritage is an outrage to them, especially since the territory taken from them lies at the ancient heart of their ancient region.

So much for the basic problem. What complicates it is the fact that the Middle East, being strategically vital because of its geographic position and its oil reserves, is a primary concern of nearly every country in the world, and above all of the superpowers. The U.S. and the Soviet Union are engaged in a constant diplomatic struggle in the Middle East, each trying to extend its own influence there and to diminish the influence of the other.

As if this were not confusing and unpredictable enough, a further complexity is added by the fact that the Arab states themselves do not always get on together. They fight over many matters—ideology, East-West alignments, and above all leadership and spheres of influence. Because the Palestine question has come to occupy such a dominant position on the Arab agenda, they fight about that too, each state seeking to upstage the others in championing this "sacred cause."

It is not surprising that this hydra-headed problem, affecting so many political relationships in the region and beyond, should have fueled 30 years of hostility and still, at the outset of the 1980s, seemed far from comprehensive solution.

But if total peace was still a distant prospect, partial peace had arrived by 1979. Egypt, the most powerful of the Arab states, had renounced war and committed itself to living with Israel. The Egyptian-Israeli peace treaty of March 1979, the logical outcome of Pres. Anwar as-Sadat's historic visit to Jerusalem in 1977 and the U.S.-inspired Camp David accords of 1978, marked a decisive breakthrough in the long and bitter history of the Arab-Israeli conflict. As 1979 drew to a close, Egypt and Israel were embarked on a slow but apparently irreversible process of normalizing relations. But the U.S. sponsorship which had helped them along this path was running out of steam. In particular, negotiations on the next scheduled issue on the agenda—autonomy for the Palestinians on the West Bank and in Gaza—were getting nowhere. Most of the Arab states bitterly criticized Sadat for going it alone, though the anti-Sadat front had not been noticeably successful, either in forcing Egypt to end its dialogue with Israel or in devising an alternative strategy of its own.

Pointers to possible movement in the early 1980s were changes in the posture and standing of the Palestinians. Gradually moving from terrorism to di-

A writer and broadcaster, Patrick Seale is correspondent on Middle Eastern affairs for The Observer, *London. His books include* The Struggle for Syria *and (with M. McConville)* French Revolution, 1968 *and* Philby: The Long Road to Moscow.

plomacy, they acquired widespread European support (from governments fearful for their oil supplies) and—most significantly—made a breach in the largely hostile U.S., and even Israeli, public opinion. Many Americans, particularly among the black community, started to question the wisdom of their government's Middle East policies, while some Israelis began to chafe at the rigidity of Prime Minister Menahem Begin's ambitions for a Greater Israel.

The stage was being prepared for a new advance toward peace, based on eventual Israeli withdrawal from the occupied territories and on Palestinian self-determination. But progress in this direction might have to wait, not only for the results of the U.S. presidential election in 1980 but also for a further, much more radical shift in Israeli attitudes.

Background to Conflict. With hindsight it is clear that the Arabs of Palestine were doomed to lose their battle with the Zionists. As long ago as 1897, European Jews founded the Zionist Organization, with the declared aim of establishing a home for the Jewish people in Palestine, while the Arabs did not awake to nationalist consciousness until a quarter of a century later. Another telling difference concerned their respective attitudes toward the dominant imperial power in the region. From the start, the Zionists tried to strike a bargain, first with the Ottoman authorities and, when that empire was defeated in World War I, with its British successor. They fell in with British imperial and strategic interests and were rewarded with the Balfour Declaration of 1917, which gave great-power legitimacy to their enterprise in Palestine.

The Arabs had hoped for independence after the Ottoman collapse. Instead, without consulting them, Britain and France carved up Arab Asia and pursued their imperial interests under the guise of League of Nations mandates. The embittered Arabs rejected the legality and authority of the British mandate in Palestine, along with the validity of Zionist rights which it confirmed. So they were forced into opposing not only the Jewish immigrants but the might of the British Empire. Their frustrations in this unequal battle erupted into repeated violence—in 1920, in 1921, in 1929, and in the Arab revolt of 1936–38.

For a long time the Zionists, as well as the British authorities, thought that, with a bit of goodwill, Jew and Arab could get along together. What was not recognized was that the Arab protests expressed an emergent nationalism, which was taking root in reaction to Zionism itself. Underlying the division between Jewish colonist and native Arab lay much mutual incomprehension, tinged with contempt on both sides. The Jews brought with them from Europe a patronizing and disparaging view of the Arabs, while the Arabs, bred in an Islamic tradition, viewed rule by (or even equality with) Jews and Christians as unthinkable.

Not only did the Jews get a head start in state building, but with each passing year their advance over the Arabs increased. A few landmarks will suffice to illustrate the point. The Jewish National Fund to finance land purchases was set up in 1901. The first *kvutza,* forerunner of the kibbutz, was founded at Deganya in 1909. The labour federation, the Histadrut, which more than any other force helped shape the future state of Israel, was established in 1920, the year in which the Haganah, embryo of Israel's defense forces, also began its clandestine operations. In 1929 the Jewish Agency replaced the Zionist Organization. Its Palestine Executive functioned more or less as a Jewish government, with a department of political affairs that was, in effect, a quasi-foreign ministry. In 1935 David Ben-Gurion, the outstanding Zionist leader of his generation, took over as chairman of this Executive. Against all this, the best the Arabs could field was a Supreme Muslim Council and, from 1936, an Arab High Committee, loose coalitions of rival notables dominated by the imprudent mufti of Jerusalem, Haj Amin al-Husayni, which proved incapable of formulating realistic political goals or of mobilizing the people in support of them.

Hitler's rise to power in Germany accelerated Jewish immigration in a way no one could have predicted, and it upgraded the Middle East in British strategic thinking. Characteristically, the Jews backed British war preparations, while the Arabs chose this moment in the late 1930s to rebel. They were crushed, their economy was ruined, and the Palestine Arab leadership was decimated.

By the outbreak of World War II, the Jewish population of Palestine had grown from less than a tenth of the total in 1918 to a third. While the Arabs stood on the sidelines, hoping an Axis victory would at last give them independence, the Jews in Palestine threw themselves into the struggle. Their economy boomed, and they learned how to make arms and use them—skills that were to stand them in good stead. In the event, these skills also came to be used against the British, first in rescuing survivors from Hitler's Europe in defiance of British immigration quotas laid down in the 1939 White Paper, and then, after the war, in a rebellion against the mandate.

Exhausted by the war, Britain gave up its mandate and passed the intractable problem of Palestine to the new United Nations, whose partition plan of 1947 was accepted by the Zionists but rejected absolutely by the Arabs. With diplomacy thus deadlocked, the Zionists took the initiative. At midnight on May 14, 1948, the moment at which Britain for-

ROBERT CAPA—MAGNUM

Nearly 1,000 Jewish immigrants arrived each day from Europe on crowded ships at Haifa Harbour after the establishment of Israel in 1948.

mally vacated power, Jewish independence was unilaterally declared and the new state of Israel came into existence.

The Arab Involvement. The proclamation of the state marked the Zionist triumph over the Palestine Arabs. It also marked a new phase in the Arab-Israeli conflict, which pitted the fledgling state against the Arab countries on its borders. The Arab world had long shared the Palestinians' rage and alarm at the growing Zionist presence, and anti-Zionism had become an essential plank in the platform of Arab nationalists. As early as 1939, the British government, eager to retain regional sympathies in view of the coming clash with Hitler's Germany, had formally recognized this wider Arab interest by inviting the Arab states, together with the Jewish Agency and the Palestine Arab leadership, to a conference in London. The conference failed to solve the problem but, by bringing in spokesmen from the Arab countries, it regionalized the issue. Henceforth, the dispute would embroil a large number of sovereign states, each with its own interests.

Immediately following the declaration of Jewish statehood, the armed forces of five Arab countries—Egypt, Transjordan, Syria, Iraq, and Lebanon—attacked Israel on all fronts, but, in a series of campaigns alternating with truces between May and December 1948, they were routed. By the summer of 1949 Israel had concluded armistices with its neighbours. It also had been recognized by more than 50 governments throughout the world, had joined the UN, and had established its sovereignty over about 20,700 km (8,000 sq mi) of mandated Palestine west of the Jordan River. The remaining 5,180 sq km (2,000 sq mi) were divided between Transjordan (the West Bank), henceforth to be known as the Hashemite Kingdom of Jordan, and Egypt (the Gaza Strip). "Palestine" ceased to exist.

The 1948 war and its aftermath set the pattern of the Arab-Israeli conflict for the next 20 years. Having achieved statehood in the teeth of Arab hostility, and after the near extermination of European Jewry, Israel was understandably obsessed with security. To be strong was the first priority, defense the overwhelming consideration. Immigrants poured in, more than doubling the population to 1.4 million by 1951. The military option, deliberately adopted, inevitably shaped the nature of the state and determined its relations in the region.

For the Arabs the war of 1948 remains to this day "the Disaster." Postwar Arab nationalism was stamped by defeat, disappointment, self-denigration, and a thirst for revenge. Because Israel was seen as the child of Western imperialism, Arab relations with the West were severely strained. Inter-Arab relations were also poisoned, in a welter of mutual recrimination. Above all, the humiliating outcome of the Palestine war discredited a whole political class, together with the Western-style parliamentary systems then operating in many Arab countries. It was in the name of Palestine that a new breed of army officers imposed dictatorships on Syria in 1949 and Egypt in 1952.

The new soldier-rulers drew their legitimacy from their pledge to continue the battle. Arab opinion was fed with the notion that Israel was no more than a temporary phenomenon that would one day be destroyed. So firm an article of faith did this become in the Arab mind that, over 30 years later, it remained a principal obstacle to peace.

If one element in the post-1948 pattern was embattled Israel and a second the unremitting hostility of its Arab neighbours, a third was the Palestinian refugees. The violent birth of Israel led to a mass exodus of Palestine Arabs. Between December 1947 and January 1949 some 700,000 took refuge in neighbouring Arab countries. They were not belligerents in the war and they were not participants in the armistice negotiations. Neither side recognized their right to a voice of their own. They became dependents on international charity, at the mercy of their host countries, housed in sprawling camps. As their numbers swelled, the young were suckled on the dream of a return to a homeland they had never seen. The abler emigrated, creating pockets of frustrated irredentism in almost every Arab country. Not until the mid-1960s did an effective Palestinian leadership emerge, giving the exiles an identity and a strategy. But the guerrilla organizations were to prove a greater threat to host countries, such as Jordan and Lebanon, than to their Israeli enemy.

The Arab-Israeli Wars. Within 25 years, the Arabs and Israel fought three more full-scale wars, in 1956, 1967, and 1973, with a good deal of skirmishing in between. Each war had its special character, giving a different twist to history and altering the balance of advantage in the region. Together they bequeathed to the future a complex legacy of interests and emotions that made it very difficult to unravel peace from the tangle of conflicting issues.

The decisive contribution of the 1956 war was to make Egypt's Pres. Gamal Abd-al Nasser the foremost Arab leader of his time and to bring about the active involvement of the superpowers in Middle Eastern affairs. Nasser was an Arab nationalist. Once in power, he sought to unite all the Arabs under Egyptian leadership and saw in the Palestine issue an excellent means of doing so. He was the first Arab statesman to try to forge a foreign policy wholly independent of the West, in which cause he turned to the Soviet bloc for arms in 1955. Israel rightly recognized him as the most formidable enemy it had yet encountered and was determined to hit him before his new weapons became operational. The opportunity came when Britain and France decided to topple Nasser after his nationalization of the Suez Canal. Israel climbed aboard, and the three countries attacked Egypt in 1956. Their military victory turned into a political fiasco when, under joint U.S. and Soviet pressure, they were forced to withdraw, leaving Nasser the undisputed hero of the Arab world.

A decade of fitful peace followed, as Arab attention was diverted from Israel to Egypt's largely unsuccessful attempts to dominate the region. But true peace was not yet a possible option. Israel still felt threatened, while the Arabs still considered Israel as unfinished business. What lit the fuse of open warfare in 1967 was a combination of many factors, the chief of which perhaps was Israel's determination to destroy Nasser. Other contributory factors were the mutual suspicions of Egypt and Syria and Nasser's mistaken belief that, with Soviet support, he could regain by bluff what Egypt had lost in 1956, notably control of the Straits of Tiran on the Red Sea. He closed the straits and gave Israel the pretext to strike at him. In six days in June, Israel not only dispatched the combined forces of Egypt, Syria, and Jordan but also overran vast tracts of Arab territory.

The Six-Day War destroyed Nasser, though he struggled on lamely for another three years until his death in 1970. It also brought crashing down the dream of Arab resurgence that he had stood for. Whatever they said after that war, the Arabs knew in their hearts that, for the foreseeable future, Israel was there to stay. As for Israel, victory transformed it into an imperial power with over a million Arabs under its rule (in addition to the 350,000 already living in the state of Israel). Its overwhelming military success bred a new arrogance and complacency. Relations with Arab neighbours were weighed only in terms of strength and weakness. The outside world, dazzled by Israel's performance, could see no end to its supremacy, and Israel was promoted to strategic partnership with the U.S. in keeping order in the Middle East.

These were not conditions to encourage Israeli statesmen to think creatively about achieving long-term harmony with the Arabs. But it was precisely this reality of Israeli domination and Arab collapse that now thrust the Palestinian guerrilla movements into the limelight. Their hit-and-run raids into Israeli-occupied territory boosted Arab morale, their spectacular hijackings and cruel killings attracted international attention to their grievance and made

MICHA BAR-AM—MAGNUM

Israeli soldiers under attack by Egyptian forces in the Sinai during the October 1973 war.

the name of the Palestine Liberation Organization famous or feared throughout the world. However reprehensible the guerrillas' tactics, they succeeded in convincing the world that the heart of the Middle East problem was not superpower rivalry or Israel's quarrels with its Arab opponents but the need for a political accommodation between the state of Israel and the people it had displaced.

After October. The current phase of the Arab-Israeli conflict may be said to date from the October 1973 war, launched against Israel by Egypt and Syria, this time not with the aim of reconquest but to restore Arab confidence, correct the imbalance between victor and vanquished, and thus prepare the way for peace negotiations. Called the Yom Kippur War by the Jews, the Ramadan War by the Arabs, it will go down in history as the occasion when the Arabs first used their oil weapon. The huge oil price rises that followed gave the Arabs stupendous, if unequally shared, purchasing power. But their newfound wealth also gave them a stake in peace, as well as the means to pressure the U.S. into helping them secure it on acceptable terms.

The road to peace, however, has proved extremely long and stony. By tireless personal diplomacy after the October war, Henry Kissinger, then U.S. secretary of state, persuaded the interlocked armies to disengage. Further progress was blocked by the 1975–76 civil war in Lebanon, a tragedy caused, in part, by those very disengagement agreements and the threat they posed to the Palestinians. The events in Lebanon drove further wedges between Israel and the Arabs, between Egypt and Syria, between Muslim and Christian Lebanese. It took all the drama of Sadat's visit to Jerusalem to get the peace bandwagon moving again.

As matters stood in 1979, three main problems blocked the way to a settlement. The first was Israel's continued land hunger. Israel agreed to give the Sinai back to Egypt in stages, but it made no such decision regarding the West Bank, the Judea and Samaria of the Bible which to mystical Zionists are the heart of their God-given homeland. The fact that this territory is presently inhabited by 700,000 Arabs has not deterred some Israeli politicians from wishing to annex it.

The second obstacle was the struggle for power, influence, and leadership among the Arab states themselves. Syria, Iraq, and Saudi Arabia rejected President Sadat's peace initiatives, not only because they feared the fundamental Palestinian problem would be passed over but also because to follow Sadat's lead would be to acknowledge Egypt's primacy in the Arab world.

The third problem takes the wheel full circle. Vast barriers—psychological, ideological, political—would have to be overcome before Israelis and Palestinians could bring themselves to recognize the legitimacy of each other's claims. For Israel, to acknowledge Palestinian nationalism would somehow cast doubt on the moral basis of the whole Zionist enterprise. For the Palestinians, to recognize Israel's right to exist meant condemning their own nation to a landlocked fraction of the former homeland.

But even if these deep and dangerous waters could be navigated, it would be a long time before Israel, still essentially the creation of European Jewry, could find tranquil acceptance in a Middle East in ferment, riven by disputes, undergoing the trauma of new wealth, with unstable political and social structures, and where Islam resurgent was more than ever the dominant cultural force.

PEOPLE OF THE YEAR

BIOGRAPHIES

The following is a selected list of men and women who influenced events significantly in 1979.

Abbado, Claudio

Claudio Abbado was in 1979 well on his way to securing a prime position among the world's orchestral conducting stars. A quiet but dedicated practitioner, with a predilection for richly flowing string lines and burnished tone-colour, Abbado in September 1979 succeeded André Previn as principal conductor of the London Symphony Orchestra (LSO), a group he had directed regularly during the previous 13 years.

Abbado's rise to prominence was unspectacular. Born in Milan, Italy, on June 26, 1933, one of a long line of musicians, he at first studied privately, entering Milan's Giuseppe Verdi Conservatory at age 16 to concentrate on piano, composition, and conducting. He then spent time further polishing his conducting skills at the Accademia Chigiano of Siena, where he worked alongside future colleagues Daniel Barenboim and Zubin Mehta and violinist Salvatore Accardo. This was followed by a spell at the Vienna Academy of Music, working with conductor Hans Swarowsky.

Abbado's first breakthrough came in 1958, when he won the Serge Koussevitzky conducting prize at the Tanglewood (Mass.) Festival. In 1963 the Vienna Mozart Association in a surprise move nominated him for the coveted Dimitri Mitropoulos conducting prize. He made his British debut in 1965, conducting Manchester's Hallé Orchestra, and in 1966 he began his association with the LSO.

From 1971 through 1976 Abbado was music director at La Scala, Milan, and in 1977 was appointed the theatre's artistic director. He made many visits to the U.S., a longtime association with the Boston and Chicago symphony orchestras leading to a host of memorable concerts and albums. His conducting of Gustav Mahler's colossal Sixth Symphony with the New York Philharmonic was described by Sedgwick Clark in the *International Music Guide* as "dynamic . . . Mahler's detailed demands leaping off the printed page with startling clarity."

(MOZELLE A. MOSHANSKY)

Alda, Alan

In a year of varied accomplishments, the actor Alan Alda made his successful debut as a major screenwriter and championed the feminist cause. Perhaps least surprising, he received an honorary M.D. degree from Columbia University's College of Physicians and Surgeons. Though he "never dissected a frog in med school, never made rounds as an intern," as *Time* magazine commented, Alda "may be everybody's favorite doctor." Since 1972 he had portrayed Capt. Hawkeye Pierce in "M*A*S*H" (for Mobile Army Surgical Hospital), a television comedy distinguished by its air of humane reality.

The perennially popular show owed much of its success to Alda as actor, occasional director and writer, and guiding sensibility. From the beginning he "worried the show would become a 30-minute commercial for the Army . . . one of those hijinks-at-the-battlefront routines." To prevent that he insisted that each episode contain at least one operating room scene. As a result he can reasonably call it "the only comedy show that's ever been done on television in which the effects of war are seen."

S. SCHAPIRO—SYGMA

Alda seems a contradiction in many respects. He rose to fame performing comedy —in a combat hospital setting. Cast as an army captain, he said offscreen, "No war has made any sense to me." Even his latest film, *The Seduction of Joe Tynan* (which he wrote and starred in), deals with a dichotomy. It focuses on a fictional U.S. senator who becomes a presidential aspirant and must try "to reconcile the feeling that family, friendship and integrity come first" with the belief that professional success is paramount. Alda describes himself as an active feminist, and he has spoken out loud and long for the Equal Rights Amendment, believing that "men are being shortchanged by a lack of equality, just as women are."

Son of Robert Alda, an actor remembered for portraying George Gershwin in the film *Rhapsody in Blue*, Alda was born in New York City on Jan. 28, 1936. He entered Fordham University intending to study medicine but switched to literature. He won a three-year acting fellowship at the Cleveland Playhouse and then went on to win critical praise and moderate success as a stage actor in New York.

(PHILIP KOPPER)

Anderson, Ottis

Ottis Anderson opened his mouth wide enough for both feet to fit inside it even before he played his first National Football League (NFL) game. He told people what a good running back he would be, adding that notoriously stingy teams like the St. Louis Cardinals need not bother choosing him in the NFL's 1979 draft of college seniors. The Cardinals chose him anyway. They paid him the money he wanted, reportedly $1.3 million for seven years, representing the largest player investment in the team's history.

Anderson returned the dividends he had promised. During the 1979 season he rambled all over the NFL's football fields and left crowds of open-mouthed spectators in his wake. While tacklers tried to catch Anderson, scouts and coaches had trouble pinning down the 6-ft 1-in, 210-lb halfback's style. Some called him a powerful runner, some pointed out his quick acceleration, and others called attention to the sprinter's speed that separated him from ordinary backs. By the time observers agreed on what he did best, Anderson had won the National Football Conference's rookie of the year and player of the year awards and had become the first rookie in NFL history to average 100 yd per game.

Anderson was born on Jan. 19, 1957, in West Palm Beach, Fla. His mother had intended his first name to be Otis, which is how it is pronounced, but the doctor who delivered him misspelled the name on his birth certificate. Survival was more important than spelling in the tenements where Anderson grew up. He began earning that tough society's respect as a third grader who played football with the older kids. With his older brother, Ottis shared the dream of making enough money from football to buy his mother a house.

His brother died in college in a swimming accident, leaving Ottis to track the dream himself. His first step as an NFL player was a giant one. Anderson ran for 193 yd in his first professional game, against the Dallas Cowboys, who were the defending conference champions. Earl Campbell and Walter Payton outgained Anderson's 1,605 yd for the season, taking away his league leadership on the final weekend, but Anderson's mother had her house by then.

(KEVIN M. LAMB)

Arkoff, Samuel Z.

Cinematically speaking, 1979 was the year of the horror show. A feature called *Alien* broke records to earn upward of $8.5 million in a fortnight. Two versions of the Dracula story came out. Ten-year-old *Night of the Living Dead* spawned a sequel, *Dawn of the Dead*. *Phantasm*, *Nightwings*, *Prophecy*, *Halloween*—all played variations on some ghoulish, ghostly, monstrous, or macabre theme. "Like junkies, the American public is clamoring for a fix of fright," *Newsweek* magazine observed, "and the Hollywood pushers are converting everybody's bloodiest nightmares into box office gold."

The major pioneer of this trend was American International Pictures, founded in 1955 by Samuel Z. Arkoff. During the next 25 years he made 150 "screamers" without much anguish, money, or artistic pretense. His low-budget quickies, aimed at adolescent audiences, cost less than $100,000 each and were completed in less than two weeks. "First we'd think of a horror title and some artwork," Arkoff remembers. "Then we wrote a script to match them." In the process his production-line studio proved to be "the boot camp of the stars." Among his trainees were Jack Nicholson, Peter Fonda, Bruce Dern, Francis Ford Coppola (*q.v.*), Peter Bogdanovich, and Woody Allen.

Born in Fort Dodge, Iowa, June 12, 1918, Arkoff attended the University of Colorado. He began producing films in 1955 because his distributing company could not find enough cheap films elsewhere. Hollywood was dying on the vine in the cold light of television. But while major studios foundered, his thrived. He catered to neighbourhood and drive-in theatres with such chestnuts as *I Was a Teenage Werewolf*, *Invasion of the Saucermen*, and a string of boy-meets-girl-on-the-beach epics.

But in 1978, ironically, he found himself swimming against the current again. For the first time AIP had closed its books in the red. The problem, wrote one analyst, was that as major producers had jumped on the bandwagon of the bizarre, they stole AIP's audience with slicker scares.

Yet Arkoff was still receiving his due. New York City's Museum of Modern Art held a month-long retrospective of AIP's repertory, and in Washington, D.C., the American Film Institute followed suit.

(PHILIP KOPPER)

Bazargan, Mehdi

The Islamic Republic of Iran's first prime minister, Mehdi Bazargan, assumed his office in revolutionary circumstances. He was appointed by Ayatollah Ruhollah Khomeini (*q.v.*) after the latter's return to Iran from 15 years of exile to universal acclaim as national leader. Khomeini exercised the supreme power through a series of committees headed by younger ayatollahs, some of which acted as summary courts-martial. When Bazargan tried to transform this revolutionary procedure into a more civilized administration of justice, Khomeini accused him of weakness. He continued to override and act apart from Bazargan administratively, and Bazargan continued to protest. On several occasions he offered his resignation, which was not accepted, and he complained, "The government has been a knife with no blade."

Bazargan represented Iran at the 25th anniversary of the Algerian nationalist uprising on Nov. 1, 1979, and met in Algiers with Zbigniew Brzezinski, U.S. Pres. Jimmy Carter's national security adviser. On his return to Teheran Bazargan was charged by the students who had seized the U.S. embassy on November 4 with having treacherously conversed with an American. On November 6 he resigned because, as he said in his letter of resignation, the interventions, inconveniences, opposition, and differences of opinion had made his and his Cabinet's position impossible for some time. Khomeini's thanks for his "backbreaking service during the revolution" dispelled thoughts that Bazargan might have to stand trial.

Bazargan was born in 1905 in Teheran, the son of a merchant. He was one of the first Iranians to study abroad. After graduating from the École Centrale in Paris, he returned to Iran in 1936 and became a professor of engineering at the University of Teheran. He supported Mohammad Mosaddeq, who as prime minister quarreled with Shah Mohammad Reza Pahlavi, and, after Mosaddeq's overthrow in 1953, Bazargan joined the National Resistance Movement. He left it in 1961 and took part in the formation of the Iranian Liberation Movement. He was sentenced four times to short periods of imprisonment. In 1963 he joined the Iranian Committee for Defense of Liberty and Human Rights founded by Ayatollah Khomeini.

(K. M. SMOGORZEWSKI)

Belushi, John

"A Mardi Gras crowd of 70,000 packed into the Super Dome to hear two white comedians from New York sing the blues?" Perplexed by the odd mix, a *Washington Post* reporter asked the rhetorical question in his incredulity over John Belushi, a most unlikely celebrity. He'd become famous pretending to be a pimple bursting in a popular college-cult film, *Animal House*. Then he went on to become the talk of Martha's Vineyard by buying World Bank Pres. Robert McNamara's sea-cliff estate for approximately $425,000.

Changing media faster than most actors change roles, Belushi appeared in New Orleans with Dan Aykroyd, a comic colleague on the "Saturday Night Live" television show. Developing a skit they had done on the show into the Blues Brothers Band, they transformed it into a musical act. Then the video team transformed that into a record. Released in time for Christmas, it was at the top of the charts by Belushi's 30th birthday, Jan. 24, 1979. By then the two charter members of the "Not Ready for Prime Time Players" had begun filming *The Blues Brothers* as a World War II satire.

Belushi's bent for the incongruous may almost be genetic. His father, an Albanian immigrant, went into the Italian restaurant business in Chicago, Belushi's birthplace. After a brief stint at the University of Michigan, Belushi joined Chicago's famous Second City improvisation troupe and then was discovered by the *New York Times* while performing in a revue called *Lemmings*.

The *National Lampoon* magazine, which produced both *Lemmings* and *Animal House*, aimed its products at the older-adolescent-to-younger-adult set, an audience as appreciative as it was affluent. At the rate of $1 million a week, the film earned back 20 times its production costs. As one observer described it, "This humor is post-'60s, post-acid and politically closest to the yippies . . . . It's anti-establishment in every way."

The reason sedate Martha's Vineyard buzzed so loudly when Belushi became a landowner was their fear that he might turn the beach estate into a hotbed of general raucousness. But evidently the man who "abuses his body in ways that would kill bulls" (his director's words) only wanted a quiet place to recover from his breakneck working pace.

(PHILIP KOPPER)

Bendjedid, Chadli

When Pres. Houari Boumédienne of Algeria fell ill in September 1978, Col. Chadli Bendjedid was appointed acting minister of defense. As senior army officer, he was an obvious successor to Boumédienne, and following the latter's death on December 27, he was selected as sole candidate during the January 1979 congress of the National Liberation Front (FLN). His election to the presidency followed on February 7.

Considered a moderate, Bendjedid successfully reconciled opponents of the late president to his government. He also maintained Algeria's nonaligned policy and its support for the Polisario Front seeking independence for Western Sahara. He clearly was not just a compromise between opposing FLN factions but quickly stamped Algerian policy with his own vision of the future. In an interview published in a French Arabic weekly in October, he warned against the dangers in a confrontation between Algeria and Morocco over Western Sahara and stressed the need for the Arab states to adopt an offensive strategy in their opposition to the Egyptian-Israeli peace treaty signed March 26.

Chadli Bendjedid was born into a poor peasant family on April 14, 1929, at Sebaa, near Annaba in eastern Algeria. He served in the French Army until 1954 when, some months after the Algerian revolution began, he joined the FLN. He rose rapidly through the ranks of the guerrilla forces in Wiliya (military region) 2, becoming commander of the 13th Battalion on the Tunisian frontier in 1960. Later he joined the staff of Colonel Boumédienne on the Moroccan border.

In 1962, shortly after independence, Bendjedid joined Boumédienne and Ahmed Ben Bella in overthrowing the Ben Khedda provisional government. He then restored order in the old Wiliya 2 area and was appointed commander of the Constantine military region in 1963. In 1964 he took over command of the Oran military region and was instrumental in Boumédienne's coup against President Ben Bella in 1965. After the coup, Bendjedid was appointed to the Revolutionary Council, but his main concern was to ensure his control over the Oran military command. In 1969 he was promoted to the rank of colonel.

(GEORGE JOFFÉ)

Bhutto, Benazir

For Benazir Bhutto, the elder daughter of the former prime minister of Pakistan, 1979 was a year of tragedy: her father, Zulfikar Ali Bhutto (*see* OBITUARIES), was executed by the military regime of Gen. Mohammad Zia-ul-Haq. Benazir played a leading role in the long struggle to save her father's life by

PAUL RAFFAELE—CAMERA PRESS/PHOTO TRENDS

touring the country and making speeches. But because of the support she drew she was placed under house arrest from February to June 1978 and from October 1978 to May 29, 1979.

Even before her father's death Benazir had become the acting head of his political party, the Pakistan People's Party (PPP), in succession to her mother, Begum Nusrat Bhutto, who had been barred from politics. After her release in May Benazir spent her time organizing the party. With elections scheduled to take place on November 17 there was the growing feeling that with Benazir at its head, the PPP would return to power with a large majority. She herself was planning to contest the elections in four constituencies, including that of her late father in her home town of Larkana in Sind. But Benazir and the PPP were banned from taking part in the elections, and soon afterward, on October 16, the elections were canceled altogether. At the same time, Benazir and her mother were once more placed under house arrest.

Born in Karachi on June 21, 1953, Benazir completed the latter part of her schooling abroad: first at Harvard University from 1969 to 1973, and then at Oxford, where she graduated with a degree in philosophy, politics, and economics in 1976. She remained at Oxford for another year to complete a foreign service course, with the intention of entering the foreign service in Pakistan. She was president of the Oxford Union in the spring of 1977, the first Asian woman to hold the office.

At the end of June 1977 she returned to Pakistan. Only days later, on July 5, her father was removed from power in a military coup by General Zia. With Bhutto under detention and then in jail, she was thrown into the turbulent life of Pakistani politics, campaigning first for his political career and then for his life. After his death she considered it her duty to continue his work for the people of Pakistan.

(VICTORIA SCHOFIELD)

Binaisa, Godfrey L.

After the overthrow of Gen. Idi Amin in April 1979, Uganda needed an experienced and impartial leader capable of firmly reestablishing law and order and of binding up the tribal and religious wounds inflicted during years of tyrannical rule. When the first man chosen to take Amin's place as president, Yusufu Lule, proved unequal to this difficult task, he was replaced in June by Godfrey Binaisa, who had been attorney general in the government of Milton Obote, the president toppled by Amin's military coup in 1971.

Binaisa was born in Kampala, Uganda, on May 30, 1920, and went to King's College, Budo, before gaining his degree from Makerere University in Kampala. He subsequently received a law degree at King's College, University of London, in 1955 and was called to the bar at Lincoln's Inn, London. He soon became involved in politics and in October 1959 founded the Uganda League, one of several parties seeking self-government for the then-British protectorate. His appointment as attorney general followed the April 1962 elections that brought Obote to the premiership and preceded Uganda's independence in October of that year. Binaisa was one of the few prominent Baganda tribal members to oppose the kabaka (king) of Buganda in the latter's resistance to the Obote government, a conflict that ended in the kabaka's defeat in 1966.

In 1967 Binaisa broke with Obote over his use of authoritarian tactics and proposals to change the constitution. As a believer in constitutional law Binaisa felt bound to resign from the government. He returned to private legal practice and in 1968 was elected chairman of the Law Development Centre and president of the Uganda Law Society. In 1970 he became a member of the Uganda Judicial Service Commission and two years later was made chairman of the organizing committee of the Commonwealth Lawyers' Conference. Unlike many of Obote's critics, Binaisa was not among those who welcomed Amin's coup in 1971. He was forced into exile and began a law practice in New York City, which he used as a base to campaign against Amin's rule.

(COLIN LEGUM)

Bishop, Maurice

One of the more surprising aspects of Grenada's March 1979 revolution was its lack of vindictiveness toward those connected with the regime of the deposed Sir Eric Gairy. There were few members of the People's Revolutionary Government who had not suffered physically at the hands of the previous administration's notorious parapolice aids, the Mongoose Gang.

The new prime minister, Maurice Bishop, probably had more reason to feel bitter than most. On the night of Nov. 18, 1973, Bishop and his companions were severely beaten by Mongoose members in full view of the police and held without medical attention in appalling conditions. Subsequently, he had to seek specialized medical attention in Barbados. Two months later, while trying to defend women and children from the police and Mongoose members, his father, Rupert Bishop, a well-liked businessman, was murdered "by persons unknown." From that point on, Maurice Bishop swore to bring down Gairy's administration.

This was attempted politically through a coalition of the Movement for Assemblies of the People and the New Jewel Movement (an acronym for Joint Endeavours for Welfare Education and Liberation). In 1976 a coalition of New Jewel and the long-established Grenada National Party and United People's Party won 6 seats, reducing Gairy's majority from 13 seats to 3. As a result of suspicions that Gairy had decided to move against New Jewel, a successful coup was mounted early in the morning of March 13, 1979. Bishop emerged as leader and, subsequently, prime minister.

Maurice Bishop was born in 1944, attended St. George's Roman Catholic Primary School, and won a scholarship to Grenada's Roman Catholic Presentation College. After working in the Grenada Civil Service for a few months, he left for England, where he entered Gray's Inn. He gained a degree in law at London University and was called to the bar in 1969. Politically, he was both a Caribbean nationalist and a socialist. Though New Jewel embraced broad Marxist-Leninist beliefs, its policy was much in line with current pragmatic Caribbean interpretations.

(DAVID A. JESSOP)

Brock, Lou

Even less than two months from his baseball retirement, Lou Brock looked ahead to the next milestone. The day was Aug. 13, 1979, and Brock had just become the 14th major league baseball player ever to hit safely 3,000 times. There seemed to be little more room for frosting on the cake of his 18 major league seasons, but Brock said, "I still keep dreaming about a man named Billy Hamilton."

Hamilton had been credited with 937 stolen bases in the late 19th century, when more lenient rules awarded a stolen base for merely advancing two bases on another man's one-base hit. Brock was eight stolen bases short of breaking that record as he spoke, making the mark look unattainable in light of his meagre 12 stolen bases in the season's first four months.

Brock had already set a single-season record for stolen bases with 118 in 1974, and he had broken Ty Cobb's modern career record with his 893rd stolen base in 1977. He had played for two St. Louis Cardinal teams that won World Series championships. And the sleek outfielder, born June 18, 1939, into a poor family in El Dorado, Ark., had been selected by Cardinal fans as the most memorable player in the team's history, a legacy that included Stan Musial and Dizzy Dean.

In an era of long-ball hitters, Brock helped to make speed fashionable again in baseball. His seven stolen bases in the Cardinals' victorious 1967 World Series set a record, and he tied it himself the next year. In 21 World Series games Brock batted .391 and tied a record with 13 hits in the 1968 Series.

He was 35 when he stole 118 bases in 1974, earning two national magazines' player of the year awards. That was one of 12 straight seasons in which he stole at least 50 bases, which set another record, and one of seven in which he batted at least .300.

But in many respects, Brock's most remarkable season was his last one. After people considered him washed up for batting .221 with only 12 stolen bases in 1978, Brock finished grandly with a .304 average. He also stole those eight bases he needed in the 1979 season's final weeks. He finished with 938 and purged Billy Hamilton from the record books. (KEVIN M. LAMB)

UPI

Byrne, Jane

When the City of Chicago was run by the late and legendary Mayor Richard J. Daley, the mayor was known by a single nickname —"Hizzoner." Jane Byrne, who is Daley's successor once removed, has, in contrast, a number of nicknames. To some she is "Ayatollah Jane" or "Calamity Jane"; to others, she is "Miss Bossy" or "Mommy Mayor."

FAVERTY—GAMMA/LIAISON

The sobriquets reflect differing views of how Byrne, who was elected mayor April 3, 1979, has been doing in Chicago's lusty political arena. Unpredictable and sometimes vindictive, she has, however, convinced just about everyone that she is a tough, skilled politician—and a force to be reckoned with.

Democrat Byrne entered politics as a Chicago volunteer in John F. Kennedy's 1960 presidential campaign. Daley, another Kennedy supporter, was impressed with her firm, no-nonsense style. Beginning in 1964 he appointed her to several relatively minor city hall jobs. In 1974 Daley named her co-chairman of the Cook County, Ill., Democratic Party.

Since Byrne's position in the party hierarchy depended almost entirely on Daley's sponsorship, Daley's death in 1976 seemed a serious blow to her career. The Daley machine's handpicked new mayor, Michael Bilandic, stripped her of her position in the party, although she kept her job as Chicago's commissioner of consumer sales, weights and measures. Then Byrne, in a remarkable reversal, turned against the machine her mentor had created. In 1977, using her consumer job as a platform, she accused Bilandic and others of attempting to "grease" the way for a taxi-fare increase. Bilandic promptly fired her.

Suddenly, Byrne had become a symbol of reform in Chicago and, ultimately, a candidate for mayor. Aided by a massive snowstorm that Chicagoans believed was dealt with poorly by the Bilandic administration, Byrne narrowly defeated Bilandic in February's Democratic mayoral primary and went on to a landslide victory in the general election.

The mayor was born Jane Burke on May 24, 1934, in Chicago and was graduated from Barat College in Lake Forest, Ill. Her first husband, William Byrne, was killed in a 1959 airplane crash. In 1978 she married Jay McMullen, a political reporter for the *Chicago Sun-Times*. (STANLEY W. CLOUD)

Carrington, Peter Alexander Rupert Carington, 6th Baron

Lord Carrington (the spelling of the family name differs from that of the title), who in 1938 inherited a peerage, a place in the House of Lords, and a title dating back to 1796, became Britain's foreign minister in the Conservative government formed in May 1979. Superficially a typecast aristocrat, born June 6, 1919, educated at Eton, soldier in the Grenadier Guards, landowner and banker, Carrington had been a full-time career politician for nearly 30 years. Had he surrendered his title and found a seat in the House of Commons, which he might have done in the 1960s, he would have been a serious contender for the leadership of the Conservative Party. As it was, he became one of the most powerful and influential members of the Conservative governments of the 1970s.

In Edward Heath's government of 1970–74 Carrington served as defense minister. One of Heath's closest confidants, he was described as "Ted's troubleshooter." He had been chairman of the Conservative Party organization—a key post—for two years during the Heath government, but he transferred his support to Margaret Thatcher when she was elected leader and was leader of the opposition in the House of Lords from 1974 to 1979.

As secretary of state for foreign affairs and Commonwealth relations, Carrington was deeply involved in the negotiations for the independence of Zimbabwe Rhodesia, and the successful outcome of the London constitutional conference was a personal triumph for him. He was a man of no-nonsense bluntness but no believer in confrontation. Indeed, in the long-drawn-out negotiations he showed qualities of realism and inexhaustible persistence. He was thought to have had an important moderating influence on Thatcher, who was inexperienced in international affairs.

Carrington had a reputation for independence of thought and action. He did not commit himself to the more extreme free market dogmas of some of his colleagues. He was on record as believing that government should intervene where market forces proved inadequate. His preoccupation with foreign affairs did not preclude his having an influential and steadying voice in the Cabinet on economic and social policy.

(HARFORD THOMAS)

Carstens, Karl

Elected president of West Germany on May 23, 1979, Karl Carstens took office on July 1. Although he had had a distinguished career as a civil servant and, subsequently, as a politician, his elevation to the highest office in the land caused controversy because of

SVEN SIMON/KATHERINE YOUNG

his former nominal membership in the Nazi Party. After studying law he trained in the German law courts and at that time was advised by a judge that he would be put at a big disadvantage if he did not join the party. In 1937 he applied for membership but delayed handing in some documents for so long that he was not accepted until 1940, after he had joined the German Army. He was cleared after World War II by a denazification court.

Carstens, who was born in Bremen on Dec. 14, 1914, studied law and political science in Germany and—after the war—in France and the U.S. He set up a law practice in Bremen in 1945, and four years later was appointed head of the Bremen "mission" to the federal government in Bonn. He joined the Foreign Service in 1954 and four years later became the foreign ministry's most senior official, with the rank of state secretary. He was subsequently state secretary in the Ministry of Defense and in the chancellor's office under Kurt Georg Kiesinger.

Elected to the Bundestag (lower house of the federal Parliament) as a Christian Democrat in 1972, Carstens served as chairman of the joint parliamentary group of Christian Democrat and Christian Social Union members from 1973 to 1976. During that time he was a vigorous opponent of the government's *Ostpolitik*, its policy toward the Soviet bloc which stressed accommodation. In December 1976 he was elected president, or speaker, of the Bundestag, a post he held until he became chief of state.

Carstens occupied a position in the Christian Democratic Union somewhat to the right of centre. But his conservatism put him on good terms with the Bavarian Christian Social Union led by Franz-Josef Strauss (*q.v.*)—an asset at all times, but especially when the two parties were on the brink of breaking their alliance.

(NORMAN CROSSLAND)

Carter, Jimmy

For U.S. Pres. Jimmy Carter 1979 might prove to have been the pivotal year of his presidency, the year in which the voters began seriously to decide if they were willing to reelect him to a second term. It was in 1979 that he began to shed the populist posture he had used so successfully as a candidate in 1976 and tried to adopt a more "presidential" stance.

By midyear, things were plainly not going at all well for Carter. Despite his success at personally mediating a peace agreement between Israel and Egypt, his public opinion ratings plummeted to record lows. The voters said that they believed Carter was personally honest but they doubted his competence to handle the details of his job and to choose his advisers wisely.

When Carter attempted to improve his image through a variety of public relations gimmicks, he did not even come close to stemming the tide of public disapproval. Indeed, some of the president's tactics—such as wholesale restructuring of his Cabinet during the summer—seemed only to hasten his decline. Thus it was hardly surprising that two of Carter's most prominent rivals for the Democratic Party's presidential nomination—Sen. Edward Kennedy of Massachusetts (*q.v.*) and Gov. Edmund ("Jerry") Brown, Jr., of California—formally announced their candidacies. Widespread doubts about their qualifications began to surface almost immediately, however, while Carter's own ratings showed some tentative improvement.

Carter's chances for reelection may also have been helped by the first major international crisis of his presidency. On November 4, after the president had approved the entrance of the ousted shah of Iran into the U.S. for cancer treatment and gallbladder surgery, antishah militants in Teheran stormed the U.S. embassy there and took more than 50 Americans hostage. They demanded that Carter extradite the shah immediately for trial as a "criminal" and said that until then they would not release the hostages. Carter refused, and a stalemate ensued. While Carter was criticized by some for not responding more boldly to the Iranian challenge, he was generally given high marks for his coolness in a highly volatile situation and his ratings in opinion polls improved markedly. The impulse to rally around the leader was intensified at year's end when the Soviet intervention in Afghanistan threatened an even more dangerous crisis.

Born Oct. 1, 1924, in Plains, Ga., Carter served as governor of Georgia from 1971 to 1974. After winning the Democratic Party nomination in 1976, he defeated Gerald Ford to gain the presidency.

(STANLEY W. CLOUD)

Casaroli, Agostino Cardinal

Appointed secretary of state—the Vatican's "foreign minister"—by Pope John Paul II on April 30, 1979, Msgr. Agostino Casaroli accordingly was made a cardinal at the consistory of June 30. The appointment as successor to Jean Cardinal Villot (*see* OBITUARIES) was a tribute to Casaroli's all-round experience. As secretary to the Council for the Public Affairs of the Church, he had been responsible for renegotiating the concordats with Spain and Italy. It was widely thought that since the pope was Polish, the secretary of state ought to be an Italian, if only so that he could help the pope disengage the papacy from Italian politics.

Agostino Casaroli was born at Castel San Giovanni in the diocese of Piacenza on Nov. 24, 1914. After completing his theological training, he went to the Accademia Pontificia, the school for Vatican diplomats. The breakthrough in his career came in 1961, when Pope John XXIII, detecting signs of détente in Communist attitudes, sought ways of entering into contact. Casaroli was sent to Vienna to head the Vatican delegation at a conference on diplomatic relations; he was back again two years later for another conference on consular relations. He made his first contacts with Communist diplomats and henceforward was identified with the Vatican's *Ostpolitik*.

Some of the landmarks along the way were the negotiation of a modus vivendi with Yugoslavia in 1966, the signing of the Treaty on the Non-proliferation of Nuclear Weapons in Moscow in 1971, and a notable speech at the Conference on Security and Cooperation in Europe at Helsinki in July 1973. He visited Eastern Europe many times, concentrating on establishing the freedom of the church to appoint its own bishops and then on the right to teach religion to children and students. Casaroli was sometimes accused of weakness in his dealings with Communists, but the election of a Polish pope in October 1978 changed the situation. John Paul II could not be accused of weakness, and his appointment of Casaroli as secretary of state, the number-two post in the Vatican, was a mark of confidence.

(PETER HEBBLETHWAITE)

Cato, (Robert) Milton

When the eastern Caribbean island of St. Vincent cast loose its links of association with Great Britain on Oct. 27, 1979, Milton Cato became its first prime minister under the new constitution, a position that was confirmed in the December 5 elections. At 64 years of age, Cato was, at the time of independence, one of the few remaining Caribbean heads of government of the old school. Though a socialist, his political convictions did not embrace modern regional interpretations, let alone the growing Marxism-Leninism in the area. He had been highly critical, in both public and private, of the effect of the revolution in neighbouring Grenada and recent developments in Jamaica and Guyana. Instead he preferred to establish closer links with the relatively conservative governments of Trinidad and Barbados, both at an economic level and through the establishment of a joint coast guard and a fisheries protection service with Barbados. Basically a pragmatist, he attempted to introduce policies that would bring employment and growth to the island's people.

Born in St. Vincent on June 3, 1915, Cato was educated at St. Vincent Grammar School and apprenticed to a local attorney. World War II intervened in his career, however, and, having joined the Canadian Army, he saw active service in Europe. After the war he attended law school in London. On his return to St. Vincent he went into private legal practice and began to identify himself with local political aspirations. He was elected a parliamentary member of the short-lived West Indies Federation. In 1955 he, along with others, founded the St. Vincent Labour Party (SVLP).

In May 1967, as leader of the SVLP, he

became chief minister and afterward prime minister when the island moved from dependency status to associated statehood. In 1972 his party lost to an opposition coalition, but in 1974, in an extraordinary turnabout, he led it to victory in conjunction with the island's other main political party. By 1976 this coalition had collapsed, but Cato retained the position of prime minister as the SVLP still had a majority in the legislative assembly. (DAVID A. JESSOP)

Chen Yun

Chen Yun (Ch'en Yün) reemerged in 1979 as one of China's most influential leaders. A close ally of First Vice-Premier Deng Xiaoping (Teng Hsiao-p'ing), he was named a vice-premier and head of the new State Finance and Economic Commission in July. Chen quickly established his authority by redesigning China's plans for modernizing the economy. Evidently feeling that the original goals were too ambitious and probably unattainable, Chen opted for less frantic development and more emphasis on light industry. His priority was to increase consumer goods and raise living standards; heavy industry would come later.

Chen, whose original name was Liao Ch'eng-yün, was born into a poor family in Jiangsu (Kiangsu) Province in 1900. As a young man he worked as a typesetter and joined the Communist Party in 1924 under the tutelage of Zhou Enlai (Chou En-lai), the late premier. He took part in the Long March (1934–35) and spent 1935–37 in the Soviet Union. During World War II he was active in organizational work for the party and from 1945 to 1949 played important roles in political and economic developments in Manchuria. He then directed China's economy after the defeat (1949) of the Nationalist government. As vice-premier (he also acted as premier during Zhou's absence), and as a member of the all-powerful Standing Committee of the party Politburo, Chen stressed sound planning and prudent policies. This approach put him at odds with Mao Zedong (Mao Tse-tung), who launched the disastrous Great Leap Forward (1958–59) in the hope that China could be transformed into an instant superpower by forcing labourers into communes and installing backyard blast furnaces throughout the land. As a consequence of his differences with Mao, Chen lost administrative posts and power. His recent return to prominence, believed to have been engineered by Deng, began late in 1978 with election to the Politburo and appointment as a vice-chairman of the Chinese Communist Party. His designation as a vice-premier in 1979 confirmed his role as undisputed czar of China's economy during the critical years that lay ahead.

(WINSTON L. Y. YANG; NATHAN K. MAO)

Civiletti, Benjamin R.

When U.S. Attorney General Griffin Bell let it be known in early 1979 that he would retire from the administration of Pres. Jimmy Carter, there was little doubt that his deputy, Benjamin Civiletti, was Bell's choice to be his successor. On August 1 the U.S. Senate confirmed the appointment, and Civiletti became attorney general of the U.S. at the comparatively young age of 44.

Born in Peekskill, N.Y., on July 17, 1935, Civiletti received an undergraduate degree

UPI

from Johns Hopkins University in Baltimore, Md., in 1957 and was graduated from the University of Maryland law school in 1961. He built a reputation as a trial lawyer while serving 2 years as an assistant U.S. attorney and 13 years in a Baltimore law firm.

Unlike many other Cabinet officers, Civiletti was not a personal friend of Carter. But he became head of the Justice Department's criminal division in 1977 on the recommendation of Charles Kirbo, an Atlanta lawyer who was one of Carter's closest advisers. Kirbo had been impressed by Civiletti's work when both were involved in an antitrust case in Baltimore.

As head of the criminal division, Civiletti handled a number of hot political problems, including the investigation of Bert Lance, former director of the Office of Management and Budget and a close personal friend of the president. Lance later was indicted on charges of bank fraud. Civiletti also supervised the investigation of Korean influence buying involving Park Tong Sun and a number of U.S. congressmen.

As attorney general Civiletti immediately encountered a fresh batch of politically sensitive cases. One involved a special prosecutor's probe of the Carter family's peanut warehouse; another investigation went into the alleged misdeeds of Hamilton Jordan (*q.v.*), the White House chief of staff. Through it all Civiletti insisted that he, and the president, were determined to keep the Justice Department free from outside influence and political pressure.

(HAL BRUNO)

Clark, Joe

On June 4, 1979, Joe Clark realized his lifelong ambition by becoming Canada's prime minister—the youngest man ever to do so. Only recently an obscure member of Parliament from Alberta, he had led the Progressive Conservative Party to victory in the May 22 elections and put an end to the 11-year reign of the Liberals under Pierre Elliott Trudeau. Observers called it a triumph for western Canada and for homey, small-town values as against Trudeau's cosmopolitan sophistication.

But whether that triumph would be sustained—or whether Joe Clark would become merely a footnote in Canadian history—was still undecided at year's end. Only six months after he took office, his minority government fell on a budget question. In new elections, set for Feb. 18, 1980, he would once again face Trudeau, called back from a brief retirement to lead the Liberal campaign.

Born in High River, Alta., on June 5, 1939, Charles Joseph Clark was the son of Charles Clark, owner of the *High River Times*. He obtained a B.A. in history (1960) and an M.A. in political science (1973) from the University of Alberta and taught political science there from 1965 to 1967. He had been active in politics since 1957, when he solicited votes door-to-door for the Conservative Party. In 1959 he became private secretary to the Alberta Conservative leader, W. J. C. Kirby, and from 1962 to 1965 he was national president of the Progressive Conservative Student Federation.

In 1967 he directed the campaign organization that brought Peter Lougheed to power as premier of Alberta. From 1967 to 1970 Clark was executive assistant to Robert Stanfield, then Conservative leader of the opposition in the House of Commons. He was first elected to Parliament in 1972 to represent Alberta's Rocky Mountain riding (district). Elected leader of his party in 1976, he was still so little known that a major Toronto newspaper headlined the story "Joe Who?"

Clark's concept of national leadership was a partnership between the federal government and the provinces. Belief in small government and free enterprise may have led to his campaign promises to dismantle or sell several government-owned corporations. He described his vision of Canada as a "community of communities" where cultural differences could flourish and small-town ideals would set the tone.

(DIANE LOIS WAY)

Coe, Sebastian Newbold

From being an athlete familiar only to track and field experts, Sebastian Coe in a sensational 41 days in 1979 became one of the most talked-about persons in sports when he set three new world records. At the Bislet Stadium in Oslo he ran 800 m in 1 min 42.4 sec on July 5 and a mile in 3 min 49 sec on July 17; then at Zürich, Switz., on August 15, he lowered the 1,500-m record by 0.10 sec to 3 min 32.10 sec. After those fireworks Coe suffered a slight hamstring injury while training near London, and he decided to sit out the rest of the 1979 season and plan a buildup for the 1980 Olympic Games.

Coe, who was born in London on Sept. 29, 1956, lived with his parents in Sheffield and was coached by his engineer-father, Peter. Unusually slight for a world record holder in the 800 m—5 ft 9½ in and 129 lb—he was unusual too in having decreased his running distances. He started as a cross-country and distance runner of note and might have been expected to graduate to 5,000 m and 10,000 m. But, as he put it, "you have to come back to speed to succeed in any event in athletics these days. You can't move up in distance to hide from it. It's all speed, speed, speed."

In 1975 Coe took a bronze medal in the European junior 1,500-m championship in Athens, clocking 3 min 45.2 sec. The next year he gained a reputation as a daredevil front runner but won nothing. In indoor competition in 1976–77 he took the European 800-m title at Nice, France, in 1 min 46.5 sec, one-tenth of a second slower than the world's indoor best.

After being sidelined by a broken foot bone, Coe in 1977 ran fourth in the Europa Cup final in Helsinki, Fin. In 1978 he was again hampered by injuries, but in August he headed the world 800-m rankings, with a 1-min 44.3-sec effort in Brussels; in the European championships in Prague, Czech., the blinding pace he set defeated him and he ran third, his chief rival and the world's leading miler, Steve Ovett, finishing second. But he got his U.K. 800-m record back from Ovett, in 1 min 44.1 sec. In 1979 Coe was faster than ever: he won the Europa Cup 800 m in Turin, Italy, ran 400 m in 46.9 sec, and produced his Oslo and Zürich records to become a favourite for the Moscow Olympics with Ovett, whom he had met only that once in Prague. Meanwhile, he was occupied with postgraduate studies in economics at Loughborough University, Leicestershire. (DAVID COCKSEDGE)

Coppola, Francis Ford

"Except for Stanley Kubrick, no other contemporary American director is as gifted as Francis Coppola . . . the only real candidate to make the definitive film about Vietnam," according to one critic. Coppola set out to make that film and in 1979 released *Apocalypse Now.* The long-awaited epic had been four years in the making; a number of cataclysms delayed it, including a typhoon that wrecked the expensive sets in the Philippines and a heart attack suffered by leading actor Martin Sheen. Originally budgeted at $12 million, it finally cost almost $20 million more than that. Even then it was not generally regarded as the "definitive" artistic statement. In one critic's view, it "may be the ultimate cinematic death trip." Many others regarded it as either a seriously flawed success or an enormously ambitious failure marred by its own magnitude.

"We made it the way Americans made war in Vietnam," said Coppola. "There were too many of us, too much money and equipment, and little by little we went insane. I thought I was making a war film and it developed that the film was making me. The jungle was making the film."

Loosely based on Joseph Conrad's short novel *Heart of Darkness,* it described the odyssey of a seeker ordered to assassinate a colonel (played by Marlon Brando) who had run amok in an isolated jungle bastion. The gruesome quest built on scenes Coppola conceived to reflect the enigmas of the war: a soldier's association of the exploding napalm's scent with victory; steak-and-beer cookouts the night before a grim assault; Playboy bunnies on tour to entertain baby-faced killers.

Born in Detroit April 7, 1939, Coppola attended UCLA film school and began working as an assistant to producer Roger Corman. As a writer, director, and producer, he went on to work on such well-respected films as *Reflections in a Golden Eye, Patton, Finian's Rainbow, The Rain People, The Conversation, The Great Gatsby, American Graffiti,* and the two *Godfather* films. In the course of this career he won five Oscars.

(PHILIP KOPPER)

Francis Ford Coppola

UPI

Cossiga, Francesco

On Aug. 4, 1979, Francesco Cossiga, a 51-year-old Sardinian, succeeded in putting together a new Christian Democrat-led coalition. In so doing, he brought to an end a six-month-long political crisis in Rome and became Italy's youngest premier since the republic was formed in 1946. A personal friend of the late Christian Democrat Party president and former premier Aldo Moro, kidnapped and murdered by the Red Brigades urban guerrillas in 1978, Cossiga held the key post of interior minister at the time of the crime and personally supervised the nationwide search for the kidnappers and their hostage.

Cossiga was born on July 26, 1928, in Sassari, Sardinia, like the Italian Communist Party leader, Enrico Berlinguer, to whom he was related (they were second cousins). A fervent Roman Catholic and a lawyer by profession, he was first elected to Parliament in 1958 on a Christian Democrat ticket and achieved Cabinet office as minister without portfolio in 1974. As interior minister from 1976, he displayed qualities of decisiveness and courage in dealing with two national emergencies—the Friuli earthquake of that year and the campaign of political terrorism culminating in the murder of Aldo Moro in May 1978.

On learning of Moro's murder, Cossiga resigned his office. He then disappeared from the limelight until he was unexpectedly called upon to try to form a government and end Italy's longest postwar political crisis. Three other leading politicians had tried and failed after the indecisive general election of June 1979, but Cossiga succeeded within 48 hours in forming a coalition of Christian Democrats, Liberals, and Social Democrats.

One of his first acts on arriving at the Palazzo Chigi (the Italian premier's office) was to install sophisticated telecommunications and computerized information-storage systems. He then dealt speedily with a number of controversial banking, political, and diplomatic appointments that had been hanging fire for months. As the year drew to a close, he embarked on a series of exploratory private meetings with heads of government of other European Economic Community members in preparation for the period (January–July 1980) when he was due to take over the chairmanship of the Community's Council of Ministers, which fell to Italy by rotation.

(DAVID DOUGLAS WILLEY)

Dacko, David

President once more of the Central African Republic following a coup that swept him to power in Bangui on Sept. 21, 1979, with the aid of French paratroops, David Dacko proclaimed the fall of Emperor Bokassa I while the latter was on a visit to Libya. Dacko thus resumed the presidency he had left when Jean-Bedel Bokassa, then a colonel and chief of staff, deposed him on the night of Dec. 31, 1965–Jan. 1, 1966. Dacko appointed Bokassa's former premier, Henri Maïdou, vice-president and on Sept. 27, 1979, formed the new regime's first government.

Born on March 24, 1930, at Bouchia in Lobaye, Dacko belonged, like former presidents Barthélémy Boganda and Bokassa, to the Mbaka tribe but came from a branch unconnected with that of his predecessors. From the upper primary school at Bambari he entered a teacher's training school, and in 1951 he became a primary school teacher in Bangui. Headmaster of Kouanga school in 1955, he became associated with Boganda and started on a political career. In March 1957 he was elected to the territorial assembly. Boganda appointed him minister of agriculture in the first government council of Oubangui-Chari, and in December 1958 he was named minister of internal and administrative affairs of the Central African Republic, which Oubangi-Chari had become.

When Boganda disappeared in a plane crash on March 29, 1959, Dacko, who claimed a family relationship, established himself as his successor. Outmaneuvering the then vice-president (head) of the government council, Abel Goumba, he had himself elected head of the government. He also took over leadership of the Mouvement d'Évolution Sociale de l'Afrique Noire (MESAN). Less than 30 years old, he now exercised sole power.

With independence on Aug. 13, 1960, Dacko moved against Goumba's opposition party, the Mouvement pour l'Evolution Démocratique de l'Afrique Centrale (MEDAC). In November 1962 he officially abolished the multiparty system, dissolving MEDAC and arresting its leaders, including Goumba, and institutionalizing MESAN as the nation's only party. Goumba was eventually allowed to live in exile.

On Dec. 31, 1965, Dacko was deposed by Bokassa, put under detention in Bangui, and then allowed to return to his village. In 1976, in an unprecedented decision,

Bokassa appointed the deposed president his personal councillor, a post that Dacko made a springboard for his coup.

(PHILIPPE DECRAENE)

dos Santos, José Eduardo

After the death in Moscow on Sept. 10, 1979, of Angola's first president, Agostinho Neto (*see* OBITUARIES), José Eduardo dos Santos, the 37-year-old minister of planning, was elected as acting president. Under the constitution dos Santos's position would only be confirmed early in 1980 after a full congress of the ruling Popular Movement for the Liberation of Angola (MPLA). Before his death Neto had promoted dos Santos to a position which marked him as his chosen successor.

The new Angolan president was born in Angola on Aug. 28, 1942. From his youth he showed himself to be a militant nationalist, joining the MPLA in 1961. He was chosen by the liberation movement to study in Moscow. There he was trained as an engineer, specializing in the problems of the oil industry, an important sector of Angola's economy. While a student in Moscow he married a Soviet woman, but the marriage apparently did not last.

Dos Santos returned from his studies in Moscow a convinced Marxist. He served for a time as an active fighter with the MPLA's Second Military Front in Cabinda, the oil province of Angola. He frequently represented the MPLA at international forums. In 1974 he was elected to the executive committee of the movement's political bureau. After the country achieved independence in 1975, he became Angola's first foreign minister. In 1978 he was switched to the post of planning minister.

Although dos Santos remained firmly committed to his Marxist ideas, he proved himself in government to be a pragmatist and flexible in his approach to the difficult problems that faced Angola after its independence. He was a firm supporter of Neto's policy of developing close economic ties with the Western nations without abandoning Angola's strong friendship with the U.S.S.R. and Cuba. (COLIN LEGUM)

Duncan, Charles W.

When he took charge of the embattled U.S. Department of Energy in the summer of 1979, businessman Charles Duncan became head of what may be the country's most controversial government agency. Prior to that he had served since the start of the Carter administration as deputy secretary of defense, in charge of that department's financial management. As the new secretary of energy Duncan left the cloistered life in the Pentagon to become embroiled in one of the nation's critical issues: the energy shortage.

From the start, his brisk businessman's approach was viewed as a sharp contrast to the sometimes chaotic rule of James Schlesinger, who had headed the Cabinet department since its creation in 1977. Schlesinger was under fire from all sides when he resigned, and the department had been severely criticized for its confusing and contradictory policies. Duncan's main asset appeared to be the professional management approach he brought to the job.

Before joining the Carter administration Duncan had been president of Coca-Cola Co., a member of the firm's board of directors, and the holder of Coca-Cola stock worth an estimated $13 million. He had to resign from the board and place his stock in a blind trust when he joined the government.

Born Sept. 9, 1926, in Houston, Texas, Duncan received a degree in chemical engineering from Rice University and did graduate work in business management at the University of Texas. After working for the Humble Oil and Refining Co., he joined his family's business, Duncan Foods, and served as president from 1958 to 1964.

Coca-Cola bought Duncan Foods in 1964, and Duncan received 170,000 shares of Coca-Cola stock and a position on the board of directors. He served as president of Coca-Cola at its Atlanta, Ga., headquarters from 1971 to 1974, the same period during which Jimmy Carter was governor of Georgia. However, Duncan was not known to be a close friend of Carter, nor was he believed to be an important Carter political supporter. It was his expertise in business management and the recommendation of mutual friends in Atlanta that led to his appointment as a deputy to Secretary of Defense Harold Brown. (HAL BRUNO)

Edwardes, Sir Michael Owen

One of the brightest and most successful of Britain's younger businessmen, Sir Michael Edwardes (knighted in 1979) was the choice in 1977 for what was seemingly Britain's most impossible job. He became executive chairman of British Leyland Ltd. (BL), the much-troubled automotive giant that was brought back from the edge of collapse and bankruptcy only by the transfusion of government money on a massive scale. Edwardes was the fifth chairman since the government took over in 1975. During recent years BL had seen its share of the U.K. car market fall from two-fifths to one-fifth by 1978. Edwardes's job was to reorganize a clumsy mammoth of a company, to prune it into a more manageable shape and size, and to bring the company back to a self-sustaining level of profit by the introduction of new models. He was to accomplish all this within the three years for which he had been appointed to hold the job.

His reputation was made with the Chloride Group Ltd., a British manufacturer of industrial batteries. Born on Oct. 11, 1930, in South Africa, where he was educated, Edwardes joined Chloride as a management trainee when he was 21. By the time he was 42, he had become chief executive, and in 1974 he took over as chairman. Under his direction the company was reorganized. Between 1970 and 1974 it quadrupled its profits.

The problem at BL was of a different order. Like other car manufacturers, it suffered from a history of chronic industrial conflict, overmanning, and low productivity. Edwardes summed it up in the phrase "far too many men producing far too few cars." With the prospect of government subsidies coming to an end, in 1979 Edwardes determined to close 13 unprofitable plants at a cost of 25,000 jobs. He put the plan to the test of a postal vote of all BL employees and secured an 87% majority vote in favour, which overwhelmed the opposition of the union officials in the affected plants. Also in 1979 Edwardes arranged with the Japanese firm of Honda for BL to manufacture a Honda model in Britain.

(HARFORD THOMAS)

Fang Yi

Fang Yi, one of China's vice-premiers and a member of its Politburo, gained new stature in 1979 when he was named administrator of the nation's program to modernize its science and technology. Fang believes China can rival the West by the year 2000 if its Four Modernizations are well planned and carried out in progressive stages.

A.G.I.P./PICTORIAL PARADE

Fang was born in Fujian (Fukien) Province in 1909. After studying in Shanghai, he became an editor at the Commercial Press and joined the Communist Party in the early 1930s. As a veteran of the Long March (1934–35), he was given various administrative posts in Communist-controlled regions. After the Communists came to power in 1949, he served as vice-governor of Fujian before being named vice-minister of finance in 1953. In 1956 he was sent to North Vietnam as foreign aid liaison and in the early 1960s was a vice-chairman of the State Planning Commisson and director of an economic commission dealing with foreign countries. In 1971, having survived the turmoil of the Cultural Revolution, he was once again called upon to handle China's economic relations with other nations, this time as minister. Fang's elevation to the Politburo in 1977 foreshadowed his 1978 appointment as vice-premier and head of the State Science and Technology Commission. During the January 1979 visit of Vice-Premier Deng Xiaoping (Teng Hsiao-p'ing) to the U.S., Fang negotiated important scientific and educational exchanges. He also concluded similar agreements with France, West Germany, and other countries. Though not trained as a scientist, Fang clearly understood the importance of both technology and basic research and impressed Western scientists with the range and depth of his comprehension. As much as any man, Fang, recently appointed president of China's Academy of Sciences, would be responsible for the success or failure of China's ambitious eight-year program to modernize its science and technology. Much was at stake, for China envisioned the next two decades as its New Long March—into the 21st century.

(WINSTON L. Y. YANG)

Galway, James

In a world dominated by rock stars and the junketings of the international jet set, it was a source of wonder in 1979 that a classical musician, a flute player hailing from modest circumstances in the U.K.'s troubled province of Northern Ireland, could rise to a similar position of celebrity and renown. Such, however, was the status awarded James Galway, one of the few "serious" musicians able to fill the world's concert halls even for thorny contemporary music programs.

An incidental miracle was that Galway was alive at all, let alone playing. For in 1977, out walking with friends near his home in Switzerland, he was run down by an out-of-control motorcycle and seriously injured. Painful months in hospital and a spell on crutches, followed by regular traction therapy, enabled him to regain his previous mastery of flute fingering and to resume a full schedule of concerts and recitals in 1978–79.

Born in Belfast on Dec. 8, 1939, Galway began his musical career when he played fife with one of the city's many pipe and drum bands. There followed a sometimes stormy period at London's Royal College of Music, where Galway's unconventional approach to certain aspects of flute practice first made themselves felt. Free-lance engagements, including work with chamber groups such as The London Virtuosi, were succeeded by a sudden stroke of fortune in 1969, when Galway auditioned at the last moment before Herbert von Karajan and succeeded Karlheinz Zöller as principal flutist with the Berlin Philharmonic.

Galway had already garnered a substantial following when, in 1975, he decided once more to free-lance. Since then an exclusive recording contract with RCA, worldwide concertizing, and radio and television series, combined with his distinctive personality and sense of humour, have made him one of music's most sought-after personalities. Still wider acclaim came in 1978, when his recording of John Denver's "Annie's Song" topped the rock charts for weeks running. (MOZELLE A. MOSHANSKY)

Garaicoechea Urriza, Carlos

President of the Partido Nacionalista Vasco (PNV), the leading Basque Christian Democrat party, and the Consejo General Vasco (CGV), Carlos Garaicoechea was one of the principal negotiators of the Basque autonomy statute signed with the central Spanish government in July. The agreement provided for measures of home rule on such matters as education, justice, taxation, and finance and was greeted with widespread relief by Spain's politicians.

The PNV acknowledged that the new agreement was better than the 1936 Basque autonomy statute but had to accept that the Basque provinces would remain under Spanish sovereignty—an essential precondition for its approval by the Army and right-wing legislators in Madrid. The PNV also endorsed plans for a special referendum to decide the status of Navarre, where loyalties to the Basques, the province, and Spain as a whole were deeply divided. Garaicoechea's election as head of the Basque government was a virtual certainty following massive Basque acceptance of the autonomy statute in an October 25 referendum. Elections to the CGV were scheduled for early 1980.

Garaicoechea announced his intention of negotiating with the militant Euzkadi ta Azkatasuna (ETA; "Basque Homeland and Liberty") and its political ally, Herri Batasuna. Both of these advocated violence until the Basques attained complete independence. To be successful he would have to show that the central government in Madrid had transferred real power to the CGV; local control of the police force and courts would be powerful symbols in his struggle to convince his opponents that their way forward lay in negotiations leading to a peaceful transfer of power. The promised referendum in Navarre would also be an important factor in determining Basque attitudes in regard to autonomy.

Carlos Garaicoechea (Garaicoetxea in Basque) was born in Navarre in 1938. He studied at Deusto University, Bilbao, and qualified as both an engineer and a lawyer. Outside the strictly political arena, his chief preoccupation was with the depressed Basque economy. He ascribed its downturn both to the continuing separatist violence and to a lack of flexibility in adapting to changes in world conditions.

(MICHAEL WOOLLER)

Giannoulas, Ted

When baseball's "chicken man" emerged from a giant egg in the San Diego Padres' infield on June 29, 1979, it was just a rehatch. He had first arrived fully fledged in Dayglow fluff five years earlier to hand out Easter eggs at the local zoo as part of radio station KGB's "promotional experiment." But the bird's inner being, 5-ft 4-in Ted Giannoulas, had bigger ideas. A communications student at San Diego State University, he suggested that KGB send him to Padres games in the fine-feathered costume. He became a fixture on and around the diamond, and the station rose from fifth to first place in local media standings.

Cavorting through the stands, lifting a web-footed leg at the umpires, smothering an occasional pretty fan's head in his yellow beak, the chicken man was soon responsible for attracting more than one out of ten spectators to the stadium. Ted Turner, the Atlanta Braves' flamboyant owner, offered Giannoulas $100,000 to turkey trot down to Georgia. But the cackling celebrity decided to keep San Diego as his home base and turn free-lance—a decision that got his suit sued off.

© 1979 EILEEN MILLER—BLACK STAR

The trouble started when he took off the vest showing KGB's call letters for an away-from-home game. The station fired him, shooed him into court claiming $250,000 in damages, and hired a substitute. But the fans threatened such mayhem that the substitute was fitted with a bulletproof vest, though nothing worse came his way than game-delaying boos. Enjoined from wearing KGB's outfit or calling himself a chicken, Giannoulas bought a new fowl suit to prance the foul lines and went to work as an attraction without a name. Offered a percentage of the gate receipts by the Padres, he was escorted by motorcycle policemen onto the field inside the styrofoam egg atop an armoured truck and emerged to the tune of *Thus Spake Zarathustra.* KGB kept the legal heat on for a while but lost listeners and ended up eating crow.

Giannoulas was not alone in the world of professional sports clowns, nor was he the first "bleacher creature." But he was the most celebrated. Now earning more than $100,000 a year, he belly flopped around the bases on national television during one All-Star Game and received the legislature's official commendation for "comedy contributions to the State of California."

(PHILIP KOPPER)

Godunov, Aleksandr

Making his princely entrance in *Swan Lake* during the Bolshoi Ballet's New York City engagement, Aleksandr Godunov smiled to the packed house like a man with a secret. Days later, on Aug. 22, 1979, the world was in on it: he had approached U.S. immigration authorities, asked for political asylum, and gotten it. Thus, the athletic dancer joined other Soviet artists—mostly musicians, writers, and dancers—who had defected to the West. Three great ballet stars had preceded him: Rudolf Nureyev, Natalia Makarova, and Mikhail Baryshnikov. But Godunov was the first to abandon the world-famous Bolshoi.

Like the others, Godunov, a native of Riga, Latvia, gave "restraint in artistic life" as his reason for defecting. Translated into less stilted language, that probably meant that he wanted to try dancing differently than the Bolshoi authorities dictated.

The Godunov incident did not end with the 29-year-old dancer's decision. A serious diplomatic row ensued. At its centre was Godunov's wife, Ludmila Vlasova, 37, another Bolshoi dancer and often his partner. Godunov told U.S. officials that she planned to seek asylum with him. But when the Bolshoi troupe boarded an Aeroflot airliner at Kennedy International Airport for the return flight to the U.S.S.R., Vlasova was with them—before U.S. authorities could learn if she was leaving by choice or under coercion. Consequently, the plane was grounded until the ballerina could be interviewed by Donald F. McHenry, deputy U.S. ambassador to the UN.

Soviet Pres. Leonid Brezhnev wired the U.S. government that the plane's effective seizure was "inexcusable." U.S Pres. Jimmy Carter wired back that a fundamental human right was at stake. McHenry wanted to interview the woman privately in the terminal but her superiors would not let her leave the plane. Finally, after three days a compromise was worked out, and McHenry met the woman in a mobile lounge. She said she was leaving voluntarily, and the plane then left with the ballerina aboard. (PHILIP KOPPER)

Hassan II

Moulay Hassan ascended the throne of Morocco on Feb. 26, 1961, and by 1979 his reign had reached a critical point. On Nov. 6, 1975, he had launched his "Green March" of 200,000 unarmed Moroccans to occupy part of Spanish, now Western, Sahara peacefully, and a week later Spain handed over the entire territory to Morocco and Mauritania. But he had not reckoned sufficiently with the hostility of Algeria and the resistance of the Saharawi and the guerrilla fighters of their Popular Front for the Liberation of Saguia el Hamra and Río de Oro (Polisario Front).

By mid-1979 Morocco's southern partner, Mauritania, had made peace with the Polisario Front and had relinquished its share of the Western Sahara, which Hassan's troops promptly occupied. But the Polisario, supported by Algeria, captured and occupied Moroccan-held towns, inflicting losses; Hassan had annexed territory he could not control after four years of fighting, and Morocco's economy was feeling the strain of the war. Furthermore, the Organization of African Unity, at its July summit, supported (as the UN General Assembly did later) a plebiscite in the Western Sahara, and King Hassan's delegation could do no more than quit the assembly in protest. But the U.S. administration's decision in October to supply new weapons to Morocco, since it was now fighting a defensive war on its own frontiers, heartened the king. On November 6, the fourth anniversary of the Green March, he reasserted his claim to Western Saharan territory and at the same time offered honourable peace to its people.

Born on July 9, 1929, of the Alawite dynasty, claiming direct descent from the Prophet Muhammad, Hassan was educated in the Muslim tradition and at the University of Bordeaux, France. He shared exile with his father, Sultan Muhammad V (for fomenting Moroccan nationalism under the French protectorate), from 1953 to 1955. In 1956 Morocco received independence. Hassan was then given the task of re-creating the Moroccan Army and restoring order. An intelligent and astute politician, both a nationalist and an autocrat, he continued his father's authoritarian rule from 1961, offering paper constitutions in 1962 and in 1970 but governing through a subservient Parliament. (GEORGE JOFFÉ)

PIERRE TOUTAIN—GAMMA/LIAISON

Hawking, Stephen

"For some people black holes seem to be the Bermuda Triangles of space." A scientist, amused and perhaps a bit annoyed, was referring to the public's faddish interest in quite serious astrophysical investigations. In the mind and mathematics of one physicist, however—Stephen Hawking of the University of Cambridge—the concept of black holes had taken on truly powerful meaning because he had made it the stepping-stone to a long-sought relationship between the physical laws that govern the universe on its smallest scale and its largest. An expert in gravitation, Hawking has been called by many of his colleagues the greatest theoretical physicist since Einstein.

Although black holes have not been (and by definition cannot be) seen directly, they have been described mathematically in great detail, and indirect evidence has convinced many scientists that some have been born in the death throes of massive stars. When a star's nuclear fuel approaches exhaustion, its inward gravitational pull exceeds the outward push of its internal fires, upsetting the balance that had allowed the star to remain stable for billions of years. The dying star collapses upon itself, and for a sufficiently massive star, this contraction is believed to continue until its size becomes infinitesimally small and its density infinitely great. The star literally crushes itself out of the observable universe, leaving behind a region in space of definite volume—a black hole—that captures both light and matter and draws them inescapably to its centre.

Hawking's mathematical probe into the workings of black holes has led him to conclude that they could have arisen not only from collapsed stars but also from the enormous forces at work during the "big bang" creation of the universe, that "mini" black holes might be no larger than an atomic particle, and that black holes "evaporate" by radiating particles of matter. In developing these concepts Hawking incorporated both Einstein's general theory of relativity, which deals with gravitational effects on large-scale objects in precisely predictable ways, and quantum mechanics, which grapples statistically with the uncertain distribution and behaviour of atoms and atomic particles. In doing so he laid the basis for what some scientists call the "Holy Grail" of physics; a unification of two heretofore irreconcilable theories, one based on certainty, the other on uncertainty.

Although Hawking's work can be admired by only a handful of specialists, his personal courage is respected by all, for Hawking is a victim of amyotrophic lateral sclerosis, an incurable wasting disease of the nervous system and muscles. Confined to a wheelchair, he cannot lift his head without difficulty, speak clearly, or write out his calculations. These he must carry in his head and communicate slowly to his secretary.

GODFREY ARGENT

Stephen Hawking was born on Jan. 8, 1942, and educated at Oxford and Cambridge. His marriage in 1965, undertaken with the knowledge that he might have only two years to live, was according to him "the turning point. . . . It gave me a reason for continuing, striving." When only 32 he was elected a fellow of the Royal Society, the highest form of honour in British scientific circles. (VICTOR M. CASSIDY)

Heng Samrin

As one observer put it, the latest invasion of Cambodia was "an abhorrent regime being overthrown by an abhorrent aggression." On Jan. 7, 1979, a force of Cambodian rebels combined with Vietnamese soldiers captured Phnom Penh, Cambodia's capital, and announced the formation of a new government with Heng Samrin as president. Heng's Soviet- and Vietnamese-backed forces had ousted the Chinese-supported regime of Pol Pot. Their military campaign, a straightforward act of aggression, amounted in effect to a war by the Soviet Union upon China waged by proxies.

Pol Pot had headed one of the most inhuman governments in history. Over a period of four years beginning in 1975, his Khmer Rouge regime had effected the deaths of approximately half the people of Cambodia. Entire cities were emptied and the inhabitants marched at gunpoint to the countryside, where they worked long hours in the fields under starvation conditions. Mass executions and other atrocities were commonplace.

In May 1978 Heng Samrin, a Khmer Rouge military leader who had risen to political power under Pol Pot, defected to Vietnam. On December 3 Hanoi radio announced the formation of the Kampuchean United Front for National Salvation and its

MTI/SYGMA

military arm, the Kampuchean Revolutionary Armed Forces. This new organization, whose goal was the overthrow of Pol Pot, moved with great swiftness, conquering Cambodia in less than a month. Pol Pot led the remainder of his forces into the jungle, where they waged guerrilla warfare against Heng during 1979.

The military activity and ensuing chaos in Cambodia swelled the steady flow of refugees into a flood. Thousands of starving people staggered out of Cambodia into Thailand, where they were placed in desperately undersupplied temporary camps. Conditions were reported to be even worse inside Cambodia, where Heng appeared to be systematically starving portions of the country in hopes of destroying the remnants of the Khmer Rouge. Until late in the year Heng refused to facilitate humanitarian assistance offered by the West.

Little was known about Heng Samrin. He was presumably a native Cambodian and was said to be 45 years old in 1979. Under Pol Pot, he was a political commissar and commander of a Khmer Rouge army division. (VICTOR M. CASSIDY)

Herrera Campins, Luis

In an election more significant as a rare example of Latin-American democracy than as a contest of opposing ideologies, Luis Herrera Campíns captured the presidency of oil-rich but financially troubled Venezuela. Perhaps the most interesting aspect of the campaign pitting Herrera of the Social Christian Party against Luis Piñerúa Ordaz of the Democratic Action Party was the importation by both sides of media experts from the United States. The candidates relied heavily on televised messages, Piñerúa promising to continue the policies of Pres. Carlos Andrés Pérez (constitutionally prevented from seeking reelection) and Herrera criticizing the Pérez regime for failing to govern efficiently and honestly and for not utilizing the nation's enormous oil revenues wisely.

Born May 4, 1925, to a middle-class family in western Venezuela, the future leader of his country's more conservative major party began his political career as a radical. While a law student at Caracas University during the 1950s, Herrera attempted to organize a strike against the despotic rule of Gen. Marcos Pérez Jiménez. He had already cofounded (with future president Rafael Caldera) the Social Christian Party, but his career came to an abrupt halt when he was arrested, jailed for four months, and then deported. He went into exile in Europe, where he forged ties between his fledgling party and the European Christian Democratic organizations.

Following the overthrow of General Pérez Jiménez in 1958, Herrera returned to Venezuela and immediately immersed himself in politics once again. He was elected to the Chamber of Deputies and served many years there as party whip before moving up to the Senate in 1973. Despite his prominence Herrera could not escape being overshadowed by fellow party leader Caldera. Caldera consistently ran as the Social Christians' presidential nominee, and when he finally won in 1968, he refused to invite Herrera into his administration.

Years of frustration were finally rewarded in August 1978 when Herrera received the overwhelming support of the party in his first bid for the Venezuelan presidency. Not an exciting campaigner, he based his appeal on a single word—"Enough!" (JEROLD L. KELLMAN)

Hockney, David

Cosmopolitan wrote of David Hockney: "If you see a bowl of tulips or a beautiful boy in a swimming pool in a different light these days, that's thanks to David Hockney's paintings. He's the Bradford boy who dyed his hair blond, made good and has given us Brits a fresh look at our lives. . . ." The most fashionable artist in Britain, Hockney startled the world of art and fashion by speaking out, seriously, in 1979. He attacked Sir Norman Reid, the retiring director of London's Tate Gallery, for filling that museum with too many examples of "minimal" art and bloodless abstracts. It was known that Hockney was one of the few fashionable artists who offered anything that could be called representational, realistic, naturalistic, or narrative, but it was not known that he cared seriously about these distinctions.

Born July 9, 1937, in Bradford, West Yorkshire, Hockney attended the town's college of art and then went on to the Royal College of Art (RCA) in London. There he became one of a group that included key figures in the development of the "Pop Art" movement in Britain. Hockney gained his diploma at the RCA in 1962, during which year he taught at Maidstone College of Art in Kent. The next five years he spent teaching at a series of U.S. universities, including the University of California's Los Angeles and Berkeley campuses, and traveling in Europe and North Africa. His first one-man show, at the Kasmin Gallery in London in 1963, was followed by a series of others there and at galleries throughout Europe and in New York. In 1970 the Whitechapel Art Gallery in London mounted a retrospective exhibition of his paintings, prints, and drawings. He also illustrated books and in 1975 designed the sets for the Glyndebourne Opera's production of *The Rake's Progress*. The same year he made a film, *A Bigger Splash*.

Describing Hockney's paintings as witty, imaginative, and autobiographical, art historian Jasia Reichardt noted that they frequently depict dramatic relationships between people in an almost theatrical setting of showers, curtains, flowers, and furniture—an implicit domesticity combined with amusing if ambiguous lines of writing and occasional disturbing undertones. (D. A. N. JONES)

Howe, Sir (Richard Edward) Geoffrey

As chancellor of the Exchequer Sir Geoffrey Howe was the principal executor of Prime Minister Margaret Thatcher's program for a radical change of direction in Britain's economic and financial policies. With a quietly courteous manner and an unexciting style as a speaker, he produced a sensational budget within six weeks of the Conservative Party government's taking office. Four months later he stunned the financial capitals of the world by removing all exchange controls on the pound sterling (except for movement of funds to Zimbabwe Rhodesia) at a single stroke.

Howe showed himself to be not only one of the committed monetarists in the Thatcher Cabinet but a decisive one as well. In his budget he cut taxes on income and at the same time raised the value-added tax (VAT) on expenditures from 8 to 15%. He set in motion plans for a sharp cutback in public expenditures. Changes that swift and far-reaching had not been seen in Britain since the World War II days. In commenting on his budget he said simply, "We promised a complete change." Looking further ahead, he said, "The reconstruction of the economy will be the task of a decade."

Howe's family background was not unlike that of Prime Minister Thatcher. Born on Dec. 20, 1926, he was the son of a solicitor in the southern Wales steel town of Port Talbot. One generation further back he could claim a working-class background, and his grandfather was an active trade unionist. But Howe had an upper-class education at Winchester College and Cambridge University, where he was chairman of the university Conservative Association. He became a successful lawyer and might well have become a judge had not politics been his primary interest. He held the post solicitor general during 1970–72, but then chose not to pursue the legal line of advancement. From 1972 to 1974 he was minister for trade and consumer affairs, then opposition spokesman on social services (1974–75) and Treasury and economic affairs (1975–79). He was knighted in 1970.

Before entering Parliament in 1964, Howe had made a considerable mark on Conservative thinking through the publications of the Bow Group, which operated as a kind of unofficial Conservative think tank. (HARFORD THOMAS)

Hussein at-Tikriti, Saddam

In mid-July 1979 Saddam Hussein at-Tikriti, vice-chairman of the Revolutionary Command Council (RCC) of Iraq and deputy secretary-general of the Iraqi Baʿath Party, demanded of Gen. Ahmad Hassan al-Bakr, chairman of the RCC (president of the republic), that he sign death sentences for "a gang of traitors" who had infiltrated the Baʿath leadership and government. Bakr declined and subsequently resigned on July 16 because of ill health. Hussein succeeded him and also became secretary-general of the Baʿath. The power behind the scene in Iraq since 1968 and now openly in charge, and the first civilian head of state since King Faisal II in 1958, Saddam Hussein appointed a special court to try the "traitors." Twenty-one were executed on August 8, and 33 others received prison sentences of up to 15 years.

The ruthless purge stemmed from the Iraqis' apparent conviction that the Syrian wing of the Baʿath Party was in league with the "conspirators." This belief was in sharp contrast to the declaration of June 19 by Presidents Hafez al-Assad of Syria and Bakr of "joint political leadership" between their two countries.

Born in Tikrit in 1935, Saddam Hussein graduated from the law faculty of Baghdad University. He joined the Baʿath Party and was elected deputy secretary-general of its Iraqi wing in 1964. On Nov. 8, 1969, he was appointed vice-chairman of the RCC. The Soviet-Iraqi treaty of friendship and cooperation having been signed in 1972, Hussein was officially received in Moscow by the Soviet leadership in March 1973. A resultant Soviet-Iraqi intelligence agreement was concluded.

Hussein also negotiated the March 1975 Iraqi-Iranian accord, which ended Iran's support of the Kurdish rebellion in northern Iraq and brought recognition by Iraq that the Iraqi-Iranian frontier along the Shatt al-Arab ran on the river's median line of maximum depth. A month later Saddam Hussein was again in Moscow. Soviet Premier Aleksey Kosygin expressed Soviet satisfaction that an agreement between the Baʿath Party and the Iraqi Communist Party, on cooperation within the National Patriotic Front, had been concluded. That cooperation, however, suffered a blow when 21 Communists were shot in May 1978 on a charge of forming secret cells within the Iraqi Army.

(K. M. SMOGORZEWSKI)

Iacocca, Lee

If a business fails to meet the demands of the marketplace, it goes bankrupt. The owners lose their money and the employees their jobs. But what if the firm has assets of $13.6 billion and thousands of employees? Perhaps then the government should provide financial assistance to avoid unemployment, financial dislocation, and reduced competition in the industry. In 1979 the U.S. Congress had to consider this question. Chrysler Corp., the nation's third largest automobile manufacturer, had suffered huge financial losses and could not pay its creditors. Consequently, it asked the federal government for over $1 billion in loan guarantees. The firm also wanted special tax concessions and relief from federal environmental regulations.

Chrysler's new chairman, Lee Iacocca, admitted that this would be the largest federal loan ever made to a private firm, but he pointed to precedents. The government had recently helped the Lockheed Corp., he said; that firm had recovered and repaid the loan. The government routinely assists many small firms as well. Iacocca added that overly stringent federal antipollution, safety, and energy standards had caused Chrysler's problems by substantially increasing its manufacturing costs. Critics, on the other hand, charged that Chrysler had recklessly overexpanded in the past and had failed to keep pace with the times. It had huge inventories of large gasoline-wasting automobiles that nobody wanted to buy.

UPI

At the end of 1979 Congress agreed to help Chrysler if the firm raised $2 billion on its own. But many believed that if the firm survived it would be because of Lido ("Lee") Anthony Iacocca. From the time he was 16 he wanted to be an automobile executive, and he had spent his entire life in the industry. Iacocca was born on Oct. 15, 1920, in Allentown, Pa., the son of Italian immigrants. After graduating from Lehigh University with an engineering degree in 1945, he joined the Ford Motor Co. Eleven years later he won his first recognition in the firm with a successful program to sell Fords and was promoted from a branch office to the firm's Dearborn, Mich., headquarters. There he made his reputation as a marketer with such money-makers as the Ford Mustang, the Mark III, the Maverick, and the Econoline truck. Iacocca was elected president of Ford in 1970.

When Henry Ford II retired as board chairman in 1978, Iacocca expected to succeed him. He was instead forced out because of personal animosities between himself and Ford. A year later Iacocca moved to the Chrysler Corp., first as president and then as chairman of the board.

(VICTOR M. CASSIDY)

Irving, John

Writing in *Vogue* in April 1979, John Irving stated, "Art is not—or is only coincidentally—news. But in the media we are all news; we are either news, or we are out of the picture." At the same time, the paperback publisher of Irving's best-selling novel, *The World According to Garp* (1978), was initiating an expensive, newsworthy media campaign, of a sort once associated only with potboilers, to promote a serious novel that had received considerable critical notice and praise. The golf caps, wrist and head sweatbands, bumper stickers, and T-shirts proclaiming "I believe in Garp" were perhaps not incompatible with a novel whose tone is one of black humour.

Reviewers paid serious attention to *Garp*. In the *New York Times Book Review*, Julian Moynahan called it "rich and humorous." R. Z. Sheppard, writing in *Time*, described it as an "extraordinary work." In 1979 *Garp* was nominated for both the National Book Critics Circle Award and the National Book Award, though it lost to *The Stories of John Cheever* on both occasions.

Irving's fourth novel concerns an eccentric mother and her son, the relationships among a husband and wife and their two children, and the process of a writer becoming a writer. Though Irving denied that *Garp* was autobiographical, certain similarities do appear between him and his protagonist, T. S. Garp. Both were born in 1942; both are novelists, having written four books; both are nonprofessional wrestlers; and both have lived in Vienna. The fictional author's fourth novel, *The World According to Bensenhaver*, can be read as Irving's parody of his own book. But Garp's life is one of extremes: slapstick, heartbreak, and violence. As Irving concludes, "In the world according to Garp, we are all terminal cases."

Irving described his own life as very ordinary. Born in Exeter, N.H., he attended Phillips Exeter Academy, the University of New Hampshire, the University of Vienna, and the University of Iowa Writers' Workshop. He taught English at Mount Holyoke College at South Hadley, Mass., and Windham College, Putney, Vt. Irving's other novels are *Setting Free the Bears* (1969), *The Water-Method Man* (1972), and *The 158-Pound Marriage* (1974).

(JOAN NATALIE BOTHELL)

Johnson, Earvin ("Magic")

From the Main Street playground in Lansing, Mich., to the Los Angeles Lakers of the National Basketball Association, Earvin Johnson took basketball on a magic carpet ride. It seemed likely that Johnson would be his sport's most influential person in the 1980s. Youngsters following his example were practicing their passing instead of slamdunks and 30-ft jump shots. Teamwork in basketball was fashionable again.

Johnson went so far as to deprecate his own shooting, telling reporters that his younger sister had beaten him in the accuracy game of horse. But he shot well enough to lead both teams with 24 points when Michigan State University became the 1979 national collegiate champion by beating Indiana State University 75–64 on March 26.

Beginning with Johnson's first game at Michigan State, the students there considered a national championship to be only a matter of time. Merchants sold paraphernalia with his name on it, and they regularly ran out of souvenir Michigan State jerseys with his number 33. But Johnson stayed in college only two years, just long enough to win one championship. He said that it was a hard decision, passing up the

UPI

1980 Olympic Games and saying good-bye to campus life, but it would have been even more difficult to pass up the Lakers' contract of $600,000 a year for four years.

Some scouts said that Johnson was ready to play professional basketball midway through his freshman year. "Whatever is happening out there," said his coach, Jud Heathcote, "he comes up with a way to win." At 6 ft 8 in he was tall enough to see passing lanes that shorter guards could not use, and he was nimble enough to navigate them before they closed, often surprising even the receivers of his passes. No wonder they called him "Magic."

Born Aug. 14, 1959, Johnson used to wake up early enough to beat everyone else to the Main Street playground so that he could play full-court games by himself. In 1979 he led the Big Ten conference in assists with 8.4 per game. He also ranked seventh in free-throw percentage and ninth in rebounding. He was named first-string All-American for the team that finished 26–6 by winning 15 of its last 16 games.

(KEVIN M. LAMB)

Jordan, Hamilton

For Hamilton Jordan, 1979 was a year of dramatic ups and downs. U.S. Pres. Jimmy Carter officially appointed him to be White House chief of staff, while the Justice Department investigated unproven charges that he had used cocaine in a New York disco club. Controversy had swirled around Jordan since he first arrived in Washington as leader of the young band of Georgians who had managed Carter's presidential campaign. Jordan supervised the organization of the Carter administration, which seemed determined to maintain its "outsider" image.

From the start, it was apparent that none of the "outsiders" from Georgia was more of a Carter "insider" than Jordan. Born Sept. 21, 1944, in Charlotte, N.C., he went to work in Carter's first gubernatorial campaign shortly after graduation from the University of Georgia, and he had conceived and engineered the plan that eventually led to Carter's presidential nomination. Aside from his immediate family, no one was closer to the president.

Unlike his predecessors, Carter had preferred not to have a designated chief of staff. The White House—as organized by Jordan—was compared to a wheel with spokes radiating out from the Oval Office, though Jordan's spoke seemed heavier and stronger than the others. His casual dress of boots and jeans, a freewheeling life-style, and alleged incidents of boorish social behaviour quickly made Jordan an ongoing item for Washington gossip columns. Fairly or unfairly, much of the blame for the legendary inefficiency of the Carter White House was placed on Jordan's young shoulders.

In August 1979, during the Cabinet shake-up that followed Carter's energy crisis meetings at Camp David, Md., Carter finally named Jordan to be his chief of staff, with all of the power and authority that had gone with the post in the past. Jordan quickly stepped into his new role. He started wearing business suits, lowered his profile as a man-about-town, and began returning phone calls. Older, experienced assistants and advisers were brought into the administration, including some Washington "insiders." While some loose ends remained to be tied up, there was general agreement in Washington that the White House was better coordinated and more efficient after Jordan was put in charge. To Washington "insiders," Jordan no longer was an "outsider." Whether he liked it or not, he had become part of the governmental and political establishment. (HAL BRUNO)

Joseph, Sir Keith Sinjohn

If any one person could claim credit for converting the British Conservative Party from Keynesian demand management to Friedmanite free market monetarism, it would be Sir Keith Joseph. He had been called Margaret Thatcher's guru, and in the Thatcher government formed in May 1979 he was made secretary of state for industry. He had been a successful industrialist as chairman of Bovis, the family building and construction firm, but it was as the intellectual conscience of the party that he qualified for the job of setting industry free from government controls—and also of removing the subsidy life belts that had kept some ailing industrial concerns afloat.

It was as an academic, donnish, and fervent apostle of the free market that Joseph had made his impact on the Conservative Party. After the collapse of Edward Heath's government in 1974 he had used the years in opposition to press the case for a radical departure from the managed (or mismanaged) mixed economy. For this purpose he set up the Centre for Policy Studies, headed by himself. When he arrived at the Department of Industry, he distributed to his civil servants a reading list that included half a dozen of his own Centre for Policy Studies pamphlets—as well as Adam Smith's *Wealth of Nations.*

In office, with the responsibility for fostering a great revival of private enterprise, his confidence as a doctrinaire economist seemed to have been undermined somewhat by his experience as a practical businessman. Committed to "reversing the trend" (the title of one of his pamphlets), he proved hesitant. He preferred "deliberate speed," he said, rather than rushing into decisions.

Born into a wealthy Leeds family on Jan. 17, 1918, Joseph (who succeeded his father as second baronet in 1944) had a brilliant career as a student of law at Oxford University, where he became a fellow of All Souls. Joseph became a member of Parliament in 1956 and was minister for health and social services in the Heath government of 1970–74. A forceful and utterly committed man of ideas, he was at the same time shy and a diffident, even apologetic, campaigner. Thus he was never in the running as possible leader of the party whose current philosophy he had done so much to shape.

(HARFORD THOMAS)

Jusuf, Mohammad

When the man who was Indonesia's defense minister in 1979, Gen. Mohammad Jusuf, was told in the early 1950s that there was no budget to cover his studies at the military staff college in Bandung, he volunteered to pay his own way. Taken aback by the suggestion, senior officers relented and Jusuf was admitted. In the years since then, Jusuf had never looked back. Now, as single-minded as ever, he was directing a major overhaul of his nation's rundown defense forces.

The son of a rebellious traditional chief, Jusuf was born on the Indonesian island of Sulawesi on June 23, 1928. He attended a Dutch elementary school, worked briefly as a clerk during World War II when Japan occupied the country, and went on to join local revolutionary forces in their struggle against the Dutch. By the time the Dutch transferred sovereignty in 1949, Jusuf realized that the future lay with those men who had a modern, Western-style education, as distinct from those who had been trained in traditional Islamic schools. For Jusuf the move paid off. After completing the basic course at the staff college, he was sent abroad for further study. Not long after his return to Indonesia, Jusuf was appointed commander of the newly formed Hasanuddin Regiment in southern Sulawesi. Later, while serving as the *panglima* (military commander) in his home province, he moved with skill and subtlety in crushing a rebellion in which the forces of Kahar Muzakar,

DAVID JENKINS

an Islamic firebrand and onetime Jusuf benefactor, had teamed up with dissident army officers. Jusuf remained in the region for eight years and was, by any yardstick, unusually successful. He not only put down an insurrection but also laid the basis for the future industrial development of the province. Most important of all, he provided an alternative focus of loyalty at a time when Kahar Muzakar was enjoying great popular support. Jusuf was a *putra daerah* (son of the region) who was establishing himself as a national figure.

In 1965 Jusuf was appointed minister of basic and light industry in the Cabinet of President Sukarno. He was 38 years old and the first man from his province ever to hold Cabinet rank. By 1979 Jusuf had been a minister longer than anyone else in the Suharto government. Three months after his return to the capital, a group of leftist junior officers spearheaded a coup in which six senior army generals were killed. In the wake of that event, Jusuf was instrumental in persuading Sukarno to transfer his executive authority to General Suharto and thus helped lay the basis for the New Order government. After 13 years in the civilian sector (as minister for industry in both the first and second Suharto Cabinets) Jusuf took over as defense minister. Sometimes criticized for his rather lacklustre past performance, he wasted no time in bringing the nation's defense establishment under his command. Jusuf, it seemed, was back in a milieu he knew and understood, and he was soon giving a new lease on life to Indonesia's 250,000-man armed forces, the biggest military force in Southeast Asia, outside Vietnam. He was now widely considered the second most powerful figure in the world's fifth most populous nation.

(DAVID JENKINS)

Kahn, Alfred

If there is a thankless job in U.S. politics, it is the one that Pres. Jimmy Carter gave in late 1978 to Alfred Kahn. An economist who had been serving as chairman of the Civil Aeronautics Board (CAB), Kahn was asked by Carter to head the administration's anti-inflation program. A year later, the outspoken, highly independent Kahn said, "I can't figure out why the president doesn't fire me. Actually, I do know. Nobody would be foolish enough to take this job."

Kahn, a 61-year-old former professor and dean at Cornell University, Ithaca, N.Y., had a direct and unconventional approach to the things he did. As CAB chairman he succeeded in helping to design and implement an airline deregulation policy, which, although partial, vastly simplified the commercial airline route structure and often provided consumers with lower ticket prices.

Similarly, when he took over the inflation job from Robert Strauss (*q.v.*), Kahn preferred to focus on what he regarded as the inflationary aspects of unnecessary government regulation instead of monitoring compliance with the administration's voluntary program of wage and price guidelines.

While his critics accused him of not doing enough, inflation continued to soar throughout 1979. Said Kahn at one point: ". . . Inflation is a situation in which we, all of us, are demanding—in rents, profits, tax

UPI

rebates—real pieces of a pie that add up to more than one pie."

Kahn's penchant for pithy, no-nonsense remarks occasionally caused him problems with the White House. For example, in May, when the administration was trying to downplay the significance of new national profits figures, Kahn called them a "catastrophe." Meanwhile, the U.S. annual inflation rate had topped 13% and, by the fall of 1979, a frustrated Kahn asked Carter to relieve him of his job—a request the president denied.

Kahn was born Oct. 17, 1917, in Paterson, N.J. After graduating from New York University he received a Ph.D. from Yale University.

(STANLEY W. CLOUD)

Kennedy, Edward Moore

On Nov. 7, 1979, Sen. Edward M. ("Ted") Kennedy officially became the third member of his family to run for president of the United States. Unofficially, Kennedy had been an undeclared candidate for two months, and the formal announcement in Boston was the climax of a yearlong guessing game about his political intentions.

The 47-year-old Massachusetts Democrat had started the year as a noncandidate, dismissing all questions with the explanation "I expect President Carter to be renominated and I expect to support him." However, the president's steady decline in the public opinion polls and a series of moves by Kennedy touched off speculation that he was getting ready to run.

Kennedy's differences with the Carter administration had been dramatically emphasized at the Democratic Party's midterm conference in Memphis, Tenn., in December 1978. Kennedy delivered an impassioned speech for his national health insurance plan, which differed sharply from the president's attempts to hold down federal government spending. Kennedy appealed to the traditionally liberal soul of the party, and his enthusiastic reception by the Democrats was a sharp contrast to their lukewarm response to Carter's austere program. A "Draft Kennedy" movement began in Iowa, New Hampshire, Florida, and other early primary states, but without overt encouragement from the senator.

The change in Kennedy's posture came after the summer energy crisis, when adverse reaction to the mass Cabinet resignations shocked Democratic politicians and sent Carter's standing in the polls plummeting. But November brought a turn-around. Kennedy's declaration coincided with the start of the Iranian crisis, which drastically raised Carter's approval rating and made criticizing the president a touchy matter. This, combined with some early mistakes and disorganization within the Kennedy campaign, made it clear that—despite the president's serious political problems—the Massachusetts senator had a hard fight ahead.

Born in Boston on Feb. 22, 1932, the youngest of the children of Joseph and Rose Kennedy, he graduated from Harvard University and received a law degree from the University of Virginia. Since his election in 1962 he has represented Massachusetts in the U.S. Senate.

(HAL BRUNO)

Khomeini, Ayatollah Ruhollah

Gathering force throughout 1978 and culminating on Feb. 1, 1979, an unprecedented revolution overturned Iran. Ayatollah Ruhollah Khomeini, a 77-year-old Iranian religious leader living in exile in France and revered for the austerity of his daily life, succeeded in overthrowing Shah Mohammad Reza Pahlavi Aryamehr of Iran, a monarch commanding the largest armed forces in the Middle East. The duel began when Ayatollah ("Gift of God," a religious term of honour) Khomeini began sending to his country taped messages to be transmitted by short-wave radio from 80,000 mosques. These messages appealed for sacrifice by the Iranian people "to protect Islam and to destroy the tyrant and his parasites." Afterward, processions marched throughout the nation shouting "Death to the shah" and "We want the return of the ayatollah." The shah's last prime minister, Shahpur Bakhtiar, insisted that the monarch leave Iran, which he did on January 16.

On February 1 Khomeini landed in Teheran, to be greeted with fervent enthusiasm by more than two million people. He refused to see Bakhtiar, whom he described as a "traitor," and on February 5 he appointed Mehdi Bazargan (*q.v.*) prime minister.

From March 1 Khomeini resided in the holy city of Qom, where he governed through his prime minister before the latter's resignation in November, and through the religious committee set up to establish an Islamic republic. The constitution for such a republic was overwhelmingly approved in a December referendum. He supported the students of Teheran when they seized the U.S. embassy in November and held the staff hostage, a disregard of international law that was to polarize Khomeini's relations with the West. Thereafter, throughout the remainder of the year, he waged an intense verbal battle against the U.S.

Khomeini was born in 1902 at Khomeyn, in central Iran, grandson and son of ayatollahs. His father, head of the Shiʿah community in the Khomeyn district, was killed by order of a landlord, and Ruhollah was brought up by his older brother Morteza. Educated in Islamic schools, he wrote 21 books on philosophical, juridical, and ethical subjects. In 1962 Khomeini moved to Qom, a stronghold of the Shiʿah sect of Islam. He was soon imprisoned for an offense against the monarch but was freed. He continued to criticize the shah, and on Nov. 4, 1964, was banished from Iran. He settled at An Najaf in Iraq, a Shiʿah holy place. In 1978 Khomeini's presence there embarrassed Iraq's government, which requested him to leave. On Oct. 6, 1978, he arrived in France and established headquarters near Paris. (K. M. SMOGORZEWSKI)

Kirkland, (Joseph) Lane

At first glance Lane Kirkland seems an unlikely labour leader: scion of Southern aristocracy, self-taught amateur archaeologist, and connoisseur of vintage wines. Yet in November 1979 he was elected to succeed George Meany as president of the 14- million-member AFL-CIO, and nobody was surprised. The *New York Times*'s dean of labour reporters, A. H. Raskin, wrote that Kirkland's "advance to the summit reflects the emergence of a new breed of union leaders . . . whose vision of unionism is shaped less by memories of sit-down strikes and private armies of scabs than by the administrative, technical and legal headaches that go with managing computerized membership records, billions of dollars in reserve funds and year-round political action and lobbying machines."

Born in tiny Camden, S.C., March 12, 1922, he came from a family that helped charter the old Confederacy (though he has been a tireless civil rights advocate within the union and nationally). Aged 16 when World War II broke out in Europe, he tried to enlist in the Canadian Army. Rebuffed, he joined the first class at the U.S. Merchant Marine Academy and spent the war years as a deck officer on ships navigating every combat zone. He worked his way through Georgetown University's Foreign Service School and on graduation took a research job at the AFL headquarters. A union staff man ever since, he became Meany's executive assistant in 1961 and in 1969 secretary-treasurer of the giant labour combine that Meany forged with the CIO.

Highly regarded by business leaders as well as the union brotherhood, Kirkland nonetheless faced a period of uncertainty. Early challenges included the union's political stance in the upcoming election year, the direction of labour toward renewed social innovation, and finally the matter of maintaining control of the 33 international unions that constituted Meany's old coalition. As Raskin observed, "Some who have chafed under the tightness of Meany's rule will be testing the mettle of the new chief."

In his first address after his unanimous election as union president on November 19, Kirkland urged unaffiliated unions to join (or rejoin) the AFL-CIO. His unnamed targets for amalgamation included the Teamsters, United Auto Workers, and National Education Association.

(PHILIP KOPPER)

Knight, Bobby

Discussions about Bobby Knight balanced his quick temper against his long list of victories and often ended in disagreement. The Indiana University basketball coach's supporters pointed to successes that included coach-of-the-year awards in 1975 and 1976. His detractors pointed to temper tantrums that antagonized referees and alienated some players, at least 13 of whom left Indiana to become starters for other schools.

Because of these qualities Knight's experience at Puerto Rico in July 1979 surprised virtually no one. He coached a U.S. national team that won the Pan American Games basketball tournament by beating all nine of its opponents by an average of 21.2 points. He also left Puerto Rico charged with aggravated assault and was later fined $500 and sentenced to six months in jail. Knight was in Indiana by the time the verdict was made; Gov. Otis Bowen did not extradite him, and university president John Ryan turned down the resignation he offered. But Knight continued to be tried by public opinion long after the morning he tussled with a security guard.

The incident started with a dispute over the use of a practice gym. Knight said that he reflexively pushed the security guard, José Silva, after Silva hit Knight in the eye while shaking a finger at him. Silva, who arrested Knight immediately, changed his story a few times before saying he never hit Knight. Michael Brooks, who played on Knight's Pan American team, summed up many people's feelings when he said, "I will treasure the experience of playing for him. On the other hand, I doubt if I would want to do it for four years."

The basketball expertise of Robert Montgomery Knight has never been an issue. Born Oct. 25, 1940, in Orrville, Ohio, he attended Ohio State University and played on the 1960 national championship team. After he became a head coach at 24, his teams at the U.S. Military Academy achieved a 102–50 record in six years even though the Army permitted nobody taller than 6 ft 6 in to attend the academy.

At Indiana Knight was named Big Ten coach of the year three times. He won four straight Big Ten championships from 1973 through 1976 and won the 1975–76 national championship with a 32–0 record, becoming the only person ever to coach and play on national championship teams.

(KEVIN M. LAMB)

Kreisky, Bruno

In May 1979 Austria's popular federal chancellor, Bruno Kreisky, led his Socialist Party of Austria (SPÖ) to victory in the third general election since coming to office in 1970. Nine years of Social Democratic government under Kreisky had brought the country prosperity, social harmony, and an international standing that reflected his extensive personal diplomacy in furtherance of Austria's "active neutrality." It was his efforts at mediation in the Middle East conflict and especially his initiative in inviting Palestine Liberation Organization (PLO) leader Yasir Arafat to Vienna that attracted most attention internationally in 1979. Paradoxically, this initiative led to Israeli accusations of anti-Semitism against Kreisky, who was himself of Jewish origin.

SVEN SIMON/KATHERINE YOUNG

Kreisky firmly believed that the PLO's involvement in negotiations was essential for any Middle East settlement. A prerequisite for such involvement was greater Western diplomatic recognition for the PLO, and Kreisky hoped that his Vienna meeting with Arafat would help to promote this. Significant also in this context was the distribution in October of the first awards of the Bruno Kreisky Foundation for Services to the Cause of Human Rights, set up in 1976 to mark Kreisky's 65th birthday. Two of the prizes went to Palestinian Isam Sartawi, Arafat's close adviser, and Israeli left-wing politician Arie Lova Eliav; the two had had secret talks in Paris in 1976–77, and the prizes were in recognition of "personal risks taken in promoting a reconciliation of the Palestinian and Israeli peoples."

Kreisky was born in Vienna on Jan. 22, 1911, the son of a rich manufacturer. He studied jurisprudence at the University of Vienna and graduated as doctor of law. A socialist from his student days, after the German annexation of Austria in 1938 he was briefly imprisoned but eventually escaped to Sweden. In Stockholm he engaged in business and journalism and from 1946 was attached to the Austrian legation. Returning to Austria in 1951, he became a secretary of state in the Foreign Ministry in 1953. A member of Parliament from 1956, he was foreign minister from 1959 to 1966. Chairman of the SPÖ from 1967, in 1976 he became vice-president of the Socialist International, in which capacity he undertook his contacts with the PLO.

(ELFRIEDE DIRNBACHER)

Kurosawa, Akira

Akira Kurosawa was a man of prodigious talents. He is also the best known and most widely admired Japanese movie director in the world. After directing such films as *Drunken Angel* (1948), which brought fame to both Kurosawa and the lead actor, Toshiro Mifune, Kurosawa gained international recognition with *Rashomon* (1950), which won the Grand Prix at the Venice Film Festival. This was but the first of many successes that included *Ikiru* (1952) and *Seven Samurai* (1954). The latter was a smash hit in Japan and provided the inspiration for a Hollywood imitation entitled *The Magnifi-*

cent Seven. Other memorable films were *Throne of Blood* (1957), *Yojimbo* (1961), *Sanjuro* (1962), and *Red Beard* (1965). These works were followed by five years of silence, partly because Kurosawa had become obsessed with perfection and found it increasingly difficult to adhere to shooting schedules and budgets as his cinematic artistry evolved. Then in 1970 his first colour film, *Dodeska-Den,* was released. It was badly timed because Japan's motion picture industry was in the doldrums and the picture flopped at the box office. The failure affected Kurosawa so deeply that he attempted suicide.

In time, however, his despondency ebbed and the master was back at work directing *Dersu Uzala,* which was shot in Siberia and financed by the Soviet Union. The film was awarded the Grand Prize at the Moscow Film Festival and an Oscar as best foreign language picture of the year. It was with renewed confidence that Kurosawa began *Kagemusha* ("Shadow Warrior"), his first samurai film in 14 years. Though it had to be bailed out by 20th Century-Fox and two American friends, directors George Lucas (*Star Wars*) and Francis Ford Coppola (*The Godfather*), the picture was hailed as Kurosawa's greatest spectacle and was scheduled for release in 1980. The 16th-century epic relates the story of a noted feudal lord whose death is kept secret by loyal retainers for three years while a look-alike *kagemusha* (double) takes his place. Kurosawa hoped the sight of 200 samurai riding into battle would surpass in excitement anything John Ford (whom he greatly admired) ever captured on film.

Kurosawa was born in Tokyo on March 23, 1910, to a samurai-ranking family. After attending art school, he took a job in a movie studio. Following tradition, he began by writing scenarios and assisting directors, mainly Kajiro Yamamoto. In 1943 Kurosawa was promoted to director. His first film, *Sugata Sanshiro* (1943), was a great success, and Kurosawa was on his way to becoming one of the greatest directors of modern times. (KAY K. TATEISHI)

Ladd, Alan, Jr.

The real life story might have been called *Son of Shane:* Hero marches into the western settlement, saves hardworking folks from evil enemies, fates worse than death, etc., then prepares to ride off into the sunset—just as Alan Ladd did in *Shane,* which profitably brought a new degree of realistic violence to the screen in 1953. As it happened in 1979, however, Alan Ladd, Jr., prepared to walk out of the 20th Century-Fox executive suite after saving the studio from terminal disaster with a series of artistic successes and outer-space spectaculars.

Young Ladd joined 20th Century-Fox in 1973 as vice-president for creative affairs. In three years he moved up to the presidency of the floundering studio. Under his low-key guidance the company produced a veritable film library of hits: *The Silver Streak, Young Frankenstein, Silent Movie, Julia* (an adaptation of a Lillian Hellman reminiscence that starred Vanessa Redgrave (*q.v.*) and Jane Fonda), and *The Turning Point* (which brought ballet star Mikhail Baryshnikov to the screen). He picked up a script two other studios had rejected, read 12 pages of it, authorized a $10 million budget, and then watched it earn back $340 million. That was *Star Wars.* Then *Alien,* his science-fiction horror film of 1979, threatened to beat even his first space epic's records. Ladd seemed a wizard; under his spell the company's earnings quadrupled.

But others in corporate management evidently quarreled with some of his policies. For example, he would share profits with mid-level production people who were crucial to a blockbuster's success. Angered by these conflicts, Ladd said that he would leave the job that paid as much as $2 million a year when his contract expired in 1980. Taking two senior executives and longtime colleagues with him, he might go to another established studio or set up his own shop.

Ladd was born in Los Angeles Oct. 22, 1937. Before joining 20th Century-Fox he worked as an agent and produced several films, including *Walking Stick* (1969) and *Nightcomers* (1971). (PHILIP KOPPER)

Lasch, Christopher

With the publication of his book *The Culture of Narcissism: American Life in an Age of Diminishing Expectations,* Christopher Lasch gained prominence in 1979. A passionate and stimulating critique of society, the book was widely read and discussed, even by the president of the United States. In it, Lasch, a historian, comments on the family, the work ethic, sports, and sexual customs, concluding that competitive individualism of the sort associated with early free enterprise capitalism has been supplanted by a neurotically dependent and directionless preoccupation with self—a pervasive social narcissism. This phenomenon, he argues, has grown out of welfare liberalism, the political ideology to which capitalism gave birth. Welfare liberalism absolves individuals of moral responsibility and calls them victims of society. People are no longer punished for their misdeeds, but are rehabilitated.

Lasch's critique represents an outgrowth of his *Haven in a Heartless World: The Family Besieged* (1977). In that work he traced the deterioration of the U.S. family structure back to the 19th century, attributing it to industrialism and to the rise of the social sciences. In earlier times, Lasch declares, the family functioned as an independent, self-directed unit. Then industry took individual work skills out of the household, collectivized them, and placed them under the control of professional managers. The weakening of the family continued as social scientists entered into the individual's personal life and took over many child-rearing tasks that previously had been performed within the household. The worst villains, Lasch maintains, were sociologists, anthropologists, and certain psychoanalysts, who proclaimed "the family's indispensability while at the same time providing a rationale for the continued invasion of the family by experts in the art of social and psychic healing."

Lasch was born on June 1, 1932, in Omaha, Neb. He was educated at Harvard and Columbia universities and taught at several schools. After 1970 he was professor of history at the University of Rochester, N.Y. (VICTOR M. CASSIDY)

Limann, Hilla

Military rule of nearly eight years ended with the inauguration of Hilla Limann as Ghana's new president on Sept. 24, 1979. A little-known figure even inside his own country, the 45-year-old former scholar and diplomat emerged as the leader of the People's National Party, which won the June elections held shortly after Flight Lieut. Jerry Rawlings (*q.v.*) and his Armed Forces Revolutionary Council had ousted the previous military government.

Born in 1934 at Gwellu in the Upper Region of what was then the British colony of the Gold Coast, Limann came from the less developed northern part of Ghana. Its people, like his own family, were mostly poor peasant farmers, or they performed menial tasks in the cities. But Limann himself was one of the best-educated men in the country. He paid his way through his early schooling by his earnings as a hunter and then, with the help of scholarships, went on to gain a science degree at the London School of Economics and Political Science, a doctorate in political science and constitutional law at the Sorbonne, and a history degree at the University of London. After this distinguished academic career, he settled for a modest diplomatic post as Ghana's representative in Switzerland.

President Limann was strongly influenced as a young man by Ghana's first

Christopher Lasch

WIDE WORLD

president, Kwame Nkrumah. Though still describing himself as a Nkrumahist, he espoused policies after coming to office that showed him to be moderate rather than militant in his economic ideas. Like Nkrumah, however, he was an ardent pan-Africanist. In his inaugural presidential address he showed himself to be a strong advocate of political tolerance, praising both Nkrumah and those who had been his bitterest critics during the earlier years of Ghana's independence.

Limann came to power at a time when his country was on the verge of bankruptcy after years of economic mismanagement. He established his first priorities as restoring Ghana's economic fortunes and, in his own words, to "cleanse" the country's public life. "Mine is a vision," he said, "of Ghana in which the majority of our people shall not be reduced to grinding poverty again."
(COLIN LEGUM)

Louisy, Allan

On July 2, 1979, Allan Louisy became prime minister of St. Lucia following the resounding defeat, in the first post-independence election, of the United Workers Party. For 16 years the UWP had held power under the leadership of John Compton (prime minister at independence on February 22).

Louisy's political career had been short. It began in October 1973 (shortly after he retired as a judge of the Associated States Appeal Court) with the then opposition St. Lucia Labour Party (SLP). It was a time of internal crisis within the SLP, and the party was split over the question of leadership. Louisy came on the scene as a mediator, to bring the warring factions together, only months before a general election was due to be held. In that time he negotiated the admission of new blood into the party and brought to it a measure of respectability that it had not known for many years.

In the elections of May 1974, Louisy made his first attempt at a House of Assembly seat, running in his home village of Laborie. The SLP lost by seven seats to ten for the UWP, but Louisy won his contest by a margin of over 1,000 votes and was selected by the party as leader of the opposition in the new Parliament.

Two years later the SLP's leadership problem, which had remained unresolved, was settled at a national party convention, and Louisy emerged triumphant in a three-way contest. One of his opponents at that time was the much younger current deputy prime minister, George Odlum, who by late 1979 appeared intent on emerging from his behind-the-scenes role.

Born in 1916, Louisy received his early education in St. Lucia. After a short spell as a civil servant, he began to study law locally and was called to the bar in 1945. He served as registrar of the Supreme Court and additional magistrate (1946–50), senior magistrate in Antigua (1951–54), and crown attorney and legal draftsman in Montserrat (1954–55) and then in Dominica (1956–58). Louisy's career then took him to Jamaica, where he was resident magistrate, then registrar of the Supreme Court and Court of Appeal until 1964, when he took up a post on the bench of the Associated States Appeal Court. (DAVID A. JESSOP)

Louly, Mohamed Mahmoud Ould Ahmed

Assuming the office of president of the Islamic Republic of Mauritania on June 3, 1979, Lieut. Col. Mohamed Mahmoud Ould Ahmed Louly, in his first message to the nation, reaffirmed Mauritania's determination to find a solution to the conflict in Western (formerly Spanish) Sahara which had increasingly sapped its resources during the past three years. Louly succeeded Lieut. Col. Mustafa Ould Salek, leader of the Military Committee for National Recovery (CMRN), that in July 1978 had ousted Moktar Ould Daddah, Mauritania's president since 1961. The change in leadership followed Ould Salek's progressive loss of authority as a result of Mauritania's worsening situation.

Louly's first act was to announce the formation of a new government, whose composition reflected the need to find solutions to the country's two most pressing problems: the disastrous state of the national finances; and the mounting tension between the Moors and the black African tribes of the south. The number of black ministers in the new 14-member government was increased from 4 to 5.

Born Jan. 1, 1943, in Tidjikja, central Mauritania, Louly joined the Army in November 1960. He was trained in French military academies and subsequently held various administrative posts on the Mauritanian general staff. He was a member of the CMRN and its successor, the Military Committee for National Salvation, formed on April 6, 1979. In Ould Salek's government Louly was successively minister in charge of inquiries and investigations, minister in charge of the CMRN permanent committee, and minister of cadre training and the civil service. Considered to be an able administrator and a man of integrity, the new head of state had some experience as an economist in addition to his military training.
(PHILIPPE DECRAENE)

MacDonald, Flora Isabel

Stamina, intelligence, integrity, and natural savvy made Flora MacDonald one of the most popular officials in the history of Canada's Progressive Conservative Party. The member of Parliament for the federal riding of Kingston and the Islands had worked in election and by-election campaigns across Canada since 1949. She tried for the party leadership herself at the 1976 convention, running a populist campaign in which she asked supporters to contribute a dollar each.

Defeated after the second ballot, MacDonald threw her support behind Joe Clark, the eventual winner. When Clark became prime minister of Canada in May 1979, MacDonald was rewarded with the Cabinet post of secretary of state for external affairs. The first Canadian woman to hold a Cabinet seat of such importance, MacDonald was proving equal to the task. At the international meeting on the Vietnamese refugee problem held in Geneva in July 1979, she was commended by other delegates for her tough stance toward the Vietnamese government.

Born June 3, 1926, in North Sydney, Nova Scotia, Flora Isabel MacDonald attended North Sydney High School and the Empire Business College. From 1952 to 1956 she worked and hitchhiked her way across Great Britain, Europe, and Canada, arriving in Ottawa in 1957. Hired as a secretary at the Progressive Conservative national headquarters, she soon became executive director and "the operational centre of the party."

In 1965 she worked for the ouster of John Diefenbaker as party leader, and in retaliation Diefenbaker had her fired in 1966. She took an administrative position in the political studies department of Queen's University, Kingston, Ont., and became a tutor in the department. But politics was her first love, and her idea of fun was a day of speeches, handshakes, and phone calls. In 1972 she was first elected to the House of Commons. Foreign affairs had also always fascinated her, and in 1972 she became the first woman to graduate from the National Defence College. When she arrived in Ottawa in 1957, her plan had been to find a position in the Department of External Affairs. It seemed only natural that, more than 20 years later, Joe Clark should give her that portfolio. (DIANE LOIS WAY)

Martens, Wilfried

On April 3, 1979, the latest and longest of Belgium's almost perennial governmental crises ended when 43-year-old Wilfried Martens became prime minister at the head of a five-party coalition that replaced Paul Vanden Boeynants's four-month-old caretaker government. Chairman of the Flemish Social Christian Party from 1972, Martens had not previously held ministerial office. A one-time organizer of Flemish marches on Brussels, he now headed a government which had as a major objective the transformation of the country's unitary political structure into a federal one based on Belgium's two main languages, Dutch (Flemish) and French.

Born at Sleidinge near Ghent on April 19, 1936, Martens studied law and Thomist philosophy at the still bilingual Roman Catholic University of Louvain (Leuven) and became chairman of the Flemish Students Association. Active in the Flemish federalist movement, he staged an unofficial "Flemish Day" at the Brussels world's fair in 1958. A member of the executive of the "Vlaamse Volksbeweging" (a federalist lobby) from 1960 until 1964, he joined the Social Christians in 1962. By 1965 he had moved up to the national committee of the party, and as a member of the personal staffs of two prime ministers he acquired firsthand political experience. Elected chairman of the Young Social Christians in 1967, he joined the staff of the then minister for community affairs, Léo Tindemans. By 1969 Martens was on the Social Christian Party executive staff and in the directorate of the party's Flemish wing. His entry into Parliament came two years after he was chosen as chairman of the Social Christians in March 1972. Together with the leaders of the other parties in the Tindemans coalition of 1974–78, Martens masterminded the Egmont and Stuyvenberg agreements on the transformation of Belgium's political structure into a federal one. As chairman of a special agreements commission, he helped

© 1979 DALE WITTNER

Nine persons were honoured with 1980 Encyclopaedia Britannica Achievement in Life Awards at a banquet in Chicago on October 16. Left to right are Col. Frank Borman (Achievement in Exploration/Business), Norman Cousins (Journalism), Hugh Downs (Television), Leonard "Red" Kelly (Sports), James Michener (Literature), Michael E. DeBakey (Science and Medicine), Edmund D. Pellegrino (Education), Mortimer J. Adler (presenter of awards for Britannica), Benny Goodman (Music), and (seated) Ella Fitzgerald (Performing Arts).

to push them through the legislature despite their many unconstitutional aspects.

A man of the centre-left, Martens relied on the Social Christian labour unions to uphold his government's stringent economic program. His successor as party chairman, Tindemans, clearly gave him only lukewarm support, and the Young Social Christians made no mystery of their dislike for the coalition. (JAN R. ENGELS)

Matsushita, Konosuke

When Konosuke Matsushita, the 84-year-old Japanese entrepreneur, announced in September 1979 that he was opening a school to train political and business leaders, no one was surprised. The self-made yen-millionaire viewed the 21st century as a time of Asian prosperity and wanted to have a hand in molding that future. In October the retired industrialist accepted 26 of 907 applicants for admission to the Matsushita School of Government and Management. The academy, located in Chigasaki, southwest of Tokyo, represented an investment of 7 billion yen (U.S. $32 million).

UPI

Matsushita, the youngest of eight children, was born near Wakayama in west central Japan on Nov. 27, 1894. When his father, a modest landowner, lost the family fortune speculating on the rice market, Matsushita had to leave school. At 9 he began working as an errand boy and at 16 joined an electric lamp company. Seven years later he formed his own company and at one time had to pawn his wife's kimono to make ends meet. The cottage industry eventually grew so large that Gen. Douglas MacArthur lumped the Matsushita enterprise together with the *zaibatsu* (financial giants) that were purged after World War II. Four years later, however, Matsushita was back in business and led his company to even greater successes. The line of electrical products was broadened to include such items as computers, television and hi-fi sets, air conditioners, and freezers. Matsushita's wife, often the first to test new home appliances, played the role of critical consumer. Matsushita's short wispy frame and homespun manner tended to mask a dynamic personality and creative mind. He was the first leading Japanese industrialist to introduce a five-day workweek, and he proved in the process that his company could become one of the largest and most profitable in the nation. Currently Matsushita, which had annual sales close to $11 billion, marketed its products overseas under such brand names as Panasonic, Technics, Quasar, and National.

After retiring as chairman of Matsushita Electrical Industrial Co. Ltd. in 1973, the much-decorated businessman maintained a lively interest in the philanthropic organization that he still headed as president. Popularly known as PHP (Peace and Happiness Through Prosperity), the organization published English and Japanese editions of a monthly magazine that promoted various ideas for improving the world. Matsushita also spent considerable time at his favourite retreat, a Japanese-style mansion called Hermitage of Truth, which was isolated by a lovely garden from the suburbs of Kyoto, the cultural capital of Japan.

(KAY K. TATEISHI)

McEnroe, John

Barging into the world of big-time tennis with a chip on his shoulder and a curse on his lips, John McEnroe stirred clouds of dust and controversy that obscured his emergence as a leading player. The brilliance of his play did not fully overcome his "bad boy" reputation until he won the U.S. Open in September 1979.

At 20 McEnroe was the youngest U.S. champion since Pancho Gonzales in 1948. He won two other major 1979 tournaments by beating Jimmy Connors in the final of the Grand Prix national and Björn Borg in the final of the World Championship Tennis (WCT) competition. Only Borg and Connors were ranked ahead of him at the end of the year, and nobody won more than his $519,042, a total achieved because McEnroe also was an accomplished doubles player. With partner Peter Fleming he won the U.S., Wimbledon, and WCT doubles titles. McEnroe finished the year by winning his 28th consecutive set in Davis Cup play in December while leading the U.S. to its second straight Cup victory.

One thing he failed to win was the hearts of his countrymen. McEnroe was booed even when he won the U.S. Open at Flushing Meadow in New York City, just a few topspin lobs away from his home neighbourhood of Douglaston. But he was used to it, having been a rebel ever since he wore denim to high school at Trinity in New York, where coats and ties were required.

© 1979 ED GOLDFARB—BLACK STAR

Tennis fans saw that side of McEnroe first, even before he captured their imaginations by becoming the youngest man ever to reach the Wimbledon semifinals when he was 18 in 1977. In his first match there he told a spectator at courtside to "get the hell out." It was clear from the outset that McEnroe wore his feelings on his wristband.

But if he sometimes sounded like a longshoreman, he played like a surgeon. He beat opponents by rushing the net and volleying, but his game did not depend so much on power as on precision. His racket, held unusually low, seemed to dangle from his left arm until his quick wrists would cause it to strike at the last possible moment.

McEnroe was born in New York City on Feb. 16, 1959. He beat six of the world's top 20 the first time he played them, including Borg in his native Sweden. McEnroe was well on his way to being ranked fifth in the world by then, having become the third freshman ever to win the U.S. collegiate singles title. He left Stanford University shortly after that victory, in time to reach the semifinals of the 1978 U.S. Open.

(KEVIN M. LAMB)

Miyake, Issey

One of the leading fashion designers of Japan was a youthful mustachioed couturier by the name of Issey (Issei) Miyake. Though a maverick of sorts, he was awarded the prestigious Mainichi Design Prize in 1976 and was hailed as one of the top ten designers in the world. Miyake said he created fashions for women as women and, therefore, had no special interest in designing clothes specifically for Japanese females. He also said he would like to see an end to the tradition that calls for new fashions every six months because the custom stifled creative development. Miyake's designs, primarily casual and deliberately timeless, were inspired by many things. His reversible linen jumpsuit, for example, was patterned after a flying squirrel, and his silk dresses and stoles that billow out when the wearers move evoke images of the spinnaker sails on old clipper ships. But Miyake fashions sometimes also embodied elements that were distinctly Japanese. These included cotton quilting used in labourers' clothes, lounging gowns, aprons traditionally worn by shopkeepers and housewives, sportswear for judo and karate, split-toe sox (*tabi*) worn with a kimono, and the body tattoo used by Japanese gangsters (*yakuza*).

Miyake was born in Hiroshima on April 22, 1938. After learning nonfashion facets of design at the Tokyo Fine Arts College, he went to Paris in 1965 to study at the Chambre Syndicale de la Couture Parisienne. A year later he became an assistant designer to Guy Laroche, then put in a stint with Givenchy. In 1970 he returned to Tokyo, where, with financial backing, he launched the Issey Miyake Design Studio. One factor in his success was the turning of fashion shows into theatrical events. He first attracted standing-room-only crowds to a noted Tokyo department store art gallery by importing 12 leggy black models to show off his creations. Record crowds also jammed an indoor Tokyo sports arena for another lively show. By 1979 Miyake owned five boutiques with annual sales estimated at $3.3 million.

(KAY K. TATEISHI)

Montebello, Philippe de

In his first year as director of New York City's prestigious Metropolitan Museum of Art, Philippe de Montebello oversaw a period of consolidation and retrenchment after a decade of vigorous expansion under his predecessor, Thomas Hoving. Under de Montebello's direction, 1979 was marked by the near completion of the museum's enormous building program, including the American Bicentennial and Michael C. Rockefeller wings. There was also a shift in emphasis away from the "blockbuster" shows lent by foreign governments and toward a concentration on the museum's own superb collection.

De Montebello's appointment as director was the beginning of a new system of management for the Metropolitan. Whereas previous directors had handled both financial and artistic matters, de Montebello was made responsible solely for curatorial and artistic concerns. Management and finance were placed under the control of the museum's new president, William B. Macomber, Jr.

De Montebello urged a reexamination of the role of the museum. By placing more emphasis on the Metropolitan's permanent collection and less on extravagant traveling shows, he hoped to change the public view of the museum as a place to visit only during special events. He called for a rethinking of the educational goals of the museum, including the attainment of a higher intellectual level of exhibitions and, at the same time, a greater degree of accessibility to the public.

De Montebello was born in Paris on May 16, 1939, and came to the United States as a child. After graduating from Harvard University, he attended New York University's Institute of Fine Arts in 1963, although he did not receive his master's degree until 15 years later.

He became associate curator of European paintings at the Metropolitan Museum in 1963. After an interlude as director of the Museum of Fine Arts in Houston, Texas, between 1969 and 1973, he returned to the Metropolitan, where he served as vice-director of curatorial and educational affairs until 1977. At that time he became acting director after Hoving's retirement. De Montebello was responsible for, among other things, the popular exhibition "Monet's Years at Giverny: Beyond Impressionism." He was named director of the museum in May 1978.

(JOAN NATALIE BOTHELL)

Muzorewa, Abel Tendekayi

On May 29, 1979, Bishop Abel Muzorewa became Rhodesia's first black prime minister after his party, the United African National Council, won 51 seats in the 100-member Parliament under a new majority-rule constitution. Only six months later he agreed to relinquish his premiership when an agreement was reached in London for the restoration of Britain's legal presence in Rhodesia, ending the 14-year-old rebellion there. He then made plans to lead his party in new elections to be held early in 1980 as a prelude to Rhodesia's independence as the new republic of Zimbabwe Rhodesia.

JEAN-MARIE SIMONET—GAMMA/LIAISON

Muzorewa first emerged as a political figure in the 1970s at a time when all the major black politicians in the country were in prison or in exile. When Lord Pearce was sent to Rhodesia by the British government to test public opinion about proposals for a settlement of the conflict, Muzorewa took a leading part in mobilizing opposition to the offered terms. At the time he appeared as a spokesman for the veteran nationalist leader Joshua Nkomo, but the two men quarreled after Nkomo's release from detention, and Muzorewa chose to lead his own party. This brought him into conflict with the established nationalist leaders grouped together in the Patriotic Front, which resorted to guerrilla warfare. Small, neat, soft-spoken, and reserved in manner, he was nevertheless a magnetic orator in his native Shona language and proved himself to be a tough negotiator during the months of difficult talks over the ending of the war; he had to face the aggressive opposition not only of the Patriotic Front leaders but also of Ian Smith, the former white Rhodesian leader with whom he had negotiated an internal settlement in 1978 that led to his short-lived government.

Muzorewa was born on April 14, 1925, in Umtali. He was educated at Methodist schools in Rhodesia and then spent five years (1958–63) at the Central Methodist College, Fayette, Mo., and at Scarritt College, Nashville, Tenn. After some years as teacher, lay preacher, youth work organizer, and pastor, he became a bishop of the United Methodist Church in 1968. A moderate in black politics, he showed himself to be as militant as the radicals on the issue of black rule.

(COLIN LEGUM)

Naipaul, Vidiadhar Surajprasad

A native of Trinidad, living in London and Wiltshire, England, novelist V. S. Naipaul remarked with practiced melancholy "The Americans do not want me because I am too British. The British do not want me because I am too foreign." Nevertheless, Naipaul, who in 1979 was teaching creative writing at Wesleyan University, Middletown,

Conn., made a considerable impact on both sides of the Atlantic with his latest novel, *A Bend in the River*. Set in Africa and compared with the work of Joseph Conrad, it was *Time* magazine's top editorial choice for several months and was among the finalists in contention for Britain's Booker Prize, which Naipaul had already won eight years previously with *In a Free State*.

Naipaul's grandfather came to Trinidad from Uttar Pradesh, India, as an indentured worker, and his father became a reporter for *The Trinidad Guardian* and a writer of short stories. Naipaul himself, born Aug. 17, 1932, was educated at Queen's Royal College, Trinidad, and University College, Oxford. His first novel, *The Mystic Masseur* (1957), concerned Indians in Trinidad—*East* Indians in the West Indies. Called a "Chekhovian delight" by one critic, it won him the 1958 John Llewelyn Rhys Memorial Prize. With *Miguel Street* (1959) he won the 1961 Somerset Maugham Award, but perhaps the most popular of his West Indian comedies was *A House for Mr. Biswas*, published in 1961.

More prizes followed. A charming novel about English suburban life, *Mr. Stone and the Knights Companion* (1963), gained him the 1964 Hawthornden Prize. Four years later he won the W. H. Smith Award with a sternly serious novel about West Indian politics, *The Mimic Men* (1967). In this he stressed a recurrent theme in his work—the idea that people in the third world, particularly in the nations once a part of the British Empire, feel like suburbanites debarred from the metropolis, while the metropolitans are inclined to patronize the suburbs in a sentimental manner. In *A Bend in the River* he seemed to be urging the Europeans of imperialist descent to feel less ashamed before the victims and pupils of their ancestors and less sentimentally tolerant of the successor states and their failings.

(D. A. N. JONES)

Nelson, Willie

"Whiskey River take my mind. . . ." Without fanfare he appears on stage and sometimes it is not until he begins to sing that the audience notices his arrival. Willie Nelson stands centre stage, looking straight ahead; he does not work the crowd. His voice, a distinctively clear, full baritone, fills the auditorium and stills the many cowboy hats that have been waving in anticipation. The dress is as individualistic as the man—T-shirt, jeans, a single diamond earring, and long auburn hair secured with a sweatband, in a ponytail, or in braids. Once he has his audience's complete attention he smiles and, whether it consists of thousands or a single interviewer, the effect is the same. An appealing blend of shyness, warmth, and innocence radiates from this man, long known as one of the "outlaws" of country music.

KATZ—BLACK STAR

In May 1979 Willie was chosen by the Country Music Association (CMA) to give U.S. Pres. Jimmy Carter a Steuben glass bowl in honour of his contributions to country music. In October the CMA presented Willie with its prestigious title "Entertainer of the Year." It was a good year for the man who had been writing and singing for over 20 years but for whom acknowledgment by his peers had been elusive.

Born April 30, 1933, Willie was raised in Abbott, Texas. He joined the Air Force and attended Baylor University in Waco before working as a disk jockey and musician in the sort of honky-tonk bars he sings about. Meanwhile, he was writing songs that were turned into hits by big-name country performers: "Hello Walls" (Faron Young), "Night Life" (Ray Price).

In 1962 Willie began to record his own songs, eventually moving to Nashville, Tenn., where he played bass in Ray Price's band and became a regular member of the Grand Ole Opry. Some hits from this period are "The Party's Over" and "Little Things." Until the 1960s it was rare for country music to cross over to the pop field. Willie's songs made the transition, but he did not.

Disillusioned by the commercialism of Nashville, Willie returned to Texas in the early 1970s, where he became affiliated with a group of musicians in Austin who were experimenting with new sounds, variously referred to as "redneck rock" and "outlaw country." As the polarization of the 1960s, musical as well as political, relaxed, more people listened to and respected his poignant renditions of traditional country blues.

(JULIE A. KUNKLER)

Newman, Paul

Celebrities travel in fast circles, but few move faster than actor Paul Newman, who drove a 650-hp twin-turbo Porsche 220 mph in 1979 in the Le Mans 24-hour auto race. He and two co-driver teammates took second place in the grueling event, one of the most difficult and dangerous on the international circuit. (Only 22 of the 55 starting cars finished in 1979.) "Perhaps now people will stop taking me for a stupid actor who is simply playing at racing and accept me as a serious racer," Newman said afterward.

One of Hollywood's perennially most popular stars, Newman came late to auto racing. Said his team's boss, veteran Dick Barbour, "If Paul had come into motor racing earlier, he might never have been an actor." But it was acting that led to his first direct contact with the sport, when he took up race driving for his role in the 1969 film *Winning*. He won his first Sports Car Club of America national race in 1973, and has competed ever since. "Racing is the best way I know to get away from all the rubbish of Hollywood," he said.

Also active in politics, Newman supported presidential candidates Eugene McCarthy in 1968 and George McGovern four years later. In 1978 U.S. Pres. Jimmy Carter appointed him to the U.S. delegation to the United Nations General Assembly Special Session on Disarmament.

Born in Cleveland, Ohio, on Jan. 26, 1925, Newman graduated from Kenyon College and studied at the Yale University School of Drama. He first gained fame in the Broadway version of William Inge's *Picnic* in 1953 and then made his film debut in the Christians-versus-lions drama *The Silver Chalice*. He was better remembered for starring roles in *Hud, Cat on a Hot Tin Roof, The Hustler, The Sting,* and *Butch Cassidy and the Sundance Kid*. An occasional behind-camera talent as well, he directed his celebrated wife, Joanne Woodward, in *Rachel, Rachel*.

(PHILIP KOPPER)

Nyad, Diana

After 27 hours and 38 minutes in the water the exhausted but exhilarated marathon swimmer Diana Nyad waded ashore on Aug. 20, 1979, at Juno Beach, Fla., to become the first person ever to swim the 89 mi between The Bahamas and the United States. Though she was aided by escort swimmers who beat away jellyfish with sticks, the swim took its toll, and Nyad emerged with one eye swollen from seawater that leaked into her goggles and a body that felt "like the F train in New York just ran over me." This successful swim followed by a year her disastrous effort to cross the more than 100 mi from Cuba to the Florida Keys.

© 1978 STERN/BLACK STAR

After the Bahamas success Nyad's announced goal was to try the Cuba swim again. Her widely publicized 1978 attempt ended after 42 hours, when Nyad was told that adverse winds had driven her so far off course that she could not hope to reach Key West. Her difficulties were compounded by strong currents, high swells, jellyfish stings, and the partial failure of her 20 × 40-ft self-propelled shark cage (a protective device that unfortunately also increased the water turbulence). After swimming a circuitous route of 76 mi and still being 60 mi from Key West, a reluctant Nyad was helped from the water.

Nyad considered the Cuba–Key West swim as her "own private Olympics," an event for which she trained for a full year and raised some $150,000 in support. Though the effort failed, she attracted an unprecedented amount of public attention to the sport of long-distance swimming.

Diana Nyad was born on Aug. 22, 1949, in New York City. She was raised in Fort Lauderdale, Fla., where she began to swim seriously in her teens. After graduating from Lake Forest College, Lake Forest, Ill., she was persuaded to enter long-distance swimming because a childhood case of endocarditis (a viral infection of the heart) had permanently reduced her swimming speed.

Nyad entered her first marathon, a ten-mile race across Lake Ontario, in 1970. She placed tenth, finishing behind nine men and setting a women's ten-mile record. In 1975 she became more widely known when she quit racing and swam a solitary course around Manhattan in 7 hours and 57 minutes. (JOAN NATALIE BOTHELL)

Nyerere, Julius

Tanzania's Pres. Julius Nyerere decisively influenced two major developments in Africa in 1979. In January he mobilized his army to invade Uganda in support of a local movement to overthrow the tyrannical Pres. Idi Amin; and in August he played a leading part at the Commonwealth heads of government meeting in Lusaka, Zambia, whose main objective was to achieve a settlement of the conflict in Zimbabwe Rhodesia. Prior to that, he played host to Queen Elizabeth II, who visited Tanzania on her way to Lusaka to open the conference.

As chairman of the "front-line" African nations (Tanzania, Zambia, Mozambique, Botswana, and Angola) opposed to white supremacist rule in southern Africa, Nyerere continued as in recent years to play a dominant role in the continent's affairs. However, his military intervention in Uganda was financially disastrous for Tanzania, and he was forced to appeal to Western and other nations for urgent economic support. His role in Uganda also brought him into conflict with an influential minority within the Organization of African Unity (OAU), of which he was one of the main founders in 1963.

When Nyerere first became president of Tanzania (then Tanganyika) in 1962, he chose to be known by the honorific title of Mwalimu, a Swahili word meaning teacher. A moralist of principle, he held that leaders should teach by example. As the founder of his nation he remained committed to the idea of creating an egalitarian socialist society based on the concept of self-reliance.

Born in March 1922, the son of a chief in Butiama, Musoma District, in Tanganyika, Nyerere became a staunch Roman Catholic. After studying at Makerere College in Uganda, he graduated from the University of Edinburgh, Scotland, and returned home to teach at the St. Francis School, Dar es Salaam, in 1952. From his early school days he was a rebel against the colonial system and a pioneer of his country's nationalist movement. Chief minister of Tanganyika in 1960 and prime minister when the country gained its independence in 1961, he became its first president the following year.

(COLIN LEGUM)

Oueddei, Goukouni

On Aug. 21, 1979, the leaders of the 11 principal political and ethnic factions in the troubled central African republic of Chad, meeting in Lagos, Nigeria, signed an agreement on national reconciliation. As a result of the agreement Goukouni Oueddei became president of the republic, and negotiations began on the formation of a "transitional government of national union"—the name being a clear indication of the extreme fragility of the country's political institutions. On September 3 an interim committee headed by Oueddei was set up to assure day-to-day government while negotiations proceeded. Finally, after a six-day gathering at Douguia, the composition of the new government was agreed upon on November 10. In a ceremony in the capital, N'Djamena, on the following day Oueddei presented to the Chadian people his administrative team, which included representatives of all the groups that had been warring with each other for a dozen years.

Born in 1944 at Zouar, in the heart of the Tibesti mountains, Oueddei was brought up in the traditional Toubou culture and had virtually no education in the contemporary sense of the word. He was one of the few sons of the Derdei, the spiritual and religious leader of the Toubou, who survived the civil war that had begun in 1967 in protest against the excesses of former president Ngarta Tombalbaye's government police. A pious Muslim, Oueddei had a wide reputation for tolerance, circumspection, and honesty and indirectly shared his father's prestige: the latter's authority was unchallenged until his death, though he was for a time an exile in Libya.

Oueddei's political career started in November 1976, when the Toubou guerrilla fighters of the National Liberation Front (Frolinat) chose him as their leader to replace his main rival, Hissen Habré. An ardent nationalist, Oueddei asserted Chad's independence from interference by Nigeria, Sudan, Libya, and France, while attempting to use France to counter all the other foreign countries involved. In March 1979 he was appointed president of the new provisional State Council and then, in May, minister of state responsible for the interior. At the Lagos meeting in August he represented the Popular Armed Forces, one of the three major combatant groups.

(PHILIPPE DECRAENE)

Peckford, (Alfred) Brian

At the convention of the Progressive Conservative Party of Newfoundland and Labrador on March 17, 1979, Brian Peckford solidly won the post of party leader, replacing the retiring Frank Moores. After succeeding Moores as premier of Newfoundland and Labrador on March 26, Peckford hastily called a provincial election in which his Conservatives defeated the Liberals under Don Jamieson. As premier, Peckford was expected to be more aggressive than his predecessor in working for the rights of the province. His platform included promises of more attention to Labrador (the mainland part of the province) and programs to preserve and promote Newfoundland culture.

Called self-assertive and even brash by some observers, Peckford first came to prominence when, during his term as Newfoundland's minister of mines and energy (1976–79), he negotiated and implemented the province's oil and gas development regulations. They were so tough that the multinational oil companies stopped their explorations in the province, but Peckford, a pragmatic man, believed that sooner or later Newfoundland's resources would be in demand no matter what the cost. Indeed, offshore exploration resumed in 1979.

After Newfoundland gave up its status as a dominion in 1949 to enter the Canadian Confederation as a province, some inhabitants, including Peckford, had felt that the province had therefore retained ownership of all its resources, whether on or off shore. Since he had been one of Prime Minister Joe Clark's early supporters, he was able to elicit from Clark a promise to consider provincial claims to natural resources in coastal waters.

Born on Aug. 27, 1942, at Whitbourne, Newfoundland, Peckford graduated from Memorial University of Newfoundland in 1966 and taught high school for several years. He first became involved in politics as a Liberal but joined the Conservative Party in 1969. In 1972 he was elected to the provincial House of Assembly and, after two years as special assistant to Premier Moores, he was appointed minister of the Department of Municipal Affairs and Housing in 1974. In 1976 he became minister of mines and energy and, in 1978, minister of rural development as well. As premier, he introduced financial programs that had distinct social overtones. Not a stereotyped Tory, Peckford described himself as "socially progressive and economically or financially conservative." (DIANE LOIS WAY)

Peurala, Alice

In a year of notable electoral triumphs for women, Alice Peurala won the presidency of Steelworkers Local 65, a 7,000-member organization that covered a one-mile stretch of Lake Michigan shoreline and included the giant U.S. Steel South Works facility at Chicago. Denying that sex differences played an important role in the election—"all anyone cares about is if I can do the job"—Peurala defeated outgoing Local 65 president John Chico. Despite her denials, Peurala was hailed as the first woman to head a major Steelworkers unit.

Born in 1928, she followed her father into the steel mills during the early 1950s,

WIDE WORLD

but her career stalled when her boss refused to promote her. "I began to see many of the men I had trained get promoted to better jobs while the women went nowhere. Then I got mad." First, she joined the union, but found it of little help. Later (1967), she filed sex discrimination charges against U.S. Steel under Title VII of the Civil Rights Act of 1964.

After a two-year investigation, the Equal Employment Opportunity Commission found that she had probable cause for her accusations that U.S. Steel had denied her a chance for promotion solely because she was a woman. When the company failed to conciliate the matter, Peurala filed suit in federal court. In an out-of-court settlement the giant steelmaker promised the next opening as product tester would go to Peurala but "I later learned that they were using supervisors to do the job rather than give it to me. I went back to court and the judge ordered me hired."

Disappointed in the lack of labour union support during her battles with U.S. Steel, Peurala decided to work toward democratizing the nearly all-male Local 65. She lost in several attempts to win election to a union office before winning the presidency. Her victory was attributed to her support of the right of union locals to vote on ratification of a labour contract. After her victory Peurala announced that she would start immediately on a campaign for improved plant safety and job security at U.S. Steel.
(JEROLD L. KELLMAN)

Pink Lady

Rolling Stone called Pink Lady "the best-selling female recording act in the world." The two young Japanese ladies who called themselves Pink Lady were indeed just that. Since they made their debut in August 1976, about $75 million had been spent buying their singles and LP's.

Mii (Mitsuyo Nemoto) and Kei (Keiko Matsuda) were both born in Shizuoka Prefecture in 1958. As middle school classmates, they took voice and dance lessons together and won a talent contest after singing on the televised program "A Star Is Born." They were immediately signed to contracts and launched their professional careers singing the pop nonsense song "Inspector Pepper." The lyrics were written by Yu Aku, the tune by Shunichi Tokura, who also selected the name Pink Lady because, like their cocktail namesake, "they sing a little, dance a little, and are visually pleasing a little." Their next hits included "SOS," "Carmen 77," "Wanted," "Chameleon Army," and the blockbuster "UFO." Pink Lady became the idol of Japan's preteen group, but older children and genuine adults were among the 70,000 persons who packed a baseball stadium to see Mii and Kei perform in their spangle-studded hot pants and silver-finished kneeboots. Thus far, they had not appeared in Japanese night clubs. For one thing, they did not want to desert—at least, not yet—the young people who were buying all those records.

With nearly every song they sang hitting the top of the charts, Pink Lady was, predictably, inundated with offers. At least ten times a day they appeared on television screens to endorse items ranging from air conditioners to ham. Their pictures also appeared on some 350 Pink Lady products. "Kiss in the Dark," Pink Lady's first American single, was disco. Mii and Kei sang English songs phonetically because neither felt at home in the language. However, after their first appearance in Las Vegas in 1978, they began to study English more seriously because, having already conquered Japan, there was still another world to conquer across the vast Pacific. On their second visit to the U.S. in 1979, their two managers, Kazuhiko Soma and Paul Drew, were no longer talking about gold records. Pink Lady, they thought, was worth its weight in platinum.
(KAY K. TATEISHI)

YAMAGUCHI-KURITA—GAMMA/LIAISON

Pink Lady

Prior, James Michael Leathes

From the start it was clear that the make-or-break issue for Britain's Conservative government elected in May 1979 would be industrial relations. One of the key Cabinet posts therefore was that of secretary of state for employment. It went to James Prior, perhaps the most moderate member of a government bent on a sharp swing to the right and pledged to curb the power of the trade unions. He had been one of Edward Heath's closest advisers in 1974 when the Heath government chose to have a showdown with the coal miners, only to be defeated at the resultant general election.

In the five years in opposition that followed, Prior set about rebuilding relationships with the unions and getting to know union leaders. By 1979 he was well prepared to take on the job of employment secretary. The Conservative election manifesto pledged the government to curb union powers in such areas as the closed shop, strike ballots, and picketing and, predictably, this triggered off a union threat of all-out opposition. Prior's response was to argue that the intention was no more than to tip the balance of power to neutrality. Meanwhile, in other aspects of labour relations, his aims were more worker participation and more effective consultation between trade unions and management. "The country does not want conflict, the shop floor does not want conflict," he insisted.

A substantial landowner and farmer of traditional Tory origins, Prior might not seem cut out for his leading role in the industrial battlefield. Born in Norwich, on Oct. 11, 1927, he was trained in estate management before he went into Parliament in 1959. His first Cabinet post, from 1970 to 1972, was as minister for agriculture and fisheries. Then, as leader of the House of Commons for the next two years, his capacity for negotiation, for lowering the temperature of dispute, was recognized. He belonged to the reformist wing of the Conservative Party, believing that inequality in Britain represented a serious threat to the fabric of society.
(HARFORD THOMAS)

Rawlings, Jerry John

In June 1979 Flight Lieut. Jerry Rawlings led a successful military coup in Ghana at the head of the Armed Forces Revolutionary Council; its aim was to purge the Army and public life of widespread corruption. Revolutionary military courts tried and executed eight top military figures, including two former heads of state, Gen. Ignatius Kutu Acheampong and Lieut. Gen. Frederick W. K. Akuffo (*see* OBITUARIES). But the young revolutionaries did not break the Army's pledge to restore Ghana to civilian rule. Two months after Pres. Hilla Limann (*q.v.*) took office, he retired Rawlings from the Army to end, at least temporarily, the career of this turbulent young officer.

Rawlings and his young coconspirators represented a new generation of Africans who felt strongly that independence had been scarred by the corruption and abuses

TERESA COLEMAN—CAMERA PRESS/PHOTO TRENDS

of power that the older generation often allowed to go unpunished. An air force pilot of mixed Ghanaian and Scottish parentage, Rawlings in 1979 was described as being about 30 years old. He attended Ghana's leading educational institution, Achimoto College. From there he went to the military academy at Teshie in 1968 and was commissioned the following year as a second lieutenant. He volunteered to serve with the 4th Squadron of Italian-trained jet fighters, which had an exceptionally high death rate in training of 50%.

Rawlings was appalled by the accumulation of wealth among Ghana's senior officers. Joined by 13 other young officers, he determined to clean up the Army's corruption in the short time remaining before the advent of new civilian rule. On May 15, 1979, he led his colleagues in a confrontation with their superior officers. Rawlings was promptly arrested; his appearances at court-martial hearings attracted considerable public interest, and he was applauded on each occasion. He was sprung from prison on June 4 and promptly took over the leadership of the successful coup, in which more than 70 soldiers were killed or wounded. Although the coup achieved its immediate purpose of dealing with those marked for special retribution, Rawlings and his colleagues failed to retain the loyalty of the Army. Thus, President Limann encountered little difficulty when he decided to retire Rawlings in November.

(COLIN LEGUM)

Redgrave, Vanessa

Star of stage and screen—and also a controversial political activist—Vanessa Redgrave was at the height of a brilliant career in 1979. Named as actress of the year by the London *Evening Standard* in 1961 and 1967, she won an Academy of Motion Picture Arts and Sciences Oscar as best supporting actress in *Julia* in 1977 and the British Academy of Film and Television Arts best actress award for the same film in 1978. In 1979 she received more critical accolades for her moving portrayal of Ellida in Ibsen's *The Lady from the Sea,* first seen in Manchester and revived at London's Round House theatre, and for the sincerity of her adulterous English wartime wife in John Schlesinger's film *Yanks.*

In the news for years as champion of the Workers' Revolutionary Party (WRP), Redgrave hit the headlines again in 1979 because of her espousal of the Palestinian cause and the consequent dispute over her agreement to play a Jewish concentration-camp inmate in Arthur Miller's TV-film version of the autobiographical *The Musicians of Auschwitz.* The author of the work, Fania Fenelon, objected to Redgrave but was overruled. Subsequently, Redgrave lost a costly libel suit, in which her brother Corin joined, against *The Observer,* a London Sunday newspaper, as well as her deposit as unsuccessful WRP parliamentary candidate for Moss Side, Manchester, in the general election.

Born in London on Jan. 30, 1937, into a renowned acting family, she followed her famous parents, Sir Michael Redgrave and Rachel Kempson, into the theatre after five years at ballet school (from 8 to 13) and after studying at the Central School of Speech and Drama. Described as "nervy, coltish, tall and shy," she made her debut in the provinces in 1957, in London in 1958, and with the Royal Shakespeare Company in 1959, playing her favourite Shakespeare role of Rosalind there, under Michael Elliott, in 1961. In 1969 she played the first of many parts for Elliott at his Manchester theatre, culminating in Ellida, a role she had done in New York in 1976. Her latest film, *Bear Island,* was made in Canada in 1979.

(OSSIA TRILLING)

Rhoodie, Eschel Mostert

Central figure in the so-called information scandal that had far-reaching political repercussions in South Africa, Eschel Rhoodie had begun a meteoric six-year career in the state hierarchy in 1972. At the age of 39—he was born in Caledon, Cape Province, on Nov. 7, 1933—he was picked by the then minister of information, C. P. Mulder, for the key post of permanent secretary of the department. His promotion over the heads of seniors in the face of opposition from the statutory public service commission drew strong criticism. It was defended on the strength of his considerable overseas experience and contacts and his book *The Paper Curtain,* in which he wrote that South

SVEN SIMON/KATHERINE YOUNG

Africa could best counter persistent international pressure by resorting to unconventional methods.

As secretary for information, Rhoodie lost no time in putting this doctrine into practice. With considerable secret funds at the department's disposal and with the overt or tacit approval of Mulder and other ministers, he developed a complex network of confidential projects and agencies at home and abroad, aimed at influencing public opinion in favour of South Africa.

In 1977 a report by the controller and auditor-general, F. G. Barrie, called attention to alleged irregularities in the appropriation of the department's funds. When investigations by judicial commissions (headed by judges Anton Mostert and R. P. B. Erasmus, respectively) substantiated a number of the allegations, there was a public outcry. The Department of Information was dissolved; Mulder resigned; Rhoodie was summarily retired on pension; and B. J. Vorster resigned as state president when findings in the final Erasmus report (May 1979) reflected on his role in the affair.

After testifying before the commission Rhoodie, with its permission, left South Africa in July 1978. His passport was later withdrawn and his assets in South Africa were frozen. He remained overseas, moving from country to country and from time to time disclosing and threatening to disclose allegedly damaging tape-recorded information. In July 1979, at South Africa's insistence, he was arrested in France and extradited to stand trial on charges of fraud. He was convicted by the Supreme Court in Pretoria on October 8 on five counts and sentenced to an effective six years' imprisonment. At year's end he was on bail while his appeal was pending.

(LOUIS HOTZ)

Rizzo, Frank

Firm law enforcement is necessary in a time of rising crime rates, but at the same time police brutality cannot be justified. In 1979 the courts had to face the decision of whether Philadelphia, Pa., in its zeal for law and order, had violated the rights of its citizens. On Aug. 3, 1979, the U.S. Department of Justice filed suit in the U.S. District Court, charging that Philadelphia Mayor Frank Rizzo and 18 high-ranking city and police officials either committed or condoned "widespread and severe" acts of police brutality.

The key figure in this case was Frank Lazarro Rizzo, who served as mayor of Philadelphia for eight years beginning in November 1971. Rizzo, who campaigned as a law-and-order Democrat, had made his name as an unusually successful and vigorous Philadelphia police commissioner between 1967 and 1971. Known as a "cop's cop," he had expanded the police force, had won the enthusiastic loyalty of his men, and had kept the crime rate in Philadelphia below that of any other major U.S. city.

The Justice Department suit alleged that Rizzo's crime-fighting techniques involved encouragement or tolerance of brutal practices such as beatings and shootings of suspects. These activities were said to have continued under Rizzo's mayoralty. Some critics charged that Rizzo throughout his career had been hostile toward minorities. Rizzo replied, however, that he prevented destructive ghetto riots in Philadelphia by

UPI

moving swiftly before minor disorders grew out of control. He also took credit for racial integration of the Philadelphia police force, for increased recruitment of black officers, and for intensive antidrug efforts in black neighbourhoods. In October a federal district judge dismissed all portions of the suit except that dealing with racial discrimination on the grounds that the government had no authority to bring it. The last charge was also dismissed, in December, because of lack of factual support.

Except for the past eight years, Rizzo had spent virtually his entire adult life in police work. He was born Oct. 23, 1920, in Philadelphia to a police family. After a brief stay in the U.S. Navy and three years in a steel mill, he joined the Philadelphia police in 1943. As he rose through the ranks, he became known as the "Cisco Kid," a tribute to his fearlessness and taste for action.

(VICTOR M. CASSIDY)

Roldós Aguilera, Jaime

Shaking off nine years of civilian and military dictatorships, Ecuadoreans joined the thin ranks of the Latin-American democracies when they gave a smashing electoral victory to Jaime Roldós Aguilera for president. The odds had seemed heavily against the ruling military government permitting a free election and—even more surprising—allowing a left-of-centre candidate such as Roldós to emerge victorious. It had established eligibility requirements for candidates so as to prevent populist Assad Bucaram from running, despite the fact that Bucaram was clearly the favourite of the Ecuadorean masses. But the government accepted the candidacy of Roldós, married to Bucaram's niece, as nominee of the Concentración de Fuerzas Populares.

Jaime Roldós Aguilera, born in Guayaquil on Nov. 5, 1940, thus emerged in the presidential spotlight as something of a surrogate. His credentials were impeccable: valedictorian of his class at Guayaquil's best college preparatory school, number one student in both his undergraduate and law school classes, and a former congressman. But he had no national political base, and he ran on the slogan "Roldós in the presidency, Bucaram in power" during his first campaign. That campaign culminated in a six-candidate contest on July 16, 1978.

It came as no surprise when none of the candidates garnered the required majority, thus necessitating a runoff. It came as a shock, however, to the military and even to his own supporters when left-leaning Roldós took a commanding lead with nearly one-third of all the votes cast. Roldós had campaigned against the military regime, blaming it for mismanaging both the country's newly found oil resources and Ecuador's overall economy.

The runoff was supposed to take place soon after the first contest, but the military leadership kept postponing it. After the U.S. warned that relations between the two nations would suffer if elections were not held, the date was set for April 29, 1979. It was no contest, Roldós capturing 68.4% of the vote. So overwhelming was the victory that it dispelled fears of the military stepping in to rob Roldós of his triumph through a recount. (JEROLD L. KELLMAN)

Runcie, the Right Rev. Robert Alexander Kennedy

In the summer of 1979, Rosalind Runcie, wife of the bishop of St. Albans, told a local newspaper reporter that the only way she wanted to leave the city was feet first, in a coffin. But leave St. Albans she would, though happily not in that mode. For just about the time she was delivering her remark, the Crown Appointments Commission was deciding that her husband was the right man to succeed Donald Coggan as archbishop of Canterbury on the latter's retirement in January 1980.

Robert Runcie was born in Liverpool on Oct. 2, 1921, the youngest of a family of four. His father was a Scottish electrical engineer, a lapsed Presbyterian, and a keen racing man with "a profound distrust of both parsons and policemen." From a local council school, the young Runcie moved up the social scale to Merchant Taylors' public school, Crosby. There, unknowingly, he set his foot on the first rung of the ladder to the loftiest position in the Anglican Communion when he allowed a friend to jolly him into attending confirmation classes. Further education at Oxford was interrupted after only a year by the outbreak of World War II. Runcie became a tank officer in the Scots Guards and won the Military Cross for two acts of bravery. Then it was back to Oxford and a first class honours degree before going on to ordination (1951).

Until his appointment as bishop of St. Albans in 1970, most of his ministry had been spent in academic posts, but there was about him none of the cool aloofness associated with certain types of academic. He had a warm, outgoing personality and a knack of commanding the affection and cooperation of those who disagreed with him. He also had a keen interest in the wider church and was cochairman of the Anglican-Orthodox Joint Doctrinal Commission for six years.

Bishop Runcie's broad sympathies did not give him a woolly approach to life. He was incisive and knew what he wanted to do with his primacy. He hoped to open up the Anglican Communion into much wider consultation, while at the same time giving it a much crisper image than it currently possessed. He disliked being labeled but when pressed described himself as a "radical Catholic." (SUSAN YOUNG)

Sá Carneiro, Francisco

Portugal's new premier-to-be following the Dec. 2, 1979, elections, Francisco Sá Carneiro, was joint leader of the Aliança Democrática (AD), which consisted of his Social Democrats (PSD), the Centre Democrats (CDS), the small Monarchist group, and several others. The right-wing coalition, which polled 45.2% of the votes cast and would hold a narrow overall majority with 128 seats in the 250-seat Assembly, was largely Sá Carneiro's creation. After the PSD split in May on whether to support a Socialist budget, Sá Carneiro left the party and began negotiations with other groups further to the right with a view to forming a coalition to contest the upcoming general and municipal elections. The PSD, needing his charisma, later welcomed him back as leader, and in July the AD was formed with Sá Carneiro and Diego Freitas do Amaral of the CDS as joint leaders.

The AD manifesto contained promises to roll back collectivization of farms south of the Tagus River, curb the size of nationalized basic industry, and push Portugal's bid for European Economic Community membership. In the medium term the AD called for reform of Portugal's Socialist constitution. After winning further support in the December 16 municipal elections, the AD was expected to nominate a presidential candidate, who, Sá Carneiro stated, must have the coalition's confidence and not be a member of the military establishment.

Born July 19, 1934, the son of a prosperous Oporto family, Sá Carneiro was graduated from law school at age 21 and became a lawyer in Oporto. Turning to politics, in 1969 he became a member of the rubber-stamp National Assembly. There he worked for liberalization of the authoritarian government, including a curtailment of the activities of the infamous secret police, but he resigned in early 1973. After the April 1974 military coup he founded the Popular Democrat Party and was its minister without portfolio in the government of Adélino da Palma Carlos during the presidency of Gen. António de Spínola. Sá Carneiro later resigned in protest against the nationalization of heavy industry, banks, and insurance companies. (MICHAEL WOOLLER)

Schreyer, Edward

While prime minister of Canada, Pierre Trudeau had always said that he would welcome Ed Schreyer in Ottawa at any time as part of the government. This was said in spite of the fact that Trudeau led the Liberal Party, while Schreyer was a member of the New Democratic Party. But Schreyer, the premier of Manitoba, preferred provincial politics. When his party lost in the 1977 Manitoba election, however, Schreyer had to step down as premier. After a period as leader of the opposition in the Manitoba legislature he accepted Trudeau's offer to move to Rideau Hall, Ottawa, as Canada's 22nd governor-general, taking office on Jan. 22, 1979. Of German extraction, he was not only the youngest but also the first person of neither English nor French descent to hold the office.

Born on a farm near Beauséjour, Manitoba, on Dec. 21, 1935, Edward Richard Schreyer at the age of four was already making speeches from the stairs of his home. After high school he was torn between careers in baseball and teaching. Choosing the latter, he attended United College in Winnipeg, from which he obtained a B.A. degree, and St. John's College, from which he gained a B.Ed. His M.A. in international relations and economics was granted by the University of Manitoba, where he served as a professor of political science and international relations from 1962 to 1965.

In 1956 Schreyer became campaign manager for Jake Schulz, federal member of Parliament for Springfield (Manitoba) and a moving force in the Manitoba Farmers' Union. As a candidate of the Co-operative Commonwealth Federation (former name of the New Democratic Party), Schreyer himself was elected to the Manitoba legislature in 1958 and represented the riding of Brokenhead until 1965. From 1965 to 1969 he was a federal member of Parliament from Manitoba. He was not happy living in Ottawa, however, and did not hesitate to return to Manitoba in June 1969, when he was chosen leader of the New Democratic Party in the province. Resigning his federal seat, he was immediately plunged into a provincial election campaign. Both he and his party were victorious, Schreyer winning the riding of Rossmere and becoming premier of Manitoba.

In assuming the office of governor-general, Schreyer became the representative of Queen Elizabeth II in Canada. As the chief of state, the governor-general must summon and dissolve Parliament, give royal assent to parliamentary bills, and read the speech from the throne at the opening of each session of Parliament.

(DIANE LOIS WAY)

Segal, George

The first retrospective of artist George Segal's work, which opened to critical acclaim at the Whitney Museum in New York City in May 1979, revealed 20 years of the development of one of the foremost sculptors in the United States. The 36 pastel drawings and 50 sculptures—including his characteristic life-size plaster figures set in commonplace environments—showed the artist discovering his unique voice in contemporary art and exploring its range.

Segal began his artistic career in the 1950s as a painter of figures but began sculpting in 1958. His first sculptural works combined painting and sculpture. For example, in the "Legend of Lot" a crudely defined plaster Lot, formed on an armature of wood, chicken wire, and burlap, stands against a background painting. In 1960, while making props for an avant-garde film, Segal realized that similar props could replace paintings as environments for his plaster figures. At about the same time he discovered a new method of creating his human figures. A student had given him some plaster-impregnated gauze, used by physicians to make casts, and Segal had his wife wrap him in the water-soaked bandages from neck to toe. The dried shell was removed (with some difficulty) and reassembled. It became "Man Sitting at a Table" (1961), and Segal had found his medium. Exhibited at a show of "New Realists" in 1962, his works began to attract attention.

WIDE WORLD

Segal gradually refined his casting method, using friends, family members, and himself as models. In part because the method itself requires long periods of motionlessness, many of Segal's figures suggest an attitude of profound introspection and isolation. His environments (diners, kitchens, buses, gas stations) grew more detailed, with props drawn from real life (Coca-Cola bottles, automobile tires, coffee cups).

In 1971 the sculptor again altered his technique. Instead of using the plaster shell for the finished form, he began using it as a mold into which liquid plaster was poured; this allowed greater realism.

Segal was born in New York City on Nov. 26, 1924. He studied at Cooper Union School of Art and Architecture, Rutgers University, the Pratt Institute of Design, and New York University. For a time he earned his living as a chicken farmer in New Jersey. His works were to be found in the permanent collections of many major museums.

(JOAN NATALIE BOTHELL)

Shagari, Alhaji Shehu

After 13 years of military rule, a civilian government was inaugurated in Nigeria on Oct. 1, 1979, with Alhaji Shehu Shagari as the new president. A strong believer in consensus and compromise rather than confrontation politics, he tried to persuade the four opposition parties to join his victorious National Party of Nigeria to provide a coalition government.

Shagari came to the presidency with some 25 years of political experience behind him. As a young teacher, he joined the Northern People's Congress and was elected to Parliament for Sokoto West in 1954. After attending a parliamentary course at Westminster, London, he became parliamentary secretary to Alhaji Abubakar Tafawa Balewa, prime minister from 1957 until the 1966 military revolt, who helped to shape Shagari's political thought. In 1959 he was made federal minister of economic development, the first of a long string of Cabinet appointments.

After the 1966 military takeover Shagari retired for a time to his farm in Sokoto and also administered the province's educational development fund. In 1970 he became federal commissioner for economic development, agriculture, and natural resources, with special responsibility for rehabilitating those parts of the country affected by the civil war. He was made federal commissioner for finance in 1971 and became a governor of the World Bank and the International Monetary Fund. He retired from government in 1975 and accepted a position as chairman of the Peugeot Automobile Co. of Nigeria. In 1978 he helped to form the National Party of Nigeria, which he led to victory in the 1979 elections.

Shagari was born at Yabo, Sokoto State, in May 1925. After completing his secondary education in 1944, he became science teacher at Kaduna College. His teaching career spanned 13 years, culminating in his appointment as headmaster of a senior primary school in Argungu in 1951. He was regarded as a distinguished poet in his native Hausa language.

(COLIN LEGUM)

Sihanouk, Prince Norodom

As Cambodia's Heng Samrin government and remnants of the fallen Pol Pot regime remained in apparent deadlock in 1979, a high-pitched voice from the country's past rose to denounce both sides and to warn that a legitimate third force must take over before the Khmer race was eliminated by war and famine. It was the voice of Prince Samdech Preah Norodom Sihanouk, whose ouster as head of state in 1970 had been the start of the nation's plunge into tragedy. He organized a Confederation of Nationalist Khmers, sent letters to various countries soliciting support, and asked for a dialogue with Vietnam on the basis that only he, Sihanouk, was in a position to unify Cambodia, end the misery of the people, and establish a government that would be legitimate, neutral, and independent enough to win international recognition.

It was no idle boast. During the decade that he was head of state, Sihanouk had followed a neutralist policy that often

LAURENT MAOUS—GAMMA/LIAISON

seemed eccentric but always kept his country out of the war that raged across its borders. The diplomatic dexterity that made this possible was a hallmark of the man considered one of Southeast Asia's most remarkable and colourful characters.

Musician, composer, and film producer as well as political leader, Sihanouk was born in Phnom Penh on Oct. 31, 1922. At 18 he became king because the French colonial authorities thought he was more pliable than other claimants. But he soon showed signs of an unusual spirit of independence. In 1955 he abdicated in favour of his father and became prime minister, foreign minister, and subsequently permanent representative to the UN. Five years later, on the death of his father, he declared himself head of state, remaining so until he was ousted in the U.S.-supported coup led by Gen. Lon Nol in 1970. He then lived in Beijing (Peking), campaigning on behalf of the Khmer Rouge underground.

Following the Communist victory in 1975, Sihanouk returned home, only to be put under house arrest by Pol Pot. He was released in January 1979 as the Pol Pot regime was falling to pro-Vietnamese forces and needed an advocate in the UN. After denouncing the Vietnamese invasion, he dissociated himself from Pol Pot as well. Setting up bases in Beijing and Pyongyang, North Korea, and embarking on a tour of Western Europe in November (with a visit to the U.S. planned for January 1980), the prince offered himself as Cambodia's only hope. (T. J. S. GEORGE)

Somoza Debayle, Anastasio

"He'll only go by force." That was the estimate made of Anastasio Somoza Debayle by one of his enemies. On July 17, 1979, Somoza did go, forced out as president of Nicaragua after months of civil war between his National Guard and the Frente Sandinista de Liberación Nacional (Sandinista National Liberation Front). He had held power far longer than most had expected and had held it under pressures that would probably have crushed others.

Somoza was one of the last Latin-American strong men. His father, Anastasio Somoza García, had ruled Nicaragua for 20 years beginning in 1936. Somoza, who was born on Dec. 5, 1925, in León, Nicaragua, was prepared for power from childhood. He went to La Salle Military Academy in Oakdale, N.Y., and from there to the U.S. Military Academy at West Point. Graduating in 1945, he returned home and rose quickly through the ranks in Nicaragua's National Guard, becoming its de facto leader by the time of his father's assassination in 1956.

Until his departure from Nicaragua, Somoza never relinquished control of the National Guard. It was his power base and, though he served only two terms as president (1967–72 and 1974–79), he was to all intents and purposes the dictator of his country from 1967 until mid-1979. He instituted agrarian reforms and health and education programs, maintained close ties with the U.S., and witnessed economic advances. He also was attacked for corruption, repression, and brutality.

The Sandinista National Liberation Front, which ultimately defeated Somoza, was founded in 1961 and waged sporadic guerrilla warfare in the countryside for many years. Somoza crushed the Sandinistas in the late 1960s, only to see them reappear a few years later. In 1974 the rebels raided the home of a prominent government official and took hostages, including members of the Somoza family. Somoza had to free 14 political prisoners and pay a $1 million ransom for the release of the hostages. In a 1978 Sandinista raid on Nicaragua's National Palace, 2,000 hostages were taken and released after more prisoners were freed and ransom paid. After that the fighting between the Sandinistas and Somoza's National Guard intensified until the entire nation was swept up in the civil war which finally toppled Somoza from power. (VICTOR M. CASSIDY)

J.P. LAFFONT—SYGMA

Stargell, Willie

Amid the jubilantly sprayed champagne, Willie Stargell sat quietly in the Pittsburgh Pirates' locker room, sipping at the wine he drinks after every baseball game. "He's Pops, my baseball father," teammate Dave Parker said. More than that, Stargell was the soul of the team that had just won the 1979 World Series championship.

"Pops" was an apt nickname for the leader of a team that calls itself a family, but Stargell was still more valuable than venerable. It was his home run that put the Pirates ahead to stay in the decisive seventh game of the World Series, and it was Stargell who set a World Series record with seven extra-base hits against the Baltimore Orioles. Voted the Series' most valuable player, Stargell batted .400, hit three home runs, and tied a World Series record with 25 total bases.

Only two years earlier there had been doubts that Stargell would ever again resume his habit of taking target practice on the farthest bleacher seats around the National League. He was 36 in 1977, becoming a relic by baseball standards. He had only 13 home runs and 35 runs batted in during that season, which was shortened for him by dizzy spells and a pinched elbow nerve. But Stargell batted in 97 runs with 28 homers the next season. In 1979 he shared the National League's most valuable player award with Keith Hernandez, hitting 32 home runs and batting in 82 runs despite frequent rests from the lineup.

All of that recognition seemed a bit much to Wilver Dornell Stargell, the self-described "big old country boy" who was born on March 6, 1941, in Earlsboro, Okla., and grew up in Alameda, Calif. He would let admirers pump his arm but not his ego. Stargell kept reminding them that the game was no different than when he played for $750 a month in 1959. The game had not changed, Stargell said, because it was something to be played: "They don't say 'Work ball!' "

Few had played it better than the Pirates' 6 ft 3 in, 225-lb first baseman. His best season was 1973, when he hit 44 of his 461 home runs, batted .299, and had an extra-base hit every 6.7 times he went to the plate. Stargell's home runs, his 43 doubles, and his 119 runs batted in led the league that year. (KEVIN M. LAMB)

Strauss, Franz-Josef

Chosen in July 1979 by the West German Christian Democratic Union and its Bavarian sister party, the Christian Social Union, as their candidate for the federal chancellorship in the 1980 election, Franz-Josef Strauss had been in the forefront of West German politics since the birth of the federal republic in 1949. A founding member of the Christian Social Union in 1945, he was the party's general secretary from 1948 to 1952. Elected to the first West German federal Parliament, the Bundestag, in 1949, he became minister without portfolio in the Cabinet of Konrad Adenauer four years later and minister for atomic affairs in 1955.

As defense minister from 1956 Strauss played a major role in building up the Bundeswehr, the country's new armed forces. He was forced to resign in 1962 for his part in the "*Spiegel* affair," in which the publisher and senior members of the staff of *Der Spiegel* magazine were arrested on suspicion of treason for publishing an article about a NATO exercise. The resignation proved to be only a temporary setback, for a court ruled that there was no basis for charges that he had misused his authority. In 1966 he became finance minister in the "grand coalition" led by Christian Democrat Kurt Georg Kiesinger and filled the post with distinction until the election of 1969, which brought the Social Democrats and Free Democrats to power. Chairman of the Christian Social Union since 1961, in November 1978 he was elected premier of Bavaria. A controversial figure and an aggressive campaigner, his position was to the right of centre in West German politics.

Strauss was born on Sept. 6, 1915, in Munich, where his father had a butcher's shop. Franz-Josef had a brilliant career at school and went on to study a variety of subjects, including German, history, and economics, at the University of Munich. (NORMAN CROSSLAND)

Strauss, Robert

For most of the first three years of the administration of U.S. Pres. Jimmy Carter, Robert Strauss was, in the eyes of many, one of the few professionals in a White House filled with amateurs. Strauss repeatedly demonstrated his loyalty to President

Carter but also managed to convey the impression that he, too, considered his broad experience to be unique.

After Strauss finished a successful term (1972–76) as chairman of the Democratic Party, Carter named him to be U.S. special trade negotiator with responsibility for bargaining with foreign trading partners. Less than two years later he was given an additional assignment: to use his and the executive branch's powers of persuasion to convince labour and business to adhere to the president's "voluntary" anti-inflation guidelines. It was a job for which Strauss, an attorney and self-made millionaire with an unquestioned gift for "jawboning," seemed highly qualified.

On April 24, 1979, the day before Egypt and Israel exchanged ratification documents in connection with their peace treaty, Strauss relinquished his trade and inflation responsibilities and became Carter's special mediator at the continuing talks between Egypt and Israel on autonomy for Palestinians in the West Bank and the Gaza Strip. Even for Strauss the new assignment proved extremely difficult. The negotiations—against the background of the U.S.'s opposition to Israeli settlement policies in the disputed areas—proceeded haltingly at best. Still, during a trip to the Middle East in September, Strauss said he had been assured by Egyptian Pres. Anwar as-Sadat that the talks were "so far down the road to success that we don't need to really worry anymore about a breakdown."

Whether that was the case or not, Strauss himself was about to get yet another job from Carter. A few weeks after returning from the Middle East, he left the government and took over the operation of Carter's reelection campaign committee.

Born in Lockhart, Texas, on Oct. 19, 1918, Strauss received a law degree from the University of Texas. He practiced law in Dallas, Texas, and also became president of Strauss Broadcasting Co.

(STANLEY W. CLOUD)

Tabai, Ieremia

When the republic of Kiribati (pronounced Kiribas), formerly the British colony of the Gilbert Islands, came into being on July 12, 1979, Ieremia Tabai, at the age of 29, became its first president. Under the Kiribati constitution, the 35 members of the House of Assembly nominate three or four candidates for a presidential election held under universal adult suffrage. In the 1978 general election—when the post was still designated chief minister—Tabai won an absolute majority over his three rivals. Now, as president under the independence constitution, he was both head of state and of government, but he could serve no more than three four-year terms.

Born on Nonouti Island in 1950, Ieremia Tabai was the son of a subsistence farmer and fisherman. After attending King George V High School on Tarawa, now the capital of Kiribati, he went to New Zealand, where he attended St. Andrew's College in Christchurch. He completed a commerce degree at Victoria University of Wellington in 1972 before returning to work in the Treasury Department of the (then) Gilbert and Ellice Islands Colony. In 1974 he was returned to the House of Assembly by the Nonouti constituency and later became the recognized "leader of the opposition" in a system characterized by loose coalitions of like-minded members rather than by formal political parties. In opposition he was a consistent critic of the centralist tendencies of Chief Minister Naboua Ratieta's government, of its somewhat extravagant plans for a costly defense force, and of increasing westernization in government and life-styles. He championed the virtues of traditional Gilbertese culture, publicized the grievances of village-dwelling copra farmers, and criticized the government expenditure on Tarawa at the expense of the "outer islands."

Prior to independence, he proved himself to be a shrewd negotiator when he led his government in discussions with the U.K. over a financial settlement. Also at issue were the demands (not met) of the Banabans that their ancestral homeland of Ocean Island, now a barren wasteland because of phosphate mining, should be separated from Kiribati. In 1979 Tabai was made a companion of St. Michael and St. George by Queen Elizabeth II.

(BARRIE MACDONALD)

Thatcher, Margaret Hilda

The Conservative victory in the United Kingdom general election of May 3, 1979, put Mrs. Margaret Thatcher into No. 10 Downing Street as Britain's first woman prime minister. Elected leader of the Conservative Party after the defeat of Edward Heath's government in 1974, she had established a remarkably firm grip on the party during five years as leader of the opposition. She had moved the Conservative position, which from the 1950s had tended toward the politics of the centre, decisively to the right.

Once in office, with a secure majority in the House of Commons, she set about steering an abrupt change of direction from that of the previous government. Keynesian demand management was discarded, to be replaced by free market monetarism; intervention in the market or in wage negotiations was taboo; most subsidies were to be phased out; and public expenditure was to be cut across the board. To carry out this drastic shake-up, she put dedicated monetarists into key positions in her Cabinet, and she masterminded it all in a distinctly autocratic style that earned her the nickname of "the iron lady." Her reputation for curt and sometimes brutal outspokenness contrasted with a conventionally ladylike appearance and style of speaking.

Margaret Thatcher's background was representative of the solid core of British middle-class conservatism. The daughter of a successful grocer who became the mayor in the small market town of Grantham, Lincolnshire, she was born on Oct. 13, 1925. She made her way to Oxford University with scholarships from the local school, studied chemistry, and was certainly the first research chemist to be a British prime minister as well as the first woman. But politics was her obsession. Elected to Parliament in 1959, she held a junior position in the Conservative government from 1964 to 1970 and reached the Cabinet in the Heath government of 1970–74 as secretary of state for education and science.

The gap in her political experience was in foreign affairs, but she quickly made herself felt at various summit meetings during 1979 by speaking her mind, however sensitive the issue might be—as in her references to the Soviet military threat and to Britain's objections to the financial mechanisms of the European Community.

(HARFORD THOMAS)

Thomas, Franklin

When he became president of the Ford Foundation in June 1979, Franklin Thomas established himself as one of the most influential black leaders in the United States. A lawyer, former police official, and urban innovator, he had turned down Pres. Jimmy Carter's invitation to be secretary of housing and urban development after deciding he couldn't "make a unique difference . . . spending half my time or more" testifying before congressional committees. But "all the vibrations felt right" when the $120,000 Ford job was offered. "The foundation can be an initiator of activities open to risk-taking. It can change directions without having to write new legislation," he said.

Founded in 1936 with a $25,000 gift, the Ford Foundation had changed directions several times in the course of becoming the nation's largest, richest, and sometimes most respected philanthropic trust. At first, it focused parochially on private charities in Michigan. Then its founders, automotive pioneer Henry Ford and his son Edsel, left huge bequests that the foundation used to broaden its scope to include higher education and projects in less developed countries. Under McGeorge Bundy, Thomas's immediate predecessor, it supported a wide range of civil rights and civil liberties causes as well, but lavish spending programs coupled with stock market reverses cut its assets by nearly half. In 1975 the foundation retrenched, and by 1979 it had assets of more than $2 billion and spent upward of $130 million in grants yearly.

Thomas promised "a shift of emphasis, more . . . than a wholesale shift" in priorities. Because of his background he was expected to broaden the foundation's role in urban affairs and community organization. For ten years he headed the Bedford-Stuyvesant Restoration Corporation, which revitalized the riot-wrecked and decayed Brooklyn, N.Y., neighbourhood where he was born on May 27, 1934.

Growing up in the Brooklyn slums, Thomas showed promise as a basketball player and went to Columbia University, where his rebounding record still stands. After receiving an undergraduate degree he served in the Air Force and then returned to graduate with honours from Columbia Law School in 1963. He worked for a federal housing agency, as an assistant U.S. attorney in New York City, and then became the city's deputy police commissioner for legal matters. He headed the Bedford-Stuyvesant organization from its creation in 1967 until 1977, when he stepped down to practice law and serve as a Ford trustee.

(PHILIP KOPPER)

Thomas, Kurt

Taking up gymnastics because he was too small for other sports, Kurt Thomas turned the United States into a giant in international gymnastics competition. The Indiana State University graduate won six medals in the 1979 world gymnastics championships and led his country to third place behind the Soviet Union and Japan, its highest finish ever. Thomas's own second-place silver medal in all-around competition was also a new high for the U.S., and he finished only 0.275 of a point behind the winner after 18 events.

Beyond his excellence, Thomas was magnetic. He was his sport's goodwill ambassador, a twirling human baton that one city passed to another to show the uninformed how exciting men's gymnastics could be. His "Thomas Flair" proved to be a showstopper on national television, although he was not sure how to explain the maneuver that involved scissor kicking while he twirled.

Thomas was born March 29, 1956, in Fort Lauderdale, Fla. In high school he spent some free time wrestling, but he had already considered quitting that sport even before the gymnastics coach discovered his talented flip-flops in a physical education class. His long arms made him a natural for gymnastics.

Thomas first gained note early in 1977 when he was the U.S. collegiate all-around champion and won the all-around gold medal in a tournament in London. That same year at a tournament in Romania he showed shocked observers that it was not impossible for a Westerner to win a gymnastics gold medal in Eastern Europe. By

© 1979 MARY ANN CARTER—BLACK STAR

October 1978 he had joined the world's elite with a gold medal for his floor exercise routine at the world championships, the first victory for U.S. men in significant international competition since 1932.

In an age of athletic specialization Thomas was an uncommon generalist. Floor exercise was perhaps his best event, but the horizontal bars was his favourite and the pommel horse was the best event for his Thomas Flair. In the 1979 world championships he won gold medals in the horizontal bars and floor exercise and silver medals in the pommeled horse and parallel bars.

(KEVIN M. LAMB)

Tuchman, Barbara

For seven years writer/historian Barbara Tuchman immersed herself in the life, and death, of 14th-century Europe. Her view of that time, of the medieval wars, plagues, political intrigues, crimes, pageantry, gallantry, and stupidity, was expressed in the title of her book on the subject—*A Distant Mirror: The Calamitous 14th Century* (1978), which remained a best seller through 1979.

Inspired at first by a curiosity about the social effects of the worst disaster of recorded history—the Black Death of 1348–50—and the parallels with our own century, Tuchman eventually came to focus on the career of one French knight. This was Enguerrand VII de Coucy, who lived from 1346 to 1397 and who played a role in many major events. The richly detailed account of life in that period made the book an immediate success with the public, although critical opinions on it were mixed. While reviewers almost unanimously praised Tuchman's fluid, lively writing, a number of historians took issue with aspects of her presentation. One such criticism was that she concentrated on events in northern France and southern England to the virtual exclusion of the rest of Europe.

Nonetheless, the overall reception of the book was enthusiastic. On Jan. 24, 1979, Tuchman became the first woman ever elected president of the prestigious American Academy and Institute of Arts and Letters, an 80-year-old honour society for creative artists. The previous year she had received a gold medal for history from the society.

Honours were not new to Barbara Tuchman. She was awarded her first Pulitzer Prize in 1963 for *The Guns of August,* a history of the early phases of World War I, from its diplomatic prelude and the invasion of Belgium on Aug. 4, 1914, to the eve of the Battle of the Marne on September 4 of that year. Her second Pulitzer was received in 1972 for *Stilwell and the American Experience in China, 1911–45.*

Barbara (Wertheim) Tuchman was born on Jan. 30, 1912, in New York City. After graduating from Radcliffe College, Cambridge, Mass., in 1933, she became a writer for *The Nation,* reporting on the Spanish Civil War from Madrid in 1937. She served as the U.S. correspondent for the *New Statesman* and, from 1944 to 1945, as editor of the Far East news desk for the Office of War Information in New York.

(JOAN NATALIE BOTHELL)

Veil, Simone Annie

The choice of Simone Veil as president of the first directly elected European Assembly at its opening session in Strasbourg, France, on July 17, 1979, came as no surprise; she had been widely considered the most likely contender for the office. Previously France's minister of health and family affairs, she resigned that post on June 11, the day after her election to the European Assembly at the head of the centre-right Union pour la France en Europe, which topped the poll in France with 27.60% of the votes cast. Her tenure of office would extend until Jan. 1, 1982.

When she was appointed minister of health in 1974—the first woman to hold full ministerial rank in France—Veil was virtu-

UZAN—GAMMA/LIAISON

ally unknown to the French, let alone to a wider European public. She soon became France's most popular political personality, widely admired and respected for her force of character and the reforming zeal with which she set about modernizing and improving the nation's health services. Her two major achievements were the enactment of bills liberalizing official policies toward contraception and legalizing abortion—both sensitive issues in a predominantly Roman Catholic society.

Simone Jacob was born on July 13, 1927, in Nice, France. Her schooling was interrupted in March 1944 by the family's deportation to Auschwitz, where her parents and brother died in concentration camps. Repatriated in May 1945, she graduated in law and gained the diploma of the Paris Institut d'Études Politiques. During 1959–65 she was an assistant public prosecutor, and in 1970 became the first woman secretary-general of the Higher Council of Judges. Appointed minister of health in Jacques Chirac's government in May 1974, she remained in office under Premier Raymond Barre until March 31, 1978, being reappointed with additional responsibility for family affairs on April 5. From 1977 she was also chairman of the Information Council for Electro-nuclear Energy.

Veil's administrative experience, natural authority, and considerable personal charm stood her in good stead as arbitrator in the procedural disputes in Europe's new Assembly. In an interview she emphasized her conviction that the president must stand above national and party political considerations.

(J. E. DAVIS)

Vickers, Jon

According to J. W. Lambert of the *Christian Science Monitor,* Canadian opera singer Jon Vickers was that rare combination—"a heroic tenor with a beautiful voice." The steely quality of his voice, called in German *Glänz,* made him famous as Aeneas in Berlioz's *The Trojans* and incomparable as Tristan in Wagner's *Tristan und Isolde.* In his performances Vickers found it essential to have a point of personal contact with the personality of each role in order to bring the character to life onstage. With Wagner's *Tannhäuser*, he could find no such point, and so in 1977 he withdrew from the revival of that opera at London's Covent Garden. The Royal Opera was forced to give Verdi's *Otello* instead, in the title role of which Vickers had been classed as "the Moor of the century."

Born Oct. 26, 1926, in Prince Albert, Sask., Jonathan Stewart Vickers had dreamed of becoming a singer from the time he was a young boy. His early working days were spent, however, as a troubleshooter for the F. W. Woolworth Co. in Manitoba. In 1947 a recording of his voice earned him a scholarship to the Royal Conservatory of Music in Toronto. There, Vickers studied lieder and opera for seven years with former operatic baritone George Lambert. He learned both cantabile and bravura, a combination rare in a heroic tenor. He sang church music and oratorio in Toronto and also with the city's symphony orchestra.

Vickers signed a contract with the Royal Opera at Covent Garden in London in 1956 and made his debut there in April 1957 as Gustavus III in Verdi's *A Masked Ball*. The major achievement of his first season in London was the role of Aeneas in *The Trojans*. During the next years Vickers learned his trade, developing a keen sense of the dramatic. Luchino Visconti's production of Verdi's *Don Carlos* at Covent Garden in 1958 marked the beginning of Vickers's international career. In that same year he appeared at the music festival in Bayreuth, West Germany, as Siegmund in Wagner's *Die Walküre*. His debut at New York City's Metropolitan Opera in 1960 was as Canio in Leoncavallo's *I Pagliacci*. Vickers's favourite role was in *Enée* by Berlioz, because of its difficult score with tessitura for four categories of tenor voice. (DIANE LOIS WAY)

Viguerie, Richard A.

When reformers in 1974 passed laws restricting the amount of money people could contribute to political campaigns in the U.S., they made small contributors the backbone of campaign financing and unwittingly created a multimillion-dollar clientele for the direct mail industry. And none of the experts prospered more than Richard A. Viguerie.

He became the leading fund raiser for conservative causes and candidates, using computerized lists of some 15 million names and addresses to bring in an estimated $15 million a year. Viguerie founded and organized some of his own best customers, a group of conservative political action committees that became a moving force within the conservative movement. His clients included the anti-Panama Canal treaty and anti-gun-control forces, presidential contenders George Wallace ($7 million in 1976) and Philip M. Crane ($2.5 million in 1979), and scores of conservative congressmen and challengers.

The 46-year-old Viguerie was born in Golden Acres, Texas, attended Texas A&I College, worked in Sen. John Tower's first campaign, and became the first executive secretary of the Young Americans for Freedom. In 1965 he founded the Richard A. Viguerie Co., Inc., which grew to include a publishing house for conservative books as well as the direct mail operation.

Operating from offices in the Washington suburb of Falls Church, Va., the interlocking companies and committees that made up the Viguerie empire became the ideological spearhead of the so-called New Right. Through the use of computers, Viguerie refined the technique of political direct mail. His machines could print two letters per second and make each look as though it had been personally written. Viguerie also perfected the art of composing the direct mail pitch so that it recruited the contributor as well as convincing him to part with his money.

Viguerie began the 1980 campaign with Illinois' U.S. Representative Crane as his presidential client-candidate, but there was a falling-out in the summer of 1979 over ideology and strategy. Despite the $2.5 million Viguerie raised for Crane, the campaign was heavily in debt. At year's end, Viguerie reportedly was favouring John Connally, though he was not an official part of the Connally campaign. (HAL BRUNO)

Viljoen, Marais

There was a touch of irony involved when Marais Viljoen became the fifth state president of the Republic of South Africa. As minister of labour (1966–75) he had firmly supported the industrial colour bar, job reservation (of certain positions for whites), and the denial of recognized trade union rights for black workers. When he was elected head of state on June 19, 1979, after the resignation of B. J. Vorster, the government of P. W. Botha was busy reversing those policies.

In 1976, at the end of a career that had begun with his appointment as a National Party organizer in Natal in 1943, he was elected president of the Senate. In that capacity he was called upon to act as state president on several occasions. His choice as Vorster's successor was seen not merely as a formality in exceptional circumstances but as a recognition of his services in an unusually wide range of administrative and executive posts. Between his first appointment in 1958 as deputy minister (and subsequently minister) of labour and his presidency, Viljoen served, either as deputy minister or as minister, in the Departments of Mines, Coloured Affairs, Immigration, Education, the Interior, and Posts and Telecommunications.

In the last-named portfolio he returned, in a sense, to his beginnings. He was born on a farm in the Cape on Dec. 2, 1915, and orphaned at the age of four. Forced to leave school before matriculation (which he obtained later by private study), he joined the Post Office as a learner telegraphist at the age of 18. In 1937 he moved on to journalism as a reporter on a newly founded Afrikaans newspaper edited by future prime minister H. F. Verwoerd, who in time would give him his first Cabinet post.

Years of service as an efficient party organizer led to his election as a member of the Transvaal provincial council in 1949 and to a seat in Parliament four years later. Having been a dedicated party politician for most of his life, he saw himself, on his election as state president, in a new role as "the representative and symbol of national unity for all population groups." (LOUIS HOTZ)

Volcker, Paul

In November 1978 the president of the New York Federal Reserve Bank, Paul Volcker, delivered a speech at Warwick University in Coventry, England. In the speech he said: "The United States no longer stands astride the world as a kind of economic colossus. . . . There has been a sense of drift, of a lack of control or direction in the monetary system, infecting and reinforcing other sources of economic instability."

Eight months after Volcker spoke those words he was given an opportunity to do something about "the lack of control or direction" of which he had complained. The opportunity came in July, when U.S. Pres. Jimmy Carter undertook a wholesale reorganization of his Cabinet. Having nominated then-Federal Reserve Board Chairman G. William Miller to succeed the ousted W. Michael Blumenthal as secretary of the treasury, Carter turned to Volcker to take over Miller's job.

Although he had not been Carter's first choice, Volcker clearly had the experience for the job. A Democrat, he had been deputy undersecretary of the treasury for monetary affairs in the administrations of John Kennedy and Lyndon Johnson and undersecretary under Richard Nixon. In the latter position he twice handled negotiations to devalue the dollar.

Just how strong Volcker's influence in his new job would be was not apparent until October. With inflation soaring at an annual rate of 13.1% in the U.S., Volcker pushed the Federal Reserve Board to take action. A sharp 1% increase in the Fed's discount rate (the interest charged to commercial banks) was announced, along with a new requirement that 8% of the money U.S. banks receive from foreign sources for relending at home—so-called Eurodollars—be held out of the loan market. Furthermore, the announcement said that the Fed, instead of concerning itself with the manipulation of interest rates, henceforth would deal with inflation by adjusting the actual supply of dollars.

Born Sept. 5, 1927, in Cape May, N.J., Volcker was graduated from Princeton University and received a master's degree from Harvard. Apart from his service with the

UPI

MONDADORI/PICTORIAL PARADE

Simon Wiesenthal

government he worked from 1957 to 1961 as an economist with the Chase Manhattan Bank in New York City.

(STANLEY W. CLOUD)

Wiesenthal, Simon

Inasmuch as Nazi criminals are to be pursued to the ends of the Earth, outstanding service has been rendered by Simon Wiesenthal, who helped to track down over a thousand of them. He took up the task soon after he emerged in 1945 from Mauthausen, the last of various camps in which he was held after the Germans seized him in 1941. Then aged 32, the son of a Jewish sugar merchant in Buczacz, Polish Galicia, he had only just graduated as an architectural engineer at Lvov Technical College. His survival, like that of his self-effacing wife Cela, was due to some Germans whose humanity he later acknowledged and rewarded.

Early in 1947 Wiesenthal set up, in Linz, Austria, a Jewish Documentation Centre to collect first-hand evidence of Nazi crimes. After an interval with the local UN refugee organization, he revived the documentation work in 1961 (the year Adolf Eichmann was put on trial) under the direction of the Jewish community in Vienna. Three years later he set up an Association of Jewish Victims of Nazi Persecution.

Financial support was found in various countries. A Wiesenthal Fund was launched in The Netherlands in 1965 and another in the U.S. in 1967. German restitution money also helped, as did the royalties of his several books. These included *I Hunted Eichmann*; an edited volume on the West German statute of limitation (*Verjährung? Nein!*); *The Murderers Among Us*; an international symposium on Nazi guilt and Jewish forgiveness, *The Sunflower*; and *Der Fall Javorska*, on the cooperation between the Gestapo and the Soviet secret service. The last-named was perhaps a reflection of his disappointment over the Eastern bloc's refusal to supply documentary evidence of Nazi crimes.

The uncompromising search for Nazi records led him to denounce a member of the Austrian government, Friedrich Peter, who was, however, shielded by Chancellor Bruno Kreisky—himself a Jew. Threats of legal action by both sides were withdrawn, but Wiesenthal decided to close his office. The larger aspect of his work was taken over by a new Simon Wiesenthal Center for Holocaust Studies in Los Angeles, Calif. He himself devoted more of his attention to the worldwide network of neo-Nazi propaganda and to the fate of political prisoners in the Soviet Union. Variously described as a Jewish James Bond or a Jewish Don Quixote, Wiesenthal probably would not object to either description. (CAESAR C. ARONSFELD)

Williams, Robin

Self-described son of a "crazy Southern belle" and an elderly, "very elegant" Ford Motor Co. vice-president whom he called "sir," Robin Williams grew up to be an alien: television's Mork from the planet Ork in the popular series "Mork and Mindy." According to a magazine account, "His two half brothers were already grown when he was born, and Robin spent hours alone in the family's immense house, tape-recording television routines of comics and sneaking up to the attic to practice his imitations."

Born in Chicago in July 1952, Williams spent his early years in a posh suburb of Detroit. His family later moved to equally posh Marin County, Calif., where "everyone was on acid and they had gestalt history classes." Disregarding his father's advice to learn a useful trade like welding, Williams tried college twice. Then he won a scholarship to New York's Juilliard School, studied acting with John Houseman and did mime in whiteface on the steps of the Metropolitan Museum of Art for loose change.

Returning to California, he met his future wife, Valerie Velardi, a modern dancer who organized his routines and pushed him around the Los Angeles improvisational circuit. He auditioned for a guest spot as a stranger from outer space in the TV situation comedy "Happy Days." The director recalls asking "if he could sit a little differently, the way an alien might. Immediately he sat on his head." Fan mail flooded the ABC network after his one-shot appearance, and "Mork and Mindy" was launched. TV's most popular series in 1978–79, it was watched by 60 million people each week.

At 26, Williams found himself earning $30,000 an episode and driving the show's writers crazy by disregarding their scripts to improvise on camera. "The pressures on TV writers are so great that they'll do the silliest things over and over. My job is to fight that voodoo repetition," he said.

A vegetarian and nonsmoker, Williams kept his wits sharp by doing stand-up nightclub comedy. Among his characters were blues singer Benign Neglect and Grandpa Funk, who reminisces, "I used to play an alien. Of course that was before the real aliens landed . . . and it wasn't so funny anymore." His future plans included playing the lead in Jules Feiffer's movie version of *Popeye*. (PHILIP KOPPER)

Young, Andrew Jackson, Jr.

A secret meeting between Andrew Young, the U.S. ambassador to the UN, and a representative of the Palestine Liberation Organization (PLO) in the summer of 1979 touched off a controversy that led to Young's resignation and a bitter dialogue between American blacks and Jews. The incident was the latest in a series of diplomatic missteps and misstatements that had marked Young's performance in the UN. Pres. Jimmy Carter was personally saddened by the events and had words of praise for Young, even as he accepted his resignation.

Andrew Jackson Young, Jr., was born in New Orleans, La., on March 12, 1932, attended undergraduate school at Washington's Howard University, and became a minister in the United Church of Christ after earning a divinity degree from Hartford Theological Seminary. He was a key aide to the Rev. Martin Luther King, Jr., during the civil rights movement of the 1960s and in 1972 became the first black elected to Congress from an Atlanta district. He was reelected to two more terms before being appointed UN ambassador by President Carter in 1977.

From the start, many in Washington believed that Young—who had been an effective and respected congressman—was miscast in the UN role. He periodically made undiplomatic statements, and on a trip through Africa managed to antagonize Great Britain, Sweden, and even the Soviet Union with charges of racism. Nevertheless, he seemed to have the strong support of President Carter, who frequently praised his work in strengthening U.S. ties to the third world. However, the president had to ask for his resignation when it was revealed that Young, contrary to U.S. policy to have no dealings with the PLO, had met secretly with its representative at the UN to discuss a forthcoming debate on Palestine.

Young's resignation prompted an immediate outcry from black leaders, especially the clergy, who charged that Carter had fired Young under pressure from American-Jewish leaders. Black clergymen, led by the Rev. Jesse Jackson of Chicago and Delegate Walter Fauntroy (Dem., D.C.), visited the Middle East, met with PLO leader Yasir Arafat, and returned to call for U.S. recognition of the PLO and for Israel to negotiate with the Palestinians. At the same time, other black leaders denounced these overtures to the PLO and attempted to heal the split between black and Jewish groups, traditional allies in the civil rights movement. Young's personal popularity in the third world was evident when the African and Asian countries voted to put off the UN debate, which the U.S. had been trying to avoid, as a tribute to him. (HAL BRUNO)

"Prizes are occasionally notable for the changes they reflect in the intellectual consensus," an editorial in the *Washington Post* began in the fall of 1979. "This year the Nobel Peace Prize and the awards in economics suggest a pattern. Currently the great public concerns in Europe, as in this country, are inflation, Middle Eastern instability and the steady accumulation of nuclear armories. But the Nobel prizes direct attention to other parts of the world and the concerns of daily life, and death."

The Prize for Peace was awarded to Mother Teresa, a Roman Catholic nun of Albanian extraction who has spent her life comforting India's destitute and dying. Not a politician, diplomat, or statesman, she is nothing more nor less than the humble and inspiring personification of selfless charity. The Prize for Economics was shared by two practical academics whose careers have centred on "human capital" (rather than monetary values) and on the importance of agriculture as a base for national economic development.

In the sciences the prizes also seemed to reward practicality instead of esoteric theory. Allan Cormack of Tufts University shared the Prize for Physiology or Medicine with British electronics innovator Godfrey Hounsfield. Working independently, the two men developed the computerized axial tomography (CAT) scanner, a device that greatly improved the ability of physicians to diagnose disorders of the brain and other organs. Herbert Brown of Purdue University and Georg Wittig of the University of Heidelberg received the Prize for Chemistry for developing boron and phosphorus compounds as organic synthesizers. Their work opened seemingly endless possibilities for compounding synthetic drugs and industrial chemicals. Only the Prize for Physics recognized purely theoretical work. It was shared by two Harvard University scientists, Sheldon Glashow and Steven Weinberg, and by Abdus Salam, who became the first Pakistani to win a Nobel award.

The Prize for Literature, awarded to Odysseus Elytis, a poet of wide popularity in his native Greece, also seemed to celebrate a kind of humane fundamentalism rather than the esoteric. In 1979 the honorarium accompanying each prize was approximately $190,000.

Prize for Peace

Mother Teresa has been called "a living saint" and "the saint of the gutters." For 30 years she has cared for the "poorest of the poor" in Calcutta's infamous slums, perhaps the most squalid in the world. She has routinely saved abandoned infants from garbage dumps, tended lepers, and sheltered the dying. Her mission has not been to perform social work or to assure her own presumed salvation. Rather, she has said, "These people are the body of Christ." In comforting and cleansing the destitute "actually we are touching His body."

A perennial candidate for the Peace Prize since her fame began to spread 20 years ago, Mother Teresa was born Agnes Gonxha Bojaxhiu on Aug. 27, 1910, in Skopje, then within the Ottoman Empire. The child of Albanian shopkeepers, she lived in reasonable comfort but found inspiration in stories of Yugoslav missionaries to India. As a teenager she joined an Irish order of nuns, the Sisters of Loretto, and embarked for Calcutta. For 20 years she taught wealthy girls at St. Mary's High School, a cloistered school within sight of one of the city's worst slums. Then, while riding a night train for Darjeeling, she heard "a call within a call," as it has been described. "The message was clear. I was to leave the convent and help the poor while living among them."

WEREK/KATHERINE YOUNG

Mother Teresa

Changing her habit for the white sari of India's poor, she began going barefoot about the city's poorest precincts. In 1948 she was authorized to establish a new sisterhood, the Missionaries of Charity, under the jurisdiction of the archbishop of Calcutta. One requirement was that she find disciples and support for her work. Declining regular government funds, she decided rather to rely on small cash donations and gifts in kind and to "depend on divine providence."

The city gave her the use of a decrepit inn near the temple of the Hindu goddess of death; 12 other nuns soon joined her ministry there. She once ministered to a dying man who turned out to be a Hindu priest. "For 30 years I have served the Goddess Kali in her temple. Now the goddess stands before me," he was reported to have said.

In 1965 her Missionaries of Charity were recognized as a pontifical congregation responsible only to the Vatican. By 1979 the order had nearly 200 branches in two dozen countries throughout the world. Besides the traditional vows of poverty, chastity, and obedience, sisters of the Missionaries of Charity also promise to welcome "free service to the poor."

Prize for Economics

Neither Sir W. Arthur Lewis nor Theodore W. Schultz has made "a major breakthrough" in economic theory. Rather, the joint winners of the Economics Prize are widely regarded as creative and practical experts whose feet are firmly planted on the original source of economic wealth, agricultural ground. Their work has involved the importance of "human capital" in any economy and the role of agrarian vitality for all less developed nations.

"Both are deeply concerned about the need and poverty in the world and engaged in finding ways out of underdevelopment," said the Swedish Academy judges who selected the laureates. "Schultz and Lewis are ready to draw daring conclusions which can lead to recommendations of changed economic policy. . . . Their widespread and profound experience of developing-country economic policies and underlying political systems makes their presentations of developing-country problems vivid and sincere."

Born on a farm near Arlington, S.D., on April 30, 1902, Schultz earned degrees at South Dakota State College and the University of Wisconsin and then taught agricultural economics at Iowa State. But he resigned in 1943 after a colleague's scholarly paper recommending margarine as a substitute for butter was censored because it might offend local dairy farmers. He then went to the University of Chicago; "Oleomargarine greased the skids that took him all the way to the Nobel Prize," said a colleague. He rose to chair Chicago's economics department in 1946 and accepted emeritus status in 1972.

During the U.S. occupation of West Germany after World War II, Schultz became intrigued with the speed of the vanquished nation's economic recovery. Physical assets and conventional "capital" had been destroyed, but "human capital" remained in abundance—talent, knowledge, energy, and the will to recover. Schultz devoted his efforts to studying this situation and became best known for defining how human resources influence overall economic development. His Nobel citation said he was the first to systematize "how investments in education can affect productivity in agriculture as well as the economy as a whole."

Sir Arthur Lewis was born Jan. 23, 1915, on St. Lucia, in the British West Indies. Moving to England as a teenage student, he earned a doctorate at the London School of Economics in 1940. On the occasion of his first appointment as a lecturer at the University of London he told colleagues "I'm the kind of person you guys like the least. I'm an educated native." A consultant as well as a scholar, he developed strong ties throughout the world's less developed nations. UN adviser to the prime minister of

BRIAN F. ALPERT—KEYSTONE

WILLIAM FRANKLIN MCMAHON

(Left) Sir W. Arthur Lewis, (right) Theodore Schultz

Ghana and a founder of the Caribbean Development Bank, he worked for a number of national governments. It was the failure of industrialization in India that confirmed his belief that successful industrialization depends on a solid agricultural base.

Author of the influential *The Theory of Economic Growth*, he became widely known for having developed the so-called Lewis Model. This tool describes how the transition from an agrarian to an industrialized economy depends more on a healthy, growing, and cheap work force than on conventional capital. Lewis was the first black to receive a Nobel award other than the Peace Prize.

Prize for Literature

Odysseus Elytis earned Nobel laurels "for his poetry, which, against the background of Greek tradition, depicts with sensuous strength and intellectual clearsightedness modern man's struggle for freedom and creativeness." In *To Axion Esti* ("Worthy It Is"), the Swedish Academy concluded, he had written "one of 20th-century literature's most concentrated and ritually faceted poems."

Born the scion of a prosperous Cretan family in 1911, he abandoned the family name Alepoudhelis to dissociate his work from the family soap business. The name he took, according to one explanation, combines elements of *Ellas* (Greek for Greece), *elpida* ("hope"), *eleftheria* ("freedom"), and *Eleni*, the mythological personification of beauty and sensuality.

Elytis studied law at Athens University and periodically worked in the family business. Intrigued by French surrealism, and particularly by the poet Paul Éluard, he began publishing verse in the 1930s, particularly in *Nea Ghrammata*. This avant-garde magazine was a prime vehicle for the "Generation of the '30s," an influential school that included George Seferis, who in 1963 became the first Greek Nobel laureate for literature. The group "shared an enthusiasm for contemporary French poetry as well as for sources in the rich Greek tradition," according to a U.S. translator, Edmund Keeley of Princeton University. "Elytis's first poems offered a surrealism that had a distinctly personal tone and a specific local habitation. The tone was lyrical, humorous, fanciful, everything that is young; the habitation was the landscape and climate of Greece, particularly the landscape of the Aegean islands."

When Nazi Germany overran Greece in 1941, Elytis joined the antifascist resistance to the Italians in Albania. He became something of a bard among young Greeks; one of his poems was regarded as a kind of anthem to freedom's cause: *Heroic and Elegiac Song for the Lost Second Lieutenant of the Albanian Campaign*. After the war he lapsed into silence, *To Axion Esti* not appearing until 1959. Reminiscent of Walt Whitman's *Song of Myself*, parts of it were set to music by Mikis Theodorakis, the composer famed for his musical scores for the films *Zorba the Greek* and *Z*. (PHILIP KOPPER)

Prize for Chemistry

Two of the elder statesmen of chemistry were honoured by being awarded equal shares of the Nobel Prize for 1979. Herbert Brown of the United States and Georg Wittig of West Germany, through decades of fruitful research, had established themselves as masters of their chosen specialties and influenced the course of the science of chemistry as a whole.

Brown, who was born in London in 1912, was taken to the United States by his parents in 1914 and attended the University of Chicago, receiving his doctorate there in 1938. Remaining at Chicago as an instructor until 1943, he then moved to Wayne State University in Detroit and finally, in 1947, to Purdue University at West Lafayette, Ind., where from 1959 he held the Wetherill research professorship (emeritus since 1978).

Brown's research activities were focused on two principal themes. One of these originated in his graduate work at the University of Chicago, when he investigated the preparation and reactions of inorganic compounds of hydrogen and boron and related compounds of hydrogen and aluminum. One of the outcomes of that research was the introduction of a new class of reducing agents that have become standard tools of the organic chemist. In later years work with the same substances led Brown to explore a group of organic compounds in which boron atoms are present. This field of research was specifically mentioned by the Nobel committee in citing him for the prize.

The second theme of Brown's research was the study of chemical reactions that take place in stages involving the appearance and disappearance of organic species that bear a positive electrical charge. The molecular structures and chemical behaviour of these so-called carbonium ions or carbo-cations was the subject of widespread and sometimes heated controversy during the 1950s and 1960s. Brown's active participation in that debate contributed to substantial advances toward one of the perennial goals of chemistry, the correlation of the molecular structure of compounds with the courses and rates of their reactions.

Wittig was born in Berlin in 1897 and as a young man displayed talents for both science and music. While retaining his love for the piano, he selected the career of the professional chemist and entered the University of Tübingen in 1916. His schooling was interrupted by military service during World War I, but he graduated from the University of Marburg in 1923 and received a doctorate there in 1926. He taught at Marburg until 1932; then, advancing through the academic ranks, he moved to the Technical College of Braunschweig and to the universities of Freiburg in 1937, Tübingen in 1944, and Heidelberg in 1956. At Heidelberg he became professor emeritus in 1965 but remained active in research.

Wittig's research interests complement those of Brown. Instead of studying compounds of boron, Wittig made his mark with compounds of phosphorus (like boron, an element uncommon in organic chemistry); instead of reactions involving positively charged intermediates, Wittig concentrated on those with negatively charged species, called carbanions. The Nobel committee picked out Wittig's achievement in employing phosphorus compounds in the synthesis of substances in which the molecules contain pairs of carbon atoms linked by the sharing of two pairs of electrons. Many compounds of this kind are difficult to prepare by other procedures, but Wittig's technique proved effective and economical; for example, a West German chemical manufacturer used it to produce vitamin A by the ton.

Prize for Physics

The Nobel Prize for Physics was shared equally by Sheldon Glashow, Steven Weinberg, and Abdus Salam for their complementary efforts in formulating a theory that encompasses both the electromagnetic interaction and the so-called weak interaction of elementary particles. Glashow and Weinberg, both 46 and both U.S. citizens, were in 1979 members of the faculty of Harvard University; Salam, a 53-year-old Pakistani, was a professor at the Imperial College of Science and Technology, London, and director of the International Centre for Theoretical Physics at Trieste, Italy.

The catalog of natural forces that govern the behaviour of minute bits of matter and energy underwent a revision during the 1970s. Since the 1930s physicists have recognized that particles can affect one another in four basic ways. Two of these have been known for centuries because their effects on ordinary objects are easily perceived: gravitation, which causes apples to fall from trees and determines the orbits of the planets, is one; electromagnetism, which explains the properties of light and the chemical behaviour of atoms, is the other. The other two became evident during the evolution of nuclear physics in the 20th century: one of them, called the strong force, operates to bind the constituents of atomic nuclei together despite the intense electric repulsion of the positively charged protons for each other; the other, the weak interaction, accounts for certain forms of radioactive decay and for reactions between the lightest of the elementary particles, electrons, neutrinos, and muons.

Gravitation has been understood since Isaac Newton's work in the 17th century. The relationship between electricity and magnetism, and their explanation as two aspects of the single phenomenon of electromagnetism, was the triumph of James Clerk Maxwell, who died in 1879, the year of the birth of Albert Einstein. Einstein, in turn, spent decades in attempts to show that the gravitational and electromagnetic interactions are manifestations of some even more fundamental influence. Though he made other great contributions to physics, this goal eluded him; indeed, during his life, the problem became more complex when the strong and weak interactions were discovered.

Physicists have persisted in their efforts to uncover some underlying general principle that would reconcile the four ways in which particles of matter affect one another. The mechanism of the mutual action of particles has been most fruitfully explored in terms of fields—the influences exerted by a particle on the surrounding space. It is considered that these fields, created by the presence of a particle, are the carriers of entities such as energy and momentum that may be transferred to another particle within range of the first. For example, an electrically charged particle sets up an electric field that is propagated through space in all directions; an uncharged particle in such a field does not respond to it, but a second charged particle will be attracted toward or repelled from the first particle with a force that depends on the magnitudes of the charges and the distance between the particles.

It has been found that the energy that the fields carry between particles is transferred only in discrete amounts called quanta, just as if the energy itself consisted of particles of a particular size. In some cases the behaviour of these field particles stretches the common meaning of the concept of a particle; for example, those called photons, the carriers of electromagnetism, have no mass, though they do possess angular momentum, or spin. Likewise, the field particle of the gravitational interaction—the yet undetected graviton—has no mass. Indeed, the absence of mass is directly connected with the infinite range of the electromagnetic and gravitational interactions. That is, gravity acts between all objects in the universe, no matter how far apart they are, and an electromagnetic wave, such as the light from even the most distant star, travels undiminished through space until it encounters some particle that can absorb it.

The strong and weak nuclear interactions are thought to operate in the same way—one particle affects a second by the exchange of a third particle (a field particle). The field particles of these interactions, called mesons, do have mass, however, and the range of these interactions is correspondingly very short: they are undetectable at distances greater than the dimensions of an atomic nucleus.

The achievement of the year's prizewinners was the selection, from among many possible theories, of one that not only explains the known facts of the electromagnetic and weak interactions, including their different ranges and otherwise discordant field particles, but also makes it possible to predict the outcome of new experiments in which elementary particles are made to impinge on one another. Physicists recently conducted several such experimental tests of the theory, using powerful accelerators, and the results agreed with the theory while discrediting alternative ones.

Glashow and Weinberg, both natives of New York City, were members of the same classes at the Bronx High School of Science there (1950) and at Cornell University in Ithaca, N.Y. (1954). Glashow went on to Harvard, receiving his Ph.D. in 1959, and then worked briefly at the Nordic Institute for Theoretical Atomic Physics in Copenhagen, the California Institute of Technology, and Stanford University. He joined the faculty of the University of California at Berkeley in 1961 and moved to Harvard in 1967.

Weinberg went from Cornell to the institute at Copenhagen for a year and then obtained his doctorate at Princeton University in 1957. He conducted research at Columbia University and at the Lawrence Berkeley Laboratory before joining the faculty of the University of California at Berkeley in 1960. During part of his last two years there, 1968–69, he was visiting professor at the Massachusetts Institute of Technology; he joined its faculty in 1969 and moved to Harvard in 1973.

Salam was born in Jhang Maghiana, now in Pakistan, and attended the Government College at Lahore. In 1952 he received his Ph.D. in mathematics and physics from the University of Cambridge, England. He returned to the Government College as professor of mathematics, 1951–54, and then went back to Cambridge as a lecturer in mathematics. He became professor of theoretical physics at the Imperial College in 1957 and the director of the institute in Trieste when it was established in 1964.

Prize for Physiology or Medicine

Allan Cormack of the United States and Godfrey Hounsfield of the U.K. shared the Nobel Prize for 1979 for the development of the computerized axial tomography (CAT) scanner, a device that produces a detailed X-ray picture of a selected section of the human body.

A conventional X-ray plate is a two-dimensional representation of a three-dimensional object, made by directing a beam of X-radiation through the object. The parts of the beam not absorbed by the object strike a sensitized plate, which is developed like a photograph to produce an image adequate for locating a fracture in a bone, especially in a flat, thin target like the hand, because it is only necessary to distinguish bone from soft tissues. A single X-ray view, however, does not solve more difficult problems, such as finding a tumour or a blood clot in the brain, a thick target composed of tissues that do not differ much in transparency to X-rays. More information can be received by taking X-rays from several directions, but often the results are vague, and efforts to improve the contrast in the plates, by injecting air or dyes, can be painful and dangerous.

In the CAT scanner electronic detectors replace the photographic plate, and the X-ray source delivers numerous short pulses of radiation as it and the detectors are rotated about an imaginary axis through, for example, the patient's head. The plane described as the X-ray beam swings around corresponds to a slice through the cranium, and the detector responses are fed to a computer that analyzes the whole set of data to produce a sharp map of that particular cross section. The process can be repeated to image as many slices as are necessary to locate a trouble spot.

Though the high price of the scanner makes it expensive to use, the technique is fast, accurate, and painless; since its introduction in 1973 it has greatly increased the reliability of the diagnosis of disorders of the brain and other organs.

Cormack was born in Johannesburg, South Africa, in 1924. Intending to become an astronomer, he studied physics and engineering at the University of Cape Town, which granted him bachelor's and master's degrees in 1944 and 1945. He then went to Cambridge University for two more years of study. Returning to Cape Town, he took a position as medical physicist at the Groote Schuur Hospital, where in 1956 he was struck by the inadequacy of conventional X-ray techniques in producing useful images of the brain. Later that year Cormack went to Harvard as a research fellow, and in 1957 he joined the physics faculty of Tufts University in Medford, Mass. He became a naturalized U.S. citizen in 1966.

During his first few years at Tufts, Cormack studied the problem of increasing the usefulness of X-rays for diagnosis and therapy, and in 1963 and 1964 he published a mathematical analysis of the process of absorption of the rays as they pass through layers of tissues that differ in density. He showed that details of a flat section could be calculated from measurements of the attenuation of X-ray beams passing through it from many different angles.

Hounsfield, born in 1919, grew up on his father's farm in Nottinghamshire, England. His tinkering with machinery eventually narrowed to electronics, and as a teenager he became skilled at building radio sets. After he enlisted in the Royal Air Force in 1939 he became proficient with radar and served part of his enlistment as a lecturer on that topic. After the war he attended the Faraday House Electrical Engineering College in London, graduating in 1951. He then joined EMI, Ltd., a conglomerate of more than 80 electronics, music, and entertainment companies. Moving from radar research to computer design, Hounsfield extended the capability of a computer so that it could interpret X-ray signals so as to form a two-dimensional image of a complex object such as the human head.

Hounsfield pursued the application of axial tomography to medical diagnosis, building a prototype head scanner and then a body scanner at EMI. When computers had evolved to the stage needed for processing the signals at the same rate they were obtained, the device was introduced commercially. (JOHN V. KILLHEFFER)

OBITUARIES

The following is a selected list of prominent men and women who died during 1979.

Acheampong, Ignatius Kutu, Ghanaian Army officer (b. Sept, 23, 1931, Kumasi, Gold Coast [now Ghana]—d. June 16, 1979, Accra, Ghana), was head of state of Ghana after overthrowing Kofi Busia's civilian government on Jan. 13, 1972. Acheampong was forced by army officers led by Lieut. Gen. Fred W. K. Akuffo (*q.v.*) to resign on July 5, 1978. After teaching at a commercial college, he was an officer cadet at Aldershot, England, and later at the General Staff College, Ft. Leavenworth, Kansas. Acheampong commanded a battalion (1969) and an infantry brigade (1971) as a lieutenant colonel in Ghana's army and was made a general in 1976. As head of state he suppressed political parties and the constitution, and under his weak and corrupting leadership Ghana reached near bankruptcy. His late attempt to promote a "union government" of military and civilians was discredited. Acheampong was executed by firing squad after a period of house arrest.

Ager, Milton, U.S. composer (b. Oct. 6, 1893, Chicago, Ill.—d. May 6, 1979, Inglewood, Calif.), produced hundreds of songs for motion pictures and the Broadway stage, including such all-time favourites as "Ain't She Sweet," composed for his daughter Shana Alexander, and "Happy Days Are Here Again," which became the theme song of Franklin D. Roosevelt's presidential campaigns and thereafter the trademark of every Democratic Party convention. In 1913 Ager left Chicago for New York, where he arranged and plugged the songs of Irving Berlin and George M. Cohan. Ager's first notable success came in 1918 when he and George W. Meyer composed "Everything Is Peaches Down in Georgia"; Al Jolson made it a hit. After World War I and the formation of the Ager, Yellen and Bornstein music publishing company, Ager continued to delight music lovers with such songs as "I Wonder What's Become of Sally" and "Could I? I Certainly Could." Other successes included the stage musicals *Rain or Shine* (1928) and *John Murray Anderson's Almanac* (1929), as well as such motion pictures as *Honky Tonk* with Sophie Tucker singing "I'm the Last of the Red Hot Mamas."

Akuffo, Fred W. K., Ghanaian Army officer (b. March 21, 1937, Akropong, Gold Coast [now Ghana]—d. June 26, 1979, Accra, Ghana), became Ghana's head of state after he led a coup that overthrew Gen. Ignatius Acheampong (*q.v.*) on July 5, 1978. Akuffo was ousted on June 4, 1979, in a coup led by Flight Lieut. Jerry Rawlings (*see* BIOGRAPHIES) and was later executed. A professional soldier who attended Britain's Sandhurst Royal Military Academy, he was also trained as a paratrooper and soon promoted. He served with the UN peacekeeping force in the Congo and commanded Ghana's parachute battalion. In 1973 he attended the National Defense College in India. A member of the ruling Supreme Military Council from 1975, he became chief of defense staff in 1976.

Allan of Kilmahew, Robert Alexander Allan, BARON, British politician and company chairman (b. July 11, 1914, Cardross, Dunbartonshire, Scotland —d. April 5, 1979, Sydney, New South Wales, Australia), was a Conservative member of Parliament for South Paddington (1951–66), party treasurer (1960–65), chairman of the party's central finance board (1961–66), and parliamentary private secretary to Prime Ministers Sir Anthony Eden and Harold Macmillan (1955–58). He was also parliamentary and financial secretary to the Admiralty (1958–59) and parliamentary under-secretary at the Foreign Office (1959–60). A naval officer with a distinguished career during World War II, he was deputy chief of naval intelligence, Washington, D.C. (1945–46). Lord Allan's business interests were mainly in publishing. He was chairman of Ladybird Books, and as a director and deputy chairman of Pearson Longman Ltd. he actively fostered the group's worldwide educational publishing activities. He was also a director of the *Financial Times* (1963–75) and a governor of the British Broadcasting Corporation (1971–76). He was created a life peer in 1973.

Amin, Hafizullah: *see* Hafizullah Amin.

Ardizzone, Edward Jeffrey Irving, British artist (b. Oct. 16, 1900, Haiphong, Indochina—d. Nov. 8, 1979, Rodmersham Green, Kent, England), skillfully carried on the tradition of English graphic art and book illustration. Unlike his 19th-century predecessors, however, he did most of his work for children's books and softened the robust satire of earlier graphic artists to produce a gentler effect of sweetness and slightly nostalgic charm. Ardizzone illustrated more than 170 books, including several he wrote himself, such as the "Little Tim" series, one of which, *Tim All Alone* (1956), won the first Kate Greenaway medal. At the age of 26, he left an office job to become a professional artist. By 1940 Ardizzone was well known as a watercolour painter and spent the next four years in Europe and North Africa as an official war artist; a collection of his works, portraying both the excitement and boredom of war, is in the Imperial War Museum, London. He was elected to the Royal Academy in 1970 and became a CBE in 1971. His autobiographical *The Young Ardizzone* appeared in 1970 and *Diary of a War Artist* in 1974.

Athenagoras, Theodoritos (THEODOROS G. KOKKINAKIS), Greek Orthodox prelate (b. 1912, Patmos, Dodecanese, Greece—d. Sept. 9, 1979, London, England), was (1964–79) head of the Greek Orthodox Church in Britain, under the title of metropolitan of Thyateira and Great Britain. Serving in this capacity he became Apokrisarios, or personal representative, from the ecumenical patriarchate of Constantinople to the archbishop of Canterbury. After training in theological seminaries, he was ordained a priest in 1940 and served in the U.S. After teaching at Pomfret (Conn.) School, he was dean and then president of Holy Cross Theological School, Brookline, Mass. During 1960–63 he was metropolitan bishop of Canada. On Dec. 29, 1963, he called on Pope Paul VI at the Vatican. This was the first official meeting between the Vatican and the ecumenical patriarchate in almost 500 years. He also represented the ecumenical patriarchate of Constantinople at World Council of Churches conferences.

Aylmer, Sir Felix, British actor (b. Feb. 21, 1889, Corsham, Wiltshire, England—d. Sept. 2, 1979, Sussex, England), portrayed upper-class characters on stage and film with unusual insight and dignity and worked untiringly to establish Equity, the British actors' union, of which he was president from 1949 to 1969. Aylmer had studied under Beerbohm Tree, Fred Terry, and Seymour Hicks, with whom he first appeared at the Coliseum in London in 1911. After naval service in World War I, he appeared in London's West End from the 1920s onward (*R. E. Lee, The Nelson Touch, The Voysey Inheritance, The Flashing Stream,* and *The Chalk Garden*), in such films as *Quo Vadis, St. Joan,* and *Separate Tables,* and in many television dramatizations until the mid-1970s. He was knighted in 1965.

Balashova, Alexandra, Russian ballet dancer (b. May 3, 1887, Russia—d. Jan. 5, 1979, Chelles, France), was one of the last surviving stars of the prerevolutionary Russian Imperial Ballet. She was less well known than most of her contemporaries among the prima ballerinas of Tsarist Russia, but her interpretation of *La fille mal gardée* was memorable for its charm and Balashova's youthful beauty. She married shortly before the Revolution and in 1922 fled with her husband to Paris, where she performed with Viktor Smoltsov at the Théâtre Fémina. From 1928 to 1972 she taught ballet, and she was for many years a prominent member of Russian émigré society.

Bandon, Percy Ronald Gardner Bernard, 5TH EARL, Irish peer and Royal Air Force officer (b. Aug. 30, 1904—d. Feb. 8, 1979, Cork, Ireland), rose in the Royal Air Force to become air chief marshal. Bandon's daring flying, practical joking, and dynamic leadership earned him an enviable reputation as "Paddy, the Abandoned Earl." After graduating (1938) from the RAF College, he commanded flying units and stations in World War II. He later served as commander in chief (1957–60) of the Far East Air Force and commander (1961–63) of the Allied Air Forces for Central Europe. He also organized the spectacular massed formation fly-bys after Queen Elizabeth II's coronation in June 1953.

Baroody, Jamil Murad, Lebanese-born diplomat (b. Aug. 8, 1905, Suq al Gharb, Lebanon—d. March 4, 1979, New York, N.Y.), was the garrulous Saudi Arabian ambassador to the UN and dean of delegates to that body's world organization. Baroody, who joined the Saudi delegation to the UN at its first meeting (1945) in San Francisco, became notorious for his verbal attacks on Zionism and for his defense of Saudi Arabia's conservatism. On more than one occasion Baroody became involved in physical encounters with fellow delegates but was given free reign by the foreign minister, Prince Saud al-Faisal, to deliver bombastic speeches without prior approval from the Foreign Ministry. During some of his more colourful orations, Baroody quoted Jesus, Robert F. Kennedy, and Mussolini and made references to miniskirts, hot dogs, and bathtubs.

Barr, John Andrew, U.S. business executive and lawyer (b. Sept. 10, 1908, Akron, Ind.—d. Jan. 16, 1979, Evanston, Ill.), became chairman (1955) of Montgomery Ward & Co., inheriting the shaky corporation's reins from Sewell Avery, a conservative autocrat. Within one year under Barr's leadership, the company opened 141 catalog stores, projected the opening of 100 others, and made plans for new retail units. Although expansion initially reduced company profits because of high operating costs, sales and profits both increased by 1962. In 1964 Barr resigned from Montgomery Ward to become dean of the Graduate School of Business at Northwestern University in Illinois. Under Barr's tutelage the school phased out undergraduate studies, expanded minority student enrollment, and established an advisory council of corporate chief executive officers to counsel and guide the school's programs. He retired from the university in 1975.

Barzani, Mulla Mustafa al-, Kurdish nationalist leader (b. *c.* 1902, Sulaymaniyah, Kirkuk Province, Iraq—d. March 2, 1979, Washington, D.C.), strove for half a century to create an independent Kurdistan for the 12 million Kurds living on the borders of Iran, Iraq, the U.S.S.R., and Turkey. The son of a landlord in northern Mesopotamia, Barzani succeeded his elder brother, Sheikh Ahmed, who led the Kurdish national struggle from World War I until the late 1930s. Barzani headed the Kurdish Democratic Party (KDP) formed in 1945 and in 1946 emerged as president of the short-lived Kurdish Mahabad Republic established with Soviet aid in northwestern Iran. After the Soviet forces withdrew, the republic collapsed, and Barzani took refuge in Soviet Azerbaijan, where he remained until he was allowed to return to Iraq by Abd al-Karim Kassem's regime. Kassem's proposal for an autonomous Kurdish area in northern Iraq was judged unsatisfactory by Barzani, and in 1960 he escaped to the mountains and started a guerrilla war against the Iraqi forces. After ten years of intermittent fighting, a 15-point cease-fire agreement was concluded on March 11, 1970, between Barzani and Pres. Ahmad Hassan al-Bakr of Iraq. A general amnesty for the insurgent Kurds was proclaimed, but it was not until March 11, 1974, that a law defining the Kurdish autonomous region was promulgated. Barzani found this unacceptable and ordered his Pesh Merga ("forward to death") forces to resume fighting. This time, however, Barzani had considerable support from Iran. When Iraq renounced its territorial claims against Iran on March 6, 1975, the shah stopped all military aid to the Kurds. Barzani took up residence in Teheran but requested political asylum in the U.S. Four years later he died of a heart attack in a Washington hospital, where he was receiving treatment for lung cancer.

Beaumarchais, Jacques Delarüe Caron de, French diplomat (b. April 16, 1913, Bayonne, France—d. Nov. 11, 1979, Paris, France), played a major role in the negotiations for British entry into the European Economic Community and served as ambassador to the Court of St. James's from 1972 to 1977. A graduate of the École des Sciences Politiques, he escaped from France to join the Free French in Algiers in 1943. Beaumarchais later was on the staff of the future foreign minister, Maurice Couve de Murville. During the 1960s Beaumarchais was head of the European Department in the French Foreign Ministry, then served as director for political affairs until his ambassadorial appointment in 1972. His period in London came at a favourable time after earlier difficulties in Anglo-French relations, and he made the French embassy a brilliant social and cultural centre.

Beckinsale, Richard, British actor (b. July 6, 1947, Nottingham, England—d. March 19, 1979, Sunningdale, England), was widely known to British television viewers as the young prison inmate Godber in BBC's prison-life comedy series "Porridge," starring Ronnie Barker. He also appeared in its sequel, "Going Straight," with Barker. Beckinsale was co-star in Yorkshire Television's "Rising Damp" series and was also a successful stage actor in such London West End plays as *Funny Peculiar* and *I Love My Wife.*

Belmont, Eleanor Robson, British-born actress and patron of the arts (b. Dec. 13, 1879, Wigan, Lancashire, England—d. Oct. 24, 1979, New York, N.Y.), charmed the theatre world with her moving performances and later became an ardent and energetic crusader for worthy causes. Before her marriage (1910) to millionaire August Belmont, a banker, owner of the Belmont racing stables, and founder of the Rapid Transit Subway Construction Co. in New York, she enjoyed rave reviews for her roles in *Arizona, Merely Mary Ann,* and her last performance in *The Dawn of Tomorrow,* which moved the audience to tears. She was besieged with letters from playwright George Bernard Shaw who confessed his admiration for her and later wrote the play *Major Barbara* specifically for her. In 1917 Belmont became actively involved in the Red Cross and crossed the Atlantic Ocean several times during World War I despite the danger of German U-boats; she was a member of the organization's central planning committee for more than 25 years. Belmont was especially relentless in her drive to keep the Metropolitan Opera alive. When she learned that the opera's old gold curtain was being sold for $100, she ingeniously had it made into eyeglass cases and bookmarks which brought $11,000 in revenue to the opera. Belmont, who was credited with the survival of the Met, was in 1933 the first woman to become a member of its board of directors. In later years she devoted herself to scores of needy causes; she died some two months short of her 100th birthday.

Beltrán, Pedro Gerado, Peruvian politician (b. Feb. 17, 1897, Lima, Peru—d. Feb. 16, 1979, Lima), was a conservative economist who became (1959) prime minister and minister of finance when the Peruvian economy was edging toward disaster. With the country's inflation rate at 11%, Beltrán, the longtime owner (1934–74) and publisher of the independent and influential Lima newspaper *La Prensa,* was appointed by Pres. Manuel Prado Ugarteche in a desperate move to rebuild the economy. During his two years as prime minister, Beltrán repaid Peru's debt of $14.5 million to the International Monetary Fund, cut inflation to 3%, and instituted a "free-exchange basis," which strengthened the country's foreign reserves and its balance of trade. Beltrán gained (1915–18) his expertise in finance at the London School of Economics and, after twice serving as president of Peru's Central Reserve Bank, he was (1944–46) ambassador to the U.S. Beltrán resigned from government service in 1961 after an unsuccessful bid for the presidency. He then returned to editing *La Prensa,* but the newspaper was expropriated (1974) by military troops supporting Pres. Juan Velasco Alvarado.

Bernac, Pierre (PIERRE BERTIN), French singer (b. Jan. 12, 1899, Paris, France—d. Oct. 17, 1979, Villeneuve-lès-Avignon, France), was a baritone best known as the interpreter of works by his composer-pianist friend Francis Poulenc. Their collaboration, which lasted 25 years, led Poulenc to compose many songs specifically for Bernac's voice, which had a wide range. In 1977 Bernac published *Poulenc et ses mélodies,* an invaluable guide to the composer's method. He also performed works by André Jolivet, Sanguet, Paul Hindemith, Lennox Berkely, and Samuel Barber. After 1945, he concentrated on teaching at the American Conservatory, Fontainebleau. Bernac gave up public performances in 1960.

Bhutto, Zulfikar Ali, Pakistani politician (b. Jan. 5, 1928, Larkana, Sind—d. April 4, 1979, Rawalpindi, Pak.), became president of Pakistan in December 1971 following the brief war with India that resulted in the secession of East Pakistan as independent Bangladesh. The son of a rich Sindhi landlord, he was educated at the universities of California and Oxford and became a barrister at the Middle Temple, London. In 1958 he entered Field Marshal Muhammad Ayub Khan's Cabinet as minister of commerce. As foreign minister (1963–66) he was instrumental in establishing close relations with China. Disillusioned with the military regime, he left the government in 1966 to form his own Pakistan People's Party (PPP), which he led in 1970 to a sweeping electoral victory in West Pakistan. After succeeding Lieut. Gen. Agha Muhammad Yahya Khan as president in late 1971, Bhutto introduced a new constitution with Islamic characteristics, while retaining martial law and, in effect, ruling by decree. From August 1973, when the new constitution took effect, he was prime minister. Sensing that the public was beginning to turn against him, Bhutto declared in March 1977 that he would "seek a new mandate from the people" by holding elections. He was opposed by the Pakistan National Alliance (PNA), an amalgam of nine separate groups. When it was announced that the PPP had captured all but 45 seats in the National Assembly, the PNA protested against "vote rigging" and demanded new elections. On July 5, 1977, Gen. Mohammad Zia-ul-Haq, the army chief of staff, seized power from Bhutto in a bloodless coup. Soon afterward Bhutto was arrested and on March 18, 1978, was sentenced to death for political murder by the Lahore High Court. Bhutto filed an appeal with the Supreme Court, which upheld the Lahore verdict. Proclaiming himself innocent, Bhutto declined to ask for clemency. He was hanged on April 4.

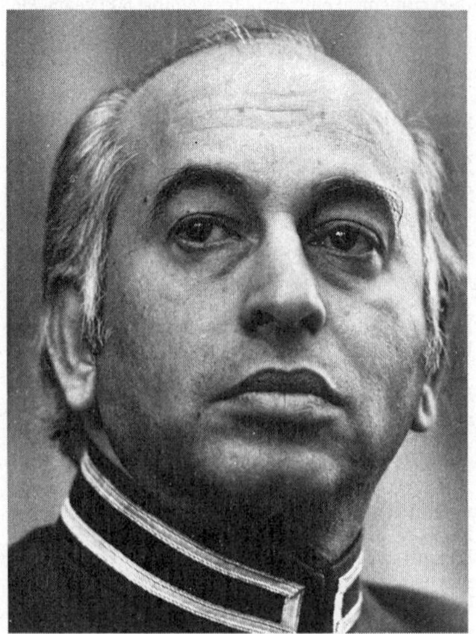

SVEN SIMON/KATHERINE YOUNG

Bishop, Elizabeth, U.S. poet (b. Feb. 8, 1911, Worcester, Mass.—d. Oct. 6, 1979, Boston, Mass.), was the author of a slim yet formidable collection of poems that earned her the admiration of both critics and fellow poets including Robert Lowell, Octavio Paz, and John Ashbery. Bishop, who won (1956) the Pulitzer Prize in Poetry for her first two volumes of poems (*North and South* [1946] and *A Cold Spring* [1955]), produced only three other volumes (*Brazil* [1962], *Questions of Travel* [1965], and *Geography III* [1977]) during a 35-year career. Her works, however, were lavishly praised for their witty verse and polished precision; Bishop often spent years revising a single poem. After graduating (1934) from Vassar College she briefly resided in Key West, Fla., and traveled to Europe, North Africa, Mexico, and Brazil, where she lived for many years and translated books from Portuguese to English. Bishop also contributed regularly to *The New Yorker* magazine, the possessor of her last complete unpublished poem. Her works are collected in *Complete Poems* (1969).

Blodgett, Katherine Burr, U.S. research scientist (b. Jan. 10, 1898, Schenectady, N.Y.—d. Oct. 12, 1979, Schenectady), developed (1938) a nonreflecting "invisible" glass that is used in automobile windshields, shop windows, telescopes, cameras, and submarine periscopes. Blodgett, who became (1918) the first woman research scientist at General Electric Co., conducted studies in both chemistry and physics with Nobel laureate Irving Langmuir. In 1926 she received the first Ph.D. in physics ever awarded to a woman by Cambridge University. After returning to General Electric, where she worked during her entire career, Blodgett invented a colour gauge, which measures the thickness of film within one microinch, and a smoke screen that saved thousands of lives during the North African and Italian invasions in World War II.

Blokhintsev, Dmitry Ivanovich, Soviet physicist (b. Jan. 11, 1908 [Dec. 29, 1907, old style], Moscow, Russia—d. Jan. 27, 1979, Moscow, U.S.S.R.), played an important role in the development of nuclear energy in the U.S.S.R. and was director of the Joint Institute for Nuclear Research at Dubna, near Moscow, from 1956 to 1965. Blokhintsev graduated from Moscow University (1930), where he later served as professor of physics (1936–56). In 1960 he chaired the Organizational Committee of the ninth International Conference on Physics and High Energies in Kiev. His major scientific contributions were in the fields of solid state quantum theory, the physics of semiconductors, quantum mechanics, theory of chain reactions, and particle physics. He was a correspondent member of the Soviet Academy of Sciences and of several foreign academies.

Blondell, Joan (ROSE JOAN BLONDELL), U.S. actress (b. Aug. 30, 1909, New York, N.Y.—d. Dec. 25, 1979, Santa Monica, Calif.), became a favourite star as a hard-boiled, wisecracking blonde in such films as *Blonde Crazy, The Public Enemy,* and *Blondie Johnson.* Blondell used *Gold Diggers of 1933, Footlight Parade,* and *Dames* as a showcase for her song and dance routines. During a span of eight years (1930–38) she appeared in nearly 50 films opposite such leading men as James Cagney and Dick Powell, her second husband. Other films in which Blondell's superiority as a character actress was evident were *Sinners' Holiday, The Crowd Roars, Three on a Match, Bullets or Ballots,* and *The Blue Veil,* for which she was nominated for best supporting actress. She also appeared on television in "Here Come the Brides" and "Banyon." Blondell's last role was as a wealthy racehorse owner in *The Champ,* a 1979 remake of the classic 1931 film that had starred Wallace Beery and Jackie Cooper.

Bolton, Guy Reginald, British playwright (b. Nov. 23, 1882, Broxbourne, Hertfordshire, England—d. Sept. 5, 1979, London, England), was the author of some 100 plays, many of which contributed substantially to the evolution of the Broadway musical as a viable theatrical form. Bolton's first play, *The Drone,* appeared on Broadway in 1911, but when he shifted to musicals during the 1920s and '30s, his career spiraled. In collaboration with P. G. Wodehouse, Bolton turned out scripts that were enlivened with songs by Jerome Kern, George and Ira Gershwin, and Cole Porter. At centre stage in such musicals as *Sally, Lady Be Good, Five O'Clock Girl, Simple Simon,* and *Anything Goes* were song and dance stars Fred Astaire, Ginger Rogers, Ethel Merman, and Jackie Gleason. In later years Bolton turned away from musicals; his drama *Anastasia* was a Broadway hit during the 1954–55 season. Bolton, who scoffed at retirement, celebrated his 95th birthday by sending yet another play to his agent.

Bomford, James, British art collector (b. 1895—d. March 26, 1979, London, England), was a private benefactor of British public art galleries and a patron of young artists. Stockbroking supported an earlier interest in motorboat racing; in 1928 Bomford won the English, Scottish, German, and Belgian championships. He took up yacht racing in 1930 but sold his schooner to help finance his mainly Impressionist collection of major French paintings, acquired under the direction of French painter André Derain. Part of his post-World War II collection of modern British paintings, which included works of the then little-known Francis Bacon, was given to the Swindon Art Gallery. In 1966 Bomford donated 100 ancient Persian bronzes to the Ashmolean Museum, Oxford, and established the Ashmolean Museum Bomford Bequest. His loan of ancient glass to the Bristol Museum and Art Gallery might be changed to a bequest.

Borgen, Johan Collett Müller, Norwegian writer (b. April 28, 1902, Oslo, Norway—d. Oct. 16, 1979, Hvaler, Østfold, Norway), a leading figure on the Norwegian literary scene for many years, was the author of some 15 novels, short story collections, stage and radio plays, and volumes of essays, letters, and literary criticism. During the 1920s and '30s Borgen was a journalist with *Dagbladet* and *Morgenbladet,* leading Oslo newspapers, and after World War II he was briefly press attaché at the Norwegian embassy in Copenhagen (1945–46). His literary debut was a collection of stories in 1925, and in 1932 he established a reputation as a bittersweet humourist and satirist with essays published under the pseudonym Mumle Gåsegg. Among his novels, *Ingen Sommar* (1944) was the first notable account of life in Norway during the German occupation, while his *Lillelord* trilogy (1955–57) stands as one of the leading works of contemporary Norwegian literature. Borgen edited the literary journal *Vinduet* from 1954 to 1960 and was a frequent broadcaster. In 1967 he was awarded the Nordic Council's Prize for Literature.

Bory, Jean-Louis, French novelist, critic, and historian (b. June 25, 1919, Méréville, France—d. June 12, 1979, Méréville), won the Prix Goncourt in 1945 with his first novel, *Mon village à l'heure allemande,* and reached a wide audience in the 1960s with film criticism in *Arts* and *Le Nouvel Observateur.* As a television scriptwriter and personality, he combined a flair for the medium with the cultured humanism of his works on Balzac and Eugène Sue and his historical study of the July 1830 Revolution. An acknowledged homosexual, he became identified with the struggle of homosexuals for acceptance. His works include a series of autobiographical novels and several books on the cinema. He died by his own hand.

Boulanger, Nadia Juliette, French music teacher and conductor (b. Sept. 16, 1887, Paris, France—d. Oct. 22, 1979, Paris), conducted leading orchestras in France, the U.S., and Britain but found her vocation as an inspired teacher of generations of performers and composers. Few men, and no other women, exercised so profound an influence on the contemporary musical scene. Her pupils included such leading 20th-century composers as Virgil Thomson, Aaron Copland, Roy Harris, Leonard Bernstein, and Lennox Berkeley, as well as her sister Lili who died at the age of 24 after showing great promise. Boulanger taught at the Paris Conservatoire, the École Normale de Musique, and the Conservatoire Américain in Fontainebleau and gave lectures and master classes in Britain and the U.S. An admirer of Stravinsky, although she studied under Gabriel Fauré, Boulanger was nonetheless active in reviving the music of earlier composers, notably Monteverdi. In 1973, despite her age and failing sight, she began a series of television appearances that revealed her forceful personality to a new audience of music lovers. Her many awards included the Légion d'Honneur, the CBE, and the gold medal of the Académie des Beaux-Arts.

Boulin, Robert, French politician (b. July 20, 1920, Villandraut, Gironde, France—d. Oct. 30, 1979, Rambouillet, France), was a minister in successive governments from his first appointment in 1961 and the longest serving minister of the Fifth Republic. A member from 1940 of the Free French and the Resistance, Boulin trained for the bar and entered politics after Gen. Charles de Gaulle's return to power in 1958. He held a variety of ministerial appointments before becoming minister of labour and participation in 1978. His wide experience, abilities as a negotiator, and conciliatory approach made him a likely candidate for the premiership to succeed Raymond Barre. But irregularities connected with some property he had bought at Val du Bois in 1974 led to a scandal in 1979 that threatened his career when reports of the deal appeared in the satirical weekly *Le Canard Enchaîné.* Though he denied the accusations, Boulin felt that he was the victim of a deliberate smear campaign and took his own life.

Bradley, Helen, British artist (b. 1900, Lees, Lancashire, England—d. July 19, 1979, Wilmslow, Cheshire, England), began to paint when she was 65 and captured the atmosphere of her Edwardian childhood for her grandchildren. Bradley lived to see her pictures sold for many thousands of pounds each. A friend of another Lancashire "primitive," L. S. Lowry, Bradley was above all an illustrator whose work is best seen in her "Miss Carter" books, which exhibit her real strengths: great personal charm, meticulous detail, and an amazing ability to reexperience the scenes and characters of her Edwardian past. She was awarded the MBE in 1979.

Brent, George (GEORGE BRENT NOLAN), Irish-born actor (b. March 15, 1904, near Dublin, Ireland—d. May 26, 1979, Solana Beach, Calif.), was a dashing leading man in more than 100 motion pictures and 300 plays during the 1930s and '40s. Brent, who played opposite such Hollywood glamour queens as Hedy Lamarr, Greta Garbo, and Joan Fontaine, was widely remembered as the surgeon who tried in vain to save the life of Bette Davis in the 1939 tearjerker *Dark Victory.* After his appearance with Ruth Chatterton in *The Rich Are Always with Us* (1932), Brent's career flourished. He and Bette Davis co-starred in 11 films, including *Front Page Woman* (1935), *The Golden Arrow* (1936), *Jezebel* (1938), *The Old Maid* (1939), and *The Great Lie* (1941). After nearly 25 years in retirement, Brent returned to the screen in 1978 for a cameo appearance as a judge in *Born Again.*

Brosa, Antonio, Spanish musician (b. June 27, 1894, Canonja, Tarragona, Spain—d. March 26, 1979, Barcelona, Spain), was an international solo violinist and leader of the Brosa String Quartet. After studies in Barcelona and Brussels, he settled in London. He toured Europe and America with his quartet until beginning his career as a solo violinist in 1938. Brosa introduced Benjamin Britten's Suite for Violin and Piano at the International Society for Contemporary Music Festival in Barcelona in 1936 and during a stay in the U.S. (1940–46) gave the first performance of Britten's Violin Concerto at Carnegie Hall in New York City, where he also led the Pro Arte Quartet. After returning to Europe in 1946, he played and broadcast in several countries.

Buchanan, (William) Edgar, U.S. actor (b. March 20, 1903, Humansville, Mo.—d. April 4, 1979, Palm Desert, Calif.), was a practicing dentist and chief of oral surgery (1929–37) at Eugene Hospital in Oregon before embarking on a highly successful acting career. He appeared in some 100 movies and gained wide popularity as a character actor in four series on television, notably as Uncle Joe, the philosophical rustic who managed Shady Rest Hotel in the long-running (1963–69) program "Petticoat Junction." In "Hopalong Cassidy" he was a comic sidekick, in "Judge Roy Bean" he portrayed the crooked judge, and in "Cade's County" he was sheriff Glenn Ford's deputy. Buchanan's movie credits include *Arizona* (1940), *Penny Serenade* (1941), *Texas* (1941), *Shane* (1953), and *Ride the High Country* (1962).

Buitoni, Giovanni, Italian businessman (b. Nov. 6, 1891, Perugia, Italy—d. Jan. 13, 1979, Rome, Italy), turned a family pasta business into the multinational food empire Industrie Buitoni Perugina. Buitonis had begun selling spaghetti in the 1820s, but it was not until Giovanni Buitoni diversified into chocolates and promoted his wares by imaginative advertising campaigns that the business began to expand. Stranded in the U.S. at the start of World War II, he launched Buitoni Foods Corp. and in the postwar period swept back into Europe, eventually capturing 60% of the French market in precooked foods.

Burgess, Russell Brian, British choirmaster (b. July 3, 1931, Leyton, Essex, England—d. Leyton, Sept. 5, 1979), was director of music at Wandsworth School in London from 1954 and both founder and director of the Wandsworth School Boys' Choir. The choir, which acquired an international reputation, made recordings with Sir Georg Solti, Zubin Mehta, and other famous conductors; its patron, composer Benjamin Britten, described it as "my favourite choir at my favourite school." Trained at the Royal Academy of Music, Burgess was associated with choral music all his adult life. Besides making recordings, accompanying choirs on European and U.S. tours, and conducting the world premiere (1969) of Britten's *Children's Crusade* in St. Paul's Cathedral in London, he also assisted (1964–71) Wilhelm Pitz, chorus master of the New Philharmonia, before succeeding him.

Camden, Archie, British musician (b. March 9, 1888, Newark-upon-Trent, England—d. Feb. 16, 1979, Wheathampstead, England), was a virtuoso performer who did much to establish the bassoon as a solo instrument; in particular, he brought the German bassoon to eminence in Britain. Camden played with many leading orchestras, including the Hallé, the BBC Symphony, and the Royal Philharmonic, and from 1954 to 1971 was a member of the London Mozart Players. He was particularly noted for his interpretation of works by Mozart, Vivaldi, and Weber.

Capp, Al (ALFRED GERALD CAPLIN), U.S. cartoonist (b. Sept. 28, 1909, New Haven, Conn.—d. Nov. 5, 1979, Cambridge, Mass.), created such immortal comic strip characters as Li'l Abner, Daisy Mae,

BOOK OF THE YEAR

UPI

and Mammy and Pappy Yokum, the outlandish residents of Dogpatch, U.S.A. Capp also introduced Joe Btsfplk, Moonbeam McSwine, Hairless Joe, and Fearless Fosdick and made Lower Slobbovia and Sadie Hawkins' Day part of the language. Capp's satirical and liberal "Li'l Abner" strip was syndicated by United Features in 1934. During the height of its popularity "Li'l Abner" appeared in over 900 newspapers, but circulation dropped to some 400 when Capp became more conservative. His conservatism became evident in the strip when he introduced the acronym SWINE to describe Students Wildly Indignant about Nearly Everything. Capp's interest in cartooning was inspired by his father, who frequently penciled cartoons for the family's enjoyment. In 1927 Capp joined Associated Press and drew Col. Gilfeather. Five years later he became the ghostwriter for Ham Fisher's "Joe Palooka" and was credited with being the genius behind the strip's success. Capp's retirement in 1977 ended the "Li'l Abner" strip that had delighted readers for over four decades.

Catlin, Sir George Edward Gordon, British political writer (b. July 29, 1896, Liverpool, England—d. Feb. 7, 1979, Hampshire, England), was a Fabian Socialist who became a leading advocate of the Atlantic alliance and was knighted in 1970 for his services to Anglo-American relations. He was professor of politics at Cornell University from 1924 to 1935 and at McGill University, Montreal, from 1956 to 1960. But it was as a leading member of the Fabian Society and as the author of many books on politics that he established his reputation as a radical thinker. *One Anglo-American Nation* (1941) set the tone for his thinking during the years following World War II. Later publications included *The Atlantic Community* (1959), *Atlanticism* (1973), and *Kissinger's Atlantic Charter* (1974).

Cesbron, Gilbert, French writer (b. Jan. 13, 1913, Paris, France—d. Aug. 12, 1979, Paris), was one of France's most popular Roman Catholic novelists of the post-World War II period, though he never obtained any major literary prize and failed to gain election to the Académie française. The artistic weaknesses of Cesbron's work, which offered an easy target for his critics, lay in the very qualities that endeared him to his readers, who recognized that the man and his books were one and that his passionate awareness of injustice and suffering made him incapable of detachment. Cesbron's novels were unashamedly propagandistic, dealing directly with contemporary problems: worker-priests (*Les saints vont en enfer,* 1952), abandoned children (*Chiens perdus sans collier,* 1954), and the handicapped (*Moi aussi je vous aimais,* 1977). A program director with Radio-Télé-Luxembourg, Cesbron was also secretary-general of the charitable organization Secours catholique.

Chain, Sir Ernest Boris, German-born biochemist (b. June 19, 1906, Berlin, Germany—d. Aug. 12, 1979, Ireland), was a joint winner of the Nobel Prize for Physiology or Medicine in 1945 for isolating and purifying penicillin. Chain trained as a chemist at the University of Berlin but left Germany in 1933 and went to Oxford, where he worked in the field of bacteriology with Sir Howard Florey. Starting from Sir Alexander Fleming's discovery of the antibacterial properties of *Penicillium notatum* mold, he managed to isolate pure penicillin and by 1941 the new drug had been tested on patients dying of staphylococcal infections. Although the first two tests failed, the third was successful and by 1945, when Chain, Florey, and Fleming were awarded the Nobel Prize, penicillin had been recognized as a dramatic advance in medical science. In 1948 Chain went to Rome as director of the International Research Centre for Chemical Microbiology, later returning (1961) to England to become professor of biochemistry at Imperial College, London. He retired in 1973 and two years later revealed his lifelong passion for music when he appeared as a concert pianist at the Wigmore Hall, London. A fellow of the Royal Society from 1949, he was knighted in 1969.

Chaliapin, Boris, Russian-born artist (b. Oct. 5 [Sept. 22, old style], 1904, Moscow, Russia—d. May 18, 1979, New York, N.Y.), was a prolific artist who gained wide recognition for the more than 400 portraits he produced for the covers of *Time* magazine during the 1940s, '50s, and '60s. Because Chaliapin could turn out a drawing in 7 to 15 hours with only a photograph to work from, editors often turned to him when big news broke and deadlines were pressing. After studying art in Moscow, Chaliapin spent ten years in Paris before immigrating (1935) to the U.S. Seven years later he sold his first (and personal favourite) cover to *Time,* a portrait of Jawaharlal Nehru, the first prime minister of independent India. Other Chaliapin covers included Russian composer Sergey Rachmaninoff; George Meany, president of the AFL-CIO; and William Scranton, former governor of Pennsylvania. Chaliapin's talents extended to figure painting, landscapes, pencil sketches, pictures of opera settings, and wood sculpture. His works are exhibited in the National Portrait Gallery in Washington, D.C.

Challe, Maurice Prosper Félix, French Air Force officer (b. Sept. 5, 1905, Pontet, Vaucluse, France—d. Jan. 18, 1979, Paris, France), was the leader of an unsuccessful rebellion against Pres. Charles de Gaulle in April 1961 to prevent Algeria's independence from France. Graduating from the French military academy at Saint-Cyr in 1925, Challe was a major on the general staff at the outbreak of World War II. In November 1942 he joined the Resistance, returning to active service in 1944 to take part in the invasion of Germany. In 1949 he was promoted to general and appointed commander in chief of the French Air Force in Morocco. In 1951 he became chief of air staff at the Air Ministry. Two years later Challe was named commandant of the École Supérieure de Guerre Aérienne and in 1955 chief of staff of the French Air Force. When General de Gaulle returned to power on June 1, 1958, he sent Challe to Algeria as commander in chief of the French forces fighting the Algerian insurgents. After de Gaulle announced in September 1959 that the Algerian people would be able to choose freely between association with France or secession, a revolt of French colons broke out in Algiers in January 1960 but quickly collapsed. A second and more serious revolt began on April 22, 1961, led by Challe with Generals André Zeller (*q.v.*), Edmond Jouhaud, and Raoul Salan. Four days later, after de Gaulle assumed extraordinary powers, Challe surrendered and returned to France to stand trial. He was sentenced to 15 years' imprisonment, but he served only five and a half years before being pardoned by de Gaulle in 1966.

Chauvel, Jean, French diplomat (b. April 16, 1897, Paris, France—d. May 31, 1979, Paris), was one of the most influential figures in French public life for more than 40 years. He joined the diplomatic service in 1921 and specialized in Far Eastern affairs, which he managed under the Vichy government during World War II. In Paris he organized (1942) a clandestine study group for foreign affairs in contact with the Resistance, then in 1944 left France secretly for Algiers, where Gen. Charles de Gaulle had appointed him head of the Foreign Affairs Commission. Under the Fourth Republic, he was head of France's permanent delegation to the UN and French representative in the Security Council (1949–52), ambassador to Switzerland (1952–54), and at the 1954 Geneva Conference played a crucial role in negotiations leading to the French withdrawal from Indochina. In 1954 he was appointed ambassador to London, a post he retained until 1963.

Cherry, (Edward) Colin, British telecommunications scientist (b. June 23, 1914, St. Albans, England—d. Nov. 23, 1979, London, England), was Henry Mark Pease professor of telecommunication at Imperial College of Science and Technology, University of London, from 1958 and a major contributor to the study of communications. After working as a laboratory assistant with the British General Electric Co., he helped develop radar during World War II, then became a lecturer at Manchester University College of Technology. He found himself in a rapidly developing field and began to apply his early studies in circuit theory and analysis to much more general problems of communication. His books *On Human Communication* (1957) and *World Communication: Threat or Promise?* (1971) reflected his increasing conviction that technology could not be divorced from sociology and psychology and that information theory had applications to many fields, including linguistics and experimental psychology. His later work was concerned with perception and the social aspects of telecommunications. In 1978 he was awarded the fourth Marconi International Fellowship.

Chiron, Louis, Monegasque racing driver (b. Aug. 3, 1899, Monaco—d. June 23, 1979, Monaco), won fame as a driver for Bugatti in grand prix motor racing before World War II. His successes in 1928 made him that year's champion driver, and he won many other victories for Bugatti. His last grand prix win was the French in 1949, but he continued to drive in rallies, winning the 1954 Monte Carlo Rally in a Lancia. He retired in 1959.

Clark, Sir George Norman, British historian (b. Feb. 27, 1890—d. Feb. 6, 1979), edited two major comprehensive histories, *The Oxford History of England* and the *New Cambridge Modern History*. The first, to which he contributed the volume on the later Stuart kings, was started in 1934; the latter, planned to include 14 volumes, first appeared in 1957. Clark was Chichele professor of economic history at Oxford (1931–43) and regius professor of modern history at Cambridge (1943–47) and a trustee of the British Museum (1949–60). He edited the *English Historical Review* from 1920 to 1925 and was president of the British Academy from 1954 to 1958. Apart from planning and editing the two multivolume histories, he wrote a number of works, particularly on 17th-century history.

Clavel, Maurice, French writer (b. Nov. 10, 1920, Frontignan, France—d. April 23, 1979, Asquins, France), followed an individual course from Gaullism to the extreme left, reconciling his politics with Christianity after his return to Catholicism in the 1960s. Though Clavel was decorated by Pres. Charles de Gaulle for his wartime Resistance activities, the two had a falling out when Clavel demanded public exposure of the role of the French government in the 1965 kidnapping and subsequent death of Mehdi Ben Barka, a Moroccan accused of treason for his support of Algeria. After the student revolt of 1968, Clavel moved further to the left and confirmed his reputation as a brilliant and controversial polemicist. Although he also wrote plays and novels, winning the 1972 Prix Médicis for his novel *Le Tiers des Étoiles*, he was best known for his contributions to the newspapers *Combat* and *Le Nouvel Observateur* and for his works of Christian philosophy, including *Dieu est Dieu, nom de Dieu* (1976).

Clore, Sir Charles, British financier (b. Dec. 26, 1904, London, England—d. July 26, 1979, London), was president of Sears Holdings Ltd. and pioneered the "takeover bid"—a tactic that brought him a huge financial empire and a personal fortune estimated at £50 million. The son of a Russian émigré, he made his first important deal when he bought, then sold, the film rights to the Tunney-Dempsey heavyweight fight (1926). But it was not until after World War II that he embarked on his seemingly endless accumulation of business properties. His career was a triumph of individual initiative and hard work, but symbolized the malaise of postwar British capitalism. He came to control main street clothing and shoe stores, betting shops, department stores, hotels, and other businesses by simply bidding well above market value for shares in a company. Clore would then sell the freeholds of its retail outlets, continue trading through them under leases, and so acquire capital that he used for further takeovers. Some of his later deals were thwarted by the business community and in 1978 he became an exile in Monaco to avoid paying tax on capital gains derived from the £20 million sale of his Hertfordshire estate. He gave large sums to charity and was said to have contributed £1 million to Israel at the time of the 1967 Arab-Israeli war. He was knighted in 1971.

Cohen, Sir John Edward, British businessman (b. Oct. 6, 1898, London, England—d. March 24, 1979, London), rose from street trading in London's East End to become multimillionaire head of Tesco Stores (Holdings) Ltd., a major British supermarket chain. His sales policy, "Pile it high, sell it cheap," carried an expanding market stall and tea sale business forward until he turned to grocery shops in the late 1920s. The name "Tesco," adopted in 1924, combined the initials of his tea supplier, T. E. Stockwell, and the first two letters of his own name. In the late 1940s his company embraced U.S. supermarket retailing techniques, and by 1978 the chain had opened 600 stores and become famous for successful price wars. Cohen was knighted in 1969 and became life president of his company the same year.

Conrad, Max, U.S. aviator (b. 1903, Winona, Minn. —d. April 3, 1979, Summit, N.J.), was a daredevil pilot who logged more than 50,000 flying hours in a 40-year career and set six small-plane distance and endurance records. Conrad, dubbed the "flying grandfather," had an insatiable desire to take to the air and flew over the Atlantic and Pacific oceans some 200 times. Among his nonstop record-setting triumphs were flights from Chicago to Rome, from New York to Sicily (both 1959), from New Jersey to Ireland (1958), and from Winona to Mexico City (1951). In 1953 he set a speed record for light planes when he flew from San Francisco to New York in 22 hours 24 minutes. Probably his most spectacular feat was his record-setting flight around the world in a twin-engine Piper Aztec in 1961. Conrad returned to his starting point in Miami, Fla., eight days 18 hours 49 minutes after his takeoff. His other interests included poetry, writing, athletics, and songwriting.

Coote, Sir Colin Reith, British journalist (b. Oct. 19, 1893—d. June 8, 1979, London, England), was managing editor of *The Daily Telegraph*, London, from 1950 to 1964. From Balliol College, Oxford, he went into the infantry in World War I, winning the Distinguished Service Order on the Italian front. He was a Coalition Liberal member of Parliament for the Isle of Ely (1917–22) and then, after working as *The Times*'s correspondent in Rome, wrote editorials for his paper specializing in foreign and political affairs. Because Coote did not share *The Times*'s support of Neville Chamberlain's policy of appeasement of Nazi Germany, he turned to home affairs and then joined (1942) *The Daily Telegraph*. He became its deputy editor in 1945 and succeeded Arthur Watson as managing editor in 1950. Coote's personal charm, social gifts, and intellect carried him into high places, and he was the personal friend of ten prime ministers. Bilingual in English and French from childhood, he also commanded a mastery of Italian. Under his editorship *The Daily Telegraph*'s circulation rose from 971,534 to 1,319,351. He was knighted in 1962. His memoirs, *Editorial*, appeared in 1965; other books were *In and About Rome* (1926), *A Companion of Honour: The Story of Walter Elliott* (1965), *The Government We Deserve* (1969), and *The Other Club* (1971).

Coste-Floret, Paul, French politician (b. April 9, 1911, Montpellier, France—d. Aug. 28, 1979, Montpellier), played a leading role in drafting the constitution of the Fourth Republic and served as a minister in several governments during the 1950s. But it was as a constitutional expert that he was most active in political life. Under the Fifth Republic, the regime introduced by Charles de Gaulle, Coste-Floret opposed the extensive powers accorded to the president over the premier. Trained as a lawyer, he was professor at the University of Algiers at the outbreak of World War II and took an active part in the overseas Resistance and the provisional government set up after the Allied landings in 1942. He was elected to the National Assembly in 1945 as a member of the Mouvement Républicain Populaire and continued to represent his home town under the Fifth Republic after 1958. He failed to win reelection in 1968 and was appointed to the Constitutional Council in 1971. In 1977 he was elected president of the University of Montpellier I.

Cotsworth, Staats, U.S. actor (b. Feb. 17, 1908, Oak Park, Ill.—d. April 9, 1979, New York, N.Y.), appeared on the stage, radio, and television in a wide variety of roles that included Banquo in Shakespeare's *Macbeth*, Tweedledee in *Alice in Wonderland*, and the lead in "Casey, Crime Photographer" on radio. Before moving to New York and the Broadway stage, Cotsworth graduated from the Philadelphia Museum School of Industrial Art. His widely acclaimed oil paintings and watercolours have been exhibited in major galleries and museums.

Coughlin, Charles Edward, Canadian-born priest (b. Oct. 25, 1891, Hamilton, Ont.—d. Oct. 27, 1979, Bloomfield Hills, Mich.), achieved notoriety during the Depression as the "radio priest," whose fiery sermons denouncing Communism, capitalism, labour unions, and "Wall Street money changers" were broadcast over 30 stations and attracted some 40 million listeners every week. Coughlin became pastor of the Shrine of the Little Flower Church in Royal Oak, Mich., in 1926. After the Ku Klux Klan burned a cross in the churchyard, Coughlin made arrangements to explain Catholicism to the community over station WJR in Detroit each Sunday. At first Coughlin restricted his sermons to religious subjects, but by the end of 1930 he turned to political topics and attacked such figures as Herbert Hoover and later Franklin D. Roosevelt, whom he called "the great liar and betrayer." After being dropped by CBS radio, Coughlin put together his own network of 29 stations and in 1936 founded the magazine *Social Justice*, which, like his broadcasts, became increasingly anti-Semitic. After the U.S. entered World War II, the church silenced Coughlin and the U.S. Post Office banned his magazine. He then quietly resumed duties as pastor of the Shrine of the Little Flower until his retirement in 1966.

Cousteau, Philippe Pierre, French oceanographer and cinematographer (b. Dec. 30, 1940, Toulon, France—d. June 28, 1979, near Alverca, Port.), was the younger son and chief protégé of Jacques-Yves Cousteau, world renowned oceanographer. As a highly respected and dedicated oceanographer in his own right, Cousteau worked with his father as a diver and photographer on the research ship "Calypso." He also filmed the television series

WIDE WORLD

"The Undersea World of Jacques Cousteau," which won ten Emmy awards. In 1965 he participated in an experiment of the Conshelf Saturation Dive Program by living 328 ft (100 m) underwater with five other aquanauts for 30 days. Cousteau also filmed that experiment for a National Geographic Society television special. Upon the creation of the Cousteau Society in 1974, Cousteau and his father became the society's executive producers for "The Cousteau Odyssey," a series of television specials. He was also co-author with his father of *Les Requins* (1970; *The Shark*). Cousteau was killed when the seaplane he was piloting crashed into a sandbank in the Tagus River.

Crockett, James Underwood, U.S. horticulturist (b. Oct. 9, 1915, Haverhill, Mass.—d. July 11, 1979, Jamaica), provided expert advice on cultivating flowers and vegetables to millions of television viewers on his popular public television show "Crockett's Victory Garden." In a 40-ft-square garden behind the television station, Crockett showed his audience how to properly grow and care for plants. After studying at the Stockbridge School of Agriculture and Texas A & M, Crockett bought a flower shop and began writing on gardening techniques. Besides his monthly pamphlets, "Flowery Talks," Crockett was the author of *Windowsill Gardening* (1958), the 12-volume Time-Life *Encyclopedia of Gardening*, *Crockett's Indoor Garden* (1977), and *Crockett's Victory Garden* (1978).

Croft-Cooke, Rupert, British writer (b. June 20, 1903, Edenbridge, Kent, England—d. June 10, 1979, Bournemouth, England), was a rolling stone whose large and diverse literary output included a 24-volume autobiographical series, more than 30 novels, plays, poems, biographies, and books on the circus, gypsies, travel, food, and wine. His travels took him to Argentina, where he edited a literary magazine (1923–24); to Madagascar and India (as an intelligence officer during World War II); and to North Africa and France. From 1929 to 1931 he was an antiquarian bookseller in London and a minor literary figure. His well-researched biographies include *Rudyard Kipling* (1948) and *Bosie* (on Lord Alfred Douglas; 1963) and his novels include *Blind Gunner* (1935) and *Wilkie* (1948).

Dard, Michel Henry, French novelist (b. Dec. 9, 1908, Aire-sur-la-Lys, France—d. July 2, 1979, Paris, France), showed a deep concern for language and the intricacies of human behaviour in his writings and played an important role in international cultural exchanges. He trained as a lawyer and taught during the 1940s at universities in the U.S.

and Romania. In 1945 he founded the periodical *Écrits de France* and from 1950 to 1964 worked for UNESCO, where he was particularly concerned with making foreign literature better known in France. *Mélusine,* his first novel, was published in 1967 and won the Prix Valery-Larbaud. He was awarded the Prix Femina in 1973 for *Juan Maldonne.* Dard's last novel, *Le rayon vert,* appeared in 1979.

Darlington, William Aubrey, British dramatic critic (b. Feb. 20, 1890, Taunton, England—d. May 24, 1979, Seaford, England), was drama critic of *The Daily Telegraph* for 48 years. During this time (1920–68) Darlington interpreted the theatre impressionistically for the ordinary playgoer. He supported both Shakespearean drama and originality in modern drama (as exemplified by John Osborne and the Royal Court Theatre) when each was struggling against the dead hand of the London West End's commercial monopoly; at the same time he also reported on more conventional entertainment. Darlington, who was a classical scholar of St. John's College, Cambridge, and read English under Sir Arthur Quiller-Couch, also wrote novels, plays, and books on the theatre. His *Alf's Button,* short stories about a little Cockney who had magical powers because one of the buttons from his uniform was melted down from Aladdin's lamp, became a novel and a play and was filmed three times.

David, Donald Kirk, U.S. educator (b. Feb. 15, 1896, Moscow, Idaho—d. April 13, 1979, Hyannis, Mass.), was dean of Harvard University's Graduate School of Business Administration from 1942 until his retirement in 1955. Davis stayed at Harvard to teach after obtaining his M.B.A. and was among the first to offer a course in marketing. After three years as executive vice-president (1927–29) and president (1929–30) of the Royal Baking Powder Co. and 11 years (1930–41) as vice-president of the Great Island Holding Co., David returned to his alma mater as dean. In 1950 he was named a trustee of the Rockefeller Foundation. He became chairman of the executive committee of the Ford Foundation in 1955 and soon after vice-chairman of its board of directors.

Davies, John Emerson Harding, British politician (b. Jan. 8, 1916, London, England—d. July 4, 1979, London), was secretary for trade and industry in the Conservative government from 1970 to 1972. Trained as an accountant, Davies left a successful career in the oil industry in 1965 to become director of the Confederation of British Industry, then a newly created national employers' organization. His experience in this essentially political post led him to seek parliamentary election in 1970. Despite rapid promotion to a major Cabinet post, his career was troubled. Believing that industry would thrive best with least government interference, Davies committed his department to a policy of nonsupport for "lame duck" companies but recanted shortly afterward to prevent the collapse of Rolls-Royce. Political realities again forced him to review his economic beliefs in 1972 when he provided aid to Upper Clyde Shipbuilders. Davies made controversial decisions on support for the Anglo-French Concorde and the siting of a third London airport; he won recognition for his skill in handling negotiations with foreign governments and for his chairmanship of the House of Commons Committee on European Common Market legislation. In November 1976 he became Conservative Party spokesman on foreign affairs, but two years later illness forced him to resign. Davies was created a life peer in 1979, but letters patent had not been issued at the time of his death.

Davis, Benny, U.S. songwriter (b. New York?, 1895? —d. Dec. 20, 1979, Miami, Fla.), was a multitalented entertainer who worked as a singer, dancer, and actor but became better known through his songs as the lyricist for such catchy tunes as "Margie" and "Baby Face." Davis, who achieved his first success with the World War I song "Goodbye Broadway, Hello France," wrote the lyrics for 22 songs that sold a million or more copies including "Carolina Moon." At the same time Davis also staged revues that featured old vaudeville stars and promoted the careers of such personalities as Ruby Keeler, Paul Whiteman, and Buddy Ebsen. In 1972 Davis was inducted into the Songwriters Hall of Fame.

De Guingand, Sir Francis Wilfred, British Army officer (b. Feb. 28, 1900, London, England—d. June 29, 1979, Cannes, France), was Gen. Bernard Montgomery's masterly chief of staff of the British 8th Army in North Africa. During World War II De Guingand rose to the rank of major general and was chief of staff of the 21st Army Group in Western Europe. Commissioned from Sandhurst in 1919, he saw service mostly abroad until he became military assistant to the war minister, Leslie Hore-Belisha, in 1939. In 1940 he was made joint planner at Middle East General Headquarters in Cairo. In 1942 he became director of military intelligence there before being chosen by Gen. Claude Auchinleck and then by Montgomery to serve as their chief of staff. De Guingand helped plan the Allied landings on Sicily in 1943. After the war he pursued a business career in South Africa. Besides his books *African Assignment* (1953) and *Generals at War* (1964), De Guingand's memoirs appeared as *Operation Victory* (1947) and *Brass Hat to Bowler Hat.* He was knighted in 1944.

Delaunay, Sonia, Russian-born painter and designer (b. Nov. 14, 1885, Gradizhsk, Ukraine—d. Dec. 5, 1979, Paris, France), was a pioneer of abstract art in the years before World War I. Delaunay blended elements of Cubism with the nonfigurative mode of expression which was developed by her husband Robert Delaunay and became known as the "Orphic" movement. Sonia Stern studied in Russia and Germany before settling in Paris. After a brief marriage to the critic Wilhelm Uhde, she married Delaunay in 1910 and their careers developed in parallel until his death in 1941. Sonia greatly influenced textile and fashion design and theatrical decor in the 1920s, particularly through the fashion house she opened in Paris when the couple returned from a five-year stay in Spain and Portugal in 1921. The Delaunays collaborated in large mural compositions for the 1937 Paris international exhibition. After Robert's death Sonia devoted herself almost exclusively to painting, developing a more personal style and producing some of her finest work in her 70s and 80s. In 1967 the National Museum of Modern Art in Paris mounted a retrospective exhibition of her work, which is represented in the Tate Gallery in London and the Museum of Modern Art in New York City.

Deller, Alfred (George), British singer (b. May 31, 1912, Margate, England—d. July 16, 1979, Bologna, Italy), revived the countertenor voice that was favoured in early music but virtually ignored in concert singing since the Baroque era. Deller began singing as a church chorister but with the encouragement of composer Sir Michael Tippet began a professional career in the 1940s and made numerous recordings of songs by Henry Purcell and Elizabethan madrigals that had been written for countertenors. He formed the Deller Consort in 1950 and ten years later appeared in Britten's opera *A Midsummer Night's Dream* as Oberon, a part written for him. Deller conducted concert tours in the U.S. and appeared at leading international festivals. He was made an OBE in 1970.

Delmer, (Denis) Sefton, British journalist (b. May 24, 1904, Berlin, Germany—d. Sept. 5, 1979, Lamarsh, Suffolk, England), was a distinguished foreign correspondent noted particularly for his reports from pre-World War II Nazi Germany. After reading history and modern languages at Lincoln College, Oxford, he returned to Berlin and in 1928 became Berlin correspondent of *The Daily Express.* While Hitler was building up his Nazi Party, Delmer cultivated the Nazi bosses. He often accompanied Hitler during his propaganda travels across Germany, reporting his speeches in *The Daily Express.* At the Reichstag fire in February 1933, Hitler singled Delmer out from waiting reporters and invited him into the burning building for an exclusive eyewitness report. From 1933 to 1936 Delmer was *The Daily Express*'s Paris correspondent, and he covered the Spanish Civil War from 1936 to 1938. During World War II he was attached to Foreign Office intelligence and became a leading broadcaster in German on BBC radio. After the war he was *The Daily Express*'s chief foreign affairs reporter until 1959. He published several books, including *Trail Sinister* (1961), *Black Boomerang* (1962), and *The Counterfeit Spy* (1971).

Deterding, Olga, Swiss heiress (b. 1923—d. Jan. 1, 1979, London, England), inherited a fortune of some $100 million from her father, Sir Henri Deterding, a founder of the Royal Dutch-Shell oil group. During the 1950s she exchanged her role in high society for that of a nurse assisting Albert Schweitzer at his leper colony in Lambaréné, Gabon. After falling ill, she returned to Europe and resumed her life in international society, traveling extensively.

Díaz Ordaz, Gustavo, Mexican politician (b. March 12, 1911, Ciudad Serdán, Mexico—d. July 15, 1979, Mexico City, Mexico), was president (1964–70) of Mexico when government troops and riot policemen engaged (Oct. 2, 1968) student demonstrators in a bloody clash that became known as the "Massacre at Tlatelolco." Although the official death toll included only 40 students killed when troops opened fire on the demonstrators, other reports claimed that hundreds died. Díaz Ordaz, a lawyer by profession, served as supreme court president in his native state before being elected to the Mexican Senate in 1946. In 1958 he was appointed interior minister by Pres. Adolfo López Mateos and took charge of internal security. His term of office as president continued to provoke strong public reactions years after he had left office. In 1977 when Díaz Ordaz was named ambassador to Spain, the novelist Carlos Fuentes resigned as ambassador to France, and Mexican newspapers again unfavourably reiterated the drastic measures taken at the Massacre at Tlatelolco. Four months after his appointment, Díaz Ordaz announced his resignation, which, he said, was "strictly due to eye trouble."

Diefenbaker, John G(eorge), Canadian politician (b. Sept. 18, 1895, Grey County, Ont.—d. Aug. 16, 1979, Ottawa, Ont.), was the crusty prime minister of Canada from 1957 to 1963 and one of the most vocal members of Parliament for nearly four decades. Diefenbaker was a proficient trial lawyer in Saskatchewan before his election to the Canadian House of Commons in 1940. In 1956 he became leader of the Progressive Conservative Party and the following year he succeeded Louis St. Laurent as prime minister, breaking the 22-year monopoly of the Liberals. In the historic 1958 election

UPI

the Conservatives won a record 208 of 265 House seats. As prime minister, "Dief the Chief" urged increased independence from the U.S. and refused to arm Canada's NATO force with U.S. nuclear weapons. Diefenbaker also pushed for the development of Canada's natural resources and its vast Arctic northlands. Often accused of running a one-man show, Diefenbaker was forced to call (1963) an election when several Cabinet members resigned during a crisis over the proposed manufacture of nuclear weapons in Canada. Even though he lost the party leadership in 1967, Diefenbaker was elected to the House of Commons for a record 13th term in May 1979.

Dodds, Eric Robertson, British classical scholar (b. July 26, 1893—d. April 8, 1979, Old Marston, Oxfordshire, England), as regius professor of Greek at the University of Oxford (1936–60), strongly upheld the need for all universities teaching humanities to include Latin and Greek courses. An undergraduate at University College, Oxford, he was professor of Greek at the University of Birmingham (1924–36), a fellow of University College, and honorary student of Christ Church, Oxford. His books include *The Greeks and the Irrational* (1951), for which he received the British Academy's Kenyon Medal, *Pagan and Christian in an Age of Anxiety* (1965), and an autobiography, *Missing Persons* (1977).

Draper, Christopher, British flying ace (b. 1892—d. Jan. 16, 1979, London, England), had a distinguished career in the Royal Naval Air Service during World War I, winning the British Distinguished Service Order and the French Croix de Guerre. In later years he gained fame with some spectacular stunts. In 1931 he flew a light plane through London's Tower Bridge and under Westminster Bridge, thereby earning the nickname "the Mad Major" and receiving a court warning. In 1953 he was given a small fine after repeating the exploit under 15 of the Thames bridges during a single flight.

Dubs, Adolph, U.S. diplomat (b. Aug. 4, 1920, Chicago, Ill.—d. Feb. 14, 1979, Kabul, Afghanistan), was a career diplomat for 30 years and a specialist in Eastern European affairs. After studying at Georgetown University in Washington, D.C., Dubs, or "Spike" as he was known to his contemporaries, became (1950) one of the first U.S. foreign service officers assigned to West Germany. He later was sent to the capital cities of Liberia and Canada, and, after learning Russian, he was assigned (1961) to the U.S.S.R. He then served in Yugoslavia and the U.S. before returning to the Soviet Union as minister counselor and acting chief of mission (1972–74). Before his appointment (1978) as ambassador to Afghanistan, Dubs was (1975) deputy assistant secretary of state for Near Eastern and South Asian affairs. On Feb. 14, 1979, he was abducted by four right-wing Muslim terrorists while riding in his car to the embassy. Dubs was shot to death in the cross fire when Afghan security police stormed the hotel where the kidnappers were holding him.

Durey, Louis(-Edmond), French composer (b. May 27, 1888, Paris, France—d. July 3, 1979, Saint-Tropez, France), was a member of "Les Six," a group that included Darius Milhaud, Arthur Honegger, Francis Poulenc, Germaine Tailleferre, and Georges Auric. Durey's musical activities and compositions, largely cantatas and other vocal works, were strongly influenced by his left-wing commitment: he was general secretary of the Fédération Musicale Populaire and vice-president of the Association Française des Musiciens Progressistes following World War II. In 1951 he wrote an arrangement of two poems by Ho Chi Minh, leader of the Vietnamese struggle against French colonialism. Besides such instrumental works as *Sinfonietta* (1966), Durey also wrote plays and contributed music criticism to the Communist press.

Dutschke, Rudi, West German political activist (b. March 7, 1940, Schönefeld, near Berlin, Germany —d. Dec. 24, 1979, Århus, Denmark), was one of the foremost leaders of the West German student movement during the 1960s. The son of a post office worker, Dutschke was influenced by the Evangelical Christian movement as a boy. Disillusioned with the version of Marxism applied in Soviet-dominated East Germany, he evaded military service by moving to West Berlin shortly before the Berlin Wall was built in 1961 and helped to found the Socialist Student League there. When the "grand coalition" of Social Democrats and Christian Democrats was formed in Bonn in 1966, he began an Extra-Parliamentary Opposition Party. Henceforth, Dutschke was in the vanguard of student demonstrations throughout West Germany. He was attracted by the theories of Herbert Marcuse, especially by his criticism of the Soviet system. Soon after returning to West Berlin from a visit to Prague in the spring of 1968, he was shot in the head and seriously wounded. The attempt to assassinate him was followed by violent student demonstrations throughout Western Europe. Having partly regained his health, Dutschke graduated as a doctor of philosophy at the West Berlin Free University. He visited Italy and then Britain, where he did research at the University of Cambridge but was expelled in 1971 for alleged subversive activity. His *Lenin, Try to Get Your Feet* (1974) outlined a program for a Marxism with a human face. More recently he became involved with the West German "green," or ecological, movement. Dutschke, who was lecturing in Denmark at Århus University, suffered a seizure—possibly resulting from his head injury—and drowned in his bath.

Earp, Charles William, British electrical engineer (b. 1905, Cheltenham, England—d. Nov. 1, 1979, Cirencester, England), laid the foundations on which aircraft direction finders and landing aids are based by his pioneering work on navigational systems. After graduating from the University of Cambridge, Earp joined Standard Telephones and Cables Ltd. and began to work on advanced telephony and electronics. During World War II he developed aircraft landing systems and later applied information theory to navigational aids. During the 1960s he became involved in the sometimes bitter struggle between rival systems, attempting unsuccessfully to gain international recognition for his own Doppler Landing Guidance System. He was made OBE in 1965 and in 1977 was awarded the first J. J. Thomson Medal of the Institution of Electrical Engineers.

Eaton, Cyrus Stephen, Canadian-born industrialist (b. Dec. 27, 1883, Pugwash, Nova Scotia—d. May 9, 1979, Northfield, Ohio), was a self-made multimillionaire whose financial empire included holdings in gas, electricity, iron mines, steel, rubber, railways, shipping, and banking. Although Eaton studied for the ministry, John D. Rockefeller, Sr., recognized Eaton's flair for business and persuaded him to join his organization. Eaton, a firm believer in capitalism, was worth some $2 million by age 30. In 1930 he helped found Republic Steel, but he lost $100 million after the crash of the stock market in 1929 and a massive court battle virtually bankrupted him by 1933. By 1942, however, he was amassing another fortune. A man of varied interests, Eaton enjoyed hunting, prize bull breeding, and studying philosophy, especially that of Bertrand Russell. In 1955, when Russell, Albert Einstein, and seven other scientists issued a manifesto urging scientists to assemble and discuss the alarming pace of the nuclear arms race, Eaton offered to finance the meeting anonymously at his home in Pugwash. In the congenial confines of Eaton's home scientists from both the East and West successfully met (July 1957) to exchange views and promote international understanding. This paved the way for future "Pugwash Conferences," in which leading scholars from around the world discussed ways of reducing armaments and examined their own social responsibilities toward economic development, population growth, and environmental destruction. Eaton was especially impressed by the sincerity of the Soviet participants and urged détente with the Soviet Union and the formal recognition of China. He became friends with Nikita Khrushchev and was awarded the Lenin Peace Prize in 1960. At the time of his death Eaton was a trustee of the University of Chicago, Denison University in Ohio, and the Harry S. Truman Library in Independence, Mo. He was also a member of the American Council of Learned Societies, the American Historical Association, the American Philosophical Association, and the American Academy of Arts and Sciences.

Eisenhower, Mamie Geneva Doud, U.S. first lady (b. Nov. 14, 1896, Boone, Iowa—d. Nov. 1, 1979, Washington, D.C.), won the special affection of the American people through the genuine warmth and friendliness that she showed in the White House while her husband, Dwight D. Eisenhower, served as 34th president of the U.S. The first lady's manner was so unaffected that even ordinary citizens felt comfortable using only her first name. She was viewed as the perfect hostess who ran the couple's household with the same efficiency that General Eisenhower used commanding the U.S. Army. The couple first met in 1915 when Mamie and her family were visiting relatives in San Antonio, Texas. On July 1, 1916, Mamie Geneva Doud and Second Lieutenant Dwight D. Eisenhower were married despite her father's (the well-to-do John Sheldon Doud) protest that she was marrying beneath her station. They had two sons,

KEYSTONE

Doud Dwight, who died of scarlet fever at age three, and John. During their 53 years of marriage the Eisenhowers lived in the Panama Canal Zone, the Philippines, France, Colorado, Kansas, Georgia, Maryland, and, when "Ike" retired, Gettysburg, Pa. After the death of her husband (March 28, 1969) Mamie spent the last decade of her life at the farm in Gettysburg. She suffered a massive stroke there on Sept. 25, 1979, and died peacefully in her sleep about a month later at the Walter Reed Army Medical Center in Washington.

Elizalde, Federico, Spanish musician (b. Dec. 12, 1907, Manila, Phil.—d. Jan. 16, 1979, Manila), trained as a classical pianist, then spent two years as a leader of a jazz band before returning to classical music as a conductor and composer. His works included *Le peintre maudit,* an opera on the life of Paul Gauguin, and concerti for violin and piano. While attending the University of Cambridge he developed an interest in jazz. This led to the composition of a ballet for Serge Diaghilev, *The Heart of a Nigger* (1928), and a spell as bandleader at the Savoy Hotel in London. Elizalde later lived in Spain and in France, where he remained throughout World War II, confined by a German order to his Bayonne estate. In 1948 he became president of the Manila Broadcasting Co. and founded the

Manila Little Symphony Orchestra. In 1951 he conducted the London Symphony Orchestra during the Festival of Britain.

Elliot, William Yandell, U.S. political scientist (b. May 12, 1896, Murfreesboro, Tenn.—d. Jan. 9, 1979, Haywood, Va.), who as professor of history and political science (1925–63) at Harvard University supervised and directed the doctoral dissertations of such eminent political figures as former U.S. secretary of state Henry A. Kissinger and former Canadian prime minister Pierre Elliott Trudeau. After earning (1923) his Ph.D. at the University of Oxford, Elliot became infamous among Harvard students for his impassioned repudiation of Marxist theory. When he left the podium, however, his reputation as an erudite scholar was secure. Besides teaching, Elliot served as an adviser to several government agencies. He was the author of *The Pragmatic Revolt in Politics* (1928) and *The Need for Constitutional Reform* (1935) and the editor of *Western Political Heritage* (with N. A. McDonald, 1949) and *Industrial Mobilization and the National Security.* After he left Harvard, Elliot taught (1963–69) literature at the American University in Washington, D.C.

Evans, Charles ("Chick"), U.S. golfer (b. July 18, 1890, Indianapolis, Ind.—d. Nov. 6, 1979, Chicago, Ill.), was a leading amateur golfer and the first person to win (1916) the U.S. Open and the U.S. Amateur championship in the same year. As an amateur Evans was prohibited from accepting prize money won in professional tournaments, so in 1930 he contributed his earnings to a college scholarship fund that benefited more than 4,000 caddies and students through the years. After caddying for two years, Evans began playing golf at the age of ten and captured his first tournament, the Western Interscholastic, in 1907. Besides being the only amateur ever to win the prestigious Western Open, Evans competed in the U.S. Amateur championships a record 50 times. He played golf well into his 70s and continued to work as a Chicago milk salesman during the blizzard of 1978–79.

Farrell, James Gordon, British novelist (b. Jan. 23, 1935, Liverpool, England—d. Aug. 12, 1979, Bantry Bay, Ireland), won the Booker Prize in 1973 for *The Siege of Krishnapur,* a historical novel set at the time of the Indian Mutiny. His first two books, *A Man from Elsewhere* (1963) and *A Girl in the Head* (1967), were praised for their wit but had little popular success. In 1970 Farrell turned to historical fiction with *Troubles,* a novel about Ireland following World War I. Though his last novel, *The Singapore Grip* (1978), was less successful than its predecessors, Farrell showed the same concern for meticulous historical research and an ability to recreate the past. He became one of the leading historical novelists of his generation.

Farrell, James T(homas), U.S. novelist (b. Feb. 27, 1904, Chicago, Ill.—d. Aug. 22, 1979, New York, N.Y.), was internationally heralded for his Studs Lonigan trilogy, a vivid and, for its time, sometimes shocking narrative of a lower middle-class Irish boy on the South Side of Chicago. The controversial trilogy (*Young Lonigan,* 1932; *The Young Manhood of Studs Lonigan,* 1934; and *Judgment Day,* 1935) depicted in realistic terms Lonigan's boyhood, degradation, and untimely death. Farrell's re-creation of the social and speech idioms of the period drew on childhood memories and was acclaimed as one of the finest examples of naturalistic writing of the 1930s. Farrell, who wrote more than 50 books, used such trilogy characters as Danny O'Neill and Bernard Clare as personalities in other works. Two of his most celebrated nonfiction works were *A Note on Literary Criticism* (1936) and *Reflections at Fifty* (1954).

Fiedler, Arthur, U.S. conductor (b. Dec. 17, 1894, Boston, Mass.—d. July 10, 1979, Brookline, Mass.), was the eminent maestro of the Boston Pops Orchestra (the Boston Symphony minus its principal players) for 50 seasons. Fiedler, whose principal aim was "to give audiences a good time," led the Pops in a combination of popular tunes, show music, and classics. From 1911 to 1915 Fiedler studied violin, piano, and conducting at the Royal Academy of Music in London before joining the Boston Symphony as a member of the second violin section. He also was proficient on the viola, celesta, piano, and organ. Fiedler's penchant for conducting prompted him to organize (1924) the Arthur Fiedler Sinfonietta when he was refused the conductorship of the Pops. In 1929 he organized the outdoor Esplanade concerts in Boston, and in 1930 he became conductor of the Pops. The scope of Fiedler's popularity was so great that he became the best-selling classical artist of all time; his recordings with the Pops sold some 50 million discs. Fiedler's greatest tribute, however, came when 400,000 devoted admirers assembled for the U.S. Bicentennial concert (July 4, 1976) on Boston's Esplanade. At the largest gathering for a classical concert in U.S. history, the crowd wildly cheered during a thunderous rendition of Tchaikovsky's *1812 Overture.* On the night of his death the Pops orchestra began its concert without direction and played Fiedler's signature piece, John Philip Sousa's "Stars and Stripes Forever."

UPI

Fields, Dame Gracie (Grace Stansfield), British music hall star (b. Jan. 9, 1898, Rochdale, Lancashire, England—d. Sept. 27, 1979, Capri, Italy), possessed a fine singing voice and a warm personality that endeared her to British audiences during the 1920s and '30s. Fields was best known for her rendering of such comic and sentimental songs as "The Biggest Aspidistra in the World," "Sally," and "Wish Me Luck As You Wave Me Goodbye." A mill girl, "Our Gracie" appeared at the Rochdale Hippodrome in 1915 and as Sally Perkins in a popular touring revue, *Mr. Tower of London* (1918–25), before captivating London audiences in such music halls as the Holborn Empire and the Alhambra. In the 1930s she enjoyed a successful film career in *Sally in Our Alley, Looking on the Bright Side,* and other films, in which she generally played a north country girl overcoming odds. In 1940 she divorced Archie Pitt and married Italian-born Monty Banks, a comedian and film director. When Britain declared Banks an undesirable alien, Fields went with him to California but voluntarily entertained thousands of Allied troops during World War II. Banks died in 1950 and Gracie settled on Capri, where she married her third husband, Boris Alperovici, in 1952. She made occasional concert appearances in England, including nine royal command performances between 1928 and 1964. Fields, who endowed an orphanage at Peacehaven, Sussex, was made a dame of the British Empire in 1979.

Flatt, Lester Raymond, U.S. singer (b. June 19, 1914, Overton County, Tenn.—d. May 11, 1979, Nashville, Tenn.), became one of the brightest stars of country music while performing with his partner, Earl Scruggs, and their Foggy Mountain Boys band. Their hard-driving bluegrass music was characterized by Scruggs's three-finger banjo style and by the "Lester Flatt G Run" on the guitar. Two of their best-known songs were "Foggy Mountain Breakdown" (the theme song for the film *Bonnie and Clyde*) and "The Ballad of Jed Clampett" (from the television comedy series "The Beverly Hillbillies"). Flatt began his professional career in 1944 as lead singer for Bill Monroe's Bluegrass Boys. In 1948 Flatt and Scruggs recorded their first album for Mercury Records. Seven years later they joined the Grand Ole Opry, where they built a reputation on such folk numbers as "Roll in My Sweet Baby's Arms" and "Old Salty Dog Blues." After the duo split up in 1969, Flatt continued to perform with the old Flatt and Scruggs band (later called The Nashville Grass).

Focke, Henrich Karl Johann, German aircraft designer (b. Oct. 8, 1890, Bremen, Germany—d. Feb. 25, 1979, Bremen, West Germany), designed the first helicopter certified as airworthy, the Fw 61 (1936). His firm, Focke-Wulf, founded with Georg Wulf in 1924, was taken from him by the Nazis in the 1930s. He therefore had no part in the design of its World War II aircraft, the famed Fw 190 fighter and the Fw 200 Condor. In 1937 he founded Focke-Achgelis & Co. to construct helicopters, and in 1942 his Fw 61 set an altitude record of 23,290 ft (7,100 m) that stood for 12 years. After the war he worked in France, Britain, The Netherlands, and Brazil. In 1958 Focke-Achgelis, later incorporated into the VFW-Fokker Co., built West Germany's first helicopter.

Forssmann, Werner, German surgeon (b. Aug. 29, 1904, Berlin, Germany—d. June 1, 1979, Schopfheim, West Germany), shared the 1956 Nobel Prize for Physiology or Medicine with André Cournand and Dickinson W. Richards. Forssmann demonstrated on himself that a catheter inserted into a vein at the elbow could safely be maneuvered all the way to the heart. This contribution to medical technology was largely ignored for nearly ten years before Cournand and Richards perfected the procedure. Cardiac catheterization, as it is now called, enables doctors both to study the conditions under which the diseased human heart functions and to make more accurate diagnoses of underlying anatomic defects. The three physicians were awarded the Nobel Prize for discoveries concerning heart catheterization and circulatory changes. Forssmann was elected a member of the American College of Chest Physicians in 1954.

Frankenfeld, Peter, German radio and television personality (b. May 31, 1913, Berlin, Germany—d. Jan. 4, 1979, Hamburg, West Germany), pioneered quiz programs on West German radio and television, becoming the country's best-known quizmaster and talk show emcee. He was a dancing teacher, magician, and commercial artist before serving in the German Army during World War II. He became an interpreter with the U.S. military government before going into broadcasting in 1948.

Fraser Darling, Sir Frank, British naturalist (b. June 23, 1903—d. Oct. 22, 1979, Forres, Scotland), was an ecologist and animal geneticist whose expertise was respected on several continents; he was also vice-president of the Conservation Foundation, Washington, D.C., 1959–72. Fraser Darling warned that man was threatening the Earth's capacity to support life. He was trained at Edinburgh University, where he became senior lecturer in ecology and conservation (1953–58); he also directed (1943–50) the major social and biological investigation published in 1955 as *West Highland Survey.* Knighted in 1970, Fraser Darling served (1970–73) on the Royal Commission on Environmental Pollution. His published surveys and ecological works include his Reith lectures, *Wilderness and Plenty* (1970), and *Impacts of Man on the Biosphere* (1969). With J. Morton Boyd, Fraser Darling wrote the classic natural history book *The Highlands and Islands* (1964).

Gabor, Dennis, Hungarian-born physicist (b. June 5, 1900, Budapest, Hung.—d. Feb. 9, 1979, London, England), was awarded the 1971 Nobel Prize for Physics for his invention of holography, a method of three-dimensional photography that allows the viewer to study an object as if he were seeing it through a window rather than on the surface of a photographic plate. Gabor worked in Berlin until 1933, then went to England where in 1947 his work on an electron microscope led to the idea of holography. He was reader in electronics (1949–58) and professor of applied electron physics (1958–67) at the Imperial College of Science and Technology, University of London. In 1967 he joined Columbia Broadcasting System Laboratories at Stamford, Conn., as a staff scientist. Gabor's publications included several books on the social implications of technological change, among them *Electronic Inventions and Their Impact on Civilization* (1959), *Inventing the Future* (1963), and *The Mature Society* (1972), warning of problems associated with nuclear weapons, overpopulation, and increased leisure.

Garner, Hugh, Canadian writer (b. Feb. 22, 1913, Batley, England—d. June 30, 1979, Toronto, Ont.), was the explosive author of biting social commentary based upon his childhood experiences in the Cabbagetown slums of Toronto during the Depression. Garner, who established a reputation in 1950 with the abridged paperback version of the novel *Cabbagetown* (unabridged edition 1968), produced ten novels, some 75 short stories, eight television dramas, and countless magazine articles. His first novel, *Storm Below* (1949), recaptured his naval experiences during World War II. Later works include *The Yellow Sweater and Other Stories* (1952), *The Sin Sniper* (1970), *Death in Don Mills* (1975), and *Murder Has Your Number* (1978). His autobiography, *One Damn Thing After Another,* appeared in 1973.

Gehlen, Reinhard, German Army officer (b. April 3, 1902, Erfurt, Thuringia, Germany—d. June 8, 1979, Bergen, Lake Starnberg, Bayern [Bavaria], West Germany), was a head of military intelligence both in the Third Reich and in West Germany. He joined the new German Reichswehr in 1920 and in 1935 became a member of Hitler's Wehrmacht general staff. At the outset of World War II he took part in the invasion of Poland. In the spring of 1942 Colonel Gehlen was appointed head of the Fremde Heere Ost (Foreign Armies East) department of the Abwehr, the military intelligence service under Adm. Wilhelm Canaris. His evaluations of Soviet military capabilities and intentions were generally correct, too correct for Hitler, who on Jan. 9, 1945, sacked Gehlen, saying that his predictions were "completely idiotic." With the end of the war in sight, Gehlen and his staff made their way south and in May gave themselves up to a U.S. unit. Gehlen was flown to Washington, D.C., where he agreed to form a German intelligence service that would get information from behind the iron curtain for the Americans. He was granted a fixed budget, and a special compound at Pullach, near Munich, was provided for the "Gehlen Organization." In May 1955 Chancellor Konrad Adenauer appointed Gehlen head of the Bundesnachrichtendienst (Federal Information Service). In 1968 he was forced to retire, mainly because two of his aides were discovered to be Soviet agents. In 1971 he published his memoirs, *Der Dienst.*

Giles, Warren Crandall, U.S. sports executive (b. May 28, 1896, Tiskilwa, Ill.—d. Feb. 7, 1979, Cincinnati, Ohio), who expertly maintained the tradition of professional baseball while keeping pace with the times as long-standing (1951–69) president of the National League. During his tenure, the league expanded from 8 to 12 teams and ended the dominance of the rival American League by winning 16 of 22 All-Star Games and 10 of 19 World Series championships. One of Giles's most outstanding achievements occurred in the 1930s when he turned the debt-ridden, last-place Cincinnati Reds into world champions. He was general manager (1936–48) of the Reds and became president in 1948 after the club achieved financial stability. Although Giles was considered a likely candidate in 1951 for baseball commissioner, he withdrew his name from the ballot when the election appeared deadlocked after 17 ballots. He was named president of the National League, and Ford Frick became commissioner.

Gould, Randall Chase, U.S. editor (b. 1897?, Minnesota—d. Oct. 23?, 1979, Mill Valley, Calif.), was a top-notch U.S. reporter in China during the mid-1920s and later served as editor and publisher (1931–49) of *The Shanghai Evening Post and Mercury,* the only American-owned newspaper in Shanghai. In the late 1930s, when a Japanese puppet regime of Chinese assumed power in Shanghai, Gould's newspaper offices were bombed and ten Chinese staff members were killed, apparently because Gould warned against Japanese aggression. In 1949, however, Gould suspended publication of the newspaper and returned to the U.S. because of growing Nationalist Chinese censorship, problems with his staff, and later Chinese Communist pressure. In 1959 he joined the staff of the *San Rafael* (Calif.) *Independent-Journal* but retired in 1963. Gould, who was apparently despondent over his own and his wife's health, killed her before turning the gun on himself.

Grand, Albert, French journalist (b. 1912—d. March 1979, Paris, France), was for many years the leading UN spokesman on the Middle East. His intellectual integrity and accurate and perspicacious information made him sought after by foreign correspondents and so respected that he could move freely between Israel and Arab countries. Having worked for French newspapers as correspondent in Britain and Spain during the Spanish Civil War, he was in New York during World War II where he issued *France Speaks,* a news bulletin on the Resistance, before serving in the French Navy. His job as a journalist after the war led to his appointment to the UN Information Services in New York. After arriving in the Middle East with Count Folke Bernadotte in 1948, he assisted UN mediator Ralph Bunche and in Jerusalem served as press officer and diplomatic councillor attached to successive commanders of the UN Truce Supervision Organization (UNTSO).

Grenfell, Joyce, British actress and author (b. Feb. 10, 1910, London, England—d. Nov. 30, 1979, London), was for 40 years one of the best-loved entertainers in British broadcasting, theatre, and cinema. Grenfell portrayed a slightly bemused middle-class Englishwoman in her stage monologues, a role that she carried over with only marginal variation into her film parts as the school mistresses of *The Happiest Days of Your Life* and the *St. Trinian's* series. The character, so instantly recognized by British and foreign audiences as an archetype of the mildly eccentric spinster, had nothing in common with its creator, who enjoyed a long and happy marriage and was an accomplished writer and journalist. Her books included *George, Don't Do That* and an autobiography, *Joyce Grenfell Requests the Pleasure* (1976). She appeared on stage in London and made frequent tours in the U.S., Canada, Australia, and New Zealand. Grenfell also enjoyed wide popularity on television, particularly as a panelist on the musical quiz "Face the Music," where she displayed a considerable knowledge of music without pretension or solemnity. During World War II she entertained the troops in North Africa, the Middle East, Italy, and India and in 1946 was made an OBE.

Griffith-Jones, (John) Mervyn Guthrie, British judge (b. July 1, 1909—d. July 13, 1979, London, England), was prosecutor in the 1960 obscenity trial against the publishers of D. H. Lawrence's novel *Lady Chatterley's Lover.* Griffith-Jones's question to the jury, whether they would want their wives or servants to read the book, unwittingly highlighted the revolution in social attitudes and behaviour taking place in British society. Educated at Eton and Cambridge and called to the bar of the Middle Temple in 1932, he served with the Coldstream Guards during World War II and was a prosecutor at the Nuremberg trials. In 1963 he appeared against Stephen Ward, the osteopath involved in the Profumo affair that rocked the British government that year. In the following year he was made common sergeant in the City of London, giving up his successful practice as crown counsel. A keen painter, he held several one-man exhibitions in London.

Guggenheim, Peggy (MARGUERITE GUGGENHEIM), U.S. art collector (b. Aug. 26, 1898, New York, N.Y.—d. Dec. 23, 1979, Venice, Italy), was a major influence on the development of Abstract Expressionism as patron of such leading painters of the genre as Jackson Pollock, Robert Motherwell, William Baziotes, and Yves Tanguy. Guggenheim, who entered the art world as a dealer, later began amassing paintings that at the time of her death were collectively estimated to be worth $30 million. Her collection, considered one of the foremost in the world, included works by Picasso, Braque, Arp, Chagall, Dalí, Miró, Klee, Kandinsky, and Pollock. Guggenheim left her collection to the New York museum named after her uncle Solomon R. Guggenheim, with the stipulation that the more than 260 pieces housed in a museum at her palazzo in Venice remain there. Her 1946 autobiography, *Out of This Century,* recounts her four marriages, to writers Lawrence Vail, John Holms, and Douglas Garman and to artist Max Ernst.

Haekkerup, Per, Danish politician (b. Dec. 25, 1915, Ringsted, Den.—d. March 13, 1979, Stubberup, Lolland, Den.), a leading figure in Denmark's Social Democrat Party during the 1960s and '70s, was his country's foreign minister (1962–66), finance minister (1971–74), minister of economics and trade (1975–77), and minister without portfolio (1978). He entered the Folketing (parliament) in 1950 and served as an exceptionally industrious Cabinet minister in five Social Democrat governments. He was also a member of the City Council of Copenhagen from 1946 to 1950 and was economics editor of the Social Democrat newspaper, *Aktuelt,* from 1956 to 1961.

Hafizullah Amin, Afghan politician (b. Aug. 1, 1929, Paghman, Afghanistan—d. Dec. 27, 1979, in or near Kabul, Afghanistan), served as president (Sept. 16, 1979 to Dec. 27, 1979) of the Revolutionary Council of Afghanistan after overthrowing Nur Mohammad Taraki (*q.v.*) in a bloody coup. After graduating from Columbia University, Amin returned to his homeland and joined the Wikh-i-Zalmayan ("awakened youth"), a reform-minded brotherhood. In 1963 Amin became a member of

UPI

the leftist Khalq ("masses") Party founded by Taraki. On April 27, 1978, Amin, who had become the Khalq strong man, engineered a coup that toppled the government of Mohammad Daud Khan. But Taraki became president of the Revolutionary Council and Amin was given a post in foreign affairs. On March 27, 1979, Amin was named prime minister, but six months later, after still another coup, he succeeded Taraki as president.

When the Soviet Union invaded Afghanistan in late December and installed Babrak Karmal as president, Amin was assassinated.

Haley, Jack (John Joseph Haley), U.S. actor (b. Aug. 10, 1899, Boston, Mass.—d. June 6, 1979, Los Angeles, Calif.), danced his way to stardom as the Tin Woodman who cavorted with Judy Garland down the yellow brick road in search of a heart in the 1939 motion picture classic *The Wizard of Oz.* In this, his most memorable role, Haley sported an outrageous metal costume with an inverted metal funnel for a hat. Early in his career Haley worked as a song plugger and also performed song-comedy routines in vaudeville. He later earned Broadway roles in *Follow Thru* (1929) and *Take a Chance* (1932) because of his bright blue eyes, handsome appearance, and unfailing sense of humour. In 1948, after appearing in some 50 films including *Sitting Pretty, Rebecca of Sunnybrook Farm,* and *Alexander's Ragtime Band,* Haley retired and turned to real estate investments. He returned to the screen in *Norwood* (1970) and made his final public appearance in April at the Academy Awards presentation which was produced by his son, Jack, Jr.

Hallpike, Charles Skinner, British otologist (b. July 19, 1900, Lahore, India—d. Sept. 26, 1979, Southampton, England), was aural physician and director of the Medical Research Council otological research unit at the National Hospital for Nervous Diseases in London (1944–65) and an international authority on hearing. Hallpike was responsible for many advances in the treatment of deafness. After working at Guy's Hospital, London, Hallpike furthered his specialized career at the Middlesex Hospital, London, which he joined in 1929. In 1938 he served in the Royal Air Force on the Flying Personnel Research Committee. He was elected a fellow of the Royal Society in 1956.

Halsman, Philippe, Latvian-born photographer (b. May 2, 1906, Riga, Latvia—d. June 25, 1979, New York, N.Y.), was a successful fashion photographer in Paris before fleeing (1940) to the U.S. in fear of the Nazis and becoming one of the most insightful portrait photographers in the world. Halsman's distinctive style and technical skill created an incessant demand for his portraits. His work appeared in *Look,* the *Saturday Evening Post,* and *Life,* for which he produced 101 covers, more than any other photographer. His subjects included such personalities as Eleanor Roosevelt, Salvador Dalí, Winston Churchill, Judy Garland, and Marc Chagall. Three of his portraits—those of Albert Einstein, John Steinbeck, and Adlai Stevenson—were so superb that they were selected for postage stamps. One of Halsman's favourite techniques was to engage his subject in conversation so that he could capture the essence of that individual. In 1945 Halsman became the first president of the American Society of Magazine Photographers, was reelected in 1954, and in 1975 was recipient of the society's Life Achievement award. He was named one of the ten greatest photographers in the world by *Popular Photography* (1958). Halsman's books include *Piccoli: A Fairy Tale* (1953), *Dali's Mustache* (1954), and the *Jump Book* (1959).

Harding, Gerald William Lankester, British archaeologist (b. Dec. 8, 1901, China—d. Feb. 11, 1979, London, England), played a crucial role in preserving the Dead Sea Scrolls as director (1936–56) of the Jordanian Department of Antiquities. With virtually no formal schooling, he worked in various jobs until his interest in Egyptian hieroglyphics induced Sir Flinders Petrie to accept his services during the 1926 excavations near Gaza, Palestine. From 1932 to 1936 he assisted J. L. Starkey at Lachish, Palestine, and deciphered inscriptions recording the destruction of the town in biblical times. When the Dead Sea Scrolls were discovered in 1947, Harding immediately recognized their importance and directed excavations at the site. He later undertook important archaeological work in Lebanon and Jordan.

Hare, (J.) Robertson, British actor (b. Dec. 17, 1891, London, England—d. Jan. 25, 1979, London), made his name with the renowned "Aldwych farce" company during the 1920s and '30s, playing in a long series of Ben Travers's farces that included *A Cuckoo in the Nest, Rookery Nook, Thark,* and *Plunder.* Hare, the much-put-upon member of a trio completed by Tom Walls and Ralph Lynn, responded to all manner of indignities, including frequent loss of his nether garments, with a woeful "Oh, calamity!"—a phrase that became his trademark. After making his West End debut in 1912 as a torchbearer in Sir John Martin Harvey's Covent Garden production of *Oedipus Rex,* he starred in the title role of *Gumpy* for two years (1914–16), then served in the British Army in France (1917–18). He first joined Walls and Lynn in the farce *Tons of Money* at the Shaftesbury Theatre, London, in 1920. Hare continued to play in farces by Travers and Vernon Sylvaine during and after World War II. During 1968–70 he played an archdeacon in BBC television's comedy series "All Gas and Gaiters."

Harris, Jed (Jacob Horowitz), Austrian-born producer and director (b. Feb. 25, 1900, Vienna, Austria—d. Nov. 15, 1979, New York, N.Y.), had a particular flair for producing and directing successful Broadway plays and for confounding his associates with outrageous behaviour. Before dropping out of Yale, Harris bluntly told a professor "I'm neither rich enough nor dull-witted enough to endure this awful place." On another occasion Harris astonished playwright George S. Kaufman by conducting a meeting in the nude. His theatrical accomplishments included such plays as *Coquette, The Royal Family, The Front Page, Broadway, A Doll's House, Our Town,* and *The Heiress,* his last significant show. After *Child of Fortune* (1956), Harris quietly retired. His autobiography, *A Dance on the High Wire,* appeared a week before his death.

Harris, Roy, U.S. composer (b. Feb. 12, 1898, Lincoln County, Okla.—d. Oct. 1, 1979, Santa Monica, Calif.), became known as "The Walt Whitman of American Music" because his musical compositions, marked by broad tonal melodies and asymmetric rhythms, were identified with U.S. nationalism. Harris worked as a truck driver before learning to compose on his own and studying music with Arthur Farwell and Modeste Altschuler in California. He then studied in Paris under Nadia Boulanger (*q.v.*), who also taught such U.S. composers as Aaron Copland and Virgil Thomson. Harris, who wrote 16 powerful symphonies and at least 185 major works, was best remembered for his Third Symphony (1939), a one-movement work that remains a standard orchestra piece, and *When Johnny Comes Marching Home* (1935), a symphonic overture based on a Civil War song, recorded by the Minneapolis Symphony under Eugene Ormandy. His reputation for homespun music was reinforced with such symphonies as the Fourth, known as the *Folksong Symphony,* which was inspired by pioneer songs; the Sixth, subtitled *Gettysburg Address;* and the Tenth, called the *Abraham Lincoln Symphony.* Harris also wrote several ballets and choral, chamber, piano, organ, and band music. From 1974 until his death Harris was composer in residence at California State University at Los Angeles.

Hartnell, Sir Norman, British couturier (b. June 12, 1901, Devon, England—d. June 8, 1979, Windsor, England), designed clothes for Queen Elizabeth II, for Queen Elizabeth the queen mother, and for other members of the royal family from 1938. Hartnell was knighted in 1977 not only for his services to the royal family but also for his contributions to the British fashion industry. From costuming the footlights revue at Magdalene College, Cambridge, he moved into dressmaking with his sister, in Bruton Street, London, in the 1920s. Patronage by royalty began with his wedding dress for the duchess of Gloucester and bridesmaid's dress for Princess Elizabeth in 1935. He designed most of Queen Elizabeth II's dresses for important occasions, including her coronation dress. Hartnell's most successful dresses were those for evening grand occasions, made of fine materials beautifully embroidered or sewn with seed pearls, sequins, or crystal. He sold ready-to-wear clothes in his boutique and to other stores and offered a perfume, "In Love," but his attempt to market men's clothes was less successful. In 1947 he received the Neiman-Marcus Award for world influence on fashion. His autobiography, *Silver and Gold,* appeared in 1955 and *Royal Courts of Fashion* in 1971.

Hathaway, Donny, U.S. singer (b. Oct. 1, 1945, Chicago, Ill.—d. Jan. 13, 1979, New York, N.Y.), whose pop hit record album "Roberta Flack and Donny Hathaway" (1972) soared to the top of the charts, sold more than 500,000 copies, and won the pair a Grammy award. In 1973 the versatile Hathaway composed, scored, and recorded the single "You've Got a Friend" in only two hours, and later in the year he recorded the hit single "Where Is the Love" with Flack. He teamed up again with Flack in 1978 and produced "The Closer I Get to You," another hit single. Hathaway, who was deeply troubled by his quick ascent to fame, plunged to his death from the 15th floor of the Essex House in New York City.

Haya de la Torre, Víctor Raúl, Peruvian statesman (b. Feb. 22, 1895, Trujillo, Peru—d. Aug. 2, 1979, Peru), was the founder (1924) of the Alianza Popular Revolucionaria Americana (APRA), better known as the Aprista movement. While studying law at San Marcos University of Lima, Haya led a mass demonstration (May 1923) protesting the dedication of Peru to the Sacred Heart of Jesus. He was jailed by the dictatorial regime of Augusto Leguía and deported (October 1923) after staging a hunger strike. Exiled to Mexico City, he founded APRA, returning to his homeland in 1931 when Leguía's regime fell. Haya's doctrine, aimed at ending imperialism and promoting Latin-American political unity, posed a threat to Peru's oligarchy, which supported Col. Luis M. Sánchez Cerro for president. In a much disputed election Sánchez became president and Haya was imprisoned until 1933. For the next 11 years he worked underground. In 1945 Aprista backed José Bustamante, who became president and outlawed the party in 1947 before being overthrown by Gen. Manuel Odría. Haya then took up residence in the Colombian embassy for five years until, under international pressure, he was allowed to leave Peru. Haya ran for president again in 1962 and led the field that included Fernando Belaúnde Terry, but the military voided the election. In the 1963 election, Belaúnde was victorious. When the military junta, which had ruled Peru since 1969, called for presidential elections for 1980, Aprista announced that Haya would be its candidate.

Hayward, Max, British linguistic scholar (b. July 28, 1924, London, England—d. March 18, 1979, Oxford, England), was a foremost Western scholar of modern Russian literature. With Manya Harari he translated Boris Pasternak's *Doctor Zhivago,* the memoirs of Nadezhda Mandelstam (*Hope Against Hope* and *Hope Abandoned*), and Olga Ivinskaya's *A Captive of Time: My Years with Pasternak.* Hayward served in the British embassy in Moscow (1947–

49) and headed the Russian department at the University of Leeds (1949–56) before joining St. Antony's College, Oxford, where he became a fellow. He was also fluent in Czech and at the time of the Hungarian rising in 1956 mastered enough Hungarian in a few days to enable him to converse with refugees.

Hearne, Richard, British comedian (b. Jan. 30, 1909, Norwich, England—d. Aug. 23, 1979, Bearstead, Kent, England), created the character of "Mr. Pastry," one of the most popular comic figures on television for 20 years. Born into a show business family, he was on stage before he could walk and on television almost before the new medium had any viewers. He trained in circus, pantomime, and musical comedy and made his television debut in 1939. "Mr. Pastry" first appeared in 1945 and became an international figure, exploiting Hearne's acrobatic training and his gift for comedy. He retired in 1970, his creator saddened by the "permissiveness" that he felt had killed family entertainment. An active worker for children's charities, Hearne was made an OBE in 1970.

Hilton, Conrad Nicholson, U.S. hotelier (b. Dec. 25, 1887, San Antonio, N.M.—d. Jan. 3, 1979, Santa Monica, Calif.), whose shrewdness, caution, and financial awareness made him the proprietor of one of the world's most prestigious hotel chains. Hilton, who purchased the 40-room Mobley Hotel in Cisco, Texas, at age 31, parlayed his original $5,000 investment into an empire. In 1946 he formed the Hilton Hotel Corp. and served as president and chairman of the board. Three years later he gained control of the Waldorf-Astoria and in 1954 the Statler Hotel chain. Hilton was also responsible for establishing the Carte Blanche credit card company and for founding Hilton International, which was acquired (1967) by Trans World Airlines and operated 75 hotels in 45 countries. Although Hilton retained his position as chairman of the board, his son Barron became president of the $500 million company with 185 inns and hotels in the U.S. Hilton's autobiography, *Be My Guest* (1957), became the bedside rival of the Gideon Bible in every one of the company's 64,000 rooms.

DESAUNOIS—SYGMA

Hitchens, (Sydney) Ivon, British painter (b. March 3, 1893, London, England—d. Aug. 29, 1979, Petworth, Sussex, England), experimented with abstraction before he began to apply his feeling for colour and horizontal planes to near-abstract landscapes. After moving to Sussex in 1940 Hitchens painted wide rectangular canvases, which are his best-known work. He also painted murals for the Folk Dance and Song Society in Cecil Sharp House and for the University of Sussex. By the 1950s Hitchens had acquired an international reputation confirmed by a major retrospective exhibition in Venice in 1956. The Tate Gallery in London held a similar exhibition in 1963 as did the Royal Academy, London, in 1979.

Hope-Wallace, Philip Adrian, British dramatic critic (b. Nov. 6, 1911, Wimbledon, Surrey, England—d. Sept. 3, 1979, Guildford, Surrey), was a London dramatic and music critic who worked for *The Times, The Daily Telegraph,* and, from 1946, the *Manchester Guardian* (later *The Guardian*) for nearly 40 years. He also wrote for weekly reviews, including *Time and Tide* and the British Broadcasting Corporation's *Listener,* besides broadcasting, notably on the "Critics" program. He was appreciated for sure judgment enlivened with urbanity and wit. From Balliol College, Oxford, he went to the International Broadcasting Company, France, in 1934. He became a correspondent for *The Times* and in World War II served in the Air Ministry press office before devoting himself to critical journalism.

Hoveida, Amir Abbas, Iranian politician (b. Feb. 18, 1919, Teheran, Iran—d. April 7, 1979, Teheran), was Iran's prime minister from January 1965 until August 1977. After taking political science degrees at the universities of Brussels and Paris, he joined the Iranian Foreign Office and served in Paris, Bonn, Ankara, and at the UN in New York. In 1958 he was appointed to the board of the National Iranian Oil Company. After becoming prime minister he organized the October 1971 festivities at Persepolis commemorating the 2,500th anniversary of the founding of the Persian Empire. As leader of the ruling Iran Novin (New Iran) Party he won a landslide victory at the 1971 general elections. Iran's financial strength enabled Hoveida to strike advantageous bargains with Western customers for Iranian oil in order to promote Iran's own economic development. Opposition at home, some of it Soviet-inspired, was never completely eradicated. In January 1974, 12 persons were brought to trial on charges of terrorist activities, including plotting to assassinate the shah. But the sovereign's gratitude proved limited and on Aug. 7, 1977, Hoveida was replaced by Jamshid Amouzegar. In November 1978 Hoveida was detained by the shah's short-lived military government. At the time of the February 1979 uprising he gave himself up to the new government appointed by Ayatollah Ruhollah Khomeini. Two months later he was sentenced to death by the Islamic Revolutionary Court and shot the same day.

Hutchison, Sir James Riley Holt, British politician (b. 1893—d. Feb. 24, 1979, London, England), helped to disrupt the German Army's response to the 1944 Normandy landings as an Allied secret agent in France during World War II. He first had to undergo facial plastic surgery because he was known to the Gestapo from his work with the French Resistance. Having served in both World Wars, he received British and French decorations for his exploits in 1945. After the war he was a Conservative member of Parliament for Glasgow divisions during 1945–50 and 1950–59 and was parliamentary undersecretary, War Office, from 1951 to 1954. In 1956 he was created a baronet. Hutchison also became a director of the Ailsa Shipbuilding Co. and was prominent in the European movement. In 1977 he published his memoirs, *That Drug, Danger.*

Hutton, Barbara, U.S. heiress (b. Nov. 14, 1912, New York, N.Y.—d. May 11, 1979, Los Angeles, Calif.), was the granddaughter of F. W. Woolworth, who founded the "5-and-10-cent store" and left a family fortune estimated at $27 million. Hutton eventually inherited $60 million, but wealth alone could not bring happiness. The "poor little rich girl" lost her mother at age four, her beloved grandfather at age seven, and her grandmother at age 12. Frequently ill and constantly protected by relatives and bodyguards, she developed a reticence and timidity that remained throughout her life. Her seven marriages, she once confessed, were attempts to ward off loneliness. Her first husband was the Russian Prince Alexis Mdivani of Georgia (1933); the next was Count Kurt Haugwitz-Reventlow of Denmark (1935), who became the father of her only child, Lance. She then successively married actor Cary Grant (1942), Lithuanian Prince Igor Troubetzkoy (1947), Dominican playboy Porfirio Rubirosa (1953), tennis ace Baron Gottfried von Cramm (1955), and Laotian Prince Raymond Doan Vinh (1964).

Illingworth, Leslie Gilbert, British cartoonist (b. Sept. 2, 1902, Barry, Wales—d. Dec. 20, 1979, Hastings, England), was a gifted draftsman whose finely drawn cartoons were familiar features of *Punch* and the *Daily Mail* for several decades. He studied at Cardiff Art School and in London at the Royal College of Art and the Slade School. In 1921 Illingworth became political cartoonist on the Cardiff *Western Mail.* After submitting his first cartoon to *Punch* in 1927 he became a regular contributor to the magazine until his retirement in 1969, supplying weekly full-page cartoons from 1937. From 1939 until his retirement he was also the *Daily Mail*'s political cartoonist. A retrospective exhibition of his original cartoons was held (1970) in the Wiggin Gallery of the Public Library in Boston, Mass.

Imamichi Junzo (b. Oct. 11, 1901, Nagasaki Prefecture, Japan—d. May 25, 1979, Tokyo, Japan), worked for 23 years with Japan's Osaka Shosen Kaisha, a famous shipping company, before joining (1952) the private broadcasting company, Radio Tokyo, as chief of the general affairs department. In 1955 Imamichi was made a director of what five years later became Tokyo Broadcasting System (TBS). For the next 20 years he nurtured the development of the company to a position of preeminence in the Japanese broadcasting industry. He became president in 1965 and chairman in 1973. Under his guidance TBS forged ahead in the public service field as well as the entertainment business. Its success demonstrated the vitality of the free enterprise approach to radio and television in Japan. In 1969 he became the founding chairman of TBS-Britannica, a company that rapidly developed due in great part to Imamichi's strong feelings for public service. In cooperation with Encyclopædia Britannica, Inc., he promoted the ambitious and unprecedented creation of a truly Japanese edition of the *Encyclopædia Britannica.* At the time of his death he remained chairman of TBS-Britannica, three years after he resigned the chairmanship of TBS itself.

Inman, Philip Albert Inman, 1ST BARON, British company director (b. June 12, 1892, Knaresborough, Yorkshire, England—d. Aug. 26, 1979, Haywards Heath, West Sussex, England), was a governor, then chairman, of Charing Cross Hospital, London, from 1921 to 1966 and raised more than £1 million in contributions to make the hospital financially secure. Inman worked his way through university and had successful careers in publishing and the hotel industry. He was made a baron in 1946 and in the following year served briefly as lord privy seal. As church commissioner Inman showed the same flair in dealing with church finances as he had as a hospital administrator. He wrote a number of books describing his life and work, including *The Human Touch.*

Isaacs, George Alfred, British trade unionist and politician (b. 1883, London, England—d. April 26, 1979, Cobham, Surrey, England), played a notable role in establishing Britain's post-World War II welfare state as minister of labour and national service (1945–51) and minister of pensions (1951) in Clement Attlee's Labour government. Isaacs was an alderman and mayor (1919–21) of Southwark before he entered Parliament in 1923 and sat as member for Southwark (1929–31 and 1939–59). As a trade unionist he was secretary (1909–49) of the National Society of Operative Printers and Assistants and in 1945 was chairman of the general council of the Trades Union Congress. Isaacs was also president of the World Trade Union Conference that year.

Jones, Preston, U.S. playwright (b. April 7, 1936, Albuquerque, N.M.—d. Sept. 19, 1979, Dallas, Texas), embarked on a writing career at the age of 37 and enjoyed instant renown with *A Texas Trilogy* (1976). When his three plays (*The Last Meeting of the Knights of the White Magnolia, Lu Ann Hampton Laverty Oberlander,* and *The Oldest Living Graduate*) were first staged on Broadway, Jones was publicized as a new Eugene O'Neill or Tennessee Williams. Though critics were not especially impressed, and after 63 rotating repertory performances the plays closed on Broadway, Jones's realistic portrayal of the residents of fictional Bradleyville, Texas, struck a sympathetic chord with audiences at the Dallas Theater Center, the John F. Kennedy Center for the Performing Arts in Washington, and regional theatres across the U.S.

Jooss, Kurt, German choreographer (b. Jan. 12, 1901, Wasseralfingen, Württemberg, Germany—d. May 22, 1979, Heilbronn, West Germany), whose Expressionist form of ballet gave a powerful impulse to modern dance. In 1932 Jooss produced two masterpieces of dance drama, *The Green Table,* a satire on the futility of war and diplomatists' peace conferences, and *The Big City*. While studying music and drama in Stuttgart, he was influenced by dance theorist Rudolf Laban, whose pupil he became. In 1924 he was appointed ballet master at the Münster City Theatre, then, founding his own company, the Neue Tanzbühne, he moved to Essen in 1927. There, as director of the Folkwang Dance Theatre Studio from 1928 and ballet master at the Essen Opera House from 1930, he was influenced by Russian ballet, which he reinterpreted in an eclectically vitalized style. After Hitler came to power Jooss in 1934 moved his company, now the Ballets Jooss, to Dartington Hall, Devon, England, but disbanded it in 1947. In 1949, as a British citizen, he returned to Essen and reestablished his school and ballet; the ballet company disbanded in 1953 and he retired as school director in 1968. In 1976 the Joffrey Ballet celebrated Jooss's 75th birthday with a program at New York's City Center devoted to his works.

Jouhandeau, Marcel Henri, French writer (b. July 26, 1888, Guéret, France—d. April 7, 1979, Rueil-Malmaison, France), spent a lifetime writing mostly autobiographical works exploring a personality molded by his provincial upbringing, his Roman Catholicism, his homosexuality, and his tormented but miraculously durable marriage. His marriage in 1929 to the dancer Caryathis (Elisabeth Toulemon) provided the material for highly personal and indiscreet works, including *Chroniques maritales* (1938). Jouhandeau was noted above all as a stylist, an aesthete who could transform into literature the most sordid of erotic adventures. His sometimes acid evocations of other writers, including André Gide, Jean Cocteau, and François Mauriac, and the novels in which, as Monsieur Godeau, he penetrates beneath the surface of provincial society ensure his place in 20th-century literature.

Kadar, Jan, Hungarian-born motion-picture director (b. April 1, 1918, Budapest, Hung.—d. June 1, 1979, Los Angeles, Calif.), was an expatriate Czech who collaborated with writer Elmar Klos to produce movies focusing on human and individual rights. His most poignant and haunting film, *The Shop on Main Street,* won an Academy Award for the best foreign film of 1965 as well as the New York Film Critics Award. Kadar's father, mother, and sister all died at Auschwitz, the Nazi concentration camp; Kadar himself was imprisoned (1938–45) by the Nazis in a labour camp near Budapest. He immigrated to the U.S. in 1968 when Warsaw-Pact forces led by Soviet tanks invaded Czechoslovakia. During the 1960s Kadar worked for Czechoslovak Film, the state-owned moviemaking monopoly, and directed such films as *Death Is Called Engelchen,* which won top honours at the 1963 Moscow International Film Festival, *The Defendant* (1964), and *The Accused* (1964). In the U.S. he directed *The Angel Levine* (1970), *Lies My Father Told Me,* which won the 1975 Golden Globe Award for best foreign film, and *Freedom Road* with Muhammad Ali.

Kahnweiler, Daniel-Henry, German-born French art dealer (b. June 25, 1884, Mannheim, Germany—d. Jan. 11, 1979, Paris, France), was a close associate of the pioneers of Cubism and an avid purchaser of paintings by Picasso, Braque, André Derain, and others before they received wide recognition. Kahnweiler settled in Paris in 1902 and opened a gallery there in 1907, the year Picasso created "Les Demoiselles d'Avignon." Kahnweiler later noted the seminal importance of this work in *Der Weg zum Kubismus* (1920; Eng. trans., *The Rise of Cubism,* 1949). He also wrote books on Picasso's sculpture and ceramics and studies of Derain, Maurice de Vlaminck, Juan Gris, and Paul Klee. Because his interest in Cubism also embraced writers connected with the movement, he published poems by Guillaume Apollinaire, Max Jacob, André Salmon, and others, with illustrations by Braque, Derain, and Picasso. A Cubist portrait of Kahnweiler painted by Picasso in 1910 is in the Art Institute of Chicago.

Kardelj, Edvard, Yugoslav politician and theorist (b. Jan. 27, 1910, Ljubljana, Slovenia—d. Feb. 10, 1979, Ljubljana), was President Tito's most loyal colleague and played a major role in shaping Yugoslavia's socialist system. A schoolteacher, Kardelj was imprisoned from 1932 to 1934 for his trade union and party activities. He then went to Moscow where he first met Tito. Kardelj fought with the Yugoslav partisans against the German occupation in World War II and from then until his death held leading posts in the League of Communists and the state: he was considered Tito's most likely successor. Kardelj lacked charisma, but he was the architect of Yugoslav self-management and the theorist of nonalignment. His main works dealt with property in the socialist state and with democracy, giving a theoretical base to the features that distinguish Yugoslav socialism from the systems of the West and of the Soviet Union.

Kelly, Emmett Lee, U.S. circus performer (b. Dec. 9, 1898, Sedan, Kan.—d. March 28, 1979, Sarasota, Fla.), enchanted children and adults alike as Weary Willie, a sad-eyed, bedraggled clown whose soulful expressions made him a leading attraction at the Ringling Bros. and Barnum & Bailey Circus from 1942 to 1956. In some of his most successful comic routines Willie could be seen thoughtfully munching a cabbage, fruitlessly chasing an elusive spotlight, or simply staring mournfully into the eyes of a spectator. Although Kelly initially pursued a career as a cartoonist, he left his job with a Kansas City advertising film company to join Howes' Great London Circus as a trapeze artist and clown. After leaving Ringling Bros. Kelly became the mascot for the Brooklyn Dodgers baseball team in 1957. His autobiography, *Clown,* was published in 1954.

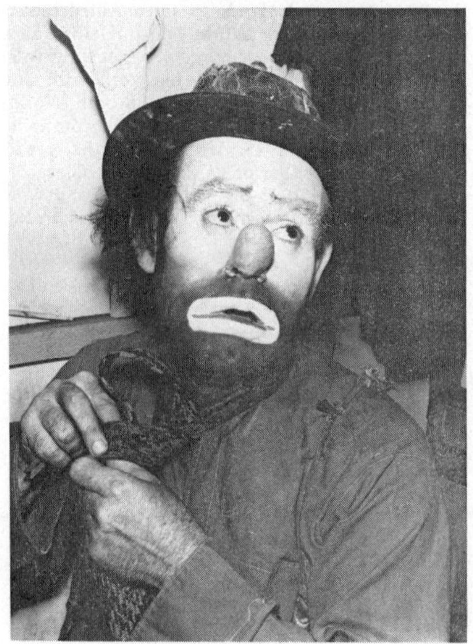
WIDE WORLD

Kenton, Stan(ley Newcombe), U.S. bandleader (b. Feb. 19, 1912, Wichita, Kan.—d. Aug. 25, 1979, Hollywood, Calif.), composed experimental arrangements using staccato saxophone ensembles and heavy rhythm accents and earned a reputation for his screaming "walls of brass." A pianist and major jazz bandleader of the big band era (1935–45), Kenton retained his musical appeal even after other bandleaders were forgotten. Kenton's band made its first appearance, introducing his innovative arrangements, in June 1941 at the Rendezvous Ballroom at Balboa Beach, Newport Beach, Calif. In 1943 his band soared to the top of wartime popularity with such Capitol records as "Artistry in Rhythm" and "Eager Beaver," and in later years it featured such crowd-pleasing singers as Anita O'Day, June Christy, and Chris Connor. In the late 1940s Kenton, who suffered from exhaustion, disbanded his group several times, and in the 1950s he reorganized a new band each year. He later offered summer music education with the establishment (1959) of the Stan Kenton Clinic, and in 1965 he helped organize the Los Angeles Neophonic Orchestra, a jazz group. In 1970 Kenton formed Creative World Records and reissued discs formerly copyrighted by Capitol Records, Inc. During the last years of his life Kenton toured extensively with his band.

Kerley, Sir Peter James, Irish radiologist (b. Oct. 27, 1900, Dundalk, Ireland—d. March 15, 1979, London, England), was an outstanding radiological authority, who specialized in heart and lung diseases and was honoured by institutions in the U.S., Canada, Australia, and the British Isles. Trained at Ireland's University College and at the University of Vienna, he became radiologist to the Westminster Hospital and the National Heart Hospital, both in London, and consultant adviser to the Ministries of Health and Aviation. Kerley attended King George VI when he developed lung cancer. With S. Cochrane Shanks he edited a six-volume *Text-book of X-Ray Diagnosis* (1938; 4th ed., 1969–72) and also edited *Recent Advances in Radiology*. Kerley was made knight commander of the Royal Victorian Order in 1972.

Kessel, Joseph, French journalist and author (b. Feb. 10, 1898, Ciara, Arg.—d. July 23, 1979, Avernes, Val d'Oise, France), was the author of more than 50 travel books and novels that reflected a life spent in the unremitting pursuit of adventure. The son of a Russian-Jewish doctor, he was educated in Russia and in France and served in the French Air Force in World War I. He then began a career as a globe-trotting reporter by covering the Irish civil war in 1920. Later assignments took him to Palestine, to the Red Sea (on Henry de Monfreid's cutter, resulting in a remarkable series of reports on the slave trade for *Le Matin*), to Berlin during the Nazis' rise to power, and to Spain during the Civil War. Active membership in the French Resistance during World War II inspired the novel *L'Armée des ombres* (1944) and the lyrics of the movement's "Chant des Partisans." After the war he resumed his travels, to India, Afghanistan, Africa, and South America. Three of his best-known novels became movies: *The Lion, The Horsemen,* and *Belle de Jour* (filmed by Luis Buñuel in 1967). Kessel also wrote film scripts and scenarios and in 1962 was elected to the Académie Française.

Kettlewell, Henry Bernard Davis, British geneticist and lepidopterist (b. Feb. 24, 1907—d. May 10, 1979, Oxford, England), achieved an international reputation for his studies on melanism in butterflies. This work, which established that black pigmentation developed in butterflies of Britain's industrial Midlands matched the polluted environments, was of importance for genetics, ecology, conservation, and the study of industrial pollution. He was co-founder of the Rothschild-Cockayne-Kettlewell Collection of British Lepidoptera (later the National Collection RCK) in the British Museum of Natural History, London. After medical training at Caius College, Cambridge, and St. Bartholomew's Hospital, London, Kettlewell became a general practitioner and in World War II served as an anesthetist. He went to South Africa in 1949 and worked for the International Locust Control Centre in Cape Town, traveling throughout tropical Africa. Returning to Britain in 1952, he was made Nuffield research fellow in the Genetics Unit of the Department of Zoology at Oxford and was the unit's senior research officer (1954–74). He wrote many papers on genetics, Lepidoptera, and ecology in specialist journals. In 1959 he was awarded the Soviet Union's Darwin Medal and in 1965 the Mendel Medal.

Knowles, John Hilton, U.S. physician (b. May 23, 1926, Chicago, Ill.—d. March 6, 1979, Boston, Mass.), was (1962–72) the iconoclastic director of Massachusetts General Hospital and the youngest doctor ever appointed to that prestigious position. Because he criticized unnecessary operations and doctors' high fees, and because he advocated preventive medicine and national health insurance, Knowles was regarded unfavourably by many in the medical profession. In 1969 he was rejected as a nominee for the post of assistant secretary of the U.S. Department of Health, Education, and Welfare, despite his impressive qualifications for the job, through the lobbying efforts of the American Medical Association. Knowles was, however, named (1972) president of the Rockefeller Foundation. Besides focusing on such domestic problems as unemployment and population stabilization, Knowles sent more than half of the foundation's grant budget abroad and helped to create international agricultural development and humanities programs.

Koeppler, Sir Heinz, German-born historian (b. June 30, 1912, Wollstein, West Prussia—d. April 1, 1979, Waco, Texas), started courses at Wilton Park, near Beaconsfield, Buckinghamshire, for German prisoners awaiting repatriation after World War II. The studies were so attractive and influential that Germans came to England to attend them. Wilton Park, of which he was warden from 1946 to 1977, was transformed into a widely attended international conference centre in 1957, after having moved to Sussex in 1950. Koeppler had studied history at German universities and at Magdalen College, Oxford, and, as an anti-Nazi, came to Britain in the 1930s. He lectured on modern history at Oxford and in World War II served in the political intelligence department of the Foreign Office. He was assistant undersecretary of state at the Foreign and Commonwealth Office (1975–77). Koeppler was knighted on retiring in 1977 and the following year became a visiting professor at Baylor University, Waco, Texas.

Kolman, Arnost (Ernst), Czech Marxist theoretician (b. Dec. 6, 1892, Prague, Bohemia—d. Jan. 22, 1979, Stockholm, Sweden), was a confidant of Lenin and survivor of the Stalinist purges. A member of a Jewish family of intellectuals, Kolman studied at the Charles University in Prague where one of his teachers was Albert Einstein. Mobilized in the Austrian Army in 1914, he deserted to the Russian side and in 1917 declared himself a Communist. He worked at the Moscow Comintern headquarters but was sent to Germany in 1919 where he was arrested and deported to Soviet Russia. He held various scientific and party posts in Moscow during the 1930s and became professor of mathematics at Moscow University. In 1945 he returned to Prague to teach at the Charles University, but in 1948 he was arrested by the Czech political police and sent to Moscow where he was imprisoned. Freed after Stalin's death in 1953, he lived in Moscow in enforced obscurity. In 1976 he was allowed to visit his daughter and son-in-law in Stockholm where he decided to stay.

Kowarski, Lew, Russian-born nuclear physicist (b. Feb. 10, 1907, St. Petersburg, Russia—d. July 27, 1979, Geneva, Switz.), was a pioneer in pre-World War II research on atomic energy and during the postwar period helped to found the European Organization for Nuclear Research (CERN). He left the Soviet Union in 1923 and studied in Belgium and France before joining the research team of Frédéric Joliot-Curie and Hans Halban. Together they realized the possibility of a chain reaction resulting from nuclear fission, but when World War II broke out Kowarski continued this work in Britain and Canada. He became a French citizen in 1939 and returned to France after the war to help build the country's first two atomic stockpiles. In 1952 he founded CERN and served as director of the scientific and technical services division. Fron 1963 he held professorships at universities in the U.S. and after his retirement in 1972 was consultant physicist to CERN.

Kuznetsov, Anatoly Vasilievich, Soviet writer (b. Aug. 19, 1929, Kurenevka, Kiev, U.S.S.R.—d. June 14, 1979, London, England), defected in 1969 while in London researching a projected book on Lenin's stay in Britain. Largely self-educated, he began work as a reporter for regional newspapers. In 1956 he went to Irkutsk to work on the construction of a power station. He used his observations to write his first novel, *Continuation of a Legend,* candidly describing the Soviet conquest of Siberia, which was heavily censored before publication. In 1966 he published *Babi Yar,* "a documentary novel" about the 1941 massacre by the German SS of Kiev's more than 70,000 Jews—also heavily censored. After this experience Kuznetsov decided to escape to the West. He obtained permission to do research in London and accompanied by a "translator"—actually a KGB agent—arrived there on July 24, 1969. After eluding his constant companion he contacted David Floyd, *The Daily Telegraph's* expert on Communist affairs, who helped him to obtain permission to stay in the U.K. His first task was to arrange the publication of *Babi Yar* in its uncensored form. It appeared in London in 1970. He then started to broadcast regularly to the Soviet Union over the U.S.-sponsored Radio Liberty.

Laguerre, André, British-born editor (b. 1915?, London, England—d. Jan. 18, 1979, New York, N.Y.), who as managing editor (1960–74) of *Sports Illustrated* turned the fledgling magazine into a publishing success by employing extensive news colour photography, restyling the format, and utilizing a talented staff of writers. At age 16 Laguerre, despondent over his father's insistence that he train for a government position, left San Francisco and eventually found a job with *The Times* (London). He joined *Time* in 1946 as a foreign correspondent and was so successful that at one time he headed both the London and Paris bureaus. In 1975 Laguerre helped found *Classic, the Magazine About Horses & Sport;* he died shortly after retiring as the magazine's editor and publisher.

La Malfa, Ugo, Italian politician (b. May 16, 1903, Palermo, Sicily—d. March 26, 1979, Rome, Italy), was leader of the small but influential Republican Party and five days before his death became deputy premier in Giulio Andreotti's coalition Cabinet. La Malfa trained for the diplomatic service and became an anti-Fascist as a young man. One of the founders (1941) of the Action Party, he fled in 1943 to Switzerland to avoid arrest but soon returned to Italy and became the Action Party representative on the National Liberation Committee. After the liberation of Italy by the Allies in 1945, La Malfa passed to the Republican Party and became minister of transport in the Ferruccio Parri government; in December 1945 he was minister of trade in the first Alcide De Gasperi coalition government. He was elected to the Constituent Assembly in June 1946. At the first parliamentary elections in April 1949 the Republican Party obtained nine seats. In the meantime, La Malfa had been assistant governor of the International Monetary Fund and later chairman of the parliamentary Commission for Finance and Treasury. From July 1960 to May 1963 he served as minister of the budget in the fourth Amintore Fanfani government. In 1965 he was elected secretary-general of the Republican Party and later became its president.

Larsen, Roy Edward, U.S. publishing executive (b. April 20, 1899, Boston, Mass.—d. Sept. 9, 1979, Fairfield, Conn.), became (1922) the first circulation manager of Time Inc. and rose to serve as the company's president from 1939 to 1960. As circulation manager, Larsen was largely responsible for the widespread distribution of *Time.* In 1929 he was named business manager and later developed the Academy Award-winning *March of Time* newsreel series that ran from 1935 to 1951. During his 56-year career, his most vital position was that of sales chief. The company's publications expanded to include such highly successful magazines as *People, Sports Illustrated, Fortune,* and *Life,* which he published from 1936 to 1946. Larsen, the only Time Inc. employee ever to be exempted from mandatory retirement at age 65, stepped down as vice-chairman of the board in April 1979.

Lauri-Volpi, Giacomo, Italian opera singer (b. Dec. 11, 1892, Lanuvio, Italy—d. March 17, 1979, Valencia, Spain), one of the great Italian singers of the 20th century, was a powerful operatic tenor who brought virility as well as sweetness to lyric roles. He was at his best during his years at the Metropolitan Opera in New York City (1923–34). He was trained at the Santa Cecilia Academy, Rome, and sang in Italian opera houses, including La Scala, and at Covent Garden, London. His notable roles in the U.S. included Radames in *Aida* and Calaf in *Turandot.*

Lawrence, Marjorie, U.S. soprano (b. Feb. 17, 1907, Dean's Marsh, Victoria, Australia—d. Jan. 13, 1979, Little Rock, Ark.), was at the height of her operatic career as a dramatic soprano when she was stricken (1941) with poliomyelitis during a rehearsal of *Die Walküre* in Mexico City. After making her singing debut (1932) in Monte Carlo in *Tannhäuser,* Lawrence sang leading Wagnerian roles at the Paris Opéra. In 1935 she made her U.S. debut at the Metropolitan Opera in *Die Walküre* and continued to command applause in such roles as Thaïs, Tosca, and Rachel in *La Juive.* Following her paralysis, Lawrence made several comeback performances confined to a wheelchair, but on March 14, 1944, she sang the part of Isolde in German while reclining on a couch, and on Dec. 11, 1947, she mesmerized the audience by standing throughout an entire performance of *Elektra.* Her autobiography, *Interrupted Melody* (1949), was made into a motion picture in 1955.

Leach, Bernard Howell, British potter (b. Jan. 5, 1887, Hong Kong—d. May 6, 1979, St. Ives, Cornwall, England), revived the potter's craft in England and greatly influenced modern ceramic design. The son of a judge, he studied art at the Slade School of Fine Art, London, and visited China and Japan. In Japan he took up ceramics under the representative of the sixth generation of Kenzans, potters in the tradition of the great Ogata Kenzan. In 1920 he settled in St. Ives. There, with the help of another great Japanese potter and his lifelong friend, Shoji Hamada, Leach established the Leach Pottery. His pottery reflected his oriental training in the simplicity, delicacy, and power of its forms. He wrote several works on pottery, including *A Potter's Book* (1940), *Kenzan and His Tradition* (1966), and *Shoji Hamada, Potter* (1976). He was made a companion of honour in 1973 and was honoured in the U.S. and in Japan, where in 1974 the Japanese Foundation awarded him a $14,000 prize and described him as "the most distinguished ceramics artist the world has today."

Lehmann, Beatrix, British actress (b. July 1, 1903, Bourne End, Buckinghamshire, England—d. July 31, 1979, London, England), became known for her powerful creation of highly charged and sometimes sinister roles. Lehmann started her career as an understudy to two of the leading actresses of the 1920s, Elsa Lanchester and Tallulah Bankhead. Though she went on to establish a solid reputation in leading Shakespearean parts her real strength lay in the emotionally intense roles in the dramas of Ibsen and O'Neill. Lehmann's left-wing political affiliations led to her banning by the British Broadcasting Corporation during the 1940s (she was president of the actors' union, Equity, in 1945), and it was only in the 1950s, with her outstanding performances in plays by Anouilh, Harold Pinter, and Tennessee Williams, that her career resumed. In later years she appeared regularly with the National Theatre and the Royal Shakespeare Company and in films and television.

L'Herbier, Marcel, French film director (b. April 23, 1888, Paris, France—d. Nov. 26, 1979, Paris), pioneered film as a means of artistic expression at a time when it was considered little more than a fairground novelty. L'Herbier continued experimenting to create a truly cinematographic language despite growing commercial pressures. He made 15 silent films, including *Eldorado* (1921) and *L'Argent* (1928), both now widely admired. He adapted readily to the coming of sound with two popular works, *Le Mystère de la chambre jaune* (1930) and *Le Parfum de la dame en noir* (1931), but continued to stress the primacy of visual expression. L'Herbier experimented with new effects and used artists like Fernand Léger for his sets. In 1936 he helped to found the Cinémathèque Française and during World War II contributed to the preservation of French cinema by establishing the Institut des Hautes Études Cinématographiques and by making one of his best films, *La Nuit fantastique* (1942). He wrote several books on the cinema and a volume of memoirs, *La Tête qui tourne* (1979).

Loughlin, Dame Anne, British trade unionist (b. June 28, 1894, Leeds, England—d. July 18, 1979, London, England), started work at the age of 12 and by 1915 had become a full-time organizer in the garment workers' trade union. In the following year she led 6,000 striking clothing workers at Hebden Bridge. A brilliant organizer and negotiator, she secured many improvements in working conditions. In 1943 she became the first woman to preside over the General Council of the Trades Union Congress and was general secretary of the National Union of Tailors and Garment Workers (1948–53). She served on many government enquiries into health and safety at work and was active in the International Labour Organization and the International Federation of Trade Unions. She was made an officer (1935) and dame commander (1943) of the Order of the British Empire.

Lubin, Germaine, French opera singer (b. Feb. 1, 1890, Paris, France—d. Oct. 27, 1979, Paris), was one of the leading sopranos in Europe before her career ended in 1944 when she was imprisoned for collaboration with the Nazis. Lubin studied at the Paris Conservatoire and made her debut in 1912. She created many roles at the Paris Opéra, sang leading parts in works by Strauss and Berlioz, and appeared at Covent Garden, London. But it was as an interpreter of Wagner that she reached the summit of her career, singing Isolde at Bayreuth in 1939. Hitler was in the audience and two years later, when his armies were occupying France, she sang the same role in Paris. Disgraced after the liberation, she was banned from public appearances for five years and except for two recitals in 1950 devoted the rest of her life to teaching.

Lyon, Ben, U.S. actor (b. Feb. 6, 1901, Atlanta, Ga.—d. March 22, 1979, aboard the "Queen Elizabeth II," Pacific Ocean), co-starred with his wife Bebe Daniels on the British radio program "Hi Gang!" during World War II. In 1950 the two began another successful series entitled "Life with the Lyons." Lyon's career began on the stage in 1918 when he appeared in *Seventeen* at the Booth Theatre in New York City. In 1923 he went to Hollywood, where he starred in *Hell's Angels* (1930), *I Cover the Waterfront* (1933), and many other films. Lyon is said to have helped select the then-unknown Jean Harlow as the leading lady in *Hell's Angels* and, as a talent director (1945–46) for 20th Century-Fox, he was credited with discovering Marilyn Monroe. In 1977 he was made an honorary officer of the British Empire for "outstanding services."

McDonald, David John, U.S. labour leader (b. Nov. 22, 1902, Pittsburgh, Pa.—d. Aug. 8, 1979, Palm Springs, Calif.), was president (1952–65) of the United Steelworkers of America when they staged (1959–60) a marathon strike that lasted 116 days and proved to be one of the costliest in U.S. history. McDonald, the son of a staunch pro-union family, often said he was born with a union spoon in his mouth. A graduate of the Carnegie Institute of Technology, he became the private secretary and protégé of Philip Murray, then vice-president of the United Mine Workers. McDonald later joined Murray when he became the first president of the steelworkers; when his mentor died, McDonald succeeded him. During his tenure as president, the union experienced a tremendous growth in power with large wage increases and recognition by steel companies. After a bitter campaign (1964) between McDonald and his deputy I. W. Abel, who accused McDonald of losing touch with the rank and file, McDonald lost the union presidency by only 10,000 votes but surrendered the office in 1965 without a recount.

Macías Nguema, Francisco, Equatorial Guinean politician (b. 1922, Nsegayong, Río Muni—d. Sept. 29, 1979, Malabo, Equatorial Guinea), assumed the presidency of Equatorial Guinea when the former Spanish colony became an independent republic in October 1968. A member of the Fang group of the Bantu tribe, Macías ruled his country as a savage dictator. Most of the 7,000 European residents fled when the Spanish garrison was evicted in 1969. Macías proclaimed himself president for life in 1972. In 1973 a UN mission was expelled and in 1976 Nigeria evacuated the last of its 45,000 cocoa estate workers after they had been mistreated and deprived of their wages. Macías was ultimately responsible for the systematic murder or exile of the small educated class, which came mostly from the rival Bubi tribe. Macías was overthrown on Aug. 3, 1979, by a military coup led by his relative, Deputy Defense Minister Teodoro Obiang Nguema Mbasogo. Accused of treason, embezzlement, and genocide, Macías was sentenced to death by a court-martial and shot.

McIntyre, James Francis Cardinal, Roman Catholic prelate (b. June 25, 1886, New York, N.Y.—d. July 16, 1979, Los Angeles, Calif.), was the dynamic archbishop of Los Angeles (1948–70) and the force behind the rapid expansion of the city's Catholic schools and churches. McIntyre was dubbed the "brick-and-mortar priest" because of the staggering increase of parishioners (from 625,000 to more than 1.6 million), schools (from 159 to 366), and parishes (from 211 to 313) under his direction. In recognition of his accomplishments, McIntyre was elevated to the cardinalate on Jan. 12, 1953. In the mid-1960s, however, the conservative prelate, who opposed the modernization of church policies and practices, drew criticism from both the clergy and laity for his silence on racial problems and for his opposition to a measure liberalizing California's abortion laws. McIntyre not only refused to speak out on civil rights but punished priests who dared to do so. His experience in a Wall Street firm before he entered training for the priesthood at 29 proved invaluable during the Depression. As chancellor of the New York archdiocese McIntyre refinanced the church's debts through low-interest loans, thereby bolstering the archdiocese's finances. In 1940 he was named titular bishop of Cyrene and auxiliary bishop of New York. During the last years of his life McIntyre was confined to St. Vincent's Hospital in Los Angeles.

Marcuse, Herbert, German-born political philosopher (b. July 19, 1898, Berlin, Germany—d. July 29, 1979, Starnberg, West Germany), gave impetus to social activists of the 1960s with such works as *Eros and Civilization* (1955) and *One Dimensional Man* (1964). Marcuse's philosophy called for a social revolution in which an elite group rejects material goals, assumes leadership, and destoys contemporary society, which he termed a "repressive monolith." His views were adopted in the 1960s by disenchanted students and other radicals, including black militant Angela Davis, but when the movement dissipated so did Marcuse's newfound popularity. He became a member of the Social Democratic Party while earning (1922) his Ph.D. at the University of Freiburg and was co-founder of the Frankfurt Institute of Social Research. When Hitler rose to power in 1933 he fled to Geneva and then to the U.S. where he lectured at Columbia University. During World War II Marcuse was an army intelligence analyst, and he headed the Central European Section of the Office of Intelligence Research after the war. He then taught (1951–54) at Columbia and Harvard universities, Brandeis University (1954–65), and the University of California at San Diego (1965–70).

Marek, Franz (Ephraim Feuerlicht), Austrian Marxist journalist (b. April 18, 1913, Przemysl, Poland—d. June 29, 1979, Neukirchen, Upper Austria), was a leading member of the Austrian Communist Party until his dismissal from its Central Committee in 1970 because of his continued criticism of the 1968 Soviet invasion of Czechoslovakia. He continued to support "Eurocommunism," with its alliance of Marxism and democracy, and to edit the independent periodical *Wiener Tagebuch*. He joined the Communist Party in 1934 while a student in Vienna but in 1938 took refuge in France, where he played an active part in the Resistance during World War II. Marek was arrested in 1944 and condemned to death but was saved by the liberation of Paris. During the postwar period, with his friend Ernst Fischer, he was his party's foremost theoretician.

Marquet, Mary, French actress (b. April 14, 1895, St. Petersburg, Russia—d. Aug. 29, 1979, Paris, France), had an immensely rich and varied career that spanned the history of the French theatre from Sarah Bernhardt to the films of the 1970s. She studied at the Conservatoire National d'Art Dramatique and made her stage debut with Bernhardt in 1915. Marquet was given leading roles in classical drama as a performer with the Comédie Française from 1923 to 1945 but left to play comedy and act in cabaret. Her first film appearance was in 1932, but her best films, including *La Grande Vadrouille* (1966), *La Vie de Château* (1966), and *La Merveilleuse Visite* (1974), were made in the post-World War II period. Poetry occupied a central place in her life: Marquet gave recitals during the German occupation and published two volumes of her own work, as well as a novel and four books of autobiography. One of the great individualists of the French stage, she triumphed over age and ill-health by sheer energy and enthusiasm.

Marx, Zeppo (Herbert Marx), U.S. theatrical agent (b. Feb. 25, 1901, New York, N.Y.—d. Nov. 30, 1979, Palm Springs, Calif.), abandoned the unrewarding job of a straight man after appearing with Chico (Leonard), Harpo (Arthur), and Groucho (Julius) in the first five Marx Brothers films: *The Cocoanuts* (1929), *Animal Crackers* (1930), *Monkey Business* (1931), *Horse Feathers* (1932), and *Duck Soup* (1933). Zeppo, who joined the act when brother Gummo (Milton) left to follow a career in the garment industry, soon became "sick and tired of being a stooge." He was given such inane lines as "The garbage man is here" while Groucho delivered the wisecracking quip: "Tell him we don't want any." After Zeppo left the comedy team he became a highly successful talent agent, an airplane parts manufacturer, and a citrus grower. He was the wealthiest of the brothers. After unsuccessful marriages to Marion Benda and Barbara Blakely, Zeppo spent the last years of his life living quietly in Palm Springs.

Massine, Léonide (Leonid Fedorovich Miassin), Russian-born dancer and choreographer (b. Aug.

9, 1895, Moscow, Russia—d. March 16, 1979, Cologne, West Germany), became a leading figure in 20th-century dance after being discovered (1913) in Moscow by Sergey Diaghilev who needed a new performer to replace Vaslav Nijinsky. Massine made his debut in Paris in 1914 in *La Légende de Joseph.* Soon he began to produce a series of ballets, including *Les Femmes de Bonne Humeur* (1917), *La Boutique Fantasque* (1919), and *Le Tricorne* (1919). *Parade* (1917), the result of his collaboration with Pablo Picasso, Jean Cocteau, and Erik Satie, turned the ballet world toward an avant-garde modernism. After Diaghilev's death Massine was artistic director, chief choreographer, and principal dancer of Colonel de Basil's Ballet Russe de Monte Carlo (1932–38). During this period he created his "symphonic ballets" set to music by Tchaikovsky, Brahms, and Berlioz. From 1941 to 1944 he directed the National Ballet Theatre, New York City. He also made ballets for, and danced in, several films, including *Carnival in Costa Rica* (1945), *The Red Shoes* (1948), *Tales of Hoffman* (1951), and *Carosello Napoletano* (1953). In all, Massine produced some 100 ballets. He had a dynamic stage presence, with the power to change instantly from comedy to poetic romanticism. Massine's autobiogrpahy, *My Life in Ballet* (1968), was followed by *Massine on Choreography* (1976).

Maudling, Reginald, British politician (b. March 7, 1917, London, England—d. Feb. 14, 1979, London), was a progressive Conservative and a Cabinet minister who lost his chance to become Britain's prime minister when he narrowly missed being elected to the leadership of his party in 1964. After attending Merton College, Oxford, he was called to the bar by the Middle Temple in 1940 but became private secretary to Air Minister Sir Archibald Sinclair during World War II. He then made a name for himself in economics in the Conservative Party's research department and entered Parliament as member for Barnet in 1950. Maudling was parliamentary secretary to the Ministry of Civil Aviation in 1952, economic secretary to the Treasury from 1952, minister of supply in 1955, and paymaster general in 1957–59. When he could not negotiate Great Britain's entry into the European Common Market because of French intransigence, he helped create the European Free Trade Association. After the 1959 general election he became president of the Board of Trade and in 1961 colonial secretary. After Prime Minister Harold Macmillan made him chancellor of the Exchequer in 1962, he worked to create an expansionist boom, but the largely mythical £800 million balance of trade deficit helped to defeat his party in the 1964 general election. During 1970–72 he served Edward Heath's government as home secretary. Maudling's career declined after his involvement in three financial scandals: he was chairman (1969) of swindler Jerome Hoffman's investment company but resigned some 17 months before its collapse; he was associated with architect John Poulson, who was tried in 1973 and convicted of bribery; and in 1965–70 he was adviser to corporation head Sir Eric Miller, who committed suicide in 1977. Maudling later served Conservative leader Margaret Thatcher as shadow foreign secretary (1974–76) before slipping to the back benches.

Merritt, H(iram) Houston, U.S. neurologist (b. Jan. 12, 1902, Wilmington, N.C.—d. Jan. 9, 1979, New York, N.Y.), co-discovered (1936) with Tracy Putnam the antiseizure drug Dilantin (diphenylhydantoin), used to combat epileptic seizures and to treat abnormal heartbeats. Merritt's discovery was an immense breakthrough because phenobarbital was the only other drug available to treat epilepsy, and its use was limited because of its sedative effect. Shortly after graduating (1926) from Johns Hopkins University, Merritt joined the faculty of Harvard University and conducted research at Boston City Hospital. In 1944 he took up residence in New York to become chief neurologist at Montefiore Hospital and a member of the faculty at Columbia University. At Columbia he became (1948) chairman of the neurology department, and from 1958 to 1970 he was dean of the College of Physicians and Surgeons and vice-president of the university. Merritt's writings include some 215 scientific papers, as well as a standard textbook on neurology and a classic book on the effects of syphilis on the brain.

Meyer, André Benoit Mathieu, French-born investment banker (b. Sept. 3, 1898, Paris, France—d. Sept. 9, 1979, Lausanne, Switz.), was for 33 years (1944–77) the energetic senior partner of Lazard Frères & Co., one of the foremost investment banking houses in the U.S., and master of a personal fortune estimated as high as $500 million. Meyer, who possessed uncanny intuitive analytical powers, adroitly used what he termed "financial engineering" to arrange mergers and corporate deals. He was subsequently dubbed "Zeus," the most powerful of gods, by awestruck associates. Under his supervision Lazard purchased Avis Rent-A-Car System for about $7 million and a few years later reaped huge profits when it sold Avis to the International Telephone and Telegraph Corp. and received $52 million in ITT stock. Meyer's philanthropic contributions included $3 million to the Metropolitan Museum of Art, New York City, for the construction of new galleries (to be completed by 1980) to house European paintings, $2.5 million to New York University, and paintings to both the Louvre in Paris and the Museum of Modern Art in New York.

Mingus, Charles, U.S. musician (b. April 22, 1922, Nogales, Ariz.—d. Jan. 5, 1979, Cuernavaca, Mexico), was an accomplished bandleader, composer, and bassist whose greatest contribution to jazz was the revolutionary introduction of the bass as a solo and melodic instrument. During the 1940s he became a prominent figure in Los Angeles playing with such music giants as Louis Armstrong and Kid Ory. After Mingus made his debut as a performer and composer with Lionel Hampton's orchestra in 1947, he moved (1951) to New York City where he worked with Billy Taylor, Charlie Parker, and Duke Ellington. In the late 1950s and early 1960s Mingus began his "Jazz Workshop." During this period Mingus became known as "jazz's angry man" because he frequently berated noisy jazz club audiences for not listening to the music and because he spoke out against racial prejudice. He semiretired in the mid-1960s but was restored to the limelight when he resumed touring and published his powerful autobiography, *Beneath the Underdog* (1971). Some of his best-known compositions include: *Black Saint and the Sinner Lady, Thrice upon a Theme,* and *Revelations.*

Mitchell, Yvonne, British actress and writer (b. July 7, 1925, London, England—d. March 24, 1979, London), cleverly combined two careers with equal success. As an actress she appeared (1940) on the stage as the child Estella in *Great Expectations,* joined Michel Saint-Denis's Old Vic Company, and then played several parts at the Shakespeare Memorial Theatre, Stratford-upon-Avon, including (1953) Cordelia in *King Lear.* In 1974 she appeared in Luigi Pirandello's *Henry IV* at Her Majesty's Theatre, London. Mitchell was twice named best actress in Britain for her roles in the films *The Divided Heart* (1954) and *Woman in a Dressing Gown* (1957). As a writer, her first play, *The Same Sky,* was produced (1951) at the Duke of York's Theatre in London, and she directed (1957) the production of a play written by her husband, Derek Monsey. Several novels, including *The Bed-sitter* (1959) and *But Answer Came There None* (1977), and such children's books as *Cathy Away* (1964) were complemented by a widely acclaimed biography, *Colette: A Taste for Life* (1975). Mitchell was also a member of the National Theatre Board from 1976.

Mohsen, Zuheir, Palestinian nationalist (b. 1936, Tulkarem, Palestine—d. July 26, 1979, Nice, France), was leader of the pro-Syrian guerrilla organization Saiqa and head of the Military Department of the Palestine Liberation Organization (PLO). A long-standing member of the Ba'ath Party and a friend of Syrian leader Hafez al-Assad, Mohsen worked as a teacher in Jordan and the Persian Gulf states before joining the Palestinian movement. He was responsible for reorganizing Saiqa and bringing it under Assad's control in 1971, at which time he became head of the organization. In 1976 the group welcomed the Syrian invasion of Lebanon and sided with Syria against other Palestinian guerrillas. Mohsen was suspended from the PLO until the Lebanese civil war ended later in the year. He was on holiday in southern France when he was assassinated, possibly by Israeli agents.

Monnet, Jean Omer Marie Gabriel, French political economist (b. Nov. 9, 1888, Cognac, France—d. March 16, 1979, Montfort-l'Amaury, France), became known on both sides of the Atlantic as the "father of Europe" for his pioneering and unceasing promotion of the idea of European integration. Monnet left school in Cognac to join the family brandy firm as a salesman in Canada. During World War I he represented the French Ministry of Commerce in the Inter-allied Maritime Commission allocating scarce commodities. In 1919 he became deputy secretary-general of the League of Nations at its Geneva headquarters. He left this post in 1923 to reorganize the family business, becoming two years later the European partner of a New York investment bank. At the start of World

PICTORIAL PARADE

War II Monnet was made chairman of the Franco-British Economic Co-ordination Committee. In June 1940, on the eve of the French collapse, he suggested to Winston Churchill a plan for a Franco-British union. During the war his relations with Charles de Gaulle were cool—to de Gaulle Monnet seemed a dreamer—but after the liberation of France he convinced de Gaulle of the importance of preparing a comprehensive plan for the reconstruction and modernization of the French economy. Monnet was appointed head of the National Planning Council and on Jan. 11, 1947, the Monnet Plan was adopted by a coalition government with Monnet as commissioner-general. In May 1950 he and Robert Schuman, then the French foreign minister, proposed the establishment of a common European market for coal and steel by countries willing to delegate their powers over these industries to an independent authority. Six countries—France, West Germany, Italy, Belgium, The Netherlands, and Luxembourg—signed the Paris treaty in April 1951 setting up the European Coal and Steel Community, Monnet served its High Authority as first president (1952–55). In 1955 he formed the Action Committee for the United States of Europe, of which he remained president until 1975.

Monsarrat, Nicholas John Turney, British novelist (b. March 22, 1910, Liverpool, England—d. Aug. 8, 1979, London, England), distilled his experiences as a World War II naval officer in *The Cruel Sea,* one of the bestselling novels of all time. By 1964, 13 years after its publication, the novel had sold more than seven million copies and had been made into an award-winning film. Monsarrat, who gave up a legal career to write during the 1930s, had only moderate success before joining the Royal Navy in 1940, where he attained the rank of lieutenant commander. He came to love the sea, and several of the almost 30 books he wrote had naval settings. For the public, he remained essentially the author of one book, though *The Story of Esther Costello* (1953) and *The Tribe that Lost Its Head* (1956) had wide success despite their relative lack of critical acclaim. From 1946 to 1956 Monsarrat was a British government press officer in South Africa and Canada, where he remained for some years before moving to Malta. He was working on a second volume of his novel *The Master Mariner* when he died; the first volume, *Running Proud*, appeared in 1978.

Morris, Sir Philip Robert, British educationalist (b. July 6, 1901, Yorkshire, England—d. Nov. 21, 1979, Rhydymain, Gwynedd, Wales), was vice-chancellor of the University of Bristol from 1946 to 1966 and played a leading role in many aspects of British and Commonwealth education. In the pre-World War II period he was an outstanding director of education with the Kent Education Authority and in 1944 was appointed to run the Army educational scheme. He took a particular interest in educational broadcasting and was vice-chairman of the British Broadcasting Corporation from 1954 to 1960. He also served on the British Council and was involved in many plans for educational exchanges, particularly with the Commonwealth countries. His energy and administrative skills allowed him to pursue an astonishing range of activities: he was president of the Library Association; he was involved with regional arts, hospitals, and the Boy Scouts Association; and he helped build Bristol into a major provincial university. He was knighted in 1946.

Morton, John Cameron Andrieu Bingham, British journalist (b. June 7, 1893, London, England—d. May 10, 1979, Worthing, England), was better known as "Beachcomber" of the *Daily Express*, for which he wrote a humorous column for over 50 years (1924–75). Educated at Harrow and Oxford, he was closely associated with those beer-drinking, ballad-writing, cricket-playing journalists who gathered round Sir John Squire and who were immortalized in A. G. Macdonell's book *England, Their England.* But the greatest influence in Morton's life was that of Hilaire Belloc, and it was shortly after meeting him that Morton became a Catholic. He joined the *Sunday Express* in 1919 and transferred to the *Daily Express* in 1922 as a reporter, but in 1924, when Wyndham Lewis left to join the *Daily Mail,* Morton took over his "By the Way" column as "Beachcomber." The characters he invented became national institutions in the course of time: Dr. Strabismus (Whom God Preserve) of Utrecht, Mr. Justice Cocklecarrot (in whose hands British justice was regularly strained to the point of destruction), a society siren called Vita Brevis, and an African potentate named M'Tralala Zogomumbozo. G. K. Chesterton called Morton's work "a huge thunderous wind of elemental and essential laughter." Morton also wrote nearly 50 books including *Sobieski, King of Poland* (1932), a series of historical essays inspired by the French Revolution, and *Hilaire Belloc: A Memoir* (1955). He was made a CBE in 1952.

Morton, Rogers Clark Ballard, U.S. politician (b. Sept. 19, 1914, Louisville, Ky.—d. April 19, 1979, Easton, Md.), was named (1969) national chairman of the Republican Party while serving (1963–71) in the U.S. Congress as a Maryland representative. In 1971 he was appointed secretary of the interior by Pres. Richard M. Nixon and in 1975 secretary of commerce by Pres. Gerald R. Ford. Morton first took an active role in politics after World War II when he ran congressional campaigns in Kentucky for his brother. His main concern, however, was the family milling and baking business until it was sold in the early 1950s to Pillsbury Co. He then moved to Maryland with his family to farm and raise cattle. In 1962 Morton was elected to the first of five consecutive terms in the House of Representatives.

Mountbatten of Burma, Louis (Francis Albert Victor Nicholas) Mountbatten, 1st Earl, British naval officer (b. June 25, 1900, Windsor, England—d. Aug. 27, 1979, Mullaghmore, County Sligo, Ireland), served as the supreme Allied commander in Southeast Asia from 1943 to 1946 and crowned his career by being the last viceroy (1947) and the first governor-general (1947–48) of India. The son of Prince Louis of Battenberg, admiral of the fleet, and Princess Victoria, Queen Victoria's granddaughter (and so a cousin of Queen Elizabeth II), he became Mountbatten when his father relinquished his title, assumed his anglicized surname in 1917, and was created marquess of Milford Haven. Mountbatten entered the Royal Navy as a cadet in 1913 and saw active service on battleships in World War I. A signals specialist, he was a captain at the outbreak of World War II in 1939, commanding a destroyer flotilla from HMS "Kelly" and then commanding the aircraft carrier HMS "Illustrious." He was made chief of combined operations, 1942–43, and a member of the British Chiefs of Staff Committee before entering upon his overall command in Southeast Asia, where he recovered Burma from Japanese forces and helped bring a swift end to the war. Appointed viceroy of India by Prime Minister Clement Attlee, he secured the desired rapid transfer of power to an independent India. Returning to the Navy, Mountbatten became commander in chief, Mediterranean (1952–54), and of all Allied forces there (1953–54). He became first sea lord of the Admiralty (1955–60), the post his Austrian-born father had had to resign, and admiral of the fleet in 1956. Service as chief of the U.K. defense staff and chairman of the Chiefs of Staff Committee (1959–65) closed his active career. He was made a viscount in 1946 and an earl in 1947.

A.G.I.P./PICTORIAL PARADE

In 1922 Mountbatten married Edwina Ashley, heiress of her grandfather Sir Ernest Cassel, who was vicereine at Mountbatten's side in India. Mountbatten was killed when his fishing boat was destroyed by an explosive charge placed on board by members of the Provisional Irish Republican Army.

Muir, Malcolm, U.S. business executive (b. July 19, 1885, Glen Ridge, N.J.—d. Jan. 30, 1979, New York, N.Y.), quickly ascended the corporate ladder to become president of McGraw-Hill Publishing Co. after beginning his career as a file clerk. In 1929 Muir helped found *Business Week*, which he established as a weekly newsmagazine. Eight years later Muir joined *News-Week*, changed its name to *Newsweek*, and revamped the four-year-old magazine by placing greater emphasis on interpretive articles and by introducing signed columns and international editions. After serving as editor in chief, publisher, and chairman of the board, Muir was named honorary chairman when the Washington Post Co. purchased the magazine in 1961.

Muir, Percival Horace, British bibliographer (b. Dec. 17, 1894, London, England—d. Nov. 24, 1979, Blakeney, Norfolk, England), helped to create the International League of Antiquarian Booksellers and served as its first president from 1948 to 1950. After a variety of jobs and military service in World War I, Muir joined (1930) the booksellers Elkin Mathews, of which he became managing director in 1939. There, as he described in his autobiography, *Minding My Own Business* (1956), he was among those who shaped the tastes and methods of the modern antiquarian book market. With his international outlook, Muir became a well-known figure in the European book trade. He was also one of the founders in 1952 of *The Book Collector* and a frequent contributor to it.

Mullard, Stanley Robert, British radio industry pioneer (b. Nov. 1, 1883, London, England—d. Sept. 1, 1979, Haywards Heath, East Sussex, England), was named head of Edison Swan's research laboratory in England in 1910 and developed high-powered thermionic valves for the Royal Navy during 1916–20. Mullard used fused silica, which withstands high temperatures, instead of glass envelopes for valves. In 1920 he formed the Mullard Valve Co., producing valves and cathode ray tubes. His company in 1924 established research connections with Philips of Eindhoven, Neth., which acquired all of Mullard's shares by 1930. Mullard, however, remained a director of the company until 1970.

Mullen, Barbara, Irish actress (b. June 9, 1914, Boston, Mass.—d. March 9, 1979, London, England), was best known for her role as a Scottish country doctor's housekeeper in the BBC television series "Dr. Finlay's Casebook" (1962–71). The series was later broadcast on radio. Mullen first appeared as a child dancer in the U.S. at the age of three and made her acting debut in London in 1939. She later starred in such productions as *Jeannie, Rebecca,* and *Murder at the Vicarage.*

Munson, Thurman, U.S. baseball player (b. June 7, 1947, Akron, Ohio—d. Aug. 2, 1979, near Canton, Ohio), was the illustrious catcher for the New York Yankees professional baseball team and their first captain since Lou Gehrig. Besides batting over .300 in five seasons, Munson played on three Yankee teams that won pennants and on two that went on to capture the World Series. Munson, who was highly respected by fellow ballplayers, was named rookie of the year in 1970, received the Golden Glove Award in 1973, 1974, and 1975, and was the American League's most valuable player in 1976. Munson was killed when his Cessna Citation twin-engine jet crashed short of the runway while he was practicing "touch and go" takeoffs and landings. His number, 15, was retired by the Yankees.

Muzrukov, Boris Glebovich, Soviet mechanical engineer (b. 1904, Lodeynoye Polye, Russia—d. Jan. 31, 1979, Moscow, U.S.S.R.), designed the T-34 medium tank that revolutionized Soviet armour during World War II. The son of a soldier, Muzrukov graduated from the Leningrad Technological Institute in 1929 and joined the heavy industry works at Kirov. In 1939 he was appointed director of the Ural Machine Building Plant, working there until 1947. With his 26-ton T-34 low silhouette tank, capable of 30 mph and armed with a 76-mm (later 85-mm) gun, the Soviet armed forces came into their own as designers, producers, and users of fighting tanks. Appointed major general during the war, Muzrukov received a Lenin Prize and other awards. A member of the Communist Party from 1938, he was a delegate to the 22nd (1961), 23rd (1966), and 24th (1971) party congresses. He was also elected three times as a deputy to the Supreme Soviet of the U.S.S.R.

Narayan, Jaya Prakash, Indian politician (b. Oct. 11, 1902, Bihar State, India—d. Oct. 8, 1979, Patna, Bihar State), founded the Indian Socialist Party, led the campaign against Prime Minister Indira Gandhi's 1975–77 state of emergency, and was the father figure of the Janata Party, a coalition formed to defeat Mrs. Gandhi's Congress Party in the elections of 1977. Narayan was known over India simply as "J.P." An early interest in politics caused him to refuse a university scholarship in accordance with Mahatma Gandhi's policy of noncooperation with the British and to go to the U.S. in 1922 to study. Narayan returned to India with Marxist views, joined the Congress Party, and helped to found its active wing, the Congress Socialist Party. He was imprisoned in 1932 and again at the beginning of World War II as a leader of the civil disobedience movement and an opponent of the war, but he escaped and organized resistance. Recaptured in 1943 and released in 1946, he left the Congress Party in 1948 and founded the Indian Socialist Party, formally constituted in 1952. But in 1954, disillusioned with Marxist politics, he joined Vinoba Bhave's pacific, social movement for land redistribution. Narayan returned to active politics in 1974. Mrs. Gandhi had him arrested in June 1975 under the state of emergency but he contracted a kidney disease in prison and was released five months later. After the victory of the Janata Party that he had helped to create, Narayan grew despondent because the apparently incurable rifts in his party were leading to its breakdown.

Natta, Giulio, Italian chemist (b. Feb. 26, 1903, Imperia, Italy—d. May 2, 1979, Bergamo, Italy), won the Nobel Prize for Chemistry in 1963, together with Karl Ziegler of West Germany, for their work on the development of high-polymer plastics. Natta studied chemical engineering in Milan and subsequently taught in Pavia, Rome, and Turin. In 1938 he was appointed professor and research director of industrial chemistry at the Milan Polytechnic Institute. It was there in 1954 that he succeeded in polymerizing propylene gas into highly ordered chains of molecules. This development proved useful in the manufacture of detergents, auto parts, fabrics, and film.

Neave, Airey Middleton Sheffield, British politician (b. Jan. 23, 1916, London, England—d. March 30, 1979, London), became the Conservative Party's parliamentary spokesman on Northern Ireland in 1975. His tough line against terrorism cost him his life when a bomb planted in his car exploded as he drove from the House of Commons' underground garage. Neave was educated at Eton and Merton College, Oxford. During World War II he was captured at Calais in 1940, but he escaped from Colditz Castle prison in Germany and returned to England to direct the escape network in Europe. He was called to the bar by the Middle Temple in 1943 and took part in the Nuremberg trials after Germany's defeat. He wrote books on all these wartime experiences. Entering the House of Commons as member for Abingdon in 1953, he rose to be joint parliamentary secretary of the Ministry of Transport and Civil Aviation (1957–59). He was parliamentary undersecretary of state for air in 1959 but resigned office because of a minor heart attack. In 1975 Neave was influential in securing Margaret Thatcher's nomination as leader of the Conservatives in opposition and was made the shadow cabinet's spokesman on Ulster. Neave was given the central post of control of the opposition leader's private office. He was a member of the Select Committee on Science and Technology from 1965 and served as its chairman (1970–75). He was also delegate to the UN High Commissioner for Refugees (1970–75).

Nervi, Pier Luigi, Italian engineer (b. June 21, 1891, Sondrio, Italy—d. Jan. 9, 1979, Rome, Italy), who revolutionized architecture with stunning and daring designs characterized by tilted arches, curved ceilings, and a feeling of space. Nervi, who considered concrete the finest construction material available, invented ferrocemento, a reinforced material of steel mesh and cement mortar. After graduating (1913) in civil engineering from the University of Bologna, Nervi began (1923) his career as an engineer and contractor in Rome. Some of his most notable designs in Italy included the Cinema Augusto in Naples; a municipal stadium in Florence; a prefabricated 309-ft-span arch for the Turin Exhibition (1949–50); the Pirelli Building (1955) in Milan, the country's first skyscraper; and two sports palaces for the 1960 Rome Olympic Games. Nervi also designed, with Marcel Breuer and Bernard Zehrfuss, the UNESCO headquarters in Paris. His last work was a massive audience hall for the Vatican. Nervi taught (1947–61) at the University of Rome and was Charles E. Norton professor (1961–62) at Harvard University. Among numerous honours he received the gold medals of the Royal Institute of British Architects (1960) and the American Institute of Architects (1964).

Neto, António Agostinho, Angolan national leader (b. Sept. 17, 1922, Bengo near Luanda, Angola—d. Sept. 10, 1979, Moscow, U.S.S.R.), became independent Angola's first president in 1975 after leading the nation in a civil war that ended Portuguese colonial rule. As a student in Portugal Neto wrote protest poetry that infuriated the authorities; it also won him recognition as an exceptionally gifted Portuguese poet. Suspected for his contacts with the illegal Portuguese Communist Party, he was arrested and imprisoned for a few months in 1952 and for two years beginning in 1955 but qualified as a doctor in 1958. He returned to Angola in 1959 and the following year was arrested for his opposition to colonial rule. Held in detention at first in Cape Verde, he was transferred in 1962 to Lisbon, but escaped to Morocco and later that year was elected president of the exiled Popular Movement for the Liberation of Angola (MPLA), based in the Congolese capital of Léopoldville (now Kinshasa). Despite Soviet support for the MPLA, Moscow's relations with Neto were uneasy and were suspended for a time but restored after the April 1974 military coup in Lisbon. In 1975 the Portuguese government agreed to grant independence to Angola, and at midnight November 10–11 Neto proclaimed the establishment of the People's Republic of Angola in Luanda with himself as president. Angola's dependence on Soviet and Cuban military help in the continuing struggle with rival nationalist movements was tempered by Neto's refusal to allow pro-Soviet hard-liners to dominate the MPLA. On Oct. 8, 1976, Neto and Soviet leader Leonid I. Brezhnev signed a Soviet-Angolan treaty of friendship and cooperation in Moscow. In May 1977 Neto survived a bloody uprising of dissident elements of the MPLA. In August 1977 he visited Havana, but he belonged neither to the East nor to the West. He arrived in Moscow in September 1979 suffering from a disease of the liver and kidneys and died there following surgery for cancer of the pancreas.

Newhouse, Samuel I(rving), U.S. communications magnate (b. May 24, 1895, Bayonne, N.J.—d. Aug. 29, 1979, New York, N.Y.), amassed holdings amounting to hundreds of millions of dollars as the owner of 31 newspapers and five broadcasting stations in 22 U.S. cities. Newhouse began building his empire in 1922 when he acquired the *Staten Island* (N.Y.) *Advance* for $98,000. He turned the anemic newspaper into a financial success and was able to purchase (1932) the *Long Island* (N.Y.) *Press* from his earnings. Newhouse, who never set up a formal office, conducted his business out of a battered briefcase. Although he was admitted to the bar, he became discouraged when he lost his first case and never practiced law. Instead, Newhouse developed a collector's fascination in the acquisition of newspapers. He held the controlling interest in such newspapers as the *Star Ledger* in Newark, N.J., the *Cleveland* (Ohio) *Plain Dealer*, and the *Portland Oregonian*; he also purchased Condé Nast Publications, which owned several magazines, including *Vogue, Bride's Magazine, Glamour,* and *House and Garden*. In 1976 Newhouse spent $305 million, the highest price ever paid in a U.S. newspaper transaction, for Booth Newspapers Inc., the publisher of eight Michigan dailies and *Parade*, a Sunday supplement.

Novaes, Guiomar, Brazilian pianist (b. Feb. 28, 1895, São João da Boa Vista, Brazil—d. March 7, 1979, São Paulo, Brazil), was called "the Paderewska of the Pampas" for her colourful, imaginative, and seemingly effortless performances of such 19th-century masters as Chopin, Schumann, and Beethoven. Novaes also played selected works of Mozart and Claude Debussy, who praised her "power of complete inner concentration." Novaes, who began playing the piano at age three, was the 17th of 19 children. Neighbours, recognizing the child's extraordinary talent, helped finance her formal musical training which began at age seven. When she was 11 Novaes gave her first recital in São Paulo and at 14 she was awarded a four-year scholarship by the Brazilian government so she could study abroad. Two years after her admission to the Paris Conservatoire, Novaes won its coveted first prize after competing against nearly 400 other musicians. The 5-ft virtuoso, who continued to enrapture audiences for over 50 years, gave her last New York performance at Hunter College in 1972.

Oberon, Merle (ESTELLE MERLE O'BRIEN THOMPSON), U.S. actress (b. Feb. 19, 1911, Tasmania, Australia —d. Nov. 23, 1979, Malibu, Calif.), portrayed the strikingly beautiful Cathy, who tormented and rejected Heathcliff (Sir Laurence Olivier) in the 1939 film classic *Wuthering Heights*. Oberon's performance was so superb that she was besieged with film offers. She played such roles as Anne Boleyn in *The Private Life of Henry VIII*, George Sand in *A Song to Remember*, and Napoleon's Josephine in *Désirée*. Oberon, who spent her childhood in India, was brought to London by her uncle, a British officer, when she was 16. She was discovered by Sir Alexander Korda, the first of her four husbands, in a studio commissary. Oberon appeared in more than 30 motion pictures and starred in *The Private Life of Don Juan, The Scarlet Pimpernel,* and *The Lodger*. Her last screen appearances were in *Hotel* (1967) and *Interval* (1973).

Ocampo, Victoria, Argentine writer and publisher (b. 1891, Buenos Aires, Arg.—d. January 1979, Buenos Aires), was the founder (1931) and longtime financial supporter of *Sur*, an avant-garde literary magazine. Ocampo, who introduced to Argentines such international authors as George Bernard Shaw, William Faulkner, Jean-Paul Sartre, and Albert Camus, was hailed as the country's "Queen of Letters" for nearly 50 years. She also was responsible for acquainting the public with the Latin-American writers Jorge Luis Borges and Gabriela Mistral. Even after a brief imprisonment in 1953—the price she paid for speaking against the regime of Juan Perón—Ocampo continued to support *Sur*.

O'Connell, Daniel Patrick, New Zealand-born international lawyer (b. July 7, 1924—d. June 8, 1979, Oxford, England), was Chichele professor of public international law, University of Oxford, from 1972. His classic textbook, *The Law of State Succession* (1956), was used as an authority at the International Court of Justice at The Hague, and he advised the British and other Commonwealth countries' governments on questions of international and constitutional law. Educated at the University of Auckland and Trinity College, Cambridge, he became (1952) reader in international law at the University of Adelaide and served (1962–72) as professor of international law there. In 1972 he became the first Roman Catholic fellow of All Souls College, Oxford, to hold a chair and from 1973 was also director of studies at the International Law Association. Besides many legal works, he produced a study of Cardinal de Richelieu in 1968.

Ogg, Sir William Gammie, British soil scientist (b. Nov. 2, 1891, Aberdeenshire, Scotland—d. Sept. 25, 1979), was director (1943–58) of the Rothamsted Experimental Station, one of the world's chief centres of agricultural research, and a leading expert in soil classification and improvement. During the 1920s, as an adviser on soils in Scotland, he introduced the system of profile classification. In 1928 Ogg was invited by a wealthy Canadian to undertake a plan for regenerating the agriculture of the Isle of Lewis in Scotland. He then became director of the experimental station named after its benefactor, the Macaulay Institute of Soil Research, and greatly extended the institute's work. An able administrator and a man with practical experience in farming, he was appointed director of the Rothamsted station during World War II and remained there until his retirement in 1958. He was knighted in 1949 and served as president of the Society of Chemical Industry (1953–1955). Ogg was a corresponding member of several foreign agricultural academies.

O'Malley, Walter Francis, U.S. baseball executive (b. Oct. 9, 1903, Bronx, N.Y.—d. Aug. 9, 1979, Rochester, Minn.), was the brusque president (1950–70) and owner (1957–79) of the Dodgers professional baseball team in both Brooklyn and Los Angeles. O'Malley, who outraged New York fans when he announced (1957) that "da bums"

UPI

were moving to Los Angeles, also persuaded Horace Stoneham to move the New York Giants to San Francisco, thereby giving the West Coast its first major league baseball teams. O'Malley demonstrated unusual business acumen when his Dodger franchise increased in value to about $50 million after the move to southern California. Under his direction, the millions of fans who jammed Ebbets Field in Brooklyn and saw the Dodgers win four pennants and one World Series were outdone by those who poured through the turnstiles in Los Angeles, first at the Coliseum and from 1962 at Dodger Stadium, to cheer teams that won seven pennants and three World Series. During the 1978 season the Dodgers broke baseball's attendance record when more than three million fans streamed through the gates.

Ortoli, Paul Ange, French naval officer (b. Sept. 19, 1900, Bastia, Corsica—d. March 29, 1979, Paris, France), was a leading supporter of Gen. Charles de Gaulle throughout World War II. After being graduated from the École Navale, he began his service in submarines. In July 1940 he joined de Gaulle's Free French Forces in London and became captain of the submarine "Surcouf," at that time the largest vessel of its type in the world. In 1941 de Gaulle appointed him head of his military Cabinet with the rank of commander. From 1942 to 1943 he commanded the light cruiser "Triomphant," serving with the Allied forces in Australian waters. In September 1943 he was appointed head of the military Cabinet of the navy commissioner in the Committee of National Liberation in Algiers. In August 1944, as rear admiral, he commanded the cruiser "Émile-Bertin" during the Allied landing in Provence, France. Soon afterward de Gaulle, then head of the French provisional government, appointed Ortoli head of his military Cabinet. From 1946 he was commandant of all French naval schools. He served as commander of the French naval forces in the Far East from 1952 and as inspector general of all French naval and naval air forces in 1955. Ortoli retired one year after his promotion to full admiral in 1960.

Ottaviani, Alfredo Cardinal, Italian prelate of the Roman Catholic Church (b. Oct. 29, 1890, Rome, Italy—d. Aug. 3, 1979, Vatican City), was an influential and autocratic head of the Holy Office during the papacy of Pius XII. Son of a poor baker, he was ordained priest in March 1916. Nineteen years later, a brilliant canon lawyer, he joined the Holy Office of which he became *proprefetto* in 1941. He enjoyed the favour of Pope Pius XII who made him a cardinal in 1953 and appointed him *prefetto* of the Holy Office (known since the second Vatican Council as the Congregation for the Doctrine of the Faith). In July 1949 Ottaviani signed a *monitum* warning parents that they might incur excommunication by permitting their children to associate with Communist influences. He was one of the very conservative quintet of cardinals known as "the Pentagon." In October 1958 Giuseppe Cardinal Siri, the "Pentagon" candidate, failed to emerge as pope, and Pius XII's successor, John XXIII, bypassed and surprised the opposition by convoking Vatican II, which opened on Oct. 11, 1962. At its first session Ottaviani spoke against liturgical reforms, but the Council rejected his main doctrinal proposals. Seen by many as a symbol of the pre-conciliar church, Ottaviani retired in 1968.

Paray, Paul, French orchestra conductor (b. May 24, 1886, Tréport-sur-Mer, France—d. Oct. 10, 1979, Monte-Carlo, Monaco), was leader of the Detroit Symphony Orchestra from 1952 to 1963 and worked with many other leading orchestras, appearing most recently with the Monte-Carlo Municipal Orchestra. After a period with the Concerts Lamoureux during the 1920s, he conducted with the Paris Opéra until 1940. His style was restrained and his repertory confined almost exclusively to classical composers. His own compositions included two symphonies, several chamber works, an oratorio, and the ballet *Artémis troublée.* He was awarded the Grand Croix of the Légion d'Honneur.

Park Chung Hee, Korean politician (b. Sept. 30, 1917, near Taegu, Son Son Province, Korea—d. Oct. 26, 1979, Seoul, South Korea), engineered a bloodless military coup in 1961 that deposed Prime Minister John M. Chang; Park then assumed power as head of a junta before being elected in 1963 to the first of three terms as president of South Korea. After graduating (1937) with top honours from Taegu Normal School, Park taught primary school before attending a Japanese military academy and serving as a second lieutenant in the Japanese Army during World War II. After Korea gained independence from Japan he was commissioned (1947) a captain in the Korean Constabulary, but a year later he was sentenced to death for taking part in a Communist revolt led by Korean officers. Park was later pardoned and returned to full rank. He also served as an officer in the Korean Army and was made a brigadier general in 1953.

As president, Park initiated a program of eco-

UPI

nomic reforms that gradually transformed both the lives and the spirit of the South Korean people. As the nation's economy expanded, exports surged to previously unimagined heights—from a few million dollars a year to some $15 billion annually, with heavy emphasis on textiles and clothing. South Korea's annual real growth rate of more than 10% was unprecedented for a less developed nation.

Politically, Park was an uncompromising anti-Communist and with U.S. support was able to keep the nation at a high level of military preparedness. Domestically, he showed little sympathy for or patience with dissenters. He was determined to reach the goals he set for the nation even though his regime was characterized as autocratic and increasingly repressive. Park was the target of two assassination attempts; in 1974 a bullet meant for him killed his wife, Yook Young Soo. Park twice oversaw revampings of the constitution. The "revitalizing" constitution of 1972, which was approved by referendum one month after martial law was declared, vastly increased the powers of the president, especially in "emergencies." The president also made extensive use of the powerful Korean Central Intelligence Agency (KCIA) to ensure domestic stability.

Park and the head of the presidential security service were shot and killed by Kim Jae Kyu, head of the KCIA, during a dinner party. Five of Park's bodyguards were killed at the same time by KCIA agents.

Parodi, Alexandre, French civil servant and diplomat (b. June 1, 1901, Paris, France—d. March 15, 1979, Paris), was a prominent member of the French Resistance during World War II and Gen. Charles de Gaulle's delegate in occupied France in 1944. During 1939–40 Parodi was director of labour and manpower at the Ministry of Labour, but he was dismissed from this post by the Vichy government. Parodi was one of four experts appointed to the clandestine Comité Général d'Études set up in July 1942 to prepare France's post-liberation constitution. In 1944 de Gaulle, then president of the Committee of National Liberation in Algiers, appointed Parodi delegate general for administration of occupied France with the rank of minister. Though his relations with Georges Bidault, chairman of the National Council of Resistance from 1943, were often tense, Parodi supported the Paris insurrection. After World War II Parodi joined the diplomatic service. In 1946 he became France's representative on the UN Security Council and in February 1949 he was appointed secretary general of the Ministry of Foreign Affairs. During 1955–57 he represented France in the North Atlantic Treaty Organization Council. In October 1960 he succeeded René Cassin as vice-president of the Conseil d'État and was its honorary vice-president from 1971.

Parsons, Talcott, U.S. sociologist (b. Dec. 13, 1902, Colorado Springs, Colo.—d. May 8, 1979, Munich, West Germany), was a controversial yet influential scholar of social thought and theory who became a towering figure in the education of three generations of sociologists. As a longtime instructor (1927–31) and professor (1931–73) at Harvard University, Parsons espoused a general theoretical system for the analysis of society. His basic premise was that all societies, simple or complex, have a shared pulse and a stable and enduring structure. Parsons received (1924) a B.A. from Amherst College in Massachusetts and studied at the London School of Economics before earning a Ph.D. from Heidelberg University in 1927. Some of his most important works include *The Structure of Social Action* (1937); *Toward a General Theory of Action* (1951), with Edward A. Shils; *The Social System* (1951); *Working Papers in the Theory of Action* (1953), with Robert F. Bales and Shils; *Economy and Society* (1956), with Neil J. Smelser; and *Politics and Social Structure* (1969).

Partridge, Eric Honeywood, New Zealand-born lexicographer (b. Feb. 6, 1894, Waimata Valley, Gisborne, New Zealand—d. June 1, 1979, Moretonhampstead, Devon, England), who was called the "word king" by critic Edmund Wilson, wrote many works on lexicography, most notably *A Dictionary of Slang and Unconventional English* (1937; revised ed., 1970). He occupied the same seat in the British Museum's rotunda Reading Room for some 40 years. He served with the Australian Infantry in World War I and with the Royal Air Force in World War II. Partridge was a Queensland traveling fellow at Oxford University (1921–23), lectured at English universities, and then ventured into publishing with his Scholartis Press (1927–31). Thereafter, he was a free-lance lexicographer and author for the rest of his life. *Usage and Abusage* (1942), *Shakespeare's Bawdy* (1947), *Origins: An Etymological Dictionary of Modern English* (1958; 4th ed., 1966), and *A Dictionary of Catch Phrases* (1977) were among his scholarly and lively books.

Perelman, S(idney) J(oseph), U.S. humorist (b. Feb. 1, 1904, Brooklyn, N.Y.—d. Oct. 17, 1979, New York, N.Y.), was a master of wordplay and a natural comic, whose books, movies, plays, and essays helped cultivate American humour. Perelman, who began writing for the early frenetic Marx Brothers films, turned out such classics as *Monkey Business* and *Horse Feathers*. He also regularly contributed essays for *The New Yorker* magazine under such absurd titles as *Beat Me, Post-Impressionist Daddy; No Starch in the Dhoti;* and *Methinks He Doth Protein Too Much.* Perelman collaborated on such plays as *One Touch of Venus* and *All Good Americans*, and for his zany *Around the World in 80 Days* he won an Academy Award as best screenwriter for 1956. Perelman, who was not opposed to poking fun at himself, expressed the following about the fate of the light satiric essay: "The handful of chumps who still practice it are as lonely as the survivors of Fort Zinderneuf; a few more assaults by television and picture journalism and we might as well post their bodies on the ramparts, pray for togetherness, and kneel for the final annihilation. Until then, so long and don't take any wooden rhetoric."

Pérez Alfonzo, Juan Pablo, Venezuelan oil czar (b. Dec. 13, 1903, Caracas, Venezuela—d. Sept. 3, 1979, Washington, D.C.), was generally regarded as "the father" and co-founder (1960) of the international association of oil producers that became known as the Organization of Petroleum Exporting Countries (OPEC). In 1941 Pérez Alfonzo helped organize the Acción Democrática Party and served as minister of mines and hydrocarbons in 1945. As Venezuela's oil minister in the late 1950s, he headed a movement to establish an oil cartel with other nations; when oil companies cut the price of Middle East oil in August 1960, Venezuela, Saudi Arabia, Iran, Iraq, and Kuwait formed OPEC. The organization was later joined by eight other countries. In 1976 another of Pérez Alfonzo's dreams was realized when Venezuela nationalized its oil industry.

Pickford, Mary (GLADYS MARY SMITH), Canadian-born actress (b. April 9, 1893, Toronto Ont.—d. May 29, 1979, Santa Monica, Calif.), became the darling of the silent screen with her golden-brown curls and innocent smile and reigned as "America's Sweetheart" at the height of her career in the 1920s. Pickford first achieved stardom in *Tess of the Storm Country* (1914), and in 1917 she further captured the hearts of her audience in *The Poor Little Rich Girl* and *Rebecca of Sunnybrook Farm.* As the first lady of Hollywood and its brightest star, Pickford smashed box office records, surpassing such stars as Lillian and Dorothy Gish, Greta Garbo, and Gloria Swanson. Like Charlie Chaplin, Pickford was a master of illusion and successfully played nymphets until well over 30 years old. In such films as *Sparrows* (1926) and *Pollyanna* (1919) she portrayed a mischievous, witty, and spunky teenager, who pulled at the audience's heartstrings. It was not until 1927 that America's idol was allowed her first romantic kiss in *My Best Girl* and in the following year she bobbed her hair, much to the dismay of her fans. Her shrewd business venture with Chaplin, Douglas Fairbanks, Sr., and director D. W. Griffith in establishing United Artists Corp. helped to make her one of the richest women in the world. (Her fortune at the time of her death was estimated at $50 million.) Pickford was married to actors Owen Moore (1911), Douglas Fairbanks, Sr. (1920), and Charles (Buddy) Rogers (1937). Before retiring from the screen in the early 1930s she won an Academy Award for *Coquette* (1929); she received another special Oscar in 1976. During the last years of her life Pickford was a recluse in her mansion, Pickfair.

PICTORIAL PARADE

Mary Pickford

Ponti, Gio, Italian architect (b. 1891, Milan, Italy—d. Sept. 15, 1979, Milan), was a spectacularly brilliant innovator who first won fame with the delicate, fish-shaped, 32-story Pirelli Rubber Company's office tower in Milan. The building, completed in 1958, was the first great success of its kind in Europe. Ponti turned away from neoclassical Fascist architecture between World Wars I and II and championed modernism. A multiform genius, he founded the Italian architectural review *Domus* in 1928, designed the interiors of such Italian liners as the "Andrea Doria," designed scenery and costumes for La Scala Theatre in Milan, and designed furniture and domestic utensils, as well as textiles. He was also an architectural historian and critic. His buildings went up in cities as far apart as Buenos Aires, Arg., Stockholm, Swed., New York, and Islamabad, Pak., and included factories, hospitals, and office buildings. They expressed a harmony of soberly balanced essential forms.

Pospelov, Pyotr Ivanovich, Soviet Communist propagandist (b. June 19, 1898, Tver, Russia—d. April 23, 1979, Moscow, U.S.S.R.), was editor in chief of *Pravda* from 1940 to 1949 and again from 1952 to 1959. He graduated from Moscow Academy of Agriculture in 1916 and joined the then-underground Communist Party. From 1920 to 1924 he was head of party agitation and propaganda in Tver Province, and for the following six years he served as an official at the party Central Committee. He was called to Stalin's secretariat in 1930, and in 1937 he became head of the Central Committee's agitation and propaganda department. During 1940–46 he was director to the Higher Party School, and in 1949 he became head of the Marx-Engels-Lenin Institute. Elected a member of the Central Committee in 1953, he was an alternate member of the Politburo from 1957 to 1961.

Quentin, Robert, British-born Australian theatrical producer (b. Aug. 3, 1917, Surrey, England—d. July 7, 1979, Sydney, New South Wales, Australia), exerted a powerful influence upon the Australian theatre, first through Eugene O'Neill's masterpiece *Mourning Becomes Electra,* which he produced during a visit in 1945–46. Quentin had worked until 1950 with the Bristol Old Vic and then was the Old Vic's company manager in London. He emigrated to Australia in 1955 and founded the Old Tote Theatre in Sydney in the 1960s. Quentin was professor of drama at the University of New South Wales and founded Australia's National Institute of Dramatic Art.

Ramanantsoa, Gabriel, Malagasy Army officer and politician (b. April 13, 1906, Tananarive [now Antananarivo], Madagascar—d. May 9, 1979, Paris, France), who, as head of government of his country from 1972 to 1975, renegotiated cooperation agreements with France and withdrew Madagascar from the franc currency area. He trained as an officer at the Saint-Cyr military academy in France and fought with the French Army in World War II and later in Indochina. He also took part in Madagascar's independence negotiations in 1960. Ramanantsoa was appointed chief of staff of the new state's armed forces and remained uninvolved in politics until asked to assume power in May 1972 during the emergency that followed student riots that year. In October a referendum confirmed him as head of state in succession to Philibert Tsiranana, the nation's first president. General Ramanantsoa's renegotiation of the cooperation agreements was seen as giving Madagascar a new independence from the former colonial power. But in 1975 he was obliged by internal unrest to hand over power to Col. Richard Ratsimandrava.

Rand, Sally (HELEN GOULD BECK), U.S. dancer (b. Jan. 2, 1904, Elkton, Mo.—d. Aug. 31, 1979, Glendora, Calif.), both shocked and delighted thousands of patrons at the 1933 World's Fair in Chicago when she performed her tantalizing fan dance at the "Streets of Paris" attraction. As Rand artfully maneuvered two large ostrich plumes to Debussy's *Clair de lune* and Chopin's Waltz in C Sharp Minor, no one could discern for sure whether she was actually nude or clothed. Rand's salary skyrocketed to $5,000 a week and signaled the start of a unique professional career that lasted more than 30 years. She first began dancing as a teenage chorus girl and was a member of the Gus Edwards juvenile vaudeville company "School Days" before becoming a circus acrobat. Rand's lovely face and

BOOK OF THE YEAR

PICTORIAL PARADE

trim figure belied her age; she last performed her original fan dance in November 1978.

Randolph, A(sa) Philip, U.S. labour and civil rights leader (b. April 15, 1889, Crescent City, Fla.—d. May 16, 1979, New York, N.Y.), was instrumental in obtaining both labour and civil rights for blacks and in the process became one of the most influential black leaders in U.S. history. In 1917 Randolph founded *The Messenger* magazine with Chandler Owen. Because the magazine questioned the rationality of Negroes fighting during World War I when they were denied freedom at home, Randolph was labeled "The most dangerous Negro in America" by an aide in Pres. Woodrow Wilson's administration. In 1925 Randolph was approached by Pullman porters who asked him to organize a union. After partial victories in 1926 and 1929, and the inclusion in 1934 of porters and maids in the Federal Railway Labor Act, the Brotherhood of Sleeping Car Porters signed its first contract with the Pullman Co. in 1937. Besides guaranteeing collective bargaining and increased wages, it cut working hours by one-third and monthly travel requirements by 4,000 mi. In later years Randolph won concessions from both Presidents Franklin D. Roosevelt and Harry S. Truman. On June 18, 1941, Randolph met with Roosevelt to discuss the barring of blacks from defense plants at the beginning of World War II. Under a threat of a march on Washington, Roosevelt signed (June 25, 1941) Executive Order 8802, which prohibited discrimination in defense industries and federal bureaus and created the Fair Employment Practices Committee. On March 22, 1948, Randolph warned Truman that blacks would not fight unless segregation in the armed forces was eliminated. Truman signed (July 26, 1948) Executive Order 9981, which barred such discrimination. In 1955 Randolph became the first black to serve on the executive council of the newly merged AFL-CIO and was named a vice-president. He also founded (1960) the Negro American Labor Council to end employment discrimination. The culmination of Randolph's career was as director of the historic "March on Washington for Jobs and Freedom" (Aug. 28, 1963) when over 200,000 persons marched on the capital; it was the largest civil rights demonstration in U.S. history.

Ratia, Armi, Finnish textile designer (b. 1912, Karelia, Fin. [now U.S.S.R.]—d. Oct. 3, 1979, Helsinki, Fin.), was the founder (1951) of Marimekko, a famous international fabric concern that introduced bold abstract prints and comfortable, easy-to-care-for clothing. Ratia's innovative designs, which are classics of freshness and simplicity, are sold as wall hangings and on Dan River sheets, Selig furniture, Motif Designs wallpaper, and Samuel Ward stationery products. In later years Ratia became more involved with the company's growth and expansion and turned over her designing to others, including Maija Isola, who created some of Marimekko's most striking patterns. The company operates offices in Japan, Australia, Western Europe, South Africa, New Zealand, and the U.S.

Ray, Nicholas (RAYMOND NICHOLAS KIENZLE), U.S. film director (b. Aug. 7, 1911, Galesville, Wis.—d. June 16, 1979, New York, N.Y.), received critical acclaim for such film classics as *They Live by Night* (1947), *Johnny Guitar* (1954), and *Rebel Without a Cause* (1955), which starkly depicted teenage alienation, loneliness, and violence. Ray attributed his dark view of human nature to novelist and moralist Albert Camus and his light, colour, and composition to architect Frank Lloyd Wright. He also directed *In a Lonely Place* (1950), *King of Kings* (1961), and *55 Days at Peking* (1963) before his career faltered. He was the subject of a feature-length documentary, *I'm a Stranger Here Myself* (1975), and appeared in the motion picture *Hair* (1978).

Rees, (Morgan) Goronwy, British writer and academic (b. Nov. 29, 1909, Aberystwyth, Wales—d. Dec. 12, 1979, London, England), was president (1953–57) of the University College of Wales, Aberystwyth, and a gifted author of novels, notably *Where No Wounds Were* (1951). He was a student at New College, Oxford, and became a fellow of All Souls, Oxford, in 1931. He resigned from Aberystwyth after being censured by the college council for a newspaper account of his friendship with the exposed spy Guy Burgess, who had fled to the Soviet Union in 1951. Devoting himself entirely to writing, he achieved success with *A Bundle of Sensations* (1960), an account of experiences in hospital and their effects; *St. Michael,* a history of the chain-store firm Marks and Spencer; *The Multi-Millionaires,* a study of six rich men; a historical guidebook, *The Rhine* (1969); and *The Great Slump* (1970).

Reitsch, Hanna, German aviator (b. March 29, 1912, Hirschberg, Lower Silesia, Germany [now Jelenia Gora, Poland]—d. Aug. 24, 1979, Frankfurt am Main, West Germany), flew the last German warplane out of Berlin in April 1945 and was the first woman to be awarded the Iron Cross. In the 1930s she trained as a flying missionary and in World War II served as a test pilot for all types of German planes, including the rocket-firing jet fighter Me 262. Reitsch set over 40 aviation records, nearly all for gliding. She was the first person to fly a glider over the Alps and her last gliding record was made in the United States in April 1979. In the early 1960s she directed the national school of gliding in Accra, Ghana, for four years. At the end of World War II Reitsch was captured by the U.S. Army and interned for 15 months, but she eventually became an honorary member of the Society of American Test Pilots. She published an autobiography, *Fliegen, mein Leben.*

Renoir, Jean, French film director (b. Sept. 15, 1894, Paris, France—d. Feb. 12, 1979, Los Angeles, Calif.), was a master filmmaker whose works were characterized by sensitivity, humanity, and artistic grace and became motion picture classics. Renoir, who was one of the foremost creators of the art of the film, wrote and directed 36 motion pictures but was most widely acclaimed for *La Grande Illusion* and *La Règle du jeu,* both produced in France during the 1930s. Renoir's father, the renowned Impressionist painter Pierre-Auguste Renoir, enjoyed painting his child because of his striking red hair. Renoir appeared as a child in four of his father's paintings, notably *Le Chasseur.* He was formally educated at the University of Aix-en-Provence, after a carefree childhood spent in the company of painters and their models. While recovering from a leg wound during World War I, Renoir spent a great deal of time in Paris movie houses viewing serials and Charlie Chaplin films. Although he studied ceramics and intended to set up a factory,

KEYSTONE

Renoir became intrigued with the evolving art of the film. In 1924 he wrote the script for his first work, *Une vie sans joie,* starring his wife. Thereafter Renoir directed his own films, which included *La Fille de l'eau* (1924), *Le Bled* (1929), and *Toni* (1934), a landmark production that influenced directors of the New Wave. After he completed *La Bête humaine* (1938), Renoir fled the Nazis and settled in Hollywood. There he turned out such works as *The Southerner* (1945) and *The River* (1951), which was filmed in India. In 1951 he returned to Europe to make *Le Carrosse d'or* (1952) and *French-Cancan* (1955) and to direct stage plays in France. He also made a number of movies for television including *Le Testament du docteur Cordelier* (1959) and *Le Déjeuner sur l'herbe* (1959). His last film was *Le Petit Théâtre de Jean Renoir* (1969).

Rhys, Jean, British novelist (b. Aug. 24, 1894, Roseau, Dominica, West Indies—d. May 14, 1979, Exeter, Devonshire, England), gained a remarkable reputation, after her work was rediscovered during the 1960s, for her powerful and individualistic portrayal of the feminine sensibility. Married during the 1920s to a songwriter, she wandered through Europe and published her first collection of stories, *The Left Bank,* in 1927. This was followed by *Postures* (1928; American title *Quartet,* 1929), *After Leaving Mr. Mackenzie* (1931), *Voyage in the Dark* (1934), and *Good Morning, Midnight* (1939), which brought critical acclaim but little popular success. After 1939 Rhys ceased to publish and remained a recluse for almost 20 years until she answered a radio producer's advertisement for information as to her whereabouts. The result of her reemergence was her novel *Wide Sargasso Sea* (1966), a fictional reconstruction of the earlier life of Mr. Rochester's mad wife in Charlotte Bronte's *Jane Eyre.* The book was a triumphant success and won several awards, including that of the Royal Society of Literature, of which she was made a fellow. Later collections of stories were *Tigers Are Better-Looking* (1968) and *Sleep It Off, Lady* (1976). She was made a CBE in 1977.

Richards, Ivor Armstrong, British literary critic (b. Feb. 26, 1893, Sandbach, Cheshire, England—d. Sept. 7, 1979, Cambridge, England), was one of the most influential literary critics of his time and a zealous promoter of Basic English, an 850-word vocabulary developed by the linguistic scholar and polymath Charles Kay Ogden. While teaching (1922–29) English and psychology at Magdalene College, Cambridge, Richards established a reputation as a critic of great merit with the publication of *The Principles of Literary Criticism* (1924) and *Practical Criticism* (1929). Richards's psychological approach to literature called for a close analysis of the text. When his student William Empson further developed this approach it became known as "The New Criticism." In the field of semantics he collaborated with Ogden on *The Foundation of Aesthetics* (1921) and *The Meaning of Meaning* (1923). Richards also wrote *Mencius on the Mind* (1931) and *Basic English and Its Uses* (1943). Later works include *Speculative Instruments* (1955) and the essay collections *Poetries* (1974) and *Complementarities* (1975). Late in life he turned to poetry and produced *Goodbye Earth and Other Poems* (1958) and *The Screens and Other Poems* (1960). He was a member of the faculty of Harvard University from 1939 to 1963 and then returned to Cambridge. Richards was made a Companion of Honour in 1964.

Riperton, Minnie, U.S. singer (b. Nov. 8, 1947, Chicago, Ill.—d. July 12, 1979, Los Angeles, Calif.), attained international recognition in 1973 when her first Epic Records album, *Perfect Angel,* co-written with her husband, Dick Rudolph, and containing the hit single "Loving You," was released. This album, produced with Stevie Wonder, stunned the world because it demonstrated Riperton's amazing and unequaled vocal range, which was reputed to be five and a half octaves. Riperton's early operatic training opened up a professional career for her at age 14 when she joined the Gems as a backup singer. She also performed with Chess Records from 1963 to 1970 and from 1966 to 1970 was a member of the Rotary Connection. Other albums include *Come to My Garden* (1970) and *Minnie* (1979). Following a mastectomy in 1976, Riperton became a representative of the American Cancer Society and in 1978 was named educational chairman of the society, becoming the first black woman to hold that position.

Robb, Inez (Inez Callaway), U.S. newspaper columnist (b. 1900?, Middletown, Calif.—d. April 4, 1979, Tucson, Ariz.), began her career as a reporter for an Idaho newspaper even before she graduated (1924) from the University of Missouri's school of journalism. After taking a job in 1927 with the *New York Daily News* as an assistant editor, she was given (1928) the post of society editor for the column that was signed Nancy Randolph. In that position, Robb showed a flair for gently teasing society without ridiculing anyone and for gaining admission to social functions by concocting disguises. On one occasion she masqueraded as a grieving widow in order to attend a prominent wedding from which reporters were barred. In 1938 she joined International News Service, served as its war correspondent during World War II, and was the author of the agency's column "Assignment: America." She also traveled in more than 40 countries and was a passenger on Pan American's first round-trip airline flight across the Atlantic Ocean in 1939. Robb later joined (1953) Scripps-Howard Newspapers and United Features Syndicate. Her column was published in some 140 newspapers until her retirement in 1969.

Rockefeller, Nelson Aldrich, U.S. politician (b. July 8, 1908, Bar Harbor, Maine—d. Jan. 26, 1979, New York, N.Y.), became (1974) the 41st U.S. vice-president after serving four terms (1959–73) as governor of New York. As a grandson of John D. Rockefeller, Sr., founder of the Standard Oil Co., Rockefeller possessed great wealth. But he chose politics over business and established remarkable rapport with voters. Even political foes admired the way "Rocky" could win supporters with as simple a greeting as "Hiya, fella." After graduating (1930) from Dartmouth College, Rockefeller learned to appreciate South American culture and speak fluent Spanish as director (1935–40) of Creole Petroleum, a Standard Oil affiliate with large holdings in Venezuela. In 1944 he was appointed assistant secretary of state for Latin-American affairs by Pres. Franklin D. Roosevelt and persuaded the Latin-American countries to sign a mutual security treaty. Rockefeller was recalled to government service in 1950 by Pres. Harry S. Truman who named him chairman of the International Development Advisory Board, a planning unit for the Point Four Program. After briefly serving (1953–55) as undersecretary in the Department of Health, Education, and Welfare and special assistant in foreign affairs to Pres. Dwight D. Eisenhower, Rockefeller was elected (1958) to the first of four consecutive terms as governor of New York. During these years he strove mightily to occupy the White House, but his reputation as a liberal irritated many Republican Party colleagues, and Rocky was denied the presidential nomination in 1960, 1964, and 1968. On Aug. 20, 1974, Pres. Gerald R. Ford nominated Rockefeller for the post of U.S. vice-president; with the approval of both houses of Congress he was sworn in on Dec. 19, 1974. Rockefeller, a lifelong patron of the arts, acquired an impressive modern art collection; he was a trustee of the Museum of Modern Art and a founder and president of the Museum of Primitive Art, both in New York City.

Rodgers, Richard, U.S. composer (b. June 28, 1902, New York, N.Y.—d. Dec. 30, 1979, New York), was a musical genius who electrified Broadway audiences with the splendid compositions he wrote for such classic musicals as *Oklahoma!* (1943), *Carousel* (1945), *South Pacific* (1949), *The King and I* (1951), and *The Sound of Music* (1959). In collaboration with librettists Lorenz Hart from 1920 to 1942 and Oscar Hammerstein II from 1942 to 1960, Rodgers effortlessly produced a glittering array of some 1,500 inspired songs. Among the most successful—and there were scores of them—were "Manhattan" and "Mountain Greenery" from *The Garrick Gaieties* (1925); "My Funny Valentine" and "The Lady Is a Tramp" from *Babes in Arms* (1937); "Oh, What a Beautiful Morning," "The Surrey with the Fringe on Top," and "People Will Say We're in Love" from the Pulitzer Prize-winning *Oklahoma!;* "Younger Than Springtime" and "Some Enchanted Evening" from his second Pulitzer Prize production, *South Pacific;* and "My Favourite Things" and "Climb Every Mountain" from *The Sound of Music.*

UPI

As a freshman at Columbia University Rodgers teamed up with Hart to compose the varsity show, *Fly with Me* (1920). The duo achieved innumerable successes with Rodgers writing the music and Hart sketching the lyrics. Their endeavours, which led to the establishment of the musical comedy as an art form, included songs for such shows as *Jumbo* (1935), *Pal Joey* (1940), and *By Jupiter* (1942). When Rodgers teamed up with Hammerstein, rumours circulated that after Hammerstein gave him the lyrics, Rodgers composed the haunting "Bali Ha'i" in a record five minutes. Other successes included melodies for *Me and Juliet* (1953), *Pipe Dream* (1955), and *Flower Drum Song* (1958). After Hammerstein's death in 1960, Rodgers worked with other librettists, notably Stephen Sondheim, for *Do I Hear a Waltz* (1965). Rodgers's last compositions were for *I Remember Mama* (1979).

Rogers, Claude Maurice, British painter (b. Jan. 24, 1907, London, England—d. Feb. 18, 1979, London), founded the Euston Road School in 1937 with William Coldstream and Victor Pasmore. When Pasmore turned to abstract painting after World War II, Rogers remained loyal to figurative and representational art. This unfashionable pursuit of realism lessened his appeal, but he continued to influence successive generations of younger artists by his example and through teaching, both at the Slade School of Fine Art and as professor of fine art at the University of Reading (1963–72). In 1973 a retrospective exhibition of his work was held at the Whitechapel Gallery, London. He is permanently represented at the Tate Gallery in London and other leading British galleries and museums. Rogers was president (1952–65) of the London Group and chairman (1961–69) of the Fine Art Panel of the National Council for Diplomas in Art and Design.

Rosenbloom, Carroll, U.S. sports executive (b. March 5, 1907, Baltimore, Md.—d. April 2, 1979, Golden Beach, Fla.), invested in the Baltimore Colts professional football team in 1953, saw them win four league championships and one Super Bowl (1971), then traded his team for the Los Angeles Rams in 1972. The unprecedented no-cash deal saved Rosenbloom more than $4 million in capital gains taxes and gave him ownership of a team that in the following years won seven consecutive division titles but never reached the Super Bowl in Rosenbloom's lifetime.

Rosse, Laurence Michael Harvey Parsons, 6th Earl, British botanist (b. Sept. 28, 1906—d. July 1, 1979, London, England), was an expert horticulturist who worked for numerous organizations that helped preserve Britain's environment and cultural heritage. The best known of these was the National Trust, which he served as deputy chairman from 1961 to 1976. He was also, at various times, chairman of the Georgian Group, the Standing Commission on Museums and Galleries, and the International Dendrology Society and president of the Ancient Monuments Society.

Rota, Nino, Italian composer (b. Dec. 3, 1911, Milan, Italy—d. April 10, 1979, Rome, Italy), wrote the music for some of the most celebrated films of the Italian post-World War II cinema and for Francis Ford Coppola's *The Godfather.* His work in this field came to overshadow his other compositions, which included symphonies and religious music. He was associated with many leading directors, including Luchino Visconti and Franco Zeffirelli, but above all with Federico Fellini; Rota wrote the haunting score for *La Strada* and was engaged on the music for *Women's City,* Fellini's latest film, when he died. He studied at the Curtis Institute of Philadelphia (1931–32) and was director of the Bari Conservatory from 1950 until his retirement in 1978.

Rovere, Richard Halworth, U.S. political writer (b. May 5, 1915, Jersey City, N.J.—d. Nov. 23, 1979, Poughkeepsie, N.Y.), was a perspicacious political author who wrote the column "Letter from Washington" (later "The Affairs of State") for *The New Yorker* magazine for some 30 years (1948–79). Rovere, who was praised for his objective, lucid, and precise writing, also published such books as *Senator Joe McCarthy* (1959), in which Rovere called McCarthy a liar, barbarian, seditionist, and cynic. In *Affairs of State: The Eisenhower Years* (1956), he described then vice-president Richard M. Nixon as "a politician with an advertising man's approach to his work. Policies are products to be sold to the public—this one today, that one tomorrow, depending on the discounts and the state of the market." After Rovere graduated (1937) from Bard College, he briefly worked for *The New Masses* magazine which espoused Communist politics. Disillusioned with Communism, Rovere left the magazine in 1939 and successively worked for *The Nation, Common Sense,* and from 1944 *The New Yorker.*

Ryan, Elizabeth, U.S. tennis player (b. 1892, Los Angeles, Calif.—d. July 6, 1979, Wimbledon, England), was one of the best women doubles players of all time and the holder of 19 Wimbledon titles, which included 12 women's doubles and seven mixed doubles titles between 1914 and 1934. During her 19-year professional career, Ryan captured 659 tournaments and was especially proficient using her chop volley and anticipating where shots would fall. Two years before her death Ryan said, "I hope I don't live to see my record broken, but if someone is to break it, I hope it is Billie Jean [King]." Ryan collapsed while watching the men's doubles finals and died the day before King won her 20th Wimbledon title.

Saltonstall, Leverett, U.S. politician (b. Sept. 1, 1892, Chestnut Hill, Mass.—d. June 17, 1979, Dover, Mass.), astutely used his old New England family name and inherited wealth to surround himself with an aura of integrity and thereby win a succession of elective offices in Massachusetts, a longtime stronghold of the Democratic Party. A graduate (1917) of Harvard Law School, Saltonstall joined his uncle's law firm before being elected a Republican alderman of Newton, a community west of Boston. In 1923 he entered the Massachusetts House of Representatives and served as speaker from 1929 to 1936. Two years later he defeated James M. Curley for the first of three terms (1939–44) in the governor's chair and became the first Republican since the Depression to hold that office. From 1944 to 1967 "Old Lev" was a U.S. senator known for his strong support of antidiscrimination legislation and foreign aid, despite his reticence and distaste for controversy. At the time of his retirement in 1967 Saltonstall was the ranking Republican on two powerful Senate bodies, the Appropriations and Armed Services committees.

Saville, Victor, British film director and producer (b. Sept. 25, 1897, Birmingham, England—d. May 8, 1979, London, England), was responsible for one of the first British talking films, *Kitty,* in 1929 and during the next decade was one of the few British directors whose work rivaled the productions of Hollywood in popular appeal. A craftsman with an eye on the box office, Saville achieved successes during this period as director or producer of such films as *I Was a Spy* (1933), *The Good Companions* (1933), *South Riding* (1938), and *The Citadel* (1938). In 1939, before leaving for the U.S., he scored a critical and popular triumph with *Goodbye, Mr. Chips,* starring Robert Donat and Greer Garson. From then until 1961 he worked in Hollywood , where he directed or produced many films, including *Kim* (1950) and *Loss of Innocence* (1961).

Sawyer, Charles, U.S. lawyer and government official (b. Feb. 10, 1887, Cincinnati, Ohio—d. April 7, 1979, Palm Beach, Fla.), was U.S. ambassador to Belgium and minister to Luxembourg before serving as secretary of commerce (1948–53) in the Cabinet of Harry S. Truman. In 1952 Sawyer, a staunch conservative and ardent defender of free enterprise, was ordered by Truman to manage the nation's steel mills, which had been seized by the government to avert a strike. In a landmark decision, the Supreme Court ruled 6–3 that the seizure violated the Constitution because it usurped the legislative powers of Congress. Sawyer then happily released the properties to their private owners and the United Steelworkers of America went on strike. Aside from his practice of law, Sawyer participated in numerous business ventures involving such diverse things as office equipment, life insurance, copper mines, newspapers, and professional sports teams.

Schenken, Howard, U.S. contract bridge master (b. 1903?—d. Feb. 20, 1979, Palm Springs, Calif.), was a skilled player of contract bridge who won a record five life master pair championships and was a member of the teams that won world titles in 1936, 1950, 1951, and 1953. During 50 years as an accomplished player, he devised such now-standard conventions as the weak two-bid, the prepared opening bid, and the forcing two-over-one response. Schenken, a prolific writer on the game, was the author of a syndicated column for 30 years and of such volumes as *Better Bidding in 15 Minutes* (1963) and *Howard Schenken's Big Club* (1968). His autobiography, *Education of a Bridge Player,* was published in 1973.

Schmid, Carlo, West German jurist and politician (b. Dec. 3, 1896, Perpignan, France—d. Dec. 11, 1979, Bonn, West Germany), played a significant role in formulating the "basic law," or constitution, of West Germany and was (1949–66 and 1969–72) vice-president of the Bundestag (parliament). The son of a German father and a French mother, he renounced French nationality at the outset of World War I and enlisted in the German Army. After the war Schmid completed his legal studies at Tübingen University, where in 1929 he became a lecturer in international law. During World War II he was a legal adviser to the German command in occupied France. In 1946 he was appointed professor at Tübingen, and the following year he became a member of the executive committee of the Social Democratic Party. Schmid was influential in bringing about the post-World War II reconciliation between West Germany and France, cemented by Gen. Charles de Gaulle and Chancellor Konrad Adenauer in 1963. From 1963 to 1966 Schmid was president of the assembly of the Western European Union. He retired in 1972.

Schmidt, Arno, German writer (b. Jan. 18, 1914, Hamburg, Germany—d. June 3, 1979, Celle, West Germany), was the author of works that seemed often perversely individualistic but bore the imprint of considerable imaginative and verbal talent. He purported to be writing for a few hundred readers who were capable of immersing themselves in his books. Schmidt's training as a mathematician was later put to use in his exploitation of puzzles and conundrums. During World War II he served with the artillery and was taken prisoner in 1945. From the 1950s he lived in virtual seclusion, writing criticism and monumental experimental novels: *Leviathan* (1949), *Die Gelehrtenrepublik* (1957), and *Zettels Traum* (1970). His last book, *Abend mit Goldrand,* appeared in 1975 and was praised for its verbal inventiveness, although some critics found the erotic theme hard to accept.

Scott-Taggart, John, British barrister and radio pioneer (b. 1897, Bolton, Lancashire, England—d. July 31, 1979, Beaconsfield, England), was a radio and radar engineer who held rights to 30 patents. In 1922 he founded the Radio Press, publishers of *Modern Wireless* and *Wireless Weekly,* from which many thousands of amateurs in the 1920s learned to build radio sets from Scott-Taggart's ST 100 design. As a radio officer in World War I, he urged the development of the thermionic valve. As a Royal Air Force wing commander staff officer during World War II, he had technical responsibility for radar stations and radar training. Scott-Taggart also continued his responsibility for Britain's radar stations after the war. Between the wars he was head of valve manufacturing for Ediswan and of patents for the Radio Communications Co. Besides numerous textbooks and articles in the technical press he also wrote books on Italian and Spanish pottery and porcelain.

Seberg, Jean, U.S.-born actress (b. Nov. 13, 1938, Marshalltown, Iowa—d. early September 1979, Paris, France), was selected from nearly 18,000 contestants for the title role in Otto Preminger's lacklustre *Saint Joan* (1957) but established her reputation in France as the star of the New Wave film *A Bout de Souffle* (1958; shown in the U.S. as *Breathless,* 1961). Seberg appeared in such motion pictures as *Bonjour Tristesse, The Mouse that Roared, Lilith, Paint Your Wagon,* and *Airport,* her last U.S. film. In 1970 Seberg became the target of a rumour circulated by the FBI which wanted to "cause her embarrassment and serve to cheapen her image with the general public" because she supported the black nationalist movement. A Hollywood gossip columnist insinuated that Seberg was pregnant by a high-ranking member of the Black Panther Party. Upon reading the article, Seberg, at that time married to Romain Gary, went into labour and gave birth to a premature baby girl who died. Seberg, who never recovered emotionally from the loss of her child, took her own life. One week after Seberg's death, the FBI acknowledged complicity in the 1970 slander.

PICTORIAL PARADE

Sheen, Fulton J. (PETER JOHN SHEEN), U.S. Roman Catholic prelate (b. May 8, 1895, El Paso, Ill.—d. Dec. 9, 1979, New York, N.Y.), was a vibrant speaker whose inspirational television show, "Life Is Worth Living" (1951–57), was carried on 123 stations and viewed by 20 million people. Sheen was endowed with piercing, deep-set blue eyes that mesmerized his audience; his ratings soared to unimaginable heights despite being slotted against such formidable rival network stars as Frank Sinatra and Milton Berle. Sheen's message, delivered without the aid of notes or cue cards, combined common sense and Christian ethics. After Sheen was ordained in 1919, he earned a Ph.D. in philosophy at the Catholic University of Louvain in Belgium and briefly served a parish before his transfer to the Catholic University of America as a teacher of philosophy. He quickly distinguished himself and rose to papal chamberlain, domestic prelate, and bishop. His broadcasting career began in 1930 on a Sunday evening radio program, "The Catholic Hour," that was heard by millions and led to his highly successful television show. Sheen also gained prominence through more than 70 books and pamphlets, including *God and Intelligence, Peace of Soul,* and *Three to Get Married.* Among his many notable converts were Louis Budenz, managing editor of the Communist *Daily Worker,* columnist Heywood Broun, and playwright-politician Clare Boothe Luce. In 1966 Sheen was appointed bishop of Rochester, N.Y., but retired in 1969 after a stormy period in that office. He then was elevated to titular archbishop but led a quiet life in a small New York apartment.

Simonov, Konstantin, Soviet writer (b. 1915, Petrograd, Russia—d. Aug. 28, 1979, Moscow, U.S.S.R.), was an eminent novelist and board secretary of the U.S.S.R.'s writers' union. Simonov celebrated the defense of his country in *The Living and the Dead,* an epic trilogy about the German invasion of Russia in World War II, the second part of which was called *Soldiers Are Not Born* and was critical of Stalin. It won him the Lenin Prize in 1974 and was translated into many languages. Simonov was a Red Army war correspondent in Outer Mongolia in 1939 and later on the German-Soviet front. His works included the novel *Days and Nights* (1944), a moving wartime account of Stalingrad; early historical poems; two wartime plays; and essays. From 1946 to 1950 Simonov was a deputy of the Supreme Soviet and edited the leading Soviet literary magazine, *Novy Mir* (1946–50 and 1954–58; the interruption was due to the magazine's temporary suspension for introducing works considered dangerous or untimely). He also edited the *Literary Gazette* (1950–53), and he received the Order of Lenin three times.

Simons, Arthur D. ("Bull"), U.S. Army officer (b. 1919?—d. May 21, 1979, Dallas, Texas), was a fearless and imaginative soldier who in 1970 commanded a daring Green Beret raid on the Sontay prisoner of war camp deep inside North Vietnam. The flawlessly executed operation was foiled, however, when Simons and his 57 men landed under heavy fire only to find that the camp had earlier been evacuated. Nevertheless, Pres. Richard M. Nixon awarded Colonel Simons the Distinguished Service Cross for his valiant effort. In 1979 industrialist H. Ross Perot enticed Simons out of retirement with a request to rescue two employees imprisoned in Iran. The mission was accomplished when Simons and his 17-man commando team reportedly instigated a riot in Teheran and stormed the prison. As Simons watched the emotional reunions of the two engineers and their families, he remarked, "I just got paid for the trip."

Skinner, Cornelia Otis, U.S. actress and author (b. May 30, 1901, Chicago, Ill.—d. July 9, 1979, New York, N.Y.), was a multitalented Broadway personality who, armed with a satirical wit, turned out light verse, monologues, anecdotes, and monodramas in which she displayed her versatile and distinctive acting skills. Skinner made her first professional stage appearance with her father, tragedian Otis Skinner, in *Blood and Sand* (1921). During the 1930s she wrote and staged her own monodramas, including *The Loves of Charles II, The Empress Eugénie,* and *The Wives of Henry VIII.* In each of these shows she played several different characters, adeptly transforming herself from one role to another. It was not until 1939 in *Candida* that Skinner established a reputation as a fine actress, and she confirmed her excellence as a dramatic actress in *Theatre* (1941). Other performances that won critical acclaim included her roles in *Lady Windermere's Fan* (1946), *Paris '90* (1952), and *The Pleasure of His Company* (1958), which she wrote with Samuel Taylor. Skinner's diverse writing ability was evident in her 1942 best-seller *Our Hearts Were Young and Gay,* written with Emily Kimbrough, and the serious and moving *Madame Sarah* (1967), which chronicled the life of Sarah Bernhardt.

Slessor, Sir John Cotesworth, British marshal of the Royal Air Force (b. June 3, 1897, Rhanikhet, India—d. July 12, 1979, Wroughton, England), was one of the architects of British air strategy during and after World War II. A childhood victim of polio, he was at first rejected for military service in World War I but managed to gain entry to the Royal Flying Corps. Slessor served as a pilot in France, Egypt, and the Sudan. During the interwar period he held staff appointments and commands in Britain and India and became director of plans at the Air Ministry in 1937. From 1942, as assistant chief of air staff and later as head of Coastal Command, Slessor used his skills as a negotiator to ensure closer Anglo-U.S. collaboration in the war effort. From 1944 to 1945 he was commander in chief, RAF, in the Mediterranean and Middle East, then served at the Air Ministry until his appointment as chief of air staff (1950–52). Slessor was firmly convinced of the need for a combined defense strategy and did much to achieve this during his period of command. After his retirement, he devoted his time to writing on defense. Slessor was knighted in 1948.

Smith, (Stanley) Patrick, British journalist (b. Sept. 7, 1915, London, England—d. Feb. 25, 1979, New Haven, Conn.), was a staff correspondent of the British Broadcasting Corporation (BBC) for 30 years and from 1945 set his stamp on its foreign news reporting as correspondent in Vienna (1945–49) and—after spells in Berlin, Bonn, Cairo, and Cape Town—in Rome (1958–70). Smith joined the BBC European Service in 1940 and was a war correspondent in Italy and Austria. His assignments included the Soviet blockade of Berlin, apartheid in South Africa, and the Mau Mau troubles in Kenya before that country became independent. In 1974 he published his memoirs, *A Desk in Rome.*

Solomons, Jack, British boxing promoter (b. 1902, London, England—d. Dec. 8, 1979, Brighton, England), earned his living as an East End London fishmonger before becoming one of Britain's more colourful and successful boxing promoters. His first big match pitted Jack London and Bruce Woodcock in 1945. He not only matched British and Commonwealth boxers but also a total of 26 world champions. In 1951 Solomons brought middleweight champion Sugar Ray Robinson and Randolph Turpin into Earls Court, London. Turpin took the title, but lost it to Robinson later in the year in a rematch in the U.S. Solomons's secondary interests included betting shops, which he owned in partnership with comedian Bud Flanagan, and the World Sporting Club, which he helped found in 1965 after surrendering the chairmanship of the British Boxing Board of Control's southern area council.

Stafford, Jean, U.S. writer (b. July 1, 1915, Covina, Calif.—d. March 26, 1979, White Plains, N.Y.), was an incisive writer whose carefully constructed *Collected Stories* (1969) won a Pulitzer Prize in 1970. After graduating from the University of Colorado at Boulder, Stafford studied at Heidelberg University in Germany from 1936 to 1937. When she returned to the U.S. and settled in Boston, she painstakingly completed a four-year effort, *Boston Adventure.* Its publication in 1944 launched Stafford's career and guaranteed her a position of prominence in literary circles. She later wrote two more novels, *The Mountain Lion* (1947) and *The Catherine Wheel* (1952), numerous short stories and children's books, and was a regular contributor to such magazines as *Kenyon Review, Partisan Review, Harper's Bazaar,* and *The New Yorker.* Stafford successively married poet Robert Lowell and writers Oliver Jensen and A. J. Liebling.

Stikker, Dirk Uipko, Dutch politician and diplomat (b. Feb. 5, 1897—d. Dec. 24, 1979), was secretary-general of NATO from 1961 to 1964, a critical period during which his conciliatory role did much to preserve the alliance. Previously, Stikker was The Netherlands' foreign minister (1948–52) and ambassador to Britain (1952–58). Receiving his doctor of laws degree from the University of Groningen, Stikker became a director of several leading Dutch companies during the 1930s. In 1946 he was a founder of the liberal Party of Freedom, later known as the People's Party for Freedom and Democracy (VVD). From 1950 to 1952 he was chairman of the Organization for European Economic Cooperation. A signatory (as Dutch foreign minister) of the North Atlantic Treaty in 1949, he was The Netherlands' permanent representative on the North Atlantic Council from 1958 until his appointment as NATO secretary-general in 1961.

Stokes, Ralph Shelton Griffin, British Army officer and mining engineer (b. July 31, 1882—d. Feb. 24, 1979, near Sherborne, Dorset, England), attained the rank of brigadier after serving in the South African (Boer) War with Paget's Horse (1901–02) and in World Wars I and II with the Royal Engineers. He took an active part in the raids on Archangel (1918–19) and Narvik (1940). In civilian life he began as a field engineer and ended as company chairman. Stokes was associated with the International Nickel Co. of New York, with De Beers Consolidated at Kimberley, South Africa, and with Trinidad Leaseholds.

Stow Hill, Frank Soskice, Baron, British lawyer and politician (b. July 23, 1902, Geneva, Switz.—d. Jan. 2, 1979), held high office in successive Labour governments after World War II, being home secretary under Harold Wilson from October 1964 until December 1965 and then lord privy seal until April 1966. The son of a Russian immigrant, Soskice was called to the bar by the Inner Temple in 1926. He entered Parliament at the 1945 election that brought Labour to power at the end of the war and was successively solicitor general (1945–51) and attorney general (April–October 1951). In 1950 he was Britain's delegate to the UN General Assembly. Soskice was knighted in 1945 and created a life peer in 1966.

Straight, Whitney Willard, U.S.-born racing driver and company chairman (b. Nov. 6, 1912—d. April 5, 1979, London, England), was a U.S. millionaire who became British by naturalization in 1936 and enjoyed a unique record as a race car driver, airman, and director of national corporations. He began his dashing career while an undergraduate at Trinity College, Cambridge, when he broke the Brook-lands track lap record in 1933 and successfully took on such ace drivers as George Easton, Kaye Don, John Cobb, and Raymond Mays. He flew his own airplane to race meetings. In 1934 he won the South African Grand Prix but gave up motor racing for aviation. He formed companies that controlled several provincial airfields and set up a chain of flying schools for both civil aviation and the Royal Air Force. During World War II he was a pilot in the RAF and received British, U.S., and Norwegian decorations. He was deputy chairman of British European Airways (1946–47) and managing director (1947–49) and deputy chairman (1949–55) of British Overseas Airways Corporation; he joined Rolls-Royce Ltd. in 1956 as executive vice-chairman, was chairman (1971–76), and thereafter chairman of Rolls-Royce Realizations Ltd. He was deputy chairman of the Post Office (1969–74).

Stypulkowski, Zbigniew, Polish politician (b. March 26, 1904, Warsaw, Poland—d. March 30, 1979, London, England), was a leader of the clandestine National Armed Forces (NSZ) in Poland during the World War II German occupation. Under his influence the major part of the 100,000-strong NSZ joined the underground Home Army in March 1944, and he became a member of the underground administration recognizing the supreme authority of the Polish government-in-exile in London. Stypulkowski graduated in 1925 from the law faculty of the University of Warsaw, joined the National Party led by Roman Dmowski, and in 1930 was elected as the youngest member of the Sejm (parliament). In 1939 he took part in the September campaign against the Germans but was taken prisoner by the Soviet army that invaded Poland from the east. In accordance with a German-Soviet agreement he was handed over to the Germans and was freed in the spring of 1940. He joined the NSZ in 1942. After the Soviet liberation of Warsaw, 16 members of the underground administration, including Stypulkowski, were put on trial in Moscow, and on June 21, 1945, all 16 were sentenced to up to ten years' imprisonment. Stypulkowski, who alone refused to recognize the right of a Soviet court to judge the political actions of Polish ministers, was given a four-month sentence. Freed, he returned to Warsaw, but he considered it safer to escape to the West and reached London in November 1945. He published a book, *Invitation to Moscow* (1951), which went into three editions and was translated into several languages. In London Stypulkowski took an active part in the Polish Political Council, which he represented in Washington, D.C., from 1959 to 1970.

Svoboda, Ludvik, Czech politician (b. Nov. 25, 1895, Hroznatin, Moravia—d. Sept. 20, 1979, Prague, Czech.), was a popular president of Czechoslovakia from 1968 to 1975. The son of a farmer, he was an agronomy student when World War I began. Drafted into the Austro-Hungarian Army, he was captured by the Russians and, switching sides, fought with them against the Central Powers. After the war Svoboda managed his father's farm and joined the Czechoslovak Army in 1921. After the German occupation of Prague in March 1939 he escaped to Poland, ending up in the U.S.S.R., where he started the formation of a Czechoslovak Army unit made up of fellow refugees. As commanding general of the Czechoslovak Army Corps

WIDE WORLD

which fought alongside the Red Army, he took part in the liberation of Czechoslovakia in May 1945. Svoboda became minister of defense in the postwar government formed by Pres. Edvard Benes. During the Communist coup of February 1948, Svoboda ordered the Army to remain neutral, and shortly afterward he joined the Communist Party. From 1955 to 1958 he headed the Czechoslovak Military Academy.

In 1968 Alexander Dubcek, the new first secretary of the Czechoslovak Communist Party, recommended Svoboda for the presidency as the man most agreeable to the U.S.S.R., and he was elected on March 30. After the Soviet-led occupation of Czechoslovakia in August, Svoboda stood firmly by Dubcek, who—with Josef Sarkovsky, Frantisek Kriegal, and Oldrich Cernik, among others—was arrested and flown to Moscow. Svoboda was called there to negotiate an agreement on the stationing of Soviet troops in Czechoslovakia, but he declared that he would not discuss the matter until the arrested leaders were released. The Soviets agreed, and on August 27 Svoboda returned to Prague with his colleagues. On May 29, 1975, Svoboda, an ailing man, was removed from office and replaced by Gustav Husak.

Taraki, Nur Mohammad, Afghan politician (b. 1917, Ghazni Province, Afghanistan—d. Sept. 16 1979, Kabul, Afghanistan), became Afghanistan's head of state and government in April 1978 after a coup in which his predecessor, Pres. Sardar Mohammad Daud Khan, was killed. Taraki was ousted in September 1979 by Hafizullah Amin (*q.v.*) and reportedly shot in a gun battle in the presidential palace. His death, announced October 9, was stated to be the result of "a severe and prolonged illness." Born into a lowly Pushtoon family, Taraki passed his matriculation by attending night school while working as a clerk in Bombay, India. In the late 1940s he worked in the press department of the Afghan government and in 1952 was appointed press attaché at the Afghan embassy in Washington, D.C. On returning to Kabul he worked as a translator for the U.S. embassy. When King Mohammad Zahir introduced a more flexible home and foreign policy in 1963, Taraki entered politics and founded the Khalq ("masses") Party. The overthrow of the monarchy in July 1963 by Mohammad Daud caused a split in the party, with one faction, known as Parcham ("banner"), supporting the Daud regime while the Taraki faction opposed it. In 1977, however, the two factions, possibly under Soviet pressure, reunited to form the People's Democratic Party with Taraki as secretary-general. The following year, with the help of Soviet-trained army units, he overthrew Daud, killing him and all his family. At the beginning of September 1979 Taraki left for Havana to represent Afghanistan at the sixth summit conference of nonaligned nations, leaving the government in the hands of Amin, who had been appointed prime minister some five months earlier. Returning via Moscow, Taraki was believed to have been advised by Soviet Pres. Leonid Brezhnev to get rid of Amin, whose anti-Islamic policy was considered dangerous. Taraki, however, failed in this and was himself overthrown by Amin.

Tate, (John Orley) Allen, U.S. poet and critic (b. Nov. 19, 1899, Winchester, Ky.—d. Feb. 9, 1979, Nashville, Tenn.), was a leading advocate of the New Criticism, which prescribed that literature be viewed contextually rather than in its historical or social context. While attending Vanderbilt University in Nashville, Tenn., Tate became a member of the Fugitives, a group of now-famous writers who shared an interest in the agrarian South and shaped 20th-century Southern literature. Their numbers included Merrill Moore, John Crowe Ransom, and Robert Penn Warren. Tate's predominant themes, in both his poetry and criticism, were the culture of the conservative agrarian South and Roman Catholicism, to which he was converted in 1950. In his best works, including "Ode to the Confederate Dead" (1926) and "The Mediterranean" (1932), he focused on the past. Tate, who acknowledged the influence of T. S. Eliot, published several collections of poetry, including *Mr. Pope and Other Poems* (1928) and *The Winter Sea* (1944), and such critical works as *Reactionary Essays on Poetry and Ideas* (1936), *Reason in Madness* (1941), and *Essays of Four Decades* (1968). Tate taught at Southwestern College in Memphis, Tenn., the University of North Carolina Women's College, New York University, and the Universities of Rome, Chicago, and Minnesota before retiring in 1968. His *Collected Poems* was published in 1977.

Teare, (Robert) Donald, British forensic scientist (b. July 1, 1911, Ramsey, Isle of Man—d. Jan. 17, 1979, Isle of Man), was professor of forensic medicine at St. George's Hospital Medical School, University of London, from 1967 to 1975 and afterward professor emeritus. Teare was frequently called as an expert witness in court cases when the outcome hinged on complex medical evidence. In 1970 his testimony helped to clear Greek shipping millionaire Stavros Niarchos of liability for the death of his wife Eugenie. His high reputation among lawyers rested on his ability to explain involved technical matters in clear and simple language. He was a fellow of the Royal College of Physicians and the Royal College of Pathologists and a leading member of other medical associations and societies.

Templer, Sir Gerald (Walter Robert), British Army officer (b. Sept. 11, 1898—d. Oct. 25, 1979, London, England), achieved the greatest success of his career when, as high commissioner and director of operations of the Federation of Malaya, 1952-54, he smashed menacing Communist guerrilla forces and restored courage and confidence to the country. Commissioned into the Royal Irish Fusiliers in 1916, he later served (1936) in Palestine during the Arab rebellion and was awarded the Distinguished Service Order. World War II saw him rapidly promoted. He was the youngest lieutenant general in the Army when commanding II Corps in 1942, but he stepped down to serve in Italy, where he was injured by a mine while in command of the 6th Armoured Division in 1944. In 1945 he was made director of military government for the 21st Army Group in Germany and sacked the lord mayor of Cologne and future chancellor of the Federal Republic, Konrad Adenauer, for "incompetence." War Office appointments followed, interrupted by service in Malaya; he ended active service as field marshal and chief of the Imperial General Staff (1955-58). Templer was made a knight of the British Empire in 1949 and of the Garter in 1963.

Thomas, Horatio Oritsejolmi, Nigerian surgeon (b. Aug. 31, 1917, Sapele, Nigeria—d. July 2, 1979, Lagos, Nigeria), was the first Nigerian to become a fellow of the British Royal College of Surgeons. He lectured in surgery at the University of Lagos from 1949 until his appointment as professor in 1962. In the same year he became dean and provost of the university's College of Medicine. From 1972 to 1975 he was vice-chancellor of the University of Ibadan. He was awarded the CBE in 1963 and the Cross of Nigeria in 1965. Besides papers in British and West African medical journals, he contributed to *Diseases of Children in the Subtropics and Tropics* (1970).

Tiomkin, Dimitri, Russian-born composer (b. May 10, 1894, St. Petersburg, Russia—d. Nov. 11, 1979, London, England), won four Academy Awards for his soaring film scores for *The Old Man and the Sea*, *The High and the Mighty*, and *High Noon* and its memorable theme song, "Do Not Forsake Me, Oh My Darlin'." Tiomkin studied under Aleksandr Glazunov at the St. Petersburg Conservatory but left for western Europe after the Revolution to begin a career as a concert pianist. After arriving in Hollywood in the 1930s with his wife, Albertina Rasch, a ballerina and choreographer, he turned to the cinema and in 1937 composed the score for *Lost Horizon*. His film scores, which became some of the most popular music of the 1950s and 1960s, included *Gunfight at the OK Corral*, *Friendly Persuasion*, *Giant*, *55 Days at Peking*, and *The Guns of Navarone*. Tiomkin's last work was as executive producer and musical director of a Soviet-U.S. film biography of Tchaikovsky.

Todman, William ("Bill") Seldon, U.S. television producer (b. July 31, 1916, New York, N.Y.—d. July 29, 1979, New York), teamed up with Mark Goodson in 1946 to produce such popular quiz and game shows as "To Tell the Truth," "I've Got a Secret," "The Price Is Right," and "What's My Line?," a Sunday night favourite for 17½ years. They also produced the late 1970s smash hit "Family Feud." The Goodson-Todman partnership capitalized on the previously unexplored realm of television quiz shows and built their success on enthusiastic audiences who eagerly competed for cash and merchandise prizes. The "Gold-Dust Twins" also formed Capitol City Publishing Co. and at one time owned 17 newspapers and a radio station.

Tomonaga, Shinichiro, Japanese physicist (b. March 31, 1906, Kyoto, Japan—d. July 8, 1979, Tokyo, Japan), was joint recipient with Julian S. Schwinger and Richard P. Feynman of the 1965 Nobel Prize for Physics for developing basic principles of quantum electrodynamics. Although the three scientists worked independently, it was learned after World War II that each had essentially reached the same conclusions, albeit using three separate approaches. Their discovery made the theory of quantum electrodynamics (the electric and magnetic effects on subatomic particles) fully consistent with the special theory of relativity. After graduating (1929) from Kyoto Imperial University, Tomonaga joined the Institute of Physical and Chemical Research and studied under Yoshio Nishina, a pioneer in nuclear physics. In 1941 he became professor of physics at Bunrika University (later Tokyo University of Education), and from 1956 to 1962 he was president of the Tokyo University of Education. Tomonaga also played a leading role in the Pugwash Conference, which campaigned against the spread of nuclear weapons. His most important work in English is *Quantum Mechanics* (1962).

Vance, Vivian (VIVIAN JONES), U.S. actress (b. July 26, 1913, Cherryvale, Kan.—d. Aug. 17, 1979, Belvedere, Calif.), was better known as Ethel Mertz, the zany neighbour, landlady, and partner in a thousand crazy schemes with Lucille Ball in the hit television series "I Love Lucy" (1951–59). Vance costarred with William Frawley, who played Fred Mertz. From 1962 to 1965 Vance again teamed up with Ball and played Viv on "The Lucy Show." Earlier in her career she appeared on Broadway in such shows as *Hooray for What!* (1937), *Skylark* (1939), *Let's Face It* (1941), and *The Cradle Will Rock* (1947). Vance succumbed to cancer.

Vanuxem, Paul, French Army general (b. July 22, 1904, Bully, France—d. Jan. 7, 1979, Paris, France), served in World War II and in subsequent French colonial campaigns before being imprisoned in 1961 for his part in the Secret Army Organization (OAS), which was formed to resist French withdrawal from Algeria. An able officer but a harsh disciplinarian, he was considered an intellectual and remained an outsider unwilling to accept the Army's noninvolvement in politics and France's abandonment of its colonial empire. He was forced to preside over the 1954 evacuation of Hanoi, the capital of French Indochina, and to witness Gen. Charles de Gaulle's granting of independence to Algeria in 1962. He always denied complicity in the OAS. After being released from prison, he turned to journalism, defending the U.S. involvement in Vietnam and confirming his reputation as a supporter of lost causes.

Velasco Ibarra, José María, Ecuadorian politician (b. 1893–d. March 30, 1979, Quito, Ecuador), was the resilient president of Ecuador who was elected repeatedly but completed only one full term of office. During his 13 intermittent years in power, Velasco held office five times (1934–35, 1944–47, 1952–56, 1960–61, and 1968–72) with 1952–56 his only completed term. As a self-proclaimed neo-liberal, he drew support from both the right and left and often disputed opponents by declaring, "Give me a balcony and I will govern Ecuador again." It was Velasco's term of office from 1952 to 1956 that became a historic landmark because he won the election by the biggest vote in Ecuador's history after campaigning as an Independent Liberal, and he became only the second president ever to complete a full term of office. Although Velasco spent nearly 30 years exiled in Argentina, he returned to Ecuador shortly before he died "to meditate and await death."

Ventura, Ray(mond), French bandleader (b. April 16, 1908, Paris, France—d. March 29, 1979, Palma, Majorca, Spain), was France's most popular jazz orchestra leader before World War II. In 1925 he founded "the Collegiate Five," the nucleus of his orchestra of Collegians. Their first recordings in 1929 included "I'm Afraid for You" and "Sweet Ella May." In the 1930s jazz violinist Stephane Grapelli joined the celebrated Collegians and they gave classical jazz concerts on a European tour. During World War II Ventura and his orchestra played throughout South America; after the war they returned to France, where their performances in concerts and films met with less success as jazz declined in popularity. Two of the band's most celebrated numbers, *Fantastique* (1932) and *Tout va très bien madame la marquise* (1935), were written by Paul Misraki. From 1948 to 1970 Ventura headed a film production company which produced some 30 films.

Viansson-Ponté, Pierre, French journalist and author (b. Aug. 2, 1920, Clisson, Loire-Atlantique, France—d. May 7, 1979, Paris, France), was a leading political commentator and a historian of the Gaullist era in France. After taking a law degree at the University of Strasbourg at the beginning of World War II, he enlisted in a tank regiment and was seriously wounded in 1940. During the German occupation he joined the Resistance and was arrested by the Gestapo in 1943. After the liberation he founded at Montpellier a weekly journal called *Homme Libre,* later joining Agence France-Presse. In 1953, with Jean-Jacques Servan-Schreiber, he founded *L'Express,* a weekly newsmagazine of which he was editor in chief (1953–58). In 1958 he became head of home affairs at *Le Monde,* becoming its editorial writer in 1972. His many political books included *L'Histoire de la République Gaullienne* (2 vol., 1970–71), probably the best appraisal of the de Gaulle era (1958–69). In *Après de Gaulle, Qui?* (1968), he enumerated three "pretenders" to the throne: Georges Pompidou, François Mitterrand, and Valéry Giscard d'Estaing. Viansson-Ponté also wrote for many French and foreign publications including *Britannica Book of the Year,* to which he contributed (1968–79) biographies of French political personalities. His last book, written with Léon Schwartzenberg, was *Changer la Mort* (1977).

Vicious, Sid (JOHN SIMON RITCHIE), British punk-rock star (b. 1958?, England—d. Feb. 2, 1979, New York, N.Y.), was the bass guitarist of the Sex Pistols, a controversial British band that gained notoriety by its outrageous behaviour, which included foul language, vomiting, spitting on audiences, and piercing the body with safety pins. The group purported to reflect the cynicism and the nihilistic attitude of Britain's working-class youth. Vicious, who was awaiting trial for the October 1978 murder of his girl friend, died of a heroin overdose some 13 hours after he was freed on bail. The Sex Pistols had disbanded early in 1978 after a disappointing U.S. tour.

Villot, Jean-Marie Cardinal, French prelate of the Roman Catholic Church (b. Oct. 11, 1905, Saint-Amant-Tallende, France—d. March 9, 1979, Vatican City), was the Vatican's secretary of state under three popes. Ordained in 1930, he completed his studies at the Angelicum University in Rome and became professor and later director of the Grand Seminary of Clermont-Ferrand (1934–39). He was then professor of moral theology at the Catholic University of Lyons (1939–42) and secretary-general of the French Episcopal Conference (1950–54). In 1954 he was appointed bishop auxiliary in Paris and in 1965 became archbishop of Lyon. On Feb. 22, 1965, Pope Paul VI created him cardinal and on May 1, 1969, appointed him secretary of state—the first Frenchman and only the third non-Italian to hold the office. Made camerlengo on Oct. 16, 1970, he administered church affairs after the deaths of Pope Paul VI and Pope John Paul I. Pope John Paul II reappointed Villot his secretary of state on Oct. 25, 1978. Villot often acted behind the scenes as a conciliator, attempting to mediate theological disputes and conflicts between church groups. He was succeeded by Agostino Cardinal Casaroli (*see* BIOGRAPHIES).

UPI

Wakeley, Sir Cecil Pembrey Grey, 1ST BARONET (b. May 5, 1892, Rainham, Kent, England—d. June 5, 1979, Chatham, England), was an eminent expert on surgery and outstanding president of the Royal College of Surgeons (1949–54). Trained at King's College Hospital, University of London, he served as a surgeon in the Royal Navy during World War I and during World War II became the Navy's senior consulting surgeon. He was consulting surgeon to many hospitals, including King's College Hospital, treasurer of the General Medical Council (1942–55), and chairman of the council of the Imperial Cancer Research Fund (1949–67). Wakeley was knighted in 1946 and made a baronet in 1952, and received numerous British and foreign honours and awards. He wrote and edited textbooks and articles on surgery and cancer.

Wallis, Sir Barnes Neville, British inventor (b. Sept. 26, 1887—d. Oct. 30, 1979, Leatherhead, Surrey, England), became known to the world at large for his invention of the rotating bouncing bomb that, when dropped from an aircraft, skipped over the water and exploded after it had sunk to the base of the retaining wall of a dam. This bomb, used during World War II by the Royal Air Force (RAF) on the Möhne and Eder dams in Germany's industrial Ruhr area, produced a devastating effect. Wallis trained as a marine engineer before joining the airship department of Vickers in 1913 as a designer. In 1930 his R100 airship flew to Canada and back but was not developed after its sister ship, the R101, was lost. Turning to aircraft, he employed his geodetic system in the RAF's Wellington bomber in World War II. His researches into detonation effects produced not only the "dambuster" bombs but also the 12,000-lb "Tallboy" and the 22,000-lb "Grand Slam." He was also responsible for the bombs that destroyed the German warship "Tirpitz," the V-rocket sites, and Germany's railway system. As chief of aeronautical research and development (1945–71) at the British Aircraft Corporation at Weybridge, Surrey, Wallis produced for supersonic aircraft the Swallow variable sweep wing and, in 1966, a new form of hollow airfoil or wing; in 1971 he designed an aircraft that could fly five times the speed of sound and needed a runway only 300 yd long. Wallis became a fellow of the Royal Society in 1954, an honorary fellow of Churchill College, Cambridge, in 1965, and was knighted in 1968.

Waltari, Mika (Toumi), Finnish author (b. Sept. 19, 1908, Helsinki, Fin.—d. Aug. 26, 1979, Helsinki), was among the most popular and prolific of modern Finnish novelists and was best known internationally for his historical novels, such as *Sinuhe, egyptiläinen* (1945; *The Egyptian,* 1949), set in ancient Egypt. *The Egyptian* was also made into a lavish Hollywood film. Other historical works were *Mikael Hakim* (1949; *The Wanderer,* 1951), about 16th-century Germany, *Johannes Angelos* (1952; *The Dark Angel,* 1953), about the fall of Byzantium, and *Turms kuolematon* (1955; *The Etruscan,* 1957). Waltari, who studied philosophy and theology at the University of Helsinki, also wrote detective novels, travel books, short stories, and plays. Sales of his books totaled around 1.5 million, and they were translated into some 30 languages. He was admitted to the Finnish Academy in 1957.

Wayne, John (MARION MICHAEL MORRISON), U.S. actor (b. May 26, 1907, Winterset, Iowa—d. June 11, 1979, Los Angeles, Calif.), attained superstardom as a rough, gruff cowboy who brought law and order to the old West by battling renegade Indians and by sending outlaws to their graves. Wayne also became a symbol of American heroism and patriotism not only in such war films as *The Sands of Iwo Jima* (1949) and *The Green Berets* (1968) but also through his unabashed patriotic fervour. During the 1970s he supported Pres. Richard M. Nixon and U.S. military involvement in Vietnam. "The Duke," as Wayne was affectionately called, was an imposing figure on the screen with his 6-ft 4-in, 225-lb frame, and to many people he seemed the embodiment of masculinity with his rugged good looks and lazy drawl. His towering presence emitted a warning—he could spring into action at a moment's notice—if he was provoked. In more than 200 films, many of them directed by John Ford and Howard Hawks, Wayne created a legendary character that was revered by his fans (his films grossed more than $400 million).

After working as a prop boy in 1927, Wayne began his career with some 40 B and C Westerns before appearing as the Ringo Kid in the motion picture classic *Stagecoach* (1939). Other films with wide appeal were *The Long Voyage Home* (1940), *Reap the Wild Wind* (1942), *Red River* (1948), *She Wore a Yellow Ribbon* (1949), *The Quiet Man* (1952), *The Man Who Shot Liberty Valance, Hatari,* and *The Longest Day* (all three in 1962), and *The Cowboys* (1972). In

1964 Wayne's many fans tearfully supported their hero when he was stricken with lung cancer; but the resilient actor survived his bout with "the big C," as he called it, and returned to the screen. His 1969 Academy Award-winning film *True Grit* portrayed Wayne as one-eyed marshal Rooster Cogburn who clamped his horse's reins between his teeth so he could gun down four outlaws with a six-gun and a repeater rifle. Wayne's last film, *The Shootist* (1976), chronicled the life of a terminally ill gunfighter and seemed to serve as an epitaph for "the Duke" when it became apparent that he was losing his last fight with cancer. Wayne was still recovering from a January 1979 cancer operation when he made an emotional final public appearance at the Academy Awards in April to present the Oscar for best picture. One week before Wayne died, Congress and Pres. Jimmy Carter authorized a special gold medal to honour one of the world's best known and most admired actors.

Westminster, Robert George Grosvenor, 5TH DUKE OF, British property magnate (b. April 24, 1910—d. Feb. 19, 1979, Ely Lodge, County Fermanagh, Northern Ireland), inherited a family fortune estimated at £500 million, including vast holdings in central London, Cheshire, Scotland, Canada, and Australia. The inheritance, managed since 1953 by a duty-dodging trust, was founded in the 17th century when Sir Thomas Grosvenor married the heiress to the Manor of Ebury, later to become Mayfair, London's most fashionable district. The 5th duke served in the Middle East during World War II and from 1955 to 1964 was an Ulster Unionist member of Parliament. He left politics to devote more time to the family business, one of the world's largest property empires, and succeeded to the title after his brother's death in 1967.

Wilding, Michael, British film actor (b. July 23, 1912, Westcliff-on-Sea, England—d. July 8, 1979, Chichester, England), starred opposite Anna Neagle in a series of lighthearted British comedies of the late 1940s as a debonair English gentleman in such films as *Piccadilly Incident, Spring in Park Lane,* and *Maytime in Mayfair.* He later appeared in more demanding roles in Alfred Hitchcock's *Under Capricorn* and *Stage Fright.* Wilding, who trained as a commercial artist, first joined the cinema as an extra hoping to find design work. He seemed one of the most promising of the young British actors, but after moving to Hollywood he found himself cast in increasingly inane parts and was later remembered chiefly for his marriage (1952–57) to Elizabeth Taylor. In 1964 he married Margaret Leighton and appeared in a few minor parts. He also worked as a film agent in Hollywood but during the last ten years of his life lived in virtual retirement.

Winegarten, Asher, British agricultural economist (b. March 26, 1922, London, England—d. Sept. 19, 1979, London), was director general of the National Farmers' Union (NFU) from April to December 1978 and enjoyed a worldwide reputation as an agricultural economist. His 1962 statistical predictions, suggesting that British food prices would rise if Britain joined the European Economic Community, aroused skepticism but were proved right. From the London School of Economics he went to the Admiralty (1942–47), became the NFU's chief economist in 1947, and was visiting professor of agricultural policy (1973–78) at Wye College, University of London. Winegarten represented NFU employers on the Agricultural Wages Board (1957–77) and was a member of the Council for International Development from 1977.

Wood, George, British comedian (b. Dec. 17, 1895, Sunderland, England—d. Feb. 19, 1979, London, England), was the last of the great music hall stars, who, because of his diminutive size (4 ft 9 in), was billed as Wee Georgie Wood. At age ten he soared to the top of the bill and even later, convincingly aided by a treble voice and appearing with his stage "mother," Dolly Harmer, continued his small-boy role. Most of his short sketches, on a waif who gets into trouble, were invented by himself. In 1936 he became head of "The Water Rats," a charitable organization run by British entertainers, and in 1946, when he was made an OBE, became chairman of the Variety Artists' Federation.

Woodcock, George, British trade union leader (b. Oct. 20, 1904, Bamber Bridge, near Preston, Lancashire, England—d. Oct. 30, 1979, Epsom, England), endeavoured to make British trade unionism as much an arm of the government as of the Labour Party while general secretary (1960–69) of the Trades Union Congress (TUC). The son of a cotton weaver, he entered the mill at age 12 and later became an official of the Weavers' Association. Woodcock won a scholarship to Ruskin College, Oxford, in 1929 and went on to New College, Oxford, where he took first-class honours in philosophy, politics, and economics. A brief period of research at Manchester University and in the civil service preceded his appointment as secretary (1936–47) to the TUC Research and Economics Department. From 1947 to 1960 Woodcock was assistant to the general secretary of the TUC. A member of the Royal Commission on Trade Unions and Employers' Associations, 1965–68, he accepted chairmanship of the subsequent Commission on Industrial Relations in 1969, hoping to achieve voluntary reform, but resigned when the commission was overshadowed by the controversial Industrial Relations Act (1971).

Woodward, Robert Burns, U.S. chemist (b. April 10, 1917, Boston, Mass.—d. July 8, 1979, Cambridge, Mass.), was awarded the 1965 Nobel Prize for Chemistry for the synthesis of sterols, chlorophyll, and other substances once thought to be produced only by living things. A giant in the field of synthetic organic chemistry, Woodward was also responsible for the synthesis of strychnine, lysergic acid, reserpine, and in 1972 vitamin B-12 (then the most intricate molecule ever constructed in a laboratory). He was instrumental in determining the structure of such complicated organic compounds as penicillin and terramycin. At an early age Woodward displayed an enthusiasm for chemistry and constructed a laboratory in his parents' basement. After earning a Ph.D. from the Massachusetts Institute of Technology at the age of 20, he joined (1941) the faculty of Harvard University. In 1944, together with William E. Doering, Woodward synthesized quinine and in 1947 protein analogues. At Harvard he was successively named professor of chemistry (1950), Morris Loeb professor (1953), and Donner professor of science (1960). At the time of his death Woodward was working on the synthesis of the antibiotic erythromycin.

Wright, John Joseph Cardinal, U.S. Roman Catholic prelate (b. July 18, 1909, Boston, Mass.—d. Aug. 10, 1979, Cambridge, Mass.), became (1969) prefect of the Congregation for the Clergy at the Vatican, in charge of some 500,000 priests, and the highest ranking American in the Curia. Wright, who was considered a theological conservative because he supported priestly celibacy and Pope Paul VI's condemnation of artificial birth control, was also known as a social liberal because he opposed the Vietnam war and supported the civil rights movement. After studies at St. John's Seminary in Brighton, Mass., Wright was ordained a priest on Dec. 8, 1935, and served in parishes in Scotland, England, and France. Wright returned to the U.S. and successively became secretary to the archbishop of Boston (1939), monsignor (1944), and auxiliary bishop of Boston (1947). He was appointed bishop of a new diocese in Worcester, Mass., and in 1958 bishop of Pittsburgh. He then established bonds wih Protestant and Jewish leaders and formed the Catholic Diocese Commission on Human Relations. In 1969 he became a cardinal and was named to the Vatican post a few days later. Suffering from cataracts and polymyositis, Wright was unable to attend the conclave that elected Pope John Paul I.

Wyn-Harris, Sir Percy, British mountaineer and colonial administrator (b. Aug. 24, 1903, London, England—d. Feb. 25, 1979, Petersfield, Hampshire, England), climbed to within 1,000 ft of the summit of Mt. Everest with L. R. Wager in the British 1933 expedition, a height unsurpassed until Sir John Hunt's successful expedition of 1953. He also helped to advance guideless climbing in the Alps and, with Eric Shipton, scaled the twin peaks of Mt. Kenya in 1929. As a Colonial Service administrator in Kenya from 1926 he furthered his work by humane common sense and red-tape cutting, spiced with humour. From 1949 to 1958 he was governor of Gambia. After World War II Wyn-Harris turned to sailing and during 1962–69 circumnavigated the globe in his 12-ton sloop "Gunning Grundel." He was knighted in 1952.

Zanuck, Darryl F., U.S. motion picture executive (b. Sept. 5, 1902, Wahoo, Neb.—d. Dec. 22, 1979, Palm Springs, Calif.), was a giant in the motion picture industry and an innovator in the use of sound and CinemaScope in films. After Zanuck joined (1924) Warner Bros. as a scriptwriter for the "Rin Tin Tin" series, he quickly became an executive producer and promoted the first successful feature film with synchronized speech and music, *The Jazz Singer* (1928), starring Al Jolson. In such films as *Little Caesar* (1931) and *Public Enemy* (1931), Zanuck popularized gangster movies and helped develop the careers of Edward G. Robinson and James Cagney. Zanuck was also instrumental in launching the careers of such superstars as Shirley Temple, Bette Davis, Tyrone Power, Betty Grable, and Gregory Peck. In 1933 Zanuck co-founded 20th Century Co. (later 20th Century-Fox) and was controlling executive when such films as *The Grapes of Wrath* (1940), *Winged Victory* (1944), *The Razor's Edge* (1946), *Viva Zapata!* (1952), and the two Academy Award winners *How Green Was My Valley* (1941) and *Gentlemen's Agreement* (1947) were released. In 1956 Zanuck retired from Fox but returned in 1962 as president and guided the studio to financial recovery with *The Sound of Music* (1965), *M*A*S*H* (1970), and *Patton* (1970). In 1971 Zanuck retired as chairman of 20th Century-Fox.

Zeller, André Marie, French Army officer (b. Jan. 1, 1898, Besançon, France—d. Sept. 18, 1979, Paris, France), was one of the four leaders of an unsuccessful rebellion against Pres. Charles de Gaulle in April 1961. A career soldier, he was one of the organizers of the Vercors resistance centre in France during World War II. In 1955 he was appointed army chief of staff, but he resigned in February 1956 to protest the government's inefficient handling of the war in Algeria. Zeller became identified with the Algérie Française movement. When de Gaulle assumed power in June 1958 he recalled Zeller as chief of staff. Zeller, then over 60, had to retire in 1959 but continued to agitate in favour of a France extending "from Dunkirk to Tamanrasset." He secretly plotted with Gen. Maurice Challe (*q.v.*) for control of Algeria and joined generals Edmond Jouhaud and Raoul Salan there. They seized power on April 22, 1961, but their revolt collapsed four days later. Zeller went into hiding but surrendered on May 6. He was sentenced to 15 years' imprisonment but was released in July 1966.

Zhang Guotao (Chang Kuo-t'ao), early Chinese Communist leader (b. Nov. 26, 1897, Jiangxi [Kiangsi] Province, China—d. Dec. 3, 1979, near Toronto, Ont.), was chairman of a secret meeting, held in Shanghai in 1921, at which 12 persons established the Chinese Communist Party. Mao Zedong (Mao Tse-tung) was among those present. Zhang visited Moscow frequently as a delegate to the Comintern and from 1928 to 1931 remained in the Soviet capital. After returning to China, he took charge of a Communist base in an area separate from that controlled by Mao. After the two Communist leaders completed the Long March (1934–35) to Shaanxi (Shensi) Province, Mao emerged as undisputed leader with Zhang second in command. After repeated bitter disputes, Zhang and Mao parted company. Zhang joined the Nationalists in 1938 and remained with them during World War II. He then moved to Hong Kong, where he lived for two decades before following his sons to Canada in 1968.

SURVEY OF THE '70s

by Andrew Hacker

The '70s were a disconcerting decade. For the first time in the memory of most Americans, people felt they had lost control over events that shaped their lives. The mood was mainly one of bewilderment. Individuals were simply unprepared for so many shocks and disappointments that came in quick succession.

- Inflation had so eroded the economy that the nation's living standard, once the highest in the world, was in fact declining by the time the decade ended.
- The country suffered its first military defeat. After 20 years of struggle and a tremendous human toll, United States forces abandoned Vietnam.
- A group of countries, once described as "underdeveloped," held the economy in thrall by controlling the price of oil. As the decade closed, energy costs continued to escalate, with no relief in sight.
- A president of the United States resigned his office under pressure, less than two years after a resounding reelection. The events that came to be known as "Watergate" bordered on the bizarre, shocking even seasoned observers.
- In society as a whole, things seemed to be falling apart. Marriage and the family, once stable social bonds, showed every sign of fraying. Divorce rates reached an all-time high, as did homes with single parents. Crime remained at record levels. Emotion-laden issues, ranging from abortion to nuclear power, embittered public debate.
- Further feelings of frustration came as the decade ended. A country 6,000 miles away, gripped by religious fervour, seized a U.S. embassy and held its occupants as hostages. Moreover, the U.S. apparently lacked the power to secure their release.

Historians will have a hard time summing up the '70s. Unlike other decades, simple phrases will not do. The '50s marked the beginning of a new postwar era. The United States assumed the mantle of world leadership, displaying confidence in its role. At home family life was celebrated, with the suburbs symbolizing a prosperity everyone could share. The '60s became a time of turmoil. Episodes of violence raised disturbing questions about the way America worked. Even so, the protests had an optimistic air. Martin Luther King, Jr. summed it up when he said, "I have a dream." So did many other Americans.

The '70s, in contrast, seemed a subdued, even chastened, decade. Many dreams had dissolved or were voiced with much less certainty. More disturbing than the actual events was the trouble people had in drawing meaning from them. For this reason, what will follow is not a year-by-year accounting but rather an analysis that puts the decade in perspective. This can best be done by focusing first on Vietnam and Watergate, followed by the advent of inflation and the energy crisis. As all this was going on, changes were occurring in the lives of individuals. The '70s witnessed some basic shifts in attitudes, in how people viewed themselves and the effect those conceptions had on the nation.

Andrew Hacker, professor of political science at Queens College, Flushing, New York, is the author of The End of the American Era *and* The New Yorkers.

During the decade . . .

. . . the total population continued to expand, but at a diminished rate. It rose by 11%, compared with a 13% increase in the '60s and 19% in the '50s.

. . . the under-5 population fell by 1.8 million, while those over 65 rose by 4.1 million.

. . . the typical woman's fertility rate (the number of children she would have in her lifetime) fell from 2.5 children to 1.8 children. The latter figure was 0.4 short of what it takes to reproduce the population. One factor was the availability of legal abortions, which exceeded 1.3 million per year and terminated more than a quarter of all pregnancies.

. . . the number of households in the nation rose by 20%, while the average number of persons per household dropped from 3.14 to 2.78. Households consisting of unmarried couples doubled, rising from 523,000 to 1,137,000. Among the latter, 24% had children on the premises.

. . . the nation's 280 central cities declined by 3.1 million people. Their surrounding suburbs grew by 9.1 million. And the rest of the country—classed as "nonmetropolitan"—also experienced a population gain, of 7.7 million people.

. . . the country's white population grew by 5.4%. Its black population rose by 11.2%. And its Hispanic population expanded by 31.2%.

The War that Was Lost. The war in Vietnam dominated the opening years of the decade. As the '70s began, the conflict was at its height—at home as well as abroad. In 1970 national guardsmen killed four students at Kent State University in Ohio. The following year over a hundred thousand demonstrators massed in Washington, and before the day was over 13,000 had been arrested. Vietnam differed from other wars in that so many citizens posed their objections in moral terms. In their eyes it was the United States that was the aggressor, raining death on a far-off people with no rational justification.

The war was mired in a stalemate. Despite a huge advantage in firepower and unchallenged command of the air, an elusive enemy could not be brought to

GEORGE W. GARDNER

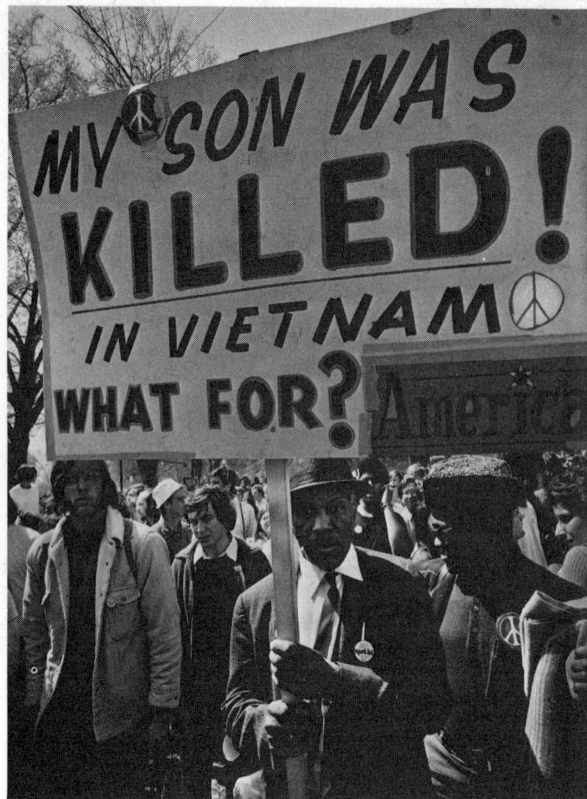

"The war was mired in a stalemate. . . . Americans might wonder if any reasons remained for carrying on the war."

bay. Even the so-called "hawk" position, asking an end to all constraints, no longer proved attractive. At the same time, the 1972 election showed that "dove" demands for immediate withdrawal were still a minority view. If Americans no longer insisted on victory, they still wanted a departure with a modicum of honour. Hence their support for the Nixon-Kissinger policy of negotiations backed by continued bombing. A cease-fire came in 1973, and the American exit began. But it soon emerged that South Vietnamese forces could not defend their capital. Hostilities were renewed, and in April 1975 Saigon fell into Communist hands. The last Americans fled in a flurry of helicopters.

What happened afterward was most revealing of all. The natural question to ask, at least at any inquest, was whether America should ever have intervened. At the outset the country had been told that containing Communism in Asia was crucial to U.S. security. Aiding South Korea, a generation earlier, was held up as the model. Were South Vietnam to fall to Communism, other nations of the region—Thailand, Burma, even India—would drop like dominoes. And China would gather up the pieces, dominating Asia and threatening the Pacific.

Yet that argument lost much of its force when, in 1971, Richard Nixon responded to an overture from China. Soon an astonished nation saw the president in Peking and learned that this long-time enemy was now to be a friend. Americans might wonder if any reasons remained for carrying on the war, but such doubts were not allowed to surface. "Containment" continued as official policy, albeit somewhat tarnished after Vietnam. As for the domino theory, only Cambodia entered the Communist orbit, with disastrous consequences for its people but little discernible effect on American security.

The aftermath of Vietnam, then, did not bring a public debate. Nevertheless, it seems clear that Americans were affected by the experience, even if they kept their feelings to themselves. Losing a war is not an easy blow to take, especially for a nation with pretensions to global power. There was also the question of how avidly anti-Communist Americans ought to be. Here, too, ritualized responses raised more questions than they answered.

And erstwhile "doves" had their share of problems as well. One of the first things the new Vietnam did was to overrun Cambodia. That Vietnam, so recently a victim, would invade a smaller neighbour was not exactly the outcome the antiwar movement had had in mind. Even more disconcerting was Vietnam's behaviour toward its citizens of Chinese origin. The plight of the "boat people" dissolved whatever sympathies were still held for the targets of American bombers. In sum, the Vietnam war and its outcome threw all sides of the ideological spectrum into a state of disarray.

Perhaps the most critical question involved America's ability to deploy military force for future missions overseas. When, in 1976, talk arose of sending American troops to Angola, Congress acted with alacrity to ban such an expedition. In fact, the United States' central strategy was to maintain a nu-

. . . employment as a whole rose by 17%. Managerial and clerical employees increased by 21%; professionals by 28%; and service workers by 30%. The ranks of blue collar workers expanded by only 8%; and agricultural employment was down 21%.
. . . occupations that experienced the most expansion were: psychologists (up 281%), college administrators (up 177%), preschool teachers (up 139%), health administrators (up 119%), real estate agents (up 112%), lawyers (up 84%), and restaurant managers (up 83%).
. . . occupations that declined were: elementary school teachers (down 8%), household servants (down 21%), telephone operators (down 24%), barbers (down 28%), and tailors (down 34%).
. . . median household income rose from $9,867 to $17,640. However, the overall gain, in noninflated dollars, was only $545—or a 3.2% growth in real purchasing power. The comparable figure for the '60s had been 34%.
. . . salaries paid to professional workers declined by 2.8%, as measured in constant dollars. So did the wages of clerical employees, by 4.4%. The real income of sales workers, however, rose by 4.4%, and so did that of managerial employees, by 1.8%. Real wages of farm workers rose by 19%.
. . . the median income of college graduates dropped from 150 to 130% of that earned by high school graduates.

HOWARD E. RUFFNER—BLACK STAR

"The war in Vietnam dominated the opening years of the decade. . . . In 1970 national guardsmen killed four students at Kent State University in Ohio."

clear standoff against the Soviet Union. But the Vietnam debacle caused concern about the country's capacity for limited operations in a hostile terrain. The issue arose once more as the '70s came to a close. Could the United States in fact carry troops to the Persian Gulf and subdue a desert nation that had outraged American honour? The decade ended with that question still in doubt.

Scandal at the Top. In the early morning hours of June 17, 1972, five men were apprehended while installing eavesdropping devices at the Democratic national headquarters in Washington's Watergate complex. After their arrest it emerged that they had been given this assignment by persons having offices in the White House. Bugging the opposition's office was one part of the overall strategy for Richard Nixon's reelection. Thus began Watergate, the most wide-ranging scandal in America's political history. It forced the resignation of a president and ended with several of the country's once most powerful officials serving terms in prison.

In fact, Watergate came to stand for a whole series of events associated with President Nixon himself and with his reelection effort. As it happened, the president had no direct foreknowledge of the break-in operation. However, he soon learned that the plan had originated in the building where he worked. At that point, the "cover-up" commenced. Put very simply, the president and his top advisers, knowing crimes had been committed, failed to pass that information on to suitable authorities. Those in the Oval Office were "obstructing justice," a felony under federal law. Moreover, in denying he knew about the break-in, the president had been lying.

The list of illegalities lengthened. There had been, for example, pressure on the Internal Revenue Service to probe the tax returns of persons critical of White House policies. The Central Intelligence Agency had provided equipment for illegal surveillance unconnected with national security. Unreported contributions were solicited from leading corporations, with the money "laundered" to conceal its origins. The president signed perjured deductions on his income tax return, reducing his liability to a token sum. Persons on his campaign payroll admitted to "dirty tricks," from printing bogus handbills to planting malicious stories in the press. There was yet another break-in, this at the office of the psychiatrist who had treated one of the persons under indictment for releasing the classified "Pentagon Papers." Various abuses by the FBI came under the "Watergate" umbrella. And so did the discovery that the vice-president of the United States had accepted bribes while he was governor of Maryland and was still receiving payments after moving to Washington.

Even hardened heads reeled as new chapters came to light. Had the president not resigned, impeachment proceedings would have been started in the House of Representatives. His resignation notwithstanding, he would probably have been indicted had not his successor granted him a "full, free, and absolute pardon" in anticipation of any charges.

But what lessons were to be gained from Watergate? It was unsurpassed as drama, from the sweep of its audacity down to every lurid detail, like the 18 minutes of missing tape. Plainly, the Nixon adminis-

> . . . overall educational enrollments fell by 3%, with elementary registrations declining by 16%. However, college enrollments rose by 33%, and nursery school attendance expanded by 66%. In the colleges, men's registrations grew by 16% and women's by 57%.
> . . . the number of Americans who had completed four or more years of college rose from 13.4 million to 21.1 million.
> . . . the median scores on the Scholastic Aptitude Tests, taken by students applying to college, dropped by 31 points on the verbal section and 20 points on the mathematical part.

PHOTOS, J. P. LAFFONT—SYGMA

(Left to right) Sen. Sam Ervin (Dem., N.C.) was the chairman of the Senate committee investigating Watergate. H. R. Haldeman, former Nixon aide, and John Mitchell, former attorney general, went to jail for their roles in the affair.

tration had grown arrogant and corrupt. Still, nobody really wanted to inquire if Watergate revealed some fatal flaws in the America of the '70s. True, there were homilies about young men sacrificing character for careers. Still, the outcries over Watergate lacked a moral edge. For one thing, a majority of Americans had voted for Richard Nixon, and they were not entirely oblivious to the manner of man he was. Nor were that many people prepared to vouchsafe that what he had done was so terribly wrong. If all he had cut was some corners, then his crime was in getting caught. In short, Watergate might have been more foreboding than Americans wished to admit. So, as with Vietnam, its perturbing implications were better left in silence. Individual Americans had to decide what their own reactions to Watergate told them about themselves.

A sombre and distraught Richard Nixon read his resignation speech to the nation on Aug. 8, 1974.

F. W. OWEN—BLACK STAR

The Declining Dollar. The end of the '70s brought double-digit inflation. Most Americans found their incomes falling behind the rising tide of prices. The president even advised people to prepare for a declining living standard. Put another way, the United States was to become a poorer nation. That had occurred before, in the depression of the 1930s. But it was not supposed to happen again.

On the whole, Americans preferred explanations that pointed precisely to particular persons or policies. The most obvious culprits were those leading the Organization of Petroleum Exporting Countries (with special emphasis on "the Arabs") who had sent the price of oil shooting through the roof. Others identified executives of the oil companies, whose profits seemed evidence enough of a skimming operation. Economists charged that the money supply was too large, setting too much cash in pursuit of too few goods. Other experts blamed governmental programs and the deficits that resulted from their increasing costs. Inflation was also attributed, in part, to rules and regulations that raised the cost of doing business. And some observers indicted the Vietnam war, for having been financed on a pay-later basis.

What was most instructive was the aura of detachment that surrounded all these explanations. If Americans felt the rising costs of gasoline, heating, and utilities, they expected increased wages and salaries to meet that inconvenience. Accustomed styles of life were still taken as given. The generous suburban home, an unaccompanied drive to work, heat and air conditioning at their usual blasts, were construed as basic rights. Congress, responding to this sentiment, refused to act on gas rationing, even of a standby sort. Nor could there be meaningful talk of an "energy policy," lest it be revealed that some American habits might face restriction. Fuel consumption went on as usual, with imports actually rising despite talk of "self-sufficiency." It was left to the '80s to show whether Americans would allow governmental action of some substantial nature.

A further impetus to inflation was that U.S. productivity, long the envy of the world, had reached a flat plateau. The problem was partly that not enough new technologies had come along to keep costs down. Even more crucial was the fact that too many Americans were on the payroll. Or they were being paid too much given their productive contribution. Indeed, with many occupations one could not easily say what their contributions were. America had created the world's largest middle class by overpaying a lot of people.

Turning Inward. One author called the '70s the "Me Decade." Another spoke of America as a "Culture of Narcissism," after the legendary youth who fell in love with his own reflection. Then came a magazine called *Self,* for those seeking personal perfection. It seemed evident that people had become preoccupied with themselves. There was much talk of "finding oneself," of "realization" and "growth" and "potential." Nor was this simply talk. People were also acting differently.

For example, the birthrate declined during the decade to below the replacement level. While no one said it in so many words, more and more adults viewed children as encumbrances. Not only had offspring become expensive; their very presence set stern limits on their parents' freedom. Hence the readiness to take advantage of legally available abortions. By the end of the decade, there were 1.3 million abortions for every 3.3 million births. And even among those who did have children, signs of self-concern showed through. A new term—"parenting"—encouraged solemn discourse about how to bring up babies. Nursery school enrollments soared, especially in those schools stressing early "development" for middle-class toddlers.

Young people were postponing marriage, with women willing to remain single much longer than before. Indeed, the 20s had turned into a period of freedom in which people could experiment and, as the saying went, try to "find themselves." The number of unmarried couples living together doubled during the '70s. And the figure would have been even higher if one counted those who kept separate residences but spent frequent nights together. Here another word—"relationship"—came into common parlance, with the opportunity it gave two people to talk about themselves. Nor did all these couples have to be of different genders. The decade saw many Americans acknowledging their homosexuality, not only to the world but to themselves as well. As it turned out, more men were apt to take this step than women, causing an arithmetic imbalance in matching up the sexes.

The most striking sign of self-concern was the rising rate of divorce. Traditionally, couples committed themselves to a lifetime marriage. Some were actually very happy. Others evolved routines that made common quarters tolerable. And fear of social censure kept many couples together. But by the '70s close to half of all marriages being contracted were destined to end in divorce. In other cases, desertion or separation would have the same result. The common element that emerged was that one or both of the spouses desired a different life. The expanded sense of self made marriage seem constricting.

JIM ANDERSON—WOODFIN CAMP & ASSOCIATES

"The end of the '70s brought double-digit inflation. Most Americans found their incomes falling behind the rising tide of prices."

. . . the number of divorces per 1,000 marriages rose from 328 to 504.

. . . the proportion of households with a husband and wife both present fell from 71% to 62%. In 1970 the typical woman heading a household was a widow. By the end of the decade, she would be more apt to be divorced, single, or separated. Among women on their own with children, 59% worked and 41% either received welfare or had some other source of income. This ratio stayed the same regardless of race.

. . . among divorced, single, and separated women raising children, only 25% received support payments from the fathers. And only 4% of all divorced women received alimony.

. . . out-of-wedlock births increased from 399,000 per year to an annual figure of 468,000. This constituted a rise from 11% of all babies born to 15%.

. . . the proportion of women over 25 who were not yet married rose from 14 to 25%.

. . . of the three million new people who joined the labour force each year, two million were women. Of the nation's 47 million wives, almost half were at work. And of these working wives, 70% had children under the age of 18 and 25% had children under the age of 6.
. . . the proportion of the nation's lawyers who were women doubled, from 5 to 10%. Among bank officers and financial managers, the proportion rose from 18 to 30%. Women went from being 11% of the professional economists to 23%. And in operations and systems research and analysis, the female quotient more than doubled, from 10 to 22%. And at the close of the '70s, women were receiving 26% of all law degrees, 22% of all medical degrees, and 23% of all degrees in veterinary medicine.
. . . taken together, the wages earned by working women came to 60% of those earned by men. And the earnings of working married women, all told, added 25% to their families' incomes.

Divorces tended to follow two general patterns. The most frequent came early, often before the arrival of children, with the initiative from either spouse or, just as easily, both. In many ways these divorces terminated what had once been proposed as "trial marriages," a period of cohabitation designed for self-discovery. The second category had more serious consequences. Such divorces usually came later on, when there were children in the home. And here the initiative was more likely to come from the husband, who wanted a fresh beginning while he had some remaining years. The most common pattern involved leaving the children with the wife, while the husband soon remarried, usually a younger woman. While many older ex-wives picked up the pieces, statistics showed that when divorced women reached their 30s they had less chance of remarrying than men in the same position. In this respect, the double standard was alive and thriving.

The '70s also placed more stress on sophistication. There was an increased concern with cuisine, both at home and in dining out. Consumption of wine and cheese increased, as did knowledge of herbs and spices. More people traveled abroad, and at home they showed greater interest in goods with foreign labels. BBC productions built up substantial audiences, from "Masterpiece Theatre" on public television to reruns of "Upstairs, Downstairs" on commercial channels. Personal health verged on an obsession: the '70s opened with tennis and skiing, to be passed by running and vendettas against tobacco. Vitamins, calories, and health foods were common topics of discussion. Sex combined exercise and enjoyment, with best-selling books depicting in graphic detail the joys of what everyone wanted to know. If the sexual revolution of the '60s started with the young, the '70s saw their elders anxious for their share.

The Women's Decade. The one group that emerged most graphically were the nation's women. The decade began with "consciousness-raising" sessions, where women would meet to share experiences and support common aspirations. Not everyone joined the National Organization for Women, or marched for the Equal Rights Amendment, or subscribed to *Ms.*, a magazine launched in 1972. Even so, a quiet revolution was taking place. Its most vivid expression was the gradual phasing out of a time-honoured occupation: the full-time housewife. By the end of the decade, only 7% of all American households consisted of a working husband, a wife at home, and two or more school-age children. Almost half of the nation's wives, including many with young children, held jobs.

Getting out of the house was the major step of the '70s. The economy certainly welcomed women, for they filled two-thirds of the new jobs created in the decade. Even so, women's wages, taken together, totaled 60% of those received by men. And despite the rise in working wives, the money they brought in tended to raise their family incomes by only 25%. The real change was psychological. Women began to see themselves in a larger light, with new realms of activity and heightened aspirations. Relations within marriages shifted in countless subtle ways.

But the decade really belonged to younger women, who were entering high school as the '70s started. Not only did they not record "housewife" as

"The Organization of Petroleum Exporting Countries . . . had sent the price of oil shooting through the roof."

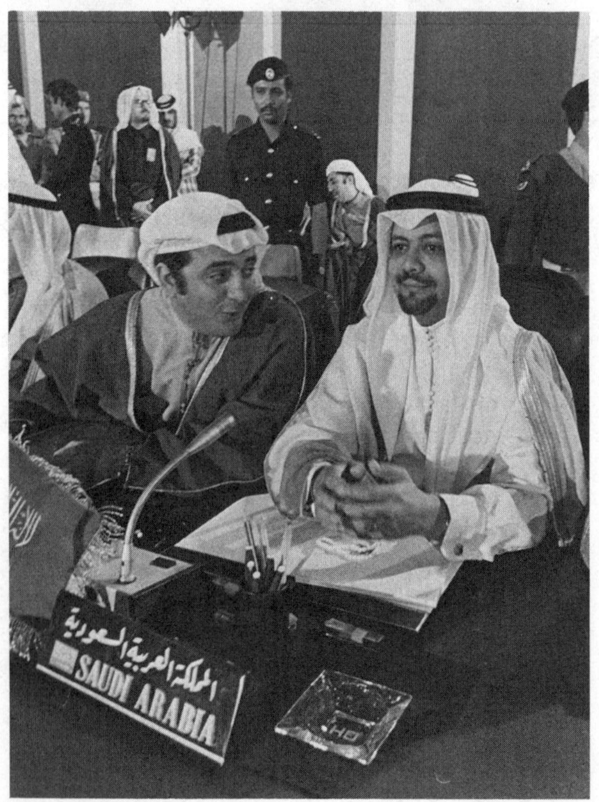

GREEN—SYGMA

MICHAEL ABRAMSON—BLACK STAR

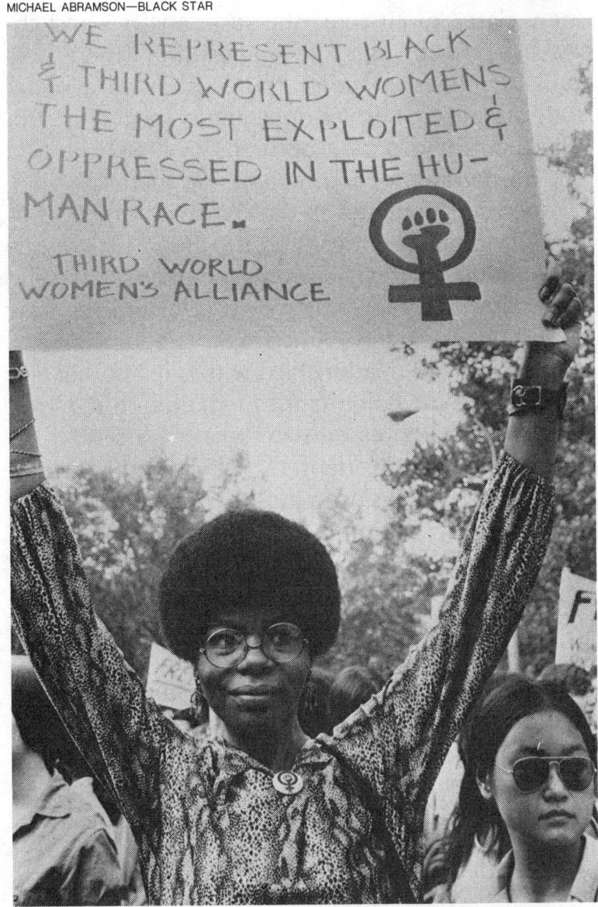

"Women began to see themselves in a larger light, with new realms of activity and heightened aspirations."

their chosen occupation, they were also bypassing "nurse," as well as "secretary" and "stewardess." Young women who entered college, as they did in record numbers, had occupational aspirations almost indistinguishable from men's. By the end of the '70s, the entering classes at many schools of medicine, law, and business came close to equal sexual representation. Even where they were still in a minority—as in science and engineering—woman applicants had as good a chance of acceptance as men and were often openly recruited. One result as the '80s advance will be that men will find they have women as their superiors, in some cases women younger than themselves and demonstrably more competent. This too will have an impact on relations between the sexes.

But there was another, more sombre, side to the story. The '70s also saw a growing number of women being left even further behind. This was mainly a class phenomenon, with overtones of race. For many young women, the sexual revolution meant getting pregnant and having a baby while still in their middle teens. The illegitimacy rate continued to climb (it would have been even higher had abortions not been available), and most of these young mothers were choosing to keep their babies. In addition, in many youthful marriages the bride was already pregnant, with the husband far from ready to support a full-fledged family. Thus the welfare rolls gained new recruits, giving a less than promising start to many American children. In all too many instances, the cycle was built in. Many teenaged girls saw becoming a mother as one possible highlight in an otherwise aimless life.

Nor did all women wish to be liberated, at least in an unequivocal way. The '70s saw Congress pass an Equal Rights Amendment, yet that proposal failed to achieve approval from the necessary legislatures. The wording of the amendment seemed innocuous enough: "Equality of rights under the law shall not be denied or abridged by the United States or by any state on account of sex." What emerged was that the legislators who opposed the amendment were supported by surprising numbers of women who agreed with their position.

It was not that these women disparaged "equal rights." Rather, they saw the amendment as symbolic. For them, it was a manifesto for the new, competitive career woman. She was the one who demanded the right to head a corporation or command a submarine. Thus the amendment had the effect of hinting that to remain a housewife was no longer an honourable estate. The country still had many women who preferred the sidelines to the career arena; who desired special protections instead of equal opportunities. The Equal Rights Amendment failed of adoption less because of male opposition than because it was seen as threatening by some of its intended beneficiaries.

Race: A Mixed Report. Relations between races showed both progress and retrogression during the '70s. In responding to polls, white Americans voiced less prejudice than in the past. The number saying they favoured integration in schools, jobs, and neighbourhoods rose during the decade. White audiences watched television programs about black life, with "Roots" setting new audience records. White voters helped elect and reelect black officials to public office. The proportion of black youths enrolled in colleges almost equaled the ratio for whites.

The '70s also saw more black Americans joining middle-class America. Among households with incomes of over $25,000, the black percentage increased by a small but visible amount. The most marked progress came for black families with a husband and wife both present. Their incomes came closest of all to the comparable figures for whites.

However, taking the races as a whole, black Americans ended the '70s worse off than they had been at the start. Overall, black income actually fell in relation to the earnings of whites. And blacks had become more heavily represented among the nation's lowest-income households. The chief reason was that at the end of the decade fewer black families had two parents present. And that, more than anything else, kept racial progress at a standstill.

Ambiguous white attitudes accompanied this two-edged development. White Americans tended to accept middle-class blacks, with relations remaining amiable even if somewhat distant. However, there was considerably less sympathy for blacks at the lower end of the scale. Here fear of how an increased black presence might affect schools, neighbourhoods, and safety played a leading role. In fact, the problem was really one of class. But people continued to find it convenient to define the issue in terms of race.

By the '70s, virtually all white Americans favoured "equal opportunity": the principle that a qualified person should not suffer discrimination for reasons of race. But during the decade another phrase appeared. "Affirmative action" asked employers and others to make their rolls more representative in racial (and sexual) terms. From this came further phrases, like "preferential hiring" and "reverse discrimination." Two Supreme Court decisions left vague whether racial "quotas" were permissible and how they differed from "goals." What was clear was that whites were less than enthusiastic over the idea that to make up for past discrimination they must be bypassed now. Tensions between the races were still very much in evidence as the '70s ended.

The Changing American. While it was the baby boom of the '50s that made education one of the nation's major industries, its full effect was not felt until the coming of the '70s. College enrollments rose by a third during the decade, as did the number of college graduates in the country. Some commentators claimed that educational standards had declined, pointing to diplomas held by semiliterates and the decline in standardized test scores. Even so, there was evidence that more people were better informed. They were buying more books, reading serious articles, and discussing subjects that required a wider range of knowledge.

Simultaneously, the economy was creating new occupations that required new kinds of skills, both technical and verbal. Among the expanding professions were psychologists and lawyers, health administrators and accountants, computer programmers and even restaurant managers. Scholars created new descriptions for these social changes. America, one said, had become a "post-industrial" society. The country, another added, had entered a "technetronic" era. A whole new stratum, "knowledge workers," had come into being: they were a "new class" of citizens, skilled in analysis and abstractions. Allowing for exaggeration, there was truth in this assessment. People showed a better understanding of topics once left to specialists. Not only that, they formed opinions of their own and had no hesitation about expressing them.

Americans emerged in the '70s with higher estimates of their own ideas and the life to which they felt entitled. In this sense, the emphasis on "self" was more than a passing fad. It reflected the new opportunities open to Americans: in education and employment, in relationships with one another and in society as a whole. As they looked in the mirror, people were impressed with what they saw.

The '70s also brought technology to maturity. America had always been innovative in engineering, honouring inventions that improved industrial methods. Indeed, it was this very emphasis that encouraged the spread of education. During the decade, technology began to make its presence felt as never before. Or it might have been that better-educated Americans had become more aware of those processes and their consequences.

Thus, for example, the '70s witnessed a serious concern over the environment. Indeed, a specialized term, "ecology," entered the common parlance. There were protests that strip-mining was raping the terrain. Industries were accused of contaminating lakes and rivers and even the rain with their harmful wastes. There was a new consciousness of chemicals, which upset the balance of nature and jeopardized human life. A huge hydroelectric project was delayed because it endangered a rare tiny fish. Spray cans with fluorocarbons were said to deplete the ozone in the atmosphere, increasing the likelihood of cancer. Hair lotions and sugar substitutes came under the same indictment. Oil spills seemed to occur on a monthly basis, as did the derailment of railroad cars carrying deadly gases. The '70s ended with a doomsday episode at a nuclear power plant, renewing public doubts about this mysterious source of energy.

These concerns did not constitute a "movement," nor were they as avowedly "political" as the protests of the '60s. Still, the ferment had an ideological

> . . . the proportion of black families among the country's high-income households (those earning more than $25,000 in constant dollars) rose from 3.8 to 4.2%. In black households with a husband and wife both present, the median income increased from 72% of white income to 77% of the white figure.
> . . . however, the black proportion among low-income households (under $7,000 in constant dollars) also increased, from 16 to 18%. In addition, husband-wife families became less prevalent among black households, declining from 68% of their total to 56%.
> . . . taken together, the median income of *all* black families fell from 61% of white income to 59%.

. . . butter consumption fell from 85 oz per person per year to 70 oz. Sugar consumption went down from 102 to 96 lb. Coffee declined from 14 to 9 lb per capita. And the typical American ate 276 eggs instead of 312.
. . . cheese consumption, however, rose from 12 to 16 lb per person. So did corn products, from 37 to 56 lb. Pork consumption went down (from 73 to 62 lb), while beef went up (114 to 126 lb). Chicken consumption remained steady, varying from 40 to 44 lb per person throughout the '70s.
. . . health expenditures rose from $309 per capita to $697, with inflation accounting for $173 of that rise. Thus, in constant dollars, the health costs of each American family of four grew by $862.
. . . the number of Americans traveling to Europe rose from 2.9 million to 3.9 million per year. However, their average stay declined from 27 days to 19 days.
. . . the number of murders rose from 16,000 to 19,000; the number of reported rapes from 38,000 to 63,000; robberies increased from 350,000 to 400,000; and burglaries from 2.2 million to 3.1 million. The number of Americans in prisons rose from 196,000 to 263,000.
. . . the proportion of eligible citizens who voted in presidential elections fell from 61% in 1968 to 56% in 1972 and 54% in 1976. In the 1978 congressional elections, 36% of those qualified actually cast ballots.

basis, even if not explicitly stated. Americans had reached a stage where they were willing to question the impact of technology on society as a whole. Implicit was a worry that the transmutation of nature —which is what technology is—had passed the safety point. At the same time, people were still apparently ready to partake of the latest products. Pocket calculators and electronic games became household staples, as did videotape recorders and microwave appliances. Americans had not given up their love of conveniences and enjoyments. If there were inconsistencies in their outlook, they tended to be overlooked.

The '70s brought a parallel rise in consumer consciousness. There were demands for full disclosure, ranging from the ingredients in a hot dog to the interest rates on loans. Attention also focused on the now-ubiquitous computer, about which every citizen had some horror story. Indeed, the computer came to stand as a symbol for the corporate organization, which spared little solace for human sensibilities. So just as Americans were feeling they merited extra attention, they found themselves encircled by impersonal institutions. One way citizens lashed back was by launching lawsuits: for negligence, malpractice, or failure to recognize a lengthening list of rights.

Still, the onward march of technology had left many Americans behind. As it happened, the '70s heard a lot less about poverty; programs begun in the '60s tended to be viewed with skepticism and often lost support. The preoccupation of the '70s was rather violent crime. What everyone knew was that the nation had an uncomfortable quotient of people who preyed on others in society. Yet for all the anger raised by these depredations, even experts said very little about solutions. No one really knew how to prevent people from committing crimes, or how to rehabilitate them if they were caught. People had grown wary of governmental programs, of the claims of social science, indeed of all authority.

What should have been the '70s' high point—the Bicentennial celebration—had a desultory air. No one really felt like celebrating. For 1976 marked America's two centuries as a *nation*. And it was no longer clear that Americans had the attributes a nation needs in its citizens. People were better educated, more widely traveled, increasingly skeptical, and strongly self-centred. And with their new sophistication came a resistance to direction. People might say they sought firm and purposive leadership, but few had the temper for being followers.

At the time of the Bicentennial, it was Henry Kissinger who remarked, "The United States has passed its historic high point, like so many earlier civilizations." This was the hard truth of the '70s, half-realized by most Americans. The United States was entering its third century less a nation than an aggregate of individuals. People may have had higher estimates of themselves than in any previous generation. But they were paying a price for this indulgence. The decade was one of those times in history when people come to understand that an era is at an end. Only then can they embark on a new beginning. That will be the task of the '80s.

The entrance of the "tall ships" into New York Harbor was one of the highlights of the Bicentennial celebration.

FRED CONRAD—SYGMA

GEORGE W. GARDNER

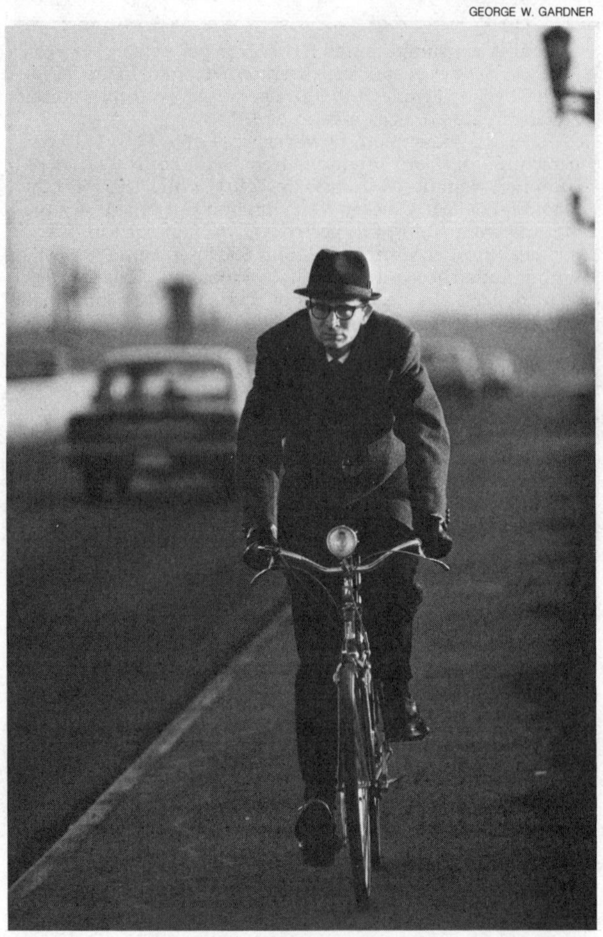

1985

by Roy C. Amara

Now that we have reached the midpoint in the decade of the 1980s, it is time to take stock of the changes that have occurred in U.S. society in the past five years, some of which could have been foreseen in 1980 and some of which have proved quite surprising. Perhaps the most basic is the perceptible trend toward more traditional life-styles and values. But before we describe these important value and life-style shifts, it is necessary to set the stage by dwelling a bit on the demographic shape of the U.S. and on the two issues that have virtually dominated all aspects of life in the early '80s: energy and the state of the economy.

Population. The expected rise in fertility (birth) rates that some demographers had forecast in the late 1970s never did materialize, although there is some evidence that the projected increase may just have been delayed by the prolonged recession of the early '80s. Instead, birthrates have remained at about the level of the late 1970s—below replacement levels at approximately 1.8 children per woman of childbearing age. Official Census Bureau estimates put the U.S. population in 1985 at slightly above 230 million.

Continuation of the so-called birth dearth into the early '80s, following the "baby bulge" of the '50s and early '60s, has had many repercussions. For example, almost a third of the U.S. population is now represented by the 25–44 age group. Fully 60% of all U.S. households consist of one or two persons, a marked change from only a decade earlier. And because of relatively high U.S. birthrates in the 1920s and the increasing longevity of senior citizens, the proportion of over-65 citizens is well above 12% of the total population.

Roy C. Amara is president of the Institute for the Future, Menlo Park, Calif. His writings include Toward Understanding the Social Impact of Computers *and* The Future as Present.

Though total U.S. population growth stood at slightly less than 1% per year in the early '80s, this growth was unevenly distributed geographically. In response to increasing disillusionment with some depressed cities and crowded suburbs, the growing attractiveness of small-town life, and the better weather in the South and West, rural and small metropolitan areas were growing at a faster rate than their larger urban and surburban counterparts. Relatively speaking, the North and East continued to lose population to the South and West. And although the rapidly rising cost of energy everywhere and concerns about water as a resource in the West deterred some from making major moves of any kind, many of America's older central cities (e.g., Detroit, Philadelphia, Cleveland, New York) continued to deteriorate. Thus, the high-growth states in the 1980s are the rural states where population had been traditionally low (Montana, Idaho, Wyoming, Colorado, New Mexico, Arizona, Utah, and Nevada), some states in the "Old South" (Virginia, the Carolinas, Georgia, and Florida), and some in the Southwest and West (Texas, Arkansas, Oregon, and Alaska).

A caveat on generalizations may be in order here. Not all of America's cities found themselves in decline in the early '80s. Boston, Pittsburgh, Chicago,

Minneapolis, San Francisco, and Seattle were strong and healthy, demographically and financially. Sound fiscal management, the influx of middle class two-wage-earner families, declining crime rates for the first time in several decades (due to sharp drops in the under-18 population), and high costs of energy all contributed to what might presage a wider urban revival in the late '80s.

During the early '80s the number of new households continued to increase at more than twice the population growth rate. This was due to the disproportionate share of the population in the prime household-forming age, to the growing tendency of many senior citizens to maintain their own households, and to children setting up their own households at earlier ages than ever before. Although high housing prices and interest rates and a prolonged recession severely depressed new housing starts in 1980 and 1981, pent-up demand has made itself felt since 1982, when interest rates moderated somewhat. Houses are smaller and often modular, sometimes built in cluster arrangements with shared common facilities. They always incorporate the increasingly strict standards on efficient energy use.

The traditional husband-wife (with or without children) family unit continued to decline—in the proportion of total households—in the early '80s. Nevertheless, it remained the dominant social unit. Indeed, there are now signs that the threat to the institution of marriage may be easing, as swinging singles and other alternative life-styles appear to be losing their attractiveness. In fact, some social scientists are detecting signs of what may become a real family revival in the mid- and late '80s.

Energy. The key concerns about energy in the early '80s continued to be cost, availability, and the difficulty of setting a national strategy that would generate hope and confidence. Virtually everyone—after about 1979—had expected energy prices to continue to escalate. Most suspected that petroleum supply and demand would remain in delicate balance worldwide. Few, however, were prepared for the confusion, vacillation, divisiveness, and absence of national purpose that has continued to plague the formation of U.S. energy policy. But we are getting a bit ahead of ourselves.

With the Organization of Petroleum Exporting Countries (OPEC) continuing to raise prices at regular intervals, and with decontrol and deregulation of oil prices in the U.S. in late 1981, the cost of a gallon of gas in the U.S. rose to the $2.50–$3 range in 1985 dollars. What has made the price at all tolerable is that engine efficiencies are now well above 25 miles per gallon for most new cars and in excess of 18 miles per gallon for all autos (new and old combined). Furthermore, at this juncture there is more concern about availability than about price, given the events of 1983 that finally forced the U.S. to go to a nationwide rationing system.

For reasons that are not difficult to understand, the dominant OPEC countries simply decided to cut supply by 5% per year until 1987, since it had become increasingly clear that such limitations would better serve their own long-term national purposes. In spite of U.S. efforts to find new domestic sources and in spite of dramatic reductions in energy growth rates (down to 1.5% per year due to conservation spurred by escalating prices), the U.S. found itself in a long-term pinch that could only be handled by a rationing system.

In many respects, these developments did not appear to change middle-class values and life-styles all that much, at least on the surface. Those hardest hit were the aged, the poor, and retired persons on fixed incomes. Dependence on the automobile (with its traditional internal-combustion engine) continued at high levels, though with increased attention to conservation. The railroads and airlines have experienced some gains at the expense of other transportation modes, and there have been some increases in light-rail (*e.g.*, electric trolley) systems and mini-buses, but in general no major shifts in transportation patterns have occurred. The price-competitive suburban electric car is just beginning to appear on the scene, and its impact may not be felt until the late '80s.

Although the availability of home heating oil is just as tight as for gasoline, price escalation here has been dampened by government-imposed price controls. Supply bottlenecks have resulted in a complex system of control and allocation formulas designed to protect fuel availability for essential government and industrial services. Needless to say, these have resulted at times in considerable shocks and dislocations to supply channels, as well as conflict and contentiousness among the many groups and organizations affected by their application.

The conflict over allocations has been overshadowed, however, by the persistent divisiveness regarding national energy policy. The best that can be said is that we have essentially backed (or been backed) into a set of energy options by default. And perhaps this is as it should be in a highly pluralistic society with fairly decentralized and democratic decision-making processes.

The essential elements of the policy follow. Starting with domestic oil, strong emphasis has been placed on maintaining or even increasing output, but to no avail, since we are simply running out of oil. Dependence on foreign crude has been cut as much as possible, but it remains at 7.5 million to 8

GEORGE W. GARDNER

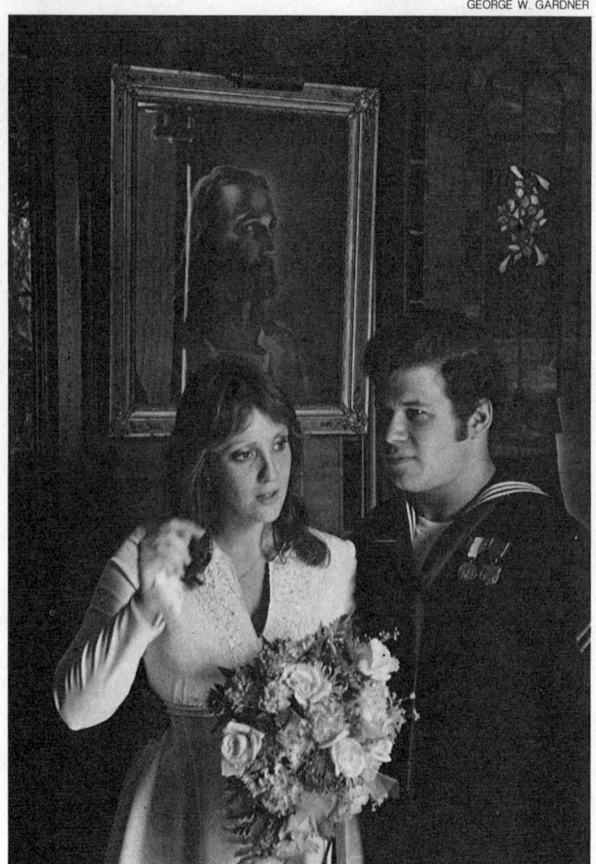

". . . there are now signs that the threat to the institution of marriage may be easing . . ."

million bbl per day. Although prospects for new domestic natural gas discoveries are reasonably good, production continues to drop. Dependence on coal (and wood or biomass) is rising 3 to 4% per year, even though the environmental problems that remain are formidable. Environmental and waste-disposal problems have kept nuclear energy's contribution to total energy production in the U.S. at the levels of the late 1970s. Solar energy has finally begun to show promise for use in space- and hot-water heating systems because of large cost reductions, resulting from increases in manufacturing capacity and government incentives. None of the more exotic forms of energy production—shale, tar sands, ocean thermal, solar satellites, hydrogen, geothermal—play any significant role. But this is not the whole story.

The truly dramatic changes are taking place in conservation. At long last, Americans—spurred by high prices and basic attitude changes—are responding behaviourally in ways that may change the traditional (and unflattering) image of the U.S. as the energy glutton of the world.

Americans have known for some time that other developed countries with comparable standards of living consume only 50 or 60% as much energy per capita as the U.S. Some of this difference is due to our greater dependence on the automobile, our larger geographic distances and particular life-styles. But some—and the residual may be considerable—is due to the lack of incentives for using energy efficiently and wisely. Attitudes and behaviour with regard to energy usage, like attitudes and behaviour generally, do not normally change overnight, particularly when they are deeply ingrained and closely associated with mobility and the freedom of individuals to make independent personal choices. But changes are occurring.

Some changes are relatively easy. As previously noted, we are now driving smaller and far more fuel-efficient cars. And since the automobile sector uses well over half the energy in the transportation sector, and the transportation sector accounts for well over half the oil consumed in the U.S. each day, the resultant savings are considerable. Without any sacrifice of personal comfort, we are also reducing energy demand substantially by making changes to our residential and commercial buildings. Spurred by increased tax incentives, insulation is being added to existing homes. Appliances—particularly air conditioners and refrigerators—have now become more energy efficient. New structures are routinely designed with better window placement and more efficient ventilation standards.

Other changes may be more painful, although they need not affect life-style radically. We are all driving a little less, cutting out some unnecessary trips, pooling cars, using public transportation a bit more. We are also setting thermostats lower in the winter and higher in the summer and wearing clothing to match. In dozens of small ways we are becoming ever so energy conscious. Some have remarked that U.S. society is becoming much more European in its outlook with respect to energy and, perhaps, resource use generally.

To round out the picture on conservation, some observations related to the industrial sector may be interesting. Significantly less energy is being used because of the slower growth of traditional industries such as steel, copper, paper, and automaking relative to less energy-intensive industries such as electronics and computers. In addition, some energy-intensive industries have been losing market shares to foreign manufacturers in recent years. Still another significant saving in industrial energy consumption is being registered through co-generation, the decentralized generation of both heat and electricity at an industrial plant site. What is happening as a result of changing energy consumption patterns —on both the personal and the industrial level—is that energy demand is now growing at only 60% of real economic growth (compared with almost 100%

prior to 1970), but without appreciable compromises in rising standards of living.

State of the Economy. Next to energy, the state of the economy has dominated U.S. societal changes in the last five years. The recession that began fairly innocuously in late 1979 persisted over a longer period and turned out to be deeper than almost anyone had forecast. Even today it is not altogether clear why this should have happened. The best guess is that it signaled the start of a long transition in the U.S. economy (and perhaps U.S. society) that continues today.

Average growth rates of the U.S. economy in the early '80s have been hovering at levels of 2% per year, just a bit better than in the 1930s. Only this year, for the first time, do we see prospects of improvement in growth, stimulated in part by the signs of a capital investment-led expansion. But again we are getting ahead of ourselves.

The real culprit in this difficult period has been inflation. Very restrictive monetary and fiscal policies by the Federal Reserve and the government were needed to bring our double-digit rates down to more tolerable levels in 1981. Even so, inflation has remained at the 7 or 8% per year level since 1981, considerably dampening the rate of recovery and aggravating the unemployment problem. What appears to have happened is that inflationary expectations continued to run very high, even when interest rates soared in late 1979 and the early '80s. This resulted in more anticipatory price increases, more militant labour demands, and a greater tendency toward short-term borrowing. As a last resort, selective wage-price controls were imposed for the limited period of 18 months in late 1981.

As the restrictive actions of government became more pronounced, consumer spending was gradually cut back, while personal savings ratios showed a sharp increase beginning in early 1980 and continuing until early 1983. The result was a prolonged slowdown in the economy starting in late 1979, creating a recessionary period that was more severe than 1974–75, if only for its length. Real gross national product (GNP) grew only at 1.5% per year in 1980–82, though the mild recovery since then has brought GNP growth above the 2% mark. Only the fact that business had been somewhat more prudent in keeping inventories at modest levels and limiting expansion of production capacity prevented the downturn from being even more severe.

The postponement or cancellation of long-term business investments until 1982–83 because of the uncertainties created by inflation was a principal factor delaying the onset of recovery. Only when inflation finally began to subside in late 1982 and early 1983 did business begin to allocate funds for long-term capital improvements. These actions were also stimulated in part by government tax and investment incentives, especially in the areas of energy, information technology, and general research and development expenditures. In addition, a growing awareness of the coming shortage of entry-level workers began to change attitudes about the need for new technologies to automate some previously labour-intensive jobs.

A glimpse at the behaviour of some key economic

GEORGE W. GARDNER

"Spurred by increased tax incentives, insulation is being added to existing homes."

indicators may be useful. As might be expected, different products experienced different rates of inflation. Some items, such as apparel, furniture, new autos, food, and housing, rose at average rates of inflation, nominally 7 or 8% per year. At the same time, many items with relatively high energy input rose at levels well above inflation, in the 12 to 15% range; these included gasoline, diesel fuel, and utility services (gas and electricity). Unemployment peaked at 8 to 9% in 1981, with particular groups—young, minority, entry-level workers—experiencing unemployment levels well in excess of 15%. The levels would have been even higher except for the rapid drop in new labour force entrants that took place, for demographic reasons, after 1982. The high rates of unemployment were particularly worrisome since the fraction of new labour force entrants represented by blacks and Hispanics was now approaching 25 to 30%. At the other end of the economic scale, almost 25% of all households were earning more than $25,000 (in 1979 dollars) and well over 75% of all such households had two wage earners. Even so, discretionary income (income in excess of that required to maintain a given standard of living) remained largely stagnant until 1984.

We cannot leave our description of the state of the economy without taking note of a fundamental measure of economic health that has gone somewhat awry in the last decade, for reasons that we do not fully understand. Growth of productivity—a measure of output per person per hour—has dropped to levels below 2% per year and stayed there, putting the U.S. close to the bottom among developed countries. This cannot be adequately explained by expenditures for environmental protection, for capital equipment, or for R & D, *or* by the level of inflation, *or* by shifts to an increasingly service-oriented economy. Only very recently has productivity growth finally shown signs of rising above the 2% level, possibly presaging a long-term movement to higher GNP growth in the late 1980s.

Employee motivation is undoubtedly one of the many complex factors playing an important but poorly understood role in productivity changes. But such motivation, in turn, stems from a much broader base of values and life-styles, and these have undergone important changes in the early 1980s.

Values and Life-styles. To understand such value and life-style shifts, it is useful to focus on the major elements that have been examined so far: the demographic *group* that is likely to influence such shifts the most; the *driving force* most responsible for changing attitudes; and the primary *culprit* (or concern) in U.S. society as viewed by a majority of Americans. The dominant group is the *"baby bulge" age cohort* born between 1945 and 1965; the principal driving force is the *cost (and availability) of energy*; and the primary culprit is *inflation*.

No single population segment in American history has had as much impact on values and life-styles as the huge group born between the mid-1940s and mid-1960s. Aside from dominating the population by its sheer size (almost 80 million), this group has consistently revolutionized the institutions in its path. In 1985 this entire group has reached adulthood, and it is continuing to have a primary influence on attitudes, values, and social issues. It is the concerns of this *adult-centred society* that are fueling the growth and emergence (and in some instances, reemergence) of certain societal features: traditionalism, self-reliance, and new forms of individual participation in societal decision making.

Heightening these adult-centred orientations is the inability of either the public or the private sector to resolve the issues of relatively slow growth and persistently high rates of inflation. There is little public confidence in the government's ability to come up with satisfactory long-term solutions for the energy and inflation problems, but the private sector is not viewed in a favourable light either. In particular, many continue to blame the large energy companies for creating—or at least taking advantage of—the tight energy situation. Distrust of government bureaucracy and the perceived self-interest of the big oil companies serve to produce a growing feeling that the only long-term hope for improving the state of affairs is to rely increasingly on oneself.

A Shift to the More Traditional. The roots of this trend go back to the tax revolts of the late 1970s that signaled a major retreat from the Great Society values of the 1960s. One indication of this changing public attitude is the *declining* share of GNP accounted for by all levels of government since 1983, after a short rise during the worst years of the recent recession. Accompanying this trend has been a continuing revival of traditional religion and reinstatement of the death penalty in several states. As a matter of fact, the general feeling has been gaining ground (confirmed by the latest national opinion poll in early 1985) that a very large majority of Americans prefer a return to more respect for traditional authority, more emphasis on the traditional family, and more emphasis on hard work. The general shift from youth values to older values (moderation, conservatism) should come as no surprise now that the baby-boom generation has matured. What may have been more surprising is that the generation born since about 1965 (the "birth dearth" group) has proved to be very traditional from the beginning, especially in contrast to its predecessors. These young people are far more materialistic and career-oriented, resembling almost a reversion to the Eisenhower years of the '50s. In spite of the lacklustre economic performance of recent years, they are not faring too badly in the job market because of the extremely small size of the age cohort.

Although U.S. society still tolerates enormous diversity in life-styles (*e.g.*, premarital sex, marijuana), the country has become decidedly more conservative with respect to the government's role in our

GEORGE W. GARDNER

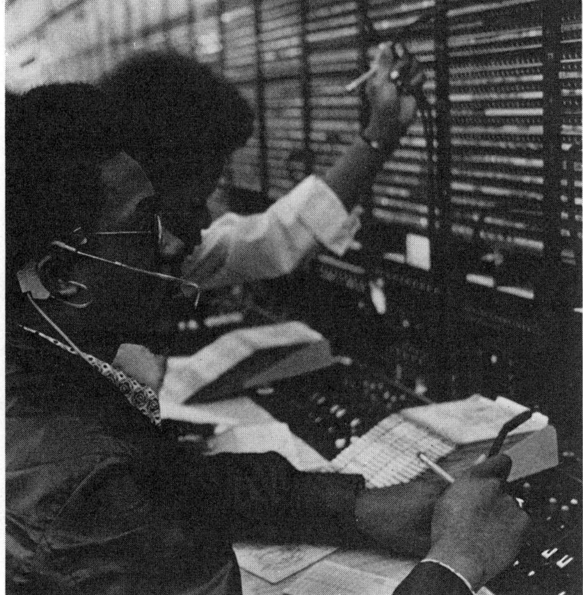

"The fraction of new labour force entrants represented by blacks and Hispanics was now approaching 25 to 30%."

lives (*e.g.*, government spending, busing, affirmative action programs, government-sponsored abortion). Thus, although individual gay rights have been widely sanctioned, the same cannot be said for their legitimization by government. The focus has shifted from the disenfranchised (minorities, women) to the traditional middle-class citizen, who had been all but forgotten in the recent past. In the past decade or more, real wages for this "forgotten man" have risen little, housing costs have escalated beyond the means of most middle-class families, and taxes have risen exponentially. The first signs of middle-class revolt appeared in the late 1970s with Proposition 13-style tax initiatives, reactions to liberal court decisions, and a conservative backlash to some of the gains of newly enfranchised groups. These movements have continued in the early '80s.

Self-Reliance. One natural reaction to the world of troubled economics, uncertain energy supplies, and ineffective institutions has been something of a movement toward individual self-reliance. As dependence on the external world has become more uncertain and chancy, a tendency has developed to rely more heavily on oneself or one's immediate neighbours.

The effects are making themselves felt in many ways. Growing one's own food, building one's own home, and making one's own repairs have achieved new status. Part of this is due to the sheer necessity of becoming more self-sufficient, imposed by inflation. But in large measure it results from the growing respect for men and women who are independent and who work for themselves.

The numbers themselves are interesting. Whereas a decade ago barely 10 million or so of the U.S. population might have been characterized as embracing the philosophy of "voluntary simplicity," the most recent estimates are that as many as 15% of the population, or about 35 million, are involved. And even this figure may underestimate the untold numbers who have simply adopted many of the attitudes and practices of self-reliance. The values of such individuals centre around self-care health practices, appropriate technology, natural foods, and general opposition to unnecessary complexity in life-style.

Increasing self-reliance—coupled with related concerns about the physical environment—has had its effect on consumer preferences. Many suppliers and retailers have been surprised at the extent of the shift toward *natural* over artificial (particularly in food products), toward *quality* over quantity, and toward *durability* over disposability. While consumers still place huge priorities on convenience and choice, conspicuous consumption is tolerated less and less. Young homemakers increasingly prefer furniture and accessories that are simple and functional. Wood is preferred over plastic imitations. Cotton and wool continue to grow in popularity. In general, mass-produced household articles are accepted only when the alternative is functionally inferior or much too expensive.

Participation. The return to traditionalism and the growth of self-reliance are being accompanied by changes in the way individuals act to influence decisions that affect their lives. Nowhere, perhaps, is this more apparent than in the workplace. The demand for more meaningful work in an environment where decisions about work organization are shared on a group basis has continued to grow. As a result, much greater efforts are being made to restructure work assignments to make them more challenging, to create smaller, more autonomous work groups, and to provide more flexible channels of communication—cutting through hierarchical structures—and, in some instances, a greater employee voice in how corporate profits are allocated. These developments have stopped short of employee representation on corporate boards, but such measures are being actively discussed, even in some union quarters, and prospects for the emergence of some form of board representation in the mid-'80s appear very high. Much of the ferment in the workplace is being hastened by the tightened labour market that has begun to develop.

The workplace is not the only arena in which broad participative changes are occurring. Alternate mechanisms—or sometimes institutions—are continuing to proliferate, aimed at influencing decisions related to government, the products we use, the environment, and the communities in which we live. Often this involves joining groups that are close to the specific concerns of the individual, such as consumer cooperatives, self-help groups, and do-it-yourself movements. Sometimes it has meant joining groups or taking actions that directly challenge traditional decision-making institutions. Inevitably it has resulted in a proliferation of lawsuits, consumer movements, environmental action groups, and single-interest lobbying organizations. Also inevitably, the increase in individual participation has made decision making slower, more complicated, and more costly.

Fortunately, as it turned out, the divisiveness in the larger society—and in the Congress reflecting that society—became so disabling that it was the central issue of the 1984 presidential election. The new president, an individual possessing unusual qualities of personal competence and leadership, has begun the long journey toward greater national consensus. This is not easy, and it will be at least another five years before we know whether we have passed the worst of what is being referred to as "the transitional decade." Indeed, it is largely because of the general disappointment in our performance in the early '80s that signs of some kind of genuine turnaround are now becoming evident. In many ways, 1985 may indeed be considered *the* pivotal year in the "decade of transition."

ARTICLES FROM THE 1980 PRINTING OF THE BRITANNICA

The world of matter can be divided, like Gaul, into three parts: the very small, the very large, and the middle size, which is the domain we ordinarily perceive with our senses. For millennia man knew only that middle realm, and based all of his science on it. The most distinctive scientific revolution of our time is our stunning new knowledge of the very large—the galaxies, the universe as a whole—and the very small—the atom, its nucleus, and the numerous particles that whirl around and within it.

New tools—aids to our senses—have had to be discovered in order to make this new knowledge possible. One of the most important new tools is the particle accelerator, which helps us see into the realm of the unimaginably tiny entities within the atomic nucleus. This new article from the 1980 printing of Encyclopædia Britannica *is a fascinating—and above all, readable—review of the accelerators that particle physicists use around the world.*

ACCELERATORS, PARTICLE

A particle accelerator is a device that produces a beam of fast-moving, electrically charged atomic or subatomic particles. The effectiveness of an accelerator usually is characterized by the kinetic energy, rather than the speed, of the particles. The unit of energy commonly used is the electron volt (eV), which is the energy acquired by a particle that has the same magnitude of charge as has the electron, when it passes between electrodes that differ in potential by one volt. Related larger units are the kiloelectron volt (keV), which is 1,000 eV; the megaelectron volt (MeV; 1,000,000 eV); and the gigaelectron volt (GeV; 1,000,000,000 eV; formerly called the BeV in the U.S.). Compared with the quantities of energy encountered in everyday experience, even the GeV is a very small amount, about that gained by a grain of salt as it drops one millimetre under the influence of gravity. The masses of the particles accelerated are so small, however, that kinetic energies in this range correspond to very high speeds: the speed of the particles in the smallest ion accelerators is about 5,000 miles (8,000 kilometres) per second, about 3 percent of the speed of light.

The particles that are accelerated are electrons, positrons (positive electrons), or ionized atoms such as protons (ionized hydrogen), deuterons (ionized heavy hydrogen), alpha particles (ionized helium), or heavier ionized atoms. Sometimes the primary beam is used; in other cases, the primary beam is directed onto a target to produce a beam of secondary particles, such as gamma rays, neutrons, mesons, hyperons, or neutrinos. A few accelerators are operated as sources of the intense radiation, called synchrotron radiation, emitted by electrons moving at almost the speed of light along curved paths.

Uses of accelerators

Physicists use accelerators in fundamental research on the structure of nuclei, the nature of nuclear forces, and the properties of nuclei not found in nature, such as the transuranic (heavier than uranium) elements and other unstable elements. Accelerators are also used for radioisotope production, industrial radiography, cancer therapy, sterilization of biological materials, and polymerization of plastics. The largest accelerators are used in research on the fundamental interactions of the elementary subatomic particles.

Every accelerator has three essential parts: a source of the particles to be accelerated, a vacuum chamber in which to accelerate them, and a source of the electric fields needed to effect the acceleration. Thermionic emission (the emission of electrons from the surface of a heated solid) is the process used to provide electrons. Positrons are produced as secondary particles by an electron accelerator and then further accelerated. Positive and negative ions are produced by electric arc or glow discharges in a gas at low pressure in a chamber; a high-voltage electrode extracts the ions from the gas through a hole in the chamber. The region in which the particles are accelerated must be highly evacuated to keep the particles from being scattered out of the beam, or even stopped, by collisions with molecules of air.

Accelerators are differentiated by the arrangements of the accelerating electric fields. In a linear accelerator, the path of the particles is a straight line, and the final energy of the particles is given by the sum of the voltages produced by the accelerating devices along that line. In a cyclic accelerator, the path of the particles is bent by the action of a magnetic field into a spiral or a closed curve that is approximately circular. In this case, the particles pass many times through the accelerating devices; the final energy depends on the magnitude of the voltages and on the number of times the particles pass through. Because the total distance travelled by the particles in a cyclic accelerator may be as much as a million miles, the cumulative effect of minute deviations from the desired trajectory would be dissipation of the beam. Therefore, the beam must be continually focussed by the magnetic fields, which are precisely shaped by powerful magnets.

HISTORY

The motivation for most of the development of the various types of particle accelerators has been their application to research into the properties of atomic nuclei and subatomic particles. Starting with Ernest (later Lord) Rutherford's discovery, in 1919, of a reaction between a nitrogen nucleus and an alpha particle, all research in nuclear physics until 1932 was performed with alpha particles from naturally radioactive elements. The natural alpha particles have kinetic energies as high as 8 MeV. It was not possible, however, to form natural alpha particles into a well-defined beam in which all the particles were of equal energy without reducing the number of particles so much that they were useless. Further experimentation required a beam of artificially accelerated ions, but there seemed little hope of generating laboratory voltages sufficient to accelerate ions to the desired energies. A calculation made by George Gamow (then at the University of Göttingen) in 1928, however, indicated that considerably less energetic ions could be useful, and this stimulated attempts to build an accelerator that could provide a beam of particles suitable for nuclear research. The first successful experiments with artificially accelerated ions were performed at the University of Cambridge, England, by J.D. Cockcroft and E.T.S. Walton in 1932. Using a voltage multiplier, they accelerated protons to energies as high as 710 keV and showed that these react with the lithium nucleus, the products being two energetic alpha particles. Other developments of that period demonstrated principles still employed in the design of particle accelerators. For example, Robert J. Van de Graaff had constructed the first belt-charged electrostatic high-voltage generator at Princeton University, in New Jersey, by 1931.

First proton accelerator

The principle of the resonance linear accelerator was disclosed by Rolf Wideröe in 1928. At the Rhenish-Westphalian Technical University in Aachen he had used alternating high voltage to accelerate ions of sodium and potassium to energies twice as high as those imparted by one application of the peak voltage. In 1931, Ernest O. Lawrence and his assistant David H. Sloan, at the University of California, Berkeley, employed high-frequency fields to accelerate mercury ions to more than 1.2 MeV; this work augmented Wideröe's achievement in accelerating heavy ions, but the ion beams were not useful in nuclear research.

The magnetic resonance accelerator, or cyclotron, was conceived by Lawrence as a modification of Wideröe's linear resonance accelerator. Lawrence's student M.S. Livingston demonstrated the principle of the cyclotron in 1931, producing 80-keV ions; in 1932, Lawrence and Livingston announced the acceleration of protons to more than 1 MeV. Later in the 1930s cyclotron energies reached about 25 MeV and Van de Graaff generators, about 4 MeV. In 1940 Donald W. Kerst, applying the results of careful orbit calculations to the design of magnets, constructed the first betatron, a magnetic-induction accelerator of electrons, at the University of Illinois.

The rapid advance in the science of accelerating particles to high energies that has occurred since the end of World War II was initiated by E.M. McMillan, at Berkeley, and V.I. Veksler, at Moscow, who in 1945 independently described the principle of phase stability, which removed an apparent limitation on the energy of resonance accelerators for protons (see below *Classical cyclotrons*) and made possible the construction of magnetic-resonance accelerators (called synchrotrons) for electrons. The principle was promptly demonstrated by the construction of a small synchrocyclotron at the University of California and an electron synchrotron in England. The first proton linear resonance accelerator was constructed soon thereafter. The large proton synchrotrons that have been built since then all depend on this principle.

In 1947 William W. Hansen, at Stanford University, California, constructed the first travelling-wave linear accelerator of electrons, exploiting microwave technology that had been developed for radar during World War II.

Developments since the 1940s

The progress in research made possible by raising the energies of protons led to the building of successively larger accelerators; the trend was ended only by the cost of fabricating the huge magnet rings required—the largest weighs nearly 40,000 tons. A means of increasing the energy without increasing the scale of the machines was provided by the demonstration, in 1952, by Livingston, E.D. Courant, and H.S. Snyder of the technique of alternating-gradient focussing (sometimes called strong focussing). Synchrotrons incorporating this principle needed magnets only 1/100 the size that would be required otherwise. All recently constructed accelerators make use of alternating-gradient focussing.

In 1956 Kerst realized that, if two sets of particles could be maintained in intersecting orbits, it should be possible to observe interactions in which one particle collided with another moving in the opposite direction with the same energy. Application of this idea requires the accumulation of accelerated particles in loops called storage rings. The highest reaction energies now obtainable have been produced by the use of this technique.

Particle storage rings

CONSTANT-VOLTAGE ACCELERATORS

The simplest type of particle accelerator is constructed by mounting a particle source on one end of an insulated, evacuated tube and creating a high voltage between the ends, with the polarity such that the particles are impelled from the source toward the far end of the tube. Such an accelerator is necessarily linear, and the electrostatic field can be applied to a given particle but once (unless, as in the tandem accelerator described below, the charge of the particle undergoes change in sign). The simplicity of concept soon gives way to complexity in execution when the electric potential exceeds 1,000,000 volts (one megavolt, or 1 MV): these high voltages produce corona discharges and lightning-like sparks outside the accelerator, which dissipate the potential needed to accelerate the particles. Even more difficult to control are sparks within the equipment and, in positive-ion accelerators, unwanted secondary beams produced when the accelerated ions strike the end of the tube.

Because these discharges and sparks generally originate at sharply curved or pointed places on the surface of an electrode, the high-voltage electrode of a modern accelerator is made in the shape of a sphere or a cylinder with rounded ends or, in the case of a low-energy device, a box with rounded edges. The insulating columns that support the terminals are meticulously designed to suppress corona or sparking. Care also is devoted to the design of the accelerator tube to ensure the uniform distribution of the voltage along its length. The voltage that a structure will withstand is increased if the pressure of the gas surrounding it is increased, so direct-voltage accelerators commonly are mounted in tanks pressurized with mixtures of nitrogen and carbon dioxide or, in certain cases, the gas sulfur hexafluoride.

Voltage multipliers (cascade generators). The source of the high voltage for Cockcroft and Walton's pioneering experiments was a four-stage voltage multiplier assembled from four large rectifiers and high-voltage capacitors. Their circuit, in effect, combined four rectifier-type direct-voltage power supplies in series. The alternating voltage supplied by a high-voltage transformer was changed to higher, direct voltages through an array of heavy-duty capacitors; a second group of capacitors kept the direct voltage constant. The final direct voltage would have been four times the peak voltage available from the transformer (200,000 volts) if corona discharge had not drained away considerable power. Nevertheless, the apparatus did accelerate protons to energies of 710 keV, sufficient to bring about the hoped-for result, a reaction with lithium nuclei. Their achievement, the first nuclear reaction effected by artificially accelerated particles, was recognized by the award of the Nobel Prize for Physics in 1951.

Cockcroft-Walton generator

Cockcroft and Walton's system for building up high direct voltages can be extended to multiplication factors many times that originally demonstrated. Commercially available accelerators that reach 4 MeV are based on this circuitry.

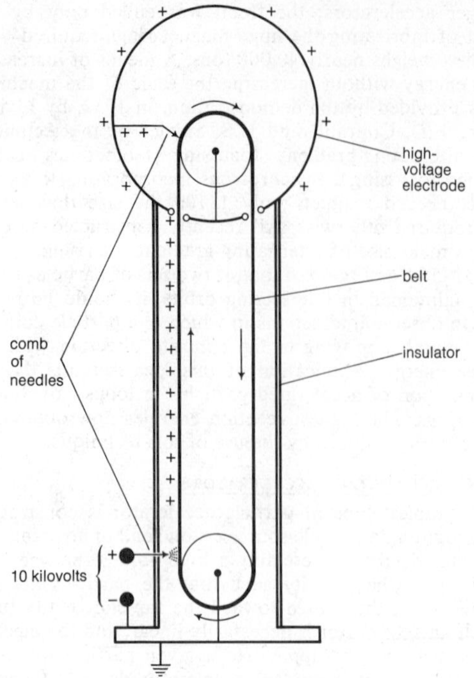

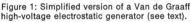

Figure 1: Simplified version of a Van de Graaff high-voltage electrostatic generator (see text).

Van de Graaff generators. In Van de Graaff generators, electric charge is transported to the high-voltage terminal on a rapidly moving belt of insulating material driven by a pulley mounted on the grounded end of the structure; a second pulley is enclosed within the large, spherical high-voltage terminal, as shown in Figure 1. The belt is charged by a comb of sharp needles with the points close to the belt a short distance from the place at which it moves clear of the grounded pulley. The comb is connected to a power supply that raises its potential to a few tens of kilovolts. The gas near the needle points is ionized by the intense electric field, and in the resulting corona discharge the ions are driven to the surface of the belt. The motion of the belt carries the charge into the high-voltage terminal and transfers it to another comb of needles, from which it passes to the outer surface of the terminal. A carefully designed Van de Graaff generator insulated by pressurized gas can be charged to a potential of about 20 MV.

Tandem Van de Graaff accelerators

In most constant voltage accelerators, Van de Graaff generators are the source of high voltage, and most of the electrostatic proton accelerators still in use are two-stage (*tandem*) accelerators. These devices provide a beam with twice the energy that could be achieved by one application of the high voltage. Figure 2 is a diagram of a tandem accelerator. An ion source yields a beam of protons, which are accelerated to a low energy by an auxiliary high-voltage supply. This beam passes through a region containing a gas at low pressure, where some of the protons are converted to negative hydrogen ions by the addition of two electrons. As the mixture of charged particles moves through a magnetic field, those with negative charge are deflected into the accelerator tube, and those with positive charge are deflected away. The beam of negative ions is then accelerated toward the positive high-voltage terminal. In this terminal, the particles pass through a thin carbon foil that strips off the two electrons, changing many of the negative ions back into positive ions (protons). These, now repelled by the positive terminal, are further accelerated through the second part of the tube. At the output end of the accelerator the protons are magnetically separated, as before, from other particles in the beam and directed to the target. In three- or four-stage tandem accelerators, two Van de Graaff generators are combined with the necessary additional provisions for changing the charge of the ions.

Van de Graaff and Cockcroft–Walton generators also are utilized for accelerating electrons. The rates at which charge is transported in electron beams correspond to currents of several milliamperes; the beams deliver energy in magnitudes best expressed in terms of kilowatts. These intense beams are used for sterilization, industrial radiography, cancer therapy, and polymerization of plastics.

Adapted from R. J. Van de Graaff, *Nuclear Instruments and Methods*, vol. 8, p. 195 (1960); North-Holland Publishing Co.

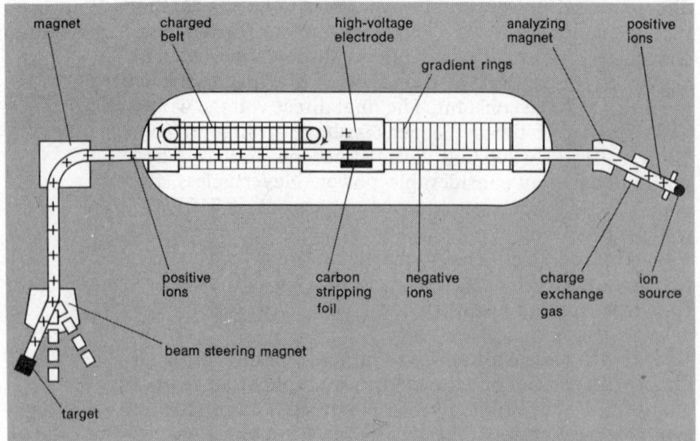

Figure 2: Two-stage tandem accelerator (see text).

BETATRONS

The name betatron connotes the most practical application of a type of accelerator that acts upon beta particles, as electrons are alternatively called. The motion of an electron in a betatron is the consequence of two forces that are exerted on it by a magnetic field that is symmetrical about the axis of the device. At any instant during its motion in a plane perpendicular to this axis, the electron is attracted toward the centre with a force that is proportional to the product of the magnitudes of its charge, its speed at that instant, and the strength of the field. The strength of the field, however, is not maintained at a constant value but is caused continuously to increase. The change induces an electric field directed along circles concentric with the axis; these fields exert a force on the electron that accelerates it along the circle. On only one such circle, termed the orbit of the electron, do the two forces act to cause the electron to remain in the circle while continuously increasing its speed. This circumstance results if the average magnetic field *inside* the orbit is always twice the magnetic field *on* the orbit. Because this so-called equilibrium orbit is circular, the acceleration chamber is made in the shape of a torus, or doughnut, as shown in Figure 3. The magnetic field is produced by a magnet designed to minimize the time lag in the response of the field to the variations in the alternating current in the windings. The poles of the magnet are tapered to cause the field near the orbit to

From *Jaderna Energie* (1958)

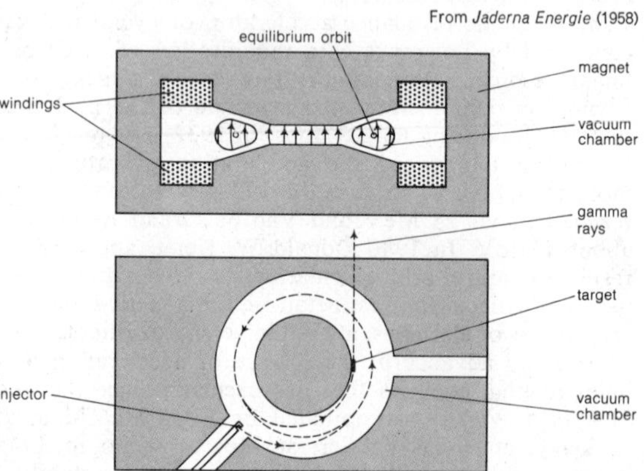

Figure 3: *Betatron.* (Top) Cross section, (bottom) plan view (see text).

decrease with increasing radius. This focusses the beam by ensuring that any particle that strays from the orbit is subjected to forces that restore it to its proper path. The theory of controlling these deviations was first worked out for the betatron; by analogy, the oscillations of particles about their equilibrium orbits in all cyclic accelerators are called betatron oscillations.

Betatron oscillations

Just as the varying magnetic field assumes the direction necessary to cause acceleration, a burst of electrons is sent into the doughnut, where—in a 20-MeV betatron—they gain about 100 eV per revolution. The acceleration lasts for one-quarter of the magnet cycle, until the magnetic field has increased to its maximum value, whereupon the orbit is caused to shrink, causing the electrons to strike a target, producing a beam of intense X-rays.

The practical limit on the energy imparted by a betatron is set by the radiation of electromagnetic energy by electrons moving in curved paths. The intensity of this radiation, commonly called synchrotron radiation (see below *Electron synchrotrons*), rises rapidly as the speed of the electrons increases. The largest betatron accelerates electrons to 300 MeV, sufficient to produce pi mesons in its target; the energy loss by its electrons through radiation (a few percent) is compensated by changing the relation between the field on the orbit and the average field inside the orbit. At higher energies this compensation would not be feasible.

Betatrons are now commercially manufactured, principally for use as sources of highly energetic ("hard") X-rays for industrial and medical radiography.

CYCLOTRONS

The magnetic resonance accelerator, or cyclotron, was the first cyclic accelerator and the first resonance accelerator that produced particles energetic enough to be useful for nuclear research. For many years the highest particle energies were those imparted by cyclotrons modelled upon Lawrence's archetype. In these devices, commonly called classical cyclotrons, the accelerating electric field oscillates at a fixed frequency and the guiding magnetic field has a fixed intensity.

Classical cyclotrons. The key to the operation of a cyclotron is the fact that the orbits of ions in a uniform magnetic field are isochronous; that is, the time taken by a particle of a given mass to make one complete circuit is the same at any speed or energy as long as the speed is much less than that of light. (As the speed of a particle approaches that of light, its mass undergoes the increase—predicted by the theory of relativity—that is called the relativistic increase.) This isochronicity makes it possible for a high voltage, reversing in polarity at a constant frequency, to accelerate a particle many times. As shown in Figure 4, an ion source is located at the centre of an evacuated chamber that has the shape of a short cylinder, like a pillbox, between the poles of an electromagnet that creates a uniform field perpendicular to the flat faces. The accelerating voltage is applied by electrodes, called dees from their shape: each is a D-shaped half of a pillbox. The source of the voltage is an oscillator—similar to a radio transmitter—that operates at a frequency equal to the frequency of revolution of the particles in the magnetic field. The

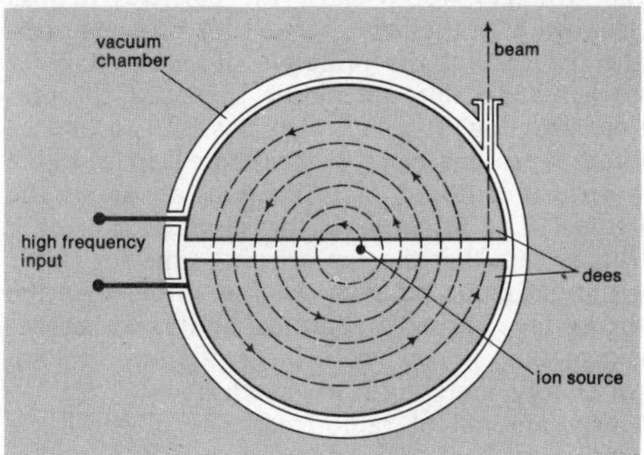

Figure 4: Plan view of the classical cyclotron.

electric fields caused by this accelerating voltage are concentrated in the gap between the dees; there is no electric field inside the dees. The path of the particle inside the dee is therefore circular. Each time the particle crosses the gap between the dees it is accelerated, because in the time between these crossings the direction of the field reverses. The path of the particle is thus a spiral-like series of semicircles of continually increasing radius.

Some means of focussing is required, as otherwise a particle that starts out in a direction making a small angle with the orbital plane will spiral into the dees and be lost. While the energy of the particle is still low, this focussing is supplied by the accelerating electric fields; after the particle has gained significant energy, focussing is a consequence of a slight weakening of the magnetic field toward the peripheries of the dees as in the betatron, but to a much smaller degree.

Cyclotron energy limitations

The energy gained by a particle in a classical cyclotron is limited by the relativistic increase in the mass of the particle, a phenomenon that causes the orbital frequency to decrease and the particles to get out of phase with the alternating voltage. This effect can be reduced by applying higher accelerating voltages to shorten the overall acceleration time. The highest energy imparted to protons in a classical cyclotron is less than 25 MeV, and this achievement requires the imposition of hundreds of kilovolts to the dees. The beam current in a classical cyclotron operated at high voltages can be as high as 5 milliamperes; intensities of this magnitude are very useful in the synthesis of radioisotopes.

Synchrocyclotrons. Cyclotrons in which the frequency of the accelerating voltage is changed as the particles are accelerated are called synchrocyclotrons, frequency-modulated (FM) cyclotrons, or, in the Soviet Union, phasotrons. Because of the modulation the particles do not get out of phase with the accelerating voltage, so that the relativistic mass increase does not impose a limit on the energy. Moreover, the magnetic focussing can be made stronger, so that the magnetic field need not be so precisely shaped.

Phase stability

Because of the phenomenon of phase stability, the frequency of the accelerating voltage need not be made to coincide with the decreasing frequency of revolution of the particles as they are accelerated. To see how phase stability affects the operation of a cyclotron, consider a particle moving in an orbit. Let the frequency of the accelerating voltage match the orbital frequency of this particle. If the particle crosses the accelerating gap at the time the accelerating voltage is zero, its energy and orbital radius will remain unchanged—it is said to be in equilibrium. There are two such times during each cycle of the accelerating voltage; only one of these (that at which the voltage is falling, rather than rising, through zero) corresponds to *stable* equilibrium. If a particle should arrive a short time before the voltage has fallen to zero, it is accelerated. Its speed therefore increases, but the radius of its orbit increases by an even larger proportion, so that the particle will take longer to reach the gap again and will next cross it at a time closer to that at which it would receive no acceleration. If, on the other hand, the particle reaches the gap a short time *after* the voltage has fallen through zero, its speed is diminished, and the radius of its orbit is diminished even more, so that it takes *less* time to reach the gap again, arriving—like the other particle—at a time closer to that at which it receives no acceleration. This phenomenon, by which the trajectories of errant particles are continually corrected, confers stability on the entire beam and makes it possible to accelerate the particles uniformly, by modulating the frequency, without dispersing them. The small periodic variations of the particles about the equilibrium values of phase and energy are called synchrotron oscillations.

Synchrotron oscillations

In the operation of a synchrocyclotron, particles are accelerated from the ion source when the frequency of the accelerating voltage is equal to the orbital frequency of the particles in the central field. As the frequency of the voltage falls, the particles, on the average, encounter an accelerating field. They oscillate in phase, but around a value that corresponds to the average acceleration. The particles reach the maximum energy in bunches, one for each time the accelerating frequency goes through its program. The intensity of the beam is a few microamperes, much lower than that of a classical cyclotron.

Large synchrocyclotrons have been constructed in many countries. They are used primarily for research with secondary beams of pi mesons. The practical upper limit of the energy of a synchrocyclotron, set by the cost of the huge magnets required, is about 1 GeV.

Sector-focussed cyclotrons. The sector-focussed cyclotron is another modification of the classical cyclotron that also evades relativistic constraint on its maximum energy. Its advantage over the synchrocyclotron is that the beam is not pulsed and is more intense. The frequency of the accelerating voltage is constant, and the orbital frequency of the particles is kept constant as they are accelerated by causing the average magnetic field on the orbit to increase with orbit radius. This ordinarily would cause the beam to spread out in the direction of the magnetic field, but in sector-focussed cyclotrons the magnetic field varies with the angular position as well as with the radius; this produces the equivalent of alternating-gradient focussing (see below *Synchrotrons*). This principle was discovered in 1938 by L.H. Thomas, then at Ohio State University, but was not applied until the alternating-gradient synchrotron was invented in 1952. Several of these devices, sometimes called azimuthally varying field (AVF) cyclotrons, have been built for use in nuclear and medical research.

LINEAR RESONANCE ACCELERATORS

The technology required to design a useful linear resonance accelerator was not developed until after 1940. These accelerators require very powerful sources of radio-frequency accelerating voltage. Further, a practical linear accelerator for heavy particles, such as protons, must make use of the principle of phase stability.

Linear accelerators fall into two distinct types: standing-wave linear accelerators (used for heavy particles) and travelling-wave linear accelerators (used to accelerate electrons). The reason for the difference is that after electrons have been accelerated to a few MeV in the first few feet of a typical accelerator, they have speeds very close to that of light. Therefore if the accelerating wave also moves at the speed of light, the particles do not get out of phase, as their speeds do not change. Protons, on the other hand, must reach much higher energies before their speeds can be taken as constant, so that the accelerator design must allow for the prolonged increase in speed.

Linear electron accelerators. The force that acts on electrons in a travelling-wave accelerator is provided by an electromagnetic field with a frequency near 3,000 MHz (1 MHz = 1,000,000 Hertz, or 1,000,000 cycles per second)—a microwave. The acceleration chamber is an evacuated cylindrical pipe that serves as a waveguide for the accelerating field. The phase velocity of an electromagnetic wave in a cylindrical pipe is greater than the velocity of light in free space, so the wave must be slowed down by the insertion of metal irises a few centimetres apart in the pipe, as shown in Figure 5. In the intense field, the electrons gain about two MeV per foot. The microwaves are produced by large klystrons (high-frequency vacuum-tube amplifiers) with power outputs of 20–30 megawatts. Because sources of radio-frequency power of this magnitude must be operated intermittently (they will not survive continuous service), the beams from these accelerators are delivered in short bursts.

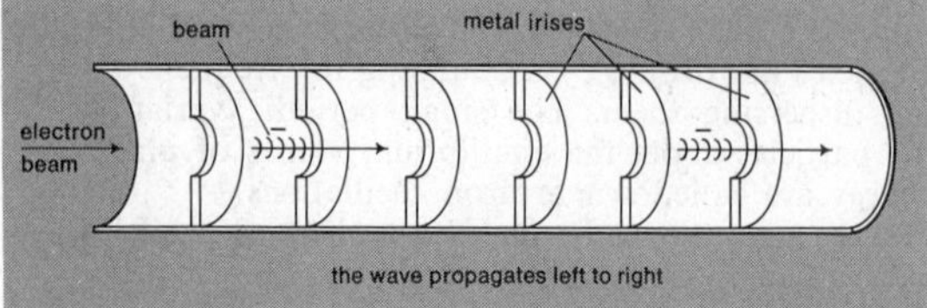

Figure 5: Waveguide acceleration chamber of an electron linear accelerator showing the irises, which decrease the phase velocity of the wave (see text).

Pulses of electrons are injected at energies of a few hundred keV (that is, speeds about half that of light). The accelerator is so designed that, during the first part of the acceleration, the electrons are caused to gather into bunches, which then are accelerated nearly to the speed of light. Subsequently, the electrons move with the crest of the electromagnetic wave.

Linear electron accelerators are manufactured commercially. They are used for radiography, for cancer treatment, and as injectors for electron synchrotrons.

The two-mile-long linear electron accelerator at Stanford University (called SLAC, an initialism for *S*tanford *l*inear *a*ccelerator *c*entre) is the source of the most energetic beams of electrons (almost 25 GeV) and positrons (almost 15 GeV) now available. Electron-beam currents of 50 microamperes and positron-beam currents of more than 1 microampere can be obtained. The accelerator is used for research on subatomic particles and for filling the electron-positron storage ring called SPEAR (*S*tanford *p*ositron-*e*lectron *a*symmetric *r*ing).

Linear electron accelerators constructed of superconducting materials were being developed in the late 1970s. The advantage offered by such a device is low power consumption, allowing production of a continuous, rather than a pulsed, beam.

Linear proton accelerators. The design principle applied in linear accelerators for protons was originated by Luis Alvarez at Berkeley in 1946. It is based on the formation of standing electromagnetic waves in a long cylindrical metal tank, or cavity, as it is sometimes called. In the design that has been adopted, the electric field is parallel to the axis of the tank. Most of these accelerators operate at frequencies of about 200 MHz.

During the time required for a proton to traverse one of these tanks, the accelerating electric fields undergo many reversals of direction. In Alvarez' design, the decelerating effect of the field during the intervals when it opposes the motion of the particles is prevented by installing on the axis of the tank a number of "drift tubes," as shown in Figure 6. The electric field is zero

Use of drift tubes

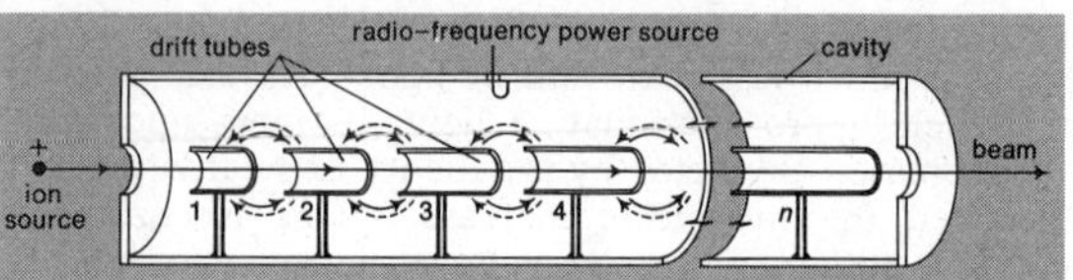

Figure 6: Proton linear resonance accelerator containing *n* metallic drift tubes (see text).

inside the drift tubes, and if their lengths are properly chosen, the protons cross the gap between adjacent drift tubes when the direction of the field produces acceleration and are shielded by the drift tubes when the field in the tank would decelerate them. The lengths of the drift tubes are proportional to the speeds of the particles that pass through them.

It would appear that any error in the magnitude of the accelerating voltages would cause the particles to lose the synchronism with the fields needed for proper operation of the device, but the principle of phase stability reduces to a manageable magnitude the need for precision in construction. It also makes possible an intense beam, because protons can be accelerated in a stable manner even if they do not cross the gaps at exactly the intended times. The principle is the same as that of a synchrotron, except that the gap-crossing time for stable phase oscillations coincides with the rise, rather than the fall, of the voltage wave. If a proton arrives at the accelerating gap late, it receives a larger-than-normal increment of energy, enabling it to "catch up."

A very large amount of radio-frequency power is required to produce the accelerating voltages. This makes it necessary for linear proton accelerators to be operated in a pulsed mode. They are supplied with protons accelerated to about 750 keV by a Cockcroft–Walton generator. The entering beam passes through an accelerating radio-frequency cavity a short distance upbeam from the main linear accelerator, so that as the particles pass through the first drift tubes, they are already bunched.

The intense pulses of protons emerging from linear accelerators make these devices ideal as injectors for proton synchrotrons. Their relatively high cost has prevented their construction except for use as meson factories. The largest linear accelerators used as injectors are located at the Brookhaven National Laboratory, Upton, N.Y., and at the Fermi National Accelerator Laboratory ("Fermilab"), Batavia, Ill. These accelerators are very similar in construction, and each is 475 feet long. The beam energy is 200 MeV, and the peak beam current is more than 100 milliamperes. They are needed as injectors only for a short time every few seconds; most of the time the beams are used for radioisotope production and medical applications.

At the Los Alamos Meson Physics Facility in New Mexico, a linear proton accelerator has been constructed for nuclear research and as a meson factory. The protons are accelerated to 100 MeV in Alvarez-type tanks and then to 800 MeV in a travelling-wave linear accelerator similar to those used for electrons but operated at a frequency of 805 MHz. The apparatus was designed to produce a beam carrying a current of 1 milliampere and a power of 800 kilowatts. The highest current yet achieved is 200 microamperes. Its intense secondary beam of low-energy pi mesons has been applied in experimental cancer therapy.

Heavy-ion linear accelerators. For research with ions more massive than the alpha particle, a relatively high energy per unit of atomic weight is desirable. The production of beams of heavy charged particles at a reasonable cost is practical only if the particles are highly ionized, because the energy gained by an ion is proportional to its charge. The SuperHILAC at Berkeley ("hilac" is an acronym from *h*eavy-*i*on *l*inear *ac*celerator) consists of two Alvarez accelerators operating at 70 MHz. The ions, after acceleration by the first of these machines, have a kinetic energy of 1.2 MeV per unit of atomic weight; this energy corresponds to a speed one-twentieth of the speed of light. These ions then pass through a thin carbon foil, which strips off many electrons. After stripping, the ions (now more highly charged) are accelerated by the second machine to an energy of 8.5 MeV per unit atomic weight, corresponding to a speed about one-seventh of the speed of light. Ions as heavy as those of uranium may be accelerated by the SuperHILAC. Heavy ion beams have been used in the search for possible stable transuranic elements.

SYNCHROTRONS

As the particles in a synchrotron are accelerated, the strength of the magnetic field is increased to keep the radius of the orbit approximately constant. This technique has the advantage that the magnet required to form the particle orbits is much smaller than that needed in a cyclotron to produce the same particle energies. The acceleration is effected by radio-frequency voltages, while the synchronism is maintained by the principle of phase stability. The rate of increase of the energy of the particles is set by the rate of the increase of the magnetic field. The peak accelerating voltage is ordinarily about twice as large as the average energy gain per turn would require, to provide the margin for phase stability. Particles can be stably accelerated with a range of energies and phases with respect to the accelerating voltage, and very intense beams can be produced.

The magnetic field must be shaped so as to focus the beam of particles. In early synchrotrons the field was caused to decrease slightly with increasing radius, as in a betatron. This arrangement resulted in a weak focussing effect that was adequate for machines in which the dimensions of the magnet gap could be appreciable in comparison with the radius of the orbit. The magnitude of the magnetic fields that may be used is limited by the saturation of the iron components that shape the field and provide a path for the magnetic flux. Therefore, if the energy of accelerators is to be increased, their radius must be increased correspondingly. For relativistic particles, the radius is proportional to the kinetic energy. The magnet of a synchrotron with weak focussing, designed to have a reasonable intensity, would have a mass proportional to the cube of the radius. It is clear that increasing the energy beyond some point—in practice, about 10 GeV—would be very expensive.

The introduction of alternating-gradient focussing provided the solution to this problem and made possible the development of synchrotrons with much higher energies. The idea was promptly incorporated in the designs of the 33-GeV proton synchrotron at the Brookhaven National Laboratory and the 28-GeV machine at the European Organization for Nuclear Research (CERN), near Geneva, Switz.

The magnetic fields in an alternating-gradient synchrotron vary much more strongly with radius than those used for weak focussing. A magnet with pole-tips shaped as shown in cross section *ab* in Figure 7 produces a magnetic field that sharply decreases with increasing radius. To the particle beam, this magnetic field acts like a lens with a very short focal length. In the vertical direction (the orbital plane is horizontal) it focusses the beam, but in the radial direction, it is almost equally defocussing. A magnet with the pole-tip shapes shown in cross section *cd* in Figure 7 produces a field that strongly *increases* with increasing radius. This field is defocussing in the vertical direction and focussing in the radial direc-

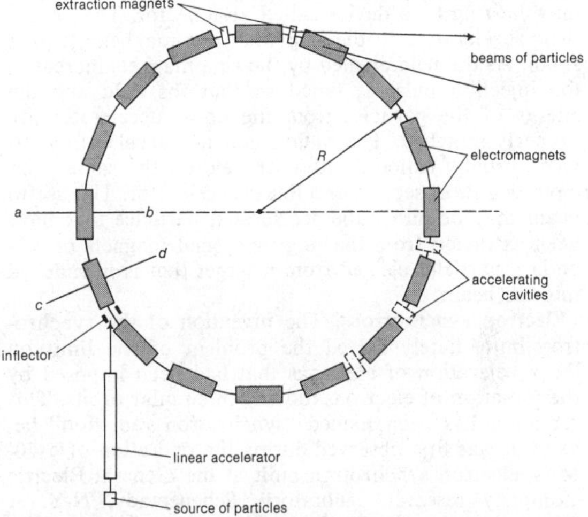

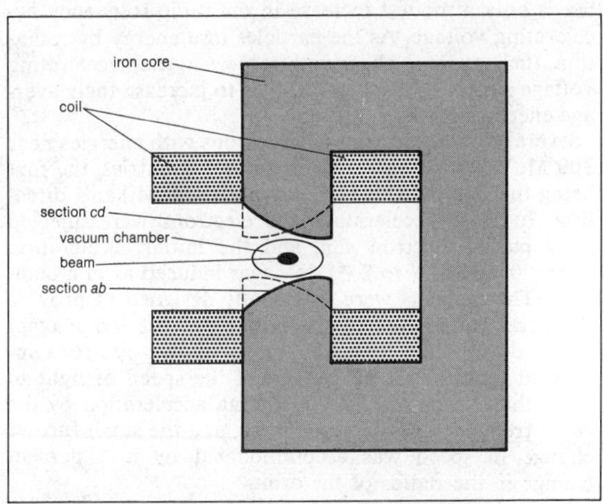

Figure 7: Synchrotron with alternating-gradient focussing, showing the placement of the two types of magnets. Shown at the bottom is a cross section of a typical magnet with the two different types of pole-tips used (see text).

Table 1: Electron Synchrotrons with Energies Greater Than 5 GeV

location	Hamburg	Daresbury, Cheshire, U.K.	Yerevan, Armenian S.S.R.	Ithaca, N.Y.
Energy (GeV)	7.5	5.2	6.1	12.2
Intensity (electrons per second)	2.5×10^{13}	1.2×10^{13}	3.5×10^{12}	1.8×10^{12}
Radius of the orbit (metres)	50.4	35	34.5	125
Repetition rate (pulses per second)	50	53	50	60
Weight of the magnets (tons)	647	400	427	125
Year of first operation	1964	1966	1967	1967

Sources: (Hamburg, Daresbury, Ithaca) *Proceedings of the IX International Conference on Accelerators*, 1974, Stanford; (Yerevan) *Proceedings of the VII International Conference on Accelerators*, 1969, Yerevan.

tion. Although pairing such magnetic fields results in partial cancellation, the overall effect is to provide focussing in both directions. The ring of magnetic field is created by a large number of magnets, with the two types of pole-tips alternating, as shown at the top of Figure 7. The beam, in effect, passes through a succession of lenses as the particles move around the ring, producing a large beam current in a vacuum chamber of small cross section.

Particles accelerated in a large synchrotron are commonly injected by a linear accelerator and are steered into the ring by a device called an inflector. They begin their acceleration in the ring when the magnetic field is small. As the field created by the ring magnets increases, the injection pulse is timed so that the field and the energy of the particles from the linear accelerator are properly matched. The radio-frequency accelerating devices, usually called cavities, operate on the same principle as a short section of a linear accelerator. The useful beam may be either the accelerated particles that have been extracted from the ring by special magnets or secondary particles ejected from a target that is introduced into the beam.

Electron synchrotrons. The invention of the synchrotron immediately solved the problem of the limit on the acceleration of electrons that had been imposed by the radiation of electrons moving in circular orbits. This radiation has been named "synchrotron radiation" because it was first observed during the operation of a 70-MeV electron synchrotron built at the General Electric Company research laboratory, Schenectady, N.Y. A betatron can accelerate electrons to 300 MeV only if the radiation is carefully compensated, but a synchrotron needs only a modest increase in the radio-frequency accelerating voltage. As the particles lose energy by radiation, their average phase with respect to the accelerating voltage simply shifts slightly so as to increase their average energy gain per revolution.

Synchrotron radiation

Several similar electron synchrotrons with energies near 300 MeV were constructed in several countries, the first being the one built at Berkeley under McMillan's direction. In these accelerators, the electrons were injected by a pulsed electron gun, and the initial acceleration from 50–100 keV to 2–3 MeV was induced as in a betatron. The magnets were specifically designed to provide the accelerating flux in the initial part of the magnet cycle; during this time, the speed of the electrons increased from about 50 percent of the speed of light to more than 95 percent. At this point, acceleration by the radio-frequency cavity supervened, and the small further change in speed was accommodated by a 5 percent change in the radius of the orbit.

Strong focussing was first applied to the electron synchrotron in the 1.2-GeV device at Cornell University, Ithaca, N.Y. All large electron synchrotrons now are equipped with linear accelerators for injectors. The practical limit on the energy of an electron synchrotron is set by the cost of the radio-frequency system needed to restore the energy the electrons lose by radiation. To minimize this energy loss, the acceleration time is made as short as possible (a few milliseconds) and the magnetic fields are kept low. Recently, superconducting radio-frequency accelerating cavities have been applied to the electron synchrotron. The characteristics of some electron synchrotrons are given in Table 1.

Proton synchrotrons. The mode of operation of a proton synchrotron is very similar to that of an electron synchrotron, but there are two important differences. First, because the speed of a proton does not approach the speed of light until its energy is well above 1 GeV, the frequency of the accelerating voltage must be modulated to keep it proportional to the speed of the particle during the initial stage of the acceleration. Second, protons do not lose a significant amount of energy by radiation at energies attainable by present-day techniques. The limit on the energy of a proton synchrotron is therefore set by the cost of the magnet ring, which increases only as the first power of the energy, or even more slowly. The highest-energy particle accelerators yet built are proton synchrotrons.

The first proton synchrotron to operate (1956) was the 3-GeV Cosmotron at Brookhaven. It, and other accelerators that soon followed, had weakly focussing magnets. The 28-GeV proton synchrotron at CERN and the 33-GeV machine at Brookhaven made use of the principle of alternating-gradient focussing, but not without complications. Such focussing is so strong that the time required for a particle to complete one orbit does not depend strongly on the energy of the particle. Therefore, for the energy range (which may extend to several GeV) within which acceleration appreciably affects the speed of the particle, phase stability operates as it does in a linear accelerator: the region of stable phase is on the rising side of the time curve of the accelerating voltage. At higher energies, however, the speed of the proton is substantially constant and the region of stable phase is on the falling side of the voltage curve, as it is in a synchrocyclotron. At the point that divides these regions, called the transition energy, there is no phase stability. At Brookhaven a model electron accelerator was built to demonstrate that the beam could be accelerated through the transition energy in a stable manner.

By courtesy of Fermilab, Batavia, Illinois

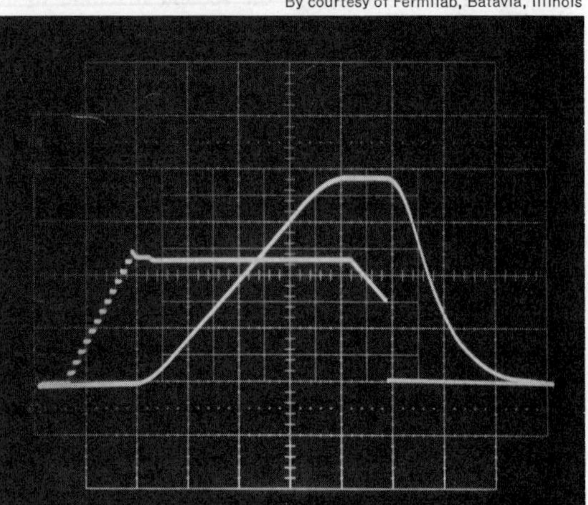

Figure 8: Oscilloscope traces representing the magnet current (which indicates the energy of the circulating protons) and the number of protons in the main accelerator ring at the Fermi National Accelerator Laboratory. One trace shows the stepwise increase in the number of protons corresponding to the injection of 13 bunches of protons from the booster. The number of circulating protons remains constant during acceleration to 400 GeV (shown by the steady rise of the other trace), slowly decreases while one-third of the protons are extracted and sent to counter experiments, then falls abruptly as the remainder of the protons are sent in a short pulse to the 15-foot bubble chamber. (The horizontal scale is one second for each large square.)

Fermilab 500-GeV proton synchrotron

The large proton synchrotron at Fermilab regularly operates at 400 GeV, though 500 GeV has been attained, accelerating 2.5×10^{13} protons in each magnet cycle. The proton beam originates in a 750-keV Cockcroft–Walton generator and is next accelerated to 200 MeV in a linear accelerator. The protons pass from the linear device into a "booster" synchrotron in which they are accelerated to 8 GeV (99.6 percent of the speed of light). While the magnetic field in the main accelerator ring is held at a strength of 400 gauss, 13 pulses of protons are injected into the ring from the booster. When the main ring has been filled in this way, the radio-frequency accelerators and the steering and focussing magnets are actuated, raising the energy of the protons from 8 GeV to 400 GeV in four seconds, or to 500 GeV in a somewhat longer time. Figure 8 shows how the magnetic field in the main accelerator ring and the intensity of the circulating beam vary during one cycle of operation, which includes injection, acceleration, and extraction of the beam of protons.

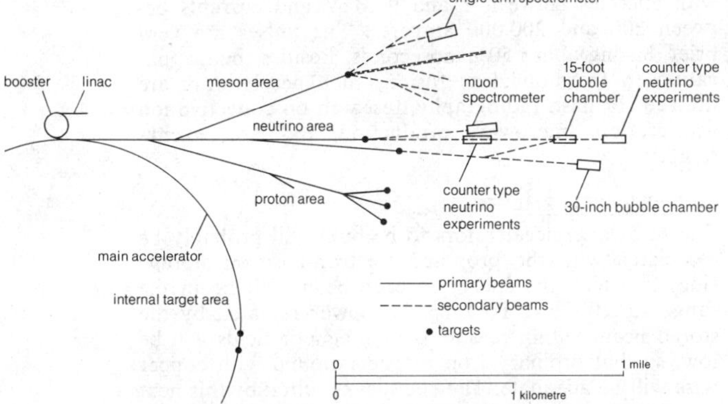

Figure 9: The plan of the Fermi National Accelerator Laboratory accelerator and experimental areas. The angles between the branches of the beam are exaggerated for clarity.
Adapted from *CERN Courier* with permission of Fermilab, Batavia, Illinois

The main accelerator ring at Fermilab is 1,000 metres in radius, making its circumference 6.3 kilometres (almost 4 miles). In this ring, the functions of bending the beam around its orbit and focussing the beam are separated. There are 774 bending magnets, each weighing 11 tons, and 180 focussing magnets, each weighing 5 tons. Injection, acceleration, and extraction of the beam take place in six straight sections, free from magnets. The beam from this accelerator is divided to serve many experimental areas. Figure 9 shows a plan of the accelerator and the experimental areas.

An accelerator very similar to that at Fermilab went into operation in 1976 at CERN, where a 28-GeV proton synchrotron serves as the booster accelerator. Proton synchrotrons are in operation in laboratories in several countries; they all are used for research into the properties of subatomic particles (see Table 2).

Table 2: Proton Synchrotrons with Energies Greater Than 20 GeV

location	Geneva, Switz.	Brookhaven, N.Y.	Serpukhov, Russian S.F.S.R.	Batavia, Ill.	Geneva, Switz.
Energy (GeV)	28	33	76	400	400
Intensity (protons per second)	3×10^{12}	4.5×10^{12}	3.4×10^{11}	2.5×10^{12}	2×10^{12}
Repetition rate (pulses per minute)	30	30	8	5	10
Radius of the orbit (metres)	100	128.5	236	1,000	1,100
Weight of the magnets (tons)	3,130	4,400	20,700	9,850	14,900
Year of first operation	1959	1960	1967	1972	1976

OTHER TYPES OF ACCELERATORS

Microtrons. Microtrons are cyclic electron accelerators that in some respects resemble cyclotrons in their operation. Their invention and early development took place in the Soviet Union. The magnetic field is constant in time, and the accelerating microwave cavity is mounted near the edge of the field, as shown in Figure 10. The source of electrons is a thermionic cathode installed in, or very close to, the cavity. After being accelerated by the electric fields in the cavity, the electrons are guided in a circular path by the magnetic field, so that they pass again through the beam aperture in the cavity and are accelerated again. The time during which an electron completes one orbit is greater than the time for its previous orbit by exactly one cycle (or a larger integral number of cycles) of the radio-frequency accelerating voltage. The synchronism depends on the principle of phase stability. The electron orbits are a set of tangent circles, the point of tangency being the acceleration gap in the cavity. To produce the high voltages in the cavity, much power is required, so that microtrons are pulsed.

Microtrons have been constructed with energies up to a few tens of MeV. They have the advantage that the beam is easily guided out of the magnetic field; for this reason, they are used as injectors for electron synchrotrons. Recently, a modified microtron has been built in which the accelerating cavity is a short superconducting linear accelerator. The magnet is divided into halves, and the orbits are semicircles joined by straight lines; the straight line common to all the orbits passes through the linear accelerator. This microtron can operate almost continuously, and it achieves 19 MeV.

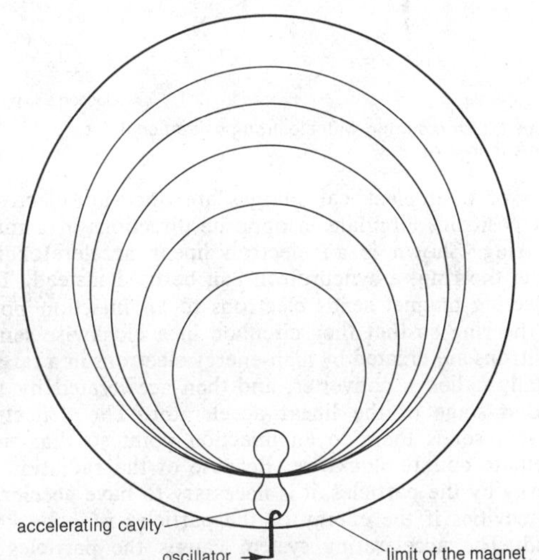

Figure 10: Typical orbits of particles in a microtron (see text).
From *Principles of Cyclic Particle Accelerators*. © 1961 by Litton Educational Publishing, Inc. Reprinted by permission of Van Nostrand Reinhold Company

Storage rings. Although particles are sometimes accelerated in storage rings, the main purpose of these rings is to make possible energetic interactions between beams of particles moving in opposite directions. When a moving object strikes an identical object that is at rest, at most half of the kinetic energy of the moving object is available to produce heat or to deform the objects: the remainder is accounted for by the motions of the objects after the encounter. If, however, the two objects are in motion in opposite directions with equal speeds, then all the kinetic energy is available to produce heat or deformation at the instant of collision. If the objects stick together, the combination is at rest after the collision. For particles with speeds close to that of light, the effect is accentuated. If a 400-GeV proton strikes a proton at rest, only 27.4 GeV are available for the interaction; the remainder produces motion of the particles. On the other hand, if two 31.4-GeV protons collide, as in the CERN storage rings, 62.3 GeV are available for the interaction (the collision is not quite "head on").

When an accelerated beam strikes liquid or solid matter, the number of particles per unit volume of the target is very large, but when the target of one beam is another beam, the number of particles interacting is very much smaller: the rate of interactions is proportional to the product of the currents in the two beams. Kerst realized in 1956 that, although the beam current in a high-energy accelerator is small, the currents circulating in the magnet rings are effectively very much larger because of the high orbital frequency of the particles. Thus, if the colliding beams are circulating in such rings, useful experiments on the interactions could be carried out. Kerst's original proposal was to accumulate a large circulating current in the same device used for the acceleration, but most colliding beams are now collected in storage rings separate from the accelerators.

Colliding beams of particles

Many storage rings have been constructed to study the interactions of electrons with positrons. The principal centres of this research are Stanford, California; Orsay, France; Hamburg, West Germany; Frascati, Italy; and Novosibirsk, Russian S.F.S.R. The only large operating proton-proton storage ring is at CERN.

The manner of operation of a typical electron-positron colliding-beam device is shown in Figure 11. Since the

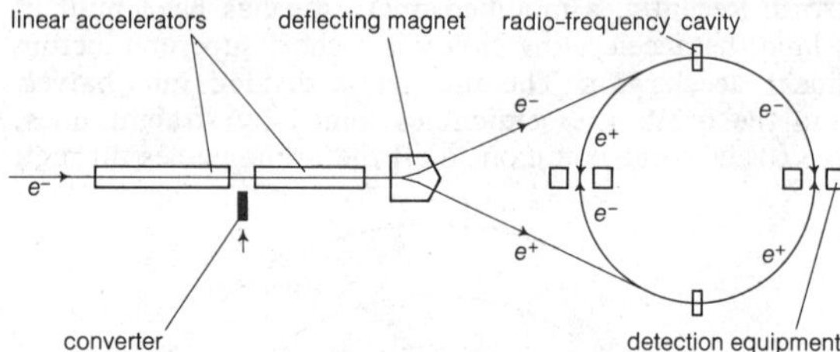

Figure 11: Storage ring with electron-positron colliding beams (see text).

signs of their electrical charges are opposite, electrons and positrons circulate in opposite directions in a magnet ring. Shown is an electron linear accelerator for filling the ring; a synchrotron can be used instead. The deflecting magnet sends electrons to an injection point on the ring so that they circulate in a clockwise sense. Positrons are created by high-energy electrons in a target, usually called a converter, and then accelerated by the second stage of the linear accelerator. The deflecting magnet sends them to an injection point so that they circulate counterclockwise. Because of the radiation of energy by the particles, it is necessary to have accelerating cavities if the energy of the particles is to be kept fixed. The accelerating system causes the particles to circulate in bunches, so that the collisions take place in only a few (commonly only two) places in the ring. This sparsity of intersections simplifies the operation by minimizing the disruption of each beam caused by interactions with the other, allowing more intense beams to be collected and used in the ring. The detection equipment for the experiments is located near the points where the beams intersect.

The highest interaction energies are at present, and will be in the future, achieved in storage rings. This places the research with them at the very forefront of man's quest for knowledge, even though many types of experiments cannot be conducted with storage rings. This is true partly because the number of interactions in a storage ring is a small fraction of that occurring in a stationary target and partly because storage rings do not produce intense beams of secondary particles.

The electrons and positrons in a storage ring emit synchrotron radiation in very large amounts—more than a megawatt in some installations. From a high-energy storage ring, the wavelength of this radiation extends into the X-ray region. Nowadays, these storage rings constitute the brightest sources of electromagnetic radiation available in the ultraviolet as well as the X-ray region. This radiation is becoming increasingly useful for research in solid-state physics, biophysics, and chemical physics; a few electron storage rings of relatively low energy are operated solely for this purpose.

Impulse accelerators. Primarily for use in research on thermonuclear fusion of hydrogen isotopes, several high-intensity electron accelerators have been constructed. One type resembles a string of beads in which each bead is a torus of laminated iron and the string is the vacuum tube. The iron toruses constitute the cores of pulse transformers, and the beam of electrons, in effect, forms the secondary windings of all of the transformers, which are connected in series. The primaries are all connected in parallel and are powered by the discharge of a large bank of capacitors. These accelerators produce beams with energies between 1 and 9 MeV and currents between 200 and 200,000 amperes. The pulses are very brief, lasting about 50 nanoseconds. Besides their application to thermonuclear fusion, such accelerators are utilized for flash radiography, research on collective ion acceleration, microwave production, and laser excitation.

FUTURE DEVELOPMENTS

The next large accelerators to be built will probably be associated with the proposed electron-positron storage rings in which the energy in each beam will lie in the range 15–20 GeV. To keep the power radiated by the stored beam within reason, their magnetic fields will be low, so that ordinary iron magnets wound with copper wire will be adequate. The energies required by this next generation of accelerators, however, will test the limits of conventional radio-frequency techniques. If the energy were to be made significantly higher, the power losses in the accelerating cavities would become prohibitive, and the use of superconducting components would be imperative.

High-energy (200–400 GeV per beam) proton-proton storage rings, with beam currents of about 10 amperes, have been seriously proposed. A small radio-frequency accelerating system would be needed to move the bunches of injected protons to the centre of the vacuum chamber; since protons radiate very little, a large system would be needed only if a part of the acceleration of the beams to high energy were to take place in the storage ring. The overall size and operating cost of such devices would be excessive if superconducting magnets were not used.

There has been a proposal for adding a superconducting ring—in the same enclosure as the main ring at Fermilab—that would be filled with 200–400-GeV protons that could be accelerated slowly to 1,000 GeV. There also has been discussion of larger accelerators, with energies up to 4,000 GeV, that could fit on the Fermilab site if superconducting magnets were used.

Future accelerators of low energy will be designed to produce more intense beams, especially in meson factories; those of higher energy will be designed for the acceleration of heavy ions. In another direction, new, higher-energy electron-storage rings will be built especially for the production of synchrotron radiation.

In a more speculative field, ways are being sought to accelerate protons to very high energies without using huge magnet rings. Veksler in 1956 suggested the formation of a very dense cloud of electrons, which would stay in a stable configuration if they had relativistic energies. In the centre of this cloud there is a point of low potential energy in which protons could be trapped; if then the cloud were to be accelerated to a very high velocity—not a particularly high energy per electron, and therefore attainable with modest energies—the protons, which are carried along, would have very high energies. So far, protons have been accelerated only to a few MeV by application of this principle.

If history can be used as a guide, one can predict that research on the properties of subatomic particles will uncover new phenomena that will require even higher energies for their study. A way will be found to produce those higher energies.

(YURI M. ADO; FRANK C. SHOEMAKER)

It is not so long ago that people in the Western world thought that places like the Seychelles did not really exist but were only prefigurements of Heaven. Islands where the Sun always shines, the gentle breezes blow, the Moon glistens on silver-white beaches and clear lagoons, the people are kind and generous: what could that be but Paradise? However, the Seychelles, a small but delightful republic in the Indian Ocean, really exists, it has a history, and this is Britannica's new article about it.

SEYCHELLES

The Republic of Seychelles is an archipelago situated between 4° and 11° south latitude and 46° and 56° east longitude in the Indian Ocean. Mahé, the main island, is about 680 miles (1,100 kilometres) northeast of Madagascar. The republic is composed of 40 central, mountainous, granitic islands of the Mahé group and 60 outer, flat, coralline islands, all spread over an area of some 150,000 square miles (400,000 square kilometres). The archipelago has a land area of 171 square miles (444 square kilometres), of which Mahé Island takes up 57 square miles. The capital is Victoria, a town with a population in 1970 of 15,600, on Mahé. Seychelles is a member of the United Nations and of the Organization of African Unity.

Physical geography, flora, and fauna. The islands of the Mahé group rise from a large, shallow, crescent-shaped submarine plateau to 3,000 feet (900 metres) above sea level in the Morne Seychellois on Mahé. The overall aspect of these islands, with their lush tropical vegetation, is that of high, hanging gardens overlooking silver-white beaches and clear lagoons. In contrast, the outer, coralline islands rise only a few feet above sea level.

The climate is tropical-oceanic, the average annual temperature varying from 24° C (75° F) to some 30° C (86° F) at sea level. Two monsoons blow over the islands, the southeast ("Suette") from May to November and the northwest ("Vents d'Nord") from November to May. Rainfall varies from island to island, tending to decline from the granitic islands to the southernmost coralline islands. On Mahé, the annual rainfall at sea level averages 92 inches (2,300 millimetres). The granitic islands have only small streams that run swiftly into the sea, hence, even short droughts produce water shortages.

The only remaining primary forests are of coco-de-mer (or sea coconut; *Lodoicea seychellarum*), which grows in protected reserves on Praslin and Curieuse islands. Aldabra Island is famed for its birdlife. The giant tortoise, once widely distributed, is now almost extinct and is protected. Hunting of the green sea turtle also is regulated. There are few insects and no animals dangerous to man on the islands, though there are sharks in abundance in the seas around.

History. Probably the Arabs were the first to see the Seychelles, but they did not settle there, and the Portuguese sighted the archipelago in the early 16th century. The first recorded landing was made in 1609 by an

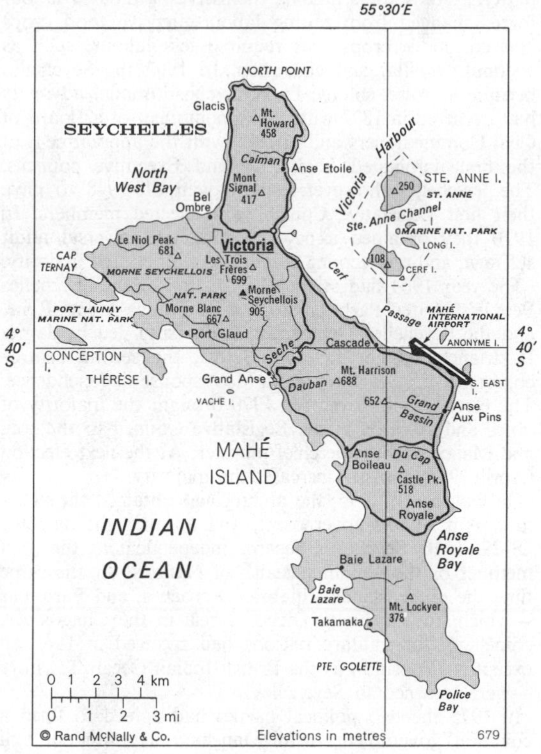

SEYCHELLES

expedition of the English East India Company, which found the islands uninhabited and abounding in water, fish, birds, and fruits. During the early 18th century they proved to be ideal hideouts for pirates.

In 1742 Bertrand-François Mahé, comte de La Bourdonnais, the French governor of Mauritius, sent Capt. Lazare Picault to explore the islands. Picault eventually anchored in a bay on the southwest coast of Mahé, which he named. The French, however, made no real attempt to annex Mahé and its surrounding islands till 1756, when a frigate was sent to take possession and forestall the British. The islands were named Séchelles, later altered by the British to Seychelles. In 1770 the first colonists began to arrive from Réunion. They so depleted the forests and the giant tortoises for exports that in 1789 they were confined to fixed areas and forbidden to trade. By the early 19th century the population had grown to more than 2,000. War between France and Britain did not affect the islands till 1794, when a British squadron appeared and demanded unconditional surrender. The Seychelles were finally ceded to Britain in 1814, by the Treaty of Paris, and were incorporated as a dependency of Mauritius, which by that time the British also had taken from France.

Seychelles, Area and Population

	area		population	
	sq mi	sq km	1960 census	1977 census
Central (granitic) group				
Mahé and satellites	59.3	153.6	33,000	54,600
Praslin and satellites	17.3	44.8	4,000	4,300
Silhouette	6.3	16.3	800	400
La Digue and satellites	5.6	14.5	2,000	1,900
Other islands	1.6	4.1	150	...
Outer (coralline) islands	81.3	210.6	1,050	700
Total Seychelles*	171.4	444.0	41,000	61,900

*Details may not add to total given because of rounding.
Source: Official government figures; René Moreux et Cie., *Marchés tropicaux et méditerranéens.*

Under British rule the Seychelles entered a long period of peaceful obscurity. The abolition of slavery in the 1830s produced a fundamental change in the agricultural pattern. The settlers, finding themselves without a labour force, changed from raising labour-intensive food crops and cotton to crops that required less labour, such as coconut, vanilla, and cinnamon. In 1903 the Seychelles became a crown colony. Previous constitutional advances had occurred in 1872 with the appointment of a Board of Civil Commissioners and in 1888 with the appointment of the first nominated Legislative and Executive councils. The Seychelles, however, had to wait till 1948 to have their first Legislative Council with elected members. In 1970 they obtained a new constitution, universal adult suffrage, and a governing council with an elected majority.

The year 1964 had seen the formation of the Seychelles People's United Party (SPUP), led by France-Albert René, and the Seychelles Democratic Party (SDP), led by James R. Mancham. The first was leftist, the second centre-conservative, but both came to espouse independence. The elections of November 1970 brought the majority of votes and 10 seats in the Legislative Council to the SDP, and Mancham became chief minister. At the next election (April 1974) the SDP increased its majority.

On October 1, 1975, the archipelago obtained the absolute right of self-government, and at midnight on June 28–29, 1976, Seychelles became independent as the 36th member of the Commonwealth of Nations. At the same time the outer islands Aldabra, Desroches, and Farquhar —which, together with Diego García in the Chagos Archipelago, for military reasons had received in 1965 an exceptional position as the British Indian Ocean Territory —were returned to Seychelles.

In 1975 the two political parties had agreed to form a coalition government, with Mancham as president and René as prime minister. On June 5, 1977, while Mancham was in London, rebels seized control of the police headquarters and other public buildings and invited René to assume the presidency. He did so, announcing that his government, while certainly not Marxist, would develop a form of socialism appropriate for the country.

The people. The original French colonists on the previously uninhabited islands, and their black slaves, were joined in the 19th century by deportees from France and by a few British. Asians from China, India, and Malaya arrived later in smaller numbers. Widespread intermarriage has resulted in a population of mixed descent.

The census of 1960 put the total population at 41,041, that of 1971 showed that the figure had risen to about 52,400, and that of 1977 showed 61,898. More than 90 percent of the people live on Mahé, a quarter in the capital, Victoria. The coral islands have no permanent population. The large increase of population during the 1970s (17 percent between 1970 and 1977) was for the most part attributable to development on Mahé.

All along the coasts of the main granitic islands are small villages, many of them populated by fishermen and their families, made up of thatched cottages clustered around a church and facing the sea. On the small islands there are only isolated cottages near the beaches.

English and French are the official languages. The mother tongue of most Seychellois, however, is Creole, a patois that is a mixture of clipped French (much of it archaic) with words from African languages and a few mutilated English words. About 90 percent of the population is Roman Catholic.

The economy. The so-called tertiary economic sector (commerce, transport, banking, insurance, tourism, administration, domestic services) is the most important in Seychelles' economic life, followed by agriculture, forestry, fishing, and the building industry. There is almost total absence of industrial plants. Tourism is of growing importance in the economy. About 15,200 visitors came to the islands in 1972, 49,500 in 1976, and the projection for 1981 is 80,000. The traditional export products that brought in foreign currency (cinnamon, copra, guano) are gradually losing importance.

Completion of the road system, the water-supply system, and the internal communications (road and air) system are planned. The harbour of Victoria has been enlarged and modernized. The international airport, near Victoria, was opened in 1971, the first modern hotel in 1972.

Administration and social conditions. The constitution of the Republic of Seychelles (1976) provides for a president of state at the head of the executive branch. He is responsible especially for foreign affairs, defense, and internal security, and he nominates and dismisses the ministers. The Cabinet consists of the prime minister and 10 other ministers, all of whom must be members of the unicameral National Assembly (25 elected members). There is a Supreme Court and a Court of Appeal for both criminal and civil matters. Since 1977 the regime has been enlarging the country's security forces.

Education standards have been rising steadily, as is shown by the literacy rate of 74 percent among persons aged 15 to 29. Though education is not compulsory, 95 percent of children of primary school age attend school. Six-year primary school is free. Children over 12 may attend secondary grammar school (admission by examination) or junior secondary school followed by technical and vocational courses. There is a teacher-training college, and scholarships are awarded for further education overseas.

Seychelles has few tropical diseases. Tuberculosis, leprosy, and filariasis, once common, are declining. The main islands have adequate hospitals and clinics.

Prospects for the future. The policy of the government is to support fishing and agriculture. The prospects for industry are negligible because the internal market is so small and the islands have no mineral resources apart from guano. An appropriate promotion of tourism and the development of the fishing industry are promising, however. In the foreseeable future, the Republic of Seychelles will be dependent upon foreign aid.

(WILHELM RUDOLF MARQUARDT)

BOOK OF THE YEAR

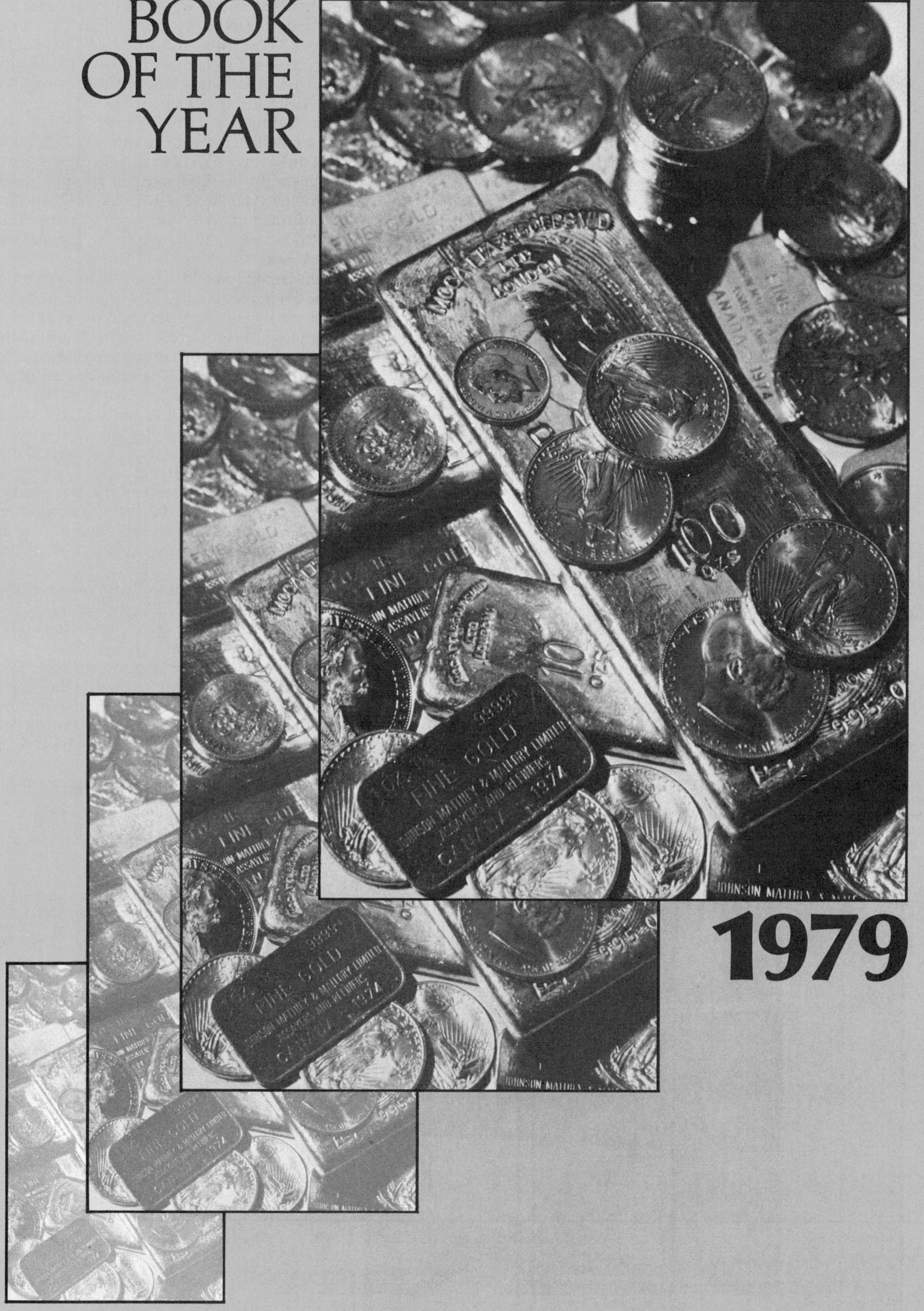

1979

Aerial Sports

The same Paul MacCready-Bryan Allen team that in 1977 won the £50,000 Kremer Prize for developing the world's first successful human-powered aircraft electrified sport aviation on June 12, 1979, with an even more spectacular feat: the first flight of a human-powered aircraft across the English Channel. For this the pair received a £100,000 prize, also established by Englishman Henry Kremer.

Allen, a Bakersfield, Calif., biochemist and bicycle racer, pedaled and piloted the team's chain-driven "Gossamer Albatross" 37 km (23 mi) from near Folkestone, England, to Cap Gris-Nez, France, in just under three hours. He never exceeded 4½ m (15 ft) in altitude and at times dipped to within inches of the Channel's heavy swells. The "Albatross," made largely of polyester, weighed approximately 9 kg (20 lb) less than the 35-kg (77-lb) "Gossamer Condor," in which Allen made his landmark 4.8-km (3-mi) flight in 1977, but had the same 29-m (96-ft) wingspan.

Though no world championship was scheduled until 1980 and the off-year Smirnoff Sailplane Derby "unofficial championship" was canceled for lack of sponsorship, there still were some exciting moments in international soaring in 1979. Flying an Astir CS N75SW sailplane over Pikes Peak in Colorado, artist and fashion model Sabrina Jackintell of the United States set a new glider altitude record for women of 12,637 m (41,460 ft). Another women's world record of 801.7 km (498.15 mi) for distance to and back from a goal was set over the Appalachian Mountains by West Germany's Hanna Reitsch (*see* OBITUARIES) in an ASW 20. A women's world record for triangular distance of 779.68 km (484.47 mi) was achieved by Great Britain's Karla Elizabeth Karel in a Glider LS-3 near Tocumwal, Australia, and a women's 100-km (62-mi) course speed record of 139.45 kph (86.65 mph) was set by Australia's Susan Martin near Waikerie, Australia, in a Planeur LS-3.

West Germany's Hans Werner Grosse set a world triangular distance record of 1,229.256 km (763.82 mi) in an ASW 17 near Alice Springs, Australia. A multiplace glider record for speed over a 750-km (465-mi) course of 122.26 kph (75.96 mph) was confirmed for West Germany's Erwin Muller and Otto Schaffner in a Janus near Bitterwasser, South Africa.

At the second world hang gliding championships at Grenoble, France, July 30 through August 12, first place in the 1st Class Division went to Josef Guggenmos of West Germany with 37,192 points. Johnny Carr of Great Britain was second with 36,688 points, and Gerard Thevenot of France was third with 35,304. In the 2nd Class Division, Rex Miller of the U.S. was first with 33,497 points, Wolfgang Hartl of Austria placed second with 32,463 points, and Hans Olschewsky of West Germany finished third with 31,993.

Despite the coldest weather the area had experienced in more than 100 years, 33 contestants were able to complete all six tasks and a "hare and hound" race at the fourth world hot-air balloon championships, held at Uppsala, Sweden, January 2–10. First place went to Paul Woessner of the U.S. with 5,274 points. Sid Cutter of the U.S. was second with 5,202 points, and Olivier Roux DeVillas of France finished third with 4,888.

The legendary Gordon Bennett Balloon Race, which had been discontinued since the start of World War II, was revived after an interruption of four decades in 1979 and held with a starting point at Long Beach, Calif., May 26 to 29. The U.S. pair

In the dim light of dawn the fragile "Gossamer Albatross," a man-powered aircraft, rises over the English Channel on the start of its trip to France. American Bryan Allen was both engine and pilot.

KEYSTONE

PAUL PROCTER—U.S. PARACHUTE ASSOCIATION

The U.S. free-fall parachute team set a new record in forming a ten-way speed star at the third World Parachute Relative Work Championships on August 31 at Chateauroux, France.

of Ben Abruzzo and Maxie Anderson, veterans of the historic "Double Eagle II" balloon crossing of the Atlantic Ocean in 1978, took first place, flying 938 km (583 mi) in 47 hours 8 minutes to Dove Creek, Colo.

Carol Davis of the U.S. set a world women's altitude record for hot-air balloons measuring between 900 and 1,200 cu m. In a Firefly over Moriarty, N.M., she reached 7,546 m (24,760 ft).

The four-member DaVinci TransAmerica team led by Vera Simons of McLean, Va., attempted the first balloon crossing of the North American continent, lifting off from Tillamook, Ore., on September 26. Despite serious difficulties over the Rocky Mountains they reached northwest Ohio, only to be knocked down by a severe thunderstorm on October 2.

At the third World Parachute Relative Work Championships on August 31 at Chateauroux, France, the eight-man team competition was won by the U.S., scoring 66 points in nine jumps. Second place went to the Canadian team, with 49 points, and third to France, with 46. The four-man team contest was won by Canada, scoring 82 points in ten jumps. Britain placed second with 77 points, and Australia finished third with 73. The U.S. team set a world record of 5.16 sec for the formation of a ten-way speed star, breaking the 8.8-sec record set by a Soviet team in 1978.

Former astronaut Neil Armstrong, the first man on the Moon, set a world altitude record for business aircraft of 15,584.6 m (51,130.56 ft) while flying a Learjet 28 N9RS between Wichita, Kan., and Elizabeth City, N.C. (MICHAEL D. KILIAN)

Afghanistan

A people's republic in central Asia, Afghanistan is bordered by the U.S.S.R., China, Pakistan, and Iran. Area: 653,000 sq km (252,100 sq mi). Pop. (1979 est.): 21,452,000, including (1978 est.) Pashtoon 50%; Tadzhik 25%; Uzbek 9%; Hazara 9%. Cap. and largest city: Kabul (pop., 1979 est., 891,700). Language: Persian and Pashto. Religion: Islam predominates. Presidents of the Revolutionary Council in 1979, Nur Mohammad Taraki to September 16, Hafizullah Amin to December 27, and Babrak Karmal; prime ministers, Taraki to March 27, Amin to December 27, and Karmal.

Political turmoil and rebellion continued to afflict Afghanistan in 1979. In a Cabinet reshuffle at the end of March, Pres. Nur Mohammad Taraki inducted Hafizullah Amin (*see* OBITUARIES) as prime minister and himself took over chairmanship of the Supreme Defense Council. On September 16 Taraki was overthrown and killed in a coup,

AFGHANISTAN

Education. (1978–79) Primary, pupils 942,817, teachers 29,789; secondary, pupils 92,401, teachers 4,503; vocational, pupils 12,118, teachers 889; teacher training, students 6,629, teachers 406; higher, students 12,480, teaching staff 1,062.

Finance. Monetary unit: afghani, with (Sept. 17, 1979) a free rate of 44 afghanis to U.S. $1 (95 afghanis = £1 sterling). Gold, SDR's, and foreign exchange (June 1979) U.S. $441 million. Budget (1976–77 est.): revenue 13,950,000,000 afghanis; expenditure 11,168,000,000 afghanis. Money supply (Feb. 1979) 28,584,000,000 afghanis.

Foreign Trade. (1978–79) Imports *c.* U.S. $378 million; exports *c.* U.S. $314 million. Import sources (1975–76): U.S.S.R. 24%; Japan 19%; West Germany 12%; India 12%; U.S. 7%. Export destinations (1975–76): U.S.S.R. 39%; Pakistan 12%; India 12%; West Germany 10%; U.K. 7%. Main exports: fruits and nuts 39%; natural gas 15%; cotton 14%; carpets 14%; karakul (persian lamb) skins 5%.

Transport and Communications. Roads (1977) 18,580 km. Motor vehicles in use (1978): passenger 26,000; commercial (including buses) 26,700. Air traffic (1977): 290 million passenger-km; freight 11 million net ton-km. Telephones (March 1978) 23,200. Radio receivers (Dec. 1976) *c.* 906,000. Television receivers (March 1979) 20,000.

Agriculture. Production (in 000; metric tons; 1978): corn *c.* 800; wheat 2,830; rice *c.* 448; barley *c.* 415; grapes *c.* 438; cotton, lint *c.* 54; wool, clean *c.* 14. Livestock (in 000; 1977): cattle *c.* 3,800; karakul sheep (1976) *c.* 6,200; other sheep *c.* 16,000; goats *c.* 3,000; horses *c.* 370; asses *c.* 1,250; camels *c.* 290.

Industry. Production (in 000; metric tons; 1977–78): coal 173; natural gas (cu m) 2,582,000; cotton fabrics (m) 76,800; rayon fabrics (m) 29,700; nitrogenous fertilizers (nutrient content) 38; cement 125; electricity (kw-hr) *c.* 810,000.

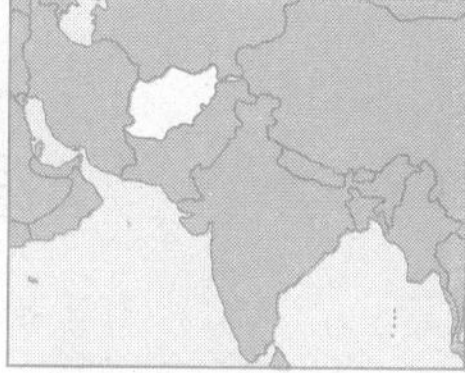

Afghanistan

Aden: *see* Yemen, People's Democratic Republic of

Advertising: *see* Industrial Review

Aerospace Industry: *see* Defense; Industrial Review; Space Exploration; Transportation

UPI

Babrak Karmal became president of Afghanistan after Soviet forces invaded the country and established him in power.

and Amin became president of the Revolutionary Council, which was nominally in charge of running the government, together with the Central Committee of the Khalq ("masses") Party and the Council of Ministers. On December 27 Amin, in turn, was overthrown and killed in a coup backed by Soviet troops. His successor, ex-deputy prime minister Babrak Karmal, had been in exile in Eastern Europe.

After the 1978 coup that overthrew Mohammad Daud, orthodox Muslims had remained hostile toward the new regime's experiment in "scientific socialism" and had been encouraged by the islamization policies undertaken in Pakistan and Iran. Skirmishes between rebels and Afghan troops spread from the countryside to the towns. In August the government had to use its massive Soviet-supplied firepower to crush a rebellion in the army fort of Bala Hissar near the capital, with several hundred casualties. Early in September a rebel force was routed near Kabul in a major battle, and later an offensive was mounted to destroy guerrillas in districts bordering Pakistan.

On September 19 a general amnesty was declared in an ineffective effort to placate the Muslims. This was followed by an administrative purge and a further attempt at reconciliation with Islam. Kabul radio accused Pakistan and Iran of sending armed infiltrators to undermine the government. Pakistan was also charged with arming the Afghan refugees and tribal rebels in the border areas with the help of Saudi Arabia, China, and the U.S. Afghan refugees in Pakistan were at one time estimated to number 140,000.

After the signing of a friendship treaty with the Soviet Union in December 1978, the Soviet presence in Afghanistan had grown steadily. Following the murder of U.S. Ambassador Adolph Dubs on February 14 in Kabul, the U.S. announced that aid to Afghanistan would be cut. As Western aid dwindled, Soviet and Eastern European trade and economic cooperation increased.

Late in December the Soviets began a massive military airlift into Kabul, and at least two motorized divisions crossed the Soviet-Afghan border. Amin, who—possibly at Soviet insistence—had moved from central Kabul to an outlying area, was captured and shot on December 27. His replacement, Karmal, whose Parcham ("flag") Party had spearheaded the coup against Daud but later lost power to the faction led by Taraki and Amin, was considered more pro-Soviet than Amin had been. At year's end reports from Kabul indicated that some 40,000 Soviet troops were fanning out through the country in an apparent attempt to crush the Muslim rebels. (GOVINDAN UNNY)

African Affairs

Far-reaching changes transformed the African continent's political configuration during 1979. Its three most notorious regimes—those of Idi Amin in Uganda, Francisco Macías Nguema in Equatorial Guinea, and Bokassa I in the Central African Empire—were swept away; the tide against military rule continued with the return of parliamentary democratic systems to Nigeria and Ghana. Crucially important was the agreement to end the 14-year-old conflict in Rhodesia and to return the country to legality under British rule as a prelude to its independence as Zimbabwe Rhodesia.

While war continued in the Western Sahara, there was hope of mediation, and the decade of conflict in Chad appeared to be over. Egypt's decision to sign a peace treaty with Israel promised to move Afro-Arab relations in a new direction. Only the conflicts in the Horn of Africa and in the south retained their menace.

The Organization of African Unity. The OAU held its 16th annual summit conference in July in Monrovia, Liberia, whose president, William R. Tolbert, became chairman for 1979–80. While the African leaders welcomed the overthrow of Uganda's President Amin, there was some criticism (led by Sudan and Nigeria) of Tanzania's military role in Uganda, on the grounds that any military attack across the border of a member state infringed a basic principle of the OAU charter. An attempt by Arab nations to denounce Egypt's peace treaty with Israel failed, but full support was given to the right of the Palestinians to an independent homeland. The right of the Western Saharans to self-determination was broadly accepted; this decision marked a substantial diplomatic defeat for Morocco. Two major new decisions were made—to adopt a human rights charter for Africa, and to hold a continental conference to discuss the now openly acknowledged failures of the economic policies of many African nations.

Southern Africa. The installation of a majority-rule government in Rhodesia under Bishop Abel Muzorewa (*see* BIOGRAPHIES), following his electoral victory in April, did not defuse the conflict inside the country and across its borders in Mozambique, Botswana, and Zambia. The world community withheld legal recognition from the Muzorewa government and continued to maintain sanctions. In August the Commonwealth conference in Lusaka, Zambia, reached agreement on a new approach to settling the dispute. This led the British government to take an initiative which brought the two parties in the conflict—Bishop Muzorewa's government and the Patriotic Front, led by Joshua Nkomo and Robert Mugabe—together, under British chairmanship, at Lancaster House, London, in September. After talks lasting more than two months, both sides agreed upon the terms of a settlement. It comprised a cease-fire, the temporary resumption by Britain of its legal authority in Salisbury, new elections to be held under Commonwealth supervision, and the promise of independence after the elections.

In Namibia the UN's initiative to achieve an internationally accepted settlement for the territory's independence made little progress in 1979. Meanwhile, the situation on the border between Namibia and Angola remained troubled, with guerrillas of the South West Africa People's Organization (SWAPO) continuing their insurgency operations and the South African Army making periodic attacks on the SWAPO bases in Angola. Along the border, too, the forces of the National Union for the Total Independence of Angola (UNITA), led by Jonas Savimbi, continued to harass the Angolan regime, which relied heavily on the support of about 20,000 Cuban combat troops.

Prime Minister Pieter W. Botha's new regime in South Africa showed itself willing to make changes in the apartheid system, but these modifications stopped short of making any concessions over the question of political rights for the black majority, which remained the principal issue at the core of South Africa's difficulties internally and abroad. Meanwhile, the South African authorities pressed forward with their policy of creating independent black homelands, Venda in 1979 becoming the third such to acquire this status.

The Horn of Africa. Ethiopia's relations with its neighbours—Somalia, Djibouti, and Sudan—remained troubled, but the fulcrum of the fighting was Ethiopia's dissident province of Eritrea, where resistance movements continued to fight for independence despite the superiority of the military forces against them. The Ethiopian military regime of Lieut. Col. Mengistu Haile Mariam remained determined to establish a Marxist-Leninist system of government, which had the committed support of the Soviet bloc and Cuba. Although Somalia had withdrawn its armed units from Ethiopia's Ogaden region in 1978, insurgent activity by local Somalis continued throughout 1979. Sporadic fighting also took place in the neighbouring provinces of Arusi and Sidamo, while security in the northern Tigre Province, adjoining Eritrea, declined. Most Arab nations, except South Yemen and Libya, supported the opposition to the Ethiopian regime. Kenya firmly supported the Mengistu regime, principally because of a possible Somali threat to its Northeastern Province.

Coups and Inter-African Relations. The successful invasion of Uganda by the Tanzanian armed forces that ended in April was the first time that an African state carried out an open military attack to overthrow a neighbouring regime. Tanzania's Pres. Julius Nyerere (*see* BIOGRAPHIES) offered as justification that he was acting in self-defense against the earlier invasion of his territory by Amin's forces and against the threat of future attacks; but he also justified his action by denouncing Amin as "a black fascist" who had brought "shame on Africa." While his action was widely applauded, it caused soul-searching within the OAU (*see* above) as well as further harming Tanzania's relations with Kenya and with Libya, which had sent several thousand soldiers in a futile attempt to save Amin from defeat. Libya's policy came in for criticism from a number of African nations because of its military intervention in the civil war in Chad, which had helped prevent the creation of a coalition government to rees-

KEYSTONE

At a military airfield near Paris, French soldiers guard the private plane of deposed Central African Emperor Bokassa I, who fled from his country in September, before he flew on to the Ivory Coast. France refused to give Bokassa asylum and he was not permitted to leave the plane. Among the charges against him was personal participation in the massacre of a group of young children.

BILL CAMPBELL—SYGMA

Joshua Nkomo addressed the heads of state in Liberia at the 16th annual summit meeting of the Organization of African Unity in July.

tablish national unity. Libya also furthered political moves to overthrow Egypt's Pres. Anwar as-Sadat because of his peace treaty with Israel.

Conflict over the Western Sahara poisoned relations between Morocco and Algeria, which supported the Western Saharans in their bid for independence. Mauritania, previously Morocco's partner in this conflict, changed its position during the year and surrendered its claims to part of the Western Sahara. The OAU threw its weight behind an initiative to persuade Morocco to accept the Saharans' right to self-determination.

There were three successful military coups during the year. In June a military administration, led by Flight Lieut. Jerry Rawlings (*see* BIOGRAPHIES), overthrew the military-civilian government in Ghana. An army coup in August put an end to the 11-year tyrannical reign of President Macías Nguema (*see* OBITUARIES). During the following month Emperor Bokassa I of the Central African Empire was deposed in a coup supported by French military forces.

Political Systems. The year witnessed some movement toward more democratic government. After the overthrow of Amin and Bokassa, both Uganda and the Central African Republic announced their intention to restore multiparty parliamentary democracy, the latter after a stabilizing period. Vigorous and free parliamentary elections in Ghana and Nigeria not only ended military rule but also set a powerful example for other West African states. Botswana's successful multiparty election resulted in an even bigger majority for the ruling party of Pres. Sir Seretse Khama. Zanzibar, the partner state in the United Republic of Tanzania, adopted a new constitution restoring the elective principle to the island.

Although Kenya was a single-party nation, its first elections since the death of its charismatic first president, Jomo Kenyatta, held in November, resulted in a peaceful political catharsis in which many unpopular older politicians were defeated. The election gave a strong mandate to Kenyatta's successor, Pres. Daniel arap Moi.

External Relations. Soviet and Cuban involvement in the continent showed no sign of increasing significantly. Their role was strongly maintained in Ethiopia but without any enlargement of their military forces; at the same time there was no reduction in the strength of Cuban troops in Angola. The Soviet-bloc countries increased the level of their technical and economic aid programs in Ethiopia but not elsewhere.

Of the Western countries, France was the most prominent in its support of certain African governments; it chaired the sixth Franco-African summit meeting at Kigali, Rwanda, in May, formed to further cooperation between the 24 African states eligible to attend and France, and it openly helped in overthrowing Bokassa. The U.S. gave additional military support to Morocco but explained its decision as being intended to assist in helping toward a peaceful solution of the Western Sahara conflict. The U.S. role in bringing about a peace treaty between Egypt and Israel was generally supported in Africa, except among some Arab states, notably Libya and Algeria.

The 44 African countries that belonged to the African, Caribbean, and Pacific (ACP) group signed the second Lomé Convention with the European Economic Community in November. The negotiations had lasted for over a year and were regarded as unsatisfactory by the ACP.

Social and Economic Conditions. Almost half the world's 8.5 million refugees were to be found in Africa. The OAU decided at its 1979 summit to deal actively with the social and economic problems of these exiles and to try to halt any increase in their numbers. The OAU also decided to mark the UN International Year of the Child by paying particular attention to the needs of African children. More than 40% of the continent's children under five experienced a period of acute malnutrition; 156 out of every 1,000 infants died before the age of one, as compared with 102 in Asia, 24 in Europe, and 19 in North America; and almost 2 million African children were classified as refugees. Illiteracy in the continent grew by 56 million during 1960–70; only 43% of children between 6 and 15 were in school. But the World Health Organization found in 1979 that smallpox had been eradicated in Africa, its last stronghold.

Thirty of the continent's 50 states had declined economically since 1974, the UN Economic Commission for Africa reported. While the 20 countries with a per capita gross domestic product (GDP) of over $300 achieved an average real annual growth rate during that period of 6.8%, the other 30 countries, with an average per capita GDP of below $200, achieved a real growth rate of barely 1% in 1976 and 2–3% in 1977. According to World Bank figures the annual GDP growth of all African countries averaged 2.6% between 1970 and 1976 and was expected to reach only 3.8% in 1985–90, as compared with Asia's average in 1970–76 of 5.1% and all the industrialized countries' 4.2%. The total external public debt of countries south of the Sahara more than tripled from $9,289,700,000 in 1971 to $30,252,000,000 in 1977. The increased cost of oil imports was a major element in the retrogression of all but the few oil-producing countries in the continent. (COLIN LEGUM)

See also Dependent States; articles on the various political units.

Agriculture and Food Supplies

World food production in 1979 fell from the record levels achieved in 1978 primarily because of a severe drop in Soviet output and substantially smaller production in India. Grain stocks, however, remained ample, although concentrated heavily in the major grain-exporting countries—particularly in the United States. Negotiations for a new international Wheat Trade Convention designed to promote world food security and market stability adjourned indefinitely early in the year without agreement, but prospects appeared better for completing a new international food aid convention.

Production Indexes. World agricultural output (excluding China) fell 2% in 1979, the first decline in seven years, according to preliminary estimates (in December 1979) of the Economics, Statistics, and Cooperatives Service of the U.S. Department of Agriculture (USDA). Drought in the U.S.S.R. and in India was primarily responsible for the reduction, although harvests were also smaller in many other parts of the world compared with the generally high level of output achieved in 1978 because of unusually widespread favourable weather conditions. Agricultural production fell 2.7% in the developed countries as a whole; a 12% drop in Soviet production and smaller declines in other regions more than offset a better than 5% increase in the U.S. Production in the less developed countries fell about 0.8%, although increases were registered in East Asia and Latin America. China appeared to have achieved a moderate increase in output.

World food production fell about 2.4%, largely reflecting the decline in grain harvests. Per capita world food production declined more than 3.5%, with output in the developed countries falling a little more and that in the less developed countries a little less.

Among the less developed regions food production fell most sharply in South Asia, influenced primarily by a 9% decline in Indian output. India was expected to cope with this shortfall by drawing on grain stocks built up in the previous two years. Although production was down again in Bangladesh, the food crisis there was easing thanks to more extensive and better organized imports and relief efforts. African food production fell only a little, but rapid population growth pushed per capita output well below the levels of the mid-1960s.

As of mid-November 1979 the United Nations Food and Agriculture Organization (FAO) listed 25 countries as affected by abnormal food shortages as a result of poor crops, the effects of war, or difficult economic situations. Sixteen of the countries were in Africa, five in Asia, two in the Middle East, and two in Latin America. The food situation was most critical in Cambodia, where a complicated political situation hampered relief efforts.

WIDE WORLD

During the record 1979 grain harvest in the U.S. even coal cars were pressed into use to haul the grain from the upper Midwest to ports on the Gulf Coast.

Table I. Indexes of World Agricultural and Food Production (excluding China)
1961–65=100

Region or country	Total agricultural production						Total food production						Per capita food production					
	1974	1975	1976	1977	1978	1979[1]	1974	1975	1976	1977	1978	1979[1]	1974	1975	1976	1977	1978	1979[1]
Developed countries	129	128	134	137	144	140	131	130	137	139	147	142	118	161	121	123	128	123
United States	117	126	129	136	136	143	122	134	137	143	144	152	109	119	120	124	125	130
Canada	112	127	139	143	146	137	112	128	142	144	148	138	95	106	117	117	118	108
Western Europe	128	125	123	129	136	134	129	125	123	129	136	134	119	116	113	118	124	122
Eastern Europe	140	138	144	144	149	147	141	138	145	145	150	148	131	128	133	132	136	132
U.S.S.R.	145	130	153	149	163	144	144	128	153	148	163	142	129	113	134	128	141	121
Japan	110	115	109	118	117	116	111	115	109	118	117	116	97	100	94	101	98	96
Oceania	119	124	124	121	135	129	127	135	138	133	152	142	104	110	111	105	119	110
South Africa	146	135	135	146	150	142	155	142	143	153	157	148	115	103	101	106	106	98
Less developed countries	134	141	144	150	155	154	135	145	149	154	159	158	103	108	108	109	110	106
East Asia	149	156	165	168	171	176	147	155	164	167	170	175	112	116	120	119	119	120
Indonesia	138	140	145	146	157	153	140	142	144	149	161	156	109	108	107	108	114	108
Philippines	146	161	172	173	175	180	147	163	173	175	177	183	108	116	121	119	118	118
South Korea	144	158	170	176	170	187	141	155	167	170	165	181	110	118	125	126	120	129
Thailand	156	162	167	167	181	180	157	167	173	169	182	180	115	119	121	115	122	117
South Asia	124	138	135	147	154	144	124	140	137	150	157	146	97	107	103	110	113	103
Bangladesh	109	122	114	126	125	123	114	128	118	130	127	124	87	95	86	92	88	84
India	122	139	135	147	156	143	122	140	137	149	158	144	96	109	104	111	115	104
Pakistan	162	155	165	184	178	192	164	161	177	193	190	200	119	114	122	129	123	126
West Asia	144	154	168	166	171	167	141	154	168	166	171	168	104	110	117	112	113	107
Iran	160	179	193	189	199	192	160	183	197	192	203	197	116	129	135	128	130	123
Turkey	136	150	163	164	164	159	131	149	160	161	162	158	100	111	116	114	112	107
Africa	125	128	129	128	131	131	125	130	132	129	133	132	95	96	95	91	91	88
Egypt	118	119	120	118	123	126	125	131	132	129	132	136	96	99	97	93	93	94
Ethiopia	111	107	104	100	95	98	109	100	97	92	88	91	84	75	71	66	61	62
Nigeria	119	121	123	125	126	125	119	121	124	126	127	126	90	89	88	87	86	83
Latin America	139	142	145	152	157	161	145	152	158	163	168	173	108	110	112	112	112	112
Mexico	143	151	147	153	159	162	150	169	164	166	175	180	103	112	105	103	105	104
Argentina	122	124	133	134	149	152	126	127	138	138	155	158	109	109	116	115	127	128
Brazil	152	153	158	170	166	176	164	168	185	193	186	197	121	121	130	132	124	128
World	131	133	138	142	148	145	132	135	141	144	151	147	113	113	117	118	122	118

[1] Preliminary.
Source: U.S. Department of Agriculture, Economics, Statistics, and Cooperatives Service.

Grains. The world grain situation tightened in 1979. The 1979–80 harvest, although the second largest on record, was forecast to be smaller than the 1978–79 crop, which had been favoured by unusually good weather. World trade in grains rose sharply, although the growth in total grain utilization slowed. Grain stocks were expected to be substantially smaller by season's end.

World grain production (wheat, coarse grains, and milled rice) was forecast—based on December estimates of crops already harvested in the Northern Hemisphere and preharvest reports in the Southern Hemisphere—to fall about 4% below the 1978–79 level of 1,450,000,000 metric tons. Output fell 63 million tons and was down in most world regions, with the United States and China the major exceptions. The U.S.S.R. reported a 58 million-ton decline from the previous year's extraordinarily good harvest of 237 million tons, resulting in the nation's smallest grain crop since 1975. World grain yields were expected to be down about 4% from the 2.08 tons per hectare in 1978–79, while harvested area was forecast to decline less than 0.5% from 718 million ha (1 ha = 2.5 ac).

World grain utilization was expected to be only slightly higher than in 1978–79 but to exceed 1979–80 production by about 2%. Larger Soviet imports, 18 million tons above the 15 million imported in 1978–79 and 7 million above the 26 million in 1975–76, were expected to be largely responsible for a nearly 12% increase in world grain trade. The U.S. was expected to supply most of the increase. Canadian and Australian exports were expected to be restricted by transportation problems, and Argentine supplies were down.

World grain stocks were expected to fall 32 million tons by the end of 1979–80, with the largest reduction, estimated at about 16 million tons, in the Soviet Union. Reductions were also forecast for both Western and Eastern Europe, India, and Japan; stocks might rise in Japan and Australia. Stocks were expected to become more concentrated in the U.S. because those held by other nations were expected to fall one-fifth while U.S. stocks remained steady at about 72 million tons.

The proportion of grain utilization that stocks represent is one commonly used rough measure of world food security. By the end of 1979–80 world grain stocks were expected to equal 14% of utilization, compared with 16% in 1978–79. The low point for the 1970s was 10.7% in 1974–75, and the preshortage range in the late 1960s was 18–21%. A possibly better measure of the world's ability to meet threats of serious food shortages, particularly in the poor countries, is the percentage that combined wheat and rice stocks represent of the consumption of those grains; wheat and rice are the predominant source of calories in most less developed countries and are the grains most likely to be imported to fill food deficits there. Wheat and rice stocks were forecast to total 16.2% of combined wheat and rice consumption at the end of 1979–80, compared with 19.7% the previous year and 12.8% in 1974–75.

World wheat production declined sharply from the 1978–79 record level because of a Soviet crop that was 35 million tons smaller and reduced Eastern European, Canadian, Australian, and Western European harvests. Total harvested wheat area in the world was only slightly reduced, but yields were smaller. The most substantial 1979–80 increases in wheat output were in the U.S., India, China, and Pakistan. However, the spring 1980 Indian wheat harvest (1980–81 crop) was forecast to be substantially smaller than in 1979 because drought reduced the availability of irrigation water; about 75% of India's wheat is irrigated.

The growth in world utilization of wheat was expected to slow in 1979–80. Consumption was likely to expand in China, North Africa, Japan,

WIDE WORLD

Glacier, a young pig, made the *Guinness Book of World Records* as the most expensive boar in history. He was sold for $42,500 for stud use because he was considered such a perfect pig.

Latin America, and Western Europe, while reductions were in prospect for Eastern Europe, South Asia, and the U.S. World use of wheat for animal feed might increase 5% because of the anticipated strong increase in Soviet wheat feeding. In attempting to maintain its livestock herds, the U.S.S.R. was able to draw upon large supplies of low-quality wheat suitable for animal feeding because of the drought.

The anticipated increase in 1979–80 world wheat trade reflects a 7 million-ton increase in the level of Soviet wheat imports from 5.1 million in 1978–79, a 50% increase by Eastern Europe, and smaller increases in North Africa, the Middle East, Bangladesh, Vietnam, and several other less developed countries. Chinese and Pakistani wheat imports were expected to be sharply reduced because of improved production. The U.S., with 48% of the forecast wheat exports, and Australia were the only major wheat suppliers expected to expand shipments.

The general decline in wheat stocks around the world would be led by an estimated 14 million-ton decline in Soviet supplies. U.S. stocks were expected to equal about 27% of the world total by the end of 1979–80, compared with 24% in 1978–79.

Most of the expected reduction in 1979–80 rice output was the result of an estimated 13 million-ton (milled basis) decline from 1978–79 in the Indian harvest because of drought, although lower production was also likely in Burma, Indonesia, Thailand, and Japan. Larger crops were forecast for China, Brazil, Vietnam, and Bangladesh. The decline in Indian rice supplies was expected to reduce Indian rice consumption enough to generate an overall world reduction in 1979–80 rice consumption even though increased use was expected in most other areas.

Total coarse grain production was expected to decline in 1979–80 despite an increase in harvested area, a U.S. crop that was 12 million tons larger than in 1978–79, and smaller increases in South Africa, Brazil, and Eastern Europe. Soviet coarse grain production was estimated to have fallen 20% (21 million tons) because of drought, and Canadian output was down 8%. Production was also considered likely to decline in Australia, Western Europe, and Argentina.

World utilization of coarse grains was expected to be little changed from 1978–79. Sharply reduced use for animal feed in the U.S.S.R. because of smaller supplies roughly offset increases in Japan, the U.S., Eastern Europe, and East and Southeast Asia. Other factors restricting feeding included a slowdown in the expansion of Western European livestock production, fewer U.S. cattle on feed in the summer of 1979, and the weakening of feed demand by the hog and poultry industries in several developed countries. The dampening influence upon demand for meat of slowing economic growth reinforced these factors.

Soviet coarse grain imports were expected to exceed the 1978–79 level of 9.9 million tons by more than 11.5 million tons, almost matching the net increase in world coarse grain trade in 1979–80. The U.S. on Oct. 3, 1979, offered the Soviet Union permission to purchase a combined total of up to 25 million tons of wheat and corn in the fourth year (October 1979–September 1980) of the U.S.–Soviet grain agreement. The U.S.S.R. did not announce the level of its intended purchases and could determine the mix of grains as long as a minimum of three million tons each of wheat and corn was taken.

Coarse grain imports were also expected to rise in 1979–80 in Eastern Europe, Japan, Western Europe, Mexico, South Korea, and Israel, but to fall in Brazil and China. U.S. coarse grain exports were expected to rise 14 million tons and to account for 70% of world trade in coarse grains in 1979–80, compared with 64% in 1978–79. Canadian and Australian exports were expected to recover from

Table II. World Production and Trade of Principal Grains (in 000 metric tons)

	Wheat			Barley			Oats			Rye			Corn (Maize)			Rice		
	Production 1961–65 average	Production 1978	Imports− Exports+ 1975–78 average	Production 1961–65 average	Production 1978	Imports− Exports+ 1975–78 average	Production 1961–65 average	Production 1978	Imports− Exports+ 1975–78 average	Production 1961–65 average	Production 1978	Imports− Exports+ 1975–78 average	Production 1961–65 average	Production 1978	Imports− Exports+ 1975–78 average	Production 1961–65 average	Production 1978	Imports− Exports+ 1975–78 average
World total	254576	441474	−65633[1] +65292[1]	98474	196123	−12837[1] +13019[1]	47775	50463	−1427[1] +1406[1]	33849	32389	−593[1] +578[1]	216429	362971	−56585[1] +56800[1]	254711	376448	−8996[1] +9187[1]
Algeria	1254	c1800	−c1380	476	c610	−156	28	c90	−3[1] −1[1]	—	—	—	4	c2	−c115	7	c2	−8[1] +1[1]
Argentina	7541	8100	+c3055	679	554	+36	676	c676	+140	422	210	+2	4984	9700	+4571	193	.310	−2[1] +122
Australia	8222	18300	+8444	978	4000	+1757	1172	1800	+306	11	c14	−3[1]	176	130	−1[1] +18	136	490	−1[1] +234
Austria	704	1195	−5 +83	563	1424	−27 +1[1]	322	304	−14	393	410	+7[1]	197	1166	−39 +1[1]	—	—	−40
Bangladesh	37	259[2]	−c1300	15	15[2]	−1[1]	—	—	−1[1]	—	—	—	4	2[2]	—	15048	18898	−281
Belgium	826	c1020	−993[3] +564[3]	485	c800	−1277[3] +407[3]	389	c140	−70[3] +10[3]	120	61[2]	−16[3] +4[3]	2	30[2]	−2012[3] +663[3]	—	—	−109[3] +40[3]
Brazil	574	c2677	−c3110	26	145	−17	20	54	−c23	17	8	—	10112	13533	−c400 +1000	6123	7242	−27[1] +168
Bulgaria	2213	c3450	−c100 +c223	694	c1500	−93[1] +c19	141	88[2]	—	58	15[2]	−17[1]	1601	c2300	−c260 +c130	37	68[2]	−4[1]
Burma	38	94	—	—	—	—	—	—	—	—	—	—	58	75[2]	+7[1]	7786	10500	+c500
Canada	15364	21146	+12629	3860	10387	+3524	6075	3621	+259	319	605	+213	1073	4215	−636 +215	—	—	−74
Chile	1082	893	−c8120	74	126	+c10	89	93	+c6[1]	7	11	—	204	257	−c110	85	105	−c20
China	22200	c53000	−c5590	14200	c20000	−c300 +c1[1]	c1600	c1000	—	c1500	c1800	—	c22500	c40000	−c2200 +c90	c86000	c160000	−c40 +c1500
Colombia	118	38	−c340	106	119	−68	—	2	−8[1]	—	—	—	826	862	−c50 +3[1]	576	1715	−25[1] +78
Czechoslovakia	1779	c5600	−c470	1556	c3600	−c180 +c80	792	c440	−c1[1] +c10[1]	897	c615	−1[1] +3[1]	474	c628	−c670	—	—	−c80
Denmark	535	c653	−23 +194	3506	c6295	−143 +642	713	c210	−30 +5	380	c326	−2[1] +73	—	—	−248	—	—	−11 +1
Egypt	1459	1933	−3601	137	132	—	—	—	—	—	—	—	1913	3197	−c550	1845	2351	+173
Ethiopia	540	423	−92	628	c760	—	5	11	—	—	—	—	743	c1079	—	—	—	−1[1]
Finland	448	241	−37 +63	400	1565	−2[1] +110	828	1082	−2[1] +73	141	74	−10[1]	—	—	−52	—	—	−13
France	12495	21057	−366 +6469	6594	11414	−185 +2918	2583	2194	−1[1] +113	367	432	−3[1] +60	2760	9473	−897 +2000	120	45	−226 +32
Germany, East	1357	3147	−c1280 +c30[1]	1291	4135	−c570	850	595	−4[1]	1741	1895	−12[1]	3	c2	−c1570	—	—	−c40[1]
Germany, West	4607	8118	−1474 +785	3462	8608	−1584 +318	2185	3202	−338 +31	3031	2457	−89 +65	55	620	−3216 +266	—	—	−171 +48
Greece	1765	c2660	+c143	248	c956	−52 +7[1]	143	c101	—	19	c6	—	239	c537	−773	88	c92	−1[1] +17[1]
Hungary	2020	c5669	−23 +c819	970	c762	−82 +4[1]	108	69[2]	−11	271	c138	−7[1] +4[1]	3350	c6700	−c940 +c430	36	35[2]	−c21
India	11191	31328	−c3550 +275	2590	2309	+10[1]	—	—	−1[1]	—	—	—	4593	c5500	−6[1]	52733	c79010	−130 +25[1]
Indonesia	—	—	−c960	—	—	—	—	—	−1[1]	—	—	—	2804	2750	−c27 +c21	12396	25739	−1450
Iran	2873	c5700	−c1330	792	c1000	−c240	—	—	—	—	—	—	24	60	−c190	851	c1650	−c380 +1[1]
Iraq	849	c910	−c750 +1[1]	851	c607	−c75	—	—	—	—	—	−2[1]	2	82[2]	−20[1]	142	c172	−191
Ireland	343	247	−c195 +c19	575	1320	−c60 +c112	357	124	−10 +1	1	c1	—	—	—	−c260	—	—	−3[1]
Italy	8857	8764	−2555 +21	276	790	−1202 +1[1]	545	440	−c120 +1[1]	87	37	−7	3633	6040	−4203 +6	612	c950	−124 +393
Japan	1332	367	−5680	1380	326	−1646	145	20	−151	2	c1	−74	96	c11	−8839	16444	16000	−41 +23
Kenya	122	c144	−51 +2[1]	15	35	−1[1]	2	7	—	—	—	—	1110	c2350	+106	14	42	−3[1]
Korea, South	170	36	−1733	1148	c1348	−242	—	—	—	18	4	—	26	138	−1160	4809	8058	−182 +13[1]
Malaysia	—	—	−386[1]	—	—	—	—	—	−4[1]	—	—	−1[1]	8	c35	−323[1] +1[1]	1140	1590	−232[1] +20[1]
Mexico	1672	2643	−254 +20	175	505	−51[1]	76	60	−3[1]	—	—	—	7369	9616	−1650 +2[1]	314	397	+15[1]
Morocco	1516	1876	−1275	1514	c2328	−39[1]	18	8[2]	—	2	c2	—	405	c390	−34	20	c27	—
Netherlands, The	606	792	−1665 +899	390	355	−373 +246	421	140	−52 +77	312	68	−47 +14	—	c5	−4541 +1979	—	—	−163 +93
New Zealand	248	357	−42 +5[1]	98	282	+c44	34	50	—	—	c1	—	16	232	+24	—	—	−7[1]
Nigeria	16	c21	−c680	—	—	—	—	—	—	—	—	—	997	c1450	−c34	207	c580	−308
Norway	19	80	−300	440	668	−67	126	367	+14[1]	3	8	−51	—	—	−77	—	—	−7
Pakistan	4153	8289	−1276	118	121	+9[1]	—	—	—	—	—	—	514	c800	+4[1]	1824	4706	+742
Peru	150	c90	−c740	185	c175	−c27	4	c1	−c6[1]	1	c1	—	490	c550	−c220 +c9[1]	324	c400	−c60
Philippines	—	—	−637	—	—	—	—	—	−c4[1]	—	—	—	1305	3333	−118	3957	6907	−67 +51
Poland	2988	c6000	−2175	1368	c3700	−1450 +25	2641	c2500	−76 +2[1]	7466	c7400	−128 +23	20	232[2]	−1496	—	—	−82
Portugal	562	252	−433	61	39	−10[1] +3[1]	87	59	−5[1]	177	102	−8	617	443	−1357 +2[1]	167	131	−75
Romania	4321	6235	−c730 +c960	415	2285	−c87	154	61[2]	−c17[1]	95	c57	−28[1]	5853	10179	−c260 +c480	40	47[2]	−c52
South Africa	834	1730	−1[1] +c106	40	99	+6[1]	107	66	+c21	10	3	—	5248	9930	−28 +2586	2	c3	−98 +1[1]
Spain	4365	4795	−130 +2[1]	1959	7953	−2[1] +74	447	542	—	385	259	−3[1]	1101	1933	−4051 +2[1]	386	411	+47
Sweden	909	c1306	−12 +729	1167	c2452	−1[1] +163	1304	c1575	−9[1] +105	142	276	+116	—	—	−44	—	—	−21
Switzerland	355	407	−363	102	216	−477	40	56	−154	52	49	−18	14	108	−253	—	—	−24
Syria	1093	c1651	−c180 +1[1]	649	c729	−2[1] +22[1]	2	2	—	—	—	—	7	c66	−17[1]	1	c1	−c60
Thailand	—	—	−c84	—	—	—	—	—	—	—	—	—	816	3030	+1936	11267	c17000	+1873
Turkey	8585	c16500	−158[1] +628	3447	c4700	−4[1] +107	495	c370	—	734	c690	+7[1]	950	c1300	—	222	280	−41
U.S.S.R.	64207	120800	−c7250 +c1839	20318	c62100	−c940 +c850	6052	c18500	−c150 +c12[1]	15093	c13600	—	13122	c9000	−c8240 +c150	390	c2100	−c350 +c10
United Kingdom	3520	c6450	−3592 +186	6670	c9830	−554 +943	1541	c715	−37 +5	21	30	−30[1] +1[1]	—	2	−3560 +45	—	—	−195 +41
United States	33040	48954	−19 +28857	8676	9736	−197 +991	13848	8649	−16 +160	828	664	−11 +8	95561	179886	−52 +42110	3084	6251	−1[1] +2172
Uruguay	465	c150	+41	28	38[2]	−7 +4	66	17[2]	−1[1] +2[1]	—	—	—	148	172	+9[1]	67	226	+110
Venezuela	1	c1	−735	—	—	−1[1]	—	—	−c7	—	—	—	477	c740	−c430	136	c600	−31 +47
Yugoslavia	3599	5355	−347 +5[1]	557	c560	−c9 +7[1]	343	284	+4	169	81	−3[1]	5618	7555	+251	23	c30	−15[1]

Note: (—) indicates quantity nil or negligible. (c) indicates provisional or estimated. [1]1975–77 average. [2]1977. [3]Belgium-Luxembourg economic union.

Sources: *FAO Monthly Bulletin of Statistics; FAO Production Yearbook 1977; FAO Trade Yearbook 1977.*

(M. C. MacDONALD)

WIDE WORLD

A Montana farmer looks at some of the 670,000 eggs that he had to destroy because they had become contaminated with PCB's, chemicals that had accidentally been mixed into poultry feed.

the low levels of the previous two years, but Argentine shipments were expected to decline.

Although total coarse grain stocks were expected to decline, it was believed that those in the U.S. might rise a little. U.S. coarse grain stocks could represent 55% of world stocks by the end of 1979–80, compared with 49% a year earlier.

Protein Meal and Vegetable Oil. The strong growth in world production of both protein meals and fats and oils was continuing in 1979–80, but the growth in demand for oilseed products was expected to weaken because of slower expansion in livestock production as a result of the slowdown in economic growth in the developed countries. The 8% rise in 1978–79 apparent world consumption (world consumption adjusted by change in world stocks) of protein meals was strongly influenced by increased feeding rates throughout the world, resulting in part from sharply increased production of pork and poultry. In addition, Europe had a long, cold winter and late spring that led to more consumption of compound feed by dairy cattle.

Large increases in U.S. soybean (18%), cottonseed (34%), and sunflower seed (99%) output were expected to account for more than 60% of the rise in world production of protein meals for 1979–80. Brazil's spring 1980 soybean crop might be up 30% following two years of drought, and the rapid expansion of Argentine soybean production was expected to continue. Anticipated reductions in output were few, mainly small declines in European rapeseed and Indian peanuts.

The combination of lower prices for meal resulting from bumper crops and higher grain prices because of tighter supplies was expected to stimulate consumption of protein meals in 1979–80. Apparent world consumption of meals seemed likely to increase 8%, and import demand for soybeans and soybean meal, 5%. The strongest expansion in use of meal was under way in some less developed and centrally planned countries. In the developed countries demand for livestock products and, hence, for animal feeds, seemed likely to be restricted by anticipated slower economic growth. In the European Economic Community (EEC), which uses one-fourth of the world's protein meal, only a small increase in livestock numbers was expected.

Prices for protein meals and vegetable oils in 1978–79 were consistently above those of a year earlier despite abundant supplies and a small increase in U.S. stocks. World meal stocks were expected to increase substantially in 1979–80 and prices to reflect lower prices for oilseeds at the farm level. The buildup in vegetable oil stocks was expected to be more rapid than for meals. Most of the stock buildup was likely to be in the form of U.S. soybeans and Canadian rapeseed.

Pulses. World production of pulses may have increased slightly in 1979, despite reduced harvests in India, southern Africa, the U.S.S.R., and Western Europe. In Asia good harvests in China,

Table III. World Oilseed Products and Selected Crops

In 000,000 metric tons

Region and product	1977–78	1978–79	79–80
Selected Northern Hemisphere crops			
U.S. soybeans	48.0	50.9	60.8
U.S. sunflower seeds	1.3	1.8	3.7
U.S.S.R. sunflower seeds	5.9	5.3	5.3
U.S. cottonseeds	5.0	3.8	5.1
Canadian rapeseeds	2.0	3.5	3.5
Indian peanuts	6.1	6.3	5.7
Senegalese peanuts	0.4	1.1	1.2
Selected Southern Hemisphere crops			
Brazilian soybeans	9.9	10.5	13.5
Argentine soybeans	2.6	3.8	4.5
Malay palm oil	1.5	2.1	2.4
World oilseed products			
Meal production[1]	79.7	85.2	96.5
Change in meal stocks[1]	1.8	0.3	4.9
Apparent meal consumption[1]	77.9	84.9	91.6
Edible vegetable oil production	35.4	37.8	41.6
Change in oil stocks	0.7	0.3	1.4
Apparent oil consumption	34.7	37.5	40.2

[1] 44% soybean meal equivalent.
Source: USDA, *Foreign Agricultural Service,* October 1979.

CHICAGO TRIBUNE—NEW YORK NEWS SYNDICATE, INC.

"Same old runaround . . . A blah-blah here and a blah-blah there. Here a blah, there a blah, everywhere a blah-blah!"

Bangladesh, Indonesia, and Thailand were expected to be offset by less favourable crops in India, Pakistan, and Afghanistan.

A larger harvest by the region's largest exporter, Morocco, together with good harvests in Nigeria and other countries of West and Central Africa, brought about an increase in African output. However, production was hurt by war in Uganda, locusts in Zaire, and drought in several countries of southern Africa. In the Middle East Iran's production was reported unchanged, while Turkey's harvest of chick-peas was up.

Latin-American production was expected to climb because of larger planted area and wider distribution of better seeds in Brazil, Mexico, and a number of the region's smaller producing countries. Output continued to decline in Western Europe because of competition from other crops, except in Portugal and Greece. Government policy supported an expansion in production for use as both feed and green fodder in Eastern Europe.

Large export supplies by the U.S., Argentina, Chile, Morocco, Thailand, and Turkey were expected to meet the strong import demand in Western Europe, the Middle East, and India. Rising prices for the main bean and lentil varieties and continuing strong, but lower, prices for chick-peas were expected to lead to increased plantings in 1980.

Meat. The expansion in world output of meat (four main types only) slowed further in 1979 according to the FAO, increasing less than 2%. High beef prices strengthened the demand for pork and poultry, and increases in their production continued to more than offset the decline in beef slaughter. Beef production was likely to fall further in 1980 as producers around the world attempted to rebuild herds by slaughtering fewer cows and holding back more heifers for breeding purposes. Several countries were likely to record larger cattle inventories by the end of 1979, including the U.S., Soviet Union, Canada, and Brazil. Cattle numbers probably remained largely unchanged in 1979 in Western Europe, New Zealand, Eastern Europe, and Argentina, although numbers might still be declining in Australia. Cattle numbers throughout the world continued their decline from the peak reached in 1975.

Both hog and poultry numbers increased sharply in most regions of the world during 1979, although hog numbers continued relatively stable in Eastern Europe and the EEC and uncertainty prevailed as to the effect of reduced grain crops on hogs and poultry in the Soviet Union. Because hogs and poultry have shorter reproductive cycles than cattle, meat supplies from these sources also increased sharply, so much so that prices softened in many areas. Added to the softened prices was the rising cost of feed in 1979 because of tighter grain supplies, and the combination reduced what had been a major incentive to pork and poultry production. Thus, the expansion of output of pork and poultry was expected to slow in 1980.

The FAO estimated that the volume of world meat trade was likely to be unchanged in 1979 at about 11 million tons, with exports of sheep, hog, and poultry meat increasing while beef exports fell. But higher meat prices, particularly for beef, were expected to boost the value of meat exports by

Table IV. World Meat Production
In 000,000 metric tons

Type of livestock	1977	1978	1979[1]
Cattle	48.4	48.4	46.7
Hogs	47.4	48.9	51.5
Poultry	24.7	25.9	27.5
Sheep and goats	7.2	7.3	7.3
Total	127.7	130.5	133.0

[1] Preliminary.
Source: FAO.

over one-fifth to about $23 billion. While total exports of beef and veal by the major exporting countries (Argentina, Australia, Mexico, Central America, Uruguay, and New Zealand) were expected by USDA to be down 6.5% from the 1978 level of 2.5 million tons, net imports by the major beef importing countries (U.S., EEC, Japan, and Canada) were expected to exceed the 1,470,000 tons imported in 1978 by almost 8%.

Dairy Products. World milk output in 36 major producing countries was forecast to increase nearly 0.6% above that in 1978. Although output was expected to be down 3% in the U.S.S.R. because of smaller grain and roughage supplies, production elsewhere was up by nearly 2%. The EEC continued its attempts to reduce milk output in order to reduce holdings of surplus dairy products and their associated costs. The target price for milk and the intervention price for milk products were frozen for the 1979–80 marketing year.

Both production and consumption of butter in the major producing countries were expected to rise only slightly in 1979, but stocks were still expected to grow 16% by the end of 1979. The EEC held about 70% of the 980,000-ton stock and adopted several measures to encourage consumption, but they appeared unlikely to solve the problem of overproduction. Output of nonfat dry milk probably fell a little in 1979, and stocks were expected to be 40% lower, at 748,000 tons. U.S. stocks fell 56,000 tons to 209,000 because of smaller production and larger consumption.

Cheese production throughout the world continued to be stimulated by strong consumer demand, particularly in the EEC and the U.S., and efforts to divert milk away from the production of butter. Output was up more than 3%, while consumption increased an estimated 2.6% and exports 3.7%. Strong increases in production were reported in the EEC, especially in France, Ireland, and the United Kingdom. More milk was expected to be directed toward cheese production from 1980–83. The strong increase in production in 1979 of casein for animal feed was expected to level off as diversion of milk away from butter production to more profitable cheese manufacture reduced the availability of skim milk.

Table V. World Milk Production[1]
In 000,000 metric tons

Region	1977	1978[2]	1979[3]
North America	70.0	69.7	70.5
United States	55.7	55.3	56.0
South America	17.7	19.0	18.7
Brazil	9.5	10.8	10.8
Western Europe	126.3	130.2	132.6
EEC	102.8	106.4	108.4
France	31.5	31.7	32.2
Germany, West	22.5	23.3	23.5
United Kingdom	14.5	15.2	15.7
Other Western Europe	23.5	23.8	24.2
Eastern Europe and U.S.S.R.	131.6	132.1	129.1
Poland	17.3	17.4	17.4
U.S.S.R.	94.7	94.5	91.5
India	24.4	25.0	25.7
Australia and New Zealand	12.6	11.4	12.5
China, Japan, South Africa	13.9	14.1	14.6
World	396.4	401.5	403.7

[1] Based on 36 major producing countries; production is very small or data are not available in most less developed countries. Countries not shown among the 36 include (North America) Canada and Mexico; (South America) Argentina, Chile, Peru, Venezuela; (EEC) Belgium, Luxembourg, Denmark, Ireland, Italy, The Netherlands; (Other Western Europe) Austria, Finland, Greece, Norway, Portugal, Spain, Sweden, Switzerland; (Eastern Europe) Czechoslovakia, Hungary, and Yugoslavia.
[2] Preliminary.
[3] Forecast.
[4] Year ending June 30 for Australia and May 31 for New Zealand.
Source: USDA, *Foreign Agricultural Service,* November 1979.

Sugar. The first decline in world sugar stocks in seven years was likely at the end of 1979–80 as the result of an estimated 4% drop in world sugar production to 87.7 million tons (raw value). Production of cane sugar, about three-fifths of global output, was expected to fall two million tons and

FRANK LODGE—THE NEW YORK TIMES

A workman examines a pile of sugar rotting in a storage building in Belle Glade, Florida. The sugar was part of a large surplus that had accumulated.

Table VI. World Production of Centrifugal (freed from liquid) Sugar
In 000,000 metric tons raw value

Region	1977–78	1978–79	1979–80
North America and Caribbean	19.2	19.3	18.5
United States	5.4	5.6	5.1
Cuba	7.2	7.0	6.5
Mexico	3.0	3.1	3.1
South America	13.9	12.5	11.8
Brazil	8.9	7.8	7.0
Europe	20.3	20.4	20.1
Western Europe	14.7	14.7	14.4
EEC	12.2	12.3	12.3
Eastern Europe	5.6	5.6	5.7
U.S.S.R.	8.8	9.0	8.5
Africa	6.2	6.4	6.7
South Africa	2.2	2.2	2.2
Asia	20.5	19.9	18.7
China	2.5	2.7	2.6
India	8.2	7.3	6.5
Philippines	2.4	2.3	2.4
Thailand	1.6	1.8	1.3
Oceania	3.7	3.3	3.4
Australia	3.3	3.0	3.0
World	92.6	90.9	87.7

Source: USDA, *Foreign Agricultural Service*, December 1979.

of beet sugar, one million. Unfavourable weather conditions in some countries and decisions in others to reduce output, some in support of International Sugar Agreement objectives, were mainly responsible.

Total sugar consumption was forecast to rise nearly 2% to 91 million tons in 1979–80; thus, stocks were expected to decline 3.3 million tons to 29.2 million. Growth in sugar consumption in recent years was greatest in the less developed and centrally planned countries but had stagnated or declined in most industrialized countries. Rising sugar prices were expected to slow consumption.

World sugar imports were about 24.7 million tons in 1978–79, about 75% from the "free market" and the remainder under special arrangements. It was believed that imports might rise one million to two million tons in 1979–80, with most of the increase by the U.S.S.R. and China.

Reduced production and stock prospects stimulated a rise in the International Sugar Agreement (ISA) indicator price for world sugar. It had fluctuated in recent years between roughly 6 and 9 cents per pound but began to climb in August 1979, reached the ISA agreed minimum of 11 cents in October, and exceeded 15 cents in December.

Although the price rise could have permitted an increase in the ISA's global export quota in late 1979, the International Sugar Council (ISC) at its November 1979 meeting decided only to relax restrictions slightly on imports from nonmembers and to redistribute 1979 quota shortfalls. It also set the 1980 quota for major exporting ISA members at 12,909,000 tons, based on estimated 1980 free market imports of 17,789,000 tons. Nonmembers were expected to ship 4.4 million tons, and smaller exporting members, 480,000. The ISC postponed until April 1, 1980, the stock financing fund provisions in the hope that the U.S. by then would have fully implemented ratification of the ISA. The U.S. Senate ratified the ISA on Nov. 30, 1979, but a bill to implement U.S. obligations under the ISA was still pending in the House of Representatives.

The rise in sugar prices also triggered a reduction in the U.S. import fee for sugar to zero; the remaining U.S. import duty of 2.8125 cents per pound could not be raised but could be lowered to 0.625 cents by presidential proclamation. Thus, the domestic U.S. sugar situation was likely to be more influenced in the future by world market forces than it had been earlier.

Coffee. World coffee production was expected to increase about 4% in 1979–80, largely because of the continued recovery in Brazilian output. A freeze at the end of May in Brazil came too late to

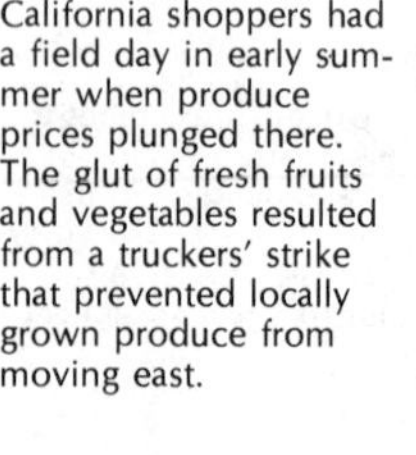
California shoppers had a field day in early summer when produce prices plunged there. The glut of fresh fruits and vegetables resulted from a truckers' strike that prevented locally grown produce from moving east.

WIDE WORLD

Table VII. World Green Coffee Production
In 000 60-kg bags

Region	1977–78	1978–79	1979–80[1]
North and Central America	14,221	15,292	15,566
Costa Rica	1,490	1,764	1,600
El Salvador	2,400	3,000	3,000
Guatemala	2,350	2,600	2,700
Mexico	3,600	3,800	3,800
South America	32,105	35,488	38,018
Brazil	17,500	20,000	22,500
Colombia	11,050	11,300	11,500
Ecuador	1,238	1,868	1,650
Africa	16,858	18,062	18,963
Cameroon	1,371	1,650	1,520
Ethiopia	3,024	3,000	3,000
Ivory Coast	3,320	4,667	4,835
Uganda	1,868	2,000	2,200
Asia and Oceania	6,958	8,075	7,691
India	2,180	1,856	1,841
Indonesia	3,241	4,652	4,200
Total	70,142	76,917	80,238

[1] Preliminary.
Source: USDA, *Foreign Agricultural Service,* October 1979.

affect the size of the country's 1979–80 crop but reduced the potential of the 1980–81 harvest from an estimated 26 million–28.5 million bags to 20 million–22 million.

Exportable world coffee production (harvested production less domestic consumption in producing countries) was also expected to rise about 4% above the 57.9 million bags in 1978–79. World coffee consumption was continuing to rise fast enough to result in perhaps a 3% decline in coffee stocks by the end of 1979–80.

The International Coffee Organization (ICO) monthly average price for green coffee rose for a few months following the August 1978 Brazilian frost, but confirmation of a large 1978–79 crop pushed prices to a low of $1.31 per pound in February 1979. The price climbed to $2 per pound in October and November following the most recent Brazilian frost.

The ICO met in London in September 1979 but once more failed to agree on a proposal to raise the 77 cents-per-pound trigger price that calls for export quotas when export prices fall below that level. Operations of the "Bogotá Group"—Brazil, Colombia, Costa Rica, El Salvador, Guatemala, Honduras, Mexico, and Venezuela—in the futures market tended to moderate downward pressure on prices.

Cocoa. World cocoa bean production in 1979–80 was forecast to reach a record high, 6% above the level of 1978–79. The world cocoa bean grind was estimated at 1,414,000 tons in calendar 1979, 2.6% above that in 1978. U.S., Dutch, and French grindings for January–September 1979 were running above the same period in 1978, while West German and British grindings were lower. Grindings were forecast to increase modestly in 1980, reflecting anticipated lower prices and more plentiful supplies, but to remain well below expected production levels. Cocoa consumption had been hurt by the use of extenders and substitutes, as well as by the effects of inflation and the slowdown in the global economy.

Table VIII. World Cocoa Bean Production
In 000 metric tons

Region	1977–78	1978–79	1979–80
North and Central America	93	95	91
South America	416	454	463
Brazil	283	314	320
Ecuador	78	83	85
Africa	938	879	962
Cameroon	108	107	110
Ghana	271	265	295
Ivory Coast	304	320	330
Nigeria	204	138	175
Asia and Oceania	61	65	70
Total	1,509	1,493	1,586

Source: USDA, *Foreign Agricultural Service,* November 1979.

Cocoa bean stocks were forecast to increase perhaps 120,000 tons in 1980, compared with increases of 116,000 and 64,000 tons in 1978 and 1979, respectively. Cocoa bean prices during the January–September 1979 period averaged $1.47 per pound, compared with the 1978 annual average of $1.53.

The International Cocoa Agreement (ICA) was extended for six months beyond the Sept. 30, 1979, expiration date. UNCTAD (United Nations Conference on Trade and Development) held a conference to renegotiate the ICA in Geneva, Switz., during November 1979. The economic provisions of the ICA had never been invoked because prices had been above the ICA's price band. Exporters were reported to be asking for a minimum price of $1.10 per pound.

Tea. World tea production in 1979 (excluding mainland China) was expected to be slightly below the record 1978 figure of 1,480,000 tons, largely because of a 13,000-ton drought-induced decline in output from India. Early indications suggested a 1980 crop of perhaps 1.5 million tons, assuming a recovery in Indian production, with world import demand remaining strong.

Table IX. World Tea Production[1]
In 000 metric tons

Region	1977	1978	1979[2]
Asia and Oceania	1,227	1,251	1,237
India	563	573	560
Japan	102	105	105
Sri Lanka	209	199	200
Turkey	84	95	95
U.S.S.R.	106	103	105
Africa	184	192	193
Kenya	86	93	102
South America	44	38	42
Total	1,456	1,481	1,472

[1] Excludes China and several small producers.
[2] Preliminary.
Source: USDA, *Foreign Agricultural Service,* October 1979.

World tea exports fell about 36,000 tons in 1978 from record 1977 shipments of 786,000 tons because importers were drawing down stocks and demand was reduced by more plentiful coffee supplies. Indian exports were expected to recover from the sharply reduced 1978 level thanks to export duty reductions. Sri Lankan exports were being hampered by the government's doubling of the minimum export price. Kenyan tea exports continued to rise; the area devoted to tea increased 5% in 1978 and was double that of a decade earlier.

Per capita tea consumption continued to decline in the U.K., totaling 2.8 kg in 1978, compared with 3.7 kg in 1976. But British imports in 1979 were expected to recover from the 1978 level of 177,811 tons, the lowest since 1950, because stocks were reduced sharply. U.S. tea imports were expected to approximate the 68,834 tons purchased in 1978.

Tea prices, as measured by the London average auction price for all teas, were stable at slightly less than $1 per pound for 1978 and 1979. They were expected to continue near that level in 1980.

Cotton. World cotton production in 1979–80 was forecast to increase almost 7% from the 1978–79 level. A sharp recovery in U.S. output was mostly responsible. Good weather was also favouring cotton growth outside the U.S.

The global demand for cotton strengthened during 1978–79 as utilization increased 2.5% to 62.8 million bales (480 lb or 218 kg per bale). But U.S. consumption fell by the same percentage to 6.4 million bales because of high interest rates, the slowdown in the U.S. economy, and the continuing trend toward greater use of man-made fibres. The growth in global utilization of cotton was expected to slow to about 0.5% in 1979–80 because of lower use in the U.S., Japan, and Hong Kong and a leveling off of Soviet, Pakistani, and Western European consumption. China was using more cotton (12.4 million bales in 1978–79) as it attempted to increase foreign exchange earnings from textile exports while meeting domestic demand. Chinese cotton imports were projected to increase to 2.5 million bales in 1979–80, approximately 300,000 above those in 1978–79.

World cotton exports totaled about 19.5 million bales in 1978–79 and were expected to increase about 2% in 1979–80. U.S. exports were expected to increase about 5% over the 6.2 million bales of 1978–79.

World stocks of cotton fell 10% during 1978–79 to 21.6 million bales but were forecast to increase about one million bales by the end of 1979–80. An expected 1.7 million-bale increase in U.S. stocks was expected to be partly counteracted by the inclination of importing nations to reduce stocks because of a possible economic slowdown and rising carrying costs as a result of climbing interest rates.

The Outlook "A" Index (average of five lowest priced of ten selected growths, cost, insurance, and freight northern Europe) for 1978–79 was 76.05 cents per pound, 17% above that for 1977–78. After peaking at 80.6 cents in November 1978, the price fell until April 1979 and then recovered to 79.4 cents by November.

Table X. World Cotton Production
In 000,000 480-lb bales

Region	1977–78	1978–79	1979–80[1]
North America	14.4	13.9	14.5
United States	12.7	12.3	13.0
Latin America and Caribbean			
Brazil	2.2	2.7	2.7
Central America	1.7	1.6	1.2
Mexico	1.6	1.5	1.5
U.S.S.R.	12.7	12.3	13.0
China	9.4	10.0	9.8
Middle East and Africa			
Egypt	1.8	2.0	2.2
Turkey	2.6	2.2	2.2
South Asia			
India	5.6	6.3	5.8
Pakistan	2.5	2.1	2.9
Other countries and regions	9.3	8.3	8.4
World	63.9	59.8	64.2

[1]Forecast.
Source: USDA, *Foreign Agricultural Service,* December 1979.

INTERNATIONAL FOOD SECURITY

Grain Reserves. A 67-country UNCTAD negotiating conference adjourned in February after failing to agree on a new Wheat Trade Convention as part of an international grains agreement. Subsequent developments offered little prospect that formal negotiations would resume in the near future. Earlier discussions within the International Wheat Council (IWC) and among exporting nations and the EEC had settled several major differences among them, but disagreements between the developed and less developed countries could not be resolved.

The UNCTAD conference achieved consensus on the basic structure of a new Wheat Trade Convention, but it could not agree on several major implementing provisions. Under that structure the world wheat market would operate within an agreed price band measured on an "indicator" scale that envisaged three "action points" in both falling and rising markets. These points called for specific responses on the part of members, but did not establish absolute price floors or ceilings beyond which prices were forbidden to move. As wheat prices began to fall or rise from the middle of the price band and the first falling or rising point was reached, members would be required to meet and to review the market situation. If prices fell or rose to the second action point, members then would attempt to agree on a program that specified obligatory accumulation or release of nationally owned reserves by individual members, tailored to the current situation; if an agreement could not be reached within a specified period, reserve actions were to be taken automatically under a program stipulated in advance in the convention. If prices continued to fall or rise to the third point because reserve actions were inadequate to stabilize the market, consultations were to be held on a joint program of measures.

The less developed countries advocated a relatively low and narrow band of price adjustments. Their position appeared largely motivated by a desire to secure access to large and relatively cheap supplies of grain. Their aims undoubtedly partly reflected their serious concern with the problems they faced in meeting growing food-grain import requirements at the same time that their energy import costs were rising even more rapidly. They were not receptive to arguments that higher prices were needed to maintain productive capacity in the developed countries, or that low world grain prices might prove a disincentive to increasing grain production in their own countries.

The developed countries generally favoured a higher and broader price band. They entered the UNCTAD negotiations with preliminary agreement among themselves to support $140 per metric ton as the point for beginning to accumulate stocks and $125 per ton as the trigger for consultations on such additional measures as production controls. Several countries, including the U.S., favoured a release point of $200 per ton in the first year of the agreement and $210 thereafter. The less developed countries for the most part advocated a much lower acquisition price—some wanted $125 per ton—and some, early in the conference, called for a re-

JAMES P. STERBA—THE NEW YORK TIMES

In an effort to modernize its agricultural methods, China began importing farm machinery from the U.S.

lease price of $140 per ton; the latter was the acquisition price proposed by the developed countries. By the end of the conference many were still supporting a release price of $160.

The advocacy of a higher and broader price band by the developed countries partly reflected the nature of their domestic grain price support policies and partly the nature of their views concerning the requirements for market stability. Some exporting countries, such as the U.S., already held large grain stocks and were finding it necessary to acquire more from their farmers as prices fell closer to $140 per ton in order to achieve domestic producer price objectives. If the acquisition price were set at $125, they believed that they would bear the brunt of stock accumulation before other countries would have to begin building stocks and that they would, thus, bear a disproportionate share of the burden of holding stocks. Rising production costs fueled by general inflation and sharply increasing energy costs were already putting pressure on domestic price support targets. Adoption of a low acquisition price would have meant large budgetary expenditures to maintain ever growing surpluses, resulting in further price-depressing effects on domestic agriculture and a reduction in future investment in productive capacity.

Similarly, the adoption of a Wheat Trade Convention stock release price lower than that for the release of domestic stocks under some producing countries' domestic price support programs could mean that such countries would also be the last to unburden themselves of unwanted grain stocks and might not have the opportunity to do so at all if prices failed to rise high enough. In addition, release prices under domestic programs are often set at a level that is regarded by farmers as just compensation for lower rates of return when prices may even have fallen below the cost of production. Any government that curtails such returns, even in consideration of broader foreign policy aims, risks the controversy that surrounds disruption of an important domestic political compromise. These examples illustrate only some of the difficulties to be met in attempting to reach an agreement that balances not only interests among countries but also among diverse groups within countries.

The conference also could not agree on the overall size or national distribution of reserves. This was an important question because the size of the total reserve would largely determine the scope and effectiveness of reserve operations. The 18 million–19 million tons provisionally pledged by participants fell far short of the 25 million–30 million tons advocated by most developed countries. Exporters accounted for 14 million–15 million tons of the pledges, but the less developed importing countries appeared willing to commit themselves to only 2 million tons; they also favoured a large stock but believed the developed countries should carry most of the burden. The U.S. proposed 5 million tons as its share, an amount in addition to the

Table XI. Official Commitments of External Assistance to Agriculture in Less Developed Countries[1]

In $000,000

	Average 1973–75	1976	1977	1978[2]
Multilateral	2,219	2,878	3,858	4,908
Bilateral	1,906	2,236	3,104	2,775
Total				
Current prices	4,125	5,114	6,962	7,683
1975 prices (UN)	4,594	5,113	6,387	6,146
1975 prices (OECD)	4,532	4,887	6,019	n.a.

[1] "Agriculture" conforms to the OECD "broad" definition.
[2] Preliminary.
Source: OECD and FAO.

U.S. farmer-owned domestic reserve (then about 11 million tons) and the component of a proposed separate U.S. reserve stock designed to guarantee U.S. food-aid commitments.

A related issue about which agreement could not be reached was concerned with special provisions to aid less developed countries in meeting stock-holding obligations. The developed nations had generally supported the establishment of a special committee that would assess reserve and reserve-related financing requirements and that would seek to mobilize and coordinate existing bilateral and multilateral sources of assistance for less developed countries that undertook to hold reserve stocks. They favoured working within the institutional framework of organizations such as the World Bank and the International Monetary Fund, both of which participated in the conference. But the less developed countries responded by calling for a reserve-stock financing fund based on compulsory contributions by developed member countries, a proposal that was unacceptable to the latter.

In the realm of reserve operations the developed nations accepted the premise that the less developed countries faced special difficulties and deserved special treatment in carrying out their obligations. For instance, it was proposed that less developed countries be given the option of postponing the accumulation of stocks until prices fell lower than the level that obligated other members to do so and that a less developed country be temporarily exempted from the duty of accumulating stocks for various reasons such as a lack of storage facilities. But the developed nations would not accept a claim by less developed countries to the unilateral exercise of such options without even review by the Wheat Trade Convention.

Other issues that remained unresolved included provisions to assure supplies to importers in times of shortage, revision of price action points to reflect factors such as inflation, and relief from stock-holding obligations by members facing special circumstances such as poor grain crops. The conference did agree to recommend extension of the International Wheat Agreement of 1971 to the IWC; it contained only consultative provisions and was extended by the IWC for two years in March.

Food Aid. The same UNCTAD conference also considered proposals to establish a new Food Aid Convention (FAC) to replace that set forth in 1971. Although the participants agreed on most of the provisions of a new FAC, they could not accept a proposal by the less developed countries—also supported by the United States—to make its entry into force independent of acceptance of a new international wheat agreement. The conference did recommend that the 1971 convention be extended. However, subsequent meetings of various international bodies concerned with food security endorsed early adoption of a new FAC, and the Food Aid Committee of the IWC voted on November 30 to call a special session to complete the negotiations in London on March 3–6, 1980. The unanimous character of the vote suggested that prospects were excellent for completion of the FAC.

The new FAC was expected to increase the pledged level of food aid in cereal grains from 4.2 million to 7.6 million tons per year, 2.4 million tons short of the 1974 World Food Conference goal. The U.S. pledged 4,470,000 tons, more than double its commitment under the 1971 FAC.

Not all cereals aid is covered by the FAC. The FAO estimated that total allocations of cereals food aid in 1979–80 would likely amount to 9.7 million tons (5.7 million by the U.S.), compared with 9.5 mil-

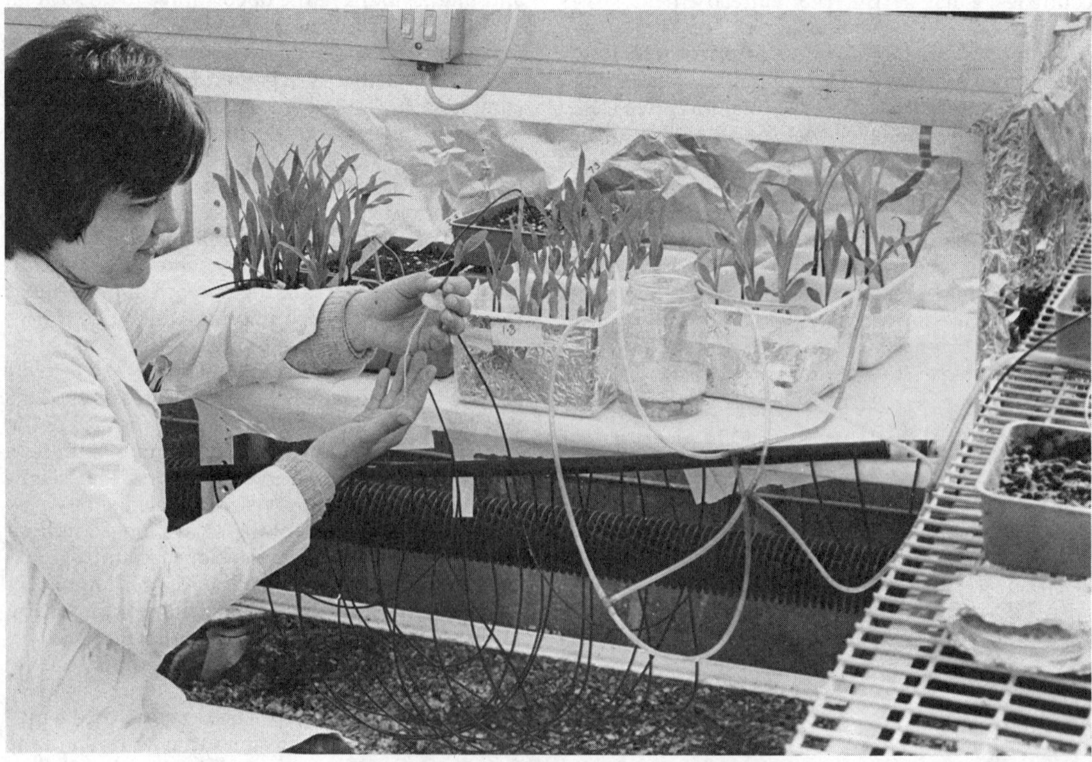

Scientists in Great Britain began work on developing a strain of corn that would be suited to the damp and cool climate of England.

KEYSTONE

lion (6.1 million by the U.S.) in 1978–79. The EEC's pledge totaled about 1.3 million tons in each of the last two years, and Canada's was one million. Japan's commitment of 680,000 tons in 1979–80 was triple its 1978–79 allocation. Contributions to the International Emergency Food Reserve by the end of October totaled 306,000 tons for 1979, compared with 325,000 for 1978. The U.S. accounted for about 40% of the total each year. The reserve was administered by the World Food Program.

AGRICULTURAL DEVELOPMENT

Foreign Assistance. Although official commitments (excluding those by the centrally planned economies) of external assistance to agriculture in the less developed countries rose 10% in 1978 in current dollars, inflation caused a small decrease in real terms from 1977 levels. Assistance to agriculture measured according to the OECD (Organization for Economic Cooperation and Development) "narrow" definition—roughly equivalent to direct use in agricultural production—rose from about $4.9 billion in 1977 to about $5.7 billion in 1978 but remained unchanged at about $4.6 billion when measured in constant 1975 prices. The U.S. devoted $556 million of its bilateral aid resources to agriculture, rural development, and nutrition in fiscal year 1978 and $610 million in 1979, and proposed $715 million in its 1980 budget. The U.S. also channeled considerable assistance to agriculture through multilateral lending institutions.

Increases in total multilateral assistance to agriculture in less developed countries roughly offset a decline from bilateral sources. Commitments in current prices by the World Bank, which accounted for about one-half of total assistance, rose 46%; those by the FAO/UN Development Program were up 26%; and those by the Organization of Petroleum Exporting Countries (OPEC) multilateral institutions increased 15%.

The International Fund for Agricultural Development (IFAD) began operation in 1978 with commitments of $118 million, but the regional development banks—especially the Inter-American Development Bank—reduced their loan activity. For 1979 IFAD targeted $375 million in commitments, including $15 million for technical assistance. Some 18–20 projects were being considered for possible co-financing with the World Bank and three regional development banks, with total commitments of about $180 million–$200 million, and an additional 10–12 projects for financing by IFAD alone, totaling $160 million–$200 million. The FAO Investment Center was expected to be responsible for more than half of the IFAD-initiated projects in 1979. With about 50% of IFAD's $1 billion capital committed, the issue of the fund's replenishment was expected to be raised in 1980.

Food Crops. The formation of a world food corps was proposed by U.S. Ambassador Andrew Young in a November 1977 speech to the FAO conference. His conception drew upon the experience of the U.S. Peace Corps in providing technical assistance at the village level by foreign volunteers. By 1979 this concept appeared to be evolving toward that of national food corps making use of voluntary village workers to introduce low-cost techniques for increasing food production; the use of foreign personnel seemed likely to be the exception rather than the rule.

The idea attracted the most interest in Africa, where pilot projects were funded in Tanzania, Mali, Upper Volta, and Senegal. The approach of these projects was partly inspired by the experience of the Puebla Plan in Mexico, the Sarvodaya Movement in Sri Lanka, and the Asian Institute of Rural Development in India.

UN Conference on Science and Technology for Development. This meeting, convened in August in Vienna, had much of the character of other North–South confrontations. A full plan of action could not be agreed upon because of differences between the developed and less developed nations. The latter called for a $2 billion–$4 billion-a-year fund devoted to science and technology for development, to be financed by assessments upon the developed countries; a worldwide computer network devoted to science and technology; free access to public and private scientific developments; and a greatly enlarged UN Secretariat to deal exclusively with such matters.

The compromise financial proposal finally adopted consisted of a $250 million voluntary interim fund to be managed by the UN Development Fund. A pledging conference was to be called later in the year by the UN, and the UN General Assembly was asked to establish a study group dealing with long-term financing arrangements. The conference agreed to recommend that some additional support for a new UN committee on science and technology for development be built into an existing UN office dealing with such matters. No agreement could be reached on the question of access to public and private science and technology.

Presidential Commission on World Hunger (CWH). Pres. Jimmy Carter established the CWH in September 1978 with a two-year charter to, among other things, determine the basic causes of international and domestic hunger and malnutrition, to identify and evaluate U.S. programs affecting them, to prepare recommendations on policies and actions to reduce hunger and malnutrition, and to assist in publicizing and implementing its recommendations. A preliminary report by the CWH was issued in December. It concluded that the major world hunger problem was the prevalence in many parts of the globe of chronic undernutrition and that the problem continued to worsen despite signs of progress. It saw poverty as "the central and most intransigent cause" of hunger. This represented a significant shift away from the advocacy in many quarters of production restraints as the central question.

The report did not minimize the many serious obstacles to increasing food production, but emphasized that rapid increases in food production would not in themselves cure widespread undernutrition if people did not acquire the purchasing power to enter the food market. It concluded that the defeat of hunger would be determined by decisions and actions well within the capacity of nations and of individuals.

The CWH made the following preliminary recommendations: (1) to make the elimination of hunger the "primary focus" of U.S. relationships with the less developed countries; (2) to give the U.S. aid agency Cabinet status; (3) to move as rapidly as possible to make 0.7% of gross national product—a target advocated by the UN—the U.S. goal for net disbursement of concessional economic assistance, and limit that to development, as opposed to security or military, assistance; (4) to prohibit the use of starvation as a method of warfare and relieve famine brought on by armed conflict through U.S. ratification on two protocols to a 1949 Geneva Convention on Humanitarian Law in Armed Conflict; and (5) to provide increased resources to successful U.S. domestic hunger programs and undertake a systematic assessment of the nutritional status of the U.S. population.

(RICHARD M. KENNEDY)

See also Environment; Fisheries; Food Processing; Gardening; Industrial Review: *Alcoholic Beverages; Textiles; Tobacco.*
[451.B.1.c; 534.E; 731; 10/37.C]

Albania

Albania

A people's republic in the western Balkan Peninsula, Albania is on the Adriatic Sea, bordered by Greece and Yugoslavia. Area: 28,748 sq km (11,100 sq mi). Pop. (1979 est.): 2,758,000. Cap. and largest city: Tirana (pop., 1976 est., 192,300). Language: Albanian. Religion: officially atheist; historically Muslim, Orthodox, and Roman Catholic communities. First secretary of the Albanian (Communist) Party of Labour in 1979, Enver Hoxha; president of the Presidium of the People's Assembly, Haxhi Leshi; chairman of the Council of Ministers (premier), Mehmet Shehu.

Haxhi Leshi and Mehmet Shehu were confirmed in their offices by the People's Assembly on Dec. 25, 1978. Following reelection, Shehu expressed his government's readiness to restore diplomatic relations with Britain if the latter would return to Albania its gold reserves valued at about £8 million. Shehu also indicated that he wished to establish ties with West Germany but stated as a precondition the payment of reparations for war damages inflicted on Albania by the German Army during World War II. Since 1974, said Shehu, the number of countries with which Albania maintained normal relations had increased by 16 to 82.

Relations with one important neighbour, Yugoslavia, developed less favourably. Shortly after China ended its "unbreakable" alliance with Albania, Enver Hoxha, ruler of the last bastion of Stalinism in Europe, published a booklet alleging that genocide was being practiced in Yugoslavia against the 1.5 million Albanians living there. Mahmut Bakhali, leader of the Albanian minority in Yugoslavia, responded by saying that Hoxha's attack "can only feed the hopes of those who want to endanger the stability, security, and independence of Yugoslavia."

A series of earthquakes that ravaged the Adriatic coastline of Albania and Yugoslavia in April caused 35 deaths in Albania.

(K. M. SMOGORZEWSKI)

ALBANIA

Education. (1973–74) Primary, pupils 569,600, teachers 22,686; secondary, pupils 32,900, teachers (1971–72) 1,318; vocational and teacher training, pupils 69,700, teachers (1971–72) 1,712; higher (1971–72), students 28,668, teaching staff 1,153.

Finance. Monetary unit: lek, with (June 30, 1979) an official exchange rate of 3.50 leks to U.S. $1 (7.50 leks = £1 sterling) and a noncommercial rate of 7 leks to U.S. $1 (15 leks = £1 sterling). Budget (1977 est.): revenue 7.7 billion leks; expenditure 7.6 billion leks.

Foreign Trade. (1964; latest available) Imports 490.6 million leks; exports 299.6 million leks. Import sources: China 63%; Czechoslovakia 10%; Poland 8%. Export destinations: China 40%; Czechoslovakia 19%; East Germany 10%; Poland 10%. Main exports: fuels, minerals, and metals (including crude oil, bitumen, chrome ore, iron ore, and copper) 54%; foodstuffs (including vegetables, wine, and fruit) 23%; raw materials (including tobacco and wool) 17%.

Transport and Communications. Roads (1971) *c.* 5,000 km. Motor vehicles in use (1970): passenger *c.* 3,500; commercial (including buses) *c.* 11,200. Railways: (1975) 302 km; traffic (1971) 291 million passenger-km, freight 188 million net ton-km. Shipping (1978): merchant vessels 100 gross tons and over 20; gross tonnage 55,870. Shipping traffic (1975): goods loaded *c.* 2.8 million metric tons, unloaded *c.* 760,000 metric tons. Telephones (Dec. 1965) 13,991. Radio receivers (Dec. 1976) 180,000. Television receivers (Dec. 1976) 4,500.

Agriculture. Production (in 000; metric tons; 1977): corn *c.* 300; wheat *c.* 400; oats *c.* 28; potatoes *c.* 122; sugar, raw value *c.* 20; sunflower seed *c.* 25; olives *c.* 47; grapes *c.* 73; tobacco *c.* 13; cotton, lint *c.* 7. Livestock (in 000; 1977): sheep *c.* 1,163; cattle *c.* 472; pigs *c.* 117; goats *c.* 674; poultry *c.* 2,307.

Industry. Production (in 000; metric tons; 1976): crude oil *c.* 2,500; lignite *c.* 950; petroleum products *c.* 2,200; chrome ore (oxide content) *c.* 340; copper ore (metal content) *c.* 10; nickel ore (metal content) *c.* 7; fertilizers (nutrient content; 1977–78) *c.* 70; cement *c.* 800; electricity (kw-hr) *c.* 2 million.

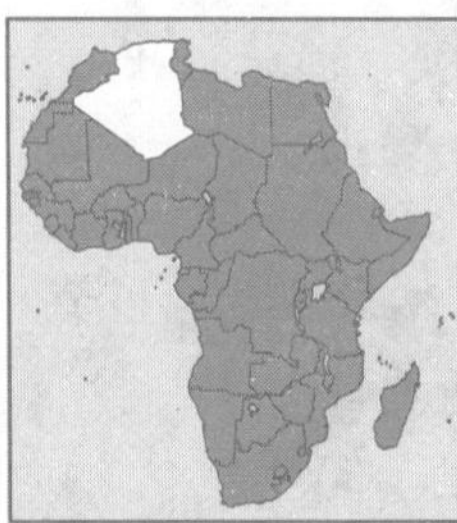

Algeria

Algeria

A republic on the north coast of Africa, Algeria is bounded by Morocco, Western (Spanish) Sahara, Mauritania, Mali, Niger, Libya, and Tunisia. Area: 2,322,164 sq km (896,592 sq mi). Pop. (1978 est.): 18,245,000. Cap. and largest city: Algiers (pop., 1977 est., 1.8 million). Language: Arabic, Berber, French. Religion: Muslim. President from Feb. 9, 1979, Chadli Bendjedid; premier from March 8, Mohamed Ben Ahmed Abdelghani.

After the death of Pres. Houari Boumédienne in December 1978, a National Liberation Front (FLN) congress on Jan. 31, 1979, nominated Chadli Bendjedid (*see* BIOGRAPHIES) as sole candidate for the presidency. This choice was approved in the February 7 national election by a 94% majority. The new government, announced on March 8, was notable for the absence of Abdel Aziz Bouteflika, former foreign minister, and for the confirmation of Mohamed Yahiaoui as FLN executive head. President Bendjedid's first moves were to heal social and political rifts. In April restrictions on former political leaders Ferhat Abbas and Ben Khedda were removed, and later that month 11 imprisoned opponents of the late President Boumédienne were released. At the same time, exit visas—long a source of popular irritation—were abolished. In July it was announced that former president Ahmed Ben Bella had been freed from house arrest.

JACQUES PAVLOVSKY—SYGMA

The new president of Algeria, Chadli Bendjedid, took the oath of office on February 9 following the death of Pres. Houari Boumédienne.

ALGERIA

Education. (1977–78) Primary, pupils 2,894,084, teachers 77,009; secondary, pupils 718,122, teachers 25,882; vocational, pupils 11,798, teachers 823; teacher training, students 12,041, teachers 1,059; higher, students 51,983, teaching staff (1976–77) 5,366.

Finance. Monetary unit: dinar, with (Sept. 17, 1979) a free rate of 3.84 dinars to U.S. $1 (8.26 dinars = £1 sterling). Gold, SDR's, and foreign exchange (June 1979) U.S. $2,084,000,000. Budget (1978 est.): revenue 32.6 billion dinars; expenditure 18.2 billion dinars (excludes 14.3 billion dinars development expenditure). Money supply (Dec. 1978) 60,628,000,000 dinars.

Foreign Trade. (1977) Imports 29,534,000,000 dinars; exports (1978) 23,215,000,000 dinars. Import sources: France 24%; West Germany 15%; Italy 10%; U.S. 9%; Japan 6%; Spain 5%. Export destinations U.S. 52%; West Germany 15%; France 13%; Italy 5%. Main exports: crude oil 87%; petroleum products 5%.

Transport and Communications. Roads (1976) 80,450 km. Motor vehicles in use (1975): passenger 286,100; commercial (including buses) 154,700. Railways: (1977) 3,890 km; traffic (1976) 1,369,000,000 passenger-km, freight 1,727,000,000 net ton-km. Air traffic (1977): 1,723,000,000 passenger-km; freight *c.* 10.5 million net ton-km. Shipping (1978): merchant vessels 100 gross tons and over 121; gross tonnage 1,152,086. Shipping traffic (1977): goods loaded 45,490,000 metric tons, unloaded 12,830,000 metric tons. Telephones (Jan. 1978) 297,700. Radio receivers (Dec. 1976) 3 million. Television receivers (Dec. 1976) 525,000.

Agriculture. Production (in 000; metric tons; 1978): wheat *c.* 1,800; barley *c.* 610; oats *c.* 90; potatoes *c.* 520; tomatoes *c.* 190; onions *c.* 91; dates 196; oranges 285; mandarin oranges and tangerines 150; watermelons (1977) *c.* 170; olives *c.* 180; wine *c.* 255. Livestock (in 000; 1977): sheep *c.* 9,540; goats *c.* 2,220; cattle *c.* 1,300; asses *c.* 443; horses *c.* 140; camels *c.* 135; chickens *c.* 16,900.

Industry. Production (in 000; metric tons; 1977): iron ore (53–55% metal content) 3,180; phosphate rock (1976) 818; crude oil (1978) 51,090; natural gas (cu m) *c.* 10,030,000; petroleum products (1976) *c.* 4,780; fertilizers (nutrient content; 1977–78) nitrogenous 42; phosphate 70; cement 1,777; crude steel (1976) 206; electricity (excluding most industrial production; kw-hr) *c.* 4,000,000.

Algeria's foreign policy was dominated by the problem of the Western Sahara. On May 7 President Bendjedid openly reaffirmed Algerian support for the Popular Front for the Liberation of Saguia el Hamra and Río de Oro (Polisario Front) and, despite Moroccan hopes for moderation, Algeria encouraged Mauritania to come to terms with the Front in August. Moroccan threats of hot pursuit and claims of Algerian aggression, made at the UN in June, were rejected. At the Organization of African Unity's summit conference in Monrovia, Liberia, in July, Algeria supported demands for a cease-fire and self-determination in the Sahara. Algeria also reestablished diplomatic relations with Mauritania on August 15, after a Mauritania-Polisario peace treaty had been signed on August 5 in Algiers.

Relations between Algeria and France did not improve significantly. France was increasingly reluctant to renew work permits for Algerians in France, and the French government was "ambivalent" over the Sahara. However, relations with Spain improved during the visit of Spanish Premier Adolfo Suárez, April 30–May 1. Algeria's nonaligned position was reaffirmed during Yugoslav President Tito's visit on May 28, before the meeting of nonaligned nations in Havana in September. During the visit of Col. Muammar al-Qaddafi of Libya on May 24, both countries restated their adherence to the 1975 mutual defense pact. Algeria also supported the decisions of the Baghdad Arab conference regarding opposition to the Egyptian-Israeli treaty.

The 1979 budget proposed in January, 14% larger than its predecessor, emphasized Algeria's commitment to development and education. The 1980 budget was to increase by a further 37%. During 1978 Sonatrach (Algeria's state hydrocarbons

Aircraft:
see Aerial Sports; Defense; Industrial Review; Transportation

Air Forces:
see Defense

Alcoholic Beverages:
see Industrial Review

group) revenue had risen 7% as the result of increases in oil and gas production. World market conditions enabled Algeria to raise oil prices by 13% in May, with further increases in October and December.

On July 1 prices of liquid natural gas sold to the U.S. consortium El Paso were increased by 400%, with the maximum price to be reached by 1983.

(GEORGE JOFFÉ)

Andorra

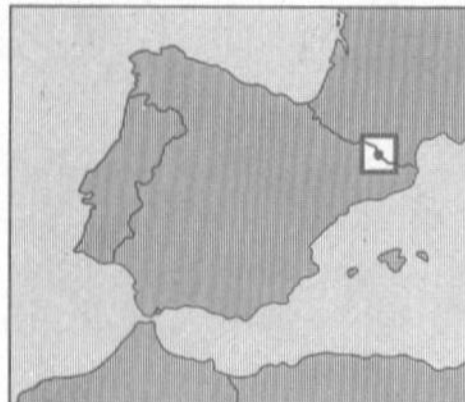
Andorra

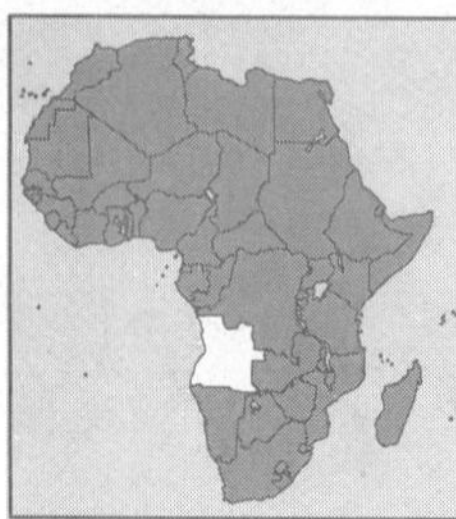
Angola

An independent co-principality of Europe, Andorra is in the Pyrenees Mountains between Spain and France. Area: 464 sq km (179 sq mi). Pop. (1977 est.): 30,700. Cap.: Andorra la Vella (commune pop., 1975 est., 10,900). Language: Catalan (official), French, Spanish. Religion: predominantly Roman Catholic. Co-princes: the president of the French Republic and the bishop of Urgel, Spain, represented by their *veguers* (provosts) and *batlles* (prosecutors). An elected Council General of 24 members elects the first syndic; in 1979, Estanislau Sangrà Font.

On Dec. 29, 1978, the Council General of the Valleys elected a new first syndic and his deputy. Estanislau Sangrà Font, an Independent, was elected by 13 votes against 11 obtained by Carlos Ribas Reig, a Conservative and nephew of the outgoing syndic, Julià Reig-Ribó. There were three blank votes and one councillor was absent. Enric Paris Torres was elected second syndic by 12 votes to 11 with four blank votes, again with one councillor absent. (The number of parishes had been increased from six to seven in June 1978; each elected four deputies to the Council General.)

At the end of March 1979, Jaume Bartumeu Cassany, one of the founders of the Andorran Democratic Association, was received at the Elysée Palace in Paris by an adviser of Pres. Valéry Giscard d'Estaing, the French co-prince. Cassany submitted a memorandum demanding the democratization of Andorra's government, the introduction of Catalan as the teaching language instead of French and Spanish, and the admission of Andorra as a full member of the Council of Europe.

From Jan. 1, 1979, Spaniards no longer needed to produce a passport for entry into Andorra.

(K. M. SMOGORZEWSKI)

ANDORRA

Education. (1975–76) Primary (including preprimary), pupils 3,802, teachers (1974–75) 142; secondary, pupils 1,753, teachers (1974–75) 120.

Finance and Trade. Monetary units: French franc and Spanish peseta. Budget (1978 est.) balanced at 1,429,000,000 pesetas. Foreign trade (1978): imports from France Fr 584,846,000 (U.S. $129.6 million), from Spain 6,410,518,000 pesetas (U.S. $83.6 million); exports to France Fr 16,008,000 (U.S. $3.5 million), to Spain 156,956,000 pesetas (U.S. $2 million). Tourism (1976) 6.5 million visitors.

Communications. Telephones (Jan. 1977) 10,400. Radio receivers (Dec. 1976) 6,600. Television receivers (Dec. 1976) 3,000.

Agriculture. Production: cereals, potatoes, tobacco, wool. Livestock (in 000; 1977): sheep *c.* 12; cattle *c.* 4.

Angola

Located on the west coast of southern Africa, Angola is bounded by Zaire, Zambia, South West Africa (Namibia), and the Atlantic Ocean. The small exclave of Cabinda, a province of Angola, is bounded by the Congo and Zaire. Area: 1,246,700 sq km (481,353 sq mi). Pop. (1979 est.): 6,901,000. Cap. and largest city: Luanda (pop., 1970, 480,600). Language: Bantu languages (predominant), Portuguese (official), and some Khoisan dialects. Religion: traditional beliefs 45%; Roman Catholicism 43%; Protestantism 12%. Presidents in 1979, Agostinho Neto to September 10 and, from September 20, José Eduardo dos Santos.

Pres. Agostinho Neto (*see* OBITUARIES) died in Moscow on Sept. 10, 1979, following an operation

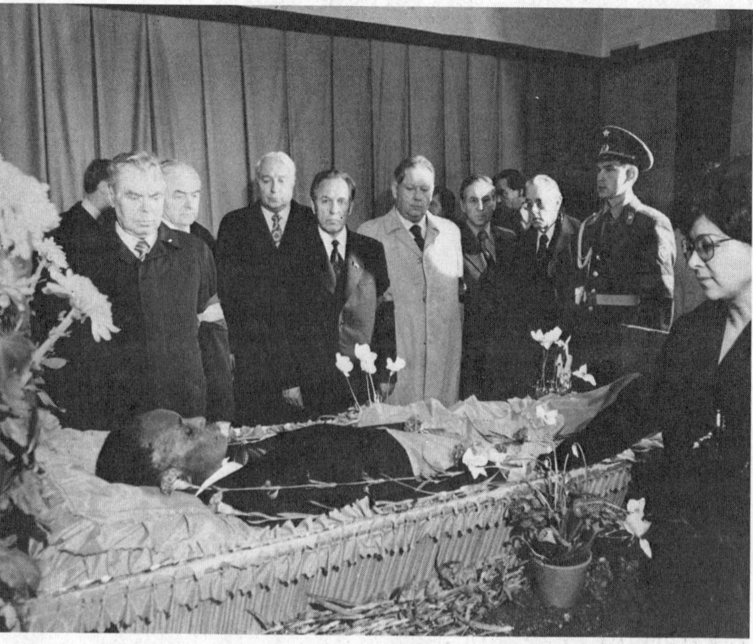
Soviet leaders view the body of Angolan President Agostinho Neto, who died in Moscow on September 10 following an operation for cancer.

ALEXEI STUZHIN—TASS/SOVFOTO

ANGOLA

Education. (1972–73) Primary, pupils 536,599, teachers 13,230; secondary, pupils 59,209, teachers 3,060; vocational, pupils 15,511, teachers 1,107; teacher training, students 3,388, teachers 330; higher, students 2,942, teaching staff 274.

Finance and Trade. Monetary unit: kwanza, with a free rate (Sept. 17, 1979) of 31.50 kwanzas to U.S. $1 (67.76 kwanzas = £1 sterling). Budget (1974 est.): revenue 23,540,000,000 kwanzas; expenditure 19,475,000,000 kwanzas. Foreign trade (1974): imports 15,853,000,000 kwanzas; exports 31,215,000,000 kwanzas. Import sources: Portugal 22%; West Germany 13%; U.S. 10%; South Africa 10%; U.K. 7%; France 7%; Italy 5%; Japan 5%. Export destinations: U.S. 38%; Portugal 27%; Canada 8%; Japan 6%. Main exports: crude oil 48%; coffee 20%; diamonds 8%.

Transport and Communications. Roads (1974) 72,323 km. Motor vehicles in use (1976): passenger 146,863; commercial (including buses) 39,270. Railways: (1975) *c.* 3,000 km; traffic (1974) 418 million passenger-km, freight 5,461,000,000 net ton-km. Air traffic (1977): 247 million passenger-km; freight *c.* 14 million net ton-km. Shipping (1978): merchant vessels 100 gross tons and over 21; gross tonnage 21,820. Shipping traffic (1975): goods loaded 15,990,000 metric tons, unloaded 2,850,000 metric tons. Telephones (Jan. 1978) 29,800. Radio receivers (Dec. 1976) 116,000.

Agriculture. Production (in 000; metric tons; 1978): corn *c.* 400; cassava (1977) *c.* 1,650; sweet potatoes (1977) *c.* 170; dry beans *c.* 65; bananas *c.* 300; citrus fruit (1977) *c.* 85; palm kernels *c.* 12; palm oil *c.* 40; coffee *c.* 54; cotton, lint *c.* 13; sisal *c.* 20; fish catch (1977) 113; timber (cu m; 1977) *c.* 8,182. Livestock (in 000; 1977): cattle *c.* 3,050; sheep *c.* 210; goats *c.* 920; pigs *c.* 365.

Industry. Production (in 000; metric tons; 1976): cement *c.* 650; diamonds (metric carats) *c.* 660; crude oil (1978) *c.* 8,200; petroleum products *c.* 670; electricity (kw-hr) *c.* 1.3 million.

for cancer. He was succeeded on September 20 by José Eduardo dos Santos (*see* BIOGRAPHIES). Despite his government's dependence on the Soviet Union and Cuba and his own Marxist principles, Neto was not unwilling to adopt a pragmatic approach to solving his country's problems. To many observers, his death seemed a setback to hopes of compromise.

Early in 1979 President Neto had announced that there were acute shortages of food, clothing, and other consumer goods in Angola. He recognized that exploitation of Angola's oil resources held out the greatest hope of economic recovery, and several Western countries displayed interest in his offer to share the profits of any venture in that field. In January a subsidiary of the French company Total signed an agreement with the Angolan government to search for offshore oil in the neighbourhood of Luanda. Neto also made it clear that he was prepared to permit further, limited extensions of private enterprise.

In August the government agreed to reopen diplomatic relations with West Germany; the main obstacle to such an arrangement had been removed when a West German rocket company was expelled from neighbouring Zaire. Angola had agreed in January to discuss the reopening of diplomatic relations with China, which had supported Holden Roberto's National Front for the Liberation of Angola (FNLA) in the struggle for power after Angola became independent. The FNLA had been inactive for some time before the proposals to China were made, but shortly afterward it reportedly renewed its guerrilla operations in the northern part of the country.

More serious from the point of view of governmental stability and economic recovery were the activities in southern Angola of Jonas Savimbi's National Union for the Total Independence of Angola (UNITA). These were closely linked with problems arising from the continuing presence in Angola of forces belonging to the South West Africa People's Organization (SWAPO). The forays of this latter group into Namibia again led to reprisal raids by South Africa, which assisted the UNITA guerrillas in an attempt to pressure Angola into restricting SWAPO's activities. Early in March South African troops and planes attacked SWAPO bases in Angola, and the following month UNITA forces occupied Cuangar on Angola's southern border. In May other UNITA forces captured the town of Calais, 90 mi east of Cuangar, after a battle with government troops. In July Angolan forces claimed to have shot down a South African fighter-bomber that was taking part in a raid over the country's southern border.

In typically pragmatic fashion, however, Neto, in the same month, adopted a more cooperative line over negotiations to solve the Namibia dispute. Following secret talks with Donald McHenry, U.S. deputy permanent representative at the UN, he proposed that there should be a 30-mi-wide demilitarized zone along the Angolan border with Namibia and that Angola should supervise SWAPO camps north of that zone to ensure that the guerrillas stayed in them. The UN would have a presence in Angola to see that the agreements were carried out. Neto's death represented a serious blow to hopes for a Namibian settlement.

The uncertain operation of the Benguela Railway because of UNITA activities continued to be a cause of economic concern and an obstacle to peaceful settlement of the southern border region. Reports of the presence of East German troops acting as instructors to the SWAPO guerrillas exacerbated the situation, and South Africa renewed air raids at the end of September.

A first summit meeting between five former Portuguese African colonies—Angola, Cape Verde, Guinea-Bissau, Mozambique, and São Tomé and Príncipe—was held in Luanda in June.

(KENNETH INGHAM)

Antarctica

The tenth Antarctic Treaty Consultative Meeting was held in Washington, D.C., site of the signing of the treaty 20 years earlier, from Sept. 17 to Oct. 7, 1979. The 13 consultative nations continued work on a proposed agreement to regulate the exploitation of living marine resources in the seas around Antarctica. They also continued discussions on exploitation of mineral resources, telecommunications policy, tourism, and improved handling of meteorological data.

Mineral resources exploitation continued to be a problem area for treaty members. Several U.S. oil companies were anxious to begin geophysical surveys and perhaps even exploratory drilling in the continental shelf. Treaty nations were expected to discourage such exploration until a greater under-

American Literature:
see Literature

Anglican Communion:
see Religion

JAMES A. RAYMOND—STATE OF ALASKA DEPARTMENT OF FISH AND GAME, FAIRBANKS

U.S. drill rigs were used to create access holes for experiments deep into the Ross Ice Shelf in Antarctica.

standing of the environmental consequences was acquired.

On November 28 an Air New Zealand DC-10 on a tourist flight over Antarctica crashed into Mt. Erebus, killing all 257 persons on board.

Cooperative International Activities. In 1978–79, the final large season for the nine-nation Ross Ice Shelf Project, U.S. drillers created three access holes through the ice shelf for experiments by Norwegian, Soviet, New Zealand, and U.S. scientists. Soviet drillers successfully took an ice core completely through the ice shelf, resulting in conclusive proof that seawater is freezing to the bottom of the Ross Ice Shelf. Geologists and glaciologists from four nations worked in the Byrd-Darwin Glaciers area seeking evidence to help explain the disintegration of a major North American Arctic ice sheet thousands of years ago. POLEX-South, an extended study of air-sea-ice interactions in the Southern Ocean, continued on Soviet and Japanese ships.

Japanese and U.S. scientists continued to gather large quantities of meteorites preserved in Antarctic ice. Some 309 were gathered during the 1978–79 season, including a 136-kg (300-lb) iron meteorite, one of the largest ever found. Laboratory studies discovered amino acids previously unknown on Earth. Five nations continued the International Antarctic Glaciological Project in East Antarctica. The U.S.S.R. and Australia continued their over-ice traverses, and France drilled additional ice cores and measured ice temperatures in the deep core hole at Dome C. U.S.-U.K. airborne radar measurements of the ice cover continued, including 11 flights to determine the boundary between East and West Antarctica. U.S. scientists began geophysical and ice strain measurements at Dome C.

The cooperative air transport system developed further. Australia joined New Zealand in making cargo flights between Christchurch and the U.S. McMurdo Station; the U.S. flew two missions to Australia's Casey Station, beginning a multiyear support arrangement; and British Antarctic Survey Twin Otters called at several Argentine bases in the Antarctic Peninsula and the U.S. Siple Station in Ellsworth Land. A U.S. ski-equipped Hercules flew an 11,400-km (7,000-mi) rescue mission to the U.S.S.R.'s Molodezhnaya Station to pick up five Soviets who had been very seriously injured in the crash of an Il-14 twin-engined airplane.

National Programs. ARGENTINA. A new research ship, the ARA "Puerto Deseado," was launched, and the "Islas Orcadas" was returned to the U.S. after a five-year loan. Family groups, including 11 women and 15 children, continued to be sent to Ft. Sargento Cabral at Esperanza Base.

AUSTRALIA. Research programs continued at three bases, and the rebuilding of Casey Station began. Sir Douglas Mawson's 1911–14 hut at Cape Denison was inspected, and it was decided to restore the hut rather than to remove it to a museum.

CHILE. The Antarctic program was reduced because of a border dispute with Argentina in Tierra del Fuego, but bases continued to be occupied.

FRANCE. Dumont d'Urville Station was resupplied and work began on an airstrip. It would take four more years to complete.

JAPAN. Research continued at Syowa and the inland Mizuho Station, especially in upper atmospheric physics. Several rockets were launched for data collection.

NEW ZEALAND. Scientists continued their studies of the Mt. Erebus volcano, and geologists surveyed the Ford Ranges in Marie Byrd Land. Work continued to rebuild Scott Base and to restore the historic huts on Ross Island from the early-20th-century Scott and Shackleton expeditions.

NORWAY. The second independent expedition since 1960 established a manned weather station on Bovet Island. The research ship "Polarsirkel" worked off the Queen Maud Land coast and in the Weddell Sea.

POLAND. A second research station, Dobrowolski, was opened along the Knox Coast. Originally the U.S.S.R.'s Oasis Station, Dobrowolski had been used by Polish scientists in 1958–59 when they were part of the Soviet Union's Antarctic Expedition.

SOUTH AFRICA. A new ice-strengthened research ship, the SA "Agulhas," made its first voyage. Construction began on a new SANAE base, while 12 scientists continued studies on the Ross seal and the upper atmosphere and recorded meteorological measurements.

UNITED KINGDOM. Research continued at the British bases despite the loss of the research ship "John Biscoe" to the shipyard for refitting. Fieldwork was conducted from the Antarctic Peninsula to the Ellsworth Mountains.

U.S.S.R. Some 560 men and women were involved in the Soviet Antarctic Expedition, 280 of whom wintered over. Russkaya Base at Cape Burke on the Marie Byrd Land coast was permanently reoccupied, bringing the number of year-round Soviet bases to seven. Construction began on a new Novolazarevskaya Station, and work on the runway at Molodezhnaya continued. When finished, the runway would be capable of handling flights from Moscow via Australia.

UNITED STATES. Some 90 projects were conducted by 305 scientists during 1978–79. Geologists discovered the potentially mineral-rich Dufek Intrusion to be much larger than previously thought, probably the same size as the Bushveld Intrusion in South Africa. Other geologists discovered that the ice flowing from West Antarctica into the Ronne and Filchner ice shelves was once at least 450 m (1,475 ft) thicker than it is today.

Algae were discovered growing near the bottom of an ice-covered lake in the Dry Valleys near McMurdo Station. Photosynthesis occurs even though only one-tenth of 1% of surface sunlight filters through the ice and water above the algae and the area is subjected to eight months of total and partial darkness each year. Scientists on board the icebreaker "Glacier" found that the Mertz and Ninnis glaciers, which had suffered major recessions between 1911 and 1958, had advanced 20 and 24 km (12 and 15 mi), respectively, in the last 21 years. Research in Palmer Station's laboratory discovered cannibalism among krill.

In midwinter a USAF C-141 jet transport delivered 3,200 kg (3.5 tons) of cargo to McMurdo Station in a parachute delivery, the first in five years. Siple Station was rebuilt, and a five-year rebuilding of McMurdo Station began. A cargo ship removed the last marginally radioactive soil from the site of the dismantled PM-3A nuclear power plant.

OTHER NATIONS. East Germany completed its 20th consecutive year of research in Antarctica with the Soviet expedition. West Germany announced plans for a major research program to begin in 1980. Press reports indicated that Peru was considering making a territorial claim, and China began discussions that might lead to joint work in Antarctica with Chile. Belgium again did not field an expedition. (PETER J. ANDERSON)

WIDE WORLD

On November 28, exactly 50 years after Comdr. Richard E. Byrd made the first flight over the South Pole, an Air New Zealand DC-10 on a sight-seeing flight over Antarctica crashed into Mt. Erebus, killing all 257 persons aboard. The crash was the fourth worst in aviation history and the third in 1979 involving a DC-10, although structural failure was ruled out in this case. Rescuers found the wreckage strewn over the slopes of the 3,780-metre volcano, about 48 kilometres north of the U.S. station at McMurdo Sound.

Anthropology

Recent research in human evolution has focused on two general areas: the morphology and taxonomy of the numerous African hominids of the Plio-Pleistocene (5.5 million–700,000 years ago), and the time and circumstances surrounding the first appearance of the hominid lineage.

Mary Leakey and Richard L. Hay announced the discovery of a remarkable series of footprints from the Laetoli site in northern Tanzania (3,750,000–3.6 million years old). Among numerous footprints of Pliocene hares, elephants, carnivores, bovids, and birds are trails of primate footprints. One of these trails is clearly that of two bipedal hominids which walked along the same line or pathway. The clear impression of the heel, arch, and toes is preserved in volcanic ash in much the same form as a modern trail left in damp sand. What was significant about this material was not that our early Plio-Pleistocene ancestors walked erect, but the antiquity of this type of locomotion. At 3.6 million–3,750,000 years, the Laetoli footprints are older than any of the previous material suggesting bipedality in our early ancestors.

Although there was no evidence in the fossil record that would provide a clue to the origin of this uniquely human activity, Stephen Gould speculated on the significance of this type of locomotion for human evolution. It had been generally assumed that the evolution of the large and complex brain was the hallmark of humanity. However, Gould suggested that bipedality may have played at least an equal, if not a more significant, role. Bipedality requires a greater sophistication in balance and muscular coordination than does locomotion employing all four limbs, and it may have been associated with the unique reorganization of the brain in the hominid line.

Left footprint of a bipedal hominid found in northern Tanzania indicates that bipedal walking was an achievement of early human ancestors between 3,750,000 and 3.6 million years ago.

FROM "PLIOCENE FOOTPRINTS IN THE LAETOLIL BEDS AT LAETOLI, NORTHERN TANZANIA," M. D. LEAKEY AND R. L. HAY, *NATURE*, VOL. 278, PP. 317-322, MARCH 22, 1979

In recent years it had been noted that, although the brain of the Plio-Pleistocene hominids is small, it is organized on a pattern more like that of modern man than that of the extant apes. Although a connection between neural reorganization associated with bipedality and the evolution of the human brain could only be suggested, freedom of the hands and forelimbs would provide a unique potential for manipulation and exploration of the environment. This could well be associated with increasing reliance on cultural solutions to adaptive problems and hence with the later development of the large brain and the sophisticated cultural activities of the later hominids.

But who were these bipedal Pliocene hominids? Beginning approximately two million years ago, there were at least two distinct lineages of hominids. One includes *Australopithecus robustus* and *Australopithecus boisei*, heavily built and with teeth and jaws suggesting an exclusively herbivorous diet. The second is represented by *Homo habilis*, smaller in size and more generalized in its dental apparatus, which is considered to be a direct human ancestor. At an earlier time period (approximately 2.5 million years ago), there was also a group of hominids known as *Australopithecus africanus*, which had been considered the most likely common ancestor for the two later hominid lineages. However, Mary Leakey suggested that the Laetoli footprints, as well as fossils of jaws and teeth from the same site and similar fossils from Hadar, Ethiopia (3.3 million–2.9 million years old), represent our own genus, *Homo*.

This implies that the two lineages diverged well before three million years ago and suggests that *Australopithecus africanus*, as well as *Australopithecus robustus* and *Australopithecus boisei*, occupy an unsuccessful side branch of the human line. However, there was by no means full consensus on this interpretation. Donald C. Johanson and Timothy D. White suggested that both the Laetoli material and the fossil material from Hadar belong to one taxonomic grouping, *Australopithecus afarensis*, ancestral to both the *Homo* lineage and the rest of the australopithecines.

There remain the basic questions of when and where the hominid line diverged from the common primate stock and the morphological form of this early ancestor. Until recently, the Miocene genus *Ramapithecus* from East Africa and Eurasia had been considered the undisputed first representative of the hominid line. However, recent discoveries of more complete dental fossils of *Ramapithecus*, as well as more fossils of contemporary Miocene Eurasian apes (*Sivapithecus*), threw doubt on this interpretation.

This entire group of fossils shows close similarity in most dental characteristics. Although the consensus is that the hominid lineage had its roots among these Miocene apes, it is not yet possible to conclude that *Ramapithecus* in either its African or its Eurasian form is the specific ancestor. Electron microscopic analyses of the enamel prism patterns of the teeth of *Ramapithecus*, the Eurasian Miocene apes, and contemporary apes suggest that *Ramapithecus* and the hominids share a unique and specific pattern. This type of analysis is still in its

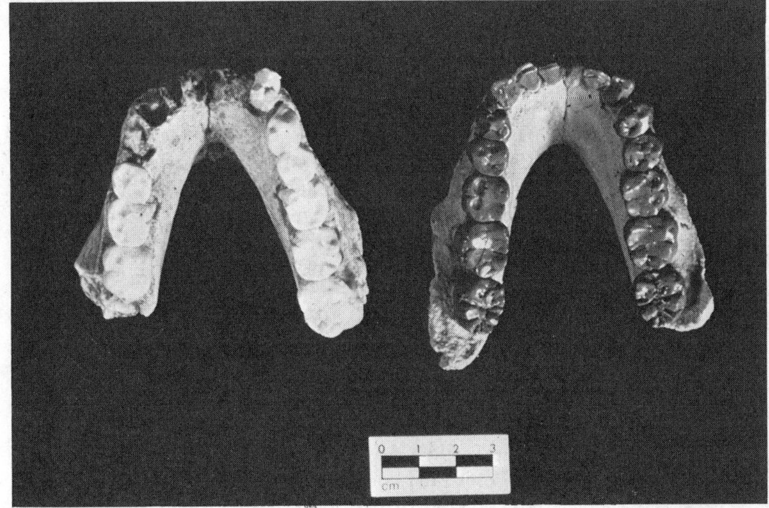

Mandibles from Laetoli (3,750,000–3.6 million years old) in Tanzania (left) and from the Hadar (3.3 million–2.9 million years old) site in Ethiopia (right) are strikingly similar. Anthropologists argue as to whether they belong to the genus *Homo* or to *Australopithecus afarensis*.

initial stages, however, and there are few if any other characteristics recognized in the currently available fossils that would unequivocally support the hypothesis that *Ramapithecus* had already separated from the ape stock. As Gould emphasized, this uncertainty, as well as the close biochemical similarity between recent apes and man, does not make it inconceivable that the hominid line appeared at a more recent date than *Ramapithecus,* perhaps between approximately 9 million and 3.5 million years ago where there is a large gap in the fossil record.

The suggestion of such a recent divergence of the hominid line poses the question of the time required to develop the efficient bipedal locomotion documented by the Laetoli footprints. This largely revolves around the question of the morphology of the trunk and limbs of the last common ancestor. Recent analyses suggest that the last common ancestor was much less specialized in its postcranial morphology than the extant great apes. Using the technique of allometry (measuring the relative growth of a part in relation to the whole organism), Leslie Aiello suggested that the modern great apes have experienced a specialized reduction of their hind limbs consistent with the mechanical requirements of locomotion for a large-bodied primate in the trees.

However, this analysis also shows that the human line is not characterized by unusually long hind limbs. The length of the human hind limbs when compared with body size is consistent with the proportions of the New and Old World monkeys. The hypothesis that the last common ancestor was more like the extant monkeys than the extant great apes was also supported by morphological analyses of the fragmentary postcranial remains from the Miocene apes, comparative morphology of extant higher primates, and aspects of the locomotor behaviour of extant apes. Surprisingly, these analyses suggest that the last common ancestor would have been more like the New than the Old World monkeys. Most likely it would have been a deliberate climber similar to the extant howler monkey of Central and South America, but lacking the prehensile tail.

A morphological analysis of the primate wrist, forelimb, and axial skeleton by Matt Cartmill and Katharine Milton also suggests that the tendency toward upright posture in apes and man is associated with a climbing form of locomotion. Therefore, the hypothetical climbing ancestor would have not only the preadaptations to upright posture gained from its climbing heritage but also a generalized skeleton. In its limb proportions, the human line is specialized from this generalized common ancestor only in having a slightly reduced forelimb and, particularly, forearm. Given a conducive adaptive situation, the only requirements for efficient erect posture would be bone and muscle rearrangements and neural reorganization. This indicates that the morphological pathway between the common ancestor and man is considerably shorter than previously thought.

(LESLIE C. AIELLO)

See also Archaeology.
[411; 10/36.B]

Archaeology

Eastern Hemisphere. The most spectacular find of 1979 appeared to have come from royal tombs at Shibarghan in northern Afghanistan. These tombs, about 2,000 years old, yielded more than 20,000 pieces of gold jewelry. These show the mixture of cultural influences—Greek, Roman, Indian, and Chinese—that prevailed at the time in that part of Asia.

Controversy, in part purely academic and in part with political overtones, continued with regard to the great find of cuneiform tablets made several years earlier at the north Syrian site of Ebla. Incomplete translations of small portions of this written evidence from about 2500 BC were taken as describing persons and places of the age of the biblical patriarchs. However, there was disagreement between the Italian excavators as to the exact dates and meanings involved, and the Syrian Antiquities Department objected to claims that ancient Ebla was "a stronghold of Hebrew cultural influence."

INGEBORG LIPPMAN—THE NEW YORK TIMES

The Iraqi government plans to spend about $36 million to excavate and restore the ancient site of Babylon. Students visiting the site sit on an ancient statue of a lion.

Since 1967 U.S. archaeologists in some foreign countries had benefited from agreements which provided that sales of U.S. grain could be paid for in local currency, the resultant sums being locally held and available for U.S. cultural and scientific enterprises. In 1979, however, the end of these sums was reached in Poland, Yugoslavia, Morocco, and Tunisia, and the money would soon be exhausted in Egypt. U.S. archaeological efforts in all of these countries thus were expected to suffer from lack of financial support.

During renovations at a Coptic monastery east of Cairo, the skeletal remains of some "13 or 14" individuals that were found were said to include the bones both of the prophet Elisha and of John the Baptist. There was not, however, any certainty in the matter.

PLEISTOCENE PREHISTORY. For the first time, stone tools were found in a Middle Pleistocene geologic context in Java, along with faunal remains of the type associated with *Homo erectus* fossils of the Java type. A Cambridge University expedition in Swaziland reported finding many new types of stone artifacts, some of which appear to have been used to form composite tools, in general association with fossil evidence of *Homo sapiens*. This was regarded as support for recent claims for the very early (before 100,000 BC) appearance of anatomically modern people in southern Africa, some 60,000 years before they appeared in Europe.

Farther south, at sites around Saldanha Bay, South Africa, shell middens of about 70,000 years of age indicate the earliest systematic human use of seafoods. In the Cantabrian region of northern Spain the La Riera cave, with its clear succession of materials from the Solutrean and Magdalenian cultures, was investigated, and a detailed examination of Late Paleolithic development in a sheltered valley near the sea was made.

NEAR EAST. In Egypt Lionel Balout reported on the detailed French restoration and study of the mummy of Ramses II, which had been sent to Paris for that purpose in 1976. Ramses was found to have died a very bent and shrunken old man affected by atherosclerosis. One curious, and not clearly explained, result of the examination was the discovery of botanical traces of tobacco—a Western Hemisphere plant—found within the mummy's abdomen.

Also from Egypt came new evidence for early kingship in Nubia. This was based on preliminary results of an archaeological survey in the Dakhleh Oasis about 644 km (400 mi) southwest of Cairo and of another archaeological survey for sites of the Persian, Greek, and Roman ages in the region between Cairo and the Suez Canal.

In Jordan a mid-2nd millennium BC burial cave north of Amman, already partially plundered, yielded an impressive variety of Mycenaean, Cypriot, and Palestinian pottery. The surrounding area was subsequently surveyed with a magnetometer in an effort to detect more graves, and positive results were indicated.

In Syria a British expedition under the direction of Peter Parr continued to work at Tell Nebi Mend, the site of Qadesh, where the Egyptians fought the Hittites. Another British expedition under David Oates, digging in northeastern Syria at Tell Brak, recovered a late Uruk cuneiform tablet, the earliest in northern Mesopotamia. French, Italian, West German, Japanese, and Dutch expeditions were also at work, the latter continuing the exposure of the important early village site of Bouqras on the middle Euphrates River. A U.S. expedition under the direction of Harvey Weiss of Yale University began excavating Tell Leilan in extreme northeastern Syria, recovering the remains of major buildings and several cuneiform tablets dating from the early 2nd millennium BC and discovering evidence of an extensive Ninevite V occupation (early 3rd millennium BC).

The Iraqi Department of Antiquities began a 15-year clearance and restoration on the site of Babylon, first generally excavated by the Germans before World War I. It seemed doubtful that remains much earlier than those of Nebuchadrezzar's time (about 600 BC) could be exposed without great difficulty due to the high water table. North of Baghdad, in the Hamrin Basin salvage project, research teams from many countries were at work, with substantial aid from the Iraq government. At Tell Razuk, dug by a joint Danish-U.S. expedition led by McGuire Gibson of the University of Chicago's Oriental Institute, there was a remarkably good preservation of mud-brick architecture of about 3000 BC. Most impressive was a large round building with the world's earliest still-intact barrel vaults.

GRECO-ROMAN REGIONS. In Turkey the now century-old work of the Germans at Pergamum was continued, as well as the work of the Austrians at Ephesus. The careful long-range archaeological investigations of these two ancient classical cities are of equivalent importance to those in the Agora of Athens. In the latter area a building identified as the state prison where Socrates spent his last days was fully exposed.

Work proceeded at various sites in Greece, Crete, and the Aegean islands on preclassical horizons. At Sesklo in Thessaly levels dating back to about 6000 BC were investigated. Greek archaeologists reported an early Helladic (3000–2500 BC) tomb with the skeletons of a pair of horses in Argo-

UNIVERSITY OF CHICAGO, ORIENTAL INSTITUTE

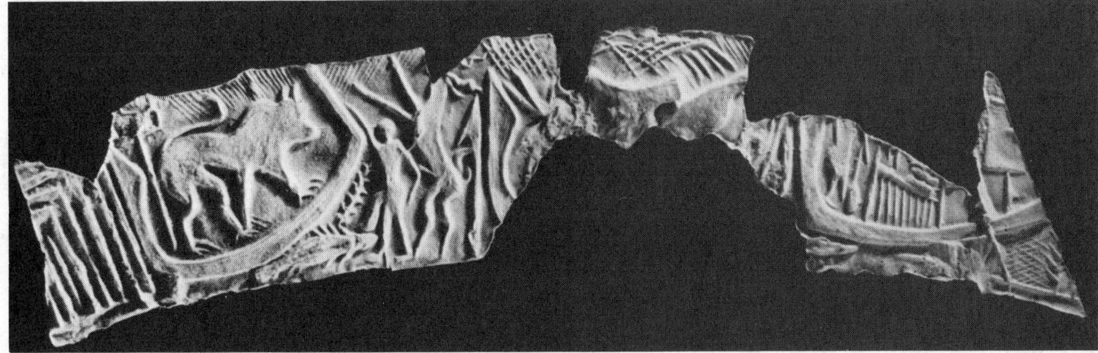

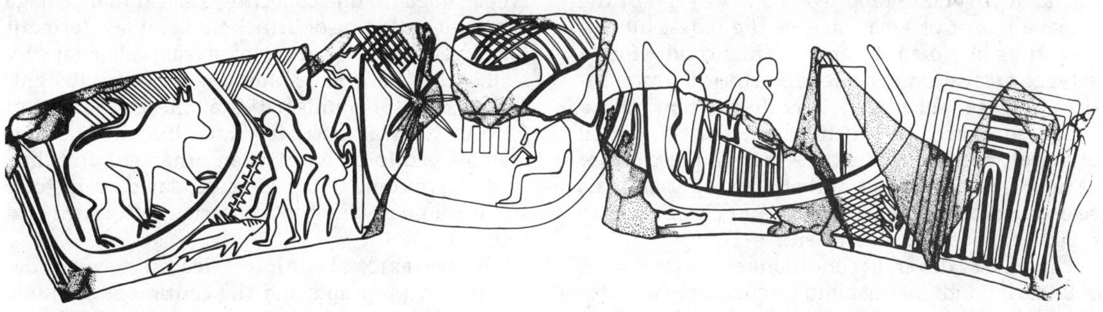

The images above (redrawn below for clarity) are from a stone incense burner used about 3300 BC in ancient Nubia in Africa.

lis. These would be the earliest evidence of horse domestication.

The usual large number of reports of Greek and Roman finds came from throughout the Mediterranean region, in western Europe, and in Asia. A 7th-century BC sanctuary to Demeter and Persephone was exposed at Cyrene in Libya with a rich yield of luxury items showing strong connections with the Levantine coast. The remains of a fine Roman villa were cleared near Siena in Italy, and the site of the Roman fortress and city of Viroconium in Shropshire, England, was being cleared.

The year's most spectacular find, that of the royal tombs at Shibarghan in northern Afghanistan, was made by a joint Afghan-Soviet expedition directed by Viktor Sarianidi. Six royal tombs, dating to between 100 BC and AD 100, yielded hoards of jewelry, including golden objects weighing up to one kilogram (about two pounds). The finds were said to rival the treasure in the tomb of King Tutankhamen in richness. Further, the artifacts involved indicate the blend of cultural influences in ancient Bactria, through which the silk and spice routes passed from east to west and where the Hellenizing influences that arrived with Alexander the Great blended with the traditions of Asia.

AFRICA AND ASIA. The journal *Science* (March 23, 1979) contained the report of an important investigation of the datings and contexts of south African rock art. This heretofore poorly dated and understood late prehistoric artistic repertoire may have begun earlier than 4,000 years ago but seems to have had major flourishes coincident with the wetter, warmer climates of about 3,000 years and again about 2,000 years before the present.

A joint Trent University-Royal Ontario Museum expedition in eastern Botswana began work on a large Iron-Age settlement that dated to around AD 900 to 1400. Another research team was making a combined ethnological and archaeological effort to study the complex iron-smelting procedures of the Haya people of northwestern Tanzania. Their highly advanced iron-smelting technology began perhaps 2,000 years ago and still persists.

A 2,400-year-old porcelain glazing kiln was reported to have been found near Hangchow, China. The oldest evidence of porcelain so far found, the kiln remains also included many fragments with bluish-gray celadon glaze.

(ROBERT J. BRAIDWOOD)

Western Hemisphere. Within the United States trends in archaeological research had to a large degree been determined by recent changes in the nature of federal legislative funding and planning programs. Since the passage in 1974 of the Moss-Bennett bill, U.S. government funding for archaeological research had increased from $15 million to $150 million per year. As a consequence U.S. archaeologists were putting nearly all their efforts into conservation and related planning programs. Over the same period National Science Foundation-supported work in the U.S. dropped from 18% of all archaeological grants in 1974 to less than 3% in 1979.

While these shifts in orientation and funding precipitated a wide range of new approaches in method and theory as well as vast increases in data, they also caused field archaeologists to jump difficult hurdles in fiscal and logistical management. The sheer volume of new cultural materials and information brought to the surface the serious limitations in the discipline's ability to process and disseminate these materials. It also pinpointed a nearly nationwide crisis in museum facilities in which the new materials could be properly conserved.

The 1979 record of the U.S. Congress was one of

mixed results for archaeology in general. On the negative side, after seven years of debate both houses of Congress again failed to reach agreement on and pass legislation to implement the UNESCO Convention on Cultural Property, designed to limit the illicit importation of plundered artifacts, for which the U.S. provides 50% of the market. In a more positive vein, in October Congress passed the Archaeological Resources Protection Act, which would alleviate one of the major causes of unregulated site destruction within the U.S. by making looting of sites a felony punishable by fines of up to $20,000 and/or two years in prison.

NORTH AMERICA. Under the direction of Carol Rector, archaeologists from the University of California at Riverside reported the discovery in the Mojave Desert of what may be the oldest human footprints in North America. While conducting a salvage excavation of a late prehistoric Serrano Indian village scheduled for destruction by a proposed sewage treatment plant, the team of 40 archaeologists found the preserved impressions of at least five individuals and at least eight animals sealed beneath three feet of silt and clay dating to 5,000 years before the present.

Under very different conditions of preservation, 300 early and pre-Eskimo archaeological sites along the coast of Labrador were identified by a joint team from the Smithsonian Institution (William Fitzhugh, Steven Cox, and Chris Nagle) and Bryn Mawr College (Richard Jordan). Excavation in several of the frozen sites yielded a well-preserved assortment of previously unknown wooden tools, carved soapstone figurines with details of prehistoric clothing, and frozen mummified human remains dating to more than 7,000 years before the present.

From 20 years of underwater explorations in the deep vertical underwater cavern of Little Salt Spring, Florida, C. J. Clausen and colleagues reported the discovery of unique wood artifacts dating to the Paleo-Indian period, between 12000 and 9000 BC. Some of the more extraordinary finds included the carcass of an extinct giant land turtle preserved with a wooden spear still in place, as well as the first reported New World occurrence of a nonreturning wooden boomerang capable of killing a deer at 50 yd.

Finally, the undisputed identification of a Norse coin dating to between 1065 and 1080 rekindled the debate over Viking visits to the New World. The coin was found in 1961 in Maine by an amateur archaeologist while collecting at an Indian village site. Thought to be of British make, it lay dormant for 20 years until a survey of private collections by staff of the Maine State Museum brought it to light. The curator of numismatics at the University of Oslo in Norway positively identified it. The coin was pierced to be worn as an ornament and thus could have come to the as-yet-undated prehistoric site through a variety of contacts, both direct and indirect.

MESOAMERICA. Within Mexico City general development programs and the continued monitoring of ongoing subway construction yielded an impressive series of new discoveries from the buried Aztec capital. Excavations on new subway lines provided new information on the boundaries of the Aztec city as well as general information on pre-Hispanic and colonial residential areas. During the last weeks of 1979, after excavating 40 ceremonial offering deposits, archaeologist Carlos González announced to the press the sensational find of a 0.9 by 1.2 m (3 by 4 ft) carved stone box,

Skeletons of baby dinosaurs were found in Montana. Princeton University scientist John Horner holds the bone from a mature animal and points to the corresponding bone of a baby.

WILLIAM E. SAURO—THE NEW YORK TIMES

found six feet below the surface and under water. It was decorated on five sides with relief sculptures showing influence from the region of Guerrero. Inside the box were four large conch shells, offerings to the god of rain, Tlaloc, and two large carved heads of semiprecious stone.

Preconstruction survey projects in other regions of Mexico were also revealing significant new information in previously little-understood culture areas of Mexico. In the Gulf Coast lowland states the archaeological survey of a proposed 12,000-km (7,500-mi) gas pipeline revealed a staggering 650 new archaeological sites.

Recent excavations at the lakeshore site of Zohapilco in the Valley of Mexico by Christine Weidenberger of the National Institute of Anthropology and History at last filled a long-standing chronological gap for human occupation there between 6000 and 2000 BC. At the same time these data altered radically the understanding of the shift to permanent village life in Mexico. The analysis of often microscopic plant and animal remains demonstrated that even without the use of irrigation agriculture, indigenous lakeshore residents were able to maintain a year-round permanent village existence in the Valley of Mexico as early as 6000 BC. Rather than irrigation, as was previously believed, the permanence was due to the abundance of plants, fish, turtles, and migratory birds.

Excavation at the site of San José de Mogote in Oaxaca by Kent Flannery and Joyce Marcus of the University of Michigan helped to alter the long-held assumption that this valley held little in the way of complex society prior to the Zapotec culture. Deeply stratified remains dating to 650–500 BC, immediately prior to the establishment of Monte Alban, yielded a complex of early superimposed tombs, houses, and public buildings.

Recent work at Pre-Classic Maya sites in the Maya lowlands of coastal Belize continued to yield new data on Maya origins. It also cast doubt on the traditional assumption that Classic Maya culture developed first in the interior Petén jungles of Guatemala. Working on the coast of Belize, David Freidl of Southern Methodist University at the Pre-Classic site of Cerros found well-preserved and very early Maya plaster masks on the sides of a platform mound as well as a possible 40-m (131-ft) docking facility for trade on the inland rivers.

South America. Declines in U.S. funds for overseas research, combined with a tightening (as of 1978 and 1979) of many Latin-American national fiscal and regulatory policies, significantly limited the nature and extent of archaeological activity in South America by research teams from other regions. By 1978 these changes had placed an increasing responsibility for prehistoric cultural research programs on Latin-American scholars and institutions. Within the last two years preconstruction archaeological planning and survey projects had been accompanying large-scale development programs in the interiors of Brazil, Argentina, and Uruguay. These were beginning to shed new light on understudied areas and cultures.

In Peru one such excavation program at the pre-Chavin and Early Horizon highland site of Huaricoto uncovered the remains of a large ceremonial centre containing white plaster floors, a multilevel stone canal system, and air-vented subterranean burnt offering pits. Dated at about 1000 BC, this centre contrasts with better-known coastal sites of the same period in that, instead of being organized in the typical Chavin pattern of U-shaped galleries and buildings around a central plaza, it appears to have been divided into elliptical precincts separated by large stone walls.

From the previously little-known interior of Uruguay a multinational team, sponsored by UNESCO and the Ministry of Culture and Education, reported a wealth of new prehistoric survey and excavation data. Salvage work prior to the construction of the Salto Grande Dam led to the identification of more than 100 new archaeological sites, together with the reconstruction of a 9,000-year sequence of prehistoric cultures. Results yielded evidence of a large population, large pre-European-contact villages, and data on climatic, riverine, and vegetation changes in conjunction with the archaeologically datable remains.

(JOEL W. GROSSMAN)

See also Anthropology.
[723.G.8c; 10/41.B.2.a.ii]

WIDE WORLD

The battered skull of a man believed killed in an Indian attack nearly 360 years ago was found in a dig near Williamsburg, Virginia.

Architecture

The importance of design quality was again highlighted in 1979 as the bedrock upon which architecture rests. Despite various problems facing architects, they were enjoined to concentrate efforts on creating quality design and workmanship as being the only way in which they could play an effective public role in changing and improving the built environment. Speaking at a series of "grass roots" meetings in the U.S., the American Institute of Architects' (AIA's) president, Ehrman Mitchell, hailed 1979 as a year of "Celebration of Architecture," challenging architects to make the public more aware of their profession's role in the contemporary world. He

Archery:
see Target Sports

said, "Our greatest failing is that we don't talk enough about architecture to the public. . . . We must begin a major thrust in building a greater public understanding of . . . the public's role in shaping the physical environment, an understanding of how it comes to be, the discernment of its quality, and the architects who design it. . . . We must build a consciousness within our ranks of the importance of design excellence and the importance of accountability. We have a responsibility to the public to create a better life through our design. We must be ever conscious of how we affect the people, the land, the cities through our design efforts. And this comes through doing—not talking."

In Britain one of the major issues facing both architects and planners—whether to rebuild or renovate Britain's decaying city centres—was spotlighted by the resignation of the chief architect and his deputy for the London borough of Camden. Until the economic slump of the mid-1970s all but halted the housing programs of local authorities, architects in public service had enjoyed more than a decade of building and redesigning major urban projects, including many civic centres. The most exciting architectural work was, as a result, to be found in the public sector, which, accordingly, attracted the best talent.

The resignation at Camden, however, was a reminder of how things had changed in the last four years. Projects for housing, schools, civic centres, and shopping districts had declined, and the public had grown increasingly critical of new large public-authority schemes. Thus the top designers frequently found themselves merely supervising programs of maintenance and minor redevelopment, while architects in private practice, after three disastrous years, were at last beginning to see a real improvement in opportunities. These were occurring especially in the Middle East, where projects for hotel complexes, commercial buildings, and hospitals abounded.

In the U.S. construction activity was expected to take a downward turn in the second half of 1979 from its high 1978 level. Total activity for the year was forecast to be about 10% below 1978 in terms of square footage built. The rise in interest rates and the general economic situation were blamed for the somewhat pessimistic forecast. Homebuilding in particular was expected to suffer as a result of higher costs of borrowing combined with the reduced availability of mortgages. The one sector that was expected to continue its spectacular growth in 1979 was office and factory construction, forecast to rise 8–10% over 1978 levels.

Awards. The AIA awarded its 1979 Gold Medal to I. M. Pei. The award was presented at the organization's national convention at Kansas City, Mo., in June. Pei also received the annual Elsie de Wolfe Award from the American Society of Interior Designers, and his achievements were further marked by his election to the post of chancellor of the American Academy and Institute of Arts and Letters. He was the first architect in the history of the predominantly literary academy to hold that position.

The 1979 Gold Medal of the Royal Institute of British Architects (RIBA) was awarded to the U.S. partnership of Charles and Ray Eames for its innovation in architecture, furniture, and communication through films, graphics, and exhibitions. The *Royal Institute of British Architects Journal* wrote, "In an age which is threatened by drabness and over-specialization, the celebration of the achievements of the Eames office is particularly appropriate."

The 1978 prizes in the Library Building Awards Program, jointly sponsored by the AIA and the American Library Association to encourage excellence in the design and planning of libraries, were announced early in 1979. First Honor Awards went to three vastly different projects. The Michigan City, Ind., Public Library, designed by C. F. Murphy Associates of Chicago, featured a central landscaped patio overlooked from the library

A gardener, not a janitor, is needed to maintain this office building near Moline, Illinois. Kevin Roche, John Dinkeloo & Associates were the architects.

KEVIN ROCHE, JOHN DINKELOO AND ASSOCIATES

building by lounge seating on three sides. The Houston, Texas, Central Library by S. I. Morris Associates of Houston was a monumental granite and glass volume connected to the old library building via a basement beneath a large plaza. The whole was a strong, bold statement. In contrast, the Sarah Lawrence College Library, Bronxville, N.Y., was almost domestic in scale and blended well into its predominantly residential setting. The plan emphasized departmentalization, a departure from the trend in library design favouring large open spaces. Architects were Warner Burns Toan Lunde of New York City.

The AIA Architectural Firm Award went to Geddes Brecher Qualls Cunningham of Philadelphia. This followed the awarding of the Silver Medal of the Pennsylvania Society of Architects to the firm for its design of the Market Street Renewal and Restoration in Corning, N.Y. The AIA award was given to the firm "to mark the high quality and consistent excellence of its designs over the last ten years."

The Italian engineer Pier Luigi Nervi, a former recipient of both the RIBA (1960) and the AIA (1964) gold medals, died in January (*see* OBITUARIES). Nervi pioneered the use of reinforced concrete to create large-scale structures with a dramatic spatial impact.

Public and Commercial Buildings. Renovation projects in 1979 were as imaginative as new structures in many instances, and preservation of old environmental areas was as important a goal as the achievement of design excellence in new buildings. A project to renovate the shopping concourse at Rockefeller Center, New York City, was announced and was expected to cost $2 million. The famous complex has an early example of an underground concourse connecting the buildings in the group. Designed to protect users from weather and traffic, such concourses became popular in multiuse centres in the 1960s and '70s. The Rockefeller Center example houses various retail outlets and is used by an estimated 250,000 people daily. Architects in charge of the revitalization project were the Walker/Group, Inc. One feature of the new design would be the removal of the walls around the sunken ice rink with its famous sculpture of Prometheus and replacement of them with full-height glazing to allow concourse users an uninterrupted vista of the rink.

Another exciting project of renovation was promised for Buffalo, N.Y., where developers acquired Louis Sullivan's turn-of-the-century Prudential Building. Improvements would include the filling in of the U-shaped centre of the structure and general modernization of services at an estimated cost of $5 million. The renovated building would also house a Sullivan museum.

"Atrium" buildings, in which large indoor glass-roofed garden spaces are created, had grown in popularity in the U.S. during recent years to the degree that an atrium was almost a requirement of any fashionable new structure, whether a shopping centre, office building, or hotel. The idea itself was not new, being an adaptation of the old glassed-in courtyard building of the traditional glazed arcade or market building. The current

COSMO VERNER—CAMERA PRESS

England's first "atrium" building, housing the Coutts Bank in London, opened in December 1978. The architects were Sir Frederick Gibberd & Partners.

revival of the atrium could be traced to John Portman's Hyatt Regency Hotel in Atlanta, Ga., built in 1967.

Late in 1978 England's first "atrium" building was completed, the new headquarters for Coutts Bank in London. Designed by architects Sir Frederick Gibberd & Partners, the building incorporated the early-19th-century facade of John Nash's West Strand improvements with its famous "pepperpots." Thus it was significant from the viewpoint of conservation as well as innovation, showing how a skillful design can incorporate a historic facade and yet create an uncompromisingly contemporary spatial quality. The site is an important one, almost opposite Charing Cross Station at the beginning of the Strand. The main entrance is a transparent glass screen midway in the flat Nash stucco facade, slightly set back into it. The atrium itself is the first-floor banking hall, the only public space in the building; it rises four stories and is toplit. This space, complete with full-size trees, is surrounded by glassed-in galleries, which alters the spatial qualities but was a requirement imposed by the fire regulations. The site is a triangular one, and the atrium occupies the centre of the triangle.

Plans were unveiled for another commercial building in London that would incorporate a glazed central space, the new headquarters for the insurance underwriters Lloyd's. The design, by Richard Rogers and Renzo Piano, the designers of the Centre National d'Art et de Culture Georges Pompidou (Centre Beaubourg) in Paris, retained the concept of the single underwriting room, which has always been a feature of Lloyd's, by creating a vast glass-roofed, steel-vaulted open space that would rise 12 stories, rather like a Victorian railway station. Galleries would open around the main space. Stairways and elevators were placed on the outside of the building to leave the centre free for the underwriting room. As at the Beaubourg, glass tubes, pipes, and ducts would become decorative features on the exterior. The Royal Fine Art Commission hailed the design as "brilliant" and expected it to be "one of the most remarkable buildings of the decade." It was welcomed as an illustration of enlightened patronage, proof that commercial buildings can be functional without being dull. The project, which would cost an estimated £45 million, was due to start in late 1979.

A vast glazed space was a feature of the Deere West building for Deere & Co. near Moline, Ill., by architects Kevin Roche, John Dinkeloo & Associates. The new building, reminiscent both of Japanese architecture with its strong horizontal emphasis and of the exploitation of glassed-in areas, was yet another example of the growing trend for business clients to commission architecture of quality and excellence. The Roche-Dinkeloo building added 200,000 sq ft of additional space to the company's headquarters. The original Deere building was designed in the late 1950s by Eero Saarinen and finished in 1964. This new addition on the company's 1,044-ac site was a three-level addition to the seven-level original and was of steel and glass construction. Inside there was an 11,000-sq-ft multilevel garden roofed by a series of gambrel-shaped glass skylights reminiscent of a glazed barn roof. This area afforded a perfect showplace for the farm, garden, and construction equipment manufactured by Deere & Co.

Landscaped interior courts also were featured in a design by U.S. architects Skidmore Owings & Merrill for the National Commercial Bank in Jidda, Saudi Arabia. In this structure no individual windows pierce the monumental marble exterior; instead, huge rectangular apertures allow light into three landscaped courts placed in alternate positions on two sides of the triangular tower. This device shields the office floors from the direct effects of the Sun and wind and adapts two traditional features of indigenous Saudi architecture: the principle of ventilation and the principle of turning the building inward. The formal structure on its prominent site overlooking the Red Sea symbolized the new urban aspirations and economic importance of Saudi Arabia in the 1970s.

The use of solar energy to provide services for buildings was again an important topic as oil prices soared. A design for a new federal prison at Bastrop, Texas, by CRS Inc. featured solar heating and cooling by means of 26,000 sq ft of solar collectors. Other innovations incorporated into the design of the facility, which would accommodate 500 inmates, included decentralized living units that would enable each prisoner to occupy his own room.

Solar heating was also a feature of the Police Services and Fire Administration Building, Mountain View, Calif., designed by architects Goodwin B. Steinberg Associates. In addition to the solar collectors, which were to be enclosed within high vertical walls, large north-facing double-glazed windows would admit cool natural light to allow an average lighting load of 1.5 w per sq ft. The solar system would provide heating, cooling, hot water, and protection against frost. The walls were to be of reinforced concrete painted white, and the steel bracing in the large clerestory windows would be painted a vivid hue to provide contrast and interest.

Architects Ulrich Franzen & Associates unveiled their design for a new corporate headquarters for Philip Morris Inc. at Park Avenue and 42nd Street in Manhattan. The 26-story, 600,000-sq-ft structure would house a midtown branch of the Whitney Museum of American Art, featuring a sculpture gallery encased in a 42-ft-high glass-enclosed pedestrian plaza. The detailing of the facade

C.F. Murphy Associates of Chicago won a First Honor Award for the design of a new public library in Michigan City, Indiana.

C. F. MURPHY ASSOCIATES

NICK WHEELER—AIA

The 1979 AIA Honor Award went to The Architect's Collaborative, Inc. for its design of the Johns-Manville World Headquarters building in Jefferson County, Colorado.

in an abstracted classical manner made reference to the Beaux-Arts detailing of neighbouring Grand Central Station but was perhaps also influenced by Philip Johnson's American Telephone and Telegraph Co. tower with its broken pediment feature.

Cultural, Religious, and Educational Buildings. The Denver Symphony Orchestra acquired a worthy new concert facility, the Boettcher Concert Hall, part of the Denver Center for the Performing Arts. The hall was the first in the U.S. to seat the audience in a 360° circle around the orchestra and was designed in such a way as to ensure that no member of the audience would be more than 85 ft from the stage. In fact, 80% of the audience can be seated within 65 ft of the stage. The aesthetic effect of the interior grows out of acoustical requirements, and the asymmetric arrangement of the banks of seats for 2,750 in itself provides visual interest. The architects, Hardy Holzman Pfeiffer Associates, were asked to try to re-create the atmosphere of an outdoor concert amphitheatre.

A fine new cathedral for the Roman Catholics in Burlington, Vt., recalled that city's historic architecture. Edward Larrabee Barnes, architect of the Cathedral of the Immaculate Conception, drew inspiration from H. H. Richardson's 19th-century Romanesque Revival Billings Library at the University of Vermont, using coloured masonry, whereby glazed bricks in green and brown are arranged in horizontal bands, and a prominent roof of seamed copper. The church replaced a large one that was destroyed by fire and translated traditional requirements into modern technology and design ideals. The plan was arrow-shaped, and inside was an impressive tentlike structure with a Greek cross of blue stained glass over the west door, reminiscent of the rose windows of Romanesque and Gothic churches.

Another fine contemporary church was that at Bagsværd, near Copenhagen, Den., by architect Jørn Utzon, designer of the Sydney Opera House. The calm yet magnificent structure is long and low with an emphatic concrete tent marking the span of the main sanctuary.

Melbourne, Australia, also sought a landmark—a city symbol that it hoped would become as famous as the Eiffel Tower in Paris or the Sydney Opera House. A competition with a prize of $100,000 was held for such a landmark, to grace an 80-ac site. (SANDRA MILLIKIN)

See also Engineering Projects; Historic Preservation; Industrial Review.
[626.A.1–5; 626.C]

Arctic Regions

Greenland adopted home rule in 1979, thereby ending 250 years of Danish colonial control. Denmark's Queen Margrethe II formally marked the change of status for the world's largest island (2.2 million sq km) and its 50,000 inhabitants by giving a copy of the Home Rule Act to the new local legislature. The official name chosen for the ice-encrusted island was Kalâtdlit Nunât, "Our Land" in Eskimo.

During the year the Alaska Highway gas pipeline, one of the largest and most publicly discussed projects in North American history, moved closer to reality. In July U.S. Pres. Jimmy Carter pledged that the nearly 8,000-km (5,000-mi) pipeline network (stretching from Prudhoe Bay in Alaska through Canada to markets as far away as Chicago and San Francisco) would be built with strong backing from the White House.

In October Soviet officials endorsed the principle of a multibillion-dollar natural-gas pipeline across the Bering Strait to serve North American markets. The plan would link production from eastern Siberian natural-gas fields via a 600-km pipeline, including 32 km between the extreme points of Siberia and Alaska. The proposal, which had been in the conceptual stage for several years, became a more viable proposition after the decision had been made to proceed with the Alaska Highway gas pipeline, with which the Siberian pipeline would be connected.

The U.S. Supreme Court in June agreed to hear a dispute between the state of Alaska and the federal government over who owns offshore areas of the Beaufort Sea. At stake were about 15% of 514,000 ac scheduled for a lease sale in December. The federal government contended that state ownership extends only to the three-mile limit. Alaskan North Slope natives and environmental groups opposed the lease sale, mostly on the grounds that exploration activity would disrupt the wildlife in the area.

In June Esso Resources Canada Ltd. confirmed the existence of a 600-million-bbl oil find at Norman Wells in the Mackenzie Valley area of the Northwest Territories. Oil was first discovered there by Imperial Oil Ltd. in 1920.

The National Energy Board of Canada began public hearings in October on applications to move Alaskan crude oil to markets in the U.S. Middle West. Foothills Oil Pipeline Ltd. was seeking to build a 34-in-diameter pipeline from the Alyeska pipeline south of Fairbanks, Alaska, to Edmonton, Alta., a distance of about 2,500 km. The oil pipeline would be constructed in the same corridor already approved for the proposed Alaska Highway gas pipeline and was estimated to cost between $1 billion and $2 billion, depending on the precise route selected. This project proposal was in direct competition with the Northern Tier Pipeline project, an all-U.S. route extending from Washington State to the East Coast, which had been favoured by U.S. Secretary of Energy James Schlesinger.

Panarctic Oils Ltd. announced in May the discovery of major new reserves of natural gas in the Arctic islands. Indications were that the well might prove to be the single largest gas accumulation yet found in the Arctic regions.

GULF CANADA/CANADIAN PRESS

A Canadian drilling rig stands silhouetted against the nighttime Arctic sky about 140 miles from the magnetic North Pole. The well produces about 8.1 million cubic feet of gas per day.

TASS/SOVFOTO

A group of seven Soviet skiers reached the North Pole after a 1,000-mile trip across the Arctic ice. It took the skiers 2½ months to complete the journey.

Twenty years after the beginning of a northern roads construction program, the Dempster Highway, Canada's first all-weather road to cross the Arctic Circle, was officially opened in August. The 671-km highway extends from the Klondike Highway in the Yukon to the Red River in the Northwest Territories.

The "M.V. Arctic," the only Canadian ice-strengthened bulk carrier capable of operating in the high Arctic for several months of the year, completed its first six months of operation in August. Tests proved its ability to operate successfully as an icebreaker and to sustain forward motion in two to three feet of ice.

In Canada a national campaign by Indian and Eskimo associations began in March to protest the federal government's lack of progress in settling native land claims. The associations also charged that the government was allowing large-scale developments to proceed in areas where native people had not surrendered their land rights.

The residents of the tiny settlement of Baker Lake in the Northwest Territories pitted themselves against the federal government of Canada and a group of mining companies that wished to explore an 80,000-sq-km (30,000-sq-mi) area surrounding the community. The natives claimed that exploration for uranium was causing changes in caribou migration patterns. The implications of a court decision could be significant, since the case would be argued on the basis of rights to hunt without disturbance on lands the Eskimos have used for hundreds of years.

Alaskan Eskimo walrus hunters agreed in May to help conduct a study of the walrus population in the Bering and Chukchi seas. A population of 200,000 had been estimated, and there was concern by some biologists that the walruses were near a state of overpopulation.

As part of a study to determine the effects of encroaching civilization on the wild musk-ox, 16 animals were captured on Nunivak Island, Alaska, and brought to the University of Alaska in February. Musk-oxen had been hunted to extinction in Alaska, and the herds on Nunivak Island were descendants of musk-oxen imported from Greenland.

Hunters on Banks Island, Northwest Territories, were permitted to hunt 150 musk-oxen under a quota established by the Northwest Territories Fish and Wildlife Service. The herd, which numbered about 6,000 animals in 1978, was estimated to be growing at an annual rate of 10%.

In June a Canadian Broadcasting Corporation program was initiated to help the Eskimos of Greenland develop a closer acquaintance with Canadian Eskimos. The Canadian program was the counterpart of a Radio Greenland version that had been in operation for several years.

In April one of the largest known expeditions to the North Pole, Project LOREX (Lomonosov Ridge Experiment), was begun in order to study the Lomonosov Ridge, a mountain range on the floor of the Arctic Ocean. One theory suggests that the ridge was once part of the European continent.

A team of seven Soviet skiers reached the North Pole after 1,600 km (1,000 mi) and 2½ months on the Arctic ice. The Soviets had left Henrietta Island in the Arctic Ocean in March.

(KENNETH DE LA BARRE)

Argentina

The federal republic of Argentina occupies the southeastern section of South America and is bounded by Bolivia, Paraguay, Brazil, Uruguay, Chile, and the Atlantic Ocean. It is the second-largest Latin-American country, after Brazil, with an area of 2,758,829 sq km (1,065,189 sq mi). Pop. (1979 est.): 26,730,000. Cap. and largest city: Buenos Aires (pop., 1978 est., 2,982,000). Language: Spanish. Religion: mainly Roman Catholic. President in 1979, Lieut. Gen. Jorge Rafael Videla.

Pres. Jorge Rafael Videla continued in office in 1979, his second three-year term scheduled to end in March 1981. José Martínez de Hoz retained his post as minister of economy and as such was architect of the program to reorganize the economy along free-market lines; despite growing criticism of these policies, his position was strengthened after Cabinet reshuffles at the end of 1978. On Jan. 25, 1979, Brig. Gen. Orlando Ramón Agosti retired as commander in chief of the Air Force and was replaced in the ruling military junta by Gen. Omar Domingo Rubens Graffigna. At the end of the year Gen. Leopoldo Fortunato Galtieri became commander in chief of the Army.

The beginning of 1979 was marked by the joint declaration on January 8 of the Chilean and Argentine governments to refrain from war to settle their conflicting claims over the Beagle Channel islands and to accept the offer of mediation by Pope John Paul II. This reduced tension between the two countries.

Criticism of the government's economic policy intensified early in 1979, when the promised decline in the inflation rate failed to materialize. The minister of economy's measures, aimed at halving inflation (170% in 1978) during 1979, consisted basically of a January–August program of predetermined devaluations of the peso (at 5% a month, then falling to 4% a month) and limited increases in incomes (at 4% a month). Excluded was the reintroduction of price controls, considered contrary to the official free-market philosophy. When Martínez de Hoz returned to Argentina after a holiday early in the year, he had to face criticism from many segments of the population. Local industrialists complained that their products were having to compete with cheaper imports; workers charged that their purchasing power was eroding rapidly; and exporters maintained that the currency was overvalued.

Signs of dissatisfaction appeared among certain sectors of the Army, particularly among those officers responsible for Fabricaciones Militares (the weapons, munitions, chemicals, and steel manufacturer run by the Army). Sensing an opening for more discussion, the press gave greater coverage to criticism and statements from party politicians of the past, despite the strict censorship rules. Former president Arturo Frondizi and Ricardo Balbín, leader of the Radical Party, were among the first to gain the limelight; the latter had been detained repeatedly but sought to win some kind of official concession because his was the largest party in opposition before the March 1976 coup. Also, the leaders of the right-wing sector of the Justicialistas, the government party in 1976, signed a joint statement calling for elections and

Argentina

UPI

Argentine publisher Jacobo Timmerman was one of those interviewed by the Inter-American Commission on Human Rights, which looked into charges of human rights violations in Argentina.

Areas:
see Demography; *see also the individual country articles*

DIEGO GOLDBERG—SYGMA

A Buenos Aires mother wears a sign demanding news of her son, one of thousands who have "disappeared" in Argentina.

changes in economic policies; this was followed by another signed petition from a wider range of politicians, including Socialists and Communists, also asking for an early return to democracy.

These events culminated in a call by a group of labour unionists, the Comisión de los 25, for a general strike on April 27. The government reacted by imprisoning the leaders of this union grouping and by announcing a 15% rise in wages and salaries above the minimum decreed for the month; moreover, negotiations with another group of trade unionists, the Comisión Nacional de Trabajo, led to their rejection of the general strike. Estimates were that only 25–30% of the workers took part in the work stoppage. All political activity on the part of unions was banned in November.

Fear of intimidation discouraged protests by the political opposition. Reports of unexplained disappearances of individuals were variously estimated at between 5,000 and 15,000 from the beginning of 1976. The government again refused to accept the validity of reports abroad, claiming they were the result of an international campaign to discredit it, and invited the Inter-American Commission on Human Rights of the Organization of American States (OAS) to investigate the allegations. President Videla did, however, state that there had been "a civil war" in Argentina and that "all wars were dirty." Local human rights organizations claimed that the government was protecting the perpetrators of this situation. The incredulity of human rights organizations was increased in August when four of their offices were entered by the police on the order of a judge and documentation on more than 3,000 cases of disappearances prepared for the Inter-American Human Rights Commission was confiscated. Nonetheless, the commission in September carried out inspections of prisons and detention centres and collected information from victims' families. The government meanwhile decreed that those reported missing should be presumed dead for legal purposes.

The armed forces, on the other hand, were able to progress, if laboriously, toward the reconciliation ("compatibilization") in one document of the three sets of political proposals prepared separately by each branch of the forces in 1978. Unofficial reports indicated that the Army's view of a gradual return to democracy would be upheld, without fundamental alterations to the constitution or restrictions as to party organization like those in Brazil, as had been suggested by the Air Force. In September, however, a right-wing general in charge of the 3rd Army Corps unsuccessfully challenged the authority of his commander in chief, Gen. Roberto Viola, for supporting what he saw as the government's increasingly "moderate" policy toward the left. General Galtieri's appointment was seen as further support for the moderate line.

The economy, meanwhile, began to grow again, with the gross domestic product increase in 1979 calculated at 7% (after a decline of approximately 4% in 1978), despite persisting inflation estimated at 140%. The recovery was concentrated in the construction sector, which helped to keep unemployment down to a minimum, as well as in the financial and farming communities. The nation's balance of trade continued to be favourable, mainly owing to the exceptionally high world price of beef. (PAUL DOWBOR)

ARGENTINA

Education. (1977) Primary, pupils 3,818,250, teachers 221,050; secondary, pupils 441,907, teachers 60,199; vocational, pupils 846,200, teachers 113,515; higher, students 536,450, teaching staff 42,500.

Finance. Monetary unit: peso, with (Sept. 17, 1979) a free rate of 1,436 pesos to U.S. $1 (3,090 pesos = £1 sterling). Gold, SDR's, and foreign exchange (May 1979) U.S. $6,873,000,000. Budget (1978 actual): revenue 3,404,000,000,000 pesos; expenditure 5,283,000,000,000 pesos. Gross national product (1975) 1,310,700,000,000 pesos. Money supply (May 1979) 10,187,900,000,000 pesos. Cost of living (Buenos Aires; 1975 = 100; May 1979) 9,217.

Foreign Trade. (1977) Imports 1,706,290,000,000 pesos; exports 2,274,040,000,000 pesos. Import sources: U.S. 19%; West Germany 10%; Brazil 9%; Japan 9%; France 5%; Italy 5%. Export destinations: The Netherlands 10%; Brazil 8%; Italy 8%; U.S. 7%; Japan 5%; Spain 5%; West Germany 5%; Chile 5%. Main exports: meat 11%; wheat 10%; corn 9%; fruit and vegetables *c.* 6%; machinery *c.* 6%.

Transport and Communications. Roads (1977) 207,367 km. Motor vehicles in use (1976): passenger 2,588,000; commercial (including buses) 1,101,000. Railways: (1977) 37,951 km; traffic (1978) 11,242,000,000 passenger-km, freight 10,370,000,000 net ton-km. Air traffic (1978): 5,295,000,000 passenger-km; freight 128.6 million net ton-km. Shipping (1978): merchant vessels 100 gross tons and over 432; gross tonnage 2,000,879. Shipping traffic (1977): goods loaded 23,807,000 metric tons, unloaded 10,619,000 metric tons. Telephones (Jan. 1978) 2,584,800. Radio receivers (Dec. 1973) 21 million. Television receivers (Dec. 1974) 4.5 million.

Agriculture. Production (in 000; metric tons; 1978): wheat 8,100; corn 9,700; sorghum 7,360; barley 554; oats *c.* 676; millet 330; rice 310; potatoes 1,593; sugar, raw value *c.* 1,397; linseed 670; soybeans *c.* 2,400; sunflower seed *c.* 1,450; tomatoes 574; oranges 650; lemons *c.* 300; apples 810; wine *c.* 2,108; tobacco 62; cotton, lint *c.* 228; cheese 245; wool, clean 85; beef and veal *c.* 3,192; fish catch (1977) 393; quebracho extract (1977) 105. Livestock (in 000; June 1978): cattle 61,280; sheep *c.* 34,000; pigs *c.* 3,800; goats *c.* 3,200; horses (1977) *c.* 3,500; chickens *c.* 32,000.

Industry. Fuel and power (in 000; metric tons; 1978): crude oil 23,233; natural gas (cu m) *c.* 8,000,000; coal 434; electricity (excluding most industrial production; kw-hr) 29,052,000. Production (in 000; metric tons; 1978): cement 6,300; crude steel 2,564; cotton yarn 84; man-made fibres (1976) 51; petroleum products (1976) *c.* 21,700; sulfuric acid 240; paper (1976) *c.* 650; passenger cars (including assembly; units) 135; commercial vehicles (including assembly; units) 45. Merchant vessels launched (100 gross tons and over; 1978) 25,300 gross tons.

Art Exhibitions

Art exhibitions in 1979 tended once again to divide into two general categories: the "theme" exhibition, devoted to a nonart topic that could be illustrated by works of art and also by everyday objects and ephemera, and the traditional large-scale retrospective. One of the outstanding examples of the first category was the exhibition held at the Victoria and Albert Museum, London, devoted to what it termed England's most popular pastime—"The Garden." The show chronicled the history of gardening (as distinct from landscape architecture) as an art form from Roman and medieval times to the formal gardens of the 16th and 17th centuries and the 19th-century "Romantic." The exhibition, which included many photographs and paintings, was imaginatively designed, with the museum's floors hidden under synthetic grass or rushes and its formal columns behind trelliswork reminiscent of a summerhouse. Throughout, larks sang and the smell of summer blossoms pervaded the air—in all, a tour de force creating an ambience of escape into another world.

An exhibition at the Royal Academy, London, was also devoted to an unconventional subject. Entitled "Derby Day 200," it was a celebration of the famous English turf classic, first run at Epsom Downs in 1779. The multimedia show encompassed paintings, drawings, prints, photographs, film shows, and ephemera, including the silver mounted hoof of one Derby winner and the tail of another. Paintings by Stubbs, J. F. Herring, and Degas were of the highest quality, while such items as posters, menus, spurs, and boots illustrated the Derby's existence as a great popular festival.

The Guggenheim Museum, New York City, mounted an important exhibition in the spring devoted to sculpture. Entitled "The Planar Dimension: Europe, 1912–1932," it concentrated on the creation of a new form of sculptural expression based on the relationship between planes in open space rather than mass and volume, one of the major and decisive events in the history of 20th-century art. Such well-known American figures as Alexander Calder and David Smith worked in the planar dimension, and to most younger artists it was the only currently valid form of sculpture. In tracing the complex history of this movement, the organizer selected objects that were at once significant yet unfamiliar. The exhibition began with a sculpture of 1912—"Guitar" by Picasso, a seminal construction of sheet metal and wire—and included works by Paul-Albert Laurens, Jacques Lipchitz, Giacomo Balla, and Alexander Archipenko. The international scope of the movement was impressively emphasized with works from France, West Germany, Belgium, Denmark, Poland, and the U.S.S.R.

"Vienna in the Age of Schubert: The Biedermeier Interior 1815–1848" was organized by the Museum für Angewandte Kunst, Vienna, and shown in the winter at the Victoria and Albert Museum. Made up of items lent from public and private collections, it described a unique period when ideals of middle-class comfort determined taste. Furniture was the main subject of the show devoted to English designer Eileen Gray (d. 1976). Her influence as a modern designer had only recently begun to receive the critical attention it deserved. She was a pioneer in the use of colour and new materials, and some of her finest pieces were executed in stark lacquerwork.

Modern design was to the forefront in one of the most ambitious exhibitions ever presented at the Hayward Gallery, London, devoted to Britain in the 1930s. Organized by the Arts Council, it encompassed every aspect of design and architecture, with nostalgic sections devoted to such figures as Frank Pick, Welles Coates, and Charles Holden. There was even a reconstruction of the bathroom designed by the painter Paul Nash for dancer Tilly Losch. Textiles, paintings, graphics, photographs, and objects were all on view.

The Metropolitan Museum of Art, New York City, mounted an exhibition devoted to Sergey Diaghilev—"Costumes and Designs of the Ballets Russes"—organized by the museum's own costume department to mark the 50th anniversary of the death of the great Russian impresario. Exam-

VICTORIA AND ALBERT MUSEUM

Historical paintings, tools, and books were included in the exhibition devoted to "The Garden," shown at the Victoria and Albert Museum in London during the summer.

Armies
see Defense

Art
see Architecture; Art Exhibitions; Art Sales; Dance; Literature; Museums; Theatre

JEANNINE DEUBEL—EB INC.

The Art Institute of Chicago mounted a show of 100 paintings and numerous drawings by French artist Henri de Toulouse-Lautrec. The core of the show was a group of 40 pictures from the Musée Toulouse-Lautrec in Albi, France.

ples included costumes by Leon Baskt for *Scheherazade* and *The Sleeping Princess*, by Golovine for *The Firebird*, and by Alexandre Benois for *Petrushka*. A separate room devoted to related works of art displayed a mask of Anna Pavlova, a Rodin bronze of Vaslav Nijinsky, and various posters and designs.

The theme of the Berlin Festival in September was "Liebermann and His Age," and the program focused on the period 1880–1900. Max Liebermann (1847–1935) was a leading figure in the revolutionary Berliner Sezession ("secession") group. The exhibition mounted for the festival at the Berlin Nationalgalerie comprised about 100 paintings and 200 drawings.

"Dearest Children: Clothes and Toys from Nineteenth-Century Royal Nurseries" at the Museum of London was one of several exhibitions marking the International Year of the Child in 1979. This small but enjoyable show drew attention to the fact that only within the previous 200 years or so had children's clothes ceased to be miniature versions of adult costumes and childhood come into its own as a legitimate subject for thought. Included in the exhibition were several dolls that belonged to Queen Victoria, as well as examples of her clothing. The evocative show demonstrated the lighter side of royal childhood.

"Treasures of the Kings of Denmark" was an exhibition displayed at the Petit Palais, Paris, in the winter of 1978–79 to mark the occasion of the state visit of Queen Margrethe II to Paris. Coloured slides showed the interiors of the Castle of Rosenborg, which was the permanent home of the collection. The centrepiece of the show was a sumptuous reconstruction of the 18th-century Salle d'Audience, resplendent with octagonal mirrors and the magnificent silver throne made for Frederick IV in 1723 by Danish silversmiths.

"Art of Norway" was the subject of an exhibition comprising painting and folk and decorative art from Norwegian museums, seen in the U.S. at Madison, Wis., Seattle, Wash., and Minneapolis, Minn.—all cities with substantial Scandinavian populations. Landscapes and seascapes predominated, and all the items were pervaded by a strong national flavour. Norwegian expressionist artist Edvard Munch, the best-known painter to emerge from Norway, was the subject of "Edvard Munch: Symbols and Images" at the National Gallery of Art, Washington, D.C. The show consisted mainly of paintings lent by Norwegian museums, including 20 major watercolours that had never before left Norway. Also included were some 20 self-portraits, giving a unique insight into the character of this artist and his highly emotional work.

An exhibition at the Grand Palais, Paris, was devoted to a little-known group of painters who worked in Florence during the 19th century and had a complex relationship with the Impressionists of a slightly later generation in France. "I Macchiaioli—Peinture en Toscane: 1856–1880" was the title of the show, which was part of a series of events that included film shows, an exhibition of photographs depicting 19th-century Tuscany from the famous Alinari art shop in Florence, a two-day colloquy, and the publication of a number of important books. The ambition of the Macchiaioli was to replace academic painting by a more personal art form taking its cue from nature. The movement had political as well as artistic motivations and was part of the movement for Italian unification, or Risorgimento. The name "Macchiaioli" was first applied to the group by a hostile critic to describe their technique of applying blobs of colour (*macchie*), but later the group adopted the name.

Anniversaries of births and deaths again provided the justification for some of the major single-subject exhibitions. The 85th birthday of the artist Joan Miró was celebrated by various exhibitions in France, although plans for a major retrospective were abandoned. The display of 100 works of sculpture from the period 1962–78 at the Musée d'Art Moderne, Paris, featured a number of charming and whimsical small-scale bronzes. Recent paintings were shown at the Galerie Maeght, and drawings and sketchbooks at the Beaubourg

ROBERT COHEN—AGIP/PICTORIAL PARADE

"Le double secret" was one of more than 200 works of René Magritte shown in an exhibit which opened at the Beaubourg in Paris in January.

(Centre National d'Art et de Culture Georges Pompidou). Miró drawings of the period 1901–78 were exhibited at the Hayward Gallery. A major exhibition devoted to the 18th-century French painter Chardin at the Grand Palais, Paris, marked the bicentenary of the artist's death. Chardin's subject matter was almost exclusively genre and still life, yet despite the limited scope of the subject matter he managed to invest his paintings with a remarkable strength and intensity. On view were nearly 140 paintings and pastels and a few drawings.

An exhibition devoted to the works of Hans Holbein the Younger was seen in London at the Queen's Gallery, Buckingham Palace. This was the first major London show devoted to the artist since 1950, and it included many fine portraits and five autograph miniatures. There were also portraits by Holbein's contemporaries, including one of Erasmus by Quentin Massys. A retrospective at the Beaubourg in Paris devoted to the works of the Belgian surrealist painter René Magritte consisted of over 200 works dating from between 1921 and 1967.

Henri Matisse was the subject of a concise and beautifully selected exhibition organized by the French Academy in Rome and shown at the Villa Medici. There had been no large-scale exhibition devoted to Matisse since the 1970 Paris show. The Rome exhibition was small—only 43 works—but admirably selected, with exhibits gathered from a variety of sources including private collections. Much of the material had not been shown in the large Paris or London retrospectives. Matisse's work had not been exhibited in Italy since 1950. One critic commented, "The exhibition is select but shows how Matisse, unlike Picasso, upheld the banner of classicism into the 20th century: nothing is unintentional, unplanned, or left to chance."

The National Portrait Gallery in London devoted a show to the 17th-century portraitist Sir Peter Lely, one of the greatest foreign-born portrait painters of the period to live and work in England. It was the first such exhibition to be devoted entirely to his work and included 59 paintings and 57 drawings. Works by the contemporary U.S. cartoonist Saul Steinberg were shown in London at the Serpentine Gallery. Style, wit, and versatility characterized these superb satirical commentaries on the social scene, familiar to readers of *The New Yorker*. The rather unsettling plaster figures of George Segal (*see* BIOGRAPHIES) were on view in a retrospective at the Whitney Museum of American Art, New York City.

"Daumier in Retrospect, 1808–1879: The Armand Hammer Collection" was shown in the spring at the Los Angeles County Museum of Art to commemorate the centenary of the artist's death. Made up of 500 lithographs supplemented by paintings, sculpture, and books, it was the most extensive Daumier show ever mounted in the U.S. All the works were selected from the Hammer collection, which included the world's largest private holding of Daumier lithographs. Fittingly enough, the show came at a time when narrative art had returned to fashion.

The first painting by Leonardo da Vinci ever exhibited on the West Coast of the U.S. was shown in Los Angeles as part of a rare loan of 11 Italian Renaissance pictures from the Hermitage in Leningrad. The show, titled "From Leonardo to Titian: Italian Renaissance Paintings from the Hermitage," was seen in Washington, D.C., New York City, and Detroit before opening in Los Angeles in November. It was the first loan of Italian Renaissance paintings permitted to leave the Soviet Union in modern times. The Leonardo canvas, "Madonna with a Flower," was thought to have been painted in 1478 and was sold to Tsar Nicholas II in 1913. Also in the exhibition were works by Titian, Correggio, and Raphael. In return, an exchange exhibition of 17 comparable pictures would be sent to the Soviet Union from the Los Angeles Museum, the National Gallery of Art, and the Detroit Institute of Arts.

A fascinating exhibition devoted to railway station architecture was organized in Paris by the

KEYSTONE

Norman St. John-Stevas, British minister for the arts, wore a pensive look as he contemplated one of "The Horses of San Marco," which was displayed at the Royal Academy in London.

Centre de Création Industrielle and seen at the Beaubourg. The show was made up of documentary and photographic material as well as sound, film images, and a series of specially commissioned works by contemporary artists to create atmosphere. Models and ephemera were also used. The exhibition would travel to Lyon and Bordeaux and then to Milan, Italy; Brussels; and Lausanne, Switz.

Also in Paris, the Musée Rodin devoted a show to the effect of Asian sculpture on Rodin, focusing on a little-known aspect of the sculptor's work. Rodin was much taken by a show of Japanese and Chinese works and by a performance given by Cambodian dancers in Marseille, which he saw at the age of 66. That inspired him to begin his own collection of Indian works late in life. The vast panorama of Indian art from ancient times to the 19th century was shown at the Petit Palais. Included in "Inde—Cinq mille ans d'art" were a number of works excavated after World War II but not previously shown outside India. Highlights of the show were the two rooms devoted to Indian miniatures. Another aspect of Indian art was the focus of "Indian Painting During the British Period, 1760–1880," organized by the American Federation of the Arts and seen in New York City, at Yale University, and at the Detroit Institute. It showed how Western techniques and tastes were assimilated as artists adapted to satisfy their newly europeanized patrons.

Some unusual objects were displayed in "Avant les Scythes, préhistoire de l'art en U.R.S.S." at the Grand Palais, a show devoted to the prehistoric period in the Soviet Union. Many of the 150 objects lent by the Hermitage had only recently been discovered. Included were beautiful bronze statuettes and jewelry from the Caucasus dating from the 1st millennium BC.

"William Carlos Williams and the American Scene, 1920–1940" was an exhibition held at the Whitney Museum of American Art and devoted to American painting of that period. Georgia O'Keefe, Marsden Hartley, Charles Sheeler, and Peter Blume were among the artists represented. The show took as its motto a line by the poet: "Everything is a picture."

Works by contemporary Yugoslav artists were the subject of an exhibition at the Kunsthalle of Nürnburg, West Germany, organized by the Museum of Contemporary Art at Belgrade and consisting of paintings, sculptures, engravings, art objects, and tapestries by 77 Yugoslav artists representing important trends in contemporary art. Their work showed the considerable influence of U.S., English, and French artistic trends. Also in West Germany, the Bavarian National Museum in Munich devoted a show to "Animal Sculpture of the Royal Nymphenburg Factory, Munich, 1905–1920." During this period the factory produced 155 models, 88 of them by the sculptor Theodor Kärner. The show demonstrated the new 20th-century attitude of German sculptors toward animals, through which they evolved a fully valid and lively intimate art form far removed from either sentimentality or bad taste.

"Crosscurrents" was the title of an exhibition of French and Italian neoclassical drawings and prints showing schemes for architecture, design, and ornament held at the Cooper-Hewitt Museum in New York City. Drawn entirely from the museum's own collection, the 140 or so drawings and prints were arranged by category; *e.g.*, architectural projects divided into executed, unexecuted, and visionary schemes. The show later traveled to the Rice Museum, Houston, Texas.

During October "The Horses of San Marco," at the Royal Academy, exhibited one of the four Byzantine bronze horses taken from Constantinople in 1204 and placed above the entrance of St. Mark's Basilica in Venice. All four had been removed for cleaning and preservation. The exhibition, organized jointly with the Olivetti Co. of Italy, comprised historical, comparative, and scientific material concerning the four horses, including paintings, drawings, sculptures, and bronzes.

(SANDRA MILLIKIN)

See also Art Sales; Museums; Photography.
[613.D.1.b]

Art Sales

Market Trends. The 1978–79 season saw a steady but for the most part unsensational advance in art prices. The top of the market was particularly strong, with intense competition for outstanding items. There seemed to be some decline in demand for the middle range in the late summer sales.

The weakening of the dollar made New York a

KEYSTONE

This ornate Louis XV cupboard was sold at auction in Monte Carlo to a representative of the Heim Gallery of London for a record $1.7 million.

more attractive buyers' market than London, making for a major increase in activity there. The revolution in Iran also had an effect on the market. Nineteenth-century Persian art, notably Qajar paintings and lacquerwork, fell significantly in value, and the market in very ornate French 19th-century furniture was seriously undermined by the withdrawal of Iranian buyers.

In London a legal battle began between art dealers and the auction houses over the buyers' premium introduced by Sotheby's and Christie's in 1975. Having been advised that the auctioneers would have been making an illegal charge under the Restrictive Trade Practices Act if they had colluded over its introduction, the British Antique Dealers' Association and the London Society of Art Dealers began legal action to prevent the auctioneers from making the charge.

Works of Art. The most sensational auction event of the year was the sale of the Wildenstein family collection of furniture, mainly of the French 18th century; the 201 lots were sold by Sotheby's in Monte Carlo for Fr 54,488,000. The furniture, from the New York home of the Wildenstein art dealing family, had been scheduled for auction in 1977, but at the last moment it was bought in its entirety by Akram Ojjeh, a Saudi Arabian businessman, for a reputed U.S. $7 million. It was auctioned on his behalf in June 1979 for some $6 million more than he had paid. Most of the finest pieces were secured by Sir Charles Clore (*see* OBITUARIES), the British financier, and Stavros Niarchos, the Greek shipowner. A new auction record price for furniture— $1.7 million (Fr 7.6 million) for a Louis XV ormolu-mounted marquetry corner cupboard surmounted by a clock, by Dubois—was paid by the Heim Gallery of London. A Louis XVI commode by J. F. Leleu made Fr 4.2 million.

A new level of prices was also set for English furniture when the collection of Gerald Hochschild was sold in London in December 1978 for £900,000 net, although some recently purchased items failed to sell. The Coombe Abbey library table, attributed to Thomas Chippendale, went for £100,000, an auction record. Andrew Constable-Maxwell's collection of ancient glass was sold by Sotheby's in June 1979 for £1.2 million. A Roman glass cage cup of *c.* AD 300, seven inches in diameter, went to Robin Symes, a London dealer, for £520,000, almost seven times the previous auction record for glass.

The family collection of Paul Rosenberg, the Paris dealer who acted for Picasso, Braque, and other artists, made $7,212,040 (£3.2 million) at Sotheby's in July. Prices were consistently high, and the $920,000 (£460,000) for Picasso's "La Bouteille de vin" was an auction record. In the same week Christie's sold the collection of Hans Mettler, a Swiss textile manufacturer, for £2.6 million (though 29% was bought back). Toulouse-Lautrec's "La Grande Loge" made a record £370,000. In April Sotheby's sold 18 pictures from the collection of Mr. and Mrs. Sydney Barlow for £2.2 million net; Monet's "Le Pont de chemin de fer à Argenteuil" made a record £420,000 and Corot's "Vénus au bain," a record £240,000.

The markets in primitive art and antiquities were both very active. A Luba carved wood stool was bought by the Metropolitan Museum of Art, New York City, for £240,000 in June. The week before, Christie's sale of Melanesian and Polynesian art from the Hooper collection included a Raratonga carved wood head at £110,000. Art Nouveau and the late 19th- and early 20th-century arts and crafts revival seemed to have become established as a major international collecting field. Christie's sold an Art Deco pendulum clock in the form of a Japanese temple gate for SFr 650,000 (a record for any clock), a Gallé marqueterie-de-verre

A Picasso, "La Bouteille de vin" from Paul Rosenberg's collection, brought $920,000 at Sotheby's in London in July. The entire Rosenberg collection brought $7,212,040.

UPI

shaped coquillage cup for SFr 370,000, and a Tiffany "Spider Web" table lamp for $150,000.

Nationalism continued to be a potent market force. In Americana, an Eastman Johnson painting, "Washington Crossing the Delaware," sold for a record $370,000 and William Harnett's "Still Life with Violin," for a record $300,000. Swiss nationalism secured an extraordinary £295,000 for Ferdinand Hodler's "Thunersee von Leissigen aus." Prices for all 19th-century paintings, including British, were affected; "An Intercepted Correspondence, Cairo" by John Frederick Lewis made £220,000 and Edward Lear's "Mount Kinchinjunga from Darjeeling," £70,000. Other notable auction prices included Matisse's "Le Jeune Marin I" at £720,000, Mondrian's "Large Composition in Red Blue and Yellow" at $800,000, a van de Cappelle seascape at £510,000, and a river landscape by Jan Brueghel the Elder at £400,000—all sold by Christie's. The London National Gallery paid $600,000 for Millet's "The Winnower" at Sotheby's in New York.

Sotheby's sold the former Gore Booth, Baron Rothschild Stradivari violoncello for £145,000 in November 1978 and the former Kreisler, Hubermann Stradivari violin in May 1979 for the same price, an auction record for any musical instrument. The seven-ton marble Warwick Vase was refused an export license from Britain and acquired by the City of Glasgow Museum for £250,000. The duke of Wellington sold a Sèvres dinner service made for the Empress Josephine to the Victoria and Albert Museum for £450,000 after having been refused a license to export it to France.

Books. The outstanding feature of the 1978–79 season was the surge in prices paid for manuscript material. The most notable event of the year was the sale to an anonymous buyer of a newly discovered Mercator atlas at Sotheby's in March 1979 for £340,000. It had been found by a Dutchman some ten years before in a Belgian print shop.

In October 1978 Christie's sold a collection of Wagner material, formed in the late 19th century by Mary Burrell, for $1,250,000. An autograph manuscript of *Tannhäuser*, complete except for the overture, made $220,000. In November 1978 a Latin treatise on divorce addressed by Friar Jacobus Calchus to Henry VIII, in a superb contemporary binding by "the King Henry binder," was sold to Clifford King, a London dealer, at Christie's in London for £60,000. The following month Christie's sold the Lyttelton family archive, containing papers stretching over 800 years, on behalf of Viscount Cobham for £164,000.

A painting, which had been carelessly hanging in a boys' school in Manchester, England, was discovered to be a missing masterpiece by the American artist Frederick Church. The 1861 painting, "Icebergs," fetched $2.5 million at Sotheby Parke-Bernet, New York City, in October.

© SOTHEBY PARKE-BERNET. AGENT: EDITORIAL PHOTOCOLOR ARCHIVES

SARA KRULWICH—THE NEW YORK TIMES

John Singer Sargent's "Millicent, Duchess of Sutherland" was part of the Benjamin Sonnenberg collection which was sold in New York City in June. The entire collection brought $4.7 million.

In June 1979 the marquess of Bath sold 180 illustrated books from the Longleat library (all duplicates) at Sotheby's for £322,865. In the same week Christie's sold books and manuscripts from the collection of Arthur Houghton, chairman of Corning Glass, for £1,555,315. A late 17th-century description of the coast between "the mouth of Calafornia and the straights of Lemaire" sold for £120,000, and a first edition of William Blake's *Songs of Innocence and of Experience*—one of the three earliest known copies—made £70,000. Also in June, a 15th-century manuscript anthology including 15 unrecorded Middle English poems sold at Sotheby's for £90,000; it was subsequently acquired by the British Library.

A major Sotheby sale of modern manuscript material in July included a diary kept by the ballet dancer Vaslav Nijinsky at £45,000. Most of the family collection of John Galsworthy letters, diaries, and manuscripts was put up for sale as a single lot and sold for £48,000.

Sotheby's received some criticism from the book trade over their outright purchase of the collection of scientific books and manuscripts formed by Robert B. Honeyman of California. A two-day sale from the collection in October made £408,691, and a second in May brought £130,000. Further sales were to be spread over four years.

In February the duke of Wellington ceded the entire papers of the first duke, valued at £740,000, to the British Library in lieu of tax.

(GERALDINE NORMAN)

SPECIAL REPORT

THE DARK SIDE OF ART

by Geraldine Norman

The market in works of art has flourished since the dawn of civilization. Wealthy Roman senators competed for Corinthian bronzes and engraved jewels. It is no coincidence that Florence, the cradle of the Renaissance, was also the banking centre of Europe. The agents of English milords scoured Europe for artworks through the 18th and early 19th centuries; the agents of American millionaires did the same in the late 19th and early 20th. But today the art market has taken a new turn. Art has come to be looked on as an investment medium and a hedge against inflation. This development has gone hand in hand with a large increase in the number of museums worldwide and in their purchasing power.

The result is a classic case of too much money chasing too few goods. Hardly a week goes by without headlines announcing new auction records in some department of art. And while huge prices have always been paid for the very good or the very fashionable, today huge prices are also paid for the second-rate. Furthermore, virtually every field of art is simultaneously in fashion as dealers desperately search for goods to meet the investors' demand.

Fakes and Frauds. If anything bursts this bubble, it will probably be the unethical practices and petty frauds that abound in the art market. They have always been around; fake Corinthian bronzes were made in ancient Rome, and the young Michelangelo is said to have buried a marble head in order to pass it off as a work of classical antiquity. But the number and financial importance of such swindles have expanded with the market itself.

Early in 1979 London's Old Bailey was the scene of the sensational trial of Tom Keating, a self-acknowledged picture faker, on charges of conspiring to pass off his fakes for financial gain. After six weeks the case was dropped on account of Keating's ill health, but not before witness after witness had explained the intricacies of art market malpractice. This condemnation of the art market itself probably influenced the attorney general's decision not to order a retrial when Keating recovered.

Geraldine Norman is saleroom correspondent for The Times *of London. She is the author of* The Sale of Works of Art *and* Nineteenth Century Painters and Paintings: A Dictionary *and co-author of* The Fake's Progress.

Not long afterward an equally sensational trial took place in Paris. Paul Petrides, 78, was found guilty of knowingly receiving stolen pictures (one had been cut from its frame with a razor) and recycling them in the art market. Petrides had been an internationally respected art dealer and the accepted expert on the work of Maurice Utrillo.

A few years earlier New York had had its big art trial with the Rothko case. Frank Lloyd, founder of the prestigious Marlborough Gallery, was found to have been involved in defrauding the heirs of the painter Mark Rothko to the tune of several million dollars. Having been Rothko's dealer during the artist's lifetime, he had also handled the sale of pictures for the estate and allegedly paid the heirs only a fraction of the pictures' value.

Sensational as they are, these court cases are only the tip of the iceberg. Rarely do art scandals get as far as the courtroom. Most are either hushed up or settled out of court. Indeed, many day-to-day malpractices are not strictly illegal—just a bit unethical.

Pricing the "Priceless." All this suggests there is something about art that fosters unethical practices. In fact, the trouble stems not from art itself but from mixing it up with money. One often reads of a "priceless masterpiece"; this is nonsense. A masterpiece or any other work of art is without price only when it is not for sale. The difficulty, which no doubt gave rise to the catchphrase, lies not with agreeing on a price but with estimating a value.

Most art market problems arise from the lack of connection between the creative process and market valuation. An artist is purely and simply attempting a visual effect, perhaps with genius and perhaps without. But once his creation reaches the marketplace, the visual effect is a relatively unimportant component of its value. The name of the artist, the size of the work, its medium, its age, the number of scholarly books or articles in which it can be "looked up," the distinction of those who have owned the artwork—all these take precedence.

It is in these areas that the fiddles and tricks are generally played. Take, for example, the whole gamut of problems concerned with picture faking. Most fakers are artists who have failed to achieve recognition in their own right; punishing the so-called experts for not recognizing their talents is usually an important part of their motivation.

The "Authentic" Touch. Once a fake is in existence, a history must be invented to authenticate it, and here art historians enter the game. The Petrides case showed that some "experts" will bend their standards for money. Indeed, one art historian, the author of several weighty tomes, is believed by insiders to have taken up art history in order to launch a whole family of fakes on the market.

THE TATE GALLERY, LONDON

This painting by George Stubbs of two hounds became so damaged in travel that the insurance company paid off the owner. Later on the picture was restored and sold to the Tate Gallery in London.

The dealing and auctioneering community are thoroughly aware of the problem, but they prefer to keep as quiet as possible about it so as not to frighten their clients. The position is exacerbated by the difficulty of attributing many old pictures and drawings to any named artist. If a picture comes into auction for sale from a dealer or collector who is likely to put more business their way, the auctioneers will probably give a dubious attribution the benefit of the doubt. Equally, a dealer who has spent good money on a picture will take a lot of convincing before he admits that his attribution is wrong.

Restorers help to confuse the issue. A very damaged picture that has been substantially repainted can still be sold as a genuine example of the master's work. A few years ago a Stubbs painting of two hounds was so damaged en route from Australia to Sotheby's in London that it was written off, and the insurance money was paid out to the owner. Some time later it reappeared on the market, fully restored, and was bought by the Tate Gallery.

Then there is the question of signatures. Over the years they have been added to many pictures to improve their market value—a practice known euphemistically in the trade as "strengthening" a signature. A leading dealer, Brian Sewell, convulsed the Keating trial with an anecdote about overhearing his restorer telephone a client because he had forgotten what signature he was supposed to be "strengthening" on a picture—and then arguing over which signature would be most suitable.

Illegal Exports. Another fertile field for malpractice concerns illegal exports. Again, this has nothing to do with art itself but reflects a kind of cultural nationalism. Many countries, notably India, Italy, and some Middle Eastern states, have tough regulations on the export of works of art or ban them altogether. Excavations normally require a government license, and important discoveries must be handed over to the state. The unintended result is that excavations are made secretly and important finds are smuggled out of the country.

In theory, major museums do not purchase items they believe were illegally exported from the country of origin. But there have been innumerable scandals in recent years. The Metropolitan Museum of Art in New York City acquired a Greek vase painted by Euphronius which is said to have been illegally excavated in Italy. A complete Greek bronze figure that the Italian authorities believe was found in shallow waters near Naples is currently on loan to the Royal Scottish Museum, Edinburgh; it is thought to be the property of the British Rail Pension Funds, which has a large art portfolio bought on the advice of Sotheby's.

Dealers and auctioneers' experts do not generally take the issue of illegal exports seriously. Most turn a blind eye even if they do not actively connive at the trade. If pressed, they will argue that art treasures are better off in a major museum than underground, in the sea, or in a poorly equipped museum in the country of origin.

Money is the root of all evil, it has been said. Certainly its exchange in large quantities tends to stimulate malpractices in any field. The special prevalence of malpractices in the art market reflects the lack of specialized knowledge of art, art history, or the art market among large purchasers, tax authorities, and law enforcement officers. It is so easy to take them for a ride.

Astronomy

Solar System. The two U.S. spacecraft Voyager 1 and Voyager 2 sped by the planet Jupiter in March and July, advancing mankind's knowledge of that planet and its satellites dramatically. Close-up photos taken from a distance of a million kilometres (620,000 mi) clearly revealed the turbulent flow of its predominantly hydrogen and helium atmosphere, including its famous Great Red Spot. In addition to such hydrocarbons as methane, acetylene, and ethane, infrared detectors aboard Voyager 1 found the atmosphere to contain ammonia, water, and phosphine. Voyager 1 also discovered a ring measuring a mere 30 km (19 mi) in thickness and lying at a distance of about 55,000 km (34,000 mi) from Jupiter's cloud tops. Perhaps the most exciting Voyager discoveries concerned the natures of the four largest Jovian satellites, each of which was found to be unique. (*See* SPACE EXPLORATION: *Special Report*.)

Shortly after the Voyager spacecraft bombarded the Earth with news of Jupiter, the much smaller Pioneer 11 encountered Saturn. Close-up photos, some taken as near as 20,200 km (12,560 mi) from Saturn's cloud tops, revealed the presence of at least one additional ring just outside the clearly visible ones. Both ultraviolet and gravitational data supported earlier speculation that the rings are composed of water ice rather than stony material. Photographs of Saturn's moon Titan—a satellite larger than Mercury and almost as large as Mars—provided some information about its atmosphere. Probably consisting mostly of methane, it includes a stratospheric layer of orange smog.

Cosmic radiation trapped by Saturn's magnetic field was found to be comparable in intensity to that in the Earth's Van Allen belts, except in the ring plane where radiation seemed negligible. After its safe traverse of the rings of Saturn, Pioneer 11 began its one-way journey out of the solar system. In 1980 and 1981 Voyagers 1 and 2 were scheduled to continue the exploration of Saturn.

Sun. That the Sun is shrinking was the recent conclusion of John A. Eddy of the Harvard-Smithsonian Center for Astrophysics in Cambridge, Mass., and Aram A. Boornazian of S. Ross and Co. in Boston. The two scientists undertook an extensive analysis of observations of the solar diameter made at the Royal Observatory at Greenwich, England, between 1836 and 1953 and at the U.S. Naval Observatory from 1846 to the present. To the astonishment of solar physicists, they found the Sun's horizontal diameter to be shrinking by about 0.1% per century, or about 1.5 metres (5 feet) per hour, and about half that vertically. Turning to old solar eclipse records, they noted that an eclipse reported by Clavius at the College of Rome on April 9, 1567, was annular rather than total as it should have been were the Sun's diameter constant. Thus, they suggested that, although the contraction is undoubtedly only temporary, it has been under way for at least four centuries.

This result has an important consequence for the origin of solar luminosity. Conventional belief holds the Sun's energy to be derived wholly from fusion of hydrogen into helium deep within the solar interior. However, as Eddy and Boornazian noted, if only the outer 20% of the Sun's radius (*i.e.*, the convective zone) is contracting, gravitational energy released by contraction could account for a significant portion of the solar luminosity—enough, in fact, to explain the puzzling shortage of neutrinos, detectable on the Earth, that had been calculated to accompany nuclear burning within the Sun.

COURTESY, MULTIPLE MIRROR TELESCOPE OBSERVATORY

A multimirrored telescope was installed on Mt. Hopkins in Arizona. This telescope uses six separate mirrors in combination with laser beams to gather in as much light as a single mirror with a 176-inch diameter.

Stars. Perhaps the most bizarre discovery in stellar astronomy during 1979 concerned an object, first studied more than a decade earlier, with the unglamorous name SS433. Late in 1978 and more fully in 1979, a group of astronomers at the University of California at Los Angeles led by Bruce Margon reported on the high-resolution spectra obtained of the object at Lick Observatory in California. Much to their surprise they found three sets of spectral lines, produced by hydrogen and helium, two of which varied in wavelength with a period of about 160 days. If the shifts are interpreted in terms of the Doppler effect in moving sources, the spectra indicate velocities of as much as 50,000 kilometres per second (31,000 miles per second) both toward and away from the observer simultaneously. By studying images of SS433 on plates in the Harvard University collection, Elaine Gottlieb and William Liller of the Harvard-Smithsonian Center for Astrophysics found that the 160-day periodicity had continued for the past 50 years. Infrared, X-ray, and radio observations all revealed the object as variable.

As usual, theorists raced in with speculations on models for the object, ranging from a supermassive black hole to an even more massive quasar. However, with the discovery by radio astronomers B. J. Geldzahler, T. Pauls, and C. J. Salter of the Max Planck Institute for Radio Astronomy in West Germany that SS433 lies in the centre of W50, a supernova remnant produced by the explosion

Association Football:
see Football

Astronautics:
see Space Exploration

of a star about 40,000 years in the past, it became clear that the object must lie within the Milky Way. Furthermore, it seemed most plausible that its peculiar variability is associated with a rotating neutron star, much like the pulsar lying at the centre of the Crab Nebula supernova remnant.

It seemed fitting in 1979, the centennial year of the birth of Albert Einstein (*see* PHYSICS: *Special Report*), that his general theory of relativity was subjected to its most precise test and, barring the perversity of nature, received its strongest confirmation to date. The object of study is a binary pulsar with the designation PSR1913+16. Discovered in 1974 by Joseph Taylor and Russell Hulse of the University of Massachusetts, it was as of late 1979 the only known pulsar to lie in a binary star system. Orbiting its companion in 7.75 hours, it pulsates with a period of about 0.059 second. With the spectacular precision possible in determining the pulse arrival times from the object, Taylor and collaborators Lee A. Fowler and Peter M. McCulloch were able to determine the change in the orbital period of the pulsar during the past five years. It amounted to about 100 microseconds (millionths of a second) per year. The general theory of relativity predicts just such a decrease due to the emission of gravitational radiation (by analogy with the emission of electromagnetic radiation by moving electric charges). The agreement between theory and observation, however, could be simply fortuitous. Whereas the theoretical value was based on calculations that assumed both components of the binary system to be collapsed stars, at year's end Philippe Crane, Jerry E. Nelson, and J. Anthony Tyson reported discovery of a very dim (21st-magnitude), probably noncollapsed star at the exact position of the binary system.

Quasars. More than 15 years after the initial discovery of quasars (quasi-stellar radio sources or QSO's) the nature of these objects of galactic physical dimensions but of stellar appearance on photographic plates remained enigmatic. Though investigations in 1979 offered no breakthroughs in understanding them, they did uncover a pair of remarkable quasars. The two quasars lie close to one another and show almost identical spectra and red shifts, placing them both at a distance from the Earth of about 6,000,000,000 light years. The observers, Dennis Walsh of the Jodrell Bank Radio Astronomy Observatory in England, Robert Carswell of the University of Cambridge, and Ray Weymann of the University of Arizona, working at Kitt Peak National Observatory in Arizona, suggested that, in fact, the two images are of one and the same quasar, produced by a splitting of its light due to the lenslike gravitational field of an intervening (but unseen) galaxy. If so, this pair of quasar images would be the most dramatic demonstration to date of the deflection of light predicted by the general theory of relativity. Subsequent radio studies of the double quasar, however, offered evidence that it consists of two very similar, yet physically separate objects. Hence, it appeared that more studies would be necessary before the true nature of this unusual object was resolved.

Cosmology. Though no dramatic new discoveries in the large-scale structure of the universe were made in 1979, several further pieces were added to the jigsaw-puzzle picture. Arno A. Penzias of Bell Laboratories in New Jersey, co-winner of the 1978 Nobel Prize for Physics for his discovery of the microwave radiation left over from the "big bang" explosion, reported discovery of molecules of hydrocyanic acid containing deuterium in the outer regions of our Galaxy. Because little nucleosynthesis is presumed to have gone on in these regions since the formation of the Galaxy, the deuterium is probably "primordial." If so, its large abundance implies an "open" universe, one slated to expand forever.

Much of the present confidence in the big-bang model derives from the belief that the 3 K microwave radiation is truly primordial. But does this radiation, in fact, have the correct spectrum to be a residual of the initial event? In 1979 David P. Woody and Paul L. Richards of the Lawrence Berkeley Laboratory in California reported precise measurements showing the overall shape of the observed spectrum to be in agreement with expectations, but with some small deviations. Whether these differences were due only to some experimental limitation or atmospheric effect or whether

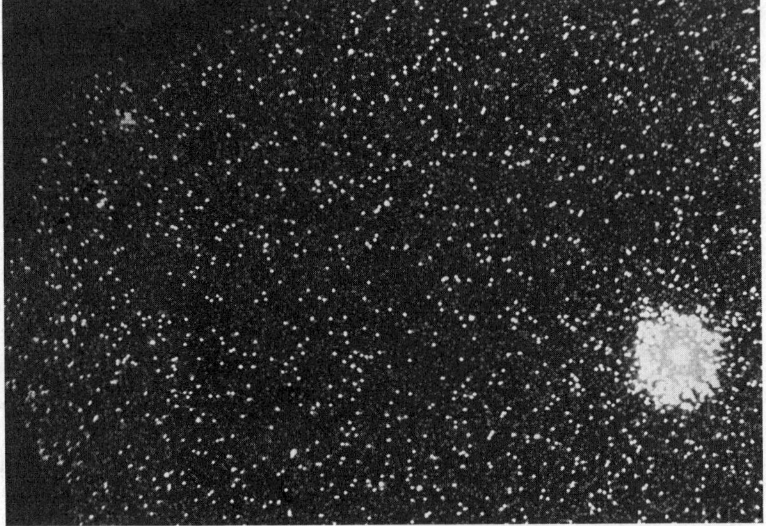

Observations made by NASA's space observatory HEAO 2 more than doubled the number of known X-ray objects in space. The X-ray photo faintly shows a newly discovered quasar in the upper left-hand corner; diagonally opposite is the much-studied quasar 3C 273.

NASA/AUTHENTICATED NEWS INTERNATIONAL

Earth Perihelion and Aphelion, 1980

January 3	Perihelion, 147,095,000 km (91,400,000 mi) from the Sun
July 5	Aphelion, 152,102,000 km (94,512,000 mi) from the Sun

Equinoxes and Solstices, 1980

March 20	Vernal equinox, 11:10[1]
June 21	Summer solstice, 05:47[1]
Sept. 22	Autumnal equinox, 21:09[1]
Dec. 21	Winter solstice, 16:56[1]

Eclipses, 1980

Feb. 16	Sun, total (begins 06:15[2]), visible E part of S. Atlantic O., Africa except NW part, N part of Indian O., Asia, excluding Japan, Indonesia except extreme E part, Philippines except SE, SW part of Soviet Union.
March 1	Moon, penumbral (begins 18:44[2]), beginning visible W part of Pacific O., Asia, Australia, part of Antarctica, Africa except W part, Europe, and Arctic; end visible Asia except E, Indian O., part of Antarctica, Africa, Europe, Atlantic O., extreme NE of N. America, E of S. America, and Arctic.
July 27	Moon, penumbral (begins 17:56[2]), beginning visible W half of Pacific O., New Zealand, Australia, most of Antarctica, Asia except N part, Indian O., Africa except NW part, and E Europe; end visible in Australia, Asia except NE part, Antarctica, Indian O., Africa, Europe except N and W part, S Atlantic O.
Aug. 10	Sun, annular (begins 16:14[2]), visible in Hawaii, E part of N Pacific O., N part of S. Pacific O., Oceania, SW N. America, West Indies, and S. America.
Aug. 26	Moon, penumbral (begins 01:42[2]), beginning visible W Indian O., Africa, extreme W part of Asia, Europe, Atlantic O., E half of N. America, S. America, and most of Antarctica, E S. Pacific O.; end visible in extreme W part of Europe, extreme W part of Africa, Atlantic O., N. America except extreme NW part, S. America, E half of Pacific O., and most of Antarctica.

[1] Universal time.
[2] Ephemeris time.
Source: *The American Ephemeris and Nautical Almanac.*

NASA

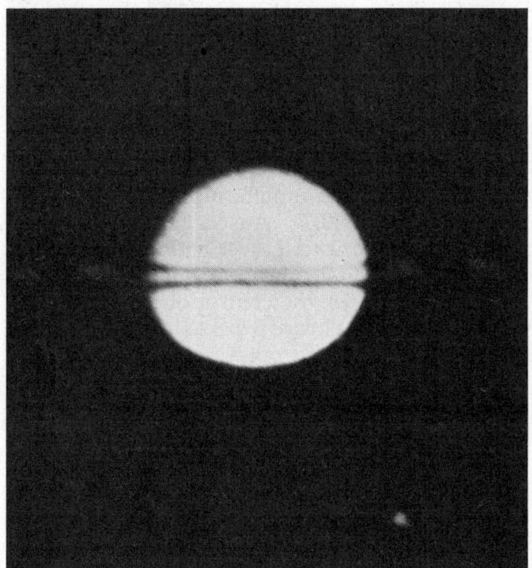

In a photograph of Saturn taken by Pioneer 11 in August, Titan, the largest of Saturn's moons, appears as a speck (lower right) even though it is almost as large as Mars.

they required a reevaluation of the entire big-bang model remained to be seen.

New Astronomies. In 1979 scientists examined data returned by two new NASA High Energy Astronomy Observatories, numbers 2 and 3 in the spacecraft series. Launched in November 1978, HEAO 2 (later named the Einstein Observatory) not only possessed about 1,000 times more sensitivity than previous instruments devoted to X-ray astronomy but also carried the first X-ray imaging telescope, allowing production of X-ray "photographs" of the universe with an angular resolution of about three arc seconds. It took pictures of many supernova remnants including the Crab, Vela, Cassiopeia A, Tycho, and SN1006. The absence of any detectable point X-ray source within the last three of these seemed puzzling in view of the widely accepted belief that supernova explosions give rise to pulsars (as they have in the Crab and Vela remnants), which should remain hot enough to detect by virtue of their X-ray emission for centuries. By late 1979 HEAO 2 had more than doubled the known number of X-ray objects. HEAO 3, launched in September 1979, was equipped to detect gamma rays and cosmic rays from distant parts of the universe.

During the year important new results were also obtained from the International Ultraviolet Explorer (IUE), launched in January 1978 by NASA and the European Space Agency (ESA). Searching the sky at ultraviolet (UV) wavelengths unobservable from the Earth's surface, IUE reported detection of outbursts of several novas, as well as an eruption of the dwarf nova VW Hyi in January. It also found stellar winds to be a common feature of hot luminous stars, detected large UV fluxes from the cores of globular clusters, and established UV spectra of distant galaxies and quasars.

(KENNETH BRECHER)

See also Earth Sciences; Space Exploration.
[131.A–B; 131.D–E; 132.D.4.b.ii; 133.B; 133.C.3.a–b]

Australia

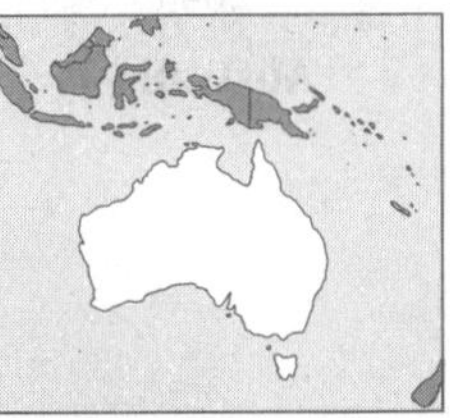

Australia

A federal parliamentary state and a member of the Commonwealth of Nations, Australia occupies the smallest continent and, with the island state of Tasmania, is the sixth largest country in the world. Area 7,682,300 sq km (2,966,200 sq mi). Pop. (1979 est.): 14,376,400. Cap.: Canberra (metro. pop., 1978 est., 215,900). Largest city: Sydney (metro. pop., 1978 est., 3,155,200). Language: English. Religion (1971): Church of England 31%; Roman Catholic 27%; Uniting Church 17%. Queen, Elizabeth II; governor-general in 1979, Sir Zelman Cowen; prime minister, Malcolm Fraser.

Domestic Affairs. Unemployment, inflation, and difficult industrial relations dominated the domestic scene in Australia during 1979. The normally quiescent public-service sector was particularly disrupted. The most visible dispute involved employees of the national telecommunications company, Telecom, a government organization run along private enterprise lines and designed to make large profits for the government. Members of the Australian Telecommunications Employees Association, charged with keeping the country's telephones, radiotelephones, teleprinters, and satellite links open, placed a series of bans and limitations on their jobs to support demands for a pay hike that the government had resisted.

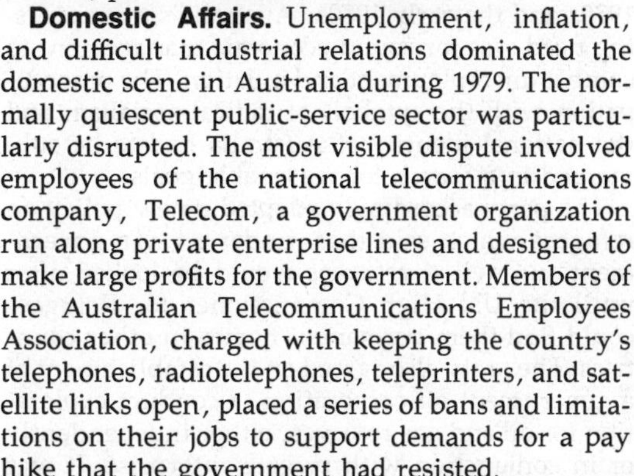

The job action was designed to cause maximum inconvenience to high-revenue business consumers and government ministers and minimum annoyance to the ordinary man in the street. This strategy worked so well that on July 13 the government was driven to proclaim the Government Employees (Employment Provisions) Act. This legislation, which had lain dormant since its passage through the upper house of Parliament during a strike by postal workers in 1977, was the last weapon in the government's arsenal. It gave the government power to suspend without pay or dismiss civil employees who took part in strikes or other job actions. As Prime Minister Malcolm Fraser explained, if trade unionists were to cause great inconvenience to the public by not working as they were employed and paid to do, they could not continue to be supported.

Once the act was proclaimed the union immediately lifted its bans. The union executive recommended a return to work. The government ceased its opposition to an Arbitration Court hearing to determine the justice of the workers' wage claim. The minister for industrial relations, Anthony Street, said that the quick end to the paralyzing dispute completely vindicated the government's action. Street's optimism proved unfounded, however, and the conflict moved from the field of telecommunications to the general arena.

The immediate cause was another new law, which affected all public servants in Australia. The Commonwealth Employees (Redeployment and Retirement) Act gave the government power to compulsorily retire civil servants without the considerable pension benefits they had counted on when choosing a civil service career. The conflict

Athletics:
see articles on the various sports

intensified when a ban was put on handling ministerial correspondence, and the ministers responded by dismissing the employees responsible. Public servants belonging to the Administrative and Clerical Officers Association led the assault on the new law, and tens of thousands of public servants held mass meetings at which it was condemned.

The Australian Labor Party (ALP) met in Adelaide in July to set out its broad objectives for the next two years. The meeting was significant insofar as it represented a turn to the right. As party leader William Hayden put it, members of the ALP had to realize that the reformist zeal of the days of Gough Whitlam's prime ministership was gone forever. In the new economic climate of the late 1970s and the early 1980s, Australia's most pressing need was for sound economic management to combat unemployment and inflation. The preoccupation with the symbols of radical socialism and the national identity of Australia had to be submerged in a search for reasonable goals.

The party accordingly adopted a new policy on refugees which said that, under an ALP government, uninvited refugees would be looked after until the UN High Commissioner for Refugees could find them permanent homes in other countries. The party also agreed on the establishment of a government oil corporation to conduct exploration for oil and gas reserves, either independently or in conjunction with private enterprise. It was envisaged that the new government company would leave the development of oil fields to private entrepreneurs. However, the ALP hoped that, by becoming involved in the oil search itself, a new Australian government could ensure a much greater rate of exploratory drilling. Currently about 50 wells were being drilled a year.

During the year the government passed legislation to set up the Barrier Reef Marine Park. The step was taken despite considerable controversy over the Queensland state government's efforts to encourage oil exploration in areas of the Great Barrier Reef.

Australians were pleased to learn in mid-1979 that the feud surrounding Kerry Packer's World Series Cricket movement, which had shattered the tranquil cricket world in 1977, was over. The peace terms suggested that at last Australia would be in a position to pick its best team in international competitions and perhaps wipe out the memories of its defeats in recent test matches and in the Prudential World Cup Series. Under the divided system of official and unofficial cricket that had pertained since 1977, Australia's international reputation as a cricket power had fallen steadily.

From 1980 all first-class cricket in Australia was to be played under the control of the Australian Cricket Board. The board expected to receive about A$1.7 million a year from a new promoter, PBL Sports. The chairman of the Australian Cricket Board, Bob Parish, said the reconciliation was great for cricket. The view was endorsed by Lynton Taylor, managing director of PBL Sports and a program executive of Packer's Channel 9 Television, Sydney, which received exclusive television rights to Australian cricket for three years.

Some Western Australians experienced a close encounter of a highly spectacular kind in July, when the derelict U.S. space station Skylab disintegrated on reentering the atmosphere and showered fiery debris widely over the state. (*See* SPACE EXPLORATION.)

The Economy. With the spectre of a possible 10.5% inflation rate and high unemployment before him, the treasurer, John Howard, introduced an early "mini-budget" into Parliament during May. Its most important features were the abandonment of tax indexation and further dismantling of the health care system, Medibank. The 40% Commonwealth medical expense rebate was abolished, and no benefits at all would be paid up to the first A$20 of medical expenses, although pensioners and the socially disadvantaged were still protected by the government. Hospital charges were increased. Educational programs were once again put under the pruning knife. The Commonwealth cut its extension service to primary industry from A$10 million to A$5 million, reduced the rural adjustment scheme from A$41 million to A$18.7 million, and halved the nitrogenous fertilizer subsidy from A$40 to A$20 per met-

AUSTRALIA

Education. (1978) Primary, pupils 1,894,654, teachers 85,273; secondary and vocational, pupils 1,115,378, teachers 77,615; teacher training, students 46,136, teachers 2,870; higher, students 263,821, teaching staff 19,087.

Finance. Monetary unit: Australian dollar, with (Sept. 17, 1979) a free rate of A$0.89 to U.S. $1 (A$1.92 = £1 sterling). Gold, SDR's, and foreign exchange (June 1979) U.S. $2,325,000,000. Budget (1978 actual): revenue A$24,589,000,000; expenditure A$27,938,000,000. Gross national product (1978) A$94.6 billion. Money supply (May 1979) A$13,004,000,000. Cost of living (1975 = 100; April–June 1979) 148.1.

Foreign Trade. (1978) Imports A$13,749,200,000; exports A$12,561,700,000. Import sources: U.S. 22%; Japan 19%; U.K. 11%; West Germany 7%. Export destinations: Japan 30%; U.S. 11%; New Zealand 5%. Main exports: coal 12%; wool 11%; beef 8%; iron ore 7%; wheat 6%; alumina 5%; nonferrous metals 5%. Tourism (1977): visitors 563,000; gross receipts U.S. $343 million.

Transport and Communications. Roads (1974) 837,866 km. Motor vehicles in use (1976): passenger 5,284,000; commercial 1,260,500. Railways: (government; 1976) 40,753 km; freight traffic (1976–77) 32,030,000,000 net ton-km. Air traffic (1977): 19,239,000,000 passenger-km; freight 413.2 million net ton-km. Shipping (1978): merchant vessels 100 gross tons and over 426; gross tonnage 1,531,739. Shipping traffic (1977–78): goods loaded 167,810,000 metric tons, unloaded 25 million metric tons. Telephones (June 1977) 5,835,000. Radio receivers (Dec. 1976) 10.5 million. Television licenses (Dec. 1976) 4,785,000.

Agriculture. Production (in 000; metric tons; 1978): wheat 18,300; barley 4,000; oats 1,800; corn 130; rice 490; sorghum 714; potatoes 734; sugar, raw value 2,945; tomatoes *c.* 160; apples 245; oranges *c.* 357; pineapples 110; wine *c.* 385; sunflower seed 139; wool, clean *c.* 400; milk 5,329; butter 112; cheese 118; beef and veal 2,130; mutton and lamb 516. Livestock (in 000; March 1978): sheep 131,510; cattle 29,379; pigs 2,219; horses (1977) *c.* 560; chickens 42,795.

Industry. Fuel and power (in 000; metric tons; 1978): coal 79,880; lignite 32,868; crude oil 21,270; natural gas (cu m) 7,240,000; manufactured gas (cu m; 1975–76) *c.* 7,160,000; electricity (kw-hr) 88,525,000. Production (in 000; metric tons; 1978): iron ore (64% metal content) 83,230; bauxite (1977–78) 24,830; pig iron 7,337; crude steel 7,590; aluminum 263; copper 153; lead 218; tin 5.1; zinc 293; nickel concentrates (metal content; 1976–77) 82; uranium (1977) *c.* 0.4; gold (troy oz) *c.* 650; silver (troy oz) *c.* 24,800; sulfuric acid 1,861; fertilizers (nutrient content; 1977–78) nitrogenous *c.* 215, phosphate *c.* 764; plastics and resins 574; cement 4,992; newsprint 210; other paper (1975–76) 920; cotton yarn 22; wool yarn 20; passenger cars (including assembly; units) 346; commercial vehicles (including assembly; units) 45. Merchant vessels launched (100 gross tons and over; 1978) 34,000 gross tons. Dwelling units completed (1978) 121,000.

ric ton as of 1980. A limit was introduced on homes that qualified for a home savings grant, with A$35,000 the limit for a full grant. Minor changes included increases in passport fees and two-way radio license fees for taxis and private couriers. Business complained when the trading stock valuation adjustment concession was abolished.

In the full budget, presented in Parliament on August 21, the economy was further tuned. The personal income tax surcharge of 2.57% was removed with effect from December 1. After protests by pensioners, their benefits were restored by the reintroduction of twice yearly increases in line with the consumer price index. Tax incentives were provided for oil exploration and for converting oil-fired industrial equipment to other energy sources. A special 20% depreciation rate was allowed for on-farm grain storage facilities, and the coal export duty was reduced from A$3.50 to A$1 per metric ton. The mildness of the August measures led to speculation that Fraser was planning an early election, since much harsher changes had been expected.

The government hoped to reduce the budget deficit to A$2,193,000,000 and accordingly maintained unrelenting pressure on public spending. Although unemployment rose to 395,700 by August 1979, no specific measures were aimed at reducing it. The unemployed were expected to wait until the economy picked up in the 1980s.

While rural incomes in 1979 were boosted by exceptionally good returns for wheat, wool, and meat exporters, the prospects for the coming season were not so promising. Government planning was based on predictions by the Organization for Economic Cooperation and Development that Australian inflation would be below the OECD average. The government was also optimistic that renewed capital inflow would continue to be attracted to Australia from overseas by the Fraser administration's firmness and the mild improvement in nonfarm productivity.

In June the Commonwealth Conciliation and Arbitration Commission delivered the 14th of its judgments in National Wage Case determinations. The commission granted Australian workers a 3.2% raise in their wages and salaries. At the same time, it called a meeting to discuss the future of wage indexation, whereby wage increases were tied to increases in the cost of living. The president of the Bench, Sir John Moore, remarked that the future of wage indexation was open to question since parties on both sides had refused to abide by the guidelines. The judgment giving workers a 3.2% increase was based on a cost-of-living increase of 4% over a six-month period, discounted by 0.8%, as the president put it, "because of increased excise on petrol [gas] and the disruptive effects of strikes in defiance of the Bench's call . . . for restraint in industrial relations."

Hayden pointed out that wage indexation at the 3.2% level, when income tax and the increases in direct taxation were taken into account, meant in effect that Australia's workers were receiving an increase of only 2.1% and thus were falling steadily behind the inflation rate. All factions immediately expressed their disquiet at the possibility that the wage indexation system might be scrapped, however. The trade unions and the Labor opposition joined to point out that, in the event of a return to the wage-fixing processes of the past, the weakest trade unionists would be at a serious disadvantage.

(TOP) UPI; (BOTTOM) KEYSTONE

Skylab's fiery trail lit up the night sky above Australia when the U.S. spacecraft crashed to Earth in July. Below: One of the larger pieces of wreckage that made it back to Earth is shown to Princess Anne of Great Britain.

Australia was not exempt from the effects of the energy crisis. After the Iranian revolution, the government acted to devise an energy policy that would help to shelter Australians from the effects of oil shortages in the future. The policy was designed to increase the use of natural gas, and to this end Prime Minister Fraser announced that the Commonwealth government intended to convert as many of its cars as practicable to run on liquefied petroleum gas rather than gasoline. He added that when the existing contract for the purchase of vehicles had expired, the Commonwealth would consider the total conversion of its fleet to liquid petroleum gas. The government also intended to cut gasoline consumption 10% by reducing the octane rating of automotive fuel from 98 to 97 and by asking the governments of New South Wales and South Australia to drop their strict requirements on exhaust emissions. To prevent noticeable fuel shortages, the oil companies were allowed to make spot purchases of petroleum on the world market at prices above the Organization of Petroleum Exporting Countries minimum and to pass the added cost on to consumers through the Prices Justification Tribunal.

The government faced a particular dilemma regarding domestic oil prices. The prime minister insisted that a move toward world parity prices was essentially designed to encourage further exploration and development of Australia's own oil fields. Critics pointed out, however, that the government had reaped a bonanza from increased oil prices. In 1979 it received 11% of its total revenue from that one commodity. Although production costs were less than A$1 a barrel for Bass Strait crude, government taxes raised the price to A$18.

Foreign Affairs. Increasing tension in Indochina, Iran, the Middle East, Afghanistan, and the Horn of Africa undermined Australia's strategic interests during 1979. In February the foreign minister, Andrew Peacock, announced on behalf of the government Australia's deep concern about the critical situation in Indochina after the Vietnamese invasion of Cambodia. Australia joined the general Western condemnation of Vietnam's aggression and called for a cease-fire and the withdrawal of Vietnamese troops. Peacock observed that the war between Vietnam and Cambodia owed much to historical and ideological rivalries, but it could have serious implications for Australia. Because the Soviets supported Vietnam, the potential existed for an intensified confrontation between the Soviet Union and China, which had close relations with Cambodia. Peacock emphasized that Australia had a fundamental interest in a peaceful and stable Southeast Asia.

An Australian foreign policy priority throughout 1979 was the influx of Vietnamese refugees. From the fall of Saigon in April 1975 to Sept. 30, 1979, Australia had accepted and resettled 24,133 Indochinese refugees. In 1979 it was receiving them at a rate of more than 1,000 a month, a figure the government claimed was better, on a per capita basis, than that of any other receiving country. By mid-1980 Australia expected to have received 37,000 refugees. A statistical breakdown of the three Indochinese national groupings showed that, of the arrivals up to 1979, 13,000 were Vietnamese, 2,500 were Laotians, and 800 were Cambodians. Small boats brought an additional 1,800 refugees to Australia. But while the refugee total was small, a Gallup Poll showed that it was overwhelmingly unpopular. Only 15% of Australians believed that Australia should take more than 10,000 refugees in 1979 for permanent settlement, and 28% recommended that the boat people should be put back to sea. (*See* REFUGEES: *Special Report.*)

Two New Guinea mudmen nonchalantly rode on a Melbourne streetcar after taking part in a promotional event for their national airline.

WIDE WORLD

In a general comment on how the government viewed its foreign policy priorities, Peacock referred to the pattern of instability in the geopolitical situation. Before 1979 international affairs had been largely dominated by economic issues. International recession, inflation, the drift toward protectionism, and the concerted pressure for economic change on the part of less developed countries meant that the traditional issues of power politics were no longer seen as being of fundamental importance. Australia, on the contrary, considered that as long as the world was organized in a system of sovereign states, power would continue to be the main arbiter in international affairs.

Prime Minister Fraser played a major role at the Commonwealth heads of government meeting in Lusaka, Zambia, in August. He had flown to the meeting desperate to succeed on the world stage as a statesman in order to counteract his low personal standing with the domestic electorate. For that reason he took a strong line on the need for fresh elections to give Zimbabwe Rhodesia not only a black majority parliament but also a black majority government. This also explained why, after the initiative to call new, U.K.-supervised elections had been agreed on by an inner hierarchy of six nations, he leaked the news of their success during a barbecue at the Australian High Commission before the agreement had been ratified by the whole caucus of 39 Commonwealth heads of government. (*See* COMMONWEALTH OF NATIONS.)

Relations with the Association of Southeast Asian Nations (ASEAN) remained shaky. The chief bone of contention during 1979 was the civil aviation agreement between Australia and the U.K. Under the new arrangements, passengers flew direct between London and Australia, being barred from stopover facilities by a low fare structure designed to stimulate through traffic. This deprived Southeast Asia of much-needed tourist revenue hitherto derived from travelers who stopped over in the region. ASEAN airlines were barred from participating in the popular low-fare scheme and protested their reduced shares of air traffic. Australia, which attached great importance to achieving a harmonious agreement with the ASEAN countries, sought to develop a stopover fare that, together with lower fares between Australia and the ASEAN region, would contribute to the development of tourism there. (A. R. G. GRIFFITHS)

See also Dependent States.

SPECIAL REPORT

THE MEMORABLE DUNSTAN

by A. R. G. Griffiths

Under Premier Donald Dunstan, the state of South Australia led the rest of the nation in the area of social reform. When he entered the state parliament of Adelaide in 1953, Dunstan thought the government restrictive, establishment-ridden, puritanical, undemocratic, prejudiced, and intolerant. In a long political career he made major changes in the social fabric that upset the provincial stability of the whole of Australian culture. Innovations enjoyed by South Australia's million and a half citizens were demanded, with varying degrees of success, elsewhere in the nation. Dunstan himself, however, despite continual urging, never moved into the federal sphere of influence, although he was told that he could follow Gough Whitlam as leader of the Labor Party in Canberra and, perhaps, become prime minister.

Dunstan's focus of activity remained deliberately local. Projecting a fierce and self-confident parochialism, he became both the darling of the intellectuals and progressives and an almost satanic figure to the conservatives.

New Laws. The key machinery that Dunstan used to accomplish his reforms was the legal system. He entered the Labor ministry in 1965 as attorney general, being at that time the only legally qualified practitioner in the party. A close appreciation of the power of law reform was etched on his consciousness, and when he became premier himself in 1967 he chose two radical attorneys general to draft his progressive legislation. Dunstan's law officers provided statutes that allowed the creation of a new style of government. Once change had achieved this respectability of legal force, a wide variety of alternative life-styles began to flourish. From a state with a deserved reputation for sabbatarianism, intolerance, and xenophobic Baptist piety, Dunstan transformed South Australia into a region where arts, culture, and dissent from accepted Australian norms were not merely tolerated but encouraged.

Dunstan first concentrated on amending the criminal law. His initial breakthrough concerned the treatment of homosexuals. He passed a law that allowed a male charged with a homosexual offense to use as a defense the fact that the act was committed in private by persons over 21. This law was later amended to abolish homosexuality as a legal offense altogether and allow charges to be made only under the heading of assault.

Behind the ponderous legal wording of the Criminal Law Consolidation Act were tremendous changes. Before the Dunstan era police had acted as agents provocateurs and obtained convictions by posing as homosexuals. In a cause célèbre George Duncan, a lecturer in law at the University of Adelaide, was thrown in the River Torrens (which runs through the centre of Adelaide) and drowned. At the time it was thought that members of the police force had thrown Duncan in, but despite an inquiry by Scotland Yard detectives seconded by the London Metropolitan Police commissioner, Sir Robert Mark, the truth was never established. In the middle of the Duncan case, Dunstan made a crucial new appointment. He chose an overseas candidate, Harold Salisbury, formerly chief constable of York and North East Yorkshire in England, to be commissioner of the South Australian police force.

The second controversial legal change occurred in 1976 when rape within marriage was made a crime. Under a new law no person was, by reason only of the fact that he or she was married to some other person, to be presumed to have consented to an indecent assault by that other person.

Dunstan's laws were not dead letters. Three policemen resigned after refusing to give evidence at the Duncan inquest; Harold Salisbury forbade the continuance of homosexual decoys; and one husband was charged with rape of his wife. Naturally the speed of such change took some citizens by surprise. A group was formed to try to counteract the new permissive liberalism, which they thought endangered community values and had a deleterious effect on community life.

Undismayed by the furor, Dunstan built up a whole infrastructure of social reform in the ten years he was premier. (From 1968 to 1970 he was leader of the opposition, resuming the premiership in the latter year.) He also was aware of the two-edged knife he wielded. Although it was racially indefensible in the 1970s for Aboriginals not to be able to drink alcohol, the sight of drunken unemployed blacks destroyed the civic amenities his government was trying to create. On the other hand, while the Lutherans wished to restrict drinking hours, the new laws enabled a boom in wine sales from which they benefited, their forefathers having established vineyards and wineries in the Barossa Valley as part of the culture transplant from their native Germany.

A. R. G. Griffiths is a senior lecturer in the School of Social Sciences, The Flinders University of South Australia. His works include Contemporary Australia *(1977).*

While it was a tenet of the civil liberties movement in South Australia that adults ought to be free to see or read whatever they liked, the new accessibility of pornography, as it seemed to Dunstan's critics, was altogether unwelcome in an area proud of its fundamentalist and Baptist origins.

Dunstan passed strict laws to protect the environment. Antilitter fines were heavy, and a deposit system was devised in 1977 to end the haphazard practice of throwing away drink cans. This reform, however, cost jobs in the can-making industries and was the first sign of the harsh wind of economic reality biting into the visionary state.

Problems with Appointees. Much of Dunstan's trouble centred on the occupant of Government House. Dunstan bravely appointed an Aboriginal, Pastor Douglas Nicholls, as governor of South Australia in 1976, the first of his race to hold viceregal office. His term as governor was short, however, as the strain of the task told on his health. Dunstan replaced him in 1977 with Keith Seaman, a minister who subsequently admitted to "a grave personal impropriety" as a clergyman; his appointment had been hotly opposed by many.

But neither Nicholls nor Seaman caused Dunstan as much heartache as his most celebrated nominee (1971) as governor, the nuclear physicist Sir Mark Oliphant. Oliphant brought the background of an academic scientist to Government House. He sided with Dunstan in early controversies, and his outspokenness as governor initially pleased Dunstan. When, however, Oliphant retired but continued to comment on South Australian politics, Dunstan felt betrayed. The chief issue that divided the two men was the dismissal in 1978 of Harold Salisbury from his post as police commissioner. To Dunstan the issues involved in the dismissal of the police commissioner were clear. Salisbury was a servant of the government who had misled its chief officers, was unrepentant, and therefore had to be removed.

The area in which Salisbury had misinformed his minister was security. Salisbury erroneously considered his duty to the federal Australian Security and Intelligence Organisation and to the federal government greater than his obligation to South Australia. The pivotal issue was whether a police state existed if the police commissioner could be sacked, an absurd proposition in Dunstan's view but not so in the eyes of Oliphant. Oliphant muddied the waters by bringing in the issue of pornography, which he said Dunstan tolerated in repellent forms.

Downfall and Aftermath. Dunstan's frankness was his Achilles' heel. At the time of the Vietnam war he opposed Australian involvement and said that had he been 20 years old he would have refused to register for conscription to the Army. When he decided that the Whitlam Labor Party government had behaved undemocratically and unconstitutionally, he did not hide his feelings. Indeed, his anger at abuse and injustice was what marked him as different in style from other politicians, and his choleric outbursts no doubt contributed to his premature retirement from the political scene.

For a quarter of a century Dunstan suffered attacks on his personality that others would have found intolerable. He was at one time said to be a half-caste Melanesian bastard and at another to be receiving shock treatment for psychiatric disorders and let out only under supervision. Personal attacks he shrugged off. Some he laughed at; others hurt him. His final crisis came at a time when his personal distress was exceptionally heavy and his political responsibilities overwhelming.

At that time, four factors combined to destroy Dunstan's equilibrium. A personal tragedy, his appointments in Government House and the police force, and the nuclear energy issue raised Dunstan's blood pressure to the extent that he collapsed dramatically in Parliament early in February 1979 and resigned a week later. He had been hard hit by the death of his young Malaysian second wife, Adele, who died abruptly of cancer on Oct. 24, 1978.

Dunstan had little time to recover from his wife's death. He took off from Adelaide to face the rigours of the European winter in a search for safeguards to the mining of South Australian uranium. Deposits of uranium at Roxby Downs station in the north of South Australia had, when mined in conjunction with copper, the potential for a multimillion-dollar industry. Dunstan's views on uranium mining were ambiguous. On the one hand he encouraged uranium exploration, but on the other he opposed the mining of uranium until it was demonstrated that it could be provided to customers safely.

In a statement from the hospital after his collapse Dunstan said that the strain of the preceding two years, combined with the loss of his wife and the grueling nature of his personal uranium inquiry, had forced his resignation. The left saw his political end as a day of doom. Others regarded it as the judgment of heaven. For South Australia a new era of consolidation, after what Dunstan described as "10 years of fairly frenzied reform legislation," began.

Dunstan packed his bags and left for Perugia in Italy to study Italian, passing into history as the mastermind behind the Festival Centre, in many ways the symbol of his period in office. He was after all the first political leader in Australia to prove that there were votes to be won from the arts and to demonstrate his theory by reading poetry—at a performance of Saint-Saëns's *Carnival of the Animals*—at the Zoological Gardens.

Austria

A republic of central Europe, Austria is bounded by West Germany, Czechoslovakia, Hungary, Yugoslavia, Italy, Switzerland, and Liechtenstein. Area: 83,853 sq km (32,376 sq mi). Pop (1978 est.): 7,508,400. Cap. and largest city: Vienna (pop., 1978 est., 1,580,600). Language: German. Religion (1978): Roman Catholic 90%. President in 1979, Rudolf Kirchschläger; chancellor, Bruno Kreisky.

The general election on May 6, 1979, resulted in a bigger overall majority for the ruling Socialist Party of Austria (SPÖ), led by Chancellor Bruno Kreisky (*see* BIOGRAPHIES). The SPÖ increased its seats by 2 to 95 in the 183-seat National Council, while the Austrian People's Party (ÖVP) lost 3, dropping its total to 77. The small Austrian Freedom Party (FPÖ) won 11 seats, a gain of one. The Communists and splinter groups remained unrepresented. (For tabulated results, *see* POLITICAL PARTIES.) The SPÖ's economic and—especially—employment policies and Kreisky's popularity were considered the main reasons for its success.

AUSTRIA

Education. (1977–78) Primary, pupils 935,091, teachers 62,435; secondary (1976–77), pupils 176,951, teachers 13,735; vocational, pupils 179,366, teachers 3,814; teacher training, students 6,050, teachers 555; higher, students 94,386, teaching staff 10,996.

Finance. Monetary unit: schilling, with (Sept. 17, 1979) a free rate of 13.05 schillings to U.S. $1 (28.07 schillings = £1 sterling). Gold, SDR's, and foreign exchange (June 1979) U.S. $4,427,000,000. Budget (1977 actual): revenue 154,610,000,000 schillings; expenditure 183,930,000,000 schillings. Gross national product (1978) 835 billion schillings. Money supply (April 1979) 130,650,000,000 schillings. Cost of living (1975 = 100; June 1979) 121.1.

Foreign Trade. (1978) Imports 231,890,000,000 schillings; exports 176,110,000,000 schillings. Import sources: EEC 65% (West Germany 43%, Italy 9%); Switzerland 6%. Export destinations: EEC 52% (West Germany 29%, Italy 9%, U.K. 5%); Switzerland 8%. Main exports: machinery 24%; iron and steel 10%; chemicals 8%; textile yarns and fabrics 7%; metal manufactures 5%; timber 5%; paper and board 5%. Tourism (1977): visitors 11,748,000; gross receipts U.S. $3,708,000,000.

Transport and Communications. Roads (1977) 106,180 km (including 781 km expressways). Motor vehicles in use (1977): passenger 1,965,250; commercial 155,844. Railways (1977): 6,492 km; traffic 6,973,000,000 passenger-km, freight 10,294,000,000 net ton-km. Air traffic (1978): 1,035,000,000 passenger-km; freight 12,490,000 net ton-km. Navigable inland waterways in regular use (1977) 358 km. Shipping (1978): merchant vessels 100 gross tons and over 10; gross tonnage 46,148. Telephones (Dec. 1977) 2,443,400. Radio licenses (Dec. 1976) 2,185,000. Television licenses (Dec. 1976) 1,772,000.

Agriculture. Production (in 000; metric tons; 1978): wheat 1,195; barley 1,424; rye 410; oats 304; corn 1,166; potatoes 1,401; sugar, raw value *c.* 337; apples 291; wine 274; meat 568; timber (cu m; 1977) 13,163. Livestock (in 000; Dec. 1977): cattle 2,547; sheep 181; pigs 3,694; chickens 14,038.

Industry. Fuel and power (in 000; metric tons; 1978): lignite 3,077; crude oil 1,793; natural gas (cu m) *c.* 2,100,000; manufactured gas (cu m) *c.* 760,000; electricity (kw-hr) 38,082,000 (58% hydroelectric in 1976). Production (in 000; metric tons; 1978): iron ore (31% metal content) 2,787; pig iron 3,077; crude steel 4,830; magnesite (1977) 1,003; aluminum 129; copper 32; zinc 22; cement 5,734; newsprint 161; other paper (1977) 1,024; petroleum products (1976) *c.* 8,660; plastics and resins 435; fertilizers (nutrient content; 1977–78) nitrogenous *c.* 265, phosphate *c.* 107; man-made fibres (1976) 131.

Kreisky's fourth Cabinet, sworn in on June 5, contained no newcomers.

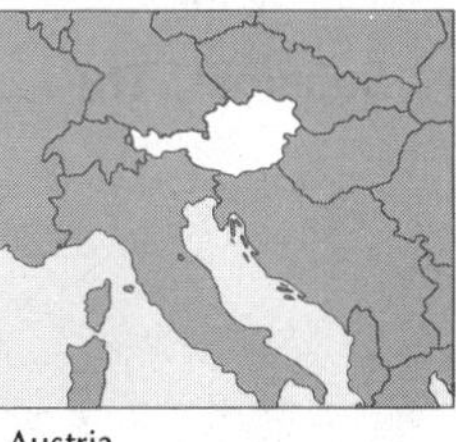
Austria

Earlier regional elections had shown varying results. In Vienna in October 1978 the SPÖ had lost four seats to the ÖVP, while the FPÖ retained three. A decline of 100,000 in the SPÖ vote was attributed to abstentions protesting the party leadership's support for nuclear power and a scandal over alleged misconduct in the city administration. However, the Vienna SPÖ still had a solid majority (57% of the poll), enabling it to continue in power; Leopold Gratz remained mayor. In the Steiermark election, held at the same time, the ÖVP lost one seat, the FPÖ gained one, and the SPÖ retained 23.

Elections in Lower Austria, Salzburg, and Kärnten in March 1979 all favoured the SPÖ, probably again reflecting the nuclear energy issue. Although the November 1978 referendum on the proposed Zwentendorf power plant had been a defeat for the SPÖ's pro-nuclear policy, the party had regained voter confidence by the rapid passage of legislation banning the use of nuclear energy. Subsequently, as the energy crisis worsened, opinion—particularly among the Socialists and also in industry—began to favour a new referendum. Kreisky insisted that repeal of the antinuclear legislation should be subject to a two-thirds majority vote in Parliament. This would pose internal problems for the ÖVP, which included pro-nuclear industrialists among its numbers.

Following his party's defeat in the election, ÖVP leader Josef Taus sought to introduce a stricter form of centralized control for the party. Failing to achieve this, he resigned. Alois Mock was elected leader in his place on July 7.

On August 23 Vienna's new International Centre—UN City—was handed over to its future occupants, the UN Industrial Development Organization, the International Atomic Energy Agency, and some lesser UN bodies. Vienna thus became the "third UN capital," after New York City and Geneva. To consolidate Vienna's position as host to large international gatherings, a conference centre accommodating 6,000 delegates was

Austrian Chancellor Bruno Kreisky (left) showed great elation when his party remained in power after the May election.

UPI

planned as an addition to UN City, to be completed by 1984.

On June 15–18 Vienna was the scene of a summit meeting between U.S. Pres. Jimmy Carter and Soviet Pres. Leonid Brezhnev, concluding with their signing of the SALT II agreement. The visit to Vienna of the Palestine Liberation Organization (PLO) leader, Yasir Arafat, on July 6–8 brought much comment in the world press. Arafat's meeting with Kreisky and Willy Brandt, respectively vice-president and president of the Socialist International, indicated a degree of Western recognition of the PLO and was bitterly criticized by Israel.

On May 8 Franz Karasek, a member of the Austrian Parliament, was elected secretary-general of the Council of Europe for a five-year term. He succeeded Georg Kahn-Ackermann of West Germany.

The economic situation remained favourable, with a higher growth rate and lower unemployment and inflation rates than the average for Organization for Economic Cooperation and Development member states. With the balance of payments showing improvement, stabilization measures were reinforced on September 7 by a 1.5% revaluation of the schilling.

(ELFRIEDE DIRNBACHER)

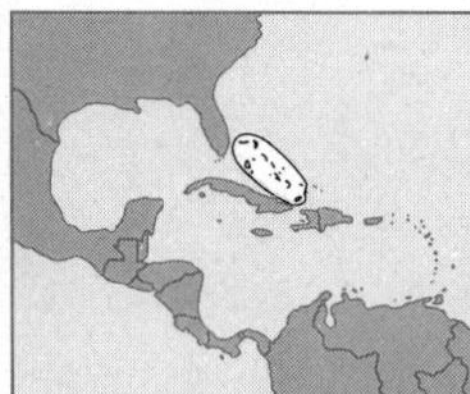

The Bahamas

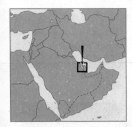

Bahrain

Bahamas, The

A member of the Commonwealth of Nations, The Bahamas comprise an archipelago of about 700 islands in the North Atlantic Ocean just southeast of the United States. Area: 13,864 sq km (5,353 sq mi). Pop. (1978 est.): 228,000. Cap. and largest city: Nassau (urban area pop., 1978 est., 133,300). Language: English (official). Religion (1970): Baptist 28.8%; Anglican 22.7%; Roman Catholic 22.5%; Methodist 7.3%; Saints of God and Church of God 6%; others and no religion 12.7%. Queen, Elizabeth II; governors-general in 1979, Sir Milo B. Butler and, from January 22 (acting), Sir Gerald Cash; prime minister, Lynden O. Pindling.

During 1979 the Bahamian government embarked on a policy aimed at reducing the unemployment rate from the existing 20–25% to about 5%. It envisioned an annual economic growth rate of 4%, holding inflation at 5%, and increasing tourist income to $1 billion by 1985.

In January the government introduced a B$253.3 million budget that placed great emphasis on improving education and health care. To fund these and other activities, a wide range of new taxes on hotels, banks, and trust companies was introduced. Stress was also placed on the development of agriculture, the small "out islands," and offshore oil exploration.

In July a major parliamentary confrontation arose between members of the ruling Progressive Liberal Party and the opposition over allegations, made to a New Jersey gambling commission, that payments had been made to senior Bahamian politicians by the U.S. firm Resorts International Inc. On March 30 the exiled shah of Iran arrived in The Bahamas. His presence was opposed by all opposition groups, and on June 10 he left for Mexico.

(DAVID A. JESSOP)

BAHAMAS, THE

Education. (1976–77) Primary, pupils 31,928, teachers (state only) 768; secondary, pupils 29,472, teachers (state only) 649; vocational (1975–76), pupils 1,823, teachers 92; teacher training (1975–76), students 731, teachers 21; higher (College of the Bahamas), students *c.* 3000.

Finance and Trade. Monetary unit: Bahamian dollar, with (Sept. 17, 1979) an official rate of B$1 to U.S. $1 (B$2.15 = £1 sterling). Budget (1978 actual): revenue B$166 million; expenditure B$186 million. Cost of living (1975 = 100; June 1979) 123.9. Foreign trade (1978): imports B$2,453,200,000; exports B$2,105,100,000. Import sources (1977): U.S. 35%; Saudi Arabia 24%; Iran 10%; Nigeria 9%; Libya 7%; Angola 5%. Export destinations (1977): U.S. 81%; Saudi Arabia 10%. Main exports (1977): crude oil 61%; petroleum products 32%. Tourism: visitors (excludes cruise passengers; 1976) 940,000; gross receipts U.S. $363 million.

Transport and Communications. Shipping (1978): merchant vessels 100 gross tons and over 93; gross tonnage 84,269. Telephones (Jan. 1978) 61,800. Radio receivers (Dec. 1976) 96,000. Television receivers (Dec. 1976) *c.* 20,000.

Bahrain

An independent monarchy (emirate), Bahrain consists of a group of islands in the Persian Gulf, lying between the Qatar Peninsula and Saudi Arabia. Total area: 662 sq km (256 sq mi). Pop. (1978 est.): 341,400. Cap.: Manama (pop., 1976 est., 105,400). Language: Arabic (official), Persian. Religion (1971): Muslim 95.7%; Christian 3%; others 1.3%. Emir in 1979, Isa ibn Sulman al-Khalifah; prime minister, Khalifah ibn Sulman al-Khalifah.

Bahrain during 1979 saw possible threats to its independence from Iran and Saudi Arabia. In February, following the revolution in Iran, 300 Bahrainis of Iranian origin demonstrated in Manama in support of Iran's religious leader, Ayatollah Ruhollah Khomeini. Furthermore, Ayatollah Sadiq Rouhani, a confidant of Khomeini, stated that Iran's 1970 renunciation of its traditional claim to Bahrain was illegal and that Bahrain was in fact Iran's 14th province. Although the Iranian Foreign Ministry contradicted the ayatollah's assertion, Bahrain's Sunni Muslim leadership became suspicious of Iranian claims that the emir, Isa ibn Sulman al-Khalifah, was "oppressing his [Shi'ah Muslim] people." (Khomeini and his lead-

BAHRAIN

Education. (1977–78) Primary, pupils 46,326, teachers 2,550; secondary, pupils 19,044, teachers 816; vocational, pupils 1,732, teachers 94; higher, students 763, teaching staff 86.

Finance and Trade. Monetary unit: Bahrain dinar, with (Sept. 17, 1979) a free rate of 0.379 dinar to U.S. $1 (0.815 dinar = £1 sterling). Gold, SDR's, and foreign exchange (June 1979) U.S. $546 million. Budget (1979 est.): revenue 255 million dinars; expenditure 280 million dinars. Foreign trade (1978): imports 792.3 million dinars; exports 733.1 million dinars. Import sources: Saudi Arabia 43%; U.K. 11%; Japan 8%; U.S. 7%; West Germany 5%. Export destinations (1977): Saudi Arabia 14%; Japan 14%; United Arab Emirates 9%; U.S. 8%; Australia 7%; Singapore 6%. Main exports: petroleum products 80%; aluminum 8%.

Industry. Production (in 000; metric tons; 1976): aluminum 122; crude oil (1978) 2,656; natural gas (cu m) 2,180,000; petroleum products (1977) *c.* 12,600; electricity (kw-hr) 682,000.

Automobile Industry:
see Industrial Review; Transportation

Automobile Racing:
see Motor Sports

Aviation:
see Defense; Transportation

Badminton:
see Racket Games

KEYSTONE

Britain's Queen Elizabeth II was greeted by Emir Isa ibn Sulman al-Khalifah when she visited Bahrain in February.

ing supporters were Shi'ah Muslims.) There was discussion of reintroducing the National Assembly (dissolved in 1975) to accede to Shi'ah demands for greater participation in government.

In June it was announced that construction of the 25-km (15.5-mi) causeway linking the country to Saudi Arabia would begin in 1980. Bahrainis feared that contact with the more traditional Sunni Muslims of Saudi Arabia would bring restraints to their comparatively liberal way of life and end progress for Bahraini women. (CHARLES GLASS)

Bangladesh

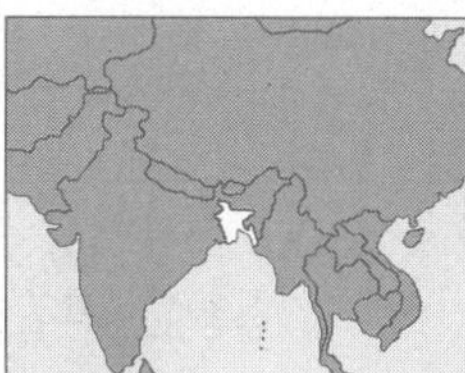

Bangladesh

An independent republic and member of the Commonwealth of Nations, Bangladesh is bordered by India on the west, north, and east, by Burma in the southeast, and by the Bay of Bengal in the south. Area: 143,998 sq km (55,598 sq mi). Pop. (1979 est.): 86,643,000. Cap. and largest city: Dacca (pop., 1974, 1,679,600). Language: Bengali. Religion: Muslim 85%, with Hindu, Christian, and Buddhist minorities. President in 1979, Maj. Gen. Ziaur Rahman.

With the lifting of martial law on April 6, 1979, Bangladesh embarked on a new course in its political history. Martial law, which had been in force since November 1975 when Maj. Gen. Ziaur Rahman seized power, was ended in pursuance of the president's promise that it would be terminated within a week of the start of the first session of the new Parliament. In the parliamentary elections, held on February 18, the newly formed Bangladesh Jatiyabadi Dal (Bangladesh Nationalist Party, or BJD) of President Zia won 207 seats in the 300-member Parliament. The once-powerful Awami League fared badly at the polls. It was split into two factions, one of which, led by Abdul Malek Ukil, emerged as the largest opposition group with 40 seats. The elections confirmed President Zia as the most powerful man in Bangladesh. His confidence was reflected in the release of large numbers of political prisoners and the relaxation of restrictions on civil liberties.

While some political stability was achieved, all was not well with the economy. The most pressing problem was a shortfall of food, officially estimated at around 2.2 million metric tons. About 1 million metric tons of this was accounted for by the failure of the *boro* (spring rice) crop as a result of drought and a shortage of diesel oil for irrigation pumps. The government proclaimed its determination "not to let anybody die of starvation," and efforts were made to obtain grain stocks. Commitments to supply grain came from a number of countries, including the U.S., India, Australia, Burma, China, and the European Economic Community. The threat of food shortages gave rise to agitation by the Awami League. However, dissensions within the opposition ranks, coupled with a vigorous propaganda drive by the government, were expected to help President Zia weather the storm.

Despite these difficulties, the authorities confidently expected an improvement in overall economic performance. The 1979–80 budget provided for the largest annual development program in the country's history, with priority being given to agriculture and rural development. The allocation for this program was put at 20 billion taka. Production targets included a forecast improvement in grain output to 14.5 million metric tons by the end of 1980. The authorities believed that jute would continue to be more profitable than rice, providing a greater incentive for farmers to adopt the intensive jute-cultivation program. An immediate aim was to extend the program to 60% of the total jute acreage, thereby raising output by an estimated seven million bales and export availability by as much as three million bales. In November the government announced an ambitious agricultural program designed to double food production within five years.

In foreign affairs, there was a further improvement in relations with India, highlighted by the visit in April of the Indian prime minister, Morarji Desai. A major point of discussion was the lack of progress being made by the joint rivers commission that came into being as a result of the Farakka barrage agreement of September 1977. The two

Balance of Payments:
see Economy, World

Ballet:
see Dance

Ballooning:
see Aerial Sports

BANGLADESH

Education. (1975–76) Primary, pupils 9,488,090, teachers 172,448; secondary, pupils 2,321,046, teachers 92,310; vocational, pupils 19,378, teachers 1,687; teacher training, students 7,610, teachers 640; higher, students 297,272, teaching staff 5,364.

Finance. Monetary unit: taka, with (Sept. 17, 1979) a free rate of 15.34 taka to U.S. $1 (official rate of 33 taka = £1 sterling). Gold, SDR's, and foreign exchange (June 1979) U.S. $359 million. Budget (1978–79 est.): revenue 13,757,000,000 taka; expenditure 10,531,000,000 taka (excludes development budget 13.9 billion taka). Gross domestic product (1977–78) 117,820,000,000 taka. Money supply (April 1979) 14,535,800,000 taka. Cost of living (1975 = 100; May 1979) 122.4.

Foreign Trade. (1978) Imports 23,337,000,000 taka; exports 8,251,000,000 taka. Import sources: U.S. 14%; Japan 12%; U.K. 9%; Canada 6%; Singapore 6%. Export destinations: U.S. 15%; U.K. 9%; Pakistan 8%; Japan 6%; U.S.S.R. 6%; Italy 5%. Main exports (1977–78): jute products 51%; jute 20%; hides and skins 10%; tea 9%.

Transport and Communications. Roads (1977) *c.* 7,000 km. Motor vehicles in use (1976): passenger 20,000; commercial 9,370. Railways: (1977) 2,874 km; traffic (1976–77) 4,634,000,000 passenger-km, freight 701 million net ton-km. Navigable waterways (1977) *c.* 8,000 km. Air traffic (1977): 519 million passenger-km; freight *c.* 17 million net ton-km. Shipping (1978): merchant vessels 100 gross tons and over 141; gross tonnage 284,496. Shipping traffic (1975–76): goods loaded 1,255,000 metric tons, unloaded 3,629,000 metric tons. Telephones (Jan. 1978) 89,200. Radio receivers (March 1969) 531,000. Television receivers (March 1970) 10,000.

Agriculture. Production (in 000; metric tons; 1978): rice 18,898; wheat (1977) 259; potatoes 863; sweet potatoes (1977) 756; sugar, raw value (1977) *c.* 520; onions *c.* 150; mangoes 255; bananas *c.* 590; pineapples *c.* 142; tea *c.* 55; tobacco *c.* 64; jute *c.* 901; meat *c.* 238; fish catch (1977) 835; timber (cu m; 1977) *c.* 11,394. Livestock (in 000; 1978): cattle *c.* 27,007; buffaloes *c.* 474; sheep *c.* 1,200; goats *c.* 8,122; chickens *c.* 52,847.

Industry. Production (in 000; metric tons; 1977–78): cement 340; crude steel 115; natural gas (cu m; 1975–76) *c.* 870,000; petroleum products 1,017; fertilizers (nutrient content) nitrogenous 106, phosphate 18; jute fabrics 546; cotton yarn 41; newsprint 28; other paper 32; electricity (kw-hr; 1976) *c.* 1,710,000.

sides made a firm commitment, announced on April 18, to take steps aimed at the best utilization of available water resources. Improved relations with Sri Lanka were marked by the signing of economic cooperation and shipping agreements during Zia's visit to Colombo in November.

Relations with another neighbour, Burma, strained for a time by the influx of an estimated 197,000 refugees from that country, improved as a result of bilateral talks aimed at the speedy return of these displaced persons. The restored friendly relations were further cemented by a visit to Dacca by Pres. Ne Win of Burma. (GOVINDAN UNNY)

Barbados

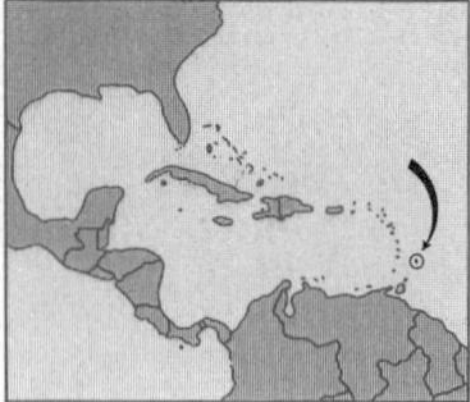
Barbados

The parliamentary state of Barbados is a member of the Commonwealth of Nations and occupies the most easterly island in the southern Caribbean Sea. Area: 430 sq km (166 sq mi). Pop. (1978 est.): 270,200; 91% Negro, 4% white, 4% mixed. Cap. and largest city: Bridgetown (pop., 1970, 8,900). Language: English. Religion: Anglican 53%; Methodist 9%; Roman Catholic 4%; Moravian 2%. Queen, Elizabeth II; governor-general in 1979, Sir Deighton Lisle Ward; prime minister, J. M. G. Adams.

BARBADOS

Education. (1976–77) Primary, pupils 33,141, teachers 1,561; secondary, pupils 25,880, teachers 1,245; vocational, pupils 679, teachers 46; teacher training, students 252, teachers 23; higher, students 2,032, teaching staff (1971–72) 111.

Finance and Trade. Monetary unit: Barbados dollar, with (Sept. 17, 1979) an official rate of Bar$2 to U.S. $1 (free rate of Bar$4.30 = £1 sterling). Budget (1977–78 est.): revenue Bar$325,670,000; expenditure Bar$378,350,000. Cost of living (1975 = 100; June 1979) 135.4. Foreign trade (1978): imports Bar$628.7 million; exports Bar$261,170,000. Import sources (1977): U.S. 24%; U.K. 19%; Trinidad and Tobago 10%; Canada 7%; Venezuela 7%. Export destinations (1977): U.S. 32%; Trinidad and Tobago 11%; Ireland 11%; U.K. 8%; Canada 6%. Main exports (1977): sugar 26%; clothing 19%; petroleum products 13%; electrical parts 9%; chemicals 6%. Tourism (1977): visitors 269,000; gross receipts U.S. $111 million.

Agriculture. Production (in 000; metric tons; 1977): sweet potatoes *c.* 4; corn *c.* 2; sugar, raw value *c.* 124.

In marked contrast to most other Commonwealth Caribbean economies, Barbados continued to prosper in 1979, as the result of an increase in the number of tourists, general economic expansion, and careful budgetary control by the government. Announcing a Bar$448 million budget containing many tax cuts, Prime Minister J. M. G. ("Tom") Adams reported at midyear a real growth of 3% in 1978 and anticipated similar progress throughout 1979. Against this, unemployment fell by only 0.4% to 15.1%, and the rate of inflation, 11.5% at the end of 1978, was expected to worsen.

The ruling Barbados Labour Party continued to pursue moderate policies, but public debate with the opposition Democratic Labour Party became more acrimonious. In the Eastern Caribbean, Barbados sought to establish closer ties between the newly independent former associated states, but by late 1979 some believed that its efforts would be doomed because of the ideological rift in the region that followed Grenada's revolution. An agreement with Trinidad and Tobago envisioned the latter's aid in developing offshore gas and oil reserves.

Barbados rejected "for the time being" a request by the Cuban government to upgrade diplomatic relations to consulate level. By contrast, permission to establish a large diplomatic mission was granted to China. (DAVID A. JESSOP)

Baseball

Major league baseball enjoyed another exceptional year in 1979, when a record 43-million-plus spectators paid to witness a season of surprises—four new teams winning division titles and the Pittsburgh Pirates capturing the 76th World Series.

World Series. The Pittsburgh Pirates defeated the Baltimore Orioles 4–1 in Baltimore on October 17 to win their fifth World Series four games to three. The Pirates won the last three games of the Series and thus became only the fourth team in history to rebound after trailing three games to one. The 1968 Detroit Tigers, 1958 New York Yankees, and 1925 Pirates had previously accomplished the feat.

"It has been one beautiful week ... this team of ours is just the most incredible group of people who love to win and love each other," said Willie Stargell (*see* BIOGRAPHIES), Pittsburgh's 38-year-old captain. "We never gave up. Surrender isn't in our vocabulary."

Stargell clubbed a two-run home run in the sixth inning of the seventh game to give the Pirates a lead they did not relinquish. Named most valuable player for the Series, Stargell had three home runs and seven extra-base hits—a Series record—and batted .400. It was "my most fun" said Stargell, respected leader of the Pirates, an earthy, uninhibited team which called itself "The Family" and espoused togetherness.

The favoured Orioles scored five runs in the first inning of the first game at Baltimore on October 10 to win 5–4. This game had been postponed one day because of cold weather and wet grounds, conditions that marred the first few games of the Series.

In the second game, at Baltimore on October 11, pinch hitter Manny Sanguillen singled in the tie-breaking run in the ninth inning as the Pirates triumphed 3–2. But in the third game, at Pittsburgh, Baltimore beat the Pirates 8–4 in a rain-delayed contest that featured lusty hitting by lesser-known Orioles such as Kiko Garcia and Benny Ayala.

The Orioles also won the fourth contest at Pittsburgh 9–6 after scoring six runs in the eighth inning on pivotal hits by pinch batters John Lowenstein and Terry Crowley. After that outburst, however, the Orioles managed only two runs in their remaining 28 innings. In the fifth game Baltimore used its best pitcher, Mike Flanagan, but the fine left-hander, who won the first game, was a 7–1 loser at Pittsburgh on October 14.

UPI

Doug DeCinces of Baltimore sent Pirates second baseman Phil Garner sprawling as DeCinces barreled into second with a steal in the fourth game of the World Series.

Willie Stargell's two-run homer in the sixth inning of the final World Series game was all the Pittsburgh Pirates needed to win the Series against the Baltimore Orioles. The Pirates went on to add two more runs to finish the game at 4–1.

WIDE WORLD

The Series then moved back to Baltimore, where interest and the weather were warming up. The Orioles, hopeful of winning their third World Series before their adoring hometown fans, were stifled 4–0 by John Candelaria and Kent Tekulve on October 16 to tie the Series at three victories each and set up the final match.

"You've got to give them credit," said Baltimore manager Earl Weaver. "We had three shots to get it over with and couldn't. Pittsburgh did what it had to do; we didn't."

Indeed, the Pirates' underrated pitching staff improved as the Series progressed, and the fearsome Pittsburgh bats achieved a .323 average for seven games, the highest in Series history.

Play-offs. The Pirates won the National League pennant by defeating the Cincinnati Reds in the best-of-five championship series. Stargell hit a three-run, 11th-inning home run to lead the Pirates to a 5–2 victory in the opening game at Cincinnati on October 2. The Pirates triumphed 3–2 in ten innings the next day and then won their first pennant since 1971 with a 7–1 romp at home on October 5.

The Orioles also achieved their first pennant since 1971 by defeating the California Angels in the American League play-offs. With Lowenstein hitting a three-run home run in the tenth inning, Baltimore won 6–3 at home on October 3. In the second game on October 4, Flanagan had a 9–1 lead after three innings but the Orioles just held on to win 9–8. At Anaheim, Calif., the Angels won 4–3 on October 5. But the Orioles trounced the Angels 8–0 on October 6 to take the series, 3 games to 1.

Banking:
see Economy, World

Baptist Churches:
see Religion

SARA KRULWICH—THE NEW YORK TIMES

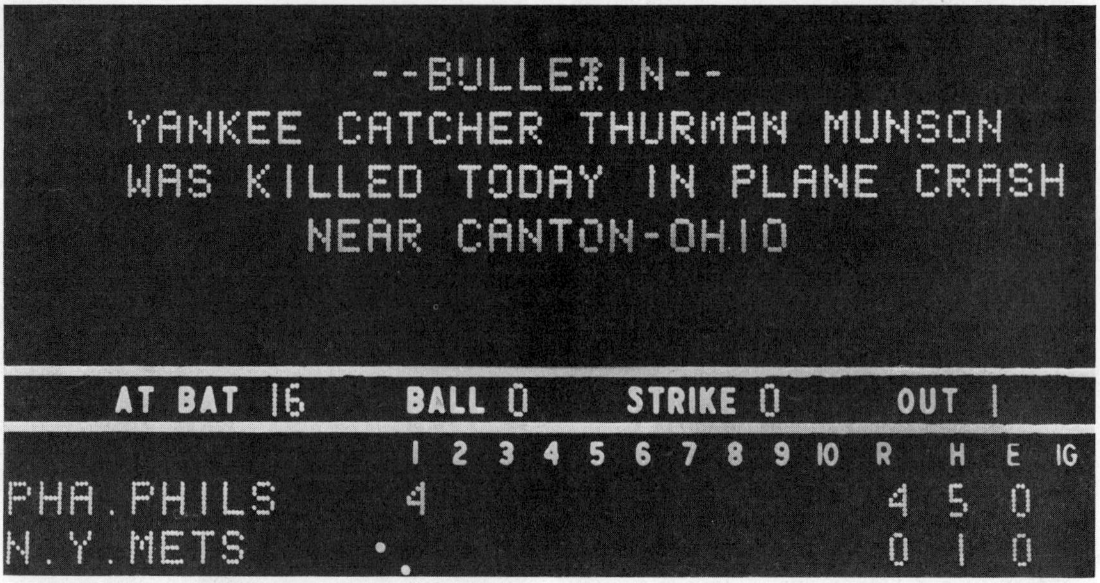

News of the death of Yankee catcher Thurman Munson was flashed on the scoreboard at Shea Stadium in New York on August 2.

Regular Season. The Pirates survived a spirited challenge by the Montreal Expos to win the East Division title in the National League. The Expos, a young team that had never had a winning record, led the East during much of the season and then, despite an arduous schedule, hung on until the last day of the regular season, when the Pirates clinched the title. The favoured Philadelphia Phillies, who acquired Pete Rose the previous winter, experienced problems with injuries and pitching and finished fourth.

The Reds, who lost Rose, won the West Division despite trailing the upstart Houston Astros at one time by ten games. Ray Knight, who replaced the popular Rose at third base, batted .318, only 13 points below what Rose hit for the Phillies. The incumbent National League champion Los Angeles Dodgers had a difficult season, especially with their pitching, and plummeted to last place early in the year. They had a respectable second half, but still finished below .500 and in third place.

The Orioles had a spectacular season, winning 102 of 159 regular season games and taking the American League East Division crown by eight games over second-place Milwaukee. After a 3–8 start the Orioles went on a tear and never looked back. The New York Yankees, world champions in 1977 and 1978, were never a factor. Rich Gossage, ace relief pitcher, broke his thumb in a clubhouse fracas during April and was out for an extended period. On August 2 Thurman Munson (*see* Obituaries), the talented Yankee catcher, was killed when his private plane crashed. The Yankees finished 13½ games behind Baltimore.

The Kansas City Royals, who had captured the West Division crown for three straight seasons, also were dethroned. The California Angels prevailed to win by three games.

Keith Hernandez, a first baseman for the St. Louis Cardinals, won the National League batting title with a .344 average. Dave Kingman of the Chicago Cubs led the league with 48 home runs; Dave Winfield of the San Diego Padres had 118 runs batted in. Brothers Joe Niekro of Houston and Phil of the Atlanta Braves each won 21 games. Houston's James Rodney Richard struck out 313 batters, while Chicago relief pitcher Bruce Sutter tied a league record with 37 saves. Lou Brock (*see* Biographies), veteran Cardinal outfielder, reached the 3,000-hit milestone in his final season.

The Orioles smashed 181 home runs, but they were paced by their brilliant pitching staff which compiled a team earned-run average of 3.28, the best in baseball. Flanagan won 23 games. Tommy John, who departed Los Angeles as a free agent and joined the Yankees, won 21 for New York. Jerry Koosman, acquired by the Minnesota Twins

Final Major League Standings, 1979

American League

East Division

Club	W.	L.	Pct.	G.B.	Balt.	Mil.	Bos.	N.Y.	Det.	Clev.	Tor.	Cal.	Chi.	K.C.	Min.	Oak.	Sea.	Tex.
Baltimore	102	57	.642	...	...	8	8	5	7	8	11	9	8	6	8	8	10	6
Milwaukee	95	66	.590	8	5	...	4	9	7	9	10	5	7	7	8	6	9	9
Boston	91	69	.569	11½	5	8	...	5	8	6	9	5	5	8	9	9	8	6
New York	89	71	.556	13½	6	4	8	...	6	8	9	5	8	7	5	9	6	8
Detroit	85	76	.528	18	6	6	5	7	...	6	9	8	9	5	4	7	7	6
Cleveland	81	80	.503	22	5	4	7	5	6	...	8	6	6	6	8	8	7	5
Toronto	53	109	.327	50½	2	3	4	4	4	5	...	5	5	3	1	8	4	5

West Division

Club	W.	L.	Pct.	G.B.	Cal.	K.C.	Tex.	Min.	Chi.	Sea.	Oak.	Balt.	Bos.	Clev.	Det.	Mil.	N.Y.	Tor.
California	88	74	.543	...	...	7	5	9	9	7	10	3	7	6	4	7	7	7
Kansas City	85	77	.525	3	6	...	6	7	8	7	9	6	4	6	7	5	5	9
Texas	83	79	.512	5	8	7	...	9	2	7	11	6	6	7	6	3	4	7
Minnesota	82	80	.506	6	4	6	4	...	8	10	9	4	3	4	8	4	7	11
Chicago	73	87	.456	14	4	5	11	5	...	5	9	3	6	6	3	5	4	7
Seattle	67	95	.414	21	6	6	6	3	8	...	5	2	4	5	5	3	6	8
Oakland	54	108	.333	34	3	4	2	4	4	8	...	4	3	4	5	6	3	4

Forfeited game: Chicago forfeited second game of doubleheader to Detroit at Chicago, July 12.

National League

East Division

Club	W.	L.	Pct.	G.B.	Pitt.	Mon.	St.L.	Phil.	Chi.	N.Y.	Atl.	Cin.	Hou.	L.A.	S.D.	S.F.
Pittsburgh	98	64	.605	...	...	11	11	10	12	10	8	4	8	8	7	9
Montreal	95	65	.594	2	7	...	10	11	12	15	9	6	5	6	7	7
St. Louis	86	76	.531	12	7	8	...	11	10	11	8	4	6	6	8	7
Philadelphia	84	78	.519	14	8	7	7	...	9	13	5	4	7	9	9	6
Chicago	80	82	.494	18	6	6	8	9	...	8	8	7	6	5	9	8
New York	63	99	.389	35	8	3	7	5	10	...	8	4	3	3	4	8

West Division

Club	W.	L.	Pct.	G.B.	Cin.	Hou.	L.A.	S.F.	S.D.	Atl.	Chi.	Mon.	N.Y.	Phil.	Pitt.	St.L.
Cincinnati	90	71	.559	...	...	8	11	6	10	12	5	6	8	8	8	8
Houston	89	73	.549	1½	10	...	10	7	14	11	6	7	9	5	4	6
Los Angeles	79	83	.488	11½	7	8	...	14	9	6	7	6	9	3	4	6
San Francisco	71	91	.438	19½	12	11	4	...	10	7	4	5	4	6	3	5
San Diego	68	93	.422	22	7	4	9	8	...	12	3	5	8	3	5	4
Atlanta	66	94	.413	23½	6	7	12	11	6	...	4	1	4	7	4	4

Tie games: Philadelphia *v.* St. Louis and Pittsburgh *v.* New York.

from the New York Mets, won 20. Mike Marshall of the Twins had 32 saves.

Fred Lynn had a splendid season for the Boston Red Sox, batting .333 to lead the American League. He also had 39 home runs and 122 runs batted in. Teammate Jim Rice had 39 home runs and 130 runs batted in. California's Don Baylor topped the league with 139 runs batted in. Gorman Thomas of Milwaukee led the league with 45 home runs. Carl Yastrzemski of Boston recorded his 3,000th hit.

Bob Lemon, who led the Yankees to their miraculous comeback in 1978, was replaced as manager by Billy Martin, who had quit a year before. After the season's end Martin was fired after getting into a fight in a bar near Minneapolis.

Baylor was voted the American League's most valuable player, while Stargell and Hernandez shared the honour in the National League, the first tie in the history of the award. Sutter became the third reliever to win a Cy Young award for best pitcher, taking the prize in the National League, and Flanagan won in the American. Rookie of the year in the National League was Los Angeles Dodger pitcher Rick Sutcliffe, while honours in the American League went to Minnesota third baseman John Castino and Toronto shortstop Alfredo Griffin. Named managers of the year were Earl Weaver of the Orioles in the American League and Bill Virdon of Houston in the National.

Before 58,905 in the Seattle Kingdome on July 17, the National League defeated the American League 7–6 in the 50th All-Star Game. The triumph was the eighth straight for the National League and its 16th in the last 17 games. The National League won it with a run in the ninth inning to snap a 6–6 tie. Dave Parker, the Pittsburgh Pirates' right fielder, was named the game's most valuable player.

Latin America. Every year several major league players matriculate to baseball teams in Venezuela, Puerto Rico, Mexico, and the Dominican Republic for about 60 games of "winter ball." The system provides extra experience for young players and for those who have not been able to play much during the regular season.

In 1979 there was a rift between the major leagues and the winter leagues because the agreement between the two had expired. Bowie Kuhn, commissioner of the major leagues, issued a temporary ban on allowing players to participate in the program. But early in October the two sides resolved the issue, and the restriction was lifted.

(ROBERT WILLIAM VERDI)

Japan. For the second time in four years the Hiroshima Toyo Carp captured the Central League pennant. Among the team's outstanding players were Yoshihiko Takahashi, a swift runner and good hitter; relief pitcher Yutaka Enatsu; home-run hitter Koji Yamamoto, and infielder Sachio Kinugasa.

In the Pacific League, the Kintetsu Buffaloes of Osaka, winners of the first half-season's competition, beat the Hankyu Braves of Nishinomiya in the play-offs with three consecutive victories. The Buffaloes' triumph was due largely to 20-year-old pitcher Tetsuharu Yamaguchi, who relieved in all three games, and to their timely hitting. It was Kintetsu's first pennant since its founding 30 years earlier.

UPI

Los Angeles pitcher Don Sutton set a new National League shutout record of 50 when he blanked the San Francisco Giants 9–0 on August 10.

In the best-of-seven Japan Series the Carp edged the Buffaloes 4–3 in the seventh game to win their first national title. The Carp had a poor start, losing the first two games, but made a dramatic comeback by winning the following three.

In the Central League Felix Millan of the Yokohama Taiyo Whales became the first foreign player to win the batting championship with a .346 average. Masayuki Kakefu of the Hanshin Tigers of Osaka was crowned as the home-run king with 48, and the runs-batted-in laurel went to Koji Yamamoto of Hiroshima with 113. Though he failed to become the home-run champion for the second consecutive year, Sadaharu Oh of the Yomiuri Giants of Tokyo hit 33 home runs to bring his lifetime record to 838.

The most valuable player award of the Central League was captured by Enatsu, who had 9 wins against 5 losses and 22 saves in 56 games.

In the Pacific League Hideji Kato of the Braves hit .364 for his second batting championship and also batted in the most runs for the third time with 104. Charles Manuel hit the most home runs with 37, winning the title for the first time. Manuel became the second foreign player to win the league's most valuable player crown since 1964.

(RYUSAKU HASEGAWA)

Basketball

United States. PROFESSIONAL. A decade of upheaval in the National Basketball Association ended with new problems replacing old ones almost as fast as new champions succeeded the incumbents. When the Seattle SuperSonics

WIDE WORLD

Elvin Hayes of the Washington Bullets grabbed a rebound and later scored against the Seattle SuperSonics in the fifth game of the NBA play-offs. The SuperSonics went on to win the championship.

dethroned the Washington Bullets in the 1979 final play-offs, it marked the tenth straight time an NBA defending champion had failed to repeat.

The Sonics did not overwhelm opponents during the regular season, compiling a 52–30 record, but their dazzling play-off performance was an indication that a long-awaited professional basketball dynasty could be shaping up in the Pacific Northwest. Their conquest of the Bullets was impressive, despite losing the first game in the best-of-seven series on a controversial last-second call. Thereafter, the Sonics were indeed "super," winning four of the next five in convincing fashion to wrest the crown from Washington.

Two brilliant young players, guard Dennis Johnson and centre-forward Jack Sikma, spearheaded the Seattle attack. Johnson edged Sikma for most valuable player honours in the championship series, but both deserved the award. The loss of centre Marvin Webster and an early-season injury to his replacement, Tom LaGarde, were overcome by Sikma's switch to that position.

Johnson and Sikma were bolstered by the arrival of burly forward Lonnie Shelton as compensation for the New York Knicks' signing of free agent Webster. Shelton was a standout for them, while Webster flopped in New York. But the award to Seattle of Shelton plus $450,000 by NBA Commissioner Lawrence F. O'Brien touched off controversy. The Knicks sued in an attempt to overturn the ruling, and the signing of free agents came to a virtual standstill for fear of excessive compensation demands.

The furor was overshadowed by the chilling gaze of television's all-seeing eye on the NBA. Ratings plummeted for nationally televised games on the CBS network, and the owners reacted with changes aimed at rekindling waning viewer interest. They adopted the "home run ball" from the defunct American Basketball Association, awarding three points for successful shots launched behind a curving line 22 to 25 ft from the basket. Purists were outraged. Franklin Mieuli, owner of the Golden State Warriors, resigned from the NBA Board of Governors, alleging that the three-point basket would "destroy the team concept."

Such immediate cosmetic surgery, however, could not hide the NBA's inability to live up to its boast of becoming "the sport of the '70s." College basketball was closer to that status, and the NBA could only hope that adding Michigan State's Earvin ("Magic") Johnson (*see* BIOGRAPHIES) to the Los Angeles Lakers and Indiana State's Larry Bird to the Boston Celtics would reverse the decline.

The return of Bill Walton, who joined the San Diego Clippers, also sparked optimism among NBA owners. Los Angeles millionaire Sam Nassi, taking over the struggling Indiana Pacers, gained national attention when he signed the first woman, Ann Meyers, to an NBA contract, but the former UCLA star was cut after only three days in training camp. She was paid $50,000 for the attempt and later joined the New Jersey Gems of the new Women's Professional Basketball League.

The WPBL survived an uneven season, ranging from success for the Chicago Hustle to failure for the Milwaukee Does. The Houston Angels won the play-offs, but the Hustle's Rita Easterling, a quick, 5-ft 7-in guard, swept individual honours, including the most valuable player award.

Collegiate basketball's two superstars, Larry Bird of Indiana State and Earvin Johnson of Michigan State, met in the NCAA finals in March. Bird gives Johnson a helping hand off the floor, but Michigan State went on to win the title 75–64.

WIDE WORLD

College. It was a year for magic in college basketball. A remarkably poised sophomore, Earvin ("Magic") Johnson, took Michigan State all the way to the 1979 National Collegiate Athletic Association (NCAA) championship, stunning previously unbeaten Indiana State 75–64 for the title March 26 in Salt Lake City, Utah.

The "dream match" was an appropriate way to end another outstanding collegiate campaign. Attendance and television ratings continued to soar. The NCAA tournament was expanded from 32 to 40 teams, an accurate reflection of the basketball boom.

Until Johnson cast his spell in the final, Larry Bird shot Indiana State to the top of the national rankings and "The Bird is the Word" became the rallying cry for his legion of fans. Bird carried the Sycamores to 33 straight victories, ultimately to the showdown with Michigan State. But he could not cope with the Spartans' vaunted "matchup zone" defense. Smothering pressure limited the All-American forward to 19 points and just 7 baskets in 21 tries. Johnson scored 24 points in the NCAA final, flashing a brilliant array of moves to open up the court for teammates. He was a decisive victor in the head-to-head confrontation with Bird, earning the tournament's most valuable player award by a wide margin.

DePaul was the sentimental favourite among the NCAA final four, mainly because of Coach Ray Meyer, who kept college basketball alive in Chicago during his 37 seasons at the Blue Demons' helm. But Indiana State prevailed over them 76–74 in a semifinal thriller, while Michigan State routed Pennsylvania 101–67 to set up the championship match.

Before reaching for NCAA glory Michigan State had to survive a Big Ten dogfight, with strong teams emerging throughout the conference. Two other Big Ten teams, Purdue and Indiana, reached the finals of the National Invitational Tournament. The Hoosiers prevailed 53–52 after a grim defensive struggle in New York City's Madison Square Garden.

Bird, acclaimed as college player of the year, and Johnson were unanimous 1979 All-America selections. Joining them on the Associated Press first team were forward David Greenwood of UCLA, centre Bill Cartwright from the University of San Francisco, and guard Sidney Moncrief of Arkansas. Meyer was named coach of the year by his colleagues in the National Association of Basketball Coaches, though some thought that Bill Hodges deserved it for taking Indiana State into the national championship game with an unblemished record.

Old Dominion won the Association for Intercollegiate Athletics for Women tournament by defeating Louisiana Tech 75–65. The Virginia school, beaten only once in 35 games, swept to the top by containing Louisiana Tech's Elinor Griffin. Inge Nissen, a native of Denmark with experience in international competition, was outstanding on defense for Old Dominion. She also scored 22 points in the championship game, with her All-American teammate, Nancy Lieberman, adding 20.

(ROBERT G. LOGAN)

UPI

The first woman ever signed with the NBA was Ann Meyers, who was given a contract by the Indiana Pacers. She was cut from the roster after three days in the training camp.

World Amateur. The eighth World Basketball Championship for Women was played in Seoul, South Korea, during April–May 1979. Seoul's new 20,000-seat basketball stadium was packed to capacity for nearly every match. The event was marred by the withdrawal of a number of Eastern European countries, which helped the U.S. women carry off the world championship for the third time. However, their progress to the title was not easy. The first day they suffered a shock when South Korea beat them 94–82, and later in the competition they scraped home with a two-point victory, 66–64, against Italy. The question remained as to whether the U.S. women would have beaten the powerful Soviet team. The final six placings were: (1) United States; (2) Korea; (3) Canada; (4) Australia; (5) Italy; (6) Japan.

In the 21st European championship for men, contested in Turin, Italy, during June, all eyes were focused on the two major rivals in basketball, the Soviet Union and Yugoslavia. The Yugoslavs, 1978 world title winners in Manila and with successive wins in the previous three European championships, were the favourites. The 12 teams were organized in three pools of four each in the preliminary rounds, and both the Soviet Union and Yugoslavia were forced into second place in groups B and C, the Soviet Union losing to Spain 101–90 and Yugoslavia surprisingly conceding first place to Israel 77–76. In the final rounds both Yugoslavia and the Soviet Union were undefeated, and the match between them decided the championship. The Soviet Union led 41–34 at halftime, and Yugoslavia could never catch up; the Soviets eventually won 96–77. The top six finishers were: (1) Soviet Union; (2) Israel; (3) Yugoslavia; (4) Czechoslovakia; (5) Italy; (6) Spain.

WIDE WORLD

Inge Nissen cut down the net after her Old Dominion team won a 75–65 victory over Louisiana Tech for the women's college basketball championship. Nissen, a 6-ft 5-in native of Denmark, scored 22 points for Old Dominion.

The 25th South American championship for men was played in Bahía Blanca, Arg., during April 1979. The outstanding teams of the tournament were Argentina and Brazil; Argentina was undefeated and Brazil finished second after losing to Argentina. At halftime Brazil was trailing by five points, 48–43, and at the final whistle was still behind by the same margin, 90–85. Final results were: (1) Argentina; (2) Brazil; (3) Uruguay; (4) Chile; (5) Venezuela; (6) Paraguay.

(K. K. MITCHELL)

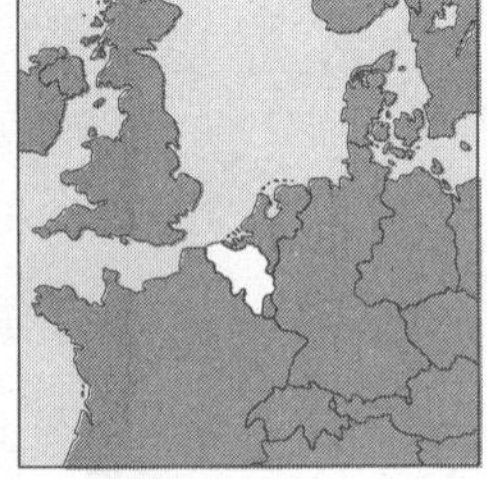

Belgium

Belgium

A constitutional monarchy on the North Sea coast of Europe, Belgium is bordered by The Netherlands, West Germany, Luxembourg, and France. Area: 30,521 sq km (11,784 sq mi). Pop. (1979 est.): 9,841,600. Cap. and largest urban area: Brussels (pop., 1979 est., commune 145,200). Language: Dutch, French, and German. Religion: predominantly Roman Catholic. King, Baudouin I; prime ministers in 1979, Paul Vanden Boeynants and, from April 3, Wilfried Martens.

The Flemish Liberals (PVV) had emerged as unquestioned gainers in the Dec. 17, 1978, election in Belgium. Results were: two Social Christian parties 82 (+ 2), two Socialist parties 58 (− 4), three Liberal parties 37 (+ 4), Walloon and Brussels Federalists (RW and Front Démocratique des Francophones; FDF) 15 (unchanged), Flemish Federalists (Volksunie) 14 (− 6), Communists 4 (+ 2), and Independents 2 (+ 2). (*See* POLITICAL PARTIES.) Protracted negotiations lasting a record 108 days dealt mainly with the proposed reform of the state structures. Following a first unsuccessful try, Wilfried Martens (*see* BIOGRAPHIES), chairman of the Flemish Social Christians (CVP), finally convinced five (Social Christians, Socialists, FDF) of the six former coalition parties to join a new coalition on April 3, 1979. Only the Volksunie stayed out, claiming that essential Flemish interests were being neglected.

The new government's program called for the creation of a series of assemblies, representing the regions and language communities. In Flanders the elected community and regional assemblies would coincide; separate community and regional assemblies were proposed for the French-speaking community and Wallonia; while Brussels would have a regional assembly only. The Flemish community and region would have a single executive, whereas separate executives were to be set up for the Walloon region and Brussels. These executives would be made up of members of the government. Martens pledged to submit to Parliament in the near future a "provisional but irreversible" second phase involving limited changes to the constitution, thus giving legal existence to the regions and extending the scope of cultural autonomy. In the third and final phase, a broad parliamentary de-

An open-air stage, intended to be used for a performance of the British Army Band, was left in ruins in Brussels after a bomb demolished it. The bombing was blamed on the Irish Republican Army.

UPI

bate would turn Belgium into a federation or confederation.

Once again these proposals were faulted by the Council of State for unconstitutionality and incoherence. Opposition to the project remained strong among Flemish associations and within the CVP, and the employers' organizations feared for the country's economic unity. The Federation of Belgian Industries (FBI) was also disturbed about the government proposals to cope with unemployment (again over 300,000). Hotly contested were the planned gradual and general introduction of the 36-hour workweek and the compulsory hiring by all firms with more than 100 employees of 3% additional personnel by 1982.

The expected deficit in the 1980 budget of close to BFr 100 billion (as grave as in 1979) prompted a warning against overspending by the National Bank. Unheedful, the government decided to cover the deficit through loans from abroad, while raising taxes on gasoline (Fr 1 more per litre), hiking the price of public transportation, and proposing a special levy for driving on expressways.

Community tensions repeatedly flared up in Voeren (Fourons), a commune of some 6,000 inhabitants, which had a French-speaking majority but had been transferred to the Flemish region in 1963. The French-speaking members of the Socialist Party set up a separate Parti Socialiste, more left-wing than its Flemish counterparts. Walloon and Brussels Liberals, on the other hand, were reunited in the Parti Réformateur Libéral (PRL). Former prime minister Léo Tindemans succeeded Martens as chairman of the CVP. As leading candidate of his party for the elections to the European Assembly, he obtained a record number of preference votes (983,000).

A major foreign venture by a Belgian consortium, the construction of two hospitals in Saudi Arabia, was jeopardized when the project's initial promoter, SA Eurosystem Hospitalier, was declared bankrupt. It was revealed that some BFr 8 billion had been paid as kickbacks in the BFr 28 billion project with the approval of the budget minister. (JAN R. ENGELS)

BELGIUM

Education. (1977–78) Primary, pupils 919,451, teachers (1976–77) 48,041; secondary and vocational, pupils 844,441, teachers (1967–68) 88,030; higher, pupils 174,151, teaching staff (universities only; 1976–77) *c.* 5,000.

Finance. Monetary unit: Belgian franc, with (Sept. 17, 1979) a free commercial rate of BFr 29.07 to U.S. $1 (BFr 62.55 = £1 sterling) and a free financial rate of BFr 30.32 to U.S. $1 (BFr 65.22 = £1 sterling). Gold, SDR's, and foreign exchange (June 1979) U.S. $6,273,000,000. Budget (1978 actual): revenue BFr 889.7 billion; expenditure BFr 1,072,500,000,000. Gross national product (1978) BFr 3,075,000,000,000. Money supply (March 1979) BFr 791.9 billion. Cost of living (1975 = 100; June 1979) 126.9.

Foreign Trade. (Belgium-Luxembourg economic union; 1978) Imports BFr 1,519,100,000,000; exports BFr 1,407,600,000,000. Import sources: EEC 69% (West Germany 23%, France 16%, The Netherlands 16%, U.K. 8%); U.S. 6%. Export destinations: EEC 72% (West Germany 23%, France 19%, The Netherlands 16%, U.K. 7%, Italy 5%). Main exports: chemicals 13%; motor vehicles 12%; machinery 12%; iron and steel 11%; food 8%; textile yarns and fabrics 6%; precious stones 6%. Tourism (1977) gross receipts (Belgium-Luxembourg) U.S. $993 million.

Transport and Communications. Roads (1977) 114,881 km (including 1,102 km expressways). Motor vehicles in use (1977): passenger 2,871,300; commercial 242,300. Railways: (1977) 4,003 km; traffic (1978) 7,137,000,000 passenger-km, freight 7,106,000,000 net ton-km. Air traffic (1978): 4,499,000,000 passenger-km; freight 386,060,000 net ton-km. Navigable inland waterways in regular use (1977) 1,539 km. Shipping (1978): merchant vessels 100 gross tons and over 268; gross tonnage 1,684,692. Shipping traffic (1977): goods loaded 38,695,000 metric tons, unloaded 57,757,000 metric tons. Telephones (Jan. 1978) 3,100,100. Radio licenses (Dec. 1977) 4,077,000. Television licenses (Dec. 1977) 2,811,000.

Agriculture. Production (in 000; metric tons; 1978): wheat *c.* 1,020; barley *c.* 800; oats *c.* 140; potatoes *c.* 1,500; tomatoes *c.* 140; apples *c.* 260; sugar, raw value *c.* 700; milk *c.* 3,750; pork *c.* 620; beef and veal *c.* 280; fish catch (1977) 45. Livestock (in 000; Dec. 1977): cattle 2,823; pigs 4,935; sheep 84; horses 44; chickens 30,951.

Industry. Fuel and power (in 000; 1978): coal (metric tons) 6,480; manufactured gas (cu m) *c.* 2,290,000; electricity (kw-hr) 50,840,000. Production (in 000; metric tons; 1978): pig iron 10,272; crude steel 12,706; copper 505; lead 125; tin 5.2; zinc 240; sulfuric acid 2,112; plastics and resins (1977) 1,471; fertilizers (nutrient content; 1977–78) nitrogenous *c.* 640, phosphate *c.* 600; cement 7,575; newsprint 80; other paper (1976) *c.* 690; cotton yarn 41; cotton fabrics 45; wool yarn 74; woolen fabrics 28; man-made fibres (1976) 49. Merchant vessels launched (100 gross tons and over; 1978) 266,000 gross tons.

Benin

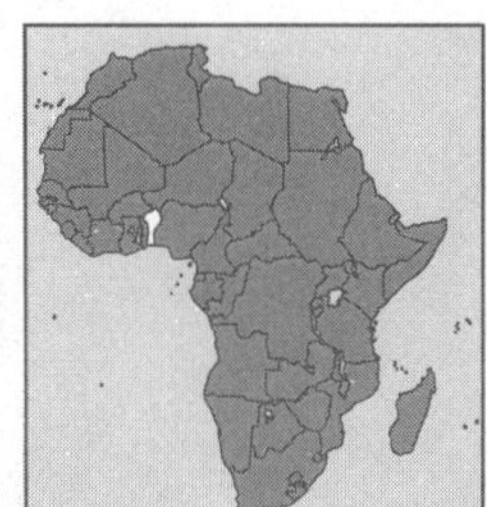

Benin

A republic of West Africa, Benin is located north of the Gulf of Guinea and is bounded by Togo, Upper Volta, Niger, and Nigeria. Area: 112,600 sq km (43,475 sq mi). Pop. (1979 est.): 3,435,000, mainly Dahomean and allied tribes. Cap.: Porto-Novo (pop., 1973 est., 97,000). Largest city: Cotonou (pop., 1973 est., 175,000). Language: French and local dialects. Religion: mainly animist, with Christian and Muslim minorities. President in 1979, Lieut. Col. Mathieu Kerekou.

After two years of strained relations between France and Benin, the former made a tentative gesture of normalization when Robert Galley, French minister of cooperation, paid a visit to Benin in May 1979. However, the Benin government took advantage of the occasion to accuse "certain highly placed French officials" of involvement in the attempted coup of Jan. 16, 1977. On May 24 Bob Denard, alias Gilbert Bourgeaud, a former French mercenary soldier in the Comoro Islands, Katanga, and Biafra and currently living in France, was

BENIN

Education. (1975–76) Primary, pupils 279,673, teachers 5,786; secondary, pupils 45,572, teachers 1,349; vocational, pupils 1,687, teachers 150; teacher training, students 170, teachers 10; higher, students 2,118, teaching staff 153.

Finance. Monetary unit: CFA franc, with (Sept. 17, 1979) a parity of CFA Fr 50 to the French franc and a free rate of CFA Fr 211.54 to U.S. $1 (CFA Fr 455.12 = £1 sterling). Budget (1978 est.) balanced at CFA Fr 23,210,000,000.

Foreign Trade. (1977) Imports CFA Fr 60,350,000,000; exports CFA Fr 7,640,000,000. Import sources: France 23%; U.K. 13%; West Germany 8%; The Netherlands 6%; U.S. 6%; Japan 5%. Export destinations: France 25%; Japan 20%; The Netherlands 13%; West Germany 8%; U.K. 8%. Main exports (1974): cotton 55%; cocoa 13%; peanuts 6%.

Agriculture. Production (in 000; metric tons; 1978): sorghum *c.* 75; corn (1977) 235; cassava (1977) 610; yams (1977) 564; dry beans *c.* 25; peanuts *c.* 60; palm kernels *c.* 80; palm oil *c.* 35; coffee (1977) *c.* 1; cotton, lint *c.* 6; fish catch (1977) 25. Livestock (in 000; 1977): cattle *c.* 833; sheep *c.* 886; goats *c.* 858; pigs *c.* 378.

Belize:
see Dependent States

condemned to death by Benin's National Revolutionary Court for his alleged role in the attempted coup, along with former president Émile Zinsou, 60 other European mercenaries, 27 African mercenaries, and 11 Benin citizens.

Relations with Gabon deteriorated after the expulsion of all Benin subjects from Gabon in July 1978, and the Organization of African Unity's summit meeting in Monrovia, Liberia, in July 1979 was the scene of violent exchanges between the delegates from the two countries.

(PHILIPPE DECRAENE)

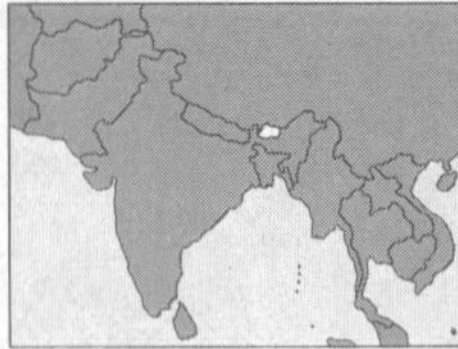
Bhutan

Bhutan

A monarchy situated in the eastern Himalayas, Bhutan is bounded by China and India. Area: 46,100 sq km (17,800 sq mi). Pop. (1979 est.): 1,269,000, including Bhutia 60%, Nepalese 25%, and 15% tribal peoples. Official cap.: Thimphu (pop., approximately 10,000). Administrative cap.: Paro (population unavailable). Language: Dzongkha (official). Religion: approximately 75% Buddhist, 25% Hindu. Druk gyalpo (king) in 1979, Jigme Singye Wangchuk.

The Bhutanese government was preoccupied during 1979 by the presence of over 4,000 Tibetan refugees who had continued to ignore appeals to become citizens. Since the discovery of a plot by Tibetan refugees to assassinate the king in 1974, the Tibetans had been a major security problem. Of an estimated 7,000 refugees who had fled their homeland in the wake of the Chinese occupation of 1949, 3,000 had accepted citizenship. A move by the Bhutanese National Assembly to extradite the rest to China was temporarily stalled by the king, who wished to explore the possibility of their being accepted by other countries. An appeal by the government to India and to some European countries went unheeded in 1979.

Following repeated requests from Bhutan, the Indian government agreed in April to allow the kingdom more trade and transit routes through third countries, especially Nepal and Bangladesh, provided the latter agreed. India undertook to consult the two governments concerned.

Rumours that Bhutan was insisting on a revision of the treaty with India to obtain more autonomy were denied by the king.

Indian Defense Minister Jagjivan Ram disavowed reports of Chinese troop movements along the 200-mi Bhutan-China border.

(GOVINDAN UNNY)

BHUTAN

Education. (1976–77) Primary, pupils 18,903, teachers 488; secondary, pupils 1,359, teachers 281; vocational, pupils 445, teachers 37; teacher training, pupils 51, teachers 16; higher, pupils 304, teaching staff 45.

Finance and Trade. Monetary unit: ngultrum, at par with the Indian rupee (which is also in use), with (Sept. 17, 1979) a free rate of 8.20 ngultrums to U.S. $1 (17.64 ngultrums = £1 sterling). Budget (1977–78): revenue 82 million ngultrums; expenditure 79 million ngultrums (excludes development expenditure of 144 million ngultrums). Most external trade is with India. Main exports: timber, fruit and vegetables, cardamom.

Bermuda:
see Dependent States

Bicycling:
see Cycling

Biographies:
see People of the Year

Biological Sciences:
see Life Sciences

Birth Statistics:
see Demography

Boating:
see Rowing; Sailing; Water Sports

Bobsledding:
see Winter Sports

Billiard Games

Billiards. At the 34th world amateur Three-Cushion Billiards Championship in Lima, Peru, during May 1979, Raymond Ceulemans of Belgium won his 16th title. Other Europeans joining him in the round-robin tournament were Johan Scherz of Austria and Egidio Vierat of France. From South America were Humberto Suguimizu and Adolfo Suarez from Peru, Alfonso Gonzales of Colombia, and Hernán Bustos of Chile. Representing Africa was Muhammad Mustapha Diab of Egypt, and from Japan were 1974 world champion Nobuaki Kobayashi and Yoshio Yoshihara. Completing the dozen finalists were Edward Robin of Las Vegas, Nev., and Allen Gilbert of Los Angeles. Robin and Gilbert were the winner and runner-up, respectively, of the tournament held by the Billiard Federation of U.S.A. in January at San Jose, Calif.

In the opening session of the world championships Kobayashi gave the best performance, averaging better than 1.000 in a win over Gonzales. Again, in the fifth round, he missed tying the world tournament high-run record of 15 by one. In the sixth round the defending champion Ceulemans and Robin fought a duel of safeties that the former eventually won in 46 innings, even though Robin averaged over 1.000 for the game. In the tenth round the best game of the tournament was played when Ceulemans bested the Peruvian champion, Suguimizu, 60–26, in just 28 innings.

In the final round the audience of 2,500 saw Gonzales tie the world high-run record of 15 in defeating Diab. Also in that round Kobayashi downed Ceulemans 60–45. However, the final standings were Ceulemans, once again champion with an average of 1.384; Kobayashi, second with 1.135; Yoshihara, third with 1.069; and Vierat, fourth with 0.939.

Pocket Billiards. Reflecting the increasing interest in billiards in the United States, more than 3,000 pool players entered the Billiard Congress of America's 1979 national Eight-Ball Tournament. The 182 finalists, of whom 44 were in the women's division, met in Louisville, Ky., from October 31 through November 3 to determine the champions.

As in the past the defending champions were unable to retain their titles in the four days of double elimination play. On the last night the "race to seven" (games won) title match began with 22-year-old Mark Wilson of Madison, Wis., facing 32-year-old professional Jimmy Reid of Royal Palm Beach, Fla. Reid had worked his way through the loser's bracket of the 142-man field to challenge the imperturbable newcomer, who had also lost an early match. Wilson won the first game and the second. Reid caught up on the third and fourth games, and forged ahead by taking the fifth. It was Wilson's turn to catch up, which he did.

At the end of 12 games the match was tied at six wins each. The 13th and deciding game started with Wilson breaking, but he experienced the first scratch of the bout. Showing no emotion, he sat down to watch Reid shoot flawlessly to clear

BILLIARD CONGRESS OF AMERICA

Jimmy Reid of Royal Palm Beach, Florida, ran the table to win the final game and the championship in BCA National Eight-Ball Tournament play in Louisville, Kentucky, in November.

the table, winning game, match, and championship.

In the women's division of the national championships the drawings for pairing of opponents put all but one of the recognized top contenders in the same flight. Only one could survive to face the winner of the other flight. As could be expected, from the opening round the competitive level of play was outstanding. By the end of four rounds leading contenders Kitty Stephens, Melodie Horn, and Vicki Frechen had fallen. Only Gloria Walker survived, having come through the loser's bracket to defeat Lori Shampo. In the championship match she faced newcomer Mary Kenniston, who had defeated Sue Warnes in their flight. Walker won the lag, broke successfully, and ran out to take the first game of a "race to five." Kenniston, under pressure, missed shots in the next two games, giving the veteran a three-game lead before she won. Walker came back, however, taking the final two games and the championship.

Twenty-nine league-winning teams of five persons each competed in the 1979 All-American Eight-Ball League Championships at Rochester, Minn., in June. The first nationwide tournament of its kind was sponsored by the Billiard Congress of America and involved 4,300 players from Oregon to Newfoundland. Of these some 200 team members won the right to represent their respective leagues.

In the 16-team men's division the Tam O'Shanter Baggins of Colorado Springs, Colo., were clearly the superior group. Team members Charles Shootman, Grady Mathews, Peter Jackson, Don Batista, Tony Cisneros, and Gary Gross cruised through the tournament with no losses. In the finals they held off an aggressive Union Center five from Albert Lea, Minn., 59–31, to take the title by showing great skill in defensive play.

The winner of the 13 women's teams was not as readily determined. On the final day of play the Tam O'Shanter Ladies, cheered on by their high-riding counterparts, overcame an earlier loss by winning five straight matches in the losers' bracket to earn the right to face the Wheel Inn Women from Billings, Mont., for the championship. Showing the strain of nine continuous hours of competition, the Tams quickly found themselves behind the rested and ready Wheelers, 25–9. Then, with one member after another winning her game, the Tams came back, making the score 33–32, with one game to go. Betty Dix of the Tams won it, 4–0, forcing the championships into a final play-off match. In the ensuing competition the Billings team – Margaret Schmittou, Gail Lave, Lorna Lacy, Pearla Moler, Tricia Alva, Beth Westrom, and Jacque Michael – reestablished its superiority, defeating the Tams 41–17 in a 6½-hour duel.

Thirty young men and women gathered at the University of Michigan at Ann Arbor to participate in the Collegiate Straight Pool Championship from April 5 to 7. They represented schools from 15 regions playing in the annual Association of College Unions-International event. Peter Lhotka, a 28-year-old graduate student at the University of North Dakota, dominated the men's division with high runs of 47 and 43 and went undefeated to take the title. Julie Fitzpatrick of the University of Wisconsin regained her crown.

(ROBERT E. GOODWIN)

[452.B.4.h.v]

Bolivia

Bolivia

A landlocked republic in central South America, Bolivia is bordered by Brazil, Paraguay, Argentina, Chile, and Peru. Area: 1,098,581 sq km (424,165 sq mi). Pop. (1978 est.): 4,886,700, of whom more than 50% are Indian. Language: Spanish 78%, Quechua 15%, Aymara 7%. Religion (1975 est.): Roman Catholic 94.2%. Judicial cap.: Sucre (pop., 1976, 63,300). Administrative cap. and largest city: La Paz (pop., 1976, 654,700). Head of the three-man military junta until Aug. 8, 1979, Gen. David Padilla Arancibia; presidents, Walter Guevara Arze from August 8, Col. Alberto Natusch Busch from November 1, and Lydia Gueiler Tejada from November 16.

Attention in Bolivia in 1979 was focused on the

nation's attempts to return to constitutional democracy. With the support of the military junta, the process was started at the end of 1978 by a commission to recommend electoral reform. The campaign for the presidency was at first contested by six ex-presidents but soon narrowed to three: Víctor Paz Estenssoro (Movimiento Nacionalista Revolucionario Histórico; MNR-H), Hernán Siles Zuazo (Unidad Democrática y Popular; UDP), and Gen. Hugo Banzer Suárez (Acción Democrática Nacionalista; ADN).

The general election took place as planned, on July 1. None of the presidential candidates gained a majority, and under the constitution the president was then to be selected by a joint sitting of the Congress of Deputies and the Senate. After seven polls in which no candidate won the necessary two-thirds majority, Walter Guevara Arze, 68-year-old president-elect of the Senate, emerged as the compromise choice and duly took office on August 8. He agreed to serve as interim president until Aug. 6, 1980.

Rumours of a military coup began to circulate almost immediately, but the takeover did not materialize until November 1. Only hours after the ninth General Assembly of the Organization of American States had ended its meeting in La Paz, troops led by Col. Alberto Natusch Busch seized the presidential palace and Natusch proclaimed himself president. Union leaders called a general strike, and on November 2 Natusch dissolved Congress and proclaimed a state of siege. Two days later planes and tanks were used in an attempt to disperse demonstrators; it was estimated that some 200 persons died in the disorders.

The military was by no means united behind Natusch. He was opposed by a right-wing faction led by Banzer and by Gen. David Padilla, head of the former junta, representing officers who favoured a return to civilian rule. On November 15, 250 officers issued a proclamation urging him to resign. Meanwhile, after several days of secret negotiations, military, congressional, and union leaders reached agreement on Natusch's removal, and on November 16 Congress selected Lydia Gueiler Tejada, its presiding officer and a member of the MNR, to succeed him as interim president.

BOLIVIA

Education. (1976) Primary, pupils 945,733, teachers (1975) 38,737; secondary, pupils 127,895, teachers (1975) 7,143; vocational (1975), pupils 18,822, teachers (1965) 1,404; teacher training, students 3,776, teachers (1973) 314; higher, students 41,408, teaching staff (universities only) 2,307.

Finance. Monetary unit: peso boliviano, with (Sept. 17, 1979) an official rate of 20 pesos to U.S. $1 (free rate of 43.03 pesos = £1 sterling). Gold, SDR's, and foreign exchange (June 1979) U.S. $193 million. Budget (1978 est.) balanced at 10,080,000,000 pesos. Gross national product (1977) 66,990,000,000 pesos. Money supply (March 1979) 8,284,000,000 pesos. Cost of living (La Paz; 1975 = 100; March 1979) 137.8.

Foreign Trade. (1978) Imports U.S. $848 million; exports U.S. $640 million. Import sources (1977): U.S. 27%; Argentina 12%; Japan 12%; Brazil 10%; West Germany 8%. Export destinations (1977): U.S. 34%; Argentina 20%; U.K. 12%; The Netherlands 5%. Main exports: tin 58%; natural gas 12%; crude oil 7%; tungsten 6%; silver 5%; zinc 5%.

Transport and Communications. Roads (1976) 38,085 km. Motor vehicles in use (1976): passenger 31,000; commercial (including buses) 41,000. Railways: (1977) 3,787 km; traffic (1976) 366 million passenger-km, freight 518 million net ton-km. Air traffic (1977): 558 million passenger-km; freight 27.8 million net ton-km. Telephones (Jan. 1978) 101,500. Radio receivers (Dec. 1976) 430,000. Television receivers (Dec. 1978) *c.* 260,000.

Agriculture. Production (in 000; metric tons; 1978): barley 75; corn (1977) 299; rice (1977) *c.* 101; cassava (1977) 294; potatoes 793; sugar, raw value (1977) *c.* 265; bananas 234; oranges *c.* 80; coffee 22; cotton, lint 17; rubber *c.* 5. Livestock (in 000; 1977): cattle *c.* 3,195; sheep *c.* 7,850; goats *c.* 2,904; pigs *c.* 1,215; horses *c.* 373; asses *c.* 744.

Industry. Production (in 000; metric tons; 1976): cement 232; crude oil (1978) 1,530; natural gas (cu m; 1977) 1,780,000; petroleum products 977; electricity (kw-hr) *c.* 1,130,000; gold (troy oz) 29; tin (1978) 16; lead ore 17; antimony ore 15; tungsten (oxide content) *c.* 4; zinc ore 49; copper ore 4.7; silver (troy oz) *c.* 5,100.

Natusch left the presidential palace quietly a short time after she took office. A minor revolt by right-wing officers ended when Gueiler agreed to appoint Gen. Rubén Rocha Patiño as army commander. Gueiler was to serve until a new presidential election, scheduled for May 4, 1980.

Meanwhile, the country faced severe economic problems. Because of declines in output of petroleum and mineral products, the growth rate of gross domestic product slowed to 1.9% during the first half of 1979, from 3.9% in the comparable 1978 period. Inflation rose sharply, and labour demand-

WIDE WORLD

As president of the Senate, Lydia Gueiler draped the presidential sash across the chest of Bolivia's incoming president, Walter Guevara Arze, in August. Three months later, after Guevara had been overthrown by military officers who were then ousted themselves, she became the country's first woman president.

ed large wage increases. During the year Bolivia became a net oil importer, placing further strains on its already weakened international reserves.

(MICHAEL WOOLLER)

Botswana

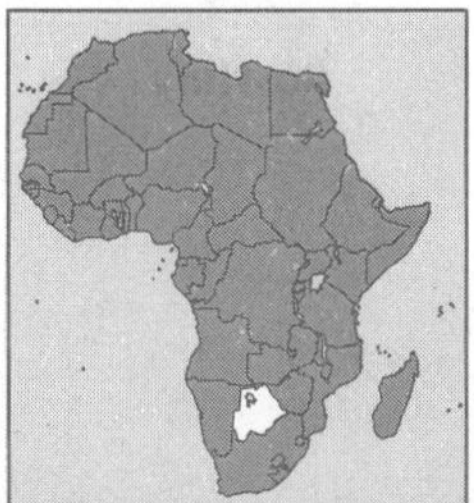

Botswana

A landlocked republic of southern Africa and a member of the Commonwealth of Nations, Botswana is bounded by South Africa, South West Africa (Namibia), Zambia, and Zimbabwe Rhodesia. Area: 576,000 sq km (222,000 sq mi). Pop. (1979 est.): 792,000, almost 99% African. Cap. and largest city: Gaborone (pop., 1976 est., 36,900). Language: English (official) and Setswana. Religion: Christian 60%; animist. President in 1979, Sir Seretse Khama.

On Oct. 20, 1979, Botswana went to the polls. Pres. Sir Seretse Khama's Botswana Democratic Party (BDP) won 29 of the 32 seats in the National Assembly. Although the turnout of eligible voters showed improvement over the record low of 33% in 1974, some doubted whether there was enough voter interest to support the nation's multiparty system. Kenneth Koma, leader of the leftist main opposition party, the Botswana National Front (BNF), declared that no opposition in Africa came to power by the ballot box. Warned of a ban if it took to violence, the BNF concentrated on advocating the severing of relations with South Africa and Zimbabwe Rhodesia and abolishing European advisers. In the voting the BNF won two seats and the Botswana People's Party one.

Although a "front-line" state in sympathy with the guerrillas in Rhodesia, Botswana, as Sir Seretse acknowledged, could not afford to cut economic ties with South Africa. South African and Rhodesian forces, seeking out the Rhodesian guerrillas and clandestine forces of the African National Congress and the Pan-African Congress operating in South Africa, made incursions into Botswana. This necessitated the strengthening of the nation's defense force from 400 men in 1977 to 3,000, placing a severe burden upon resources.

(MOLLY MORTIMER)

BOTSWANA

Education. (1978) Primary, pupils 145,459, teachers 4,653; secondary, pupils 16,086, teachers 731; vocational, pupils 2,222, teachers 340; teacher training, students 669, teachers 55; higher, students 762, teaching staff 85.

Finance and Trade. Monetary unit: pula, with (Sept. 17, 1979) an official rate of 0.83 pula to U.S. $1 (free rate of 1.78 pula = £1 sterling). Budget (1978–79 est.): revenue 102.9 million pula; expenditure 89.7 million pula (excludes development expenditure of 76.2 million pula). Foreign trade (1977): imports 239.6 million pula (80% from South Africa in 1975); exports 156.7 million pula (47% to U.K., 24% to South Africa, 22% to U.S. in 1975). Main exports: diamonds 31%; meat and products 27%; copper-nickel ore 26%.

Agriculture. Production (in 000; metric tons; 1977): sorghum 33; corn *c.* 42; millet *c.* 5; peanuts *c.* 7; beef and veal *c.* 31. Livestock (in 000; 1977): cattle *c.* 2,400; sheep *c.* 450; goats *c.* 1,100; chickens *c.* 580.

Industry. Production (in 000; metric tons; 1976): coal 224; diamonds (metric carats) 2,361; copper ore (metal content) 12; nickel ore (metal content) 13; electricity (kw-hr) 332,000.

Bowling

Tenpin Bowling. WORLD. At the end of the 1978–79 season the Fédération Internationale des Quilleurs (FIQ) reported a record membership of 62 national federations with a combined membership of 10.5 million men and women. The 62 member federations represented 59 nations, there being separate membership for ninepins and tenpins in Belgium, Denmark, and The Netherlands. Cyprus, Korea, and Uruguay had provisional memberships.

After two decades of efforts the FIQ application for recognition was approved at the 81st session of the International Olympic Committee (IOC) in Montevideo, Uruguay. This approval did not automatically include nine- and tenpin bowling in the Olympic Games program, but the recognition offered prestige and paved the way for participation in regional games recognized by the IOC.

The regional Olympic organizations in Asia included tenpin bowling in the Asian Games in December 1978 in Bangkok, Thailand. The ladies' division was dominated by the local Thai women and visitors from the Philippines. Olivia Bong Coo (Phil.) won the ladies' singles with a score of 1,270 for six games and 404 for the two-game match-play finals. In the doubles Thailand scored 2,263, defeating runner-up Japan by 24 pins. The trios championship was also won by Thailand, 3,267, by a margin of only 3 pins over second-place Philippines. In the ladies' fives Philippines did not meet serious competition, defeating runner-up Thailand by 170 pins after having scored a six-game series of 5,536 pins. In the men's singles, Masami Hirai (Japan) rolled 1,220 to defeat the second, third, and fourth finishers by 7, 8, and 9 pins, respectively. In the doubles Hirai was paired

AMERICAN BOWLING CONGRESS

Winners of the American Bowling Congress Classic were the Robby's Automatic Positioner team consisting of (from left to right): Butch Soper, Fred Conner, Capt. Jack Andolina, Tom Laskow, and Boysie Huber.

Bonds:
see Stock Exchanges

Books:
see Art Sales; Literature; Publishing

Bophuthatswana:
see South Africa

Botanical Gardens:
see Zoos and Botanical Gardens

Botany:
see Life Sciences

with Kiyoshi Taneda to win first place with 2,437, with the Hong Kong pair second at 2,419. Trios competition was won by Thailand, 3,669, with Japan runner-up at 3,530. The vice-president of the FIQ Asian Zone, P. S. Nathan (Malaysia), led his own team to victory in the fives event, with 5,763 pins over runner-up Thailand, 5,643. The "dark horse" of the eighth Asian Games, Ahn Byung-Ku (South Korea), rolled 427 in the match-play finals to defeat Hirai by 23 pins.

The international finals of the amateur singles tournament, Bowling World Cup, were held in Bogotá, Colombia. Samran Banuen (Thailand) mastered the men's division and Lita de la Rosa (Phil.) the ladies'. In the 17th annual Bowling Tournament of the Americas in July 1979 in Miami, Fla., Mexico won the women's singles, mixed foursomes, and both junior singles; the U.S. won mixed doubles, men's doubles, men's singles, and men's all-events; Canada won the women's doubles and Bermuda the women's all-events.

(YRJÖ SARAHETE)

UNITED STATES. A family tradition was maintained when brothers Nelson Burton, Jr., and Neil Burton of St. Louis, Mo., captured the Classic Division doubles championship with a 1,413 score in the American Bowling Congress (ABC) tournament in Tampa, Fla. The Burtons' father, Nelson, Sr., had won the ABC doubles title in 1937, with partner Virgil Gibbs. Nelson, Jr., one of the sport's leading professionals, also won the Classic all-events championship with a nine-game score of 2,079, giving him a lifetime total of eight ABC titles. Ed Biro, Kingston, N.Y., won the singles honours with 739, and the team title went to Robby's Automatic Positioner No. 1 of Glendale, Calif., which rolled 3,110. Delegates at the ABC's convention in Tampa voted to discontinue the professionals' Classic Division and in the future permit professionals to compete only in the Masters tournament, a match-play meet held in conjunction with the ABC.

ABC Regular Division winners included: singles, Rick Peters, Franklin, Ohio, 761; doubles, Mike Turnbull and Jack Wilson, Akron, Ohio, 1,388; team, Hal Lieber Trophies, Gary, Ind., 3,202; all-events, Bob Basacchi, Detroit, 2,097. Doug Myers of El Toro, Calif., won the Masters championship.

There were plenty of onlookers as Nelson Burton, Jr., rolled his 12th strike for a 300 game in the ABC Classic doubles competition in Tampa, Florida.

AMERICAN BOWLING CONGRESS

In Professional Bowlers Association (PBA) play Mark Roth of North Arlington, N.J., who was voted Bowler of the Year in 1977 and 1978, appeared to be headed toward a third such honour. With several events remaining on the 1979 schedule, Roth led in number of tournaments won (six) and prize money ($117,617). He had won 22 PBA championships in five years.

Perfection was achieved at the Women's International Bowling Congress (WIBC) tournament, in Tucson, Ariz., when Lori Gensch, a 25-year-old Milwaukee, Wis., bowler, became the first competitor in the 59-year history of the WIBC meet to shoot a 300 game. Miss Gensch's feat occurred in Open Division doubles play. She and her partner, Linda Sherwood, Overland Park, Kan., placed fourth with 1,253. First place in Open doubles went to Mary Ann Deptula and Geri Beattie of Detroit, who totaled 1,314. Betty Morris, Stockton, Calif., led the singles with 699 and the all-events with 1,945. Alpine Lanes, Euless, Texas, bowled 3,096 to place first in Open team competition. The winner of the Queens tournament, staged on the WIBC meet lanes, was Donna Adamek of Monrovia, Calif., who defeated Shinobu Saitoh of Tokyo 216–181 in the final game.

Duckpins. A 2,271 score by Eastport Shell, Annapolis, Md., won the men's championship in the team division of the 1979 National Duckpin Bowling Congress tournament. Osthimer Florist, Richmond, Va., topped the women's teams with 2,008, and the mixed team title was taken by Cannon YMCA, No. 2, Kannapolis, N.C., which bowled 2,156.

Other winners in the tournament included: men's singles, Dave Moody, Silver Spring, Md., 583; men's doubles, Wayne Wolthouse and Gary Hamilton, Baltimore, Md., 1,008; women's singles, Doris Holshouser, Kannapolis, N.C., 508; women's doubles, Brenda Willig and Elaine Green, Baltimore, 886.

(JOHN J. ARCHIBALD)

Lawn Bowls. In January 1979 an inaugural Embassy Indoor Bowls world championship was launched at Coatbridge, Scotland. David Bryant (England), who won the inaugural outdoor world title in 1966, also became the first indoor world champion. In the Kodak International Masters at Worthing, England, Bryant retained his singles title, the pairs going to David McGill of Scotland. In England David Cutler became the youngest person ever to win a major national singles championship when he captured the English title 23 days after his 25th birthday.

The English Indoor Bowling Association took the step of amending the rule to award prizes in kind and not in cash so as to permit the award of premium and other savings bonds, immediately convertible into cash, thus opening the way to open professionalism in place of increasingly devious amateurism. It remained to be seen whether the International Bowling Board would expel the British Isles national associations or recognize professionalism as inevitable. (C. M. JONES)

Brazil

A federal republic in eastern South America, Brazil is bounded by the Atlantic Ocean and all the countries of South America except Ecuador and Chile. Area: 8,512,000 sq km (3,286,500 sq mi). Pop (1979 est.): 119,670,000. Principal cities (pop., 1975 est.): Brasília (cap.; federal district) 763,300; São Paulo 7,198,600; Rio de Janeiro 4,857,700. Language: Portuguese. Religion: Roman Catholic 91%. Presidents in 1979, Gen. Ernesto Geisel and, from March 15, Gen. João Baptista da Figueiredo.

Domestic Affairs. Almost 44 million people participated in the general elections that took place Nov. 15, 1978. The government-sponsored party, ARENA (National Renewal Alliance), won a majority of seats in both houses of Congress and in most of the state assemblies, although the opposition party, MDB (Brazilian Democratic Movement), increased the number of its seats in the lower house. Prior to the elections greater freedom to express their views had been allowed the candidates of both parties. Previously, under the provisions of the so-called Falcão Law, a candidate appearing on radio or television could state only his name and that of his party.

It had been announced that Pres. Ernesto Geisel would permit the constitutional reforms adopted by Congress in September 1978 to go into effect after the November 15 elections. Among these were restoration of the writ of habeas corpus and a guarantee of autonomy for the judicial and legislative branches of government. On Dec. 29, 1978, Geisel repealed all emergency legislation, including the presidential decree (of 1969) providing for the banishment of persons accused of political crimes. These persons, known as *banidos* ("banished ones"), were said to total 128 and included such political leaders as Miguel Arraes and Leonel Brizzola, former governors, respectively, of the states of Pernambuco and Rio Grande do Sul. All the *banidos* were allowed to return to Brazil after Jan. 1, 1979.

After his election as president (by an electoral college on Oct. 15, 1978), Gen. João Baptista da Figueiredo declared that he was willing to offer "his hand of conciliation" to all those who had opposed his election. He wanted, he said, to make Brazil a "genuine democracy," to eliminate inequalities in the distribution of wealth among citizens and regions of the country, and to improve internal markets without diminishing exports. He also stated that he was determined to continue to improve Brazil's relations with the other countries of South America as well as with the new nations of Africa.

On Jan. 19, 1979, two months before his inauguration, Figueiredo repeated these promises in another address to the nation in which he announced the names of his Cabinet. He also pledged to continue the political reforms initiated by President Geisel. As provided by the constitution, Figueiredo and his vice-president, Antônio Aureliano Chaves de Mendonça, were duly inaugurated on March 15, 1979, in Brasília.

The new administration was immediately confronted with several serious problems. Numerous strikes plagued the nation, paralyzing public services. Among the political problems were how to provide for free elections of municipal officers (1980) and state governors (1982) and whether or not to grant amnesty to the *cassados* (those who had lost their political rights under a previous decree) and to persons accused of political crimes. On June 27 a bill was introduced in Congress providing for the amnesty of all *cassados* except persons convicted of acts of terrorism, assault, kidnapping, or personal attacks.

Brazil

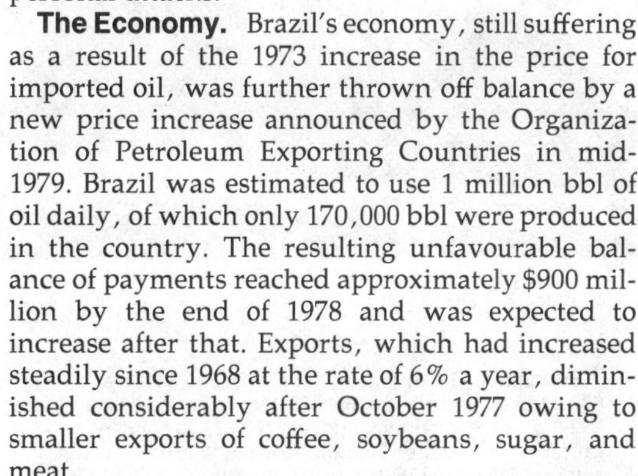

The Economy. Brazil's economy, still suffering as a result of the 1973 increase in the price for imported oil, was further thrown off balance by a new price increase announced by the Organization of Petroleum Exporting Countries in mid-1979. Brazil was estimated to use 1 million bbl of oil daily, of which only 170,000 bbl were produced in the country. The resulting unfavourable balance of payments reached approximately $900 million by the end of 1978 and was expected to increase after that. Exports, which had increased steadily since 1968 at the rate of 6% a year, diminished considerably after October 1977 owing to smaller exports of coffee, soybeans, sugar, and meat.

Frost in the winter of 1978 severely affected the coffee crop, already previously hurt by drought. More than 30% of the crop was said to be lost. In August 1979 exports of coffee were temporarily suspended.

GHISLAINE MOREL—GAMMA/LIAISON

Brazil's outgoing president, Ernesto Geisel (right on podium), listened to the words of incoming president João Baptista da Figueiredo (at podium) during inauguration ceremonies on March 15.

Boxing:
see Combat Sports

WIDE WORLD

Brazil's alcohol-powered fleet of motorcars is increasing. By 1981 it is expected that 16% of the automobiles built in the country will burn alcohol made from locally grown sugarcane.

BRAZIL

Education. (1974) Primary, pupils 19,286,611, teachers 887,424; secondary, pupils 628,178; vocational, pupils 782,827; teacher training, students 270,723; secondary, vocational, and teacher training, teachers 156,174; higher, students (1976) 1,316,640, teaching staff (1975) 120,550.

Finance. Monetary unit: cruzeiro, with a free rate (Sept. 17, 1979) of 28.92 cruzeiros to U.S. $1 (62.22 cruzeiros = £1 sterling). Gold, SDR's, and foreign exchange (April 1979) U.S. $11,236,000,000. Budget (1978 actual): revenue 349,218,000,000 cruzeiros; expenditure 344,346,000,000 cruzeiros. Gross national product (1978) 3,386,300,000,000 cruzeiros. Money supply (April 1979) 489,050,000,000 cruzeiros. Cost of living (São Paulo; 1975 = 100; May 1979) 391.9.

Foreign Trade. Imports (1977) 181,480,000,000 cruzeiros; exports (1978) 224,114,000,000 cruzeiros. Import sources: U.S. 20%; Saudi Arabia 11%; Iraq 9%; West Germany 9%; Japan 7%. Export destinations (1977): U.S. 18%; West Germany 9%; The Netherlands 8%; Japan 6%; Italy 6%. Main exports: coffee 16%; soybeans and products 12%; iron ore 8%.

Transport and Communications. Roads (1976) 1,489,064 km. Motor vehicles in use (1976): passenger 6,348,600; commercial 737,400. Railways: (1976) 30,300 km; traffic 11,638,000,000 passenger-km; freight 63,246,000,000 net ton-km. Air traffic (1978): 8,724,000,000 passenger-km; freight 477.6 million net ton-km. Shipping (1978): merchant vessels 100 gross tons and over 565; gross tonnage 3,701,731. Shipping traffic (1977): goods loaded 81,863,000 metric tons, unloaded 62.1 million metric tons. Telephones (Dec. 1977) 4,708,000. Radio receivers (Dec. 1975) 16,980,000. Television receivers (Dec. 1976) 10,525,000.

Agriculture. Production (in 000; metric tons; 1978): wheat *c.* 2,667; corn 13,533; rice 7,242; cassava (1977) 26,511; potatoes 2,015; sweet potatoes (1977) 1,815; sugar, raw value *c.* 7,780; tomatoes 1,452; dry beans 2,188; soybeans 8,970; coffee 1,200; cocoa 257; bananas 6,176; oranges 7,818; cotton, lint 460; sisal 212; tobacco 402; rubber *c.* 30; beef and veal *c.* 2,250; pork *c.* 850; fish catch (1977) *c.* 790; timber (cu m; 1977) 152,274. Livestock (in 000; 1978): cattle *c.* 89,000; pigs *c.* 37,600; sheep *c.* 17,200; goats *c.* 7,200; horses (1977) *c.* 5,100; chickens *c.* 310,000.

Industry. Fuel and power (in 000; metric tons; 1978): crude oil 8,067; coal (1977) 3,864; natural gas (cu m) *c.* 2.5 million; manufactured gas (cu m; 1977) *c.* 440,000; electricity (kw-hr; 1977) 99,869,000 (92% hydroelectric in 1976). Production (in 000; metric tons; 1978): pig iron *c.* 10,000; crude steel 12,145; iron ore (68% metal content) 65,770; bauxite (1977) *c.* 1,040; manganese ore (metal content; 1976) 900; gold (troy oz) *c.* 420; cement *c.* 23,300; wood pulp (1976) 1,515; paper (1976) 2,010; fertilizers (nutrient content; 1977–78) nitrogenous 232, phosphate 1,122; passenger cars (units) *c.* 540; commercial vehicles (units) *c.* 520. Merchant vessels launched (100 gross tons and over; 1978) 442,000 gross tons.

Fuel was the great problem. Measures adopted resulted in a 4% reduction of consumption. The authorities promoted various types of fuel, including alcohol from sugarcane, rice husks, and wood shavings. It was estimated that by 1981 more than 16% of the automobiles built in Brazil would be equipped with motors to burn pure alcohol.

Inflation was estimated at more than 42% for 1978, and during 1979 it was said to be running at an annual rate of 65%. This was reflected in the value of the cruzeiro. It was officially set at 20.37/20.47 cruzeiros per U.S. dollar on Dec. 8, 1978; following a series of "mini-devaluations," a 30% devaluation announced in December 1979 lowered its value to about 42.5 to the dollar.

Foreign Relations. On the occasion of Brazil's Independence Day commemoration (Sept. 7, 1978), U.S. Pres. Jimmy Carter sent a telegram to President Geisel declaring that Brazil should be justly proud of its accomplishments and of the prestige it enjoyed among nations. He referred to the close friendly relations that had existed between the two countries for more than a century. This friendship had been well expressed, he added, during his recent official visit to Brazil (March 1978). It was again evident during U.S. Vice-Pres. Walter Mondale's visit to Brazil (March 21–23, 1979), which resulted in an extension of the compromise agreement (reached at the end of 1978) on Brazilian textile exports to the United States.

In a speech to political and military leaders (Jan. 19, 1979) before his inauguration, President Figueiredo declared that his foreign policy would be inspired by nonintervention in other nations' internal affairs. At about the same time, his minister-to-be of foreign relations, Ramiro Elísio Saraiva Guerreiro, declared in a press interview that Brazil had no ambitions to dominate other nations in South America. Existing controversies with Argentina would be resolved in an effort to harmonize the interests of both nations.

It was announced in August that President Figueiredo had accepted President Carter's invitation to visit the U.S. in an official capacity. The date was to be set later. (RAUL D'ECA)

Bulgaria

A people's republic of Europe, Bulgaria is situated on the eastern Balkan Peninsula along the Black Sea, bordered by Romania, Yugoslavia, Greece, and Turkey. Area: 110,912 sq km (42,823 sq mi). Pop. (1978 est.): 8,822,600, including 85.3% Bulgarians (but excluding some 210,000 Macedonians classified as Bulgarian according to official statistics), 8.5% Turks, 2.6% Gypsies, and 2.5% Macedonians. Cap. and largest city: Sofia (pop., 1978 est., 996,500). Language: chiefly Bulgarian. Religion: official sources classify 35.5% of the population as religious, although this figure is suspect since the regime promotes atheism. Of those who practice religion, it is estimated that 85% are Bulgarian Orthodox, 13% Muslim, 0.8% Jewish, 0.7% Roman Catholic, and 0.5% Protestant, Gregorian-Armenian, and others. First secretary of the Bulgarian Communist Party and chairman of the State Council in 1979, Todor Zhivkov; chairman of the Council of Ministers (premier), Stanko Todorov.

The year 1979 began with a five-day state visit to Sofia by Pres. Leonid I. Brezhnev of the Soviet Union, who characterized Soviet-Bulgarian relations as an example of socialist internationalism in action. The close relationship had been significantly emphasized by the opening in November 1978 of a direct ferry service between the ports of Ilyichevsk, near Odessa, U.S.S.R., and Varna, Bulg.

A Polish party and state delegation led by Edward Gierek visited Bulgaria in February, and in July Gierek was the guest of Bulgaria's chief of state, Todor Zhivkov. Chancellor Helmut Schmidt of West Germany visited Bulgaria officially in May. In April Zhivkov spent two days in Athens for talks with the Greek prime minister, Konstantinos Karamanlis, and in July he visited Ankara, where he was the guest of Turkey's prime minister, Bulent Ecevit. At the end of July Ilie Verdet, the Romanian premier, visited Stanko Todorov, his Bulgarian opposite number. They discussed bilateral economic collaboration, especially the new trade agreement for 1981–85 and the building of a joint hydroelectric power station on the Danube River between Turnu Magurele, Rom., and Nikopol, Bulg.

On September 9 Bulgaria celebrated the 35th anniversary of its socialist revolution with the inauguration of a nuclear power station at Kozloduy on the Danube, built with Soviet help and the first of its kind in Eastern Europe.

(K. M. SMOGORZEWSKI)

Bulgaria

BULGARIA

Education. (1976–77) Primary and secondary, pupils 1,095,791, teachers 57,177; vocational, pupils 279,663, teachers 19,406; teacher training, students 23,230, teachers 2,325; higher (1975–76), students 128,593, teaching staff 12,230.

Finance. Monetary unit: lev, with a free exchange rate of 0.89 lev to U.S. $1 (1.92 lev = £1 sterling). Budget (1978 est.): revenue 10,274,000,000 leva; expenditure 10,249,000,000 leva.

Foreign Trade. (1977) Imports 6,062,000,000 leva; exports 6,022,000,000 leva. Main import sources: U.S.S.R. 57%; East Germany 7%; West Germany 5%. Main export destinations: U.S.S.R. 55%; East Germany 8%; Poland 5%. Main exports (1976): machinery 33%; tobacco and cigarettes 11%; transport equipment 9%; fruit and vegetables *c.* 8%; iron and steel 6%; wines and spirits *c.* 6%. Tourism: visitors (1977) 4,570,000; gross receipts (1975) U.S. $230 million.

Transport and Communications. Roads (1976) 36,091 km (including 20 km expressways). Motor vehicles in use (1976): passenger *c.* 218,000; commercial (including buses) *c.* 47,000. Railways: (1977) 4,415 km; traffic (1978) 7,000,000,000 passenger-km, freight 17,148,000,000 net ton-km. Air traffic (1977): 555 million passenger-km; freight 7.9 million net ton-km. Navigable inland waterways (1973) 471 km. Shipping (1978): merchant vessels 100 gross tons and over 189; gross tonnage 1,082,477. Telephones (Jan. 1978) 946,023. Radio licenses (Dec. 1976) 2,750,000. Television licenses (Dec. 1976) 1,546,000.

Agriculture. Production (in 000; metric tons; 1978): wheat *c.* 3,450; corn *c.* 2,300; barley *c.* 1,500; potatoes *c.* 390; sunflower seed *c.* 448; tomatoes *c.* 750; grapes *c.* 1,257; apples *c.* 335; tobacco *c.* 126; meat *c.* 606. Livestock (in 000; Jan. 1978): sheep 10,145; cattle 1,736; goats 326; pigs 3,399; horses (1977) 128; asses (1977) 320; chickens 39,024.

Industry. Fuel and power (in 000; metric tons; 1978): lignite *c.* 25,000; coal 280; crude oil *c.* 240; natural gas (cu m; 1976) 37,000; electricity (kw-hr) 31,790,000. Production (in 000; metric tons; 1978): iron ore (33% metal content) *c.* 2,400; manganese ore (metal content; 1976) *c.* 11; copper ore (metal content; 1977) 57; lead ore (metal content; 1977) 115; zinc ore (1977) *c.* 80; pig iron 1,490; crude steel 2,469; cement 5,149; sulfuric acid 974; nitric acid (1976) 783; soda ash (1976) 1,025; fertilizers (nutrient content; 1977) nitrogenous 705, phosphate 279; cotton yarn 84; cotton fabrics (m) 350,000; wool yarn (1977) 33; woolen fabrics (m) 33,000. Merchant vessels launched (100 gross tons and over; 1978) 146,000 gross tons.

Burma

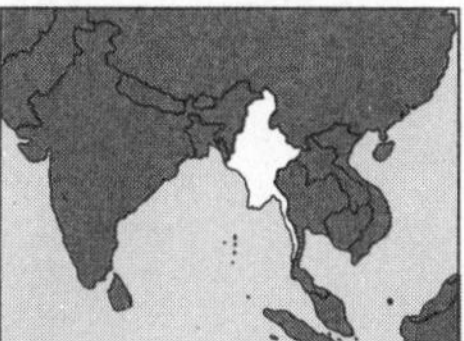

Burma

A republic of Southeast Asia, Burma is bordered by Bangladesh, India, China, Laos, Thailand, the Bay of Bengal, and the Andaman Sea. Area: 676,577 sq km (261,288 sq mi). Pop. (1979 est.): 34,361,000. Cap. and largest city: Rangoon (pop., 1973, 2.1 million). Language: Burmese. Religion (1977): Buddhist 80%. Chairman of the State Council in 1979, U Ne Win; prime minister, U Maung Maung Kha.

Burma recorded no significant change in 1979 in either its economic or its political situation. Reports of corruption in high circles provoked a government decree requiring all 250 members of the ruling Burma Socialist Program Party Central Committee to declare their assets in cash, business interests, and estates. The decree was also made applicable to 300 party executives throughout the country.

There were indications that Burma was becoming more receptive to an expansion of foreign investment in its economy. As of 1979 major aid donors for economic development were the Asian Development Bank with $26 million for a fisheries project and a rice-processing project and the International Development Association with $34 million for agricultural development.

Relations with neighbouring Bangladesh, normalized in 1978 with an agreement on phased repatriation to Burma of Muslim refugees, were further cemented by a visit to Bangladesh by Pres. U Ne Win early in 1979. By March an estimated 67,800 of the 197,000 refugees who had earlier fled the border region to Bangladesh had returned.

Brazilian Literature: *see* Literature

Bridge: *see* Contract Bridge

Bridges: *see* Engineering Projects

British Commonwealth: *see* Commonwealth of Nations; *articles on the various member states*

Brunei: *see* Dependent States

Buddhism: *see* Religion

Building and Construction Industry: *see* Engineering Projects; Industrial Review

BURMA

Education. (1976–77) Primary, pupils 3,686,773, teachers 79,653; secondary, pupils 1,038,898, teachers 29,361; vocational, pupils 8,141, teachers 714; teacher training (1974–75), students 4,428, teachers 301; higher, students 84,981, teaching staff 3,319.

Finance. Monetary unit: kyat, with (Sept. 17, 1979) a free rate of 6.73 kyats to U.S. $1 (14.47 kyats = £1 sterling). Gold, SDR's, and foreign exchange (June 1979) U.S. $180 million. Budget (1976–77 est.): revenue 16,677,000,000 kyats; expenditure 17,318,000,000 kyats.

Foreign Trade. (1978) Imports 2,114,000,000 kyats; exports 1,665,900,000 kyats. Import sources (1977): Japan 25%; Singapore 12%; U.K. 8%; West Germany 7%; South Korea 6%; China 6%; U.S. 6%. Export destinations (1977): Singapore 15%; Indonesia 14%; Bangladesh 14%; Sri Lanka 10%; Japan 9%; Hong Kong 6%; Mauritius 5%. Main exports: teak 35%; rice 30%.

Transport and Communications. Roads (1975) 21,956 km. Motor vehicles in use (1976): passenger 37,700; commercial (including buses) 40,500. Railways: (1976) 4,347 km; traffic (1978) 3,500,000,000 passenger-km, freight 507 million net ton-km. Air traffic (1977): 178 million passenger-km; freight 1.3 million net ton-km. Shipping (1978): merchant vessels 100 gross tons and over 73; gross tonnage 70,848. Telephones (Jan. 1978) 32,600. Radio licenses (Dec. 1976) 665,000.

Agriculture. Production (in 000; metric tons; 1978): rice 10,500; dry beans *c.* 186; onions 136; bananas (1977) *c.* 239; sesame seed *c.* 103; peanuts *c.* 444; cotton, lint *c.* 6; jute *c.* 43; tobacco *c.* 77; rubber 20; fish catch (1977) 519; timber (cu m; 1977) 22,474. Livestock (in 000; March 1978): cattle *c.* 7,865; buffalo *c.* 1,855; pigs *c.* 1,915; goats *c.* 615; sheep *c.* 221; chickens *c.* 17,300.

Industry. Production (in 000; metric tons; 1978): crude oil 1,410; electricity (excluding most industrial production; kw-hr) *c.* 960,000; cement 250; lead concentrates (metal content; 1976) 3.8; zinc concentrates (metal content) 4.8; tin concentrates (metal content) 0.5; tungsten concentrates (oxide content; 1976) 0.4; nitrogenous fertilizers (nutrient content; 1977–78) *c.* 55; cotton yarn 14.

The insurgency menace posed by the Burmese Communist Party and the Karen separatists was still a problem, but guerrilla activities were in a low key compared with previous years. There was general agreement that assistance to Communist guerrillas from China had dwindled because of that nation's preoccupation with developments in Cambodia and Vietnam.

On September 28 Foreign Minister Myint Maung told the UN General Assembly that Burma was leaving the nonaligned movement because of "disillusionment" with the movement's summit meeting in Havana. (GOVINDAN UNNY)

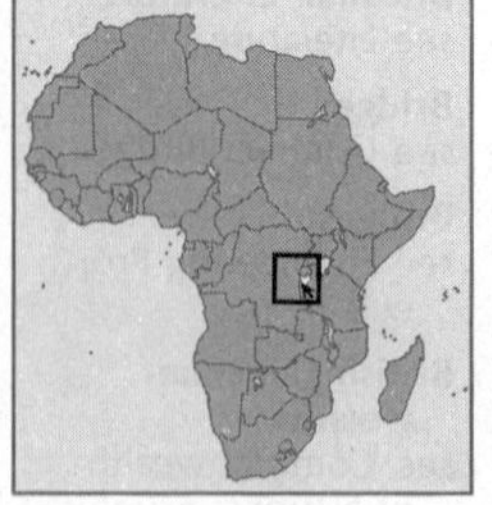
Burundi

Burundi

A republic of eastern Africa, Burundi is bordered by Zaire, Rwanda, and Tanzania. Area 27,834 sq km (10,747 sq mi). Pop. (1979 est.): 4,176,000, mainly Hutu, Tutsi, and Twa. Cap. and largest city: Bujumbura (pop., 1977 est., 162,600). Language: Rundi and French. Religion: Roman Catholic 55%; animist 38%; Protestant 6%; Muslim 1%. President in 1979, Lieut. Col. Jean-Baptiste Bagaza.

Pres. Jean-Baptiste Bagaza's military government (which he headed following abolition of the post of prime minister in October 1978) caused a small stir in 1979 when it expelled 52 Roman Catholic and Protestant missionaries for allegedly inciting civil war against the ruling Tutsi minority. At the same time, the government claimed progress toward eradicating tribal and feudal prejudice and

BURUNDI

Education. (1976–77) Primary, pupils 130,739, teachers 4,224; secondary (1975–76), pupils 5,773, teachers 326; vocational (1975–76), pupils 2,871, teachers 398; teacher training (1975–76), students 5,381, teachers 398; higher (1975–76), students 1,002, teaching staff 223.

Finance. Monetary unit: Burundi franc, with (Sept. 17, 1979) an official rate of BurFr 90 to U.S. $1 (free rate of BurFr 193.63 = £1 sterling). Gold, SDR's, and foreign exchange (June 1979) U.S. $64.8 million. Budget (1978 actual): revenue BurFr 9,762,800,000; expenditure BurFr 9,762,600,000.

Foreign Trade. (1978) Imports BurFr 8,842,000,000; exports BurFr 6,029,000,000. Import sources: Belgium-Luxembourg 23%; West Germany 10%; France 9%; Japan 7%; Iran 7%; Kenya 7%. Export destinations: U.S. 47%; China 6%. Main exports: coffee 85%; cotton 7%.

Agriculture. Production (in 000; metric tons; 1978): sorghum *c.* 110; corn *c.* 140; cassava (1977) *c.* 902; potatoes (1977) *c.* 151; sweet potatoes (1977) *c.* 873; dry beans *c.* 162; bananas *c.* 950; coffee *c.* 23; cotton, lint (1977) *c.* 2. Livestock (in 000; Dec. 1976): cattle 779; sheep *c.* 312; goats 571; pigs 47.

initiating agricultural reform. Burundi, however, remained one of the world's poorest countries, with a per capita annual income of approximately $70, average life expectancy of 40 years, and an infant mortality rate of about 150 per 1,000; more than 90% of the people depended on subsistence farming. The nation continued to lean heavily on external aid, Belgium and France being the chief donors. Following a mineral survey that revealed large nickel deposits, U.S. interests became visible in Bujumbura.

Relations with Tanzania improved after the final payment by Burundi as compensation for raids into Tanzanian territory, and Burundi took a full part in Kagera River basin development with Rwanda and Tanzania. It also joined with Rwanda, Tanzania, and Zaire in the Community of the Great Lakes. The war in Uganda caused problems for Burundi by blocking its communications with East African ports.

In April Burundi was visited by Romanian Pres. Nicolae Ceausescu in the course of his African tour, and a treaty of friendship and cooperation between the two countries was signed. Agreement was also reached on Romanian aid for the exploitation of Burundi's nickel ore. (MOLLY MORTIMER)

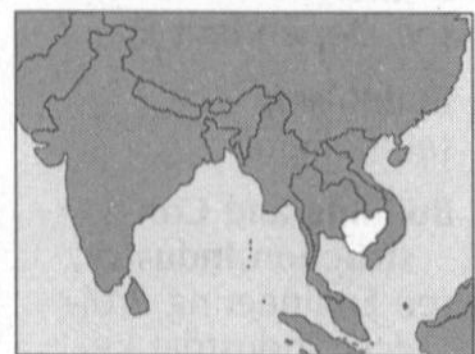
Cambodia

Cambodia

A republic of Southeast Asia, Cambodia is the southwest part of the Indochinese Peninsula, on the Gulf of Thailand, bordered by Vietnam, Laos, and Thailand. Area: 181,035 sq km (69,898 sq mi). Pop. (1979 est.): between 4.5 million and 5 million according to official figures. It is estimated to comprise: Khmer 93%; Vietnamese 4%; Chinese 3%. Cap.: Phnom Penh (urban area pop., 1979 est., 270,000). Language: Khmer (official) and French. Religion: Buddhist. Head of state to Jan. 7, 1979, Khieu Samphan; premier to January 7, Pol Pot; head of the People's Revolutionary Council from January 7, Heng Samrin.

On Jan. 7, 1979, rebel guerrillas backed by Vietnam seized power in Phnom Penh and set up a People's Revolutionary Council headed by Heng

CAMBODIA

Education. (1973–74) Primary, pupils 429,110, teachers 18,794; secondary, pupils 98,888, teachers 2,226; vocational, pupils 4,856, teachers 202; teacher training, students 553, teachers 18; higher, students 11,570, teaching staff 276.

Finance. Monetary unit: riel, with (Sept. 17, 1979) a nominal free rate of 1,200 riels to U.S. $1 (2,582 riels = £1 sterling); the general internal use of currency was suspended from 1975, a system of rationing being in use. Budget (1974 est.): revenue 23 billion riels; expenditure 71 billion riels.

Foreign Trade. (1973) Imports 14.2 billion riels; exports 2.7 billion riels. Import sources: U.S. *c.* 69%; Thailand *c.* 11%; Singapore *c.* 5%; Japan *c.* 5%. Export destinations: Hong Kong *c.* 23%; Japan *c.* 22%; Malaysia *c.* 18%; France *c.* 12%; Spain *c.* 10%. Main export: rubber 93%.

Transport and Communications. Roads (1976) *c.* 11,000 km. Motor vehicles in use: passenger (1972) 27,200; commercial (including buses; 1973) 11,000. Railways: (1977) *c.* 612 km; traffic (1973) 54,070,000 passenger-km, freight 9,780,000 net ton-km. Air traffic (1977): 42 million passenger-km; freight 400,000 net ton-km. Inland waterways (including Mekong River; 1977) *c.* 1,400 km. Telephones (Dec. 1975) 71,000. Radio receivers (Dec. 1975) 110,000. Television receivers (Dec. 1976) 35,000.

Agriculture. Production (in 000; metric tons; 1978): rice *c.* 1,750; corn *c.* 80; bananas *c.* 94; oranges *c.* 32; dry beans *c.* 15; rubber (1977) *c.* 18; tobacco *c.* 8; jute (1977) *c.* 4. Livestock (in 000; 1978): cattle *c.* 1,300; buffalo *c.* 580; pigs *c.* 750.

Samrin (*see* BIOGRAPHIES), president of the Kampuchean United Front for National Salvation (KUFNS). There were conflicting reports about the fate of the fallen regime's leaders. Former foreign minister Ieng Sary was said to have been rescued by a Thai helicopter while head of state Khieu Samphan apparently escaped in a Chinese aircraft. From bases in China the Pol Pot group quickly organized military resistance and a diplomatic offensive against the new regime.

Heng Samrin lost no time in announcing an eight-point program that pledged restoration of freedom to the people. This liberalization and the end of the Pol Pot regime, which had become known as one of the cruelest in modern times, seemed to mark a turn for the better in Cambodia. But political realities pointed otherwise. The fact that Pol Pot's ouster was the result of a Vietnamese invasion raised fears in Southeast Asia of an expansionist Hanoi. China, resentful of Vietnam's hegemony in Indochina, continued its support of the fallen Pol Pot. Influential U.S. circles argued against normalizing relations with an aggressive Hanoi government.

The result was that Pol Pot continued to receive diplomatic recognition at the UN (confirmed by a General Assembly vote on September 21) and substantial Chinese assistance in organizing a guerrilla campaign. Cambodia slipped into a new civil war, with the Pol Pot faction claiming to have killed or captured 40,000 among an estimated 200,000 Vietnamese troops in the country and the Heng Samrin government claiming 42,000 Pol Pot guerrillas as casualties.

A further diplomatic complication for Heng Samrin was provided by former head of state Prince Norodom Sihanouk (*see* BIOGRAPHIES). After keeping him under house arrest for the three years it was in power, the Pol Pot government had released Sihanouk on January 6. He was given the task of speaking for Cambodia in the UN Security Council, where a complaint against Vietnamese "aggression" had been filed. But after denouncing Vietnam's policy of "annexation and hegemony," Sihanouk turned on his former tormentors and rejected all attempts by the Pol Pot group to enlist him as an ally. From Beijing (Peking) and Pyongyang, North Korea, he launched his own diplomatic campaign on the basis that he alone had the recognition and legitimacy to end the fighting and establish an independent government.

Neither the diplomatic ballyhoo nor the punitive war China unleashed on Vietnam on February 17 seemed to shake Heng Samrin or Hanoi's backing of him. In February Vietnamese Premier Pham Van Dong paid an official visit to Phnom Penh and signed a peace and friendship treaty. In August a special People's Revolutionary Tribunal in Phnom Penh sentenced Pol Pot and Ieng Sary to death, after a trial in absentia, on charges of systematic massacre, evacuation of urban populations, forced establishment of communes, and extermination of monks, religious believers, and the intelligentsia. The following month the government won a point when the summit meeting of nonaligned nations in Havana left the Cambodian seat vacant.

Through all the political maneuvers, the extent of the human tragedy in Cambodia kept growing. Refugees flowed into Thailand, sometimes to be driven back by Thai authorities. More than two million people were believed to be starving. Phnom Penh at first refused to allow international aid lest the Pol Pot forces also benefit from it, but by September, Red Cross and UN Children's Fund assistance began to flow into the country. Opening the second congress of the KUFNS in September, Heng Samrin admitted the famine conditions but blamed the Pol Pot regime. Noting that agriculture and industry had been reduced to zero, he said thousands of tons of food and other aid were pouring in from the Soviet Union and Vietnam. Meanwhile, Vietnam began an all-out military campaign to wipe out the remnants of Pol Pot's supporters. Heavy fighting near the Thai border forced more refugees to flee into Thailand, further

Two small Cambodian children tried to revive their mother after she collapsed while trying to flee from strife in Cambodia.

UPI

straining that country's ability to care for them. On December 27 the former regime's ambassador to China announced that Khieu Samphan had become premier in place of Pol Pot, who was now commander in chief of the guerrilla forces.

(T. J. S. GEORGE)

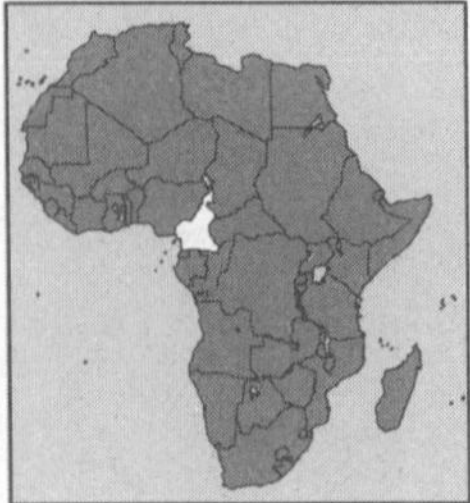
Cameroon

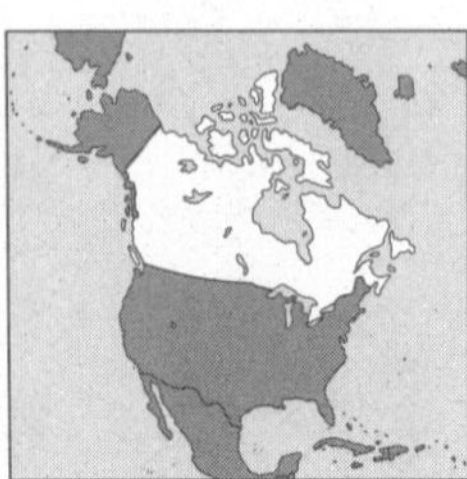
Canada

Cameroon

A republic of west Africa on the Gulf of Guinea, Cameroon borders on Nigeria, Chad, the Central African Republic, the Congo, Gabon, and Equatorial Guinea. Area: 465,054 sq km (179,558 sq mi). Pop. (1978 est.): 7,980,700. Cap.: Yaoundé (pop., 1976, 313,700). Largest city: Douala (pop., 1976, 458,400). Language: English and French (official), Bantu, Sudanic. Religion: mainly animist, with Roman Catholic (25.5%), Protestant, independent Christian, and Muslim minorities. President in 1979, Ahmadou Ahidjo; prime minister, Paul Biya.

Cameroon in 1979 took part in negotiations concerning the conflict in Chad, meeting with Nigeria, Libya, and Sudan in particular. During the third conference of Chadian national reconciliation, held in Lagos, Nigeria, in May 1979, the Cameroon delegates tried to secure acceptance of moderate proposals advanced by elements close to France. While the Nigerians practically blockaded N'Djamena, the capital of Chad, and deprived it of food and oil, Cameroon enabled supplies to reach it by the trans-Cameroon railway and through Douala. In September part of the French force stationed in Chad was evacuated by that route.

The overthrow of Pres. Francisco Macías Nguema, dictator of Equatorial Guinea, was welcomed in Yaoundé. Thousands of Equatorial Guinea's political refugees lived in Cameroon, but few returned home after what they believed to be only a palace revolution.

In October a revolt in the village of Dollé in the northern region was suppressed by the Army, with more than 100 villagers reportedly being killed.

(PHILIPPE DECRAENE)

CAMEROON

Education. (1976–77) Primary, pupils 1,156,199, teachers 22,763; secondary, pupils 120,207, teachers (1975–76) 3,309; vocational, pupils 39,652, teachers (1975–76) 1,364; teacher training, students 1,310, teachers (1975–76) 185; higher, students 8,207, teaching staff (1975–76) 376.

Finance. Monetary unit: CFA franc, with (Sept. 17, 1979) a parity of CFA Fr 50 to the French franc and a free rate of CFA Fr 211.54 to U.S. $1 (CFA Fr 455.12 = £1 sterling). Budget (total; 1977–78 est.) balanced at CFA Fr 137 billion.

Foreign Trade. (1978) Imports CFA Fr 237 billion; exports CFA Fr 182 billion. Import sources (1977): France 43%; U.S. 7%; West Germany 7%; Japan 6%; Italy 5%. Export destinations (1977): France 27%; The Netherlands 26%; West Germany 10%; Italy 8%. Main exports: cocoa 20%; coffee 30%; timber 12%.

Transport and Communications. Roads (1975) 43,500 km. Motor vehicles in use (1976): passenger 59,500; commercial (including buses) 51,200. Railways (1977): 1,173 km; traffic 238 million passenger-km, freight 506 million net ton-km. Shipping (1978): merchant vessels 100 gross tons and over 29; gross tonnage 83,777. Telephones (June 1973) 22,000. Radio receivers (Dec. 1974) 603,000.

Agriculture. Production (in 000; metric tons; 1978): corn *c.* 350; millet *c.* 370; sweet potatoes (1977) *c.* 160; cassava (1977) *c.* 810; bananas *c.* 105; plantains (1977) *c.* 1,020; peanuts *c.* 164; coffee *c.* 90; cocoa *c.* 100; palm kernels *c.* 49; palm oil *c.* 84; rubber *c.* 19; cotton, lint *c.* 15; timber (cu m; 1977) *c.* 7,865. Livestock (in 000; 1977): cattle 2,917; pigs *c.* 700; sheep *c.* 2,100; goats *c.* 1,553; chickens *c.* 9,300.

Industry. Production (in 000; metric tons; 1976): cement 210; aluminum (1977) 57; electricity (kw-hr) 1,336,000.

Canada

Canada is a federal parliamentary state and member of the Commonwealth of Nations covering North America north of conterminous United States and east of Alaska. Area: 9,976,139 sq km (3,851,809 sq mi). Pop. (1979 est.): 23.6 million, including (1971) British 44.6%; French 28.7%; other European 23%; Indian and Eskimo 1.4%. Cap.: Ottawa (metro pop., 1977 est., 702,200). Largest cities: Toronto (metro pop., 1977 est., 2,849,000); Montreal (metro pop., 1977 est., 2,809,900). Language (mother tongue; 1976): English 61%; French 26%; others 13%. Religion (1971): Roman Catholic 46%; Protestant 42%. Queen, Elizabeth II; governors-general in 1979, Jules Léger and, from January 22, Edward R. Schreyer; prime ministers, Pierre Elliott Trudeau and, from June 4, Joe Clark.

Domestic Affairs. Pierre Elliott Trudeau, who had dominated Canadian politics for 11 years, fell from power in 1979. In a general election on May 22, Trudeau's Liberal Party lost office to the Progressive Conservatives, led by a 39-year-old MP from Alberta, Charles Joseph ("Joe") Clark (*see* BIOGRAPHIES). Sworn into office on June 4, Clark became the 16th prime minister of Canada and the youngest man ever to hold the post.

The Clark government in turn met a dramatic check on December 13, when its first budget was defeated in the House of Commons. Under the parliamentary system, loss of confidence on a budget requires the resignation of the government. On this occasion, the 133 Conservatives present were outnumbered by 112 Liberals and 27 New Democratic Party (NDP) members for a total of 139 votes. On three previous confidence motions the minority Clark government had been sustained by the five Social Credit members from Quebec, but they refused to accept parts of the budget. Clark asked Governor-General Edward Schreyer (*see* BIOGRAPHIES) to grant a dissolution of Parliament, and an election was called for Feb. 18, 1980. Trudeau, who had announced his resignation as leader of the Liberal Party on November 21, was urgently requested by his caucus to reconsider his decision and fight the next election. On December 18 he reluctantly agreed to stay on as leader.

The Conservative victory in May demonstrated the truth of an old political maxim: people vote against sitting governments rather than for alternative ones. After 11 years in office, Trudeau and his ministers appeared tired, unable to formulate fresh policies, and, to many Canadians, lacking in credibility. Their handling of Canada's economic problems contributed to this impression. Trudeau had won the last election, in 1974, partly on the assertion that the wage and price controls advocated by the Conservatives would be bad for the economy. A little more than a year later he had imposed mandatory restraints. Another factor worked against Trudeau in English-speaking Canada. The election of the separatist Parti Québécois in 1976 had produced a wave of support for Trudeau as the leader best able to deal with this challenge. As time went on and Quebec made no overt moves toward separation, anxiety over the issue waned. Trudeau's emphasis on constitutional changes to hold the country together seemed less relevant. Economic problems became dominant.

Against a lacklustre Liberal image, Clark presented the appeal of a team leader determined to cut back "big government" by controlling public spending and trimming public services. He promised a more cooperative approach toward the ten provinces, seven of which were now headed by governments drawn from his own party. He offered to share some of the central government's powers with the provinces and to allay the claims of the West that the federal government showed a bias toward central Canada. Tax cuts were promised, especially by making mortgage interest and real estate taxes deductible from income tax. The economy would be stimulated by encouraging private business.

Although Clark lacked Trudeau's personal flair, his claim that he could deal more effectively with the country's current problems proved popular, especially in English-speaking Canada. The Conservatives won over half the seats in the four Atlantic provinces, more than doubled their standing in Ontario, held their own in the Prairies, and gained heavily in British Columbia. The Liberals retained their political base in Quebec but lost in the large urban ridings of Ontario and were virtually wiped out from the Great Lakes to the Pacific. Thirteen of Trudeau's ministers were defeated, eight of them from Ontario. The third major party, the socialist NDP, although it increased its strength in the West, did not register the gains it had expected in industrial Ontario. The Social Credit Party, confined to Quebec and campaigning under a new leader, dropped from nine to six.

CANADIAN PRESS

Canada's new prime minister, Joe Clark, gave a happy victory salute to his followers after his party's victory on May 22. His government lasted only until December 14.

The Conservatives' 136 seats fell short of the 142 necessary for a working parliamentary majority, but absenteeism and the de facto support of the Social Credit members assured them control of the new House of Commons. On September 23 a Social Credit MP quit his party to join the Conservative caucus, and on the eve of the opening of Parliament, Clark announced that the former Liberal speaker in the House would continue in the chair, thus depriving the opposition of one vote. Two by-elections on November 19 changed the standings slightly, as the Conservatives lost the seat of the late John Diefenbaker (*see* OBITUARIES) to the

Election Results, May 22, 1979
(1974 results in parentheses)

Area	Progressive Conservatives	Liberals	New Democratic Party	Social Credit	Independent
Atlantic region (Nfld., N.S., N.B., P.E.I.) 32 (32)	18 (17)	12 (13)	2 (1)	0 (0)	(1)
Quebec 75 (74)	2 (3)	67 (60)	0 (0)	6 (11)	
Ontario 95 (88)	57 (25)	32 (55)	6 (8)	0 (0)	
West (Man., Sask., Alta., B.C.) 77 (68)	57 (49)	3 (13)	17 (6)	0 (0)	
North (N.W.T., Yukon) 3 (2)	2 (1)	0 (0)	1 (1)	0(0)	
Total 282 (264)	136 (95)	114 (141)	26 (16)	6 (11)	(1)

CANADA

Education. (1978–79) Primary, pupils 3,455,608; secondary, pupils 1,820,620; primary and secondary, teachers 271,106; higher, students 616,795, teaching staff 52,373.

Finance. Monetary unit: Canadian dollar, with (Sept. 17, 1979) a free rate of Can$1.16 to U.S. $1 (Can$2.50 = £1 sterling). Gold, SDR's, and foreign exchange (June 1979) U.S. $3,687,000,000. Budget (1978–79 actual): revenue Can$43,550,000,000; expenditure Can$51,050,000,000. Gross national product (1978) Can$230,410,000,000. Money supply (May 1979) Can$29,460,000,000. Cost of living (1975 = 100; June 1979) 137.6

Foreign Trade. (1978) Imports Can$52,711,000,000; exports Can$54,749,000,000. Import sources: U.S. 71%; Japan 5%. Export destinations: U.S. 70%; Japan 6%. Main exports: motor vehicles 24%; machinery 7%; nonferrous metals 6%; timber 6%; chemicals 6%; newsprint 6%; cereals 5%; metal ores 5%. Tourism (1977): visitors 12,703,000; gross receipts U.S. $1,616,000,000.

Transport and Communications. Roads (main; 1975) 872,021 km. Motor vehicles in use (1976): passenger 9,016,300; commercial 2,266,400. Railways (1977): 69,967 km; traffic 2,660,000,000 passenger-km, freight 200,900,000,000 net ton-km. Air traffic (1978): 25,967,000,000 passenger-km; freight 675.8 million net ton-km. Shipping (1978): merchant vessels 100 gross tons and over 1,289; gross tonnage 2,954,499. Shipping traffic (includes Great Lakes and St. Lawrence traffic; 1977): goods loaded 119,770,000 metric tons, unloaded 58,882,000 metric tons. Telephones (Dec. 1977) 14,488,000. Radio receivers (Dec. 1976) 23.4 million. Television receivers (Dec. 1976) 9,895,000.

Agriculture. Production (in 000; metric tons; 1978): wheat 21,146; barley 10,387; oats 3,621; rye 605; corn 4,215; potatoes 2,453; tomatoes *c.* 470; apples 453; rapeseed 3,357; linseed 533; soybeans 512; tobacco 115; beef and veal 1,040; pork 615; fish catch (1977) 1,280; timber (cu m; 1977) 149,415. Livestock (in 000; Dec. 1977): cattle 12,877; sheep 392; pigs 6,714; horses (1976) *c.* 345; chickens 77,068.

Industry. Labour force (Dec. 1978) 10,871,000. Unemployment (Dec. 1978) 7.9%. Index of industrial production (1975 = 100; 1978) 115.2. Fuel and power (in 000; metric tons; 1978): coal 25,568; lignite 5,034; crude oil 64,275; natural gas (cu m) 77,200,000; electricity (kw-hr) 335,708,000 (73% hydroelectric and 6% nuclear in 1976). Metal and mineral production (in 000; metric tons; 1978): iron ore (shipments; 61% metal content) 41,942; crude steel 14,898; copper ore (metal content) 640; nickel ore (metal content) 127; zinc ore (metal content) 1,245; lead ore (metal content) 366; aluminum (exports; 1976) 508; uranium ore (metal content) 9.3; asbestos 1,422; gold (troy oz) 1,666; silver (troy oz) 40,168. Other production (in 000; metric tons; 1978): cement 10,443; wood pulp 19,013; newsprint 8,811; other paper and paperboard (1976) 3,455; sulfuric acid (1977) 3,140; plastics and resins 701; synthetic rubber 246; fertilizers (nutrient value; 1977–78) nitrogenous *c.* 1,342, phosphate *c.* 651, potash *c.* 206; passenger cars (units) 1,143; commercial vehicles (units) 675. Dwelling units completed (1978) 247,000. Merchant vessels launched (100 gross tons and over; 1978) 136,000 gross tons.

NDP. The popular vote did not show the same swing to the Tories. Of 11.2 million votes cast, the Conservatives won 36%, fractionally more than they had obtained in 1974, while the Liberals fell three points, to 40%.

The Clark government assumed office on June 4. Thirty ministers were appointed, but eight were given double portfolios. A notable feature of the Cabinet was its lack of strong representation from Quebec. Disappointed in his efforts to bring Quebecers from outside Parliament into the ministry, Clark fell back on the two Conservatives elected from the province and two Quebec senators who had sat in the former Conservative Cabinet of Diefenbaker. The most important appointments were those of John Crosbie (Finance); Flora MacDonald (External Affairs; *see* BIOGRAPHIES); Walter Baker (Privy Council president and National Revenue); Sinclair Stevens (Treasury Board); Robert de Cotret (Industry, Trade, and Commerce), and David Crombie (Health and Welfare).

Parliament did not meet until October 9, when the Clark government presented its legislative program. Many of the Conservatives' election promises were repeated, including a freedom of information law and the tax credit plan for homeowners. Eight studies into different areas of policy were promised. On key issues, such as inflation, the impending Quebec referendum on the province's future, and energy policy, the speech from the throne was silent. (*See* Special Report.)

There were four provincial elections in 1979, two in the West and two in Atlantic Canada. The results in Alberta on March 14 came as no surprise. Premier Peter Lougheed's Conservative government won 74 of the 79 seats in the legislature and polled 57% of the popular vote. In office since 1971, the Lougheed government was seen as providing sound leadership during the province's oil-based economic growth. In adjoining British Columbia, another administration of a conservative persuasion was returned. Premier William ("Bill") Bennett led his Social Credit government to a narrower victory on May 10, winning 31 of the 57 seats in the legislature. The New Democratic Party took the remainder, increasing its standing by 8 members. The old-line parties were wiped out, giving British Columbia a true two-party legislature for the first time in decades.

Canada's new governor-general, Edward R. Schreyer, and his wife, Lily, left Parliament Hill in style after his installation on January 22.

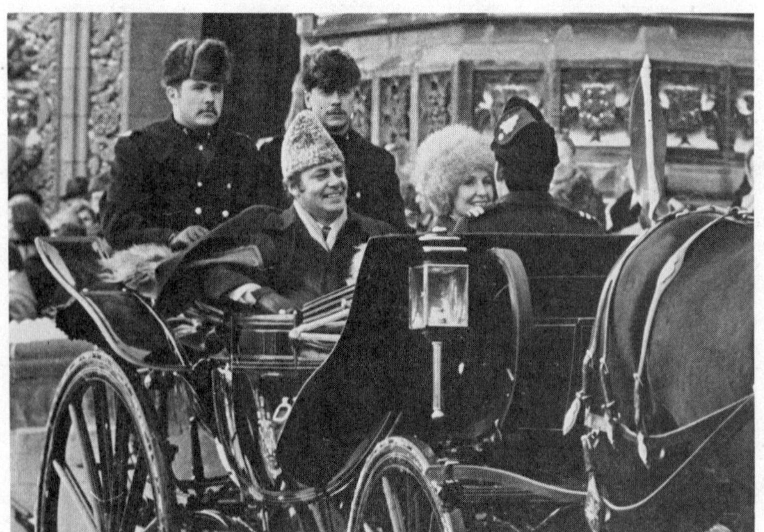

JOHN MAHONEY—OTTAWA JOURNAL/CANADIAN PRESS

The elections on the other side of Canada also revealed a trend away from the Liberals. In tiny Prince Edward Island, on April 23, the Liberal government went down to defeat, leaving Canada without a Liberal provincial government for the first time since Confederation in 1867. The Conservatives under J. Angus MacLean took 21 of the legislature's 32 seats, the Liberals under former premier Bennett Campbell the remainder. The Conservatives held their own in Newfoundland on June 18. Under a new young leader, Brian Peckford (*see* BIOGRAPHIES), who had succeeded Frank Moores as premier in March, the Conservatives were continued in power with a substantial majority. They won 33 of the legislature's 52 seats, with the Liberals, also under a new leader (Donald Jamieson, formerly Trudeau's minister for external affairs), gaining the rest.

Canada gained its 22nd governor-general when Edward R. Schreyer, former New Democratic premier of Manitoba, was sworn into office on January 22. Schreyer was the fifth native-born Canadian to hold the viceregal office.

The Economy. To no one's surprise, the economy showed a mediocre performance in 1979. Finance Minister Crosbie in September saw a real increase of between 1.5 and 3% as possible, although in fact there was a decline in real growth in the second quarter—the first such decline in three years. The gross national product was expected to rise to about Can$257 billion for the year. Inflation for the year ended in October was running at 9.3%, fueled by higher oil prices and food costs. The seasonally adjusted unemployment rate, at 7.4% in October, represented an improvement over 1978.

The slide into recession in the U.S. during 1979 hurt the Canadian economy. Exports of wood, newsprint, aluminum, and automotive products were affected, causing the merchandise trade surplus to fall to an expected $2.1 billion for the year. The current account deficit of about $7 billion was one of the largest ever recorded. In an effort to keep capital flowing into the country and to prop up the 86-cent (U.S.) Canadian dollar, the Bank of Canada raised the bank rate to 14% on October 25. This was the tenth increase in less than two years and was immediately felt in higher interest charges and mortgage rates. On September 5 Canada began issuing a bullion coin, the gold Maple Leaf, with a face value of $50 but containing one ounce of pure gold and hence with much higher market value.

In advance of its first budget, the new Conservative government revealed one of its fiscal policies, the promised plan to provide an income tax credit for mortgage interest and property tax payments to homeowners. The scheme would go into partial effect in the 1979 tax year.

The Conservative administration presented its first budget on December 11. Crosbie, stating that Canada would have to face "an era of new realism," introduced higher taxes in a number of areas, including an immediate excise tax of 18 cents a gallon on gasoline. He announced that the price of oil and natural gas would begin rising steeply for the next four years beginning on July 1, 1980. The increase in government spending was to be held to 10% with the objective of reducing the current $11.2 billion federal deficit by about $2 billion by 1983–84.

Foreign Affairs. Prime Minister Clark was introduced to summit diplomacy a few weeks after taking office. On June 24 he flew to Japan to attend an economic summit conference of the seven leading Western industrial nations. At the meeting, held June 28–29, he played a discreet role, helping, on a number of occasions, to work out compromises between U.S. and European positions. He committed Canada to reducing its annual average increase in oil consumption between 1980 and 1985 to 1%. The next month he was off to Africa—the first Canadian prime minister to visit that continent—to attend the 39-nation Commonwealth heads of government meeting in Lusaka, Zambia. The main topic of the sessions was another attempt to find a solution to the bitter conflict in Zimbabwe Rhodesia. Clark's role in the August 1–7 meeting was that of facilitator, endeavouring to promote consensus among the presidents and prime ministers in attendance.

A promise made by Clark during the heat of the election campaign haunted the new government during its first months in office. This was his pledge to move the Canadian embassy in Israel from Tel Aviv to Jerusalem. Arab states threatened an economic boycott of Canada if the government went ahead with the move. A number of contracts were affected, including a $1 billion order given to a Canadian firm to build a communications system in Saudi Arabia. As the furor grew, Clark asked his predecessor as leader of the party, Robert L. Stanfield, to conduct a fact-finding mission to the Middle East. On October 29, after Stanfield had firmly recommended against the move, Clark backed away from his election promise.

The Canadian nuclear industry suffered a severe blow on October 1 when Argentina announced that it had awarded a contract to build the first of four 600-Mw heavy water nuclear reactors to a West German-Swiss combine. Atomic Energy of Canada Ltd., with its efficient Candu reactor, had hoped to win the contract. Canada's stringent safeguards on the use of nuclear materials and technology, as well as higher-than-expected costs on a nuclear reactor sold earlier to Argentina, were believed to lie behind the decision.

The new minister for external affairs, Flora MacDonald, showed a personal commitment to human rights when she addressed the UN General Assembly on September 25. She called on the world body to establish an office of undersecretary-general to deal with gross violations of human rights. Earlier, the Clark government had announced that Canada would take up to 50,000 Indochinese refugees during 1979–80.

Reciprocal fishing in Canadian-U.S. border waters was resumed in 1979 following a "fish war" the previous year, in which each country closed its waters to the other's fishermen. An interim agreement was reached in January looking toward resolution of the differences through treaty action. The waters would be reopened, and a joint U.S.-Canada commission would set each nation's shares of an annual maximum catch for each of the major fish species. A second treaty would submit the dispute over the boundary line across the Gulf of Maine to international arbitration. The treaties were signed in late March, but ratification by the U.S. Senate was delayed because of the long hearings over the SALT II agreement. In the meantime, Canadian and U.S. fishermen continued to use their accustomed waters. In late August another dispute broke out, this time over U.S. fishermen taking albacore tuna within Canada's 200-mi fishing zone on the Pacific. U.S. tuna boats were seized, leading to a U.S. ban on tuna imports from Canada. In September the two countries agreed that they could not settle the issue before the end of the 1979 season, and, accordingly, would continue discussions into 1980.

Energy was also on the Canadian-U.S. agenda. As part of his program to reduce U.S. reliance on foreign oil, U.S. Pres. Jimmy Carter announced on July 16 that he would "insist personally" that the $14 billion Alaska Highway gas pipeline be built without further delay. The 7,680-km (4,800-mi) pipeline was already two years behind its original schedule, which called for completion in 1983. While the U.S. government was interested in a gas pipeline through Canadian territory, it was less certain about a future oil route paralleling the Alaska Highway gas line. Prime Minister Trudeau suggested this possibility on a visit to Washington to see President Carter on March 3, together with an alternative route that would connect Valdez with Skagway on the Alaskan Panhandle and then follow the Alaska Highway through the Yukon. Shortly before he left the post of U.S. energy secretary, James Schlesinger advised against a Canadian oil pipeline on the grounds that it would be more costly than a tanker route from Valdez to Port Angeles, Wash., from which oil could be transported to the East Coast via all-U.S. pipelines. Schlesinger's Northern Tier project was opposed by residents of British Columbia worried about possible environmental damage from oil spills along their coast.

Another problem on the Canadian-U.S. horizon was acid rain, caused by acid-filled clouds that drifted across the border from coal-fired power plants and industries in both countries. The toxic precipitation that resulted threatened to pollute as many as 50,000 lakes in northern Ontario and Quebec, as well as lakes in New England, over the next 20 years. Canadian and U.S. environmental officials met during the year to discuss an air-pollution agreement, but President Carter's desire to encourage conversion from oil to coal made the achievement of a treaty on the subject more difficult. (*See* ENVIRONMENT.)

Kenneth M. Curtis, a former Democratic governor of Maine, was sworn in as U.S. ambassador to Canada on September 29. President Carter's first visit to Canada was scheduled for November 9 and 10. However, the crisis over the seizure of the U.S. embassy in Teheran by Iranian militants and the holding of American hostages there forced Carter to postpone his visit to 1980. (D. M. L. FARR)

SPECIAL REPORT

CANADA—FACING THE '80s

by Peter Ward

Canada prepared to enter the decade of the 1980s with a political face radically changed from that of the 1970s. Public concern over the possible separation of Quebec from the rest of Canada had diminished considerably, and Quebec separatism had been replaced as the overriding national issue by the oil-price-induced recession that was stifling economic growth. At the same time, higher oil prices were dramatically altering Canada's economic map as the centre of prosperity shifted to the oil-rich western provinces, most notably Alberta. There had been a definite swing to the political right, exemplified by the May 22, 1979, election of a Conservative federal government headed by Prime Minister Joe Clark (*see* BIOGRAPHIES).

Canada had begun the 1970s with a Liberal administration in Ottawa and with Liberal governments in five of the ten provinces. As the 1980s dawned there was not one provincial Liberal government left, although Quebec's separatist Parti Québécois government was being threatened by a rejuvenated provincial Liberal Party. Seven of the provinces had Conservative administrations and British Columbia was headed by a right-wing Social Credit government; the left-wing New Democrats were in power in Saskatchewan.

On the federal level, Joe Clark was only the second Conservative leader to win power in Canada since 1935. Liberals had governed the country continuously from 1935 to 1979 except for 1957–63, when John Diefenbaker (*see* OBITUARIES) was prime minister. Pierre Elliott Trudeau, the man Clark defeated, had been Liberal prime minister since 1968. Clark would face the voters again on Feb. 18, 1980, following the defeat of his government in Parliament—by the combined Liberal and New Democratic Party opposition—over his austerity budget. Trudeau had announced on November 21 that he would retire, but he revoked that decision at the request of his party and would oppose Clark again in the February election.

Clark's small-town, western Canadian background —he is from High River, Alta.—was reflected in his back-to-basics value system, and his rough-hewn style contrasted strongly with Trudeau's urbane polish. He had campaigned on the basis of promises to allow more power to the provincial governments, although most analysts agreed that growing distrust of Trudeau among the electorate had been an important factor in the Liberal defeat.

Clark was sworn into office as head of a minority Conservative government on June 4, the day before his 40th birthday, making him the youngest prime minister in Canadian history. He waited until October 9 to face Parliament with his Cabinet, but even before that his government had begun to make significant changes, imprinting his administration with his small-town values. But he also made several major mistakes, and by the time defeat in Parliament came on December 13, his stock with the voters had plummeted. Public opinion polls in December showed his party 19 percentage points behind the Liberals. Discontent was highest in urban southern Ontario, which had the heaviest concentration of parliamentary seats in Canada. At year's end his immediate task was to reverse this feeling. The alternative was defeat at the hands of the Liberals.

Economics and Oil. The new federal government, with virtually no experienced ministers, had faced a grim economic prospect, especially since Conservative policies, whatever their long-term merits, could well deepen the expected recession. By late 1979 tight money policies had pushed interest rates beyond 13%, and inflation, at 9.3%, was barely under control. Canada had a gross national debt in excess of $100 billion and an expected federal deficit in 1979–80 of $10 billion.

Clark was pledged to slash 60,000 jobs from the federal payroll in three years, and he had moved to tighten Canada's generous unemployment insurance system, which costs $5 billion annually to operate. Against stiff political opposition, he planned to sell many of the large government-owned companies to private industry, including the Liberal-created, $5 billion oil company Petro-Canada. Opponents of the Petro-Canada sale insisted that the company could be used as a powerful tool in dealing with Canada's most severe problem: energy supply and pricing. Clark wanted to give one-third of the company to Canadians in the form of shares, sell another third to Canadians with a limit of 3% ownership for any individual or institution, and retain a third in the hands of the government. He claimed that Petro-Canada in its new form would be a far more effective answer to many of Canada's energy problems.

Canada is more insulated from the international oil crisis than other Western nations, because of domestic production and promising new discover-

Peter Ward operates Ward News Service in the Parliamentary Press Gallery, Ottawa.

GEORGE HUNTER—MILLER SERVICES

Harnessing the tides in the Bay of Fundy to produce electrical power has been proposed by the Canadian government as a means of reducing oil consumption.

ies. Clark set a goal for Canada of energy self-sufficiency by 1990, but his methods of attaining that goal were not popular. They included a controlled increase in the price of gasoline and diesel fuel of roughly 35 cents a gallon during the next year.

As of 1979, Canada's domestic oil production totaled 1.3 million bbl per day. Of this, 250,000 bbl per day of heavy crude were sold to the Midwestern states of the U.S. at world prices. At the same time, Canada imported 800,000 bbl per day of foreign crude, also at world prices. There was one controlled price for crude in Canada, which was $10 a barrel lower than the world price. The federal government made up the difference by subsidizing foreign oil purchases, at a cost of $5 million daily. Clark intended to raise the Canadian oil price rapidly to 85% of world levels, keeping it 15% lower than the price in Chicago.

The tactic would save the federal treasury immense amounts of money, but it would also create problems. It would mean comparable increases in the prices of other forms of energy. It would also mean billions of dollars in extra revenue for oil companies and for the producing provinces. The oil-generated wealth of the producing provinces had already given rise to regional imbalances. Alberta, by far the largest oil- and natural-gas-producing province, could afford the nation's lowest taxation rate. British Columbia and Saskatchewan had also profited from higher energy prices, but the traditional industrial regions of Ontario and Quebec, where most of the country's people live, had suffered as a result of the massive revenue transfers. The challenge facing the federal government was to find some method of using the extra energy funds for the benefit of all Canada, but without violating each province's jurisdiction over its own resources.

Critics claimed that Clark had been unwise in conceding offshore mineral resources to provincial jurisdiction. Oil and gas finds made off Newfoundland and Nova Scotia gave promise of major commercial development within ten years. Other oil and gas discoveries made above the Arctic Circle in the Beaufort Sea would also probably be developed within a decade, but Clark had pledged provincial status for the Yukon Territory, and northern Canadians could be expected to claim these new finds. Ottawa already faced hard bargaining with northern natives over land claims.

Clark had hoped to recycle large portions of oil and gas revenue into the construction of refineries to extract oil from the Athabaska Tar Sands in northern

CANADIAN PRESS

Quebec's Liberal leader Claude Ryan sparked a resurgence of the Liberal Party in the province by winning a seat in the Quebec National Assembly on April 30.

Alberta, which have an estimated potential of some 700,000,000,000 bbl. Two extraction plants were already operating, with a combined production of 200,000 bbl of oil daily, and two more were being developed. Part of Clark's energy strategy included switching domestic energy consumption away from oil to natural gas. Canada has a surplus of natural gas in the West, and large contracts were approved in late 1979 for the sale of gas to the U.S.

The federal government also hoped to reduce oil consumption substantially by substituting such renewable energy sources as solar power and hydropower. There was no intention of abandoning plans for the future growth of nuclear power. Other energy schemes likely to be started within ten years included harnessing the tides in the Bay of Fundy, exploitation of geothermal power in the Prairie Provinces, and shipment of liquefied natural gas from Arctic deposits to southern markets by tanker. A successful energy policy would be vital to Canadian economic recovery and national unity.

The Quebec Problem. In the spring of 1980, Quebec's separatist premier, René Lévesque, would hold a provincial referendum on the negotiation of a "sovereignty association" with Canada. Militant Parti Québécois backers who favoured outright separation of the province from the Canadian confederation lacked sufficient support among the Quebec electorate to gain approval for independence without some form of economic association. However, Lévesque and his Cabinet felt they might win a referendum mandate giving them power to negotiate economic association combined with political sovereignty.

Even with the referendum taking shape, the Quebec situation appeared less volatile than in previous years. A public opinion survey taken in August 1979 showed that only 29% of Quebecers thought Canada would break up, compared with 47% who held that opinion in 1969. Gallup reported that only 18% of Canadians coast to coast believed Canada would split, the smallest number to foresee the country's breakup since 1945.

Part of the reason for the change was the resurgence of the Quebec Liberals under Claude Ryan, who espoused a form of Catholic conservatism. Ryan had succeeded in exorcising the old image of corruption in the Quebec Liberal Party, and many considered him to be the potential winner in the next Quebec election, which would have to be held before the end of 1981. In many ways, Ryan was as much of a Quebec nationalist as Lévesque, but he wanted increased powers for Quebec within a federal system—an idea that meshed well with Clark's ideas about increased provincial rights.

Outlook for the Future. Assuming Clark's minority government could regain power—at dissolution he held 133 seats in the 282-seat House of Commons—a considerable decentralization of Canadian federal power could be expected, along with a withdrawal of federal influence from business. Clark pledged more Canadian support for NATO, but his defense policy would be inhibited by lack of funds for new weapons as his government sought to end deficit spending. Social programs constructed by Liberal governments were also likely to suffer, although Clark has the reputation of being a left-wing Conservative. He hoped to involve back-bench members of Parliament more directly in the decision-making process through committee work, thereby moving Canada more toward the U.S. style of government.

The most visible change for Canadians during the brief Clark term was the switch in leadership, from a highly charismatic international figure—Pierre Trudeau—to a younger man who drinks Coke with dinner and considers as his greatest asset the ability to bring opposing points of view together into constructive compromise. The ability of all Canadians to effect compromise would be put to the test in 1980, with Canada's future at stake.

Cape Verde

An independent African republic, Cape Verde is located in the Atlantic Ocean about 620 km (385 mi) off the west coast of Africa. Area: 4,033 sq km (1,557 sq mi). Pop. (1979 est.): 317,000. Cap.: Praia (pop., 1970, 21,500). Largest city: Mindelo (pop., 1970, 28,800). Language: Portuguese. Religion: mainly Roman Catholic. President in 1979, Aristide Pereira; premier, Maj. Pedro Pires.

Pres. Aristide Pereira of Cape Verde attended the first meeting of heads of state of five former Portuguese African colonies, which ended in Luanda, Angola, on June 11, 1979. At the summit the leaders of Cape Verde, Angola, Mozambique, Guinea-Bissau, and São Tomé and Príncipe sought more effective cooperation to overcome their countries' economic dependence and agreed to adopt identical plans for economic and social development. A ministerial coordinating committee was to be set up, based in Luanda.

President Pereira visited East Berlin in May and signed two cooperation agreements. In the same month a similar agreement was made with a French aid agency.

The first national assembly of women of Guinea-Bissau and Cape Verde was held at Bissau in June. Its aim was to campaign for improvement in the conditions for women, including an end to forced and early marriages.

The 1979 budget was 50 million escudos higher than the 1,277,000,000 escudo budget for 1978 but was more austere. The islands had suffered from repeated droughts, and the banana crop, the sole export, had declined. (R. M. GOODWIN)

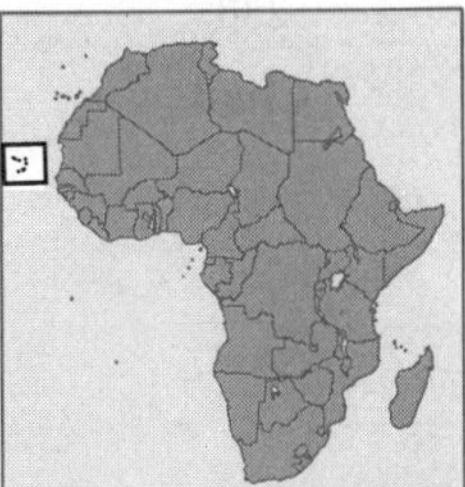
Cape Verde

CAPE VERDE

Education. (1977–78) Primary, pupils 55,406, teachers 1,269; secondary, pupils 6,045, teachers 256; vocational, pupils 782, teachers 43; teacher training, pupils 198, teachers (1976–77) 32.

Finance and Trade. Monetary unit: escudo Caboverdiano, with (Sept. 17, 1979) a free rate of 36.51 escudos to U.S. $1 (78.55 escudos = £1 sterling). Budget (total; 1974 est.): revenue 683.9 million escudos; expenditure 903.2 million escudos. Foreign trade (1976): imports 911.4 million escudos; exports 48,030,000 escudos (excluding transit trade). Import sources: Portugal 58%; The Netherlands 5%. Export destinations: Portugal 63%; Angola 14%; Zaire 5%; U.K. 5%. Main exports: fish 29% (including shellfish 16%); bananas 19%; salt 9%.

Transport. Shipping traffic (1976): goods loaded 18,000 metric tons, unloaded 161,000 metric tons.

Central African Republic

The landlocked Central African Republic is bounded by Chad, the Sudan, the Congo, Zaire, and Cameroon. Area: 624,977 sq km (241,305 sq mi). Pop. (1979 est.): 2,305,000. Cap. and largest city: Bangui (pop., 1979 est., 350,000). Language: French (official); local dialects. Religion: animist 60%; Christian 35%; Muslim 5%. Emperor until Sept. 20, 1979, Bokassa I; president from September 26, David Dacko; premiers, Henri Maïdou and, from September 26, Bernard Ayandho.

CENTRAL AFRICAN REPUBLIC

Education. (1975–76) Primary, pupils 221,412, teachers 3,329; secondary, pupils 21,509, teachers 515; vocational, pupils 1,771, teachers (1973–74) 141; teacher training, students 615, teachers 47; higher, students 555, teaching staff 85.

Finance. Monetary unit: CFA franc, with (Sept. 17, 1979) a parity of CFA Fr 50 to the French franc and a free rate of CFA Fr 211.54 to U.S. $1 (CFA Fr 455.12 = £1 sterling). Budget (total; 1977 est.) balanced at CFA Fr 21,975,000,000.

Foreign Trade. (1978) Imports CFA Fr 12,776,000,000; exports CFA Fr 16,182,000,000. Import sources (1977): France 55%; West Germany 7%; Japan 5%. Export destinations (1977): France 63%; Belgium-Luxembourg 16%. Main exports (1976): coffee 34%; timber 24%; diamonds 17%; cotton 17%.

Agriculture. Production (in 000; metric tons; 1978): millet *c.* 40; corn (1977) *c.* 37; sweet potatoes (1977) *c.* 62; cassava (1977) *c.* 900; peanuts *c.* 133; bananas *c.* 74; plantains (1977) *c.* 61; coffee *c.* 10; cotton, lint *c.* 11. Livestock (in 000; 1977): cattle *c.* 620; pigs *c.* 63; sheep *c.* 77; goats *c.* 577; chickens *c.* 1,276.

Industry. Production (in 000; 1976): diamonds (metric carats) *c.* 405; cotton fabrics (m; 1974) 6,000; electricity (kw-hr) 53,000.

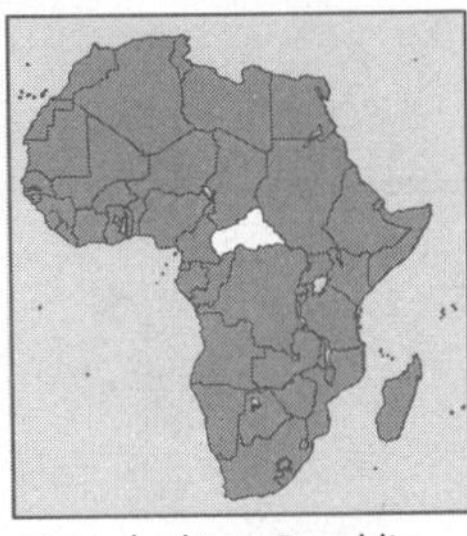
Central African Republic

Nearly 14 years of Central African tyranny ended on Sept. 20, 1979, when French paratroops restored former president David Dacko (*see* BIOGRAPHIES) as chief of state in place of Emperor Bokassa I, who was absent in Libya and flew to France before finding refuge in the Ivory Coast. The government set up on September 26 by Dacko, with Bernard Ayandho as premier, reestablished the republic. Popular discontent in the capital, Bangui, was serious. In spite of its renewed aid France was disliked, because of the manner of Dacko's reinstatement, the continued presence of French troops, France's refusal at first to allow former premier Ange Patassé to return from Paris, and the exposure of the close relations between Bokassa and French Pres. Valéry Giscard d'Es-

A statue of Jean-Bédel Bokassa, who called himself Emperor Bokassa I, was pulled from its pedestal in Bangui after Bokassa was overthrown in September.

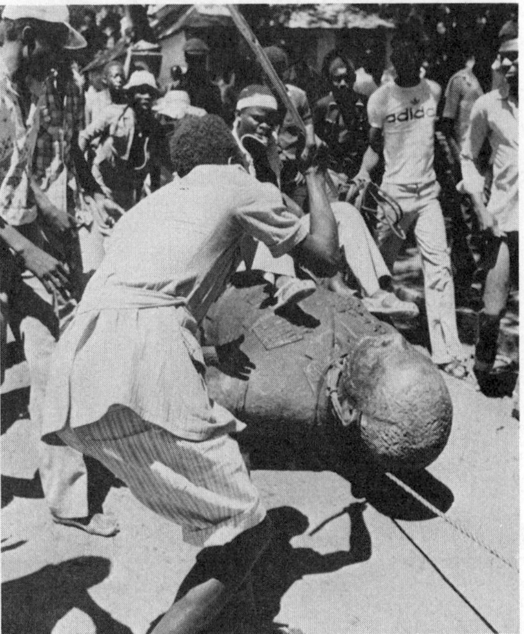
NADAL—SIPA PRESS/BLACK STAR

Canadian Literature: see Literature

Canoeing: see Water Sports

Catholic Church: see Religion

Cave Exploration: see Speleology

Census Data: see Demography; *see also the individual country articles*

Central America: see Latin-American Affairs; *articles on the various countries*

Ceramics: see Materials Sciences

Ceylon: see Sri Lanka

taing. Dacko also was strongly criticized because he did not summon Abel Goumba, in opposition in exile in Benin, and because, after a trial of strength at the end of October between government and Patassé supporters, he ordered Patassé's imprisonment.

The downfall of Bokassa's empire began with demonstrations by students and schoolchildren on January 19 and 20 against an order to wear new uniforms (made in a factory owned by the emperor); the Army intervened, and many died and many more were wounded. In March Barthélémy Yangongo, minister of information, was imprisoned, and Bokassa escaped an attempt on his life.

On May 14 Amnesty International denounced the massacre of over 100 schoolchildren in Bangui by the Imperial Guard on April 18. Bokassa denied that any massacre had occurred, but Gen. Sylvestre Bangui, Central African ambassador in Paris, confirmed it and gave up his post. By July four opposition movements had coordinated themselves in Paris. Bokassa's last vestiges of credit disappeared when five African judges visited Bangui and concluded in August that the personal participation of the emperor in the assault, which had caused "between 50 and 200 deaths," was "almost certain." (PHILIPPE DECRAENE)

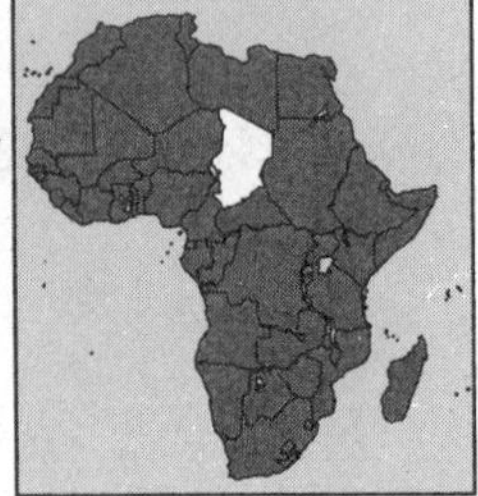

Chad

Chad

A landlocked republic of central Africa, Chad is bounded by Libya, the Sudan, the Central African Republic, Cameroon, Nigeria, and Niger. Area: 1,284,000 sq km (495,755 sq mi). Pop. (1978 est.): 4,309,000, including Saras, other Africans, and Arabs. Cap. and largest city: N'Djamena (pop., 1978 est., 281,000). Language: French (official). Religion: Muslim 45%; animist 45%; Christian 10%. President in 1979, Brig. Gen. Félix Malloum until March 23; premier, Hissen Habré until March 23; chairmen of the provisional government, Goukouni Oueddei from March 23, Lol Mohamed Shawa from April 29, and, from August 22, Goukouni Oueddei.

The political and military conflict in Chad, intensified by foreign interference, reached new heights in 1979. In January Premier Hissen Habré, a Muslim from northern Chad, and Pres. Félix Malloum, a Christian from the south, quarreled over the provisions of the August 1978 reconciliation charter. An attack by the national police on Habré's house in N'Djamena on February 12 led to violent fighting between the Chad National Army (ANT) and Habré's Armed Forces of the North

CHAD

Education. (1976–77) Primary, pupils *c.* 220,700, teachers *c.* 2,620; secondary, pupils 18,382, teachers 590; vocational, pupils 649, teachers (1965–66) 30; teacher training, students 549, teachers (1973–74) 26; higher, students (1975–76) 547, teaching staff (1974–75) 94.

Finance. Monetary unit: CFA franc, with (Sept. 17, 1979) a parity of CFA Fr 50 to the French franc and a free rate of CFA Fr 211.54 to U.S. $1 (CFA Fr 455.12 = £1 sterling). Budget (total; 1978 est.) balanced at CFA Fr 17,084,000,000.

Foreign Trade. (1976) Imports CFA Fr 28,111,000,000; exports CFA Fr 14,861,000,000. Import sources (1975): France 37%; Nigeria 10%; The Netherlands 7%; U.S. 6%; U.K. 5%; Cameroon 5%. Export destinations (1975): Nigeria 20%; France 7%; Congo 5%. Main exports (1975): cotton 69%; meat 6%.

Agriculture. Production (in 000; metric tons; 1978): millet *c.* 580; sweet potatoes (1977) *c.* 46; cassava (1977) *c.* 59; peanuts *c.* 85; beans, dry *c.* 45; dates *c.* 25; mangoes *c.* 29; cotton, lint *c.* 54; meat *c.* 50; fish catch (1977) *c.* 115. Livestock (in 000; 1977): horses *c.* 145; asses *c.* 300; camels *c.* 316; cattle *c.* 3,716; sheep *c.* 2,448; goats *c.* 2,448.

Thousands of non-Muslims fled from N'Djamena when violence broke out between warring factions.

DANIEL SIMON—GAMMA/LIAISON

(FAN). This conflict spread beyond N'Djamena to the countryside, where the guerrillas of the National Liberation Front (Frolinat), itself divided, controlled three-quarters of the nation. After the death of four French civilians, French paratroops intervened, joining the 2,000 French troops and 400 permanent military advisers with ANT in N'Djamena. On February 19, a truce between ANT and FAN was signed, the French now supporting Habré. In the face of Frolinat demands, France agreed on March 20 to withdraw its forces gradually.

The truce could not resolve the deep tribal and religious crisis. Conferences at Kano, Nigeria, in March and April, and at Lagos, Nigeria, in May and August were variously attended by 11 Chad groups and by Niger, Nigeria, Cameroon, Central African Republic, Libya, and Sudan. The meeting at Kano produced a cease-fire and an agreement by Malloum and Habré to resign their offices and turn the government over to a provisional state council headed by Frolinat leader Goukouni Oueddei (*see* BIOGRAPHIES), a Muslim. This government was formed on March 23. It was succeeded by a provisional government headed by Lol Mohamed Shawa on April 29. At Lagos on August 21 the 11 Chad groups signed an agreement providing for a transitional government of national union under Oueddei's presidency. After further negotiations this was formed on November 10.

Meanwhile, in May Nigeria refused to supply Chad with petroleum. In late June Libyan troops began an offensive into Chad, but they were driven back early in July. (PHILIPPE DECRAENE)

Chemistry

Solar energy research sparked a surge of activity in photoelectrochemistry during the past year. Many new applications were found for lasers, and chemists made important discoveries concerning the origin of life on Earth.

Organic Chemistry. Several important scientists were in the news. U.S. chemist and Nobel laureate Robert Woodward died in July (*see* OBITUARIES), but his major contributions, including the synthesis of quinine, cortisone, chlorophyll, and vitamin B_{12}, would not be forgotten. Another Nobel laureate, Italian polymer chemist Giulio Natta (*see* OBITUARIES), died in May. In October Georg Wittig of the University of Heidelberg in West Germany and Herbert Brown of Purdue University, West Lafayette, Ind., won the Nobel Prize for Chemistry for their development, respectively, of synthetically useful phosphorus compounds

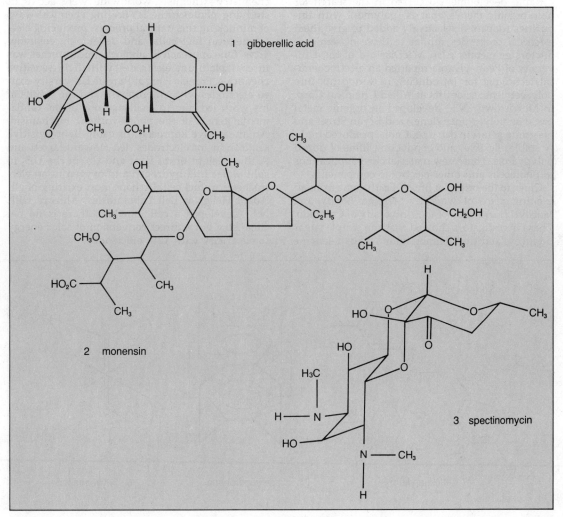

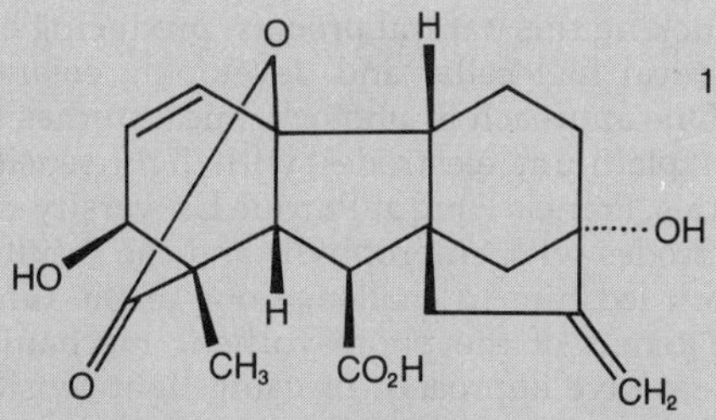

1 gibberellic acid

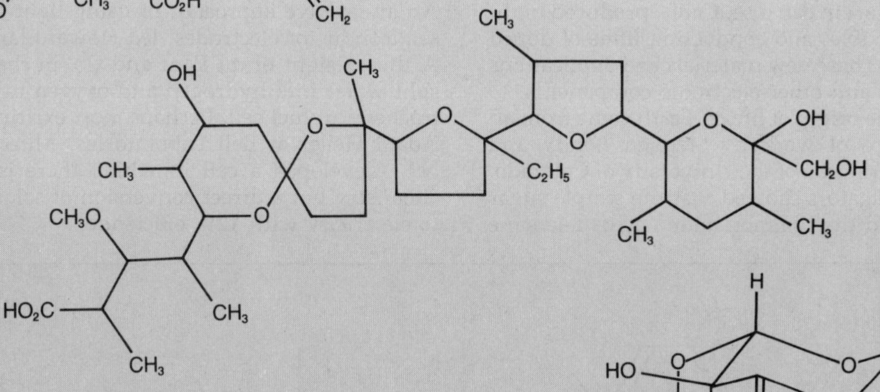

2 monensin

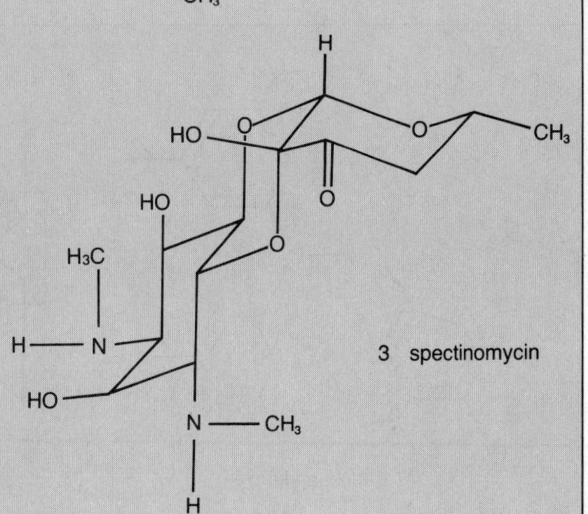

3 spectinomycin

Chemical Industry: *see* Industrial Review

(ylids) and boron reagents, particularly sodium borohydride (*see* NOBEL PRIZES).

The most imaginative syntheses of recent months came from Harvard University: Elias Corey and collaborators prepared gibberellic acid (1), a plant hormone that controls stem elongation, and Yoshito Kishi and his team cleverly engineered the construction of monensin (2), a polyether antibiotic that alleviates the effects of cardiac muscle failure during heart attacks. Other newly synthesized drugs include the anti-tumour agents adriamycin and daunomycin. Spectinomycin (3), prepared by David R. White of Upjohn Co., Kalamazoo, Mich., is a drug often used for treating penicillin-resistant gonorrhea.

Syntheses of exciting and unusual structures that helped in understanding chemical bonding included those of a hexaarylethane (4) by Anton Rieker and co-workers at the University of Tübingen in West Germany and Virgil Boekelheide's remarkable molecule superphane (5), which the University of Oregon chemist compared to two insects joined through their legs. James Marshall of Northwestern University, Evanston, Ill., christened his new class of compounds betweenanenes (6) because the double bond is sandwiched between two methylene bridges on opposite sides of the molecule.

Rapid development occurred in the search for new organic metals; that is, polymers with impurities (dopants) selectively added to give them electrical properties similar to those of semiconductors or metals. Alan MacDiarmid of the University of Pennsylvania reported an electrochemical technique for introducing new dopants into polyacetylene; scientists at Allied Chemical Corp. in Morristown, N.J., developed an organic metal based on poly(*p*-phenylene); and Bryan Street and his group at IBM in San Jose, Calif., produced highly stable, flexible, and conducting films of doped polypyrrole. These new materials had applications to photocells and other electronic components.

Clues to the origin of life on Earth came from an exciting piece of work by Stephen Bondy and Marilyn Harrington of the University of Colorado. These investigators showed that the simple sugar D-glucose and the common amino acids L-leucine and L-aspartate bind stereospecifically (*i.e.*, with great dependence on the spatial arrangement of the atoms in the molecule) to a colloidal clay, bentonite, whereas no binding was evident for the biologically uncommon enantiomers, such as L-glucose, which are the mirror images of their more abundant twins. The difference in the ability to be absorbed onto a solid surface was thought to increase the possibility that certain isomers were selected to participate in the complex chemistry preceding the first appearance of living organisms.

Prebiological formation of amino acids has been the subject of study for more than 20 years. In May, Allen Bard of the University of Texas at Austin reported that reactions involving the illumination of semiconductor pellets (platinized n-TiO_2), in an ammonia solution through which methane was being bubbled, amazingly produced the amino acids glycine, alanine, serine, aspartic acid, and glutamic acid. Bard suggested that, although such "molecular cells" of platinum and titanium dioxide would not have been around eons ago, semiconducting oxides of iron or tungsten might have served as a rudimentary form of photosynthesis until biological photosynthetic systems based on chlorophyll evolved.

Physical Chemistry. The need for novel energy sources stimulated research into photoelectrochemistry. Chemists worldwide were active in studying photosynthesis, finding chemical ways of mimicking this natural process, producing electrochemical fuel cells, and developing solar devices. One approach in photochemical studies was to coat platinum electrodes with light-sensitive chemicals. Francis Fong at Purdue University coated electrodes with chlorophyll, and the results of his work led him to challenge one of the fundamental tenets of the photosynthetic mechanism. An alternative approach, of using light-sensitive semiconductor electrodes, led Howard Jarrett and Arthur Sleight of du Pont and Co. in the U.S. to split water into hydrogen and oxygen in an electrochemical fuel cell. Perhaps most exciting of all, Adam Heller at Bell Laboratories, Murray Hill, N.J., developed a cell in which there is no net chemistry but a direct conversion of solar energy to electricity with 12% efficiency.

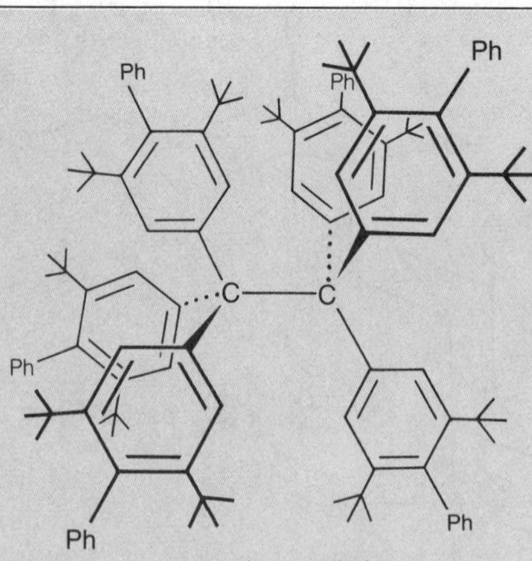

Ph Ph Ph C C Ph Ph Ph

$(CH_2)_a$ C C $(CH_2)_b$

4 hexaarylethane 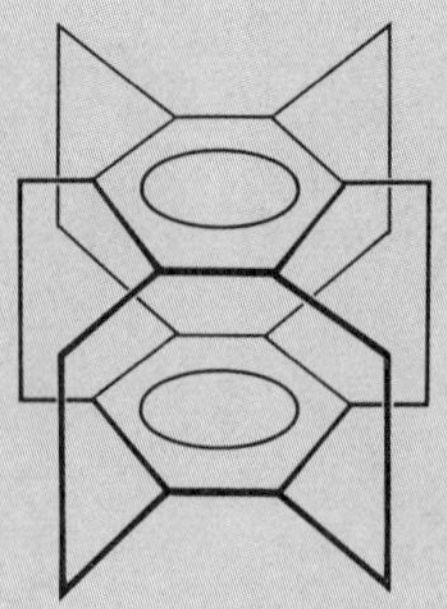 5 superphane 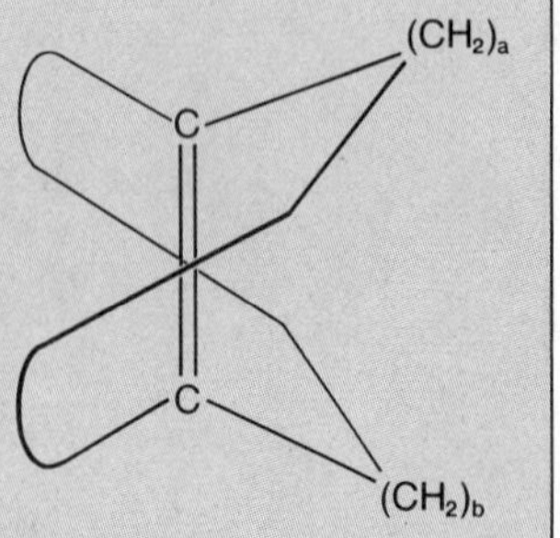 6 betweenanene

Ph = phenyl group

Despite numerous studies into solar energy conversion, efforts were not spared to improve the utilization of such sources as coal. Robert Coughlin and Mohammad Farooque of the University of Connecticut made news in June with their announcement of a room-temperature electrochemical process that generates high-purity hydrogen from a coal/water slurry at costs competitive with conventional coal gasification.

Inorganic Chemistry. Progress was made in understanding noble gas chemistry when Konrad Seppelt and Dieter Lorenz of the University of Heidelberg synthesized the xenon compound $Xe(OTeF_5)_6$. Its red-violet colour was a key to the bonding in many of the approximately 80 other xenon compounds that had been made since 1962. These chemists also proposed that KrF_2 is likely to be the only stable compound of krypton.

In the field of nonaqueous chemistry, chemists were examining applications for alkalide salts—those containing singly negative ions of sodium, potassium, rubidium, or cesium—in semiconductor or photoelectric devices. Late in 1978, William Peer at the University of Texas persuaded gold, which normally forms Au^{2+} in solution, to become Au^- in a liquid ammonia solution containing cesium. A fascinating variety of ions with curious oxidation states was found by Gary Schrobilgen of Guelph University in Ontario, who dissolved tellurium and selenium in disulfuric acid (65% fuming sulfuric acid). Nuclear magnetic resonance (NMR) studies confirmed the existence of such ions as $Te_2Se_4^{2+}$, Te_4^{2+}, and Te_6^{4+} with $\frac{1}{3}$, $\frac{1}{2}$, and $\frac{2}{3}$ oxidation states and helped solve the 150-year-old mystery of the nature of these brightly coloured solutions.

Emphasis in transition metal chemistry remained on metal cluster compounds, which are molecules containing metal atoms bonded together into triangular or polyhedral arrays. Leading this field were Earl Muetterties at Cornell University, Ithaca, N.Y., who carried out a major review of the known cluster compounds, especially their relationship to the surfaces of bulk metal in chemisorption and catalytic properties, and F. Albert Cotton of Texas A&M University, College Station, who was searching for compounds, such as $Cr_2[(CH_2)_2P(CH_3)_2]_4$, with an extremely short chromium-chromium quadruple bond.

A new understanding of the nature of perhaps the most important inorganic chemical known to man, water, could come from the work of Wolfram Saenger at the Max Planck Institute in Göttingen, West Germany. Using X-ray and neutron scattering techniques he found five- and six-membered hydrogen-bonded rings in crystals of alpha-cyclodextrin$\cdot 6H_2O$, a complex of six linked glucose molecules and six water molecules. He suggested that these rings might help explain the flickering cluster structure of liquid water. Also of interest was the characterization, by Gheorghe Mateeson and George Benedikt of Case Western Reserve University, Cleveland, Ohio, of the structure of protonated water, H_3O^+. Its arrangement had been thought to be tetrahedral, but this new work confirmed a planar arrangement of hydrogens around the central oxygen.

Inorganic chemists at the Library of Congress Preservation Office made news by developing a process, using diethyl zinc vapour, that could deacidify old paper. A successful large-scale treatment technique based on this process could extend the lives of the millions of books that are deteriorating (by acid hydrolysis of the cellulose in the paper) in libraries throughout the world.

Analytical Chemistry. In recent years the combination of lasers with optical, acoustical, and electronic instrumentation has produced extremely sensitive analytical techniques. Laser microprobe techniques were used to analyze fluid inclusions in geological samples, study the quality of industrial glass, and assist in pollution monitoring. Laser fluorimetry was employed by Richard Zare and colleagues at Stanford University to detect a mere 750 femtograms (750×10^{-15} g) of a toxin, the potent carcinogen aflatoxin B_{2A}, in moldy corn sent to them by the U.S. Department of Agriculture. One laser technique of possible use to police in forensic analysis was developed by Control Laser Corp. of Orlando, Fla., and can reveal, by luminescence, fingerprints on many substances, including human skin.

In the past year chemists mapped the distribution of organic compounds in tiny samples of plant tissue, monitored concentrations of the radioactive gas radon in groundwater to help in earthquake predictions, and determined if 20,000-year-old flint implements had been heated to improve their working properties. They also confirmed that the Plate of Brass, a postcard-sized relic discovered in California in 1936 that bears an inscription by Sir Francis Drake, was of an alloy unknown in the 16th century and, therefore, a fake.

Most newsworthy was the analysis of a mere three millilitres of water on April 11 at Oak Ridge (Tenn.) National Laboratory. The sample was primary coolant water from the nuclear reactor at Three Mile Island in Pennsylvania, which had experienced accidental overheating of the reactor core. Within 36 hours Oak Ridge analytical chemists had used several instrumental techniques to determine levels of uranium, boron, plutonium, sodium, and lithium; the isotopic distributions of uranium, plutonium, and lithium; the pH; gross radioactivity; activities of 20 radioisotopes; and the presence and concentrations within certain limits of 23 other elements. It was from the results of these analyses that the severity of the accident could be scientifically assessed by the U.S. Department of Energy and the Nuclear Regulatory Commission and early corrective action taken to safeguard nearby populated areas.

(GORDON WILKINSON)

See also Materials Sciences; Nobel Prizes.
[121.B.1.e; 121.B.9; 122.A; 122.D–E; 122.G–H; 312.A.2]

Chess

It had become apparent in the late 1970s that the Soviet Union was no longer producing the wealth of young chess talent that it had in the previous quarter of a century. True, in September 1978, the Soviet master Sergey Dolmatov won the world ju-

WIDE WORLD

Peter Biyiasas (left), grand master from San Francisco, matched his skills against a computer in games played in Chicago. The computer was monitored by David Cahlander (top right) of Control Data Corp. (of Minneapolis, Minn., where the computer was located) and David Slate (right) of Northwestern University. Biyiasas won one game and the computer won one.

nior championship, but in the same month England won the first world youth (under 26) team championship at Mexico City ahead of the U.S.S.R. and beat the Soviet team in their individual match by 3–1.

Also in September 1978 the second Interpolis Grandmaster tournament at Tilburg, Neth., was won by Lajos Portisch (Hungary). Whereas Anatoly Karpov (U.S.S.R.) was so tired that he refrained from chess activity for some months after his narrow victory in the world championship in 1978 over Viktor Korchnoi, the latter resumed play immediately and, playing for Switzerland in the Olympiad at Buenos Aires, Arg., made the best score on top board (9 out of 11). However, Hungary won the Olympiad.

The Soviet championship tournament, held in December 1978, resulted in a tie between ex-world champion Mikhail Tal and Vitaly Tseshkovsky. But the most impressive performance was that of the 15-year-old schoolboy Garry Kasparov, who finished ninth; in April 1979 Kasparov won first prize at Banja Luka, Yugos., two points ahead of Ulf Andersson (Sweden) and Jan Smejkal (Czech.). Andersson had a good tournament year, finishing first at the Clarin tournament at Buenos Aires after the Olympiad there in November. He also won the Hastings Premier Tournament (December 1978–January 1979).

The European junior championship at Groningen, Neth., was won by John van der Wiel (Neth.), ahead of Dolmatov. The under-17 world championship, also held at that time at Sas van Gent, Neth., was won by Paul Motwani (Scotland) with the 14-year-old English boy prodigy Nigel Short finishing third.

Lev Polugaevsky (U.S.S.R.) won the Wijk aan Zee grand master tournament in The Netherlands in January 1979. Two international tournaments played at Tallinn, U.S.S.R., in January and February were won by Soviet grand master Boris Gulko and ex-world champion Tigran Petrosian (U.S.S.R), respectively. Korchnoi tied for first place with Ljubomir Ljubojevic (Yugos.) at São Paulo, Brazil, in February. An international tournament at Munich, West Germany, in March resulted in a four-way tie for first place between Vladimir Liberzon (Israel), Florian Gheorghiu (Rom.), Svetozar Gligoric (Yugos.), and Vlastimil Hort (Czech.).

Karpov did play in one of the strongest tournaments ever to be held, at Montreal from April 10 to May 7. This was a double-round event and was rated category 15, the highest rating ever. The world champion tied with Tal for first place with 12 points, followed by Portisch 10½, Ljubojevic 9, and Boris Spassky (U.S.S.R.) and Jan Timman (Neth.) 8½. On May 11–12 Werner Hug (Switz.) broke the simultaneous display record by playing against 560 opponents at Emmenbrücke, Switz., winning 385, drawing 126, and losing 49 games. Another strong tournament, held in June at Bled-Portoroz, Yugos., was won by Timman, a point ahead of Zoltan Ribli (Hung.) and Bent Larsen (Den.). A strong tournament, the World Open, was held in New York City from June 30 to July 4 and ended in a seven-way tie for first place between Tony Miles (England), Walter Browne, Arthur Bisguier, John Fedorowicz, and Bernard Zuckerman (all U.S.), Gheorghiu, and Haukur Angantysson (Iceland).

England won the Clare Benedict (West European) Team Tournament held at Middlesborough, England, in July. There was a tie for first place at the world under-17 championship at Belfort, France, between Marcelo Temponi (Arg.) and Short. The title went to Temponi on a superior point count. Karpov won a quadrangular grand master tournament at Waddinxveen (Neth.).

The 1979 world junior championship tournament took place at Skien, Norway, in July–August and was won by Yasser Seirawan (U.S.). In August Short figured in a three-way tie between Robert Bellin and John Nunn in the British championship

English Opening Riga Interzonal, 1979.

White	Black	White	Black
L. Polugaevsky	M. Tal	L. Polugaevsky	M. Tal
1 N–KB3	P–QB4	16 R–QN1	B–N2 (e)
2 P–B4	N–KB3	17 N–N5	QxP
3 N–B3	P–Q4	18 Q–K3 (f)	KR–B1
4 PxP	NxP	19 R–B1	P–N5
5 P–K4	N–N5 (a)	20 N–R4	NxP
6 B–B4	B–K3	21 N–N6 (g)	R–Q6
7 BxB	N–Q6 ch (b)	22 N–R3	Q–R5
8 K–B1	PxB	23 Q–K1	R(Q6)–KB6
9 N–KN5	Q–N3 (c)	24 NxR	N–Q6
10 Q–K2? (d)	P–B5	25 Q–Q1 (h)	QxP
11 P–QN3	P–KR3	26 RxR	PxR ch
12 N–B3	N–B3	27 K–B1	Q–B4
13 PxP	0–0–0	28 K–N1	B–Q5 ch
14 P–N3	P–N4	White resigns	
15 K–N2	Q–B4		

(a) 5 ..., NxN; 6 NPxN, P–KN3; used to be played, leading to a type of Grunfeld Defense after 7 P–Q4; but it was then discovered that 6 QPxN, QxQ ch; 7 KxQ, N–B3; 8 B–K3, P–K3; 9 K–B2, was in White's favour. (b) And not 7 ..., PxB; 8 0–0, QN–B3; 9 N–KN5, Q–Q2; 10 Q–N4, N–Q5; 11 P–B4, P–KN3; 12 P–K5, Q–B3; 13 N–K2, NxN ch; 14 QxN, N–B7; 15 R–N1, N–Q5; 16 Q–K4, when White has a considerable advantage (Golombek-Dykstra, Leeuwarden, 1947). (c) An innovation suggested to Tal by his trainer Kapengut. Simple development leaves the initiative in White's hands, *e.g.*, 9 ..., N–B3; 10 NxKP, Q–Q2; 11 NxP! NxN; 12 Q–R5 ch, P–N3; 13 QxN, Q–Q6 ch; 14 K–N1, B–N2; 15 Q–QN5, R–Q1; 16 QxQ, RxQ; 17 K–B1, 0–0; 18 K–K2, R–Q2; 19 P–B3 (Rimman-Stean, Amsterdam, 1978). (d) This obvious move is bad; instead correct was 10 Q–B3. (e) Black, with all his pieces in attacking positions, has emerged from the opening in complete control of the initiative, a situation in which Tal is in his element. (f) Black was threatening to win the Queen by N–B5 ch. (g) If 21 RxN, RxR ch; 22 QxR (22 KxR, R–B1 ch wins for Black) 22 ..., QxP ch; picks up the White Rook. (h) If 25 Q–K2, then comes the delightful variation 25 ..., N–Q5; 26 Q–Q1, QxQ; 27 RxQ, R–B7 ch; 28 K–R1, N–B6 with mate to follow.

at Chester, but the title went to Bellin on a superior point count.

In the first interzonal tournament from each of which three players would qualify for the candidates' matches in 1980, at Riga, U.S.S.R., in August and September, Tal won with the high total of 14; other qualifiers were Polugaevsky and Andreas Adorjan (Hung.). In the second, at Rio de Janeiro, Brazil, in September and October, Portisch, Petrosian, and Hubner qualified. In the women's interzonal at Rio de Janeiro, Nana Joseliani (U.S.S.R) easily outdistanced the field with 14½ points, and the other two qualifiers were Zsuzsa Veroci (Hung.) and Nana Alexandria (U.S.S.R.). The qualifiers from the other women's interzonal, held at Alicante, Spain, in October and November, were Elena Ahmilovskaya (U.S.S.R.), Tatiana Lematchko (Bulg.), and Nino Gurieli (U.S.S.R.). (HARRY GOLOMBEK)

Chile

A republic extending along the southern Pacific coast of South America, Chile has an area of 756,626 sq km (292,135 sq mi), not including its Antarctic claim. It is bounded by Argentina, Bolivia, and Peru. Pop. (1979 est.): 10,917,500. Cap. and largest city: Santiago (metro. pop., 1979 est., 3,763,400). Language: Spanish. Religion: predominantly Roman Catholic. President in 1979, Gen. Augusto Pinochet Ugarte.

In a joint declaration on Jan. 8, 1979, Chile agreed with Argentina to accept the mediation of Pope John Paul II in their Beagle Channel islands dispute and to refrain from hostilities in connection with it. During the same month Gen. David Padilla, head of the Bolivian military junta, stated that about 30 Chileans had been expelled from his country on suspicion of espionage. The year 1979 was the 100th anniversary of the war in which Bolivia lost territory and access to the sea to Chile. Bolivia had been attempting to reacquire some of this territory by negotiation.

On January 3 Chile's military government, through its new labour minister, José Piñera Echenique, offered a plan to restore normal labour union activities, restricted since the September 1973 coup that brought the military to power. The offer was an apparent attempt to avert an international boycott of Chilean trade. The measures included abrogation of a five-year ban on scheduling union meetings without police approval, the holding of new union elections, and the permitting of collective bargaining for new contracts after June 30.

Subsequently, the Inter-American Regional Labour Organization (ORIT), active in 28 countries, put off indefinitely a trade boycott of Chile, Nicaragua, and Cuba. Although union leaders in Chile protested that the reforms were being selectively implemented, ORIT decided to give Chile's president, Gen. Augusto Pinochet Ugarte, time to put them into effect.

Despite continued criticism of the government's conservative fiscal policies, both from domestic opponents and from international organizations that claimed such policies placed an undue burden on the poor, the government enjoyed substantial success in this area. A number of multinational companies that had either had their factories nationalized or had left the country during the leftist government of former president Salvador Allende, began to return to Chile. Most prominent among them was Anaconda Co., which in May announced the purchase of a $20 million copper ore property, Los Pelambres, in the Andes Mountains. A company spokesman said that Anaconda planned a two-year exploration program to determine whether further investment would be warranted.

In general economic terms Chile's foreign debt was estimated at $6.5 billion, the highest per capita in the world except for that of Israel. But economic growth averaging 6.2% annually in recent years and an inflation rate estimated at a respectable 25% for 1979, along with increased foreign investment, considerably improved the economic outlook.

On January 9 three Cuban exiles went on trial in a U.S. court on charges stemming from the 1976 assassination in Washington, D.C., of former Chilean diplomat Orlando Letelier. The three,

CHILE

Education. (1978) Primary, pupils 2,368,005, teachers 93,271; secondary, pupils 324,379, teachers 41,666; vocational, pupils 166,092, teachers (1976) 11,509; higher, students (universities only) 130,208, teaching staff (1974) 22,211.

Finance. Monetary unit: peso, with (Sept. 17, 1979) an official rate of 39 pesos to U.S. $1 (free rate of 83.26 pesos = £1 sterling). Gold, SDR's, and foreign exchange (May 1979) U.S. $1,624,000,000. Budget (1977 est.): revenue 120,747,000,000 pesos; expenditure 108,607,000,000 pesos. Gross national product (1977) 313,377,000,000 pesos. Money supply (Dec. 1978) 30,578,000,000 pesos. Cost of living (Santiago; 1975 = 100; June 1979) 1,079.3.

Foreign Trade. (1978) Imports U.S. $3,002,000,000; exports U.S. $2,408,000,000. Import sources: U.S. 23%; Brazil 8%; Japan 7%; Argentina 7%; West Germany 7%; Iran 5%; Venezuela 5%. Export destinations (1977): West Germany 14%; Brazil 13%; U.S. 12%; Japan 12%; Argentina 7%; U.K. 5%. Main exports: copper 50%; metal ores *c.* 10%.

Transport and Communications. Roads (1977) 74,898 km. Motor vehicles in use (1977): passenger 294,600; commercial 164,600. Railways: (1976) 10,819 km; traffic (1978) 2,030,000,000 passenger-km, freight 2,038,000,000 net ton-km. Air traffic (1977): 1,433,000,000 passenger-km; freight 107.7 million net ton-km. Shipping (1978): merchant vessels 100 gross tons and over 146; gross tonnage 446,319. Telephones (Jan. 1978) 483,200. Radio receivers (Dec. 1976) 1.8 million. Television receivers (Dec. 1976) 710,000.

Agriculture. Production (in 000; metric tons; 1978): wheat 893; barley 126; oats 93; corn 257; potatoes 981; rapeseed 52; dry beans 112; tomatoes *c.* 172; sugar, raw value (1977) 315; apples *c.* 160; wine *c.* 520; wool, clean *c.* 11; beef and veal *c.* 184; fish catch (1977) 1,285; timber (cu m; 1977) 9,024. Livestock (in 000; 1978): cattle 3,492; sheep (1977) *c.* 5,700; goats (1977) *c.* 600; pigs *c.* 951; horses *c.* 450; poultry (1977) *c.* 19,500.

Industry. Production (in 000; metric tons; 1978): coal 1,051; crude oil 840; natural gas (cu m) *c.* 1,330,000; petroleum products (1976) 4,084; electricity (kw-hr) 10,167,000; iron ore (61% metal content) 9,683; pig iron (1977) 425; crude steel (ingots; 1977) 506; copper ore (metal content) 1,024; copper 639; nitrate of soda (1977) 562; manganese ore (metal content; 1976) 8.6; sulfur (1976) 18; iodine (1977) 1.9; molybdenum concentrates (metal content; 1976) 10.9; gold (troy oz; 1977) 116; silver (troy oz; 1977) 8,460; cement (1977) 1,140; nitrogenous fertilizers (1977–78) 96; newsprint 132; other paper (1976) 128; woven cotton fabrics (m; 1976) 50,000; fish meal (1976) 253.

Chile

WIDE WORLD

In May Israel Bórquez, head of the Chilean Supreme Court, rejected a U.S. appeal for extradition of three Chilean army officers wanted in Washington, D.C., for the assassination of former Chilean diplomat Orlando Letelier.

Guillermo and Ignacio Novo Sampol and Alvin Ross Díaz, were members of the U.S.-based anti-Castro Cuban Nationalist Movement. On February 14 Guillermo Novo and Alvin Ross were convicted of murdering Letelier on orders from the now-disbanded Chilean secret police agency, DINA. The prosecution evidence in the case was based primarily on testimony, given in exchange for immunity on some charges and reduced sentence on others, of Michael Vernon Townley, a U.S. citizen who worked for DINA and admitted planning the assassination on orders from superiors within that organization. Five others were indicted in the case: two Cubans who could not be found and three Chileans, including former DINA head Gen. Juan Manuel Contreras Sepúlveda and two other Chilean army officers.

Following the conviction of the Cubans, the U.S. turned over evidence in the case to the Chilean government and asked it to extradite the three Chilean army officers to stand trial in the U.S. The head of the Chilean Supreme Court was appointed to study the case and on May 14 rejected the extradition request on grounds of insufficient evidence based on "paid accusations" in the form of Townley's testimony. The U.S. temporarily recalled its ambassador to Chile as a result. Relations between the two countries were described by both sides as "severely strained," and U.S. State Department officials said that they would reserve final action pending a further review of the case by the full Chilean Supreme Court.

Meanwhile, on June 14 Pinochet recalled his own ambassador to Washington "to consider the state of Chile's relations with the United States." On October 1 the full Supreme Court ruled that the evidence contained in the U.S. request was insufficient either to extradite the three or to hold them for trial in Chile. They were subsequently released from house arrest, where they had been held since the case began. The U.S. expressed its severe displeasure with the decision and once again recalled its ambassador to Chile for "consultations."

In his September 11 speech to the nation on the anniversary of the military coup that overthrew Allende, Pinochet rejected opposition demands that he set a timetable for elections and the restoration of representative government. In the area of human rights, press restrictions were relaxed considerably and a number of political exiles, including members of the Communist Party who had fled following the coup, returned quietly to the country. In February and again in October, however, discoveries were made of mass graves believed to contain the remains of persons who disappeared while in government custody immediately after the coup. The Pinochet government repeatedly denied claims by domestic opponents, the Roman Catholic Church, various international organizations, and other governments that political prisoners were killed at that time. (KAREN DEYOUNG)

China

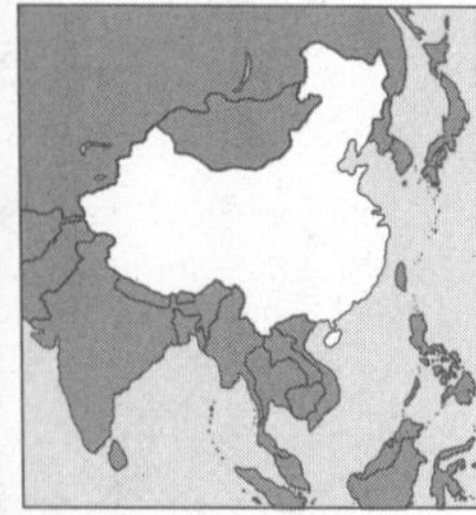
China

The most populous country in the world and the third largest in area, China is bounded by the U.S.S.R., Mongolia, North Korea, Vietnam, Laos, Burma, India, Bhutan, Nepal, Pakistan, and Afghanistan and also by the Sea of Japan, the Yellow Sea, and the East and South China seas. From 1949 the country has been divided into the People's Republic of China (Communist) on the mainland and on Hainan and other islands, and the Republic of China (Nationalist) on Taiwan. (*See* TAIWAN.) Area: 9,561,000 sq km (3,691,521 sq mi), including Tibet and excluding Taiwan. Population of the People's Republic (1978 est.): 960 million, according to official figures; unofficial estimates ranged upward to 1,003,900,000 in 1978. Capital: Beijing (Peking; metro. pop., 1975 est., 8,487,000). Largest city: Shanghai (metro. pop., 1975 est., 10,888,000). Language: Chinese (varieties of the Beijing dialect predominate). Chairman of the Permanent Standing Committee of the National People's Congress (nominal chief of state) in 1979, Ye Jianying (Yeh Chien-ying); chairman of the Communist Party and premier, Hua Guofeng (Hua Kuo-feng).

Oct. 1, 1979, marked the 30th anniversary of the founding of the People's Republic of China, proclaimed by the first session of the Chinese People's Political Consultative Conference, forerunner of the National People's Congress (NPC), the nominal legislature. The first session of the congress in 1954 had elected Communist Party Chairman Mao Zedong (Mao Tse-tung) as president, with vast undefined powers. In the years that followed, the leadership struggle in the party and government passed through a series of phases epitomized by distinctive slogans: A Hundred Flowers Bloom followed by the Antirightist Struggle of 1954–57, the 1958 Great Leap Forward, the shift from revolution to development and modernization in 1959–

65, the Great Proletarian Cultural Revolution, the fall of the "gang of four" (Mao's widow, Jiang Qing [Chiang Ch'ing], and three leaders of the Cultural Revolution) immediately after Mao's death in 1976, and the Four Modernizations (agriculture, industry, science and technology, and defense) in 1978–79. In the leadership struggle, broadly speaking, the Maoist revolutionists attempted to create a utopia by the spiritual remolding and transformation of the masses while the pragmatists considered the building of an economic infrastructure as the first essential in the transition to Communism. The Maoists were discredited by the economic chaos of the Great Leap Forward, and in 1959 the second People's Congress almost unanimously elected Liu Shaoqi (Liu Shao-ch'i) as president. With the assistance of Premier Zhou Enlai (Chou En-lai) and party secretary-general Deng Xiaoping (Teng Hsiao-p'ing), Liu's administration succeeded in bringing about an economic recovery. However, its "revisionist" policies alarmed Mao, who struck back by launching the Cultural Revolution. In 1969 the ninth party congress purged Liu, Deng, and many other moderates.

The Cultural Revolution decimated the party as an effective organ of power and weakened the national defense. In the face of internal turmoil and increasing Soviet threats, the Cultural Revolution ended without having fulfilled Mao's objectives. Deng and other former Politburo members were restored by the tenth party congress and, with Zhou playing an indispensable role, the rebuilding of the party and government was begun. Zhou's death in January 1976 weakened the position of the moderates, and Deng was ousted once again. Soon, however, the radical leftists lost their protector with Mao's passing on September 9. A week later the so-called gang of four was put under arrest. In July 1977 the third plenum of the tenth party congress approved retroactively the appointment of Hua Guofeng (Hua Kuo-feng) as party chairman and reinstated Deng for the second time. In the ensuing months, Deng became a driving force for modernization. Economic success rather than ideological purity dominated the national policy and the mood of the nation.

UPI

U.S. Treasury Secretary Michael Blumenthal raised the American flag when a U.S. liaison office in Beijing became an embassy on March 1.

Pinyin: The New Chinese Spelling

Early in 1979, at the request of the Chinese government, numerous magazines and newspapers around the world introduced their readers to Pinyin, a new system for "spelling the sounds" of Mandarin Chinese by means of the roman alphabet. Because the editors of the *Britannica Book of the Year* support the notion of worldwide uniformity in the spelling of Chinese, Pinyin will be used in this issue for the first time. To better assist readers in making the transition to Pinyin, traditional spellings also will be given in parentheses whenever it seems advisable to do so.

Though Pinyin was adopted by China in 1958, the English-speaking world by and large continued to use the time-honoured system of romanization devised by Thomas F. Wade, a 19th-century British scholar, and later modified by H.A. Giles. In time, English-speaking scholars, librarians, and publishers accepted Wade-Giles as standard, with a few notable exceptions such as Chiang Kai-shek, Sun Yat-sen, and Peking.

In a fair number of instances, the Pinyin and Wade-Giles spellings are identical. However, unlike Wade-Giles, Pinyin makes frequent use of *x* and *q* and gives them values that are perplexing to those whose native tongue is English. What appears in Wade-Giles as *hsi*, for example, becomes *xi* in Pinyin; *ch'ing* becomes *qing*; and so on. Other obvious changes include the substitution of *zhang* for *chang*, *da* for *ta*, etc. The distinctive Wade-Giles hyphen used between two personal names disappears in Pinyin because personal names are run together. Thus Mao Tse-tung, Chou En-lai, and Liu Shao-ch'i become, respectively, Mao Zedong, Zhou Enlai, and Liu Shaoqi.

In some instances, Pinyin seems to bear no resemblance whatever to traditional spellings. This is especially true in cases where commonly accepted spellings preserved local pronunciations. Pinyin makes no concessions to local dialects because its basis is Mandarin, the language of northern China. Thus Canton, located in southern China, becomes Guangzhou in Pinyin, and Amoy becomes Xiamen.

It should also be noted that the use of Pinyin is limited to mainland China. The *Book of the Year* continues to use traditional spellings for Taiwan and other areas outside China proper.

WIDE WORLD

Asserting the greater freedom of speech being allowed in China, an army veteran stood up during a rally in September to complain to the crowd that he was unable to find a job.

CHINA

Education. (1978–79) Primary, pupils 146,240,000, teachers (1964–65) *c.* 2.6 million; secondary, pupils 65,480,000; vocational, pupils 880,000; higher, students 850,000.

Finance. Monetary unit: yuan, with (Sept. 17, 1979) a free rate of 1.55 yuan to U.S. $1 (3.33 yuan = £1 sterling). International reserves (Aug. 1978 est.) U.S. $2.5 billion. Total industrial and agricultural output (1978) 569 billion yuan. Gross national product (1977 est.) U.S. $346 billion.

Foreign Trade. (1978) Imports 18,740,000,000 yuan; exports 16,760,000,000 yuan. Import sources: Japan 30%; West Germany 10%; U.S. 8%; Australia 5%; North Korea *c.* 5%. Export destinations: Hong Kong 20%; Japan 19%; North Korea *c.* 6%. Main exports: food (fruits and vegetables, meat and products, cereals) *c.* 30%; textiles and clothing *c.* 25%; crude oil *c.* 15%.

Transport and Communications. Roads (1978) 890,000 km. Motor vehicles in use (1976): passenger *c.* 50,000; commercial 1,044,000. Railways: (1978) 50,000 km; traffic (1959) 45,670,000,000 passenger-km, freight (1978) 533,300,000,000 net ton-km. Air traffic (1977): *c.* 1,500,000,000 passenger-km; freight (1978) 97 million net ton-km. Inland waterways (including Chang Jiang [Yangtze River]; 1978) 136,000 km. Shipping (1978): merchant vessels 100 gross tons and over 713; gross tonnage 5,168,898. Telephones (Dec. 1977) *c.* 5 million. Radio receivers (Dec. 1977) *c.* 45 million. Television receivers (Dec. 1977) *c.* 1 million.

Agriculture. Production (in 000; metric tons; 1978): rice *c.* 160,000; corn *c.* 40,000; wheat *c.* 53,000; barley *c.* 20,000; millet *c.* 25,000; potatoes *c.* 42,000; beetroot 2,702; dry peas *c.* 5,000; soybeans *c.* 13,000; peanuts *c.* 2,800; rapeseed *c.* 1,400; sugar, raw value *c.* 3,500; tobacco *c.* 950; tea 268; cotton, lint 2,167; jute 1,088; cow's milk *c.* 4,700; beef and buffalo meat *c.* 2,200; pork *c.* 14,000; fish catch 4,660; timber (cu m) 51,620. Livestock (in 000; 1978): horses *c.* 6,500; asses *c.* 11,500; cattle and buffaloes 93,890; sheep 169,940; pigs 301,290; goats *c.* 70,000; chickens *c.* 1,370,000.

Industry. Fuel and power (in 000; metric tons; 1978): coal (including lignite) 618,000; crude oil 104,050; electricity (kw-hr) 256,550,000. Production (in 000; metric tons; 1978): iron ore (metal content) *c.* 40,000; pig iron 34,790; crude steel 31,780; bauxite (1976) *c.* 1,100; aluminum (1976) *c.* 200; copper *c.* 200; lead *c.* 100; zinc *c.* 100; magnesite *c.* 1,000; manganese ore *c.* 300; tungsten concentrates (oxide content) *c.* 12; cement 65,240; sulfuric acid 6,610; plastics 679; fertilizers (nutrient content) 8,693; soda ash 1,329; caustic soda 1,640; cotton yarn 2,380; cotton fabrics (m) 11,029,000; man-made fibres 285; paper 4,390; motor vehicles (units) 149.

Domestic Affairs. The third plenum of the 11th party congress, held Dec. 12–23, 1978, with 281 members in attendance, was called to give formal approval to the sweeping policy changes initiated under the new leadership. The decisions to embark on the program of Four Modernizations and to rehabilitate practically all victims of the Cultural Revolution represented a watershed in the country's political history. The plenum also proclaimed important changes in the country's economic course, including the acceleration of agricultural production by the adoption of sound economic measures; emphasis on improved living standards; and expansion of economic cooperation with industrial democracies in order to obtain advanced technologies and equipment. Finally, "in order to safeguard people's democracy," it proposed to draft a full-fledged legal code to replace the previous system of arbitrary justice.

Among those elected to the Politburo were Chen Yun (Ch'en Yün; *see* BIOGRAPHIES), Hu Yaobang (Hu Yao-pang), and Wang Zhen (Wang Chen), all Cultural Revolution victims, and Deng Yingchao (Teng Ying-ch'ao), the widow of Zhou Enlai. Chen Yun, the top economic planner in 1950, was made a vice-chairman of the party and a standing member of the Politburo, next in line to Deng and outranking Wang Dongxing (Wang Tung-hsing), Mao's former bodyguard and security chief. Chen was also named to head a newly formed 100-member Central Commission for Inspecting Discipline, with the task of enforcing party rules and regulations. Hu Yaobang, the youngest Politburo member and a longtime associate of Deng, was appointed to the re-created post of secretary-general of the party and, concurrently, as chief of the party's Propaganda Department. As a result of the reshuffle, Deng emerged as the single most powerful leader, although Hua continued to retain the positions of party and government head.

Shortly before the meeting of the plenum, the regime had loosened restrictions on travel, both inside China and abroad, and on religious worship. These moves, together with the new leadership's call for the emancipation of the mind and the decision to draft a new legal code, encouraged a wall poster campaign and some demonstrations in Beijing (Peking) and other major cities demanding democracy and individual rights. The outburst caused some concern to the authorities. On March 18 Deng was reported to be very critical of those who had complained about human rights violations in letters sent to U.S. Pres. Jimmy Carter and Leonard Woodcock, the U.S. ambassador to China. On March 29 the authorities announced that any rally, poster, or publication opposing the Communist Party and its leadership or Marxism-Leninism-Mao Thought would be banned. The "democracy wall" in the centre of Beijing, where dissident posters and petitions had been allowed for over a year, was abolished on December 6, and the space for posters, guaranteed by the 1978 constitution, was moved to an outlying district. In October Wei Jingsheng (Wei Ching-sheng), the most prominent of the dissidents, was sentenced to 15 years in prison for giving military secrets to a foreigner and counterrevolutionary activities.

Despite their personal and ideological differences, the avowed Maoists and the pragmatists in the new leadership seemed to share the view that the vehement demand for a Western-style democracy challenged the party's leadership. In mid-April, in the deliberations of a working conference in preparation for the second session of the fifth NPC, it was agreed that enhancement of democracy and liberation of thinking should not affect the structure of the present regime.

The second sessions of the fifth NPC and the fifth National Committee of the Chinese People's Political Consultative Conference (CPPCC) were held simultaneously. The CPPCC, a front organization with over 2,000 members, met from June 15 to July 2 to rally and unite the people in support of the decisions of the third plenum on socialist modernization. Over 100 members were newly rehabilitated veteran cadres, including Wang Guangmei (Wang Kuang-mei), widow of Liu Shaoqi.

In the midst of rising demands for human rights and better living conditions, the second session of the fifth NPC, consisting of 3,471 deputies, opened on June 18. In his report to the Congress, Hua stated that the focus of the work of the whole nation had shifted to socialist modernization. Discussing socialist democracy and the legal system, Hua said that the Four Modernizations would not work "without a high degree of political democracy" and that to bring greater order it was essential to strengthen the socialist legal system. On economic planning, Hua reported that the original goals of the ten-year plan announced in February 1978 were too ambitious. Instead, it had been decided to devote three years (1979–81) to readjusting, reconstructing, consolidating, and improving the economy. Hua's report was in line with the reordering of the modernization program to avoid overdependence on purchases abroad for building heavy industry. The modification gave priority to agriculture, light industry, coal, oil, transportation, and communications. Reviewing the international situation, Hua attacked the expansionist policies of social imperialism and expressed disappointment in SALT II, which could neither check the arms race nor provide a fundamental solution to the question of world peace.

At the plenary meeting on June 21, Vice-Premier Yu Qiuli (Yü Ch'iu-li), minister in charge of the State Planning Commission, and Finance Minister Zhang Jingfu (Chang Ching-fu) reported on the 1979 national economic plan and the state budget, respectively. According to Yu, the total value of agricultural and industrial production in 1978 was the current equivalent of U.S. $362 billion ($93 billion for agriculture and $269 billion for industry). Zhang revealed that 1978 revenue amounted to $70,770,000,000 and total expenditure to $70,130,000,000. Revenue and expenditure for 1979 would total about $72 billion each. These reports on the actual size of the national budget, the value of industrial and agricultural output, and other key economic indicators—previously considered to be state secrets—reflected the new leadership's more open approach and signaled its intention to seek the seats in the World Bank and the International Monetary Fund occupied by Taiwan. After two weeks of deliberation, the Congress approved Chairman Hua's report and appointed three experienced economists, Chen Yun, Bo Yibo (Po I-po), and Yao Yilin (Yao I-lin), to be vice-premiers. Chen was also made head of a newly formed State Finance and Economic Commission.

Before it closed on July 1, the Congress adopted seven laws dealing with the organization of local people's congresses, the election of deputies to the People's Congress, the organization of people's courts and people's procuratories, codes of criminal court procedure and criminal law, and joint Chinese-foreign investment. The first legal code in the regime's 30-year history prohibited extorted confessions and arbitrary arrests and was expected to lend some support to the independence of the judicial system. The electoral ordinance introduced a system of direct popular elections for local offices. The joint Chinese-foreign investment and management law would permit foreign firms to enter into joint ventures with Chinese companies. (*See* Feature Article: *China's Future.*)

The Economy. For the first time the government officially acknowledged such problems as unemployment, housing shortages, and hunger, previously deemed impossible in the Communist

state. Vice-Premier Li Xiannian (Li Hsien-nien) revealed that China had 20 million unemployed and 100 million who were undernourished. The economy was being made more consumer-oriented, both domestically and on the foreign trade front in order to earn foreign exchange. Tourism, long shunned for fear of foreign influence, was being promoted. A system of incentives was introduced to spur lagging productivity.

The official statistics showed considerable economic recovery during the past two years. Despite a devastating drought in the northern wheat belt, total grain output in 1978 reached 304,750,000 tons, 22 million tons more than in 1977. The 1979 plan called for an increase in grain output of 7,750,000 tons. However, China still expected to import substantial amounts of grain from the U.S. and other countries in the next few years. A significant increase in foreign trade was reported. Chinese exports reached $10,680,000,000 in 1978, a gain of 20% over 1977, while imports, at $11,950,000,000, had risen 41%. Statistics for the first six months of 1979 showed imports up 60% compared with the first half of 1978, and exports up 27%. Much of the increase in imports consisted of advanced technology.

According to official figures, 1978 output in several key industries had risen significantly over 1977 levels. Steel production increased 55.3%, from 20,460,000 to 31,780,000 tons; coal rose 28% to 618 million tons; crude oil was up 19.5% to 104 million tons; and electric power reached 256 billion kw-hr, a gain of 26%.

Foreign Affairs. China's foreign policy also assumed a more pragmatic and outward-looking stance. Fear of Soviet-Vietnamese encirclement and disillusionment with the nonaligned movement, especially the links between certain third world countries and the U.S.S.R., moved China to consolidate closer ties with Japan, Western Europe, and the U.S. Chinese leaders visited dozens of countries during the year, and the Chinese government played host to leaders from scores of countries. In mid-October Hua, accompanied by Foreign Minister Huang Hua and trade experts including Vice-Premier Yu Qiuli, left Beijing for a three-week tour of France, West Germany, the U.K., and Italy, the first such visit by a top Chinese Communist leader since the founding of the People's Republic.

After 30 years of estrangement, the U.S. extended full diplomatic recognition to the People's Republic as of January 1. In the joint communiqué on the establishment of diplomatic relations, both sides opposed hegemonism and neither sought hegemony. China established diplomatic relations with Djibouti on January 8 and with Portugal on February 8, and in June Ireland recognized Beijing as the sole legal government of China. The total number of countries having diplomatic relations with China increased to just over 120.

First Vice-Premier Deng arrived in Washington, D.C., on January 28 for a nine-day visit. The Carter administration received him with a 19-gun salute, traditionally reserved for a head of government. At the arrival ceremony on the White House

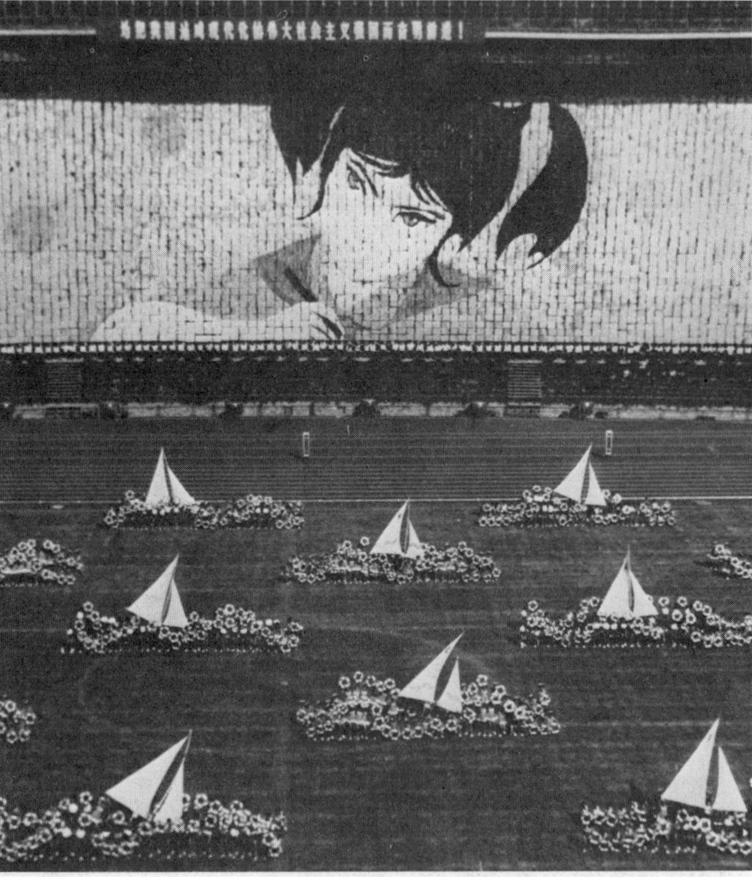

Chinese youngsters practiced calisthenics in preparation for the fourth National Games which began in Beijing on September 15. In one demonstration a group holding white sails danced like surging waves.

UPI

Chinese Literature:
see Literature

Christian Church (Disciples of Christ):
see Religion

Christianity:
see Religion

Churches of Christ:
see Religion

Church Membership:
see Religion

Church of England:
see Religion

Cinema:
see Motion Pictures

Cities:
see Environment

Clothing:
see Fashion and Dress

Coal:
see Energy

Coins:
see Philately and Numismatics

Colleges:
see Education

lawn, Deng lost no time in stating China's desire to seek closer cooperation with the U.S., both to help his country's development and to check Soviet expansionism. On January 31, Deng and President Carter signed a cultural agreement, an agreement on scientific and technical cooperation, a high-energy physics agreement, and a consulate agreement.

Several U.S. Cabinet-level missions were sent to China, including one in February, headed by Treasury Secretary Michael Blumenthal, to settle outstanding property claims between China and the U.S. This paved the way for Secretary of Commerce Juanita M. Kreps to initial, on May 14, a long-term U.S.-China trade treaty that included a most-favoured-nation clause and would open the way for low-interest Export-Import Bank credits to China. The treaty was formally signed on July 7 in Beijing by Ambassador Woodcock and Chinese Foreign Trade Minister Li Qiang (Li Ch'iang). However, to the annoyance of the Chinese, Carter waited four months before sending it to the Senate for ratification. It was made known that, to keep relations with Moscow and Beijing in balance, Washington would like to grant most-favoured-nation treatment to China and the U.S.S.R. at about the same time. Carter had received assurances from Beijing that it would conform to the Jackson-Vanik Amendment, which made granting of most-favoured-nation status contingent on the lifting of restrictions on emigration.

Reciprocating Deng's visit to Washington, U.S. Vice-Pres. Walter Mondale arrived in Beijing on August 25. Following "extremely productive and friendly" talks with Hua and Deng, he joined the latter in signing an accord on the details of the cultural exchange program and a protocol on hydroelectric power projects that would involve as much as $2 billion in credits over five years. In Guangzhou (Canton) on August 31, Mondale opened the first U.S. consulate in China in 30 years.

The normalization of Sino-U.S. relations opened the way for even closer relations between China and Japan. On his way home from the U.S. in February, Deng spent three days in Japan, where he had talks with Prime Minister Masayoshi Ohira. In March the eight-year bilateral trade agreement signed by the two countries in 1978 was extended by five years. In May China concluded agreements under which Japan would lend it more than $10 billion for development.

The border dispute between China and Vietnam erupted into war on February 17, when China invaded Vietnam in retaliation for Vietnam's invasion of Cambodia. (*See* CAMBODIA; VIETNAM.) "Having attained the goal in self-defense counterattack against the aggressor," China began to withdraw its forces from Vietnam on March 5, and by the end of March the foreign ministries of both sides had agreed to begin high-level talks. The meetings continued through most of the year, but little was accomplished except for an agreement in May to exchange prisoners. Each side charged the other with preparing for a new war and attempting to dominate Laos and Cambodia.

On April 3 Beijing informed Moscow that it would not renew the 30-year Sino-Soviet treaty of friendship and alliance when it expired in April 1980. Both Beijing and Moscow expressed an interest in improving relations, however, and talks on diplomatic, trade, and cultural exchange topics were scheduled for September, China having dropped its longstanding precondition that Soviet troops be withdrawn from disputed border areas. Despite a minor border incident in Xinjiang (Sinkiang) in June, a delegation headed by Vice-Foreign Minister Wang Youping (Wang Yu-p'ing) arrived in Moscow on September 24. On September 26 the Chinese diplomats met with a Soviet team headed by Deputy Foreign Minister Leonid Ilyichev and began to work out an agenda and procedures. A 1979 Sino-Soviet trade agreement was signed in August. (HUNG-TI CHU)

UPI

The face of Charlie Chaplin gazes out at Jinan (Tsinan), Shantong (Shantung) Province, from a poster advertising his film *Modern Times*.

Colombia

Colombia

A republic in northwestern South America, Colombia is bordered by Panama, Venezuela, Brazil, Peru, and Ecuador and has coasts on both the Caribbean Sea and the Pacific Ocean. Area: 1,138,-914 sq km (439,737 sq mi). Pop. (1979 est.): 26,587,000. Cap. and largest city: Bogotá (pop., 1979 est., 4,055,900). Language: Spanish. Religion: Roman Catholic (96%). President in 1979, Julio César Turbay Ayala.

Pres. Julio Turbay Ayala had inherited several political problems when he took office in 1978, and these persisted into 1979. Chief among them were the suppression of active guerrilla groups and control of the drug trade. The president was criticized by his own Liberal Party and by the left regarding the security statute of Sept. 6, 1978, which provided for stiffer sentences for crimes connected with terrorism and subversion. Murders, bombings, and kidnappings by the M-19 (Marxist-Leninist) guerrilla group and the FARC (Colombian Revolutionary Armed Forces) increased, provoking an army counteroffensive, mainly in the Santander region. A raid on an army arsenal in Usaquén on Jan. 2, 1979, by the M-19 group was followed by many arrests, including those of Tony López Oyuela, a former chief of police, Col. Genaro Ñungo Méndez, a senior military prosecutor, and several foreign businessmen. In June–July President Turbay Ayala undertook an extensive tour, largely in Europe. In part, this was designed to improve his country's image, which had been tarnished by alleged human rights violations.

A study by the Asociación Nacional de Instituciones Financieras (ANIF) indicated that some 150,000 people were involved in marijuana production in Colombia. At the end of 1978 a campaign to suppress production of the drug in La Guajira, Magdalena, and César provinces was successful enough to generate U.S. offers of financial aid to continue the program. However, illegal exports of marijuana in the first half of 1979 were estimated at $200 million, 30% more than during the same period in 1978.

The economy performed well during 1978, with gross domestic product growing at a rate of 8%. However, the rate of inflation was 17.8%, possibly increasing to 25% during 1979. In 1978 the peso had been devalued by 8%. Coffee production for 1978–79 (October–September) was estimated at 10.8 million bags, compared with 10,350,000 in 1977–78, and 1979–80 production was forecast at a record 12 million bags. Exports for calendar 1978 were valued at $1,701,000,000, but the value of exports during 1979 would depend on world coffee prices. The external sector performed well during 1978, providing a current account surplus of $841 million and an overall balance of payments surplus of $655 million. The tight monetary policy of 1978 was continued into 1979, but the Turbay administration took a more liberal attitude toward foreign investment than its predecessor.

Earthquakes on November 23 and December 12 caused severe damage and some 150 deaths, mostly at El Charco. (CHRISTINE MELLOR)

COLOMBIA

Education. (1975) Primary, pupils 3,953,242, teachers 131,211; secondary, pupils 1,045,312, teachers 55,227; vocational, pupils 260,467, teachers 14,894; teacher training, students 67,664, teachers 3,995; higher (1977), students 279,475, teaching staff 27,287.

Finance. Monetary unit: peso, with (Sept. 17, 1979) a free rate of 42.55 pesos to U.S. $1 (91.54 pesos = £1 sterling). Gold, SDR's, and foreign exchange (June 1979) U.S. $3,189,000,000. Budget (1978 actual): revenue 84,065,000,000 pesos; expenditure 78,084,000,000 pesos. Gross national product (1977) 706,170,000,000 pesos. Money supply (May 1979) 132,760,000,000 pesos. Cost of living (Bogotá; 1975 = 100; May 1979) 230.

Foreign Trade. Imports (1978) 114,914,000,000 pesos; exports (1977) 80,478,000,000 pesos. Import sources (1977): U.S. *c.* 42%; Japan *c.* 12%; West Germany *c.* 10%; Venezuela *c.* 7%; France *c.* 7%. Export destinations: U.S. *c.* 32%; West Germany *c.* 19%; Venezuela *c.* 6%; Japan *c.* 5%. Main exports: coffee 62%; textile yarns and fabrics *c.* 6%. Tourism (1976): visitors 522,000; gross receipts U.S. $208 million.

Transport and Communications. Roads (1977) 50,987 km. Motor vehicles in use (1977): passenger 387,500; commercial 67,400. Railways: (1976) 3,403 km; traffic (1977) 391 million passenger-km, freight 1,216,000,000 net ton-km. Air traffic (1977): 3,376,000,000 passenger-km; freight 176.1 million net ton-km. Shipping (1978): merchant vessels 100 gross tons and over 61; gross tonnage 271,953. Telephones (Jan. 1978) 1,396,600. Radio receivers (Dec. 1977) *c.* 2.9 million. Television receivers (Dec. 1977) *c.* 1.8 million.

Agriculture. Production (in 000; metric tons; 1978): corn 862; rice 1,715; barley 119; sorghum 517; potatoes 1,996; cassava (1977) 2,113; soybeans 137; onions *c.* 230; tomatoes 261; bananas *c.* 1,500; sugar, raw value *c.* 1,014; palm oil *c.* 55; coffee *c.* 648; tobacco 63; sisal (1977) *c.* 42; cotton, lint 82; beef and veal *c.* 431; timber (cu m; 1977) *c.* 24,083. Livestock (in 000; Dec. 1977): cattle *c.* 25,294; sheep 2,255; pigs 1,966; goats 632; horses (1976) 1,535; chickens *c.* 61,800.

Industry. Production (in 000; metric tons; 1978): crude oil 6,600; natural gas (cu m; 1976) *c.* 1,710,000; coal (1976) *c.* 3,620; electricity (kw-hr; 1977) *c.* 15,100,000; iron ore (metal content; 1977) 460; crude steel *c.* 260; gold (troy oz) *c.* 290; emeralds (carats; 1973) 109; salt (1976) 1,112; cement 4,155; caustic soda 32; fertilizers (nutrient content) nitrogenous *c.* 72, phosphate *c.* 33; paper (1976) 283.

Combat Sports

Boxing. In 1979 Muhammad Ali relinquished the World Boxing Association (WBA) heavyweight title and announced his retirement. A professional boxer for 19 years, and the only man to win the world heavyweight title three times, Ali lost only 3 decisions in 59 contests and avenged them all. He took part in 24 championship contests. The WBA paired Leon Spinks (U.S.) with Gerrie Coetzee (South Africa), and John Tate (U.S.) with Kallie Knoetze (South Africa) in elimination contests for the vacant title. Tate stopped Knoetze, while Coetzee knocked out Spinks. The two winners met in Pretoria, South Africa, and 81,000 spectators saw Tate win on points to become WBA champion. The World Boxing Council (WBC) continued to recognize Larry Holmes (U.S.) as the champion, and he stopped challengers Osvaldo "Jaws" Ocasio (Puerto Rico) in 7 rounds, Mike Weaver (U.S.) in 12, and Earnie Shavers (U.S.) in 11. Among the light heavyweights, Matthew Saad Muhammad (U.S.), formerly Matthew Franklin, won the WBC championship by knocking out Marvin Johnson (U.S.) in eight rounds and then outpointed John Conteh (England). Victor Galíndez (Arg.) regained the WBA crown from Mike Rossman (U.S.) in ten rounds but then lost it to Johnson by a knockout in the 11th round.

The middleweight title changed hands when New York-based Vito Antuofermo (Italy) outpointed Hugo Corro (Arg.). Antuofermo later retained his title in a disputed draw with Marvin Hagler (U.S.). In junior middleweight competition, Maurice Hope (England) became WBC champion, stopping titleholder Rocky Mattioli (Australia) and Mike Baker (U.S.), while Denmark-based Ayub Kalule (Uganda) took the WBA title from Masashi Kudo (Japan). Wilfred Benítez (Puerto Rico) gained the WBC welterweight crown from Carlos Palomino (U.S.) and beat Harold Weston (U.S.), but in November Sugar Ray Leonard (U.S.) knocked him out in the 15th round to win the championship. José Cuevas (Mexico) retained the WBA title by stopping Scott Clark (U.S.), outpointing Randy Shields (U.S.), and knocking out Angel Espada (Puerto Rico). Sang Hyun Kim (South Korea) won the WBC junior welterweight title from Saensak Muangsurin (Thailand) and then outpointed Fitzeroy Giussipi (Trinidad and

Colonies:
see Dependent States

UPI

WBC heavyweight champion Larry Holmes hit the canvas in the seventh round of a bout with Earnie Shavers on September 28. Holmes got up, however, and stopped Shavers on a TKO in the 11th round.

Tobago); Antonio Cervantes (Colombia) remained WBA champion, outpointing Miguel Montilla (Dominican Republic).

Roberto Durán (Panama) relinquished the lightweight championship to move up to a higher weight division, and the WBA recognized Ernesto España (Venezuela) when he knocked out Claude Noel (Trinidad and Tobago); España later stopped Johnny Lira (U.S.). Jim Watt (Scotland) became WBC champion by defeating Alfredo Pitalúa (Colombia); Watt then beat Roberto Vásquez (U.S.). Alexis Argüello (Nicaragua), WBC junior lightweight champion, knocked out Alfredo Escalera (Puerto Rico) and Rafael Limón (Mexico); Sam Serrano (Puerto Rico), WBA champion, beat Julio Valdez (Dominican Republic) and Nkosana Mgxaji (South Africa).

In featherweight competition, Danny "Little Red" López (U.S.), WBC king, beat Roberto Castañón (Spain) and Mike Ayala (U.S.); Eusebio Pedroza (Panama), WBA champion, stopped Royal Kobayashi (Japan), Héctor Carrasquilla (Panama), and Ruben Olivares (Mexico). Wilfredo Gómez (Puerto Rico), WBC junior featherweight champion, stopped Nestor Jiménez (Colombia), Julio Hernandez (Nicaragua), and Nick Perez (U.S.); Ricardo Cardona (Colombia), WBA champion, outpointed Chung Sun Hyun (South Korea) and Yukio Segawa (Japan). Carlos Zárate (Mexico) beat Mensah Kpalogo (Togo) but then lost the WBC bantamweight title to Lupe Pintor (Mexico); Jorge Luján (Panama), WBA champion, stopped Cleo García (Nicaragua). Miguel Canto (Mexico) lost the WBC flyweight title to Chan Hee Park (South Korea), who then outpointed Tsutomu Igarashi (Japan) and knocked out Gustavo Espadas (Mexico). Betulio González (Venezuela), WBA champion, was held to a draw by former champion Shoji Oguma (Japan) and lost to Luis Ibarra (Panama). The WBC junior flyweight crown was retained by Kim Sung Jun (South Korea) with wins over Héctor Ray Meléndez (Dominican Republic) and Siony Carupo (Phil.); Yoko Gushiken (Japan) held the WBA crown with victories over Rigoberto Marcano (Venezuela), Alfonso López (Panama), and Rafael Pedroza (Panama).

In Europe Lorenzo Zanon (Italy) became heavyweight champion with a victory on points against

Table I. Boxing Champions
as of Dec. 31, 1979

Division	World	Europe	Commonwealth	Britain
Heavyweight	Larry Holmes, U.S.* John Tate, U.S.†	Lorenzo Zanon, Italy	John L. Gardner, England	John L. Gardner, England
Light heavyweight	Matthew Saad Muhammad, U.S.* Marvin Johnson, U.S.†	Rudi Koopmans, The Netherlands	Lottie Mwale, Zambia	Bunny Johnson, England
Middleweight	Vito Antuofermo, Italy*†	vacant	Ayub Kalule, Uganda	Kevin Finnegan, England
Junior middleweight	Maurice Hope, England* Ayub Kalule, Uganda†	Marijan Benes, Yugoslavia	Kenny Bristol, Guyana	Pat Thomas, Wales
Welterweight	Sugar Ray Leonard, U.S.* José Cuevas, Mexico†	Jorgen Hansen, Denmark	Clyde Gray, Canada	Kirkland Laing, England
Junior welterweight	Sang Hyun Kim, South Korea* Antonio Cervantes, Colombia†	Jo Kimpuwani, France	Obisia Nwankpa, Nigeria	Clinton McKenzie, England
Lightweight	Jim Watt, Scotland* Ernesto España, Venezuela†	Charlie Nash, N. Ireland	Hogan Jimoh, Nigeria	vacant
Junior lightweight	Alexis Argüello, Nicaragua* Sam Serrano, Puerto Rico†	Rodolfo Sánchez,Spain	Johnny Aba, Papua New Guinea	...
Featherweight	Danny López, U.S.* Eusebio Pedroza, Panama†	Roberto Castañón, Spain	Eddie Ndukwu, Nigeria	Pat Cowdell, England
Junior featherweight	Wilfredo Gómez, Puerto Rico* Ricardo Cardona, Colombia†	...	...	...
Bantamweight	Lupe Pintor, Mexico* Jorge Luján, Panama†	Juan Francisco Rodríguez, Spain	John Owen, Wales	John Owen, Wales
Flyweight	Chan Hee Park, South Korea* Luis Ibarra, Panama†	Charlie Magri, England	vacant	Charlie Magri, England
Junior flyweight	Kim Sung Jun, South Korea* Yoko Gushiken, Japan†	...	...	...

*World Boxing Council champion. †World Boxing Association champion.

WIDE WORLD

U.S. wrestler Lee Kemp (left) succeeded in taking down West German Martin Knosp to win his second straight world title in the 74-kilo class.

Alfredo Evangelista (Spain). Rudi Koopmans (Neth.) took the light-heavyweight championship from Aldo Traversaro (Italy) and later stopped Robert Amory (France). The junior middleweight title was captured by Marijan Benes (Yugos.) from Gilbert Cohen (France); Benes then stopped Adoni Amana (Spain). The welterweight title changed hands twice. Dave Green (England) stopped Henry Rhiney (England) but lost to Jorgen Hansen (Denmark). Jo Kimpuwani (France) became junior welterweight champion, beating José Heredia (Spain). Charlie Nash (Northern Ireland) took the lightweight title by outpointing André Holyk (France). Rodolfo Sánchez (Spain) won the junior lightweight crown from Carlos Hernández (Spain), while Roberto Castañón and Juan Francisco Rodríguez, both of Spain, retained their featherweight and bantamweight titles, and Charlie Magri (England) took the flyweight title from Franco Udella (Italy).

After the death of middleweight Willie Classen of injuries sustained in a fight in Madison Square Garden on November 23, the New York State Athletic Commission suspended boxing in the state. New safety procedures were to be instituted early in 1980. (FRANK BUTLER)

Wrestling. Two major international wrestling tournaments were held in 1979, the world wrestling championships and the competition at the Pan-American Games. In the world championships at San Diego, Calif., in August, the U.S.S.R. again won first place in both freestyle and Greco-Roman competition. The U.S. showed marked improvement in both types of wrestling, placing second in freestyle and fourth behind Hungary and Bulgaria in Greco-Roman. At the Pan-American Games in San Juan, P.R., the U.S. won the freestyle, taking all ten gold medals. Cuba finished second and Canada third. Cuba won the Greco-Roman with the U.S. second and Canada third.

In the National Collegiate Athletic Association tournament, Iowa, with 122½ points, won for the second straight year. Iowa State was second with 88 points, and Lehigh finished third with 69¾ points. (MARVIN G. HESS)

Fencing. In the world championships held in August at Melbourne, Australia, the Soviet Union won six of the tournament's eight gold medals. Because Australia is distant from many countries, the turnout of national teams was not as great as in recent years. In dominating the championships the Soviet fencers triumphed individually in foil and sabre, captured all three men's team title events, and finished first in women's team foil. As a result they were awarded the Prince Rainier Cup, symbolic of the overall team crown.

The powerful showing by the Soviets lent credence to the pre-tournament report that their fencers had gone through intensive training for the competition. This conclusion was borne out in particular by their strong performance in the team events, in which they showed their depth with each of the three weapons.

Philippe Riboud of France and Cornelia Hanisch of West Germany captured the individual épée and women's foil events, respectively. By doing so they prevented the Soviets from making a sweep of all eight titles. The strongest Soviet showing in the individual events was in the sabre. Vladimir Nazlymov led an onslaught that earned all three of that event's medals for his team. Viktor Krovopouskov, the 1978 titleholder, was second while Mikhail Voursev finished third. In the foil Aleksandr Romankov, second in 1978, topped France's Pascal Jolyot. In the épée, Riboud outdueled Hungary's Imre Kolzonay.

The success by Hanisch in women's foil marked a step upward for her. In 1978 she had been able to place only third. Second to Hanisch was Valentina Sidorova of the U.S.S.R.

Once among the world's greatest fencers, the Hungarians were particularly disappointed. In 1978 they had shown signs of making a great comeback in men's sabre and épée, but in Australia they succeeded in acquiring only a sixth place in the sabre while earning a second in épée. (MICHAEL STRAUSS)

Judo. The year's activities in judo were highlighted by the 11th World Judo Championships at Paris in December, with Japan winning four of the

Table II. World Wrestling Champions

Weight class	Freestyle	Greco-Roman
48 kg (105.5 lb)	Serge Kornilaev, U.S.S.R.	Constantin Alexandru, Romania
52 kg (114.5 lb)	Yuji Takada, Japan	Lajos Racz, Hungary
57 kg (125.5 lb)	Hideaki Tomiyama, Japan	Chamil Serikov, U.S.S.R.
62 kg (136.5 lb)	Vladimir Yumin, U.S.S.R.	Istvan Toth, Hungary
68 kg (149.5 lb)	Mikhail Charachura, U.S.S.R.	Andrezej Supron, Poland
74 kg (163 lb)	Lee Kemp, U.S.	tie { Ferec Kocsis, Hungary Iyanko Chopov, Bulgaria
82 kg (180.5 lb)	Istvan Kovacs, Hungary	Gennady Korban, U.S.S.R.
90 kg (198 lb)	Khasan Ortzuev, U.S.S.R.	Frank Andersson, Sweden
100 kg (220 lb)	Ilia Mate, U.S.S.R.	Nikolay Balboshin, U.S.S.R.
100+ kg	Salman Chasimikov, U.S.S.R.	Aleksandr Tomov, U.S.S.R.

eight titles at stake. Sumio Endo won the open weights, Yasuhiro Yamashita took the heavyweight, Shozo Fujii captured his fourth world championship title, the light-middleweight, and Kiyoto Katsuki won the lightweight title. The Soviet Union took two titles: light-heavyweight by Temor Khubuluri and bantamweight by Nicolai Solodukhin; France won one gold (and four silvers): flyweight by Thierry Rey; and East Germany captured its first world title: middleweight by Detley Ultsch.

In the 1979 All-Japan Championships—the world's only major judo tournament without weight classes—21-year-old Yasuhiro Yamashita won an unprecedented third consecutive title, pinning Sumio Endo by *kamishiho-gatame* for *ippon*, or full-point victory. The 127-kg (282-lb) Tokai University student also won the open-weights competition for the third straight time during the 12th All-Japan Weight Class Championships, while two-time national champion Haruki Uemura took the heavyweight title in the seven-weight-class competition. Led by Yamashita's victory in the over-95-kg class, Japan won five of the seven titles at stake in the Paris International Meet in February, while France's Jean-Luc Rouge and Thierry Rey won the under-95-kg and under-60-kg classes, respectively. Rouge also won the over-95-kg title in the European Championships in Brescia, Italy, but the Soviets edged France for the team title. Soviet *judokas* also dominated the Spartakiade in August by winning six of the eight titles. Shozo Fujii won the 78-kg contest and Yasuhiko Moriwaki the 60-kg competition.

Karate. In 1979 Wado-kai *kumite* (free fighting) specialist Hsiao Murase was the top karate performer for the second year in a row. Japan's all-styles champion won the Wado-kai national championship in June at Tokyo's Nippon Budokan for the second time in the past four years and then captured the open-weights title in the National Athletic Meet in September on the strength of his superlative *jodan-zuki* punch. Tokyo won the team title. More than 261 *karateka* from 39 prefectures competed. In December 1978 Murase again finished first in the third Asian-Pacific Tournament. Japan beat Taiwan 2–1 in the finals to win the team title for the third year in a row. In the annual Shotokan (Japan Karate Association) tourney in June at the Budokan, the *kumite* and *kata* (prescribed forms) individual titles were won, respectively, by Fujikiyo Omura and Yoshiharu Osaka; the team title went to Tokyo. In the national Goju-kai Championships in September, Akio Takahashi won the individual title and the Wakayama Prefecture "A" team took the team title. Shigeru Takada of the Mexico branch of Shito-kai won the individual title in the All-Japan Shito-kai Championships in July. Yoji Ebihara won both the All-Japan Rembu-kai Championships and the national *bogu* (protective equipment) tournament in June at Tokyo Gymnasium. Japan beat a U.S. team 4–1 in an exchange contest in August at the 17th All-Japan Rengo-kai Championships in Osaka. Akira Isozaki captured the individual title.

More than 1,200 *karateka*, including 16 foreign contenders from the U.S., Brazil, Hong Kong, and Macao, competed in the 54th All-Japan Seigo-kai Championships in August. Keikichi Kawasaki won first place in the *dan* (degree) contest, while Koto Dojo took the team title. In other national tournaments, Koji Sugita won the Butoku-kai individual title and Saitama Prefecture the team title in July in Tokyo; Makoto Ozaki took the Itosu-kai individual title and Ichikawa Prefecture the team title in August at Kobe. In the final major tournament of the year, Makoto Nakamura defeated Keiji Sanpei in the Kokushin-kai's second World Open tournament. It is Japan's only full-contact karate tournament.

MARILYN K. YEE—THE NEW YORK TIMES

Pascal Trinquet of France (right) remained unbeaten through five bouts to win the International Invitational Fencing Tournament in New York in April. In this photo, she is battling Louise Marie LeBlanc of Canada.

UPI

East German contender Heinke (left) tangled with Soviet Harabelli in the under-78-kilo class judo competition in May. Heinke won the match.

Sumo. *Yokozuna* (grand champion) Kitanoumi's dominance of sumo declined somewhat in 1979, although he won three of the six annual 15-day *basho* (tournaments) and was named *rikishi* (wrestler) of the year for the fifth time, with a total of 77 wins and 13 losses. The 26-year-old powerhouse boosted his *yusho* (tournament championships) to 17. In a surprise promotion, 31-year-old Mienoumi was elevated to the top rank of *yokozuna* in July after two consecutive runner-up performances. Asahikuni, who held the second-highest rank of *ozeki*, retired at age 32 after suffering a severe shoulder injury in the autumn tournament. Hawaiian-American Jesse Kuhaulua, who fights under the name Takamiyama, set a new all-time record for consecutive appearances in the top (*makunouchi*) division. The 35-year-old *rikishi* had fought 1,065 bouts in a row by the end of the year.

In tourney action, Kitanoumi won the Hatsu *basho* (New Year's tournament) with a 14–1 record for his sixth *yusho* in seven tourneys, and he had a perfect 15–0 mark in the Haru (spring) *basho* that followed in March. But just when it seemed he might repeat his incredible feat of the previous year by winning five of the six tournaments, Kitanoumi lost to *ozeki* Mienoumi in the Natsu (summer) *basho* in May to end his 32-bout winning streak, paving the way for *yokozuna* Wakanohana to capture the *yusho* with a 14–1 record. Kitanoumi and Mienoumi tied for second place with 13–2 marks. In the Nagoya *basho* in July, *yokozuna* Wajima won his first title in 18 months with a brilliant 14–1 record, beating Mienoumi in a play-off. As a result of his two straight *jun-yusho* (runner-up) performances, Mienoumi was promoted as the 57th *yokozuna*, thus bringing to four the number of currently active grand champions. The Aki (autumn) *basho* championship went to Kitanoumi with a 13–2 record in a ragged tournament that saw the four *yokozuna* upset a total of no less than nine times. In the final Kyushu *basho* in November, newly promoted *yokozuna* Mienoumi grabbed the *yusho* with a fine 14–1 record and compiled the year's second-best mark of 73–17. Wakanohana, who won one title and was second three times, finished behind Mienoumi with 71 wins and 19 losses, but ahead of Wajima, who captured one *yusho* and one *jun-yusho* while earning 68 wins in 90 bouts. With Mienoumi moving up to *yokozuna* and Asahikuni retiring, 29-year-old Takanohana was the only active *ozeki*; he set a new record during the year by holding his rank for 43 *basho*. Two-time *ozeki* Kaiketsu retired during the January tournament as a *maegashira no. 9*. The former Nihon University *judoka* had won two *yusho* and received the Fighting Spirit Prize a record seven times. In the Kyushu *basho*, *maegashira no. 1* Tochiakagi upset three *yokozuna* in the same tourney.

Kendo. As expected, Japan dominated the action in the fourth World Kendo Championships in August at Sapporo, Japan. The Japanese beat the South Koreans 4–0 to capture the team title, while Hironori Yamada, a 31-year-old policeman from Kumamoto Prefecture, defeated 25-year-old Kazuo Furukawa 2–0 with two *kote* strikes to his opponent's forearm guard to win the individual title. Yamada was a semifinalist in the 1978 national championships. More than 300 kendoists from 20 countries competed. Japan thus retained the team and individual titles it had held since the triennial world event started in 1970 in Tokyo. In the men's national championships held at Tokyo's Nippon Budokan in December, all-Japan runner-up Eiji Sueno of Kagoshima Prefecture edged Furukawa by two *men* (helmet) strikes to one. Furukawa eliminated Yamada 2–0 in the semifinals in a rematch of their World Championship finals contest.

A 24-year-old martial arts instructor, Ritsuko Komatsu, beat high school student Y. Hasegawa by *do* and *men* strikes to the breastplate and helmet to win the 18th All-Japan Women's Championships in May. Hasegawa upset two-time national champion C. Nemoto in the semifinals. The national men's team title went to Aichi Prefecture.

(ANDREW M. ADAMS)

[452.B.4.h.v11]

SPECIAL REPORT

THE MARTIAL ARTS: AN INSIDE VIEW

by Donn F. Draeger

Millions of people presume they have a rather clear notion of the martial arts. Actually, genuine martial arts are rarely seen and, at best, are only imperfectly known by the vast majority of people. This is so because those who lack technical competence in the field have disseminated widespread misconceptions. When martial and nonmartial entities are mixed together indiscriminately, however, they impose inappropriate meanings and values upon one another. The purpose of this report, therefore, is to present a professional "view from the inside" of man's combative culture and in the process explain the true nature of martial arts. To this end we will discuss and delimit some typical East Asian forms of combative arts and show something of their innermost workings. The end result will not be a precise definition of martial arts, but it will dramatically change our way of thinking about them.

Martial Arts. Not all fighting arts are martial arts. It is equally true, but not so immediately evident, that martial arts embrace more than fighting techniques. Martial arts are systems of combat designed by and for professional warriors (who are a specially educated hereditary elite) and have an inherent sociopolitical base. The primary purpose of any martial system is to ensure the security and ascendancy of the warrior group for which it is designed. Such systems manifest an adaptive response to the problem of group survival or extinction. Given the fact that warriors considered martial arts to be their exclusive privilege conferred under divine sanction, it is understandable that they would proscribe the learning of martial skills to persons in the lower levels of their societies. Not recognizing this exclusivity has contributed to a wide misunderstanding of the true nature of the martial arts.

In India, China, Korea, and Japan—countries where a warrior elite once prevailed—a moral dimension intruded and commonly circumscribed each respective warrior ethos. In all cases there has been a deep concern with the inner man and with the introspective approach to truth as contrasted with outer things and values. It was not enough that a warrior wage combat successfully. What mattered most was that he wage combat honourably. Combat lost with honour carried no stigma, but victory gained through dishonour was despicable. The importance of nobility of character, self-restraint, benevolence, and courage was promulgated through systematic education. However, because individual ethnic, racial, or national warrior groups had different views on how reason and passion might bind courage to benevolence, each unit formulated its own ethical standards. These not only differed from one another but were substantially different from the ethics then prevailing in the civil segments of their respective societies.

Donn F. Draeger is director of the International Hoplological Research Center in Honolulu.

Belief Systems. The martial ethics of India, China, Korea, and Japan were strongly conditioned by their respective indigenous belief systems, *i.e.*, by superstitions, dogmas, rituals, and institutions. Whereas Indian martial arts were steeped in animistic lore and fortified with Brahmanic-Hindu, Buddhist, and Islamic concepts, Chinese and Korean martial cultures were permeated with animistic, Taoist, Confucian, and Buddhist teachings. In Japan it was not Zen Buddhism, as is so popularly believed, but indigenous Shinto and esoteric Buddhist doctrine (*mikkyo*) that profoundly influenced Japanese martial culture. Buddhism in India tended toward peace; it made few condemnations of warfare. It did, however, draw the very vital line between legitimate combat waged by the professional warrior caste (*kshatriya*) and the socially damaging acts of combative violence perpetrated by random individuals. Buddhist doctrine placed the warrior above the priest (*brahman*) and encouraged an altruistic system of morality that was a corollary of its position on fundamental truths regarded in a psychological rather than a metaphysical or theological manner. The responsibility for martial matters was entrusted to the monopoly of the warrior caste with the further proviso that it was sacrilegious for a lower social order to assume the duties of a higher one.

Whether a system is an actual method of battlefield fighting or whether it is regarded as an adjunct to such combat, the system is designated a martial art. In Japan, for example, more than 50 different martial systems have been identified. *Kenjutsu* is the major component system within what experts call *ko bujutsu*, classical martial arts. *Kenjutsu* (as opposed to *iai-jutsu*) embraces combat made with the sword already drawn and was the primary art of the classical warrior (*bushi*). *Ko bujutsu* is extant today in its centuries-old forms as an exercise in ethnic identity and cultural preservation articulated by thousands of group "styles" (*ryu-gi*). It also has a modern counterpart in the new martial arts (*shin *bujutsu*), taught only to the armed forces and to members of law enforcement agencies.

Unarmed Fighting. Other discrete features of a martial art define a technical horizon that is beyond the scope of civil arts of combat and usually of no immediate interest to exponents of such arts. No ethnic, racial, or national warrior group has ever been known to reject weapons in favour of unarmed fighting men who rely on punches, kicks, and twist-of-the-wrist techniques. Training with weapons has always been included in the martial curricula of all ages. It was reliance on the bow and the blade as major weapons, and on some means of conveyance (an adjunct system) such as a chariot or horse, that determined the martial orbit of aristocratic warriors. The point is that in East Asia the possession of bow, blade, and transport has always implied social and economic superiority and was a combination well contrived to establish and maintain an emphasis on aristocratic group unity such as clearly divided the noble of birth from the common peasant. Similarities and affinities aside, it should now be clear how unrealistic it is to equate the martial art of any single ethnic, racial, or national source with that of any other. Thus the search for a unitary, all-pervading corporate rationale among martial arts of different East Asian countries is futile.

The worthwhile objectives envisioned by promoters of the civil arts as physical education in which competitions and mass entertainment themes dominate have no place in martial systems. Martial arts are always combatively functional because they are based on mutual suspicion and distrust among groups for whom the only game to be "played" involves the ultimate risk of life or death. Japanese-created disciplines such as judo, kendo, karate-do, aiki-do, and others and Okinawan karate-like combative arts are, from the historical point of view, clearly plebeian-derived systems, *i.e.*, civil arts that have never served a warrior ethos. Moreover, with the exception of some Okinawan systems, none of the aforementioned *do*-form disciplines is primarily a system of self-defense, being exercised either as a vehicle of cultism in pursuance of the Way (*michi*)—here self-perfection, not self-protection—or as physical education in the form of competitive sport.

A civil art of self-defense is exactly what its name implies—*self*-defense—concerned primarily with the individual's response to combative emergencies, not those of the group, which is always the concern of martial arts. Moreover, civil systems are self-*defense* systems by which the operator responds to aggression. The much acclaimed "no offense" (*sente nashi*) approach to combat that is the basis of all Japanese karate-do is a case in point. Exponents of karate-do must necessarily operate under conditions of severely curtailed maneuver and initiative, but both of these are essential elements in martial combat.

China. Pristine Chinese combative systems, once influential on the Asian landmass, have not always assumed the forms that are today generically classified as martial arts (*wu shu*). No longer extant are martial systems of combat that featured the bow, crossbow, halberd, and various types of swords, spears, and shields wielded by armoured fighting men who were either ground deployed or mounted on horses or riding in chariots. In the wake of these truly martial arts there developed numerous systems of combat, of physical education, and of theatrical performance, based on both unarmed and armed methods, that are today referred to as "martial arts." Apparently forgotten is the crucial fact that scores of generations of influential Chinese have taught that even to consider the subject of martial matters is a sure sign of ignorance and low breeding. It was the civil bureaucrat, the scholar-gentry, who qualified by academic ability to replace the martial men in roles of governmental leadership, and it is his brand of "martial arts," taught and practiced as a civilian endeavour, that has most deeply influenced the disciplines we now enjoy: *shaolin*, *taijichuan* (*t'ai chi ch'uan*), *xingyi* (*hsing-i*), and *bagua* (*pa-kua*).

Korean combative arts also developed as an intermix of martial and civil forms and, despite considerable indigenous autogeneity, bear the indelible imprint of Chinese and Mongolian influences. Korean weapons systems never reached technical maturity for various reasons, including the Chinese civil influence of "favouring arts and despising arms." This is evident in such popular disciplines as Tang Soo Do and Tae Kwon Do, both of which are inadequate to deal with battlefield realities.

Modern East Asian combative arts are, by virtue of the mass participation of millions of civilian exponents, securely divorced from any martial parentage they once may have had. The ancients believed that martial arts must be exclusively the privilege of persons who were by the strictest standards of moral integrity biosocially "fitted" to assume the responsibility entrusted to them. This same precaution is needed today to prevent the misuse of fighting techniques by those who would use their knowledge and training to the detriment of society. If properly used, these arts can serve to enrich the culture of every nation. But participants should seek in them the guiding principles of life that not only are necessary to any wholesome civil endeavour but are capable of providing deeper insights and perhaps even wisdom to those who comprehend their true meaning.

Commonwealth of Nations

The 22nd meeting of Commonwealth heads of government in Lusaka, Zambia, on Aug. 1–7, 1979, promised to be divisive because of its concentration on Zimbabwe Rhodesia, but in the event it passed off calmly. After touring Tanzania, Malawi, and Botswana, Queen Elizabeth II, despite fears for her safety because of possible terrorist action, opened the Lusaka conference of 39 nations. (Though St. Lucia and Kiribati brought the Commonwealth total to 41, Nauru and Tuvalu, as special members, do not attend the meetings.) Later in the year, St. Vincent and the Grenadines became the 42nd member.

After an uneasy start a group consisting of leaders of Britain, Zambia, Tanzania, Nigeria, Jamaica, and Australia produced a nine-point declaration that committed the British government to submitting a new constitution for Zimbabwe Rhodesia to an all-party London conference. This was accepted, and the conference broke up a day early. The London conference opened on September 10, and after weeks of difficult negotiations, agreement was reached on a plan leading to new elections and eventual legal independence. As part of the arrangement, Zimbabwe Rhodesia reverted to the status of a British colony on December 12, with Lord Soames as governor. A cease-fire, to be monitored by British and other Commonwealth troops, was signed in London on December 21.

In the Pacific, Australia and New Zealand reassessed their roles. Australia submitted a report on Pacific relations, stressing local culture and environment as well as island trade and aid. Australia continued to support the Papua New Guinea budget by more than A$200 million a year. New Zealand produced a defense and strategy review of 1978 based on the ANZUS security treaty between Australia, New Zealand, and the U.S. (and for the first time chose a Maori, Brian Poananga, as Army chief of staff) and expressed concern at Chinese and Soviet expansion in the South Pacific.

Some concern was felt in the British Caribbean when the first left-wing coup, bypassing ballot boxes, took place in Grenada; in Dominica Oliver Seraphine replaced Patrick John, and in St. Lucia, after elections marked by violence, Allan Louisy (*see* BIOGRAPHIES) defeated John Compton. Fresh vigour was infused into the Caribbean Community and Common Market by a new secretary and a $112 million loan sponsored by the World Bank.

With regard to the Commonwealth economy, the Commonwealth Development Corporation (CDC) in 1979 expanded into French-speaking Africa, having achieved a record for new enterprises in 1978, mainly in the poorest countries. As of 1979 total CDC revenue stood at £31 million, with total commitments of £379 million. The only setback was Nigeria's indigenization policy, which, with a 60% capital takeover, meant the CDC could no longer operate there.

British aid estimates for 1979–80 rose by £75 million to £790 million (£843 million gross). A breakdown of 1978 (£733 million) figures showed that more than 95% consisted of grants and aid to Commonwealth countries, India topping Asian recipients with £119 million, while Kenya (£29 million) and Zambia (£33 million) received the most in Africa and Jamaica (£19 million) in the Caribbean. In 1979 £145 million was pledged to India and £80 million to Kenya. A new Commonwealth plan to speed industrialization was approved at a Commonwealth ministerial meeting in Bangalore, India, in March, and a team of Commonwealth experts flew to Uganda in May to help rehabilitate that nation's economy.

(MOLLY MORTIMER)

See also articles on the various political units.
[972.A.1.a]

BILL CAMPBELL—SYGMA

The Rhodesian question was high on the agenda when the 22nd Commonwealth Conference opened in August at Lusaka, Zambia.

Comecon: *see* Economy, World

Commerce: *see* Economy, World

Commodity Futures: *see* Stock Exchanges

Common Market: *see* Economy, World; European Unity

Communications: *see* Industrial Review; Television and Radio

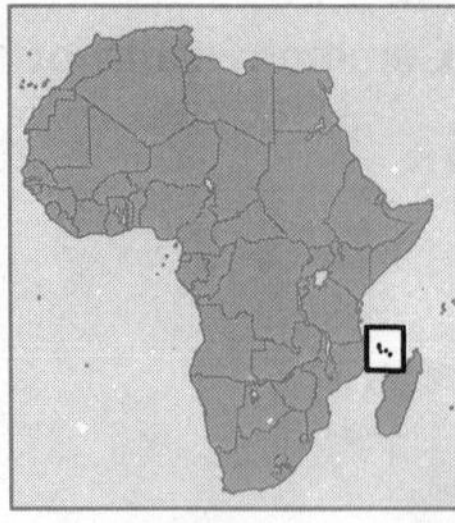

Comoros

Comoros

An island state lying in the Indian Ocean off the east coast of Africa between Mozambique and Madagascar, the Comoros in 1979 administratively comprised three main islands, Grande Comore (Ngazídja), Moheli (Mohali), and Anjouan (Dzouani); the fourth island of the archipelago, Mayotte, continued to be a de facto dependency of France. Area: 1,792 sq km (692 sq mi). Pop. (1978 est.): 311,000. Cap. and largest city: Moroni (pop., 1976 est., 18,300), on Grande Comore. Language: Comorian (which is allied to Swahili), Arabic, and French. Religion: Islam (official). President in 1979, Ahmed Abdallah; premier, Salim Ben Ali.

The Comoros was readmitted to the Organization of African Unity on Feb. 26, 1979. It had been expelled in July 1978 after the coup, led by French mercenary Robert Denard, that overthrew Pres. Ali Soilih. In February and March, Pres. Ahmed Abdallah visited France, with which he had very close relations. In an attempt to crush opposition among the young, he ordered the arrest of a number of students and schoolboys in August and September.

Air Tanzania inaugurated a weekly direct flight to the Comoros on March 12. The conference of foreign ministers of 42 Islamic countries at Fez, Morocco, in May decided to give urgent financial aid to the Comoros to assist recovery from natural disasters, including an eruption of the Kartalha volcano. The conference of nonaligned countries in Cuba in September demanded that the Comoro island of Mayotte, which remained French, be reunited with the rest of the archipelago.

(PHILIPPE DECRAENE)

COMOROS

Education. (Including Mayotte; 1976–77) Primary, pupils 34,181, teachers 849; secondary, pupils 2,541, teachers 115; teacher training, students 45, teachers 3.

Finance and Trade. Monetary unit: CFA franc, with (Sept. 17, 1979) a parity of CFA Fr 50 to the French franc and a free rate of CFA Fr 211.54 to U.S. $1 (CFA Fr 455.12 = £1 sterling). Budget (1976 est.) balanced at *c.* CFA Fr 1 billion. Foreign trade (including Mayotte; 1976): imports U.S. $13 million; exports U.S. $9 million. Import sources (1973): France *c.* 40%; Madagascar *c.* 16%; Kenya *c.* 5%. Export destinations (1973): France *c.* 75%; Madagascar *c.* 9%; Italy *c.* 7%; West Germany *c.* 6%. Main exports (1972): vanilla 41%; essential oils 33%; cloves 11%; copra 6%.

Computers

Smaller, cheaper, faster. Those bywords of the computer industry since its inception, especially since the advent of the silicon semiconductor chip early in the 1970s, remained the key descriptive terms for data processing during 1979. The major consequence of the continuing trend toward more computer power at less cost was the continued penetration of computers into all levels of business, government, and other realms of society.

This penetration, so omnipresent that few failed to recognize to some degree the electronic revolution occurring all about them, evoked fear as well as celebration. While few denied the benefits computers had wrought, many worried about computer-related crime and the threat to personal privacy posed by huge data banks accessible to many thousands of people.

Technological Advances. The silicon chip took a step forward late in 1978 with IBM's announcement that an experimental high-density microcircuit had been produced by electron-beam technology. The density of the circuits generated with the new technology is ten times greater than the density of circuits in conventional silicon chips, since the new circuitry operates with just one-tenth the energy dissipation of previous field-effect transistor circuits. Sure to lead to yet smaller and faster computers, the IBM microcircuit is produced by using a computer-controlled electron beam to project patterns on one presensitized silicon wafer; after each projection the wafer is developed much like film.

Bubble memories constituted another field of major technological advance during 1979. Smaller, more reliable, and potentially (they have been in commercial production only since 1978) less costly than the semiconductor disk memory systems in current use, bubble memories store bits of information in oval-shaped magnetic domains measuring one-sixteenth the diameter of a human hair. Capable of storing far greater amounts of information (one introduced during the year can store up to one million bits in contrast to the 64,000-bit maximum of a semiconductor memory chip), the bubble memory also enjoys advantages in terms of nonvolatility and imperviousness to dust and temperature fluctuations.

Nonvolatility is a property of bubble memories that prevents them from losing their contents when cut off from a power supply, thereby eliminating the need for expensive backup systems (such as batteries) that semiconductor memories require. Their imperviousness to environmental conditions allows computers equipped with bubble memories to be moved out of the air-conditioned, dust-free rooms to which they were formerly confined and to take their place on the factory floor right next to the machine tools they control. Bell Telephone Laboratories, IBM, and Texas Instruments, Inc., had been the industry leaders in bubble memory research.

IBM also scored a major advance with the introduction of its 6670 Information Distributor. A photocopying machine and a printer for word-processing systems, the 6670 is also able to communicate with distant computers, terminals, and other machines like itself in order to create an electronic mail system. It will be, analysts predict, a pivotal component of the "office of the future"—an integrated system of computers, word processors, printers, copiers, and other electronic apparatuses. The 6670 can print as many as 36 pages a minute in up to four typefaces per page, and it can both "talk" to and receive stored data from other computers over ordinary telephone lines.

Texas Instruments captured another market for itself with the TI-59 programmable calculator. A pocket-sized instrument that sells for about $300, the TI-59 resembles far more expensive microcomputers in its ability to remember automatically the keystroke sequence required to solve a problem. Sequences can be stored either on tiny magnetic cards or in semiconductor memory chips. The cards and chip modules (one of the latter holds the information equivalent of about 24 cards) can be inserted easily into the calculator.

At the other end of the size spectrum, the Cray 1 supercomputer exercised technological dominance over all its electronic counterparts. Ten times faster than the biggest IBM computer and with six times more memory capacity, the Cray 1 sold for $8 million. By the end of 1979 scarcely more than a dozen of the huge machines (six and a half feet high, five feet wide) had been sold; the price and the fact that a Cray 1 requires another computer on-line as an input-output device just to make efficient use of its capabilities certainly inhibited its sales potential. Nevertheless, the creator of the Cray 1, Seymour Cray of Chippewa Falls, Wis., was already working on the Cray 2, intended to be twice as fast and four times as efficient as his original supercomputer.

Business. It was another year of excellent growth for mainframe manufacturers, the builders of huge computers frequently costing a million dollars or more each. Led by IBM, mainframe makers enjoyed a 15% growth rate over 1978 sales. And yet the mainframe computer business was by far the most sluggish segment of the computer industry, an industry estimated to have sold close to $48 billion worth of goods and services during 1979.

The main activity was in minicomputers, paced by industry leader Digital Equipment Corp., and by small business systems. The annual growth rate was better than 30%, as declining prices combined with enhanced performance to lure many small businesses into the computer revolution. What many of these businesses wanted—and what minicomputers made possible—was a system of distributed data processing. In such a system a network of small computers and terminals spread out through offices and factory floors can handle data processing locally rather than requiring a centralized mainframe.

In January IBM introduced new mainframe central processors, the 4300 models. Analysts agreed that the price/performance ratio of the 4300 computers was at least three to four—perhaps five—times better than that of the 370 line. Other mainframe makers, especially the numerous plug-compatible manufacturers (PCM's) who had proliferated and profited by marketing cheaper computers capable of operating with IBM software, were most grievously affected. Some industry experts predicted the total demise of the PCM's, believing that they would be unable to undersell the amazingly inexpensive 4300s.

Applications. Computers were put to work in a variety of ways beyond their predominant business-oriented functions. Among the more unusual (but timely) applications was the creation by a private company of an up-to-the-minute data log of terrorist acts throughout the world. A new firm called Risks International, Inc. maintained the

PHOTOS, IBM CORP.

LLATV-3

Experimental silicon chip (top), an extremely dense field-effect transistor (FET) integrated circuit developed by IBM scientists, measures four millimetres (one-sixth of an inch) square. Scanning electron micrograph reveals a highly magnified view of several circuits comprising part of one of the chip's registers (left). The development represented several years of work at IBM to reduce the widths of individual circuits in chips to one micrometre (1/25,000 of an inch) or less.

data on a Radio Shack TRS-80 microcomputer and sold the information to firms whose executives could be threatened by terrorist activities.

It was in the home and car, however, that new computer applications were most noteworthy. Viewdata, a system of electronic services capable of transforming an ordinary television set into a computer terminal, seemed ready to enter the U.S. Already established in Great Britain, France, and Canada, the system allows subscribers to receive travel, educational, and financial advice, recipes, etc.; to buy department store goods and airline tickets; and to get all sorts of computerized information on a TV screen merely by calling a central data bank over standard telephone lines.

Meanwhile, U.S. automobile manufacturers were solidifying plans to add computers to the majority of their products. "By 1981," the president of General Motors predicted, "we expect virtually all GM cars sold in this country will be equipped with an on-board computer as standard equipment."

Social Issues. John G. Kemeny, president of Dartmouth College, predicted that the nation's ability to nurture a "computer literacy" would become a fundamental issue of the next decade. He noted that more than 90% of Dartmouth graduates had gained some computer experience, and that the vast majority could at least create a simple program. But what would become of those who lacked such literacy? *Saturday Review*, in a cover story entitled "Computer Shock" (June 23, 1979), dealt with the possibility of a social bipolarization involving a small minority of technologically oriented elitists on the one hand and a new huge "underclass" of people who would be nearly unemployable due to their lack of computer skills.

Automation had long been feared as a threat to employment, but the situation took a new turn as the electronic "office of the future" became more of a reality. Computer-driven word and data processors, electronic mail equipment, and other telecommunications devices threatened to eliminate jobs for secretaries and clerical personnel, as well as some middle-management positions.

Computer crime continued to pose major problems. Data-processing equipment owned by government and private industry made vulnerable targets for sabotage, terrorism, and subversion, but it was theft by computer that constituted the most frequent crime. Moreover, in contrast to ordinary armed robberies, which rarely netted more than $10,000, computer thefts averaged about $500,000. (JEROLD L. KELLMAN)

[735.D; 10/23.A.6–7]

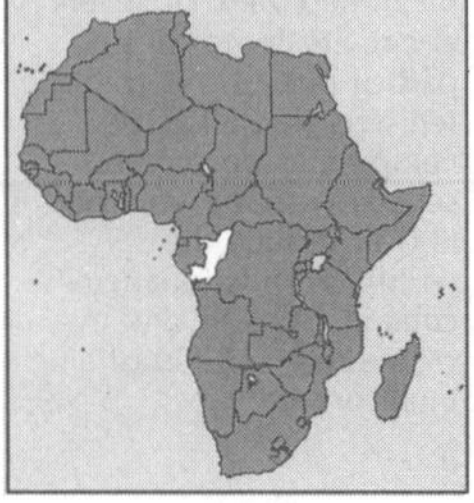
Congo

Congo

A people's republic of equatorial Africa, the Congo is bounded by Gabon, Cameroon, the Central African Republic, Zaire, Angola, and the Atlantic Ocean. Area: 342,000 sq km (132,047 sq mi). Pop. (1978 est.): 1,454,000, mainly Bantu. Cap. and largest city: Brazzaville (pop., 1974 prelim., 299,-000). Language: French (official) and Bantu dialects. Religion: Roman Catholic 39.3%; most of the remainder are animist. Presidents in 1979, Gen. Joachim Yhombi-Opango to February 5 and, from February 8, Col. Denis Sassou-Nguesso; premier, Col. Louis Sylvain Ngoma.

Pres. Joachim Yhombi-Opango and his governing Military Committee (all later imprisoned) surrendered their powers at a full session of the Congolese Labour Party (PCT) Central Committee on Feb. 5, 1979. The committee named the former defense minister, Col. Denis Sassou-Nguesso, head of state three days later, and his nomination was confirmed on March 27 by a special party congress. Col. Louis Sylvain Ngoma remained as premier. The new government favoured the strengthening of relations with the Soviet Union.

On July 8 an overwhelming majority of voters approved adoption of a new socialist constitution and elected a docile National Popular Assembly.

CONGO

Education. (1975–76) Primary, pupils 319,101, teachers 5,434; secondary, pupils 94,276, teachers 2,042; vocational, pupils 7,129, teachers 337; teacher training, students 705, teachers 34; higher, students 3,249, teaching staff 165.

Finance. Monetary unit: CFA franc, with (Sept 17, 1979) a parity of CFA Fr 50 to the French franc and a free rate of CFA Fr 211.54 to U.S. $1 (CFA Fr 455.12 = £1 sterling). Budget (1978 est.) balanced at CFA Fr 60,249,000,000.

Foreign Trade. (1977) Imports CFA Fr 50,450,000,000; exports CFA Fr 50,110,000,000. Import sources: France 49%; West Germany 6%; U.S. 5%. Export destinations: Italy 30%; France 12%; U.S. 7%; Spain 7%; The Bahamas 6%. Main exports: crude oil 52%; timber 15%; chemical fertilizer (1976) 9%.

Transport and Communications. Roads (1977) *c.* 11,-000 km. Motor vehicles in use (1976): passenger 20,000; commercial (including buses) 13,000. Railways: (1977) 803 km; traffic (1978) 294 million passenger-km, freight 478 million net ton-km. Air traffic (including apportionment of Air Afrique; 1977): 152 million passenger-km; freight 14.2 million net ton-km. Telephones (Jan. 1978) 13,400. Radio receivers (Dec. 1976) 83,000. Television receivers (Dec. 1976) 3,300.

Agriculture. Production (in 000; metric tons; 1977): cassava 769; sweet potatoes *c.* 105; peanuts 24; sugar, raw value *c.* 35; bananas 25; plantains *c.* 33; coffee *c.* 1; cocoa *c.* 2; palm oil *c.* 5; tobacco 2. Livestock (in 000; 1977): cattle *c.* 50; sheep *c.* 52; goats *c.* 102; pigs *c.* 44; chickens *c.* 843.

Industry. Production (in 000; metric tons; 1976): cement 52; crude oil (1978) 1,610; natural gas (cu m; 1977) 9,000; lead concentrates (metal content) 2.5; zinc ore (metal content) 5.1; potash (oxide content) 445; potash fertilizers (nutrient content; 1977–78) *c.* 81; electricity (kw-hr; 1977) 120,000.

An amnesty was decreed in August for persons condemned for having taken part in the 1977 assassination of Pres. Marien Ngouabi. Nevertheless, various humanitarian organizations claimed the government was still holding many political prisoners. (PHILIPPE DECRAENE)

Consumerism

In a speech delivered at a consumer seminar in Jakarta, Indon., early in 1979, Anwar Fazal, president of the International Organization of Consumers Unions (IOCU), noted that over the last decade the consumer movement, which had originated in the U.S. and Europe, had taken firm root in the Asian and Pacific regions. He said that consumerism was a dynamic social movement, a part of the larger movement for human rights and economic justice, a critical part of the development process for a better quality of life. He called upon consumers everywhere to speak out effectively and gave them five general principles—critical awareness, assertive action, social responsibility, ecological responsibility, and solidarity—as guidelines to follow.

International Cooperation. In the debates and discussions of the international organizations, consumerism played a larger part than ever before. Consumer protection was a major issue at the second regular session of the UN Economic and Social Council (Ecosoc) meeting in Geneva in July, where a resolution called on the UN secretary-general to draft a comprehensive report on carrying out work on consumer protection within the UN system. Under provisions in the draft, Ecosoc would recognize that consumer protection had an

Congregational Churches: *see* Religion

Conservation: *see* Environment

Construction Industry: *see* Engineering Projects; Industrial Review

UPI

Joseph Highland (left) and Robert Rauch of the Environmental Defense Fund demonstrate models of hand-held hair dryers which the U.S. government ordered recalled because of suspected harmful amounts of asbestos.

important bearing on economic and social development, as well as on the health, safety, and welfare of the people of all countries. It would also recognize that international cooperation in this area was important in promoting the economic and social development of the less developed countries.

Statements made by the delegates following adoption of the resolution by consensus indicated the complexity of their concerns. Japan, for example, made it clear that it reserved the right to determine consumer protection measures for its own consumers, nor did it interpret "consumer protection related to trade" to compel it to give access to its markets. The U.S. and U.K. stated their conviction that national governments had the primary responsibility for their consumers; the U.S.S.R. expressed its opposition to the setting up of any new departments to deal with consumer protection; and the representative of the Nordic countries noted that the adoption of the resolution was a significant step in helping less developed countries protect their consumers.

Also of consumer concern was the decision of the International Energy Agency (IEA) to designate October 1979 as International Conservation Month, during which a variety of exhibitions, conferences, and competitions were planned to promote awareness of the need for conservation and the means by which it could be achieved. In seeking to restrain energy demand, the IEA did not mean to interfere with normal economic growth or to depress living standards; the aim of its conservation policy was to use energy better, to eliminate wastage, and to utilize every unit of energy with the maximum efficiency.

The lot of consumers—especially children—in the less developed countries was the subject of a statement presented by IOCU to the UNICEF Executive Board in May. The indiscriminate consumption of "junk" foods, it was claimed, resulted in an unbalanced diet for children of all ages and social levels, and this particularly affected the health of those who were least protected economically. In children it generated arteriosclerosis, a predisposition to hypertension, and, in many young people, hyperactivity and poor concentration.

National Policies. In 1979 there was a dramatic increase in consumer complaints in the U.S. about many products and services. There was a massive recall of asbestos-lined hair dryers because of the potential danger that they might cause cancer. Automobile complaints topped the list with housing coming in second.

Gasoline rationing programs and whether service stations should be allowed to charge by the half gallon were the two concerns most often voiced by consumers to state regulatory agencies. The U.S. Federal Trade Commission (FTC) proposed a rule that would prescribe the method for the certification and posting of octane ratings in gasoline. A label supplied by the refineries showing the octane number would be placed on the face of every gasoline pump, assisting the consumer in matching the right gasoline to the specifications suggested by the car manufacturer.

The Federal Home Loan Bank Board during the year adopted new regulations that allowed its member institutions to offer alternative mortgages, including "graduated payment," "variable rate," and "reverse annuity" plans. These gave consumers more options in the financing of their homes. Uniform procedures were adopted by a number of federal agencies for the enforcement of truth-in-lending laws. All federally insured savings and loan associations, commercial banks, credit unions, and mutual savings banks were or-

"It's my observation that more and more consumers are looking after their own interests these days."

DRAWING BY BOOTH; © 1979 THE NEW YORKER MAGAZINE, INC.

WIDE WORLD

Although there are no other identical items that may be substituted for Static Guard... We recommend the use of a fabric softener, either liquid or sheets, because of Static Guards recent unjustifiable unit price increase!
purex
purex

In the wake of soaring prices some supermarkets posted signs advising customers to choose alternative products. This supermarket in Boston advises customers to select a fabric softener as an alternative.

dered to use the same guidelines so that consumers could make better comparisons of loan rates.

The FTC expanded its "energy labeling" system by including the manufacturers of refrigerators, freezers, dishwashers, water heaters, room air conditioners, clothes washers, and furnaces. Under the new regulations energy labels would have to be prominently placed on all new appliances. These labels would include average operating costs, energy usage, and efficiency.

In 1979 several government agencies, including the FTC and the Consumer Product Safety Commission, increased their spending to reimburse witnesses who testified before them on matters of concern to consumers. This allowed consumers who could not normally afford to appear before these agencies the chance to voice their opinions and recommendations on new legislation.

A 1979 FTC report concluded that life insurance companies generally pay returns far below the rate available in equally secure investments. Consequently, the FTC called for tough disclosure rules for life insurance companies, though its recommendations had no legal weight because all insurance regulation takes place at the state level.

In France the Union Fédérale des Consommateurs (UFC) warned consumers against three drugs, available freely on the French market without prescription, which, the UFC suggested, contain potentially cancer-causing mineral fibres of minute diameter. UFC called for the withdrawal of these drugs from the market. In Belgium the Association des Consommateurs opened its first Information Centre for Consumers; it was hoped that this centre, situated in a busy new shopping area in the heart of Brussels, would enable members of the public to obtain free advice on consumer problems.

In India the Karnataka Consumer Service Society produced a film on consumer education and protection for local distribution. The Consumer Protection Association of Turkey, with the support of the United Nations Industrial Development Organization and IOCU, organized a seminar in February on the promotion of the consumer protection movement in that land. The Central Consumers' Authority in Israel prepared a survey on baby equipment, aimed at helping a family to choose articles of good quality at moderate prices.

During the year Australia introduced further provisions to limit the maximum noise levels of cars and motorcycles and to speed up the introduction of date-stamping of prepacked goods. A federal investigation into products unsafe for children resulted in the banning of some from the market, and the government also planned an effort to convince schoolchildren of the dangers of smoking.

Ireland had a director of consumer affairs for the first time in 1979, and in Norway a law on the handling of disputes relating to consumer sales gave consumers further protection in the marketplace. In Spain a new self-regulatory body began to draw up a checklist of standards to protect children from harmful and misleading advertisements.

In the U.K. new regulations introduced in July required restaurants and similar establishments to display prices so that they might be seen by potential customers before entering the premises. The government also decided to introduce regulations under which upholstered furniture, including imported pieces, would have to be resistant to ignition from smokers' materials.

(ISOLA VAN DEN HOVEN; EDWARD MARK MAZZE)

See also Economy, World; Industrial Review: *Advertising*.

[532.B.3; 534.H.5; 534.K]

Contract Bridge

In 1979 the Bermuda Bowl, the official World Team Championship, was for the first time contested by the champions from all six zones. Moreover, during the year a seventh zone was established. It was the Bridge Federation of Asia and Middle East, members of which were India, Sri Lanka, Bangladesh, Pakistan, Iran, and Lebanon, with the United Arab Emirates under consideration.

The 24th Bermuda Bowl took place in Rio de Janeiro in October 1979. North America, the defending champion, was represented by a wholly U.S. team; South America by the host country, Brazil; Europe by Italy, 13-time champions; the Far East by Taiwan; Central America by a composite team from Guadeloupe and Venezuela; and the Antipodes by Australia. The six teams met three times in a round-robin contest to determine the two finalists. At the outset few expected any final other than a rematch of the old antagonists, North America and Italy, but as it happened both teams were hard pressed by Australia, which almost to the end was capable of dislodging one or the other. Australia finally won a well-earned third place behind North America and Italy, which finished first and second, respectively.

Italy began the final with a lead of 37 points over the U.S. team, a carry-over from the earlier meetings between the two countries. After 16 deals it had increased the lead to 43, but after a further 16, in which North America scored 71 points against 3, North America led by 25. When play began in the last 16 deals, North America led by 66 points and there had been nothing in the Italians' performance to suggest that they might recover from such a decisive disadvantage. But Giorgio Belladonna, 13 times world champion and playing for the last time in a championship contest, had other ideas. He was determined to retire on a winning note and led a magnificent fight in which the Italians (Belladonna, Benito Garozzo, Arturo Franco, Vito Pittala, Dano De Falco, Lorenzo Lauria) came back to within striking distance with four hands to play. On the next to the last hand they had the chance to bring off a remarkable win:

NORTH
♠ 3
♥ A 9 8 7 3
♦ 6 5
♣ Q 10 9 5 3

WEST
♠ J 9
♥ K 4 2
♦ A J 9 8
♣ J 8 7 6

EAST
♠ A K 10 8 6 2
♥ Q J 10
♦ Q 7 3
♣ K

SOUTH
♠ Q 7 5 4
♥ 6 5
♦ K 10 4 2
♣ A 4 2

Dealer, East. North-South game.

At both tables West was declarer in three no trumps with North having to choose between a club and a heart lead. Belladonna led the ten of clubs and the contract had no chance. The defense began with three club tricks before conceding a fourth club to declarer. South ducked the first spade and eventually declarer lost a heart and a diamond in addition to four club tricks to go two down.

When the hand appeared on the Vu-Graph screen, the audience knew that Italy could win if it was able to make three no trumps. Billy Eisenberg for North America led the seven of hearts. De Falco overtook with the king and led the jack of spades. Eddie Kantar ducked and declarer continued with a second spade, winning with the king when North failed to follow.

The queen of diamonds was covered by the king and ace, and declarer led a low heart. Eisenberg won with the ace and switched to a low club for Kantar's ace. Kantar returned the four of clubs for Eisenberg's nine, and when Eisenberg returned a third heart declarer was in a winning position. On the third heart South discarded the two of clubs and his original hand could now be counted as four spades, two hearts, three clubs, and four diamonds.

To win declarer should finesse the eight of diamonds, cash the jack of diamonds, and exit with a fourth diamond. South, Kantar, would then be obliged to lead into the dummy's spade, giving declarer the last two tricks and the contract. Unfortunately, De Falco made an error; he cashed his third spade winner after winning the third heart at trick 8 and now there was no escape from South's queen. Declarer thus was one down, a slight gain for Italy but not enough. Had De Falco made his contract Italy would have gained 11 points instead of 2 and would have won the tournament by four points instead of losing by five.

Belladonna was the star player of the match, and Malcolm Brachman, a Texas oil millionaire, the most controversial. Brachman, a modest and unassuming man, had a burning ambition to become a bridge expert. To help him achieve this aim he hired five top professionals to form a team with him, Billy Eisenberg, Eddie Kantar, Bobbie Goldman, Paul Soloway (all past world champions), and Mike Passell. Together they qualified to represent North America in the Bermuda Bowl, Brachman having played the requisite number of hands in the trials to qualify as a playing member.

In the Bermuda Bowl the team captain, Ed Theus, took the view that the team's chances of winning would be improved if Brachman did not play. The other five members of the team all wanted him to play. Theus, in response to this demand, played Brachman for the first 32 hands of the final and, in the event, North America gained 62 points when he was at the table and lost 20 when he was not playing. Nonetheless, there was every likelihood that the American Contract Bridge League would legislate to prevent a recurrence of this situation. (HAROLD FRANKLIN)

[452.C.3.a.i]

Costa Rica

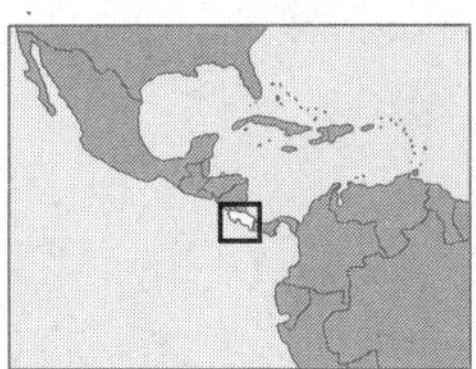

Costa Rica

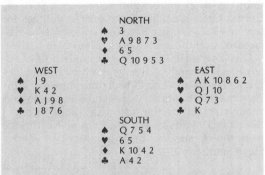

A Central American republic, Costa Rica lies between Nicaragua and Panama and has coastlines on the Caribbean Sea and the Pacific Ocean. Area: 50,898 sq km (19,652 sq mi). Pop. (1979 est.): 2,224,000, including white and mestizo 98%. Cap. and largest city: San José (metro. pop., 1978 est., 584,700). Language: Spanish. Religion: predominantly Roman Catholic. President in 1979, Rodrigo Carazo Odio.

Costa Rica's diplomatic relations with Nicaragua, broken off on Nov. 21, 1978, were resumed on July 21, 1979. Costa Rican support for the ultimately successful Sandinista guerrilla movement in Nicaragua adversely affected relations with El

COSTA RICA

Education. (1976) Primary, pupils 365,957, teachers 10,965; secondary, pupils 93,862, teachers 4,264; vocational, pupils 22,175, teachers 1,651; higher, students (1975) 32,928, teaching staff (1974) *c.* 3,500.

Finance. Monetary unit: colón, with (Sept. 17, 1979) an official rate of 8.57 colones to U.S. $1 (free rate of 18.50 colones = £1 sterling). Gold, SDR's, and foreign exchange (June 1979) U.S. $103.5 million. Budget (1978 actual): revenue 4,111,000,000 colones; expenditure 5,426,000,000 colones. Gross national product (1978) 28,915,000,000 colones. Money supply (May 1979) 5,678,000,000 colones. Cost of living (San José; 1975 = 100; May 1979) 121.5.

Foreign Trade. (1978) Imports 10,151,000,000 colones; exports 7,231,000,000 colones. Import sources (1977): U.S. 34%; Japan 13%; Guatemala 6%; West Germany 5%; El Salvador 5%; Nicaragua 5%. Export destinations (1977): U.S. 29%; West Germany 12%; Nicaragua 7%; The Netherlands 7%; Guatemala 6%; El Salvador 6%. Main exports: coffee 36%; bananas 17%; beef 7%. Tourism (1977): visitors 328,000; gross receipts U.S. $60 million.

Transport and Communications. Roads (1976) 24,674 km (including 665 km of Pan-American Highway). Motor vehicles in use (1975): passenger 59,800; commercial (including buses) 42,700. Railways: (1978) 1,003 km; traffic (main only; 1974) 81 million passenger-km, freight 14 million net ton-km. Air traffic (1978): 360 million passenger-km; freight 19.1 million net ton-km. Telephones (Jan. 1978) 145,100. Radio receivers (Dec. 1976) *c.* 400,000. Television receivers (Dec. 1976) *c.* 155,000.

Agriculture. Production (in 000; metric tons; 1978): sorghum *c.* 55; corn (1977) *c.* 61; rice (1977) *c.* 130; potatoes (1977) *c.* 25; bananas 1,170; oranges *c.* 74; sugar, raw value (1977) 194; coffee 95; cocoa *c.* 9; palm oil *c.* 24. Livestock (in 000; 1977): cattle 1,920; horses *c.* 109; pigs *c.* 215; chickens *c.* 5,200.

Industry. Production (in 000; metric tons; 1976): petroleum products 247; cement 362; nitrogenous fertilizers (1977–78) 32; electricity (kw-hr; 1978) *c.* 1,800,000 (88% hydroelectric in 1976).

Cosmetics:
see Fashion and Dress

Cost of Living:
see Economy, World

Salvador, Guatemala, and Honduras, especially after a provisional Sandinista junta was set up in Costa Rica in June, before the guerrillas overthrew Nicaragua's Pres. Anastasio Somoza on July 17.

Pres. Rodrigo Carazo lost some political support during the year. Costa Rica faced labour problems, with major strikes in February at the Costa Rican Banana Co. and in July at the Pozuela cookie factory. After workers were evicted from the latter, they occupied the cathedral and invaded the Ministry of Labour, before the strike collapsed at the end of August. On August 18 a ten-day strike by the Puerto Limón Labour Federation (Fetral) was declared illegal, but it spread and produced violent clashes with the Civil Guard. The government gave in on August 23 and granted concessions to the strikers. The minister of labour, Estela Quezada, resigned in August.

The economy grew by 5% in 1978, but declining coffee prices and increases in the price of petroleum made 1979 a year of readjustment. The balance of trade deficit at the end of 1978 stood at U.S. $207.6 million and by June 1979 had increased to $246 million. At the same time, the trade balance with the Central American Common Market fell from a surplus of $7.4 million in 1977 to a deficit of $27.5 million in 1978. The balance of payments deficit at the end of 1978 stood at $51.7 million, and international reserves fell from $295.2 million at the end of June 1978 to $87.5 million at the end of July 1979. (CHRISTINE MELLOR)

Court Games

Handball. Naty Alvarado of Los Angeles won his second U.S. National Open handball title in 1979 by defeating defending champion Fred Lewis of Miami, Fla., 21–20, 21–11, at the Coliseum Sportrooms in Coral Gables, Fla. The win, Alvarado's seventh major title of the handball season, made him the leading money winner on the Spalding professional handball tour for 1978–79. His official prize money for the season totaled $16,300.

Naty Alvarado (left) takes the ball off the back court in the U.S. National Open handball competition against defending champion Fred Lewis. Alvarado defeated Lewis and won his second National Open title, thus becoming the leading money winner in the Spalding professional handball tour of 1978–79.

TERRY MUCK—UNITED STATES HANDBALL ASSOCIATION

In the United States Handball Association (USHA) open doubles competition, Stuffy Singer (Los Angeles) and partner Marty Decatur (New York) defeated Chicago's Vern Roberts and Dave Dohman for their second straight open doubles title, 21–14, 18–21, 11–9. In masters play for men over 40 Jim McKee of Memphis, Tenn., defeated Dick Miller of Vienna, Va., 13–21, 21–6, 11–9 for the singles title, and Ron Earl and Marty Goffstein of San Jose, Calif., defeated Chuck Schildmeyer and Bernie Coffee, also of California, 21–16, 20–21, 11–7. In golden masters play for men over 50 Jack Briscoe of St. Louis, Mo., won his third singles title in a row by defeating San Francisco's Rudy Stadlberger 21–11, 21–16. Briscoe had won this event every year since he became eligible in 1977. In golden masters doubles Alvis Grant (Dallas, Texas) and Chuck Harris (Kansas City, Mo.) defeated Ken Kidd and Marv Gurian (both of San Jose, Calif.) 21–8, 21–14. Lee Shinn and Ralph Stapper, Salem, Ore., won the super master doubles for men over 60, beating Rod Rodriquez and Joe Kaloustian, both of Los Angeles, 21–6, 21–5.

Lake Forest (Ill.) College won its sixth USHA intercollegiate handball title by winning the doubles (Fran Harvey and Bob Martin) and showing sufficient overall strength in the A and B singles to gain enough points for the team title. Gary Stedman from the University of California at Northridge won the A singles, defeating Montana Tech's Steve Stanisich 21–20, 21–7.

(TERRY CHARLES MUCK)

Jai Alai. U.S. players continued in 1979 to enter the ranks of professionals, long dominated by the Basques. The 1978 U.S. champion Mike McGee joined the Fort Pierce, Fla., roster, while Mike Faedo began to play for Ocala, Fla. Gilbert Trujillo was signed as a professional at the Milford, Conn., fronton, and Cary Sargent entered the pros at the Las Vegas, Nev., fronton. Teenager Freddie Griffin became the first black player to enter professional jai alai, playing for Fort Pierce.

Hurricane David, which swept through Florida in September, did considerable damage to jai alai frontons. The Melbourne fronton lost its roof and had a late start for its season. The Palm Beach fronton, which was under construction due to a fire earlier in the year, was completely leveled by the hurricane.

In U.S. amateur competition a tournament was held to determine the national champions. The semifinals took place in November at Fort Pierce, and the finals were scheduled to be held in Miami in January 1980. Those qualifying for the final round were, in the front court, Bobby Hirsh, Mitch Rappaport, Dwayne Owens, and Scott King. Backcourt players who made it to the finals included Peter Stock, Greg Benjamin, Jimmy Ryder, and Tracy Moore.

Miami was scheduled to have a summer professional jai alai season for the first time in 1980. The fronton in Dania, Fla., was undergoing a $6 million renovation. When completed, the fronton would include a new court, players' quarters, and dining and banquet facilities. Capacity would be increased to 11,000 spectators.

(ROBERT H. GROSSBERG)

Volleyball. The year 1979 was one of regional activity in volleyball as teams attempted to qualify

ALEXANDER YAKOVLEV—TASS/SOVFOTO

The U.S. women's volleyball team defeated Leningrad in the seventh summer Spartakiade of the U.S.S.R. The U.S. team placed third in the games behind Japan and the Soviet Union.

for the 1980 Olympic Games. The U.S. women secured a place at the Olympics by finishing second to Cuba in the North Central and Caribbean America championships held in Havana in April. Because they were the 1978 world champions, the Cuban women were already qualified for the Olympics.

In men's competition Cuba won the North Central and Caribbean America championship and thereby qualified for the Olympics. The U.S. men would have to participate in the final Olympic qualification tournament in Bulgaria in January 1980 to gain a berth at Moscow.

In South America the Peruvian women and the Brazilian men earned positions in the 1980 Olympics. Qualifying for the Olympics from the European zone were Yugoslavia in the men's tournament and East Germany in women's competition. A tournament for Olympic qualifiers from the Far East resulted in victories for China in both men's and women's competition.

There were a number of other significant volleyball tournaments throughout the world during 1979. One of the most notable was the Soviet Spartakiade, a quadrennial event in the U.S.S.R. normally open only to Soviet athletes but in 1979 conducted as a pre-Olympic competition. The victories by the Japanese women and the Soviet men at the Spartakiade clearly established both those perennial powers as the favourites for the 1980 Olympic gold medals.

The U.S. women finished third in this competition, behind Japan and the Soviet Union but ahead of a number of other world powers. The U.S. men did not participate.

The first U.S. world invitational volleyball tournament was held in Colorado Springs, Colo., in August. The nations represented were Japan, Korea, Canada, the Soviet Union, and the U.S. The Korean men and the U.S. women earned first place honours in what might become an annual event. (ALBERT M. MONACO, JR.)

Cricket

The most important event in the 1978–79 cricket season was a six-test series in Australia. England defeated the home team 5–1, the most one-sided victory ever recorded in competition between the two. Australia, deprived of its leading players under contract to Kerry Packer's World Series, was outplayed in matches dominated by England's fast bowlers R. G. D. Willis, M. Hendrick, and I. T. Botham. England also demonstrated brilliant catching and fielding. J. M. Brearley was a skillful captain and R. W. Taylor a stylish wicket-keeper and batsman. All England's chief batsmen played at least one big innings, D. I. Gower and D. W. Randall making centuries. Australian fast bowler R. M. Hogg achieved the remarkable record of 41 wickets. His main allies were fast-medium A. G. Hurst and leg-spinner J. D. Higgs. Australian captain G. N. Yallop, K. J. Hughes, and G. M. Wood all made centuries.

India and Pakistan met in a three-match series in India, won 2–0 by Pakistan. After a draw in the first test, Pakistan won the next two by eight wickets each, establishing superiority. For Pakistan Zaheer Abbas was the supreme batsman with scores of 176, 96, 235 not out, 34 not out, and 42 in his five innings. Javed Miandad made 154 not out, 35, 100, and 63 not out, and the captain, Mushtaq Mohammad, and Asif Iqbal also enjoyed themselves with big innings. Fast bowlers Imran Khan and Sarfraz Nawaz were the most successful. For India S. M. Gavaskar made a century in each innings in the third test and other scores of 97 and 89; G. R. Viswanath made 145 in the first test, and others to bat well were D. B. Vengsarkar and C. P. S. Chauhan: As usual the Indian spinners B. S. Bedi and B. S. Chandrasekhar did the bulk of the work, and a young fast-medium bowler, Kapil Dev, showed promise with bat and ball.

India played a six-match series against the West Indies, captained by A. I. Kallicharran and without their Packer players, in India. India won the only test finished, by three wickets. Lifeless pitches produced high scores against toiling bowlers. For India, the captain, Gavaskar, made four centuries and a 93, Viswanath two centuries, and Vengsarkar, Dev, A. D. Gaekwad, and M. Amarnath one each. India had a strong opening bowling pair in Dev and left-arm K. D. Ghavri, but Bedi lost some of his effectiveness and so a big burden fell on off-spinner S. Venkataraghavan and the erratic Chandrasekhar. For West Indies Kallicharran made 187, 98, and 71; left-handed opening bat S. F. A. Bacchus had scores of 250, 96, and 61; and A. B. Williams 111.

Pakistan, with a full complement of Packer players, undertook a short tour of New Zealand and Australia. Pakistan won the first test in New Zealand by 128 runs, Mushtaq taking 4 for 60 and 5 for 59, and Wasim Raja 4 for 68 on a pitch (field) ideal for spin. The other two tests were spoiled by rain. Pakistan's star batsman was Miandad with scores of 81 and 160 not out, and other century-makers were Majid Khan (119 not out), Asif (104), and

Council for Mutual Economic Assistance: *see* Economy, World

Test Series Results, November 1978–September 1979

Test	Host country and its scores		Visiting country and its scores		Result
1st	India	462 for 9 wkt dec	Pakistan	503 for 8 wkt dec and 34 for no wkt	Match drawn
2nd	India	199 and 465	Pakistan	539 and 128 for 2 wkt	Pakistan won by 8 wkt
3rd	India	344 and 300	Pakistan	481 and 165 for 2 wkt	Pakistan won by 8 wkt
1st	Australia	116 and 339	England	286 and 170 for 3 wkt	England won by 7 wkt
2nd	Australia	190 and 161	England	309 and 208	England won by 166 runs
3rd	Australia	258 and 167	England	143 and 179	Australia won by 103 runs
4th	Australia	294 and 111	England	152 and 346	England won by 93 runs
5th	Australia	164 and 160	England	169 and 360	England won by 205 runs
6th	Australia	198 and 143	England	308 and 35 for 1 wkt	England won by 9 wkt
1st	India	424 and 224 for 2 wkt	West Indies	493	Match drawn
2nd	India	371	West Indies	437 and 200 for 8 wkt	Match drawn
3rd	India	300 and 362 for 1 wkt dec	West Indies	327 and 197 for 9 wkt	Match drawn
4th	India	255 and 125 for 7 wkt	West Indies	228 and 151	India won by 3 wkt
5th	India	566 for 8 wkt dec	West Indies	179 and 179 for 3 wkt	Match drawn
6th	India	644 for 7 wkt dec	West Indies	452 for 8 wkt	Match drawn
1st	New Zealand	290 and 176	Pakistan	271 and 323 for 6 wkt dec	Pakistan won by 128 runs
2nd	New Zealand	402	Pakistan	360 and 234 for 3 wkt dec	Match drawn
3rd	New Zealand	254 and 281 for 8 wkt	Pakistan	359	Match drawn
1st	Australia	168 and 310	Pakistan	196 and 353 for 9 wkt dec	Pakistan won by 71 runs
2nd	Australia	327 and 236 for 3 wkt	Pakistan	277 and 285	Australia won by 7 wkt
1st	England	633 for 5 wkt dec	India	297 and 253	England won by an innings and 83 runs
2nd	England	418 for 9 wkt	India	96 and 318 for 4 wkt	Match drawn
3rd	England	270	India	223 for 6 wkt	Match drawn
4th	England	305 and 334 for 8 wkt dec	India	202 and 429 for 8 wkt	Match drawn

Zaheer (135). For New Zealand B. A. Edgar made 129, G. P. Howarth 114, J. G. Wright 88, J. V. Coney 82 and 69, and the captain, M. G. Burgess, 71. Fast bowler Imran took 5 for 106 for Pakistan in the second test, and for New Zealand R. J. Hadlee took 5 for 62, 4 for 101, and 5 for 104.

In Australia Pakistan won the first test by 71 runs, but Australia responded in the second with a seven-wicket win. In Pakistan's victory Majid Khan made 108 and Zaheer 59, and fast bowler Sarfraz took 9 for 86, including a record spell of 7 for 1. For Australia A. R. Border made 105 and the captain K. J. Hughes 84. In Australia's win Border made 85 and 66 not out, R. Darling made 75 and 79, and Hurst took 9 for 155, in two innings. For Pakistan Miandad and Asif made not out centuries.

West Indies retained the World Cup at Lord's, London, in June where they beat England by 92 runs, thanks primarily to a great innings of 138 by I. V. A. Richards and the fast bowling of J. Garner (5 for 38). In England afterward, India played and lost a four-test series 1–0. England won the first test by an innings and 83 runs, the second and third were drawn, and in the fourth India made a wonderful effort after being set to score 438 runs to win in the fourth innings. They made 429 for 8, Gavaskar making 221, Chauhan 80, and Vengsarkar 52, and at the end they needed only 9 runs to tie the series with 2 wickets left. In the first test Gower made 200 not out for England, G. Boycott 155, G. A. Gooch 83, and G. Miller 63 not out in a record total of 633 for 5 declared. Dev took all 5 wickets for 146. In India's reply Gavaskar (61 and 68) and Viswanath (78 and 51) were in a class alone. At the second test at Lord's, after being bowled out for 96, Botham taking 5 for 35, India saved the game by fine batting by Viswanath (113) and Vengsarkar (103). The third test was remarkable for an astonishing 137 by Botham out of England's total of 270. He hit 5 sixes and 16 fours in 200 minutes.

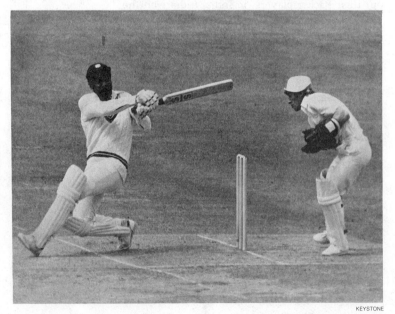

I. V. A. Richards (left) was instrumental in helping the West Indies defeat England by 92 runs to retain the Prudential World Cup in June.

KEYSTONE

In England Essex won the county championship from Worcestershire and Surrey, and the Benson and Hedges Cup by beating Surrey by 35 runs. Somerset won the Gillette Cup by beating Northamptonshire by 45 runs, and the John Player League from Kent and Worcestershire. In the first-class averages Boycott headed the batting with 102.53 runs, and J. Lever (106) and D. L. Underwood (105) were the only bowlers to take more than 100 wickets.

In Australia Victoria won the Sheffield Shield, and in New Zealand Otago won both the Shell Cup and the Shell Trophy. In South Africa Transvaal won the Castle Currie Cup, Northern Transvaal won the Castle Bowl, and Transvaal "B" the President's Cup. In the West Indies Barbados won the Shell Shield, and in India Delhi won the Ranji Trophy and North Zone the Duleep Trophy. In Pakistan National Bank won the Qaid-I-Azam Trophy and the Patron's Trophy.

The Australian Cricket Board and Packer's World Series Cricket (WSC) signed an agreement in May to phase out WSC; Packer would televise Australian cricket for three years on Channel 9 of his network, while one of his companies would promote the board's cricket for ten years. The agreement was approved by the International Cricket Conference. (REX ALSTON)

See also Australia.
[452.B.4.h.ix]

Crime and Law Enforcement

Violent Crime. TERRORISM. Nowhere was the scourge of terrorism felt more keenly than in strife-torn Northern Ireland where, during a decade of bitter conflict between Protestant and Catholic extremists, nearly 2,000 persons had died and more than 20,000 had been injured. On Aug. 27, 1979, the most illustrious victim to date, Lord Mountbatten of Burma (*see* OBITUARIES), died with several companions when a remotely detonated bomb blew up his fishing boat as it left the harbour of Mullaghmore on Ireland's northwest coast. Only a few hours later at least 18 British soldiers were killed in another bomb explosion near Warrenport just across the Ulster border.

Responsibility for both acts was claimed by the Provisional wing of the Irish Republican Army, and in November a 31-year-old member of the Provisional IRA was found guilty of Mountbatten's murder and sentenced to life imprisonment. The same terrorist group was thought to have gunned down the British ambassador to The Netherlands, Sir Richard Sykes (*see* OBITUARIES), outside his residence in The Hague on March 22. Later in March a splinter faction of the Provisional IRA, the Irish National Liberation Army, was believed to have been responsible for the bombing death of a senior member of the British Parliament, Airey Neave (*see* OBITUARIES).

The deaths of these eminent figures raised fears that other prominent persons could become targets for assassination. A visit by Pope John Paul II to Northern Ireland was canceled, and during his stay in Ireland, the pontiff was guarded by a massive security operation that included a number of helicopter gunships borrowed from West Germany. Meanwhile, the British and Irish governments reached agreement on new measures to combat terrorist activities, including more intensive border patrols and improved communications between their respective police and security forces. The British government appointed Sir Maurice Oldfield, reputedly the model for the character of "M" in Ian Fleming's James Bond novels, as chief security coordinator for Northern Ireland.

Elsewhere in Europe attempts to curb terrorism met with mixed success. Italian police, in a sweep that began in February, netted some 150 alleged terrorists, including most of those thought to have taken part in the kidnapping and murder of former premier Aldo Moro in 1978. However, in early May, in the biggest terrorist attack since the Moro killing, a dozen Red Brigades members took over the Rome offices of the ruling Christian Democrat Party, holding the staff prisoner and planting bombs that later destroyed the building. During their getaway they killed a policeman and wounded two others.

In West Germany in May, police shot down Elisabeth von Dyck, allegedly one of the participants in the 1977 kidnapping and murder of the German industrialist Hanns-Martin Schleyer, when she reportedly drew a gun on them as they closed in on her apartment. On June 25, Gen. Alexander Haig, then NATO commander, narrowly escaped death when a land mine exploded just behind his car as he drove through the Belgian countryside. A left-wing terrorist group based in West Germany, the Red Army Faction, was thought to have been responsible.

In Spain another high-ranking military officer was less fortunate. In a savage assault with submachine guns and hand grenades, terrorists believed to be members of the Basque separatist movement cut down Lieut. Gen. Luis Gomez Hortigüela and several aides as the general left his Madrid apartment. Basque separatists were also thought to have been responsible for bomb explosions at Madrid's airport and railway stations during the peak summer holiday season. The attacks, which resulted in the deaths of at least five people and injuries to more than 100 others, were said to be part of a "vacation war" directed at the profitable Spanish tourist industry. In Israel, which had long experienced the brunt of terrorist violence, Menahem Begin became the first Israeli prime minister to advocate introduction of the death penalty for terrorist acts "of inhuman cruelty." Begin's statement followed a terrorist attack on a family in the small town of Nahariya during April.

During a Moscow visit in June by U.S. Attorney General Griffin Bell, Soviet officials requested the U.S. to share information on international terrorists who might disrupt the 1980 Moscow Olympics. The Soviets wished to avoid a repetition of

KEYSTONE

Jacques Mesrine, regarded by police as France's Public Enemy No. 1, was killed in a police ambush in Paris in November.

the 1972 Olympics at Munich, West Germany, when Palestinian terrorists killed 11 Israeli athletes.

MURDER AND VIOLENCE. Following a widely publicized trial in San Francisco for the November 1978 murders of Mayor George Moscone and Supervisor Harvey Milk, an avowed homosexual, former supervisor Dan White was found guilty of voluntary manslaughter, a verdict that rendered him liable to a maximum sentence of seven years eight months in prison. White's lawyers had employed a diminished mental capacity defense, based in part on the contention that White had become deranged as a result of his penchant for junk food. After the jury's verdict, which required more than a week of deliberation, thousands of persons, many of them homosexuals, rampaged through San Francisco inflicting an estimated $1 million damage in a protest against the jury's leniency.

After a month-long, nationally televised trial in Miami, Fla., Theodore Robert Bundy, a former law student, was found guilty of murdering two women in a Tallahassee sorority house, bludgeoning three others, and burglarizing two houses. He was sought for questioning in as many as 36 other murders in five states and had been indicted for the rape-murder of a 12-year-old girl in Lake City, Fla. Bundy was sentenced to death following his murder convictions. More prisoners were awaiting execution in Florida than in any other state.

In September Amnesty International, a London-based human rights organization, issued a report calling on all governments to work toward immediate and total abolition of capital punishment. Amnesty also called for an emergency meeting of the UN Security Council to halt what it described as a worldwide wave of political killings. It singled out for special attention the revolutionary regime in Iran which, following the removal of the shah from power, summarily put to death hundreds of his former supporters. (*See* IRAN.)

Pakistani Pres. Mohammad Zia-ul-Haq refused to grant executive clemency to former prime minister Zulfikar Ali Bhutto (*see* OBITUARIES), whose final judicial appeal against a death sentence imposed upon him in 1978 was rejected by the nation's supreme court. Despite pleas for mercy from world leaders, Bhutto was hanged in the precincts of Rawalpindi jail in April. Subsequently, Bhutto's daughter Benazir (*see* BIOGRAPHIES) claimed that her father had actually died in his cell following an assault by officials.

In the U.K. another politician, Jeremy Thorpe, former leader of the Liberal Party, was aquitted of conspiring, with three co-defendants, to murder his alleged homosexual lover. Media coverage of what the British press labeled "the trial of the century" prompted questions about fairness in the reporting of pretrial proceedings in sensational cases, as well as the practice of purchasing, for substantial sums, the stories of key witnesses for possible future publication. Similar concerns prompted the U.S. Supreme Court in July to decide, by a five to four majority, that the Constitution did not give the public, including the press, any right to attend criminal pretrial hearings. (*See* PUBLISHING.)

HELP US STOP THE RIPPER
FROM KILLING AGAIN.
LOOK AT HIS HANDWRITING.
LISTEN TO HIS VOICE.
PHONE LEEDS
(0532) 464111.
IF YOU RECOGNISE EITHER, REPORT IT TO YOUR LOCAL POLICE
LONDON

UPI

Police in Leeds, England, utilized billboards in an attempt to track down the murderer believed responsible for the killing of 12 women, 9 of them prostitutes, in Yorkshire.

Nonviolent Crime. WHITE COLLAR AND POLITICAL CRIME. In March the effect of white collar crime on U.S. society came under scrutiny in hearings before the House of Representatives Subcommittee on Crime. The chairman of the committee, Rep. John Conyers (Dem., Mich.), charged that the U.S. Law Enforcement Assistance Administration (LEAA) had spent only a "minuscule portion" of its money on white collar offenses. Testifying before the same subcommittee, an expert in white collar crime, Marshall Clinard, stated that in 1975 and 1976 almost two-thirds of America's largest corporations were guilty of violating federal laws, but fewer than 1% of all federal enforcement actions against such corporations had involved criminal sanctions against a corporate officer.

Not all countries showed similar leniency to white collar offenders. In Switzerland in July, two bank managers were sentenced to 4½ years' imprisonment in a banking scandal that cost the Swiss bank Credit Suisse a reputed U.S. $717 million.

In South Africa in October, following a series of sensational disclosures about a multimillion-dollar propaganda and influence-buying scheme, former propaganda chief Eschel Rhoodie (*see* BIOGRAPHIES) was found guilty of various fraud charges and sentenced to six years' imprisonment. The so-called "Muldergate Scandal," involving a scheme whereby foreign organizations and politicians were bribed to support South Africa and foreign news media were purchased for use as propaganda organs, had led to the resignations of Information Minister Cornelius Mulder; Gen. Hendrik Van Den Bergh, head of South Africa's secret service; and the country's president and former prime minister, B. J. Vorster. (*See* SOUTH AFRICA.)

THEFT AND FRAUD. The theft of art treasures continued to be a major problem for law enforcement authorities. In February a Grecian marble head, over 2,500 years old, was removed from New York City's Metropolitan Museum of Art. Earlier, while the San Francisco art museum was closed for the Christmas vacation, thieves made off with paintings by Rembrandt and other Dutch masters worth several million dollars. A few days later, the theft of more than $3 million worth of paintings by Cézanne was discovered at the Art Institute of Chicago. The thefts appeared to be the work mainly of individuals rather than international rings. However, it was also believed that well-known works, which could not easily be resold, were stolen "to order" and destined for black markets in the Middle East, South America, or Japan.

The energy crisis, and particularly the gasoline shortage, brought a new rash of crimes. U.S. law enforcement authorities reported a major increase in gasoline thefts, ranging from the hijacking of tank trucks to the siphoning of fuel from the tanks of individual automobiles. In July Los Angeles police discovered an illegal tap that had siphoned thousands of gallons of gasoline from a refinery pipeline. These thefts were seldom solved because of the difficulty in tracing the stolen goods.

Bank robberies in the U.S. were on the increase. The FBI reported that there were 22% more such crimes in the first six months of 1979 than in the corresponding period of 1978. In New York City five banks were robbed in one hour on August 20, and there were ten bank robberies the following day. According to law enforcement authorities, the typical bank robber was no longer a skilled professional but an unemployed petty criminal in his 20s who often robbed on impulse. Among reasons cited for the increase were the difficult economic situation, the proliferation in many states of small branch banks with poor security, and elimination of the old-fashioned teller's cage in favour of open counters.

The burgeoning demand for birds as pets brought with it a reported substantial rise in the number of birds smuggled into the U.S. The Fish and Wildlife Service estimated that the illegal traffic in birds was at least equal to the 350,000 that were legally imported each year. In October the Australian police broke up a large bird-smuggling racket that involved the clandestine importation into the U.S. of hundreds of rare birds each year.

The continuing increase in computer-related crimes was also of concern to law enforcement authorities. Researchers from the Stanford Research Institute in California reported that they had recorded more than 600 computer-assisted crimes throughout the world since 1967. A particular problem in combating these offenses was that there was usually a gap of two to three years between the commission of a computer crime and the time it was reported to investigative agencies.

Law Enforcement. Serious reported crime in the U.S. increased 2% overall during 1978, according to the FBI's *Uniform Crime Reports.* This was the first increase in two years. Violent offenses showed the greatest rate of growth, with rape rising by nearly 7%, robbery by 3%, and aggravated assault by 7%. Preliminary figures showed a much greater increase for the first quarter of 1979. The National Crime Survey, based on interviews with persons aged 12 and over, showed that from 1973 to 1977 personal property losses rose by nearly 7% and household losses by 15%.

WIDE WORLD

Theodore Bundy was found guilty in July of the murder of two Florida coeds. He was considered also to be a strong suspect in 18 to 36 other murders.

State and local authorities reported difficulties in dealing with the crime of arson. According to the National Fire Prevention Association, losses in arson-caused fires had risen from $74 million in 1965 to $634 million a decade later, and that figure had more than doubled by 1979. FBI Director William Webster ordered a stepped-up enforcement effort by his agency, while the LEAA and the U.S. Fire Administration announced that they would coordinate a nationwide antiarson campaign. Much of the arson was believed to be the work of organized crime, which profited from insurance claims on the burned properties.

In New York City police specialists in organized crime began investigating the assassination in July of crime syndicate boss Carmine Galante. Galante and two colleagues died in a hail of gunfire while dining at an Italian restaurant in Brooklyn. It was feared that Galante's 1920s-style execution, presumably by rival mobsters, might touch off a war among the five New York crime "families." In 1972 the death of Joseph ("Crazy Joe") Gallo under similar circumstances had led to a war in which at least 16 people were killed.

The use of deadly force by and against U.S. police came under scrutiny during the year in a special report issued by the United Methodist Church. The church reported that in the period 1967–74, the average number of persons killed by police each year rose from 245 to 359, 50% of whom were black. FBI figures for 1977 indicated that 93 police officers had been killed while on duty, the lowest number since 1969. The church's report noted that the use of deadly force by police could be reduced. Following the introduction of stricter firearms guidelines and revised training procedures for police, the number of civilians killed by police in New York City had been lowered from 90 in 1971 to 54 two years later.

Concern about the use of deadly force and other alleged abuses by Philadelphia police led the U.S. Justice Department in August to file an unprecedented lawsuit against the city's mayor, Frank

Rizzo (*see* BIOGRAPHIES) and 20 other city and police officials. The suit charged police with violating the civil rights of racial and ethnic groups, asked for a court order barring the mayor and the police department from continuing the brutal behaviour, and sought to cut off all federal funds from the city's police services unless its policies were changed. However, all portions of the suit except those involving racial discrimination were dismissed by a federal district judge on the grounds that the attorney general lacked standing to sue. Later, the last charge was dismissed for lack of factual support. Earlier, the Justice Department had stated that it was investigating similar charges against police departments in Houston, Texas, Memphis, Tenn., and Mobile, Ala.

As the FBI continued efforts to rebuild its image following highly publicized revelations of earlier misconduct, Pres. Jimmy Carter sent to Congress a proposed charter for the agency designed to establish standards of conduct. On August 9 the bureau experienced the worst day for loss of life in its history when two agents in El Centro, Calif., and one in Cleveland, Ohio, were killed, apparently in unrelated incidents.

In India, where policemen had traditionally supplemented their low salaries by various forms of corruption and extortion, an official commission recommended improved conditions of service, including increases in pay. When the increases were not forthcoming, police began to go on strike, and the agitation spread to include the crack paramilitary Central Reserve Police and the Central Industrial Security Force. Prime Minister Morarji Desai called in the Army to disarm the police, and at least 25 people were killed in the resultant fighting.

In October the British police launched a £4 million advertising campaign aimed at catching the "Yorkshire Ripper," believed to have murdered 12 women and attacked several others in northern England during the past four years. In an attempt to track down the Ripper, nine of whose victims were prostitutes, police had mounted the biggest manhunt in British history. Among the clues was a tape-recorded message mailed in June by the Ripper to the assistant chief constable in charge of the West Yorkshire police.

During 1979 the British police and public celebrated the sesquicentennial of the London Metropolitan Police Force with a series of exhibitions and displays depicting the history of this famous body. Since its establishment in 1829 by Sir Robert Peel, the force had grown from 1,000 members to more than 22,000. (DUNCAN CHAPPELL)

See also Prisons and Penology.
[522.C.6; 543.A.5; 552.C and F; 737.B; 10/36.C.5.a]

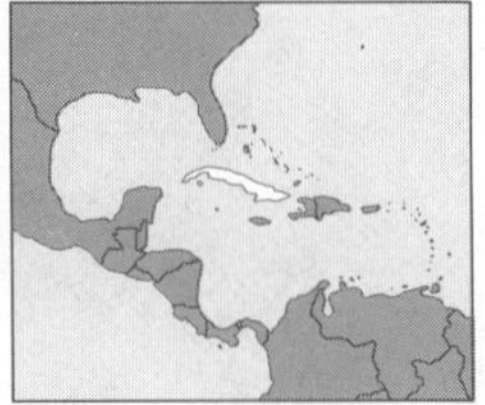

Cuba

Cuba

The socialist republic of Cuba occupies the largest island in the Greater Antilles of the West Indies. Area: 110,922 sq km (42,827 sq mi), including several thousand small islands and cays. Pop. (1978 est.): 9,648,900, including (1953) white 72.8%; mestizo 14.5%; Negro 12.4%. Cap. and largest city: Havana (pop., 1978 est., 1,981,300). Language: Spanish. Religion: Roman Catholic (49%). President of the Council of State in 1979, Fidel Castro Ruz.

UPI

Pres. Fidel Castro addressed two thousand members of the National Assembly on January 1 when Cuba celebrated the 20th anniversary of the Castro regime.

Cuba experienced political stability in 1979 but made little economic progress. Changes continued to be made in the institutional framework to bring it into line with those of other member countries of the Council for Mutual Economic Assistance (CMEA or Comecon). On April 8 elections were held for 10,660 representatives to municipal assemblies; the assemblies were the basic organ of *Poder Popular*, the process of decentralizing power that had been continuing since 1974.

Cuba's role in Africa was the principal impediment to improved commercial and diplomatic links with the U.S. The continuing strained relations between the two countries were underscored by Pres. Fidel Castro's strong attack on Washington's policies in a speech in January, on the occasion of the 20th anniversary of the Cuban revolution. He condemned in particular the normalization of U.S.-China relations. Late in April U.S. Pres. Jimmy Carter said that a strengthening of ties between the two countries would not take place while Havana's African involvement persisted and the issue of U.S. claims for compensation for property expropriated in 1959 and 1960, estimated at about $2 billion, remained unresolved.

Havana's growing influence in the Caribbean alarmed the U.S. administration, especially following the coup in Grenada in March and during the Nicaraguan civil war in June and July. In September the alleged presence in Cuba of a Soviet combat brigade, estimated at 2,000–3,000 men and including motorized rifle battalions, tank and artillery battalions, and combat and service support units, caused a major furor in the U.S., though the Soviets insisted there had been no change in their Cuban presence. On October 1 President Carter, in a televised address to the nation, announced countermeasures: a new, full-time U.S. military task force would operate in the Caribbean area; air surveillance of Cuba would be resumed; and exercises would be staged at the U.S. base at Guantánamo Bay. He added, however, that assurances had been received from Moscow that Soviet forces in Cuba would never threaten the U.S.

There was some movement in dealings between the U.S. and Cuba during the year. About 100,000 exiles were expected to visit Cuba during 1979 following the ending of the travel ban against them on January 1. At the end of March the University of Minnesota announced that it would exchange teachers and students, the first academic exchange to take place since 1959. In August Associated Press reporters returned to Cuba for the first time in ten years.

In September delegates from 92 countries attended the sixth summit meeting of the nonaligned movement in Havana, the first such conference to be held in Latin America. The meeting was dominated by disagreement between Cuba and Yugoslavia, along with their respective supporters, over the principles of nonintervention and noninterference. Other points of contention included the representation of Cambodia, Egyptian membership, and the dispute between Morocco and Algeria over the Western Sahara. Six new members attended: Nicaragua, Grenada, Bolivia, Suriname, Pakistan, and the South West Africa People's Organization. Cuba was to chair the movement until 1982, and there was concern that it would endeavour to direct the movement toward the ideas and aims of the U.S.S.R. rather than independence from the two main power blocs.

There was little sign of a diminution in the Cuban military presence in Africa. Official U.S. sources reported in August that between 2,000 and 3,000 of the troops sent to Ethiopia in late 1977 and early 1978 to help repel an incursion from Somalia had been withdrawn; however, it was estimated that between 11,000 and 14,000 remained. A military force of about 30,000, along with 2,000–3,000 civilians, continued to be maintained in Angola.

In May President Castro paid an official visit to Mexico for talks with Pres. José López Portillo, principally on education, sugar, technology, and oil. Castro was also invited by the new Nicaraguan government to visit Managua at his own convenience. In October he addressed the UN General Assembly in New York City as chairman of the nonaligned movement.

Economic development was still dominated by the key role of sugar as a hard-currency earner. World prices remained at a low level. The 1978–79 sugar crop was estimated at about 8 million tons, compared with 7,450,000 in 1977–78. In a speech early in July, President Castro criticized recent economic failings, especially the grave deterioration in the transportation network, shortcomings in education and public health, and lack of discipline among workers. He stated that Cuba faced another two decades of austerity. However, a little

CUBA

Education. (1976–77) Primary, pupils 1,845,075, teachers 82,520; secondary, pupils 642,624, teachers 49,586; vocational, pupils 187,819, teachers 11,503; teacher training, students 118,000, teachers 4,200; higher, students 122,456, teaching staff 9,934.

Finance. Monetary unit: peso, with (Sept. 17, 1979) a free rate of 0.76 peso to U.S. $1 (1.63 peso = £1 sterling). Budget (1975 est.) balanced at *c.* 4.5 billion pesos. Gross national product (1977 est.) U.S. $8.7 billion.

Foreign Trade. (1977) Imports 3,443,000,000 pesos; exports 2,902,000,000 pesos. Import sources (1975): U.S.S.R. 40%; Japan 12%; Spain 5%; West Germany 5%. Export destinations (1975): U.S.S.R. 56%; Spain 8%; Japan 8%. Main exports (1975): sugar 90%; nickel and copper ores 5%.

Transport and Communications. Roads (1975) 29,543 km. Motor vehicles in use (1976): passenger 80,000; commercial (including buses) 40,000. Railways: (1977) 14,730 km; traffic (1976) 767 million passenger-km, freight 1,848,000,000 net ton-km. Air traffic (1977): 773 million passenger-km; freight 11 million net ton-km. Shipping (1978): merchant vessels 100 gross tons and over 331; gross tonnage 779,187. Telephones (Jan. 1978) 321,000. Radio receivers (Dec. 1976) 2.1 million.Television receivers (Dec. 1976) 650,000.

Agriculture. Production (in 000; metric tons; 1978): rice *c.* 460; cassava (1977) *c.* 262; sweet potatoes (1977) *c.* 257; tomatoes *c.* 240; sugar, raw value *c.* 7,457; bananas *c.* 142; oranges *c.* 138; coffee *c.* 27; tobacco *c.* 46; jute *c.* 6; beef and veal *c.* 143; fish catch (1977) 185. Livestock (in 000; 1978): cattle *c.* 5,700; pigs *c.* 1,800; sheep *c.* 350; goats *c.* 97; horses (1977) *c.* 840; chickens *c.* 20,000.

Industry. Production (in 000; metric tons; 1976): crude oil 234; natural gas (cu m) 21,000; petroleum products *c.* 6,240; electricity (kw-hr) *c.* 7,198,000; copper ore (metal content; 1977) 2.6; chrome ore (oxide content) *c.* 10; nickel ore (metal content) 37; salt 150; paper *c.* 123; sulfuric acid 383; nitrogenous fertilizers (1977–78) *c.* 47; cement (1977) 2,657; crude steel 250; cotton yarn (1977) 24; cotton fabrics (sq m) 134,060.

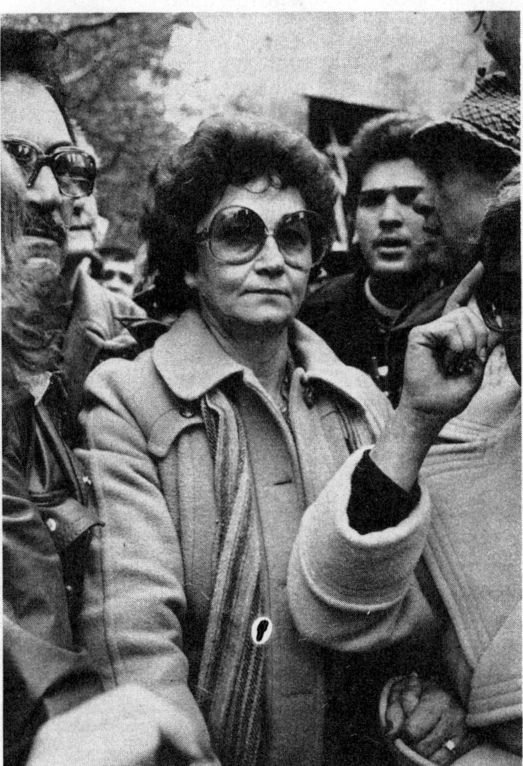
UPI

The younger sister of Fidel Castro, Juanita Castro, joined an anti-Castro demonstration in New York City when the Cuban leader addressed the United Nations on October 12.

Crops:
see Agriculture and Food Supplies

more competition was to be permitted, with managers of state concerns expected to make profits.

In April Cuba and the U.S.S.R. signed a 1979 trade agreement providing for mutual trade valued at 4 billion rubles, the same as in 1978. Meanwhile, the Havana authorities continued to do everything possible to develop commercial and financial relations with non-Communist sources. In June international banks granted Cuba a seven-year loan of DM 220 million, the largest credit raised in Western financial markets for some years. Borrowing in 1978 totaled $60 million, against $11 million in 1977. A five-year trade agreement was signed with Spain in February, providing for Spanish imports of coffee, tobacco, and fish in return for purchases by Cuba of capital goods, ships, and machinery. (ROBIN CHAPMAN)

Cycling

The Netherlands dominated the 1979 world cycling championships by taking six gold medals, two on the Valkenburg road circuit and four at the Olympic Stadium in Amsterdam. Most impressive was the victory of Jan Raas in the 275-km professional road race, watched by a crowd of 250,000. Dutch women contributed to the national triumph, 17-year-old Petra de Bruin winning on the road and, in her last season of competition, Keetie van Oosten-Hage taking her fourth 3,000-m track pursuit title. In tandem sprinting the dominance of the defending champions and four-time winners, Vladimir Vackar and Miroslav Vymazal (Czech.), ended when they were beaten in the semifinal by Yave Cahard and Franck Depine (France); the latter pair went on to win the final.

Dutch cyclist Joop Zoetemelk crosses the finish line to win the third Climbers Criterium at Chanteloup-Les-Vignes, France, in February.

A.F.P./PICTORIAL PARADE

1979 Cycling Champions

Event	Winner	Country
WORLD AMATEUR CHAMPIONS—TRACK		
Men		
1,000-m time trial	L. Thoms	East Germany
Sprint	L. Hesslich	East Germany
Tandem sprint	Y. Cahard and F. Depine	France
Individual pursuit	N. Marakov	U.S.S.R.
Team pursuit		East Germany
50-km points	J. Slama	Czechoslovakia
50-km motor-paced	M. Pronk	The Netherlands
Women		
Sprint	G. Tsareva	U.S.S.R.
Individual pursuit	K. van Oosten-Hage	The Netherlands
WORLD PROFESSIONAL CHAMPIONS—TRACK		
Sprint	K. Nakano	Japan
Individual pursuit	B. Oosterbosch	The Netherlands
One-hour motor-paced	M. Venix	The Netherlands
WORLD AMATEUR CHAMPIONS—ROAD		
Men		
100-km team time trial		East Germany
Individual road race	G. Giacomini	Italy
Women		
Individual road race	P. de Bruin	The Netherlands
WORLD PROFESSIONAL CHAMPION—ROAD		
Individual road race	J. Raas	The Netherlands
WORLD CHAMPIONS—CYCLO CROSS		
Amateur	V. di Tano	Italy
Professional	A. Zweifel	Switzerland
MAJOR PROFESSIONAL ROAD-RACE WINNERS		
Het Volk	R. de Vlaeminck	Belgium
Milan–San Remo	R. de Vlaeminck	Belgium
Paris–Roubaix	F. Moser	Italy
Amstel Gold Race	J. Raas	The Netherlands
Ghent–Wevelghem	F. Moser	Italy
Flèche Wallonne	B. Hinault	France
Liège–Bastogne–Liège	D. Thurau	West Germany
Tour of Flanders	J. Raas	The Netherlands
Grand Prix of Frankfurt	D. Willems	Belgium
Bordeaux–Paris	A. Chalmel	France
Autumn Grand Prix	J. Zoetemelk	The Netherlands
Tour of Lombardy	B. Hinault	France
Grand Prix des Nations time trial	B. Hinault	France
Tour de France	B. Hinault	France
Tour of Italy	G. Saronni	Italy
Tour of Spain	J. Zoetemelk	The Netherlands
Tour of Switzerland	W. Wesmael	Belgium
Tour of Britain	Y. Kachinin	U.S.S.R.
Tour of Luxembourg	L. Didier	Luxembourg
Four Days of Dunkirk	D. Willems	Belgium
Dauphiné Libéré	B. Hinault	France
Paris–Nice	J. Zoetemelk	The Netherlands
Paris–Brussels	L. Peeters	Belgium

Professional road racing followed the usual pattern, with "town to town" and short stage races early in the season building up to the big national tours of Spain, Italy, and France and to several important one-day tests. Established stars took most of the honours, exceptions being André Chalmel (France), first in the Bordeaux–Paris, and 21-year-old Giuseppe Saronni (Italy), who defeated his compatriot, ex-world champion Francesco Moser, in the Tour of Italy.

In June Bernard Hinault (France) was favoured to win the Tour de France, having succeeded in 1978 at his first attempt. Hinault triumphed in style, though halfway through the 3,700-km event he briefly lost the race leadership to Joop Zoetemelk of The Netherlands, who eventually finished second.

Soviet roadmen dominated the three main amateur stage races. Yuri Kachinin won the 14-day Tour of Britain ("Milk Race") and led the winning U.S.S.R. team, and Sergey Sukhorutchenkov achieved a remarkable double triumph by finishing a clear winner in both the Prague–Warsaw–Berlin "Peace Race" and the Tour de l'Avenir, the amateur version of the Tour de France.

(J. B. WADLEY)

Curling:
see Winter Sports

Cyprus

An island republic and a member of the Commonwealth of Nations, Cyprus is in the eastern Mediterranean. Area: 9,251 sq km (3,572 sq mi). Pop. (1978 est.): 616,000, including Greeks 82%; Turks 18%. Cap. and largest city: Nicosia (pop., 1978 est., 160,000). All these population figures should be considered unreliable, as they do not take into account the extensive internal migration or the recent and reportedly extensive Turkish immigration and Greek emigration, for which authoritative data are not available. Language: Greek and Turkish. Religion: Greek Orthodox 77%; Muslim 18%. President in 1979, Spyros Kyprianou.

Efforts to resolve the five-year-old dispute that kept the island divided into Greek and Turkish Cypriot sectors continued throughout 1979, but no real progress was made. What at first appeared to be a breakthrough came in May with the arrival of UN Secretary-General Kurt Waldheim, who organized a two-day summit between Pres. Spyros Kyprianou and the Turkish Cypriot leader, Rauf Denktash. On May 19 a ten-point agreement was reached that called for resumption of the stalled intercommunal talks.

The talks resumed on June 15, as arranged, but broke down a week later. The Greeks demanded immediate resettlement of the Famagusta suburb of Varosha, once a popular vacation resort, but the Turks wanted simultaneous consideration of their territorial and security problems. Numerous behind-the-scenes attempts by the UN and various foreign powers failed to narrow the differences, and what little improvement in relations the Kyprianou-Denktash summit had brought quickly vanished.

The appalling economic situation in the Turkish-occupied north was seen by many as an obstacle to peace. The Denktash administration, in a bid to halt soaring prices, imposed severe restrictions on shopkeepers and caused an uproar by banning the importation of many goods from countries other than Turkey. Experts agreed that there could be no real solution as long as the economy of the self-proclaimed Turkish Federated State of Cyprus was tied to that of the mainland.

In the south the once enviable economic picture began to fade, and inflation seemed certain to end the year in double figures. The fuel crisis did not help, and the government was forced to introduce numerous restrictions in an effort to cut consumption, apart from increasing prices by an average 25%. The biggest income earner, tourism, continued to break all records, however, despite the loss of the best hotels and resorts.

A scandal broke in September with the discovery by police of over 100 priceless antiquities in the home of Austrian Prince Alfred zur Lippe-Weissenfeld, the local representative of the UN High Commissioner for Refugees. They were believed to have been looted in the north, and Greek Cypriots were outraged by the thought that the man who was in charge of the welfare of nearly 200,000 refugees should himself be profiting from their losses.

CYPRUS

Education. Greek schools (1978–79): primary, pupils 54,309, teachers 2,260; secondary, pupils 42,441, teachers 2,266; vocational, pupils 6,445, teachers 504; teacher training, students 113, teachers 16; higher, students 1,342, teaching staff 136. Turkish schools (1976–77): primary, pupils 18,220, teachers 593; secondary, pupils 10,504, teachers 514; vocational, pupils 811, teachers 134; teacher training, students 68, teachers 4.

Finance. Monetary unit: Cyprus pound, with (Sept. 17, 1979) a free rate of C£0.35 to U.S. $1 (C£0.75 = £1 sterling). The Turkish lira is also in use in North Cyprus (Turkish Federated State). Gold, SDR's, and foreign exchange (June 1979) U.S. $383 million. Budget (1978 est.): revenue C£91,478,000; expenditure C£87,542,000. Excludes budget of Turkish Federated State (1978 est.): revenue U.S. $72 million; expenditure U.S. $89 million.

Foreign Trade. (South only; 1978) Imports C£283 million; exports C£128 million. Import sources: U.K. 22%; Italy 12%; West Germany 7%; Greece 6%; U.S. 6%; Japan 5%; Iraq 5%; France 5%. Export destinations: U.K. 23%; Lebanon 9%; Saudi Arabia 9%; Syria 5%. Main exports: clothing 13%; cigarettes 9%; potatoes 8%; wine and spirits 7%; cement 7%; footwear 6%; citrus fruit 5%. Tourism (South only; 1977): visitors 178,000; gross receipts U.S. $58 million.

Transport and Communications. Roads (1977) 9,885 km. Motor vehicles in use (1977): passenger 71,600; commercial 15,500. Air traffic (1978): 525 million passenger-km; freight 20.7 million net ton-km. Shipping (1978): merchant vessels 100 gross tons and over 793; gross tonnage 2,599,529. Telephones (Dec. 1977) 86,000. Radio licenses (Dec. 1976) 200,000. Television licenses (Dec. 1974) 85,000.

Agriculture. Production (in 000; metric tons; 1978): barley 81; wheat (1977) 36; potatoes (1977) *c.* 235; grapes *c.* 170; oranges *c.* 109; grapefruit (1977) *c.* 65; lemons *c.* 38; olives *c.* 15. Livestock (in 000; 1977): sheep *c.* 490; cattle *c.* 35; pigs 155; goats *c.* 395.

Industry. Production (in 000; metric tons; 1977): asbestos *c.* 35; iron pyrites (exports) 172; copper ore (exports; metal content) *c.* 5.6; chromium ore (oxide content) *c.* 5.2; gypsum (exports) 34; petroleum products (1976) *c.* 370; cement (1978) 1,107; electricity (kw-hr; 1978) 920,000.

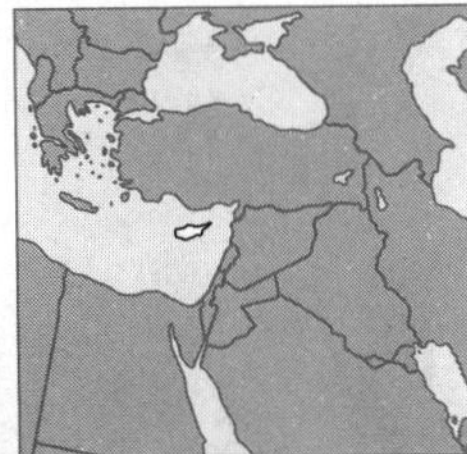
Cyprus

The prince was allowed to leave the island, and the UN apologized for his actions.

Relations with Egypt remained severed, having been broken off on Feb. 22, 1978, after a shoot-out between local police and Egyptian commandos trying to capture an aircraft where two Palestinians held a number of hostages. However, direct flights between the two countries were resumed on November 1. (CHRIS DRAKE)

Czechoslovakia

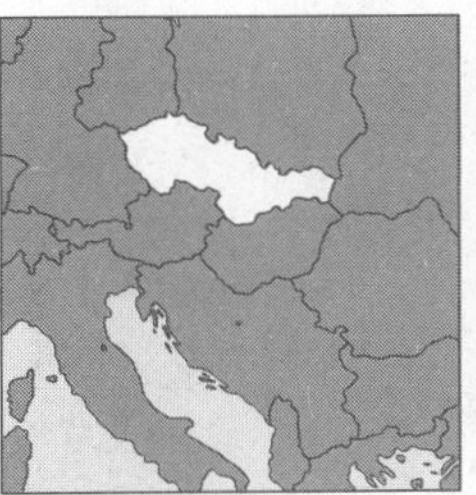
Czechoslovakia

A federal socialist republic of central Europe, Czechoslovakia lies between Poland, the U.S.S.R., Hungary, Austria, and East and West Germany. Area: 127,881 sq km (49,375 sq mi). Pop. (1979 est.): 15,184,300, including (1978 est.) Czech 64%; Slovak 30%. Cap. and largest city: Prague (pop., 1979 est., 1,188,600). Language: Czech and Slovak (official). General secretary of the Communist Party of Czechoslovakia and president in 1979, Gustav Husak; federal premier, Lubomir Strougal.

The dominant theme of Czechoslovak politics during 1979 was the state of the economy—a matter of central importance in a country where political stability depended on the maintenance of a high standard of living to a far greater degree than in societies where the government's right to rule was based on consent. The legacy of the forcible

CZECHOSLOVAK NEWS AGENCY/KEYSTONE

Former waste dumps and coal mines are being recultivated in Czechoslovakia. This park outside Most used to be the waste dump of the Smeral mine.

ending of the 1968 reform program was that Czechoslovakia was depoliticized, and political decision-making was concentrated in the hands of a small and self-selected elite. In exchange for popular acquiescence in this depoliticization, the leadership guaranteed the population an absence of police terror and a steady rise in material consumption. This latter component of the government's policy was being seriously jeopardized by mounting economic difficulties.

The authorities were fully aware of the wider implications of an economic downturn and devoted a great deal of attention to finding ways of avoiding it. In the period between the Communist Party congress in April 1976 and the December 1978 session of the party's Central Committee, no fewer than 7 out of 12 plenary sessions of the Central Committee had concerned themselves with economic questions. The problems raised at the December 1978 session focused on the worsening situation in Western markets, a serious matter since Czechoslovakia depended on imports from the West not only for high technology goods but also for some raw materials. The engineering goods industry, which had made important contributions to the country's export earnings, was singled out for its late deliveries and poor quality control.

The country's energy deficit proved to be an even greater problem. Czechoslovakia was relatively poor in domestic energy resources—coal was the only one in abundance—and had relied on the Soviet Union for both oil and natural gas. However, the price of Soviet energy had risen steadily during the second half of the 1970s, and the Soviet Union had served notice that Czechoslovakia would have to look elsewhere for some of its energy requirements in the 1980s. The country had already experienced grave shortages in the winter of 1978–79, when there were power cuts to both domestic and industrial users. This underlying situation was exacerbated by the crisis in Iran, with which Czechoslovakia had signed barter agreements for oil, and by breakdowns in domestic coal production.

Dams:
see Engineering Projects

Speaking to the National Assembly on March 28, Premier Lubomir Strougal warned that the consumption of energy in industry was too high. Strougal also warned industrial managers that the quality of output was too low, that innovation was slow, and that productivity would have to be raised. The party newspaper *Rude Pravo* commented on the same theme on August 15, when it declared that the era of cheap energy was over and that the state could no longer be expected to subsidize energy costs, whether for industrial or domestic users. The government introduced massive price increases precisely for this purpose. On July 20 price rises averaging 50% were announced, affecting fuel oil, gasoline, electricity, children's clothing, telephone charges, and postage, although food subsidies were not withdrawn. The popular response to these warnings and measures was hoarding and panic buying. The entire position was made worse by the rather poor harvest in 1979—a shortfall of two million tons of grain, which effectively made it impossible for the country to reach its declared goal of self-sufficiency in grain by 1980.

The authorities believed that nuclear energy was the most viable alternative to oil, and development of the country's nuclear energy program was pressed forward. In this context, the publication of a report by the opposition group Charter 77 on nuclear energy was highly unwelcome, in that it claimed the power station at Jaslovske Bohunice, Slovakia, had suffered two accidents, in 1976 and 1977, and had had to be temporarily shut down. The report sparked off considerable anxiety in neighbouring Austria, but the Charter report and the Austrian reaction were both dismissed as exaggerated.

Within the party, there was almost complete immobility. The projected exchange of party cards—a review of the party's membership—was undertaken in the hope that party supervision of the economy and economic management would improve. Party cadres were warned that their responsibility for adequate functioning of the economy was substantial.

Charter 77 continued to function, despite growing harassment by the authorities. After some months of relatively light-handed treatment—Jaroslav Sabata, a charter spokesman, was given a sentence of nine months on trumped-up charges in January—the authorities evidently decided that a major crackdown was necessary. At the end of May house searches were initiated and well-known individuals were detained, among them the dramatist Vaclav Havel. Despite massive Western protests, Havel and five others were put on trial in October and given prison sentences ranging up to five years. What appeared to have angered the authorities most was the activity of the unofficial Committee for the Defense of the Unjustly Persecuted (VONS), which had been responsible for a steady stream of well-informed reports on police excesses. A number of charter documents did appear during the year, however, notably discussions of nuclear safety, restrictions

CZECHOSLOVAKIA

Education. (1977–78) Primary, pupils 1,941,089, teachers 98,779; secondary, pupils 127,188, teachers 8,333; vocational and teacher training, pupils 565,809, teachers 28,209; higher, students 137,629, teaching staff 17,559.

Finance. Monetary unit: koruna, with (Sept. 17, 1979) a commercial rate of 5.25 koruny to U.S. $1 (11.30 koruny = £1 sterling) and a tourist rate of 9.20 koruny to U.S. $1 (19.78 koruny = £1 sterling). Budget (1977 est.): revenue 260.4 billion koruny; expenditure 260.2 billion koruny. Gross national product (1977 est.) U.S. $61,470,000,000.

Foreign Trade. (1978) Imports 68,074,000,000 koruny; exports 66,772,000,000 koruny. Import sources (1977): U.S.S.R. 34%; East Germany 11%; Poland 8%; West Germany 6%; Hungary 5%. Export destinations (1977): U.S.S.R. 33%; East Germany 12%; Poland 9%; Hungary 6%; West Germany 5%. Main exports (1977): machinery 39%; iron and steel 9%; motor vehicles 8%; chemicals 6%.

Transport and Communications. Roads (1974) 145,455 km (including 79 km expressways). Motor vehicles in use (1977): passenger 1,692,300; commercial 289,800. Railways (1977): 13,190 km (including 2,830 km electrified); traffic 19,180,000,000 passenger-km, freight (1978) 72,358,000,000 net ton-km. Air traffic (1978): 1,584,000,000 passenger-km; freight 18,250,000 net ton-km. Navigable inland waterways (1977) *c.* 480 km. Shipping (1978): merchant vessels 100 gross tons and over 15; gross tonnage 150,770. Telephones (Dec. 1977) 2,863,000. Radio licenses (Dec. 1976) 3,928,000. Television licenses (Dec. 1977) 3,903,000.

Agriculture. Production (in 000; metric tons; 1978): wheat *c.* 5,600; barley *c.* 3,600; oats *c.* 440; rye *c.* 615; corn *c.* 628; potatoes *c.* 3,837; sugar, raw value *c.* 710; rapeseed *c.* 170; beef and veal *c.* 393; pork *c.* 815; timber (cu m; 1977) 17,200. Livestock (in 000; Jan. 1978): cattle 4,758; pigs 7,510; sheep 841; chickens 42,986.

Industry. Index of industrial production (1975 = 100; 1978) 117. Fuel and power (in 000; metric tons; 1978): coal 28,255; brown coal 95,298; crude oil 119; petroleum products (1976) 16,036; natural gas (cu m) *c.* 1,070,000; manufactured gas (cu m) 7,950,000; electricity (kw-hr) 68,936,000. Production (in 000; metric tons; 1978): iron ore (26% metal content) 2,023; pig iron 10,090; crude steel 15,293; magnesite (1975) 2,885; cement 10,220; sulfuric acid 1,196; plastics and resins 810; caustic soda 311; fertilizers (nutrient content; 1977) nitrogenous 605, phosphate 433; cotton yarn 129; cotton fabrics (m) 593,400; woolen fabrics (m) 61,760; man-made fibres 152; paper (1977) 857; passenger cars (units) 176; commercial vehicles (units) *c.* 80. Dwelling units completed (1977) 138,000.

on foreign travel, the black market economy, and the problem of the Gypsies. Shortly before the trial, the playwright Pavel Kohout was stripped of his citizenship while in Austria and refused reentry to Czechoslovakia.

Gen. Ludvik Svoboda, president at the time of the Soviet invasion in 1968, died on Sept. 20, 1979 (*see* OBITUARIES). (GEORGE SCHÖPFLIN)

Dance

The American Ballet Theatre (ABT), founded as the Ballet Theatre in 1939 and with its debut taking place Jan. 11, 1940, in New York City, came perilously close to going out of existence on the eve of its 40th birthday. Contract negotiations between the dancers and management had broken down on Oct. 29, 1979, resulting in a lockout (not a strike) of the dancers. A December season at the Kennedy Center for the Performing Arts in Washington, D.C., was canceled, and a gala anniversary performance at New York City's Metropolitan Opera House, scheduled for Jan. 11, 1980, was on the brink of cancellation when a new contract proposal was accepted by the dancers late on December 20. The new contract provided for substantial salary increases, a guaranteed 40 weeks per year of employment, management payment of hotel bills during tours (plus $20 a day for food), and supplemental unemployment benefits for dancers whose contracts might be terminated before the end of the 40-week guaranteed employment.

During the year ABT's Ballet Theatre Foundation (the company's funding-management entity) engaged dancer Mikhail Baryshnikov as director of ABT. He was to start in the fall of 1980, succeeding longtime directors Lucia Chase and Oliver Smith. Chase, patroness of the company since its inception and co-director since 1945, stated that she would relinquish her title but that she would not leave the company. ABT production and performing highlights during the year included Glen Tetley's *Contredances* (to music of Anton von Webern), created especially for Britain's Anthony Dowell, who had just joined the company, and Natalia Makarova; a revival of Agnes de Mille's *Fall River Legend* with Cynthia Gregory dancing the principal role of The Accused for the first time; the premiere of Gregory's first choreography, a solo to Bach's "Air for G String"; the premiere of a new ballet by Antony Tudor, *The Tiller in the Fields* (Dvorak); a revival of Ben Stevenson's *Three Preludes* (Rachmaninoff) as a starring piece for Gelsey Kirkland, with John Meehan as her partner; Rudolf Nureyev in a guest appearance in Tetley's *Pierrot Lunaire*; and guest performances by West Germany's Peter Breuer and France's Charles Jude.

Aleksandr Godunov (*see* BIOGRAPHIES), who defected from the Bolshoi Ballet in New York City during the Soviet troupe's tour, was engaged by ABT but during the lockout period resigned with-

MARTHA SWOPE

Mikhail Baryshnikov and Patricia McBride starred in the "Fall" segment of Jerome Robbins's *The Four Seasons,* performed by the New York City Ballet in January.

out ever having danced with the U.S. company. The resignation came about because he believed his reported annual $150,000 ABT salary (or guarantee) symbolized a divisive factor between corps de ballet dancers and management. Godunov's wife (Ludmila Vlasova) returned to the U.S.S.R. after being detained for several days while U.S. government officials tried to learn if she was returning of her own free will. (Subsequently, in Los Angeles, Leonid Kozlov and his dancer wife, Valentina Kozlova, also defected from the Bolshoi.)

The New York City Ballet (NYCB), which had engaged Baryshnikov as a company member, lost him before his contract was due to expire. A tendinitis condition was given as the reason for his leaving. Company premieres included Jerome Robbins's *The Four Seasons* (to music of Verdi) and *Opus 19* (Prokofiev). The former featured Patricia McBride and Baryshnikov (later replaced by Peter Martins), and the latter also used McBride and Baryshnikov. An excerpt from Robbins's first major ballet, *Fancy Free* (created in 1944 for the Ballet Theatre), by the School of American Ballet for its annual concert, heralded the mounting of the full ballet (slated for 1980) for the NYCB itself. A new ballet by Peter Martins, *Sonate di Scarlatti* (initially titled *Giardino di Scarlatti*), starring Heather Watts and Bart Cook, was added to the repertory. George Balanchine, the company's artistic director and principal choreographer, briefly curtailed his duties while he underwent heart treatment and, ultimately, heart surgery. An extensively abridged version, by himself, of his historic *Apollo* was staged, first for Baryshnikov. The NYCB, in addition to its regular New York City, Washington, D.C., and Saratoga Springs, N.Y., seasons, toured Europe.

The Joffrey Ballet, faced with major deficits and requiring new funding, suspended its repertory seasons in New York and its regular touring schedule. Instead, it served as a sort of backup company for Nureyev in two New York engagements featuring a program consisting of *Le Spectre de la rose*, *Petrushka*, *Parade*, and *L'Après-midi d'un faune*. Joffrey II, however, under the direction of Sally Brayley Bliss, continued to be active with productions of new ballets and a touring program.

Among the other U.S. ballet troupes of major size and stature that were active in resident seasons in their home cities and on touring programs were the Pennsylvania Ballet, with new works by Ben Harkarvy (the artistic director), Dane LaFontsee, and Rodney Griffen; the Pittsburgh Ballet Theatre, which added the full-length *The Sleeping Beauty* to its repertory; the Houston Ballet, also with a new *The Sleeping Beauty*; and the San Francisco Ballet, with new ballets by Michael Smuin (its co-director with Lew Christensen).

Troupes visiting the U.S. from other countries came from the U.S.S.R., the U.K., Belgium, The Netherlands, Venezuela, West Germany, Denmark, Cuba, and Canada. The Ballet Nacional de Cuba, starring Alicia Alonso, featured several ballets by Alberto Mendez, Cuba's principal junior choreographer; a full-length *Swan Lake*; Brian MacDonald's *Prologue for a Tragedy* (to music of Bach); and Alonso herself dancing *Giselle* for the 36th year. Britain's Royal Ballet was seen in Kenneth MacMillan's *La Fin du jour*, a new production of *The Sleeping Beauty*, and a revival of Sir Frederick Ashton's *A Birthday Offering*. The National Ballet of Canada presented a revival of Roland Petit's *Le Loup* and its production of *The Sleeping Beauty* (with Nureyev as guest star).

UPI

A prominent guest artist for the Joffrey Ballet, Rudolf Nureyev, danced with Denise Jackson in *Le Spectre de la rose* in New York in March.

Maurice Béjart's Ballet of the 20th Century highlighted new versions of *Petrushka*, *Gaîté Parisienne*, and *Le Spectre de la rose* (with Judith Jamison as guest artist) plus the full-length *Amor di poeta* and, in *Life*, a return to the U.S., after an absence of more than 20 years, of Jean Babilée. Moscow's Bolshoi Ballet was seen in a repertory of ballets choreographed by its artistic director, Yuri Grigorovich. These included his new version of *Romeo and Juliet* (Prokofiev) and the first U.S. showing of his earlier classic, *Legend of Love*.

A large number of modern dance companies, headed by the groups representing the works of Martha Graham, the late José Limon, Merce Cunningham, Paul Taylor, Pearl Lang, Alwin Nikolais, Murray Louis, Louis Falco, Twyla Tharp, Don Redlich, Dan Wagoner, Bella Lewitzky, and others, performed extensively. Some of these appeared on such series as New York's Riverside Dance Festival, the Dance Umbrella, the Dance Theatre Workshop, and the American Theater Laboratory.

The all-black Dance Theatre of Harlem and the multiracial Alvin Ailey American Dance Theater increased their activities in both performance schedules and creative ventures. The Puerto Rican Dance Theatre and Ballet Hispanico, both based in New York City, offered programs stressing Hispanic and Caribbean themes and characteristics, and wholly ethnic dance troupes and ensembles from Japan, India, Taiwan, China, and European nations visited the U.S.

The Jacob's Pillow Dance Festival in Massachusetts ranged in its presentations from performances by soloists of the Royal Danish Ballet to a revival of the all-male *Brahms Rhapsody*, created almost 50 years earlier by the late Ted Shawn, longtime director of Jacob's Pillow. Norman Walker, the Pillow's director for several years, retired from the post following the summer season, and Liz Thompson was appointed the new director.

Among special events were a televised performance at the White House by members of the NYCB with Baryshnikov and McBride starring, and a program by Jacques d'Amboise's National Dance Institute, dedicated to the task of getting young American males interested in ballet, at Madison Square Garden's Felt Forum. In the latter more than 350 boys between the ages of 8 and 14 danced. (WALTER TERRY)

Both the Royal Ballet companies in London staged special programs to mark the 75th birthday (on Sept. 17, 1979) of Sir Frederick Ashton, the ballet's founder-choreographer; at Covent Garden there was a triple bill of his ballets *The Dream* (1964), *Symphonic Variations* (1946), and *A Wedding Bouquet* (1937), while the Sadler's Wells Royal Ballet presented *Les Rendezvous* (1933) and *The Two Pigeons* (1961). Ashton added no new work but earlier made a short solo of excerpts from the many roles he created for Dame Margot Fonteyn to perform at a special gala five days after her own 60th birthday (May 18). It was set to the music of Sir Edward Elgar's *Salut d'amour*, and Ashton himself joined her onstage for the last few bars. She received belated official bestowal (by the Royal Ballet) of the title "prima ballerina assoluta," but reports of her "farewell" proved premature when, a month later, she appeared at the London Coliseum with Rudolf Nureyev and the London Festival Ballet in Vaslav Nijinsky's *L'Après-midi d'un faune* and for two unannounced performances in Michel Fokine's *Le Spectre de la rose*.

The main Royal Ballet, which toured Washington, D.C., Montreal, the U.S. West Coast, and Mexico during the summer, was mostly occupied with existing repertory works at Covent Garden, adding only Balanchine's *Liebeslieder Walzer* (music by Brahms) and MacMillan's new one-act *La Fin du jour* (Ravel). MacMillan created another new work for the Sadler's Wells Royal Ballet: *Playground* (Gordon Crosse), on a theme of mental instability. It was premiered at the Edinburgh Festival, together with a pantomime comedy by David Bintley, *Punch and the Street Party* (Lord Berners), but after further performances in London neither was retained in the following tour repertory. Peter Wright, director of the company, staged a new production of *Coppélia* with some additional choreography of his own; the classic was also newly staged by Brenda Last for the Norwegian National Ballet in Oslo and by Ulf Gadd for the Göteborg (Sweden) Ballet.

After 11 years as artistic director of the London Festival Ballet, Beryl Grey was succeeded by John Field, director of the Royal Academy of Dancing. Before the changeover the company in May undertook an artistically successful but financially problematic visit to China for performances at Beijing (Peking) and Shanghai. Earlier, it premiered a popular new three-act ballet by Ronald Hynd, *Rosalinda*, based on the Johann Strauss operetta *Die Fledermaus*. This also provided the French choreographer Roland Petit with the subject and music for another balletic version under the title *La Chauve-souris*, successfully premiered by his Ballets de Marseille at Monte Carlo, with his wife, Zizi Jeanmaire, in the Rosalinda role.

Petit had previously made a new ballet based on Aleksandr Pushkin's *The Queen of Spades* for the Paris International Dance Festival, with Baryshnikov in the central role of Hermann the gambler. It was typical of a marked trend throughout Europe of "literary" ballets, which during the year embraced Dumas's *Lady of the Camellias* by John Neumeier at Stuttgart, West Germany; Dostoyevsky's *The Idiot* by Valery Panov at West Berlin; Byron's *Manfred* by Nureyev at Paris; Synge's *Playboy of the Western World* by Joan Denise Moriarty for the Irish Ballet at Dublin; the Orpheus myth, by Domy Reiter-Soffer in *Timetrip Orpheus*, also for the Irish Ballet, and by William Forsythe in *Orpheus* at Stuttgart. Another classic legend was featured in Rudi van Dantzig's *Ulysses*, which inaugurated an unprecedented 14 consecutive nights of ballet by the resident company at the Vienna State Opera.

Shakespeare, moreover, furnished Glen Tetley with his first full-length (two-act) ballet, *The Tempest*, for Britain's Ballet Rambert. This premiered at the Schwetzinger Festival in West Germany in May and afterward was seen in Paris and London and on tour throughout Britain. With original music by Norway's Arne Nordheim and designs by

UPI

The first U.S. appearance of Soviet Bolshoi Ballet defectors Leonid and Valentina Kozlov was in New Orleans in October when they performed in *These Fascinating Sounds* during the Ballet Galaxie '79.

WIDE WORLD

England's Royal Ballet, which toured North America during the summer, performed a number of works, including *La Fin du jour.* Julian Hosking and Merle Park headlined the performance in Montreal.

Nadine Baylis, it was not so much a translation of the play into dance as a series of choreographic poems on it.

Tetley further had the distinction of a triple bill of his ballets given by the Royal Danish Ballet at Copenhagen, where *Greening* (Nordheim), *Voluntaries* (Poulenc), and *The Rite of Spring* (Stravinsky) comprised the first new program presented by the company's new director, Henning Kronstam. His major project for the year was a week-long festival in November celebrating the centenary of August Bournonville, with eight ballets by this founder of the Danish classical school. Danish dancer Peter Schaufuss anticipated the festival by turning producer for the first time in a new version of Bournonville's *La Sylphide* (1836) for the London Festival Ballet at the Royal Festival Hall. It lovingly preserved the original but restored several previously cut passages in the Lövenskjold music.

Scottish Ballet, with *La Sylphide* already in its repertory, brought this to London with another Bournonville classic, *Napoli* (1842), at Sadler's Wells Theatre. The two London seasons overlapped, and balletic history was made on one night (August 29) when *La Sylphide* was performed by both companies on their respective stages. The Scottish company, celebrating its own tenth anniversary, looked in a new direction by commissioning music for two ballets from members of well-known pop groups, Yes and Jethro Tull, with choreography by Royston Maldoom (*Ursprung*) and Robert North (*The Water's Edge*). They were given with director Peter Darrell's *Such Sweet Thunder* (Duke Ellington) as a triple bill collectively titled *Underground Rumours* and attracted new young audiences. London Contemporary Dance Theatre continued to appeal primarily to youth and devised a new program especially for performance on the new full-circular stage at London's Round House, with works by director Robert Cohan and associate choreographers Siobhan Davis and Robert North.

Another tenth anniversary celebrant was Manchester's Northern Ballet Theatre, which staged a balletic version of *Madam Butterfly* by resident choreographer Jonathan Taylor, using the Puccini music reorchestrated without voices. Other new works were created by company member David Radford with *Incognita* (songs by Strauss and Mahler) and by U.S. choreographers Charles Czarny with *Rustic Variations* (Goldmark) and Daryl Gray, making his U.K. debut with *Ten Easy Pieces* (Stravinsky). *Cinderella* became the inescapable Christmas subject in Britain, with a new ballet by director Robert de Warren for Northern Ballet, using a little-known score composed for the subject by Johann Strauss; another new version by Peter Darrell for Scottish Ballet used an arrangement of Rossini's music from *La Cenerentola,* and the Royal Ballet at Covent Garden revived Ashton's 1948 version to music of Prokofiev.

London was host during the year to an unprecedented procession of visiting companies. At Covent Garden the National Ballet of Canada was followed in turn by the Martha Graham Dance Company from New York City and by the New York City Ballet, warmly acclaimed after 14 years since its last visit. The Ballet of the Finnish State Opera House appeared at Sadler's Wells, as did the all-black Dance Theatre of Harlem, which was rapturously received. Israel's Kibbutz Dance Company paid its first visit (at Logan Hall), and the Edinburgh Festival presented Alicia Alonso and the Ballet Nacional de Cuba for the first time in Britain. The Alvin Ailey American Dance Theater toured other European countries, including the Eastern bloc.

Other developments in Europe included the rebirth of France's former Ballet Théâtre Contemporain as Ballet Théâtre Français based at Nancy, and the debut of Théâtre Chorégraphique de Rennes directed by Romanian-born Gheorghe Caciuleanu. Netherlands Dance Theater celebrated its 20th anniversary while rapidly recovering its former reputation for adventure and character under Czechoslovakian-born Jiri Kylian as director; his *Symphony of Psalms* (Stravinsky) and *Glagolitic Mass* (Janacek) were much acclaimed. The Dutch National Ballet continued to prosper, as did the national companies in Sweden and Hungary, where Antal Fodor had the distinction of a program comprising four of his ballets. Hamburg continued to flourish under Neumeier, whose new *Dreams* comprised a double bill of *Don Quixote* and *The Legend of Joseph,* both to music by Richard Strauss.

Three outstanding choreographers died in 1979: Léonide Massine, creator of *The Three-Cornered Hat, La Boutique fantasque,* and many other classics of the 20th century; Walter Gore, creator of the title role in *The Rake's Progress* for Ninette de Valois (1935) and subsequently choreographer of numerous works for companies in Britain, West Germany, The Netherlands, Norway, and elsewhere; and Kurt Jooss, founder of the Ballets Jooss and creator of *The Green Table, The Big City,* and other works of sociodramatic character. (*See* OBITUARIES.) (NOËL GOODWIN)

See also Music; Theatre.

Danish Literature:
see Literature

Deaths:
see Demography; *see also obituaries of prominent persons who died in 1979 listed under* People of the Year

Defense

The two most significant developments in defense in 1979 were ominous in themselves and suggested, in addition, that the 1980s would be much less stable than the 1970s. The first of these trends was regional instability; the second was the emergence of potential instability in Europe.

In many regions of the world, force was being used internally and externally to change political structures, and in most cases the new power structures were less secure than the old ones. The most dramatic instance was the overthrow of the shah of Iran in a revolution led by a 78-year-old religious leader, Ayatollah Ruhollah Khomeini (*see* BIOGRAPHIES), who himself seemed, by year's end, to have only the shakiest control over the country. Farther south, the remaining conservative Persian Gulf oil producers faced a future the uncertainties of which were emphasized by the continuing low-level conflict between Soviet-supported Yemen (Aden; South Yemen) and Western-supported Yemen (San'a'; North Yemen). On Iran's southeastern frontier, Pakistan's development of a nuclear capability was proceeding faster than expected, and it seemed likely that the "Islamic" nuclear weapon would be tested within a matter of months. In Afghanistan the struggle between conservative guerrillas and the Soviet-supported government escalated into an international crisis at year's end when Soviet troops entered the country in force, ostensibly to assist the Afghans in putting down the rebels; the initial result, however, was the installation of new rulers in Kabul, presumed to be more amenable to Soviet direction. (*See* AFGHANISTAN.) At the other end of what Zbigniew Brzezinski, U.S. Pres. Jimmy Carter's assistant for national security affairs, called the "arc of crisis," Turkey was experiencing domestic instability and its disputes with Greece, especially over Cyprus, remained unsettled.

Other areas of the world were equally unstable. In Southeast Asia, Vietnam invaded Cambodia on Dec. 27, 1978, and succeeded in overthrowing the genocidal Khmer Rouge government of Pol Pot, believed to have killed some two million people since 1975. The Vietnamese completed their occupation of Cambodia in January 1979, but on February 17 China, which had allied itself with Pol Pot, launched a divisional-level punitive expedition against Vietnam that lasted until March-April. Meanwhile, remnants of the Khmer Rouge continued to hold out in remote areas of the country.

In Africa two notable tyrants were overthrown with external assistance. Idi Amin of Uganda fell in April to a Tanzanian invasion, while in September the self-styled Emperor Bokassa I of the Central African Empire was ousted in a coup engineered by France and supported by French forces. In Zimbabwe Rhodesia, where Patriotic Front guerrillas continued their attacks throughout the year, the threat of South African intervention to protect the white minority—leading in turn to the involvement of Angola and Mozambique, where Cuban forces were stationed, and of Zambia—receded in December with agreement on a British-supervised cease-fire at the conclusion of the London constitutional conference. In Latin America the overthrow of Pres. Anastasio Somoza Debayle of Nicaragua by the left-wing Sandinista guerrillas in July raised fears that unrest would spread to other Central American countries. On August 31 the U.S. announced that the Soviet Union had a combat brigade of 2,000–3,000 men in Cuba, in violation of the spirit if not the letter of the post–1962 Cuban missile crisis understandings between the U.S. and the Soviets, but the matter was subsequently papered over.

The second trend, the emergence of potential instability in Europe, affected what had been for nearly two decades the most stable area in the world. Essentially, Western Europe's security had rested on a conventional defense by NATO forces, backed by U.S. willingness to use tactical nuclear weapons to defeat a Warsaw Pact invasion and, if this failed, to initiate strategic nuclear war with the Soviet Union. As long as the U.S. enjoyed strategic and tactical nuclear superiority, this strategy had worked well. It had also enabled NATO to economize on conventional forces and so hold down defense spending.

The emergence of Soviet strategic parity and/or superiority vis-à-vis the U.S. on the one hand and of unprecedented Warsaw Pact conventional superiority on the other underlined the crucial importance of tactical, theatre nuclear forces (TNF) for NATO. These, however, would require major modernization, both quantitatively and qualitatively, in the face of an apparent Soviet drive for TNF superiority, epitomized by the Soviet SS-20

In a show of force, U.S. troops stormed ashore on the beach at Guantanamo Bay, Cuba. The U.S. was demonstrating its military potential in the face of Soviet troops in Cuba.

UPI

intermediate-range ballistic missile (IRBM) and the Backfire bomber. To counter these, the NATO Council meeting in December accepted, with some reservations, a proposal to install 108 Pershing II IRBM's and 464 cruise missiles in Western Europe in the early 1980s.

The arms control implications of these innovations in military technology and strategy were far-reaching. The kind of TNF modernization undertaken by the Soviet Union, if followed by the U.S. and NATO, meant that it would no longer be possible to divorce the European theatre nuclear balance from the strategic nuclear balance, as had been done in SALT I and SALT II. A SALT III would thus have to include tactical (nuclear) arms limitation talks, which would try to address these questions as well as those posed by the modernization and expansion of the independent British and French nuclear forces. (*See* Special Report.)

The political future of Europe seemed as uncertain as its military future. The post-Brezhnev Soviet leadership was expected to try to translate its military superiority into political gains before its domestic oil shortages became too much of a handicap, probably before 1982. One potential flashpoint was Yugoslavia, where President Tito's imminent retirement could create both opportunity and incentive for a Soviet intervention which NATO would have to counter. This was the scenario used by a retired British general, Sir John Hackett, in his book *The Third World War*. Its remarkable popularity (over 500,000 copies sold in a year) emphasized the general expectation of increased conflict inside, as well as outside, Europe in the 1980s.

UNITED STATES

Although U.S. defense spending was expected to reach a record $122.7 billion in fiscal 1980, continued inflation meant that it had actually been decreasing as a percentage of gross national product (GNP), from 5.2% in 1977 to 5% in 1978. As a result of the all-volunteer recruiting system, over half was spent on personnel. The U.S. was expected to increase defense spending significantly, with or without a SALT II treaty, and there was pressure to reintroduce some form of conscription.

The most important defense decision was President Carter's approval of procurement of a totally new intercontinental ballistic missile (ICBM) system, the MX mobile ICBM. This would be larger and more accurate than any ICBM currently deployed by the U.S., with 10 × 370-kiloton warheads (10 warheads, each with a yield of 370 kilotons), large enough to destroy Soviet ICBM silos. Since all fixed-silo ICBM's would be vulnerable by 1981, the MX would utilize a multiple arm points/multiple protective structures (MAPS/MPS) system, whereby individual missiles would be moved between several widely separated hardened shelters. The Soviets would have to target all the shelters, since they would never know which ones were empty, thus absorbing much larger numbers of Soviet warheads and making it much more difficult for them to execute a successful disarming first strike. Carter chose the so-called racetrack system, whereby the MX would be moved around lightly protected oval roads, with spurs running off to the MPS. The roads and shelters would be opened periodically so the Soviets could verify that the number of MX's did not exceed the SALT II ceilings.

It was uncertain whether such a system could actually be built. Liberal critics argued that it was too expensive ($33 billion) and would be destabilizing, since it threatened the Soviet ICBM force. Conservatives attacked the president's delay in deploying the MX, which could not become operational before 1989. But the president faced a dilemma: nondeployment would ensure defeat of SALT II in the Senate, but deployment would alienate liberals and highlight SALT II's failure to restrain the strategic arms race. Delays in the construction of the first seven Ohio-class nuclear-powered ballistic missile submarines (SSBN's), each carrying 24 Trident C-4 submarine-launched ballistic missiles (SLBM's), had further narrowed the president's options. The first Ohio SSBN would not enter service until late 1980. The Trident SLBM (6,500-km [4,000-mi] range; 8 × 100 kiloton multiple independently targetable reentry vehicles [MIRV]) had also suffered development problems, delaying its retrofitting into 12 older SSBN's currently deployed with Poseidon SLBM's (4,635-km [2,880-mi] range; 10 × 50 kiloton warheads).

In conventional forces, U.S. numbers remained about the same, with new equipment being introduced in insufficient quantities to offset the overall low levels. The Army of 750,800 (56,840 women) was slowly being reoriented for use in a European conflict; one of the five infantry divisions was being mechanized, to add to the existing five mechanized and four armoured divisions. That left four infantry divisions of little use on a sophisticated armoured battlefield, plus one airmobile and one airborne division. The first 110 XM-1 medium tanks were delivered, but the new armoured fighting vehicle (AFV) was canceled as too expensive, and 1,207 more M-113 armoured personnel carriers (APC's) were ordered instead. Tanks remained at about 10,500, the same as a decade earlier. TOW and Dragon antitank guided weapons (ATGW's) were being procured in large numbers, despite doubts about their effectiveness in Europe.

U.S. Army strength in Western Europe had risen to 202,400 personnel, with 3,000 medium tanks. Reinforcements in a crisis would comprise two armoured, two mechanized, three infantry, and one airmobile divisions. The only other major overseas deployment consisted of 33,400 personnel in South Korea. President Carter's plans to withdraw most or all of these forces had been canceled as destabilizing. There was one weak division (14,000 personnel) in Hawaii.

The Air Force was deploying new tactical fighters, including 312 F-15 Eagles and F-16s, while the F-18 was under development. Also being deployed were 112 A-10A ground-attack aircraft. Three squadrons were equipped with 14 E-3A airborne warning and control system (AWACS) aircraft to greatly increase their effectiveness; eight more AWACS aircraft were on order, plus 18 for NATO. Older aircraft included 282 F-111A/D/E/F bombers, 1,100 F-4 Phantoms, and 72 A-7D fighter-bombers. Major deployments outside the

U.S. included 74,300 personnel with U.S. Air Force, Europe and 23,000 with the Pacific Air Forces in Japan, South Korea, and the Philippines.

Ironically, given President Carter's naval background, the U.S. Navy fell to a record postwar low of 172 major surface combat vessels in 1978, although the number did rise to 180 in 1979. There were also 80 attack submarines (73 nuclear). The 13 aircraft carriers had a total of 1,100 aircraft, including 168 F-14A Tomcats and 144 F-4 fighters, plus 110 A-6E Intruders and 300 A-7E strike aircraft. Congress again authorized a fourth nuclear carrier (CVN), to cost over $2 billion, although the president had vetoed similar authorizations in previous years.

The bulk of the ex-World War II ships had finally been retired, so the Navy was based on modern types. Whether there were enough of them was questionable, however, as was the adequacy of their missile armament, despite the entry into service of the Harpoon antiship missile (100-km [60-mi] range). The Tomahawk SLCM was being developed for use with surface vessels and submarines. The U.S. Marine Corps remained a large (184,000 personnel) and expensive force of amphibious infantry. Its value in a major European war was limited, but it could form a useful intervention force in certain situations.

U.S.S.R.

Soviet defense spending continued to rise steadily, accounting for at least 11–14% of GNP (over U.S. $150 billion) and perhaps as much as 18% (Western estimates varied). Contrary to widespread expectations, a decade of arms control had brought no reductions. There was no evidence that the Soviet economy could not maintain this burden indefinitely.

The impressive qualitative buildup of the strategic forces continued, with little decrease in quantity. The last of the old SS-7 and SS-8 ICBM's were retired, but the 230 new ICBM's (SS-17/18/19) that were deployed had accuracies comparable to U.S. ICBM's and larger and more numerous warheads. At sea, the Soviets had reached or exceeded their SALT I Interim Agreement ceiling of 950 SLBM's in 64 SSBN's, with the SS-N-18 SLBM (8,000+-km [5,000+-mi] range; 3 × 1–2-megaton MIRV) replacing the SS-N-8. Intensive Soviet development of antiballistic missile (ABM) systems continued, including the charged particle beam (CPB). Within the U.S., intense controversy continued over whether the theoretical potential of the CPB could be translated into an operational weapons system, but it was clear that the U.S. was far behind in CPB research and was making a major effort to catch up.

Soviet general purpose forces increased only slightly to about 3,658,000 personnel, but they continued to receive increased quantities of modern equipment equal or superior to anything in the West. The Army of 1,825,000 personnel comprised 47 tank, 118 motor rifle, and 8 airborne divisions, an increase of 4 divisions. Armoured vehicle holdings improved, notably with additions of the new T-64 and T-72 main battle tanks (MBT's) and BMP mechanized infantry combat vehicles (MICV), but total holdings remained at about 50,000 MBT's and 55,000 MICV/AFV's. Roughly one-fourth of the Army (46 divisions) was stationed on the Sino-Soviet border, but this included only 6 tank divisions, emphasizing that Soviet ground forces were primarily targeted against Western Europe. In the crucial northern and central European area, the Soviets and the Warsaw Pact could muster 20,500 MBT's against NATO's 7,000. In divisional equivalents, allowing for the smaller Soviet and Pact divisions of 11,000–13,000 men (which still had as many tanks as the larger U.S. divisions), the Soviets could field 47 divisions to NATO's 27. Two new battlefield tactical nuclear weapons were introduced, the SS-21 and SS-22 (100–160-km [65–100-mi] range; kiloton-range warhead).

The 475,000-strong Air Force had 4,350 combat aircraft. These included increasing numbers of newer types, notably the Su-17 Fitter C (640), MiG-23/27 Flogger B/D (1,400), and Su-19 Fencer (230). Attack helicopters were appearing in significant numbers, especially the Mi-24 Hind (580). Long-range air transport capabilities also increased. In northern and central Europe the Sovi-

The diagram shows three road loops resembling racetracks, each containing one MX missile. To provide secrecy of location, each missile would be moved at random into any one of 23 shelters on the road loops. After a missile had been brought into each loop, a barrier would be erected, preventing another missile from being brought in. The Soviets could monitor the barriers and be assured of compliance with the arms control agreements.

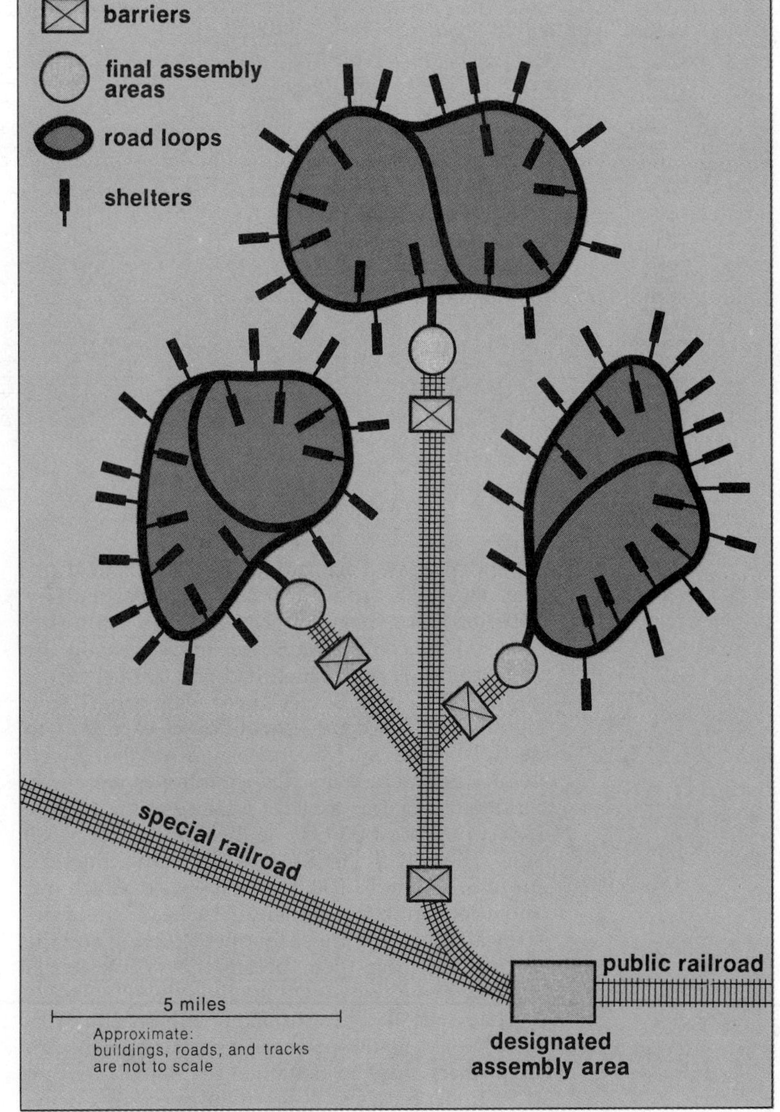

Approximate Strengths of Regular Armed Forces of the World

Country	Military personnel in 000s: Army	Navy	Air Force	Warships[1]: Aircraft carriers/cruisers	Submarines[2]	Destroyers/frigates	Jet aircraft[3]: Bombers and fighter-bombers	Fighters/reconnaissance	Tanks[4]	Defense expenditure as % of GNP
I. NATO										
Belgium	62.3	4.4	20.1	—	—	4 FFG	90 FB	42, 18 R	396	3.5
Canada	29.3	14.2	36.5	—	3	4 DDG, 19 FF	—	120	114	1.8
Denmark	21.4	6.1	7.1	—	6 C	2 FFG	58 FB	39, 16 R	320	2.4[5]
France[6]	326.8	70.2	103.6	2 CV, 1 CVH, 1 CG	23, 4 SSBN	17 DDG, 25 FF	33 SB, 274 FB	145, 45 R	1,060	3.3
Germany, West	335.2	36.5	106.0	—	24 C	7 DDG, 4 DD, 6 FF	425 FB	90 R	3,779	3.4
Greece	145.0	17.0	22.6	—	7	12 DD, 4 FF	132 FB	79, 40 R	1,320	4.7
Italy	254.0	42.0	69.0	1 CVH, 2 CAH	9	4 DDG, 3 DD, 2 FFG, 10 FF	162 FB	72, 36 R	1,650	2.4
Luxembourg	0.6	—	—	—	—	—	—	—	—	1.1[5]
Netherlands, The	75.0	16.8	19.0	—	6	2 DDG, 7 DD, 8 FFG	108 FB	36, 18 R	800	3.3
Norway	20.0	9.0	10.0	—	15 C	5 FFG	72 FB	16, 12 R	116	3.2[5]
Portugal	37.0	14.0	9.5	—	3	17 FF	24 FB	—	81	2.8[5]
Turkey	470.0	45.0	51.0	—	13	12 DD, 2 FF	213 FB	56, 34 R	3,500	4.5
United Kingdom	163.7	72.9[7]	86.3	2 CVH, 1 CVV, 2 LPH, 2 CAH	16, 10 SSN, 4 SSBN	13 DDG, 53 FFG	48 SB, 50 B, 120 FB	109, 126 R	900	4.7
United States	934.8[7]	524.2	563.0	3 CVN, 10 CV, 8 CGN, 20 CG, 3 LHA, 7 LPH, 19 LPD, 33 LSD/T	7, 73 SSN, 41 SSBN	37 DDG, 35 DD, 7 FFG, 58 FF	381 SB, 282 B, 2,078 FB	637, 252 R	10,500	5.0
II. WARSAW PACT										
Bulgaria	115.0	10.0	25.0	—	4	2 FF	64 FB	78, 24R	1,800	. . .
Czechoslovakia	140.0	—	54.0	—	—	—	155 FB	252, 55 R	3,400	3.8
Germany, East	107.0	16.0	36.0	—	—	2 FF	35 FB	300	2,500	5.8
Hungary	80.0	—	24.0	—	—	—	—	150	1,250	2.4
Poland	210.0	22.5	85.0	—	4	1 DDG	220 FB	378, 81 R	3,400	3.0
Romania	140.0	10.5	30.0	—	—	—	70 FB	240, 18 R	1,500	1.7
U.S.S.R.	1,825.0	433.0[7]	1,480.0[8]	2 CV, 2 CVH, 8 CG, 24 CA	138, 41 SSN, 71 SSBN, 19 SSB, 45 SSGN, 24 SSG	50 DDG, 50 DD, 33 FFG, 103 FF	156 SB, 868 B, 3,320 FB	2,600, 795 R	50,000	11–14
III. OTHER EUROPEAN										
Albania	30.0	3.0	10.0	—	3	—	—	100	100	. . .
Austria	34.0	—	4.0	—	—	—	34 FB	—	270	1.2
Finland	34.4	2.5	3.0	—	—	2 FF	—	52	—	1.5
Ireland	12.5	0.6	0.7	—	—	—	—	—	—	. . .
Spain	240.0	40.0[7]	41.0	1 CV	8	13 DD, 8 FFG, 8 FF	38 FB	77, 27 R	670	1.8
Sweden[9]	44.5/750.0	11.8	9.6	—	14	3 DDG	108 FB	306, 54 R	660	3.4
Switzerland[9]	10.5/580.0	—	8.0/45.0	—	—	—	270 FB	33, 26 R	840	1.9
Yugoslavia	190.0	25.0	44.0	—	5	1 DD	122 FB	126, 46 R	2,150	. . .
IV. MIDDLE EAST AND MEDITERRANEAN; SUB-SAHARAN AFRICA; LATIN AMERICA[10]										
Algeria	78.0	3.8	7.0	—	—	—	24 B, 100 FB	90, 6 R	500	3.0
Egypt	272.0	20.0	103.0	—	12	5 DD	23 B, 432 FB	130	1,600	. . .
Iran[11]	285.0	30.0	100.0	—	1	3 DD, 4 FFG	356 FB	77, 14 R	1,735	. . .
Iraq	190.0	4.0	28.0	—	—	—	22 B, 190 FB	115	1,800	. . .
Israel[9]	138.0/375.0	6.6/10.0	21.0/27.0	—	3	—	558 FB	18 R	3,050	24.5
Jordan	60.0	—	7.0	—	—	—	32 FB	41	500	. . .
Lebanon[12]	8.0	—	0.5	—	—	—	7 FB	—	—	. . .
Libya	35.0	3.0	4.0	—	3	—	24 B, 110 FB	24, 5R	2,000	2.4
Morocco	90.0	2.0	6.0	—	—	—	50 FB	—	140	. . .
Saudi Arabia	35.0	1.5	8.0	—	—	—	65 FB	20	350	15.0
Sudan	60.0	1.4	1.5	—	—	—	36 FB	—	130	. . .
Syria	200.0	2.5	25.0	—	—	2 FF	174 FB	215	2,600	. . .
United Arab Emirates	23.5	0.9	0.7	—	—	—	9 FB	32	—	. . .
Yemen, North	35.0	0.6	1.0	—	—	—	—	3	232	. . .
Yemen, South	19.0	0.5	1.3	—	—	—	12 B, 47 FB	50	260	. . .
Angola[13]	35.0	2.5	2.5	—	—	—	—	31	235	. . .
Ethiopia[14]	215.0	2.0	4.6	—	—	—	94 FB	—	630	. . .

ets and Warsaw Pact could field 4,200 tactical aircraft against NATO's 2,350 and were particularly superior in interceptors (2,050 versus 400). This reflected the continuing Soviet investment in the Air Defense Force, which had 550,000 personnel and 2,600 aircraft. Soviet forces were acquiring a significant "look-down, shoot-down" capability to destroy targets, such as cruise missiles, flying well below the interceptors. Cruise missiles were also vulnerable to the massive surface-to-air missile (SAM) network of 10,000 launchers at over 1,000 sites. The new Soviet SA-10 SAM, with a range of up to 3,200 km (2,000 mi) at speeds of Mach 4–5 and a conventional or nuclear warhead, could destroy air-launched cruise missiles (ALCM's) and the aircraft carrying them before they could reach their targets.

The Soviet Navy continued to enhance its ability to project Soviet power at a distance, although its primary mission remained sea denial, cutting U.S. supply routes to Western Europe and destroying U.S., British, and French SSBN's before they could launch their SLBM's. Its 85 amphibious warships included the new Ivan Rogov class. The two Kiev-class 43,000-ton through-deck carriers each carried 12 vertical takeoff and landing (VTOL) strike aircraft and antisubmarine warfare (ASW) assault helicopters, plus 8–16 SS-N-3/12 surface-to-surface missiles (SSM's; 520–725-km [324–450-mi] range; kiloton-range warhead). Two more of these large multipurpose weapons platforms were being built, and an escorting nuclear-powered cruiser was nearing completion. Other major units were two Moskva-class helicopter carrier/cruisers with 18 helicopters, 6 Kara-class cruisers (more building), 10 Kresta II-class ASW cruisers, four Kresta I- and four Kynda-class guided weapons cruisers, and 23 Krivak I/II ASW destroyers with SS-N-14 ASW missiles (more building).

The submarine force remained the world's largest, including 41 nuclear attack submarines (SSN's) and 138 diesel submarines. The new A-class SSN

Country	Military personnel in 000s			Warships[1]			Jet aircraft[3]			
	Army	Navy	Air Force	Aircraft carriers/ cruisers	Submarines[2]	Destroyers/ frigates	Bombers and fighter-bombers	Fighters/ reconnaisance	Tanks[4]	Defense expenditure as % of GNP
Mozambique[15]	22.8	0.7	0.5	—	—	—	—	—	240	...
Nigeria	160.0	6.0	7.0	—	—	—	21 FB	—	—	...
Somalia	45.0	0.5	1.0	—	—	—	3 B, 15 FB	7	80	...
South Africa[9]	48.5/404.5	4.7	10.0	—	3	1 DD, 3 FF	15 B, 37 FB	32	270	...
Tanzania[16]	50.0	0.7	1.0	—	—	—	—	20	20	...
Uganda[16]	20.0	—	1.0	—	—	—	—	31	35	...
Zaire	18.5	1.0	1.0	—	—	—	—	13	—	...
Zimbabwe Rhodesia	20.0	—	1.5	—	—	—	7 B, 27 FB	—	—	...
Argentina	80.0	32.9[7]	20.0	1 CVH, 1 CAH	4	1 DDG, 7 DD, 2 FFG	11 B, 159 FB	25	100	3.3
Brazil	182.0	49.0[7]	50.0	1 CVH	8	6 DDG, 10 DD	39 FB	14	60	1.0[5]
Chile	50.0	24.0	11.0	3 CA	3	2 DDG, 4 DD, 2 FFG, 3 FF	34 FB	—	70	...
Colombia	55.0	8.0[7]	4.5	—	2	3 DD	19 FB	—	—	1.0
Cuba	160.0	9.0	20.0	—	2	—	40 FB	128	600	8.3
Mexico	80.0	15.0[7]	5.0	—	—	2 DD, 6 FF	—	—	—	0.5
Peru	70.0	12.0	10.0	2 CG, 2 CA	8	2 DDG, 4 DD, 2 FFG, 2 FF	32 B, 51 FB	10	310	...
V. FAR EAST AND OCEANIA[10]										
Afghanistan[17]	80.0	—	10.0	—	—	—	30 B, 104 FB	35	800	...
Australia	31.9	16.5	21.8	1 CV	6	3 DDG, 1 DD, 6 FFG	21 B, 48 FB	13	103	2.7[5]
Bangladesh	70.0	3.5	3.0	—	—	2 FF	27 FB	—	30	...
Burma	153.0	9.0	7.5	—	—	2 FF	—	—	—	...
China	3,600.0	360.0[7]	400.0	—	91, 1 SSN, 1 SSB	11 DDG, 14 FFG	540 B, 500 FB	4,275	11,000	10.0
India	950.0	46.0	100.0	1 CV, 1 CA	8	6 FFG, 16 FF	50 B, 333 FB	252, 6 R	1,850	3.2
Indonesia	180.0	39.0[7]	20.0	—	3	11 FF	16 FB	—	—	...
Japan	155.0	42.0	44.0	—	13	18 DDG, 14 DD, 11 FFG, 4 FF	59 FB	288, 14 R	690	0.9
Korea, North	600.0	27.0	45.0	—	15	3 FF	85 B, 60 FB	420	2,150	11.4
Korea, South	520.0	47.0	32.0	—	—	16 FF	212 FB	12 R	860	5.6
Laos	46.0	0.5	2.0	—	—	—	—	10	—	...
Malaysia	52.5	6.0	6.0	—	—	2 FF	16 FB	—	—	4.7
New Zealand	5.6	2.8	4.2	—	—	4 FFG	13 FB	—	—	1.9
Pakistan	400.0	12.0	17.0	—	6	7 DD	11 B, 235 FB	10 R	1,000	5.7
Philippines	65.0	22.0[7]	16.0	—	—	8 FF	53 FB	—	—	3.4
Singapore	30.0	3.0	3.0	—	—	—	116 FB	—	—	5.5
Taiwan	439.0[7]	35.0	65.0	—	2	7 DD, 15 DDG, 11 FF	—	353, 8 R	175	7.7
Thailand	145.0	28.0[7]	43.0	—	—	4 FF	38 FB	—	20	3.7
Vietnam[18]	1,000.0	3.0	20.0	—	—	1 FF	10 B, 305 FB	180	1,400	...

Note: Data exclude paramilitary, security, and irregular forces. Naval data exclude vessels of less than 100 tons standard displacement. Figures are for July 1979.

[1] Aircraft carrier (CV); helicopter carrier (CVH); medium (V/STOL aircraft) carrier (CVV); general purpose amphibious assault ship (LHA); amphibious transport dock (LPD); amphibious assault ship (helicopter) (LPH); dock landing ship (LSD); heavy cruiser (CA); guided missile cruiser (CG); helicopter cruiser (CAH); destroyer (DD); guided missile destroyer (DDG); frigate (FF); guided missile frigate (FFG); N denotes nuclear powered.
[2] Nuclear submarine (SSN); ballistic missile submarine (SSB); guided (cruise) missile submarine (SSG); coastal (C); N denotes nuclear powered.
[3] Bombers (B), fighter-bombers (FB), strategic bombers (SB), reconnaissance fighters (R); data exclude light strike/counter-insurgency (COIN) aircraft.
[4] Main battle tanks (MBT), medium and heavy, 31 tons and over.
[5] Gross domestic product.
[6] French forces were withdrawn from NATO in 1966, but France remains a member of NATO.
[7] Includes marines.
[8] Figure includes the Strategic Rocket Forces (375,000) and the Air Defense Force (550,000), both separate services.
[9] Second figure is fully mobilized strength.
[10] Sections IV and V list only those states with significant military forces.
[11] Iranian figures refer to pre-revolutionary situation.
[12] Figures approximate, given Lebanon's civil war and division.
[13] Plus 20,000 Cubans and 2,500 East Germans serving with Angolan forces.
[14] Ethiopia also has 17,000 Cuban plus other Soviet bloc troops and a 150,000-strong People's Militia.
[15] Plus Cuban, Warsaw Pact, and Chinese advisers and technicians in Mozambique.
[16] Figures are before the Tanzanian-Ugandan war when Ugandan forces disintegrated.
[17] Figures approximate, given civil war in Afghanistan. Exclude Soviet and Warsaw Pact advisers and/or troops.
[18] Figures include substantial equipment of former South Vietnamese forces.

Sources: International Institute for Strategic Studies, 18 Adam Street, London, *The Military Balance 1979–80, Strategic Survey 1978.*

was reported to be faster and to dive deeper than any U.S. counterpart. The Soviets were alone in having submarines designed to carry cruise missiles; of the 45 nuclear and 24 diesel cruise missile submarines, 53 carried the SS-N-3 Shaddock SLCM, now being replaced by the SS-N-12. The Naval Air Force, which provided land-based air power under naval control, totaled 870 combat aircraft, including 30 Tu-22M Backfire B, 40 Tu-22 Blinder C, and 295 Tu-16 Badger C/G medium bombers.

NATO

The tactical nuclear balance in Europe was even more uncertain than the superpowers' strategic nuclear balance, largely because the relevant information was politically sensitive and hence highly classified. Moreover, many of the forces involved, especially strike aircraft, were dual-capable, that is, they could deliver either conventional or nuclear warheads. NATO's nuclear warheads could be released for use by the national command authorities of the U.S., Britain, and France. U.S. nuclear weapons supplied under the two-key arrangement could be delivered by nonnuclear NATO countries with the consent of the U.S. and of the Western European country providing the delivery system. All estimates of the TNF available emphasized how devastating their use could be for both Western and Eastern Europe. On a small, crowded continent, "tactical" nuclear warheads would be strategic in their effect.

TNF in Europe fell into three categories: long-range (1,900–8,850-km [1,200–5,500-mi] range), often called Eurostrategic or gray-area weapons systems; medium-range (320–1,900-km [200–1,200-mi] range); and battlefield TNF with ranges under 320 km. The last two were often grouped together, inaccurately, as short-range TNF. The Soviet advantage was particularly marked in long-range TNF. The Soviets had deployed 120 of an expected 1,000 SS-20 IRBM's that would replace the

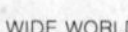

The nuclear submarine "Ohio," lead ship in the Trident series, was launched at Groton, Connecticut, in April; the strategic ship would carry 24 ballistic missiles with a range of over 4,000 miles.

existing 500 SS-4 medium-range ballistic missiles (MRBM's) and 90 SS-5 IRBM's. Medium-range bombers included 50–80 Backfire B's (8,850-km [5,-500-mi] range; 8,000-kg [17,500-lb] weapons load), 135 Tu-22 Blinders, and 318 older Tu-16 Badgers. NATO's major long-range TNF was supposed to consist of four U.S. SSBN's, each with 16 Poseidon SLBM's, but only two SSBN's would normally be on patrol at any given time, and it was doubtful whether they could be spared from the U.S. strategic nuclear strike force. This left 222 U.S. FB-111A/F-111E/F medium-range bombers, 48 British Vulcan B2 and 50 Buccaneer bombers, and, from the French, 18 SSBS S-2 IRBM's and 33 Mirage IVA bombers. The British and French strategic forces totaling 8–10 SSBN's with 16 SLBM's each would be retained for strategic strikes against Soviet cities.

Soviet medium-range TNF consisted mostly of new, deep-interdiction strike aircraft deployed from 1970–74 onward. They included 1,000 MiG-21 Fishbed J/K/L/N's, 1,400 MiG-23/27 Flogger B/D's, 640 Su-17 Fitter C/D's, and 230 Su-19 Fencers. There were also 335 older Su-7 Fitter A's. Soviet short-range ballistic missiles (SRBM's) included 500 SS-12 Scaleboards plus 18 SS-N-4 Sark SLBM's in 6 G-I-class diesel submarines, 39 SS-N-5 Serb SLBM's in 13 G-II-class diesel submarines, and 21 SS-N-5's in 7 H-II SSBN's. Six SS-N-8 SLBM's in one H-III-class SSBN were also available. All these submarines were based in the Baltic, and neither they nor the SLBM's they carried were limited by SALT II. NATO medium-range TNF were older, having been first deployed between 1958 and 1962. They included 367 F-104 Starfighters and 500 F-4 Phantoms, 60–100 A-6E's and A-7E's on U.S. carriers, and 24–48 Étendard IVM strike aircraft on French carriers. There were also 200–500 British and French Jaguar aircraft and 100 French Mirage 5F strike aircraft. The only NATO S/M/IRBM's currently deployed were 108 U.S. Pershing I's and 72 West German-operated Pershing I's with U.S.-controlled warheads. The Pershing II, planned to have a range of 2,400–3,200 km (1,500–2,000 mi) and multiple-kiloton-range warheads, would be able to reach western U.S.S.R. from West Germany.

Very short-range (battlefield) nuclear weapons included, on the Soviet side, the SS-1b/c Scud A/B and FROG 7 SRBM, plus the SS-21 SRBM introduced in 1978, all with kiloton-range warheads. The 324 SS-N-3 Shaddock medium-range cruise missiles on ships and submarines were being replaced by the SS-N-12. NATO had 36 U.S. Lance and 32 French Pluton SRBM's, plus 54 Lance and 91 obsolete Honest John SRBM's deployed under the two-key system, also with kiloton-range warheads. In addition, the U.S. had nuclear shells with yields of up to two or more kilotons for 155-mm and 203-mm howitzers owned by the U.S. and most of its NATO allies. The Soviets certainly deployed comparable nuclear artillery, and the British and French had the capability to develop such shells and might have done so. The U.S. was also producing the components to transform existing tactical nuclear warheads into enhanced radiation weapons (ERW) within hours, as a compromise between producing the controversial ERW's (neutron bombs) and canceling them. Such weapons would destroy Warsaw Pact armour and troops by radiation rather than by blast.

It was clear that there were enough nuclear weapons on both sides of the iron curtain to destroy Europe in a "tactical" nuclear war. It was also clear that whichever side struck first could destroy most of its opponents' tactical nuclear weapons on the ground or in their storage areas before they could be used. NATO TNF would have to be modernized unless suitable nuclear arms-control arrangements could be reached for Europe, as was sought by NATO's new European arms control body. The political problems TNF force modernization would cause showed every sign of being as bad as if not worse than any in NATO's history.

UNITED KINGDOM

British defense spending, while expected to rise to $17,572,000,000 for 1979–80, fell once again in terms of GNP to 4.7%, although as a percentage of GNP it was still the highest in Western Europe. Total personnel rose slightly, to 322,891. The new Conservative government moved rapidly to implement its campaign pledge to upgrade Britain's defense forces in the face of what Prime Minister Margaret Thatcher regarded as a very real Soviet threat. Service pay was substantially increased to halt the severe decline in morale, and defense spending was raised by 3% in real terms.

The most important decision facing the government was how, and at what cost, to modernize Britain's nuclear deterrent, currently centred on four aging Resolution-class British-built SSBN's armed with 16 U.S.-supplied Polaris A-3s (4,635-km [2,880-mi] range; 3 × 200-kiloton multiple reentry vehicles [MRV]). Surprisingly, the Thatcher option was the most ambitious and expensive: to seek Trident C-4 SLBM's from the U.S. under the 1962 Nassau agreement, together with assistance in building SSBN launchers. Alternatively or in addition, Britain, in cooperation with France, would develop cruise missiles that could be launched from a wide variety of platforms, including the new Tornado multirole combat aircraft developed by Britain, West Germany, and Italy and just entering service. British TNF, about which little was known, would also presumably be upgraded.

The Army of 163,681 personnel was still drained by the need to provide troops for service in Northern Ireland, and the 55,000-strong British Army of the Rhine (BAOR) was below strength and short of modern equipment. Reorganization had abolished the brigade and replaced it with formations known as field forces, of varying strength depending on their roles. The 86,310-strong Royal Air Force was being reoriented back toward an air defense role; 165 air defense versions of the Tornado were on order, to counter the Soviet Backfire bomber and deep-interdiction fighter-bomber threat. Current air defense relied on Lightnings and Phantoms plus, for attack, Vulcan and Buccaneer bombers and Jaguar and Harrier vertical/short takeoff and landing (V/STOL) strike planes. These were mostly obsolete or aging types. The Royal Navy of 72,900 personnel had 72 major surface combat vessels. An important new type was the Invincible class, a 16,000-ton, through-deck/mini carrier with 8 VTOL aircraft and 10 helicopters, usable for defense, especially against air- or ship-launched missiles, or for short-range strikes. The Navy also had 13 guided weapons destroyers, 53 frigates, and 10 nuclear submarines (SSN's), with 4 SSN's on order.

FRANCE

French forces increased slightly, to 509,300 personnel, as did defense spending, to 3.3% of GNP in 1978 and $18,776,000,000 in 1979. In the nuclear *force de frappe,* the four SSBN's with 16 MSBS M-20 SLBM's (4,800-km [3,000-mi] range; 1 × 1-megaton warhead) were being joined by two SSBN's under construction, each with 16 MSBS M-4 SLBM's (5,600-km [3,500-mi] range; high-kiloton-range MIRV). The 18 land-based, fixed-silo S-2 IRBM's were being replaced by the longer-range and more powerful S-3. The 33 Mirage IVA strategic bombers were supplemented by 105 Mirage IIIE's, plus 40 Mirage F-5 and 105 Jaguar strike aircraft and 24 Super Étendard and Étendard IVM carrier strike fighters. The idea of Franco-German cooperation in nuclear forces, with West Germany providing economic and technical assistance for the construction of delivery vehicles for French nuclear weapons, was again raised by influential political and military figures. Officially, Paris and Bonn rejected the idea, but its inherent logic was inescapable, especially given doubts about the credibility of the U.S. nuclear guarantee.

The French Army of 326,800 personnel was still active overseas, especially in Africa. Total overseas deployment for all services was about 19,000. The 70,250-strong Navy had 48 major surface combat vessels, including two Clemenceau-class medium attack carriers with 40 aircraft each, and 23 diesel submarines; the first French SSN was planned. The Air Force, with 103,650 personnel, had 477 combat aircraft including 30 Mirage IIIC and 90 Mirage F-1C interceptors.

WEST GERMANY

In terms of numbers and quality, West Germany's armed forces were the key to Western Europe's defense. Personnel totaled 495,000 and could be increased to about 1,250,000 on total mobilization. At $24,391,000,000, defense expenditure was still only 3.4% of GNP. The 335,200-strong Army had been reorganized into 16 armoured and 12 armoured infantry (mechanized) brigades of 4,500–5,000 men each, plus 3 light infantry, 2 mountain, and 3 airborne brigades. Armour included 1,342 M-48A2/A4 and 2,437 Leopard 1 MBT's, with 1,800 Leopard 2 MBT's on order, plus 2,136 Marder MICV's and 4,030 M-113 APC's. The Army had 65 Honest John and 26 Lance SSM's.

The 106,000-strong Air Force had 480 combat aircraft, with an additional 132 in the naval air force. The aircraft included 217 F/TF-104G Starfighter fighter-bombers (being replaced by 210 Tornadoes), 60 F-4F Phantom fighter-bombers, and 18 Alpha Jet strike aircraft. The air defense command had 60 F-4F interceptors, plus 216 Nike Hercules and 216 Improved HAWK SAM's. The coast defense Navy of 36,500 personnel included 24 coastal submarines.

DISARMAMENT AND ARMS CONTROL

The already slim chances of achieving arms control receded still further in 1979, and it appeared that the UN's Disarmament Decade of the 1970s had really been an Armament Decade. Apart from SALT II, the Carter administration's attempts to secure effective arms control had also failed. Negotiations on a three-power (U.S.-U.K.-Soviet) comprehensive nuclear test ban (CTB) were stalemated over Soviet rejection of Western proposals for verification and the question of whether all tests should be banned (a zero-yield treaty) or only those above a specified threshold. The Soviets continued to conduct very large underground nuclear tests like the one in November 1979, well in excess of the 150-kiloton limit that had been established by the 1974 Threshold Test Ban Treaty and the 1976 Peaceful Nuclear Explosions Treaty. Senate ratification of those treaties had been postponed by President Carter because they did nothing to restrain test-

Some Soviet tanks were withdrawn from East Germany in December as part of a partial troop withdrawal announced by Soviet Pres. Leonid Brezhnev.

WIDE WORLD

ing, although the U.S. was acting as if they were in force.

Attempts to secure limitations on antisatellite weapons through the antisatellite arms talks had failed because the Soviets wanted to preserve their lead in antisatellite weapons while the U.S. was trying to catch up. The U.S. had also failed to secure any limitations on arms sales to the third world, except by U.S. firms. The resultant sales opportunities had been eagerly snapped up by other Western arms suppliers, notably Britain and France, and by the Soviets. Third world countries rejected any suggestion of restraint as a form of neocolonialism.

The Vienna negotiations on mutual (and balanced) force reductions (M[B]FR), under way since 1973, had made no real progress and seemed unlikely to do so. They were too limited geographically (the NATO guidelines area covered only Belgium, Luxembourg, The Netherlands, East and West Germany, Poland, and Czechoslovakia) and in terms of weapons systems covered (essentially tanks and personnel, plus a few aircraft). The West's 1975 Option III proposal (so-called because it was their third major proposal) had included TNF, offering a Western reduction of 29,000 troops, 1,000 tactical nuclear warheads, 54 nuclear-capable strike aircraft, and 36 Pershing SRBM's in exchange for Soviet withdrawal of 68,000 troops and 1,700 tanks, constituting a Soviet tank army. By 1979, however, Option III appeared unwise, given NATO's TNF modernization plans. So did NATO's 1978 modification of the proposal, which would allow the Soviets to withdraw 1,700 tanks from anywhere in the guidelines area instead of a tank army, since this would do much less to reduce Soviet offensive capabilities. The well-publicized withdrawal of some Soviet tanks and personnel from East Germany in December was more effective politically, although militarily it was worthless. Soviet Pres. Leonid Brezhnev's October announcement that the U.S.S.R. was prepared to withdraw some forces had been accompanied by an offer to negotiate a reduction in SS-20 IRBM's stationed in the western U.S.S.R. The offer was withdrawn after the NATO Council's mid-December decision to install Pershing II's and cruise missiles in Western Europe, although, to meet objections from the Dutch and Belgians, this had been accompanied by an agreement to seek new arms-reduction talks.

The likelihood of further nuclear weapons proliferation, despite moderately effective efforts to stop or slow it, was highlighted in October by the U.S. report of a possible South African nuclear test. South Africa denied the allegation and the evidence was ambiguous, but it had the technical resources to develop nuclear weapons, and there had been reports in 1977 of South African preparations for testing. Pakistan was also attempting to join the nuclear club, having evaded the nonproliferation treaty suppliers' safeguards to acquire a gaseous centrifuge producing enriched uranium. Most observers expected a Pakistani nuclear test at any time. Other likely new nuclear weapons powers included South Korea, Taiwan, Japan, Argentina, Brazil, and Chile. West Germany's agreement to supply Brazil with a complete nuclear energy cycle, giving Brazil a weapons option, was still in effect despite intense U.S. opposition. The Geneva disarmament negotiations, now known as the Committee on Disarmament, failed to produce a single agreement in 1979.

THE MIDDLE EAST

The first year of the separate Israeli-Egyptian peace failed to produce the hoped-for moves toward a broader Israeli-Arab settlement that would include the Palestinians, while Egypt remained an outcast in the Arab world. (*See* MIDDLE EASTERN AFFAIRS.) Indeed, the security problems of Israel and Egypt had increased significantly with the fall of the shah of Iran and his replacement by the unpredictable government of the Ayatollah Khomeini. In broader terms, the stability of the entire Middle East was threatened by the passing of Iran as a military and political power.

Iran had provided a conservative, pro-U.S. balance to the left-wing revolutionary forces in the area, notably Syria, Iraq, and the Palestine Liberation Organization (PLO), while providing security for the militarily weak, oil-rich states of the Persian Gulf. Both the left- and right-wing Arab countries were anti-Israeli, but it had been hoped that the conservative group would support Egypt enough to provide the basis for a broader peace settlement. Instead, the shah's fall forced them into an uneasy alliance with the left-wing rejectionist states. The Persian Gulf, the world's largest oil-producing area, also lost its major protector, the Iranian Army. The inability of the U.S. to influence events in Iran, and its impotence in the face of the seizure of embassy personnel by Iranian militants gave rise to the perception, both within and outside the Middle East, that it had become a weak, indecisive power. The Israeli hard-liners, in particular, were strengthened in their view that Israel must look after its own security, defined in a narrow military rather than a broad political sense.

As a percentage of GNP, Israeli defense spending remained one of the highest in the world, although the 1978 military budget, at 24.5% of GNP, represented a decrease from the 1976 level of 36.3% of GNP ($4,214,000,000). Defense spending in 1979 was expected to drop still further to $1,624,000,000. The armed forces totaled 165,000, including 138,000 in the Army, but could be increased to over 400,000 within 24 hours of mobilization. The first 40 Israeli-produced Merkava tanks with 105-mm guns joined the armoured force of 3,050 MBT's and 4,000 AFV's. Israeli tactical doctrine now stressed the use of combined teams of armour, infantry, artillery, and ATGW to suppress enemy ATGW and conduct the mobile armoured warfare at which the Israelis excelled. The 21,000-strong Air Force had 576 combat aircraft, including 48 of the latest U.S. F-15 fighters. The F-15 scored its first kill in action against a Syrian MiG-21 at a distance of about 15 mi. The Syrians lost at least nine MiG-21s and 23s during air battles over Lebanon in the fall. Officially, Israel denied the existence of a nuclear weapons stockpile, but it was widely believed to comprise 20–30 15-kiloton fission weapons.

KWANG FILM SYNDICATE/AUTHENTICATED NEWS INTERNATIONAL

Units of the Taiwan armed forces staged full-scale exercises to demonstrate their military preparedness in spite of the termination of its mutual defense treaty with the U.S.

Israel retained effective control over the southern third of Lebanon, while Syria occupied the rest with 30,000 men of the Arab Deterrent Force. (*See* LEBANON.) Syrian forces totaled 227,500 personnel. The Army of 200,000 was equipped with 1,500 T-54/55 and 900 T-62 MBT's, 1,600 APC's, and 800 guns and howitzers. The Air Force had 389 combat aircraft, including 60 Su-7, 16 MiG-23, and 48 MiG-27 fighter-bomber/interceptors, plus 215 MiG-21PF/MF interceptors. Syrian defense expenditure had doubled, to $2,036,000,000 or over 30% of GNP. Jordan's defense spending also rose, to $381 million in 1979. This provided an army of 60,000 men with 500 MBT's and an air force of 7,000 with 73 combat aircraft, including 56 F-5A–F's.

Egypt's 395,000-man armed forces cost $2,168,000,000, but their combat value had been sharply reduced by a shortage of spare parts for Soviet equipment, only partly offset by new British, French, and U.S. supplies. The Army of 350,000 men had 850 T-54/55 and 750 T-62 MBT's, 200 BMP-76PB MICV's, and 2,500 APC's, plus 1,300 guns and howitzers. Outside Egypt, 50,000 troops were deployed to assist Sudan and 200 were stationed in Oman. The 25,000-man Air Force had 563 combat aircraft. Two MiG-23s had reportedly been transferred to the U.S. for evaluation.

Iran's armed forces had ceased to exist as a fighting organization. Over 60% of the personnel had reportedly deserted, and most of the equipment was unserviceable. This included 875 Chieftain heavy MBT's, 860 M-47/48/60 MBT's, 825 APC's, 710 guns and howitzers, 190 F-4D/E and 166 F-5E/F fighter-bombers, and 77 F-14A Tomcat interceptors. The highly secret F-14 electronics and Phoenix air-to-air missile (AAM) had probably been acquired by the Soviets. The eventual fate of this billion-dollar stockpile was uncertain, but Iran was largely defenseless even against its rebel Kurdish population.

Iraq, Iran's traditional enemy, had an army of 190,000, with 1,700 T-54/55/62 MBT's, 200 BMP MICV's, 1,500 AFV's, and 800 guns and howitzers. The 28,000-man Air Force fielded 340 combat aircraft. On the Arabian Peninsula, the Soviet-supported forces of South Yemen—20,800 strong with 260 MBT's and 47 fighter-bombers—were waging a guerrilla war against North Yemen, with its 36,600-man armed forces and 232 MBT's. Although Saudi Arabian defense spending had nearly doubled since 1977, to $14,184,000,000 or 15% of GNP, its forces totaled only 44,500 personnel with little armour, plus 65 F-5E fighter-bombers and 18 Lightning F-53 interceptors.

AFRICA SOUTH OF THE SAHARA

Tanzania's successful attack on Uganda underlined the fact that most African armies were really semitrained police forces, lacking both the equipment and the ability to move beyond their borders without great difficulty. They were neither intended nor able to fight well-equipped and disciplined forces, like the Cubans in Mozambique and Angola (20,000) and in Ethiopia (17,000).

On paper, Tanzania had superior armed forces totaling 51,700 men, with 20 MBT's and 20 jet fighters, versus Uganda's 21,000 men, 35 MBT's, and 31 jet fighters. But the real difficulty both sides faced was logistical: transporting troops to the fighting area and supplying them with food and armament. Discipline was also a problem. Uganda apparently expected its October 1978 occupation of the disputed Kyaka border area to go unchallenged, especially since Idi Amin was receiving considerable military aid from Libya. However, Tanzanian Pres. Julius Nyerere mustered 10,000 troops, drove out the 2,000–3,000 Ugandan invaders by December 1978, and in February 1979 combined an internal uprising against Amin with a Tanzanian offensive. By mid-April the Ugandan Army had disintegrated and Amin had fled. Casualty levels were unclear but relatively light.

The guerrilla war in Zimbabwe Rhodesia was in its seventh year. Although the country's seven million blacks shared in Bishop Abel Muzorewa's multiracial government, the 200,000-strong white population retained basic political control, a situation that was unacceptable to the Patriotic Front guerrillas. The two main Front leaders, Robert Mugabe and Joshua Nkomo, had combined forces to fight the war, but they remained fierce political rivals. About 8,000 men each were provided by Mugabe's Zimbabwe African National Union (ZANU), based in Mozambique, and

Nkomo's Zimbabwe African People's Union (ZAPU), based in Zambia. Neither of the host countries was able to stop Zimbabwe Rhodesian raids on the guerrilla bases. Zambia, with only 14,300 men under arms, suffered heavily, especially after Zimbabwe Rhodesia cut off its vital grain imports in November.

Despite significant losses (about 70,000) within the white population, Zimbabwe Rhodesia's 21,500-strong armed forces were still more effective than the guerrillas. They were reinforced by the 43,000-man paramilitary British South African Police, and their elderly air force of 7 Canberra light bombers and 9 Hunter FGA9 and 18 Vampire FB9 fighter-bombers provided relatively complete air superiority. Defense expenditure was only $400 million, probably about 12% of GNP. The danger was that the Patriotic Front leaders would turn to the Soviets for increased assistance. If this had included Cubans or threatened the white population, South Africa would almost certainly have intervened. This prospect was averted by the successful outcome of the London constitutional conference. (*See* ZIMBABWE RHODESIA.)

South Africa had underscored its hard-line policy by refusing to relinquish control over Namibia and increasing defense spending to $2,118,000,000. The South African armed forces totaled 63,250 personnel and could be increased to 404,500 on mobilization. The Army of 48,500 had 250 Centurion MBT's, 1,280 AFV's, and 200 guns and howitzers. The 10,000-man Air Force would certainly be able to deliver nuclear weapons if, indeed, South Africa possessed them. Its 9 Canberra and 6 Buccaneer bombers and 23 Mirage III fighter-bombers were all nuclear capable. Other aircraft included 32 Mirage F1-AZ interceptors and 14 Mirage F1-CZ fighter-bombers.

SOUTH, SOUTHEAST, AND EAST ASIA

Indochina was still torn by conflicts as Vietnam, supported by the Soviets and opposed by China, continued its attempt to gain control over neighbouring Laos and Cambodia. The worst sufferers were the Cambodians, whose population was estimated to have fallen from 7.4 million in 1974 to less than 4 million. Those not killed directly or indirectly by the Pol Pot regime were caught in the further devastation caused by Vietnam's December 1978 invasion and the subsequent famine.

Vietnam's Army of one million men was now the most powerful in Southeast Asia, with 1 armoured, 28 infantry, 2 artillery, and 1 antiaircraft divisions. Its armament of 1,400 MBT's, 600 light tanks, 1,800 AFV/APC's, and about 2,500 guns and howitzers included large quantities of U.S. equipment captured from South Vietnam. The 20,000-man Air Force had 110 MiG-17, 30 MiG-23/27, 60 Su-7/20, 35 F-5A, and 70 A-37B fighter-bombers plus 60 MiG-19 and 120 MiG-21 interceptors. The Pol Pot forces had had a nominal strength of 12 divisions (120,000 men) with only light equipment and were short of food and supplies. The Vietnamese invasion began on Dec. 27, 1978, and succeeded in gaining effective control of the country by Jan. 7, 1979. Some 120,000 troops were retained in Cambodia as an army of occupation, like the 40,000 Vietnamese in Laos. The Chinese invasion of Vietnam in February failed to divert Vietnamese troops from Cambodia. The Vietnamese resistance was sufficiently effective to inflict an estimated 20,000 Chinese casualties, although Vietnamese losses were also heavy.

The limited nature of China's attack on Vietnam emphasized its relative weakness in all military resources except personnel, a weakness the Chinese were trying to remedy by purchasing Western equipment and technology. The Army of 3.6 million had only 11,000 MBT's, mostly outdated Soviet T-34s and Chinese-produced Type-59/63s, for 11 armoured divisions, and its 1,500 APC's were supplemented by horse cavalry. Artillery totaled 16,000 guns and howitzers. In contrast, the 46 Soviet divisions on the Sino-Soviet border had about 13,000 MBT's and 10,000 MICV/APC's for 550,000 personnel. The Chinese Air Force had 400,000 men and 4,700 combat aircraft. China's nuclear and thermonuclear weapons stockpile was probably adequate, but delivery capabilities were limited to about 70 CSS-2 IRBM's and 50 CSS-1 MRBM's (2,800/1,100-km [1,750/700-mi] range; warhead about one megaton) plus the first two Chinese ICBM's (the CSS-3; 11,000-km [7,000-mi] range), 90 Tu-16/B-6 Badger bombers, and some F-9 fighter-bombers. The Chinese would have difficulty in maintaining their strike capabilities in the 1980s unless they could acquire weapons systems like the long-range cruise missile. The Navy of 360,000 remained a coastal defense force.

The assassination of South Korea's Pres. Park Chung Hee underlined South Korea's continuing security problems. New intelligence assessments indicated that North Korea had increased its combat divisions to 40, although without significantly altering its previously underestimated military manpower of 632,000–672,000. Its Army of 600,000, with 2,150 MBT's and 3,500 guns and howitzers, was supported by an air force of 45,000 with 565 combat aircraft. South Korea's forces might not be able to defeat a North Korean invasion, although it had an army of 520,000 with 860 MBT's and 2,100 guns and howitzers and a 32,000-man air force with 254 combat aircraft, including 37 F-4D/E, 135 F-5E, and 50 F-86 fighter-bombers. Defense budgets were high: $1,231,000,000 (11.4% of GNP) for the North and $3,219,000,000 (about 5.6% of GNP) for the South.

Taiwan spent 7.7% of GNP (over $1.7 billion) to maintain armed forces of 539,000, with 800 medium and light tanks and 388 combat aircraft. Japan's defense spending remained extremely low as a percentage of GNP—0.9%—but this still amounted to $10,083,000,000. The 241,000-strong armed forces had 690 MBT's, 361 combat aircraft, and a large navy of 42,000 men with 13 submarines. India and Pakistan maintained their armed truce. India's armed forces totaled 1,096,000 personnel with 1,850 MBT's and 620 combat aircraft, maintained at a cost of $3,724,000,000 (3.2% of GNP). Pakistan's 429,000-man armed forces, with 1,000 MBT's and 256 combat aircraft, cost over $1 billion (5.7% of GNP). (ROBIN RANGER)

See also Space Exploration.
[535.B.5.e.ii; 544.B.5–6; 736]

SPECIAL REPORT

THE SALT II DEBATE

by Robin Ranger

For the U.S. Senate, the crucial issues in the debate on ratification of the second strategic arms limitation talks agreement (SALT II) were political rather than technical. In terms of foreign policy, the question was whether approval of SALT II would, as the Carter administration urged, re-create the mutually self-reinforcing and beneficial relationship that had existed between SALT I and détente, or whether, as its critics argued, it would sacrifice substantial U.S. and allied strategic interests to appease an expansionist Soviet Union.

Domestically, SALT II was seen not only as a major test of the Carter administration's ability to secure passage of an important piece of legislation but also as a test of strength between the previously dominant bipartisan liberal coalition and the emerging forces of neoconservatism. With an eye on the 1980 presidential election, the Republican Party used the ratification debate to test the Democratic Party's cohesiveness and as a proving ground for its own contenders for the presidential nomination. The fact that the final vote on ratification was significantly delayed, first by the official announcement that the Soviet Union had a combat brigade in Cuba and then by the Iran and Afghanistan crises, emphasized just how political the SALT II debate had been.

Advice and Consent. Under the U.S. Constitution, the Senate had to give its advice and consent to SALT II, as to any treaty, by a two-thirds majority of senators present and voting; if all 100 members were present, this would mean 67 votes. In addition, the Senate could attach understandings and amendments to a treaty. The legal distinction between the two was a fine one but, for practical purposes, "understandings" were Senate interpretations of SALT II's terms that would be binding on the administration, although they would still constitute unilateral U.S. interpretations. Amendments would be more far-reaching, requiring Soviet acceptance. So-called killer amendments were those the Soviet Union could not accept.

Robin Ranger is an associate professor in the Department of Political Science, St. Francis Xavier University, Antigonish, Nova Scotia, and a Department of National Defence Fellow in Strategic Studies.

The Soviets appeared incapable of understanding that the Senate had a legitimate role in debating SALT II, as evidenced by their insistence that they would not accept any changes in, or understandings or amendments to, the treaty. If they persisted in this view, it would mean the end of this particular treaty and of the SALT process in general. But the U.S.'s allies, especially in Western Europe, also had difficulty in realizing that SALT II might be rejected, modified, or postponed—until 1980 or indefinitely.

The contrast with the almost unanimous approval of the 1972 SALT I agreement by the U.S. Senate and by the American public was particularly sharp. Even the public mood in the U.S. was difficult to gauge. Opinion polls showed that the public wanted an agreement limiting strategic arms, but the respondents were unclear as to whether this particular treaty did, in fact, accomplish that end and, in broader terms, whether it was desirable given the current unsettled state of Soviet-U.S. relations.

The Agreements. Even the basic terms of the SALT II agreements were far more complex than those of SALT I, and their precise effects were subject to widely differing interpretations. As an arms control treaty, SALT II was a remarkable achievement, pushing arms control by treaty as far as it could go if not further. The agreements fell into four parts: the treaty proper; the Protocol; Soviet Pres. Leonid Brezhnev's statement on the Backfire bomber (see TABLE); and a Statement of Principles on SALT III.

The SALT II treaty established a series of quantitative sublimits on launchers for strategic delivery vehicles (SDV's) equipped with multiple independently targetable reentry vehicles (MIRV) and hence most suitable for attacking the other side's strategic forces. The objective was to defer the day when both sides' land-based intercontinental ballistic missile (ICBM) forces would become vulnerable to attack. This could create an incentive, in a crisis, for each side to take out the other's ICBM's or, still worse, to gamble that an attack on the opposing side's total strategic forces (ICBM's, submarine-launched ballistic missiles [SLBM's], and bombers) would leave it with insufficient forces to threaten retaliation. Accordingly, unlike SALT I, SALT II gave both sides freedom to move to seaborne deterrent forces within each sublimit, placing no limit on the number of submarine launch vehicles (SSBN's) either side could have. SALT I had limited the U.S. to 41 SSBN's and the Soviets to 61 modern SSBN's.

The additional qualitative constraints on both sides' strategic forces were also intended to limit their counterforce capabilities. It was unclear, however, whether the SALT II ceilings were low enough, or the limitations precise enough, to achieve this objective. Liberal critics like Sen. George McGovern

(Dem., S.D.) argued that the SALT II ceilings were too high, simply legitimizing both superpowers' planned strategic force buildups through 1985. Hard-line conservative critics, notably Senators Jake Garn (Rep., Utah), Henry Jackson (Dem., Wash.), and John C. Stennis (Dem., Miss.; chairman of the Senate Armed Services Committee), took the opposite view. To them, SALT II represented unilateral restraint by the U.S.—restraint which the Soviet Union was not reciprocating and which would leave U.S. strategic forces dangerously vulnerable in the 1980s. As Jackson put it, SALT II was appeasement of the Soviets.

Conservative critics also attacked the Protocol ban on U.S. deployment of ground/sea-launched cruise missiles (G/SLCM's), needed for the defense of NATO-Europe, until 1981. They were skeptical, furthermore, that the administration would let the Protocol lapse in 1981, especially if the Soviets demanded its extension. They derided Brezhnev's letter of assurances on the Backfire bomber as worthless and doubted that the Statement of Principles would produce a worthwhile SALT III, given SALT II's defects. SALT II supporters took the opposite view: the Protocol was a useful attempt to limit the potentially destabilizing long-range cruise missile technology before it got out of hand, while Brezhnev's assurances on Backfire were adequate, as was the Statement of Principles.

A Last, Best Hope. The Senate debate thus ignored the technical minutiae of SALT II and focused on the politically salient and popularly intelligible aspects. Essentially, its supporters, numbering 25–30 senators led by Edward Kennedy (Dem., Mass.), argued that, whatever its defects and however far short of the ideal it might fall, SALT II was the best SALT agreement the U.S. was likely to get. It offered the best, and also the last, hope of preserving strategic stability and Soviet-U.S. détente. Administration witnesses, notably Secretary of Defense Harold Brown and Secretary of State Cyrus Vance, stressed this theme in testimony before the Senate Foreign Relations and Armed Services committees. It was expounded by Ambassador Marshall D. Shulman, special adviser on Soviet affairs to the secretary of state. The superpowers were bound together in a limited adversary relationship from which they could not escape, but the adversary aspects could be reduced by cooperation.

Such cooperation was inevitable, because neither side could benefit from a nuclear exchange or even from a large-scale conventional war. Both sides could now, as in the past, benefit from cooperation to lessen the pace of the strategic arms race and reduce the risks of inadvertent conflict through misunderstanding or misperception. Ultimately, therefore, SALT II was of transcendent importance, since it contributed to the survival of humanity. Pres. Jimmy Carter constantly stressed this point, together with his administration's belief in minimal deterrence, that is, in the sufficiency of very low levels of nuclear weapons to deter aggression. The president suggested that one Poseidon submarine would suffice. The arcane calculations of nuclear strategists about the possibilities of limited nuclear counterforce strikes were, in this view, unrealistic theological exercises, ignoring the fact that both superpowers had far more nuclear weapons than they needed.

Secretary of Defense Brown's term "essential equivalence" reflected the same view, that the U.S. required only those strategic weapons that it deemed sufficient for deterrence, regardless of the size of the Soviet forces, except where these threatened the survivability of the U.S. Minuteman ICBM forces. The vulnerability of Minuteman had not

Weapons Systems Subject to SALT II Limits

		Currently deployed			
		United States		Soviet Union	
Weapons system	SALT II limit	No.	Type	No.	Type
Strategic delivery vehicles (SDV) with MIRV[1]					
Heavy ICBM[2]	308[3]	0	—	200	SS-18
Light ICBM		550	Minuteman III	100	SS-17
				300	SS-19
Total ICBM	820	550		600	
SLBM[4]		496	Poseidon C-3	144	SS-N-18
ASBM[5]		0	—	0	—
Total ICBM, SLBM, ASBM	1,200	1,046		744	
Heavy bombers able to carry long-range ALCM[6]		3	B-1 (prototypes)	0	—
Total SDV with MIRV	1,320	1,049		744	
Strategic delivery vehicles (SDV) without MIRV					
Heavy ICBM		0	—	100	SS-9
Light ICBM		54	Titan II	638	SS-11
		450	Minuteman II	60	SS-13
Total ICBM		504		798	
SLBM		160	Polaris A-3	528	SS-N-6
				266	SS-N-8
				12	SS-NX-17
Total SLBM		160		806	
Heavy bombers		196	B-52D/F	113	Tu-195 Bear
		311[7]	B-52G/H	43	Mya-4 Bison
Total heavy bombers		507		156	
Total SDV without MIRV	1,080[8]	1,171		1,760	
Total SDV	2,400[9]	2,220		2,504	

[1] Multiple independently targetable reentry vehicles.
[2] Intercontinental ballistic missiles.
[3] Applies to all heavy ICBM whether MIRVed or not.
[4] Submarine-launched ballistic missiles.
[5] Air-to-surface ballistic missiles; experimental concept; none projected.
[6] Air-launched cruise missiles.
[7] 120 of these are scheduled for conversion to ALCM carriers.
[8] 930 after Jan. 1, 1981; applies if limits on SDV with MIRV reached.
[9] 2,250 after Jan. 1, 1981.

Additional Treaty Limitations: (1) MIRV "fractionation" limit: No ICBM may carry *more* than 10 warheads; no SLBM may carry *more* than 14 warheads. (2) "Heavy bomber" is defined as: (a) U.S. B-52 and B-1 and Soviet Bear and Bison (not Backfire); (b) any new bombers able to execute similar missions; (c) aircraft carrying LRCM with ranges over 600 km, or (d) carrying ASBM's. (3) No heavy bomber currently deployed can carry more than 20 LRCM's; *average* LRCM deployment may not exceed 28 LRCM's per heavy bomber. (4) Additional ICBM limitations: Key parameters of existing tested ICBM's may not vary by more than 5%; only one new type of ICBM may be deployed by each side (U.S. MS-X; Soviet SS-?). (5) Long-range air-launched cruise missiles (LR-ALCM) and long-range cruise missiles (LRCM): cruise missiles with a range capability of over 600 km. (6) "Light" ICBM: any ICBM with a launch-weight or throw-weight not greater than that of the Soviet SS-19 ICBM; "heavy" ICBM: any ICBM with a launch-weight or throw-weight greater than that of the SS-19. (7) Aircraft carrying LR-ALCM must be distinguished by functionally related observable differences (FROD's) to assist verification. In a written statement on June 16, 1979, Pres. Leonid Brezhnev promised not to increase the radius of action of the Backfire bomber in strikes against the U.S. territory (*sic*) and not to exceed the current Backfire production rate of 30 per year. Backfire, first deployed in 1974, has a range of 8,850 km (5,500 mi) and a weapons load of 7,900 kg (17,500 lb), nearer to 66 U.S. FB-111A (9,600 km, 12,500 kg [6,000 mi, 27,500 lb]) than to B-52D (first deployed 1956; 16,100–20,100 km, 27,200–31,800 kg [10,000–12,500 mi, 60,000–70,000 lb]).

SVEN SIMON/KATHERINE YOUNG

U.S. Pres. Jimmy Carter and Soviet Pres. Leonid Brezhnev exchanged copies of the SALT II agreement after the documents were signed in Vienna in June.

been created by SALT II and could not be solved by it. Instead, the U.S. would have to take appropriate unilateral action, as the Carter administration had by deciding to develop the MX mobile ICBM. Rejecting SALT II would mean rejecting any hope of stabilizing the strategic balance and of providing both superpowers with a relatively certain strategic environment in the 1980s.

A One-Sided Bargain. SALT II's hard-core opponents, numbering 15–20 senators, viewed it as a one-sided bargain that favoured the Soviet Union. They particularly criticized the U.S. refusal to count Backfire as a strategic bomber, although it had all the performance characteristics of one, and its acceptance of the Soviets' unilateral advantage in heavy ICBM's, suitable only for a first strike. The critics therefore proposed killer amendments that would reduce the Soviet heavy ICBM force or allow the U.S. to have the same number of heavy ICBM's as the Soviets.

Technically, the heavy ICBM issue was not sufficiently important to justify the attention it received, but it was more understandable than most and hence politically relevant. Similarly, the Backfire bomber really added very little to the Soviet strategic forces targetable against the U.S. population; it was essentially a Eurostrategic system designed for use against Western European and Chinese targets. However, excluding all Backfire from the SALT II ceilings while including U.S. B-52s in storage and the three B-1 bomber prototypes appeared inequitable and unbalanced. The Protocol restraints on G/SLCM's also seemed to represent a unilateral U.S. and allied sacrifice, as did the limitations on the long-range air-launched cruise missile, which the very old B-52 bombers could carry.

Brezhnev's assurances on Backfire were of doubtful value, since they could not be verified or enforced. Amendments were therefore proposed to include Backfire in the Soviet totals of SDV's; to ensure that the Protocol expired on Dec. 31, 1981, and was not renewed or kept in force by unilateral U.S. action; and to secure firmer limitations on Backfire's performance and production. Not all these amendments were intended as killer amendments, but the Soviets' apparent refusal to consider even the smallest changes to SALT II threatened to make them such. Yet to get ratification some changes would have to be made in the agreements, as the Carter administration reluctantly recognized. Even so, it seemed doubtful whether the three very different sets of requirements of the U.S. Senate, the U.S. president, and the Soviets could be met.

Political Issues. Here again, the issues were political. President Carter apparently believed that, in the last resort, the Senate would not dare reject so important a treaty, but it had defied presidents on foreign policy matters before—most notably in 1919–20 when it defeated Woodrow Wilson's proposal for U.S. membership in the League of Nations. The right-wing lobby against SALT, spearheaded by the Committee on the Present Danger under Paul Nitze (U.S. Department of Defense representative to the SALT negotiations in 1969–74), was noticeably more effective than the pro-SALT lobby organized by the administration. The general trend within the defense and foreign policy community in both the U.S. and Europe was also running against SALT, in the sense that there were few strong supporters of the SALT II agreements as negotiated. There was also considerable skepticism about the ability of any SALT II (or SALT III) to contribute to strategic stability.

The contrast with the virtually unanimous analytical and political support for SALT I in 1972 was striking. The old liberal coalition supporting détente through arms control had disappeared. Instead, there was a deep division between SALT's supporters and its opponents, both of whom clearly believed that the survival of America—and, indeed, of humanity—would be threatened if their opponents won. Feelings ran high, and the majority of senators, accordingly, delayed making a commitment. This was especially true of those who were up for reelection in 1980. Frank Church (Dem., Idaho), chairman of the Senate Foreign Relations Committee, typified their dilemma. As a liberal Democrat he personally favoured SALT II, but he faced a major right-wing challenge in his home state.

Nevertheless, a consensus had emerged within the Senate by the mid-August recess. It favoured ratification of SALT with some amendments (but not killers) and understandings, provided that, in return, the Carter administration accepted a mandated increase in the defense budget of 3 to 5% in real terms (at least $35 billion–$55 billion after inflation). This idea was introduced by Sen. Sam Nunn (Dem., Ga.) and received the influential support of former secretary of state Henry Kissinger in his August testimony before the Foreign Relations Committee. He argued that the SALT process was of such paramount importance that ratification of SALT II, with such modifications as the Senate found necessary, was preferable to its rejection, provided the U.S. simultaneously moved to counter the rising tide of Soviet political and military power.

Questions for the '80s. Paradoxically, there was a growing feeling in the Senate that SALT II per se was largely irrelevant to the real issues facing the U.S.: the level and nature of its strategic forces for the 1980s; their costs; and the nature of the Soviet-U.S. relationship. The verification issue, stressed by Sen. John Glenn (Dem., Ohio), receded in importance, despite the controversy over whether or not the loss of the U.S. monitoring stations in Iran was crucial. It seemed likely that the U.S. could monitor Soviet compliance with SALT II adequately. What was more important was to determine what the U.S. response would be to evidence that the Soviets had violated SALT II or had exploited its ambiguities.

Would the U.S. act on such evidence or suppress it, as appeared to have happened with SALT I? How would the U.S. act to deter the Soviets from such violations? Would it, for example, abrogate SALT II and/or the 1972 treaty banning antiballistic missile systems? Here, as elsewhere, the real questions about SALT II were political. If one agreed with the Carter administration's assessments of Soviet intentions and capabilities, then one would agree with its case for SALT II. If one did not, one could argue for modification of SALT II and an increase in U.S. defense spending or for rejection of SALT II.

By late 1979 the corrosive absence of trust in the Carter administration had become a major obstacle to SALT II's ratification. There was, for example, little confidence in the president's intention to proceed with the MX mobile ICBM system once ratification had been secured. In the case of the almost purely symbolic issue of Soviet troops in Cuba, the presidential response was generally seen as inappropriate. The seizure of the U.S. embassy in Teheran by Iranian militants and the Soviet incursion into Afghanistan raised considerations of U.S. power and policy in an area of vital interest to both the U.S. and the Soviets.

The management of a limited adversary relationship as delicately balanced as that between Washington and Moscow required a willingness to define and assert Washington's legitimate interests that President Carter had seemed unwilling or unable to provide—at least to the satisfaction of a majority in the Senate and, to judge by the public opinion polls, in the country. Thus the prospects of securing a vote on SALT II ratification before the 1980 presidential election year had been slight, even before the year-end crises. Even a favourable vote on ratification would depend for its effectiveness on Soviet acceptance of such amendments and understandings as might be attached. This seemed highly questionable, especially given Brezhnev's health, his age (73 in December 1979), and the uncertainties surrounding the identity and policies of his successor(s).

SALT II thus seemed unlikely to contribute much to strategic stability in the 1980s, because the combined pressures of military technology and political rivalry had made obsolete the arms control processes and agreements of the 1970s. Stability would henceforth be harder and more expensive to obtain, while its maintenance would be much less sure.

Demography

World population in 1978–79 was characterized by three principal features: an annual increase of over 70 million persons to a world total of 4,400,000,000; a general decline in fertility somewhat offset by a decline in mortality; and an escalation of the problem of international migration. The annual world growth rate of 1.7% threatened to add another 375 million persons in five years, more than the entire population of Latin America. The projected median population of the world by the year 2000 was estimated by the Population Division of the U.S. Census Bureau at 6,400,000,000.

The considerable problem of international migration was intensified by the flight of thousands of Cambodians and Vietnamese from their homelands. (*See* REFUGEES: *Special Report*.) Widespread interest in the International Year of the Child provided additional incentives to obtain accurate statistical data relating to children under 15, who numbered 1,400,000,000 in 1975. The mid-1979 populations of the "big four" countries were estimated to be (in millions): China 960, India 660, U.S.S.R. 264, and the U.S. 220.

Birth Statistics. An estimated 3,329,000 live births occurred in the U.S. in 1978, slightly more than the final total of 3,326,632 in 1977. The birthrate nonetheless declined from 15.4 per 1,000 population in 1977 to 15.3 in 1978. The rate for the six-month period ended June 1979 was 15.2, compared with 14.8 for the corresponding period ended June 1978. The fertility rate, 66.4 births per 1,000 women of childbearing age (15–44), was 2% lower than that for 1977 (67.8), despite the fact that the number of women in this group had increased. It was anticipated that the number of women in the childbearing years would grow about 10% by 1985. The projected figures, however, show a greater increase of women in their 30s than of women in their 20s, the ages of highest fertility; this might hold down the number of births.

According to final data for 1977, there were 635,562 nonwhite births in the U.S., representing 19.1% of all births. Of these, 544,221, or 85.6%, were to black mothers. The birthrate for blacks was 21.7 live births per 1,000 population, as compared with 14.4 for whites. Between 1970 and 1977 the white birthrate declined 17.2% and the nonwhite, 12.7%. The fertility rate for blacks was 89.8 per 1,000 women aged 15–44, compared with 64 for whites. Both rates had dropped since 1970, the white by 23.9% and the black by 22.2%.

Birthrates rose from 1976 to 1977 for mothers having their first through fourth births, with third-order births showing the greatest increase (5%). Rates for higher orders continued to drop; fifth-order births fell 5.9% and eighth- and higher-order births, 16.7%. Among blacks there was an increase in the rate of the first- through fourth-order births, while sixth- and higher-order births declined. Significant decline in higher-order births for both whites and blacks occurred between 1970 and 1977. For example, birthrates for black mothers having their fifth child dropped 52% and corresponding rates for white mothers fell 59%. For all races, sixth- and seventh-order birthrates dropped over 60% and eighth- and higher-order rates over 70% in this period.

There were an estimated 515,700 births to unmarried women in 1977, an increase of 10% over 1976. The National Center for Health Statistics related this to the rising number of single women in the population and their rate of childbearing. There was a decline in the number of births to unmarried girls under 15 and an increase in births

OT KRAIPIT—SIPA PRESS/BLACK STAR

Refugees fleeing Cambodia were herded into makeshift camps just across the border in Thailand.

to mothers aged 15–39; this was greatest for women aged 20–24 years (16%). While the numbers of births to both white and black unmarried women rose, the increase was greater for whites (11.7%) than for blacks (8.8%). Fertility rates reflected similar differentials; for unmarried white women aged 15–44 the increase was 7.9% and for black women it was 1.6%. Of every 1,000 live births, 155 were to unmarried women. The ratio was 82 for white women and 517 for black women.

The total fertility rate in 1977 was 1,826 births per 1,000 women, or an average of 1.8 children per woman. In 1970 women had an average of 2.5 children. The total fertility rate for whites was 1,735 and for blacks, 2,309.

Natural increase (the excess of births over deaths) added an estimated 1,405,000 persons to the U.S. population in 1978; the rate of increase was 6.5 persons per 1,000 population, the same as in 1977. The world rate of natural increase averaged 19 per 1,000 population in the period 1970–77. Estimated UN regional rates were: Africa 27, northern America 9, Latin America 28, Asia 22, Europe 6, Oceania 20, and the U.S.S.R. 10. Many countries in Western Europe were approaching a balance of births and deaths; in some, deaths exceeded births. In West Germany there were 121,000 more deaths than births in 1977. In August China announced a plan to reduce its birthrate to 5 per 1,000 by 1985 (23.4 in 1971 and 12.05 in 1978) but admitted this would be difficult.

Death Statistics. There were an estimated 1,924,000 deaths in the U.S. in 1978, with a rate of 8.8 deaths per 1,000 population. The provisional death rate for the 12-month period ended June 1979 was 8.6. The age-adjusted death rate, with controls for changes in age composition, dropped from 6.3 per 1,000 population in 1976 to 6.1 in 1977–78, a record low. Differentials by colour and sex remained significant. In 1978 the age-adjusted death rate was 35% higher for nonwhites than for whites and 79% higher for males than for females.

The ten leading causes of death in 1978, accounting for 83% of all deaths, are shown below. The first three leading causes, heart disease, cancer, and stroke, accounted for 67% of all deaths.

Cause of death	Estimated rate per 100,000 population
Diseases of the heart	333.0
Malignant neoplasms	181.9
Cerebrovascular diseases	79.1
Accidents	47.8
Influenza and pneumonia	26.7
Diabetes mellitus	15.0
Cirrhosis of the liver	13.7
Arteriosclerosis	13.4
Suicide	11.9
Certain causes of mortality in early infancy	10.3

An influenza epidemic early in 1978 caused a 16% rise in the rate for influenza and pneumonia (26.7, compared with 23.1 in 1977). Increases also occurred for malignant neoplasms (2%) and motor vehicle accidents (6%). There were decreases for cerebrovascular diseases (6.3%) and infections of the kidney (18%).

Expectation of Life. Life expectancy at birth for the U.S. population rose to a new high of 73.3 years in 1978. It was 73.9 for white persons and 69.4 for nonwhite persons. On the average, females were expected to outlive males; life expectancy was 77.7 years for white females, 70.2 years for white males, 73.7 years for nonwhite females, and 65.3 years for nonwhite males.

Average world life expectancy was put at 60 years; it was 71 years for persons in developed countries and 56 years for those in less developed countries. Countries in which both sexes had a life expectancy at birth of over 70 years included Cyprus, Israel, Japan, Denmark, Iceland, The Netherlands, Norway, Sweden, and Switzerland.

Infant and Maternal Mortality. Infant mortality continued to decline in the U.S. and several other countries. There were an estimated 45,300 deaths of infants under one year in the U.S. in 1978, 4% less than in 1977. The infant mortality rate was 13.6 infant deaths per 1,000 live births, the lowest ever recorded in the U.S. and 3.5% lower than in 1977. Infant deaths continued to decline in 1979; for the 12-month period ended June 1979, the infant mortality rate was 13.3. Final data for 1977 show that among white infants the mortality rate decreased 7.5% (from 13.3 in 1976 to 12.3), while among nonwhites the decrease was 7.7% (from 23.5 to 21.7). A significant factor was the 5% drop in the neonatal mortality rate (deaths under 28 days), from 9.9 per 1,000 live births to 9.4. Infant mortality rates in Europe in 1977 ranged from 8 in Sweden to 35.2 in Yugoslavia. The average rate for the less developed countries was over 100.

In 1978 there were an estimated 320 maternal deaths associated with childbearing in the U.S.; of these, 61% were to nonwhite women. The provi-

continued on page 298

Table I. Birthrates and Death Rates per 1,000 Population and Infant Mortality per 1,000 Live Births in Selected Countries, 1978[1]

Country	Birth-rate	Death rate	Infant mortality	Country	Birth-rate	Death rate	Infant mortality
Africa				Norway	12.7	9.9	9.2
Egypt	37.6	10.5	101.3[2]	Poland	19.0	9.3	22.5
Mauritius[2]	26.8	7.9	45.6	Portugal	16.8	9.8	38.9[4]
Nigeria[2]	49.2	20.7	...	Romania[2]	19.7	9.7	31.2
South Africa[3]	43.1	13.9	...	Spain	17.2	7.9	15.0
Tunisia[2]	36.4	7.9	54.9[4]	Sweden	11.3	10.8	8.0[2]
Asia				Switzerland	11.2	9.0	9.8[2]
Cyprus	19.3	8.4	17.5	United Kingdom	12.3	11.7	14.2
Hong Kong	17.5	5.2	11.6	Yugoslavia	17.4	8.7	35.2[2]
Israel	24.8	6.8	16.5	North America			
Japan	15.0	6.0	8.9[2]	Antigua[2]	19.7	6.8	24.5
Kuwait[2]	41.5	4.8	39.1	Bahamas, The[2]	22.1	4.9	28.3
Philippines[4]	26.7	6.3	58.9[5]	Barbados[2]	16.0	8.0	25.0
Singapore	16.9	5.2	12.6	Canada	15.2	7.3	12.4[2]
Syria[4]	50.4[2]	14.8	112.5	Costa Rica[6]	29.3	4.6	33.6
Taiwan	19.2	4.7	12.9[6]	Cuba[6]	19.8	5.6	22.9
Thailand[6]	24.1	5.5	25.5	El Salvador[2]	41.7	7.8	59.5
Europe				Guatemala[6]	42.6	13.1	76.5
Austria	11.3	12.5	16.9[2]	Jamaica[6]	29.8	7.1	20.4
Belgium	12.4	11.7	11.6	Mexico[6]	34.6	6.5	54.7
Bulgaria	15.5	10.5	23.7[2]	Panama[2]	28.8	4.8	28.5
Czechoslovakia	18.4	11.5	18.7	Puerto Rico[2]	22.6	6.0	20.1
Denmark	12.2	10.4	8.9	United States	15.3	8.8	13.6
Finland	13.5	9.2	12.0[2]	Oceania			
France[2]	14.0	10.1	11.4	American Samoa[2]	36.5	4.4	18.8
Germany, East	13.9	13.9	13.1[2]	Australia	15.7	7.6	12.5[2]
Germany, West	9.3	11.8	15.5[2]	Fiji[2]	27.0	3.9	14.5
Greece	15.6	8.7	19.3	Guam[6]	32.8	5.0	18.0
Hungary	15.7	13.1	24.3	New Zealand[2]	17.4	8.4	14.2
Iceland	18.6	6.5	10.8	Pacific Islands,			
Ireland[2]	21.4	10.5	15.7	Trust Terr. of[2]	29.2	4.3	31.2
Italy	12.5	9.4	17.6[2]	Western Samoa	14.0	2.6	16.3
Netherlands, The	12.6	8.2	9.5	U.S.S.R.	18.3	9.8	27.7[5]

[1] Registered births and deaths only.
[2] 1977.
[3] 1975–1980 UN estimate.
[4] 1975.
[5] 1974.
[6] 1976.
Sources: United Nations, *Population and Vital Statistics Report*; various national publications.

Table II. World Populations and Areas[1]

Country	AREA AND POPULATION: MIDYEAR 1978 Area in sq km	Total population	Persons per sq km	POPULATION AT MOST RECENT CENSUS Date of census	Total population	% Male	% Female	% Urban	Age distribution (%)[2] 0–14	15–29	30–44	45–59	60–74	75+
AFRICA														
Algeria	2,322,164	18,245,000	7.9	1977	17,272,000	49.7	50.3	52.0	47.5	—40.1—			—12.4—	
Angola	1,246,700	6,831,000	5.5	1970	5,646,166	52.1	47.9	14.2	...	...	...	...	...	...
Benin	112,600	3,341,000	29.7	1961	2,082,511	49.0	51.0	9.3	46.0	22.7	16.4	9.3	—5.6—	
Botswana	576,000	760,000	1.3	1971	574,094	45.7	54.3	8.4	46.1	21.7	12.8	9.0	5.0	5.4
British Indian Ocean Territory	60	—	—	1971	110	...	...	...	...	...	...	...	...	...
Burundi	27,834	4,068,000	146.2	1970–71	3,350,000	47.6	52.4	3.5	44.1	25.0	17.0	9.8	3.0	1.0
Cameroon	465,054	7,981,000	17.2	1976	7,663,246	49.0	51.0	28.5	43.4	—48.3—			—8.3—	
Cape Verde	4,033	313,000	77.6	1970	272,071	48.2	51.8	19.7	47.0	20.8	14.2	8.7	6.2	3.0
Central African Republic	624,977	2,120,000	3.4	1975	2,088,000	...	...	...	...	...	...	...	...	...
Chad	1,284,000	4,309,000	3.4	1975	4,030,000	...	...	...	...	...	...	...	...	...
Comoros[3]	1,792	311,000	173.5	1966	244,905	49.2	50.8	13.5	44.1	23.6	15.7	8.7	4.2	3.8
Congo	342,000	1,454,000	4.3	1974	1,300,120	48.7	51.3	39.8	...	...	...	...	...	...
Djibouti	23,000	242,000	10.5	1960–61	81,200	...	...	57.4	...	...	...	...	...	...
Egypt	997,667	39,939,000	40.0	1976	38,228,180	51.0	49.0	43.9	31.6	—65.5—			—2.9—	
Equatorial Guinea	28,051	327,000	11.7	1965	277,240	52.8	47.2	...	53.1	—48.5—		—16.4—		
Ethiopia	1,221,900	29,705,000	24.3	1970	24,068,800	50.7	49.3	9.7	43.5	27.0	16.3	8.8	3.7	0.7
French Southern and Antarctic Lands	7,366	—	—	—	—	—	—	—	—	—	—	—	—	—
Gabon	267,667	1,300,000	4.9	1970	950,009	47.9	52.1	26.9	35.4	19.2	22.2	16.3	6.3	0.6
Gambia, The	10,403	569,000	54.7	1973	493,499	51.0	49.0	15.0	41.3	—44.1—		—14.6—		
Ghana	238,533	10,775,000	45.2	1970	8,559,313	49.6	50.4	28.9	46.9	24.4	15.8	7.5	3.8	1.6
Guinea	245,857	4,762,000	19.4	1972	5,143,284	...	...	...	43.1	—56.9—				
Guinea-Bissau	36,125	777,000	21.5	1979	777,214	51.7	48.3	...	...	...	...	...	...	...
Ivory Coast	322,463	7,205,000	22.3	1975	6,702,866	52.0	48.0	32.4	44.6	—55.4—				
Kenya	580,367	14,856,000	25.6	1969	10,942,705	50.1	49.9	9.9	48.4	25.1	13.6	7.5	3.9	1.5
Lesotho	30,355	1,280,000	42.2	1976	1,216,815	...	...	...	...	...	...	...	...	...
Liberia	97,790	1,717,000	17.6	1974	1,503,368	51.0	49.0	...	41.0	—59.0—				
Libya	1,749,000	3,014,000	1.7	1973	2,249,222	53.0	47.0	60.2	48.8	22.2	15.3	8.2	4.0	1.6
Madagascar	587,041	8,776,000	14.9	1974–75	7,568,600	49.5	50.5	16.4	44.2	26.3	14.4	9.8	4.2	1.1
Malawi	118,484	5,670,000	47.9	1977	5,561,821	48.0	52.0	...	...	...	...	...	...	...
Mali	1,240,142	6,290,000	5.1	1976	6,035,272	49.0	51.0	...	...	...	...	...	...	...
Mauritania	1,030,700	1,540,000	1.5	1976–77	1,419,939	...	...	21.9	...	...	...	...	...	...
Mauritius	2,040	920,000	451.0	1972	851,334	50.0	50.0	42.9	40.3	28.6	14.5	11.0	4.9	0.7
Mayotte	378	47,000	124.3	1978	47,246	49.9	50.1	...	50.2	23.4	13.9	7.0	3.8	1.7
Morocco	458,730	18,906,000	41.2	1971	15,379,259	50.1	49.9	35.4	46.2	22.4	16.0	8.3	5.3	1.8
Mozambique	799,380	9,940,000	12.4	1970	8,168,933	49.4	50.6	...	45.3	22.5	19.1	9.1	3.8	0.3
Niger	1,186,408	4,994,000	4.2	1977	5,098,657	49.3	50.7	11.8	...	...	...	...	...	...
Nigeria	923,800	80,627,000	87.3	1973	79,760,000	...	...	...	...	...	...	...	...	...
Réunion	2,512	493,000	196.3	1974	476,675	48.5	51.5	...	42.6	25.8	15.6	10.0	4.8	1.2
Rwanda	26,338	4,820,000	183.0	1978	4,820,000	49.0	51.0	...	...	...	...	...	...	...
St. Helena & Ascension Islands	412	5,000	12.9	1976	5,866	52.0	48.0	29.4	34.2	27.7	16.3	10.8	8.4	2.6
São Tomé & Príncipe	964	83,000	86.1	1970	73,811	50.8	49.2	...	...	...	...	...	...	...
Senegal	196,722	5,380,000	27.3	1976	5,085,388	49.2	50.8	...	...	...	...	...	...	...
Seychelles	443	62,000	140.0	1977	61,950	50.0	50.0	37.1	39.9	26.3	14.0	10.8	6.8	2.1
Sierra Leone	71,740	3,200,000	44.6	1974	2,729,479	39.6	60.4	...	36.7	27.2	19.4	9.0	—7.6—	
Somalia	638,000	3,446,000	5.4	—	—	—	—	—	—	—	—	—	—	—
South Africa	1,133,759	23,833,000	21.0	1970	21,794,328	49.2	50.8	47.9	40.8	26.1	16.7	10.0	5.0	1.3
Bophuthatswana[4]	40,430	1,245,000	30.8	1970	880,312	46.9	53.1	14.2	44.7	26.4	12.5	—13.5—		1.3
Transkei[4]	41,002	2,178,000	53.1	1970	1,745,992	41.2	58.8	3.2	46.4	22.8	14.1	—15.3—		1.2
Venda[4]	7,184	357,000	49.7	1970	265,129	38.8	61.2	0.2	48.1	22.7	13.7	6.4	7.6	1.5
South West Africa	824,268	953,000	1.2	1970	763,630	50.8	49.2	24.9	...	...	...	...	...	...
Sudan	2,503,890	17,380,000	6.9	1973	14,819,000[5]	50.4	49.6	...	46.7	—48.4—			—4.9—	
Swaziland	17,364	540,000	19.6	1976	494,534	45.6	54.4	15.2	47.7	25.2	13.7	7.9	3.7	1.7
Tanzania	945,050	16,308,000	17.3	1967	12,313,469	48.8	51.2	5.5	43.9	24.7	15.4	8.6	4.1	3.3
Togo	56,785	2,404,000	42.3	1970	1,953,778	48.1	51.9	...	49.8	21.5	15.1	8.0	3.6	2.0
Tunisia	154,530	6,075,000	39.3	1975	5,588,209	50.8	49.2	49.0	43.7	25.6	14.7	10.0	4.9	0.9
Uganda	241,139	12,780,000	53.0	1969	9,548,847	50.5	49.5	7.7	46.2	24.0	15.7	8.3	4.2	1.6
Upper Volta	274,200	6,464,000	23.6	1975	5,638,203	50.2	49.8	0.7	...	...	...	...	...	...
Western Sahara	266,769	152,000	0.6	1970	76,425	57.5	42.5	45.3	42.9	27.2	16.3	7.4	4.4	1.8
Zaire	2,344,885	27,080,000	11.5	1974	24,327,143	...	...	...	52.5	—47.5—				
Zambia	752,614	5,472,000	7.3	1969	4,056,995	49.0	51.0	26.9	46.3	24.0	16.6	9.4	3.0	0.7
Zimbabwe Rhodesia	390,272	6,930,000	17.8	1969	5,099,350	50.3	49.7	16.8	47.2	25.4	15.7	8.4	—3.3—	
Total AFRICA	30,142,133	451,551,000	15.0											
ANTARCTICA total	14,244,900	[6]	—	—	—	—	—	—	—	—	—	—	—	—
ASIA														
Afghanistan	653,000	20,882,000	32.0	—	—	—	—	—	—	—	—	—	—	—
Bahrain	662	278,000	419.9	1971	216,078	53.8	46.2	78.1	44.3	25.3	16.9	9.0	3.7	0.8
Bangladesh	143,998	84,655,000	587.9	1974	71,479,071	51.9	48.1	8.8	48.1	22.0	15.6	8.7	4.6	1.1
Bhutan	46,100	1,262,000	27.4	1969	931,514	...	...	...	...	...	...	...	...	...
Brunei	5,765	201,000	34.9	1971	136,256	53.4	46.6	63.6	43.4	28.0	15.7	8.1	3.9	0.9
Burma	676,577	32,205,000	47.6	1973	28,885,867	49.7	50.3	...	40.5	—53.4—			—6.0—	
Cambodia	181,035	4,500,000	24.9	1962	5,728,771	50.0	50.0	10.3	43.8	24.9	16.8	9.8	4.1	0.6
China	9,561,000	960,000,000	100.4	1953	574,205,940	51.8	48.2	13.3	35.9	25.1	18.8	12.9	6.3	1.0
Cyprus	9,251	616,000	66.6	1976	612,851	...	...	...	...	...	...	...	...	...
Hong Kong	1,050	4,606,000	4,386.6	1976	4,420,390	51.0	49.0	...	30.0	30.2	15.4	14.9	7.3	1.7
India	3,287,782	638,388,000	194.2	1971	547,949,809	51.8	48.2	19.9	41.9	24.1	17.8	10.2	4.9	1.1
Indonesia	1,919,558	134,563,000	70.1	1971	119,817,706[7]	49.3	50.7	17.5	44.0	23.9	18.6	9.1	3.8	0.7
Iran	1,648,000	35,213,000	21.4	1976	33,591,875	51.0	49.0	46.8	46.2	—49.6—			—4.2—	
Iraq	437,522	12,330,000	28.2	1977	12,171,480	51.0	49.0	63.5	...	...	...	...	...	...
Israel	20,700	3,696,000	178.6	1972	3,147,683	50.3	49.7	85.3	32.6	26.9	15.6	13.6	9.2	2.0
Japan	377,643	114,898,000	304.2	1975	111,939,643	49.2	50.8	75.9	24.3	24.9	23.1	15.9	9.2	2.5
Jordan	95,396	2,212,000	23.2	1961	1,706,226	50.9	49.1	43.9	45.4	26.1	13.7	7.5	5.1	1.8

Table II. World Populations and Areas[1] *(Continued)*

Country	AREA AND POPULATION: MIDYEAR 1978 Area in sq km	Total population	Persons per sq km	POPULATION AT MOST RECENT CENSUS Date of census	Total population	% Male	% Female	% Urban	Age distribution (%)[2] 0–14	15–29	30–44	45–59	60–74	75+
Korea, North	121,200	17,070,000	140.8	—	—	—	—	—	—	—	—	—	—	—
Korea, South	98,914	37,019,000	374.2	1975	34,678,972	50.0	50.0	48.4	38.0	28.2	17.9	10.2	4.6	1.0
Kuwait	16,918	1,198,000	70.8	1975	994,837	54.7	45.3	85.9	31.3	60.0	43.0	16.8	—0.9—	
Laos	236,800	3,546,000	15.0	—	—	—	—	—	—	—	—	—	—	—
Lebanon	10,230	3,152,000	308.1	1970	2,126,325	50.8	49.2	60.1	42.6	23.8	16.7	9.1	—7.7—	
Macau	16	276,000	17,250.0	1970	248,636	51.4	48.6	100.0	37.6	28.9	15.0	11.3	5.9	1.1
Malaysia	329,747	12,737,000	38.6	1970	10,434,034[8]	50.4	49.6	26.1	44.9	25.5	15.2	9.2	—5.2—	
Maldives	298	143,000	479.9	1978	143,046	52.6	47.4	20.7	...	...	...	...	...	...
Mongolia	1,565,000	1,577,000	1.0	1979	1,594,800	...	...	...	...	...	...	...	...	...
Nepal	145,391	13,420,000	92.3	1971	11,555,983	49.7	50.3	13.8	40.5	25.5	18.7	9.7	—5.6—	
Oman	300,000	843,000	2.8	—	—	—	—	—	—	—	—	—	—	—
Pakistan	796,095	75,620,000	95.0	1972	64,892,000	53.0	47.0	25.5	44.0	—56.0—				
Philippines	300,000	46,351,000	154.5	1975	42,070,660	50.6	49.4	31.6	44.0	28.0	14.9	8.4	3.9	0.8
Qatar	11,400	200,000	17.5	—	—	—	—	—	—	—	—	—	—	—
Saudi Arabia	2,240,000	7,870,000	3.5	1974	7,012,642	...	...	...	...	...	...	...	...	...
Singapore	616	2,334,000	3,789.0	1970	2,074,507	51.2	48.8	100.0	38.8	28.1	16.9	10.5	4.9	0.8
Sri Lanka	65,610	14,184,000	216.2	1971	12,689,897	51.3	48.7	22.4	39.3	27.8	15.9	10.5	5.2	1.3
Syria	185,180	8,328,000	45.0	1970	6,304,685	51.3	48.7	43.5	49.3	22.4	14.3	7.5	4.8	1.7
Taiwan	35,990	16,950,000	471.0	1975	16,206,183	51.8	48.2	...	36.7	29.8	16.4	11.7	4.6	0.8
Thailand	542,373	45,100,000	83.2	1970	34,397,374	49.6	50.4	13.4	45.5	24.9	16.1	8.6	—4.9—	
Turkey	779,452	43,144,000	55.4	1975	40,347,719	50.1	49.9	41.8	39.8	26.8	16.1	9.4	5.8	1.3
United Arab Emirates	83,600	860,000	10.3	1975	655,973	...	...	...	...	...	...	...	...	...
Vietnam	329,465	51,450,000	156.2	—	—	—	—	—	—	—	—	—	—	—
Yemen (Aden)	287,680	1,853,000	6.4	1973	1,590,275	49.5	50.5	33.3	47.3	20.8	15.8	8.6	—6.6—	
Yemen (San'a')	200,000	5,648,000	28.2	1975	5,237,893	47.6	52.4	8.2	46.7	—53.3—				
Total ASIA[9,10]	44,596,144	2,529,758,000	56.7											
EUROPE														
Albania	28,748	2,608,000	90.7	1960	1,626,315	51.4	48.6	30.9	42.7	—57.3—				
Andorra	464	31,000	66.8	1975	26,558	...	...	...	...	...	...	...	...	...
Austria	83,853	7,508,000	89.5	1971	7,456,403	47.0	53.0	51.9	24.4	20.5	18.3	16.5	15.5	4.8
Belgium	30,521	9,840,000	322.4	1970	9,650,944	48.9	51.1	...	23.5	21.0	19.4	17.1	14.4	4.6
Bulgaria	110,912	8,814,000	79.5	1975	8,727,771	49.9	50.1	58.0	21.8	22.4	20.6	18.8	13.0	3.4
Channel Islands	194	130,000	670.1	1971	126,363	48.5	51.5	...	21.8	21.4	18.4	18.1	14.9	5.3
Czechoslovakia	127,881	15,138,000	118.4	1970	14,344,987	48.7	51.3	55.5	23.1	24.8	18.4	16.7	13.6	3.4
Denmark	43,075	5,100,000	118.4	1976	5,072,516	49.5	50.5	82.6	22.4	22.5	19.4	16.8	13.8	5.1
Faeroe Islands	1,399	41,000	29.3	1970	38,612	52.2	47.8	27.8	31.8	23.0	16.5	16.0	9.4	3.4
Finland	337,032	4,753,000	14.1	1978	4,758,088	48.4	51.6	59.7	20.8	25.2	21.0	16.8	12.4	3.8
France	543,965	53,299,000	98.0	1975	52,655,802	48.9	51.1	70.0	22.6	24.4	17.8	16.2	13.3	5.6
Germany, East	108,328	16,756,000	154.7	1971	17,068,318	46.1	53.9	73.8	23.3	19.9	20.1	14.7	16.9	5.1
Germany, West	248,651	61,310,000	246.6	1970	60,650,599	47.6	52.4	...	23.2	21.3	19.7	16.6	15.0	4.2
Gibraltar	6	29,000	4,833.3	1970	26,833	48.1	51.9	91.9	22.9	22.7	21.1	18.7	11.2	3.4
Greece	131,990	9,360,000	70.9	1971	8,768,641	49.8	50.2	53.2	24.9	20.4	21.9	16.5	12.5	3.8
Hungary	93,032	10,690,000	114.9	1970	10,322,099	48.5	51.5	45.2	21.1	23.6	20.5	17.7	13.6	3.5
Iceland	103,000	224,000	2.2	1970	204,930	50.6	49.4	...	32.3	25.1	16.4	13.7	9.0	3.5
Ireland	70,283	3,221,000	45.8	1979	3,364,881	...	...	...	...	...	...	...	...	...
Isle of Man	572	64,000	111.9	1976	61,723	47.5	52.5	51.8	20.5	19.1	15.6	17.3	20.2	7.3
Italy	301,262	56,779,000	188.5	1971	54,136,547	48.9	51.1	...	24.4	21.2	20.7	17.0	12.8	3.9
Jan Mayen	373	—	—	1973	37	...	...	—	...	...	...	...	...	...
Liechtenstein	160	25,000	156.2	1970	21,350	49.7	50.3	...	27.9	27.1	18.6	14.5	9.3	2.6
Luxembourg	2,586	356,000	137.7	1970	339,841	49.0	51.0	68.4	22.1	20.5	21.4	17.5	14.6	3.9
Malta	316	311,000	984.2	1967	314,216	47.9	52.1	94.3	29.8	25.9	17.6	13.8	10.2	2.7
Monaco	1.90	26,000	13,684.2	1975	25,029	45.2	54.8	100.0	12.9	17.5	18.4	20.9	21.2	9.1
Netherlands, The	41,160	13,937,000	338.6	1971	13,060,115	49.9	50.1	54.9	27.2	24.6	17.9	15.6	10.9	3.7
Norway	323,895	4,059,000	12.5	1978	4,066,000	...	...	...	...	...	...	...	...	...
Poland	312,677	35,010,000	112.0	1974	33,635,900	48.5	51.5	54.1	24.3	27.5	19.0	15.3	11.1	2.7
Portugal	91,632	9,798,000	106.9	1970	8,663,252	47.4	52.6	37.2	28.4	21.9	19.0	16.2	11.2	3.3
Romania	237,500	21,855,000	92.0	1977	21,657,569	49.3	50.7	47.8	25.7	23.7	19.6	17.2	10.9	3.0
San Marino	61	21,000	344.3	1947	12,100	49.3	50.7	...	28.4	—71.6—				
Spain	504,750	37,109,000	73.5	1970	34,032,801	48.9	51.1	54.7	27.8	22.0	19.9	16.1	10.8	3.4
Svalbard	62,050	—	—	1974	3,472	...	...	...	...	...	...	...	...	...
Sweden	449,964	8,278,000	18.4	1975	8,208,544	49.7	50.3	82.7	20.7	21.3	18.8	18.1	15.4	5.7
Switzerland	41,293	6,340,000	153.5	1970	6,269,783	49.3	50.7	52.0	23.4	23.7	20.2	16.3	12.5	3.9
United Kingdom	244,102	55,822,000	288.7	1971	55,515,602	48.5	51.5	76.9	24.1	21.0	17.6	18.3	14.3	4.7
Vatican City	.44	1,000	2,272.7	—	—	—	—	—	—	—	—	—	—	—
Yugoslavia	255,804	21,914,000	85.7	1971	20,522,972	49.1	50.9	38.6	27.2	24.6	22.7	13.5	9.8	2.2
Total EUROPE[10]	10,504,493	673,746,000	64.1											
NORTH AMERICA														
Anguilla	91	7,000	76.9	1974	6,519	...	...	...	...	...	...	...	...	...
Antigua	440	72,000	163.6	1970	64,794	47.2	52.8	33.7	44.0	24.2	12.0	11.7	—8.0—	
Bahamas, The	13,864	228,000	16.4	1970	168,812	50.0	50.0	71.4	43.6	24.3	16.8	9.8	4.4	1.1
Barbados	430	270,000	627.9	1970	235,229	48.0	52.0	3.7	35.9	27.2	12.9	12.8	8.7	2.5
Belize	22,965	132,000	5.6	1970	119,934	50.6	49.4	54.4	49.3	22.5	13.0	8.7	5.0	1.5
Bermuda	46	58,000	1,260.9	1970	52,330	50.2	49.8	6.9	30.0	25.8	20.5	14.4	7.7	2.0
British Virgin Islands	153	12,000	78.4	1970	10,484	53.0	47.0	21.9	39.0	29.1	14.7	10.0	5.1	1.9
Canada	9,976,139	23,498,000	2.4	1976	22,992,604	49.8	50.2	75.5	25.6	28.3	18.4	15.1	9.3	3.3
Cayman Islands	288	14,000	48.6	1970	10,068	46.8	53.2	61.1	37.1	21.7	16.0	11.1	7.4	2.9
Costa Rica	50,898	2,111,000	41.5	1973	1,871,780	50.1	49.9	40.6	43.3	27.0	14.2	8.4	4.4	2.7
Cuba	110,922	9,728,000	87.7	1970	8,569,121	51.3	48.7	60.3	27.0	25.0	16.9	12.1	6.8	2.2
Dominica	772	81,000	104.9	1970	70,302	47.4	52.6	46.2	49.1	21.2	11.2	10.0	6.3	2.2
Dominican Republic	48,442	5,124,000	105.8	1970	4,006,405	50.4	49.6	40.0	47.2	24.8	15.2	7.8	3.8	1.2
El Salvador	21,041	4,354,000	206.9	1971	3,554,648	49.6	50.4	39.4	46.2	25.1	15.2	8.2	4.3	1.0
Greenland	2,175,600	49,000	.02	1976	49,630	54.1	45.9	74.7	...	...	...	...	...	...
Grenada	344	111,000	322.7	1970	96,542	46.2	53.8	...	47.1	23.0	11.6	9.4	6.6	2.2
Guadeloupe	1,705	317,000	185.9	1974	324,500	...	...	41.9	41.2	22.8	14.3	10.4	5.3	1.7
Guatemala	108,889	6,836,000	62.8	1973	5,160,221	50.0	50.0	33.6	45.1	26.7	15.1	8.3	—4.8—	

Table II. World Populations and Areas[1] *(Continued)*

Country	AREA AND POPULATION: MIDYEAR 1978 Area in sq km	Total population	Persons per sq km	POPULATION AT MOST RECENT CENSUS Date of census	Total population	% Male	% Female	% Urban	Age distribution (%)[2] 0–14	15–29	30–44	45–59	60–74	75+
Haiti	27,750	4,833,000	174.2	1971	4,329,991	48.2	51.8	20.4	41.5	25.8	16.5	9.5	5.0	1.7
Honduras	112,088	3,438,000	30.7	1974	2,656,948	49.5	50.5	37.5	48.1	25.8	13.9	7.8	3.6	0.9
Jamaica	10,991	2,133,000	194.1	1970	1,813,594	49.8	50.2	41.4	37.5	25.1	15.2	12.4	7.5	2.3
Martinique	1,079	316,000	292.9	1974	324,832	48.2	51.8	55.6	39.5	25.0	14.2	11.8	7.3	2.2
Mexico	1,972,546	66,944,000	33.9	1970	48,225,238	49.9	50.1	58.7	46.2	25.6	14.6	8.0	4.4	1.2
Montserrat	102	12,000	117.6	1970	11,458	46.9	53.1	31.7	37.9	20.6	9.8	12.1	10.7	8.9
Netherlands Antilles	993	246,000	247.7	1972	223,196	48.8	51.2	...	38.0	26.7	16.7	10.3	6.4	1.8
Nicaragua	128,875	2,395,000	18.6	1971	1,877,972	48.3	51.7	48.0	48.1	25.6	14.1	7.4	3.6	1.1
Panama	77,082	1,826,000	23.7	1970	1,472,082	52.3	47.7	26.7	37.6	28.7	17.5	11.9	3.3	1.1
Puerto Rico	8,897	3,358,000	377.4	1970	2,712,033	49.0	51.0	58.1	36.5	26.1	15.9	11.9	7.1	2.5
St. Christopher-Nevis (-Anguilla)[11]	269	50,000	185.9	1970	45,327	46.9	53.1	31.7	48.4	18.9	9.5	12.1	8.7	2.4
St. Lucia	623	118,000	189.4	1970	99,806	47.2	52.8	36.9	49.6	21.3	11.6	9.8	5.5	2.2
St. Pierre & Miquelon	242	6,000	24.8	1974	5,840	49.4	50.6	...	33.8	24.7	18.0	12.9	—10.5—	
St. Vincent & the Grenadines	389	118,000	303.3	1970	89,129	47.4	52.6	...	51.2	21.7	11.0	8.8	—7.2—	
Trinidad and Tobago	5,128	1,133,000	220.9	1970	931,071	49.4	50.6	...	42.1	26.2	14.2	10.8	—6.8—	
Turks and Caicos Islands	500	7,000	14.0	1970	5,558	47.4	52.6	—	47.1	20.4	12.0	11.1	7.0	2.5
United States	9,363,123	218,059,000	23.3	1970	203,211,926	48.7	51.3	73.5	28.6	24.0	17.0	16.3	10.4	3.7
Virgin Islands (U.S.)	345	101,000	292.7	1970	62,468	49.9	50.1	24.4	35.7	28.3	19.4	10.8	4.4	1.4
Total NORTH AMERICA	24,244,051	358,095,000	14.8											
OCEANIA														
American Samoa	197	31,000	157.4	1974	29,190	50.5	49.5	...	44.9	25.7	15.5	9.5	3.5	0.9
Australia	7,682,300	14,213,000	1.8	1976	13,915,500	50.0	50.0	86.0	27.2	25.5	18.3	15.7	9.8	3.2
Canton and Enderbury Islands	70	—	—	1970	0	—	—	—	—	—	—	—	—	—
Christmas Island	135	3,000	22.2	1970	2,691	64.4	35.6	0	30.8	34.6	22.0	10.8	1.4	0.4
Cocos Islands	14	1,000	71.4	1971	618	49.0	51.0	0	27.3	38.6	21.8	8.9	3.3	0.2
Cook Islands	241	17,000	70.5	1976	18,128	51.3	48.7	...	49.8	22.1	12.9	9.2	4.9	1.1
Fiji	18,272	607,000	33.2	1976	588,068	50.5	49.5	37.2	41.1	29.8	16.2	8.8	3.3	0.8
French Polynesia	3,265	146,000	44.7	1977	137,382	52.5	47.5	39.7	42.0	27.2	17.0	8.9	4.0	0.8
Guam	549	109,000	198.5	1970	84,996	55.7	44.3	25.5	39.7	29.1	19.3	8.9	2.5	0.5
Johnston Island	3	1,000	333.3	1970	1,007	...	...	0	...	...	...	...	...	...
Kiribati	713	55,000	77.1	1973	52,837	49.3	50.7	29.7	44.1	24.8	15.3	9.7	5.1	1.1
Midway Islands	5	2,000	400.0	1970	2,220	...	...	0	...	...	...	...	...	...
Nauru	21	8,000	381.0	1977	7,254	52.1	47.9	0	44.2	33.1	11.4	8.5	—2.8—	
New Caledonia	19,079	138,000	7.2	1976	133,233	52.0	48.0	42.1	38.6	26.3	18.6	10.4	4.9	1.2
New Hebrides	11,870	102,000	8.6	1967	77,988	52.1	47.9	12.0	45.6	26.0	15.5	8.5	—4.4—	
New Zealand	268,704	3,107,000	11.6	1976	3,129,383	49.9	50.1	83.0	29.1	26.0	17.3	14.5	10.0	3.1
Niue Island	259	4,000	15.4	1976	3,843	50.2	49.8	24.8	46.2	23.8	13.6	7.9	5.8	2.6
Norfolk Island	35	2,000	57.1	1971	1,683	49.0	51.0	0	25.2	20.7	19.7	18.9	12.5	2.9
Pacific Islands, Trust Territory of the	1,880	134,000	71.3	1973	114,973	51.7	48.3	43.9	46.2	25.8	12.7	9.1	—5.9—	
Papua New Guinea	462,840	2,990,000	6.5	1971	2,489,935	52.0	48.0	11.1	45.2	24.5	17.4	9.9	1.4	1.6
Pitcairn Island	4	65	16.2	1977	74	...	...	0	...	...	...	...	...	...
Solomon Islands	28,896	214,000	7.4	1976	196,823	52.2	47.8	...	47.8	24.1	14.5	8.4	3.6	1.3
Tokelau	10	2,000	200.0	1974	1,574	46.1	53.9	...	48.2	18.3	14.3	9.4	—9.6—	
Tonga	750	93,000	124.0	1976	90,128	51.1	48.9	...	44.4	26.2	14.8	9.5	4.0	1.1
Tuvalu	26	7,000	269.2	1973	5,887	46.3	53.7	...	40.8	23.3	14.5	13.4	6.4	1.6
Wake Island	8	2,000	250.0	1970	1,647	...	...	...	...	...	...	...	...	...
Wallis and Futuna	255	9,000	35.3	1976	9,192	50.0	50.0	...	46.6	23.6	14.0	9.9	5.1	0.8
Western Samoa	2,849	154,000	54.0	1976	151,983	51.7	48.3	21.1	48.2	26.0	12.6	8.7	3.5	1.0
Total OCEANIA	8,503,250	22,151,000	2.6											
SOUTH AMERICA														
Argentina	2,758,829	26,393,000	9.6	1970	23,390,050	49.7	50.3	80.4	29.3	24.6	19.9	15.4	8.6	2.2
Bolivia	1,098,581	4,887,000	4.4	1976	4,647,816	49.1	50.9	...	41.6	26.8	15.6	9.6	4.7	1.7
Brazil	8,511,965	115,397,000	13.6	1970	93,139,037	49.7	50.3	55.9	42.2	26.7	16.3	9.4	—5.1—	
Chile	756,626	10,848,000	14.3	1970	8,884,768	48.8	51.2	75.1	39.0	25.5	16.6	10.4	5.6	2.9
Colombia	1,138,914	25,867,000	22.7	1973	22,551,811	48.6	51.4	63.6	44.1	27.3	14.9	8.5	4.1	1.0
Ecuador	281,334	7,814,000	27.8	1974	6,521,710	50.1	49.9	41.3	44.6	26.5	14.7	8.4	4.6	1.3
Falkland Islands	16,265	2,000	0.1	1972	1,957	55.2	44.8	44.7	26.7	22.4	—51.9—			
French Guiana	89,000	60,000	0.7	1974	55,125	52.1	47.9	76.5	37.9	27.7	16.7	10.7	5.5	1.5
Guyana	215,000	819,000	3.8	1970	699,848	49.7	50.3	33.3	47.1	25.1	13.4	9.0	4.4	1.0
Paraguay	406,752	2,888,000	7.1	1972	2,357,955	49.6	50.4	37.4	44.9	25.4	14.5	9.2	4.5	1.5
Peru	1,285,216	16,819,000	13.1	1972	13,538,208	50.0	50.0	59.6	43.9	25.8	15.6	8.7	—5.9—	
Suriname	181,455	374,000	2.1	1971	384,903	50.0	50.0	...	48.0	—52.0—				
Uruguay	176,215	2,864,000	16.3	1975	2,782,000	49.0	51.0	83.0	27.0	22.6	19.2	16.9	10.8	3.5
Venezuela	899,180	13,122,000	14.6	1971	10,721,522	50.0	50.0	75.0	35.1	31.7	17.5	10.0	4.4	1.3
Total SOUTH AMERICA	17,815,332	228,154,000	12.8											
U.S.S.R.[10]	22,402,200	261,569,000	11.7	1979	262,400,000	...	...	62.3	...	...	...	...	...	...
in Asia[10]	16,831,000	68,380,000	2.3											
in Europe[10]	5,571,000	193,189,000	34.7											
TOTAL WORLD[12]	150,050,303	4,263,455,000	31.4											

[1]Any presentation of population data must include data of varying reliability. This table provides published and unpublished data about the latest census (or comparable demographic survey) and the most recent or reliable midyear 1978 population estimates for the countries of the world. Census figures are only a body of estimates and samples of varying reliability whose quality depends on the completeness of the enumeration. Some countries tabulate only persons actually present, while others include those legally resident, but actually outside the country, on census day. Population estimates are subject to continual correction and revision; their reliability depends on: number of years elapsed since a census control was established, completeness of birth and death registration, international migration data, etc.
[2]Data for persons of unknown age excluded, so percentages may not add to 100.0.
[3]Excludes Mayotte, shown separately.
[4]Transkei received its independence from South Africa on Oct 26, 1976; Bophuthatswana on Dec. 6, 1977; Venda on Sept. 13, 1979. All are Bantu homeland states whose independence is not internationally recognized.
[5]Sudan census excludes three southern autonomous provinces.
[6]May reach a total of 2,000 persons of all nationalities during the summer.
[7]Includes 1970 census for Portuguese Timor, now part of Indonesia.
[8]West Malaysia only.
[9]Includes 18,130 sq km of Iraq-Saudi Arabia neutral zone.
[10]Asia and Europe continent totals include corresponding portions of U.S.S.R.
[11]Excludes Anguilla, shown separately.
[12]Area of Antarctica excluded in calculating world density.

Table III. Life Expectancy at Birth, in Years, for Selected Countries[1]

Country	Period	Male	Female
Africa			
Burundi	1975–80	41.4	44.6
Egypt	1975–80	53.7	56.1
Liberia	1975–80	44.4	47.6
Madagascar	1975–80	44.4	47.6
Nigeria	1975–80	41.9	45.1
Upper Volta	1975–80	37.5	40.6
Asia			
Hong Kong	1976	68.0	75.5
India	1976–81	53.8	52.6
Indonesia	1975–80	48.7	51.3
Israel[2]	1977[3]	71.9	75.4
Japan	1977[3]	73.1	78.2
Korea, South	1975	66.0	70.0
Pakistan	1975–80	52.4	52.1
Taiwan	1976[3]	68.8	73.7
Thailand	1975–80	57.6	63.2
Europe			
Albania	1975–80	68.0	70.7
Austria	1975–80	68.7	75.5
Belgium	1968–72	67.8	75.5
Bulgaria	1974–76	68.9	73.9
Czechoslovakia	1977[3]	66.7	73.6
Denmark	1976–77[3]	71.2	77.1
Finland	1976[3]	67.5	76.1
France	1976[3]	69.2	77.2
Germany, East	1976	68.8	74.4
Germany, West	1975–77	68.6	75.2
Greece	1970	70.1	73.6
Hungary	1974	66.5	72.4
Iceland	1975–76[3]	73.0	79.2
Ireland	1974–76[3]	66.8	70.7
Italy	1970–72	69.0	74.9
Netherlands, The	1976[3]	71.5	78.0
Norway	1975–76	71.8	78.1
Poland	1977[3]	69.2	74.6
Portugal	1975–80	66.1	72.7
Romania	1975–77	67.5	72.1
Spain	1970[3]	69.6	75.1
Sweden	1976[3]	72.1	77.9
Switzerland	1968–73	70.3	76.2
United Kingdom	1974–76	69.4	75.6
Yugoslavia	1970–72	65.4	70.2
North America			
Barbados	1975–80	68.0	73.0
Canada	1975–80	69.6	75.6
Costa Rica	1975–80	68.5	72.1
Cuba	1970[3]	68.5	71.8
Guatemala	1975–80	54.9	56.6
Mexico	1975–80	63.6	67.4
Panama	1975–80	66.3	69.5
Puerto Rico	1975–80	70.6	75.3
United States	1977[3]	69.7	77.1
Oceania			
Australia	1975–80	69.7	76.0
New Zealand	1975–80	69.4	75.6
South America			
Argentina	1975–80	66.1	72.9
Brazil	1975–80	60.7	66.7
Chile	1975–80	61.3	67.6
Peru	1975–80	56.3	60.0
Suriname	1975–80	64.8	69.8
Uruguay	1975–80	67.3	73.3
Venezuela	1975–80	64.6	68.3
U.S.S.R.	1971–72[3]	64.0	74.0

[1] Projection.
[2] Jewish population only.
[3] Actual.
Sources: United Nations, *Selected World Demographic Indicators by Countries, 1950–2000;* official country sources.

continued from page 294

sional maternal mortality rate was 9.9 deaths per 100,000 live births, a considerable drop from the rate of 22.2 in 1969. Denmark, in 1976, reported a new low rate of 1.5 maternal deaths per 100,000 live births. In areas of the world where maternal mortality remained a major health problem, estimated rates frequently exceeded 200.

Marriage and Divorce Statistics. In the U.S. marriages peaked in 1973, reached a low point in 1975, and then increased. According to provisional reports, 2,243,000 marriages occurred in 1978, a 3% increase over the 2,178,367 marriages in 1977. The marriage rate was 10.3 per 1,000 population, compared with 10 in 1976. For the 12-month period ended June 1979, the marriage rate was 10.4, compared with 10.1 for the corresponding period ended June 1978. Final figures for the data year 1977

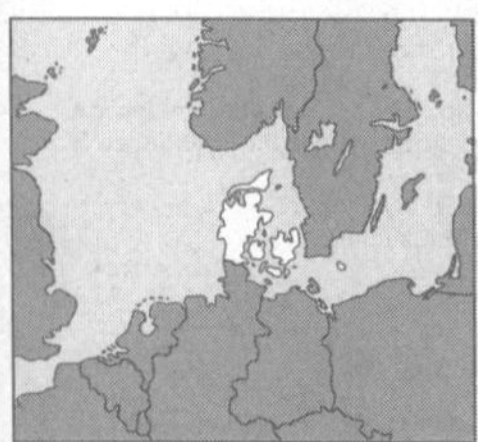
Denmark

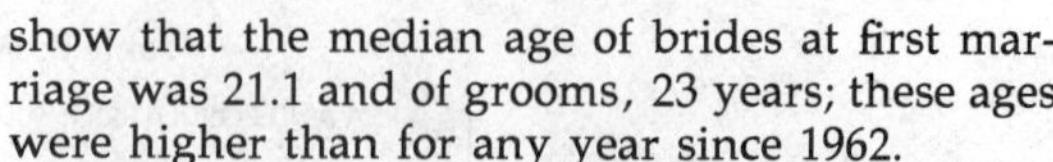
show that the median age of brides at first marriage was 21.1 and of grooms, 23 years; these ages were higher than for any year since 1962.

Remarriages comprised an increasing proportion of all marriages. Between 1971 and 1977 the proportion of marriages involving previously married brides rose from 24 to 32%. The median age at remarriage after divorce remained about the same as in prior years: 30.2 years for brides and 33.6 years for grooms. From 1968 to 1977 the median age of widowed brides rose from 50.6 years to 53.1 years and for widowed grooms, from 57.9 years to 60.1 years.

The estimated number of divorces in 1978 (1,122,000) was 2.9% more than in 1977 and 75.6% more than were granted a decade earlier (639,000 in 1969). The provisional divorce rate was 5.1 per 1,000 population, a 2% increase over 1977 and a 59.4% increase since 1969. For the 12-month period ended June 1979, the divorce rate was 5.2 per 1,000 population, compared with 5.1 for the corresponding period ended June 1978.

Final data for 1977 showed that the divorce and annulment rate was 21.1 per 1,000 women aged 15 years and over, an increase of 69% since 1968. The median duration of marriage ending in divorce was 6.6 years. An estimated 1,095,000 children under 18 were involved in divorces in 1977, a drop of 2% from 1976. The average number of children per divorce declined from 1.34 in 1968 to 1 in 1977, probably because of the lowering of birthrates. Comparative divorce rates for 1976–77 were available for only a few countries, such as Belgium (1.3), Japan (1.3), Norway (1.5), Sweden (2.5), and the U.S.S.R. (3.4).

Surveys and Censuses. Under the direction of the International Statistical Institute at The Hague, Neth., the World Fertility Survey was under way in 35 countries. A total of 25 major country reports would be published by 1980. For a number of countries the years 1979–81 represented a census-taking period. Most, like the U.S., had geared up for a census in 1980. (ANDERS S. LUNDE)

[338.F.5.b; 525.A; 10/36.C.5.d]

Denmark

A constitutional monarchy of north central Europe lying between the North and Baltic seas, Denmark includes the Jutland Peninsula and 100 inhabited islands in the Kattegat and Skagerrak straits. Area (excluding Faeroe Islands and Greenland): 43,075 sq km (16,631 sq mi). Pop. (1979 est.): 5,111,500. Cap. and largest city: Copenhagen (pop., 1978 est., 662,500). Language: Danish. Religion: predominantly Lutheran. Queen, Margrethe II; prime minister in 1979, Anker Jørgensen.

The general election on Oct. 23, 1979, brought little change. In August 1978 Prime Minister Anker Jørgensen had broadened the Danish government by including the Liberal Democrat (Venstre) Party, thus expanding its support in the 179-seat Folketing (Parliament) from the 66 seats held by his Social Democrat Party to 88. The coalition existed uneasily until Jørgensen called for the election. Winning 69 seats (a gain of 3), the Social Democrats were prepared to form a minority government. The Conservatives won 22 seats (+7), but Mogens Glistrup's maverick "antitax" Progress Party (20 seats) lost 6, and the Communist Party lost all of its 7. The Liberal Democrats remained stable at 23 (+1).

The government had fallen out over a scheme of "economic democracy," under which, in return for two years of income and wage restraint, a system of industrial profit sharing would be inaugurated. The scheme had been put forward by the Danish trade unions and, in a modified form, was supported by the bourgeois parties. It was rejected by the Liberal Democrats, however, and Jørgensen had no choice but to resign, on September 28.

During 1979 the "unnatural" coalition nevertheless settled some important issues. By prolonging a modified wages agreement for two years on March 28, it averted strikes after the breakdown of wage negotiations. In June the value-added tax was raised 20–25% and gasoline and tobacco taxes were increased sharply. The government also carried through Denmark's largest-ever business transaction, with a consortium of petroleum companies on utilization of the natural gas reserves in Denmark's North Sea sector. This would involve an investment of 8 billion kroner over 5 years and sales of the product over 20 years possibly amounting to 30 billion kroner.

Denmark faced serious economic difficulties in 1979. Between 1975 and 1979 its foreign debt had risen from 14% of the gross national product to 25%, partly because of the need to cover balance of payments deficits. Inflation, fed by petroleum price rises, had been running at a minimum annual rate of 7–8% and was increasing. The remedy was seen to be stimulation of export industries and of home industries that competed against imports. Reduction of expenditure in the public sector was also called for. From 1973 to 1978 agriculture and industry had lost 30,000 of their labour force while public services throughout the country had increased by 150,000. Income tax had reached levels

DENMARK

Education. (1976–77) Primary, pupils 561,132; secondary, pupils 254,708; primary and secondary, teachers 58,954; vocational, pupils 38,602, teachers (1974–75) *c.* 5,290; teacher training (1975–76), students 15,934, teachers 1,216; higher, students (1975–76) 110,271, teaching staff (1971–72) 10,467.

Finance. Monetary unit: Danish krone, with (Sept. 17, 1979) a free rate of 5.21 kroner to U.S. $1 (11.20 kroner = £1 sterling). Gold, SDR's, and foreign exchange (June 1979) U.S. $3,934,000,000. Budget (1978–79 est.): revenue 89,517,000,000 kroner; expenditure 101,203,000,000 kroner. Gross national product (1978) 303,710,000,000 kroner. Money supply (May 1979) 68,670,000,000 kroner. Cost of living (1975 = 100; June 1979) 144.

Foreign Trade. (1978) Imports 81,402,000,000 kroner; exports 65,313,000,000 kroner. Import sources: EEC 49% (West Germany 21%, U.K. 11%, The Netherlands 6%); Sweden 13%; U.S. 5%. Export destinations: EEC 47% (West Germany 17%, U.K. 14%, Italy 5%, France 5%); Sweden 13%; Norway 7%; U.S. 6%. Main exports: machinery 20%; meat 15%; chemicals 7%; dairy produce 6%; fish 5%. Tourism: visitors (1976) 16,232,000; gross receipts (1977) U.S. $940 million.

Transport and Communications. Roads (1977) 66,550 km (including 408 km expressways). Motor vehicles in use (1977): passenger 1,374,900; commercial 263,200. Railways: (1976) 2,511 km; traffic (1976–77) 3,460,000,000 passenger-km, freight 1,920,000,000 net ton-km. Air traffic (including apportionment of international operations of Scandinavian Airlines System; 1978): 2,833,000,000 passenger-km; freight 136.1 million net ton-km. Shipping (1978): merchant vessels 100 gross tons and over 1,397; gross tonnage 5,530,408. Shipping traffic (1978): goods loaded 8,244,000 metric tons, unloaded 34,521,000 metric tons. Telephones (including Faeroe Islands and Greenland; Jan. 1978) 2,743,800. Radio receivers (Dec. 1977) 1,826,000. Television licenses (Dec. 1977) 1,719,000.

Agriculture. Production (in 000; metric tons; 1978): wheat *c.* 653; barley *c.* 6,295; oats *c.* 210; rye *c.* 326; potatoes *c.* 1,009; rutabagas (1977) 1,238; sugar, raw value *c.* 441; apples *c.* 130; rapeseed *c.* 71; butter 140; cheese 183; pork 812; beef and veal 237; fish catch (1977) 1,807. Livestock (in 000; July 1978): cattle *c.* 3,095; pigs *c.* 7,920; sheep (1977) 56; chickens (1977) 14,943.

Industry. Production (in 000; metric tons; 1978): crude steel 863; cement (1977) 2,309; fertilizers (nutrient content; 1977–78) nitrogenous 117, phosphate 99; plastics and resins (1976) 145; crude oil 432; petroleum products (1976) 7,824; manufactured gas (cu m) 300,000; electricity (kw-hr) 20,360,000. Merchant vessels launched (100 gross tons and over; 1978) 399,000 gross tons.

WIDE WORLD

Newly reelected Prime Minister Anker Jørgensen (wearing coat) presented his new Cabinet to Queen Margrethe II of Denmark following the formation of a new government in October.

higher than in any other Western country. In 1979, 60% of the country's gross national income of some 300 billion kroner went to public expenditure, half of it for health and social welfare. It was recognized that the country's standard of living would have to suffer some diminution in order to make industry more competitive, redress the balance of payments, and relieve unemployment.

On November 29 the government announced a 5% devaluation of the krone against the other currencies of the European Monetary System and on December 4 put before Parliament an emergency economic plan. This included stringent price and income controls, increased corporation and wealth taxes, and a compulsory profit-sharing scheme. However, the plan was strongly opposed and to avert defeat the government had to modify it considerably.

On June 7, in a low (47%) turnout of voters, two-thirds voted for pro-European parties which won 10 of mainland Denmark's 15 seats in the European Assembly; 3 of them went to each party in the right-centre coalition. The opposition to the European Economic Community (EEC) won 5 seats. A 16th seat, belonging to Greenland under home rule, went to an anti-EEC candidate. (The Faeroe Islands, which also had home rule, had elected to stay out of the EEC.)

(STENER AARSDAL)

See also Dependent States.

Dependent States

In 1979 three dependent states, St. Lucia and St. Vincent in the Caribbean and the Gilbert Islands (renamed Kiribati) in the Pacific, were granted independence. (*See* SAINT LUCIA; SAINT VINCENT AND THE GRENADINES; KIRIBATI.)

Europe and the Atlantic. On May 1 Greenland achieved home rule. After a general election on April 4, the moderate left-wing party Siumut obtained 13 of the new Landsting's (Parliament's) 21 seats. The government comprised Prime Minister Jonathan Motzfeldt and four secretaries, all members of Siumut. No foreign secretary was appointed because foreign relations were conducted by Denmark. In the Faeroe Islands the three-party coalition, formed with difficulty in January, entered into crisis at the end of July. The Social Democrats, who numbered Prime Minister Atli Dam among their members, and the left-wing Republicans announced at the opening of a new session of Parliament on July 30 that they wished to break up the coalition because its third member, the Popular Rally, opposed the purchase of a ferryboat deemed necessary to support the single vessel plying between Thorshavn and Norway, Britain, and The Netherlands. However, the crisis was overcome and the coalition saved.

British aid to Gibraltar for 1978–81 totaled more than £14 million. Anglo-Spanish talks on practical cooperation and a cessation of Spanish harassment developed during Spain's application to join the European Economic Community. Moreover, Spain's difficulties with its Ceuta and Melilla enclaves in North Africa, which were claimed by Morocco and which were scenes of violence during 1979, and with the Canary Islands, for which the Organization of African Unity demanded independence, also took Spanish attention away from Gibraltar.

In the Atlantic Ocean the Falkland Islands' determination to stay British was emphasized by the illegal Argentine occupation of South Thule since December 1976. The British Conservative Party government sent a senior minister to the Falklands in May to observe the implementation of a 1976 economic survey, consider the possible exploitation of fish and oil, and evaluate the huge dependency in Antarctica.

Caribbean. In 1979 the remaining British dependencies and associated states were principally concerned with the political changes taking place within the eastern Caribbean and the effects of increased energy prices on their already near-subsistence economies. By the end of 1979 only two associated states remained, St. Vincent and St. Lucia having achieved independence during the course of the year.

In Antigua discussions were held with the British government on achieving independence in 1980, but these ran into difficulty over opposition objections and the desire of Antigua's island ward, Barbuda, to secede. Though manufacturing continued to expand, only tourism proved profitable, and during the year the government approached Trinidad and Venezuela for economic assistance. Following an international political storm a locally based Canadian company, Space Research Corp., was expelled from Antigua for allegedly breaking the United Nations embargo on arms shipments to South Africa.

Discussions were also held in St. Kitts-Nevis and Anguilla on independence. Though the eventual right of Anguilla to remain a British dependency was accepted by all parties, the Nevisians' local representatives demanded complete independence from St. Kitts. This was, however, rejected by the government of the associated state, and the issue was not resolved. Prime Minister Paul Southwell died on May 18 and was replaced by Lee Moore,

Puerto Rican nationalists gave a defiant clenched fist salute after their sentences were commuted by U.S. Pres. Jimmy Carter in September. The four had served long jail terms, one for an attack on the residence of Pres. Harry S. Truman in 1950, three for an attack on the House of Representatives in 1954.

UPI

KEYSTONE

A new headquarters building for British forces in Hong Kong was officially opened on March 4.

the attorney general and minister of external affairs. In November 1978, at a general election, St. Kitts's opposition People's Liberation Movement took all seven seats. Led by John Osborne, a local businessman, the new government espoused a free-enterprise philosophy and decreased state intervention. By mid–1979 it had become clear that because of the island's small financial base, overseas investment was unlikely without counterpart funding, via the island government, from the British. Public expenditure cuts made it apparent by late 1979 that such funds would not be available, nor would there be money for promised salary increases to the island's civil servants.

In the smaller dependencies the government of the Turks and Caicos Islands continued to argue with the British government over its desire to approve legislation locally, the chief minister indicating to Britain in May that his government hoped to proceed to full internal self-government. In contrast, neither the British Virgin Islands nor the Cayman Islands sought any such change. Both continued to prosper, with their tourist-based economies showing steady improvement. Following talks on independence, the government of Bermuda stated that because the majority of the island's people had no wish to take such a step it would be rejected but regularly reviewed.

In Belize little progress was made toward solving the border dispute with Guatemala. The issue was discussed at the Commonwealth heads of government conference in Lusaka, Zambia, and later the Barbados government sought clarification of reports that Britain and Guatemala had agreed to the territory's independence in 1980. This was denied. In the general election on November 21 Prime Minister George Price's People's United Party, seeking independence without surrender of territory to Guatemala, won a clear victory. Meanwhile, offshore and onshore oil exploration began.

The French government made clear to its overseas départements of Martinique, Guadeloupe, and French Guiana that it was reversing its policies and intended to make them economically self-sufficient. A ten-year economic plan to create a technologically oriented work force was outlined. The proposals were criticized by the extreme right and far left. Though calls for full independence continued from the Communist and left-leaning parties, the labour unions wanted most to separate from France. Attempts were made to forge closer links between the French overseas territories and Dominica, St. Lucia, Barbados, and Trinidad. The trail of damage left in Guadeloupe and Martinique by Hurricane David at the end of August was reckoned at Fr 800 million.

In the Netherlands Antilles a joint Dutch-Antillean working party planned to make recommendations on the constitutional structure of the territory after it achieved independence. The 26-member team, which included delegations from The Netherlands and each island, was charged with determining the extent of independence and post-independence relationships.

Puerto Rico was preoccupied with the 1980 elections and a possible seeking of statehood with the U.S. Separatists were a minority, but the return of four Puerto Rican nationalists, granted clemency by U.S. Pres. Jimmy Carter after long imprisonment in the U.S. for terrorist acts, was greeted by a crowd of 5,000 at San Juan airport on September 12. Earlier, in April, William Morales, a Puerto Rican nationalist, was sentenced in the U.S. to ten years in prison for possessing weapons; he was said to be a member of a pro-independence group claiming responsibility for 100 bombing incidents in the U.S. Later a New York state court sentenced him to 29–89 years for his part in a bombing in New York City. In December terror-

continued on page 305

Dentistry: see Health and Disease

ANTARCTIC

Claims on the continent of Antarctica and all islands south of 60° S remain in status quo according to the Antarctic Treaty, to which 19 nations are signatory. Formal claims within the treaty area include the following: Australian Antarctic Territory, the mainland portion of French Southern and Antarctic Lands (Terre Adélie), Ross Dependency claimed by New Zealand, Queen Maud Land and Peter I Island claimed by Norway, and British Antarctic Territory, some parts of which are claimed by Argentina and Chile. No claims have been recognized as final under international law.

AUSTRALIA

CHRISTMAS ISLAND

Christmas Island, an external territory, is situated in the Indian Ocean 1,410 km NW of Australia. Area: 135 sq km (52 sq mi). Pop. (1978 est.): 3,100. Cap.: The Settlement (pop., 1971, 1,300).

COCOS (KEELING) ISLANDS

Cocos (Keeling) Islands is an external territory located in the Indian Ocean 3,685 km W of Darwin, Australia. Area: 14 sq km (5.5 sq mi). Pop. (1977 est.): 447.

NORFOLK ISLAND

Norfolk Island, an external territory, is located in the Pacific Ocean 1,720 km NE of Sydney, Australia. Area: 35 sq km (13 sq mi). Pop. (1978 est.): 1,800. Cap. (de facto): Kingston.

DENMARK

FAEROE ISLANDS

The Faeroes, an integral part of the Danish realm, are a self-governing group of islands in the North Atlantic about 580 km W of Norway. Area: 1,399 sq km (540 sq mi). Pop. (1979 est.): 42,800. Cap.: Thorshavn (pop., 1977 census, 11,600).

Education. (1978–79) Primary, pupils 6,052; secondary, pupils 2,424; primary and secondary, teachers (1977–78) 466; vocational, pupils (1977–78) 1,129, teachers (1966–67) 88; teacher training, students 115, teachers (1966–67) 12; higher, students 19.

Finance and Trade. Monetary unit: Faeroese krone, at par with the Danish krone, with (Sept. 17, 1979) a free rate of 5.21 kroner to U.S. $1 (11.20 kroner = £1 sterling). Budget (1977–78 est.): revenue 377,187,000 kroner; expenditure 377,029,000 kroner. Foreign trade (1977): imports 910 million kroner; exports 863 million kroner. Import sources: Denmark 72%; Norway 12%. Export destinations: U.S. 25%; Denmark 22%; U.K. 11%; Italy 9%; France 8%; Spain 6%. Main exports: fish 82%; fish meal 9%; ships 5%.

Transport. Shipping (1978): merchant vessels 100 gross tons and over 177; gross tonnage 60,939.

Agriculture and Industry. Fish catch (1977) 310,000 metric tons. Livestock (in 000; 1977): sheep 61; cattle 2. Electricity production (1976–77) *c.* 95 million kw-hr (*c.* 58% hydroelectric).

GREENLAND (Kalâtdlit-Nunât)

An integral part of the Danish realm, Greenland, the largest island in the world, lies mostly within the Arctic Circle. Area: 2,175,600 sq km (840,000 sq mi), 84% of which is covered by ice cap. Pop. (1979 est.): 49,300. Cap.: Godthaab (Nûk; pop., 1978 est., 8,500).

Education. (1978–79) Primary, pupils 7,990; secondary and vocational, pupils 3,049; primary, secondary, and vocational, teachers 1,061; higher, students 538.

Finance and Trade. Monetary unit: Danish krone. Budget (1976 est.): revenue 109.1 million kroner; expenditure 95.7 million kroner. Foreign trade (1977): imports 965 million kroner; exports 555 million kroner. Import sources: Denmark 82%; U.K. 8%; The Netherlands 7%. Export destinations: Denmark 45%; Finland 17%; West Germany 15%; U.S. 14%; France 7%. Main exports: fish 51%; zinc ore 28%; lead ore 13%.

Agriculture. Fish catch (1977) 60,000 metric tons. Livestock (in 000; Nov. 1977): sheep 17; reindeer 2.

Industry. Production (in 000; metric tons; 1976): lead ore (metal content) 31; zinc ore (metal content) 88; electricity (kw-hr) *c.* 125,000.

FRANCE

FRENCH GUIANA

French Guiana is an overseas département situated between Brazil and Suriname on the northeast coast of South America. Area: 90,000 sq km (34,750 sq mi). Pop. (1978 est.): 60,000. Cap.: Cayenne (pop., 1978 est., 32,900).

Education. (1977–78) Primary, pupils 10,838, teachers 600; secondary and vocational, pupils 5,834, teachers (1975–76) 338; teacher training, students 39.

Finance and Trade. Monetary unit: French (metropolitan) franc, with (Sept. 17, 1979) a free rate of Fr 4.23 to U.S. $1 (Fr 9.10 = £1 sterling). Budget (total; 1976 est.) balanced at Fr 190,578,000. Foreign trade (1978): imports Fr 860,920,000; exports Fr 33,310,000. Import sources (1977): France 65%; Trinidad and Tobago 13%; U.S. 5%. Export destinations (1977): U.S. 57%; France 15%; Martinique 7%. Main exports (1977): shrimp 54%; timber 17%.

FRENCH POLYNESIA

An overseas territory, French Polynesia consists of islands scattered over a large area of the south central Pacific Ocean. Area of inhabited islands: 4,182 sq km (1,615 sq mi). Pop. (1979 est.): 150,000. Cap.: Papeete, Tahiti (pop., 1977, 65,600).

Education. (1976–77) Primary, pupils 28,883, teachers 1,295; secondary, pupils 7,727, teachers 478; vocational, pupils 1,821, teachers 177; teacher training, students 120, teachers 6.

Finance and Trade. Monetary unit: CFP franc, with (Sept. 17, 1979) a parity of CFP Fr 18.18 to the French franc and a free rate of CFP Fr 76.92 to U.S. $1 (CFP Fr 165.50 = £1 sterling). Budget (1978) balanced at CFP Fr 13.5 billion. Foreign trade (1977): imports CFP Fr 29,187,000,000 (50% from France, 19% from U.S.); exports CFP Fr 1,464,000,000 (82% to France, 8% to Italy in 1976). Main exports (1976): nuclear material *c.* 70%; coconut oil 21%. Tourism (1976): visitors 117,000; gross receipts U.S. $49 million.

GUADELOUPE

The overseas département of Guadeloupe, together with its dependencies, is in the eastern Caribbean between Antigua to the north and Dominica to the south. Area: 1,705 sq km (658 sq mi). Pop. (1978 est.): 317,000. Cap.: Basse-Terre (pop., 1977 est., 15,800).

Education. (1976–77) Primary, pupils 63,934, teachers (1975–76) 2,018; secondary and teacher training, pupils 38,057; vocational, pupils 7,554; secondary, vocational, and teacher training, teachers 2,147; higher, students 1,400.

Finance and Trade. Monetary unit: French (metropolitan) franc. Budget (total; 1977 est.) balanced at Fr 1,199 million. Cost of living (Basse-Terre; 1975 = 100; April 1979) 137. Foreign trade (1978): imports Fr 1,909,700,000 (74% from France in 1977); exports Fr 498,830,000 (80% to France, 15% to Martinique in 1977). Main exports (1977): bananas 36%; sugar 36%; wheat meal and flour 7%; rum 7%.

MARTINIQUE

The Caribbean island of Martinique, an overseas département, lies 39 km N of St. Lucia and about 50 km SE of Dominica. Area: 1,079 sq km (417 sq mi). Pop. (1979 est.): 311,900. Cap.: Fort-de-France (pop., 1974, 98,800).

Education. (1976–77) Primary, pupils 80,342, teachers 3,353; secondary, pupils 46,280, teachers 2,865; teacher training, students 1,364, teachers 14.

Finance and Trade. Monetary unit: French (metropolitan) franc. Budget (1977 est.): revenue Fr 594 million; expenditure Fr 531 million. Cost of living (Fort-de-France; 1975 = 100; March 1979) 145. Foreign trade (1978): imports Fr 2,241,000,000; exports Fr 459,970,000. Import sources (1977): France 62%; Venezuela 9%; Saudi Arabia 5%. Export destinations (1977): France 63%; Guadeloupe 24%; Italy 9%. Main exports (1977): bananas 56%; petroleum products 20%; rum 9%.

MAYOTTE

An African island dependency of France that was formerly a part of the Comoros, Mayotte lies in the Indian Ocean off the east coast of Africa. Area: 378 sq km (146 sq mi). Pop. (1978): 47,200. Cap.: Dzaoudzi (pop., 1978, 4,100).

Education. (1978–79) Primary, pupils 7,253, teachers 170; secondary, pupils 667, teachers 34; vocational, pupils 62.

Finance and Trade. Monetary unit: French (metropolitan) franc. Main exports: vanilla, essential oils, copra.

NEW CALEDONIA

The overseas territory of New Caledonia, together with its dependencies, is in the South Pacific 1,210 km E of Australia. Area: 19,079 sq km (7,366 sq mi). Pop. (1978 est.): 137,500. Cap.: Nouméa (pop., 1976, 56,100).

Education. (1979) Primary, pupils 33,939, teachers 1,450; secondary, pupils 8,660, teachers 557; vocational, pupils 3,038, teachers 275; higher, students 396, teaching staff 53.

Finance and Trade. Monetary unit: CFP franc. Budget (1977 rev. est.): revenue CFP Fr 13,795,000,000; expenditure CFP Fr 12,645,000,000. Foreign trade (1978): imports CFP Fr 23,933,000,000; exports CFP Fr 18,160,000,000. Import sources (1977): France 39%; Bahrain 20%; Australia 10%; Singapore 9%; U.S. 5%. Export destinations (1977): France 50%; Japan *c.* 30%; U.S. *c.* 15%; West Germany *c.* 5%. Main exports (1976): ferronickel 44%; nickel castings 27%; nickel 24%.

RÉUNION

The overseas département of Réunion is located in the Indian Ocean about 720 km E of Madagascar and 180 km SW of Mauritius. Area: 2,512 sq km (970 sq mi). Pop. (1979 est.): 493,300. Cap.: Saint-Denis (pop., 1978 est., 111,900).

Education. (1977–78) Primary, pupils (1979) 96,123, teachers 4,401; secondary and vocational, pupils (1979) 73,844, teachers 2,828; teacher training (1973–74), students 319, teachers 22; higher, students 1,901, teaching staff 62.

Finance and Trade. Monetary unit: French (metropolitan) franc. Budget (1977 est.) balanced at Fr 2,941,000,000. Cost of living (Saint-Denis; 1975 = 100; March 1979) 135.8. Foreign trade (1978): imports Fr 2,684,510,000; exports Fr 519,020,000. Import sources (1977): France 64%; South Africa 6%. Export destinations (1977): France 66%; U.K. 28%. Main export (1977): sugar 87%.

SAINT PIERRE AND MIQUELON

The self-governing overseas département of Saint Pierre and Miquelon is located about 20 km off the south coast of Newfoundland. Area: 242 sq km (93 sq mi). Pop. (1978 est.): 6,200. Cap.: Saint Pierre, Saint Pierre.

Education. (1978–79) Primary, pupils 768, teachers 41; secondary, pupils 511, teachers 42 (including vocational); vocational, pupils 130.

Finance and Trade. Monetary unit: French (metropolitan) franc. Budget (1976 est.) balanced at Fr 28.6 million. Foreign trade (1977): imports Fr 125,000,000; exports Fr 16,860,000. Import sources (1976): Canada 64%; France 27%. Export destinations (1976): ship's bunkers and stores 53%; Canada 30%; U.S. 13%. Main exports (1974): petroleum products 53%; cattle 30%; fish 12%.

WALLIS AND FUTUNA

Wallis and Futuna, an overseas territory, lies in the South Pacific west of Western Samoa. Area: 255 sq km (98 sq mi). Pop. (1977 est.): 9,000. Cap.: Mata Utu, Uvea (pop., 1976, 558).

NETHERLANDS, THE

NETHERLANDS ANTILLES

The Netherlands Antilles, a self-governing integral part of the Netherlands realm, consists of an island group near the Venezuelan coast and another group to the north near St. Kitts-Nevis. Area: 993 sq km (383 sq mi). Pop. (1979 est.): 246,500. Cap.: Willemstad, Curaçao (pop., 1970 est., 50,000).

Education. (1973–74) Primary, pupils 38,170, teachers 1,492; secondary and vocational, pupils

12,104, teachers 631; higher (university only), students *c.* 150, teaching staff *c.* 15.

Finance. Monetary unit: Netherlands Antilles guilder or florin, with (Sept. 17, 1979) a par value of 1.80 Netherlands Antilles guilders to U.S. $1 (free rate of 3.85 Netherlands Antilles guilders = £1 sterling). Budget (1972 rev. est.): revenue 122 million Netherlands Antilles guilders; expenditure 121 million Netherlands Antilles guilders. Cost of living (Aruba and Curaçao; 1975 = 100; Nov. 1978) 124.4.

Foreign Trade. (1977) Imports 5,630,000,000 Netherlands Antilles guilders; exports 4,762,000,000 Netherlands Antilles guilders. Import sources (1976): Venezuela 45%; Saudi Arabia 34%; U.S. 5%. Export destinations (1976): U.S. 47%; Ecuador 5%; U.K. 5%. Main export (1976): petroleum products 92%. Tourism (1976): visitors 368,000; gross receipts U.S. $240 million.

Transport and Communications. Roads (1972) 1,150 km. Motor vehicles in use (1975): passenger 50,136; commercial 5,650. Shipping traffic (1975): goods loaded *c.* 24,490,000 metric tons, unloaded *c.* 31,890,000 metric tons. Telephones (Jan. 1978) 49,600. Radio receivers (Dec. 1976) 150,000. Television receivers (Dec. 1976) *c.* 36,000.

Industry. Production (in 000; metric tons; 1976): petroleum products *c.* 31,970; phosphate rock 54; electricity (kw-hr) *c.* 1,500,000.

NEW ZEALAND

COOK ISLANDS

The self-governing territory of the Cook Islands consists of several islands in the southern Pacific Ocean scattered over an area of about 2.2 million sq km. Area: 241 sq km (93 sq mi). Pop. (1978 est.): 19,600. Seat of government: Rarotonga Island (pop., 1976, 9,800).

Education. (1977) Primary, pupils 4,962; secondary, pupils 2,210; primary and secondary, teachers (1975) 360; teacher training, students 48.

Finance and Trade. Monetary unit: Cook Islands dollar, at par with the New Zealand dollar, with (Sept. 17, 1979) a free rate of CI$1.005 to U.S. $1 (CI$2.16 = £1 sterling). Budget (1977–78 est.): revenue CI$12,134,000; expenditure CI$12,514,000. Foreign trade: imports (1973) CI$4,947,000 (83% from New Zealand, 5% from Japan); exports (1976) CI$2,203,000 (96% to New Zealand). Main exports: fruit preserves 50%; clothing 20%; fruit 9%; oilseeds 5%.

NIUE

The self-governing territory of Niue is situated in the Pacific Ocean about 2,400 km NE of New Zealand. Area: 259 sq km (100 sq mi). Pop. (1978 est.): 3,900. Capital: Alofi (pop., 1976, 1,007).

Education. (1976) Primary, pupils 1,038, teachers (1975) 65; secondary, pupils 286, teachers (1975) 22.

Finance and Trade. Monetary unit: New Zealand dollar. Budget (1977–78): revenue NZ$3,140,000 (excluding New Zealand subsidy of NZ$2.8 million); expenditure NZ$6,310,000. Foreign trade (1977): imports NZ$2,109,000 (83% from New Zealand); exports NZ$255,000 (92% to New Zealand). Main exports (1976): fruit 44%; plaited ware 18%; copra 15%; vegetables 15%; honey 6%.

TOKELAU

The territory of Tokelau lies in the South Pacific about 1,130 km N of Niue and 3,380 km NE of New Zealand. Area: 10 sq km (4 sq mi). Pop. (1978 est.): 1,600.

NORWAY

JAN MAYEN

The island of Jan Mayen, a Norwegian dependency, lies within the Arctic Circle between Greenland and northern Norway. Area: 373 sq km (144 sq mi). Pop. (1973 est.): 37.

SVALBARD

A group of islands and a Norwegian dependency, Svalbard is located within the Arctic Circle to the north of Norway. Area: 62,050 sq km (23,957 sq mi). Pop. (1978 est.): 3,500.

PORTUGAL

MACAU

The overseas territory of Macau is situated on the mainland coast of China 60 km W of Hong Kong. Area: 16 sq km (6 sq mi). Pop. (1978 est.): 276,200.

Education. (1977–78) Primary, pupils 22,173, teachers 780; secondary, pupils 10,756, teachers 596; vocational, pupils 2,731, teachers 215; teacher training, students 50, teachers 6; higher, students 3,233, teachers 99.

Finance and Trade. Monetary unit: pataca, with (Sept. 17, 1979) a free rate of 5.31 patacás to U.S. $1 (11.42 patacás = £1 sterling). Budget (1978 est.) balanced at 195 million patacás. Foreign trade (1977): imports 1,102,400,000 patacás; exports 1,221,500,000 patacás. Import sources: Hong Kong 64%; China 27%. Export destinations: West Germany 20%; U.S. 17%; France 16%; Hong Kong 10%; U.K. 6%; Italy 5%; The Netherlands 5%. Main exports (1976): clothing 83%; textile yarns and fabrics 6%.

Transport. Shipping traffic (1977): goods loaded 592,000 metric tons, unloaded 509,000 metric tons.

SOUTH WEST AFRICA (NAMIBIA)

South West Africa has been a UN territory since 1966, when the General Assembly terminated South Africa's mandate over the country, renamed Namibia by the UN. South Africa considers the UN resolution illegal. Area: 824,268 sq km (318,251 sq mi). Pop. (1979 est.): 980,000. National cap.: Windhoek (pop., 1975 est., 77,400). Summer cap.: Swakopmund (pop., 1975 est., 13,700).

Education. (1978) Primary and secondary, pupils 173,316, teachers 5,388.

Finance and Trade. Monetary unit: South African rand, with (Sept. 17, 1979) an official rate of R 0.83 to U.S. $1 (free rate of R 1.77 = £1 sterling). Budget (total; 1976–77 est.): revenue R 242 million; expenditure R 310 million. Foreign trade (included in the South African customs union; 1977 est.): imports *c.* R 400 million (*c.* 80% from South Africa in 1972); exports *c.* R 650 million (*c.* 50% to South Africa in 1972). Main exports: diamonds *c.* 40%; karakul pelts *c.* 10%; fish *c.* 10%; uranium *c.* 10%; copper *c.* 10%; cattle and meat *c.* 10%.

Agriculture. Production (in 000; metric tons; 1977): corn *c.* 15; millet *c.* 20; beef and veal *c.* 141; sheep and goat meat *c.* 25; fish catch 460. Livestock (in 000; 1977): cattle *c.* 2,875; sheep *c.* 5,085; goats *c.* 2,026; horses *c.* 43; asses *c.* 63.

Industry. Production (in 000; metric tons; 1976): copper ore (metal content) 39; lead ore (metal content) 42; zinc ore (metal content) 48; tin concentrates (metal content) 0.7; vanadium ore (metal content) 0.7; uranium (1977) 2.8; diamonds (metric carats; 1977) 2,001; salt *c.* 210; electricity (kw-hr; 1963) 188,000.

UNITED KINGDOM

ANGUILLA

Formally a part of the associated state of St. Kitts-Nevis-Anguilla, the island of Anguilla comprises a separate administrative entity, having received a constitution separating its government from that of St. Kitts-Nevis in 1976. Area: 91 sq km (35 sq mi). Pop. (1977 est.): 6,500.

Education. (1979) Primary, pupils 1,610, teachers 68; secondary, pupils 450, teachers 20.

Finance and Trade. Monetary unit: East Caribbean dollar, with (Sept. 17, 1979) an official rate of ECar$2.70 to U.S. $1 (free rate of ECar$5.81 = £1 sterling). Budget (1977 est.) balanced at ECar$3,285,000 (including U.K. grant of ECar$1,262,000). Foreign trade (included with St. Kitts–Nevis; 1976 est.) exports *c.* ECar$1 million. Main export destinations: Trinidad and Tobago *c.* 40%; Puerto Rico *c.* 30%; Guadeloupe *c.* 14%; U.S. Virgin Islands *c.* 10%. Main exports: salt *c.* 40%; lobster *c.* 36%; livestock *c.* 14%.

ANTIGUA

The associated state of Antigua, with its dependencies Barbuda and Redonda, lies in the eastern Caribbean approximately 60 km N of Guadeloupe. Area: 440 sq km (170 sq mi). Pop. (1977 est.): 72,400. Cap.: Saint John's (pop., 1974 est., 23,500).

Education. (1976–77) Primary, pupils 13,285, teachers 477; secondary, pupils 6,458, teachers 271; vocational, pupils 153, teachers 21; teacher training, students 89, teachers 9.

Finance and Trade. Monetary unit: East Caribbean dollar. Budget (1977 est.): revenue ECar$32 million; expenditure ECar$41 million. Foreign trade (1975): imports ECar$145,140,000; exports ECar$59,920,000. Import sources: U.K. 19%; U.S. 19%; Trinidad and Tobago 11%; The Bahamas 11%; Venezuela 9%; Iran 7%; Canada 5%. Export destinations: bunkers 57%; U.S. 10%; Guyana 5%. Main export: petroleum products 87%.

BELIZE

Belize, a self-governing colony, is situated on the Caribbean coast of Central America, bounded on the north and northwest by Mexico and by Guatemala on the remainder of the west and south. Area: 22,965 sq km (8,867 sq mi). Pop. (1980 est.): 140,612. Cap.: Belmopan (pop., 1980 est., 4,508).

Education. (1977–78) Primary, pupils 34,111, teachers 1,226; secondary, pupils 5,662, teachers 358; vocational, pupils 598; higher, students 439, teaching staff 20.

Finance and Trade. Monetary unit: Belize dollar, with (Sept. 17, 1979) an official rate of Bel$2 = U.S. $1 (free rate of Bel$4.30 = £1 sterling). Budget (total; 1978 est.) balanced at Bel$110 million. Foreign trade (1975): imports Bel$185.5 million; exports Bel$129.6 million. Import sources: U.S. 39%; U.K. 22%. Export destinations: U.S. 51%; U.K. 41%. Main exports: sugar 76%; clothing 8%; citrus products 5%.

BERMUDA

The colony of Bermuda lies in the western Atlantic about 920 km E of Cape Hatteras, North Carolina. Area: 46 sq km (18 sq mi). Pop. (1979 est.): 57,200. Cap.: Hamilton, Great Bermuda (pop., 1973 est., 3,000).

Education. (1976–77) Primary, pupils 6,614, teachers 374; secondary, pupils 5,393, teachers 466; vocational (1974–75), pupils 510, teachers 49.

Finance and Trade. Monetary unit: Bermuda dollar, at par with the U.S. dollar (free rate, at Sept. 17, 1979, of Ber$2.15 = £1 sterling). Budget (1977–78 est.): revenue Ber$78.3 million; expenditure Ber$78.4 million. Foreign trade (1977): imports Ber$185.6 million; exports Ber$39.1 million. Import sources: U.S. 47%; U.K. 19%; Netherlands Antilles 10%; Canada 6%. Export destinations: bunkers 27%; Jamaica 18%; U.S. 11%; Spain 10%. Main exports: petroleum products 42%; drugs and medicines 41%. Tourism (1977): visitors 573,000; gross receipts U.S. $230 million.

Transport. Roads (1977) *c.* 240 km. Motor vehicles in use (1976): passenger 12,100; commercial 1,900. Shipping (1978): merchant vessels 100 gross tons and over 99; gross tonnage 1,814,455.

BRITISH INDIAN OCEAN TERRITORY

Located in the western Indian Ocean, this colony consists of the islands of the Chagos Archipelago. Area: 60 sq km (23 sq mi). No permanent civilian population remains. Administrative headquarters: Victoria, Seychelles.

BRITISH VIRGIN ISLANDS

The colony of the British Virgin Islands is located in the Caribbean to the east of the U.S. Virgin Islands. Area: 153 sq km (59 sq mi). Pop. (1977 est.): 12,000. Cap.: Road Town, Tortola (pop., 1973 est., 3,500).

Education. (1975–76) Primary, pupils 2,251, teachers 123; secondary and vocational, pupils 821, teachers 48.

Finance and Trade. Monetary unit: U.S. dollar (free rate, at Sept. 17, 1979, of U.S. $2.15 = £1 sterling). Budget (1978 est.): revenue U.S. $7,759,000; expenditure U.S. $7,890,000. Foreign trade: imports (1976) U.S. $14,295,000; exports (1975) U.S. $497,200. Import sources: U.S. 28%; Puerto Rico 24%; U.K. 15%; U.S. Virgin Islands 12%; Trinidad and Tobago 11%. Export destinations (1974): U.S. Virgin Islands 53%; Anguilla

22%; St. Martin (Guadeloupe) 9%; U.K. 5%. Main exports (mainly reexports; 1974): motor vehicles 16%; timber 14%; beverages 10%; fish 7%; iron and steel 6%; machinery 6%.

BRUNEI

Brunei, a protected sultanate, is located on the north coast of the island of Borneo, surrounded on its landward side by the Malaysian state of Sarawak. Area: 5,765 sq km (2,226 sq mi). Pop. (1978 est.): 201,300. Cap.: Bandar Seri Begawan (pop., 1978 est., 70,000).

Education. (1977) Primary, pupils 34,360, teachers 1,824; secondary, pupils 15,204, teachers 936; vocational, pupils 422, teachers 84; teacher training, students 527, teachers 61.

Finance and Trade. Monetary unit: Brunei dollar, with (Sept. 17, 1979) a free rate of Br$2.15 to U.S. $1 (Br$4.62 = £1 sterling). Budget (1978 est.): revenue Br$2.4 billion; expenditure Br$944 million. Foreign trade (1978): imports Br$639,250,000; exports Br$4,195,210,000. Import sources: Japan 24%; Singapore 22%; U.S. 15%; U.K. 11%; Malaysia 5%. Export destinations: Japan 74%; U.S. 9%; Singapore 5%; South Africa 5%. Main exports: crude oil 62%; natural gas 31%.

Agriculture. Production (in 000; metric tons; 1977): rice *c.* 10; cassava *c.* 3; bananas *c.* 2; pineapples *c.* 2; rubber *c.* 1. Livestock (in 000; 1977): buffalo *c.* 17; cattle *c.* 3; pigs *c.* 15; chickens *c.* 941.

Industry. Production (in 000; 1977): crude oil (metric tons) 10,540; natural gas (cu m) 10,511,000; electricity (kw-hr; 1976) *c.* 240,000.

CAYMAN ISLANDS

The colony of the Cayman Islands lies in the Caribbean about 270 km NW of Jamaica. Area: 288 sq km (111 sq mi). Pop. (1978 est.): 14,000. Cap.: George Town, Grand Cayman (pop., 1970 census, 3,800).

Education. (1978–79) Primary, pupils 2,216, teachers 94; secondary, pupils 1,524, teachers 105.

Finance and Trade. Monetary unit: Cayman Islands dollar, with (Sept. 17, 1979) an official rate of CayI$0.83 to U.S. $1 (free rate of CayI$1.79 = £1 sterling). Budget (1977 est.): revenue CayI$12,759,000; expenditure CayI$11,817,000. Foreign trade (1977): imports CayI$29 million; exports CayI$1,268,000. Most trade is with the U.S. (about two-thirds) and Jamaica. Main export (1976): turtle products 98%. Tourism (1977): visitors 108,600; gross receipts U.S. $20 million.

Shipping. (1978) Merchant vessels 100 gross tons and over 135; gross tonnage 169,100.

FALKLAND ISLANDS

The colony of the Falkland Islands and dependencies is situated in the South Atlantic about 800 km NE of Cape Horn. Area: 16,265 sq km (6,280 sq mi). Pop. (1978 est.): 1,800. Cap.: Stanley (pop., 1978 est., 1,100).

Education. (1977–78) Primary, pupils 206, teachers 23; secondary, pupils 110, teachers 16.

Finance and Trade. Monetary unit: Falkland Island pound, at par with the pound sterling, with (Sept. 17, 1979) a free rate of U.S. $2.15 = FI£1. Budget (excluding dependencies; 1978– 79 est.): revenue FI£1,787,000; expenditure FI£1,767,000. Foreign trade (1976): imports FI£1,063,000 (83% from U.K. in 1971); exports FI£2,374,000 (93% to U.K. in 1971). Main export: wool 83%.

GIBRALTAR

Gibraltar, a self-governing colony, is a small peninsula that juts into the Mediterranean from southwestern Spain. Area: 5.80 sq km (2.25 sq mi). Pop. (1978 est.): 29,300.

Education. (1977–78) Primary, pupils 2,706, teachers 150; secondary, pupils 1,644, teachers 113; vocational, pupils 472, teachers 18.

Finance and Trade. Monetary unit: Gibraltar pound, at par with the pound sterling. Budget (1976–77 est.): revenue Gib£18,440,000; expenditure Gib£19,462,000. Foreign trade (1977): imports Gib£35,590,000 (67% from U.K.); reexports Gib£13,859,000 (31% to EEC, 16% to U.K. in 1971). Main reexports: petroleum products 82%; tobacco and manufactures 13%. Tourism (1976) 125,000 visitors.

Transport. Ships entered (1976) vessels totaling 18,896,000 net registered tons; goods loaded 8,000 metric tons, unloaded 358,000 metric tons.

GUERNSEY

Located 50 km W of Normandy, France, Guernsey, together with its small island dependencies, is a crown dependency. Area: 78 sq km (30 sq mi). Pop. (1973 est.): 50,600. Cap.: St. Peter Port (pop., 1971, 16,300).

Education. (1977–78) Primary and secondary, pupils 8,071, teachers 457.

Finance and Trade. Monetary unit: Guernsey pound, at par with the pound sterling. Budget (1977): revenue £27,574,000; expenditure £22,190,000. Foreign trade included with the United Kingdom. Main exports (1976): manufactures *c.* 50%; tomatoes *c.* 35%; flowers *c.* 14%. Tourism (1977) 306,000 visitors.

HONG KONG

The colony of Hong Kong lies on the southeastern coast of China about 60 km E of Macau and 130 km SE of Canton. Area: 1,050 sq km (405 sq mi). Pop. (1979 est.): 4.9 million. Cap.: Victoria (pop., 1976, 501,700).

Education. (1978–79) Primary, pupils 553,530, teachers 18,321; secondary, pupils 441,785; vocational, pupils 11,761; secondary and vocational, teachers 15,064; higher, students 25,231, teaching staff 2,643.

Finance. Monetary unit: Hong Kong dollar, with (Sept. 17, 1979) a free rate of HK$5.04 to U.S. $1 (HK$10.83 = £1 sterling). Budget (1978–79 est.): revenue HK$11,483,000,000; expenditure HK$11,677,000,000.

Foreign Trade. (1978) Imports HK$62,839,000,000; exports HK$53,740,000,000. Import sources: Japan 23%; China 17%; U.S. 12%; Taiwan 7%; Singapore 5%; U.K. 5%. Export destinations: U.S. 30%; West Germany 9%; Japan 8%; U.K. 7%; Singapore 5%. Main exports: clothing 30%; textile yarns and fabrics 9%; watches and clocks 7%; telecommunications apparatus 6%; plastic toys and dolls 5%. Tourism (1977): visitors 1,756,000; gross receipts U.S. $786 million.

Transport and Communications. Roads (1977) 1,092 km. Motor vehicles in use (1977): passenger 122,900; commercial 42,800. Railways: (1977) 35 km; traffic (1978) 324 million passenger-km, freight 62 million net ton-km. Shipping (1978): merchant vessels 100 gross tons and over 150; gross tonnage 874,850. Shipping traffic (1978): goods loaded 6,895,000 metric tons, unloaded 20,945,000 metric tons. Telephones (Dec. 1977) 1,252,000. Radio receivers (Dec. 1977) 2.5 million. Television receivers (Dec. 1977) 840,000.

ISLE OF MAN

The Isle of Man, a crown dependency, lies in the Irish Sea approximately 55 km from both Northern Ireland and the coast of northwestern England. Area: 572 sq km (221 sq mi). Pop. (1979 est.): 64,000. Cap.: Douglas (pop., 1976, 20,300).

Education. (1977–78) Primary, pupils 5,771; secondary, pupils 3,935; vocational, pupils 3,350.

Finance and Trade. Monetary unit: Isle of Man pound, at par with the pound sterling. Budget (1978–79): revenue £37.53 million; expenditure £37.51 million. Foreign trade included with the United Kingdom. Main exports: fish, cereals, livestock. Tourism (1978) 487,900 visitors.

JERSEY

The island of Jersey, a crown dependency, is located about 30 km W of Normandy, France. Area: 117 sq km (45 sq mi). Pop. (1976): 71,000. Cap.: St. Helier (pop., 1976, 25,100).

Education. (1977–78) Primary, pupils 6,914; secondary, pupils 5,450; primary and secondary (1976–77), teachers 670.

Finance. Monetary unit: Jersey pound, at par with the pound sterling. Budget (1977): revenue £63,981,000; expenditure £48,860,000.

Foreign Trade. (1978) Imports £176,094,000 (88% from U.K.); exports £64,579,000 (76% to U.K.). Main exports: motor vehicles 13%; potatoes 9%; tomatoes 8%; tea 8%; telecommunications apparatus 7%; musical instruments 7%; knitted fabrics 5%; clothing 5%. Tourism (1977): visitors 775,000; gross receipts U.S. $141 million.

MONTSERRAT

The colony of Montserrat is located in the Caribbean between Antigua, 43 km NE, and Guadeloupe, 60 km SE. Area: 102 sq km (40 sq mi). Pop. (1977 est.): 12,200. Cap.: Plymouth (pop., 1974 est., 3,000).

Education. (1976–77) Primary, pupils 2,356, teachers 95; secondary, pupils 702, teachers 48; vocational, pupils 62, teachers 8.

Finance and Trade. Monetary unit: East Caribbean dollar. Budget (1978 est.) balanced at ECar$9,150,000 (including U.K. aid of ECar$1,672,000). Foreign trade (1977): imports ECar$18,933,000; exports ECar$1,643,000. Import sources: U.K. 25%; U.S. 23%; Trinidad and Tobago 11%; Canada 5%. Export destinations: U.S. 31%; St. Kitts-Nevis 23%; Barbados 14%; Guadeloupe and Martinique 9%; Antigua 7%; Jamaica 5%; U.S. Virgin Islands 5%. Main exports (domestic only): packaging 19%; fishing materials 17%; cotton 12%; cattle 8%; postage stamps 7%; tomatoes 7%; textile yarns and fabrics 6%.

PITCAIRN ISLAND

The colony of Pitcairn Island is in the central South Pacific, 5,150 km NE of New Zealand and 2,170 km SE of Tahiti. Area: 4.53 sq km (1.75 sq mi). Pop. (1979 est.): 65, all of whom live in the de facto capital, Adamstown.

ST. HELENA

The colony of St. Helena, including its dependencies of Ascension Island and the Tristan da Cunha island group, is spread over a wide area of the Atlantic off the southwestern coast of Africa. Area: 412 sq km (159 sq mi). Pop. (1978 est.): 5,300. Cap.: Jamestown (pop., 1978 est., 1,500).

Education. (1978–79) Primary, pupils 831; secondary, pupils 490; primary and secondary, teachers 74; vocational, pupils 15, teachers 2; teacher training (1975–76), students 5, teachers 2.

Finance and Trade. Monetary unit: St Helena pound, at par with the pound sterling which is also used. Budget (1977–78 est.): revenue St.H£2,245,000; expenditure St.H£2.2 million. Foreign trade (1977–78): imports St.H£1,758,000 (61% from U.K., 28% from South Africa in 1968); exports nil.

ST. KITTS-NEVIS

This associated state consists of the islands of St. Kitts and Nevis (Anguilla received a separate constitution in 1976). Area: 269 sq km (104 sq mi). Pop. (1977 est.): 49,700. Cap.: Basseterre, St. Kitts (pop., 1975 est., 16,800).

Education. (1977–78) Primary, pupils 8,900, teachers 339; secondary, pupils 5,305, teachers 316; vocational, pupils 120, teachers 21; higher, students 69, teaching staff 12.

Finance and Trade. Monetary unit: East Caribbean dollar. Budget (1978 est.): revenue ECar$27 million; expenditure ECar$30 million. Foreign trade (1977): imports ECar$59.1 million; exports ECar$40.5 million. Import sources (1975): U.S. 29%; U.K. 20%; Trinidad and Tobago 10%; Canada 7%; The Netherlands 5%; Japan 5%. Export destinations (1975): U.S. 51%; U.K. 42%. Main exports (1975): sugar 61%; television and parts 34%.

TURKS AND CAICOS ISLANDS

The colony of the Turks and Caicos Islands is situated in the Atlantic southeast of The Bahamas. Area: 500 sq km (193 sq mi). Pop. (1977 est.): 7,100. Seat of government: Grand Turk Island (pop., 1977 est., 2,900).

Education. (1978) Primary, pupils 1,849, teachers 90; secondary, pupils 708, teachers 38.

Finance and Trade. Monetary unit: U.S. dollar. Budget (1978 est.) balanced at $4,713,000. Foreign trade: imports (1976) $4,939,000; exports (1977) $2,447,000. Main exports: crayfish 67%; conch meat 33%.

UNITED KINGDOM and FRANCE

NEW HEBRIDES

The British-French condominium of the New Hebrides is located in the southwestern Pacific about 800 km W of Fiji and 400 km NE of New Caledonia. Area: 11,870 sq km (4,583 sq mi). Pop. (1978 est.): 101,600. Cap.: Vila (metropolitan area pop., 1976 est., 17,400).

Education. (1977) Primary, pupils 21,805, teachers (1976) 595; secondary and vocational, pupils 2,051, teachers (1976) 107; teacher training (1976), students 137, teachers 12.

Finance. Monetary units: Australian dollar and New Hebrides franc, with (Sept. 17, 1979) a parity of NHFr 16.16 to the French franc and a free rate of NHFr 68.38 = U.S. $1 (NHFr 147.11 = £1 sterling). Condominium budget (1977 est.): revenue NHFr1,033,000,000; expenditure NHFr 829 million. British budget (1976–77 est.): revenue A$6,923,000; expenditure A$7,138,000. French budget (1976 est.): revenue NHFr 1,496,000,000; expenditure NHFr 1,497,000,000.

Foreign Trade. (1977) Imports NHFr 3,164,000,000; exports NHFr 2,525,000,000. Import sources (1975): Australia 30%; France 25%; Japan 8%; New Caledonia 7%; U.K. 5%. Export destinations (1975): France 43%; U.S. 28%; Japan 15%; New Caledonia 8%. Main exports: copra 43%; fish 42%; cocoa 7%.

Agriculture. Production (in 000; metric tons; 1977): bananas *c.* 1; copra *c.* 37; cocoa 1; fish catch *c.* 8. Livestock (in 000; 1977): cattle *c.* 115; pigs *c.* 64; chickens *c.* 134.

Industry. Production: manganese ore (metal content; exports; 1977) 23,000 metric tons; electricity (1976) *c.* 17 million kw-hr.

UNITED STATES

AMERICAN SAMOA

Located to the east of Western Samoa in the South Pacific, the unincorporated territory of American Samoa is approximately 2,600 km NE of the northern tip of New Zealand. Area: 197 sq km (76 sq mi). Pop. (1977 est.): 34,000. Cap.: Pago Pago (pop., 1974, 4,700).

Education. (1978) Primary, pupils 6,464, teachers 274; secondary, pupils 2,777, teachers 121; higher, students 836, teaching staff (1971–72) 32.

Finance and Trade. Monetary unit: U.S. dollar. Budget (1977 est.) balanced at $55.4 million (including U.S. federal grants of $46 million). Foreign trade (1976-77): imports (excluding fish for canneries) $51 million (74% from U.S., 10% from Japan in 1974); exports $65 million (95% to U.S. in 1970). Main export: canned tuna 90%.

GUAM

Guam, an organized unincorporated territory, is located in the Pacific Ocean about 9,700 km SW of San Francisco and 2,400 km E of Manila. Area: 549 sq km (212 sq mi). Pop. (1978 est.): 109,000. Cap.: Agana (pop., 1974 est., 2,500).

Education. (1977-78) Primary, pupils 24,303, teachers 1,186; secondary and vocational, pupils 6,083; teachers 509; higher, students 4,343, teaching staff (1971–72) *c.* 140.

Finance and Trade. Monetary unit: U.S. dollar. Budget (1976-77 est.): revenue $250.3 million; expenditure $204.2 million. Foreign trade (1976): imports $268 million (32% from U.S., 5% from Japan); exports $25 million (35% to Taiwan, 25% to U.S. Trust Territories, 21% to U.S.). Main exports: petroleum products, copra, watches, scrap metal. Tourism: visitors (1977) 246,000; gross receipts (1973) U.S. $90 million.

Agriculture and Industry. Production (in 000; metric tons; 1977): copra *c.* 1; eggs *c.* 1; fish catch 0.1; petroleum products (1976) *c.* 1,060; electricity (kw-hr; 1976) *c.* 1,040,000.

PUERTO RICO

Puerto Rico, a self-governing associated commonwealth, lies about 1,400 km SE of the Florida coast. Area: 8,897 sq km (3,435 sq mi). Pop. (1979 est.): 3,378,000. Cap.: San Juan (pop., 1976 est., mun., 516,500).

Education. (1978) Primary, pupils 509,000; secondary, pupils 156,000; primary and secondary, teachers 27,320; higher, students 119,970, teaching staff (1971-72) *c.* 4,400.

Finance. Monetary unit: U.S dollar. Budget (1976–77 actual): revenue $3,075,000,000; expenditure $2,797,000,000. Gross domestic product (1977–78) $10,903,000,000. Cost of living (1975 = 100; May 1979) 117.

Foreign Trade. (1977–78) Imports $6,529,000,000 (59% from U.S., 8% from Venezuela); exports $4,850,000,000 (85% to U.S.). Main exports (1974–75): chemicals 25%; petroleum products 14%; clothing 11%; machinery 11%; fish 8%. Tourism (1977–78): visitors 1,474,000; gross receipts $482 million.

Transport and Communications. Roads (paved; 1976) 10,690 km. Motor vehicles in use (1977): passenger 672,500; commercial 115,100. Railways (1977) 96 km. Telephones (Jan. 1978) 560,700. Radio receivers (Dec. 1976) 1,765,000. Television receivers (Dec. 1976) 631,000.

Agriculture. Production (in 000; metric tons; 1978): sugar, raw value 182; pineapples 37; bananas 111; oranges 34; coffee 12; tobacco (1977) 2; milk 438; meat (1977) 60; fish catch (1977) 59. Livestock (in 000; Jan. 1978): cattle 562; pigs 280; chickens 5,803.

Industry. Production (in 000; metric tons; 1978): cement 1,330; beer (hl) 474; rum (hl; 1977) *c.* 600; petroleum products (1976) 11,567; electricity (kw-hr) 13,832,000.

TRUST TERRITORY OF THE PACIFIC ISLANDS

The Trust Territory islands, numbering more than 2,000, are scattered over 7,750,000 sq km in the Pacific Ocean from 720 km E of the Philippines to just west of the International Date Line. Area: 1,880 sq km (726 sq mi). Pop. (1979 est.): 132,300. Seat of government: Saipan Island (pop., 1973 census, 12,400).

Education. (Including Northern Marianas; 1977–78) Primary, pupils 28,026, teachers 1,502; secondary, pupils 7,982, teachers 566; vocational (1976–77), pupils 257, teachers (1973–74) 13; higher, students 581.

Finance and Trade. Monetary unit: U.S. dollar. Budget (including Northern Marianas; 1976–77 est.): revenue $78,631,000 (including U.S. grant of $71.2 million); expenditure $117,231,000. Foreign trade (including Northern Marianas; 1977): imports $44 million (*c.* 50% from U.S., *c.* 27% from Japan in 1972); exports $10.9 million (54% to Japan in 1972). Main exports: coconut products 54%; fish 32%.

VIRGIN ISLANDS

The Virgin Islands of the United States is an organized unincorporated territory located about 60 km E of Puerto Rico. Area: 345 sq km (133 sq mi). Pop. (1978 est.): 101,130. Cap.: Charlotte Amalie, St. Thomas (pop., 1970, 12,200).

Education. (1978) Primary, pupils 20,000; secondary, pupils 5,000; primary and secondary, teachers 1,600; higher (1977–78), students 2,061, teaching staff 58.

Finance. Monetary unit: U.S. dollar. Budget (1976–77 est.): revenue $114 million; expenditure $113 million.

Foreign Trade. (1976) Imports $2,678,800,000; exports $2,010,200,000. Import sources: Iran 43%; Nigeria 14%; Qatar 10%; United Arab Emirates 9%; U.S. 8%; Libya 8%. Export destinations: U.S. 96%. Main exports (1973): petroleum products 50%; alumina 31%. Tourism (1976): visitors 613,000; gross receipts U.S. $152 million.

continued from page 301

ists attacked a busload of U.S. Navy personnel in the countryside, killing two and wounding several others.

Voters in the U.S. Virgin Islands on March 6 rejected a constitution that would have increased their self-government. Their primary reason for doing so was fear of tax increases.

Africa. The Organization of African Unity (OAU) continued to press for the independence of Ceuta, Melilla, and the Canary Islands from Spain. In the Canary Islands a nationalist candidate won the islands' seat in the Spanish Parliament in the March elections. In the the Western Sahara the Popular Front for the Liberation of Saguia el Hamra and Rio de Oro (Polisario Front), the movement for self-determination by the peoples of the Western Sahara, scored important successes in 1979. It secured the withdrawal of Mauritania from the war when the two sides signed a peace treaty on August 5 (after which Morocco annexed Mauritania's share of the Western Sahara) and also gained notable victories in battle against Morocco, capturing and temporarily holding several desert towns. The Polisario was openly supported by Algeria and received consideration from Spain, its secretary-general having a private meeting with Spain's premier on April 30. At its July summit the OAU called for a UN-supervised referendum on the future of the Western Sahara, and Morocco's representative quit the meeting in protest.

No conclusion was reached on the future of Namibia (South West Africa). The Constituent Assembly elected in December 1978 established a National Assembly on May 21, 1979. The assembly, dominated by the Democratic Turnhalle Alliance (DTA), was approved by the South African government but was not recognized by the UN or by the internal wing of the black nationalist South West Africa People's Organization (SWAPO). Meanwhile, SWAPO's external wing continued to raid Namibia from its bases in Angola, attracting

South African military reprisals. In November UN Secretary-General Kurt Waldheim invited representatives of all political parties, the five mediating Western nations of the UN, and the South African government to a conference on Namibia's future. Later there was disagreement between South Africa and SWAPO about the proposed demilitarized strip between Namibia and Angola, and at the end of November the DTA also expressed skepticism as to its practicability.

Indian Ocean. At a session of the OAU's Coordinating Committee for the Liberation of Africa at Dar es Salaam, Tanzania, on January 15, Pius Msekwa, chief executive of Tanzania's ruling party, said that as a colonized area Réunion deserved the committee's support. At an earlier agenda-planning meeting the committee had urged any liberation groups to come forward and negotiate to receive aid. Mayotte Island, in the Comoros, maintained its status as a French dependency, and the metropolitan French Gaullist party, the Rassemblement pour la République, strengthened its political links there after winning 91% of Mayotte's votes in the June elections for the European Assembly.

On Australia's Christmas Island, an Australian arbitration officer, James Taylor, was forcibly prevented from leaving after he had inserted layoff clauses in employees' agreements with the British Phosphate Commission. The islanders demanded that both he and the island's administrator be replaced so that better terms could be obtained for the commission's Malaysian workers.

Pacific. In July 1979 the Gilbert Islands, Britain's last Pacific colony, became the independent republic of Kiribati, leaving only Pitcairn as a British dependency. In the Franco-British New Hebrides condominium a government of national unity was formed in December 1978. But in the elections on Nov. 19, 1979, the pro-British Vanuaaku ("Our Land") Party won 26 of the 39 seats in the Assembly (the French "moderate" federal party won 13), and its president, Walter Lini, became prime minister of a government expected to take the colony into independence in 1980. The first full census in January 1979 showed a population of 112,596. Early in 1979 plantations and houses on Ambrym Island were devastated by ash from Benbow volcano.

French Pres. Valéry Giscard d'Estaing and his wife were greeted with tribal ceremonies on their visit to New Caledonia.

KEYSTONE

France's presence in French Polynesia continued to cause controversy. In February Charlie Ching, nephew of the former nationalist leader Pouvanaa A Oopa, was jailed for ten years for involvement with terrorists. In August the Territorial Assembly called for the suspension of all nuclear tests pending investigation of two incidents: an explosion of decontamination fluid that killed two workers and injured others on July 6; and the injury of two people by a tidal wave that coincided with a nuclear test on July 25. Despite official denials a team of experts subsequently showed that on July 25 a bomb was exploded when it became lodged in a shaft at 800 m (2,640 ft) and could not be lowered to the full depth of 1,000 m (3,300 ft).

In July Pres. Valéry Giscard d'Estaing visited the French Pacific. In French Polynesia he made firm reference to that country's enduring relationship with France, but he indicated to the New Caledonians (whose government had been suspended in March) that they could decide their own future electorally. Radical change by the vote was unlikely because the indigenous Melanesians constituted only 40% of the population. The French government also made moves toward a ten-year "contract" with New Caledonia under which territorial status would be maintained, with emphasis on economic development and, in the political sphere, a requirement that parties must receive at least 10% of the overall vote to be able to return members to the Council of Government. The latter was an attempt to disenfranchise the small pro-independence and predominantly Melanesian parties. On July 1 election coalitions of conservative and centrist parties outpolled (58 to 34%) the five parties of the Independence Front.

In the U.S.-administered Trust Territory of the Pacific Islands, the Marianas in January became a commonwealth of the U.S. tied to the mainland by defense and security arrangements, and the districts of Truk, Yap, Ponape, and Kosrae joined to form the Federated States of Micronesia with their capital at Palikir, Ponape. In elections for the new Congress of the Federated States in March, Tosiwo Nakayama of Truk was voted president. Negotiations over future political status continued with Palau and the Marshalls, which had rejected federation in July 1978. Discontent in the latter district was heightened by a long-standing dispute over compensation for the U.S. defense presence. The U.S. drew hostile comment from Pacific nations in July, when it became known that in order to prevent reprocessing of nuclear reactor wastes in Southeast Asia the government was considering the purchase of uninhabited Palmyra Island in the northern Line group as a dump for radioactive material.

The U.S. Pacific Islands Development Commission in January held a meeting at Pago Pago, on Tutuila Island in American Samoa, which was attended by American Samoa, Guam, Hawaii, and Micronesia, with Tonga, Tuvalu, Western Samoa, and French Polynesia invited as observers. A treaty with Tuvalu settled U.S. claims to four of the nation's nine islands.

In the Cook Islands former premier Sir Albert Henry, dismissed for the bribery of voters through the offer of very cheap "fly a voter" flights from New Zealand for the 1978 election, along with some Cook Islands associates and U.S. businessman Finbar Kenny, who ran the philatelic bureau, were charged with conspiracy to defraud the crown (stamp revenue was diverted to pay for the flights). All pleaded guilty. Henry was fined and placed on probation for three years without participation in politics, preventing his involvement in the 1982 election.

Norfolk Island was given a degree of self-government by Australia. After elections in August a chief minister and Executive Council were chosen from among the nine elected members of the Legislative Council.

East Asia. The pressure of immigration into Hong Kong, not only from mainland China but also from Southeast Asia, intensified in 1979. (*See* MIGRATION, INTERNATIONAL.) It was reported that Chinese secret societies had organized syndicates to provide transportation for immigrants into Hong Kong or Macau for up to HK$60,000 a head. The British colony's governor, Sir Murray MacLehose, whose tenure of office had been extended three times, visited Beijing (Peking) in March–April to discuss the problem and also the colony's future. Hong Kong's huge economy remained a miracle of prosperity.

In May Japan and the Soviet Union discussed the Kuril Islands, occupied by the Soviet Union after World War II but formerly Japanese, as a preliminary to a formal peace treaty between the two countries. No progress was made.

A 1978 agreement between Britain and Brunei for British support until probable independence in 1983 was reinforced by an offer to Brunei of membership in the Association of Southeast Asian Nations. Singapore also offered support. The sultan of Brunei was concerned about possible Indonesian or Malaysian annexation of his state and also about left-wing dissension fomented from outside.

(PHILIPPE DECRAENE; DAVID A. JESSOP; BARRIE MACDONALD; MOLLY MORTIMER)

See also African Affairs; Commonwealth of Nations; United Nations.

Djibouti

An independent republic in northeastern Africa, Djibouti is bordered by Ethiopia, Somalia, and the Gulf of Aden. Area: 23,000 sq km (8,900 sq mi). Pop. (1978 est.): 242,000, most of whom are Cushitic Afars or Somali Issas; there are smaller Arabic and European communities. Capital: Djibouti (pop., 1978 est., 160,000). Language: Arabic and French (official); Saho-Afar and Somali are spoken in their respective communities. Religion: predominantly Muslim. President in 1979, Hassan Gouled Aptidon; premier, Barkat Gourat Hamadou.

Tension in Djibouti resulting from hostility between the Afar and Issa peoples continued during 1979. Amnesty International was concerned over the fate of some 15 young Afar militants of the Mouvement Populaire de Libération (MPL), arbitrarily detained since 1977. In March, 20 fresh arrests were made following an attack by the regime's opponents against a barracks at Randa, and another 50 Afars were imprisoned after an attempt on the life of a member of the Cabinet on June 17. The MPL merged with another opposition party to form an underground Afar opposition, the Front Démocratique pour la Libération de Djibouti. On March 4 the Rassemblement Populaire pour le Progrès (RPP) was founded to succeed the Ligue Populaire Africaine pour l'Indépendance, with Pres. Hassan Gouled Aptidon as chairman.

The presence of some 10,000 refugees from Eritrea and the Ogaden region of Ethiopia aggravated Djibouti's difficulties. Forced to seek foreign aid, the government turned above all to the "brother states" of the Arab League and to France, which in January reinforced its military presence in Djibouti by basing ten Mirage III aircraft there.

(PHILIPPE DECRAENE)

DJIBOUTI

Education. (1975–76) Primary, pupils 10,469, teachers 336; secondary, pupils 1,644, teachers 96; vocational, pupils 690, teachers 59; teacher training, students 11, teachers 4.

Finance. Monetary unit: Djibouti franc, with (Sept. 17, 1979) a par value of DjFr 177.72 to U.S. $1 (free rate of DjFr 365 = £1 sterling). Budget (1979 est.) balanced at DjFr 9,650,000,000.

Foreign Trade. (1976) Imports DjFr 21,284,000,000; exports DjFr 2,919,000,000. Import sources (1973): France 49%; Ethiopia 12%; Japan 6%; U.K. 6%. Export destinations (1973): France 84%. Main exports: ships and boats 16%; skins and leather 7%.

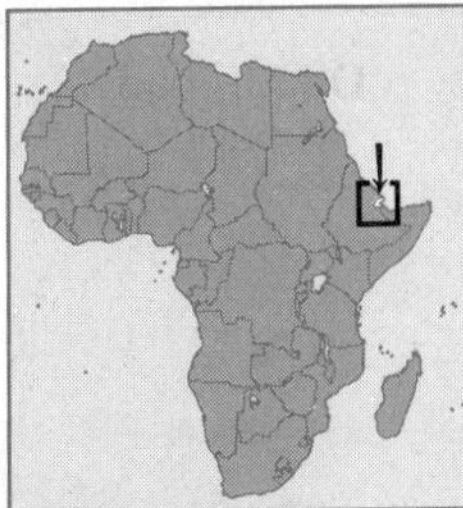

Djibouti

Dominica

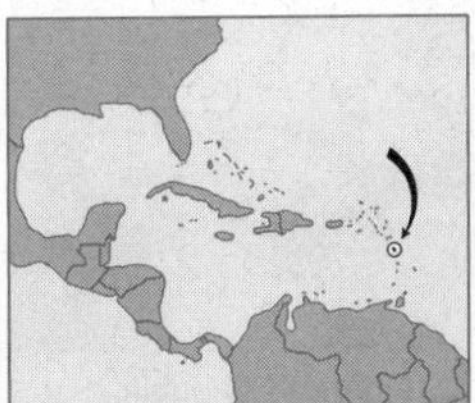

Dominica

A republic within the Commonwealth of Nations, Dominica, an island of the Lesser Antilles in the Caribbean Sea, lies between Guadeloupe to the north and Martinique to the south. Area: 772 sq km (300 sq mi). Pop. (1977 est.): 80,000. Cap.: Roseau (pop., 1978 est., 16,800). Presidents in 1979, Sir Louis Cools-Lartigue (interim) to January 16 and (acting) from June 15 to 16, Fred Degazon from January 16 to June 14, and Lenner Armour (acting) from June 21; prime ministers, Patrick R. John and, from June 21, Oliver Seraphine.

In early 1979 Patrick John's government was rumoured to be party to a plan to mount a mercenary invasion of Barbados, and in May a British television program alleged the invasion plan was part of a scheme involving South African investment in Dominica. An attempt to introduce legislation to halt local publication of the revelations and ban strikes in essential services brought a crowd of

Disasters: see page 54

Disciples of Christ: see Religion

Diseases: see Health and Disease

Divorce: see Demography

DOMINICA

Education. (1978–79) Primary, pupils 15,220, teachers 423; secondary, pupils 9,814, teachers 299; vocational, pupils 400, teachers 21; higher, students 154, teachers 8.

Finance and Trade. Monetary unit: East Caribbean dollar, with (Sept. 17, 1979) an official rate of ECar$2.70 to U.S. $1 (free rate of ECar$5.81 = £1 sterling). Budget (1976–77 est.): revenue ECar$28,517,000; expenditure ECar$30,984,000. Foreign trade (1976): imports ECar$49.8 million; exports ECar$29.1 million. Import sources (1975): U.K. 30%; U.S. 10%; Canada 10%. Export destinations (1975): U.K. 78%. Main exports (1975): bananas 58%; grapefruit 11%.

some 13,000 demonstrators to the government headquarters. It was broken up by Defence Force members, who shot indiscriminately into the crowd, leaving two dead and nine wounded. Within a month members of the ruling Labour Party had deserted the government, but John retained power until June 21, when Lenner Armour was sworn in as acting president with all-party support. Oliver Seraphine was appointed prime minister on the same day and announced that elections would be held within six months.

On August 30 Dominica was hit by Hurricane David, which ravaged the island for five hours with winds gusting up to 150 mph. At least 40 people died, 9,000 were injured, and 60,000 were made homeless. Essential services were knocked out, and almost all the banana plantations, Dominica's economic mainstay, were destroyed. Sixty percent of the already poor road system was destroyed, along with 80% of the schools. Much of the ground cover was stripped away, causing concern about long-term ecological damage. First estimates were that $185 million would be needed to rebuild the island. Though aid poured in from all over the world, recovery would probably take at least 20 years.

Earlier, the island's interim government signed the Declaration of St. George's, which established greater cooperation between St. Lucia, Grenada, and Dominica. (DAVID A. JESSOP)

Dominican Republic

Dominican Republic

Covering the eastern two-thirds of the Caribbean island of Hispaniola, the Dominican Republic is separated from Haiti, which occupies the western third, by a rugged mountain range. Area: 48,442 sq km (18,704 sq mi). Pop. (1979 est.): 5,275,400, including mulatto 75%; white 15%; Negro 10%. Cap. and largest city: Santo Domingo (pop., 1979 est., 1,103,400). Language: Spanish. Religion: mainly Roman Catholic (95%), with Protestant and Jewish minorities. President in 1979, Antonio Guzmán Fernández.

During 1979 there was much dissent and conflict within the Dominican Republic's ruling Partido Revolucionario Dominicano (PRD), and Pres. Antonio Guzmán Fernández was criticized for not carrying out the party's economic and monetary policies. After a Cabinet reshuffle in February–March, only two PRD members remained. The country's economy encountered difficulties during the first half of the year; depressed world prices affected its main export commodity, sugar, and oil imports were expected to cost up to $300 million. In midyear a balance of payments deficit of $100 million and a trade deficit of $400 million were forecast for 1979. In October the Rosario gold mines were nationalized. Unrest followed several local price rises for gasoline, and in August Guzmán decreed that public transportation would be taken over by the state.

At the end of August and early in September,

DOMINICAN REPUBLIC

Education. (1976–77) Primary, pupils 903,521, teachers 17,932; secondary, pupils 136,570, teachers 4,417; vocational, pupils 5,326, teachers 299; teacher training, students 1,353, teachers 49; higher, students 42,395, teaching staff 429.

Finance. Monetary unit: peso, at parity with the U.S. dollar, with a free rate (Sept. 17, 1979) of 2.15 pesos to £1 sterling. Gold, SDR's, and foreign exchange (June 1979) U.S. $223.6 million. Budget (1978 actual): revenue 596.2 million pesos; expenditure 663.6 million pesos. Gross national product (1977) 4,343,600,000 pesos. Money supply (March 1979) 462.3 million pesos. Cost of living (Santo Domingo; 1975 = 100; April 1979) 131.3.

Foreign Trade. (1978) Imports 1,018,400,000 pesos; exports 675 million pesos. Import sources: U.S. 43%; Venezuela 15%; Japan 8%; Netherlands Antilles 6%. Export destinations: U.S. 55%; Switzerland 9%; Venezuela 8%; Puerto Rico 6%; The Netherlands 6%. Main exports: sugar 25%; coffee 13%; cocoa 13%; ferronickel 11%; gold and alloys 11%; tobacco 7%; chemicals 5%.

Transport and Communications. Roads (1975) 11,844 km. Motor vehicles in use (1977): passenger 82,700; commercial 39,500. Railways (1977) *c.* 590 km. Telephones (Jan. 1978) 139,400. Radio receivers (Dec. 1977) 210,000. Television receivers (Dec. 1976) 160,000.

Agriculture. Production (in 000; metric tons; 1978): rice *c.* 308; sweet potatoes (1977) *c.* 65; cassava (1977) *c.* 175; sugar, raw value *c.* 1,150; dry beans *c.* 37; tomatoes *c.* 125; peanuts *c.* 68; oranges *c.* 71; avocados (1977) *c.* 131; mangoes *c.* 169; bananas *c.* 315; plantains (1977) *c.* 550; cocoa *c.* 34; coffee *c.* 45; tobacco *c.* 57. Livestock (in 000; June 1977): cattle 2,487; sheep 22; pigs 831; goats 285; horses 198; chickens *c.* 7,580.

Industry. Production (in 000; metric tons; 1977): cement 862; bauxite 576; nickel ore 25; gold (troy oz) 343; silver (troy oz) 1,852; petroleum products *c.* 1,190; electricity (kw-hr) *c.* 2,671,000.

An islander looks at the rubble that was left after Hurricane David leveled a Catholic church at San Cristóbal early in September.

UPI

Drama:
see Motion Pictures; Theatre

Dress:
see Fashion and Dress

Earthquakes:
see Earth Sciences

Hurricane David, followed by Hurricane Frederic, brought devastation to the country, killing more than 600 people and leaving 225,000 homeless. Floods were extensive, communications cut, and relief supplies hindered. Damage was estimated at $1 billion. Foodstuffs had to be imported to compensate for losses to the corn, sorghum, bean, plantain, and yucca crops. The 1979–80 sugar crop was estimated to have been cut by 30%. Financial aid came from international bodies and Venezuela, and the U.S. provided medical aid and helicopters.

(SARAH CAMERON)

Earth Sciences

GEOLOGY AND GEOCHEMISTRY

The U.S. Geological Survey celebrated its centennial in 1979. The original responsibility of the organization was to classify public lands and to examine the geologic structure, mineral resources, and products of the national domain. It expanded greatly after 1950 and in the late 1970s exerted a powerful influence on geologic and geochemical research, ranging from the ocean floor to other planets. Survey members were deeply involved with development of such natural resources as water, minerals, and energy, as well as with preservation of environmental quality.

The essential starting point in most geologic research is an accurate map, and the U.S. Geological Survey has become the nation's largest civilian mapmaking agency, producing many kinds of maps including those derived from satellite imagery. The Survey recently started a new computerized national Map and Chart Information System that offered greatly expanded and quicker service to map users. The new system could provide overnight listings from about 160,000 maps and charts, with coverage expected to expand to about one million maps by 1985.

The origin of mountain ranges continued to be a central theme in geology. Shortening of the crust by 100–200 km (1 km is 0.62 mi) during mountain building was commonly demonstrated by structural and stratigraphic analyses, which derive information, respectively, from the internal structure and layering of rocks. Significant advances in understanding have resulted in recent years from a combination of the traditional stratigraphic and paleogeographic approaches (paleogeography is the geography of the geologic past) with modern structural analysis techniques, including the analysis of strain in deformed rocks by X-ray goniometry, which reveals the responses of constituent minerals in the rocks to the deforming forces. There were advocates for the primary role of gravity in the development of mountain structures, but many investigators assigned a minor role to the former dogma of gravity sliding or spreading in connection with the development of belts of thrust and nappe structures, in which there has been overriding movement of one rock mass over another.

A major thrust structure was discovered by Cocorp, a consortium project for determination of the deep structure of continents by seismic methods, beneath the Appalachian mountain chain, which was formed when North America and Africa approached and collided between 450 million and 250 million years in the past. It appears that old crystalline rocks were pushed westward in three or four episodes over the top of younger sedimentary rocks. The buried sedimentary layer, 1–5 km thick, was traced for 250 km along the mountain range, at a depth of 6–10 km below the surface.

U.S. spacecraft Voyager 1 and Voyager 2 provided the first view of volcanic eruptions on an extraterrestrial body, Io, a satellite of Jupiter which is about the same size as the Earth's Moon. Voyager 1 revealed eight active volcanic vents, fountaining greenish gas and solid material to heights of 70–280 km, with ejection velocities of 1,800–3,300 km per hour. Each eruption continued for at least several hours, and some were apparently under continuous eruption during the entire 6.5-day observation period. Four months later Voyager 2 revealed that at least six of the volcanoes were still active, with plumes about the same size, but no new eruption sites were observed. Dozens of calderas were photographed, with surface temperatures more than 150° C (270° F) above the average surface temperature of Io. Dark areas on the surface were interpreted as lava flows and possibly recent flows of molten sulfur. The eruptions on Io are comparable in intensity with the greatest, rarest eruptions on the Earth, taking into account differences in gravity and atmospheric drag. Preliminary calculations suggested that gravitational interaction between Jupiter and Io may produce sufficient tidal heating within Io to create and power the volcanoes. (*See* SPACE EXPLORATION: *Special Report*.)

Explorers in the deep-sea submersible vessel "Alvin" discovered a special kind of eruption on the Earth's ocean floor, 2.5 km below the ocean surface. Along the crest of the submarine rise between the Pacific and Riviera lithospheric plates off Central America was found a series of chimney-like hydrothermal water vents several metres high, resembling miniature volcanoes, which are built from particles of metallic sulfides. Similar heaps of sulfide deposits, rich in silver, copper,

Scientists probing the ocean bottom were startled to find huge red tube worms nearly two miles below the surface of the ocean. These tube worms and other strange forms of life are supported by nutrients and hot water spewing out of vents in the Pacific Ocean floor.

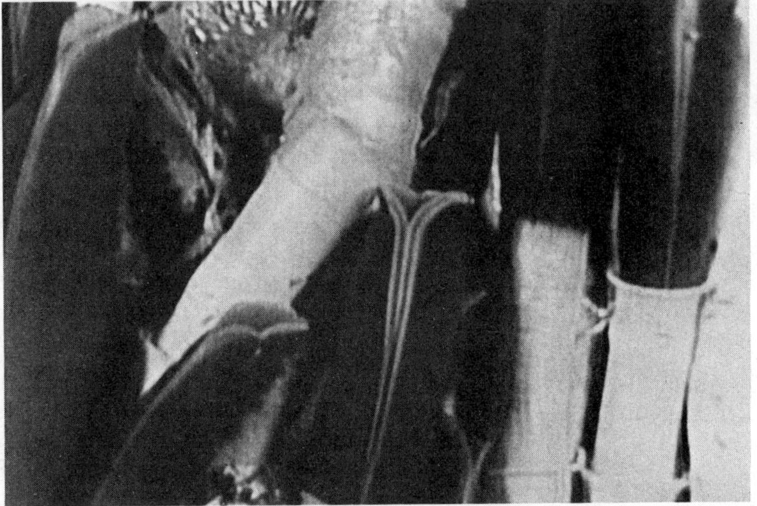

WIDE WORLD

UPI

At least 17,000 people had to be evacuated from villages on St. Vincent in the West Indies after Soufrière volcano erupted and spewed tons of ash and boulders high into the air on April 13.

zinc, cobalt, and lead, may extend for thousands of kilometres along other submarine divergent plate boundaries, the sites of seafloor spreading. In these regions ocean water percolates through cracks down to depths of 1.5 km or more, where it is heated by magma chambers and dissolves metallic elements from the surrounding rock. These elements are subsequently precipitated as insoluble compounds as the hot solutions (as much as 350° C, or 660° F) are sent fountaining through geysers on the ocean floor into the cool ocean water.

In these same environments, where the water temperature may be 15° C (59° F) in contrast with the normal 2° C (36° F) of surrounding ocean water, unique oases of marine life were first discovered in 1977. Subsequent dives found additional colonies, with species previously unknown. The most striking creature is a red sea worm 2.5 m (8 ft) long enclosed by a white, plasticlike tube. Each self-contained community appears to be sustained by geothermal energy instead of sunlight, with bacteria and a suitable concentration of hydrogen sulfide required to sustain the colony. The community dies if the hot-water geyser that supplies it ceases to flow.

In contrast with these local events, extinction of the dinosaurs and other animal species about 65 million years in the past occurred on a global scale. Recent geochemical evidence was found compatible with the hypothesis that the extinctions were associated with some extraterrestrial event, perhaps even a supernova. Trace-element studies of limestones from northern Italy revealed a 25-fold increase in the element iridium at the Cretaceous/Tertiary boundary. It was difficult to explain this abrupt increase by known geochemical processes, but iridium abundance in extraterrestrial material was known to be about 1,000 times that in the Earth's crust.

Paleontologists must also consider extraterrestrial sources for the origin of life. The brown and yellow colours pictured by Voyagers 1 and 2 for the clouds of Jupiter resemble the colours produced by organic compounds generated in laboratory experiments involving electrical discharges through gases corresponding to Jupiter's atmosphere. The pristine meteorites recovered recently from Antarctic ice were found to contain amino acids with properties suggesting that they are from pre-life chemical reactions somewhere in space.

Innovative ideas in paleontology keep the topics of the origin, evolution, and extinction of species in lively debate. Differences of opinion about the rise and diversification of new species relate to differences in approach. The classical view, based on the fossil record, is that species are merely segments in a linear progression of slow, continuous evolution. Frustration with the imperfect fossil record led to new approaches, using computer simulations for random generation of evolutionary patterns based on the equilibrium theory of modern ecology, without using the historical record of the fossils. Similarities were found between the computer-generated evolutionary patterns and real events in the fossil record.

In recent years many paleontologists favoured the model of punctuated equilibrium. In this view species normally evolve slowly, and most changes occur when small populations diverge rapidly into new forms during short intervals of time. Some of the species produced during these periods of adaptive radiation survive as distinctive new species. The episodes are rarely documented in the geologic record because they occur locally in place and time. The new theory and the appearance of major syntheses were stimulating more detailed examination of the fossil record.

The application of new techniques has extended the scope of experimental studies of minerals and rocks at high pressures and temperatures. For example, many recent studies were concentrating on the fractionation of trace elements between coexisting minerals and between minerals and melts. Analysis of elements present in trace amounts in the phases of a quenched heterogeneous sample (*i.e.*, a sample that has solidified into a mixture of distinct mineral regions) is very difficult for the small samples used in most high-pressure apparatus. Nevertheless, a successful method was developed using a beta-track technique. The trace element to be measured is labeled with a radioactive isotope that emits beta particles (electrons) as it decays, and the distribution and concentration of the element in the sample after the experiment is determined by counting the tracks left by beta particles in a layer of specially prepared plastic. Less than a thousandth of a gram of sample is needed for the analysis.

In addition to trace-element distributions, the technique was adapted to measure the percentage of melt produced as a function of temperature above the solidus, the temperature at which melting begins, of peridotite (the rock composing the Earth's upper mantle) at various pressures. Such measurements were fundamental to an understanding of the process of igneous rock formation, but they had defied conventional techniques. The experiments were also conducted in the presence of water or carbon dioxide, and the beta-track method provided values for the solubility of carbon dioxide in the liquid of partially melted rocks as a function of pressure and temperature.

(PETER JOHN WYLLIE)

[212.F.2.b–c; 214.A.5; 214.B.1.c; 231.D.1.b; 231.G; 241.D–G; 312.A and D]

WIDE WORLD

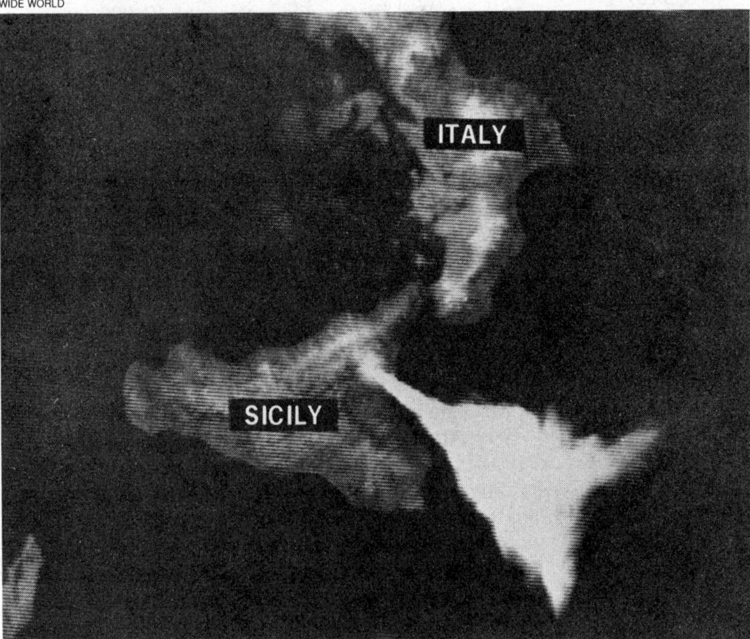

A satellite photograph clearly shows a huge plume of smoke arising from Mount Etna in Sicily in August.

GEOPHYSICS

Among significant earthquakes of the year, none was of magnitude 8 or greater and only ten were in the magnitude range of 7–8. Deaths numbered in the hundreds, including at least 199 persons as a result of an earthquake of magnitude 6.7–7.5 on January 16 in Iran, more than 100 by a shock of magnitude 7.2 in Yugoslavia and Albania on April 15, and 41 in eastern China on July 9 by a relatively small shock of magnitude 5.3–6. On November 14 another earthquake in Iran, of magnitude 6.7, damaged 14 mud-brick villages and killed several hundred persons. The largest shock reported in recent months, of magnitude 7.8, took place off the coast of Oaxaca, Mexico, on Nov. 29, 1978, while the second largest, of magnitude 7.7, occurred on Feb. 28, 1979, in southeastern Alaska. Early reports gave a magnitude of 7.7–8.1 to an earthquake that rocked the Colombia-Ecuador border region on December 13. The two most damaging earthquakes were the magnitude 6.4 shock on June 2, which resulted in $1.5 million in damage to the town of Cadoux, Western Australia, and the magnitude 6.4 earthquake of July 1, which resulted in $2 million in damage to petroleum-loading facilities at Puerto Armuelles in Panama.

A promising method for long-range earthquake forecasting was gaining acceptance. It involved the identification of seismic gaps in the thousands of kilometres of known seismic belts around the world. A seismic gap is a normally active area that has not experienced a large earthquake for an extended period. Successful forecast of the large earthquake off the coast of Oaxaca in 1978 illustrates the approach. First, an unusual absence of moderate earthquakes in the magnitude range of 4–7 was noted. Second, a seismic gap was identified in which a major earthquake had not occurred for many years. These conditions seemed so promising near Oaxaca that a local network to monitor minor seismic activity was installed and operating prior to the main shock. Monitoring revealed a familiar, though not necessarily indicative, pattern of no activity followed by 12 hours of intensive minor shocks (less than magnitude 3.6), and then an 18-hour quiet period immediately preceding the large shock.

Prognostication by identification of seismic gaps cannot be called prediction because the time of occurrence cannot be foreseen except in a very general way. Efforts were being concentrated, however, on the search for recognizable short-range precursors. Such things as cessation of intermediate shocks in the area, duration of quiescence to date, determination of unusually high crustal stress, possible migration patterns in which some space/time sequence can be identified, and volcanic activity along lithospheric plate boundaries were all regarded as promising indicators. Two of the problems that remained were whether the existence of a gap necessarily presages the occurrence of a large shock and whether the absence of a gap precludes one. Until definitive precursors were identified, these problems would remain persist.

At least 15 large volcanoes around the world were observed in continuous or nearly continuous activity throughout the year. Along with general eruptions, lava flows, ash falls, and pumice islands were recorded several tragic occurrences resulting in loss of life and property. On February 21 poisonous gas and lava from the Dieng volcanic complex in Indonesia killed at least 175 persons

WIDE WORLD

Scientists placed delicate sensing instruments at Terrapin Point at Niagara Falls in July after there were indications of an earth shift on the Horseshoe Falls side of the cataract.

and resulted in the evacuation of 17,000 from six nearby villages. On April 29 heavy rainfall mobilized volcanic material on the flanks of Merapi volcano in Sumatra, causing extensive landslides that killed 80 persons and severely damaged seven villages. Karkar volcano, off the northern coast of New Guinea, had been the scene of varied and sometimes severe activity for many months. On March 8 a severe eruption, accompanied by a blast of hot gas and ejecta, devastated the southeast quadrant of the caldera, killing two veteran volcanologists who were camping just below the rim.

Two well-known volcanoes, Soufrière on St. Vincent in the West Indies and Etna in Sicily, exhibited nearly constant activity throughout the year. The former reached a peak of activity during early April, resulting in the evacuation of at least 17,000 residents who were not allowed to return home until May 14. Mount Etna, which was under extensive study by volcanologists and others, was also a tourist attraction due to its long and colourful history. For these reasons a number of persons were close to the crater when on September 12 a severe and unexpected explosion killed at least 9 persons and severely injured 20.

Because the crust of the Earth is produced from the mantle and because convection cells in the mantle are postulated as the driving force for continental migration, it is especially important to determine mantle structure and history. Geochemists were studying the composition of basalts, which are the primal rocks derived directly from the mantle. Of special significance were determinations of the isotopic ratios of rubidium-strontium, uranium-lead, and samarium-neodymium in order to postulate evolution of the mantle. Until recently, variations in the results were explained on various grounds that still left the mantle as a homogeneous entity. However, subsurface exploration in the Atlantic, particularly along the mid-ocean ridges, and studies conducted on Atlantic islands and in the U.S. in Yellowstone Park and on Hawaii were indicating a marked differentiation within the mantle. Research was continuing to determine which of the current theories best fit the data. Candidates included a two-layer model of the mantle comprising an asthenosphere, which is a partially molten layer lying 75–250 km (45–150 mi) below the surface, and another deeper source connected to the surface by plumes of partially melted rock. The shallower source would produce the basaltic magmas of the mid-ocean ridges, whereas the plumes would be evidenced by such islands as Hawaii, Iceland, and the Azores. A second model was postulated by those who maintained that at least three sources were needed to explain the new data. (RUTLAGE J. BRAZEE)
[212.D.4; 213.A.2; 213.B and D; 241.D]

HYDROLOGY

Flooding in the U.S. and Puerto Rico during 1979 caused more than 100 deaths and $3 billion in property damage. Records dating back to 1925 indicate that 1979 ranks second in monetary losses in the nation due to flooding. Some of the worst flooding in their history occurred in April in central

NATIONAL CLIMATIC CENTER—NOAA

Satellite photo captured the intensity of Hurricane David as the storm traveled northward past Palm Beach, Florida, on September 3. Dotted lines outline Florida, Cuba, and The Bahamas and depict lines of latitude and longitude.

Mississippi and Alabama. Tidal flooding caused by Hurricanes Frederic and David resulted in major damage along the Gulf Coast in Alabama, Florida, and Mississippi. During September the combined flow of the five largest U.S. rivers—the Mississippi, St. Lawrence, Columbia, Ohio, and Missouri—averaged 764,000,000,000 gal a day, which was 25% above normal and 8% higher than 1978.

Major spring flooding in Canada resulted in heavy property damage in Saskatchewan, Manitoba, and Ontario. Heavier-than-normal winter snow accumulation and low temperatures during early April combined with rains and rapid warming to cause severe flooding in the Red River basin south of Winnipeg, Man. It was estimated that 12,000 people were affected by the April 25 flood in the Red River basin.

The International Joint Commission, a bilateral governmental body established to solve problems relating to the U.S.-Canadian frontier, reported a further decline in total phosphorus concentrations in Lake Michigan and Lake Ontario. The most noticeable decline was along the north shore of Lake Ontario. Although improvement of water quality in the Great Lakes was sought from upgrading of municipal sewage treatment plants, only about 60% of municipal sewage received complete treatment. A topic of current concern in the Great Lakes region was long-range transport of air pollutants and "acid rain." The increasing acidity of rain and snow was related to burning of fossil fuels.

A U.S. Geological Survey report pointed out that about 310 sq km (120 sq mi) of land near Phoenix, Ariz., had subsided more than 3.1 m (7 ft) since 1952 because of a lowering of groundwater levels as a result of groundwater withdrawal. Water levels declined as much as 120 m (400 ft) from 1923 to 1979. The land subsidence produced many narrow fissures that subsequently widened into deep gullies from erosion and damaged highways, railroad beds, farmlands, irrigation supply systems, and private residences.

Industrial and domestic wastes in the New River as it flows from Mexico into the U.S. at Calexico, Calif., were causing major water-quality problems. High levels of bacteria and organic solids and absence of dissolved oxygen were killing fish and lowering recreational value along the U.S. reach of the river. The problem was under investigation by the International Boundary and Water Commission, a joint U.S.-Mexican effort.

In 1979 many technical symposia covered topics of concern for hydrologists. Noteworthy international symposia were presented in India on hydrologic aspects of droughts, in Australia on hydrology of regions of low precipitation, in Mexico City on water for human survival, and in the U.S.S.R. on methods for estimating groundwater resources. The American Water Resources Association meeting in Las Vegas, Nev., dealt with water policy, water use, and use of scientific information in water resources planning. The National Water Well Association meeting in Oklahoma City highlighted hydrology of regions that yield coal, oil, and uranium. The Geological Society of America meeting in San Diego sponsored a symposium on water-quality management. The American Geophysical Union sponsored a symposium in San Francisco on organic contaminants in groundwater. (JOHN E. MOORE)

[222.A.2.b; 232.C.1–2]

UPI

Streets in Chicago resembled an Arctic village after more than 20 inches of snow hit the city on January 14.

METEOROLOGY

In the continuing effort to "do something about the weather" the World Meteorological Organization (WMO) and its 151 constituent member nations and territories expanded their operations, promoted research programs and technological improvements, and extended cooperation with other leading scientific institutions and universities. In February the World Climate Conference convened in Geneva under WMO auspices, and in April and May the eighth Congress of WMO provided authority and financing for new programs in meteorology during the ensuing four-year period.

International cooperation in weather reporting and forecasting and in establishment of meteorologic agencies and institutions has been very successful for longer than a century, effective often during wartime when other fields of cooperation among nations have broken down. The worldwide systems of communications for weather reports, forecasts, and storm warnings are vital to the day-to-day planning and operations of the business and social world, and this relationship grew stronger during 1979 as world problems became more complex and public concern about air pollution, variations in weather and climate, and kindred threats to human survival increased.

Among the grave problems brought into focus by the February conference was man's unintentional modification of climate. Evidence available in 1979 indicated that stratospheric pollution by carbon dioxide from uncontrolled burning of fuels and by other contaminants that could change the Earth's radiation balance was inevitable unless practical corrective ways could be devised.

The Global Atmospheric Research Program (GARP) embraced the greatest approach ever undertaken toward comprehensive scientific analysis and broad understanding of meteorologic phenomena and the Earth's weather. This grand concept was the logical outgrowth of the International Geophysical Year of 1957–58 and the consequent interest and optimism among scientists and

WIDE WORLD

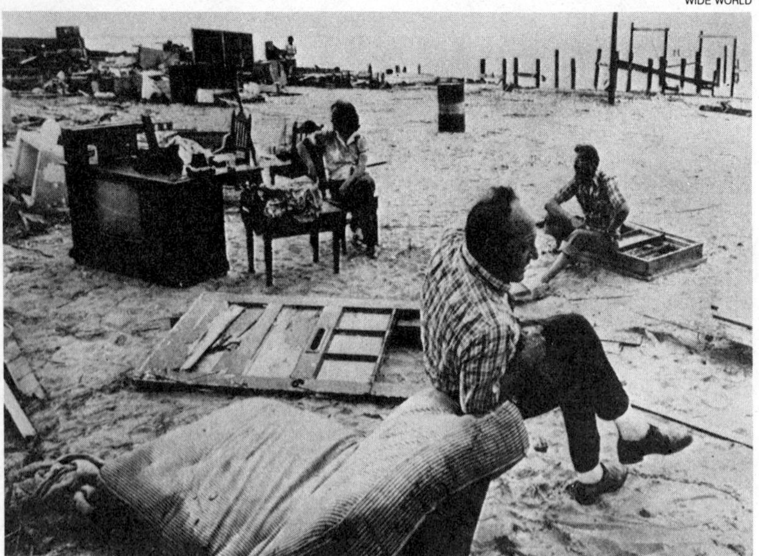

Residents guarded what was left of their possessions after Hurricane Frederic leveled their homes on Dauphin Island, Alabama, in September.

world leaders. The scope and intellectual depth of its conception and organization for worldwide cooperation among nations were unparalleled. With the participation of more than 140 countries, GARP began its field operational phase (data gathering) in December 1978; its intensive analysis and research studies were expected to run at least through the 1980s.

The activities of GARP during 1979 were designated by GWE, an acronym for the Global Weather Experiment (previously termed FGGE, for First GARP Global Experiment). Its descriptions in various journals, among them the *Bulletin of the American Meteorological Society* for June 1979, cited important roles for the World Weather Watch (WWW), geostationary satellites and other space orbiting systems, the European Space Agency (SPA), aircraft dropsonde systems (parachuted measuring instruments), ocean weather stations (specially equipped ships), automatic data-recording buoys, constant-level high-altitude balloons, and other observational and data-recording systems. Huge gaps in data from the atmosphere and oceans of the Southern Hemisphere and polar regions have prevented accurate analysis in the past; these gaps would be filled in part by data obtained by floating constant-level balloons.

The success of numerous programs based on international or interagency cooperation during the year was most encouraging. The policy of seeking comprehensive and wholly objective analysis and knowledge was evident in the joint supervision of GARP programs by WMO and the International Council of Scientific Unions (ICSU). Whereas WMO is the organization of weather service operating bodies, mostly governmental, ICSU is made up mostly of nongovernmental members from universities, institutes, and other centres of research.

In August and September two major Atlantic tropical storms took heavy tolls in life and property in the Caribbean and along the Atlantic and Gulf coasts of the U.S. Hurricane David, which formed off the Cape Verde Islands in late August, achieved winds of 240 kph (kilometres per hour; 150 mph) before dissipating itself inland along the U.S. East Coast. Its swath of destruction crossed the Caribbean island of Dominica on August 30, leaving at least 40 persons dead and 60,000 homeless. The next day David's winds and tides wreaked their greatest damage in the Dominican Republic, causing 600 deaths and more than $1 billion in losses to industry and agriculture. After battering Haiti, Cuba, and The Bahamas, the hurricane struck Florida on September 3 and Georgia and the Carolinas a day later with approximately 140-kph (90-mph) winds; at least 16 deaths in the U.S. were blamed on the storm.

Within two weeks another storm of hurricane status, christened Frederic, began hampering disaster relief efforts that had been mounted in the wake of David. On September 12 Frederic ravaged the U.S. Gulf Coast with 210-kph (130-mph) winds, destroying homes, highways, and coastal industries along a broad front in Florida, Alabama, and Mississippi and causing at least eight deaths. (F. W. REICHELDERFER)

[221.B.5.b; 224.C; 224.D.2.c.iii]

Eastern European Literature:
see Literature

Eastern Non-Chalcedonian Churches:
see Religion

Eastern Orthodox Churches:
see Religion

Ecology:
see Environment; Life Sciences

OCEANOGRAPHY

On Oct. 10, 1978, a short circuit in its power supply system caused the first U.S. oceanographic satellite, Seasat, to cease operation after only three months in orbit. During this time it had scanned 95% of the world's oceans every 36 hours from a height of 800 km (500 mi), and in 1979 the data that it returned were subjected to detailed analysis.

Seasat carried five sensors on board. A radar altimeter, designed to measure the distance from the satellite to the sea surface with a precision of less than ten centimetres (five inches), readily detected ocean tides over the Patagonian Shelf (off the Atlantic coast of Argentina) as well as the roughly one-metre (three-foot) rise in sea level across the Gulf Stream flow and perpendicular to the rotation of the Earth. A microwave scatterometer, designed to measure surface winds by scattering microwaves from the shortest wind-driven ocean-surface waves, proved able to map surface winds with an accuracy of several metres per second provided that there was no rainfall and that the overall pattern of the wind was already known (from surface observations or satellite cloud images). A synthetic aperture radar, which combines into a single high-resolution image all returning radar echoes received from each point of the sea surface during the entire time that the point is visible from the satellite, yielded images of the sea surface on which individual ships were readily visible. These images showed not only systems of wind-driven surface waves and internal waves but also large-scale patterns of unknown origin.

A radiometer aboard Seasat provided images of the sea surface in both visible and infrared light; the infrared images could be converted into maps of sea surface temperature showing horizontal temperature variations as small as a few degrees Celsius. A multichannel microwave radiometer imaged the sea surface by recording its emission of several kinds of microwaves in order to estimate sea surface temperature and surface winds. An important by-product of the use of this instrument, so far not completely studied, was the ability to estimate the amount of water vapour and liquid water in the air between satellite and ocean.

In spite of Seasat's premature demise, the mission was a noteworthy success in demonstrating the potential of remote sensing of the ocean from space. It was a forerunner of much future research, with practical applications ranging from wave forecasts to climate prediction.

Remote sensing is not the only tool needed in studying the ocean, the depths of which are opaque to visual, infrared, and microwave radiation. The oceans, however, are transparent to sound waves, and during the fall of 1979 scientists were attempting to measure ocean currents by examining their effects on sound waves passed through them. An array of buoys roughly 160 km (100 mi) across, with acoustic receivers on some buoys listening to acoustic transmitters on others, was set out in the western Atlantic. Currents within the array would be deduced using techniques borrowed from geophysicists, who probe the structure of the Earth by measuring the travel times of seismic waves, and from medical scientists, who build up a detailed picture of the portion of the body they wish to study by combining many X-ray images in a process called tomography. Its oceanic adaptation, acoustic tomography, could prove valuable in long-term monitoring of ocean currents and their variation. Such monitoring was essential in plans to understand ocean circulation and its role in global climate.

The specially outfitted deep-sea drilling ship "Glomar Challenger" has spent the past decade drilling into the seafloor at locations around the globe in an effort to confirm and amplify the hypothesis of seafloor spreading. According to this concept oceanic crust is continuously being formed at mid-ocean ridges from which it spreads laterally toward ocean trenches; there it plunges beneath other portions of the seafloor. En route, the seafloor becomes covered with sediments deposited from the ocean above. Their thickness and composition contain a history of the Earth, which scientists were learning to read.

At the beginning of the year, the "Glomar Challenger" completed a study in the Gulf of California. Using a new sampling tool, a hydraulic piston corer, which penetrates the sediment with minimal disturbance, the ship's crew recovered a core section 200 m (660 ft) long in which sedimentary layers laid down in successive years could be identified year by year. Widespread use of such a corer could open the way for reconstruction of global climate and its variations over long periods of the past. Subsequent work in the vicinity of the Middle America Trench, along the Pacific coast of Mexico and Central America, suggested that the former connection between the Pacific Ocean and Caribbean Sea may not have been as large as was once believed. Thereafter, drilling progressed over the Galápagos Rift, a centre of seafloor spreading where seawater is known to percolate through the crust in a slow circulation driven by subcrustal heating. (MYRL C. HENDERSHOTT)

[223; 231.D.1.b; 231.G; 241.G]

See also Disasters; Energy; Life Sciences; Mining and Quarrying; Physics; Space Exploration; Speleology.

Economy, World

The most prominent feature of the world economy during 1979 was an acceleration in inflation. This, in turn, led to the reemergence of cautious and, in some cases, restrictive monetary policies on the part of the authorities, a development that became particularly pronounced during the second half of the year. As a result, by late 1979 the tempo of business activity was slowing down in most developed countries, and the prospects were for a further loss of momentum in 1980.

Although the rate of price increases was beginning to accelerate as early as the autumn of 1978, faster inflation during 1979 was not the result of the pressure of demand but of the large increase in the cost of raw materials. Although this was true of most commodities, the major offender was oil. Nor was the rise in oil prices a consequence of a significant expansion in the developed world's oil consumption. While the various conservation policies were not, in general, working well, in the autumn of 1979 it was estimated that net oil imports into the large developed countries would be some 1% higher during the year than in 1978. The principal cause of the hike in oil prices was the Iranian revolution and the consequent reduction in supplies from that country. At the same time some oil producers were determined to offset the effect of the fall in the value of the dollar on their revenues. As a result of these factors the 14.5% rise that originally was to be implemented by the end of 1979 was already a reality by April. Further

CHART 1

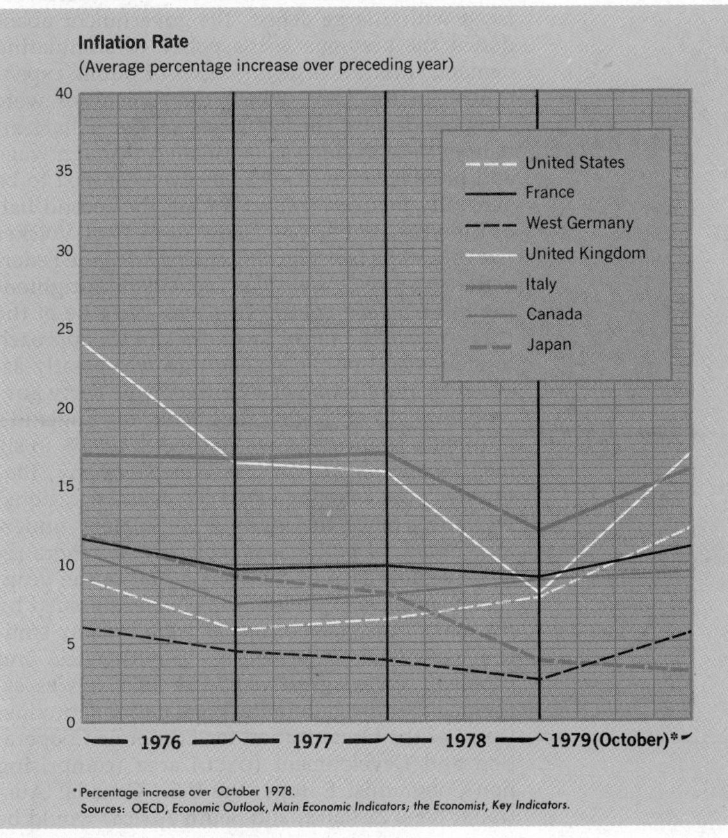

Table I. Real Changes in Gross National Products of OECD Countries

% change, seasonally adjusted at annual rates

Country	Average 1965–66 to 1975–76	Change from previous year 1978	1979*
Canada	4.7	3.4	3.50
France	4.7	3.3	3.00
Germany, West	3.3	3.4	3.75
Italy	4.1	2.6	4.25
Japan	8.2	5.6	5.50
United Kingdom	2.1	3.2	1.25
United States	2.7	4.0	2.75
Total major countries	4.0	4.0	3.50
Australia	4.6	2.7	4.00
Austria	4.5	1.5	3.25
Belgium	4.1	1.6	2.50
Denmark	3.3	1.0	2.50
Finland	4.6	2.5	4.50
Greece	6.2	6.2	3.25
Ireland	4.0	7.0	4.25
Netherlands, The	4.7	2.5	3.00
New Zealand	3.2	0.5	2.75
Norway	4.6	3.5	2.00
Spain	6.3	2.9	3.25
Sweden	3.1	2.8	4.75
Switzerland	2.2	0.9	1.25
Total OECD countries	4.3	2.4	3.00

*Estimate.
Source: Adapted from OECD, *Economic Outlook*, July 1979.

increases took place in subsequent months, and it was calculated in late 1979 that by the start of 1980 oil prices would have risen in a year by approximately 40% to about $23 per barrel. The prices of other commodities also rose, although less rapidly. At the end of November *The Economist* dollar commodity index (which excludes oil) was 24.8% higher than in the corresponding period of 1978.

Faced with this situation, most countries were forced to tighten their monetary and fiscal policies. In Japan the official discount rate was increased as early as April and again in July. Furthermore, faced with a large deficit, the government abandoned the previous year's policy of stimulating demand through large injections of public expenditure. In the U.S., where the difficulties were compounded by the weakness of the dollar, attempts were made to slow inflation through wage and price policies. These, however, proved to be generally ineffective, and during the second half of the year, under the influence of Paul Volcker (*see* BIOGRAPHIES), the new chairman of the Federal Reserve Board, there was a considerable tightening in monetary policy. This was also true of the U.K., where the move toward a stricter approach to money and public expenditure was greatly assisted by the election of a Conservative Party government. As a result the Bank of England's minimum lending rate was increased by 5% in six months to a record 17%. In West Germany, too, interest rates were increased on several occasions, while in France the initially stimulatory undertone of official policy was replaced by a more restrictive approach in the second half of the year.

Nevertheless, although the policies pursued by the major developed countries were broadly similar, individual performances, growth rates, and problems varied greatly. In late 1979 it was estimated that the gain in the gross national product (GNP) of the Organization for Economic Cooperation and Development (OECD) area (comprising non-Communist Europe, the U.S., Canada, Australia, New Zealand, and South Africa) would be about 3.5%, marginally below the advance of 3.8% recorded in 1978. As in previous years the star performer was Japan with a GNP growth of 5.5–6%. In contrast to the previous year, however, the distinction for the slowest advance went to the United Kingdom (approximately 1.3%). In West Germany there was a modest acceleration from 3.5% in 1978 to approximately 4%. Elsewhere in Europe Italy appeared to be heading for a gain of some 4%, compared with the previous year's 2.2%, while in France the indications were that the 1978 growth rate of 3% would be exceeded by a small margin. In the U.S. growth was highly uneven during the year; the late 1979 estimates pointed to a gain of between 2 and 2.5%, representing a considerable decline from the 4% growth rate chalked up in 1978.

In contrast to GNP, industrial production was thought to have done a little better than in 1978 in most OECD countries. This resulted in a modest decline in the number of jobless; in the U.K. unemployment (expressed as a percentage of the labour force) fell from 5.6% in January to 5.2% in September; in the U.S. it was down to 5.6% in the second quarter from 5.9% 12 months previously, but by October it was back to 6%; in West Germany the October figure was 3.6%, compared with 4.3% a year previously. France, however, did not share in this trend; although industrial growth was faster than in 1978, structural changes led to an increase in the unemployment rate from 6.1% in October 1978 to 6.7% in the autumn of 1979. The highest rates, over 7.5%, were experienced in Canada and Italy, although in the case of Canada this represented a decrease from the previous year.

Despite the almost universal preoccupation with prices, the rate of inflation exhibited marked variation from country to country, with the effect of higher oil and commodity prices being dampened or exacerbated by changes in the external value of individual currencies. One of the weakest currencies was the dollar (although its trade-weighted index rose from 83.5 in January to 85.1 in December), which ensured that consumer prices were registering a 13% annual rate of increase by late autumn. The Japanese yen also fell rapidly in the wake of the large appreciation in 1978, but up to the end of 1979 only a small part of the resulting price effect found its way into consumer prices, which were rising at an annual rate of only about 4%. The West German and French currencies also faced some pressure, but in the case of West Germany consumer prices in late 1979 exceeded the previous year's level by only about 5.5%, whereas for France the comparable figure stood at nearly 12%. Paradoxically, sterling was one of the strongest currencies during the year, and yet the inflation rate in the U.K. was approximately 17% by late 1979. However, a significant part of this, perhaps as much as 5–6%, was due to the increase in value-added tax introduced in the June budget to cover the cost of reductions in personal taxation. All in all, the evidence was that the average level of inflation for the OECD area would show a significant acceleration; in 1978 the figure was 7.9%, but the latest indications were that the 1979 result would be somewhat in excess of 10%.

KEYSTONE

Ministers of 13 OPEC member countries voted to increase crude oil prices an average of 16% when they met June 28 in Geneva.

In 1978 the less developed countries faced serious problems, including high rates of inflation in the developed world and a deterioration in their terms of trade. Nevertheless, their economic growth rate was in excess of that of the OECD area. The initial indications for 1979 pointed to a broadly similar picture. Although non-oil-producing countries were seriously affected by the high price of oil, this was partially offset by the relatively fast rise in the prices of other commodities, especially metals and some foodstuffs. Nevertheless, many countries of the less developed world faced serious balance of payments deficits, which, once again, appeared to have depressed their growth to somewhat below the historical trend.

NATIONAL ECONOMIC POLICIES

Developed Market Economies. UNITED STATES. Following four years of vigorous expansion, the U.S. economy during 1979 was widely expected to enter into a "growth recession" phase before picking up again in 1980 in time for the presidential election. Although the first half of the year broadly fitted this pattern, by the summer the economic indicators began pointing upward, and the third-quarter figures for the GNP confirmed the sharp rebound. This period also coincided with strong demand for credit, which, coupled with the accelerating inflation at home and the weakness of the dollar on the foreign exchange markets, led to the adoption of an increasingly restrictive monetary stance by the authorities. The year drew to a close amid exaggerated fears that the punitive interest rates and the monetary squeeze were pushing the economy into a sharp recession, which could—if it turned out to be virulent and long lasting—drag down the rest of the world as in the 1973–75 recession.

The opening period of the year was influenced on the one hand by the surprising buoyancy of the economy in late 1978 and on the other by the restrictive measures introduced in November 1978 that were beginning to take effect. On balance a slowdown was quite likely, but the meagre increase of 0.4% registered by the GNP in the first quarter was surprisingly low. This was followed by shocking figures for the second quarter, which showed that the economy had declined at an annual rate of 2.3%. The recession appeared to have arrived earlier than expected, contradicting the government's view held at the start of the year that GNP would grow by 3.3% during 1979. The weakness of the economy was particularly in evidence in the personal sector, where, following the Christmas 1978 spending spree, consumers' resolve to rebuild savings was reinforced by a decline in real incomes. Sales of both nondurable and durable goods were sluggish. Automobile sales in the spring and early summer were a major casual-

Table II. Percentage Changes in Consumer Prices in Selected OECD Countries

Country	Average 1961–70	Average 1971–76	1977	1978	Latest month* 1979
Canada	2.7	7.4	8.0	9.0	9.5
France	4.0	8.9	9.4	9.1	11.0
Germany, West	2.7	5.9	3.9	2.6	5.3
Italy	3.9	12.2	17.0	12.1	16.0
Japan	5.8	11.1	8.1	3.8	3.1
United Kingdom	4.1	13.6	15.9	8.3	17.0
United States	2.8	6.6	6.5	7.7	12.2
Australia	2.5	10.2	12.3	7.9	9.2
Austria	3.6	7.3	5.5	3.6	3.7
Belgium	3.0	8.5	7.1	4.5	4.6
Denmark	5.9	9.2	11.1	10.0	12.8
Finland	5.0	12.1	12.2	7.8	7.7
Greece	2.1	12.5	12.1	12.6	20.9
Iceland	11.9	26.0	29.9	44.9	41.9
Ireland	4.8	14.0	13.6	7.6	13.6
Luxembourg	2.6	7.6	6.7	3.1	5.1
Netherlands, The	4.1	8.7	6.4	4.1	3.9
New Zealand	3.8	11.3	14.3	12.0	15.2
Norway	4.5	8.5	9.1	8.1	3.5
Portugal	3.9	16.0	27.2	22.6	25.8
Spain	6.0	13.0	24.5	19.7	15.5
Sweden	4.0	8.3	11.4	10.0	7.9
Switzerland	3.3	6.7	1.3	1.1	4.9
Turkey	5.9	18.4	26.0	61.9	56.4
Total OECD	3.4	8.6	8.9	7.9	11.8

*Twelve-month rate of change.
Sources: OECD, *Economic Outlook*, July 1979; OECD, *Main Economic Indicators*; The Economist, *Key Indicators*.

Table III. Total Employment in Selected Countries
(1975=100)

Country	1976	1977	1978	1979 First quarter	1979 Second quarter	1979 Third quarter
Australia	103	105	105	105	106	106
Canada	102	104	107	106	111	116
France	99	99	97	97	96	97
Germany, West	99	99	100	100	100	...
Italy	101	102	102	101	102	105
Japan	101	102	104	102	106	106
Sweden	101	101	101	101	103	104
United Kingdom	99	100	100	115	117	...
United States	103	107	111	112	114	116

Source: OECD, *Main Economic Indicators.*

ty. Even growth in consumer credit tapered off, having held up reasonably well until the spring. Residential investment, however, followed a different profile. Having declined early in the year, it recovered strongly in the spring. In spite of the high cost of housing and the rising cost of mortgages, demand remained buoyant, as it represented a hedge against inflation.

Industrial production reflected the demand pattern fairly closely, with output of consumer goods following an erratic but downward trend while the production of business equipment and materials remained fairly strong. Against a background of weakening company profits and high interest rates, orders for capital goods remained flat. On a more encouraging note the decline in industrial production did not result in a sharp inventory buildup, indicating that the manufacturers could read the economic signs adequately and adjust production levels accordingly. As production slowed down and businessmen grew more cautious in the face of a retreat by the consumers, unemployment bottomed out at 5.2% in May—the lowest point reached in five years—and then began a gradual but steady climb to reach 6% in November.

Meanwhile, inflation, which was to dominate the economic scene for the remainder of the year, rose steadily, leaving the price guidelines of Pres. Jimmy Carter well behind. In the first half of the year consumer prices increased at an annual rate of 13.2%. As in other OECD countries the main culprit was oil prices. However, other factors such as housing costs also contributed.

Given the economic forecasts of the government at the start of the year, it was not surprising that the stance of fiscal policy, as unveiled in the January budget for the fiscal year beginning in October 1979, was mildly restrictive. It attached a high priority to reducing inflation and accordingly proposed virtually no increase in real expenditure except for defense, which was expected to rise by 3%. New spending programs and tax initiatives were restrained or deferred. The proposed deficit of $29 billion was in line with the commitment made in the counterinflation program and compared favourably with a deficit of $37.5 billion then projected for 1978–79.

Apart from the budget the counterinflation program represented the administration's other policy instrument for controlling inflation. The price guidelines were modified in March to prevent companies from making all the allowable increases in the second half of the fiscal year. In April, in the first major test of the pay guidelines, the trucking industry reached an agreement with the Teamsters Union that provided for an increase of 30% over three years. The agreement came in the wake of a ten-day strike and, although by some nimble arithmetic the administration claimed it was within the guidelines, it was far in excess of the 22.5% normally allowable and weakened the program. A second major blow came in May when a federal court ruled that the withholding of federal government contracts from companies that did not follow the wage/price guidelines was unconstitutional.

Thus, monetary policy again became the first line of defense against inflation. Although in the spring the money supply was expanding in excess of the Federal Reserve Board's target, it was judged not to be excessive taken over a six-month period. During the summer, however, both money supply and inflation raced ahead, the latter reaching 13% on an annual basis. At the same time demand for credit remained strong. During the first month of his tenure as chairman of the Federal Reserve Board, Paul Volcker made a series of decisive moves. He raised the federal funds rate (the rate banks charge each other for overnight loans) to 11.5% and the discount rate (the rate the board charges to its member banks) to a record 10.5%. The commercial banks responded by increasing their prime rates to 13%. However, these measures, harsh as they seemed at the time, proved to be insufficient to dampen the demand for credit, strengthen the dollar, and defuse the explosive rise in the price of gold, which rose from $250 per troy ounce in June to more than $500 per troy ounce by the year's end.

Leaving the International Monetary Fund (IMF) annual meeting in Belgrade, Yugos., before it was finished, Volcker rushed home to announce on October 6 a stunning three-point package. The discount rate was raised from 11 to 12% (having gone up from 10.5 to 11% only two weeks previously). This bombshell was accompanied by a rise in reserve requirements on any increase in a broad range of bank liabilities, including Eurodollar borrowings. The third point was the most radical one: the Federal Reserve Board announced that from then on it was shifting the focus of monetary policy away from the interest rate for federal funds and toward curbing bank reserve growth and thus credit creation. In a nutshell the significance of the October package was that the board had implicitly admitted that the basic causes of the dollar's weakness were domestic. Furthermore, the steps taken to rectify a number of basic weaknesses in its own methods of monetary control confirmed the growing ingenuity of the U.S. banks in finding new ways to finance credit expansion outside the officially defined money supply.

The immediate effect of the Volcker package was a leapfrogging increase in the prime rates of commercial banks to the dizzy heights of 15¾% by mid-November. Interest rates were expected to peak at about that level, and when the economic statistics published in December showed a slowdown in loan demand it led to a cautious 0.5% drop in the prime rates.

United Kingdom. In 1979 the British economy was characterized by sluggish growth and a radical change in economic policy. Although the preceding year recorded a relatively good gain of 2.7% in the volume of gross domestic product, 1979 opened on a fairly gloomy note. This was largely the result of extensive labour disputes and industrial action arising out of the authorities' attempt to implement yet another round of incomes policy. This attempt was unsuccessful, and the resulting dislocation led to a decline in output in the opening quarter of the year as well as the emergence of a large balance of payments deficit. This, together with signs of an acceleration in inflation, weakened the already precarious position of the Labour Party government, and in the May general election a Conservative Party government, led by Margaret Thatcher, was returned to power with a substantial majority.

But this was a Conservative government with a difference. Unlike its predecessors, its strategy was, and continued to be, based on a reduction in direct government influence in the economy, a large cut in public expenditures, a shift from direct to indirect taxation, and a greater reliance on monetary as opposed to fiscal methods of controlling the economy. Thatcher's new team wasted no time in putting these principles, which represented a fundamental departure from the policy pursued by all postwar governments, into effect. Accordingly, in the June budget the chancellor of the Exchequer announced substantial cuts in income tax, to be compensated for by a large increase in value-added tax, a reduction in government spending, an increase in the Bank of England's minimum lending rate from 12 to 14%, and a generally tighter monetary policy.

Although it was expected that initially the new measures would have an adverse effect on business activity, as the government was making its budget announcements the economy appeared to be staging a recovery. Thus, gross domestic product rose by 2.1% between the first and second quarters, the volume of exports increased rapidly, and the current account deficit was cut back by nearly 40%. However, this was largely a reaction to the artificially depressed performance of the winter quarter, and by late summer the underlying trend of the economy became basically flat. The effects of the new government's economic policy were also beginning to be felt. Because of the large increase in value-added tax, the rise in the retail price index jumped from an 11.4% annual gain in June to one of 15.6% in July. At the same time higher interest rates and tighter money were starting to exert an adverse influence on business confidence and corporate profitability. Partly as a result of this but also because of sustained strikes in the manufacturing sector, output fell in the third quarter. Nevertheless, the level of wage settlements remained undesirably high, and the growth of the money supply continued to outstrip the government's target range. Faced with this situation, the Bank of England announced yet another increase in the minimum lending rate to a record 17% in November. The indications were that this had an adverse effect on some areas of domestic demand toward the end of the year. Also, by this time the decision to cut back public expenditure was beginning to have an effect, making the closing quarter of the year a period of relatively weak growth.

All in all the total output of the economy was thought to have risen by some 1–1.5% during 1979, approximately half the rate of the previous year. In spite of this, there was a reduction in the level of unemployment. At the start of the year 5.6% of the labour force was out of work, but by September the figure was down to 5.2%. Nevertheless, by late 1979 there were strong indications of a change in trend, and it was widely expected that because of the anticipated decline in output there would be higher levels of unemployment in 1980. During 1979 all major areas of demand were weaker than in the previous year.

Private consumption—which benefited from the cut in income tax but suffered as a result of the higher value-added tax—was relatively buoyant, recording a volume increase of just over 3.5%. Investment activities, however, suffered from the general uncertainty and pessimism about the future as well as the high cost of money. As a result the volume of investment expenditure may have fallen by as much as 3.5%, one of the poorest performances in several years. Public consumption was estimated to have risen by less than 1%, largely because of the new government's determination to contain its borrowing requirement. The relatively fast rate of domestic inflation and the sustained strength in the exchange value of sterling led to a loss of competitiveness of British exports in world markets, with the result that their volume growth for the entire year was estimated at only some 2.5%.

At the same time the external strength of sterling made imports more attractive. These were also encouraged by the dislocation caused by the various labour disputes and the consequent failure of British industry to satisfy demand. The combined effect of these factors was a gain of about 11% in the volume of imports, which was some 2½ times as large as the increase recorded in the previous year. Not surprisingly, the balance of payments situation deteriorated markedly. Although performance was beginning to improve in the second half of the year, the current account deficit for all of 1979 was provisionally estimated at approximately £2,500 million, compared with a surplus of £1,032 million in 1978.

Throughout the year inflation was on a sharply rising trend. In January 1979 the annual gain in the retail price index stood at 9.3%. Then, partly because of rising oil prices, an increase in earnings of about 15–16%, and the relatively fast monetary expansion allowed by the Labour government, a steady acceleration took place during the first half of the year. In July the effect of the increase in value-added tax was felt, and this, added to pressures mentioned earlier, caused the subsequent months to be on a steadily rising trend. Thus, indications were that the year would end at a rate of 18–19%.

Despite Britain's poor balance of payments performance, sterling remained strong in world foreign exchange markets. This was partly a reflection of the weakness of the dollar and high British interest rates (particularly toward the end of the year), but overseas holders of British currency were also impressed with the new government's apparent determination to pursue a strict monetary policy as well as the support that the growing North Sea oil production was providing for virtually all areas of the economy. In January 1979 £1 sterling bought $1.98, but by the end of November the rate was at $2.16.

JAPAN. Japanese economic policy during 1979 contrasted sharply with that pursued in the preceding year. In 1978 the total output of the economy grew by 5.5%. Although this was well in excess of the growth rates managed by most other developed countries, domestically it was regarded as unsatisfactory. Accordingly, the government went to considerable lengths to stimulate the economy, largely by higher public spending and relaxed monetary conditions. In spite of these measures the economy in 1979 appeared to have recorded a similar growth of about 5.5%. Yet for much of the year the principal official preoccupation was the fear of overheating the economy, which resulted in the adoption of a marginally restrictive approach to economic management. There were three principal reasons for this change in policy. First, though not the most important, there was a new prime minister and a radically reshuffled government. In November 1978 the expansion-minded Prime Minister Takeo Fukuda was ousted by Masayoshi Ohira, who was clearly not concerned with boosting the growth rate above 6%. Second, by the end of 1978 renewed inflationary pressures appeared, which, given the elections scheduled for the second half of 1979, had a powerful effect in changing the orientation of official policy from growth to stability. Finally, during most of 1978 the Japanese were under fire from their trading partners for having a large surplus in their foreign trade, and it was felt that rapid domestic growth would provide at least a partial solution by stepping up the volume of imports. However, by the end of the year there were signs that the rapid rise in the external value of the yen to November 1978 was beginning to cut back Japan's export growth. A further weakening in export performance took place in 1979, thereby removing the need to maintain a high rate of economic growth for balance of payments reasons.

CHART 2

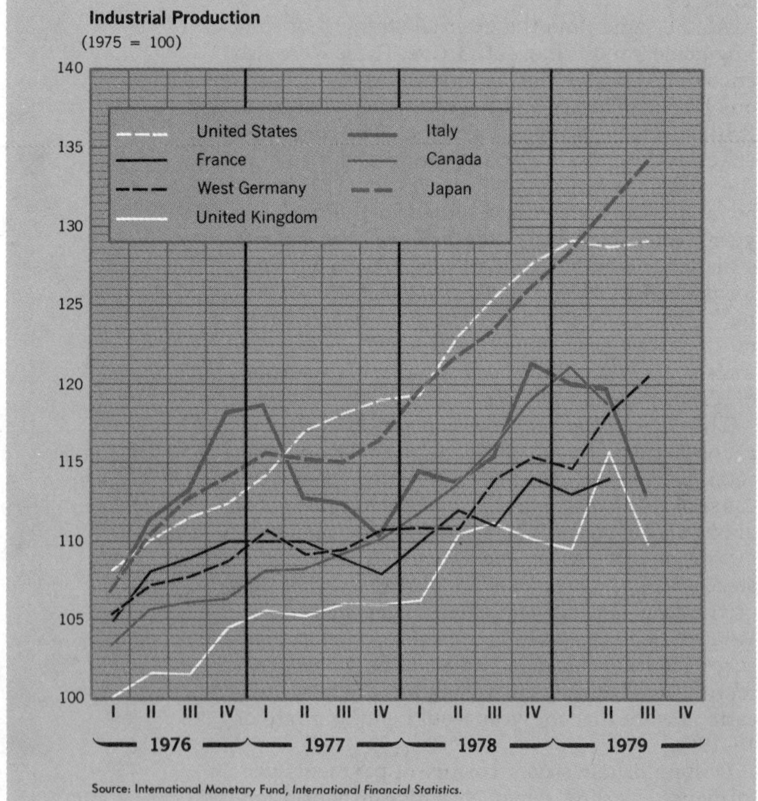

Source: International Monetary Fund, *International Financial Statistics*.

Partly as a result of the stimulus provided by the Fukuda government up to late 1978, the first quarter of 1979 (the last three months of Japan's 1978–79 fiscal year) had a high level of business activity. Gross national product rose at an annual rate of 6.9%, with private and public consumption and private plant and equipment investments providing much of the impetus. Exports also recorded a good volume growth but, mainly because of the program of emergency imports instituted earlier in response to foreign criticisms of the country's trade surplus, this was greatly exceeded by the growth of imports. This was sufficient to produce a small deficit in the current account of the balance of payments for the first time in several years.

Although it was clear that in the absence of further stimulatory action the growth rate would moderate as the year progressed, the evidence pointed to a continuing acceleration in inflation. The politically all-important retail price index showed no appreciable advance over the previous quarter, but rising oil prices, the fall in the exchange value of the yen, and the emergence of demand/supply imbalances in some areas led to an accelerating increase in the index of wholesale prices. Partly because of this but also in order to encourage bond sales to cover the large public deficit built up by previous governments, the Bank of Japan raised its discount rate from 3.5 to 4.25% in April and took action to hold down lending by commercial banks. This was the first increase in the discount rate since the spring of 1975, and it was hoped it would also provide some support for the yen, which was continuing downward.

As expected, in the second quarter of the year there was a somewhat weaker rate of overall economic growth (6.3% at an annual rate), largely because the policy of heavy government spending that was a feature of the 1978–79 budget had been abandoned by the new government. Also, because of the phasing out of the various import-boosting measures, the growth of merchandise imports fell back in comparison with the preceding three months. As a result there was a trade surplus of rather modest proportions. However, this was not sufficient to offset the traditional deficit on invisible transactions (those, such as tourism, not reflected in foreign trade statistics), and the current account registered the second quarterly deficit in succession. The trend of prices showed no improvement. On the contrary, owing to the continued weakness of the yen and overseas price pressures, import prices halfway through the year were approximately 21% higher than they had been 12 months previously. This was reflected in the wholesale index, which went up by about 3% in the second quarter (equivalent to an annual rate of 12.5%), bringing its level in July to 8.3% above the figure registered in the corresponding month of 1978. Retail prices also started to move upward, and by July the 12-month comparison yielded a gain of 4.3% as against 2.1% in March.

Faced with this situation (and rising interest rates overseas) the authorities tightened the monetary screw once again. The official rate was increased by a full percentage point to 5.25% in July, and the central bank established stricter limits on the growth of bank lending. Judging by the preliminary indicators, these measures did not appear to have a serious effect on economic growth during the third quarter of the year. Most major components of demand, including private consumption and private plant and equipment investments, recorded further advances; exports appeared to have gained a little from the improvement in competitiveness that occurred as the yen weakened, and gross national product was thought to have risen at an annual rate of 5.5–6%. The trend of prices, however, remained unsatisfactory. Wholesale prices continued to rise relentlessly and pushed the appropriate index in October to 14.5% higher than a year earlier. At the same time, despite the modest improvement in the overseas trade performance, the current account was once again in deficit.

As in the preceding quarters the yen continued to lose ground on the foreign exchange markets. Indeed, just as in 1978 one of the major problems of the Japanese economy was the continuous appreciation of the currency, the principal problem in 1979, which aggravated many other potential weaknesses, was the rapid decline in its value. In the ten months to October 1978 the yen appreciated by some 28% to $1 = 176 yen. Although this was helpful in holding down domestic inflation, it also had the effect of boosting the foreign exchange value of Japan's exports. This, in turn, inflated the dollar value of its current account surplus, which, apart from giving rise to further criticism from abroad, led to a further hardening in the exchange rate. From November 1978, however, the yen pursued a downward course. At first the authorities welcomed this development, but by the spring of 1979 the Bank of Japan was supporting the currency in order to slow down its decline, which was beginning to have an adverse effect on prices and reduced the dollar value of the country's exports. Nevertheless, the drop continued, and by the middle of November 1979 one dollar was worth 243 yen, representing a depreciation since November 1978 of approximately 30%.

By this time it was clear that the year as a whole would register a large external payments deficit and that, despite further domestic deflationary moves, the currency could drop to an even lower level. The government, therefore, announced a series of measures to encourage the inflow of funds into the country. The immediate reaction was one of a small improvement in the exchange rate, although there were fears that this would prove to be of a temporary nature. At the year's end the outflow of capital was still largely unhindered by government regulations, although officials made little secret of the fact that some tightening to provide further support for the yen might become necessary.

The final quarter of the year was characterized by considerable uncertainty. It was widely expected that, under the cumulative influence of the measures taken to date, the tempo of economic growth would falter without any clear sign of an improvement in prices, the external sector, or the underlying strength of the currency. For the year as a whole GNP was expected to rise by 5.5–6%, with private consumption and investment, exports, and imports showing a good increase but with public investment falling below the previous year's level. Industrial output appeared to be heading for a 7% increase with a consequent cut in unemployment. Wholesale price inflation by the year's end was expected to be running at some 17%, and the current account seemed to be heading for a deficit of some $1 billion–$3 billion, compared with a surplus of $16.5 billion in 1978.

West Germany. The economic situation in West Germany during 1979 remained satisfactory. Economic growth was likely to have been in the region of 4%, representing a slight increase from 1978 (3.5%). The expansionary policy followed by the government in 1978 was generally accepted as the main factor leading to improved domestic demand and output. This was accompanied by improved capacity utilization, higher profits, and reduced unemployment.

The opening months of the year, however, were marred by sluggish industrial output, which was held back by the severe winter weather, and by the uncertainty caused by the Iranian revolution. By the summer the economy shrugged off these worries and rebounded strongly. Industry's order books lengthened appreciably and toward the close of the year stood nearly 8% higher in real terms. Similarly, orders in hand were 15% (at current prices) higher during the first half of 1979.

As indicated by the state of the order books, industrial production expanded at a healthy pace, comfortably exceeding the government's forecast of a 3–4% rise in 1979. The rate at which industrial capacity was utilized, mirroring the higher level of activity, increased from about 80% at the start of the year to more than 85% by the autumn. All this led to an improved business climate and confidence, which resulted in a rise in investment in new plant and machinery aimed at expanding productive capacity rather than at improving and replacing old plant, which had characterized investment in recent years.

Another development giving rise to satisfaction was the steady decline in the number of unemployed. The jobless rate, having started the year at over 5%, steadily dropped to 3.3% in June. At the same time job vacancies reached a five-year peak. Not surprisingly, there was a severe shortage of skilled workers in industry. Although in the second half of the year the reduction in unemployment leveled out, there was no indication that unemployment was about to rise rapidly provided inflation was not given another upward push by large wage demands. In fact, throughout 1979 the main economic worry was the dent in the exemplary inflation record of recent years, which caused a marked shift in economic policy away from engineering high economic growth toward strong action to check the rise in prices. Although the West German inflation rate during 1979, at about 5%, ranked the lowest among the major OECD countries, it nevertheless represented a doubling of the previous year's mark. Apart from the strong surge in the economy and the high money supply growth at the end of 1978 and in early 1979, powerful external factors were at play, the most significant one being the oil price hike. This period also witnessed a relative weakness of the mark, which exaggerated the firmness in the world market price for imported raw materials. Too, a long-planned increase in value-added tax came into effect in the summer, giving an immediate upward push to consumer prices.

As the measures adopted in 1978 aimed at strengthening demand began to bear fruit during 1979, but at the expense of a rising rate of inflation, the economic policymakers were quick to adopt a progressively restrictive monetary policy. The Bundesbank served notice of its determination to keep the growth of the money supply within its target rates (between 6 and 9%) when as early as January it raised the Lombard rate from 3.5 to 4%. At the same time the bank's minimum reserve ratios were raised by 5%, effective from February 1. At the end of March the Bundesbank moved again and raised the discount rate by one percentage point to 4%. The Lombard rate was also raised to 5% and was further increased by another half a percentage point at the end of May. During the summer months, as both inflation and the demand for bank loans appeared not to respond to earlier rises in interest rates, the Bundesbank was left with little alternative but to act again to restore credibility to its monetary targets in the fight against inflation. Thus, both the discount rate and the Lombard rate were raised by one percentage point on July 13, to 5 and 6%, respectively.

In recent years West Germany had been criticized by its major trade partners for having an economic growth rate lower than the average for Western industrialized countries but running huge trade (and current) account surpluses. During 1979 this situation was reversed. The West German growth rate was higher than that of its major partners, and its current account surplus disappeared in the first eight months. The current account figures for that period were a deficit of DM 4.4 billion, compared with a surplus of DM 7.4 billion for the corresponding period of 1978.

FRANCE. In many ways the performance of the French economy during 1979 was similar to that of the previous year. It experienced a slight slowdown which was accompanied by rising inflation and higher unemployment. The balance of payments improvement in 1978 fell victim to high oil prices. In spite of the intensifying inflationary pressures, economic policymakers, with one eye on the rising tide of unemployment and the other on the 1981 presidential election, judged it appropriate to give the economy a mild stimulus in the spring and again in the late summer. This, however, was soon followed by a credit tightening aimed at containing the rapidly expanding money supply and the accelerating inflation.

The year 1978 closed on an encouraging note with industrial production rising, inflation easing, and demand for exports strengthening. Against this cheerful background the official forecasts for 1979 were for a 3.5% growth in GNP, after a rise of only 3% in 1978. By the summer it became clear that the economy was expanding more slowly than had seemed likely a few months earlier, but a strong export demand was expected to underpin the second half. Official estimates released toward the close of the year showed that there was some recovery and that economic growth could after all be slightly in excess of 3%.

Rapid inflation was a feature of the French economy in 1979. During the opening months the increase in the services component was particularly strong, mainly because of higher transport charges, but later in the year prices of manufactured goods also rose strongly. As in other parts of the world higher oil prices played a large role in stoking inflation. In July the annual rate of inflation stood at 13%, compared with the revised official target for the year as a whole of 9.5%. The final outcome was thought likely to be not less than 12%. The progress made in the balance of payments during 1978 was not maintained. Although exports remained buoyant for most of the year, imports expanded faster on account of higher oil prices. Thanks to a strong performance by invisibles, however, the current account was expected to remain in the black at the year's end by about Fr 4 billion.

The tenor of economic policy in France during 1979 was broadly similar to that of the previous year: it was aimed at bringing inflation under control, protecting the balance of payments, and improving the employment situation. Another aim was to stimulate investment, and to this end in early April a modest Fr 5.8 billion package of measures was announced. It took the form of a tax incentive scheme and low-interest loans for job-creating investments. Another mild stimulus followed in October (amounting to Fr 2.5 billion) to put new life into public works and housing schemes. The budget deficit, following the small stimuli given to the economy, was expected to be nearly Fr 40 billion, compared with Fr 30 billion in the previous year.

Given the weakness of demand, monetary policy was not intended to be too restrictive. However, in the autumn, as money supply continued to race ahead of the official targets and inflation became a political issue, the government tightened its monetary stance by introducing restrictions and announcing a lower target for money growth in 1980. These measures also coincided with the publication of the 1980 budget proposal, which envisioned a deficit of Fr 31 billion. However, given a likely slippage of between Fr 10 billion and Fr 20 billion, this would have added to inflationary

SYGMA

The fifth annual economic summit of industrialized oil-consuming nations, meeting in Tokyo in June, worked on strategies for countering OPEC's oil price increases.

pressures. Thus, by restricting credit growth at this stage the economic policymakers hoped to mop up the expected surplus liquidity.

Developing Countries. As in the past few years, during 1978 and 1979 the developing countries continued to be affected by the relatively sluggish economic activity and high rates of inflation in the developed world. In addition to these external problems, many developing countries also had to contend with a number of home-produced difficulties, including inadequate policies. Despite this discouraging backdrop, the aggregate growth rate of the developing countries, at 5.2% in 1978 (the latest year for which figures are available), was again in excess of that of the industrialized nations. However, the deceleration in the growth rate, which has been in evidence since 1976, continued in 1978. (From a low of 4.9% in 1975, economic growth recovered to 5.7% in 1976 but declined to 5.5% in 1977.)

More Developed Countries. These nations consist of two main groups: primary producers, such as Australia, New Zealand, and South Africa, and certain European countries, such as Greece, Yugoslavia, Turkey, and Ireland. As a whole they experienced a slightly faster growth rate during 1978 compared with the previous year. A marginal improvement in the rate of inflation was also in evidence. Gross domestic product (GDP) growth of 3% was again less than that of industrialized countries and non-oil-producing developing countries. The continuing weak feature of their economies could in the main be attributed to three factors: the slow recovery of the industrialized countries from the 1974–75 recession, a sharp deterioration in the terms of trade, and the tight fiscal and monetary policies that had to be followed by many in order to fight inflation. Several countries within this group, including Austria, Finland, and Ireland, succeeded in achieving single-figure inflation rates after several years in double digits. Significant reductions were also achieved by New Zealand, Portugal, and Spain. Iceland and Turkey were the two notable exceptions that went against the trend and experienced sharply higher inflation rates.

The major oil-producing countries experienced a further deceleration in their economic growth rates during 1978, mainly because of a 4.5% decline in oil output. By 1978 oil production accounted for 40% of the group's total GDP, and so any cyclical changes in the demand/supply equation could produce large fluctuations in total economic output. The fact that nonoil output of this group expanded by 8% in 1978 underlines this point effectively. Measures taken by oil producers since 1975 to contain inflation and expand their capacity to absorb imports continued to have favourable effects on their consumer prices. Viewed from many aspects, 1979 was unlikely to have been an equally good year for this group because of the problems in Iran. However, individual countries were likely to have fared better as the demand for—and the price of—oil was much higher.

Less Developed Countries. The world's less developed nations continued during 1978 to register more or less the same economic growth rates experienced in the previous two years. This meant that the short-term average (1975–78) of 5% was below that of the medium-term average (1967–72) of 6.1%. Economic growth was smallest in the countries where the per capita incomes were lowest. Most of those countries were in Africa. By contrast, in Asia favourable economic policies coupled with rapid expansion of exports of manufactured goods resulted in continued economic growth rates far in excess of the 1967–72 average.

Inflation remained high among the less developed countries, with wide regional differences ranging from 7% in Asia to more than 40% in Latin America and the Caribbean. A noticeable acceleration in the rate of inflation was seen in the first half of 1978, and the same trend was likely to have continued during the remainder of the year.

The World Bank in its 1979 annual report, commenting on the fact that during 1978 the less developed countries achieved a higher rate of economic growth than the industrialized nations, pointed out that this was no cause for rejoicing since it was due to slow growth in the industrialized countries rather than to any real improvement in the less developed ones. The bank also painted a gloomy picture of the gap between the rich and the poor countries. It postulated that "even if the less developed countries were to double their per capita growth rates while the developed countries merely maintained theirs, it would take almost a century to close the absolute income gap between them."

Total aid as a share of the combined GNP of the donor countries stood at 0.32% (0.31% in 1977), far short of the target of 0.7%. Only Sweden, The Netherlands, and Norway reached or exceeded the latter level. Preliminary data suggested that the 1979 level of official development aid was in the region of $20 billion, which, if confirmed, would represent a slowdown in the rate of increase. The flow of nonconcessionary aid, including export credits and direct portfolio investments, leveled out at $38.3 billion in 1978, a gain of only $3.5 billion. Aid provided by the Organization of Petroleum Exporting Countries (OPEC), after growing sharply from $1.7 billion in 1973 to $8.1 billion in 1976, declined to $7.5 billion in 1977 and $6.7 billion in 1978. This reflected OPEC's declining gross income and diminishing current account surpluses during this period.

The balance of payments of the non-oil-producing developing countries, having shown a modest recovery during 1976 and 1977, worsened in 1978. Their combined deficit rose from $21 billion in 1977 to $31 billion in 1978. This was accounted for mainly by higher inflation in the industrialized world, causing prices of the imports of the developing countries to outstrip gains in export prices. This process gained momentum in 1979 and was expected by the IMF to lead to a year-end deficit of $43 billion. These countries borrowed abroad

CHART 3

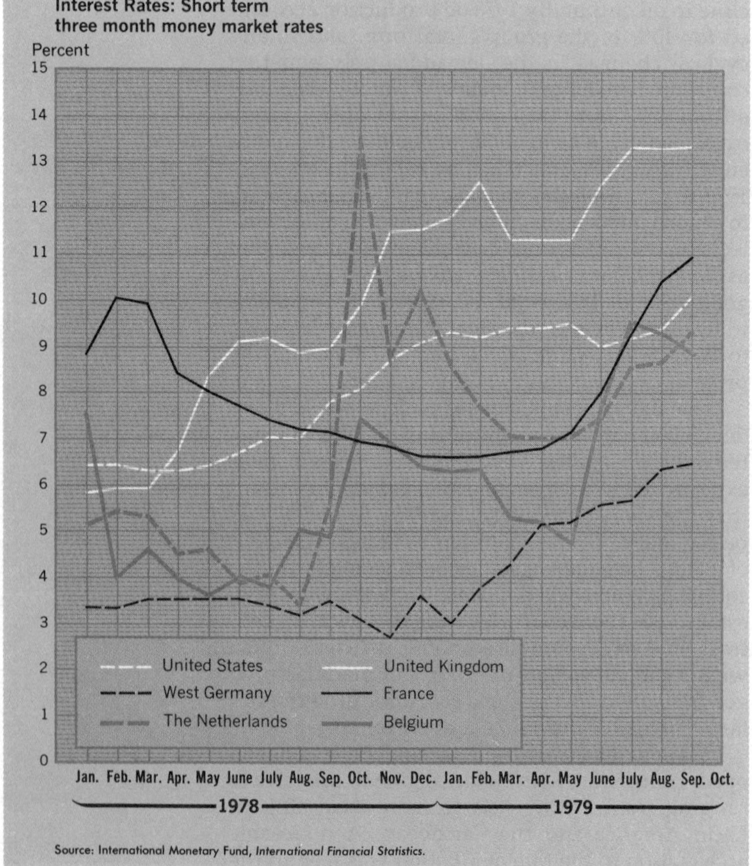

Source: International Monetary Fund, *International Financial Statistics.*

Table IV. Flow of Financial Resources from DAC Countries to Developing Countries and Multinational Institutions, 1967–69 to 1978

In $000,000,000

	Average 1967–69	1970	1976	1977	1978*
Total flow of resources†	12.80	15.80	40.70	49.50	56.60
as % of GNP	0.75	0.78	0.98	1.05	1.00
Official development assistance (net)	6.50	6.80	13.70	14.70	18.30
as % of GNP	0.38	0.34	0.33	0.31	0.32
Non-concessional flows	6.30	9.00	27.00	34.80	38.30
as % of GNP	0.37	0.44	0.65	0.74	0.68

*Preliminary.
†Includes grants by private voluntary organizations.
Note: Details may not add to totals because of rounding.
Source: World Bank, *Annual Report 1979.*

Table V. Changes in Output in the Developing Countries, 1967–78

% changes in real GNP or GDP

Area	Annual average 1967–72	Change from previous year 1975	1976	1977	1978
Major oil exporting countries*	9.0	−0.3	12.8	6.2	2.6
More developed primary producing countries	6.1	2.0	3.3	2.6	3.0
Europe†	6.5	2.4	3.6	3.5	3.2
Australia, New Zealand, South Africa	5.1	1.2	2.6	0.4	2.6
Less developed countries	6.1	4.1	5.0	5.1	5.2
Africa	5.0	2.3	4.7	4.0	3.7
Asia	4.8	6.1	5.8	6.6	6.9
Latin America and the Caribbean	6.8	2.6	4.8	4.3	4.3
Middle East	8.8	8.4	2.8	5.9	6.5

*Algeria, Indonesia, Iran, Iraq, Kuwait, Libya, Nigeria, Oman, Qatar, Saudi Arabia, United Arab Emirates, and Venezuela.
†Finland, Greece, Iceland, Ireland, Malta, Portugal, Romania, Spain, Turkey, and Yugoslavia.
Source: Adapted from the International Monetary Fund, *Annual Report 1979.*

Table VI. Changes in Consumer Prices in the Developing Countries, 1967–78

In %

Area	Annual average 1967–72	Change from previous year 1974	1975	1976	1977	1978
Major oil exporting countries*	8.0	17.0	18.8	16.4	15.1	9.9
More developed primary producing countries	6.0	16.7	16.9	14.4	17.8	16.6
Europe†	6.8	18.6	18.2	15.0	20.9	20.8
Australia, New Zealand, South Africa	4.6	13.6	14.6	13.2	12.2	8.7
Less developed countries	10.1	33.0	32.9	29.9	29.7	24.6
Africa	4.8	18.6	16.4	17.4	24.4	21.2
Asia	5.4	27.8	11.5	0.9	9.0	6.8
Latin America and the Caribbean	15.9	40.9	54.6	62.4	51.6	43.1
Middle East	4.3	21.8	20.3	20.2	19.2	21.7

*Algeria, Indonesia, Iran, Iraq, Kuwait, Libya, Nigeria, Oman, Qatar, Saudi Arabia, United Arab Emirates, and Venezuela.
†Finland, Greece, Iceland, Ireland, Malta, Portugal, Romania, Spain, Turkey, and Yugoslavia.
Source: Adapted from the International Monetary Fund, *Annual Report 1979.*

heavily in 1978 and were able to add $12.5 billion to their international reserves. The higher level of reserves was likely to have been useful in financing their larger deficit in 1979, when the cost of external borrowing was much higher. One inevitable consequence of higher external borrowings is the increased burden of debt servicing. Consequently, the number of countries experiencing arrears on current account payments or conducting or seeking debt renegotiation increased to 12, compared with only 3 in 1974.

The combined current account balance of the oil-exporting countries plunged from a $32 billion surplus in 1977 to $6 billion in 1978, reflecting the sharp fall in the value of oil exports and continuing growth in imports of both goods and services. During 1979, thanks to a 50% rise in the price of oil, the terms of trade changed dramatically, leading to expectations of a surplus of about $43 billion.

In contrast to the other subgroups, the more developed developing countries succeeded in cutting back their current account deficits by nearly 50% in 1978. The IMF attributed this favourable state of affairs to the more restrictive fiscal and monetary policies that these nations followed, to adjustments to exchange rates, and, in the case of the Mediterranean countries, to increased earnings from tourism. In 1979, however, under the impact of higher oil prices and increased imports, a significant deterioration in the current account balance was taken for granted.

Centrally Planned Economies. From June 26 to 28, 1979, the 33rd plenary session of the Council for Mutual Economic Assistance (CMEA or Comecon) was held in Moscow. This was an anniversary session celebrating 30 years of the existence of this organization, which includes the U.S.S.R., Poland, East Germany, Czechoslovakia, Romania, Bulgaria, Hungary, Mongolia, Vietnam, and Cuba. Soviet Premier Aleksey Kosygin, who chaired the meeting, told the other CMEA leaders that the Soviet bloc "was the only industrially developed area in the world which had avoided the heavy blows suffered by the capitalist economies as a result of the energy crisis." Referring to the "principles of socialist internationalism," Kosygin also stated that "within a short historical period the CMEA countries have turned themselves into a monolithic group of states with a progressive economic structure."

These declarations were designed to celebrate the occasion rather than to represent reality. In fact, the energy crisis was the dominant issue for all countries of the CMEA, including the U.S.S.R. Little was said, however, about the current needs or immediate plans to improve the energy situation. Instead, the session concentrated on long-term programs up to the year 2000. The session also spent considerable time discussing various aspects of the five-year plans due to start in 1981 and the five long-term programs for economic cooperation and integration. These programs were to be implemented during the next ten years.

It was characteristic that the CMEA sessions dealt with problems and issues that had supposedly been settled at previous meetings. Thus, three years earlier in East Berlin, at the 30th CMEA session, it had been decided to embark on five long-term programs of collaboration between the member countries. During the 31st session these programs were narrowed down to three, covering fuel, energy, and raw materials; machine building; and agriculture and food. In 1978 it was stated that the plans for the implementation of these programs had finally been completed. In 1979, however, the plans were again put on the agenda, together with two additional projects dealing with industrial consumer goods production and transportation.

It seemed that in spite of great economic difficulties experienced by all countries of the Soviet bloc, the 1979 conference dealt only with side issues and avoided major immediate problems. The communiqué issued at the end of the meeting did not reveal whether there was any discussion of the energy and raw material problems nor did it reveal whether the urgent problem of food shortages or that of the growing indebtedness to the West was dealt with.

One important agreement was completed, however. This concerned cooperation in the development of nuclear energy. Again, this was a long-term project, and even if it was implemented fully and on schedule its benefits would not be felt before 1990. By that year the share of electric power produced by nuclear energy in the European part of CMEA and Cuba combined was expected to reach some 35% of the total electricity generated.

In 1979 the energy problems of the CMEA countries other than the U.S.S.R. were acute. In response, Premier Kosygin said that during the current five-year plan (1976–80) these countries would receive from the U.S.S.R. 370 million tons of crude oil, 46 million tons of petroleum products, and 88,000,000,000 cu m of gas. During the next five-year period these deliveries were to be increased by 20%.

Shortages of power in CMEA countries were

Table VII. Output of Basic Industrial Products in Eastern Europe, 1978

In 000 metric tons except for natural gas and electric power

Country	Hard coal	Brown coal	Natural gas (000,000 cu m)	Crude petroleum	Electric power (000,000 kw-hr)	Steel	Sulfuric acid	Cement
Bulgaria	...	...	...	...	31,788	2,472	974	5,148
Czechoslovakia	28,260	95,292	...	120	66,060	15,288	1,200	10,200
Germany, East	...	253,272	...	...	95,952	6,972	966	12,516
Hungary	2,952	22,716	66,252	2,196	25,416	3,876	643	4,764
Poland	192,624	40,968	66,156	...	115,560	19,248	3,312	21,648
Romania	...	...	...	...	...	...	...	...
U.S.S.R.	723,996	...	3,101,976	572,460	1,200,000	150,996	22,404	129,267

Source: UN, *Monthly Bulletin of Statistics.*

causing severe disruptions in production and transport. The communiqué issued at the end of the 1979 session stated that the long-term program envisioned modernization of major international railway lines in the European part of the CMEA and the reconstruction of the Moscow–Warsaw–Berlin and Bucharest–Sofia, Bulg., expressways. Kosygin drew attention to the necessity of developing Soviet-style, broad-gauge railway lines. Two such lines, linking the U.S.S.R. with Romania and Czechoslovakia, already existed, and a third, linking the U.S.S.R. with Poland, was near completion.

Of the main problems not dealt with at the CMEA conference, the most important was the shortage of food, which was most severely felt in 1979 in the U.S.S.R. and Poland. The exceptionally severe winter and spring floods destroyed many crops. As a result harvests in both those countries were poor. Grain, edible fats, meat, and fodder had to be imported, mainly from the West, and in most cases bought on credit. It was estimated that the indebtedness of the CMEA countries to Western creditors in 1979 amounted to $56 billion and could reach $80 billion by 1980. This rapid growth of indebtedness occurred at a time when the rate of economic growth in all CMEA countries was steadily decreasing. While in 1977 growth was estimated to be 5%, it declined in 1978 to 4%. There were, however, considerable differences in national figures; for example, Romania's economy grew at a rate of 9.9% and Hungary's at 6.4%.

CHART 4

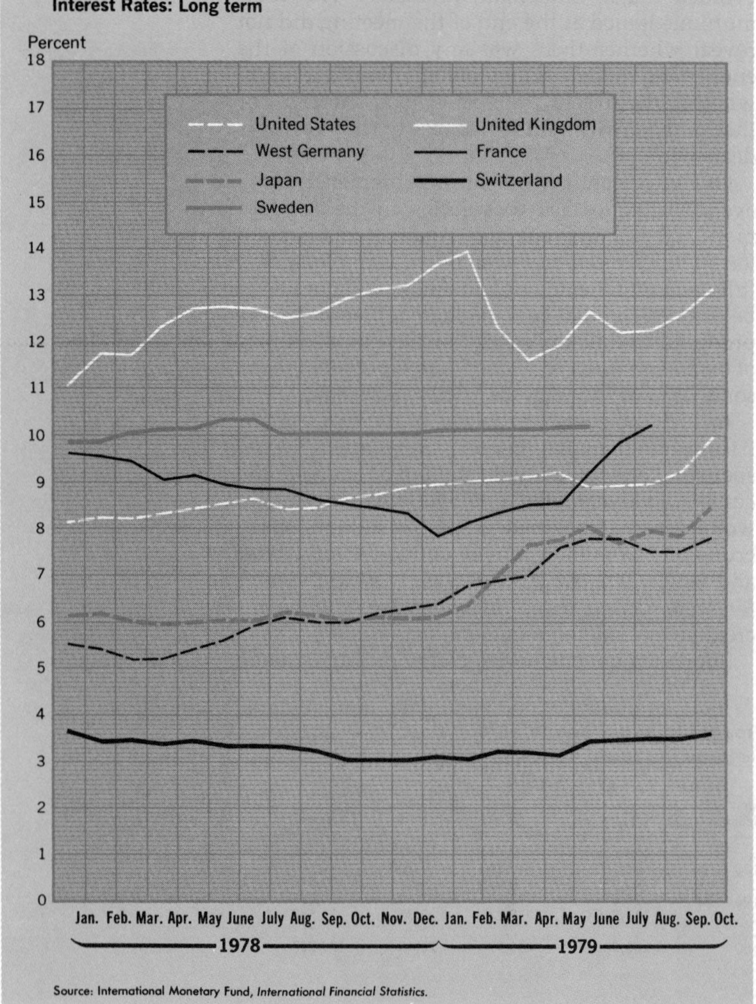

Source: International Monetary Fund, *International Financial Statistics*.

Table VIII. Rates of Industrial Growth in Eastern Europe*

Country	1956–60	1966–70	1971–75	1976	1977
Bulgaria	15.9	11.2	9.0	8.0	5.9
Czechoslovakia	10.5	6.3	6.7	5.5	5.5
Germany, East	9.2	6.4	6.3	5.9	5.2
Hungary	7.5	6.1	6.3	4.1	6.4
Poland	9.9	8.3	10.5	10.7	6.2
Romania	10.9	11.8	13.1	11.5	9.9
U.S.S.R.	10.4	8.5	8.5	4.8	5.2

*Yearly average percentages.
Source: *Ekonomicheskaya Gazeta*.

Table IX. Foreign Trade of Eastern Europe

In $000,000

	Exports			Imports		
Country	1976	1977	1978	1976	1977	1978
Bulgaria	5,382	6,329	7,448	5,626	6,329	7,617
Czechoslovakia	9,035	10,818	12,322	9,706	11,149	12,560
Germany, East	11,361	12,024	13,267	13,196	14,334	14,572
Hungary	4,932	5,832	6,350	5,528	6,522	7,898
Poland	11,050	12,336	13,361	13,867	14,674	15,121
Romania	6,100	7,021	. . .	6,100	7,018	. . .
U.S.S.R.	37,169	45,161	52,176	38,108	40,817	50,546

Source: UN, *Monthly Bulletin of Statistics*.

The European CMEA countries continued to make a determined effort to increase their exports to and decrease their imports from the West. But these efforts were only partly successful, and on the whole their trade deficit with the West was growing. In 1978 it rose by $2.5 billion and amounted to over $10 billion.

INTERNATIONAL TRADE

Though the tightening of economic and fiscal policies in most countries, developed and less developed, brought down the overall pace of growth in output in 1979, international trade was less affected than the other components of the world's economy. The rise in many commodity prices, especially of oil, exaggerated the expansion in trade expressed in value terms, but, nevertheless, the volume of goods traded on international markets was between 4 and 6% higher in 1979 than in the previous year. World production, on the other hand, was unlikely to have risen by more than 3.75% in real terms during 1979.

To a considerable extent, however, the annual totals mask a changing trend within each year. In 1978 there was a general acceleration in economic activity and in trade between countries as the year progressed, which carried over into the early months of 1979. But by the end of the first quarter of the latter year it was clear that the rate of increase in world trade was slowing. The available evidence indicates that the slackening in the volume of international transactions continued into the closing months of 1979, reflecting the overall deterioration in business conditions except in those countries that were oil exporters. A special additional factor late in the year was the effective withdrawal of Iran from its normally substantial role as a dominant oil exporter and major importer of foodstuffs and industrial products.

At the beginning of the year there were hopes

that the fifth meeting of the United Nations Conference on Trade and Development (UNCTAD), held in Manila in May, would produce results that would benefit the non-oil-producing developing nations. However, these countries took the view that the conference's outcome was fundamentally negative in terms of its effect in practice. No real progress was made toward reducing protectionist policies in foreign trade, which in 1979 contributed to the acceleration of inflation in developing countries that depend on supplies from abroad.

The debate on how the developing countries might avoid being forced into the unwelcome role of becoming mere suppliers of industrial inputs for the highly industrialized countries was bitter. Policy decisions by the developed economies were seen as determining the growth patterns of the less developed countries, which were becoming increasingly dependent on events in the dominant industrialized areas. In particular, the multinational corporations found themselves accused at the UNCTAD conference of controlling about half of the developing countries' foreign trade in raw materials and using their influence to obstruct those countries' access to world markets.

Given the rapid increase in the international price of oil in 1979, the developing countries also found themselves with inflated import bills and consequent balance of payments problems. The UNCTAD conference thus became a forum for the non-oil-producing less developed countries to attempt to persuade the OPEC members to find ways of mitigating the effects of higher oil prices, but without significant success.

Among other arrangements the International Tin Agreement exhausted its buffer stock and thus was unable to function as an effective force in 1979. The International Coffee Agreement continued to be locked in disputes on price targets and allocation of quotas, while the cocoa agreement was inoperative because prices in 1979, though relatively weak, were above the agreement's ceiling level. The International Sugar Agreement was unable to introduce any order into international trade in this commodity in the absence of the U.S., which had not ratified the pact, and the European Economic Community (EEC) countries, which maintained their refusal to become members. Progress was made during the year in achieving a formula for an international rubber agreement. The main intention was to defend a reference price for rubber by means of a reserve stock and thus safeguard producers' interests.

The general configuration of world trade in 1979 was otherwise approximately the same as in 1978, though with slower expansion. The swing into deficit of many countries' payments accounts emphasized the slowing of expansion in imports. Higher oil prices, as well as playing an important part in the deterioration of payments accounts, were also instrumental in curbing the volume of oil imports, with production limits in OPEC countries also playing their part.

Industrialized Nations. The developed OECD countries showed an increase of about 6% in their exports in 1979. It was notable that trade among members grew faster than that with less developed countries. However, this overall pattern concealed a 2% drop in OECD exports to OPEC countries, compared with an 8% rise in sales to the non-oil-producing less developed countries. A broadly similar pattern was evident in OECD imports.

Table X. Soviet Trade with Eastern European Countries

In 000,000 rubles, current prices

Country	Exports 1976	Exports 1977	Exports 1978	Imports 1976	Imports 1977	Imports 1978
Bulgaria	2,276.7	2,658.7	3,144.4	1,663.5	2,494.6	2,997.4
Czechoslovakia	2,320.5	2,680.4	3,002.0	1,648.6	2,436.9	3,058.6
Germany, East	3,217.9	3,661.2	3,982.0	2,275.9	3,066.2	3,711.2
Hungary	1,771.3	2,066.5	2,396.4	...	2,872.1	3,600.0
Poland	2,750.1	3,195.9	3,449.6	2,485.0	1,021.9	979.0
Romania	770.2	1,003.5	971.3	529.8	...	2,429.9

Source: U.S.S.R. Foreign Trade Statistics/Moscow, 1977/2079.

Table XI. Soviet Crude Petroleum and Products Supplied to Eastern Europe

In 000 metric tons

Country	1973	1974	1975	1976
Bulgaria	9,322	10,855	11,553	11,868
Czechoslovakia	14,340	14,836	15,965	17,233
Germany, East	12,985	14,424	14,952	16,766
Hungary	6,294	6,729	7,535	8,435
Poland	12,376	11,855	13,271	14,073

Source: U.S.S.R. Foreign Trade Statistics/Moscow, 1977/2079.

The U.S. benefited from sustained demand from Europe, and for 1979 as a whole its volume of exports of goods and services was likely to have risen by 8.5% over 1978. However, the rising cost of imports prevented the improvement in exports from showing up in full in the trade account and thus offset part of the advantage of the depreciation of the dollar against most major trading currencies. In addition, inflation in the U.S. economy was also passed on into export prices. Nevertheless, the nation's 1979 trade deficit seemed likely to be the lowest in three years.

Though Japan's once massive balance of payments surplus became a deficit in 1979, the trade account remained in surplus. The decline in the value of the yen helped to restore the competitiveness of Japanese exports during the year, but still left 1979 exports as a whole lower in volume terms than in 1978 or 1977. In July, however, the volume of overseas sales began to increase. Imports tapered off in the second half of the year, reflecting slower growth in the economy as a whole.

The growing strength of sterling, a consumer spending boom, and restocking by industry and the distributive trades probably produced a 6% rise in the United Kingdom's imports of goods and services in 1979. But the strength of the pound was also instrumental in pushing up British export prices faster than those of its main international competitors. As a result the volume of exports increased by no more than 2%, notwithstanding a recovery from July onward. These trends swung the trade account massively into deficit.

The effects of the rise in oil prices were especially marked in West Germany. Though exports were remarkably buoyant, rising by about 12% in value terms, there was a massive surge in imports (over 17% in the first half year). However, a trade surplus was maintained, even though a net outflow of services produced the unusual situation for West Germany of a current account deficit.

Table XII. Payments Balances on Current Account, 1973–79

In $000,000,000

Area	1974	1975	1976	1977	1978	1979*
Industrial countries	−4	25	7	4	33	10
More developed primary producing countries	−14	−15	−14	−13	−6	−10
Major oil exporting countries	68	35	40	32	6	43
Non-oil developing countries	−30	−38	−26	−21	−31	−43
	20	7	8	2	2	—

*International Monetary Fund projections.
Source: International Monetary Fund, *Annual Report 1979.*

In France the trade account deteriorated as 1979 progressed as a result of the OPEC oil price rises combined with precautionary buying by the French oil companies. For the year as a whole the extra import bill came to about Fr 18 billion. Exports of capital goods did well, taking the overall growth in exports to nearly 7%. A continued rise in external sales of agricultural products also had a beneficial effect. But because of the cost of oil the trade account went into deficit, though it was probably kept within Fr 10 billion.

Strong demand from the home market in Italy led to some shift into domestic consumption of goods that otherwise would probably have been exported. However, overseas sales still grew strongly, by about 8% in volume. This was a result of the depreciation of the lira, which gave Italian goods a competitive edge. Import growth accelerated under the influence of strong investment and inventory building demand, resulting in a likely 10% increase in volume in 1979. As a result the trade surplus was cut to about $750 million, well under half the previous year's figure.

Developing Countries. The substantial increases in the price of oil emphasized even more in 1979 the fundamental difference in trade performance between those developing countries that had petroleum resources and those that did not. The oil exporters' current balance of payments surplus rose sharply, though to a considerable extent the price increases in the early part of 1979 no more than offset the deterioration in the terms of trade of those countries in 1978. Despite a decline in oil production levels, of which Iran probably accounted for about 40%, the OPEC members probably raised their total export revenues by about one-third compared with 1978.

Imports did not rise in line with the expansion in export revenues. This resulted partly from efforts to control inflation in the oil-producing countries and partly from lack of absorptive capacity for industrial goods. On the other hand, imports of foodstuffs continued at a high level, reflecting in most cases deficiencies in local agricultural output. The leading suppliers of all categories of goods were the U.S., West Germany, and Japan. Among specific oil-producing countries the most notable development was the sharp absolute fall in imports into Nigeria and, particularly, Iran. The latter country also experienced a major decline in its exports.

Those developing countries without oil resources found themselves in acute difficulties in 1979 as oil prices rose. The total current account deficit of the nations in this group worsened by an estimated $10 billion during the year. As a result the poorer countries were obliged to curb their imports substantially. In addition, they suffered from a weakening of demand from commodity buyers in the industrial countries, where economic activity also was adversely affected by the increase in the price of oil.

The improvement in world prices for its main commodity exports enabled Malaysia to increase its trade surplus by 5% in 1979 even though the volume of exports showed no significant growth overall. Rubber, palm oil, tin, sawn logs, and, above all, oil revenue all rose strongly.

The broad base of Brazil's economy inevitably meant that it was affected strongly by the three main issues of world commodity arrangements, oil, and protectionism in its export markets. The combined effect of these forces was to increase the trade deficit further. Together with an adverse balance on most invisibles, this probably raised the current account deficit to more than $10 billion for 1979 as a whole.

Relatively weak growth in consumer demand helped to keep down growth in imports in Australia. At the same time export sales were strong as a result of overseas interest in Australia's mineral resources, taking estimated growth to more than 12% in volume terms. In an important move reorienting its foreign trade position, Australia in 1979 switched away from the assumption that its interests necessarily lie with the developed nations and decided to encourage trade with third world countries.

Centrally Planned Economies. There was a sharp increase in imports in 1978, the latest period for which data were available in any detail. Exports also rose strongly, but by only 14% for the centrally planned economies as a whole as against the 20% increase in total imports.

Table XIII. Current Balances of Payments

In $000,000,000

Country	1973	1974	1975	1976	1977	1978	1979*
Canada	+0.1	−1.5	−4.6	−3.8	−3.8	−4.6	−5
France	−0.6	−5.8	+0.1	−5.9	−3.3	+4.0	+4
Germany, West	+4.7	+9.9	+3.6	+3.5	+3.8	+8.8	−3
Italy	−2.2	−8.0	−0.6	−2.9	+2.3	+6.4	+9
Japan	−0.1	−4.7	−0.7	+3.7	+10.9	+16.6	−6
United Kingdom	−2.1	−7.7	−3.6	−1.5	+0.5	+2.0	−6
United States	+7.1	+2.1	+18.3	+4.6	−14.0	−13.9	−5
OECD total	+10.9	−26.6	+2.6	−16.8	−23.5	+11.5	−28
Other developed countries	+0.6	−3.8	−4.9	−2.5	−1.7	−0.2	+1
Centrally planned economies*	+1.0	−0.1	−6.0	−3.5	+2.3	+0.2	+2
Oil exporting countries*	−3.4	+59.9	+48.9	+46.2	+42.1	+13.5	+67
Other less developed countries*	−9.1	−29.4	−40.6	−23.4	−19.2	−24.9	−42
at 1975 prices†							
OECD total	+14.9	−29.9	+2.6	−16.6	−21.6	+9.2	−20
Other developed countries	+0.8	−4.3	−4.9	−2.5	−1.6	−0.2	+1
Centrally planned economies*	+1.4	−0.1	−6.0	−3.5	−2.1	+0.2	+1
Oil exporting countries*	−4.7	+67.3	+48.9	+45.7	+38.6	+10.8	+47
Other less developed countries*	−12.5	−33.0	−40.6	−23.2	−17.6	−19.9	−30

*Estimate.
†In terms of export prices of manufactured goods.
Sources: International Monetary Fund, *International Financial Statistics;* UN, *Monthly Bulletin of Statistics;* national sources.

A striking development in trade with the developed industrial countries was the sharp increase in China's trading activity. Imports rose by 50% and exports by 25%. Most dramatically, purchases from non-Communist industrial countries reached $7 billion, an increase of over 65% from the 1977 level. Japan continued to be the major supplier, followed by Western Europe. These developments brought China's trade deficit with those partners to about $3 billion in 1978, three times larger than in the previous year. Steel, machinery and equipment, and foodstuffs together accounted for three-quarters of China's total imports.

Imports by the Soviet Union and European members of the CMEA from Western industrial countries rose faster than exports to those markets. In consequence the deficit on this area of East–West trade increased to nearly $10 billion in 1978 from the previous year's $7 billion.

Commodities. Commodity prices in 1979 were subject to considerable speculative activity. Initially centred mainly on precious metals, this speculation subsequently spread to other raw materials. It was a powerful factor in pushing up prices and was strong enough to distort normal supply and demand factors.

To some extent because of increases in wheat output in countries that normally import large quantities, world trade in wheat fell slightly in 1978–79. Though the main exporting countries in the Americas and Australia shipped smaller quantities than in the previous season, the EEC sharply increased its exports. However, wheat prices rose, largely as a result of U.S. farm price policies.

World production of corn (maize), sorghum, millet, barley, oats, and rye increased in 1978–79. These gains, which were spread widely throughout the producing countries (though the U.S.S.R.'s corn crop fell considerably), contributed to a buildup of stocks since international trade in coarse grains rose by only 4%. The price of corn rose strongly from 1978 into 1979. Trade in rice contracted following good harvests, which reduced the need for imports in the countries that normally import heavily in order to make up the local production deficit. Nevertheless, prices were rising in 1979. International trade in oils and fats was 15% higher in 1978–79 than in the previous season, and prices showed few major increases.

Though sugar output in 1978–79 was slightly lower than in the previous year, demand was weak and prices declined. Wherever practicable, exporters tried to hold back sugar from the international market. The main factor influencing the market was the massive decline in imports by the U.S. and the EEC from less developed countries.

There were considerable uncertainties in the coffee market, where frosts in Brazil cut the harvest, and in consequence world prices rose sharply. Latin-American producers in the Bogotá Group used their support fund to boost prices by operating in the futures market. Cocoa producers found themselves with a smaller 1978–79 crop, partly a result of bad weather in West Africa. Even so, demand from the main importing countries was weak, and a cocoa surplus built up. The decision by Ghana to abolish its cocoa marketing board introduced an element of uncertainty that led to some precautionary buying late in 1979 and thus contributed toward a stabilizing of international price levels.

VADILLO—EL SOL DE MEXICO/ROTHCO

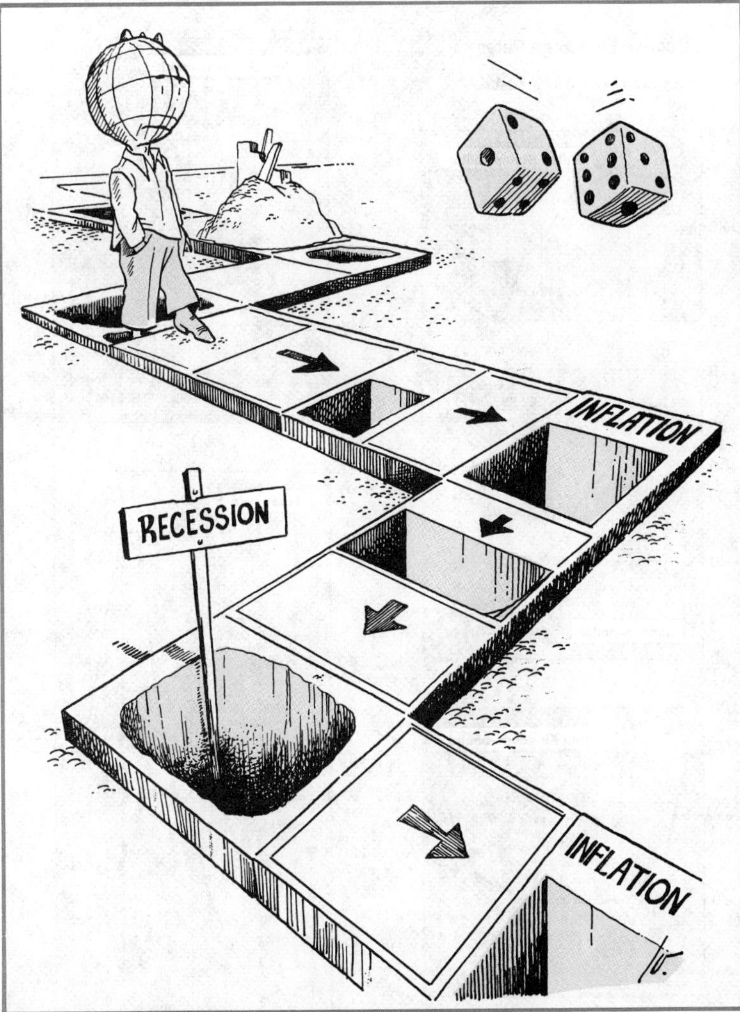

ECONOMIC FORECAST

On balance, 1979 was a year in which the start of a recovery in world trade was undermined by the rapid increase in the price of oil. Though OPEC clearly obtained a large increase in export revenues, non-oil-producing developing countries in particular found their external positions under pressure. Weakening business activity in the main industrial countries also produced lower demand for commodity producers. Thus, trade deficits outside the OPEC countries increased dramatically and had a wide destabilizing effect. (EIU)

INTERNATIONAL EXCHANGE AND PAYMENTS

There was a large transfer of income in 1979 from importers of oil to oil exporters. The main cause was the rise in oil prices, but this was reinforced by the fall in the volume of imports by some oil-exporting countries, notably Iran and Nigeria. The changes in areas' current balances between 1978 and 1979 were remarkably similar to those between 1973 and 1974 (TABLE XIII) and, although the 1979 changes were smaller when allowance was made for inflation, this was because the main

CHART 5

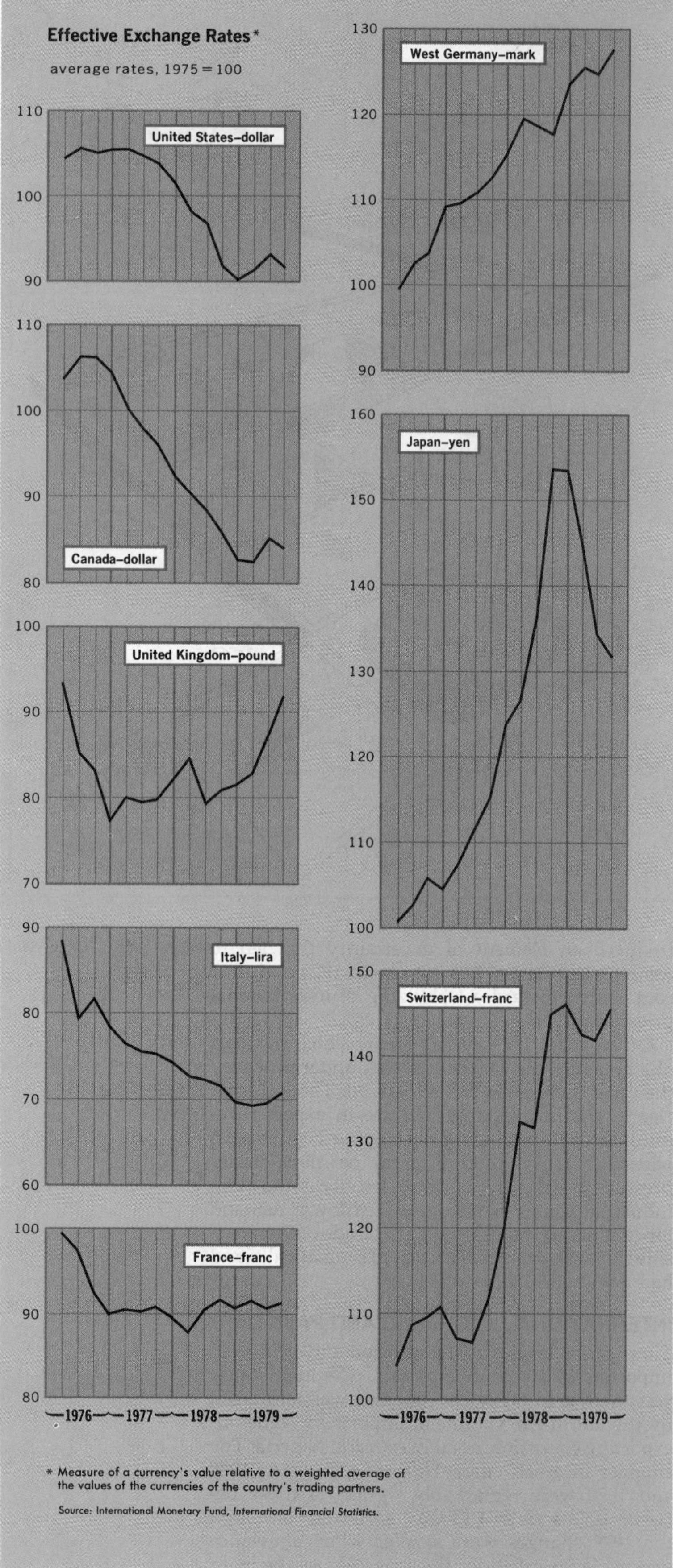

* Measure of a currency's value relative to a weighted average of the values of the currencies of the country's trading partners.

Source: International Monetary Fund, *International Financial Statistics.*

rise in the oil price did not occur until almost halfway through the year instead of at the beginning as in 1974. Changes estimated at constant prices for a year from mid-1979 would be similar to 1974.

The other major difference between 1979 and earlier years was the increased intervention in exchange rate movements by all governments and particularly by the U.S. The change in U.S. policy meant that there was no longer any major country or area without a target for its exchange rate. This necessarily increased the probability that the targets would prove irreconcilable, as there was no longer a country willing to fit in with others' policies. Two other aspects of exchange-rate policy in 1979 guaranteed inconsistent aims and consequently unstable rates. Since "floating" rates became common in the early 1970s, many governments had believed that it is right to smooth out day-to-day fluctuations in order to avoid uncertainties that can damage trade and have no long-term advantages to the adjustment of the economy; at the same time they accepted that a clear trend in the rate should not be permanently resisted. But the period over which resistance is attempted might be increasing; governments began trying to prevent movements that might last several months if they believed such changes reflected only a short-term aspect of the economy. The formation of the European Monetary System (in January 1979) institutionalized this type of policy by avoiding large day-to-day fluctuations but permitting periodic realignments. The only full realignment, at the end of September, was extremely small (the largest relative move was 5%).

If governments differ over whether a relative movement of their countries' exchange rates is temporary or a trend, their intervention policies will be temporarily inconsistent. A more important difficulty, both because it might last indefinitely and because it led to escalating and directly opposed intervention, was the increasing importance attached to controlling inflation as the major goal of economic policy and the consequent preference of the major countries for an appreciating, or at least stable, exchange rate to minimize the effects of external price rises. In 1978 attention seemed to have shifted back toward growth, but the rise in the oil price brought a reaction against inflation. The 1974 oil price rise, which occurred when growth was still a major goal, was accompanied by recognition that "competitive devaluation" to increase output growth could lead to an unstable cycle of policies, with potentially serious effects on both trade flows and inflation, and most countries avoided it. However, recognition of the dangers to trade and growth from "competitive revaluation" to control inflation appeared to have been weaker in 1979, and the course of exchange and interest rates indicates that some governments did not completely avoid it. Increasing concern to set common international policies clearly carries the risk that all countries will be simultaneously attempting either to devalue or to revalue.

Current Balances. The OECD countries moved from a surplus of about $12 billion to a deficit of almost $30 billion in 1979. The moves of Japan and West Germany into deficit accounted for more than one-half and almost one-third of this, respectively. There was also a large deterioration in the position of the U.K., from a small surplus to a $6 billion deficit. There was, however, a large reduction in the U.S. deficit. With France and Italy in substantial surplus, the pattern of surpluses and deficits was very different from that in 1974.

There was little change in Canada's deficit, although its interest payments on borrowing to finance past deficits continued to rise. More than half the improvement for the U.S. came from a smaller trade deficit, but there were also a $7 billion improvement in its balance on profits (Table XIV) and a reduction of perhaps $1 billion in its travel deficit. Although there was a small improvement in Japan's balance on profits, its deficit on other services increased. The massive rise in the French balance on services that occurred in 1978 because of travel receipts and construction and engineering services in the Middle and Far East appeared to have continued in 1979; a rise of $3 billion offset a small deterioration in the balance on trade. Perhaps $4 billion–$5 billion of the West German change from 1978 could be attributed to a higher deficit on nontrade items, including a small fall in profit income, a rise of $2 billion in spending on travel, and higher remittances home by foreign workers. The entire improvement in the Italian current balance resulted from higher income from services. Most of the change in Britain's nontrade balance was the result of the virtual elimination of its surplus of $1.5 billion on profits, though there were also higher contributions to the EEC budget and a smaller surplus on services.

The deficit of the non-oil-producing developing countries increased from the level of the last three years, about $20 billion, to more than $40 billion, a level comparable, even after allowing for inflation, to that in 1974. South Africa accounted for the surplus of the developed countries outside the OECD; it benefited by perhaps $2 billion from the rise in the price of gold. The centrally planned economies appeared to have restrained their imports to avoid any increase in their deficits.

The surplus of the oil exporters probably rose more than $50 billion. In 1978 probably only Iraq was in current surplus on official figures, although Saudi Arabia was in surplus after allowance for its receipts of profits; Kuwait does not publish figures but was probably in surplus. The average 40% increase in the value of their exports with almost no change in the value of their imports probably gave surpluses in 1979 to Ecuador, Indonesia, Libya, Nigeria, and Trinidad and Tobago, considerably broadening the spread of the surplus.

Capital Flows. Total identified long-term capital flows from the major lenders fell back in 1979 because of the inflow into West Germany, encouraged by the rise in West German interest rates. The level of U.S. net outflows remained high. Direct investment abroad rose from $17 billion in 1978 to an annual rate of more than $25 billion in the first half of 1979, while direct investment from abroad in the U.S. changed little in the same period, a departure from the rises of the last few years. The long-term outflow was accompanied by an outflow of short-term capital, especially foreign

UPI

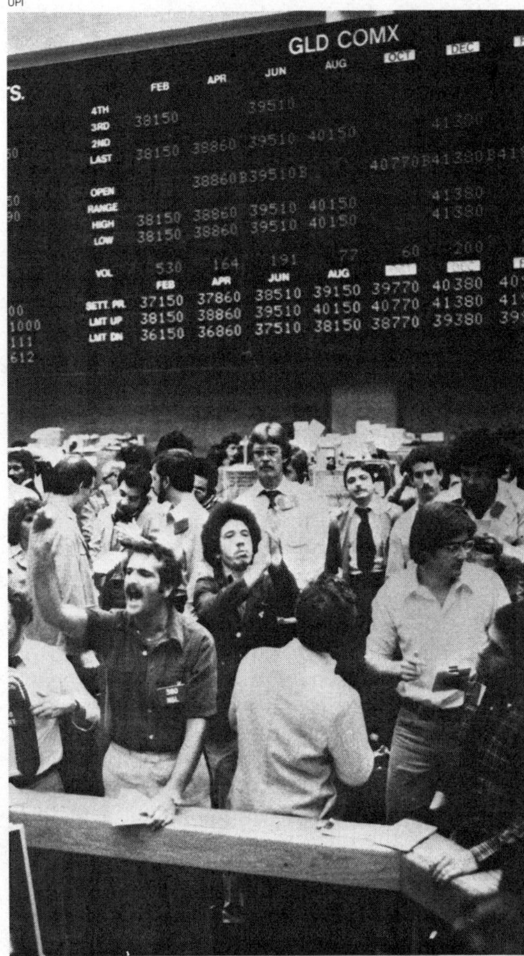

Bidding was frantic at the New York Commodity Exchange as gold prices soared during September.

official holdings by European countries and Japan; OPEC assets rose. The change in the Japanese balance followed successive relaxations of the restrictions on foreign capital inflows into Japan during the first half of the year, applying to foreign bank deposits in Japan and then to foreign purchases of yen bonds. There was also a repayment of a loan from Saudi Arabia dating from 1974. There was an increase in foreign direct investment in the U.K. There was an unusual net outflow of direct investment from Canada in 1979 because of Canadian purchases of foreign holdings in Canada.

Switzerland, like Japan, used the decline in up-

Table XIV. Foreign Investment by Major Countries

In $000,000

Country	1973	1974	1975	1976	1977	1978	1979*
Long-term capital flows							
Germany, West	+4,846	−2,231	−6,840	−126	−5,562	−1,132	+10,709
Japan	−9,750	−3,881	−272	−984	−3,184	−12,389	−9,500
United Kingdom	+2,021	+6,718	+2,157	+3,013	+6,671	−3,710	−1,400
United States	−7,696	−7,217	−19,939	−18,083	−15,367	−15,750*	−20,000
Total	−10,579	−6,611	−24,894	−16,180	−17,442	−32,981	−20,191
Net interest, dividends, and profits							
Germany, West	+582	−67	+408	+905	+184	+2,278	+1,400
Japan	+490	−451	−273	−204	+115	+900	+2,200
United Kingdom	+3,090	+3,328	+1,693	+2,346	+351	+1,605	—
United States	+12,153	+15,503	+12,787	+15,975	+17,989	+21,645	+29,000
Total	+16,315	+18,313	+14,615	+19,022	+18,639	+26,428	+32,600

*Estimate.
Source: National sources.

ward pressure on its exchange rate as an opportunity to reduce its restrictions on capital inflows. It changed from active intervention to prevent the franc from becoming a reserve currency to permitting limited official purchases of Swiss liabilities. The West German central bank also accepted that the mark is in practice a reserve asset. These changes facilitated the shift in the composition of countries' foreign exchange reserves from dollars. The process was led by the oil producers, which made large deposits in dollars and pounds after the 1974 oil price rise, and was continued in 1977 and 1978 by the non-oil-producing developing countries. It was the result of fears about the level of the dollar and the pound, greater use of exporters' own currencies in trade in place of dollars or pounds combined with the growing share of West Germany and Japan in trade, and fears of the political risks of placing a large part of a country's assets in a single country. In mid-1979 60–65% of foreign exchange reserves could be identified by currency. Of this, dollars still totaled 75%, but marks were at least 15% and Swiss francs and yen, perhaps 3–4% each; sterling fell to under 2%. The main problem in identifying the rest was large unrecorded holdings on Eurocurrency markets. It seemed probable that most of these were in the same currencies (excluding sterling).

Ecuador

There was an allocation of the IMF's reserve asset, the Special Drawing Right (SDR), at the beginning of 1979, but this accounted for less than one-third of the increase in reserves in 1979, and total holdings of SDR's were only about 5% of holdings of foreign currencies. Changes in reserves by areas in 1979 did not show the effects of the balances. There was only a small increase for the oil exporters, while the non-oil-producing developing countries continued to increase reserves through borrowing. The developed countries also increased their reserves substantially, but their changes reflected exchange-rate intervention more than balances of payments.

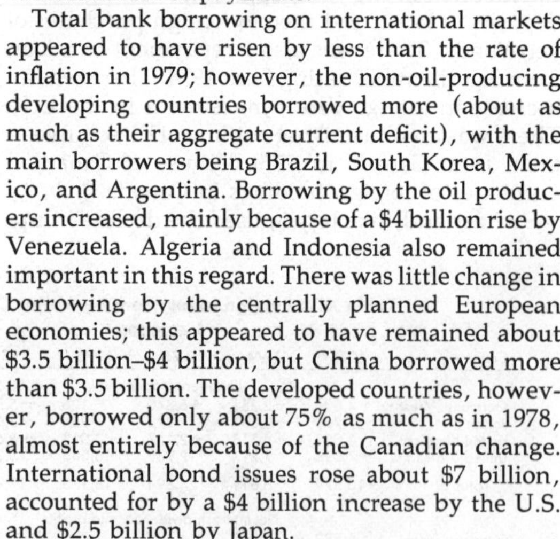

Total bank borrowing on international markets appeared to have risen by less than the rate of inflation in 1979; however, the non-oil-producing developing countries borrowed more (about as much as their aggregate current deficit), with the main borrowers being Brazil, South Korea, Mexico, and Argentina. Borrowing by the oil producers increased, mainly because of a $4 billion rise by Venezuela. Algeria and Indonesia also remained important in this regard. There was little change in borrowing by the centrally planned European economies; this appeared to have remained about $3.5 billion–$4 billion, but China borrowed more than $3.5 billion. The developed countries, however, borrowed only about 75% as much as in 1978, almost entirely because of the Canadian change. International bond issues rose about $7 billion, accounted for by a $4 billion increase by the U.S. and $2.5 billion by Japan.

Exchange and Interest Rates. The most important changes in effective exchange rates in 1979 were the large and persistent fall in the yen and the rise in the pound. West German and Swiss rates changed little after large rises in 1978, while the U.S., Italy, and Canada did not recover from 1978 falls; France remained flat. In contrast to the past, when exchange rates moved roughly with changes in trade, this does not seem to have been important in 1979 except for effects from the level of oil imports. In the first half of 1979 the risk of a shortage of oil helped to strengthen the dollar because the U.S. is a major oil producer. The Canadian dollar also rose. When the problem changed to price, the effect of the cost of oil on balances became more important; this helps to explain the strength of sterling. Both quantity and price fears weakened the yen, as did the general deterioration in the Japanese current balance. Neither the U.K. nor the West German move into deficit was accompanied by an exchange rate fall.

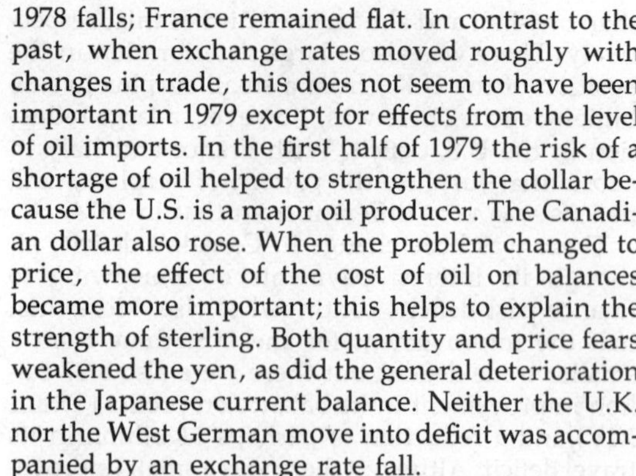

Monetary policy differences, indicated by relative interest rates, were important, and many interest rate changes appeared to be for exchange-rate motives as well as internal ones. U.K. interest rates remained well above those of other countries throughout the year. U.S. rates, after a rise at the end of 1978, changed little until the autumn, when they rose. Until then the fall of the dollar relative to European currencies had been resisted by a decline of more than $2.5 billion (25%) in U.S. foreign exchange reserves in the summer. (SHEILA A. B. PAGE)

Ecuador

A republic on the west coast of South America, Ecuador is bounded by Colombia, Peru, and the Pacific Ocean. Area: 281,334 sq km (108,624 sq mi), including the Galápagos Islands (7,976 sq km), which is an insular province. Pop. (1979 est.): 8,047,000. Cap.: Quito (pop., 1978 est., 742,900). Largest city: Guayaquil (pop., 1978 est., 1,022,000). Language: Spanish, but Indians speak Quechuan and Jivaroan. Religion: predominantly Roman Catholic. In 1979 the country was ruled by a military junta including Vice-Adm. Alfredo Poveda Burbano (Navy), Gen. Guillermo Durán Arcentales (Army), and Gen. Luis Leoro Franco (Air Force) until August 10; president from August 10, Jaime Roldós Aguilera.

A peaceful transfer of power from Ecuador's military junta to a democratic civilian government took place in 1979. Two candidates participated in the second round of presidential elections on April 29: Jaime Roldós Aguilera (*see* BIOGRAPHIES) of the Concentración de Fuerzas Populares (CFP) and Sixto Durán Ballén Cordovez of the Frente Nacional Constitucionalista (FNC). The second round was held together with the legislative elections, and Roldós achieved an overwhelming victory with 68.4% of the vote. Eleven political parties participated in the congressional elections for 12 national and 57 provincial representatives, and the CFP won predominance in Congress, with 45 seats overall. Roldós, who took office as president on August 10, met opposition in the new populist Congress led by Assad Bucaram. He had to veto several bills, and the division between the executive and the legislative branches widened. On the day Roldós took office a new constitution went into effect. It extended the length of the president's

ECUADOR

Education. (1976–77) Primary, pupils 1,278,402, teachers 33,567; secondary and vocational, pupils 429,124, teachers 25,954; teacher training, pupils 2,191, teachers 153; higher, students 180,813, teaching staff (1970–71) 2,867.

Finance. Monetary unit: sucre, with (Sept. 17, 1979) an official rate of 25 sucres to U.S. $1 (free rate of 60.20 sucres = £1 sterling). Gold, SDR's, and foreign exchange (June 1979) U.S. $615 million. Budget (1978 actual): revenue 19,054,000,000 sucres; expenditure 22,986,000,000 sucres. Gross national product (1978) 174,770,000,000 sucres. Money supply (May 1979) 38,253,000,000 sucres. Cost of living (Quito; 1975 = 100; June 1979) 155.2.

Foreign Trade. (1978) Imports U.S. $1,582,700,000; exports U.S. $1,531,700,000. Import sources (1977): U.S. 38%; Japan 16%; West Germany 8%. Export destinations (1977): U.S. 36%; Panama 10%; Peru 9%; Chile 7%. Main exports (1977): crude oil 54%; cocoa and products 18%; coffee 13%; bananas 11%.

Transport and Communications. Roads (1973) 21,490 km (including 1,392 km of Pan-American Highway). Motor vehicles in use (1975): passenger 51,300; commercial (including buses) 77,200. Railways: (1977) 965 km; traffic (1975) 65 million passenger-km, freight 46 million net ton-km. Air traffic (1977): 551 million passenger-km; freight 9.8 million net ton-km. Telephones (Jan. 1978) 222,000. Radio receivers (Dec. 1971) *c.* 1.7 million. Television receivers (Dec. 1978) *c.* 400,000.

Agriculture. Production (in 000; metric tons; 1978): rice 285; corn (1977) 218; potatoes *c.* 498; cassava (1977) *c.* 350; sugar, raw value *c.* 340; bananas *c.* 2,375; pineapples *c.* 119; oranges *c.* 520; coffee *c.* 89; cocoa *c.* 73; fish catch (1977) 475. Livestock (in 000; 1976): cattle *c.* 2,725; sheep *c.* 2,150; pigs *c.* 2,700; horses *c.* 265; chickens *c.* 7,500.

Industry. Production (in 000; metric tons; 1977): cement 623; crude oil (1978) 10,182; natural gas (cu m) 44,308; petroleum products *c.* 1,970; electricity (kw-hr) *c.* 2,145,000; gold (troy oz) 8; silver (troy oz) *c.* 30.

term from four to five years and provided for a legislature with only one house rather than two.

Ecuador's gross domestic product was expected to grow by about 5% in 1979, compared with 6.8% in 1978. The decline was caused partly by political uncertainties surrounding the transition from military to civilian rule and partly by the prolonged drought which affected both agricultural production and hydroelectric output. The external public debt caused concern; it was estimated at about $4.6 billion, of which $1 billion was for arms purchases. Nevertheless, Ecuador benefited greatly from the rise in oil prices and sold its oil on the spot market at record high levels.

(SARAH CAMERON)

Education

Continued constraint on both expenditure and expectations was a pervading feature of education in most advanced industrial countries in 1979, certainly compared with the explosive years of the 1960s. For both economic and demographic reasons, the prospect for the 1980s appeared to be one of contraction. Even in China there were signs that the heady promises of expansion voiced soon after the expulsion of the "gang of four" in 1976 would have to come to terms with economic reality. In Western Europe the most dramatic application of the brakes was in the U.K., where the new Conservative government announced an immediate reduction in educational spending of some 3% overall, with a further 5% cut scheduled for the following year. In France as well there were indications that spending would be held back because of falling enrollments.

Enrollments were also down in the U.S., but expenses continued to climb, in large measure because of inflation. The $161 billion that went for education in the U.S. accounted for 7.3% of all the money Americans spent. Education cost more than any other public service. There were 58.4 million students in U.S. classrooms at the beginning of the 1979–80 school year, some 3 million fewer than in 1975. Even so, 30% of the population, or 66 million people, were involved in education as students, teachers, or administrators.

At the 50th anniversary conference of the International Bureau of Education in Geneva, held in July, particular emphasis was placed on the need to raise standards of efficiency in educational systems. UNESCO, under whose aegis the International Bureau operated, put special stress on the avoidance of wastage, particularly through the repetition of grades. In a paper presented to the conference, it was estimated that the 2% repetition in the U.S. in 1971–72 cost between $740 million and $900 million. For some less developed countries, which were spending up to a quarter of their national budgets on education, this was a grave problem, especially in Africa where "repetition" at the primary level was common. The average level of repetition in the latest years for which figures were available was estimated at 17.7% for Africa, 10.9% for Latin America, 9.9% for Asia and Oceania, and 3.5% for Europe and the U.S.S.R.

World illiteracy continued to decline. UNESCO estimated the total number of functional illiterates at 814 million, or approximately 30% of the adult population. Nonetheless, because of the increase

WHITE HOUSE PHOTO

Marilyn Black, a teacher from Hanover, New Hampshire, was congratulated at a White House ceremony by Pres. Jimmy Carter on being elected 1979 National Teacher of the Year. The annual event is sponsored by the Encyclopædia Britannica companies, *Ladies' Home Journal* magazine, and the Council of Chief State School Officers.

Ecumenical Movement:
see Religion

in population, there seemed little hope of reducing the absolute number. Indeed, UNESCO forecast that it would rise to 954 million by the year 2000. The number of functionally illiterate persons in the U.S. was increasing, according to a Ford Foundation report. Skills once satisfactory for day-to-day living were no longer adequate in an increasingly complex society, and more and more persons were falling behind. Estimates of the number of adults in the U.S. considered to be functionally illiterate ranged from 18 million to 64 million.

Most of the oil-rich countries were making continued—indeed, relentless—efforts to improve their literacy rates. Mexico announced plans to invest $9 billion in education by 1982. In Saudi Arabia in 1979 the proportion of the national budget devoted to education rose to 13.5%, or some 18 billion riyals, compared with 168 million riyals in 1951. It was planned to extend elementary education (ages 6–12) to all boys and to 60% of girls by 1980. In Qatar a ten-year "master plan" to improve the lower levels of education involved the building of some 156 new schools.

The U.S. Congress enacted a major Carter administration proposal establishing a separate Cabinet-level Department of Education. The department would have a $14.2 billion budget and more than 17,000 employees. To head the new department, Carter picked the highest-ranking woman jurist in the nation, Shirley M. Hufstedler, formerly on the 9th U.S. Circuit Court of Appeals, resident of California and a graduate of the Stanford University Law School. In her writings, Hufstedler had discussed the limitations of litigation which, for example, could eliminate racial discrimination in schools but not racial hatred. With the appointment, Carter began to reassemble his education team, decimated during the summer by the resignations of Ernest Boyer as U.S. commissioner of education and Patricia A. Graham as director of the National Institute of Education. Having taken the "E" out of the Department of Health, Education, and Welfare (HEW), Congress renamed the agency the Department of Health and Human Services.

Congressional appropriations for HEW were again delayed by controversies over the use of federal funds to pay for abortions for women on welfare. In the final $72.5 billion departmental budget, gains were registered for some education programs. Education of the handicapped got an additional $72 million for a total of $1,050,000,000 (but personnel development for the handicapped lost $2 million). Women's equity gained $1 million; bilingual education, $8,360,000; basic skills improvement, $7,250,000; and the Fund for the Improvement of Post-secondary Education, $500,000. Two new projects, PUSH for Excellence and law-related education, received $1 million each. Appropriations for higher education totaled $5.1 billion and for elementary-secondary education, $3.3 billion.

South Africa increased its expenditure on education in 1979–80 by R 38 million for Africans and by R 28 million for whites. This did little to equalize provisions for the two races, however, since the total for African education ran to R 182 million and for white, R 354 million. In June the new minister of education, T. N. H. Jenson, announced the long-term aim of introducing compulsory schooling for blacks, but he promised that no funds would be allocated for this purpose at the expense of white education.

Primary and Secondary Schools. In Western Europe the country being followed with the greatest interest by educators was newly oil-rich Norway. In this it replaced Sweden, which had been the pioneer in establishing a universal system of comprehensive secondary education, as distinguished from a system of specialized schools. Norway in 1979 was well along in its effort to use the educational system as the means of preserving and strengthening small communities. The Norwegians insisted that the remotest localities be provided with schools and even with universities, though in most Western European countries universities with fewer than 1,000 students would be considered uneconomic.

Spain's two-year Education Investment Program was completed during the year. Over 1.5 million new school places had been created between July 1977 and the middle of 1979, at a cost of some £280 million. Technical training courses, which had been somewhat neglected in the crash education program, were upgraded and 125,000 new places were provided. It was estimated that the annual cost to the state of keeping a child in primary school was £238, in secondary school, £420, and in a university, £600.

In both Great Britain and France there was fierce opposition on the part of teachers and trade unions to government economy measures. In England and Wales the new Conservative minister for education, Mark Carlisle, encountered organized resistance to his economy proposals, particularly in view of the fact that, in addition to cutting state aid, he wished to increase government assistance to private schools by subsidizing school places in private schools that joined an "assisted places scheme." In France the minister of education, Christian Beullac, had even greater difficulty applying the cuts the French government believed were necessary, given the expected 500,000 drop in primary school enrollment over the next four years. Some 30,000 teaching posts were to be eliminated, and many schools, especially in rural areas, were to be closed. The Ministry of Education set about redrawing the *carte scolaire*—France's school map—and Beullac proposed a reduction from 2,720 to 1,310 in the number of auxiliary teachers without permanent appointments. The measures led to massive demonstrations in Paris.

Falling enrollments and economic constraints inevitably affected teacher employment and teacher training. The vague hopes of greater teacher interchange within the European Economic Community failed to materialize. However, initiatives were begun by the Nordic Council to bring about a common labour market for teachers in Sweden, Denmark, Norway, Finland, and Iceland, involving common acceptance of teacher qualifications.

Twenty-five years after the U.S. Supreme Court decision in *Brown* v. *Board of Education of Topeka* outlawed separate school systems for blacks and

Inflation Is Worst U.S. Enemy—Students

Overwhelming lack of confidence in the ability of the federal government to solve the problems facing the U.S. was apparent in a poll of high school seniors conducted by the Encyclopædia Britannica Educational Corp. Fewer than 10% of the students surveyed expressed confidence that the president and Congress could meet the nation's needs.

"Can these people . . . really be trusted as our leaders with the mess they have created?" was how one student put it, citing foreign affairs, energy, and deficit spending as areas where the government had failed. Another called the U.S. government the laughing stock of the world.

Inflation was named as the country's greatest problem by 62% of those polled (compared with 47% in a similar survey conducted a year earlier), while the oil shortage was second with 31%. Contradicting the beliefs of many economists, most of the students thought that inflation could be brought under control in a relatively short time if the government attacked the problem seriously; for example, by curtailing spending. Some rather cynical respondents felt this would be done after the presidential election.

Turning to foreign affairs, nearly two-thirds believed the U.S. would be involved in a major war before the end of the century, and 51% thought war would come within the next decade. Nevertheless, fewer than 10% planned to volunteer for military service. Passage of the SALT II agreement was favoured by about two to one.

Asked who they preferred among potential presidential candidates (before the Iranian crisis), the students picked Ted Kennedy (48%) and Jimmy Carter (39%) among the Democrats and, on the Republican side, Ronald Reagan and Gerald Ford (tied with approximately 38% each).

In the more personal realm, a majority listed their parents and other family members as having the greatest influence on their lives. Television continued to suffer an apparent decline. Named as the single greatest influence by most of the students taking part in a 1975 poll, it fell to 20% in 1978 and was not even mentioned in 1979.

Another continuing trend was the absence of public heroes. Asked who they thought was the greatest person in the world, a sizable number voted for themselves and 43% named their mothers and/or fathers. Less than 1% of the vote went to any U.S. political or government leader. Among the few public figures named were Pope John Paul II (6%) and Egyptian Pres. Anwar as-Sadat (2.6%).

Finally—reflecting, perhaps, a distinction between the disillusioning and disturbing outer world and personal life—89% said their high school years had been happy.

whites, one of the nation's biggest desegregation cases was set in motion by HEW Secretary Patricia Roberts Harris, who said that she could not in good conscience continue the stalled negotiations with Chicago's school board. HEW formally asked the Justice Department to undertake legal action to force the huge school system to desegregate. HEW officials charged that for 40 years the school system had perpetuated segregation and systematically avoided desegregation. Chicago's Access to Excellence program, which included some voluntary busing to schools offering special programs, was considered to be inadequate. The Chicago system faced further difficulties late in the year when its bond rating was downgraded, making borrowing impossible and threatening severe cash flow problems. The superintendent, the president of the board, and the board's financial officers resigned amid accusations of financial mismanagement.

The Supreme Court determined that federal judges could order systemwide busing even if school board policies had resulted in segregated schools in only part of a district. In a decision involving the Dayton, Ohio, schools, it reaffirmed the power of judges in Northern districts and continued a trend started in 1973 in a decision concerning Denver, Colo. The intent of the court was to require school districts to take affirmative action to remove all vestiges of discrimination, as well as to eliminate official actions that create segregated schools. Busing had been the major means of desegregating Northern school districts.

Several other court decisions had major implications for U.S. schools. A federal judge in San Francisco ruled that IQ testing is unconstitutional if it results in placing a disproportionate percentage of black and other minority children in classes for the mentally retarded. He held that the tests discriminated against minority groups because test items were based on what white students would be expected to know. In Florida, one of 38 states requiring high school students to pass a functional literacy test before graduating, a federal judge ruled that the test was academically valid but could not be used to determine readiness for graduation until all graduating seniors had attended desegregated schools. It would be four years before Florida met this standard.

A federal judge in Detroit sided with black parents in Ann Arbor, Mich., who claimed that "black English" is not merely substandard English but a bona fide language that must be recognized by teachers. However, the judge refused to reject school officials' methods of classifying students for "learning disabled" classes. The attorney for the parents had claimed that proficiency in black English was not recognized in the determination of verbal skills, which were a factor in class placement.

The Internal Revenue Service backed away from its proposed restrictions on the eligibility of private schools for tax-exempt status. The schools were given greater latitude in proving they did not discriminate against minority group children. The regulations covered only private elementary-secondary schools that had been found to be discriminatory or that had expanded as a result of school desegregation.

A year after California passed Proposition 13 cutting property taxes by $7 billion, there had been no appreciable decline in public services in the state. Local governments received 96% of the revenue they had expected before Proposition 13 was passed. The state continued to run a fiscal surplus, fees added some income, and citizens and businesses contributed hundreds of thousands of dollars to schools, parks, and other public services. However, Howard Jarvis, a leader in the campaign to pass Proposition 13, was working to reduce the high state personal income tax, and this, if successful, could seriously change the local budget situation.

Some 45,000 teachers in 15 U.S. states went on strike at the start of the 1979–80 school year, causing more than 800,000 students to miss the opening of school. The key demand was for more pay. Despite the fact that they were illegal in many jurisdictions, the number of teacher strikes was about 20 times what it had been in the 1960s.

Continuing a ten-year trend, Scholastic Aptitude Test (SAT) scores fell again, although the drop was small. One million U.S. students, about two-thirds of those planning to enter college, took the test, the most widely used college entrance examination in the country. Males again did better than females in both verbal and mathematical skills, particularly mathematics. A record 17% of students taking the SAT belonged to minorities, and more than half of these were black. A national survey indicated that, while most students could do mechanical mathematical operations, such as addition and multiplication, their ability to understand mathematical concepts and solve problems had declined since 1973. This coincided with the movement to eliminate the "new math" and emphasize "basics" in mathematics instruction.

In India yet another attempt was made to draft a national policy on education, with the aim of giving every boy and girl in the 6-to-14 age group eight years of elementary education within the next decade. The original target date—1960 under the constitution enacted in 1950—had been repeatedly postponed. The government also announced that it planned to attain universal literacy through the National Adult Education Program by the same deadline. Among the features of the new policy were the specifications that there should not be more than three public examinations and that schoolchildren were not to be examined in more than 7 out of 14 subjects. Also, the curriculum was to be made more relevant and would include "socially useful productive work." Other proposals included the introduction of more vocational education at the higher secondary stage and bringing industry into active collaboration with technical schools and colleges.

While many countries were showing interest in computer education, France appeared to be making the most vigorous efforts to introduce it into the school system. The Ministry of Education announced that over the next five years all upper secondary schools would be provided with their own mini-computers. In all, some 10,000 mini-computers were to be made available, at an estimated cost of £35 million. The aim was to give all students a basic understanding of computers and thereby expand the program of technological education introduced by former minister of education René Haby in 1977. It was also hoped that the program would help the French computer industry, which was thought to be in a somewhat precarious position. The proposals met some resistance from teachers, who feared that computer-assisted learning might replace them in the classroom. The minister denied this, though it seemed possible that the later stages of the program might involve some experimentation with computer-assisted instruction.

The Williams Committee presented its report on education and training in Australia. Established in October 1976 and chaired by Bruce Williams, vice-chancellor of Sydney University, the committee was charged with examining the whole range of educational provision in the country. Although it saw no need for fundamental structural alterations, the panel called for a more streamlined and cost-effective school system. The need to prepare young people for work was underlined by the fact that the unemployment rate for persons aged 14 to 19 was about three times that for the labour force as a whole. Secondary schools, therefore, were urged to help pupils in the transition from school

Pres. Jimmy Carter in October signed legislation creating a new Department of Education. In the photo he is applauded by supporters of the legislation.

TERESA ZABALA—THE NEW YORK TIMES

to work, to extend work-experience programs, and to improve career guidance. As in other debates on education in the English-speaking world, much was said about the need for schools to be accountable and to clarify their objectives and relate them to the needs of the community.

Ever since the 1960s, there had been a growing interest in the participation of parents, members of the community, and even pupils in the government of schools. In Western Europe, participation had advanced furthest in Denmark, which had changed its local government system in 1970 and in the process created governors for every school. The governors included parents, elected for a period of four years, with, in addition, a councillor from the local municipality, the head teacher, a representative of the teachers' council, and, in the case of the secondary schools, a representative of the pupils' council. These governors, in turn, elected representatives to the local education authority. By 1979 it was clear that this administrative invention had become a significant political element.

In Italy the recently established school councils were part of a movement that also attempted to decentralize educational administration by creating local provincial advisory bodies. However, bureaucratic control remained in the hands of the Italian civil service, and the new bodies had no real power. Art. 27 of Spain's new constitution called for more participation in the control of education, but its vague wording led to varying interpretations and considerable dispute. This came to a head early in 1979 when the headmistress of a school in Madrid was suspended for initiating a democratic system of school management.

In Ireland the boards of management of national schools, introduced some three years earlier, were still being boycotted by primary school teachers because the Roman Catholic Church had a majority of nominees. In Northern Ireland the Astin report, published in July, sought to reduce representation by church nominees—both Protestant and Catholic—in school government. In England and Wales legislation to implement the Taylor report, which recommended representation of parental and community interests on school governing bodies, was delayed by the fall of the Labour government, though the Conservative Party promised to work toward more parental involvement in the schools.

Higher Education. Intense pressure on places in higher education was endemic in the less developed countries, but China faced a particularly serious situation. University education had virtually ceased to develop during the Cultural Revolution. Before 1949 China had some 207 universities and colleges with about 155,000 students. By 1966, just before the Cultural Revolution, the number had increased to 435 institutions with 670,000 students. Ten years later the number of student places was virtually the same, although by 1978 some 850,000 were crammed into them. By 1979 it was reported that approximately 7 million students in middle schools were waiting to take examinations for the universities, and additional large numbers were hoping to make up for opportunities lost during the Cultural Revolution. It was clear that higher education would remain accessible to only a fraction of the population for some time to come.

WIDE WORLD

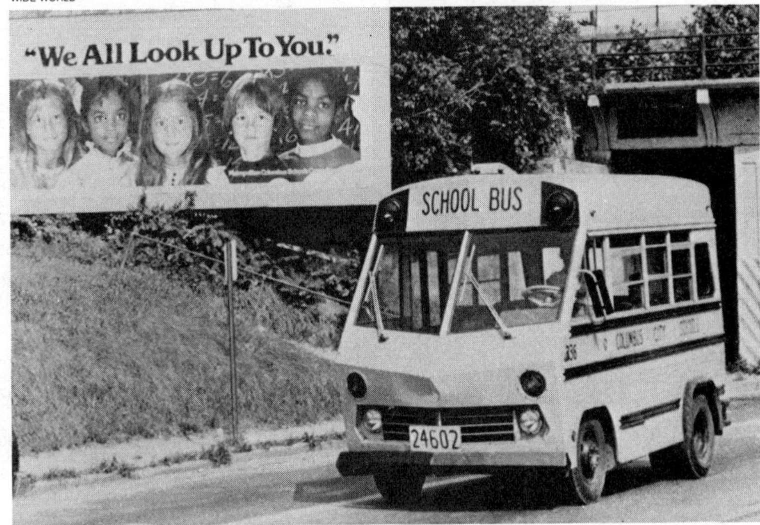

Billboards promoting school busing went up in Columbus, Ohio, when schools began a court-ordered busing program in September.

In Malaysia there were signs of dispute between the Chinese and Malay populations over university places. Between 1975 and 1979 the proportion of Chinese in the universities had dropped from 36% —some 15,000 places—to 29%, while the Malay proportion increased correspondingly. The Chinese community objected, but the Malays, infected to some extent with Islamic revivalism, emphatically rejected the Chinese protests.

Most Western European countries were attempting to contain the expansion of higher education, despite demographic pressures. A conference of West German university rectors proposed that 500 new university teaching posts be created to keep pace with student expansion up to 1988, when a peak was expected, but that existing posts should lapse when the holder retired. Estimates by the U.K. Department of Education and Science indicated that the number of students in higher education by 1985 would be much lower than previously forecast, and it was expected that many institutions of higher education, though not universities, might be forced to close.

Boston University became the first major private university in the U.S. to experience a faculty strike. After a bitter round of negotiations, agreement had been reached to increase faculty salaries and involvement in academic decision-making in the nation's fourth-largest private institution. The trustees then called for changes in the agreement, and the faculty struck. Unionized clerical, library, and maintenance workers supported the faculty's pay demands.

In the 1978 Bakke decision, the U.S. Supreme Court had struck down quota systems used to admit specific numbers of minority students to the medical school of the University of California at Davis. After the court made its ruling, the federal government provided specific guidance on what institutions could and could not do. The guidelines permitted setting numerical goals for the number of minority students an institution would like to admit, but not precise quotas. Race or national

World Education

Most recent official data

Country	1st level (primary)			General 2nd level (secondary)			Vocational 2nd level			3rd level (higher)			Literacy	
	Students (full-time)	Teachers (full-time)	Total schools	Students (full-time)	Teachers (full-time)	Total schools	Students (full-time)	Teachers (full-time)	Total schools	Students (full-time)	Teachers (full-time)	Total schools	% of population	Over age
Afghanistan	942,817	29,789	3,417	92,401	4,530	318	12,118	889	26	19,109	1,468	20	8.0	15
Albania	569,600	22,686	1,374	32,900	1,318	46	69,700[1]	1,712[1]	85	28,668	1,153	5	71.0	9
Algeria	2,894,084	77,009	8,209	718,122	25,882	939	23,839[1]	1,882[1]	52	51,983	5,366	15	26.4	15
Angola	536,599	13,230	5,585	59,209	3,060	177	18,899[1]	1,437[1]	73	2,942	274	1	30.0	...
Argentina	3,818,250	221,050	20,590	441,907	60,199	1,679	846,200	113,515	3,718	536,450	42,500	412	92.6	15
Australia	1,894,654	85,273	8,007	1,115,378[2]	77,615[2]	2,239	46,136[3]	2,870[3]	...	263,821	19,087	100	...	...
Austria	935,091	62,435	5,573	176,951	13,735	291	185,416[1]	4,369[1]	267	94,386	10,996	36	98.0	15
Bangladesh	9,488,090	172,448	40,313	2,321,046	92,310	9,304	26,988[1]	2,327[1]	122	297,272	5,364	396	22.2	15
Bolivia	945,733	38,737	...	127,895	7,143	...	22,598[1]	1,718[1]	80	41,408	2,307	16	39.8	15
Botswana	145,459	4,653	377	16,086	731	35	2,891	395	25	762	85	1	18.4	15
Brazil	19,286,611	887,424	186,563	628,178	156,174[4]	9,323	1,053,550[1]	...	...	1,316,640	120,550	...	79.8	15
Brunei	34,360	1,824	172	15,204	936	27	949	145	4[5]	...	...	...	64.0	15
Bulgaria	1,095,791[6]	57,177[6]	...	...	...	...	302,893[1]	21,731[1]	...	128,593	12,230	...	91.4	8
Burma	3,686,773[6]	79,653[6]	...	1,038,898	29,361	...	12,569[1]	1,015[1]	...	84,981	3,319	...	68.3	8
Cambodia	350,000	7,500	1,333	...	...	...	...	...	...	11,570	276	35	36.1	...
Cameroon	1,156,199	22,763	4,506	120,207	3,309	253	40,962[1]	1,549[1]	130	8,207	376	10	12.0	...
Canada	3,455,608	271,106[6,7]	16,500	1,820,620	...	...	...	...	...	616,795	52,373	235	95.6	14
Chile	2,368,005	93,271	4,120	324,379	41,666	525	166,092	11,509	234	130,208	22,211	8	89.0	15
China	146,240,000	2,600,000	...	65,480,000	...	...	880,000	...	...	850,000	...	...	40.0	...
Colombia	3,953,242	131,211	32,230	1,045,312	55,227	3,252	328,131[1]	18,889[1]	932	279,475	27,287	70	98.5	15
Congo	319,101	5,434	...	94,276	2,042	...	7,834[1]	371[1]	...	3,249	165	2	28.8	...
Costa Rica	365,957	10,965	...	93,862	4,264	...	22,175	1,651	...	32,928	3,500	5	84.7	15
Cuba	1,845,075	82,520	13,310	642,624	49,586	1,024	305,819[1]	15,703[1]	439	122,456	9,934	27	...	...
Czechoslovakia	1,941,089	98,779	8,860	127,188	8,333	349	556,809[1]	28,209[1]	1,516	137,629	17,559	36	99.5	15
Denmark	461,839	53,401	2,234	290,499	58,957	2,558	95,124	...	124	117,656	7,215	...	100.0	15
Dominican Republic	903,521	17,932	5,487	136,570	4,417	175	6,679[1]	348[1]	20	42,395	429	6	67.3	15
Ecuador	1,278,402	33,567	...	429,124[2]	25,954[2]	...	2,191[3]	153[3]	...	180,813	2,867	...	62.6	15
Egypt	4,211,345	132,728	10,297	1,935,088	59,729	2,402	474,017[1]	42,896[1]	448	518,630	...	12	43.4	10
El Salvador	853,811	16,563	...	72,898[2]	1,491[2]	...	868[3]	25[3]	...	31,351	2,015	...	49.0	15
Fiji	132,440	4,209	644	32,955	1,662	124	2,421[1]	242[1]	31	1,448	150	1	79.0	15
Finland	422,638	25,096	4,299	343,759	19,430	1,051	93,916[1]	12,337[1]	544	122,427	5,787	20	100.0	15
France	5,014,682	214,795	54,229	5,137,794	300,839	7,382	1,106,554[1]	52,328[1]	3,801	1,041,916	17,646[8]	17,718	100.0	7
Germany, East	2,599,596[6]	161,477[6]	5,593[6]	...	...	...	446,209	29,975	977	382,204	33,570	287	100.0	15
Germany, West	6,019,128	243,725	17,848	3,486,612	176,108	5,149	479,764	29,246	4,628	1,065,900	114,654	3,202	99.0	15
Greece	938,597	32,665	9,743	562,695	21,797	2,106	131,521	...	1,733	122,833	6,521	33	86.0	15
Guatemala	792,843	18,475	6,010	137,370[4]	6,237[4]	493	...	...	...	22,881	1,411	5	36.7	15
Honduras	522,710	14,479	5,088	76,776	...	...	24,032[1]	...	...	21,227	...	...	59.5	10
Hong Kong	550,530	18,321	882	441,785	15,064[1]	399	11,761	...	26	25,231	2,643	20	80.9	...
Hungary	1,107,000	71,925	4,214	352,000	14,954	...	...	...	...	106,000	13,450	48	98.2	15
India	55,772,018	1,354,460	477,037	40,702,098	1,505,565	141,600	273,504[1]	...	2,045	3,716,350	...	9,805	34.2	15
Indonesia	22,389,796	709,511	114,741	3,380,458	212,405	14,204	1,089,460[1]	78,492[1]	3,879	304,025	21,802	639	64.0	15
Iran	4,768,588	167,457	38,585	2,109,381	84,092	6,336	247,497[1]	12,303[1]	644	154,215	13,952	372	36.2	15
Iraq	2,459,870	87,148	10,560	781,766	25,254	1,579	68,674[1]	4,212[1]	155	89,197	5,207	62	52.0	15
Ireland	561,931	18,448	3,561	280,682	16,966	832	7,428	220	70	36,798	3,207	63	100.0	15
Israel	602,535	32,225	2,041	78,954	5,731	368	75,305	7,981	359	83,910	1,365	54	92.8[9]	14[9]
Italy	4,580,616	255,267	32,060	2,928,157	249,777	12,721	1,687,355[1]	131,145[1]	4,060	756,922	43,277	60	93.9	15
Ivory Coast	740,375	15,358	2,697	113,366	3,959	...	9,165	620	...	8,701	368	...	20.0	...
Japan	11,146,859	445,719	24,876	9,463,367[2]	481,668[2]	15,875	...	...	...	2,289,197	117,934	1,016	99.7	...
Jordan	431,107	13,351	1,076	221,822	10,354	1,297	9,266	582	16	20,317	996	22	67.6	15
Kenya	2,974,849	89,773	8,896	320,310	12,696	1,486	559[3]	64[3]	2	14,264	1,500	20	40.0	15
Korea, South	5,640,712	117,290	6,450	3,282,151[2]	80,472[2]	2,780	677,824	19,993	574	406,087	25,603	222	88.5	13
Kuwait	120,504	7,920	177	156,496	11,804	199	6,025[1]	1,216[1]	16	9,318	606	5	64.0	10
Laos	442,000	7,248	2,125	59,200	607	37	14,413[1]	497[1]	27	1,000	152	3	58.8	...
Lebanon	497,723	32,901[6]	2,319	167,578	...	1,241	7,133[1]	1,059[1]	159	50,803	2,313	13	88.0	15
Lesotho	225,960	4,235	1,081	17,433	621	60	1,213[1]	851[1]	11	601	95	9	56.5	15
Liberia	129,776	7,360[6]	843	108,077	...	275	1,173[1]	119[1]	6	2,694	190	3	21.5	15
Libya	574,770	26,182	2,150	194,866	12,792	2,150	30,420[1]	2,455[1]	106	17,174	1,922	19	52.4	15
Luxembourg	33,638	1,821	...	8,438	860	15	15,482[1]	941	42	446	137	2	100.0	15
Malawi	675,740	11,115	2,371	15,140	725	61	2,525[1]	175[1]	13	1,836	122	4	16.5	15
Malaysia	1,929,914	61,267	6,370	961,288	34,315	1,179	21,740	993	82	40,755	2,686	23	60.8	10
Mali	370,000	9,413	...	20,000	511	...	4,444[1]	458[1]	...	6,000	327	4	2.2	...
Mauritius	136,019	6,269	236	78,038	2,452	130	1,565[1]	113[1]	10	967	100	2	61.6	12
Mexico	12,600,620	274,717	55,618	2,999,456	160,532	8,778	454,658[1]	32,438[1]	1,494	599,920	30,865	149	76.2	9
Morocco	1,925,187	50,829	2,236	650,796	40,507	644	26,223	...	...	76,054	...	19	22.2	...
Mozambique	577,997	8,345	...	36,155	1,682	...	18,485[1]	1,106[1]	...	2,621	326	...	7.0	...
Nepal	643,835	20,775	...	243,231	10,609	...	19,517[1]	1,451[1]	...	23,504	1,516	...	12.5	15
Netherlands, The	1,521,037	62,956	9,564	811,998	52,116	1,527	549,335[1]	45,100[1]	1,847	261,188	28,000	382	100.0	15
New Zealand	519,431	21,110	2,553	234,705	13,744	395	5,960	1,872	17	35,911	3,459	15	100.0	15
Nicaragua	373,948	9,759	2,334	85,192	2,631[2]	197	20,237	...	78[1]	23,566	1,052	8	57.0	15
Nigeria	4,889,857	144,351	14,676	498,744	19,409	1,343	71,333	3,480[1]	217[1]	32,971	5,019	13	25.0	15
Norway	397,700	20,543	2,998	260,389	20,758[2]	1,413	87,618	10,332	...	66,710	6,679	130	100.0	15
Pakistan	5,877,880	148,059	53,246	2,079,863	117,210	7,997	45,752[1]	2,976[1]	356	340,858	18,129	546	26.7	10
Panama	368,738	13,032	2,260	95,682	3,712	77	43,509	2,240[1]	115[1]	35,444	1,808	2	81.3	15
Papua New Guinea	268,136	8,590	1,994	35,105	1,369	94	8,408[1]	1,076[1]	107	9,804	1,235	46	32.1	10
Paraguay	477,237	16,869	2,799	92,437[2]	8,825[2]	...	...	...	...	20,032	1,846	...	79.7	15
Peru	3,019,624	75,491	20,126	699,547	26,987	1,537	190,559	7,568	329	190,635	12,113	58	71.6	15
Philippines	7,861,641	270,764	33,180	2,696,460	82,191	2,445	182,196	...	284	946,860	26,003	...	76.4	15
Poland	4,111,656	189,342	12,590	389,319	24,502	885	1,403,733[1]	73,219[1]	6,507	401,233	76,556	90	97.8	15
Portugal	1,284,862	67,051	13,448	417,112	13,272	458	90,784[1]	9,590[1]	223	84,911	8,198	267	71.0	...
Puerto Rico	520,000	27,360[6]	1,357	158,000	...	476	...	3,097	71	100,885	1,042	13	87.1	15
Romania	3,153,016	148,922	14,608	1,020,608	49,898	934	171,831[1]	5,554[1]	726	182,337	13,575	...	100.0	8
Rwanda	434,150	8,161	1,606	8,870	820[4]	56	3,700[1]	...	...	1,069	184	4	23.0	15
Saudi Arabia	686,108	35,139	2,711	203,314	13,875	749	19,483[1]	1,853[1]	78	26,437	2,133	20	5.2	...
Senegal	345,198	9,496	...	78,384	1,758	...	14,090[1]	820[1]	124	8,213	412	...	45.6	6
Singapore	300,398	11,112	364	179,811	7,828	135	9,342[1]	767[1]	13	15,861	1,040	4	77.4	10
South Africa	4,122,079	145,132[2,11]	4,784[6]	979,193	...	...	20,773	...	179	136,293	10,597	52	89.0	...
Soviet Union	34,300,000	2,641,000[6]	167,000	10,400,000	...	...	4,662,000[1]	227,000[1]	4,302	5,109,600	336,000	865	99.7	10
Spain	6,640,246	211,037	201,226	783,964	51,466	2,242	407,812	28,075	1,878	647,298	31,160	232	90.1	15
Sri Lanka	1,492,147	50,665	6,970	1,076,502	57,854	1,673	11,587[1]	1,845[1]	39	14,568	1,860	...	78.1	10
Sudan	1,217,510	33,783	4,440	313,185	12,880	1,075	13,858[1]	1,197[1]	1,069	21,342	1,420	20	20.0	9
Sweden	697,000	37,740	4,934	567,000	46,994	...	...	...	...	149,000[1]	...	...	100.0	15
Syria	1,326,414	41,550	7,169	362,885	30,143	1,150	32,753[1]	3,399[1]	75	85,474	1,332	3	46.6	10
Taiwan	2,319,342	66,954	2,378	1,563,321[2]	64,327[2]	...	...	...	...	308,583	15,275	101	85.9	15
Tanzania	1,954,443	39,245	...	56,481	2,930	...	11,695[1]	786[1]	...	3,064	434[8]	...	...	...
Thailand	6,810,747	270,567	32,445	1,049,360	34,450	1,043	209,722[1]	15,050[1]	320	81,696	7,757	27	81.8	10
Togo	395,381	6,528	1,199	74,567	1,832	112	6,807[1]	329[1]	23	2,186	177	2	10.5	...
Tunisia	1,004,144	25,342	2,469	247,299[2]	10,711[2]	202	...	...	...	23,339	2,282	...	32.2	10
Turkey	5,499,456	182,314	...	1,030,746	28,908	2,933	323,521[1]	18,804[1]	563	339,692	16,981	...	54.7	6
Uganda	1,139,420	32,554	4,022	58,816	2,665	198	11,295[1]	644[1]	44	5,474	617	4	32.0	15
United Kingdom	5,572,523	237,699	27,102	4,844,165[2]	285,106[2]	5,882	...	...	...	735,800	33,100	105	100.0	15
United States	32,600,000	1,320,000	...	15,600,000[2]	1,120,000[2]	...	...	...	...	11,600,000	830,000	...	98.8	14
Uruguay	382,759	15,679	2,327	138,000	13,980	261	55,034[1]	4,541[1]	23	39,927	2,149	3	90.5	15
Venezuela	1,990,123	63,198	...	583,163	35,671[4]	...	48,047	...	...	213,542	15,792	...	83.4	...
Western Samoa	41,463	1,471	152	9,290	492	38	664[1]	70[1]	4	207	38	6	98.3	10
Yugoslavia	1,456,809	58,801	13,333	1,786,330	83,377	5,905	493,504[1]	41,206[1]	1,630[1]	256,420	16,202	319	83.5	10
Zaire	3,538,257	80,481	5,924	225,606	14,483[4]	2,511	109,597	...	...	21,021	2,550	36	15.0	15
Zambia	907,867	19,300	2,743	78,805	3,538	121	8,172[1]	710[1]	24[1]	3,447	412	5	38.3	15
Zimbabwe Rhodesia	829,039	23,844	3,172	76,743	3,810	192	4,034	325	20	4,913	489	15	34.3	15

[1]Includes teacher training. [2]Includes vocational. [3]Teacher training only. [4]General includes vocational and teacher training. [5]Excludes teacher training.
[6]Data for primary include secondary. [7]Includes preprimary education. [8]Universities only. [9]Jewish population only. [10]Kenyans only. [11]Public schools only. [12]Excludes teachers' colleges.

origin could be used as a positive criterion in making admissions decisions.

Regulations on intercollegiate athletics issued under Title IX of the Education Amendments of 1972 became effective at the start of the 1979–80 academic year. They required that expenditures on athletics, including athletic scholarships, be proportional to the number of men and women athletes. A proposed regulation mandating equal expenditure per capita was dropped, but athletic benefits were to be made available to women "in an equitable way" and the interests and abilities of both sexes were to be taken into account in planning athletic programs. The 1972 legislation prohibited sex discrimination in any institution that received federal funds, and Congress required HEW to develop guidelines.

Several groups representing the handicapped organized to oppose a Supreme Court decision that handicapped persons are protected from discrimination only if they can participate in an educational program in spite of the handicap. In its first ruling under sec. 504 of the 1973 Rehabilitation Act, the court held that a handicap can be taken into account in an institution's decision to refuse admission and that an institution does not have to substantially change its standards to admit a handicapped person to a collegiate program.

The job market for U.S. college graduates was mixed. Job offers to bachelor's degree holders were up 30% from 1978, but master's degree students received 9% fewer job offers, and doctorate holders experienced a 23% drop. Offers to some graduate-level students increased, however, most notably in engineering and computer sciences. Job opportunities expanded more rapidly for women than for men. Liberal-arts graduates were the least sought after.

After more than a decade of grade inflation, U.S. college and university faculty were beginning to assign lower grades. In some cases, administrators applied pressure to return grades to a more normal distribution.

Research. The most influential research paper to appear in Western Europe was the so-called Rutter report, entitled *Fifteen Thousand Hours* (the time most English children spend in school). Michael Rutter, a psychiatrist, and his colleagues analyzed records of attendance, behaviour, and examinations at 12 secondary schools in London in an effort to determine how much the school, as an institution, actually affects a child's progress in these areas. The effects of schooling had been seriously challenged by James Coleman and others in the U.S., but *Fifteen Thousand Hours* came out unequivocally in favour of the school as a highly significant influence on the child's progress.

The Rutter team found that schools differed in attendance rates, pupil behaviour (at school and outside), and examination results, and that these differences were not simply a product of family circumstances, the local environment, or the achievement of the feeder primary schools. The report emphasized the need for a structured framework in the school and for properly balanced intakes. "The outcomes are likely to be most favourable when there is a reasonable balance of academically successful children who . . . are more prone to identify with the school goals. . . ."

Another noteworthy document was the report by Torsten Husén of a series of seminars run by the Aspen Institute. The seminars began in Aspen, Colo., in 1976 and were later followed by discussions at the Aspen Institute in Berlin. Husén, a professor of education in Stockholm, undertook to write a book based on the findings, which he titled *The School in Question: A Comparative Study of the School and Its Future in Western Societies.*

The book concluded, among other things, that schools are remarkably resistant to change. Husén quotes Philip Jackson as saying that U.S. schools during the past 15 years had "lived through a spirit of reform that did not materialize." Turning his attention to the shape of things to come, Husén concluded that by the end of the century the time devoted to formal full-time schooling would be reduced. Formal classroom teaching would continue to age 15, after which all young persons would have "drawing rights" to another four to six years of education in institutions of their own choosing. Thus there would be a system of lifelong or recurrent education related to career patterns and changes. (JOEL L. BURDIN; TUDOR DAVID)

See also Libraries; Motion Pictures; Museums.

Egypt

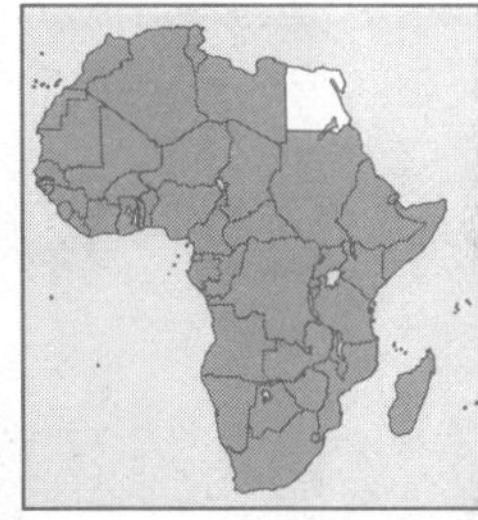

Egypt

A republic of northeast Africa, Egypt is bounded by Israel, Sudan, Libya, the Mediterranean Sea, and the Red Sea. Area: 997,667 sq km (385,201 sq mi). Pop. (1979 est.): 41,065,000. Cap. and largest city: Cairo (pop., 1979 est., 5,423,000). Language: Arabic. Religion (1976): Muslim 94%, according to official figures; non-Muslims, however, may be undercounted. President in 1979, Anwar as-Sadat; prime minister, Mustafa Khalil.

Foreign Relations. In 1979 Egypt became the first Arab nation to sign a peace treaty with Israel. Because of this it suffered throughout the year the opposition of most other Arab countries. Financial aid to Egypt was suspended, diplomatic relations were severed, and the regime of Pres. Anwar as-Sadat was condemned. President Sadat sought compensatory aid from the United States and took measures to silence political and religious opposition to his rule.

In January negotiations between Egypt and Israel under the terms of the 1978 Camp David accords appeared to have reached an impasse. Mediation efforts in the Middle East by Alfred Atherton, special envoy of U.S. Pres. Jimmy Carter, between January 16 and 28 collapsed over the question of Egypt's treaty obligations to come to the defense of other Arab states should they be attacked by Israel. Discussions continued in the U.S. between Israeli and Egyptian delegations, led, respectively, by Foreign Minister Moshe Dayan and Prime Minister Mustafa Khalil. Egyptian delegation member Osama al-Baz expressed his government's unwillingness to abandon its Arab allies: "If the price of peace with Israel is the isolation of Egypt from the Arab world, then Egypt chooses to remain in the Arab fold."

CLAUDE SALHANI—SIPA PRESS/BLACK STAR

U.S. Pres. Jimmy Carter and Egyptian Pres. Anwar as-Sadat acknowledged the cheers of throngs which lined the streets when Carter arrived in Cairo for a state visit in March.

The negotiations seemed to be in imminent danger of collapsing at the end of February, as a result of the Israelis' refusal to recognize Egypt's prior treaty obligations, when President Carter personally intervened. He invited Israeli Prime Minister Menahem Begin to Washington at the beginning of March and presented him with U.S. compromise proposals, which Begin accepted on March 5. Carter flew to Egypt on March 8 to present the measures to President Sadat. Several thousand students at Alexandria University demonstrated their opposition to Carter's visit and the proposed treaty, and arrests by police followed. Carter flew to Israel on March 10 for final discussions on the proposals. He stopped in Cairo again on March 13, meeting Sadat at Cairo International Airport and announcing that he had achieved the formula for an Egyptian-Israeli peace treaty. On his return to Washington Carter dispatched his national security adviser, Zbigniew Brzezinski, to Egypt, Saudi Arabia, and Jordan in an effort to win "moderate" Arab support for the treaty.

On March 26 Begin and Sadat signed the peace treaty between Egypt and Israel on the White House lawn in Washington, ending the state of war between their two countries that had existed since 1948. Differences between the two sides emerged, however, even before the signing ceremony, and both Begin and Sadat lobbied for public and congressional sympathy in Washington. Under the terms of the treaty Israel would return the Sinai Peninsula to Egypt through phased withdrawals over a period of three years, and Egypt would grant Israel full diplomatic recognition. The treaty left out the thorny issues of Syrian and Jordanian territories occupied by Israel, Israeli colonization of the West Bank and Gaza, self-determination for the Palestinians, and the status of Jerusalem.

On May 25 Israel returned El Arish to Egypt and in the succeeding months gave back other parts of the Sinai, including St. Catherine's Monastery on Mt. Sinai. Despite the steady Israeli withdrawals there was no progress in discussions between Egypt and Israel on Palestinian "autonomy" in the Israeli-occupied West Bank and Gaza Strip. The U.S. negotiator, Robert Strauss (*see* BIOGRAPHIES), was unable to persuade either Egypt or Israel to accept the U.S. compromise proposals for limited Palestinian self-rule.

A demonstration of the new era in Egyptian-Israeli relations occurred in August when the first Israeli tour group arrived in Cairo to visit the pyramids and other attractions in the once-forbidden land. Israel, in response, began approving visas for visiting Egyptians.

The Arab League Council met in Baghdad, Iraq, at the end of March to suspend Egypt's League membership and to transfer Arab League headquarters from Cairo to Tunis. By the end of April all Arab states except Sudan, Oman, and Somalia had severed diplomatic relations with Egypt. In May the Conference of Islamic States met in Fez, Morocco, to suspend Egyptian membership in that organization. Although private Arab businessmen were permitted to trade with Egypt, the Arab oil-producing nations ended their substantial subsidies to the Egyptian government. Saudi Arabia, Qatar, and the United Arab Emirates withdrew from the Arab Organization for Industrialization (AOI), the main function of which had been the funding of Egyptian arms manufacture. Egypt in retaliation froze the AOI's U.S. $1.4 billion assets. On July 6 Saudi Arabia canceled an agreement to purchase for Egypt 50 F-5E jet fighters from the U.S.

President Sadat in 1979 turned to the U.S. for the aid he had forfeited from the Arab countries. He announced in January that Egypt would need another "Marshall Plan" and U.S. aid of $21 billion over five years for the country to find its way out of its economic difficulties. To improve his standing with the U.S., Sadat in February offered to make Egypt the "watchdog" of Western interests in the region. He gave refuge to the deposed shah of Iran for one week in January and offered him permanent asylum in November, when the Mexican government refused to readmit him and the U.S. government was seeking a friendly nation to accept him. He offered to send Egyptian troops to Oman to support the sultan against left-wing insurgents and to Morocco in defense of King Hassan's claims to the Western Sahara. Relations with neighbouring Libya and with the revolutionary regime in Iran became especially strained in 1979, and Egypt's political isolation in the region intensified throughout the year. Sadat, however, maintained Egypt's membership in both the Organization of African Unity and the nonaligned movement, over strong Arab objections.

Relations with the Soviet Union improved during the year. In November Egypt announced the appointment of one of its leading diplomats, Muhammad Samih Anwar, as ambassador to the U.S.S.R. Previously, for more than two years, the Egyptian embassy in Moscow had functioned under the leadership of a lower-ranking chargé d'affaires. Other indications of the improvement in relations included deliveries of Soviet spare parts for Egyptian military aircraft and an increase in commercial activity. Analysts believed that the Soviet Union was making an effort to increase its limited influence in the Middle East, while Egypt was trying to win Soviet support in the UN should the Palestinian autonomy question be brought before that forum.

Domestic Affairs. The treaty with Israel appeared to be popular with most Egyptians, who viewed it as the only means of relieving the country of its large military commitments, and Sadat attempted to build a consensus at home that he lacked in the rest of the Arab world. He nevertheless encountered both religious and political hostility to the treaty and to his other policies. A referendum of Egyptian voters on April 19, the accuracy of which was hotly contested in Egypt, gave a 99.95% vote in favour of the treaty. In the June parliamentary elections the pro-government National Democratic Party won 330 of 360 People's Assembly seats. The opposition Unionist Progressive Party, led by Khalid Mohieddine (one of the original Free Officers who led the 1952 revolution), won no seats; it accused the government of irregularities in the balloting and complained of the arrest and harassment of its members. Fifty-six alleged members of the Egyptian Communist Party were arrested on August 17, and in December Muslim fundamentalist demonstrators were arrested at Cairo University.

On January 9 the government announced a record budget of $18,489,900,000. Anticipated revenue was $14,657,500,000, leaving a deficit of $3,832,400,000 (30% of national income). The anticipated deficit, the increase in Egypt's national debt to $12 billion (excluding previous debts to the Soviet Union), and a deficit in the balance of trade led to continuing difficulties with the International Monetary Fund. The IMF conditions of 1978 for a three-year loan of $730 million were not met, and Egypt received only $90 million. The World Bank lent Egypt $219 million, and Japan lent $145 million in 1979. Although the U.S. pledged $1.8 billion in military and civilian aid to Egypt, this fell far short of Sadat's goal of $21 billion over five years.

The Egyptian economy, however, continued to expand in 1979 at a rate of about 8%, with growth attributed to an increase in Sinai oil income, Suez Canal revenues, and tourism. The inflation rate in 1979 was about 37%. (CHARLES GLASS)

EGYPT

Education. (1976–77) Primary, pupils 4,151,956, teachers 125,397; secondary, pupils 1,828,090, teachers 52,700; vocational, pupils 408,540, teachers 25,215; teacher training, students 32,744, teachers 2,830; higher, students 717,053, teaching staff 24,987.

Finance. Monetary unit: Egyptian pound, with (Sept. 17, 1979) an official rate of E£0.70 to U.S. $1 (free rate of E£1.58 = £1 sterling). Gold, SDR's, and foreign exchange (June 1979) U.S. $414 million. Budget (1978 est.) balanced at E£6,516 million. Gross national product (1977) E£7,139 million. Money supply (June 1979) E£4,097.7 million. Cost of living (1975 = 100; June 1979) 148.

Foreign Trade. (1978) Imports E£2,632.2 million; exports E£679.8 million. Import sources: U.S. 16%; West Germany 11%; Italy 8%; U.K. 8%; France 7%; Japan 5%. Export destinations: U.S.S.R. 17%; Italy 12%; U.S. 5%; The Netherlands 5%; France 5%; Japan 5%. Main exports: crude oil 21%; cotton 19%; cotton yarn and fabrics 17%; fruit and vegetables 7%; petroleum products 7%; aluminum 5%.

Transport and Communications. Roads (1976) 26,596 km. Motor vehicles in use (1977): passenger 283,200; commercial (including buses) 64,000. Railways (1976): 4,856 km; traffic 8,748,000,000 passenger-km, freight 2,201,000,000 net ton-km. Air traffic (1978): 2,325,000,000 passenger-km; freight 25.8 million net ton-km. Shipping (1978): merchant vessels 100 gross tons and over 205; gross tonnage 456,291. Telephones (Jan. 1975) 503,200. Radio licenses (Dec. 1976) 5,250,000. Television licenses (Dec. 1975) 620,000.

Agriculture. Production (in 000; metric tons; 1978): wheat 1,933; barley 132; millet 656; corn 3,197; rice 2,351; potatoes *c.* 950; sugar, raw value *c.* 680; tomatoes 1,505; onions 503; dry broad beans (1977) *c.* 237; watermelons (1977) *c.* 1,250; dates 460; oranges 700; grapes 250; cotton, lint *c.* 375; cheese *c.* 234; beef and buffalo meat 234. Livestock (in 000; 1978): cattle *c.* 2,150; buffalo *c.* 2,300; sheep 1,800; goats 1,380; asses (1977) *c.* 1,574; camels (1977) *c.* 101; chickens *c.* 26,986.

Industry. Production (in 000; metric tons; 1978): cement 3,033; iron ore (metal content; 1977) 704; crude oil 24,383; natural gas (cu m; 1977) 1,470,000; petroleum products (1977) 10,466; sulfuric acid 235; fertilizers (nutrient content; 1977–78) nitrogenous 195, phosphate 80; salt (1977) 701; cotton yarn 212; cotton fabrics (m) 728,000; electricity (kw-hr; 1977) *c.* 13 million.

El Salvador

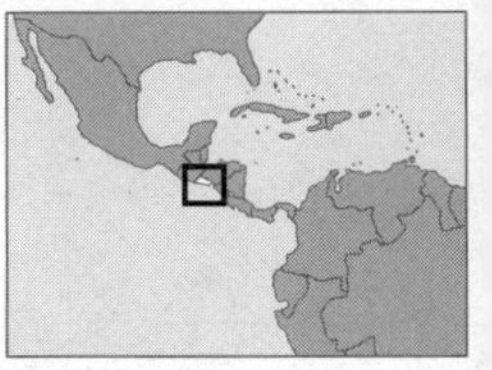
El Salvador

A republic on the Pacific coast of Central America and the smallest country on the isthmus, El Salvador is bounded on the west by Guatemala and on the north and east by Honduras. Area: 21,041 sq km (8,124 sq mi). Pop. (1979 est.): 4,663,000. Cap. and largest city: San Salvador (pop., 1975 est., 378,100). Language: Spanish. Religion: Roman Catholic. President in 1979, Gen. Carlos Humberto Romero until October 15; after October 15 the country was governed by a military junta headed by Col. Jaime Abdul Gutiérrez and Col. Adolfo Arnoldo Majano.

On Oct. 15, 1979, a "moderate" military junta, headed by Col. Jaime Abdul Gutiérrez and Col.

Eire:
see Ireland

Electrical Industries:
see Energy; Industrial Review

Electronics:
see Computers; Industrial Review

EL SALVADOR

Education. (1978) Primary, pupils 858,811, teachers (1976) 16,563; secondary and vocational, pupils 72,898, teachers (1975) 1,491; teacher training (1976), students 868, teachers (1975) 25; higher, students 31,351, teaching staff (1976) 2,015.

Finance. Monetary unit: colón, with (Sept. 17, 1979) a par value of 2.50 colones to U.S. $1 (free rate of 5.33 colones = £1 sterling). Gold, SDR's, and foreign exchange (June 1979) U.S. $298 million. Budget (1978 actual): revenue 1,048,000,000 colones; expenditure 1,184,000,000 colones. Gross national product (1978) 7,612,000,000 colones. Money supply (June 1979) 1,099,000,000 colones. Cost of living (1975 = 100; June 1979) 145.

Foreign Trade. (1978) Imports 2,552,800,000 colones; exports 1,571,800,000 colones. Import sources (1977): U.S. 29%; Guatemala 13%; Japan 11%; Venezuela 9%; West Germany 6%; Costa Rica 5%. Export destinations (1977): U.S. 33%; West Germany 19%; Guatemala 13%; The Netherlands 9%; Japan 6%; Costa Rica 5%. Main exports (1977): coffee 63%; cotton 8%.

Transport and Communications. Roads (1974) 10,972 km (including 625 km of Pan-American Highway). Motor vehicles in use (1977): passenger 70,100; commercial (including buses) 35,500. Railways (1977) 602 km. Air traffic (1977): 219 million passenger-km; freight *c.* 25 million net ton-km. Telephones (Jan. 1978) 70,400. Radio receivers (Dec. 1976) 1.4 million. Television receivers (Dec. 1976) 136,000.

Agriculture. Production (in 000; metric tons; 1978): corn 540; sorghum 176; dry beans 43; sugar, raw value 297; bananas (1977) *c.* 53; oranges *c.* 51; coffee 132; cotton, lint 74. Livestock (in 000; 1977): cattle *c.* 1,162; pigs *c.* 430; horses *c.* 83; chickens *c.* 3,400.

Industry. Production (in 000; metric tons; 1977): cement 334; petroleum products 715; cotton yarn 6.4; electricity (kw-hr; 1978) *c.* 1,450,000.

Adolfo Arnoldo Majano, overthrew and exiled Pres. Carlos Humberto Romero and promised reform, establishment of order, and free elections. However, the coup failed to end the unrest and extremist violence that plagued the country throughout the year.

Earlier, in response to the growing unrest, Romero's government had proposed liberalizing reforms. In March a law giving the government extraconstitutional powers was repealed, and later the president promised free congressional elections in 1980.

Despite these measures, extremist violence, along with active political opposition, increased dramatically. Coalitions of peasant, student, and labour union groups occupied embassies and churches to protest economic and political conditions. Twenty-three people died on May 8 after police fired on a demonstration in support of the Popular Revolutionary Bloc's occupation of the San Salvador cathedral. On May 22 police shot and killed 14 students marching toward the Venezuelan embassy, which had been taken over by the same group. The government subsequently imposed a month's state of siege.

Guerrilla kidnapping of businessmen for ransom continued, and prominent individuals, including the education minister, the Swiss chargé d'affaires, and the brother of the president, were killed by antigovernment forces. Three Roman Catholic priests were assassinated, allegedly by government-backed paramilitary organizations. In the most serious of a series of strikes, electrical workers virtually paralyzed San Salvador on March 19–20 when they turned off city electricity.

Within two weeks of the coup, violence escalated once again. At least 45 persons died during three days in late October, more than 25 of them in a five-hour battle with national security forces in downtown San Salvador. On November 6 the Popular Revolutionary Bloc reached a truce with the junta and vacated two government ministries, where they had been holding some 30 hostages. Other leftist groups vowed to continue their resistance. (KAREN DEYOUNG)

Energy

Two events regarding energy made headlines throughout the world in 1979. One concerned nuclear power, the other oil, and the repercussions of both continued throughout the year.

Three Mile Island. On March 28 an operating nuclear power reactor at Three Mile Island in the Susquehanna River, near Harrisburg, Pa., experienced the most serious accident in the history of the nuclear power industry in the United States. (*See* Sidebar.) During a period of three days a combination of faulty information, poor communications, overlapping authority, and some sensationalism in the handling of the event by the media came close to creating public panic. The public was led to believe at one time that the most dreaded of all nuclear accidents—the meltdown of a reactor core—was imminent. This was followed by the announcement of a possible hydrogen explosion in the reactor, with the possible consequent release of large amounts of radioactivity over a wide area. Pregnant women and children were advised to leave the immediate surrounding area, and many people did so.

As it turned out, by the time the accident became publicly known the danger of core meltdown was already past, and the danger of a hydrogen explosion never existed. It was determined that the radioactivity actually released did not constitute a threat to the general public. The consequences of the accident were, nevertheless, widespread and profound. They included:

1. Several investigations, including one by a presidential commission, hearings in both houses of Congress, and others by the nuclear and electric utility industries.
2. The immediate closing of seven operating reactors like that at Three Mile Island and the delayed restarting of five other similar reactors currently shut down for maintenance. These reactors were not allowed to operate until the Nuclear Regulatory Commission was satisfied that they had been modified so as to prevent a recurrence of the Three Mile Island event. (The last of the reactors was restored to operation in August.)
3. A moratorium on the licensing of all new nuclear reactors by the Nuclear Regulatory Commission, which lasted until September.
4. The cancellation of three nuclear reactor projects by other utilities.
5. A flood of lawsuits against the utility operating the Three Mile Island reactor by local residents who had fled the area during the incident or who claimed psychic trauma from the fear it generated.
6. An intensification of the campaign against nuclear power by its opponents.

Other governments nervously reassessed their own nuclear power plants and programs in the

Employment:
see Economy, World

light of Three Mile Island, as nuclear opponents stepped up their efforts. Sweden scheduled a national referendum on nuclear power for March 1980. Only in Japan did the accident result in plant closings. The government temporarily shut down one reactor and postponed the restarting of nine others that were shut down for maintenance.

The presidential commission made its report in October. It concluded that although no one had been harmed, the accident was far too serious to permit another similar occurrence. Its recommendations called for, among other things, a restructuring of the Nuclear Regulatory Commission, much greater emphasis on safety in the design and operation of nuclear reactors and in operator training, and better emergency planning at all levels of government and the electric utility industry.

In the first few months after the event its long-term effect on the future of nuclear power in the U.S. was much debated. Nuclear opponents contended that a full-fledged disaster had been narrowly averted and that it demonstrated the inherently intolerable danger of nuclear power. Proponents argued that, to the contrary, all safety systems had operated as designed, the danger had been unduly sensationalized, no one had been harmed, and the lessons learned from the incident would ensure that it could never recur. By the end of the year it appeared that the setback to nuclear power was temporary and that orders for new reactors would eventually be resumed. No one could say, however, how long it would be before that occurred.

That new capacity of some kind would be needed was made clear by the repeated setting of records for weekly consumption of electricity during the year. The record set in the summer of 1978 was broken during a week of cold weather in January. This in turn was broken during two consecutive weeks in August. The new record was 49,500,000,000 kw-hr for one week's use. This occurred despite voluntary conservation efforts and federal restrictions on thermostat settings for air conditioning in publicly used buildings.

Iranian Revolution. The oil event of outstanding importance was the Iranian revolution. As part of the disorders that led to the flight of Shah Mohammad Reza Pahlavi on January 16, strikes by the oil workers had cut off Iranian oil exports at the end of 1978. Although the Ayatollah Ruhollah Khomeini (*see* BIOGRAPHIES) ended his exile on February 1, exports did not resume until the first week in March and then were only a trickle. Since Iran had been providing nearly 12% of the oil supply of the non-Communist world, the cutoff of exports had far-reaching repercussions. Taking advantage of the situation, the Organization of Petroleum Exporting Countries (OPEC) decreed in December 1978 an increase in prices beginning with a 5% rise on Jan. 1, 1979, and continuing with increases on April 1, July 1, and October 1 that would amount to a total of 14.5% for the year.

By the time Iran's exports were resumed, world oil markets were in a state of disruption approaching that occasioned by the Arab oil embargo of 1973–74. Other OPEC countries, notably Saudi Arabia, increased their exports, so a full-fledged

WIDE WORLD

More than 400 service stations in Iowa began pumping gasohol, a mixture of alcohol and gasoline. The alcohol was made from Iowa corn.

crisis was averted. Amid uncertainty as to how long this policy would be maintained and the degree to which Iran could resume its former level of output and export, importing nations scrambled to obtain supplies and avoid serious shortages. The International Energy Agency, the organization of the major oil importing countries, laid plans to share available supplies among its members if any of them experienced a serious shortage, and all countries took steps to conserve supplies.

For the OPEC countries the opportunity afforded by the continuing absence of Iranian exports was irresistible. By late February first one and then another of the OPEC members began to increase their prices over the levels established on January 1 by adding "surcharges." An OPEC meeting in late March raised the base price of crude oil by 9% effective April 1, bringing the price to the level previously scheduled to take effect on October 1. At the same time OPEC broke precedent by officially approving the right of its members to add individual surcharges to the base price. As a result the actual price increases on April 1 averaged 17%.

The resumption of Iranian exports at less than half their previous level was followed by production cutbacks by some OPEC members and additional "surcharges" on export prices. At its June meeting OPEC responded to this pressure by approving yet another increase. This time, however, there was a split in OPEC ranks over the size of the increase. In a compromise that set another precedent, OPEC established a floor price to accommodate the moderates, such as Saudi Arabia, and a ceiling to satisfy the radicals, such as Iran. As of July 1 Saudi light crude, the official benchmark, was priced at $18 per barrel, compared with $13.34 on January 1, and other producers could charge as high as $23.50 per barrel.

Continued high prices on the spot market, however, led to still further announcements of price increases by individual OPEC countries during the fourth quarter. With spot prices of $30 to $40 per barrel being reported, Kuwait led the move with a 10% increase, followed by Libya, Iran, Nigeria, and Iraq. Non-OPEC producers such as Mexico and the Soviet Union joined in. At the December OPEC meeting, the members failed to reach agreement; each country was left free to fix its own price, with the $24 a barrel for Saudi light crude near the low end of the scale.

Shortage of Gasoline. Meanwhile, a gasoline supply shortage erupted in California with startling suddenness in early May. All of the phenomena that occurred during the shortages caused by the oil embargo in 1974 reappeared—long lines of waiting motorists at service stations, short station hours, and station shutdowns as their supplies were exhausted. In mid-June the California shortage disappeared as suddenly as it had begun, to be followed almost immediately by a shortage on the East Coast from Washington, D.C., to Boston. By mid-August the lines there, too, had disappeared.

No adequate explanation of these events was forthcoming from either government or industry. Supplies of crude oil in the U.S. were actually higher in the first half of 1979 than in the corresponding period of 1978. The culprit appeared to be the U.S. Department of Energy in its allocation of gasoline supplies to different regions of the country, since most of the nation was totally unaffected. Very small local shortfalls in supply were quickly magnified into long lines of waiting cars by public panic. When regional supplies were reshuffled, the lines just as quickly disappeared.

These local phenomena were accompanied by an equally unpleasant development on a national scale. As crude oil prices rose during the first half of the year, these increases began to be felt in product prices. Profiteering during the gasoline shortages brought the first dollar-a-gallon gasoline in U.S. history, and by the end of the year the dollar level was being reached and exceeded throughout the country in prices for all types of gasoline.

Other Developments. Although overshadowed by the preceding, other events regarding petroleum took place during the year. In the course of development of Mexico's new oil fields in the Gulf of Mexico, a well blew out of control in early June and began gushing oil at the rate of 30,000 bbl a day. Early attempts to cut off the flow were unsuccessful, but the dumping of steel balls and other materials in the well succeeded in reducing the flow to 10,000 bbl a day. In October a device was lowered over the well that captured much of the escaping oil. By that time, however, the well had gained the unpleasant distinction of having created the largest oil spill in history.

Negotiations begun early in the year finally culminated in September in an agreement between the United States and Mexico for the sale of natural gas by Mexico. An original agreement in 1977 on the export of 2,000,000,000 cu ft a day at a price of $2.60 per 1,000 cu ft had been vetoed by the U.S. secretary of energy, an action that led to a deterioration in Mexico-United States relations. The new agreement was for 300 million cu ft a day at a price of $3.625 per 1,000 cu ft, subject to escalation through an index tied to crude oil costs.

In the unconventional energy field one of the results of the gasoline shortages and high prices was the introduction of "gasohol" (a blend of 10% ethyl alcohol with gasoline) as a commercial motor fuel marketed by service stations. In July the world's largest electricity-generating windmill, with a capacity of 2,000 kw and two 100-ft blades, was dedicated at Boone, N.C.

U.S. Pres. Jimmy Carter proposed two new energy programs during the year. The first, announced in April, included: mandatory standards for thermostat settings in nonresidential buildings of no higher than 65° F in winter and no lower than 80° F in summer; a 5% reduction in federal government energy use; the decontrol of crude oil prices, with progressively higher prices permitted until final decontrol by Sept. 30, 1981; a windfall profits tax on oil production; and the establishment of an Energy Security Fund to use the proceeds from the windfall profits tax for assistance to low-income families to offset higher energy costs, for the funding of mass transit programs, and for research and development in new energy technologies and sources.

The second program, announced in July, included creation of an Energy Security Corporation to bring about the development of 2.5 million bbl a day of oil substitutes by 1990; establishment of an Energy Mobilization Board empowered to expedite the granting of permits and construction of critical energy facilities; provision of new incentives for the development of heavy oil, unconventional natural gas, and oil shale; a mandatory 50% reduction of oil consumption by electric utilities by the year 1990; the provision of $2.4 billion annually in assistance to low-income families; and provision of $16.5 billion over ten years for improvements in mass transportation systems and automobile fuel efficiency. Carter estimated that enactment of his two programs, together with already established programs, would permit the U.S. to reduce its oil imports by 50% by 1990. However, the only final action taken by Congress in the energy field during the year was a $1,350,000,000 authorization to help the poor and elderly meet fuel bills.

In August President Carter decontrolled the price of heavy crude oil in an attempt to stimulate domestic oil production. This action, it was hoped, would make possible prompt exploitation of the large reserves in California of such oil, which is difficult and expensive to produce.

(BRUCE C. NETSCHERT)

The Accident at Three Mile Island

At the nuclear power facility at Three Mile Island in Pennsylvania the evolution of a single minor event into a major accident was due to a combination of factors: (1) equipment malfunction, (2) errors in operating procedure, (3) instrument malfunction, (4) consequent lack of sufficient information by the operators, and (5) consequent decisions based on mistaken assumptions.

The event began at 4 AM on March 28 with the automatic closing for no reason of a valve, which interrupted the water supply to the steam system. This caused the automatic shutdown of the main pumps supplying the water, and the resulting low steam pressure caused the automatic shutdown of the steam turbine. With heat no longer being removed by steam flow to the turbine, pressure built up in the reactor cooling system and an automatic relief valve opened to reduce the pressure. The valve stuck open (and remained so for almost 2½ hours). The high pressure, however, had caused the nuclear reactor to shut down automatically. All of this happened within the first minutes.

With the main pump to the steam generator out of operation, auxiliary pumps had automatically started up to maintain the water supply. Unknown to the operators, however, two valves had been manually closed during routine testing two days earlier and had not been reopened after the test (contrary to regulations). Thus, no water was supplied to the steam system. As a consequence rising temperature and declining pressure caused the emergency core cooling system to come into operation automatically. Water poured into the cooling system and, with the relief valve stuck in the open position, vented into the tank designed to accumulate excess water. As the flow continued the tank filled, and 15 minutes after the initial event its relief disk ruptured, spilling water onto the floor of the reactor building. This in turn actuated sump pumps, which transferred the water to a tank in an auxiliary building; when this tank subsequently overflowed, radioactive gases began to escape into the atmosphere.

In an attempt to retain control of the system, the operators shut off the emergency cooling and several minutes later restored it as pressure started to recover. Between one and two hours after the accident began, cooling water pumps were cut off as the operators continued trying to shut down the reactor. Unknown to the operators this led to the exposure of fuel elements, the reaction of the zirconium cladding on the elements with steam and the resultant formation of hydrogen, and probable partial melting of the fuel.

By 16 hours after the initial event cooling water circulation had been restored and temperature and pressure were stable, although still far from complete shutdown conditions. Well before this time it had become fully apparent that the problem was no ordinary one. In the following days a team of experts was assembled to diagnose the situation and recommend procedures. The apparent occurrence of a small hydrogen explosion in the reactor building and the recording of high radiation levels led to the conclusion, during the next two days, that the top of the reactor vessel was filled with a "bubble" of hydrogen and fission product gases. This meant that temperatures and pressures must be carefully manipulated to prevent further core damage and breakdown of the cooling water pumps.

Strategies to eliminate the hydrogen and regain full water circulation were quickly applied and the emergency was controlled. The stable conditions of "cold shutdown" were not attained, however, until April 27.

COAL

In 1979 the uncertainty of future oil supplies increased the interest in coal in many countries. The temporary moratorium on the licensing of nuclear power plants in the U.S. and difficulties in obtaining planning approval for nuclear stations in other countries heightened the importance of maintaining and expanding coal production in the short, as well as the long, term. World hard coal production in 1978 reached an estimated 2,614,830,000 metric tons, 5.8% above 1977, with increases reported from China, the U.S.S.R., Poland, South Africa, and Australia. Production in Western Europe fell just under 1%, but in Eastern Europe it increased by 2.5%.

CHINA. In 1978 China produced more than 618 million metric tons of coal, 96% coming from underground operations. The coal industry employed over three million workers. Previous estimates of annual coal production had been on the low side. China was making strenuous efforts to raise production through mechanization, development of new coalfields throughout the country to avoid transportation difficulties, and expansion of existing mines. China planned to produce one billion tons a year by 1985, and exports to Japan were expected to reach three to four million tons annually by 1980. With probable reserves totaling about 1,500,000,000 metric tons, coal was likely to play a major role in supplying China's energy needs for many years.

U.S.S.R. In 1978 a total of 724 million metric tons of raw coal and lignite were produced in the Soviet Union, a slight increase over 1977. About one-third came from opencut operations. Bituminous coal totaled 478 million tons and anthracite 79 million tons. Lignite production increased 3% over 1977 to reach 168.4 million tons. Annual capacity increased by 26 million tons. In 1979 the construction of one of the largest surface mines in the U.S.S.R., at Berezovka, was well under way; the mine was expected to produce 55 million metric tons annually when in full operation.

UNITED STATES. In 1979 U.S. bituminous coal production was expected to rise 10% over the 1978 level, with electric utilities, which consume about two-thirds of the coal mined in the U.S., expected to increase their coal burn by 6%. Total coal production in 1978 amounted to 598,974,264 metric tons, compared with 615,300,000 tons in 1977. The decline was attributed to the United Mine Workers' strike in the first quarter of the year and a rail workers' strike later in the year that affected production in the eastern states. Bituminous coal and anthracite output amounted to 560,468,160 tons and 5,846,904 tons, respectively; 32,659,200 tons of lignite were also produced. Exports of bituminous coal and anthracite totaled 36.3 million tons, compared with 48.7 million tons in 1977, the shortfall being attributed to the strikes. U.S. coal producers were concerned about environmental constraints that might prevent them from increasing output to the level required for the 1980s.

EUROPEAN ECONOMIC COMMUNITY. Total hard coal production in 1978, at 238,065,000 metric tons, was 2.5 million tons below that of 1977. The decline in production continued despite strenuous efforts in all member countries to stabilize or increase output. Belgium's 6.6 million tons in 1978 was a decline of 6.8% from 1977. In France production dropped by 1,653,000 tons to 19,639,000 tons; lignite production dropped by 11.3% to 2.7 million tons. Hard coal production in West Germany dropped 1.2 million tons to 90.1 million tons, although lignite production increased slightly to 123.6 million tons as West Germany remained the world's third largest lignite producer.

The United Kingdom's National Coal Board (NCB) recorded a drop of 1 million tons during the financial year 1978–79 to 119.9 million tons, almost all attributed to lost deep-mine production caused by the hard winter and transportation difficulties during the last quarter of the financial year. Deep-mined output of 105.3 million tons was down 800,000 tons. Opencut operations and licensed mine production remained at about the same level as in 1977–78, at 13.5 and 1.1 million tons, respectively. Productivity improved significantly, this being associated with the first full year of an incentive scheme. Coal consumption rose by nearly 1 million tons, with power station coal burn at a record 83.3 million tons representing more than 70% of total power station fueling. Overall accident rates in the 1978–79 financial year were the lowest on record, but two major incidents at Bentley and Colborne collieries claimed 17 lives. Plans submitted by the NCB to the U.K. Department of Energy in December 1978 provided for expansion of deep-mined output to 111 million metric tons in 1983–84, with opencut production rising to 15 million tons.

POLAND. Hard coal production in Poland increased by 3.5% over the 1977 level to reach a record 192,662,000 metric tons; brown coal output during the same period amounted to 41 million tons and was expected to double by 1985. Poland planned to have its coal production reach more than 200 million tons in 1979 and 240 million tons annually by 1985, with the developing Lublin coalfield producing 7 million tons. Poland exported 402 million tons of hard coal in 1978, a rise of 900,000 tons over 1977, and the nation remained the world's second largest coal exporter.

JAPAN. Production of coal in 1978 rose slightly, to just under 19 million metric tons, thus continuing to stabilize at about 20 million tons a year in accordance with government policy. The indigenous colliery coal was twice as expensive as imported coal, resulting in increased stockpiles of the domestic product. Imports decreased 14.2% to 52,180,000 tons in 1978. The most noticeable drop was in coal from the U.S., down 6,310,000 tons to 8,870,000 tons, though the U.S. maintained its position as Japan's third largest supplier. Australian imports remained the largest at 25,180,000 tons, down 1,270,000 tons; Canada, in second place, increased supplies by 126,599 tons to reach 10,960,000. During the first four months of 1979 increases in supplies from the U.S. and slightly lower levels from Australia and Canada were reported.

INDIA. Production during the fiscal year ended March 31, 1979, amounted to 101,320,000 metric tons, about the same level as in the previous year and substantially below the original target of 113.5 million tons. Shortages of power and explosives, industrial unrest, and unprecedented floods in the Bengal and Bihar coalfields caused the shortfall. Production picked up by the end of the first quarter of 1979, and pithead stocks stood at about 14 million tons. Although India's hard coal and lignite reserves were estimated at 87,000,000,000 tons, only 5,600,000,000 tons were prime coking coals, 50% of which were considered recoverable. Concerned about these limited reserves, compared with the planned development of the steel industry, India decided to acquire leases in overseas countries for the development of coking coal mines. Imports of coking coal from Canada and Australia were begun in 1978 for the first time to conserve indige-

The energy crunch gave impetus to experiments in producing gas from coal. This plant in Homer City, Pennsylvania, a joint venture by the American Gas Association and the U.S. government, could produce 2.4 million cubic feet of gas from 120 tons of coal daily.

WIDE WORLD

nous reserves. By the year 2000 India planned to produce 395 million tons of coal annually.

South America. Coal production in 1978, at 9,610,000 metric tons, showed a modest increase of 74,000 tons over 1977. Colombia, with the largest known coal reserves in South America, was the largest producer at 4.2 million tons and planned to increase production to 12 million tons by 1990. Brazil produced 3.9 million tons and Chile 1.4 million tons.

Africa. Of the estimated total of 94,958,000 metric tons of hard coal mined in Africa in 1978, some 90.6 million tons were produced by South Africa, an increase of 5.2 million tons over 1977 and a new record. Zimbabwe Rhodesia's production, at 2.2 million tons, dropped 300,000 tons. South African exports rose 18%, reaching 14.9 million tons during 1978. Most of the coal was exported through the new Richards Bay port facility, where expansion plans were already under way. South Africa planned to increase its exports to 44 million tons annually by 1985. By the year 2000 exports could reach 55 million tons with a total annual production of 155 million tons. South Africa still produced some of the world's cheapest coal, but mining costs were rising with increased mechanization.

Australia. Australia, a major exporter of low sulfur and coking coals, exported 38 million metric tons in fiscal 1977–78, and exports were scheduled to rise to 200 million tons annually by the year 2000. Brown coal production from Victoria increased by an estimated 3 million tons to 33,150,000 tons. With the completion of several large new power stations by the late 1980s, demand for brown coal was expected to rise to 54 million tons a year. Investigations into the conversion of brown coal into other fuels was being actively pursued.

Canada. In 1978 total coal production increased from 31,438,287 short tons mined in 1977 to 33,594,972 short tons. Both bituminous and sub-bituminous coal production increased, though lignite production in Saskatchewan fell slightly to 5,570,000 short tons. Exports rose 13.2% to 15 million short tons, with Japan taking some 80%. Canada was seeking to develop other export markets, and trial shipments were sent to France in 1978. Production in British Columbia increased 500,000 tons to just under 10 million short tons. Alberta's total coal production of all types increased by 1.5 million tons. Bituminous coal output in Nova Scotia increased to just under 3 million tons, and the output from New Brunswick remained unchanged, 350,000 tons for 1978. To maintain compliance with environmental regulations, greater movement of western coal (with its characteristically lower sulfur content) to eastern Canadian markets was to be expected in the future. (R.J. FOWELL)

ELECTRICITY

With new oil price increases, the virtual stoppage of oil exports from Iran, and with opposition to nuclear power in many countries intensified by the accident at Three Mile Island, Pennsylvania, in March (*see* above), there was worldwide debate in 1979 on energy policy in general and electricity supply in particular. World consumption of electricity in 1978 rose by about 3.4% over that in 1977. Even at this comparatively low rate of increase in electricity demand and assuming an expanding use of nuclear power, electricity supply authorities throughout the world would face difficult fuel problems during the next 20 years or so. In the Arab oil-producing countries the problem was less severe; they foresaw the increased use of gas turbines for electricity generation as a major aid in the solution of their problem of dealing with the increasing demand for electricity.

Other countries were busy with plans for expanding coal production. Ministers from 20 members of the International Energy Agency decided to encourage the construction of new coal-fired power stations and to stimulate investment in their coal-mining industries. The EEC countries also decided to encourage coal production and to promote the use of solid fuels in power stations. Australia was expanding coal production not only to meet domestic demand but in the hope of exporting coal to Japan, which was planning to build, during the next two years, new coal-fired stations having an aggregate output capacity of about 20,000 Mw. Japan's own coal industry was incapable of fulfilling its requirements.

Even the U.K., with huge undeveloped coal resources, was unable to satisfy the demand from British coal-burning power stations and was importing coal. This resulted mainly from a past policy of building oil-fired stations and closing down coal mines when supplies of oil were relatively cheap and plentiful. British oil production from offshore wells in the North Sea was approaching the level at which it would be able to satisfy domestic oil demand, and so electricity production was not likely to be affected by any possible shortage of imported oil. North Sea supplies were not used to any appreciable extent for electricity generating stations, and the prospect of increased domestic coal production, together with the commissioning of more nuclear stations now under construction, left Britain in a relatively comfortable situation. As of the end of 1979 nuclear power provided about 12% of Britain's electricity, and this would rise to about 20% in 1982.

The growing concern with energy shortages was not confined to the developed, industrialized countries. At a conference in London dealing with third world energy shortages, it was broadly agreed that nuclear power should be used in the developed world in substitution for fossil fuels. Such a policy would free liquid fuels for electricity generation and transportation purposes in the third world until their technical development had reached a level commensurate with a wide application of nuclear power.

New Zealand, although not in the third world, shared many of its problems as well as some of those of the industrialized nations. The country had little coal or natural gas; some geothermal steam was used for small generating stations, and the hydroelectric installations on which much of the country's electricity production depended suffered from frequent droughts. After studying the possibilities of wind power, tidal power, solar power, magnetohydrodynamic generation of electricity, and the many other methods of power generation

In an effort to encourage the use of solar energy, U.S. Pres. Jimmy Carter had solar panels installed on the West Wing of the White House. He spoke at a rooftop ceremony to dedicate the panels in June.

PICTORIAL PARADE

Installed Capacity and Production of Electric Power in Selected Countries, 1976–77

Country	Hydroelectric power: Operating plants: Installed capacity (000 kw)	Hydroelectric power: Operating plants: Production (000,000 kw-hr)	Total electric power: Installed capacity (000 kw)	Total electric power: Production (000,000 kw-hr)
World	. . .	. . .	. . .	6,916,700
Algeria	300*	500*	1,160	3,960*
Argentina†‡	1,745	5,000	9,856	27,336*
Australia	5,535*	15,595	19,957*	82,464
Austria	6,533	20,511	10,537	37,680
Bangladesh	110	505	915*	1,380*
Barbados	—	—	99	252*
Belgium†‡	502	334	10,942	47,100
Brazil	18,411	81,468	21,796	88,380
Bulgaria†‡	1,887	2,954	7,210	29,700
Burma	181	470	441	912*
Cameroon	199	1,278	227	1,332
Canada†‡	40,052	213,049	65,566	316,548
Central African Empire	11*	51*	17*	53*
Chad	—	—	23*	58*
Chile	1,462	6,234	2,661	9,864
Colombia	2,420	10,000	3,850	13,416*
Congo	17*	65*	34*	120*
Costa Rica	239	1,456	406	1,644
Cyprus	—	—	269	888
Czechoslovakia†‡	1,805	3,465	14,552	66,300
Denmark	9	24	6,570	22,488
Dominican Republic	96*	175*	443	2,690
Egypt	2,550*	7,000*	3,900	11,000
El Salvador	108*	436*	305	1,332
Ethiopia	206	360	320	480*
Finland	2,374	9,379	8,042	31,872
France†‡	18,705	48,200	50,266	210,348
Gabon	—	8*	58*	228*
Germany, East†‡	727	1,174	16,735	91,992
Germany, West†‡	6,175	14,052	81,631	335,316
Ghana	792	4,174	900	4,226
Greece	1,415*	1,870*	4,740	17,400*
Guatemala	103*	305*	333	1,250
Guyana	—	—	95*	396
Hong Kong	—	—	2,919*	8,280*
Hungary	40	163	4,666	23,388
Iceland§#	392	2,349*	523	2,604*
India†‡	9,029	34,827	23,689	90,840*
Iran	804*	3,974	5,130	17,311
Ireland	531*	892*	2,162*	9,312*
Israel	—	—	2,157*	11,112
Italy†‡§#	17,163	40,953	44,831	166,572
Ivory Coast	224*	380*	360*	960*
Jamaica	15*	145*	685	1,404
Japan†‡§#	25,955	88,373	116,871	511,776
Kenya	171	694	284	1,044*
Korea, South	711*	1,789*	5,340	26,556*
Kuwait	—	—	. . .	5,208*
Lebanon	246	800	608	1,248
Libya	—	—	796*	1,488*
Luxembourg	932*	. . .	1,157	1,308
Madagascar	40	171*	95	276*
Malawi	59	283	105	276*
Malaysia	. . .	. . .	1,361	7,200
Mauritania	—	—	40*	96*
Mauritius	25	55	143	312
Mexico§#	4,616	17,179	12,847	50,052
Morocco	396*	978*	980	3,444*
Mozambique	514*	1,510	793	1,752*
Netherlands, The†‡	—	—	15,009	58,296
New Zealand§#	3,471*	14,922*	5,125*	21,264*
Nigeria	420*	2,525*	960	3,396
Norway	16,959	82,106	17,121	72,492
Panama	15*	110*	363	1,236*
Papua New Guinea	86	260	275	1,039
Philippines	1,138	4,860	3,507	11,412*
Poland	797	2,098	20,131	109,368
Portugal	2,338	4,887	3,588	13,872
Rhodesia (Zimbabwe)	705	4,856	1,192	4,608
Romania	2,705	8,107	12,323	58,272
Senegal	—	—	130*	456*
Singapore	—	—	1,390*	5,112*
South Africa	329*	1,876	15,344	80,196
Spain†‡	11,955	22,508	24,534	93,708
Sri Lanka	195	1,134	281	1,202
Suriname	21	1,176	301	1,335
Sweden†‡	12,497	54,856	26,591	87,576
Switzerland†‡	10,410	26,622	12,016	44,124
Syria	—	—	842	1,788
Thailand	910*	3,637*	2,775	10,296
Togo	2	4	24	76*
Trinidad and Tobago	—	—	454	1,572
Tunisia	29*	53*	426	1,524*
Turkey	1,873	8,360	4,350	20,520
U.S.S.R.†‡	43,131	135,735	228,307	1,149,996
U.K.†‡	2,456	5,121	78,597	283,476
U.S.†‡§#	68,422	286,883	550,369	2,185,404
Yugoslavia	5,143	20,555	10,073	48,636
Zaire	1,159	3,400	1,217	3,502
Zambia	989	6,784	1,261	7,044

*Public sector only. †Includes nuclear (in 000 kw): Argentina 340; Belgium 1,666; Bulgaria 880; Canada 2,666; Czechoslovakia 150; France 2,928; East Germany 950; West Germany 6,328; India 640; Italy 670; Japan 7,441; The Netherlands 524; Spain 1,120; Sweden 3,314; Switzerland 1,006; U.S.S.R. 7,000; U.K. 5,734; U.S. 42,919. ‡Includes nuclear (in 000,000 kw-hr): Argentina 2,527; Belgium 10,037; Bulgaria 4,989; Canada 16,430; Czechoslovakia 442; France 15,100; East Germany 5,271; West Germany 24,262; India 3,253; Italy 3,807; Japan 34,079; The Netherlands 3,872; Spain 7,555; Sweden 15,993; Switzerland 7,561; U.S.S.R. 14,000; U.K. 36,155; U.S. 191,108. §Includes geothermal (in 000 kw): Iceland 3; Italy 421; Japan 55; Mexico 75; New Zealand 192; U.S. 559. #Includes geothermal (in 000,000 kw-hr): Iceland 19; Italy 2,523; Japan 400; Mexico 550; New Zealand 1,233; U.S. 3,616.

Sources: United Nations, *Statistical Yearbook, 1977*; *Monthly Bulletin of Statistics*.

UPI

The world's largest wind turbine went into operation in Boone, North Carolina, in July. The giant windmill can, ideally, provide electricity for about 500 homes.

that were being suggested by antinuclear and environmental groups in Europe and the U.S., a New Zealand government fact-finding committee concluded that nuclear power was the only practicable alternative to importing fuel for oil-burning stations. Interestingly, New Zealand made an intensive study of tidal power based on the only two examples in operation, one a 240-Mw plant in the estuary of the Rance River in France and the other a 400-Mw installation near Murmansk in the Soviet Union. The latter was a pilot installation for a 600-Mw scheme proposed by the U.S.S.R. A tidal scheme on the River Severn in England had been under consideration for many years, and the current power crisis brought it once more into the realm of possibility.

Investigations were proceeding into ways of modernizing hydroelectric power stations. Following the published results of the reconstruction of the generating plant in the power station at Horksheim in West Germany, the Swiss Water Economy Board estimated that the increased electricity production obtainable from modernization of existing Swiss hydroelectric plants would cover about 6% of the estimated increase in electricity consumption up to the year 2000. The World Bank announced a change of policy by which it would assist less developed countries with their energy plans and stated that about 60 oil-importing countries needed such assistance. Over the next five years 25–30% of World Bank lending to these countries for energy purposes would be for hydroelectric projects, 15–20% for thermal stations, and 30–40% for transmission and distribution.

The question of power transmission was receiving a great deal of attention, with the aim of establishing larger pools of generating capacity in order to obtain security of supply and maximum efficiency of generating plant. There were already grid systems in Western Europe, in the Council for Mutual Economic Assistance (Comecon) bloc, and in the U.K. The British grid system was linked to Europe by an underwater power cable between Britain and France, but it carried only 160 Mw in either direction. There was now a proposal to link the Comecon grid with the Western European grid by a 750-kv transmission line running through Poland, West Berlin, and East Germany. There were also plans for a stronger link to carry 2,000 Mw between Britain and France by an underwater cable in a deep trench dug in the seabed of the English Channel.

Linking large transmission systems requires the provision of buffers to take care of sudden peaks in demand. These may take the form of pumped storage hydroelectric plants. Several of these were in operation, notably in Wales and in Scotland. A pumped storage installation consists of two reservoirs, an upper and a lower, and reversible motor-generator-turbine pumps. Motors drive the pumps at off-peak periods to fill the upper reservoir, and at peak demand periods the water is released. The pumps then act as turbines to drive the generator motors and supply power to the electricity network within seconds of the opening of water valves.

Combined heat and power projects where power stations are a source of heat as well as of electricity were a means of achieving increased efficiency in the production and utilization of electricity. Such schemes were common in Europe, the U.S.S.R., the U.S., and the U.K., and while the generating efficiency of electricity was reduced there was an increase in the overall efficiency of energy in its final use. Electricity suppliers in all the EEC countries including Britain were being urged to encourage such projects wherever possible.

In spite of the widespread popular opposition in many countries to the development of nuclear power it seemed that there was no alternative. Development of the fast breeder reactor, one that breeds as well as consumes fissionable material, was proceeding in the U.K., France, West Germany, and the U.S.S.R., and it was certain to become increasingly important in electricity production. After many years of U.S., British, and Soviet research work on magnetohydrodynamic (MHD) generation, a plant was operating in the U.S.S.R., using U.S. magnets, and another plant was being built in the U.S. But it was likely to be some years before MHD (in which electricity is generated by passing a superheated stream of ionized gas through a magnetic field) was used on a large scale.

Another research project that seemed to be speeding up was that concerning nuclear fusion, which was international in its scope although the U.S. and the U.S.S.R. were in the lead. European nuclear fusion research was to be carried out at Culham in Oxfordshire, England. The research project, known as JET (Joint European Torus), was funded by the EEC countries together with Switzerland and Sweden, and it would work closely with U.S. and Soviet organizations. It would help in the international search for a feasible alternative method to produce electricity. (JAMES F. AMOR)

NATURAL GAS

World gas reserves on Jan. 1, 1979, were estimated at 68,854,000,000,000 cu m (68,854 billion cu m or bcm), equivalent to 47 years of supply at 1978 rates of commercial production. In 1978 world commercial natural gas production rose by 40.98 bcm to 1,458.38 bcm, the most significant increases being in the U.S.S.R., Norway, Mexico, and Algeria. Production fell in the U.S., The Netherlands, and Iran. Gross natural gas production was an estimated 1,754 bcm.

Several major gas discoveries were announced in 1979, although few details were released. The discovery of a gas field some 125 km (77.5 mi) off the west coast of South Africa and Namibia was reported. Exxon announced a "significant" discovery off the coast of Trengganu, Malaysia, and India discovered an offshore field 120 km (77.4 mi) northwest of Bombay. Two offshore gas discoveries were announced in Venezuela, one of which tested gas at rates up to 680,000 cu m a day. In the Dutch North Sea, additional reserves were found in block P/6, making commercial development appear likely. In the U.S. gas was discovered for the first time in Oregon, and there was continued interest in the Baltimore Canyon region in the Atlantic Ocean off the coast of New Jersey. Although there were further disappointments in the area, Tenneco Corp. reported an encouraging find, and the U.S. Geological Survey reported a "significant" amount of natural gas discovered by a test well in very deep waters.

Two offshore discoveries were reported as being particularly significant. In the Persian Gulf, off the coast of Abu Dhabi, what was said to be a major new gas field was found by drilling through the Umm Shaif oil reservoir to reach a deeper rock formation. This deeper level had already been shown to contain gas in Qatar. In the Norwegian North Sea the gas discovery by Shell Oil Co. in block 3½ was surrounded by mystery. No official figures were released, but there were widespread reports that the discovery contained several times the reserves of the Frigg field, which would make it one of the world's largest.

The Iranian revolution had widespread repercussions because of prior arrangements for Iran to sell gas to the U.S.S.R. in exchange for an equivalent volume to be piped from the U.S.S.R. to West Germany, France, Czechoslovakia, and Austria. The Igat-1 pipeline extending from the fields in southern Iran to the Soviet border was to be supplemented by Igat-2, due to be completed in 1981. In January 1979 Iranian gas supplies through Igat-1 were stopped, causing severe fuel shortages in the Caucasian republics of the U.S.S.R., and work on Igat-2 was halted. Deliveries of gas to the U.S.S.R. were resumed in March, but at a lower rate than previously because gas production is linked to oil production, which had been cut. In July Iran confirmed that the Igat-2 project had been canceled and announced that there were to be no new plans for gas exports. This appeared to put an end to the proposal for exports of liquefied natural gas (LNG) from Iran to Japan and the U.S. The price and volume of future exports to the U.S.S.R. were still being negotiated.

The Soyuz gas pipeline, to carry gas from the Orenburg fields in the U.S.S.R. to Eastern Europe, was completed in January 1979. The Soviet Union also reported further progress on the project to develop the gas resources of Yakutia in Siberia. The proven reserves of the Yakutia fields reached 825 bcm and were expected to be confirmed at 1,000 bcm by the end of 1980. That level was considered to be the minimum necessary for the project to deliver the planned supplies of 10 bcm a year to Japan and the U.S. for 25 years.

After two years of acrimonious negotiations, the U.S. and Mexico reached agreement in September 1979 on sales of natural gas. With Mexico's gas production rising and new reserves being proved, this agreement had the potential to make a much greater contribution to U.S. gas supplies than the 300 million cu m a day agreed upon. The price to be paid for Mexican gas was indexed to the price of crude oil. Some progress was also made on the arrangements for another potentially important source of gas for the U.S., Alaska. The Atlantic Richfield Co. and Standard Oil Co. (Ohio) reached separate agreements for the sale of their shares of gas production from the Prudhoe Bay field, with reserves estimated at 750 bcm. The U.S. Federal Energy Regulatory Commission approved a formula for determining the costs of building a pipeline from Alaska to the lower 48 states, a step forward in the lengthy administrative and legal process necessary before the pipeline could actually be built.

Final agreement was reached in March 1979 on the delivery of Algerian LNG to West Germany and The Netherlands. Instead of the 160 bcm originally proposed, it was agreed that Algeria would supply 224 bcm over 20 years, half going to the Dutch company Gasunie and half to West German gas companies. The Dutch Parliament approved plans for the LNG terminal to receive Algerian gas to be built at Emshaven, rather than Rotterdam. An increase in the volume of the other major Algerian gas export project, the pipeline to Italy, was also reported to be under consideration. The 2,500-km (1,550-mi) pipeline from Algeria, through Tunisia, under the Mediterranean to Sicily and then north through the Italian mainland to Bologna, currently under construction, had a capacity of 12.4 bcm a year. This could be raised to 18 bcm by additional compression, or a second pipeline could be installed beside the first. Interest in taking the additional supplies from Algeria via Italy was shown by Switzerland and Greece. Greece was also interested in a pipeline link to Bulgaria, giving it access to Soviet gas.

Several proposals for international LNG projects made some progress during the year. The Iranian crisis, and the apparent collapse of plans for LNG exports from Iran, increased Japanese interest in other areas, including Australia, Sarawak, and Indonesia. In New Zealand it was decided that gas from the Maui field should be used as feedstock for a methanol plant rather than being exported as LNG. In October 1979 the U.S. Department of Energy at last gave its approval for the project to import Indonesian LNG, although the proposed terminal at Point Conception in California still faced considerable opposition. A significant omen for the future was the decision by the Organization of Petroleum Exporting Countries (OPEC) to discuss a uniform price for gas exports at their meeting in December, but no published conclusions were reached. OPEC countries had proven reserves of 23,000 bcm—one-third of world proven gas reserves—and apparently were interested in bringing gas prices into line with those for oil. (RICHARD J. CASSIDY)

PETROLEUM

During 1979 the international oil scene was in disarray over prices, supplies, and consumption. The spotlight was on the U.S., which toward the end of 1979 was importing more oil than it was producing, a situation Pres. Jimmy Carter described in July as "intolerable." The fall of the shah of Iran and the cessation of Iranian petroleum exports from December 1978 to March 1979 upset the oil markets, whose turbulence remained not just factual but also, perhaps more significantly, psychological.

There was a growing realization on the part of consumers and producers of the need for a more orderly market and a better global energy program, but the shock waves from Iran and market opportunism managed paradoxically to turn reasonable increases over 1978 of 3% in consumption and 5% in production into a scramble for supplies. By October prices of crude oil had increased some 60% since the beginning of 1979. Even the increased OPEC ceiling of $23.50 for light Arabian crude, set in June at Geneva, was breached in October by Kuwait, Libya, and the U.K. OPEC's December meeting failed to agree on a new price structure, leaving the members free to act on their own. Commenting on the situation, the Saudi oil minister, Sheikh Ahmad Zaki Yamani, urged the consuming nations to act "before it is too late."

WIDE WORLD

An unusual spectacle in Switzerland was the appearance of an oil drilling rig which started operation in October. Two West German firms were drilling test holes near Finsterwald for oil believed to be 6,000 metres (20,000 feet) underground.

In the first six months of 1979 world production was up by an estimated 5% over the same period in 1978. Iranian production was almost halved, the difference being made up by increased production from Saudi Arabia, Iraq, Kuwait, Nigeria, Libya, and Venezuela, but these increases were not guaranteed to last. U.K. production from the North Sea rose by 55%, practically allowing Britain to become self-sufficient in oil. Venezuelan production recovered from 1978 levels by 14%, and Mexico's expansion continued by about 25% in spite of a spectacular uncontrolled blowout offshore (*see* above).

Reserves. There was a minor decrease in the total world "published proved" reserves at the end of 1978, to a total of 649,000,000,000 bbl, compared with 653,700,000,000 bbl the year before. The Western Hemisphere share was much the same at 12.9% of the total, but the Middle East share rose 1% to 56.9%. The Chinese share was the same, 3.1%, but the U.S. at 5.2%, Western Europe at 3.7%, the U.S.S.R. at 10.9%, and Africa at 8.9% were all marginally lower.

Production. World oil production increased by only 0.7% in 1978, compared with 3.6% in 1977 and 8.5% in 1976, and averaged 62,965,000 bbl a day. OPEC production declined by 4.9% to 30,155,000 bbl a day. The Western Hemisphere had a larger production increase than in 1977, 4.2% (1977, 1.1%) to 16,805,000 bbl a day, as did northern North America, up 3.6% with a 4.5% U.S. increase but a Canadian decline of 1.7%. Latin-American production rose by 5.5%, with Mexico (22.9%) and Ecuador (9.8%) registering the largest increases and Colombia and Venezuela having decreases.

Middle Eastern production as a whole declined by 5.6% but increased its share of the world total from 32.6 to 34.1%, with Sharjah (−21.4%), Abu Dhabi (−12.8%), Saudi Arabia (−10.3%), and Iran (−8.2%) all having lower production levels. The Neutral Zone (+29%), Dubai (+13.5%), and Qatar (+10.8%) registered increases. Total African production was also down in comparison with 1977 by 2.7%; though Egypt (+15.2%) and Algeria (+7%) had increases, their share of the world total declined to 9.8% from 10.2%. China (+6.7%), the Soviet Union (+5.9%), and Eastern Europe increased production. Indonesian output, which had increased 11.9% in 1977, decreased by 2.9%. In 1978 the Soviet Union was the largest single producer, with 18.6% of world production, or 11,705,000 bbl a day, followed by the U.S. (15.8%; 10,265,000 bbl a day), Saudi Arabia (13.2%; 8,270,000 bbl a day), Iran (8.4%), Iraq (4.1%), Venezuela (3.7%), and Nigeria and Libya (both 3.1%). The OPEC share of total world oil production was 48.3%, 30,155,000 bbl a day, a decline of 4.9% from 1977. Over the decade 1968–78 world production increased by an annual average of 4.5%.

Consumption. During 1968–78 world consumption increased annually by an average 4.8%. In 1978 it rose 3.3% over 1977 and reached its highest level, 63,120,000 bbl a day. Reductions occurred only in Turkey (8.5%), Sweden (5.6%), Denmark (3.2%), Norway (1.7%), The Netherlands (1%), and Australasia (0.8%). Consumption in the Western Hemisphere rose 2.9% (24,370,000 bbl a day), in Western Europe 2.5% (14.6 million bbl), and in the Eastern Hemisphere 3.6% (38,750,000 bbl). The U.S. consumption increase declined from 5.5 to 2.5% (18,345,000 bbl). Canadian consumption increased slightly to 1,835,000 bbl a day. Countries and areas with increases of 5½% and above were Greece (12.1%), Southeast Asia (10.2%), Austria (8.3%), Yugoslavia (7.7%), South Asia (7.6%), and Eastern Europe, the Middle East, and Ireland (5.6%). The major consuming countries remained in the same order as in 1977: the U.S. (18,345,000 bbl a day, 28.9%); the U.S.S.R. (8,385,000 bbl a day, 13.5%); Japan (5,420,000 bbl a day, 8.5%); and West Germany (2,955,000 bbl a day, 4.6%).

Refining. In 1978 the increase in world oil refining capacity (4.2%, 79,155,000 bbl a day) was in line with that of 1973–78 (4.1%) but less than the 1968–78 average (6.1%). In all areas capacity increased: North America by 2.9%; the Western Hemisphere, 4.4%; Western Europe, 2.3%; the Middle East, 8.5%; Africa, 15%; South Asia, 13.3%; Southeast Asia, 2.8%; Japan, 2%; and the U.S.S.R., Eastern Europe, and China, 5.1%.

Mexico had an outstanding increase of 55.8%, followed by Iraq with 22.6% and Spain with 14.9%. The U.S. had the highest share of world capacity, 22%, the same as in 1977 and amounting to 17,375,000 bbl a day, followed by the combined capacity of the U.S.S.R., Eastern Europe, and China (17.8%), Japan (6.9%), Italy (5.4%), and France (4.4%). West German and U.K. capacity remained virtually the same at 3,090,000 and 2,655,000 bbl a day, respectively. World refinery output totaled 60,790,000 bbl a day.

Tankers. At the end of 1978 there was a significant reduction in the size of the world tanker fleet of 4% to 328.5 million tons deadweight (dw), mostly accounted for by a decline of 4.1% in Liberian tonnage to 103.4 million tons dw. Liberia continued to own the largest share of world tonnage (31.5%), followed by Japan (8.9%), the U.K. (8.6%), and Norway (8.1%). The U.S. registered the largest increase, 1.3%, for its biggest recent world share of 4.4%, just behind France. Voyages from the Middle East continued to account for most tanker movements, 74.5%. Interarea tanker movement in 1978 was down 2.5% compared with 1977. The tonnage on order in 1978 was the least since 1972, 12.4 million tons dw, of which one-quarter was for ships over 285,000 tons dw. However, an improvement in the tanker market was observable in mid-1979 with 90 new orders being placed in the first six months. (R. W. FERRIER)

See also Engineering Projects; Industrial Review; Mining and Quarrying; Transportation.
[214.C.4; 721; 724.B.2; 724.C.1–2; 737.A.5]

Engineering Projects

Bridges. A problem facing engineers with greater frequency than ever before was that of structural damage to bridges crossing highways or waterways, caused by heavy trucks, truck-mounted cranes, etc., or by ships going off course. The frequency of such accidents was increasing faster than the growth in traffic. To offset the risk, bridge piers had to be made stronger and protected by barriers, even though the likelihood of such an accident at any particular bridge was small.

The possibility of ships hitting bridge piers was one that faced authorities and their engineers considering the practicability of bridging any busy sea route. The growth of international road traffic meant that a number of very long fixed sea crossings became desirable. Such crossings included the Great Belt between the islands of Fyn and Sjælland in Denmark; across the English Channel between England and France; between Spain in Europe and Morocco in Africa across the Strait of Gibraltar; and across the Río de la Plata between Calonia, Uruguay, and Buenos Aires, Arg. In these cases tunnels were not feasible for road traffic because, for the lengths required, they could not be adequately ventilated. Technically, bridges were feasible in each case, but they necessarily had to satisfy maritime requirements for the safe passage of the world's largest ships.

The largest vessels afloat had a length of some 366 m, a beam of 55 m, and drew up to 27.5 m (1 m = 3.3 ft). Clearance required above high water was 61 m. The longest stayed girder bridges being built had spans of 450 m, and the world's longest span suspension bridge, the Humber Bridge in the U.K., expected to be completed during 1980, had a main span of 1,410 m. For the English Channel and the Great Belt a continuous run of large suspension bridges, each with a span of 2,000 m, was proposed. Such bridges would offer a clearance nearly 40 times the beam of the largest ships and much more for most of the ships passing up the channels.

Still longer spans were being designed, and models were successfully tested in wind tunnels; one example was the 3,000-m span for the Strait of Messina between the toe of Italy and Sicily. This very long span would allow the main towers to be located on dry land, thereby minimizing their cost; any shorter span would mean that the towers would have to be built above piers with foundations in very deep water, which would be both difficult to construct and costly. For the sea crossings mentioned above, however, the piers would have to be sited in deep water (though nowhere so deep as the Strait of Messina); the piers would therefore be expensive, and to achieve a minimum cost structure the optimum span was reduced to the 2,000 m proposed. The piers would have to be protected against an off-course ship.

Maritime interests were opposed to these proposals, insisting that such bridges would offer an unacceptable hazard to ships, despite the considerable clearance that would exist. But they were opposed to any fixed crossing, bridge or tunnel, road or rail, because it would eliminate cross-channel shipping services and reduce international shipping. There could be no doubt, though, that bridges able to carry road vehicles were more suited to predicted traffic growth than either railways or seaborne services. Somehow, stronger measures had to be enforced so that ships would maintain their allotted courses, thereby removing objections to the proposed bridges.

Construction began on the world's most ambitious bridge scheme, joining the island of Shikoku to the main island of Japan, Honshu. Three crossings were planned. The first to be built would be the Sakaide to Okayama route, where the sea distance was 10 km (1 km = 0.62 mi). It would consist of two suspension bridges over the main channels and a series of truss bridges and viaducts between small islands and rock outcrops. The suspension bridges would have main spans of 990 m and 1,100 m. Each would have two decks, the upper carrying four road lanes for automobile traffic and the lower four rail tracks. The piers for the suspension bridges had foundations in granite under fast flowing tidal waters 27 m deep.

Another notable bridge under construction was a concrete arch in Yugoslavia with a span of 390 m and a rise of 67 m. The previous longest concrete arch was the Gladesville Bridge in Australia, with a main span of 305 m. (DAVID FISHER)

Buildings. Awareness of the need to conserve energy resources continued to inhibit the imagination of building designers, a state of affairs exacerbated by the effect of the Iranian revolution upon world oil prices. There were, however, welcome signs that the pronouncements of doom and announcements of panaceas so prevalent in recent years were giving way to a more mature realization that the strain upon energy resources could be eased, if not solved, by diverse and unspectacular methods. More frequently than not, these involved the adaptation of existing technologies rather than the employment of wholly new ones.

Reevaluation of the role of each building profession also seemed likely to result in buildings designed for maximum energy conservation. It had traditionally been the function of the services engi-

A bridge nearly a mile long was completed to connect the Adriatic island of Krk to the mainland of Yugoslavia via St. Marco Island. The bridge was completed during the year.

KEYSTONE

neering specialists—mechanical, electrical, heating, and ventilating—to inject their expertise at a late stage into an already completed architectural and structural design. More and more, however, design teams consisting of all the building professions were being set up at the beginning of projects, with the result that architects and structural engineers were being made more aware of the energy implications of their conceptions.

A good example of this teamwork in practice was the Felmore housing program at Basildon, Essex, England, in which 4,000 dwellings as well as ancillary facilities would ultimately be provided. Energy conservation was laid down by the client as a guiding principle for all the architects involved, and they established design teams that took into account such factors as climate, site layout, environmental conditions, the shape of the buildings, and internal planning in the preparation of their schemes. Energy savings as great as 50% could be achieved by careful attention to insulation, ventilation, orientation of the buildings on the site, the arrangement of windows and doors, and building shape, all without any increase in capital cost.

Even greater energy savings were anticipated for two big office building projects planned in Chicago and in Chattanooga, Tenn. The former was a three-story, semicircular, glass-clad structure to house, appropriately enough, the Chicago branch of the U.S. Department of Energy. The glass walls and the clear plastic roof vaults would allow natural lighting on most of the floor space, while solar collectors on the straight south-facing wall would provide heating for storage in winter and energy for the refrigeration plant in summer. The Tennessee Valley Authority, 800 km (500 mi) to the south, expected to cut the energy costs of an office complex of 92,950 sq m (1 million sq ft) by using mirrors to capture light and heat from the Sun and underground water to supply cooling. The building would have virtually no windows on its east and west faces, the large windows and positioned mirrors being concentrated on the north and south faces to make the most use of solar heat and natural light.

The Bitsa equestrian complex began to take shape in Moscow. The field would be the site of equestrian events during the 1980 Olympic Games.

VASILI YEGOROV—TASS/SOVFOTO

Another symptom of the search for energy conservation was the belief, belatedly gaining ground in the U.S., that tall buildings are less efficient in terms of energy and cost than short squat ones. A Chicago firm of developers went so far as to ask architects Skidmore Owings & Merrill to redesign a projected tall office building. The new 28-story design was claimed to save $1 million, the economics being effected in the foundations, superstructure, and exterior walls and in the heating, ventilating, and air-conditioning system; the savings that would be made in future operating costs were not included.

The relatively new techniques of lightweight structures continued to fuel the imaginations of designers faced with the task of providing very large enclosures or covering extensive areas. The tented enclosure for Hajj pilgrims at the new Jidda international airport in Saudi Arabia would have, when completed, the largest fabric roof in the world—a vast double rectangle of 210 tentlike units covering a total area of 42 ha (104 ac). Each tented roof would be 14 m square, rising conically to a height of 35 m.

In Moscow work continued on the buildings for the 1980 Olympic Games. The Prospekt Mira complex, close to the Kremlin, comprised a 15,000-seat swimming pool and a 45,000-seat drum-shaped indoor stadium. The latter, covered with a diaphanous steel membrane measuring 224 by 182 m, was the largest such hall in Europe.

(PETER DUNICAN)

Dams. The International Commission on Large Dams (ICOLD), a voluntary nongovernmental body that fosters links between dam engineers in all parts of the world and promotes the interchange of professional expertise, held its 13th triennial congress in India in 1979. The statistics contained in ICOLD's *World Register of Dams* relate only to large dams exceeding 15 m in height. The 13,000 dams listed thus represent only a small percentage of all dams. In the case of the U.K., for example, of a known total of some 5,000 dams only 500 qualified for inclusion in the register. As a further measure of the extent of dam-building activity over the years, a recent national survey in the U.S., which made use of satellite recording techniques to assist in providing adequate coverage, identified some 50,000 dams.

The huge scale of the largest projects is immediately apparent from the accompanying table of dams currently under construction that exceed either 150 m in height and/or 15 million cu m in volume or that impound in excess of 14,800,000,000 cu m of water. In terms of dam-building activity, national size or wealth can be seen to be no criterion. Nations that are heavily committed to water resource development and, therefore, have extensive dam-construction programs range from such relatively small countries as Austria and Switzerland through Spain and Mexico to the subcontinent of India. As an example from a small nation, the planned Boruca hydroelectric project in Costa Rica (population 2.2 million) would include construction of a 260-m-high rockfill embankment dam to create a lake with a surface area of some 220 sq km.

A further illustration of the scale and impact of individual projects in less developed countries was provided by the Temengor (Malaysia) and Magat (Philippines) projects. Temengor Dam, now completed and having a height of 127 m, had a flood storage capacity of 850 million cu m and an installed generating capacity of 348 Mw. Magat, on which work began during the year, would irrigate some 1,050 sq km of land and, it was estimated, would increase the available rice yield by 300,000 metric tons a year.

Economic and technical considerations combined to ensure that the overwhelming majority of modern dams, including those mentioned, were embankment structures. Constructed of compacted earthfill and/or rockfill, such dams could be safely located on sites where concrete dams were either unsuitable or uneconomic. Recent advances in embankment dam engineering included raising dams "in the wet," that is, in flowing water, and the use of bituminous materials for construction of the watertight membrane or core. An interesting example of the latter technique was in progress in the U.K. at the site of the 56-m-high Megget Dam.

August 1979 was marked by a major dam disaster. The collapse of Machhu II Dam in India was reported to have killed as many as 5,000 people, and published accounts of the incident suggested that hydrologic factors might have been responsible. Events at Machhu illustrated how much still had to be learned regarding flood prediction and also stressed the burden of responsibility carried by the dam engineer. However, awareness of the importance of proper surveillance of dams had increased to such an extent that the already good record of performance of large dams was being steadily bettered. (A. I. B. MOFFAT)

Roads. Worldwide inflation, coupled with rapidly escalating costs of highway construction, reduced tax revenues, and scarcity and high prices of asphalt and other petroleum products, combined to hamper construction of new highways,

Major World Dams Under Construction in 1979[1]

Name of dam	River	Country	Type[2]	Height (m)	Length of crest (m)	Volume content (000 cu m)	Gross capacity of reservoir (000 cu m)
Agua Vermelha	Grande	Brazil	E, G	90	3,990	19,640	11,000,000
Amaluza	Paute	Ecuador	A	170	410	1,157	120,000
Atatürk	Euphrates	Turkey	E, R	180	1,915	75,000	48,000,000
Baishan	Songhuajiang	China	G	150	670	1,630	6,215,000
Canales	Genil	Spain	E, R	156	340	4,733	7,070,000
Chicoasen	Grijalva	Mexico	E, R	263	480	15,000	1,705,000
Dabaklamm	Dorferbach	Austria	A	220	350	950	235,000
Dongjiang	Laishui	China	A	157	438	1,389	8,120,000
Dry Creek	Dry Creek	U.S.	E	110	915	23,000	310,000
Emborcacao	Paranaíba	Brazil	E, R	158	1,500	23,300	17,600,000
Finstertal	Nederbach	Austria	E, R	150	652	4,500	60,000
Foz do Areia	Iguaçu	Brazil	E, R, G	153	830	13,700	7,320,000
Grand Maison	Eau d'Olle	France	E, R	155	550	12,000	140,000
Gura Apelor Retezat	Riul Mare	Romania	E, R	168	460	9,000	225,000
Guri (final stage)	Caroni	Venezuela	E, R, G	162	9,404	77,846	139,000,000
Inguri	Inguri	U.S.S.R.	A	272	680	3,880	1,100,000
Itaipú	Paraná	Brazil / Paraguay	E, R, G	185	7,900	27,000	29,000,000
Itaparica	São Francisco	Brazil	E, R, G	105	4,700	16,000	12,000,000
Itumbiara	Paranaíba	Brazil	E, G	106	6,262	35,600	17,000,000
Karakaya	Euphrates	Turkey	A, G	180	420	2,000	9,580,000
Kenyir	Trengganu	Malaysia	E, R	150	900	16,000	14,000,000
Kishau	Tons	India	E, R	253	360	NA	2,400,000
La Grande No. 2	La Grande	Canada	E, R	160	2,835	23,000	61,720,000
La Grande No. 3	La Grande	Canada	E, R	100	3,855	22,187	60,020,000
La Grande No. 4	La Grande	Canada	E, R	125	3,100	20,000	19,390,000
Lakhwar	Yamuna	India	G	192	440	2,000	580,000
Las Portas	Camba	Spain	A	152	484	747	751,000
Lonyangxia	Hwanghe	China	G	172	342	1,300	24,700,000
Mihoesti	Aries	Romania	E, R	242	242	180	6,000
Nurek	Vakhsh	U.S.S.R.	E	300	704	58,901	10,500,000
Oosterschelde	Vense Gat Oosterschelde	The Netherlands	E	45	9,000	70,000	2,900,000
Oymapinar	Manargat	Turkey	A	185	360	575	310,000
Revelstoke	Columbia	Canada	E, R, G	153	1,620	13,000	5,180,000
Rogun	Vakhsh	U.S.S.R.	E	325	660	75,500	11,600,000
São Felix	Tocantins	Brazil	E, R	160	1,950	34,000	50,600,000
Sayano-Shushensk	Yenisei	U.S.S.R.	A	242	1,068	9,117	31,300,000
Sobradinho	São Francisco	Brazil	E, R, G	43	3,900	13,200	34,200,000
Sterkfontein	Nuwejaarspruit	South Africa	E	89	3,050	15,500	2,660,000
Tedorigawa	Tedori	Japan	E, R	153	420	10,120	231,000
Tehri	Bhagirathi	India	E, R	261	570	22,750	3,539,000
Thomson	Thomson	Australia	E, R	165	1,275	12,500	1,100,000
Tucurui	Tocantins	Brazil	E, G	86	4,200	43,000	34,000,000
Upper Wainganga	Wainganga	India	E	43	181	NA	50,700,000
Ust-Ilimsk	Angara	U.S.S.R.	E, G	105	3,565	8,702	59,300,000
Wujiangdu	Wujiang	China	G	165	368	1,930	2,300,000
Yacambu	Yacambu	Venezuela	E	158	107	300	427,000
Yacyreta-Apipe	Paraná	Paraguay / Argentina	E, G	33	69,600	61,200	21,000,000
Zillergründl	Ziller	Austria	A	180	505	980	90,000
Major World Dams Completed in 1978 and 1979[1]							
Balimela	Sileru	India	E	75	4,363	18,788	3,610,000
Dartmouth	Mitta-Mitta	Australia	R	180	670	14,100	4,000,000
Fierze	Drin	Albania	E, R	158	400	700	2,620,000
Hasan Ugurlu	Yesil Irmak	Turkey	E, R	175	435	9,042	1,078,000
Kolyma	Kolyma	U.S.S.R	E, R	130	750	12,550	14,800,000
Nader Shah	Marun	Iran	E	175	220	7,200	1,620,000
São Simão	Paranaíba	Brazil	E, R, G	120	3,611	27,387	12,540,000
Takase	Takase	Japan	E, R	176	362	11,600	76,000
Toktogol	Naryn	U.S.S.R.	G	215	293	3,345	19,500,000

[1] Having a height exceeding 150 m (492 ft); or having a total volume content exceeding 15 million cu m (19.6 million cu yd); or forming a reservoir exceeding 14,800 × 10^6 cu m capacity (12 million ac-ft).
[2] Type of dam: E = earth; R = rockfill; A = arch; G = gravity.
NA = not available.

(T. W. MERMEL)

A.F.P./PICTORIAL PARADE

Pierre Dumas, president of the French Society for the Fréjus road-tunnel, spoke at dedication ceremonies on the completion of the French part of the tunnel that would connect France and Italy. The tunnel would carry traffic underneath the French Alps.

especially in the industrialized nations. This situation was somewhat alleviated by technological breakthroughs in the area of substitute construction materials, and by improved production methods for asphalt and portland cement concrete used in new construction and maintenance procedures. The year 1979 was also marked by the completion or near completion of a number of significant highway projects on several continents.

In the United States highway construction costs climbed 11.6% in one three-month period in 1979. Of the 68,260-km Interstate System, 93.1% was now in service. The estimated total cost of the Interstate System was revised to $112.9 billion, of which $41 billion would finance the 6.9% yet to be built. The cost of construction of urban interstate highways was illustrated by the engineering estimate of $891 million for an 11-km segment of I–90 through metropolitan Seattle, Wash., authorized in late 1979. This figure included relocation expenses for residents who would be displaced by the new highway.

The major step forward in the completion of the Pan-American Highway, which would eventually stretch from the northern border of Canada to the southernmost tip of South America, was taken with the paving of a 37-km section of the Darien Gap Highway between Tocumen and Chepo in Panama. The Darien Gap Highway, 400 km long in Panama and Colombia, was the only remaining section of the Pan-American Highway still to be built.

A full-scale example of the recycling of pavement material to reconstruct worn-out highways was the reconstruction of the 25-km Edens Expressway in metropolitan Chicago. Approximately 350,000 tons of the original pavement were scheduled to be crushed and recycled in the $113 million project.

Recycling of existing materials was dictated not only by the growing scarcity of aggregates and the environmental considerations implied in quarrying them but also by the high costs of transporting them for long distances to the construction site. The result of this situation was an upsurge of interest in alternative paving materials and additives, ranging from sulfur to pulverized rubber tires and phosphogypsum, the latter a by-product of the fertilizer and mining industries. Development of thin bonded concrete overlays for highway construction, as well as more efficient and environmentally acceptable methods of producing hot-mix asphalt and portland cement concrete, were significant factors in reducing the costs of building and maintaining roads.

In Canada, where provincial expenditures for road and bridge construction and maintenance were expected to reach $3,145,000,000 in fiscal year 1979–80, construction was begun on a 388-km two-lane road to link British Columbia with the Northwest Territories. The existing Alaska Highway, much of which was still dirt road, was also to be upgraded and expanded over the next ten years in a joint Canadian-U.S. program. Mexico planned to spend $145 million to build a network of rural roads intended to encourage agricultural settlement and reduce urban congestion in Mexico City, Guadalajara, and Monterrey.

In Europe the last segment of the La Turbie–Roquebrune–Cap Martin Motorway was opened in France, connecting Paris with the Italian border. The 6-km section, which contained a 300-m bridge and three tunnels, cost approximately $64 million.

Cuts in government spending in the U.K. affected highway construction and improvements in rural areas. Essential expenditures were being used to finance routes carrying heavy industrial traffic, especially to Britain's ports. Completion of the M25 orbital route around London was considered the most important project in the U.K. In West Germany the 119-km auto route between Stuttgart and Singen was opened, completing an unbroken limited-access highway from the Danish border to the Swiss border.

In the Middle East Kuwait embarked on a major upgrading of its existing expressway system. The State Organization of Roads and Bridges began construction of Expressway One in Iraq, which was to stretch for 1,000 km from the Jordanian and Syrian borders to the Kuwait border, bypassing Baghdad. In Asia the Taiwan Highway Bureau planned 14 major highway development and improvement programs over the next ten years at a total cost of $1.4 billion, including a 22-km extension of the North-South Freeway from Kao-hsiung to P'ing tung. The Pan-Philippine Highway was now open from the northern tip of the archipelago to the southern part of the country.

Japan's eighth five-year road improvement program was under way, at a cost of $125,330,000,000. It was to include the construction of 3,200 km of expressways and the 32-km Honshu–Shikoku bridge system. (HUGH M. GILLESPIE)

Tunnels. At the fifth annual meeting of the International Tunneling Association, at Atlanta, Ga., in June 1979, China was admitted as a member. It was reported that, of 15 countries studied over the previous four years, Japan was a clear leader in the construction of soft-ground shield tunnels, having constructed 353 km, with West

England:
see United Kingdom

English Literature:
see Literature

Entertainment:
see Dance; Motion Pictures; Music; Television and Radio; Theatre

Entomology:
see Life Sciences

Germany in a distant second place at 52 km. Both these countries were also leaders in the research of methods for eliminating dependence upon the use of compressed air for tunneling in noncohesive ground. The West German bentonite shield in use at Antwerp, Belgium, achieved a world record daily advance by driving 23 m of a 5.7-m-diameter tunnel for the town's new subway.

The presence of boulders is a hazard that can cause disruption to the progress of a slurry shield. A Japanese contractor helped to solve the problem in a 3.6-m-diameter tunnel by installing a 500-mm-wide jaw crusher into which were fed boulders from the face via a 250-mm pipeline. Japanese engineers believed that the earth-pressure balancing shield, a development of the slurry shield, would ultimately prove to be more economical than current slurry shields because it had the significant advantage of eliminating plant required to separate slurry from excavated material. For the first time a Japanese shield of this type was to be used in the U.S. for the construction of a new 2.7-m-diameter sewer in San Francisco.

West German tunneling engineers devised a unique method for equalizing side movement against the lining of a tunnel driven through ground liable to mining subsidence. The system used special segments into which were fixed heavy-duty precompressed steel springs. Four such special segments to each ring of conventional cast-iron lining were being used in the construction of a 6.9-m-diameter running tunnel for the new subway at Gelsenkirchen in the Ruhr.

In the U.K. the first drive in Europe's longest machine-bored rock tunnel was completed at Kielder when the 2.85-m-diameter Wear Tees Tunnel holed out after 14.4 km of driving. On the second drive a U.S. Robbins tunneling machine established record progress on the contract by driving 670 m in one month. The biggest underground development for the Coal Board in Britain was the construction of a new mine at Selby in North Yorkshire. There two drifts of 4.7-m diameter, each 800 m long and lined with spheroidal graphite cast-iron segments, were being driven down a grade of 1 ft vertical for every 4 horizontal by boom-type tunneling machines mounted in shields. The driving of tunnels by this method at such a gradient through water-bearing ground represented a major achievement for mechanical tunneling methods.

The construction of large-diameter tunnels using shields was another feature of tunneling in 1979. In Switzerland driving began on the Rosenberg Tunnel using a shield 11.8 m in diameter equipped with four road-header-type rotary excavators. In Egypt, 14 km north of Suez, the halfway mark was reached in the driving of the first road tunnel under the Suez Canal. An 11.8-m-diameter shield was being used on the precast-concrete-lined tunnel, which was expected to be completed at the end of 1980.

The second longest road tunnel in Europe was completed at the end of 1978 when the 14-km-long Arlberg Tunnel in Austria was opened seven months ahead of schedule. In May 1979 another major Alpine road tunnel was fully excavated when the 12.8-km Fréjus II Tunnel between France and Italy was holed out from the Italian side after four years of tunnel driving.

(DAVID A. HARRIES)

[733; 743.A]

Environment

As the economic difficulties of the industrial nations deepened, governments found themselves under pressure to relax environmental controls. In the U.S. it seemed probable that pollution caused by the burning of coal would be tolerated because an increase in the use of coal would reduce pressure on oil supplies. Dow Chemicals expressed the feeling of much of the business community when it opposed measures to protect the environment that it saw as rigid and inhibiting.

Despite this, the environmental movement remained active, and some gains were made. The U.S. Environmental Protection Agency (EPA) secured an agreement with United States Steel Corp. that promised to yield a dramatic improvement in air and water quality in Pittsburgh, Pa. Probably the most important environmental achievement of the year came in June, when delegates from countries bordering the Mediterranean agreed to an Action Plan that would reduce polluting discharges into rivers that flow into one of the world's most badly polluted seas.

The most serious environmental accident of the year was the blowout of the Ixtoc 1 oil well, off the coast of Mexico, on June 3. The most controversial issue was still nuclear power, more so than ever after the Three Mile Island, Pennsylvania, incident in March. (*See* ENERGY.)

INTERNATIONAL COOPERATION

UN Environmental Program. At the seventh session of the UNEP governing council, held in Nairobi, Kenya, from April 18 to May 3, about 300 delegates were told that the failure of some mem-

Antinuclear protesters paraded on New York City's Wall Street in October in a futile attempt to blockade the New York Stock Exchange.

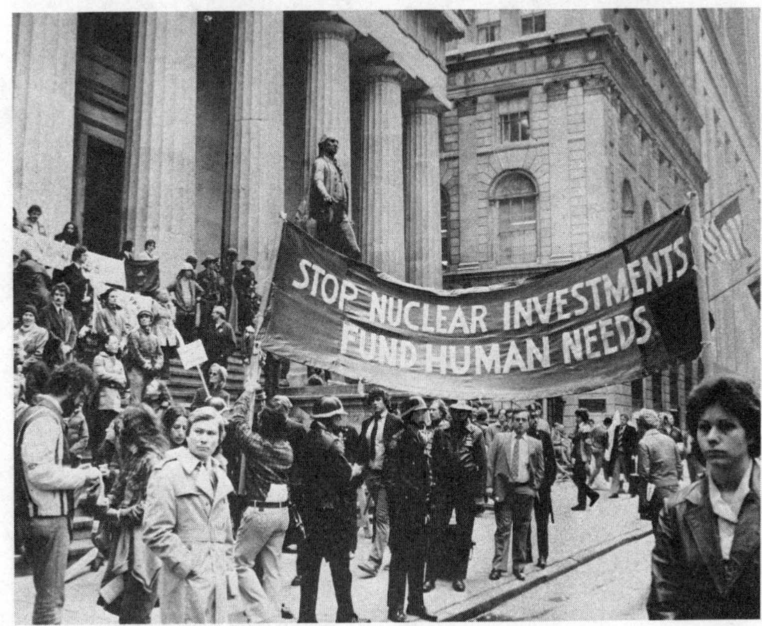

UPI

bers to pay their dues had left UNEP U.S. $28 million short of its budget target of $150 million. The council urged UNEP to participate in the New International Development Strategy and the World Climate Program and to collaborate with other organizations in developing a plan of action for reducing emissions of carbon dioxide and defining a policy to protect soils from erosion and degradation.

The Coordinating Committee on the Ozone Layer, formed in 1977, met in Bonn, West Germany, in December 1978. In attendance were delegates from UNEP, the World Health Organization (WHO), the European Economic Community (EEC), the International Council of Scientific Unions, the Council of Europe, the Manufacturing Chemists' Association, eight national governments, and several nongovernmental organizations. The committee recommended that a comprehensive environmental assessment of the effects of ozone depletion be considered, including the economic aspects of corrective actions.

In September UNEP considered a report it had commissioned from a British firm of environmental and planning consultants, Atkins Research and Development, which was published later in the year. The 300-page report advocated the use of environmental impact assessment procedures in less developed countries, covering the social and cultural effects of development as well as the effects on the physical environment.

On February 11 delegates from 17 of the 18 countries bordering the Mediterranean concluded a week-long meeting by approving a budget for the Mediterranean Action Plan called for in the Barcelona Convention. They did not resolve the problem of controlling pollutants from sources miles inland, which include the most toxic of industrial wastes. It was expected that agreement on this complex issue would not be reached until late in the year, but at a meeting in Geneva in June, 14 of the Mediterranean countries agreed on the text of a treaty and adjourned, with no further session planned until the formal signing, scheduled for April 1980.

The treaty covered factory wastes, sewage, and agricultural chemicals. Its approach was pragmatic, recognizing the wide economic differences between the northern and southern Mediterranean states. Each country was required to monitor conditions in its own territory. At half-yearly intervals UNEP would circulate the data, and every two years scientists from the treaty nations would meet to discuss them and devise improvements. The treaty called for a complete halt to discharges of lubricating oils, plastics, radioactive substances, carcinogens, arsenic, and cadmium.

World Environment Day was celebrated in many countries on June 5, often featuring children to mark the International Year of the Child.

World Health Organization. At a WHO Symposium on Environmental Protection Programs in Industrial Areas, held at Katowice, Poland, in November 1978, delegates from 13 countries concluded that too little was known of the relationships between environmental and economic factors to permit a wholly scientific approach to pollution control. It was agreed that effective monitoring and enforcement procedures were essential, and that the long-term aim must be to modify industrial processes so as to reduce the amount of waste they produce.

Workers ready a 30-ton steel cone in an attempt to seal off the runaway Ixtoc 1 oil well off the coast of Mexico. Efforts made in September and October to cap the well were unsuccessful, and oil continued to be released into the Gulf. Map at left shows movement of the oil slick from June 3 to Nov. 1, 1979.

UPI

In January 1979 the Greek government announced plans to build sewage-treatment facilities to reduce marine pollution caused by discharges from Athens. The first stage of the project, estimated to cost $20 million, would be financed by the UN Development Program and implemented by WHO. Work was to begin in 1980 and should be completed by 1982. The first stage would provide primary treatment for normal dry-weather flow. Subsequent stages would increase the treatment capacity.

UN Conference on the Law of the Sea. The eighth session of UNCLOS was held in Geneva from March 19 to April 27, when it adjourned to reconvene later in New York. The delegates, from more than 140 countries, again failed to agree on ways to regulate the mining of seabed minerals or to control marine pollution. The most difficult problem proved to be the definition of the extent and nature of the power of coastal states. The urgency with which agreement had been sought on seabed mining had been reduced by the failure of the U.S. Senate to pass the Deep Seabed Hard Mineral Resources Act before its session ended in October 1978. This meant that several consortia which had hoped to begin mining were forced to postpone their plans.

Organization for Economic Cooperation and Development. The first OECD report on the state of the environment in its member states was published on May 1, 1979. *The State of the Environment* dealt with many environmental problems, including the rate at which wild species were becoming extinct and noise levels which, it said, exceeded the acceptable limit of 65 decibels for about 100 million citizens of OECD countries, or 15 to 20% of the population. The report estimated that in 1975, private industry investment in antipollution measures amounted to 4.6% of gross domestic product in Japan, 3.4% in the U.S., 1.7% in the U.K., and 0.7% in Norway. In the days following its publication, the report was discussed by OECD environment ministers in Paris. Members were urged to cooperate more closely, and the chairman of the meeting, Doug Costle of the EPA, pointed out that prevention of pollution was about ten times cheaper than its cure. Ministers noted that environmental issues had become politically significant.

European Economic Community. In July the EEC Council of Ministers agreed to introduce a labeling system for industrial chemicals produced in amounts exceeding one metric ton a year. The introduction of new chemicals had to be reported, and as production increased the new regulations required more complex toxicological data about them. The reporting requirements were related to production thresholds of 10, 100, and 1,000 metric tons a year, or five times those amounts cumulatively. By the time the final threshold was crossed, manufacturers would have had to supply information on the effects of the chemical on human fertility and fetuses and the results of cancer tests on animals.

In its *State of the Environment Report,* published in March, the European Commission predicted that a new range of environmental laws would be enacted in the 1980s. The report favoured a requirement for environmental impact assessments before major industrial or construction projects were permitted. It also foresaw the introduction of stricter safety standards in industry to prevent the recurrence of disasters like that at Seveso, Italy, in 1976, when dioxin escaping from a chemical plant contaminated a wide area.

Council of Europe. Some 200 representatives of local and regional authorities attended a congress on the prevention of transfrontier pollution, sponsored by the Council and held at Aachen, West Germany, April 3–5. The congress called for the immediate adoption by national governments of the draft European outline convention on transfrontier cooperation, and for greater decentralization of powers to local authorities. National governments were urged to harmonize their environmental policies, to allow equal access to information to citizens on either side of a frontier, and to apply the "polluter pays" principle in cases of transfrontier pollution.

The Rhine was the subject of a Public Parliamentary Hearing held in Strasbourg, France, on May 29. About 70 parliamentarians heard and questioned experts on the scientific examination of the river, the legal aspects of controlling pollution, and the activities of bodies charged with this control. It was agreed that, although some progress had been made, much remained to be done.

The third European Ministerial Conference on the Environment, held in Bern, Switz., September 19–21, concentrated on the environmental effects of modern farming and forestry.

NATIONAL DEVELOPMENTS

Nuclear Power. On March 28, 1979, the failure of a water pump began the train of events that led to the accident at the Metropolitan Edison nuclear plant at Three Mile Island, in the Susquehanna River near Harrisburg, Pa. Nuclear power had long been the major target for environmentalist campaigns, and the Harrisburg incident had repercussions throughout the world.

In the U.S. opinion polls published in April showed a strengthening of the opposition to nuclear power, and during the course of the year a number of antinuclear demonstrations were held reminiscent of the anti-Vietnam war protests of the 1960s. On June 30 several thousand people gathered to protest the opening of the Diablo Canyon power plant near San Luis Obispo, Calif., and in October an attempt to occupy the site of two plants under construction at Seabrook, N.H., was held back by national guardsmen and police. On October 29 demonstrators tried unsuccessfully to block entrance to the New York Stock Exchange in a protest against support of the nuclear power industry by the nation's financial community.

On October 30 the President's Commission on the Accident at Three Mile Island, chaired by John Kemeny, president of Dartmouth College, Hanover, N.H., submitted to Pres. Jimmy Carter a report highly critical of the nuclear industry and the government's attempts to regulate it. Not only was Metropolitan Edison found guilty of poor maintenance and deficient staff training, but these failings were said to be widespread throughout the industry. Although several members reportedly favoured a moratorium on the construction of nuclear plants, the commission as a whole did not recommend such a drastic measure. It did, however, recommend that construction or operation of new plants be allowed only in states that had satisfactory plans for dealing with a nuclear emergency and that the government regulatory apparatus be overhauled to provide more stringent controls.

On June 3 European environmental groups held simultaneous antinuclear demonstrations in West Germany, France, Britain, Sweden, Finland, The Netherlands, Belgium, Luxembourg, Italy, Spain, and Switzerland. Two of the three nuclear plants in Switzerland, and a fourth that had not yet opened, were of the Harrisburg type. On February 17–18 a national referendum defeated by 51 to 49% a proposal by environmental groups that would have required existing plants to be reexamined and new plants to be approved by the cantons where they were built. The government responded with proposals of its own, which included many new safety precautions, and these were accepted by more than two-thirds of the voters in a referendum held on May 19–20.

West German plans to build a fuel reprocessing plant at Gorleben, Lower Saxony, encountered strong opposition, and at the end of March an inquiry into the proposal began in Hanover. A public demonstration had been arranged for April 2, and the Harrisburg accident a few days before ensured that it would be the largest antinuclear protest the country had yet seen; 40,000 people paraded through Hanover in a procession six miles long. On May 16 the Lower Saxony government announced that the plant would not be built. On the same day, Chancellor Helmut Schmidt said the country's nuclear program would continue, and that arrangements had been made for German spent fuel to be reprocessed at the French Cap de la Hague plant. In April a report from the Hydrographic Institute, Hamburg, West Germany, showed that radioisotopes, almost certainly from Cap de la Hague, had been found in the English Channel and the North Sea.

In February the British government decided to allow the Anglo-West German-Dutch consortium Urenco to double to 2,000 metric tons a year the capacity of its uranium enrichment plant at Capenhurst, Cheshire. This led to protests and a demand for a full public discussion, which was refused. During a demonstration at Capenhurst on July 15, some demonstrators chained themselves to the gates of the plant while others obstructed police. The previous evening a torchlight procession was held in Chester.

Damage estimated at £20,000 resulted from the occupation by demonstrators of the Torness, East Lothian, site of a proposed advanced gas-cooled reactor on May 4–7. On July 6 the secretary of state for Scotland, George Younger, was urged to abandon the Torness scheme in a letter from the Scottish Campaign to Resist the Atomic Menace (SCRAM), accompanied by a petition bearing 20,000 signatures. The petition was rejected. According to an opinion poll of residents in the Torness area, conducted by a residents' group, 65% of the 5,000 people interviewed opposed the scheme and 25% wanted work to be stopped until guarantees could be given concerning safety and the environmental effect of the plant. Of the 10% in favour, all either worked on the site or were over 50 years of age. On September 15 an anti-Torness march was held in Edinburgh.

There was strong opposition in Britain to plans for drilling test holes as part of the search for nuclear-waste-disposal sites in Europe. The Kyle and Carrick Council refused permission for drilling in the Galloway Hills, and when the U.K. Atomic Energy Authority (UKAEA) appealed to the secretary of state for Scotland, the Scottish Conservation Society replied with a petition to the queen bearing the signatures of 100,000 local people. The Scottish secretary ordered a public inquiry and, since 15 sites in Britain were being considered for test drilling, the Town and Country Planning Association urged that all of them be debated at a single inquiry, preferably in the spring of 1980. The government promised only a local planning inquiry, but environmentalists suspected that its terms of reference might be wider than usual.

The problem of nuclear-waste disposal was reaching serious proportions in the U.S. During the year the dump site at Beatty, Nev., was closed and that at Hanford, Wash., was temporarily closed. The only other nonmilitary site accepting low-level radioactive wastes was at Barnwell, S.C., and access to it was severely restricted. This posed a problem not only for power plants but also for the medical profession, which needed to dispose of radioactive materials used in medicine. In the absence of any decision on how to store highly radioactive wastes, they were being kept in pools near the reactors, but many pools were running out of space, and there was strong local opposition to increasing their size.

In September, Friends of the Earth criticized a plan by the UKAEA to ship radioactive materials from the Dounreay development establishment in Caithness to the reprocessing plant at Windscale,

World's 25 Most Populous Urban Areas[1]

Rank	City and country	City proper: Most recent population	City proper: Year	Metropolitan area: Most recent population	Metropolitan area: Year
1	Tokyo, Japan	8,468,200	1978 estimate	28,043,000	1978 estimate
2	New York City, U.S.	7,414,800	1979 estimate	16,369,200	1978 estimate
3	Osaka, Japan	2,707,100	1978 estimate	16,047,000	1978 estimate
4	Mexico City, Mexico	8,988,200	1978 estimate	14,200,000	1979 estimate
5	London, U.K.	6,918,000	1978 estimate	11,517,000	1977 estimate
6	Shanghai, China	5,700,000	1970 estimate	10,888,000[2]	1975 estimate
7	Los Angeles, U.S.	2,795,000	1979 estimate	10,800,200	1978 estimate
8	São Paulo, Brazil	8,107,500	1979 estimate	10,473,000	1976 estimate
9	Ruhr, West Germany[3]	—	—	10,278,000	1975 estimate
10	Rio de Janeiro, Brazil	5,394,900	1979 estimate	8,601,000	1976 estimate
11	Paris, France	2,155,200	1978 estimate	8,549,900	1975 census
12	Buenos Aires, Argentina	2,982,000	1978 estimate	8,498,000	1975 estimate
13	Peking, China	...	...	8,487,000[2]	1975 estimate
14	Calcutta, India	3,148,700	1971 census	8,297,000	1977 estimate
15	Moscow, U.S.S.R.	7,644,000	1977 estimate	7,819,000	1977 estimate
16	Nagoya, Japan	2,085,300	1978 estimate	7,781,000	1978 estimate
17	Chicago, U.S.	2,940,000	1979 estimate	7,678,100	1978 estimate
18	Bombay, India	...	...	7,605,000[2]	1977 estimate
19	Seoul, South Korea	...	...	7,525,600[2]	1977 estimate
20	Cairo, Egypt	5,247,000	1978 estimate	7,066,900	1976 estimate
21	Jakarta, Indonesia	...	...	6,178,500[2]	1977 estimate
22	Manila, Philippines	1,479,100	1975 census	5,900,600	1979 estimate
23	Philadelphia, U.S.	1,765,000	1979 estimate	5,747,300	1978 estimate
24	Bangkok, Thailand	...	...	4,870,500	1978 estimate
25	San Francisco, U.S.	657,000	1979 estimate	4,711,200	1978 estimate

[1]Ranked by population of metropolitan area.
[2]Municipality or other civil division within which a city proper may not be distinguished.
[3]A so-called industrial conurbation within which a single central city is not distinguished.

KEYSTONE

Hundreds of tons of high explosives and poisonous gases left over from World War II were found in an abandoned chemical plant in Hamburg, West Germany. The containers of deadly gas were discovered after an eight-year-old boy playing at the site was killed.

Cumbria, through the Pentland Firth and around Cape Wrath. The substance to be shipped was plutonium nitrate, which had contaminated a Windscale worker in May.

The Windscale complex remained controversial. In March a leak at the complex was disclosed, and on April 19 local authorities were told that it amounted to 30,000 curies of radioactivity, the largest spillage in the history of British Nuclear Fuels Ltd. On May 16 the report of the inquiry into the incident by the Nuclear Safety Executive ordered the company to find ways to contain or recover the discharged wastes. On July 16 a fire broke out in the cave where the casing is stripped from fuel rods, and after routine screening eight workers were detained for more detailed examination to see whether they had been exposed to dangerous levels of radiation.

Following Harrisburg, there were antinuclear demonstrations at 15 British nuclear plants on April 8 to protest the introduction into Britain of the pressurized water reactor. In June a group called Alternative to Nuclear Technology said it was advising people to deduct 15% from their electricity bills and to send the amount to the Department of Energy with a note requesting that it be devoted to research into alternatives to nuclear power. On the weekend of June 2–3, Arthur Scargill, president of the Yorkshire miners' union and chairman of Energy 2000, a group composed of environmentalists, miners, and other antinuclear groups, called on the energy lobby to mount a national campaign against the pro-nuclear policies of the Conservative government. This led to the formation of a new organization launched at a conference on November 10, which aimed to campaign within the trade union movement, the churches, the political parties, and among academics. At the Trades Union Congress, held in Blackpool in September, a number of unions expressed doubt about the country's nuclear program, although several of the larger unions remained pro-nuclear.

The antinuclear movement was growing in Ireland, where the government planned to build the country's first nuclear plant at Carnsore Point, County Wexford. Environmentalists pointed out that the site was 12 mi from Wexford, exactly the same distance as that between Three Mile Island and Harrisburg. The weekend of August 18–19 saw the occupation of the site by thousands of demonstrators, including many who took the opportunity to promote their own—not necessarily related—causes.

On June 8 mining for uranium began officially at the Ranger and Nabarlek mines in the Northern Territory of Australia. The Australian Council of Trade Unions and the opposition Labor Party opposed uranium mining, but rising unemployment led two of the largest unions, representing general and miscellaneous workers, to compete to supply labour to the mines. The unions representing metalworkers, railwaymen, and electrical tradesmen said they would not work at the mines and would try to stop vital equipment from reaching them.

The only Eastern European country to witness the emergence of a popular antinuclear movement was Yugoslavia, where plans to build the country's second nuclear plant on the island of Vir off the Dalmatian coast in the Zadar region met strong local opposition from residents who feared damage to their fishing and tourist industries.

Although most of the controversy over the effects of radiation on the environment centred around the power industry, other industries were involved as well. In July the state of Arizona closed a plant in Tucson that manufactured self-illuminating signs and digital watches. Tritium, a radioactive isotope of hydrogen, had been leaking from the plant for some months, contaminating much of the neighbourhood including a school kitchen and a senior citizens' centre. The tritium was removed from the plant and taken by truck to a military installation west of Flagstaff.

Oil at Sea. The interim report of the Liberian investigation into the March 1978 sinking of the "Amoco Cadiz," published in March 1979, placed much of the blame for the disaster on the tanker's captain, Pasquale Bardari, because of his long delay before summoning help. The "Amoco Cadiz" had released 1.6 million bbl of oil into the sea off the coast of Brittany in the worst oil pollution disaster to that time. The record was broken when a blowout on June 3 at the Ixtoc 1 well off the coast of Yucatán, Mexico, sent oil gushing into the Gulf of Mexico at the rate of 30,000 bbl a day. Despite all efforts to cap the well, it continued to release oil, which drifted toward Texan and Mexican beaches. In October Pemex, the Mexican oil monopoly, announced that a steel cone had been fitted over the well to capture much of the oil, but the flow could not be stopped until relief wells had been completed. Damage to the Texas coast was not as great as had been feared, although the tourist industry claimed it had suffered losses. However, it might be years before the full extent of the effect on the environment could be assessed.

Two large tankers, the "Atlantic Express" and the "Aegean Captain," collided in the Caribbean off Tobago on July 19. The former sank, and the latter was towed to Curaçao for repairs. Fires caused by the collision killed 27 seamen. Strong currents, the warm water, and hot weather helped to break up slicks. As a result, although the "Atlantic Express" was thought to have lost about 90,000 metric tons of oil, pollution was not severe.

The Shetland Islands suffered pollution that killed some 3,700 seabirds, 50 sheep, and oiled a further 2,000 sheep when the "Esso Bernicia" spilled 1,160 metric tons of heavy fuel oil after a collision with a jetty as it approached the Sullom Voe terminal on January 1. The terminal was not opened officially until January 20, by which time the "Esso Bernicia" incident had totally defeated the antipollution preparations and further pollution had been caused by tankers dumping ballast at sea. The Baltic Sea experienced what was said to be its worst oil-pollution incident in March when a Soviet tanker ran aground near the port of Ventspils, Latvia, releasing between 5,000 and 20,000 metric tons of crude.

Urban Problems. Overcrowding and poor hygiene in Naples, Italy, were popularly blamed for an outbreak of respiratory diseases, including infection with respiratory syncytial virus (RSV), that killed more than 40 children during the 1978–79 winter. On Feb. 21, 1979, WHO reported that, of the 38 deaths counted as of February 13, most were under two years of age and all came from poor and crowded homes. The report, however, offered no evidence of malnourishment in the victims, unsanitary surroundings, or local conditions that were unusual for Naples. For a time these deaths were erroneously grouped with an earlier rash of infant deaths, the causes of which had no connection with respiratory illness.

In Britain the plight of the inner cities had led the Labour government to change its urban improvement policies, which previously had favoured the New Towns and other resettlement areas. This policy was continued by the Conservative government, but expenditure was curtailed as part of the general reduction in public spending. On September 2 the chairman of the Association of Metropolitan Authorities called for an injection of capital into the big cities. Echoing similar plaints by U.S. urbanologists, he pointed out that migrants from the older areas tended to be workers who paid taxes, leaving the authorities with reduced revenues and an aging and deprived population in need of care.

In the U.S. success in luring middle-class families back to some parts of the inner cities brought its own set of problems. In areas undergoing "gentrification," property values tended to soar, squeezing out the original residents and sometimes changing the character of the neighbourhood that had made it desirable in the first place. In many cities this trend, plus a variety of tax benefits, was leading to wholesale conversions of rental buildings to condominiums or cooperatives. While this form of property ownership could bring increased stability, it also depleted the rental market and often worked a hardship on the aging and less affluent. (*See* Special Report.)

Urban and Industrial Pollution. Mexico City was reputed to be among the world's most polluted urban areas. In December 1978 UNEP announced that the Mexican government had accepted in principle the recommendations of a group of scientists who had studied the problem. The proposed reforms would bring pollution levels down to acceptable limits in two to three years. (*See* MEXICO: *Special Report.*)

Also in December 1978, the London Brick Co., maker of about half the bricks used in Britain, announced plans to build a new factory, which it wished to locate out of sight in a deep clay pit. Nearby villagers, supported by the Alkali Inspectorate, objected, arguing that this would increase air pollution. The company maintained that it was impracticable to reduce this pollution and that in any case it was harmless. A decision was postponed until the company completed further experiments into ways of reducing pollution. In February the Health and Safety Executive ordered tests to be carried out in the Bedfordshire brickfields to determine if fluoride emissions from the kilns were dangerous.

Britain's largest pit for the disposal of toxic wastes, occupying 600 ha (1,500 ac) at Pitsea, Essex, was the subject of a prolonged fight between its owners, Land Reclamation Ltd., a subsidiary of Redland-Purle, and the Basildon Council. The company wished to keep the pit open and the council, supported by local residents, sought to close it by blocking the only access road. This would have prevented the use of the pit for industrial wastes but would have allowed domestic wastes from London to be brought in by river. On May 24 the company lost the fight to keep the road open but was allowed to appeal against the council's refusal to permit an alternative road to be built.

In November a House of Representatives subcommittee released a list of 3,383 sites in the U.S. where chemical wastes were stored, although it said not all of them were necessarily hazardous. Texas led the list with 319 sites, followed by Ohio with 253 and New Jersey with 223.

On May 26 a factory owned by Dow Chemicals at Pittsburgh, Calif., was closed after an explosion that released a cloud of chlorine gas and killed two workers. Dow had been campaigning against the Toxic Substances Control Act, which required manufacturers to supply details of their products to the EPA and which Dow believed inhibited the development of new products and processes.

In Pittsburgh, Pa., the EPA concluded an agreement with the U.S. Steel Corp., which agreed to spend $400 million on improving nine of its plants so that they would conform to federal air and water regulations by the end of 1982. The EPA said this would halve the amount of particulate emissions in the area and reduce pollution of the Monongahela River by 90%.

Acid rain, reported in areas as far apart as Sweden and Canada and in parts of the U.S. from New England to Texas, was receiving increasing attention. Canada's minister of the environment, John Fraser, described it as the most serious environmental problem Canada had ever faced. The phenomenon occurred when sulfur dioxide and nitrogen oxides from the burning of fossil fuels combined with water vapour in the atmosphere. The resultant acidic precipitation was damaging to water, forest, and soil resources in the affected areas; it was blamed for the disappearance of fish from many lakes in the Adirondacks; and recent reports indicated that it could corrode buildings and might be hazardous to human health. Because the contaminants could be carried long distances, the sources of acid rain were hard to pinpoint and hence difficult to control. In his August 2 environmental message, President Carter announced a ten-year study of the problem, with a $10 million budget for the first year. However, Canadian officials feared that a proposed U.S.-Canadian treaty on the subject might be postponed because of U.S. concern with energy independence and conversion to coal.

Heavy Metals. Inhabitants of the English village of Shipham, Somerset, were told on January 19 that county council analysts had found from 11 to 100 parts per million (ppm) of cadmium in soil samples collected in the village and that a few had contained 998 ppm. Green vegetables grown in the soil contained 0.02 to 3.3 ppm, and root vegetables 0.05 to 1.3 ppm. Cadmium is associated with zinc, and until a century ago there had been a zinc mine

DENNIS ROBINSON—THE GLOBE AND MAIL, TORONTO

The entire 240,000 population of Mississauga, Ontario, had to be evacuated after a freight train derailment threatened to spread chlorine gas over a wide area.

at Shipham. Tests conducted under the supervision of J. H. Fremlin of the University of Birmingham showed that some villagers had 10 to 20 times the normal amount of cadmium in their livers.

A further cadmium warning was contained in a report published on February 5 by the Avon and Somerset county councils, which said that sludge containing large amounts of cadmium was being dumped in the Bristol Channel from zinc smelting works and that shellfish could be contaminated. According to a Swedish study published early in March, exposure to polychlorinated biphenyls (PCB's) might increase the amount of cadmium that is absorbed by the kidneys. A study of airborne dust and soils near a scrap-metal plant in Islington, London, which began in 1976, found significant but probably harmless amounts of cadmium. On March 1, 1979, it was announced that scientists of the Greater London Council were considering a survey of all London scrap-metal plants.

The finding that scrap-metal plants also contribute lead to the atmosphere was made by members of the Environmental and Medical Sciences Division of the U.K. Atomic Energy Research Establishment, Harwell, whose report was published late in January. The study had been commissioned by Associated Octel, a manufacturer of lead additives for gasoline, which was being sued by the parents of three children for damage alleged to have been caused by lead.

The March 29, 1979, issue of the *New England Journal of Medicine* reported on the most thorough investigation ever made into the effects of lead poisoning on children. A team from the Children's Hospital Medical Center and the Harvard Medical School, both in Boston, led by Herbert L. Needleman, examined dentine from the milk teeth of 3,329 Massachusetts children, subjected the children to psychological tests, and received behavioural reports from their teachers. The study showed that children with large amounts of lead in their bodies performed less well than those with little lead. These findings were confirmed by a much smaller study carried out by G. Winneke of Düsseldorf (West Germany) University, who published his results on April 30, and by an Australian study published in July. In the latter, 1,200 Sydney children were examined by a team from the University of New South Wales and the Prince of Wales Hospital, Sydney, led by Lloyd Smythe. Smythe concluded that the safety levels for lead exposure proposed by the American Academy of Pediatrics and the EPA were too high.

The British government was urged by the Conservation Society to improve on its plan to reduce the lead content of gasoline from 0.45 grams per litre to 0.40 grams per litre by 1981. On August 1 a new group, Parents Against Lead, held a meeting attended by about 70 people living close to London's Shell Centre. In May the Mole Valley Council, Surrey, offered to buy the produce of gardeners living within 25 mi of the proposed route of the M25 expressway so that it could be subjected to analysis.

Studies with rats, reported in the *Journal of Physiology* in February, suggested that a large proportion of lead entering the body is derived from food and drink. In May Michael Moore of the University of Glasgow told a London meeting of the Conservation Society that his experiments showed lead was absorbed into food from cooking water. In some parts of Glasgow where old plumbing produced heavy lead pollution of water, people could be ingesting 50% more lead than the limit recommended by WHO and the Food and Agriculture Organization.

Agricultural Chemicals. The herbicide 2,4,5-T was banned for most uses throughout the U.S. in March, following an EPA investigation into miscarriages among women in three areas of Oregon. The investigation arose from a letter written by Mrs. Bonnie Hill on behalf of herself and seven other women, all of whom had miscarried after being exposed to 2,4,5-T sprayed on nearby forests. In the last week in September forests in southern Oregon were sprayed with 2,4-D amid widespread protests, but the spraying of the Six Rivers National Forest in California, scheduled for late September, was abandoned because of public opposition. The campaign to prevent aerial spraying spread into all the West Coast states.

The EPA's Oregon findings were considered by British government scientists but rejected. Replying to a question in the House of Commons on July 26, Jerry Wiggin, parliamentary secretary at the Ministry of Agriculture, Fisheries, and Food, said the EPA had not established a correlation, scientifically or statistically, between exposure to 2,4,5-T and miscarriage. The herbicide remained on sale in Britain. However, the seventh report of the Royal Commission on Environmental Pollution, published on September 18, advised the British authorities to remain closely in touch with the EPA on the effects of 2,4,5-T, and it criticized the use of pesticides in Britain as unnecessarily extravagant.

(MICHAEL ALLABY)

WILDLIFE CONSERVATION

In Great Britain the Grey Seal Group, organized by the Council for Nature and financed by the People's Trust for Endangered Species and the World Wildlife Fund, appointed two investigators to consider whether a proposed 15–20% reduction of the North Sea gray seal population was justified. Following their May 1979 report, the government decided that further inquiries were needed and that the proposed slaughter of 30,000 seals under a six-year program would be held in abeyance. The traditional kill of 2,000 seal pups annually by fishermen would be allowed to continue.

In December 1978 a helicopter pilot flying over Doubtful Sound, an extremely remote area in southwestern New Zealand, saw signs of *Stigops habroptilus*, the owl parrot or kakapo, a flightless parrot that is one of the world's rarest birds. Wildlife officers rushed to the spot, where they located four birds—all apparently males. This appeared to confirm the extraordinary fact that all recently discovered kakapos seemed to be males. A report on another of the world's rarest birds, *Himantopus novazealandiae*, the New Zealand black stilt, indicated that only 20 breeding pairs and 10 young remained, a drop of 25% in six years. Several black stilt breeding grounds had been lost to hydroelectric developments, and the proposed Ahuriri power scheme, if implemented, would be a further threat. There was good news concerning another endangered bird, *Notiomystis cincta,* the stitch bird. Protection on Little Barrier Island had been so successful that the New Zealand Wildlife Service was seeking other predator-free islands on which to establish further populations.

Exceptionally severe weather in much of western Europe during early 1979 caused heavy bird casualties. Bans on wildfowl shooting were introduced in most affected countries, and by January 15 the only places in northwestern Europe where such shooting was allowed were southern France and the British Isles. Finally, the British government, without the approval of all sporting organizations but prompted by the Royal Society for the Protection of Birds (RSPB), banned the shooting of wildfowl and waders from January 26 onward. In August the RSPB announced that it had purchased 2,000 ha (5,000 ac) of salt marsh and mudland in the Dee estuary. This acquisition, combined with the previous purchase of part of the Ribble estuary by The Nature Conservancy at a cost of £1,750,000, laid the foundation for a chain of protected sites for migratory birds in northwest England.

In February, at a symposium on tigers in New Delhi, India, Zias Gairizhu of the Northeast China Forestry College in Harbin gave an estimate of 150 for the number of Manchurian tigers living in China. He gave no estimate for the subspecies of tiger found in southern China. Other estimates of tiger numbers, of various subspecies, were: in the U.S.S.R., 150; Bangladesh, 430; Nepal, 170 to 220; and Sumatra, 400 to 500. Tiger numbers in India were estimated at 2,484, a substantial increase over the 1,800 estimate made before Operation Tiger was launched in 1974. In Nepal radio tracking of young tigers was being used to determine the best shape for a tiger reserve, given the young tigers' propensity for dispersal. North Korea had created national parks to protect tigers and excavated caves to encourage breeding; 50 tigers were reported to be living in these protected areas.

In March the second meeting of parties to the Convention on International Trade in Endangered Species of Wild Fauna and Flora (CITES) was held in Costa Rica. All birds of prey except New World vultures were added to Appendix 2 of the CITES convention, and all parties to the convention were called on to produce better reports on the wildlife trade in their countries. An example of the cruelty involved in this trade occurred in Rome on September 20, when a cargo of 54 wild animals carried by British Cargo Airlines and intended for various places in Italy arrived at Rome airport from South Africa. Because their veterinary certificates were unacceptable, they remained in the aircraft until September 26, when they were flown on to Bahrain. By that time 22 animals had died, and five further deaths occurred shortly afterward.

The Advisory Committee on Oil Pollution of the Sea reported that in 1978 more than 500 oil spills had occurred around the coasts of Britain and Ireland and more than 10,000 seabirds had been affected. Following the Ixtoc 1 blowout, nearly all Canadian waterfowl, including the world population of wild whooping cranes, found oil directly in their path as they moved down the Mississippi flyway to winter around the Gulf of Mexico.

In July Costa Rica legislated to reduce the seaward limits of the Tortuguero national park from 12 to 3 mi, thus allowing fishermen to kill breeding green turtles off their only nesting beach in the western Caribbean. Experts said that this would frustrate the effort of neighbouring Nicaragua, which had protected the green turtle. It was clearly intended to allow resumption of the export trade in the turtles, abandoned when Costa Rica joined CITES, and representations were made by conservation bodies to Costa Rica's president, Rodrigo Carazo Odio.

On September 25 President Carter signed, "with regret," legislation permitting completion of the Tellico Dam on the Little Tennessee River. The dam had been held up for some five years under the provisions of the Endangered Species Act because it would destroy the only known habitat of the snail darter, a species of tiny perch. In the fight over Tellico, environmentalists had been joined by landowners whose property had been condemned because of the project and others who opposed the dam as wasteful and unnecessary. After they were upheld by the Supreme Court, Congress had amended the Endangered Species Act to create a high-level review board which, however, also decided for the snail darter. Finally, led by Sen. Howard Baker (Rep., Tenn.), Congress passed an amendment to an energy and water development appropriations bill making a special exemption for Tellico. Carter was said to be reluctant to use his veto power because he favoured the appropriations bill as a whole and because a veto might prompt Congress to further vitiate the Endangered Species Act, which was due for review. Meanwhile, some of the snail darters had been transferred to the Hiwassee River, where they were said to be doing well.

In July the London meeting of the International Whaling Commission (IWC) was preceded by a rally of 10,000 people in Trafalgar Square demanding a total ban on commercial whaling. The IWC made some progress toward protecting whales by adopting a Seychelles proposal to designate the whole Indian Ocean as a whale sanctuary and by establishing a moratorium on whaling from factory ships—both considerations excluding the minke whale. It also acknowledged that cruelty in whaling was an acceptable subject for consideration. Earlier in the year the Australian government had announced that it would ban all whaling within its impending 200-mi fishing zone and, from January 1981, would ban importation of all whale products. A new and rather strange threat to whales materialized in Hawaii, where nearly half the whales of the North Pacific breed, and in Baja California, the breeding place of the Californian gray whale. Tourists used boats and aircraft to observe and photograph these whales, with the result that mothers and young often became separated. (C. L. BOYLE)

See also Agriculture and Food Supplies; Energy; Fisheries; Historic Preservation; Life Sciences; Transportation. [355.D; 525.A.3.g and B.4.f.i; 534.C.2.a; 724.A; 737.C.1]

Epidemics:
see Health and Disease

Episcopal Church:
see Religion

SPECIAL REPORT

WHEN HOME IS NOT A HOUSE

by Alan S. Oser

Housing in the United States can be looked upon from a variety of perspectives: the quality of shelter it provides, the soundness of the investment it affords for the owner, the contribution its production makes to the dynamics of the national economy, and the effect it has upon the physical and fiscal stability of the community in which it is located. These aspects of housing and their interactions vary from region to region. Even within the regions they vary—between well-to-do neighbourhoods and poorer ones, between city and suburb, and between investor-owned and owner-occupied housing. In general there were more problems with rental housing than with owner-occupied housing in 1978 and 1979, and the older northern cities had more troubles than the developing Sunbelt of the Southwest.

The year 1978 might be termed "normal" in the sense that some of the longer-term characteristics of the housing market were sustained. From the production standpoint, for example, there were about two million housing starts. In view of continuously rising interest rates in the late 1970s and the inflation in construction costs, this was a considerable achievement and a continuation of the production gains from the low point of about 1.2 million starts during the recession year of 1975.

But when figures are measured against some standard of "housing need" in the nation, they are less impressive. The strongest potential pool of home buyers, those in the 25-to-34-year-old age group, rose from 27 million in 1972 to approximately 33 million in 1978 and was expected to keep rising through 1990. By no means was production moving at a rate to satisfy the housing needs of this group, at a price it could afford.

New Mortgage Arrangements. Trying to help matters, the U.S. government introduced graduated-payment mortgages. These enable buyers obtaining mortgages insured by the Federal Housing Administration to reduce their monthly mortgage payments in the initial years of ownership. As the years go on, with their incomes presumably rising, their payments increase.

Alan S. Oser is real estate editor of the New York Times.

There was also growth in variable-rate mortgages, especially in California, probably the nation's "hottest" housing market. In these mortgages interest rates periodically rise and fall in accordance with changes in the amount of mortgage funds available in savings and loan institutions. This provides a stronger inducement to lenders to grant mortgages than does the conventional fixed-rate system.

Another step that helped keep the U.S. housing market humming was the federal government decision to allow savings and loan associations and savings banks to offer their depositors a six-month savings certificate paying a return competitive with instruments offered by commercial banks. This restrained the sharp outflow of funds from these savings institutions that had seriously depleted their mortgage-lending capacities during another period of rising interest rates in 1973–74.

Rising Values. From an investment standpoint housing continued to be a sound long-term buy for the average American. The resale value of homes continued to rise with the inflation rate, generally even a couple of percentage points ahead of it, statistics collected by the National Association of Realtors suggested. The median sale price of an existing single-family house rose to $48,700 during 1978, an increase of 13.5% over the preceding year. In volume, resales experienced a banner year. There were 3.9 million transactions, up 9.3% from the year before.

Congress moved to allow older Americans to reap more of the reward of this rise in value. In the Revenue Act of 1978 it increased to $100,000 the amount of profit on a house sale that taxpayers can exclude from their income in computing their federal income taxes and lowered to 55 from 65 the age at which taxpayers would be eligible for this exclusion.

The national figures in production and resales concealed striking regional and local disparities. The Southwest and California had especially strong years, thereby skewing the figures, while the Northeast and North Central states continued to lag. Population was slowly moving away from the industrial centres of the Northeast and Middle West. The drastic increase in the cost of imported fuel had the most adverse effect upon those regions, from which industry continued the slow withdrawal that began during World War II.

Rental Housing Shortage. In housing, the segment of the market that was suffering was the immense stock of old multifamily rental apartments, where many moderate- and low-income people live. Since the atmosphere of economic stringency of the late 1970s afforded little possibility of producing replacement housing for this population, the major challenge became how to preserve and ex-

FRED R. CONRAD—THE NEW YORK TIMES

The rental housing shortage led to the renovation of many older apartment buildings. Above, an apartment house on 89th Street near Third Avenue in Manhattan was being reclaimed from decay.

tend this older housing stock. Accordingly, the tendency of owners to abandon rental housing in older urban neighbourhoods was a disturbing phenomenon. Such structures were often left to decay to such an extent that they had to be torn down. Nowhere was this more pronounced than in the South Bronx area of New York City, where Pres. Jimmy Carter dramatized the problem by a widely publicized visit to the most devastated locations.

But government was basically unable to build a vast quantity of new housing for moderate- and low-income people. Congressional hearings established that its principal weapon for such an effort—rent subsidies for new and substantially rehabilitated housing under the so-called Section 8 program of the National Housing Act—was generating projected annual subsidy costs averaging $4,200 per year in 1978. Clearly the nation was finding it too expensive to solve the housing problems of such people by building new housing for them.

That fact, coupled with the deterioration and abandonment of existing rental housing, was creating the great housing crisis of the older cities in the late 1970s. Much of the older housing needed new investment to maintain its desirability. But weakening rent-paying capacity, fears of rent controls, and declining housing demand as a result of population shrinkage made many owners reluctant to spend the necessary amount of money on their units.

At the same time, however, a reverse trend was under way. In many of the older cities there were areas in which people, often young middle-income couples, were buying old houses in declining neighbourhoods at relatively low prices. They would then renovate the houses, increasing their value and attractiveness and making the neighbourhoods more desirable. These middle-class people were bringing the capacity and will to improve neighbourhoods to the central cities, though the prices of such renovated dwellings usually put them beyond the reach of low-income buyers. Increased gas prices also were likely to strengthen housing in or near cities.

Condominiums. A major feature of the past year was the continued rise of the condominium and cooperative forms of ownership, in which people own only their own interior space or the land immediately around their unit and depend on an association for the maintenance of common spaces and ground. In areas where the market for such forms of housing was strong, owners of rental housing moved increasingly to convert their buildings to condominiums and other homeowner-association arrangements. This added to the shortage of rental units, although some condominiums were bought as investments and offered for rent.

Meanwhile, the increasing mobility of Americans was having a strong effect on the role of the single-family house as an ideal. Traditionally, home ownership has been one of the "dreams" of Americans. But the increasing mobility of the U.S. population seemed to be reshaping that ideal. Although no statistics were available on the average life of a conventional mortgage, people in the home-mortgage business were suggesting a figure of about seven years, and probably less in California.

In many cases the new housing developments directed toward first-time buyers emphasized social amenities, such as clubhouses and swimming pools, and low-maintenance characteristics. The decline in average family size contributed to making these features more attractive to many buyers than, for example, large backyards and extensive floor space. Much new construction in 1978 and 1979 was directed either toward older "empty nesters" or young "families" with few if any children. And a pale beginning of attention was being paid to lowering the fuel-consumption needs in the operation of homes; however, these efforts were hindered by the considerable decentralization of the building industry.

Future Outlook. The notion of a high level of housing production as an important social goal seemed to be in eclipse in the late 1970s, with the U.S. facing other more pressing domestic problems. The emerging issue was the need to maintain existing housing and bring its cost in line with people's ability to pay for it. This presented a formidable challenge for the 1980s.

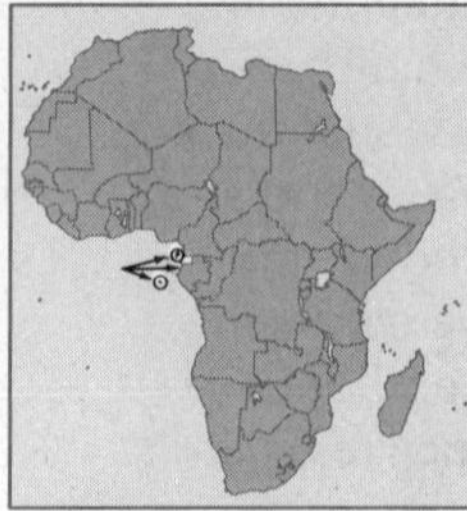

Equatorial Guinea

Equatorial Guinea

The African republic of Equatorial Guinea consists of Río Muni, which is bordered by Cameroon on the north, Gabon on the east and south, and the Atlantic Ocean on the west; and the offshore islands of Bioko and Pagalu. Area: 28,051 sq km (10,831 sq mi). Pop. (1979 est.): 333,000. Cap. and largest city: Malabo, on Bioko (pop., 1970 est., 19,300). Language: Spanish. President to Aug. 3, 1979, Francisco Macías Nguema; chief of state after that date, Lieut. Col. Teodoro Obiang Nguema Mbasogo.

The second of three tyrannical heads of state to be deposed in Africa in 1979, Pres. Francisco Macías Nguema (*see* OBITUARIES) was overthrown on August 3 in a coup led by his defense minister and relative, Lieut. Col. Teodoro Obiang Nguema Mbasogo. The trial of Macías and his henchmen began in Malabo on September 24, and five days later he and six others were convicted of mass murder and executed.

The new chief of state, Lieut. Col. Nguema, named a Supreme Military Council consisting of two vice-presidents and ten presidents of commissions. An amnesty for all political prisoners, the reopening of Roman Catholic missions, and an early return to democracy were announced. Spain (from which Equatorial Guinea gained independence in 1968), the first country to recognize the new government, denied complicity but admitted foreknowledge of the coup.

The most recent of several reports deploring gross violations of human rights in Equatorial Guinea, that of Swedish anthropologist Robert Klinteberg, described the country as Africa's concentration camp. Over 125,000 of its population had fled, and its economy remained utterly stagnant. (MOLLY MORTIMER)

Deposed president Francisco Macías Nguema of Equatorial Guinea being taken out of the courtroom where he was tried for genocide in September. He was later executed.

WIDE WORLD

EQUATORIAL GUINEA

Education. (1973–74) Primary, pupils 35,977, teachers 630; secondary (1975–76), pupils 3,984, teachers 115; vocational (1975–76), pupils 370, teachers 29; teacher training (1975–76), students 169, teachers 21.

Finance and Trade. Monetary unit: ekuele, with (Sept. 17, 1979) a free rate of 69 ekuele to U.S. $1 (148 ekuele = £1 sterling). Budget (1970): revenue 709.4 million ekuele; expenditure 589.3 million ekuele (excludes capital expenditure of 650.7 million ekuele). Foreign trade (1976): imports *c.* 930 million ekuele (80% from Spain in 1970); exports *c.* 2.9 billion ekuele (91% to Spain in 1970). Main exports (1974): cocoa *c.* 69%; coffee *c.* 12%.

Agriculture. Production (in 000; metric tons; 1977): sweet potatoes *c.* 32; cassava *c.* 50; bananas *c.* 15; cocoa *c.* 7; coffee *c.* 6; palm kernels *c.* 2; palm oil *c.* 5. Livestock (in 000; 1977): sheep *c.* 33; cattle *c.* 4; pigs *c.* 8; goats *c.* 7; chickens *c.* 83.

Equestrian Sports

Thoroughbred Racing and Steeplechasing. UNITED STATES AND CANADA. Harbor View Farm's four-year-old colt Affirmed and Hawksworth Farm's three-year-old colt Spectacular Bid, leaders of their respective divisions the previous season, again were acclaimed champions in 1979. In addition, Affirmed, voted best two-year-old colt in 1977 and horse of the year in 1978, again was named horse of the year.

Other Eclipse Award winners in voting conducted by the Thoroughbred Racing Associations, the National Turf Writers Association, and staff members of the *Daily Racing Form* were: Harry A. Oak's Rockhill Native, two-year-old colt or gelding division; Ryehill Stable's Smart Angle, two-year-old filly; Calumet Farm's Davona Dale, three-year-old filly; Peter M. Brant and George Strawbridge, Jr.'s Waya, older filly or mare; Greentree Stable's Bowl Game, male grass horse; Edward I. Stephenson and Nelson Bunker Hunt's Trillion, female grass horse; C. J. Lancaster's Star De Naskra, sprinting; and William L. Pape and Jonathan Sheppard's Martie's Anger, steeplechasing.

Lázaro Barrera was named outstanding trainer for a record fourth consecutive year. Jockey Laffit Pincay, Jr., who established a one-year record of $8,183,535 in money won by his mounts, also earned his fourth Eclipse Award. The previous record total of $6,188,353 was set in 1978 by Darrel McHargue. Cash Asmussen, based in New York, was voted best apprentice jockey. The Harbor View Farm of Louis Wolfson repeated as outstanding owner. Claiborne Farm in Paris, Ky., operated by Seth W. Hancock, 30, was named outstanding breeder.

The 1½-mi Jockey Club Gold Cup at Belmont Park late in the season was the only confrontation between Affirmed and Spectacular Bid. Affirmed's victory gave him horse-of-the-year honours. At that point each had clinched divisional titles.

Spectacular Bid began his campaign by winning seven consecutive stakes, including the Kentucky Derby and the Preakness. He failed in the third leg of the Triple Crown, finishing third to Coastal and Golden Act in the Belmont. Willie Shoemaker subsequently replaced Ron Franklin as Spectacular

Bid's jockey. After a 2½-month rest Spectacular Bid resumed competition with a 17-length victory in an allowance race at Delaware Park, running the 1$\frac{1}{16}$ mi in track record time of 1 min 41.6 sec. Spectacular Bid then won the Marlboro Handicap by five lengths, defeating older rivals as well as Coastal.

After Affirmed failed as the odds-on favourite in his first two starts at Santa Anita, Pincay replaced Steve Cauthen as the colt's jockey and rode him to seven consecutive victories including his career-ending race in the Jockey Club Gold Cup. In that event Affirmed took a short lead early and never lost it while repulsing several challenges by Spectacular Bid and one by Coastal. Spectacular Bid came almost abreast of Affirmed late in the stretch, but the older horse rallied to win by three-quarters of a length over a dull racing surface. Afterward Wolfson remarked: "Affirmed was the champion two-year-old and he was the champion three-year-old. But it wasn't until this year, at four, that he convinced me he was a great horse."

Affirmed earned $1,148,800 in 1979 to increase his career total to a world record $2,393,818. Kelso had held the mark of $1,977,896 since 1966. Spectacular Bid won the Meadowlands Cup Handicap in his final start of the season to increase his earnings to $1,279,333 and establish a one-year record.

Trillion, who raced in France prior to her U.S. campaign late in October, was voted a champion though she failed to win a race in America. Within 21 days the five-year-old mare finished second in four consecutive starts against male rivals, but she was a strong contender always. The five-year-old gelding Bowl Game captured five of ten starts, ending the season with consecutive wins in the Arlington Handicap, Man o'War, Turf Classic, and the Washington (D.C.) International.

Davona Dale won eight consecutive stakes, including the trio of races that comprises the Triple Crown for three-year-old fillies: the Acorn, Mother Goose, and Coaching Club American Oaks. She also annexed the Kentucky Oaks and the Black-Eyed Susan to become the first filly to sweep those five fixtures. Her earnings of $555,723 broke the record for most money earned by a filly or mare in one year. Rockhill Native's most important victories came in the Sapling, Futurity, and Cowdin, none farther than seven furlongs. In his final start, the one-mile Champagne contested in mud, the gelding ran second to Joanie's Chief. Smart Angle took six of nine starts, including the Matron, Frizette, and Selima. She lost by a nose to Genuine Risk in the 1$\frac{1}{16}$-mi Demoiselle while conceding 5 lb to her rival.

In the triple crown events for Canadian-foaled three-year-olds sponsored by the Ontario Jockey Club, Steady Growth won the Queen's Plate, Mass Rally triumphed in the Prince of Wales Stakes, and Bridle Path was victorious in the Breeders' Stakes. Golden Act was winner of the $200,000 Canadian International. (JOSEPH C. AGRELLA)

EUROPE AND AUSTRALIA. There was no outstanding horse in National Hunt racing in Britain in 1978–79, and the weather did its worst—frost, snow, and flood caused the cancellation of more meetings than the previous record of 113 in 1976–77. At Cheltenham the Champion Hurdle featured an epic duel for the second year in a row between the winner, Monksfield from Ireland, and Sea Pigeon; the Gold Cup was won by Alverton, trained by M. H. Easterby and ridden by J. J. O'Neill; and the Triumph Hurdle went to Pollerton.

The Grand National Steeplechase was won for the first time in its 134 years by a Scottish-trained horse, Rubstic, owned by John Douglas, trained at Hawick by John Leadbetter, and ridden by Maurice Barnes. Zongalero was second, 1½ lengths behind. The Mackeson Gold Cup was won by Man Alive. The Hennessy Gold Cup at Newbury was won by Fighting Fit, and Gay Spartan took the King George VI Steeplechase at Kempton Park from Jack of Trumps. At Sandown Park Diamond Edge won the Whitbread Gold Cup from Master Smudge. John Francome was National Hunt champion jockey. In France the Grand Steeplechase de Paris at Auteuil was won by Chinco.

In flat racing a good crop of three-year-olds generally got the better of their elders in both England and France. Steve Cauthen from the U.S. brought his talent to Britain for the first time and, working for trainer Barry Hills, quickly adapted himself, riding the winner of the second classic race of the season, the Two Thousand Guineas. Unfortunately his mount, Tap on Wood, and the narrowly beaten Kris were never to meet again. Kris, trained by Henry Cecil, was unbeaten afterward, winning the St. James's Palace Stakes at Royal Ascot, the Sussex Stakes at Goodwood, the Waterford Crystal Mile and the Queen Elizabeth II Stakes at Ascot, and the Bisquit Cognac Challenge Stakes at Newmarket. Tap on Wood was incapacitated by a virus infection in Hills's stable (the virus also did much to spoil the season for Peter Walwyn's big stable and affected others), but returned to win an autumn race at Doncaster commandingly.

Many considered Kris to be the best miler in Europe, although he did not meet France's Irish River, whose victories included the Prix du Marois at Deauville and Longchamp's Prix d'Ispahan and Prix du Moulin, as well as the Poule d'Essai des Poulains. An even greater hero of the English sea-

BARTON SILVERMAN—THE NEW YORK TIMES

Affirmed, with Laffit Pincay in the saddle, outran Spectacular Bid to win the Jockey Club Gold Cup in October.

son was Troy, trained by W. R. Hern. Troy took the 200th running of the Derby from Ireland's Dickens Hill and France's Northern Baby by the astonishing margin of seven lengths; he won the Irish Sweeps Derby, also from Dickens Hill, the King George VI and Queen Elizabeth Diamond Stakes from Gay Mécène, and the Benson & Hedges Gold Cup. But in Longchamp's Prix de l'Arc de Triomphe the sparkle and acceleration had gone, and Troy, an odds-on favourite, had to be content with third place behind Three Troikas and Le Marmot. In the St. Leger the French produced the winner, Son of Love, and the runner-up, Soleil Noir. Cecil-trained Le Moss, perhaps the best stayer in Europe, notched victories in the Ascot Gold Cup, the Goodwood Cup, and the Doncaster Cup, but then lost in the Jockey Club Cup at Newmarket. Among the older sprinters Thatching and Double Form were outstanding, notably in the July Cup at Newmarket and the King's Stand Stakes at Royal Ascot, respectively. In the William Hill Sprint Championship, won by Ahonoora, Thatching was first easily but was disqualified for interference. Double Form took France's Prix de l'Abbaye at Longchamp. Absalom took Ascot's Diadem Stakes and wound up his career with a victory in Italy. Beaten only once, by Odeon, in seven outings, Quay Line won Doncaster's Park Hill Stakes from Odeon; Connaught Bridge won the Yorkshire Oaks.

Of the two-year-olds Sonnen Gold won the Gimcrack Stakes, Lord Seymour the Mill Reef Stakes, Final Straw Doncaster's Champagne Stakes, and Known Fact the Middle Park Stakes; Monteverdi won the Dewhurst Stakes from Tyrnavos, and Hello Gorgeous took the William Hill Futurity Stakes. The filly Mrs. Penny won the Lowther Stakes and the Cheveley Park Stakes.

Trainer Cecil's horses won a record £682,189; but Hern, including his victories outside of England, netted about £700,000. Cecil established a record for the number of winners trained in an English season, 128. J. Mercer, Cecil's stable jockey, was champion jockey.

Horses and jockeys found the going rough during the Grand National at Aintree, England, in March. Rubstic, ridden by Maurice Barnes, was the winner.

KEYSTONE

In France Top Ville, trained by François Mathet, won France's Derby equivalent, the Prix du Jockey Club, in record time and thereby gave his jockey, Yves Saint-Martin, his sixth success in that race, equaling the record. But a more unusual feat was the victory by Three Troikas in the Arc de Triomphe; she was owned by trainer Alec Head's wife Ghislaine, was trained by her daughter Christiane, and was ridden by her son Freddie. Niniski, trained by Hern, won France's St. Leger equivalent, the Prix Royal Oak, although in 1979 the character of the race was altered when older horses were admitted into it.

Australia's Melbourne Cup, run over 3,000 m, was won by the six-year-old horse Hyperno, ridden by Harry White and trained by Bart Cummings, from Salamander. In New Zealand women jockeys were allowed to ride for the first time in 1978–79, and Linda Jones rode Holy Toledo to a head victory over Drum Short in the Wellington Derby on January 22, the first success in a major race for a woman rider. (R. M. GOODWIN)

Harness Racing. In the greatest speed year ever in the U.S. just about every record was broken in 1979 except Steady Star's 1 min 52 sec time trial. Abercrombie paced the fastest race mile ever (1 min 53 sec); Niatross finished his two-year-old season undefeated and with earnings of $602,901, which included the richest-ever Woodrow Wilson Pace; and Sonsam produced a new three-year-old figure of 1 min 53.4 sec in winning the $750,000 Meadowlands Pace. Tender Loving Care took a time trial of 1 min 52.8 sec at Lexington to become the fastest pacing mare ever. Hot Hitter won the Little Brown Jug and the Adios Stake in earning over $700,000—a record figure for one season.

Happy Motoring beat Sonsam in the $336,420 Cane Pace. The Fox Stake for pacers went to Storm Damage. The $200,000 Roosevelt International Trot was won by the U.S. entry Doublemint from Express Gaxe (Sweden). In other major U.S. trotting events the Kentucky Futurity went to Classical Way; the "Colonial" trot was won by Chiola Hanover; and Legend Hanover won the Hambletonian. Canada's Maple Leaf Trot was won by Cold Comfort. The world drivers' championship was won by Kevin Holmes of New Zealand.

In Australia Run Joe Run took the Australian pacing Derby and was the first three-year-old there to win $100,000 in one season. Top Western Australian two-year-old San Simeon remained unbeaten, while Hanover Schell won the Sydney $29,020 Waratah Stakes for colts and Frisco Turnkey took the $22,200 fillies' division. Australia's fastest mare, Roma Hanover (1 min 57.8 sec), returned barren from stud to win the Italian Cup and other races at Moonee Valley. Toliver Gigi won the New South Wales Oaks, and Rhett the Victorian pacing Derby. Top-class two-year-old Thomas Adios won the Inaugural New South Wales Sires Stake for colts and geldings, while Kiaroa took the fillies' division. Dual Brigade won the $35,000 Lord Mayor's Cup. The 1978 New Zealand Cup was won by Trusty Scot, while the 1978 New Zealand pacing Derby went to Sovereign, Scotch Tar taking the Dominion Handicap for trotters. Christchurch was host to the 1979 Inter-Dominion Championships where Rondel won the $125,000 pacers' final and No Response the trotters' final. The filly Minilima won the New Zealand Oaks.

The top European trotter Pershing (U.S.-bred) earned $350,000 by the end of September, winning in France, Sweden, West Germany, and elsewhere. The $120,000 Swedish Derby was won by the filly May Björn and the Swedish sprinting championship of $23,000 by Active Bowler. The top trotter in Sweden was Express Gaxe (2 min). Swedish trotter Duke Iran retired with 51 victories and earnings of more than $390,000. The Danish Criterium for three-year-olds was won by Captain Bogo from Christa U and Cili Rog; and trotter Nevele won the Tuborg championship from Torok. In the Grand Prix at Oslo, Norway, French trotter Hillion Brillouard was victorious.

Hillion Brillouard won the Prix Centenaire de Vincennes at Paris from Hadol du Vivier, whose wins included the Prix de France. High Echelon won the $200,000 Prix d'Amérique in Paris from French-bred Idéal du Gazeau, then defeated Idéal du Gazeau in the Prix de Sélection and proved his versatility by winning the Prix des Centaures under saddle. At Milan, Italy, Speed Expert established a new 1,600-m record of 1 min 58.7 sec. The $130,000 Lotteria Nazionale was won by Last Hurrah. Vulcan won the Austrian Trotting Derby in Vienna. (NOEL SIMPSON)

Show Jumping. At Rotterdam, Neth., in August 1979, the British show jumping team of Carolyn Bradley (with Tigre), David Broome (Queensway Big Q), Malcolm Pyrah (Law Court), and Derek Ricketts (Hydrophane Coldstream) won the European Team Championship, with 24.7 penalty points as against West Germany's 30.95 and Ireland's 34.1. Gerd Wiltfang won the individual title for West Germany, riding Roman, with 8.95; his compatriot Paul Schockemöhle (Diester, 9.10) won the silver medal, and Hugo Simon (Gladstone, 10.85) the bronze for Austria.

The European Three-Day Event Championship, at Luhmühlen, West Germany, was won by an Irish team of John Watson (Cambridge Blue), Alan Lillingston (Seven Up), Lieut. David Foster (Inis Meain), and Helen Cantillon (Wing Forward). Great Britain was second and France third. Nils Haagensen, the lone Dane, won the individual gold medal while Rachel Bayliss took the silver for Britain and Rudiger Schwartz the bronze for West Germany. The U.S. National Horse Show in New York City in November was won by the U.S. with Great Britain second and Canada third. Mike Matz of the U.S. was individual champion followed by Harvey Smith (U.K.) and Terry Rudd (U.S.). (PAMELA MACGREGOR-MORRIS)

Polo. In the 1979 $150,000 Michelob World Cup, held at Palm Beach, Fla., U.S.-Texas, represented by B. Evans (handicap 7), T. Wayman (9), Red Armour (9), and Joe Barry (9), beat Coronel Suarez of Argentina 8–7. Coronel Suarez was represented by E. Trotz (7), H. Araya (8), C. Garros (9), and J. C. Harriott (10).

The Coronation Cup in England produced a first-time win for the home country by 9–7 over Mexico. England was represented by J. Horswell (6), P. Withers (7), J. Hipwood (8), and H. Hip-

Major Thoroughbred Race Winners, 1979

Race	Won by	Jockey	Owner
United States			
Acorn	Davona Dale	J. Velasquez	Calumet Farm
Alabama	It's in the Air	J. Fell	Harbor View Farm
Amory L. Haskell	Text	W. Shoemaker	Elmendorf Farm
Arlington-Washington Futurity	Execution's Reason	E. Delahoussaye	Howard B. Noonan
Beldame	Waya	C. Asmussen	Peter M. Brant, George Strawbridge Jr.
Belmont	Coastal	R. Hernandez	William Haggin Perry
Blue Grass	Spectacular Bid	R. Franklin	Hawksworth Farm
Brooklyn	The Liberal Member	R. Encinas	Ogden Phipps
Californian	Affirmed	L. Pincay Jr.	Harbor View Farm
Champagne	Joanie's Chief	R. Hernandez	Peter Barbarino
Coaching Club American Oaks	Davona Dale	J. Velasquez	Calumet Farm
Delaware	Likely Exchange	M. Sellers	G. Watts Humphrey Jr.
Delaware Oaks	It's in the Air	W. Shoemaker	Harbor View Farm
Demoiselle	Genuine Risk	L. Pincay Jr.	Mrs. Bertram R. Firestone
Flamingo	Spectacular Bid	R. Franklin	Hawksworth Farm
Florida Derby	Spectacular Bid	R. Franklin	Hawksworth Farm
Frizette	Smart Angle	S. Maple	Ryehill Farm
Futurity	Rockhill Native	J. Oldham	Harry A. Oak
Gulfstream Park	Sensitive Prince	J. Vasquez	Joseph Taub, Dr. Dennis Milne, Hilary Boone
Hollywood Derby	Flying Paster	D. Pierce	B. J. Ridder
Hollywood Gold Cup	Affirmed	L. Pincay Jr.	Harbor View Farm
Hollywood Invitational	Johnny's Image	S. Hawley	Mrs. Meryl Ann Tanz, Edmund Gann
Hollywood Oaks	Prize Spot	S. Hawley	Glen Hill Farm
Hopeful	J. P. Brother	J. Imparato	John P. Campo
Jockey Club Gold Cup	Affirmed	L. Pincay Jr.	Harbor View Farm
Kentucky Derby	Spectacular Bid	R. Franklin	Hawksworth Farm
Kentucky Oaks	Davona Dale	J. Velasquez	Calumet Farm
Ladies	Spark of Life	J. Cruguet	Rokeby Stable
Laurel Futurity	Plugged Nickel	B. Thornburg	John M. Schiff
Man o' War	Bowl Game	J. Velasquez	Greentree Farm
Marlboro	Spectacular Bid	W. Shoemaker	Hawksworth Farm
Matchmaker	Warfever	J. L. Samyn	Mrs. Shirley Sucher
Matron	Smart Angle	S. Maple	Ryehill Farm
Metropolitan	State Dinner	C. McCarron	C. V. Whitney
Monmouth Invitational	Coastal	R. Hernandez	William Haggin Perry
Monmouth Oaks	Burn's Return	J. Vasquez	Ivanhoe Stables
Mother Goose	Davona Dale	J. Velasquez	Calumet Farm
Oak Tree Invitational	Balzac	C. McCarron	Mrs. Howard B. Keck
Preakness	Spectacular Bid	R. Franklin	Hawksworth Farm
Ruffian	It's in the Air	L. Pincay Jr.	Harbor View Farm
Santa Anita Derby	Flying Paster	D. Pierce	B. J. Ridder
Santa Anita Handicap	Affirmed	L. Pincay Jr.	Harbor View Farm
Sapling	Rockhill Native	J. Oldham	Harry A. Oak
Selima	Smart Angle	S. Maple	Ryehill Farm
Sorority	Love Street	J. Tejeira	Dan Lasater
Spinaway	Smart Angle	S. Maple	Ryehill Farm
Spinster	Safe	E. Fires	Elizabeth Brisbine
Suburban	State Dinner	J. Velasquez	C. V. Whitney
Sunset	Sirlad	D. McHargue	Abram S. Hewitt
Swaps	Valdez	L. Pincay Jr.	Aaron U. Jones
Top Flight	Waya	A. Cordero Jr.	Peter M. Brant, George Strawbridge Jr.
Travers	General Assembly	J. Vasquez	Bertram R. Firestone
Turf Classic	Bowl Game	J. Velasquez	Greentree Stable
United Nations	Noble Dancer II	J. Vasquez	Haakon Fretheim
Vanity	It's in the Air	W. Shoemaker	Harbor View Farm
Washington (D.C.) International	Bowl Game	J. Velasquez	Greentree Stable
Widener	Jumping Hill	J. Fell	El Peco Ranch
Wood Memorial	Instrument Landing	A. Cordero Jr.	Pen-Y-Bryn Farm
Woodward	Affirmed	L. Pincay Jr.	Harbor View Farm
Yellow Ribbon	Country Queen	L. Pincay Jr.	Mrs. Maribel G. Blum, Mr. and Mrs. George Sarant, Arnold Winick
Young America	Koluctoo Bay	J. Velasquez	Lightning Stable
England			
One Thousand Guineas	One in a Million	J. Mercer	Helen Springfield Ltd.
Two Thousand Guineas	Tap on Wood	S. Cauthen	A. Shead
Derby	Troy	W. Carson	Sir Michael Sobell
Oaks	Scintillate	P. Eddery	J. Morrison
St. Leger	Son of Love	A. Lequeux	A. Rolland
Coronation Cup	Ile de Bourbon	J. Reid	D. McCall
Ascot Gold Cup	Le Moss	L. Piggott	C. d'Alessio
Eclipse Stakes	Dickens Hill	A. Murray	Mme J.-P. Binet
King George VI and Queen Elizabeth Diamond Stakes	Troy	W. Carson	Sir Michael Sobell
Sussex Stakes	Kris	J. Mercer	Lord Howard de Walden
Benson & Hedges Gold Cup	Troy	W. Carson	Sir Michael Sobell
Champion Stakes	Northern Baby	P. Paquet	Mme A. d'Estainville
France			
Poule d'Essai des Poulains	Irish River	M. Philipperon	Mme R. Adès
Poule d'Essai des Pouliches	Three Troikas	F. Head	Mme A. Head
Prix du Jockey Club	Top Ville	Y. Saint-Martin	Aga Khan
Prix de Diane	Dunette	G. Dolenze	Mme H. A. Love
Prix Royal Oak	Niniski	W. Carson	Lady Beaverbrook
Prix Ganay	Frère Basile	J.-L. Kessas	J.-P. Binet
Prix Lupin	Top Ville	Y. Saint-Martin	Aga Khan
Prix du Cadran	El Badr	H. Samani	Mahmoud Fustok
Grand Prix de Paris	Soleil Noir	H. Samani	Baron Guy de Rothschild
Grand Prix de Saint-Cloud	Gay Mécène	F. Head	J. Wertheimer
Prix Vermeille	Three Troikas	F. Head	Mme A. Head
Prix de l'Arc de Triomphe	Three Troikas	F. Head	Mme A. Head
Ireland			
Irish Two Thousand Guineas	Dickens Hill	A. Murray	Mme J.-P. Binet
Irish One Thousand Guineas	Godetia	L. Piggott	R. Sangster
Irish Guinness Oaks	Godetia	L. Piggott	R. Sangster
Irish Sweeps Derby	Troy	W. Carson	Sir Michael Sobell
Irish St. Leger	Niniski	W. Carson	Lady Beaverbrook
Italy			
Derby Italiano del Galoppo	Marracci	D. Depalmas	Dormello-Olgiata Stud
Gran Premio del Jockey Club	Scorpio	M. Depalmas	G. Oldham
West Germany			
Deutsches Derby	Königsstuhl	P. Alafi	Zoppenbreuch Stud
Grosser Preis von Baden	M-Lolshan	B. Taylor	E. Alkhalifa
Grosser Preis von Berlin	Nebos	L. Mäder	Countess Batthyany
Preis von Europa	Nebos	L. Mäder	Countess Batthyany

KEYSTONE

Carolyn Bradley of England, riding Tigre, was the winner of the French Grand Prix at Longchamp.

wood (8) and Mexico by J. Rodríguez (6), M. Gracida (7), A. Herrera (9), and P. Gallardo (6). In the supporting Silver Jubilee Cup England II defeated France 5–2. The British Open championship was won by Songhai.

In the Argentine Open Championships Coronel Suarez (A. Heguy, H. Heguy, J. Harriott, and A. Harriott—all 10) defeated Mar del Plata 16–4. In the U.S. International Open Retama beat Tulsa 7–5, and the U.S. Gold Cup also went to Retama, which defeated Abercrombie and Kent 9–8.

In Europe the Deauville Gold Cup was won by the Falcons, who beat Les Diables Bleus 10–8; Retama won Spain's Sotogrande Gold Cup; and in West Germany the BB's were again the major cup winners. (COLIN J. CROSS)

[452.B.4.h.xvii; 452.B.4.h.xxi; 452.B.5.e]

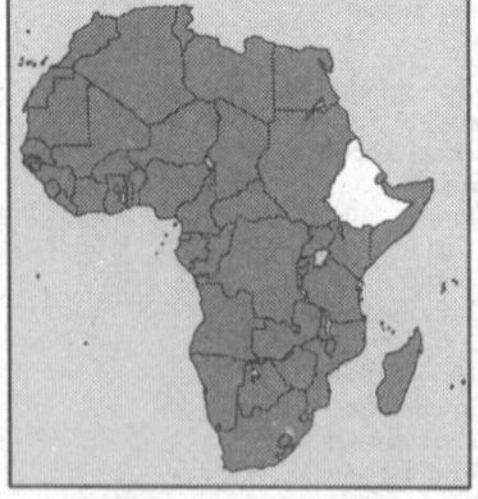

Ethiopia

Ethiopia

A socialist state in northeastern Africa, Ethiopia is bordered by Somalia, Djibouti, Kenya, the Sudan, and the Red Sea. Area: 1,221,900 sq km (471,800 sq mi). Pop. (1979 est.): 30,017,000. Cap. and largest city: Addis Ababa (pop., 1979 est., 1,179,000). Language: Amharic (official) and other tongues. Religion: Ethiopian Orthodox and Muslim, with various minorities. Head of state and chairman of the Provisional Military Administrative Council in 1979, Lieut. Col. Mengistu Haile Mariam.

Toward the end of 1978, the Ethiopian Revolutionary Armies, with backing from Soviet and Cuban personnel, succeeded in occupying most of the major settlements and towns previously held by secessionist groups in the northern province of Eritrea. By late January 1979 the focus of activity was in the northern subprovince of Sahel, where the towns of Afabet, Nakfa, and Karora remained in secessionist hands. Afabet was captured on January 30, and during the year the campaign against the remaining rebel strongholds was reinforced by attacks launched from the Red Sea coastline north of Massawa, which had been brought under government control by February. By the middle of 1979, the focal point of the fighting was the town of Nakfa, capital of the Sahel subprovince.

Although trouble continued in the southeastern region of Ogaden, where incursions by the West Somalia Liberation Front persisted, the limitation of the areas under rebel control in the north permitted a refocusing of national effort on problems of development. In February the Provisional Military Administrative Council (PMAC) announced the launching of the "National Revolutionary Development Campaign." It was celebrated in Addis Ababa on February 2 at a mass rally, the highlight of which was a parade of agricultural equipment acquired as a result of the visit of the PMAC chairman, Lieut. Col. Mengistu Haile Mariam, to Eastern Europe in November 1978. In his speech on this occasion, Mengistu declared that "where tanks and artillery were deployed yesterday, tractors and bulldozers will rumble in the future."

The Development Campaign, which stressed the economic and cultural sectors, was directed at the eradication of long-standing basic problems of hunger, disease, illiteracy, unemployment, and prostitution. It was linked to the government target of an increase in the economic growth rate to 6.7% by 1979–80. The new agricultural machinery was being employed in an extension of state farm activity that aimed at putting an additional 82,600 ha under cultivation and increasing agricultural output from this sector by 164,000 metric tons in 1979. In addition, a 45.6% increase in industrial production and a 33% increase in coffee exports (the most important foreign exchange earner) were projected for the year.

Another component of the campaign was to initiate transformation of the peasants' associations, formed from groupings of small farmers, into producers' cooperatives. Directives for this operation were issued in July; 1,000–2,000 sq m of land would be retained by individual farmers, while the rest of the land under each association would be farmed on a cooperative basis. By August 1, 33 such cooperatives had been formed in the southern province of Sidamo. The Tatek Military Camp near Addis Ababa, previously used for training militia, was now being used for the training of production cadres to support the formation of production cooperatives in agriculture and small-scale industry.

During March and April, Lieutenant Colonel Mengistu made a tour of the southern provinces in personal support of the Development Campaign. This resulted in a widespread shake-up of state farm management. It also had repercussions in the form of an extensive reorganization of the ministries and agencies for agriculture, state farms, coffee and tea development, settlement and relief, domestic and foreign trade, and tourism and hotels, which was announced in May.

On the cultural front, considerable success was achieved in the campaign against illiteracy, initiated in July as part of the broader development campaign. The pilot phase, from July to September, was planned for 1.3 million participants. In September it was announced that 4.6 million had been enrolled in literacy classes and would take their literacy test in October before proceeding to the follow-up courses in health, agriculture, and community living. The immediate effect of the campaign was felt in the urban areas, where the target for eradication of illiteracy was mid-1980. After that date, the campaign would focus on the remaining 15 million illiterates in rural areas. The target for universal literacy was September 1984. In the health sector, efforts centred on a primary health care program, based on the training of recruits from peasant associations in basic preventive medicine. The target was health for all by the year 2000. In April the eradication of smallpox from Ethiopia was officially confirmed.

In recent years investment in development projects had been limited by the government's preoccupation with internal political problems and the mobilization of resources against secessionist groups. However, national development efforts continued to be supported by both East and West. Agricultural machinery and trucks were supplied by Eastern European countries; Soviet aid was given for a dairy farm and milk-processing plant in the Bahir Dar region and for a projected additional cement plant in Dire Dawa; the European Economic Community, through the European Development Fund, was financing a 4 million birr inland fisheries project in the Rift Valley region, low-cost housing development, rural water development, coffee improvement schemes in the southwest, and an extensive program of assistance to the education sector. In April 1978 the International Development Association had approved a development credit of $24 million for a grain storage and marketing project.

Economic and financial relations with other socialist economies were strengthened in 1979. An extensive tour of Eastern Europe made by Mengistu early in the year was followed by the signing of a number of new economic and cultural agreements. As trade with Eastern Europe increased, there was a marked change in the pattern of manufactured consumer goods and other products available in Ethiopia. Meanwhile, cultural and educational delegations from a number of socialist countries, including Cuba, laid the foundation for increasing assistance. Cuba received a large number of Ethiopian students; Cuban students were now enrolled in the postgraduate centre of the Addis Ababa University, and Cuba was providing staff for the establishment of a school of veterinary science. East Germany and the U.S.S.R. provided staff for the university, and East Germany supplied a team of experts for the Ministry of Education.

Political developments included the strengthening of popular associations or mass organizations following formation of the All-Ethiopia Peasants' Association in 1977 and replacement of the All-Ethiopia Trade Union leadership in January 1979. In July the process of reestablishing the Ethiopian Teachers' Association was completed with the formation of a national committee. Similar moves were under way to set up national associations for women and youth.

These developments were linked to the question of establishing a "working class party," which had been expected for some time. At the fifth anniversary celebrations of the revolution in September, Mengistu announced the decision of the PMAC to set up a commission that would be "the only legal revolutionary political body that will be entrusted with the task of organizing the party." Earlier at-

ETHIOPIA

Education. Primary, pupils (1975–76) 1,050,334, teachers (1973–74) 18,646; secondary, pupils 229,365, teachers (1973–74) 6,181; vocational (1973–74), pupils 5,533, teachers 554; teacher training (1973–74), students 3,126, teachers 194; higher (1973–74), students 6,474, teaching staff 434.

Finance. Monetary unit: birr, with (Sept. 17, 1979) a par value of 2.07 birr to U.S. $1 (free rate of 4.46 birr = £1 sterling). Gold, SDR's, and foreign exchange (June 1979) U.S. $123 million. Budget (1975–76 actual): revenue 775 million birr; expenditure 1,141,000,000 birr. Money supply (April 1979) 1,255,400,000 birr. Cost of living (Addis Ababa; 1975 = 100; May 1979) 197.9.

Foreign Trade. (1978) Imports 942.7 million birr; exports 633.6 million birr. Import sources (1977): Japan 16%; Italy 10%; Saudi Arabia 10%; U.S. 9%; West Germany 8%; Iran 7%; U.K. 6%. Export destinations (1977): U.S. 26%; East Germany 15%; West Germany 9%; Saudi Arabia 8%; Japan 7%; Djibouti 5%; Italy 5%. Main exports: coffee 79%; hides and skins 10%.

Transport and Communications. Roads (1977) 23,000 km. Motor vehicles in use (1976): passenger 43,300; commercial 8,900. Railways: (1977) 988 km; traffic (including Djibouti traffic of Djibouti-Addis Ababa line, excluding Eritrea; 1976) 132 million passenger-km, freight 260 million net ton-km. Air traffic (1978): 512 million passenger-km; freight 26 million net ton-km. Telephones (Jan. 1978) 78,700. Radio receivers (Dec. 1977) *c.* 215,000. Television receivers (Dec. 1977) *c.* 25,000.

Agriculture. Production (in 000; metric tons; 1978): barley *c.* 760; wheat 423; corn *c.* 1,079; millet *c.* 207; sorghum 611; potatoes (1977) *c.* 177; sugar, raw value (1977) *c.* 135; sesame seed *c.* 40; chick-peas *c.* 95; dry peas *c.* 87; dry broad beans (1977) *c.* 337; bananas *c.* 70; coffee *c.* 190; cotton *c.* 15. Livestock (in 000; 1978): cattle *c.* 27,500; sheep *c.* 23,150; goats *c.* 17,120; horses (1977) *c.* 1,520; mules (1977) *c.* 1,431; asses (1977) 3,875; camels (1977) 966; poultry *c.* 52,100.

Industry. Production (in 000; metric tons; 1975–76): cement 100; petroleum products (1977) *c.* 530; cotton yarn 9.8; cotton fabrics (sq m) 81,000; electricity (kw-hr; 1976–77) *c.* 682,000.

tempts to form a single party had been made through EMALEDH, the Union of Ethiopian Marxist-Leninist Organizations, created in mid-1977, but this approach was now condemned as having "been a platform for certain petty-bourgeois opportunists." The position was underlined at a meeting of military commissars, cadres, and discussion forum leaders, where it was declared that there was no alternative to Lieutenant Colonel Mengistu as head of the commission, and that the commission would "consist of comrades with unquestioned revolutionary accomplishment and commitment."

European Unity

January 1979 should have seen the start of the most radical initiative yet taken by the countries of the European Economic Community (EEC) to achieve greater financial and economic integration. The European Council, consisting of the heads of government of the nine Common Market countries, had decided the previous month in Brussels to launch the new European Monetary System (EMS) to link the currencies of the EEC. In the event, the British government decided to stay out, but it had been expected that at the start of 1979 the EMS would get under way with the support of the other Community countries.

In fact, inauguration of the EMS was delayed, largely because of the Common Market's complicated system of farm trade subsidies and levies.

Simone Veil of France (centre dais) was elected president of the European Parliamentary Assembly at a meeting in Strasbourg in July.

GILBERT UZAN—GAMMA/LIAISON

These operated so as to compensate food importers and exporters for movements in exchange rates among EEC currencies. The French made their participation in the EMS conditional on the abolition of the subsidies and levies—called monetary compensatory amounts—which, Paris was convinced, worked against the interests of French farmers.

After months of technical negotiations, a compromise was found that enabled the EMS to get under way in March. Its launching was hailed by its most important architects—Pres. Valéry Giscard d'Estaing of France and Chancellor Helmut Schmidt of West Germany—as "a historic decision." But while the election of a Conservative government in the U.K. in May resulted in a general shift of U.K. policies toward more enthusiastic acceptance of the Community, U.K. membership in the EMS still seemed unlikely.

In September the finance ministers of the Nine decided the EMS was working smoothly enough to rule out the need for any change in the rules of operation. Within a week, however, the same ministers, together with central bank leaders, had to meet in Brussels to deal with mounting pressures inside the system. These arose partly from the backwash created by the worldwide movement away from the U.S. dollar, but they also reflected the growing economic gap between currencies such as West Germany's, which benefited from low inflation rates and a strong balance of payments, and currencies such as the Danish krone that were plagued by high inflation rates and a weak balance of payments. The mark was revalued by 2% and the Danish krone devalued by 3%. But as the U.S. dollar's troubles continued, another weak currency, the Belgian franc, remained under pressure, and questions began to be raised about future EEC policy toward the dollar.

As a milestone on the Community's road to closer integration, the launching of the EMS was inevitably overshadowed by the holding of the first direct elections to the European Assembly in June. (*See* Special Report.) The campaign failed to excite the imagination of most electorates, and the turnout in some countries was low, falling to under 50% in Britain and Denmark, where skepticism toward EEC membership persisted.

The opening of the Assembly in Strasbourg, France, on July 17 was the major highlight of the year for the Community. Simone Veil (*see* BIOGRAPHIES), former French minister of health, was elected president of the Assembly. The opening sessions in July and September were accompanied by procedural wrangling, exacerbated by the different parliamentary traditions of the members. While the Socialists remained the largest single group in the Assembly, there was a broad centre-right majority. The first serious confrontation between the Assembly and the two other decision-making Community institutions, the Council of Ministers and the Commission, developed in the autumn over the proposed Common Market budget for 1980. Guided by declarations made by past European Councils, the Commission proposed a budget for 1980 in which increases in obligatory spending for agriculture were matched by larger increases in nonfarm spending.

KEYSTONE

Chinese Premier Hua Guofeng (centre) reviewed an honour guard with French Pres. Valéry Giscard d'Estaing (left) when Hua visited Paris in October.

The overwhelming share of EEC budgets traditionally taken by agriculture had been a source of growing controversy and discontent, particularly in countries—notably the U.K.—that benefited very little from EEC farm spending. Members of the Assembly made it clear that they disapproved of the Council of Ministers' decision to slash the proposed increases in nonfarm spending while leaving the agricultural budget virtually intact. Under current rules members of the Assembly had very limited powers to amend the annual EEC budget, but some members in different political groups began canvassing support for outright rejection of the budget. These efforts proved successful for on December 13, after much negotiating, the Assembly voted 288–64 to reject the budget.

The contents and the future of the EEC budget provided an important talking point throughout 1979. Reports of the growing imbalance between national payments to and receipts from the budget had caused a particular sensation in Britain just before the new year, when it was suggested that the U.K. would take over from West Germany as the principal net contributor to EEC finances. Initial British complaints about this prospect were at first rejected by the Commission and by officials from other EEC governments. In March, however, the Commission produced figures showing that the U.K. had indeed emerged as by far the largest net contributor to the budget, though it was the third poorest of the nine member states.

The issue of British payments to the EEC budget was taken up energetically by both the Labour government of James Callaghan and the new Conservative government led by Margaret Thatcher. At the Strasbourg meeting of the European Council in June, Thatcher persuaded her fellow heads of government that the Commission should be instructed to investigate the entire question and come up with potential remedies in time for consideration by the November 29–30 European Council in Dublin. The Commission suggested a reduction in the British contribution of some £350 million ($700 million), plus increased EEC spending in Britain. However, Giscard wanted the £350 million to constitute a "full and final settlement," and this proved unacceptable to Thatcher, who had originally asked for a reduction of £1 billion ($2.2 billion). A serious rupture was avoided by postponing the question until the next European Council meeting in the spring.

Overshadowing the issue of national payments and receipts was the question of the prospective exhaustion of finance for the budget. EEC spending was financed from agricultural levies, customs duties, and a payment by member states equalling up to 1% of value-added tax. Thanks to the rapid growth in spending on the common agricultural policy (CAP), it seemed in the autumn of 1979 that these sources would be exhausted by 1981. Unless some additional source of revenue was discovered, an absolute ceiling would be imposed on Community spending. Obligatory spending on farm policy—notably on financing the Community's massive surpluses of milk and other food products—would continue to take precedence over spending on regional, social, and industrial alternative energy developments. As a result, all nonfarm spending might eventually have to be sacrificed.

The Commission continued to recommend a "prudent price" policy in an attempt to limit and eventually reduce the output of surplus agricultural products, particularly in the dairy sector, but such a policy remained dependent on the support of farm ministers from the Nine. To strengthen the hand of those who wanted more consideration given to consumers and to the interests of budgetary discipline, the Assembly considered recommendations that the annual EEC farm-price-fixing meetings be attended by finance as well as farm

European Economic Community:
see Economy, World; European Unity

A.G.I.P./PICTORIAL PARADE

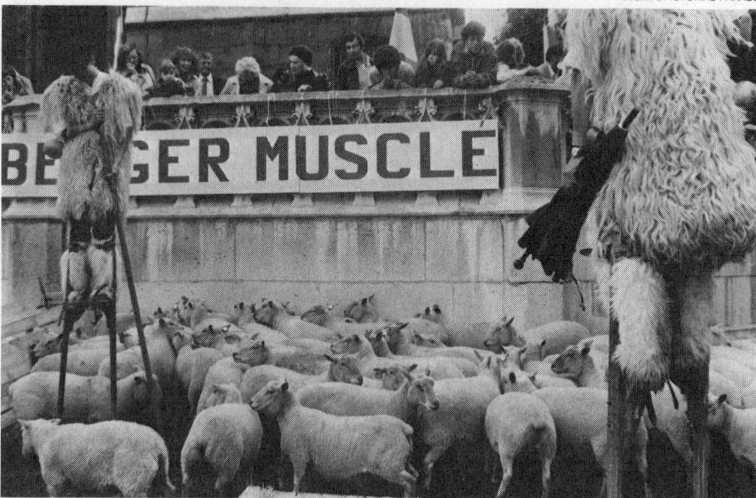

French shepherds massed their flocks in the city of Cherbourg in an attempt to prevent the importation of lamb from England.

ministers. In October France relaxed, but did not lift, its ban on imports of British lamb, which it had enacted to protect its own farmers but which was against EEC rules. Meanwhile, Britain, in the interests of conservation, arrested French fishermen for trawling with nets that were too small, although this did not contravene EEC rules.

Under French presidency, the EEC completed negotiations on the accession of the tenth member state, Greece. The treaty of accession was signed in Athens on May 28, and Greece was expected to become a formal member of the Community on Jan. 1, 1981, after the treaty was ratified by the parliaments of Greece and the nine existing member states. The Commission began exploratory talks with Spain on its application to join, while official negotiations with Portugal, begun in 1978, continued at a pace made all the more leisurely by Portugal's economic and political difficulties. Meanwhile, Turkey made clear its discontent with the association agreement it had had with the EEC since 1963. In the autumn of 1979 there were suspicions in Brussels that, despite the massive economic problems faced by the government in Ankara, Turkey might see merit in pressing its entitlement to apply for full membership, if only to improve the terms of its association agreement.

The economies of most of the Nine appeared to be in good shape at the outset of 1979, but the picture had altered by midyear. In part this was due to the exhaustion of the modest but prolonged recovery after the recession that began in 1973. But it also obviously owed much to the new round of oil price increases announced by members of the Organization of Petroleum Exporting Countries in June. At the June meeting of the European Council, the Nine agreed for the first time to limit future imports of oil for the years to 1985.

Later that month, the situation was complicated by the decision of the Tokyo summit conference of the seven major non-Communist industrial powers to fix individual national oil import targets. This left unresolved the question of whether British oil from the North Sea sold to EEC countries should be included in their import ceilings or be treated as an indigenous source of energy. A compromise formula limiting the extent to which North Sea oil could be excluded from national oil import targets by other EEC countries was agreed on at a meeting of energy ministers of the Tokyo summit governments in Paris during September.

The gloomier world economic and energy outlook made for particularly difficult negotiations between the EEC and its international trading partners in the General Agreement on Tariffs and Trade (GATT) Tokyo Round of multilateral trade talks. After 5½ years of negotiations, a draft agreement was concluded in April. But a question mark remained over whether the GATT agreement would permit the EEC to introduce selective import controls when imports from third countries caused serious disruption in domestic markets.

Disagreement about trade policy was also the source of friction between the Community and Japan, as well as between the EEC and a number of rapidly industrializing less developed countries and exporting nations in Eastern Europe. There were complaints about dumping of foreign industrial exports in the Common Market and complaints about growing trade protectionism in the EEC from some of the Community's trading partners. Despite objections to aspects of EEC policies on imports, the Nine did sign, in October, a five-year trade, aid, and development agreement renewing the 1975 Lomé Convention with 57 countries in the group of associated African, Caribbean, and Pacific countries.

In view of the deteriorating world energy outlook, it was not surprising that there was renewed interest in strengthening ties with the Middle East. The Irish presidency of the Council of Ministers, which took over from France at the end of June, made it known that the EEC wanted to broaden the Euro-Arab dialogue. The Nine also moved closer to recognizing the Palestine Liberation Organization (PLO). The acting president of the Council, Michael O'Kennedy, the Irish foreign minister, referred to the PLO in an address given on behalf of the Nine before the UN in September. Organizations representing the Palestinians, he said, should be involved in negotiations for a Middle East peace settlement. (JOHN PALMER)

See also Defense; Economy, World.
[534.F.3.b.iv; 971.D.7]

Evangelical Churches:
see Religion
Exhibitions:
see Art Exhibitions; Museums; Photography
Faeroe Islands:
see Dependent States
Falkland Islands:
see Dependent States
Farming:
see Agriculture and Food Supplies

SPECIAL REPORT

THE EUROPEAN ASSEMBLY: A NEW STEP

by Edward Heath

The direct elections of members of the European Assembly held in the nine countries of the European Economic Community between June 7 and 10, 1979, marked a major step forward in the life of the Community. As a result, the Community can claim that it has begun the process of becoming a truly democratic organization. Hitherto the members had been indirectly elected—in other words, appointed by the party managers of the national parliaments.

The treaties that established the Community and its two related organizations, the European Coal and Steel Community and the European Atomic Energy Community, always required that direct elections to the Assembly should eventually take place, but only after the Council of Ministers had approved a proposal from the Assembly itself. This development took longer than anticipated by those who originally created the three communities. Now, despite the fact that the elections were not carried out on a unified system (as is also required by the treaties), the last of the Community's institutions to be established has begun to assume its intended form.

A Democratic Institution. The significance of this, not only for the European Community but for the rest of the world, and especially for those countries with which it has close relations, is considerable. In the eyes of its own citizens, the Community has become democratically respectable, an important matter for those living in its free, democratic member countries. The members of the indirectly elected Assembly had no direct responsibility to the voters in a European capacity. All that has now been changed. During the campaign every citizen had the opportunity of getting to know the candidates, of hearing them speak, and of asking them questions. Those elected will now have to remain in constant touch with the voters. They can be lobbied by industrialists, financiers, traders, farmers, housewives, and every organization which considers its interests to be affected by the actions of the Community. All these groups will be able to press their points of view and ask for support for their policies from the Assembly members. This should serve to bridge the gap between the Community and the citizen. The Community was not devised to suit the needs of ministers and bureaucrats; it was created for the benefit of the peoples of Europe. The new Assembly can make this a reality.

That the Community has become democratic is also important in the eyes of its friends, particularly those across the Atlantic, as well as those in the 58 countries with which it has close commercial and financial arrangements under the Lomé Convention. It took the U.S. Senate over 120 years before its members became subject to direct elections. The Community has achieved this in less than 30 years, a feat of which it can rightly be proud. Although many of those with whom it deals may have one-party states, they too take confidence from the fact that they are in contact with a democratic organization. The Community has an advantage in the modern world in that, as an entity, it has no colonial past. Some of its member countries had the greatest empires the world has ever known, but that era is over. The formation of the Community brought about a fresh start. This aspect of its life has been reinforced by the direct elections to the Assembly.

Powers and Influence. The elections have not changed in any way the actual powers of the Assembly which are laid down in the treaties. Any increase in its powers requires not only the approval of the Council of Ministers but also ratification by each national parliament. Only one such change has so far occurred in the life of the Assembly, in 1975 when additional budgetary powers were approved for it. What is important is that its new democratic status can give it greatly increased influence, in particular over the commissioners and the Council of Ministers. To what extent this will become so will depend on the way in which the Assembly handles its affairs and the impact it makes on public opinion. This in turn will depend both on the quality of the members and on their success in capturing the attention of television, radio, and the press.

The constitutional power of the Assembly enables it to dismiss the commissioners as a whole, a major act comparable to bringing about the downfall of a government in a national parliament and one that is seldom likely to be used. As a result of the amendment of the treaties in 1975, the Assembly is also allowed to make changes in the budget. In the case of agriculture and other "compulsory" expenditures, these amendments can only be rejected by a qualified majority vote in the Council of Ministers.

The Rt. Hon. Edward Heath, MBE, MP, was Conservative prime minister of the United Kingdom from 1970 to 1974, during which time negotiations were completed for the country's entry (Jan. 1, 1973) into the European Economic Community.

They can be sustained by a minority blocking vote. For all other Community expenditure, the Assembly can overrule the Council of Ministers—as when it rejected the draft budget for 1980.

There are also requirements for the commissioners to place regulations and other proposals before the Assembly for discussion and debate so that its views may be expressed and taken account of by those responsible. The budgetary powers of the Assembly will become more important as the Community reaches the present limit of its expenditure, probably in 1980. This will give the Assembly the opportunity of voting to change the balance inside the budget; for example, between the amount of money going to the common agricultural policy and that allocated to other purposes.

Members will be able to exert their influence mainly in two ways: first through their work in committees, and second through their debates in the chamber. The committees which meet to formulate and discuss policy can set out their proposals in a detailed report presented to the Assembly as a whole by their rapporteurs. This is a positive aspect of the Assembly's work. Such committee documents can be used to instigate action by the Commission and Council of Ministers in the direction required by the Assembly. Full debates in the chamber, not only on such reports but on every major issue of the day affecting the Community, can capture the imagination of the public.

In any parliamentary system the exercise of such influence can be even more important than the exercise of constitutional powers. If the European Assembly is wise, it will concentrate on developing its influence to the utmost, proving itself to be in tune with public opinion and mindful of the needs of the citizen, before it considers requesting an increase in its powers under the treaties. It is, of course, true that most representative bodies have spent their history gradually absorbing power from the more autocratic authorities which preceded them. It would be in keeping with precedent if the European Assembly also moved along such lines. The position on this occasion, however, is complicated by the fact that not only may the European Assembly find itself from time to time in conflict with the Commission or the Council of Ministers or both; it may also find itself confronted by jealous national parliaments of the member countries.

Political Groupings. In order to exert their full influence, it will be necessary for some parties to align themselves with others to form permanent working groups. The Social Democrats, with 112 seats, are the largest single party in the 410-seat Assembly, closely followed by the Christian Democrats (108). The British Conservative members form the largest single national party (60), and it is customary for them to work with the two Danish Conservatives. In the past it has proved impossible to secure general agreement among the Christian Democrats to work together with the British Conservatives. Although the West German Christian Democrats were always willing to do so, some others, in particular the Italians, disliked, for internal political reasons, being associated with the name Conservative. This particular difficulty has now been resolved by both parties changing their names. The Christian Democrats have become the European People's Party; the Conservatives have become the European Democratic Group.

There are, however, still some differences of philosophy and policy between the two groups, particularly over certain moral issues such as abortion. In the European Democratic Group these questions are normally left to the individual conscience of the member; in the European People's Party they are governed by the basic philosophy of the party itself. This difference in approach on certain moral questions need not, however, prevent the groups from working together on major policy questions affecting the future of Europe. Indeed, they have already done so on a wide range of issues in the nominated Assembly, and this cooperation has deepened in the directly elected Assembly. The European People's Party and the European Democratic Group together, with 172 members, have a substantial majority over the Social Democrats, even though the 44 Communists might on occasion support them. There is also a part to play for the 40 Liberal members and 22 European Progressive Democrats drawn from France, Ireland, Scotland, and Denmark, for on particular issues they might very well hold the balance of power.

The fact that no party will be able to dominate the Assembly on its own and that the members will have to form groupings of this kind means that they will have to establish a working basis as a result of compromises. No party will be able to get everything it wants. All will have to make concessions in order to achieve some of their own objectives. Although some members may feel that working out such compromises is objectionable to their principles, the formulation of the consensus necessary to carry a vote on a particular issue should be beneficial in two ways. First, it will mean that the attitudes and policies of the main groupings will be moderated. On most occasions, the more extreme ideas, of the left or of the right, which may well have been included in a manifesto to satisfy a particular wing of the party, will have to be jettisoned in the common interest to try to ensure that the vote on the major items is successful.

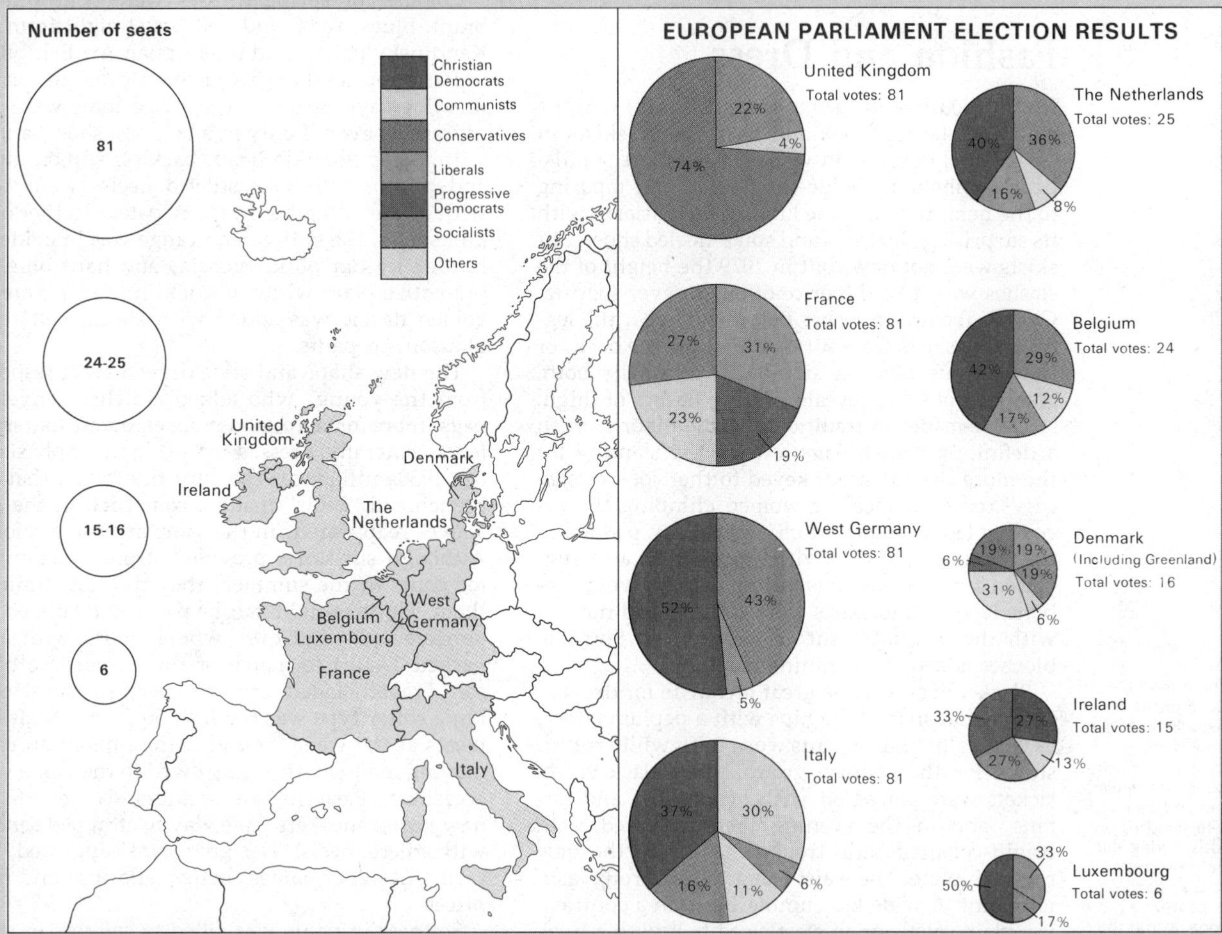

The second consequence of such party groupings is that the members will be forced to think and act in a European way. Of course there will be some national interests on which it is vital for them to stand firm. But the process of conciliation and concession-making will lead members to see another country's point of view. More and more, they will come to recognize that individual national problems cannot be solved in isolation. They can only be resolved in a European context. More and more, members will realize that, in fact, we all share many problems in common.

The task of the Community is to work out common solutions which take into account national characteristics and individual differences. That is why the Community was formed. That is what it is about—to find common solutions to common problems. These party alignments, therefore, will gradually bring about a more intensive European approach to the life of the Community.

Closer Union? If the members of the Assembly, through their committee system and their debates, concentrate on the great issues facing the Community today, this in itself will contribute toward the development of a greater European unity. They should press for a common energy policy, which is urgently required. They should encourage the development of an industry policy which will provide the legal infrastructure on which private enterprise can unite its activities within the Community. They should also press for governments to rationalize their activities in those fields in which there is public ownership, research, and development.

Above all, they should press for a common foreign policy within the Community so that Europe can exercise its influence in other continents where danger threatens. As the United States relinquishes part of the role it has played for 25 years as the world's policeman, it becomes more necessary for Europe in the West and Japan in the Pacific to undertake wider obligations. This is not to say that the Community should acquire its own military organization, although it should make a greater contribution toward procuring the arms NATO needs. It should, however, use its economic power to help the less developed world and resolve the tensions and conflicts which arise there. If the Assembly devotes its energies and experiences to the pursuit of these policies, it will play a major part in the future development of European unity.

Fashion and Dress

It was good-bye in 1979 to the ethnic era, with its cluttered, layered look and its gathered skirts in small floral designs. In walked a far more sophisticated silhouette. Wide-shouldered and tapering to the hem, the new line kindled enthusiasm with its surprising skirt slits and spike-heeled shoes. Slit skirts were not new, but in 1979 the height of the slashes was, like the price of oil, forever soaring. Cut off about two inches below the knee, the leg-revealing skirts were slit up the front, the back, or the side—usually one side but occasionally both. Any gust of wind revealed daring flashes of thigh.

Tailor-mades in traditional woolen fabrics with a definitely British flavour were the standby for the more elegant style, keyed to the "look of success" recommended for women climbing the executive ladder. Squared off and lightly padded at the shoulders, they invited movement and suggested a body-conscious feeling. Jackets were hip-bone length, and skirts were straight and narrow with the inevitable slit or wrap effect. Soft silk blouses added the feminine touch.

Black velvet was the great favourite for dressier jackets that shaped the hips with a peplum effect, as well as for knicker suits worn with white ruffled shirts. For the younger group, plain black velvet jackets were paired off with plaid skirts and tartans, and in the evening they appeared with bright-coloured satin trousers featuring the new roomy hipline. The waist was another strong fashion point. A wide kid cummerbund in a contrasting plain colour or an elasticized belt with a hook fastening at the front was a must with summer dresses.

The suit line for 1979 emphasized broad shoulders, a belted waist, and narrow skirts, freed for walking by deep slits. Little hats were popular, and three- and four-inch heels were standard on city sandals; spring suit (below left) by James Galanos. Gray flannel gave the pantsuit a more formal tone, as did the return of the classic pump; pantsuit (below right) by Kasper.

(LEFT) FRED R. CONRAD—THE NEW YORK TIMES; (RIGHT) FREDRIC STEIN—CHICAGO SUN-TIMES

Colours for spring dresses were bold and vibrant. Blues, reds, and yellows straight from the Kandinsky palette and the Russian Art Exhibition in Paris appeared in tiny geometric designs on the first fine days. Strong, explosive colours were omnipresent, even if only in a belt or a shoe. Sandals with instep or ankle strap, backless slip-on mules and pumps—all with stiletto heels—went wild with colour. Whether in shiny patent leather or in dull suede, the entire neon range was in evidence headed by hot pink, fuchsia, and hard blue. To dramatize plain white or khaki in midsummer, a golden dazzle was added with shoes, belt, bag, blouson, or pants.

The new shape and style drew a swift response from the young, who added clutch or envelope bags, more makeup, and more elaborate hairstyles for a generally dressed-up feeling. Emphasizing the 1950s influence, the tiny tilted hats that the French call "bibis" made a comeback in the fall. Gloves reappeared, in the same explosive colours. Although slit skirts provided strong competition for pants in the summer, they did not eliminate them. Tight-as-tight-can-be pants that cupped the derriere were still everywhere, worn with a V-necked T-shirt to match or the all-purpose blouson. Frayed, faded jeans still walked the streets, but a softer type was the fashion favourite. It had pleats at the waist, rounded the hips in an easy-moving manner, then narrowed to the ankle with occasional Eastern-style softness. To set off the new jeans, sneakers gave way to strapped sandals with stiletto heels. "Designer jeans" appeared, featuring designer names, better tailoring, and high prices.

Softness in pants was allied to softness in tops, often resulting in a roomy pajama look. An alternative was the long slim tunic over clinging pants. All white was the favourite for this outfit. All white, too, was the cotton jogging outfit, now a classic and not worn exclusively for training. Separate tops came in all shapes: tank tops, strapless, form-revealing "bustiers" in stretch fabrics, camisoles with a loose "underwear" fit. All competed with the cotton jersey T-shirt, and young women everywhere continued to serve as billboards for everything from U.S. universities to Skylab. Some plain V-necked T-shirts were elongated to mid-thigh level and caught up in a huge knot on one side. The Saint-Tropez summer evening fashion fad was for discothèque glitter, with bare tops and matching shorts in bright-coloured, shiny satin.

Shorts came in all shapes and lengths—bermuda length with cuffs, extra brief and bound in contrasting braid. Jump shorts were worn with a wide, elasticized belt for roller skating, often accompanied by a square-shouldered bolero without fastenings or a navy nautical jacket. Aside from linen sneakers with rubber soles, the most usual footwear was a low-heeled canvas sandal with a rope wedge sole or a perforated leather or suede sandal with a thick, ridged rubber sole in natural colour. Sports sandals were often worn with socks.

In beachwear, one-piece bathing suits featured the lingerie look. The all-black suit with narrow black lace edging a plunging neckline, cutouts, and even long, clinging sleeves was well designed for playing the bathing beauty on the edge of the pool. Other hints of 1950s Hollywood glamour were apparent in draped and gathered effects that required a perfect figure and in bared backs. Colours were mostly bright, with alternatives of pure white and occasionally gold lamé—obviously less for swimming than for dancing at the disco with the addition of a skirt or shorts. Camisole tops with two narrow shoulder straps and plain, fitted tops with a single asymmetrical strap across one shoulder were also part of the 1979 scene. On windy Atlantic beaches, coverups and windbreakers in orange or yellow ciré were welcome.

Foremost among summer fads was the terry cloth headband inspired by tennis champion Björn Borg, worn dead straight, Indian fashion. Headbands were also popular for town wear, usually in sheer jersey matched to a dress or T-shirt. An idea for fun jewelry adopted by teenagers was a set of dominoes, pierced and threaded on an elastic band and worn as a necklace.

Even in summer, the long, windblown hair style was being disciplined. Rolled or braided hair was dressed with ornaments, little fancy combs, and flowers. But in the fall the broad-shouldered silhouette required a long neck to avoid topheaviness. The 1950s influence gave way to the '60s with the reintroduction of short hair and the elfin small head made famous by Audrey Hepburn.

Autumn coats were designed with deep roomy armholes to allow for suits worn underneath. A more juvenile silhouette was provided by the classic redingote style, waisted and full-skirted, with sleeves puffed at the shoulders and velvet trim or frogging down the front. Quilted, down-filled outerwear, originally designed for winter sports and a staple among the young for several years, entered the fashion mainstream. In the winter a basic for the fashion-conscious woman turned out to be the old familiar twin sweater set, pullover and cardigan, if possible in real cashmere and preferably from Scotland. To go with it, another old-timer was revived—the pearl necklace with one to four strands, sometimes even accompanied by pearl drop earrings. Diamond-studded brooches and barrettes, rejected by the young for many years as too matronly, brought dazzle to a suit or an otherwise unassuming jersey dress.

In keeping with the more sophisticated approach to fashion, the suntanned, natural look of previous seasons gave way to a far more delicate use of makeup. Complexions were intended to be light, even pale, perhaps with an application of talcum powder or Canon's "Opalescent" powder with mother-of-pearl pigment for evening. Lips were outlined. The warm and glowing colours of "Cognac" inspired Helena Rubinstein's new shades of "Lipstick International" matched to nail polish. Use of an eyeliner gave more emphasis to the eyes. "Silver-Fox" and "Champagne Plum" were Estée Lauder's eye-shadow suggestions.

(THELMA SWEETINBURGH)

Men's Fashions. The shoulder became a focal point of men's fashions in 1979. Jackets introduced at the leading menswear trade shows in Europe featured a wide and square, unmistakably masculine shoulder line, an easy, slimmer body shape, and a narrow waistline.

PHOTOS, UPI

For evening, Bill Blass showed a knockout cascade of ruffles in hot pink taffeta. A more casual evening look teamed a mohair sweater with the new padded shoulders with jewel-studded georgette evening trousers, by Donna Karan and Louis Dell'olio for Anne Klein.

The previous year's trend to double-breasted styling continued on an international scale, from Australia to America and throughout Europe. It was apparent in business and leisure suits and in separate jackets. Double-breasted blazers and blazer suits were also fashionable. Some blouson jackets incorporated both wider shoulders and double-breasted styling. No longer the prerogative of younger, fashion-conscious men, blousons had become standard garments in most wardrobes.

Man-made fibres were used as alternatives to the traditional terry toweling for track suits, another garment now worn by almost all age groups and for many occasions other than active sports.

Two famous names in British fashion, Tommy Nutter and Bill Gibb, designed new menswear collections for the Austin Reed shops in Britain and Europe. Austin Reed, through the acquisition of Chester Barrie, became associated with Hickey Freeman Inc., and the two groups jointly provided the U.K. and the U.S. with the world's highest quality and highest priced ready-to-wear suits. Hornes Menswear lifted the curtain on what might be the menswear shop of the future when it coordinated groups of head-to-foot outfits for special occasions in their redesigned Oxford Street, London, shop.

At the London jubilee conference of the International Wool Textile Organization, its president commented: "We shall shortly leave behind us the

AUTHENTICATED NEWS

Yves Saint Laurent's double-breasted two-button suit for spring featured an unconstructed look in 100% cotton. The tapered trousers were finished with a narrow cuff.

'slob' '70s to enter what I hope will be the 'elegant' '80s. There is a distinct, recognizable and often predictable relationship between the fashion of the day and the social pattern of life of that period. I believe there is now a renewed appreciation of quality." British wool cloths continued to find favour throughout the world; 90% of all participants at the 18th World Congress of Master Tailors in Munich, West Germany, used mainly British cloths for their show entries.

(STANLEY H. COSTIN)

See also Industrial Review: *Furs*.
[451.B.2.b and d.1; 629.C.1]

Field Hockey and Lacrosse

Field Hockey. In preparing for the 1980 Olympic Games, men's field hockey had its first major tournament in November 1978 at Lahore, Pakistan. The host country won this inaugural Champions Trophy with Australia second and Great Britain third.

JAMES DRAKE—"SPORTS ILLUSTRATED" © TIME INC.

Dave Huntley scores one of his three goals of the day, aiding Johns Hopkins University in defeating the University of Maryland. Johns Hopkins won its second straight NCAA lacrosse championship.

In March 1979 the Hockey Association's annual international tournament was held on the artificial turf at the Crystal Palace, London, because of bad weather. Great Britain beat Belgium, but the next day Belgium defeated an inexperienced England team. At Perth, Australia, in April, Pakistan won a ten-nation tournament, also played on artificial turf. Australia finished second and The Netherlands third. Belgium won a four-nation tournament at Zagreb, Yugos., in May, defeating England, Czechoslovakia, and Yugoslavia. At Brussels in September West Germany defeated The Netherlands in a four-nation tournament on goal average, each team having defeated Belgium and England. Earlier, The Netherlands had tied a six-match series at home with Pakistan, the world champion. A Junior World Cup, for players under 21, was held at Versailles, France. This 12-nation event was won by Pakistan, which defeated West Germany in the final.

Indoors, England for the first time won the U.K. home countries championship at Belfast in January. As a result England went to Eindhoven, Neth., to play against The Netherlands, Austria, Italy, Switzerland, and Belgium for places in the European Championship tournament, to be held at Zürich, Switz., in early 1980. England qualified along with Austria and The Netherlands.

In women's outdoor competition 18 nations took part in the second World Cup tournament at Vancouver, B.C., in August 1979. The event, run by the International Federation of Women's Hockey Associations, was won by The Netherlands, which beat West Germany in the final. The U.S. placed third, Australia fourth, Wales fifth, and England sixth.

After the World Cup Great Britain defeated Australia but lost to New Zealand. Before the World Cup New Zealand toured Australia and won all three matches, and at Edinburgh, Scotland, Britain defeated both The Netherlands and the U.S. Scotland won the U.K. home international championship, and England tied its annual match with Ireland. (SYDNEY E. FRISKIN)

Lacrosse. MEN. International lacrosse benefited from the 1978 world championship, all countries afterward reporting an increase in the number of players. To assist both international players and referees the International Federation of Lacrosse encouraged the use of international rules at the national level. Following the success of Canada in the 1978 world championship, Canadian box lacrosse, a six-to-a-side version of the field game, had its local popularity challenged.

In the U.S. Johns Hopkins University of Baltimore, Md., once again won the National Collegiate Athletic Association championship. The Maryland club was winner of the club competition, and the college superstars beat the club superstars 12–10, with Mike Buzzell (Navy) voted as the best U.S. attack player. For the fifth straight year the North defeated the South, 21–15.

In Australia, where lacrosse is essentially a club game, Williamstown was the champion of the Victoria State League, defeating Surrey Park 23–12, and in the South Australia state championship Glenelg defeated East Torrens 14–13. In the Three-State Competition, Victoria triumphed over South Australia 19–9 in the final play-off.

In England Lancashire beat Cheshire 11–10, but Cheadle, a Cheshire club, took all the other honours. The club was North of England League champion, North of England flag winner (defeating Mellor 15–8), and the English Club champion (beating Hampstead 28–5). The South of England flag was won by Hampstead, and Oxford was the Southern League champion.

(CHARLES DENNIS COPPOCK)

WOMEN. In Britain in 1978–79 bad weather caused many cancellations of matches and prevented the completion of the territorial championship, which was left undecided for the second successive year. The highlight of the season was the arrival of the U.S. national team to play Great Britain in a series of three matches. Great Britain, having defeated Australia in five test matches in the summer of 1978, saw this as an opportunity to regain the world championship. The first test, a 4–4 draw in Cardiff, showed the effectiveness of U.S. zoning techniques. The team feeling, fitness, and relaxed stickwork of the U.S. then led the team to success in five matches, beating England Reserves 6–3, Wales 10–3, Scotland 7–3, Scottish President's XII 8–4, and British Universities 10–3. However, the England team with its speed, accuracy, and inventiveness managed to win 7–4, and this paved the way for Great Britain's victories in the last two tests by scores of 8–6 and 8–4.

At the club level in the U.S. Philadelphia I reclaimed the title by winning the 1979 national championship. In England, Purley, a club in existence for only one season, won the Clubs and Colleges Tournament. Middlesex won the counties championship, and the South Reserves the territorial reserve tournament. The experienced England team remained supreme by defeating Wales 16–1, Scotland 11–3, and the Celts 13–3, and an England squad was being prepared for a tour to the U.S. in the spring of 1980. An encouraging sign was the recognition of a junior England team which, after training sessions, beat Wales 22–0.

(MARGARET-LOUISE FRAWLEY)

Fiji

An independent parliamentary state and member of the Commonwealth of Nations, Fiji is an island group in the South Pacific Ocean, about 3,200 km E of Australia and 5,200 km S of Hawaii. Area: 18,272 sq km (7,055 sq mi), with two major islands, Viti Levu (10,388 sq km) and Vanua Levu (5,535 sq km), and several hundred smaller islands. Pop. (1979 est.): 624,000, including (1976) 49.8% Indian, 44.2% Fijian. Cap. and largest city: Suva (pop., 1976 census, 63,600). Language: English, Fijian, and Hindi. Religion: Christian and Hindu. Queen, Elizabeth II; governor-general in 1979, Ratu Sir George Cakobau; prime minister, Ratu Sir Kamisese Mara.

With the economic outlook improved by the discovery of copper on Viti Levu and favourable offshore oil prospects, and with inflation for 1978 down to 6.1%, the Fijian government in 1979 brought in a status quo budget with only minor increases in duty on a few items. Sugar production was expected to reach an all-time high of 450,000 metric tons.

FIJI

Education. (1977) Primary, pupils 132,440, teachers 4,209; secondary, pupils 32,995, teachers 1,662; vocational, pupils 1,678, teachers 177; teacher training, students 743, teachers 65; higher (1979), students 1,448, teaching staff 150.

Finance and Trade. Monetary unit: Fiji dollar, with (Sept. 17, 1979) a free rate of F$0.83 to U.S. $1 (F$1.80 = £1 sterling). Budget (1978 est.): revenue F$158.5 million; expenditure F$171.1 million. Foreign trade (1978): imports F$300,890,000; exports F$170.7 million. Import sources: Australia 30%; Japan 16%; New Zealand 15%; U.K. 9%; Singapore 7%; U.S. 5%. Export destinations: U.K. 40%; Australia 11%; U.S. 10%; New Zealand 9%. Main exports (1977): sugar 57%; petroleum products 14%; fish 6%; coconut oil 5%. Tourism (1977): visitors 173,000; gross receipts U.S. $80 million.

Transport and Communications. Roads (1975) 2,976 km. Motor vehicles in use (1977): passenger cars 19,300; commercial (including buses) 11,000. Railways (1976) 644 km (for sugar estates). Shipping traffic (1977): goods loaded 528,000 metric tons, unloaded 785,000 metric tons. Telephones (Jan. 1978) 32,700. Radio receivers (Dec. 1977) 300,000.

Agriculture. Production (in 000; metric tons; 1978): sugar, raw value c. 316; rice (1977) 18; cassava (1977) c. 92; copra c. 30. Livestock (in 000; Sept. 1977): cattle c. 156; pigs c. 32; goats c. 55; horses c. 36; chickens c. 820.

Industry. Production (in 000; 1977): cement (metric tons) 80; gold (troy oz) 49; electricity (kw-hr) c. 290,000.

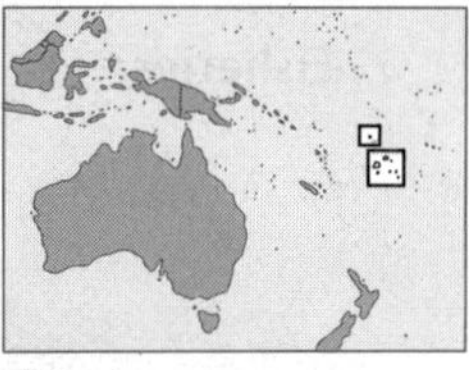
Fiji

In January a new contract was offered to sugar growers. They would receive 70% of returns (with 30% to the Fiji Sugar Corporation) when production was below 325,000 metric tons, and higher percentages in better years. The contract became binding when two-thirds of the growers accepted it. However, James Shankhar Singh, minister of communications and works in the predominantly Fijian Alliance Party (AP) government, spoke against the contract and resigned from the Cabinet.

Attorney General Sir Vijay Singh became embroiled in controversy when a flour-milling company he had represented as a lawyer and dealt with as a minister was convicted of defrauding its shareholders and the government. In 1979 Fiji celebrated the 100th anniversary of the first arrival of indentured Indian immigrants. During August–September Fiji was host to the South Pacific Games.

(BARRIE MACDONALD)

Finland

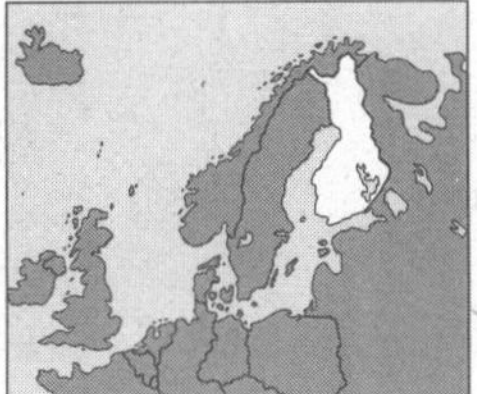
Finland

The republic of Finland is bordered on the north by Norway, on the west by Sweden and the Gulf of Bothnia, on the south by the Gulf of Finland, and on the east by the U.S.S.R. Area: 337,032 sq km (130,129 sq mi). Pop. (1979 est.): 4,764,400. Cap. and largest city: Helsinki (pop., 1979 est., 483,600). Language: Finnish, Swedish. Religion (1976): Lutheran 98.1%; Orthodox 1.2%. President in 1979, Urho Kaleva Kekkonen; prime ministers, Kalevi Sorsa and, from May 26, Mauno Koivisto.

Finland's general election of March 18–19, 1979,

Fencing: *see* Combat Sports

produced a 3% rightward swing in the popular vote and some marked changes in the composition of the 200-seat, single-chamber Parliament. While the Social Democrats' representation was reduced from 54 to 52, the National Coalition (Conservatives) increased theirs from 35 to 47. The Centre Party lost three seats and the Finnish People's Democratic League (largely Communist), five. (For tabulated results, *see* POLITICAL PARTIES.)

Pres. Urho Kaleva Kekkonen first called on victorious Conservative chairman Harri Holkeri to form a new government and then, when his efforts foundered, on Social Democratic vice-chairman Veikko Helle. On May 11 Mauno Koivisto (Social Democrat), governor of the Bank of Finland and prime minister during 1968–70, was appointed prime minister-designate. His Cabinet, sworn in 15 days later, contained nine non-Socialist and eight Socialist ministers (including Koivisto). It differed on two scores from the previous administration led by Social Democratic chairman Kalevi Sorsa: the Swedish People's Party replaced the Liberals, and the coalition's parliamentary base was narrowed from 142 to 133 (122 excluding dissenting Communists, or well below the two-thirds majority required for much key legislation).

In May Kekkonen paid a state visit to West Germany which set the seal on the eight-year process of normalizing relations with both Germanys. In a speech meant to eradicate misconceptions about Finnish neutrality, Kekkonen asked his German audience: "Is it really so difficult to grasp . . . that we do not seek security in membership of a military alliance, but rather in international cooperation founded on broad consensus?"

On June 20 the president publicly castigated parliamentary speaker and Centre Party chairman Johannes Virolainen for "causing the nation damage." This followed publication in West Germany of a magazine interview in which Virolainen hinted that Finland's Conservatives had been excluded from the government because of their record in the "Night Frost" administration of 1958–59, when relations with Moscow were strained. Before the March election, the Soviet press had declared that Conservatives in power could endanger Finnish-Soviet relations. Since the Conservatives increased their share of the vote from 18.4 to 21.7%, the campaign evidently misfired, possibly accounting for the transfer of the Soviet ambassador in Helsinki to other duties. The most prestigious Chinese politician ever to set foot in Finland, Vice-Premier Geng Biao (Keng Piao), signed a bilateral industrial and commercial agreement during a visit in May.

After four lean years, a 7% economic growth rate was expected for 1979—possibly the highest in the Organization for Economic Cooperation and Development region. Unemployment, though still persistent, fell from 8.8% of the work force in January to 5.1% in August. At the same time, the first eight months of the year yielded a 629 million markkaa (*c.* U.S. $165 million) trade surplus to go with the 2,869,000,000 markkaa (*c.* $760 million) surplus for the whole of 1978. But trends abroad suggested that the boomlet could not be sustained, and there was stress on keeping inflation below the levels in competing countries. For the first time ever, the markka—devalued ten times since World War II—was revalued on September 21 by 2%. The move was meant to reduce imported inflationary pressures and to encourage another restrained centralized wage settlement to match the 13-month accord reached on January 9.

The internationally known writer Mika Waltari died in August (*see* OBITUARIES). A fire at an old people's home at Virrat on January 23 cost the lives of at least 26 of the residents (*see* DISASTERS).

(DONALD FIELDS)

FINLAND

Education. (1976–77) Primary, pupils 438,804, teachers 27,414; secondary, pupils 341,421, teachers 21,399; vocational, pupils 88,771, teachers 9,292; teacher training, students 898, teachers 108; higher, students 119,274, teaching staff 5,780.

Finance. Monetary unit: markka, with (Sept. 17, 1979) a free rate of 3.85 markkaa to U.S. $1 (8.28 markkaa = £1 sterling). Gold, SDR's, and foreign exchange (June 1979) U.S. $1,978,000,000. Budget (1979 est.): revenue 43,515,000,000 markkaa; expenditure 43,513,000,000 markkaa. Gross national product (1978) 128,330,000,000 markkaa. Money supply (May 1979) 12,435,000,000 markkaa. Cost of living (1975 = 100; June 1979) 148.6.

Foreign Trade. (1978) Imports 32,338,000,000 markkaa; exports 35,206,000,000 markkaa. Import sources: U.S.S.R. 19%; Sweden 14%; West Germany 13%; U.K. 9%; U.S. 5%. Export destinations: U.S.S.R. 18%; Sweden 15%; U.K. 13%; West Germany 10%; Norway 5%. Main exports: paper 24%; machinery 13%; ships 9%; timber 9%; wood pulp 5%; clothing 5%; iron and steel 5%.

Transport and Communications. Roads (1977) 74,149 km (including 194 km expressways). Motor vehicles in use (1977): passenger 1,075,400; commercial 136,200. Railways: (1977) 6,089 km; traffic (1978) 2,984,000,000 passenger-km, freight 6,328,000,000 net ton-km. Air traffic (1978): 1,645,000,000 passenger-km; freight 41.9 million net ton-km. Navigable inland waterways (1977) 6,675 km. Shipping (1978): merchant vessels 100 gross tons and over 341; gross tonnage 2,358,623. Telephones (Jan. 1978) 2,032,300. Radio licenses (Dec. 1976) 2,179,000. Television licenses (Dec. 1977) 1,454,500.

Agriculture. Production (in 000; metric tons; 1978): wheat 241; barley 1,565; oats 1,082; rye 74; potatoes *c.* 746; sugar, raw value (1977) *c.* 71; rapeseed *c.* 40; butter *c.* 73; cheese *c.* 65; eggs *c.* 76; meat (1977) 267; fish catch (1977) 117; timber (cu m; 1977) 33,970. Livestock (in 000; June 1978): cattle 1,779; sheep 106; pigs 1,245; reindeer 177; horses 25; chicken 9,032.

Industry. Production (in 000; metric tons; 1978): pig iron 1,960; crude steel 2,336; iron ore (metal content) 691; cement 1,796; sulfuric acid 856; petroleum products (1977) 11,061; plywood (cu m; 1977) 360; cellulose (1977) 3,228; wood pulp (1977) mechanical 1,774, chemical 3,472; newsprint 1,126; other paper and board (1977) 3,641; electricity (kw-hr) 34,200,000; manufactured gas (cu m) 25,000.

Fisheries

World fisheries continued to be dominated by the effects of rising fuel costs, shrinking stocks of the more popular fish species, and the still relatively new concept of a 200-mi exclusive economic zone (EEZ). By early 1979, more than 90 nations had claimed jurisdiction and prior rights over what previously had been international waters.

In introducing a U.S. $35 million program designed to help less developed coastal states set up proper management measures in their new fishery zones, Kenneth C. Lucas, head of the Fisheries Division of the UN Food and Agriculture Organization (FAO), called the 200-mi regime "the most important development in the history of world fisheries." Fish already accounted for about 55% of the animal protein consumed in Asia and 24% in Africa; by the year 2000 demand could well have doubled, with 75% of the increase coming from less developed countries. By that time, the cost of a program like that proposed by the FAO might well have risen to at least $30 billion.

While extended jurisdiction might usher in a golden age for less developed coastal states, it was not seen by Norway as the answer to its problems. Even with more exclusive access to its once prolific fishing grounds, Norway was faced with a drop in production amounting to over 800,000 tons. Much of this shortfall was accounted for by the almost total ban on herring fishing, imposed in an effort to build up decimated stocks. Norway was also short of cod which, as a major export, was almost equivalent to an internationally hard currency.

Norway's problem was one that increasingly affected the more technologically advanced fishing nations, namely, that fishing had become too efficient. During the preceding 25 years, fishing vessels had acquired a vastly increased capability for locating and catching fish, but this had not been matched by a decrease in numbers of vessels. Sometimes, as in the case of purse seiners and big pelagic trawlers, catch potential had risen by a factor of more than ten. As a result, even when catching power was diverted to less valuable and more plentiful species such as blue whiting and capelin, the stock could be diminished so rapidly that it became endangered before scientists had time to issue warnings.

Norway reacted to this situation during the year by drastic catch restrictions and fleet reductions. This, in turn, required a relatively large injection of state funds to maintain the liquidity of fishing enterprises until such time as stocks might recover. More than 10% of the 300-strong purse seiner fleet was sold during the year. A proportion of these vessels found their way into British ownership, where they circumvented the government's efforts to restrict catching power by refusing grants and loan aid. To the buyers, they represented a short-term, quick-money investment, primarily in the west of England mackerel fishery. But as the fleet buildup began in the fall, fears grew that this fishery, too, would prove to be yet another victim of the industry's failure to match catching capacity to stock availability—or to control man's greed.

Europe's problems were watched with some concern by other nations. One of these was Canada, whose 200-mi zone takes in some of the world's most famous fishing grounds. Following the Conservative victory in May, Roméo LeBlanc was replaced as fishery minister by the more cautious James McGrath, whose stated aim was greater stability, more long-term planning, and an end to the "gold rush panic" into fishing. One of his first acts was to follow the advice of the new North Atlantic Fishing Organization and announce a temporary closure, in 1980, of the Grand Banks cod fishery. A five-year, $250 million program for Newfoundland included a shore complex, "Harbour Grace," which by 1985 would handle 250,000 metric tons of fish a year—one-quarter of the province's anticipated 1-million-metric-ton catch. On the Pacific coast, a new fisheries harbour was planned for Vancouver, B.C. Meanwhile, Canada's new EEZ was the source of a dispute with the U.S., as Canada seized a number of U.S. vessels fishing for albacore tuna within the Canadian zone. The U.S. claimed the albacore tuna was migratory and therefore subject to international rather than national control.

In the U.S. a new mood of optimism stimulated investment in vessels and shore plant. The Marco shipyard at Seattle, Wash., was busy building a series of 122-ft steel vessels for the Alaskan crab and salmon fisheries, while the launching of the 160-ft trawler "American No. 1" was seen as a move into the big trawler league and the start of a "U.S. boats in, foreign boats out" policy. A new National Aquaculture Council was set up to stimulate inland production, and on the North Pacific coast several floating fish factories were deployed to handle the increased catch. The aim was an annual fish production of 5.5 million tons by 1990. This compared with 3 million tons in 1978, when a record value of $1.6 billion, despite a poor tuna season off Africa, suggested that the target was not

KEYSTONE

Boxes of herring were found stacked on the docks at Boulogne, France, despite a Common Market ban on herring fishing.

Table I. Whaling: 1977–78 Season (Antarctic); 1977 Season (Outside the Antarctic)
Number of whales caught

Area and country	Fin whale	Sei/ Bryde's whale	Hump-back whale	Minke whale	Sperm whale	Total	Percentage assigned under quota agree-ment[1]
Antarctic pelagic (open sea)							
Japan	–	254	–	2,378	36	2,668	49.6
U.S.S.R.	–	311	–	2,600	2,124	5,035	50.4
Total	–	565	–	4,978	2,160	7,703	100.0
Outside the Antarctic[2]							
Japan	–	500	–	–	3,078	3,578	
U.S.S.R.	–	275	–	–	3,266	3,727[3]	
Peru	2	392	–	–	799	1,193	
Australia	–	–	–	–	624	624	
Iceland	144	132	–	–	110	386	
Greenland	9	–	10	–	–	19	
Others	–	230	–	–	2,098	2,328	
Total	155	1,529	10	–	9,975	11,855[3]	

[1] Antarctic only.
[2] Excluding small whales.
[3] Including 186 gray whales.
Source: The Committee for Whaling Statistics, *International Whaling Statistics*.

unrealistic. However, it was expected that this would involve the exploitation of presently underutilized species such as Alaskan bottom fish and East Coast squid.

In the Southern Hemisphere, New Zealand had found plenty of applicants for licenses to fish within its 200-mi zone, in which new stocks of fish and prawns had been discovered. New Zealand had never seriously exploited its distant waters, where the Japanese and Koreans, among others, had enjoyed years of good fishing. They now found themselves having to pay for the privilege, while the U.S.S.R. had been allowed to deploy seven large vessels under a "joint venture" agreement. Relative newcomers were West Germany and Spain, the latter with an eye on New Zealand's well-stocked squid and skipjack tuna resources. New Zealand continued a cautious buildup of its own fleet, with import restrictions on foreign-built vessels currently being waived.

Australia's entry into the 200-mi league had been bedeviled by difficulties in reaching agreement with Japan, one of the ten nations that, between them, had made more than 40 applications for fishing licenses or joint ventures. By mid-1979 Japan had withdrawn on the grounds that the Australian price was too high and New Zealand complained that the cost of policing the new zone swallowed up the income from fishing licenses.

Member nations of the European Economic Community (EEC) still showed no sign of reaching agreement on a common fisheries policy, making any concerted conservation effort difficult, especially in view of the disparity of interests and fish preferences among the nations concerned. Britain, whose waters contained about 65% of the Community's fish, maintained a modified but firm position on preferential rights despite the change of government in the spring. Once again, Britain took unilateral conservation action, contrary to EEC policy, when the minimum size of certain trawl net meshes was increased in an effort to reduce the catch of immature fish.

The EEC had already stated its intention to reduce the numbers of certain types of "less efficient" artisanal boats by scrapping and sale subsidies and retraining schemes for unemployed fishermen. The opposite policy was being promoted for less developed nations, where the social implications of employment and community were seen as paramount. In countries with distant-water fisheries—Britain, France, and West Germany for example—there was a disastrous "natural wastage" of big trawlers, now excluded from their traditional grounds and either sold, scrapped, or idle. Britain's Associated Fisheries took a staggering loss, blamed in part on an unsuccessful venture in Australian waters and the lack of a firm EEC policy on which investment could be based.

Trawling operations can consume one ton of fuel for every ton of fish caught, and with fuel costs rising rapidly, attention was turned to less energy-intensive ways of fishing. The more static fishing methods such a gillnetting were reviewed, and attempts were made to mechanize the handling and baiting of longlines, on which hooks are fixed every few metres. There was renewed interest in such fuel-saving devices as electronic monitoring units and propeller nozzles. In the U.S. experiments were carried out with a 57-ft boat fitted with hydraulically controlled sails.

Table II. World Fisheries, 1977[1]
In 000 metric tons

Country	Catch		Trade	
	Total	Freshwater	Imports	Exports
Japan	10,733.3	268.4	941.7	582.9
U.S.S.R.	9,352.2	919.7	50.5	459.1
China	6,880.0	4,568.0	...	...
Norway	3,562.2	1.5	39.9	899.2
United States	3,101.5	230.5	1,027.9	226.0
India	2,540.0	953.1	2.0	65.0
Peru	2,530.0	6.5	0.3	489.6
South Korea	2,419.0	21.4	31.3	513.9
Denmark	1,806.6	18,3	195.0	611.3
Thailand	1,778.1	146.9	19.2	180.3
North Korea	1,600.0	...	...	...
Indonesia	1,545.0	389.9	15.6	48.4
Philippines	1,510.8	198.2	62.5	13.7
Spain	1,454.8	18.8	128.6	190.1
Iceland	1,374.4	0.5	3.6	396.0
Chile	1,285.3	...	0.4	231.0
Canada	1,280.4	123.1	86.3	442.0
Vietnam	1,013.5	176.3	3.2	4.3
Bangladesh	835.0	740.0	...	3.7
Brazil	790.1	135.0	64.8	26.3
France	760.3	1.5	450.7	123.8
Mexico	670.1	15.5	16.4	64.5
Poland	664.7	30.9	159.1	96.9
South Africa	602.9	0.1	11.2	107.0
England, Wales	525.2	...	606.1 [2]	186.0 [2]
Burma	518.7	138.9	0.1	0.2
Nigeria	505.7	335.9	63.1	3.6
Malaysia	499.2	2.5	135.7	114.0
Ecuador	475.5	...	...	94.6
Scotland	451.6	1.3	[3]	[3]
West Germany	432.1	15.8	790.9	199.4
Italy	427.0	24.8	321.7	64.0
Namibia (South-west Africa)	404.2	0.1	...	...
Argentina	392.8	10.4	0.9	140.0
Ghana	382.7	50.1	76.6	2.2
Netherlands, The	313.0	3.6	287.5	232.9
Portugal	310.3	0.3	102.1	50.1
Faeroe Islands	310.3	...	4.1	87.5
Senegal	288.8	6.5	9.4	46.6
Morocco	260.6	0.6	0.1	68.1
Tanzania	250.0	200.0	5.2	0.4
Pakistan	248.5	43.0	0.3	25.8
Panama	228.0	...	1.7	32.9
East Germany	209.4	17.9	140.1	...
Oman	198.0	...	...	...
Sweden	192.1	13.1	158.4	84.9
Other	5,587.1	...	...	...
World total	73,501.0	11,323.3 [4]	7,886.1 [4]	7,963.3 [4]

[1] Excludes whaling.
[2] Includes Scotland.
[3] Included with England, Wales.
[4] Includes unspecified amounts in Other category.
Source: United Nations Food and Agriculture Organization, *Yearbook of Fishery Statistics*, vol. 44 and 45.

The picture in South America had improved, although the Peruvian anchoveta harvest was still a disappointing one-fifth of what it had once been. This was offset by increased food-fish production, however, and it was thought that the catch could be increased considerably over the current 1.4 million tons. An FAO/UN Development Program scheme, covering 23 countries from Bermuda to Brazil, aimed at total production of 4.7 million tons. Aquaculture was to be promoted in South America under a plan backed by the Inter-American Development Bank, with a production goal of 1.5 million tons.

Another small step was taken in 1979 toward saving the whale. Although the International Whaling Commission's annual meeting failed to achieve a complete moratorium on whaling, factory ship whaling was banned for all species except minke whales. A move was also made to control the activities of "pirate" whalers. (H. S. NOEL)

See also Food Processing.
[731.D.2.a]

Floods:
see Earth Sciences; Engineering Projects

Food Processing

The health, safety, and nutritional aspects of foods received increasing attention during 1979. The detection of cancer-producing nitrosamines at levels of parts per billion in some foods posed questions of their elimination from the diet, since this would necessitate the exclusion of cured and smoked meats and fish and most vegetables. Several U.S. scientists asserted that pepper, foods baked to a brown colour such as pizza, and fried and broiled foods also produced cancer and should be avoided, but other scientists considered such fears exaggerated because objective appraisal was hampered by uncertainties concerning the interpretation of animal experiments and the significance of minute amounts of toxic substances.

Claims that food additives caused hyperactivity in young children were investigated by U.S. authorities. The results were not conclusive but did suggest that an additive-free diet could alter the behaviour of a few children; a food colour (tartrazine) was particularly suspect. However, according to responsible British medical opinion there were few if any indications to justify the use of a rigorous additive-free diet in the treatment of hyperactivity.

A World Health Organization/UNICEF Working Paper criticized the baby food industry for the harm it had allegedly caused in discouraging breast-feeding in less developed countries, but some considered that there was oversimplification of the issues and that more detailed studies were needed. An Australian consumer organization condemned "fast foods" as contributing to obesity, diabetes, heart disease, and hypertension on the grounds that they were too high in calories, fat, and salt. The Italian authorities reported on an occurrence of breast enlargement in a school that affected 213 boys and 110 girls. It was attributed to estrogen in meat or poultry from an uncontrolled source.

A European Economic Community (EEC) directive required that manufacturers be liable for faults in their products, including foods (except agricultural products), even if these faults were unforeseeable at the time of manufacture. The EEC announced a review of flavourings, surface sprays on fruit and vegetables, baby foods, frozen foods, and pesticide residues, as well as information exchange on food contamination, consultative procedures with various interested parties, and legal redress. The Codex Alimentarius Commission circulated recommendations on the sterilization of foods by irradiation to the governments of 118 countries.

Processing and Packaging. Food manufacturers achieved some substantial energy savings, especially in waste heat recovery from refrigeration units, evaporators, driers, ovens, and in sterilization processes. Energy economies exceeding 50% were reported by Japanese food companies, and a British firm manufacturing confectionary products was able to eliminate supplementary space heating with an annual saving of about £100,000 by utilizing waste heat from the bakery ovens. Realization of the economic advantages of using natural gas for direct instead of indirect heating in food-drying processes was impeded in various countries by legislative problems. Use of food wastes as boiler fuel made progress.

A feasibility study by U.S. scientists of wave-power systems for the purification of seawater by reverse osmosis indicated a cost of $1.29 per 1,000 gal. A French manufacturer of dried milk demonstrated that concentration of milk by ultrafiltration was an economic alternative to evaporation. A Swiss plant for pasteurizing cheese milk by solar energy was installed in Afghanistan. Pending EEC regulations specifying average weight of contents led to the development of new automatic computerized weighing machines capable of determining and controlling the average weight of the contents and providing a statistical analysis of deviations from the mean.

Fruit, Vegetable, and Confectionary Products. Investigations in many countries into the causes and control of fruit and vegetable deterioration were reviewed by a British research organization, which emphasized the need for new techniques and plant. It commented that the Japanese were currently the most original and dynamic in this area. Damage to tomatoes dropped into trucks from mechanical harvesters was reduced by an ingenious U.S. technique utilizing an inflated plastic cushion from which air was released as the load increased, thus maintaining a minimum fall. Improvements were made in the pitting of peaches by rotating them between blades, which cut them in half and gripped the stone while resilient pneumatic cups rotating in opposite directions engaged the halves and separated them from the stone. U.S. scientists also investigated the sorting of apples to eliminate bruised fruit and found that the use of infrared reflectance with measurement of electrical conductance was the best means of automatic selection.

COURTESY INFACT; PHOTO, NICK ALLEN

Producers of infant formula were accused of pushing their products in less developed countries without fully informing mothers of the problems involved in their use. Nestlé agreed to withdraw advertising such as this billboard in Zimbabwe Rhodesia.

SUMMERS—FAYETTEVILLE TIMES, N. C./ROTHCO

A Swiss machine for making a wide range of comminuted (reduced to fine particles) and emulsified products combined in one unit a colloid mill, dissolver, stripper, strainer, and vacuum deaerator. French scientists developed a continuous process for fermenting and drying cocoa beans to replace the traditional fermentation between banana leaves and sun drying. A machine developed in France for extracting olive oil was claimed to process 850 kg (1,870 lb) of olives hourly with extremely low oil losses; the olives were crushed, and the stones, pulp, aqueous portions, and oil were then separated.

A West German beet sugar company commissioned a unique computer-controlled sugar plant with a peak intake of 15,000 tons of beets a day from 3,700 growers. Each load had an identification card upon which, when inserted into a reader terminal, were recorded delivery details, weight, and, subsequently, data on sugar content and trash for accounting purposes. All subsequent manufacturing operations including pulp drying were under computer control.

Dairy Products. Declining butter consumption and problems of whey disposal stimulated international collaboration. The utilization of whey, the separation of whey proteins, and the applications of hydrolyzed lactose as a sweetener were investigated. Australian scientists studied the acid, enzymatic, and ion-exchange hydrolysis of lactose and concluded that the method of choice depended largely on the end use. A French company removed the proteins from whey by ultrafiltration and then demineralized and hydrolyzed the lactose in the permeate by ion-exchange. This solution was concentrated to a syrup for use as a sugar replacer. British scientists investigated the preparation of alcoholic beverages from whey.

There was much research, especially in Australia, on alternative outlets for butter including the fractionation of butterfat and blending with vegetable oils. Low-calorie spreads of reduced butterfat content were developed in many countries for weight-control regimens. Pizzas gained great popularity in Japan, and a special cheese was developed to facilitate the production of pizzas by automated methods.

Meat, Unconventional Protein, and Seafood. There were some noteworthy developments in meat and poultry technology. Meat chilled too soon after slaughter, before rigor mortis takes place, becomes tough. Australian scientists invented an electrical treatment to accelerate rigor mortis and thus freezing, thereby reducing losses and improving quality; the first appliance was installed in New Zealand for lamb processing. British scientists developed a novel process for the "hot" deboning of beef carcasses immediately after slaughter instead of after the traditional 18-hour cooling. Deboning was followed by vacuum packing and cooling under controlled conditions. A U.S. company developed a machine for deboning whole cooked poultry and raw turkeys and ducks. It was claimed to give yields of 80–85%, compared with 60% by manual means, and to be more hygienic than manual removal or previous mechanical processes. A Swiss organization began a systematic investigation of the reforming of scraps of meat, poultry, and fish in order to improve their utilization.

In spite of much debate on the protein needs of less developed countries and general increases in meat, poultry, and fish prices, the utilization of alternative sources of protein made little progress outside the U.S., where the Department of Defense authorized their use up to 20% in meat products. A range of imitation cheese and other dairy-type products was developed from peanut protein, and a spray-dried glandless cottonseed protein isolate was also produced.

Efforts continued in various countries to improve the utilization of fish resources. Australian fishery experts reported that out of some 2,500 species only a few were known to the public. Previous optimistic assessments of British fishery experts concerning the great potential of blue whiting as an alternative to cod were not fulfilled. Commercial users found that their small size and the unsuitability of existing machines for deboning made their use too costly. The world's first turtle farm, in the Cayman Islands, began to export turtle steaks.

New Foods. Various new dairy products were introduced during the year, including a number of carbohydrate-free preparations obtained by fermenting milk with yeasts. New beverages included one made from buttermilk and concentrated fruit juices (Brazil); carbonated drinks from deproteinized whey (Hungary) and fermented whey and beetroot juice (Yugoslavia); a whey/milk combination that could also be used to make yogurt and cheeselike products (South Africa); and a combination of coconut milk with skim milk powder (Mozambique).

In view of the reaction of some consumers to the high fat content of butter, numerous spreads of lower fat content were developed: in Britain, a spread from vegetable fat and casein; in Czechoslovakia, one containing 35% butterfat; in Sweden, one containing 40% butterfat and 7.5% protein; and in the U.S.S.R., a similar preparation containing casein coprecipitated with whey protein. U.S. technologists developed a cheese substitute from casein and vegetable oil for use in frozen pizzas at half the cost of mozzarella. Its substitution for up to 50% of the total amount of cheese was authorized in school lunches.

Continuing interest in the potential of krill resulted in the successful introduction of a number of new products, including canned krill paste, a frankfurter-type krill sausage, a smoked krill spread, and a soup. Other new products included a cheeselike product from small pelagic fish from Denmark; canned shark meat and a frankfurter-type shark-meat sausage from Mozambique; a shark-meat steak that proved an acceptable alternative to fried fish from Australia; and a spread from squid and small cephalopods from Britain. Mexican fishery experts developed a type of fish cake that did not require refrigeration, made from small fish that accompany the shrimp trawl and are usually discarded. (H. B. HAWLEY)

See also Agriculture and Food Supplies; Fisheries; Health and Disease; Industrial Review: *Alcoholic Beverages.*
[451.B.1.c.ii; 731.E–H]

Football

Association Football (Soccer). The year following the World Cup finals is usually one of introspection, the departure of some national team managers, and the application of lessons learned from the finalists. During 1979 there were no outstanding lessons to be applied from the spectacular 1978 finals in Argentina, though among those who left the active soccer scene were manager Helmut Schoen of West Germany and player Berti Vogts (Borussia Mönchengladbach). Some Argentine stars left their native land for fortunes elsewhere, following the path to Europe already trodden by Mario Kempes. Osvaldo Ardiles and Ricardo Villa both went to Tottenham Hotspur in England, while Alberto Tarantini had a spell with Birmingham City and Daniel Bertoni, like Kempes, went to Spain.

The 1982 World Cup finals, to be held in Spain, were scheduled to have 24 finalists in a tournament of 52 games played over a month. Six groups of four teams each would contest the opening rounds, after which the top two in each group would be split into four further groups of three each. The winning four teams of the latter groups would then play in the semifinals. Europe would have 13 places, plus host nation Spain. There would be three South American representatives—in addition to defending champion Argentina—and two each from Africa, Asia, and Central-North America.

EUROPEAN CHAMPIONS' CUP. Nottingham Forest made sure the cup for European champion clubs stayed in England for another year by defeating FC Malmö, Sweden, by a single goal in Munich, West Germany, on May 30. The crucial goal was scored by Trevor Francis when he ducked in to head home a cross from Scottish winger John Robertson in the final minute of the first half. That goal and Francis's talented all-around performance in his first European Cup match underlined the wisdom of Nottingham manager Brian Clough's decision to pay a record British transfer fee of £1 million ($2 million) to Birmingham City for his services. But as a spectacle the final was substandard. The Swedish part-timers, managed by Englishman Bob Houghton, became enmeshed in their defensive strategy to such an extent that they seldom broke out of their own half. Nottingham Forest had opportunities created by Francis, John McGovern, and Ian Bowyer, but their main strikers, Gary Birtles and Tony Woodcock, failed to exploit them.

Malmö had the misfortune to lose its ex-

Kevin Keegan of England (right) struggles to put the ball past the Scottish goalkeeper George Wood as England defeated Scotland 3–1 on May 26 for the U.K. Home International Championship.

CENTRAL PRESS/PICTORIAL PARADE

perienced midfield man Staffan Tapper, who limped off after 34 minutes. Much of the team's momentum went with him, though in the final game there was no denying the superiority of the English side. Nottingham Forest goalkeeper Peter Shilton must have been extended to maintain his concentration, he had so little to do. Nottingham Forest tried in vain to add to the tally but was repeatedly caught in the Swedes' offside trap. Had Malmö not suffered so many injuries shortly before the final, the game in the giant Munich stadium could well have been a better balanced and brighter spectacle. As it was, with Tapper out – he broke a toe during training the previous evening – there was little support from midfield for the strikers. And in truth the Swedes were not in the same class as the professionals from Nottingham, whose performance was highlighted by the brilliance of Francis against a backdrop of solid teamwork.

European Cup-Winners' Cup. Barcelona, so often the bridesmaid, gained the Cup-Winners' Cup in 1979 by defeating West Germany's Fortuna Düsseldorf 4–3 in a sparkling game in extra time in Basel, Switz., on May 16. As might be expected of a seven-goal final, some of the defensive work left much to be desired, but the 58,000 spectators, including some 35,000 who had traveled from Spain, were delighted with such a nail-biting display. The turning point in the game occurred when Gerd Zimmerman, the man who put the brake on Barcelona's Austrian World Cup striker Hans Krankl, limped off six minutes before the end of extra time. That left the Spaniards with an extra advantage in attack, which just swung the balance. Thus Barcelona triumphed in a very fast game that was kept flowing by the Hungarian referee Karoly Palotai.

Table I. Association Football Major Tournaments

Event	Winner	Country
European Champions' Cup	Nottingham Forest	England
European Cup-Winners' Cup	Barcelona	Spain
UEFA Cup	Borussia Mönchengladbach	West Germany
Libadores (South American Champions' Cup)	Olympia	Paraguay
World Youth Championship	Argentina	

Table II. Association Football National Champions

Nation	League winners	Cup winners
Albania	Partizan Tirana	Vlaznia
Austria	Austria WAC	SW Innsbruck
Belgium	Beveren	Beerschot
Bulgaria	Levski Spartak	Levski Spartak
Cyprus	Omonia	Apoel
Czechoslovakia	Dukla Prague	Locomotiv Kosice
Denmark	Vejle	Frem
England	Liverpool	Arsenal
Finland	Helsinki	Lahlen Reipas
France	Strasbourg	Nantes
Germany, East	Dynamo Berlin	Magdeburg
Germany, West	SV Hamburg	Fortuna Düsseldorf
Greece	AEK Athens	Panionios
Hungary	Ujpest Dozsa	Raba Gyor
Iceland	Valur	IK Akranes
Ireland	Dundalk	Dundalk
Italy	AC Milan	Juventus
Luxembourg	Red Boys	Red Boys
Malta	Hibernians	Sliema Wanderers
Netherlands, The	Ajax	Ajax
Northern Ireland	Linfield	Cliftonville
Norway	IK Star	Lillestrøm
Poland	Ruch Chorzow	Arka Gdynia
Portugal	FC Porto	Boavista
Romania	Arges Pitesti	Steaua Bucharest
Scotland	Celtic	Rangers
Sweden	Öster Vaxjö	FC Malmö
Switzerland	Servette Geneva	Servette Geneva
Turkey	Trabzonspor	Fenerbahce
U.S.S.R.	Dynamo Tbilisi	Dynamo Kiev
U.S.	Vancouver Whitecaps	
Wales		Shrewsbury
Yugoslavia	Hajduk Split	Rijeka

UPI

A member of the French rugby team struggles to hang onto the ball in a game in New Zealand. The French team played the New Zealand team twice, losing the first game 23–9 but winning the second 24–19.

José Sanchez opened the scoring for the Spanish side, but the brothers Klaus and Thomas Alloffs bundled the ball over the line after Barcelona goalkeeper Pedro Artola had dropped a shot from Rudi Bommer. Thomas Alloffs was credited with the goal. Juan Asensi then scored for Barcelona, but Wolfgang Seel made Fortuna's second goal and sent the game into overtime. In the first extra period Barcelona's Carlos Rexach, who had earlier missed converting a penalty with a weak shot, sent in a fierce drive to make it 3–2; then came the eventual winning goal by Krankl. But the resilient Germans struck back with another goal by Seel to bring the score to 4–3; Barcelona held out and so ended their ten-year barren period without a European trophy to their credit.

UEFA Cup. A penalty kick by Danish striker Allan Simonsen brought Borussia Mönchengladbach its second UEFA Cup victory in three finals. The West German side thus beat Red Star Belgrade by an aggregate of 2–1 after the first leg in Yugoslavia on May 9 had been tied 1–1. In the first leg Red Star produced much good football and deservedly took the lead when Slavoljub Muslin triggered off a move that led to his sending in a short centre for Milos Sestic to turn into the German goal. In the second half of the contest the Yugoslavs seemed more inclined to defend their lead than to increase it. Finally, Simonsen moved past a couple of Red Star defenders and slipped the ball to Horst Wohlers, who curved it in to tie the game at 1–1. So ended the scoring as the final 30 minutes produced chances for both sides but no takers.

In the return match at Düsseldorf, West Germany, on May 23 there was plenty of passion among the players, but the coolness of the veteran captain Berti Vogts helped Borussia through some sticky periods. Red Star's Ivan Jurisic was responsible for the penalty after 18 minutes when he brought down Simonsen. The Dane made the kick himself, and Aleksandar Stojanovic in the Red Star goal had no chance to stop it. In the closing minutes Muslin slammed a shot that beat goalkeeper Wolfgang Kneib, but the ball crashed against the goal frame. Thus the cup went to the West Germans, who survived a tremendous battering from Red Star.

U.K. HOME INTERNATIONAL CHAMPIONSHIP. England won the U.K. Home title by defeating Scotland 3–1 at Wembley, London, on May 26 in a match that was something of a personal tragedy for the Scottish goalkeeper George Wood of Everton. In the second half he let a shot by Ray Wilkins (Chelsea) drop from his hands, and Steve Coppell of Manchester United swooped onto the ball and sent it into the net for a 2–1 England lead. From that moment England was in the driver's seat as the Scots lost much of their rhythm and cohesion. In the first half the Scots had hammered at the English defense but had just one goal by John Wark (Ipswich Town) to show for their efforts. During that first half an overenthusiastic Scot raced onto the field and held up play for some time, waving a tartan scarf. The Scots claimed that this upset their rhythm, and in the closing minutes of the half England's Peter Barnes (Manchester City) tied the score at 1–1. Kevin Keegan (SV Hamburg) rounded off England's victory in the second half by capping a fine interpassing movement with Trevor Brooking (West Ham) by cracking the ball just inside the post.

England had made a flying start toward its title defense by comfortably beating Northern Ireland 2–0 at Windsor Park, Belfast, on May 19 with goals by Dave Watson (Manchester City) and Coppell. The same day at Ninian Park, Cardiff, Wales dented the pride of Scotland with a hat trick by John Toshack, the Swansea player-manager, as the new-look Scots defense failed. Wales held England to a goalless draw at Wembley on May 23, just 24 hours after the Scots had defeated Northern Ireland 1–0 with a goal by Arthur Graham (Leeds) at Hampden Park, Glasgow. The night before the England-Scotland match Northern Ireland had tied Wales 1–1 in Belfast.

NORTH AMERICAN SOCCER LEAGUE. Canada's Vancouver Whitecaps ended the monopoly of the New York Cosmos in the NASL championship when they eliminated the Cosmos in the semifinals. The Whitecaps then went on to win the title in the New York Giants' stadium at East Rutherford, N.J., on September 8, by defeating the Tampa Bay Rowdies 2–1. Both Whitecap goals came from Trevor Whymark, formerly of Ipswich, England, and the game was very much influenced by English-born players, including Whitecap Alan Ball, who won a World Cup medal with England in 1966. Whymark's opening goal was answered

WIDE WORLD

Trevor Whymark (right) of Vancouver gets off a shot that went past the Tampa Bay goalkeeper in 1979 NASL soccer bowl competition in September.

for Tampa Bay by Jan Van Der Veen (ex-Antwerp, Belgium). Whymark then scored the winner with a deflected shot off defender Barry Kitchener, another Englishman. (TREVOR WILLIAMSON)

Rugby. RUGBY UNION. The major event of the 1978–79 season was the New Zealand All Blacks' 18-match tour of the British Isles in October, November, and December 1978. They won 17 of those matches, losing only to Munster (12–0), and they achieved the unprecedented feat of defeating all four home countries on one tour.

The All Blacks, managed by Russ Thomas, coached by Jack Gleeson, and captained by Graham Mourie, toured Britain in place of the South African Springboks, whose scheduled tour did not take place for political reasons. The New Zealanders beat Ireland 10–6, Wales 13–12, England 16–6, and Scotland 18–9. They were much too good for England, but in each of the other games the All Blacks clinched their victory only in the last few minutes.

The All Blacks were preceded by the Pumas of Argentina, who played six matches in England, one in Wales, one in Ireland, and one in Italy. Led by Hugo Porta, a gifted standoff half and goal kicker, the Pumas held an England XV (with two or three exceptions the full England team) to a score of 13–13 at Twickenham.

The home international championship was again won by Wales even though it had lost the services of Gareth Edwards, Gerald Davies, Phil Bennett, and Terry Cobner through retirement from international rugby. This was Wales's fourth championship in five seasons, and they also achieved an unprecedented fourth triple crown (defeating England, Scotland, and Northern Ireland) in four years. The only team that managed to match them was France, which defeated them 14–13 in Paris. The French, however, could only draw 9–9 with Ireland in Dublin, and they also went down to an unexpected defeat to England, 7–6, at Twickenham. Ireland had an encouraging season in that it beat England 12–7 in Dublin, tied with both France and Scotland, and put up a tough fight against Wales at Cardiff. But England and Scotland had disappointing seasons, Scotland finishing in last place with two draws and two losses.

Following the home internationals, England traveled to Japan and the South Pacific, Ireland to Australia, and France to New Zealand. England had a hard struggle before winning the first of two internationals against Japan by 21–19 in Osaka, but it won the second more easily 38–18 in Tokyo. The English team then went on to beat Fiji 19–7 and Tonga 37–17.

Ireland had a successful tour of Australia, winning its two internationals against the Wallabies 27–12 at Brisbane and 9–3 at Sydney. The French were crushed 23–9 in the first of their two internationals in New Zealand, but they played spectacular attacking rugby in winning the second 24–19. The New Zealanders then went to Sydney and were defeated 12–6 by the Wallabies, the Australians' first victory over New Zealand in Australia since 1934. New Zealand got back some self-respect by beating the Pumas 18–9 in Dunedin and 15–6 at Wellington, even with a deliberately weakened team.

RUGBY LEAGUE. Australia dominated the season, winning its test series in Britain 2–1 and then beating Great Britain 3–0 in a series in Australia. The Australians won the first test in Britain 15–9 at Wigan; the British managed to win the second 18–14 at Bradford, but the Australians led 19–0 at halftime in the decisive third test and won it 23–6 at Headingley. When the British team then went to Australia, they began the test series by losing the first match 35–0. They did better in the second, losing 24–16, but were again overwhelmed in the third, 28–2. This was the first time Great Britain had ever lost all three tests of a series in Australia. Great Britain went on to win its first two tests in New Zealand, 16–8 and 22–7, but New Zealand won the third 18–11. The Australians received a setback when they visited France at the end of their tour of the British Isles. The French won both tests, 13–10 at Carcassonne and 11–10 at Toulouse.

(DAVID FROST)

U.S. Football. PROFESSIONAL. For the second straight year the Pittsburgh Steelers won the championship of U.S. professional football, defeating the Los Angeles Rams 31–19 in the Super Bowl on Jan. 20, 1980, in Pasadena, Calif. The Steelers thus became the first team to win four Super Bowls. Named the most valuable player of the game was Pittsburgh quarterback Terry Bradshaw, who passed for two of his team's touchdowns. One of them, 73 yd to John Stallworth, was the longest touchdown pass in Super Bowl history. Given little chance to win, the Rams extended the Steelers fully and were in the lead 19–17 at the end of three quarters.

Probably the most surprising development of U.S. professional football in 1979 was that Tampa Bay was among the National Football League's play-off teams. No professional team's fortunes had reversed any more suddenly than those of the Buccaneers, a four-year-old expansion team that had lost its first 26 games. But in 1979 it won the Central Division championship in the National Football Conference. The victory did not come easily. The Buccaneers had three chances to clinch a play-off berth before finally winning their last game, 3–0.

The National Conference play-off teams besides Tampa Bay, which had a 10–6 record, were Western Division winner Los Angeles (9–7), Eastern Division winner Dallas (11–5), and "wild-card" teams Philadelphia (11–5) and Chicago (10–6), the two best runners-up. In the wild-card play-off contest Philadelphia rallied behind the passing of quarterback Ron Jaworski to overcome a Chicago lead and win 27–17. The next play-off round featured an upset as Los Angeles defeated Dallas 21–19 on three touchdown passes by Vince Ferragamo. Tampa Bay stopped Philadelphia 24–17 as Ricky Bell ran for 142 yd and two touchdowns. In the National Conference championship Los Angeles qualified for the Super Bowl for the first time with a 9–0 triumph over Tampa Bay.

In the American Football Conference, whose teams won 36 of their 52 games against National Conference opponents, Pittsburgh (12–4) won the Central Division, San Diego (12–4) the Western Division, and Miami (10–6) the Eastern Division; Houston (11–5) and Denver (10–6) were the wild-card teams. The play-offs began with a 13–7 win by Houston over Denver, in which the winners lost quarterback Dan Pastorini, star running back Earl Campbell, and wide receiver Ken Burrough through injuries. In the next round Houston, playing without all three, achieved one of the year's major upsets with a 17–14 triumph over San Diego. The Oilers were led by their defense, notably Vernon Perry, who had four interceptions and blocked a field-goal attempt. Meanwhile, Pittsburgh, led by quarterback Bradshaw, routed Miami 34–14. In the conference championship

WIDE WORLD

Houston Oiler Mike Renfro's apparent end-zone catch in the Oilers-Steelers AFC play-off game was ruled incomplete by side judge Donald Orr, who said Renfro did not have control of the ball in the end zone.

Table III. NFL Final Standings and Play-offs, 1979

	W	L	T
AMERICAN CONFERENCE			
Eastern Division			
*Miami	10	6	0
New England	9	7	0
Jets	8	8	0
Buffalo	7	9	0
Baltimore	5	11	0
Central Division			
*Pittsburgh	12	4	0
*Houston	11	5	0
Cleveland	9	7	0
Cincinnati	4	12	0
Western Division			
*San Diego	12	4	0
*Denver	10	6	0
Oakland	9	7	0
Seattle	9	7	0
Kansas City	7	9	0
NATIONAL CONFERENCE			
Eastern Division			
*Dallas	11	5	0
*Philadelphia	11	5	0
Washington	10	6	0
Giants	6	10	0
St. Louis	5	11	0
Central Division			
*Tampa Bay	10	6	0
*Chicago	10	6	0
Minnesota	7	9	0
Green Bay	5	11	0
Detroit	2	14	0
Western Division			
*Los Angeles	9	7	0
New Orleans	8	8	0
Atlanta	6	10	0
San Francisco	2	14	0

*Qualified for play-offs.

Play-offs

Wild-card round
Houston 13, Denver 7
Philadelphia 27, Chicago 17

American semifinals
Houston 17, San Diego 14
Pittsburgh 34, Miami 14

National semifinals
Los Angeles 21, Dallas 19
Tampa Bay 24, Philadelphia 17

American finals
Pittsburgh 27, Houston 13

National finals
Los Angeles 9, Tampa Bay 0

Super Bowl
Pittsburgh 31, Los Angeles 19

Pittsburgh stopped Houston 27–13 to qualify for a defense of its NFL title.

Washington of the NFC complained about being left out of the play-offs because of the procedure the league used to break its tie with Chicago. Because both teams had 10–6 records and 8–4 records within their conference, the play-off berth hinged on point differential, points scored minus points allowed. Chicago trailed by 33 going into its last game but squeaked into the Super Bowl tournament by winning that game 42–6.

The performance was uncharacteristic of the Bears, who built their offense around conference rushing leader Walter Payton (1,610 yd) and ranked third from the bottom in passing, but it was typical of the NFL season. Offense, especially passing, increased dramatically, a result of 1978 rules that permitted offensive linemen to use their hands more in protecting the quarterback and limited the contact allowed by pass defenders. Total offense increased by 10.6% over 1977, scoring by 16.9%, and passing yards by 22.8%.

NFL players threw 536 touchdown passes in 1979, compared with 469 in 1978 and 385 in 1977, and they had 44 individual 300-yd passing games, compared with 5 in 1977. Twelve gained at least 1,000 yd on receptions, three times as many as in 1978, and the same number of players ran for 1,000 yd in 1979.

Pittsburgh averaged 391.1 yd per game, the most ever by an NFL team, largely because Bradshaw averaged a league-leading 7.89 yd per pass attempt. The Steelers also led the AFC in defense, yielding only 266.9 yd a game.

San Diego was the most spectacular passing team, leading the league with 244.7 passing yards per game and making the play-offs for the first time in 14 years. Charger quarterback Dan Fouts set NFL records with 4,082 yd passing and four straight 300-yd games. He had two 1,000-yd receivers, Charlie Joiner and John Jefferson.

Dallas became the first NFL team ever with three 1,000-yd gainers, Tony Dorsett on the ground and Tony Hill and Drew Pearson through the air. Quarterback Roger Staubach, who threw 27 touchdown passes and only 11 interceptions, was the NFL's highest rated passer. The Cowboys led the NFC with 373 yd and 23.2 points per game.

Los Angeles won a league-record seventh consecutive division title after a challenge from New Orleans, which had its first .500 season ever. For Houston Earl Campbell won his second NFL rushing crown in two seasons with 1,697 yd and tied a league record with 19 rushing touchdowns. He was later voted the league's most valuable player.

St. Louis Cardinal management was disappointed enough to make the only mid-season coaching change, firing former college legend Bud Wilkinson. But the Cardinals had the consolation of running back Ottis Anderson (*see* BIOGRAPHIES), who became the first rookie to average 100 rushing yards per game with 1,605.

Ending their splendid careers voluntarily were halfback O. J. Simpson of San Francisco and defensive end Jim Marshall of Minnesota. Both were part-time players in 1979, but Simpson remained the NFL's second most prolific rusher with 11,236 yd and Marshall had played 20 seasons and a record 282 consecutive regular season games.

WIDE WORLD

USC running back Charles White waves the football triumphantly after scoring a touchdown in the fourth quarter to tie Ohio State in the Rose Bowl on Jan. 1, 1980. The extra point gave USC a 17–16 victory. White was earlier named winner of the Heisman Trophy.

The New York Jets' 165.4 rushing yards per game led the league, as did Denver's defensive yield of 105.8 rushing yards a game and Tampa Bay's defensive averages of 246.9 total yards and 129.8 passing yards.

COLLEGE. Alabama, Ohio State, Southern California, and Florida State went into the New Year's Day bowl games undefeated, but only two survived. Alabama, which defeated Arkansas 24–9 in the Sugar Bowl, was voted the 1979 national champion over Southern California, the Rose Bowl winner by 17–16 against previously unbeaten Big Ten champion Ohio State. Although Alabama's schedule was less demanding, Southern California's record was blemished by a 21–21 tie with Stanford. Florida State, the other team that lost its first game on the first day of 1980, was Oklahoma's victim 24–7 in the Orange Bowl.

Ohio State's 11–0 regular-season record was familiar, but the Buckeyes reached it in an unfamiliar way. They made extensive use of the forward pass, which Woody Hayes considered a four-letter word during his 28 years as coach. Quarterback Art Schlichter became the school's all-time leading passer after only two seasons. Hayes had been fired after punching an opponent at the end of Ohio State's 1978 Gator Bowl defeat. He was replaced by Earle Bruce, whose offense ranked fourth in scoring and threw only five interceptions, the country's second fewest.

Brigham Young quarterback Marc Wilson led college passers with 250 completions, 3,720 yd, 29 touchdowns, and 325.5 yd of total offense per game, helping his school rank first nationally with 40.6 points per game, 521.4 yd of total offense per game, and 368.3 passing yards per game. Quarterback Ed Luther of Pacific Coast Conference champion San Jose State (6–4–1) had the year's most successful passing game with 467 yd, helping his team rank second in passing.

Big Eight champion Oklahoma (10–1) ranked second in scoring and second in rushing offense to

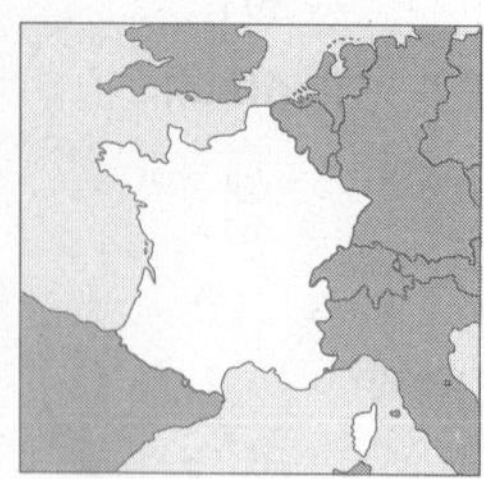

France

East Carolina (7–3–1), which also ranked second in total offense and third in scoring. Billy Sims, the 1978 Heisman Trophy winner as college player of the year, led the country with 22 touchdowns and had the year's best rushing game with 282 yd. But Sims lost the Heisman Trophy and the national rushing title to Charles White of Pacific Ten champion Southern California (10–0–1), who averaged 180.3 yd a game.

Alabama, the 11–0 Southeast Conference champion, led the country by allowing only 5.3 points per game and also ranked second in total yards allowed, second in passing yards allowed, and fourth in rushing offense. Western Carolina (6–5) was the pass defense leader with an average of 77.5 yd allowed. Pittsburgh (10–1) ranked fifth in scoring defense and limited one opponent to a season-low −17 yd rushing.

Yale led the country in total defense, giving up 175.4 yd per game, and in rushing defense, with an average yield of 75 yd. But even Yale's Ivy League championship was hollow because its only loss was against traditional rival Harvard.

Arkansas and Houston, both 10–1, tied for the Southwest Conference title, and Houston went on to win the Cotton Bowl 17–14 over Nebraska. Other conference winners were North Carolina State (7–4) in the Atlantic Coast, Boise State (10–1) in the Big Sky, Murray State (9–1–1) in the Ohio Valley, Tennessee-Chattanooga (9–2) in the Southern, Boston University (8–1–1) and Massachusetts (6–4) in the Yankee, and Grambling (8–2) in the Southwestern. Navy defeated Army for the sixth time in seven years, tying the service academies' 80-game series.

Individual national leaders included Turk Schonert of Stanford, with 67.58% pass completions and also the highest passing efficiency; Rick Beasley of Appalachian State, with 6.7 catches per game; and Clay Brown of Brigham Young, with a 45.3 yd punting average. Jim Ritcher, a North Carolina State centre, won the Outland Trophy, given to the country's best lineman.

Canadian Football. The Edmonton Eskimos won their second consecutive Grey Cup by beating the Montreal Alouettes 17–9 in the Canadian Football League's championship game, even though Montreal won all the game's individual awards. Montreal running back David Green, who led CFL rushers with 1,678 yd and 11 touchdowns, was the most valuable player of the game, and kicker Don Sweet was named Canadian player of the game for kicking three field goals. Linebacker Tom Cousineau of Montreal was named the championship game's best defensive player, giving his eventful season a fruitful finish. Cousineau played in Canada even though the National Football League had made him the first player chosen in the NFL's draft of college seniors. He replaced Montreal's previously most popular player, Carl Crennel, who was traded.

Edmonton, which won the Western Conference with a 12–2–2 record and outscored its opponents 495–219, also had its share of stars during the season. Waddell Smith led pass receivers with 74 catches, 1,214 yd, and 13 touchdowns, and Brian Kelly was second with 61 catches, 1,098 yd, and 11 touchdowns. Warren Moon's 20 touchdown passes as a reserve quarterback also led the league, and Larry Highbaugh tied Mike Nelms of Ottawa with a league-high 10 interceptions.

(KEVIN M. LAMB)

Foreign Aid:
see Economy, World

Foreign Exchange:
see Economy, World

France

A republic of Western Europe, France is bounded by the English Channel, Belgium, Luxembourg, West Germany, Switzerland, Italy, the Mediterranean Sea, Monaco, Spain, Andorra, and the Atlantic Ocean. Area: 544,000 sq km (210,040 sq mi), including Corsica. Pop. (1979 est.): 53,383,000. Cap. and largest city: Paris (pop., 1978 est., 2,155,-200). Language: French. Religion: predominantly Roman Catholic. President in 1979, Valéry Giscard d'Estaing; premier, Raymond Barre.

Domestic Affairs. Throughout 1979, Premier Raymond Barre's government, under pressure from Pres. Valéry Giscard d'Estaing, endeavoured to adapt to the "new state of the world," in the face of soaring oil prices, inflation, strikes, and unemployment, while pursuing its aim of a society marked by less glaring inequalities. The cantonal elections confirmed the electorate's swing toward the left, and the year also saw the election (for the first time by direct universal suffrage) of French representatives to the European Assembly in Strasbourg.

From the start of the year, rising unemployment, strikes, and inflation created a difficult social and economic situation. Support for a day of national strike action in protest against government plans to cut 21,000 jobs in the steel industry varied according to region. In the north and in Lorraine the strikes spread to other economic sectors; roads and railways were blocked and factories shut down. The situation cooled after incidents in Denain that resulted in some 40 injured among strikers and police on March 7–8. A march through Paris organized by the Confédération Général du Travail (CGT) in support of the steelworkers' demands brought out tens of thousands of demonstrators, but the atmosphere was calm. The only incident occurred at the end of the day, when radicals politically unconnected with the march broke windows on the Place de l'Opéra and the main boulevards and clashed with the police. For several weeks a strike at the Société Française de Productions, the state television production centre, practically shut down all television channels. There were also stoppages on the railways, phased strikes in the post office, and power cuts. After lengthy negotiations, the unions and the employers' organization reached an agreement on a reform of unemployment compensation that was described by both sides as "an immense effort of solidarity" and "a social revolution."

After a month-long strike by clerical employees, work resumed at the Paris stock exchange at the end of March, but the profession had experienced one of its most bitter conflicts. The government put forward measures that would help provide 400,000 jobs for young people over the next three years. This Third National Pact on Unemployment

A.F.P./PICTORIAL PARADE

Nearly 80,000 people, calling for an end to joblessness, marched peacefully through Paris during a demonstration in March. Radicals later used the march as an excuse to stage a riot in which hundreds were injured.

would cost Fr 10 billion and included a 50% exemption from social insurance contributions for employers who hired young people, the extension of apprenticeships, and the renewal of practical, long-term vocational courses.

The cantonal elections to fill half the seats in the *conseils généraux* resulted in a clear victory for the left-wing opposition, which considerably improved its position. François Mitterrand's Socialist Party, after making gains in the first round on March 18, emerged from the second round on March 25 as the main victor. Out of 1,847 vacant seats (half the seats in each département being up for election every three years), the Socialists gained 158 for a total of 558, compared with their previous 400. The Communist Party also improved its position, taking 32 additional seats for a total of 228 (196 previously). On the other hand, the Union pour la Démocratie Française (UDF), the pro-Giscard party, which made the best showing among the parliamentary majority parties, lost 64 seats, falling from 494 to 430. The various moderates lost 51 seats (down to 276 from 327) and Jacques Chirac's Rassemblement pour la République (RPR) lost 43 (198 against 241).

After the 1977 municipal elections in which it had captured two-thirds of the town halls in cities of over 30,000 inhabitants, the left now controlled nearly half of the *conseils généraux* (45 as against 49 for the majority parties, representing a loss of 8 for the latter). In 1978 the left, unable to agree on a common program, had gone down to defeat in the parliamentary elections. The cantonal election results seemed to show that the left was seen as better fitted to govern at the city and departmental level than at the national, and that the electorate, while apprehensive of giving the Communist Party governmental responsibility nationally, with all the risks it would entail, had no such reservations when it came to awarding it local power.

The political lessons of the cantonal elections could not be ignored, especially since there was a high turnout of voters (about 63%). Even in the first round, the Socialists, Communists, and Mouvement des Radicaux de Gauche (MRG) achieved a combined total of 51% of the poll, while the UDF, RPR, and "moderates supporting the majority" managed only 43%. The result was, in fact, a massive opinion poll of nearly 17 million voters in all parts of the country except Paris.

The Socialist Party, internally divided, had no illusions about its chances of reaching another joint program with the Communist Party. The Socialist Party congress, meeting in April at Metz, achieved no basis for compromise between the draft resolutions sponsored by Mitterrand (46.97%), Michel Rocard (21.25%), Pierre Mauroy (16.8%), and the Centre d'Études, de Recherches et d'Éducation Socialistes (CERES; 14.98%). At the end of October there was agreement on a "Socialist plan," but this did not mean that the splits among the candidates had been healed, though Mitterrand remained the favourite for the 1981 Socialist presidential candidacy.

The Communist Party held its 23rd congress at Saint-Ouen, a working-class Paris suburb, in May. Through its leader, Georges Marchais, its members were invited to "give preference to the unity of the base," while Mitterrand and the Socialist Party organization were violently criticized. At the party's National Council in October, Marchais warned the working class against "supporters of class collaboration." At the 79th congress of the Radical Party, the deputy from Paris, Didier Bariani, replaced Jean-Jacques Servan-Schreiber as president; the party was to "resume its total freedom of expression toward the government."

WIDE WORLD

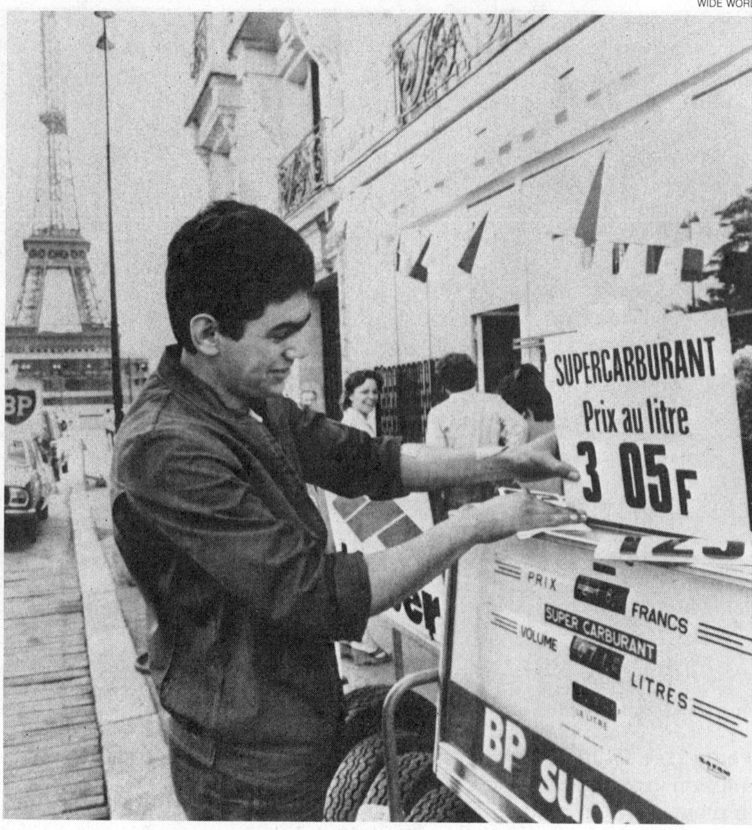

Paris gas stations raised their prices in August to approximately $2.82 per gallon, making French gasoline the most expensive in the EEC.

Elections to the European Assembly took place in France on June 10. The 60% turnout contrasted with, for example, the very high level of abstention in the U.K. France's 81 seats in the Assembly would be held by 26 UDF members from the list of Simone Veil (*see* BIOGRAPHIES), 22 Socialists and MRG members from the Mitterrand list, 19 Communists from the Marchais list, and 15 RPR members from the Chirac list. Thus the four major political groupings won 17,746,580 of the 20,176,135 votes cast (87.95%). None of the minor parties succeeded in attaining the magic 5%, below which they could not be represented. On July 17 Veil was elected president of the new Assembly.

A few weeks earlier, a technical reshuffle of the government had been brought about by Veil's resignation as minister of health. At least four members of the government would have responsibility for health and social security, which were experiencing increasingly large deficits. The new minister of health was Centrist Party member Jacques Barrot. He was to be assisted by two secretaries of state, Jean Farge, inspector general of finance, in charge of social security as such, and Daniel Hoeffel, responsible for health. Finally, Monique Pelletier, minister-delegate for women, would be concerned with family problems under the direct authority of the premier. Maurice Charretier replaced Barrot in the Ministry of Trade and Crafts.

At the beginning of July, there were price increases, first for milk, rents, and public transport, and then for gasoline and domestic fuels. Electricity prices also rose, and gas prices were expected to follow. By the end of the month the number of those seeking work rose above 1.4 million for the first time. The resolution of two major industrial disputes had a calming effect, however. The union federations signed a steel industry compact designed to lessen the effects of the planned restructuring, and a dispute in the ports that had lasted for seven months moved toward settlement.

With inflation continuing to run at more than 10%, Barre proposed a package of economic and social measures to support the economy. Involving some Fr 4.5 billion, they were designed to benefit those most affected by the price rises and to aid the construction and public works industries. But the 1980 budget introduced in the autumn session of Parliament showed a heavy deficit of Fr 35 billion —expected to increase to Fr 50 billion—while growth in 1980 would rise by at least 2.5%. After vigorous debate and three unsuccessful motions of censure, the budget was passed by the National Assembly on November 20. On December 24, however, the Constitutional Council declared the budget void because of unconstitutional irregularities in its presentation. Parliament approved an emergency measure that permitted the government to continue collecting revenue pending resubmission of the budget in January.

On September 13 Barre offered the unions "an agreement on national solidarity to favour employment and the low-paid and on preferences of every type." This proposal, set out in a letter, resulted in a series of discussions in October between unions, the government, and employers that stressed four themes: low wages, working hours, workers' say in industry, and the role of management. However, the CGT refused to take part and called for strikes in the public sector that hit electricity, gas, transport, and postal services. They were condemned by the government as a series of blows against the economy. An unusual one-day strike by French doctors added to the confusion.

The circumstances surrounding the suicide on October 30 of Robert Boulin (*see* OBITUARIES), minister of labour and participation, aroused strong feelings throughout the country. In a suicide note, Boulin accused the minister of justice, Alain Peyrefitte, of deliberately failing to check malicious disclosures from a magistrate's files concerning a questionable purchase of land by Boulin in 1973. Boulin was succeeded by Jean Matteoli, previously chief of the French National Coal Board.

Popular opposition to nuclear power continued, and Mitterrand called for a halt in its development pending safety studies. Nevertheless, by October the French Electricity Generating Board had decided to prepare two new nuclear power stations for operation.

There was a rash of bomb explosions in Paris and other cities. In May a number of bombs were exploded in Paris by extremists and separatists, including 22 set off at various points in the capital by the Corsican Liberation Front. The Corsicans also claimed credit for the bomb explosions at the Army's biggest gasoline depot in the Paris region on October 25. The fugitive Jacques Mesrine, France's most-wanted criminal, was tracked down by police and shot dead in Paris on November 2.

Foreign Affairs. Thanks to the unremitting activity of President Giscard, France played an important role in international affairs during 1979. The year began with a Western summit conference in Guadeloupe, at which U.S. Pres. Jimmy Carter, Giscard, Prime Minister James Callaghan of Britain, and Chancellor Helmut Schmidt of West Germany examined changes in the world balance of power. The French president subsequently visited countries as varied as Cameroon, where he launched an appeal to Africa, and Romania, where he met with Pres. Nicolae Ceaucescu. In Mexico he had talks with Pres. José López Portillo on the "new world economic order," and in the U.S.S.R. he signed several documents with Pres. Leonid Brezhnev, including a "Program for the Development of Cooperation Between France and the Soviet Union in the Interests of Détente and Peace."

In May Giscard went to Kigali, the capital of Rwanda, for a two-day official visit and to participate in the sixth Franco-African summit conference, where he suggested the establishment of a "trilogue" between Europe, Africa, and the Arab world. On his way home, in Khartoum, Sudan, he gained the approval of Pres. Gaafar Nimeiry for this project. In July, after a stopover in Abu Dhabi for talks with Sheikh Zaid ibn Sultan An-Nahayan, president of the United Arab Emirates, he paid an official visit to the French territories in the Pacific, stopping at Nouméa in New Caledonia and Papeete in Polynesia. In the autumn, France played host to Edward Gierek, first secretary of the Polish United Workers' Party, Portuguese Pres. António Ramalho Eanes, and Premier Hua Guofeng (Hua Kuo-feng) of China. Queen Elizabeth II paid a private visit to France at the invitation of the president.

In September Emperor Bokassa I was deposed and replaced as leader of the Central African Republic by the country's former president, David Dacko (*see* BIOGRAPHIES). France's decision to send a unit of paratroopers to Bangui to effect the coup was strongly condemned by the opposition as "interference in the affairs of a foreign country." Giscard rejected the accusation and called the idea that France was seeking economic advantage in Africa "insulting and stupid."

Giscard saw the establishment of the European Monetary System as a fundamental necessity for Europe. The system came into existence on March 13, with all the European Economic Community (EEC) countries taking part except the U.K., which signed the agreement but would continue to allow its currency to float. Six months later the finance ministers of the Nine met in Brussels and concluded that the system was working satisfactorily. In May, at Hoerdt, near Strasbourg, Giscard outlined the future of France in Europe, stating that never had consensus on Europe been so strong in France.

FRANCE

Education. (1978–79) Primary, pupils 5,014,682, teachers 214,795; secondary, pupils 5,137,794, teachers 300,839; vocational, pupils 27,947, teachers 2,877; teacher training, students 27,947, teachers 2,877; higher, students 1,041,916.

Finance. Monetary unit: franc, with (Sept. 17, 1979) a free rate of Fr 4.23 to U.S. $1 (Fr 9.10 = £1 sterling). Gold, SDR's, and foreign exchange (June 1979) U.S. $18,474,000,000. Budget (1979 actual): revenue Fr 441.3 billion; expenditure Fr 458.5 billion. Gross national product (1978) Fr 2,135,100,000,000. Money supply (Dec. 1978) Fr 566,440,000,000. Cost of living (1975 = 100; June 1979) 143.5.

Foreign Trade. (1978) Imports Fr 368,590,000,000; exports Fr 357.6 billion. Import sources: EEC 51% (West Germany 19%, Italy 10%, Belgium-Luxembourg 9%, The Netherlands 6%, U.K. 6%); U.S. 7%; Saudi Arabia 5%. Export destinations: EEC 53% (West Germany 17%, Italy 11%, Belgium-Luxembourg 10%, U.K. 7%, The Netherlands 5%); U.S. 6%. Main exports: machinery 21%; motor vehicles 13%; food 12%; chemicals 12%; iron and steel 7%. Tourism (1977): visitors 26,265,000; gross receipts U.S. $4,377,000,000.

Transport and Communications. Roads (1977) 799,380 km (including 4,283 km expressways; excluding *c.* 690,000 km rural roads). Motor vehicles in use (1977): passenger 16,990,000; commercial 2,175,000. Railways: (1977) 34,150 km; traffic (1978) 53,460,000,000 passenger-km, freight 67,328,000,000 net ton-km. Air traffic (1978): 30,215,000,000 passenger-km; freight 1,809,600,000 net ton-km. Navigable inland waterways in regular use (1977) 6,969 km; freight traffic 11,266,000,000 ton-km. Shipping (1978): merchant vessels 100 gross tons and over 1,317; gross tonnage 12,197,354. Telephones (Jan. 1978) 17,519,000. Radio licenses (Dec. 1976) 17,442,000. Television licenses (Dec. 1976) 14.5 million.

Agriculture. Production (in 000; metric tons; 1978): wheat 21,057; barley 11,414; oats 2,194; rye 432; corn 9,473; potatoes 7,459; sorghum 381; sugar, raw value 4,065; rapeseed *c.* 628; tomatoes 709; cauliflowers (1977) *c.* 440; carrots (1977) *c.* 400; green peas (1977) *c.* 596; apples 3,022; peaches (1977) *c.* 319; wine 5,882; tobacco 54; milk 29,930; butter 545; cheese 1,010; beef and veal *c.* 1,677; pork *c.* 1,670; fish catch (1977) 760; timber (cu m; 1977) *c.* 29,127. Livestock (in 000; Dec. 1977): cattle 24,133; sheep 11,543; pigs 11,797; horses (1977) 375; chickens *c.* 163,870.

Industry. Index of production (1975 = 100; 1978) 112. Fuel and power (in 000; 1978): coal (metric tons) 19,640; electricity (kw-hr) 222,551,000; natural gas (cu m) 7,900,000; manufactured gas (cu m; 1977) 6,040,000. Production (in 000; metric tons; 1978): iron ore (30% metal content) 33,456; pig iron 19,189; crude steel 22,839; bauxite 1,988; aluminum 552; lead 144; zinc 245; cement 28,015; cotton yarn 220; cotton fabrics 168; wool yarn 137; man-made fibres 334; sulfuric acid 4,580; petroleum products (1977) 111,923; fertilizers (nutrient content; 1977–78) nitrogenous *c.* 1,470, phosphate *c.* 1,560, potash 1,669; passenger cars (units) 3,621; commercial vehicles (units) 452. Merchant shipping launched (100 gross tons and over; 1978) 644,000 gross tons.

In June Margaret Thatcher, Britain's new Conservative prime minister, visited Paris and assured Giscard of her attachment to France and to the idea of European unity. Immediately afterward, at the European Council meeting, the heads of government of the Nine agreed on the stand which, at France's suggestion, Europe would adopt at the Tokyo "summit" of the seven major Western industrial countries later in the month.

The energy crisis and European affairs were once again at the heart of the discussions between Giscard and Chancellor Schmidt at the semiannual Franco-West German summit in October. Paris and Bonn decided to build a joint satellite television system, but they found progress was slow toward an agreement to allow the U.K. some leeway in its payments toward financing of the Common Market. France in October refused to end its ban on imports of British lamb, though this contravened EEC rules. Disagreement on the issue was not resolved by Giscard's visit to London in November. At the end of October, Giscard made an official visit to West Berlin, the first by a French head of state to the former German capital since the time of Napoleon I. (JEAN KNECHT)

See also Dependent States.

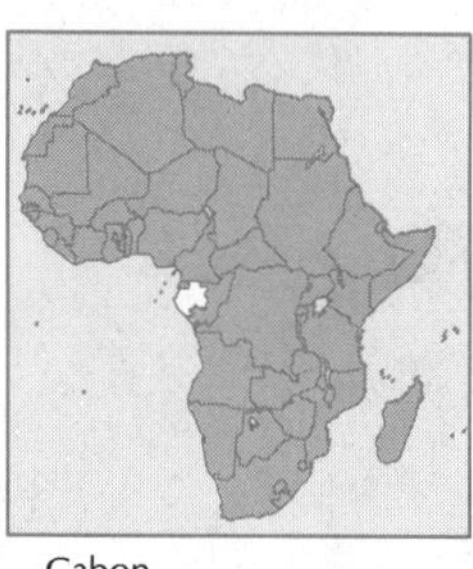
Gabon

Gabon

A republic of western equatorial Africa, Gabon is bounded by Equatorial Guinea, Cameroon, the Congo, and the Atlantic Ocean. Area: 267,667 sq km (103,347 sq mi). Pop. (1978 est.): 1,300,200. Cap. and largest city: Libreville (pop., 1978 est., 225,200). Language: French and Bantu dialects. Religion: traditional tribal beliefs; Christian minority. President in 1979, Omar Bongo; premier, Léon Mébiame.

In 1979 Gabon's relations with France were both happier and closer than ever. Pres. Omar Bongo and France's Pres. Valéry Giscard d'Estaing met several times during the year.

President Bongo had intervened without success to try to secure the abdication of Emperor Bokassa I of the Central African Empire, but the latter refused to surrender power voluntarily. In the conflict in Chad, Bongo acted as a mediator, and in February Libreville became a staging post for the evacuation by air of French civilians domiciled in Chad's capital, N'Djamena.

At the end of December 1978 the 187-km (116-mi) first section of the trans-Gabon railway, which was to cross the country for a distance of 654 km (406 mi), was inaugurated. The event was attended by France's economy minister, whom the president thanked for his government's financial contribution.

The fall of Pres. Francisco Macías Nguema of Equatorial Guinea in August was followed with close attention in Libreville inasmuch as there were several thousand refugees from Equatorial Guinea living in Gabon. Their presence had created considerable tension.

Bongo was reelected to a second term without opposition December 30. (PHILIPPE DECRAENE)

GABON

Education. (1977–78) Primary, pupils 140,632, teachers 2,866; secondary, pupils 21,614, teachers 1,011; vocational, pupils 3,405, teachers 246; teacher training, students 1,323, teachers 84; higher, students 1,284.

Finance. Monetary unit: CFA franc, with (Sept. 17, 1979) a parity of CFA Fr 50 to the French franc (free rate of CFA Fr 211.54 = U.S. $1; CFA Fr 455.12 = £1 sterling). Budget (1978 est.) balanced at CFA Fr 242,451,000,000.

Foreign Trade. (1977) Imports *c.* CFA Fr 163 billion; exports CFA Fr 269 billion. Import sources (1976): France 69%; U.S. 6%. Export destinations (1976): France 42%; U.S. 17%; U.K. 10%; The Bahamas 10%. Main export: crude oil 79%.

Transport and Communications. Roads (1977) 6,897 km. Motor vehicles in use (1974): passenger *c.* 10,100; commercial (including buses) *c.* 7,300. Railways (1979) *c.* 150 km (part of 935 km planned). Air traffic (1977): 129 million passenger-km; freight 8.6 million net ton-km. Telephones (Dec. 1973) 11,000. Radio receivers (Dec. 1976) 93,000. Television receivers (Dec. 1976) 8,500.

Agriculture. Production (in 000; metric tons; 1977): cassava *c.* 182; corn *c.* 2; peanuts *c.* 2; bananas *c.* 10; plantains *c.* 80; palm oil *c.* 3; coffee *c.* 1; cocoa *c.* 3; timber (cu m) *c.* 2,487. Livestock (in 000; 1977): cattle *c.* 5; pigs *c.* 5; sheep *c.* 60; goats *c.* 66.

Industry. Production (in 000; metric tons; 1977): uranium 0.6; crude oil (1978) 11,386; natural gas (cu m) 684,300; manganese ore (metal content) 1,000; petroleum products *c.* 1,470; electricity (kw-hr) 443,000.

The Gambia

Gambia, The

A small republic and member of the Commonwealth of Nations, The Gambia extends from the Atlantic Ocean along the lower Gambia River in West Africa and is surrounded by Senegal. Area: 10,403 sq km (4,016 sq mi). Pop. (1979 est.): 584,-500, including (1973) Malinke 37.7%; Fulani 16.2%; Wolof 14%; Dyola 8.5%; Soninke 7.8%; others 15.8%. Cap. and largest city: Banjul (pop., 1977 est., 51,700). Language: English (official). Religion: predominantly Muslim. President in 1979, Sir Dawda Jawara.

During the May 1979 congress of the ruling People's Progressive Party, Pres. Dawda Jawara was reelected secretary-general of the party, and general aims for economic policy were established (including condemnation of corruption). Pressure for the establishment of a one-party state was resisted by the government, which called for greater decentralization and participation in administration. Following the virtual demise of the old opposition United Party, there were moves to set up a new "provincial" party under Sheriff Dibba (once vice-president of The Gambia and close to Jawara but later expelled from his party as a "tribalist").

GAMBIA, THE

Education. (1977–78) Primary, pupils 27,560, teachers 1,094; secondary and vocational, pupils 6,994, teachers 387; teacher training, students 193, teachers 15.

Finance. Monetary unit: dalasi, with (Sept. 17, 1979) a free rate of 1.86 dalasis to U.S. $1 (par value of 4 dalasis = £1 sterling). Budget (1978-79 est.): revenue 66,132,000 dalasis; expenditure 69,424,000 dalasis.

Foreign Trade. (1978) Imports 209,780,000 dalasis; exports 82,890,000 dalasis. Import sources: U.K. *c.* 33%; China *c.* 10%; France *c.* 7%; West Germany *c.* 7%. Export destinations: France *c.* 27%; U.K. 25%; Switzerland *c.* 18%; Ghana *c.* 7%; Italy *c.* 6%. Main exports: peanuts and by-products 76%.

French-Canadian Literature:
see Literature

French Guiana:
see Dependent States

French Literature:
see Literature

Friends, Religious Society of:
see Religion

Fuel and Power:
see Energy

Furniture Industry:
see Industrial Review

Furs:
see Industrial Review

As a result of a visit by President Jawara to Conakry, Guinea, in March, Guinea agreed to join The Gambia and Senegal in the Gambia River Development Organization. Jawara also visited Dakar, Senegal, to meet officials from Senegal and Guinea-Bissau to discuss both legitimate trade and smuggling.

Foreign aid included an undertaking by China to build a 27 million dalasi sports stadium in Banjul. The Gambia's main trade and aid partner, Britain, offered a new £10 million grant to help finance development during 1980–83, to replace the exhausted £6 million grant of 1976.

(MOLLY MORTIMER)

Gambling

A state commission studying the possibility of legalized casino gambling in New York recommended in August 1979 that casinos be permitted to operate and that they should be confined to four areas: New York City, Long Beach on Long Island, the Catskill Mountains resort area, and the Buffalo-Niagara Falls region. The total number of casinos should not exceed 40. The commission also proposed that state and local governments take from the casinos 20% of the projected $3 billion in annual gross revenues.

In New Jersey, where the first legal casino outside Nevada opened in Atlantic City in 1978, the state Senate passed a bill in August that would increase temporarily the tax on gambling-casino profits. Proceeds would go to a "lifeline" program that would help some of the state's elderly citizens pay their fuel bills for the winter of 1979–80. The tax would be raised from 8 to 11% and would decrease one percentage point for each new casino that began operation; after five were licensed, the tax would return to 8%, where it would remain. Opponents of the bill claimed that it would prevent new casinos from opening in the state. A month earlier Resorts International Inc. had announced that it was planning to build its second casino in Atlantic City along with a 1,000-room hotel. As of the end of 1979 there were two casinos operating in New Jersey, both in Atlantic City.

A record amount of money was wagered at the horse-race meeting at Saratoga Springs, N.Y., during the summer. The 24-day meet attracted a crowd of 504,603 persons who bet $59,350,382, a 12% increase over 1978.

As of the end of 1979 bingo had become legal in all states of the U.S. except 12. It was estimated that bettors gambled approximately $4.5 billion on the game in 1979, as much as was spent on motion pictures and phonograph records.

Illegal wagering in the U.S. was estimated at more than $67 billion annually in the late 1970s. Much of this was bet on athletic contests, with games in the National Football League believed to have accounted for some $20 billion of the total. State lotteries had been expected to reduce the amount of illegal betting, especially that wagered on policy wheels and numbers games, but they did not seem to be having that effect. In fact, some state games suffered from declining revenues during 1979. Critics maintained that illegal gambling with its tax-free gains would continue to flourish as long as the winnings from legal bets were taxed.

Gambling continued during 1979 to be one of the major leisure activities in the United Kingdom. During 1978 nearly £10,000 million was bet, principally on horse and dog racing, football pools, bingo, slot machines, lotteries, and in casinos. The most popular form of gambling in terms of the number of participants was football (soccer) pool betting; approximately 15 million people staked

UPI

A $3 million surveillance system permits Resorts International Inc. to monitor every patron and every dealer on the floor in its Atlantic City, New Jersey, casino.

some £290 million. Casino gambling, largely attracting the wealthy, continued at about the same level of popularity and accounted for more than half the total amount of money bet during the year.

Lotteries continued to be one of the major forms of gambling in Great Britain in 1979. The instant lottery game became firmly established and helped to account for the increase in the popularity of this kind of betting. By the end of the year some 260 local authorities and 950 societies had lottery schemes registered with the Gaming Board of Great Britain. (DAVID R. CALHOUN; GBGB)

See also Equestrian Sports.
[452.C.2]

Games and Toys

Microelectronic chips invaded the games and toys market in 1979 to an even greater extent than in earlier years and seemed likely to bring about important changes in its structure. In the first place, electronic games were being bought by and for a much wider age group than was the case with traditional toys; second, the price range was extending far above the $10 or so previously considered a safe upper limit for toys and games, reaching up to more than $300; and third, sales, previously heavily concentrated in the pre-Christmas period, were now being spread more evenly throughout the year. According to a market research survey, the U.S. market for microchip-based games and toys would top $802 million in 1979, about 55% above 1978, and would reach $1.4 billion by 1984. This compared with total toy sales in the U.S. in 1979 of about $5.5 billion.

Among the great variety of flashing, buzzing, and bleeping electronic gadgetry that crammed the store counters, some of the year's best-sellers seemed as likely to end up in the executive suite as in the toy cupboard. Among them were a talking Chess Challenger; hand-held bridge and backgammon players; electronic dice; Microvision (a miniature liquid-crystal screen console, programmable with several games); as well as the previous year's Simon, a memory game using coloured lights and sounds; and the versatile, multigame Merlin. Electronic toys more specifically geared to the younger end of the market included Big Trak, a fairly unwarlike six-wheeled tank; Superstar 3000, an all-electronic stringless guitar with the doubtfully advantageous ability to remember tunes played on it and to play them back; and a number of "teaching games," such as Speak & Spell, Race Teacher, and Little Professor.

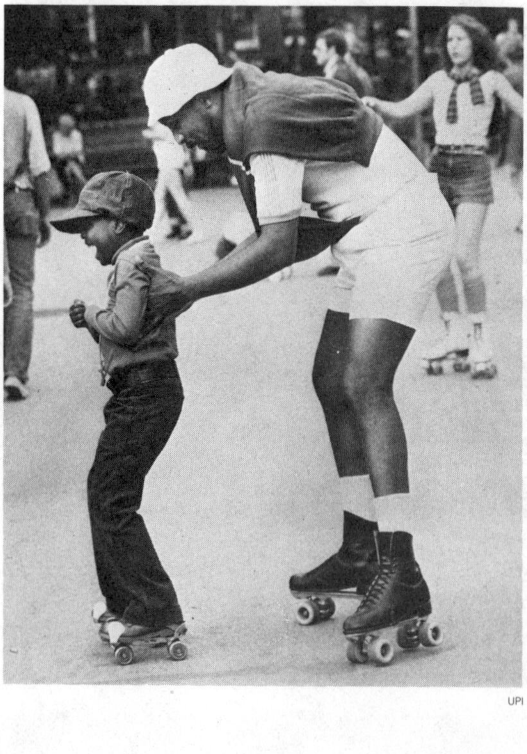

In New York a father introduces his son to the roller skating craze with obviously happy results.

UPI

In Britain, where the 1979 toy market was estimated at $600 million, electronic toys were expected to account for only about $40 million, indicating a certain resistance to the newcomers in favour of more traditional toys. Mail-order houses and large stores reported bicycles, wheeled toys, and billiards and pool tables as best-sellers in the pre-Christmas period.

Other established favourites that continued to be popular were the three-inch-high Playpeople, originally from West Germany and now selling in 50 countries; model railways; and a variety of model car racing circuits. The British National Association of Toy Retailers' "Toy of the Year" title went to the Legoland Space range of constructional kits on the space travel theme.

Roller skating enjoyed great popularity in the U.S. during the year, with skate sales averaging about 300,000 pairs per month. The new skates came in a variety of styles and featured polyurethane wheels, which were much quieter than their metal predecessors. A combination of two booms was "roller disco," and new rinks with elaborate light and sound systems were being built to accommodate the increasing numbers of dancing skaters.

When a Michigan State student disappeared briefly in August, it was at first surmised that he had gotten lost in the university's maze of underground steam tunnels while playing Dungeons and Dragons. This game, first devised in 1974, was especially popular among college students and had an estimated 300,000 followers throughout the U.S. Played with books, paper, miniature figures, and sets of dice with as many as 20 sides each, it is basically a fantasy adventure game in which each participant, equipped with preset strengths and weaknesses, sets out on an adventure against such daunting obstacles as demons and dragons.

Sadly, Meccano, the pioneer constructional toy that had entertained and educated generations of budding engineers since its invention by Frank Hornby in 1901, was one of the casualties in what was financially a bad year for some of the major toy manufacturers. Airfix Industries, owners of Meccano since 1971, reported losses of nearly £1 million for the half year March–September 1979 and decided to close down the Meccano factory. Afterward it was occupied by the more than 900 workers employed there, who hoped to continue production as a cooperative. Two other British-based manufacturers, Dunbee-Combex-Marx Ltd.

and Lesney Products Ltd. (makers of Matchbox cars and race tracks), reported slumping profits.

Early Meccano sets would undoubtedly become collectors' items, fetching high prices in the thriving market for antique and "vintage" toys. German tinplate toys from the turn of the century were currently selling at from $50 to $4,000.

Hong Kong and Taiwan continued to lead as exporters of toys and games. The value of Hong Kong's exports in 1979 was estimated at $1 billion, 50% going to the U.S., 10% to the U.K., and 8% to West Germany. Taiwan's exports were valued at $500 million. (GORDON A. WEBB)

[452.B.6; 452.C–D]

Gardening

It was estimated that the number of home vegetable gardeners in the U.S. increased 10 to 20% in 1979, mostly as a result of high food costs. Coping with insect pests was one of the major problems for new gardeners. Tests at the University of California showed that spraying a weak solution of soap and water or detergent and water could keep garden pest insects at nondamaging levels. Such sprays were also less damaging to beneficial insects than most synthetic insecticides.

Frequent rains in many parts of the eastern U.S. made blackspot, a serious disease of roses, difficult to control. Peter Semeniuk, a U.S. Department of Agriculture (USDA) scientist, reported the development of three hybrid roses with resistance to seven strains of the blackspot fungus native to areas in the East, South, and Midwest. Budwood of the new roses had been released to interested commercial and amateur breeders.

Three roses won 1980 All-America Rose awards, all of them developed by William Warriner, research director of Jackson & Perkins: Love, a grandiflora with brilliant red blooms; Honor, a glistening white hybrid tea that had already received six awards from all over the world; and, Cherish, a floribunda that produces shell pink flowers the size of hybrid teas. It was the first time that all of the rose awards had gone to one person.

A full-petaled white floribunda, Margaret Merril (Harkness; called Harkuly in the U.K. where it was classified as a floribunda/hybrid tea type), won 1978 gold medals at Rome and Geneva and, in the U.K., the Royal National Rose Society's Henry Edland medal for most fragrant rose. The Golden Rose at The Hague, Neth., in 1978 went to the floribunda Milrose (Delbard) and the Golden Rose at West Flanders, Belg., to another floribunda, Meigavesol (Meilland). A hybrid tea, Mullard Jubilee (McGredy), won the fragrance award at The Hague.

Two vegetables and three flowers were 1980 All-America award winners: Gold Rush hybrid squash, with bright golden skin and excellent zucchini flavour; Holiday Time, an ornamental pepper that grows only six to eight inches tall and bears edible hot peppers that are yellow when young and turn orange and red as they mature; Peter Pan Flame, a vibrant flame-red zinnia; Sangria verbena, whose wine-red colour changes with the angle of the sun; and Janie dwarf French marigold, with deep golden-orange blooms that appear earlier than those of other marigolds of its class.

All-America Rose Selections

All-America Selections

A 1980 All-America Rose Selections winner was Cherish (left), a floribunda. A marigold, Janie (right), won a bronze medal for All-America Selections.

Charles R. Krause, plant pathologist with the USDA Science and Education Administration, found that the scanning electron microscope, which magnifies images up to 200,000 times, shows plant leaf characteristics clearly enough to identify specific cultivars. He believed this "fingerprinting" method might soon become a part of plant patent applications, supplementing the traditional morphological descriptions.

Gypsy moth damage in the northeastern U.S. in 1979 was only half that in 1978, according to preliminary USDA estimates. The figures, compiled each year from aerial surveys, showed that approximately 260,222 ha (643,000 ac) of trees were defoliated in the Northeast in 1979, compared with 514,774 ha (1,271,990 ac) in 1978. Among the causes of the decline were the wet, cold weather, caterpillar diseases, gypsy moth parasites released through state and federal programs, and spraying of areas where the heaviest damage was expected. For the first time, 40 ha (100 ac) were defoliated in Michigan and 4 ha (10 ac) in Delaware.

In Britain, following the massive buildup during 1978 in the population of the ladybird (ladybug) beetle, a predator of aphids, the balance in 1979 tilted in favour of the aphids. Most crops were affected, but the potato cultivar Pentland Crown, widely used for french fries (chips), was especially hard hit.

Conservation, both of gardens of historical interest and of vanishing plant species, remained a matter of concern. At a conference organized by the Royal Horticultural Society in London, it was agreed that urgent action was needed to halt the decline in garden maintenance and to encourage the propagation and distribution of rare species and of the older cultivars of popular garden plants now threatened with extinction. The cost of maintaining gardens and opening them to the public was seen as the basis of the problem.

"The Garden: a Celebration of One Thousand Years of British Gardening" was the title of an exhibition staged in London to mark 1979 as the

"Year of the Garden." (*See* ART EXHIBITIONS.) The U.S. Forest Service planned to celebrate its 75th birthday in 1980 by promoting an $80 million program entitled "Plant a Birthday Tree."

(J. G. SCOTT MARSHALL; TOM STEVENSON)

See also Agriculture and Food Supplies; Environment; Life Sciences.
[355.C.2–3; 731.B.1]

German Democratic Republic

German Democratic Republic

A country of central Europe, Germany was partitioned after World War II into the Federal Republic of Germany (Bundesrepublik Deutschland; West Germany) and the German Democratic Republic (Deutsche Demokratische Republik; East Germany), with a special provisional regime for Berlin. East Germany is bordered by the Baltic Sea, Poland, Czechoslovakia, and West Germany. Area: 108,328 sq km (41,826 sq mi). Pop. (1979 est.): 16,751,400. Cap. and largest city: East Berlin (pop., 1979 est., 1,129,000). Language: German. Religion: (1969 est.): Protestant 80%; Roman Catholic 10%. General secretary of the Socialist Unity (Communist) Party and chairman of the Council of State in 1979, Erich Honecker; president of the Council of Ministers (premier), Willi Stoph.

After a raw spell in the relationship between East and West Germany, it seemed by October 1979 that tentative preparations were at last being made for an all-German summit. For most of the year the circumstances for such summitry were hardly favourable. The muzzle on East German dissidents was tightened, Western correspondents based in East Berlin were put on a leash, and harsh amendments to the penal code came into effect. But East Germany's 30th anniversary celebrations in October, attended by Soviet Pres. Leonid Brezhnev and most of the Warsaw Pact leaders, brought with them the prospect of a modest thaw.

Among the 30th anniversary presents to the people were an increase in basic pensions, an undertaking to hold down rents and the prices of essential commodities, and an amnesty for an unspecified number of certain categories of prisoners. The terms of the amnesty gave rise to doubts about the fate of political prisoners, of whom there were thought to be about 4,000 in East Germany. But on October 11 two of East Germany's most famous political prisoners were set free: economist Rudolf Bahro (whose book *The Alternative*, published in the West, strongly criticized the East German system), sentenced in 1978 to eight years in prison for "spying"; and Nico Hübner, who had served 15 months of a five-year sentence for "hostility to the state," having refused to serve in the army. Both were expelled to West Germany.

The restrictions on Western journalists, introduced in April, were the most stringent yet imposed by any of the Eastern bloc countries. They compelled Western correspondents based in East Berlin to give at least 24 hours' notice of their plans to travel within East Germany, stating their precise destination and the reasons for the trip. Furthermore, correspondents had to obtain prior permission to interview East German citizens. Ostensibly the regulations applied to all correspondents from the "capitalist industrial countries," but in fact they were directed against West German correspondents, especially against representatives of West German television.

Early in April the East German authorities had accused West German journalists of meddling in East German domestic affairs by interviewing people in line outside Intershops, where Western goods could be bought for Western currency. The authorities had just announced that in the future East German citizens would not be able to pay for their goods in cash but only with vouchers, for which they must change their Western money at a bank. Many people were suspicious, sensing — wrongly, as it turned out—that the privilege of Intershopping was about to be removed. There

Soviet leader Leonid I. Brezhnev (left) gave a kiss of friendship to Erich Honecker (right) when Brezhnev arrived in East Berlin in October to celebrate the 30th anniversary of East Germany as a Soviet bloc nation.

MINGAM—GAMMA/LIAISON

Garment Industry: *see* Fashion and Dress

Gas Industry: *see* Energy

Gemstones: *see* Industrial Review

Genetics: *see* Life Sciences

Geochemistry: *see* Earth Sciences

Geology: *see* Earth Sciences

Geophysics: *see* Earth Sciences

German Literature: *see* Literature

GERMAN DEMOCRATIC REPUBLIC

Education. (1977–78) Primary and secondary, pupils 2,527,788, teachers (1976–77) 161,477; vocational, pupils 452,817, teachers 15,213; higher (1975–76), students 386,000, teaching staff 34,566.

Finance. Monetary unit: Mark of Deutsche Demokratische Republik, with (Sept. 17, 1979) an official rate of M 1.81 to U.S. $1 (M 3.90 = £1 sterling). Budget (1977 est.): revenue M 124,543,000,000; expenditure M 124,103,000,000. Net material product (at 1975 prices; 1977) M 155.2 billion.

Foreign Trade. (1977) Imports M 49,882,000,000; exports M 41,844,000,000. Import sources: U.S.S.R. *c.* 35%; Czechoslovakia *c.* 8%; Poland *c.* 8%; West Germany *c.* 7%; Hungary *c.* 6%. Export destinations: U.S.S.R. *c.* 32%; Czechoslovakia *c.* 9%; West Germany *c.* 9%; Poland *c.* 8%; Hungary *c.* 6%. Main exports (1975): machinery 37%; transport equipment 12% (ships 5%); chemicals; textiles.

Transport and Communications. Roads (1977) *c.* 117,300 km (including 1,619 km autobahns). Motor vehicles in use (1977): passenger 2,236,700; commercial 262,500. Railways: (1977) 14,215 km (including 1,511 km electrified); traffic (1978) 22,263,000,000 passenger-km, freight 53,104,000,000 net ton-km. Air traffic (1977): 1,586,000,000 passenger-km; freight 67.8 million net ton-km. Navigable inland waterways in regular use (1977) 2,538 km; goods traffic 2,215,000,000 ton-km. Shipping (1978): merchant vessels 100 gross tons and over 452; gross tonnage 1,539,994. Telephones (Dec. 1977) 2,860,100. Radio licenses (Dec. 1977) 6,261,000. Television licenses (Dec. 1977) 5,450,000.

Agriculture. Production (in 000; metric tons; 1978): wheat 3,147; barley 4,135; rye 1,895; oats 595; potatoes 10,770; sugar, raw value *c.* 730; cabbages (1977) 371; rapeseed 320; apples *c.* 295; pork 1,174; beef and veal 427; fish catch (1977) 209. Livestock (in 000; Dec. 1977): cattle 5,549; sheep 1,927; pigs 11,757; goats 34; poultry 48,258.

Industry. Index of production (1975 = 100; 1978) 116. Production (in 000; metric tons; 1978): lignite 253,266; electricity (kw-hr) 95,955,000; iron ore (39% metal content) 80; pig iron 2,561; crude steel 6,976; cement 12,520; sulfuric acid 971; petroleum products (1977) 18,893; fertilizers (nutrient content; 1977): nitrogenous 839, phosphate 403, potash 3,229; synthetic rubber 155; passenger cars (units) 171; commercial vehicles (units) 37.

was a run on the shops to beat the deadline, and some people had voiced their complaints when interviewed by West German television about the change in the system. Opening a window to the West by allowing foreign journalists relative freedom had been a demonstration of self-confidence, but evidently the leadership concluded that its generosity had gone too far. Communist Party leader Erich Honecker, generally regarded in the West as a cautious dove, was persuaded by his hawkish colleagues to restore order.

East German escapes to the West continued. On September 16 two families, eight people in all, fled in a homemade hot-air balloon from Thuringia in East Germany to Bavaria in the West, exhibiting great ingenuity and courage. Since the Berlin Wall was built in August 1961 nearly 180,000 people had left East Germany for West Germany illegally. Nearly 52,000 of them got out in the first five months after the wall was built, and in recent years numbers had fallen to about 5,000 annually, most of whom came by way of third countries. One reason for the decrease was that the fortifications along the wall were much more difficult to overcome. But another important factor was that improved relations between the two German nations had probably made the idea of escaping less compelling for many East Germans. Some 50,000 East Germans below pensionable age were allowed to visit West Germany annually on compassionate grounds, and since the conclusion of the East-West German treaty in 1972 about 5,000 East Germans each year had been permitted to join their families permanently in West Germany.

Changes in the penal code which came into effect on August 1 gave the courts the power to sentence dissident writers to five years in prison for passing to Western publishers manuscripts that were likely to "damage the interests of the German Democratic Republic." A new offense was the transmission of nonsecret but "damaging" information to foreign intelligence services or to other unspecified foreign organizations and their helpers; this was punishable by prison sentences of from 2 to 12 years. Previously, authors who published in the West without permission received relatively small fines. But early in the year novelist Stefan Heym (*see* LITERATURE: *German*) had to pay approximately $4,500 for dodging the censor. (NORMAN CROSSLAND)

Two couples and their four children pose beside their makeshift hot air balloon which enabled them to escape from East Germany to West Germany in September. The two families floated over the militarized border at night.

KEYSTONE

Germany, Federal Republic of

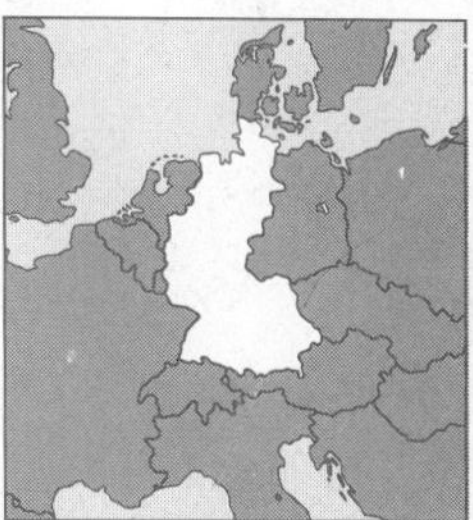

Federal Republic of Germany

A country of central Europe, Germany was partitioned after World War II into the Federal Republic of Germany (Bundesrepublik Deutschland; West Germany) and the German Democratic Republic (Deutsche Demokratische Republik; East Germany), with a special provisional regime for Berlin. West Germany is bordered by Denmark, The Netherlands, Belgium, Luxembourg, France, Switzerland, Austria, Czechoslovakia, East Germany, and the North Sea. Area: 248,651 sq km (96,004 sq mi). Pop. (1979 est.): 61,321,700. Provisional cap.: Bonn (pop., 1979 est., 285,100). Largest city: Hamburg (pop., 1979 est., 1,664,300). (West Berlin, which is an enclave within East Germany,

RÉGIS BOSSU—SYGMA

West Germans protested in Bonn against the election of Karl Carstens as president of West Germany. The protesters objected to Carsten's having been a member of the Nazi Party during his student days in the 1930s.

had a population of 1,909,700 in 1979.) Language: German. Religion (1970): Protestant 49%; Roman Catholic 44.6%; Jewish 0.05%. Presidents in 1979, Walter Scheel and, from July 1, Karl Carstens; chancellor, Helmut Schmidt.

In 1979, its 30th anniversary year, West Germany presented a picture of economic strength and political stability. Unemployment was substantially reduced from previous years; the rate of inflation, though higher than usual, remained among the lowest in the Western world; and there was little trouble on the labour front except for a serious strike in the steel industry. Karl Carstens (*see* BIOGRAPHIES) succeeded Walter Scheel as federal president on July 1.

Domestic Affairs. By the autumn the number of unemployed had fallen to about 800,000, compared with well over a million in the corresponding period of 1978. Inflation passed the 5% mark in September, but this was largely due to special factors. For instance, a long-planned increase in value-added tax came into effect in July, giving an immediate upward push to prices. Still more inflationary was the steep rise in the prices of oil and raw materials. Even so, the country was experiencing an economic upswing, and real economic growth was likely to reach 4% or more for the year. A six-week strike in the steel industry was settled in January. The main aim of the labour union involved, IG Metall, was to start a phased introduction of the 35-hour workweek. Instead, it agreed to accept an offer of longer vacations and more time off for night shift workers and workers over 50.

Politically, attention was focused for much of the year on the activities of the Christian Democratic Union (CDU) and the Bavarian Christian Social Union (CSU), the two opposition parties in the federal Parliament. In May the chairman of the CDU, Helmut Kohl, announced that he would not campaign for the chancellorship a second time, although he remained at least nominal leader of the opposition. At the last federal election, in 1976, the CDU-CSU under Kohl's leadership polled 48.6% of the total vote, achieving its second best result since the formation of the republic. But Kohl's unconvincing performance since then had caused mounting criticism. Indeed, the CDU-CSU was so concerned with its own affairs that it lacked the time and energy to offer a serious challenge to the government.

But Kohl did not intend to leave the field open to his arch detractor, Franz-Josef Strauss (*see* BIOGRAPHIES), chairman of the CSU and, since November 1978, premier of Bavaria. So, unknown to Strauss, Kohl and his friends hatched a plan to nominate Ernst Albrecht, the premier of Lower Saxony, to be their chancellor candidate. Kohl considered that Albrecht was the best available advocate of centrist policies and that he had a special appeal to women and first-time voters.

The plan became known publicly, and within hours Strauss, said to have been persuaded not only by his fellow Bavarians but also by friends in the CDU to enter the race, announced that he would be ready to campaign for chancellor if the call came. He had been increasingly mentioned as a possible contender, and though he himself had over the years usually been coy and evasive when asked about his ambitions he had recently allowed that he was one of several opposition politicians who were "capable" of doing the chancellor's job.

Ignoring the rumblings from Bavaria, the CDU executive committee decided to propose to the CSU that Albrecht be chosen chancellor candidate for the two parties. The CSU merely took note of this move and gave a unanimous welcome to Strauss's consent to his own candidacy. It soon became clear that Strauss would not back down in Albrecht's favour. The existence of the CDU-CSU as a united force was at stake. Finally, on July 2, Strauss was accepted as candidate by the leadership of both parties.

Resistance to Strauss's candidacy turned out to be weaker than expected. The Christian Democratic leaders who most bitterly opposed him—Kohl among them—quickly decided to grin and bear it. But the support of the Protestant north, which Strauss so desperately needed, was less than wholehearted. Moreover, Strauss was being sharply reminded that the union was a coalition, encompassing a broad spectrum of political views. Its powerful lobby representing the interests of industrial and white-collar workers reacted with great suspicion to Strauss's statements about the "limits of the welfare state."

Strauss favoured a system of retirement pension insurance that offered more scope for "self-help"; tightening the regulations on eligibility to receive unemployment benefits; and cutting back expenditures on health services. The workers' lobby on the other hand considered that even the present government was neglecting the development of the welfare state. Strauss was advised to listen carefully to these arguments; approximately 27% of the people who supported the CDU-CSU union at the last election were classed as workers, and more than 40% of the rest were salaried staff and their families.

Federal Chancellor Helmut Schmidt was becoming increasingly impatient with the opponents of nuclear energy and, amid the encircling gloom of an oil crisis, calculated that most people shared his views. He believed that whatever progress might be achieved in the search for alternative sources, nuclear energy would be essential at least for a transitional period lasting several decades. Schmidt would be grudgingly satisfied if his Social Democratic Party (SPD) could be pushed into line on the nuclear energy issue with their junior partner in the coalition, the Free Democratic Party (FDP). At its conference in June the FDP gave "skeptical, conditional" approval to the development of nuclear energy as a transitional solution until it could be replaced by other forms of power. Schmidt told his Cabinet colleagues that he could hardly stay in office if his party failed to go along with that.

At a conference in July the Social Democrats of Baden-Württemberg approved a resolution calling for a ban on the building of further nuclear power stations in their state for at least the next five years. Since the Social Democrats were not in power in the state parliament at Stuttgart, the decision had no practical effect, but it gave the chancellor a chilling reminder of the strength of the antinuclear lobby. At the federal conference of the SPD in December, the party approved cautious expansion of nuclear power but gave priority to coal.

It seemed that Schmidt had probably more to fear in the 1980 federal election from people who professed to support him than from his political opponents. Just how bizarre the result could be was shown by a poll in October. According to this, some 70% of the people who were inclined to vote for "green," or ecological, candidates would prefer Schmidt's reelection to his replacement by Strauss. Yet by taking votes away from the government parties they could put in the man they did not want. Schmidt's Social Democrats could not hope to stay in power without the help of the FDP. And the Free Democrats, judging by the results of state elections, were particularly susceptible to the call of the "greens."

Encouraged by their performances (3.2% in the election to the European Assembly, 5.1% in the state election in Bremen, and 11.7% in a local election in Tübingen), over 1,000 delegates from ecological and other groups attended a conference in October to lay the foundations of a countrywide "green" party. This, they hoped, would be formally constituted in January 1980, well in time for the federal election. But there were problems. The conference hardly presented a picture of unity. Mingling with the opponents of nuclear energy and of economic growth at all costs was a motley collection of people for whom protection of the environment was not a first priority, including members of extreme Communist groups and of vague sects that wished to change the social system.

By September the nuclear energy industry was reporting that it was almost on its knees. It had not received a domestic order for a reactor since 1975 and none from abroad since 1977. Jobs in a sector that employed about 150,000 people were in danger, and there was an immediate risk that West Germany would fall behind in nuclear technology. The specialists reckoned that to secure energy supplies the country must build two to three power stations a year, each of 1,300-Mw capacity, until the end of the century. At the end of 1979 only ten plants were in operation, with a total capacity of 8,950 Mw. Plans for new stations were held up by the courts, and the federal government still had to solve the problem of nuclear waste disposal.

The federal coalition was justifiably relieved by

GERMANY, FEDERAL REPUBLIC OF

Education. (1977–78) Primary, pupils 6,019,128, teachers 243,725; secondary, pupils 3,486,612, teachers 176,108; vocational, pupils 479,764, teachers 29,246; higher, students 1,066,100, teaching staff 114,654.

Finance. Monetary unit: Deutsche Mark, with (Sept. 17, 1979) a free rate of DM 1.81 to U.S. $1 (DM 3.90 = £1 sterling). Gold, SDR's, and foreign exchange (June 1979) U.S. $47,989,000,000. Budget (federal; 1978 actual): revenue DM 171,230,000,000; expenditure DM 196,910,000,000. Gross national product (1978) DM 1,282,600,000,000. Money supply (June 1979) DM 223.9 billion. Cost of living (1975 = 100; June 1979) 116.3.

Foreign Trade. (1978) Imports DM 243,710,000,000; exports DM 284,910,000,000. Import sources: EEC 49% (The Netherlands 13%, France 12%, Italy 10%, Belgium-Luxembourg 8%, U.K. 5%); U.S. 7%. Export destinations: EEC 46% (France 12%, The Netherlands 10%, Belgium-Luxembourg 8%, Italy 7%, U.K. 6%); U.S. 7%; Austria 5%; Switzerland 5%. Main exports: machinery 30%; motor vehicles 14%; chemicals 12%; iron and steel 6%; textiles and clothing 5%. Tourism (1977): visitors 8,423,000; gross receipts U.S. $3,804,000,000.

Transport and Communications. Roads (1977) 474,303 km (including 6,711 km autobahns). Motor vehicles in use (1977): passenger 20,377,200; commercial 1,298,300. Railways: (1977) 31,721 km (including 10,886 km electrified); traffic (1978) 38,251,000,000 passenger-km, freight 57,267,000,000 net ton-km. Air traffic (1978): 17,572,000,000 passenger-km; freight 1,410,560,000 net ton-km. Navigable inland waterways in regular use (1977) 4,456 km; freight traffic 49,254,000,000 ton-km. Shipping (1978): merchant vessels 100 gross tons and over 1,999; gross tonnage 9,736,667. Shipping traffic (1978): goods loaded 35,029,000 metric tons, unloaded 104,562,000 metric tons. Telephones (Dec. 1977) 22,931,700. Radio licenses (Dec. 1977) 20,646,000. Television licenses (Dec. 1977) 18,909,000.

Agriculture. Production (in 000; metric tons; 1978): wheat 8,118; barley 8,608; oats 3,202; rye 2,457; potatoes 10,510; sugar, raw value *c.* 2,975; apples 1,783; wine 671; cow's milk 23,291; butter *c.* 564; cheese 721; beef and veal *c.* 1,400; pork *c.* 2,620; fish catch (1977) 432. Livestock (in 000; Dec. 1977): cattle 14,763; pigs 21,386; sheep 1,135; horses used in agriculture (1976) 355; chickens 90,295.

Industry. Index of production (1975 = 100; 1978) 112. Unemployment (1978) 4.4%. Fuel and power (in 000; metric tons; 1978): coal 83,935; lignite 123,560; crude oil 5,059; coke (1977) 28,959; electricity (kw-hr) 353,400,000; natural gas (cu m) 20,300,000; manufactured gas (cu m) 12,530,000. Production (in 000; metric tons; 1978): iron ore (32% metal content) 1,599; pig iron 30,280; crude steel 41,210; aluminum 1,152; copper 396; lead 306; zinc 474; cement 33,508; sulfuric acid 4,677; newsprint 524; cotton yarn 163; woven cotton fabrics 160; wool yarn 53; man-made fibres 880; petroleum products (1977) 99,300; fertilizers (1977–78) nitrogenous 1,305, phosphate 722, potash 2,445; synthetic rubber 421; plastics and resins 6,743; passenger cars (units) 3,902; commercial vehicles (units) 293. Merchant vessels launched (100 gross tons and over; 1978) 599,000 gross tons. New dwelling units completed (1978) 368,000.

the outcome of state elections in West Berlin and Rhineland-Palatinate in March. True, the elections brought no change; an alliance of Social Democrats and Free Democrats continued to govern West Berlin, and a Christian Democratic government with an absolute majority stayed in power in Mainz. But in both cases the Free Democrats improved their representation. They had obviously recovered from the shocks of the previous year, when they were swept out of the parliaments of Hamburg and Lower Saxony.

The West Berlin election had unique features. The relatively youthful mayor, Dietrich Stobbe, had been elected less than two years earlier, having been dispatched by SPD headquarters to clean up the Berlin party that was worn out by long service—it had been in power since 1950—and torn by scandals. Stobbe had evidently stopped the rot. The party was gaining strength and polled as well as at the previous election in 1975.

The arrest in June of Rolf Heissler, a founder member of a group called the Munich Tupamaros, reduced to 14 the number of known top West German terrorists still on the run. Heissler was the seventh urban guerrilla to be captured alive since the kidnapping and subsequent murder of the president of the employers' federation, Hanns-Martin Schleyer, in 1977. Two others were shot dead by the police, Willy Peter Stoll in a Düsseldorf restaurant in September 1978, and Elisabeth von Dyck in an apartment in Nürnberg in May 1979.

The increasing strength and militance of neo-Nazis caused concern. In August a court in West Berlin passed stiff sentences on ten men, aged between 21 and 47, for setting up a local branch of the forbidden Nazi Party. The ringleader was sent to prison for three years, two others were jailed for 18 months and 14 months, respectively, and the rest got suspended sentences of between six months and a year. Earlier in the year the screening on West German television of the U.S. series "Holocaust" prompted the biggest public debate on the country's Nazi past since the end of World War II. (*See* Special Report.)

Foreign Affairs. In the eyes of the federal government, the Chinese leader Hua Guofeng (Hua Kuo-feng), who paid a week's visit to West Germany during his Western European tour in October, was the perfect guest. He scrupulously avoided making attacks on his country's archenemy, the Soviet Union. Indeed, in his speeches he managed not to mention the Soviets by name at all. Hua's moderate tone was just what the West German government had asked for, or rather ordered; they did not want a repetition of Hua's performance on the French leg of his European tour when he attacked the Soviets with no holds barred. Before the Chinese leader arrived in Bonn the German government spokesman said that no doubt Hua would consider it inadvisable to continue the conflict with the Soviet Union on West German territory.

Significantly, a trip to West Berlin was not included in the busy program arranged for the Chinese delegation, an omission which the guests accepted without protest. The West Germans felt that the sight of Hua peering over the Berlin Wall would be an unnecessary affront to the Soviets. In short, the West German government wanted to maintain good relations with China, but not at the expense of its relationship with the Soviet Union. Accordingly, Hua's visit was considerably less than spectacular. An economic cooperation pact, which established a six-year framework for the development of bilateral trade, provided some window dressing, but the agreement was vague in many respects.

The relationship between West Germany and the Soviet Union was under enough strain without having the Chinese make it worse. West Germany was bearing the brunt of the Soviet propaganda campaign against NATO plans for deployment of a new generation of U.S. nuclear missiles in Western Europe. Publicly, Schmidt was less skeptical than most other Western leaders about the Soviet offer—made in a speech by Leonid Brezhnev in East Berlin in October—to withdraw up to 20,000 Soviet troops and 1,000 tanks from East Germany. The chancellor was nonetheless adamant that NATO must be prepared if necessary to establish a force of medium-range nuclear missiles comparable to that of the Soviet Union. The West German government proposed that NATO should decide to produce such weapons but that their deployment should depend on progress in arms limitation negotiations. Further, the government insisted that the missiles should not be based only in West Germany but should be accepted by at least one other nonnuclear NATO country.

Israeli suspicions about West German policy in the Middle East were aroused by a series of visits paid to Arab countries by Foreign Minister Hans-Dietrich Genscher. During the year he was in Libya, Iraq, Saudi Arabia, Lebanon, Jordan, and Egypt. According to the West German government the purpose of these trips was to assist in obtaining a Middle East settlement, although bilateral questions also played an important role.

The Israelis said that the West Germans were obviously much more interested in securing oil supplies than in supporting Israeli interests. It was notable that Schmidt showed no inclination to take up a four-year-old invitation to visit Israel. There were informal contacts between leading West German politicians and the Palestine Liberation Organization (PLO), and in July SPD Chairman Willy Brandt met with the PLO leader, Yasir Arafat, in Austria.

At a price Poland was observing the agreement under which many of its citizens of German origin were allowed to leave the country to settle in West Germany. Under a "money for people" deal, ratified by the federal Parliament in 1976, West Germany agreed to grant Poland a large loan and to cover Polish citizens' claims against West Germany. In return the Polish government would issue exit visas to 125,000 ethnic Germans over a four-year period. By August about 115,000 had already arrived in West Germany, and the Polish leader Edward Gierek gave an assurance that applications would still be considered after the agreement had expired. It was thought that at least another 100,000 ethnic Germans wished to settle in the West. (NORMAN CROSSLAND)

SPECIAL REPORT

THE NAZI HUNT GOES ON

by Norman Crossland

On July 3, 1979, the Bundestag, West Germany's federal parliament, voted to abolish the statute of limitations for murder. Under the statute, proceedings in murder cases could not be opened if the crime was committed 30 or more years earlier. Had the statute not been scrapped, it would have meant that from Jan. 1, 1980, Nazi murderers who were not already on the wanted list would not, if discovered, be brought to trial. The issue was a controversial one. The abolition of the statute was approved on a free vote by 255 votes to 222.

The "Holocaust" Shock. Undoubtedly, the decision of the Bundestag was influenced by the showing in West Germany in January 1979 of the U.S. television film "Holocaust." This dramatized story of the Nazi extermination of the Jews stirred the German conscience as had nothing before. During the past 30 years more than 100 documentary films about the Nazi period have been shown on West German television, bringing the most horrific concentration-camp scenes into the living room. Millions of printed words have recorded the evidence of war crimes trials, which still drag painfully on. Yet it took this film, criticized by reviewers in several countries for triviality and tasteless emotionalism, to inspire the first widespread public debate on a subject that so many Germans would prefer to forget.

Presumably, the film caused such a reaction because "Holocaust," unlike the documentaries, used the technique of popular journalism. It focused the story on the fate of one Jewish family, people with whom the viewer could identify. Ghastly as it sounds, six million dead are a statistic that numbs the imagination, while extermination of one family that we have come to know and like is comprehensible. Although it was shown on the third television channel, which usually puts out regional programs for minority audiences, and although the four-part series did not start until 9 PM, "Holocaust" got the kind of viewer ratings that some light entertainment shows would be lucky to achieve.

Norman Crossland is the Bonn correspondent for The Economist, *London.*

The viewing quota climbed during the week to reach 41% for the final episode of the tragedy, which meant that that part was seen by 15 million people. Millions of viewers stayed up to hear the discussion that followed each installment—among historians, psychologists, writers, and former inmates of concentration camps. During the week more than 30,000 people telephoned the discussion panel to ask questions or to express views. At the beginning of the week negative and positive reactions were roughly balanced. "How did it all happen?" "How many people knew what was going on?" "The film tells only half the truth—what about the hostile attitude of European Jews toward National Socialism [*sic*]?" "I'm 35 and innocent, and I don't want to be burdened by the past"—these were some typical reactions.

But as the series continued, the proportion of viewers approving of the film increased to about two-thirds. The discussion of Nazi crimes was taken up in schools, universities, and factories. Advertisements appeared in the personal columns of newspapers proposing the setting up of "Holocaust" discussion groups. Awkward questions were asked within families about the wartime experiences of fathers and grandfathers. Henri Nannen, editor of *Stern* magazine, publicly admitted: "I knew that in the name of Germany defenseless people were being slaughtered like vermin. And without shame I wore the uniform of the Luftwaffe." But not everybody knew that the Jews were being exterminated, and many of those people who were told either could not or did not want to believe it.

The Third Reich in Popular Myth. The ignorance of many young Germans about this darkest chapter in their country's history should not have caused surprise. In 1977 a teacher in Kiel compiled a selection of schoolchildren's essays about Hitler that produced some alarming howlers. One 13-year-old boy wrote: "I heard he came from Holland," and another: "Adolf Hitler was an Italian." According to one lad Hitler's opponents were called Nazis, and Hitler had them put in the gas chambers. A girl was nearer the mark: "He came from Austria . . . such a fool, coming from another country and simply taking over the government." All schools are supposed to include the Third Reich in their history lessons, but evidently it is not taught thoroughly everywhere. Nor can a lot of the children expect much enlightenment from their parents, since more than half the population were born after World War II.

Moreover, many older people who still have vivid personal memories of the Nazi period are not prepared to condemn Hitler out of hand. A television series called "We Germans and the Third Reich," screened in August 1979 as a follow-up to "Holo-

NBC PHOTO

Meryl Streep, playing the role of a Catholic woman married to a Jew in the U.S. TV mini-series "Holocaust," screams as her husband is taken away by the Nazis. The program was credited with helping to spur Germany into abolishing the statute of limitations for Nazi war criminals.

caust," showed that some people were nostalgic for at least the prewar part of Hitler's dictatorship. "He was right, was Adolf," said one man; "he built the autobahns—and at a stroke the unemployment problem was solved." A woman fondly recalled jolly times as a member of the Bund Deutscher Mädchen (the girls' branch of the Hitler Youth Movement). "In my view," she said, "it was a time when life's truly noble virtues were cultivated." Most of the anecdotes contained nothing about the politics of the period. What still most impressed people was the "orderliness" and the "cleanliness" and the Nazis' economic solutions.

Even so, relatively few Germans appear to be still susceptible to extremist political appeals from either the right or the left. For many years extremist parties have received minute support at elections, and by mid–1979 the membership of the once powerful National Democratic Party had dropped to a mere 8,500. Though the government has been concerned about the increasing strength and militance of neo-Nazi groups, their total membership in 1979 was only about 1,300. This "new right" could not be described as a movement. It was split, disorganized, and had no common ideology. Extreme right-wing publications, on the other hand, had a considerable readership, and the most significant of them, the weekly *Deutsche National Zeitung,* boasted a circulation of about 100,000. Clearly, a lot of people like to read that the horrors of Auschwitz never really happened.

A Nation's Conscience. But this was a small minority, and its view amounted to no more than a shrill heckling in the searching public debate about the past. Most Germans, and especially the country's youth, were plunged into an orgy of introspection by "Holocaust" and by other films and books about the Hitler period. Yet why had it taken so long for the Germans, en masse, to react in this way? There are several possible explanations. Many millions of Germans themselves suffered terribly during the war and in the immediate postwar years. Their cities were almost totally destroyed, and after 1945 some ten million Germans were expelled from their homes in the Eastern territories and had to make their way under appalling conditions to the West.

Many Germans were so preoccupied with the fight for their own survival that they were disinclined to face up to stories about Nazi crimes. Some people tended to put the Allied firebombing of Dresden and the brutality of Soviet occupation on a par of immorality with the extermination camps. At that time the question "Who started it all?" was of secondary importance. Then came the cold war, which led to West Germany's rapid integration in the Western camp. Simultaneously, the Germans were working like beavers at the task of reconstruction, and the world marveled at the *Wirtschaftswunder*—the "economic miracle." West Germany's leaders made solemn and sincere statements admitting the Germans' collective responsibility for Nazi crimes, and as soon as it was able to do so, West Germany began paying huge sums of money to the victims who had survived. But busy decades went by before a new generation of Germans became engaged in an *Auseinandersetzung,* a thorough analysis of Nazism and its roots. As one girl student, monitoring the reaction to the "Holocaust" series, put it: "It's as if an entire nation is laying bare its soul."

No Let-Off for Nazi Criminals. The July 1979 debate on the statute of limitations was the third time the Bundestag had had to face the problem. When it first arose, in 1965, members voted for a neat, if legally questionable, solution. The statutory period in those days was only 20 years, but it was decided to bring forward the starting date to the end of 1949; *i.e.,* when German courts began to try war criminals. The Free Democratic minister of justice, Ewald Bucher, thought that this was a fiddle and resigned. The matter had to be resolved again in 1969. This time Parliament extended the period to 30 years and fervently hoped that that would be the end of the affair. Opponents of a further extension or of an abolition of the statute argued that as the years went by, the task of the courts became impossibly difficult. Memories fade; proceedings are held up because witnesses or prisoners are ill; and defense counsel become masters of delaying tactics.

Moreover, a refusal to tamper again with the statute would not necessarily have meant that there would have been no more trials after the end of 1979. Cases already in the pipeline could end up in the courts. But the pressure on the West Germans from abroad, notably from Israel and Poland, to continue the hunt for Nazi criminals was as strong in 1979 as it had been in 1965 and 1969. And most members of the government coalition of Social Democrats and Free Democrats were haunted by the fear that after January 1980 former Nazis in West Germany might boast publicly about their crimes and go unpunished. Their views were summed up by the justice minister, Hans Jochen Vogel, who said that after Auschwitz there could be no statute of limitations in Germany for murder.

The West German authorities cannot say precisely how many Germans have been convicted of war crimes—by foreign as well as German courts—since the war. This is because reliable statistics from the Soviet Union, Yugoslavia, and Czechoslovakia are not available. But it is estimated that the figure is about 70,000. West German prosecutors have investigated some 85,000 cases, but German courts have in fact convicted and sentenced only about 6,500 people for war crimes. This relatively low rate of conviction is due to various factors. Many of the suspects could not be traced. Thousands of people whose crimes were well documented died in the war or in prison camps immediately afterward. Many had been sentenced to death by courts of the Allied powers and executed. Several thousand others had been convicted by the Allies and could not be tried in Germany again on the same charges.

Still at Large. An unknown but probably large number of Germans fled after the war to South America or to Arab countries and managed to lie low. Some whose whereabouts were discovered have managed to escape justice because extradition applications were rejected. At the top of the wanted list is Josef Mengele, the former camp doctor at Auschwitz, who is reliably believed to be in Paraguay. Another is Gustav Wagner, a former senior official at the extermination camp of Sobibor, who is in Brazil. But the possibility that as-yet-unnamed Nazi criminals of this calibre will be added to the files of the German prosecuting authorities becomes increasingly remote.

Most likely the last of the major war crimes trials is the case in the Düsseldorf assize court against former members of the staff of the Majdanek concentration camp near Lublin in Poland. This trial began in November 1975 and was still making slow progress four years later. Originally, there were 14 people in the dock, accused of taking part in the murder of 250,000 Jews. Four of the defendants were dismissed from the case in April 1979 for lack of evidence. The trial provided a striking example of the delaying tactics of defense lawyers. The central office for the investigation of Nazi war crimes in Nürnberg complained in 1979 that defense counsel in a number of cases were more concerned with playing for time or having their clients declared medically unfit to stand trial than with contesting the prosecution evidence. In the first 15 years that war crimes trials were held in West German courts, the conviction rate was about 10%. It has since dropped to less than 2%. This is a consequence of Germany's late start in facing up to its past.

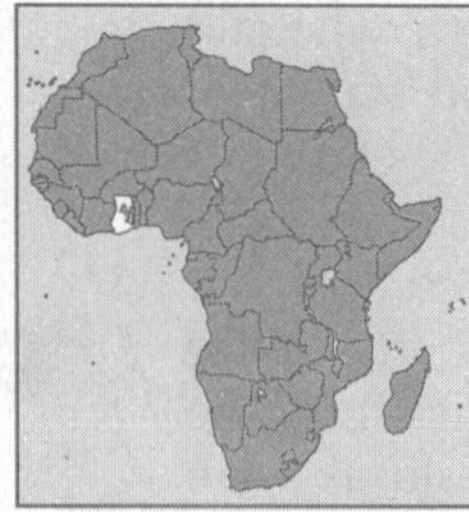
Ghana

Ghana

A republic of West Africa and member of the Commonwealth of Nations, Ghana is on the Gulf of Guinea and is bordered by Ivory Coast, Upper Volta, and Togo. Area: 238,533 sq km (92,098 sq mi). Pop. (1979 est.): 11,103,000. Cap. and largest city: Accra (pop., 1975 est., 716,600). Language: English (official); local Sudanic dialects: Akan 44%, Mole-Dagbani 16%, Ewe 13%, and Ga-Adange 8%. Religion: Christian 43%; Muslim 12%; animist 38%. Chairman of the National Redemption Council and of the Supreme Military Council until June 4, 1979, Lieut. Gen. Fred W. K. Akuffo; head of the Armed Forces Revolutionary Council until September 24, Lieut. Jerry Rawlings; president from September 24, Hilla Limann.

Lieut. Gen. Fred Akuffo (*see* OBITUARIES), who took over the country in July 1978 with the aim of cleaning up after Gen. Ignatius Acheampong's (*see* OBITUARIES) "seven years of mismanagement," raised the ban on political parties on Jan. 1, 1979. He planned elections in June that would return the country to civilian rule. Events overtook him, however. He was overthrown in a coup on June 4 (after an unsuccessful attempt in May) by 32-year-old Flight Lieut. Jerry Rawlings (*see* BIOGRAPHIES), who also intended to cleanse the country with the help of his Armed Forces Revolutionary Council.

GHANA

Education. (1976–77) Primary, pupils 1,213,291, teachers 41,407; secondary, pupils 551,899, teachers 25,081; vocational, pupils 21,204, teachers 1,064; teacher training, students 3,867, teachers 909; higher (1975–76), students 9,079, teaching staff 1,103.

Finance. Monetary unit: cedi, with (Sept. 17, 1979) a free rate of 2.83 cedis to U.S. $1 (6.09 cedis = £1 sterling). Gold, SDR's, and foreign exchange (June 1979) U.S. $242 million. Budget (1978–79 est.): revenue 3.2 billion cedis; expenditure 2.9 billion cedis. Gross domestic product (1975) 6,044,000,000 cedis. Money supply (May 1979) 3,662,300,000 cedis. Cost of living (Accra; 1975 = 100; Dec. 1978) 822.

Foreign Trade. (1977) Imports 1,176,000,000 cedis; exports 1,106,000,000 cedis. Import sources (1975): U.S. 16%; U.K. 15%; West Germany 11%; Nigeria 7%; Japan 6%; Libya 5%. Export destinations (1975): U.K. 15%; U.S. 11%; The Netherlands 10%; Switzerland 8%; West Germany 8%; Japan 7%; U.S.S.R. 7%; Yugoslavia 5%. Main exports: cocoa 61%; timber 8%.

Transport and Communications. Roads (1977) 32,200 km. Motor vehicles in use (1976): passenger 64,000; commercial (including buses) 46,000. Railways: (1976) 953 km; traffic (1972) 431 million passenger-km, freight 305 million net ton-km. Air traffic (1977): 234 million passenger-km; freight 3.6 million net ton-km. Shipping (1978): merchant vessels 100 gross tons and over 85; gross tonnage 186,079. Telephones (Jan. 1978) 66,400. Radio receivers (Dec. 1976) 1,080,000. Television receivers (Dec. 1976) 35,000.

Agriculture. Production (in 000; metric tons; 1978): corn *c.* 350; cassava (1977) *c.* 2,500; taro (1977) *c.* 1,400; yams (1977) *c.* 800; millet *c.* 120; sorghum *c.* 120; tomatoes *c.* 110; peanuts *c.* 80; oranges *c.* 150; cocoa *c.* 270; palm oil *c.* 21; meat (1977) *c.* 80; fish catch (1977) 383; timber (cu m; 1977) *c.* 13,060. Livestock (in 000; 1977): cattle *c.* 850; sheep *c.* 1,500; pigs *c.* 380; goats *c.* 1,800; chickens *c.* 10,500.

Industry. Production (in 000; metric tons; 1977): bauxite 244; petroleum products *c.* 1,160; gold (troy oz) 484; diamonds (metric carats) 2,300; manganese ore (metal content) *c.* 107; electricity (kw-hr) *c.* 4,300,000.

Gibraltar:
see Dependent States

Gilbert Islands:
see Kiribati

Glass Manufacture:
see Industrial Review

Gliding:
see Aerial Sports

Rawlings promptly executed his three military predecessors: Akuffo, Acheampong, and Lieut. Gen. Akwasi Afrifa, along with several senior officials, but international pressure and a threatened Nigerian oil embargo halted further executions. Elections were held on June 18, and Ghana returned to civilian government under the presidency of Hilla Limann (*see* BIOGRAPHIES) on September 24. Though accused of electoral malpractice, Limann's People's National Party won 71 of the 140 parliamentary seats. In November the new government retired Rawlings from the armed forces.

(MOLLY MORTIMER)

Golf

For the third successive year Tom Watson in 1979 ranked far ahead of his rivals on the United States professional golf tour. He won four tournaments and a record $462,636 that brought his total for three years to well over $1 million, but his showing in major championships was disappointing.

The only time Watson came close to victory in a major event was when he lost a play-off for the Masters title in April at Augusta, Ga., to Fuzzy Zoeller after one of the most unexpected finishes in the history of a tournament where the extraordinary is commonplace. Not since Horton Smith and Gene Sarazen won the first two Masters had anyone succeeded at his first attempt.

When Ed Sneed, whose handsome style and great golf had given him a five-stroke lead after 54 holes, left the 15th green in the last round, he was three strokes ahead. Then his agony began. Three putts on the 16th and three from the edge of the 17th left him a par four to win, but his putt on the 18th stopped on the brink of the hole, and he was condemned to a sudden-death play-off, the first of its kind in the Masters, with Watson and Zoeller. Zoeller, who had holed difficult putts on the 17th and 18th to stay in the hunt, then showed the courage to attack. After Watson missed a likely putt to win on the first extra hole, Zoeller hit an enormous drive on the second, pitched inside the others, and holed out for a remarkable victory.

After his great Masters victory in 1977 Watson had twice finished second, only a stroke behind the winner. Many thought that Jack Nicklaus had not competed enough to be in peak form for the Masters, but had he not slightly overhit an approach shot on the 17th he probably would have tied with the others.

Since Hale Irwin won the 1974 U.S. Open, the golfing world had wondered when one of the purest styles and coolest minds in the game would win another major title. Although often in contention, he could not sustain the challenge. Then at Inverness Club in Toledo, Ohio, in June the lean years ended, but not without anxiety. In trying to protect a lead of five strokes during the last round, he lost his driving tempo on the closing holes. His pursuers could not take advantage of this, however, and Irwin won by two strokes with a par total of 284. Gary Player, with a great final round of 68, shared second place with Jerry Pate. This was typical of the deathless resolve of Player, a man who had won his first major championship 20 years earlier. Pate, whose swing is a model of smoothness, maintained his challenge in courageous fashion. Tom Weiskopf, Irwin's closest competitor for the first three rounds, developed problems with his swing at the finish that cost him a share of second place. Nicklaus had a strange Open, eventually sharing ninth place, but only because his final 36 holes were 11 strokes better than the first 36. While Nicklaus just managed to qualify for the tournament, Watson failed by a stroke. A fault had crept into his driving, and so the strongest favourite was out early.

The outcome must have been a relief to the U.S. Golf Association, which had been concerned that several Opens in recent years had not produced champions of the highest world class. It had also been accused of making the courses too severe, but no such criticism could fairly be aimed at Inverness. The course demanded straight driving but the rough was not as fierce as at some other links. The greens were fast but not too hard, and the balance between reward and punishment was right.

Irwin began the British Open in July as if destined to become only the fifth golfer—along with Bobby Jones, Sarazen, Ben Hogan, and Lee Trevino—to win both Opens in the same summer. In cold, windy weather at the Royal Lytham and St. Annes Golf Club in St. Annes, England, a pair of 68s left him two strokes ahead of Severiano Ballesteros of Spain, who finished his second round with four birdies in five holes over the toughest part of the course. Both had 75s the next day and by then Ben Crenshaw and Nicklaus were close behind. Ballesteros's strategy on the last day was to attack almost without restraint. Vast drives soared into all kinds of unlikely places, but he well knew that the rough had been trampled by the largest crowds ever to watch the championship. In fact, he hit only one fairway from the tee, but so great was his confidence in his short game and putting that he never became defensive. Such driving on a U.S. course would have swept him into the 80s, but he knew what he was about and had the courage to play the old links as he found it.

Isao Aoki of Japan gratefully kisses his golf ball after it plopped into the hole on one shot to win him a $120,000 home in Scotland. Aoki hit the hole in one during World Match Play Championship competition in Wentworth, England, in October.

PRESS ASSOCIATION

None of the great players whom he beat, including Crenshaw and Nicklaus, who finished three strokes behind him, could claim that he was unlucky to lose. All made mistakes for which the condition of the course was not responsible. Had Crenshaw not taken a six on the 71st hole, Ballesteros would have been under severe pressure. Crenshaw's second-place finish was his second in a row in the British Open, Nicklaus beating him in 1978. So Ballesteros became the youngest Open champion of the century and the first golfer from the continent of Europe to win the British Open since Arnaud Massy in 1907.

The Professional Golfers' Association (PGA) championship at Oakland Hills Country Club near Detroit brought near disaster before eventual triumph for David Graham of Australia, who had played for many years in the U.S. Standing on the 18th tee he needed only a par to equal Johnny Miller's record last round of 63 in a major championship and to clinch the victory. Then the pressure hit him. A bad drive led to a six and a tie with Crenshaw. On the first extra hole Graham seemed doomed to defeat, but the putter that had served him magnificently throughout did not fail and he holed in from 25 ft. A birdie two on the third hole gave Graham the win his skilled golf deserved and condemned Crenshaw to yet another runner-up finish, his fourth within six weeks. Watson, who led with a 66 after the first round, fell back in the final round, while Nicklaus finished 22 strokes behind Graham.

The climax to the U.S. season brought victory and the year's largest prize of $100,000 to Lon Hinkle in the World Series of Golf. Heavy September rains had softened the giant Firestone Country Club course at Akron, Ohio, and the difficult par of 70 was frequently broken, notably by Hinkle with three rounds of 67. With two holes to play Larry Nelson, who had played consistently well throughout the year, seemed certain to win, but a badly hit pitch to the 17th green cost him two strokes. Bill Rogers, who broke 70 in every round, also lost a stroke at the 17th, and Watson's final drive went into the trees. Trevino made a fine attempt to tie with a birdie at the last hole that just failed, and Hinkle was safe. It was only his third victory on the tour.

U.S. teams were victorious on two international fronts, winning the Ryder Cup 17–11 at White Sulphur Springs, W.Va., and the Walker Cup 15½–8½ at Muirfield in Scotland. But for the second successive year the U.S. club professionals were beaten by a team from Great Britain and Ireland, losing by 12½–4½ in the Isle of Man.

UPI

Severiano Ballesteros of Spain waves to the crowd after winning the British Open in July.

The Ryder Cup contest was closer than the score suggests. After two days of foursomes and singles the U.S. team, for which Lanny Wadkins and Nelson played formidably good golf in winning all their four matches together, led by only one point with 11 18-hole singles matches to play. For the first time the visitors included players from the continent of Europe in addition to Britain and Ireland. Ballesteros and Antonio Garrido of Spain were on the team but could win only one point, having the misfortune to be drawn more often than not against Wadkins and Nelson. The Europeans were given a great start in the singles when Bernard Gallacher, their outstanding player, beat Wadkins, but Nelson then overcame Ballesteros and the Americans won the next four matches on the last green. Tom Kite came from behind against Tony Jacklin, as did Mark Hayes against Garrido, and Hubert Green finished with two birdies to beat Peter Oosterhuis. When Andy Bean and Hale Irwin cruised easily home, the U.S. had won for the 19th time in 23 encounters.

Midway through the last session of the Walker Cup match the issue seemed certain to be desperately close. The U.S. players needed four points from the eight singles to win and were given an inspiring start by Scott Hoch, who played the strongest golf of the whole contest in beating Peter McEvoy, the leading British player. But at one time the U.S. team was ahead in only one match. Then, as the pressure mounted, the British began to falter. Although no match was decided before the 16th green, the U.S. won seven.

In the British Amateur championship, which followed at Southport, Merseyside, Jay Sigel of the U.S. played effortless, beautiful golf in reaching the final, where, fittingly as an amateur of permanent status, he disposed of Hoch. The whole U.S. Walker Cup team competed in the U.S. Amateur championship at Canterbury Golf Club near Cleveland, Ohio, together with John Cook, the defending champion, and Bobby Clampett, the outstanding amateur of 1978. Cook lost his form in the final match and was defeated 8 and 7 by Mark O'Meara.

The European tour was notable for the play of Sandy Lyle, aged 21, who had been a professional for less than two years. His three wins included the European Open by seven strokes, and he finished at the head of the Order of Merit with almost £40,000. Ballesteros, who had been first the previous three years, finished second.

Isao Aoki of Japan made a brave defense of his World Match Play title at Wentworth, Surrey. After a memorable contest with Bill Rogers of the U.S. he lost on the last green of a 36-hole final.

Once again Nancy Lopez dominated the Ladies' Professional Golfers' Association (LPGA) competition in the U.S. Her victories included the last Colgate European Open, and her official prize money of $197,488 beat her record of the previous year. In September she joined with Jo Ann Washam to win the LPGA team championship in Portland, Ore., by one stroke over Susie Berning and Carole Jo Skala. In July Jerilyn Britz won the U.S. Women's Open by two strokes over Debbie Massey at Fairfield, Conn. Others who enjoyed success during the season included Jane Blalock, JoAnne Carner, Sandra Post, and Amy Alcott.

For the first time a major competition was held in Greece, on the Glyfada course near Athens, where the World Cup was won by the U.S. (Irwin and J. Mahaffey). (P.A. WARD-THOMAS)

JoAnne Carner exhibits joyous relief after sinking a 15-foot putt during the final round of the Honda Civic Golf Classic on March 18 in San Diego, California, which she won by three strokes.

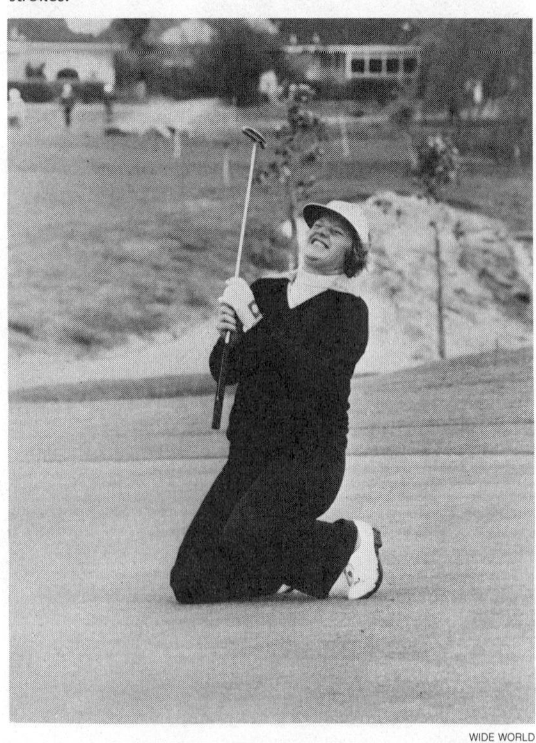

WIDE WORLD

Greece

A republic of Europe, Greece occupies the southern part of the Balkan Peninsula. Area: 131,990 sq km (50,962 sq mi), of which the mainland accounts for 107,194 sq km. Pop. (1979 est.): 9,360,-000. Cap. and largest city: Athens (pop., 1971, 867,000). Language: Greek. Religion: Orthodox. President in 1979, Konstantinos Tsatsos; prime minister, Konstantinos Karamanlis.

Three developments dominated Greece's international relations in 1979: the signing of the treaty of accession to the European Economic Community (EEC); Prime Minister Konstantinos Karamanlis's official visit to Moscow, the first by the head of a Greek government; and a marked deterioration in relations with the U.S. and NATO.

Negotiations with the EEC were concluded in December 1978, and the treaty of accession was formally signed in Athens on May 28. The Greek Parliament ratified the agreements, although the Panhellenic Socialist Movement (Pasok) and the Communist Party of Greece (KKE), which opposed Greek entry, boycotted the debate. In October the prime minister traveled to four EEC countries to press for early ratification of the treaty so Greece could become a full member, the tenth, on Jan. 1, 1981, as scheduled.

Greece's entry into the EEC became the most important aspect of the "multidimensional," Western-oriented but more independent foreign policy that Karamanlis enunciated at the opening of the International Trade Fair of Thessaloniki on September 8. Greece drew closer to its Western European partners as its relations with the U.S. deteriorated. Greece resented Washington's pronounced pro-Turkish tilt after the revolution in Iran, and U.S. unwillingness to curb Turkey's veto on Greece's unconditional military reintegration into NATO froze U.S.-Greek bilateral relations.

Greece sought reentry into NATO's integrated military command (after its walkout in 1974) mainly because it feared Turkey's filling in the jurisdictional gap created in the Aegean by Greece's withdrawal. NATO offered compromise formulas for reentry that were espoused by the U.S. but rejected by Greece as an encroachment on its national sovereignty. Greece boycotted NATO's autumn exercise "Display Determination '79" because it did not conform to the Greek demand for exclusive operational control of the Aegean air space. At the same time, the Greek government called off another NATO exercise, "Athlete Express," in which NATO's multinational mobile force would have been airlifted to northern Greece to help the Greeks confront a simulated attack by Warsaw Pact forces. This maneuver would have coincided with Karamanlis's visit to Moscow, October 1–5.

On September 6, quite unexpectedly, a Greek-Soviet deal was signed enabling Soviet Navy ships to undergo repairs at Neorion shipyards on the Aegean island of Syros. The news caused a sensation in the West since it made Greece the first NATO country to grant the Soviet Mediterranean Fleet logistical support. The Greek government gave assurances that the deal was private, commercially motivated, and concerned only unarmed supply vessels. Still, when it emerged that the agreement made no clear mention of unarmed ships, the Greek Foreign Ministry announced that the contract was being renegotiated. In October Karamanlis visited Moscow (and later Budapest and Prague), where he signed an innocuous political document on cooperation and consultation and an agreement for economic and technical cooperation. The latter would be the basis for such joint ventures as the building of an alumina plant in Greece by the Soviets and for the sale to Greece of Soviet electricity, natural gas, and larger quantities of crude oil.

Repeated bilateral diplomatic encounters achieved little progress toward a settlement of disputes with Turkey. The main difficulty was Turkey's decision to block the resumption of Greece's full role in NATO. The failure to make progress in solving the Cyprus question, as well as the inherent weaknesses and subsequent fall of the government of Prime Minister Bulent Ecevit in Turkey, also impeded any rapprochement.

GREECE

Education. (1976–77) Primary, pupils 938,597, teachers 32,665; secondary, pupils 562,695, teachers 21,797; vocational, pupils 131,521; higher, students 122,833, teaching staff 6,521.

Finance. Monetary unit: drachma, with (Sept. 17, 1979) a free rate of 37.42 drachmas to U.S. $1 (80.52 drachmas = £1 sterling.) Gold, SDR's, and foreign exchange (June 1979) U.S. $1,089,000,000. Budget (1978 actual): revenue 243,150,000,000 drachmas; expenditure 286,340,000,000 drachmas. Gross national product (1978) 1,182,300,-000,000 drachmas. Money supply (Feb. 1979) 200.6 billion drachmas. Cost of living (1975 = 100; June 1979) 168.9.

Foreign Trade. (1978) Imports 280,310,000,000 drachmas; exports 123,730,000,000 drachmas. Import sources: EEC 44% (West Germany 16%, Italy 10%, France 6%, U.K. 6%); Japan 13%; Saudi Arabia 5%. Export destinations: EEC 51% (West Germany 21%, Italy 11%, France 7%, The Netherlands 5%); Saudi Arabia 6%. Main exports: fruit and vegetables 18%; textile yarns and fabrics 10%; petroleum products 9%; clothing 7%; tobacco 6%; iron and steel 6%; cement 5%; nonferrous metals 5%. Tourism (1977): visitors 3,961,000; gross receipts U.S. $981 million.

Transport and Communications. Roads (1977) 36,812 km (including 91 km expressways). Motor vehicles in use (1977): passenger 618,600; commercial 261,200. Railways (1977): 2,479 km; traffic 1,622,000,000 passenger-km, freight 856 million net ton-km. Air traffic (1978): 4,630,000,000 passenger-km; freight 60,440,000 net ton-km. Shipping (1978): merchant vessels 100 gross tons and over 3,666; gross tonnage 33,956,093. Telephones (Jan. 1978) 2,319,800. Radio receivers (Dec. 1976) 2,750,000. Television receivers (Dec. 1976) 1,160,000.

Agriculture. Production (in 000; metric tons; 1978): wheat *c.* 2,660; barley *c.* 956; oats *c.* 101; corn *c.* 537; rice *c.* 92; potatoes *c.* 944; sugar, raw value (1977) *c.* 271; tomatoes *c.* 1,751; onions *c.* 127; watermelons (1977) *c.* 600; apples *c.* 174; oranges *c.* 600; lemons *c.* 169; peaches (1977) *c.* 346; olives *c.* 1,470; olive oil 262; wine *c.* 435; raisins *c.* 150; tobacco 113; cotton, lint 138. Livestock (in 000; Dec. 1977): sheep *c.* 8,004; cattle (1976) 1,116; goats *c.* 4,489; pigs (1976) 819; horses (1976) 149; asses (1976) 279; chickens 31,517.

Industry. Production (in 000; metric tons; 1978): lignite 22,367; electricity (kw-hr) 19,460,000; petroleum products (1977) 10,465; iron ore (43% metal content) 1,707; bauxite 2,640; aluminum 146; magnesite (1977) 1,363; cement 11,-439; sulfuric acid 1,111; fertilizers (1977–78) nitrogenous 278, phosphate 180; cotton yarn 100. Merchant vessels launched (100 gross tons and over; 1978) 25,000 gross tons.

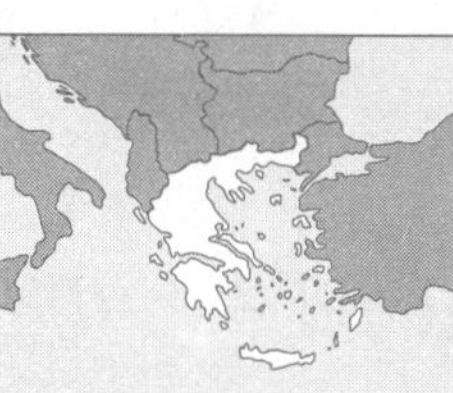

Greece

Great Britain:
see United Kingdom

WIDE WORLD

The first of nearly 1,500 women inducted into the Greek Army reported to training camp in January.

In November Karamanlis visited China, while official visits by Greek ministers to Arab capitals (Karamanlis himself went to Saudi Arabia and Syria in February) resulted in interstate deals that secured the bulk of Greece's crude oil requirements for 1980. Karamanlis visited the presidents of Yugoslavia and Romania on March 16–18. On April 29 he received the president of Bulgaria in Corfu and induced him to lift his objections to the resumption of efforts for multilateral Balkan cooperation. As a result, experts from five Balkan states (Albania abstained) met in Ankara, Turkey, in November to discuss regional cooperation in communications and telecommunications.

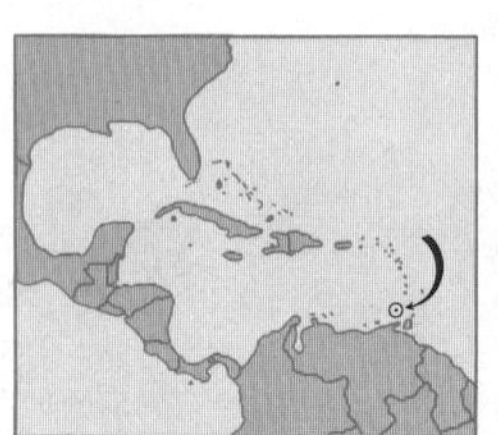

Grenada

On the home front, the government's stringent economy measures, aimed at dealing with the energy crisis and restraining excessive consumerism and waste, did not halt inflation. The cost of living soared between 22 and 25% in 1979. These developments incited labour unrest, while the continuing dearth of productive private investment checked the rate of growth and threatened unemployment. The formation of a right-wing Progressive Party by Spyros Markezinis, prime minister under the former military junta, was announced in November.

A government decision to send a selection of Greek antiquities abroad on loan to museums, in exchange for other art treasures to be shown in Greece, provoked angry reactions, especially in Crete where people massed outside the museum of Herakleion on February 28 and set up barricades. The crisis reached explosive proportions, but an eruption was averted when Karamanlis ordered the Herakleion exhibits to be omitted from the first shipment to the Louvre. The 1979 Nobel Prize for Literature was awarded to Odysseus Elytis (*see* NOBEL PRIZES), the second Greek poet (after the late George Seferis in 1963) to be so honoured.

Relations between the state and the Orthodox Church of Greece were strained by the government's decision to establish diplomatic relations with the Holy See (July 14), which the Orthodox prelates opposed. Also, some bishops refused to enforce a new law passed by Parliament in February granting divorce to couples separated for more than six years. Another source of contention was the government's plan to introduce civil marriage in Greece, where only religious marriage had been valid. (MARIO MODIANO)

Grenada

A parliamentary state within the Commonwealth of Nations, Grenada, with its dependency, the Southern Grenadines, is the southernmost of the Windward Islands of the Caribbean Sea, 161 km N of Trinidad. Area: 344 sq km (133 sq mi). Pop. (1978 est.): 111,200, including Negro 53%, mixed 42%, white 1%, and other 4%. Cap.: Saint George's (pop., 1974 est., 6,600). Language: English. Religion: Christian. Queen, Elizabeth II; governor-general in 1979, Sir Paul Scoon; prime ministers, Sir Eric Gairy and, from March 13, Maurice Bishop.

The Commonwealth Caribbean's first full-scale coup took place on March 13, 1979, when members

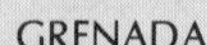

GRENADA

Education. (1971–72) Primary, pupils (1972–73) 28,745, teachers 884; secondary, pupils (1972–73) 4,773, teachers 182; vocational, pupils 497, teachers 10; teacher training, students 101, teachers 6.

Finance and Trade. Monetary unit: East Caribbean dollar, with (Sept. 17, 1979) a par value of ECar$2.70 to U.S. $1 (free rate of ECar$5.81 = £1 sterling). Budget (1978 est.) balanced at ECar$75 million. Foreign trade (1978): imports ECar$95.8 million; exports ECar$45.7 million. Import sources (1973): U.K. 27%; Trinidad and Tobago 20%; U.S. 9%; Canada 8%. Export destinations (1973): U.K. 33%; West Germany 19%; The Netherlands and possessions 14%; U.S. 8%; Belgium-Luxembourg 5%. Main exports (1977): nutmeg 34%; cocoa 23%; bananas 22%; fish 16%. Tourism (1977): visitors 28,500 (excludes 108,500 excursionists); gross receipts (1976) *c.* U.S. $15 million.

of the opposition New Jewel Movement, led by Maurice Bishop (*see* BIOGRAPHIES), seized power. The takeover, which occurred when Prime Minister Sir Eric Gairy was away from the island, was nearly bloodless and had widespread support.

Other Caribbean states and major powers with interests in the area hesitated to recognize the new regime, for fear of encouraging further coups within the region. Eventually Jamaica, Guyana, and Barbados recognized the new People's Revolutionary Government (PRG). Britain, the U.S., Canada, and other Western nations followed. Cuba, which established diplomatic relations in April, supplied arms to counter a possible mercenary invasion mounted by Gairy, together with substantial medical and other assistance under a two-year agreement.

Grenada's delegates to the Commonwealth heads of government conference in Lusaka, Zambia, and to the Havana summit of the nonaligned movement, which Grenada joined, played a significant part in behind-the-scenes discussions. The PRG revealed that no statistics or records had been kept by the previous administration, that many international loans had "disappeared," and that the economy was in ruins. In October, 20 people were arrested on charges of plotting to murder Prime Minister Bishop. (DAVID A. JESSOP)

Guatemala

A republic of Central America, Guatemala is bounded by Mexico, Belize, Honduras, El Salvador, the Caribbean Sea, and the Pacific Ocean. Area: 108,889 sq km (42,042 sq mi). Pop. (1979 est.): 6,835,900. Cap. and largest city: Guatemala City (pop., 1978 est., 814,800). Language: Spanish, with some Indian dialects. Religion: predominantly Roman Catholic. President in 1979, Fernando Romeo Lucas García.

Guatemala

After Pres. Fernando Lucas García took office in Guatemala in July 1978, there was an official move toward more political liberalization, with recognition of several new parties, but there also was a great increase in political violence, with deaths estimated as high as 2,000 in the first half of 1979. Several notable personalities were assassinated, including Alberto Fuentes Mohr, former minister for finance and for foreign affairs, in January and Manuel Colom Argueta, a former mayor of Guatemala City, in March, both seemingly by right-wing factions. In June, in apparent retaliation from the left, Gen. David Cancinos Barrios, the army chief of staff, was assassinated. Labour unrest also increased as higher oil prices resulted in a rise in the cost of living, and there was violence against several prominent trade union leaders. In foreign affairs Guatemala still laid claim to Belize, which effectively prevented the British colony from gaining its independence.

The economy showed a satisfactory growth rate of 5.2% in 1978, although it slowed down from the 8% registered in 1977 as coffee prices fell from the high levels of previous years. The government's 1979–82 four-year plan emphasized agricultural, industrial, and infrastructure projects, and the industrial sector was expected to play a major role in future growth. However, the 1979 growth rate was forecast as declining to between 3 and 4%, and inflation was causing problems as oil prices continued to rise. (CHRISTINE MELLOR)

GUATEMALA

Education. (1977) Primary, pupils 792,843, teachers (1975) 18,475; secondary, vocational, and teacher training, pupils 137,370, teachers 6,237; higher (University of San Carlos only; 1975), students 22,881; teaching staff 1,411.

Finance. Monetary unit: quetzal, at par with the U.S. dollar (free rate, at Sept. 17, 1979, of 2.15 quetzales to £1 sterling). Gold, SDR's, and foreign exchange (June 1979) U.S. $782 million. Budget (1978 actual): revenue 735 million quetzales; expenditure 728 million quetzales. Gross national product (1977) 5,529,000,000 quetzales. Money supply (June 1979) 790 million quetzales. Cost of living (1975 = 100; June 1979) 147.8.

Foreign Trade. (1977) Imports 1,083,500,000 quetzales; exports 1,182,100,000 quetzales. Import sources: U.S. 39%; Japan 11%; West Germany 7%; Venezuela 6%. Export destinations: U.S. 32%; West Germany 13%; El Salvador 9%; Japan 8%; The Netherlands 6%. Main exports: coffee 45%; cotton 13%; sugar 7%; chemicals *c.* 7%.

Transport and Communications. Roads (1977) 17,139 km (including 824 km of Pan-American Highway). Motor vehicles in use (1976): passenger 82,700; commercial (including buses) 50,100. Railways: (1977) 1,828 km; freight traffic (1976) 117 million net ton-km. Air traffic (1978): 153 million passenger-km; freight 7.1 million net ton-km. Telephones (Jan. 1978) 70,600. Radio licenses (Dec. 1978) *c.* 280,000. Television receivers (Dec. 1978) *c.* 150,000.

Agriculture. Production (in 000; metric tons; 1978): corn 760; sugar, raw value *c.* 410; tomatoes *c.* 76; dry beans *c.* 80; bananas *c.* 566; coffee 139; cotton, lint *c.* 133; tobacco 10. Livestock (in 000; 1977): sheep 612; cattle *c.* 2,220; pigs 667; chickens 11,239.

Industry. Production (in 000; metric tons; 1977): cement 491; petroleum products *c.* 720; electricity (kw-hr) 1,291,000.

Guinea

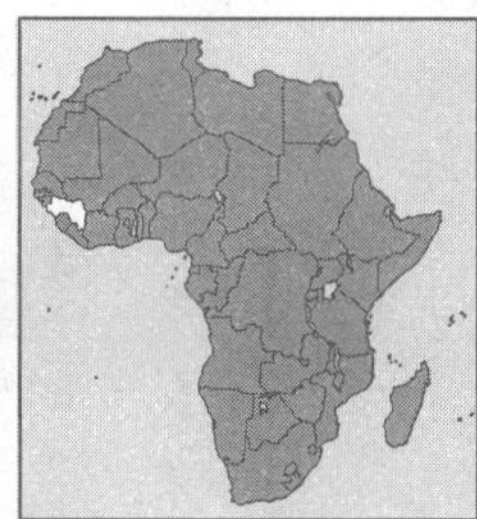
Guinea

A republic on the west coast of Africa, Guinea is bounded by Guinea-Bissau, Senegal, Mali, Ivory Coast, Liberia, and Sierra Leone. Area: 245,857 sq km (94,926 sq mi). Pop. (1979 UN est.): 4,887,000. Cap. and largest city: Conakry (pop., 1974, 412,000). Language: French (official). Religion: mostly Muslim. President in 1979, Ahmed Sékou Touré; premier, Louis Lansana Beavogui.

Guinea's long period of diplomatic isolation having ended in 1978, Pres. Ahmed Sékou Touré paid several visits abroad in 1979 – to Morocco in January, Ivory Coast in February, Yugoslavia in July, the U.S. in August, and Senegal in October.

GUINEA

Education. (1971–72) Primary, pupils 169,132, teachers 4,698; secondary, pupils 68,410, teachers (1970–71) 2,360; vocational (1970–71), pupils 2,013, teachers 150; teacher training (1970–71), students 1,478, teachers 275; higher (1970–71), students 1,974, teachers (1965–66) 95.

Finance. Monetary unit: syli, with (Sept. 17, 1979) a free rate of 18.94 sylis to U.S. $1 (40.74 sylis = £1 sterling). Budget (1976–77 est.): revenue 5,283,000,000 sylis; expenditure 3,904,000,000 sylis (excludes capital expenditure of 3,089,000,000 sylis).

Foreign Trade. (1977) Imports *c.* 6.6 billion sylis; exports *c.* 6,630,000,000 sylis. Import sources: France *c.* 20%; U.S.S.R. *c.* 11%; U.S. *c.* 6%; Italy *c.* 6%. Export destinations: U.S. *c.* 18%; France *c.* 13%; West Germany *c.* 12%; U.S.S.R. *c.* 12%; Spain *c.* 12%; Canada *c.* 7%; Italy *c.* 7%. Main exports (1975–76): bauxite *c.* 57%; alumina *c.* 31%.

Greek Orthodox Church:
see Religion

Greenland:
see Dependent States

Guiana:
see Dependent States; Guyana; Suriname

Premier Raymond Barre of France received Louis Lansana Beavogui, the Guinean premier, in Paris in June as a preliminary to Sékou Touré's expected visit to France later.

Before Sékou Touré was received by Pres. Jimmy Carter in Washington, D.C., he freed Msgr. Raymond Marie Tchidimbo, archbishop of Conakry, imprisoned for over eight years for "plotting." Amnesty International claimed that Guinea's dictator held several thousand political prisoners in detention. The Guinean opposition abroad asserted that exiles who had returned to Guinea under amnesty had been arrested.

In April the president's half brother Ismael Touré, minister of economy and finance, was accused of factional activities and dropped from the Cabinet and the ruling party political bureau, but in June he was back again as minister of geology and mines. Under a nonaggression and mutual defense treaty concluded between Guinea and Liberia on Jan. 23, 1979, some hundred Guinean soldiers intervened in Liberia in April to help Pres. William Tolbert reestablish control after serious rioting in Monrovia. (PHILIPPE DECRAENE)

Guinea-Bissau

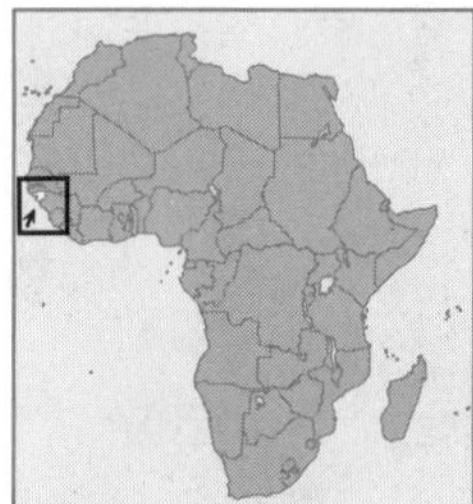

Guinea-Bissau

An independent African republic, Guinea-Bissau has an Atlantic coastline on the west and borders Senegal on the north and Guinea on the east and south. Area: 36,125 sq km (13,948 sq mi). Pop. (1979) 777,200. Cap. and largest city: Bissau (metro. area pop., 1979, 109,500). President in 1979, Luis de Almeida Cabral; premier, João Bernardo Vieira.

In February 1979 Pres. António Eanes of Portugal visited Guinea-Bissau and was warmly received by Pres. Luis Cabral. This was the first visit by a Portuguese head of state to a former colony and was part of Portugal's attempt to reestablish ties with its former dependencies. As far as Guinea-Bissau was concerned, the effort was meeting with considerable success. Although Guinea-Bissau was accepting aid from a number of countries, it had agreements with Portugal covering almost every aspect of the country's cultural and economic development. Portuguese far outnumbered all other foreign-aid workers in Guinea-Bissau and, while financial assistance from the UN Development Program and Sweden contributed to the building of schools and the provision of books and equipment, Portugal provided the teachers. Similarly, a new high school underwritten by The Netherlands was designed by a Portuguese architect and built by a Portuguese contractor.

Militant women of Guinea-Bissau and Cape Verde held their first national assembly in Bissau in June to campaign against early and forced marriages and the practice of female circumcision. They also demanded "real conditions for children's security." Committees were set up to study how to combat such evils as prostitution and alcoholism. (KENNETH INGHAM)

See also Cape Verde.

GUINEA-BISSAU

Education. (1977–78) Primary, pupils 93,256, teachers 2,620; secondary, pupils 4,612; vocational, pupils 76; teacher training, students 284; secondary, vocational, and teacher training, teachers 540.

Finance and Trade. Monetary unit: Guinea-Bissau peso, with (Sept. 17, 1979) a free rate of 33.74 pesos to U.S. $1 (72.60 pesos = £1 sterling). Budget (1976 est.): revenue 463 million pesos; expenditure 907 million pesos. Foreign trade (1977): imports 1,235,000,000 pesos; exports 428 million pesos. Import sources: Portugal 40%; Sweden 8%; U.S.S.R. 8%; France 7%. Export destinations: Portugal 59%; Egypt 18%; Senegal 11%. Main exports: peanuts 60%; fish 19%; copra 12%.

Agriculture. Production (in 000; metric tons; 1977): rice *c.* 40; plantains *c.* 23; peanuts *c.* 30; palm kernels *c.* 7; palm oil *c.* 5; copra *c.* 5; timber (cu m) *c.* 530. Livestock (in 000; 1977): cattle *c.* 260; pigs *c.* 172; sheep *c.* 71; goats *c.* 181.

Guyana

Guyana

A republic and member of the Commonwealth of Nations, Guyana is situated between Venezuela, Brazil, and Suriname on the Atlantic Ocean. Area: 215,000 sq km (83,000 sq mi). Pop. (1979 est.): 865,000, including (1970) East Indian 51.8%; African 31.2%; mixed 10.3%; Amerindian 4.9%. Cap. and largest city: Georgetown (pop., 1970, 63,200). Language: English (official). Religion (1970): Hindu 37%; Protestant 32%; Roman Catholic 13%. President in 1979, Arthur Chung; prime minister, Forbes Burnham.

The attempts of the ruling People's National Congress (PNC) to implement still greater austerity in 1979 led to considerable political unrest. In July bauxite workers struck for five weeks, engendering other sympathy strikes. After violent confrontations with the police and the murder of Bernard Darke, a Jesuit priest and journalist, some strikers' demands were met. Education Minister Vincent Teekah was murdered in October. The University of Guyana was closed for a term, and there was a reshuffle in the security forces.

The life of Parliament was again extended by 12 months, to October 1980. Opposition groups suggested that the Constituent Assembly, established to prepare a new constitution, was not proceeding with urgency. A new political coalition, the Work-

GUYANA

Education. (1975–76) Primary and secondary, pupils 196,269, teachers 7,144; technical, pupils 2,956, teachers 126; teacher training, pupils 640, teachers 89; higher, students 1,752, teaching staff 157.

Finance. Monetary unit: Guyanan dollar, with (Sept. 17, 1979) a par value of Guy$2.55 to U.S. $1 (free rate of Guy$5.49 = £1 sterling). Budget (1976 est.): revenue Guy$446 million; expenditure Guy$605 million.

Foreign Trade. (1978) Imports Guy$710 million; exports Guy$753.8 million. Import sources (1977): U.S. 27%; Trinidad and Tobago 23%; U.K. 21%. Export destinations (1977): U.K. 33%; U.S. 18%; Trinidad and Tobago 6%; Norway 6%; Jamaica 6%; Canada 5%. Main exports (1977): bauxite 38%; sugar 28%; alumina 11%; rice 10%.

Agriculture. Production (in 000; metric tons; 1978): rice *c.* 300; sugar, raw value *c.* 342; bananas and plantains *c.* 19; oranges (1977) *c.* 11; copra *c.* 3. Livestock (in 000; 1977): cattle *c.* 290; sheep *c.* 116; goats *c.* 64; pigs *c.* 131; chickens *c.* 10,800.

Industry. Production (in 000; 1977): bauxite (metric tons) 3,223; alumina (metric tons; 1976) 247; diamonds (metric carats) *c.* 40; electricity (kw-hr) *c.* 416,000.

ing People's Alliance, emerged. The economy remained in a parlous state, with low prices for Guyana's bauxite, alumina, and sugar. The International Monetary Fund made a fresh Guy$206,450,000 three-year loan.

Prime Minister Forbes Burnham met Suriname's Prime Minister Henck Arron in Barbados in April to resolve the border dispute. The issue was deferred, but further discussions were begun later.

(DAVID A. JESSOP)

Gymnastics and Weight Lifting

Gymnastics. A new generation of gymnasts competed in the 1979 world gymnastics championships at Fort Worth, Texas, Dec. 2–9, 1979. The new all-around combination champions were Nelli Kim and Aleksandr Ditiatin, both of the U.S.S.R. The bid of Romania's Nadia Comaneci for the gold medal in the women's all-around competition was thwarted when she was hospitalized with an infected wrist.

In the team competition the Soviet men's team supplanted long-reigning Japan, and the Romanian women scored a remarkable upset by dethroning the U.S.S.R. The U.S. men's team won the bronze medal, the first such medal ever gained by the U.S. in world gymnastics championships. The U.S. women's team finished sixth following a series of injuries, illnesses, and form reversals. It had been expected that the U.S. women would challenge for the first three places.

The Soviet Union continued its supremacy in the sport by accounting for 17 out of a total of 43 medals available, of which 5 were gold. Eastern Europe as a whole won 33 medals, of which 11 were gold. China won its first gold medal ever when Ma Yanhong tied East Germany's Maxi Gnauck for the women's uneven parallel bars title.

The U.S. won three gold medals in the individual exercises. Kurt Thomas (*see* BIOGRAPHIES) retained his title in the floor exercise by tying with East Germany's Roland Bruckner and won the horizontal bar competition outright. Bart Conner won the other U.S. gold medal by nosing out Thomas on the parallel bars. Thomas, second in the men's all-around combination, also was silver medalist in the individual pommel horse. The final medal for the U.S. was earned by Conner when he tied for third in the vault.

Although Comaneci was expected to be a strong contender for top honours in the 1980 Olympic Games and to repeat her 1976 triumphs, an era ended in the men's world championships when the former world and Olympic champion, Nikolai Andrianov of the U.S.S.R., won only one silver medal, in the vault. Thomas and Ditiatin were the outstanding men. The latter won the rings and the vault and placed third in the horizontal bar. Among the women Emillia Eberle led the Romanian team to the title and also was the gold medalist in the floor exercise, winning by 0.005 point over Kim. Eberle also placed third on the uneven parallel bars. The surprise victor in the balance beam competition was Verna Cerna of Czechoslovakia, with a slight margin over Kim.

The distribution of the medals was wide. In the women's competition ten different gymnasts shared in the medals as four countries won the five gold medals, none of which went to the U.S.S.R. Romania, the team champion, had two individual winners in Eberle in the floor exercise and Dumitrita Turner in the vault. For the U.S. Christa Canary was fifth in the vault, Suzy Kellems eighth in the vault, defending champion Marcia Frederick seventh in the uneven parallel bars, and Leslie Pyfer eighth in the floor exercise. Ten different men were among the 19 medalists in the six men's individual events. In addition to Thomas in the floor exercise the only other holdover champion was Hungary's Zoltan Magyar on the pommel horse, winner every year since 1973.

Weight Lifting. Because of internal problems in Iran the 1979 world weight lifting championships were transferred to Thessaloníki, Greece, and held November 3–11. The U.S.S.R. dominated the competition by capturing six world titles; all but one of the ten Soviet lifters placed in the top three.

The only world record for total lift was recorded

1979 World Weight Lifting Champions

Weight class	Winner, country	Performance
52 kg	[1] Kanybek Osmonaliev, U.S.S.R.	242.5 kg
56 kg	Anton Kodjabasev, Bulgaria	267.5 kg
60 kg	Marek Seweryn, Poland	282.5 kg
67.5 kg	[1] Yanko Russev, Bulgaria[2]	332.5 kg
75 kg	[1] Roberto Urrutia, Cuba	345 kg
82.5 kg	[1] Yuri Vardanian, U.S.S.R.	370 kg
90 kg	Gennadi Bessonov, U.S.S.R.	380 kg
100 kg	Pavel Sirchine, U.S.S.R.	385 kg
110 kg	Sergei Arakelov, U.S.S.R.	410 kg
110+ kg	Soultan Rachmanov, U.S.S.R.	430 kg

[1] Retained 1978 world title.
[2] World record for total lift.

WIDE WORLD

Nadia Comaneci, now a 17-year-old, became the first person ever to win the Women's European Gymnastic Championships three times in a row with a victory at Copenhagen in May.

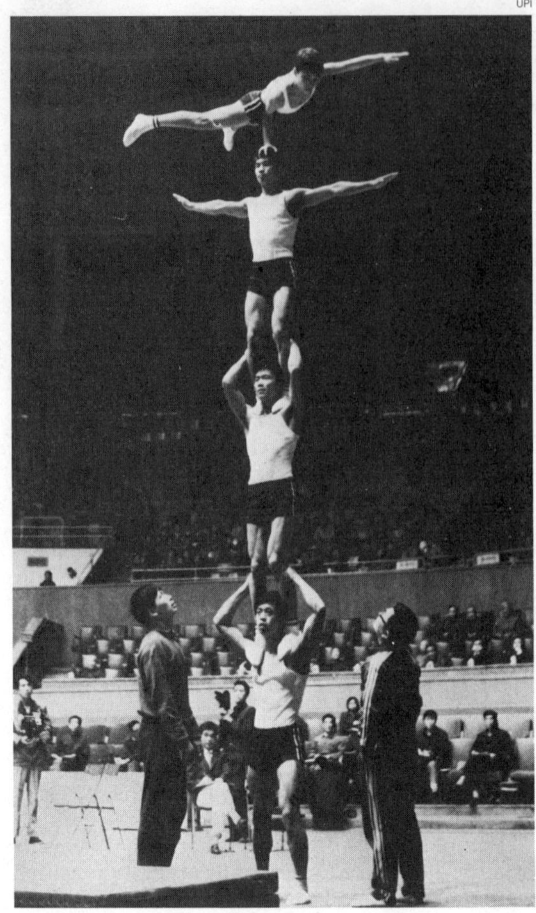

UPI

The Shanghai Acrobatic Gymnastic Team won the team title during the fourth Chinese Games in Beijing in September.

by defending champion Yanko Russev of Bulgaria in the 67.5-kg class, who broke his own record by pushing up the total from 325 kg (715 lb) to 332.5 kg (731.5 lb). He also set a new world mark for the clean and jerk of 187.5 kg (412.5 lb). In the 56-kg class Anton Kodjabasev, the other Bulgarian to win a world title in Greece, equaled the recognized world record of 267.5 kg (588.5 lb) for the total lift.

The Soviet athletes clearly dominated the competition, scoring 286 points in the team competition. They were followed by, in order, Bulgaria, East Germany, Poland, Cuba, and Hungary.

China continued to make progress in weight lifting and promised to challenge for Olympic medals in the lighter weights at Moscow in 1980. The highest finisher for the U.S. was Mark Cameron, sixth in the 100-kg class.

(CHARLES ROBERT PAUL, JR.)

[452.B.4.f]

Haiti

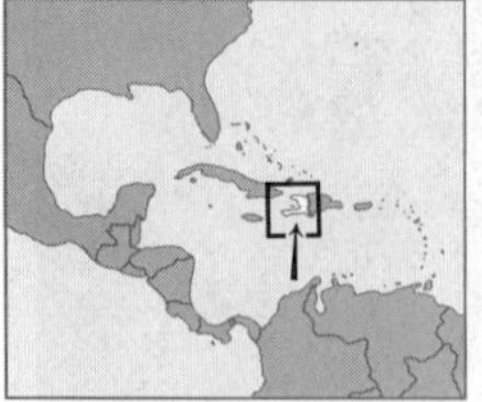

Haiti

The Republic of Haiti occupies the western one-third of the Caribbean island of Hispaniola, which it shares with the Dominican Republic. Area: 27,750 sq km (10,715 sq mi). Pop. (1979 est.): 4,919,700, of whom 95% are Negro. Cap. and largest city: Port-au-Prince (pop., 1978 est., 703,100). Language: French (official) and Creole. Religion: Roman Catholic; Voodooism practiced in rural areas. President in 1979, Jean-Claude Duvalier.

HAITI

Education. (1976–77) Primary, pupils 608,348, teachers 12,140; secondary, pupils 55,818, teachers 3,324; vocational (1975–76), pupils 5,356, teachers 474; higher, students 5,195, teaching staff 697.

Finance. Monetary unit: gourde, with (Sept. 17, 1979) a par value of 5 gourdes to U.S. $1 (free rate of 10.76 gourdes = £1 sterling). Gold, SDR's, and foreign exchange (Dec. 1978) U.S. $36 million. Budget (1977–78 est.) balanced at 387 million gourdes. Cost of living (Port-au-Prince; 1975 = 100; April 1979) 124.1.

Foreign Trade. (1977) Imports 1,127,000,000 gourdes; exports 746.5 million gourdes. Import sources (1976): U.S. 56%; Netherlands Antilles 7%; Canada 6%; Japan 6%. Export destinations (1976): U.S. 61%; France 10%; Italy 6%; Belgium-Luxembourg 5%. Main exports: coffee 45%; bauxite 12%.

Transport and Communications. Roads (1977) *c.* 4,000 km. Motor vehicles in use (1976): passenger 18,700; commercial (including buses) 2,400. Railways (1977) *c.* 250 km. Telephones (Jan. 1977) 17,800. Radio receivers (Dec. 1976) 95,000. Television receivers (Dec. 1976) 14,000.

Agriculture. Production (in 000; metric tons; 1978): rice *c.* 105; corn (1977) *c.* 250; sorghum *c.* 155; sweet potatoes (1977) *c.* 95; cassava (1977) *c.* 145; sugar, raw value (1977) *c.* 48; dry beans *c.* 46; bananas (1977) *c.* 51; plantains (1977) *c.* 198; mangoes *c.* 285; coffee *c.* 32; sisal *c.* 13. Livestock (in 000; 1977): cattle *c.* 755; pigs *c.* 1,800; goats *c.* 1,400; sheep *c.* 83; horses *c.* 392.

Industry. Production (in 000; metric tons; 1977): cement 266; bauxite (exports) 701; electricity (kw-hr) 215,000.

The main political event in Haiti during 1979 was the election for 58 members of the National Assembly, held—with much fraud—on February 11. All the seats were obtained by pro-government candidates except for one independent, Alexander Lerouge, who stood in Cap Haïtien.

Early in the year there were signs that four years of U.S. encouragement to permit some political liberalization was having effect. Three centrist political parties were formed, and two fielded candidates in the election. Journalists and writers formed trade unions, and plays were staged in Port-au-Prince indirectly criticizing the regime. By October, however, hard-liners surrounding the president's mother, Simone Duvalier, and the deputy defense and interior minister, Wéber Guerrier, had resumed full power. A meeting of some 6,000 human rights activists in Port-au-Prince on November 9 was disrupted by men believed to be government agents. In a Cabinet reshuffle four days later, 8 of the 14 members were replaced by military men and Duvalier loyalists.

Pres. Jean-Claude Duvalier, addressing 15,000 "national security volunteers" (successors to the notorious Tontons Macoutes) in September, stated they were the regime's basis and that Haiti rejected foreign political models. Some 200 arrests were reported, media censorship was tightened, and a new law licensed all journalists. Nonetheless, restoration by the U.S. Senate of $18.4 million in aid for 1979–80, previously canceled, eased pressure on the regime. The continuing outflow of Haitians escaping to The Bahamas and southern Florida, often in unseaworthy boats, received national attention in the U.S. in August when panicky smugglers forced their passengers into the sea off Palm Beach. A woman and five children died, and the two smugglers were charged with murder.

(ROBIN CHAPMAN)

Health and Disease

General Developments. The 31st Assembly of the World Health Organization (WHO) passed a resolution aimed at improving the supply of "essential" drugs to less developed countries. WHO produced a list of such drugs to encourage both manufacturers and importing nations to concentrate upon providing a cheap supply of medicines that had been shown to save lives and reduce suffering, rather than many costly products that have small effect on well-being.

The idea that the supply and use of drugs should be restrained was not directed only to the third world. In Great Britain a Royal Commission appointed to report on the workings of the country's National Health Service recommended that British doctors be encouraged to prescribe from a limited list of drugs proved to be useful or essential. The government rejected this suggestion, to the relief of the drug industry.

In 1978 and early 1979 more than 60 children under four years of age met unexplained deaths in Naples, Italy, sending the Italian government and an international team gathered by WHO on a search for what the local press was soon calling the "mystery disease." Although some of the earliest deaths had followed a government diphtheria-tetanus vaccination effort, in February 1979 WHO investigators concluded that the "disease" was really two or three separate problems. They found that the largest number of deaths, which had occurred from December to mid-February, had been caused by an unusually virulent outbreak of common winter respiratory diseases. Deaths between August and December, however, could not be so explained. In these the "commonest clinical presentation" was brain damage, and about one-quarter of the victims had received diphtheria-tetanus vaccinations just before their illnesses began. Although Naples's squalid and unsanitary living conditions had earned for it the epithet "the Calcutta of Europe," the investigators uncovered no evidence of malnourishment in the victims or of factors in their everyday environment that differed from those of the city as a whole.

In a report on the state of the nation's health the U.S. Public Health Service sought to shift the focus of health care to prevention and away from treatment. It stated that many of the degenerative diseases responsible for chronic illness are preventable. Simple measures to enhance the prospect of longer life include elimination of cigarette smoking; reduction of alcohol misuse; reduction in dietary calories, fat, salt, and sugar; moderate exercise; and periodic screening for such disorders as high blood pressure and certain cancers.

A new 1,200-page report by the U.S. surgeon general's office marshaled for the first time all the evidence to show overwhelmingly that cigarette smoking causes not only lung cancer but an array of other diseases, including heart disease and cancer of the mouth, larynx, and esophagus, and is associated with cancer of the bladder, kidney, and pancreas, as well as with peptic ulcers. Smoking

YALE UNIVERSITY SCHOOL OF MEDICINE, PHOTO BY WILLIAM CARTER

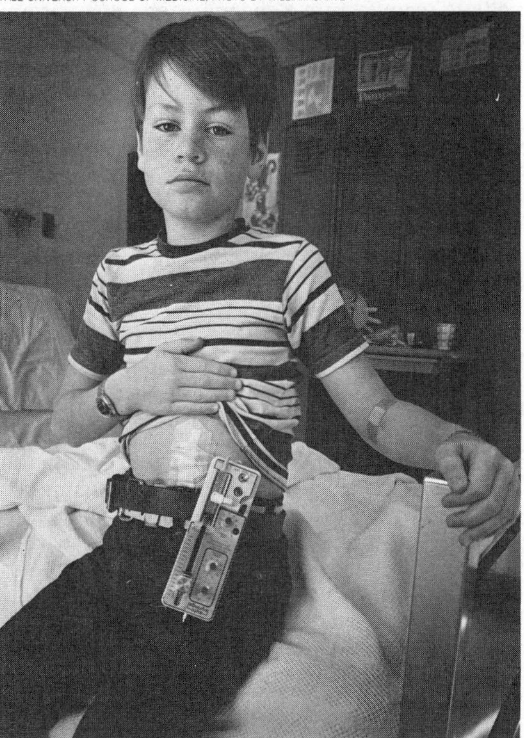

A small pump that continuously injects insulin into patients who have severe diabetes was being developed at Yale University School of Medicine.

had decreased markedly among men since the first report on smoking was issued in 1964, but it maintained the same level among adult women and rose sharply among girls. In 1979 three in ten American adults smoked, compared with four in ten in 1964. More blacks smoked than did whites and blue-collar workers smoked more than white-collar workers. Workers in such industries as asbestos, chemical, rubber, and uranium were at a much greater risk of developing lung cancer than nonsmokers. Six million Americans under the age of 20 smoked; 100,000 were 12 years old or younger.

In late 1978 Joseph Califano, secretary of the Department of Health, Education, and Welfare (HEW), announced that a new federal study had indicated that 20% of future cases of cancer in the U.S. were likely to result from exposure to carcinogens at work. Exposure to asbestos alone could cause two million premature deaths from cancer among U.S. citizens during the next 30 years.

Interest grew in the possible virtues of interferons as an effective approach to cancer therapy. Interferons are antiviral proteins secreted by cells infected by viruses. They were shown to restrict cell growth and to produce remissions in patients with bone cancer and with cancer of the cells of the bone marrow. Because interferons are natural substances with virtually no adverse side effects, there was at least some expectation that they could provide the basis for treating some forms of cancer.

There was growing support for the idea that "coronary deaths" usually result from the formation of a blood clot in one of the arteries supplying the heart muscle and that the best preventive measures against such a happening are those that reduce the blood's tendency to clot. It was known, for example, that aspirin reduces the clotting power of blood. It does so by reducing the ability of the

Handball
see Court Games

Harness Racing:
see Equestrian Sports

body to manufacture a chemical, one of a variety of powerful regulatory substances called prostaglandins, involved in the clotting mechanism. In August an advisory committee to the U.S. Food and Drug Administration (FDA) unanimously agreed that there was good evidence that four aspirin tablets per day constitute a safe and effective deterrent against strokes and heart attacks. Some medical investigators also believed that, like aspirin, the diet may have an important effect upon the manufacture within the body of prostaglandins involved in the blood clotting mechanism. It appeared that certain so-called essential fatty acids are necessary for the production of a prostaglandin that induces clotting, and other fatty acids are needed for the synthesis of a prostaglandin that "dissolves" clots. Hence, a proper balance of the two kinds of fatty acids in the diet reduces both the risk of dangerous bleeding and an undue tendency for clots to form inside vessels.

The Center for Disease Control (CDC) in Atlanta, Ga., found no evidence of any increase in the incidence of birth defects in babies conceived while their mothers were wearing intrauterine contraceptives. It also reported that the death rate from legal abortions was declining because women were requesting abortions earlier in their pregnancies. An Ethics Advisory Board set up to assist HEW recommended that basic research in laboratory fertilization and implantation of human embryos is ethically acceptable if the goal is to produce children for infertile married couples.

Measles could be eliminated from the U.S. by 1982 because of widespread immunization, said Surgeon General Julius Richmond. Of 46 states surveyed in the fall of 1978, 29 reported that at least 90% of children entering school for the first time had received measles vaccine. In 1978, 26,795 cases were reported, a decline of 53% from the previous year. In the first 26 weeks of 1979, only 10,686 cases were reported, an all-time low.

The CDC stated that U.S. physicians were administering smallpox vaccinations needlessly, with many patients suffering reactions. About 2.5 million doses of vaccine were used in the nation in 1978 even though there had not been a case in the U.S. since 1949 or in the world since 1977. Routine smallpox vaccination was discontinued in children in 1971, and vaccination was no longer required of any traveler entering the country. In late October WHO officially declared the world free of smallpox and announced that it would advise its member nations to cease vaccinating for the disease and to drop requirements for travelers' vaccination certificates.

Rabies continued to spread in Europe, with newly infected areas being confirmed in Italy, Denmark, Austria, Switzerland, France, and Czechoslovakia. Foxes remained the principal animal vectors of the disease. The infection also spread inland from the borders of Rhodesia, probably as a result of the disruption of the dog vaccination program caused by the war. Twelve human cases were seen in 1977–78, compared with an average incidence of less than two a year during the previous quarter century. In the U.S. an Idaho woman died of rabies seven weeks after receiving a corneal transplant, and investigations revealed that the infection had been carried by the transplant. This incident not only demonstrated a unique mode of transmission of the disease but also supported the idea that humans can be infected with rabies virus without becoming ill, since the donor of the transplant clearly had not shown signs of an overt rabies infection.

In Great Britain a new program of heart transplants was launched at Papworth Hospital near Cambridge in January when a 44-year-old man received a heart graft from a traffic accident victim. Unfortunately the recipient failed to recover from anesthesia and died shortly after the operation for reasons not specific to the procedure. Another heart transplant was undertaken some six months later, and the patient was still alive and well in early autumn. It was announced that efforts would be made to raise money in order to ensure that the U.K. could suppport a "centre of excellence" for the performance of such surgery. Some critics, however, felt the money might be better spent in discovering and eliminating the causes of heart disease. (*See* PHYSICS.)

Regulation and Legal Matters. As was becoming customary, the British Parliament was asked to consider a bill that would greatly reduce the number of abortions performed legally in the U.K. This particular piece of legislation, which was not a government measure but the proposition of a private member, sought to hamstring the activities of the country's various charities, which handle about half of all British abortions. Although intended as an attempt to curb abuses of the present abortion law, it was, in fact, only an incident in the continuing struggle between pro- and anti-abortionist groups. In the U.S. both houses of Congress reached agreement on a bill that would permit federally financed abortions when the mother's life is endangered by pregnancy and in cases of rape or incest.

During the course of the year the British Medical Association (BMA) waged a running battle with the government concerning a proposed "child health computing scheme." The idea was to record every birth on a machine that would then produce, at appropriate times, memoranda regarding immunizations and similar routine procedures. The central records would also note significant facts concerning the health of the children on file for the purpose of ensuring their adequate medical care. The BMA was concerned that such a system would destroy traditional doctor-patient confidentiality. Cynical observers of the dispute suggested that doctors were only fearful that their own performances would be monitored by relentlessly efficient, government-owned electronic "auditors." In a similar vein the BMA and Britain's Royal College of Nursing objected to police requests that doctors and nurses keep alert for "wanted" persons and otherwise use their special knowledge of individuals and the community to assist the police. These disputes typified the growing conflict between the duty of medical personnel to their patients and their duty to the state, upon which in many nations they were becoming increasingly dependent for their training and income.

For almost a decade many attempts had been made, particularly in the U.S. and the U.K., to use the power of the law to restrain the activities of molecular biologists in their experiments with genes because of a somewhat vague, yet powerful feeling that "genetic engineering" makes a reality of the old fiction of the "mad scientist" brewing up techniques capable of changing the nature of life. During the year a fascinating reaction to this attitude ensued, with many authorities throughout the world stating their views that controls should not be applied and that attempts to restrict research were ill advised.

In December 1978 HEW published a new set of guidelines, effective at the start of 1979, that lifted or downgraded previously imposed restrictions on most categories of genetic engineering research. Secretary Califano said that the relaxation of controls was "the result of decreased concern in the scientific community about the potential hazard of the research." In Great Britain the Genetic Manipulation Advisory Group stated that "the possible hazards have been grossly overstated and that the term *genetic manipulation* has a high emotive content." In April a major international gathering, partly organized by the Royal Society of London, decided that regulations governing genetic engineering research should be substantially relaxed, if not abolished altogether. One possible explanation for this change in attitude was the fact that genetic engineering was experiencing growing commercial importance. It appeared likely that bacterial genes could be so manipulated that large-scale cultures of microorganisms would become economical biological factories for the production of insulin and other invaluable molecules.

The American Medical Association (AMA) withdrew the label "unscientific cult" from chiropractic, a system of healing involving spinal manipulation. The action came after chiropractors in New Jersey and Chicago filed antitrust suits charging organized medicine with conspiracy to drive chiropractors out of business. A third suit was filed by the attorney general of New York. In rescinding its 1966 statement on chiropractic, the AMA also ended its policy of branding as "unethical" any professional association of physicians with chiropractors. It stopped short of endorsing chiropractic, however, and said that it would continue to warn the public against entrusting diagnosis and treatment to "practitioners who rely upon the theory that all diseases are caused by misalignment of spinal vertebrae." The American Osteopathic Association also took steps to remove itself from antitrust vulnerability by ending a 15-year-old prohibition on its 18,000 members from joining the AMA if they so chose.

A report by a committee of the U.S. National Academy of Sciences concluded that saccharin is a potential human carcinogen of probable low efficacy but did not endorse the FDA's recommendation that the artificial sweetener be banned. The report urged a revision of food safety laws to give the FDA a flexible policy which would replace the present requirement that food or cosmetic additives causing cancer in man or animals be eliminated.

In the first lawsuit to be won by a plaintiff claiming harm from the hormone diethylstilbestrol (DES), a six-member jury in New York City awarded $500,000 to a 25-year-old woman who developed vaginal cancer, allegedly because she was exposed while in the womb to DES, which was given to her mother to prevent miscarriage. The entire pharmaceutical industry was held liable.

Although no conclusive evidence existed that exposure to low levels of radiation constituted a health hazard, after comprehensive review an HEW health task force reported that the incidence of leukemia produced by such radiation as received in medical and dental X-rays could be higher than formerly believed. Consequently HEW ordered new guidelines for common X-ray procedures and for certification of X-ray machines and of technicians in nuclear medicine and radiation therapy. About 50% of low-level radiation comes from man-made sources, of which 90% is from dental and medical X-rays and use of radioactive materials in diagnosis and treatment.

After almost two years of study HEW decided against reclassifying marijuana to permit its medical use, stating that the drug could lead to psychological or physical dependence. As of 1979 several states had approved marijuana for research on glaucoma or cancer patients. HEW had been under a federal appeals court order to give scientific consideration to reclassification. The Supreme Court upheld the agency's decision.

Economic Aspects. The 96th Congress failed to follow predictions that 1979 would be the year for enactment of a national health insurance program in the U.S. Ten health insurance proposals

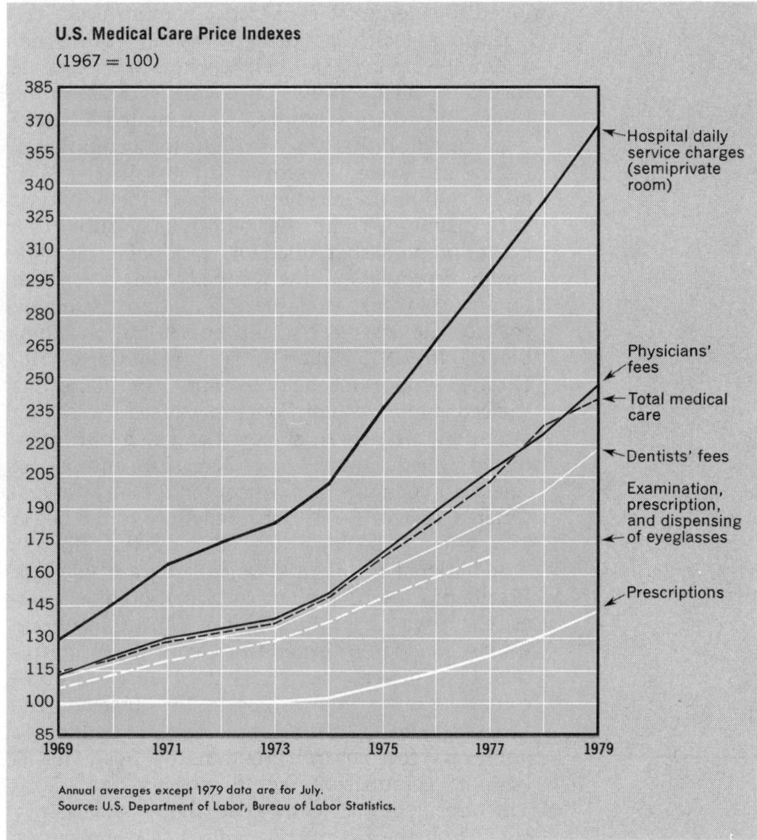

ZIMMER U.S.A., INC.

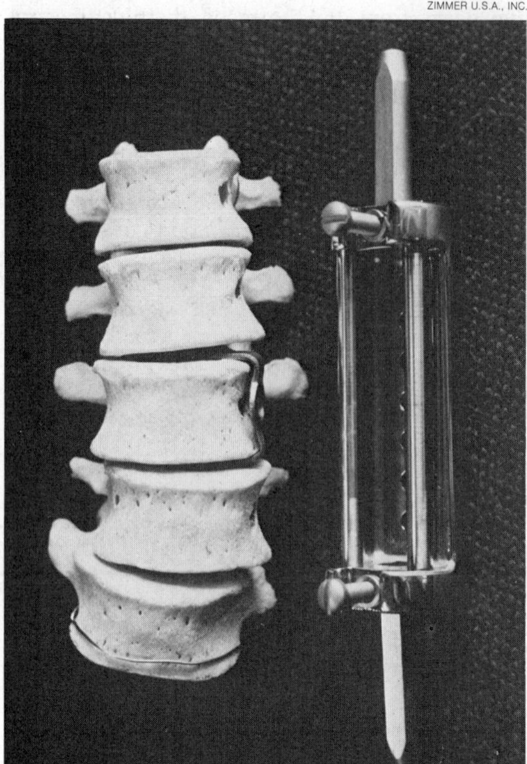

Orthopedist Charles C. Edwards designed this metal device to replace several vertebrae that had to be removed from the spine of a cancer patient. The spinal cord passes through the device and is protected by it.

were introduced in Congress, ranging from simple tax-deductible allowances to two comprehensive measures sponsored by Pres. Jimmy Carter and Sen. Edward M. Kennedy (Dem., Mass.). Both failed to emerge from reference committees.

Carter's HealthCare proposal would require that all employers provide their workers with private insurance plus a provision covering catastrophic illness. Kennedy's proposal represented a sharp departure from his ten-year fight for a completely federalized system resembling those in the U.K. and Scandinavia. His new approach included private insurance companies as carriers. Unlike the Carter proposal that called for a gradual implementation of provisions, the Kennedy measure called for a total package effective on adoption. Estimated cost for the first year would be $30 billion, compared with a $15 billion outlay for the Carter bill. Divided support for the two competitive plans plus the economic mood of Congress caused increasing attention to be given at year's end to a bill introduced by Sen. Russell Long (Dem., La.) and calling solely for coverage of catastrophic illness at an estimated cost of $4 billion. Benefits would begin after a family outlay of $2,000 in doctor bills.

A national health insurance program was not President Carter's top health priority. His strongest effort was made in behalf of a bill that would impose mandatory expenditure controls on hospitals, but this was rejected by the House of Representatives by a vote of 234 to 166. Instead, the House adopted a substitute measure that endorsed voluntary cost control programs by hospitals. A national commission would monitor the effort. The president had contended that a mandatory control on the rate of hospital costs was basic to any national health insurance program and to the fight against inflation. He wanted federal controls imposed if hospitals' annual rate of spending increased by more than 11.6% a year.

The cost cap was opposed by the hospital industry and physicians' organizations. To forestall federal controls the hospital industry and the health professions renewed their emphasis on a Voluntary Effort (VE) campaign to hold down spending. In 1978, the first year of the VE drive, the rate of increase in hospital spending dropped from 15.6 to 12.8%, with savings estimated at $1,480,000,000. The goal for 1979 was 11.6%.

In his annual budget message to Congress, Carter asked that spending for health be kept at a mimimum. He noted that rising costs of health care plus inflation would add an estimated $18.7 billion, largely in social security funds. The $100 billion HEW budget was described as the third largest in the world, behind only the total government budgets of the U.S. and the Soviet Union. Among exceptions to recommended cutbacks were mental health, health maintenance, and preventive health programs. Major cuts were recommended for medical education, aimed at minimizing the oversupply of doctors. Congress, however, restored some of the education funds.

In its annual report on the state of the nation's health, HEW said that health care costs rose at an average annual rate of 8.1% between 1950 and 1975 and an average of 12.7% per year thereafter. The number of operations per 10,000 persons increased by almost 25% during the period from 1965–66 to 1975–76 and did so despite a decline for 14 consecutive years in the number of hospital beds.

(DONALD W. GOULD; ARTHUR J. SNIDER)

[424.A.7.c; 424.B.1.a; 424.C.1; 425.C.2; 425.D.3; 425.I.2.e.i; 425.J; 10/35.C.2]

MENTAL HEALTH

The mental health field experienced some excitement when scientists at a major clinical research centre in the U.K. linked schizophrenia with viral infection. In a published paper workers in the communicable diseases and psychiatry divisions at the Clinical Research Centre, Northwick Park Hospital, London, reported that cerebrospinal fluid (the fluid surrounding the brain and spinal cord) in 13 of 38 patients diagnosed as suffering from schizophrenia showed evidence of viral infection. Similar evidence of viral presence was discovered in fluid from 8 of 11 patients suffering from other serious diseases of the nervous system. By contrast, only one in 25 "controls" (patients with medical or surgical conditions apparently unrelated to the mind) yielded cerebrospinal fluid showing any evidence of viral infection. This report typified the continuing effort to establish some organic basis for mental disorders, although research during the year made only small advances toward a biochemical understanding of the problem.

In the absence of such understanding, doctors struggled to do the best they could for the millions of mentally ill whose existence demanded some kind of treatment. Unsurprisingly, many of their efforts attracted criticism. Just before it was toppled in May, and in spite of strong opposition from the medical profession, the British Labour government stated its intention of pressing ahead with plans for setting up new multidisciplinary panels to confirm and approve any proposals to impose hazardous or irreversible treatment on the mentally ill. With the change of government implementation of such a requirement became less likely, but the proposals did reflect a growing awareness that psychiatrists and others responsible for the care of the mentally ill exercised a large influence over the welfare and fate of the patients involved.

In the U.S., in the case of *Geis* v. *Mark and Ervin,* two physicians were sued for $2 million because 12 years earlier they had subjected the son of the plaintiff to a series of neurosurgical procedures with the aim of curbing his violent behaviour. The court heard testimony that these procedures had led to the patient's "total incapacitation." Helen Geis, the mother of the patient, Leonard Kille, contended that her son did not give consent to the operation and held further that the risks entailed in the brain surgery were inadequately explained. The two physicians were acquitted in February.

In a study of the distribution of the incidence of stress diseases in the British Isles, mental illness was shown—perhaps unsurprisingly—to be more prevalent in the more undesirable areas of land. This geographical account of the incidence of depression, schizophrenia, and other disorders supported the idea that both environment and genetic constitution are important in determining the likelihood of any individual requiring the care of a psychiatrist. However, the question of how to treat depressions and other disturbances of the mind that are generated by life in sad societies remained unresolved.

Anxiolytics—more popularly known as tranquilizers—remained the most commonly prescribed drugs in Western nations, but a study of the effect of Librium (chlordiazepoxide) upon anxious rats suggested that the beneficial effects of such medicines may wear off within days of continued use. Two researchers working in the School of Pharmacy in the University of London induced anxiety in rats by placing them in unfamiliar surroundings under a very strong light. After five days spent in unpleasant circumstances, drugged rats were found to be "much more sociable" than undrugged animals. After two or three weeks, however, there was little difference in behaviour between treated and untreated animals. The results of this research project offered a message for doctors who strive to keep their patients calm for months and even years on the products of the pharmaceutical industry: psychotropic (mind-affecting) drugs may be an invaluable "first aid" treatment for emotional disorders, but they are likely no substitute for actions that reduce or remove the stressful circumstances that generate neuroses, anxiety, and depression.

Regardless of the results of studies with rats, the availability of tranquilizing drugs did not seem to be lifting the mood of nations. Japan, for example, experienced a high incidence of multiple suicides involving parents and their offspring. Such "family suicides" were attributed to business failures and to money worries related to the fact that in Japan interest rates on loans ranging between 20 and 100% were commonplace. Earlier reports noted the high incidence of suicides among children in Japan, and the suggestion was made that this was the result of intensive competition in the schools. (DONALD W. GOULD)
[432.A.1; 438.D]

DENTISTRY

During 1979 the dental profession in the U.S. launched a concerted effort to increase access to comprehensive dental care for all segments of the public. Accordingly, the American Dental Association (ADA) was studying blueprints for access programs directed at those categories of individuals who were not covered by existing dental care programs. ADA officials pointed out that, in general, access programs should be tailored (1) to allow patients to obtain treatment, (2) to maximize the number of persons treated, and (3) to place responsibility on the state legislatures for funding and implementing programs for persons entitled to government support.

Dentist Ronald E. Goldstein of Atlanta, Ga., reported that discolorations in teeth caused by food, tobacco, drugs, or other agents could be bleached successfully in some cases, thus obviating the need to crown them. Noting a success rate of about 75%, Goldstein said that the technique could produce overall lightening and, in some cases, reduce or eliminate dark yellow or orange-brown traces. A short series of treatments using a bleaching agent activated by heat and light was required.

Recent advancements in denture technology offered at least some patients the chance of better denture fit and retention. Raymond Willen of Cleveland, Ohio, indicated that in some patients tooth roots were being saved to help support a complete denture. In spite of badly decayed teeth, many patients still have some solid roots, which can be saved to act as support and retention for the denture. Willen compared such root retention to the use of pilings driven deep into solid rock to support a construction on soft earth. Just as the pilings supply the construction with a firm foundation, the natural roots retained in bone provide a similar service.

The meteoric rise in gold prices had only a slight effect on the cost of dental restorative treatment utilizing gold, reported dentist Chester J. Gibson of McMinnville, Ore. The use of gold constitutes only a small part of the overall restorative dental treatment and thus a small part of the overall cost. Nevertheless, the trend of increasing gold prices accelerated research aimed at exploring the use of alloys with lower gold content and base metal alloys such as mixes of chromium and nickel. Gibson noted that although these alloys cost less, the dentist or laboratory would need to spend more time with them because they are harder to work than precious metals. The additional preparation time in some cases might make these alloys more expensive than gold. (LOU JOSEPH)
[422.E.1.a.ii; 10/35.C.1]

See also Demography; Life Sciences; Nobel Prizes; Social Security and Welfare Services.

SPECIAL REPORT

TO RUN OR NOT TO RUN

by Richard Whittingham

Not too many years ago the only person found running down a city street either was a child blessed with boundless energy, someone trying to catch a bus, or someone fleeing in fear. Nowadays, however, millions of people of all ages and both sexes are running for their health, to condition their bodies, for diversion from the stresses of everyday life, or just for pleasure.

How did all this happen? Where and when did it all begin? Some say it was simply a natural progression. In the 1950s people were preoccupied with the sedentary joys provided by television. In the 1960s they got up from in front of the TV set and took to walking, marching for some things, like civil rights, and against others, like the war in Vietnam. According to those who reason this way, it would follow that the 1970s would be the decade of running, which it surely did turn out to be.

Aerobics. The roots of the running phenomenon actually were planted a little more than a decade ago when two track coaches, Arthur Lydiard in New Zealand and Bill Bowerman at the University of Oregon, devised programs of jogging as aids to the health, fitness, and well-being of the average person, and then spread the word. Shortly after that, Kenneth Cooper, a consultant on physical fitness to the U.S. Air Force, developed a program he called "aerobics." He published it in a book, *Aerobics*, which since has multiplied into *The New Aerobics*, *Aerobics for Women* (of which his wife, Mildred, was co-author), and *The Aerobics Way*. The foundation of Cooper's program is that if exercise for the average person is to be effective it must contribute to cardiovascular fitness; that is, it has to benefit the heart, the rest of the circulatory system, and the respiratory system.

For an exercise to do this, however, it must be sustained (for a minimum period of 15 minutes, gradually increasing to longer times). Because of their stops and starts, play and rest, such sports as tennis or golf do not qualify. Sports that do include running, rapid walking, bicycling, continuous swimming, and cross-country skiing. Cooper's book on aerobics provided a precise program of exercise to follow, utilizing any one of those activities.

Other books followed along with seemingly countless new programs of running, running clubs, marathon races, and fun runs (noncompetitive races). A sort of cliquelike camaraderie developed among those who took to the streets and paths for the purpose of jogging long distances. The proverbial "loneliness of the long-distance runner" had suddenly been revoked.

Not for Everyone. Authorities generally agree that running is good for the hearts and lungs of most people, if done within the proper limits for each individual. The American Heart Association supports jogging, as does the President's Council on Physical Fitness and Sports. But all preach common sense in both approach and application. There is a consensus that anyone who has been leading a relatively sedentary life or is in or beyond his or her 30s should not take up running without first having a physical examination and consulting with a physician about an exercise program.

The need for such caution indicates the strenuousness of this form of exercise, an aspect that is often lost in the ringingly evangelistic approach of many of the more committed proponents and/or authors of running programs. Some programs are simply not for everybody. Thomas Cureton, professor emeritus at the University of Illinois, for example, warns older people not to take up such strenuous regimes as Cooper's aerobics and suggests milder alternatives instead. Other prospective runners may have various characteristics or ailments that require personal modifications in their running programs.

There is also concern with the way in which a person runs. Warming up beforehand, cooling down afterward, dressing properly, and not trying to run too fast and too far are just some of the rules that runners should follow.

Running also involves more than just the heart and lungs. There are the muscles and bones of the body and their related joints, cartilages, tendons, and ligaments. These are taxed, often severely so, in long, rigorous runs. Orthopedic specialists are not always as enthusiastic in their outlook on running as are cardiologists. Knee, ankle, and foot-bone problems are not uncommon as a result of protracted running, some serious enough to have enduring debilitating effects. A number of bone specialists suggest the possibility that running continuously in the age brackets of the 30s, 40s, and 50s may lead to some long-term physical problems in the 60s, 70s, and later years.

Richard Whittingham has written on many subjects. His books include Martial Justice *and* The Chicago Bears.

GEORGE W. GARDNER

Running for health and relaxation, and for pleasure, has become in just a few years a major leisure sports activity in the U.S.

It is too early to tell, however, what any of the long-term results of serious jogging in the middle and older years will yield. The activity has only recently become a widespread phenomenon, and scientists, physicians, and health experts have not had a chance to study it in its entirety. Only time will tell if there is something the advocates have overlooked or misinterpreted.

The Jogging Industry. Along with the sport itself a bevy of new products for the runner's market have appeared, enabling many runners and nonrunners to trot to the bank, figuratively speaking, with their sudden windfalls. The publishing industry is a first-class example. Virtually hundreds of books on the subject of running have invaded bookstore shelves and paperback racks in the last few years. Most are "how-to" books, but there are also motivational tomes, almanacs, logbooks, and atlases of places to run. There is even something for those who want to go beyond the mere physical experience of running and into its more mysterious and metaphysical regions; for example, there are such titles as *Zen Running; Beyond Jogging: The Innerspaces of Running; Holistic Running: Beyond the Threshold of Fitness;* and *Running and Being.*

The ultimate prize has been taken by James Fixx, whose elementary manual on the activity, *The Complete Book of Running*, first published by Random House in 1977, has sold approximately 750,000 copies in hardback alone and remained on the best-seller lists more than a year and a half. It has proved to be one of the most successful ventures in hardbound book publishing in modern times. Even a paperback satire of it, *The Non-Runner's Book*, established itself on the best-seller lists.

Several magazines aimed solely at runners are now in national distribution. The most popular, *Runner's World*, claims a readership of 1.2 million each month.

Then there is the apparel industry. Banished is that dull gray sweat suit worn by yesterday's athlete. Warm-up suits or jogging outfits have proliferated in an abundance of colours, styles, and fabrics—some from the creative spirits of the world's foremost clothing designers. Accessories have run the gamut from a sweatband with a built-in radio to unisex jogging underwear.

And consider also running shoes. It used to be that if a person wanted a pair of shoes for running, he or she would have a simple choice. If the person were truly serious, he would opt for a pair of those lightweight, black leather track shoes with needle-sharp spikes; if only casual, there was always a pair of gym shoes. Not any more. Today there are runner's shoes, both imported and domestic, for ordinary running and for marathoning, without cleats and with them—a dazzling array for the customer to choose from. There are even stores that specialize solely in running shoes and other equipment for the runner.

Future Outlook. Whether running is here to stay is an unanswerable question. The fact that it is here, in ever increasing proportions, is undeniable. Whether it will help or harm a person is mostly a result of the way that person goes about the activity.

Running may bring good health, a body that is fit and perhaps trim (though it will not of itself achieve that), and a mind that is unclouded, free of anxiety and stress, and filled with self-accomplishment. But it will not bring immortality. It may prevent us from dying of a heart attack, as columnist William F. Buckley pointed out, but what then is the alternative: "Cancer. Leprosy. Creutzfeldt-Jakob disease." There are quite obviously more painful and less desirable ways to pass from this Earth than by the swift and often painless failure of the heart. "A question," Buckley suggests, "to consider during those hours we do not spend jogging."

WIDE WORLD

The beautiful Shir-dor is one of 54 monuments being restored in Samarkand, an ancient city in the southern part of the U.S.S.R. whose golden age in the 14th century was ushered in by Timur.

Historic Preservation

By September 1979, 47 countries had ratified or accepted the International Convention Concerning the Protection of the World Cultural and Natural Heritage. Payments to the World Heritage Fund amounted to U.S. $1 million. Among the projects financed was the contribution of equipment for the restoration of historic buildings in Antigua, Guatemala, which had been severely damaged in a series of earthquakes in 1976. The World Heritage Committee also approved a contribution for the preservation of Swayambhunath Temple in the Kathmandu Valley of Nepal.

In Egypt work on the transfer of the complex of ancient buildings from the island of Philae (located in the Nile between the High Dam and the Aswan Dam) to the island of Agilkia was completed during 1979. Formal dedication was planned for March 1980.

In Haiti work began on the preservation and restoration of the Citadelle Laferrière, the massive fortified castle built by Henri Christophe during 1804–13, 28 km (17 mi) to the south of Cap-Haïtien. Looted after Christophe's death in 1820 and damaged by the earthquake of 1842, it had since suffered from weathering and neglect. The Citadelle, the Baroque palace of Sans Souci, and the site of Ramiers were being proposed for an international campaign to be carried out by UNESCO on behalf of the Haitian government.

In Greece an announcement that an aluminum plant would be built in Kamiotissa and a cement plant in Itea, in the vicinity of Delphi, aroused considerable opposition. As a result of the protests, the government announced that the plants would be located elsewhere. The celebrated grove of olive trees in the valley below Delphi was classified as a "nationally important site."

UNESCO

After heavy monsoon rains washed away supporting soil, workers installed rock bolts to preserve a 5th century AD temple complex on a hill in the Kathmandu Valley of Nepal.

While tourism was an important source of the funds needed to finance conservation and restoration—and in some countries was one of the main resources of the economy—the sheer numbers of visitors contributed to the wear and tear of the buildings and sites involved. A case in point was the plight of Pompeii in Italy, revealed in a recent report. About two-thirds of the city had been cleared of the ash that covered it during the eruption of Vesuvius in AD 79. The buildings of brick faced with marble or plaster were unroofed—with the exception of a few where roofs had been installed to protect mural paintings—and suffered considerably from exposure to the elements. At the same time, the flagstone streets were being worn by the tread of 1.3 million visitors a year. The staff was inadequate to meet the need for maintenance and control. During the year four valuable statues and six wall paintings were stolen. The Italian Parliament adopted a special $4 million budget for conservation, but a much larger budget evidently was required.

Terrorism continued to threaten important historic buildings. On April 20, 1979, a bomb caused serious damage to the Palace of the Senators, one of a complex of buildings designed by Michelangelo, located on the Capitoline Hill in Rome. The bomb caused wide cracks in the Hall of Julius Caesar, the halls of the Palace of the Conservators, and the Capitoline Museum. Large patches of stuccoed and decorated ceilings fell, and many frescoes were damaged. It was estimated that it would take at least a year to repair the damage, at a cost of $1.2 million.

In England the Civic Trust was carrying out a pilot project for the revitalization and regeneration of a small historic town, Wirksworth, near Derby. Its original prosperity was based on lead mining during the 17th and 18th centuries. When the ore played out it entered a period of stagnation and remained virtually unchanged. Many buildings were now either vacant or underused, and the town suffered from lack of employment and loss of population. Under the guidance of the trust and with the aid of grants from the Department of the Environment, improvement projects were begun. Old residences were bought, restored with added modern amenities, and resold. The principal monuments were also being restored, and there were encouraging signs that the process of abandonment had been reversed.

In the U.S. projects to renovate the deteriorating inner cores of cities by turning old commercial buildings and industrial plants into social and small market centres had in recent years included the conversion of the Ghirardelli chocolate factory in San Francisco and renovation of Quincy Market (Faneuil Hall) in Boston. In Washington, D.C., a large-scale project was under way in Georgetown, where such landmarks as Rive Gauche, City Tavern, and the Old Car Barn located across the Chesapeake and Ohio Canal would be converted into a shopping mall, town houses, and apartments. The Old Car Barn (originally a tobacco warehouse) would have a furniture mart on the ground floor and condominium apartments on the upper floors.

A study by the U.S. Advisory Council on Historic Preservation showed that approximately one-third of all the energy consumed in the U.S. involved the construction and use of buildings. The study noted that "once energy is embodied in a building, it cannot be recovered and used for another purpose. . . . Preservation saves energy by taking advantage of the non-recoverable energy embodied in an existing building and extending the use of it." In addition, the renovation of historic centres and quarters of cities would lessen the use of private cars and reduce energy consumed in commuting between cities and the surrounding suburbs. (HIROSHI DAIFUKU)

See also Architecture; Environment; Museums.

After $5 million was spent on restoration of the building, the main lobby of Radio City Music Hall in New York City was glistening again as it did when it first opened its doors in 1932.

JACK MANNING—THE NEW YORK TIMES

Honduras

Honduras

A republic of Central America, Honduras is bounded by Nicaragua, El Salvador, Guatemala, the Caribbean Sea, and the Pacific Ocean. Area: 112,088 sq km (43,277 sq mi). Pop. (1980 est.): 3,691,000, including 90% mestizo. Cap. and largest city: Tegucigalpa (pop., 1977 est., 316,800). Language: Spanish; some Indian dialects. Religion: Roman Catholic. In 1979 Honduras was governed by a three-man military junta headed by Gen. Policarpo Paz García.

The military government of Honduras met with increased opposition in both urban and rural areas

HONDURAS

Education. (1977) Primary, pupils 502,749, teachers 14,010; secondary, pupils 65,309, teachers 2,601; vocational (1975), pupils 12,936; teacher training, students 1,011, teachers 115; higher (university only), students 15,464, teaching staff 825.

Finance. Monetary unit: lempira, with (Sept. 17, 1979) a par value of 2 lempiras to U.S. $1 (free rate of 4.29 lempiras = £1 sterling). Gold, SDR's, and foreign exchange (June 1979) U.S. $182 million. Budget (1978 actual): revenue 549.5 million lempiras; expenditure 579.2 million lempiras. Gross national product (1978) 3,417,000,000 lempiras. Money supply (April 1979) 569.6 million lempiras. Cost of living (Tegucigalpa; 1975 = 100; June 1979) 128.8.

Foreign Trade. (1978) Imports 1,386,200,000 lempiras; exports 1,193,700,000 lempiras. Import sources (1977): U.S. 43%; Japan 11%; Guatemala 6%; Venezuela 5%; Trinidad and Tobago 5%. Export destinations (1977): U.S. 49%; West Germany 18%; Japan 6%; The Netherlands 5%. Main exports: coffee 35%; bananas 23%; timber 7%; beef 7%.

Transport and Communications. Roads (1977) 7,678 km. Motor vehicles in use (1977): passenger 14,300; commercial (including buses) 24,900. Railways (1976) 1,780 km. Air traffic (1977): 270 million passenger-km; freight 5.5 million net ton-km. Shipping (1978): merchant vessels 100 gross tons and over 70; gross tonnage 130,831. Telephones (Dec. 1976) 19,000. Radio receivers (Dec. 1976) 161,000. Television receivers (Dec. 1976) 48,000.

Agriculture. Production (in 000; metric tons; 1978): corn *c.* 340; sorghum *c.* 48; sugar, raw value (1977) *c.* 107; dry beans *c.* 50; bananas *c.* 1,338; plantains (1977) *c.* 125; oranges *c.* 27; pineapples *c.* 28; palm oil *c.* 11; coffee *c.* 59; cotton, lint (1977) *c.* 10; tobacco *c.* 7; beef and veal (1977) *c.* 44; timber (cu m; 1977) 4,175. Livestock (in 000; 1977): cattle *c.* 1,770; pigs *c.* 525; horses *c.* 285; chickens *c.* 8,000.

Industry. Production (in 000; metric tons; 1977): cement 247; petroleum products *c.* 530; lead ore (metal content) 21; zinc ore (metal content) 20; electricity (kw-hr) *c.* 701,000.

Hebrew Literature:
see Literature

Highways:
see Engineering Projects; Transportation

Hinduism:
see Religion

Hockey:
see Field Hockey and Lacrosse; Ice Hockey

Holland:
see Netherlands, The

in 1979, causing it to cancel the elections scheduled for April 1980. Relations with the labour unions deteriorated, and in an open clash between unions and police at the Bemis Handal textile plant in March, 3 workers died, 100 people were arrested, and the plant was set afire, causing damage estimated at U.S. $10 million. The agricultural unions also were militant, occupying land in December 1978 in the northwestern areas of Santa Barbara and Yoro.

In foreign relations Honduras discreetly supported the regime of Pres. Anastasio Somoza in Nicaragua. After Somoza was overthrown in July, many troops loyal to him fled across the border into Honduras.

The economy performed well during 1978, with a gross domestic product growth rate of 8.9%. This was expected to slow to about 6.5% in 1979. The rate of inflation increased 5.7% during 1978 based on the official cost-of-living index, but the actual rates were probably much higher. Economic results for 1979 would depend very largely on commodity price movements, especially for coffee and bananas, which constituted Honduras's main exports. (CHRISTINE MELLOR)

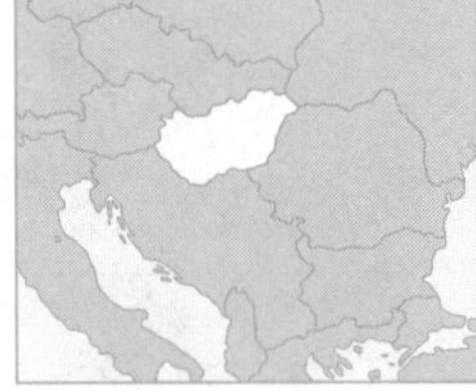

Hungary

Hungary

A people's republic of central Europe, Hungary is bordered by Czechoslovakia, the U.S.S.R., Romania, Yugoslavia, and Austria. Area: 93,032 sq km (35,920 sq mi). Pop. (1979 est.): 10,698,800, including (1970) Hungarian 95.8%; German 2.1%. Cap. and largest city: Budapest (pop., 1979 est., 2,093,200). Language (1970): Magyar 95.8%. Religion (1970): Roman Catholic about 60%, most of the remainder Protestant or atheist. First secretary of the Hungarian Socialist Workers' (Communist) Party in 1979, Janos Kadar; chairman of the Presidential Council (chief of state), Pal Losonczi; president of the Council of Ministers (premier), Gyorgy Lazar.

The Hungarian finance minister, Lajos Faluvegi, in February 1979 visited Washington, D.C., where he and U.S. Secretary of the Treasury W. Michael Blumenthal signed an agreement excluding double taxation (which ensures that a person or corporation earning certain kinds of income in more than one country will not have to pay the full taxes of each country). In statements at the signing ceremony both ministers stressed the importance of the 1978 agreement by which the U.S. granted Hungary most-favoured-nation status. In March it was announced that Hungary was seeking a loan of approximately $300 million from U.S. banks. It was the first time Hungary had entered the U.S. capital market since World War II.

Hungary's most important foreign visitor in 1979 was Soviet Pres. Leonid Brezhnev, who flew to Budapest on May 30 accompanied by four other prominent party officials and left on June 1. Formally, the Soviet leader was returning the visit to Moscow at the beginning of March by Hungarian Communist Party leader Janos Kadar. The essence of the long joint communiqué published on June 3 was that as long as Hungary conformed to the Soviet foreign policy line and retained Communist rule it could relax political and economic controls at home.

The journey of West German Chancellor Helmut Schmidt to Hungary in September was the first visit there by a West German head of government. Economic questions played a part in his talks with Kadar, but other matters were also discussed, especially the prospects for further East-West détente. In October Prime Minister Konstantinos Karamanlis visited Hungary, the first Greek statesman to do so since the end of World War II.

During the year there were significant exchanges of visits between Hungary and Romania. In April Frigyes Puja, the Hungarian foreign minister, visited Stefan Andrei, his Romanian counterpart; in July Ilie Verdet, the Romanian premier, paid a visit to Hungarian Premier Gyorgy Lazar; and on August 31 Romanian Pres. Nicolae Ceauses-

West German Chancellor Helmut Schmidt, on a visit to Budapest in September, viewed a tablet containing the names of Jews killed by the Nazis in Hungary.

SVEN SIMON/KATHERINE YOUNG

Hong Kong:
see Dependent States

Horse Racing:
see Equestrian Sports; Gambling

Horticulture:
see Gardening

Hospitals:
see Health and Disease

cu received Sandor Gaspar, a member of the Hungarian Socialist Workers' Party Politburo and deputy chairman of the Presidential Council. In all three meetings the situation of the Magyar minority in Romania was believed to have been discussed. On May 14–15 the foreign ministers of the Warsaw Treaty member states met in Budapest to discuss urgent tasks related to "consolidating peace and security in Europe."

Laszlo Cardinal Lekai, archbishop of Esztergom and primate of Hungary, visited Poland in June to witness Pope John Paul II's triumphal tour. In May Donald Coggan, archbishop of Canterbury, visited Hungary.

Peter Veress, a former deputy minister of foreign trade, was appointed minister of that department on March 30. He took over from Jozsef Biro, who had retired.

The construction of a nuclear power station, the first in Hungary, began at Paks, on the Danube River; when ready it would have a capacity of 1,760 Mw and would supply 25% of the country's electricity consumption. In January the prices of many consumer goods shot up: beer by 20%, gasoline by 25%, tobacco by 30%, and rice by 50%. In July the price of bread, unchanged for many years, rose by 50%. The Hungarian people appeared to accept these rises with equanimity. In February new foreign exchange and customs regulations were introduced with the aim of reducing black market activity, especially by visitors from other Eastern European countries. Western tourists would receive some 25% more when changing money at the official rate.

(K. M. SMOGORZEWSKI)

HUNGARY

Education. (1978–79) Primary, pupils 1,107,000, teachers 71,925; secondary, pupils 352,000, teachers 14,954; higher, students 106,000, teaching staff 13,450.

Finance. Monetary unit: forint, with (Sept. 17, 1979) a commercial free rate of 35.93 forints to U.S. $1 (77.30 forints = £1 sterling) and a noncommercial (tourist) rate of 20.53 forints to U.S. $1 (44.17 forints = £1 sterling). Budget (1978 est.): revenue 385.9 billion forints; expenditure 389.7 billion forints. Net material product (1977) 479.2 billion forints.

Foreign Trade. (1978) Imports 300,933,000,000 forints; exports 240,707,000,000 forints. Import sources: U.S.S.R. 28%; West Germany 12%; East Germany 8%; Czechoslovakia 5%; Austria 5%. Export destinations: U.S.S.R. 30%; West Germany 8%; East Germany 8%; Czechoslovakia 7%; Poland 5%; Yugoslavia 5%. Main exports: machinery 22%; motor vehicles 11%; chemicals 9%; meat and meat preparations 6%; fruit and vegetables 5%; clothing 5%.

Transport and Communications. Roads (1977) 99,612 km (including 181 km expressways). Motor vehicles in use (1977): passenger 744,685; commercial 136,679. Railways: (1977) 8,063 km; traffic (1978) 12,605,000,000 passenger-km, freight 23,915,000,000 net ton-km. Air traffic (1977): 653 million passenger-km; freight 5.5 million net ton-km. Inland waterways in regular use (1977) 1,302 km. Telephones (Jan. 1978) 1,103,800. Radio licenses (Dec. 1977) 2,577,000. Television licenses (Dec. 1977) 2,557,000.

Agriculture. Production (in 000; metric tons; 1978): corn *c.* 6,700; wheat *c.* 5,669; barley *c.* 762; rye *c.* 138; potatoes *c.* 1,700; sugar, raw value *c.* 530; cabbages (1977) *c.* 220; tomatoes *c.* 460; onions *c.* 160; sunflower seed *c.* 240; rapeseed *c.* 123; green peas (1977) *c.* 250; plums (1977) *c.* 200; apples *c.* 980; wine *c.* 480; tobacco *c.* 24; milk *c.* 2,380; beef and veal *c.* 145; pork *c.* 880. Livestock (in 000; Dec. 1977): cattle 1,949; pigs 7,850; sheep 2,619; horses 144; chickens *c.* 61,116.

Industry. Index of production (1975 = 100; 1978) 116. Production (in 000; metric tons; 1978): coal 2,955; lignite 22,719; crude oil 2,201; natural gas (cu m) 7,350,000; electricity (kw-hr) 25,417,000; iron ore (24% metal content) 534; pig iron 2,332; crude steel 3,882; bauxite 2,895; aluminum 71; cement 4,764; petroleum products (1977) 9,789; sulfuric acid 644; fertilizers (1977) nitrogenous 572, phosphate 196; cotton yarn 63; man-made fibres 28; commercial vehicles (units) 15.

Ice Hockey

North American. The seven years of rivalry between the National Hockey League and the World Hockey Association ended in March when the NHL absorbed four teams from the upstart WHA, which then dissolved. The four new entries, the Winnipeg Jets, Edmonton Oilers, Quebec Nordiques, and New England Whalers (to be called the Hartford Whalers) paid $6 million each to join the league, expanding it to 21 teams.

The Montreal Canadiens won the NHL Stanley Cup for the fourth consecutive season, defeating a

Table I. NHL Final Standings, 1978–79

	Won	Lost	Tied	Goals	Goals against	Pts.
Prince of Wales Conference						
JAMES NORRIS DIVISION						
Montreal	52	17	11	337	204	115
Pittsburgh	36	31	13	281	279	85
Los Angeles	34	34	12	292	286	80
Washington	24	41	15	273	338	63
Detroit	23	41	16	252	295	62
CHARLES F. ADAMS DIVISION						
Boston	43	23	14	316	270	100
Buffalo	36	28	16	280	263	88
Toronto	34	33	13	267	252	81
Minnesota	28	40	12	257	289	68
Clarence Campbell Conference						
LESTER PATRICK DIVISION						
New York Islanders	51	15	14	358	214	116
Philadelphia	40	25	15	281	248	95
New York Rangers	40	29	11	316	292	91
Atlanta	41	31	8	327	280	90
CONN SMYTHE DIVISION						
Chicago	29	36	15	244	277	73
Vancouver	25	42	13	217	291	63
St. Louis	18	50	12	249	348	48
Colorado	15	53	12	210	331	42

Table II. World Ice Hockey Championships, 1979

	Won	Lost	Tied	Goals	Goals against	Pts.
Group A Championship Section						
U.S.S.R.	6	0	0	51	12	12
Czechoslovakia	3	2	1	25	30	7
Sweden	1	4	1	20	38	3
Canada	1	5	0	20	36	2
GROUP A Relegation Section						
Finland	4	1	1	23	17	9
West Germany	3	2	1	27	21	7
United States	2	2	2	22	20	6
Poland	0	4	2	15	29	2
GROUP B Promotion Section						
Netherlands, The	3	0	0	15	6	6
East Germany	2	1	0	16	9	4
Romania	1	2	0	8	9	2
Norway	0	3	0	5	20	0
GROUP B Relegation Section						
Switzerland	3	0	0	14	6	6
Japan	2	1	0	17	10	4
Austria	1	2	0	8	13	2
Denmark	0	3	0	8	18	0
GROUP C						
Yugoslavia	7	0	0	83	10	14
Italy	6	1	0	64	17	12
France	5	2	0	59	27	10
Bulgaria	4	3	0	35	28	8
Great Britain	2	5	0	23	68	4
Spain	2	5	0	25	48	4
South Korea	1	5	1	16	67	3
Australia	0	6	1	13	53	1

Hydroelectric Power: *see* Energy; Engineering Projects

Hydrology: *see* Earth Sciences

UPI

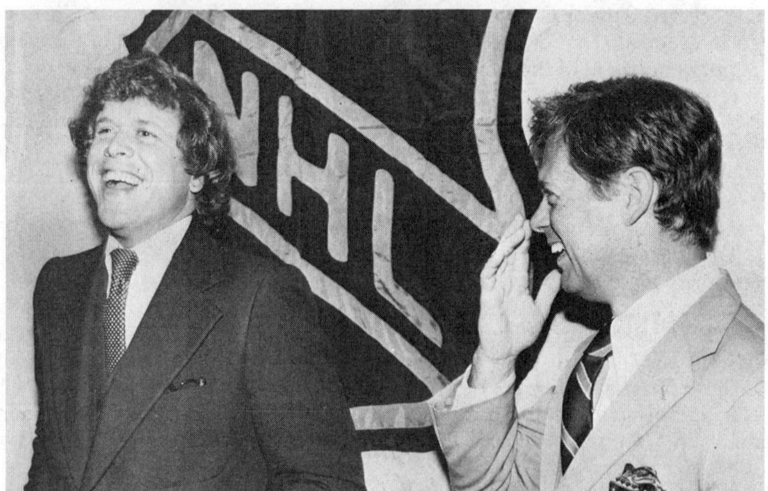

Howard Baldwin (left), president of the World Hockey Association, and John Ziegler, president of the National Hockey League, shared a light moment after the NHL voted in March to admit into its ranks the four remaining teams of the WHA.

plucky, young New York Ranger team in the final, four games to one. The decisive game was played at the Montreal Forum, enabling the Canadiens to win the Cup before their home fans for the first time since 1968. They had won their last six Stanley Cups on the road.

The Rangers had been fueled during the 1978–79 season by the addition of two Swedes, Anders Hedberg and Ulf Nilsson, and by a new general manager, the charismatic Fred ("the Fog") Shero. Although they had finished only third in the Patrick Division, their youthful defensive corps suddenly matured in the play-offs and created an emotional semifinal series against the neighbouring New York Islanders, winning in six games before standing-room-only crowds. The Rangers reached the final for only the third time since 1940.

The Conn Smythe Trophy for the most valuable player in the play-offs went to Bob Gainey, a hard-working forward for the Canadiens. Bryan Trottier, the 22-year-old centre for the New York Islanders, won the Hart Trophy as the most valuable player to his team. He was the youngest forward and second-youngest player ever to receive the award. Trottier also won the Art Ross Trophy as the leading scorer during the regular season. Denis Potvin of the Islanders won the Norris Trophy as the league's outstanding defenseman for the third time.

Bob MacMillan of the Atlanta Flames won the Lady Byng Memorial Trophy as the most gentlemanly player. Bobby Smith of the Minnesota North Stars won the Calder Trophy for rookie of the year, and Bob Gainey won the Frank Selke Trophy as the outstanding defensive forward. Ken Dryden and Michel ("Bunny") Larocque of the Canadiens won the Vezina Trophy for the best goaltending for the fourth straight season.

In the World Hockey Association the Winnipeg Jets, under former Ranger general manager John Ferguson and Tom McVie, former coach of the Washington Capitals, won the AVCO World Trophy as the last WHA champions. They won eight of their ten postseason contests, sweeping Quebec in four straight games in the semifinal series before upsetting the league champion Edmonton Oilers in six games.

After the Canadiens won the NHL's championship, they lost a number of important people from their organization. Ken Dryden, the 32-year-old goalkeeper, announced his retirement after eight years and six Stanley Cups to pursue a law career. Jacques Lemaire, the 34-year-old centre for wingers Guy Lafleur and Steve Shutt, left for Switzerland, where he had signed to be coach and general manager of a team. Scotty Bowman, who led the Canadiens to five Stanley Cups in his seven years as coach of the team, joined the Buffalo Sabres as head coach and general manager, a job he had hoped for with the Canadiens following the retirement of Sam Pollock the previous season. Bowman hired Roger Neilson, the former coach of Toronto, as his assistant at Buffalo.

There were many other moves in the NHL management ranks prior to the 1979–80 season. Bernard ("Boom Boom") Geoffrion took over as coach of the Canadiens. Floyd Smith was named coach at Toronto, where his former boss, George ("Punch") Imlach, became general manager after being dismissed by Buffalo. Eddie Johnston became coach of Chicago. Don Cherry, the Boston coach, moved to the same post at Colorado. Fred Creighton, released from his coaching job in Atlanta, took over Cherry's job at Boston. Al MacNeil, former director of player personnel for Montreal, replaced Creighton at Atlanta.

In addition to Dryden, the NHL lost another of its star goalkeepers in Bernie Parent of Philadelphia. He retired at the age of 34 after 14 years in the league because of an eye injury suffered in a Feb. 17, 1979, game against the New York Rangers. Parent had helped the Flyers win successive Stanley Cups in 1973–74 and 1974–75.

The most shocking event of the year was the defeat of an NHL all-star team by the Soviet Union's national team in a three-game series in February billed as the inaugural Challenge Cup. The Soviet team won the last two games of the series in New York City's Madison Square Garden, including a startling 6–0 victory in the final contest. The Soviets' swarming tactics and extraordinary stamina enabled them to overwhelm the hastily assembled NHL team.

Helmets became compulsory in the NHL in the

UPI

Yvon Lambert (left), of the Montreal Canadiens, watches teammate Rick Chartraw's scoring shot bounce back out of the goal in the last game of the Stanley Cup competition. The Canadiens beat the New York Rangers four games to one to win the championship.

1979–80 season for players who had signed professional contracts after June 1, 1979; this covered most rookies. Players who had signed before then and who endorsed a waiver were to be allowed to play without helmets. Helmets remained compulsory in junior, college, and international hockey.

In the American Hockey League the Maine Mariners swept both league and play-off titles, taking the Calder Cup for the second straight year. They defeated New Haven, four games to one. In the Central Hockey League the Dallas Black Hawks won the Adams Cup by defeating Salt Lake City four games to one. (ROBIN CATHY HERMAN)

European and International. The acceptance of Luxembourg increased the number of member nations in the International Ice Hockey Federation (IIHF) to 31 in 1979, a year that marked closer cooperation between amateur and professional officials and players.

The 46th world championships were contested in three groups by 24 nations, the eight title contenders competing in Group A during April 5–25 in Moscow. Preliminary matches split the eight into two sections, the top four teams contesting the championship and the other four deciding which one would be relegated to Group B. The Soviet Union retained the title with the first undefeated performance in four years, twice overwhelming the Czechoslovak runners-up, 11–1 early on and 6–1 in the final game. In the latter contest Gregg Madill became the first North American professional referee to officiate in a championship match. It was the 16th championship for the U.S.S.R., whose main goalkeeper, Vladislav Tretiak, had a fairly easy time.

Only one non-Soviet was selected among the six outstanding players of the tournament, traditionally chosen by accredited journalists. They named Tretiak, defensemen Valerij Vassiliev and Jiri Bubla (Czechoslovakia), and forwards Boris Mikhailov, Vladimir Petrov, and Sergey Maharov. The Golden Stick award for the best player went to Mikhailov, the Soviet right-winger and captain. Sweden took the bronze medal, reversing the previous season's order with fourth-placed Canada. The U.S. and Canada again fielded squads well below each nation's best, owing to Stanley Cup and other NHL commitments. This made their challenges less meaningful, true world supremacy remaining a matter of guesswork until fully representative sides from the NHL could be pitted against the cream of Europe. At the bottom end, Poland failed to win any of its six games and dropped out of the first group.

The Netherlands earned the right to move up to Group A by winning Group B in convincing style at Galati, Romania, on March 16–24, toppling the East German favourites 4–3 in the crucial match. This was a remarkable performance by the Dutch, who had won promotion to Group B only the previous season. Denmark and Austria, the bottom teams in Group B, were demoted and replaced by Yugoslavia and Italy; the latter were, respectively, victor and runner-up of the Group C matches contested in Barcelona, Spain, on March 16–25. Australia, although last in Group C, made a welcome appearance in the tournament to underline that country's progress in the sport.

The long-cherished idea of the Stanley Cup champion meeting the top European club to contest an annual world club trophy came nearer to reality after favourable talks between NHL president John Ziegler and IIHF president Gunther Zabetzki. A four-game series, two on either side of the Atlantic, was proposed for 1980.

The annual senior international tournament for the Izvestia Cup, in Moscow in December 1978, included a North American entry representing the NHL. Although this team did not include the league's star players, by its very appearance it stressed a continuing improvement in the sport's transatlantic relations. Highlight of the series was a 3–3 tie between the U.S.S.R. and Czechoslovakia in a final game that left the two equal in points, the Soviet side winning the cup because of scoring more goals. The NHL team finished third.

The world junior (under 21) championship, ended Jan. 4, 1979, in Karlstad, Sweden, was retained by the U.S.S.R., with Sweden runner-up, Finland third, Czechoslovakia fourth, and Canada fifth of the eight contestants. It was the fourth successive Soviet victory. (HOWARD BASS)

Iceland

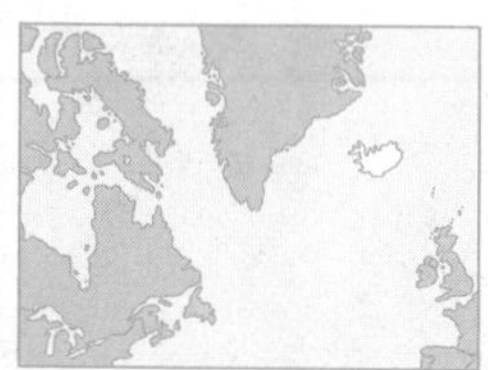

Iceland

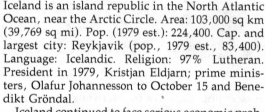

Iceland is an island republic in the North Atlantic Ocean, near the Arctic Circle. Area: 103,000 sq km (39,769 sq mi). Pop. (1979 est.): 224,400. Cap. and largest city: Reykjavik (pop., 1979 est., 83,400). Language: Icelandic. Religion: 97% Lutheran. President in 1979, Kristjan Eldjarn; prime ministers, Olafur Johannesson to October 15 and Benedikt Gröndal.

Iceland continued to face serious economic problems in 1979, as inflation accelerated to an annual rate of over 55% in the second half of the year. The sharp rise in world oil prices was partly responsible; Iceland was especially hard hit by the oil-price increases because it purchased nearly all its oil from the Soviet Union on a long-term contract but at Rotterdam spot market prices. The average price of oil for Iceland increased by about 120% between 1978 and 1979, or twice as much as the world price. But the principal source of inflation in 1979, as previously, was the system of adjusting wages to price increases every quarter. The government made repeated efforts in 1979 to mitigate the effect of wages on prices, but differences within the coalition made it impossible to do much and eventually led to the government's downfall.

The leftist government coalition of the Progressive Party, the Social Democrats, and the People's Alliance had taken office on Aug. 31, 1978, under the premiership of Olafur Johannesson, on the strength of its pledge to restore full adjustment of wages to price increases, partially cut by the previous government. But it became difficult to keep that promise and at the same time curb inflation, especially in view of the increases in the price of oil. The government was overwhelmed with problems of monetary and fiscal policy and could not agree on measures to be taken.

In the autumn of 1979, no agreement could be reached by the coalition partners on the presentation of the 1980 statement for the coming year, a fact that caused the Social Democrats to withdraw their support from the coalition in early October. On October 15 Johannesson's government resigned, and a minority caretaker government of the Social Democrats headed by Benedikt Gröndal, protected from a no-confidence vote by the Independence Party, took office. It dissolved Parliament and called new elections for December 2–3.

The elections, fought largely on the issue of inflation, produced indecisive results. The Independence Party won the largest block of seats, 21 in the 60-seat legislature, followed by the Progressive Party with 17, the People's Alliance with 11, and the Social Democrats with 10. It was expected that negotiations to form a new government would be prolonged.

In the course of the year, it became apparent that the stock of capelin, a vital factor in the fish-dominated economy, was being overfished by both Iceland and Norway. The Icelandic and Norwegian governments negotiated on catch limits in the summer but could not reach agreement. During autumn negotiations between Iceland and the Soviet Union on a new long-term trade agreement, the Icelandic government endeavoured unsuccessfully to persuade the Soviet Union to stop basing its oil sales to Iceland on Rotterdam prices. Iceland sought new suppliers of oil but found none willing to sell below the spot market price.

At the beginning of 1980, all protective tariffs on industrial products traded between Iceland and both the European Free Trade Association (EFTA) and the European Economic Community (EEC) were to be eliminated. The Johannesson government foresaw difficulties for the small Icelandic manufacturing sector and instituted a temporary 6% extra protective tariff on imported manufactured products that competed with Icelandic products. This measure would expire in 1980. It was tolerated, although not with formal consent, by the EFTA and EEC countries.

ICELAND

Education. (1975–76) Primary, pupils 26,418, teachers 1,380; secondary, pupils 20,292, teachers 1,538; vocational, pupils 5,351, teachers 819; teacher training, pupils 210, teachers 30; higher, students 2,970, teaching staff 575.

Finance. Monetary unit: króna, with (Sept. 17, 1979) a free rate of 377.2 krónur to U.S. $1 (811.5 krónur = £1 sterling). Gold, SDR's, and foreign exchange (June 1979) U.S. $136 million. Budget (1978 est.): revenue 139,496,000,000 krónur; expenditure 138,473,000,000 krónur. Gross national product (1978) 550.7 billion krónur. Money supply (June 1979) 54,997,000,000 krónur. Cost of living (Reykjavik; 1975 = 100; May 1979) 326.7.

Foreign Trade. (1978) Imports 184,321,000,000 krónur; exports 176,286,000,000 krónur. Import sources: West Germany 11%; U.K. 11%; Denmark 10%; Sweden 9%; U.S.S.R. 8%; Norway 8%; The Netherlands 8%; U.S. 7%. Export destinations: U.S. 29%; U.K. 17%; West Germany 8%. Main exports: fish and products 76%; aluminum 13%.

Transport and Communications. Roads (1977) 11,525 km. Motor vehicles in use (1977): passenger 65,700; commercial 6,700. There are no railways. Air traffic (1978): 2,118,000,000 passenger-km; freight 37.1 million net ton-km. Shipping (1978): merchant vessels 100 gross tons and over 383; gross tonnage 175,097. Telephones (Dec. 1977) 95,500. Radio licenses (Dec. 1977) 65,000. Television receivers (Dec. 1977) 56,000.

Agriculture. Production (in 000; metric tons; 1978): potatoes 13; hay c. 360; turnips 1; milk 134; mutton and lamb 16; fish catch 1,558. Livestock (in 000; Dec. 1978): cattle 63; sheep 891; horses 51; poultry 369.

Industry. Production (in 000): electricity (public supply only; kw-hr; 1978) 2,660,000; aluminum (metric tons; 1977) 71.

Ice Skating:
see Winter Sports

Iceland's weather conditions took an unusual turn in the summer of 1979, when the northern part of the country was hit by extremely cold weather, creating difficulties for agriculture there.

(BJÖRN MATTHÍASSON)

India

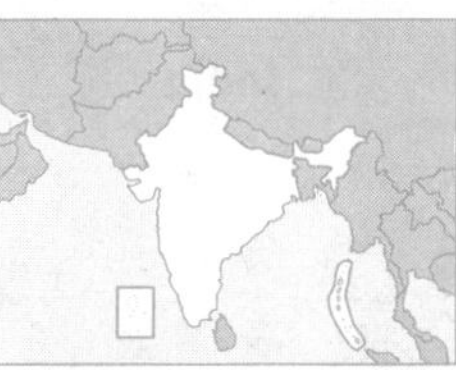

India

A federal republic of southern Asia and a member of the Commonwealth of Nations, India is situated on a peninsula extending into the Indian Ocean with the Arabian Sea to the west and the Bay of Bengal to the east. It is bounded (east to west) by Burma, Bangladesh, China, Bhutan, Nepal, and Pakistan; Sri Lanka lies just off its southern tip in the Indian Ocean. Area: 3,287,782 sq km (1,269,-420 sq mi), including the Pakistani-controlled section of Jammu and Kashmir. Pop. (1978 est.): 638,388,000; Indo-Aryans and Dravidians are dominant, with Mongoloid, Negroid, and Australoid admixtures. Cap.: New Delhi (pop., 1971, 301,800). Largest cities: Calcutta (metro pop., 1977 est., 8,297,000) and Greater Bombay (metro pop., 1977 est., 7,605,000). Language: Hindi and English (official). Religion (1971): Hindu 83%; Muslim 11%; Christian 3%; Sikh 2%; Buddhist 0.7%. President in 1979, N. Sanjiva Reddy; prime ministers, Morarji Desai until July 15 and, from July 28, Charan Singh.

The year 1979 was one of drought and drift for India. The Janata Party split and lost power at the centre. Its patron saint, Jayaprakash Narayan (*see* OBITUARIES), died on October 8. The Lok Sabha (lower house of Parliament) was dissolved halfway through its life of five years, and the country hoped against hope that a viable government would emerge from the general election scheduled to be held in the first week of January 1980.

Domestic Affairs. Charan Singh returned to the union Cabinet on January 24 as finance minister and deputy prime minister, but his reentry did not put an end to factional fights within the ruling party. In June Raj Narain quit the Janata Party, and in July several other pro-Charan Singh members resigned when a no-confidence motion introduced by the Congress Party was being debated. The Janata Party was thus reduced to a minority within the government, and Prime Minister Morarji Desai resigned on July 15. Jagjivan Ram was elected leader of the Janata parliamentary party in his place.

Meanwhile, the leader of the opposition, Y. B. Chavan, was unable to form a government, and so Pres. N. Sanjiva Reddy invited Charan Singh to do so; Charan Singh had by then secured the support of several opposition groups. His government, which took office on July 28, included representatives of the Congress, the Congress for Democracy, the Muslim Majlis, and the All-India Anna Dravida Munnetra Kazhagam. But before he could obtain a confidence vote in the Lok Sabha the Congress (I)—I for Indira—withdrew its support, reportedly because Charan Singh refused to drop the court cases against Indira Gandhi, her son Sanjay, and associates. Charan Singh resigned on August 20 and asked for a new election. The president then dissolved the Lok Sabha. Charan Singh continued to head a caretaker government, and his party took the name Lok Dal. In late October the chief election commissioner announced that the parliamentary poll would be held on January 3 and 6, 1980. The exit of H. N. Bahuguna, finance minister, further weakened the government. Toward the end of the year the political picture was confused, with loyalties and alliances being made and unmade with ease.

The Congress (I) was not without its share of troubles. Devraj Urs, the Karnataka state chief minister, broke with Mrs. Gandhi in June and moved over to the other Congress, of which he was elected president. In spite of dissensions, however, all the nation's parties agreed to elect M. Hidayutullah, a former chief justice, as the vice-president of the republic in succession to B. D. Jatti.

Defection having become a national pastime, many state governments fell. In Uttar Pradesh, R. N. Yadav made way for Banarsi Das as chief minister. In Bihar, Karpoori Thakur was voted out and Ram Sundar Das formed a government. Devi Lal was forced out of office in Haryana, and his place was taken by Bhajan Lal. The Union Territory of Goa, Diu, and Daman came under president's rule, and there were changes of government in Assam, Meghalaya, and Arunachal Pradesh. In October the Kerala government headed by P. K. Vasudevan Nair of the Communist Party of India resigned over a local issue, and C. H. M. Koya of the Kerala Muslim League formed a new coalition government. Elections were held in October in Sikkim; the Janata Party was defeated, and a government was formed by N. B. Bhandari. Earlier, in May, the Mizo People's Conference won elections in Mizoram, and Brig. T. Sailo formed a government. Insurgent activities continued in that territory, and the Mizo National Front was outlawed. Its leader, Laldenga, was arrested in July but freed on bail by a court in October.

Mrs. Gandhi strove to convert Janata difficulties to her advantage by vigorous campaigning

Supporters joyfully raised portraits of Charan Singh when he was sworn in as the new prime minister of India on July 28.

BALDEV—SYGMA

throughout India. A commission investigating the affairs of Sanjay Gandhi's Maruti Co. held that Mrs. Gandhi had used undue influence to promote the business interests of her son. Sanjay Gandhi and V. C. Shukla were found guilty of having destroyed the film *Kissa Kursi Ka* and were sentenced to two years in prison. Parliament adopted a bill providing for the establishment of special courts to try cases involving excesses during the state of emergency (June 1975–January 1977) imposed by Mrs. Gandhi's government. Prosecutions were launched against Mrs. Gandhi for her part in the alleged harassment of four officials and against V. C. Shukla for alleged misuse of office in having election posters prepared by officials. A contempt charge against Mrs. Gandhi was dismissed on December 20. Charges of favouritism against Morarji Desai and Charan Singh were referred to a former Supreme Court judge.

The 44th constitution amendment bill, which had been adopted by Parliament earlier, came into force on receiving approval of the required number of state legislatures. Another bill was introduced to amend the constitution so as to transfer the subject of cow protection from control by the states to the joint control of the states and the union government. This was in pursuance of an assurance to Acharva Vinoba Bhave, who had undertaken a fast in April demanding a total ban on cow slaughter. A private member's bill in the Lok Sabha to curb religious conversions caused disquiet among the minorities. Parliament also voted a bill to give pensions to former members. Ordinances were issued by the president to provide for preventive detention to check hoarding and profiteering and to ban donations from companies to political parties.

A major disaster occurred in August in the town of Morvi in Gujarat when a dam collapsed, killing an estimated 5,000 persons. Earlier, in March, landslides caused 230 deaths in Himachal Pradesh. A cyclone struck the Andhra coast in May. A plane crash near Bombay in August resulted in 45 deaths. Religious clashes occurred in Aligarh, Jamshedpur, and Ahmedabad. There was continuing unrest in various police organizations such as the Central Reserve Police and the Central Industrial Security Force. The Army was called in to put them down, and in the process 24 were killed in Bokaro and 3 in Delhi in June.

Tanker trucks distributed drinking water to residents in Morvi, about 515 kilometres northwest of Bombay, after a dam burst, killing an estimated 5,000 people in the area.

BALDEV—SYGMA

A Press Council was formed early in the year. The government also introduced a bill to give a measure of autonomy to All India Radio and Television, but the bill lapsed with the dissolution of the Lok Sabha. The assassination of Lord Mountbatten (*see* OBITUARIES), the last British viceroy, was widely mourned. An Albanian-born Indian nun, Mother Teresa, was awarded the Nobel Peace Prize for her work in Calcutta and elsewhere.

The Economy. Inflation returned, in double-digit form. The general price level on October 6, according to the Reserve Bank of India, was 220.8, or 17.5% above the level on Oct. 7, 1978. The rise since the end of March was 15.6%. Although grain production in the agricultural year July 1978–June 1979 was as high as 130.1 million metric tons, it was feared that the next year's output might show a decline of 10 million to 13 million metric tons owing to the failure of rains. Some 218 districts in the country were affected by drought, fully or partially. The "food for work" program was expanded, and steps were initiated to cut nondevelopmental expenditure. The union government's budget, presented by Charan Singh on February 28, gave priority to agriculture, rural development, and labour-intensive industries.

Taxation to bring in an additional Rs 6,650,000,000 was proposed, to be shared between the union government and the states. The union government's revenue receipts in 1979–80 were placed at Rs 112,090,000,000 and expenditure at Rs 113,960,000,000. With capital receipts of Rs 59,620,000,000 and capital expenditure of Rs 71,300,000,000, the overall deficit was Rs 13,550,000,000. Total allocation for defense was Rs 30,550,000,000 and for development, Rs 125,510,000,000. The fertilizer subsidy was increased, as was the provision for irrigation. Procurement prices of grain and sugarcane were increased to help farmers. The 1977–78 gross national product was placed at Rs 731,570,000,000 at current prices. The growth rate in 1978–79 was estimated at 3.7%, compared with 7.4% for 1977–78. The World Bank pledged aid of $3 billion for 1979–80. Loan agreements were signed with the U.K. for Rs 1,044,000,000, with the U.S. for Rs 1,760,000,000, and with Japan for Rs 740 million.

Among major factories that went into production during the year was the Rs 4 billion Indian Petrochemical Ltd. plant at Baroda. An agreement was signed between Punjab and Himachal Pradesh on the Rs 2.5 billion Thein Dam project. Sanction was also given for work on a 1,100-kw superthermal station at Farakka.

There were demands for the abrogation of the agreement signed with Britain for the Jaguar deep-penetration strike aircraft. However, the first of the aircraft began to be made during the year. An India-built space satellite, Bhaskara, weighing 444 kg, was put into orbit at a Soviet launching station in June, and an agreement was signed with the U.S.S.R. for the launching of another satellite in 1980. In August an attempt by the Indian Space Research Organization to send up a satellite launch vehicle failed.

Foreign Affairs. A. B. Vajpayee, foreign minister in the Desai Cabinet, visited China in February. Although statements were made by both sides favouring closer relations, the visit was cut short owing to the Chinese attack on Vietnam. Prime Minister Desai visited Sri Lanka, Bangladesh, the Soviet Union, Poland, Czechoslovakia, and Yugoslavia. Later in the year, because of the change of government, the Indian delegations to the Commonwealth conference in Zambia and the summit meeting of nonaligned nations in Cuba weres led not by the prime minister but by the new foreign minister, S. N. Mishra.

In his speech on Independence Day Charan Singh cautioned that if Pakistan went ahead with any plan to make a nuclear bomb, India might be forced to reconsider its decision not to produce nuclear weapons. Virginity tests carried out on Asian fiancées seeking entry to the U.K. caused much resentment; a British minister visited New Delhi in October for talks on immigration. Among notable foreign dignitaries to visit the country during the year were Soviet Premier Aleksey Kosygin, East German leader Erich Honecker, and Australian Prime Minister Malcolm Fraser.

(H. Y. SHARADA PRASAD)

INDIA

Education. (1977–78) Primary, pupils 55,772,018, teachers 1,354,460; secondary, pupils 40,702,098, teachers 1,505,565; vocational, pupils 185,251, teachers (1970–71) 14,024; teacher training, pupils 88,253, teachers (1970–71) 1,534; higher, students 3,716,350, teaching staff (1970–71) 119,000.

Finance. Monetary unit: rupee, with (Sept. 17, 1979) a free rate of Rs 8.20 to U.S. $1 (Rs 17.64 = £1 sterling). Gold, SDR's, and foreign exchange (May 1979) U.S. $7,403,000,000. Budget (1978–79 est.): revenue Rs 107,824,000,000; expenditure Rs 108,992,000,000. Gross domestic product (1977–78) Rs 871.2 billion. Money supply (May 1979) Rs 217.1 billion. Cost of living (1975 = 100; June 1979) 107.5.

Foreign Trade. (1978) Imports Rs 60,632,000,000; exports Rs 52,481,000,000. Import sources (1977–78): U.S. 13%; West Germany 9%; Iran 9%; U.K. 8%; U.S.S.R. 7%; Japan 7%; Iraq 6%. Export destinations (1977–78): U.S. 13%; U.S.S.R. 12%; U.K. 10%; Japan 9%; West Germany 5%. Main exports (1977–78): textile yarns and fabrics 14%; tea 10%; precious stones 10%; clothing 6%; iron and steel 5%.

Transport and Communications. Roads (1974) 1,232,300 km. Motor vehicles in use (1976): passenger 799,500; commercial 415,200. Railways: (1978) *c.* 60,700 km; traffic (1977–78) 168,300,000,000 passenger-km, freight 161,600,000,000 net ton-km. Air traffic (1978): 9,070,000,000 passenger-km; freight 323.3 million net ton-km. Shipping (1978): merchant vessels 100 gross tons and over 591; gross tonnage 5,759,224. Telephones (March 1978) 2,247,200. Radio licenses (Dec. 1976) 14,848,000. Television licenses (Dec. 1976) 280,000.

Agriculture. Production (in 000; metric tons; 1978): wheat 31,328; rice *c.* 79,010; barley 2,309; corn *c.* 5,500; millet *c.* 10,500; sorghum *c.* 12,000; potatoes 8,153; cassava (1977) 6,480; sugar, raw value 7,030; sugar, noncentrifugal (1977) *c.* 8,500; chick-peas 5,451; mangoes *c.* 9,149; bananas *c.* 3,853; cottonseed *c.* 2,500; rapeseed 1,618; sesame seed *c.* 489; linseed 504; peanuts *c.* 6,200; tea *c.* 565; tobacco 445; cotton, lint *c.* 1,173; jute (including substitutes) 1,482; meat *c.* 849; fish catch (1977) 2,540. Livestock (in 000; 1978): cattle *c.* 181,651; sheep *c.* 40,432; pigs *c.* 8,834; buffalo *c.* 61,043; goats *c.* 70,704; poultry *c.* 144,200.

Industry. Production (in 000; metric tons; 1978): coal 101,542; lignite 3,613; crude oil 11,270; natural gas (cu m) 1,680,000; iron ore (63% metal content) 37,660; pig iron 9,728; crude steel 9,948; bauxite 1,644; aluminum 206; gold (troy oz) 90; manganese ore (metal content; 1977) 665; cement 19,625; cotton yarn 911; woven cotton fabrics (m; 1977) 6,900,000; man-made fibres 186; petroleum products (1977) 22,472; sulfuric acid 2,220; caustic soda 547; electricity (excluding most industrial production; kw-hr) 100,920,000; passenger cars (units) 46; commercial vehicles (units) 49.

Indonesia

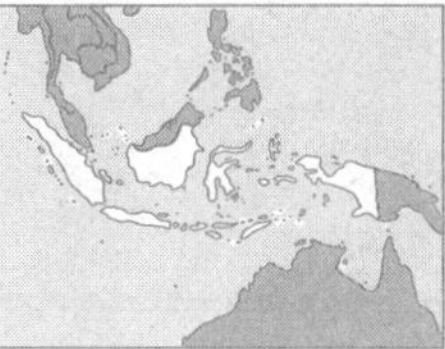
Indonesia

A republic of Southeast Asia, Indonesia consists of the major islands of Sumatra, Java, Kalimantan (Indonesian Borneo), Celebes, and Irian Jaya (West New Guinea) and approximately 3,000 smaller islands and islets. Area: 1,919,558 sq km (741,145 sq mi). Pop. (1979 est.): 144,912,000. Area and population figures include former Portuguese Timor. Cap. and largest city: Jakarta (pop., 1977 est., 6,178,500). Language: Bahasa Indonesia (official); Javanese; Sundanese; Madurese. Religion: mainly Muslim; some Christian, Buddhist, and Hindu. President and prime minister in 1979, Suharto.

Vietnam's invasion and occupation of Cambodia and the arrival in the Indonesian archipelago of "boat people" fleeing Vietnam were characterized by President Suharto in a national address in 1979 as "a fearsome development." Alarm over these events was coupled with growing anxiety at home, particularly in regard to land disputes and to the Islamic community.

In domestic affairs Islamic unrest vied with the land issue for national attention. The resurgence of Islam appeared to some Indonesian commentators as a backlash against Indonesia's modernization and had features in common with the militant Islamic upheaval in Iran. Police, for example, confiscated portraits of Iran's Ayatollah Ruhollah Khomeini. (*See* Feature Article: *Islam Resurgent.*)

Land disputes spread chiefly on Java and Sumatra, a consequence of the government's policy of land reform. The redistribution of land often placed the government at odds with peasant "squatters" on land that in the past had been unclaimed or where the ownership was in doubt. Members of Parliament urged the government to give the issue top priority and to avoid the use of force to resolve it. Lieut. Gen. Amir Machmud, minister for home affairs, warned that the land disputes could provide the outlawed Indonesian Communist Party (PKI) with an opportunity to exploit the situation and stage a comeback. (The PKI had been banned and dissolved in 1965 following an abortive Communist coup in which six members of the army general staff were murdered.) Admiral Sudomo, the director of national security, appealed to press and Parliament to avoid inflammatory statements on the problem but admitted that 80% of the cases handled by his agency involved land disputes.

Against this background, for the first time since General Suharto filled the power vacuum left by the unsuccessful PKI coup, voices were raised within and without the Army suggesting that the next president—scheduled to be elected in 1983—not come from the Army. Vice-Pres. Adam Malik, the highest ranking civilian in the government, conceded publicly that there was an undercurrent of restlessness in the country and appealed for the resolution of internal conflicts by due process and the electoral system.

In foreign affairs Indochina held stage centre. Indonesia joined with Malaysia, the Philippines, Singapore, and Thailand, its partners in the Association of Southeast Asian Nations (ASEAN), in calling upon China to withdraw its expeditionary force from Vietnam (which China did) and upon Vietnam to withdraw its invading troops from Cambodia (which Vietnam did not do). In a humanitarian gesture Indonesia provided a temporary haven for more than 40,000 refugees fleeing the repressive Communist regime in Vietnam. Indonesia, however, declined to accept refugees on a permanent basis on the grounds that it was already saddled with one of the lowest standards of living in Asia. (*See* REFUGEES: *Special Report*.)

China's short-lived attack on Vietnam caused a postponement of full restoration of Sino-Indonesian diplomatic relations. Indonesia thus remained one of the few countries in the world that had not exchanged ambassadors with China. In 1966 Indonesia had suspended diplomatic relations with China, accusing the Chinese Communists of complicity in the attempted coup by the PKI.

INDONESIA

Education. (1978) Primary, pupils 22,389,796, teachers 709,511; secondary, pupils 3,380,458, teachers 212,405; vocational, pupils 877,129, teachers 64,486; teacher training, students 212,331, teachers 14,006; higher, students (1977) 304,025, teaching staff 21,802.

Finance. Monetary unit: rupiah, with (Sept. 17, 1979) a free rate of 625 rupiah to U.S. $1 (1,345 rupiah = £1 sterling). Gold, SDR's, and foreign exchange (June 1979) U.S. $3,116,000,000. Budget (1979–80 est): revenue 5,467,000,000,000 rupiah (excluding foreign aid of 1.5 billion rupiah); expenditure 6,900,000,000,000 rupiah. Gross national product (1977) 18,420,000,000,000 rupiah. Money supply (Jan. 1979) 2,588,200,000,000 rupiah. Cost of living (Jakarta; 1975 = 100; June 1979) 174.3.

Foreign Trade. (1978) Imports U.S. $6,690,000,000; exports U.S. $11,643,000,000. Import sources: Japan 30%; U.S. 12%; West Germany 9%; Singapore 7%; Taiwan 5%. Export destinations: Japan 39%; U.S. 25%; Singapore 11%; Trinidad and Tobago 5%. Main exports: crude oil 60%; timber 9%; food 8%; rubber 6%; natural gas 5%.

Transport and Communications. Roads (1978) *c.* 115,000 km. Motor vehicles in use (1977): passenger 479,300; commercial (including buses) 327,100. Railways: (1974) 7,610 km; traffic (1977) 3,810,000,000 passenger-km, freight 853 million net ton-km. Air traffic (1977): 3,917,000,000 passenger-km; freight 56.9 million net ton-km. Shipping (1978): merchant vessels 100 gross tons and over 1,093; gross tonnage 1,272,387. Telephones (Jan. 1978) 324,500. Radio licenses (Dec. 1976) 5.1 million. Television receivers (Dec. 1976) 325,000.

Agriculture. Production (in 000; metric tons; 1978): rice 25,739; corn 2,750; cassava (1977) 12,169; sweet potatoes (1977) 2,453; sugar, raw value 1,350; bananas *c.* 1,764; tea *c.* 73; copra *c.* 950; soybeans *c.* 530; palm oil *c.* 505; peanuts *c.* 687; coffee *c.* 191; tobacco *c.* 70; rubber *c.* 870; fish catch (1977) 1,545. Livestock (in 000; 1978): cattle 6,167; buffalo 2,222; pigs 2,976; sheep 3,710; goats 7,119; horses (1977) 649; chickens 107,493.

Industry. Production (in 000; metric tons; 1978): crude oil 80,450; natural gas (cu m) 23,230,000; petroleum products (1977) *c.* 21,370; coal 261; tin concentrates (metal content) 24; bauxite 1,009; electricity (excluding most industrial production; kw-hr; 1977) *c.* 4,380,000.

On the economic front Indonesia in April launched its third (1979–84) five-year plan. It postulated an economic growth rate of 6.5% annually. Although the nation produced a record rice harvest in 1979, approximately 17.5 million tons, it was still compelled to import this basic food. Accordingly, the new plan placed greater emphasis on agricultural output.

As an expression of confidence in Indonesia's economic future, Japan and the Western capitalist countries announced grants and loans of almost $1 billion in economic aid for 1979–80. An additional $1.4 billion came from the World Bank, the Asian Development Bank, and the UN Development Program. (ARNOLD C. BRACKMAN)

Industrial Relations

Industrial relations in 1979 were heavily influenced by the continuing gloomy world economic situation. Economic growth was again disappointing, and unemployment generally continued to be high. Yet inflationary pressures persisted, worsened appreciably for most countries by the substantial increase in oil prices. In wage bargaining, workers in industrialized countries commonly maintained the expectation that their wages should be raised to cover the increased cost of living.

Wages apart, the principal issues in industrial relations in 1979 were unemployment, job security, and working hours. Labour efforts in these areas took three main forms. First, unions pressed governments to adopt policies aimed at maintaining or creating jobs; second, they endeavoured to stave off, or mitigate the consequences of, plant closings or reductions in work forces; and third, they sought to reduce working hours, partly as a worthy goal in itself but largely in the hope of creating additional job opportunities. The aim of a 35-hour week rapidly gathered strength during the year as an international labour union objective. This goal met fierce opposition from employers, who doubted that reduction of hours would lead to many more jobs becoming available and who felt unable to face the substantial costs involved in even a small reduction in working time. There were no appreciable general reductions in standard weekly working hours during the year, although a considerable number of union agreements provided for some extension of vacations or holidays or for earlier retirement, and a few envisioned small reductions in hours at some future date.

Britain and Ireland. In Britain industrial relations were a major national issue. During the early weeks of the year, particularly, there was a series of major strikes for wage increases, notably in road haulage, the health service, and local government. Settlements rose to a level far beyond what the Labour Party government had striven hard to secure as part of its counterinflationary policy. In February the government and the Trades Union Congress reached a "concordat" and issued a joint statement (*The Economy, the Government and Trade Union Responsibilities*) including guidance on the conduct of industrial relations and consideration of economic prospects and the special problems of public service workers, concerning whom a standing commission on pay comparability in relation to the private sector was quickly set up. These actions did much to cool a heated situation, but the strikes—and some features of them that disturbed wide sections of public opinion—were clearly not forgotten in the general election of May and played a part in ensuring Labour's defeat.

Although apparently fairly quiet, the situation when the Conservative Party took office contained some potentially difficult elements. Wage and price increases were running at a much higher level than in 1978; labour productivity continued to be comparatively low; and there was deep mistrust among trade unions about what the government might do. While the government lost no time in putting forward its promised electoral program of modest adjustments to existing industrial relations legislation concerning picketing, the closed shop, and union ballots, its approach was conciliatory and cautious. However, consistent with its basic economic philosophy, it made clear its belief in free collective bargaining; if workers made claims that resulted in unemployment, if employers made concessions that led to bankruptcy, it was their own responsibility and not that of government.

A national dispute in the engineering industry, involving strikes of first one day and then two days a week from early August to the beginning of October, centred on the unions' insistence on a reduction in working hours. In the end the package conceded by employers included a 39-hour week to begin in November 1981 and additional holidays.

In Ireland a proposed *National Understanding for Economic and Social Development*, arrived at between government, unions, and employers, was published in April. It was not endorsed, but in July a new agreement on wages was finally worked out, on the basis of government commitments on a number of employment, fiscal, and other social policies. In a heavy year for strikes, one concerning postal and telephone workers that lasted 18 weeks was particularly notable.

United States. On September 28 George Meany, the 85-year-old former plumber from the Bronx, New York City, who had been president of the American Federation of Labor-Congress of Industrial Organizations (AFL-CIO) since the inception of the merged organization in 1955—and president of the AFL for three years before that—made known that he did not intend to seek reelection. Tough, irascible, shrewd, an implacable anti-Communist, he had long seemed to dominate the U.S. labour movement. Lane Kirkland (*see* BIOGRAPHIES), secretary-treasurer of the AFL-CIO, was elected to replace him at the organization's convention in November. The two men were close enough in outlook to suggest that no sharp change in the orientation of U.S. unions was to be expected, although some movement seemed likely.

The rise in inflation in the U.S. put added strains on the administration's voluntary wage and price guidelines, which were also under pressure from union claims in some industries. A scheme to provide tax incentives for those who conformed to the guidelines foundered. The guidelines were relaxed slightly; in September an accord was made with labour, and a new Pay Advisory Committee, chaired by former secretary of labour John T. Dunlop and including union, employer, and public members, was established.

Though some important contracts could only with difficulty be reconciled with the guidelines, U.S. wage settlements were more moderate than in

KEYSTONE

Nearly 100,000 British public service workers rallied in Hyde Park, London, in January demanding higher pay.

UPI

Lane Kirkland (left), incoming president of the AFL-CIO, accepts the gavel from outgoing president George Meany, who served in the post for 24 years.

some other countries, and no major, long-drawn-out confrontations occurred. There were problems in trucking and in the rubber industry, but for the first time in many years long-term agreements were negotiated in the automobile industry without a strike.

Continental Europe. West Germany continued to be a relative bastion of economic stability. Wage settlements were again moderate. The one really major industrial dispute was the strike and lockout in the steel industries that had started in North Rhine-Westphalia in November 1978, the key issue being a demand for movement toward a 35-hour week. The dispute ended in January; the 40-hour week was maintained, but provision was made for increased holidays and vacations over a period up to 1982.

On March 1 the West German Constitutional Court delivered its keenly awaited decision on the 1976 codetermination law, which gave workers in large companies seats on corporate boards. Employers had argued that the law was unconstitutional, but the court confirmed its constitutionality in a judgment which, without completely satisfying either employers or unions, contained elements to the taste of each. Another legal question much discussed during the year, and which remained in dispute, was the right of employers to lock out workers in an industrial dispute (there having been several major lockouts in recent years).

In 1977 the West German unions had withdrawn from the national "concerted action" meetings in protest against the employers' questioning of the constitutionality of the codetermination law. The issue now being disposed of, the way was clear for a resumption of national consultations, and a first "summit" meeting between union and employer representatives took place in July.

In France the government continued its policies aimed at economic stability, including a measure of wage restraint, throughout the year. Premier Raymond Barre carried out a series of talks with union and management leaders with a view to seeing what could be done to create a better climate for industrial relations. The main immediate focus of attention, however, was on employment. New unemployment benefit arrangements were legislated in January, followed by a central agreement between the employers and the major trade unions in March. The most serious single problem, which produced violent confrontations in the early part of the year, was in the steel industry. An overall plan devised to make the industry economically viable could not prevent an estimated loss of more than 20,000 jobs, but it did include retraining and early retirement provisions. It was reluctantly accepted by the unions in July.

In Denmark it again proved impossible to negotiate a central wage settlement, and in March Parliament extended the current arrangements for another two years. It also added special provisions to help low-paid workers and for extended vacations. Also in March the country experienced an unprecedented walkout of civil servants and public employees, related to pay negotiations. Union and Social Democratic proposals for a share in industrial ownership for workers continued to cause considerable controversy.

A number of important agreements were made in Italy, notably the metal industry agreement of July. It provided for wage increases, a 40-hour reduction in annual working time to take place in 1981, the reinstatement of certain national holidays, and consultation rights for union workers on new company investments and employment changes.

The new industrial relations systems of Portugal and Spain continued to evolve. In Portugal, where the new non-Communist trade union centre, the União Geral de Trabalhadores, gathered strength, the government introduced a comprehensive measure confirming the right of association and establishing rules for union elections and voting by secret ballot. In January a decree in Spain established an institute for mediation, arbitration, and conciliation. The major development in Spain, however, was a comprehensive package of legislative proposals covering individual employment rights, collective agreements, and the rights and obligations of works councils. Also, in July, the major employers' organization and the Socialist trade union centre, the Unión General de Trabajadores, signed a noteworthy agreement concerning pay, the handling of disputes, questions regarding employment, and the rights of workers at the workplace.

South Africa. The wind of change blew strongly through South African industrial relations when the Wiehahn Commission issued its first report in May. The commission recommended the recognition of black workers' trade unions; providing apprenticeship opportunities for black workers; abolishing statutorily enforced separate facilities for white and black workers; and scrapping the statutory reservation of certain jobs for particular races. The government's subsequent proposals did not go so far but were later somewhat liberalized in legislation that took effect in October.

(R. O. CLARKE)

The views expressed in this article are the author's own and should not be attributed to any organization with which he may be connected.

See also Economy, World; Industrial Review.
[521.B.3; 534.C.1.q; 552.D.3 and F.3.b.ii]

Industrial Review

World manufacturing production in 1978 rose at about the same rate as in 1977. The rate of growth of output accelerated marginally in the advanced industrial countries as well as in the less developed areas but did not change in the centrally planned economies. Although provisional estimates indicated a somewhat more rapid advance in 1979, it became increasingly clear that world manufacturing production had so far been unable to return from the 1975 recession to the fast growth of the long post-World War II period to 1973.

On the demand side the greatest stimulus to industrial activity came from the current spending on goods and services by public authorities. This was partly due to the easing of financial difficulties in which state and local authorities in the United States had previously found themselves, as well as to the fair measure of success achieved by the attempts on the part of some countries, such as Japan and West Germany, to stimulate their economies via the public sector.

On the supply side one feature of 1978 was that the heavy industries, as a group, grew at about twice the rate of the light industries. Although the growth of the heavy industries after their enormous decline in the 1975 recession exceeded that in the light industries in 1976 and 1977 as well, this discrepancy became even more pronounced in 1978. The production of base metals, including steel, recovered from its stagnation in 1977 and grew by about 5%; other heavy industries, such as metal products, building materials, and chemicals, advanced at a similar rate. The growth rate of the light industries was only about 3%; the food-drink-tobacco and the paper-printing sectors grew faster than that, but the textile-clothing-footwear trades and the wood industries experienced considerably slower growth than the average.

In both the less industrialized countries and the centrally planned economies, manufacturing activity grew faster than in the advanced industrial nations, both overall and in almost all industries except for base metals and paper-printing. Especially depressed was the textile-clothing-footwear group in the advanced countries, which had been stagnating for some years. In quite a few types of manufacturing there was rapid progress in newly industrialized countries in the less developed areas (such as South Korea, Brazil, Hong Kong, Singapore, and Taiwan) as well as in southern Europe (Spain, Portugal, and Greece). The industries of some of those countries were competing successfully in world markets in fields that are technologically demanding, such as consumer electronics.

Outstanding among the advanced countries was the performance of the U.S. manufacturing industries; their output rose by more than 6% in 1978. This was matched by the Japanese and Canadian industries, but none of the major European industries came near to that rate of growth. Manufacturing production in Western Europe rose by less than 2% in 1978. The growth of the "big four" in Europe was also less than 2%, with Italy and West Germany slightly above, France fractionally below, and the United Kingdom well below that average.

Among the other countries in the European

CHICAGO TRIBUNE—NEW YORK NEWS SYNDICATE, INC.

Community, Ireland's output rose rapidly, but progress in the Benelux countries (Belgium, The Netherlands, and Luxembourg) and Denmark was modest. Similarly slow was the growth of manufacturing production in the Alpine republics (Austria and Switzerland) and in Finland. Output actually fell in Sweden and Norway, while it rose rapidly in the somewhat less advanced industrial countries in southern Europe: Spain, Portugal, Greece, and Yugoslavia. It appeared, however, that in 1979 the roles might have changed: manufacturing output appeared to be growing more slowly in North America and more rapidly in Western Europe.

Australian industry progressed moderately, while growth in South Africa was faster than in 1977. Trends in the less industrialized world were mixed; some Asian countries raised their manufacturing output (India +7%), but production in Pakistan fell. Output in Latin America rose by only about 3% despite a growth rate of 9% in Mexico, and that in Africa and Oceania increased even less.

In most industrial countries some measures were in force to restrain domestic demand. In general, these were enacted in order to keep inflation in check and took various forms, such as tight monetary policy and strict control of public expenditures. Because of the general weakness of demand, aggravated by isolated cases of protectionism, world trade in manufactures grew by only 5% in volume; although this was marginally higher than in 1977, it remained far below the 9% average of the ten years ended in 1976.

Industrial (and other) unemployment fell in the United States but remained high elsewhere. Despite the high overall unemployment, shortages in certain skills were nevertheless reported in many industrial countries. Productivity advanced slowly. As measured by output per hour worked in manufacturing, it rose relatively rapidly in Japan (8%) and France (5%), but only 2–3% in the United States, West Germany, and Italy, and 1% in the United Kingdom.

The centrally planned economies maintained their previous growth rate in 1978. Their strict control of imports helped those industries, such as textiles and clothing, that in the other advanced nations were experiencing competition from the less developed countries. Among the centrally planned economies, output in Bulgaria rose fastest and that of the U.S.S.R. was the slowest (4½%); growth in the manufacturing industries in the other Eastern European countries was satisfactory and in any case higher than that in most areas of Western Europe.

(G. F. RAY)

Table I. Index Numbers of Production, Employment, and Productivity in Manufacturing Industries

1970=100

Area	Relative importance[1] 1970	Relative importance[1] 1978	Production 1977	Production 1978	Employment 1977	Employment 1978	Productivity[2] 1977	Productivity[2] 1978
World[3]	1,000	1,000	130	136	...	...	...	...
Industrial countries	896	869	126	132	...	...	...	...
Less industrialized countries	104	131	161	172	...	...	...	...
North America[4]	409	417	131	140	...	...	...	...
Canada	27	29	131	142	103	104	127	137
United States	381	388	130	138	101	105	129	131
Latin America[5]	59	69	155	160	...	...	...	...
Mexico	13	15	146	159	...	...	...	...
Asia[6]	137	154	140	152	...	...	...	...
India	11	12	135	144	117	...	115	...
Japan	99	98	126	134	98	97	128	138
Pakistan[7]	3	3	129	120	...	...	...	...
Europe[8]	365	335	121	123	...	...	...	...
Austria	6	7	130	133	101	99	129	134
Belgium	11	11	120	124	...	...	...	...
Denmark	5	4	117	120	88	87	133	137
Finland	4	4	124	127	105	103	118	123
France	67	65	127	129	99	97	129	134
Germany, West	104	90	115	117	90	90	128	130
Greece	3	4	169	182	132	137	128	133
Ireland	1	1	137	158	99	...	139	...
Italy	37	35	122	125	113	111	108	112
Netherlands, The	13	11	118	120	84	81	140	148
Norway[9]	4	3	116	114	105	102	103	105
Portugal	3	4	156	166	...	...	...	...
Spain	12	17	172	184	...	...	...	...
Sweden	13	10	111	109	101	97	110	113
Switzerland	12	9	101	102	80	80	127	128
United Kingdom	54	43	105	106	88	88	119	121
Yugoslavia	13	17	168	184	139	144	121	128
Rest of the world[10]	30	26	112	113	...	...	...	...
Australia[7]	14	12	109	112	90	88	121	128
South Africa	6	5	117	122	116	...	101	...
Centrally planned economies[11]	...	...	177	189	...	...	...	...

[1] The 1970 weights are those applied by the UN Statistical Office; those for 1978 were estimated on the basis of the changes in manufacturing output since 1970 in the various countries.
[2] This is 100 times the production index divided by the employment index, giving a rough indication of changes in output per person employed.
[3] Excluding Albania, Bulgaria, China, Czechoslovakia, East Germany, Hungary, Mongolia, North Korea, North Vietnam, Poland, Romania, and the U.S.S.R.
[4] Canada and the United States.
[5] South and Central America (including Mexico) and the Caribbean islands.
[6] Asian Middle East and East and Southeast Asia, including Japan.
[7] Years beginning July 1.
[8] Excluding Albania, Bulgaria, Czechoslovakia, East Germany, Hungary, Poland, Romania, and the U.S.S.R.
[9] Employment and productivity based on 1972=100.
[10] Africa and Oceania.
[11] These are not included in the above world total and consist of Albania, Bulgaria, Czechoslovakia, East Germany, Hungary, Poland, Romania, and the U.S.S.R.

Table II. Pattern of Output, 1975–78

Percent change from previous year

	World[1]				Developed countries				Less developed countries				Centrally planned economies			
	1975	1976	1977	1978	1975	1976	1977	1978	1975	1976	1977	1978	1975	1976	1977	1978
All manufacturing	−7	9	5	5	−8	9	4	5	3	7	6	7	9	7	7	7
Heavy industries	−10	10	5	6	−10	10	5	5	0	10	7	8	10	9	8	8
Base metals	−14	9	0	5	−16	8	0	6	3	6	8	6	7	8	3	5
Metal products	−8	9	6	5	−10	9	6	5	4	9	6	9	12	9	9	9
Building materials, etc.	−7	10	5	5	−8	8	5	5	6	10	7	8	7	6	4	4
Chemicals	−8	12	7	5	−8	13	6	5	−5	11	8	6	10	8	7	6
Light industries	−3	8	3	3	−4	7	3	3	5	5	4	5	6	3	6	4
Food, drink, tobacco	1	5	4	5	0	5	3	4	4	7	7	7	5	2	5	4
Textiles	−3	7	0	1	−6	9	−1	0	5	6	1	4	6	5	4	4
Clothing, footwear	−1	9	1	2	−3	9	0	0	11	10	2	6	7	6	5	4
Wood products	−8	10	3	2	−9	11	4	2	0	4	5	−2	8	4	5	5
Paper, printing	−9	7	3	4	−9	8	4	4	−6	−7	3	1	8	6	5	4

[1] Excluding centrally planned economies.
Source: UN, *Monthly Bulletin of Statistics.*

Table III. Output per Hour Worked in Manufacturing

1970=100

Country	1970	1973	1974	1975	1976	1977	1978
France	100	121	125	121	135	139	146
Germany, West	100	117	121	126[1]	135[1]	140[1]	144[1]
Italy	100	125	130	123	134	143[1]	146[1]
Japan	100	133	136	131	143	153	166
U.K.	100	118	119	119	124	124	125
U.S.	100	113	116	118	124	126	129

[1] Not strictly comparable with earlier years.
Source: National Institute, *Economic Review.*

Table IV. Manufacturing Production in the U.S.S.R. and Eastern Europe[1]

1970=100

Country	1976	1977	1978
Bulgaria[2]	164	175	188
Czechoslovakia	148	156	164
East Germany[2]	145	152	159
Hungary	143	152	159
Poland	184	197	206
U.S.S.R.	152	161	168

[1] Romania not available.
[2] All industries.
Source: UN, *Monthly Bulletin of Statistics.*

ADVERTISING

The single largest account change in advertising history took place in 1979 when Kenyon and Eckhardt switched from the Ford Motor Co. to the Chrysler Corp. Kenyon received some unique incentives, including a five-year, no-cut contract, the right to have its personnel on Chrysler planning and marketing committees, and control of advertising for all Chrysler cars.

A Harris Poll showed that 85% of U.S. consumers interviewed thought television advertising was misleading, and 80% thought newspaper and magazine advertisements were misleading or untrustworthy. Major advertisers attempted to remedy this situation by spending more money on public interest advertising; for example, oil companies were advertising how to save fuel. Advocacy advertising was on the rise in 1979. Companies such as Chrysler, Bethlehem Steel, and Aetna Life and Casualty sponsored magazine and newspaper advertisements urging readers to write Congress in support of various economic issues. Many of the advertisements presented both sides. The Federal Trade Commission (FTC) distributed a report in September recommending that, instead of detailed regulations, advertisers be provided with incentives to disseminate better information voluntarily.

FTC hearings on advertising during children's TV programs continued through the first half of the year. The proposals presented ranged from a total ban on advertising aimed at anyone younger than eight to creating an advertisers' fund for "affirmative" ads that would promote good nutrition. The major issues debated were whether children can effectively evaluate advertising claims, whether parents should be more involved in the process of evaluating advertisements aimed at their children, and whether the government or industry should place more control on advertising to this segment of the market.

While the FTC was deciding on its final recommendations, the effects of the hearings were already apparent in the 1979–80 television season. Many ads aimed at children stressed discussing the products with parents. The television industry created a series of public service messages designed to show children the difference between cartoon "reality" and the normal world. Advertisements were also addressed to parents pointing out the need to monitor their children's TV viewing.

A potential new medium for advertisers opened up when the Federal Communications Commission (FCC) removed the exclusive market rule limiting communities to one over-the-air pay-TV station apiece. This was the last barrier to paid subscription television in the U.S. Paid subscription television differs from cable systems in that the signal is broadcast in a scrambled manner, and only a set equipped with a decoder provided to subscribers can receive the program. Six such stations were already in existence in the U.S.

FTC regulations proposed in 1979 would require all food advertisers to substantiate any claims made for products with regard to fat, calories, or cholesterol content. Drug manufacturers would be required to display prominently in advertisements all warnings currently on drug labels. In a precedent-setting decision, the commission ordered an advertising agency to present scientific evidence to support advertising claims for a gasoline-saving device. The agency could not misrepresent any test or survey used to support energy claims or misrepresent the energy-saving characteristics of the product. Scientific evidence would have to be presented by two independent sources not connected with the advertisers and with no economic interest in the product or service.

Taylor Wine Co., with the permission of the FCC and the Bureau of Alcohol, Tobacco, and Firearms, was allowed to use advertisements that compared its wines with named competitors. This was the first time that any alcoholic beverage had been allowed to use comparative taste tests in its advertisements since a 1954 policy banned taste tests in beer advertising. Advertising by banks offering "free checking" services and big-ticket premiums to attract savers came under close scrutiny by bank regulators in 1979. Many of the advertisements were found to be so complex that it was difficult for consumers to comparison shop among financial institutions.

Since 1976 advertising had grown at a faster rate each year than the U.S. economy. Estimated advertising expenditures in 1979 totaled $49 billion, compared with $43 billion in 1978. The top 100 national advertisers accounted for $10.3 billion. Television advertising rates rose an average of 55% over the three-year period 1975–78. This compared with increases of 24% for radio, 30% for newspapers, and 23% for magazines over the same period.

According to statistics published by *Advertising Age*, the top 100 national advertisers increased their expenditures in measured media in 1978 by 17% over 1977. Procter & Gamble continued to hold first place with expenditures of $554 million, followed by Sears, Roebuck, General Foods, General Motors, and K Mart. Procter & Gamble increased its advertising expenditures by 20% in 1978 because of heavy commitments to new products. Two entertainment companies, Warner Communications and MCA, were newcomers to the top 100 list, while Goodyear and Shell were dropped. Automobile companies took over three of the first five places in spot radio advertising. Chrysler led with a 300% increase in spot radio, while General Motors and Nissan ranked second and fifth, respectively. The leading users of network TV advertising were Procter & Gamble, General Foods, American Home Products, Bristol-Myers, and General Motors.

ABC obtained television rights to the 1984 Olympic Games in Los Angeles with a record bid of $225 million, substantially larger than the $87 million paid by NBC for rights to the 1980 Moscow Olympics. Advertisers paid an average of $150,000 a minute for commercials on these athletic events.

(EDWARD MARK MAZZE)

Comparative advertising—in which rival brands are listed by name rather than by such terms as "Brand X"—was advanced in August when the Taylor Wine Co. was allowed by the FCC and the Bureau of Alcohol, Tobacco, and Firearms to publish results of comparative taste tests.

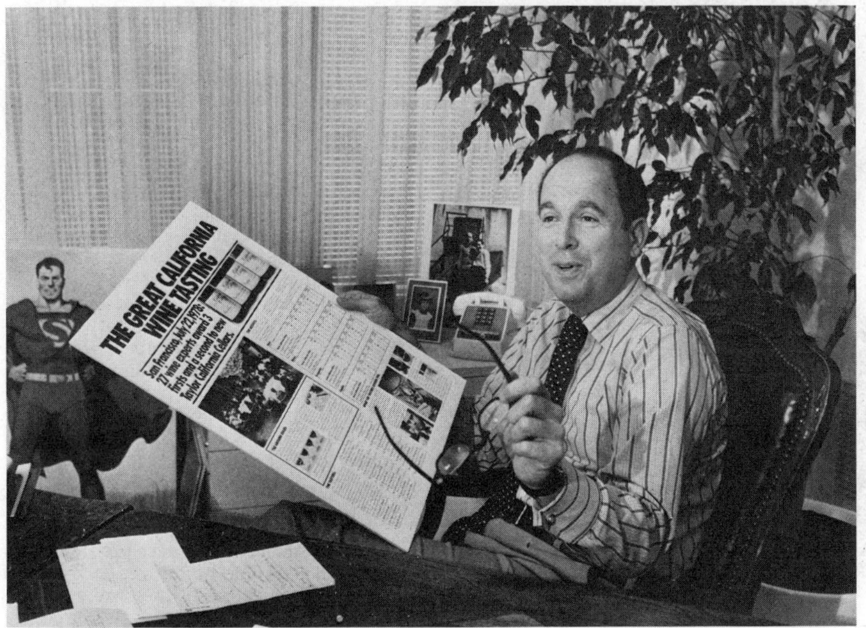

AEROSPACE

Reequipment, record demand for seats, another fuel crisis, and a disastrous accident were the principal ingredients of the 1979 air transport scene. Confidence in the management of both airlines and aircraft manufacturers received a severe jolt when an American Airlines DC-10 crashed near Chicago's O'Hare International Airport in May, killing 274 people. It was the worst accident in U.S. civil aviation history, and the Federal Aviation Administration (FAA) took the rare step of grounding all 138 U.S. DC-10 aircraft and, by extension, many of those operated by foreign companies. The FAA grounded, ungrounded, grounded again, and finally released the DC-10s for flight, and was torn between the airlines (which wanted to get the planes into the air again) and the powerful Airline Passengers Association (which wanted them grounded). DC-10s accounted for some 12% of U.S. internal capacity, and the grounding had considerable impact. European operators, with the assent of their own air-safety bodies, lifted their self-imposed bans and were flying long before the U.S. lines. (*See* TRANSPORTATION.)

The revolution in Iran triggered the second fuel crisis in a decade. Since the 1973–74 shortages most major airlines had organized long-term agreements with suppliers, but even so there were shortages, and spot market supplies were in demand. Shortages would have cut deeper had it not been for the 37-day grounding of the DC-10s, but they did create planning headaches for airlines facing generally great demand for capacity; for the first time since World War II domestic airlines in the U.S. were operating at as high as 70% of capacity.

All four Western wide-body airliners—Boeing 747, McDonnell Douglas DC-10 (despite the accident that lost the U.S. manufacturer an order from Italy's Alitalia), Lockheed L-1011 TriStar, and Europe's A300 Airbus—continued to sell well. The giant Boeing plant at Everett, Wash., was gearing up to build seven 747s a month, its maximum capacity for the world's biggest civilian transport. (An indication of the health of the U.S. industry was that, in 1978, Boeing took orders for a staggering 490 aircraft.)

But there was even greater interest in the developing replacement market for the current fleets of short- and medium-haul, narrow-body types such as the Boeing 707 and 727, Douglas DC-8, Hawker Siddeley Trident, and Sud-Aviation Caravelle. In 1978 Boeing launched its long-awaited 707 and 727/737 replacements in the shape, respectively, of the 767 and 757.

Meanwhile, a new and significant development took place in March when United Airlines announced a $400 million program to replace the noisy and thirsty 1950s-vintage engines in its DC-8 airliners with new, quiet, and economical Franco-U.S. CFM56 engines. The move was followed by several other operators of the long-range DC-8 variants.

Europe continued to work on the Airbus Industrie A310, a cut-down version of the A300. In late 1978 Britain rejoined the Airbus consortium, paying a $50 million reentry fee, together with a £50 million contribution toward the A310. This move came just in time to capitalize on orders for the A310 from Lufthansa and KLM, which planned to spend, between them, $1,575,000,000 on 35 aircraft plus options on another 35. Total orders and options for the A300 and A310 neared 400 by November 1979. The A300 and A310 had General Electric engines, and the demonstrator A300 powered by Pratt & Whitney was shown off at the Paris Air Show in June. A further indication of confidence in the 260-seat, 1,675-mi (2,695-km)-range, wide-body twinjet came from Rolls-Royce, which in June announced that it would provide engines for an RB.211-powered version. But the Paris show pointed up Europe's inability to develop a medium-range, narrow-body type; Airbus Industrie's JET (Joint European Transport) and A200 and Fokker's F-29 were still at the research stage, with no breakthrough yet in sight.

The last of the 16 Concorde supersonic transports authorized by the British and French governments flew in April. The 17-year program was terminated in September, although the two countries agreed to provide operational maintenance costs during the next four years. In January two Concordes of British Airways and Air France touched down at the Dallas–Fort Worth, Texas, airport, inaugurating the new Braniff service connecting Europe with the central U.S. via Washington, D.C. Three months later the Braniff operation, with five flights a week, was said to be profitable. The U.S.S.R., after withdrawing its Tupolev Tu-144 supersonic transports following two crashes, reintroduced them on the 3,800-mi (6,100-km) Moscow–Khabarovsk route (the earlier, Moscow–Alma Ata route was significantly shorter, at 2,025 mi [3,260 km]).

A new fighter plane for the U.S. Navy and the Marines was the McDonnell Douglas/Northrop F-18. The services planned to procure 1,377 of the planes.

UPI

There was also considerable activity concerning military aircraft. In June the McDonnell Douglas F-15 Eagle, the top Western fighter, went into action for the first time. Flown by Israeli pilots and vectored toward their targets by a Hawkeye airborne command post, they engaged MiG-21s of the Syrian Air Force while flying cover for Israeli forces attacking suspected Arab terrorist positions in southern Lebanon; at least five out of eight MiG-21s were downed with no loss to the Israelis. A few weeks later Libyan leader Col. Muammar al-Qaddafi offered to send some of his Soviet-supplied MiG-25 Foxbats to help the Syrians. By late October Israeli pilots were reporting the presence of another Soviet fighter, the swing-wing MiG-23 Flogger, also flying for the Syrians.

The U.S. technical press in February reported the existence of two new Soviet bomber designs and followed this up in March by describing three new Soviet fighters. The rapidly increasing strength and improving quality of the Warsaw Pact military machine finally obliged the North Atlantic Treaty Organization to make up its mind on the U.S. Airborne Warning and Control System, and 18 of the hugely expensive aircraft were ordered.

In the U.S. a famous fighter, the diminutive Skyhawk, went out of production after 26 years. Likely contenders for longevity records of the future were the McDonnell Douglas/Northrop F-18, which made its first flight in November 1978, and the General Dynamics F-16, principal aircraft in a multibillion-dollar U.S.-European coproduction program. The first European F-16s, replacements for the F-104G Starfighters, took to the air during the year.

On June 12, just before the 70th anniversary (July 25) of Louis Blériot's first flight across the English Channel, Bryan Allen of California pedaled the U.S.-designed and built "Gossamer Albatross" over the same route to win for the plane's designer, Paul MacCready, the £100,000 prize offered by British businessman Henry Kremer; the same team had in 1977 won the £50,000 prize for the first man-powered flight over a one-mile course in the "Gossamer Condor." But British prestige was at least partially restored in September when, in commemorating the 60th anniversary of the world's first scheduled passenger flight, a British-designed powered hang glider flew from Biggin Hill, near London, to Saint-Cyr, near Paris.

(MICHAEL WILSON)

ALCOHOLIC BEVERAGES

Beer. Estimated world beer production in 1978, at 835 million hectolitres (hl), was 15 million hl above that of the previous year. Once again the U.S. was the world's largest producer, although the year's output of 190,296,000 hl was nearly 5% below that of 1977. West Germany was the second largest producer, but its 91,656,000 hl represented a drop of 2.8% from the 94,336,000 hl of 1977, while the U.K. retained third place with a modest increase of 1.8% to 66,415,000 hl. In terms of per capita consumption West Germans remained the world's heaviest beer drinkers, but Australians replaced Czechoslovaks in second place and the Irish moved up from eighth to third place. (*See* Table V.)

In most countries of the world malting barley is the grain principally used for brewing. In some countries modern farming methods had led to a rise in recent years in the nitrogen content of the marketed grain. This was an unwelcome development because the nitrogenous material in the grain is incapable of being fermented. Thus, either more grain must be used to produce a given barrelage or less beer must be accepted from a given tonnage. However, there was an improvement in this respect in the U.K. and other European countries in the past two seasons, attributable to farmers timing their additions of fertilizer to ensure that the nitrogen was fully utilized by the plant and was not held in the grain.

Low-nitrogen barley is important to the brewer for other reasons besides yield. The use of additional grain adds to cost and also to fuel utilization. In a few countries, of which the U.K. is the best example, beer attracts a high rate of duty and, where this duty is imposed on the original gravity of the beer, the addition of malt increases the duty as well as the production cost. In the U.K. the duty currently paid was about one-third of the retail price of beer at the bar. (ARTHUR T. E. BINSTED)

Spirits. The world trend toward light spirits continued, with whiskey losing its market share in North America, where vodka, white rum, and tequila all gained ground. In the U.K. whiskey still accounted for 51% of the total spirits market, but gin had slipped from 18 to 15% and vodka had advanced from 5 to 12% over the past seven years.

The world market for Scotch whisky was expected to increase at 3–5% a year over the next five to ten years. World exports were worth a record £661.3 million in 1978 against £512 million in 1977. Exports to the U.S. jumped by 71% in volume in April 1978 alone, and for the first four months of 1978 were up by 27.7% in volume to 11,760,000 proof gal and 26.5% in value to £57.2 million. The U.S. share of total world consumption of Scotch whisky was about 29%, nearly twice the U.K. share. Bulk exports of Scotch whisky in 1978 totaled 9.6 million proof gal (14.3% above 1977), of which 65.6% went to Japan, where it was blended and sold under local labels. Scotch malt-based whiskies were also being made in Japanese-owned factories in Brazil and Mexico.

French cognac exports represented 80% of total sales of the beverage, with the U.K. second after the home market, the U.S. third, and West Germany fourth. The countries of the European Economic Community together took more than 50% of total production.

Manifestations of a growing antiliquor lobby in several countries included a ban in Sweden on all advertising of alcoholic beverages as from July 1. There were calls for a similar ban in the U.K., and tighter restrictions were imposed in Spain and France. Public drinking on the streets was banned in New York City.

(ANTONY C. WARNER)

Wine. Because of especially favourable conditions, estimated world production of wine in 1979 reached 340 million hl. Volume was comparable to the record years of 1973 and 1974. Quality was good and in many cases excellent throughout Europe. European production, including that of the U.S.S.R., totaled 270 million hl, representing 79% of world production; countries of the EEC alone produced 156 million hl, or 58%.

In the Western Hemisphere steadily growing U.S. production reached a new record total of 19 million hl, and Argentina's harvest, also increasing, was about 25 million hl. There were no significant variations in production in the rest of the world except in North Africa, where harvests were diminishing yearly.

France produced 73,850,000 hl of wine. In the Bordeaux area the quantity produced exceeded the average, and the quality was considered very high, possibly exceptional. In Burgundy, too, volume and quality were higher. The Beaujolais harvest was no greater than that of 1978, but quality was very good. In Alsace quantity and quality were good. In the Champagne region the improvement over 1978 was particularly marked: an unusually abundant harvest and wine of outstanding quality.

Italian production rose to more than 72 million hl, of which 48 million were of red or rosé wine. The harvest was markedly greater than that of 1978, and the wine produced in many regions, particularly those of northern Italy, was of very high quality. Spain had one of its best harvests, 42 million hl, as compared with 28.5 million in 1978. Portugal's increase was less notable, but the *vinhos verdes* region benefited from excellent climatic conditions to produce 40% more wine than in 1978.

West German viticulture suffered from a cold winter. Later, conditions were better and production was satisfactory, at more than 9 million hl (8 million in 1978). The U.S.S.R. enjoyed a good year with a wine production of 28 million hl, making it the world's fourth-greatest producer.

Australian production continued to increase, and the 1979 harvest was 3,453,920 hl. (PAUL MAURON)

Table V. Estimated Consumption of Beer in Selected Countries
In litres[1] per capita

Country	1976	1977	1978
West Germany	150.9	148.7	145.6
Australia[2]	139.9	136.2	137.7
Ireland	123.0	126.2	131.8
East Germany	124.5	126.4	130.0
Czechoslovakia	139.7	134.3	129.0
New Zealand	119.8	122.5	127.4
Belgium[3]	138.0	130.1	125.5
United Kingdom	118.9	119.5	121.3
Luxembourg	130.0	120.0	121.0
Denmark	118.83	116.32	116.9
Austria	102.0	103.1	100.9
United States	82.5	85.9	88.6
Hungary	76.4	80.6	86.0
Canada[4]	87.0	85.1	85.5
Netherlands, The	83.87	83.90	85.18
Switzerland	71.1	68.3	68.0
Finland	54.6	55.3	54.96
Spain	47.9	46.9	52.1
Venezuela	50.0	50.0	...
Sweden	59.1	53.6	48.9
Norway	44.72	45.47	46.04
France	48.66	46.21	45.25
Bulgaria	45.0	45.0	...
Colombia	39.9	40.0	40
Yugoslavia	40.4	38.7	...

[1]One litre = 1.0567 U.S. quart = 0.8799 imperial quart.
[2]Years ending June 30.
[3]Excluding so-called household beer.
[4]Years ending March 31.

Table VI. Estimated Consumption of Potable Distilled Spirits in Selected Countries
In litres[1] of 100% pure spirit per capita

Country	1976	1977	1978
Poland	5.4	5.8	5.6
Luxembourg	4.1	4.7	5.5
Hungary	4.0	4.62	4.55
East Germany	3.7	3.7	3.7
Czechoslovakia	3.0	3.48	3.6
Canada[2]	3.34	3.42	3.45
U.S.S.R.	3.3	3.3	3.3
United States	3.12	3.14	3.17
Netherlands, The	2.48	2.91	3.01
Spain	3.1	3.0	3.0
West Germany	3.33	2.92	2.99
Sweden	3.08	2.97	2.99
Finland	3.0	2.99	2.82
Yugoslavia	2.6	2.7	...
France[3]	2.5	2.5	2.5
Belgium	1.95	2.1	2.38
Ireland	2.03	2.16	2.36
Iceland	2.31	2.46	2.25
Switzerland	1.80	1.88	2.00
New Zealand	2.00	2.00	2.00
Romania	2.00	2.10	2.0
Bulgaria	2.00	2.00	...
Italy	1.9	2.0	2.0
Cyprus	1.6	1.7	1.9
United Kingdom	1.66	1.42	1.72

[1]One litre = 1.0567 U.S. quart = 0.8799 imperial quart.
[2]Years ending March 31.
[3]Including aperitifs.

Table VII. Estimated Consumption of Wine in Selected Countries
In litres[1] per capita

Country	1976	1977	1978
France[2]	101.27	102.10	98.00
Portugal	97.8	97.0	91.3
Italy	98.0	93.5	91.0
Argentina	84.8	88.5	85.0
Spain	71.0	65.0	70.0
Chile	47.84	52.30	47.7
Switzerland[3]	43.5	44.9	45.9
Luxembourg	45.8	49.3	43.3
Greece	39.8	39.6	42.0
Austria	36.3	36.1	35.0
Hungary	35.3	34.0	34.0
Romania	30.0	30.0	33.1
Yugoslavia	28.0	27.9	...
Uruguay	25.0	25	...
West Germany	23.6	23.4	23.8
Bulgaria	20.0	22.0	...
Belgium	15.7	17.5	17.8
Czechoslovakia	16.5	17.2	17.5
Australia[4]	11.2	13.7	14.3
U.S.S.R.	13.4	13.3	14.0
Denmark	12.53	11.67	12.22
Netherlands, The	11.35	11.73	12.18
New Zealand	9.7	9.4	9.5
Poland	8.5	9.1	9.3
Sweden	8.47	9.50	9.06
South Africa	9.89	9.00	8.80

[1]One litre = 1.0567 U.S. quart = 0.8799 imperial quart.
[2]Excluding cider (*c.* 20 litres per capita annually).
[3]Excluding cider (*c.* 5.6 litres per capita 1977–78).
[4]Years ending June 30.

Source: Produktschap voor Gedistilleerde Dranken, *Hoeveel alcoholhoudende dranken worden er in de wereld gedronken?*

AUTOMOBILES

The major development in the automobile industry in 1979 involved the Chrysler Corp. The third largest U.S. automaker was plagued by a variety of troubles which eventually forced its chairman to seek financial assistance from the U.S. government. Chrysler asked the government for loan guarantees totaling about $1.2 billion, claiming that the growing burden of meeting federal safety, emission, and fuel economy laws was forcing it to spend more money than it could make.

After considerable negotiation and a marathon session in Congress just before adjournment, a bill was passed providing $1.5 billion in federal loan guarantees on condition that the firm raise $2 billion in assistance and concessions from workers, dealers, creditors, and other parties. A requirement that union employees give up $462.5 million in raises over the next three years would necessitate renegotiation of the current contract. In seeking federal funds, the troubled automaker disclosed that its losses for calendar 1979 would total more than $1 billion, the greatest loss in corporate history. It also said that it would continue to lose money in 1980—about $450 million.

The year started out with promise for Chrysler. The new president, Lee Iacocca (*see* BIOGRAPHIES), the man who had been fired as president of Ford Motor Co. in 1978, was expected to lead the company back into a profitable posture. He could not do so. The company soon was burdened with huge inventories of nonselling big cars and was forced to offer a rebate of $400 per car in order to entice buyers into showrooms.

Chrysler finally admitted that it had made a major mistake for years. Unlike its domestic rivals, it had built cars at its factories without having orders for them first from its dealers. By contrast, General Motors, Ford, and American Motors only built cars when they had firm orders. Chrysler vowed to stop the practice.

John Riccardo, citing poor health and his fear that a continued association with Chrysler might jeopardize its chances of receiving a federal loan, retired as chairman of Chrysler. He named Iacocca to succeed him. Paul Bergmoser, who had been a top purchasing executive with Ford, was named Chrysler president to succeed Iacocca. By the end of the year Iacocca had lured more than half a dozen former Ford executives, some of whom had been in early retirement, to join him at Chrysler.

While able to attract key personnel, Chrysler instituted an executive pay cut. Most executives took up to a 10% reduction in salary, while both Riccardo and Iacocca chose to receive token $1 salaries for two years unless Chrysler was able to return to profitability.

In seeking labour union support for its federal loan guarantees and as a means of getting the United Auto Workers to accept a contract settlement somewhat less bountiful than that agreed upon with both General Motors and Ford, Chrysler agreed to name UAW president Douglas Fraser to the Chrysler board of directors. While union representation on a company's board had been common practice in Europe for many years, it was a precedent-setting measure by Chrysler and it was believed the union would eventually seek the same treatment from the other automakers.

UPI

Workers at the General Motors Willow Run Assembly Plant attach a bumper to a Buick of the new "X-body" series—downsized front-wheel-drive models.

As a further means of obtaining federal assistance, Chrysler announced its plans for the 1980s, saying that it would convert all its cars to front-wheel drive by 1985 and reduce the types of vehicles offered to basically a trio of subcompact, compact, and midsize only slightly larger than compact. It also said that it would offer diesel engines in its cars by 1985, making it the second U.S. producer after General Motors with plans to do so.

The Chrysler financial predicament nearly overshadowed the fact that the entire U.S. industry had an off year in sales. For the 1979 model year ended Sept. 30, 1979, industry sales declined 7.2% to 8,602,640 units from 9,274,811 in 1978. General Motors sales were down 2.5% to 5,152,900 units, while Ford declined 13.5% to 2,274,292 units. Chrysler was off 10.9% to 1,029,370 units, and American Motors sales fell 26.2% to only 146,078 units.

Despite the overall sales decline, GM was able to increase its share of the total market from 57 to 59.9%, while Ford's share fell to 26.4 from 28.4%; Chrysler's share declined to 12 from 12.5% in 1978; and American Motors was down to a meagre 1.7 from 2.1% in 1978.

For the 1979 calendar year, sales by GM, Ford, and Chrysler were off 12.1% to slightly over 8 million units from 9.1 million in the previous calendar year. Sales for the 1980 model year also started poorly, with the total for October down more than 20% from October 1978. As a result thousands of auto workers were laid off.

The automakers were particularly concerned about the sales decline because several new models had been introduced during the 12-month period. The most successful of the new cars were the downsized, restyled, front-wheel-drive compacts from GM that came to be known as the X-body cars. These included the Chevrolet Citation, Buick Skylark, Oldsmobile Omega, and Pontiac Phoenix, cars built on 104-in wheelbases in comparison with the 111-in wheelbase of the cars that they replaced. The X-cars were brought to market in April 1979 but were designated as 1980 models. They became so popular so quickly that GM was forced to increase production at a third plant, and still dealers had to quote buyers a wait of six months to one year from order to delivery.

In the fall of 1979, when the 1980 models were introduced, GM had little to offer in the way of new cars other than a dramatically restyled Cadillac Seville with what was referred to as a "bustle" rear deck lid treatment that seemed to copy heavily from the Bentley of the early 1930s. And Seville, establishing a first for GM, offered a diesel engine as standard equipment.

GM greatly expanded the use of diesel engines and turbocharging of its gasoline-engine cars for 1980. It also brought out five new gasoline engines that were in fact smaller cubic-inch-displacement versions of its previous big block V-8s.

Though it did not bring out many new 1980 models, GM made news around the world when it said that it had made a major technological breakthrough in batteries that might allow it to produce electric vehicles by 1985. GM claimed that the breakthrough consisted of its ability to get longer life—prolonged charge/discharge cycles—out of a zinc/nickel oxide battery to replace the lead acid battery it had been experimenting with since the mid-1960s. A production model electric car, which GM said would be either a small two-passenger commuter car or a small commercial van, would be an industry first and had been talked about for nearly two decades.

At Ford the last of the so-called gas guzzlers, the big Lincoln and Mark, were downsized by about a foot in length and 900 lb in weight while still retaining the same basic exterior styling. These models, brought out in October 1979, included an all-new entry, the Continental Mark VI four-door luxury car. The Mark VI designation was all-new as well.

Ford downsized its Thunderbird to slightly larger than a compact car as well as the T-Bird's companion car, the Mercury Cougar XR-7. It dropped the LTD II midsize models.

Chrysler brought out several new models in the midsize range. Cordoba, its specialty intermediate, was reduced by three inches in wheelbase and six inches in overall length; it was also some 350 lb lighter, while at the same time getting all-new sheet metal. Its companion car was the Dodge Mirada, a replacement for the Dodge Magnum that had only lasted two years on the market.

Chrysler restyled its midsize Dodge Diplomat and Chrysler LeBaron and brought out a new full-size model, the Plymouth Gran Fury. The firm also announced in the fall that by 1981 the Imperial name would be brought back on a new luxury model slightly larger than compact size.

At American Motors a first for a U.S. manufacturer was the introduction of the four-wheel-drive Eagle, a conversion of the compact Concord car to four-wheel drive. AMC also let it be known that more such vehicles would follow, namely, a four-wheel-drive version of the subcompact Spirit in the 1981 model year.

AMC also made news when it decided that, rather than being just friends with Renault, it would let the French automaker become family. AMC said that it would allow Renault to buy up to a 22.5% equity interest in the U.S. auto manufacturer. Under terms of the agreement Renault also said it would provide AMC with up to $150 million in funds to help the firm begin producing, in 1982, a Renault-designed/AMC-built family of front-wheel-drive economy cars in Kenosha, Wis., for the 1983 model year. Renault also concluded a coproduction agreement with Volvo of Sweden whereby it would acquire a 20% interest in Volvo's automobile division by 1986.

During the year AMC also announced that it was reinstating its dividend of 7½ cents a share payable quarterly. It last paid a dividend in 1974.

Automakers outside the U.S were also bringing new cars to market. Toyota produced its first front-wheel-drive model, the subcompact Tercel. Datsun completely restyled its subcompact sports car, the 200-SX, while Honda restyled the mini Civic for the first time in seven years. Volkswagen brought out a new Rabbit (Golf) convertible in the fall of 1979 as well as a subcompact pickup truck that offered eight four-cylinder gasoline or diesel engines. It also introduced a new replacement for the old VW bus that was called the Vanagon because it was a cross between a van and a bus. The truck was being built at Volkswagen's plant in New Scranton, Pa., and the company said it would have to add a second plant in the U.S. to build vehicles soon since its sales goal was 500,000 units annually and New Scranton only had capacity for production of 225,000 units.

In the U.K. in September, British Leyland (BL) chairman Sir Michael Edwardes (*see* BIOGRAPHIES) announced plans to end production of the MG sports car, lay off 25,000 workers, and close all or part of 13 plants. Other moves to salvage the financially ailing government-owned firm included a coproduction deal with Honda of Japan.

Amid the flurry of new cars came a flurry in new car prices. The U.S. automakers agreed to a voluntary ceiling of 5.5% in price increases in the Oct. 1, 1979, to Sept. 30, 1980, time period. In the Oct. 1, 1978, to Sept. 30, 1979, period the automakers had agreed to a 6% ceiling, but an analysis of prices showed the average base price of a domestic car rose by $1,065, or 18.7%, during that time. The average base price for a U.S. car at the outset of the 1980 model year was $6,731, compared with $5,666 at the outset of the 1979 model year.

In the fall of 1979 the U.S. Environmental Protection Agency tightened its federal corporate average fuel economy standards and called for U.S. manufacturers to produce a mix of vehicles that averaged 20 mpg for the 1980 model year. That was up from 19 mpg in the 1979 model year.

When the EPA released its mileage ratings on the 1980 models in the fall of 1979, non-U.S. cars once again dominated the field. However, a debate ensued because the Volkswagen Rabbit made in the U.S. topped the EPA ratings. The EPA decided to call the car an import because about 50% of its components were shipped from West Germany for assembly in the U.S.

(JAMES L. MATEJA)

BUILDING AND CONSTRUCTION

In the United States the value of new construction, seasonally adjusted, was $221,-483,000,000 in June 1979. Throughout the first half of the year construction outlays continued at a higher annual rate than the $206,224,000,000 total during 1978. However, as 1979 drew to a close there were clear indications that the construction industry was headed toward a substantial curtailment in activity. Despite this indicated downturn, it appeared that the total outlays for the year would exceed the level achieved in 1978.

During the five-year period ending with 1979, dollar outlays for new construction moved up sharply in each successive year, but when expenditures were shown in constant 1972 dollars, it was apparent that much of the increase had been due to inflation. The general inflationary trend during the 1970s had stimulated construction of all types, as people viewed buildings for businesses or homes as a hedge against inflation. However, the onset of the recession in 1979, accompanied by high interest rates and a sharp reduction in the availability of mortgage funds, reduced the ability of buyers to utilize this hedge.

The level of dollar outlays for residential building, an important component of construction, was higher during 1979 than in 1978 despite the high interest rates and the continuing upward spiral in construction costs. Data published by the U.S. Department of Commerce on new privately owned housing units authorized by permit-issuing agencies revealed, however, that fewer units were authorized each month in 1979 than in the corresponding month of 1978.

The inflationary conditions continuing into 1979 were revealed in the various indexes of construction costs. In June 1979 the composite construction cost index of the U.S. Department of Commerce stood at 196.1 (1972=100), a rise of 12% over June 1978. Among the construction materials showing the greatest cost increases were: building wire, up 42%; copper water tubing, up 35%; nonmetallic sheathed cable, up 35%; steel reinforcing bars, up 28%; selected hardwood lumber, up 23%; Douglas fir, up 18%; building blocks, up 17%; and building brick, up 14%. As a result of all these cost increases, the average price of a single-family house rose until it was approximately $68,000 in 1979.

In the U.S. during 1979 the detached single-family house continued to be the major type sought in the market. In 1978 completions of such units were reported by the U.S. Department of Commerce to be 73% of all residential construction, and in 1979 it appeared that the proportion would be only slightly lower. A survey of the characteristics of single-family houses built during the 1970s revealed that more than 80% had central warm-air heating systems; an increasing number had central air-conditioning systems and used electricity for heating. By 1977, 61% of the new homes had fireplaces. During the 1970s two-thirds of the houses built had three bedrooms; by 1977 more than 70% had two or more bathrooms. The proportion of houses with exterior walls built of wood or wood products increased during the 1970s; in 1977 the distribution revealed 38% with walls of wood or wood products, 31% with brick, 12% with stucco, 11% with aluminum siding, and 3% with other types.

In Canada residential construction declined 3.5% in the last quarter of 1978 and remained at a low level of activity into 1979. While higher business profits were expected to stimulate business investment in 1979 and 1980, consumer expenditures were expected to remain depressed and government policy restrictive. There were no signs to indicate a renewal in building and construction.

Economic conditions in Western Europe improved during the last half of 1978, but the outlook in 1979 was clouded by possible serious dislocations of oil supplies from Iran. The economies of the developed countries reflected the prevailing uncertainty regarding the economic outlook. In the U.K. private housing investment was down during the last half of 1978, and while some recovery was expected during the early part of 1979, the forecast was that activity during the year would be 20% lower than in 1978. In West Germany the construction industry was extremely active in 1978, and it was anticipated that building activity would remain strong until the middle of 1979 helping to keep the country's economy in high gear. In France private investment was low in 1978, but plans for capital expenditure in 1979 suggested that a substantial rise would occur. Elsewhere in Western Europe, building and construction generally remained depressed.

In Japan during 1978 the government sought to stimulate the economy by a substantial increase in expenditures on public works and publicly financed housing. These efforts met with moderate success, and the government decided that in the 1979–80 budget period it would continue to concentrate expenditures on those two areas.

(CARTER C. OSTERBIND)

CHEMICALS

With few exceptions, chemical industries in the industrialized countries throughout the world shed the remnants of their sluggish performances in 1977 and rebounded smartly in 1978. The pace of production, sales, and profits during the first three quarters of 1979 indicated that at least for that period 1979 would prove to be an even better year.

Shipments of chemicals and allied products in the U.S., as tabulated by the U.S. Department of Commerce, amounted to $126,445,000,000 in 1978, 11% above the total in 1977. For the first half of 1979 chemical shipments rose to $71,931,000,000, 16% higher than for the first half of 1978.

Though higher prices were responsible for part of the increase, most of it was real. The U.S. Federal Reserve Board index of chemical production rose from 185.7 in 1977 (1967=100) to 197.4 in 1978, an increase of 6.3%. Preliminary figures for the first six months of 1979 revealed that the index averaged 208, 5.4% higher than it was for the full year 1978.

In the meantime chemical prices rose only 3.1% in 1978, according to the U.S. Department of Labor's index of producer prices. The index increased from 192.8 (1967=100) in 1977 to 198.8 in 1978. For the first half of 1979 it averaged 212.3, 6.8% higher than it was for 1978. Because of higher costs for feedstocks and energy, the prices for chemicals rose rapidly in 1979. By July the index had reached 224.3.

Higher oil prices imposed by the Organization of Petroleum Exporting Countries (OPEC) during 1979 did help the U.S. chemical industry's balance of trade, however. The U.S. was producing considerable amounts of crude oil that was being transferred to domestic industries at controlled prices below the world market level. That gave U.S. chemical companies a competitive edge against nations more dependent upon imported OPEC oil. Also contributing to the U.S. industry's healthy exports were a generally high demand for chemical products and a currency that was depressed against those of its major trading partners. In 1978 U.S. chemical exports, as compiled by the U.S. Department of Commerce, were valued at $12,618,300,000, while imports totaled $6,427,400,000. The net value of exports, $6,190,900,000, was 6% higher than in 1977. During the first six months of 1979 net value of chemical exports shot up 38.6% to $8,037,300,000, while net imports rose only 12.3% to $3,638,400,000. Net exports, therefore, were worth $4,398,900,000, which was 71.9% more than in the same period of 1978. McGraw-Hill's fall survey of preliminary plans for capital spending indicated that U.S. chemical companies expected to raise spending for plant and equipment in 1980 by more than 14%.

In Japan the chemical industry in 1978 recovered from a prolonged slump, thanks to an improved economy in general and a determined effort to streamline and restructure. Chemical sales during calendar 1978 were approximately $62 billion. The country's Ministry of International Trade and Industry (MITI) reported that for fiscal 1978 (which ended March 31, 1979), the chemical production index averaged 122.2 (1975=100). By March 1979 it had risen to 129.7.

MITI also reported that 391 chemical and man-made fibre makers planned to increase capital spending from $1,980,600,000 in fiscal 1978 to $2,243,900,000 in fiscal 1979, the first such increase since 1975. Most of the money was destined for energy conservation.

West Germany's chemical industry registered a 5% increase in physical output in 1978, but the value of sales rose only 2.7% to $46.6 billion. One of the principal reasons was the strength of the mark, which gained 13% against the U.S. dollar in 1978. Also contributing was European overcapacity for the production of many chemicals.

Chemical business improved slightly in the last quarter of 1978 and then moved up 12% in the first quarter of 1979. Early in the year chemical executives were predicting a 4% increase in sales for the year. By the end of June it appeared as though the first-half increase would be at least 12% and that the full year would outperform expectations. The industry was taking a cautious attitude, however. It was concerned over possible inventory building by customers, and it was worried about high costs for feedstocks and wages and about slim profit margins. High costs would normally dampen exports. However, the West German chemical industry imported $10.5 billion worth of chemicals in 1978, while it exported $19.2 billion for a favourable balance of trade of $8.7 billion.

Chemical sales in the United Kingdom in 1978 amounted to about $31.3 billion. A strike by truck drivers in January 1979 hurt the chemical industry. The British Chemical Industries Association said that the strike would cost the industry $597 million in total sales and $498 million in exports. By the start of the fourth quarter it appeared that chemical sales would rise 15% in 1979 to $36 billion. Only 1.2% of the increase would be real, however, the rest being caused by inflation.

During the year, the British government gave its long-awaited approval to a $1.3 billion complex to process natural gas liquids at Mossmoran, Fife, Scotland. Considered a key part of the long-range development of the U.K. petrochemical industry, it would include a plant to extract liquids from natural gas and a plant to make ethylene from the liquids. Although a local group was seeking to overthrow the approval in court, groundwork for the gas separation unit and detailed design on the ethylene plant had started by the fourth quarter of 1979.

(DONALD P. BURKE)

ELECTRICAL

The average annual growth rate in the world electrical market in the 1970s was 7%, compared with 9% in the 1960s; a rate of 6% was predicted for the 1980s.

A market shift from heavy electrical equipment toward electronic goods began in the 1950s, and by 1978 heavy electrical equipment comprised 34.5% of the world electrical market, compared with 25% for electronic goods. With the development of the microprocessor and microelectronics generally the trend was expected to continue, and by 1990 the predicted market proportions were 28.4% for heavy electrical equipment and 27.5% for electronic goods, including microprocessor-based systems. (See *Microelectronics,* below.) The electrical consumer goods market had been steady at about 19.5% of the total market for 20 years, and no change was expected over the next decade.

Competition among the industrialized nations in the world electrical market became more intense as less developed countries began international trading. Japan increased its market share from 14.7% in 1970 to 16% in 1977, while the U.S. retained 17.8% in 1977, compared with 20.1% in 1970. During the same period the less developed countries increased their share from 4.1 to 8%.

In Europe the changes were relatively minor. France and the U.K. each retained 7% of world electrical exports, while West Germany was still second in the world with 16.1% in 1970 and 16.2% in 1977, although hard pressed by Japan. West Germany's share of world electrical equipment manu-

General Electric's Electronic Halarc light bulb, shown in a cutaway model at left, is said to last up to five years in normal use while consuming less energy than a conventional tungsten-filament bulb. The new bulb, developed by miniaturizing the metal halide lamp commonly used in sports stadia, would cost $10.

GENERAL ELECTRIC

facture was 10%. In 1978 exports of electrical equipment grew by 6.5%, but imports were 11.3% above the previous year. Imports of electrical equipment in 1978 accounted for 5% of the domestic market in Japan; 11% in the U.S.; 28% in West Germany; 30–36% in France, the U.K., and Italy; 56% in Sweden; 63% in Switzerland; and 69% in Austria.

Most of the multinational companies in the electrical industry reported good business during 1978. General Electric of the U.S. announced increases of 13% in net earnings and 12% in sales over the previous year, and the French Compagnie Général d'Électricité group had a 12.5% increase in sales. However, West German-based companies such as Siemens, Allgemeine-Elektrizitäts-Gesellschaft, and Brown Boveri suffered from lack of power station orders and heavy involvement in Iranian contracts and had to be content with a range from a 5% increase to a decline of 2%.

In Britain the General Electric Co. (no relation to the U.S. General Electric) reported a 7% rise in turnover in 1978 and a 16% increase in pretax profits. The electronics side of the business experienced the most growth, followed by the heavy industry sector.

A growing number of new product developments from the electrical industry were related to energy conservation. Exxon Corp., the U.S. oil giant, grabbed the headlines in May 1979 with the announcement that it had developed a black box device that would improve the efficiency of electric motors and that it was bidding for Reliance Electric to exploit the energy-saving device. The device turned out to be a form of variable speed control of AC motors using power transistors instead of the more usual thyristors, diodes, and smoothing circuits. Variable-speed control not only could result in 50% savings in energy but would also allow for the elimination of energy wastage in secondary control equipment such as valves in pumping applications. The main advantage of the Exxon motor controller was its cheapness. It was two to five times less expensive to make than existing variable-speed controllers, and if it were widely applied, the energy saved in industry would be equivalent to one million barrels of oil a day in the U.S. alone.

Another energy-saving development, described as the most important in lighting since the fluorescent tube, was announced by General Electric in May 1979. Called the Electronic Halarc, it was a replacement for the common tungsten-filament electric light bulb. The Halarc, which had five times the life and five times the efficiency of the ordinary bulb, used a small arc tube instead of a tungsten filament.

(T. C. J. COGLE)

FURNITURE

Prompted by gloomy government predictions of recession and rising inflation in 1979, the U.S. home furnishings industry reduced inventory levels and slowed production. Instead of the anticipated downturn, however, sales remained at 1978 levels and some regions, including the Sunbelt states, enjoyed better than average results.

In 1978 U.S. furniture manufacturers increased their volume of shipments by 13% over 1977, to an estimated $21 billion at retail. Based on U.S. Census Bureau reports, estimated sales in 1979 totaled $17.6 billion. This did not include sales of imported furniture or of furniture made by manufacturers classified as belonging to other industries (such as metal). Shipment values for the first nine months of 1979 reflected inflation. According to the National Association of Furniture Manufacturers, bedroom and dining room volume during this period was up 12%, tables 22%, recliners 11%, upholstery 4%, and metal dinettes 2%; summer and casual furniture volume was unchanged.

Probably the most dramatic style development was the emergence of brass furniture, notably beds, dinettes, and even baby cribs. Some plastic simulated woods, made of increasingly costly petroleum, were being replaced by genuine hardwoods, particularly oak. The U.S. Department of Agriculture's Forest Resources Laboratory reported that 3,400,000,000 bd-ft of hard- and softwood lumber were used for furniture in 1978.

The growing acceptance of modular wall units continued, apparently spurred by the need for vertical storage in increasingly smaller homes and apartments. Conversely, the popularity of multipurpose furniture for family rooms, now called "great rooms," also continued to grow. Considered a style experiment, "Hi-Tech," a trend toward the industrial look in home furniture and accessories, featured steel cases, wire baskets, and office-type seating. Action chairs, such as recliners, gained in popularity. A newer product, called the incliner, had a seat within a seat that moved with the body. Casual and easily transportable "life-style" furniture accounted for another growing market segment.

While the U.S. consumer price index rose 22.7% between July 1978 and July 1979, furniture wholesale prices increased by only 11%. This could be attributed in part to the reaction of a highly competitive industry to an anticipated recession, causing it to absorb much of the estimated 34% increase in labour and material costs. The lower value of the U.S. dollar in foreign markets brought an increase in U.S. furniture exports, estimated at $200 million in 1978. However, the U.S. continued to import 2½ times more furniture than it exported.

(ROBERT A. SPELMAN)

FURS

Prices for nearly all furs continued to rise in international markets in 1979. Average increases were in the neighbourhood of 15–20%, but some long-haired items advanced as much as 50%. Once again the increases were sharpest for U.S. and Canadian buyers, whose dollars were eroded by inflation and fluctuations in the international currency market.

After climbing steadily for nearly a decade, retail fur sales declined somewhat in North America. Although furs were still important in the fashion picture, double-digit inflation, soaring interest rates, and fear of recession caused many consumers to reexamine their priorities. In Europe, on the other hand, retail sales were excellent, especially in West Germany, Italy, Switzerland, and France. Business in Japan and Hong Kong reportedly set new records. While Japan was a fur consumer, Hong Kong was a net producer and exporter; its 1979 shipments were at twice the rate of the previous year and were expected to approach $200 million.

The first American International Fur Fair was held in New York City in March and drew nearly 22,000 visitors, almost the same as the well-established event in Frankfurt, West Germany. Officials estimated that the U.S. fair generated some $40 million in wholesale sales.

Nations belonging to the International Convention on Trade in Endangered Species met in Costa Rica to formulate a clearer definition of the responsibilities of individual governments in controlling their own resources; improve policing of commercial and tourist traffic in products made from endangered species; and suppress the "laundering" of certain wildlife products through the issuance of false documents. A U.S. proposal for permission to export alligator skins after a ten-year moratorium and to ease restrictions on bobcat was withdrawn.

There was an increase in antifur activity. In California an Animal Bill of Rights, the first of its kind anywhere, was enacted by the state legislature. In Washington a broad campaign was launched by the Humane Society of the United States to ban leg-hold traps and discourage fur buying.

There was a revival of interest in karakul, also known as persian lamb. More than ten million karakul skins were produced each year on ranches in the Soviet Union, Afghanistan, South Africa, and South West Africa (Namibia). Renewed demand was attributed to the widespread use of karakul by internationally famous designers.

(SANDY PARKER)

GEMSTONES

There was a definite tapering off of diamond sales during the first half of 1979. The sluggish market forced De Beers, major supplier of the world's diamonds, to order sharp cuts in sales of rough diamonds to dealers. Israel and Belgium received only half their expected supply, while India's was reduced to a quarter, producing a crisis in that country's diamond industry. As a result of De Beers's actions, however, prices for finished diamonds over a quarter of a carat remained firm. Larger diamonds were already becoming scarce in the first half of the year, leading inevitably to price increases in the last half.

In August De Beers increased prices by 13%, and this helped trigger a rise in the prices of larger and better quality diamonds of from 38 to 45%. By October, when New York diamond dealers raised prices of such diamonds by 28%, the spectacular price surge of 1978 had resumed. Even such actions as the stringent tightening of credit to diamond cutters by Israeli banks did little to slow price increases. Despite diamond-related problems, the U.S. jewelry industry enjoyed considerably increased sales, although profits were somewhat lower than in 1978. Spectacular diamond sales included an old 17.47-carat light pink diamond which brought $660,000, or about $37,800 per carat, at Christie's in London.

Among coloured gems, there was general market acceptance of beautiful bright blue topaz coloured permanently by irradiation. Apparently much of the good blue sapphire entering the market was also treated. Dealers in the great gem centre of Bangkok, Thailand, estimated that 90% of all sapphires originating in Australia, Sri Lanka, and Thailand were heat-treated to intensify the colour. At a time when better quality emeralds were in short supply, green garnet (tsavorite) also gained acceptance. Cubic zirconia, the best man-made substitute for diamond, was much more widely distributed. Ruby supplies reportedly continued to drop, as did supplies of amethyst from Zambia, aquamarine and tourmaline from Mozambique, and sapphire, garnet, and tanzanite from Tanzania. Pearls staged something of a comeback, and the U.S. took second position, after West Germany, as a buyer of pearls from Japan.

France, attempting to regain its position of importance in the market, opened a large new Precious Stones Centre in Paris, with complete facilities for the trade. Israel tripled the size of its large and modern Diamond Exchange. (PAUL E. DESAUTELS)

GLASS

Glass production registered a small increase in 1979, in line with growth rates over the last few years. Moves toward consolidation and rationalization within the industry continued. Saint-Gobain-Pont-à-Mousson of France reorganized the management and organizational structure of both its holding company and its operating divisions. Owens-Illinois Inc. and Domglas Inc. (Montreal) planned to form a joint company—Libbey-St. Clair—which would manufacture glass tableware.

Pilkington Brothers Ltd. of the U.K. invested £70 million in a new float glass line at its St. Helens factory. Its Reflectafloat 33/52 glass was the first monolithic solar-control glass with a reflective coating to be produced by the firm. With a reflective capacity of up to 43%, it was one of the most efficient solar-control glasses so far available. A £120 million bid enabled Pilkington to take over a large part of the operations of the French firm BSN-Gervais Danone and a 54.8% stake in the West German Flachglas company. In one of its most spectacular moves, Pilkington also gained complete control of Glaverbel (Belgium) and Machinale Glasfabriek De Maas (The Netherlands). This made Pilkington the largest flat-glass producer in the world.

In the U.S. Corning Glass Works was producing ultraflat glass photomasks that were a vital component in the production of semiconductor integrated circuits. A flatness rate of 2.3 microns over a surface more than 100 mm in diameter was achieved.

Western European manufacturers were becoming concerned about the increasing volume of glassware imported into the EEC from Eastern Europe. It arrived mainly through the low tariff wall between East and West Germany and led to accusations of dumping. The problem of imported lamps was already under investigation by the EEC Commission.

In the U.K. glass-container manufacturers fought back competition from alternative forms of packaging with the wide-mouth bottle and 1½-litre glass bottle. The trend toward lighter-weight glass containers continued. New weights and measures legislation being introduced in the U.K. gave rise to the concept of bottles that could also be used as measuring containers. Since—so far at least—only glass containers could be used in this way, a beneficial effect on the demand for glass was expected.

United Glass Ltd. of the U.K., partly owned by Owens-Illinois, installed the world's biggest bottle-making machine at its Alloa, Scotland, factory, to be used in the manufacture of whisky bottles. Because of the unusually large width between the centres of its ten molds (6¼ in), it would be able to manufacture bottles of one quart size and above. The research and development division of United Glass, in conjunction with Owens-Illinois, used a computer in Ann Arbor, Mich., to help design new bottles. A visual display terminal at St. Albans was linked via satellite to the computer, which produced a diagram of the initial mold shape needed for press-and-blow operations.

The practice of recycling glass containers in order to cut down waste and save energy continued to grow in many parts of the world. In the U.K. £750,000 was invested in plants to process glass collected from local authorities. Based on the proportion of waste glass recovered, Switzerland continued to lead the field, with 35% of the nation's glass waste recycled by Vetropack. (MARTHA H. MINA)

INSURANCE

Global premium volume of private insurance exceeded $300 billion in 1979; annual sales had more than tripled in the past decade. Divided approximately 40% for life and 60% for nonlife insurance, these sales represented about 5% of world gross national product. The figures exclude social security taxes and premiums for government insurance plans, as well as insurance in Eastern Europe and in countries such as Iran where insurance had been nationalized.

By 1979 life insurance premium income in the U.K. was increasing at an annual rate of 17% and general insurance by 7%. Lloyd's of London added 3,000 new underwriting members, bringing its membership to 17,000 and its premium income to more than £1,000 million. However, in response to heavy losses by several syndicates, Lloyd's system of self-regulation was under review. A £35 million loss occurred with the disappearance of the German barge carrier "München" in early 1979, and even larger marine losses were expected from the July collision of two supertankers off Tobago. In addition, claims estimated to exceed £100 million were made under insurance contracts guaranteeing computer leases in the U.S.; this might become the worst one-line loss in Lloyd's 300-year history.

To meet the growing insurance needs of multinational firms, financial alliances were instituted between the principal U.K. and U.S. brokers. An EEC directive in 1979 permitted life insurers to open establishments in any EEC country, but full freedom to transact all insurance services across frontiers was progressing only slowly.

The growth of U.S. life insurers was strong. Assets approached $400 billion and life insurance in force neared the $4 trillion mark. Health insurance and annuities registered the largest sales increases, with percentage gains of 15% or more. Total life, health, and annuity premiums amounted to approximately $90 billion in 1979.

U.S. life insurers were heavily criticized in a 1979 report from the FTC, which summarized their rate of return on whole life insurance as very low. Although statistically misleading because canceled policies were included in the data, the report increased support for government price disclosure rules designed to provide greater consumer protection. Hearings held by the President's Commission on Pension Policy were also expected to result in proposals for more federal regulation of pension funding, benefit, and investment practices.

During the first half of 1979, U.S. property and liability insurance suffered underwriting losses of almost $1 billion on $44 billion of written premiums. Fortunately, this was offset by investment income of more than $4 billion. A record 30 catastrophe losses (each involving more than $1 million) during this period caused $600 million in insured damages, a figure exceeded for the full year during only 3 of the previous 30 years. Furthermore, this did not include losses of $120 million from Hurricane David in September and the all-time single-catastrophe losses from Hurricane Frederic, mostly in Alabama and Mississippi, which were expected to total $750 million. Other disasters resulting in high insurance losses included tornadoes in Kansas and Texas early in the year; the crash of a DC-10 aircraft at Chicago in May, which claimed 274 lives; the collapse of roofs on arenas in Kansas City, Mo., and Rosemont, Ill.; and the nuclear accident at the Three Mile Island power plant in Pennsylvania.

Arson continued to be a pressing problem in fire insurance, and the insurance industry was cooperating with government to obtain tougher laws and investigations. The Insurance Services Office announced revision of general liability contracts; many of its simplified "readable" homeowners', business owners', and automobile policies were adopted in a number of states.

Auto rating classification systems were the subject of considerable discussion. Although a midyear report by the National Association of Insurance Commissioners rejected elimination of current classifications, several states passed laws forbidding the use of sex and marital status (and sometimes age) as rating criteria. Many insurers would begin to use auto-model year as an additional basis for rates in 1980, and others were experimenting with increased emphasis on such factors as years of driver experience and accident records.

No-fault automobile liability insurance made little progress in 1979, and Nevada became the first state to repeal its no-fault law. In a significant change of sales technique, Allstate Insurance Companies adopted a dual system of marketing by appointing more than 1,000 "independent" agents to add to their "exclusive" agency force. (DAVID L. BICKELHAUPT)

WIDE WORLD

Nearly 13,000 U.S. Steel Corp. employees lost their jobs in November when the steelmaker closed 16 unprofitable plants in eight states.

IRON AND STEEL

In a year of recovery for world steel in output terms, production in 1979 was likely to rise to a new record level of around 750 million metric tons, some 6% above that of 1978. All producing countries would probably make more than in 1978 except perhaps France and Italy (affected by strikes) and India (various shortages associated with climatic conditions). The prospect for 1980 was not good, however, with reduced demand expected in many major industrial regions.

There was a generally modest improvement in financial performance as a result of higher utilization of plant capacities and some price rises. This improvement was most evident in the case of industries based mainly on solid home market demand and which were not seriously undermined by import pressures: for example, those in the U.S., Japan, and Australia. In the countries of the EEC, however, the financial improvement shown by most companies was only in terms of slightly reduced, though still very large, losses.

Tables VIII and IX illustrate the changing patterns of world steel activity. While the major traditional Western producers (including Japan) produced no more during the steel recession and in most cases sharply less than five years earlier, the Eastern European countries continued to advance at a steady rate. The Soviet Union had topped the list in terms of country output of crude steel by a wide margin for the last six years, and Poland and Czechoslovakia were now major producers by any standard. Much more strikingly, however, a number of smaller producers—by no means exclusively less developed countries—showed appreciable and in some cases dramatic production gains, despite the recession. Among these nations were South Korea, Taiwan, Finland, South Africa, Brazil, Mexico, India, and Canada. Spain continued to maintain the high levels achieved there in recent years.

The U.S. industry enjoyed a reasonably good year with some increase in domestic demand and a capacity utilization rate averaging 88%. Profits rose but not to a level appropriate to investment costs in so capi-

Table VIII. World Production of Crude Steel
In 000 metric tons

Country	1974	1975	1976	1977	1978	1979 Year to date	1979 No. of months	1979 Percent change 1979/78
World	708,900	645,630	676,770	674,070	715,350	—	—	—
U.S.S.R.	136,200	141,330	144,810	146,660	151,400	74,820	6	—
U.S.	132,200	105,820	116,120	113,700	124,000	95,220	9	+ 4.1
Japan	117,130	102,310	107,400	102,410	102,110	83,300	9	+10.4
West Germany	53,230	40,410	42,410	38,980	41,250	34,800	9	+ 8.3
France	27,020	21,530	23,230	22,090	22,840	16,800	9	− 3.1
China*	26,000	26,000	21,000	23,400	31,000	†		
Italy	23,800	21,870	23,460	23,340	24,280	17,590	9	− 2.6
United Kingdom	22,380	19,770	22,400	20,470	20,260	16,230	9	+ 8.2
Belgium	16,230	11,580	12,150	11,260	12,600	10,230	9	+13.7
Poland	14,560	15,010	15,640	17,840	19,250	7,900	5	—
Czechoslovakia	13,640	14,320	14,960	15,050	15,290	3,780	3	—
Canada	13,620	13,020	13,290	13,630	14,900	11,900	9	+ 8.0
Spain	11,500	11,100	10,980	11,170	11,340	9,000	9	+ 9.5
Romania	8,840	9,550	10,970	11,460	11,780	†		
Australia	7,810	7,870	7,790	7,340	7,600	5,980	9	+ 4.8
Brazil	7,520	8,390	9,250	11,250	12,200	10,230	9	+15.8
India	7,070	7,990	9,360	10,010	10,100	6,980	9	− 1.2
Luxembourg	6,450	4,620	4,570	4,330	4,790	3,690	9	+ 2.0
East Germany	6,170	6,480	6,740	6,850	6,980	1,090	2	—
Sweden	5,990	5,610	5,140	3,970	4,330	3,370	9	+ 9.6
South Africa	5,840	6,830	7,110	7,300	7,850	6,600	9	+12.6
Netherlands, The	5,840	4,820	5,180	4,920	5,580	4,390	9	+ 7.4
Mexico	5,120	5,280	5,290	5,550	6,740	5,300	9	+ 6.2
Austria	4,700	4,070	4,480	4,090	4,340	3,660	9	+12.7
Hungary	3,470	3,670	3,650	3,720	3,770	1,920	6	—
North Korea*	3,200	2,900	3,000	4,000	5,080	†		
Yugoslavia	2,840	2,920	2,750	3,180	3,460	2,570	9	− 0.8
Argentina	2,350	2,210	2,410	2,680	2,790	2,400	9	+22.2
Bulgaria	2,190	2,270	2,460	2,590	2,470	1,070	5	—
South Korea	1,950	1,990	3,520*	4,350	4,970	5,540	9	+53.6
Finland	1,660	1,620	1,650	2,200	2,330	1,790	9	+ 5.9
Turkey	1,590	1,700	1,970	1,900	2,170	1,840	9	+ 9.4
Greece	930	900	1,110	1,000*	1,000*	†		
Taiwan	900	1,010	1,630	1,770	3,430	3,210	9	+35.2

*Estimated. †1979 figures not yet available.
Source: International Iron and Steel Institute; British Steel Corp.

Table IX. World Production of Pig Iron and Blast Furnace Ferroalloys
In 000 metric tons

Country	1974	1975	1976	1977	1978
World	504,640	468,410	484,270	480,550	497,740
U.S.S.R.	99,870	102,970	105,380	107,370	110,700
Japan	90,440	86,880	86,580	85,890	78,590
U.S.	87,010	72,510	78,810	73,780	79,550
West Germany	40,220	30,070	31,850	28,980	30,160
France	22,520	17,920	19,020	18,260	18,500
China*	22,000	22,000	18,000	20,000	26,000
United Kingdom†	13,940	11,940	13,910	12,270	11,340
Belgium	13,150	9,070	9,870	8,910	10,130
Italy	11,760	11,410	11,630	11,410	11,340
Canada	9,580	9,310	10,030	9,660	10,340
Czechoslovakia	8,910	9,290	9,480	9,720	9,940
Poland	7,790	7,750	8,040	9,650	11,240
Australia‡	7,520	7,510	7,310	6,730	7,280
India‡	7,410	8,440	9,780	9,800	9,270
Spain	6,910	6,840	6,630	6,640	6,250
Romania	6,080	6,600	7,650*	7,780	8,160
Brazil	5,850	7,050	8,170	9,380	10,040
Luxembourg‡	5,470	3,890	3,760	3,720	3,720
Netherlands, The‡	4,800	3,970	4,270	3,920	4,610
South Africa	4,660	5,210	5,850	5,810	5,900
Austria	3,440	3,060	3,320	2,970	3,080
Mexico	3,210	2,050	2,330	3,000	3,510
Sweden‡	2,980	3,310	2,950	2,330	2,360
North Korea*	2,700	2,900	3,000	4,000	5,000
Hungary	2,290	2,220	2,220	2,320	2,330
East Germany	2,280	2,460	2,530	2,630	2,560
Yugoslavia	2,130	2,000	1,920	1,930	2,080
Bulgaria‡	1,530	1,510	1,550	1,610	1,490
Finland‡	1,380	1,370	1,330	1,760	1,860
Turkey‡	1,320	1,340	1,680	1,620	1,720
Argentina‡	1,080	1,030	1,280	1,100	1,440
South Korea‡	990	1,190	2,010	2,430	2,740
Norway	660	640	650	500	550

*Estimated. †Estimated adjustment to calendar-year basis.
‡Excluding ferroalloys.
Source: International Iron and Steel Institute.

tal-intensive an industry as steel. The strength of home demand was broadly based, with particularly active markets in nonresidential construction, durable goods machinery, and domestic equipment. Imports for the year were expected to decline to approximately 14 million metric tons. However, some weakening in the market became evident during the second half of 1979, and the prospect for 1980 was for a possible decline of about 5% in domestic shipments.

The "trigger price" system designed to reduce the potentially disruptive effect of imports on the U.S. market continued in operation during 1979, the government issuing quarterly-reviewed import price levels based on Japanese costs. Any imports arriving at lower prices would be liable to accelerated antidumping procedures. The quotas on stainless and tool steel imports first introduced in mid-1976 were to be phased out by February 1980.

In Japan output was likely to reach 110 million metric tons in 1979, still well below the 1974 level but the highest since then. The economy was especially active during the first half of the year, with an upturn experienced even in shipbuilding and a large rise in apparent steel consumption. On the other hand, export demand from China was much lower than previously expected because of the major restructuring of China's industrial modernization program. The overall prospect for the Japanese steel industry in 1980 was for a stationary situation at best.

The Davignon Plan of steel market support measures, comprising import restraint agreements with the governments of the major non-EEC steel-supplying countries, mandatory and recommended minimum prices set by the European Commission for sales within the European Coal and Steel Community, and recommended tonnages for deliveries of each main product, was maintained in the European Community throughout the year. Economic activity improved in several Community countries, with demand from investment sectors rising and the building of stocks by consumers and merchants resulting in increased output and some market strengthening. However, oversupply of flat products with associated price weakness persisted, and the prospect for 1980 was of a decline in consumption. Restructuring measures designed to restore the international competitiveness of the EEC steel industry were being undertaken in most countries and were expected to be further developed in the following year.

The Steel Committee formed within the Organization for Economic Cooperation and Development (OECD) in October 1978 met on a number of occasions during 1979, and was expected to sponsor a steel symposium early in 1980. The committee was studying the market prospects in a number of particularly sensitive product areas with the broad objectives of maintaining as free trade as practical in steel during the crisis; seeking to ensure that any protective measures that might be adopted were as limited and equitable as possible; and encouraging restructuring designed to resolve the steel problem in the longer term. If the expected further market downturn took place in 1980, the OECD Steel Committee could prove valuable as a vehicle for alleviating the international tensions that could arise in the field of steel trade regulation.

(TREVOR J. MACDONALD)

MACHINERY AND MACHINE TOOLS

The latest (1977) Census of Manufactures report, published by the U.S. Department of Commerce, revealed that the machine tool industry in the United States consisted of about 1,300 firms, mostly small in size, with two-thirds of those employing fewer than 20 people. At the other end of the size scale there were estimated to be ten firms that employed more than 1,000 people. Total industry employment was about 90,000. Fewer than 400 of the firms accounted for more than 90% of the total U.S. machine tool output.

In a recent study of machine tools installed in U.S. metalworking plants, it was determined that approximately 34% of them were more than 20 years old and only about 31% were less than 10 years old, a situation that almost certainly contributed to a reduction in the productivity growth of the U.S. compared with that in many of the other industrialized countries. By contrast, fully 60% of the machine tools installed in Japan were less than ten years old, as were 42% of those installed in Italy. Reports indicated that 54% of the machine tools installed in the U.S.S.R. were also less than ten years old.

Machine tools are typically subdivided into two categories, metal-cutting and metal-forming. The former includes milling machines, lathes, drill presses, and other machines used to shape the workpiece by chip-removal techniques. The metal-forming machines include punch presses, bending machines, and shears. Each class is reported separately in U.S. Department of Commerce and National Machine Tool Builders' Association statistics. These figures showed 1979 U.S. shipments of metal-cutting machines to be about $2.7 billion, while those of metal-forming machines totaled approximately $900 million.

In spite of the high cost of borrowed capital for machine-tool purchases, orders for new machine tools were placed at near record levels during the year. Orders in 1979 for metal-cutting machines were approximately $4.5 billion and for metal-forming machines, approximately $1 billion. With new orders considerably exceeding shipments, a sizable backlog existed on the books of those companies engaged in the manufacture of this machinery. Current production levels indicated a 12–16-month backlog depending on machine type. The size of this backlog made it unlikely that the machine tool industry would be severely affected by any temporary downturn in the U.S. economy.

As a further hedge against the effects of fluctuating domestic economic growth, the U.S. machine tool industry was attempting to increase its share of the worldwide market. This effort was being aided by currency exchange rates favourable to U.S. exporters. At the same time, the effect of the importation of machine tools made outside the U.S. was being moderated by the greater dollar cost of such imports under the current exchange rates.

A major exhibition of machine tools from throughout the world was scheduled to take place in September 1980 at the McCormick Place exhibition hall in Chicago. More than 100,000 prospective buyers were expected to view the latest in metal-cutting and metal-forming tools and related control techniques. Covering more than 750,000 sq ft of exhibit area, this convention was held every other year to bring machine tool buyers and sellers together in a single convenient location.

(JOHN B. DEAM)

Heavy machinery and tools from all over Europe were on display at an international fair in Barcelona.

EFE/PHOTO TRENDS

MICROELECTRONICS

Among the fastest growing industries in the world in 1979, microelectronics was characterized not only by its high technical content but also by its tremendous impact on other products. These ranged from calculators, watches, radios, and television to highly sophisticated computer systems.

Memories. The value of memory consumption worldwide was expected to grow from approximately $100 million in 1970 to tens of billions of dollars in 1990. This explosive growth would almost certainly be accompanied by dramatic decreases in cost per bit, which would allow memories to be used in a wide variety of consumer products. In the early 1970s the price of one type of memory was approximately 1 cent per bit. By 1990 the price of a comparable memory would be 1 millicent per bit.

The memory sold in highest volume in 1979 was the 16-K dynamic random access memory (RAM; K=1,024 bits). In 1979 a new type of 16-K dynamic RAM was successfully manufactured in high volume. (In a dynamic RAM, data must be refreshed periodically or it will be lost.) This was the single-power-supply 16 K, and the leader was Intel Corp. Formed in 1968, Intel was expected to have sales of more than $1 billion in 1980. There was also evidence in 1979 of high-volume production of the next generation of dynamic RAM's, the 64-K dynamic RAM. In addition to the improvements in the dynamic RAM's there was even more rapid progress with static RAM's. In 1979, 16-K static RAM's were in production, and by 1990 it was expected that static RAM consumption would exceed that of the dynamic RAM and that the price per bit of the static RAM would be lower than that of the dynamic RAM.

As microelectronics progressed into the 1980s, the metal oxide semiconductor (MOS) was expected to dominate the technologies, and the performance of MOS with scaling down to the 1.5 micron level would exceed that of the older bipolar technology. MOS also had the advantage of lower power dissipation and higher packing density.

In addition to the high growth in RAM's there would also be very high growth in read only memories (ROM's), in which information is read out but not altered in operation. The driving force behind the growth in ROM's would be the continued incorporation of software into hardware.

Logic. Logic in 1979 was increasingly dominated by the microprocessor, which was evolving into the microcomputer. It was in the area of microcomputers that the explosive impact of microelectronics would be mainly felt. Whereas memory products perform the passive function of storage of information, the logic and microcomputer form the active sector, such as the processing of the data. This processing can range from control of a microwave oven to very large computers.

In 1979 the 16-bit microprocessor became a reality. A 16-bit microprocessor such as the Motorola 68000 was equivalent to a minicomputer that in the mid-1970s sold for a few hundred thousand dollars. Within a few years it would be possible, using microcomputer technology, to build such a minicomputer for about $100. The effect of such a development would be great. Among the expected specific applications were: the increased incorporation of microprocessors in automobiles to improve fuel economy; the use of microprocessors in two-way television sets for voice selection of stations and other applications; and the use of microprocessors in computers for small businesses and homes.

IBM CORP

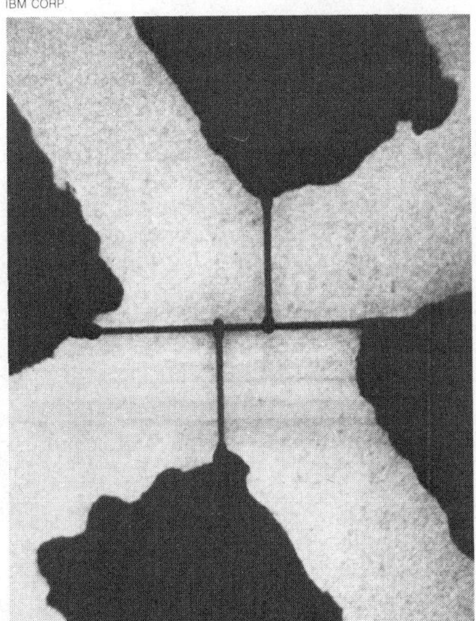

Tiny electronic circuit elements (black lines) from IBM Research Division, only 50-billionths of a metre wide, are far thinner than human nerve fibre.

One measure of the impact of microelectronics was that in 1970 the consumption of microelectronic products within the electronic industry was approximately 1% of the total sales. In 1980 that percentage had risen to approximately 6%, and by 1990 it was projected to reach 12%. Not only would microelectronics have a major impact on the cost structure of the electronics industry, but, more important, the performance of microelectronic products would determine the performance of the end system. (HANDEL H. JONES)

NUCLEAR INDUSTRY

The nuclear industry suffered its most serious setback yet as a result of the accident at Three Mile Island near Harrisburg, Pa., on March 28, 1979. (*See* ENERGY.) The accident had important political repercussions in many countries. The most significant in the U.S. was the appointment of a presidential commission under John G. Kemeny.

The Kemeny Commission's report, published on October 30, called for the nuclear industry to "dramatically change its attitude toward safety." It did not, as some commission members wished, propose a moratorium on all further construction pending the enactment of suggested reforms, but it recommended that no licenses for new plants be issued before the state government concerned had devised satisfactory emergency plans. While laying most of the blame for the accident on the Three Mile Island plant's operators, Metropolitan Edison, the report also criticized the role of the Nuclear Regulatory Commission and recommended that the NRC be abolished and replaced by a new agency headed by a single, presidentially appointed director. With regard to the health hazard produced by radiation released during the incident, the commission concluded that this was negligible.

Two significant steps in practical research on the effects of loss of coolant in reactors were made during the year: one was the beginning of experiments at the Loss-of-Fluid Test Facility at the Idaho National Engineering Laboratory, which had already given encouraging results on the performance of water-cooled reactors under these conditions; the second was the conclusion of engineers working on Britain's prototype fast breeder reactor at Dounreay that the controversial faster breeder would not reach dangerous temperature levels if the liquid sodium coolant pumps failed. The natural circulation of the sodium would be ample to cool the reactor while it shut down.

In Britain the new Conservative Party government quickly made clear its belief in the need to rejuvenate the country's nuclear industry and nuclear power plant construction program. A new grouping composed of Rolls-Royce and Northern Engineering Industries from Britain and Combustion Engineering, one of the leading U.S. reactor constructors, was announced. Its objective was to develop home and export markets for nuclear power stations incorporating the Combustion Engineering System 80 design of pressurized water reactor (PWR). Later in the year the Central Electricity Generating Board made its first move toward beginning the first British PWR project by asking the Nuclear Power Co. (the reactor constructor) to negotiate with Westinghouse Electric Corp. of the U.S. for a 1,200-Mw PWR.

The progress of France's nuclear power program excelled that of any other country, although agitation over cracks discovered by Électricité de France in parts of the water coolant circuit caused union workers to refuse to fuel the Gravelines and Tricastin plants. Although agreeing that the cracks were not serious, the unions maintained that it would be easier to repair them at once rather than by using special techniques after radioactivity had contaminated the components. Also during the year the French constructor Framatome received two blows with the loss of prospective orders from China and Iran.

Nuclear waste disposal had particular importance in West Germany because part of the licensing procedure for each nuclear plant involved determining how the waste from the plant was to be disposed of finally. A proposed waste reprocessing and storage centre at Gorleben was the subject of a public inquiry in March at Hanover. In May, however, the Lower Saxony government blocked the proposal pending further research on waste disposal.

The West German constructor Kraftwerk Union gained an order for a second heavy-water reactor at the Atucha power station in Argentina. This $1.5 billion contract was won against stiff competition from Atomic Energy of Canada Ltd. (AECL). The Canadian company's bid was reputedly 30% less than the West German offer, and AECL blamed the loss of the order on the Canadian government's continuous changes of policy on safeguards requirements. The Argentines also ordered a heavy-water production plant from Sulzer of Switzerland, also in competition with AECL.

Construction of the 1,200-Mw Bushehr power station in Iran was halted following the revolution there. The new authorities alleged that the plant was being built below the requisite "workmanship standards." The constructor, Kraftwerk Union, in turn, demanded payment for work already completed, but without success. In Spain two plants previously held up pending governmental authorization were given the go-ahead. These were the 1,020-Mw Trillo station and the two-unit, 1,950-Mw plant at Valdecaballeros.

In perhaps the most far-reaching reaction to the Three Mile Island incident outside the U.S., the previously pro-nuclear Social Democratic opposition party in Sweden changed its view on the need for a public referendum on the nuclear power issue; this question had already caused the collapse of Thorbjörn Fälldin's Centre-Conservative government in 1978. It was decided that a referendum would be held early in 1980, and the result would be upheld by the government even if it favoured continuing the Swedish nuclear program, which Fälldin, again prime minister after the September 1979 election, personally opposed. In Switzerland a referendum in February 1979 produced a close vote in favour of continuing that country's nuclear program.

Although losing the Argentine order, the Canadian industry clinched its long-negotiated deal to supply the first of two 600-Mw Candu heavy-water reactors to Romania. But Canadian hopes of sales to Japan were dashed when the Japanese postponed a decision between the Canadian and Japanese designs of heavy-water, pressure-tube reactors. The prototype of the Japanese design, the 165-Mw Fugen reactor, was commissioned during the year.

The Japanese centrifuge-type uranium enrichment plant at Ningyo-Toge began production in the first section to be commissioned. Japan continued its active participation in the Australian uranium mining industry with a A$56,250,000 loan to Queensland Mines for development of the Narbalek deposit in the Northern Territory, and two leading Japanese utilities were among the prospective buyers of the Australian government's 50% share of the Ranger project, also in the north.

Figures for nuclear energy production and capacity in 1978 released in 1979 showed that 17 new reactors were commissioned worldwide. The total number of power reactors (over 150 Mw) in service at the beginning of 1979 was 169, with a total capacity of 110,095 Mw, including: 74 PWR's (56,944 Mw); 10 pressurized heavy-water reactors (5,375.2 Mw); and 4 other types (1,718 Mw). (RICHARD A. KNOX)

PAINTS AND VARNISHES

Skyrocketing costs for raw materials, many of them oil-derived, hit the paint industry in most countries in 1979. Some key materials soared by 50% within a few months, and even pigments derived from minerals, such as titanium dioxide, were affected by sharply higher energy costs. In some markets raw-material suppliers also sought to improve their profit margins. In the summer the Paintmakers Association of Great Britain warned of price increases exceeding 30% for industrial coatings.

Among European producers, Italy showed the greatest growth, with sales up some 4% by volume and 15% by value. The Netherlands ranked next, followed by West Germany. The French, Swedish, and Belgian paint industries all suffered declines in real terms, although the value of sales advanced. Total sales in the U.K. ran some 3% by volume ahead of the previous year, with value up about 13%.

Antinuclear demonstrators marched on the Barseback nuclear power plant, north of Malmö, Sweden, in September. The power plant is in the background.

WIDE WORLD

The picture was somewhat brighter elsewhere. Output in North America was estimated to be up about 6% by tonnage and 14% by value. The Japanese paint industry seemed to be shrugging off the lingering business recession, with sales rising as much as 11%; this had to be compared, however, with an annual growth of 20% before the 1973 oil crisis.

The industry's profitability in many countries was influenced by factors other than economic activity. European manufacturers, having largely come to terms with tighter health and safety regulations, prepared for expensive relabeling of most products in conformity with the EEC paints directive. Originally published in 1977, the directive was due to be implemented by national regulations as of November 1979. In the event, some countries acted before the deadline, while the U.K. deferred implementation until 1981 to await the outcome of revisions already in progress in Brussels. Implementation of the related solvents and substances directives was similarly untidy, so the EEC's declared aim of "harmonization" still seemed to be some years away.

The paint industry in North America was involved in the latest round of negotiations under the General Agreement on Tariffs and Trade (GATT). Imports into Canada had been liable to an average duty rate of 15%, while the U.S. applied an effective rate of around 30%. Partly because of this, imports accounted for some 15% of Canadian paint sales while imports to the U.S. were only a fraction of 1%. Following the Tokyo Round of GATT negotiations, the Canadian tariff was to be reduced in eight stages to 9.2% and the U.S. tariff would come down to 10%.

(LIONEL BILEFIELD)

PHARMACEUTICALS

Despite indications of recession in other segments of the economy, the U.S. pharmaceutical industry's vital signs continued especially strong in 1979. Major companies reported record sales and profits through at least the first three quarters. One reporting source (*Product Marketing* magazine) estimated retail prescription sales in 1978 at about $12.4 billion, with over-the-counter (OTC) drugs accounting for another $8.5 billion. Market observers expected that in 1979 these figures would be up about 11% for prescription drugs and 8% for OTC drugs.

Prospects for the cheaper generic (non-trade-named) drugs were brightening. International Resource Development Inc. of Norwalk, Conn., estimated that such drugs currently accounted for 25 cents of every dollar spent on prescription drugs (about $2.3 billion in 1978 figures). Four factors had helped to accelerate this trend: (1) strong support for generics by the Department of Health, Education, and Welfare, as typified by support for the "maximum allowable cost" prescription reimbursement schedule, the drive to publish a national compendium of drug prices, and reinforcement of the bioequivalence of similar drugs; (2) action by state legislatures to encourage dispensing of generic drugs by pharmacists; (3) an accelerated effort by several large pharmaceutical companies to build up their business in so-called branded generics; and (4) expiration of many

WIDE WORLD

William Lijinsky (left) and Joseph Highland of the Environmental Defense Fund called for a ban on sleep aids, which they said contained carcinogens.

pharmaceutical patents, especially for antibiotics and tranquilizers.

Some significant regulatory and/or legislative developments threatened to add to manufacturer (and eventually consumer) costs into the 1980s. The U.S. Senate passed a watered-down version of the Drug Reform Act, which was proposed as one way to reduce the "drug lag" by decreasing the time and red tape required before a new drug could be put on the market. Manufacturers, however, expressed concern about the government's increased powers, granted by the bill, to remove established products from the market when side effects or consumer safety became an important concern. Another provision would mandate package inserts in most prescription drugs explaining their possible risks and benefits. Opponents claimed this would cost millions and would discourage full use of medications by the consumers for whom they were prescribed.

For OTC drug makers in the U.S. the most startling happening in 1979 was the recall of two major product categories: sleep aids (because of the discovery that a key ingredient, methapyrilene, is carcinogenic) and sunscreens (when 6-methylcoumarin, a perfuming material, was found to be a sensitizer in strong sunlight). Especially for the sleep aids, the size of the recall surprised even the Food and Drug Administration (more than 600 products were involved). In both cases, once the recall was completed the manufacturers were able to reformulate the products.

(DONALD A. DAVIS)

PLASTICS

Renewed oil shortages and another round of major price rises precluded any return to commercial stability in the world plastic industry in 1979. In Western Europe the price of the naphtha fraction rose about twice as much as that of the actual crude oil. This was because of intense competition between its alternative uses for gasoline and for petrochemical feedstocks and hence plastics manufacture.

Despite price rises averaging 20–30% in the first half of 1979, sales boomed. Plastics processors built up large material stocks in an attempt to keep ahead of the increases, which, on the whole, they succeeded in passing on to their customers. Most European plastics material suppliers, having seized the opportunity to reintroduce some profitability into their pricing, reported very good results for the early part of the year. Later on, sales slackened with the end of the stock-building phase. Disregarding this distorting factor, it was estimated that the true increase in consumption over the year continued at a modest annual rate of 3–5%.

The outlook for the immediate future would depend on whether ever increasing oil prices led to world recession, and this, in turn, would be determined largely by the performance of the U.S. economy. The U.S. had traditionally used natural or liquefied petroleum gases to make plastics, rather than naphtha. The prices of the former were largely unaffected in 1979 and, in addition, U.S. oil prices were government-controlled and thus remained much lower than elsewhere. Not only was growth in plastics greater in the U.S. than in Europe, but European producers were becoming increasingly concerned over the ability of U.S. exporters to sell plastics far more cheaply.

There was considerable discussion of the possibilities for making plastics from materials other than oil. Coal and "biomass" (vegetable) sources were theoretically feasible, but the huge quantities that would be needed for anything approaching a complete changeover would require prohibitively large capital investment and would also create major environmental problems. Nevertheless, some movement toward the reestablishment of a coal-based chemicals industry (as had already occurred in South Africa) was expected to take place.

Most of the obvious substitutions of plastics for traditional materials had been made, but the possibilities were by no means exhausted. Even the oil shortage was boosting demand for plastics because their lightness saved energy in some applications. Most energy-saving projects favoured the use of plastics, and some opened up new areas, for example, solar heating. Higher standards of thermal insulation were being achieved with the use of very large amounts of such materials as polyurethanes and expanded polystyrene.

The massive Kunststoffe exhibition held in Düsseldorf, West Germany, in October amply confirmed the underlying health of the industry. Modified forms of known plastics, rather than completely new materials, were in the forefront, particularly where they offered greater rigidity, heat and impact resistance, nonflammability, or

E. I. DU PONT DE NEMOURS & COMPANY

Bennett N. Epstein of Du Pont holds bicycle wheel made of Zytel ST-801, a new super-tough nylon.

other qualities needed to satisfy increasingly complex legislative safety requirements. The main developments in the packaging sector were the increased use of polypropylene (still the fastest-growing material) in general and the great interest in polyethylene terephthalate (PET) for clear, rigid bottles for carbonated drinks. Many new grades of engineering plastics were introduced; some varieties of thermoplastic polyesters had novel elastomeric properties, combining the strength of plastics with the extensibility of rubber. Polycarbonate technology also widened with the entry of new manufacturers following expiration of the original patents.

(ROBIN C. PENFOLD)

PRINTING

Although computer-assisted typesetting, electronic colour scanning, and digital facsimile transmission had been in use for many years, 1979 saw the first real advances toward true automation by the printing industry. Laser plate-making units coupled with electronic picture-transmission systems were introduced by a growing number of newspapers in North and South America and Europe. In Britain, Crosfield Electronics started field testing of Lasergravur cylinder making; combined with electronic colour scanning and the Magnascan 570 system, it permitted complete filmless reproduction from copy directly onto the cylinder. In West Germany, Dr.-

Ing. Rudolf Hell, celebrating its 50th anniversary, sold several Chromakom integral copy-with-text systems that enabled direct plate or cylinder making via electronic storage and control. The company also continued experiments with electron beam cylinder engraving.

The Soviet Union bought two Helprint-Optronics systems for rapid direct picture production during the 1980 Olympic Games. Optronics made its first U.S. installation with Standard Gravure and announced joint development plans with Klimsch of West Germany, one of the oldest specialists in reproduction equipment. Sci-Tex of Israel announced computerized systems for producing printing forms direct from copy that were compatible with other manufacturers' scanners, plate makers, or engravers. Coulter-Stork introduced the KC silverless copy-to-form system using digital equipment. As a spin-off from space technology, several newcomers announced printing systems derived from methods of producing weather charts from satellite signals.

In Sweden the world's biggest web-offset book press, built by GMS, started operation; it produced 384-page books at the rate of 4,000 complete bound copies an hour. In Britain, Richard Clay claimed to have started up the largest completely integrated paperback production line in the world. The automatic transfer press design from Harris Corp., which allows continuous nonstop running of a web offset press in book publication, came to Europe. The ingenious design of the machine allows plating up for sequential work while one or two press units are running at full speed. Idle units are then electronically brought to full speed and take over from printing units. A similar system, described as "flying plate change," was introduced by Albert of West Germany, now under effective control of the world's oldest printing-machine maker, König & Bauer. The world's second-oldest printing-machine maker, MAN, also in West Germany, took over Wood-Hoe in the U.S. and renamed its Roland offset subsidiary MAN-Roland.

Press automation progressed further. Electronic inking control was advanced by the Roland CCI system and Harris Densicontrol. Complete press-control systems were introduced, and the first such Harris system went on a newspaper press destined for Yugoslavia. Eight-page web offset presses became best-sellers. Zirkon machines from East Germany remained the market leaders, but Harris was a close second with Albert just behind.

In gravure, photolitho-to-gravure conversion systems attracted increasing attention. Toppan of Japan and its European chief licensee, Conzett & Huber of Switzerland, gained additional sublicensees for their process in Austria, Britain, The Netherlands, and South Africa. The greatest expansion of gravure continued to take place in the U.S. The possibility of printing on lighter-weight papers made gravure economically attractive, and several new plants were opened.

(W. PINCUS JASPERT)

RUBBER

For the first time in many years a major strike was averted by negotiations between the major rubber companies and the United Rubber Workers. Because of a misunderstanding Uniroyal was struck, but the issues were quickly resolved. The increase in wages and fringe benefits was substantial, about 26% spread over three years. Adjustments other than wages were quite comprehensive, covering the cost of living, added pay for skilled tradesmen, an additional paid holiday, pensions, life and medical insurance, vacations, and areas of company-union relations. The settlement was borderline in meeting government guidelines, but approval was granted on condition that the small excess over the guidelines was not passed on to the consumer in the form of higher prices.

The first international agreement on regulating trade in natural rubber was reached on October 5. Under its terms, effective on Oct. 1, 1980, a buffer stock of 550,000 metric tons of natural rubber was to be used to maintain prices within a range of 68–124 cents per kilogram (2.2 lb).

Profitability of rubber manufacturing concerns varied widely in 1979. Inability to pass on oil-related costs was only one factor decreasing profitability. The massive recall of the "500" radial tire affected the earnings of the Firestone Tire & Rubber Co. adversely. Uniroyal reported losses for each quarter. Of the "big five" rubber manufacturers, only B. F. Goodrich Co. reported an increase in third-quarter earnings over 1978. Several firms ceased bias tire production in 1979, and others reduced the production of bias tires to balance production and demand.

The price of oil not only affected fuel costs but also the cost of all rubber products, because many of the materials used in rubber manufacture are derived from oil. A study made by Goodyear Tire & Rubber Co. showed that every $1 increase in the cost of oil increased the cost of industrial rubber goods by as much as 2.5%.

The U.S. Department of Transportation cited rolling resistance of tires as a key area in making automobiles more fuel efficient. The major rubber companies were working to reduce rolling resistance of the radial tire, which already had markedly lower rolling resistance than the bias tire. Early versions of such tires were used on the X-car, introduced by General Motors in the spring of 1979. Further improvements in both tire construction and low-energy-loss rubber compounds were expected to produce even more fuel-efficient tires.

Natural rubber was just one of the raw materials used in rubber manufacture to show a marked increase in price during the year. On Oct. 1, 1978, the New York spot price was 56½ cents per pound for smoked sheets, and on Oct. 1, 1979, it was 68 cents, a 20% increase. The price of the most widely used synthetic rubber rose from 37 cents per pound to 50 cents, an increase of 35%, as a result of cost increases in raw materials such as benzene.

World production of natural rubber in 1978 was estimated at 3,715,000 metric tons, an increase of 110,000 tons over 1977. Production for 1979 was estimated at 3,750,000 tons, an increase of 35,000 tons over 1978.

The U.S. continued to be the largest single buyer of natural rubber, purchasing 764,654 tons in 1978. World consumption of natural rubber latex (dry basis) was estimated at 284,500 tons. Statistics on world consumption of synthetic latices were incomplete, but U.S. consumption was 157,000 tons (dry basis) of the styrene butadiene type. Consumption of both natural and synthetic rubber worldwide was estimated at 12,415,800 tons in 1978.

Production of reclaimed rubber in 1978 was equal to or slightly above that of 1977 (about 200,000 tons). This was the second

B. F. Goodrich Co. and United Rubber Workers Union officials in June announced a new labour agreement which would affect about 55,000 tire industry workers.

WIDE WORLD

Table X. Natural Rubber Production
In 000 metric tons

Country	1976	1977	1978
Malaysia	1,612	1,613	1,606
Indonesia	848[1]	835[1]	900[1]
Thailand	412	431	467
India	148	152	133
Sri Lanka	152	146	156
Liberia	82	80[1]	78[1]
Philippines	58	60[1]	63
Nigeria	53[1]	59[1]	58[1]
Zaire	29[1]	30[1]	26[1]
Brazil	20	23	24
Others	161[1]	176[1]	204[1]
Total	3,575[1]	3,605[1]	3,715[1]

[1] Estimate, or includes estimate.
Source: The Secretariat of the International Rubber Study Group, *Rubber Statistical Bulletin.*

Table XI. Synthetic Rubber Production
In 000 metric tons

Country	1976	1977	1978
United States	2,425	2,528	2,473
Japan	941	971	1,029
France	437	479	492
Germany, West	373	414	407
United Kingdom	320	329	294
Netherlands, The	247	240	223
Italy[1]	250	240	250
Canada	210	238	248
Brazil	164	188	206
Germany, East	145	150[1]	155[1]
Belgium[1]	115	125	130[1]
Romania	95	136	140[1]
Poland	117	119	126
Mexico	69	78[1]	80[1]
Spain	79	77	79[1]
Korea	35	43	62
Czechoslovakia	57	59	60[1]
Australia	42	44	44
Argentina[1]	45	36	36
South Africa	35	27	32
Others	1,829[1]	2,038[1]	2,154[1]
Total	8,030[1]	8,500[1]	8,720[1]

[1] Estimate, or includes estimate.
Source: The Secretariat of the International Rubber Study Group, *Rubber Statistical Bulletin.*

consecutive year that output of the reclaimed product increased slightly. The U.S. Department of Energy had a preliminary study made concerning the reuse of scrap rubber in rubber products. The scrap could be utilized as either ground scrap or reclaimed rubber. The study could have far-reaching effects on the volume of reclaimed rubber used.

Tire quality grading for bias and belted-bias tires was implemented during the year in the U.S. and radial tires also were required to have grade numbers by April 1, 1980. The grading label on passenger tires was to list the relative wear resistance, traction, and heat resistance. The National Highway Traffic Safety Administration sponsored grade labeling to inform the tire-buying public of the level of performance it could expect. (JAMES R. BEATTY)

SHIPBUILDING

In the quarter ended June 30, 1979, the world shipbuilding order book showed its first increase since March 1974—a modest 272,925 gross registered tons (grt), which in the past would have represented a single very large crude oil carrier. At the end of July there were 2,704 vessels of over 100 grt on order worldwide, representing a little over 53 million tons deadweight (dw), or 25.4 million grt, a considerable reduction from the mid-1978 figure of 61 million tons dw. Estimates of annual world demand for new tonnage, which ranged from 10 million to 14 million grt, evened out at approximately 13 million grt. Some experts were predicting that by the mid-1980s demand would have risen to about 23 million grt a year.

Despite clear indications that world shipbuilding capacity was still well in excess of demand, there was little further reduction. The world's yards (including those in Eastern Europe) could produce 30 million grt. The EEC gave official approval to the proposed international scrap-and-build scheme, subject to certain conditions that would preclude exploitation by unscrupulous operators. Basically, the scheme involved the scrapping of large tankers, with one new vessel constructed to replace every two that were scrapped. The problem had been reaching agreement on the level of subsidy required to induce an owner to scrap a vessel with a market value in excess of the current scrap price.

Because tanker freight rates gradually improved in 1978, more tankers came out of lay-up. Owners began to place orders for new 80,000–100,000 tonners that would meet the new international safety regulations calling for segregated ballast tanks. As these regulations began to bite, more owners of older tonnage would have to decide whether to scrap their vessels or bring them into line with international requirements.

State assistance to EEC and Scandinavian shipyards continued to make ship prices unrealistic. In Belgium, France, The Netherlands, West Germany, and the U.K. the financial help was significant—and essential for the industry's survival. British Shipbuilders, the state shipbuilding group, revealed details of its plan to reduce manpower in the country's merchant shipbuilding yards by 25,000 in order to achieve commercial viability. The U.K. order book stood at 992,000 grt, compared with a capacity—unchanged since 1972—of at least 1.5 million grt.

After several years of successful operation, shipyards in Spain, South Korea, and Brazil began to suffer from steep increases in the cost of labour and materials. As productivity in Brazilian yards decreased, the backlog of orders was held up, so the country continued to maintain second place in the world shipbuilding order table with 4.5 million tons dw (2.5 million grt). The leader, Japan, had just over 13 million tons dw (7 million grt). The order book of the South Korean yards was reduced to 805,491 grt, but in Poland the state yards increased theirs to a total of 1.8 million grt. In the U.S. the volume of orders on which work had not yet started approached the 500,000-grt level.

World marine-engine-building capacity was nearly double the current requirement, and several companies faced cash liquidity problems. It had been hoped that many owners would convert tonnage of a suitable age from steam-powered turbines to diesel engines in order to reduce fuel costs. Only seven orders were placed for such conversions, however, the bulk of them going to Japan. One of the major Swedish yards reduced the size of two tankers from 250,000 tons dw to 150,000 tons by cutting out a midship section, and it was believed that more such orders would be forthcoming. Several large vessels were purchased for conversion to suit their new owners. Among them, two former transatlantic liners changed flag: the 66,000-ton "France" became the "Norway" and the 18,000-ton "Kungsholm" was renamed "Sea Princess." Multipurpose cargo liners with roll-on/roll-off container and bulk-carrying facilities continued to attract attention, and new orders were placed for more than 40 vessels of this type. (W. D. EWART)

TELECOMMUNICATIONS

In 1979 telecommunications technology advanced fastest in the application of fibre optics, the technique of transmitting messages through long glass fibres in the form of light waves. For example, fibre optic cables appeared in tests of the public telephone network and television-based information systems for the home and office.

The world's longest passenger liner, the "France," was purchased by new owners and renamed the "Norway."

WIDE WORLD

As expected, the battle between American Telephone and Telegraph Co. (AT&T), IBM Corp., and Xerox Corp. over which should be allowed by the U.S. Federal Communications Commission (FCC) to tap the office-of-the-future market continued with no end in sight. Complicating matters, the 1978 proposed revision of the Communication Act of 1934 (which established the FCC and the regulation of telecommunications in the U.S.) died in Congress due to lack of support.

Telephones. Experimenting on a fibre-optic cable of the type that might be used in a future telephone line, Bell Telephone Laboratories scientists demonstrated digital information transmission at the unheard-of rate of 200 gigabits per second (1 gigabit = 1 billion bits). The system thus far was being used for experimenting with the remarkable bandwidth capabilities of glass fibres.

This Bell development has bandwidth far in excess of that needed by any currently practical communications system. For example, it is 2,000 times wider in bandwidth than the system used in the Bell Telephone fibre-optics test in Chicago in 1978.

Continuing the trend of earlier years to use fibre-optic telephone systems when new facilities are required, the Bell System announced in 1979 that it would install its first standard-design light-wave communications system. It would handle both voice and data communications on telephone lines in Atlanta, Ga., in 1980.

In the world's first field trial of an information system for home telephones based on fibre optics, Bell Canada began a two-year test of a voice, video, and data service to 35 homes in Toronto. The $1,750,000 installation employed 1.2 km of fibre. And, unlike some other systems, the fibre actually went directly to the customer's telephone.

Also in Canada Manitoba Telephone—independent of Bell—planned to wire 150 homes with glass fibre in the rural town of Elie. The $6.1 million installation would offer multichannel television, FM radio, and a variety of other services. A major purpose of this test was to solve the communications problems of rural Canadian residents. Fibre cable with its wide bandwidth could bring many different kinds of services into a home on one connection, allowing the cost to be distributed among many suppliers.

Regulations. Bringing modern electronics technology into the office was a dream of AT&T, which hoped to do it through its telephone-based Advanced Communication Service. ACS was designed to allow all the data-handling machines in one office to communicate with those in any other office that had a telephone. IBM, the Satellite Broadcasting System with its satellite-based technology, and Xerox with a system based on combining terrestrial microwave links and satellites also hoped to share in this business.

Legal problems abounded for all of these suppliers, and AT&T's case was typical. In 1979 controversy continued with charges that Bell's service would involve computer-like data-processing activities. The FCC had maintained that Bell would not be allowed to engage in such activities. Moreover, competitors claimed that Bell could charge artificially low prices by subsidizing its service from the profits of its standard telephone business unless strong measures were taken to prevent such a practice.

Table XII. Countries Having More Than 100,000 Telephones

Telephones in service, 1978

Country	Number of telephones	Percentage increase over 1968	Telephones per 100 population	Country	Number of telephones	Percentage increase over 1968	Telephones per 100 population
Algeria	297,689	90.8	1.6	Kuwait	152,517	198.1	13.1
Argentina	2,584,801	66.4	9.9	Lebanon[3]	227,000	51.0	7.4
Australia[1]	5,835,330	83.6	41.5	Luxembourg	185,549	89.4	52.3
Austria	2,443,412	110.1	32.0	Malaysia	374,676	139.6	2.9
Belgium	3,100,109	76.8	31.5	Mexico	3,712,407	255.5	5.5
Bolivia	101,500	214.2	2.1	Morocco	210,000	31.0	1.2
Brazil	4,708,000	219.7	4.0	Netherlands, The	5,845,894	115.3	42.1
Bulgaria	946,023	180.0	10.7	New Zealand	1,715,343	53.2	54.5
Canada	14,505,728	73.0	63.2	Nigeria	128,352	69.1	0.2
Chile	483,225	54.9	4.5	Norway	1,562,500	58.3	38.6
Colombia	1,396,591	171.2	5.6	Pakistan[4]	239,600	35.5	0.3
Costa Rica	145,069	189.6	6.9	Panama	156,668	167.3	8.8
Cuba	321,054	32.7	3.3	Peru	402,459	143.7	2.6
Czechoslovakia	2,863,307	70.6	19.0	Philippines	567,321	173.3	1.3
Denmark	2,743,758	86.7	52.9	Poland	2,925,450	91.1	8.4
Dominican Republic	139,412	290.1	2.8	Portugal	1,174,853	90.7	12.0
Ecuador	221,578	151.8	2.9	Puerto Rico	560,724	134.1	16.1
Egypt[2]	503,947	38.1	1.3	Romania[2]	1,133,154	106.0	5.2
Finland	2,032,280	113.9	42.8	Saudi Arabia	185,000	318.1	2.4
France	17,518,813	150.3	32.9	Singapore	455,120	281.9	19.6
Germany, East	2,860,069	60.6	17.1	South Africa	2,319,558	75.4	9.8
Germany, West	22,931,683	122.2	37.4	Spain	9,527,781	182.0	26.3
Greece	2,319,797	251.4	25.1	Sweden	5,930,276	50.7	71.7
Hong Kong	1,251,021	253.5	27.4	Switzerland	4,145,169	63.6	65.9
Hungary	1,103,843	74.0	10.3	Syria	193,044	99.8	2.5
India	2,247,187	126.2	0.4	Taiwan	1,685,132	631.9	10.0
Indonesia	324,546	78.9	0.2	Thailand[5]	366,862	220.6	0.8
Iran	828,571	276.5	2.5	Tunisia	144,116	132.7	2.5
Iraq	319,590	181.9	2.6	Turkey	1,378,620	222.3	3.3
Ireland	519,000	89.3	16.1	U.S.S.R.	19,600,000	115.4	7.5
Israel	929,837	171.5	25.5	United Kingdom	23,182,239	91.6	41.5
Italy	16,118,928	128.4	28.5	United States	161,448,000	56.2	74.4
Jamaica	111,192	82.2	5.6	Uruguay	268,026	30.6	9.6
Japan	50,625,589	177.9	44.2	Venezuela	847,318	159.1	6.4
Kenya	143,768	119.7	1.0	Yugoslavia	1,555,663	207.4	7.1
Korea, South	1,978,366	369.8	5.2	Zimbabwe Rhodesia	196,750	56.3	2.9

[1] As of June 30, 1977. [2] 1977. [3] 1972. [4] As of June 30, 1976. [5] As of Sept. 30, 1977.
Sources: American Telephone and Telegraph Company, *The World's Telephones, 1978*; Statistical Office of the United Nations, *Statistical Yearbook, 1969*.

The FCC started to deal with this problem in 1979. It indicated that it would allow the telephone company to engage in every kind of service provided Bell set up a separate division with entirely separate accounting procedures. Typical of this new attitude was a decision in July to allow the telephone company to use satellites for private special services such as cable television transmission. Until then, Bell had been prohibited from using satellites for anything but the transmission of standard telephone conversations. By this and other acts the FCC indicated a trend toward a more competitive, less regulated communications industry. (HARVEY J. HINDIN)

TEXTILES

Awareness of the past shortcomings of the world's textile industry was sharpened by the continuing energy crisis and the realization that probably never again would energy be cheap. A series of textile mill surveys carried out in Britain revealed certain areas where obvious economies could be made. The main area was in the sector known as wet processing, which includes bleaching, dyeing, printing, and finishing textiles. Controlling the application of water to the textiles not only saved water but also meant that there was less water to remove at a later stage, which also saved energy, usually in the form of heat. Using less water also brought about a reduction in the wastes produced, and this allowed a reduction in effluent treatment requirements. Recovery of heat from waste liquors also proved effective in reducing the power requirements of the dyehouses. As the waste left the processing machinery, it was taken through economizers and heat-exchangers so that much of the heat was extracted and reused in closed systems within the factory.

Several new systems of spinning yarns were under intensive development, while in weaving the acceptance of shuttleless looms continued but with a growing emphasis on the so-called air jet looms. These simply transport the weft yarns across the looms in a concentrated jet of air or, for certain materials, water. These machines were much faster than shuttle looms and were also quieter and required less power.

(PETER LENNOX-KERR)

Wool. Two main upturns in wool values during 1979, in February and October, were separated by a more static spell, with actual price movements varying according to the currency concerned. Floor prices were raised for the 1978–79 season, but support for growers was not needed. World production during the season was provisionally estimated at 1,456,000 metric tons clean, 1% more than in 1977–78.

Increased demand stemmed mainly from the less developed countries in the Far East, from certain state trading countries, and from some members of the EEC. The changing balance of world wool consumption and

PETER MARCUS—BUSINESS WEEK

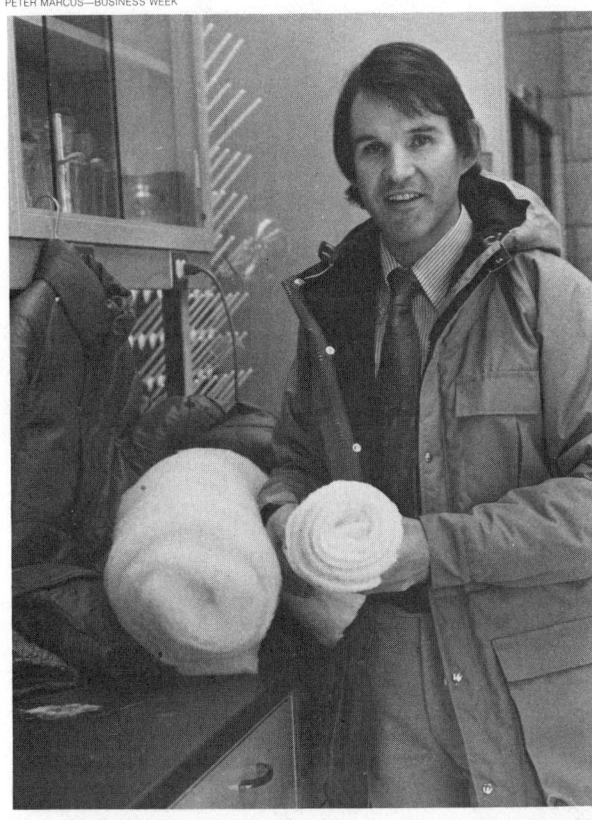

A new material, Thinsulate, which provides the same amount of warmth as the best insulating materials but with half the thickness, was produced by 3M Co. The new material was being used to insulate winter garments.

wool textile production, coupled with currency movements, continued to affect parts of the older established wool-consuming countries adversely. The U.K. in particular experienced difficulties due to increased imports of wool textiles and problems related to exports because of high rates for the pound sterling.

Wool grower stockpiles, notably in Australia, declined rapidly when prices improved in February and continued to do so afterward until, by the closing months of the year, the level reached had limited market significance. Rises in the price of oil, affecting man-made fibre prices and availability, had no obvious and immediate effect on demand but raised the possibility of a relative increase in the proportion of natural fibre consumed.

(H. M. F. MALLETT)

Cotton. During the 1978–79 season the world area devoted to growing cotton declined by more than 2 million ac, accompanied by a reduction in average yield of 12 lb per acre. Production fell from 64.1 million bales in 1977–78 to 60.2 million bales. Bad weather and severe insect damage in some major cotton-producing areas caused the decline in average yield, which was down by 20% in the U.S. and as much as 60% in the Sudan. Reduced output, together with sharply improved demand, resulted in the end-of-season carry-over falling by 2.3 million bales to an estimated 22.5 million bales. Stocks were much lower in the U.S. and in certain other net exporting countries such as the Sudan and Argentina.

World consumption of raw cotton in 1978–79 rose by 2 million bales to a record 62.7 million bales, with mill usage remaining steady. Preliminary estimates showed consumption in the U.S. down from 6.5 million bales to 6.3 million, but elsewhere, apart from the Eastern bloc, it was up from 30 million bales to 31.9 million. In the U.S.S.R., China, and Eastern Europe output reached 22.5 million bales and consumption 24.5 million.

Global production in 1979–80 was expected to rise by some 4 million bales to 64 million bales through higher acreage planted and larger yields. U.S. output was estimated at over 14 million bales, compared with less than 11 million bales in 1978–79.

The average price of raw cotton in Liverpool during 1978–79 rose from about 72 cents per pound to more than 80 cents before declining in the early months of 1979 to below 73 cents. A subsequent recovery brought the cost back to 78 cents. Exporters such as the U.S. and importers such as Japan opposed any international agreement to regulate world rates, but 16 less developed countries representing about 30% of the world cotton trade and some 60% of third-world cotton exports called for a reserve stock system.

(ARTHUR TATTERSALL)

Silk. After the Japanese government reluctantly imposed in August 1974 what amounted to a ban on raw silk imports, traders strove to find loopholes through which to import silk in forms other than those decreed. Each loophole in its turn was plugged. Confident in its intrinsic evaluation of silk as well as in its ability through technology and research to come to terms with the consumer, the government had stood firm. Its policy had survived five years and recently had gained rather than lost credibility. Consumption was recovering, and despite the weight of imports, whether officially negotiated or not, the imbalance of trade was not significant. Funds were made available in May 1979 to promote silk at home, and the government's determination to preserve cocoon farmers, throwsters, weavers, and, in particular, domestic consumers was manifest to all.

Meanwhile, China raised the price of 3A 20/22 denier from 44.50 yuan to 49.20, and a minimum of 51.70 was announced for 1980. The advance was considerable but still far from closing the gap with Japan. Raw silk from Brazil was becoming scarce, as the government there adjusted subsidies to favour the export of fabric. Indeed, supplies of silk available to weavers in the West were not plentiful nor were new sources immediately apparent, though schemes were afoot in a number of less developed countries. India was carrying out a program of growth, again aimed at augmenting exports of fabric rather than of raw material.

(PETER W. GADDUM)

Man-Made Fibres. The rising cost of oil, the industry's main raw material, made man-made fibre producers reconsider their products in 1979. A number of plants closed during the year, having become unprofitable. Despite regular increases throughout the year, the prices being asked for the main man-made fibres—polyester, polyamide (nylon), and acrylic—still did not cover the rises in the cost of the oil-based derivatives used in their manufacture.

One alternative to oil-derived fibres was viscose rayon, made from the cellulose extracted from rapidly growing softwood trees. Viscose rayon also had the advantage of being biodegradable, whereas the synthetic oil-based fibres are difficult to destroy.

Another man-made fibre being given greater consideration was polypropylene. This is based on a version of propylene, the gas that previously was burned off at the top of the chimneys of oil cracking plants as a waste product. Polypropylene fibre had the major disadvantage of being exceedingly difficult to dye, but its "wicking" properties—that is, the ability to transmit moisture from, say, the surface of the skin to the outside of the fabric—made it particularly suitable for some specialized uses such as "dry liners" in babies' diapers.

(PETER LENNOX-KERR)

TOBACCO

Moves during 1979 to carry the smoking and health controversy into less developed countries where it was not yet a live issue for consumers did not prevent world cigarette production from rising by just under 2%, to about 4.3 trillion. To make these cigarettes, and lesser quantities of other tobacco products, more than 100 countries grew some 12,200,000,000 lb of tobacco—fractionally less than in 1978. Overall supply was in line with demand, but imbalances affecting certain types of leaf persisted. In particular, the Balkans and Italy were still growing more oriental tobacco than the world needed and had huge accumulated stocks. Greece, which in 1979 produced 11.3% of the world's oriental, faced a special problem; it had to liquidate its surplus by the time it joined the EEC in 1981.

Less developed countries of East Asia, Latin America, and Africa, which had been exporting more tobacco since sanctions curtailed Rhodesian trade, were fearful that a sanctions-free Zimbabwe Rhodesia could become an intensely tough competitor in world markets. Documented world trade in leaf tobacco, 3,100,000,000 lb in 1979, though below the all-time record of 1974, was still healthy because price levels were moderate. If sanctions-dodging Rhodesian exports were visible, total trade in leaf would be approximately 6% higher.

Producer and consumer countries had common interest in trials with a new, nonsynthetic type of filler material for cigarettes. Experimental acreages in several countries were providing exceptional per-acre yields by means of dense planting and reaping regrowth after the main harvest. Not only the usual leaves but the tops of the stalks as well were being gathered and, after curing, homogenized into paperlike sheet tobacco that could go straight into manufacture. This technique could eliminate the 15–20 months of storage that leaf tobacco normally needs to mature before it can enter the manufacturing process; it would be of great economic significance because of the cost of warehousing and stock financing.

Antitobacco legislation led in 1979 to more bans on smoking in public places, an increase in the number of countries requiring warnings on cigarette packs, and further advertising restraints. Campaigns shifted from saving the smoker from harming himself to saving nonsmokers from the discomfort or annoyance of smoke-laden air. Tobacco interests and private groups, long inert under attack, were starting to fight back, in the name of individual freedom, against the more intemperate actions and doctrines of their critics. No significant new evidence linking smoking with disease emerged during the year, but earlier claims were becoming ever more widely accepted.

There was further reduction in the average "tar" content of cigarettes in the developed countries; 59% of the brands now on the U.S. market were "low-tar," but in West Germany—pioneer of mild cigarettes—more robust blends were in rising demand. Manufacturers everywhere sought blend formulas that married low "tar" with full flavour, with varying success. Achieving this was extremely difficult because all smoke dilution methods in current use to lower "tar" and nicotine levels simultaneously reduced the taste and some of the aroma conveyed in the smoke.

(MICHAEL F. BARFORD)

TOURISM

Tourism's worldwide growth continued at a moderate pace in 1979. International arrivals reached 275 million, 6% more than in 1978. Receipts totaled $75 billion, up 15%. Overall, the volume increase in world travel in 1979 was similar to that in 1978, but the rise in money spent was less than the 24% registered in 1978 over 1977.

There were big increases in expenditures abroad of Japanese (80%) and Spanish (50%) travelers in 1979. The world's largest tourism spender, West Germany, expected a 20% rise and the U.S., 10%.

Table XIII. Major Tourism Earners and Spenders in 1978
In $000,000

Major Spenders	Expenditure
West Germany	$14,397
United States	8,364
France	4,272
Japan	3,717
Netherlands, The	3,401
Canada	2,968
United Kingdom	2,813
Austria	2,462
Belgium/Luxembourg	2,177
Switzerland	1,668
Sweden	1,401
Italy	1,206

Major Earners	Receipts
United States	$7,070
Italy	6,285
France	5,903
Spain	5,488
West Germany	4,813
Austria	4,716
United Kingdom	4,464
Switzerland	2,446
Canada	1,722
Greece	1,326
Belgium/Luxembourg	1,310
Netherlands, The	1,254
Denmark	1,125
Mexico	1,117
Hong Kong	1,103

Source: World Tourism Organization.

Although the continuing development of tourism seemed inevitable, certain major issues affecting the outlook remained unresolved. These concerned inflation, energy supply, and world economic growth. Escalating costs in popular receiving countries pointed to a change in the direction of tourist flows in the 1980s. The energy outlook remained overcast, with airlines posting fare increases to compensate for higher jet fuel costs and automobile users facing higher pump prices in most countries and occasional gasoline shortages in North America. Though the threat of a deep U.S. recession faded, unemployment remained high; the only glimmer of hope lay in calls for increased paid holidays and shorter hours. The continued weakness of the dollar made some European destinations appear prohibitive in cost to U.S. travelers. On the brighter side, railroad investment continued strong, while the airlines—after a record year—could offer a wider-than-ever spread of low-cost air fares to tap the pleasure travel market.

On a country-by-country basis, early results pointed to a successful season in a number of Mediterranean areas. Cyprus welcomed 40% more visitors and Malta 30% more, while Italy set its sights on a 15% growth rate (although a series of kidnappings in Sardinia brought cancellations from some intending to visit the island). On the other hand, as the pound sterling climbed to more than U.S. $2.20, travel to Britain stagnated. During 1978 the U.K. had welcomed 12.6 million overseas visitors, bringing more cash into the country than North Sea oil, reported the British Tourist Authority (BTA). But BTA chairman Sir Henry Marking warned: "London may well have to look to its laurels, as its share of business has fallen consistently."

Britain was not the only victim of a strong currency. Tourism in Belgium and West Germany showed no growth, while in Austria it fell 5% and in Switzerland 10% after a disappointing winter season. Spain made a good start in 1979 with first-half arrivals up by 14%, but hotel strikes and isolated terrorism at major resorts adversely affected the peak season; arrivals in August were 1.2 million less than during the previous year. Thanks to currency devaluation, Spain's neighbour, Portugal, was reported to be heading toward a 24% increase in visitors.

Australia reported 10% growth, with the operating budget of the Australian Tourist Commission doubled to A$8.2 million. In Hong Kong growth was 13% and in Indonesia and Singapore, 14%. But the Association of Southeast Asian Nations countries was disquieted by Australia's new International Civil Aviation Policy, which they claimed would lead to tourists flying over Asia at very low fares on the

A group of determined travelers left London in February for a 40-day rail trip that would take them to Hong Kong by way of the U.S.S.R. and China, a journey of 9,000 miles.

KEYSTONE

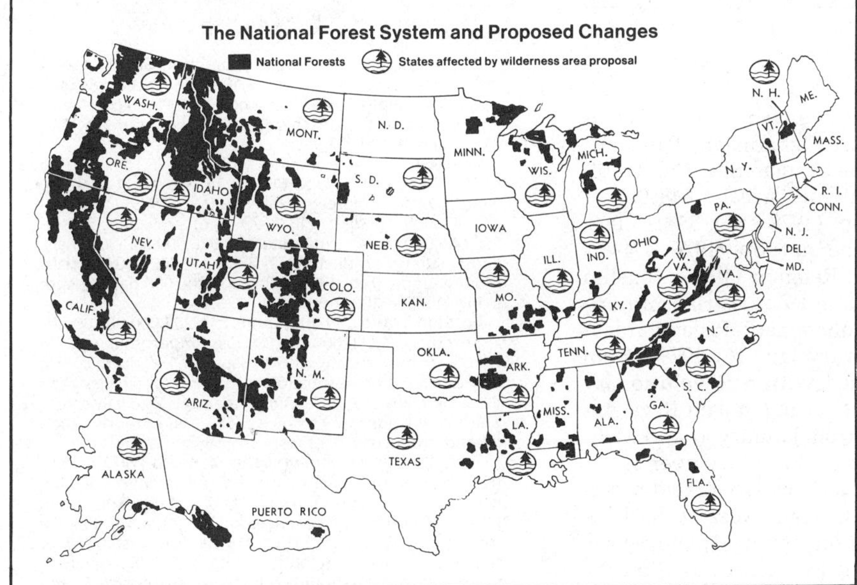

Europe-Australia route. Travel to India increased 5%, while Egypt was the scene of a hotel boom, a brisk trade in Nile River cruises, and a 16% growth rate. In the Persian Gulf nations business travel was active, though a potential for oversupply of hotel rooms loomed.

In Kenya tourism was reported to be picking up in 1979, while in Zambia there was hope that a political settlement in neighbouring Zimbabwe Rhodesia would give impetus to a 45 million-kwacha tourism master plan launched by the Zambia National Tourist Bureau with the aid of Irish Tourist Board experts and EEC funds. Tunisia's tourism grew by 12% with more than 1.2 million visitors, four-fifths from Europe.

Although a Caribbean Tourism Research Centre seminar in December 1978 had underscored the major market potential of Europe for Caribbean travel, the subregion enjoyed an uncertain season. An inhibiting factor was the U.S. Tax Reform Act of 1976, limiting allowable tax deductions for convention expenditures outside the U.S. There were pressures in the U.S., however, to ensure special status for Caribbean destinations, while there was equal determination in the region to reduce its dependence on North American travelers. Though much damage was wrought to smaller Caribbean islands by Hurricane David in the autumn, a back-to-normal situation was quickly restored at many resorts. An oil spill missed scenic Tobago, and Bermuda chalked up a 9% increase in arrivals. A major hotel training school opened in Cuba as part of a move to tap the island's vast tourism potential.

The U.S. welcomed 21 million foreign visitors in 1979, a 6% increase. Hotel occupancies were steady at 65–67%, but there was anxiety over the effects of gas shortages on pleasure travel by car. In spite of its devalued dollar, Canada's 1979 tourist season began hesitantly, though there was moderate growth of occupancies in business centres.

With emphasis on energy conservation growing, the world's railroads promoted the energy efficiency of rail travel. Modernization schemes continued, among them a major project for Greece, while two new members, Saudi Arabia and China, joined the International Union of Railways.

In the retail field much interest focused on the attempts of such tour operators as Tjæreborg (Denmark) to bypass the travel agent and sell directly to the public. Tjæreborg's fully computerized operation claimed to sell cheaper packages through the elimination of the middleman's profit. The possibility of linking potential travelers to a computer through their domestic telephone and television set was offered by teletext systems, which became generally available in Europe during 1979. Such systems were held to offer prospects not only for furnishing consumers with timetable and destination information but also for making instant reservations—a possibility regarded with some apprehension by the travel trade. (CAMILLE SHACKLEFORD)

WOOD PRODUCTS

Important decisions made in 1979 would have lasting effects on the U.S. forest products industry. The Senate ratified the multilateral trade agreements negotiated under GATT. When approved by the other countries concerned, they would open up new U.S. export opportunities by lowering tariffs in the EEC, Japan, and Canada, all large buyers of wood, paper, and paperboard products. The U.S. forest industry was also likely to gain from agreements on nontariff barriers to trade, especially those relating to subsidies, standards, and customs valuation. The U.S. exported some $2.6 billion worth of pulp, paper, and paperboard annually, and at least $5 billion worth of paper was used to package other exports. The U.S. was the largest paper and paperboard producer and the second largest lumber-producing country, after the U.S.S.R.

Domestically, one of the most significant events affecting the forest industry was the conclusion of a lengthy U.S. Forest Service study of 153 million ha (62 million ac) of unroaded lands in the national forests. From 1970 these areas had been treated as Federal Wilderness Preserves, where no trees could be planted or harvested. Motorized vehicles and permanent shelters were banned and, in general, only backpackers could enter. The Roadless Area Review and Evaluation (RARE II), the second of two such studies, was concluded in April, after comprehensive public involvement. It indicated that Americans, three to one, supported using the forest resource rather than preserving it as wilderness.

The Carter administration recommended that 38 million ha (15.4 million ac) be added to the existing 46 million-ha (19 million-ac) federal wilderness system and that another 89 million ha (36 million ac) be released for nonwilderness uses (*e.g.*, timber harvesting, recreation, and grazing). The rest—24.7 million ha (10 million ac)—would be studied further. The final decision would be made by Congress. Some 23% of the nation's softwood sawtimber, used for building homes, came from the national forests.

Production, sales, and earnings in the U.S. paper industry appeared to be headed toward record highs in 1979. Production of paper and paperboard was calculated at approximately 64.5 million tons, compared with 61.5 million tons in 1978. Capital spending plans for 1979 indicated a 40% increase in outlays, to $4.8 billion, more than three times the average rate of increase of all other industries.

Continued strength in home building and other wood-using industries, together with increased exports, kept lumber production high during the first half of 1979. However, production dropped as housing construction began to decline later in the year. Lumber production for all of 1979 was estimated at 36,600,000,000 bd-ft, about 4% below 1978. Softwood lumber accounted for about 78% of the total and hardwood lumber for about 22%. The value of lumber shipments was estimated at approximately $13 billion, 9% above 1978.

Shipments of plywood were estimated to be down about 4% in 1979. Growth in substitute products, such as wafer board, a composite panel made by bonding wood chips together, was spurred by new plants in the upper Midwest. Wafer board facilities planned in 1979 would more than double previous combined U.S. and Canadian capacity. U.S. lumber imports consisted almost entirely of softwoods from Canada. In 1979 such imports represented about 24% of total U.S. lumber consumption, slightly less than in 1978.

Energy from wood increased in importance in the minds as well as the fireplaces of many Americans as the energy crunch worsened. Wood in 1979 furnished slightly more than 2% of the country's heat and energy. The U.S. Department of Energy estimated that by the end of the 1980s wood—a renewable resource—would provide about 10% of the nation's energy needs. (TAIT TRUSSELL)

See also Agriculture and Food Supplies; Computers; Consumerism; Economy, World; Energy; Food Processing; Games and Toys; Industrial Relations; Materials Sciences; Mining and Quarrying; Photography; Television and Radio; Transportation.

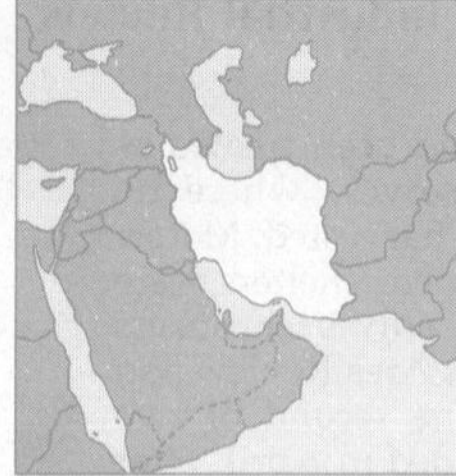

Iran

Iran

An Islamic republic of western Asia, Iran is bounded by the U.S.S.R., Afghanistan, Pakistan, Iraq, and Turkey and the Caspian Sea, the Arabian Sea, and the Persian Gulf. Area: 1,648,000 sq km (636,000 sq mi). Pop. (1978 est.): 35,213,000. Cap. and largest city: Teheran (pop., 1976, 4,496,000). Language: Persian. Religion (1976): Muslim 99%; Christian, Jewish, and Zoroastrian minorities. Shah-in-shah, Mohammad Reza Pahlavi Aryamehr (left the country Jan. 16, 1979); from February 3 power resided with a Revolutionary Council; prime ministers, Gen. Gholam Reza Azhari, Shahpur Bakhtiar from January 4, and Mehdi Bazargan from February 5 to November 6.

Iran's slide into political chaos accelerated rapidly in early 1979. Gen. Gholam Reza Azhari resigned as prime minister on January 1, ending the shah's attempts to impose his political will on the country and signaling the loss of authority by the regime. Shahpur Bakhtiar was appointed prime minister, but he insisted that the shah leave Iran immediately after the formation of an acceptable Cabinet. The shah ultimately departed on January 16 after urging the Army to remain loyal to the prime minister.

The shah's removal opened the way for the return from exile of Ayatollah Ruhollah Khomeini (*see* BIOGRAPHIES), who during 1978 had become the chief symbol of opposition to the regime. Combining religious preeminence with political respectability, Khomeini by early 1979 had no rival in the Iranian popular imagination. In the weeks preceding the shah's flight, Khomeini had promised that he would establish an Islamic republic. A relentlessly growing tide of popular opinion in favour of his return forced Bakhtiar to concede the issue, and the ayatollah made a triumphant entry into the capital on February 1. Bakhtiar attempted to hold the constitution against the religious authorities, but he was opposed by the National Front, the main antishah coalition, and failed to gain adequate support from the Army or the people at large. He was forced into hiding and later into exile.

Forces loyal to Ayatollah Khomeini executed nine Kurdish rebels following an uprising in August.

UPI

IRAN

Education. (1976–77) Primary, pupils 4,768,588, teachers 167,457; secondary, pupils 2,109,381, teachers 84,092; vocational, pupils 201,472, teachers 10,041; teacher training, students 46,025, teachers 2,262; higher, students 154,215, teaching staff 13,952.

Finance. Monetary unit: rial, with (Sept. 17, 1979) a free rate of 71.46 rials to U.S. $1 (153.75 rials = £1 sterling). Gold, SDR's, and foreign exchange (May 1979) U.S. $10,118,000,000. Budget (1978–79 est.): revenue 2,796,000,000,000 rials; expenditure 2,936,000,000,000 rials. Gross national product (1977–78) 5,347,600,000,000 rials. Money supply (Feb. 1979) 1,348,000,000,000 rials. Cost of living (1975 = 100; April 1979) 178.

Foreign Trade. (1978) Imports *c.* 1,208,000,000,000 rials; exports *c.* 1,580,000,000,000 rials. Import sources: U.S. *c.* 20%; West Germany *c.* 19%; Japan *c.* 15%; U.K. *c.* 8%; Italy *c.* 6%. Export destinations: Japan *c.* 17%; U.S. *c.* 13%; West Germany *c.* 9%; U.S. Virgin Islands *c.* 7%; Italy *c.* 6%; The Netherlands *c.* 6%; France *c.* 5%. Main exports: crude oil and products 97%.

Transport and Communications. Roads (1975) *c.* 52,000 km. Motor vehicles in use (1977): passenger 932,700; commercial 204,000. Railways: (1977) 4,604 km; traffic (1976) 3,511,000,000 passenger-km, freight 4,627,000,000 net ton-km. Air traffic (1977): 4,116,000,000 passenger-km; freight *c.* 83 million net ton-km. Shipping (1978): merchant vessels 100 gross tons and over 208; gross tonnage 1,194,675. Telephones (Jan. 1978) 828,600. Radio receivers (Dec. 1976) 2.1 million. Television receivers (Dec. 1976) 1,720,000.

Agriculture. Production (in 000; metric tons; 1978): wheat *c.* 5,700; barley *c.* 1,000; rice *c.* 1,650; potatoes *c.* 680; sugar, raw value *c.* 630; onions *c.* 250; tomatoes *c.* 300; watermelons (1977) *c.* 890; melons (1977) *c.* 460; dates *c.* 300; grapes *c.* 917; apples *c.* 450; soybeans *c.* 130; tea *c.* 27; tobacco *c.* 16; cotton, lint *c.* 150. Livestock (in 000; 1978): cattle *c.* 6,650; sheep *c.* 33,660; goats *c.* 13,500; horses (1977) *c.* 350; asses (1977) *c.* 1,800; chickens *c.* 65,000.

Industry. Production (in 000; metric tons; 1976–77): cement 6,100; coal *c.* 900; crude oil (1978) 261,770; natural gas (cu m; 1977) 57,336,000; petroleum products (1977) *c.* 36,680; lead concentrates (metal content; 1977–78) 40; chromium ore (oxide content; 1977–78) *c.* 80; electricity (kw-hr; 1977) *c.* 18,000,000.

Following the ayatollah's return, street fighting against the security forces intensified, while deep divisions appeared between the Army and the Air Force. Severe unrest culminated on February 11 when the generals recalled their troops to barracks and mass civilian and guerrilla attacks overran the major Army bases in the Teheran area, completing the disintegration of the armed forces' morale. Large quantities of arms fell into the hands of the guerrillas, the Muslim militia, and others, and power effectively moved to the ayatollah. Khomeini appointed Mehdi Bazargan (*see* BIOGRAPHIES), a respected member of the National Front and a dedicated Muslim, as prime minister to manage an interim Cabinet.

The form of government adopted from mid-February was unstructured. The Cabinet had little real power, and political authority rested with Khomeini and his Revolutionary Council. The latter's membership was kept secret, but it was led by a senior ayatollah, Mahmoud Taleghani. Power was manifested through control of the revolutionary militia and the ability of Khomeini to appeal directly to the mass of the population in support of his policies. Khomeini's strength was demonstrated in a referendum called for March 30 and 31 to decide on the adoption of an Islamic republic, which was accepted by an overwhelming majority. After being debated in the Revolutionary Council and submitted to a council of experts, elected on August 3, for ratification, a new constitution was approved by the voters on December 2–3. It provided for a president and a representative assembly to be elected by universal suffrage, although the assembly's powers of initiating legislation would be limited. A council of guardians, composed of religious authorities, would oversee the presentation and passage of legislation, while final authority, including the command of the armed forces, would be vested in a *faqih*, the leading theologian of the country. The *faqih* was not specifically named in the constitution; however, it was assumed that the post would go to Khomeini. Elections were scheduled for early 1980.

Once the armed forces had ceased to be a convincing organization, the ayatollah faced few serious challenges. The left-wing groups that had participated in the fighting against the shah were beaten in their attempts to expand their own power base in the revolution's aftermath. The ranks of the shah's supporters were reduced by defection, exile, and execution. In the period to Oct. 4, 1979, 623 persons were executed by the revolutionary authorities. Bakhtiar set up a centre of opposition to Khomeini in Paris, but it had little influence on Iranian political affairs. The Revolutionary Council reduced the opportunities for domestic opposition by taking over the headquarters of the main left-wing parties and closing down newspapers that published views discordant with government or Muslim policies.

Opposition to the new leadership developed in provincial and tribal areas where Sunni Islam prevailed and where there were long-standing linguistic and ethnic claims to separatism. Fighting between government forces and Turkoman tribes broke out on March 26 and lasted until April 2. Violence in Kurdistan (Kordestan) began in February and reached serious proportions in March, when clashes between Kurdish autonomists and government forces occurred in Sanandaj and Naqadeh. An attempt at outright rebellion by the Kurds in late August was crushed by September 3, though the main Kurdish groups took to the hills and guerrilla activity continued.

The government faced further problems from the Arabic-speaking tribes of the south, where there was street fighting in May and June. A campaign of sabotage directed against oil installations and public utilities began in July. The arrest of Arab perpetrators, execution of those found guilty of murder, and the extradition of the Arab spiritual leader, Ayatollah Mohammed Taher Khaghani, from Khuzestan failed to bring quiet. Strikes and noncooperation by Arabs employed in the oil industry inhibited petroleum output. The country's major ports were also periodically affected by strikes and closings.

During the year divisions became apparent between Khomeini and other senior Shiʿite religious leaders. Khomeini's view that state and religion are inseparable caused theological unease in the main religious centre of Qom. Ayatollah Taleghani rejected Khomeini's view that only pro-Muslim parties should be accepted and promoted open democracy until his death on September 10. Ayatollah Seyed Kazem Shariat-Madari totally opposed the direct involvement of the religious establishment in day-to-day politics, and late in the year there were serious disorders among his followers in northwestern Iran, with open revolt flaring at times in Tabriz. Nevertheless, Khomeini succeeded in holding the Shiʿite religious establishment together behind him. A number of prominent clergymen were assassinated by terrorists of the Forghan group, including Ayatollah Morteza Motahari on May 1 and Mohammad Mofateh on December 18; the same extremist group injured Ayatollah Hashemi Rafsanjani on May 25.

The revolution brought important changes in foreign policy. The new regime was highly nationalistic and showed antipathy to both the U.S. and the U.S.S.R. Support for the Palestinian cause dominated foreign policy, together with support for Muslim political movements, especially those with a Shiʿite bias. Shiʿite minorities in Afghanistan, Iraq, and the Persian Gulf states received unofficial but clear encouragement to revolt, and this led to deteriorating relations with those countries. Iranian claims to the island of Bahrain were renewed and diplomatic relations with Egypt severed.

A major confrontation with the U.S. was precipitated when the shah, who after brief stays in Egypt, Morocco, and The Bahamas had been granted a six-month visa by Mexico, was admitted to the U.S. on October 22 for medical treatment. Iran, which had condemned him to death in absentia, demanded his extradition, which the U.S. refused. On November 4 militants seized the U.S. embassy in Teheran and announced that the occupants would be held hostage until the shah was returned. The exact number of hostages was a matter of dispute; after the release of some non-U.S. nationals, women, and blacks, the U.S. State Department set it at 50 plus three senior officials being detained at the foreign ministry. The identity of the militants was also a matter of conjecture. They claimed to be students loyal to Khomeini, but the degree to which he controlled them was unclear, and at times they disagreed openly with the Revolutionary Council.

The seizure was condemned by the UN Security Council (*see* UNITED NATIONS) and by a wide spectrum of governments, but U.S. efforts to secure the hostages' release were frustrated by the difficulty in finding responsible officials with the authority to negotiate, a situation that was compounded by a series of rapid turnovers in the post of foreign minister. U.S. moves, including an embargo on Iranian oil imports, the freezing of Iranian assets, and the movement of a naval force to the area, proved ineffective. The departure of the shah to Panama failed to defuse the situation, which remained extremely tense at year's end. (For a chronology of the Iranian-U.S. crisis, *see* page 48.)

The country's economy underwent an accelerating decline. Petroleum output, which averaged 1,181,000 bbl a day in the first quarter of the year, recovered sharply to almost 4 million bbl a day in

Information Science and Technology:
see Computers

Insurance:
see Industrial Review

International Bank for Reconstruction and Development:
see Economy, World

International Law:
see Law

International Monetary Fund:
see Economy, World

Investment:
see Economy, World; Stock Exchanges

the second quarter. However, sabotage and technical problems caused production to falter in July–September, and production in the first week of September was reported at less than 3 million bbl a day. The forced resignation of the head of the National Iranian Oil Company on September 28 led to further disruption. Immediately after the revolution, the role of the foreign consortium that produced most of Iran's oil was terminated.

Private banks were taken over by the government on June 7, insurance companies on June 25, and all major industries on July 5. A rapid rundown of industry occurred as foreign enterprises and capital withdrew, discipline among the work force declined, and difficulties arose in obtaining raw materials and spare parts. New government industrial policies were slow in taking shape. Most major projects begun by the shah lapsed or were considerably reduced in scale.

(KEITH S. MCLACHLAN)

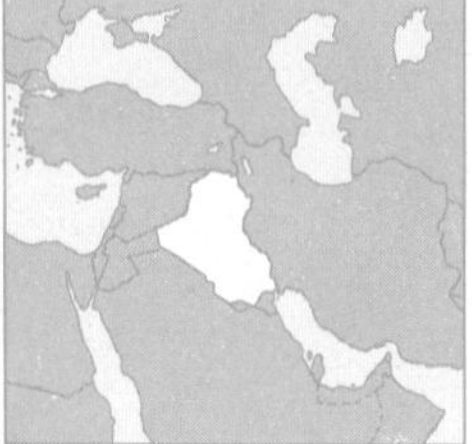

Iraq

Iraq

A republic of southwestern Asia, Iraq is bounded by Turkey, Iran, Kuwait, Saudi Arabia, Jordan, Syria, and the Persian Gulf. Area: 437,522 sq km (168,928 sq mi). Pop. (1977): 12,171,500, including Arabs, Kurds, Turks, Aramaic-speakers, Iranians, and others. Cap. and largest city: Baghdad (pop., 1977, 3,205,600). Language: Arabic. Religion: mainly Muslim, some Christian. Presidents in 1979, Gen. Ahmad Hassan al-Bakr and, from July 16, Saddam Hussein at-Takriti; prime minister from July 16, Saddam Hussein at-Takriti.

Iraq in 1979 regained leadership of the Arab opposition to Egyptian negotiations with Israel. On March 14 it called for a meeting of Arab foreign and economy ministers in Baghdad to coincide with the signing of the Egypt-Israel treaty on March 27. The Palestine Liberation Organization and 18 Arab states—excluding Egypt, Sudan, and Oman—attended the stormy conference which resolved on March 31 to: withdraw ambassadors from Cairo; deprive Egypt of membership rights in the Arab League; transfer Arab League headquarters from Cairo to Tunis; and suspend aid, loans, and oil shipments to Egypt.

Pictures of Iraq's outgoing president, Ahmad Hassan al-Bakr (right), and his successor, Saddam Hussein at-Takriti (left), adorned walls and shop windows in July.

SVEN SIMON/KATHERINE YOUNG

IRAQ

Education. (1978–79) Primary, pupils 2,459,870, teachers 87,148; secondary, pupils 781,766, teachers 25,254; vocational, pupils 48,186, teachers 3,273; teacher training, students 20,488, teachers 939; higher, students 89,197, teaching staff 5,207.

Finance. Monetary unit: Iraqi dinar, with (Sept. 17, 1979) a par value of 0.295 dinar to U.S. $1 (free rate of 0.642 dinar = £1 sterling). Budget (1979 est.) balanced at 9,467,000,000 dinars. Gross national product (1976) 4,736,800,000 dinars. Cost of living (1975 = 100; Sept. 1978) 130.2.

Foreign Trade. Imports (1977) 1,151,300,000 dinars; exports (1978) 3,250,900,000 dinars. Import sources: West Germany 18%; Japan 18%; U.K. 7%; France 6%; Italy 5%; U.S. 5%. Export destinations: France *c.* 17%; Italy *c.* 16%; Brazil *c.* 9%; U.K. *c.* 8%; Japan *c.* 6%; U.S.S.R. *c.* 5%; Spain *c.* 5%. Main export: crude oil 99%.

Transport and Communications. Roads (suitable for vehicles; 1975) 9,692 km. Motor vehicles in use (1977): passenger 150,400; commercial (including buses) 74,500. Railways: (1975) 1,990 km; traffic (1976) 797 million passenger-km, freight 2,254,000,000 net ton-km. Air traffic (1978): 1,333,000,000 passenger-km; freight 41.4 million net ton-km. Shipping (1978): merchant vessels 100 gross tons and over 115; gross tonnage 1,305,907. Telephones (Jan. 1978) 319,600. Radio receivers (Dec. 1975) 1,252,000. Television receivers (Dec. 1976) 425,000.

Agriculture. Production (in 000; metric tons; 1978): wheat *c.* 910; barley *c.* 607; rice *c.* 172; cucumbers (1977) *c.* 107; watermelons (1977) *c.* 300; onions *c.* 103; tomatoes *c.* 405; dates *c.* 581; grapes *c.* 76; tobacco *c.* 10; cotton, lint (1977) *c.* 13. Livestock (in 000; 1978): cattle *c.* 2,500; sheep *c.* 11,488; goats *c.* 3,620; camels (1977) *c.* 228; asses (1977) *c.* 450.

Industry. Production (in 000; metric tons; 1977): cement *c.* 2,500; crude oil (1978) 129,076; natural gas (cu m) 1,580,000; petroleum products *c.* 5,400; electricity (excluding most industrial production; kw-hr) 5,000,000.

Iraq's relations with neighbouring Syria improved steadily until July 16, when Pres. Ahmad Hassan al-Bakr resigned because of ill health and was succeeded by Saddam Hussein at-Takriti (*see* BIOGRAPHIES). On January 15 Iraqi Foreign Minister Saadoun Hammadi and Defense Minister Air Marshal Adnan Khairalla Tulfah went to Damascus for the first meeting of the military coordination committee, and two weeks later Saddam Hussein attended the first conference of the Higher Joint Political Committee in Damascus. The first practical benefit was the reopening on February 24 of the Iraqi oil pipeline from Kirkuk to the Syrian port of Banias. The first oil deliveries were for Syrian domestic use, but the Syrians were expected to earn $100 million in transit fees in 1979. The governments in Baghdad and Damascus stated that their countries would soon be united as a single political entity and that their respective ruling Baʿath parties would become one. On April 22 Iraqi Revolutionary Command Council (RCC) member Naim Haddad said that Iraq had submitted its proposals for constitutional unity with Syria. The high point of unity efforts came on June 16 when Syrian Pres. Hafez al-Assad arrived in Baghdad for discussions with President Bakr.

A month later Saddam Hussein's accession to power following Bakr's resignation was accompanied by a bloody purge of the RCC, the military command, the Baʿath Party, and the labour union leadership. On August 8, after arrests that began the day Hussein took office, 21 people, including the minister of industry and minerals and the minister of state for Kurdish affairs, were executed for their alleged involvement in a conspiracy to overthrow the new president. It was widely reported that Saddam Hussein believed that Syria had been behind the conspiracy, and no further unity talks took place in 1979.

The regime's treatment of members of the Iraqi Communist Party (ICP) put a severe strain on relations with the Soviet Union. The last remaining Communist ministers in government were dismissed on April 25 and May 5. The ICP claimed in February that 31 of its members had been executed and another 1,900 members and sympathizers had "disappeared."

Other internal opposition came from Kurdish rebels in northern Iraq, who intensified their war against the Baghdad regime. In January Masoud al-Barzani, son of Kurdish leader Mulla Mustafa al-Barzani (*see* OBITUARIES), survived an assassination attempt in Vienna before returning to Iraq as a rebel leader. Fighting between Pesh Merga rebels and Iraqi troops led on June 4 and 14 to Iraqi bombing of Kurdish villages in Iran. This, combined with the arrest in Iraq of Shi'ah leader Ayatollah Sayed Mohammad Bakr as-Sadr, caused relations with Iran to deteriorate.

Iraq adopted an unusually moderate line within the Organization of Petroleum Exporting Countries (OPEC) over oil prices. In February it joined Saudi Arabia in freezing prices for the year's first quarter and refused to take advantage of the shortfall in Iranian oil. In June the cost of Basra crude was raised to $17 a barrel, and in October that of Iraq's highest quality crude delivered at Banias rose to the OPEC ceiling of $23.50 a barrel. In late December Iraq joined Venezuela, Libya, and Indonesia in raising prices 10 to 15%.

(CHARLES GLASS)

Ireland

Separated from Great Britain by the North Channel, the Irish Sea, and St. George's Channel, the Republic of Ireland shares its island with Northern Ireland to the northeast. Area: 70,283 sq km (27,136 sq mi), or 84% of the island. Pop. (1979 est.): 3,364,900. Cap. and largest city: Dublin (pop., 1979 est., 543,600). Language (1971): mostly English; 28% speak English and Irish or Irish only. Religion: 94% Roman Catholic. President in 1979, Patrick J. Hillery; prime ministers, John Lynch and, from December 11, Charles J. Haughey.

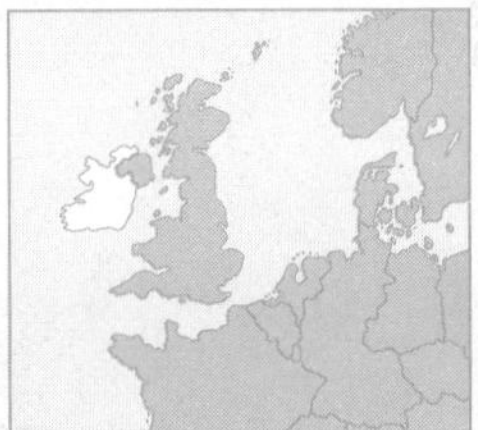

Ireland

Ireland faced a major energy crisis in 1979 which coincided with one of the worst winters since the keeping of meteorological records began. The government detached the punt (Irish pound) from the stronger pound sterling in March and, for the first time in 150 years, the country had its own currency. Together with other European currencies, the punt fluctuated downward against sterling. These difficulties were offset by the remarkably successful visit of Pope John Paul II in the early fall. In December Ireland gained a new prime minister as John Lynch resigned and was replaced by Charles Haughey, known as an ardent Irish nationalist.

LONDON DAILY EXPRESS/PICTORIAL PARADE

Smoke rose 3,000 feet in the air from the French oil tanker "Betelgeuse," which exploded and burned in Bantry Bay in January.

In common with other Western countries, Ireland suffered from the oil shortage that followed Iran's revolution. Since Ireland's was a growth economy, the effect was more extensive than in many other nations, and the situation was aggravated by the unusually cold and prolonged winter. By Easter there was an acute shortage of gasoline, while supplies of heating oil and factory fuels were substantially reduced or even cut off. There were several fuel price rises. However, the government, despite considerable pressure, did not introduce rationing. Conditions improved in the summer, and the minister for industry, commerce, and energy, Desmond O'Malley, negotiated a bilateral oil deal with Iraq.

During the same period, from February to the end of June, postal services were suspended as the result of a long-standing labour dispute. The combined effect of this and the energy crisis on tourism, a major industry, was considerable, as was the effect on industry and commerce generally. Growth predictions and job creation targets were continually revised downward while inflation prospects were continually revised upward.

After introducing a budget that aimed at some reform of the taxation system by placing a heavier burden on the farming community, the government was faced with urban protests against the Pay-As-You-Earn (PAYE) system of taxation. Two marches through Dublin took place in March, with an estimated 200,000 taking part. The government promised further reforms, but the episode had a prejudicial effect on protracted talks aimed at formulating the National Understanding on Wages and Employment. This was finally achieved on July 25, when the parties agreed on a 15% wage increase in two phases over 15 months.

On June 7 Ireland went to the polls to choose 15 members of the European Assembly and to vote in local government elections. In the wake of the energy crisis, the postal strike, and the protests about taxation, the government did badly. Instead of the predicted eight or nine seats in the European Assembly, it won only five. Fine Gael and Labour won four each, and there were two Independents. The government also did badly in the local elections. The holding of both polls on the same day somewhat distorted the turnout, which, at 55%, was high by European standards.

The gloom that persisted through the first part of the year was lifted when rumours of a visit to Ireland by Pope John Paul II were confirmed in May. The visit took place from September 29 to October 1. After a mass in Phoenix Park, Dublin, attended by 1,250,000 people, the pope went to Drogheda in the archdiocese of Armagh, where he made a passionate appeal for peace to the men of violence in Northern Ireland. He visited Clonmacnoise, the Marian Shrine at Knock, and held a youth mass in Galway and a further mass in Limerick before flying to the United States. He urged the Irish people to stand firm against divorce, abortion, and contraception.

Contraception was the subject of the year's most controversial piece of legislation, the government's Family Planning Bill. In extremely cautious terms, the bill enacted the already established constitutional right to artificial methods of contraception. One member of John Lynch's government declined to vote in favour of any part of the bill and declined to resign as well. The party treated it as a matter of conscience, and the possibility of a government crisis was averted.

IRELAND

Education. (1977–78) Primary, pupils 561,931, teachers 18,448; secondary and vocational, pupils 280,682, teachers 16,966; higher, students 36,798, teaching staff 3,207.

Finance. Monetary unit: Irish pound (punt), with (Sept. 17, 1979) a free rate of I£0.48 to U.S. $1 (I£1.04 = £1 sterling). Gold, SDR's, and foreign exchange (June 1979) U.S. $2,117,000,000. Budget (1978 actual): revenue £2,076 million; expenditure £2,932 million. Gross national product (1977) £5,359 million. Money supply (June 1979) £1,447.5 million. Cost of living (1975 = 100; May 1979) 159.8.

Foreign Trade. (1978) Imports £3,706.5 million; exports £2,959.2 million. Import sources: EEC 70% (U.K. 49%, West Germany 7%, France 5%); U.S. 8%. Export destinations: EEC 77% (U.K. 47%, France 9%, West Germany 8%, Belgium-Luxembourg 5%; The Netherlands 5%); U.S. 6%. Main exports: machinery 13%; chemicals 12%; beef and veal 11%; dairy products 8%; textile yarns and fabrics 6%; cattle 5%. Tourism (1977): visitors 1,447,000; gross receipts U.S. $323 million.

Transport and Communications. Roads (1975) 89,006 km. Motor vehicles in use (1977): passenger 572,700; commercial 53,300. Railways (1977): 2,004 km; traffic 794 million passenger-km, freight 534 million net ton-km. Air traffic (1978): 1,835,000,000 passenger-km; freight 85,950,000 net ton-km. Shipping (1978): merchant vessels 100 gross tons and over 110; gross tonnage 212,143. Telephones (Jan. 1978) 519,000. Radio receivers (Dec. 1976) 949,000. Television licenses (Dec. 1977) 595,000.

Agriculture. Production (in 000; metric tons; 1978): barley 1,320; wheat 247; oats 124; potatoes 1,070; sugar, raw value *c.* 185; cabbages (1977) *c.* 139; cow's milk *c.* 4,640; butter *c.* 119; cheese *c.* 51; beef and veal 384; pork *c.* 132; fish catch (1977) 96. Livestock (in 000; June 1978): cattle *c.* 7,154; sheep 3,378; pigs 1,031; horses (1977) *c.* 82; chickens *c.* 8,434.

Industry. Production (in 000; metric tons; 1977): cement 1,600; coal (1978) 36; petroleum products 2,287; electricity (kw-hr; 1978) 9,973,000; manufactured gas (cu m) 270,000; beer (hl; 1976–77) 4,400; wool fabrics (sq m) 3,000; rayon, etc., fabrics (sq m; 1976) 16,700.

On August 27 Lord Mountbatten of Burma (*see* OBITUARIES) was killed off the coast of Mullaghmore, County Sligo, by a bomb placed in his fishing boat by the Provisional Irish Republican Army (IRA) and detonated by remote control. It marked a new low point in Anglo-Irish relations, with exceptionally bitter recriminations against Ireland appearing in the British press. Increased security measures were taken along the border during August and September. In November Thomas McMahon, said to be the Provisional IRA's chief expert on remote-controlled bombs, was convicted of the murder and sentenced to life imprisonment. A survey published in October showed that one in five people in Ireland supported the aims of the Provisional IRA. Though much criticized, it underlined the complex attitudes in the republic about North-South relations.

Early in November Prime Minister Lynch visited the U.S., where he urged Americans not to support IRA terrorists. A month later he surprised the country by resigning, citing, among other reasons, the loss of two by-elections in Cork and the end of the Irish presidency of the European Council. On December 7 Haughey, then serving as health minister, defeated Finance Minister George Colley for the Fianna Fail leadership, and he was confirmed as prime minister by Parliament on December 11. Haughey, who once stood trial for smuggling arms to the IRA, was expected to take a harder line than Lynch on reunification.

On January 8 a French oil tanker, the "Betelgeuse," blew up at the Whiddy Island Oil Terminal, in Bantry Bay, killing 50 people. It was one of the worst fire disasters in the history of the state. A measure of light relief continued at the Wood Quay Viking site in the centre of Dublin, where politicians and protesters took over the site. The 18-month effort to save the remnants of the Viking settlement was in vain, however. After a decision by the Irish Supreme Court on March 7, development of a civic office complex was going ahead as planned. (MAVIS ARNOLD)

See also United Kingdom.

Israel

A republic of the Middle East, Israel is bounded by Lebanon, Syria, Jordan, Egypt, and the Mediterranean Sea. Area (not including territory occupied in the June 1967 war): 20,700 sq km (7,992 sq mi). Pop. (1979 est.): 3,776,000. Cap. and largest city: Jerusalem (pop., 1978 est., 376,000). Language: Hebrew and Arabic. Religion: predominantly Jewish (1979 est., 84%) with Muslim, Christian, and other minorities. President in 1979, Yitzhak Navon; prime minister, Menahem Begin.

Israel

Domestic Affairs. No one would have thought it possible in the dramatic days of March 1979, as the "peace process" was approaching its climax with U.S. Pres. Jimmy Carter addressing the Knesset (parliament) in Jerusalem and helping to put the finishing touches on the peace treaty between Egypt and Israel, that six months later Israel would have withdrawn into an altogether different and far more parochial preoccupation with the

W. KAREL—SYGMA

Israel's highest court ruled that Elon Moreh, an Israeli settlement being established on the West Bank near Nablus, was not vital to national security and must be abandoned.

state of the economy and the ineffectiveness of the government. During this time opinion polls revealed a dramatic decline in the popularity of the government. After the conclusion of the peace treaty with Egypt, Prime Minister Menahem Begin's Likud coalition had improved its position in relation to the opposition Labour Alignment, but by May the Labour preference was equal to that of Begin's party. By November the Labour Alignment, even though beset internally by leadership conflicts, was shown to be well ahead of the Likud coalition.

This was not, however, a renewal of the country's confidence in Labour. The inconstancy of the electorate, so evident in 1979, was a new feature of Israeli politics, where ingrained party loyalties had been almost immovable for 30 years. No party had convincing answers for 1979's twin problems: how to restructure Israel's economy so as to overcome the runaway inflation and the imbalance between productivity and expenditure, and how to transform a war economy into a peace economy that still had to maintain all the military options.

Instead, the government and the opposition spent most of their energies on fighting what could be described as media issues—secondary problems that provided useful publicity at home and often adverse comment abroad. Most of the conflicts with Egypt and the U.S. in the working out of the peace process turned out to be ephemeral. These developments were not helped by the widespread replacement of former officials, envoys, and administrators by new men, loyal to the new government and rewarded at last for party service. In this, Begin's government was no more than following the example of its Labour predecessors. What was unfortunate, however, was the indiscriminate replacement of some of Israel's most outstanding officeholders.

The high hopes entertained when Begin took charge of the government that henceforth there would be a firm hand at the helm did not materialize. For a man who had been so completely accepted by his party as leader, Begin was singularly ineffective in ensuring the cohesion of his Cabinet members. Enormous energy was expended, and much ill will induced among friends and allies, on questions such as the West Bank settlements and relations with the Carter administration that did not affect the security or the well-being of Israel.

The Economy. But for most Israelis 1979 was a year of peace. Despite terrorist attacks on civilians inspired by the Palestine Liberation Organization (PLO), continuing long periods of military service for the young, and a runaway inflation that had reached an annual rate of more than 100% by November, the people prospered. Private consumption in real terms increased by 8% in 1979 over the previous year. Costly and highly taxed television sets, refrigerators, and automobiles recorded unprecedentedly high sales.

The national budget did not, however, reflect the burgeoning well-being suggested by outward appearances. Industry and even more so the public sector were beset by crippling strikes, including those by teachers, postal workers, bank clerks, government attorneys, and Israel's national airline, El Al. The main concern was to ensure that Israel's wage structure would remain linked to the rapid rate of inflation. But below the surface the more pressing cause was the economic insecurity induced by the combination of inflation and devaluation of the national currency.

The government failed in 1979 to keep to the course that it had charted in 1977 of doing away with government controls in order to increase exports and attract more foreign investment. Previously, it had succeeded to some extent on both counts. Exports increased by some 25%, but much of this was accounted for by the sale of Israeli-manufactured arms. Foreign investment also rose by more than 50% in 1978 and continued to improve throughout 1979. But other aspects of the new economic policy met with failure. Imports increased. Public-sector spending was not reduced. There was no restructuring of the labour force, and government borrowing—mainly in the U.S.—soared to a point where the national debt stood at

Ireland, Northern: *see* United Kingdom

Iron and Steel Industry: *see* Industrial Review

Islam: *see* Religion

some U.S. $15 billion at the end of 1979. The interest paid by Israel for the year exceeded $2 billion.

In economic terms the peace settlement with Egypt was a costly affair for Israel. Even with U.S. assistance the relocating of defense installations in the Sinai to areas in the Negev, the loss of relatively cheap oil, and the cost of restructuring the entire defensive system would add considerably to the budget for 1979. In the budget was a dramatic decrease in defense expenditure, the total of $1,624,000,000 being barely half that spent in either 1977 or 1978. The proportion of gross national product spent on defense dropped from 36% in 1976 to less than 20% in 1979. However, it was the political implication of Israel's defense effort that overshadowed the often debatable statistics. At the end of 1979 Israel was more dependent economically and politically on the U.S. than ever before.

Foreign Relations. The hoped-for rapprochement with African countries leading to a resumption of the once-flourishing relationship between Israel and black Africa did not materialize in the face of increasing Arab and third world hostility to the Israeli-Egyptian peace settlement. Movement toward peace and normalization with Egypt also lost its initial drive. It was often accompanied by petty and unimaginative bickering on both sides. Foreign Minister Moshe Dayan (until his resignation) and Defense Minister Ezer Weizman rose above this norm and matched Egyptian Pres. Anwar as-Sadat and his prime minister in a more imaginative approach. They were unable, however, to influence the Israeli Cabinet.

The overthrow of the shah in Iran in January removed a balancing factor to unrelieved Arab hostility on Israel's northern and eastern front. The shah had accepted Israeli help in organizing Iran's agriculture and recognized that there was a community of interest in preserving the Middle East peace. Iran was moreover the supplier of half of Israel's oil imports and a valuable market for some $200 million of its exports. During the revolution Israel evacuated about 1,000 Jews from Teheran.

The peace negotiations with Egypt had run into an impasse at the end of 1978. Israel's principal negotiators, Dayan and Weizman, had repeatedly been overruled by a hard-line Cabinet majority. However, on Feb. 11, 1979, Israel and Egypt accepted President Carter's invitation to resume peace talks in Washington, D.C. There, on March 5, Begin accepted Carter's peace formula, which involved Carter himself going to Jerusalem and to Cairo. On March 8 Carter met Sadat in Cairo. After intensive talks between the presidents and their advisers and an address to the Egyptian People's Assembly, Carter left for Jerusalem on March 10. There he met in full session with Israel's Cabinet on March 12 and addressed the Knesset together with Prime Minister Begin. But there remained unresolved issues on which Begin and the hard-line majority of the Cabinet would not agree. This was resolved in a night session between U.S. Secretary of State Cyrus Vance and Foreign Minister Dayan. It was accepted by Begin at a breakfast meeting on March 13 with Carter, who carried the proposals to Cairo for Sadat's approval.

On the following day Israel released 66 Palestinian prisoners in exchange for one Israeli soldier held by the PLO. On March 15 the Egyptian Cabinet approved the treaty terms. Four days later the Israeli Cabinet did likewise after the National Religious Party had threatened to leave the Cabinet unless Israel retained control of the West Bank. The treaty terms were put before the Knesset the following day. Begin assured members that "in

Palestinian guerrillas Halad Hussein (left) and Hussein Fiad were convicted in Israel in October for a 1978 terrorist attack on an Israeli bus that left 37 Israelis dead and 82 wounded.

UPI

ISRAEL

Education. (1977–78) Primary, pupils 602,535, teachers 32,225; secondary, pupils 78,954, teachers 5,731; vocational, pupils 75,305, teachers 7,981; higher, students 83,910, teaching staff (1974–75) 13,981.

Finance. Monetary unit: Israeli pound, with (Sept. 17, 1979) a free rate of I£28.07 to U.S. $1 (I£60.40 = £1 sterling). Gold, SDR's, and foreign exchange (June 1979) U.S. $2,958,000,000. Budget (1978–79 est.) balanced at I£182,000 million. Gross national product (1978) I£223,855 million. Money supply (May 1979) I£28,888 million. Cost of living (1975 = 100; June 1979) 434.

Foreign Trade. (1978) Imports I£129,335 million (including I£26,768 million military goods); exports I£68,510 million. Import sources: U.S. 19%; Switzerland 11%; West Germany 10%; U.K. 9%; The Netherlands 8%; Italy 5%. Export destinations: U.S. 17%; West Germany 9%; Hong Kong 8%; U.K. 7%; The Netherlands 5%; Belgium-Luxembourg 5%; Japan 5%; France 5%. Main exports: diamonds 38%; chemicals 10%; metal manufactures 10%; machinery 5%; citrus fruit 5%. Tourism (1977): visitors 893,900; gross receipts U.S. $461 million.

Transport and Communications. Roads (1977) 11,669 km. Motor vehicles in use (1977): passenger 312,777; commercial 101,400. Railways (1976): 786 km; traffic 280 million passenger-km, freight (1977) 535 million net ton-km. Air traffic (1978): 4,885,000,000 passenger-km; freight 205,019,000 net ton-km. Shipping (1978): merchant vessels 100 gross tons and over 55; gross tonnage 420,933. Telephones (Jan. 1978) 929,800. Radio receivers (Dec. 1976) 655,000. Television licenses (Dec. 1976) 475,000.

Agriculture. Production (in 000; metric tons; 1978): wheat *c.* 175; potatoes *c.* 221; watermelons (1977) 97; tomatoes *c.* 230; onions *c.* 60; oranges *c.* 919; grapefruit *c.* 456; grapes *c.* 70; apples *c.* 110; olives *c.* 9; bananas *c.* 62; cotton, lint *c.* 67; cheese *c.* 55; poultry meat *c.* 177; fish catch (1977) 24. Livestock (in 000; 1977): cattle 335; sheep 218; goats 142; pigs *c.* 80; camels 11; chickens *c.* 12,000.

Industry. Production (in 000; metric tons; 1978): cement 1,996; crude oil 24; natural gas (cu m) 57,000; phosphate rock (1977) 1,228; petroleum products (1977) *c.* 6,990; sulfuric acid 183; fertilizers (nutrient content; 1977–78) nitrogenous 51, phosphate 47, potash 683; paper (1977) 96; electricity (kw-hr) 11,800,000. New dwelling units completed (1978) 35,600.

Judea, Samaria, and Gaza there will never be a Palestinian state" and that Jerusalem "will never be divided again." On March 22 the Knesset approved the treaty terms by a vote of 95 to 18.

The treaty was formally signed on March 26 on the White House lawn in Washington, D.C., by President Sadat and Prime Minister Begin. President Carter witnessed the signatures; meanwhile, in Beirut PLO chairman Yasir Arafat vowed that he would ensure that "the hands of the signatories would be chopped off." A month later Egypt and Israel exchanged the instruments of ratification at Umm Khashiba in the Sinai desert.

Dayan had expressed strong dissatisfaction about the manner in which the negotiations for the implementation of the next stage of the agreement were to be conducted. On April 22 the Executive and the Knesset portion of Begin's Herut Party demanded that Dayan be sacked. It was the beginning of Dayan's long battle for what he regarded as a more realistic foreign policy, which ended with his resignation on October 21.

In his letter of resignation to Begin, Dayan reviewed the conduct of negotiations for Palestinian autonomy, which were an integral part of the peace treaty with Egypt. They had been conducted by the hard-line National Religious Party leader, Interior Minister Yosef Burg, in an evident Cabinet rebuff to Dayan in mid-April. Dayan told Begin about his reservations on the conduct of the autonomy negotiations. He was certain that it was an urgent problem that could be solved without damage to Israeli interests. He linked his remarks with his opposition to the requisition of private land for the establishment of the settlement at Elon Moreh. On the following day, October 22, the Supreme Court ruled that the Gush Emunim settlement at Elon Moreh was illegally established and would have to be evacuated. On December 9 construction was begun on a new settlement for the residents of Elon Moreh, near the village of Dayr al Hatab. Four days earlier, after a month of growing unrest among the West Bank Arabs, Israel abandoned its attempt to deport Bassam al-Shaka, the Palestinian mayor of Nablus, for having allegedly expressed sympathy for PLO terrorism.

The talks on Palestinian autonomy dragged on inconclusively through the remainder of the year. Meanwhile, Israel handed over El Arish to Egypt ahead of time, and President Sadat went to Beersheba in May. In July the second stage of Israel's withdrawal from Sinai was concluded, and Sadat received Begin in Alexandria. On September 4 Sadat was enthusiastically welcomed when he sailed into Haifa port on yet another state visit. Finally, in November, Israel handed back to Egypt a 1,503-sq km (580-sq mi) region, which included the Monastery of St. Catherine on Mt. Sinai and the Alma oil fields in the Gulf of Suez.

After much soul-searching Begin brought back into the Cabinet on November 7 a hard-line administrator and politician to take charge of the Treasury and to seek to restore Israel's economic balance; he appointed Yigal Hurwitz, who had resigned from the Cabinet because of his disagreement over the settlement with Egypt.

(JON KIMCHE)

Italy

Italy

A republic of southern Europe, Italy occupies the Apennine Peninsula, Sicily, Sardinia, and a number of smaller islands. On the north it borders France, Switzerland, Austria, and Yugoslavia. Area: 301,263 sq km (116,318 sq mi). Pop. (1979 est.): 56,828,500. Cap. and largest city: Rome (pop., 1979 est., 2,914,600). Language: Italian. Religion: predominantly Roman Catholic. President in 1979, Alessandro Pertini; premiers, Giulio Andreotti and, from August 5, Francesco Cossiga.

From January to August 1979, Italy underwent its longest political crisis since World War II. The Italian Communist Party decided at the beginning of the year to end two years of parliamentary power-sharing experiments with the ruling Christian Democrats and returned to the opposition. A general election in June produced no substantive political changes. During the crisis two party leaders, Ugo La Malfa (Republican) and Bettino Craxi (Socialist), tried and failed to form coalitions not led by Christian Democrats. Finally, in August, Francesco Cossiga (*see* BIOGRAPHIES), a Christian Democrat, formed a new coalition composed of Christian Democrats, Social Democrats, and Liberals.

Domestic Affairs. The Italian Communists triggered the long government crisis by withdrawing from a ten-month-old parliamentary pact on the grounds that they were not being adequately consulted by the ruling party and that the govern-

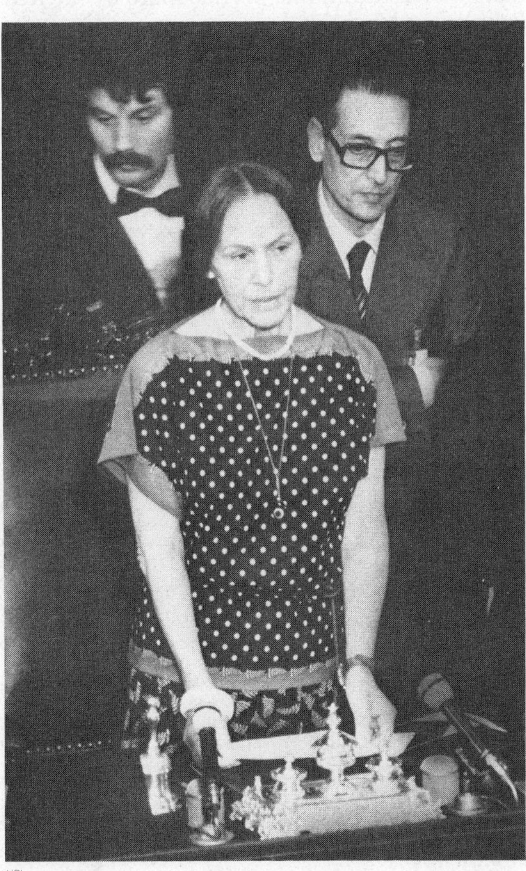

UPI

Nilde Jotti became the first woman to serve as president of Italy's Chamber of Deputies after her election on June 20.

Italian Literature: *see* Literature

ment was failing to tackle basic problems, including terrorism and unemployment. Premier Giulio Andreotti resigned on January 31. Although both the main political parties said that they wished to avoid a premature general election (Parliament had another two years to run), an attempt by the veteran Republican Party leader, Ugo La Malfa, to form a new coalition failed, and Pres. Alessandro Pertini dissolved Parliament on April 2. This was the third time in succession that an Italian Parliament had not run its full five-year course.

In the election campaign the Communists demanded equality of treatment as potential Cabinet members in the next government, while the Christian Democrats maintained their veto on Communist power-sharing at Cabinet level. The result of the vote held on June 3 and 4 varied so little from the 1976 general election (Christian Democrats 38.3% of the vote, as compared with 38.7% in 1976, and Communists 30.4%, as compared with 34.4%) that the political stalemate appeared likely to continue. (For tabulated results *see* POLITICAL PARTIES.) The 4% drop in the Communist vote was read as a sign of dissatisfaction expressed by some Communist supporters with the party's failure to take advantage of the gains scored in 1976 by pressing for effective social and economic reforms.

Finally, after further abortive attempts by Andreotti, Craxi, and Christian Democrat Filippo Maria Pandolfi, former treasury minister, to form a government, Cossiga became Italy's youngest-ever premier at the age of 51. Cossiga, a Sardinian, had served from 1976 to 1978 as interior minister and had resigned his Cabinet post as a point of honour after the murder of Aldo Moro by the Red Brigades in May 1978.

The Red Brigades continued its campaign of political terrorism, though for most of the year it was less intensive than in 1978. Victims included civil servants, industrialists, police officers, and magistrates. On January 29 Emilio Alessandrini, a Milan public prosecutor, was ambushed and shot dead, the sixth leading magistrate to be assassinated in two years. On July 13 Police Col. Antonio Varisco, head of security at Rome's central courts, was murdered by terrorists. On September 21 a high-ranking executive of the Fiat automobile firm in Turin, Carlo Ghiglieno, was shot dead by the Red Brigades. Four days later a Sicilian judge, Cesare Terranova, was murdered in Palermo. The level of violence rose toward year's end. In one of the most spectacular incidents, on December 11, members of the Front Line, a group linked to the Red Brigades, entered the business school of the University of Turin in midafternoon, rounded up students and faculty, and shot ten victims in the legs. On December 15 the government asked for new powers of search and arrest to combat the increase in guerrilla activity.

Judicial investigations into the murder of Aldo Moro proceeded slowly. Two left-wing university professors, Antonio Negri of Padua and Franco Piperno of Cosenza, were charged in connection with the kidnap and murder of the former premier. Both denied the charges. Piperno was arrested in Paris in August and was extradited to Rome.

Prospero Gallinari, one of the Red Brigades terrorists accused by police of having actually taken part in the kidnap of Moro and the murder of his bodyguards, was arrested after being seriously wounded by police during a gunfight in a Rome suburb in September. A parliamentary inquiry was ordered into the Moro murder, but no date was set.

An unprecedentedly long criminal trial ended in Catanzaro, southern Italy, on February 24. Three extreme right-wingers, Franco Freda, Giovanni Ventura, and Guido Gianettini, were sentenced to life imprisonment for their part in Italy's worst postwar terrorist attack—the Milan bank bombing of December 1969 in which 16 people were killed and more than 80 injured.

An important judgment was handed down by Italy's Constitutional Court. For the first time a former Cabinet minister was jailed on corruption charges. Mario Tanassi, former defense minister, was sentenced to two years and four months in prison for accepting kickbacks from the U.S. Lockheed Aircraft Corp. in exchange for military aircraft contracts. Tanassi was paroled after six months, however.

Italy's largest private employer, the Fiat au-

ITALY

Education. (1978–79) Primary, pupils 4,580,616, teachers (1975–76) 255,267; secondary, pupils 2,928,157, teachers (1975–76) 249,777; vocational, pupils 1,469,776, teachers (1975–76) 112,246; teacher training, students 217,579, teachers (1975–76) 18,899; higher, students 756,922, teaching staff (1976–77) 43,277.

Finance. Monetary unit: lira, with (Sept. 17, 1979) a free rate of 814 lire to U.S. $1 (1,751 lire = £1 sterling). Gold, SDR's, and foreign exchange (June 1979) U.S. $21,683,000,000. Budget (1978 actual): revenue 53,851,000,000,000 lire; expenditure 80,897,000,000,000 lire. Gross national product (1978) 220,599,000,000,000 lire. Money supply (March 1979) 120,972,000,000,000 lire. Cost of living (1975 = 100; June 1979) 173.5.

Foreign Trade. (1978) Imports 47,836,000,000,000 lire; exports 47,487,000,000,000 lire. Import sources: EEC 45% (West Germany 17%, France 15%); U.S. 7%. Export destinations: EEC 48% (West Germany 19%, France 14%, U.K. 6%); U.S. 7%. Main exports: machinery 22%; motor vehicles 9%; chemicals 6%; textile yarns and fabrics 6%; clothing 6%; petroleum products 6%; iron and steel 6%; food 5%; footwear 5%. Tourism (1977): visitors 17,549,000; gross receipts U.S. $4,762,000,000.

Transport and Communications. Roads (1976) 291,864 km (including 5,529 km expressways). Motor vehicles in use (1977): passenger 16,650,000; commercial 1,244,500. Railways: (1976) 19,923 km; traffic (1978) 38,950,000,000 passenger-km, freight 16,320,000,000 net ton-km. Air traffic (1977): 12,793,000,000 passenger-km; freight 527.6 million net ton-km. Shipping (1978): merchant vessels 100 gross tons and over 1,694: gross tonnage 11,491,873. Telephones (Jan. 1978) 16,118,900. Radio licenses (Dec. 1977) 13,193,000. Television licenses (Dec. 1977) 12,646,000.

Agriculture. Production (in 000; metric tons; 1978): wheat 8,764; corn 6,040; barley 790; oats 440; rice *c.* 950; potatoes 2,856; sugar, raw value *c.* 1,350; cabbages (1977) 599; cauliflowers (1977) 554; onions 520; tomatoes 3,653; grapes *c.* 10,900; wine *c.* 6,650; olives *c.* 2,400; oranges 1,400; mandarin oranges and tangerines 305; lemons 652; apples 1,770; pears (1977) 1,260; peaches (1977) 1,187; tobacco 104; cheese *c.* 567; beef and veal *c.* 1,022; pork *c.* 955; fish catch (1977) 427. Livestock (in 000; Dec. 1977): cattle 8,806; sheep 8,694; pigs 9,467; goats 960; poultry *c.* 119,440.

Industry. Index of production (1975 = 100; 1978) 117. Unemployment (1978) 7.2%. Fuel and power (in 000; metric tons; 1978): lignite *c.* 1,000; crude oil 1,420; natural gas (cu m) 13,709,000; manufactured gas (cu m) 3,240,000; electricity (kw-hr; 1977) 166,550,000. Production (in 000; metric tons; 1978): iron ore (44% metal content) 353; pig iron 11,578; crude steel 24,278; aluminum 281; lead 45; zinc 186; cement 38,232; cotton yarn 160; man-made fibres 492; fertilizers (nutrient content; 1977–78) nitrogenous 1,029, phosphate 494, potash 134; sulfuric acid 2,946; petroleum products (1977) 102,501; passenger cars (units) 1,510; commercial vehicles (units) 146. Merchant vessels launched (100 gross tons and over; 1978) 184,000 gross tons. New dwelling units completed (1978) 153,800.

tomobile company, with a payroll of some 250,000 workers, took the unprecedented step of firing 61 workers in October for persistently disrupting production by means of violence on the shop floor. Between 1975 and 1979 three Fiat managers had been murdered and 19 injured in acts of political terrorism which Fiat said originated inside the factories. The sackings brought immediate protests by the militant metalworkers' union, but a series of strikes received only patchy support.

A work stoppage by more than 1,000 military air traffic controllers brought all flights to and from Italy to a halt for 12 hours on October 19. The controllers demanded transfer to civilian employment in order to enable them to negotiate higher wages and better conditions of service. The government agreed after the intervention of President Pertini in his role of commander of Italy's armed forces. Other public service employees subject to military discipline, including the customs police (Guardia di Finanza) and public security police (Pubblica Sicurezza), also demanded civilian status.

Foreign Affairs. The approaching Italian chairmanship of the Council of Ministers of the European Economic Community (for the six-month period beginning January 1980) led Premier Cossiga to embark on a series of meetings with European heads of government. He received the British prime minister, Margaret Thatcher, in Rome and visited West Germany and France for talks with West German Chancellor Helmut Schmidt and French Pres. Valéry Giscard d'Estaing.

Italy encountered pressure from the Soviet Union not to sell military equipment to China. A letter from Soviet Pres. Leonid Brezhnev warned of "serious consequences" if reported arms sales were made, and this was followed up by a verbal warning during the visit to Rome of Soviet Foreign Minister Andrey Gromyko in January. The Soviet Union also tried to dissuade the Italian government from accepting U.S. cruise and Pershing missiles on Italian territory in the 1980s as part of the overall NATO defense of Western Europe. The Chinese leader Hua Guofeng (Hua Kuo-feng) visited Italy at the end of his four-country European tour in November.

A U.S. official, Dominic Perrone, was expelled from Italy on February 14 after a secret report he wrote on Italy's intelligence services was leaked and published in full in an Italian newspaper. The report was critical of the military and antiterrorist intelligence departments.

Voting in the election for the European Assembly took place on June 10, one week after the Italian general election. The European election campaign was completely overshadowed by the domestic vote, but the turnout (85.5%) was among the highest recorded in the Community. The results paralleled those of the national election, with both Christian Democrats and Communists experiencing fractional losses.

President Pertini paid official visits to West Germany and Yugoslavia during the year. He also attended an informal lunch at the Vatican with Pope John Paul II on October 23, an event described in the Italian press as "unprecedented."

WIDE WORLD

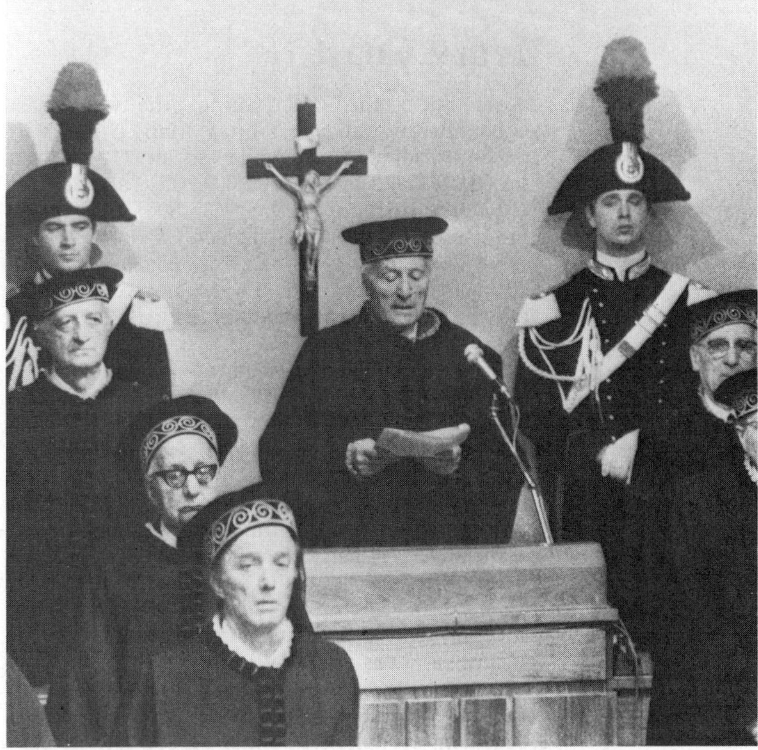

In March, the president of Italy's Constitutional Court, Paolo Rossi, read the finding of conviction of former defense minister Mario Tanassi of corruption in a Lockheed bribery scandal.

The Economy. Italy joined the European Monetary System when it came into operation in March, and the lira stood up well on international exchange markets. The Bank of Italy was alleged to have failed to report irregularities in the granting of large credits from public funds to a large private chemical company that got into financial difficulties. The much-respected governor of the bank, Paolo Baffi, was taken before a judge to explain how he exercised his discretionary powers, while the deputy governor was arrested and kept in jail for 12 days. Industrialists, bankers, and the government rallied around Baffi, and little damage appeared to have been done to the international image of Italy's central bank. But Baffi resigned and was replaced by Carlo Azeglio Ciampi, formerly the bank's director general.

Industrial production slowed down as the year advanced, while inflation continued. The September rise of 2.5% resulted in a yearly average rate of 15.3%, well above 1978. Industrial wages rose faster than inflation, and the unemployment rate increased to 8.3%. The official unemployment total in July was 1,880,000, but the true figure was believed to be over 2 million.

The trade deficit increased sharply to 1,345,000,000,000 lire in the first six months of 1979, mainly because of higher non-oil imports. The outlook was for a growing deficit as higher oil prices came into force. Italy's reserves reached a record U.S. $36.2 billion at the end of August. The three-year economic stabilization plan for 1979–81 was shelved as the Cossiga government embarked on policies that appeared to lead to higher rather than lower public spending. Italy's growth rate, about 4% for 1979, was expected to slow to 2.5% in 1980.

(DAVID DOUGLAS WILLEY)

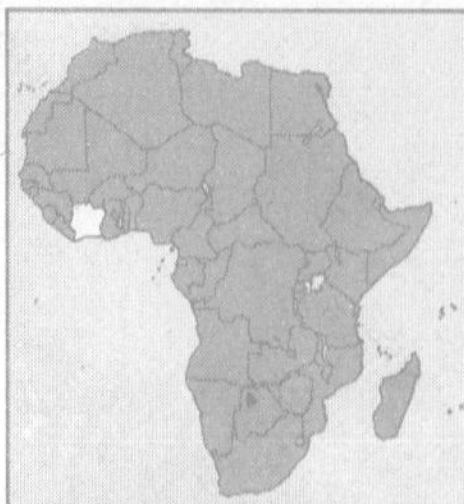

Ivory Coast

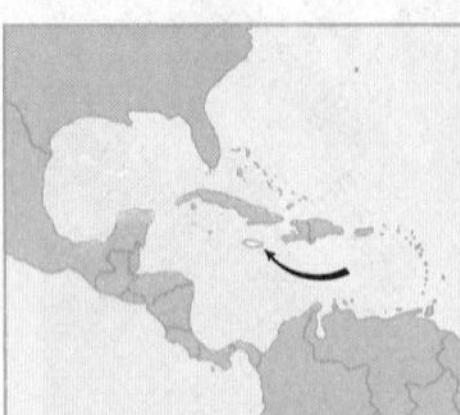

Jamaica

Ivory Coast

A republic on the Gulf of Guinea, the Ivory Coast is bounded by Liberia, Guinea, Mali, Upper Volta, and Ghana. Area: 322,463 sq km (124,504 sq mi). Pop (1978 est.): 7,205,000. Cap. and largest city: Abidjan (pop., 1975, 685,800). Language: French (official) and local dialects (Akan 41%, Kru 17%, Voltaic 16%, Malinke 15%, Southern Mande 10%). Religion: animist 65%; Muslim 23%; Christian 12%. President and premier in 1979, Félix Houphouët-Boigny.

The Ivory Coast remained politically and economically stable in 1979 and maintained its traditional friendships abroad. Relations with France, which remained close, were marked by the retirement in January of Jacques Raphaël-Leygues, French ambassador to Ivory Coast, after an exceptionally long tenure of 15 years.

In May Pres. Félix Houphouët-Boigny received King Juan Carlos of Spain and Queen Sofia on an official visit. During the year the president spent several weeks in Switzerland, and there were persistent rumours of his failing health.

At the request of France and after consultation with members of his country's political party, President Houphouët-Boigny agreed late in September to grant asylum to former Central African emperor Bokassa I. Bokassa had been deposed in a bloodless coup on September 20. The reconciliation with Guinea that had been initiated in 1978 was sealed on March 1 by the official visit of Pres. Ahmed Sékou Touré of Guinea to Yamoussokro, the Ivory Coast birthplace of Houphouët-Boigny.

Economic expansion continued in all sectors. In 1978 cotton production for the first time exceeded 100,000 metric tons of fibre, and the Ivory Coast overtook Ghana as the world's leading cocoa producer. (PHILIPPE DECRAENE)

IVORY COAST

Education. (1976–77) Primary, pupils 740,375, teachers (1975–76) 15,358; secondary, pupils 113,366, teachers (1974–75) 3,959; vocational, pupils 9,165, teachers (1974–75) 620; higher, students 8,701, teaching staff (1973–74) 368.

Finance. Monetary unit: CFA franc, with (Sept. 17, 1979) a parity of CFA Fr 50 to the French franc (free rate of CFA Fr 211.54 = U.S. $1; CFA Fr 455.12 = £1 sterling). Gold, SDR's, and foreign exchange (May 1979) U.S. $321 million. Budget (1978 est.) balanced at CFA Fr 223.2 billion. Money supply (April 1979) CFA Fr 437,590,000,000. Cost of living (Abidjan; 1975 = 100; June 1979) 194.8.

Foreign Trade. (1978) Imports CFA Fr 522.5 billion; exports CFA Fr 524,380,000,000. Import sources: France 39%; Japan 7%; West Germany 7%; U.S. 5%. Export destinations: France 23%; The Netherlands 19%; U.S. 15%; Italy 6%; West Germany 5%. Main exports: cocoa and products 39%; coffee 25%; timber 14%.

Agriculture. Production (in 000; metric tons; 1978): rice *c.* 480; corn (1977) *c.* 140; millet *c.* 45; yams (1977) *c.* 1,700; cassava (1977) *c.* 689; peanuts *c.* 50; bananas *c.* 190; plantains (1977) *c.* 764; pineapples *c.* 300; palm kernels *c.* 38; palm oil *c.* 135; coffee 198; cocoa 297; cotton, lint 37; rubber *c.* 20; fish catch (1977) 83; timber (cu m; 1977) 10,682. Livestock (in 000; 1977): cattle *c.* 650; sheep *c.* 1,050; goats *c.* 1,100; pigs *c.* 222; poultry *c.* 8,145.

Industry. Production (in 000; metric tons; 1977): cement 875; petroleum products *c.* 1,600; cotton yarn 7; diamonds (metric carats; 1976) 60; electricity (kw-hr) 1,212,000.

Jamaica

A parliamentary state within the Commonwealth of Nations, Jamaica is an island in the Caribbean Sea about 145 km (90 mi) S of Cuba. Area: 10,991 sq km (4,244 sq mi). Pop. (1979 est.): 2,137,400, predominantly African and Afro-European, but including European, Chinese, Afro-Chinese, East Indian, Afro-East Indian, and others. Cap. and largest city: Kingston (pop., 1974 est., 169,800). Language: English. Religion: Christian, with Anglicans and Baptists in the majority. Queen, Elizabeth II; governor-general in 1979, Florizel Glasspole; prime minister, Michael Manley.

Throughout 1979 Jamaica faced economic difficulties and further polarization of political opinion. The government passed with difficulty the quarterly tests imposed by the International Monetary Fund (IMF) before it could obtain further portions of the island's U.S. $330 million three-year standby credit. It soon became clear, however, that these sums were insufficient, and short-term commercial loans and an additional $80 million from the IMF in 1980 were sought.

The People's National Party (PNP) clashed acrimoniously with the opposition Jamaica Labour Party over, among other subjects, the alleged presence of Soviet, Cuban, and U.S. agents on the island. In January a National Patriotic Movement organization fostered a strike, ostensibly connected with gasoline price increases, that virtually paralyzed the country and resulted in at least six deaths. Relations with the U.S. and the U.K. became increasingly strained, while relations with Cuba and the U.S.S.R. improved. Jamaica assisted the new Grenada government. Relations with Trinidad deteriorated after a request for a $25 million loan was badly mishandled. Flooding in western Jamaica in June left 50,000 people homeless. (DAVID A. JESSOP)

JAMAICA

Education. (1976–77) Primary, pupils 431,882, teachers 10,002; secondary, pupils 224,817, teachers 8,377; vocational, pupils 5,321, teachers 355; teacher training, students 6,017, teachers 201; higher, students 10,305, teaching staff (1973–74) 638.

Finance. Monetary unit: Jamaican dollar, with (Sept. 17, 1979) a par value of Jam$1.78 to U.S. $1 (free rate of Jam$3.84 = £1 sterling). Gold, SDR's, and foreign exchange (June 1979) U.S. $51 million. Budget (1978 actual): revenue Jam$854.1 million; expenditure Jam$1,428,400,000.

Foreign Trade. (1978) Imports Jam$1,278,000,000; exports Jam$1,096,300,000. Import sources (1977): U.S. 36%; Venezuela 16%; Netherlands Antilles 11%; U.K. 10%; Canada 6%. Export destinations (1977): U.S. 44%; U.K. 20%; Norway 11%; Canada 9%. Main exports: alumina 52%; bauxite 20%; sugar 8%. Tourism (1977): visitors 387,000; gross receipts U.S. $116 million.

Agriculture. Production (in 000; metric tons; 1978): sugar, raw value *c.* 307; bananas *c.* 150; oranges *c.* 22; grapefruit *c.* 20; sweet potatoes (1977) *c.* 17; yams (1977) *c.* 130; cassava (1977) *c.* 21; corn (1977) *c.* 10; copra *c.* 7. Livestock (in 000; 1977): cattle *c.* 282; goats *c.* 330; pigs *c.* 240; poultry *c.* 3,840.

Industry. Production (in 000; metric tons; 1978): cement 294; bauxite 11,732; alumina (1977) 2,015; gypsum (1977) 206; petroleum products *c.* 1,000; electricity (kw-hr) *c.* 2,400,000.

Jai Alai: *see* Court Games

Japan

A constitutional monarchy in the northwestern Pacific Ocean, Japan is an archipelago composed of four major islands (Hokkaido, Honshu, Kyushu, and Shikoku), the Ryukyus (including Okinawa), and minor adjacent islands. Area: 377,643 sq km (145,809 sq mi). Pop. (1979 est.): 115,920,000. Cap. and largest city: Tokyo (pop., 1978 est., 8,468,200). Language: Japanese. Religion: primarily Shinto and Buddhist; Christian 0.8%. Emperor, Hirohito; prime minister in 1979, Masayoshi Ohira.

Japan

Domestic Affairs. On Jan. 25, 1979, in his first speech as prime minister before the reconvened 87th Diet, Masayoshi Ohira declared that Japan had entered a new "age of culture." He contrasted this with the preceding era, which had stressed economic growth, and pledged to steer the nation toward a "just welfare society."

One reason for the shift in emphasis was the slowdown in growth. A 1978 fiscal year (ended March 1979) White Paper reported that during 1978 the economy had moved toward equilibrium, on both the international and the domestic front. Domestic demand rather than exports had become the prime mover in the economy. Japan's industrial production had risen modestly in December 1978 so that the year ended with a 6.1% gain. The consumer price index in calendar 1978 averaged 122.6 (1975 = 100), marking an 18-year-low annual increase of 3.8%. Unemployment set a record at an annual average of 1,240,000; the jobless rate (2.2%) was the third largest in the postwar era.

Despite Japan's previous pledge to attain a 7% growth rate in fiscal 1978, the actual increase was smaller. On June 30 Prime Minister Ohira told the nation that, despite increases in oil prices by the Organization of Petroleum Exporting Countries (OPEC), Japan should be able to achieve targets of 6.3% economic growth and less than 5% inflation in fiscal 1979. Early in August the Economic Council presented a new seven-year plan (to replace that expiring in 1980), calling for an inflation-adjusted average annual growth rate of 5.7%.

Meanwhile, inflation began once again to disrupt economic plans. In July the Bank of Japan announced that the wholesale price index had risen 1.9% over the June level (an annual rate of 25.3%), the most rapid rate of increase in more than five years. One result was a rise in the consumer price index for Tokyo's 23 wards of 1.6% to 129.6 (1975 = 100). On July 23 the Bank of Japan announced that the prime interest rate would be raised 1% to 5.25% per annum, the highest level in two years.

With only a paper-thin majority in the Diet, Ohira's Liberal-Democratic Party (LDP) government faced increasing legislative opposition. On January 15 the Cabinet completed its 1979 budget, providing for a 38,610,000,000,000 yen general account. This represented an appropriation increase of 12.6%, the lowest annual rise in 14 years. On March 14, the (lower) House of Representatives of the Diet passed the budget by a slim majority, reversing a budget committee decision against it earlier in the day. The committee rejection marked the first time in three decades that a government-sponsored budget had been disapproved.

In addition to difficult economic problems, Prime Minister Ohira's slim LDP majority leadership was tested by continued disclosures of official corruption in procurement and sales of U.S. aircraft in Japan. On February 28, in a Tokyo district court hearing involved in the trial of former prime minister Kakuei Tanaka, a startling deposition taken in July 1976 in Los Angeles for the Japanese prosecutors was revealed. A former Lockheed Corp. vice-president, A. C. Kotchian, testified that he had paid the Marubeni Corp. 500 million yen, with the knowledge that the sum would be paid to Tanaka for favourable consideration of Lockheed's L-1011 (TriStar) aircraft. Meanwhile, in December 1978, the U.S. Securities and Exchange Commission (SEC) had made equally dramatic disclosures.

Japanese law-enforcement officials quickly began investigations of SEC charges to the effect that McDonnell Douglas Corp. had paid commissions through its agent, Mitsui Co., to help the sales of its aircraft. In January the SEC further disclosed payments by another U.S. aircraft manufacturer, Grumman Corp., to its Japanese agent, Nissho-Iwai Co. On April 2 Hachiro Kaifu, an executive at Nissho-Iwai, was arrested on charges of violating provisions of the foreign exchange law. Prosecutors also searched the home of Mitsuhiro Shimada, a former director of Nissho-Iwai, who committed suicide in February. On May 28 Raizo Matsuno, former chief of the nation's defense agency, insisted before a Diet select committee that sums paid to him were "donations."

The aircraft investigations had a direct effect on the Diet, which ended its 175-day session in mid-June. Many bills in the legislature had to be scrapped because of quarrels over opposition demands that Matsuno, an LDP member, be charged with perjury for his testimony.

LDP management of the Diet was also severely hampered by the necessity for coalition politics. The party held only 252 of the 511 seats in the lower house. With the death on March 9 of Tomomi Narita, long chairman of the Japan Socialists

WIDE WORLD

Japanese Prime Minister Masayoshi Ohira listened glumly to October election results which left his Liberal-Democratic Party eight seats short of a clear majority. The party, nevertheless, retained control of the government.

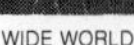

(JSP), the chief opposition party commanded 117 seats. The remaining seats were distributed among the Komeito (56); Democratic Socialists (DSP; 28); Japan Communists (JCP; 19); and minor parties, independents, and vacancies (39). In September the LDP gained a one-seat edge over the combined opposition in the (upper) House of Councillors, when two opposition members and only one LDP member resigned to run in the lower house election. Seats in the upper house were then distributed as follows: LDP, 124; JSP, 52; Komeito, 28; JCP, 16; DSP, 10; and minor parties, independents, and vacancies, 22 (total, 252).

LDP leaders were encouraged by the results of quadrennial local elections held on April 8, when conservative forces in alliance with centrists regained control in Tokyo and in Osaka (after 12 and 8 years, respectively). Such coalitions won in ten other gubernatorial races, and the LDP won outright in three prefectures. In Tokyo the former deputy governor of the metropolis, Shunichi Suzuki, defeated Kaoru Ohta, former chairman of the General Council of Trade Unions (Sohyo). In additional elections held later in April, 103 of 152 mayors elected were either backed by the LDP or supported by conservative-centrist coalitions.

Nationwide public opinion polls conducted by Kyodo News Service in late August showed that 48.7% of those polled supported the LDP (the highest figure since the 49.6% in support of Prime Minister Eisaku Sato in 1964). The JSP had the support of only 15% (a drop of 2% since the March poll). On the other hand, nonsupporters outnumbered supporters of the Ohira Cabinet (46.1% nonsupport, 44.8% support). Nonetheless, Ohira exercised his prerogative under art. 7 of the constitution and on September 7 dissolved the House of Representatives in favour of a general election scheduled for October 7. The LDP announced that it would strive to attain a "stable majority" of more than 271 seats.

Results of the 35th general election, the first held since 1976, gave the LDP only 248 seats (8 seats less than the 256 needed for a majority). Ten elected independents, however, announced that they would join the party, thus allowing the LDP to retain a slim majority in the lower house. The JSP also lost ground (from 123 to 107 seats). The biggest gain—from 19 to 39 seats—was made by the Communists.

Ohira acknowledged his "responsibility" for the LDP's poor showing but struggled to retain his office during the political infighting that preceded the special session of the Diet, called in early November to elect the prime minister. The first vote in the lower house was indecisive, but in the runoff—the first in Japanese history between two members of the same party—Ohira defeated former prime minister Takeo Fukuda 138–121. In the new 20-member Cabinet formed November 8, economist Saburo Okita became foreign minister and Noboru Takeshita, finance minister.

Foreign Affairs. Japan's gold and foreign exchange reserves reached an all-time high of U.S. $33.1 billion in January (second in the world to West Germany's $52 billion). At that time, however, forces leading to equilibrium (mainly appreciation of the value of the yen) were slowing exports as imports increased. During the first six months of 1979 exports rose only 6%, while imports soared 35%. As a result Japan's current account balance showed a $1.7 billion deficit, the first loss in four years (in sharp contrast to the $8.5 billion surplus from January to June 1978).

Despite these long-range corrections, short-run trade problems placed a strain on Japanese-U.S. relations. In 1978 the largest volume of bilateral trade in history produced a record U.S. deficit of $11.5 billion in merchandise exchange with Japan (about half of Japan's global surplus and 40% of the U.S. world deficit). U.S. Pres. Jimmy Carter pledged his efforts to ease subsequent economic friction in a letter delivered to Prime Minister Ohira by U.S. Secretary of the Treasury Michael Blumenthal, who arrived from China for a stopover in Tokyo March 4–5.

One symptom of the growing friction, which in fact threatened reciprocal summit meetings, was the issue of procurement of supplies by Japan's public corporations. In March Prime Minister Ohira sent trade representative Nobuhiko Ushiba to Washington, D.C., to discuss this issue, as well

JAPAN

Education. (1978) Primary, pupils 11,146,859, teachers 445,719; secondary and vocational, pupils 9,463,367, teachers 481,668; higher, students 2,289,197, teaching staff 117,934.

Finance. Monetary unit: yen, with (Sept. 17, 1979) a free rate of 224 yen to U.S. $1 (481 yen = £1 sterling). Gold, SDR's, and foreign exchange (June 1979) U.S. $23.6 billion. Budget (1979–80 est.) balanced at 38,600,000,000,000 yen. Gross national product (1978) 206,300,000,000,000 yen. Money supply (June 1979) 67,674,000,000,000 yen. Cost of living (1975 = 100; June 1979) 127.1.

Foreign Trade. (1978) Imports 16,725,000,000,000 yen; exports 20,569,000,000,000 yen. Import sources: U.S. 19%; Saudi Arabia 11%; Australia 7%; Indonesia 7%; Iran 5%. Export destinations: U.S. 26%; South Korea 6%. Main exports: machinery 27% (telecommunications apparatus 5%); motor vehicles 21%; iron and steel 14%; instruments 8%; ships 7%; chemicals 7%; textiles 5%.

Transport and Communications. Roads (1977) 1,088,254 km (including 2,024 km expressways). Motor vehicles in use (1978): passenger 19,942,500; commercial 11,369,600. Railways: (1977) 26,849 km; traffic (1978) 301,911,000,000 passenger-km, freight 40,270,000,000 net ton-km. Air traffic (1978): 25,654,000,000 passenger-km; freight 1,316,500,000 net ton-km. Shipping (1978): merchant vessels 100 gross tons and over 9,321; gross tonnage 39,182,079. Telephones (March 1978) 50,625,600. Radio receivers (Dec. 1977) 64,978,000. Television licenses (Dec. 1977) 27,495,000.

Agriculture. Production (in 000; metric tons; 1978): rice 16,000; wheat 367; barley 326; potatoes *c.* 3,305; sweet potatoes (1977) *c.* 1,279; sugar, raw value *c.* 620; onions *c.* 1,080; tomatoes *c.* 960; cabbages (1977) *c.* 3,801; cucumbers (1977) *c.* 1,045; aubergines (1977) *c.* 650; watermelons (1977) *c.* 1,169; apples *c.* 837; pears (1977) *c.* 533; oranges *c.* 353; mandarin oranges and tangerines *c.* 3,097; grapes *c.* 340; tea *c.* 105; tobacco *c.* 173; milk 6,100; timber (cu m; 1977) 34,390; fish catch (1977) 10,733. Livestock (in 000; Feb. 1978): cattle 3,891; sheep *c.* 11; pigs *c.* 8,344; goats *c.* 79; chickens *c.* 300,000.

Industry. Index of production (1975 = 100; 1978) 122.8. Fuel and power (in 000; metric tons; 1978): coal 18,990; crude oil 541; natural gas (cu m) 2,900,000; manufactured gas (cu m) 6,990,000; electricity (kw-hr; 1977–78) 532,609,000. Production (in 000; metric tons; 1978): iron ore (54% metal content) 597; pig iron 80,171; crude steel 102,103; aluminum 1,061; petroleum products (1977) 214,336; cement 84,882; cotton yarn 448; woven cotton fabrics (sq m) 2,316,000; newsprint 2,482; man-made fibres 1,847; sulfuric acid 6,435; caustic soda 2,764; plastics and resins 5,870; fertilizers (nutrient content; 1977–78) nitrogenous 1,446, phosphate 696; cameras (35 mm; units) 8,071; wristwatches (units) 49,192; radio receivers (units) 16,278; television receivers (units) 13,117; passenger cars (units) 5,975; commercial vehicles (units) 3,265; motorcycles (units) 6,000. Merchant vessels launched (100 gross tons and over; 1978) 4,801,000 gross tons. New dwelling units started (1978) 1,754,000.

WIDE WORLD

A government scandal involving millions of dollars worth of aircraft contracts inspired labour activists to carry a model of an airplane in Tokyo's May Day parade.

as that of U.S. access to Japanese markets. He was followed in early April by Foreign Minister Sunao Sonoda, who in turn paved the way for Ohira's eight-day tour of the U.S. from April 30 to May 7. On May 3, speaking to Japanese reporters in Washington just after meetings with President Carter, Ohira promised that the two countries would work out an agreement on public corporation procurement prior to the June summit meeting of seven world industrial powers in Tokyo. On June 1, at the Foreign Ministry in Tokyo, Ushiba and U.S. trade representative Robert Strauss announced settlement of the long-pending procurement issue on a basis of "mutual reciprocity." The agreement cleared the way for President Carter's state visit to Japan later in June, on the eve of the summit meeting.

Carter and his wife, Rosalynn, were officially welcomed to Japan on June 25 in an elaborate ceremony held at the government guest house in Akasaka. The 78-year-old Emperor Hirohito greeted the Carters and, together with the empress, received the state visitors in audience at the Imperial Palace. Later the same day Ohira and Carter agreed on the need for oil-consuming nations to curb imports as well as to conserve petroleum products. They also announced that the two governments would inaugurate a "wisemen's group" to coordinate economic policies.

In Tokyo, June 28–29, the leaders of the major industrial nations met in a summit conference chaired by Prime Minister Ohira. They included President Carter, French Pres. Valéry Giscard d'Estaing, British Prime Minister Margaret Thatcher, West German Chancellor Helmut Schmidt, Italian Premier Giulio Andreotti, Canadian Prime Minister Joe Clark, and European Commission Pres. Roy Jenkins.

On June 28 the summit leaders denounced OPEC oil price increases as "unwarranted rises," which would have serious consequences for both developed and less developed nations. Japan (with Canada and the U.S.) promised to maintain oil import levels in 1980 no higher than they had been in 1979. In art. 2 of the Tokyo Declaration, the delegates warned of inflation, which had been subsiding but was regaining momentum.

Further strains in the U.S.-Japanese relationship appeared toward the end of the year during the crisis over the seizure of hostages in the U.S. embassy in Teheran. The Carter administration accused Japan of buying up Iranian oil that had been earmarked for the U.S. before Carter cut off Iranian imports, thereby undermining U.S. efforts to bring economic pressure on Iran. Prime Minister Ohira asked importing companies not to increase their oil purchases from Iran and ordered a study of Japanese policies regarding Iranian oil.

As to relations with Communist nations, Japan experienced difficulties with both China and the Soviet Union during the year. On February 14 Chinese Vice-Premier Deng Xiaoping (Teng Hsiao-p'ing) aroused alarm in Tokyo with his emphasis on "necessary punitive action" to be taken against Vietnam for its "aggression" against Cambodia. On February 19, after fighting on the border between China and Vietnam erupted, Japan urged China to withdraw its troops and appealed to Vietnam to cease action in Cambodia. In an unprecedented statement, chairman Ichio Asukata of the JSP stated in March that China's military action against Vietnam ran counter to his party's principles of peace and stability in the world. Prime Minister Ohira paid a five-day visit to China in December, during which agreements were completed involving over $1.5 billion in Japanese credits for energy-related projects.

Normalization of relations between Japan and

China had served only to heighten concern in the Soviet Union. At the UN in New York, Foreign Minister Sonoda agreed with Soviet Foreign Minister Andrey Gromyko that the two nations should improve economic relations, but Gromyko charged that Japan was moving toward "militarism." Sonoda responded that many Japanese were concerned about the Soviet military buildup in East Asia. Specifically, the issue of Japan's northern territories had flared up again.

In regard to this issue, Japan in February had filed an official protest against an increase in the number of Soviet troops located on two (Etorofu, Kunashiri) of four islands in the southern Kurils, which were regarded by Tokyo as Japanese territory. Late in September Japan learned from U.S. intelligence sources that Soviet troops on the islands were being increased to division strength (10,000 men) and that the buildup extended to Shikotan, just 100 km (60 mi) north of Hokkaido. This development was alarming because the U.S.S.R., in the joint communiqué by which the two nations had normalized relations in 1956, had promised to return Shikotan and the smaller Habomai group to Japan after a peace treaty was signed. On October 2 Vice-Minister Masuo Takashima conveyed a strong protest to Soviet Ambassador Dmitry Polyansky in Tokyo. The latter flatly rejected the claim, saying that it constituted "reckless interference" in the internal affairs of the Soviet Union.

(ARDATH W. BURKS)

Jordan

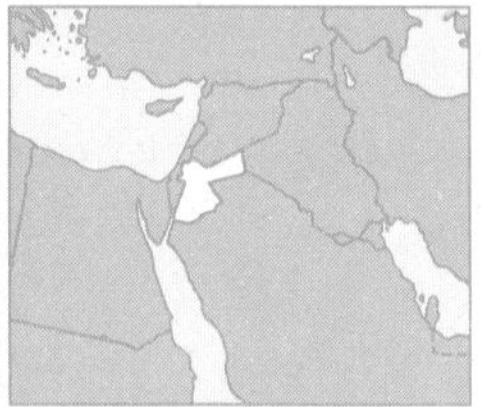

Jordan

A constitutional monarchy in southwest Asia, Jordan is bounded by Syria, Iraq, Saudi Arabia, and Israel. Area (including territory occupied by Israel in the June 1967 war): 95,396 sq km (36,833 sq mi). Pop. (1979 est.): 3,085,000. Cap. and largest city: Amman (pop., 1978 est., 775,800). Language: Arabic. Religion (1961): Muslim 94%; Christian 6%. King, Hussein I; prime ministers in 1979, Mudar Badran and, from December 19, Sharif Abdul Hamid Sharaf.

Jordan's King Hussein (left) greets Palestine Liberation Organization leader Yasir Arafat as the latter arrives at Mafraq air base near Amman in March.

UPI

Jordanian foreign policy in 1979 abandoned its traditionally pro-Western orientation in favour of nonalignment. Despite U.S. attempts to persuade King Hussein to support U.S. Middle East policy, especially the Egyptian-Israeli peace treaty of March 26, the Jordanian monarch actively promoted rejection of the treaty. U.S. congressional obstruction of arms and aid for Jordan led Hussein to diversify his sources of military supply.

U.S. Secretary of Defense Harold Brown flew to Amman on February 12 as part of his post-Iranian revolution tour of the region, and U.S. national security adviser Zbigniew Brzezinski followed on March 18. Brzezinski failed to persuade Hussein to participate in negotiations with Israel and Egypt over the future of the occupied West Bank, and Hussein in a press interview on March 20 accused the Carter administration of "arm-twisting" over the treaty. The U.S. House of Representatives Foreign Affairs Committee then made $880 million in military aid for Jordan dependent on Jordanian cooperation with U.S. Middle East policy.

Jordanian and U.S. officials attempted to preserve good mutual relations, with visits to Amman by U.S. Assistant Secretary of Defense David McGiffert on April 7 and Rear Adm. H. S. Packer, commander of U.S. Mideast Forces, on May 6. Pres. Jimmy Carter's special envoy, Robert Strauss (*see*

JORDAN

Education. (1978–79) Primary, pupils 431,107, teachers 13,351; secondary, pupils 221,822, teachers 10,354; vocational, pupils 9,266, teachers 582; higher, students 20,317, teaching staff 996.

Finance. Monetary unit: Jordanian dinar, with (Sept. 17, 1979) a free rate of 0.30 dinar to U.S. $1 (0.64 dinar = £1 sterling). Gold, SDR's, and foreign exchange (June 1979) U.S. $1,017,000,000. Budget (1978 actual): revenue 250 million dinars (including foreign aid and loans of 87 million dinars); expenditure 356 million dinars. Gross national product (1978) 716.6 million dinars. Money supply (June 1979) 433,780,000 dinars. Cost of living (1975 = 100; June 1979) 151.8.

Foreign Trade. (1978) Imports 458,780,000 dinars; exports 90,970,000 dinars. Import sources (1977): U.S. 15%; West Germany 14%; Saudi Arabia 9%; U.K. 7%; Japan 6%; Italy 6%. Export destinations (1977): Saudi Arabia 30%; Syria 11%; Iran 9%; Iraq 6%; Lebanon 6%; Kuwait 5%. Main exports (1977): phosphates 21%; oranges 12%; vegetables 8%; chemicals 7%; machinery 5%; aircraft 5%. Tourism (1977): visitors 1,773,000; gross receipts (1976) U.S. $208 million.

Transport and Communications. Roads (excluding West Bank; 1977) 4,837 km. Motor vehicles in use (1977): passenger 53,300; commercial 18,400. Railways (1977) *c.* 380 km. Air traffic (1978): 1,754,000,000 passenger-km; freight 51.6 million net ton-km. Telephones (Jan. 1978) 53,100. Radio receivers (Dec. 1976) 531,000. Television licenses (Dec. 1976) 125,000.

Agriculture. Production (in 000; metric tons; 1977): wheat *c.* 53; barley *c.* 12; tomatoes *c.* 88; aubergines *c.* 43; watermelons *c.* 19; olives (1978) *c.* 37; oranges *c.* 5; lemons *c.* 9; grapes *c.* 14. Livestock (in 000; 1977): cattle *c.* 36; goats *c.* 490; sheep *c.* 820; camels *c.* 19; asses *c.* 50; chickens *c.* 2,960.

Industry. Production (in 000; metric tons; 1977): phosphate rock 1,759; petroleum products 1,146; cement 501; electricity (kw-hr) 601,000.

Biographies), was in Amman on July 7 in another attempt to involve Hussein in the faltering West Bank "autonomy" talks. The Carter administration attempted to salvage the sale of 300 M60A tanks to Jordan in August by promising Congress that the sale would not affect the balance of power in the Middle East. In the face of the conditions put on the purchase of U.S. weaponry by Congress, Hussein turned to Britain to buy Chieftain tanks originally built for the shah of Iran and to France for 36 Mirage F-1 fighter-bombers.

On July 18 the Jordanian commander in chief, Lieut. Gen. Zaid Bin Shaker, led the country's first military delegation to the Soviet Union amid speculation that Jordan was about to purchase Soviet weapons. On September 17 Prime Minister Mudar Badran announced that Jordan would consider purchasing arms from the Soviet Union. King Hussein attended the summit conference of nonaligned nations in Havana at the beginning of September and on September 23 announced the establishment of diplomatic relations with Cuba.

Jordan improved its relations with the Palestine Liberation Organization (PLO) in 1979. In March the UN Security Council approved a Jordanian-sponsored resolution to establish a commission to examine Israeli policy regarding settlements in the West Bank. PLO Chairman Yasir Arafat met Hussein at Mafraq air base north of Amman on March 17, and the two sides issued a joint communiqué in support of the Baghdad resolutions of November 1978 that had rejected Egyptian Pres. Anwar as-Sadat's negotiations with Israel. Hussein and Arafat met again at Mafraq on August 21, and on September 19 Arafat made his first visit to Amman since 1970, when the Jordanian Army crushed PLO forces in Jordan and drove them out of the country.

On March 28, Jordan became the first Arab country to sever diplomatic relations with Egypt. In May Egyptian newspapers were banned and all trade with Egypt was prohibited. In August Hussein attempted to mediate between Syria and Iraq after an alleged coup attempt in Baghdad for which the Iraqi leadership blamed Syria.

The rate of inflation declined in 1978 and early 1979 to about 7%, according to the Department of Statistics. But later price rises forced the central bank to impose monetary controls in June.

On December 19 the king formed a new government with Sharif Abdul Hamid Sharaf, former ambassador to the U.S., replacing Mudar Badran as prime minister. (CHARLES GLASS)

See also Middle Eastern Affairs.

Kenya

An African republic and a member of the Commonwealth of Nations, Kenya is bordered on the north by Sudan and Ethiopia, east by Somalia, south by Tanzania, and west by Uganda. Area: 580,367 sq km (224,081 sq mi), including 11,230 sq km of inland water. Pop. (1979 est.): 15,780,000, including (1969) African 98.1%; Asian 1.5%. Cap. and largest city: Nairobi (pop., 1978 est., 820,000). Language: Swahili (official) and English. Religion: Protestant 36%; Roman Catholic 22%; Muslim 6%; other, mostly indigenous, 36%. President in 1979, Daniel arap Moi.

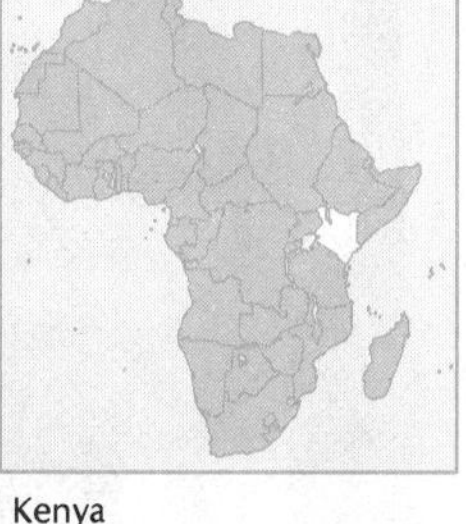

Kenya

KENYA

Education. (1977) Primary, pupils 2,974,849, teachers 89,773; secondary and vocational, pupils 320,310, teachers 12,696; teacher training, students 8,986, teachers 672; higher, students 5,837, teachers 892.

Finance. Monetary unit: Kenyan shilling, with (Sept. 17, 1979) a free rate of KShs 7.33 to U.S. $1 (KShs 15.77 = £1 sterling). Gold, SDR's, and foreign exchange (June 1979) U.S. $464 million. Budget (1977–78 actual): revenue KShs 9,166,000,000; expenditure KShs 10,037,000,000. Gross national product (1978) KShs 40,951,000,000. Cost of living (Nairobi; 1975 = 100; May 1979) 139.3.

Foreign Trade. (1978) Imports KShs 13,215,000,000; exports KShs 7,914,000,000. Import sources: U.K. 22%; West Germany 13%; Japan 10%; Iran 7%; U.S. 6%; Italy 5%; France 5%. Export destinations: West Germany 14%; U.K. 14%; Uganda 10%; The Netherlands 6%; Italy 5%; U.S. 5%. Main exports: coffee 32%; petroleum products 18%; tea 16%; fruit and vegetables 6%. Tourism (1977): visitors 300,800; gross receipts U.S. $121 million.

Transport and Communications. Roads (1976) 50,091 km. Motor vehicles in use (1977): passenger 114,100; commercial (including buses) 83,900. Railways (1976): 2,426 km; freight traffic 3,653,000,000 net ton-km. Air traffic (1977): 563 million passenger-km; freight 16 million ton-km. Telephones (Jan. 1978) 143,800. Radio receivers (Dec. 1976) 514,000. Television receivers (Dec. 1976) 50,000.

Agriculture. Production (in 000; metric tons; 1978): corn *c.* 2,350; wheat *c.* 144; millet *c.* 130; potatoes 361; sweet potatoes (1977) *c.* 540; cassava (1977) *c.* 750; sugar, raw value (1977) *c.* 175; bananas 120; coffee *c.* 70; tea *c.* 93; sisal *c.* 31; cotton, lint *c.* 6; fish catch (1977) 39. Livestock (in 000; 1977): cattle *c.* 7,350; sheep *c.* 3,900; pigs *c.* 70; goats *c.* 4,300; camels *c.* 540; chickens *c.* 16,500.

Industry. Production (in 000; metric tons; 1977): cement 1,130; soda ash (1976) 115; petroleum products *c.* 2,460; electricity (kw-hr) *c.* 1,120,000.

In an attempt to counter Kenya's large trade deficit, the government on Jan. 4, 1979, imposed restrictions on overseas travel and on imports, except for agricultural and industrial machinery financed from abroad. A new five-year plan was announced in March, to cover 1979–83. In it, the government hoped to avoid some of the overoptimistic policies that had proved ineffective in the previous plan and to overcome difficulties left by the collapse of the East African Community (EAC), which had included Kenya, Tanzania, and Uganda. The new plan envisaged the expenditure of U.S. $10 billion to encourage small farmers, rural communities, the landless, the poorly paid, and the youth of the country to make the best use of available resources. Schemes were drafted to reduce unemployment, to assist in family planning, and to increase the number of doctors. One relic of the EAC was disposed of when the assets of the former East African Airways on Kenyan soil were liquidated and the proceeds distributed to the creditors.

Relations with neighbouring Uganda gave rise to a variety of problems. The fighting that led to the overthrow of Pres. Idi Amin of Uganda brought a flood of Ugandan refugees into Kenya. Among them were some who had collaborated with Amin, and the Kenyan authorities tried to sift them out. The Kenya government welcomed the new government of Uganda. After a visit to Nairobi in April by a Ugandan delegation led by the foreign minister, Otema Alimadi, Kenya promised $250,000 as immediate help for Pres. Yusufu Lule's government. It was a shock to Ken-

Japanese Literature:
see Literature

Jazz:
see Music

Jehovah's Witnesses:
see Religion

Jewish Literature:
see Literature

Journalism:
see Publishing

Judaism:
see Israel; Religion

Judo:
see Combat Sports

Kampuchea:
see Cambodia

Karate:
see Combat Sports

Kashmir:
see India; Pakistan

Kendo:
see Combat Sports

WIDE WORLD

Robert Astles, British-born aide to ousted Ugandan dictator Idi Amin, was taken into court in Kenya in June to face extradition to Uganda on murder charges.

ya, therefore, when Lule was overthrown by members of his own government after only two months in office. There were fears in Kenya that his successor, Pres. Godfrey Binaisa (*see* BIOGRAPHIES), might incline more toward Tanzania than to Kenya. Another symptom of Kenya's concern was the request of Pres. Daniel arap Moi to Pres. Julius Nyerere (*see* BIOGRAPHIES) in July to withdraw Tanzanian troops from Uganda. At about the same time, some 2,500 Ugandans were expelled from Kenya after a crime wave in which, it was alleged, some of them had been involved.

Large numbers of refugees, not only Ugandans but also Ethiopians, Somalis, Rhodesians, South Africans, Mozambiquans, Rwandans, and Rundi (from Burundi), were unable to find employment. Resettlement areas were established in the Coast Province where food and other supplies were provided. The government agreed to cooperate in trying to find employment for refugees who were already well trained.

In January President Moi met the Ethiopian leader, Lieut. Col. Mengistu Haile Mariam, in Addis Ababa. The two leaders expressed similar views on the situation in the Horn of Africa. In September Moi paid a visit to Saudi Arabia, during which an attempt was made to reconcile Kenya and Somalia; he also received assurances of aid worth $55 million. In June the president made a state visit to Great Britain.

In elections held November 8, Moi was overwhelmingly reconfirmed as president. About half the incumbent members of the National Assembly, including a number of ministers who had served under former president Jomo Kenyatta, were voted out of office. Members of the ruling Kenya African National Union (the sole party) were permitted to run against each other, and most seats were contested. Philip Leakey, son of the anthropologists Louis and Mary Leakey, became the first white to be elected since independence and was appointed assistant minister for natural resources and the environment.

(KENNETH INGHAM)

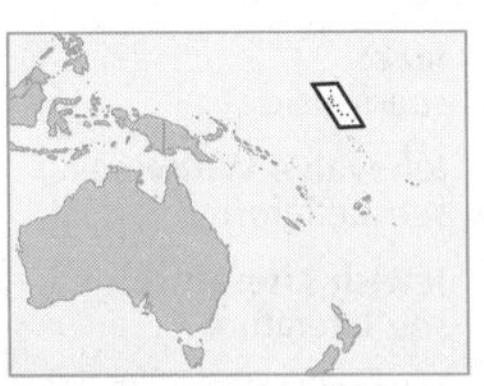

Kiribati

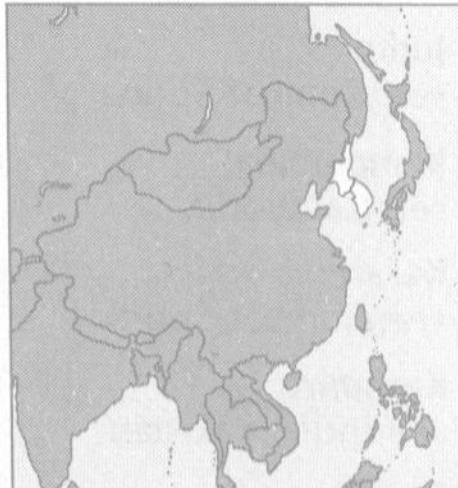

Korea

Kiribati

An independent republic in the western Pacific Ocean and member of the Commonwealth of Nations, Kiribati comprises the former Gilbert Islands, Ocean Island (Banaba), the Line Islands, and the Phoenix Islands. Area: 713 sq km (275 sq mi). Pop. (1979 est.): 56,000, including Micronesian 91%, Polynesian 4%, other indigenous 4%, others 1%. Cap.: Bairiki (pop., 1973, 1,800) on Tarawa atoll (pop., 1973, 17,100). Language: English (official). Religion (1973): Roman Catholic 48%; Protestant 45%. President (*beriti-tenti*) in 1979, Ieremia Tabai.

Kiribati, formerly the Gilbert Islands, became an independent republic in full association with the Commonwealth of Nations in ceremonies attended by Princess Anne, representing Queen Elizabeth II, on July 12, 1979. As Kiribati's first president, Ieremia Tabai (*see* BIOGRAPHIES) became head of state and of government. Under Kiribati's constitution, 35 members are elected by universal (18 years) suffrage to the House of Assembly for four-year terms. The House then nominates three or four candidates for the presidential election. The president, who can serve no more than three terms, appoints a vice-president and Cabinet of ten from within the House.

As an independence settlement, the U.K. agreed to provide a grant-in-aid of approximately A$2.5 million a year for 1979–82. This would help Kiribati to cover the loss to national income when phosphate mining ceased at Banaba (Ocean Island) and to keep its A$68 million phosphate reserve fund intact. The Banabans continued to demand increased compensation for phosphate mined from their land and independence from Kiribati. They had yet to fill the Kiribati House of Assembly seat reserved for them. Just before independence the U.S. renounced its claim to Canton atoll, which had been a British-U.S. condominium since 1939.

(BARRIE MACDONALD)

KIRIBATI

Education. (1977) Primary, pupils 13,679, teachers 435; secondary, pupils 1,000, teachers 71; vocational, pupils 183, teachers 28; teacher training, students 73, teachers 12.

Finance and Trade. Monetary unit: Australian dollar, with (Sept. 17, 1979) a free rate of A$0.89 to U.S. $1 (A$1.92 = £1 sterling). Budget (1977 est): revenue A$11,771,000; expenditure A$9,724,000. Foreign trade (1977): imports A$11,693,000; exports: A$18,212,000. Import sources (1976): Australia 51%; New Zealand 11%; U.K. 9%; Japan 6%; U.S. 5%. Export destinations (1976): Australia 63%; New Zealand 31%; U.K. 5%. Main exports: phosphates 87%; copra 13%.

Industry. Production (in 000; 1977): phosphate rock (metric tons) 425; electricity (kw-hr) *c.* 5,000.

Korea

A country of eastern Asia, Korea is bounded by China, the Sea of Japan, the Korea Strait, and the Yellow Sea. It is divided into two parts roughly at the 38th parallel.

WIDE WORLD

The funeral cortege of slain South Korean Pres. Park Chung Hee moved slowly to the capital building for funeral services November 3.

Murder and mystery brought the Park Chung Hee era in Korea to an abrupt end in 1979. The shattering climax of the president's death in October was in sharp contrast to the note of optimism with which the year opened. Within a month of the resumption of diplomatic relations between the U.S. and China on Jan. 1, 1979, North and South Korea sent each other formal proposals and counterproposals for a conference to achieve peace. South Korean President Park suggested a dialogue without any conditions "anywhere and at any level." The North's Democratic Front for Reunification of the Fatherland proposed a congress of popular representatives from both sides.

Nothing much came of the peace feelers, however. In March the North Koreans took umbrage at a massive joint U.S.-South Korean military exercise named Team Spirit '79. They called it "an unbearable insult," while the South maintained that the war game had been planned long before and had nothing to do with the new North-South contacts. Three meetings took place between the two countries, but they led to a deadlock over how to resume full-fledged reunification talks. By early April each side was boycotting the other.

On July 1 the U.S. and South Korea issued a joint statement calling for a three-way meeting between them and North Korea to find ways of reducing tension in the peninsula. The North called it a "confused proposal" and rejected it as "utterly unfeasible." It said that the problem of Korean unification should be solved by the Koreans themselves without foreign interference, but that it would keep a door open for a dialogue with the U.S.

Republic of Korea (South Korea). Area: 98,914 sq km (38,191 sq mi). Pop. (1979 est.): 37,605,000. Cap. and largest city: Seoul (pop., 1978 est., 7,823,000). Language: Korean. Religion: Buddhist; Christian; Confucian; Tonghak (Chondokyo). Presidents in 1979, Gen. Park Chung Hee and, from October 26, Choi Kyu Hah; prime ministers, Choi Kyu Hah and, from December 10, Shin Hyon Hwak.

The visit by U.S. Pres. Jimmy Carter to Seoul from June 29 to July 1 generated political pressures that shook the Park government even before the assassin struck. Park appeared to interpret the visit as a sign of tacit approval of his internal policies, while his many critics argued that Carter was concerned about the suppression of dissenters. Leading critic Kim Dae Jung, who had been released in December 1978 after serving two-thirds of a five-year sentence, was under interrogation again by February 1979 in connection with the formation of a new political organization, the National Alliance for Democracy and National Unification.

The big showdown, however, was with Kim Young Sam, newly elected leader of the major opposition group in Parliament, the New Democratic Party (NDP). In July he delivered a keynote speech in the National Assembly bitterly accusing President Park of staying in power too long. He attacked the suppression of basic rights, demanded the release of prisoners of conscience, and declared that the most effective way of fighting Communism was by promoting freedoms.

A week after the Assembly speech Moon Bu-shik, the editor of the NDP party organ, was arrested for publishing it. In August, when women textile workers used the NDP's premises to protest layoffs, a massive force of riot policemen raided the headquarters and violently dispersed them; one woman was killed and scores were injured. U.S. officials described the action as "excessive and brutal." In October Kim himself was expelled from Parliament by a two-thirds majority vote as provided by the constitution. The ruling Democratic Republican Party, which controlled 161 seats in the 231-seat legislature, listed nine charges against him, including attempts to break down the constitutional order and seeking foreign interference in the country's internal affairs.

Noting that since the Carter visit "there has been a definite retrogression in the state of human rights in South Korea," the U.S. recalled Ambassador William Gleysteen "for consultations." The NDP for its part announced a boycott of the National Assembly and then the resignation en masse of its parliamentarians.

Suddenly tension erupted into violent antigovernment riots in Pusan, the home constituency of Kim Young Sam. They spread quickly to neighbouring Masan, with students and workers going on a rampage. The government cracked down with a heavy hand; moving in tanks and armoured cars, it suppressed the riots by the third day.

But the calm that was restored was an uneasy one, and, as later events showed, dissension developed among Park's closest advisers. On the night of October 26 he met with some of them at a private dinner given at a restaurant maintained by the Korean Central Intelligence Agency. There, halfway through the meal, he was shot dead by KCIA chief Kim Jae Kyu. Five aides of the president, including the influential chief bodyguard, Cha Chi Chol, were also killed. Kim was arrested several hours later at Army headquarters. The government initially put out a statement claiming that the president had been accidentally shot. Subsequently, it admitted there had been a conspiracy. The final report issued by the authorities said that Kim had been plotting for five months to remove the president.

Early apprehensions that anarchy would follow Park's killing proved wrong. Immediately after the incident Prime Minister Choi Kyu Hah was sworn in as acting president. In December he was elected president by the 2,560-member National Conference for Reunification. The apparent smoothness of the transition and Choi's first acts—the lifting of the controversial Emergency Decree No. 9 and the release of 68 political prisoners—spread the impression that a liberalization program was about to be put into effect.

At first the political parties also appeared to be engaged in a policy of domestic détente. The ruling DRP elected longtime Park associate Kim Jong Pil as leader. In a surprise show of goodwill, he called on opposition leader Kim Young Sam at the latter's NDP headquarters. The two announced they would start a "bipartisan dialogue."

By mid-December, however, the mood had changed. Just before the new prime minister, Shin Hyon Hwak, was to announce a caretaker Cabinet, the powerful martial law commander, Gen. Chung Sung Hwa, was arrested for alleged complicity in Park's murder on orders given by Gen. Chon Too Hwan, head of the Army Security Command, an army intelligence unit. Defense Minister Ro Jae Hyun was dismissed from his post, and the top military commanders were reshuffled. When the Cabinet lineup was finally announced, the key portfolios of defense, home, and justice went to hard-line generals.

The reason for the "countercoup" was widely believed to be a power struggle between the military leaders. Conservative and nationalistic elements headed by Chon were said to have acted to block what they considered too rapid liberalization which, according to them, would create chaos in the country. At the same time the Army Security Command charged that Chung Sung Hwa and ten other top generals had conspired with the KCIA to topple Park. They were reported to have been implicated by Kim Jae Kyu in secret testimony.

Democratic People's Republic of Korea (North Korea). Area: 121,200 sq km (46,800 sq mi). Pop. (1979 est.): 17,498,000. Cap.: Pyongyang (metro. pop., 1976 est., 1.5 million). Language: Korean. Religion: Buddhist; Confucian; Tonghak (Chondokyo). General secretary of the Central Committee of the Workers' (Communist) Party of Korea and president in 1979, Marshal Kim Il Sung; chairman of the Council of Ministers (premier), Li Jong Ok.

Keeping a relatively low profile, North Korea reportedly tried to establish contacts with the U.S. in 1979, but with little apparent result. With regard to China it welcomed "the fact that our brotherly neighbour ended long hostile relations and established diplomatic ties with the U.S." But it was angry when Japan's Defense Agency chief, Gen. Ganri Yamashita, visited South Korea in July. The visit, it charged, was "to strengthen Japan-South Korea military conspiracy."

In the same month South Korea claimed that an

KOREA: Republic

Education. (1979) Primary, pupils 5,640,712, teachers 117,290; secondary, pupils 3,282,151, teachers 80,472; vocational, students 677,824, teachers 19,993; higher, students 406,087, teaching staff 25,603.

Finance. Monetary unit: won, with (Sept. 17, 1979) an official rate of 485 won to U.S. $1 (free rate of 1,048 won = £1 sterling). Gold, SDR's, and foreign exchange (June 1979) U.S. $5,113,000,000. Budget (1978 actual): revenue 4,657,900,000,000 won; expenditure 4,548,500,000,000 won. Gross national product (1978) 22,255,700,000,000 won. Money supply (June 1979) 2,538,200,000,000 won. Cost of living (1970 = 100; June 1979) 174.3.

Foreign Trade. (1978) Imports 7,246,400,000,000 won; exports 6,152,100,000,000 won. Import sources (1977): Japan 36%; U.S. 23%; Saudi Arabia 10%; Kuwait 5%. Export destinations (1977): U.S. 31%; Japan 21%; Saudi Arabia 7%; West Germany 5%. Main exports (1977): clothing 21%; textile yarns and fabrics 11%; electrical machinery and equipment 9%; fish 7%; metal manufactures 6%; footwear 5%; ships 5%. Tourism (1977): visitors 950,000; gross receipts U.S. $370 million.

Transport and Communications. Roads (1977) 45,663 km (including 1,224 km expressways). Motor vehicles in use (1977): passenger 125,600; commercial 119,100. Railways (1978): 5,732 km; traffic 20,140,000,000 passenger-km, freight 10,719,000,000 net ton-km. Air traffic (1977): 5,475,000,000 passenger-km; freight 402 million net ton-km. Shipping (1978): merchant vessels 100 gross tons and over 1,148; gross tonnage 2,975,389. Telephones (Jan. 1978) 1,978,400. Radio receivers (Dec. 1976) *c.* 10,050,000. Television receivers (Dec. 1978) *c.* 4,630,000.

Agriculture. Production (in 000; metric tons; 1978): rice 8,058; barley *c.* 1,348; potatoes *c.* 360; sweet potatoes (1977) 1,844; soybeans 293; cabbages (1977) *c.* 1,079; watermelons (1977) *c.* 190; onions *c.* 129; apples *c.* 369; oranges *c.* 116; tobacco 134; fish catch (1977) 2,419. Livestock (in 000; Dec. 1977): cattle 1,492; pigs 1,482; goats 216; chickens 30,224.

Industry. Production (in 000; metric tons; 1978): coal 18,056; iron ore (56% metal content) 587; crude steel 3,140; cement 15,133; tungsten concentrates (oxide content; 1977) 3.5; zinc concentrates 65; gold (troy oz; 1977) 20; silver (troy oz; 1977) 2,042; sulfuric acid 1,441; petroleum products (1977) 20,820; man-made fibres 468; electricity (excluding most industrial production; kw-hr) 31,510,000; radio receivers (units; 1977) 6,404; television receivers (units; 1977) 2,990. Merchant vessels launched (100 gross tons and over; 1978) 402,000.

KOREA: People's Democratic Republic

Education. (1976–77) Primary, pupils 2,561,674; secondary and vocational, pupils *c.* 2 million; primary, secondary, and vocational, teachers *c.* 100,000; higher, students *c.* 100,000.

Finance and Trade. Monetary unit: won, with (Sept. 17, 1979) a nominal exchange rate of 0.91 won to U.S. $1 (1.96 won = £1 sterling). Budget (1976 est.) balanced at 12,513,000,000 won. Foreign trade (approximate; 1978): imports *c.* 1.4 billion won; exports *c.* 1.2 billion won. Import sources: China *c.* 50%; U.S.S.R. *c.* 18%; Japan *c.* 13%. Export destinations: China *c.* 40%; U.S.S.R. *c.* 25%; Japan *c.* 9%; West Germany *c.* 5%. Main exports (1972): zinc and ore *c.* 30%; lead and ore *c.* 15%; magnesite *c.* 15%; iron and steel *c.* 15%; iron ore *c.* 12%; cement *c.* 8%.

Agriculture. Production (in 000; metric tons; 1978): rice *c.* 4,500; corn *c.* 1,850; barley *c.* 350; millet *c.* 430; potatoes *c.* 1,450; sweet potatoes (1977) *c.* 360; soybeans *c.* 320; apples *c.* 430; tobacco *c.* 42; fish catch (1977) *c.* 1,600. Livestock (in 000; 1977): cattle *c.* 820; pigs *c.* 1,580; sheep *c.* 275; goats *c.* 210; chickens *c.* 17,632.

Industry. Production (in 000; metric tons; 1977): coal *c.* 45,100; iron ore (metal content) *c.* 3,800; pig iron *c.* 3,100; steel *c.* 3,100; lead *c.* 70; zinc *c.* 136; magnesite *c.* 1,500; silver (troy oz) *c.* 1,600; tungsten concentrates (oxide content) *c.* 2.7; cement *c.* 7,000; electricity (kw-hr; 1965) 13.3 million.

army officer from the North, Lieut. Kim Hyung-soon, 25, defected by crossing the demilitarized zone to the South. It said that Kim was a member of the Army's powerful political security department. The North struck back in October by attacking Kim Young Sam's ouster from the South Korean Parliament. It was described as "another premeditated and organized fascist outrage" that would "only hasten the Park Chung Hee clique's destruction."

U.S. intelligence sources reported in October that the North Korean Army had become the fifth largest in the world (after China, the Soviet Union, the U.S., and India). It was in a position, according to one U.S. congressman, to seize the city of Seoul before the U.S. could intervene. Fighting personnel were estimated at between 550,000 and 600,000, compared with 450,000 in 1977. It was pointed out that the increased strength was not a sudden spurt by North Korea but the result of U.S. intelligence acquiring more information than it had had in the past. Critics countered by saying that the administration had merely provided new figures to back up a moratorium on U.S. troop withdrawals from the South, as had been demanded by influential congressional circles.

Pres. Kim Il Sung presented a financial report as part of his 1979 New Year's message. He claimed that the industrial growth rate in 1978 was 17%, 4.9% higher than the 12.1% set for the second seven-year plan (1978–84). He listed electricity, steel, chemical fertilizers, and cement as the sectors that registered high production increases.

(T. J. S. GEORGE)

Kuwait

An independent constitutional monarchy (emirate), Kuwait is on the northwestern coast of the Persian Gulf between Iraq and Saudi Arabia. Area: 16,918 sq km (6,532 sq mi). Pop. (1979 est.): 1,272,200. Cap.: Kuwait (pop., 1975, 78,100). Largest city: Hawalli (pop., 1975, 130,600). Language: Arabic. Religion (1975): Muslim 94.9%; Christian 4.5%. Emir, Sheikh Jabir al-Ahmad al-Jabir as-Sabah; prime minister in 1979, Crown Prince Sheikh Saad al-Abdullah as-Salim as-Sabah.

On Jan. 8, 1979, it was announced that Kuwait's oil production of two million barrels a day would not be increased in 1979 to compensate for the suspension of Iranian oil exports. Soon afterward, however, the Oil Ministry said it would permit short-term increases of 5 to 10% in oil supplied to companies suffering from the loss of Iranian oil. Kuwait raised its oil prices in line with the Organization of Petroleum Exporting Countries (OPEC) minimum rates, set at Geneva on March 27, but added its own surcharge of $1.20 a barrel. On October 8 Kuwait unilaterally raised its price to $21.43 per barrel. Following the December OPEC meeting, which failed to agree on a new price structure, Kuwait again raised its price, to $25.50.

Although Kuwait condemned the March treaty between Egypt and Israel and severed diplomatic relations with Egypt on April 22, the country pursued its traditional policy of mediation in inter-

KEYSTONE

Britain's Queen Elizabeth II arrived in Kuwait on February 12 at the start of her Mideast tour.

Arab disputes. Kuwait sponsored an emergency session of the Arab League Council, March 4–6, which ended the border war between Yemen (San'a') and Yemen (Aden). The leaders of the two Yemens signed an agreement in Kuwait on March 29 for unification of their two countries. In February Kuwait became the first Arab Persian Gulf state to support the new Iranian regime. The foreign minister visited Teheran on July 21.

The newly formed opposition Democratic Coalition-Kuwait published its manifesto in Paris in February. It sought the return of the National Assembly, dissolved in 1976. (CHARLES GLASS)

KUWAIT

Education. (1977–78) Primary, pupils 120,504, teachers 7,920; secondary, pupils 156,496, teachers 11,804; vocational, pupils 4,988, teachers 1,010; teacher training, pupils 1,037, teachers 206; higher, students 9,318, teaching staff 606.

Finance. Monetary unit: Kuwaiti dinar, with (Sept. 17, 1979) a free rate of 0.28 dinar to U.S. $1 (0.59 dinar = £1 sterling). Gold, SDR's, and foreign exchange (June 1979) U.S. $2,105,000,000. Budget (1978–79 est.): revenue 2,301,000,000 dinars; expenditure 1,950,000,000 dinars. Gross national product (1976–77) 3,672,000,000 dinars. Money supply (June 1979) 675 million dinars. Cost of living (1975 = 100; March 1979) 127.9.

Foreign Trade. (1978) Imports 1,268,900,000 dinars; exports 2,874,200,000 dinars. Import sources (1977): Japan 20%; U.S. 14%; U.K. 10%; West Germany 9%; South Korea 5%; Italy 5%. Export destinations (1977): Japan 25%; U.K. 9%; The Netherlands 7%; Italy 7%; Taiwan 7%; South Korea 7%. Main exports: crude oil 75%; petroleum products 16%.

Transport. Roads (1977) c. 1,920 km. Motor vehicles in use (1977): passenger 285,800; commercial (including buses) 95,100. Air traffic (1978): 1,355,000,000 passenger-km; freight 41.2 million net ton-km. Shipping (1978): merchant vessels 100 gross tons and over 251; gross tonnage 2,240,030. Shipping traffic (1975): goods loaded 107,233,000 metric tons, unloaded 2,532,000 metric tons.

Industry. Production (in 000; metric tons; 1977): petroleum products 17,062; crude oil (1978) c. 105,180; natural gas (cu m) 10,134,000; electricity (kw-hr) 6,018,000.

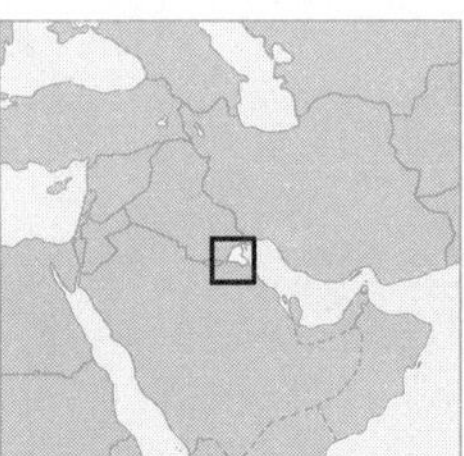

Kuwait

Labour Unions:
see Industrial Relations

Lacrosse:
see Field Hockey and Lacrosse

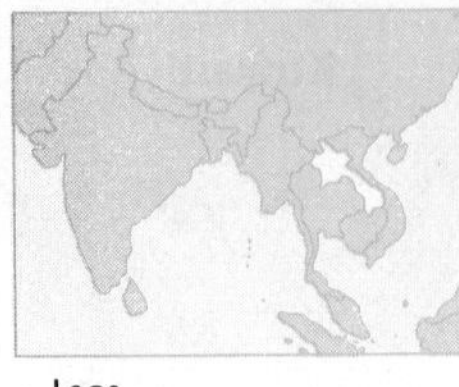

Laos

Laos

A landlocked people's republic of Southeast Asia, Laos is bounded by China, Vietnam, Cambodia, Thailand, and Burma. Area: 236,800 sq km (91,400 sq mi). Pop. (1979 est.): 3,633,000. Cap. and largest city: Vientiane (pop., 1978 est., 200,000). Language: Lao (official); French and English. Religion: Buddhist; tribal. President in 1979, Prince Souphanouvong; premier, Kaysone Phomvihan.

In low-key style, Laos slipped into the diplomatic structure Vietnam had apparently designed for the Indochinese states. The orchestrated moves were completed when President Souphanouvong visited Cambodia in March 1979. Although it was considered a low-level delegation (since Premier Kaysone Phomvihan was the real power in the country) and there was no mention of the grandiose Indochina Federation, Souphanouvong signed cultural, scientific, and economic cooperation agreements which the Laotian text of the joint communiqué described as treaties. At the same time, Kaysone visited Bangkok and on April 4 signed an agreement with Thailand on the elimination of guerrilla bases along their common frontier.

Concurrently, Laos moved further away from China. The size of the Chinese embassy in Vientiane was progressively reduced, and several Chinese journalists and road builders were asked to leave. One result was that, for most of the year, the shadow of a possible Chinese "punishment" of Vientiane remained a matter of concern. It was reported that Chinese agents in the border regions were instigating local people to rise against Vietnamese domination. Many Laotian refugees in Thai camps were said to have asked for resettlement in China in the hope that the Chinese government would help them fight the "occupation forces" in Laos. By midyear Vientiane spoke of China massing troops near the frontier. In September Hanoi publicly proclaimed that artillery battles were taking place across the border and that China had designs on Laos.

There was evidence of mounting domestic problems. In an unusually candid report to the Council of Ministers early in the year, Kaysone admitted substantial losses of foreign aid and equipment as a result of bureaucratic muddles; poor and sometimes unfair distribution of goods; prices that were not "well-managed"; and accounting that was "inadequate." Under pressure from international agencies as well as its socialist allies, the government decided to give priority to a review of current projects and long-term plans, improvement of management practices, and streamlining of the bureaucracy.

The biggest problem was the lack of qualified personnel. Many educated people had fled the country, while others were caught up in charges of corruption and misuse of funds. Untrained and inexperienced people were consequently given jobs as agriculturists, soil technicians, engineers, and farm administrators—with disastrous results. The government asked for an increased flow of experts from Vietnam and the Eastern European countries. A crash educational program was introduced, and some headway was apparently being made with the construction of schools across the land and a literacy drive embracing young adults as well as primary school children.

There were indirect references to a serious food shortage. Even with normal production, a shortfall of 133,000 tons of grain was projected for 1979. Among the reasons listed by official sources were lack of initiative by members of cooperatives, a shortage of modern tools, and "belief in ghosts, spirits, and superstitions." (T. J. S. GEORGE)

LAOS

Education. (1977–78) Primary, pupils 442,000, teachers (1974–75) 7,248; secondary, pupils 59,200, teachers (1972–73) 607; vocational, pupils 10,500, teachers (1972–73) 270; teacher training (1972–73), students 3,913, teachers 227; higher, students 1,000, teaching staff (1974–75) 152.

Finance. Monetary unit: kip, with (Sept. 17, 1979) an official exchange rate of 400 kip to U.S. $1 (free rate of 861 kip = £1 sterling). Budget (1978 est.): revenue 46.3 billion kip (including foreign aid of 31 billion kip); expenditure 49.4 billion kip.

Foreign Trade. (1974) Imports 1,950,000,000 new kip; exports 330 million new kip. Import sources: Thailand 49%; Japan 19%; France 7%; West Germany 7%; U.S. 5%. Export destinations: Thailand 73%; Malaysia 11%; Hong Kong 10%. Main exports: timber 81%; tin 11%.

Transport and Communications. Roads (1978) *c.* 8,000 km. Motor vehicles in use (1974): passenger 14,100; commercial (including buses) 2,500. Air traffic (1977): 10 million passenger-km; freight *c.* 500,000 net ton-km. Inland waterways (total; 1978) *c.* 4,600 km. Telephones (Dec. 1973) 5,000. Radio licenses (Dec. 1976) 200,000.

Agriculture. Production (in 000; metric tons; 1977): rice 847; corn 35; onions *c.* 30; melons *c.* 22; oranges *c.* 18; pineapples *c.* 28; coffee *c.* 2; tobacco *c.* 4; cotton, lint *c.* 3; timber (cu m) *c.* 3,298. Livestock (in 000; 1978): cattle *c.* 534; buffalo *c.* 1,303; pigs *c.* 1,576; chickens (1977) *c.* 16,744.

Industry. Production (1977): tin concentrates (metal content) 600 metric tons; electricity (excluding most industrial production) *c.* 250 million kw-hr.

Latin-American Affairs

The revolution in Nicaragua shook the Americas in 1979; it had wider repercussions than might have been expected from a straightforward overthrow of a dictatorship. For example, it showed that a popular uprising could succeed in bringing down a military-backed regime, despite the latter's superior firepower and equipment. It served as a shock to other such regimes and gave heart to their opponents; indeed, the subsequent overthrow of another dictatorship in El Salvador by junior army officers proclaiming themselves to be left-wing followed the Nicaraguan revolution. Moreover, it moved the governments of the Andean Group countries and Mexico to support the Nicaraguan revolutionaries actively and demonstrated that Cuba, at least in Latin America, would stand on the sidelines and provide only moral support to the insurgents. It also put to the test the U.S. government policy of nonintervention and concern for human rights.

After the Nicaraguan revolution practical matters of reconstruction drew more attention than the sort of government that was established; the legislation nationalizing banks, insurance, and the principal industrial and agricultural concerns that had been the property of the Somoza family was considered of minor importance. Nevertheless, these moves represented steps toward the formation of a socialist state, the second, after Cuba, to appear in Latin America.

External Relations. Latin America's commercial relations with the U.S. and the European Economic Community (EEC) worsened in 1979. Toward the end of 1978 the U.S. government imposed countervailing duties on those exports from Latin America which it thought were being subsidized unfairly; Colombian textiles and Uruguayan leather products were among the goods affected by this measure. The EEC tightened its policy during 1979 by way of import quotas; iron-ore exports from Brazil and Chilean fruit exports were forbidden access on the grounds that they were being "dumped."

This spate of trade barriers on Latin-American exports gave rise to considerable protest. The gravity of the situation increased following the decision by the Organization of Petroleum Exporting Countries (OPEC) in June to raise the price of petroleum by 33%. Crude-oil importing countries in Latin America (particularly Brazil, Chile, Uruguay, and the Central American republics) were expected to go further into debt in order to finance their resulting balance of payments deficits.

Attempts by Latin Americans to resist the spreading restrictions on their exports all but failed. However, the urgency of the situation was emphasized more than ever before in the inter-American and other international conferences held in 1979; a need to organize a united trading front was recognized. Probably the most important conference held in this connection was that organized in April by the Economic Commission for Latin America of the UN; there it was proposed to set up a regional financial agency to aid countries with balance of payments difficulties, something that the Andean Group had already started to do in 1978. Moreover, it was recommended that an advisory service be established to monitor protectionist measures adopted by developed nations. At a March conference held by members of the UN Conference on Trade and Development (UNCTAD) in Geneva, a commodity fund was established with strong Latin-American support that would allow international commodity cartels to obtain financial backing in order to support the prices of their products in the event of an economic downturn. In September Latin Americans joined with Spain and the Philippines to propose, at the annual conference of the International Monetary Fund, a thorough reform of that organization's operations so that it would give greater consideration to poor non-oil-producing nations.

The package of measures that emerged in early 1979 from the "Tokyo Round" of talks held by General Agreement on Tariffs and Trade (GATT) member countries did little to satisfy the main concerns of Latin America. In fact, the U.S. government agreed at the talks to dismantle the special tariff reductions that had applied to certain exports from poor countries. Known as the Generalized System of Preferences, these concessions, which provided an opportunity for Latin-American countries to develop their export trade in their vast neighbouring markets, would be phased out beginning in 1980. Moreover, certain countries, such as Argentina, Brazil, and Mexico, were classed as countries that had reached an "intermediate" stage of development and therefore had to accept reductions in their own protectionist barriers. As a result, Brazil announced that it would start phasing out its system of import deposits. Argentina had already embarked on a program of tariff reductions.

Mexican-U.S. relations became a focus of interest as a result of the discoveries of even greater deposits of petroleum off the Mexican coast in the Gulf of Mexico. In February presidents Jimmy Carter of the U.S. and José López Portillo of Mexico met as a gesture of goodwill. The meeting, however, failed to speed up notably the long-drawn-out negotiations for a gas-supply contract. The Mexicans tried to include in the negotiations the issues of restrictions on Mexican immigrant labour in the U.S. and U.S. farmers' moves against importation of cheap Mexican tomatoes into the U.S. Finally, in September an agreement was reached, with the U.S. paying $3.62 per 1,000 cu ft for a daily supply of 300 million cu ft of natural gas.

Integration. The Andean Group (Bolivia, Colombia, Ecuador, Peru, and Venezuela) alone made significant progress in 1979 toward establishing the foundations of a common market. During the year, it concentrated on developing the basis of an integrated regional motor-vehicle industry. Under the Motor-Vehicle Sectorial Program, as agreed upon in 1977, each member country would have exclusive manufacturing rights for specific categories of automobiles and

WIDE WORLD

Argentine Pres. Jorge Rafael Videla announced in January that his country and Chile had agreed to submit their dispute over the three Beagle Islands off the tip of South America to Vatican mediation.

UPI

Former New York Yankee slugger Joe DiMaggio (holding bat) was on hand in April to congratulate Venezuelan Pres. Luis Herrera Campins (left) and officials of the newly formed Triple-A Inter-American Baseball League.

trucks and would be able to supply these vehicles to other group members free of import duties. International companies formed joint ventures with local firms to submit bids for the installation of motor-vehicle manufacturing plants; Volkswagen, Volvo, Renault, and General Motors offered contracts to begin production in 1980 on this basis. However, differences arose over the allocation among member countries of rights in regard to the metalworking and petrochemical programs; Venezuela wanted to ensure that its already-established industries would benefit from these new programs; Bolivia and Ecuador were mostly concerned about the tendency of the more sophisticated industries to gravitate to the bigger markets and leave them neglected. Doubts arose as to whether Bolivia and Ecuador had the financial resources or manpower and technology to erect sophisticated industries in the short period of time required by the needs of Venezuela's fast-growing economy. In July, nevertheless, a compromise agreement was reached on a metalworking program that included electrical equipment.

Moreover, the important process of establishing a common external tariff was begun by the Andean Group in 1979, and intraregional tariffs on goods in general (including those outside sectorial programs) were reduced. The presidents of the member countries met in Cartagena, Colombia, in May to celebrate the tenth anniversary of the Andean Pact. At the meeting they decided to create an Andean Tribunal to settle disputes within the organization.

The Latin American Free Trade Association (LAFTA), in contrast, failed to achieve significant new initiatives during the year. Brazil disregarded the opportunity of negotiating accords with the most likely nations, Argentina, Chile, and Uruguay, all of which were intent on progressively reducing tariffs. Indeed, Brazil appeared to be more interested in strengthening its links with the Andean Group by way of the Amazon Pact. This was seen as the logical outcome of its recent political policy favouring those nations over the military governments of Argentina, Chile, and Uruguay, a stance confirmed when the Brazilian government supported the candidacy of Carlos Alzamora of Peru at the August elections for a permanent secretary of the Sistema Económico Latinoamericano.

In the River Plate Basin, on the other hand, developments took a more concrete shape. The giant 1,890-Mw Salto Grande hydroelectric dam on the Uruguay River, built jointly by Argentina and Uruguay, began operating in June 1979, when the first of 14 Soviet-made generating turbines was started. The project included a series of locks that would make the Uruguay River navigable for 1,200-metric-ton barges as far as the Brazilian village of São Pedro, as compared with the previous upper limit of Concordia (Argentina) and Saltos (Uruguay). A final treaty was signed by Argentina and Paraguay for the design, position, and construction of the even larger 2,700–3,400-Mw Yacyretá-Apipé Dam on the Paraná River, now scheduled to begin operating in 1986 instead of 1983. Earlier, the Paraguayan government had sought to change the position of the dam so that the reservoir would flood less Paraguayan territory. A compromise was reached, and Argentina agreed to pay Paraguay an annual indemnity for the land flooded.

Meanwhile, the massive (by far the world's largest hydroelectric generating dam) 12,600-Mw Brazilian-Paraguayan Itaipú Dam, 478 km (296 mi) farther upstream, was being built at a rapid pace. It was scheduled to start operating in 1983 and to be completed by 1986; however, at the beginning of 1979, the Brazilians announced that the Itaipú would have 2 extra turbines added to the 18 planned in 1978. This led to the breaking off of negotiations between Argentina and Brazil over the question of making the Itaipú project compatible with Corpus, another Argentine-Paraguayan dam planned 288 km (179 mi) farther downstream from Itaipú with a potential capacity of 6,000 Mw. The Corpus Dam would create a reservoir that would flood Brazilian territory and reach the Itaipú Dam, possibly reducing the latter's capacity. An agreement between the two countries was concluded late in the year, providing Corpus with a capacity of 4,400 Mw and only slightly diminishing Itaipú's generating output. (PAUL DOWBOR)

See also articles on the various political units.
[971.D.8; 974]

Latin-American Literature:
see Literature

Latter-day Saints:
see Religion

Law

Court Decisions. The most significant judicial decisions in 1979 emanated from the United States Supreme Court, reflecting the fact that the Constitution of the United States vests tremendous powers in its courts and also the role of the Supreme Court in that arrangement. Some of the mystique of that court, however, was lifted at the year's end by the publication of an investigative book about the court's private foibles, *The Brethren*, by Bob Woodward and Scott Armstrong. This revelation about the decision-making processes of the court tended to make its decisions even more interesting and speculative to legal scholars.

LEGISLATIVE IMMUNITY. If the demystifying of the court caused some to doubt the continuing force of the "rule of law" in the U.S. legal system, the court itself reiterated that principle in two cases involving a U.S. senator and a congressman. In *Davis* v. *Passman* the court held that Otto Passman, formerly a congressman from Louisiana, could be sued for allegedly firing his secretary because she was a woman, and that a suit in federal court under the Fifth Amendment to the Constitution for money damages was an appropriate remedy against Passman. *Hutchinson* v. *Proxmire* was a libel action brought by a research scientist who, while conducting a federally funded project, received a "Golden Fleece of the Month" award from Sen. William Proxmire of Wisconsin. The award was made by the senator to publicize allegedly wasteful government spending. The research in question was aimed at developing an objective measure of aggression by studying particular animal behaviour, such as the clenching of jaws, screaming, kicking, and so forth. In a speech to the Senate announcing the Golden Fleece Award for this research, Proxmire said, "The funding of this nonsense makes me almost angry enough to scream and kick or even clench my jaws. . . . Dr. Hutchinson's studies should make the taxpayers as well as his monkeys grind their teeth." The essence of this speech was then released by the senator to the press and transmitted by him through a newsletter to his constituents.

In suing Senator Proxmire, Hutchinson had to overcome two substantial hurdles. First, he was confronted with the proposition that public figures cannot prevail in libel suits unless they establish actual malice on the part of the defendant in uttering or publishing the allegedly defamatory remarks. Second, he faced the "Speech or Debate Clause" privilege that gives legislators immunity for statements made on the floor of the legislature. The court held that Hutchinson was not a public figure and thus did not have to show that Senator Proxmire had maliciously defamed him. Second, it held that the Speech or Debate Clause only protects legislative activities. Thus, while Senator Proxmire's speech on the Senate floor was immune, that immunity did not extend to the press release or newsletter that repeated the speech.

ABORTION. The U.S. Supreme Court held unconstitutional a Massachusetts statute that made illegal the performance of an abortion on an unmarried woman under the age of 18 unless she had obtained the consent of her parents or a court order authorizing the operation. In handing down the decision Justice Lewis Powell, Jr., stated that there is a constitutional right to seek an abortion and that this right had been unduly burdened by the legislation in question, primarily because "it permits judicial authorization for an abortion to be withheld from a minor who is found by the superior court to be mature and fully competent to make (the) decision independently." He pointed out that the Massachusetts statute was also defective in that it required the unmarried minor to consult and notify her parents of her desire for an abortion before an independent judicial determination could be sought. This requirement, in Justice Powell's view, imposed an undue burden on the young woman because many parents hold strong views on abortion and can effectively dominate their children.

In England the High Court awarded damages of £20,000 to a woman who had undergone an abortion that proved unsuccessful in that a healthy child was subsequently born. The judgment, considered large in Great Britain, was seen by some legal and medical observers as placing on physicians a "guarantee of success" when they perform an abortion.

LEGITIMACY. The civil law countries of the world commonly have made a distinction between legitimate and illegitimate children for purposes of inheritance and other family rights, whereas most common law (English-speaking) countries have tended to abolish this difference. Many civil law countries also have been giving illegitimate children greater rights by way of legislation. In 1979 this tendency received added impetus from the European Court of Human Rights. The court in *Marchx* v. *Belgium* held that provisions of the Belgian civil code under which an illegitimate child must be legally recognized by his or her mother in

Actor Lee Marvin appeared greatly relieved after a California court awarded Michelle Triola Marvin only $104,000 in a "palimony" suit. She had asked for half of the $3.6 million he had earned during the time they lived together.

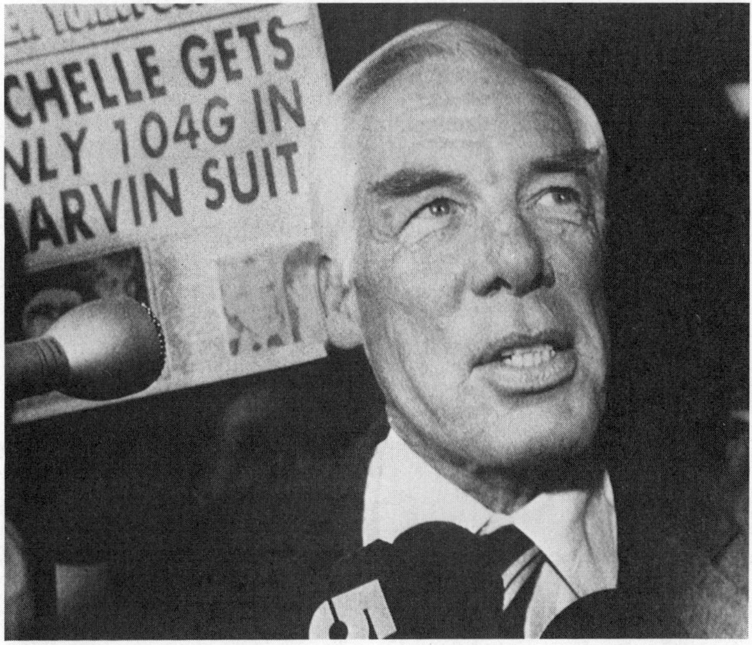

WIDE WORLD

order for "affiliation" to be established were in contravention of the European Convention on Human Rights. Affiliation is a civil law concept concerning the act of determining paternity of a bastard child and of assuming the obligation to support it.

The court reasoned that the requirement of affiliation discriminated against illegitimate children because legitimate children obtain rights without any such legal activity. Moreover, the court opined that the concept of affiliation was repugnant to "family life" because it forced the parents either to recognize their illegitimate offspring and thus diminish their own rights of inheritance from one another and their rights of voluntary disposition, or to disown the child and thus stigmatize all persons involved.

RACE RELATIONS. The U.S. Supreme Court has consistently held since 1954, when it handed down the landmark decision of *Brown* v. *Board of Education*, that public schools may not be intentionally segregated along racial lines. It has also held that the disparate impact on students and foreseeable consequences of public school practices respecting race do not, by themselves, prove that such practices are motivated by considerations of racial discrimination. In 1979 the court clarified these competing notions by holding that school board "actions having foreseeable and anticipated disparate impact are relevant evidence to prove the ultimate fact, forbidden purpose."

The cases involved the school systems of Columbus and Dayton, Ohio, both of which were highly segregated along racial lines. Half of the public schools in Columbus were either 90% black or 90% white, while in Dayton 51 of the 69 public schools were virtually all white or all black. Moreover, it was found that both school systems considered race in making teacher assignments and apparently in establishing attendance zones and sites for new construction. This evidence convinced a majority of the court that the two cities were guilty of "de jure" (and not merely "de facto") racial segregation in violation of the Equal Protection Clause of the Fourteenth Amendment.

The most celebrated case handed down by the Supreme Court in 1979 was *United Steelworkers of America* v. *Weber*. In this decision the court held that an employer and a labour union did not violate Title VII of the Civil Rights Act of 1964 by implementing a joint plan under which they reserved one-half of the positions in their craft training program for blacks. The decision, handed down exactly one year to the day after the *Regents of the University of California* v. *Bakke* judgment, surprised many observers who had construed the latter case to mean that racial quota systems are unconstitutional irrespective of the purposes that motivate them. Moreover, Title VII of the 1964 Civil Rights Act forbids discrimination "because of race" in employment, fortifying the view that so-called affirmative action plans of hiring had been outlawed by Congress as well.

Justice William Brennan, Jr., writing for a five-to-two majority, nevertheless held that not all affirmative action plans are unconstitutional or violative of the Civil Rights Act. He declined to "define in detail the line of demarcation between permissible and impermissible affirmative action plans," but he held that it was acceptable to employ affirmative action to "break down old patterns of racial segregation and hierarchy." Quoting from the late Sen. Hubert Humphrey, Justice Brennan stated that a basic purpose of Title VII was "to open employment opportunities for Negroes in occupations which have been traditionally closed to them." Based on this statement, Justice Brennan thought, "It would be ironic indeed if a law triggered by a nation's concern over centuries of racial injustice . . . constituted the first legislative prohibition of all voluntary, private, race-conscious efforts to abolish traditional patterns of racial segregation. . . ."

Chief Justice Warren Burger dissented. He said that the court's result was one that he would be inclined to support if he were in Congress voting on an amendment to Title VII to achieve that end, but that he could not support the judgment because "it is contrary to the explicit language of the statute and arrived at by means wholly incompatible with long-established principles of separation of powers." The reference to separation of powers apparently was an allusion to the fact that the majority of the court had, in Burger's view, disregarded the plain meaning of the statute, thus ignoring Congress, and had substituted its own legislative judgment by reliance on the "spirit" of the statute. "In passing Title VII," he wrote, "Congress outlawed all racial discrimination. . . . With today's holding, the Court introduces into Title VII a tolerance for the very evil that the law was intended to eradicate. . . ."

ALIENS. The U.S. Supreme Court sustained the constitutionality of a New York state education law forbidding certification as a public school teacher of any person who is not a citizen of the United States unless that person has manifested an intention to apply for citizenship. The Federal Constitutional Court of West Germany held that it is not unconstitutional to order the deportation of an alien for carrying a gun without a license. The deportation had been ordered on general preventive grounds. The court held that such orders are valid so long as "the principle of proportionality" is observed.

WIRETAPS. In *Malone* v. *Commissioner of the Metropolitan Police* the High Court of England held that it is legal to tap a telephone when authorization has been obtained from the home secretary. The court acknowledged that there seemed to be no limits on the discretion of the home secretary in authorizing wiretaps but suggested that this was a problem that should be addressed by the House of Commons and not the court. It also refused to rule on the possible impact of the European Convention on Human Rights on this matter, stating that the convention imposed a treaty obligation on the state that was not justifiable in the courts.

The Federal Supreme Court of Switzerland held that it was legal to tap the phone of a person in custody on criminal charges. The court pointed out that Swiss criminal law permitted the interception of mail and telegrams to prisoners and said that telephones should be treated as telegrams.

(WILLIAM D. HAWKLAND)

International Law. The two great international law themes in 1979 were war and peace and large-scale multilateral organization. Both had a high political content and seemed to reflect the major structural change in the world community that had been discernible since ex-U.S. president Richard M. Nixon's initiative toward China. The significant feature of many of these events was precisely that they were not allowed to remain merely local affairs of concern only to the participants. The political world forces were merging into organizational structures—some ad hoc, some permanent—through which those forces were being increasingly channeled. Even the concept of international taxation emerged tentatively into print, a concept that necessarily presupposed a higher degree of political structure than had yet been seen in the family of nations.

WAR AND PEACE. Of these events the most important was clearly the signing of the peace treaty between Egypt and Israel in Washington, D.C., on March 26, 1979. This treaty was opposed by many of the Arab states, but, together with the virtual destruction of Lebanon as an independent state, it forced the political dispute centred on Israel and the Arab world away from war and into more complex, and hence more negotiable, channels. A new actor in this drama during 1979 was the Israeli Supreme Court, which, for the first time, ruled in October that the expulsion of Arab landowning villagers from a district of the West Bank to make way for an Israeli settlement was unlawful.

A second event of major importance concerned the invasion of the U.S. embassy in Teheran, Iran, by a group of Iranian students who subsequently took embassy personnel hostage. The U.S. asked the International Court of Justice to take "the quickest possible action" to ensure the release of the hostages. On December 15 the court unanimously ordered the release of all the hostages, but Iran refused, claiming that the court had no jurisdiction. (*See* IRAN.)

At the western end of the Mediterranean a peace agreement was concluded in August between Mauritania and the Polisario guerrillas in the formerly Spanish territory of Rio de Oro (Western Sahara). The subsequent withdrawal of Mauritanian personnel from the southern part of the territory was immediately followed by an assertion of Moroccan sovereignty over that area.

In December Zimbabwe Rhodesia returned temporarily to British rule as Southern Rhodesia with the installation of Lord Soames as governor. The British presence would be maintained until the election of a majority government and implementation of the republican constitution under the terms of the London settlement conference. (*See* ZIMBABWE RHODESIA.)

One consequence of the breakdown of law and order in these and other areas of the world (the Horn of Africa, the Indochinese Peninsula) was the reemergence of a traditional form of international lawlessness. Although air hijacking remained quiet, true piracy at sea became widespread off Lebanon (linked to smuggling) and in the Gulf of Thailand (where pirates in fast motor launches assaulted and robbed the refugees from

WIDE WORLD

U.S. Attorney General Benjamin Civiletti presented the U.S. case for the release of hostages in the U.S. embassy in Teheran to the International Court of Justice at The Hague. The court later ruled unanimously in favour of the U.S., but Iranian authorities ignored the ruling.

Vietnam). On the level of high policy, the SALT II treaty between the U.S. and the U.S.S.R. was signed in Vienna in June. However, the ratification debate in the U.S. Senate was prolonged, and action was further delayed by the successive international crises involving Iran and Afghanistan. (*See* DEFENSE: *Special Report*.)

INTERNATIONAL ORGANIZATION. In matters of more peaceful intercourse the practice of institutionalizing multi-state collaboration grew significantly. The importance of this action lay in the development of habits of organized joint consultation and action.

The Tokyo Round of the General Agreement on Tariffs and Trade talks resulted in April in important agreements on technical barriers to trade and on government procurement. Especially significant were two codes on antidumping and on subsidies and countervailing duties. The package was ratified quickly by the U.S., which passed implementing legislation later in the year.

The institutional future of the European Economic Community (EEC) came under increasing study during the year, particularly as a result of Greece's signing of the Treaty of Accession to the Community in May and the realization that after it became a full member in January 1981 many of the implications of further enlargement of the organization (languages, voting, political agreement, economic rivalry) would have to be faced and more permanent solutions found. Not only did the supreme administrative court of France, the Conseil d'État, refuse in December 1978 to accept the binding nature of rulings of the European Court of Justice (preceded only a short while before by a vicious attack on the court by Michel

Debré in the French Parliament) but also, in October 1979, the French government flatly refused to act upon a judgment of the court that had been specifically directed to it. This was an action brought against France by the European Commission holding that customs restrictions on the import of British lamb were unlawful. Also in the autumn the court delivered judgment in favour of France in the first case brought by one member state against another (by France against the U.K. for breach of the common fisheries policy). Earlier in the year two other judgments were delivered against the U.K., for banning the import of EEC potatoes and for refusing to implement and enforce the requirement for commercial road vehicles to carry and use tachographs. Of worldwide significance, the Lomé II Convention was signed in October to extend the existing arrangement between the EEC and nearly 50 third world countries in Africa, the Caribbean, and the Pacific.

Although the UN Conference on Trade and Development (UNCTAD) meetings in Manila did not produce any important or firm result, they did provide the stimulus to the EEC to adopt a position in favour of the Convention on a Code of Conduct for Liner Conferences (providing for sharing the trade on certain sea routes between the two end ports, with only 20% of the business left available for other traders); promised ratification by the EEC would provide a sufficient proportion of shipping nations to bring the convention into force. UNCTAD's long-running discussions on transfer of technology made noticeable progress, and the draft of an eight-part convention on international multi-modal transport was completed.

TERRITORY. The tendency toward greater organization of states was also to be seen in some of the territorial issues of the year. The Antarctic Treaty powers agreed in October on a draft convention on the exploitation of living resources in Antarctic waters south of the "Antarctic convergence" (the line where the warmer water overlies the near-freezing Antarctic surface water). Currently, this agreement was important only with regard to fishing for krill, the staple diet of the whale, but it could in the future include minerals as well.

The Panama Canal treaties encountered a last-minute obstacle in September when the U.S. House of Representatives unexpectedly defeated a bill to implement the treaties 11 days before they were due to go into effect; however, the disagreement was settled in time for the Canal Zone to be formally transferred to Panamanian sovereignty on October 1 and for control of the canal to pass from the U.S.-owned Panama Canal Co. to a joint U.S.-Panama commission.

A sudden flurry of activity also occurred in regard to outer space. The UN Committee on the Peaceful Uses of Outer Space approved the draft of a treaty proclaiming the Moon and other celestial bodies to be the common heritage of mankind and subject to no exclusive rights, whether economic or political; it even went so far as to envision an international regime to manage development of space resources. The Scientific and Technical Sub-Committee of the same committee concluded that the use of nuclear power resources in outer space posed no danger if certain safeguards were followed, and it called for a second UN conference on exploration and peaceful use of outer space to be held within five years. The Canadian government in January submitted to the U.S.S.R. a claim for compensation for damage caused by the crash-landing of the Soviet Cosmos 954 satellite on Canadian soil in January 1978, a crash that deposited radioactive debris. The claim was made on the basis of general international law and the 1972 UN Convention on International Liability for Damage Caused by Space Objects. Immaterial passage through space was the subject of the World Administrative Radio Conference. (*See* TELEVISION AND RADIO.)

MARITIME AFFAIRS. The year's two sessions of the UN Conference on the Law of the Sea resulted in a revised version of the Informal Composite Negotiating Text on 304 draft articles. However, several important issues still awaited full discussion. A date of August 1980 was set for completion of the work on this vast convention.

In May the final ratifications were deposited of the 1974 Safety of Life at Sea Convention, laying down stringent construction and equipment requirements for oil tankers. It replaced the 1960 convention and was to come into force in May 1980. Other developments within the Intergovernmental Maritime Consultative Organization were the establishment of working groups to prepare draft guidelines on procedures for reporting incidents involving harmful substances and for the collection of casualty data and the preparation of draft guidelines on marine pollution.

The annual acceleration of oil pollution incidents continued. Following the Mexican Ixtoc-1 oil rig blowout in June, damage claims were filed by local fishermen, the Texas government, and the U.S. government. These totaled some $360 million against various companies involved, but a Mexican inquiry concluded that no one was at fault on the rig. A UN Environmental Program meeting of 17 coastal states approved in February a two-year program to fight pollution in the Mediterranean, and a treaty was signed between Greece and Italy on protection of the Ionian Sea from environmental threats. An amendment to the London anti-dumping convention of 1972 was adopted in December 1978 for settlement of disputes relating to the dumping and incineration of toxic wastes at sea, and new control regulations for the latter came into force in March 1979.

Apart from steps toward a declaration that the Indian Ocean should become a "zone of peace," slight adjustments to the world whaling pattern, and changes in the Northwest Atlantic and North Pacific Fisheries conventions, most of the remaining maritime developments related to boundaries. Of these, two concerned the International Court of Justice, which declined jurisdiction in December 1978 in the Aegean Sea continental shelf dispute between Greece and Turkey and that same month received a new continental shelf boundary dispute between Tunisia and Libya.

(NEVILLE MARCH HUNNINGS)

See also Crime and Law Enforcement; Prisons and Penology; United Nations.

SPECIAL REPORT

WOMEN AND THE LAW

by June Sochen

During the 1960s and 1970s, American women experienced significant changes in their adult expectations, education, and experiences. The climate of opinion under Presidents John F. Kennedy and Lyndon B. Johnson encouraged the rights of individuals and minorities to express themselves and to work for their freedom. When the Vietnam war became a national issue in the mid-1960s, the antiwar movement engaged many young women who later transferred their energies to the women's liberation movement. Meanwhile, women professionals, many of whom had worked quietly for women's equality in the 1950s, joined together in 1966 to form the National Organization for Women (NOW).

By the early 1970s, previously unknown words such as *feminism, consciousness raising,* and *male chauvinism* had entered the public's vocabulary. Contemporary rhetoric declared that women had been treated as second-class citizens, defined as wives and mothers, and never given full opportunity to develop their individual potentials. While the '60s witnessed important presidential and congressional initiatives promoting women's equality, the 1970s became the interpretive decade, when the judiciary, including the Supreme Court, analyzed and assessed the meaning and enforcement possibilities of the previous decade's executive actions and legislation.

The Presidential Commission. Early in his administration, President Kennedy accepted the recommendation of Esther Peterson, director of the Women's Bureau of the Department of Labor, to create a President's Commission on the Status of Women. Peterson, a career government worker and the highest-ranking woman in Kennedy's administration, was keenly aware of the fact that, while American women were going to work in increasing numbers, they were largely employed in low-paying jobs. Among the topics to be studied by the commission were differences in the legal treatment of men and women regarding political and civil rights, property rights, and family relations.

President Kennedy appointed Eleanor Roosevelt honorary chairman, while Peterson became executive vice-chairman. Of the 25 members, 14 were women, including Sen. Maurine Neuberger and Rep. Edith Green of Oregon. The commission's report, issued in October 1963 and later published in book form as *American Women,* reviewed American women's educational, occupational, and legal status and concluded that much needed to be done to improve the situation.

The Legislative Foundation. In June 1963 the Equal Pay Act, sponsored by Representative Green, was signed into law. The act, the first major piece of legislation to address the problem of economic equality for women, provided for equal pay for women working for any company that was subject to the Fair Labor Standards Act. The Civil Rights Act of 1964, perhaps the most important legislation affecting American minorities, barred sex discrimination in employment (Title VII) as well as discrimination against anyone on the basis of race, colour, or national origin. The explicit reference to sex discrimination, though introduced by a Southern senator intent on defeating the bill, eventually became women's major legal weapon in the struggle for equal treatment in employment.

While the Civil Rights Act of 1964 became the basis for most subsequent legislation regarding employment opportunities for women and minorities, the two education acts of 1965—the Elementary and

GEORGE W. GARDNER

June Sochen is professor of history at Northeastern Illinois University in Chicago. Her books include Movers and Shakers: American Women Thinkers and Activists, 1900–1970 *and* Herstory: A Woman's View of American History.

Secondary Education Act and the Higher Education Act—provided the foundation for later legislation on eliminating discrimination in schools. In 1972 the Education Amendments Act took a major step in that direction by forbidding sex discrimination against students and employees in federally assisted educational programs.

One sensitive area concerned school athletic programs. Under Title IX, high schools and colleges were required to make self-studies of their institutions and develop appropriate programs by July 1978. The law does not require young men and women to play contact sports together or to have integrated locker rooms, but it does require schools to provide adequate programs, facilities, and equipment for women's athletics and to have coeducational programs where this is reasonable. This legislation continued to cause a great deal of excitement and, as of 1979, its implementation was far from complete. However, the rise of women's tennis and golf, as well as the beginnings of coeducational athletic programs in the nation's elementary and secondary schools, gave promise of doing much to alter traditional views of women.

Though the social consequences of national legislation usually take a while to make themselves felt, in this case, the vigorous, new nondiscriminatory laws coincided with a period of unprecedented growth in the youth population. Consequently, there were more young women than ever before ready to embrace the new possibilities available to them. By 1979 the number of full- and part-time women college students equaled the number of male students for the first time in U.S. history. Women college graduates began attending graduate and professional schools in greater numbers. In 1890 women doctors constituted about 5% of all doctors in the country; in 1970 the figure was 6.7%; in 1979 it was 11.2%—a spectacular increase over a single decade.

In traditionally male fields such as engineering and the natural sciences, women also increased their share, though not as dramatically. While 0.8% of all engineers were women in 1960, they represented 2.7% of the profession in 1977. Only 9.2% of physical scientists were women in 1960, a figure that had risen to 15.6% by 1977. In all professions combined, women went from a 32.8% share in 1960 to 40.5% in 1977. Despite these gains, as of 1976, on average, women with five or more years of college earned slightly less than men with four years of high school.

Judicial Enforcement. The Supreme Court also played an important role in expanding women's rights during the last two decades. In the area of reproductive freedom, the court, in the landmark *Roe* v. *Wade* decision handed down in 1973, declared that a woman has the right to obtain an abortion in the first trimester of pregnancy with no restrictions. Though the abortion issue had long been—and continued to be—extremely controversial, the court later upheld a woman's right, including a minor female's right, to a legal abortion. In a 1971 decision of the California Supreme Court, it was declared that women, even if they were not the wives or daughters of bar owners, could tend bar. This had been one of the last occupations that excluded women, as women.

Two cases challenging affirmative action programs designed to help women and minorities were decided by the Supreme Court. In *The Regents of the University of California* v. *Bakke* (1978), Allan Bakke, a white male, claimed he had been excluded from the university's medical school while less qualified minority applicants were accepted. The court ruled that Bakke should be admitted but that race (and possibly sex) could be a consideration when schools were devising admissions programs. In *United Steelworkers of America, AFL-CIO* v. *Weber et al.* (1979), the court positively upheld Kaiser Aluminum's skilled training program designed primarily for black workers. (*See* LAW.) Both cases have important implications for women desiring to enter special training programs or professional schools. Since women traditionally marry and raise families before completing their education and occupational training, they often seek admittance to schools and jobs at a later age than males. Furthermore, their life experience differs from that of males, a factor also requiring consideration.

The last two decades have not been without their share of failures and frustrations. The Equal Rights Amendment, first proposed in 1923, finally received a favourable hearing in Congress in 1972. Thirty-five states quickly ratified it, but the remaining three state ratifications needed to make it part of the Constitution could not be obtained. In 1978, in an unprecedented action, Congress extended the time allowed for ratification to 1982. While many states have passed equal rights laws, and the laws already noted are working to eliminate sex discrimination, advocates of ERA argue that it would be the first constitutional recognition of sex equality and would require, in one comprehensive move, that all state governments review their laws and eliminate any vestiges of discrimination. While both sexes have shown an increased awareness of and sympathy for women's rights, most women, young and old, continued to experience cultural stereotyping, limited job opportunities, and lack of encouragement in seeking their individual goals. Much work remained to be done.

Lebanon

A republic of the Middle East, Lebanon is bounded by Syria, Israel, and the Mediterranean Sea. Area: 10,230 sq km (3,950 sq mi). Pop. (1979 est.): 3,254,-000. Cap. and largest city: Beirut (metro. pop., 1975 est., 1,172,000). The populations of both Lebanon and its capital city, Beirut, are thought to have declined since the outbreak of civil war in 1974, but reliable figures are not available. Languages: Arabic predominates; Armenian-, Kurdish-, and French-speaking minorities. Religion: available estimates show Christians comprising variously from 40 to 55% of the population and Muslims from 45 to 60%; there is a Druze minority. President in 1979, Elias Sarkis; prime minister, Selim al-Hoss.

Lebanon continued to suffer in 1979 from sporadic violence between rival religious and political groups and from major outbreaks of fighting in the south between Palestinian commandos and the Israeli Army. Refugees from southern Lebanon exacerbated economic and social difficulties in the capital city of Beirut, and the country moved no closer in 1979 toward economic reconstruction or political reconciliation. Syrian troops of the Arab Deterrent Force (ADF) continued their peacekeeping role in most of Lebanon, while the United Nations Interim Force in Lebanon (UNIFIL) attempted with only limited success to separate forces in the south.

The government in January announced plans costing U.S. $7 billion to rebuild the areas destroyed during the 1975–76 civil war, but political uncertainty and lack of security made investment unlikely. Random killing of civilians in January was the first sign that violence would continue in 1979 as it had in 1978. Fighting between Christian Falangist militiamen and Syrian ADF troops erupted on February 14. The ADF shelled the southern suburbs of Beirut, and on February 15 snipers began shooting in the centre of the capital.

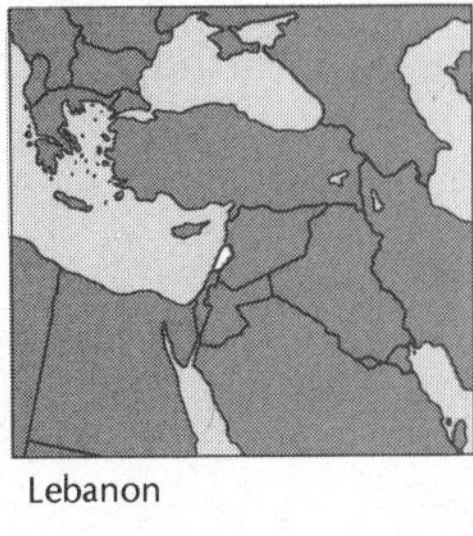

Lebanon

The next day the Falangists (led by Pierre Gemayel) and the National Liberal Party (the other main Christian grouping, led by former president Camille Chamoun) announced a reorganization of their forces to meet the Syrian threat. Despite their past cooperation during the civil war, the Christian leadership remained badly divided in 1979, and relations between their militias were marked by violence and attempted assassinations. Clashes between Falangists and Christian militiamen from the northern town of Zghorta, home of former president Suleiman Franjieh, recurred throughout 1979.

The main threat to Lebanon's security and fragile unity came, however, from the southern portion of the country, where UNIFIL troops were attempting to separate the Palestinian commandos and their Lebanese leftist allies from the Christian rightist forces of former Lebanese Army major Saad Haddad and his Israeli armourers. On April 18, after four months of shelling between the two sides, as well as Israeli attacks against Lebanese villages located north of the UNIFIL buffer line, Haddad declared the 900-sq km (350-sq mi) border area under his control to be the independent state of "Free Lebanon."

The Lebanese government dismissed Haddad's action as illegal partition and issued a warrant for his arrest. On the same day 500 Lebanese Army troops moved into south Lebanon in an attempt to assert central government authority there for the first time since 1976. Haddad's forces prevented them from entering the Christian zone and proceeded to shell UNIFIL headquarters at Naqoura.

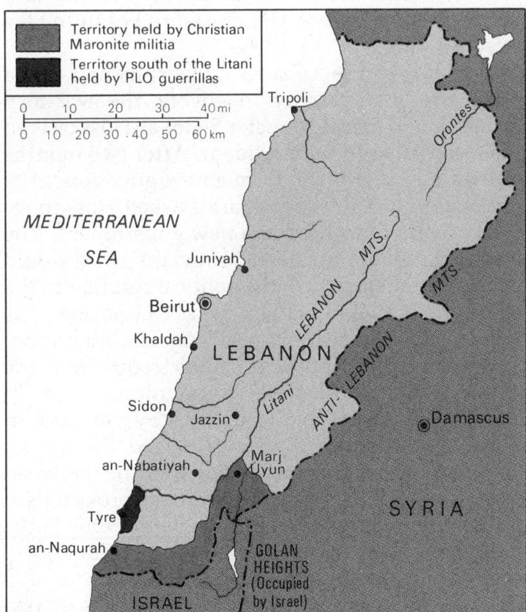

LEBANON

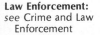

Education. (1972–73) Primary, pupils 497,723; secondary, pupils 167,578; primary and secondary, teachers 32,-901; vocational, pupils 3,898, teachers (1970–71) 508; teacher training, students 3,235, teachers (1971–72) 551; higher, students 50,803, teaching staff 2,313.

Finance. Monetary unit: Lebanese pound, with (Sept. 17, 1979) a free rate of L£3.26 to U.S. $1 (L£7.02 = £1 sterling). Gold and foreign exchange (June 1979) U.S. $2,-051,000,000. Budget (1978 est.): revenue L£1,403 million; expenditure L£2,083 million.

Foreign Trade. (1978) Imports *c.* L£4,640 million; exports *c.* L£1,849 million. Import sources: Italy *c.* 12%; France *c.* 9%; U.S. *c.* 7%; Saudi Arabia *c.* 7%; West Germany *c.* 6%; U.K. *c.* 6%. Export destinations: Saudi Arabia *c.* 41%; Syria *c.* 8%; Jordan *c.* 7%; Kuwait *c.* 6%; United Arab Emirates *c.* 5%. Main exports (1973): machinery 14%; fruit and vegetables 12%; chemicals 8%; aircraft 6%; clothing 6%; textile yarns and fabrics 5%; motor vehicles 5%.

Transport and Communications. Roads (1977) *c.* 7,-100 km. Motor vehicles in use (1977): passenger 229,900; commercial (including buses) 27,100. Railways: (1977) *c.* 425 km; traffic (1974) 2 million passenger-km, freight 42 million net ton-km. Air traffic (1978): 1,397,000,000 passenger-km; freight 514.1 million net ton-km. Shipping (1978): vessels 100 gross tons and over 189; gross tonnage 277,846. Telephones (Jan. 1973) 227,000. Radio receivers (Dec. 1976) 1.6 million. Television receivers (Dec. 1976) 425,000.

Agriculture. Production (in 000; metric tons; 1978): potatoes *c.* 90; wheat (1977) *c.* 30; tomatoes (1977) *c.* 70; grapes *c.* 100; olives *c.* 65; bananas (1977) *c.* 43; oranges *c.* 192; lemons *c.* 82; apples *c.* 80; tobacco *c.* 5. Livestock (in 000; 1977): cattle *c.* 84; goats *c.* 330; sheep *c.* 237; chickens *c.* 7,723.

Industry. Production (in 000; metric tons; 1977): petroleum products *c.* 1,710; cement *c.* 1,360; electricity (kw-hr) *c.* 1,600,000.

Law Enforcement: *see* Crime and Law Enforcement

Lawn Bowls: *see* Bowling

Lawn Tennis: *see* Tennis

WIDE WORLD

Palestinian guerrilla security chief Abu Hassan and several companions were killed when their car was attacked in Beirut in January. The PLO blamed Israel for the deaths.

On April 21 Chamoun announced his support of Haddad's "independence," further weakening the effort of Pres. Elias Sarkis to restore government authority.

On June 19 Israeli forces launched an attack on south Lebanon, and fighting between the Israelis and Palestinian commandos continued for five days until an informal cease-fire was arranged through U.S. mediation. The UN Security Council on January 19 had issued Resolution 444, which called for the installation of UNIFIL troops in the area under the control of Haddad and Israel. The Israelis, however, refused to allow UNIFIL troops into the area, and they continued to hit Palestinian targets and Lebanese villages.

On June 8 Israeli jets bombed the town of Nabatiyah. On June 27, in the most serious escalation of fighting, Israeli and Syrian jets clashed, with at least four planes shot down in the first Israeli-Syrian encounter since 1974. Israeli attacks on south Lebanon were deplored by the U.S. Department of State. UNIFIL commanders complained in July that their force was inadequate to the task before them. Finally a UN cease-fire began to take effect in August.

On May 16 the Lebanese government faced a crisis over its inability to govern the war-torn country, and Prime Minister Selim al-Hoss offered his resignation to the president. After two months of fruitless attempts to form a new government of national unity, President Sarkis asked Hoss to return on July 16 as head of a new government. The new government included politicians, who would ostensibly attempt to find a political solution to the country's problems, rather than "technocrats," as had been the case in the previous administration.

With the withdrawal of Saudi troops from the ADF in March and United Arab Emirate troops in April, the ADF became virtually a Syrian force in Lebanon. Christian leaders criticized the Syrian "occupation" of Lebanon, and fighting between the Lebanese Army and Syrian troops broke out on June 20 in the mountains outside Beirut. One Lebanese soldier was killed and three were wounded. A cease-fire took effect two days later.

(CHARLES GLASS)

Lesotho

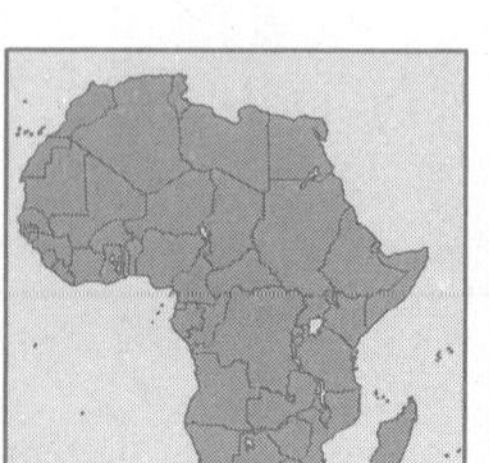

Lesotho

A constitutional monarchy of southern Africa and a member of the Commonwealth of Nations, Lesotho forms an enclave within the republic of South Africa. Area: 30,355 sq km (11,720 sq mi). Pop. (1976): 1,216,800. Cap. and largest city: Maseru (pop., 1976 prelim., 14,700). Language: English and Southern Sotho (official). Religion: Roman Catholic 38.7%; Lesotho Evangelical Church 24.3%; Anglican 10.4%; other Christian 8.4%; non-Christian 18.2%. Chief of state in 1979, King Moshoeshoe II; prime minister, Chief Leabua Jonathan.

Lesotho continued to navigate the difficult course between the economic realities of its relations with South Africa and the political pressures exerted by the Organization of African Unity. At the 20th anniversary of his ruling Basuto National Party (BNP) in April, Chief Leabua Jonathan condemned South African policies and claimed large parts of the Orange Free State. At the same time, over 50% of his country's manpower (some 200,000) continued to work in South Africa.

Internal politics were roiled by the activities of the exiled opposition Basuto Congress Party leader, Ntsu Mokhehle, in Zambia, who had won the

LESOTHO

Education. (1977) Primary, pupils 225,960, teachers (1976) 4,235; secondary, pupils 17,443, teachers (1976) 621; vocational (1976), pupils 835; teacher training (1976), students 378; vocational and teacher training, teachers 851; higher (1976), students 601, teaching staff 95.

Finance and Trade. Monetary unit: maloti, at par with the South African rand, with (Sept. 17, 1979) a free rate of 0.83 malotis to U.S. $1 (1.77 malotis = £1 sterling). Budget (1977–78 est.): revenue R 48,906,000; expenditure R 34,465,000 (excludes development expenditure of R 56.4 million). Foreign trade: imports (1976) R 179.6 million; exports (1977) R 12.2 million. Main exports: wool 21%; mohair 16%; diamonds 10%. Most trade is with South Africa.

Agriculture. Production (in 000; metric tons; 1977): corn *c.* 90; wheat *c.* 55; sorghum *c.* 50; dry peas *c.* 7; wool *c.* 1.3. Livestock (in 000; 1977): cattle *c.* 600; goats *c.* 920; sheep *c.* 1,680.

1970 elections (annulled by Jonathan) and still claimed to be the legitimate leader of Lesotho. Armed incursions and bomb explosions occurred in May, and clashes with police were reported in November. Gerard Ramoreboli, leader of the official opposition, denounced the violence, but it strengthened demands that the ruling BNP declare its support for a one-party state. In July Jonathan announced that Lesotho's paramilitary force would be expanded into a full-scale army.

(MOLLY MORTIMER)

Liberia

A republic on the west coast of Africa, Liberia is bordered by Sierra Leone, Guinea, and Ivory Coast. Area: 97,790 sq km (37,757 sq mi). Pop. (1978 est.): 1,716,900. Cap. and largest city: Monrovia (pop., 1978 est., 229,300). Language: English (official) and tribal dialects. Religion: mainly animist. President in 1979, William R. Tolbert, Jr.

Liberia's normal stability was shaken by riots on April 14, 1979, the worst outbreak of violence in the country's history. The riots were caused by a proposed increase in the price of rice and by inflation, but they also had political overtones. In an effort to reach the target of self-sufficiency in rice projected for 1980 and to encourage the nation's 137,000 small farmers, a rise in price from 12 to 18 cents per pound had been recommended. This was still barely cost price to the farmer.

The ruling True Whig Party claimed that the resulting violence was stirred up by Gabriel Matthews' Progressive Alliance of Liberia (a U.S.-based socialist body). Troops from Guinea were flown in under the January 23 nonaggression and mutual defense treaty, and people were arrested for treason and held under emergency powers declared on April 24. There were more than 40 deaths and 500 injuries, and damage from fire and looting amounted to about $30 million–$40 million. Pres. William Tolbert called the affair a "national tragedy" perpetrated by wicked and evil men aided by foreign powers. He expelled three Soviet officials.

LIBERIA

Education. (1978) Primary, pupils 129,776; secondary, pupils 108,077; primary and secondary, teachers 7,360; vocational, pupils (1975) 851, teachers (1970) 66; teacher training (1975), students 322, teachers 53; higher, students 2,694, teaching staff *c.* 190.

Finance. Monetary unit: Liberian dollar, at par with the U.S. dollar, with a free rate (Sept. 17, 1979) of L$2.15 = £1 sterling. Budget (total; 1978–79 est.) balanced at L$340 million (including development expenditure).

Foreign Trade. Imports (1977) L$463.5 million; exports (1978) L$486.4 million. Import sources: U.S. 26%; West Germany 9%; Japan 9%; The Netherlands 9%; U.K. 7%; Sweden 6%; Spain 5%. Export destinations (1977): West Germany 24%; U.S. 21%; Italy 13%; France 8%; The Netherlands 7%; Belgium-Luxembourg 6%; Spain 6%. Main exports (1977): iron ore 61%; rubber 13%; coffee 10%; timber 7%; diamonds 5%.

Transport and Communications. Roads (1977) 11,218 km. Motor vehicles in use (1977): passenger 15,800; commercial 5,900. Railways (1977) 493 km. Shipping (1978): merchant vessels 100 gross tons and over 2,523 (mostly owned by U.S. and other foreign interests); gross tonnage 80,191,329. Telephones (Jan. 1978) 8,420. Radio receivers (Dec. 1976) 265,000. Television receivers (Dec. 1976) 8,900.

Agriculture. Production (in 000; metric tons; 1978): rice *c.* 264; cassava (1977) *c.* 270; bananas (1977) *c.* 67; palm kernels *c.* 13; palm oil *c.* 25; rubber *c.* 85; cocoa *c.* 3; coffee *c.* 9. Livestock (in 000; 1977): cattle *c.* 36; sheep *c.* 180; goats *c.* 180; pigs *c.* 95.

Industry. Production (in 000; metric tons; 1977): iron ore (metal content) *c.* 11,960; petroleum products *c.* 530; cement *c.* 100; diamonds (metric carats) 326; electricity (kw-hr) *c.* 887,000.

Liberia

In June a general amnesty was declared, a commission of inquiry was set up, and a rice subsidy established instead of the price increase.

Liberia was host to the July summit conference of the Organization of African Unity (OAU) and, in December, to an OAU "mini-summit" on the Western Sahara conflict.

(MOLLY MORTIMER)

Libraries

Important trends in 1979 were: (1) improvement in the training of library users; (2) service to children in the International Year of the Child, for which the International Federation of Library Associa-

FRED R. CONRAD—THE NEW YORK TIMES

The John Fitzgerald Kennedy Library in Boston, designed by I. M. Pei & Partners, was dedicated in ceremonies in October.

LANDESBILDSTELLE BERLIN

An interior view of the Staatsbibliothek Preussischer Kulturbesitz which was opened in West Berlin in December 1978.

tions and Institutions (IFLA) published *Library Service to Children: an International Survey*, by Colin Ray; (3) increased services to ethnic minorities; and (4) further development of information networks. The *Unesco Bulletin for Libraries* (after January superseded by *Unesco Journal of Information Science, Librarianship and Archives Administration*) carried numerous informative articles on these trends. UNESCO's *General Information Programme* stated that the final goal of all libraries was to serve users and published *Guidelines for Developing and Implementing a National Plan for Training in Information Use*, by T. C. Wilson. Also relevant was *User Education in Libraries* (1978), by Nancy Fjällbrant and Malcolm Stevenson.

IFLA held its General Council in Copenhagen in August, at which the theme was library legislation. The president, Preben Kirkegaard, head of the Danish School of Librarianship, retired, and Else Granheim, director for public and school libraries, Norway, was elected in his place. UAP (Universal Availability of Publications) was promoted by the IFLA Office for International Lending under M. B. Line of the British Library, who described recent advances in the March-April 1979 *Unesco Journal of Information Science, Librarianship and Archives Administration*. International lending was an essential backup to Euronet, the European information network, inaugurated in mid-1979. Meanwhile, UNESCO published for ISORID (International Information System on Research in Documentation) two international directories, one of institutions and one of specialists active in research on information, libraries, and archives. WIPO (World Intellectual Property Organization) was working on the standardization of patent documents and on new retrieval methods for patent information.

The seventh Cranfield Conference on mechanized storage and retrieval systems was held in England in July. A bibliography of English-language references to library automation, 1973–77, was published in the December 1978 *Journal of Library Automation*. In Canada Conser (Conservation of Serials) continued to build up its data base for serial titles, using the computer facilities of the Ohio College Library Center; the base involved 15 large libraries, including the Library of Congress, Washington, D.C., and the National Library of Canada, Ottawa.

In France the Centre National de Prêt at the Bibliothèque Nationale became one of five centres for library coordination, while the CNRS (Centre National de Recherche Scientifique), with its more than 16,000 sets of periodicals, was able to satisfy over 300,000 requests for information from throughout France and from other nations. The Bibliothèque de Documentation Internationale Contemporaine at the Nanterre branch of the University of Paris published a catalog of its approximately 4,500 periodicals, including more than 600 in Cyrillic alphabets, and thus established itself as the leading French library on international affairs. A pioneer step in international training was taken in July with the first course for 25 French librarians at the College of Librarianship Wales, Aberystwyth, Wales.

In West Germany the striking building of the Staatsbibliothek Preussischer Kulturbesitz in West Berlin, designed by architect Hans Scharoun, was officially opened in December 1978. It cost more than DM 1 billion. In the U.K. the government's demand for economy dominated all libraries. The British Library's budget was cut by £600,000, while its plans for a new building in London were severely criticized as extravagant.

Nordinfo continued its work for 1977–80 in Scandinavia on policy and coordination, acquisition, data bases, and education of staff and users. It assumed responsibility for Scannet, the inter-Scandinavian data network.

In the U.S. the Association of American Publishers had set up the Copyright Clearance Center, but libraries resisted the demand to register and pay for photocopying. The Council on Library Resources announced a new attempt to coordinate library networks. Service to ethnic minorities expanded in the South for those speaking Spanish, encouraged by the American Library Association's Task Force on Ethnic Materials. In California the public library service was reduced owing to the revolt against paying local property taxes.

The tailoring of reader guidance to readers' needs continued to develop in the U.S.S.R. Cooperative instruction of students in library use and in bibliography was introduced in 11 technical colleges in Novosibirsk. In the third world libraries struggled to develop. For example, there was an attempt in Indonesia to form a network of scientific libraries, but it received no government support. The July-August 1978 *Unesco Bulletin for Libraries* contained summaries of reports by 39 librarians in French-speaking Africa.

Publications during the year included the second edition of *Anglo-American Cataloguing Rules;* the 19th edition of the *Dewey Decimal Classification;* the full Italian edition of the *Universal Decimal Classification* (UDC); and an excellent brief introduction to the UDC by G. Robinson of the British Standards Institution. (ANTHONY THOMPSON)

[441.C.2.d; 613.D.1.a; 735.H]

Libya

A socialist republic on the north coast of Africa, Libya is bounded by the Mediterranean Sea, Egypt, the Sudan, Tunisia, Algeria, Niger, and Chad. Area: 1,749,000 sq km (675,000 sq mi). Pop. (1978 est.): 3,014,100. Cap. and largest city: Tripoli (pop., 1978 est., 800,000). Language: Arabic. Religion: predominantly Muslim. Secretaries-general of the General People's Congress in 1979, Col. Muammar al-Qaddafi and, from March 1, Abdul Ali al-Obeidi.

The December 1978 General People's Congress in Tripoli witnessed the ostensible withdrawal of Col. Muammar al-Qaddafi from national leadership and the inauguration of a system of elected regional people's congresses, each of which would send elected representatives to an annual general congress. Elected officials from regional congresses would represent local interests in all the national government bureaus except those responsible for petroleum, foreign affairs, and heavy industries. By February the elections had been completed. In addition to the people's congresses, revolutionary committees were appointed to serve in key institutions, such as the University of Libya, where Qaddafi considered supervision and strong leadership necessary.

The new system of government notwithstanding, Qaddafi remained the nation's leader. His main exercise in international affairs was an ill-fated expedition by Libyan troops to assist the doomed Idi Amin, president of Uganda, in April. The extent of the casualties was secret. Idi Amin was given refuge for a time in a Tripoli hotel in May. On July 25 it was reported in Chad that a Libyan military force had been encountered there and defeated. Libya maintained its claim to a deep strip of territory south of its border with Chad, a region that probably contained uranium resources. Relations with Egypt remained poor, with closed borders and no air traffic. The participation of Egyptians in Libya's work force continued to decline but remained substantial, probably more than 30,000. Qaddafi was somewhat less strident toward the West and other Arab countries than in the past. Relations with the U.S. were strained when a mob stormed the U.S. embassy on December 2, but Qaddafi later gave assurances that such an episode would not happen again. He also condemned Iran for seizing American hostages in the U.S. embassy in Teheran. At the same time, he attacked the Palestine Liberation Organization and said Libya would stop contributing to it. Palestinians in Libya complained of pressures evidently designed to split them from the PLO.

Oil continued to finance the economy, and price increases by the Organization of Petroleum Exporting Countries (OPEC), together with premiums charged on Libya's high-quality and well-located crude, caused national revenues to rise again without any increase in production. An announcement at the end of June that Libya proposed an oil export ban was taken as a propaganda ploy. Libya needed its oil revenues and

Libyan leader Col. Muammar al-Qaddafi spoke to followers in June during ceremonies commemorating the ninth anniversary of the removal of U.S. bases from Libya.

WIDE WORLD

LIBYA

Education. (1977–78) Primary, pupils 574,770, teachers 26,182; secondary, pupils 194,866, teachers 12,792; vocational, pupils 6,267, teachers 487; teacher training, students 24,153, teachers 1,968; higher, students 17,174, teaching staff 1,922.

Finance. Monetary unit: Libyan dinar, with (Sept. 17, 1979) a par value of 0.296 dinar to U.S. $1 (free rate of 0.637 dinar = £1 sterling). Gold, SDR's, and foreign exchange (June 1979) U.S. $3,868,000,000. Budget (total; 1975 actual): revenue 1,997,575,000 dinars (including petroleum revenue of 1,283,995,000 dinars); expenditure 2,323,530,000 dinars (including development expenditure of 841,843,000 dinars). Gross national product (1977) 5,182,000,000 dinars. Money supply (March 1978) 1,718,000,000 dinars. Cost of living (Tripoli; 1975 = 100; June 1978) 141.5.

Foreign Trade. (1978) Imports (fob) *c.* 1,653,000,000 dinars; exports 2,813,300,000 dinars. Import sources (1977): Italy 27%; West Germany 13%; France 8%; Japan 7%; U.K. 6%; U.S. 5%; Greece 5%. Export destinations (1977): U.S. 40%; West Germany 17%; Italy 17%; Spain 5%. Main export: crude oil 100%.

Transport and Communications. Roads (including tracks; 1976) *c.* 20,000 km (including 8,700 km surfaced). Motor vehicles in use (1977): passenger 386,000; commercial (including buses) 181,600. Air traffic (1977): 815 million passenger-km; freight 7.5 million net ton-km. Shipping (1978): vessels 100 gross tons and over 75; gross tonnage 885,362. Shipping traffic: goods loaded (1977) 92,892,000 metric tons, unloaded (1975) 9,619,000 metric tons. Telephones (Dec. 1974) 102,000. Radio licenses (Dec. 1976) 110,000. Television licenses (Dec. 1975) 10,000.

Agriculture. Production (in 000; metric tons; 1978): barley *c.* 200; wheat (1977) *c.* 70; potatoes (1977) *c.* 80; watermelons (1977) *c.* 110; tomatoes *c.* 220; onions *c.* 57; oranges *c.* 32; olives *c.* 165; dates *c.* 85. Livestock (in 000; 1977): sheep *c.* 3,000; goats *c.* 1,250; cattle *c.* 152; camels *c.* 60; asses *c.* 73.

Industry. Production (in 000; metric tons; 1977): petroleum products *c.* 4,990; crude oil (1978) 120,700; electricity (Tripolitania; excluding most industrial production; kw-hr) *c.* 1,500,000.

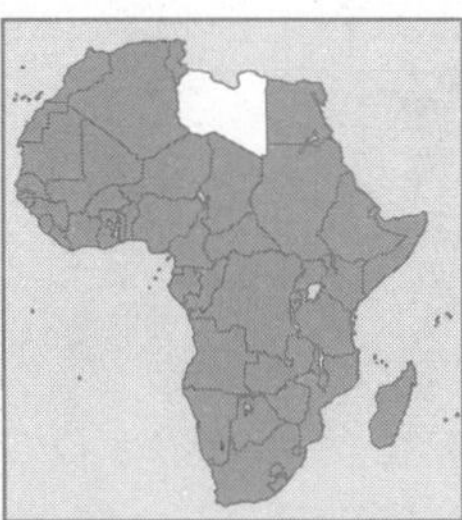

Libya

could no longer manipulate the world markets as it did in 1970–71. Emphasis in internal investment was being given to agriculture and industry. In June international consultants were asked to examine the condition of agriculture in the densely farmed coastal strip close to the capital, where water resources had been irreversibly depleted.

(J. A. ALLAN)

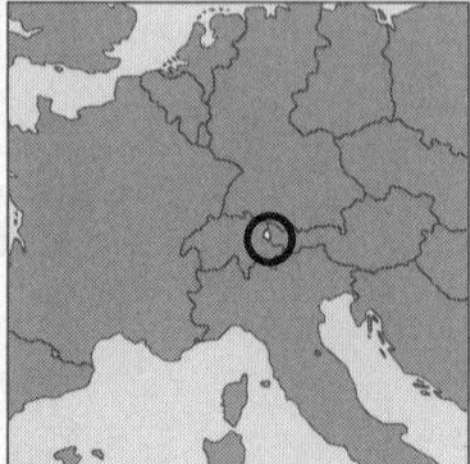
Liechtenstein

Liechtenstein

A constitutional monarchy between Switzerland and Austria, Liechtenstein is united with Switzerland by a customs and monetary union. Area: 160 sq km (62 sq mi). Pop. (1978 est.): 24,700. Cap. and largest city: Vaduz (pop., 1976 est., 4,620). Language: German. Religion (1976): Roman Catholic 84%. Sovereign prince, Francis Joseph II; chief of government in 1979, Hans Brunhart.

Liechtenstein was shaken during 1979 by the so-called Chiasso affair. It was discovered that the Chiasso branch of the Crédit Suisse had been issuing guarantees unknown to and unauthorized by the bank's headquarters in Zürich, Switz. Most of the guarantees had gone to finance investments by a Liechtenstein company, the ownership of which was obscure. The Crédit Suisse was forced to write off some U.S. $400 million, and Switzerland urged Liechtenstein to put its house in order. The principality could not afford to ignore this request in view of the 1923 customs treaty that aligned its import and export regulations with those of Switzerland. Liechtenstein officials said much of the money never actually went to the principality but had been credited to bank accounts elsewhere—in Switzerland, The Bahamas, Panama, or the Cayman Islands—where bank accounts were secret and few questions were asked.

Prince Francis Joseph II and Princess Gina were among the royal mourners who attended the funeral service of Lord Mountbatten at Westminster Abbey, London, on September 5.

(K. M. SMOGORZEWSKI)

LIECHTENSTEIN

Education. (1979–80) Primary, pupils 2,008, teachers 91; secondary, pupils 1,720, teachers 93.

Finance and Trade. Monetary unit: Swiss franc, with (Sept. 17, 1979) a free rate of SFr 1.63 to U.S. $1 (SFr 3.51 = £1 sterling). Budget (1978 est.): revenue SFr 199,-976,000; expenditure SFr 195,575,000. Exports (1977) SFr 668.9 million. Export destinations: Switzerland 37%; EEC 29%; EFTA (other than Switzerland) 8%. Main exports: metal manufactures, chemicals, furniture, pottery. Tourism (1977) 80,425 visitors.

Life Insurance:
see Industrial Review

Life Sciences

Research into the origins of life on Earth made some exciting, if not definitive, advances during the year. Representative was a report in September by an international group of scientists, headed by Cyril Ponnamperuma of the University of Maryland, of what it believed to be the oldest evidence of life yet found: organic molecules extracted from Greenland rocks dated at 3,830,000,000 years. When analyzed for carbon isotope content, a certain fraction of the chemicals—which were hydrocarbons, including compounds resembling benzene and napthalene—showed a ratio of carbon-12 to carbon-13 that suggested a living origin. Unlike simple chemical reactions, biological processes favour incorporation of carbon-12 over the heavier isotope in organic molecules. Although far from certain, Ponnamperuma's conclusions offered to add another 400 million years to a record that many scientists held to have been established by the discovery in 1977 of microfossils resembling cells of blue-green algae (cyanobacteria) in sediments from southern Africa dated at 3,400,000,000 years.

The uncertainty in these findings exemplified the ambiguous nature of much of recent research into primitive evolution. Investigators in the field worked immersed in lively debate concerning the specific sequence and timing of events that spawned life and even the kind of evidence that should be accepted as biological in origin. In contrast with the work described above, H. D. Pflug of the Justus Liebig University in West Germany and H. Jaeschke-Boyer of the Laboratoire d'Application Jobin Yvon in France reported in August their discovery of about 100 complete cell-like bodies preserved in Greenland rocks dated at an age comparable to those studied by Ponnamperuma's group. Microscopic examination and microanalytical results convinced the two investigators that the bodies are the remains of an organism—perhaps a yeast, but probably a more primitive cell because "the time span of roughly half a billion years [between the age of the bodies and the time that conditions on Earth first became favourable to life] appears too short for the evolution from a simple organic compound to a eukaryotic organism to have occurred." As the search for life's beginnings continued, there seemed little doubt that both studies would come under fire from investigators with differing interpretations of the evidence.

(CHARLES M. CEGIELSKI)

[312.A.1–4]

ZOOLOGY

During 1979 a pair of interesting reports appeared regarding the physiology and behaviour of fossil animals. In one, P. A. Johnston of the University of Alberta described his study of the growth rings in dinosaur teeth to obtain further information on the possibility that dinosaurs were warm-blooded (endothermic) rather than cold-blooded (ectothermic). In recent years the possibility that dinosaurs were warm-blooded had been advanced by some experts. In general, growth rings have been found to a greater degree in the skeletal tissues of ectotherms than in endotherms, because ectotherms are more sensitive to the effects of seasonal feeding variations. Thus, if dinosaurs were warm-blooded, growth rings should not be found, as had been the case. Johnston, however, found growth rings in the teeth of various Late Cretaceous Albertan dinosaurs, which lived about 70 million years ago. He interpreted his results as indicating that the dinosaurs he studied were cold-blooded, as are living reptiles. Indeed, growth rings have been found in endotherms living under climatic extremes, but climatic conditions of the Late Cretaceous were rather uniform in Alberta. Although Johnston's results supported the traditional view that dinosaurs were cold-blooded, controversy about possible endothermy was expected to continue.

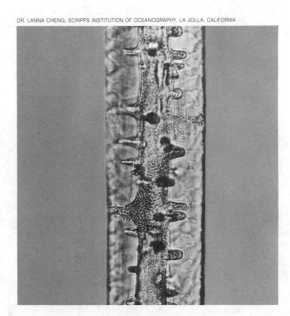

A second study of fossils dealt with the feathers of the first known bird, *Archaeopteryx*. Recently it had been suggested that this bird was strictly terrestrial and unable to fly, with its feathers possibly being used as insect traps. Alan Feduccia of the University of North Carolina and H. B. Tordoff of the University of Minnesota, who studied the fossilized wing feathers of this bird, found that the vanes conform to the asymmetric pattern present in those of flying birds. A typical feather has a tapered central support called a rachis; it separates the interlocking barbs on each side into two sheets known as vanes. In general, the typical body feathers of birds are symmetric, whereas the primary wing feathers of flying birds show asymmetry, with the rachis lying toward the leading edge. On the other hand, the wing feathers of flightless birds are symmetric. The investigators drew attention to the highly asymmetric wing feathers of *Archaeopteryx*, supporting the traditional concept that it could glide and perhaps fly.

Another group of investigations concerned aspects of animal reproduction. J. K. Waage of Brown University, Providence, R.I., found that the male damselfly (*Calopteryx maculata*) uses its penis to remove sperm deposited in the female's sperm storage organs from previous matings, in addition to the usual function of transferring its own sperm. This report was apparently the first in which sperm removal has been attributed to the male of any animal. Waage first observed that, prior to mating, females carry large amounts of sperm derived from previous matings. He then noted that during mating the male engages in undulatory movements that result in the removal of about 90% of the stored sperm from the female. These movements are followed by the transfer of his own sperm. Waage also observed horns on the head of the penis that function in sperm removal, as well as other characteristics. These results may shed light on the established fact that insect eggs are usually fertilized by stored sperm from the most recent previous mating, although some mixing naturally occurs.

Another finding showed an association between declining pesticide residues and increased success of osprey reproduction. P. R. Spitzer of Cornell University, Ithaca, N.Y., and his co-workers studied the breeding of ospreys (*Pandion haliateus*) in Connecticut and eastern Long Island. Previous studies had shown that osprey numbers declined during the late 1950s and throughout the next decade. This decline was caused mainly by failure of eggs to hatch and was associated with abnormally thin shells. It was also established that pesticides cause such eggshell thinning. Spitzer's group collected unhatched eggs from representative nests between 1969 and 1976 and determined the extent of their contamination with insecticide and mercury residues. The average concentration in the eggs of the pesticide residue DDE declined fivefold between 1969 and 1976 and approximately threefold since 1973, following the decline in DDT use in the 1960s and its virtual cessation in North America since 1972. Average eggshell thickness increased from 412 μm (micrometres) in 1970 to 446 μm in 1976, although this increase was not statistically significant. They also found a marked increase in the number of eggs hatching, as well as a decline in the pesticide residues in these eggs. Thus, it was concluded that the osprey comeback was caused by the termination of DDT use.

A third reproductive study, conducted by P. D. Moehlman of the University of Wisconsin, concentrated on the role of helpers in the rearing of blackbacked jackals (*Canis mesomelas*). Helpers are defined as offspring that aid in the feeding and guarding of subsequent litters. With monogamous parents, helpers are necessarily full siblings to the pups. Moehlman found that families with helpers had a significantly higher survivorship of offspring than those without helpers. Eleven out of 15 litters that she observed had nonparent adult help-

DR. LANNA CHENG, SCRIPPS INSTITUTION OF OCEANOGRAPHY, LA JOLLA, CALIFORNIA

Zoologists at the San Diego Zoo noticed that their polar bears' fur had a decidedly green tint; microscopic examination revealed that algae were living not on the surface of the hairs but inside them, in the hollow medulla, at the centre of the hair shaft.

COURTESY OF PAUL A. JOHNSTON, DEPT. OF GEOLOGY, UNIVERSITY OF ALBERTA

Whether the presence of growth rings in dinosaur teeth indicate that the creatures were cold-blooded rather than warm-blooded was a subject of controversy among scientists. The dinosaur tooth pictured is about 73 million years old and was found in Alberta.

Moroccans spread poison bait in an effort to reduce the number of huge swarms of locusts. Locusts continued to be a severe agricultural problem in Africa and parts of the Middle East, and unsettled political conditions in these areas often hampered efforts to control the insects.

ers. In general, older parents had more helpers than younger parents, because they had more older offspring available to serve. She determined that food supply (grass rats) was adequate and that helpers provided food either directly or by regurgitation to the pups. She calculated that a helper gained more by being a helper (yield one pup per adult) than it would have by raising pups with its own mate (yield one-half pup per adult). In addition, helpers probably benefit themselves by increasing their experience on the home territory, by long-term reproductive success, and by acquisition of a piece of the home territory. Parents also benefit from the presence of helpers, owing to increased pup survival and in other ways. Moehlman felt that, although it is in the parents' best interest to retain helpers, the benefits to be accrued from them are potentially limited by the availability of food resources.

During 1979 new information became available about the sex attractant of dogs. M. Goodwin and co-workers at Purdue University, West Lafayette, Ind., found that the chemical substance methyl-*p*-hydroxybenzoate is present in the vaginal secretions of female dogs in heat (estrus), but not when they are unreceptive. When this chemical was rubbed on the vulvas of unreceptive females, male dogs attempted to mate with them and persisted despite resistance of the females with barks and snaps. The investigators pointed out that vaginal secretions are extremely complex chemically and that the compound they studied, in fact, might not be the sex attractant; however, related chemicals proved only partially effective.

Of two significant discoveries dealing with animal movements, the first was reported by P. H.-S. Jen and J. K. McCarty of the University of Missouri, who compared the ability of bats to avoid moving and stationary objects. Frames containing six wires were placed in the centre of a room and either were kept stationary or were moved by an oscillator. Little brown bats (*Myotis lucifugus*) were then made to fly across the room, and the percentage of successful avoidance of the wires was recorded. A hit was tallied if the body or arm of a bat collided with the wires. Unexpectedly, the bats were found to be significantly better at avoiding moving wires than stationary ones. As a control, artificial "model bats" were thrown at the frames to establish that the simple motions of unguided objects could not account for the difference in the bats' performance with stationary and moving wires. When confronted with a moving barrier, the bats were seen to hesitate at the side of the room before flying across it; however, they negotiated the stationary barrier almost immediately. The investigators theorized that greater success in flying across the moving obstacle was due to the fact that insectivorous bats normally rely on moving prey and thus would be expected to concentrate more intently on a moving object.

In another investigation, S. A. Wainwright and co-workers at Duke University, Durham, N.C., found that the internal pressure of lemon sharks (*Negaprion brevirostris*) increases more than tenfold in the transition from slow to fast swimming and that this increase is accompanied by a stiffening of the skin. Because the shark's muscles are attached to the skin as securely as they are attached to the vertebral column, the skin can act as an "external tendon," transmitting muscular force and displacement to the tail. This view, which contrasts with the usual concept of the skin as a relatively inert body covering, means that the shark's skin should be regarded as an exoskeleton, comparable to the cuticles of nematodes and caterpillars. This group also showed that the elastic recoil of shark skin provides energy for subsequent swimming movements. Energy is stored in the stretched skin on the convex side of a fast-swimming shark and then is released to accelerate the unbending of the fish that results from muscular contraction on the convex side, thereby increasing the power output at the start of a fast swimming stroke.

(RONALD R. NOVALES)

[242.B.2.b.xiii and xiv; 333.B.1.b.v; 342.A.6; 342.C.3.a]

Entomology. The desert locust (*Schistocerca gregaria*) has threatened the crops of northern Africa, the Near East, and the Indian subcontinent throughout recorded history. Even with modern technological resources, control of the insect depends on constant international surveillance and cooperation, especially at the ultimate source of the plagues, an area bordering the Red Sea and Gulf of Aden. When unusually good spring rains provide a favourable flush of plant growth, more than the usual number of young hoppers survive, and these, crowding together, cause in each other a physiological transformation into the gregarious form of the insect—the true locust. As adults, they have the capacity to fly for hundreds of kilometres in coherent, migrating swarms. The migrants may breed and their progeny continue to devastate new environments, but populations do not persist indefinitely outside the ancestral breeding grounds.

Unfortunately, however, these regions are not always accessible to locust control workers, and the birth of a new plague in Ethiopia in late 1977 coincided with human warfare that prevented early warning and control. As a result, swarms invaded Sudan, Somalia, Saudi Arabia, Iran, Pakistan, and India in 1978 and 1979, and some outfliers were seen in Mauritania, Mali, and Niger. In most areas, swarms were treated successfully, but it was strongly suspected that breeding had continued in Ethiopia and southern Iran, and the UN Food and Agricultural Organization reported that a resurgence of the plague was still a possibility.

Chemicals remained man's principal weapon against insects, but the World Health Organization warned of the dangers of pesticide misuse, especially in the third world. An estimated 500,000 people a year were killed or incapacitated by pesticides, mostly farmers in less developed countries who knew little of safety regulations and who continued to mix pesticides with bare hands.

Meanwhile, the UN Environment Program (UNEP) reported that more than 200 insect species had become resistant to nine major groups of pesticides, including such important agricultural pests as the cotton bollworm, boll weevil, rice stem borer, brown plant hopper, Colorado potato beetle, spider mites of fruit and greenhouse crops, cutworms, and weevils of cereals. Perhaps the most worrying of all were the more than 100 insecticide-resistant vectors of disease, including mosquitoes, houseflies, black flies, and fleas. Already, massive resurgence of malaria had occurred in some countries. Where resistance had developed, it had probably resulted from regular exposure of a major portion of a pest's breeding population to the pesticide. Simply switching to a new pesticide thus provided only short-term solutions. During the year UNEP urged worldwide research into new techniques that integrated several different approaches to insect control. Judicious and restricted use of chemicals might be combined with, for example, environmental control of breeding habitats, biological control, behavioural control with pheromones, and efforts to breed resistance to pests into crops and animals.

Honeybees excel at finding things by means of their ability to memorize and interpret the "dance message" of scout bees. On return from reconnoitering for food, the scout waggles her abdomen while proceeding in a straight line along a vertical surface in the hive, then circles back to begin again. The orientation of the line with the vertical corresponds with the horizontal direction of the food source in relation to the Sun, and the length of the line indicates the distance from the hive. Recently W. G. Wellington and D. Cmiralova of the University of British Columbia discovered that scouts must somehow signal the height of the source, too. When several sources were placed on a vertical ladder, experiments with marked bees showed that a scout directed foragers to the source she herself had found, not to others. The researchers argued that any animal species that engages in finding food or a nest above ground must be able to gauge height, presumably through sensitivity to pressure. Some flies detect pressure with their antennae, which in both flies and bees are also sensitive to sound. Scout bees "buzz" while dancing, and Wellington and Cmiralova suggested that the rhythm accompaniment provided the additional information about height.

Some reported sightings of unidentified flying objects (UFO's) were probably clouds of insects, according to Philip Callahan and R. W. Mankin of the U.S. Department of Agriculture. Moths can provide a source of electrons in certain electric

Japanese beetles will refuse to eat plants treated with extract from the seed of the East Indian neem tree. When the extract was painted on the soybean leaf below to spell out the letters "NM," the beetles ate all around the treated area.

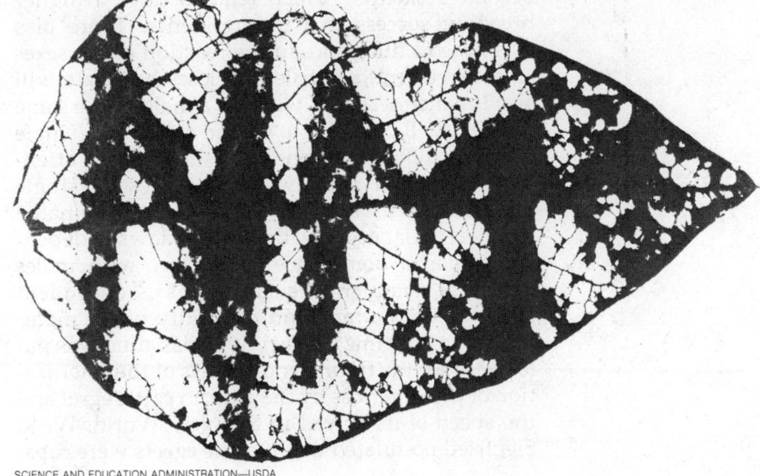

SCIENCE AND EDUCATION ADMINISTRATION—USDA

fields—including some climatic conditions—that excite atmospheric gases to emit visible light. Although the light generated by a single insect would be barely visible, a swarm of the spruce budworm moth, for example, could be as much as 100 × 25 km (60 × 15 mi) in extent and emit enough light to be seen far away. Callahan and Mankin suggested that UFO records might, if nothing else, provide data on insect migrations.

(PETER W. MILES)

[313.H.5.d and n; 321.E.2.a]

Ornithology. As of 1979 four species of birds were known to bait fish deliberately. The green heron of North America was observed to use bread or other food, which had been thrown to fish by humans, to lure those fish within range of its beak. When the fishing was bad at a particular point on the bank of a freshwater or tidal pool, the heron picked up the bait in its bill and walked some way with it before replacing it on the water surface. One bird even used a feather—a "fly"—for this purpose. In Africa the ecological counterpart of the North American green heron, the green-backed heron, was seen behaving in exactly the same way by the river at Hunter's Lodge in Kenya, where a pied kingfisher also baited fish by swooping to take bread from the water surface and then dropping pieces from a perch overhanging the water. In captivity, a sun bittern was watched placing grubs that had been put out by humans for passerine birds, with whom it shares its aviary, in a small artificial pond and then grabbing the swordtails thus attracted.

Another example of sophisticated object use concerns a common crow in California that was observed to use automobiles as nutcrackers. The bird drops palm fruits (*Washingtonia* species) onto a busy road and waits for passing cars to break them open, whereupon the bird swoops down to pick up suitable fragments. Crows in the Shetland Islands off Scotland were reported to drop large seashells on roads to be cracked by passing trucks.

Jackdaws are social birds, but A. Roell observed two degrees of sociality. Resident birds defend their nest sites throughout the year and spend more time in the vicinity of the colony. Nonresidents defend their nest sites only during the breeding season. These categories are not static, but apparently only adult and mated individuals may become residents, which tend to have a higher breeding success than nonresidents. There also was noted a difference in the reaction of the sexes to bereavement: a female that loses her mate will also lose her nest site, whereas a male in the same position will continue to defend the site. A single male has difficulty defending a site from the attentions of paired jackdaws, but successful single males seem to be very attractive to unmated females. Social organization of jackdaws is dependent upon a dominance hierarchy, with males generally dominant. Female status is dependent partly upon the rank and proximity of the mate.

For the first time a plausible explanation was put forward for the timing and success of the colonization of the Americas by the African cattle egret and the speed of its spread in the New World. W. R. Siegfried postulated that if cattle egrets were capable of crossing the Atlantic Ocean unaided by man, then it is reasonable to suppose that many such flights must have been made over the centuries. But not until the turn of this century did the species establish a bridgehead and then fan out. Prior to colonization by Europeans the Americas did not offer a habitat suitable for cattle egrets. In particular, unlike Africa with its water buffalo, there were no large grazing ungulate residents of floodplains and other wetland areas. It was man's artificial creation of short-grass meadow on moist substrate that proved a crucial factor in facilitating the cattle egret's recent establishment on the western side of the Atlantic.

Timothy C. Williams and Janet Williams of Swarthmore (Pa.) College analyzed the migration of songbirds and small shorebirds that takes place each fall from the east coast of North America to the Caribbean and South America. The birds' crossing of the ocean, for example, from Halifax, Nova Scotia, to Antigua in the West Indies, about 2,800 km (1,700 mi), is 47% shorter than a route via Florida. Moreover, these blackpoll warblers, white-rumped sandpipers, and others take advantage of both northwest offshore winds and the northeast trades as tail winds; another advantage is that the route is presumably without predators. The trip, however, does require a degree of exertion not matched by any other vertebrate animal. The flight to Antigua takes 64 hours. For a man the metabolic equivalent would be to run four-minute miles for 80 hours.

A species of bird new to science was found in highland Ethiopia by John S. Ash. It was named the Ankober serin and is a species of streaked seedeater. On the average, only one or two new kinds of bird are discovered each year.

(JEFFERY BOSWALL)

[313.J.6; 342.B.1.b.vi; 352.A.5.a]

MARINE BIOLOGY

With the increased need to provide baseline data on coastal environments, from which could be assessed changes attributable to pollution, the dynamics of shore communities were being more fully evaluated. Rocky shore communities exhibit a mosaic distribution of their component organisms, and the format of the mosaic changes cyclically over a period of years. Overall composition of communities also changes, as was observed after the grounded tanker "Torrey Canyon" spilled several tens of thousands of tons of oil off Cornwall, England, in 1967. Massive deaths of plants and animals were followed by cycles of abundance of a few interacting species, and return to the normal mosaic of a wide variety of species took as long as eight to ten years.

Work in the English Channel threw doubt on the classic theory that the spring phytoplankton outburst ceases when such simple inorganic nutrients as nitrates are exhausted. Instead, other species of phytoplankton that directly utilize organic nitrogen compounds come to dominate after those that use nitrate decline in numbers. Thus there need not be a drop in total productivity.

Ctenophores, commonly known as comb jellies, are among the most delicate of plankton animals;

their fragility and solubility in the preservative solution formalin cause them to be grossly under-represented in plankton samples and, hence, in schemes of marine ecosystems. From the U.S. submersible "Alvin," deep-living ctenophores were observed directly to be much more abundant and diverse than their surface-living relatives, and several species were new to science.

Statoliths, the grains of calcium-based mineral in the statocysts that function as organs of orientation in squids and cuttlefish, are important in studies of fossil cephalopods that lack shells. New studies, which described the structures in detail for the first time, suggested that they also would become important in the identification of living species, in food analyses of cephalopod predators, and in the study of deep-sea deposits.

The deep sea is probably the most physically constant of all marine environments, lacking changes in light and temperature; in such surroundings it had been supposed that seasonality of breeding would not occur. Many fish inhabiting the continental slope in temperate latitudes, however, were found to have a seasonal reproductive cycle that is probably cued by seasonal changes in food supply deriving from organisms in the upper layers of the sea.

Pogonophora, or beardworms, are poorly studied bottom-living invertebrates that are unusual in possessing no internal digestive system. Investigation of the pogonophoran *Siboglinum fiordicum* showed that it accumulates amino acids and glucose across the body wall; however, uptake from measured concentrations of these food substances in the environment would be insufficient to support the life of that species. It was hypothesized that the immediate vicinity of the animals must have higher concentrations of dissolved organic matter, possibly deriving from associated microorganisms, anaerobic animals, or both.

The scales of fish exhibit growth rings, and "scale reading" is perhaps the most powerful tool available to the biologist in estimating the rate of fish growth. New work refined this technique by measuring the rate at which a radioactively labeled amino acid, glycine, is incorporated into fish scales to give an "instantaneous growth rate" of the fish at the time of sampling. Though there were early reports of sounds being emitted by fish, only recently had sophisticated underwater listening apparatus become generally available. Work with this equipment indicated that a variety of fish make sounds and that the cod family (Gadidae) includes a number of particularly vocal forms. Calls are divisible into brief pulses of low-frequency sound repeated at different rates and in different groupings. Sounds are emitted particularly during brief aggressive encounters, and they occur most commonly in large species, which are less susceptible to predators that have good low-frequency hearing, such as seals and dolphins.

(ERNEST NAYLOR)

[313.G.2.d; 313.I.1.d; 333.B.1.b.iv; 354.B.2 and 4]

BOTANY

Two of the characteristic features of plant cells, chloroplasts and vacuoles, were among the focal points of recent research in plant biology. The chloroplasts, of course, are of ultimate importance to life today because it is within these structures that occur the processes of photosynthesis, whereby solar energy is captured and transformed into forms that cells can use. In contrast to earlier ideas that chlorophyll, the crucial light-absorbing pigment, was simply embedded in the lipid matrix of the chloroplast membranes, it has become clear that chlorophyll-protein complexes are important in the functional organization of these membranes. Indeed, with improved analytical techniques, it was demonstrated that no free chlorophyll is present in membranes but that all is complexed with proteins. Four major chlorophyll-protein complexes were obtained, and it appeared that a clearer picture of the molecular architecture of photosynthetic membranes was emerging.

Relationships between the partially autonomous chloroplasts, which contain their own genetic material, and the cells within which they function also attracted attention. One of the proteins associated with chlorophyll to form a light-harvesting complex is coded for by genes of the plant cell nucleus and synthesized on cytoplasmic ribosomes outside the chloroplast. Upon illumination of leaves of plants grown in the dark, there is an increase in synthesis of chlorophyll and in the amount of chlorophyll/protein complex inserted in the membranes. In addition, as recent work with barley leaves demonstrated, illumination of the leaves results in the appearance in the cell of the messenger RNA (mRNA) carrying the code for the protein component of the light-harvesting complex. Thus, both the amount of chlorophyll and the amount of protein are regulated by light. There appeared to be distinct mechanisms of control. However, it was also shown that in a mutant lacking one of the basic types of chlorophyll molecules, chlorophyll b, and in which the complex is missing from the membranes, the same mRNA species appeared following illumination of the leaves.

Another protein unique to chloroplasts is ribulose-1,5-biphosphate (RuP_2) carboxylase, the enzyme responsible for fixing carbon from atmospheric carbon dioxide. Two separate types of subunits, a large one coded for by chloroplast genes and a small one coded for by nuclear genes, associate to form the functional protein in the chloroplast. As was the case for the chlorophyll-complexing protein above, illumination of dark-grown *Lemna* plants caused an increase in the amount of mRNA coding for the small subunit of RuP_2 carboxylase. Furthermore, in both cases the protein subunit coded for was shown to be considerably longer than the final functional unit within the chloroplast. Other experiments showed that this longer precursor molecule, when mixed with chloroplasts, was transported inside the chloroplast, trimmed to its final size, and associated with the large subunits already present.

Another prominent feature of plant cells is the vacuole, a membrane-enclosed compartment containing many kinds of molecules in solution and occasionally crystalline deposits. The development of procedures for isolating vacuoles led to recent investigations on the metabolic activity of vac-

FRANK HANES—THE CHICAGO TRIBUNE

A new weapon being tested in the fight against Dutch elm disease is the intravenous feeding of a chemical into the vascular system of the trees to ward off the disease. The experiment was being conducted at Chicago's Grant Park.

uoles, which also contain various hydrolytic enzymes. (A hydrolytic enzyme effects chemical breakdown of a molecule by splitting bonds and "patching" the severed ends with the elements of a water molecule.) During germination of castor-bean seedlings, a protein called the crystalloid storage protein becomes enclosed by the vacuolar membrane, or tonoplast, and eventually the protein disappears. Recent analyses of the protein composition in isolated vacuoles showed that enzymatic hydrolysis of the crystalloid protein does occur within the vacuoles and continues following isolation. These results provided evidence for a role for these structures in protein breakdown, confirming earlier suggestions that the plant cell vacuole can function in the same way as the packets of enzymes, called lysosomes, that are found in animal cells.

Vacuoles also contain much of the sucrose found in plant cells, and an active role for the vacuolar membrane in the accumulation of sucrose in the sugar-storing cells of red beets was demonstrated in 1979. Isolated vacuoles from this tissue were able to accumulate sucrose against a concentration gradient, and the rate of the uptake was stimulated by ATP, the "energy currency" of cells. Activity of ATP-ase, the enzyme that allows the energy stored in ATP to be made available, was also shown to be associated with the vacuoles, and the results also suggested the possibility that the enzyme was located on the inner surface of the tonoplast.

(PETER L. WEBSTER)

[322.A; 323.A; 331.A.2.c]

MOLECULAR BIOLOGY

Diphtheria, Cholera, and Seed Poisons. Pressing problems are usually first solved by trial and error methods; these give some control, but without understanding. True understanding of the problem and of its workable solutions usually comes much later when there is opportunity for careful experimentation. Thus mankind learned to smelt, alloy, and work metals centuries before anything was known about the role of crystal structure in determining hardness and ductility. Similarly, procedures for making leather were perfected long before anyone understood the protein chemistry of tanning.

Diphtheria and cholera have ravaged mankind for millennia. Diphtheria was a major cause of death among small children until the beginning of the 20th century, and severe outbreaks of cholera still occur periodically. The central European curse "May cholera take you" evokes some appreciation of the universal fear of this affliction. Discovery of a few of the basic properties of these diseases in the 19th century allowed them to be brought under control. Thus, in 1854 English physician John Snow traced a London outbreak of cholera to the water from a fouled well, and in 1883 the pioneer bacteriologist Robert Koch identified the responsible microbe, *Vibrio cholerae*. Simple improvements in personal hygiene and in sewage disposal then eliminated this disease from most of the world.

Diphtheria was traced to *Corynebacterium diphtheriae*. Culture of this organism in artificial medium led to the discovery that it secreted a soluble toxin that actually caused the symptoms of the disease. Injected into horses, this toxin induced the production of a circulating antitoxin, which was first used in treating a sick child on Christmas Eve in 1891. Thirty-two years later it was found that the toxin itself could be made harmless while retaining its antigenicity—*i.e.*, its capacity to stimulate the body's immune system—by treating it with dilute formaldehyde. The toxoid so produced, when administered to young children, conferred an active immunity to the disease.

In recent years some intriguing complexities of diphtheria have been brought to light. Diphtheria toxin is a medium-sized protein: 62,000 daltons (units of atomic weight). It is incredibly effective in killing susceptible animals, being lethal at only one ten-millionth of a gram per kilogram of body weight. Although secreted by the bacterium as a single polypeptide chain, it is functionally two separate components called A and B. The B component comprises two-thirds of the toxin molecule and serves to bind it to specific sites on the membrane of susceptible cells. The B component then somehow creates a channel in the membrane through which the A component extends into the cell. In the cell, protein-splitting enzymes sever the A component so that it is then free to diffuse about inside the cell, while the B fragment remains outside. The A fragment is actually an enzyme, and it catalyzes a reaction in which a portion of a coenzyme, nicotinamide adenine dinucleotide, is transferred onto a specific protein. The protein that is modified and inactivated by this action of the A fragment is called the elongation factor, which normally catalyzes an essential step in protein synthesis within the cell. The net effect of its inactivation is that protein synthesis in the affected cell comes to a halt and the cell dies.

Diphtheria toxin can be cleaved into its A and B fragments outside the cell, and these can be separated. The B fragment is then found to possess all of the antigenicity of the intact toxin but none of its lethality. The A fragment exhibits its full catalytic activity in the absence of the B fragment and can inhibit protein synthesis in the test tube, but it has little effect on intact cells because, without the aid of the B fragment, it cannot enter them. Toxin-resistant cells have been found to differ from susceptible cells in that they lack the surface features that bind the B component. Immunized animals have antibodies that combine with the B component and so prevent it from binding to cell surfaces.

All bacteria require iron for growth, and many have evolved elaborate mechanisms, involving the synthesis and secretion of potent iron-trapping agents (siderophores) and the subsequent active uptake of the iron-siderophore complexes, to facilitate getting the needed iron into the bacterial cell. Bacterial hosts have evolved numerous defenses against bacterial infection, one of which involves the synthesis of certain proteins that bind iron very tightly. These compete with the bacterial siderophores and so prevent the bacteria from getting the iron needed for growth.

C. diphtheriae has a countermeasure to this host defense. When starved for iron, and only then, it secretes its toxin, which causes host cells to leak iron compounds as they die. Synthesis of the toxin is ordinarily repressed by an iron-containing protein that binds onto the bacterial chromosome at a location adjacent to the toxin gene and so prevents its transcription. When iron is in short supply, this repressor protein cannot be made and the toxin gene is unmasked. When cultures of *C. diphtheriae* are starved for iron, they devote a large portion of their total protein synthesis to the making of toxin. This phenomenon is exploited by man in the commercial production of this toxin.

The ability to produce toxin is clearly useful to *C. diphtheriae*, yet there are strains that cannot make the toxin. These strains gain the ability to make toxin only when infected with a particular virus. Upon entering the bacteria this virus incorporates its own small complement of genetic material into the larger one of the host cell. The gene coding for the toxin actually belongs to the virus. Here then is a case of a virus collaborating with a bacterium in an attack upon a larger host; *i.e.*, man.

The situation described above for diphtheria toxin applies to the actions of other protein toxins, including cholera toxin and the plant toxins abrin and ricin, which are found in the seeds of the rosary pea and castor bean, respectively. In each case, one component of the toxin serves to insert the other component into susceptible cells, and the inserted portion exerts a catalytic activity detrimental to the cells. In fact, it has been possible to produce hybrid toxins in which the active component is carried into the cell by an unnatural partner. Thus, a subunit of a toxin from wisteria seeds, when combined with fragment A of diphtheria toxin, enabled the latter to gain entry into mouse cells and kill them.

Gaining real understanding of the details of mechanism is a luxury compared with working out the rules of thumb that provide immediate solutions to problems, but it provides a vantage point from which more effective solutions can often be seen. (IRWIN FRIDOVICH)

Crown Gall. Recent developments in molecular biology have led to reconsideration of the significance and extent of transfer of genetic information between species. Extensive breeding work by agricultural geneticists has generated hardier and more productive plant and animal food sources. Nevertheless, success in such ventures has generally resulted from the breeding of closely related species, with the probability of a fertile mating decreasing as the species difference between the mating pair increases.

Barriers to genetic exchange also exist among the simplest of organisms, the bacteria. It has been known for some years that under certain conditions transfer of DNA, the substance of which genes are made, can occur between bacteria. Again, however, barriers exist that markedly reduce DNA transfer between certain bacterial species or strains. Given the existence of such barriers, two questions come to mind. First, to what extent does genetic exchange, even of limited nature, occur between unrelated organisms in nature? Secondly, if some exchange occurs, what molecular mechanisms are responsible for such phenomena? Unfortunately, general answers to both questions were unavailable as of the late 1970s. Nevertheless, recent work on a disease that afflicts a variety of plants provided a specific example of genetic exchange between unrelated species, the consequence of which is quite remarkable.

Crown gall disease results in the production of tumours near the crown of dicotyledonous plants.

Research during the early 1900s demonstrated that the primary causative agent was the bacterium *Agrobacterium tumefaciens,* which infects wounded areas of the plant. It was subsequently shown, however, that the presence of this bacterium was required only for some early event in plant tumour formation. Exposure of the plant to *A. tumefaciens* for only a few hours to a few days was found to be sufficient to induce tumours that would continue to grow and proliferate in the absence of the bacterial pathogen. This indicated that the bacterium was producing a factor, called the tumour-inducing principle, that could permanently transform normal plant cells into tumour cells.

Before considering the nature of the tumour-inducing principle, it is appropriate to consider the nature of the tumour state and possible reasons why it is advantageous for *A. tumefaciens* to induce such a state in plant tissue. As in all higher organisms, most cells in a normal well-developed plant are in a so-called resting state. Chromosome (DNA) replication and cell division are highly regulated by hormones and growth factors, and these events occur only as necessary to achieve the adult state or to replace old cells that are continually being sloughed off. Tumour growth reflects an aberration of such regulatory mechanisms in which cell growth and division become independent of normal controls.

For example, in the case of crown gall disease, tumour cells multiply in the absence of kinetin and naphthalene acetic acid, two hormones required for growth of normal plant cells. This, however, is not the only difference between crown gall tumour and normal plant tissue. Crown gall cells typically synthesize and excrete large quantities of octopine or nopaline, unusual amino acids that are derivatives of the common amino acid arginine that is found in most proteins. Moreover, strains of *A. tumefaciens* have the unique ability to utilize either octopine or nopaline as sources of energy, and of carbon and nitrogen for biosynthetic purposes. Thus, it would appear that tumour induction by *A. tumefaciens* reflects a remarkable parasitic adaptation by the bacterium that permits it to establish a favourable environment uniquely suited to its own growth and proliferation.

What then is the nature of the tumour-inducing principle of *A. tumefaciens* that is capable of causing such a profound transformation of plant cells? The first clue to its identity came in 1974 with the demonstration by H. Teuchy, M. Van Montagu, J. Schell, and their colleagues in Ghent, Belgium, that tumour-inducing strains of *A. tumefaciens* contain a large plasmid with a molecular weight of about 120 million daltons. Plasmids, which are circular DNA molecules frequently found in bacterial cells, can be considered to represent a class of secondary bacterial chromosomes. Each bacterial cell contains one very large DNA molecule, or chromosome, which contains all the genetic information necessary for the cell's survival. Under certain circumstances, however, the bacterium can acquire a plasmid as a second chromosome.

Although plasmids are generally not necessary for survival, they can provide growth advantages under certain conditions. Indeed, this is the case for the class of plasmid associated with tumorogenic strains of *A. tumefaciens.* Work in a number of laboratories demonstrated that the genes required for tumour induction, as well as the genes necessary for the bacterium to grow on tumour-produced octopine or nopaline, are located on the plasmid DNA molecule. Thus, the plasmid not only permits the bacterium to induce plant tumours but also endows it with the unique ability to grow on the unusual amino acids elaborated by the host tumour.

The most remarkable feature of crown gall disease came to light in 1977 with a surprising discovery by Eugene Nester and his colleagues at the University of Washington in Seattle that suggested how the *A. tumefaciens* plasmid acted as the tumour-inducing principle. Their experiments demonstrated that crown gall tumour cells, but not normal plant cells, contain a DNA segment that is identical to part of the plasmid found in virulent strains of the *A. tumefaciens* bacterium. This DNA segment is present at about 18 copies per plant cell and has a molecular weight of about six million daltons, corresponding to about 5% of the genetic information encoded within the plasmid DNA molecule. This finding implies that *A. tumefaciens* can bring about transfer of at least part of its plasmid chromosome into the plant cell, with the six million dalton DNA segment then being stably inherited by daughter tumour cells.

Moreover, it was found that at least some of the genetic information residing on this DNA segment is expressed in the tumour cell. The first step in expression of the master information encoded in a DNA molecule is synthesis of an RNA copy. This working copy of the gene then typically directs the synthesis of a protein, which may function in the cell as an enzyme or structural element. In the case of crown gall disease, Nester and his colleagues demonstrated that tumour cells contain RNA copies of a portion of the plasmid DNA segment that is present in such cells. These findings indicate that transformation of plant cells to the tumour state is associated with transfer of genes from bacterium to plant. The stable inheritance of the DNA segment containing these genes and their expression within the tumour cell can readily account for the early observation that, once induced, the tumour state can persist in the absence of infecting bacteria.

The mechanism by which gene transfer occurs from bacterium to plant in crown gall disease was not yet understood at the end of 1979, nor was it clear how the presence of the plasmid DNA segment is able to induce such a profound change in the physiology of the host plant cell. Indeed, the location of the plasmid DNA segment within the tumour cell was not yet known. Nevertheless, it seemed likely that information on these points would be forthcoming. Moreover, it was not clear to what extent crown gall is representative of a general phenomenon in nature. The type of genetic exchange associated with crown gall could be rare, or this disease could be merely the first example of a widespread phenomenon.

(PAUL LAWRENCE MODRICH)

[321.E.3; 339.C.1–3]

See also Earth Sciences; Environment.

Liquors, Alcoholic:
see Industrial Review

Literature

The 1979 Nobel Prize for Literature was awarded to Odysseus Elytis, a Greek poet. Although his work had been translated not only into Swedish but also into Russian and Spanish, he was relatively unknown to the English-speaking world, and little effort was made to introduce his poetry to the general reader. (*See* NOBEL PRIZES.)

On the BBC's "Book Programme," a list of Nobel Prize winners was recited, with the implication that these writers were unknown to most readers, and deservedly so; there was no suggestion that the general ignorance might be the fault of the readers rather than the writers. Political and national considerations were apparent in the reaction to Elytis's success. His cool reception contrasted with the warmth of 1978, when Isaac Bashevis Singer won the prize. Singer's work was available in excellent English, he was American and Jewish and he wrote about Eastern Europe; to the English-speaking world, therefore, his work was pleasingly exotic but not alien or alienating. Furthermore, he was not involved in the conventional politics of capitalism, Communism, and imperialism, but concerned with the religious or supernatural side of life, in an ethnic context. This tendency seemed relevant to the modern world, as seen by readers aware of conditions in Ireland, Iran, and Islam in general.

The English-speaking world was little influenced by Western European work in other languages. The literature of Eastern Europe, as usual, made a mark only insofar as it pointed to Communist oppression of the artist. There was no Pasternak, no Solzhenitsyn, in 1979; but an edited version of the memoirs of Dmitry Shostakovich, the Soviet composer (denounced as a forgery in Moscow), was discussed from the anti-Communist point of view. So were Aleksandr Zinoviev's satire *The Yawning Heights* and Georgy Vladimov's *Faithful Ruslan*, a story about a prison-camp guard dog, presented as a caricature of the Soviet bureaucracy's blind ruthlessness and servile obedience to orders. (See *Expatriate Russian Literature*, below.)

Odysseus Elytis

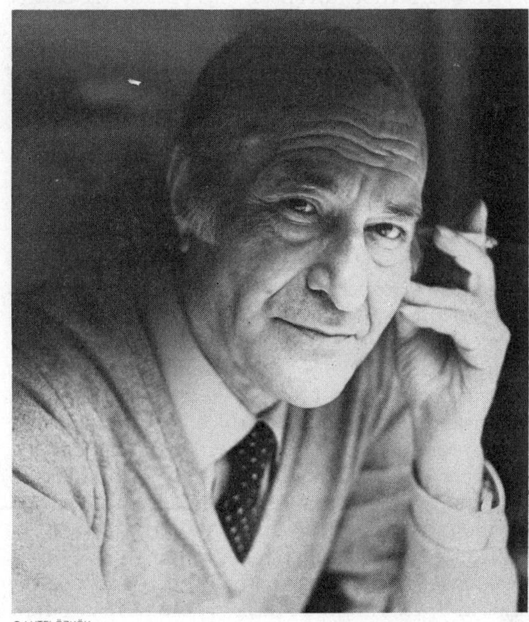

The insularity of the English-speaking world was encouraged by the absence during most of the year of the *Times Literary Supplement* (*TLS*), the only "journal of record" that attempted to survey world literature and review new books in foreign languages, besides offering a comprehensive survey of new books in English. The disappearance of the *TLS* caused dismay in U.S. universities and encouraged discussion of the old question: "What *is* literature?" Terry Eagleton, writing in the *New Statesman*, suggested that Marxists had followed Western tradition in making a "fetish" of literature: "Marxism has blandly assumed that there is indeed something called 'literature,' privileged bits of writing distinguishable by certain immutable properties, which can thus become the object of a critical science. . . . In accepting the fetish of literature, Marxist criticism underwrites the ideologically significant divisions which a recent phase of class-society has enforced between different levels of writing—between those granted the gold seal of 'literary merit' and those relegated to the outer darkness. . . ."

ENGLISH

United Kingdom. The director of the Cheltenham Festival of Literature, A. C. H. Smith, announced: "Literature is a posthumous word, a medal we confer upon the few books and plays which survive their own generation, and testify to posterity what it was like to be alive, and writing, then." As if to challenge "the fetish of literature," he chose to describe the concerns of the festival in pragmatic language—"the production of writing now," including songs and crime fiction. More grandly, he promised that "the empire of the English language will be mapped by distinguished visitors from Ireland, America, and Australia," but this was an exaggeration. The American was Allen Ginsberg, to remind the audience of the Beat Generation of the 1950s. The Irishman and the Australian both came from London, being the editor in chief of *The Observer* and the television critic of the same paper, Clive James, whose contribution was a rhymed satire on London literary journalists.

James's editor, Conor Cruise O'Brien, restored nobility to the concept of "literature" while firmly relating it to other areas of life. His lecture, "The Ikons—Religion, Politics and Literature," attempted to show a kinship between achievements of the human imagination, whether engaged in political, religious, or literary activity.

The principal debate at Cheltenham was entitled "Has literature got anything to do with selling books?"—illustrating the doubts about the meaning of "literature" and its relationship to "the production of writing now." For instance, proponents of Public Lending Right (the scheme for compensating authors for lendings of their books from public libraries) sometimes spoke reverently of books, making reference to literary and artistic merit, and sometimes of fair treatment for authors, making reference to popularity and consumer demand. The Booksellers Association Service House (BASH) produced a "Book of the Season" project, whereby a chosen book, priced at £4.95, was assiduously promoted for three months, after which the price went up to £7.95.

No new hardback book bridged the gap between quality and popularity. There was more eager discussion of the previous year's hardbacks, by such as Graham Greene and John Irving (*see* BIOGRAPHIES), now out in paperback. Similarly, the television version of John Le Carré's *Tinker, Tailor, Soldier, Spy* evoked an intelligent public interest in an ambitious modern book.

Three attempts were made, rather late in the day, to provide substitutes for the missing *TLS*. One came from Edinburgh, reviving that city's literary rivalry with London. Another, *The London Review of Books*, edited by Karl Miller, was presented as a supplement to the *New York Review of Books*. The third, *Quarto*, was produced by *Vole* magazine, a young-minded journal of conservation and ecology, edited by a former *TLS* man, Richard Boston. The young editor of *Quarto* (also a former *TLS* man) pointed out that his own generation was not reading the traditional "little magazines" but journals that took a serious interest in popular songs or rock lyrics.

As if to support this point, a veteran of London literature, Tambimuttu, brought out *Poetry London/Apple Magazine*. This 65-year-old Ceylonese had a great success with *Poetry London* in the 1940s; the "Apple" derived from his association with the Beatles in the 1960s. His new magazine offered verse by normal, literary poets and also by such rock lyricists as Leonard Cohen and Bob Dylan.

In conventional publishing there was a strong tendency to look back to the past. Historical novels and dramas mingled with biographies and collections of letters. The feminist movement, notably the Virago Press, unearthed several good books by women whose feminist tendencies had not been much remarked. Selma James spoke at Cheltenham about "Ms. Jane Austen," presenting her as "a fierce feminist," and Germaine Greer, in *The Obstacle Race*, wrote interestingly about women's contribution to painting and sculpture. Jeannette Kupfermann produced *The Ms.Taken Body*, a synthesis of ideas and arguments about the female body reflecting her own versatility as social anthropologist, antenatal teacher, actress, and model. Two other unusual successes, outside the normal categories, were Ronald Blythe's study of old age, *The View in Winter*, and *The Discipline of Law*, an influential defense of the traditional English distinction between law and justice by Lord Denning, master of the rolls.

Penelope Fitzgerald

COLLINS

FICTION. The narrow confines of the British Isles seemed to inspire less lively fiction than the old empire. In *Burger's Daughter*, Nadine Gordimer continued to explore the problems of liberal English-speaking South Africans in Afrikaner territory. No less impressive was *A Bend in the River*, another novel of Africa, by the Trinidadian author V. S. Naipaul (*see* BIOGRAPHIES). Hovering round the fringe of the U.K. and the Commonwealth was *The Mangan Inheritance* by Brian Moore—first an Ulsterman, then a Canadian, and now writing about an Irish-American's return to the old country. *The Old Jest* was Jennifer Johnston's name for Ireland; her novel of that name was awarded the Whitbread Prize.

Ireland and its history were prominent in serious fiction, notably Thomas Flanagan's *The Year of the French*, about a French-backed Irish uprising in 1798. Two historical novels were contenders for the Booker Prize. *The Confederates* by Australian Thomas Keneally concerned attempts to involve Britain in the American Civil War. *Joseph* by Julian Rathbone introduced the figure of Napoleon into his story of the Peninsular War. In the event, the Booker Prize went to *Offshore*, a quiet English novel by the little-known Penelope Fitzgerald.

Among senior novelists, C. P. Snow (*A Coat of Varnish*) and Muriel Spark (*Territorial Rights*) published quietly interesting novels which critics found slight. But William Golding, after a long silence, presented the horrendous and apocalyptic *Darkness Visible* to a public rather weary of the sinister and macabre. "Feed the heart on fantasies," warned Yeats, "and it grows brutal."

LETTERS, LIVES. Biographies, memoirs, and collected letters were both popular and successful. Alethea Hayter's selection from Edward FitzGerald's correspondence, *FitzGerald to His Friends*, was an engaging miniature, as were the 20th-century letters of C. S. Lewis (*They Stand Together*, edited by Walter Hooper) and Rupert Hart-Davis (*The Arms of Time*) to personal friends. The latest volume in many a scholarly edition offered the correspondence of John Locke, Lewis Carroll, Byron, Hazlitt, D. H. Lawrence, and Virginia Woolf. In this area of literature there was untroubled confidence in a continuing tradition.

There were popular biographies of *Charles: Prince of Wales* by Anthony Holden and of *King Charles II* by Antonia Fraser. There were also new volumes on George Orwell, the Burma policeman; Lord Lytton, the viceroy of India; and Wilfrid Scawen Blunt, the Victorian anti-imperialist. Moving to domestic politics, unusual studies of statesmen and politicians included C. E. Lysaght's *Brendan Bracken,* on that elusive acolyte of Winston Churchill, and Geoffrey Goodman's *The Awkward Warrior,* on Frank Cousins, one of the new breed of trade union statesmen.

Among the former prime ministers turned author were Lord Home, irritating the humane with his memoirs of blood sports in *Border Reflections,* and Harold Wilson, arguing the case for his premiership in *Final Term.* Also offered were *Memoirs* by Jo Grimond, former leader of the Liberals, and a biography of Hugh Gaitskell, Labour's former leader, by Philip Williams. *Hugh Gaitskell* was reckoned as the biography most relevant to the current condition of British politics. The trial of Jeremy Thorpe, another former Liberal leader (successor to Grimond), for incitement to murder inspired much writing but no literature, in the high sense of the word. In the low sense of consumer-oriented literature, the "production of writing now," the Thorpe trial was relevant to publishers' activities. Witnesses were discredited on the ground that they had contracted to write books about themselves.

Poetry. An important literary event was the petition to the General Synod of the Church of England, asking that the poetry (and music) of the church not be withdrawn from general circulation in the interest of modernity. The new translation of the Bible and the variant versions of the Book of Common Prayer were the principal targets of this campaign. It was sponsored by a poetry journal, *PN Review,* and secured the signatures of 649 writers, scholars, statesmen, and servicemen of national distinction. A natural response from the modernizing churchmen was: "How many of these signatories are regular churchgoers? How many of them support the idea of *The Bible Designed to Be Read as Literature?*" A similar response was evident when the poet Geoffrey Hill (one of the signatories) used Christian language in his 1978 collection, *Tenebrae.* Religion or just "literature"?

Another signatory, Kingsley Amis, published his *Collected Poems* in 1979, while Robert Conquest brought out a striking new selection of poems, *Forays.* Both suffered from their versatility, their involvement with fiction and politics. As a poet, G. S. Fraser suggested, Kingsley Amis "has not an agreed reputation. . . . A poet of great talent but, sadly, with a vulgar streak." Other senior poets publishing in 1979 were Douglas Dunn, P. J. Kavanagh, and Terence Tiller. Ted Hughes, influential because he was the favourite of the schoolteachers, offered two books, *Remains of Elmet* and *Moortown.* Sincerity became an issue in considering the verse of Seamus Heaney, a powerful poet of Northern Irish Catholic stock. D. J. Enright produced a set of short poems called *A Faust Book,* using Christian language—but for religious or "literary" reasons?

It was a year in which the government favoured private sponsorship rather than public money for the arts. There was fear that the Poetry Society would lose its Arts Council grant, but it transpired that the council merely wished to transfer responsibility for this London-based organization to the Greater London Arts Association.

(D. A. N. JONES)

United States. Fiction. The major novels of 1979 continued to deal not so much with the lives of men in society as with the life of the solitary hero, alone and wrestling with himself. They blueprinted with bitterness and violence the complex fate of being an American. Abstracted, alienated from the society of their times, surrounded by an envelope of emptiness, these heroes had an almost mythic quality. The characteristic hero was irreconcilably opposed to society; and the novel, like an interior drama, bodied itself forth in symbolic terms by narrative put-ons, ethnic melodrama, or by pseudo or authentic fictional autobiography.

Few critics could resist the conclusion that Norman Mailer scored his greatest success with *The Executioner's Song,* probably the year's most masterful entry. This "nonfiction novel," a 1,056-page leviathan, featured the life story of double-murderer Gary Gilmore. Goodbye, self-advertising, two-fisted clown-drunk Mailer. Hello, relentlessly objective, ventriloquist Norman, as if Mailer, always his own existential hero, had discovered one with even stronger credentials. Speaking as witness, narrator, and voice of the times, Mailer's "fiction" became not only a metaphor of reality but also a metaphor of itself—a compelling projection of Mailer's own nature through that of a truly doomed man.

The Ghost Writer was Philip Roth's sonata-like masterwork, his best novel in years. The theme, twisting through twirled narrative threads, was the artist's conflict between the obsessive demands of his calling and the separate but equal demands of family and human contact: hero E. I. Lonoff (famous Jewish writer) surrenders totally to his

Norman Mailer

© THOMAS VICTOR

UPI

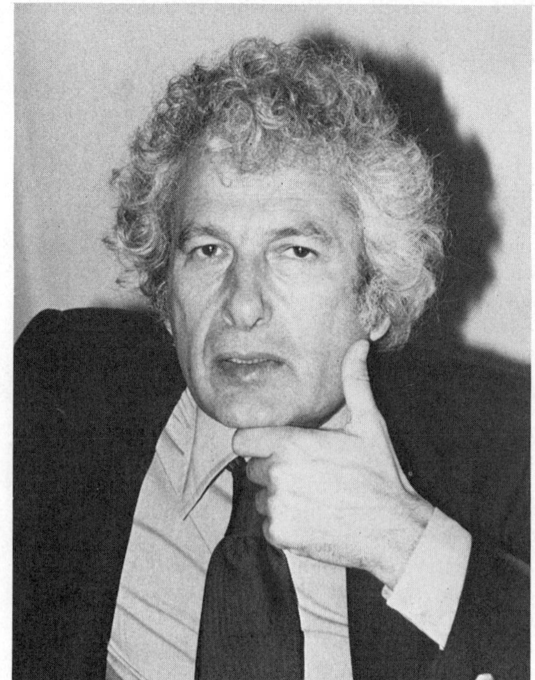

Joseph Heller

obsession of driving his well-bred wife crazy with gentle, helpless, selfish inhumanities.

Bernard Malamud's *Dubin's Lives* was a seemingly autobiographical novel whose monumentally sad hero—a biographer of Twain and Thoreau—wonders if he has "given up life to write lives." Like Malamud, Dubin is a Jewish man of letters who married at 31, has two grown children, and lives in Vermont. The kitchen/bedroom exchanges provide the most genuinely hurtful combat since Strindberg: "He lived in six sheets of glass, shouting soundless pleas for freedom."

Elizabeth Hardwick

© THOMAS VICTOR

Sophie's Choice, by William Styron, was a smugly pouting autobiographical novel artificially heaped with import by making one of the characters (Sophie) a concentration-camp survivor, the only other non-Jewish tenant in the Flatbush boarding house where narrator "Stingo," the young Styron, comes to attempt his first novel in 1947 after a brief nightmare as a reader at McGraw-Hill.

Joseph Heller atoned for his ethnic cover-up in *Something Happened* with *Good as Gold*, an assaulting work of impolite comic energy. Bruce Gold, a bored writer of books of "fiery caution and crusading inertia," comes to the attention of the White House and is offered a position anywhere on the scale from "close Presidential source" to secretary of state. The White House here plainly stands for archetypal WASP stupidity, the way the Army stood for confusion and lunacy in *Catch-22*, with the same effect: manic plenitude.

Two other autobiographical novels were notable: *Just Above My Head*, by James Baldwin, a sour lip-chewing work of churchly and outcast anger, talking around and beyond white readers about the injuries of being good of heart, black, musical, and homosexual; and *Sleepless Nights*, by Elizabeth Hardwick, a dazzling and difficult memoir/novel/poem in which the author locates "lost things," the singularity of places, and the images of those she has cared about since the '30s.

The ideas of creative cruelty (both mythic and real) were explored in a number of important novels about the estranged self acting as a predator in order to discover the limit of its own possibilities and thus to escape itself. In these works society was perceived as the dead weight of custom, the repressive force of abstract horror from which man must escape.

"When we disbelieve what others do, we end up disbelieving what we could do ourselves" was the credo of *Passion Play*, Jerzy Kosinski's latest pageant of lust and cruelty. Kosinski's current alter-ego brute is immigrant polo player Fabian, "an outlaw from the league of crusaders, inquisitors, and censors of sexual conduct." In *The Living End* Stanley Elkin fiendishly toys with religious myths and Minneapolis—all culminating in God's explanations of Everything ("He explained why children suffered and showed them how to do the latest disco steps") and with the revelation that Goodness has nothing to do with the way history has been arranged.

Kurt Vonnegut's *Jailbird* took capitalism, labour history, McCarthyism, and Watergate and put them all into the memoirs of Walter Starbuck, a chauffeur's son and minor Watergate convict. Most compelling compressed metaphor: all of America is like a minimum-security prison.

King of the Jews, by Leslie Epstein, was a major work of extravagant pain and horrible imagination: only the iron-hearted came away unshaken. An unnamed Polish city during World War II creates its walled ghetto, and under the direction of the Nazis ("the Others") forms a *Judenrat*, a self-governing council to oversee the Jews' own decimation. Chosen council leader is Trumpelman, a quack doctor and insurance swindler. Epstein's operatic account of the Holocaust is affecting—it

© THOMAS VICTOR

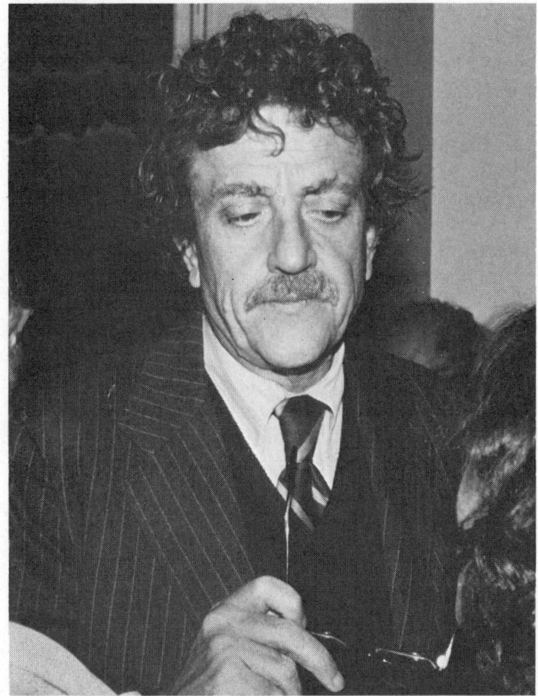

Kurt Vonnegut

apes Trumpelman's own desperate attempts to hold onto life—and the vividness makes the pity and tragedy pulse.

On the tamer side, straight from the ivory tower, were two academic novels by major writers. John Barth, in a grand gesture of self-advertisement, took characters from five of his six previous books and had them all write *Letters*; while Joyce Carol Oates's *Unholy Loves* viewed morbid-shallow academics with a satiric curl of the lip.

In the genre of historical fiction the major offering was *Hanta Yo* by Ruth Beebe Hill, a *Roots*-wise mammoth simulation of Plains Indian culture circa 1835. This was the story of the Dakotah/Mahto band—their migrations; warriors galloping home with scalps, horses, captive women; ceremonies of grief and celebration with trilling women and kill-tales; the lonely quests of the seer—a magnetic work of exotic authenticity.

Two powerful collections of short fiction appeared. *Old Love* by Nobel laureate I. B. Singer deadpanned sin, greed, and mystic doings; and John Updike's *Problems* had divorce as its tonic note.

History, Biography, and Belles Lettres. The connection between history and truth, or the apprehension of truth and its communication by means of history, was the central problem of a number of significant works during the year. Why study history? was the question posed by Harvard University professor Oscar Handlin's *Truth in History*. The answer: to discover the truth, even "though it takes a whole world of knowledge" to do so.

Truth was also the subject of William Shawcross's *The Sideshow: Nixon, Kissinger and the Destruction of Cambodia*. A decade after the secret bombing of Cambodia Nixon was a president driven from office and Cambodia a devastated country. Shawcross vividly reconstructs the process that led to this dismal two-part denouement, for it was the secret bombing which necessitated the illegalities that culminated in Watergate. The "sideshow" is what Cambodia came to be contemptuously called in Washington, where its destruction served not only U.S. aims in Vietnam but also the career interests of key Americans, of whom Henry Kissinger looms the largest. The publication of Kissinger's own version, *White House Years*, was something of a historical event. No overall assessment of his foreign policy mission is offered, but overwhelming detail illustrates progress: in China, the Middle East, and in détente with the Soviet Union. But there is no inkling that the domestic cost of playing tough may sometimes come too high.

Another account of a determined search for truth, justice, and the American Way was *To Set the Record Straight*, by Judge John Sirica, perhaps the strongest candidate for unmitigated hero status produced by the Watergate scandal. For five years Sirica was the axis around which Watergate revolved. When confronted by a sloppy prosecution of the Watergate burglars, Sirica responded with a determination that blew the scandal wide open.

More contemporary was *Energy Future: The Report of the Harvard Business School Energy Project*, edited by Robert Stobaugh and Daniel Yergin. In it Harvard puts its seal of approval on proposals previously associated with more radical thinkers like Barry Commoner: "The cornerstone of our thinking is that conservation and solar energy should be given a fair chance in the market system to compete with imported oil and the other traditional sources."

The Powers That Be was David Halberstam's new incarnation of preeminence, where the real powers that be, the president-makers and policy-shapers, are the prime media magnates—William Paley of CBS, Henry Luce of *Time*, the proprietors of the *New York Times, Los Angeles Times*, and *Washington Post*. It was a smashing imaginative projection, based on interviews with everyone. Ubiquitous intellectual John Kenneth Galbraith scored with *The Nature of Mass Poverty*, provocatively asserting poverty to be self-perpetuating, a matter of realistic "accommodation to the culture of poverty."

Several major theoretical offerings appeared: *Reinventing Womanhood*, embodying Carolyn Heilbrun's thesis that in literature as in life women have generally shown an amazing incapacity to imagine themselves as autonomous beings and that "Woman must learn to call whatever she is or does female"; *Optimism*, by noted sociologist Lionel Tiger, arguing that a force of optimism exists in humans which has a biological urgency underlying much of human action—bearing children, sowing crops, believing in God, falling in love, acting charitably; and *The Culture of Narcissism*, by Christopher Lasch, which commented on the trivialization of emotions, the confessional mode as literary development, the devaluation of the American past, and the hollowness of new prescriptions.

It was also time for a de-romanticized, de-mythified, close-up retelling of the launching of the U.S.

Space Program by radical sheik Tom Wolfe. *The Right Stuff* was the inside italicized true story of those first seven astronauts (referred to as "The True Brothers") obsessed with having "the right stuff"—that certain blend of guts and smarts that spells pilot success.

John Keats's insight that "a man's life of any worth is a continual allegory, and very few eyes can see the Mystery" continued to challenge writers of biography. *The Rise of Theodore Roosevelt* by Edmund Morris detailed everything that, in time, made the man an irresistible force—the curiosity and concentration, the energy, the ardour, the dramatic flair, the fun he had being a great, boyish nuisance. Frank Sulloway's closely argued *Freud*, an impressively documented intellectual biography, was a tour de force of unabashed revisionist psychoanalysis, which, while not diminishing Freud's genius, elicited objections and rebuttal as much as admiration. Prizewinning biographer Ernest Samuels offered *Bernard Berenson*, a remarkable study of the cicerone of Italian Renaissance painting and his pursuit of "perfect culture."

The second installment of B. F. Skinner's autobiography, *The Shaping of a Behaviorist*, was a dense, methodical reconstruction of Skinner's advance from an earlier Pavlovian impulse to a refined search for the laws of operant behaviour. *As It Happened*, a memoir by CBS chairman William Paley, traced the network's development lovingly and exhaustively, leaving no doubt that he was in control all along the way. In *Breaking Ranks*, a political memoir by Norman Podhoretz, the editor explained his disillusion with radicalism and the New Left and his resolve, as of 1968, to wage all-out war on the "armies of the alienated." And finally, in *Disturbing the Universe*, Freeman Dyson traced the course of 50 years of contact with pivotal scientific figures and momentous events, focusing on the moral dilemmas posed by those who disturb the universe.

Lewis Thomas

COURTESY MEMORIAL SLOAN-KETTERING CANCER CENTER: PHOTO, ALAN S. ORLING

Notable belletristic volumes included: *On Lies, Secrets, and Silence*, essays supporting Adrienne Rich's conviction that male-dominated society quashes the "life-expanding impulses" of both sexes; Flannery O'Connor's *The Habit of Being*, an astonishingly brilliant collection of letters; and Lewis Thomas's *The Medusa and the Snail*, an enlightened rondo of essays on biology and medicine.

POETRY. Two major collections of poetry appeared. *The Poems of Stanley Kunitz* was the record of a poet's 50 fruitful years and very personal voice, and *Collected Earlier Poems* by Denise Levertov deepened our understanding of a poet who may be the finest writing in English today. *The Oresteia of Aeschylus*, translated by Robert Lowell, was a fine posthumous work, the poet at his unfrilliest, bringing the bold grandeur and terror of the original tragedies to a modern unstressed idiom without slighting either drama or language. And Robert Penn Warren garnered praise with *Brother to Dragons*, a dazzling work in multiple voices occasioned by the real-life crime in 1811 in which two nephews of Thomas Jefferson hacked to death a Negro slave. (FREDERICK S. PLOTKIN)

Canada. Several well-known Canadian novelists had new books out in 1979. Margaret Atwood made another of her satirical forays among Toronto's intelligentsia in *Life Before Man*. In Jack Hodgins's *The Resurrection of Joseph Bourne*, life in a Vancouver Island logging town becomes a comic pageant peopled by characters all slightly larger than life. *Me Bandy, You Cissie* was another comic work in which the author, Donald Jack, uses the setting of the Algonquin Round Table to show off his verbal dance of puns, double and single entendres, and other semantic tricks and postures. Robert Harlow uses a horse race as an extended metaphor in *Making Arrangements*, while William Weintraub makes some out-in-left-field prophecies about the life of the English minority in Quebec 20 years after separation in *The Underdogs*.

Reservoir Ravine, the third in Hugh Hood's cycle of 12 novels, *A New Age*, leapfrogs backward to present the life of the hero's parents. In *Latakia*, Audrey Thomas ponders the paradox that between a man and a woman who know each other all too well there can be so deep a chasm, while in *Nights in the Underground*, newly translated from the French, Marie Claire Blais chronicles the passions and the pains of a group of gay women. Another recent translation was Gabrielle Roy's *Children of My Heart*, which won a Governor General's Award for fiction in French. b. p. Nichol, better known as a poet, published two novels during the year: *Craft Dinner*, a complicated work built around a strong story line, and *Journal*, in which writing and being a writer are the focus of attention. Matt Cohen further demonstrated his growth as a novelist in *The Sweet Second Summer of Kitty Malone*, while Marilyn Bowering worked both sides of the line between prose and poetry in *The Visitors Have All Returned*. A voice from the past was Isabella Valancy Crawford's *The Halton Boys*, describing growing up in a small Ontario town in the late 19th century.

Biographies ranged from *A Hundred Different Lives*, the second volume of Raymond Massey's au-

CAMERA PRESS/MILLER SERVICES

Marie Claire Blais

tobiography, to *Peter Lougheed: A Biography* by Allan Hustak, which never quite answers the question of what economic and social circumstances allowed a virtual stranger to become leader of the Alberta Conservatives. *Stefansson and the Canadian Arctic* by Richard J. Diubaldo makes it very clear why he was Canada's most hated explorer-hero at home and its most prestigious in the U.S. and Europe. Histories included *Go Do Some Great Thing* by Crawford Kilian, describing how blacks fleeing persecution in San Francisco settled in British Columbia upon the invitation of Sir James Douglas, its first governor. *Queen's University*, vol. i, *1841–1917* by Hilda Neatby details the first 75 years of that remarkable institution.

Experimental poetry appeared to be on the increase, as indicated by the appearance of such books as the *International Anthology of Concrete Poetry*, vol. i, edited by John Jessop, in which geometric designs, word collages, ink stamp designs, and pen and ink graphics are used by poets to break down and playfully manipulate the basic elements of their art. *In England Now That Spring* by Steven McCaffery and b. p. Nichol, with its polaroid poems, found texts, and visionary collaborations, serves as an eccentric record of a journey through England and Scotland. Paul Dutton's *Right Hemisphere, Left Ear* includes drawn and typewritten visual poems among found and sound poems. *The Canadian Haiku Anthology* edited by George Swede, the first Canadian anthology of this form, includes examples by Eric Amann, LeRoy Gorman, and Rod Willmot, among others.

More conventional in their treatment of language were poets like Susan Musgrave in *A Man to Bury, A Man to Marry*, which treats age-old sexual dilemmas with humour and innocence, and Michael Ondaatje in *There's a Trick with a Knife I'm Learning to Do*, which attempts to dissect how we see what we see. Dennis Lee brought out *The Gods*, his first book for adults since *Civil Elegies* won the Governor General's Award in 1972. Irving Layton also had a new book, *Droppings from Heaven*.

(ELIZABETH WOODS)

FRENCH

France. As the decade, politically uninspiring and clouded by threats of economic recession, drew to a close, the past seemed to offer a refuge from uncertainty. Month after month the literary best-seller lists consisted almost entirely of historical novels, led by Jeanne Bourin's *La Chambre des dames*. Set in the 13th century, it was spiced with the violence and sexual passion that are the usual ingredients of popular fiction, but it had qualities that raised it well above the average gore-and-gibbet romance. Unfortunately, it stumbled over a recurrent dilemma of the historical novel, failing to discover a language that was appropriate without being pretentiously archaic. The same problems faced Robert Merle in *En nos vertes années*, but the Prix Goncourt winner, Antonine Maillet's *Pélagie-la-Charrette*, evaded it, drawing strength from the still-living dialect of 18th-century settlers in Canada.

The attraction of such works seemed to lie partly in the depiction of a society that was believable, yet remote from the reader's experience. This condition was also fulfilled by *Fausse Rivière*, Maurice Denuzière's sequel to an earlier novel about 19th-century Louisiana, and by Claude Poulain's saga of France and Spain in the 10th century, *Les Chevauchées de l'an mil*. But one could not help feeling that there was something unhealthy in this hunger for an imaginary past, which asked no urgent questions of the reader. The same was true of excursions into more recent periods: the title and 1930s-style jacket of Pierre-Jean Remy's *Orient Express*, promising an easy ride to nostalgia, probably did much to explain its success.

The past, however, could provide inspiration for works of a different kind, like Christiane Singer's *La Mort viennoise*, where the theme of an outbreak of plague in 17th-century Vienna was the starting point for a profound and beautifully written novel. Jacques Teboul's *Cours, Hölderlin!* hardly came into the category of historical fiction. Through the metaphor of the German poet's "wanderings" during his 37-year confinement, it examined society's fear of madness, inspiration, and the power of the imagination.

As in previous years, childhood and adolescence were favourite themes, and women writers like Marie Chaix (*L'Age du tendre*), Viviane Villamont (*Le Guêpiot*), Béatrix Beck (*La Décharge*), and Valérie Valère (*Malika, ou un jour comme les autres*) brought a feminine sensibility to their treatment. The year also saw the publication of volumes of reminiscences by distinguished writers of an earlier generation. Michel Mohrt, describing his dour Breton upbringing in *La Maison du père*, wrote directly of experiences he had drawn on in his novels, while Marcel Arland, in *Ce fut ainsi*, looked

Marcel Arland

back on an intellectual class broken against the disaster of 1940.

Poetic fantasy was once more the keynote in several works, especially by younger writers. Jean-Marc Roberts won the Prix Renaudot with *Affaires étrangères*, the story of one man's domination over another. Others of the same type included Serge Bramly's *Un Piège à lumière* and Marc Cholodenko's *Les Pleurs, ou le grand oeuvre d'Andrea Bajarsky*. Another well-received poetic novel was Jeanne Champion's sombre and dream-like study of a family, *Les Frères Montaurian*.

Two novels successfully broke the monopoly of historical fiction. Vladimir Volkoff used the conventions of the spy story to unconventional ends in *Le Retournement*, and Simone Schwartz-Bart's *Ti-Jean l'Horizon* helped demonstrate the importance of French literature from outside France.

It was not a year of great innovation. Jean Cayrol published *Histoire du ciel*, one of a series of novels begun in 1969 which took as their central "character" a place or element and channeled its history and mythology through human protagonists. Another experimental novel, Hélène Cixous's *Ananké*, had a mixed critical reception but confirmed her as one of the most interesting writers in her field. Roger Peyrefitte, writing for a quite different and wider public, also confirmed a well-established reputation with *Roy*, the deliberately sensational story of an American adolescent, while Yves Navarre, who published two novels during the year (*Portrait de Julien devant la fenêtre* and *Le Temps voulu*), was finding a style that combined lucidity and tenderness. The prolific Pierre-Jean Remy drew on his experiences as a diplomat in *Cordelia, ou l'Angleterre*, and Daniel Boulanger published a further collection of short stories, *Un Arbre dans Babylone*. Only Pascal Lainé, with *Tendres cousines*, seemed willing to break new ground, adopting an unfamiliar setting and a lighter tone than in his earlier novels.

In poetry, as in fiction, it was hard to find evidence of radically new directions. Alain Bosquet's *Poèmes, un* were his collected works up to 1967. Pierre Emmanuel published *Una, ou la mort, la vie*, Guillevic, *Etier*, and André Pieyre de Mandiargues, *L'ivre Oeil*. Among interesting books by younger poets was Patrick Reumaux's *Repérages du vif*. Much contemporary poetry seemed to be moving toward total silence, broken only by a word or two carelessly left behind on an otherwise blank page.

The literary year in France was thus characterized by an absence of any compelling and unifying sense of purpose. The explanation was perhaps to be found in Régis Debray's analysis of the intellectual climate of the country, *Le Pouvoir intellectuel en France*, which sought to establish the shift of power from literature to the media. It was a depressing analysis, and its Marxist author was not consoled by the wider popular appeal of television and the press.

In February the novelist Michel Déon was made a member of the Académie Française. Among writers who died during the year were Gilbert Cesbron, Michel Dard, Jean-Louis Bory, Maurice Clavel, and Marcel Jouhandeau (*see* OBITUARIES).

(ROBIN BUSS)

Canada. Of the abundant French Canadian literature produced during 1979, three titles were especially deserving of attention. In *Naissances: De l'écriture québécoise*, Philippe Haeck pursues and further develops the train of inquiry begun in 1975 with *L'Action restreinte: De la littérature*. Using the format of a dialogue with students, the author analyzes a variety of French-Canadian texts, dealing not only with their aesthetic and emotive value but also with their social relevance for the college student. In the second part of the book, Haeck develops this topic more didactically by articulating his theory of literature, including his thoughts on the creative literary process and on the teaching of literature. In speaking of his belief in the power of the written word, he states: "It is not really a question of the writer's respecting the way a given language works but rather of his inventing a new language with which to make his voice heard over the wall of standardized speech." This passage as well as the entire book were sure to cause controversy.

Madeleine Gagnon's *Lueur roman archéologique* contains no trace of what is usually understood as the traditional novel, yet throughout there is a first-person narrator who, through various games of transferal, association, split personality, mimesis, remembrance, dream, unveiling, and recovering, seeks to express her "other self" in the spaces that separate her words. This is a disconcerting novel, but once the vertigo of the writing style has been overcome, the reader is drawn in as an accomplice to the work's sensitivity, eroticism, and urgent desire to unravel its tale.

One can hardly speak of Louis-Philippe Hébert's collection of short stories, *Manuscrit trouvé dans une valise*, without quoting from the piece "Prière d'insérer": "We temporarily have the power to control mirrors and time." Each story in the work falls victim to this power of displacement, and the text itself is a subterfuge by virtue of its continuous elusiveness. The collection, which evokes in some aspects the works of Borges, Joyce, or the surrealists, is fascinating because it demonstrates with such virtuosity the art of pretense.

(ROBERT SAINT-AMOUR)

GERMAN

The 30th anniversary of the two German states produced a rich harvest of books, in which almost all the major authors, in both West and East, were represented.

Martin Walser followed his previous year's success with what was generally regarded as his most important work yet, *Seelenarbeit*, an immaculately written study of exploitation and conformism, awareness of history in good and bad senses, and much else besides. Max von der Grün's *Flächenbrand* had similar themes but was more direct in its method, using an exciting and somewhat implausible plot to warn against neo-Nazism and collaboration of the ruling Social Democrats with capitalism. Heinrich Böll's first major work in five years, *Fürsorgliche Belagerung*, was disappointing. Its subject matter, the atmosphere of totalitarianism and suspicion created by the terrorist attacks of 1977, was highly topical, but the elegiac style was a serious flaw.

Contrasting with these political novels were Peter Handke's *Langsame Heimkehr*, another story of a search for the self, and Max Frisch's *Der Mensch erscheint im Holozän*, a study of old age in which fragile human civilization is confronted by the might of natural forces. In Rolf Hochhuth's first novel, *Eine Liebe in Deutschland*, the story of an illicit wartime love affair between a German woman and a Polish prisoner is interrupted, sometimes overpointedly, by historical analysis.

Max von der Grün

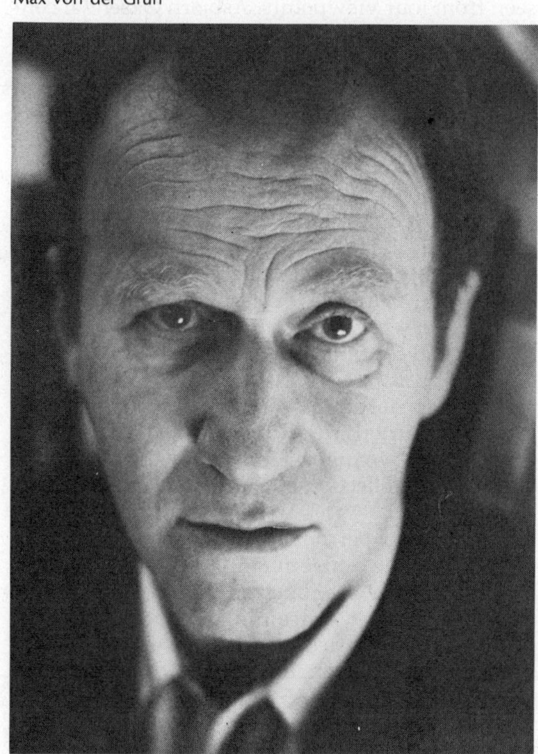

© LUTFI ÖZKÖK

© LUTFI ÖZKÖK

Peter Handke

History appeared in a number of important autobiographies, some of them disguised as "fiction." Foremost was Helga Novak's universally praised *Die Eisheiligen*, on growing up in the decade 1939–49. Wendelgard von Staden's *Nacht über dem Tal* described a childhood spent in the neighbourhood of one of Hitler's concentration camps. Hermann Stahl's *Das Pfauenrad* was a more egocentric account of the painter's life up to 1945, while Christian Ferber's *Die Seidels* portrayed the history of the author's family from the year 1811. More difficult to classify was Günter Grass's *Das Treffen in Telgte*, a thank offering to Hans Werner Richter, founder of the influential postwar "Gruppe 47." Grass's predilections for the "baroque" were apparent in this study of the function of literature, in which the author imagined a comparable "Gruppe 1647" meeting at the close of the Thirty Years' War.

An interesting feature of the year was the number of major collections of anecdotal or discursive short prose pieces. Helmut Heissenbüttel's *Eichendorffs Untergang* was his most accessible work to date, an entertaining series of scurrilous, absurd, or grotesque "Märchen." Thomas Bernhard's *Der Stimmenimitator* owed much to Kleist and Hebel, while Wolfdietrich Schnurre received critical acclaim for *Der Schattenfotograf*. More conventional were Wolfgang Bächler's *Stadtbesetzung*, W. E. Richartz's *Der Aussteiger*, Ludwig Fels's *Mein Land*, and Guntram Vesper's *Nördlich der Liebe*.

Lyric poetry was well represented with collections by Ilse Aichinger (*Verschenkter Rat*), Michael Krüger (*Diderots Katze*), and Klaus Konjetzky (*Die Hebriden*). Paul Wühr's long cycle, *Rede*, with its leitmotiv of "May," the month of poets, lovers, and revolution, was well received, but the major work was Hans Magnus Enzenberger's *Der Untergang der Titanic*, in which the "Titanic" seemed to stand both for the doomed bourgeoisie and for modern technological socialism.

In East Germany strained relations between

writers and party officials led to a number of expulsions from the writers' union, notably of Stefan Heym and Rolf Schneider, both of whom had published works in the West that were held to be hostile to the socialist state. Heym's *Collin* attacked the failures and injustices of the Communist Party since the Spanish Civil War, while Schneider's *November* treated the expulsion of the protest singer Wolf Biermann in 1976. These romans à clef found their officially approved counterpart in Harry Thürk's *Der Gaukler*, in which the exiled Soviet writer Aleksandr Solzhenitsyn appears as a CIA agent. More reputable examples of "socialist realism" included vol. ii of Erik Neutsch's *Der Friede im Ostem* and Dieter Noll's *Kippenberg*. Of greater interest to Western readers were Christa Wolf's *Kein Ort. Nirgends*, a deeply melancholy portrayal of a fictitious encounter between two unhappy writers of the early 19th century; Gunter de Bruyn's *Märkische Forschungen*, a mildly satirical account of historical scholarship in its uneasy relationship to ideology; and Ulrich Plenzdorf's *Legende vom Glück ohne Ende*, a lively, colloquially narrated allegory on the theme of individuality and conformism.

(J. H. REID)

SCANDINAVIAN

Danish. During 1978–79 Danish literature was marked by some outstanding individual successes and by some quite distinct literary trends. Thorkild Hansen's *Knut Hamsun* (1978), which raised a storm of protest and discussion, was described as some of the most compelling reading in Danish for many years. Despite its apparent biographical nature, it was probably best seen as a continuation of the documentary novel at which Hansen was so adept. The other success story was that of Vita Andersen, whose poems *Tryghedsnarkomaner* from 1977 suddenly swept Denmark in 1978 and were followed by a volume of short stories, *Hold Kæft og vær smuk* (1978), and a further volume of poems, *Næstekærlighed eller Laila og de andre* (1978). Her striking popularity seemed to be due to her fearless personal revelations and the apparent simplicity of her approach.

Thorkild Hansen

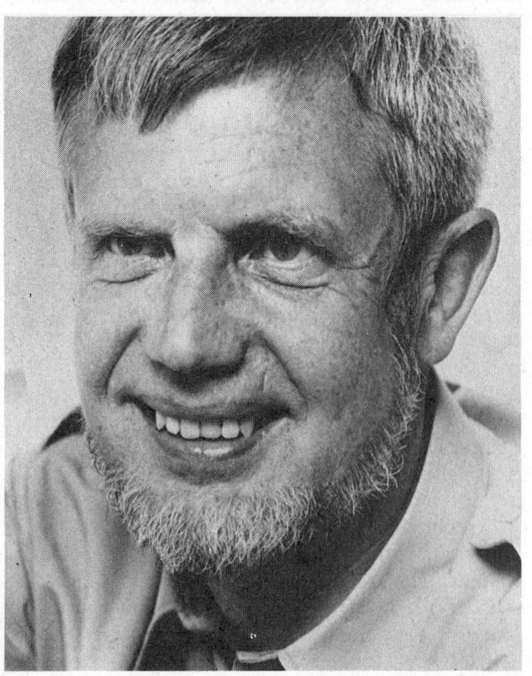

© FOTO BORGE WALTHER

Vita Andersen's work was related to the literature of intimate personal confessions that had been part of the Danish literary scene for some years. Klaus Rifbjerg was thought by some to have started the genre with *Marts 70* (1970), and in 1979 he tried to stop it from getting out of hand with an amusing parody, *Dobbeltgænger*. There was wit, too, in his weightier but somewhat uneven *Joker*, a novel centred on a journalist's tragedy.

Anders Bodelsen's *År for år* (1978) was a broader analysis of modern Denmark and its society; based on two characters and their families, it had symbolic overtones sufficient to give it general significance. A very different approach to modern culture was found in Poul Vad's vast *Kattens anatomi* (1978), full of fantasy and imagination, humour, and serious philosophy. It was largely for this novel that Vad was awarded the Danish Academy's 1979 literature prize. William Heinesen, whose early novel *Blæsende gry* was republished, was deservedly awarded the H. C. Andersen Prize.

Charlotte Strandgaard wrote a new volume of poetry, *Brændte Børn*, dealing with relations between men and women from a woman's point of view. Jesper Jensen's *Mand Mand* was called a male counterpart to Vita Andersen's work. Away from specific problems, Henrik Nordbrandt's *Rosen fra Lesbos* was lyrical poetry of great linguistic beauty.

(W. GLYN JONES)

Norwegian. Among much serial fiction being produced by Norwegian writers, Nils Werenskiold's *Familien Meyer og friheten* analyzed with humour and irony the shortcomings of a marriage seen from four viewpoints. Asbjørn Øksendal continued his Olav Trygvesson serial with *Olav fra Gardarike*, a lively account of the king's Viking raids in Russia and northern Europe at the end of the 10th century. Vera Henriksen's *Dronningsagaen* told the story of the widow of St. Olav. Sissel Lange-Nielsen provided a well-researched account of the Second Crusade in *Korstog*, the first volume of a projected series, *Under fiskenes tegn*. A 13th-century pilgrimage to the Holy Land opened a new sequence by Ragnhild Magerøy, *De som dro sudr*. Karin Bang launched a collection of novels about Norwegian whaling, Jutøy, with *Havet ble blo*, and Dag Solstad continued his handling of the 1940–45 German occupation with *Krig. 1940*. Terje Stigen returned to northern Norway in *Rekviem over en sommer*, a witty third volume devoted to the development of a young writer. Finn Havrevold also continued a collection of childhood experiences in *Fars hus*.

The complex personality of a vanished archaeologist was at the centre of Finn Carling's *Tårnseileren*. Dag Sundby examined sexual problems in the novel *Abelsmerket*, concerning the fatal attempt of a 41-year-old married bisexual to seek fulfillment of his homosexual longings. An outstanding debut was Truls Øra's *Romanen om Helge Hauge*, portraying the frustrating life of an industrial worker. Odd Eidem's *Pieter og jeg* depicted a confrontation

GYLDENDAL NORSK FORLAG

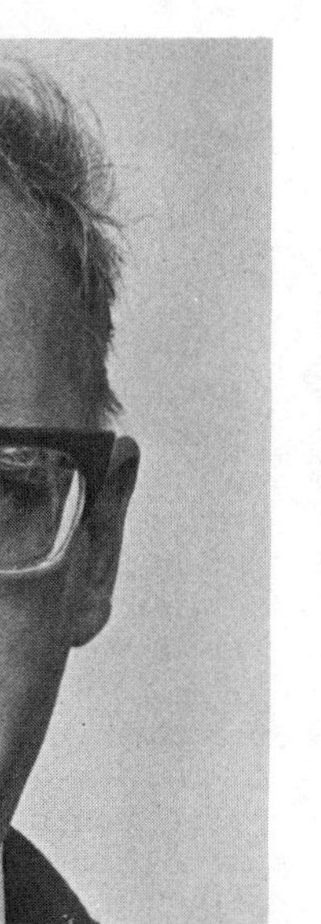

Nils Werenskiold

© LUTFI ÖZKÖK

Kerstin Ekman

between two generations of radicals, while a mental breakdown provided the material for Carl Frederik Prytz's *De vindskeive.* Petter Mørk's *Variasjoner på G-strengen* was a retrospective selection of short stories by a leading contributor to the genre over the last ten years. Short stories were also contributed by Bjørg Vik in *En håndfull lengsel.*

A feeling of impending death characterized Rolf Jacobsen's collection of poems *Tenk på noe annet.* A wide spectrum of human emotions was covered in Carl Frederik Prytz's *Dikt om kjærlighet på godt og vondt,* while Sigmund Skard's *Skymingssong* was a bittersweet farewell to life. Love was a central theme in Stein Mehren's *Vintersolhverv.* Tor Obrestad's *Songar* was a selection of his poems written between 1966 and 1978.

Johan Borgen, a central figure in Norwegian literature, died on Oct. 16, 1979 (*see* OBITUARIES).

(TORBJØRN STØVERUD)

Swedish. Although social concern was still an obvious ingredient in the books published during 1979, narrative skill and imagination appeared to have reasserted themselves after the vogue of the documentary genre. *Snöljus* by the promising young Lars Anderson combined melodrama (top-secret microbiological experiments leading to the hushed-up loss of three innocent lives) with quiet realism and was clearly intended as a warning against governmental silence on dangerous issues. Another imaginative response to the threat of impersonal collectivization was offered in Björn Runeborg's *Baccara,* in which the hero—a subservient executive—suddenly wakes up when a crisis hits his firm and sees life in an entirely new and electrifying way.

A group chronicle spanning several generations was the approach adopted by two leading woman writers in their desire to shed light on sociopolitical realities; in *Vredens dag* Sara Lidman continued to follow the fortunes of an isolated Norrland community a century ago, and in *Änglahuset* Kerstin Ekman completed her trilogy examining women's relationships to each other, their own bodies, their work, and their families. In *Linneas resor* Ann-Charlotte Alverfors wrote of a young woman writer's search for independence, and in *Gyllene röda äpplen* Anna Westberg continued to chart the careers of two working-class girls. Kristina Hasselgren's interior monologue in *Känslokapitalisterna* provided a key to a foster daughter's problems.

The highly topical question of sex roles was also illuminated by Sven Delblanc in *Kära Farmor,* with the narrator trying to find his existential bearings after the funeral of his domineering grandmother. Polish-born Rita Tornborg was aware of the problems besetting men and women but, compassionate and humorous as always, she infused her Stockholm novel *Salomos namnsdag* with a joyous belief in people's power to help each other. Göran Tunström demonstrated a similar conviction in *Ökenbrevet,* his text supposedly written by Jesus himself before taking up his ministry.

Ivar Lo-Johansson reached vol. 2, *Asfalt,* of his autobiography, and poet-cum-critic Olof Lagercrantz published his long-awaited biography of *August Strindberg.* Four leading poets published works: Karl Vennberg, *Från ö till ö;* Lars Norén, *Den ofullbordade stjärnan;* Göran Sonnevi, *Språk, verktyg, eld;* and Kjell Espmark, *Försök till liv.*

(KARIN PETHERICK)

ITALIAN

While Italian readers were absorbed in *Il perduto amore,* an uncomplicated and delicate love story by Mario Tobino, and the translation of Gerald Green's *Holocaust,* critics acclaimed *Centuria* by Giorgio Manganelli, an intriguing series of absurd, interwoven little tales. Structurally similar was Italo Calvino's *Se una notte d'inverno un viaggiatore,* possibly the cleverest book of the year, where the reader becomes the protagonist in a vain quest for a plot that constantly eludes him.

The recently developed interest in apocalyptic themes was confirmed by Carlo Cassola with *Il superstite* (and later with *Il paradiso degli animali*), in which the price of a genuine concern for the survival of mankind in the face of a nuclear catastrophe was some very poor fiction. More convincing was *L'allegria dell'orco* by Luigi Compagnone, a surreal and witty story set in a world bereft of life, where objects take over and organize themselves in an epic march toward some obscure destination.

Neohistorical fiction was the true novelty of the year, however, and it revealed the impatience of many Italian intellectuals with both self-indulgent formal experimentation and the country's apparently incurable and everlasting turmoil. The Middle Ages, providing a setting for both *L'ordalia* by Italo A. Chiusano and *Sveva* by Gian Luigi Piccioli, was, perhaps, the favoured period. However, Giulio Del Tredici set his *Tarbagatai* among primitive "Lombard" river pirates who side with Hannibal's invading troops against Roman imperialism; Ferruccio Ulivi with *Le mani pure* rewrote the story of Brutus, seen as the prototype of the intellectual whose intervention in history is doomed to failure; Giuseppe Berto, who died in 1978, wrote *La gloria*, about the life of Christ seen through the eyes of Judas; and Barbara Alberti with the delicate and poetic *Vangelo secondo Maria* turned Christ's mother into a candid feminist.

Mario Rigoni Stern's short and simple novel *Storia di Tönle*, set between 1866 and 1917, brought to life one of the most memorable characters of the year's fiction; Tönle, a shepherd of the Veneto highlands, obstinately affirms his freedom beyond state borders, official languages, and bureaucracies till he dies. The same dignity pervaded *La chiave a stella*, an unusual novel by another nonprofessional writer, Primo Levi, in which a Turin worker relates, in a language that perfectly suits him, his work experiences throughout the world. Amid so many cries of decaying values and impending doom, this was an encouraging and salutary book presenting a concrete character in a vital, imaginative, and impassioned relationship with his job.

The year also saw the publication of *Quaderno a cancelli*, a diary that Carlo Levi wrote mainly while blind and in a clinic two years before his death in 1975. Another posthumous book was *Il giorno del giudizio*, the only novel by Salvatore Satta, a Sardinian magistrate who died in 1975. Received by some critics as the Sardinian *Gattopardo*, it narrates in a tense, masterful style the vicissitudes of a Nuoro middle-class family. But its true protagonist is the Sardinian obsession with death or the variety of ways in which death consistently defeats the living.

Poetic production was less rich, the main event being the publication of *Poeti italiani del Novecento*, a new anthology by Pier Vincenzo Mengaldo. Although individual poets were for once presented without the straitjacket of schools and movements, the structure of the anthology remained firmly historical and authors and poems were selected according to the taste and judgment of its editor. Heated polemics greeted its appearance.

Nonfiction works included the topical *L'affare Moro* by Leonardo Sciascia, on the events that led to the death of the Italian politician, and *Libro bianco sull'ultima generazione* by Alberto Ronchey, an alarming analysis of the so-called generation of terror. More important were two eminently readable biographies, *Vita di Gabriele D'Annunzio* by Piero Chiara and *Vita di Pasolini* by Enzo Siciliano. Their remarkable success was due not only to their merits but, mainly perhaps, to what D'Annunzio and Pasolini represent in the tormented history of 20th-century Italy. (LINO PERTILE)

SPANISH

Spain. The Premios de la Crítica, the most prestigious prizes in the four languages of Spain, were awarded for works in Castilian to the exiled Chilean José Donoso, for *Casa de campo*, a political fable, and in poetry to Angel García López for *Mester Andalusí*. Among the three other languages the awards were given in Catalán, to Ramón Pinyol, for *Alicates*; in Gallego, for *Tempo de Compostela* by Salvador García-Bondaño; and in Basque, for *Bale Denborak* by Augustín Zubikarai.

The Premios Nacionales de Literatura included one to the appropriately named Félix Grande, one of the finest poets writing in Spanish, for his formidable *Las Rubaiyatas de Horacio Martín*. Another of these awards was presented to Carlos Bousoño for the critical *El irracionalismo poético*.

After 23 years of vigorous and colourful existence, the typographically luxurious magazine *Los papeles de Son Armandans*, directed by the equally colourful Camilo José Cela, went out of existence. It had carried out a unique role in bringing into print in Franco's Spain almost all the nation's scattered creative writers, notably the men of letters who went into exile at the republic's fall in 1939 and their associates and descendants. Jaime Salinas, son of the exiled poet Pedro Salinas, restructured the publishing house of Alfaguara, the press founded by Cela, and became the miracle publisher of the year. From a foundering enterprise he created what many believed to be the best publishing firm in Spain.

Titles from the excellent *El Bardo* verse series included *Usuras y figuraciones*, by the highly cultured Carlos Barral, and a definitive edition of the Cuban José Lezama Lima's *Fragmentos a su imán*, a posthumous contribution by the most baroque of classicists. The same Lezama's *Cartas*, also published in Spain, were not allowed in Cuba. They showed his total exile from contemporary island politics and policy; in the letters to his family, already in external exile as opposed to his own internal exile, he notes the eternal pressure from the ideologues. (ANTHONY KERRIGAN)

Latin America. The major writers who have placed Latin-American literature in the international spotlight continued to enhance its reputation. Renowned fiction writers Alejo Carpentier (Cuba), José Donoso (Chile), Julio Cortázar (Argentina), and Manuel Puig (Argentina) published notable works. It was also a year in which literary prizes such as the Casa de las Américas in Cuba and the Premio de Novela Plaza y Janés in Colombia, as well as the publication of first novels by young writers, attested to the vitality of Latin-American letters.

The most important novels were Carpentier's *La consagración de la primavera* (late 1978) and *El arpa y la sombra*, Donoso's *Casa de campo*, and Puig's *Pubis angelical*. Carpentier's two novels reflected his lifelong preoccupation with history and the fine arts, whereas Donoso and Puig demonstrated more of a rupture with their previous work. Donoso's notably self-conscious novel turned to a 19th-century setting. Puig moved further from a strictly Argentine context, novelizing problems of morality and sexuality on a more international level.

The Casa de las Américas prizes were dominated by natives of two countries where literature was censored, Uruguay and Argentina. Argentina's Humberto Constantini shared the novel prize with Luis Britto García of Venezuela. Constantini, the author of *Háblenme de Funes,* won the prize with *De dioses, hombrecitos y policías.* Britto García's *Abrapalabra* was an audacious experiment with language. The other prizewinners were Fernando Butazzoni of Uruguay for *Los días de nuestra sangre* (short story), María Gravina Telechea of Uruguay for *Lázaro vuela rojo* (poetry), and the Guatemalan Arturo Arias for *Ideología, literatura y sociedad de la Revolución Guatemalteca 1944–1954* (essay), along with the Puerto Rican Juan Flores for *Insularismo o ideología burguesa en Antonio Pedreira.* The Premio de Novela Plaza y Janés went to Plinio Apuleyo Mendoza for *Años de fuga,* a novel dealing with the relationship of two generations of Latin-American intellectuals with the political realities of their respective countries.

Younger novelists whose recent contributions deserved attention were Cuba's Severo Sarduy, a theoretician of the novel influenced by the French, who published *Maitreya;* the Mexican Ignacio Solares, who published his second novel, *Anónimo* (considered by many critics the best Mexican novel of the year); and the Colombians Héctor Sánchez, Flor Romero de Nohra, and Fanny Buitrago. New writers from Peru were Isaac Goldemberg, whose *La vida a plazos de Don Jacobo Lerner* appeared for the first time in Spanish (at the end of the previous year), and Laura Riesco, author of *El truco de los ojos.*

Mexico and Colombia were especially productive in fiction. José Agustín remained at the forefront of the young, rebellious writers in Mexico with *El rey que se acerca a su templo.* Arturo Azuela, also Mexican, published *Manifestación de silencios.* Two Mexican writers dealt with the clash between troops and students at a Mexico City housing project in 1968: Agustín Ramos in *Al cielo por asalto* and José Revueltas in *Mexico 1968: juventud y revolución.* In addition, Jorge Aguilar Mora wrote his second novel, *Si muero lejos de ti,* and the prolific Luis Spota published *El rostro de sueño.* Besides Héctor Sánchez (*El tejemaneje*), Flor Romero de Nohra (*Los sueños del poder*), and Fanny Buitrago (*Los pañamanes*), other somewhat established young Colombian writers who published were Benhur Sánchez Suárez with *A ritmo de hombre* and Darío Ruiz Gómez with *Hojas en el patio.*

The remainder of Latin America offered several noteworthy novels. Three of Argentina's most recognized writers produced new works: Julio Cortázar (*Un tal Lucas*), Adolfo Bioy Casares (*El héroe de las mujeres*), and Mario Benedetti (*Cotidianas,* poems). Cuba's José Lezama Lima's letters were published (*Cartas [1939–1976]*; see *Spain,* above), along with his compatriot César Leante's *Los guerrilleros negros* and Cintio Vintier's *De peña pobre.* Ecuador's Demetrio Aguilera Malta published *Réquiem para el diablo.*

Given the regimes in power in much of Latin America, many writers worked and published abroad, especially Uruguayans, Argentines, and Chileans. Chile's Antonio Skármeta continued writing fiction concerning precisely the problem of the Latin American in exile, a theme of growing importance. In addition to the fascination with French literary theory, a trend of the '70s, criticism focused on the writings of the earlier 20th century and the literature of the avant-garde. Thus numerous critical studies and editions appeared on the work of the Peruvian poet César Vallejo, and an edition of the *Revista Iberoamericana* (edited by René de Costa) was dedicated to the Chilean avant-garde poet Vicente Huidobro.

(RAYMOND L. WILLIAMS)

PORTUGUESE

Portugal. The year's major literary event was the posthumous publication of Jorge de Sena's novel *Sinais de Fogo,* on which he had worked intermittently for over a decade. The nature of its subject—the effect of the Spanish Civil War on the author's generation, at a time when the Salazar regime was already firmly established in Portugal—would have precluded its publication before 1975, but with the change in political climate Sena was encouraged to continue the novel, the first of an intended cycle.

Sinais de Fogo was much more than a novel about political unawareness and self-deception. By centring the action of his story on a small group of people whiling away the summer of 1939 in a seaside resort north of Lisbon, the author unveils moral and social tensions not dissimilar to those that will be unleashed on a gigantic scale by the war. The plot is spun around the clandestine preparation of a voyage of republican sympathizers to the territories held by the Madrid government. In the symbolic texture of the book, the voyage soon stands as a metaphor for the discovery of the self. This turns gradually into a descent into hell, where all the libidinal and primeval forces are let loose in anticipation of an existential anguish that only art can redeem.

Herberto Helder was probably the most distinguished innovator among authors to take the path opened up by Sena. In *Vox e Photomaton* he crosses the frontiers that divide the conscious from the unconscious and subverts the order of literary discourse normally associated with each of them. Innovation came also from the least expected quarter—the regional novel. In *Vindima de Fogo,* Cristóvão de Aguiar forged a new style, enlivened by local speech, to create an admirable and humorous fresco of the rural society of São Miguel, one of the islands of the Azorean archipelago caught between its Portuguese traditions and the lure of North America. (L. S. REBELO)

Brazil. Brazilian theatre began to flourish once again in 1979. Dias Gomes published his second play in two years; *As primícias* from late 1978 was followed by *O rei de Ramos.* Both are fables about power and oppression, but the first is intensely dramatic, while the second is based on popular traditions and has music by Chico Buarque. Buarque also wrote his own play, based on *The Beggar's Opera*. Márcio Souza published two plays about life in the "colonized " Amazon state. Censorship was lifted on Oduvaldo Viana's *Rasga Coração.*

Silviano Santiago's volume of poetry, *Crescendo Durante a Guerra numa Província Ultramarina*, censures the role of an intellectual elite that popularizes an imported culture. The poetry of Adélia Prado's *Solte os cachorros* approaches fiction with rhyme as she recalls carnal and mystic pleasures. The complete poems of the late Joaquim Cardozo appeared. Carlos Nejar and Antônio Fantinato, a younger poet, also published new collections.

Clarice Lispector's posthumous novel *Um sopro da vida (Pulsações)* was pervaded by music and thematic repetition, suggesting a medieval song. Changes that occurred in Brazil during the 1960s were a concern of fiction. Luiz Vilela turned to the novel to criticize life on a São Paulo newspaper, in *O inferno é aqui mesmo.* Other novels about that decade were José Louzeiro's *O estranho hábito de viver* and Antônio Marcello's *Ensaio Geral.* In *Na Barra de Catimbó,* Plínio Marcos recounted the founding of a new *favela* in an impressive sociopolitical statement.

Julieta de Godoy Ladeira, Geraldo Ferraz, and Luiz Vilela published new volumes of short fiction. The title novella of Domingos Pellegrini's *As sete pragas* deals with the success and decline of a land manipulator in Paraná state. Sônia Coutinho's characters in *Os venenos de Lucrécia* are torn between desire for yesterday's traditions and life in today's Copacabana. The stories of the "Dominican Frei Betto," a "militant for the theology of liberation," concern torture and injustice in contemporary Brazil.

Souto Maior's long-suppressed *Dicionário do palavrão e termos afins*, with well over 3,000 regional euphemisms culled from literary and popular sources, was finally published. New collections of socioliterary criticism were published by Gilberto Mendonça Teles and Roberto Schwarz. Studies of Clarice Lispector and Marcos Konder Reis appeared, as did the final volume of Wilson Martins's *História da inteligência brasileira* and an unusual "Freudian" interpretation of the Brazilian cultural movement *tropicalismo* by Celso Favaretto.

(IRWIN STERN)

Leonid Lenonov

V. SAVOSTYANOV—TASS/SOVFOTO

RUSSIAN

Soviet Literature. Although 1979 was not a year for presentation of the biennial Lenin Prizes, the Soviet Union's highest literary awards, an exception was made with the award of a Lenin Prize to Pres. Leonid I. Brezhnev for his trilogy *Little Land, Rebirth,* and *Virgin Lands,* published the previous year.

"I write of things I know best. . . ." These words spoken by Konstantin Simonov (*see* OBITUARIES) in an interview published in the May 9 (Victory Day), 1979, issue of *Literaturnaya Gazeta* indicated that he remained faithful to the theme of the military feats of the Soviet people to the end of his life; he died on August 28, aged 63. During the year a start was made on the publication of a ten-volume edition of his collected works.

The magazine *Druzhba Narodov* celebrated its 40th anniversary during the year. From a modest publication originally intended for Russian translations of works by writers in Soviet national republics and autonomous regions, it had developed into one of the U.S.S.R.'s most popular magazines. In 1979 it carried the reminiscences of Simonov and short stories by Sergey Zalygin, a poem by Eduardas Mieželaitis (translated from Lithuanian), and a cycle of poems by Irakly Abashidze (translated from Latvian) and Tulepbergen Kaipbergenov (translated from Kara-Kalpakian). It also carried many translations of Ukrainian works in connection with the 325th anniversary of the Ukraine's reunification with Russia.

The 180th anniversary of Aleksandr Pushkin's birth was marked by celebrations in Moscow, Leningrad, Kishinev, Odessa, Tbilisi, and other towns and localities connected with his life. The great Russian poet was one of the most widely published authors in the Soviet Union. In 1979 alone, volumes of works by Pushkin had a total printing of over 18 million.

Leonid Leonov, the venerable Soviet writer and public figure, was 80 in 1979. His novels *Barsuki, The Thief, Sot, Skutarevsky, Road to the Ocean,* and *Russian Forest* and his plays and other writings—all showing a profoundly humanistic approach to the problems facing man in an era of scientific and technological revolution—had become classics. Many new editions of his works and books dedicated to his literary activity were published in honour of his birthday. Among the latter were V. Kovalev's *Studies of Leonid Leonov,* F. Vlasov's *Epic of Courage,* an anthology of literary and critical articles entitled *Learning from Leonov,* and a collection of papers entitled *The World Significance of Leonid Leonov's Writings.*

Oak Roots: Impressions and Meditations on England and Englishmen, notes by Vsevolod Ovchinnikov, a *Pravda* journalist, were serialized in three issues of the magazine *Novy Mir.* They followed his successful *A Branch of Sakura,* published after an earlier visit to Japan. (MAYA Y. ISKOLDSKAYA)

Expatriate Russian Literature. Two outstanding novels by Soviet authors out of favour with the Moscow regime became available in English in 1979, Aleksandr Zinoviev's *The Yawning Heights* and *Faithful Ruslan* by Georgy Vladimov. These two writers, the first a brilliant philosopher and professor of logic, the second a professional novelist, provided typical examples of the fate that befalls those in the U.S.S.R. who dare to "think (and write) otherwise," to deviate from the carefully laid down precepts of official dogma.

Zinoviev, a wartime fighter pilot, worked in the Institute of Philosophy of the Soviet Academy of Sciences for 22 years and was a member of Moscow University's faculty of philosophy for 14 years. Once his novel was published in the West, all his past services to the nation counted for nothing. He was sacked from all his posts and expelled from the Communist Party, and he and members of his family were subjected to constant harassment and persecution. Zinoviev was forced to leave his country and now lived in Munich, West Germany. His *Yawning Heights* was a massive work of 830 pages in the tradition of Swift and Gogol, a sustained satirical onslaught on the closed society and the closed minds of those who run it, described by one reviewer as "the bitterest attack on the Soviet system to appear in Russian."

Vladimov was until 1975 a popular novelist, having started his working life as a journalist in 1953. From 1956 to 1959 he worked as an editor under Aleksandr Tvardovsky on the influential literary journal *Novy Mir*. He began writing *The Dogs*, which was later to develop into *Faithful Ruslan*, in 1963, but the fall of Nikita Khrushchev prevented its publication. The appearance of the novel in the West in 1975 put an end to Vladimov's successful career. In 1977 he wrote a scathing letter of resignation to the Soviet writers' union.

Faithful Ruslan was a parable, the story of a guard dog that became unemployed when Khrushchev closed down the labour camps that were part of Joseph Stalin's monstrous legacy. Seen entirely through its canine hero's eyes, this was a tragic story of misplaced loyalty, treachery, and human degradation. Trained all his life to guard convicts, Ruslan suddenly has nowhere to go. He attaches himself to one of his former charges, living in anticipation of the day when the camp will reopen and he can resume his faithful service.

Several other popular and previously widely published authors, including Vasily Aksyonov, Fazil Iskander, Andrey Voznesensky, and Bella Akhmadulina, fell out with the regime. They were among the 23 writers who, in January 1979, submitted a 700-page literary almanac to the writers' union, demanding that this antidote to the "nauseating inertia in our literary journals and publishing houses" be published, uncensored. Needless to say, their request was rejected and they were accused of trying to embarrass the authorities. The almanac, called *Metropol*, was later published in the West. (GEORGE THEINER)

EASTERN EUROPEAN LITERATURE

The cultural climate throughout Eastern Europe grew distinctly colder in 1979, particularly in Czechoslovakia and East Germany. In the latter the regime, no doubt worried by the increasing number of books that managed to cross the Berlin Wall and the ease with which East Germans could watch West German television programs, passed a new law severely restricting contacts with foreigners and making the passing of manuscripts or written statements "harmful to the interests of the State" punishable by five years in prison. That the law was intended not to prevent potential spies from passing on state secrets but rather to stop writers from publishing in the West was made clear by earlier action taken against such people as Stefan Heym, who was fined M 9,000 for "violating currency regulations" by publishing his latest novel, *Collin*, in West Germany without official permission. (See *German* above.)

Another trend in East Germany was the increased emigration of troublesome authors, whom the authorities seemed only too pleased to allow to settle in the "other" Germany. One of the most recent arrivals in the West was Jurek Becker, whose novel *Sleepless Days* was published in the U.K. at the end of the year. It dealt with the gradual disillusionment and political awakening of a schoolteacher who discovers that the system he once believed in is built on lies, fear, intimidation, and cruelty.

In Czechoslovakia writers were prominent among those who suffered constant harassment and worse for their continued adherence to ideals of democracy. Vaclav Havel, whose one-act plays *Audience* and *Private View* had already been widely performed in Britain and throughout Europe, managed to make these into a trilogy with *Protest* before being placed under house arrest in December 1978. The following May he and nine other members of VONS (Committee for the Defense of the Unjustly Persecuted) were arrested, and in October he was found guilty of "subversion" and sent to prison for 4½ years.

Another leading Czechoslovak playwright, Pavel Kohout, was allowed to spend a year working with the Viennese Burgtheater. Then, in October 1979, he was prevented from returning home. He was later deprived of his citizenship, as was Milan Kundera, who had been living in France since 1975. Kundera's novels and books of short stories (such as *Laughable Loves, Life Is Elsewhere, The Farewell Party*, and the most recent *Livre du rire et de l'oubli*) had won him international acclaim. Kohout's latest novel, *The Hangwoman*—a macabre fantasy about the only female recruit in a state institute for the training of master executioners—was published in West Germany.

Jiri Grusa, arrested in 1978 for writing *The Questionnaire*, was released after three months in custody and had the charges against him withdrawn. Another of the "nonconformist" Prague authors, Alexander Kliment, had much success with his novel, *Boredom in Bohemia*, published in Austria, West Germany, Switzerland, and Sweden. And last but not least, Jaroslav Seifert, the grand old man of Czechoslovak poetry, unexpectedly produced a new collection of verse called *Umbrella from Piccadilly*.

The Hungarian dissidents at the end of 1979 displayed unprecedented boldness and demonstrated how their ranks had grown by the impressive array of signatures on protests against the Prague trial of Havel and his friends. They also published *0.1%*, a compilation of articles and essays that was brought out in a French translation in Paris. Its title referred to the number of Hungarians the dissidents believed were willing to "stand up and be counted."

Poland boasted many more such people, its unofficial publishing exceeding by far any comparable activity in the other countries of Eastern Europe. In 1979 some 20,000 pages of such publications were in circulation. One of the best known, *Zapis*, brought together the "unpublishable" work of some of the best Polish writers. Two of its issues were novels by Tadeusz Konwicki, *The Polish Complex* and *Minor Apocalypse*.

Published during the year in the U.S. in the series "Writers from the Other Europe" were two remarkable volumes from the pen of a long-dead Polish author, Bruno Schulz. A Jewish schoolteacher executed by the Nazis in 1942, Schulz produced only three finished works before his death; the two now available in English were both collections of prose pieces, *The Street of Crocodiles* and *Sanatorium Under the Sign of the Hourglass*.

(GEORGE THEINER)

JEWISH

Hebrew. The year 1979 was a microcosm of Israeli literature's perennial preoccupations: the old, the current, and new directions. As to the old, four significant publications appeared: *Korot Beytenu*, S. Y. Agnon's ninth posthumous (and most autobiographical) work; a collection of poetry by Uri Zvi Greenberg and a reprint of his *Sefer Hakitrug Veha'emuna*; and a reissue of S. Yizhar's pre-1948 novella *Befa'atei Negev*. As to the new, a divergent voice in Israeli fiction was noted in the first novels of Ya'akov Botchan and David Shitz. Botchan's work was a grim testimony of alienation in the post-Yom Kippur War period, and Shitz's a historical novel of Germany's pre-Holocaust generation.

Current works included volumes of fiction by Y. Orpaz, D. Tselka, D. Shahar, and Sandbank; a new play by N. Aloni; poetry by Gouri, M. Wieseltier, Hourvitz, E. Megged, D. Avidan, and Y. Pinkas; and essays and criticism by A. Oz, Balaban, and D. Miron. G. Kressel published his important reference book *Guide to the Hebrew Press* (1691–present). Three books of poetry (by Atar, N. Yonathan, and Pen) were best-sellers, and *100 Poems for Soldiers* also sold well—ample testimony to the Israelis' continued interest in Hebrew poetry.

Beyond these publications, the literary scene reflected two significant trends. Heightened by the signing of the Israeli-Egyptian peace agreement, there was an increasing awareness of Arabic literature and of the Arab problem. At the same time, several authors began to look back on the "'48 generation" of Israeli literature, to determine its roots and motivations and to evaluate its aesthetic and cultural effects. Finally, the periodical *Moznayim* celebrated its 50th anniversary with a special, expanded issue.

(WARREN BARGAD)

Yiddish. The award of the 1978 Nobel Prize for Literature to Isaac Bashevis Singer produced an entire industry of criticism, largely in English, but most discussed only those works that had appeared in English translation. A number of his most important works remained in the columns of the *Jewish Daily Forward*, and some critics expressed chagrin over his reluctance to revise and prepare these novels and stories for publication in Yiddish in book form.

Chaim Grade, author of *Tsemakh Atlas* and *The Agunah*, was publishing the novel *From Under the Earth* in the *Forward*; it describes the heroism and tragedy of a group of Holocaust survivors who return to Vilnius and attempt to rebuild their lives. Abraham Sutzkever's collection of stories, *Where the Stars Spend the Night*, brilliantly re-creates the horror and suffering of the Holocaust. His short anthology of poems, *First Night in the Ghetto*, is overwhelming in its moving simplicity and clarity. Itzhak Janosowicz was represented by *Container of Spices and Other Stories*, about Jewish life and experiences in wartime Russia.

Important poetic anthologies appeared by Rochelle Keprinsky, Motl Saktzier, and Hirsh Osherovitch. Chanan Kiel's *A Shepherd in Exile* tells of the sufferings of Jewish refugees during World War II and of his attitude and mystical feelings about Israel. Isaiah Spiegal published his *Collected Poems*. Uri Zvi Greenberg, considered the most important Hebrew poet in Israel today, published all his Yiddish poems in two volumes. *The Man of Forty* by the martyred Soviet Yiddish poet Perets Markish appeared at last in the original and became the object of much discussion. Parts of it had been published in *Sovetish Heymland* in 1965, and a Russian translation had appeared in 1969.

Three volumes of criticism and literary scholarship were published: the late Moyshe Starkman's *Collected Writings*; Leyzer Podriachik's *In Profile of the Times*; and Elias Schulman's *Portraits and Studies*, an overview of Yiddish literary history and personalities.

(ELIAS SCHULMAN)

CHINESE

China. In 1979 China continued the cultural and literary thaw initiated in 1977 following the downfall of the radical "gang of four." Outlining the latest official policy at a congress of writers and artists in October, Vice-Premier Deng Xiaoping (Teng Hsiao-p'ing) stressed artistic workers' freedom to choose subject matter and method of presentation, as well as the requirement to educate the people in Communist ideology. Many purged writers and critics were rehabilitated, and even works of dissent literature began to appear. (*See* CHINA.)

Some writers felt free to write about love, which had been condemned as a vestige of bourgeois decadence in the late 1960s and early '70s. A good example was *A Place for Love* by Liu Xinwu (Liu Hsin-wu). Tragic tales and satirical plays designed to expose the dark side of Communist society were allowed to appear. Xing Yixun's (Hsing Yi-hsün's) play *Power and the Law* became popular for its revelation of the evil doings of a party secretary. Zhao Zixiong's (Chao Tzu-hsiung's) drama *The Call of the Future* pitted Communist against Communist rather than the stereotyped conflict between good Communist and corrupt reactionary. Despite its somewhat wooden characters and disjointed plot, it presented believable people, satirical attacks on certain Communist officials, and the world of personal relationships and human emotions. It was one of the latest literary works to break through some of the conventions imposed on literature during the Cultural Revolution, which had permitted only superhumanly good or infernally evil characters.

Another important development of 1979 was the rising interest in history. The historical play *Wang Zhaojun* (*Wang Chaochün*) by the recently rehabilitated veteran playwright Cao Yu (Ts'ao Yü), with its emphasis on personal sacrifice and unity among China's ethnic groups, attracted much attention in China. One more volume of Yao Xueyin's (Yao Hsüeh-yin's) monumental historical novel *Li Zicheng* (*Li Tzu-ch'eng*) was published.

Taiwan. In contrast to China's cultural and literary thaw, Taiwan seemed to have tightened its control over political and other activities. Nevertheless, Taiwan literature continued to demonstrate vitality and diversity. Political satires became very popular; the best example was probably Huang Fan's story *Lai So*, which satirized not only the Communists and the Taiwan Independence Movement but the Nationalist government and the ruling party, the Kuomintang, as well. The lives of Taiwan's capitalists and businessmen became an important theme, best represented by Chang Hsi-kuo's novel *The Water of the Yellow River*.

The movement to create a Taiwan "nativist" literature (*hsiang-t'u wen-hsüeh*) continued to be a literary issue, despite reservations in official circles. Its advocacy of a native Taiwanese literature, written in the local dialect and with emphasis on local themes, gained more acceptance. Its leaders rejected both traditional "literati" literature and Western modernist influences. A good example was Chung Chao-cheng's *The Story of the Heroes of Ma-li-k'o-wan*, a novel dealing with life among the mountain tribes in Taiwan.

Taiwan writers residing abroad also attracted attention. Among them were Pai Hsien-yung, whose *The Prodigal Sons*, a novel dealing with conflicts between fathers and sons and other themes in the Taiwan of the 1970s, appeared to be a major literary contribution. Ch'en Jo-hsi's recent stories, based on her experiences in China during the Cultural Revolution, were widely read in both Taiwan and the West.

(WINSTON L. Y. YANG; NATHAN K. MAO)

JAPANESE

The craze for newness was one of the most salient features of Japanese literary life; hence the journalistic fuss about the recipients of the Akutagawa literary prize, awarded biennially to the "most promising" young authors. The 1979 winners were Yoshiko Shigekane, a middle-aged housewife, and So Aono, whose novelette (*Nights of a Fool*) seemed to be based on his own experiences as a cosmopolitan hippie. Shigekane's literary background consisted almost exclusively of creative writing courses given at the Culture Centre, a kind of inexpensive private school providing courses in such subjects as archaeology, English conversation, and the tea ceremony. Naturally, Shigekane's acquisition of the prize was acclaimed as a "brilliant achievement" for the centre, and Yomiuri Press and NHK were establishing new centres on a huge scale.

CHINA PHOTO SERVICE/EASTFOTO

Cao Yu

Even among established authors, the female imagination was the more active and successful. Fumiko Enchi's *Home Without a Dining Table* was based on the actual experiences of several families whose sons joined the Red Army terrorist group. Though it suffered from catering to the popular taste for melodrama (it was originally serialized in the newspapers), it remained an exciting novel of social and psychological analysis. Ayako Sono's *Room of Absence* was another impressive achievement, remarkable for its vivid evocation of life in a Japanese Roman Catholic convent. Starting as a novel of intense piety and ending as a comical, even satirical, novel of manners, it successfully conveyed the contemporary predicament of Catholicism, even though the change in tone seemed a little artificial. Tsuneko Nakasato's fine collection of short stories, *Tagasode-so*, developed the theme of female loneliness with graceful subtlety. In Yuko Tsushima's *Spheres of Light*, with its skillful vignettes about a young divorcée with a baby daughter, the theme of the independent woman was toned down by the author's poetical style.

Japanese male authors were not inactive. Otohiko Kaga's *Sentence* was a voluminous novel of documentation, dealing with the psychology of a young murderer under sentence of death. Kaga was trained as a psychoanalyst and served as police doctor for several years, so his descriptions were accurate and convincing, although the novel was somewhat too heavy and theoretical. Tetsuro Miura's *Rider of a Rocking Horse*, an excellent collection of short stories, dealt mainly with the emotional responses of children. Among works of biography and criticism were Fujio Noguchi's *Shusei Tokuda*, Koichi Isoda's *Kafu Nagai*, Hideaki Oketani's *Dostoevsky*, and Shoichi Saeki's *Narrative Art*.

(SHOICHI SAEKI)

See also Art Sales; Libraries; Nobel Prizes; Publishing.
[621]

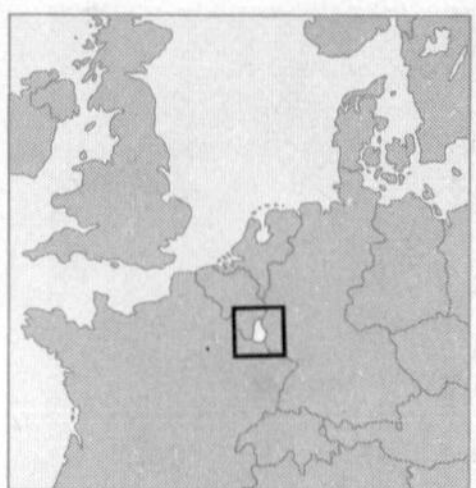

Luxembourg

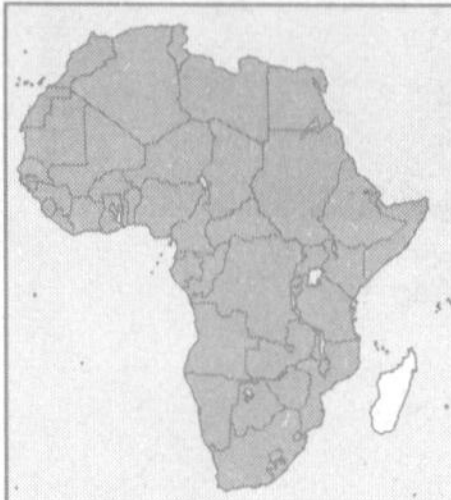

Madagascar

Luxembourg

A constitutional monarchy, the Benelux country of Luxembourg is bounded on the east by West Germany, on the south by France, and on the west and north by Belgium. Area: 2,586 sq km (999 sq mi). Pop. (1978 est.): 360,000. Cap. and largest city: Luxembourg (pop., 1977 est., 76,500). Language: French, German, Luxembourgian. Religion: Roman Catholic 93%. Grand duke, Jean; prime ministers in 1979, Gaston Thorn and, from July 19, Pierre Werner.

A general election held June 10, 1979, resulted in defeat for the Liberal-Socialist government of Prime Minister Gaston Thorn, who resigned the following day. The Liberals actually increased their strength from 14 to 15 seats, but their ally, the Workers' Socialist Party, lost 3, reducing its representation to 14. The Christian Socialist parliamentary group rose from 17 to 24 members, while the Social Democrats and the Communists each lost 3 seats and retained 2. Two new independent groups won one seat apiece.

After consulting the various party leaders, on June 19 Grand Duke Jean asked Pierre Werner, the 66-year-old leader of the Christian Socialist Party, to form a new government. Lacking a majority in the 59-member Chamber of Deputies, Werner asked Thorn to join him in a coalition. After month-long negotiations, Werner announced the composition of a Cabinet of five Christian Socialist and four Liberal ministers, with himself as prime minister and Thorn as foreign minister. The new government was sworn on July 19, but its durability appeared uncertain to political observers.

In June the government announced that it had abandoned plans for a nuclear power plant to be built at Remerschen and had opted for a coal-fired plant instead. Grand Duke Jean and Duchess Josephone Charlotte visited China in September.

(K. M. SMOGORZEWSKI)

LUXEMBOURG

Education. (1977–78) Primary, pupils 33,638, teachers 1,821; secondary, pupils 8,438, teachers (1975–76) 860; vocational, pupils 15,382, teachers (1975–76) 941; teacher training, students, 100; higher, students (1976–77) 446, teaching staff (1975–76) 137.

Finance. Monetary unit: Luxembourg franc, at par with the Belgian franc, with (Sept. 17, 1979) a free rate of LFr 29.07 to U.S. $1 (LFr 62.55 = £1 sterling). Budget (1979 est.): revenue LFr 41,212,000,000; expenditure LFr 42.1 billion. Gross domestic product (1978) LFr 106,570,000,000. Cost of living (1975 = 100; June 1979) 125.8.

Foreign Trade: *see* BELGIUM.

Transport and Communications. Roads (1977) 4,971 km (including 27 km expressways). Motor vehicles in use (1977): passenger 141,400; commercial 10,100. Railways: (1977) 274 km; traffic (1978) 296 million passenger-km, freight 649 million net ton-km. Air traffic (1977): 175 million passenger-km; freight 300,000 net ton-km. Telephones (Jan. 1978) 185,500. Radio licenses (Dec. 1976) 205,000. Television licenses (Dec. 1976) 105,000.

Agriculture. Production (in 000; metric tons; 1977): barley 57; wheat 25; oats 20; potatoes 55; wine *c.* 15. Livestock (in 000; May 1977): cattle 212; pigs 86; chickens 185.

Industry. Production (in 000; metric tons; 1978): iron ore (29% metal content) 835; pig iron 3,721; crude steel 4,791; electricity (kw-hr) 1,389,000.

Madagascar

Madagascar occupies the island of the same name and minor adjacent islands in the Indian Ocean off the southeast coast of Africa. Area: 587,041 sq km (226,658 sq mi). Pop. (1979 est.): 9,048,000. Cap. and largest city: Antananarivo (pop., 1976 est., 468,000). Language: Malagasy (national) and French (official). Religion: animist 57%; Roman Catholic 20%; Protestant 18%; Muslim 5%. President in 1979, Didier Ratsiraka; prime minister, Lieut. Col. Désiré Rakotoarijaona.

A neurotic fear of plots raged like an almost permanent epidemic in 1979 in Antananarivo, where Pres. Didier Ratsiraka continually ordered arrests, expulsions of foreigners, and alerts. Even strikes were repressed as being the consequence of "imperialist maneuvers."

In March Ratsiraka proposed to South Africa an exchange of "foreign mercenaries" detained in Madagascar for 51 South African political prisoners, including the black nationalist leader Nelson Mandela; the offer was rejected. Among Madagascar's detainees in question were two South Africans and one U.S. subject arrested in January 1977 for an unauthorized landing on Madagascar and sentenced in April 1978 to five years in prison.

It was learned in August 1979 that Maj. Richard Andriamaholison, former minister of information under the Richard Ratsimandrava government, and Capt. Marson Rakotonirina had been held without trial since their arrest in October 1977.

President Ratsiraka on May 16, 1979, attended the state funeral at Antananarivo to honour Maj.

MADAGASCAR

Education. (1976) Primary, pupils 1.1 million, teachers (1975) 18,688; secondary, pupils 114,468, teachers (1975) 5,088; vocational, pupils 7,000, teachers (1973) 879; teacher training (1973), students 993, teachers 63; higher, students 11,000, teaching staff (1972) 411.

Finance. Monetary unit: Malagasy franc, at par with the CFA franc, with (Sept. 17, 1979) a parity of MalFr 50 to the French franc (free rates of MalFr 211.54 = U.S. $1 and MalFr 455.12 = £1 sterling). Gold, SDR's, and foreign exchange (Feb. 1979) U.S. $28.3 million. Budget (1978 est.) balanced at MalFr 158 billion.

Foreign Trade. (1977) Imports MalFr 85,210,000,000; exports MalFr 82,630,000,000. Import sources (1976): France 37%; Qatar 9%; West Germany 9%. Export destinations (1976): France 29%; U.S. 16%; Japan 7%; West Germany 7%; Reunion 6%. Main exports (1976): coffee 43%; cloves and clove oil 9%; vanilla 7%; petroleum products 7%.

Transport and Communications. Roads (1976) 27,507 km. Motor vehicles in use (1977): passenger 57,400; commercial (including buses) 52,300. Railways: (1977) 884 km; traffic (1978) 296 million passenger-km, freight 211 million net ton-km. Air traffic (1977): 280 million passenger-km; freight 7.8 million net ton-km. Shipping (1978): merchant vessels 100 gross tons and over 45; gross tonnage 40,303. Telephones (Jan. 1978) 28,700. Radio receivers (Dec. 1976) 609,000. Television receivers (Dec. 1976) 8,000.

Agriculture. Production (in 000; metric tons; 1978): rice 1,981; corn (1977) *c.* 135; cassava (1977) 1,300; sweet potatoes (1977) *c.* 287; potatoes (1977) *c.* 120; mangoes *c.* 190; dry beans *c.* 42; bananas *c.* 450; oranges *c.* 80; pineapples *c.* 45; peanuts 35; sugar, raw value (1977) *c.* 110; coffee 87; cotton *c.* 14; tobacco 5; sisal 17; beef and veal *c.* 106; fish catch (1977) *c.* 56. Livestock (in 000; Dec. 1977): cattle *c.* 9,000; sheep (1976) *c.* 744; pigs *c.* 560; goats (1976) *c.* 1,376; chickens (1976) *c.* 13,628.

Livestock
see Agriculture and Food Supplies

Lumber
see Industrial Review

Lutheran Churches:
see Religion

Macau:
see Dependent States

Machinery and Machine Tools:
see Industrial Review

Gen. Gabriel Ramanantsoa (*see* OBITUARIES), virtual head of state from May 18, 1972, when Pres. Philibert Tsiranana gave him full powers, to Feb. 5, 1975. At the end of September President Ratsiraka paid a state visit to Paris.

(PHILIPPE DECRAENE)

Malawi

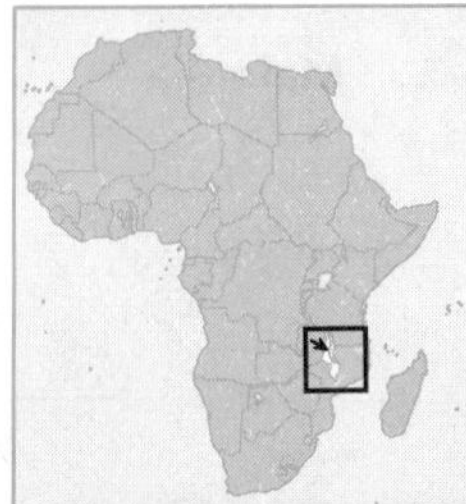

Malawi

A republic and member of the Commonwealth of Nations in east central Africa, Malawi is bounded by Tanzania, Mozambique, and Zambia. Area: 118,484 sq km (45,747 sq mi). Pop. (1977 prelim. census): 5,561,821. Cap.: Lilongwe (pop., 1977 prelim. census, 102,900). Largest city: Blantyre (pop., 1977 prelim. census, 222,200). Language: English (official) and Chichewa (national). Religion: Christian 33%; remainder predominantly traditional beliefs. President in 1979, Hastings Kamuzu Banda.

Pres. Hastings Banda attended the Commonwealth heads of government conference in Zambia in August 1979, but his continuing refusal to take sides in the political disputes in southern Africa prevented him from having a significant role in the discussions about the future of his neighbour, Zimbabwe Rhodesia. Queen Elizabeth II received a friendly welcome when she visited Malawi on her way to the conference in July. Pres. Daniel arap Moi of Kenya paid an official visit to Blantyre in July when Malawi celebrated the 15th anniversary of its independence.

President Banda made changes in his Cabinet in January and again in July. In February he told Parliament that his agents had been responsible for the attempted assassination by a letter bomb of Attati Mpakati, an opposition leader exiled in Mozambique.

After the fluctuations of 1978 the prices of Malawi's main exports, tobacco and tea, remained reasonably stable, but this could not prevent the accumulation of a sizable trade deficit. Fortunately, plentiful supplies of hydroelectric power prevented the soaring prices of oil products from having as serious an impact on Malawi as on some other African countries.

(KENNETH INGHAM)

MALAWI

Education. (1977–78) Primary, pupils 675,740, teachers 11,115; secondary, pupils 15,140, teachers 725; vocational and teacher training, students 2,525, teachers 175; higher (1976–77), students 1,836, teaching staff 122.

Finance. Monetary unit: kwacha, with (Sept. 17, 1979) a free rate of 0.81 kwacha to U.S. $1 (1.75 kwacha = £1 sterling). Gold, SDR's, and foreign exchange (June 1979) U.S. $42.4 million. Budget (1978 actual): revenue 136 million kwacha; expenditure 186.9 million kwacha.

Foreign Trade. (1978) Imports 285.2 million kwacha; exports 157.1 million kwacha. Import sources (1977): South Africa 37%; U.K. 19%; Japan 9%; U.S. 5%. Export destinations (1977): U.K. 42%; U.S. 10%; The Netherlands 7%; South Africa 7%. Main exports: tobacco 56%; tea 19%; sugar 7%.

Transport and Communications. Roads (1977) 15,745 km. Motor vehicles in use (1977): passenger 11,500; commercial 15,500. Railways: (1977) 566 km; traffic (1978) 67 million passenger-km, freight 223 million net ton-km. Air traffic (1978): 138.5 million passenger-km; freight 7.2 million net ton-km. Telephones (Jan. 1978) 22,600. Radio receivers (Dec. 1976) 130,000.

Agriculture. Production (in 000; metric tons; 1978): corn *c.* 1,400; cassava (1977) *c.* 90; sorghum *c.* 110; sugar, raw value (1977) *c.* 98; peanuts *c.* 100; tea *c.* 32; tobacco *c.* 56; cotton, lint (1977) *c.* 8. Livestock (in 000; 1977): cattle 729; sheep *c.* 89; goats *c.* 763; pigs *c.* 190; poultry *c.* 8,484.

Malawian Pres. Hastings Kamuzu Banda and citizenry dressed in costume were on hand to greet Britain's Queen Elizabeth II when she visited Malawi in July.

CHRISTIANE CHOMBEAU—GAMMA/LIAISON

Malaysia

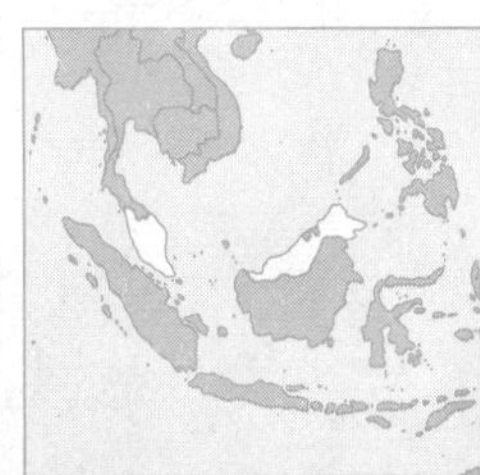

Malaysia

A federation within the Commonwealth of Nations comprising the 11 states of the former Federation of Malaya, Sabah, Sarawak, and the federal territory of Kuala Lumpur, Malaysia is a federal constitutional monarchy situated in Southeast Asia at the southern end of the Malay Peninsula

Magazines:
see Publishing

Malagasy Republic:
see Madagascar

WIDE WORLD

The previously uninhabited island of Bidong, eight miles off the coast of Malaysia, was thronged with refugees during the year when "boat people" from Vietnam began arriving there.

(excluding Singapore) and on the northern part of the island of Borneo. Area: 329,747 sq km (127,316 sq mi). Pop. (1978 est.): 12,736,600, including (1970) Malays 47.1%, Chinese 33.9%, Indians 9.1%, and Dayaks 3.5%. Cap. and largest city: Kuala Lumpur (pop., 1975 UN est., 557,000). Language: Malay (official). Religion: Malays are Muslim; Indians mainly Hindu; Chinese mainly Buddhist, Confucian, and Taoist. Supreme heads of state in 1979, with the title of *yang di-pertuan agong*, Tuanku Yahya Putra ibni al-Marhum Sultan Ibrahim and, from March 29, Sultan Haji Ahmad Shah al-Musta'in Billah ibni al-Marhum Sultan Abu Bakar Ri'ayatuddin al-Mu'adzam Shah; prime minister, Datuk Hussein bin Onn.

From the very beginning of 1979 the Malaysian government expressed concern about the increasing influx of refugees from Vietnam. In January more than 50,000 were concentrated in temporary camps on islands off the east coast of the Malay Peninsula. The vast majority of the refugees were ethnic Chinese, providing Malay opponents of the government with an opportunity to charge that the racial balance in the country was under threat.

The issue was brought to a head in June when the deputy prime minister, Dato Seri Mahathir Mohamed, announced that in the future the government would not only expel the Vietnamese "boat people" but would also seek to pass legislation giving powers to shoot them on sight. Although the shooting policy was later rescinded by Prime Minister Datuk Hussein bin Onn, this statement, along with a policy of towing away incoming refugee boats, served to defuse political tension within the country prior to the annual assembly of the United Malays National Organization. It also galvanized the international community into holding a further conference on refugees in Geneva in July, at which Vietnam agreed to a moratorium on departures and Western countries made improved offers of resettlement. (*See* REFUGEES.)

Malaysia demonstrated solidarity with its fellow members of the Association of Southeast Asian Nations (ASEAN) in refusing to endorse the removal of the Pol Pot government in Cambodia by Vietnamese force of arms. In August the foreign ministers of ASEAN met in Kuala Lumpur and reaffirmed their position strongly deploring Vietnam's armed intervention against Cambodia's independence and territorial integrity. In September the chief of staff of the armed forces, Tan Sri Mohamed Sani Ghafar, announced a military expansion in the 1980s to meet the external threats posed by developments in Indochina.

The annual assembly of the Malayan Chinese Association was dominated by the contest for leadership between its president, Datuk Lee San Choon (minister of works and utilities), and its deputy president, Datuk Michael Chen (minister of housing and local government). In the voting the incumbent held onto office 901 to 686. The defeated challenger was immediately dropped from all party posts. He also resigned his ministerial portfolio and announced his decision to form a new Chinese-based party.

In January an industrial dispute over salary negotiations occurred between the government-controlled Malaysian Airline System (MAS) and the airline employees' union. In February all flights were grounded temporarily after a government spokesman claimed that some employees had tampered with aircraft equipment. The detention of some union employees followed, as well as the deregistration of some unions. The detainees included Donald Uren, Asian representative of the International Transport Workers' Federation, which prompted Australian union members to refuse to release an MAS DC-10 aircraft at Sydney Airport. It was released eventually through the action of the Australian government, but a boycott of the refueling of MAS aircraft ended only when Uren was released from detention.

Elections were held for the state assembly in

MALAYSIA

Education. (1977) *Peninsular Malaysia.* Primary, pupils 1,609,335, teachers 50,531; secondary (1976), pupils 838,-968, teachers 29,924; vocational (1975), pupils 21,134, teachers 930; higher, students (1976) 39,658, teaching staff (1974) 2,624. *Sabah.* Primary, pupils 127,555, teachers 5,-032; secondary (1976), pupils 52,153, teachers 1,978; vocational (1976), pupils 300, teachers 35. *Sarawak.* Primary, pupils 193,024, teachers 5,704; secondary (1976), pupils 70,167, teachers 2,413; vocational (1974), pupils 306, teachers 28; higher, students (1976) 1,097, teaching staff (1974) 62.

Finance. Monetary unit: ringgit, with (Sept. 17, 1979) a free rate of 2.15 ringgits to U.S. $1 (4.62 ringgits = £1 sterling). Gold, SDR's, and foreign exchange (June 1979) U.S. $3,781,000,000. Budget (1978 est.): revenue 8,-277,000,000 ringgits; expenditure 8,058,000,000 ringgits. Gross national product (1978) 34,608,000,000 ringgits. Money supply (May 1979) 7,642,000,000 ringgits. Cost of living (Peninsular Malaysia; 1975 = 100; April 1979) 115.2.

Foreign Trade. (1978) Imports 13,690,000,000 ringgits; exports 17,094,000,000 ringgits. Import sources: Japan 23%; U.S. 14%; Singapore 9%; U.K. 7%; Australia 6%; West Germany 6%. Export destinations: Japan 22%; U.S. 19%; Singapore 16%; The Netherlands 6%; U.K. 5%. Main exports: rubber 21%; timber 15%; crude oil 13%; tin 12%; palm oil 11%.

Transport and Communications. Roads (1975) 25,133 km. Motor vehicles in use (1977): passenger 572,100; commercial (including buses) 196,200. Railways: (1977) 2,375 km; traffic (including Singapore; 1978) 1,270,000,000 passenger-km, freight 1,293,000,000 net ton-km. Air traffic (1978): 2,533,000,000 passenger-km; freight 86.8 million net ton-km. Shipping (1978): merchant vessels 100 gross tons and over 182; gross tonnage 552,456. Telephones (Jan. 1978) 374,700. Radio receivers (Dec. 1976) 1,450,000. Television licenses (Dec. 1977) 599,200.

Agriculture. Production (in 000; metric tons; 1978): rice 1,590; rubber *c.* 1,580; copra *c.* 207; palm oil 1,778; tea *c.* 3; bananas *c.* 460; pineapples *c.* 280; pepper (Sarawak only; 1977) 27; tobacco *c.* 10; meat (1977) *c.* 145; fish catch (1977) 619; timber (cu m; 1977) *c.* 37,500. Livestock (in 000; Dec. 1976): cattle 412; buffalo 212; pigs 1,308; goats 333; sheep 47; chickens *c.* 46,600.

Industry. Production (in 000; metric tons; 1978): tin concentrates (metal content) 63; bauxite 595; cement 2,-194; iron ore (56% metal content) 319; crude oil 10,320; petroleum products (Sarawak only; 1977) *c.* 800; electricity (kw-hr) 8,202,000.

Sarawak in September. The National Front coalition gained 45 of the 48 seats contested, the remaining 3 going to independent candidates. Within the coalition, Party Pesaka Bumiputera Bersatu won 18 seats, the Sarawak United People's Party 11, and the Sarawak National Party 16.

The elected king, or *yang di-pertuan agong*, of Malaysia, Tuanku Yahya Putra ibni al-Marhum Sultan Ibrahim of Kelantan, died on March 29 at the age of 62. He was succeeded by Sultan Haji Ahmad Shah al-Musta'in Billah ibni al-Marhum Sultan Abu Bakar Ri'ayatuddin al-Mu'adzam Shah, the sultan of Penang. (MICHAEL LEIFER)

Maldives

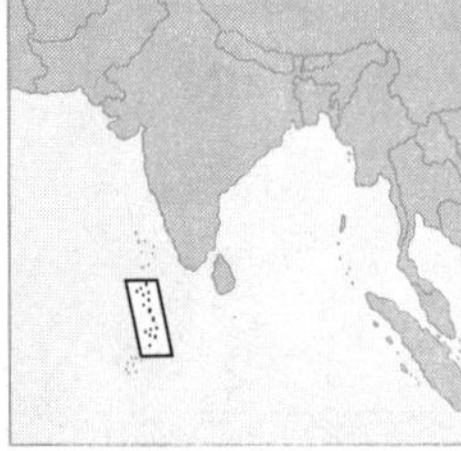
Maldives

Maldives, a republic in the Indian Ocean consisting of about two thousand small islands, lies southwest of the southern tip of India. Area: 298 sq km (115 sq mi). Pop. (1978): 143,000. Cap.: Male (pop., 1978, 29,600). Language: Divehi. Religion: Muslim. President in 1979, Maumoon Abdul Gayoom.

During 1979 Pres. Maumoon Abdul Gayoom made his first presidential journeys abroad, to the U.S., Kuwait, Libya, and the meeting of nonaligned countries in Cuba. As minister of transport in 1978, Gayoom had been responsible for major airport expansion in the Maldives, and as president he energetically continued the islands' development. He established a corporation to compete with foreign companies fishing within the Maldives' 200-mi economic zone, concluded an agreement with Sri Lanka for the resumption of Maldivian fish exports (the first consignment left in September), and negotiated to acquire two larger ships for general trade.

MALDIVES

Education. (1977) Primary, pupils 2,747, teachers 29; secondary, pupils 641, teachers 55; teacher training, students 30, teachers 11.

Finance and Trade. Monetary unit: Maldivian rupee, with (Sept. 17, 1979) a par value of MRs 3.93 to U.S. $1 (MRs 8.46 = £1 sterling). Budget (1976): revenue MRs 17.2 million; expenditure MRs 35.7 million. Foreign trade (1977): imports MRs 35.8 million; exports MRs 14.5 million. Main import sources: Japan, U.K., Thailand, Sri Lanka, India. Main export destinations: Japan, Sri Lanka, Thailand. Main exports (1976): Maldive (dried) fish 46%; raw fish 44%; shells 5%.

Hong Kong Orient Express Airways conducted a feasibility study on Gan for airport and tourist development there. Schools were established in all 19 atolls, doubling the school population to 5,000. Abroad, Gayoom improved relations with the Maldives' oldest allies, Sri Lanka and Great Britain. Though Saudi Arabia still supplied the most aid to the Maldives, increased British involvement was arranged, and Gayoom moved generally closer to the West.

In February armed Maldivians boarded a U.S. oceanographic survey vessel and allegedly kidnapped three crew members. The details remained unclear, but in March the two countries signed a statement agreeing that the Maldivians had thought the ship was illegally fishing in Maldivian waters. (MOLLY MORTIMER)

Mali

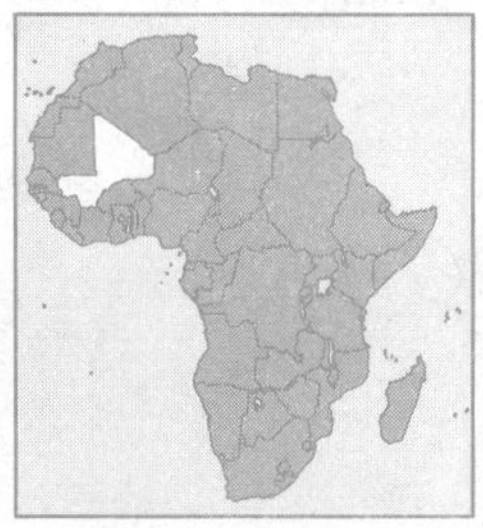
Mali

A republic of West Africa, Mali is bordered by Algeria, Niger, Upper Volta, Ivory Coast, Guinea, Senegal, and Mauritania. Area: 1,240,142 sq km (478,832 sq mi). Pop. (1978 est.): 6,290,000. Cap. and largest city: Bamako (pop., 1976, 404,000). Language: French (official); Hamito-Semitic and various tribal dialects. Religion: Muslim 65%; animist 30%. Head of the military government in 1979, Gen. Moussa Traoré.

As a first step toward the promised early establishment of civilian government in Mali, the nation's rulers set up at Bamako on March 30, 1979, a new political party, the Union Démocratique du Peuple Malien (UDPM), with a National Council comprising 137 members, 104 of them civilians. On June 19 Gen. Moussa Traoré, sole candidate, was reelected president of the republic by an almost unanimous vote, and the 82 UDPM candidates were similarly elected.

Nevertheless, unrest spread throughout Mali and met with severe repression, arousing the concern of such organizations as Amnesty Interna-

MALI

Education. (1976–77) Primary, pupils 291,966, teachers 8,280; secondary, pupils 8,915; vocational, pupils 2,609; secondary and vocational, teachers 540; teacher training (1974–75), students 1,839, teachers 126; higher, students 2,920, teaching staff 435.

Finance. Monetary unit: Mali franc, with (Sept. 17, 1979) a par value of MFr 100 to the French franc and a free rate of MFr 423 to U.S. $1 (MFr 910 = £1 sterling). Budget (1978 est.) balanced at MFr 61 billion.

Foreign Trade. (1978) Imports MFr 91.3 billion; exports MFr 42.5 billion. Import sources (1976): France 40%; Ivory Coast 14%; Senegal 10%; China 7%; West Germany 6%. Export destinations (1976): France 31%; Ivory Coast 13%; West Germany 11%; China 10%; U.K. 9%; Senegal 6%. Main exports (1976): cotton 50%; livestock 13%; peanuts 12%; cereals 6%.

Agriculture. Production (in 000; metric tons; 1978): millet and sorghum *c.* 1,035; rice *c.* 270; corn *c.* 85; peanuts 146; sweet potatoes (1977) *c.* 36; cassava (1977) *c.* 40; cottonseed *c.* 75; cotton, lint *c.* 43; beef and veal (1977) *c.* 42; mutton and goat meat (1977) *c.* 31; fish catch *c.* 100. Livestock (in 000; 1977): cattle *c.* 4,076; sheep *c.* 4,437; goats *c.* 4,057; camels *c.* 188; horses *c.* 160; asses *c.* 429.

tional. The trial of former leaders of the junta (Kissima Doukara, Tiecoro Bagayoko, Karim Dembele, and Joseph Mara) for corruption began on February 27. Doukara was sentenced to death for embezzlement, but on June 11 the Supreme Court annulled the sentences. Abroad, opposition grouped itself around the Union Démocratique Révolutionnaire Malienne, whose leader, Didi Demba Medina, lived in Libya.

(PHILIPPE DECRAENE)

SYNDICATION INTERNATIONAL/PHOTO TRENDS

On April 1 the British flag was lowered for the last time on the island of Malta when the British closed their bases there. Libyan leader Col. Muammar al-Qaddafi attended the ceremonies.

Malta

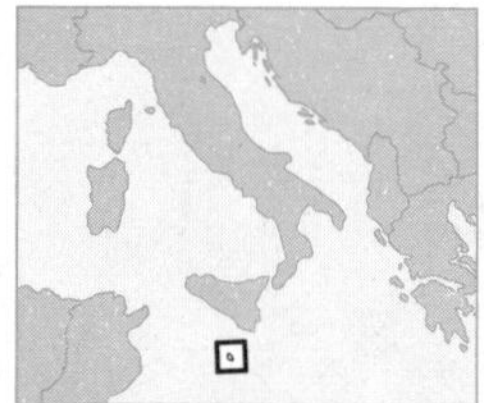

Malta

The Republic of Malta, a member of the Commonwealth of Nations, comprises the islands of Malta, Gozo, and Comino in the Mediterranean Sea between Sicily and Tunisia. Area: 320 sq km (124 sq mi), including Malta, Gozo, and Comino. Pop. (1979 est.): 311,400. Cap.: Valletta (pop., 1978 est., 14,000). Largest city: Sliema (pop., 1978 est., 20,100). Language: Maltese and English. Religion: mainly Roman Catholic. President in 1979, Anton Buttigieg; prime minister, Dom Mintoff.

The highlight of 1979 was the end of the seven-year military facilities agreement with Great Britain and NATO on March 31 and the closing of the British base in Malta after a presence of 179 years. Malta would thenceforth be nonaligned, and the government proclaimed that its energies would be directed toward the attainment of peace and unity in the Mediterranean.

No decisive progress was made in negotiations with neighbouring countries to make up the loss of M£28 million annually resulting from the expiration of the facilities agreement. With an expenditure of M£112.9 million, the budget forecast a deficit of M£15 million. Agreement was reached in June on Malta's textile quotas within the European Economic Community. In consequence, the ban on British textile imports imposed in 1978 was lifted.

On October 15 a man was wounded and taken into custody after forcing his way into the offices of the prime minister's staff and firing several shots. Prime Minister Dom Mintoff was in his own office at the time, and no one was hurt. In the evening, during a Socialist demonstration to celebrate Mintoff's 30th anniversary as leader of the Labour Party, a group of supporters ransacked and looted the house of the leader of the opposition, Edward Fenech Adami, and beat up his wife. They

MALTA

Education. (1976–77) Primary, pupils 30,863, teachers 1,529; secondary, pupils 25,953, teachers 1,994; vocational, pupils 4,904, teachers 447; higher, students 1,757, teaching staff 285.

Finance. Monetary unit: Maltese pound, with (Sept. 17, 1979) a free rate of M£0.35 = U.S. $1 (M£0.76 = £1 sterling). Gold, SDR's, and foreign exchange (June 1979) U.S. $903 million. Budget (1977–78 est.): revenue M£97.3 million; expenditure M£93 million.

Foreign Trade. (1978) Imports M£221.5 million; exports M£131,950,000. Import sources: U.K. 26%; Italy 20%; West Germany 13%; U.S. 6%; France 5%. Export destinations: West Germany 33%; U.K. 21%; Libya 8%; China 5%; The Netherlands 5%. Main exports (1977): clothing 42%; machinery 7%; food 7%; petroleum products 6%; printed matter 5%. Tourism (1977): visitors 362,000; gross receipts (1976) U.S. $67 million.

Transport and Communications. Roads (1977) 1,273 km. Motor vehicles in use (1977): passenger 60,700; commercial 12,500. There are no railways. Air traffic (1978): 531 million passenger-km; freight 4.2 million net ton-km. Shipping (1978): merchant vessels 100 gross tons and over 47; gross tonnage 101,541. Shipping traffic (1978): goods loaded 164,600 metric tons, unloaded 1,178,000 metric tons. Telephones (March 1978) 67,250. Radio licenses (Dec. 1977) 70,000. Television licenses (Dec. 1977) 66,200.

Manufacturing:
see Economy, World; Industrial Review

Marine Biology:
see Life Sciences

also wrecked three Nationalist Party clubs, attacked the office of a church newspaper, and gutted the premises of *The Times*, an independent daily newspaper. Scanty police protection was completely ineffective and no arrests were made.

(ALBERT GANADO)

Materials Sciences

Ceramics. The year 1979 was marked by continuing emphasis on ceramics for heat engines, nuclear waste disposal, energy conservation, and several specialty applications. Under the direction of the U.S. Department of Energy (DOE) and the Defense Advanced Research Projects Agency, programs on ceramics for turbine engines moved into their feasibility demonstration test phases. Great progress was made in design with brittle materials and the fabrication and rig testing of individual ceramic components and engine stages. But engineering difficulties remained in the design and construction of complex, multistage engines, in which unpredicted loading patterns and time-dependent effects were causing major component failures.

In view of the significant progress made to date, DOE was negotiating with two U.S. industry teams to develop advanced gas turbine engines for demonstration in an automobile by 1984. Increasing engine temperatures from 925° to 1,300° C (from 1,700° to 2,400° F) with uncooled ceramics could increase efficiencies by 25–55%.

Though concern for nuclear safety following the Three Mile Island reactor incident in Pennsylvania in March (*see* ENERGY) threatened to delay new fission plant sites in the U.S., other countries moved ahead with plant site planning and construction. One major concern in the operation of nuclear plants is the safe disposal of radioactive wastes. The search for suitable storage schemes intensified, with ceramic glasses and canisters emerging as leading candidates for the immobilization of these potentially dangerous materials.

By the late 1970s the technology for incorporating nuclear wastes in specially formulated glasses was well advanced. France, Great Britain, and Canada had already stored vitrified nuclear wastes for almost 20 years to test their stability under real burial conditions. France built the world's first production-scale facility for immobilizing nuclear waste in glass in mid-1978. Most countries considered the use of multiple barriers for waste isolation highly desirable. Waste masses that produce low heat can be stored in cement or concrete canisters. The ASEA company in Sweden developed a hot isostatically pressed alumina container that could safely store even high-temperature wastes.

Many systems, including the electric car, depend on batteries with very high energy densities. Although batteries based on lithium-sulfur dioxide (SO_2) and lithium-thionyl chloride ($SOCl_2$) have great potential for these applications, their development has been slowed by difficult safety problems. The Altus Corp. in Palo Alto, Calif., recently developed ceramic seals that withstand internal erosion of the lithium cell chemistry and also protect these batteries from external damage with a high safety factor. Their cells have shown long shelf life and high resistance to abuse.

The U.S. space shuttle, scheduled for its first flight in 1980, suffered several setbacks during the year, including difficulties with the ceramic thermal-protection tiles that cover a large fraction of its exterior skin. In response, Lockheed Missiles and Space Co. was speeding development of a second-generation thermal protection tile material. Called fibrous refractory composite insulation (FRCI), it uses some higher strength, larger diameter fibre containing a minute amount of boron ("Nextel" fibres made by the 3M Co.) as well as the pure silica fibre used in the first-generation material. Following successful qualification tests, FRCI tiles could find application in critical locations on the second flight orbiter. (NORMAN M. TALLAN)

[721.B.2.d.iii; 721.C.4; 724.C.5]

Metallurgy. As in the mid-1970s, the main influences in metallurgy in 1979 were energy and material shortages, rising costs, and government regulation. The cobalt shortage, arising from political problems, was one of the most serious among materials. The best high-temperature alloys containing cobalt were being replaced, albeit at decreased serviceability, by high-nickel alloys. In magnetic materials samarium was being substituted for cobalt, and it was possible that in the near future less expensive rare-earth metals would be used. The substitution is satisfactory in permanent magnets but not in magnetically soft alloys.

A special ceramic material designed as armour for vehicles transporting radioactive materials is able to withstand the impact of a .30 calibre armour-piercing projectile.

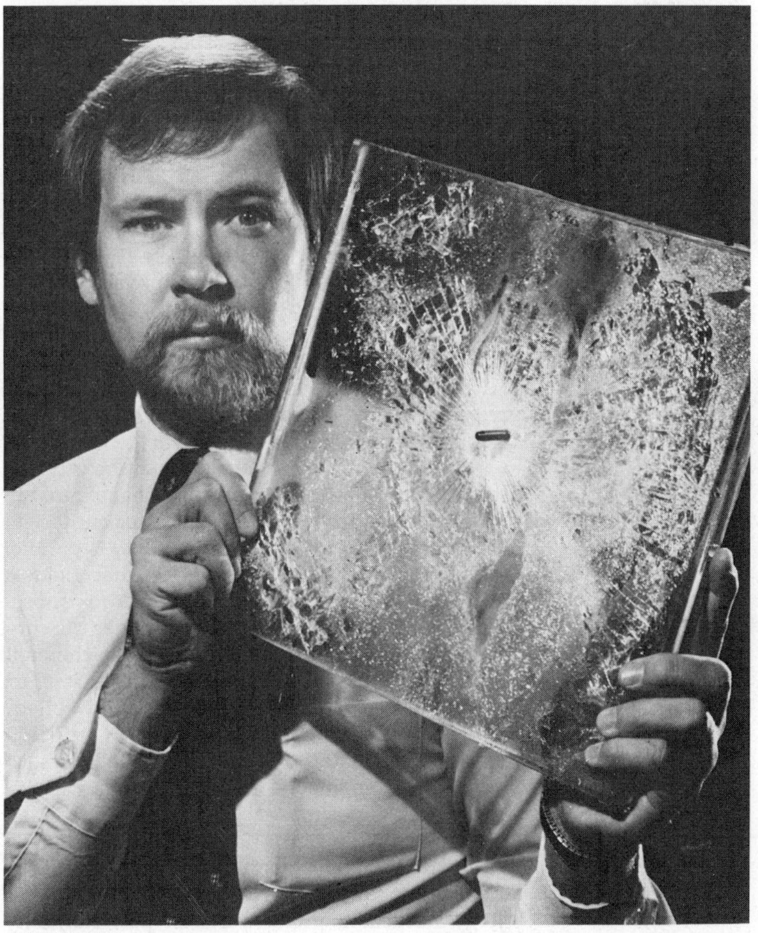

SANDIA LABORATORIES

GENERAL ELECTRIC AIRCRAFT ENGINE GROUP

General Electric technician uses laser drill to vaporize holes in hard-alloy aircraft engine component. Drilling a total of 70,000 cooling holes per engine, this advanced technique offers a savings of several thousand dollars over other methods.

To date, no good substitute had been found for cobalt in cemented carbide cutting tools.

Reducing the amount of energy being consumed in metal production was making slow progress. From 1972 to 1978 energy needed for aluminum production in the U.S. was reported to have decreased by 10.8%, excluding the energy consumed in pollution control. Die-casting energy requirements were reduced by 21% in three years, with improvements coming particularly in the process of holding liquid metal ready for casting.

Short on both metallurgical coke and energy, Japan reduced the coke required to produce a ton of pig iron from an average of 497 kg (1,096 lb) in 1973 to a record low in one blast furnace of 445.5 kg (982 lb) during 1978. As in many other cases the savings resulted not from major changes but from many small improvements in the process.

Use of continuous casting continued to expand partly because of energy savings, which for steel amounted to as much as 50% over conventional ingot practice. A process developed in the U.S.S.R. uses an electromagnetic field rather than a mold to contain the solidifying metal and direct impingement of the water for cooling. Heat flow is parallel to the surface of the metal, an effect that yields a particularly favourable grain structure for subsequent working. Another new development, a continuous rod caster, pulls the rod up from the melt through a water-cooled mold. The metal is then immediately hot rolled, quenched, cold rolled, and coiled, achieving in 40 seconds what ordinarily would keep material in the plant for 40 days for production from ingots. A product yield of 99% was claimed.

Powder metallurgy continued as one of the most rapidly growing developments in metallurgy. One auto manufacturer reported a 50% reduction in energy needed to produce a steel part normally requiring extensive machining by forming the part to near-net shape from steel powder; less energy is needed to produce steel powder than bars and to machine a nearly finished final shape.

Aluminum is so easy to form that very often powder metallurgy offers little advantage. Preparation of powders of high-strength aluminum alloys by atomizing and rapid freezing, however, produces a very fine dendrite structure and makes fine dispersions and supersaturated solid solutions possible. Parts with superior combinations of strength, corrosion resistance, and other properties can thus be produced. Very finely shredded aluminum scrap was shown to have better flow properties than spherical-particle powders, offering such advantages as greater uniformity of structure in parts of complex shape and simplified recycling of selected scrap.

The auto industry was turning to high-strength, low-alloy (HSLA) steels for necessary weight reduction without greatly increased cost. These steels, sometimes called microalloyed steels, achieve high strength with a combination of small amounts of several alloying elements rather than with the much higher alloy content needed with a single additional element. A microscopic distribution of two phases that can be developed in some grades of HSLA steel by heat or mechanical treatment gives formability comparable to conventional lower strength carbon steel sheet; hence these steels adapt readily to existing production processes.

(DONALD F. CLIFTON)

[721.B.5.a; 725.B]

See also Industrial Review: *Glass; Iron and Steel; Machinery and Machine Tools;* Mining and Quarrying.

Mathematics

In 1979, for the second time since its recent establishment, the prestigious Alan T. Waterman Award of the U.S. National Science Foundation was conferred on a mathematician, topologist William P. Thurston of Princeton University. This $150,000 award, established by Congress in 1975 to commemorate the 25th anniversary of the creation of the National Science Foundation, is made each year to a scientist under 35 years of age who shows exceptional promise for significant future achievement.

Thurston's work revolutionized mathematicians' understanding of the way surfaces interleave and the way space curves, not just in two and three dimensions but in higher dimensions as well. He developed an extensive theory of "foliations," leaflike structures that fit together like the pages of a book, and classified all possible foliations of an important class of surfaces called "compact manifolds." In addition, he introduced a new geometric object rather like a geodesic on a globe (the path of shortest distance) that enabled him to describe the changes that these compact surfaces can undergo.

Two other men who made extensive contributions to geometry and topology also received major awards in 1979. French mathematicians Jean Leray and André Weil shared the $100,000 Wolf Prize in

Mathematics, Leray for his pioneering work in applying topological methods to differential equations and Weil for his inspired introduction of algebraic geometry into the classical subject of number theory. The Wolf prizes, awarded annually in agriculture, physics, chemistry, medicine, mathematics, and occasionally in art, were a new endeavour (established in 1976) with worldwide objectives and endowment similar to the Nobel prizes.

Leray was honoured for work that took the most abstract part of mathematics—algebraic topology—and applied it to very specific problems "taken from amongst the most challenging of the science of our times." His theories not only opened up solutions to whole classes of differential equations but also altered the direction of research in algebraic topology. Weil, "a formidable scholar of classical mathematics whose historical insight . . . is unequaled among mathematicians today," is largely responsible for the development of algebraic geometry with its attendant applications in analysis, number theory, and algebra.

Breakthroughs in mathematics research have recently come most often from the frontier of computer science and mathematics. Research during the past year followed the same pattern. Perhaps the most exciting development—and certainly the one with greatest potential effect on the many users of mathematics—was a new algorithm (*i.e.*, a step-by-step problem-solving method) for solving the famous "linear programming" problem. This problem is solved repeatedly by every major industrial firm as it tries to minimize cost or maximize profit subject to the constraints of labour, capital, and various resources.

For 30 years the standard method of solving this problem has been the simplex algorithm invented by George Dantzig of Stanford University. This algorithm searches for a solution by moving along the edges of a high-dimensional polyhedron, at each step picking the available path that most rapidly increases profit (or reduces cost). Because the method might eventually search all corners of the polyhedron, it always yields a solution. But because there are so many places to wander, it can take unconscionably long for the solution to emerge.

In 1979 Soviet mathematician L. G. Khachian proposed a new method that is guaranteed to work in a reasonable amount of time and is simple enough to program on a hand calculator. His method, which was subsequently confirmed by Hungarian mathematicians Peter Gács and Laszlo Lovász, uses a sequence of high-dimensional ellipses to approximate a solution. Whereas the simplex method progresses incessantly uphill, always gaining on its objective as it searches for the best point, Khachian's much more rapid algorithm permits temporary sacrifice, a digression from the objective, if a greater subsequent gain can be obtained in that way. The new algorithm is able to "look ahead," much as a mountain climber may descend into a valley in order to reach a slope from which he then can launch his final assault on the summit.

The importance of this new result is not just that it guarantees a quick solution and is easy to program but also that it behaves in an "intelligent" way that may presage future breakthroughs in algorithms. Its intelligence lies not in actual perception or foresight but in clever application of high-dimensional geometry.

(LYNN ARTHUR STEEN)

Mauritania

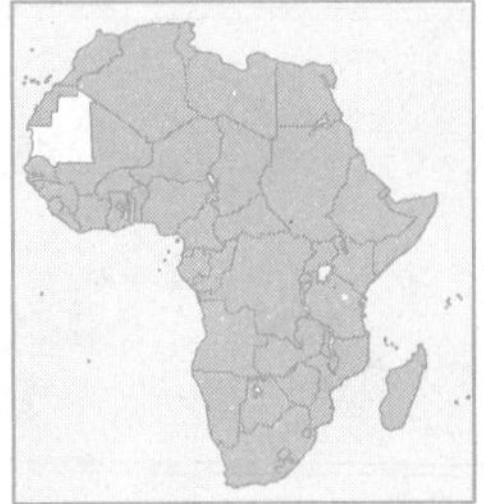

Mauritania

The Islamic Republic of Mauritania is on the Atlantic coast of West Africa, adjoining Western Sahara, Algeria, Mali, and Senegal. Area: 1,030,700 sq km (398,000 sq mi). Pop. (1977): 1,420,000. Cap.: Nouakchott (pop., 1977, 135,000). (Data above refer to Mauritania as constituted prior to the purported division of Spanish Sahara between Mauritania and Morocco.) Language: Arabic, French. Religion: Muslim. Head of the Military Committee for National Recovery in 1979 and, from March 20, head of state, Col. Mustafa Ould Salek; on June 3 Ould Salek resigned both positions and was replaced as head of state by Lieut. Col. Mohamed Mahmoud Ould Louly; premiers, Lieut. Col. Ahmed Ould Bouceif from April 6 until May 27 and, from May 31, Lieut. Col. Mohamed Khouna Ould Kaydalla.

Endowed with full powers as Mauritania's leader on March 20, 1979, Col. Mustafa Ould Salek then dismissed four ministers who favoured negotiating on the conflict in the former Spanish Sahara with the Polisario Front guerrillas. On April 6 Lieut. Col. Ahmed Ould Bouceif became premier and sought "peace with honour" in the Sahara, but on May 27 he was killed in an air crash. Four days later the Military Committee for National Salvation nominated Lieut. Col. Mohamed Khouna Ould Kaydalla to take his place. On June 3 the moves toward a reversal of policy were completed when Ould Salek was replaced as head of state by Lieut. Col. Mohamed Mahmoud Ould Louly (*see*

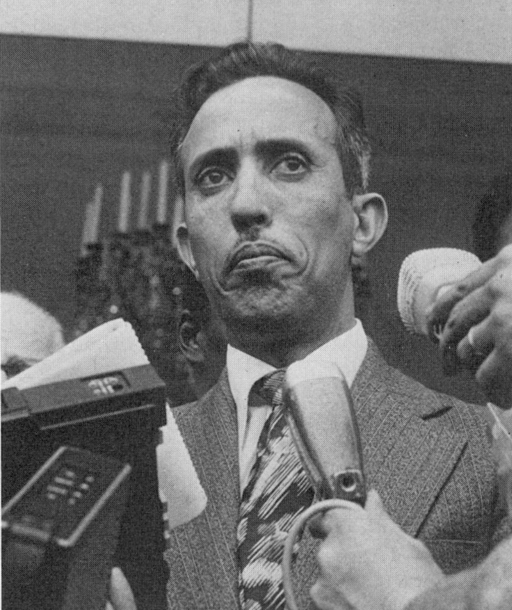

A.G.I.P./PICTORIAL PARADE

Premier Ahmed Ould Bouceif answered journalists' questions on the problem of Western Sahara during his visit to Paris in early May.

Biographies), and the situation was deemed sufficiently stable for former Pres. Moktar Ould Daddah to be freed and allowed to go to France for medical treatment in October.

Mauritania signed a peace treaty with the Polisario Front on August 5 in Algiers and resumed diplomatic relations with Algeria on August 14. Afterward it broke its 1975 defense alliance with Morocco. When Mauritania renounced sovereignty over Tiris el Gharbia province (its share of former Spanish Sahara), Morocco annexed it. Although its troops left Mauritania proper in September, Morocco became as much a menace as the Polisario guerrillas had been.

The black community in Mauritania agitated against racial discrimination, and in March and May black leaders were arrested for subversion but soon freed. On March 30 the 17 black members (there were 81 Arab-Berbers) of the newly created National Consultative Council resigned.

(PHILIPPE DECRAENE)

See also Morocco.

MAURITANIA

Education. (1974–75) Primary, pupils 47,000, teachers 1,768; secondary, pupils 5,493, teachers (1973–74) 200; vocational, pupils 1,591, teachers (1973–74) 117; teacher training (1971–72), students 145.

Finance. Monetary unit: ouguiya, with (Sept. 17, 1979) a free rate of 42.28 ouguiya = U.S. $1 (90.96 ouguiya = £1 sterling). Gold, SDR's, and foreign exchange (June 1979) U.S. $88.7 million. Budget (1978 est.) balanced at 10,195,000,000 ouguiya.

Foreign Trade. (1978) Imports 8,362,000,000 ouguiya; exports 5,499,000,000 ouguiya. Import sources: France *c.* 28%; Belgium-Luxembourg *c.* 12%; West Germany *c.* 9%; Spain *c.* 9%; Senegal *c.* 5%. Export destinations: France *c.* 26%; Italy *c.* 17%; Japan *c.* 13%; U.K. *c.* 10%; Spain *c.* 9%; West Germany *c.* 8%; Belgium-Luxembourg *c.* 7%. Main exports: iron ore 76%; fish 21%.

Mauritius

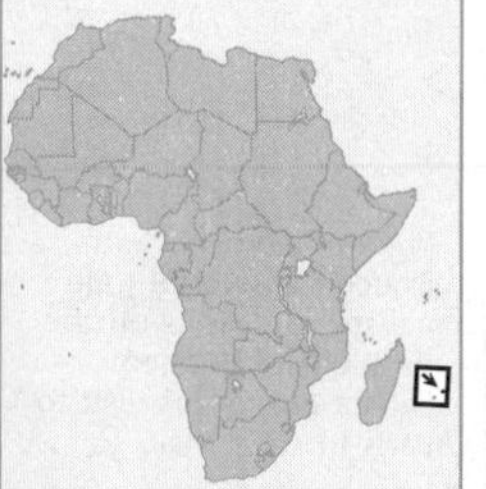

Mauritius

The parliamentary state of Mauritius, a member of the Commonwealth of Nations, lies about 800 km E of Madagascar in the Indian Ocean; it includes the island dependencies of Rodrigues, Agalega, and Cargados Carajos. Area: 2,040 sq km (787.5 sq mi). Pop. (1979 est.): 938,600, including (1977) Indian 69.3%; Creole (mixed French and African) 28%; others 2.7%. Cap. and largest city: Port Louis (pop., 1979 est., 144,800). Language: English (official); French has official standing for certain legislative and judicial purposes; and Creole is the lingua franca. Religion (1974 est.): Hindu 51%; Christian 30%; Muslim 16%; Buddhist 3%. Queen, Elizabeth II; governor-general in 1979, Sir Abdul Rahman Muhammad Osman; prime minister, Sir Seewoosagur Ramgoolam.

The minority coalition Labour government of Sir Seewoosagur Ramgoolam continued to steer a course between Gaetan Duval's right-wing Social Democratic Party and the left-wing Mauritius Militant Movement (MMM) of Paul Bérenger. The resignation of two ministers following the Glover Commission report on corruption increased demands for a further inquiry and a general election. External policy veered leftward when the government joined the Conference of Progressive Parties of the Southwest Indian Ocean. The move brought objections from the MMM, already a member, which believed the government was coopting its position by demanding that the U.S. and France abandon their bases on the islands of Diego Garcia and Réunion.

The economy's excessive dependence on sugar remained a cause for concern, despite long-term contracts negotiated under the Lomé Convention. Sugar accounted for 35% of labour, 80% of export earnings, and 40% of the gross national product (GNP). The government continued to encourage diversification, mainly light industry (now 30% of GNP) and tourism. Over 30,000 persons were unemployed.

(MOLLY MORTIMER)

MAURITIUS

Education. (1977) Primary, pupils 136,019, teachers 6,269; secondary, pupils 78,038, teachers 2,452; vocational, pupils 1,141, teachers 93; teacher training, students 424, teachers (1976) 20; higher, students 967, teaching staff *c.* 100.

Finance and Trade. Monetary unit: Mauritian rupee, with (Sept. 17, 1979) a free rate of MauRs 5.92 to U.S. $1 (MauRs 12.73 = £1 sterling). Gold, SDR's, and foreign exchange (June 1979) U.S. $45.5 million. Budget (1978–79 est.): revenue MauRs 1.5 billion; expenditure MauRs 1,602,000,000. Foreign trade (1978): imports MauRs 3,076,400,000; exports MauRs 1,987,300,000. Import sources (1977): U.K. 18%; France 11%; South Africa 11%; Japan 8%; Australia 5%; West Germany 5%. Export destinations (1977): U.K. 67%; France 8%; U.S. 6%. Main exports (1977): sugar 70%; clothing 13%. Tourism (1976): visitors 93,000; gross receipts U.S. $28 million.

Agriculture. Production (in 000; metric tons; 1978): sugar, raw value *c.* 695; bananas (1977) *c.* 7; tea *c.* 4; tobacco *c.* 1; milk (1977) *c.* 23. Livestock (in 000; 1977): cattle *c.* 54; pigs *c.* 6; sheep *c.* 4; goats *c.* 68; chickens *c.* 1,200.

Mexico

Mexico

A federal republic of Middle America, Mexico is bounded by the Pacific Ocean, the Gulf of Mexico, the U.S., Belize, and Guatemala. Area: 1,972,546 sq km (761,604 sq mi). Pop. (1978 est.): 66,944,000, including about 55% mestizo and 29% Indian. Cap. and largest city: Mexico City (pop., federal district, 1978 est., 8,988,200; metro. area, 1979 est., 14.2 million). Language: Spanish. Religion: predominantly Roman Catholic. President in 1979, José López Portillo.

Pope John Paul II visited Mexico Jan. 26–31, 1979, to open the third General Conference of the Latin-American Episcopate in Puebla. Just before the visit the nation's attorney general, Oscar Flores Sánchez, reported on government investigations into the cases of 314 missing persons. He explained that the majority had died in confrontations with the law or with rival groups, while some were in hiding. This explanation was not generally accepted, however, and in August a group of activists occupied the Swiss embassy for seven days, demanding the release of political prisoners. The building was cleared on August 10 by riot police. An amnesty was granted to 919 prisoners and exiles in mid-1979 under the 1978 amnesty law, bringing the total released to 1,539.

Late in November Mexico announced that it

MEXICO

Education. (1976–77) Primary, pupils 12,600,620, teachers 274,717; secondary, pupils 2,999,456, teachers 160,532; vocational, pupils 316,318, teachers 23,121; teacher training, students 138,340, teachers 9,317; higher, students 599,920, teaching staff (1975–76) 30,865.

Finance. Monetary unit: peso, with (Sept. 17, 1979) a free rate of 22.62 pesos to U.S. $1 (48.66 pesos = £1 sterling). Gold, SDR's, and foreign exchange (May 1979) U.S. $2,012,000,000. Budget (1978 actual): revenue 407 billion pesos; expenditure 507 billion pesos. Gross domestic product (1977) 1,639,500,000,000 pesos. Money supply (Jan. 1979) 246,720,000,000 pesos. Cost of living (1975 = 100; June 1979) 203.9.

Foreign Trade. (1978) Imports 183,329,000,000 pesos; exports 135,845,000,000 pesos. Import sources: U.S. 60%; Japan 8%; West Germany 7%. Export destinations: U.S. 63%. Main exports (1977): crude oil 21%; coffee 10%; metals and ores 8%. Tourism (1977): visitors 3,247,000; gross receipts U.S. $2,373,000,000.

Transport and Communications. Roads (1977) 200,060 km (including 1,062 km expressways). Motor vehicles in use (1977): passenger 2,682,000; commercial (including buses) 1,077,600. Railways (1977): 24,434 km; traffic 5,040,000,000 passenger-km, freight 36,230,000,000 net ton-km. Air traffic (1977): 8,520,000,000 passenger-km; freight 96.2 million net ton-km. Shipping (1978): merchant vessels 100 gross tons and over 336; gross tonnage 727,201. Telephones (Jan. 1978) 3,712,400. Radio receivers (Dec. 1974) 17,514,000. Television receivers (Dec. 1978) 5.5 million.

Agriculture. Production (000; metric tons; 1978): corn 9,616; wheat 2,643; barley 505; sorghum 4,185; rice 397; potatoes 837; sugar, raw value *c.* 3,049; dry beans 940; soybeans 324; tomatoes 1,117; bananas 1,137; oranges *c.* 2,400; lemons *c.* 440; cottonseed 548; coffee *c.* 270; tobacco 72; cotton, lint 332; beef and veal *c.* 600; pork 414; fish catch (1977) 671. Livestock (in 000; Dec. 1977): cattle 29,333; sheep 7,856; pigs 12,321; goats 8,193; horses 6,612; mules 3,270; asses 3,282; chickens 152,816.

Industry. Production (in 000; metric tons; 1978): cement 14,100; crude oil *c.* 60,830; coal (1977) 6,610; natural gas (cu m) *c.* 29.2 million; electricity (kw-hr) 55.2 million; iron ore (metal content) 3,514; pig iron 5,002; crude steel 6,571; sulfur (1977) 1,856; petroleum products (1977) *c.* 37,700; sulfuric acid 2,200; fertilizers (nutrient content; 1977–78) nitrogenous 611, phosphate 282; aluminum 43; copper 74; lead 150; zinc 172; manganese ore (metal content; 1977) 175; gold (troy oz) *c.* 200; silver (troy oz) *c.* 53,000; cotton yarn (1975) 158; woven cotton fabrics 67; man-made fibres (1977) 192; radio receivers (units; 1977) 976; television receivers (units; 1977) 699; passenger cars (units) 253; commercial vehicles (units) 106.

would refuse to readmit the deposed shah of Iran, who had lived in the country on a six-month tourist visa from June to late October. Though Mexico had closed its embassy in Iran, there was speculation that it feared reprisals from other Muslim countries if the shah were allowed to return.

On July 1, in the first congressional elections held since the political reform of 1978, three minority parties, the Mexican Communist Party (PCM), the Workers' Socialist Party, and the Mexican Democratic Party, gained formal registration with 5% of the vote for the PCM and 1.5% for each of the other two parties. The Institutional Revolutionary Party (PRI), the ruling faction, won 70% of the total votes and 291 out of 300 directly elected seats, while 4 seats went to the National Action Party (PAN). Five seats were successfully challenged in the Electoral Court, and all went to the PRI in new elections. However, some seats were still being contested at year's end. A further 100 seats were distributed proportionally among minority parties, with 39 going to the PAN and 18 to the PCM.

In his annual message to the nation in September, Pres. José López Portillo stated that Mexico's proven petroleum reserves totaled 45,800,000,000 bbl (oil equivalent), probable reserves 45,000,000,000 bbl, and potential reserves 200,000,000,000 bbl, assuring supplies for 60 years. Current production amounted to about 1,700,000,000 bbl a day of products, with exports approximating 500,000 bbl a day. Major discoveries were made in the Chicontepec, Bermudez, and Cantarell fields.

After 21 months of negotiations Mexico finally agreed in September to sell approximately 300 million cu ft of natural gas a day to the U.S. at $3.625 per 1,000 cu ft, to be revised every quarter and following prices of the Organization of Petroleum Exporting Countries. Agreements were signed or discussed to sell oil to France, Spain, and Canada (100,000 bbl a day each), Japan (100,000 to 200,000), Sweden (70,000), and Brazil (20,000 bbl more) from 1980 or 1981 onward. Stated policy was that production would not be increased after the target of 2,250,000 bbl a day was reached in 1980, with half of this output available for export. Meanwhile, Pemex, the national petroleum monopoly, had a major blowout on June 3 at the Ixtoc 1 well in the Bay of Campeche, spilling oil at a rate of 30,000 bbl a day. Efforts to cap the well and drill relief wells were unsuccessful at year's end, and some of the oil reached the coast of Texas, causing frayed relations with the U.S.

Various trade agreements were signed, mainly for technical cooperation, with Spain, Czechoslovakia, France, and Sweden. U.S. Pres. Jimmy Carter visited Mexico on February 14–16 to discuss oil, gas, illegal Mexican immigration to the U.S., trade control, and drug smuggling; in September President López Portillo visited the U.S. Cuban Pres. Fidel Castro made his first visit to Mexico since 1959 in May, to discuss exchanges of technology and tourism. (BARBARA WIJNGAARD)

MELLOUL—SYGMA

Storage facilities and oil pipelines symbolize the oil boom that was taking place in Mexico during the year.

Medicine: see Health and Disease

Mental Health: see Health and Disease

Merchant Marine: see Transportation

Metallurgy: see Materials Sciences

Metals: see Industrial Review; Materials Sciences; Mining and Quarrying

Meteorology: see Earth Sciences

Methodist Churches: see Religion

SPECIAL REPORT

MEXICO CITY: A TROUBLED GIANT

by Sergio Sarmiento

The cleanest, clearest air in Mexico once was found over the valley where Mexico City stands. Today it has been replaced by a haze of smog, generated by the city and trapped by a surrounding string of mountains and hills. Owing to its stately colonial architecture, the Mexican capital was once dubbed "the city of palaces." But now sprawling slums and shantytowns encircle and threaten the mansions of yesteryear as well as the modern townhouses and condominiums of the emerging middle class.

Population Woes. By mid-1979 it was officially estimated that 14.2 million people lived in the metropolitan area of Mexico City, and its population growth was calculated at a hefty 5.5% annually. This urban area is now thought to be the most populous in any less developed country, and by some estimates it will become the most heavily populated in the world by the end of the century. As a whole, Mexico's population growth has slowed down from 3.5 to 2.9% annually during the past few years, and birthrates in the capital have actually been lower than in the countryside. Immigration accounts for the city's faster growth.

Every day more than 1,000 newcomers arrive in the city to stay. They ride in buses and travel light—very often carrying only a battered canvas suitcase. The men come first. They stay with relatives or sleep in the open until a job and suitable living quarters are found. Wives and children—and sometimes grandparents, uncles, aunts, and cousins—follow, usually a few months later. Often they all settle in the northeastern outskirts of the city, where rents are cheapest; sometimes they become squatters. Other immigrants are temporary. For instance, young Indian women, often carrying their offspring, go to the city for a few days to beg and thus supplement their husbands' income.

Life in the capital is not easy. The few available jobs for unskilled people generally require hard physical work with long hours. Wages for such labour are seldom higher than the legal minimum, $180 per month. To make things worse, the jobs are usually located far from the working-class living areas, and the city's public transportation system is notoriously inefficient. It is not unusual for a worker to spend five or six hours every day in crowded buses and subway trains traveling to and from his place of employment.

Many immigrants in the city have attempted at one time or another to cross the Río Grande into the United States. But although wages and working conditions are much better across the border, there are often bitter memories of the U.S. sojourns. In Mexico City, at least, there are no immigration police to hound the *ilegales*, or illegal workers, and one need not submit to blackmail or ill treatment for fear of being revealed. The possibility of returning to the countryside is out of the question. Industrialization has basically touched only the nation's urbanized areas, and so there are few jobs to be had outside the cities. Furthermore, the agrarian reform, which for years has been one of the government's main concerns, has failed to provide every deserving peasant with land—there is simply not enough arable land in the country.

Living in the City. *Comercio*, a publication of Mexico's National Chamber of Commerce, recently indicated that the metropolis is the second noisiest in the world and the third most polluted. Food processing and distribution are often unsanitary. Half the population is said to be suffering from gastrointestinal, respiratory, or nervous diseases. In addition, traffic is a major problem. Exasperated by the perennial congestion of streets and expressways, motor vehicle drivers are aggressive and careless. Little consideration is shown to the numerous bicycle riders or to pedestrians. The latter must usually run to cross some of the city streets. Traffic accidents claim 3,000 lives a year.

Although the minimum wage is higher than in most less developed countries, many have to make ends meet with less than that. Unemployment among the city's economically active population (only 34.8% of the total population) was officially estimated to stand at 6.3% in mid-1979, but even government sources acknowledge that 4.4% of the economically inactive population over 12 years old should, in fact, be considered unemployed. Some university sources guess that 30–40% of the truly economically active population are not fully employed and, indeed, high underemployment among unskilled and semiskilled workers visibly plagues the city. Education is compulsory only through the sixth grade, and so thousands of 12-year-olds join the work force every year. Unable to obtain regular jobs for lack of marketable skills, they turn to wash-

---

Sergio Sarmiento is editor in chief of the Spanish-language Enciclopedia Barsa, *published in Mexico City by Encyclopædia Britannica Publishers, Inc.*

PHOTOS, GEORGE W. GARDNER

ing cars, shining shoes, or peddling an extraordinary variety of goods for a few pesos a day.

Food is expensive in relation to individual incomes. A kilogram (2.2 lb) of a regular grade of beef sold for about $4 ($1.80/lb) in late 1979, while top-grade beef was fetching close to $7 ($3.18/lb). Milk cost about 32 cents a litre ($1.21 per U.S. gallon) and eggs about $1 a kilo (80 cents per dozen). Even so, discontent within the food industry was widespread, and its spokesmen openly criticized the government for forcibly keeping prices for these products "artificially low."

Rental housing is critically scarce. High real-estate taxes and legislation hampering the eviction of delinquent tenants have made the construction of rental units unattractive. On the other hand, inflated building costs—brought about in part by excessive government demand for materials—have quashed the dreams of many Mexico City residents of ever owning a home. Even small government-subsidized condominiums, without heating and erected in the crime-ridden traditionally working-class areas of the city centre, easily fetched $20,000 per unit in 1979. Middle-class apartments started at $40,000; houses, at $60,000. Architects and engineers have lowered their professional standards so as not to price their products out of the market. Significantly, many new buildings sustained damage during the earthquakes of late 1978 and early 1979, while older structures suffered hardly a crack.

Mexico City is a metropolis of dramatic contrasts. The rich live in palatial splendour, while the children of the poor are reduced to spending their days on the sidewalks of the city's slums.

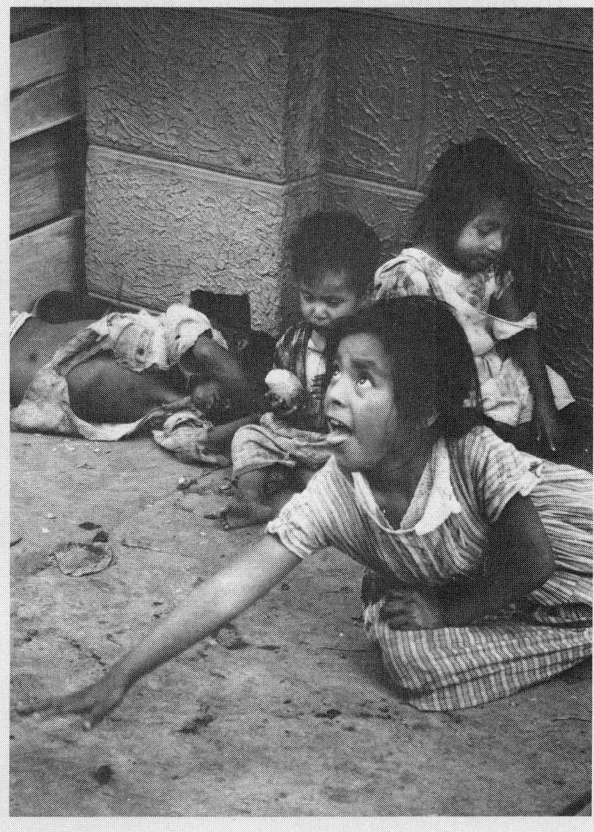

A City of Two Worlds. Despite everything, few *chilangos*—Mexico City dwellers—seem willing to move out. Complaining about the inconveniences of living in the metropolis has long become a national hobby, but many share the opinion of a middle-class housewife who asked at a party: "Is there any other place where you'd rather be?"

And indeed Mexico City has some qualities that can make life in its midst quite pleasant. The average temperature is 18° C (64° F), and variations are relatively small. Since it lies at an altitude of 2,240 m (7,350 ft) above sea level, the city does not suffer from the humidity and high temperatures that make working so difficult along the country's coasts. Rains are often heavy in the summer, but they clean the air and allow *chilangos* much-treasured smogless glimpses of the Sun. More important still is the fact that violent crimes are relatively few, in comparison with other cities of the same size.

From a cultural point of view, two worlds have a claim on Mexico City. On the one hand, the city is Latin American and proud of its heritage; on the other, its proximity to the United States has conferred on it a distinctive North American character. Some of its areas could easily be thought to belong to Dallas or Los Angeles. "El hot dog," "la hamburguesa," "el pent-house," and "la Coca Cola" have become part of the language and tradition of the city much more than in other regions of the world outside the U.S. and Canada.

The cultural life is surprisingly rich. Art exhibitions open almost every day; a wide variety of Mexican, U.S., and European films are shown; the Mexican theatre ranks high in the Spanish-speaking countries and indeed in the world. The city boasts four full-fledged symphony orchestras, and there is virtually one concert of classical music every day. Mexico City has wrested from Buenos Aires the claim to being the cultural capital of Latin America; artists and writers from all over the continent have flocked to it in search of a freedom of expression that has become rare elsewhere in Latin America.

Saving the City. The future of the Mexican capital clearly depends on its population growth, and some official measures have already been taken to curb it. The federal government has adopted a National Plan for Urban Development, which aims, among other things, at decentralizing the administrative and productive activities of the country. A decision was made in the first half of 1979 to transfer 25 state-owned firms out of Mexico City, a move that was supposed to establish close to 3,000 jobs in the provinces. The relocation of 70 other government enterprises was being considered. Moreover, it was expected that 70,000 bureaucrats would be resettled outside of the city by 1982. Tax breaks were being granted to private companies willing to move to priority areas, but takers were few and a wait-and-see attitude was prevalent in business circles.

Within Mexico City the Federal District Department initiated massive works in 1978 in an attempt to speed up motor vehicle movement, which then averaged, according to the city's mayor, 10 km per hour (6.25 mph). A total of 133 km (82.4 mi) of new boulevards had been built by June 1979 at a cost of $362 million. The flow of vehicles improved noticeably, and it was expected to be even better when a citywide, computer-regulated traffic-light system became operational by the end of the year. With 400 new vehicles entering the city streets every day, however, critics maintained that the improvement would be only temporary. Furthermore, pedestrians were finding it difficult to cross the new multilane boulevards. Only the young and able-bodied could be expected to do so at the busiest intersections. An elderly woman living alone in a small apartment in the south side of the city complained: "They've cut my world in two!"

An example of the sort of problems faced by the authorities in their attempts to improve life is provided by the dispute over city buses. Noisy, dirty, and polluting to an extreme, the privately owned buses have seemed for years to fall outside the scope of the municipality's laws and regulations. They roar down streets and come to screeching halts, blocking traffic and causing falls among the passengers tightly packed inside. Seldom do the drivers stop long enough to allow all passengers to descend at ease, and the frequency of service is erratic. For years nobody dared to take on the bus owners and drivers, who had become a law unto themselves, until Mayor Carlos Hank González announced in 1979 that the buses would be replaced in the new cross-city boulevards by silent, nonpolluting trolley buses to be run by the city. The association of bus owners, though, soon flexed its political muscles and compelled the mayor to scale down his plans. By late 1979 the buses' privileges were still in full force.

The Air's Most Transparent Region. It is difficult to predict what will become of the city. Official measures are bound to curb its growth to some extent, but there is always the danger of increasing joblessness even more among unskilled workers. Yet *chilangos* are not overly concerned. Like those living in urban areas in other parts of the world, they have for the most part grown indifferent to their own environment. Their disinterest seems to echo the closing sentences of Mexican writer Carlos Fuentes's 1958 novel, *La región más transparente*: "Our fate lies here. What can we do about it ? In the air's most transparent region."

Middle Eastern Affairs

The revolution in Iran and the March 26 treaty between Egypt and Israel dominated the political life of the Middle East in 1979. The Iranian revolution in particular threw into sharp relief the main issues of the year: Islamic resurgence (*see* Feature Article: *Islam Resurgent*), sectarian and national divisions, provocative oil policies, rapid modernization, insecurity in the Persian Gulf region, and an Arab-Israeli dispute which persisted despite the U.S.-sponsored Egyptian-Israeli treaty of peace. The response of the governments and peoples of the region to the overthrow of the shah of Iran revealed the potential of that issue for destabilizing the area.

Soviet activities in Ethiopia to the west and Afghanistan to the east caused further anxiety to the conservative and pro-Western regimes of the Persian Gulf. Egypt's isolation from the rest of the Arab world damaged its economic position, but the Arab states without Egypt no longer posed a credible military threat to Israel. Israel and the Palestine Liberation Organization (PLO) continued their war of attrition on Lebanese soil in 1979, and the PLO enhanced its diplomatic status in Europe and won valuable support from Iran.

Arab-Israeli Relations. The U.S. began the year with vigorous efforts to secure a peace treaty based on the September 1978 Camp David accords between Egypt and Israel. U.S. Pres. Jimmy Carter personally visited both countries to overcome the remaining obstacles to a treaty. On March 26 Egyptian Pres. Anwar as-Sadat and Israeli Prime Minister Menahem Begin signed a treaty formally ending the state of war that had existed between their two countries since 1948. The Carter administration pledged $3 billion in military aid to Israel and $1.8 billion in military and civilian aid to Egypt.

At the same time the U.S. attempted to win Arab support for the treaty from such "moderate" U.S. allies as Saudi Arabia and Jordan. By the end of April, however, all Arab states except Oman, Sudan, and Somalia had severed diplomatic relations with Egypt, and the Arab oil states had ended their economic assistance to the Sadat government. The Arab League suspended Egypt's membership at the end of March and moved its headquarters from Cairo to Tunis. In May Egypt was suspended from the Conference of Islamic States in Fez, Morocco. The Arab states and Iran condemned Sadat's "separate peace" and accused him of abandoning the Palestinian people.

Borders between Israel and Egypt were formally opened on May 27 following the Israeli withdrawal from El Arish in Sinai. Negotiations between Egypt and Israel on the sensitive issue of Palestinian autonomy continued throughout 1979, but they failed to achieve any results due to the unwillingness of any Palestinians to support proposals to which they were not a party and to Israeli settlement policies in the occupied territories. The year's last round of negotiations ended in Cairo on December 19. Delegates said that they had reached agreement on some of the technical matters regarding election of a self-governing authority for the 1.2 million Palestinians in the Israeli-occupied West Bank and Gaza Strip. But significant issues still not resolved included the extent of power to be granted the Palestinians and the right of East Jerusalem Arabs to participate in the elections. (*See* Feature Article: *Two Peoples—One Land.*)

Sadat held a referendum on April 19 in which he asked the Egyptian people to support the treaty with Israel. The percentage in favour of the treaty was 99.95%, but there were accusations of ballot irregularities. He silenced opposition to the treaty from both the religious right and the political left through a series of arrests of his opponents. The loss of Arab aid and investment money hurt the Egyptian economy in 1979, and U.S. aid of $1.8 billion was less than Sadat had sought in compensation. The economy grew by 8%, however, due to revenues from the newly recovered Sinai oil wells, the Suez Canal, and tourism. Israel's de-

WILLIAM KAREL—SYGMA

Egyptian Pres. Anwar as-Sadat, U.S. Pres. Jimmy Carter, and Israeli Prime Minister Menahem Begin joined hands in the White House garden after Sadat and Begin signed a peace treaty on March 26 ending the war between the two nations.

Microbiology:
see Life Sciences

mand for full diplomatic relations with Egypt had not been met by Sadat by the end of 1979.

The PLO made considerable progress in 1979 toward achievement of diplomatic recognition in Europe. PLO chairman Yasir Arafat held a widely publicized meeting with Austrian Chancellor Bruno Kreisky (*see* BIOGRAPHIES) and with former West German chancellor Willy Brandt in Vienna July 6–8. He also visited Spain in September and Portugal in November. His earlier meetings in Teheran in February with Iran's religious leaders were equally significant in that Iranian support for the PLO increased the organization's independence with regard to the Arab states. Relations with Libya deteriorated, however, and Libya suspended aid to the PLO in December.

Arafat's reception by European leaders was sharply criticized by Israel, but the unofficial meeting in New York City between PLO United Nations observer Zehdi Labib Terzi and the U.S. ambassador to the UN, Andrew Young (*see* BIOGRAPHIES), drew the loudest Israeli protests. Although the U.S. Department of State admitted that other U.S. diplomats had met privately with PLO officials, Young was forced to resign on August 15. His resignation aroused indignation in the U.S. black community, led to further political estrangement between U.S. Jews and blacks, and produced black support for the PLO. The PLO continued in 1979 to seek U.S. diplomatic recognition, but the Carter administration honoured the secret commitment made by former U.S. secretary of state Henry Kissinger to Israel not to deal with the PLO.

Israel suffered internal political and economic crises in 1979, but Prime Minister Begin's government remained in power and managed to win Israeli support for the treaty with Egypt despite some opposition from his own Likud alliance. Inflation in 1979 exceeded 100%, and the policy of constructing Israeli settlements on occupied Arab land came under increasing domestic criticism. In June the Israeli Supreme Court prohibited further work on the West Bank settlement of Elon Moreh near Nablus, and on October 22 it declared the settlement to be illegal and ordered it to be dismantled. Israeli settlers opposed this decision, and controversy over settlements policy raged into 1980. Foreign Minister Moshe Dayan resigned on October 21 over the government's intransigence in discussions with Egypt over Palestinian "autonomy" and the future of Israeli colonization of the territories. The failure of the government's economic policies to reduce the rate of inflation or to satisfy the demands of the labour unions forced Begin on November 7 to remove Simcha Ehrlich from his post as finance minister.

Israel continued in 1979 to adopt an aggressive posture toward Palestinians in Lebanon and to retaliate in force after Palestinian commando attacks inside Israel. On April 10 Israeli jets bombed Palestinian targets near Beirut, and on June 8 they bombed the town of Nabatiyah in southern Lebanon. Also in southern Lebanon the Israelis supported Lebanese Christian militia leader Maj. Saad Haddad against Palestinians and Lebanese leftists. Haddad and the Israelis prevented both UNIFIL (United Nations Interim Force in Lebanon) troops and contingents of the regular Lebanese Army from entering the Christian border enclave under the terms of UN resolutions. On June 27 aerial combat between Israeli F–15s and Syrian MiGs led to fears of a major war. A UN-imposed truce began to take effect in August, but it was violated regularly by both sides.

The Arab World and Iran. The revolution in Iran and the accession to power there of the Shiʿah Muslim clergy in February led to fears of Iranian support for Shiʿah Muslim groups in Arab states led by Sunni Muslims, particularly Bahrain and Iraq. (Iran's repression of its own Arab minority, who had demanded regional autonomy, was condemned by the Arab world.) Iran's Ayatollah Sadiq Rouhani in July reasserted historic Iranian claims to Bahrain and in August accused the island's rulers of oppressing the Shiʿah majority. Ayatollah Ruhollah Khomeini (*see* BIOGRAPHIES) became a popular figure for the generally poorer Shiʿah Muslims in many Arab nations. Iranian propaganda called on the Shiʿah of Iraq to assert themselves against the Sunni leadership in Baghdad. For its part Iraq in June bombed Kurdish villages in Iran as part of its campaign against Kurdish Pesh Merga guerrillas. The Iraqi government also arrested the Shiʿah leader Ayatollah Sayed Mohammad Bakr as-Sadr in Najef, and this led to Iranian demands for his release.

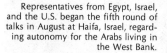

Representatives from Egypt, Israel, and the U.S. began the fifth round of talks in August at Haifa, Israel, regarding autonomy for the Arabs living in the West Bank.

WIDE WORLD

Libyan chief of state Col. Muammar al-Qaddafi attempted to establish good relations with Iran's new leaders; their religious fundamentalism and appeals to democracy bore some resemblance to his own rule in Libya. But Qaddafi's overtures were rejected when he could not explain satisfactorily the circumstances surrounding the disappearance of the Iranian-born Lebanese Shi'ah leader Imam Musa Sadr in Libya in 1978.

Militant Iranian students seized the U.S. embassy in Teheran on November 4 and took the embassy personnel hostage. By the year's end they continued to hold some 50 hostages, having released some blacks and women. The U.S. sought to negotiate for the release of all the captives, but the students maintained that this could not be achieved until the deposed shah was returned to Iran. With the failure of negotiations the U.S. threatened military intervention and economic sanctions. These threats led to concern that anti-U.S. sentiment might be aroused in parts of the Middle East sympathetic to Iran. Consequently, in late November wives and children of U.S. diplomats and businessmen in Bahrain, Kuwait, Qatar, the United Arab Emirates, Oman, and Iraq were encouraged to evacuate those areas.

Fighting between Yemen (San'a') and Yemen (Aden) erupted late in February when each side accused the other of aggression. The U.S. sent arms to Yemen (San'a'), while the Soviets supported Yemen (Aden), where they already had a substantial presence. Saudi Arabia presented peace proposals on February 27, which led to a cease-fire and the signing of a unity agreement between the two Yemens in Kuwait in March.

Negotiations between Syria and Iraq on unification of their two countries under the terms of the Joint Action Charter of October 1978 made considerable progress in the first six months of 1979. Oil supplies from Iraq through the pipeline to the Syrian port at Banias resumed on February 24, and Syrian Pres. Hafez al-Assad went to Baghdad on July 16 to publicize the intended unity of the two countries and their two Ba'ath parties (which had split in 1966). Moves toward Iraqi-Syrian union came to an abrupt halt in July, however, when Iraqi Pres. Ahmad Hassan al-Bakr resigned and was replaced by Revolutionary Command Council vice-chairman Saddam Hussein at-Takriti. Hussein purged his Cabinet when he assumed power, executed 21 people for suspected conspiracy against his rule, and accused Syria of sponsoring a plot against him. No further unity talks took place in 1979. Iraq and Saudi Arabia relations improved however, largely because of their common suspicions of Iranian intentions.

Saudi Arabia was rocked at the end of the year by the seizure of the Grand Mosque in Mecca by Sunni Muslim fundamentalists on November 20 and demonstrations by the Shi'ah minority in the Eastern Province in December. Both expressions of opposition were quickly dealt with, but their occurrence raised serious doubts about the security of the Saudi state. U.S. press reports about rifts within the ruling family over the succession, oil policies, and attitudes toward the U.S. were contradicted by Saudi officials.

Oil and OPEC. The price of oil produced by the member states of the Organization of Petroleum Exporting Countries (OPEC) in 1979 rose an average of 113%. Saudi Arabia, despite strong objections from Iran, managed to keep the dollar as the international medium of exchange for oil and to compensate the U.S. in July, August, and September for a shortfall of Iranian oil of 2 million bbl a day. In June OPEC created a two-tier pricing system in which Saudi oil cost $18 a barrel and the OPEC ceiling was $23.50. Iranian exports resumed in the autumn, at which time the price per barrel of OPEC oil averaged $21.50.

After the OPEC oil ministers' meeting in Caracas, Venezuela., in December, there was no agreement on an OPEC price ceiling. Saudi crude would cost $24 a barrel, Indonesian $26.50, and Iranian $28.50; Libya's price of $30 was raised by a further $4.72 at year's end. Despite calls by the PLO for an oil embargo against the U.S. in response to the Egyptian-Israeli treaty, Saudi Arabia backed by Syria prevented any such move at the March Arab League Council meeting. (CHARLES GLASS)

See also Energy; articles on the various political units.
[978.B]

Migration, International

On Oct. 4, 1979, it was reported that the number of illegal immigrants caught trying to reach Hong Kong from China had risen to about 180 a day. Increased police activity on both sides of the border followed an exodus from China in the spring, and the figure dropped from an estimated 600 a day to 20 in July. In May 14,400 would-be immigrants were apprehended, and in July 658. By September, however, the total had risen again to 5,330, with approximately 75% now coming by water instead of land. Many were paying $3,000 a head to organized syndicates for a place in a fast boat from Macau.

Large-scale migrations continued throughout the year in Indochina. Cambodians fleeing the

Laotian refugees who had fled from the pro-Communist Pathet Lao into Thailand were transported to a camp at Nong Khai.

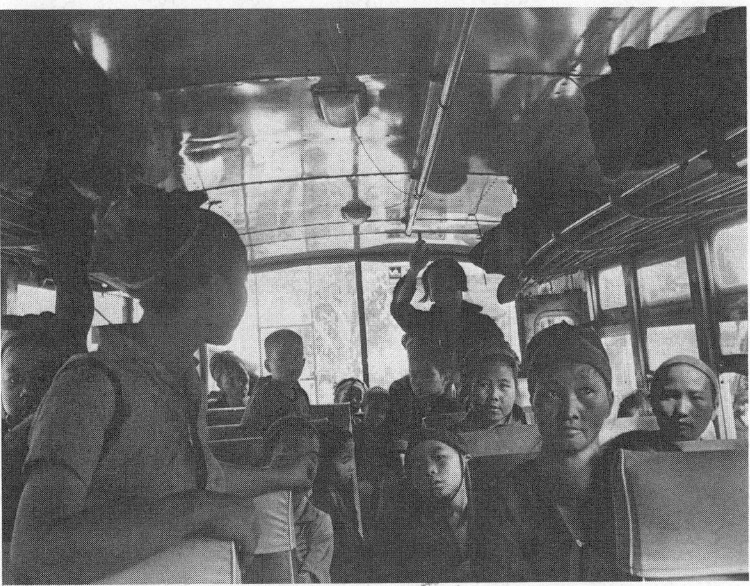
BRIAN EADS—CAMERA PRESS/PHOTO TRENDS

Vietnamese invasion settled in large numbers in Thailand, and thousands of Vietnamese left their own country by boat. (*See* REFUGEES: *Special Report*.) Many people of Chinese ancestry living in Vietnam were forced to resettle in China.

Illegal or undocumented workers entering the U.S. were estimated in January 1979 to have reached 800,000 annually. Most came from Mexico (about 60%) and Central and South America, but some arrived from as far as South Korea and the Philippines. One million apprehensions of such immigrants were recorded in 1978. Unscrupulous syndicates were organizing much of the illegal immigration in the Americas; in 1978 more than 15,000 smugglers were apprehended trying to smuggle 192,000 persons into the U.S. Mexico's Pres. José López Portillo pledged his country's determination to deal with the problem.

It was estimated that industrialized Argentina had attracted more than 2.5 million workers from outside the country. They included 700,000 Paraguayans, 700,000 Chileans, 650,000 Bolivians, 400,000 Uruguayans, and 200,000 Brazilians.

In Zimbabwe Rhodesia official statistics showed that in November 1978 a record 2,057 whites left the country and only 223 arrived. In the first quarter of 1979, 2,916 whites left the country, more than half of them settling in South Africa.

Recruitment of foreign workers by European

CAMERAPIX/KEYSTONE

Refugees fled from Uganda across the White Nile when Tanzanian troops and Ugandan insurgents attacked the forces of Idi Amin early in the year.

Economic Community (EEC) countries had virtually ceased by 1979. The 12.5 million already there from North Africa, Spain, Portugal, Turkey, Yugoslavia, and Greece lived mainly in ghettos, often exploited by employers and landlords and sometimes harassed by the police; they represented 5% of the EEC's labour force. European Commission Vice-Pres. Henk Vredeling, in charge of social and employment affairs, in March announced programs that would deal with training for workers returning to their homelands, illegal entry, and reunification of families.

The French government approved harsh new measures to control foreigners' movements and length of stay in France. On April 19 the National Assembly law commissions discussed the new measures, which would affect more than 4 million foreign persons. Of this figure, 800,000 were Algerian and 700,000 were citizens of EEC countries. Soon after Pres. Valéry Giscard d'Estaing was elected in 1974, a police crackdown on foreigners began, and the number who were expelled rose. Meanwhile, on Jan. 3, 1979, Jean-Marc Lech, director general of the Institut Français d'Opinion Publique, admitted faking the results of an immigration survey commissioned by the Immigration Ministry by reducing the number of people in favour of sending immigrants home from 77 to 57%.

In the U.K. Alex Lyon, a former Home Office minister and chairman of the U.K. Immigrants' Advisory Service (UKIAS), called for an objective scrutiny of immigration procedures. UKIAS joined a number of organizations calling for an inquiry into immigration procedures after newspaper revelations on February 1 that a gynecological examination had been carried out on an Indian wom-

Immigration and Naturalization in the United States

Year ended June 30, 1976

Country or region	Total immigrants admitted	Quota immigrants	Nonquota immigrants: Total	Nonquota immigrants: Family—U.S. citizens	Aliens[1] naturalized
Africa	7,723	5,735	1,988	1,797	2,894
Asia[2]	149,881	102,258	47,623	44,239	56,465
China[3]	18,823	14,404	4,419	4,036	11,145
Hong Kong	5,766	5,002	764	674	...
India	17,487	16,462	1,025	839	5,574
Iran	2,700	1,825	875	857	836
Iraq	3,432	3,264	168	164	483
Israel	2,982	2,134	848	731	1,548
Japan	4,258	2,062	2,196	1,862	1,549
Jordan	2,566	2,074	492	471	1,381
Korea, South	30,803	20,011	10,792	10,045	10,446
Lebanon	2,840	2,346	494	466	1,154
Philippines	37,281	20,978	16,303	15,601	16,145
Thailand	6,925	1,782	5,141	4,805	985
Vietnam	3,048	1,027	2,021	1,787	1,412
Europe[4]	72,411	51,374	21,037	18,798	47,480
Germany, West	5,836	1,613	4,223	3,796	4,856
Greece	8,417	6,338	2,079	1,938	6,151
Italy	8,380	6,202	2,178	1,956	7,891
Poland	3,805	2,742	1,063	973	2,768
Portugal	10,511	9,309	1,202	1,065	3,739
Spain	2,254	1,341	913	788	886
U.S.S.R.	8,220	7,998	222	188	535
United Kingdom	11,392	6,649	4,743	4,186	9,345
Yugoslavia	2,820	2,253	567	527	2,447
North America	142,307	107,110	35,197	29,879	43,085
Canada	7,638	3,475	4,163	3,463	3,759
Cuba	29,233	27,999	1,234	476	20,506
Dominican Republic	12,526	10,464	2,062	1,799	1,904
El Salvador	2,363	1,667	696	642	470
Haiti	5,410	4,805	605	553	1,870
Jamaica	9,026	7,398	1,628	1,490	3,849
Mexico	57,863	39,459	18,404	15,392	6,301
Trinidad and Tobago	4,839	4,040	799	724	1,179
Oceania	3,591	2,381	1,210	1,066	760
South America	22,699	15,914	6,785	6,240	8,302
Argentina	2,267	1,663	604	513	1,574
Colombia	5,742	3,542	2,200	2,024	2,029
Ecuador	4,504	3,633	871	824	880
Guyana	3,326	2,895	431	407	980
Peru	2,640	1,624	1,016	977	850
Total, including others	398,613	284,773	113,840	102,019	159,873

Note: Immigrants listed by country of birth; aliens naturalized by country of former allegiance.
[1]Year ended Sept., 30, 1977. [2]Includes Turkey. [3]Taiwan and People's Republic.
[4]Includes U.S.S.R.
Source: U.S. Department of Justice, Immigration and Naturalization Service, 1976 Annual Report and unpublished data from 1977 Annual Report.

an entering the country and that at least 34 such examinations had taken place at the British High Commission in New Delhi. On June 2 the UN Human Rights Commission passed a resolution expressing concern at "indignities and hardships suffered by nonwhite immigrants" in Britain. The home secretary agreed that the new Conservative Party government's proposed changes in immigration rules to restrict the entry to Britain of fiancés and husbands of women not born in Britain was sexual discrimination but claimed that such entry had abused the system of immigration control. The changes were approved by Parliament on December 4. However, 19 Conservative members abstained from voting to protest their discriminatory nature, one of them resigning his post of parliamentary private secretary. (STUART BENTLEY)

See also Refugees.
[525.A.1.c]

Mining and Quarrying

Mining and quarrying in the United States in 1979 continued at an even pace, but plans for new mines and expansions of existing facilities were restrained. This was imposed by the interrelated threat of economic inflation and energy shortage, which caused planners to take a wait-and-see attitude.

One area of greatly accelerated interest was prospecting for gold, a result of the astronomical rise in the price of that commodity to more than $500 per troy ounce at year's end. Many prospectors reexamined old mining areas such as those at Cripple Creek, Colo.; Nome, Alaska; and Grass Valley, Calif. The only major development was the initiation of engineering by Freeport Minerals Co. for its Jerritt Canyon, Nev., gold discovery.

The rising cost of imported fuel appeared to be giving impetus to the production in the U.S. of synthetic fuels from oil shale, coal, and tar sands. The technology for such production existed and had been used before, but the great expense of such projects continued to be a formidable hurdle to overcome. The recovery of uranium from low-grade deposits by a process of leaching at the site increased during 1979 and was expected to add to the conservation of resources in the U.S.

Industry Developments. A $25 million expansion of the lead-zinc mining and concentration operations of Ozark Lead Co. in southeast Missouri was announced. Crude ore from the underground mine, currently produced at a rate of 1.5 million tons annually, was to be boosted by one-third. The project included construction of two additional 1,200-ft shafts and the driving of nearly two miles of underground tunnels. Since the mine opened in 1968, more than ten miles of underground roadway had been built. The metal output after expansion was expected to amount to approximately 96,000 tons per year of lead and more than 10,200 tons of zinc, along with some copper, silver, and cadmium.

Kerr-McGee Coal Corp. began operations in August at the Clovis Point mine, eight miles east of Gillette, Wyo. During 1979 about 700,000 tons of coal were mined there and shipped to Cajun Electric Cooperative in Louisiana. By 1981 the mine was scheduled to be producing at the rate of 4.5 million tons per year. Approved reclamation programs for this surface mine would, it was hoped, make the surrounding grasslands more productive than before the mining began.

Anaconda Co. was ordered by the U.S. Federal Trade Commission to divest itself of its part ownership of the Twin Buttes mine in Montana and its 20% interest in the Inspiration mine in Arizona. However, the company was allowed to retain the new Carr Fork copper mine near Bingham, Utah, and the Berkeley pit in Montana. The first copper concentrate was shipped after midyear from the Carr Fork mine. This event climaxed five years of construction and the expenditure of $200 million. The property has the capacity of producing 56,000 tons per year of metallic copper.

In July the Cleveland Cliffs Iron Ore Co. closed the last underground iron ore mine in the Lake Superior district, the Mather B Mine near Negaunee, Mich. Opened in 1947, the mine had produced 50 million tons of ore during its peak month of May 1975.

The extraction of uranium from phosphoric acid continued to proceed rapidly. The International Minerals and Chemical Corp. was building a plant at its New Wales, Fla., complex that was expected to produce 750,000 lb of uranium oxide (U_3O_8) per year beginning in 1979. Close to 4 million lb of U_3O_8 were scheduled to be recovered annually from Florida phosphate when plans for new recovery units were completed by 1980.

A new mine was to be developed in northwestern Quebec by Canadian interests. In accordance with the Quebec government's policy regarding mining towns, no new town was to be created for this project. Mine employees would live instead at an existing town, Moutel, and a road would be constructed to the mine. This policy resulted from the problem of dealing with ghost towns after mines were exhausted.

Late in the year the government of Jamaica appeared ready to sign an accord with North American aluminum producers that would reduce the levy on bauxite, the ore from which aluminum is extracted. It was anticipated that the move would cause producing companies to reopen Jamaican mining and refinery operations that had been curtailed because of the high cost of production due to the levy.

After a three-year development period and the expenditure of $300 million, the first shipment of bauxite was loaded in August by Mineração Rio do Norte S.A. from its Trombetas mine in Brazil. The deposit is one of the major world reserves, situated in the Amazon River basin some 300 mi northeast of Manaus. The project included mine development, processing facilities, a railroad, a port, and a townsite in Para State. The company was owned by an international consortium in which the principal partners were Companhia Vale do Rio Doce of Brazil and Alcan of Canada.

The Anaconda Co. was the successful bidder for the Los Pelambres copper deposit in Chile, an undeveloped property near the border with Argentina. Anaconda was formerly owner of large Chilean copper mines, which were nationalized in 1969 and then taken over without compensation in 1971 by the regime of Salvador Allende.

The world's largest coal mine was planned to be producing 27 million metric tons per year by 1982 to feed Sasol III, the South African government's synthetic oil facility. In 1979 the mine had a capacity of 12 million metric tons per year to serve the Sasol II synthetic oil plant.

Technological Developments. It is not well-known that normally only about one-third of the petroleum in an oil field is ever recovered. The best industry estimates are that the producing fields of the U.S. contain more than 300,000,000,000 bbl of oil that will remain in the ground if tapped by conventional drilling methods. In the late 1970s interest was revived by the U.S. Bureau of Mines in recovery of this oil by mining, a method used in recent times by several European nations.

Several mining techniques have been considered. Surface mining of shallow deposits is feasible, and there are many reservoirs amenable to this method. Actual underground mining and extraction of the reservoir rock did not appear attractive because of environmental or economic factors. However, utilization of mining techniques to enter the underlying or overlying rocks followed by close-spaced penetration of the reservoir by drill holes held promise. In this system, once the mining development work has been completed, the petroleum engineer takes over and forces the oil out by steam inducement or water flooding. In either case the oil is drained from the reservoir. Thus, the method consists of conventional oil production augmented by many close-spaced producing wells.

An experimental test of gasifying coal in place underground was successfully concluded by U.S. Department of Energy researchers at a site near Pricetown, W.Va. About 1,000 tons of coal were gasified, producing gas that could be burned under boilers. Two 900-ft-deep boreholes 40 ft apart were drilled into a coal seam. The coal was ignited at the base of one borehole and air injected under high pressure at the other. The air passed through the steam cracks and pores until it met the flame front, which then followed a path to the high-pressure borehole. The combustion gases were forced up this borehole and then directed to a point of utilization. Similar tests had been conducted in western U.S. coal beds, but it was hoped that these tests in the East presaged new sources of heating gas near dense population centres.

Work continued during the year in the effort to develop oil shale in Colorado. A partnership of Standard Oil Co. of Indiana and Gulf Oil Corp. was developing the Rio Blanco oil shales near Rangely, Colo. A 971-ft shaft was sunk, and tunnels were being driven to five blocks that were to be fragmented by shrinkage stoping. Broken shale was to be drawn from the stopes to create a working chamber. For the retorting process superheated, inert, oxygen-free gases at temperatures of up to 870° C (1,600° F) were to be injected through a casing to heat the top of the chamber. Oil would separate from the shale and percolate down through the broken shale in the chamber to a collecting drift at the bottom of the chamber from which it could be pumped to the surface. Gas was also to be collected and brought to the surface for generating purposes. The advantages of such a retorting method are the environmental benefits of leaving the waste product in the ground and containment of the retorting activity below the surface. (JOHN V. BEALL)

Production. The overall mining production index, as calculated by the United Nations, showed growth of only about 1.7% during 1978 (*see* Table), reflecting the continued caution of an industry that depends heavily on energy supplies. Indeed, since 1975 only petroleum could be said to have shown strong and sustained growth (and that totaled only 12.8% since 1975); coal, on the other hand, by the first quarter of 1979 was barely 5% above production levels of 1975. A steep decline in the petroleum sector during the first quarter of 1979 was attributable in large part to the consequences of the political situation in Iran.

Price increases for many commodities outran inflation during 1978 and 1979, permitting a number of mining operations to extend (or plan extension of) operations into areas too marginal for profitable exploitation in the past. Gold mining in South Africa was probably the most successful utilization of lower-yield ore bodies, although other commodities, especially coal and cobalt-bearing ore bodies, could be expected to reap similar rewards from international prices.

Among the important developments was a conference held in Jurica, Mexico, during December 1978 on the subject of small-scale mining. Representatives from approximately 70 countries attended and found a broad measure of agreement on the nature and importance of small operations: small mines can be brought into production rapidly, employ local (often unskilled) labour, produce little environmental damage, provide seasonal employment, and do not require large expenditures of capital (and time) to provide such support facilities as housing and roads. Also, many types of deposits cannot be worked economically on a large scale.

Domestically in the U.S., the value of mining output in 1978 rose 13% over 1977, totaling about $19.7 billion in 1978 (and valued at some $200 billion after the processing of these same materials). Of 22 metals for which the U.S. Bureau of Mines maintained statistics, 11 showed an increase in production levels; of 48 nonmetallic commodities, 35 had increased output. Among the nonmetals particularly strong performances were shown by barite (up 14%), pumice and volcanic cinder (up 14%), cement, rock phosphate, and crushed stone.

Aluminum. World production of bauxite, the primary ore of aluminum, was estimated to have declined slightly, by about 1.3%, from 84,242,000 metric tons in 1977 to 83,122,000 tons in 1978. This reflected reductions in all of the three leading producing countries: Australia, at 24.3 million tons (−6.8%); Jamaica, 11,736,000 (−2.7%); and Guinea, 11 million (−2.7%). Output of alumina (aluminum oxide, the concentrated intermediate stage in the production of aluminum metal) rose slightly during 1978, reaching 29,976,000 tons; major producers were Australia (6,676,000 tons), the United States (5,960,000 tons), the Soviet Union (an estimated 2.6 million tons), and Jamaica (2,142,000 tons). Output of aluminum metal rose by about 2.6% during 1978, totaling 14,052,000 tons, with the U.S. accounting for some 31% despite both cutbacks of electrical power to major producers and price increases for power actually supplied. World aluminum refining capacity rose to more than 17 million tons annually, with new facilities or additional capacity beginning operations in the U.S.S.R. and Yugoslavia, in particular.

Antimony. In terms of contained metal, world production of antimony was estimated to have declined by approximately 6.3% in 1978 to about 66,900 metric tons, most of the decline being attributable to reduced consumption in the industrialized countries. The major producers continued to be Bolivia, with 12,672 tons, China, with an estimated 12,000 tons, and South Africa, with 10,478 tons. Smelter production in the U.S., however, rose by 10%, supplied in part by large export increases to the U.S. by China and South Africa.

Arsenic. Recovery from the precipitous production declines of 1975 and 1976 stagnated during 1978, with production remaining at about 34,500 metric tons; production statistics, although mostly estimates, indicated that the major producers were relatively unchanged from the preceding year. The U.S.S.R. led with 7,400 tons, followed by South West Africa (Namibia) at 7,250 tons, France at 6,900 tons, and Sweden at 6,800 tons.

Cadmium. Preliminary data from the U.S. Bureau of Mines indicated that cadmium smelter production in 1978 declined about 7% from 17,585 metric tons to 16,403. The major producers were the U.S.S.R. (an estimated 2,800 tons), regaining first place from Japan, and Japan (2,531 tons). As with arsenic, concern about environmental effects of the metal led to reduced dispersion via industrial flue dust and similar means; the U.S. Environmental Protection Agency promulgated final regulations regarding allowable concentration of the metal in effluents of mine, mill, and industrial operations.

Cement. The worldwide total of cement production for 1976–78 was estimated to have varied by not more than one million tons against an overall figure of about 711 million metric tons. The major producer in 1978 was the U.S.S.R. with 127 million tons; it lost ground, however, to second-place Japan, which increased its production by more than 16%, to 84.9 million tons; the U.S. fell to third place with about 76.1 million tons. China was fourth at 65.2 million tons, a 17.2% increase over the preceding year.

Chromium. World mine production of chromite, the principal ore of chromium, rose slightly (by about 1.4%) during 1978 from an estimated 9.8 million tons to some 9,940,000 tons; the major producing countries continued to be South Africa (3,145,000 tons) and the U.S.S.R. (estimated to be about 2.1 million tons), together accounting for some 53% of the world total. Continuation of the trade embargo against Zimbabwe Rhodesia, continued dependence of U.S. consumers on foreign (particularly South African) supplies, and the growth of the South African ferrochrome industry brought complaints by ferrochrome producers in the U.S., Japan, and the EEC, although, with the reduction of supply and quality of chromite shipments from the U.S.S.R., consuming industries were obliged to locate alternate sources of the material.

Cobalt. The recovery of the cobalt mining industry brought production levels back to those of 1974, the all-time high year. Hard production figures, often withheld for strategic reasons, were sparse, but it appeared that growth of about 4.3% took place in 1978. Zaire continued as the leading producer, with about 10,400 metric tons of a world total of about 30,800; the second leading producer was New Caledonia, with about 4,200 tons. Zaire's monetary and economic difficulties and the place occupied in the strategic industries of client countries by cobalt and other metals mined in Zaire led the International Monetary Fund to approve in September 1979 a standby line of credit intended to stabilize the Zairian economy.

Copper. According to data of the Intergovernmental Council of Copper Exporting States (CIPEC) world mine production fell in 1978 by approximately 3%, from 7,983,000 metric tons to about 7,743,000 tons. The major producers were the U.S. with about 1,352,000 tons, followed by the U.S.S.R. with an estimated 1.1 million tons, Chile with 1,036,000 tons, Canada 658,000 tons, and Zambia 643,000 tons. CIPEC members together accounted for about 40% of total world production. Primary smelter production of blister copper was estimated to have declined by about 1.7% to some 7,998,000 tons, the major producers of which were the U.S. (1,343,000 tons) and the Soviet Union (an estimated 1.1 million tons). Output of refined metal was estimated, however, to have risen slightly (0.4%), with the U.S. and U.S.S.R. also the leaders, at 1,780,000 and 1,440,000 tons, respectively, followed by Japan at 959,000 tons. World consumption showed a healthy growth of 3.9%.

Gold. Production of gold was thought, on the basis of preliminary estimates by the U.S. Bureau of Mines, to have risen only slightly during 1978. However, the astonishing price increases of 1979 were thought likely to generate strong industry growth, as the metal continued to prove attractive to many types of purchasers as a hedge against inflation. Mine production was about 39.6 million troy ounces during 1978; the leading producer, South Africa, accounted for about 22,649,500 oz, or 57% of the total, up 4.7% over 1977. Lesser producers included the U.S.S.R. at about 7.9 million oz, Canada 1.7 million oz, and the U.S. 965,000 oz. Gold production for 1979 in South Africa was expected to be substantially above 1978 levels both because of the opening of three new mines and because of the extension of many existing mines into areas that only become economically productive if the world price is above $200 per ounce.

Iron. World production of iron ore was estimated to have declined about 4% during 1978 and to have begun rising again in 1979, based on results for the first two quarters of 1979. Total production in 1978 amounted to approximately 804.5 million metric tons, of which the major producers were the Soviet Union, with 244 million tons, about 30% of the world total, followed by the U.S. (82,080,000 tons), Australia (81,660,000 tons), China (an estimated 65 million tons), Canada (39,622,000 tons), India (35,122,000 tons), and France (33,776,000 tons). Pig-iron production was estimated to have risen by a relatively slight 2.1%, to an estimated total of 496.6 million tons; the leading producers were the U.S.S.R. with 110,702,000 tons, followed by the U.S. at 79,541,000 tons, Japan's import-based industry with 78,589,000 tons, China 34,790,000 tons, and West Germany 30,148,000 tons.

Lead. World mine production of lead ore was estimated to have remained virtually unchanged between 1977 and 1978, rising only 1,000 metric tons to 3,246,000 tons. The leader was the U.S. with 531,000 tons, off about 1% from the preceding year; other important producers included Australia with 415,000 tons and Canada with 308,311 tons. Preliminary estimates by the U.S. Bureau of Mines indicated that world smelter production of lead rose some 2.5% during 1978 to an estimated 3,720,000 tons. The leading producer was the U.S. with 499,000 tons, a 10% decline from 1977, mostly attributable to a ten-week strike at AMAX Lead Co., Buick, Mo. The Soviet Union was thought to be smelting about the same amount as the U.S., but no hard figures were available; following these two the major producers were West Germany (294,000 tons), Australia (217,000 tons), Japan (196,000 tons), and Canada (194,000 tons). Apparent consumption in the U.S., the largest consuming country, was up about 4%.

Manganese. World production of manganese fell again in 1978, to about 22.5 million metric tons, according to preliminary data. The Soviet Union was thought to be the world's major producer with an estimated 8.5 million tons, or about 38% of the world total. The second-leading producer, South Africa, suffered a 21% decline, although opening of a new mine at Middelplaats (production began in January 1979) was expected to add about one million tons per year of new capacity to South Africa's 1978 production of 4,180,000 tons. Other major producers included Australia, showing a 50% increase in 1978 to 2,085,000 tons, and Gabon, with 1,567,000 tons. Brazil's production dropped to 783,000 tons, less than one-third of what it had been as recently as 1971.

Mercury. World production of mercury was estimated to have fallen by about 11.4% during 1978, continuing a trend that began in 1971 when mercury production reached a high of 10,364 metric tons. Output in 1978 was only about 6,067 tons, as few major producers showed increases. The leader continued to be the U.S.S.R. with an estimated 2,070 tons, followed by Spain with some 1,070 (an 11% decrease from the preceding year) and Algeria with 1,034.

Molybdenum. Mine production of molybdenum in 1978 was estimated to have increased by about 4.7%, reaching a new high

Indexes of Production, Mining, and Mineral Commodities

(1975=100)

	1974	1975	1976	1977	1978	1979 I	1979 II
Mining (total)							
World[1]	106.1	100.0	108.4	114.6	116.5	113.2	...
Centrally planned economies[2]	94.2	100.0	104.5	108.5	112.1	114.6	117.4
Developed market economies[3]	101.5	100.0	103.2	108.9	112.8	115.8	118.1
Less developed market economies[4]	112.8	100.0	112.6	119.9	120.1	109.6	...
Coal							
World[1]	96.7	100.0	101.4	102.4	101.6	105.0	...
Centrally planned economies[2]	96.7	100.0	101.9	103.9	105.4	105.4	108.0
Developed market economies[3]	97.0	100.0	100.9	101.1	98.7	103.8	108.1
Less developed market economies[4]	91.6	100.0	104.2	105.2	107.0	118.4	...
Petroleum							
World[1]	108.5	100.0	110.5	116.3	119.1	112.8	...
Centrally planned economies[2]	93.0	100.0	107.0	112.4	118.6	123.3	126.1
Developed market economies[3]	99.8	100.0	104.5	115.7	126.4	138.0	129.2
Less developed market economies[4]	113.3	100.0	112.6	117.1	117.3	104.6	...
Metals							
World[1]	105.6	100.0	102.3	103.4	101.8	103.9	...
Centrally planned economies[2]	100.8	100.0	101.9	103.2	104.0	103.6	107.4
Developed market economies[3]	105.2	100.0	101.9	101.8	98.1	96.8	100.6
Less developed market economies[4]	109.5	100.0	103.5	106.2	106.6	116.1	...
Manufacturing (total)	104.0	100.0	108.2	113.3	118.8	122.6	...

[1]Excluding Albania, China, North Korea, Vietnam.
[2]Bulgaria, Czechoslovakia, East Germany, Hungary, Poland, Romania, U.S.S.R.
[3]North America, Europe (except centrally planned), Australia, Israel, Japan, New Zealand, South Africa.
[4]Caribbean, Central and South America, Africa (except South Africa), Asian Middle East, East and South East Asia (except Israel and Japan).
Source: UN, *Monthly Bulletin of Statistics* (November 1979).

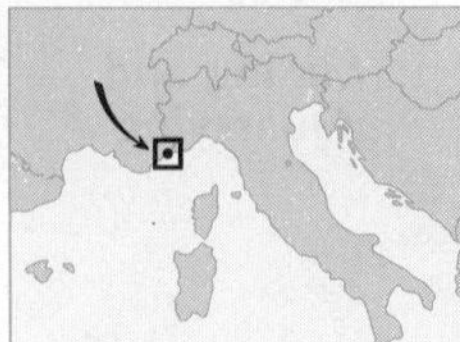
Monaco

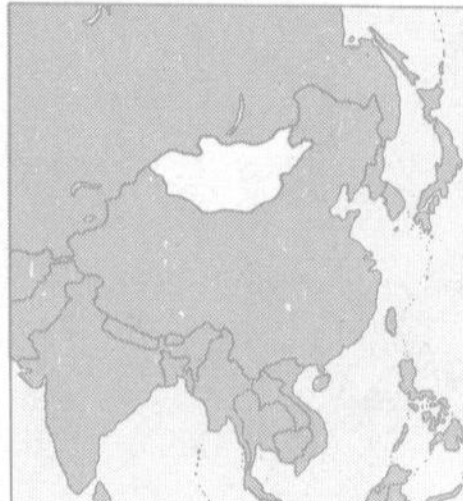
Mongolia

of about 97,800 metric tons. The U.S., the world leader at 59,803 tons, or about 61% of the world total, showed an 8.2% increase, attributable to initial output from the Henderson Mine in Colorado. U.S. output through the first nine months of 1979 showed a further 7% growth. Other major producers included Canada, Chile, and the U.S.S.R.

Nickel. World production of nickel was estimated by the U.S. Bureau of Mines to have declined during 1978 by almost 24%, primarily because of a nearly 45% decline in Canadian production to about 130,055 metric tons, which was still some 22% of the world total of about 588,000 tons. Other major producers included the U.S.S.R. at an estimated level of under 100,000 tons, down about a third from only two years earlier, and New Caledonia at 63,000 tons, an estimated 60% decline from the preceding year. It was estimated that, worldwide, producers were operating at about 65% of capacity. Long-term consumption prospects of the metal were raised in mid-1979 by demonstration of the possibility of extensive use of nickel as a component of batteries for electric automobiles, some 700 of which were to be purchased by the U.S. Department of Energy for demonstration in 1980.

Platinum-Group metals. Production of the platinum-group metals (platinum, palladium, iridium, osmium, rhodium, and ruthenium) was estimated to have remained approximately constant in 1978 with respect to the preceding year, at about 6.4 million troy ounces. About 93% of the production originated in two countries, the U.S.S.R. at about three million ounces and South Africa at 2,950,000 oz; the only other important producer was Canada, at 279,000 oz.

Silver. According to preliminary U.S. Bureau of Mines data, silver production worldwide increased by about 2.6% in 1978, evenly distributed among the major producers. Total output was some 334 million troy ounces; the world leader was Mexico with 53,642,000 oz, followed by the U.S.S.R. (about 45 million oz), Canada (38,760,000), and the U.S. (38,571,000). World consumption, according to Handy & Harman, rose about 3% to a total of about 423 million oz (excluding centrally planned countries), of which 159.5 million oz was utilized in the U.S. Particular increases occurred in photographic applications and production of silver flatware.

Tin. World mine production of tin was estimated to have risen slightly during 1978, from 231,400 metric tons to 235,000 tons. Malaysia was the leading producer at 60,698 tons, showing its first increase in six years, followed (it was estimated) by the U.S.S.R. (33,000 tons), Bolivia (30,827), Indonesia and Thailand (both about 26,000), and China (about 20,000). Smelter production fell slightly, according to preliminary estimates, to 228,900 tons, of which the leading producers were Malaysia, the U.S.S.R., Indonesia, and China, probably in that order. Although smelting capacity already exceeded world output by 50%, new smelting plants were planned for Rwanda, South Africa, and Thailand. The fifth International Tin Agreement, of which the U.S. was a member, tried to raise production levels, but supplies fell short of demand, and prices rose about 15% during 1978.

Titanium. World output of titanium rutile concentrates was estimated to have fallen to about 234,000 metric tons (−10.5%) and that of titanium ilmenite concentrates to have risen 8.5% to 4,436 tons in 1978. Consumption and market conditions in the U.S., the primary consuming country, were strong in 1978. During 1979 the trial of several companies and their executives on charges of price fixing during 1970–76 was completed, with one plea of guilty and eight of no contest. Demand for titanium oxide (white) pigments continued to be strong into 1979.

Tungsten. World mine production of tungsten was thought to have risen slightly in 1978 to a new high of about 38,550 metric tons; the two leading producers were thought to be China at about 8,900 tons and the U.S.S.R. at some 8,000 tons, followed by the U.S. (3,270 tons), Bolivia (3,106), and Australia and South Korea (both about 2,500 tons).

Uranium. Another strong increase in production levels of uranium was shown in 1978, with a 12.3% increase in non-Communist world production to about 30,600 metric tons. Data were unavailable for centrally planned economies, but the leading producer was thought to be the U.S. with almost 50% of output at 16,800 tons; other major producers for which data were available included Canada (9,440 tons), and South Africa (4,531 tons). Particularly energetic exploration programs were under way in Madagascar and Zambia.

Zinc. World mine production of zinc was estimated to have fallen about 4.1% during 1978 to a total of about 4,524,000 metric tons. The leading producers included Canada with 1,032,358 metric tons (about 23% of world production), Australia (470,400 tons), the U.S. (302,669 tons), Japan (275,078 tons), Mexico (246,080 tons), and Poland (just under 240,000 tons). Smelter production was not much changed from 1977 and was led by Japan at about 768,000 tons, followed by the Soviet Union (estimated at about 750,000 tons), Canada (495,000 tons), West Germany (474,000 tons), and the U.S. (436,000 tons). (WILLIAM A. CLEVELAND)

See also Earth Sciences; Energy; Industrial Review: *Gemstones; Iron and Steel;* Materials Sciences.

Missiles:
see Defense

Molecular Biology:
see Life Sciences

Monetary Policy:
see Economy, World

Money and Banking:
see Economy, World

Monaco

A sovereign principality on the northern Mediterranean coast, Monaco is bounded on land by the French département of Alpes-Maritimes. Area: 1.90 sq km (0.74 sq mi). Pop. (1979 est.): 25,000. Language: French. Religion: predominantly Roman Catholic. Prince, Rainier III; minister of state in 1979, André Saint-Mleux.

In November 1979 Prince Rainier celebrated the 30th anniversary of his enthronement. During his reign the casino of Monte Carlo and the issue of postage stamps had ceased to be the principal sources of Monaco's revenue, which now came mainly from the tourist trade.

In July the prince appointed a Paris-born naturalized U.S. citizen, Bernard F. Combemale, as chief executive of the Société Anonyme des Bains de Mer et du Cercle des Étrangers, the company that runs almost everything in Monaco and that has an annual revenue estimated at some U.S. $250 million. An international investment expert who had begun his career as a clerk at the Chemical Bank of New York, Combemale said of his relations with Prince Rainier: "It is just the same as reporting to the chairman of a corporation."

(K. M. SMOGORZEWSKI)

MONACO

Education. (1977–78) Primary, secondary, and vocational, pupils 4,904, teachers (1976–77) 357.

Finance and Trade. Monetary unit: French franc, with (Sept. 17, 1979) a free rate of Fr 4.23 to U.S. $1 (Fr 9.10 = £1 sterling). Budget (1977 est.): revenue Fr 596 million; expenditure Fr 515 million. Foreign trade included with France. Tourism (1977) 209,000 visitors.

Mongolia

A people's republic of Asia lying between the U.S.S.R. and China, Mongolia occupies the geographic area known as Outer Mongolia. Area: 1,565,000 sq km (604,000 sq mi). Pop. (1979 est.): 1,623,000. Cap. and largest city: Ulan Bator (pop., 1977 est., 345,000). Language: Khalkha Mongolian. Religion: Lamaistic Buddhism. First secretary of the Mongolian People's Revolutionary (Communist) Party in 1979 and chairman of the Presidium of the Great People's Hural, Yumzhagiyen Tsedenbal; chairman of the Council of Ministers (premier), Zhambyn Batmunkh.

"The Soviet people set great store by their tried and tested alliance with the Mongolian people," said a message of greetings sent on July 11, 1979, by Pres. Leonid I. Brezhnev and Premier Aleksey Kosygin of the U.S.S.R. to the leaders of Mongolia on the occasion of the 58th anniversary of the Mongolian People's Republic. On August 23 Yumzhagiyen Tsedenbal, first secretary of the Mongolian People's Revolutionary Party, was received by Brezhnev at Oreanda, Crimea, where they examined Soviet-Mongolian economic cooperation during the 1981–85 period and discussed the "hegemonistic" tendencies of China. Signifi-

MONGOLIA

Education. (1977) Primary and secondary, pupils 373,500; vocational, pupils 18,000; primary, secondary, and vocational, teachers 13,500; higher, students 17,800, teaching staff 1,000.

Finance. Monetary unit: tugrik, with (Sept. 17, 1979) a nominal exchange rate of 3.04 tugriks to U.S. $1 (6.54 tugriks = £1 sterling). Budget (1979 est.): revenue 3,772,000,000 tugriks; expenditure 3,762,000,000 tugriks.

Foreign Trade. (1976) Imports 1,007,000,000 tugriks; exports 775 million tugriks. Import source: U.S.S.R. *c.* 93%. Export destinations: U.S.S.R. *c.* 81%; Czechoslovakia *c.* 6%. Main exports (1975): livestock 27%; meat 19%; wool 16%.

Transport and Communications. Roads (1977) *c.* 75,000 km (including *c.* 9,000 km main roads). Railways: (1978) 1,710 km; traffic (1977) 227 million passenger-km, freight 2,542,000,000 net ton-km. Telephones (Dec. 1978) 35,800. Radio receivers (Dec. 1978) 140,300. Television receivers (Dec. 1978) *c.* 40,800.

Agriculture. Production (in 000; metric tons; 1978): wheat *c.* 400; oats *c.* 70; barley *c.* 72; potatoes (1977) *c.* 32; milk (1977) *c.* 235; beef and veal (1977) *c.* 68; mutton and goat meat (1977) *c.* 126; wool *c.* 12. Livestock (in 000; Dec. 1976): sheep 13,906; goats 4,548; cattle 2,417; horses 2,205; camels 607.

Industry. Production (in 000; metric tons; 1978): coal and lignite 3,787; fluorspar 438; cement (1977) 100; electricity (kw-hr) 1,156,000.

cantly, the Soviet and Mongolian press published commemorative articles devoted to the Soviet-Mongolian victory over the Japanese at the Khalkyn River in 1939. In September a consultative meeting of deputy foreign ministers of socialist countries was held in Ulan Bator. During the same month the Mongolian minister of defense and the chief of Mongolia's general staff visited Poland.

As a member of the Council for Mutual Economic Assistance (CMEA, or Comecon), Mongolia was prospering. Its foreign trade in 1978 amounted to some 500 million rubles, or about U.S. $335 million. Of this total, approximately 84% represented exchanges with the U.S.S.R. and 12.8% with other Comecon members. (K. M. SMOGORZEWSKI)

Morocco

A constitutional monarchy of northwestern Africa, on the Atlantic Ocean and the Mediterranean Sea, Morocco is bordered by Algeria and Western Sahara. Area: 458,730 sq km (177,117 sq mi). Pop. (1978 est.): 18,906,000. Cap.: Rabat (pop., 1977 est., 704,100). Largest city: Casablanca (pop., 1978 est., 2,113,100). (Data above refer to Morocco as constituted prior to the purported division of Western Sahara between Morocco and Mauritania.) Language: Arabic (official), with Berber, French, and Spanish minorities. Religion: Muslim. King, Hassan II; prime ministers in 1979, Ahmed Osman and, from March 22, Maati Bouabid.

The worsening Saharan situation clouded Moroccan horizons during 1979. After Mauritania signed a peace treaty with the Popular Front for the Liberation of Saguia el Hamra and Río de Oro (Polisario Front) on August 5, Morocco occupied Dakhla, in formerly Mauritanian-controlled Sahara. The Polisario Front had begun attacks inside Morocco, assaulting Tan Tan on January 28 and again on June 13 and 27 and temporarily capturing Lebouirate on August 24. In October a Polisario Front claim that it had captured Semara (Smara) in the Western Sahara and killed 1,200 Moroccan soldiers was denied by Morocco, which countered with the claim that it had killed more than 1,000 guerrillas.

MOROCCO

Education. (1979) Primary, pupils 1,925,187, teachers 50,829; secondary, pupils 650,796, teachers 40,507; vocational, pupils 14,985; teacher training, students 11,238, teachers (1975–76) 486; higher, students 76,054, teaching staff (1975–76) 1,642.

Finance. Monetary unit: dirham, with (Sept. 17, 1979) a free rate of 3.88 dirhams to U.S. $1 (8.35 dirhams = £1 sterling). Gold, SDR's, and foreign exchange (June 1979) U.S. $661 million. Budget (1979 est.): revenue 13 billion dirhams; expenditure 12.8 billion dirhams (excludes capital expenditure of 8.7 billion dirhams). Gross national product (1978) 53,450,000,000 dirhams. Money supply (June 1979) 22,237,000,000 dirhams. Cost of living (1975 = 100; April 1979) 144.1.

Foreign Trade. (1978) Imports 12.4 billion dirhams; exports 6,260,000,000 dirhams. Main import sources: France 26%; Spain 10%; U.S. 8%; West Germany 7%; Italy 7%; Iraq 6%. Main export destinations: France 27%; West Germany 11%; Spain 7%; Italy 6%; Belgium-Luxembourg 5%. Main exports: phosphates 32%; citrus fruit 13%; textiles 12%; vegetables 6%. Tourism (1977): visitors 1,427,000; gross receipts U.S. $375 million.

Transport and Communications. Roads (1976) 26,702 km. Motor vehicles in use (1976): passenger 347,400; commercial 121,600. Railways: (1976) 1,756 km; traffic (1977) 835 million passenger-km, freight 3,474,000,000 net ton-km. Air traffic (1978): 1,901,000,000 passenger-km; freight 23.2 million net ton-km. Shipping (1978): merchant vessels 100 gross tons and over 117; gross tonnage 341,410. Telephones (Jan. 1978) 210,000. Radio receivers (Dec. 1976) 1.5 million. Television receivers (Dec. 1976) 522,000.

Agriculture. Production (in 000; metric tons; 1978): wheat 1,876; barley *c.* 2,328; corn *c.* 390; potatoes *c.* 190; sugar, raw value *c.* 363; tomatoes *c.* 465; grapes *c.* 215; oranges *c.* 643; mandarin oranges and tangerines *c.* 142; olives *c.* 300; dates *c.* 73; fish catch (1977) 261. Livestock (in 000; 1978): sheep *c.* 14,300; goats *c.* 5,700; cattle (1977) *c.* 3,650; horses *c.* 310; mules *c.* 370; asses *c.* 1,200; camels *c.* 210; poultry *c.* 21,300.

Industry. Production (in 000; metric tons; 1978): coal 720; crude oil *c.* 30; petroleum products (1977) *c.* 2,610; electricity (excluding most industrial production; kw-hr) 3,592,000; cement 2,819; iron ore (55–60% metal content) 63; phosphate rock (1977) 17,572; manganese ore (metal content; 1977) 58; lead concentrates (metal content; 1977) 109; zinc concentrates (metal content; 1977) 11.

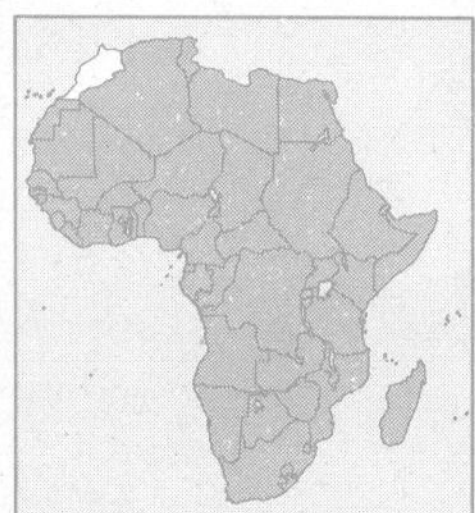
Morocco

Morocco had accused Algeria of instigating Polisario attacks and claimed that the guerrillas were Algerian-paid mercenaries. On March 12 Muhammad Abrouk was appointed Morocco's commander in chief, while domestic support was mobilized through the creation of a Defense Council headed by King Hassan (*see* BIOGRAPHIES) and including representatives of all political parties. In May and June, pressure on Spain to moderate its policy favouring self-determination for the Western Sahara culminated during King Juan Carlos's visit to Rabat. In June, after the second attack on Tan Tan, Morocco formally complained to the UN Security Council about Algerian aggression, and in July it walked out of the Organization of African Unity's summit meeting in Monrovia, Liberia, to protest a call for a Saharan cease-fire and referendum. In October the U.S. decided to resume arms supplies, and in November Morocco launched a major offensive in the Sahara.

Relations with Egypt were disrupted when the Moroccan ambassador was recalled from Cairo, in keeping with decisions made at the Baghdad Arab

Mormons: *see* Religion

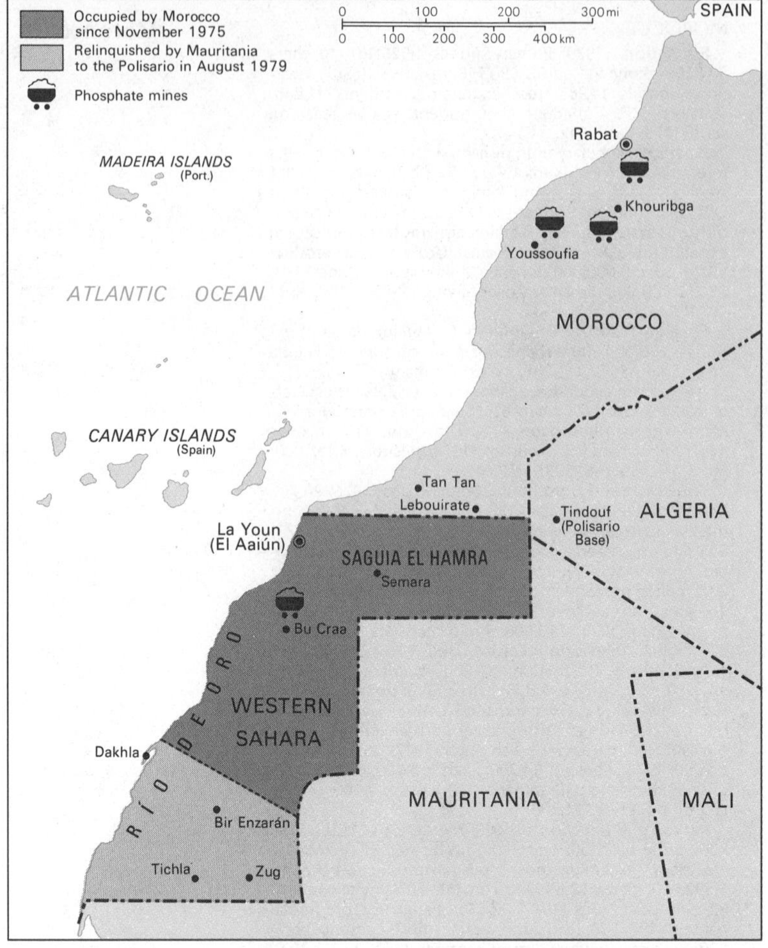

summit. However, Egyptian Pres. Anwar as-Sadat still supported Morocco over the Sahara and offered military aid in September. Continued Saudi financial and political support was assured after King Khalid's visit in May. Morocco reluctantly offered hospitality to the shah of Iran from January 22 to March 30, though it recognized the new Iranian government in February.

The Soviet Union signed a seven-year trade agreement on July 3, despite earlier Moroccan protests over Soviet aid to Algeria for iron ore extraction at Gara Djebilet. At home, inflation continued, and there were a number of disruptive strikes. Wage increases of up to 40% were announced on April 27, but inflation and defense costs necessitated tax increases in July. On March 22 the veteran prime minister, Ahmed Osman, was replaced by Maati Bouabid, who had support in the labour unions. (GEORGE JOFFÉ)

Motion Pictures

At the close of the 1970s the mood of the commercial cinema in many Western countries was cautiously jubilant. Audience decline seemed at last to have been arrested, thanks partly to the steady flow of U.S.-originated box-office infallibles such as *Alien, The Deer Hunter*, and *Superman*. Even the energy crisis was reckoned to have certain compensations; it was anticipated that it would tend to take people out of their cars and into the local movie houses.

English-Speaking Cinema. UNITED STATES. Several of the major distribution companies enjoyed record turnovers (Warner Brothers for the first time in history topped $200 million), in each case due to the performance of individual films. Paramount, for instance, was enjoying the profits of *Grease* and *Saturday Night Fever*; 20th Century-Fox, *Star Wars*; Universal Pictures, *Jaws, Jaws 2*, and *National Lampoon's Animal House*; Warner Brothers, *Superman* and *Every Which Way But Loose*. Although these big box-office successes tended to be "family films," which succeeded in winning back a part of the long-lost older adult audience, the film industry continued anxiously to scan the tastes of the teenagers and under-25s, who remained the most significant market for films. Recent successes like *Coming Home, The Deer Hunter*, and *Apocalypse Now* began to lead one to the conclusion that the new generation of filmgoers was attracted by political content, even though in the past Hollywood had regarded any kind of politics as box-office poison.

In retrospect, Michael Cimino's *The Deer Hunter*, one of the great box-office successes of the year and winner of the Academy Award for best picture of 1978, seemed specious and shallow (it was voted by British critics "the Most Disappointing Film of the Year," despite favourable initial reaction). Charged with racism, it seemed to respond more to national self-pity than to attempt real analysis of the Vietnam war and its significance to Americans. The film was not favoured by inevitable comparisons with the epic *Apocalypse Now* of Francis Ford Coppola (*see* BIOGRAPHIES), which emerged in 1979 after four years of costly work. For two-thirds of its length the film's vision of war was astonishing and horrific; after that it was diminished by a return to its narrative origins in Joseph Conrad's story *Heart of Darkness*.

Other films of political slant included James Bridges's *China Syndrome*, an intelligent, frightening speculation about what might happen in the event of an accident in a nuclear reactor, the impact of which was considerably heightened by the accident at the nuclear power plant at Three Mile Island, Pennsylvania, that occurred soon after the film's release; Martin Ritt's *Norma Rae*—closely enough based on fact to attract legal threats from a woman claiming to be the original of the title character—about a girl who becomes involved in labour union organization in a Southern cotton mill; and *The Seduction of Joe Tynan*, written by and starring Alan Alda (*see* BIOGRAPHIES) and contemplating some hazards of political life.

Walter Hill's *The Warriors*, set in the Bronx in the 1960s, enjoyed a succès de scandale on account of its violence and established a new vogue for "gang" films—generally set in the 1950s. Some examples were Michael Pressman's *Boulevard Nights*, Philip Kaufman's *The Wanderers*, Jonathan Kaplan's *Over the Edge*, and Robert Collins's *Walk Proud*.

Alongside this new Hollywood style, old genres were perpetuated in sequels, imitations, and "prequels." *Superman* inspired *Buck Rogers in the 25th Century*, *Star Wars* led to *Star Trek*, a filmed version of the 1960s television serial with the original TV cast. Irwin Allen directed, *Beyond the Poseidon Adventure* to follow *The Poseidon Adventure*; Sylvester Stallone, who had written and starred in *Rocky*, wrote, directed, and starred in *Rocky II*; Richard Lester's *Butch and Sundance: The Early Days* provided an introduction to the 1969 success *Butch Cassidy and the Sundance Kid*.

Remakes included *The Champ*, a shamelessly sentimental revisiting of King Vidor's 1931 "weepie," this time directed by Franco Zeffirelli. The vogue for horror and the occult was represented by *Alien* and *The Amityville Horror*; the style was satirized in John Badham's *Dracula* and Stan Dragoti's *Love at First Bite*.

One of the most distinguished U.S. films of the year was *Wise Blood*, from Flannery O'Connor's novel about religious fanaticism in the rural South, directed with masterly style by the veteran John Huston. A little heralded movie that gained both critical acclaim and box-office success was Peter Yates's *Breaking Away*, a wry and touching comedy about coming of age in the working class in a university town. James Frawley brought Jim Henson's Muppets to film with *The Muppet Movie*, which featured appearances by Dom DeLuise, Steve Martin, and Milton Berle. Ted Kotcheff's *North Dallas Forty* was a critical look at the bruising world of U.S. professional football, and in *The Onion Field* Harold Becker brought to the screen Joseph Wambaugh's powerful nonfiction book about the killing of a policeman. Released in mid-December were Steven Spielberg's slapstick *1941* and Robert Benton's *Kramer vs. Kramer*, a look at divorce in the 1970s. Woody Allen confirmed his position as the most gifted of the younger U.S. directors with *Manhattan*, a funny and perceptive portrait of the bourgeois intellectual world of New York, seen with the love-hate of a resident. John Carpenter, one of the brightest new hopes of the U.S. cinema, made an effective horror film, *Halloween*, and an honourable hagiography, *Elvis*.

Several great Hollywood veterans died in 1979, including Mary Pickford, one of the first and biggest movie stars, John Wayne, George Brent, John Cromwell, a director-actor who had recently made a comeback as a comic actor in the films of Robert Altman, Jack Haley, Zeppo Marx, Merle Oberon, Joan Blondell, and directors Robert Florey and Nicholas Ray. (*See* OBITUARIES.)

At the annual awards ceremony of the U.S. Academy of Motion Picture Arts and Sciences, honouring works of 1978, Cimino's *The Deer Hunter* won prizes for best film, best director, best supporting actor (Christopher Walken), best editing (Peter Zinner), and best sound. Jon Voight and Jane Fonda were voted best actor and actress for their performances in *Coming Home*; and Maggie Smith was best supporting actress for her role in *California Suite*. The best foreign-language film was the French *Préparez vos Mouchoirs* (*Get Out Your Handkerchiefs*), directed by Bertrand Blier.

BRITAIN. The British cinema did not share the euphoria of other Western motion picture industries. There was the inevitable new James Bond film, Lewis Gilbert's *Moonraker*, and also John Guillermin's *Death on the Nile*, a follow-up to *Murder on the Orient Express* in bringing Agatha Christie's mystery novels to the screen. There was an unwise attempt to recapture old glories, with remakes of two of Alfred Hitchcock's most memorable 1930s thrillers, *The Thirty-nine Steps* and *The Lady Vanishes*.

The gang film spilled over into Britain with Franc Roddam's *Quadrophenia*. Its re-creation of the psychology of a period and class—the "Mods" and "Rockers" who staged their wars in English seaside resorts in the early 1960s—made it one of the better British pictures of the year. Other noteworthy productions were Kenneth Loach's endearing children's film *Black Jack*; and Terry Jones's startling *Monty Python's Life of Brian*, which attracted to itself angry charges of blasphemy (its comic hero is an exact contemporary of Christ and follows a parallel career) and large audiences in both Britain and the U.S.

Two literary adaptations of distinction were Roman Polanski's *Tess*, a Franco-British co-production, adapted, conscientiously, from Thomas Hardy's *Tess of the d'Urbervilles*; and *The Europeans*, a quiet, sensitive, and witty adaptation from Henry James by U.S. director James Ivory.

As in other recent years the most encouraging signs of life in British cinema came from young directors working outside the commercial establishment, often on small budgets. Derek Jarman's version of *The Tempest* was at once one of the most successful efforts to capture Shakespearean poetry and a film of enormous visual invention. His Prospero's island was dominated by a cobwebby man-

BOB PENN—CAMERA PRESS/PHOTO TRENDS

Dracula, played by Frank Langella, together with his latest victim, Lucy Seward, played by Kate Nelligan, in the movie *Dracula*.

sion of a style, which, like the costumes, defied period identification. With the support of the British Film Institute and the National Film Finance Corp., and in co-production with West German television, Chris Petit made *Radio On*, a stylish first work, if too heavily influenced by the "road films" of Wim Wenders in West Germany.

AUSTRALIA. The recent spectacular renascence of Australian cinema showed signs of decline, in artistic terms at least. With economic recession, the Canberra government reduced its support of film development, preferring to help promote sure box-office success. With this discouragement added to the audiences' apparent lack of enthusiasm for films on Australian subjects, filmmakers abandoned indigenous themes in order to compete with low-budget U.S. production for international sales (for instance, George Miller's highly successful *Mad Max*). Some exceptions were the attractive first feature film of Gillian Armstrong, *My Brilliant Career*, based on the autobiography of a bright, poor girl in the early 1900s; Jim Sharman's realist horror film *The Night, the Prowler*; and Donald Crombie's *Cathy's Child*, based on the true story of the abduction of a child by her Greek father and the effect exerted upon the case by the local press.

CANADA. The Canadian cinema, both English- and French-speaking, had another disappointing year. The best works to emerge were both modest films made by woman directors. Anne-Claire Poirier's *Mourir à tue-tête* was an elaborately structured discussion of rape, using fiction, documentary, and debate. Diane Létourneau made a touching cinema verité account of a community of nuns, *Les Servantes du Bon Dieu*.

Western Europe. FRANCE. The death of the great director Jean Renoir (*see* OBITUARIES) at the age of 85 severed a significant link with the classic French film of the 1930s and '40s. The new French cinema seemed to be in the doldrums. The major creative figures of recent years, such as François Truffaut, Claude Chabrol, Alain Resnais, and Eric Rohmer, released no new films, and for the most part the French cinema presented an impression of bourgeois farce (Michel Vocoret's *Nous Maigrirons Ensemble*; Patrick Schulmann's *Et la Tendresse? . . . Bordel!*) and mediocre detective stories. A veteran, André Cayatte, made one of his characteristic courtroom dramas in *L'Amour en question*. Henri Costa-Gavras adapted Romain Gary's novel *Clair de Femme*. Joseph Losey broke new ground in his career with an Italo-Franco-German co-production of *Don Giovanni*. Two women directors made their debuts, Catherine Breillat with *Tapage nocturne* and Christine Pascal with *Félicité*.

Francis Ford Coppola's *Apocalypse Now* often used incongruous images to convey the horror of war. Here American soldiers make their escape after destroying a Vietnamese village to gain access to a beach for surfing.

ITALY. Four of the year's most notable films, by Federico Fellini, Francesco Rosi, Jean-Marie Straub, and a group of Italian directors that included Marco Bellocchio, were all made possible by co-production with television. Fellini's *Prova d'Orchestra* was a film metaphor, which, behind a deceptive simplicity, hid a mischievous ambiguity that angered many critics. An orchestra rehearsal is made to symbolize a social organism in breakdown and then in retreat, under the pressure of external threat, into paternalism and dictatorship. Francesco Rosi's adaptation of Carlo Levi's autobiographical novel *Cristo si è fermato a Eboli*, even in the shortened version prepared for cinema exhibition (it was originally designed for television), was flaccid compared with the tension of Rosi's recent films. Jean-Marie Straub and Danièle Huillet, in *From the Cloud to the Resistance*, adapted two works by Cesare Pavese to create a dialogue marginally more accessible than their last film, *Fortini-Cani*. *The Cinema Machine* was a remarkable documentary about addiction to making motion pictures. Besides Bellocchio, its directors were Silvano Agosti, Stefano Rulli, and Sandro Petraglia.

Much had been expected from *La Luna*, Bernardo Bertolucci's first film since *1900*, and perhaps in consequence the unfavourable reaction was exaggerated when it turned out to be only a sentimental melodrama, consciously operatic in treatment, about the relationship of a young widow, preoccupied with her career, and her vulnerable young son. One of the least expected and most agreeable debuts of the year was that of Maurizio Nichetti, who appeared, as it seemed, from nowhere to triumph at the newly revived Venice Festival as director, writer, and co-star of *Ratataplan*, a zany comedy, shamelessly derivative and yet still full of its own inventions, vitality, gags, and funny characters.

WEST GERMANY. The indefatigable Rainer Werner Fassbinder celebrated his 33rd year with three new feature films. *The Marriage of Maria Braun* was the ironic portrait of a marriage constantly frustrated of consummation by German history from World War II to the "economic miracle." *In a Year with 13 Moons* was a melancholy tale of exploitation, the victim a hefty and suicidal transsexual. *The Third Generation* was an ambivalent anecdote on the mindlessness of contemporary urban terrorism. Fassbinder's contemporary, Werner Herzog, had less critical success with two adaptations, one from F. W. Murnau's 1922 Dracula film *Nosferatu*, the other from Georg Büchner's *Woyzeck*. In each case the major distinction of the film was the central performance of Klaus Kinski.

Volker Schlöndorff's loyal adaptation of Günter Grass's *The Tin Drum*, marvelously evoking the visual aspect of between-wars Danzig, shared the Grand Prix at the Cannes Film Festival and won worldwide commercial success. Schlöndorff's wife, Margarethe von Trotta, made her second feature film, *Sisters, or the Balance of Happiness*, about a young woman who seeks to fulfill her dreams first through her sister and, after the sister's suicide, through a young girl.

AUSTRIA. There was evidence of a new movement among young movie enthusiasts making feature films on tiny budgets. Lepeniotis's *Operation Hydra* used the formula of a conventional war thriller to explore the wartime psychology of the Austrian *haute bourgeoisie*. Manfred Kaufmann's *Gefischte Gefühle* sensitively charted the shifting sentiments of a group of young professional people. Encouragement was given to this new Austrian cinema by the shooting in Vienna of Maximilian Schell's ambitious West German-Austrian co-production of *Tales from the Vienna Woods*, based on his fine stage production of Odon von Horvath's play at London's National Theatre.

SCANDINAVIA. Internationally established directors seemed to be inactive or out of form. Kjell Grede's maudlin *My Beloved* and Bo Widerberg's appalling adaptation of Knut Hamsun's *Victoria* were debacles for Sweden's previously most promising directors. Perhaps the most memorable new Swedish film was Stefan Jarl's *A Respectable Life*, a sequel to *They Call Us Misfits*, which Jarl had codirected with Jan Lundqvist ten years earlier and which was a report on the lives of a group of near-delinquent Stockholm teenagers. In the latest movie Jarl found the once jolly boys terrifyingly demoralized or destroyed by drink and drugs; one of the principal figures actually died from a drug overdose during the filming.

From Norway Anja Breien's *Next of Kin* was an intelligent and deft feminist comedy about the bickering heirs of a fortune; and *Says Who . . . ?!*—co-produced, co-written, directed by, and starring Petter Vennerød—looked at contemporary society through the eyes of a former 1960s flower child.

Eastern Europe. U.S.S.R. The big "official" production of the year was Andrey Mikhalkov-Konchalovsky's *Siberiade*, evidently the Soviet Union's reply to Bertolucci's *1900* but in the outcome a turgid nationalist hymn. Konchalovsky's more talented half brother, Nikita Mikhalkov (who appeared as an actor in *Siberiade*), directed an altogether more modest and attractive film, the direct transference of a five-act stage play, *Five Evenings*, to the screen. The film dealt with a man's revisiting of his past and was distinguished as much by its historical pertinence as by its outstanding "chamber" performances. Other films that stood out from the generally conventional Soviet production were Georgy Daniela's *Autumn Marathon*, about the trials of an incorrigible philanderer, and Lana Gogoberdize's *Some Interviews on Personal Problems*, about the personal and public life of an investigative journalist.

POLAND. The country's senior director, Andrzej Wajda, was in the vanguard of a vigorous renascence in Polish cinema. His *Man of Marble*, a highly critical reappraisal of recent history, was for a time withheld; but after its release, and in a more tolerant atmosphere, Wajda made *Without Anaesthetic*, a fierce account of the punishment by ostracism that can afflict those who do not conform in a socialist society. *The Maids of Wilko* was in a gentler mood: a literary exercise, based on a novel by Jaroslav Iwaskiewicz about a young man who revisits the scenes of a lost love.

NEW YORKER FILMS

Woyzeck, played by Klaus Kinski, confronts Drum Major, played by Josef Bierbichler, in Werner Herzog's film *Woyzeck*.

Largely fired by Wajda's example, a whole new young generation, unencumbered by the fears of the past, came into evidence, displaying a spirit of social criticism practically unprecedented in the Eastern bloc. The Moscow International Film Festival Grand Prix was won by Krzysztof Kieslowski's *Camera Buff*, ostensibly a light comedy but accurately demonstrating the processes that produce censorship and artistic dogma. Feliks Falk's *Chance*, set in a boys' school, attacked competitive pedagogical methods. Agnieska Holland's *Provincial Actors* dealt with the issues of careerism in a socialist society. Ryszard Filipski's *Flying High* and Janusz Kijowski's *Kung Fu* both attacked corrupt, time-serving bureaucracy.

HUNGARY. In Hungary also there was evidence of a more positive critical attitude to society and recent history. Pal Gabor's *Vera's Training* mercilessly exposed the corruption of a young enthusiast in 1948 by a Stalinist "education." Andras Kovacs's *Stud Farm* presented in symbolic terms other problems of the change to socialism in the first post-World War II years. Janos Rozsa's *The Trumpeter*, in the guise of a period adventure story set in the years after Hungary's "liberation" by the Austrians from Turkish rule, feelingly explored the disappointment of a young man looking for a political ideal.

The most ambitious film of the year, indeed the costliest film ever made in Hungary, was Miklos

Annual Cinema Attendance[1]

Country	Total in 000	Per capita
Afghanistan	19,200	1.1
Albania	9,000	4.1
Algeria	45,000	2.7
Angola	3,700	0.6
Argentina	82,200	3.2
Australia	32,000	3.0
Austria	17,800	2.4
Bahrain	2,000	8.2
Barbados	1,200	4.9
Belgium	23,300	2.4
Benin	1,200	0.4
Bolivia	3,200	0.9
Brazil	275,500	2.6
Brunei	2,500	17.0
Bulgaria	113,500	12.9
Burma	222,500	8.1
Cambodia	20,000	3.0
Cameroon	6,500	1.0
Canada	95,400	4.1
Chile	44,600	5.0
Colombia	163,600	6.8
Cuba	124,300	14.2
Cyprus	6,100	9.5
Czechoslovakia	86,300	5.7
Denmark	18,600	3.7
Dominican Republic	5,200	1.2
Ecuador	38,700	5.6
Egypt	65,000	1.9
El Salvador	14,100	3.5
Finland	9,600	2.0
France	176,000	3.3
Germany, East	84,100	5.0
Germany, West	126,000	2.0
Ghana	1,100	0.1
Grenada	1,100	11.5
Guam	1,000	10.3
Guatemala	15,400	2.8
Guyana	8,600	10.9
Haiti	1,500	0.3
Hong Kong	60,000	13.3
Hungary	76,000	7.1
Iceland	2,300	10.8
India	2,260,000	3.8
Indonesia	107,500	0.8
Iran	110,000	3.3
Iraq	8,300	1.3
Ireland	38,000	13.0
Israel	22,000	6.1
Italy	515,700	9.2
Ivory Coast	10,000	1.5
Japan	165,000	1.4
Jordan	4,300	1.6
Kenya	5,700	0.4
Korea, South	69,000	1.9
Kuwait	4,700	4.7
Lebanon	49,700	18.0
Liberia	1,000	0.6
Libya	23,000	9.4
Luxembourg	1,100	3.2
Macau	2,200	8.0
Madagascar	2,900	0.4
Malawi	2,500	0.5
Malaysia	108,800	9.1
Mali	2,500	0.5
Malta	3,200	9.7
Martinique	2,100	6.0
Mauritius	17,000	18.9
Mexico	251,200	4.2
Morocco	32,000	1.8
Mozambique	4,600	0.5
Netherlands, The	28,300	2.1
New Zealand	15,000	4.9
Nicaragua	7,700	7.7
Norway	18,500	4.6
Pakistan	195,000	3.0
Panama	7,100	4.8
Philippines	318,000	7.6
Poland	131,600	3.8
Portugal	39,100	4.0
Puerto Rico	6,800	2.2
Romania	183,500	8.5
Senegal	3,800	0.7
Singapore	38,900	17.1
Somalia	4,700	1.7
Spain	249,300	6.8
Sri Lanka	55,500	4.0
Sudan	24,000	1.4
Suriname	1,700	5.0
Sweden	23,200	2.8
Switzerland	23,000	3.6
Syria	42,000	5.5
Taiwan	175,000	10.5
Tanzania	3,500	0.2
Thailand	71,000	1.7
Trinidad and Tobago	8,400	8.0
Tunisia	12,500	2.3
Turkey	246,700	6.7
Uganda	1,300	0.1
U.S.S.R.	4,000,000	15.4
United Kingdom	103,900	1.9
United States	1,032,800	4.8
Upper Volta	1,000	0.2
Venezuela	36,100	3.1
Yemen (Aden)	3,500	2.4
Yugoslavia	75,900	3.5
Zaire	1,700	0.1

[1] Countries having over one million annual attendance.

Jancso's *Vitam et Sanguinem*. It dealt with the life of a historical figure, a right-wing aristocrat whose nationalism finally brought him, in World War II, into uneasy alliance with the Communists. The pictorial brilliance seemed often designed to evade the political trickiness of the theme.

YUGOSLAVIA. Filmmakers in Yugoslavia were also tackling delicate subjects. Fadil Hadzik's *The Journalist* showed frankly the processes of gagging the press. Milos Radivojevic, in *Breakdown*, dealt with the growing social conflicts of a television reporter, using telling absurdist comedy techniques. Less accomplished in technique but politically even more remarkable was Besim Sahatciu's *The Wind and the Oak*, the first cinematic discussion of the repressions suffered by Yugoslavia's Albanian minority.

CZECHOSLOVAKIA. In an atmosphere of continuing political repression, one of the best remaining directors of the pre-1968 generation, Jiri Menzel, retreated into nostalgia and sheer prettiness with *Those Wonderful Movie Cranks*. This likable, picturesque comedy was dedicated to the early days of movies in and around Prague.

BULGARIA. One of the best films to emerge from Bulgaria for some years was Ranghal Vulghanov's *The Unknown Soldier's Patent Leather Shoes*. Largely played by nonprofessional actors, it was a very personal recollection of a village childhood. The same skeptical spirit noted in other socialist countries was also evident in Georgy Diulgenov's *Swap*, which dealt with the moral double-talk that characterized political and social life in the 1950s.

EAST GERMANY. Among a generally indifferent production Heiner Carow's *Ikarus* was outstanding. A film evidently intended for the International Year of the Child, it dealt with the eight-year-old son of divorced parents and the wider sociological and psychological implications of the case.

Asia. JAPAN. Although new sources of finance were being developed through collaboration with television and sponsorship by large industrial companies, and Akira Kurosawa was at work on his first Japanese film for more than a decade, no films of any real note emerged from Japan during the year.

HONG KONG. King Hu, the acknowledged master of the Hong Kong historical film, toured the international festivals with two visually magnificent works, *Legend of the Mountain*, a Sung-dynasty ghost story, and *Raining in the Mountain*, about the power struggle in a Ming-dynasty monastery. Hu, having shown the possibilities of giving an aesthetic substance to a traditional commercial genre, had evidently inspired a new generation: Hark Tsui made a distinguished debut with *The Butterfly Murders*, a kind of medieval science fiction thriller.

INDIA. The best films of the year came from established directors. Shyam Benegal's *Junoon* bridged the gulf between "art" and "commercial" films with an epic treatment of an incident from the period of the Indian Mutiny about the doomed passion of a Pathan noble for an English girl. Girish Karnad's *Once Upon a Time and Once Again* outdid the martial arts pictures of the Far East in visual and narrative treatment. Mrinal Sen's *Parasuram* was a stylized, ironic, bitter account of pavement dwellers in Calcutta.

Africa and the Middle East. Throughout Africa there were signs of newly emerging cinemas. Promising films appeared from Benin (Richard de Meideros's *The Newcomer*) and from Nigeria (Ola Balagun's folk saga, *Fight for Freedom*). In Senegal, which had already produced a director of international status in Ousmane Sembene, a woman director, Safi Faye, made an admirable film about the changing ways of life in a little African village, *Grandfather*.

EGYPT. Youssef Chahine's *Alexandria . . . Why?* took a Silver Bear award at the Berlin Festival. Unpolished and unassuming, and irresistibly attractive, it was an unusually revealing recollection of a boyhood in Alexandria between 1942 and 1945, when personal affections and ambitions seemed more important than the other man's war raging about Egypt. Daringly generous in its sentiments, it was banned in most of the Arab world.

ISRAEL. A shoestring first feature, Ilan Moshenson's *The Wooden Gun* investigated Israeli history and national attitudes through the story of two opposed groups of children. Another attractive first film, *Moments*, directed by the actress Michal Bat-Adam, dealt discreetly and lightly with a lesbian attraction within a sexual triangle. The year's most ambitious Israeli film, however, was a coproduction with West Germany, Manahem Golan's adaptation of Isaac Bashevis Singer's novel *The Magician of Lublin*. (DAVID ROBINSON)

Nontheatrical Motion Pictures. One of the most honoured films of the year was *The Flight of the Gossamer Condor* by Ben Shedd, distributed by Churchill Films. The intriguing tale documents the struggle to make aviation history by building a man-powered aircraft capable of flying a difficult course to win an international prize. The film won an Academy Award for a documentary, was honoured by the American Science Film Association as an outstanding science story, received the Golden Eagle for CINE (The Council on International Nontheatrical Events), and was awarded the American Film Festival blue ribbon in the sciences and mathematics category.

The top film of the American Film Festival (sponsored by the Educational Film Library Association) captured three principal awards, an unusual feat. *With Babies and Banners—The Story of the Women's Emergency Brigade*, produced by Lorraine Gray, Anne Bohlen, and Lyn Goldfarb and distributed by New Day Films, won a blue ribbon, the Emily Award for highest rating, and the John Grierson Award. Using rare historical footage, the film portrays the role of Flint, Mich., women in a 1937 General Motors sitdown strike.

Winner in the visual essays category was *Fire!* by Film Polski, distributed by Encyclopædia Britannica Educational Corp. The idyllic forest life is shattered by a roaring forest fire, destroying birds, animals, trees, and greenery. After a rain ends the fire a single plant emerges and life renews itself. (THOMAS W. HOPE)

See also Photography; Television and Radio.
[623; 735.G.2]

Motor Sports

Grand Prix Racing. New cars and engine developments, splendid driving by top contenders, and the retirement of Great Britain's James Hunt and Austria's Niki Lauda were highlights of the 1979 season of Formula One racing. Renault again campaigned its turbocharged cars with compression ratios of 1½–1 against others' 3–1 machines and enjoyed some success.

The season opened at Buenos Aires in January with the Argentine Grand Prix, which attracted many new cars but suffered from a starting-line accident involving eight drivers that eliminated the Ferrari of Jody Scheckter of South Africa. The winner was Jacques Laffite of France in a Ligier; he also made the quickest lap at 200.968 kph, a record for the circuit (1 mph = 1.61 kph). In the Brazilian Grand Prix at Interlagos, Ligier did it again, with Laffite first and Patrick Depailler of France second, followed by Carlos Reutemann of Argentina in a Lotus 79. Again Laffite had the fastest lap at 190.548 kph. In unexpected rain, and therefore much drama, the Ferraris triumphed in the South African Grand Prix at Kyalami, French-Canadian Gilles Villeneuve winning from his teammate Scheckter and setting a new lap record of 198.540 kph. Jean-Pierre Jarier of France finished third in a Tyrrell. The race was stopped early because of heavy rain and then restarted.

The U.S. Grand Prix West at Long Beach, Calif., was dominated by the Michelin-tired Ferraris, Villeneuve lapping fastest at 144.283 kph and leading Scheckter home. Alan Jones from Australia was third, the beginning of the great showing by this driver for the Williams team. In the Spanish Grand Prix at Jarama, Depailler's Ligier led home Reutemann in a Lotus 79 and Mario Andretti of the U.S. in the new Lotus 80. Although it showed promise in this race, the new Lotus never did as well again. After a stop to fit special tires, Villeneuve set a new lap record of 160.329 kph. In the Belgian Grand Prix at Zolder an exciting race was won by Scheckter for Ferrari; Laffite was second for Ligier, and Villeneuve, after setting a new course record of 184.658 kph, lost third place to Didier Pironi of France in a Tyrrell when the Ferrari ran out of fuel. Scheckter won another close-fought race at Monaco, after Villeneuve had retired with transmission failure; Clay Regazzoni of Switzerland in a Williams came in second, only 0.44 sec behind, third place being filled by Reutemann in a Lotus 79. Depailler's Ligier made the fastest lap, at 134.240 kph.

The Swedish Grand Prix was canceled for financial reasons. The French Grand Prix was held on July 1 at the Dijon-Prenois circuit, and to the delight of the French a Renault driven by Jean-Pierre Jabouille of France was the victor, as Renault had been in the first French Grand Prix in 1906. Moreover, René Arnoux of France, in the other Renault RS, set a new lap record of 197.802 kph. The Ferrari of Villeneuve was second, with Arnoux third after a stupendous last-lap duel. In the 1979 British Grand Prix at Silverstone, Regazzoni won for the Williams team. Arnoux's Renault took second place, with Jarier's Tyrrell third. The winner had the fastest lap, at a record 228.320 kph.

UPI

Gilles Villeneuve of Canada swings into the lead on his way to winning the U.S. Grand Prix East at Watkins Glen, New York, in October.

The superiority of the Williams FW's with Cosworth V8 engines and on Goodyear tires was endorsed in the German Grand Prix at the little Hockenheim circuit. Jones won from Regazzoni, leaving third place to Laffite in a Ligier. In Austria the Österreichring was used for the Grand Prix, and there the Williams team achieved its third 1979 victory, Jones keeping ahead of Villeneuve's Ferrari, with Laffite's Ligier third; Arnoux in the Renault had a record lap at 223.378 kph. Jones scored his third successive victory at Zandvoort, in the Dutch Grand Prix. The Italian Grand Prix was run at the much-improved Monza course, where Scheckter and Villeneuve finished a popular first and second in Ferraris. Regazzoni was third in a Williams that had broken the circuit lap record at 218.410 kph. The triumph clinched the 1979 world driving championship for Scheckter, as well

WIDE WORLD

The 63rd running of the Indianapolis 500 was won by Rick Mears of Bakersfield, California, in only his second year at Indy.

Motorboating: *see* Water Sports

Motor Industry: *see* Industrial Review

KEYSTONE

South African Kork Ballington won the 250-cc world championship with his victory at the French Grand Prix in September. It was his second successive year as world champion in both the 350-cc and 250-cc classes.

as the championship of makes for Ferrari. In the Canadian Grand Prix at Montreal, Jones (Williams) made best lap and beat Villeneuve by about one second; Regazzoni was third in another Williams. Last of all came the United States Grand Prix East at Watkins Glen, N.Y. A faulty wheel change caused Jones to shed a wheel on the circuit; Villeneuve had failing oil pressure but nursed his Ferrari home first, ahead of Arnoux's Renault and Pironi's Tyrrell.

Other Races. Villeneuve won the Race of Champions at Brands Hatch for Ferrari, at 189.452 kph. The Le Mans 24-hour race suffered again from lack of entries and too-specialized competing "sports cars." It was won by a turbocharged Porsche 935, Porsche taking the first four places. In the Spa 24-hour race a Ford Capri proved victorious. Before the 1979 season was over Ford of Britain had won the rally championship, with its rear-drive Escort RS saloons making a last appearance. Hannu Mikkola of Finland, driving for Ford, proved himself the top driver. The Tourist Trophy, held at Silverstone, went to a BMW CSL.

(WILLIAM C. BODDY)

U.S. Racing. In the United States the racing season was dominated by old names and new battles. The war between the United States Auto Club (USAC) and the fledgling Championship Auto Racing Teams Inc. (CART) for control of single-seater "champ car" competition continued throughout the 1979 season. The Indianapolis Motor Speedway kept its 500-mi race with USAC, but Rick Mears, a CART adherent, won, while USAC backer A. J. Foyt finished second.

This schism, which began ostensibly over the turbocharging philosophy of USAC, had hardened by the time of the Indianapolis race into a clash of personalities. The result was a fairly successful 14-race CART season, while USAC—whose other types of racing flourished—was limited to seven champ-car contests. CART had the advantages of running on tracks owned or controlled by Roger Penske. Also, CART's affiliation with the Sports Car Club of America (SCCA) and its ability to convince such stock-car tracks as those at Atlanta, Ga., and Charlotte, N.C., to try its brand assured it the larger number of races.

In any case Foyt won a record seventh USAC champ-car crown, while Mears won the CART title. At the 63rd annual Indianapolis 500, which for the first time in decades was forced by the courts to start 35 cars instead of 33, the controversies almost overshadowed the race. Yet it was one of the safest and quickest of the 500s. Mears, who won $270,401 for averaging 255.827 kph (158.899 mph), inherited the lead 19 laps from the finish from Penske teammate Bobby Unser, who had a balky fourth gear and fell to fifth. Runner-up Foyt won $107,291; third-place Mike Mosley won $65,031; and fourth-place Danny Ongais, who was a lap behind, won $41,197.

In other USAC racing categories Foyt also won the stock-car division. Greg Leffler managed a close victory in sprint cars, and Mel Kenyon and Steve Lotshaw battled to the final race before Lotshaw won the midget-car crown.

There was controversy of a different sort in the National Association for Stock Car Auto Racing (NASCAR) competition, and the ultimate beneficiary seemed to have been the most successful stock-car driver of all time, Richard Petty. The Winston Cup series crown went down to the final race, the Los Angeles Times 500 at Ontario, Calif., between Petty and money-winning champion Darrell Waltrip ($465,870). Benny Parsons won the race, and Petty won the championship.

But the title may have been decided at the Daytona 500 in February. Donnie Allison and Cale Yarborough tangled and crashed on the next-to-last turn of the final lap, letting Petty slip by for the win. Afterward, Yarborough, Allison, and Allison's brother Bobby engaged in fisticuffs before a national television audience, drawing fines and warnings of suspension from NASCAR. Waltrip finished second, only a car length back, and Foyt was third. Buddy Baker won the pole position with a record lap of 315.639 kph (196.049 mph).

U.S. road racing was more staid, although SCCA lost executive director Tom Duval, professional racing director Burdette Martin, and club racing director Tex Arnold in surprise resignations, while IMSA (International Motor Sports Association) lost the Winston Co., its main sponsor, in an equally surprising move. Jackie Ickx of Belgium won the Can-Am Challenge Cup and $117,052 by winning at Riverside, Calif. He drove a Lola T33CS. In SCCA Trans Am Category II John Paul, driving a Porsche 935, won the title and $60,700. In Category I Gene Bothello in a Corvette won the title and $37,357.

Peter Gregg and his Porsche Turbo won his seventh Winston GT championship but lost in the premier IMSA event, the 24-Hour Pepsi Challenge at Daytona Beach. That was won by a three-man Porsche Turbo team of Ted Field, Danny Ongais, and Hurley Haywood. The Sebring 12-Hour race went to a Porsche Turbo driven by Rob McFarlin, Bob Akin, and Roy Woods.

(ROBERT J. FENDELL)

Formula One Grand Prix Champions, 1979

Race	Driver	Car	Average speed
Argentine	J. Laffite	Ligier S	197.587 kph
Brazilian	J. Laffite	Ligier S	188.669 kph
South African	G. Villeneuve	Ferrari 312T4	188.600 kph
U.S. West	G. Villeneuve	Ferrari 312T4	141.312 kph
Spanish	P. Depailler	Ligier S	154.449 kph
Belgian	J. Scheckter	Ferrari 312T4	179.018 kph
Monaco	J. Scheckter	Ferrari 312T4	130.901 kph
French	J.-P. Jabouille	Renault RS	191.315 kph
British	C. Regazzoni	Williams FW	223.370 kph
German	A. Jones	Williams FW	216.092 kph
Austrian	A. Jones	Williams FW	219.708 kph
Dutch	A. Jones	Williams FW	187.674 kph
Italian	J. Scheckter	Ferrari 312T4	212.185 kph
Canadian	A. Jones	Williams FW	169.536 kph
U.S. East	G. Villeneuve	Ferrari 312T4	171.401 kph

WORLD DRIVERS' CHAMPIONSHIP: Scheckter, 51 pt, Villeneuve, 47 pt, Jones, 40 pt
CHAMPIONSHIP OF MAKES: Ferrari, 113 pt, Williams-Ford, 75 pt, Ligier-Ford, 61 pt

Motorcycles. Kenny Roberts of the U.S., riding a Yamaha, in spite of early injuries overcame the challenges of Virginio Ferrari of Italy (Suzuki) and Barry Sheene of the U.K. (Suzuki) to remain 500-cc world champion in 1979. Kork Ballington of South Africa (Kawasaki) was again world champion in the 350-cc and 250-cc classes; Angel Nieto of Spain (Minarelli) won in the 125-cc; Eugenio Lazzarini of Italy (Kreidler) in the 50-cc; Rolf Biland and K. Waltisperg of Switzerland in the B2A (conventional) sidecar; and B. Holzer and C. Meierhans of Switzerland in the B2B (enclosed) sidecar.

At the British Silverstone meeting in August, senior riders prepared to set up a "World Series" road-race program, breaking away from the Fédération Internationale Motocycliste (FIM) and its promoters' low rates of pay. The FIM congress in October condemned the scheme but increased its 1980 prize money sevenfold.

In Tourist Trophy (TT) races Ron Haslam of the U.K. took the Formula One world title. In the Isle of Man TT, Scotland's Alex George (Honda) was Formula One and Classic races champion, while Mike Hailwood of the U.K. (Suzuki) won the senior race.

Motocross world champions were Britain's Graham Noyce (Honda), 500-cc; Sweden's Håkan Carlqvist (Husqvärna), 250-cc; and Harry Everts of Belgium (Suzuki), 125-cc. The Motocross des Nations was won by Belgium from Great Britain and West Germany, while Italy triumphed in the International Six Days' Trial. Ivan Mauger of New Zealand won speedway racing's world championship. (CYRIL J. AYTON)

See also Water Sports.
[452.B.4.c]

Mountaineering

In 1978–79 ascents of Everest again figured prominently. In the post-monsoon season of 1978 a Franco-West German expedition placed 16 people on the summit via the South Col route but drew unfavourable criticism because of its size and elaborate organization. More notable was a Yugoslav expedition's first ascent by the west ridge in 1979. After the 1979 monsoon the normal route was repeated by a West German party; on the descent the summit pair (one of them the wife of the leader) died after a forced bivouac.

In post-monsoon 1978 the U.S. ascent of K2 was noteworthy. The route followed the northeast ridge and then traversed to the original route (above the Abruzzi ridge) for the final pyramid. The first ascent of Langtang Lirung was made by a Japanese-Nepalese expedition, and of Dhaulagiri by the southeast ridge by a Japanese expedition, the leader of which was killed during the descent. Changabang was climbed by the south buttress by an Anglo-Polish party, by a route of very great difficulty. Annapurna I was climbed by the Dutch route by an all-woman expedition, with two deaths.

Before the 1979 monsoon a first northwest face ascent of Kangchenjunga was made by a four-man British party. A U.S.-Nepalese expedition made the first ascent of Gaurishankar, by the southwest face. Peak 29 in Nepal was ascended by the west face; this was the first certain ascent of the mountain since a Japanese party that may have reached the summit disappeared.

Fears for the natural environment increased restrictions on mountaineering throughout the world in 1979. It became increasingly difficult to obtain permission to climb in the Himalayas in India. In the U.S. the Antiquities Act invoked by Pres. Jimmy Carter in 1978 made millions of acres in Alaska subject to access control by the National Park Service for climbing (in addition to the 5 million ac of the Mount McKinley National Park area). In Britain those wishing to protect birds sought the prohibition of climbing on all seacliffs except where specifically allowed.

In the Alps there were an increasing number of cases in which surviving members of parties involved in climbing accidents were made subject to legal action. In 1979, for example, four British, three West German, and one French climber were killed in a multiple accident in the Mont Blanc group. Ten parties were descending when a member of a British party slipped and pulled down his companions, who carried another British and a French and a West German party with them. Charges of manslaughter against the sole survivor of the second British party, Christopher Marsh, aged 17, were being considered by the examining magistrate. (JOHN NEILL)

Mozambique

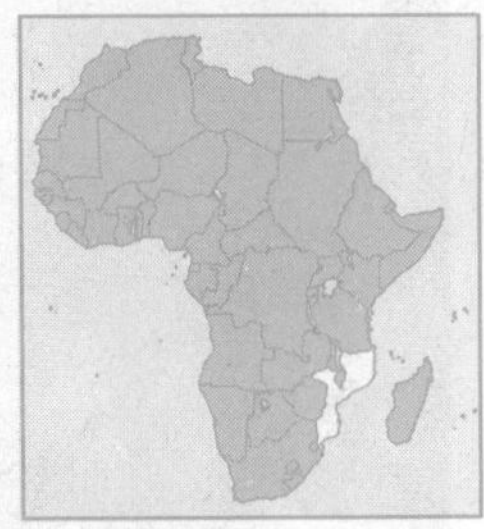
Mozambique

An independent African state, the People's Republic of Mozambique is located on the southeast coast of Africa, bounded by the Indian Ocean, Tanzania, Malawi, Zambia, Zimbabwe Rhodesia, South Africa, and Swaziland. Area: 799,380 sq km (308,642 sq mi). Pop. (1979 est.): 12 million. Cap. and largest city: Maputo (pop., 1970, 354,700). Language: Portuguese (official); Bantu languages predominate. Religion: traditional beliefs 70%, Christian about 15%, Muslim 13%, with Hindu, Buddhist, and Jewish minorities. President in 1979, Samora Machel.

Early in January 1979 the permanent political committee of the Mozambique Liberation Front (Frelimo) announced that the country was in a state of war as a result of increased guerrilla activi-

MOZAMBIQUE

Education. (1972–73) Primary, pupils 577,997, teachers 8,345; secondary, pupils 36,155, teachers 1,682; vocational, pupils 17,216, teachers 984; teacher training, students 1,279, teachers 122; higher (1976–77), students 906, teaching staff 164.

Finance and Trade. Monetary unit: Mozambique escudo, with (Sept. 17, 1979) a free rate of *c.* 33 escudos to U.S. $1 (*c.* 70 escudos = £1 sterling). Budget (1977 est.): revenue 6,530,000,000 escudos; expenditure 10,030,000,000 escudos. Foreign trade (1977): imports 10,658,000,000 escudos; exports 4,908,000,000 escudos. Import sources: South Africa 20%; West Germany 15%; Zimbabwe Rhodesia *c.* 13%; Portugal 10%; Iraq 9%; U.K. 7%; Japan 5%. Export destinations: U.S. 27%; Portugal 16%; U.K. 7%; South Africa 6%; The Netherlands 6%; Japan 5%; Zimbabwe Rhodesia *c.* 5%. Main exports: cashew nuts 30%; textiles 9%; tea 8%; cotton 6%; sugar 5%.

Transport and Communications. Roads (1974) 39,173 km. Motor vehicles in use (1977): passenger 107,900; commercial (including buses) 24,700. Railways (1975): 4,161 km; traffic 210 million passenger-km, freight (1974) 2,180,000,000 net ton-km. Air traffic (1977): 378 million passenger-km; freight 5.4 million net ton-km. Telephones (Jan. 1977) 52,300. Radio licenses (Dec. 1976) 225,000.

Agriculture. Production (in 000; metric tons; 1978): corn *c.* 400; sorghum *c.* 200; cassava (1977) *c.* 2,450; peanuts *c.* 80; sugar, raw value *c.* 150; copra *c.* 75; bananas *c.* 65; cashew nuts (1977) *c.* 200; tea *c.* 14; cotton, lint *c.* 26; sisal *c.* 18. Livestock (in 000; 1977): cattle *c.* 1,350; sheep *c.* 95; goats *c.* 350; pigs *c.* 185; chickens *c.* 16,500.

Industry. Production (in 000; metric tons; 1977): petroleum products *c.* 390; bauxite *c.* 5; cement *c.* 220; beer (hl; 1976) 655; electricity (kw-hr) *c.* 4,940,000.

ty by the Mozambique National Resistance. The MNR had carried out a number of successful operations in the four central provinces of the country. Two months later, on February 28, the death penalty was introduced for "enemies of the working masses" found guilty of offending, endangering, hindering, prejudicing, or perturbing the independence, integrity, and sovereignty of the country, and of the organization of Frelimo and the state and their normal operations, the normal conduct of the national economy, the political, economic, and social stability of the country, and international peace.

Suspected guerrillas based in Mozambique were captured by Rhodesian forces in September.

WIDE WORLD

On March 23 guerrillas started a damaging fire among oil storage tanks in the Beira port area, and the government was forced to call in South African experts to deal with it. Eight days later—possibly as a reaction to this latest guerrilla activity—ten men, including two black Rhodesians, were executed after being charged with spying for Rhodesia. Also among those executed was a Portuguese national, Manuel da Silva. A visiting Portuguese trade delegation walked out of talks with Mozambican leaders in protest against the summary nature of the trial and the refusal to give the defendants an opportunity to appeal. The Portuguese government also handed a letter of protest to the Mozambique ambassador in Lisbon, to which Pres. Samora Machel responded by canceling a meeting with the visiting Portuguese industry minister.

In mid-April ten more persons, four Rhodesians and six Mozambicans, were executed for treason, terrorism, and espionage. Nevertheless, antigovernment guerrilla forces continued their attacks on the Army. Several times during the year, units of the Rhodesian ground and air forces attacked Patriotic Front guerrilla bases in Mozambique, inflicting heavy casualties. In late October the MNR claimed capture of the town of Macossa in central Mozambique.

President Machel's government also felt itself under attack from both Christianity and Islam. The president personally criticized the Muslim community on a number of occasions; although the government's hostility to Islam gained less publicity outside Mozambique than did the campaign against Christianity, it was no less concentrated. Early in the year several Anglican and Roman Catholic churches were closed in Gaza Province bordering South Africa, and religious services were banned. Missionaries in the northern province of Cabo Delgado were confined to the coastal town of Pemba. No reason was given, but some of the Christians had undoubtedly shown sympathy for "liberation movements."

President Machel still claimed to belong to the nonaligned movement, though at a meeting of the movement's Coordinating Bureau in Maputo at the end of January he called on the members to give economic, financial, political, and military support to the armed struggle in southern Africa. He also condemned the attempts by unnamed powers to achieve a solution to southern Africa's problems by other means. Nevertheless, Mozambique's economic links with South Africa remained strong. The purchase by South Africa of electricity from the Cabora Bassa Dam provided a valuable source of income to Mozambique. The number of Mozambicans employed in South Africa had fallen since independence, but the gold they earned was another important source of revenue. In February senior executives of the Mozambican railways, harbours, and airways signed an agreement with their South African counterparts to update the arrangements made in 1970, with the prospect of doubling South African traffic on Mozambique's railways by 1980–81. (KENNETH INGHAM)

Museums

The opening in May 1979 of London's new Tate Gallery extension was a major event in the museum world. The new gallery gave the Tate 50% more exhibition space. From an architectural point of view, it was less exciting than the East Building of the National Gallery of Art in Washington, D.C., which opened in 1978. The galleries were toplit by means of an ingenious form of light-reflecting pyramid, which ensured an even spread of light while protecting sensitive watercolours, drawings, and oils from too much harmful ultraviolet radiation. The galleries were split into bays about 30 ft square, with partitions creating square galleries within each bay. Architects were Llewelyn-Davies, Weeks, Forestier-Walker, & Bor in association with the Department of the Environment.

At the same time it was announced that James Stirling and Partners, architects, had been selected by the trustees of the Tate to carry out a feasibility and design study on development of the old military hospital site adjacent to the gallery. The aim of the study would be to consider new building on the site, to be carried out in phases as money became available. In the meantime, some of the existing hospital buildings would be used to house prints, archives, and parts of the collection.

In the U.S. the Art Institute of Chicago celebrated its hundredth anniversary, as did the Smith College Museum of Art, Northampton, Mass., while the Museum of Modern Art, New York City, reached its 50th year. Major openings included the Institute of Contemporary Art at the Virginia Museum of Fine Arts—the first traditional art museum in the U.S. to open a contemporary museum within its original structure. The Museum of Contemporary Crafts reopened at a new location in New York City, while nearby the Fine Arts Museum of Long Island was formed. Reflecting the renewed interest in representational art, a group of the foremost realist artists in the U.S. established the Artist's Choice Museum, to include a permanent exhibition area in New York City and traveling shows. In Chicago the 12-year-old Museum of Contemporary Art reopened after renovation and expansion. Thanks to an anonymous gift, the Fogg Art Museum at Harvard University neared its goal of $17.2 million for a new building.

A new museum at Jarrow, Tyne and Wear, England, was devoted to the history of the Saxon and medieval monastery of St. Paul's, Jarrow, best known for its association with the Venerable Bede. To mark the opening, some of the original manuscripts produced in the area were displayed, including an illuminated copy of Bede's *Ecclesiastical History of the English People* lent by the authorities in Leningrad. In October 1978 the Musée de Neuilly, France, was opened to house a collection of "toys" (clockwork automatons) donated by Jacques Damiot, who, at the request of the mayor of Neuilly, also became the museum's first curator. In 1979 Damiot opened an extension to his museum dedicated to "La Femme," containing such memorabilia as Marie Antoinette's corset and Katherine Dunham's feet cast in bronze.

Acquisitions. The largest public collection of the paintings of Andrew Wyeth was established when the Greenville County (S.C.) Art Museum was given 26 works purchased by Mr. and Mrs. Arthur Magill, worth about $4.5 million. Of the $30 million worth of art left by the late Nelson Rockefeller, the Museum of Modern Art would receive 23 paintings and 4 sculptures, all of the 20th century, worth about $8.5 million, while the Metropolitan Museum of Art, New York City, would get 1,610 primitive works worth about $5 million. The Justin K. Thannhauser collection of 75 French works, on view at the Guggenheim Museum in New York City for more than a decade, was donated to the museum; the collection included 34 important Picassos. The National Gallery of Art acquired what was thought to be the only surviving set of portraits of the first five presidents, by Gilbert Stuart. The proposed sale of Stuart's portraits of George and Martha Washington to the National Portrait Gallery by the Boston Athenaeum sparked a chorus of protest in Boston, and a fund was started to keep the portraits in that city.

The National Gallery, London, purchased two "modern" paintings, a Cubist work by Picasso of 1914 titled "Fruit Dish, Bottle and Guitar" and a Fauve work by Matisse of 1908, "Portrait of Greta Moll." Justifying the purchases of works by artists not previously represented in the gallery's collection, the chairman of the trustees said, "Our collection should not stub its toes, as it were, on an artificial chronological barrier: today's geniuses will become, in the process of time, Old Masters."

The old castle at Dorenburg in Grefrath near Düsseldorf, West Germany, which had been converted into an open-air museum illustrating local history and culture, received a large collection of toys, consisting of about 2,000 items from three centuries, on permanent loan by a Cologne antique dealer. Included were French 19th-century lady dolls with original costumes, jewelry, and

Galleries in the newly built "extension" were opened to visitors at London's Tate Gallery in the spring.

TATE GALLERY

TOM VAN EYNDE

Chicago's Museum of Contemporary Art reopened in the spring after a program of renovation and expansion. Among the first exhibitions was a group of wall paintings that were scheduled to be destroyed when the show closed.

hairstyles; mechanical tin toys; and even religious toys such as a group of 17th-century glass figures showing the Last Supper.

Administration. The long-awaited report of a working party set up by the Standing Commission on Museums and Galleries to devise a new system for local museums in the U.K. was published in January. Under the system suggested, only a small number of museums would receive direct government grants; the rest would be administered by area councils. A bilateral central policy-making body would be established consisting of a Museums Commission, responsible for overseeing the area councils and certain specified museums, and a Museums Council that would represent museum interests countrywide and report to the Museums Commission. It was estimated that about £6 million a year would be needed to implement the suggested plans.

Although bolstered by continued rising attendance, the more than 5,500 museums in the U.S. still faced financial crisis. Federal government support, which had risen gradually during the '70s, was expected to reach $80 million by 1982. At the same time, however, private sources had diminished and operating costs had risen by about 90% in a decade. Adding to the problem were the serious rise in art thefts, necessitating additional expenditures for security; increased maintenance costs as a result of higher attendance; and declining support from local governments attempting to cut their spending.

Concern was expressed in some quarters that the popularizing gestures so prevalent in the museum world might affect the importance of the permanent collections. Encouraged by the financial and popular success of such "blockbuster" exhibitions as the treasures of Tutankhamen, museums were experimenting with other means of establishing a new image: programs for continuing education; sponsorship of domestic and foreign tours; and outreach programs, such as the Indianapolis Museum of Art's program in which objects would be available for handling. A growing involvement with business was evident in such projects as the Whitney Museum of American Art's plan to open a branch in the new Manhattan headquarters of the Philip Morris Corp. and the Boston Museum of Fine Art's 12,000-sq-ft branch in Faneuil Hall, donated by the developers.

Four days of discussions on "The History of Museums and Collections in Natural History," held in London in April, attracted 160 delegates from 15 countries. Special emphasis was placed on the problems of locating and saving collections and their associated documentation. University collections were particularly likely to suffer from neglect. (JOSHUA B. KIND; SANDRA MILLIKIN)

See also Art Exhibitions; Art Sales.
[613.D.1.b]

Music

Classical. In the U.S. Zubin Mehta's first round as music director of the New York Philharmonic dominated the season. Critical response was generally positive, complaints about interpretative blandness being offset by praise for the warm, clean playing Mehta elicited from the orchestra. In Los Angeles Carlo Maria Giulini's tenure as conductor of the Philharmonic got off to an impressive start, with transparent, reverential readings of symphonies by Beethoven, Schubert, and Brahms that emphasized Giulini's roots in the European tradition. Maurice Abravanel resigned as conductor of the Utah Symphony after 32 years and some ambitious album projects, including the complete symphonies of Gustav Mahler. Neville Marriner, founder of London's acclaimed Academy of St. Martin in the Fields chamber orchestra, assumed control of the Minnesota Symphony from Stanislav Skrowaczewski, while Michael Gielen, conductor at the Frankfurt Opera and deputy to Gennady Rozhdestvensky at the BBC Symphony in London, was appointed successor to the late Thomas Schippers in Cincinnati. Leonard Slatkin took over the St. Louis Symphony from Jerzy Semkow, and, in a surprise move, Julius Rudel replaced Michael Tilson Thomas at the Buffalo Philharmonic. With the death of Arthur Fiedler, at 84 (*see* OBITUARIES), the future of Boston's celebrated "Pops" concerts was uncertain pending appointment of a new conductor.

In the U.K. Claudio Abbado (*see* BIOGRAPHIES) succeeded André Previn as conductor of the London Symphony, Previn's increasing commitment to a much improved Pittsburgh Symphony and various compositional activities making heavy demands on his time. Despite speculation that Previn or even Giulini might succeed a sadly declining Antal Dorati as conductor of the Royal Philharmonic (now headed by former Edinburgh Festival director Peter Diamand), the post went to Walter Weller, onetime Vienna Philharmonic concertmaster and outgoing conductor of the Royal Liverpool Philharmonic. At Liverpool Weller was replaced by Simon Rattle. Paavo Berglund stepped down as conductor at the Bournemouth Symphony and made guest debuts with the London Philharmonic and one of Eastern Europe's premier orchestras, the Dresden State. James Loughran divided his time between conductorship of the Manchester-based Hallé Orchestra and a similar post at the Bamberg Symphony. Bernard Haitink was succeeded by Sir Georg Solti as conductor of the London Philharmonic.

One of music's greatest losses in 1979 was the death at age 93 of Nadia Boulanger, perhaps the world's leading teacher and, during the 1930s, in the forefront of the Monteverdi revival. Among other deaths were those of the bassoon player Archie Camden, violinist Antoni Brosa, composers Louis Durey and Roy Harris, choirmaster Russell Burgess, and conductor-composer Paul Paray. (*See* OBITUARIES.)

OPERA. Greatest interest was reserved for the production at the Palais Garnier in February by the Paris Opera of Alban Berg's unfinished opera *Lulu,* in a scholarly completion by Friedrich Cerha. Teresa Stratas sang the title role to wide acclaim, Pierre Boulez conducted, and Patrice Chéreau, enfant terrible of past Bayreuth seasons, directed a production that, after a sticky opening scene, had great impact. Reviews were detailed and enthusiastic, the long-embargoed third act being seen as an essential facet in 20th-century music.

The season was a generally good one for opera in New York City, with the Metropolitan and City operas playing full schedules (interrupted briefly, in the case of the City Opera, by a musician's strike). The Met's roster began well with Placido Domingo singing his first New York *Otello,* a performance that was telecast live by the Public Broadcasting Service. The program was shown throughout the U.S. and also in Mexico, the homeland of Gilda Cruz-Romo, who sang Desdemona. A revival of the 1978 production of Wagner's *Tannhäuser* was theatrically unadventurous but musically exciting. Teresa Zylis-Gara, Tatyana Troyanos, and Kurt Moll (the latter making his Metropolitan debut) strengthened a previously unremarkable cast and offset the sudden loss of James McCracken, who walked off stage complaining that favourable treatment was being accorded other company members. James Levine's conducting was again considered to be of high calibre—more so than in the subsequent Metropolitan Wagner productions, *The Flying Dutchman* and *Parsifal.* In the former especially, Levine's fondness for uptempo speeds and blown-out dynamics led to considerable critical dissent. Other new productions were two by John Dexter: Smetana's *The Bartered Bride* in a new translation by Tony Harrison, con-

WIDE WORLD

Spanish tenor Placido Domingo sang the lead role in Verdi's *Otello* with Gilda Cruz-Romo as Desdemona at the Metropolitan in New York City.

ducted by Levine and featuring Teresa Stratas, Nicolai Gedda, Martti Talvela, and Jon Vickers (*see* BIOGRAPHIES); and—less impressive—Donizetti's *Don Pasquale*, the principal flaw being the limp conducting of Nicola Rescigno.

Most imaginative of the New York City Opera's new productions was the premier of Dominick Argento's *Miss Havisham's Fire*, starring Rita Shane in the title role and conducted by Julius Rudel. A potentially imaginative double bill pairing Purcell's *Dido and Aeneas* with Richard Strauss's ballet *Le Bourgeois Gentilhomme* (the latter choreographed by George Balanchine) was disappointing, while a revival of Victor Herbert's *Naughty Marietta*, with Gianna Rolandi and conducted by John Mauceri, was considered amusing but lightweight.

In Europe Jean-Pierre Ponnelle's witty staging for the Salzburg Festival of Mozart's *The Magic Flute*, with Eric Tappy's lithe Tamino and zestful playing by the Vienna Philharmonic under James Levine, was highly praised. The production at the Salzburg Landestheater of Cesar Bresgen's opera *The Angel from Prague*, a lavish staging based on a novel by Leo Perutz, was also noted, both inside and outside Austria. Despite patchy direction from Karlheinz Haberland, the work was considered to provide further proof of a previously largely unknown composer's imaginative abilities.

In Finland Aulis Sallinen's latest opera, *The Red Line*, created a stir. Completed in only a few months, it was seen to be a sparse and sombre successor to the more dramatic *The Horseman*. Soloists included Jorma Hynninen, Taru Valjakka, and Usko Viitanen. In Sweden Handel's *Xerxes* was revived in a highly successful production by Leif Söderström at the 18th-century Drottningholm court theatre near Stockholm.

DON McPHEE—THE GUARDIAN

The Beijing Opera Company, once again in favour after having been banned in China for more than ten years during the Cultural Revolution, opened at the Coliseum in London during an overseas tour.

Prague had its first taste of Benjamin Britten's *Peter Grimes*, in a clean-cut production by Ladislav Stros. Expressive rather than dramatic, Ivo Zidek was considered a capable Grimes, while Antonin Svork and Jaroslav Horacek as, respectively, Captain Balstrode and Swallow, displayed decisive characterization and ringing voices. Josef Kuchinka conducted the National Theatre Orchestra and Chorus.

Notable productions in West Germany included an unplanned staging at Frankfurt of Franz Schreker's *Die Gezeichneten* conducted by Michael Gielen, which won something of a cult following. Götz Friedrich's production for the Deutscher Oper, Berlin, of Mozart's *The Marriage of Figaro* proved an unexpected delight. A star cast was headed by Dietrich Fischer-Dieskau, José Van Dam, Julia Varady, and Barbara Hendricks. Daniel Barenboim conducted.

In London the Royal Opera lumbered from crisis to crisis, Terry Hands's new production of Wagner's *Parsifal*, conducted by Solti, being adjudged Covent Garden's most disastrous flop in years. Richard Strauss's *Der Rosenkavalier* was canceled owing to disputes over fees and overspending of rehearsal time on Puccini's *La Bohème*. Happiest news from the Royal Opera House was August Everding's production, borrowed from the Munich Opera, of *The Magic Flute*, conducted by Colin Davis, and a revival of Stravinsky's *The Rake's Progress*.

The English National Opera, by contrast, enjoyed a fine season. Highlights were a gaudy, bucolic production of Poulenc's *Les mamelles de Tirésias* and, as Christmas fare, a Charles Mackerras/Colin Graham production of Janacek's *Adventures of Mr. Broucek*. Sets, lighting, and vocal and orchestral standards continued excellent at the company's home, the London Coliseum.

SYMPHONIC MUSIC. In New York Peter Pears, Galina Vishnevskaya, and John Shirley-Quirk joined with Mstislav Rostropovich and the Washington National Orchestra and Chorus in a moving performance of Britten's *War Requiem*. Other highlights of the New York season included three concerts featuring Rozhdestvensky, making his debut with the Philharmonic; the second of these constituted the strangest in any recent season—an overture by Giovanni Paisiello, Prokofiev's Second Symphony, three short works by Johann Strauss the younger, and two minor Shostakovich pieces, one of them his *Tahiti Trot*, a reorchestration of the "Tea for Two" foxtrot from Vincent Youmans's 1925 musical comedy *No, No, Nanette*. Also noteworthy were a dynamic Mahler Sixth Symphony from Claudio Abbado, numerous tributes to composer Elliot Carter, celebrating his 70th birthday, and an outstanding recital by pianist Maurizio Pollini that succeeded in getting New Yorkers out of their seats to applaud as thorny a modern piece as Pierre Boulez's Piano Sonata No. 2.

In Boston Seiji Ozawa's conducting with the Boston Symphony and Tanglewood Festival Chorus of Schoenberg's *Gurrelieder* was the highlight of the season. In March 1979 the Boston Symphony was the first U.S. orchestra to visit China, with a widely publicized tour to Shanghai and

UPI

The Bee Gees (left to right, Maurice, Barry, and Robin Gibb) donated their talents in a benefit concert for UNICEF as part of the observance of the International Year of the Child.

Beijing (Peking). In Chicago Carlos Kleiber made an explosive debut with the Chicago Symphony in gripping performances of Weber and Beethoven. In Los Angeles Hans Werner Henze's Second Violin Concerto was played by Soviet virtuoso Gidon Kremer and conducted by Giulini.

Elsewhere, London continued to be judged musical capital of the world. Andrew Davis directed the Philharmonia in an Elgar series at the Royal Festival Hall, while Lorin Maazel completed a Mahler symphony cycle with the same orchestra. Yehudi Menuhin celebrated the 50th anniversary of his concert debut with recitals and concerts, including a warmhearted reading of the Mendelssohn Concerto with Antal Dorati and the Detroit Symphony, making their first visit to the U.K. Sergiu Celibidache returned to direct the London Symphony in readings that veered alarmingly between the inspired and the wildly eccentric. The 1979 season of Henry Wood Promenade Concerts at the Albert Hall was considered the best for many years. Works of particular interest included Schumann's neglected *Faust,* exquisitely conducted by Michael Gielen, Sibelius's *Kullervo* under Rozhdestvensky, and a mixed media evening that featured orchestral and choral works by Ravel and Messiaen and staged dancing by a Balinese Gamelan team. The Israel Philharmonic under Zubin Mehta was visiting orchestra, giving a warm if slightly colourless reading of Mahler's Fifth Symphony and the European premiere of the impressive Third Symphony by Joseph Tal of Israel.

Sir Robert Mayer, organizer of children's concerts during well over half a century and founder of the Youth and Music movement, celebrated his 100th birthday on June 5. The many tributes to his pioneer work in the musical education of young people included a concert at the Royal Festival Hall.

RECORDINGS. Notable disk releases for the year included the first of two volumes containing the complete works of Webern, directed by Boulez (Columbia CBS); the premier recording by the Amadeus Quartet of Britten's Third String Quartet (London Decca); first recordings of Brian Ferneyhough's *Transit* (London Decca), Aribert Reimann's opera *Lear* (Polydor), and Peter Maxwell Davies's *Symphony* (London Decca); first-ever complete recordings of Grieg's *Peer Gynt* (Unicorn) and Vaughan Williams's *Hugh the Drover* (Angel EMI); a complete cycle of Haydn's 43 piano trios by the Beaux Arts Trio (Philips); a recording directed by Wolfgang Gönnenwein of Beethoven's *Missa Solemnis,* played on original instruments and sung by a chamber choir (Harmonia Mundi); only the second recording to be made of Britten's *Peter Grimes,* conducted by Colin Davis (Philips); a welcome new recording, again from Davis, of Berlioz's opera *Beatrice and Benedict* (Philips); the beginnings of fine Tchaikovsky (Philips) and Shostakovich (London Decca) symphony cycles from Bernard Haitink, and of Schumann songs from Fischer-Dieskau (Polydor); complete recordings of hitherto unavailable operas by Shostakovich (*Lady Macbeth of the Mtsensk District,* Angel EMI) and Richard Strauss (*The Silent Woman,* Angel EMI; and *The Egyptian Helen,* London Decca); remarkable all-Liszt folder from veteran pianist Ervin Nyiregyházi (Columbia CBS); the continuation of London Decca's complete Janacek opera cycle, with *The Makropoulos Case;* the first of Angel EMI's sessions with the Philadelphia Orchestra; a mass of reissues by conductor Sir Thomas Beecham, the centenary of whose birth was celebrated in 1979, from Angel EMI, CBS U.K., and RCA; and a batch of fine issues of neglected English music from the independent British company Lurita, featuring works by Rawsthorne, Frank Bridge, Malcolm Arnold, Finzi, Joseph Holbrooke, Cyril Rootham, and others.

(MOZELLE A. MOSHANSKY)

Jazz. By the end of the 1970s jazz had undergone such far-reaching renovations that it was doubtful whether many of the founding fathers would recognize the music at all. Experiments in abstruse time signatures, in esoteric harmonic sequences, and in revolutionary technology all contributed to the transformation of what had once been an earthy art into something with a fiercely specialized appeal. By the end of the 1970s the electrifying of instruments had become commonplace. The process that had begun in the 1930s with the emergence of the vibraphone and the electric guitar suddenly took a surge forward with the emergence of electrified keyboard techniques that required a drastic rethinking on the part of established players. It was revealing that one of the best recorded performances of 1979 on an electric piano, by Oscar Peterson, was the fruit of a complete year of practice and experiment.

The final year of the decade was not a particularly distinguished one in terms of the emergence of fresh talent or of any upsurge in public interest, although Europe continued to be the host to a proliferating number of jazz "festivals." In the U.S. the Newport Jazz Festival proceeded on its venerable way, but by the end of the decade the promoters' problem of finding ways to rearrange familiar talents into original alignments had become a severe one, given the continued prominence of more and more stars of a pensionable age.

During 1979 many of them ceased to be pensionable and became posthumous instead. The saddest loss was that of the bassist-composer Charles Mingus (*see* OBITUARIES), an unrepentant iconoclast whose contribution to the evolving art of jazz composition had yet to be assessed. Mingus, born in Nogales, Ariz., in 1922, sometimes obscured the ingenuity of his own music with the rhetoric of his public pronouncements. But none of this ever really detracted either from his accomplished technique as a bassist or from his genuine originality as a composer for groups varying in size from trio to full orchestra.

In August there occurred the death of bandleader-composer Stan Kenton (*see* OBITUARIES), who in the late 1940s and early 1950s enjoyed a worldwide reputation as a progressive leader that his actual performances never quite justified. Among the identifying marks of his best work were pyrotechnics from the brass section, portentous orchestrations that often camouflaged inconsequential themes, and a restlessness that manifested itself in constant re-formings of the orchestra. Ironically, for so spectacular a lion of the avant garde, Kenton himself was a pianist of a genially dixieland disposition.

Other deaths in the year included those of the trombonist Bill Rank, who 50 years earlier had been a pioneer in the ranks of the white jazzmen grouped around leaders like Frank Trumbauer; trombonist Vernon Brown, who began in the same environment as Rank and went on to be featured in the heyday of the big bands as a soloist with Artie Shaw and Benny Goodman; the tenor saxophonist Patrick "Corky" Corcoran, whose entire playing career was dominated by his long association with the Harry James orchestra; tenor saxophonist Albert "Happy" Caldwell, prominent at one time as a sideman with Thomas "Fats" Waller and Fletcher Henderson; and, in a slightly different category, Fred Elizalde (*see* OBITUARIES), a Philippine-born pianist-composer whose connections with jazz had long since withered but who in the later 1920s had come to Britain and helped to pioneer the art of composing and orchestrating inside a jazz context.

During 1979 there were virtually no outstanding new recordings, but at least two ambitious reissue projects were worth mention. By 1979 the series issued by French CBS to commemorate the World War II recordings of Duke Ellington had been completed, while in the U.S. five important albums were issued on the Arista label preserving the music created by Charlie Parker during his connection with the Savoy label. (BENNY GREEN)

Popular. The record industry faced crisis in 1979, a sharp drop in sales marking the end of 25 years of expansion. All the major companies were forced to cut back on personnel, promotions, and artist rosters. Increased prices encouraged already widespread illegal taping.

This depression did not deter newcomers, many of whom signed with small independent labels. They included women singer/songwriters Rickie Lee Jones and Judie Tzuke, three-piece rock band The Police, blues guitarist George Thorogood, and the futuristic Gary Numan. Punk rock was disintegrating; its leaders, the Sex Pistols, disbanded in the U.S. in January, and in February bassist Sid Vicious died in New York while on bail after being charged with murdering his girl friend. Lead singer Johnny Rotten formed Public Image, Ltd., a more experimental band. The Pistols' film *The Great Rock'n'Roll Swindle* remained unreleased, but some recordings were salvaged from the collapse of the group's management company, Glitterbest.

The extreme punk style found little success in the U.S., where audiences preferred the music-hall humour of Ian Dury, Wreckless Eric's comical anarchy, and the guitar-based harmonies of Dire Straits and Rockpile, incorporating hit soloists Nick Lowe and Dave Edmunds. Some British artists, for example, Nick Gilder, fared better in the U.S. than at home; conversely, Blondie, the New York band whose singer Debbie Harry was a pin-up favourite, twice topped the U.K. singles and album charts. A "New Mod" style claimed to succeed New Wave; its perpetrators wore smarter clothes, but their music, though more conventional than punk, remained aggressive. The urban humour of Squeeze and Chas & Dave provided contrast, as did two chart-topping romantic duets: "Reunited" by Peaches & Herb and "You Don't Bring Me Flowers" by Barbra Streisand and Neil Diamond.

It was an eventful year for several established artists. Stevie Wonder's long-awaited album, *Journey Through the Secret Life of Plants,* was released in October. Mike Oldfield, previously a reluctant performer in live concerts, toured Europe with a large ensemble of musicians. Cliff Richard, celebrating 21 years in show business, had a British top hit, "We Don't Talk Anymore," in August. Bob Dylan testified to his Christian conversion in his new album *Slow Train Coming*. The Who, with Kenny Jones replacing the late Keith Moon, played in arenas throughout the world; in a concert at Cincinnati, Ohio, 11 fans were trampled to death at the entrance to the stadium. The Bee Gees could hardly be expected to top their 1978 successes, but their new album yielded a U.S. top tune, "Tragedy," and they organized an all-star concert to benefit the International Year of the Child. George Harrison did return to recording, but Paul McCartney remained the only ex-Beatle musically active; in February he signed a £10 million record

Namibia:
see Dependent States; South Africa

NATO:
see Defense

Navies:
see Defense

deal jointly with EMI and CBS, making him one of the world's wealthiest pop stars. While still refusing to play together, the four did unite in protesting against the British presentation of *Beatlemania,* a multimedia stage show based on the Beatles' career that used impersonators.

Internationally, disco was the dominant style, so popular that relatively unknown artists could produce top hits, such as Anita Ward's "Ring My Bell." Older songs such as "Knock on Wood" were given the disco beat. The music was complemented by flamboyant presentation, such as that of the Village People, whose "YMCA" was an international hit.

In June Donna Summer became the first female singer in 15 years to top both singles and album charts in the U.S.; behind her powerful voice, producer Giorgio Moroder used synthesizers to create a hypnotic pulse. Crisp rhythms and subtle arrangements distinguished the music of Chic, whose writers Nile Rogers and Bernard Edwards also produced a hit album for the four-sister group Sister Sledge.

Memorable concerts included Led Zeppelin's two performances at Knebworth, visits to the U.S.S.R. by Boney M. and Elton John, the Grateful Dead's three-night sellout of Madison Square Garden, and Kate Bush's debut tour featuring magicians, mime, and spectacular staging. On New Year's Eve San Francisco's Winterland closed with a concert by the Grateful Dead. An attempt to present a tenth-anniversary Woodstock Festival failed, but some of the original artists, including Arlo Guthrie and Country Joe McDonald, organized a tour. For the second straight year Israel won the Eurovision Song Contest. Two famous British television pop shows were revived, "Juke Box Jury" and "Oh Boy!"

Reggae remained esoteric, with Bob Marley still a dominating musician. His former colleague in the Wailers, Peter Tosh, established himself as a solo artist, playing some successful U.S. concerts. The lighter "Bluebeat" style regained popularity in Britain, played by mixed-race bands such as The Specials.

In September Dame Gracie Fields, the British singer/comedienne who became a worldwide favourite, died at her Capri home. Richard Rodgers, composer of many successful musical comedies with partners Lorenz Hart and Oscar Hammerstein, Jr., died in December. Other deaths included those of Norrie Paramor, producer for Cliff Richard, the Shadows, and many other British stars; bluegrass guitarist Lester Flatt; Lowell George, founder of the band Little Feat; composer Van McCoy; singers Minnie Riperton and Donny Hathaway; and former Wings guitarist Jimmy McCulloch. (*See* OBITUARIES.)

An end-of-decade view of popular music showed the evaporation of the Woodstock peace/love ideal and the rise of a violence exemplified in one of the year's best-selling singles: The Boomtown Rats' "I Don't Like Mondays," a dramatic ballad based on a shooting incident in San Diego, Calif., in January. Subjective singer/songwriters had given way to garish theatrics and elaborate staging, and torpid 1960s nostalgia had been exploded by the New Wave. Out of this melée identifiable sounds had emerged: disco and an updated pop music combining instant appeal with the knowingness of its audience.

(HAZEL MORGAN)

See also Dance; Motion Pictures; Television and Radio; Theatre.

Nauru

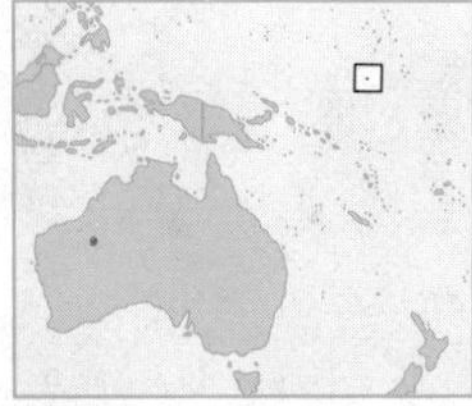
Nauru

An island republic in the Pacific Ocean, Nauru lies about 1,900 km (1,200 mi) E of New Guinea. Area: 21 sq km (8 sq mi). Pop. (1977 census): 7,254, including Nauruan 57%; Pacific Islanders 26%; Chinese 9%; European 8%. Capital: Yaren. Language: Nauruan and English. Religion (Nauruans only): Protestant 60%; Roman Catholic 33%. President in 1979, Hammer DeRoburt.

After the drama of the 1978 election, Nauruan politics were quiet in 1979. The process of economic diversification continued from Nauru House in Melbourne, Australia, where Nauru's portfolio of investments was being built up as a hedge against the time when the phosphate ran out. During May and June negotiations were completed to increase Nauruan–New Zealand air traffic. Both governments were to set up an air service which (subject to a secret capacity agreement) allowed one return service per week between Yaren and Auckland, N.Z., via Port Vila. Both carriers had traffic rights throughout the route and to points beyond.

The major political controversy concerned Pres. Hammer DeRoburt's protracted U.S. $7.5 million libel suit against a Pacific publishing group. The journalists had printed in a Guam newspaper, *The Pacific Daily News,* a story that said a separatist group in the Marshall Islands had been obtaining funds from Nauru. This, said DeRoburt, was untrue in every respect. (A. R. G. GRIFFITHS)

NAURU

Education. (1978) Primary and secondary, pupils 2,139, teachers 129; vocational, pupils 61, teachers 4; teacher training (1977), students 6, teacher 1.

Finance and Trade. Monetary unit: Australian dollar, with (Sept. 17, 1979) a free rate of A$0.89 to U.S. $1 (A$1.92 = £1 sterling). Budget (1978–79 est.): revenue A$40,610,000; expenditure A$33.6 million. Foreign trade (1975–76): imports A$13.8 million (*c.* 58% from Australia, *c.* 30% from The Netherlands in 1974); exports A$37.3 million (*c.* 51% to Australia, *c.* 41% to New Zealand, *c.* 5% to Japan). Main export: phosphate *c.* 100%.

Industry. Production (in 000): phosphate rock (exports; metric tons; 1976–77) 929; electricity (kw-hr; 1977) 26,000.

Nepal

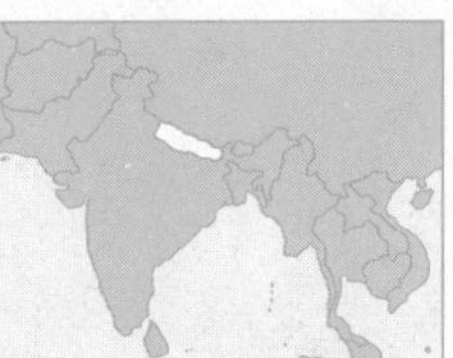
Nepal

A constitutional monarchy of Asia, Nepal is in the Himalayas between India and the Tibetan Autonomous Region of China. Area: 145,391 sq km (56,136 sq mi). Pop. (1978 est.): 13,420,000. Cap. and largest city: Kathmandu (pop., 1976 est., 171,400). Language: Nepali (official) 52.5%, also Bihari (including Maithili and Bhojpuri) 18.5%, Tamang 4.8%, Tharu 4.3%, and Newari 3.9%. Religion

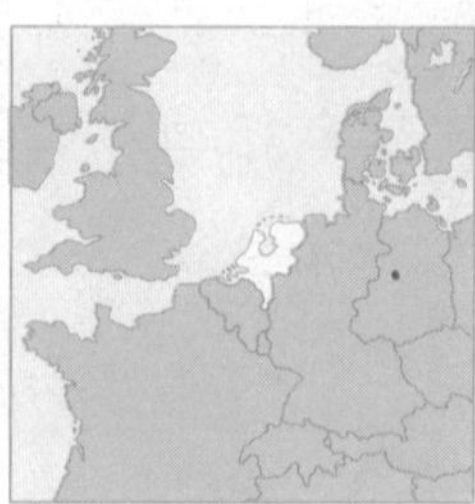
The Netherlands

NEPAL

Education. (1976) Primary, pupils 643,835, teachers 20,775; secondary, pupils 243,231, teachers 10,609; vocational, pupils 16,815, teachers 513; teacher training, students 2,702, teachers 173; higher (1975), students 23,504, teaching staff 1,516.

Finance. Monetary unit: Nepalese rupee, with (Sept. 17, 1979) a par value of NRs 12 to U.S. $1 (free rate of NRs 25.82 = £1 sterling). Gold, SDR's, and foreign exchange (June 1979) U.S. $172 million. Budget (total; 1977–78 actual): revenue NRs 1,554,000,000 (excludes foreign aid of NRs 467 million); expenditure NRs 2,675,000,000.

Foreign Trade. (1978) Imports NRs 2,677,100,000; exports NRs 1,099,700,000. Import sources: India *c.* 31%; Japan *c.* 16%. Export destinations: India *c.* 48%; Japan *c.* 8%; U.S. *c.* 5%; West Germany *c.* 5%. Main exports (1974–75): jute goods *c.* 33%; raw jute *c.* 13%; curio goods *c.* 11%; jute cuttings *c.* 7%. Tourism: visitors (1977) 129,000; gross receipts (1974) U.S. $9 million.

Agriculture. Production (in 000; metric tons; 1978): rice *c.* 2,400; corn *c.* 750; wheat *c.* 401; millet *c.* 130; potatoes *c.* 300; jute *c.* 58; tobacco *c.* 5; buffalo milk *c.* 470; cow's milk *c.* 210. Livestock (in 000; 1978): cattle *c.* 6,753; buffalo *c.* 4,070; pigs *c.* 353; sheep *c.* 2,350; goats *c.* 2,450; poultry *c.* 21,000.

(1971): Hindu 89.4%; Buddhist 7.5%. King, Birendra Bir Bikram Shah Deva; prime ministers in 1979, Kirti Nidhi Bista and, from May 30, Surya Bahadur Thapa.

The long-smoldering demand in Nepal for democratic reforms finally erupted in the form of violent student revolts during April and May 1979 and led to the dramatic announcement by King Birendra on May 24 that he would hold a referendum on whether the nation should continue the partyless panchayat system of government or switch to a multiparty system. The announcement was widely acclaimed, especially by the leaders of the Nepalese Congress Party, whose main spokesman, former prime minister Bisheswar Prasad Koirala, had been placed under house arrest on April 27; Koirala subsequently was released on May 9. He had returned to Nepal in March after medical treatment in the U.S. The king also released from prison a large number of Koirala's colleagues and other dissidents and granted amnesty to about 200 other politicians and student leaders held in custody during the two-week-long student agitation, which cost more than 20 lives.

On May 30 the government of Prime Minister Kirti Nidhi Bista was replaced by a new 28-member Council of Ministers headed by Surya Bahadur Thapa, considered a moderate. The king also lifted restrictions on the press and on campaigning for the referendum, which was expected to take place early in 1980. (GOVINDAN UNNY)

Netherlands, The

A kingdom of northwest Europe on the North Sea, The Netherlands, a Benelux country, is bounded by Belgium on the south and West Germany on the east. Area: 41,160 sq km (15,892 sq mi). Pop. (1979 est.): 14,013,300. Cap. and largest city: Amsterdam (pop., 1979 est., 718,600). Seat of government: The Hague (pop., 1979 est., 458,200). Language: Dutch. Religion (1971): Roman Catholic 40.4%; Dutch Reformed 23.5%; no religion 23.6%; Reformed Churches 9.4%. Queen, Juliana; prime minister in 1979, Andreas van Agt.

On Jan. 12, 1979, the Dutch government, with the agreement of Parliament, placed a battalion of 700 men at the disposal of the United Nations peace force in Lebanon. The minister of foreign affairs, Christoph van der Klaauw, paid a visit to Israel February 24–27 and spoke with Prime Minister Menahem Begin about the Dutch battalion's role in Lebanon and the Arab states' trade boycott of Israel. Begin urged the need for legal measures against the boycott, but van der Klaauw refused to commit himself. A report by an investigatory committee showed that many Dutch companies were giving in to the Arabs' trade conditions, including declarations that company employees were not Jews. A majority of Parliament voted against these practices.

Van der Klaauw visited China in January and discussed the problem of the refugees from Indochina and also the possibility of economic cooperation. The Chinese leadership showed interest in joint ventures with Dutch companies on a 51–49% basis, especially with regard to offshore industry.

At the end of August Parliament discussed the Willem Aantjes affair. Almost all parties criticized

Britain's ambassador to The Netherlands, Sir Richard Sykes, was shot and killed in his automobile outside his home in The Hague on March 22.

WIDE WORLD

NETHERLANDS, THE

Education. (1977–78) Primary, pupils 1,521,037, teachers 62,956; secondary, pupils 811,998, teachers 52,116; vocational, pupils 539,238, teachers 44,000; teacher training, students 10,097, teachers 1,100; higher, students 261,188, teaching staff 28,000.

Finance. Monetary unit: guilder, with (Sept. 17, 1979) a free rate of 1.99 guilders to U.S. $1 (4.29 guilders = £1 sterling). Gold, SDR's, and foreign exchange (June 1979) U.S. $8,727,000,000. Budget (1978 actual): revenue 99.8 billion guilders; expenditure 105.4 billion guilders. Gross national product (1978) 282,450,000,000 guilders. Money supply (June 1979) 66,040,000,000 guilders. Cost of living (1975 = 100; June 1979) 124.9.

Foreign Trade. (1978) Imports 116,118,000,000 guilders; exports 108,207,000,000 guilders. Import sources: EEC 57% (West Germany 25%, Belgium-Luxembourg 13%, France 8%, U.K. 7%); U.S. 9%. Export destinations: EEC 71% (West Germany 31%, Belgium-Luxembourg 15%, France 11%, U.K. 7%, Italy 5%). Main exports: food 20%; chemicals 15%; machinery 15%; petroleum products 10%; natural gas 6%. Tourism (1977): visitors 2,788,000; gross receipts U.S. $1,110,000,000.

Transport and Communications. Roads (1974) 104,480 km (including 1,839 km expressways). Motor vehicles in use (1977): passenger 3,920,000; commercial 295,000. Railways: (1977) 2,850 km (including 1,731 km electrified); traffic (1978) 8,190,000,000 passenger-km, freight 2,886,000,000 net ton-km. Air traffic (1978): 12,382,000,000 passenger-km; freight 823,020,000 net ton-km. Navigable inland waterways (1977) 4,342 km; freight traffic 32,127,000,000 ton-km. Shipping (1978): merchant vessels 100 gross tons and over 1,238; gross tonnage 5,180,392. Shipping traffic (1978): goods loaded 73,044,000 metric tons, unloaded 246,456,000 metric tons. Telephones (Jan. 1978) 5,845,900. Radio licenses (Dec. 1977) 4,105,000. Television licenses (Dec. 1977) 3,878,000.

Agriculture. Production (in 000; metric tons; 1978): wheat 792; barley 355; oats 140; rye 68; potatoes 6,231; tomatoes 365; onions *c.* 450; sugar, raw value *c.* 950; cabbages (1977) *c.* 246; cucumbers (1977) *c.* 343; carrots (1977) *c.* 165; apples *c.* 430; rapeseed 23; milk 11,346; butter *c.* 211; cheese *c.* 418; eggs *c.* 346; beef and veal *c.* 374; pork *c.* 1,053; fish catch (1977) 313. Livestock (in 000; May 1978): cattle 4,990; pigs 9,172; sheep 841; chickens *c.* 70,365.

Industry. Index of production (1975 = 100; 1978) 108. Production (in 000; metric tons; 1978): crude oil 1,402; natural gas (cu m) 88,730,000; manufactured gas (cu m) 960,000; electricity (kw-hr) 61,706,000; pig iron 4,612; crude steel 5,592; cement 3,916; petroleum products 60,515; sulfuric acid 1,680; plastics and resins 1,358; fertilizers (nutrient content; 1977–78) nitrogenous 1,453, phosphate *c.* 262; newsprint 128; synthetic rubber 2,231. Merchant vessels launched (100 gross tons and over; 1978) 202,000 gross tons. New dwelling units completed (1978) 106,000.

the Cabinet's handling of the accusation by the director of the Institute of War Documentation, Lou de Jong, that Aantjes, formerly leader of the Christian Democrats, had been a member of the German SS during World War II. Although further investigation proved that the accusation was not quite correct, a majority voted against Aantjes's return to public life. Before this debate Joseph Kotälla, the convicted second-in-command of the concentration camp at Amersfoort, died in prison at Breda.

During the debate on government policy the differences between the two major coalition parties, the Christian Democrats and the Liberals, became clearer. The Liberals did not share the Christian Democrats' view that the purchasing power of the typical employee should be maintained at the same level as in the previous year and that taxation of higher income groups should be raised. During a discussion on the "modernization" of NATO's nuclear weapons, the Christian Democratic Party argued that the decision on the deployment of new missiles ought to be part of the East-West negotiations on disarmament and control of nuclear weapons; the Liberal Party sought a decision before East-West negotiations began. On December 6 ten Christian Democrats voted with the opposition on a nonbinding motion urging rejection of the missiles at the NATO Council meeting later in the month. To help meet Dutch objections, NATO linked its approval of new missiles with an offer to renew East-West negotiations. The Dutch told NATO they would wait two years before deciding whether to permit deployment of missiles in The Netherlands, and the ten deputies backed the government's position in a confidence vote on December 20.

In August tugmen and dockworkers in Rotterdam harbour struck for better wages and working conditions. A few weeks before the strike the trade unions had signed a collective labour agreement with the shipping companies, and they refused to support the tugmen's strike. Through the mayor of Rotterdam, André van der Louw, the shipping companies and the tugmen reached agreement after six weeks. The dockworkers had struck before the negotiations between their trade unions and the dock companies began; the unions did not support most wage demands of these workers, believing that their realization would result in a loss of jobs in the near future. The strike was accompanied by violence and bitterness between those dockworkers who wanted to work and those who wished to continue the strike. After four weeks the strike committee decided that it was irresponsible to continue it and ordered the men to return to work. (DICK BOONSTRA)

See also Dependent States.

New Zealand

New Zealand

New Zealand, a parliamentary state and member of the Commonwealth of Nations, is in the South Pacific Ocean, separated from southeastern Australia by the Tasman Sea. The country consists of North and South islands and Stewart, Chatham, and other minor islands. Area: 268,704 sq km (103,747 sq mi). Pop. (1979 est.): 3,105,800. Cap.: Wellington (pop., 1979 est., 137,600). Largest city: Christchurch (pop., 1979 est., 171,300). Largest urban area: Auckland (pop., 1979 est., 805,900). Language: English (official), Maori. Religion (1976): Church of England 35%; Presbyterian 22%; Roman Catholic 16%. Queen, Elizabeth II; governor-general in 1979, Sir Keith Holyoake; prime minister, Robert David Muldoon.

Firm plans, announced in 1979, to divert natural gas from an offshore field to replace more than half its oil imports gave New Zealand hope of relief from the oil costs that had been dragging down its economy. These plans would not take effect until 1987, however. Meanwhile, a newly established economic monitoring group of the nation's Planning Council observed in September that, unless trade recovered unexpectedly or production increased markedly, New Zealand could only expect continuance of a pattern of low growth, high inflation and unemployment, high external deficits and borrowing, and persistent industrial strife.

The budget, presented in June, was an extension of policies aimed at enlarging the export sector, renewing the confidence of farmers, making the domestic economy more stable and manageable, and to some extent returning to a private enterprise philosophy. Tax relief was provided for

Netherlands Overseas Territories: *see* Dependent States

New Guinea: *see* Indonesia; Papua New Guinea

New Hebrides: *see* Dependent States

Newspapers: *see* Publishing

NEW ZEALAND

Education. (1978) Primary, pupils 519,431, teachers 21,110; secondary, pupils 234,705, teachers 13,744; vocational, pupils 5,960, teachers 1,872; higher, students 35,911, teaching staff 3,459.

Finance. Monetary unit: New Zealand dollar, with (Sept. 17, 1979) a free rate of NZ$1 to U.S. $1 (NZ$2.16 = £1 sterling). Gold, SDR's, and foreign exchange (June 1979) U.S. $654 million. Budget (1977–78 actual): revenue NZ$5,068,000,000; expenditure NZ$5,429,000,000. Gross national product (1977–78) NZ$14,979,000,000. Cost of living (1975 = 100; 2nd quarter 1979) 166.2.

Foreign Trade. (1978) Imports NZ$3,359,400,000; exports NZ$3,603,900,000. Import sources: Australia 22%; U.K. 16%; U.S. 14%; Japan 13%; West Germany 7%. Export destinations: U.K. 18%; U.S. 15%; Japan 14%; Australia 12%. Main exports: wool 18%; lamb and mutton 11%; beef and veal 11%; butter 7%. Tourism (1977): visitors 390,000; gross receipts U.S. $155 million.

Transport and Communications. Roads (1976) 96,034 km. Motor vehicles in use (1978): passenger 1,251,600; commercial 245,000. Railways: (1977) 4,688 km; traffic (1976–77) 497 million passenger-km, freight (1977–78) 3,402,000,000 net ton-km. Air traffic (1978): 4,115,000,000 passenger-km; freight 145.7 million net ton-km. Shipping (1978): merchant vessels 100 gross tons and over 109; gross tonnage 211,112. Telephones (March 1978) 1,715,300. Radio receivers (Dec. 1976) 2,715,000. Television licenses (Dec. 1978) 863,100.

Agriculture. Production (in 000; metric tons; 1978): wheat 357; barley 282; oats 50; corn 232; potatoes (1977) *c.* 257; dry peas *c.* 65; tomatoes *c.* 71; wine *c.* 41; apples 185; milk 6,069; butter 234; cheese 78; wool 222; sheepskins (1977) *c.* 113; mutton and lamb 500; beef and veal 549; fish catch (1977) 111; timber (cu m; 1977) 9,742. Livestock (in 000; Jan. 1978): cattle 9,129; sheep *c.* 60,300; pigs 546; chickens *c.* 6,461.

Industry. Production (in 000; metric tons; 1978): coal 1,974; lignite 164; crude oil (1977) 686; natural gas (cu m) 1,340,000; manufactured gas (cu m) 64,000; electricity (excluding most industrial production; kw-hr) 21,352,000; cement 798; aluminum (1977) 145; petroleum products (1977) *c.* 3,120; phosphate fertilizers (1977–78) *c.* 398; wood pulp (1977) 882; newsprint (1977–78) 276; other paper (1977–78) 365.

intermediate-range earners, between NZ$4,500 and NZ$11,000. Export incentives were in the form of tax rebates or cash refunds. Estate duty exemption began an annual rise that would take it from NZ$25,000 to NZ$250,000 in four years.

The export incentives seemed to be a significant factor in the revitalizing of manufactured exports and the recovery of the domestic economy that was apparent by September. Inflation continued, however, and in the year ended June 1979 it reached 12.4%, compared with 12.2% for the preceding year (14.1% in 1976). The outlook was for further increases. The increase in the consumer price index stood at 4.5% for the second quarter and threatened to reach 16% for the year ending March 1980. A government curb on free wage bargaining in September resulted in a 24-hour general strike, only the second in New Zealand's history. As of mid-September, 26,191 were registered as unemployed, and migration of the disenchanted to Australia continued.

In Parliament one seat changed hands as the result of a commission inquiry into voting procedures, leaving the ruling National Party with 51 seats to 40 for Labour and 1 for the Social Credit Party. The investigation led to a further, more general inquiry into the state of the electoral rolls and the rules for marking ballots.

Illicit drug peddling was a major problem for the police. Several murders were believed to have been committed by gang members as a means of maintaining discipline within the illegal drug trade. An effort by the parliamentary opposition to set up a select committee to inquire into the matter was defeated by the government majority.

Laws designed to restrict therapeutic abortions were proving widely ineffective as many doctors declined to cooperate. Nevertheless, the number of illegitimate births in New Zealand was reported to be increasing. Centralization of control and programming of the two television channels, both publicly owned but previously in competition, proved controversial. In particular, criticism was directed at the removal of the news editing operation from Wellington to Auckland. Worldwide media attention was directed to reports of unidentified flying objects, although scientists looking into the matter discounted the purported UFO's as atmospheric reflections of the lights from squid fishing boats.

Jim Knox was appointed to succeed Sir Tom Skinner as president of the Federation of Labour. Knox, who had been secretary of the organization for some years, introduced a more direct style to industrial relations. Jim Anderton succeeded Arthur Faulkner as president of the Labour Party. In the Cabinet, Barry Brill became undersecretary of energy; and in Parliament, which convened May 17, Prime Minister Robert Muldoon relinquished the role of leader of the House in favour of Minister of State David Thomson. (JOHN A. KELLEHER)

See also Dependent States.

Nicaragua

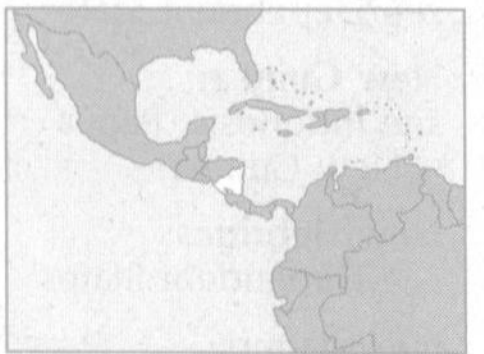

Nicaragua

The largest country of Central America, Nicaragua is a republic bounded by Honduras, Costa Rica, the Caribbean Sea, and the Pacific Ocean. Area: 128,875 sq km (49,759 sq mi). Pop. (1978 est.): 2,395,000. Cap. and largest city: Managua (pop., 1978 est., 517,700). Language: Spanish. Religion: Roman Catholic. Presidents in 1979, Anastasio Somoza Debayle and, on July 17–18, Francisco Urcuyo Maliaños; from July 20 the nation was governed by a five-member Government Junta of National Reconstruction.

The 46-year rule of Nicaragua by the Somoza family ended on July 17, 1979, when Pres. Anastasio Somoza Debayle (*see* BIOGRAPHIES) resigned and fled to the U.S. following seven weeks of civil war against his government by the Sandinista National Liberation Front. An interim president selected by Somoza, Francisco Urcuyo Maliaños, resigned after two days in office, and a five-member Sandinista-appointed junta was installed in Managua on July 20. Although the Sandinistas had fought against the Somoza family for nearly two decades, stepping up their offensive into a short-lived nationwide insurrection in September 1978, it was not until early in 1979 that their victory seemed likely.

On January 19 Somoza rejected the final plan of an Organization of American States (OAS) team, including the United States, Guatemala, and the Dominican Republic, to help find a political solution for the Nicaraguan situation. The plan called for a plebiscite on the presidency, with Somoza resigning if he lost.

During the first five months of the year the Sandinistas operated out of bases in neighbouring Costa Rica and Honduras and from clandestine camps within Nicaragua, engaging in hit-and-run strikes against the National Guard and gradually winning support. On May 29 about 300 Sandinistas attacked from Costa Rica, beginning a full-scale offensive. Somoza accused Venezuela, Panama, and Costa Rica of plotting his overthrow by aiding the rebels and unsuccessfully tried in the OAS to invoke an inter-American mutual defense pact against the Sandinistas. On June 4 a Sandinista-organized general strike, to last until Somoza resigned, closed 80% of the businesses in Nicaragua.

By early June guerrillas and Sandinista-led civilians were fighting the National Guard, the latter equipped with artillery and aircraft, in most Nicaraguan cities. The government gradually lost ground. Although a U.S. proposal on June 21 that an OAS peacekeeping force be sent to Nicaragua was rejected by that organization as interventionist, the OAS two days later called for Somoza's "immediate and definitive replacement." Somoza resigned and left for Miami, Fla., on July 17. Nicaragua was momentarily thrown into confusion when his successor, former Senate president Urcuyo, announced his intention to remain in office, but he too fled, to Guatemala on July 18.

The Sandinistas entered Managua on July 19, and the next day the Government Junta of National Reconstruction formally took power. The five-member junta included businessman Alfonso Robelo Callejas, poet and professor Sergio Ramírez Mercado, physicist and union leader Moisés Hassan Morales, Sandinista leader Daniel Ortega Saavedra, and Violeta Barrios de Chamorro, widow of slain newspaper publisher Pedro Joaquín Chamorro. The Sandinistas offered Somoza's troops asylum. As many as 1,000 National Guardsmen were subsequently held for civil trial on war crimes charges, but most of those who sought asylum were released. An 18-member Cabinet was drawn from political and professional groups. The Cabinet resigned on December 4 to give the junta freedom "to confirm, substitute, or relocate according to the conveniences and necessities of the Sandinista revolutionary process." Late in the year special tribunals were formed to try some 7,000 persons accused of war crimes and collaboration with the Somoza regime.

Some foreign governments, particularly the U.S., feared that the new government, which quickly established close ties with Cuba, would move sharply to the left. Among the junta's first acts were expropriation of the property of Somoza and members of his government and sympathizers who fled the country with him and nationalization of local banks and insurance companies and of Nicaragua's mineral and forestry resources. The import and export of foodstuffs were also put under government control, and a Sandinista Army was established. The Sandinistas, however, said that they intended to establish a pluralist democracy in Nicaragua and promulgated a number of laws guaranteeing civil and political rights. While

UPI

Sandinista rebels rode triumphantly into Managua after former president Anastasio Somoza's forces capitulated in July.

NICARAGUA

Education. (1977–78) Primary, pupils 373,948, teachers 9,759; secondary, pupils 85,192; vocational, pupils 18,549; secondary and vocational, teachers (1976–77) 2,631; higher, students (including teacher training) 25,254, teaching staff (1976–77) 1,052.

Finance. Monetary unit: córdoba, with (Sept. 17, 1979) a par value of 10 córdobas to U.S. $1 (free rate of 21.35 córdobas = £1 sterling). Gold, SDR's, and foreign exchange (Dec. 1978) U.S. $52 million. Budget (1977 actual): revenue 1,790,000,000 córdobas; expenditure 1,505,000,000 córdobas (excludes capital expenditure of 1,438,000,000 córdobas). Gross national product (1978) 14,670,000,000 córdobas. Money supply (April 1979) 2,011,700,000 córdobas. Cost of living (Managua; 1975 = 100; Sept. 1978) 123.

Foreign Trade. (1978) Imports 4,187,600,000 córdobas; exports 4,538,700,000 córdobas. Import sources (1977): U.S. 30%; Venezuela 12%; Japan 9%; Costa Rica 8%; Guatemala 7%; West Germany 7%; El Salvador 5%. Export destinations (1977): U.S. 22%; West Germany 13%; Japan 11%; Costa Rica 8%; The Netherlands 6%; Guatemala 5%; El Salvador 5%; Belgium-Luxembourg 5%. Main exports: coffee 31%; cotton 23%; meat 10%; chemicals (1976) 8%.

Transport and Communications. Roads (1977) 17,941 km (including 384 km of Pan-American Highway). Motor vehicles in use (1977): passenger *c.* 38,000; commercial (including buses) *c.* 30,000. Railways: (1977) 373 km; traffic (1972) 28 million passenger-km, freight 14 million net ton-km. Air traffic (1977): 77 million passenger-km; freight 2 million net ton-km. Telephones (Jan. 1978) 55,800. Radio receivers (Dec. 1974) 126,000. Television receivers (Dec. 1976) 90,000.

Agriculture. Production (in 000; metric tons; 1978): corn *c.* 209; rice *c.* 82; sorghum *c.* 58; dry beans *c.* 51; sugar, raw value (1977) *c.* 224; bananas *c.* 157; oranges *c.* 55; cottonseed 237; coffee 60; cotton, lint 144. Livestock (in 000; 1977): cattle 2,768; pigs *c.* 690; horses *c.* 270; chickens 4,288.

Industry. Production (in 000; metric tons; 1977): petroleum products *c.* 730; cement 221; gold (exports; troy oz) 61; electricity (kw-hr) 1,180,000.

they established relations with Communist-bloc nations, they retained ties with the West.

The government's principal concern was to reconstruct the war-devastated country and to revitalize its economy, now left with nearly $600 million in foreign debt due in 1979 and only $3.5 million in the treasury. Talks aimed at refinancing the debt opened in Mexico City in December. The junta made numerous appeals for international aid. Projected per capita income for 1979 would reach only 1962 levels, and export earnings from agricultural commodities that traditionally supplied most of Nicaragua's foreign exchange were severely reduced. Worst, nearly 500,000 people were left homeless, and estimates of those killed, primarily civilians caught in National Guard air and artillery attacks, ranged from 10,000 to 40,000.

(KAREN DEYOUNG)

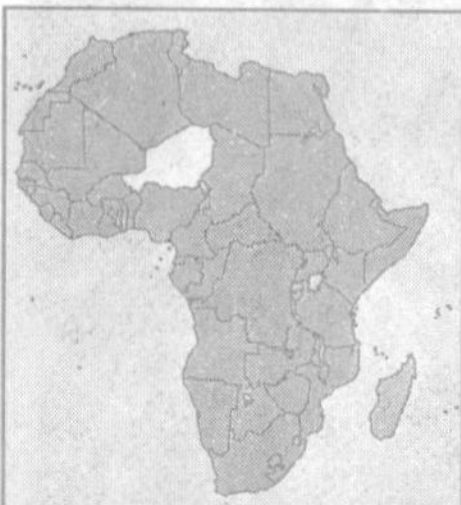

Niger

Niger

A republic of north central Africa, Niger is bounded by Algeria, Libya, Chad, Nigeria, Benin, Upper Volta, and Mali. Area: 1,186,408 sq km (458,075 sq mi). Pop. (1979 est.): 5,126,000, including (1972 est.) Hausa 53.7%; Zerma and Songhai 23.6%; Fulani 10.6%; Beriberi-Manga 9.1%. Cap. and largest city: Niamey (pop., 1977 prelim., 225,-300). Language: French (official) and Sudanic dialects. Religion: Muslim 85%; animist 14.5%; Christian 0.5%. President in 1979, Col. Seyni Kountché.

Pres. Seyni Kountché paid a private visit to Paris in July 1979, as a prelude to a proposed official visit to Niamey by Pres. Valéry Giscard d'Estaing of France in February 1980. In August President Kountché was promoted from lieutenant colonel to colonel.

Niger's government was much concerned by events in neighbouring countries and regions. In the Sahara the Polisario guerrilla forces, who were trying to gain control of the Western Sahara, were increasing their recruitment among the Tuaregs, who were numerous in Niger. The conflict in Chad was disturbing because there were sizable Chadian Toubou minorities in Niger territory, and Niger was involved in the conferences about Chad held in Nigeria at Kano and Lagos from March to August. There was also anxiety over Libyan leader Col. Muammar al-Qaddafi's increasingly active policy in Africa.

(PHILIPPE DECRAENE)

NIGER

Education. (1977–78) Primary, pupils 177,620, teachers 4,215; secondary, pupils 21,944, teachers 831; vocational, pupils 333, teachers 34; teacher training (1976–77), students 731, teachers 42; higher (1975–76), students 541, teaching staff 74.

Finance. Monetary unit: CFA franc, with (Sept. 17, 1979) a par value of CFA Fr 50 to the French franc (free rate of CFA Fr 211.54 = U.S. $1; CFA Fr 455.12 = £1 sterling). Gold, SDR's, and foreign exchange (May 1979) U.S. $107 million. Budget (1977–78 rev. est.): revenue CFA Fr 44.8 billion; expenditure CFA Fr 46 billion.

Foreign Trade. (1978) Imports *c.* CFA Fr 78 billion; exports *c.* CFA Fr 36 billion. Import sources: France *c.* 41%; U.K. *c.* 8%; Japan *c.* 8%; U.S. *c.* 7%; Ivory Coast *c.* 6%; West Germany 6%. Export destinations: France *c.* 75%; Nigeria *c.* 11%; West Germany *c.* 6%. Main exports (1975): uranium 61%; livestock 19%; peanut oil 5%.

Transport and Communications. Roads (1977) 7,587 km. Motor vehicles in use (1977): passenger 18,800; commercial 3,320. There are no railways. Inland waterway (Niger River; 1977) *c.* 300 km. Telephones (Jan. 1977) 8,100. Radio receivers (Dec. 1971) 150,000.

Agriculture. Production (in 000; metric tons; 1978): millet 1,091; sorghum 361; rice 34; cassava (1977) *c.* 200; onions *c.* 64; peanuts 74; goat's milk *c.* 123. Livestock (in 000; 1977): cattle *c.* 2,900; sheep *c.* 2,560; goats *c.* 6,200; camels *c.* 265.

Industry. Production (in 000; metric tons; 1977): uranium 1.6; tin concentrates (metal content) *c.* 0.1; cement 40; electricity (kw-hr) *c.* 70,000.

Nigeria

Nigeria

A republic and a member of the Commonwealth of Nations, Nigeria is located in Africa north of the Gulf of Guinea, bounded by Benin, Niger, Chad, and Cameroon. Area: 923,800 sq km (356,700 sq mi). Nigeria's total population is extremely uncertain; in 1979 calculations ranged from a UN estimate of 74,595,000, to a Nigerian government estimate of 83.4 million that excludes adjustment for estimated overenumeration, to an unofficial estimate of 100,075,000, including Hausa 21%; Yoruba 20%; Ibo 17%; Fulani 9%. Cap. and largest city: Lagos (metro. pop., 1977 est., 3.5 million). Language: English (official), Hausa, Yoruba, and Ibo. Religion (1963): Muslim 47%; Christian 34%. Head of the provisional military government until

NIGERIA

Education. (1973–74) Primary, pupils 4,889,857, teachers 144,351; secondary, pupils 498,744, teachers 19,409; vocational, pupils 22,117, teachers 1,120; teacher training, students 49,136, teachers 2,360; higher (1975–76), students 32,971, teaching staff 5,019.

Finance. Monetary unit: naira, with (Sept. 17, 1979) a free rate of 0.59 naira to U.S. $1 (1.27 naira = £1 sterling). Gold, SDR's, and foreign exchange (June 1979) U.S. $2,-497,000,000. Federal budget (1978–79): revenue 6,-830,000,000 naira; expenditure 7,230,000,000 naira (including 5,250,000,000 naira development expenditure). Gross domestic product (1977–78) 20,791,000,000 naira. Money supply (March 1979) 5,292,300,000 naira. Cost of living (Lagos; 1975 = 100; Jan. 1979) 192.6.

Foreign Trade. (1978) Imports *c.* 6,524,000,000 naira; exports 6,688,700,000 naira. Import sources (1977): U.K. 22%; West Germany 16%; U.S. 11%; Japan 11%; Italy 7%; France 7%. Export destinations (1977): U.S. 40%; Netherlands Antilles 15%; The Netherlands 11%; U.K. 8%; France 7%; West Germany 6%. Main export: crude oil 90%.

Transport and Communications. Roads (1977) 105,000 km. Motor vehicles in use (1977): passenger 133,-700; commercial 23,600. Railways: (1975) 3,524 km; traffic (1974–75) 785 million passenger-km, freight 972 million net ton-km. Air traffic (1978): 1,268,000,000 passenger-km; freight 10.3 million net ton-km. Shipping (1978): merchant vessels 100 gross tons and over 101; gross tonnage 324,-024. Telephones (Jan. 1978) 128,400. Radio receivers (Dec. 1976) 5.1 million. Television receivers (Dec. 1977) 450,-000.

Agriculture. Production (in 000; metric tons; 1978): millet *c.* 3,100; sorghum *c.* 3,800; corn *c.* 1,450; rice *c.* 580; sweet potatoes (1977) *c.* 200; yams (1977) *c.* 15,000; taro (1977) *c.* 1,800; cassava (1977) *c.* 10,600; tomatoes *c.* 250; peanuts *c.* 500; palm oil *c.* 670; cocoa *c.* 180; cotton, lint 37; rubber *c.* 90; fish catch (1977) 506. Livestock (in 000; 1978): cattle *c.* 11,566; sheep *c.* 8,254; goats *c.* 24,188; pigs *c.* 973; poultry *c.* 97,210.

Industry. Production (in 000; metric tons; 1978): crude oil 94,897; natural gas (cu m; 1977) *c.* 500,000; cement (1977) 1,260; tin concentrates (metal content) 2.8; petroleum products (1977) *c.* 2,350; electricity (kw-hr; 1977) *c.* 3,500,000.

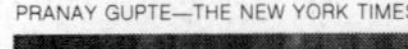
PRANAY GUPTE—THE NEW YORK TIMES

Former U.S. ambassador to the UN Andrew Young (right) and members of a U.S. trade delegation talked with then President-elect Alhaji Shehu Shagari when the trade mission visited Lagos in September.

Oct. 1, 1979, Lieut. Gen. Olusegun Obasanjo; president from October 1, Alhaji Shehu Shagari.

Before civilian Alhaji Shehu Shagari (*see* BIOGRAPHIES) was sworn in as Nigeria's president on Oct. 1, 1979, five elections were held to mark Nigeria's peaceful return to civilian government after 13 years of military rule. The transition went as planned by the retiring head of the military government, Lieut. Gen. Olusegun Obasanjo. Under the new constitution agreed upon by the 1978 Constituent Assembly, 48 million voters were asked to consider the claims of five accepted parties. The parties had to be nationwide and nonethnic. All emphasized economic development, education, and varying degrees of public control. They were the People's Redemption Party (PRP; leader, Alhaji Aminu Kano), Unity Party of Nigeria (UPN; Chief Obafemi Awolowo), Great Nigeria People's Party (GNPP; Alhaji Waziri Ibrahim), Nigerian People's Party (NPP; Nnamdi Azikiwe), and National Party of Nigeria (NPN; Alhaji Shehu Shagari).

Voting, in a low poll and sometimes on ethnic lines, took place in July and August. For the Senate, 95 senators were elected; the NPN won 36 seats, UPN 28, NPP 16, GNPP 8, and PRP 7. The NPN gained seats in 12 of the 19 states. For the National House of Assembly 455 members were chosen, and the results were: NPN 168, UPN 111, NPP 79, GNPP 48, and PRP 49. Elections for 1,347 members of the 19 state assemblies gave the NPN 36.2% of the overall vote, with the UPN next at 24.7%. Elections for state governors gave the NPN 7, UPN 5, NPP 3, PRP 2, and GNPP 2.

The presidential election was disputed. Although Shagari received a majority vote (5.7 million, as against 4.9 million for his nearest rival, the UPN's Awolowo) and more than a quarter of the votes in 12 states (a majority in 9 of them), it was argued that two-thirds of 19 states should be reckoned as 13. On August 16 the Federal Electoral Commission upheld the election, and the NPN emerged as the leading party nationwide.

Externally, Nigeria, with its 250,000-man Army and economic potential as the world's fifth largest oil producer, continued to assert a right to African leadership. During the year this was seen in its initiative concerning Chad. Meetings with groups from Chad and with other nearby nations held at Kano and Lagos resulted in the establishment of a transitional government in Chad in August. Nigeria also maintained peacekeeping troops in Chad and took a strong anti-South Africa stance, which included the offer of aid and a military presence to Transkei.

Nigerian oil politics caused a greatly increased U.S. involvement in Nigerian affairs, since Nigeria had become the U.S.'s second largest oil supplier; Nigeria also halted oil supplies to Ghana in protest against the execution of former military leaders and to Chad in disapproval of the transitional government's actions there. On July 31 Nigeria nationalized British Petroleum's facilities, thereby putting African pressure on British policies in southern Africa. Although Nigeria remained an important trading partner of Great Britain, 1979 figures as of June were 60% below those of the corresponding period in 1978.

Oil itself brought difficulties of imbalance, inflation, and unemployment, despite increasing revenues. Oil provided 75% of the nation's revenue and 95% of its exports. However, the 1979 budgetary deficit rose to 3,239,000,000 naira, the latest increase in a steady rise after the surplus year of 1974. Although federal revenue had quadrupled since 1974, expenditures in the same period had risen from 1,562,000,000 naira to 9,510,000,000 naira. Agricultural exports, which had provided four-fifths of the total in 1960, fell to 5% in 1979, and the production of peanuts, once the chief export, virtually ceased, leaving the country unable to feed itself. Obasanjo in his budget speech in March stressed the need to work for self-sufficiency. He promised defense cuts of 76 million naira, agricultural expansion, the banning of luxury imports, and control of inflation. Later in the year Shagari's civilian government found it hard to meet the economic and social expectations of a growing population. (MOLLY MORTIMER)

Nobel Prizes:
see People of the Year

Norway

Norway

A constitutional monarchy of northern Europe, Norway is bordered by Sweden, Finland, and the U.S.S.R.; its coastlines are on the Skagerrak, the North Sea, the Norwegian Sea, and the Arctic Ocean. Area: 323,886 sq km (125,053 sq mi), excluding the Svalbard Archipelago, 62,048 sq km, and Jan Mayen Island, 373 sq km. Pop. (1979 est.): 4,074,000. Cap. and largest city: Oslo (pop., 1979 est., 457,200). Language: Norwegian. Religion: Lutheran (94%). King, Olav V; prime minister in 1979, Odvar Nordli.

Developments at home and abroad were generally favourable in 1979. The upsurge in world petroleum prices that followed the Iranian revolution raised the value of oil and gas on the Norwegian continental shelf. Petroleum output from Norwegian fields already in production—Ekofisk and Frigg—increased from 30 million metric tons in 1978 to more than 40 million tons, raising state revenue from this source to some 6.6 billion kroner (3.8 billion kroner in 1978). Toward the end of the year the giant Statfjord development, containing both oil and gas, also came on stream.

While output from Frigg and Ekofisk was rising, exploration drilling by the oil companies revealed the existence of several new fields, among them a gas field northwest of Bergen that was believed to be even larger than Frigg. The new finds seemed to ensure that offshore petroleum would continue to play an important role in the economy.

The government's ambitious plan to buy a 40% stake in Volvo, the Swedish automobile manufacturer, was rejected in January by the company's Swedish shareholders. As a result, Volvo's newly created oil subsidiary, Volvo Petroleum, was not among the companies selected when Norway awarded eight new oil exploration concessions in April. Statoil, the Norwegian State Oil Company, got a 50% stake in all eight concessions, or blocks; depending on the size of eventual discoveries, this could rise to between 70 and 80%.

There was controversy over the government's decision, approved by Parliament in May, to allow exploration drilling off northern Norway starting in 1980. So far, the search for petroleum in Norwegian waters had taken place only below the 62nd parallel. Drilling farther north had been postponed because of the rich fishery resources in those waters and the harsh Arctic weather conditions. An earlier decision to allow northern drilling, starting in 1978, had been temporarily shelved after the 1977 Ekofisk blowout. The government promised that, to limit pollution in case of an accident, effective Norwegian equipment for checking oil spills would be stockpiled near the intended drilling sites. In June, however, opponents of the plan found ammunition in the poor performance of Norwegian equipment flown to Mexico to help fight the spill from the Ixtoc-1 blowout in the Gulf of Mexico.

The prices and incomes freeze imposed in the fall of 1978 continued, as planned, throughout 1979. It helped to curb domestic demand and stimulate saving, while bringing costs more into line with those of Norway's competitors. At the same time, there was a revival of world demand for key Norwegian exports such as metals and wood products. For the first time in many years it appeared that the balance of trade (in goods and services) would show a small surplus. The payments balance continued in deficit, however, reflecting the burden of servicing the large foreign debt.

Unemployment averaged below 2% through most of the year—far less than in most Western industrial nations. In the October speech from the throne, the government appealed to all sectors of the population to show "moderation and solidarity" in 1980 wage demands, so that employment could be maintained and costs kept under control even when the prices and incomes freeze ended.

The ruling Labour Party suffered heavy losses in local elections in September, when its share of the vote dropped by 2% to just over 36%. The Conservative Party, on the other hand, secured 29.7%, compared with 22.6% in the 1975 local elections. Most other parties lost ground, except for the

NORWAY

Education. (1977–78) Primary, pupils 397,700, teachers 20,543; secondary, pupils 260,389, teachers 20,758; vocational, pupils 87,618, teachers (1975–76) 10,332; higher, students 66,710, teaching staff 6,679.

Finance. Monetary unit: Norwegian krone, with (Sept. 17, 1979) a free rate of 5.01 kroner to U.S. $1 (10.77 kroner = £1 sterling). Gold, SDR's, and foreign exchange (June 1979) U.S. $3,716,000,000. Budget (1979 est.): revenue 61,753,000,000 kroner; expenditure 78,118,000,000 kroner. Gross domestic product (1978) 207,550,000,000 kroner. Money supply (May 1979) 38,550,000,000 kroner. Cost of living (1975 = 100; June 1979) 134.6.

Foreign Trade. (1978) Imports 59,879,000,000 kroner; exports 52,627,000,000 kroner. Import sources: Sweden 18%; West Germany 14%; U.K. 12%; U.S. 7%; Denmark 7%; Japan 5%. Export destinations: U.K. 37%; Sweden 11%; West Germany 8%; Denmark 6%; U.S. 5%. Main exports: ships and rigs 20%; crude oil 18%; machinery 8%; aluminum 8%; chemicals 7%; fish 6%; iron and steel 5%.

Transport and Communications. Roads (1977) 78,889 km (including 182 km expressways). Motor vehicles in use (1977): passenger 1,106,600; commercial 143,100. Railways: (1977) 4,241 km (including 2,440 km electrified); traffic (1978) 2,060,000,000 passenger-km, freight 2,716,000,000 net ton-km. Air traffic (including Norwegian apportionment of international operations of Scandinavian Airlines System; 1978): 3,787,000,000 passenger-km; freight 144.8 million net ton-km. Shipping (1978): merchant vessels 100 gross tons and over 2,646; gross tonnage 26,128,428. Shipping traffic (1977): goods loaded 29,765,000 metric tons, unloaded 21,794,000 metric tons. Telephones (Jan. 1978) 1,562,500. Radio licenses (Dec. 1976) 1,318,000. Television licenses (Dec. 1977) 1,120,200.

Agriculture. Production (in 000; metric tons; 1978): barley 668; oats 367; potatoes 576; apples *c.* 58; milk (1977) 1,874; cheese 65; beef and veal (1977) *c.* 70; pork (1977) *c.* 85; timber (cu m; 1977) *c.* 8,081; fish catch (1977) 3,562. Livestock (in 000; June 1977): cattle 942; sheep 1,779; pigs 702; goats 69; chickens *c.* 3,798.

Industry. Fuel and power (in 000; metric tons; 1978): crude oil 17,275; coal (Svalbard mines; Norwegian operated only) 459; natural gas (cu m; 1977) 264,000; manufactured gas (cu m) 16,000; electricity (kw-hr) 81,103,000. Production (in 000; metric tons; 1978): iron ore (65% metal content) 3,715; pig iron 1,261; crude steel 808; aluminum 640; copper 15; zinc 71; cement 2,150; petroleum products (1977) 8,512; sulfuric acid 384; fertilizers (nutrient content; 1977–78) nitrogenous 336, phosphate 126; fish meal (1977) 465; wood pulp (1977) mechanical 763, chemical 863; newsprint 464; other paper (1977) 741. Merchant vessels launched (100 gross tons and over; 1978) 354,000 gross tons. New dwelling units completed (1978) 39,600.

Norwegian Literature:
see Literature

Nuclear Energy:
see Defense; Energy; Industrial Review

Numismatics:
see Philately and Numismatics

Obituaries:
see People of the Year

Oceanography:
see Earth Sciences

Oil:
see Energy

Opera:
see Music

Organization of African Unity:
see African Affairs

Organization of American States:
see Latin-American Affairs

Ornithology:
see Life Sciences

Orthodox Churches:
see Religion

Painting;
see Art Exhibitions; Art Sales; Museums

Paints and Varnishes:
see Industrial Review

ecology-conscious Liberal Party and a small rightist antitax party. Indecisive leadership and disagreement on key issues within the party were blamed for Labour's defeat. In October Prime Minister Odvar Nordli carried out a Cabinet reshuffle apparently aimed at restoring unity. The shake-up brought prominent representatives of the party's left and right wings into the government and put leading trade unionists in the key posts of industry and finance. (FAY GJESTER)

Oman

An independent sultanate, Oman occupies the southeastern part of the Arabian Peninsula and is bounded by the United Arab Emirates, Saudi Arabia, Yemen (Aden), the Gulf of Oman, and the Arabian Sea. A small part of the country lies to the north and is separated from the rest of Oman by the United Arab Emirates. Area: 300,000 sq km (120,000 sq mi). Pop. (1979 est.): 864,000; for planning purposes the government of Oman uses an estimate of 1.5 million. No census has ever been taken. Cap.: Muscat (pop., 1973 est., 15,000). Largest city: Matrah (pop., 1973 est., 18,000). Language: Arabic. Religion: Muslim. Sultan in 1979, Qabus ibn Sa'id.

During 1979 there was a resumption of Oman's war against insurgents in the southern Dhofar Province. At the same time, the country was isolated from most of its Arab neighbours because of Sultan Qabus ibn Sa'id's decision to support the Egyptian-Israeli peace treaty. Fighting resumed in Dhofar in May with an attack by the Popular Front for the Liberation of Oman (PFLO), which claimed to have killed a British officer and six Omani soldiers. This attack, the first engagement in more than a year, was followed on June 1 by the assassination of the Omani governor of Dhofar.

The U.S. Senate rewarded Sultan Qabus for his loyalty to Egyptian Pres. Anwar as-Sadat by increasing military aid to $15 million. In April President Sadat promised to send troops to Oman if its security was threatened.

Oman increased its oil prices in 1979, in line with the policy of the Organization of Petroleum Exporting Countries. An increase of 16% over 1978 revenues of $1.2 billion was anticipated.

(CHARLES GLASS)

OMAN

Education. (State only; 1978–79) Primary, pupils 77,974; secondary, pupils 7,963; primary and secondary, teachers, 4,286; vocational, pupils 346, teachers (1976–77) 48; teacher training, students 115, teachers 16.

Finance and Trade. Monetary unit: rial Omani, with (Sept. 17, 1979) a par value of 0.345 rial to U.S. $1 (free rate of 0.741 rial = £1 sterling). Gold, SDR's, and foreign exchange (June 1979) U.S. $381 million. Budget (1978 actual): revenue 509 million rials; expenditure 560 million rials.

Foreign Trade. (1978) Imports 327.2 million rials; exports 522.3 million rials. Import sources: U.K. 21%; United Arab Emirates 16%; Japan 16%; West Germany 6%; U.S. 6%. Export destinations: Japan 57%; U.S. 15%; Norway 7%; The Netherlands 6%; Trinidad and Tobago 6%. Main export: crude oil 99%.

Industry. Production (in 000): crude oil (metric tons; 1978) 15,705; electricity (kw-hr; 1977) 538,000.

Oman

Pakistan

A federal republic, Pakistan is bordered on the south by the Arabian Sea, on the west by Afghanistan and Iran, on the north by China, and on the east by India. Area: 796,095 sq km (307,374 sq mi), excluding the Pakistani-controlled section of Jammu and Kashmir. Pop. (1978 est.): 75,620,000. Cap.: Islamabad (pop., 1972, 77,300). Largest city: Karachi (metro. area pop., 1975 est., 4,465,000). Language: Urdu and English. Religion: Muslim 97%, Hindu and Christian minorities. President in 1979, Gen. Mohammad Zia-ul-Haq.

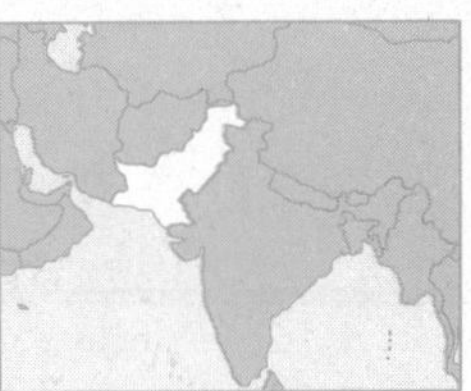

Pakistan

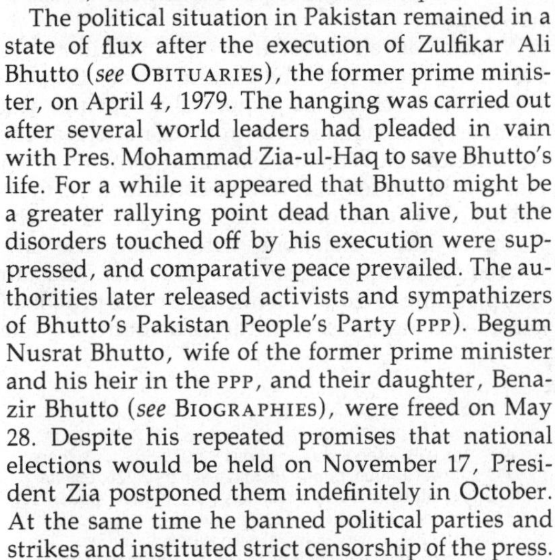

The political situation in Pakistan remained in a state of flux after the execution of Zulfikar Ali Bhutto (*see* OBITUARIES), the former prime minister, on April 4, 1979. The hanging was carried out after several world leaders had pleaded in vain with Pres. Mohammad Zia-ul-Haq to save Bhutto's life. For a while it appeared that Bhutto might be a greater rallying point dead than alive, but the disorders touched off by his execution were suppressed, and comparative peace prevailed. The authorities later released activists and sympathizers of Bhutto's Pakistan People's Party (PPP). Begum Nusrat Bhutto, wife of the former prime minister and his heir in the PPP, and their daughter, Benazir Bhutto (*see* BIOGRAPHIES), were freed on May 28. Despite his repeated promises that national elections would be held on November 17, President Zia postponed them indefinitely in October. At the same time he banned political parties and strikes and instituted strict censorship of the press.

The Pakistan National Alliance (PNA), which had been participating in General Zia's military government, formally ended its relationship with the Army on April 15. A coalition of six (originally nine) opposition parties, the PNA had been forged to oppose Bhutto during the 1977 elections and continued after the military coup. The ostensible reason for the withdrawal was that the PNA had achieved its objectives of introducing Islamic reforms and obtaining a date for new elections. The PNA promised continued support for the government from outside. In its place, a new federal Cabi-

UPI

Supporters of Zulfikar Ali Bhutto wept openly when they heard the news on April 4 that the former Pakistani prime minister had been executed by the regime that had ousted him in a military coup.

net of 15 ministers was appointed by the president on April 21.

Another development was the ushering in of islamization. On February 10, the Prophet Muhammad's birthday, General Zia issued a series of measures considered fundamental for islamization of the economy and the combating of crime.

On the economic front, there was a fall in the growth rate of the gross domestic product from 7 to 5.9% and of the gross national product from 10 to 6.3%. Prices continued to be a matter of concern. Although the government claimed that the inflation rate was being contained, the sensitive price index for 28 essential items recorded a rise of 7.3%. The trade and balance of payments deficits rose to new highs.

A major development in foreign relations was Pakistan's break with the Central Treaty Organization on March 12 and its formal acceptance as a member of the nonaligned group of nations at the nonaligned movement's summit conference in Havana in September. China continued to meet Pakistan's defense needs and to support it on the Kashmir issue. Relations with India also improved, although persistent reports that Pakistan was planning to explode a nuclear device provoked sharp exchanges between the two countries. The U.S. also showed concern over reports of the "Islamic bomb."

Although Pakistan condemned the holding of hostages in the U.S. embassy in Teheran, it maintained a sympathetic attitude toward Iran's revolutionary government. On November 21 two Americans were killed when a crowd stormed and burned the U.S. embassy in Islamabad, and some 100 persons were trapped for five hours before being rescued by Pakistani troops. On the same day U.S. installations were attacked in three other cities, according to some reports because of rumours implicating the U.S. in the takeover of the Grand Mosque in Mecca. (*See* SAUDI ARABIA.) The Pakistani government subsequently expressed regret over the incidents, but relations with the U.S. were severely strained. Late in December, however, after Soviet troops entered Afghanistan, the U.S. warned that it would use "armed force" to defend Pakistan if the fighting in Afghanistan spilled over the border. Earlier, the U.S.S.R. had accused Pakistan of aiding the Afghan rebels in their struggle against the Marxist regime in Kabul. (*See* AFGHANISTAN). (GOVINDAN UNNY)

PAKISTAN

Education. (1977–78) Primary, pupils 5,877,880, teachers 148,059; secondary, pupils 2,079,863, teachers 117,210; vocational, pupils 29,391, teachers 2,226; teacher training, students 16,361, teachers 750; higher, students 340,858, teaching staff 18,129.

Finance. Monetary unit: Pakistan rupee, with (Sept. 17, 1979) a par value of PakRs 9.90 to U.S. $1 (free rate of PakRs 21.07 = £1 sterling). Gold, SDR's, and foreign exchange (June 1979) U.S. $466 million. Budget (1978–79 est.): revenue PakRs 28,591,000,000; expenditure PakRs 27,670,000,000. Gross national product (1977–78) PakRs 179,970,000,000. Money supply (May 1979) PakRs 50,405,000,000. Cost of living (1975 = 100; June 1979) 134.5.

Foreign Trade. (1978) Imports PakRs 32,998,000,000; exports PakRs 14,781,000,000. Import sources (1977–78): Japan 13%; U.S. 11%; U.K. 9%; West Germany 8%; Saudi Arabia *c.* 5%. Export destinations (1977–78): Japan 9%; Iran *c.* 8%; U.K. 7%; Hong Kong 6%; West Germany 6%; U.S. 5%; United Arab Emirates *c.* 5%. Main exports (1977–78): rice 19%; cotton fabrics 13%; carpets 9%; cotton 8%; cotton yarn 8%; leather 5%; petroleum products 5%.

Transport and Communications. Roads (1977) 87,472 km. Motor vehicles in use (1976): passenger 202,800; commercial 60,537. Railways: (1978) 8,815 km; traffic (1977–78) 12,993,000,000 passenger-km, freight (1976–77) 8,677,000,000 net ton-km. Air traffic (1978): 4,648,000,000 passenger-km; freight 199.8 million net ton-km. Shipping (1978): merchant vessels 100 gross tons and over 80; gross tonnage 442,401. Telephones (June 1977) 269,300. Radio licenses (June 1978) 1,540,000. Television receivers (June 1978) 520,000.

Agriculture. Production (in 000; metric tons; 1978): wheat 8,289; corn *c.* 800; rice 4,706; millet *c.* 322; sorghum *c.* 286; potatoes 294; sugar, raw value 857; sugar, noncentrifugal (1977) *c.* 1,450; chick-peas 614; onions 325; rapeseed 236; cottonseed *c.* 1,130; mangoes *c.* 600; dates *c.* 210; oranges *c.* 530; tobacco 74; cotton, lint *c.* 548; beef and buffalo meat *c.* 337; mutton and goat meat 266; fish catch (1977) 248. Livestock (in 000; 1978): cattle 14,946; buffalo 11,069; sheep 22,291; goats 25,597; camels (1977) 656; chickens 42,144.

Industry. Production (in 000; metric tons; 1978): cement 3,103; crude oil 484; coal and lignite 1,180; natural gas (cu m; 1976–77) 4,816,000; petroleum products (1977) *c.* 2,960; electricity (kw-hr; 1976–77) *c.* 11,050,000; sulfuric acid 53; caustic soda 36; soda ash (1977–78) 69; nitrogenous fertilizers (nutrient content; 1977–78) 307; cotton yarn 315; woven cotton fabrics (sq m) 375,000.

Panama

A republic of Central America (from Oct. 1, 1979, including the Canal Zone), Panama is bounded by the Caribbean Sea, Colombia, the Pacific Ocean, and Costa Rica. Area: 77,082 sq km (29,762 sq mi). Pop. (1979 est.): 1,891,000. Data for area and population include the Canal Zone. Cap. and largest city: Panama City (pop., 1978 est., 439,900). Language: Spanish. Religion (1978 est.): Roman Catholic 86.2%. President in 1979, Aristides Royo.

Aristides Royo, elevated to the presidency of Panama on Oct. 11, 1978, retained many of his predecessor's advisers. He also inherited such problems as unemployment, poor housing, inflation, and violence. A student demonstration, a destructive riot sparked by high fuel costs, and resentment aroused by the unchanged minimum wage impelled the government to keep tight control over the populace. Police authority continued to rest with the National Guard under the command of former dictator Omar Torrijos, who, however, receded from the public view. The plight of the poor and the new president's Marxist taint prompted the issuance of a pastoral letter of protest and warning from the archbishop and the nine bishops of the Roman Catholic Church in Panama.

Panama's foreign relations centred on Nicaragua and the U.S. Torrijos had long harboured a strong dislike for Nicaragua's Pres. Anastasio Somoza, and in the fall of 1978 he stationed military forces along the Costa Rica-Nicaragua border, although the U.S. government persuaded him to go no further. As the anti-Somoza revolution gathered force, he provided sanctuary for Sandinista guerrillas, forwarded weapons, and offered military advice and training. These policies culminated in Panamanian recognition of the Sandinista government. (*See* NICARAGUA.)

Panama looked to the transfer of the canal from

Panama

Panamanians celebrated as their country took over the Panama Canal Zone in October.

the U.S. to offset its economic woes and provide backing for a more aggressive foreign policy. Obstacles emerged, however, chiefly in the U.S. House of Representatives, which was considering legislation to implement the canal treaties. Panamanians were disturbed by plans to eliminate U.S. military assistance and foreign aid and by proposals that would require Panama to pay all canal transfer costs, impose tighter congressional controls over property conveyance, institute U.S. military control if foreign troops found lodgment in Panama, and cut off money payments if Panama aided revolts in other countries.

Royo journeyed to Washington in mid-May to protest these measures and warn of their rejection in Panama. However, some of them were implanted in the law passed by Congress on September 26. Among its provisions were the creation of an operating commission having a majority of American members and subject to annual congressional appropriations, and the stipulation that future property transfers proceed only after Congress had been notified of them in advance. Language was also included to preclude the transfer of the canal itself before the year 2000 and to place the canal under U.S. military control in case foreign troops appeared in Panama. Formal transfer of the Canal Zone took place on October 1, when some 150,000 Panamanians poured into the Zone to begin a day of joyful celebration.

On December 16 the former shah of Iran, whose trip to the U.S. for medical treatment had sparked the holding of hostages in the U.S. embassy in Teheran, was admitted to Panama and took up residence on the resort island of Contadora. His presence in the country gave rise to demonstrations in which a number of people were injured. (*See* IRAN.) (ALMON R. WRIGHT)

PANAMA

Education. (1978) Primary, pupils 368,738, teachers 13,032; secondary, pupils 95,682, teachers 3,712; vocational, pupils 42,660, teachers 2,167; teacher training, students 849, teachers 73; higher, students 35,444, teaching staff 1,808.

Finance. Monetary unit: balboa, at par with the U.S. dollar, with a free rate (Sept. 17, 1979) of 2.15 balboas to £1 sterling. Gold, SDR's, and foreign exchange (June 1979) U.S. $194 million. Budget (1978 actual): revenue 436 million balboas; expenditure 511 million balboas. Gross national product (1977) 2,173,900,000 balboas. Cost of living (Panama City; 1975 = 100; April 1979) 119.8.

Foreign Trade. Imports (1977) 861.2 million balboas; exports (1978) 242.2 million balboas. Import sources: U.S. 31%; Ecuador 15%; Venezuela 8%; Saudi Arabia 7%; Japan 5%. Export destinations (1977): U.S. 45%; Canal Zone 10%; West Germany 8%; The Netherlands 5%. Main exports: bananas 29%; petroleum products 25%; shrimps 12%; sugar 8%.

Transport and Communications. Roads (1977) 7,885 km. Motor vehicles in use (1977): passenger 71,700; commercial 17,700. Railways (1977) *c.* 490 km. Air traffic (1977): 384 million passenger-km; freight 4.2 million net ton-km. Shipping (1978): merchant vessels 100 gross tons and over 3,640 (mostly owned by U.S. and other foreign interests); gross tonnage 20,748,679. Telephones (Jan. 1978) 156,700. Radio receivers (Dec. 1977) 280,000. Television receivers (Dec. 1977) 206,000.

Agriculture. Production (in 000; metric tons; 1978): rice *c.* 211; corn *c.* 83; sugar, raw value (1977) *c.* 182; mangoes *c.* 26; bananas 742; oranges 62; coffee *c.* 5; fish catch (1977) 228. Livestock (in 000; 1977): cattle 1,372; pigs 185; horses *c.* 164; chickens *c.* 4,300.

Industry. Production (in 000; metric tons; 1977): petroleum products *c.* 2,790; cement 331; manufactured gas (cu m; 1978) 1,200; electricity (kw-hr) *c.* 1,640,000.

Papua New Guinea

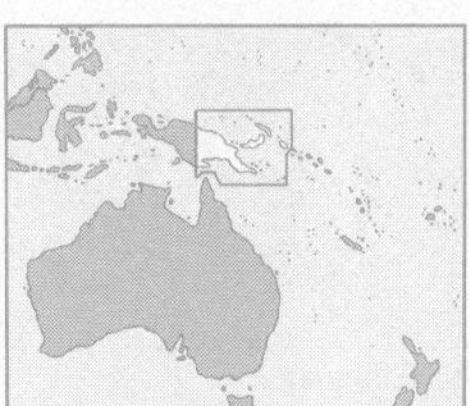

Papua New Guinea

Papua New Guinea is an independent parliamentary state and a member of the Commonwealth of Nations. It is situated in the southwest Pacific and comprises the eastern part of the island of New Guinea, the islands of the Bismarck, Trobriand, Woodlark, Louisiade, and D'Entrecasteaux groups, and parts of the Solomon Islands, including Bougainville. It is separated from Australia by the Torres Strait. Area: 462,840 sq km (178,704 sq mi). Pop. (1979 est.): 3,078,500. Cap. and largest city: Port Moresby (pop., 1979 est., 121,600). Language: English, Hiri or Police Motu (a Melanesian pidgin), and Pisin (also called Pidgin English or Neo-Melanesian) are official, although the latter is the most widely spoken. Religion (1966): Roman Catholic 31.2%; Lutheran 27.3%; indigenous 7%. Queen, Elizabeth II; governor-general in 1979, Sir

Palestine:
see Israel; Jordan

Panama Canal Zone:
see Dependent States; Panama

PAPUA NEW GUINEA

Education. (1978) Primary, pupils 268,136, teachers 8,-590; secondary, pupils 35,105, teachers 1,369; vocational, pupils 6,362, teachers 949; teacher training, students 2,046, teachers 127; higher, students 9,804, teaching staff 1,235.

Finance. Monetary unit: kina, with (Sept. 17, 1979) a free rate of 0.71 kina to U.S. $1 (1.53 kinas = £1 sterling). Gold, SDR's, and foreign exchange (June 1979) U.S. $457 million. Budget (1978 est.): revenue 483 million kinas; expenditure 476 million kinas.

Foreign Trade. (1978) Imports 568.7 million kinas; exports 551.2 million kinas. Import sources (1977): Australia *c.* 43%; Japan *c.* 17%; Singapore *c.* 10%. Export destinations (1977): Japan 25%; West Germany 19%; Australia 12%; U.S. 10%; U.K. 5%. Main exports: copper concentrates 40%; coffee 19%; cocoa 11%; coconut products 6%.

Transport. Roads (1977) 17,241 km. Motor vehicles in use (1976): passenger 17,700; commercial (including buses) 19,200. There are no railways. Shipping (1978): merchant vessels 100 gross tons and over 67; gross tonnage 16,718.

Agriculture. Production (in 000; metric tons; 1978): bananas *c.* 885; cassava (1977) *c.* 88; taro (1977) *c.* 230; yams (1977) *c.* 180; palm oil *c.* 80; cocoa 32; coffee *c.* 47; copra *c.* 132; tea *c.* 6; rubber *c.* 6; timber (cu m; 1977) 6,296. Livestock (in 000; 1977): cattle *c.* 161; pigs *c.* 1,184; goats *c.* 15; chickens *c.* 1,107.

Industry. Production (in 000; 1977): silver (troy oz) 1,-500; copper ore (metal content; metric tons) 182; gold (troy oz; 1978) *c.* 750; electricity (kw-hr; 1977–78) 1,145,-000.

Tore Lokoloko; prime minister, Michael T. Somare.

During 1979 Papua New Guinea experienced a series of strikes by trade unionists, including air traffic controllers, bus drivers, dockworkers, and copper miners. Noting that Papua New Guinea was a developing country and had to get its people to work, Prime Minister Michael Somare said he would not allow unions to run the country. He added that if Parliament decided there should be no trade unions in Papua New Guinea, he would be only too glad to support the move. Law and order constituted a major problem. Tribal warfare in the western highlands took an estimated 400 lives, and a state of emergency was proclaimed.

However, the government was strengthened in 1979 by the presence of John Kaputin as minister of national planning and development. Kaputin aimed to stabilize private-sector incomes and pursue an exchange rate policy that would maintain the purchasing power of the kina.

(A. R. G. GRIFFITHS)

Paraguay

Paraguay

A landlocked republic of South America, Paraguay is bounded by Brazil, Argentina, and Bolivia. Area: 406,752 sq km (157,048 sq mi). Pop. (1979 est.): 2,974,000. Cap. and largest city: Asunción (pop., 1977 est., 460,800). Language: Spanish (official), though Guaraní is understood by more than 90% of the population. Religion: Roman Catholic (official). President in 1979, Gen. Alfredo Stroessner.

Gen. Alfredo Stroessner's position in the Latin-American community became prominent when Paraguay alone supported Pres. Anastasio Somoza of Nicaragua at the meeting of the Organization of American States that demanded his resignation on June 23, 1979. Somoza, who was overthrown in July, later went to Paraguay. Acuerdo Nacional, an opposition front seeking a democratization process, was formed in February. It consisted of the Partido Liberal Radical Auténtico, the Febreristas, the Christian Democrats, and the Movimiento Popular Colorado.

Opposition to current economic policies also arose inside the ruling Colorado Party and the pro-government union association, the Confederación Paraguaya de Trabajadores. Two Asunción daily newspapers under the control of the Colorado Party, *Ultima Hora* and *La Tribuna*, were critical of the official policy and were closed by the government in June, reappearing early in August.

The country showed a high rate of economic growth (10%) in 1978; this was expected to be reduced in 1979 because of severe flooding of the Paraguay River early in the year and because of the increase in international oil prices. The inflation rate was expected to rise to 25%.

(MARTA BEKERMAN DE FAINBOIM)

PARAGUAY

Education. (1977) Primary, pupils 477,237, teachers 16,-869; secondary and vocational, pupils 92,437, teachers 8,-825; higher, students 20,032, teaching staff 1,846.

Finance. Monetary unit: guaraní, with (Sept. 17, 1979) a par value of 126 guaranís to U.S. $1 (free rate of 266 guaranís = £1 sterling). Gold, SDR's, and foreign exchange (June 1979) U.S. $564 million. Budget (1978 actual): revenue 34,716,000,000 guaranís; expenditure 27,892,000,000 guaranís. Gross national product (1977) 259 billion guaranís. Money supply (June 1979) 48,776,-000,000 guaranís. Cost of living (Asunción; 1975 = 100; June 1979) 158.2.

Foreign Trade. (1978) Imports 48,368,000,000 guaranís; exports 31,830,000,000 guaranís. Import sources: Brazil 20%; Argentina 15%; Algeria 11%; U.K. 10%; U.S. 9%; West Germany 8%; Japan 8%. Export destinations: West Germany 15%; Japan 13%; The Netherlands 10%; Argentina 9%; Brazil 8%; U.S. 7%; Switzerland 6%; U.K. 6%. Main exports: cotton 39%; soybeans 15%; meat 9%; timber 8%; vegetable oils 7%.

Transport and Communications. Roads (1978) *c.* 12,-000 km. Motor vehicles in use (1977): passenger 26,800; commercial 8,400. Railways: (1978) 498 km; traffic (1977) 23 million passenger-km, freight 17 million net ton-km. Navigable inland waterways (including Paraguay-Paraná River system; 1978) *c.* 3,000 km. Telephones (Jan. 1977) 41,600. Radio receivers (Dec. 1976) 180,000. Television receivers (Dec. 1976) 55,000.

Agriculture. Production (in 000; metric tons; 1978): corn *c.* 410; cassava (1977) *c.* 1,700; sweet potatoes (1977) *c.* 130; soybeans *c.* 300; dry beans *c.* 57; sugar, raw value (1977) 70; tomatoes *c.* 55; oranges *c.* 140; bananas *c.* 282; palm kernels *c.* 18; tobacco *c.* 40; cottonseed *c.* 160; cotton lint *c.* 81; beef and veal (1977) *c.* 119. Livestock (in 000; 1977): cattle *c.* 5,670; sheep *c.* 372; pigs *c.* 1,110; horses *c.* 328; chickens *c.* 9,500.

Industry. Production (in 000; metric tons; 1977): petroleum products *c.* 220; cement 200; cotton yarn 73; electricity (kw-hr) 626,300.

Peru

Peru

A republic on the west coast of South America, Peru is bounded by Ecuador, Colombia, Brazil, Bolivia, Chile, and the Pacific Ocean. Area: 1,285,-215 sq km (496,224 sq mi). Pop. (1979 est.): 17,291,000, including approximately 52% whites and mestizos and 46% Indians. Cap. and largest city: Lima (metro. area pop., 1978 est., 4,376,100). Language: Spanish and Quechua are official; Indians also speak Aymara. Religion: Roman Catholic. President of the military government in 1979, Francisco Morales Bermúdez.

In 1979 a series of strikes, many ending in violence, reflected popular dissatisfaction with the economic austerity measures adopted by the Peruvian military government to qualify for international loans. The government interpreted much of the labour turmoil as politically motivated, and it became more intense as the May 1980 scheduled date for Peru's first general election since the 1968 military takeover drew nearer. On February 2 Gen. Pedro Richter Prada became prime minister in a government shuffle giving more power to conservatives within the military.

Following several years of fiscal difficulties, the government in early January succeeded in rescheduling nearly $800 million in interest and amortization payments due to 283 foreign commercial banks in 1979–80. As part of an economic austerity package agreed on with its creditors, the government on January 3 decreed a 20% increase in the price of some foodstuffs and gasoline. Union federations called a general strike for January 9. Their demands included raises of at least $50 a month to offset a 1978 inflation rate of 75% (workers had been granted increases of $10 a month at the beginning of 1979). In response, the government declared a state of emergency on January 5, suspended constitutional guarantees, arrested several hundred labour and political leaders, and closed seven news magazines (three others were added later). Peru's Constituent Assembly, a 100-member body elected in 1978 to write a new constitution for the proposed civilian government, joined in denouncing the strike, which began on January 9 but failed after two days when most workers refused to join.

Wage increases of as much as 50% were demanded by workers at the Toquepala copper mine and Ilo copper smelter in a strike that began March 13. Workers at the Cuajone mine soon joined; and production amounting to about 75% of Peru's copper exports was suspended. The government declared such strikes illegal, imposed a state of emergency in the mining region, and jailed some union leaders. Most of the workers were back by the end of March, but not before Peru's fragile economy had been damaged. Although the January-imposed state of emergency expired in early March, leading magazines were still forbidden to publish. On March 19 five prominent journalists and publishers led a hunger strike, which ended several days later when the government agreed to meet them and subsequently allowed them to publish again.

Aeroperu, the country's national airline, went on strike in May. On June 4 nearly 50,000 teachers struck for salary increases; dozens were arrested during demonstrations in Lima, and most had gone back to work by early October. In July another government-imposed price increase brought a 24-hour general strike. Troops and riot police patrolled major cities and at least one person was killed in Iquitos. Once again, the government declared such strikes illegal.

Although the Constituent Assembly voted to disband in July when the military rejected portions of the constitution it had written, the dispute was resolved, and the government scheduled general elections for May 18, 1980. More than 20 political parties registered for the elections, but the likely outcome was substantially changed by the death in August of 84-year-old Víctor Raúl Haya de la Torre (*see* OBITUARIES), founder of the Alianza Popular Revolucionaria Americana (APRA).

Peru's shaky economic prospects were somewhat improved by the discovery, announced by the government on February 9, of a major new oil field that could raise the country's proven petroleum reserves by 18% to 559 million bbl. Even so, Petroperú, the state oil concern, joined most other nearly bankrupt government-run businesses in seeking to reschedule its substantial foreign debt. (KAREN DEYOUNG)

PERU

Education. (1977) Primary, pupils 3,019,624, teachers 75,491; secondary (1976), pupils 699,547, teachers 26,987; vocational (1976), pupils 190,559, teachers 7,568; higher (1976), students 190,635, teaching staff 12,113.

Finance. Monetary unit: sol, with (Sept. 17, 1979) a free rate of 234 soles to U.S. $1 (504 soles = £1 sterling). Gold, SDR's, and foreign exchange (June 1979) U.S. $575 million. Budget (1978 actual): revenue 263,743,000,000 soles; expenditure 346,383,000,000 soles. Gross national product (1978) 1,615,000,000,000 soles. Money supply (April 1979) 297 billion soles. Cost of living (Lima; 1975 = 100; April 1979) 437.8.

Foreign Trade. Imports (1977) 157,539,000,000 soles; exports (1978) 313,217,000,000 soles. Import sources: U.S. 29%; Ecuador 10%; Venezuela 9%; Japan 7%; West Germany 7%. Export destinations (1977): U.S. 30%; Japan 12%; Italy 5%. Main exports: copper 21%; fish meal 11%; coffee 9%; silver 7%; lead 6%; zinc 6%.

Transport and Communications. Roads (1976) 56,940 km. Motor vehicles in use (1977): passenger 300,400; commercial (including buses) 166,200. Railways (1976): 2,125 km; traffic 528 million passenger-km, freight (1977) 612 million net ton-km. Air traffic (1977): 1,353,000,000 passenger-km; freight 36 million net ton-km. Shipping (1978): merchant vessels 100 gross tons and over 686; gross tonnage 574,718. Telephones (Jan. 1978) 402,500. Radio receivers (Dec. 1976) 2,068,000. Television receivers (Dec. 1976) 600,000.

Agriculture. Production (in 000; metric tons; 1978): rice *c.* 400; corn *c.* 550; wheat *c.* 90; barley *c.* 175; potatoes *c.* 1,650; sweet potatoes (1977) *c.* 160; cassava (1977) *c.* 450; sugar, raw value 881; onions *c.* 158; oranges *c.* 150; lemons *c.* 80; coffee *c.* 66; cotton, lint *c.* 81; fish catch (1977) 2,530. Livestock (in 000; 1978): cattle 4,167; sheep *c.* 14,000; pigs 2,030; goats *c.* 2,070; horses (1977) *c.* 643; poultry *c.* 37,000.

Industry. Production (in 000; metric tons; 1977): cement 1,970; crude oil (1978) 7,709; natural gas (cu m) *c.* 520,000; iron ore (metal content) 4,021; pig iron 244; crude steel 379; copper 150; lead 79; zinc 67; tungsten concentrates (oxide content) 0.7; gold (troy oz) 96; silver (troy oz) 30,100; fish meal 497; petroleum products *c.* 5,780; electricity (kw-hr) 8,557,000.

Philately and Numismatics

Stamps. Continuing inflation and the pressure of investment buying by nonphilatelists during 1979 were reflected in the steadily rising prices for rare stamps and items of postal history. An example was the $100,000 paid at Sotheby Parke Bernet in New York City in November 1978 for a mint single of the U.S. 24-cent airmail stamp of 1918 with inverted centre. A new record price of $145,000 for

Paper and Pulp: see Industrial Review

Parachuting: see Aerial Sports

Penology: see Prisons and Penology

Pentecostal Churches: see Religion

Petroleum: see Energy

Pharmaceutical Industry: see Industrial Review

An all-time record price of $430,000 was paid for a doubloon minted in 1787 by New York goldsmith Ephraim Brasher.

WIDE WORLD

a U.S. cover was set at the Siegel Gallery in New York in April 1979.

Stanley Gibbons International Ltd., the only publicly owned philatelic company, was acquired by Letraset International Ltd. at a valuation of £18.5 million and continued its expansion by taking over the Swedish firm of Frimärkshuset AB for £387,500. A major purchase by Gibbons was the Marc Haas collection of U.S. postal history for more than $10 million, thought to be the biggest single philatelic purchase ever made. A new auction record for a one-country collection was achieved by Harmers, whose London and New York salesrooms together realized £531,089 for the Sir Henry Tucker collection of Bermuda. The claim of Edgar Mohrmann of Hamburg, West Germany, to a world record auction result for a single stamp (the Swedish 1855 three-skilling error of colour) was disputed by two New York auctioneers, who suggested that the published figure of DM 1 million was the "knockdown" price and that no sale actually took place.

There were two major omnibus issues in 1979: the International Year of the Child and the centenary year of the death of Sir Rowland Hill, a British pioneer in postal reform. The International Philatelic Federation's major exhibition was Philaserdica 79, held at Sofia, Bulg. The three main awards were: Grand Prix d'Honneur, Fritz Heimbüchler (West Germany) for Romania 1822–72; Grand Prix National, Vassil Karaivanov (Bulg.) for classic Bulgaria; and Grand Prix International, Enrique M. de Bustamente (Spain) for classic Peru. At the Harrogate congress of the British Philatelic Federation, new signatories to the Roll of Distinguished Philatelists were Hans Hunziker (Switz.), John H. Levett (U.K.), James J. Matejka, Jr. (U.S.), and John L. Messenger (U.K.). The Philatelic Congress Medal was awarded to John C. W. Field of Sutton Coldfield, England. The Lichtenstein Medal of the Collectors Club of New York went to Enzo Diena (Italy).

On September 23 the U.S. released a 15-cent John Paul Jones commemorative stamp, the first U.S. postage stamp not printed by the government. In

Riders saddled up for the 1979 Pony Express Race from St. Joseph, Missouri, to Sacramento, California, the original route of the Pony Express. The race was sponsored by the British Post Office to commemorate the invention of the adhesive postage stamp.

UPI

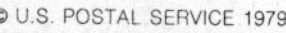

© U.S. POSTAL SERVICE 1979

A commemorative stamp to mark the International Year of the Child was issued by the U.S. Postal Service in February.

August the Kenny International Corp. of New York pleaded guilty in a U.S. federal court to using $337,000 of the funds of its subsidiary, the Cook Islands Development Corp., to promote the electoral aims of then prime minister Sir Albert Henry. The funds came from the sale of Cook Islands stamps to philatelists and were earmarked for the Cook Islands government. Kenny International was fined $50,000 for violating the U.S. Foreign Corrupt Practices Act, and Finbar Kenny agreed to reimburse the Cook Islands government and to plead guilty to one charge of fraud before the Cook Islands courts. (KENNETH F. CHAPMAN)

Coins. The small-size, nonsilver U.S. dollar coin, popularly known as the Susan B. Anthony dollar, was released by commercial banks on July 2, 1979. Intended to replace the one-dollar bill and effect savings amounting to millions of dollars annually, the new coin was not well accepted by the public. The main objections were that it too closely resembled the popular quarter dollar and was unattractive.

The U.S. Mint announced that it expected to produce one-ounce and half-ounce gold medallions in 1980 for sale to the public. Of interest to collectors was the Mint's intention to place a "P" mint mark on the dimes, quarters, and half dollars produced by the Philadelphia Mint in 1980. The mark appeared on all Susan B. Anthony dollars struck there.

The market for collector coins and related items was influenced by the speculative demand for gold and silver. An 1895 (Philadelphia Mint) silver dollar that was auctioned in mid-1978 for $10,750 brought $16,500 just a year later, while a 1902 special collector set of six U.S. coins, one cent to $1, that sold for $2,100 in the same 1978 sale went for $9,000. An all-time record price for an American coin at public auction was established with the sale of a Brasher doubloon for $430,000. The privately minted coin was made in 1787 by New York goldsmith Ephraim Brasher.

Numismatists who had formed good libraries relating to the hobby were finding some of their books much appreciated in value. An 1858 book on contemporary banknote production that brought $26 at auction 25 years earlier was sold to a book dealer for $1,000 in 1979.

In spite of efforts to detect and expose false collector coins, the unwary continued to be duped. Counterfeiting was most prevalent in the gold coin series, but even less expensive coins were not exempt. During 1979 the certification service of the American Numismatic Association discovered excellent counterfeits of relatively common 1867 and 1868 U.S. Indian head cents.

The terminal illness of the actor John Wayne (*see* OBITUARIES) prompted the U.S. Congress to authorize a president's gold medal in his honour. Within three months of the medal's announcement, the Mint had received 60,000 orders, equally divided between the 3-in and the 1$\frac{5}{16}$-in pieces, and over 5,000 inquiries for duplicates of the 3-in gold presentation piece. Among special Israeli state medals was one noting the centenary of Albert Einstein's birth, another "The Ark and the Covenant" based on the biblical narrative of Noah's Ark, and one observing the 50th anniversary of the Jerusalem Rotary Club.

Representative new coins included: Canada, 1979, silver dollar depicting the first voyage by commercial ship on the Great Lakes, a 100-dollar International Year of the Child gold coin, and a one-ounce gold bullion piece; Czechoslovakia, 1978, two silver commemorative coins; Egypt, several new designs, one in memory of singer Um Kalthoum who died in 1975; Isle of Man, 1979, several coins, including a crown observing the tercentenary of the island's coinage; Jamaica, 1979, a silver 10-dollar coin depicting a giant native butterfly; Macau, 1978 silver 100- and gold 500-pataca coins depicting a modern racing car, and 1979 silver 100- and gold 500-pataca coins celebrating the year of the goat; Soviet Union, several new coins added to the sets of 28 silver, 6 gold, and 5 platinum coins being issued in observance of the 1980 Olympic Games to be held in Moscow.

(GLENN B. SMEDLEY)

[452.D.2.b; 725.B.4.g]

Philippines

Situated in the western Pacific Ocean off the southeast coast of Asia, the Republic of the Philippines consists of an archipelago of about 7,100 islands. Area: 300,000 sq km (115,800 sq mi). Pop. (1979 est.): 47,719,400. Cap. and largest city: Manila (pop., metro. area, 1979 est., 5,900,600). Language: Pilipino (based on Tagalog), English, Spanish, and many dialects. Religion (1970): Roman Catholic 85%; Muslim 4.3%; Aglipayan 3.9%; Protestant 3.1%; others 2.4%. President and premier in 1979, Ferdinand E. Marcos.

The eighth year of martial law rule by Pres. Ferdinand E. Marcos began Sept. 23, 1979, with growing economic, political, and security problems facing the Philippines. Marcos continued to postpone the ending of martial law and the holding of national elections. He said on September 21 that he believed martial law should not be lifted for the next 18 months because "we are facing danger" from economic problems and from two separate guerrilla wars, one with Muslim separatists and the other against Communists.

The rate of inflation was more than 20%, and there was labour unrest over the failure to receive officially decreed pay raises from businesses that said they could not afford them. Malnutrition and other signs of poverty were reported from many areas. Economic growth slowed from the 5.8% rate of 1978 as foreign investment declined and borrowing abroad became more difficult. The balance of payments deficit rose sharply because of the increased cost of oil and other imports, while export prices were generally stagnant.

Economic problems as well as political opposition to Marcos led to demonstrations in defiance of a ban on them. Marcos conceded that there were problems. He said that he was disappointed by the "return to the same cynicism that started the proclamation of martial law" in 1972, by "the same corruption, the same dishonesty, and the same self-centred selfishness." The most serious problem under martial law, Marcos said, was complacency of those who had forgotten the reasons he had imposed it.

The crime rate rose toward the high level of 1972, and the guns that Marcos had tried to restrict then were again commonplace. Complaints of abuses of power by the armed forces were numerous. Defense Minister Juan Ponce Enrile said that he was trying to stop them, noting also that military morale was low.

Military abuses prompted complaints of human rights violations, although Marcos charged the Muslims and Communists with "posing in uniforms of the military" to commit crimes. Some clergymen of the Roman Catholic Church and some

PHILIPPINES

Education. Primary (1977–78), pupils 7,861,641, teachers 270,764; secondary (1978–79), pupils 2,696,460; vocational, pupils 182,196; secondary and vocational, teachers (1977–78) 82,191; higher, students 946,860, teaching staff 26,003.

Finance. Monetary unit: peso, with (Sept. 17, 1979) a free rate of 7.35 pesos to U.S. $1 (15.81 pesos = £1 sterling). Gold, SDR's, and foreign exchange (June 1979) U.S. $2,067,000,000. Budget (1978 actual): revenue 30,146,000,000 pesos; expenditure 32,602,000,000 pesos. Gross national product (1978) 170.9 billion pesos. Money supply (June 1979) 16,502,000,000 pesos. Cost of living (1975 = 100; June 1979) 145.8.

Foreign Trade. (1978) Imports 37,885,000,000 pesos; exports 24,567,000,000 pesos. Import sources: Japan 27%; U.S. 21%; Saudi Arabia 6%. Export destinations: U.S. 33%; Japan 24%; The Netherlands 8%. Main exports: coconut oil 18%; metal ores 14%; clothing 10%; fruit and vegetables 7%; electrical equipment 7%; timber 7%; sugar 6%.

Transport and Communications. Roads (1977) 119,220 km. Motor vehicles in use (1977): passenger 440,500; commercial (including buses) 327,100. Railways: (1976) 1,069 km; traffic (1977) 692 million passenger-km, freight 49 million net ton-km. Air traffic (1978): 4,430,000,000 passenger-km; freight 126.6 million net ton-km. Shipping (1978): merchant vessels 100 gross tons and over 577; gross tonnage 1,264,995. Telephones (Jan. 1978) 567,300. Radio receivers (Dec. 1976) 1,875,000. Television receivers (Dec. 1976) 800,000.

Agriculture. Production (in 000; metric tons; 1978): rice 6,907; corn 3,333; sweet potatoes (1977) *c.* 750; cassava (1977) *c.* 679; sugar, raw value *c.* 2,400; bananas *c.* 2,435; pineapples *c.* 500; copra *c.* 2,600; coffee *c.* 82; tobacco *c.* 52; rubber *c.* 154; pork *c.* 387; fish catch (1977) 1,511; timber (cu m; 1977) 34,188. Livestock (in 000; March 1978): cattle 1,820; buffalo *c.* 5,300; pigs *c.* 9,700; goats *c.* 1,410; horses *c.* 330; chickens 58,892.

Industry. Production (in 000; metric tons; 1977): coal 285; chrome ore (oxide content) 162; copper ore (metal content) 273; gold (troy oz) 558; silver (troy oz) 1,621; cement 4,112; petroleum products *c.* 9,210; sulfuric acid 257; cotton yarn 31; electricity (kw-hr) *c.* 15,800,000.

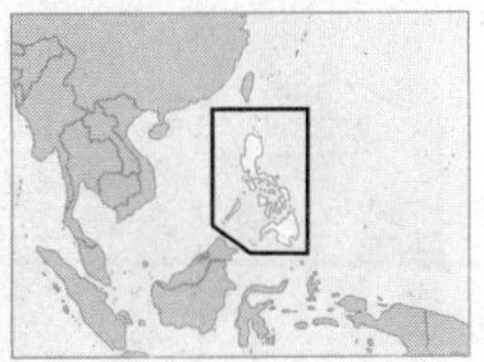

Philippines

political leaders from before the 1972 declaration of martial law led opposition to the violations, corruption, and other abuses. The head of the Roman Catholic Church in the Philippines, Jaime Cardinal Sin, emerged as the main public opponent of Marcos. Sin warned on September 4 of a danger of civil war, but he said that it could be averted if Marcos held free, orderly, and peaceful national elections. Marcos contended that talk of any broader civil war than the regionally limited Muslim and Communist rebellions was ridiculous, "a figment of the imagination."

In the first significant Cabinet reshuffle since the beginning of martial law, Marcos on July 23 appointed more technocrats to his government. He created a new Commission on Islamic Affairs for liaison between the Philippines and two semiautonomous regional governments established for Muslim areas in Mindanao and the Sulu Archipelago. Some Muslims, however, said they were no longer just seeking autonomy within the nation but now wanted independence.

The second guerrilla war, against the Maoist New People's Army, also continued. The Communists slowly extended their power in widely scattered areas, including north-central Luzon Island and Samar Island.

After development work carried on since 1962, the first power from natural underground steam was obtained January 11 at Tiwi in southern Luzon. The geothermal power potential of the country was estimated at 200,000 Mw in 25 separate fields. (HENRY S. BRADSHER)

Photography

As the decade of the 1970s closed, the mark of electronic technology on still photography was strikingly evident. Both amateur and advanced professional cameras—in fact, virtually all but the least expensive instant and 110 styles—featured some kind of microelectronic automation of functions that had been manually performed at the beginning of the decade. Several major retrospectives reaffirmed the vitality of photography as a means of creative expression, as did continuing emphasis on the photograph in many established and newly launched periodicals.

This photograph of a man fleeing from authorities after holding his family hostage was part of a series that won a Pulitzer Prize for spot news photography for Thomas J. Kelly III of the *Pottstown* (Pa.) *Mercury*.

WIDE WORLD

Photo Equipment. A notable example of the attempt by manufacturers to provide utmost user convenience in a compact format at relatively low cost was the Canon AF-35M, introduced late in 1979. A nonreflex 35-mm camera small enough to fit into a jacket pocket, it included focusing from three feet to infinity that was handled automatically by a new Canon-developed system utilizing an infrared-emitting diode. With this system, distance was measured by electronically evaluating the intensity of infrared light reflected back to a built-in sensor. In addition, the AF-35M provided programmed automatic exposures from *f*/2.8 at 1/8 sec to *f*/16 at 1/500 sec, a built-in "pop-up" electronic flash, and a built-in motor for automatic film advance and rewinding.

Other manufacturers including Konica, Fuji, and Chinon utilized the previously introduced Honeywell Visitronic autofocus system, which analyzed differences in subject contrast to gauge distance, in compact 35-mm cameras that won popular acceptance. Polaroid provided a number of its cameras with its Sonar OneStep autofocusing device, which utilized ultrasonic "chirps" much like a flying bat. As yet only in prototype stages were more precise, sophisticated autofocus systems designed for eventual use with advanced single-lens-reflex (SLR) cameras.

The category of medium-to-low-priced automatic-exposure 35-mm SLR's experienced a great boom and intense competition during 1979. Manufacturers not already producing such models rushed to get them on the market, and those already active in this endeavour expanded their lines. A common feature of most of these new models, designed for amateur photographers just entering the 35-mm SLR field, was an increased use of specialized plastics for some components, with resulting advantages of lighter weight and lower cost.

Of particular interest was the Nikon EM, from a company whose reputation was based on advanced amateur and professional 35-mm equipment. An ultracompact and lightweight SLR, it provided aperture-priority exposure automation (user sets the aperture; shutter speed is chosen electronically) and emphasized simplicity of operation. An electronically governed metal-bladed shutter provided stepless speeds from 1 to 1/1000 sec, but there was no external shutter-speed control except B and a single "M90" setting that allowed 1/90-sec exposure. Automatic devices to prevent user mistakes included audible and visual warning signals if the selected aperture required the shutter speed to drop below 1/30 sec or overshoot the scale above 1/1000 sec. Nikon supplied a new line of lightweight, compact, economical Nikon Series E lenses for the EM including a 50-mm *f*/1.8, a 35-mm *f*/2.5, and a 100-mm *f*/2.8.

Lenses of all kinds, but particularly zooms and telephoto designs for 35-mm SLR's, continued to proliferate. Among long-range zooms in the longer ranges of focal length the trend was toward those providing continuous operation into the extreme close-focusing range without the need to shift manually into a so-called macro mode. Canon introduced a new line of more compact, lighter weight FD lenses with a redesigned bayonet mount that offered quicker, easier interchangeability. Fuji, the last Japanese manufacturer of 35-mm cameras to utilize a screw-mount lens, introduced its own Fujica-X bayonet mount.

Most of the new SLR's introduced during the year were available with an accessory motor autowinder and a matching electronic flash unit that provided automatic flash exposure control through the camera's built-in metering system.

After a promising start sales of instant films and cameras lagged during 1979, with Polaroid and Kodak vying for shares of the market. Konishiroku and Fuji in Japan and Agfa in West Germany, all of which had instant systems of their own under development, chose not to enter the market in 1979. Polaroid demonstrated an improved SX-70 "time zero" colour film, which developed in one minute rather than the approximately four minutes required by former material. As the year ended, however, it was not yet available on the market in quantity. Despite the brilliant technology involved, Polaroid's unique Polavision system for "instant" colour movies proved to be a marketing disaster, and the company announced that it was phasing out the product.

The rising cost of silver intensified concern for developing practical nonsilver imaging techniques, and there was much speculation during 1979 about the feasibility of an all-electronic still camera using a CCD (charge-coupled device) array rather than conventional film to record the image. Such a device was demonstrated by Fairchild Camera & Instrument Corp. in the U.S. but remained in the early developmental stage. Cost reduction and improvement of image quality would be needed before the technique could become practical for all but highly specialized applications. Nevertheless, a crew for *National Geographic* magazine produced remarkable still images in colour using a CCD-equipped video camera while photographing the seafloor off the Galápagos Islands.

Cultural Trends. In terms of photographic books and exhibitions, 1979 in many ways was a year of retrospectives, led in the U.S. by homage to western landscape photographer Ansel Adams. Tributes to Adams included a cover story in *Time*, a major exhibition at New York City's Museum of Modern Art, and publication of a $75 book whose quality of reproduction did justice to the virtuoso printing of Adams. A tribute on another level was the sale at auction of "Moonrise, Hernandez, New Mexico," perhaps the most popular Adams image, for $12,000. Among other photographers honoured by retrospectives and books during the year were Henri Cartier-Bresson and Philippe Halsman. The latter, famed for his "psychological" portraiture, 101 *Life* covers, and his images of celebrities jumping, died shortly after completing work on his exhibition (*see* OBITUARIES). New work was shown by another master of portraiture, Arnold Newman. His "Great British" exhibit portrayed 50 notable Britons in his distinctive "environmental" style, which often incorporates portions of the surroundings as symbolic and graphic elements of the picture.

The International Center of Photography in New York City, founded by Cornell Capa, celebrated its fifth anniversary with an ambitious program of exhibitions, courses, workshops, and seminars. One of its major activities during the year was the organization of a summer-long program of photography, in cooperation with UNESCO, for the city of Venice. During Venezia '79—la Photografia, as the festival was called, 25 exhibitions were displayed in various museums and galleries.

After a promising start as a twice-monthly picture newsmagazine early in 1979, the reborn *Look* foundered and ceased publication. The new monthly *Life*, however, which emphasized photographic essays rather than fast-breaking news events, established a comfortable, if unexciting, position for itself among the magazine-buying public. A U.S. edition of the highly successful West German magazine *Geo* made lavish use of excellent colour photography in its attempt to compete with the huge *National Geographic*. New magazines like *Omni*, which blended science fiction with nonfictional articles oriented to the "space age," used photographs extensively. Despite the dominance of television, the still picture on the printed page continued to be in demand.

In 1979 the Pulitzer Prize for spot news photography went to Thomas J. Kelly III of the *Pottstown* (Pa.) *Mercury* and for feature photography to the staff photographers of the *Boston Herald-American*. At the Pictures of the Year awards, co-sponsored by the National Press Photographers Association and the University of Missouri School of Journalism, Chris Johns of the *Topeka* (Kansas) *Capital-Journal* was chosen as Newspaper Photographer of the Year and *National Geographic*'s James Sugar as Magazine Photographer of the Year.

(ARTHUR GOLDSMITH)

See also Motion Pictures.
[628.D; 735.G.1]

Physics

Magnetism in the Health Sciences. The effects of magnetism have found application for some thousands of years. For example, the lodestone swinging as a compass in the Earth's magnetic field was one of the earliest scientific instruments. The Earth's field, however, has always been considered to be weak, and the possibilities of using even weaker magnetic fields have been virtually ignored. In the past two decades exploitation of the phenomenon of superconductivity—the loss of electrical resistance in materials at very low temperatures—has resulted in techniques and devices for detecting and measuring magnetic fields many orders of magnitude weaker than the Earth's field. This advance has opened up a whole new vista of science, and the applications to medicine in particular are both exciting and challenging.

Weak magnetic fields are known to emanate from the human body. They are produced by two separate mechanisms: by metal contaminants, mainly in the lungs and digestive system, and by electrical body currents. Magnetic fields of the former kind are generally about a million times weaker than the Earth's field, whereas those originating from the traveling signals of nerve cells are even more feeble, some hundred million times less than the Earth's field at their strongest.

Measurement of these very weak fields first requires cancellation of the Earth's field, followed by elimination of background fields generated by, for example, metal objects in the laboratory or passing urban traffic. These sources of magnetic noise can produce fields as large as one-hundredth or one-thousandth of the Earth's field, much stronger than the fields to be detected. Two techniques have been developed for canceling such magnetic interference in the locality of the patient under observation. The first involves use of a room shielded with five separate metal walls to prevent penetration of fluctuating fields, after which any steady magnetic field still present can be balanced out. The second, a much cheaper and more convenient approach, is to use multiple superconducting pick-up loops, rather than a single loop, to detect the magnetic field. These loops (called SQUID's, for superconducting quantum interference devices) are wound in such a way and are fixed sufficiently close to each other that fields from distant sources induce equal but opposite signals, which cancel out; yet they are sufficiently separated that localized body fields induce unequal signals, which provide information concerning the location, strength, and fluctuation of the local field.

Physicist David Blair of the University of Western Australia examines vacuum chamber constructed to house an extremely sensitive gravitational wave antenna. Once fabricated, the antenna—a large bar of the rare element niobium—will join existing detectors in the search for gravitational field vibrations believed to be produced during stellar explosions and other violent cosmic events.

LONDON DAILY EXPRESS/PICTORIAL PARADE

Detection of the presence of magnetic particles has been under study for several years by David Cohen and co-workers at the Massachusetts Institute of Technology National Magnet Laboratory. As an example of the sensitivity of their shielded-room approach, the static magnetic fields produced by particles of metal in the stomach resulting from eating canned food were readily detected. Even more revealing were measurements reported by Cohen's group in May on the long-term expulsion of contaminants from the lungs. Twelve subjects breathed in a small quantity of magnetite dust (a magnetic form of iron oxide), which settled in the lungs and produced a measurable external magnetic field. The decay of this field was studied for a year, and the field strength at a particular time was used to deduce the fraction of particles remaining in the lungs. It was found that after a year the nine nonsmokers in the group had eliminated about 90% of the particles, whereas the three heavy smokers still had more than 50% present in the lungs. Obviously the sample tested was very small, yet the results indicated strongly that smoking impairs the ability of the lungs to remove foreign bodies and offered a reason why heavy smokers are more susceptible to a wide range of carcinogenic particles in the environment.

The ability to detect the magnetic fields produced by nerve currents in the body could be even more useful in the future. For example, Samuel Williamson and co-workers at New York University detected the magnetic fields that originate in the eye, muscles, heart, and brain. It was possible, for example, to differentiate between healthy and faulty heart operation by a study of the magnitude and variation of the magnetic field produced.

Perhaps the most promising development was the ability to study the electrical activity of the brain using a probe totally external to the body. In the late 1970s the only comparable technique was electroencephalography (EEG), which measures electrical skin potentials in the scalp resulting from underlying electric currents. Studies of the brain using EEG are very imprecise because the high electrical resistivity of the skull (80 times that of the brain itself) smears out the effects being studied. However, with magnetoencephalography (MEG), as the new technique was called, measurement was claimed to be much more precise.

Experiments in the past on patients undergoing brain surgery had revealed that sensory information from one side of the body is received on the opposite side of the brain. For example, a small electric shock to a specific finger of the right hand produces a detectable electric current within a particular, well-defined area on the left hemisphere of the brain. Williamson's group applied similar stimulation to human test subjects while they were being probed nonsurgically using MEG. They detected the magnetic field produced by brain currents and determined that its spatial distribution corresponded to the area of the brain indicated by the earlier electrical measurements. In addition, the magnetic field response pattern shifted by two centimetres when the stimulus was moved from the little finger to the thumb. Such resolution

Continued on page 575

SPECIAL REPORT

THE MAN EINSTEIN

by Ernst Gabor Straus

March 14, 1979, marked the 100th anniversary of the birth of Albert Einstein, an event that was celebrated all over the world. His ideas profoundly changed and deepened mankind's basic concepts of space, time, matter, energy, and the laws that describe the physical world. Since verification of the general theory of relativity by observations during the solar eclipse of 1919, not only his fellow scientists but the general public as well had come to regard him as the embodiment of scientific greatness.

He is probably the only scientist—and one of very few people—whose face is familiar to virtually everyone. On one occasion a letter whose only address was a pencil sketch of Einstein's face was promptly delivered to him by the post office. Einstein himself was bewildered by the adulation and interest of people who had only a vague inkling of his work. But the public was right in choosing this man of striking appearance with the deep and serious eyes, the kindly and often mischievous smile, and the unconventional hair and clothing. For it chose a man who not only made one of the greatest advances in human thought but also unceasingly and uncompromisingly pursued truth wherever it led, in human affairs as well as in science.

The Special Theory. Einstein felt that he had the basis for his special theory of relativity when at the age of 16 he asked himself: "What does a man see when he rides on a light wave?" This line of thinking was typical of Einstein's "thought experiments," which guided his intuition—he called it his nose—in his search for the correct concepts and laws of physics. In this case the problem was a conflict with Newton's law of inertia, which states that as far as the laws of mechanics are concerned there is no such thing as absolute motion; that is, a physicist in a laboratory cut off from contact with the outside universe has no way of detecting whether he is in motion or at rest. On the other hand, it is reasonable to assume that a person riding the crest of a wave, light waves included, does not perceive the wave oscillations that would be apparent to another person who is not riding the wave crest. For this latter situation motion does not appear relative. Einstein's solution consisted in elevating Newton's law of inertia to a fundamental principle of physics, the principle of relativity, valid not only in mechanics but in all of physics. Pursued to its logical implications it showed that familiar—and seemingly unassailable—concepts like distance, time, mass, and simultaneity were not absolutes but depended on the relative speed of the observer. By contrast, the speed of light assumed an absolute role as the "speed limit of the universe."

The most famous and fateful consequence of the special theory of relativity is the equation $E=mc^2$; *i.e.*, energy equals mass multiplied by the square of the velocity of light. This relation shows that mass is a form of energy and that, in view of the magnitude of the velocity of light, there is enormous energy stored in even a small amount of matter. This equation forms the basis for the explanation not only of the source of energy of the Sun and other stars but also of atomic energy and the atomic bomb. Thus the search for a deeper understanding of the nature of space, time, and matter put vast powers for good or ill into human hands and indirectly led within 40 years to the devastation of Hiroshima and Nagasaki.

Einstein's connection with those events was not purely scientific. In 1939, alarmed by reports that Nazi Germany was working on atomic weapons, he wrote to U.S. Pres. Franklin D. Roosevelt, alerting him to the possibility of such weapons. His reaction to their use by the U.S. in 1945 was that, had he known how little progress Germany had made toward an atomic bomb, he would never have written that letter. He was very active, both alone and through organizations, warning of the dangers of the proliferation of atomic arms and urging the nations of the world to establish a supranational authority for their control.

Gravity and Acceleration. Almost immediately after its conception Einstein perceived an unsatisfactory feature in his special theory of relativity, a problem that had already concerned Newton. While it explained in a satisfactory manner how the laws of nature are independent of the uniform motion of the observer (motion of constant direction and speed), it did not deal in a satisfactory way with accelerated motion. Another thought experiment led him to his successful ten-year search, the "elevator experiment." A man in a closed elevator suddenly finds himself and all objects floating about weightlessly. There are two possible explanations: he has been shot into orbit and is free of the Earth's gravity, or someone has cut the cables putting him and the elevator in free-fall.

Ernst Gabor Straus, a friend of and former assistant to Einstein, is professor of mathematics at the University of California at Los Angeles.

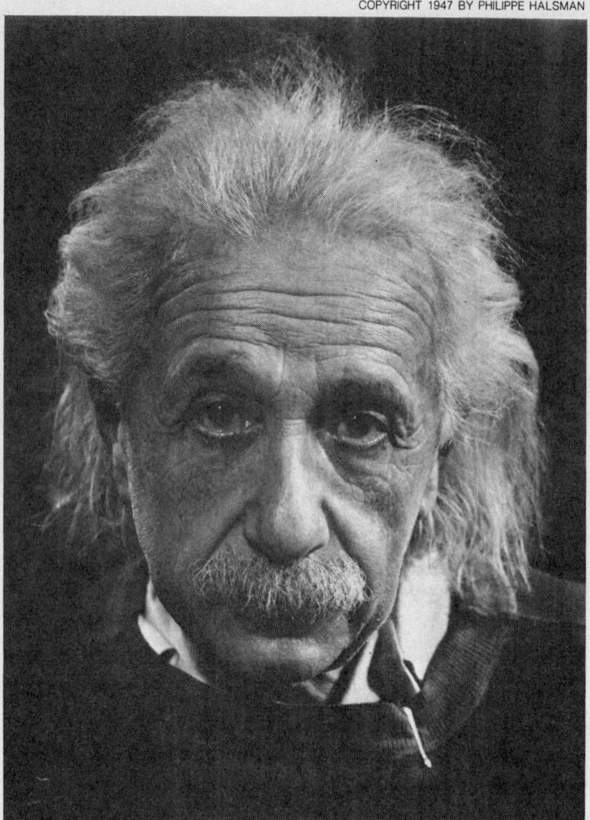

"Einstein's spirit of humanity and opposition to all imposed authority made him a convinced pacifist and an outspoken opponent of militarism . . ."

In the course of his investigations Einstein went to his mathematician friend Marcel Grossmann and asked him whether there was a mathematical formalism suitable for the study of such accelerated frameworks. Grossmann told him that the German mathematician Bernhard Riemann had indeed developed such a geometry more than 50 years earlier, but that the mathematical complexity made the theory unsuitable for physical application. Einstein asked only if there were any alternative theories; when the answer was "no," he proceeded to build the general theory of relativity on the foundations of Riemannian geometry.

This crowning achievement of Einstein's work recognized the identity between the law of gravity and the law of inertia and extended the principle of relativity to motions of every kind. In the realm of low energy densities, such as the solar system, deviations from Newton's laws are slight and difficult to detect, but the theory gave a natural explanation for the deviation of the precession of the orbit of Mercury from the value predicted from Newtonian physics and accurately predicted the gravitational bending of starlight by the mass of the Sun. It formed the foundation of consistent models for cosmology, accounting for the expansion of the universe that had been observed by means of the red shift of light from distant galaxies and other remote objects. In recent years new cosmic observations have supported many predictions of Einstein's cosmology. Such currently active topics as the "big bang" theory of cosmic creation, black holes, and gravitational waves have their origin in the general theory of relativity.

Philosopher and Humanitarian. Einstein's search was always for the ultimate laws of the universe, and he believed that the criterion for the correct concepts and laws was essentially an esthetic one. He called it "logical simplicity." He would say: "This is so beautiful, God would not have passed it up" or "For a musical man this is convincing."

The years from 1916 to his death in 1955 were devoted to the search for a "unified field theory," one that would weld the forces of gravity and electromagnetism into an organic whole and would in the process explain the observed quantization of matter and energy into certain discrete magnitudes. Unable to accept the probabilistic foundations of quantum theory that dominated the work of his contemporaries, he felt that "God does not play dice." His own attempts were based on various geometric models in the spirit of the Riemannian model that had served so well. Although these models have not had the conspicuous success of the general theory of relativity, there is an active resurgence of interest in geometric models in current attempts to unify the fundamental forces of nature and in other fields of research.

Einstein's spirit of humanity and opposition to all imposed authority made him a convinced pacifist and an outspoken opponent of militarism in World War I. His hero in political life was Indian leader Mahatma Gandhi, whose inspired use and advocacy of nonviolence he admired. He abandoned pacifism in the face of the horrors of Nazism but returned to the advocacy of supranational authority and national disarmament after World War II. He supported Socialist and Zionist causes and was among the founders and early supporters of the Hebrew University of Jerusalem.

The one pleasure he derived from his great fame was the ability it gave him to help others. He enabled many hundreds of people to escape Nazi and other persecution. He never hesitated to write letters, finding employment and support for the many who were in need of his help.

He never lost his enthusiasm for his great search, and he was blessed with the ability to work until his last day. Among his final written words appeared the statement: "What I seek to accomplish is simply to serve with my feeble capacity truth and justice at the risk of pleasing no one."

Continued from page 572
was impossible to achieve by conventional electrical detection external to the skull.

Lasers. Although the laser has become a very versatile and widely used piece of equipment, one of its major drawbacks is that any given type operates within very narrow ranges of frequency. The dye laser, an exception, is tunable over a range that is restricted only by the absorption band of the dye, but it does not give the power output or the efficiency required in many applications.

Collaborative research at Columbia University in New York City and the Naval Research Laboratory in Washington, D.C., recently led to the development of a laser with high power, tunability, and possible high efficiency. Rather than using electron transitions between atomic or molecular energy levels, the new laser uses free electrons moving in a magnetic field that varies in intensity along the axis of the magnetic coil. During early development its output was in the far-infrared at a wavelength of 400 micrometres (millionths of a metre). Emission, however, could be changed by varying either the energy of the electrons, which are provided by a particle accelerator, or the period of the undulating magnetic field. A research group at Stanford University, which was pursuing similar ideals, reported the development of a free-electron laser at a wavelength of about three micrometres, in the near-infrared.

High-Energy Physics. In the complicated world of high-energy physics the elementary building blocks of neutrons, protons, and certain other formerly "fundamental" particles were thought to be quarks. Quarks have the mystifying properties of carrying either $\pm \frac{1}{3}$ or $\pm \frac{2}{3}$ of the charge on the electron and probably of being unable to exist independently. This latter characteristic was making the task of demonstrating their presence very difficult.

Among the more recent bits of evidence in support of the quark concept were the results of two experiments at the German Electron Synchrotron (DESY) in Hamburg, West Germany. Both experiments, which observed the creation of new particles from colliding beams of electrons and positrons, reaffirmed the existence of the upsilon meson and of one of its excited (higher energy) states. These two particles, first detected in 1977 in proton-nuclei collision experiments at the Fermi National Accelerator Laboratory in the U.S., were held by quark theory to consist of a quark and its antimatter counterpart, an antiquark, both of which carry a distinguishing quantum property, or "flavour," variously called beauty or bottom. Augmenting these results, a collaboration of scientists working at the European Organization for Nuclear Research (CERN) in Geneva reported evidence in mid-1979 supporting the predicted existence of a meson composed of two quarks—but of which only one carries the flavour of beauty. The experiment involved collision of negative pi mesons with metal nuclei; confirmation awaited searches in other types of experiment, most likely the colliding-beam variety.

Another aspect of quark theory supposes quarks to be held together in elementary particles by means of a force arising from the rapid exchange of yet another hypothetical particle, the gluon. Like quarks, gluons may also be prohibited from existing independently of their associated particles, or at least long enough to be detected directly, but during the spring and summer some indirect evidence of their presence was reported from electron-positron colliding-beam experiments at DESY. Three separate sprays, or jets, of particles were detected emerging from the collisions. Whereas two-jet events, which had been observed in previous experiments, were ascribed to the decay of newly created quark-antiquark pairs into detectable particles, appearance of the third jet was interpreted as an indication of the momentary creation of gluons, followed almost instantaneously by their quarklike decay into other particles. The physics community was far from unanimous in supporting the experimenters' interpretation of these three-jet events, and more widespread agreement would probably come only after resolution of jet structure was improved with the use of higher energy colliding beams. (S. B. PALMER)

See also Nobel Prizes.
[111.H; 112.E; 125.D.8; 127.C; 128.B.4]

Poland

Poland

A people's republic of eastern Europe, Poland is bordered by the Baltic Sea, the U.S.S.R., Czechoslovakia, and East Germany. Area: 312,677 sq km (120,725 sq mi). Pop. (1979 est.): 35,048,700. Cap. and largest city: Warsaw (pop., 1979 est., 1,552,300). Language: Polish. Religion: predominantly Roman Catholic. First secretary of the Polish United Workers' (Communist) Party in 1979, Edward Gierek; chairman of the Council of State, Henryk Jablonski; chairman of the Council of Ministers (premier), Piotr Jaroszewicz.

Meetings in Warsaw on Jan. 24, 1979, between Edward Gierek, first secretary of the ruling Polish United Workers' Party (PUWP), and Stefan Cardinal Wyszynski, primate of Poland and chairman of the Polish Episcopal Conference, and between Pope John Paul II and Andrey Gromyko, member of the Soviet Politburo and minister of foreign affairs of the U.S.S.R., at the Vatican almost certainly initiated the pope's visit to Poland. Gierek wished to know how far the outspoken pope would go in his sermons as defender of human rights and of the rights of the Polish Catholic Church. He also objected to the pontiff's desired date for his visit to Krakow—May 8, the 900th anniversary of St. Stanislaw's death—because that day was also the 34th anniversary of the unconditional surrender of Germany; on that day both the Polish government and its armed forces would be celebrating the Allied victory over the Third Reich. The pope agreed to a month's postponement of his visit, and on February 22 Cardinal Wyszynski invited Pope John Paul II to Poland.

The pope landed in Warsaw on June 2. First kissing the soil of his country, he then conveyed his "due respect" for the state authorities and his "warm thanks" for their sympathetic attitude to his visit. At the Belweder Palace he was cordially

Pipelines:
see Energy; Transportation

Plastics Industry:
see Industrial Review

Poetry:
see Literature

POLAND

Education. (1978–79) Primary, pupils 4,111,656, teachers 189,342; secondary, pupils 389,319, teachers 24,502; vocational and teacher training, pupils 1,403,733, teachers 73,219; higher, students 401,233, teaching staff 52,300.

Finance. Monetary unit: zloty, with (Sept. 17, 1979) a commercial and tourist rate of 32.10 zlotys to U.S. $1 (69.10 zlotys = £1 sterling). Budget (1978 est.): revenue 1,059,900,000,000 zlotys; expenditure 1,057,100,000,000 zlotys. Net material product (1977) 1,736,000,000,000 zlotys.

Foreign Trade. (1978) Imports 50,919,000,000 exchange zlotys; exports 44,724,000,000 exchange zlotys. Import sources: U.S.S.R. 30%; East Germany 8%; West Germany 7%; Czechoslovakia 6%; U.K. 6%. Export destinations: U.S.S.R. 34%; East Germany 8%; Czechoslovakia 7%; West Germany 7%. Main exports (1977): machinery 35%; coal 13%; transport equipment 11%; chemicals 9%; food 7%.

Transport and Communications. Roads (1977) 299,725 km (including 139 km expressways). Motor vehicles in use (1977): passenger 1,547,300; commercial 509,500. Railways: (1977) 23,953 km (including 6,308 km electrified); traffic (1978) 46,715,000,000 passenger-km, freight 138,072,000,000 net ton-km. Air traffic (1978): 2,087,000,000 passenger-km; freight 18,390,000 net ton-km. Navigable inland waterways (1977) 3,734 km. Shipping (1978): merchant vessels 100 gross tons and over 796; gross tonnage 3,490,587. Telephones (Jan. 1978) 2,925,400. Radio licenses (Dec. 1977) 8,348,000. Television licenses (Dec. 1977) 7,170,000.

Agriculture. Production (in 000; metric tons; 1978): wheat *c.* 6,000; rye *c.* 7,400; barley 3,700; oats *c.* 2,500; potatoes *c.* 46,600; sugar, raw value *c.* 1,840; rapeseed *c.* 700; cabbages (1977) *c.* 1,500; onions *c.* 350; tomatoes *c.* 370; carrots (1977) *c.* 400; cucumbers (1977) *c.* 300; apples *c.* 920; tobacco *c.* 115; butter *c.* 290; cheese *c.* 356; hen's eggs *c.* 476; beef and veal *c.* 750; pork *c.* 1,833; fish catch (1977) 665; timber (cu m; 1977) 22,020. Livestock (in 000; June 1978): cattle 13,115; pigs 21,717; sheep 4,248; horses (1977) 2,062; chickens (adult birds) 76,229.

Industry. Index of industrial production (1975 = 100; 1978) 122. Fuel and power (in 000; metric tons; 1978): coal 192,622; brown coal 41,000; coke (1977) 19,054; crude oil (1977) 460; natural gas (cu m) 7,990,000; manufactured gas (cu m; 1977) 7,811,000; electricity (kw-hr) 115,558,000. Production (in 000; metric tons; 1978): cement 21,678; iron ore (30% metal content) *c.* 500; pig iron 11,668; crude steel 19,250; aluminum (1977) 104; copper (1977) 307; lead (1977) 85; zinc (1977) 228; petroleum products (1977) *c.* 14,830; sulfuric acid 3,316; plastics and resins 596; fertilizers (nutrient content; 1977) nitrogenous 1,529, phosphate 966; cotton yarn 225; wool yarn 107; man-made fibres 240; cotton fabrics (m) 917,000; woolen fabrics (m) 124,000; passenger cars (units) 325; commercial vehicles (units) 69. Merchant vessels launched (100 gross tons and over; 1978) 679,000 gross tons. New dwelling units completed (1977) 276,000.

welcomed by members of the party and government headed by Gierek, who expressed confidence that the pope's visit would serve the cause of unity. The pope called for peace and rapprochement between nations. He said that the church was not asking for privileges but for freedom in the fulfillment of its mission.

The triumphal nine-day visit continued to Gniezno, historical see of Polish primates; to Czestochowa with its shrine of the Virgin Mary; to Krakow (June 6–10), whose bishop Stanislaw was martyred in 1097; and to Oswiecim (Auschwitz) and its extermination camp. The pope addressed gatherings of more than a million, whom he urged to be strong in faith, love, and hope. The visit passed without incident, and the authorities received praise for their civility and restraint.

Shortly after the pontiff's visit the PUWP organized the celebration of the 35th anniversary of the Lublin Manifesto published on July 22, 1944, by the Soviet-sponsored Polish Committee of National Liberation. On September 1 there followed the commemoration of the 40th anniversary of the German invasion of Poland. On both occasions official speeches stressed the role of the U.S.S.R. as the sole liberator of Poland.

On October 19 the Central Committee of the PUWP adopted "Draft Directives for Further Development of Socialist Poland and Prosperity of the Polish Nation." In his introductory speech Gierek affirmed that during the 1970s the country "was lifted to a new qualitative level," achieved by a great program of investments, the opening of new workshops for the exceptionally large generation of young people, and the modernization of productive potential. He also admitted that during the second half of the 1970s "external causes" and unfavourable weather conditions had slowed down economic growth and added that certain errors in planning had been committed. As an example of the latter, the supply of electric power could not keep up with the demand.

Speaking in the Sejm (parliament) on October 25, Jan Szydlak, a Politburo member and deputy premier, revealed that the main reason for the power shortage was that, though the installed capacity of power stations was 24 million Mw, only three-quarters of it was serving consumers at any given time because 25% of the units were constantly under repair. To remedy this, the Draft Directives for 1981–85 foresaw an increase of hard coal extraction to 235 million tons and of brown coal to 90 million tons; this was to increase the generation of electric power by 28%. Production of steel was to reach 25 million tons and that of the chemical industry was to increase by 32%. Agricultural production was expected to rise by 13%, while the number of cattle would reach about 15.5 million and of pigs, 23.5 million. Gierek insisted in his speech that a large increase in the production of grain and feed for livestock was the key task. (K. M. SMOGORZEWSKI)

Police:
see Crime and Law Enforcement

Political Parties

The following table is a general world guide to political parties. All countries that were independent on Dec. 31, 1979, are included; there are a number for which no analysis of political activities can be given. Parties are included in most instances only if represented in parliaments (in the lower house in bicameral legislatures); the figures in the last column indicate the number of seats obtained in the last general election (figures in parentheses are those of the penultimate one). The date of the most recent election follows the name of the country.

The code letters in the affiliation column show the relative political position of the parties within each country; there is, therefore, no entry in this column for single-party states. There are obvious difficulties involved in labeling parties within the political spectrum of a given country. The key chosen is as follows: F-fascist; ER-extreme right; R-right; CR-centre right; C-centre; L-non-Marxist left; SD-social democratic; S-socialist; EL-extreme left; and K-Communist.

The percentages in the column "Voting strength" indicate proportions of the valid votes cast for the respective parties, or the number of registered voters who went to the polls in single-party states.

[541.D.2]

COUNTRY AND NAME OF PARTY	Affiliation	Voting strength (%)	Parliamentary representation
Afghanistan			
Pro-Soviet government since April 27, 1978	—	—	—
Albania (November 1978)			
Albanian Labour (Communist)	—	99.9	250 (250)
Algeria (February 1977)			
National Liberation Front	—	99.95	261
Angola, People's Republic of			
Movimento Popular de Libertaçao de Angola (MPLA)	—	—	—
Argentina			
Military junta since March 24, 1976	—	—	—
Australia (December 1977)			
National Country	R	...	19 (23)
Liberal	C	...	67 (65)
Australian Labor	L	...	38 (36)
Other	—	...	0 (3)
Austria (May 1979)			
Freiheitliche Partei Österreichs	R	6.06	11 (10)
Österreichische Volkspartei	C	41.90	77 (80)
Sozialistische Partei Österreichs	SD	51.03	95 (93)
Bahamas, The (July 1977)			
Progressive Liberal Party	CR	55.0	30 (30)
Bahamian Democratic Party	L	...	5 (8)
Free National Movement	L	...	2 —
Bahrain			
Emirate, no parties	—	—	—
Bangladesh (February 1979)			
Jatiyabadi Dal (Nationalist Party)	R	49.0	207
Awami League	CR	...	40
Muslim League	C	...	20
Jatiya Samajtantrik Dal (National Socialist)	L	...	9
Others	—	...	24
Barbados (September 1976)			
Democratic Labour	C	...	7 (18)
Barbados Labour	L	...	17 (6)
Belgium (December 1978)			
Vlaams Blok	ER	...	1 (0)
Volksunie	R	...	14 (20)
Front Démocratique Francophone	R	...	10 (11)
Rassemblement Wallon	R	...	5 (4)
Parti Libéral { Flemish	CR	...	22 (17)
Parti Libéral { Wallon	CR	...	15 (16)
Parti Social-Chrétien { Flemish	C	...	57 (56)
Parti Social-Chrétien { Wallon	C	...	25 (24)
Parti Socialiste Belge { Flemish	SD	...	26 (27)
Parti Socialiste Belge { Wallon	SD	...	32 (35)
Parti Communiste	K	...	4 (2)
UDRT (Brussels anti-tax)	—	...	1 (0)
Benin (Dahomey)			
Military government since 1972	—	—	—
Bhutan			
A monarchy without parties	—	—	—
Bolivia (July 1979)			
Acción Democrática Nacionalista	R	...	21
Unidad Democrática y Popular	CR	...	37
Movimiento Nacionalista Revolucionario	C	...	43
Alianza por Integración Nacional	L	...	6
Partido Socialista	SD	...	6
Three other parties	—	...	4
Botswana (October 1979)			
Botswana Democratic Party	C	...	29 (27)
Botswana People's Party	L	...	1 (2)
Botswana National Front	EL	...	2 (2)
Brazil (November 1978)			
Aliança Renovadora Nacional (ARENA)	CR	...	231 (199)
Movimento Democrático Brasileiro (MDB)	L	...	189 (165)
Bulgaria (May 1976)			
Fatherland Front	—	99.9	400 (400)
Burma (January 1978)			
Burma Socialist Program Party	—	99.0	464 (451)
Burundi (October 1974)			
Tutsi ethnic minority government	—	—	—
Cambodia (Kampuchea)			
Civil war during 1979	—	...	—
Cameroon (May 1978)			
Cameroonian National Union	—	99.98	120 (120)
Canada (May 1979)			
Social Credit	R	4.5	6 (11)
Progressive Conservative	CR	36.0	136 (95)
Liberal	C	39.9	114 (141)
New Democratic	L	18.0	26 (16)
Independents	—	1.5	0 (1)
Cape Verde Islands (June 1975)			
African Party for the Independence of Guinea-Bissau and Cape Verde	—	84.0	56
Central African Republic			
Provisional military government since Sept. 26, 1979	—	...	—
Chad			
Military government since 1975	—	—	—
Chile			
Military junta since Sept. 11, 1973	—	—	—
China, People's Republic of (February 1978)			
Communist (Kungchantang) National People's Congress	—	...	3,500
Colombia (February 1978)			
Partido Conservador	R	...	86 (66)
Partido Liberal	C	...	109 (113)
Unión Nacional de Oposisión	L	...	4 (20)
Comoros (December 1974)			
Single party rule from Aug. 3, 1975	—	—	—
Congo			
Military government since Sept. 1968	—	—	—
Costa Rica (February 1978)			
Partido de Liberación Nacional	R	...	25 (27)
Partido de Unidad	C	...	27 (16)
Three left-wing parties	L	...	5 (8)
Cuba (November 1976)			
Partido Comunista Cubano	—	...	481
Cyprus (September 1976)			
Greek Zone: Pro-Makarios three-party alliance	—	...	34
Independent	—	...	1
Turkish Zone: National Unity Party	—	...	30
Communal Liberation Party	—	...	6
Populist Party	—	...	2
Republican Turkish Party	—	...	2
Czechoslovakia (October 1976)			
National Front	—	...	200
Denmark (October 1979)			
Conservative	R	12.5	22 (15)
Liberal Democratic (Venstre)	CR	12.5	23 (22)
Christian People's	CR	2.6	5 (6)
Progress (M. Glistrup)	C	11.0	20 (26)
Radical Liberal (Radikale Venstre)	C	5.4	10 (6)
Justice (Retsforbund)	C	2.6	5 (6)
Centre Democrats (E. Jakobsen)	C	3.2	6 (10)
Social Democrats	SD	38.3	69 (66)
Socialist People's	EL	5.9	11 (8)
Left Socialists	EL	3.6	6 (5)
Communist	K	1.9	0 (7)
Others	—	...	2 (2)
Djibouti (May 1977)			
Ligue Populaire Africaine pour l'Indépendance (mainly Somali)	C	...	33
Front de Libération de la Côte des Somalis	L	...	30
Dominica (November 1978)			
Dominica Freedom Party	C	...	3
Dominica Labour Party	L	...	16
Independents	—	...	2
Dominican Republic (May 1978)			
Partido Reformista	C	...	42 (86)
Partido Revolucionario	SD	...	49 ...
Others	—	...	... (5)
Ecuador (April 1979, figures incomplete)			
Partido Conservador	R	...	10
Concentración de Fuerzas Populares	C	...	30
Izquierda Democrática	L	...	14
Unión Democrática Popular	EL	...	3
Egypt (November 1976)			
Arab Socialist Union	—	...	350
El Salvador			
"Moderate" provisional government since Oct. 15, 1979	—	...	—
Equatorial Guinea			
Provisional military government since Aug. 3, 1979	—	...	—
Ethiopia			
Military government since 1974	—	—	—
Fiji (September 1977)			
Alliance Party (mainly Fijian)	—	...	36 (24)
National Federation (mainly Indian)	—	...	15 (26)
Others	—	...	1 (2)
Finland (March 1979)			
National Coalition Party (Conservative)	R	21.7	47 (35)
Swedish People's	R	4.3	10 (10)
Centre Party (ex-Agrarian)	C	17.4	36 (39)
Liberal	C	3.7	4 (9)
Christian League	C	4.8	9 (9)
Rural	L	4.6	7 (2)
Social Democratic	SD	24.0	52 (54)
People's Democratic League (Communist)	K	17.9	35 (40)
Others	—	1.75	0 (2)
France (March 1978)			
Centre-Right:			
Gaullists (Rassemblement pour la République)	R	25.84	148 (185)
Giscardians (Union pour la Démocratie Française)	CR	23.18	137 (54)
Other	—	1.64	6 (36)
Union of Left:			
Parti Radical	L	2.02	10 (12)
Parti Socialiste	SD	28.46	103 (89)
Parti Communiste	K	18.83	86 (73)
Others	—	...	1 (9)
Gabon (February 1973)			
Parti Démocratique Gabonais	—	...	70
Gambia, The (April 1977)			
People's Progressive Party	C	...	29 (28)
United Party	L	...	2 (3)
German Democratic Republic (October 1976)			
National Front (Sozialistische Einheitspartei and others)	—	99.9	500 (434)
Germany, Federal Republic of (October 1976)			
Christlich-Demokratische Union	R	38.0	190 (177)
Christlich-Soziale Union	R	10.6	53 (48)
Freie Demokratische Partei	C	7.9	39 (41)
Sozialdemokratische Partei Deutschlands	SD	42.6	214 (230)
Deutsche Kommunistische Partei	K	0.3	0 (0)
Ghana (June 1979)			
People's National Party	—	...	71
Popular Front Party	—	...	43
Action Congress Party	—	...	10
United National Convention	—	...	13
Social Democratic Party	—	...	3
Greece (November 1977)			
National Rally	R	6.82	5 (0)
New Democracy Party	CR	41.85	172 (215)
Democratic Centre Union	C	11.95	15 (57)
New Liberals (mainly in Crete)	C	1.08	2 (0)
Panhellenic Socialist Movement	SD	25.33	93 (15)
Left Alliance (Eurocommunist)	EL	2.72	2 (6)
Greek Communist Party (pro-Moscow)	K	9.36	11 (5)
Others	—	0.89	— (2)
Grenada			
People's Revolutionary Government since March 13, 1979	—	...	—

COUNTRY AND NAME OF PARTY	Affiliation	Voting strength (%)	Parliamentary representation
Guatemala (March 1978)			
Movimiento de Liberación Nacional	CR	...	20
Partido Institucional Democrático	CR	...	17
Partido Demócrata Cristiano	C	...	7
Partido Revolucionario	L	...	14
Others	—	...	3
Guinea (December 1974)			
Parti Démocratique de Guinée	—	100.0	150
Guinea-Bissau (1975)			
African Party for the Independence of Guinea-Bissau and Cape Verde	—	...	92
Guyana (July 1973)			
People's National Congress	C	...	37 (30)
People's Progressive Party	EL	...	14 (19)
Others	—	...	2 (4)
Haiti			
Presidential dictatorship since 1957	—	—	—
Honduras			
Military junta since Dec. 4, 1972	—	—	—
Hungary (June 1975)			
Patriotic People's Front	—	97.6	352
Iceland (December 1979)			
Independence (Conservative)	R	35.4	21 (20)
Progressive (Farmers' Party)	C	24.9	17 (12)
Social Democratic	SD	17.4	10 (14)
People's Alliance	K	19.7	11 (14)
Independent	—	...	1 (0)
India (March 1977)			
Janata (People's) Party and allies:			
Janata (including Jan Sangh, Opposition Congress, Swatantra, Samyukta, and Praja Socialist parties)	—	...	295 (53)
Akali Dal (Sikh Party)	C	...	9 (1)
Dravida Munnetra Kazhagam	R	...	1 (23)
Communist-Marxist (pro-Chinese)	K	...	22 (25)
Five other parties	—	...	14 (3)
Congress Party and allies:			
Congress	C	...	150 (350)
Anna Dravida Munnetra Kazhagam	R	...	19 —
Communist (pro-Soviet)	K	...	7 (23)
Four smaller parties	—	...	7 (9)
Four independent parties	—	...	14 (28)
Indonesia (May 1977)			
Sekber Golkar (Functional Groups)	—	62.1	232 (236)
United Development Party (merger of four Islamic parties)	—	29.3	99 (94)
Partai Demokrasi Indonesia (merger of five nationalist and Christian parties)	—	8.6	29 (30)
Iran			
Provisional government since February 1979	—	...	—
Iraq			
Military and Ba'ath Party governments since 1958	—	...	...
Ireland (June 1977)			
Fianna Fail (Sons of Destiny)	C	...	84 (69)
Fine Gael (United Ireland)	C	...	43 (54)
Irish Labour Party	L	...	17 (19)
Sinn Fein (We Ourselves)	—	...	0 (0)
Others	—	...	4 (2)
Israel (May 1977)			
Likud	R	33.4	43 (39)
Torah Front	CR	4.8	5 (5)
National Religious	C	9.2	12 (10)
Democratic Movement for Change	C	11.6	15 —
Independent Liberal	C	1.2	1 (4)
Civil Rights Movement	L	1.2	1 (3)
Labour Alignment	SD	24.6	32 (51)
Democratic Front for Peace and Equality (pro-Soviet)	K	4.6	5 (4)
United Arab List	—	1.2	1 (3)
Others	—	8.0	5 (1)
Italy (June 1979)			
Movimento Sociale Italiano	F	5.3	30 (35)
Partito Liberale Italiano	CR	1.9	9 (5)
Democrazia Cristiana	C	38.3	262 (262)
Partito Repubblicano Italiano	C	3.0	16 (14)
Partito Social-Democratico Italiano	L	3.8	20 (15)
Partito Socialista Italiano	SD	9.8	62 (57)
Partito d'Unità Proletaria	EL	1.4	6 (6)
Partito Radicale	EL	3.4	18 (4)
Partito Comunista Italiano	K	30.4	201 (228)
Südtiroler Volkspartei	—	0.6	4 (3)
Others	—	2.1	2 (1)
Ivory Coast (November 1970)			
Parti Démocratique de la Côte d'Ivoire	—	99.9	100
Jamaica (December 1976)			
People's National Party	L	...	48 (35)
Jamaica Labour Party	S	...	12 (18)
Japan (October 1979)			
Liberal-Democratic	R	44.6	248 (249)
Komeito (Clean Government)	CR	9.8	57 (55)
Democratic-Socialist	SD	6.8	35 (29)
Socialist	S	19.7	107 (123)
Communist	K	10.4	39 (17)
Independents and others	—	8.7	25 (38)
Jordan			
Royal government, no parties	—	—	60
Kenya (November 1979)			
Kenya African National Union (158 elected, 12 nominated, 2 ex-officio)	—	...	172 (158)
Kiribati (ex. Gilbert Islands, July 1979)			
House of Assembly	—	...	35
Korea, North (November 1977)			
Korean Workers' (Communist) Party	—	100.0	579
Korea, South (February 1973)			
Democratic Republican	CR	38.7	73
New Democratic	L	32.6	52
Democratic Unification	S	10.1	2
Independents	—	18.6	19
Kuwait			
Princely government, no parties	—	—	30
Laos, People's Democratic Republic of			
Lao People's Revolutionary Party	—	...	...
Lebanon (April 1972)			
Maronites (Roman Catholics)	—	...	30
Sunni Muslims	—	...	20
Shi'ite Muslims	—	...	19
Greek Orthodox	—	...	11
Druzes (Muslim sect)	—	...	6
Melchites (Greek Catholics)	—	...	6
Armenian Orthodox	—	...	4
Other Christian	—	...	2
Armenian Catholics	—	...	1
Lesotho			
Constitution suspended Jan. 30, 1970	—	—	—
Liberia (October 1975)			
True Whig Party	—	...	41
Libya			
Military government since Sept. 1, 1969	—	—	—
Liechtenstein (February 1978)			
Vaterländische Union	CR	...	8 (7)
Fortschrittliche Bürgerpartei	C	...	7 (8)
Luxembourg (June 1979)			
Parti Chrétien Social	CR	34.5	24 (18)
Parti Libéral	C	21.3	15 (14)
Parti Ouvrier Socialiste	SD	24.3	14 (17)
Parti Social Démocratique	S	6.0	2 (5)
Parti Communiste Luxembourgeois	K	5.8	2 (5)
Independents	—	...	2 (0)
Madagascar (June 1977)			
Avant-garde de la Révolution Malgache	C	...	112
Parti du Congrès de l'Indépendance	L	...	16
Others	—	...	9
Malawi (June 1978)			
Malawi Congress Party	—	...	87
Malaysia (July 1978)			
Barisan Nasional	—	...	131 (120)
Democratic Action Party (mainly Chinese)	L	...	16 (9)
Party Islam	—	...	5 (14)
Maldives (February 1975)			
Presidential rule since 1975	—	—	—
Mali			
Military government since Nov. 19, 1968	—	—	—
Malta (September 1976)			
Nationalist Party	R	48.7	31 (27)
Labour Party	SD	51.3	34 (28)
Mauritania			
Military government since July 10, 1978	—	—	—
Mauritius (December 1976)			
Independence Party (Indian-dominated)	C	...	28 (39)
Parti Mauricien Social-Démocrate	L	...	8 (23)
Mauritius Militant Movement	K	...	34
Mexico (July 1979, results incomplete)			
Partido Revolucionario Institucional	CR	...	291
Partido Acción Nacional	C	...	4
Partido Auténtico de la Revolución Mexicana	L	...	...
Partido Popular Socialista	S	...	...
Partido Comunista Mexicano	K	...	...
Monaco (January 1978)			
Union Nationale et Démocratique	—	...	18 (17)
Mongolia (June 1977)			
Mongolian People's Revolutionary Party	—	99.99	354 (295)
Morocco (June 1977)			
Independents (pro-government)	CR	44.7	141 (159)
Popular Movement (rural)	CR	12.4	44 (60)
Istiqlal (Independence)	C	21.6	49 (8)
National Union of Popular Forces	L	14.6	16 (1)
Others	—	...	14 (12)
Mozambique (December 1977)			
Frente da Libertação do Moçambique (Frelimo)	—	...	210
Nauru (November 1977)			
Nauru Party (Dowiyogo)	—	...	9
Opposition Party (DeRoburt)	—	...	8
Independent	—	...	1
Nepal			
Royal government since December 1960	—	—	—
Netherlands, The (May 1977)			
Christian Democratic Appeal (Anti-Revolutionaire Partij, Christelijk-Historische Unie, and Katholieke Volkspartij)	CR	31.9	49 (48)
Boerenpartij (Farmers' Party)	CR	0.8	1 (3)
Volkspartij voor Vrijheid en Democratie	C	18.0	28 (22)
Democrats 1966	C	5.4	8 (6)
Democratische-Socialisten '70	L	0.7	1 (6)
Partij van de Arbeid	SD	33.8	53 (43)
Communistische Partij van Nederland	K	1.7	2 (7)
Seventeen other parties	—	...	8 (15)
New Zealand (November 1978)			
National (Conservative)	CR	39.5	51 (54)
Labour Party	L	40.5	40 (32)
Social Credit	C	16.4	1 (1)
Nicaragua			
Provisional government since July 20, 1979	—	...	—
Niger			
Military government since April 17, 1974	—	—	—
Nigeria (July-August 1979)			
National Party of Nigeria	—	...	168
Unity Party of Nigeria	—	...	111
Nigerian People's Party	—	...	79
Great Nigeria People's Party	—	...	48
People's Redemption Party	—	...	49

COUNTRY AND NAME OF PARTY	Affiliation	Voting strength (%)	Parliamentary representation
Norway (September 1977)			
Høyre (Conservative)	R	24.7	41 (29)
Kristelig Folkeparti	CR	12.1	22 (20)
Senterpartiet (Agrarian)	C	8.6	12 (21)
Venstre (Liberal)	C	3.2	2 (1)
New People's Party	C	1.7	0 } (2)
Party of Progress	C	1.9	0 }
Arbeiderpartiet (Labour)	SD	42.5	76 (62)
Sosialistisk Venstreparti (Socialist Left)	S	4.1	2 } (16)
Kommunistiske Parti	K	0.4	0 }
Oman			
Independent sultanate, no parties	—	—	—
Pakistan			
Military government since July 5, 1977	—	—	—
Panama (August 1978)			
National Union Assembly	—	...	505
Papua New Guinea (June–July 1977)			
Pangu Party	—	...	39 (22)
United Party (chief opposition)	—	...	38 (34)
People's Progress Party	—	...	18 (12)
National Party	—	...	3 (10)
Country Party	—	...	1 —
Papua Besena	—	...	5 (2)
Other	—	...	5 —
Paraguay (February 1977)			
Partido Colorado (A. Stroessner)	R	69.0	...
Opposition parties	—	31.0	...
Peru (June 1978)			
Partido Popular Cristiano	CR	27	25
APRA (Alianza Popular Revolucionaria Americana)	CR	35.3	37
FOCEP (Frente Obrero, Campesino y Estudiantino Popular)	L	...	12
Socialists	S	...	6
Communists	K	...	6
Others	—	...	14
Philippines			
Martial law since Sept. 23, 1972	—	—	—
Poland (March 1976)			
Front of National Unity	—	99.4	460 (460)
Portugal (December 1979)			
Aliança Democrática: Popular Monarchists	R		5 (0)
Aliança Democrática: Centre Democrats	CR		42 (71)
Aliança Democrática: Social Democrats	C	45.2	75 (42)
Aliança Democrática: Reformists	C		5 (2)
Aliança Democrática: Independents	—		1 (0)
Partido Socialista Portugues	SD	27.4	74 (107)
União Democrática Popular	EL	2.2	1 (1)
Partido Comunista Portugues	K	19.0	44 (40)
Movimiento Democrático Popular	EL	6.2	3 (0)
Qatar			
Independent emirate, no parties	—	—	—
Romania (March 1975)			
Communist-controlled Socialist Unity Front	—	99.9	349
Rwanda (July 1975)			
National Revolutionary Movement	—	—	—
Saint Lucia (July 1979)			
United Workers' Party	C	...	5
St. Lucia Labour Party	S	...	12
Saint Vincent and the Grenadines (December 1979)			
St. Vincent Labour Party	—	...	11
New Democratic Party	—	...	2
San Marino (May 1978)			
Partito Democratico-Cristiano	CR	42.2	26 (25)
Partito Social-Democratico	SD	...	9 (9)
Partito Socialista Unitario	S	...	8 (8)
Partito Comunista	K	25.1	16 (15)
Others	—	...	3 (3)
São Tomé and Príncipe (1975)			
Movimento Libertaçao	—	—	—
Saudi Arabia			
Royal government, no parties	—	—	—
Senegal (February 1978)			
Parti Socialiste	CR	82.5	83
Parti Démocratique Sénégalais	L	17.1	17
Seychelles			
People's Progressive Front (alone in power after the June 5, 1977, coup)	—	—	—
Sierra Leone (June 1978)			
All People's Congress	CR	...	85 (70)
Singapore (December 1976)			
People's Action Party	CR	...	69 (65)
Solomon Islands			
Independent Group	C	...	...
National Democratic Party	L	...	...
Somalia (December 1979)			
Somalian Revolutionary Socialist Party	—	...	171
South Africa (November 1977)			
Herstigte Nasionale Partij	ER	3.2	0 —
National Party	R	64.8	134 (122)
South African Party	CR	1.7	3 —
New Republic Party	C	11.8	10 —
United Party	C	—	— (41)
Progressive Federal Party	L	16.7	17 —
Progressive Reform Party	L	—	— (7)
Others	—	—	— (1)
Spain (March 1979)			
Coalición Democrática	R	5.0	9 (16)
Unión Centro Democrático	CR	34.0	168 (165)
Partido Socialista Obrero Español	SD	29.0	121 (118)
Partido Comunista Español	K	10.0	23 (20)
Catalans (two parties)	—	...	9 (13)
Basques (three parties)	—	...	12 (9)
Others	—	...	8 (9)
Sri Lanka (July 1977)			
United National Party	R	...	139 (19)
Freedom Party	C	...	8 (91)
Tamil United Liberation Front	C	...	17 (12)
Communists and others	—	...	2 (44)
Sudan (February 1978)			
Sudan Socialist Union	—	...	304
Suriname (November 1977)			
National Party Combination (H. Arron)	—	...	24 (22)
United Democratic Party (J. Lachmon)	...	...	15 (17)
Swaziland			
Royal government, no parties	—	—	—
Sweden (September 1979)			
Moderata Samlingspartiet	R	20.4	73 (55)
Centerpartiet	CR	18.2	64 (86)
Folkpartiet (Liberal)	C	10.6	38 (39)
Socialdemokratiska Arbetarepartiet	SD	43.5	154 (152)
Vänsterpartiet Kommunisterna	K	5.6	20 (17)
Switzerland (October 1979)			
Christian Democrats (Conservative)	R	...	44 (46)
Republican Movement } National Action (V. Ochen) }	R	...	3 (6)
Evangelical People's	R	...	3 (3)
Swiss People's (ex-Middle Class)	CR	...	23 (21)
Radical Democrats (Freisinnig)	C	...	51 (47)
League of Independents	C	...	8 (11)
Liberal Democrats	L	...	8 (6)
Social Democrats	SD	...	51 (55)
Socialist Autonomous	EL	...	3 (1)
Communist (Partei der Arbeit)	K	...	3 (4)
Others	—	...	3 (0)
Syria (August 1977)			
National Progressive Front	—	...	159
Others	—	...	36
Taiwan (Republic of China)			
Nationalist (Kuomintang)	—	...	773
Tanzania (October 1975)			
Tanganyika African National Union	C	93.2	218
Zanzibar Afro-Shirazi (nominated)	L	...	52
Thailand (April 1979)			
Social Action Party	—	...	82
Thai Nationalist Party	—	...	38
Democratic Party	—	...	32
Thai People's Party	—	...	32
Serithan (Socialist) Party	—	...	21
Others	—	...	96
Togo			
Military government since 1967	—	—	—
Tonga (June 1972)			
Legislative Assembly (partially elected)	—	—	21
Trinidad and Tobago (September 1976)			
People's National Movement	C	...	24 (36)
Democratic Action Congress	—	...	2
United Labour Front	L	...	10
Tunisia (November 1979)			
Parti Socialiste Destourien	—	...	121 (112)
Turkey (June 1977)			
National Action (A. Turkes)	ER	6.4	16 (3)
National Salvation (N. Erbakan)	R	8.6	24 (48)
Turkish Justice (S. Demirel)	CR	36.9	189 (149)
Democratic	C	1.8	1 (45)
Republican Reliance (T. Feyzioglu)	C	1.9	3 (13)
Republican People's (B. Ecevit)	L	41.4	213 (185)
Others	—	...	4 (7)
Uganda (October 1979)			
Members of district councils created by National Liberation Front	—	...	61
Representatives from Uganda National Liberation Army	—	...	10
Others	—	...	56
Union of Soviet Socialist Republics (March 1979)			
Communist Party of the Soviet Union	—	99.99	1,500 (767)
United Arab Emirates			
Federal government of seven emirates			
United Kingdom (May 1979)			
Conservative	R	43.9	339 (276)
Liberal	C	13.8	11 (13)
Labour	L	36.9	268 (319)
Communist	K	...	0 (0)
Scottish National Party	—	...	2 (11)
Plaid Cymru (Welsh Nationalists)	—	...	2 (3)
Ulster Unionists (four groups)	—	...	10 (10)
Others	—	...	3 (3)
United States (November 1978)			
Republican	CR	...	159 (143)
Democratic	C	...	276 (292)
Upper Volta (April 1978)			
Union Nationale pour la Défense de la Démocratie	CR	...	13
Union Démocratique Voltaïque	C	...	28
Union Progressiste Voltaïque	S	...	9
Uruguay			
Rule by Council of State from 1973	—	—	—
Venezuela (December 1978)			
COPEI (Social Christians)	CR	...	88 (64)
Acción Democrática	L	...	88 (102)
Movimiento al Socialismo	SD	...	11 (9)
Movimiento Electoral del Pueblo	S	...	3 (8)
Movimiento Institucional Revolucionario	EL	...	4 (2)
Partido Comunista Venezuelano	K	...	1 (2)
Vietnam, Socialist Republic of (April 1976)			
Communist Party	K	...	...
Yemen, People's Democratic Republic of			
National Liberation Front	—	—	—
Yemen Arab Republic			
Military government since 1974	—	—	—
Yugoslavia (May 1978)			
Communist-controlled Federal Chamber	—	...	220
Zaire (October 1977)			
Legislative Council of the Mouvement Populaire de la Révolution	—	...	268
Zambia (December 1973)			
United National Independence Party	—	80.0	125
Zimbabwe Rhodesia			
Temporarily returned to British rule as Southern Rhodesia December 1979	—	—	—

(K. M. SMOGORZEWSKI)

Portugal

Portugal

A republic of southwestern Europe, Portugal shares the Iberian Peninsula with Spain. Area: 91,632 sq km (35,379 sq mi), including the Azores (2,335 sq km) and Madeira (796 sq km). Pop. (1979 est.): 9,819,600, excluding about 550,000 refugees (mostly from Africa). Cap. and largest city: Lisbon (pop., 1979 est., 861,500). Language: Portuguese. Religion: Roman Catholic. President in 1979, Gen. António dos Santos Ramalho Eanes; premiers, Carlos Mota Pinto to June 7 and, from August 1, Maria de Lurdes Pintassilgo.

Political events continued to dominate news in Portugal throughout 1979. On Dec. 13, 1978, Carlos Mota Pinto's government of technocrats had survived a no-confidence motion presented by the Communist Party, or PCP (45 votes). The motion was defeated by the combined votes of the Social Democrat (PSD) and Centre Democrat (CDS) parties (109), while the Socialists (PSP) abstained. Although the Mota Pinto program contained many points of similarity with those of the three previous constitutional governments, it differed on the question of the role of the private and public industrial sectors, advocated a faster pace for the return of agrarian land or payment of an indemnity to former owners, and represented the application of orthodox economic doctrine to solve the country's main economic and structural problems.

Political opposition to the program from parties of the left mounted, and on March 22, following the defeat in the Assembly of the government's medium-term plan and the 1979 budget (43 for, 46 against, 116 abstentions), the premier submitted the resignation of his Cabinet to Pres. António Ramalho Eanes. The offer was refused, and the government agreed to resubmit a new budget in May. It passed with the support of the CDS and 37 former members of the Social Democrat Party; the Socialists and the Social Democrat rump abstained, while the Communists and extreme-left parties voted against. However, 70 amendments to the budget were introduced, raising the projected deficit to 82 billion escudos. The deputies accepted the need for increased government revenues through higher rates on industry and property but rejected a proposal to tax Christmas bonuses.

In view of this second effective failure of the government's budget strategy, and in the knowledge that the Socialists and Communists would probably succeed in their censure motions, President Eanes accepted the resignation of the administration on June 7. In theory, the president had three options: to appoint another independent administration (opposed by the Socialists); to encourage the emergence of a workable parliamentary majority; or to dissolve the Assembly and call elections within a 90-day period. On July 13, following consultations with the Council of the Revolution, the president decided on calling elections, which were set for December 2. Portugal now faced four elections over two years, since municipal elections were due on December 16 and general and presidential elections in 1981. President Eanes appointed Maria de Lurdes Pintassilgo to head an impartial caretaker government to serve from August 1 until the results of the December 2 poll were known.

SAMUEL IAVELBERG—GAMMA/LIAISON

Maria de Lurdes Pintassilgo took office August 1 as interim prime minister of Portugal. Following elections held on December 2, her replacement by Francisco Sá Carneiro, leader of the Democratic Alliance, was awaited at year's end.

The result of the elections to the Assembly was a clear swing to the right, in the shape of the Democratic Alliance (AD) led by Francisco Sá Carneiro (*see* BIOGRAPHIES). The AD won an overall majority of 128 seats in the 250-seat Assembly, while the Socialists' representation was reduced from 107 to 74. Within the AD, Sá Carneiro's own Social Democrats gained 75 seats and the Centre Democrats 42. (*See* POLITICAL PARTIES.) Pintassilgo resigned December 27 but remained as caretaker premier pending the formation of a new government by Sá Carneiro early in 1980. Support for the AD was confirmed in the municipal elections on December 16.

Agrarian reform, a strong factor in the fall of four governments since 1976, once again became a political issue in 1979 and figured prominently in the AD's election manifesto. The Mota Pinto administration had continued the first constitutional government's policy of returning land illegally expropriated between 1974 and 1976. Tension in the Alentejo between farming cooperatives and the National Guard was high as a result of the enforced removal of peasants from illegally occupied farms. The policy was restarted under the Pintassilgo administration on September 27, after the interim government was accused of stalling on the issue. Tragedy struck on September 28 when two farm workers resisting eviction were shot by the National Guard, and the return of land was suspend-

Polo:
see Equestrian Sports; Water Sports

Populations:
see Demography; *see also the individual country articles*

PORTUGAL

Education. (1976–77) Primary, pupils 913,613, teachers 39,844; secondary (1975–76), pupils 612,371, teachers 35,-682; vocational (1975–76), pupils 131,441, teachers 14,998; teacher training (1975–76), students 10,362, teachers 1,377; higher (1975–76), students 79,702, teaching staff 7,891.

Finance. Monetary unit: escudo, with (Sept. 17, 1979) a free rate of 49.57 escudos to U.S. $1 (106.65 escudos = £1 sterling). Gold, SDR's, and foreign exchange (June 1979) U.S. $1,621,000,000. Budget (1978 est.): revenue 219,571,-000,000 escudos; expenditure 219,521,000,000 escudos. Gross national product (1978) 767.4 billion escudos. Money supply (March 1979) 301,340,000,000 escudos. Cost of living (Lisbon; 1975 = 100; June 1979) 215.7.

Foreign Trade. (1978) Imports 227,180,000,000 escudos; exports 107.2 billion escudos. Import sources: EEC 46% (West Germany 14%, U.K. 10%, France 9%, Italy 5%); U.S. 12%; Spain 5%; Iraq 5%. Export destinations: EEC 55% (U.K. 18%, West Germany 13%, France 9%, Italy 6%); U.S. 7%; Sweden 5%. Main exports: textile yarns and fabrics 17%; clothing 13%; machinery 10%; food 8%; cork and manufactures 7%; wine 7%; chemicals 5%. Tourism (1977): visitors 1,410,000; gross receipts U.S. $404 million.

Transport and Communications. Roads (1976) 46,945 km (including 66 km expressways). Motor vehicles in use (1976): passenger 1,034,300; commercial 111,000. Railways: (1977) 3,592 km; traffic (1978) 5,163,000,000 passenger-km, freight 933 million net ton-km. Air traffic (1978): 3,380,000,000 passenger-km; freight 111.8 million net ton-km. Shipping (1978): merchant vessels 100 gross tons and over 342; gross tonnage 1,239,963. Telephones (Jan. 1978) 1,174,900. Radio licenses (Dec. 1976) 1,525,-000. Television licenses (Dec. 1977) 1,137,000.

Agriculture. Production (in 000; metric tons; 1978): wheat 252; oats 59; rye 102; corn 443; rice 131; potatoes 1,160; tomatoes 679; figs (1977) *c.* 200; apples 117; oranges *c.* 116; wine 557; olives *c.* 230; olive oil *c.* 35; cow's milk *c.* 735; meat 391; fish catch (1977) 310; timber (cu m; 1977) 8,010. Livestock (in 000; 1978): sheep *c.* 3,-657; cattle (1977) *c.* 1,140; goats *c.* 740; pigs (1977) *c.* 2,120; poultry *c.* 17,268.

Industry. Production (in 000; metric tons; 1978): coal 183; petroleum products (1977) 5,596; manufactured gas (Lisbon; cu m) 137,000; electricity (kw-hr) 13,499,000; iron ore (50% metal content) 53; crude steel 435; sulfuric acid *c.* 260; fertilizers (nutrient content; 1977–78) nitrogenous *c.* 180, phosphate *c.* 101; plastics and resins 101; cement 5,121; kaolin (1977) 73; preserved sardines (1977) 29; wood pulp (1977) 616; cork products (1977) 270; cotton yarn 78; woven cotton fabrics 51.

ed on October 17. A bombing campaign against government representatives continued until November.

Following the acceptance by the European Economic Community (EEC) of Portugal's application for membership in October 1978, relations drew closer, and Portugal was expected to begin its transition period in 1983. In October President Eanes made a state visit to France, where he received expressions of support from Pres. Valéry Giscard d'Estaing and talks on French investment, particularly an expansion of Renault's Portuguese operation, were held. At home the far left opposed EEC and NATO membership and wished to strengthen ties with Portuguese-speaking Africa; the far right adopted the opposite posture, while the Socialists wished to have a closer relationship with both Africa and the EEC.

Growth in the domestic economy continued to slow (unemployment was estimated at 12% at the end of 1978). Lack of demand and the slow growth of world trade led to low utilization of productive capacity, which in mid-1979 averaged 76%, slightly below 1977 levels. The outlook for the balance of payments improved considerably, but that for the local economy was worsened by a bank credit squeeze, higher taxes, and charges for public-sector services, as well as by the results of the program—inspired by the International Monetary Fund (IMF)—that set lower economic growth targets for 1978 and 1979. New loans from the IMF were stalled by the political crisis.

The year started badly for agriculture. In January bad weather delayed planting and the application of fertilizers, so that sown areas were reduced by 11% from 1978 levels. In February northern and central Portugal suffered the worst flooding in more than a century when the country's four major rivers burst their banks. Harvests in the south were affected by early frost and hail in September and October.

Portugal's worker-control law was declared constitutional in mid-September. Depending on company size, between 3 and 11 committee members were to be elected to serve on worker's commissions by April 1980. Elections had to be called 15 days in advance by at least 20% of a company's work force or a minimum of 100 workers.

(MICHAEL WOOLLER)

See also Dependent States.

Prisons and Penology

In a number of countries, including the U.K., crime figures went down in 1979, although the U.S. reported an increase, especially in crimes of violence. It was doubtful whether any penal or correctional system had much effect on the incidence of crime. A large percentage of offenses did not even come to the notice of the police and, of those that did, only a minority were cleared up and the perpetrators brought to trial. The risk of being caught, found guilty, and punished, though it varied according to type of offense and the circumstances in which it was committed, remained comparatively slight.

Nevertheless, arguments continued about the nature of the penal system in pluralistic, liberal democracies. Some penologists believed that the criminal law was based on a broad consensus of generally agreed attitudes within society. Sanctions imposed by the courts upheld these common values. There had to be a penal system, though it should be run justly and efficiently. Conflict theorists rejected this view and held that laws were

While anguished demonstrators protested outside the Florida state prison, John Spenkelink was led into the execution chamber on May 25. His sister, Carol, is at right.

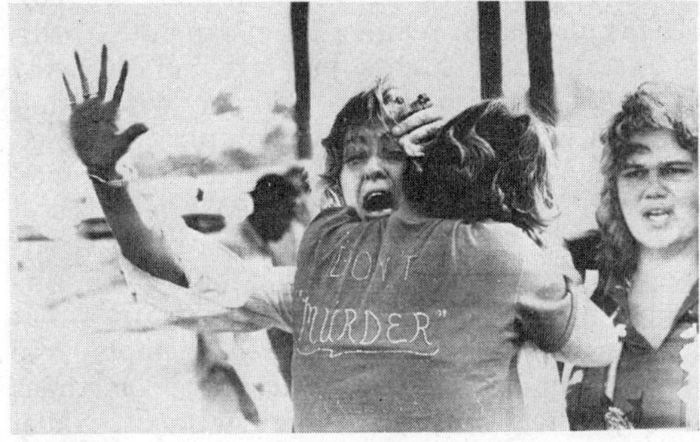

WIDE WORLD

Portuguese Literature:
see Literature

Power:
see Energy; Engineering Projects; Industrial Review

Presbyterian Churches:
see Religion

Prices:
see Economy, World

Printing:
see Industrial Review

EFE/PHOTO TRENDS

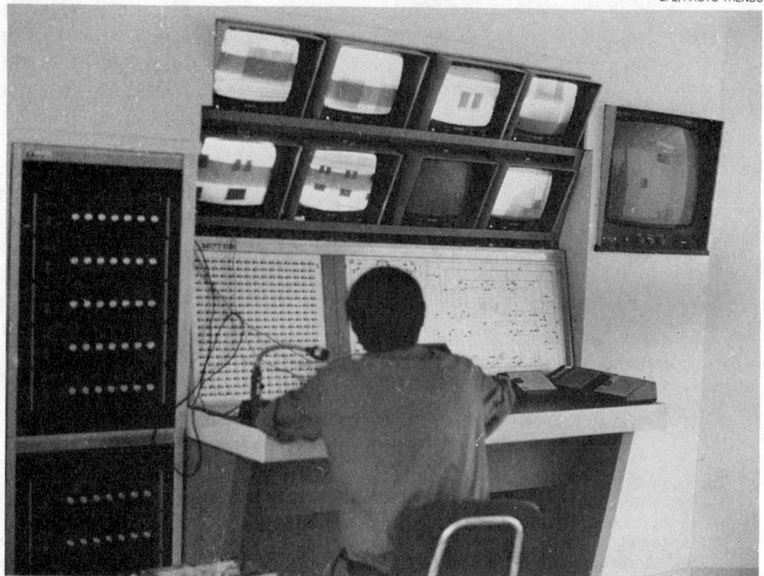

Guards check on activities through TV monitors in Spain's most modern prison in Ciudad Real. Surrounded by a desert, the prison is considered almost escape-proof.

designed to help the haves against the have-nots; that the penal system was one of the instruments whereby the ruling class kept the rest down; that courts were oppressors in a class war; that offenders were at the mercy of social forces beyond their control; and that theft of private property was a good way of undermining the system.

Opinions about the use of the death penalty diverged sharply. At the Florida state prison in Starke, on May 25, John Spenkelink became the first individual in the U.S. in 12 years to be executed against his will. (Gary Gilmore, executed at Utah state prison on Jan. 17, 1977, had repudiated all efforts on his behalf for a stay of execution; so too did Jesse Bishop, executed at the Nevada state prison on Oct. 22, 1979.) A month earlier, the Israeli government decided, by a bare majority, to introduce the death penalty for particularly vicious terrorist murders. No execution had taken place as of year's end. In late 1978, by contrast, the Spanish government, under the terms of its new constitution, abolished the death penalty except for military crimes committed in time of war. In July 1979 a parliamentary motion to make capital punishment available to the courts once again was heavily defeated in the U.K. In France, one of the few Western European countries retaining the death penalty, the National Assembly held a full-scale debate on capital punishment in June, but no vote was taken.

There were still major differences among countries in the number of persons in custody per 100,000 population. In Western Europe the U.K., with 78.3, still had the highest proportion of convicted prisoners, followed by West Germany with 69 and Belgium with 63.8. Most other countries hovered between 40 and 30, while The Netherlands stood out with only 9.4. These figures were only rough indications, however, because strict comparisons were impossible. The proportion for the U.S. was higher than for Western European countries, but so was the crime rate. Continued attempts were made to cut down prison populations, sometimes simply by reducing the average length of custodial sentences for different offenses, as the Dutch had done. But sanctions also represent a moral judgment. Thus the newly elected government in the U.K. indicated that it would introduce, for certain types of young, physically and mentally robust offenders, a form of detention that, while short, would involve a strict, demanding, and disciplined regime.

There were comparatively few major prison riots in 1979, but the many smaller disturbances served to undermine morale among both staff and prisoners. The U.S. expert Hans Toch, in his book *Living in Prison* (1977), isolated environmental factors that are important to inmates. High among these were privacy and the need for peace and quiet. There was also a strong concern for safety and protection, but these two primary needs were hard to satisfy. With increasing numbers of lesser offenders being dealt with in the community, a proportionately larger residue of unstable and violent inmates remained in custody. Steve Twinn, of the Officer Training School, Leyhill, England, analyzed the psychological effect on staff of violent attacks by inmates. The mere possibility of such events required that staff be reassured about their personal value as well as their safety. When an explosion did occur, it represented more than a physical assault, especially if an apparently positive relationship between an inmate and a staff member was thus abruptly shattered.

Such problems, together with overcrowding, bad conditions, long working hours, and lack of public recognition, were behind the strike actions by some prison personnel. In Belgium a strike in June 1979 led to the escape of prisoners. In New South Wales, Australia, staff stopped work in 24 prisons in August. In the U.K. in March, 500 of the 1,600 inmates of Walton Prison, Liverpool (designed to accommodate 800), demonstrated against the effects of a prison officers' work-to-rule action and the severe overcrowding that caused it; prolonged industrial action had resulted in the setting up of a committee of inquiry under Sir John May, a judge of the High Court. Lack of funds was at the root of many of the difficulties in correctional systems. Imprisonment was expensive, but effective alternatives for dealing with less serious but frequently very deprived offenders in the community were not cheap either. These people often lacked even such basic skills as literacy and numeracy. At the same time, they often had a variety of personal problems, including alcoholism and drug addiction.

Social skill training proved helpful to some offenders. Often they were organized in groups, where the emphasis was placed on sharing problems and jointly working out solutions. Simulation of crisis situations—interviews, frictions at home or with actual or potential employers—was also useful. But such programs required appropriate accommodations and a dedicated staff. The National Institute of Law Enforcement and Criminal Justice of the U.S. Department of Justice developed a useful scheme of making successful projects widely known by publicizing them in *Exemplary Projects.* An attempt to deal with young offenders by confining them to their own homes was started in New Brunswick. It remained to be seen whether this simple substitute for other and more costly types of detention would work.

Research continued to demonstrate that no penal system, unless it used intolerably draconian methods, could do much to lower the crime rate. For those who were not adherents of conflict theory, early prevention appeared to be a more promising method. At the local level, certainly, it had proved possible for parents, schools, police officers, youth leaders, and others to cooperate in reducing juvenile delinquency. Merely mobilizing community awareness could help, as in the Seattle (Wash.) Community Crime Prevention Program, which decreased burglaries by 30%. But the formulation of broad, practical, national strategies for crime prevention was still a long way off.

(HUGH J. KLARE)

A sizable cache of weapons was discovered when guards conducted a shakedown at the Stateville Correctional Center in Joliet, Illinois, in September.

CHICAGO SUN-TIMES PHOTO BY R. B. LEFFINGWELL

See also Crime and Law Enforcement; Law.
[521.C.3.a; 543.A.5.a; 10/36.C.5.b]

Publishing

In 1979 the publishing industry in general felt the effects of deteriorating world economic conditions. Reappearance of *The Times* of London was a notable exception among frequent closings of newspapers. A feature of the year was an upswing in censorship and official control of information in many parts of the world; authors and journalists were subjected to increasingly severe repression in some countries, among which post-revolutionary Iran featured prominently. In the U.S.S.R. a call by *Pravda* for a return of political satire did not mark any sort of change in Soviet attitudes toward the role of the press. In China hopes of liberalization faded when Wei Jingsheng (Wei Ching-sheng), editor of the dissident *Exploration,* was sentenced to 15 years in prison in October. In Pakistan Salamat Ali, correspondent of the Hong Kong-based *Far Eastern Economic Review,* was sentenced to a year's hard labour under the country's martial law. Jacobo Timerman, former editor of *La Opinion,* was expelled from Argentina after 29 months in prison or under house arrest; and Robert Cox, editor of the English-language *Buenos Aires Herald,* which protested the spread of violence under Argentina's military rulers, decided to leave the country because of threats against his family.

In South Africa new government pressures were seen as efforts to impose self-censorship on the press after further legal restraints were shelved because of resistance to them. In Britain reaction to the Anthony Blunt espionage disclosures (*see* UNITED KINGDOM) caused the government to drop its proposed new "protection of information" legislation.

African ministers of information meeting in Addis Ababa, Ethiopia, in May agreed to establish a Pan-African News Agency. In November the Nonaligned News Pool, grouping agencies in some 60 countries, met in Belgrade, Yugos., and adopted a "plan of action" aimed at the "decolonization" of information. The year ended without agreement among members of the UNESCO press commission headed by Sean MacBride on the text of a final report.

Newspapers. On Tuesday, Nov. 13, 1979, edition No. 60,473 of *The Times* of London appeared, almost one year after No. 60,472. On the following Sunday its sister, *The Sunday Times,* also returned, marking the end of a remarkable episode in the troubled history of British newspaper publishing.

Although the return of two major newspapers

Profits:
see Economy, World

Protestant Churches:
see Religion

Psychiatry:
see Health and Disease

was generally acclaimed, opinion was divided over the merits of the strategy of confrontation of Times Newspapers Ltd. (TNL) with the printing unions. In editorials and other comment some other Fleet Street houses expressed the view that the cost – close to £30 million – had been great and the gain inadequate. *The Times*'s management had been forced to make numerous concessions, and the major issue, that of manning new computerized technology, was set aside for negotiation during the year ahead.

The short-term effects of the absence of *The Times* and *The Sunday Times* on their rivals were, predictably, beneficial. The *Telegraph* newspapers, *The Observer*, and *The Guardian* achieved new peaks, with circulation gains of 50% and more, during the year *The Times* and *The Sunday Times* did not publish. But it was notable that while *The Times*'s rivals – *The Guardian*, *The Daily Telegraph*, and the *Financial Times* – had between them added more copies than *The Times* had been selling, *The Sunday Telegraph* and *The Observer* had added only about one million copies, against the 1¼ million or more sold by *The Sunday Times*. Nevertheless, balance sheets gained substantially from advertising that would normally have gone to the dominating TNL titles as well as from extra sales, and these newspapers faced the return of competition and the increasingly imminent recession with a welcome bonus in their reserves.

The *Daily Star* tabloid, launched by Express Newspapers Ltd.'s new management in November 1978 as a brash sister to the *Daily Express*, achieved a circulation of about one million by mid-1979 but was still confined to a Manchester printing, with no union agreement for the extension to London that might permit a bigger impact. Meanwhile, the other four popular nationally distributed dailies lost about half a million sales against the previous midyear average, most of that shared by the *Daily Mirror* and *The Sun*.

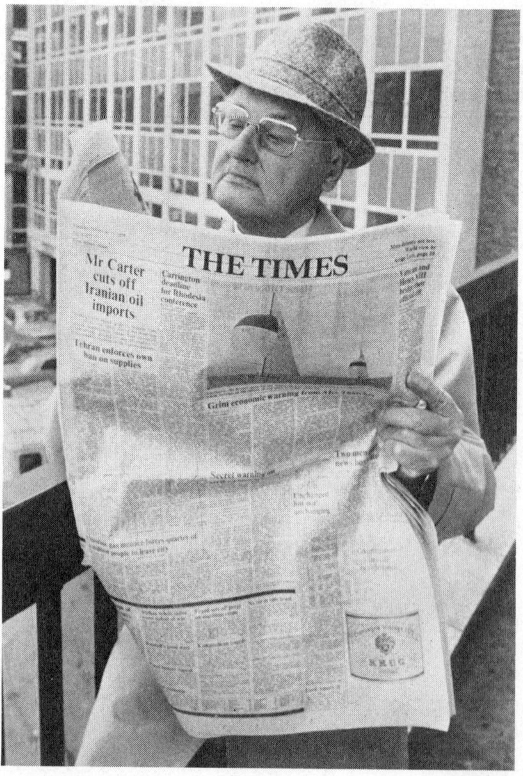

The aim of reaching people who had never before bought newspapers was behind the launching on October 10 of Italy's first popular tabloid in the Fleet Street style; in fact, the publishers of *L'Occhio* ("The Eye") brought in a designer from the *Daily Mirror*. Editor Maurizio Costanzo discounted bare bosoms as not suitable for a family readership but believed there was a large market for pictures, gossip, sports, and simplified news in a nation whose total sales of daily newspapers were reckoned equivalent to the circulation of just one British popular tabloid.

In January the London *Financial Times* launched an international edition printed in Frankfurt, West Germany. Its distribution was to extend to most of Western Europe, New York City and other leading U.S. cities, and Canada.

In France *L'Aurore* was integrated more closely into Robert Hersant's press empire, and an eventual merger of its masthead into that of *Le Figaro* seemed likely. More surprisingly, the independent *Le Quotidien de Paris* reappeared in November after closing down in June 1978. *Le Monde* and *Le Matin*, two Parisian papers that increased their sales in 1979 against an overall loss of circulation among the capital's eight dailies, both launched Sunday supplements during the year.

In Australia the intervention of the Trade Practices Commission caused Rupert Murdoch to withdraw his bid to take over the *Melbourne Herald* and *Weekly Times*. (PETER FIDDICK)

In the United States newspaper circulation continued its unbroken path of recovery from the recession-caused lows of the early 1970s, though many publishers were worried that the nation's new economic downturn would end that streak. Total daily circulation for the year rose nearly 1% to 61,989,997, a five-year high, according to the 1979 *Editor & Publisher International Yearbook*. Morning circulation leaped 3.4% to a record 27,656,739, while evening circulation dropped by 1.2% to 34,-333,258, the lowest figure in 20 years. There were 1,756 daily newspapers, a net gain of 3 for the year. There were 355 morning papers, 8 more than a year earlier, and 1,410 evening papers, 5 fewer. (The nation's 18 "all day" papers, those with editions throughout the day, are counted in both morning and evening categories.)

Much of the gain in morning circulation and the decline in evening circulation resulted from a significant new trend: evening papers with dwindling readership were adding morning editions. One of the nation's largest evening dailies, the decorous but declining *Philadelphia Bulletin* (circulation 500,000), entered the morning market just as the year began. Another, the financially ailing *Washington Star* (circulation 329,000), made the switch a few months later. Though evening newspapers were more numerous and more widely read than their morning counterparts, the evening was becoming a difficult time of day to publish a newspaper. The reasons included heightened competition from evening television news broadcasts and

A Londoner catches up on the news after *The Times* resumed publication in November following a dispute between management and labour unions that lasted 347 days.

KEYSTONE

WIDE WORLD

The new owners of *Esquire* are Phillip Moffitt (left) and Christopher Whittle, who bought the magazine in April.

from suburban evening papers, traffic jams that hampered midday delivery, and the habits of readers. *Dallas Times Herald* publisher Lee Guittar, whose paper added a morning edition late in 1978, commented that "people are acclimated to having their newspaper with their morning coffee."

One evening paper that made the transition from evening to morning in 1979—to no avail—was the *Montreal Star* (circulation 114,000), which shut down in September after 110 years of publication. The paper had been weakened by an eight-month strike of printers and by the flight from Quebec of English-speaking Canadians, worried about the rising militancy of the province's French-speaking majority. Montreal was thus left with only one English-language paper, the morning *Gazette* (circulation 168,000).

A standard feature in more than 1,100 U.S. newspapers during the year was the national and international reporting of United Press International, the world's second largest wire service, after the Associated Press. Yet UPI, which was owned jointly by the Scripps-Howard and Hearst newspaper chains (the Associated Press is a cooperative owned by its clients), had been losing money heavily for nearly two decades. To stave off financial collapse in 1979 the wire service invited 100 of its largest newspaper and broadcasting customers to buy a total of 90% of its stock. The sale would provide the service with as much as $4.5 million in new funds.

The press continued to suffer setbacks at the hands of the U.S. Supreme Court in 1979. In *Herbert* v. *Lando*, the court ruled that journalists must answer questions about what they were thinking when they prepared reports that provoked libel suits. Despite protests by some journalists that the decision would have a "chilling effect" on editorial

World Daily Newspapers and Circulations, 1977–78[1]

Location	Daily newspapers	Circulation per 1,000 population
AFRICA		
Algeria	4	13
Angola	5	18
Benin	2	...
Botswana	1	31
Cameroon	1	2
Central African Republic	1	...
Chad	3	0.3
Congo	5	...
Egypt	16	...
Equatorial Guinea	2	...
Ethiopia	5	2
Gabon	2	1
Ghana	4	42
Guinea	1	2
Guinea-Bissau	1	11
Ivory Coast	2	6
Kenya	3	12
Lesotho	1	1
Liberia	2	8
Libya	3	...
Madagascar	12	...
Malawi	2	6
Mali	2	...
Mauritius	12	96
Morocco	9	21
Mozambique	2	4
Niger	1	0.2
Nigeria	21	...
Réunion	3	98
Senegal	1	6
Seychelles	2	58
Sierra Leone	2	...
Somalia	1	...
South Africa	23	45
Sudan	4	...
Tanzania	2	9
Togo	1	4
Tunisia	5	38
Uganda	1	2
Upper Volta	3	...
Zaire	4	3
Zambia	2	20
Zimbabwe Rhodesia	2	16
Total	180	
NORTH AMERICA		
Antigua	2	146
Bahamas, The	3	138
Barbados	1	101
Belize	2	43
Bermuda	1	203
Canada	117	229
Costa Rica	5	90
Cuba	16	...
Dominican Republic	10	42
El Salvador	11	54
Guadeloupe	1	56
Guatemala	9	37
Haiti	7	20
Honduras	7	52
Jamaica	3	58
Martinique	1	80
Mexico	256	...
Netherlands Antilles	5	206
Nicaragua	6	49
Panama	6	81
Puerto Rico	4	140
Trinidad and Tobago	3	121
United States	1,756	284
Virgin Islands (U.S.)	3	...
Total	2,236	
SOUTH AMERICA		
Argentina	176	...
Bolivia	14	35
Brazil	280	39
Chile	47	...
Colombia	40	...
Ecuador	29	49
French Guiana	1	21
Guyana	3	150
Paraguay	5	46
Peru	35	...
Suriname	5	...
Uruguay	30	...
Venezuela	47	...
Total	712	
ASIA		
Afghanistan	15	...
Bangladesh	30	4
Burma	7	10
Cambodia	17	10
China	392	...
Cyprus	13	127
Hong Kong	111	350
India	875	15
Indonesia	172	...
Iran	28	25
Iraq	5	26
Israel	25	180
Japan	180	385
Jordan	4	27
Korea, North	11	...
Korea, South	30	173
Kuwait	6	179
Laos	8	...
Lebanon	33	...
Macau	7	...
Malaysia	31	87
Mongolia	2	77
Nepal	29	...
Pakistan	102	...
Philippines	18	...
Saudi Arabia	12	...
Singapore	12	239
Sri Lanka	11	25
Syria	7	...
Taiwan	31	...
Thailand	18	42
Turkey	450	...
Vietnam	6	...
Yemen (Aden)	3	...
Yemen (San'a')	2	...
Total	2,508	
EUROPE		
Albania	2	48
Austria	31	...
Belgium	61	...
Bulgaria	14	250
Czechoslovakia	30	255
Denmark	49	359
Finland	59	...
France	156	182
Germany, East	39	...
Germany, West	411	404
Gibraltar	2	173
Greece	106	107
Hungary	29	223
Iceland	6	586
Ireland	10	246
Italy	78	113
Liechtenstein	2	393
Luxembourg	6	365
Malta	5	...
Netherlands, The	95	315
Norway	72	405
Poland	44	237
Portugal	30	70
Romania	34	145
Spain	134	116
Sweden	145	553
Switzerland	97	385
U.S.S.R.	686	...
United Kingdom	130	251
Vatican City	1	...
Yugoslavia	26	87
Total	2,590	
OCEANIA		
American Samoa	2	320
Australia	70	394
Cook Islands	1	40
Fiji	2	70
French Polynesia	4	...
Guam	1	165
New Caledonia	2	81
New Zealand	35	322
Niue	1	60
Papua New Guinea	1	6
Total	119	

[1]Only newspapers issued four or more times weekly are included.
Sources: UN, *Statistical Yearbook, 1977* (1978); *Editor & Publisher International Year Book* (1979); *Europa Year Book 1979, A World Survey;* various country publications.

decision making, others believed that the press still had considerable protection against libel suits. In fact, some press lawyers noted that journalists sometimes win libel cases by testifying about their state of mind, specifically by demonstrating that they had not lied or had serious doubts about the accuracy of their reports. Though the practical effect of the ruling appeared to be modest, many journalists felt that the Supreme Court was becoming increasingly hostile to their needs.

That suspicion gained when the court ruled later in the year, in *Gannett* v. *DePasquale*, that criminal proceedings could be closed to the public in some circumstances. The case involved a pretrial hearing on suppression of evidence, but the wording of several justices' opinions left the impression that actual criminal trials could be closed as well—a notion that seemingly contradicted the U.S. tradition of open criminal proceedings. Unlike *Herbert* v. *Lando*, the decision had an immediate and widespread effect. Within a few weeks of the ruling local judges had granted half of 50 requests to exclude the press and, in some cases, the public at large from their courtrooms. The issue of whether the decision applied only to pretrial hearings or to trials themselves became further confused when several Supreme Court justices took the unusual step of trying to explain the decision publicly. Their remarks only added to the uncertainty. Late in the year the court accepted for decision a similar case, in apparent hope of finally reaching a clear-cut decision.

The Gold Medal for Public Service, the most prestigious of the Pulitzers, went to the tiny *Point Reyes* (Calif.) *Light* (circulation 2,700) for its articles on Synanon, a local drug-rehabilitation program that was described as having turned into an authoritarian cult.

James Risser of the *Des Moines Register* won his second Pulitzer for national reporting, this time for a series on pollution by farmers. The entire staff of the *San Diego Evening Tribune* received the general local reporting prize for coverage of a midair plane collision over San Diego that killed 144 persons.

Erwin Knoll, editor of *The Progressive* magazine, stirred up a national debate when he proposed to publish an article detailing the working of the hydrogen bomb. After a lengthy dispute, a federal court approved publication.

UPI

Gilbert Gaul and Elliot Jaspin of the *Pottsville* (Pa.) *Republican* won the award for special local reporting for an inquiry into the involvement of organized crime in a local coal company. Some Pulitzer jurors thought the prize should have gone instead to the *Chicago Sun-Times* for its articles on corruption among city officials, but other jurors disapproved of the paper's methods, which involved opening a local tavern where reporters posed as bartenders and managers and secretly recorded the attempts of city employees to solicit illegal payoffs from the business. That ruse was criticized by some Pulitzer judges as journalistically unethical. Richard Ben Cramer won the international reporting prize for his dispatches from the Middle East for the *Philadelphia Inquirer*, that paper's fifth Pulitzer in as many years. The prize for commentary went to a writer who is basically a humour columnist, Russell Baker of the *New York Times*. (DONALD MORRISON)

Magazines. Despite the generally buoyant consumer economy in Britain the September debut of *Now!* was met with skepticism. It marked the arrival on the British publishing scene, after several attempts, of Sir James Goldsmith, head of the French-based multinational food company Générale Occidentale and more recently owner of *L'Express*, a French newsmagazine. Doubts primarily centred on the appetite of the British public for a weekly newsmagazine, whether on the model of *L'Express* or of the leading U.S. journals *Time* and *Newsweek*, given the great strength of national daily newspapers and network television in Britain. A more specific problem was that the magazine was introduced at the same time that a long strike blacked out the commercial television channel, making the planned saturation advertising campaign impossible. In fact, however, the launch went well, and within two months *Now!* was claiming to have settled at weekly sales around 250,000, at which level it might be viable.

Activity in the business magazine sector included the February launching of *Financial Weekly* by the Trafalgar House group, under former *Punch* editor William Davies. Among literary magazines *The New Review* closed after four years of publication because of mounting debts and the withdrawal of its Arts Council subsidy. The absence until November of the *Times Literary Supplement* (*TLS*) stimulated the appearance of several new titles in the field, but it seemed doubtful whether all would long survive the *TLS*'s return. (*See* LITERATURE: *United Kingdom*.)

The French satirical weekly *Le Canard Enchaîné* boosted its circulation toward the million mark—and incurred legal action on charges of receiving stolen documents—with a series of political exposés. One deeply embarrassed Pres. Valéry Giscard d'Estaing over a gift of diamonds from the former Central African emperor, Bokassa I. Another provoked a scandal over a land deal that led to the suicide of Robert Boulin, the labour minister. (PETER FIDDICK)

Restrained in March from publishing a controversial article on hydrogen weapons, *The Progressive* won U.S. federal court approval to issue the piece in November. The 40,000-circulation monthly journal of liberal political reporting was the first publication in U.S. history to be placed under prior restraint of publication in a national security case. The U.S. Department of Justice asked that its case against the magazine be dismissed after a Wisconsin daily newspaper in late September published a long letter that contained much the same material as in the article, "The H-Bomb Secret, How We Got It—Why We're Telling It."

The trend of more and more people in the U.S. to read more and more magazines continued in 1979, much to the joy of publishers who reported advertisement revenue up once again. By midyear it had risen 14% over the corresponding period of 1978. The upward move began in 1976 and seemed likely to continue through the early 1980s.

In seeking an explanation for this boom in sales, publishers agreed that magazines had met the challenge of television by developing specialized titles for narrow-interest audiences, as opposed to TV's broad-gauge approach to viewers. In addition, higher cover and subscription prices were meeting the actual costs of publication and distribution, and so publishers no longer had to engage in mad drives for more and more readers to get more advertisers to pay higher rates. The question that remained was how high magazine prices could be raised before buyers would throw up a resistance line.

Advertising continued to be a major part of the success or failure of magazines, and *Time* won the advertising plum of the year. A new record for a single advertisement charge was set in the Feb. 5, 1979, issue when Gulf & Western Industries, Inc. paid *Time* $3.8 million for a special 64-page insert.

Among countless takeovers in 1979, the most publicized was the sale of *Esquire* to two young Tennessee publishers, Christopher Whittle and Phillip Moffitt. The new owners planned to rework the magazine to appeal to men between 25 and 45.

One of the briefest revivals in the history of magazine publishing was made by *Look*. Resurrected in February by the owner of Paris *Match*, the magazine had lost $10 million by July under the editorship of *Rolling Stone* publisher Jann Wenner. While the publisher continued to claim that the magazine would again be issued, it seemed unlikely since in midsummer most of the staff were fired.

The other major casualties included *Viva*, the five-year-old monthly directed to career women, published by Bob Guccione of *Penthouse*. It failed to dent the lead of *Cosmopolitan*, *Vogue*, and *Glamour*. The liberal newsmagazine *New Times* went under, although at the same time the publisher brought out the highly successful *The Runner*. And Harcourt Brace Jovanovich, Inc., which started *Human Nature* in November 1977, closed it in February 1979.

Working on the premise that 2.1 million U.S. museum members have a specialized interest, McGraw-Hill, Inc. brought out a pilot issue of *Muse* magazine in 1979. With hope for an eventual circulation of one million, *Muse* featured articles and departments on museums specializing in art, science, natural history, and even sport and gardening. The estimated 275–300 other new titles issued in 1979 included, among others: *Working Mother*, a bimonthly from the publisher of *McCall's*; *New Technology*, a liberal interpretation of science and industry; *Science Fiction and Fantasy Book Review*; *Geo*, a general monthly with identity problems and a rich format; *Stage*, from the American Stage Guild; and such specialized titles as *Clocks* and *Kite Lines*.

Instead of taking excerpts from new books and periodicals, as did *New Harvest*, the latest 1979 entry in this field, one publisher came up with the original idea of simply reprinting first chapters. In the aptly titled *Chapter One*, the first chapters of four novels and six nonfiction works were offered to readers.

The book of the year concerning magazines, particularly *Time*, was David Halberstam's *The Powers That Be*. The controversial study praised *Time* publisher Henry Luce to excess, according to some critics. Others hailed the author as having given an accurate portrayal of *Time* as a newsmagazine that helped shape U.S. politics and society.

One of the National Magazine Awards for 1978 (presented in the spring of 1979) went to *New West* magazine for public service. This West Coast version of *The New York Magazine* won the award for an article about defects in steel-belted radial tires. The seven other winners were: *The American Journal of Nursing*, *The Atlantic Monthly*, *Audubon*, *Life*, *The National Journal*, *Progressive Architecture*, and *Texas Monthly*. (WILLIAM A. KATZ)

Books. There was continuing improvement in relations between Western publishers and those in China and the Soviet Union in 1979. Delegations from both countries visited Britain during the year, and visits were made to China by groups of U.S. and West German publishers. A British Book Exhibition was held in China in the latter half of the year. Britain also signed a cultural agreement with China and a protocol with the Soviet Union. However, the Moscow International Book Fair in September was marred by the confiscation of some U.S., British, and Swedish publications by the Soviet authorities.

As a result of unfavourable economic circumstances the 31st Frankfurt (West Germany) Book Fair, held October 10–15, was quieter and more sober than many of its predecessors. The number of exhibitors, 5,014, was slightly below the previous year's (revised) total of 5,098, but the number of countries represented increased from 78 to 81. In all, approximately 280,000 titles, including 84,000 new ones, were shown. After West Germany, the largest national contingent of exhibitors was from the U.K. (547), followed by the U.S. (524) and France (189).

The advent of new technology had several implications for publishers. The European Commission introduced Euronet, a document delivery service within the Common Market countries. Teleordering systems for books were installed in both Britain and the U.S. In the U.K. initial moves were made to resolve the problem of photocopying books in educational institutions. Examples of piracy in third world countries proliferated. In Australia a new amended Copyright Act was implemented, and an investigation into book prices

UPI

Thousands of bibliophiles jammed 52nd Street and Fifth Avenue to view books on display at 173 bookstalls during the New York Book Fair in September.

began. In France retail price maintenance for books was abolished.

British publishers did not have a good year in 1979. Sales were affected by the economic recession. Cutbacks in government spending damaged institutional spending at home and threatened to disrupt the work overseas of such valuable agencies as the British Council. Exports were hurt by the strength of the pound, and overseas postal rates quadrupled in a short period of time.

The British Publishers Association formed the Book Marketing Council in an effort to improve sales of books on the home market. A national committee of inquiry was formed to investigate problems in schoolbook supply. A working party of teachers and others working in education convened by the National Book League reported that spending levels were inadequate and that twice as much money should be spent on schoolbooks.

Total sales of British books in 1978 topped the £500 million mark for the first time. Turnover on the home market was £310 million, while exports totaled £212 million. Wage settlements in the printing industry seemed likely to cause an increase of up to 20% in the price of British books by the end of 1979. *The Guinness Book of Records* was able in October to print its own record, the first copyrighted book to sell more than 40 million copies. (JOHN DAVIES)

Book publishing in the U.S., which grew at a healthy rate in 1978, seemed in 1979 to be in the early stages of a recession-induced slowdown, according to sources in the Association of American Publishers. AAP chairman Alexander Hoffman noted in mid-July that in the past "publishing had been remarkably recession proof" but that now "it could be running into meaningful price resistance." Small increases and some dips seemed to characterize AAP's monthly sales reports.

Categories of books showing declining sales through the first nine months of 1979, according to AAP figures, were adult trade hardcover, off 1% on sales of $172 million, and juvenile paperbacks, which suffered a 19.7% loss on sales of $11.9 million. Mass-market paperbacks showed a 6.9% increase through September on sales of $359.5 million; adult trade paperback sales showed a 2.8% gain for the nine months on sales of $54.9 million, although sales for September were off 1.5%. Juvenile hardcover sales for the first nine months were up 4.2% on sales of $65 million.

Also ahead for the first nine months of 1979 were mail-order publications, up 4.8% on sales of $160.6 million. Technical, scientific, business, and medical books showed strong sales through the nine months, up 28% on sales of $148.9 million. Book club sales in the same period rose 11.8%. College textbooks and materials posted a 5.5% gain through September on sales of $361.5 million. Elementary and high school textbooks and materials rose 10.2% through the first three quarters on sales of $536.1 million.

For 1978 AAP estimated that book sales increased 12.6% to a total of $5.8 billion, compared with 1977 sales of $5.1 billion. Largest increases were posted by the trade book category, in which a 16.5% rise to $940.5 million was reported. Professional books enjoyed the next highest percentage of increase, up 15.2% with total sales reaching $807.9 million. College textbook sales increased by 13.1% to $749.2 million, while elementary-secondary textbook sales rose 10.2% to $823.5 million. Mass-market paperbacks increased 12.2% to $608.1 million.

U.S. book title output in 1978, as reported by R. R. Bowker Co., was 41,216 titles of all kinds (new books and new editions), 3.8% below the 1977 total. In only a few areas were there increases, notably in business book titles, which were up nearly 16%, and new fiction listings, which increased about 5%. The average price of hardcover volumes rose less than 1%; mass-market paperback prices rose about 10.5%; and trade paperback prices increased approximately 6%.

The trend toward dominance of conglomerates in the publishing world continued to arouse concern in the publishing community. According to W. T. Grimm and Co., a Chicago-based merger specialist, mergers increased 14% in the publishing and printing industry in 1978 compared with 1977. The 1978 total was 65, up from 57 in 1977.

Interestingly, in 1979 the big merger stories were the ones that never took place. A seven-week legal battle to repulse a takeover bid was the result of the offer in January by the American Express Co. of $830 million (about $34 per share) for McGraw-Hill, Inc., one of the largest publishing companies in the U.S. McGraw-Hill's board of directors contested the attempted takeover, citing the importance of maintaining the independence of its operations, which included *Business Week*, a leading business magazine, and Standard & Poor's, an investment advisory board that issues widely accepted ratings on bonds. McGraw-Hill and American Express also traded lawsuits.

Subsequently, American Express withdrew the $34 per share offer and raised the ante to $40 per share, but this time only if the majority of the board of directors of McGraw-Hill recommended the offer or agreed not to oppose it. McGraw-Hill's 13-member board unanimously rejected the offer, and American Express withdrew the second bid.

American Broadcasting Co. withdrew in November from an agreement for it to acquire Macmillan, Inc. in a $340 million transaction shortly after the boards of both companies had approved the plan. Earlier, in accepting ABC's offer, Macmillan broke off talks with Mattel Inc., a toy manufacturer.

ABC was successful with another merger attempt; it bought a 51.6% interest in the Chilton Book Co., a publisher of magazines and books. Mattel acquired Western Publishing Co. for $120.8 million in cash and stock. Western publishes the Golden Book series and Whitman Books.

Record-breaking sales of paperback rights continued to be set each year, and in 1979 the price surpassed $3 million. Bidding $3,208,875, Bantam Books topped seven other paperback houses for reprint rights to *Princess Daisy*, the second novel by Judith Krantz, author of the best-seller *Scruples*.

In yet another record-breaking rights sale the film rights to the forthcoming nonfiction book *Thy Neighbor's Wife* by Gay Talese, to be published by Doubleday & Co., Inc. in 1980, were sold to United Artists for $2.5 million. The sum surpassed the $2,150,000 paid by Zanuck-Brown earlier in the year for Peter Benchley's *The Island*, also a Doubleday book. (DAISY G. MARYLES)

See also Literature.
[441.D; 543.A.4.e]

Qatar

An independent monarchy (emirate) on the west coast of the Persian Gulf, Qatar occupies a desert peninsula east of Bahrain, with Saudi Arabia and the United Arab Emirates bordering it on the south. Area: 11,400 sq km (4,400 sq mi). Pop. (1978 est.): 200,000. Capital: Doha (pop., 1978 est., 160,000). Language: Arabic. Religion: Muslim. Emir in 1979, Sheikh Khalifah ibn Hamad ath-Thani.

Oil price increases by the Organization of Petroleum Exporting Countries (OPEC) in December 1978 and in 1979, coupled with surcharges and sales on the world spot market well above OPEC prices, increased Qatar's revenues in 1979. The Qatari finance and petroleum minister, Sheikh Abdul Aziz ibn-Khalifah ath-Thani, announced in January that the increase would merely compensate Qatar for the drop in the value of the U.S. dollar.

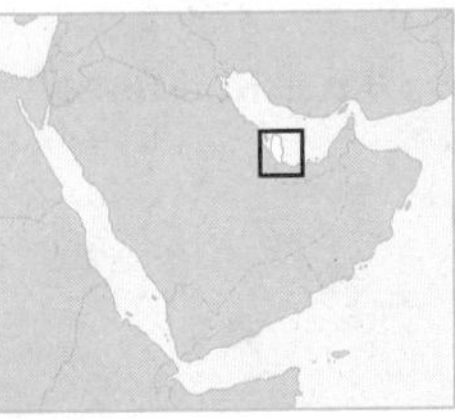
Qatar

Exploitation of natural gas in the North-West Dome gas field proved too expensive, at an estimated $3 billion, for Qatar to undertake alone. Thus, the government announced in May that it would sponsor a joint study with Royal Dutch Shell on exploitation of the proven reserves of 31 million cu ft of gas.

On May 5 Qatar revalued the riyal 2% against the U.S. dollar. The revaluation ended the interchangeability of the riyal with Bahraini and United Arab Emirates currencies. Qatar agreed in February, after the visit of the emir, Sheikh Khalifah ibn Hamad ath-Thani, to Paris, to sell France one million metric tons of oil in exchange for French weaponry.

Qatar joined other Arab nations in rejecting the March 26 Egyptian-Israeli treaty and in severing diplomatic relations with Egypt. Qatar planned to contribute $320 million annually to Syria, Jordan, and the Palestine Liberation Organization to enable them, without Egypt's support, to confront Israel. (CHARLES GLASS)

QATAR

Education. (1976–77) Primary, pupils 25,266, teachers 1,377; secondary, pupils 9,716, teachers 791; vocational, pupils 375, teachers 75; teacher training, students 256, teachers 59; higher (1975–76), students 779, teaching staff 69.

Finance. Monetary unit: Qatar riyal, with (Sept. 17, 1979) a free rate of 3.73 riyals to U.S. $1 (8.02 riyals = £1 sterling). Gold, SDR's, and foreign exchange (Dec. 1978) U.S. $203 million. Budget (1978 est.): revenue 8,564,000,000 riyals; expenditure 8,280,000,000 riyals.

Foreign Trade. (1978) Imports 4,589,700,000 riyals; exports 8,982,200,000 riyals. Import sources: Japan 20%; West Germany 19%; U.K. 16%; U.S. 10%; France 7%; Italy 5%. Export destinations: Japan *c.* 22%; France *c.* 19%; U.S. *c.* 13%; Thailand *c.* 9%; Madagascar *c.* 8%; Italy *c.* 7%; Belgium-Luxembourg *c.* 5%; Netherlands Antilles *c.* 5%. Main export: crude oil 99%.

Industry. Production (in 000; metric tons): crude oil (1978) 23,200; petroleum products (1977) 281; nitrogenous fertilizers (1977–78) 76; electricity (kw-hr; 1977) *c.* 900,000.

Race Relations

Relations between dominant and subordinate ethnic groups deteriorated significantly during 1979 in many parts of the world. Often conflict resulted from subordinate groups challenging previously agreed or imposed resolutions to issues of power, privilege, or status. The process of decolonization precipitated perhaps the most intractable of social and political problems in which black and white confronted each other; reverberations of the process spread throughout the globe.

Europe. In Britain the annual report of the Institute of Race Relations identified "a high incidence of racial violence, compounded by police disregard of, or hostility to, black communities." The Commission for Racial Equality took up a similar theme on April 5 in an inquiry into violence in an area in eastern London, maintaining that local police "appear to have condoned organised attempts to incite racial hatred."

Electoral support for an avowedly racist political party in the U.K. declined during the year. The National Front contested a record 303 seats in the May parliamentary elections, but its performance was poor in every constituency when compared with its modest but encouraging results in February and October 1974; on average the party polled 1.25% of votes cast in the 303 constituencies.

Reports from Sweden in March of racist attacks on black people and some of the country's 700,000 resident foreigners linked such activity with neofascist organizations. An attack upon a school and the daubing of racist slogans in Olofström in early March by a self-styled "new Nazi party" coincided with assaults by motorcycle gangs on the 9,000–10,000-strong Assyrian immigrant community in Stockholm's suburbs.

Puerto Rico:
see Dependent States

Quakers:
see Religion

Quarrying:
see Mining and Quarrying

Increased action by French police checking the residence permits of black people on the Paris subway provoked opposition from labour unions and many legislators. At a protest meeting in March on the platform of a railway station, a new Committee for a Metro (subway) Free from Racism distributed green stars of David, reminiscent of badges Jews were obliged to wear by the Nazis. The Metro Workers Union said that police activity was clearly linked to the policy of sending back unwanted immigrants to their home countries.

Middle East. In Iran the victorious forces who caused the shah and his supporters to flee were as unwilling to accede to demands from minority groups for self-government as their deposed predecessor had been. Minority ethnic groups, including Baluchis, Arabs, Kurds, and Azerbaijanis, were estimated to constitute at least half of Iran's 35 million population. Fighting between the revolutionary government and each of the minorities lasted intermittently throughout the year.

Attention was diverted from this situation following the invasion by students of the U.S. embassy in Teheran on November 4. Members of the embassy staff were taken hostage while their captors demanded the extradition of the shah from the U.S. Ayatollah Ruhollah Khomeini (*see* BIOGRAPHIES), leader of the country's revolutionary government, stated on November 17 that women enjoyed special privileges under Islam and blacks were "an oppressed minority" who may have been sent to Iran "under compulsion." Two days later the students released two black marines and one woman, and a second group of six black men and four women was released on November 20. A leading black activist in the U.S., Vernon Jordan, described the move as "a cynical attempt to divide the American people."

Asia. Open conflict between Mizos fighting for independence from India in Mizoram broke out again in June and continued throughout August as supporters of the Mizo National Front attacked Indian security forces. The inhabitants of the small hill state on India's northeastern border differed in language, race, and religion from their neighbours in Assam. Since the disastrous 1958 famine the conflict between the central Indian government and the secessionists had never been far from the surface. On August 9 secessionists attacked a police station in the adjoining territory of Tripura, leaving a policeman dead and several injured.

Students from several African and Arab countries attending the Shanghai Textile Institute in China were involved in three days of fighting with local Chinese and fellow students. Arguments developed on July 3 when a foreign student refused to turn down his radio at night and quickly escalated into pitched battles at the foreign students' dormitory; 16 students were admitted into the hospital as a result of the fighting. Posters appeared describing the foreigners as "black devils" and criminals. Third world student sources reportedly said they would not return to their classes "as we fear for our lives."

Africa. In South Africa the ruling National Party's policy of creating black homelands within the country's borders continued with the establishment of Venda on September 13. The creation of Venda, along with that of Transkei and Bophuthatswana, was condemned in a statement agreed to by all members of the UN Security Council on September 21. The statement called on all governments to deny recognition to the so-called independent homelands. The establishment of Venda was described as being "designed to divide and dispossess the African people and establish client states under its domination in order to perpetuate apartheid."

A strike by the white Mine Workers Union began on March 7 when 120 white workers in the O'Kiep copper mine in northern Cape Province struck to protest the employment of two Coloured (mixed race) miners. When it became clear that the minister of labour was not going to intervene, the union ordered its 10,000 members to return to work on March 14. A government White Paper on May 8 proposed that black workers "permanently employed" and "permanently resident" in urban

Ku Klux Klansmen in Decatur, Alabama, knelt before a burning cross at the site where a clash on May 25 left two blacks and two whites wounded. Klansmen demanded that blacks who had been arrested be charged with attempted murder.

UPI

areas be allowed to join officially sanctioned labour unions and that "job reservation" be abolished. (*See* SOUTH AFRICA.)

In Zimbabwe Rhodesia the war between the Patriotic Front's guerrilla forces and government troops cost the lives of many combatants before the cease-fire agreed at the end of 1979; most of these casualties, inevitably, were Africans. Under the terms of the settlement reached at the London constitutional conference, Zimbabwe Rhodesia's future republican constitution would incorporate a comprehensive declaration of rights providing protection against discrimination by reason of race, colour, or creed. In elections to the new House of Assembly to be held two months after implementation of the cease-fire, 20 members would be elected by whites and the balance of 80 by blacks. The whites would only be able to form a government in coalition with the black party holding the largest number of seats.

Whites had been leaving the country at a steady pace. During the first quarter of 1979 there was a net loss of 2,916 whites; almost half of the 18,071 who left in 1978 settled in South Africa.

North America. On May 19–20 racial violence erupted in California's Folsom prison as members of the white supremacist Aryan Brotherhood, the Black Guerrilla Family, and Nuestra Familia, a Latino group, clashed with each other. One prisoner died, and 17 others were injured. The large numbers of blacks and Latinos in the prison population would inevitably lead to increased racial violence in the future, claimed Philip Guthrie, a spokesman for the prison authorities in California. On August 27 the UN Subcommission on Human Rights received a submission from a group of eight international lawyers alleging that black prisoners in U.S. jails were victims of "flagrant racism" and suffered violation of their human rights.

On June 27 the U.S. Supreme Court, in *United Steelworkers of America* v. *Weber*, ruled that an employer can promote black employees rather than white employees with greater work experience as part of an affirmative action program to offset racial discrimination. The decision reversed that of a New Orleans court of appeal. (*See* LAW.)

The white supremacist Ku Klux Klan held an abortive "white power" march in Montgomery, Ala., on August 11–12; an estimated 300 Klansmen succeeded in staging one on June 9 in Decatur, Ala. But Klan activity of an altogether more horrific nature occurred in Greensboro, N.C., on November 3. An anti-Klan rally at a predominantly black housing project was attacked by Klan members shooting indiscriminately into the crowd; five people were killed and ten wounded.

Tension between Jews and blacks in the U.S. increased during the year. A precipitating factor was the dismissal of the U.S. representative to the UN, Andrew Young, a black (*see* BIOGRAPHIES), after he met with a UN observer from the Palestine Liberation Organization, contrary to official U.S. policy. The incident led some blacks to express sympathy for the Palestinians, and some U.S. Jews withdrew their financial support from black organizations.

In June 300 Canadian Indian chiefs traveled to London to petition Queen Elizabeth II to recognize treaties and promises made to the tribes on July 1, 1867, and enshrined in Canada's basic law, the British North America Act. Chief Noel Starblanket, leader of the National Indian Brotherhood of Canada delegation, pointed out that since the Canadian government had excluded Indians from full participation (they had observer status only) in discussions on new constitutional arrangements, they were effectively denied any avenues to make their views known.

WIDE WORLD

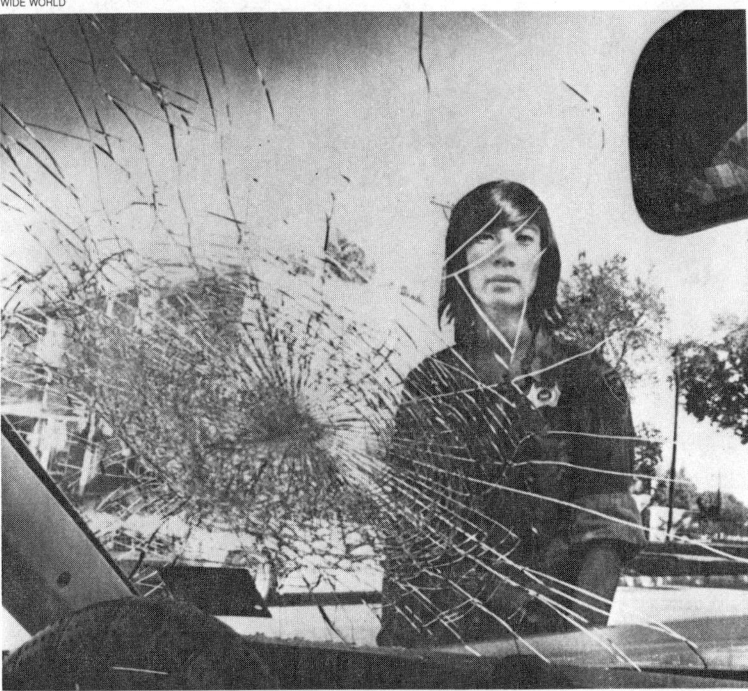

A Vietnamese immigrant views the smashed windshield of his automobile in Denver, Colorado. The city has witnessed numerous racial conflicts between Vietnamese and Chicanos.

South America. In January the Latin America Bureau exposed the deep-seated racial prejudice of Guatemala's white ruling class; at least 50% of the population are Mayan and they "are treated at best as second class citizens, deemed to have an inferior culture."

Patrick Montgomery, representing the Anti-Slavery Society of London before the UN, reported that actions of the Brazilian government and tin mining companies threatened the existence of the country's indigenous peoples. He reported that experts believed "the largest surviving Amerindian tribe in South America, the Yanoama, numbering some 17,000 people would cease to exist within twenty years." In southern Brazil in May Caingang Indians attacked white farmers occupying two-thirds of the 15,000 ha (37,000 ac) of land officially designated as theirs. (STUART BENTLEY)

[522.B]

Racket Games

Badminton. In the All-England tournament held in London during March 1979, Liem Swie King of Indonesia won his second straight title by defeating Flemming Delfs of Denmark 15–7, 15–8 in the final round. Lene Koppen of Denmark won the women's championship with an 11–9, 1–11,

LONDON DAILY EXPRESS/PICTORIAL PARADE

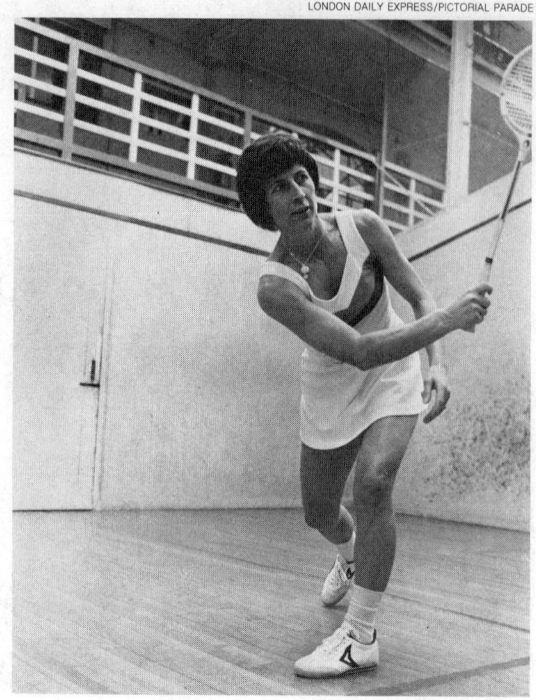

Heather McKay of Australia defeated Britain's Sue Cogswell to retain the women's World Open squash championship.

11–8 triumph over Saori Kondo of Japan. Indonesian pairs won the doubles championships. Tjun Tjun and Johan Wahjudi took the men's event with a 17–16, 15–3 victory over Stefan Karlsson and Cless Nordin of Sweden, and Imelda Wiguno and Verawaty Wiharjo won the women's title 15–3, 10–15, 15–7 over Mikiko Takada and Atsuko Tokuda of Japan.

The U.S. championships took place in Omaha, Neb., in April. In the men's singles Chris Kinard of California defeated Gary Higgins of California 6–15, 15–11, 15–12. Pam Brady of Michigan won the women's title 12–9, 2–11, 12–9 over Utami Kinard of California. Jim Poole and Mike Walker of California teamed up to win the men's doubles 15–17, 17–16, 15–11 over fellow Californians John Britton and Charles Coakley. Pam Brady and Judianne Kelly of California defeated Cheryl Carton and Diana Osterhues of California 15–5, 15–7 in women's doubles, and Kelly joined with Mike Walker to defeat John and Traci Britton in the mixed doubles 15–12, 15–12.

(JACK H. VAN PRAAG)

Squash Rackets. The International Squash Rackets Federation at its general meeting in Brisbane, Australia, in October 1979 unanimously agreed to adopt the principle of open squash, in which amateurs and professionals compete against one another in the same tournaments, as of Sept. 1, 1980. But member countries that might lose government grants if they abolished amateur status could retain the distinction. Efforts by Nigeria to get South Africa expelled from the federation were again defeated.

The World Open championship, held in Toronto in September 1979, resulted in a third successive victory for Geoffrey Hunt (Australia), who beat Qamar Zaman (Pakistan) with astonishing ease in straight games in 26 minutes. Hunt had also beaten Zaman in the final of the British Open championship in five games—his sixth win in this event—and thus confirmed his position as the world's leading player. Hashim Khan returned from Pakistan to England to defend his Open Vintage (over 55) title and won again. In the final he beat J. H. Giles (Great Britain), a much younger man who scored only 11 points against the winner.

In the European Championships in February, England won the men's event for the seventh time, beating Sweden in the final. England's women were also successful, with Ireland as runner-up.

In the U.S. Amateur championship final, M. Sánchez (Mexico) beat Tom Page (U.S.). Sharif Khan of Pakistan won the North American Open championship for the tenth time in 11 years. In the seemingly last Amateur International championships, held in Brisbane, Great Britain defeated Pakistan 2–1 in the final to win the team event. Jehanigir Khan of Pakistan beat P. Kenyon of Great Britain in individual competition.

Heather McKay of Australia retained the women's World Open championship, beating Sue Cogswell (U.K.). Great Britain won the first world women's team championship, defeating Australia in the final. (JOHN H. HORRY)

Rackets. William Surtees retained the world rackets championship by beating challenger William Boone 5–0 in New York City and at Queen's Club, London, in February 1979. At the start of the second leg at Queen's Club, Boone was already four games down.

Boone avenged his 3–0 defeat by John Prenn in the British amateur singles final in January by defeating him in the final of the Louis Roederer British Open championship at Queen's Club in March. Howard Angus and Andrew Milne won the British amateur doubles championship for the second straight year.

The rehabilitation of the rackets court in Gibraltar was celebrated with an unofficial European Open championship meeting in October 1978. Boone won the singles title, and he and Tom Pugh gained the doubles.

Real Tennis. Howard Angus retained the real tennis world championship at the Royal Court, Hampton Court, near London, on April 19, 1979. Angus beat Chris Ronaldson, the Troon professional, who had earned the right to challenge by winning an elimination competition 7–0 in only two legs.

Angus won the British amateur singles for a record 14th successive year, beating Alan Lovell in the final at Queen's Club in February. Angus won the Marylebone Cricket Club gold racket, also for the 14th straight year, at Lord's, London, in June, beating Lovell 3–1. (CHRISTINA WOOD)

Racquetball. The year 1979 was a banner one in the rapidly expanding world of racquetball. Still the fastest growing participatory sport in the United States, racquetball was growing at a rate comparable to those of tennis and bowling at parallel stages of development. Statistics placed racquetball's growth at more than 40% in 1979 (over 1978) and an amazing 283% over 1976. Approximately ten million participants spent nearly $550 million on racquetball and racquetball equipment during the year.

Competitively, 20-year-old Marty Hogan again won not only the U.S. national championship but also eight of the nine tour stops. His closest rival was 19-year-old Mike Yellen, who was runner-up in the national championships.

(CHARLES S. LEVE)

Refugees

Refugees were more than ever in the news headlines during 1979. Most noteworthy were the dramatic plight of the "boat people" from Vietnam, who arrived in Malaysia, Thailand, Hong Kong, Indonesia, Macau, and other parts of Southeast Asia in large numbers, and the flight of thousands of Cambodians into Thailand. (*See* Special Report; CAMBODIA.) In an effort to cope with the gigantic problem of Indochinese refugees, the UN High Commissioner for Refugees, Poul Hartling, in December 1978 called a full-scale international consultative meeting in Geneva, appealing for resettlement places in countries of permanent asylum no less than for funds.

A strong resettlement drive was mounted, but the continuing and indeed increasing outflow of boat people and other Indochinese refugees made it impossible to bridge the gap between arrivals in camps and departures from them. By mid-1979 the refugee population of Laotians, Cambodians, and Vietnamese in camps in the region surpassed 350,000, excluding tens of thousands of Cambodians arriving overland in Thailand and those who had fled to Vietnam earlier. In May 1979, for example, more than 50,000 boat people arrived in Southeast Asian countries of temporary asylum; the number who left the region to be resettled during the same month was less than 9,000. Since 1975 more than 185,000 Indochinese refugees had been resettled in the U.S., France, Australia, Canada, and other countries, apart from some 130,000 Indochinese who went to the U.S. in mid-1975.

In May the UN High Commissioner for Refugees (UNHCR) concluded a Memorandum of Understanding with the Vietnamese government to facilitate the "orderly departure" of Vietnamese who wished to leave their country, under certain conditions (including the availability of places for permanent resettlement). However, events in that region assumed an alarming character after Malaysia and Thailand turned back refugees entering from Vietnam and Cambodia, respectively. In July an international meeting was called in Geneva by the UN secretary-general, Kurt Waldheim, with the purpose of obtaining maximum support for concrete measures designed to ameliorate the tragic situation of refugees and displaced persons in Southeast Asia.

The continent with the highest number of refugees, however, continued to be Africa, where during 1979 there were approximately four million refugees and displaced persons. These originated mostly from the Horn of Africa and southern Africa; they were spread throughout different African countries, such as Angola, Botswana, Djibouti, Kenya, Mozambique, the Sudan, Zaire, and Zambia. In Uganda, following an urgent appeal from the new government, UNHCR extended emergency assistance to the returning Ugandan refugees and exiles and also to Ugandans who had become displaced inside their own country. Some 30,000 other Ugandans sought refuge in the Sudan. Another international meeting on refugee problems took place in Arusha, Tanzania, in May. This meeting reviewed the conditions of refugees in Africa with a view toward establishing greater intergovernmental and humanitarian cooperation on their behalf.

WILLIAM CAMPBELL—SYGMA

The Agabar camp in Somalia provided shelter for 28,000 refugees who fled from strife in the Ogaden desert region of Ethiopia. There were an estimated 350,000 Ethiopian refugees in Somalia in 1979.

In Latin America the resettlement of refugees, mainly from Chile, continued during the year. The largest UNHCR program was on behalf of Nicaraguan refugees, more than 100,000 of whom arrived in Honduras, Costa Rica, and other countries in Central America. In Europe a regular flow to the Western part of the continent from Eastern Europe was again recorded.

During 1979 two major repatriation operations were concluded. About 160,000 Zairians returned to their former villages in Zaire from Angola and neighbouring countries and about as many Burmese returned to the state of Arakan in Burma from Bangladesh. Some 17,000 non-Bengalis (not included in the mass airlift undertaken by UNHCR in the subcontinent during 1973–74) were being moved from Bangladesh to Pakistan in 1979. Figures issued by the Pakistan government in November showed that the number of Afghans seeking refuge in Pakistan from the civil war in Afghanistan had risen to 255,000, the largest concentration of refugees in any Asian country except for Vietnamese in China.

From October 1977 seven more states ratified the 1951 Convention and the 1967 Protocol Relating to the Status of Refugees, the latest one being Suriname in November 1978. This would make it easier for UNHCR to deal with aspects of refugee problems in those countries.

There were substantial increases in the budget and staff of UNHCR. It was estimated that the overall budget for general program in 1979 would be more than $210 million, as compared with $112 million in 1978.

(UNHCR)

See also Migration, International.

Radio:
see Television and Radio

Railroads:
see Transportation

Real Tennis:
see Racket Games

Recordings:
see Music

Reformed Churches:
see Religion

SPECIAL REPORT

THE BOAT PEOPLE

by John E. McCarthy

Throughout recorded history an enduring tragedy has been the displacement of persons from their homes because of their political ideology, race, or religious beliefs. In 1979 there were, according to the United Nations High Commissioner for Refugees, more than 13 million such people. One of the most tragic of these movements is that of the "boat people" fleeing by sea from Vietnam.

It is almost impossible to envision what changes could occur in a nation that would force thousands of its citizens to take to the seas in small boats, leaving all worldly possessions behind, with only one definite belief: that despite the dangers that faced them they could not turn back. The stories of the hardships endured by these people—boats attacked by pirates, sunk in storms, stranded on coral reefs, and turned away by other nations—are repeated time and time again. Many of those who set out from Vietnam died at sea.

Flight from the Communist Regime. This refugee flow started when the government of South Vietnam collapsed with the fall of Saigon in April 1975. Frightened because of the military occupation by North Vietnam and the uncertainty of their future under a Communist government, more than 150,000 Vietnamese decided to leave their homes and risk their lives on the open sea in their search for freedom.

Since the installation of the new government in Ho Chi Minh City (the new name for Saigon), seabound refugees have continued to slip away by the hundreds from Vietnam. In late 1978 it became apparent that the Vietnamese government had added to the flow by deciding to rid the country of ethnic Chinese and others who seemingly could not adjust to the new social and economic order. These people were encouraged to leave.

Their departure was recently accelerated by the threat of enforced movement to the newly created economic zones. On the basis of interviews with refugees, it appears that these zones are primitive agricultural endeavours where survival is difficult. Of the 300,000 desperate people who have fled by sea and managed to secure asylum in nearby nations, 140,000 were believed to have made the journey during the first six months of 1979.

An additional horror is added to this story when one realizes that parents who could not secure boat space for their entire families often sent their young children on alone, with the hope that they might join them at a later date. Thousands of these unaccompanied children are now the most unprotected of the unprotected in the refugee camps throughout Southeast Asia. Also in these camps are the children who survived pirate attacks during which the adult passengers were killed. Special programs have been instituted by the United States and other nations to facilitate the movement of these children to places of safety.

Repeatedly, Vietnam's officials stated at international conferences that they could not control the outflow of these people. In spite of their protestations, however, this movement was apparently organized at the highest level of the Vietnamese government. Escaping refugees have said that government officials accepted fees paid in gold for departure, secured boats, and even towed these vessels with their sad human cargo out to sea.

The number of boat people who have lost their lives because of poorly constructed and equipped boats, storms, and pirates is incalculable. Representatives of the Hong Kong and French governments put the figure at 50% of the total number of refugees, while the U.S. Department of State estimated the rate at between 40 and 70%. The real loss of life will never be known, and the only figures available refer to the number of refugees who survive.

The sadness of this movement has been intensified and complicated by the tremendous animosity and internal problems of the countries of first asylum, particularly Thailand and Malaysia. Both of these nations, by means of police action and military force, have returned tens of thousands of the boat people to the seas. Those refugees who were permitted to land were generally sent to dismal camps to exist in spartan surroundings or were forced to live on deserted islands.

The physical and mental health of these displaced persons is of serious concern to the world community. The longer these refugees remain in camps, the greater the likelihood that they will fall victim to illnesses of all types, particularly those that relate to malnutrition and unsanitary conditions.

While limited health facilities are available in the Philippines, Hong Kong, and Japan, organized programs of health care are almost totally lacking in other Southeast Asian refugee camps. A recent sur-

---

John E. McCarthy is president of the International Catholic Migration Commission and executive director of Migration and Refugee Services at the United States Catholic Conference.

vey by the Center for Disease Control of the U.S. Public Health Service indicated that the major afflictions in the camps are tuberculosis, parasitic infections, and malaria. The seriousness of this medical problem can be well illustrated in that approximately 25% of those eligible for emigration are deemed inadmissible to other countries on health grounds. Many such people, however, have been admitted to other countries after undergoing intensive medical treatment.

Search for Solutions. The fate of the boat people was addressed at the United Nations Conference on Refugees in Geneva in July 1979. Commitments were obtained from some nations to increase their resettlement efforts. During the meeting the Vietnamese government again repeated that it had no control over the refugee flow; however, Vietnam did commit itself to placing a temporary moratorium on the movement of small boats away from its shores. The Vietnamese government's pledge to stop the flow of boat refugees was based on the assumption that an orderly departure would be allowed for those who wished to leave Vietnam and for those whom the government wished to expel. Since the Geneva conference, officials in Vietnam have stated that they would permit up to 10,000 of their nationals to emigrate each month.

Number of Indochinese Refugees Permanently Resettled from April 25, 1975, to Sept. 30, 1979

Recipient country	Number	Recipient country	Number
Argentina	86	Italy	640
Australia	24,133	Japan	100
Austria	450	Luxembourg	52
Belgium	1,334	Netherlands, The	838
Canada	27,451[1]	New Caledonia	96
Denmark	792	New Zealand	1,037
Finland	100	Norway	1,107
France	51,016[2]	Sweden	647
Germany, West	7,971	Switzerland	2,109
Greece	52	Taiwan	64
Guam	51	United Kingdom	3,260
Hong Kong	113	United States	261,446[3]
Ireland	109	Others[4]	208
Israel	169		
		Total	385,431

[1]Resettled as of Nov. 15, 1979.
[2]Includes 524 refugees resettled in French Guiana.
[3]Resettled as of Oct. 31, 1979.
[4]Includes 19 countries.
Sources: Canadian Department of Employment and Immigration; U.S. Department of State; Intergovernmental Committee for European Migration; UN High Commissioner for Refugees.

Any organized departure program from Vietnam

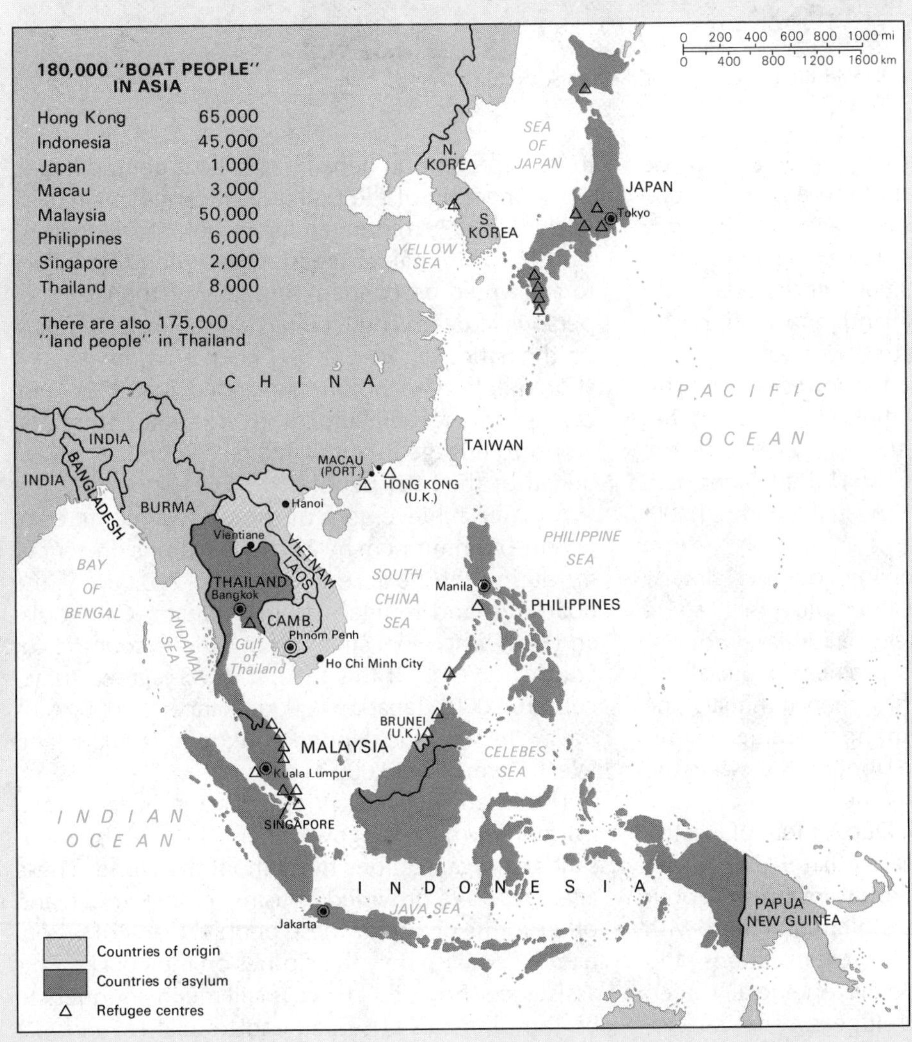

JULIEN QUIDEAU—CAMERA PRESS/PHOTO TRENDS

Children of the boat people cluster behind the barbed wire of the Songkla refugee camp on the Gulf of Thailand. Thailand has 14 such camps.

will have to relate to the ongoing project to provide permanent resettlement for the more than 180,000 boat people now stranded in areas of temporary asylum. These locations include Hong Kong with 65,000; Malaysia with 50,000; Indonesia with 45,000; and Singapore, Thailand, the Philippines, Macau, Japan, and Korea with fewer numbers.

Much has been accomplished in recent months, with resettlement opportunities provided for the refugees in many areas of the world. Among the major recipient countries are the United States with 260,000; France with 51,000; Australia with 24,000; and Canada with 27,000.

Because many of the receiving countries already suffered from high rates of unemployment, some questions arose as to whether the admission of refugees would exacerbate this problem. From all reports, however, the effect has been minimal. The main reason for this is that among the refugee families only one or two enter the labour force, while the remaining members are consumers.

A recent survey by the U.S. Department of Health, Education, and Welfare revealed that 94.5% of the heads of the refugee households are in the labour force. In view of this work ethic, combined with humanitarian concerns, labour organizations and unions throughout the world have generally been sympathetic to accepting refugees. The AFL-CIO, in its statement on behalf of the boat people issued at the meeting of the Executive Council in Chicago in August 1979, reiterated its support for the admission of additional refugees, maintaining that failure to act would be condemning tens of thousands of persons to death and would create an indelible stain on the national conscience. The International Longshoremen's Association responded in a like vein, calling on the U.S. and other free nations of the world to engage in a massive rescue endeavour on behalf of the boat people.

A major achievement of the Geneva conference was the commitment by 23 of the nations present to try during the next year to resettle 260,000 of the boat and land refugees from Vietnam, Cambodia, and Laos who were stranded in various countries of Southeast Asia. Of this total, the U.S. agreed to accept 168,000; Canada, 36,000; France, 17,000; Australia, 14,000; the United Kingdom, 10,000; and West Germany, 10,000.

The boat people of Vietnam have been helped not only by national governments but also by thousands of organizations throughout the world. These agencies have provided housing, employment, and other forms of aid for these people, many of whom had to flee with only the clothes on their backs. This assistance shows that there is still much goodness to be found in this unsettled and troubled world.

Religion

What belongs to God and what belongs to Caesar? An ancient question, it was asked anew and answered afresh in 1979 in nearly every part of the world.

At the beginning of the year, the relationship between the state and religious authorities became sharply focused in Iran. Many rejoiced and many wailed as the Ayatollah Ruhollah Khomeini, a zealous leader of Islam's Shiʿa branch, returned from exile in Paris to become the dominant figure in Iranian political and religious life. Written off as a fundamentalist and fanatic by cosmopolitan Muslim leaders, the Ayatollah nevertheless commanded the support of millions in Iran as he sought to make Islamic law the foundation of a theocratic society. (See *Islam*, below.)

Polish-born John Paul II, the enormously popular new spiritual leader of the world's 600 million Roman Catholics, faced delicate church-state issues every time he traveled outside of Italy. (*See* Sidebar: *The Traveling Pope.*)

Addressing the Latin-American bishops at Puebla de los Angeles, Mexico, in January, the pope made the first major policy statement of his young regime. Faced with a church divided over "liberation theology," which interprets salvation in terms of political action, the pontiff took a middle way. He carefully avoided making a wholesale indictment of liberation theology while, at the same time, taking pains to state that the church must not interpret Christ as merely a political figure or revolutionary.

Visiting his Polish homeland in June, "the first Slav pope," a veteran of church-state battles under a Communist regime, never mentioned the Communist Party or the Soviet Union by name, but he seized every opportunity to insist that the church must be free to accomplish its mission in the world. In his UN speech and in several other addresses during his U.S. trip in October, he emerged as a critic of the arms race, a strong advocate of human rights, and a spokesman for those suffering from an "unjust distribution" of the world's resources.

Although, near the end of his stay in the U.S., John Paul became the first pope to visit a U.S. president in the White House, he stressed throughout his pilgrimage that he had come primarily as a pastor, not as a political leader or chief of state. In dealing with ecclesiastical issues, he displayed conservative theological credentials. Addressing the nation's Catholic bishops, he "ratified" the stand against artificial means of birth control taken by Pope Paul VI in his 1968 encyclical *Humanae Vitae*. In addition, he reaffirmed the tradition of a male, celibate priesthood, called upon theologians to stay within the boundaries of church teaching as interpreted by the hierarchical magisterium, and reiterated church opposition to "homosexual practices" and sex outside of marriage. By year's end, in fact, there were clear signs in Western Europe and the U.S. that the pope's concern for strict doctrine was arousing some fears among Catholic intellectuals. Progressives were especially concerned about papal "crackdowns" calling for greater obedience to Vatican authority on the part of theologians (the influential scholar Hans Küng was declared to be no longer a Catholic theologian); universities and seminaries under direct pontifical control; and the vast Society of Jesus. (See *Roman Catholic Church*, below.)

As soon as the Vatican announced plans for a papal trip to the Philippines in December, new church-state tensions emerged there. When Imelda Romualdez Marcos, wife of Philippines Pres. Ferdinand Marcos, claimed credit for persuading the pope to visit her country, Jaime Cardinal Sin, archbishop of Manila, told the press that the pope was coming in response to an invitation from the nation's bishops. The contretemps dramatized the tenseness of church-state relations in the islands. Subsequently, the trip was postponed to a later date.

Religious issues continued to aggravate the long-standing tensions in the Middle East. As the struggle for Palestinian autonomy in areas currently occupied by Israel went on, many Jews and Arab Muslims based their claims for land rights on theological principles. The Palestinian-Israeli conflict spilled over into American religious life. In LaGrange, Ill., a national conference of Christian leaders in May issued "The LaGrange Declaration," calling for "political self-determination and justice for the Palestinian people." Immediately, the conference was described by Jewish leaders as a "one-sided propagandistic conference that completely ignored the question of Israeli security and Jewish human rights."

Not long afterward, Jewish and black religious leaders found themselves on opposite sides in the uproar that ensued when Andrew Young (*see* BIOGRAPHIES), the U.S. ambassador to the UN, was fired for making unauthorized contacts with the Palestine Liberation Organization. After the heat of the battle died down a bit, some of the same leaders stepped forward to heal the new rifts that jeopardized black-Jewish collaboration on issues of common concern.

In many other ways, the God-Caesar question was raised during 1979.

As the year began, the U.S. was still recovering from the shock inflicted by news of the mass suicide of 913 cultic followers of the Rev. Jim Jones in a Guyana commune. Public outrage led to legislative investigations into the practices of religious cults. They were defended by those who contended that the guarantee of religious freedom in the First Amendment to the U.S. Constitution does not make religious groups immune to punishment when they violate civil laws. At the same time, civil libertarians and a number of religious leaders condemned the investigations as "witch-hunts."

Rulings in recent years by certain U.S. regulatory agencies prompted some denominations, notably the Roman Catholic Church and major Lutheran bodies, to form new committees to monitor church-state issues. Especially worrisome to church officials were a ruling that required religious schools to pay federal unemployment insurance taxes and another that appeared to threaten

The Traveling Pope

John Paul II's first trip abroad after his election took him to Mexico in January for the third Latin-American Bishops' Conference. He combined his attendance at the bishops' meeting with a pastoral pilgrimage to Mexico City, Puebla, Oaxaca, Guadalajara, and Monterrey. Wherever he went, hundreds of thousands greeted him warmly with shouts of "Viva el Papa!"

The journey home to Poland in June had originally been planned for May, when the 900th anniversary of the martyrdom of St. Stanislaw was due to be celebrated. The saint, a medieval predecessor of the pope in the see of Krakow, was regarded as the symbol of the church's right to remind the state of its moral obligations. The Polish authorities asked the pope to choose a less politically provocative date.

He went, in fact, on June 2. Everywhere the crowds were huge and well disciplined; public order was left in the hands of volunteers organized by the church—a wholly unprecedented event in a Communist country. It was obvious that the Polish government dreaded the papal visit, but it was powerless to contain the enthusiasm of the devout as the pope traveled from Warsaw to the Jasna Gora monastery in Czestochowa and on to Krakow, his hometown of Wadowice, the Nazi concentration camp at Auschwitz-Birkenau, and Nowy Targ. There were memorable scenes in Victory Square, Warsaw, where the pope was interrupted for ten minutes by applause, patriotic songs, and the chanting of "We want God."

On September 29 the pope flew to Ireland for a two-day visit. Tentative plans for a side visit to Northern Ireland were canceled after the assassination of Lord Mountbatten (*see* OBITUARIES), allegedly by Irish Republican Army terrorists. But at Drogheda near the Ireland-Northern Ireland border, John Paul delivered a powerful appeal for peace in the troubled country. (*See* IRELAND.)

From Ireland the pontiff flew to the U.S. for a seven-day visit that included Boston, New York City, Philadelphia, Des Moines, Iowa (in response to an invitation from a farmer), Chicago, and Washington, D.C. The visit came in response to an invitation to address the UN General Assembly and an invitation from the National Conference of Catholic Bishops. Some Vatican officials would have preferred a 1980 date, but the pontiff decided on 1979 in order to avoid the U.S. presidential election campaign. Maintaining an almost superhuman schedule, the pope was greeted by crowds estimated in the many hundreds of thousands.

In November John Paul flew to Turkey to meet with Dimitrios I, spiritual leader of Orthodox Christians. His chief purpose was to initiate steps toward "full unity" of the two branches of Christendom, divided since the schism of 1054.

the tax-exempt status of religious schools if they failed to meet criteria regarding racial discrimination. These and other government policies, church officials said, represented dangerous government "incursions" into religious affairs.

U.S. Pres. Jimmy Carter came under fire from the press and some religious leaders after he disclosed to the adult Bible class at First Baptist Church in Washington, D.C., that, during a visit to South Korea, he had "witnessed" to "our faith" in a conversation with Pres. Park Chung Hee. Critics charged that Carter had stepped out of his proper role as head of state when he allowed himself to become a champion of the Christian faith in his dealings with the leader of a predominantly Buddhist country.

Religious leaders collaborated with the president on two important issues, however. As he prepared for his July 15 speech on energy policy, Carter invited a variety of national leaders to the presidential retreat at Camp David, Md. They included, on one occasion, a cluster of leading religious officials who came to be called the "God Squad." After the session, the God Squad issued a statement supporting the intent of Carter's program, though other religious leaders criticized them for allowing themselves to be used as part of a political strategy. Less controversial was the important role played by religious agencies in helping the government resettle thousands of Indochinese "boat people." (*See* REFUGEES.)

Elsewhere, Christians viewed with satisfaction mounting evidence indicating that the government of China was relaxing some of its restrictions on religious activities. In India, on the other hand, Christians viewed with alarm efforts to introduce in Parliament a bill banning the use of force or gifts as a means of converting persons from one religious faith to another. (See *Hinduism*, below.)

In Nicaragua the Roman Catholic Church was caught in the middle of the revolution that eventually ousted Pres. Anastasio Somoza. Some observers said there were "two churches" in Nicaragua—one that supported the old order and another that openly sided with the revolutionaries. In the aftermath of the revolution, it became apparent that insurgent priests and lay Catholics had played an important role in ending the Somoza dynasty.

Apart from church-state issues, other noteworthy events in the world of religion included:

The selection of Bishop Robert Runcie as the new archbishop of Canterbury, succeeding Donald Coggan as the titular leader of worldwide Anglicanism.

The final adoption of a new Book of Common Prayer by the Episcopal Church in the U.S. (See *Anglican Communion*, below.)

The election of Adrian Rogers, an archconservative defender of "biblical inerrancy," as president of the 13-million-member Southern Baptist Convention. (See *Baptist Churches*, below.)

A world assembly on religion, science, and technology, sponsored by the World Council of Churches at the Massachusetts Institute of Technology, that attracted theologians and scientists from five continents.

(ROY LARSON)

PROTESTANT CHURCHES

Anglican Communion. The main event of the year was the appointment of Robert Runcie (*see* BIOGRAPHIES), bishop of St. Albans since 1970, to succeed Donald Coggan as archbishop of Canterbury in January 1980. This was the first appointment of an archbishop to be made through the recently appointed Crown Appointments Commission, which gave the Church of England a greater (and the state a lesser) say than hitherto in the selection of its bishops and archbishops.

The new archbishop saw as his task the steering of the Communion away from the fuzziness and ambivalence that baffled so many people and toward a state in which it would be clear "where we stand in faith and what our decision-making processes are." This was a theme similar to that which emerged at the fourth meeting of the Anglican Consultative Council, held in Canada in May. The emphasis was on developing family ties between the member churches of the Communion and on building procedures for consultation.

However, the Council did consider some less domestic matters. It passed a resolution asking churches to study human rights issues and to make appropriate responses. It also urged member churches to ensure that conditions for their own employees did not conflict with these rights. Concern over the spread of Islam was discussed, but in the end delegates favoured a diplomatic statement calling for greater dialogue between Anglicans and Muslims. An unexpected and poignant arrival at the meeting was a lone representative from the church in Uganda, signifying the emergence of that church from the Dark Age imposed on it by former president Idi Amin.

In July the General Synod in England followed up its 1978 refusal to ordain women at home with a refusal to allow women legally ordained overseas to officiate during visits to England. There were signs that this was causing resentment among Anglican churches that did ordain women.

The new archbishop of Canterbury, Robert Runcie, was to assume office in January 1980. He had been bishop of St. Albans since 1970.

WIDE WORLD

In the U.S. the Episcopal Church held its triennial General Convention in September. Despite some opposition at the local level, the convention gave overwhelming approval to the new Book of Common Prayer endorsed by its predecessor in 1976 (a step also taken by the Church of England, which approved the Alternative Services Series in November despite a vigorous petition campaign). Drama was reserved for the debate on whether homosexuals ought to be ordained. Three years earlier the convention had endorsed full civil rights for homosexuals, but this time it reaffirmed the church's traditional teaching on sexual morality and said that it was inappropriate to ordain practicing homosexuals. Twenty-three bishops signed a statement declaring that they would not accept or implement the resolution, which in any case was not legally binding.

(SUSAN YOUNG)

Baptist Churches. The most spectacular if not the most significant news in the Baptist world in 1979 was the exchange of Soviet spies for political prisoners, among whom was Georgi Vins, a Baptist minister. Vins had been imprisoned because of his involvement with the illegal Council of Churches of Evangelical Christians—Baptists (CCECB). The situation in the U.S.S.R. was confusing. Even as the Vins exchange was taking place, Joseph Bondarenko, a Baptist minister from Riga, Latvia, was sentenced to three years in a strict-regime labour camp for organizing a demonstration and resisting an official. On the other hand, Soviet authorities approved the constituting of a Second Baptist Church of Moscow in the suburb of Mitischi and lifted the ban on the importation of Bibles.

The 111 member bodies of the Baptist World Alliance reported a total of 29,596,-529 baptized believers in 115,563 churches as of the beginning of 1979, a gain of 1,436 churches and 415,174 members since the 1978 reporting period. The BWA estimated that the total number of people bearing the name of Baptist exceeded 34 million. Baptist unions and conventions in less developed countries had made great gains in recent years. In Burma, BWA reports indicated that the number of baptized believers had grown from 207,345 in 1966, when missionaries were ejected, to 344,135 in 1979.

In the U.S. the Southern Baptist Convention elected an avowedly conservative president, Adrian Rogers of Memphis, Tenn., at its annual meeting in Houston, Texas. Reportedly, the issues that led to Rogers's election were biblical inerrancy and the alleged "liberalism" of certain professors at the Convention's seminaries. Rogers said he would not favour a "witch hunt" but indicated he would support an investigation of the seminaries if it were conducted by a "fair and balanced" committee. Illustrating their diversity, the Southern Baptists also voted to back SALT II and endorse studies on arms control.

At its biennial meeting in Carbondale, Ill., the American Baptist Churches, U.S.A., elected William Keucher of Detroit to a two-year term as president. Statements of concern were passed about hunger, domestic violence, the regulation of broadcasting, and small-farm policy. From January to October 1978, the ABC,USA National Ministries parish witness program had coordinated the placement of 1,259 refugees. M. William Howard, a black Baptist, was elected president of the National Council of Churches. The largest black Baptist convention in the U.S., the National Baptist Convention, U.S.A., was planning the celebration of its centennial in 1980.

(NORMAN R. DE PUY)

Christian Church (Disciples of Christ). Shaken by the fact that the People's Temple and the Rev. Jim Jones, who led Temple members to mass suicide in Guyana in 1978, were linked to it, the Christian Church (Disciples of Christ) nevertheless reaffirmed the congregational freedom that is a heritage of the denomination. The church's Administrative Committee asserted that the tragedy was unique and decided not to initiate a policy for ousting errant congregations. Disciples, however, did move to tighten controls over who could be considered a minister of the denomination.

Disciples from 20 nations gathered in Jamaica for the first-ever meeting of official representatives of national church bodies. The Disciples Ecumenical Consultative Council was new in that U.S. and Canadian Disciples had had no national authority until about a decade earlier. Also, because of the church's ecumenical stance outside North America, there had been few national bodies that were identifiably Disciples.

Following similar action by the United Church of Christ, the Disciples' General Assembly approved six additional years of study and work leading to a decision in 1985 on whether to enter formal union negotiations. The church declined to endorse ordination of homosexuals, reiterating that regions had the final say in such matters. (ROBERT LOUIS FRIEDLY)

Churches of Christ. Growth characterized the Churches of Christ in 1979, especially in Latin America, Asia, and Africa. Currently, there were 10,000 members of the church in 173 congregations in South Africa and 6,000 in 86 churches in South Korea. In its six years of ministry to national and ethnic groups in New York City, the International Mission in the World Trade Center reported conversions of representatives of 20 nations.

Busing played a major role in growth in the U.S. According to a national survey, some 3,600 of 15,000 local congregations were involved in bus ministries. There was growing emphasis on family ministry, with family counseling centres and ministries begun in many churches. The daily devotional guide *Power for Today* began a family section. Prison ministries were also being stressed. Since 1970, when Chaplain Frank Butler arranged for a baptistery at the San Quentin (Calif.) prison, almost 500 men had been baptized.

The Broadway church in Lubbock, Texas, with 3,000 members, reported a record one-Sunday contribution of over $2 million toward the cost of an enlarged educational building. (M. NORVEL YOUNG)

Religion

Church of Christ, Scientist. Christian Scientists marked their church's centennial in the spirit of quiet rededication to Christian healing. At the denomination's June annual meeting at the First Church of Christ, Scientist, in Boston, members were reminded of their church's founding purpose—to "commemorate the word and works of our Master [Christ Jesus], which should reinstate primitive Christianity and its lost element of healing" (Mary Baker Eddy, 1879).

Harvey W. Wood, chairman of the Christian Science board of directors, noted the "growing interest in Christian healing by people of different faiths." Other church officers reported a slight increase in members seeking accreditation for full-time healing service as Christian Science practitioners. Also, despite a decline in overall membership, new congregations in Africa and Latin America were growing. Financial contributions had increased, and the *Christian Science Monitor* Endowment Fund had grown steadily since its inception in 1978.

Mrs. Ada Reynolds Jandron, a Christian Science practitioner from Boston, was elected to a one-year term as president of the church. (ALLISON W. PHINNEY)

Church of Jesus Christ of Latter-day Saints. The thousandth Latter-day Saint stake (diocese) was established in February 1979 with headquarters in Nauvoo, Ill., highlighting the recent growth of the church, whose members were expelled from Nauvoo in 1846. That growth included approximately 1,700 conversions to the Mormon faith in Nigeria and Ghana in the first year of exploratory missionary contact there. This marked the beginning of proselytizing among the blacks of Africa, in the wake of the June 1978 revelation giving all worthy male members access to priesthood offices.

The church's First Presidency reaffirmed opposition to the Equal Rights Amendment to the U.S. Constitution, and members were encouraged to exercise their rights as citizens in taking political action against ratification of ERA. Such action was opposed by a small but articulate minority of pro-ERA church members. In December Sonia Johnson, an outspoken advocate of ERA, was excommunicated because she was "not in harmony with church doctrine . . . ," but she planned to appeal to a higher church court. All Latter-day Saints were encouraged to conserve energy resources, and many small congregations were given increased flexibility, reducing the need for travel by supervisory personnel.

The organization of stakes in Bolivia and Paraguay (January and February) and the first area conference held in Canada (August) were among major events for the church. Effective in January 1979, for the first time, seven General Authorities of the church were given "emeritus" status in order to relieve them of administrative responsibilities for health reasons.

(LEONARD J. ARRINGTON)

Jehovah's Witnesses. A society of Christians who offer home Bible instruction free of charge, Jehovah's Witnesses in 1979 numbered 2,186,075 individuals in 205 lands. During the year the Witnesses conducted an average of 1,261,735 free home Bible studies, in which they emphasized the beliefs that the Bible is the inspired word of God, that Jehovah is the only true God, that salvation comes through faith in God's Son, Jesus Christ, that the Bible is the only sound guide to a successful and happy life, and that the functioning of God's heavenly kingdom through Christ will soon restore the Earth to peaceful, paradisiacal conditions. In 1979, 113,672 new Kingdom proclaimers were baptized. Altogether, the Witnesses devoted 318,974,347 hours to promoting Bible education and adherence to Christian standards of honesty and morality.

A series of 109 four-day "Living Hope" conventions were held in the U.S., Great Britain, and Canada, with a combined attendance of over one million. The principal discourse was "Mankind's Only Hope—God's Unshakable Kingdom." The convention also highlighted the hundredth year of the Witnesses' chief journal, *The Watchtower—Announcing Jehovah's Kingdom.*

(FREDERICK W. FRANZ)

Lutheran Churches. Ways to move Lutheran churches toward a greater unity—and toward more active involvement on the ecumenical scene—were under discussion in many quarters in 1979. The subject was stimulated by preparations for celebrations in 1980 of the 450th anniversary of the Augsburg Confession, the historic Reformation document that is basic to Lutheran belief. Especially in the U.S. and Germany, Roman Catholic leaders were encouraging priests and parishioners to join Lutherans in a mutual examination of the meaning of the confessional writings for Christianity today.

Within the Geneva-based Lutheran World Federation (LWF), representing some four-fifths of the world's approximately 70.5 million Lutherans, new theological examinations of the meaning of "confessionality" were under way. The LWF and the World Council of Churches agreed to form a joint committee to examine ways of cooperating more closely in theological, pastoral, and sociological programs.

In the U.S. Lutheran unity talks took on a new dimension as many district presidents of the conservative Lutheran Church-Missouri Synod joined discussions with leaders of the American Lutheran Church, Lutheran Church in America, and Association of Evangelical Lutheran Churches—though only on an unofficial basis. Officially, the Missouri Synod held to its separatist line. In Asia Lutheran churches formed a new "coordination and information board." Preparations were under way in Latin America for a seventh Latin America Lutheran Congress in 1980. In East Germany Lutherans were preparing to join a new Protestant federation.

Church-state relations were a dominant concern for many Lutherans. In Namibia churches remained firm in their fight against apartheid. In Latin America there were questions about the role of multinational firms in socioeconomic development. A series of conferences sponsored by the Lutheran Council in the U.S.A. concluded with a warning against excessive government intervention in the life of churches.

Lutherans remained in theological dialogue on a variety of fronts. The LWF continued talks with the Roman Catholic Church, renewed a dialogue with Anglicanism, and prepared for discussions with Orthodox bodies. U.S. Lutheran-Catholic conversations moved into their 15th year.

A 60-minute television production by Lutheran Film Associates of the U.S., "The Joy of Bach," celebrated the life and work of the great Lutheran composer with premiere showings over the Public Broadcasting Service during the 1979 Christmas season.

(NEIL B. MELLBLOM)

Methodist Churches. The major emphasis throughout 1979 was on evangelism and church growth. Alan Walker, director of evangelism for the World Methodist Council (WMC), introduced a "Creative 10-point Plan of Evangelism" to the Executive Committee. National conferences and local churches were invited to set targets for membership growth. Many of the churches in Southeast Asia were reporting large increases in membership, and the rate of the decline in the U.S. and Britain was slowing.

The ten-point plan also included a call to prayer, teaching in personal witness, plans for an international youth conference in 1980, and a renewed emphasis on justice, freedom, and peace. At a special service in Athens, Methodists from all over the world covenanted together to take the program to their churches.

The second WMC Peace Award went to Pres. Anwar as-Sadat of Egypt in recognition of his bold initiative in visiting Jerusalem to break the deadlock in relations between Israel and Egypt.

The continuing joint international commission of Roman Catholics and Methodists, meeting in Rome, discussed the doctrine and person of the Holy Spirit. They affirmed that "more unifies us than divides us in our mutual understanding of the Holy Spirit in the life of the individual Christian and in the shared life of the community of faith." New conversations between the Lutheran World Federation and the WMC began in Dresden, East Germany, where representatives from each church discussed the "authority of the Bible and the authority of the church" in relation to the confessions and to historical criticism.

The British Conference debated a report on the "Christian Understanding of Human Sexuality," which included recommendations on the church's attitude to homosexual as well as heterosexual relationships. The report suggested that "if mankind is made in the image of God, the only ultimate scandal is that of lovelessness." The conference referred the report back for further consideration.

In November 1729 the Holy Club first met in Oxford, with John and Charles Wesley as leading members. A special service to commemorate the 250th anniversary of this meeting, at which the name "Methodist" was first used, was held in Oxford.

(PETER H. BOLT)

Pentecostal Churches. Ecumenical initiatives and activities marked the year for North American Pentecostals. In May Pentecostals and other charismatics initiated a worldwide celebration of Pentecost as the birthday of the church. Called "Jesus 79," these celebrations drew some 250,000 persons in 26 U.S. cities. Similar celebrations were held in several other nations.

The highlight of the year for the Pentecostal movement was the convening of the 12th Pentecostal World Conference (PWC) in Vancouver, B.C., attended by over 15,000 delegates from 64 nations representing more than 300 denominations. Among delegates from Communist nations was a group from Cuba, the first to attend the triennial gathering since 1958. For the first time representatives from the charismatic movement in the traditional churches spoke from the PWC platform. These included Episcopalian Dennis Bennett and Roman Catholic Archbishop Arokiaswamy of Bangalore, India.

Elsewhere during the year, General Overseer Ray Hughes announced a "Double in a Decade" program for the 400,000-member Church of God (Cleveland, Tenn.). The Open Bible Standard Churches elected Ray Smith to take the place of retiring leader Frank Smith. In June the Pentecostal Church of God celebrated its 60th anniversary at its national convention in Oklahoma City, and in August the Assemblies of God celebrated its 65th anniversary at its 38th General Council in Baltimore, Md. Also in August, the Pentecostal Holiness Church (mostly white) and the Original United Holy Church of the World (mostly black) announced an affiliation, the first significant ecumenical move across racial lines among Pentecostals for over 50 years. (VINSON SYNAN)

Presbyterian, Reformed, and Congregational Churches. As in previous years, the World Alliance of Reformed Churches (WARC) saw human rights as one of its priority areas of concern. The WARC pursued studies on the "Theological Basis of Human Rights" in close cooperation with churches from other traditions and, at the same time, endeavoured to assume its responsibilities in a very practical way.

One example of this was the consultation, held under the auspices of the WARC regional group and through the good offices of the Federation of Swiss Protestant Churches, of ten WARC member churches in Pretoria, South Africa, March 12–16. These churches all originated from the missionary endeavours of European churches, but they represented white, black, Coloured, and Indian people and were seriously divided on the question of apartheid. This was the first time they had met together to discuss political, economic, social, and racial issues.

The WARC executive committee met September 2–8 in Seoul, South Korea, a venue chosen to show support for the Korean member churches. The committee's agenda called for decisions about the next General Council, to be held in August 1982 in Ottawa, Ont., under the theme "Thine Is the Kingdom, the Power and the Glory." The executive committee also received three new churches into Alliance membership: the Evangelical Congregational Church in Argentina, the Evangelical Presbyterian Church in Chile, and the Evangelical Christian Church in Halmahera, Indonesia. WARC membership stood at 145.

A new step in ecumenical dialogue was made when a Reformed delegation paid an official visit to the ecumenical patriarchate of Constantinople in Istanbul, Turkey, at the end of July for preliminary conversations on an Orthodox-Reformed theological dialogue. This was the first such official visit, at world level, since the Reformation in the 16th century. Evaluation of earlier dialogues with the Baptist World Alliance and the Secretariat for Promoting Christian Unity of the Roman Catholic Church was well under way. Preparations for the next round in the Anglican-Reformed dialogue were also well advanced.

(INGRID T. TRINDADE)

Religious Society of Friends. The Quaker faith sees no division between "religion" and the things of the world, so it was not surprising that the main concerns of Quakers during 1979 were shared with others inside and outside the churches.

Having been closely identified for years with opposition to nuclear armaments, Quakers were now turning their attention to the less cataclysmic dangers latent in the development of nuclear power. Among some U.S. Quaker groups, notably the American Friends Service Committee, this resulted in a campaign of vigorous opposition. British Friends, although they shared the general anxiety, did not take a decided stance. The refugee situation in Southeast Asia also engaged the attention of Friends in many countries. British Friends joined other churches in expressing abhorrence of the racist activities of the small National Front party before the May general election.

Two gatherings brought together Quakers from all over the world. In January the third International Mission and Service Conference was held in Guatemala, and in August the Friends World Committee for Consultation held its triennial meeting at Gwatt, Switz., attended by Friends from 29 countries. (DAVID FIRTH)

Salvation Army. During 1979 the Salvation Army was among those agencies working to alleviate the suffering of displaced persons around the world. Since September 1978 Salvationists had been running two camps in Costa Rica for Nicaraguan refugees. Currently, some 1,300 people were under the Army's care.

Gen. Arnold Brown, head of the Salvation Army, views a statue of the Army's founder, William Booth, in London.

KEYSTONE

While the Costa Rican government took responsibility for health problems, the Army was providing medical care for children separated from their parents. Food, clothing, and schooling were also being provided, at a cost of about U.S. $20,000 monthly. Substantial aid for the Army's program came from the Dutch government, various charitable agencies, and the Army's National Headquarters and Southern Territory Headquarters in the U.S.

Salvationists in Hong Kong were ministering to the huge numbers of Vietnamese "boat people" there. The Army was also asked to provide welfare service in a camp being set up on the island of Lamtau, where thousands of Indochinese refugees were reportedly housed in a prison with a capacity for 600 and in hastily erected corrugated-iron shelters. A sizable rehabilitation program for refugees was begun in Africa.

(JENTY FAIRBANK)

Seventh-day Adventist Church. The growth rate of the SDA church accelerated during 1979, from 4.95 to almost 6%. World membership reached some 3.2 million at midyear. Growth in South America was so rapid that 250 churches and chapels were constructed. "The Voice of Prophecy," the church's major radio program, was being broadcast on 1,213 stations.

In China SDA churches in Shanghai and near Swatow were opened for regular services. All SDA churches in Uganda were reopened after the fall of Idi Amin, and the hospital at Ishaka was returned to the church. *The Adventist Review,* the church's official organ, added a Portuguese-language edition.

Ministry to the world's needy was expanded by Seventh-day Adventist World Service. Medical supplies were distributed to 28 countries, and supplemental food was supplied daily to 350,000 people in Chile, Haiti, Rwanda, and Peru. Appropriations for the 1979 world budget topped $125 million, exceeding 1978 appropriations by $10 million.

In January Neal C. Wilson took office as president of the world church, succeeding Robert H. Pierson, who resigned after 12 years in office. (KENNETH H. WOOD)

Unitarian (Universalist) Churches. The 18th annual General Assembly of the Unitarian Universalist Association (UUA), held at Michigan State University June 25–30, 1979, was dedicated to the theme "To Everything a Season—A Time to Grow." Among numerous resolutions passed were calls for the establishment of a comprehensive government health care plan; support for SALT II, decisive nuclear weapons cutbacks, and reductions in defense spending; emphasis on solar heating research; and concern about irresponsible marketing of infant formula in less developed countries. Eugene Pickett, parish minister and headquarters administrator, became the fourth president of the UUA following the death of Paul Nathaniel Carnes on March 17.

Manchester, England, was the site of the 51st annual meeting of British Unitarians, April 6–9. Nearly 1,000 delegates—a record for recent years—installed Roy Smith as their new general secretary. He replaced Brian Golland, who retired after ten years' service.

Reflecting changing times, the national Laymen's League, founded in 1919, was dissolved on July 1. It was once a major fund raiser and ministerial recruiter. On the other hand, the international Church of the Larger Fellowship, which tied together isolated religious liberals by publishing and ministry-by-mail programs, celebrated its 35th anniversary. It had members in 90 countries and all states and provinces of the U.S. and Canada.

Scholars from several disciplines gathered at Harvard Divinity School, Cambridge, Mass., May 1–3, to discuss "Religion, Science, and the Sources of Ethical Motivation and Religious Experience." The first UUA Center City Church Conference met June 22–24 in Detroit to deliberate "The Paradox of Churches in the Inner City."

Over the next five years the UUA was to receive a $20 million endowment from the Unitarian Society of Plandome, N.Y. For the third time in five years, the UUA's Annual Program Fund achieved its goals.

(JOHN NICHOLLS BOOTH)

The United Church of Canada. Preparations for the 28th General Council, scheduled for Aug. 15–24, 1980, constituted a priority task for national and regional offices during the year. Plans to hold the council in Quebec had to be abandoned when facilities were found to be unavailable, and it would meet instead at Dalhousie University, Halifax, Nova Scotia. The theme of the meeting would be "Affirming Our Heritage—Claiming God's Future."

Major reports to be presented at the council would include: "Project Ministry," a four-year study on the role of clergy and laity; "Human Sexuality"; "Science, Technology and Ethics"; "Abortion"; "Ethics and Genetics"; and a recommended theologically based salary structure for church employees. If approved by the council, implementation of the recommendations in these reports would be studied with a view to their implications for change in the '80s.

Many of the 2,300 congregations across Canada were participating in the reception of refugees from Vietnam, as well as providing support for other victims of natural and human disasters. Church members were also responding to a $500,000 appeal for funds to aid the Vietnamese refugees. This was over and above the budgeted figure of $750,000 for World Development Service and Relief.

The executive of General Council voted $200,000 from special funds for the production of television materials. It was hoped that all necessary research and production would be completed in time for televising in the fall of 1980. Following this initial effort, there would be a thorough evaluation of audience response before further production was undertaken. The theme of the national TV project was "These Things We Share."

In December 1978 the editor of *The Observer*, A. C. Forrest, died suddenly. He had been editor of the church's national publication for 23 years.

(NORMAN K. VALE)

United Church of Christ. The 12th General Synod of the United Church of Christ met in Indianapolis, Indiana, June 22–26, 1979. The delegates voted to support SALT II; reaffirmed opposition to the death penalty; and expressed determination to press for passage of the Equal Rights Amendment and for full vindication of the "Wilmington Ten," civil rights activists arrested in 1971 in Wilmington, N.C. They also endorsed the ecumenical boycott of Nestlé products, organized to protest that firm's marketing of infant formula in less developed countries. The delegates responded to the energy crisis by passing pronouncements and other resolutions urging action by local churches and mission agencies.

In a historic action, the General Synod voted to participate in a six-year covenant with the Christian Church (Disciples of Christ) to explore the possibility of beginning formal union negotiations. Noting the changing face of pluralistic America, the UCC voted to develop at least 15 new churches each year over the next ten years and to fund the effort through an all-church campaign. After receiving reports of a churchwide study of human sexuality, the delegates created a Task Force on Human Sexuality, representing divergent viewpoints, to continue churchwide study for four years. A new process providing for local churches and conferences to participate in the selection of denominational priorities was adopted.

Yvonne V. Delk of New York and Alice B. Snow of Sedona, Ariz., received the Antoinette Brown Award honouring the service of women in ministry. Nathanael M. Guptill of Connecticut was elected to a two-year term as moderator, and Joseph H. Evans was reelected to a four-year term as secretary of the church.

(AVERY D. POST)

[827.D; 827.G.3; 827.H; 827.J.3]

ROMAN CATHOLIC CHURCH

Any account of the Roman Catholic Church in the year 1979 had to begin, and probably end, with the vigorous personality of John Paul II. Though the church was no longer quite so Rome-centred as it used to be—much less pope-centred—he both captured the headlines and touched on all the important questions.

His popular base was in Rome itself. Audiences were so crowded that they had to be moved first into St. Peter's and then onto the square outside, creating traffic problems for the Rome municipality. He was described, not inaccurately, by Norman St. John Stevas, a British Cabinet minister, as "the pop-pope." Through his journeys he reached an even vaster public. Paul VI ceased to travel outside Italy after his tour of the Far East in 1970. By the end of 1979 John Paul II had already made three major journeys, and more were planned. (See *Introduction*, above.)

Each of his journeys posed theological and political problems: the "theology of liberation" in Latin America; church-state relations under a Communist regime in Poland; the church's mission in tormented Northern Ireland; its contribution to international affairs at the UN; its answers to the demands for a loosening of old restraints among many groups in the U.S. Partial answers to these questions could be gathered from what had actually been happening.

The successful Vatican mediation between Chile and Argentina in the Beagle Straits dispute was the first such instance since the 19th century. Critics pointed out that by it the Vatican had lent credence to the idea that the military leaders of the two nations could be regarded as Christian statesmen. The simple response was that peace was preferable to war. Nicaragua showed that the church was capable of leaning in the other direction. Although the Vatican was not directly involved in the Sandinista campaign that overthrew Anastasio Somoza, the local church most certainly was. After the Sandinista victory, a Jesuit, Fernando Cardenal, became minister for culture and education.

The new pope's Polish background inevitably meant a reappraisal of the Vatican's *Ostpolitik*. He seized the initiative by his visit to Poland and in many other ways showed that he would pursue a more activist policy. Vatican Radio began to broadcast a weekly mass to Poland. The Hungarian bishops received a letter from the pope designed to stiffen their resolve.

Internal church matters also received the pope's attention. In December 1978 he had talked with the dissident traditionalist Archbishop Marcel Lefebvre, and later there were three meetings with Franjo Cardinal Seper, prefect of the Congregation for the Doctrine of Faith. Lefebvre reported that he found a "new atmosphere" in the Vatican, but in May he soured it somewhat by unilaterally publishing the 17 questions on which Seper had demanded satisfaction. He then went ahead with further ordinations in June, despite an express order to the contrary.

The most important document of the year was the encyclical *Redemptor Hominis* (March 4). Commentators hunted through it for "condemnations," but they were missing the point. The pope was not issuing condemnations. He was trying to share his personal vision of humanity renewed in Christ, the Second Adam. He was turned not toward the past but toward the year 2000, a date that seemed to exert a fascination over him. He spoke as though the crises of the last 15 years had been resolved.

One crisis that had not been resolved was that of the priesthood, as was evident from the reactions to the papal letter dated Palm Sunday (April 8). It was not an official document but a personal letter from the pope to his fellow priests in which, writing in the first person, he shared his own experience of the ministry. Yet to many the letter seemed to put the clock back. It held out no hope for the ordination of married men and still less for the ordination of women. Administrative measures, meanwhile, had shown that the pope would be a rigorist on the question of the priesthood. Those who wished to resign were bluntly offered a choice between staying put and breaking church law.

Moves were made to defend traditional doctrine. Toward year's end Hans Küng, perhaps the most widely known among liberal theologians, was censured and forbidden to teach. A similar action was taken against Jacques Pohier, a French Domini-

UPI

Pope John Paul II signed the most important papal document of the year, the encyclical *Redemptor Hominis,* in March.

can, and Edward Schillebeeckx of the Catholic University of Nijmegan, Neth., was closely questioned by experts from the Congregation for the Doctrine of Faith. The Congregation also condemned a liberal book on human sexuality published two years earlier by the Catholic Theological Society of America.

The Anglican-Roman Catholic International Theological Commission published a document called *Elucidations* in which it replied frankly to objections to its work. On June 27 Basil Cardinal Hume, archbishop of Westminster, speaking at a service in Westminster Abbey for the annual Methodist Conference, wondered aloud whether the ecumenical movement was not entering a phase "which is characteristic of the spiritual life, the dark night of the soul." But he added that it would be "a purifying and refining process."

A similar ambivalence marked Orthodox-Catholic relations. A delegation from the ecumenical patriarch visited Rome on June 29, and the pope paid a three-day visit to Constantinople in late November. An official dialogue was to begin between the two churches. But the long-standing dialogue with the Russian Orthodox Church met unexpected obstacles. A meeting arranged for Odessa in April was canceled "because of organizational difficulties."

The theme of the abandoned meeting was to have been: "The Local Church in Its Relationship with the Universal Church." It was the theme of the year. The new and immensely energetic pope claimed all the attention, while the local churches struggled with intractable problems. The optimism of John Paul II sometimes helped and sometimes had no effect. He was the youngest pope since Pius IX in 1846, the most active in a century, the most interesting, and the most unpredictable. (*See* VATICAN CITY STATE.)

(PETER HEBBLETHWAITE)

[827.C; 827.G.2; 827.J.2]

THE ORTHODOX CHURCH

In the Soviet Union, the official antireligious policy of the government was softened somewhat in favour of officially recognized Orthodox institutions. The number of students admitted into theological schools reached 1,500, almost double the 1975 figure. However, groups of Orthodox young people, seeking answers to contemporary problems independently, faced brutal repression.

Departing from his usual silence about his relations with the Turkish government, Patriarch Dimitrios of the ecumenical patriarchate in Istanbul charged Turkish authorities with "illegal activities" directed against Greek Orthodox churches and institutions in Turkey. The minority status of the Greek community was dramatized by the visit of Pope John Paul II in November, under tight security and arousing little interest in the Muslim population. The pope, whose avowed purpose was to hasten reunification of the two churches, joined Dimitrios in a Eucharistic service on the feast of St. Andrew.

In Greece open conflict arose between the hierarchy of the Orthodox Church and the Greek government concerning laws liberalizing divorce and abortion that were passed by Parliament against bitter opposition from the church. In an article published in October 1978, the influential bishop of Piraeus, Kallinikos, expressed himself in favour of formal separation of church and state in Greece.

The small but respected Orthodox Church in Finland, which enjoys the status of a state religion together with the majority Lutheran Church, took steps toward obtaining autocephaly (total administrative independence). The General Assembly decided on the creation of a third diocese and establishment of an auxiliary episcopate, both steps fulfilling canonical conditions for autocephaly.

In the U.S. the Orthodox Church seemed to be increasing its appeal to a broader and less ethnic constituency. A conservative Protestant denomination, with headquarters in Santa Barbara, Calif., assumed the name Evangelical Orthodox and expressed formal interest in historic Orthodoxy. At the same time, the monastery of New Skete, Cambridge, N.Y. (formerly a Roman Catholic monastic community of the Eastern rite), was received into the Orthodox Church by Metropolitan Theodosius of New York.

Two American-born priests—Boris Geeza of Chicago and Mark Forsberg of Boston—were elected to the episcopate in the autocephalous Orthodox Church in America. Another American, Christopher Kovacevich, from Pittsburgh, Pa., was elected bishop in the Serbian American jurisdiction. The Greek Archdiocese in America received a new charter, approved by its ecclesiastical authority in Istanbul, which gave greater independence to its local bishops.

On July 2 one of the most vocal spokesmen for Orthodox unity, Ignatius Hazim, was elected patriarch of Antioch, with residence in Damascus, Syria. The election followed the death of Patriarch Elias IV on June 21. (JOHN MEYENDORFF)

EASTERN NON-CHALCEDONIAN CHURCHES

The major event in 1979 was the visit made to Western Europe by the most influential leader of Eastern Non-Chalcedonian churches, Patriarch Shenouda III of the Coptic Church. In Geneva, on February 7, he met with the representatives of the Orthodox Commission and declared himself ready for union conversations "anywhere and at any time." He noted that an eventual union should imply mutual recognition of separate developments within the churches since their formal separation in AD 451. Most theologians agreed that no real theological differences now exist between the two sides.

Political difficulties represented an obstacle, however. In Ethiopia, Patriarch Theophilus and other bishops had been deposed and imprisoned by the revolutionary government, so the representative character of Ethiopian ecclesiastical delegates at international meetings was in doubt. This included particularly the meeting of the Central Committee of the World Council of Churches at Kingston, Jamaica (Jan. 1–11, 1979), where the Ethiopian delegates were seated only conditionally.

(JOHN MEYENDORFF)

[827.B; 827.G.1; 827.J.1]

JUDAISM

The peace treaty between Egypt and the state of Israel in 1979 brought with it less spiritual exultation than might have been expected. The uncertainties of peace overshadowed the fulfillment of a 36-year dream, for none knew whether, in fact, peace had come at all. But the treaty did underline the tendency of American Jews to turn inward and to focus upon the inner life of their own community. For once peace did come to the state of Israel, those long sequences of crises that had kept alive and sustained Jewish community life in the Diaspora for nearly half a century would draw to a close.

When it turns inward, as it did in 1979, American Jewry sees some obvious facts. Jews take their place along a continuum, from Orthodoxy, through Conservatism, to Reform, and from a maximum commitment of behaviour and belief to a minimum one. Orthodoxy, the group with the deepest ties to Judaism, is declining in numbers, since it remains essentially a commitment of the first generation of immigrants. But, as Orthodoxy declines in numbers, its conservatism becomes stronger, interpreting the requirements of Judaism ever more strictly, treating other Jews with ever diminishing tolerance.

The recognition was growing, in the words of *Moment Magazine* (January 1979), that neither money nor organization can secure a future for Judaism in America. What Judaism in America lacks is a "corpus of intellectually consequential ideas about what it means to be a Jew, here and now, in this time and in this place." As *Moment* phrased matters, "If the theology and ideology for contemporary Jewry were merely what people pretend—a conventional apologetic, a ritual of excuses—it might not matter. But ideas do move people; without ideas, people will not move. . . ."

In this regard, the surrogates of religion in Jewry found themselves particularly in need of ideas. Charles Liebman, in his landmark article on the New York Federation of Jewish Philanthropies, published in the *1979 American Jewish Yearbook*, quotes a Jewish leader as saying, "For many Jews, Federation is . . . a vehicle by which the individual expresses a major part of his own Jewish fulfillment." By "Federation" is meant participation in Jewish philanthropy. For significant numbers of Jews, it is the Federation that is primary, the synagogue secondary. A principal theory behind the raising of money in Jewish philanthropy has had to do with the needs of the state of Israel and its recurring crises. But if all that draws Jews to Jewish activity is the state of Israel, and if the needs of that state no longer appear so urgent, what important programs or activities remain to render "being Jewish" important and immediate?

There could be no doubt that the Jews form a stable and continuing group. As Liebman wrote, "Jews were now viewed as a distinctive group with distinctive group interests. Such a conception carried political overtones and affected the individual's understanding of what it means to be a Jew." On the other hand, that understanding scarcely included the substance of Jewish belief, learning, and practice. Liebman describes the response of the New York Jewish Federation Board of Trustees, in rejecting a 1968 proposal to strengthen the funds for Jewish education, as follows: "Nor could the Board accept the notion that Jewish education was an essential ingredient for Jewish survival when most Federation leadership had none."

As Daniel Elazar observed ("What Indeed Is American Jewry?" *Forum*, winter 1978), the Jewish community "is thoroughly unideological." But no ideas also constitute an ideology and, as Liebman says, "In sacrificing too much for the sake of consensus, when it is not clear that all the elements in Federation are committed to Jewish survival as an operative goal," considerable difficulties are raised. Liebman concludes, "If Federation is to create and lead a Jewish community, it will not do so by shifting Jewish loyalties to itself, but rather by serving as an instrument for shaping loyalties. In the last analysis, Federation is an instrument, and not an end, in the creation of a Jewish community."

It was that fact which, in 1979, rendered all the more urgent the issue of ideology or theology. A community without an ideal for its own existence may last but has no life worth having. This, it would appear, was the challenge of the end of decades of war and, perhaps, the beginning of a time of peace. Could Judaism survive the end of crisis and torment? That question would, one hoped, be the one to dominate the 1980s. (JACOB NEUSNER)
[826]

BUDDHISM

Probably the most important event for Buddhism in 1978–79 was the 12th general conference of the World Fellowship of Buddhists (WFB), held in October 1978 in Tokyo, Japan. Concurrently, the World Fellowship of Buddhist Youth also held its general conference.

Because the WFB embraces the three main branches of Buddhism, the Theravada (southern), Mahayana (northern), and Tibetan traditions, its conference theme, "Buddhist Contribution to the Future," and the discussions and resolutions could be taken as good indicators of the pulse of today's Buddhism. The 350 delegates headed by Princess Poon Pismai Diskul of Thailand, president of the Fellowship, expressed a wide range of concerns: how to overcome the historic divisions and other barriers to unity within the worldwide Buddhist community; the Buddhist view of future society, including the obligation to cooperate with other world religions and humanitarian groups in striving toward world peace and harmony; and the education of Buddhist youth and the necessity of social action.

Notwithstanding the optimistic mood of the WFB, the picture in Asia was far from encouraging. Especially tragic was the situation in Indochina, where Communist regimes had effectively destroyed Buddhist institutions. (*See* CAMBODIA; LAOS; VIETNAM.) Thailand, too, was beset by internal problems that undercut the influence of Buddhism. The Chinese government established four Institutes for Research on World Religions, including one on Buddhism. In Japan, Daisaku Ikeda, the dynamic president of Soka-gakkai, the largest Buddhist-related "new religion," resigned.

Buddhism fared better in the West, as illustrated by the fact that, of the eight new regional centres admitted to the WFB, five were from the West. Scholarly activities increased in the West, as evidenced by the Seminar of Young Tibetologists, held at the University of Zürich, Switz.; the conference of the International Association of Buddhist Studies, held at Columbia University, New York City; and the Calgary (Alta.) Buddhist Conference. Western interest was also reflected in the media attention given to the U.S. tour of the exiled Tibetan Buddhist leader, the Dalai Lama, in the fall. This was the first time a Dalai Lama had visited the U.S.

(JOSEPH M. KITAGAWA)
[824]

The Dalai Lama was greeted by Terence Cardinal Cooke on a visit to St. Patrick's Cathedral in New York City. The exiled leader of Tibetan Buddhists spent seven weeks touring the U.S.

FRANK MASTRO—PICTORIAL PARADE

HINDUISM

The year 1979 saw the eruption of violence between the Hindu and Muslim communities in India on a scale scarcely known since 1947, when the subcontinent was partitioned between India and Pakistan. In one incident, in April, over 300 people were killed, 500 seriously wounded, and 600 arrested when Hindus in Jamshedpur, Bihar, attempted to take a religious procession through the Muslim quarter. Implicated in the violence was the Rashtriya Swayam Sevak Sangh (RSS or National Volunteer Corps), an extremist Hindu group.

Communal feeling also flared between Hindus and Christians over a "Freedom of Religion Bill" introduced into the Indian Parliament. The proposed legislation would make punishable by imprisonment any activity leading to "forced conversion"; *i.e.*, that obtained by the use of force, threat, or gift. Christians feared that education, health care, or even the promise of salvation might be construed as an attempt at "forced conversion."

Another occasion for communal tension was the effort of the Hindu leader Vinoba Bhave to have the Indian government ban all slaughter of cows, regarded as sacred by Hindus and forbidden as food. The slaughter of older cows and those unfit for use was permitted in Kerala and West Bengal, where the state governments insisted that total prohibition could not be enforced because beef is an important item in the diet of the sizable non-Hindu population. In April Bhave began a fast "to death," but he ended it after five days upon being assured by Prime Minister Morarji Desai that a nationwide ban would be enacted.

Communal conflict was among the concerns of the second World Hindu Conference, held at Allahabad in January. Thirty thousand delegates from 17 countries met for three days to work out a 12-year plan for the revival and modernization of Hinduism. Organized by a religious group affiliated with the RSS, the conference resolved to promote a stronger and more dynamic Hindu society in which communal conflicts and untouchability would be eradicated and castes would remain "only for the purpose of marriage."

Two archaeological discoveries added to an understanding of the historical development of Hinduism. In Goa 15 cave temples dedicated to the god Siva were found, identifying Goa as an important centre of the early cult of the god and possibly the homeland of early Hindu cave architecture. In Panna, West Bengal, a find of important sculpture further identified that site as a cultural and religious centre of the Gupta period (*c.* AD 500).

In the U.S. an impressive temple was dedicated to the god Krishna in the hills of West Virginia in September. Under construction for six years, the temple was built by members of the International Society for Krishna Consciousness.

(H. PATRICK SULLIVAN)

[823]

ISLAM

Muslims everywhere were caught up by the revolution in Iran, which overthrew the shah and brought to power the Ayatollah Ruhollah Khomeini (*see* BIOGRAPHIES). A number of conservative religious developments occurred under the Khomeini regime. In March Iranians voted overwhelmingly for an Islamic republic, which allowed religious leaders to veto prospective laws. Coeducation in primary and secondary schools was outlawed, and boys were to be segregated from girls in many youth activities. Nightclubs were closed; motion pictures were banned if they were considered at all provocative; men and women swimming together were attacked by militant Islamic groups; and a number of prostitutes were executed.

In November younger followers of Khomeini occupied the U.S. embassy in Teheran, taking its personnel hostage. While the diplomatic negotiations centred on whether the U.S. would return the former shah to Iran, a strong feeling of anti-Westernism and Islamic revivalism underlay the statements and actions of Iranian leaders. Also in November, a group of Muslims occupied the Grand Mosque at Mecca for several days and were dislodged only by force of arms resulting in a number of deaths. A news blackout made it difficult to determine the membership or goals of the group, although the action appeared unrelated to the takeover of the embassy in Iran. However, the occupation of the Grand Mosque triggered attacks on U.S. diplomatic posts in Pakistan. (*See* IRAN.)

The Iranian revolution pointed up Islam's growing power and attractiveness in the modern world. In recent years Muslim countries, including those with military regimes, had become more overtly deferential to the Shariʿah, the classical Law of Islam. In 1979 Pakistan revamped its civil and criminal codes to conform more closely to the Shariʿah; so did Kuwait; and in other countries, for example, Egypt, parliamentary debates centred on the same issues. In November 1978 about two million people went on the Hajj, the sacred pilgrimage to Mecca, compared with one million only a few years earlier.

In the Soviet Union more attention was being paid to the Muslim areas. More Soviet Muslims were going on the Hajj, and a few Muslims from outside the Soviet Union were allowed to visit there. The Muslim population in the U.S.S.R. was not much smaller than the ethnic Russian, and its birthrate was increasing. Muslim influence in India led to an announcement in late April that many old mosques, some closed for decades, would be reopened and refurbished as funds allowed. An example of blending traditional law with contemporary trends was the rapid growth of mutual funds, such as those of the Islamic Investment Company in Saudi Arabia, which allowed return on investment without violating laws against taking of interest. (*See* Feature Article: *Islam Resurgent.*)

Interfaith relations remained active. King Hassan II's efforts to restore harmony between Jews and Muslims resulted in the return of some Moroccan Jews. In 30 years the Moroccan Jewish community had declined from 400,000 to 22,000. In May the American Jewish Congress, remarking on the increase of the Muslim population in the U.S., called for interfaith talks among American Jews, Christians, and Muslims.

(REUBEN W. SMITH)

[828]

WORLD CHURCH MEMBERSHIP

Reckoning religious adherence throughout the world is a precarious exercise. Different religions and even different Christian churches vary widely in their theories and methods of counting and reporting. Some simply depend on government population figures; for others, "numbering the people" is forbidden by religious law. Some faith communities number only adults or heads of families; others count children, retainers, servants. Where religious liberty obtains, some count contributors; others estimate communicants or constituents.

Procedures vary from country to country even within the same religion. Quite reliable statistics are available on the mission fields, for Buddhism, Islam, and Hinduism as well as Christianity. In areas where a religion has prevailed for many centuries (Christianity in Europe, Hinduism in India), official figures usually report whole populations as adherents, although the rise of antireligious ideologies rebukes the casual assumption implicit in that procedure.

Although Albania is the only officially atheist state, the 20th century has produced a number of governments hostile to religion in theory and/or practice. It is difficult if not impossible to get any reliable religious statistics from the peoples they control.

The traditional listing of religions, used by scholars since the study of world religions became an academic discipline, makes no provision for several religions now numerous and important—Baha'i, Cao Dai, Ch'ondogyo, Jainism, the Spiritualist Church of Brazil. Finally, each year brings reports of new genocides or substantial movements of refugees. The recent flight of millions from persecution in Uganda, Cambodia, Vietnam, and Equatorial Guinea adds uncertainty to figures often only two or three years old.

The reader is therefore advised to reflect carefully upon the statistics and to refer to articles discussing the different countries and religions when pursuing the subject in depth.

(FRANKLIN H. LITTELL)

Estimated Membership of the Principal Religions of the World

Religions	North America[1]	South America	Europe[2]	Asia[3]	Africa	Oceania[4]	World
Total Christian	235,109,500	177,266,000	342,630,400	95,987,240	129,717,000	18,063,500	998,773,640
Roman Catholic	132,489,000	165,640,000	176,087,300	55,077,000	47,224,500	4,395,500	580,913,300
Eastern Orthodox	4,763,000	517,000	57,035,600	2,428,000	14,306,000 [5]	414,000	79,463,600
Protestant[6]	97,857,500	11,109,000	109,507,500	38,482,240	68,186,500 [7]	13,254,000	338,396,740
Jewish	6,155,340	635,800	4,061,620	3,212,860	176,400	76,000	14,318,020
Muslim[8]	371,200	251,500	14,145,000	427,266,000	145,214,700	87,000	587,335,400
Zoroastrian	250	2,100	7,000	254,000	650	–	264,000
Shinto[9]	60,000	92,000	–	57,003,000	200	–	57,155,200
Taoist	16,000	10,000	–	31,261,000	–	–	31,287,000
Confucian	97,100	70,150	–	157,887,500	1,500	80,300	158,136,550
Buddhist[10]	171,250	192,300	192,000	254,241,000	14,000	30,000	254,840,550
Hindu[11]	88,500	849,300	350,000	473,073,000	1,079,800	499,000	475,939,600
Totals	242,069,140	179,369,150	361,386,020	1,500,185,600	276,204,250	18,835,800	2,578,049,960
Population[12]	365,314,000	242,560,000	749,373,000	2,460,380,000	447,905,000	23,035,000	4,288,567,000

[1] Includes Central America and the West Indies.
[2] Includes the U.S.S.R. and other countries with established Marxist ideology where religious adherence is difficult to estimate.
[3] Includes areas in which persons have traditionally enrolled in several religions, as well as China with an official Marxist establishment.
[4] Includes Australia and New Zealand as well as islands of the South Pacific.
[5] Includes Coptic Christians.
[6] Protestant statistics usually count "full members," that is adults, rather than all family members or baptized infants and are therefore not comparable with the statistics of ethnic religions or churches counting all constituents of all ages.
[7] Including many new sects and cults among African Christians.
[8] The chief base of Islam is still ethnic, although some missionary work is now carried on in Europe and America (viz. "Black Muslims"). In countries where Islam is established, minority religions are frequently persecuted and their statistics are hard to come by.
[9] A Japanese ethnic religion, Shinto has declined since the Japanese emperor gave up his claim to divinity (1947). Neither does it survive well outside the homeland.
[10] Buddhism has produced several modern renewal movements which have gained adherents in Europe and America and other areas not formerly ethnic-Buddhist. In Asia it has made rapid gains in recent years in some areas, and under persecution it has shown greater staying power than Taoism or Confucianism. It transplants better.
[11] Hinduism's strength in India has been enhanced by nationalism, a phenomenon also observable in Islam. Modern Hinduism has also developed renewal movements that have won converts in Europe and America.
[12] United Nations, Department of Economic and Social Affairs; data refer to midyear 1979.

(FRANKLIN H. LITTELL)

SPECIAL REPORT

RESURGENT FUNDAMENTALISM

by Martin E. Marty

Pres. Jimmy Carter of the United States recently told his Baptist Bible class in Washington that too many religious people were taking the sword in the name of God, but "obviously not with God's approval." He spelled out some sore spots: "Within the sects of the Moslem world—in Syria, Iraq, Saudi Arabia, Iran—the tensions that exist because people worship God in a slightly different way cause death." Then, in order not to appear prejudiced against one religion, he turned closer to home: "In Northern Ireland, you see terrorism and murder in the name of Christ, religion, God."

That Carter singled out Iran was no surprise. The overthrow of Shah Mohammad Reza Pahlavi by militant religious forces led the media to speak of "resurgent fundamentalism" in Islam. The revolutionaries, led by the uncompromising Ayatollah Ruhollah Khomeini, rallied around the symbols of a hard-line Shi'ite version of Islam, one that did not even recognize other Islamic sects as being faithful to the Muslim tradition. "Our frame of reference," said Khomeini, "is the time of the Prophet and Imam Ali." He meant that all aspects of life are settled in terms of 1st-century Islam (7th century AD). (*See* Feature Article: *Islam Resurgent*.)

Once Khomeini's followers had conquered, they set out to apply Islamic law from the sacred book, the Qur'an, in literal fashion. Since their leader had been in exile and their movement in eclipse for some years, their fervour and their early successes led observers to inquire about the precise way in which faith was resurgent. Some analysts began to find parallels in other great religions of the world. Is this truly a time of "fundamentalist" renewal?

Differences and Similarities. Forceful religious leaders like to think their causes are unique, and they resist comparisons. Thus Salem Azzam, the Saudi secretary-general of the European Islamic Council, complained that Westerners confuse Islamic events with revived Christian fundamentalism. "Not only is this a baseless and arrogant assumption," he said, but it is like a "return to colonialism—indirect but of a more profound type." This means that to him the choice of words one uses to describe a situation can lead to confusion and even misrepresentation.

Still, the religious vocabulary is limited, and it is difficult for people in one culture to conceive what is happening elsewhere without some reference points. So it is that words like conservatism, traditionalism, and, most of all, fundamentalism serve as codes for complex realities. Of course, the details of antimodernist movements differ in each religion and region. The content of faith is not the same in Islam, Judaism, and Christianity, even where there are some similarities of form. What Westerners call militant fundamentalism in Islam had different applications in diverse Islamic cultures, but this form of traditionalism insists everywhere that the faithful must let every part of their life be dominated by their religion.

An outlook like that inevitably leads to political pressure, even in cultures whose religions are not open to fundamentalism. Hinduism, for example, is a faith that seeks to embrace and to absorb other faiths more than to rule them out. But in today's India there are some intransigent movements among Hindus that resist modernization as much as do the followers of Khomeini. One major issue troubling India is the sacred cow. In Kerala and West Bengal, non-Hindus want to kill cattle for their beef, but Hindus want them protected on religious grounds. Rajendra Singh, general secretary of the Rashtriya Swayam Sevak Sangh (RSS or National Volunteer Corps), suggests a belligerent side of the Corps when he reminds outsiders of the daily prayer its members intone: "God make us so strong that nobody should be able to subdue us, but make our character so noble that the world should bow down before us." Whether or not the world will bow down, governments can be brought down in the face of such militancy, and India's ruling power, which favours more pluralism, is worried.

In much of the rest of Asia it is harder to discern fundamentalisms, especially where religions have no messianic or missionary impulses. In some cases, as in China, Buddhism and the philosophical faiths of Taoism and Confucianism were so set back by modern political regimes that it is hard to speak of recovery at all. But in Japan militancies have developed in the form of Nichiren-sho-shu and one of its spawns, Soka-gakkai, the "value-creating society," which has forged uncompromising millions, especially the young, into a spiritual and political force.

Movements in the West. Carter also pointed to Northern Ireland, where Protestant fundamentalism is one of many voices supporting one side in a dis-

---

Martin E. Marty is Fairfax M. Cone distinguished service professor at the University of Chicago and associate editor of The Christian Century.

pute that involves religious loyalties alongside economic and ethnic grievances. While ecumenically minded leaders in the strife-torn region are working to overcome differences, a fundamentalist group like the Rev. Ian Paisley's independent Presbyterians sounds exactly like the forces of Khomeini or the RSS in wanting to be sure that "nobody should be able to subdue us."

Israel has what might be called fundamentalist orthodoxy as well. Akin to Islam and Christianity as a "religion of the book" and the oldest of the three, Judaism has survived many political changes and outlasted many misfortunes. But with the restoration of Israel in 1948 it became possible for militants to reread the scripture and apply it literally in what look to others like political causes. The Gush Emunim there would qualify as fundamentalist, since its literal reading of the Bible compels it fervently to protest the notion of surrendering any of the West Bank territories. In August the tensions reached the highest levels when Israel's two chief rabbis split over this interpretation. Rabbi Ovadia Yosef of the Sephardic (formerly Spanish) Jews was flexible, but Rabbi Shlomo Goren, the Ashkenazic ("northern" European) leader, said: "We are one nation with our faith and our land. Our charter to the Holy Land is the Bible." He meant every inch of land, every letter of the Bible. (*See* Feature Article: *Two Peoples—One Land*.)

American Christianity has also seen resurgent fundamentalism, which is not to be equated with all conservative Protestantism and Catholicism. In the political realm it has shown up in a new lobby called Christian Voice. This organization intends to rally support through the "electronic church"—evangelistic television—and work for the passage of laws it favours and the selection of fundamentalist candidates for public office. Its leadership thinks of America as "the last stronghold of the Christian faith on this planet . . . under increasing attack from satanic forces." Christian Voice people read the Bible literally and want to apply its findings and positions in a culture where the adherents of such fundamentalism are only a minority.

A Resurgent Force. What is the origin of this term "fundamentalism" against which Salem Azzam protests but which more and more people use? Azzam is right; it grew up in American Protestantism. Europe has no such party. The name came from a series of booklets called *The Fundamentals*. By the mid-1920s the fundamentalist party had caused splits in a number of American denominations, but it was largely defeated and went more or less underground. The climate of the '70s made its reappearance possible.

Catholics do not usually speak of fundamentalism, though a version of it has begun to appear in certain pentecostal circles. In August 1979 Humberto Cardinal Medeiros of Boston attacked the intellectual side of the movement: the church "cannot be fundamentalist in her approach to the word that God has inspired and revealed." The truer Catholic counterpart of fundamentalism elsewhere is the traditionalism of Archbishop Marcel Lefebvre, who desires to return the church to the practices it followed before the reforms of the Second Vatican Council, including the use of the Latin Mass. But this fundamentalism is not much of a political force. Some have suggested that the very staunch conservatism of Polish Catholicism has a fundamentalist tinge, because it is uncompromising in the face of the Communist regime and literal about the tradition. But whoever observes its best-known exemplar, Pope John Paul II, can see that this version of Catholicism has an expansiveness and openness that historic fundamentalism lacks.

The resurgence of fundamentalism has surprised many observers and triggered many questions. Two or three centuries ago, when skeptics began to prophesy the end of religion as the human race grew increasingly rational, some moderates prophesied that the only religion that could survive would be very compromising and adaptive. So liberalisms and modernisms emerged in successive waves. But they have turned out to be too open-ended, too full of ambiguity for many believers. Today there is a strong search for identity, and hard-line groups better define people than do more relaxed ones. In the midst of the questionings that have come along with modernity, many people seek authority. Fundamentalism is absolutely certain about its appeal to the authority of the Bible, the Qur'an, or other scriptures.

Fundamentalism is also a useful form of religion in power relations because it organizes all of people's energies in a holy cause. They waste no time being distracted by shades of gray in a world that they want to believe is made up of blacks and whites. They want to know instantly who belongs to their group and who does not, who is loyal and who is not. And if they have an enemy—be it the shah of Iran, the Arab world, the Protestants or Catholics of Ireland, the liberals of America—nothing rallies people more than a fundamentalist outlook of absolutes and total demands. Far from killing off fundamentalism, then, the perils of modernity have served to enhance it. Whether scholars like Salem Azzam like it or not, and whether the term applies perfectly across cultures or not, it is likely that Americans will continue to use it to make sense of a force that gives hope to millions and is profoundly disturbing to millions more.

CALGARY HERALD

Jack Hannum, of Ogden, Utah, was named all-around cowboy at the Calgary Stampede in July.

Rodeo

The highlight of 1979 for the Professional Rodeo Cowboys Association (PRCA) was the completion of a new headquarters building and rodeo hall of champions in Colorado Springs, Colo. The 27,000-sq ft hall filled with rodeo memorabilia was expected to become a major tourist attraction in the area.

The PRCA sanctioned 628 rodeos during the year, with record prize money of more than $9 million. The association's National Finals Rodeo, held in December at Oklahoma City, Okla., was also a record-breaker; the finals were moved to the city's big Myriad sports complex, and the nine-day event was sold out for the sixth consecutive year. The contest was also the richest rodeo in history, with nearly $500,000 awarded in prize money.

Tom Ferguson of Miami, Okla., won his sixth consecutive world all-around champion cowboy title at the conclusion of the finals. Ferguson's year-end arena winnings totaled $96,272; added to that were various bonus checks, including $10,000 from the Winston Rodeo Awards enabling Ferguson to top the $100,000 mark in rodeo prize money for the fourth straight year. The 29-year-old cowboy competed in rodeo's timed events—calf roping, steer wrestling, steer roping, and team roping.

Runner-up for the all-around title was Paul Tierney of Rapid City, S.D., who won $92,201 and also emerged as world champion calf roper with $59,294 earned in that event. Other champions included Bruce Ford of Evans, Colo., $80,260 in bareback riding; Bobby Berger of Lexington, Okla., $41,709 in saddle bronc riding; Don Gay of Mesquite, Texas, $59,999 in bull riding; Stan Williamson of Kellyville, Okla., $44,864 in steer wrestling; Allen Bach of Queen Creek, Ariz., $27,887 in team roping; Gary Good of Elida, N.M., $18,338 in steer roping; and Carol Goostree of Verden, Okla., $43,100 in barrel racing, an event sanctioned by the Girls Rodeo Association (GRA) in conjunction with PRCA contests. The GRA also continued to hold its own "all-girl" rodeos during the year, culminating with a final in San Antonio, Texas, in October. GRA all-around champion was Jennifer Haynes of Albuquerque, N.M.

For the Canadian Rodeo Cowboys Association (CRCA), 1979 became a year of turmoil when the famed Calgary Stampede broke away from the association. The dispute between Stampede officials and the CRCA centred on proposed purse increases, and the Stampede subsequently decided to feature competition between various teams formed by regional rodeo associations. The Stampede viewed the team concept as successful for its purposes, and it planned to continue under that format. However, interest waned in team rodeo held under the auspices of Major League Rodeo (MLR), which was never associated with the Stampede, and the MLR folded early in the season, only its second year of operation.

The International Rodeo Association, which is similar to the PRCA but smaller in terms of prize money, enjoyed a successful year and again scheduled its finals for Tulsa, Okla., in January 1980. Going into that event, reigning champion Dan Dailey of Franklin, Tenn., was leading in the competition for all-around title with $32,804 in earnings. (RANDALL E. WITTE)

Rhodesia:
see Zimbabwe Rhodesia

Roads:
see Engineering Projects; Transportation

Rockets:
see Defense; Space Exploration

Roman Catholic Church:
see Religion

Romania

A socialist republic on the Balkan Peninsula in southeastern Europe, Romania is bordered by the U.S.S.R., the Black Sea, Bulgaria, Yugoslavia, and Hungary. Area: 237,500 sq km (91,700 sq mi). Pop. (1979 est.): 21,953,000, including (1977) Romanian 88.1%; Hungarian 7.9%; German 1.6%. Cap. and largest city: Bucharest (pop., 1977, 1,807,000). Religion: Romanian Orthodox 70%; Greek Orthodox 10%. General secretary of the Romanian Communist Party, president of the republic, and president of the State Council in 1979, Nicolae Ceausescu; chairmen of the Council of Ministers (premiers), Manea Manescu and, from March 29, Ilie Verdet.

On Aug. 1, 1979, Pres. Nicolae Ceausescu of Romania was received at Oreanda, in Crimea, by Soviet Pres. Leonid Brezhnev, who presented him with the Order of Lenin, conferred upon him in 1978 by the Presidium of the Supreme Soviet of the U.S.S.R. The Oreanda ceremony suggested that the Soviet leadership had forgiven the absence of Romanian troops at the joint maneuvers of the Warsaw Treaty forces held in May in Hungary. On October 12, Ceausescu and Col. Gen. Ion Coman, minister of national defense, received in Bucharest Marshal V. G. Kulikov, commander in chief of the armed forces of the Warsaw Treaty powers, and Army Gen. A. I. Gribkov, Kulikov's deputy and chief of staff. On November 11 *Krasnaya Zvezda*, the Soviet armed forces newspaper, printed an article by Maj. Gen. Dumitru Penescu, deputy chief of staff of the Romanian Army, in which he declared that his country would fight with the Warsaw Treaty forces "against imperialistic aggression in Europe" but reaffirmed that the Romanian Army would stay under national control, which meant that it would not go beyond the Romanian frontiers. On November 4, in Bucharest, Ceausescu and President Tito of Yugoslavia signed a joint declaration proclaiming that, in certain circumstances, it was necessary to fight against all forms of domination and hegemonism.

The 12th congress of the Romanian Communist Party (CPR) was held in Bucharest from November 19 to 23. It was attended by 2,656 delegates and 148 delegations of the left-wing parties from 98 countries. Ceausescu reported on the party's activities between the 11th congress (November 1974) and the current one and also on future tasks. He stressed that the Romanian people's development of the country's economic potential was a great achievement. In spite of the severe earthquake of March 1977, the current five-year plan had been completely implemented. Industrial production was expected to increase by some 70% over the plan period and by a yearly rate of 9 to 10%. Actual production increases in agriculture above the levels of the 1971–75 plan would average five million tons of grain, two million tons of sugar beets, and more than one million tons of vegetables. Livestock numbers and the volume of animal production were also expected to rise. In 1980 the national income was expected to be 16 times higher than in 1938 and the national wealth to be about 7.6 times greater.

Ceausescu proclaimed that with the 1981–85 plan Romania, formerly almost entirely agrarian, would enter a period that would take it beyond the stage of a developing socialist country and transform it into a nation with a medium level of development. He said that the next plan would require sacrifice and austerity to expand the national raw materials base, increase the coverage of the needs of national economy from home resources, and reduce imports. He revealed that crude petroleum had been found on the continental shelf of Romania's Black Sea coast in deposits possibly large enough to further the Romanian goal of self-sufficiency in energy by 1990.

Romania

On the last day of the congress 84-year-old Constantin Pirvulescu, one of the founders of the CPR in 1921, accused Ceausescu of being "undemocratic" and added that the congress was merely a gathering that was agitating for Ceausescu's reelection as general secretary. Ceausescu called Pirvulescu a "provocateur" and a "foreign agent," and after a motion from the floor, Pirvulescu was stripped of his mandate as a delegate. The incident produced a triumphal demonstration in favour of Ceauses-

ROMANIA

Education. (1977–78) Primary, pupils 3,153,016, teachers 148,922; secondary, pupils 1,020,608, teachers 49,898; vocational, pupils 153,389, teachers 3,967; teacher training, students 18,442, teachers 1,587; higher, students 182,-337, teaching staff 13,575.

Finance. Monetary unit: leu, with (Sept. 17, 1979) an official rate of 12 lei to U.S. $1 (free rate of 26.77 lei = £1 sterling). Budget (1979 est.): revenue 344.2 billion lei; expenditure 341.9 billion lei.

Foreign Trade. (1977) Imports 34,879,000,000 lei; exports 34,893,000,000 lei. Import sources: U.S.S.R. 19%; West Germany 8%; East Germany 7%; Czechoslovakia 5%. Export destinations: U.S.S.R. 19%; East Germany 7%; West Germany 7%; Czechoslovakia 5%. Main exports (1973): machinery 9%; transport equipment 8%; petroleum products 7%; meat 7%; chemicals 7%; clothing 6%; timber 5%.

Transport and Communications. Roads (1975) *c.* 95,-000 km (including 96 km expressways). Motor vehicles in use (1977): passenger *c.* 220,000; commercial *c.* 110,000. Railways: (1976) 11,080 km; traffic (1977) 23,206,000,000 passenger-km, freight 70,035,000,000 net ton-km. Air traffic (1978): 1,109,000,000 passenger-km; freight 13.2 million net ton-km. Inland waterways in regular use (1975) 1,628 km. Shipping (1978): merchant vessels 100 gross tons and over 239; gross tonnage 1,428,041. Telephones (Dec. 1977) 1,133,000. Radio licenses (Dec. 1977) 3,086,-000. Television receivers (Dec. 1977) 3,161,000.

Agriculture. Production (in 000; metric tons; 1978): wheat 6,235; barley 2,285; corn 10,179; potatoes *c.* 4,450; cabbages (1977) *c.* 840; onions *c.* 383; tomatoes *c.* 1,353; sugar, raw value *c.* 670; sunflower seed *c.* 792; soybeans *c.* 230; linseed *c.* 40; plums (1977) *c.* 545; apples *c.* 524; grapes *c.* 1,325; tobacco *c.* 47; cheese *c.* 139; beef and veal *c.* 306; pork *c.* 772; timber (cu m) *c.* 20,587. Livestock (in 000; Jan. 1978): cattle *c.* 6,306; sheep 14,463; pigs 9,744; horses (1977) 576; poultry 89,019.

Industry. Fuel and power (in 000; metric tons; 1977): coal 7,368; lignite 19,416; coke 3,184; crude oil 14,652; natural gas (cu m) *c.* 34,080,000; manufactured gas (cu m) *c.* 1,300,000; electricity (kw-hr) 59,858,000. Production (in 000; metric tons; 1977): cement 13,875; iron ore (metal content) 640; pig iron 7,784; crude steel 11,457; petroleum products *c.* 21,260; sulfuric acid 1,523; fertilizers (nutrient content) nitrogenous 1,381, phosphate 548; cotton yarn 171; cotton fabrics (sq m) 703,000; wool yarn 61; woolen fabrics (sq m) 119,000; man-made fibres *c.* 170; newsprint 98; other paper *c.* 605. New dwelling units completed (1977) 145,000.

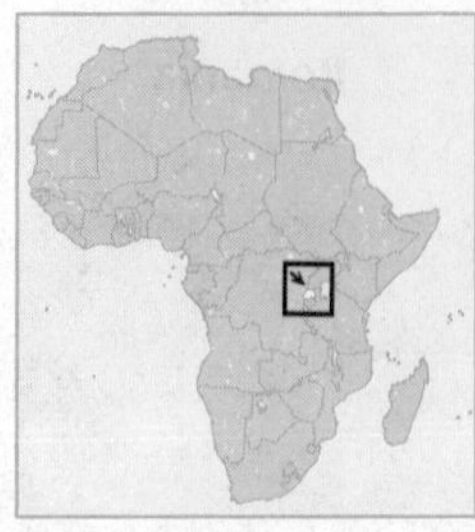

Rwanda

cu, who was unanimously reelected for five years. The congress also elected a Central Committee of 245 members and 163 alternates. The committee then elected the Executive Political Committee of 27 members and 18 alternate members, which in turn elected a Standing Bureau of 15 members headed by Ceausescu and including Elena Ceausescu, Colonel General Coman, Ilie Verdet (premier since March 29), and Stefan Andrei (foreign minister). (K. M. SMOGORZEWSKI)

Rowing

Five nations shared the 14 men's and women's titles in the 1979 world rowing championships held on Lake Bled in Yugoslavia. East Germany won medals in every class, dominating the men's competition with six championships and also winning three of the women's events. Finland and Norway won the other two men's titles. The Soviet Union won two of the remaining women's championships, the other winner being Romania.

The East Germans defeated the Soviet Union by 1.99 sec in coxed fours for the first of their gold medals in the men's championships. They then beat the Soviet Union by more than 3 sec in coxless pairs. In coxed pairs they were given a close run by Czechoslovakia before winning by 0.6 sec, but their coxless four had over 5 sec to spare as Czechoslovakia again finished second.

East Germany finished nearly 3½ sec ahead of West Germany in quadruple sculls and then scored its sixth win at the expense of New Zealand by a similar margin in eights. In both single and double sculls the East German entries placed third; the winners were Norway in double sculls and Pertti Karppinen of Finland in singles.

In the women's championships East Germany took three gold and three silver medals. The two Soviet Union winners were, rather unusually, their country's only medalists. The other gold medal country was Romania, which also won a silver and three bronze medals. Bulgaria finished with a pair of silver medals.

Great Britain, Norway, Spain, and the U.S. were the gold medal winners in the four lightweight championships, also held on Lake Bled. However, The Netherlands—with two silvers and a bronze—was the only country to win more than one medal.

Yale University was a strong finisher but lost the final round for the Grand Challenge Cup at the Henley Regatta in England in July.

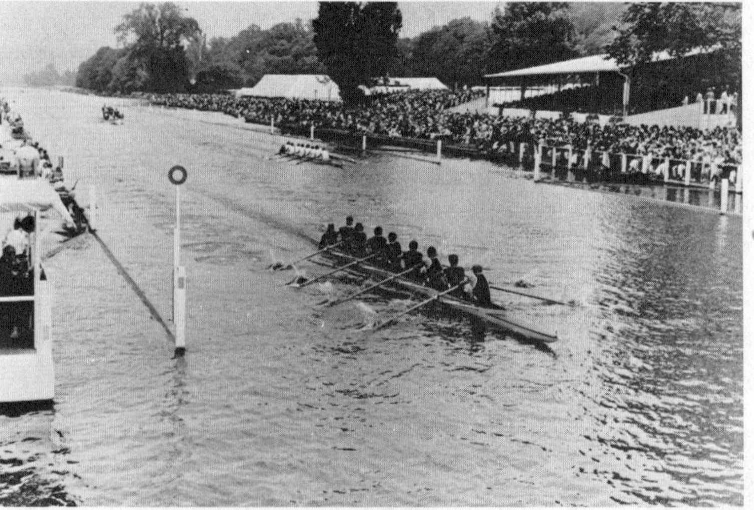

WIDE WORLD

In Moscow, on its home waters on the course for the 1980 Olympic Games Regatta, the Soviet Union retained its position as world leader in junior rowing. The Soviets even improved on their impressive 1978 record of three gold and two silver medals by adding two more golds. West Germany finished with one gold, four silver, and two bronze medals, while East Germany did nearly as well with one gold, two silvers, and two bronzes. The other gold medal went to Bulgaria.

After the successful introduction of women's junior championships in 1978, the number of classes was increased to six. East Germany provided three of the winners, and the other three were Bulgaria, Canada, and Romania. The Soviet Union won four of the silver medals.

In the International Rowing Federation veteran meeting (for competitors aged 27 years and over) at Nottingham, England, 20 countries celebrated the 50th anniversary of veteran rowing in the U.K. Great Britain and West Germany won most of the events. Other nations with winners were Australia, France, The Netherlands, Norway, Sweden, Switzerland, and the U.S.

Also in England, at the Henley Royal Regatta only 3 of the 12 open events were won by non-British competitors. Yale University from the U.S. won the Ladies Plate (eights), while Ridley College, Canada, scored its third win in five years in the Princess Elizabeth Cup (eights). The third overseas winner was Garda Siochana, Ireland, in the Prince Philip Cup (coxed fours). Oxford won the 125th University Boat Race, which marked the 150th anniversary of the first challenge in 1829, by 3½ lengths and thereby reduced Cambridge's lead in the series to 68–56. (KEITH OSBORNE)

Rwanda

A republic in eastern Africa and former traditional kingdom whose origins may be traced back to the 15th century, Rwanda is bordered by Zaire, Uganda, Tanzania, and Burundi. Area: 26,338 sq km (10,169 sq mi). Pop. (1978 census): 4,820,000, including (1970) Hutu 90%; Tutsi 9%; and Twa 1%. Cap. and largest city: Kigali (pop., 1978 census, 118,000). Language (official): French and Kinyarwanda. Religion: Roman Catholic 41%; most of the remainder are animist; there are small Protestant and Muslim minorities. President in 1979, Gen. Juvénal Habyarimana.

In a referendum held Dec. 17, 1978, Rwanda accepted a new constitution (replacing the 1962 version) by an 89.9% majority. This marked a return to "normal institutions" following the military takeover in 1973. The National Revolutionary Development Movement remained the sole legal party, and Pres. Juvénal Habyarimana was reelected to another five-year term on Dec. 24, 1978, by a 98.99% vote. The new constitution guaranteed Habyarimana immunity from censure and prosecution. His regime gained prestige when it was

RWANDA

Education. (1976–77) Primary, pupils 434,150, teachers 8,161; secondary, pupils 8,870; vocational, pupils 2,097; teacher training, pupils 1,603; secondary, vocational, and teacher training, teachers 820; higher, students 1,069, teaching staff 184.

Finance. Monetary unit: Rwanda franc, with (Sept. 17, 1979) a par value of RwFr 92.84 to U.S. $1 (free rate of RwFr 208.73 = £1 sterling). Gold, SDR's, and foreign exchange (June 1979) U.S. $89.5 million. Budget (1976 actual): revenue RwFr 7,318,000,000; expenditure RwFr 5,898,000,000.

Foreign Trade. (1978) Imports RwFr 7,354,300,000; exports RwFr 6,522,800,000. Import sources (1977): Belgium-Luxembourg 21%; Japan 12%; Kenya 11%; West Germany 8%; Iran 8%; France 7%; U.S. 5%. Export destinations (1977): Kenya 81%; Belgium-Luxembourg 6%. Main exports: coffee 72%; tea 9%; tin ore 6%.

Agriculture. Production (in 000; metric tons; 1978): sorghum 160; corn *c.* 72; potatoes *c.* 175; sweet potatoes (1977) *c.* 695; cassava (1977) *c.* 416; dry beans *c.* 173; dry peas *c.* 62; pumpkins (1977) *c.* 61; plantains (1977) *c.* 1,902; coffee *c.* 21; tea *c.* 6. Livestock (in 000; July 1977): cattle *c.* 668; sheep *c.* 248; goats *c.* 682; pigs *c.* 71.

host to the sixth Franco-African Conference at Kigali during May 1979, attended by Pres. Valéry Giscard d'Estaing of France.

Half of Rwanda's budget of RwFr 9,214,300,000 was covered by foreign aid for public expenditure, and political stability and low costs continued to attract foreign investment. Close technical and economic relations with Belgium were maintained, with Belgian aid for 1979 amounting to BFr 900 million. European Economic Community aid was guaranteed to help recoup losses arising from the war in Uganda, which barred landlocked Rwanda's access to East African ports.

Eleven Belgians, allegedly mercenaries intending to take part in attacks on Zaire, were sentenced to terms of imprisonment of one to nine years by a Rwandan court in June. (MOLLY MORTIMER)

Sailing

Sailing suffered one of its worst disasters in 1979, at the Fastnet race off the coast of Great Britain in August. The event attracted 306 starters and was won by Ted Turner of the U.S. in "Tenacious," but it ended in tragedy for many. A violent Atlantic storm struck the fleet when most yachts were in the Irish Sea between Land's End and the Fastnet. Only 85 yachts finished the race, 23 were lost or abandoned, and 18 competitors lost their lives. The scale of the disaster and of the rescue operation, with more than 100 yachtsmen being rescued by helicopter, lifeboat, and ship, led to a full-scale inquiry. Many questions regarding safety still had to be answered, and the question of abandoning a yacht in severe conditions had to be considered. Doing so was clearly a hazardous operation, but one discovery that emerged from the storm was that sailing yachts do not sink very readily and might well be safer than life rafts.

The first big race of 1979 was, as always, the classic Sydney–Hobart. For a number of years the new generation of lightweight yachts had ruled the roost. But with some drastic modifications made to the International Ocean Racing (IOR) rules, aimed, it would seem, particularly at the

World Class Boat Champions

Class	Winner	Country
18-ft skiff	Iain Murray	Australia
Star	Bud Melges	U.S.
Tempest	Rolf Bahr	West Germany
Contender	Peter Newlands	New Zealand
Finn	Cam Lewis	U.S.
International 14	John Gallagher	U.S.
Fireball	Crispin Read-Wilson	U.K.
Enterprise	Mike Holmes	U.K.
Hornet	Jeremy Newman	U.K.
O.K.	Richard Dodson	New Zealand
Cadet	Rodney Behrens	Australia
Flying 15	John Cassidy	Australia
Dragon	Rob Porter	Australia
Flying Dutchman	Marc Bouet	France
Tornado	Reg White	U.K.
505	Steve Taylor	U.S.
6-m	Pelle Petterson	Sweden
Sunfish	Dave Chapin	U.S.
Laser	Lasse Hjortnaes	Denmark
Women's 420	Cathy Foster	U.K.
Women's Laser	Marit Söderström	Sweden
WORLD TON CUP CHAMPIONS		
2-ton	Baron Edmund de Rothschild	France
1-ton	John MacLaurin	U.S.
¾-ton	Lars Nylinder	Sweden
½-ton	Tony Bouzaid	New Zealand
¼ ton	Jacques Faroux	France
Mini-ton	Maletto	Italy
Micro-ton	Jacques Faroux	France

British Navy helicopters rescued crewmen after a storm struck during the Fastnet race in the English Channel and Irish Sea. Eighteen persons were drowned.

SYNDICATION INTERNATIONAL/PHOTO TRENDS

New Zealand designers, things changed in 1979. First, a number of top yachtsmen with older boats decided to revamp their heavier-displacement yachts. New sails and a good crew could do wonders for these older heavier-displacement craft, as was shown by Peter Kurts when he won the Sydney–Hobart in his 1973 Sparkman and Stephens 47-ft "Love and War." Until the last few hours John Garner in his 1968 "Margaret Rintoul" (once Sid Fischer's "Ragamuffin," which led the Fastnet race in 1971) was close behind. Jack Rooklyn's "Apollo" crossed the finish line first, although Rolly Tasker in his new 77-ft "Siska" actually completed the course in some 20 hours less; however, a provisional rating of 74.5 ft put "Siska" over the IOR upper limit, which was 70 ft. After the race was over the yacht's new rating came through at 68.5 ft, but by then it was too late to affect the outcome of the race.

The British, as defending champions, started as

Rubber:
see Industrial Review

Rugby Football:
see Football

Russia:
see Union of Soviet Socialist Republics

Russian Literature:
see Literature

Sabah:
see Malaysia

WIDE WORLD

"Independent Endeavour," a 62-foot ketch skippered by American Skip Novak, sailed over 11,000 nautical miles to win the Parmelia race from Plymouth, England, to Fremantle, Western Australia, in November. The course followed the original route of the "Parmelia," which brought the first settlers from England to Western Australia in 1829.

favourites for the Admiral's Cup under the leadership of Edward Heath. But the gods and some self-inflicted wounds put an end to their success. As it turned out, the Australia team of "Impetuous," "Police Car," and "Ragamuffin" won the event by a comfortable margin over the U.S. and Hong Kong. A new Peterson 39 owned by Jeremy Rogers of the U.K. was the highest individual scorer, with "Police Car," a Dubois-design craft owned by Peter Cantwell of Australia, second and the Ron Holland-designed 77-ft "Imp" finishing third for the U.S. With this event Ed Dubois, a young British designer, put himself into the big league.

Some of the Ton Cup championships were disappointing. Several races in the one-ton series were abandoned due to near-hurricanes and missing buoys. The three-quarter-ton series ended in a shambles when a sudden storm decimated the fleet, leaving only two boats fit to struggle to the finish, while in the half-ton long race nearly half the fleet failed to finish in the rough going. All the series were interesting, however, with New Zealand's Laurie Davidson creating something of a record with two of his designs. His "Pendragon," which in 1978 won the three-quarter-ton series, was uprated by adding five feet to the mast and carried off the One-Ton Cup. In the half-ton class "Waverider" won for the second successive season, as did the Italian-owned mini-tonner "Wahoo." Jacques Faroux won the quarter-ton and micro-ton series as both designer and helmsman for France. (ADRIAN JARDINE)

[452.B.4.a.ii]

Saint Lucia

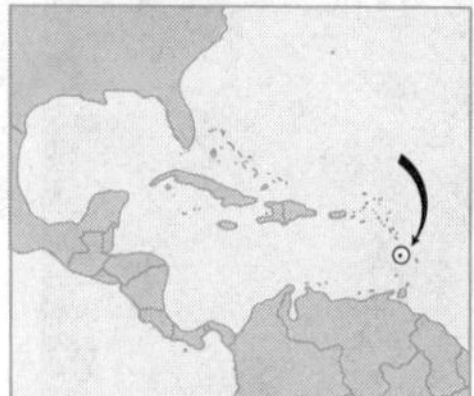

Saint Lucia

A parliamentary democracy and a member of the Commonwealth of Nations, St. Lucia, the second largest of the Windward Islands in the Eastern Caribbean, is situated 20 mi NE of St. Vincent and 25 mi S of Martinique. Area: 622 sq km (240 sq mi). Pop. (1979 est.): 130,000, predominantly of African descent. Cap. and largest city: Castries (pop., 1979 est., 45,000). Language: English and a local French dialect. Religion: Roman Catholic 86%; remainder Anglican, Methodist, and others. Queen, Elizabeth II; governor-general in 1979, Sir Allen Montgomery Lewis; prime ministers, John G. M. Compton and, from July 2, Allan Louisy.

After a number of procedural difficulties, St. Lucia finally achieved full independence on Feb. 22, 1979. The ceremonies were boycotted by the opposition St. Lucia Labour Party (SLLP), which had wanted a referendum regarding independence.

On July 2 the new state's first prime minister, John Compton, called a general election in which his ruling United Workers Party was resoundingly defeated by the SLLP, by 12 House of Assembly seats to 5. The SLLP's victory was attributed to a vast increase in the number of young people eligible to vote, a critical unemployment situation, and the failure of many on the island to benefit from its rapid economic development. Though the SLLP was led to victory by 63-year-old former judge Allan Louisy (see BIOGRAPHIES), it was widely believed that the real architect of its success was the deputy prime minister, George Odlum.

The new government, though following broadly socialist policies, accepted the continuation of a mixed economy and placed major emphasis on agricultural self-sufficiency. It immediately set about widening its diplomatic relations by attending the Commonwealth heads of government conference in Lusaka, Zambia, and applying for membership in the nonaligned movement. In July it was a joint signatory to the Declaration of St. George's, establishing closer cooperation among Dominica, Grenada, and St. Lucia. In August diplomatic relations were established with Cuba. (DAVID A. JESSOP)

ST. LUCIA

Education. (1978–79) Primary, pupils 30,295, teachers 863; secondary, pupils 4,584, teachers 173; vocational, pupils 169, teachers 24; teacher training, students 125, teachers 11.

Finance and Trade. Monetary unit: East Caribbean dollar with (Sept. 17, 1979) a par value of ECar$2.70 to U.S. $1 (free rate of ECar$5.81 = £1 sterling). Budget (1977 est.): revenue ECar$57,842,000; expenditure ECar$58,269,000. Foreign trade (1976): imports ECar$125,710,000; exports ECar$49,911,000. Import sources: U.K. 25%; U.S. 20%; Trinidad and Tobago 15%; Canada 12%. Export destinations: U.K. 45%; Leeward and Windward Islands 17%; Trinidad and Tobago 12%; Barbados 8%; Jamaica 5%. Main exports: bananas 42%; cardboard boxes 17%; coconut oil 10%; clothing 7%. Tourism (including cruise passengers; 1977) 137,100 visitors.

Saint Vincent and the Grenadines

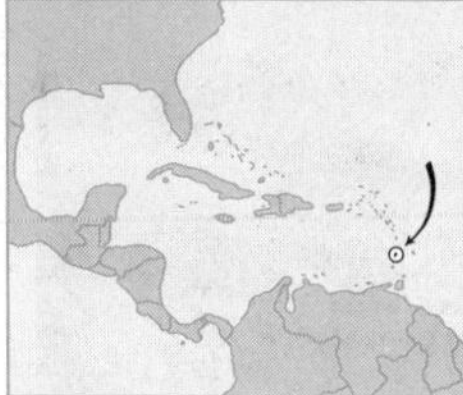

Saint Vincent and the Grenadines

A constitutional monarchy within the Commonwealth of Nations, St. Vincent and the Grenadines (islands of the Lesser Antilles in the Caribbean Sea) lies southwest of St. Lucia and west of Bar-

ST. VINCENT

Education. (1977–78) Primary, pupils 25,181, teachers 1,087; secondary, pupils 5,219, teachers 284; vocational, pupils 135; teacher training, students 227; vocational and teacher training, teachers 35.

Finance and Trade. Monetary unit: East Caribbean dollar, with (Sept. 17, 1979) a par value of ECar$2.70 to U.S. $1 (free rate of ECar$5.81 = £1 sterling). Budget (1978–79 est.): revenue ECar$32.4 million; expenditure ECar$31.3 million. Foreign trade (1977): imports ECar$81.9 million; exports ECar$27 million. Import sources (1974): U.K. 30%; Trinidad and Tobago 15%; Canada 13%; U.S. 9%; Barbados 5%. Export destinations (1974): U.K. 66%; Barbados 15%; Trinidad and Tobago 9%. Main exports (1975): bananas 58%; arrowroot 7%; mace 6%; coconut oil (1974) 6%.

bados. Area (including Grenadines): 388 sqs km (150 sq mi). Pop. (1978 est.): 117,600, predominantly of African descent. Cap. and largest city: Kingstown (pop., 1978 est., 22,800). Language: English (official). Religion (1970): Anglican 47%; Methodist 28%; Roman Catholic 13%. Queen, Elizabeth II; governor-general in 1979, Sir Sidney Gun-Munro; prime minister, Milton Cato.

St. Vincent became an independent nation on Oct. 27, 1979. Following independence, it became a member of the Commonwealth and of the Organization of American States, and Prime Minister Milton Cato (*see* BIOGRAPHIES), who was returned to power in a general election on December 5, declared for an independent policy within those groups.

The island's dormant La Soufrière volcano erupted on April 13. Ash, steam, and dust rose over 6,100 m (20,000 ft), polluting water and damaging the main banana and arrowroot crops and livestock. Tourism was seriously affected, and 15,000 people remained in evacuation centres until June. Overseas assistance was received in particular from the U.K., U.S., Canada, Venezuela, and Trinidad.

The ruling St. Vincent Labour Party pursued a relatively conservative line in 1979. It was concerned over the changes taking place in Grenada, St. Lucia, and Dominica and sought closer links with the more moderate governments of Trinidad and Barbados. The December election was followed by a secessionist revolt on two islands of the group. (DAVID A. JESSOP)

San Marino

A small republic, San Marino is an enclave in northeastern Italy, 5 mi SW of Rimini. Area: 61 sq km (24 sq mi). Pop. (1979 est.): 21,000. Cap. and largest city: San Marino (metro. pop., 1978 est., 8,300). Language: Italian. Religion: Roman Catholic. The country is governed by two *capitani reggenti*, or co-regents, appointed every six months by a Grand and General Council. Executive power rests with three secretaries of state: foreign and political affairs, internal affairs, and economic affairs. In 1979 the positions were filled, respectively, by Giordano Bruno Reffi, Alvaro Selva, and Emilio della Balda.

On Oct. 1, 1978, Ermenegildo Gasperoni, a 73-year-old Communist, and Adriano Reffi, a 41-year-old Socialist, became co-regents of San Marino, causing a Polish Communist weekly to proclaim that there was now a state in Western Europe under Communist rule. As of 1979 the Communist-Socialist coalition held 31 seats in the Grand and General Council against 26 Christian Democrats and 3 Independents. Gasperoni had fought during the Spanish Civil War in the International Brigade, while Reffi, a medical man, was a personal friend of Lord Thorneycroft, chairman of the British Conservative Party and proprietor of a villa in San Marino.

In August 1979 eight industrial companies of San Marino participated for the first time in the international "Life and Fashion" exhibition in Moscow. Glauco Benato, president of the San Marino Industrial Association, expressed confidence that trade with Soviet organizations would develop. (K. M. SMOGORZEWSKI)

SAN MARINO

Education. (1977–78) Primary, pupils 1,623, teachers 132; secondary, pupils 1,209, teachers (1976–77) 108.

Finance. Monetary unit: Italian lira, with (Sept. 17, 1979) a free rate of 814 lire to U.S. $1 (1,751 lire = £1 sterling); local coins are issued. Budget (1977 est.) balanced at 34,039,000,000 lire. Tourism (1977) 2,565,000 visitors.

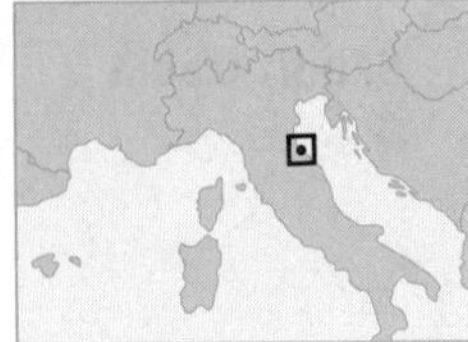

San Marino

São Tomé and Príncipe

An independent African state, the Democratic Republic of São Tomé and Príncipe comprises two main islands and several smaller islets that straddle the Equator in the Gulf of Guinea, off the west coast of Africa. Area: 964 sq km (372 sq mi), of which São Tomé, the larger island, comprises 854 sq km. Pop. (1979 est.): 84,000. Cap. and largest city: São Tomé (pop., 1977 est., 20,000). Language: Portuguese. Religion: mainly Roman Catholic. President in 1979, Manuel Pinto da Costa; premier, Miguel Trovoada.

In April 1979 São Tomé and Príncipe and Portugal ratified trade, cultural, and other agreements that had been reached during a visit to São Tomé by the Portuguese foreign minister in July 1978. The two countries also accorded each other most-favoured-nation status with regard to trade. Portugal remained São Tomé's principal customer and supplier of goods.

São Tomé and Príncipe

SÃO TOMÉ AND PRÍNCIPE

Education. (1976–77) Primary, pupils 14,162, teachers 527; secondary, pupils 3,012, teachers 81; vocational, pupils 155, teachers 30.

Finance and Trade. Monetary unit: dobra, with (Sept. 17, 1979) a free rate of 34.70 dobras to U.S. $1 (74.66 dobras = £1 sterling). Budget (1977 est.) revenue 180 million dobras; expenditure 454 million dobras. Foreign trade (1975): imports 288,469,000 dobras; exports 180,432,000 dobras. Import sources: Portugal 61%; Angola 13%. Export destinations: The Netherlands 52%; Portugal 33%; West Germany 8%. Main exports (1973): cocoa 87%; copra 8%.

Agriculture. Production (in 000; metric tons; 1978): cocoa *c.* 7; copra *c.* 5; bananas *c.* 1; palm kernels *c.* 3; palm oil *c.* 1. Livestock (in 000; 1977): cattle *c.* 2; pigs *c.* 3; sheep *c.* 1; goats *c.* 1.

Salvador, El: *see* El Salvador

Salvation Army: *see* Religion

Samoa: *see* Dependent States; Western Samoa

São Tomé's representative at the sixth Franco-African Conference in Kigali, Rwanda, in May 1979 was Maria do Nascimento da Graca Amorim, appointed foreign minister in an extensive Cabinet reshuffle carried out by Pres. Manuel Pinto da Costa in October 1978.

President Costa himself attended the first summit conference of the heads of the five former Portuguese African colonies, held in Luanda, Angola, in June 1979. It was agreed that the five (Angola, Mozambique, Cape Verde, Guinea-Bissau, and São Tomé and Príncipe) should adopt identical economic and social development plans.

(KENNETH INGHAM)

Saudi Arabia

Saudi Arabia

A monarchy occupying four-fifths of the Arabian Peninsula, Saudi Arabia has an area of 2,240,000 sq km (865,000 sq mi). Pop. (1978 est.): 7,866,000. Cap. and largest city: Riyadh (pop., 1976 est., 667,000). Language: Arabic. Religion: Muslim. King and prime minister in 1979, Khalid.

In 1979 Saudi Arabia joined most other Arab states in condemning Egypt's peace treaty with Israel. Despite strains in its traditionally friendly relationship with the United States, the kingdom pursued a policy of oil price restraint, production increases, and support of the U.S. dollar. Internally, the kingdom showed its first deficit budget since 1974. The regime faced the first serious opposition to its leadership when young Muslim fundamentalists seized the Grand Mosque in Mecca on November 20.

Saudi Arabia had refrained from outright rejection of Egyptian Pres. Anwar as-Sadat's peace initiative in 1978, but the March 26, 1979, Egyptian-Israeli treaty forced the Saudis to join their fellow Arabs in severing diplomatic relations with Egypt and condemning Sadat's "separate peace." On March 16 U.S. Pres. Jimmy Carter's national security adviser, Zbigniew Brzezinski, flew to Riyadh in an abortive attempt to persuade the kingdom's leaders to support the treaty. According to U.S. officials, the Saudis were especially disturbed because the treaty failed to include a commitment by the Israelis to withdraw from occupied Arab territory, including Jerusalem, and did not guarantee a homeland for the Palestinians.

Thick smoke rose from the Grand Mosque at Mecca after about 300 Muslim fanatics seized the mosque on November 20. Saudi Arabian troops later recaptured the shrine after several days of fighting.

UPI

In February Crown Prince Fahd canceled a scheduled trip to the U.S., and the Saudi representatives at the Arab League Council meeting in Baghdad, Iraq, on March 27 supported economic and political sanctions against Egypt. Despite their obvious displeasure with U.S. policy, the Saudis successfully defeated a Palestine Liberation Organization (PLO) resolution calling for a trade embargo against the U.S. The Saudis were further offended by the publication, on April 14, of a controversial report by the U.S. Senate Subcommittee on International Economic Policy which stated that Saudi oil reserves could be depleted within 20 years. The study, which had been produced by the subcommittee staff, contained information which the Saudis considered to be highly confidential.

Saudi Arabia broke off diplomatic relations with Egypt on April 23. On May 7 the Saudi foreign minister, Prince Saud al-Faisal, said the Egyptian-Israeli treaty had not affected U.S.-Saudi relationships, but the following day U.S. Secretary of State Cyrus Vance, testifying before the Foreign Affairs Committee of the U.S. House of Representatives, said there were "clear and sharp differences" between the two countries over the treaty. Later in May Prince Sultan ibn Abdel-Aziz, the Saudi defense and aviation minister, announced that the Arab Organization for Industrialization would be dissolved. The organization, established in 1975, had been formed to manufacture various types of military hardware, using Egyptian factories and labour and financial backing from Saudi Arabia, Qatar, and the United Arab Emirates.

Saudi Arabia expressed concern about U.S. commitments to Persian Gulf security in light of the revolution in Iran and the war in Yemen in February. The kingdom was anxious to maintain a careful distance from U.S. policies, which had become increasingly unpopular in the region since the signing of the Egyptian-Israeli treaty, and it rejected an offer in early March of 18 U.S. F-15 jet fighters with U.S. crews, to be based in Saudi Arabia for possible use in Yemen. In May, however, Prince Sultan announced that the kingdom would purchase 60 F-15s from the U.S.

In June Crown Prince Fahd told the *New York Times* that it was "incumbent on the United States to talk to the PLO." Nevertheless, despite the U.S. government's refusal to negotiate with the Palestinian leaders, the Saudis agreed in July to increase oil production by one million barrels a day for three months. A week later the U.S. State Department announced the sale of $1.2 billion worth of arms to the Saudi National Guard.

During the year, Saudi Arabia sought to improve its relations with Western Europe and Japan. There were rumours in early 1979 that the kingdom would permit the establishment of diplomatic relations with the U.S.S.R. However, Saudi fears of Soviet involvement in Ethiopia, Afghanistan, and South Yemen prevented the establishment of diplomatic relations between the two countries.

The turn of events in Iran was a matter of serious concern to the Saudi government. On January 6 Crown Prince Fahd said his country supported the shah, but after the shah was overthrown the foreign minister told a Kuwaiti newspaper that the kingdom would take no position on Iran as long as events there remained a purely internal affair. Possible Iranian influence on Saudi Arabia's Shi'ah minority did not become a public concern until December, when Shi'ah demonstrations took place in the Eastern Province.

The brief war between Yemen (San'a') and Yemen (Aden) in February prompted swift Saudi diplomatic action. The Saudis proposed a four-point peace plan on February 27, which led to a cease-fire and an agreement on unity between the two Yemens. Saudi Arabia put its own forces on alert and at the same time withdrew its troops from the Arab Deterrent Force in Lebanon. Relations with Iraq, traditionally hostile, improved in 1979. The two countries found common cause in their support of the Baghdad resolutions against President Sadat, as well as their mutual fear of the new regime in Iran and its stated intentions of expanding in the Gulf. The two states agreed to cooperate in matters of Gulf security, and Iraq altered its radical posture on oil prices and production in favour of Saudi Arabia's "moderate" approach.

The Saudi government anticipated a budget deficit of U.S. $8.3 billion in 1979 and an increase of 27% in government spending, from $38.7 billion to $47.6 billion. On May 26 the finance and economy minister, Muhammad Ali Abu Khail, announced that the budget would include expenditures of $14.5 billion on defense, $7.2 billion on communications, $5.5 billion on education and vocational training, and $2.5 billion on internal security. The country imported $23.2 billion in foreign goods and in 1978–79 registered its first balance of payments deficit ($58.3 million) since the 1974 increase in oil revenues.

The first serious incident involving opposition to the government since the Mecca riots of September 1978 began at dawn on November 20, the beginning of the year 1400 in the Islamic calendar, when approximately 300 Muslim fundamentalists seized the Grand Mosque in Mecca. Coming at a time of high religious excitement in the Islamic world and shortly after the seizure of American hostages in the U.S. embassy in Teheran, the takeover of Islam's holiest shrine gave rise to rumours that Iranian Shi'ah militants and/or the U.S. was involved. However, Saudi authorities later indicated that the dissidents were mainly Saudis, some of them former theology students, although non-Saudi Muslims also took part in the assault.

After receiving a ruling from the country's religious leaders (the 'ulama') that the seizure was an "ignoble crime and an act of atheism in the House of God," Saudi forces blasted open the doors of the mosque and charged the dissidents. However, it took the National Guard and the Army more than a week to recapture the mosque, locate the worshipers who had been taken hostage, and remove the attackers from the catacombs below the mosque where many of them had taken refuge. It was reported that 156 people died in the fighting. The Saudi dissidents were said to be members of the Bedouin 'Utaibah tribe who had proclaimed one of their number as the mahdi (messiah) on the eve of the new Muslim century.

In December the Eastern Province was shaken by demonstrations among the Shi'ah minority, who demanded reforms and a decrease in oil production. Saudi troops opened fire on the demonstrators, and 15 people were reportedly killed. The two incidents raised doubts about the security of the Saudi state. The governor of Mecca subsequently resigned, and the army command was reshuffled.

The official ceiling on oil production in 1979 was 8.5 million bbl a day, but cuts in Iranian oil production led the Saudis to raise their ceiling to 9.5 million bbl a day for three months, beginning July 1, to enable the U.S. to weather the crisis, and later to extend the increase to the end of the year. The price of Saudi crude oil rose from $14.54 a barrel in March to $17.87 in May. The Saudi prices were below those of other members of the Organization of Petroleum Exporting Countries, and at the meeting of OPEC oil ministers in Caracas, Venezuela, in December the Saudis pushed for price restraint. No agreement on oil prices resulted from the meeting, but the Saudi oil minister, Sheikh Ahmad Zaki Yamani, announced that Saudi Arabia would maintain its price at $24 a barrel, below most other OPEC rates.

(CHARLES GLASS)

SAUDI ARABIA

Education. (1975–76) Primary, pupils 686,108, teachers 35,139; secondary, pupils 203,314, teachers 13,875; vocational, pupils 4,832, teachers 697; teacher training, students 14,651, teachers 1,156; higher, students 26,437, teaching staff 2,133.

Finance. Monetary unit: riyal, with (Sept. 17, 1979) a free rate of 3.35 riyals to U.S. $1 (7.20 riyals = £1 sterling). Gold, SDR's, and foreign exchange (June 1979) U.S. $16,355,000,000. Budget (1978–79 est.) balanced at 130 billion riyals. Gross domestic product (1977–78) 185,384,000,000 riyals. Money supply (April 1979) 49 billion riyals. Cost of living (1975 = 100; 4th quarter 1978) 148.

Foreign Trade. (1978) Imports (fob) *c.* 67 billion riyals; exports 128.7 billion riyals. Import sources (1977): U.S. 19%; Japan 12%; West Germany 8%; U.K. 6%; Italy 6%. Export destinations (1977): Japan 19%; U.S. 10%; France 10%; Italy 7%; The Netherlands 5%. Main exports: crude oil 93%; petroleum products 7%. Tourism (1976) gross receipts U.S. $611 million.

Transport and Communications. Roads (1976) 26,267 km. Motor vehicles in use (1977): passenger *c.* 376,400; commercial (including buses) *c.* 500,400. Railways: (1976) 612 km; traffic (1974) 72 million passenger-km, freight 66 million net ton-km. Air traffic (1977): 4,923,000,000 passenger-km; freight 109 million net ton-km. Shipping (1978): merchant vessels 100 gross tons and over 154; gross tonnage 1,246,112. Telephones (Jan. 1978) 185,000. Radio receivers (Dec. 1976) 260,000. Television receivers (Dec. 1976) 130,000.

Agriculture. Production (in 000; metric tons; 1978): sorghum *c.* 95; wheat *c.* 150; barley *c.* 15; tomatoes *c.* 140; onions (1977) *c.* 50; grapes *c.* 45; dates *c.* 300. Livestock (in 000; 1977): cattle *c.* 170; sheep *c.* 1,410; goats *c.* 775; camels *c.* 620; asses *c.* 103; poultry *c.* 9,800.

Industry. Production (in 000; metric tons; 1978): crude oil 410,500; petroleum products (1977) *c.* 24,860; natural gas (cu m) *c.* 9,400,000; electricity (excluding most industrial production; kw-hr; 1977) *c.* 2,500,000; cement (1976) 1,104.

Scandinavian Literature: *see* Literature

Schools: *see* Education

Scotland: *see* United Kingdom

Sculpture: *see* Art Exhibitions; Art Sales; Museums

Securities: *see* Stock Exchanges

Seismology: *see* Earth Sciences

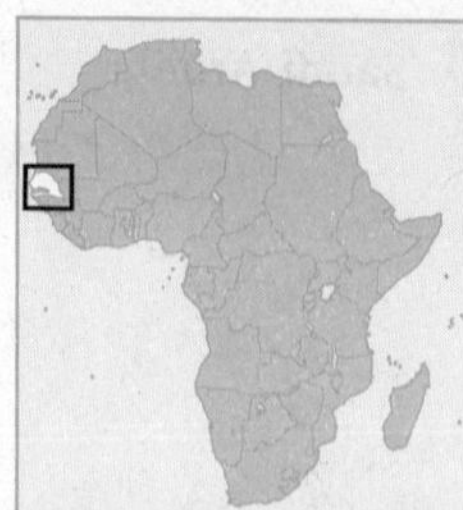

Senegal

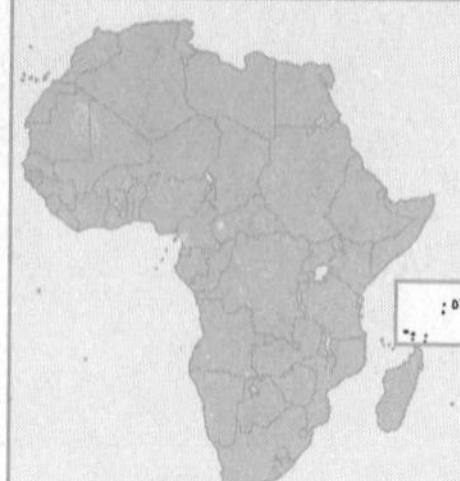

Seychelles

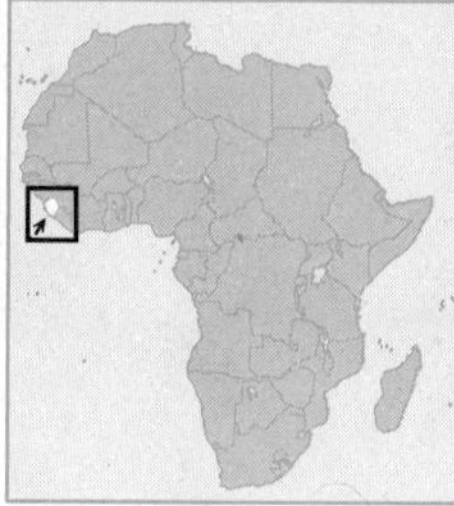

Sierra Leone

Senegal

A republic of northwestern Africa, Senegal is bounded by Mauritania, Mali, Guinea, and Guinea-Bissau and by the Atlantic Ocean. The independent nation of The Gambia forms an enclave within the country. Area: 196,722 sq km (75,955 sq mi). Pop. (1979 est.): 5,518,000. Cap. and largest city: Dakar (pop., 1976 prelim., 798,800). Language: French (official); Wolof; Serer; other tribal dialects. Religion: Muslim 80%; Christian 10%. President in 1979, Léopold Sédar Senghor; premier, Abdou Diouf.

Senegal's standing as the most democratic of the French-speaking West African nations was reinforced in 1979 in three ways: it had no political prisoners, a fact publicly confirmed by Pres. Léopold Senghor in January at a UNESCO-sponsored conference in Dakar on the rights of man; a fourth political party, the Mouvement Républicain Sénégalais of Boubacar Gueye, was created in February; and, also in February, the second congress was held of the Parti Africain de l'Indépendance, reconstituted in 1976 and increasing its membership in March 1979 with the accession to it of three other, smaller Marxist-Leninist groups.

Cooperation with France remained close, and President Senghor met French Pres. Valéry Giscard d'Estaing in Paris twice, in March and August. Senegal attended the Franco-African Conference at Kigali, Rwanda, in May and was the first to call for the setting up of a commission of inquiry into events in the Central African Empire. Under the presidency of a Senegalese judge, the commission decided that a massacre of children involving Emperor Bokassa had occurred there, and in July Senegal became the only African nation to recall its ambassador from Bangui.

President Senghor, together with Mali's president and the Mauritanian premier, broke ground on December 12 for the three countries' joint Senegal River project. (PHILIPPE DECRAENE)

SENEGAL

Education. (1977–78) Primary, pupils 345,198, teachers 9,496; secondary, pupils 78,384, teachers 1,758; vocational and teacher training, pupils 14,090, teachers 820; higher (1975–76), students 8,213, teaching staff 412.

Finance and Trade. Monetary unit: CFA franc, with (Sept. 17, 1979) a par value of CFA Fr 50 to the French franc (free rate of CFA Fr 211.54 = U.S. $1; CFA Fr 455.12 = £1 sterling). Budget (total; 1977–78 est.) balanced at CFA Fr 151 billion. Foreign trade (1977): imports CFA Fr 187.5 billion; exports CFA Fr 152.9 billion. Import sources: France *c.* 45%; The Netherlands *c.* 7%; Italy *c.* 6%; U.S. *c.* 5%; West Germany *c.* 5%. Export destinations: France *c.* 49%; U.K. *c.* 10%; Italy *c.* 6%; Nigeria 5%. Main exports (1975): petroleum products 20%; peanut oil 19%; phosphates 18%; fish and products 6%; peanut oil cake 5%.

Seventh-day Adventist Church:
see Religion

Ships and Shipping:
see Industrial Review; Transportation

Seychelles

A republic in the Indian Ocean consisting of 89 islands, Seychelles lies 1,450 km from the coast of East Africa. Area: 443 sq km (171 sq mi), 166 sq km of which includes the islands of Farquhar, Desroches, and Aldabra. Pop. (1977): 61,950, including Creole 94%, French 5%, English 1%. Cap.: Victoria, on Mahé (pop., 1977, 23,000). Language: English and French are official, creole patois is also spoken. Religion: Roman Catholic 91%; Anglican 8%. President in 1979, France-Albert René.

A new constitution was proclaimed March 26, 1979, and took effect on June 5, the second anniversary of Pres. France-Albert René's coup. It entrenched the one-party state declared by René the previous June. The president, assisted by a council of ministers, would serve a five-year term as head of state and commander in chief. The Seychelles People's Progressive Front's presidential nominee would be subject to approval by popular vote. Quadrennial elections would be held to choose 23 members of the People's Assembly, to which an additional 2 members would be appointed by the president.

The first elections, on June 23–26, duly confirmed René in office with 97.99% of the votes cast. Previously, in May, a tense situation, with rumours of a rice shortage and sabotage, led René to threaten a state of emergency. Tanzanian troops joined a Malagasy contingent already in Seychelles for "joint maneuvers," remaining until after the elections. In November René announced that an attempted coup had been quashed.

During the year a 200-mi economic zone around the archipelago was declared, and British aid was sought against incursions by Soviet and Japanese fishing vessels, estimated to take some 250,000 tons of fish a year (compared with the Seychelles' own catch of about 6,000 tons). At Seychelles' instigation the International Whaling Commission at its conference in July voted to make the Indian Ocean a whale sanctuary. Whale-watching was one of the tourist attractions of Seychelles. (KENNETH INGHAM)

SEYCHELLES

Education. (1977) Primary, pupils 10,001, teachers 424; secondary, pupils 4,252, teachers 193; vocational, pupils 159, teachers 20; teacher training, students 150, teachers 22; higher (1976), students 142, teaching staff 16.

Finance and Trade. Monetary unit: Seychelles rupee, with (Sept. 17, 1979) a free rate of SRs 6.20 to U.S. $1 (par value of SRs 13.33 = £1 sterling). Budget (1978–79 est.) balanced at SRs 205 million. Foreign trade (1977): imports SRs 349.7 million; exports SR 77.8 million. Import sources: U.K. 27%; Kenya 12%; South Africa 9%; Japan 7%; Singapore 6%; Australia 5%. Export destinations: ship and aircraft bunkers and stores 63%; Pakistan 18%. Main exports: petroleum products 45% (jet fuel 32%, marine diesel fuel 10%); copra 19%; aircraft engine parts 11%. Tourism (1978): visitors 64,000; gross receipts U.S. $29 million.

Sierra Leone

A republic within the Commonwealth of Nations, Sierra Leone is a West African state on the Atlantic coast between Guinea and Liberia. Area: 71,740 sq km (27,699 sq mi). Pop. (1979 est.): 3,305,000, including (1963) Mende and Temne tribes 60.7%; other tribes 38.9%; non-African 0.4%. Cap. and largest city: Freetown (pop., 1974, 314,340). Language: English (official); tribal dialects. Religion:

SIERRA LEONE

Education. (1976–77) Primary, pupils 218,379, teachers 6,700; secondary, pupils 50,455, teachers 2,297; vocational, pupils 1,690, teachers 154; teacher training, students 1,269, teachers 121; higher, students 2,077, teaching staff 327.

Finance and Trade. Monetary unit: leone, with (Sept. 17, 1979) a free value of 1.09 leones to U.S. $1 (2.35 leones = £1 sterling). Budget (1978–79 est.): revenue 147.8 million leones; expenditure 133.2 million leones. Foreign trade (1977): imports 206,250,000 leones; exports 140,270,000 leones. Import sources: U.K. *c.* 18%; China *c.* 13%; Nigeria *c.* 10%; U.S. *c.* 7%; Japan *c.* 6%; France *c.* 5%; West Germany *c.* 5%. Export destinations: U.K. *c.* 40%; U.S. *c.* 36%; The Netherlands *c.* 7%; West Germany *c.* 7%. Main exports: diamonds 44%; coffee 25%; cocoa 13%; bauxite 6%.

Agriculture. Production (in 000; metric tons; 1978): rice *c.* 500; cassava (1977) *c.* 89; palm kernels *c.* 30; palm oil *c.* 45; coffee *c.* 4; cocoa *c.* 7; fish catch (1977) 80. Livestock (in 000; 1977): cattle *c.* 318; sheep *c.* 70; goats *c.* 185; pigs *c.* 38; chickens *c.* 3,424.

Industry. Production (in 000; metric tons; 1977): bauxite 760; petroleum products *c.* 310; diamonds (metric carats) 771; electricity (kw-hr) *c.* 200,000.

animist 66%, Muslim 28%, Christian 6%, according to outdated statistics; it appears that Islam is rapidly gaining converts from animism, however. President in 1979, Siaka Stevens.

Although the one-party state approved by referendum in 1978 brought political stability to Sierra Leone, the nation's ailing economy in 1979 faced its worst crisis since independence. In large part this was caused by inflation, corruption, and heavy dependence on the International Monetary Fund (IMF) and other creditors. The governor of the Bank of Sierra Leone painted a bleak picture in his February address; the May mini-budget admitted a failure to cut public expenditure and to accept the IMF's demand for a 20% currency devaluation for fear of resulting social and political problems. In his June budget Finance Minister F. M. Minah announced a 113.6 million leone deficit. Lack of economic discipline and the expense of large-scale development projects, including preparations for Sierra Leone to be host to the Organization of African Unity's (OAU's) 1980 summit conference, accounted for much of this.

At the opening of Parliament in June, Pres. Siaka Stevens claimed success for the first year of the one-party government, noting that there had been less tribal friction. He asserted that many of the nation's economic troubles were due to lack of government control (citing the Rice Corporation's mismanagement, which resulted in large imports instead of self-sufficiency). He believed that the costs of playing host to the OAU would be recouped by permanent assets developed for the occasion.

(MOLLY MORTIMER)

Singapore

Singapore, a republic within the Commonwealth of Nations, occupies a group of islands, the largest of which is Singapore, at the southern extremity of the Malay Peninsula. Area: 616 sq km (238 sq mi). Pop. (1979 est.): 2,362,700, including 76% Chinese, 15% Malays, and 7% Indians. Language: official languages are English, Malay, Mandarin Chinese, and Tamil. Religion: Malays are Muslim; Chinese, mainly Buddhist; Indians, mainly Hindu. President in 1979, Benjamin Henry Sheares; prime minister, Lee Kuan Yew.

SINGAPORE

Education. (1978) Primary, pupils 300,398, teachers 11,112; secondary, pupils 179,811, teachers 7,828; vocational, pupils 7,902, teachers 654; teacher training, students 1,440, teachers 113; higher, students 15,861, teaching staff 1,040.

Finance. Monetary unit: Singapore dollar, with (Sept. 17, 1979) a free rate of Sing$2.15 to U.S. $1 (Sing$4.62 = £1 sterling). Gold, SDR's, and foreign exchange (May 1979) U.S. $5,401,000,000. Budget (1978–79 est.): balanced at Sing$3,668,000,000 (including transfer to development fund of Sing$666 million). Gross national product (1978) Sing$17,406,000,000. Money supply (May 1979) Sing$5,117,000,000. Cost of living (1975 = 100; June 1979) 108.3.

Foreign Trade. (1978) Imports Sing$29,602,000,000; exports Sing$22,986,000,000. Import sources: Japan 19%; Saudi Arabia 13%; Malaysia 13%; U.S. 13%. Export destinations: U.S. 16%; Malaysia 14%; Japan 10%; Hong Kong 7%. Main exports: petroleum products 23%; machinery 17%; rubber 11%; food 6%; ship and aircraft stores 5%. Tourism (1977): visitors 1,682,000; gross receipts U.S. $322 million.

Transport and Communications. Roads (1978) 2,267 km. Motor vehicles in use (1978): passenger 146,400; commercial 55,600. Railways (1978) 38 km (for traffic *see* Malaysia). Air traffic (1978): 9,752,000,000 passenger-km; freight 419,970,000 net ton-km. Shipping (1978): merchant vessels 100 gross tons and over 954; gross tonnage 7,489,205. Shipping traffic (1978): goods loaded 28,963,000 metric tons, unloaded 46 million metric tons. Telephones (Dec. 1977) 455,000. Radio licenses (Dec. 1978) 410,500. Television licenses (Dec. 1978) 353,200.

Singapore

Singapore's ruling People's Action Party (PAP) retained all seven seats in by-elections held in February 1979, two candidates being returned unopposed. In a subsequent Cabinet reshuffle the major change of portfolio involved Deputy Prime Minister Goh Keng Swee, who transferred from defense to education. He subsequently announced the introduction of a new education policy that involved streaming (placing pupils of approximately equal ability in the same classes) at an early age with the object of combating high dropout and failure rates. A major emphasis also was placed on formal moral education—teaching students to be good citizens.

In April Goh Chok Tong was elevated from the position of senior minister of state for finance to that of minister of trade and industry. At age 38, he thus became the youngest member of the Cabinet. Political significance was attached to his appointment in February as second secretary-general of the PAP.

In August the government indicated a major change in its industrial policy, expressed by wage increases and by imposing obligations on employers to contribute to employee pension funds. The object was to use the rising cost of labour to force industry to set up more capital-intensive and complex operations. This commitment to high technology represented a recognition of the problems of competing with regional neighbours in low-cost labour-intensive industrial operations.

At the meeting of foreign ministers of the Association of Southeast Asian Nations (ASEAN) in Bali, Indon., in June, Sinathamby Rajaratnam of Singapore took a strong stand against the installation by Vietnam of a new government in Cambodia. This position was sustained at the conference of nonaligned nations at Havana in September and reinforced by the Singapore delegation to the UN General Assembly, which supported the retention of the Cambodian seat by the ousted government of Pol Pot. In September President Suharto of Indonesia paid a two-day visit to Singapore, where he discussed Indochina and the implications for the ASEAN states of the Sino-Vietnamese conflict with Prime Minister Lee Kuan Yew.

(MICHAEL LEIFER)

Social Security and Welfare Services

During 1979 social security and welfare services in Western countries were affected in one way or another by the need of governments to reduce public expenditure—a need increased by the continuing rise in oil prices.

International Developments in Social Security. Various countries reviewed their arrangements for adjusting benefits. West Germany passed legislation in 1978 suspending for a period of three years the mechanism linking pensions to gross earnings; instead of keeping pace with earnings, pensions would rise in 1979 by 4.5% and by 4% in 1980 and 1981. This was expected to yield a substantial saving to the government. In Italy the government decided that the formula for adjusting pensions introduced in 1975 and extended to cover special schemes in 1978 was proving too expensive to operate; under the 1979 Finance Act the coefficient adjusting pensions for the rise in wages was reduced from 5.9 to 2.9%, and the government intended to reform the entire adjustment mechanism at a later date.

In its 1979 budget the new Conservative Party government in the U.K. also announced its intention to alter the arrangements for adjusting pensions; currently, pensions rose in line with prices or wages, whichever was higher, but the government proposed that future adjustments should have to compensate for price increases only. In The Netherlands, where social security benefits were normally adjusted in line with earnings, the government decided to reduce the benefit increase payable in July 1979. Such restrictions often met with opposition from the public; in Australia the government had decided to move from twice yearly to annual pension adjustments, but in 1979 this decision was reversed.

Health care was another major target for governments seeking to curb public expenditure. In the U.K. the National Health Service had for some time been subjected to a system of cash limits, and the shortage of resources available to the service caused adverse comment among health workers and patients. Events took a dramatic turn in mid-1979 when an area health authority refused to implement cuts in its budget of approximately £5 million, saying that this would mean cutting essential services and putting human life at risk. As a result the minister for health suspended the members of the authority and appointed five commissioners in their place.

In France a substantial deficit reappeared in health insurance at midyear, just six months after the government had decided on a package of measures designed to ensure the financial stability of the scheme for the following three years. This was explained as being two-thirds due to a rapid growth in expenditure and one-third due to a shortfall in revenue. The government's remedy was to impose cash limits on public hospital expenditure, to freeze prices charged to health insurers by private hospitals during 1979, to suspend the rise in doctors' and dentists' pay due in October, and to reduce expenditure on pharmaceuticals. An additional contribution was to be levied on all persons insured under the general scheme from August 1979 till the end of 1980.

At the beginning of 1979 an early retirement scheme came into operation in Denmark. Workers aged 60 and over might choose to stop work and to receive benefits, which amounted to 90% of earnings for 2½ years, 80% for two years, and 60% for the remaining period up to 67, the normal retirement age. In France the employers' federation and the labour unions renewed for an additional two years the agreement first concluded in 1977 under which all workers aged 60 and over might choose to stop work and to receive a "pre-pension," provided that they had been covered by unemployment insurance for at least ten years. However, the new agreement went further than the old one, extending the scheme to cover workers aged 55 and over who were unemployed.

At the same time, French employers and unions agreed on the reform of unemployment insurance, after long, hard negotiation and under some pressure from the government. Special benefits for workers losing their jobs for economic reasons, previously equal to 90% of earnings, were reduced, while standard benefits were improved, particularly for the low paid. Unemployment assistance was incorporated into standard insurance benefits, and the unemployment insurance scheme received a state subsidy.

In spite of the difficulties facing social security, there were positive developments in certain areas. One of these was the equal treatment of men and women. Toward the end of 1978 the Council of Ministers of the EEC approved a directive on this subject. The directive's impact on sex equality would be limited, though by no means negligible. Survivors' benefits, family allowances, and nonstatutory or private schemes were not covered. Furthermore, member states might make certain exceptions to the principles of equal treatment laid down in the directive. For example, they might decide to have different retirement ages for men and women, to discriminate with regard to social benefits related to the bringing up of children, or to have discriminatory provisions with respect to pension supplements for dependent spouses. However, supplements for dependent children could not be discriminatory. Member states would have up to six years to bring their legislation into line with the directive, a much longer period than had been proposed by the Commission.

The directive would lead to changes in three countries in particular: Ireland, The Netherlands,

Skating:
see Ice Hockey; Winter Sports

Skeet Shooting:
see Target Sports

Skiing:
see Water Sports; Winter Sports

Soccer:
see Football

and the U.K. In Ireland and the U.K. it was still difficult for a married woman receiving sickness or unemployment benefits to get dependents' supplements for her children or spouse. In Ireland both the amount and the duration of benefits were less in the case of married women. In The Netherlands a married woman did not qualify for a pension at age 65 if her husband had not yet attained that age.

Social assistance was covered by the directive if it was designed to complement or supplement social security proper. This was the case in the U.K. with its extensive system of supplementary benefi ts; at present such benefits could not be claimed by married women. In Ireland unemployment assistance was payable to married women only if they had at least one dependent child; no such condition applied to men. In The Netherlands a married woman could obtain unemployment assistance only if she was the breadwinner.

Also accomplished during the year were important reforms in health care, work injury insurance, benefits for the elderly, and the financing of social security. Italy's national health service came into effect at the beginning of the year, replacing the old system run by numerous health insurance funds. These funds had recently suffered severe financial problems, and there was also considerable concern regarding the very different standards of care in different areas of the country and under different occupational funds. The new service was a unified system, financed out of general taxation and administered mainly at the regional and local levels. Most of its facilities, hospitals, clinics, and pharmacies were publicly owned, but private, religious, and university facilities might remain independent and provide services under contract to the regional health authorities.

In the U.S.S.R. people who became employees after working on a collective farm would benefit substantially from legislation passed in June 1979. Previously such people had been unable to qualify for a pension under the scheme for collective farms and, because many had been in wage employment for a relatively short time, their pensions as employees were correspondingly small. However, as of the beginning of 1980 they would qualify for a farmer's pension and their period of employment would be counted as if they had continued to work on the collective farm.

While many systems raised contribution rates and ceilings, Ireland made an important qualitative change in April 1979 when it eliminated flat-rate contributions (paid at different rates for men and women) and replaced them with wholly pay-related contributions. After the U.K. changed to earnings-related contributions in 1975, Ireland had been the only major industrialized country left in the world in which employed persons paid flat-rate contributions. (ROGER A. BEATTIE)

U.S. Developments. As the War on Poverty marked its 15th anniversary, the United States marked time in the social welfare field in 1979. There was considerable discussion about reform, several proposals were made, but little was accomplished in the way of concrete action. Typical was the experience in three key areas—Social Security, national health insurance, and welfare. The need for change in all three was widely proclaimed, but agreement could not be reached on specific plans.

A major source of concern was the Social Security system, which paid out about $125 billion in benefits to some 35 million Americans in 1979. Congress had enacted the biggest Social Security tax hike in history in 1977, but the deteriorating economy caused unanticipated problems and brought renewed warnings and calls for further revision.

U.S. Pres. Jimmy Carter proposed to save money by eliminating, reducing, or replacing several Social Security benefits, such as payments to post-secondary students, disability benefits, and lump-sum death benefits. The Congressional Budget Office warned that inflation and recession threatened the short-term financial soundness of the system by decreasing revenues and driving up benefits at an accelerated pace. It said that increased payroll taxes or new sources of revenue would be needed or a lid would have to be placed on automatic cost-of-living increases for beneficiaries (the 9.9% increase in June was the largest ever).

On the other hand, there were calls to reduce or postpone the large payroll tax increases scheduled to take effect in coming years. Employees and employers would pay taxes on the first $25,900 of a worker's wages in 1980 at a rate of 6.13%. The rate was slated to rise to 6.65% in 1981 and to 6.7% in 1982, while maximum wages subject to taxation would go up to $29,700 and $31,800 in those years. This meant that the maximum tax was scheduled to rise about 33%, from $1,587.67 in 1980 to $2,130.60 in 1982.

Despite the warnings, studies, and proposals, no major revisions were made in the Social Security system in 1979. One part of the Carter plan, a cut in future benefits to disabled workers, got as far as passage by the House of Representatives.

More debate than action also was generated over national health insurance, as three different plans were proposed—one by the Carter administration, another by Sen. Edward Kennedy (Dem., Mass.), and a third by Sen. Russell Long (Dem., La.). Most

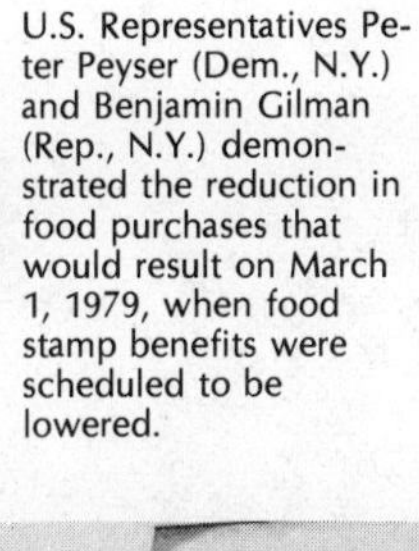

U.S. Representatives Peter Peyser (Dem., N.Y.) and Benjamin Gilman (Rep., N.Y.) demonstrated the reduction in food purchases that would result on March 1, 1979, when food stamp benefits were scheduled to be lowered.

UPI

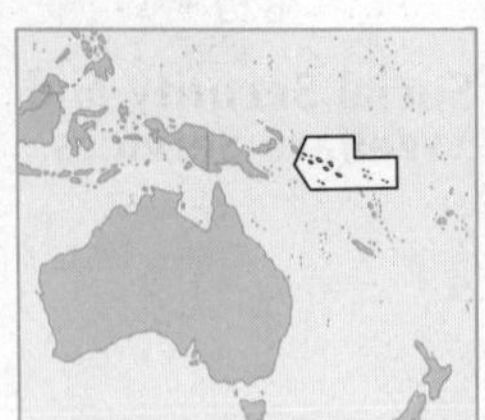
Solomon Islands

Somalia

ambitious of the three was Kennedy's, which would start in 1983, cost an estimated $35.7 billion the first year, and provide comprehensive coverage and substantial benefits. It would rely on private insurers as intermediaries but would put stringent new controls on both the insurance industry and physicians' fees.

The administration's proposal, which would go into effect in stages starting in 1983, would cost an estimated $18.3 billion in its first phase. It would cover extremely high medical bills for everyone, upgrade public programs for the poor and elderly, and merge Medicaid and Medicare into a new program with uniform benefits and a single national standard for eligibility. Individuals and families would pay up to $2,500 a year in medical bills, plus part of the insurance costs. Most limited of the plans was Long's, which would provide catastrophic coverage only at an estimated cost of $5 billion to $10 billion a year. It was the only one that made some headway in Congress.

An exception to the general lack of activity occurred in November when the House of Representatives approved a scaled-down version of President Carter's plan to restructure the largest welfare program, Aid to Families with Dependent Children. The measure would establish for the first time minimum benefits to poor families with children, setting them at 60% of the official poverty level as of Jan. 1, 1981, and 65% after Oct. 1, 1981. It also would guarantee benefits to two-parent families when the principal wage earner was unemployed. The cost of the plan was estimated at about $3 billion a year.

While few innovations were achieved in the three major areas of social welfare, one new program did emerge in response to rapidly rising fuel costs: $1,600,000,000 in federal funds was authorized to help some 7 million poor and the elderly pay winter heating bills. Congress also provided an emergency appropriation of $620 million to keep the food stamp program operating at its normal level through the fiscal year ended Sept. 30, 1979. The need for additional money arose because soaring food prices pushed costs beyond the $6.2 billion statutory limit. That ceiling would almost certainly present a problem again in 1980, when food stamp costs were expected to soar well above $8 billion. New regulations for food stamp recipients went into effect in 1979. They established tighter restrictions on eligibility, thus eliminating marginally poor families, but they also did away with the cash requirement for the purchase of stamps, thereby bringing in more of the very poor. Approximately 18.5 million people were receiving food stamps at year's end.

Despite a slowdown, the War on Poverty had had some success. The Bureau of the Census reported that in 1978, 24,497,000 Americans–11.4% of the population–lived below the poverty level (defined as $6,662 a year for a nonfarm family of four). This compared with 36,055,000 Americans, or 19%, below the poverty line in 1964.

(DAVID M. MAZIE)

See also Education; Health and Disease; Industrial Review: *Insurance*.
[522.D; 535.B.3.e; 552.D.1]

Soil Conservation:
see Environment

Solomon Islands

The Solomon Islands is an independent parliamentary state and member of the Commonwealth of Nations. The nation comprises a 1,450-km (900-mi) chain of islands and atolls in the western Pacific Ocean. Area: 28,896 sq km (11,157 sq mi). Pop. (1978 est.): 214,000 (Melanesian 93.8%; Polynesian 4%; Gilbertese 1.4%; others 1.3%). Cap. and largest city: Honiara (pop., 1978 est., 16,500). Language: English (official), Pidgin (lingua franca), and some 90 local languages and dialects. Religion: Anglican 34.2%, Roman Catholic 18.7%, Seventh-day Adventist 9.7%, other Protestant 30.7%. Queen, Elizabeth II; governor-general in 1979, Baddeley Devesi; prime minister, Peter Kenilorea.

Tensions reflecting interdistrict rivalries continued during the Solomon Islands' first year of independence. The government tried to counter the spread of separatist tendencies by charging three people with sedition (one was convicted) for making statements likely to provoke ill will and hostility.

The budget presented in December 1978 was defeated by 19 votes to 18, but the government was not called on to resign. Instead, Parliament approved the use of consolidated funds while a new budget was prepared and then, in February, passed a slightly amended version of the original.

Parliament gave the government power to extend the territorial limit from 3 to 12 mi offshore and to declare a 200-mi exclusive economic zone. A 200-mi fishing zone had been established earlier and, for an annual license fee of A$350,000, Japanese fishing associations had been given the right to remove up to 6,000 metric tons of skipjack tuna.

Having been admitted to full membership in 1978, the Solomon Islands was host to the 1979 meeting of the South Pacific Forum in July.

(BARRIE MACDONALD)

SOLOMON ISLANDS

Education. (1976) Primary, pupils 27,021, teachers 975; secondary, pupils 1,528, teachers 90; vocational, pupils 1,260, teachers 57; teacher training, students 171, teachers 18.

Finance and Trade. Monetary unit: Solomon Islands dollar with (Sept. 17, 1979) a par value of SI$0.95 to 1 Australian dollar (free rate of SI$0.88 = U.S. $1; SI$1.90 = £1 sterling). Budget (1977 est.): revenue SI$11.7 million; expenditure SI$10.3 million. Foreign trade (1977): imports SI$25.8 million; exports SI$29.8 million. Import sources (1976): Australia 36%; Singapore 14%; Japan 12%; U.K. 10%; New Zealand 5%; U.S. 5%. Export destinations (1976): Japan 34%; U.S. 26%; U.K. 13%; The Netherlands 8%. Main exports (1976): fish 37%; timber 31%; copra 18%; palm oil 6%.

Somalia

A republic of northeast Africa, the Somali Democratic Republic, or Somalia, is bounded by the Gulf of Aden, the Indian Ocean, Kenya, Ethiopia, and Djibouti. Area: 638,000 sq km (246,300 sq mi). Pop. (1979 est.): 3,542,000, mainly Hamitic, with

SOMALIA

Education. (1977–78) Primary, pupils 167,339, teachers 5,401; secondary, pupils 69,831, teachers 3,618; vocational, pupils 3,607, teachers 208; teacher training, students 2,281, teachers 148; higher, students 299.

Finance. Monetary unit: Somali shilling, with (Sept. 17, 1979) a par value of 6.30 Somali shillings to U.S. $1 (free rate of 12.96 Somali shillings = £1 sterling). Gold, SDR's, and foreign exchange (June 1979) U.S. $116 million. Budget (1978 est.): revenue 1,174,000,000 Somali shillings; expenditure 1,107,000,000 Somali shillings. Cost of living (Mogadishu; 1975 = 100; April 1979) 155.9.

Foreign Trade. Imports (1977) 1,432,800,000 Somali shillings; exports (1978) 689.1 million Somali shillings. Import sources: Italy *c.* 29%; U.K *c.* 10%; India *c.* 9%; West Germany *c.* 5%; Iraq *c.* 5%; The Netherlands *c.* 5%. Export destinations (1977): Saudi Arabia *c.* 35%; Italy *c.* 19%; U.S.S.R. *c.* 9%; Japan *c.* 6%. Main exports: livestock 83%; bananas 9%.

Transport and Communications. Roads (1973) *c.* 17,100 km. Motor vehicles in use (1972): passenger 8,000; commercial (including buses) 8,000. There are no railways. Air traffic (1977): 19 million passenger-km; freight 300,000 net ton-km. Shipping (1978): merchant vessels 100 gross tons and over 19; gross tonnage 72,961. Telephones (Jan. 1971) *c.* 5,000. Radio receivers (Dec. 1976) 69,000.

Agriculture. Production (in 000; metric tons; 1978): corn *c.* 100; sorghum *c.* 130; cassava *c.* 30; sesame seed *c.* 25; sugar, raw value *c.* 30; bananas *c.* 150; goat's milk *c.* 288. Livestock (in 000; 1977): cattle *c.* 2,654; sheep *c.* 7,212; goats *c.* 8,212; camels *c.* 2,000.

Arabic and other admixtures. Cap. and largest city: Mogadishu (pop., 1976 UN est., 286,000). Language: Somali spoken by a great majority (Arabic also official). Religion: predominantly Muslim. President of the Supreme Revolutionary Council in 1979, Maj. Gen. Muhammad Siyad Barrah.

For Somalia the outstanding event of 1979 was the adoption of the new constitution, which had been promised ever since Pres. Muhammad Siyad Barrah's regime suspended the original postcolonial constitution in 1969. This took place against a background of serious problems. A poor country still suffering from the effects of the unsuccessful 1977 military campaign against Ethiopia, Somalia had to accommodate more than half a million refugees from the battle areas in the disputed Ogaden region. Meanwhile, guerrilla activity continued in the Ogaden. Exiles hostile to the Barrah regime took refuge in Ethiopia and Kenya, where their efforts to undermine Barrah, particularly by hostile broadcasting, were tolerated or encouraged.

Development projects continued at a slowed pace. A three-year development plan was projected with an expenditure of 7 billion Somali shillings on, among other things, agricultural and animal husbandry projects and a television network. There seemed no prospect, however, of the Somali Army's regaining the strength achieved, with Soviet backing, before the 1977 campaign. The Western powers, to whom Barrah turned after rejecting the Soviet alliance, provided economic but not military aid, and the Iranian revolution removed another source of support. The Army eventually relied mainly on Egypt and Iraq for equipment.

Meanwhile, there were moves to repair the breach with the Soviet Union. Somalia campaigned in the UN and the Organization of African Unity to have the future of the disputed Ogaden territory decided by a plebiscite of its—mainly Somali—inhabitants. A rapprochement with Kenya, the other neighbour with whom Somalia disputed territory, was hinted at when Presidents Barrah and Daniel arap Moi of Kenya visited Saudi Arabia together in September.

The new constitution, drafted by the Somali Revolutionary Socialist Party, was submitted to a national referendum in August, and 99.96% of the electorate registered approval. It provided for a one-party socialist state, with a People's Assembly to be elected every five years and a president elected by the members of the Assembly every six years. It further provided for freedom of religion and the press and for a unified economic system, based on socialist planning, comprising four sectors: public; cooperative; state and private joint enterprise; and private. The constitution committed Somalia to supporting "the liberation of Somali territories under colonial occupation" (Djibouti and the ethnically Somali areas of Ethiopia and Kenya) "by peaceful and legal means." This was a theme pursued by President Barrah at a military parade on October 21 to mark the tenth anniversary of his coming to power, when he also appealed for international aid to help cope with the refugee problem. First elections to the People's Assembly were held on December 30, all 171 seats being filled by the ruling Somalian Revolutionary Socialist Party.

(VIRGINIA R. LULING)

See also Ethiopia.

South Africa

South Africa

The Republic. Occupying the southern tip of Africa, South Africa is bounded by South West Africa (Namibia), Botswana, Zimbabwe Rhodesia, Mozambique, and Swaziland and by the Atlantic and Indian oceans on the west and east. South Africa entirely surrounds Lesotho and partially surrounds the three former Bantu homelands of Transkei (independent Oct. 26, 1976), Bophuthatswana (independent Dec. 6, 1977), and Venda (independent Sept. 13, 1979), although the independence of the latter three is not recognized by the international community. Walvis Bay, part of Cape Province since 1910 but administered as part of South West Africa since 1922, was returned to the direct control of Cape Province on Sept. 1, 1977. Area (including Walvis Bay but excluding the three former homelands): 1,133,759 sq km (438,073 sq mi). Pop. (1979 est.): 24,116,000, including (1978 est., excluding the three homelands) black (Bantu) 67%, white 19%, Coloured 11%, Asian 3%. Executive cap.: Pretoria (pop., 1978 est., 650,600); judical cap.: Bloemfontein (pop., 1978 est., 174,500); legislative cap.: Cape Town (pop., 1978 est., 892,200). Largest city: Johannesburg (pop., 1978 est., 1,416,700). Language: Afrikaans and English (official); Bantu languages predominate. Religion: mainly Christian. State presidents in 1979, B. J. Vorster to June 4 and, from June 19, Marais Viljoen; prime minister, P. W. Botha.

DOMESTIC AFFAIRS. Upon publication of the Erasmus Commission of Inquiry's final report on the irregularities committed by the disbanded De-

KEYSTONE

South Africa's President B. J. Vorster resigned on June 4 after he had become implicated in a government scandal. From 1966 to 1978 he had served as prime minister of the country.

partment of Information, State President B. J. Vorster resigned on June 4. The commission had found that, as prime minister, he had been aware of the irregularities and jointly responsible for their continuance. He was succeeded as state president by Marais Viljoen (*see* BIOGRAPHIES), president of the Senate, on June 19. Viljoen's place in the Senate was taken by J. T. Kruger, the minister of justice. The key Department of Plural Relations and Development was renamed Cooperation and Development, with P. G. Koornhof as minister. In public statements, Prime Minister P. W. Botha reiterated the government's intention to eliminate racially discriminatory practices as far as possible and to promote a constellation of states in southern Africa, to include independent black states, autonomous homelands, and possibly urban black communities within South Africa.

Government policy on separate development (the word apartheid having been officially discarded) included consolidation of the homelands; modification or possibly eventual repeal of such "hurtful" laws as the Mixed Marriages Act and provisions of the Immorality Act barring intercourse across the colour line; and greater self-government in the urban black townships. A Central Consolidation Committee was appointed, with attention to the fragmented independent homeland of Bophuthatswana; large-scale exchanges of land were envisaged, as well as the optional buying out of white landowners.

Venda (*see* below), the northernmost black area, became a republic on the Transkei model. The QwaQwa (Basotho), Ndebeli, and Swazi moved closer toward homeland self-government and legislative authority. In the Ciskei the feasibility of independence for the territory was investigated. In other homelands, notably Lebowa and KwaZulu, sentiment was against a move toward independence before a final consolidation. The Inkatha movement, whose moving spirit was Gatsha Buthelezi, chief minister of KwaZulu, and which had been founded for cultural purposes, widened into a political alliance extending beyond KwaZulu. A clash of interests developed between Inkatha and other black-oriented movements such as Black Consciousness, centred mainly in the white urban areas and universities. Black Consciousness inspired the establishment of the Soweto Civic Association and the first congress of the Azanian People's Organization, both with political aims at the local and national levels.

The position of the urban black population, especially in such major residential complexes as Soweto, preoccupied the administration. Their permanence within the "white" areas was officially recognized, and a network of elected community councils was established. In the case of Soweto (pop. *c.* 1 million), powers comparable to those of the average municipality were granted or envisioned. Regional committees were also appointed throughout the country to advise on urban black problems, complementing the work of the community councils and the race relations committees. Yet basic grievances remained. The operation of in flux control, the pass laws, the generally low standard of wages, aggravated by mounting inflation, and, above all, massive unemployment among urban blacks served to create immediate problems, quite apart from fundamental political issues.

SOUTH AFRICA

Education. (1979) Primary, pupils 4,112,079; secondary, pupils 979,193; vocational, pupils 20,773; primary, secondary, and vocational, teachers 145,132; higher, students 136,293, teaching staff 10,597.

Finance. Monetary unit: rand, with (Sept. 17, 1979) a free rate of R 0.83 to U.S $1 (R 1.77 = £1 sterling). Gold, SDR's, and foreign exchange (June 1979) U.S. $1,004,000,000. Budget (1978–79 est.): revenue R 7,668,000,000; expenditure R 9,811,000,000. Gross national product (1978) R 38,077,000,000. Money supply (June 1979) R 5,425,000,000. Cost of living (1975 = 100; June 1979) 151.2.

Foreign Trade. (Excluding crude oil and products; 1978) Imports R 6,622,000,000; exports R 11,196,000,000. Import sources: West Germany 20%; U.K. 17%; U.S. 16%; Japan 13%; France 8%. Export destinations (excluding gold): U.S. 19%; U.K. 17%; Japan 10%; West Germany 9%; Switzerland 6%. Main exports: gold specie *c.* 35%; food 11%; gold coin 9%; diamonds 8%; iron and steel 7%; nonferrous metals and ores 6%.

Transport and Communications. Roads (excluding tracks; 1977) 202,922 km. Motor vehicles in use (1977): passenger 2,163,500; commercial 821,200. Railways: (excluding Namibia; 1977) 20,124 km; freight traffic (including Namibia; 1978) 80,963,000,000 net ton-km. Air traffic (1978): 7,243,000,000 passenger-km; freight 239,510,000 net ton-km. Shipping (1978): merchant vessels 100 gross tons and over 295; gross tonnage 660,735. Telephones (March 1978) 2,320,000. Radio receivers (Dec. 1976) 2.5 million. Television receivers (Dec. 1978) *c.* 1,250,000.

Agriculture. Production (in 000; metric tons; 1978): corn 9,930; wheat 1,730; sorghum 611; potatoes *c.* 750; tomatoes *c.* 340; sugar, raw value *c.* 2,000; peanuts 318; sunflower seed 447; oranges *c.* 590; grapefruit *c.* 90; pineapples *c.* 185; apples *c.* 320; grapes *c.* 1,130; tobacco *c.* 39; cotton, lint *c.* 47; wool 56; milk *c.* 2,550; meat 958; fish catch (1977) 603. Livestock (in 000; June 1978): cattle *c.* 13,000; sheep *c.* 31,400; pigs *c.* 1,450; goats *c.* 5,270; horses (1977) *c.* 225; chickens *c.* 28,000.

Industry. Index of manufacturing production (1975 = 100; 1978) 98. Fuel and power (in 000; 1978): coal (metric tons) 90,370; manufactured gas (cu m; 1977) *c.* 3,500,000; electricity (kw-hr) 84,765,000. Production (in 000; metric tons; 1978): cement 6,824; iron ore (60–65% metal content) 23,901; pig iron 7,096; crude steel 7,892; antimony concentrates (metal content; 1977) 12; copper 134; chrome ore (oxide content; 1977) 1,460; manganese ore (metal content; 1977) 2,338; uranium (1977) 6.7; gold (troy oz) 22,710; diamonds (metric carats; 1977) 8,033; asbestos (1977) 380; petroleum products (1977) *c.* 12,690; fertilizers (nutrient content; 1977–78) nitrogenous *c.* 414, phosphate *c.* 403; newsprint 240; fish meal (including Namibia; 1977) 176.

A significant development was the government's acceptance, in principle and largely in practice, of recommendations by two commissions, on labour legislation and on race and other laws affecting utilization of labour and urban black living conditions. In its first report, the Wiehahn Commission on the labour laws recommended the extension of full trade union rights to black workers. It also recommended equal pay for equal work, training and retraining schemes for black workers, apprenticeship training for all races, and the right (previously withheld from blacks) to become indentured as apprentices. Repeal of the compulsory separation of facilities for different races in shops, offices, and factories was recommended. A national manpower commission and an industrial court were established. The phasing out of job reservation, whereby certain jobs were reserved for whites, was an objective of the new labour structure.

The Riekert Commission's report contained wide-ranging recommendations on restrictive race and related laws, aimed at their relaxation or, where possible, their scrapping and at changes in their administration, the ending of unjustifiable discrimination, and more efficient use of resources, including labour. It emphasized easing of interrace relations and covered such matters as influx control, separation of families under the migrant labour system, the "white by night" curfew, and opportunities for the development of an African middle class. For the most part the recommendations were accepted by the government.

The Wiehahn and Riekert reports were opposed in some political quarters and by some white workers, notably the South African Mineworkers' Union, which objected to the proposals on black trade union membership and the elimination of job reservation. There was also disagreement over the new Bantu land consolidation policy, amendment of controversial apartheid laws, mixed sport, and the sharing of public amenities, which were reflected in parliamentary by-elections. The ruling National Party lost ground, not least to the right-wing Herstigte Nasionale Party (HNP), and in November lost a by-election for the first time, to the Progressive Federal Party in Natal.

In November the former minister of information, V. P. ("Connie") Mulder, who had resigned from the Cabinet and later was expelled from the National Party after the Department of Information affair, formed his own new National Conservative Party, to preserve the traditional policies of the National Party. (Eschel Rhoodie [*see* BIOGRAPHIES], Mulder's former subordinate, was convicted of fraud on October 8.) The Progressive Federal Party leader, Colin Eglin, was replaced by F. van Zyl Slabbert, who thus became leader of the official opposition. Although Parliament on March 30 refused to debate the introduction of a new constitution, plans to restructure the South African constitution to accommodate the Coloured and Indian populations moved forward with the appointment of an all-party commission of both houses of Parliament to draft a constitution based on the Cabinet's proposals. Coloured and Indian opinion generally reacted against the proposals, calling instead for a unitary system with a parliament representing all races.

A new Coloured Party, the South African Alliance under W. Bergins, was formed to end statutory racial discrimination and promote unity between all racial groups. A new Indian party, the Democratic Party of South Africa with J. B. Patel as chairman, was founded to work for peaceful change and cooperation with all racial groups short of an alliance.

FOREIGN RELATIONS. Early in the year there was disagreement between South Africa and the five countries (U.S., Great Britain, France, West Germany, and Canada) charged by the UN Security Council with formulating a plan for independence for South West Africa (Namibia). South Africa rejected UN Secretary-General Kurt Waldheim's proposal that, during the transition period leading to a general election and independence, the South West Africa People's Organization (SWAPO) should be permitted to have bases in Namibia and its forces outside should be monitored not by the UN Transition Assistance Group (UNTAG) but by the Angolan authorities. Fresh proposals submitted to South Africa provided for the creation of an UNTAG-patrolled demilitarized cease-fire zone 50 km (30 mi) wide, running along the Angola-Namibia border. Meanwhile, sporadic hostilities between the South African border forces and SWAPO continued.

In Namibia itself the 50-member multiracial Constituent Assembly, elected in December 1978 but repudiated by the UN, converted itself in May into a National Assembly with legislative powers sanctioned by the administrator general, M. T. Steyn, and implicitly endorsed by South Africa. The action was taken at the request of the dominant Democratic Turnhalle Alliance (DTA) under Dirk Mudge. The assembly legislated to abolish racial discrimination and then demanded executive powers and control of administrative services. Its establishment was opposed by the white Aktur group, led by A. H. du Plessis, which boycotted proceedings in the assembly. Aktur's seats were declared vacant after it made an abortive attempt to have the assembly declared illegal. Steyn resigned and was succeeded in August by Gerrit Viljoen, head of the influential Afrikaner Broederbond. In November the UN set up a conference on Namibia attended by the various political parties and South Africa.

The Botha government's foreign policy was realigned toward Africa rather than toward the West. It aimed to steer clear of involvement in the East-West power struggle and to restore détente with moderate leaders among its neighbours in southern Africa. Government spokesmen emphasized the concept of a "constellation of states" based on the socioeconomic and strategic interdependence of the region, with South Africa providing the leadership and technological expertise.

South Africa's handling of its race problems was attacked at the UN and elsewhere with threats of economic sanctions, disinvestment, and isolation within the international community. South Africa reacted by calling attention to its mineral wealth, development potential, credit-worthiness, and

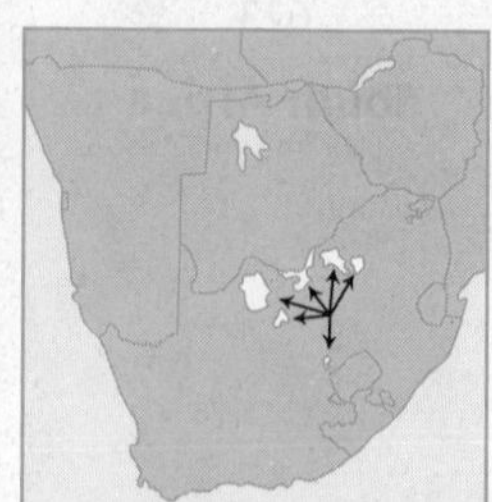
Bophuthatswana

Transkei

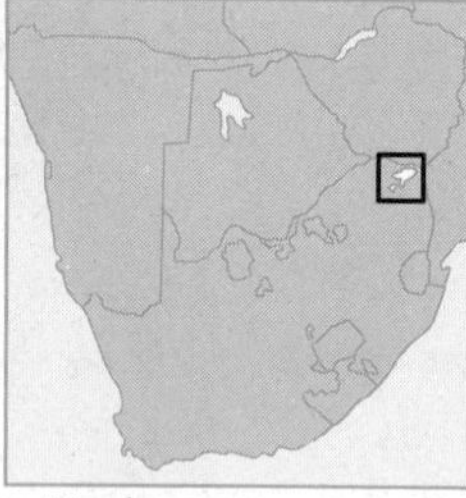
Venda

relative political stability. After several years of nonparticipation, South Africa appointed an ambassador to the UN, A. Eksteen. Relations with the U.S. were disturbed for a time by allegations of U.S. aerial espionage over sensitive South African security areas. In the fall the U.S. claimed to have detected a low-yield nuclear explosion in the South African region, but South Africa denied any nuclear weapons testing. In international sport, South African teams were barred from a number of countries. South Africa played an indirect part in British negotiations for Zimbabwe Rhodesia's independence. The possibility of active intervention was envisioned if Rhodesian developments menaced South Africa.

THE ECONOMY. Presenting the 1979 budget on March 28, Minister of Finance Owen Horwood declared that the government's policy of "disciplined growth from a position of strength" would enter Phase III. This was indicated by an exceptionally large surplus in the current balance of payments account; a steadily rising upswing in the gold and foreign exchange reserves; effective control of government spending, bank credit, and the money supply; freedom of national resources to expand; and further improvement in South Africa's international credit rating.

Inflation rose, largely because of increased fuel prices and a new sales tax, while consumer spending and productivity lagged. There was widespread unemployment, particularly among blacks. However, aided by stimulatory measures, the economy was expected to grow by up to 4%. Taxes were reduced, interest rates lowered, and bank credit facilities relaxed. A system of managed floating of the rand was introduced, together with a new financial rand to encourage foreign investment. Streamlining of the state administrative machinery was announced in October. Defense expenditure was increased by 20%, and arms production expanded.

Bophuthatswana. The republic of Bophuthatswana consists of six discontinuous, landlocked geographic units, one of which borders Botswana on the northwest; it is otherwise entirely surrounded by South Africa. Area: 40,430 sq km (15,610 sq mi). Pop. (1978 est.): 1,245,000, including 99.6% Bantu, of whom Tswana 69.8%, Northern Sotho 7.5%. Cap.: Mmabatho. Largest city: Ga-Rankuwa (pop., 1973 est., 64,200). Languages (official): Central Tswana, English, Afrikaans. Religion: predominantly Christian (Methodist, Lutheran, Anglican, and Bantu Christian churches). President in 1979, Lucas Mangope.

Makeshift arrangements with South Africa continued to operate by mutual agreement, enabling Bophuthatswana to maintain trade and other contacts over its fragmented parts, but the country needed to be consolidated as soon as possible. The South African (Van der Walt) commission on the consolidation of the homelands tentatively proposed large-scale exchanges of land and the buying out, at great cost, of farms owned by whites who did not wish to remain. Also at issue was the future of the border town of Mafeking, located in South Africa but claimed by Bophuthatswana on historic and economic grounds.

Transkei. Bordering the Indian Ocean and surrounded on land by South Africa, Transkei comprises three discontinuous geographic units, two of which are landlocked. Area: 41,002 sq km (15,831 sq mi). Pop. (1978 est.): 2,178,000, including (1970) Bantu 99%, of whom 95% were Xhosa. Cap. and largest city: Umtata (pop., 1978 est., 30,000). Language: Xhosa (official); English and Sesotho may be used for official purposes as well. Religion: Christian 65.8%, of which Methodist 25.2%; non-Christian 13.8%; 10.4% unspecified. President from Feb. 20, 1979, Kaiser Daliwonga Matanzima; prime minister, George Matanzima.

Diplomatic relations with South Africa, ruptured in 1978 over the land question, would not be restored until Griqualand East was transferred from South Africa, according to a statement by Prime Minister George Matanzima in October. Despite this, Transkei remained on good terms with South Africa,on which its financial dependence increased during 1979.

Many Transkei Xhosas living in South Africa who had not taken out Transkei citizenship were given until October 1980 to do so, although a South African plan to grant dual citizenship in such cases might alter the position.

Transkei, still denied international recognition outside South Africa, maintained informal ties with various countries. Air services with South Africa were improved, and a radio station was opened at Port St. Johns. Detention without trial of political opponents and labour unrest were reported. In November the government banned 34 political, religious, and journalistic organizations, including Buthelezi's Inkatha movement and the South African Council of Churches.

Venda. The independent republic of Venda comprises two geographic units in extreme northeastern South Africa separated by a narrow corridor belonging to its eastern neighbour, the

BOPHUTHATSWANA

Education. Primary, pupils (1976) 326,826, teachers (1973) 4,537; secondary, pupils (1976) 55,895; vocational (1973), students 471, teachers 37; teacher training, students (1976) 3,035; secondary and teacher training, teachers (1973) 771; higher, students (1973) 167.

Finance and Trade. Monetary unit: South African rand. Budget (1977–78) balanced at R 72 million. Foreign trade included with South Africa.

TRANSKEI

Education. (1978) Primary, pupils 647,985, teachers 12,627; secondary, pupils 33,636, teachers 1,179; vocational, pupils 908, teachers 59; teacher training, students 3,034, teachers 126; higher, students 503, teaching staff 96.

Finance and Trade. Monetary unit: South African rand. Budget (total; 1978–79 est.): revenue R 225 million; expenditure R 328 million. Most trade is with South Africa.

VENDA

Education. (1978) Primary, pupils 107,711, teachers 2,300; secondary, pupils 23,460, teachers 555; vocational, pupils 323; teacher training, students 674.

Finance and Trade. Monetary unit: South African rand. Budget (1979): balanced at R36.7 million. Most trade is with South Africa.

Gazankulu homeland. Area: 7,184 sq km (2,448 sq mi). Pop. (1978 est.): 357,000, including (1970) 90% Venda, 6% Shangaan, and 3% Northern Sotho. Cap.: Thohoyandou (replacing Sibasa). Largest town, Makearela (pop., 1976 est., 1,972). Language (official): Venda, English, and Afrikaans. Religion: traditional religions predominate; Christian minority. President in 1979, Patrick Mphephu.

Venda became a republic on Sept. 13, 1979. There was virtual unanimity on the South African-backed move to independence, though Venda was denied international recognition. In pre-independence elections for the Legislative Assembly, the traditionalist Venda National Party (NDP), led by Patrick Mphephu, was opposed by the Venda Independence People's Party. The VIPP advocated modernization, and its leader, Baldwin Mudau, was detained for a time before independence. The VIPP won the most seats, but the NDP secured a majority with the help of the chiefs and nominated tribal representatives. (LOUIS HOTZ)

See also Dependent States.

Southeast Asian Affairs

War worries triggered by events in Indochina and the mass exodus of refugees from the Communist countries to neighbouring non-Communist states kept Southeast Asia in crisis throughout 1979. At the centre was Vietnam, which was invaded by China in February after it had sent troops into Cambodia to defeat the Pol Pot regime. Vietnam's action in Cambodia led it into an antagonistic relationship with member countries of the Association of Southeast Asian Nations (ASEAN). These developments gave a new cohesion to ASEAN and thus to the collective attitudes of non-Communist Southeast Asia. There was vague talk about ASEAN developing a military profile, but there was no official move apart from ongoing bilateral joint exercises. What did develop was a new political strength born of shared views on Indochina.

ASEAN and Vietnam. ASEAN's new unity of policy superseded previous differences in approach. When North Vietnam won the war against South Vietnam in 1975, Indonesia and Malaysia had shown interest in coming to terms with it, perceiving China as a more serious long-term problem for the region. On the other hand, Singapore had argued against close cooperation with Vietnam. In the wake of Vietnam's push into Cambodia in December 1978, senior Indonesian leaders continued to caution against an attitude of belligerency against Hanoi or moves that would isolate it. Singapore's Prime Minister Lee Kuan Yew, however, said in November that Europe, the U.S., and Japan should impose economic sanctions against Vietnam and deny it the political support it badly needed. But despite such divergence in perceptions, ASEAN stood solidly together in demanding the withdrawal of Vietnamese troops from Cambodia and in criticizing Hanoi's policy toward refugees.

The Vietnamese action in Cambodia caused alarm in Southeast Asian capitals because it was seen as a precedent for military intervention by one country in another. ASEAN foreign ministers met hurriedly in Bangkok, Thailand, and issued a terse joint communiqué deploring the intervention and calling for "the immediate and total withdrawal of the foreign forces from Kampuchean territory." They also strongly urged the UN Security Council to take the "necessary and appropriate measures to restore peace, security, and stability in the area."

Much of ASEAN's resentment stemmed from fears that Vietnam had reneged on assurances, personally given by Premier Pham Van Dong during a high-profile tour of the region four months earlier, that it would not interfere in the affairs of other countries. ASEAN members refused to recognize the new Hanoi-backed regime of Heng Samrin (*see* BIOGRAPHIES) in Cambodia and continued their recognition of the fallen Pol Pot government.

Vietnam for its part turned against ASEAN after the group's UN resolution calling for the with-

Cambodian revolutionary forces moved into a deserted Phnom Penh on January 7. The city had previously been evacuated during the Pol Pot regime.

INTERFOTO MTI/SYGMA

LIAISON

Vietnamese regional militiamen move toward the border to repel Chinese troops who invaded Vietnam in February. The Chinese said that they were "punishing" Vietnam for its invasion of Cambodia, a Chinese ally.

drawal of forces from Cambodia was vetoed by the Soviet Union in March. The resolution, as well as reports that Thailand was letting military supplies go to anti-Vietnam rebels in Cambodia, caused Hanoi to abandon its year-old wooing of ASEAN and denounce it instead. "ASEAN actions," it said, "are detrimental to the interests of the three Indochina countries, to the ASEAN countries, and to the peace and stability of Southeast Asia and the rest of the world." Toward the end of the year, however, Hanoi softened its stand and came up with assurances of goodwill and noninterference in Thailand.

China's Intervention. If Southeast Asian countries were alarmed by Vietnam's thrust into Cambodia, they were even more disturbed by China's incursion into Vietnam in February. The general impression at the end of that war was that neither side had won, that the Chinese had inflicted on Vietnam a wound Hanoi would not forget, and that the overall effect was unfavourable to peace in the region.

The widespread concern was reflected in a flurry of top-level meetings. In late March, Thailand's Prime Minister Kriangsak Chamanand traveled to northern Sumatra to discuss the events with Indonesia's President Suharto. He then flew to Singapore for talks with Lee. Suharto and Lee in turn met with Malaysia's home affairs minister, Ghazalie Shafei. Suharto announced that he would proceed to Manila to confer with Pres. Ferdinand E. Marcos of the Philippines. All leaders seemed to recognize Thailand's special position as a frontline state facing Indochina.

The mood grew grim by September with Vietnam intensifying its military operation in western Cambodia and the flow of refugees into Thailand breaking all previous records. There were fears across the region that the war could spill into Thailand. Kriangsak warned of a "mighty storm" if "political and diplomatic action" were not quickly taken to stabilize the Indochina situation. ASEAN countries presented a joint resolution before the UN in November appealing for an end to outside interference in Cambodia's affairs. Ironically, Vietnam's allies also presented a resolution calling on all nations to refrain from any activity that would "constitute interference in Cambodia's internal affairs." The ASEAN resolution was passed with an overwhelming majority, but it seemed to have little effect on the situation.

One result of the growing concern for the security of the region was increased U.S. military assistance. Thailand topped the list of recipients; during a one-year period U.S. military sales to Bangkok quadrupled to $411 million. In Malaysia in the course of a Southeast Asian tour in October, U.S. Assistant Secretary of State Richard C. Holbrooke said that increased military supplies would be made available to that country as well. Declaring that the U.S. would react appropriately if Vietnam crossed the border into Thailand, he said that "Thailand is the key to ASEAN and ASEAN is the key to Southeast Asia." He added that the period of "trauma, withdrawal, and guilt" that followed the U.S. retreat from South Vietnam was over as proved by the fact that during the past year Congress had backed all the aid proposals made for the region by the Carter administration.

The Indochinese Exodus. Worries over the military situation were aggravated by Southeast Asia's human tragedy of the year—the refugee exodus. Although refugees had been fleeing Vietnam for several years, the exodus in 1979 developed into a major region-wide crisis because of the vast numbers involved and the intractable political issues with which it was intertwined. The widespread impression that authorities in Vietnam were conspiring to push out its citizens produced considerable resentment in neighbouring countries. The fact that the bulk of the refugees were ethnic Chinese created special problems for such countries as Malaysia and Indonesia, which were in no mood to upset their own delicate racial balances. The result was that distress signals from flimsy refugee boats in Southeast Asian seas were ignored by many passing ships, while Malaysia announced a tough policy of towing refugees who reached its shores back into the open sea. The tragedy that developed was widely recognized as one of the worst in modern times. (*See* REFUGEES: *Special Report*.)

Economic Developments. For all the turmoil caused by war worries and refugees, per capita gross national product (GNP) and growth rates in Southeast Asia, along with East Asia, remained the highest in the third world and higher than in many developed countries. Noting that GNP growth had been "accompanied by broad advances in the satisfaction of basic needs in health, nutrition, education, and other services," the World Bank said in September that the record of socioeconomic progress was attributable to "political stability, generally strong commitment to development, a large increase in investment levels, high priority given to the agriculture and export sectors, an unprecedentedly rapid increase in international trade and, last but not least, generally sound and pragmatic economic management." The Bank cautioned, however, that the distribution of the benefits of growth had remained generally unequal and that "such unequal distribution is also occurring between regions within a number of countries, where, most notably, areas dependent on rainfed agriculture often lag behind."

The year's sharp rise in oil prices had a damaging effect on the region's current account balance. ASEAN members reiterated their resolve to help one another in any oil crisis that developed, especially if Thailand came under pressure from outside forces. But the continuing dependence of the region on imported oil was emphasized when Iran suspended its supplies to the Philippines in October, charging that the Philippine government was persecuting its Muslim citizens. Another blow to Southeast Asia's current account was expected from slower growth in the U.S. and other industrialized countries and consequent reduction in their imports. (T. J. S. GEORGE)

See also articles on the various countries.
[976.B]

Space Exploration

Clearly the space spectacular of 1979 was the dramatic reentry of Skylab into the Earth's atmosphere during its 34,981st orbit. The 69,750-kg (155,000-lb) space station plunged into the denser regions of the atmosphere on July 11 several hundred miles off the southern coast of Western Australia. Portions of it fell into the Indian Ocean, but many pieces dropped onto Australia with objects weighing as much as 850 kg (1,870 lb) falling near towns such as Kalgoorlie and Rawlinna. Untold numbers continued eastward along a 6,400-km (4,000-mi) corridor into Australia's Great Victorian and Great Sandy deserts. Prior to the impact the U.S. National Aeronautics and Space Administration (NASA) had predicted that the chances of anyone being killed were extremely remote, and there were no reported casualties. The Skylab space station had cost $293 million out of a program with a total cost of $2.5 billion. Launched on May 14, 1973, it was visited by three crews of three men each during its six-year lifetime.

On January 31 U.S. Pres. Jimmy Carter and Vice-Premier Deng Xiaoping (Teng Hsiao-p'ing) of China signed a protocol to the Agreement on Cooperation in Science and Technology. It included plans for the establishment of satellite communications, ground receivers, and transmitters. The cost of the satellite and ancillary equipment in the U.S. could be as much as $500 million. A group of ten high-ranking U.S. space experts toured Chinese space facilities during the summer and discussed a possible purchase by the Chinese of a Landsat satellite ground-receiver station.

Manned Flight. The Soviet Union announced that it had made an offer to France to train and fly a French astronaut aboard a resupply Soyuz to the Salyut 7 space station in 1983. The French accepted the offer and were said to be considering a woman as the nation's first person in space. The Soviets also revealed that a Vietnamese astronaut was in training for a similar mission.

Soyuz 32 was launched on Feb. 25, 1979, from

NASA/AUTHENTICATED NEWS INTERNATIONAL

Assembled space shuttle "Enterprise" —orbiter, external fuel tank, and twin booster rockets—rolled out of Kennedy Space Center's vehicle assembly building in April for launch pad tests. Problems with its main engines, skin insulation, and other components were postponing first launch of its sister ship, "Columbia," from 1979 to at least the following summer.

South West Africa: *see* Dependent States; South Africa

Soviet Literature: *see* Literature

Soviet Union: *see* Union of Soviet Socialist Republics

the Soviet space centre at Tyuratam with Lieut. Col. Vladimir A. Lyakhov and Valery V. Ryumin aboard. On the following day the spacecraft docked with the Salyut 6 space station. The two cosmonauts immediately began rehabilitating the craft, which had been in orbit for a year and a half and had been unoccupied since the previous November. They also began a series of medical experiments. One included a number of houseflies, several of which escaped into the space station and thereby added a familiar feature of life on Earth to life in space. On March 14 Progress 5, a cargo spacecraft, docked with the Salyut 6, delivering additional rocket-engine propellants, repair parts, food, and other supplies.

As the cosmonauts entered their second month in space, they increased the length of their exercise period to 2.5 hours per day, indicating that they were planning a long stay. On April 3 Progress 5 was separated from the Salyut and reentered the atmosphere. Seven days later Soyuz 33, manned by Nikolai Rukavishnikov and Georgy Ivanov, a Bulgarian, was launched from Tyuratam to visit Salyut 6. Propulsion system problems with the Soyuz 33 prevented rendezvous and docking. The crew then aborted the mission and returned to Earth on April 12.

Further resupply of the Salyut 6 took place on May 15 with the arrival of the Progress 6 cargo spacecraft, and Ryumin and Lyakhov continued with a variety of scientific and engineering experiments, including Earth resources observations of the Soviet landmass and location of fishing grounds. Biological experiments included observations of the growth of plants in weightlessness. On June 9 the unmanned Soyuz 34 docked with the Salyut 6, later moving from the aft docking port to the forward port to make room for the future arrival of Progress 7. Also on June 9 Progress 6 was undocked and reentered the atmosphere.

Progress 7 was launched on June 28 and docked with the space station on June 30. Included in its cargo were 46 kg (105.6 lb) of air, a radiotelescope, and a variety of foodstuffs that permitted the crew to plan their meals according to personal preference. Progress 7 separated from the space station on July 18.

Once Progress 7 was safely away, Lyakhov and Ryumin installed the radio telescope and deployed its 10-m (33-ft)-diameter antenna by remote control through an airlock in the Salyut 6. However, the antenna snagged on the aft end of the space station, preventing further docking of Soyuz or Progress vehicles at that end. Maneuvers with the attitude-control engines of the Salyut 6 failed to dislodge the ensnared antenna. Both crewmen donned space suits and went outside to free it. Like earlier U.S. astronauts on Skylab, the two men quit working while the space station passed into the night side of its orbit. Once daylight returned, they cut the balky antenna loose with a pair of wire cutters.

On August 19, Lyakhov and Ryumin returned to Earth after 175 days and 36 minutes in space. This was a new record, breaking that of 139 days, 14 hours, and 48 minutes set by two of their fellow cosmonauts on Nov. 2, 1978.

At the end of August, the 35 astronaut candidates of NASA, who had been selected in January 1978, completed their training at the Johnson Space Center in Houston, Texas, and became eligible for assignment to flight crews on forthcoming space shuttle missions. The group included 15 pilots and 20 mission specialists. Among the latter were six women, the first female U.S. astronauts. With the selection of the new astronauts the total in the U.S. space program reached 62. Concerning the selection of future astronauts, NASA announced a change in practice. Astronaut candidates would be selected annually to fill vacancies.

Unmanned Satellites. An international cooperative launching took place on Oct. 24, 1978, when the U.S.S.R. launched Intercosmos 18 containing experiments provided by not only its own scientists but also those from Czechoslovakia, Hungary, East Germany, Poland, and Romania. Launched piggyback with it was Magion 1, Czechoslovakia's first satellite, which stayed attached to Intercosmos 18 until it was separated on Nov. 14, 1978. In coordination with Intercosmos 18, Magion was to monitor and report on very-low-frequency radiowaves occurring in the outer atmosphere.

Launched on Nov. 13, 1978, HEAO 2 (High Energy Astronomy Observatory; later named the Einstein Observatory) went to work almost immediately, supplying especially valuable data to scientists on X-ray sources in space. It discovered what is believed to be a black hole in Cygnus X-1, a binary star some 6,000 light-years from the Earth. By mid-1979 HEAO 2 had observed some 20 known quasars and discovered several more. In observing supernovas the satellite reported the existence of ionized sulfur, calcium, magnesium, and argon in their X-ray spectra. Previously only silicon and iron had been detected. HEAO 2 also obtained the first X-ray images of a rare celestial object known as an X-ray burster. These objects, less than 48 km (30 mi) in diameter, can emit as much energy in 10 seconds as the Sun does in a week.

On Jan. 9, 1979, HEAO 1 ended its mission after having been launched in August 1977. During that period it discovered about three new X-ray sources per day, including what probably is a black hole in the constellation Ara. The last in the highly successful HEAO series was launched from Kennedy Space Center in Florida on September 20. HEAO 3 achieved an almost perfectly planned orbit at an altitude of about 500 km (300 mi).

For the first time, in November 1978, a satellite returned radio altimeter measurements sufficient to produce contour maps of the Earth's surface that compared in accuracy with the best man-made ones using geodetic measurements. GEOS 3 (Geodynamics Experimental Ocean Satellite) provided the data from an altitude of 840 km (520 mi) during 19 orbits over the San Joaquin Valley of southern California.

Launch Vehicles. An analysis made during 1979 of Soviet space launch vehicle failures since 1970 indicated a rate of under 10%. The two most trouble-prone were the nation's two largest boosters, the A II used for the Soyuz and Progress laun-

Major Satellites and Space Probes Launched Oct. 1, 1978–Sept. 30, 1979

Name/country/ launch vehicle/ scientific designation	Launch date, lifetime*	Weight in kg†	Physical characteristics Shape	Diam- eter in m†	Length or height in m†	Experiments	Orbital elements Perigee in km†	Apogee in km†	Period (min)	Inclination to Equator (degrees)
Progress 4/U.S.S.R./A II/ 1978-090A	10/3/78 10/26/78	7,000 (15,432)	sphere and cone	2.3 (7.55)	8 (26.25)	Supply vehicle for Salyut 6 space station	187 (116)	356 (221)	89.88	51.6
NavStar (GPS 3)/U.S./ Atlas F/1978-093A	10/7/78	450 (992)	cylinder with four panels	1.23 (4.04)	1.8 (5.91)	Satellite in global positioning network for U.S. armed forces	20,283 (12,603)	20,310 (12,620)	722.6	62.8
Tiros 11/U.S./Atlas Centaur/ 1978-096A	10/13/78	734 (1,618)	cylinder	1.8 (5.91)	3.7 (12.14)	Polar orbiting meteorological satellite	849 (528)	864 (537)	98.9	102.13
Nimbus 7/U.S./Delta/ 1978-098A	10/24/78	715 (1,576)	truncated cone with two panels	1.5 (4.92)	3 (9.84)	Oceanographic and meteorological satellite	943 (586)	955 (593)	104.09	99.28
Intercosmos 18/U.S.S.R./ C I/1978-099A	10/24/78	550 (1,213)	octagonal elipsoid (probably)	1.8 (5.91)	1.5 (4.92)	Studies of ionosphere and magnetosphere by E. Ger., Hung., Pol., Rom., Czech., and the U.S.S.R.	414 (257)	761 (473)	96.49	82.97
Magion 1/Czechoslovakia/ C I/1978-099C	10/24/78	15 (33)	cylinder	‡	‡	Study of ionosphere and magnetosphere	404 (251)	722 (449)	93.6	82.9
Radio 1/U.S.S.R./C I/ 1978-100B	10/26/78	‡		‡	‡	Part of first Soviet amateur radio satellite	1,685 (1,047)	1,706 (1,060)	120.4	82.5
Radio 2/U.S.S.R./C I/ 1978-100C	10/26/78	‡		‡	‡	Part of first Soviet amateur radio satellite	1,685 (1,047)	1,706 (1,060)	120.4	82.5
Prognoz 7/U.S.S.R./A IIe/ 1978-101A	10/30/78	950 (2,094)	sphere with four panels	1.8 (5.91)		Study of solar plasma and electromagnetic radiation and of Earth's magnetic fields	483 (300)	202,965 (126,117)	5,888	65
HEAO 2/U.S./Atlas Centaur/ 1978-103A	11/13/78	3,100 (6,834)	tapered octagonal prism	3 (9.84)	5.8 (19.01)	Detection of X-ray sources in the sky	523 (325)	542 (337)	95.08	23.5
NATO 3-C/NATO/Delta/ 1978-106A	11/19/78	375 (827)	cylinder	2.2 (7.22)	3.1 (10.17)	Communications satellite	35,460 (22,034)	35,814 (22,254)	1,428.5	4.3
Anik 4/Canada/Delta/ 1978-116A	12/16/78	544 (1,199)	cylinder	1.7 (5.58)	1.5 (4.92)	Communications satellite	35,782 (22,234)	35,791 (22,239)	1,436.1	0
Horizon 1/U.S.S.R./D Ie/ 1978-118A	12/19/78	‡	cylinder with two panels	‡	‡	Communications satellite	22,581 (14,031)	48,365 (30,053)	1,420	11.3
Molniya-3 (11)/U.S.S.R./ A IIe/1979-004A	1/18/79	1,500 (3,307)	cylindrical cone with six panels	1.6 (5.25)	4.2 (13.78)	Communications satellite	474 (295)	40,806 (25,356)	736	62.8
Meteor-1 (29)/U.S.S.R./A I/ 1979-005A	1/25/79	2,750 (6,063)	cylinder with two panels	1.5 (4.92)	5 (16.4)	Weather satellite	617 (383)	642 (399)	97.2	97.9
Scatha/U.S./Delta/ 1979-007A	1/30/79	659 (1,452)	cylinder	2 (6.56)	2 (6.56)	Identification and measurement of sources of build-up of electrical charge on spacecraft	27,581 (17,138)	43,214 (26,852)	1,416.2	7.8
Ayame/Japan/N/ 1979-009A	2/6/79	260 (573)	cylinder	1 (3.28)	1.5 (4.92)	Experimental communications satellite	33,966 (21,105)	35,421 (22,010)	1,380.6	0.4
SAGE/U.S./Scout/ 1979-013A	2/18/79	147 (324)	six-sided polygon	1.02 (3.33)	1.62 (5.31)	Effort to obtain data on aerosols and ozone in upper atmosphere	545 (339)	655 (407)	96.9	54.9
Hakuchoh (CORSA 8)/Japan/ Mu-3C/1979-014A	2/21/79	96 (211)	cylinder	1 (3.28)	0.5 (1.64)	Study of the soft X-ray region of the spectrum	538 (334)	568 (353)	95.7	29.9
Soyuz 32/U.S.S.R./A II/ 1979-018A	2/25/79 6/13/79	6,600 (14,551)	sphere and cone	2.3 (7.55)	7.5 (24.61)	Delivered scientific experiments from Salyut 6 space station to Earth	244 (152)	283 (176)	90.7	51.6
Intercosmos 19/U.S.S.R./C I/ 1979-020A	2/27/79	550 (1,213)	octagonal elipsoid (probably)	1.8 (5.91)	1.5 (4.92)	Scientific satellite with payloads supplied by Soviet-bloc nations	500 (311)	991 (616)	99.7	73.9
Meteor-2 (4)/U.S.S.R./A II/ 1979-021A	3/1/79	2,750 (6,063)	cylinder with two panels	1.5 (4.92)	5 (16.4)	Advanced weather satellite	857 (533)	908 (564)	102.2	81.2
Progress 5/U.S.S.R./A II/ 1979-022A	3/12/79 4/5/79	7,000 (15,432)	sphere and cone	2.3 (7.55)	8 (26.25)	Supply vehicle for cosmonauts in Salyut 6 space station	296 (184)	324 (201)	88.8	51.65
Soyuz 33/U.S.S.R./A II/ 1979-029A	4/10/79 4/12/79	6,600 (14,551)	sphere and cone	2.3 (7.55)	7.5 (24.61)	Aborted attempt to ferry two cosmonauts to the Salyut 6 space station	194 (121)	261 (162)	89	51.6
Raduga 5/U.S.S.R./D Ie/ 1979-035A	4/25/79	5,000 (11,023)	cylinder	‡	‡	Communications satellite	35,902 (22,308)	35,902 (22,308)	1,442	0.3
Progress 6/U.S.S.R./A II/ 1979-039A	5/13/79 6/9/79	7,000 (15,432)	sphere and cone	2.3 (7.55)	8 (26.25)	Resupply vehicle for Salyut 6 space station	193 (120)	268 (167)	88.8	51.6
Ariel 6/U.K./Scout D/ 1979-047A	6/2/79	154 (340)	cylinder with hemispherical end and four panels	0.696 (2.28)	1.388 (4.55)	Scientific studies of high-energy radiation	600 (373)	654 (406)	97	55
Soyuz 34/U.S.S.R./A II/ 1979-049A	6/6/79 8/19/79	6,600 (14,551)	sphere and cone	2.3 (7.55)	7.5 (24.61)	Unmanned ferry for Soyuz 32 crew	198 (123)	270 (168)	88.9	51.6
Bhaskara/India/C I/ 1979-051A	6/7/79	444 (979)	24-sided polyhedron	0.94 (3.08)	0.66 (2.17)	Earth resources experiments	512 (318)	557 (346)	95.2	50.7
NOAA 6/U.S./Atlas E/ 1979-057A	6/27/79	723 (1,594)	cube with three panels	1 (3.28)	1.2 (3.94)	Environmental monitoring satellite	807 (501)	824 (512)	102.2	98.8
Progress 7/U.S.S.R./A II/ 1979-059A	6/28/79 7/18/79	7,000 (15,432)	sphere and cone	2.3 (7.55)	8 (26.25)	Resupply vehicle for Salyut 6 space station	395 (370)	405 (252)	92.2	51.6
Horizon 2/U.S.S.R./D Ie/ 1979-062A	7/5/79	‡	cylinder with two panels	‡	‡	Communications satellite	36,550 (22,711)	36,550 (22,711)	757	0.8
HEAO 3/U.S./Centaur/ 1979-082A	9/20/79	2,948 (6,499)	octagonal prism	2.4 (7.87)	5.8 (19.03)	Effort to study cosmic rays and gamma rays	494 (307)	505 (314)	94.6	43.6

*All dates are in universal time (UT).
†English units in parentheses: weight in pounds, dimensions in feet, apogee and perigee in statute miles.
‡Not available.

(MITCHELL R. SHARPE)

TASS/WIDE WORLD

Soviet cosmonauts Valery Ryumin and Vladimir Lyakhov returned to Earth on August 19 after a record 175 days in space.

ches and the DI used for Salyut, interplanetary probes, and geosynchronous communications satellites.

The U.S. space shuttle encountered its share of troubles during the year. In September 1978 both the main engine and the orbital maneuvering engine achieved successful static firings. In October, however, a main oxygen valve failed, and in December the main engine heat exchanger exploded. On February 17 the last of four full-scale test firings of the shuttle's solid-propellant booster rocket took place successfully. However, troubles with the liquid-propellant main engine continued to plague the shuttle's development.

The U.S.S.R. announced in the fall of 1978 that it, too, was developing a space shuttle. Such development had been reported in the West for some time. The Soviet shuttle was believed to be much smaller than the U.S. model, having room for only two or three crewmen.

During the year European Space Agency announced that it would build five production models of the Ariane launch vehicle, for a total cost of some $200 million. After three failures, the first successful launching took place December 4 from the Kourou space centre in French Guiana.

Space Probes. As 1978 drew to a close, the U.S. probe Pioneer 10 neared the outer reaches of the solar system. It found that beyond a distance of some 16 astronomical units from the Sun the incidence of cosmic radiation becomes unpredictable and erratic. (One astronomical unit equals approximately 93 million mi) After becoming the first space probe to investigate Jupiter, Pioneer 10 on July 11 crossed the orbit of Uranus on its way out of the solar system and into intergalactic space. Launched on March 3, 1972, the probe returned the first close-up picture of Jupiter's famed Great Red Spot and made major contributions toward understanding the planet's magnetic field and radiation belts as well as its weather.

During 1979 the U.S. probes Voyager 1 and Voyager 2 also visited Jupiter. They then were programmed to swing past Saturn, Voyager 1 in November 1980 and Voyager 2 in June 1981. Voyager 2 was also targeted to rendezvous with Uranus in January 1986. For a discussion of their discoveries as they flew past Jupiter, *see* Special Report.

Pioneer 11 kept its rendezvous with Saturn on September 1 and survived the hazardous voyage through the rings of the planet, passing within 20,200 km (12,560 mi) of its cloud top. Images returned by the probe were not as clear as scientists had expected and much beneath the quality of those made of Jupiter by the Voyagers. The pictures did, however, reveal the structure of Saturn's rings in greater detail, indicating that they are probably composed of ices rather than other matter. The photographs also disclosed the existence of a new ring. Other instruments proved that the planet's atmosphere is warmer than had been supposed and that the planet has a magnetic field. Pioneer 11 also returned information that led scientists to speculate that three of Saturn's moons, Iapetus, Rhea, and Titan, have a low density; this indicates ice rather than other solid matter.

In December 1978 Pioneer Venus 1 and 2 transmitted important new information about Venus. Among the new findings were unexpectedly high amounts of molecular oxygen and argon-36 in the atmosphere, a surface temperature of 480° C (900° F), and a surface similar to that of Earth or Mars.

Two Soviet probes of Venus also visited the planet late in 1978. Venera 12 reached the planet on December 21 and released an atmospheric probe. The probe descended to the surface on a parachute. Data from it indicated a pressure of 88 atmospheres and a surface temperature of 460° C (860 ° F). The probe transmitted information from the surface for 1 hour and 50 minutes.

Venera 11's probe entered the Venusian atmosphere on Dec. 25, 1978, and landed some 800 km (497 mi) from where its companion probe had touched down. It returned practically identical data from the surface for 95 minutes. Both Soviet probes confirmed the high concentration of argon-36 in the Venusian atmosphere noted by the earlier U.S. missions. (MITCHELL R. SHARPE)

See also Astronomy; Defense; Earth Sciences; Industrial Review: *Aerospace; Telecommunications;* Television and Radio.
[738.C]

OUR FAR OUT NEIGHBOURS

by Edward C. Stone

In 1979, 369 years after Galileo's discovery that four satellites were orbiting Jupiter, two Voyager spacecraft flew past the giant planet, returning close-up views of what Galileo saw only as points of light. The NASA spacecraft, built and controlled by the Jet Propulsion Laboratory of the California Institute of Technology, were launched in 1977. Voyager 1 encountered Jupiter on March 5, 1979, with Voyager 2 following on July 9. The two flybys yielded more than 200 days of intensive measurements, providing a wealth of information about the planet.

The Atmosphere. Jupiter's appearance is dominated by layers of coloured clouds near the top of a very deep atmosphere composed mainly of hydrogen and helium. An unexpected number of vortical or rotational features were observed in the atmosphere. Of these the Great Red Spot, with counterclockwise wind speeds of about 400 kph (250 mph), is the most obvious. The winds immediately above the Great Red Spot are also counterclockwise, indicating that there is a rotating vertical column of gas extending downward to an unknown depth in the atmosphere. The slow upwelling of material within the column may be the source of the chemicals that produce the red colour of the cloud.

Because dozens of other features exhibit similar counterclockwise winds, the Great Red Spot appears to be just the largest of many similar atmospheric structures. Auroral activity—like the Earth's northern lights—and lightning were also observed in Jupiter's atmosphere.

The Ring and the Galilean Satellites. With the discovery by Voyager 1 of a ring, Jupiter joined Saturn and Uranus as the ringed planets of the solar system. The bright outer region in the Jovian ring is 7,000 km wide with an outer edge about 55,000 km above the cloud tops (1 km=0.62 mi). There is much fainter ring material extending inward, probably all the way to the planet.

A small satellite, temporarily called 1979-J1, was discovered just beyond the outer edge of the ring. The satellite is about 30 km in diameter and circles Jupiter every 428 minutes, the shortest period of any known natural satellite.

The two Voyager flybys provided detailed observations of all four of the satellites discovered by Galileo. Voyager 1 discovered eight active volcanoes on Io, with plumes extending up to 280 km above the surface. At least six of the volcanoes were still active four months later during the Voyager 2 flyby. The detection of a tenuous sulfur-dioxide atmosphere, along with the red, orange, and yellow of the surface flows on Io, suggests the importance of sulfur in the volcanic processes.

The surface of Europa was found to be covered with a thin layer of water ice crisscrossed by numerous broad, darker bands that create the visual impression of a global ice pack. The dark bands, perhaps ancient fractures in the ice crust that subsequently were filled with fluid from below, exhibit little relief above or below the remarkably smooth surface. Three impact craters and narrow bright ridges less than a few hundred metres high provide the major relief in the surface, which may be as young as 100 million years old.

Ganymede's surface appears to be much older and is characterized by large, dark polygons separated by brighter grooved terrain. The dark regions, more heavily cratered than are the bright, are probably remnants of Ganymede's original crust, which, through expansion or spreading, was broken into regions separated by the younger grooved terrain. Such tectonic activity may have lasted a few hundred million years as the interior of Ganymede cooled.

Apparently Callisto's surface was not modified by such internal processes. It is densely cratered, indicating that it must be some 4,000,000,000 years old. The most distinctive features on Callisto, two bull's-eye patterns, one of which is 3,000 km in diameter, are the residual imprints of two very large impacts by meteorites.

Magnetosphere. Jupiter's magnetic field, first directly detected by the Pioneer 10 spacecraft in 1973, extends a minimum of three million kilometres from the planet and is the largest discrete structure in the solar system, dwarfing even the Sun. The magnetosphere is large enough that all four Galilean satellites sweep through Jupiter's magnetic field as they orbit the planet.

Io is the source of some of the particles trapped in Jupiter's magnetic field. Sulfur dioxide gas from the satellite's volcanoes gives rise to a cloud of electrically charged sulfur and oxygen ions with temperatures of 100,000 ° C. The cloud, shaped like a doughnut around Jupiter, causes intense auroral activity in Jupiter's polar regions.

Edward C. Stone is a Voyager Project scientist and a professor of physics at the California Institute of Technology.

PHOTOS, COURTESY JPL/NASA

Voyagers 1 and 2, each launched in 1977, flew past Jupiter on different trajectories toward Saturn in 1979. Each provided close-up views of the giant planet and its satellites, detecting a ring around Jupiter for the first time.

Jupiter is photographed by Voyager 1 from a distance of 55 million kilometres (34 million miles). The dominant feature on the planet is the Great Red Spot, an atmospheric system larger than the Earth and having rotational wind speeds of 400 kph (250 mph).

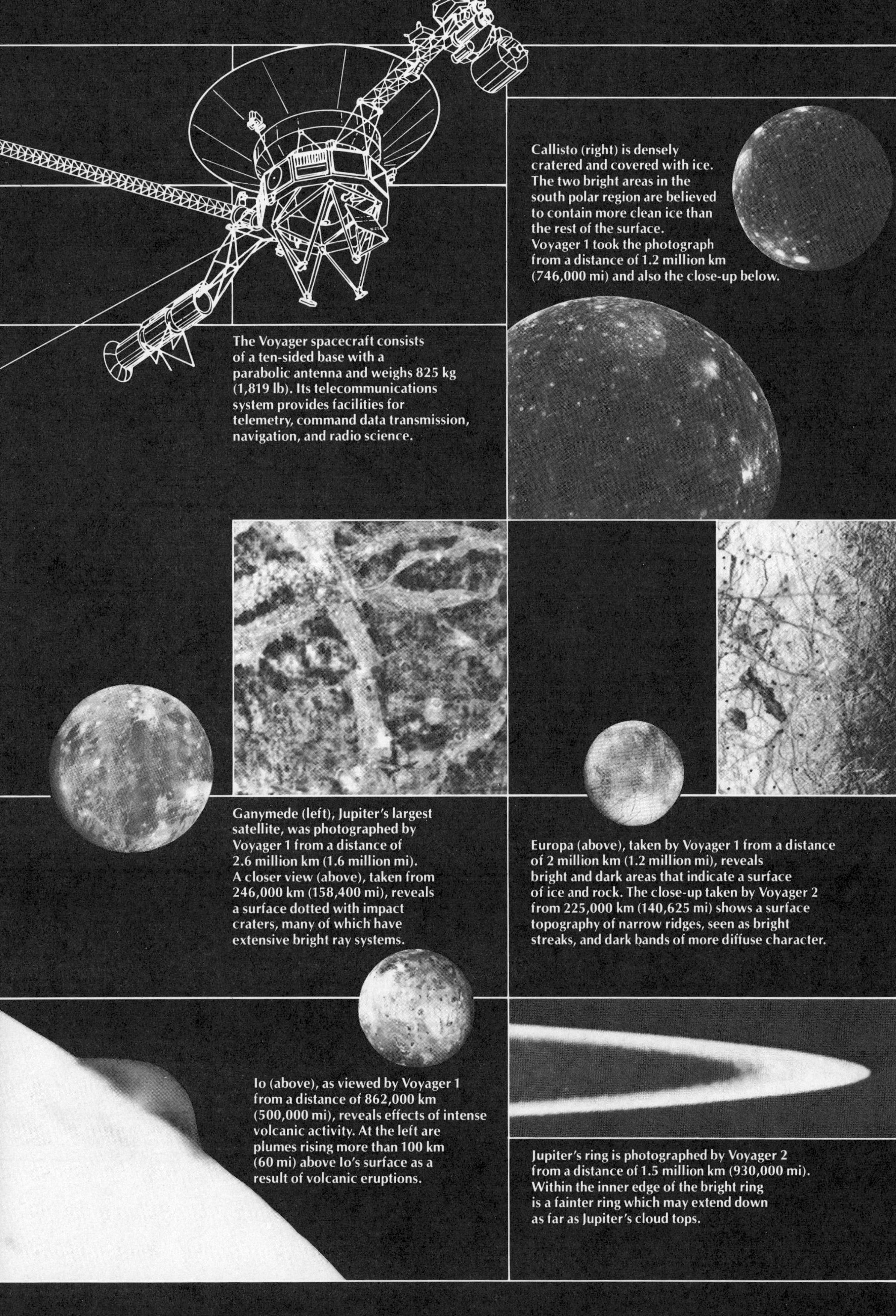

Callisto (right) is densely cratered and covered with ice. The two bright areas in the south polar region are believed to contain more clean ice than the rest of the surface. Voyager 1 took the photograph from a distance of 1.2 million km (746,000 mi) and also the close-up below.

The Voyager spacecraft consists of a ten-sided base with a parabolic antenna and weighs 825 kg (1,819 lb). Its telecommunications system provides facilities for telemetry, command data transmission, navigation, and radio science.

Ganymede (left), Jupiter's largest satellite, was photographed by Voyager 1 from a distance of 2.6 million km (1.6 million mi). A closer view (above), taken from 246,000 km (158,400 mi), reveals a surface dotted with impact craters, many of which have extensive bright ray systems.

Europa (above), taken by Voyager 1 from a distance of 2 million km (1.2 million mi), reveals bright and dark areas that indicate a surface of ice and rock. The close-up taken by Voyager 2 from 225,000 km (140,625 mi) shows a surface topography of narrow ridges, seen as bright streaks, and dark bands of more diffuse character.

Io (above), as viewed by Voyager 1 from a distance of 862,000 km (500,000 mi), reveals effects of intense volcanic activity. At the left are plumes rising more than 100 km (60 mi) above Io's surface as a result of volcanic eruptions.

Jupiter's ring is photographed by Voyager 2 from a distance of 1.5 million km (930,000 mi). Within the inner edge of the bright ring is a fainter ring which may extend down as far as Jupiter's cloud tops.

Spain

Spain

A constitutional monarchy of southwest Europe, Spain is bounded by Portugal, with which it shares the Iberian Peninsula, and by France. Area: 504,750 sq km (194,885 sq mi), including the Balearic and Canary islands. Pop. (1979 est.): 37,-551,000, including the Balearics and Canaries. Cap. and largest city: Madrid (pop., 1979 est., 4,120,900). Language: Spanish. Religion: Roman Catholic. King, Juan Carlos I; premier in 1979, Adolfo Suárez González.

Following approval by both houses of the Cortes and in a referendum, Spain's new constitution became law on Dec. 27, 1978, and was promulgated two days later. Premier Adolfo Suárez González then dissolved the Cortes and announced general elections for March 1, 1979, and provincial and municipal elections for April 3.

In the general elections, in which two-thirds of the electorate voted, there was little change among leading parties. The ruling Unión Centro Democrático (UCD) won 168 seats in the Congress of Deputies in the Cortes, 3 more than in 1977 but 8 short of an overall majority. The Partido Socialista Obrero Español (PSOE) and its Catalan and Basque wings, the PSC and PSE, respectively, together gained 121 seats (3 more than in 1977), while the Partido Comunista Español (PCE) won 23 (3 more than in 1977). The right-wing Coalición Democrática (CD) secured only 9 seats (16 held in 1977). In the 208-seat Senate, "a chamber of territorial representation," the UCD and PSOE, respectively, held 120 and 68 seats.

In the lower house the Partido Nacionalista Vasco (PNV) was reduced to seven from eight seats in 1977; Herri Batasuna (United People), closely linked with the Basque separatist organization Euzkadi ta Azkatasuna (ETA), won three seats but then refused to take them in protest against the lack of progress on the Basque autonomy issue. Four other regional parties—from Navarre, Aragon, Andalusia, and the Canary Islands—won seats for the first time. The UCD gained a vote of confidence (183–149) on March 30, and Suárez named his Cabinet on April 5.

Preliminary results of the April 3 provincial and municipal elections showed that the UCD elected 29,614 councillors; PSOE 12,220; PCE 3,608; PNV 1,084; Herri Batasuna 260; and the BNPG (Galician Nationalists) 253. On April 18 the PSOE and PCE agreed to join forces wherever they had a combined majority, and with the help of the Socialist Party of Andalusia and of Convergéncia i Unió in Catalonia this placed the left in control in many of the cities.

The government announced that a ceiling of 11–14% on wage increases in the public sector would be in force in 1979. The limit was subject to revision if after the first six months of the year prices

SPAIN

Education. (1977–78) Primary, pupils 6,-640,246, teachers 211,037; secondary, pupils 783,964, teachers 51,466; vocational, pupils 407,812, teachers 28,075; higher, students 647,-298, teachers 31,160.

Finance. Monetary unit: peseta, with (Sept. 17, 1979) a free rate of 66.02 pesetas to U.S. $1 (142.05 pesetas = £1 sterling). Gold, SDR's, and convertible currencies (April 1979) U.S. $11,-560,000,000. Budget (1978 actual): revenue 1,461,000,000,000 pesetas; expenditure 1,-590,000,000,000 pesetas. Gross domestic product (1977) 8,744,000,000,000 pesetas. Money supply (June 1979) 3,400,000,000,000 pesetas. Cost of living (1975 = 100; June 1979) 196.2.

Foreign Trade. (1978) Imports 1,431,500,-000,000 pesetas; exports 1,001,400,000,000 pesetas. Import sources: EEC 35% (West Germany 10%, France 9%, U.K. 5%, Italy 5%); U.S. 13%; Saudi Arabia 9%; Iran 5%. Export destinations: EEC 46% (France 17%, West Germany 11%, U.K. 6%, Italy 5%); U.S. 9%. Main exports: machinery 13%; fruit and vegetables 11%; motor vehicles 10%; iron and steel 10%; chemicals 7%; textiles and clothing 6%. Tourism (1977): visitors 34,267,000; receipts U.S. $4,003,000,000.

Transport and Communications. Roads (1977) 145,997 km (including 1,442 km expressways). Motor vehicles in use (1977): passenger 5,944,900; commercial 1,117,000. Railways: (1977) 15,799 km (including 5,362 km electrified); traffic (1978) 16,758,000,000 passenger-km, freight 10,876,-000,000 net ton-km. Air traffic (1978): 14,601,000,-000 passenger-km; freight 386,148,000 net ton-km. Shipping (1978): merchant vessels 100 gross tons and over 2,753; gross tonnage 8,056,080. Telephones (Jan. 1978) 9,527,800. Radio receivers (Dec. 1976) c. 9.3 million Television receivers (Dec. 1976) 6,640,000.

Agriculture. Production (in 000; metric tons; 1978): wheat 4,795; barley 7,953; oats 542; rye 259; corn 1,933; rice 411; potatoes 5,316; sugar, raw value 1,115; tomatoes 2,153; onions 930; cabbages (1977) 450; melons (1977) 686; watermelons (1977) 379; apples 951; pears (1977) 231; peaches (1977) 213; oranges 1,648; mandarin oranges and tangerines 852; lemons 239; sunflower seed 539; bananas 390; olives 2,051; olive oil 510; almonds (1977) 134; wine 2,903; tobacco 32; cotton, lint c. 33; cow's milk 5,-763; hen's eggs 581; meat 2,226; fish catch (1977) 1,455. Livestock (in 000; 1978): cattle 4,545; pigs c. 9,230; sheep c. 15,463; goats c. 2,200; horses (1977) 256; mules (1977) 269; asses (1977) 242; chickens c. 53,330.

Industry. Index of industrial production (1975 = 100; 1977) 119. Fuel and power (in 000; metric tons; 1978): coal 12,050; lignite 8,250; crude oil 874; manufactured gas (cu m) c. 2,700,000; electricity (kw-hr) 99,267,000. Production (in 000; metric tons; 1978): cement 29,305; iron ore (50% metal content) 8,221; pig iron 6,620; crude steel 11,258; aluminum (1977) 211; copper (1977) 149; zinc (1977) 157; petroleum products (1977) 46,137; sulfuric acid (1977) 3,274; fertilizers (nutrient content; 1977–78) nitrogenous c. 904, phosphate c. 450, potash 552; cotton yarn (1977) 82; wool yarn (1977) 35; man-made fibres (1977) 222; passenger cars (units) 989; commercial vehicles (units) 150. Merchant vessels launched (100 gross tons and over; 1978) 643,000 gross tons.

rose by more than 6.5%. Consumer prices did rise by 7.3% in the first half of the year, and the Cabinet recommended a wage increase of 1.7%. The Spanish employers' federation and the Unión General de Trabajadores (UGT) had signed an agreement in July defining negotiating procedures, salary revisions, and recourse to official arbitration. But in spite of this the Confederation of Workers' Commissions called a demonstration on October 14 in Madrid against the 1.7% wage increase ceiling, charging that it did not meet price increases.

In March the government outlined its economic plan. Its final implementation was delayed until August by changes in the prices of oil charged by the Organization of Petroleum Exporting Countries and forecasts of world recession. The August plan contained elements of the October 1977 Moncloa Pact, with labour and social laws to put the new constitution into effect. Also included were measures to control the growth of the money supply and the public sector's deficit, to stimulate competition in financial and stock markets, to promote domestic savings, and to encourage investment in order to help overcome increasing unemployment caused by the recession. Measures to ready the country for eventual EEC membership were to be taken, including adoption of value-added and wealth taxes. At the end of July the Cortes approved an energy plan up to 1987, under which Spain would install 10,500 Mw of nuclear capacity. As of 1979 only about 3% of the nation's energy came from three nuclear power stations, but seven others were under construction. Coal-fired electricity generation was also to be encouraged.

Approximately 60 deaths were attributed to terrorism in 1978, and there was an upsurge with more deaths in the first nine months of 1979. After attacks by ETA on police, Army, and government representatives in the Basque country, the ETA campaign was broadened in July to include Madrid. Bombs were exploded at the city's airport and main railway stations, and also at tourist resorts outside the Basque country. Attacks on French property and nationals were also intensified after France suspended the political refugee status of exiled Basques in France on the grounds that Spain was now a democracy.

The government signed autonomy agreements with the PNV, led by Carlos Garaicoechea (*see* BIOGRAPHIES), in July, and with an all-party commission from Catalonia on August 7. Both agreements were subjected to referendums on October 25, in which both the Basque country and Catalonia voted approval by about 90%. Both Basques and Catalans were granted regional parliaments, and their languages would have official status alongside Spanish; they would also have responsibility for local education, taxation, and finance, and eventually control of their own police forces. Elections for a Basque assembly were to take place early in 1980, while in Catalonia there would be a six-year transition period during which power would be steadily transferred by the central government to the Generalitat of Catalonia, to which elections would also be early in the new year. Nevertheless, the ETA published a communiqué after

FIEL/PHOTO TRENDS

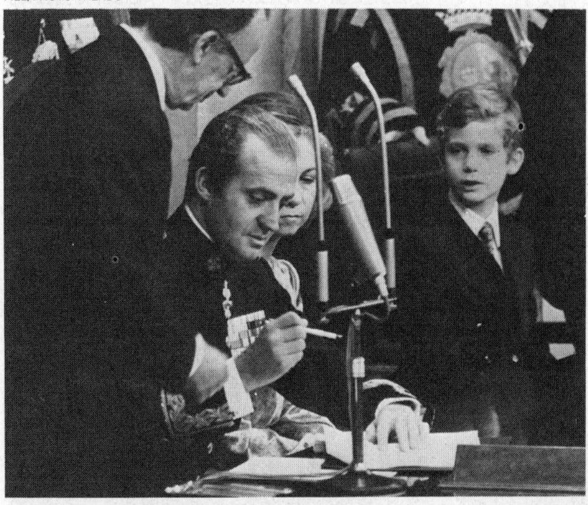

King Juan Carlos I signed the new Spanish constitution on December 27, 1978.

the referendum stating that it would continue its fight.

Spain was the first country to recognize the new government in Equatorial Guinea after the overthrow of Francisco Macías Nguema, and in December King Juan Carlos visited the former Spanish colony. (MICHAEL WOOLLER)

Speleology

A small but significant discovery was made in the world's longest cave, the 306.9-km (190.7-mi)-long Mammoth Cave/Flint Ridge system in Kentucky. A new passage extended the cave to beneath yet a third limestone ridge (Joppa Ridge), where it was expected to connect with other large caves. The world's second longest, the Hölloch in Switzerland, was also lengthened, to 135.5 km (84.2 mi). Exploration was continuing in Jewel Cave, South Dakota, where the mapping exceeded 100 km (62.1 mi). The record British cave length exceeded 45 km (28 mi) after Bob Hryndyj dived through a newly discovered sump and linked all the major systems of Casterton Fell and Leck Fell, including Lancaster Hole, Link Pot, and Pippikin Pot.

Several of the world's deepest caves were extended even farther. Belgian explorers in the Schneeloch near Salzburg, Austria, were stopped at 902 m (2,959 ft) at the head of a pitch leading down to a river. An upward branch brought them 132 m (433 ft) above the entrance, giving a total vertical extent of 1,034 m (3,392 ft). Shortly afterward another expedition increased the depth to 1,086 m (3,563 ft), and the cave became the fourth deepest in the world. As in the previous year, it was again a Polish group that extended the Austrian Lamprechtsofen, this time to 1,024 m (3,360 ft) and sixth place among the world's deepest caves. Another Austrian cave, the Hochlecken Grosshöhle, was explored to 1,022 m (3,353 ft) and became the seventh deepest.

Mexican caves received much attention. Peter Sprouse discovered a link between Cueva del Brinco and Cueva del Infiernillo, giving a combined depth of 900 m (2,953 ft) and a length of more than 20 km (12.4 mi). The connection itself, below 816 m (2,677 ft), was claimed to be the deepest such linkup in the world. The combined system,

ASSOCIATION FOR MEXICAN CAVE STUDIES; PHOTO BY TERRY RAINES

A connecting link was discovered between Cueva del Brinco (pictured) and Cueva del Infiernillo in Mexico, making the combined system more than 12 miles long.

known as Sistema Purificación, was later explored to a new depth of 914 m (2,999 ft) and thus became the deepest in the Americas.

In England Oliver Statham and Geoffrey Yeadon set a world record for length of a dive, 1,829 m (6,000 ft), from Kingsdale Master Cave to the river's resurgence at Keld Head. Much of the dive was filmed by the divers themselves using miniature equipment, and this film, together with their conversation transmitted through the rock by speleophone, was subsequently shown on television.

The first international symposium to be devoted to the history of speleology was held in Vienna, and another international historical conference marked the 160th anniversary of Postojnska Jama in Yugoslavia as a major tourist cave. An important publication was the much enlarged new edition of Paul Courbon's *Atlas des grands gouffres du monde.* (T. R. SHAW)

[232.A.5.a]

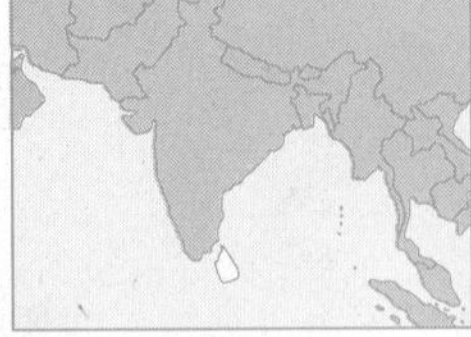

Sri Lanka

Sri Lanka

An Asian republic and member of the Commonwealth of Nations, Sri Lanka (Ceylon) occupies an island in the Indian Ocean off the southeast coast of peninsular India. Area: 65,610 sq km (25,332 sq mi). Pop. (1978 est.): 14,184,000, including Sinhalese about 72%; Tamil 21%; Moors 7%. Cap. and largest city: Colombo (pop., 1977 est., 616,000). Language: Sinhalese (official), Tamil, English. Religion (1971): Buddhist 67%; Hindu 18%; Christian 8%; Muslim 7%. President in 1979, J. R. Jayawardene; prime minister, Ranasingle Premadasa.

The Sri Lankan economy had made significant gains by 1979 under the government of Pres. J. R. Jayawardene. Adoption of a realistic exchange rate, liberalization of trade, and concentration on major development projects contributed. In 1978 the country achieved a growth rate of 8.2% in real terms, more than twice the average rate during the previous decade.

In industry, overall output increased by 11% in real terms. Performance in the vital plantation sector was mixed, with tea production declining while rubber and coconut output increased. Progress was made on such development projects as the free trade zone, the Mahaweli River diversion scheme, and housing investment and urban development programs, while trade liberalization brought more goods into the shops. The Sri Lanka Aid Consortium pledged an aid commitment of SLRs 11 billion for 1979. Cooperation agreements with Bangladesh were signed during a visit by Pres. Ziaur Rahman in November.

The Tamil minority's demand for a separate state continued. The government declared a state of emergency in July to combat terrorism by militant Tamil youth. An all-party presidential commission to consider the Tamils' problems was set up on August 10, but the opposition Sri Lanka Freedom Party refused to cooperate.

The Coordinating Bureau of the nonaligned nations met in Colombo in early June. Its deliberations were torn by the problem of representation for Cambodia and by an Arab move to suspend Egypt for signing a peace treaty with Israel. The bureau decided to refer these issues to the nonaligned summit meeting, held in Havana, Cuba, in September. (GOVINDAN UNNY)

SRI LANKA

Education. (State only; 1977–78) Primary, pupils 1,492,147, teachers 50,665; secondary, pupils 1,076,502, teachers 57,854; vocational (1976–77), pupils 4,778, teachers 1,239; teacher training (1976–77), students 6,809, teachers (1974–75) 606; higher (universities only; 1974–75), students 14,568, teaching staff 1,860.

Finance. Monetary unit: Sri Lanka rupee, with (Sept. 17, 1979) a free rate of SLRs 15.41 to U.S. $1 (SLRs 33.15 = £1 sterling). Gold, SDR's, and foreign exchange (June 1979) U.S. $420 million. Budget (1978 actual): revenue SLRs 11,633,000,000; expenditure SLRs 17,775,000,000. Gross domestic product (1978) SLRs 38,550,000,000. Money supply (May 1979) SLRs 6,670,000,000. Cost of living (Colombo; 1975 = 100; June 1979) 123.2.

Foreign Trade. (1978) Imports SLRs 14,581,000,000; exports SLRs 13,295,000,000. Import sources: Japan 11%; U.K. 10%; Saudi Arabia 10%; India 9%; U.S. 8%; Iran 6%; Australia 5%; France 5%. Export destinations: U.K. 7%; U.S. 7%; Japan 6%; Pakistan 5%; Saudi Arabia 5%. Main exports: tea 48%; rubber 16%; coconut products 7%.

Transport and Communications. Roads (1977) 24,736 km. Motor vehicles in use (1976): passenger 93,770; commercial 34,690. Railways: (1976) 1,498 km; traffic (1976–77) 2,792,000,000 passenger-km, freight 214 million net ton-km. Air traffic (1977): 404 million passenger-km; freight 2.5 million net ton-km. Telephones (Jan. 1978) 74,200. Radio receivers (Dec. 1976) 800,000.

Agriculture. Production (in 000; metric tons; 1978): rice 1,992; cassava (1977) c. 750; sweet potatoes (1977) c. 220; onions c. 60; mangoes c. 58; lemons c. 51; pineapples c. 54; copra 146; tea c. 215; coffee c. 9; rubber c. 154; fish catch (1977) 139. Livestock (in 000; June 1977): cattle c. 1,745; buffalo c. 854; sheep c. 30; goats c. 570; pigs c. 41; chickens c. 5,973.

Industry. Production (in 000; metric tons; 1977): salt 46; cement (1978) 575; graphite (exports) 8.9; petroleum products c. 1,510; cotton yarn 5; electricity (kw-hr) 1,331,000.

Squash Rackets: see Racket Games

Stamp Collecting: see Philately and Numismatics

Stock Exchanges

Stock markets throughout the world in 1979 generally were influenced by conflicting internal and international economic trends which often generated wide fluctuations in equity prices. For the most part countries insulated from higher oil prices or those with stock markets that tend to benefit from inflation experienced higher equity prices. Conversely, countries unable to fill their energy needs from domestic sources or those lacking natural resources generally had weak stock markets. Altogether, 11 of the 17 major stock price indexes for which weekly data were available registered gains for 1979 as a whole (TABLE I).

Worldwide economic recovery continued in 1979, though at a slower rate than in 1978. A constant flow of negative news with regard to inflation and interest rates, energy price increases and shortages, and turbulence in international currency markets was counterbalanced by strong gains in real gross domestic product, industrial output, and employment. However, nearly all the major industrialized nations were forced to initiate restrictive economic policies. Moreover, the slowdown in growth of the global economy was occurring with full realization that any steps to counter recessionary forces would tend to revive inflationary pressures.

The rush by investors to put their wealth in tangible assets, such as real estate, gold, and diamonds—while ignoring equity securities—enhanced the relative attractiveness of stocks. As the underlying worth of equities increased considerably more than the prices of the stocks themselves, many companies found that buying existing firms was much cheaper than building new facilities. Consequently, merger activity was a bullish influence in several markets. At the same time, the mood of investors toward equities often wavered from euphoria to pessimism, depending on their interpretation of news developments. For example, escalation of oil prices by the Organization of Petroleum Exporting Countries (OPEC) and reports of spot shortages in major petroleum markets increased incentives to expand production of oil, natural gas, coal, and other alternative energy sources. This was particularly bullish for petroleum, natural resource, and oil service companies. On the other hand, the same news promised continuation of persistent inflation and rising interest rates, which was bearish for financial-related firms and those in regulated industries.

At the end of 1979 the global economy faced major uncertainties over the effects on world trade and the international monetary system of rising oil prices. As a result the overall direction of equity markets in the 1980s would probably be determined by whether the potential financial strains inherent in the transfer of real purchasing power from oil-consuming to oil-exporting countries could be avoided. (ROBERT H. TRIGG)

United States. The stock market's overall performance in 1979 was impressive despite some sluggishness among the blue-chip stocks. The Dow Jones industrial average closed at 838.74, only 4.2% above its 1978 close of 805.01, but the broader measures did better. Standard & Poor's 500-stock index was up 12.2%, and the New York Stock Exchange (NYSE) composite index rose 15.4%, while average stock prices on the American Stock Exchange and in over-the-counter markets showed much more substantial gains.

The broad rise in stock prices occurred despite pessimistic economic forecasts based on disrupted

Table I. Selected Major World Stock Price Indexes*

Country	1979 range† High	1979 range† Low	Year-end close 1978	Year-end close 1979	Percent change
Australia	740	546	542	740	+37%
Austria	69	62	63	69	+10
Belgium	109	99	98	103	+ 5
Denmark	97	86	89	87	− 2
France	113	82	88	103	+17
Germany, West	840	705	817	716	−12
Hong Kong	879	494	496	879	+77
Italy	94	68	69	82	+19
Japan	6,591	5,926	6,002	6,570	+ 9
Netherlands, The	86	66	81	68	−16
Norway	142	74	75	135	+80
Singapore	435	346	349	435	+25
South Africa	451	271	269	451	+68
Spain	112	81	100	84	−16
Sweden	401	331	362	351	− 3
Switzerland	329	294	289	303	+ 5
United Kingdom	559	406	471	414	−12

*Index numbers are rounded, and limited to countries for which at least 12 months' data were available on a weekly basis.
†Based on the daily closing price.
Sources: *Barron's, The Economist, Financial Times,* and the *New York Times.*

Table II. U.S. Stock Market Prices

Month	Railroads (10 stocks) 1979	Railroads (10 stocks) 1978	Industrials (400 stocks) 1979	Industrials (400 stocks) 1978	Public utilities (40 stocks) 1979	Public utilities (40 stocks) 1978	Composite (500 stocks) 1979	Composite (500 stocks) 1978
January	44.45	46.13	111.15	99.34	50.33	52.40	99.71	90.25
February	44.92	44.69	109.49	97.95	50.74	51.60	98.23	88.98
March	46.64	43.61	111.66	97.65	50.62	51.72	100.11	88.82
April	49.75	44.77	113.95	102.07	50.09	52.16	102.07	92.71
May	49.88	46.05	111.24	107.70	48.65	51.71	99.73	97.41
June	52.60	44.92	112.98	107.96	50.57	52.25	101.73	97.66
July	54.73	43.97	113.63	107.39	51.73	52.32	102.71	97.19
August	57.62	47.26	118.93	114.99	52.52	53.35	107.36	103.92
September	56.00	48.19	121.06	115.11	51.16	52.54	108.60	103.86
October	...	47.63	...	111.56	...	51.28	...	100.58
November	...	43.56	...	105.23	...	49.04	...	94.71
December	...	43.37	...	106.92	...	49.32	...	96.11

Sources: U.S. Department of Commerce, *Survey of Current Business;* Board of Governors of the Federal Reserve System, *Federal Reserve Bulletin*. Prices are Standard and Poor's monthly averages of daily closing prices, with 1941–43 = 10.

Table III. U.S. Government Long-Term Bond Prices and Yields
Average price in dollars per $100 bond

Month	Average 1979	Average 1978	Yield (%) 1979	Yield (%) 1978	Month	Average 1979	Average 1978	Yield (%) 1979	Yield (%) 1978
January	47.97	53.74	8.43	7.50	July	48.39	49.97	8.35	8.09
February	47.97	53.09	8.43	7.60	August	48.01	51.32	8.42	7.87
March	47.84	52.90	8.45	7.63	September	...	51.67	8.68	7.82
April	47.89	52.15	8.44	7.74	October	...	50.11	...	8.07
May	47.24	51.34	8.55	7.87	November	...	49.54	...	8.16
June	48.61	50.91	8.32	7.94	December	...	48.38	...	8.36

Source: U.S. Department of Commerce, *Survey of Current Business*. Average prices are derived from average yields on the basis of an assumed 3% 20-year taxable U.S. Treasury bond. Yields are for U.S. Treasury bonds that are taxable and due or callable in ten years or more.

Table IV. U.S. Corporate Bond Prices and Yields
Average price in dollars per $100 bond

Month	Average 1979	Average 1978	Yield (%) 1979	Yield (%) 1978	Month	Average 1979	Average 1978	Yield (%) 1979	Yield (%) 1978
January	52.8	57.2	9.25	8.41	July	53.4	54.5	9.20	8.88
February	52.6	56.9	9.26	8.47	August	53.0	56.1	9.23	8.69
March	52.2	57.0	9.37	8.47	September	51.8	56.1	9.44	8.69
April	52.3	56.3	9.38	8.56	October	...	54.7	...	8.89
May	51.9	55.5	9.50	8.69	November	...	54.3	...	9.03
June	53.5	55.2	9.29	8.76	December	...	53.3	...	9.16

Source: U.S. Department of Commerce, *Survey of Current Business*. Average prices are based on Standard and Poor's composite index of A1+ issues. Yields are based on Moody's Aaa domestic corporate bond index.

oil flows due to the Iranian revolution; record high inflation rates; runaway gold, silver, and commodities prices; and a weak dollar. OPEC doubled the cost of oil in 1979, creating inflationary pressures that were partially arrested by monetary restraints by the Federal Reserve Board. These restraints caused interest rates to rise sharply during the last half of the year. The best stock market gains were made in issues related to oil and other natural resource industries. Gold stocks rose by more than 70% during the year. Bond prices, moving inversely with yields, declined during 1979 across a broad front with the prime rate moving from 11.5% in July to 15.5% in November and ending the year at 15%.

The volume of trading on the New York Stock Exchange rose sharply in 1979 to a record turnover of 8,155,915,314 shares, a gain of 13% over the 7,205,054,539 figure for 1978; trading in warrants rose by 106%, increasing from 31,606,800 in 1978 to 65,102,200 in 1979. The NYSE had its busiest trading day in history on October 10, when 81.6 million shares were sold. Turnover was also up on the American Stock Exchange with 1,099,990,000 shares being traded, a gain of 11% over the previous year. The biggest gain was recorded in the over-the-counter markets, where the National Association of Securities Dealers reported sales of 3,651,213,900 shares, up from the 1978 level of 2,762,498,900 by 32%.

Bond turnover continued to decline on the New York Stock Exchange, falling to $4,087,890,000 in 1979, down 10% from 1978 after a 2% drop between 1977 and 1978. Bond sales on the American Stock Exchange fell 15% in dollar volume to $226,060,000 in 1979 from the 1978 level of $265,550,000. Bond yields rose sharply during 1979 in all market sectors, with an average drop in corporate prices of approximately 13% from the previous year's Dow Jones bond averages. The price-earnings ratio for the Dow Jones industrials ended 1979 at 6.2 times average earnings as compared with 7.9 times for 1978.

The price of a seat on the New York Stock Exchange rose sharply from approximately $80,000 bid at the end of 1978 to $195,000 by November 1979. On the American Stock Exchange a membership sold for $40,000 in 1978 and increased by 113% to $85,000 in November 1979. Reflecting the increased activity on that market, a seat on the Chicago Board Options Exchange was sold for $100,000 in December 1979.

As a result of widespread commission competition, there was a continuing consolidation among brokerage houses with mergers of major firms and increased sharing of facilities among smaller companies set up to provide specialized research services. The larger firms branched out into unrelated activities such as life insurance sales, real estate and oil tax shelter programs, and the management of money market funds. The Securities and Exchange Commission chairman expressed concern in a number of speeches about the dangers of overdiversification away from the areas of greatest expertise of the leading brokerage firms.

The Standard & Poor composite index of 500 New York Stock Exchange stocks (TABLE II) began the year at 99.71, dipped slightly to 98.23 in February, climbed to 100.11 in March and 102.07 in April, dropped to 99.73 in May, and thereafter rose steadily to a level of 108.60 in September. The low for the year was 96.13 on February 27, and the high was 111.27 achieved on October 5. The all-time high for this index was 125.85 recorded Jan. 11, 1973. The 400 industrials in the index entered 1979 at an average of 111.15, dipped in February, and then rose slowly in March and April. After a decline in late May the index climbed briskly to 121.06 in September. The high for the year was 124.49 on May 10; the low was 107.08 on February 27. Public utility stocks traded within a narrow range between 48.65 and 52.52. Railroad stocks moved steadily upward in price during 1979, rising from 44.45 in January to 57.62 in August before falling back to 56 in September.

The best gains among stock groups were golds, more than 70%; followed by oils, 60%; oil-service stocks, 42%; and international oils, about 30%. Other large advances were made by aerospace stocks, 35%; semiconductors, 25%; chemicals, 32%; forest products, 20%; and textiles, 30%. Automobile, beverage, cosmetics, household prod-

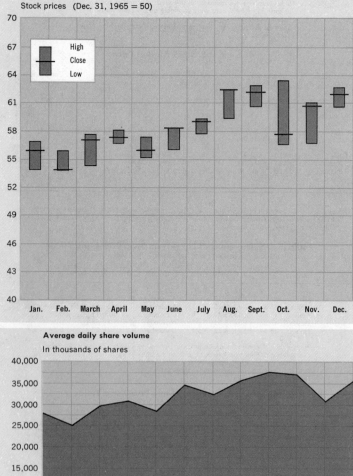

New York Stock Exchange Composite Index, 1979

Stock prices (Dec. 31, 1965 = 50)

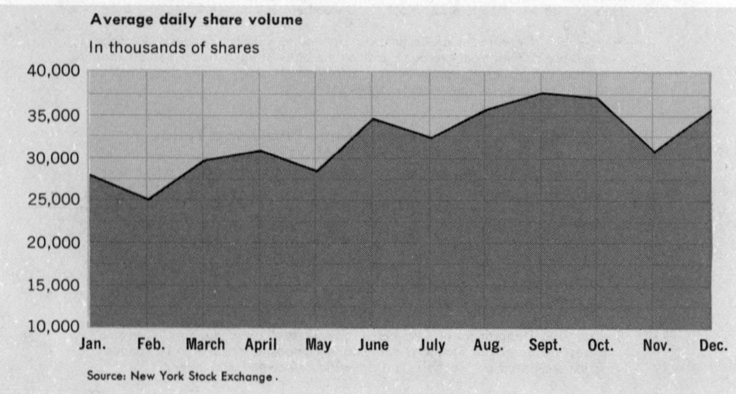

Source: New York Stock Exchange.

ucts, restaurant, tire, and airline stock groups sustained losses of from 10 to 15%.

United States government long-term bond prices were relatively steady in 1979 (Table III), although they were well below the levels of corresponding months in 1978. In January, at 47.97, the average was 11% below the corresponding figure of 53.74 in 1978. By August 1979 the average was 48.01, down from the 51.32 level of the previous year. Short-term issues were far more volatile as interest rates fluctuated widely in 1979. During November the U.S. Treasury sold an issue with a 10.44% average return, the highest ever for any bond sold by the agency since 1865.

Corporate bond prices (Table IV) averaged $52.80 per $100 bond in January 1979, down from $57.20 in January 1978. The average declined in February and March, recovered slightly in April, dropped back in May, and peaked in June. During the second half of the year prices slid fairly regularly to 51.8 in September and lower thereafter. Yields on the highest quality corporate bonds fluctuated between 9.25% in January and 9.5% in May, slipped to 9.29% in June and 9.20% in July, and then increased to 9.23% in August and 9.44% in September. After the Federal Reserve Board's policy decision on October 6 to shift from interest-rate stabilization to control of the money supply through greater emphasis on the level and growth of bank reserves, the monetary base declined, credit tightened up, and interest rates jumped almost immediately. The net effect was to increase effective yields on corporate bonds to the highest levels in several years.

The boom in the options markets continued in 1979 with an increase of 34% in the number of futures contracts traded. The frenzy in gold and silver prices, with new all-time record price levels being set, brought tens of thousands of new customers into options trading, giving this market much more prominence in the U.S. than ever before. The Futures Industry Association estimated that 11.5 million futures contracts were traded in 1970 and 77 million in 1979, illustrating an industry gain of 570% over the decade. New futures contracts were authorized by the Commodity Futures Trading Commission, and the industry began to suffer from severe growing pains. Problems of coping with a heavy flow of orders, keeping accurate records, preventing market irregularities, providing adequate trading space, recruiting and training skilled market makers to provide the liquidity that attracts outside customers, and preventing "corners" or "squeezes" were major concerns in 1979. The Commodity Futures Trading Commission investigated five instances of unusual trading called "squeezes," in which supplies of commodities appeared to be temporarily insufficient to meet delivery requirements on futures exchanges. To overcome squeezes in coffee, copper, silver, potatoes, and wheat, new positions were temporarily banned, margin requirements were raised, and other steps were taken. The NYSE prepared to begin a futures exchange, following the example of the American Stock Exchange.

The Securities and Exchange Commission took an aggressive role in 1979, with more emphasis on improved accounting techniques and reporting than on any substantial increase in disciplinary activity. In April the SEC proposed rules, which, if adopted, would require all companies that register with it to include in annual reports to stockholders and in certain reports to the commission a management statement and an auditor's opinion on certain internal accounting controls. The commission also pressed auditors to join the "SEC practice section" of the American Institute of Certified Public Accountants in order to step up a program of peer reviews. At the same time that more stringent reporting requirements were being suggested for the accounting and legal professions, steps were taken to make it easier for small firms to obtain access to the public market by reducing the requirements for registration of small issues.

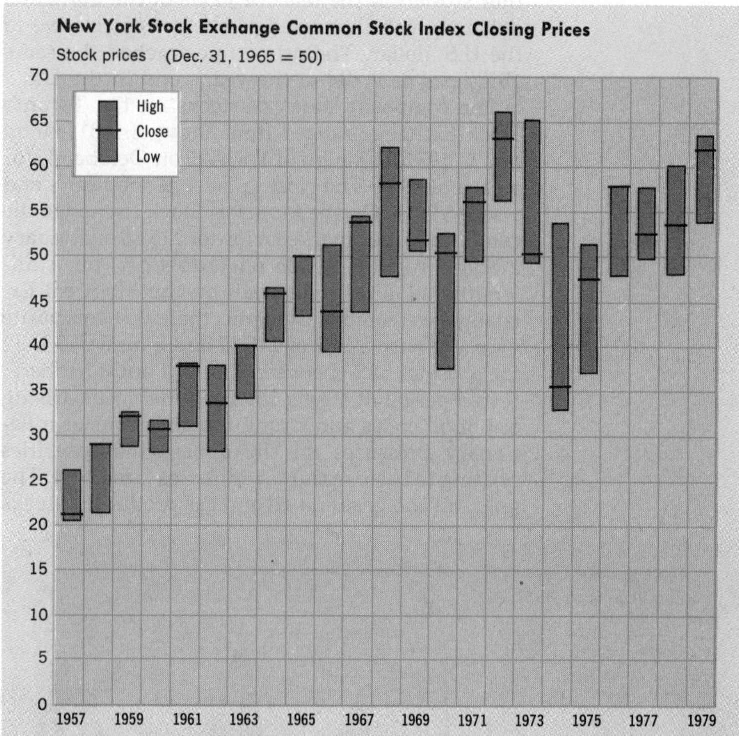

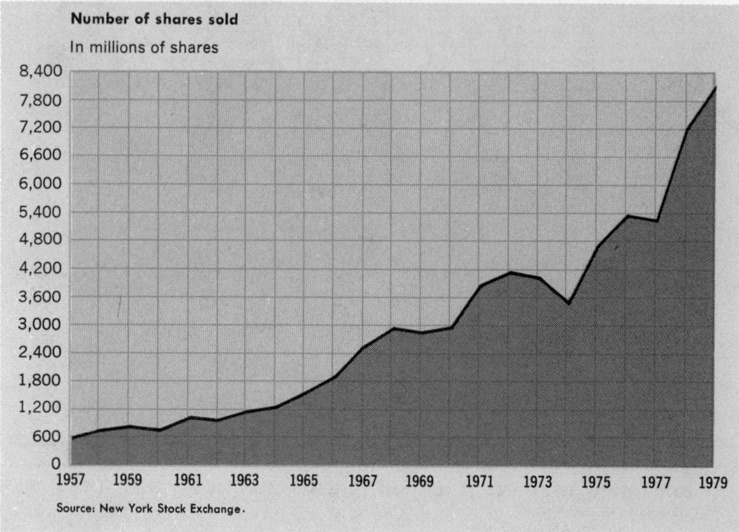

Source: New York Stock Exchange.

Canada. The Canadian stock market had a good year in 1979 as stock prices rose rapidly but irregularly during the year. The economy was healthy, with a rise in overall real growth of between 2.5 and 3%, an increase in employment of 3.9%, and a decline in the unemployment rate from 8.1% in January to 7.1% in September. New orders and shipments in the manufacturing sector registered 12-month gains of more than 20% in most months of the year. Retail sales gained 12.4%. Recessionary influences were seen in housing starts, which were down, and consumer inflation, which continued at a high level of 9% for the year.

The most dramatic economic events of the year related to the historically high interest rates, which were boosted in the summer and fall to record levels. Canadian rates were forced to remain in line with those of the U.S. in order to prevent further erosion in the relative value of the Canadian dollar, which fluctuated at about 0.85 relative to the U.S. dollar. The prime rate reached the same 15% level as it did at the year's end in the U.S.

The composite index of stocks on the Toronto Stock Exchange ranged from a low of 1,315.80 on Jan. 2, 1979, to a high of 1,814.95 on October 5, for a gain of 38%. The closing level at the year's end was 1,811.13. On the Montreal Stock Exchange the combined index marked a low of 225.80 on January 2 and a high of 314.35 on October 5, for a differential of 40%. Industrials on the Montreal Exchange were more dynamic than the composite average, with a low of 219.19 and a high of 332.12 for a rise of 52% between January and October.

In a period of strong international focus arising out of oil crises and strong transmissions of inflationary pressures on the dollar, the securities relating to basic resource industries fared best. The gold, oil and gas, and oil and gas producers' stocks rose dramatically in 1979. Golds were up 68%; oil and gas, 103%; and oil and gas producers' shares, 104% during 1979. The bond markets in Canada were relatively stable in regard to the long-term issues of both government of Canada and major corporations. The short-term market moved in tandem with the prime rate and followed the pattern of the U.S. interest rate movements closely, with a steep rise in the last half of the year.

(IRVING PFEFFER)

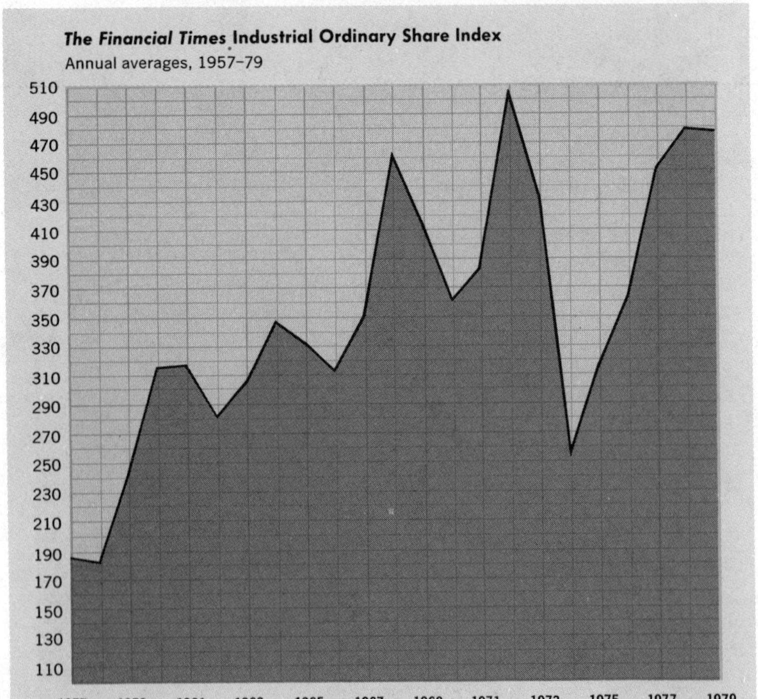

Western Europe. The trend of stock markets throughout Western Europe was generally mixed in 1979. The two most economically powerful countries in the region, Great Britain and West Germany, experienced lower stock prices. Bear markets also prevailed in The Netherlands, Spain, Sweden, and Denmark. On the bullish side Norway, Italy, and France enjoyed relatively strong equity markets. Stock prices in Austria, Switzerland, and Belgium were also able to post a gain over the year.

In Great Britain the *Financial Times* index of 30 industrial shares traded on the London Stock Exchange fell for the second year in a row. From the end of 1978 to the end of 1979 the index was down 12%. The stock market had to contend with a variety of bearish factors, including continuing high inflation, eroding corporate profits, growing labour unrest, and financial disturbances due to spiraling oil prices. Offsetting influences included the return to power of the Conservative Party, the relative strength of sterling in foreign exchange markets, and the prospect that North Sea oil would enable Britain to achieve an energy surplus by the end of 1980.

After weakness in the first six weeks of 1979 stock prices turned stronger on news of Prime Minister James Callaghan's call for general elections on May 3 and continued in that direction following his replacement by Margaret Thatcher after the election. From April 6 to May 4 stock prices advanced 6% to a new all-time high. However, Prime Minister Thatcher's announced program, although reducing the role of government in the British economy in the long run, offered the immediate likelihood of slower industrial output, higher interest rates, and lower exports. Between early May and early August stock prices plunged 18%. But then, because of the strength of the British pound in international currency markets, stock prices rose nearly 3% for August as a whole and added another 3% during September and early October. The subsequent bearish trend was triggered by the Bank of England's boost in its minimum lending rate to a record 17% and investor expectations that Britain's inflation rate would hit 20% before the end of the year. Further fuel was added to bearish sentiment when turmoil in Iran reduced the flow of oil to industrialized nations and OPEC announced its intention to raise oil prices. The decline in equity values from October 5 to November 23 amounted to 15%.

As 1979 drew to a close, investors' hopes that Britain's North Sea oil reserves might ultimately insulate the country from severe economic hardship were counterbalanced by fears of looming recession in the world economy and uncertainty

The *Financial Times* Industrial Ordinary Share Index
Annual averages, 1957–79

Source: *The Financial Times*.

surrounding the ability of the less developed countries to pay for oil exports. As a result stock prices finished 26% below the spring highs and only 2% above the November bottom.

The West German stock market was generally weak in 1979. The Commerzbank index of 60 issues traded on the Frankfurt Stock Exchange fell 12% from the end of 1978 to the end of 1979. The index reached its 1979 high on January 16, and the low was set on November 7. Stock prices rallied in early January on the belief that inflation, which in 1978 had dropped to its lowest level since the early 1970s, would continue to be held in check. However, the cumulative effects of a surging money supply, higher oil prices following the revolution in Iran, and costly wage settlements arising from the first major strike among West German steelworkers in 50 years dashed expectations that inflation could be controlled. To cool down a booming economy with accelerating inflationary trends, the West German central bank initiated a series of increases in interest rates and imposed restrictions on the credit expansion activities of commercial banks. From January 16 to June 30 the drop in stock prices amounted to 13%.

Stock prices in July and August recovered about 5% of the earlier losses. Although stock prices were virtually unchanged in September, the market entered a sharp decline beginning in mid-October. The central bank again was forced to tighten monetary policy and raise interest rates following the U.S. Federal Reserve Board's measures to bolster the U.S. dollar and fight inflation. Equity values skidded 5% in October and reached a three-year low in November before stabilizing. As the decade ended investors seemed discouraged over the ominous implications of OPEC price increases that raised the cost of oil to nearly double that of a year earlier, and also by the unrest in Iran and Afghanistan.

The Dutch stock market finished 1979 with a loss of 16%. Prices on the Amsterdam Stock Exchange reached their highest point on January 24, nearly 6% above the 1978 close, but declined over the next four months. At the end of May equity values were 15% below the January high. The large government deficit and the Dutch guilder's persistent weakness against the West German mark meant that interest rates would be forced to stay at very high levels. That not only discouraged capital investment and delayed the much needed modernization of Dutch manufacturing plant and equipment but also reduced incentives to invest in equity securities. The market remained in a relatively narrow trading range during June and July before turning upward in August. The ensuing rally added only 4% to equity values and soon gave way to a new selling wave. The Dutch central bank's discount rate rose from 8% at the end of September to 9.5% on December 12. During that period alone equity prices fell 11%.

The stock market in Spain was lower for the fourth year in a row. The decline in the price index of shares traded on the Madrid Stock Exchange was 16% for the year as a whole. After the index reached its high on March 8, equity prices fell on average until late November before turning upward. While two-thirds of Spain's energy needs came from oil and gas, only 2% of its oil was produced by domestic sources. Thus, the relentless upward pressure on oil prices raised doubts that the country could improve its growth rate (2–2.5%) and lower its inflation rate (16–17%).

The stock market in Norway experienced the largest increase in equity prices in 1979 (80%) among the major world indexes. Surging oil prices added significantly to the equity values of companies with stakes in the oil and gas fields in the Norwegian sector of the North Sea. Moreover, the ominous news from the oil-price front ensured that royalties to the Norwegian government from offshore oil-drilling licenses would continue to grow rapidly. In addition to the oil boom Norwegian investors were also heartened by the repeal of the 5% tax on investments imposed on mining and manufacturing companies and also by the success of the government's wage/price freeze, which held inflation under 5%. After a low on January 16 the Oslo Stock Exchange index reached its 1979 high on December 13.

In Italy prices on the Milan Stock Exchange generally followed a bullish pattern. Beginning with the first trading session of 1979 the stock market entered an upward phase of considerable proportions. The market reacted positively to the country's ability to cut its annual inflation rate to 12% from 23% and to post a trade surplus in 1978 for the first time since World War II. Equity values jumped 13% from the end of 1978 to the end of March, despite the fall of Premier Giulio Andreotti's government on January 31. Moreover, the market not only stayed on the plus side until the caretaker government was replaced in August by a new one under Francesco Cossiga but actually added 5% to equity values. The index then chalked up a rise of nearly 10% in August and gained another 2% in September. Throughout this period Italy's central bank maintained interest rates that were more than double those of West Germany. This policy attracted large inflows of capital, which caused a sharp increase in the country's currency reserves. The stock market's rise, however, was blunted in the final quarter of 1979 by news of Saudi Arabia's suspension of crude oil shipments to a government agency, higher spot prices in petroleum markets, and fears of oil shortages. Nevertheless, equity values managed to finish with a gain of 19% for the year as a whole.

The stock market in France was also a star performer in 1979. Despite a French economy deeply troubled by a combination of relatively slow growth, persistent high inflation, increasing government deficits, and high unemployment, the general index of shares traded on the Paris Bourse advanced 17%. This bullish performance was attributable to good earnings by French companies and government programs to promote savings and investment.

The Austrian stock market rose 10%. Industrial output in the second quarter of 1979 was 5% higher than the comparable figure a year earlier, while consumer prices rose a modest 3.2%. As for interest rates, the Austrian central bank was able to maintain its discount rate below the levels prevailing at the end of 1978, the only free world country with that distinction.

In Switzerland the price of stocks rose 5% on average. The market was up 11% in January, extending the upward trend established in November 1978. That rally was triggered by the drop in the value of the Swiss franc. Such a decline promised to help Swiss export industries regain some of their competitiveness in foreign markets, which they had lost due to the 38% gain in the value of Swiss currency in 1978. Nevertheless, as the year wore on it became evident that the cost of accumulating U.S. dollars to keep the lid on the franc's value was an increase in annual inflation from about 1% to nearly 4%. The stock market's severest monthly declines occurred in May, October, and November. The freezing of Iranian assets by the U.S. in November posed unsettling questions for the Swiss banking system, which is characteristically an international financial haven. As the year ended stock prices were at a point 8% below the May 2 high and 3% above the 1978 close.

Other Countries. The stock markets in the British crown colony of Hong Kong and in Singapore both experienced bull markets in 1979. The index of 33 stocks traded on the Hong Kong Exchange gained 77% after rising 23% in 1978. The vigorous upswing was spurred by an excess of liquidity in the economy and the belief that equities were undervalued because they failed to reflect the true worth of their underlying assets. The latter view also triggered a boom in merger and acquisition activity. Much the same sentiment that prevailed in Hong Kong also affected the stock market in Singapore. However, there the overall gain in equity values for the year as a whole was not as large (+25%).

In South Africa the *Financial Mail* industrial share price index of issues traded on the Johannesburg Stock Exchange jumped 68% in 1979 to its highest level ever recorded. The primary forces behind the market's move were the spectacular rise in the price of gold, the efforts of Prime Minister P. W. Botha's government to stimulate economic growth, and the improved outlook for investment capital.

The strong Australian stock market reflected the energy surplus of the country and the influence of higher prices for raw materials. The boost in oil prices by OPEC, surging prices for precious metals, and accelerating demand for alternative energy resources all tended to focus investor attention on Australia's vast natural resources and mineral wealth. The All Ordinaries Index of the Sydney Stock Exchange surpassed its previous peak year of 1970 and finished 1979 some 37% higher than at the end of 1978.

Prices on the Tokyo Stock Exchange began 1979 in a bullish atmosphere. Widespread expectations of relatively strong growth in economic activity fueled the advance. By the end of January the Tokyo Dow industrials index recorded a new historic high. Prices dropped on average in February and were weak in March, as concern grew over announcements by several OPEC members of large hikes in the prices they charged for crude oil, news that large U.S. petroleum companies would be forced to cut crude oil supplies to Japan, and the possibility of tighter credit to combat inflation. However, continued reports of higher corporate profits sent stock prices sharply higher. The 6,300 barrier of the 225-stock index was pierced in May. Twice during that month margin requirements on stocks had to be boosted in order to reduce speculation and control the volume of trading. Over the next two months equity prices settled into a relatively narrow range as investors were torn between the bullish prospects for many companies, including energy and natural resource issues, and realization that the monetary policy was definitely tightening.

After steadily appreciating through August and September the index spurted to a new all-time high in early October. However, the unexpectedly poor showing by Japan's ruling Liberal Democrats in the October national elections sent stock prices tumbling. The decline also was reinforced by soaring commodities prices and credit-tightening moves that caused interest rates to climb. Nevertheless, as the 1970s ended the Tokyo stock market was surprisingly strong, having finished 1979 with a net gain of 9% despite the country's heavy reliance on imported oil.

Commodity Markets. World commodity price indexes experienced sharp gains in 1979, while price movements of individual commodities were extremely volatile as near-panic speculative fever gripped several markets. *The Economist*'s commodity price index, which measures spot prices in terms of the U.S. dollar for 29 internationally traded foodstuffs, fibres, metals, and other raw materials, climbed 25% from the end of 1978 to mid-December 1979. The index at mid-December achieved an all-time high, more than 75% above its previous peak in August 1973.

Gold fever reached epidemic proportions as prices soared to dazzling highs. At the end of 1978 gold closed in the London market at $226 an ounce. By early February the price had reached the $250 level. It then took seven months to climb from $250 to $350 an ounce, but only three months to move from $350 to $450. By the end of December the London gold quotation reached $524, for a net gain of 132% for 1979 as a whole.

The speculative intensity in gold, however, was exceeded in the silver market, where an ounce of silver quintupled from the end of 1978 to the end of 1979. Skyrocketing gold and silver prices also spilled over into copper and other metal markets. Some foodstuffs, especially sugar, were also affected. However, profit taking kept most gains well below those of gold and silver.

The 1979 strength in commodity prices was attributable to a number of factors. The flight from paper currencies into tangible assets as a way to safeguard wealth from rising inflation played a major role. The demand for gold, in particular, reflected that metal's ability to hold its value when inflation has robbed paper currencies of their value. Moreover, as the price of gold and silver exploded, spectators looked for attractive substitutes as inflation hedges. (ROBERT H. TRIGG)

See also Economy, World.
[534.D.3.g.1]

Strikes:
see Industrial Relations

CAMERAPIX/KEYSTONE

A tank decorated with portraits of Sudan's Pres. Gaafar Nimeiry led a parade marking the tenth anniversary of his administration. Nimeiry became president of Sudan on Oct. 28, 1969.

Sudan

A republic of northeast Africa, the Sudan is bounded by Egypt, the Red Sea, Ethiopia, Kenya, Uganda, Zaire, the Central African Republic, Chad, and Libya. Area: 2,503,890 sq km (966,757 sq mi). Pop. (1979 est.): 17,865,000, including Arabs in the north and Negroes in the south. Cap. and largest city: Khartoum (pop., 1977 est., 1,089,-300). Language: Arabic, various tribal languages in the south. Religion: Muslim in the north; predominantly animist in the south. President in 1979, Maj. Gen. Gaafar Nimeiry; prime minister, Rashid Bakr.

Pres. Gaafar Nimeiry, who in May received the rank of field marshal, endured in 1979 the most troubled of his ten years of power. The country had reached a condition of economic crisis, caused mainly by going ahead too fast with an ambitious development program. The situation was aggravated by an influx of refugees from Ethiopia and Uganda, possibly numbering half a million. In addition, floods caused widespread damage in the south of the country. In these circumstances, great hopes were raised by reports of a major oil strike in western Sudan.

Disaffection toward the regime grew, encouraged by various groups including the Communist Party and, at the other end of the political spectrum, the pro-Arab Muslim Brotherhood. In April an attempted coup of uncertain political origin was crushed, and 14 people were subsequently convicted and imprisoned on charges of subversion. Matters came to a head in August, when a sudden raise in gasoline prices triggered riots and a nationwide railwaymen's strike. Nimeiry lowered oil prices again, reestablished controls over bread and grain prices, and announced pay increases for government workers. At the same time he made major changes in both the Cabinet and the Sudan Socialist Union (SSU), the country's one party. Seven ministers were dismissed, including the vice-president, Gen. Abu al-Qusain Muhammad Ibrahim, who also lost his position of secretary-general of the SSU, taken over by Nimeiry. The defense minister, Gen. Abdul Magid Hamid Khalil, became vice-president.

Progress was made toward integration with Egypt. This, however, provoked strong opposition in the non-Muslim south Sudan.

(VIRGINIA R. LULING)

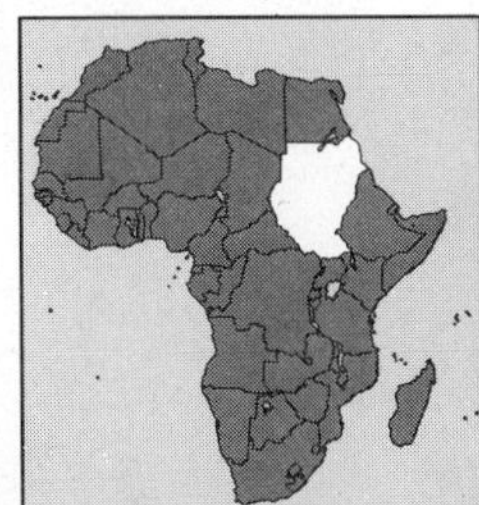

Sudan

SUDAN

Education. (1976–77) Primary, pupils 1,217,510, teachers 33,783; secondary, pupils 313,185, teachers 12,880; vocational, pupils 9,151, teachers 777; teacher training, students 4,707, teachers (1975–76) 420; higher (1975–76), students 21,342, teaching staff 1,420.

Finance. Monetary unit: Sudanese pound, with (Sept. 17, 1979) a par value for a commercial rate of Sud£0.50 to U.S. $1 (free rate of Sud£1.08 = £1 sterling) and a par value for other transactions of Sud£0.80 to U.S. $1 (free rate of Sud£1.72 = £1 sterling). Gold, SDR's, and foreign exchange (June 1979) U.S. $27.4 million. Budget (1977–78 est.): revenue Sud£553 million; expenditure Sud£489 million. Gross domestic product (1976–77) Sud£2,091 million. Money supply (June 1979) Sud£738,880,000. Cost of living (1975 = 100; Dec. 1978) 153.

Foreign Trade. (1977) Imports Sud£368,980,000; exports Sud£230,180,000. Import sources: U.K. 14%; West Germany 12%; Japan 11%; Iraq 10%; France 8%; U.S. 7%; India 5%; Italy 5%. Export destinations: Italy 12%; India 9%; China 9%; Japan 8%; West Germany 7%; Yugoslavia 6%; France 6%. Main exports: cotton 60%; peanuts 11%; sesame seed 7%; gum arabic 5%.

Transport and Communications. Roads (1978) *c.* 50,-000 km (mainly tracks, including *c.* 560 km asphalted). Motor vehicles in use (1977): passenger *c.* 55,000; commercial (including buses) *c.* 30,000. Railways: (1978) 4,734 km; freight traffic (1973–74) 2,324,000,000 net ton-km. Air traffic (1977): 555 million passenger-km; freight 10.4 million net ton-km. Inland navigable waterways (1978) *c.* 4,-100 km. Telephones (Jan. 1978) 62,300. Radio receivers (Dec. 1977) *c.* 1,125,000. Television receivers (Dec. 1975) 100,000.

Agriculture. Production (in 000; metric tons; 1978): wheat *c.* 370; millet *c.* 520; sorghum *c.* 2,400; sesame seed *c.* 267; cottonseed *c.* 290; peanuts *c.* 850; sugar, raw value (1977) *c.* 151; dates *c.* 109; cotton, lint *c.* 167; cow's milk *c.* 906; beef and veal *c.* 170; mutton and goat meat *c.* 123; timber (cu m; 1977) 27,450. Livestock (in 000; 1978): cattle *c.* 16,567; sheep *c.* 15,670; goats *c.* 11,974; camels (1977) 2,813; asses (1977) *c.* 675; chickens *c.* 25,072.

Industry. Production (in 000; metric tons; 1977): petroleum products *c.* 1,210; electricity (kw-hr) *c.* 810,000; salt 92; cement *c.* 178.

Suriname

Suriname

A republic of northern South America, Suriname is bounded by Guyana, Brazil, French Guiana, and the Atlantic Ocean. Area: 181,455 sq km (70,-060 sq mi). Pop. (1977 est.): 448,000, including (1971) Hindustanis 37%, Creoles 30.8%, Indonesians 15.3%, Bush Negroes 10.3%, Amerindians 2.6%. Cap. and largest city: Paramaribo (pop., 1971, 102,300). Language: Dutch (official); English and Sranan (a creole) are lingua francas; Hindi, Javanese, Chinese, and various Amerindian languages are used within individual ethnic communities. Religion: predominantly Hindu, Christian, and Muslim. President in 1979, Johan Ferrier; prime minister, Henck Arron.

Early in 1979 two events undermined the position of Prime Minister Henck Arron's Cabinet. First, the Javanese political party (KTPT) broke with Arron's National Party Combination (NPK), and the three Javanese ministers resigned. This reduced support for the government to 20 of the 38

Sumo:
see Combat Sports

Surfing:
see Water Sports

SURINAME

Education. (1977–78) Primary, pupils 85,250, teachers 3,077; secondary, pupils 26,945, teachers 1,290; vocational, pupils 4,078, teachers 240; teacher training, students 3,065, teachers 174; higher (university only; 1976–77), students 938, teaching staff 113.

Finance. Monetary unit: Suriname guilder, with (Sept. 17, 1979) a par value of 1.785 Suriname guilders to U.S. $1 (free rate of 3.85 Suriname guilders = £1 sterling). Gold, SDR's, and foreign exchange (June 1979) U.S. $152 million. Budget (1978 est.): revenue 623 million Suriname guilders; expenditure 650 million Suriname guilders.

Foreign Trade. (1977) Imports *c.* 710 million Suriname guilders; exports *c.* 585 million Suriname guilders. Import sources: U.S. *c.* 31%; The Netherlands *c.* 21%; Trinidad and Tobago *c.* 14%; Japan *c.* 7%. Export destinations: U.S. *c.* 40%; Norway *c.* 14%; The Netherlands *c.* 11%; U.K. *c.* 8%; West Germany *c.* 7%. Main exports: alumina 48%; bauxite 20%; aluminum 16%; rice 6%; shrimps 5%.

Transport and Communications. Roads (1977) *c.* 2,500 km. Motor vehicles in use (1976): passenger 28,800; commercial 6,900. Railways (1977) 152 km. Navigable inland waterways (1977) *c.* 1,500 km. Telephones (Jan. 1978) 20,800. Radio receivers (Dec. 1976) 112,000. Television receivers (Dec. 1976) 38,000.

Agriculture. Production (in 000; metric tons; 1978): rice *c.* 190; oranges *c.* 10; grapefruit *c.* 6; bananas *c.* 41; palm kernels *c.* 9; sugar, raw value *c.* 9. Livestock (in 000; 1977): cattle *c.* 24; pigs *c.* 7; goats *c.* 5; chickens *c.* 946.

Industry. Production (in 000; metric tons; 1977): bauxite 4,860; alumina 1,215; aluminum 50; electricity (kw-hr) 1,421,000 (86% hydroelectric).

seats in Parliament. Second, it appeared that NPK election-campaign leader Caesar Seedorf had practiced fraud in 1977 to secure his party's victory.

In April the Dutch minister of development aid, Jan de Koning, visited Suriname to report the disapproval by the Dutch lower house of Parliament of the way in which development aid from The Netherlands was being spent. In April Arron and Forbes Burnham, prime minister of Guyana, agreed to reopen negotiations on their border problems. This was important because the World Bank insisted on the settlement of the New River Triangle territorial dispute as a precondition for the financing of a Surinamese hydroelectric project. (DICK BOONSTRA)

Swaziland

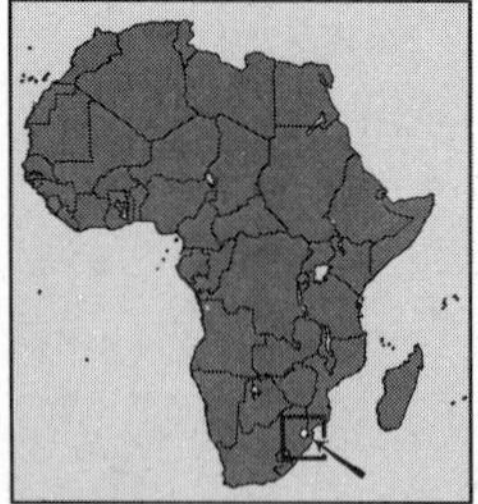

Swaziland

Sweden

A landlocked monarchy of southern Africa, Swaziland is bounded by South Africa and Mozambique. Area: 17,364 sq km (6,704 sq mi). Pop. (1976 prelim. census): 494,500. Cap. and largest city: Mbabane (pop., 1976 prelim. census, 23,100). Language: English and siSwati (official). Religion: Christian 60%; animist 40%. King, Sobhuza II; prime minister in 1979, Maj. Gen. Maphevu Dlamini.

A new Parliament (Libandla), resulting from the elections in 1978 of 20 senators and 50 deputies (10 of each chosen by the king), was opened by King Sobhuza II on Jan. 19, 1979. Under the new constitution political parties were forbidden, and Parliament's role in government was limited to debate and advice.

Although the country's stability was faintly ruffled in 1979 by the entry of political refugees from Mozambique and South Africa, Swaziland remained a haven of economic success in Africa, a success furthered by technical aid from Israel and the development of export routes to Richards Bay, South Africa. Anticipated revenue in 1979, at 115 million emalangeni, would be 32% over 1978, while expenditures on statutory and recurrent accounts, at 68 million emalangeni, would be up 20%; education would account for 12 million emalangeni, an increase of 20%; and capital expenditure was estimated at 101 million emalangeni. Swaziland remained an African star for Britain's Commonwealth Development Corporation (CDC), which transferred its southern African office from Johannesburg to Mbabane during the year. The nation continued to be the centre of the CDC's most successful operations, in particular the Royal Swaziland Sugar Corp., for which Tate and Lyle, a British sugar company, built a third mill at Simunye. (MOLLY MORTIMER)

SWAZILAND

Education. (1976) Primary, pupils 92,721, teachers 2,513; secondary, pupils 17,396, teachers 885; vocational, pupils 480, teachers (1975) 43; teacher training, students 451, teachers 52; higher, students 446, teaching staff (1975) 75.

Finance and Trade. Monetary unit: lilangeni (plural emalangeni), at par with the South African rand, with (Sept. 17, 1979) a free rate of 0.83 lilangeni to U.S. $1 (1.77 emalangeni = £1 sterling). Budget (1978–79 est.): revenue 87 million emalangeni; expenditure 61 million emalangeni (excludes capital expenditure of 108 million emalangeni). Foreign trade (1976): imports 168.6 million emalangeni; exports 163,340,000 emalangeni. Export destinations (1970): U.K. 25%; Japan 24%; South Africa 21%. Main exports (1975): sugar 54%; wood pulp 9%; iron ore 9%; asbestos 7%; timber 5%.

Agriculture. Production (in 000; metric tons; 1977): corn 85; rice *c.* 5; potatoes *c.* 5; sugar, raw value (1978) *c.* 262; pineapples *c.* 18; cotton, lint *c.* 6; timber (cu m) *c.* 2,511. Livestock (in 000; 1977): cattle *c.* 640; sheep *c.* 37; pigs *c.* 22; goats *c.* 280.

Industry. Production (in 000; metric tons; 1977): coal 129; iron ore (metal content; 1978) 770; asbestos 38; electricity (kw-hr) *c.* 173,000.

Sweden

A constitutional monarchy of northern Europe lying on the eastern side of the Scandinavian Peninsula, Sweden has common borders with Finland and Norway. Area: 449,964 sq km (173,732 sq mi). Pop. (1979 est.): 8,297,500. Cap. and largest city: Stockholm (pop., 1979 est., 653,900). Language: Swedish, with some Finnish and Lapp in the north. Religion: predominantly Lutheran. King, Carl XVI Gustaf; prime ministers in 1979, Ola Ullsten and, from October 9, Thorbjörn Fälldin.

Sweden ended 1979 on a strong economic surge even though it was afflicted with a weak coalition government. The non-Socialist parties were returned to power in September with 175 seats in the single-chamber Parliament, a majority of one. These elections amounted to a serious setback for the powerful Social Democratic Party, which until 1976 had ruled Sweden for a consecutive 44 years. The political future of party leader Olof Palme was uncertain. The new government was led by Thorbjörn Fälldin, leader of the Centre Party, in uneasy coalition with the Conservative and Liberal parties. (*See* POLITICAL PARTIES.)

SWEDEN

Education. (1977–78) Primary, pupils 697,000, teachers (1976–77) 37,740; secondary, pupils 567,000, teachers (1976–77) 46,994; higher (including teacher training), students 149,000.

Finance. Monetary unit: krona, with (Sept. 17, 1979) a free rate of 4.22 kronor to U.S. $1 (9.08 kronor = £1 sterling). Gold, SDR's, and foreign exchange (June 1979) U.S. $3,840,000,000. Budget (1978–79 est.): revenue 111,677,000,000 kronor; expenditure 141,616,000,000 kronor. Gross national product (1978) 390,490,000,000 kronor. Money supply (April 1979) 43,550,000,000 kronor. Cost of living (1975 = 100; June 1979) 143.5.

Foreign Trade. (1978) Imports 92,735,000,000 kronor; exports 98,201,000,000 kronor. Import sources: West Germany 18%; U.K. 11%; U.S. 7%; Denmark 7%; Finland 6%; Norway 5%. Export destinations: West Germany 11%; U.K. 11%; Norway 10%; Denmark 9%; U.S. 6%; Finland 6%; France 5%; The Netherlands 5%. Main exports: machinery 26%; motor vehicles 12%; paper 9%; iron and steel 8%; wood pulp 5%; chemicals 5%; timber 5%.

Transport and Communications. Roads (1977) 128,873 km (including 776 km expressways). Motor vehicles in use (1977): passenger 2,857,140; commercial 169,100. Railways (1977): 12,082 km (including 7,479 km electrified); traffic 5,586,000,000 passenger-km, freight 14,782,000,000 net ton-km. Air traffic (including Swedish apportionment of operations of Scandinavian Airlines System; 1978): 4,064,000,000 passenger-km; freight 202.7 million net ton-km. Shipping (1978): merchant vessels 100 gross tons and over 696; gross tonnage 6,508,255. Telephones (Jan. 1978) 5,930,300. Radio licenses (Dec. 1977) 3,264,600. Television licenses (Dec. 1977) 3,050,900.

Agriculture. Production (in 000; metric tons; 1978): wheat *c.* 1,306; barley *c.* 2,452; oats *c.* 1,575; rye 276; potatoes 1,420;sugar, raw value *c.* 339; rapeseed 343; apples *c.* 122; milk *c.* 3,255; butter 61; cheese *c.* 96; beef and veal *c.* 148; pork *c.* 306; fish catch (1977) 192; timber (cu m; 1977) 47,370. Livestock (in 000; June 1978): cattle 1,892; sheep (1977) 390; pigs *c.* 2,600; chickens (1977) *c.* 12,000.

Industry. Index of industrial production (1975 = 100; 1978) 95. Production (in 000; metric tons; 1978): cement 2,304; electricity (kw-hr) *c.* 90,200,000 (59% hydroelectric in 1977); iron ore (60–65% metal content) 21,486; pig iron 2,364; crude steel 4,221; aluminum 79; petroleum products (1977) 14,503; sulfuric acid (1976) 767; man-made fibres (1977) 33; wood pulp (1977) mechanical 1,527, chemical 6,129; newsprint 1,258; other paper (1977) 3,949; passenger cars (units) 258. Merchant vessels launched (100 gross tons and over; 1978) 1,305,000 gross tons. New dwelling units completed (1978) 53,700.

Vital political and economic decisions were being delayed by a raging debate over the future of nuclear power in Sweden, which cut across party lines. With Sweden having northern Europe's most powerful environmental lobby, there was a good chance that voters in a nuclear referendum in March 1980 would reject nuclear development. Sweden had six operating nuclear power stations, and another six awaited the go-ahead signal in a nation heavily dependent upon Middle East oil. Sweden used more energy per capita than any other nation in Europe. Many companies were said to be sitting on investment plans while awaiting the outcome of the referendum as well as wage negotiations with labour unions. In 1978 unions accepted a deal whereby real incomes declined, in view of the nation's runaway inflation and soaring deficit in the balance of payments. But union compliance in 1979 was proving more difficult.

Economic growth surged on a healthy tide of exports, and real disposable income reached record heights. The gross national product (GNP) climbed at an estimated 4% against a backdrop of low unemployment and manageable inflation. The Organization for Economic Cooperation and Development (OECD) noted that in a 12-to-18-month period the Swedish inflationary rate "nearly halved, falling well below the OECD average, the competitiveness of Swedish industry had improved, and the current external deficit has been greatly reduced while unemployment has remained low."

The prosperity of Sweden was so patently evident that it came as a shock to find economists speaking cautiously about national "recovery" after the country's worst economic crisis since the 1930s. The cold fact was that during 1975–78 important industrial sectors suddenly stagnated or even collapsed. The bottom fell out of shipbuilding, partly as a result of high production and wage costs. Export-oriented industries such as timber and special steels were suffering because of uncompetitive costs. Sharp krona devaluations totaling 18% and the decision (in December 1978) to leave the European currency arrangement put Swedish products on the road to recovery. Still, the level of foreign borrowing remained high because of oil imports. Government lending to industry was exceeding commercial bank lending, and increased government expenditures were not being matched by higher revenues.

The National Institute of Economic Research predicted GNP growth in 1980 of just over 4% and believed domestic demand and private consumption were likely to grow despite the recessionary climate in other OECD countries. However, the troubled balance of current accounts was expected to show a major deterioration, largely because of higher oil bills. Oil imports in 1979 were estimated at 6.5 billion kronor more than expected. Consumer prices, influenced by oil prices, rose by 8.5% in 1979. In November the Swedish central bank raised the discount rate by 1% to 9% to move Sweden closer to the international discount level.

Volvo in 1979 became the first Swedish company ever to make estimated annual pretax profits of 1 billion kronor. In 1978 the firm arranged a deal whereby 40% of the company would have been sold to the Norwegian government to raise badly needed investment capital, but the plan was vetoed early in 1979 by a group of Volvo shareholders. A cooperation agreement between Volvo's auto division and Renault of France was concluded in December. (ROGER NYE CHOATE)

Swimming

International swimming matches in 1979 provided the last tune-up for the 1980 Olympic Games. For the first time the Fédération Internationale de Natation Amateur (FINA), the world governing organization for amateur aquatics, conducted a Cup championship. That, combined with the quadrennial Pan American Games, turned what should have been a relatively quiet pre-Olympic year into an exciting one, though it failed to produce the usual number of world records.

The VIII Pan American Games, held July 1–8 at San Juan, Puerto Rico, with 20 nations competing, were completely dominated in swimming by the United States, which won 28 gold, 12 silver, and 6 bronze medals out of 29 races. Runner-up Canada won 1 gold, 12 silver, and 15 bronze medals. The U.S. men won all their races, with Canada's Anne Gagnon winning the 200-m breaststroke to prevent the U.S. women from duplicating the men's feat. Highlight of the Pan American Games was

Swedish Literature: *see* Literature

the performance of Cynthia "Sippy" Woodhead from Riverside, Calif., who won three individual gold medals plus anchoring the winning 400-m freestyle and medley relays.

In Europe the Soviet Union staged the VII Summer Spartakiade, July 25–August 2, to rehearse for the forthcoming Olympic Games, scheduled for Moscow in July 1980. Swimmers from 11 nations participated, and though the tournament failed to produce world records one European and eight Soviet national marks were achieved. Soviet swimmers completely dominated the competition.

The first FINA World Cup championship for swimming was held in Tokyo September 1–3. The tournament was attended by national teams from the U.S., Canada, Australasia, the Soviet Union, Sweden, and Japan and by two combined groups, one from remaining European nations and one from Mexico and Central and South America. Noticeably absent were the team from East Germany and the Soviet Union's number-one squad.

Each team was limited to one entry per event, with points awarded toward the championship. Despite the absence of many of the U.S. champions the U.S. won the championship with 258 points. Second was the combined European team with 209.5, and Canada finished third with 192. Cynthia Woodhead was named the outstanding swimmer, winning three individual gold medals and anchoring the winning freestyle relay. She lost a possible fifth gold medal when the medley team was disqualified because of a team member's early start.

The Pan American Games, FINA Cup, U.S. AAU (Amateur Athletic Union) championships at Fort Lauderdale, Fla., August 16–19, and a U.S.-Great Britain dual meet in August provided a showcase for the resurgence of U.S. women's swimming. Following up their dominance at the 1978 world championships, the U.S. women in 1979 were responsible for six of the nine world record performances. Woodhead twice lowered the 200-m world record. At the Pan American Games on July 3 she lopped off 0.1 sec (1 min 58.43 sec), and two months later at the FINA Cup meet she lowered the mark to 1 min 58.23 sec.

On October 19 Diana Nyad became the first person to swim the 60-mile distance from The Bahamas to Florida. The journey, which lasted 27 hours and 38 minutes, was her second try within a month; on her first attempt, stings from a Portuguese man-of-war forced her to leave the water.

UPI

World Swimming Records Set in 1979

Event	Name	Country	Time
MEN			
200-m freestyle	Sergey Kopliakov	U.S.S.R.	1 min 49.83 sec
400-m freestyle	Vladimir Salnikov	U.S.S.R.	3 min 51.41 sec
400-m freestyle	Vladimir Salnikov	U.S.S.R.	3 min 51.40 sec
800-m freestyle	Vladimir Salnikov	U.S.S.R.	7 min 56.49 sec
200-m individual medley	Jesse Vassallo	U.S.	2 min 3.29 sec
WOMEN			
200-m freestyle	Cynthia Woodhead	U.S.	1 min 58.43 sec
200-m freestyle	Cynthia Woodhead	U.S.	1 min 58.23 sec
1,500-m freestyle	Tracey Wickham	Australia	16 min 6.63 sec
1,500-m freestyle	Kim Linehan	U.S.	16 min 4.49 sec
200-m breaststroke	Svetlana Varganova	U.S.S.R.	2 min 31.09 sec
200-m breaststroke	Lina Kachushite	U.S.S.R.	2 min 28.36 sec
200-m butterfly	Mary T. Meagher	U.S.	2 min 9.77 sec
200-m butterfly	Mary T. Meagher	U.S.	2 min 8.41 sec
200-m butterfly	Mary T. Meagher	U.S.	2 min 7.01 sec

The U.S. unveiled another new star, Mary T. Meagher, a 14-year-old from Louisville, Ky. Ranked 53rd in the world in 1978, Meagher at the Pan American Games on July 7 swam the 200-m butterfly in 2 min 9.77 sec to break the old record by 0.1 sec. On August 16 in a preliminary race she lowered that mark to 2 min 8.41 sec, and several hours later in the AAU finals she again set a record by swimming the distance in 2 min 7.01 sec.

In the women's 1,500-m freestyle, a non-Olympic event, Australia's Tracey Wickham at Perth, Australia, on February 25 was timed in 16 min 6.63 sec to erase her world mark (16 min 14.93 sec). On August 19 at the AAU meet, Kim Linehan from Austin, Texas, broke Wickham's mark with a time of 16 min 4.49 sec. Jesse Vassallo, a native Puerto Rican who lived and trained in the U.S., set a new men's 200-m individual medley world record with a 2 min 3.29 sec performance at the Pan American Games.

The U.S.S.R. served notice that its crash four-year training program, set to peak at the 1980 Olympics, was on schedule. During the year Soviet swimmers set six world records. Vladimir Salnikov in a dual meet with East Germany on April 6 at Potsdam, East Germany, set a world record of 3 min 51.41 sec for the 400-m freestyle, slicing 0.15 sec from the old mark, and on August 19 at Moscow he again lowered the mark to 3 min 51.40 sec. In the 800-m freestyle, a non-Olympic event, Salnikov set a world record of 7 min 56.49 sec. Teammate Sergey Kopliakov lowered the 200-m freestyle world record to 1 min 49.83 sec.

The Soviet women also achieved world-record performances. Svetlana Varganova on March 30 at Minsk lowered the 200-m breaststroke mark to 2 min 31.09 sec, and a week later at Potsdam Lina Kachushite stroked the same event in 2 min 28.36 sec to regain the record.

Diving. At the Pan American Games divers from the U.S. won all four events. The men were led by world champion Greg Louganis of Mission Viejo, Calif., who triumphed in both the 3-m springboard and the 10-m platform. Phil Boggs of Miami, Fla., the 1976 Olympic Games champion, finished second in the springboard and third behind Mexico's Carlos Giron in the platform. In the women's springboard Denise Christensen of Tucson, Ariz., edged Janet Ely Thorburn of Dallas, Texas, and in the platform Barbara Weinstein of

BARTON SILVERMAN—THE NEW YORK TIMES

This S-shaped formation won a gold medal for the U.S. synchronized swimming team in July during the Pan American Games, which took place in San Juan, Puerto Rico.

Cincinnati, Ohio, slipped by Thorburn for a U.S. sweep.

The World University Games heralded the return of China to international competition for the first time since 1958. Soviet 1976 Olympic champion Irina Kalinina won the springboard, but a pair of young Chinese girls were runners-up. Chen Xiaoxia and Shi Meiqin won the silver and bronze medals. In the platform Chen surprised Kalinina for the gold with Chen Xi taking third. In the men's competition Aleksandr Kosenkov of the Soviet Union won the springboard, followed by Rolando Pedreguera of Cuba and Li Kongzheng of China. Vladimir Aleynik of the U.S.S.R. won the platform with teammate David Ambartsumian second and Li Hongping of China third.

(ALBERT SCHOENFIELD)

[452.B.4.a.i]

Switzerland

A federal republic in west central Europe consisting of a confederation of 23 cantons (three of which are demi-cantons), Switzerland is bounded by West Germany, Austria, Liechtenstein, Italy, and France. Area: 41,293 sq km (15,943 sq mi). Pop. (1979 est.): 6,297,600. Cap.: Bern (pop., 1979 est., 142,900). Largest city: Zürich (pop., 1979 est., 376,400). Language (1970): German 65%; French 18%; Italian 12%; Romansh 1%. Religion (1970): Roman Catholic 49.4%; Protestant 47.7%. President in 1979, Hans Hürlimann.

In the October 1979 elections to Switzerland's Federal Parliament, the percentage of those who did not vote (over 50%) reached an all-time high. Of the 200 seats in the National Council (lower chamber), the Socialists obtained 51 (down 3 from the preceding Council), the Radicals 51 (+4), the Christian Democrats 44 (−2), and the Centrists 23 (+1); the rest went to a few minority parties. The Social Democrat, Radical, Christian Democrat, and Centrist coalition continued to govern. The Council of States, composed of two deputies from each of the cantons, also preserved its stability. (*See* POLITICAL PARTIES.)

There were plebiscites on no less than 17 initiatives in 1979, while 7 parliamentary draft laws risked the referendum. In mid-February 933,676 enfranchised citizens approved the proposal to lower the voting age on federal issues to 18 years, but 964,105 opposed it; a proposal to create and maintain a nationwide network of pedestrian paths was approved by more than 3 to 1; one for the prohibition of advertising for alcoholic beverages and tobacco products was rejected by 1,114,485 to 772,842; an "antinuclear" initiative was defeated by 965,271 to 919,923.

On May 20 voters were again called upon, this time to decide three issues. The second government-sponsored attempt to modify the pattern of federal taxes by the introduction of the value-added tax (previously rejected in 1977) in order to reduce the escalating federal deficit was defeated (by 939,751 to 496,637); the government proposal on nuclear power production, taking some restrictions demanded by critics into consideration, was accepted (982,723 to 444,156); and an initiative for "democratic control" of motor highway construction was massively defeated. The law on nuclear power became effective on July 1, but opposition to the development of nuclear energy in the country continued.

In November the Ministry of Public Finance announced a plan proposing economies in federal expenditures, increased taxes, and a shift of financial responsibilities from federal to cantonal authorities. The six half-cantons (each of them half of a demi-canton) of the federation demanded the right to accede to the status of full canton (Jura had become a full canton on January 1). Proceeding slowly was the preparation of the plebiscite to decide for or against Switzerland's entering the United Nations.

Iran's revolutionary government demanded that the shah's funds deposited in Swiss banks be frozen. The Federal Council replied that this was not a political but a legal matter to be presented in the courts. In the face of criticism the Political Department pursued a policy of personal contacts with foreign governments, and its head visited a number of capitals, including those of six African countries. In July a ten-year program of economic, industrial, and scientific cooperation was signed with the U.S.S.R. A similar agreement was concluded with China.

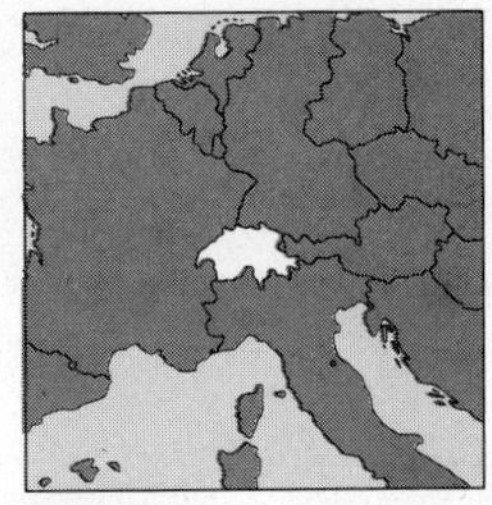

Switzerland

In September a commission studying the country's economic situation reported that private investment was increasing and that export industries were doing well. Only the watch and

SWITZERLAND

Education. (1978–79) Primary, pupils 524,500, teachers (excluding craft teachers; 1961–62) 23,761; secondary, pupils 424,400, teachers (full time; 1961–62) 6,583; vocational, pupils 206,000; teacher training, students 9,300; higher, students 71,500, teaching staff (universities and equivalent institutions only; 1975–76) 5,414.

Finance. Monetary unit: Swiss franc, with (Sept. 17, 1979) a free rate of SFr 1.63 to U.S. $1 (SFr 3.51 = £1 sterling). Gold and foreign exchange (June 1979) U.S. $18,858,000,000. Budget (1980 est.): revenue SFr 15,045,000,000; expenditure SFr 17,342,000,000. Gross national product (1978) SFr 157 billion. Money supply (April 1979) SFr 75,220,000,000. Cost of living (1975 = 100; June 1979) 108.5.

Foreign Trade. (1978) Imports SFr 42.3 billion; exports SFr 41,779,000,000. Import sources: EEC 68% (West Germany 29%, France 12%, Italy 10%, U.K. 8%); U.S. 8%. Export destinations: EEC 47% (West Germany 18%, France 9%, U.K. 7%, Italy 6%); U.S. 7%; Austria 5%. Main exports: machinery 31%; chemicals 20%; watches and clocks 8%; precious metals and stones 7%; textile yarns and fabrics 5%. Tourism (1977): visitors 8,341,000; gross receipts U.S. $1,943,000,000.

Transport and Communications. Roads (1977) 62,206 km (including 704 km expressways). Motor vehicles in use (1977): passenger 1,932,800; commercial 168,600. Railways: (1976) 4,973 km (including 4,944 km electrified); traffic (1978) 8,094,000,000 passenger-km, freight 6,218,000,000 net ton-km. Air traffic (1978): 10,147,000,000 passenger-km; freight 430.7 million net ton-km. Shipping (1978): merchant vessels 100 gross tons and over 27; gross tonnage 230,762. Telephones (Jan. 1978) 4,145,200. Radio licenses (Dec. 1977) 2,133,900. Television licenses (Dec. 1977) 1,845,600.

Agriculture. Production (in 000; metric tons; 1978): wheat 407; barley 216; oats 56; corn 108; potatoes 893; rapeseed 28; apples 320; pears (1977) *c.* 125; sugar, raw value (1977) 85; wine *c.* 122; milk 3,515; butter 33; cheese 119; beef and veal 152; pork *c.* 263. Livestock (in 000; April 1978): cattle 2,024; sheep 379; pigs 2,115; chickens (1977) 6,053.

Industry. Index of industrial production (1975 = 100; 1978) 107. Production (in 000; metric tons; 1977): aluminum 80; cement 3,649; petroleum products 4,389; man-made fibres (1977) 81; cigarettes (units) 30,537,000; watches (exports; units) 44,053; manufactured gas (cu m) 65,000; electricity (kw-hr; 1978) 41,000,000.

tourist industries were suffering from the high value of the Swiss franc. The rate of inflation, about 5%, remained one of the lowest among industrialized countries; more than half of the price increases during the year were the result of the increased cost of oil.

The new legislature first met at the end of November and rejected the production of an all-Swiss armoured car for the Army as far too expensive. Preference was given to a West German model. It also decided by a narrow margin to postpone the decision concerning the introduction of Daylight Saving Time, thus turning the country into an island within the European system of transportation and communication. Georges-André Chevallaz, minister of finance, became president of the federation for 1980 by routine election.

(MELANIE STAERK)

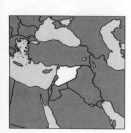

Syria

Syria

A republic in southwestern Asia on the Mediterranean Sea, Syria is bordered by Turkey, Iraq, Jordan, Israel, and Lebanon. Area: 185,180 sq km (71,498 sq mi). Pop. (1978 est.): 8,328,000. Cap. and largest city: Damascus (pop., 1978 est., 1,113,000). Language: Arabic (official); also Kurdish, Armenian, Turkish, Circassian, and Syriac. Religion: predominantly (over 80%) Muslim. President in 1979, Gen. Hafez al-Assad; premier, Muhammad Ali al-Halabi.

SYRIA

Education. (1977–78) Primary, pupils 1,326,414, teachers 41,550; secondary, pupils 362,885, teachers 30,143; vocational, pupils 22,645, teachers 2,472; teacher training, students 10,108, teachers 927; higher, students 85,474, teaching staff (universities only; 1975–76) 1,332.

Finance. Monetary unit: Syrian pound, with (Sept. 17, 1979) a par value of S£3.925 to U.S. $1 (free rate of S£8.44 = £1 sterling). Gold, SDR's, and foreign exchange (Dec. 1978) U.S. $456 million. Budget (total; 1979 est.) balanced at S£22,591 million. Gross domestic product (1977) S£25,993 million. Money supply (Dec. 1978) S£13,867 million. Cost of living (Damascus; 1975 = 100; June 1979) 134.

Foreign Trade. (1978) Imports S£9,650 million; exports S£4,160 million. Import sources: West Germany 11%; Italy 8%; France 8%; Iraq 7%; Romania 7%; Japan 5%. Export destinations: West Germany 10%; France 10%; The Netherlands 9%; U.S. 9%; U.S.S.R. *c.* 9%; Italy 8%; Greece 7%; Saudi Arabia 5%. Main exports: crude oil 62%; cotton 16%.

Transport and Communications. Roads (1976) *c.* 16,339 km. Motor vehicles in use (1976): passenger 62,800; commercial 50,200. Railways: (1976) 1,672 km; traffic (1977) 269 million passenger-km, freight 426 million net ton-km. Air traffic (1977): 795 million passenger-km; freight 9.4 million net ton-km. Telephones (Jan. 1978) 193,000. Radio receivers (June 1976) 1,232,000. Television receivers (Dec. 1976) 230,000.

Agriculture. Production (in 000; metric tons; 1978): wheat *c.* 1,651; barley *c.* 729; potatoes (1977) *c.* 135; pumpkins (1977) *c.* 155; cucumbers (1977) *c.* 187; tomatoes *c.* 560; onions *c.* 164; watermelons (1977) *c.* 500; melons (1977) *c.* 200; grapes *c.* 353; olives 252; cottonseed *c.* 236; cotton, lint *c.* 145. Livestock (in 000; 1978): sheep *c.* 7,397; goats *c.* 1,039; cattle (1977) *c.* 639; horses (1977) *c.* 55; asses (1977) *c.* 235; chickens *c.* 4,673.

Industry. Production (in 000; metric tons; 1977): cement 1,395; crude oil (1978) 10,008; natural gas (cu m) *c.* 120,000; petroleum products 3,714; cotton yarn 28; electricity (kw-hr) 2,043,000.

The first tangible fruits of the October 1978 Joint Action Charter between Syria and Iraq were agreements signed on Jan. 8, 1979, for the creation of a single Syrian-Iraqi tourist company and the resumption of Iraqi crude oil supplies through Syria's pipeline. Discussions on full unity of the two countries, their armies, and their separate Ba'ath Party structures achieved considerable progress in the first half of 1979. The two defense ministers met in Damascus on January 15 to consider the merger of their armed forces. Iraq's Revolutionary Command Council vice-chairman, Saddam Hussein at-Takriti, met Syria's Pres. Hafez al-Assad in Damascus January 28–30, and plans for the unification of foreign, defense, and information ministries were announced. The culmination of the unity discussions between the two former antagonists took place on June 16 when President Assad was received with full honours in Baghdad by Iraqi Pres. Ahmad Hassan al-Bakr. No implementation of unity agreements followed, however, and relations between the two Ba'athist regimes deteriorated after the resignation in July of President Bakr and his replacement by Saddam Hussein. (*See* IRAQ.) Hussein accused Syria of having supported an abortive coup against him, but on August 27 President Assad officially denied Syrian involvement.

Syria was left with virtual control of the Arab

Deterrent Force in Lebanon in 1979 when both the United Arab Emirates and Saudi Arabia withdrew their contingents. Lebanese Pres. Elias Sarkis went to Damascus on May 14 to discuss the future of the 30,000-man Syrian force in Lebanon, which some Lebanese Christian leaders had come to view as a force of occupation. On June 27 Israeli warplanes bombed the Lebanese coastal town of Damur and were intercepted by Syrian MiG-21s. At least four Syrian planes were shot down by Israeli F-15s in the first Israeli-Syrian air encounter since their disengagement agreement of May 29, 1974.

Syria, along with most Arab nations, opposed Egypt's March 26 treaty with Israel and severed diplomatic relations with Cairo. It pursued a relatively moderate policy vis-à-vis the U.S. over the treaty, with Syrian Foreign Minister Abdel-Halim Khaddam stating in March that Syria would not support an Arab oil embargo of the U.S. Nonetheless, Syria's opposition to the U.S.-sponsored treaty led the U.S. House of Representatives on April 7 to withhold the U.S. $45 million in aid to Syria requested by the administration. On May 22 the U.S. Senate restored the amount to the foreign aid bill. At the same time Syria improved its relations with the Soviet Union. Soviet Foreign Minister Andrey Gromyko flew to Damascus on March 24 to discuss Syria's response to the treaty. The Syrian-Soviet rapprochement came to light on January 4 when Defense Minister Gen. Moustapha Tlas went to Moscow with requests for improved Soviet arms. On January 26 Syria signed a protocol on maritime navigation with the Soviet Union, and in February there were reports of the sale to Syria of Soviet MiG-23 fighter jets.

On the home front Syria in 1979 experienced serious intercommunal violence and underground opposition to the regime of President Assad. Religious tension between the majority Sunni Muslim population and the Alawite military and civilian leadership of President Assad led to the assassination of the Alawite attorney general of the State Security Court, Adel Mini, on April 11, the killing of three Alawite secret police agents in June, and the murder of an Alawite religious leader on August 30. In June there were anti-Alawite demonstrations in the Sunni towns of Hama, Homs, and Aleppo, and on June 16, 32 Alawite military cadets were murdered and 54 wounded at the Aleppo artillery school. Many of those wounded later died. Interior Minister Brig. Gen. Adnan Dabbagh on June 22 blamed the banned Sunni fundamentalist Muslim Brotherhood for the killings, and 300 suspected Muslim Brothers were arrested. Fourteen men, 12 of them in absentia, were sentenced to death for the Aleppo killings. A Muslim Brotherhood leader in Jordan denied the organization was implicated. (CHARLES GLASS)

Syrian Pres. Hafez al-Assad (left) greeted King Hussein of Jordan at the airport when Hussein arrived in March to discuss the Egyptian-Israeli peace treaty.

WIDE WORLD

Table Tennis

The 35th biennial world table tennis championships were held in Pyongyang, North Korea, from April 25 to May 6, 1979. Men's teams representing 54 associations competed for the Swaythling Cup, which was won by Hungary. China was runner-up, Japan third, and Czechoslovakia fourth. The Chinese women's team retained the Marcel Corbillon Cup. North Korea finished second, Japan third, and the U.S.S.R. fourth. In individual competition, Seiji Ono of Japan won the men's singles title by defeating Guo Yuehua of China. Ge Xinai of China took the women's crown with a victory over Li Song Suk of North Korea. Veterans Dragutin Surbek and Anton Stipancic of Yugoslavia won the men's doubles by defeating Istvan Jonyer and Tibor Klampar of Hungary in straight sets. In the all-China women's doubles final, Zhang Li and Zhang Deying triumphed over Ge Xinai and Yan Guili. In the mixed doubles, which also featured two Chinese teams, Liang Geliang and Ge Xinai beat Li Zhenshi and Yan Guili.

During the tournament, Ichiro Ogimura of Japan was elected deputy president of the International Table Tennis Federation (ITTF), replacing Hisao Kido. The Council of the ITTF—which for the first time was appointed by representatives from Africa, Asia, Europe, Latin America, North America, and Oceania—granted two options to organize world championships. The first was given to Yugoslavia for 1981, the other to Japan for 1983. The Council also admitted Qatar and Laos to ITTF membership, bringing the total number of associations to 122.

The fourth Asian championships were held in Kuala Lumpur, Malaysia, from Nov. 22 to Dec. 2, 1978. As expected, China overwhelmed the other 18 participating associations by capturing both team titles and monopolizing the men's and women's singles finals. Guo Yuehua, who was later runner-up in the 1979 world championships, defeated Liang Geliang in four sets to win the men's singles crown. Cao Yanhua won the women's singles final, defeating Yang Ying in

1979 World Rankings

MEN	WOMEN
1. Seiji Ono (Japan)	1. Ge Xinai (China)
2. Guo Yuehua (China)	2. Li Song Suk (North Korea)
3. Tibor Klampar (Hungary)	3. Zhang Deying (China)
4. Gabor Gergely (Hungary)	4. Tong Ling (China)
Li Zhenshi (China)	5. Pak Yung Sun (North Korea)
6. Liang Geliang (China)	6. Zhang Li (China)
7. Dragutin Surbek (Yugos.)	7. Gabriella Szabo (Hungary)
8. Milan Orlowski (Czech.)	8. Kayoko Kawahigashi (Japan)
9. Istvan Jonyer (Hungary)	9. Jill Hammersley (England)
Norio Takashima (Japan)	10. Judit Magos (Hungary)

straight sets. North Korea won both the men's and women's doubles championships, but Japan took the mixed doubles with a four-set victory over China.

The fifth Commonwealth championships took place in Edinburgh, Scotland, in mid-April 1979. Hong Kong players were clearly the stars of the tournament, winning both team titles and both singles championships. In all these events England finished second. England, however, won the women's and mixed doubles crowns, and Australia the men's doubles.

The Europe Top Twelve Players tournament was played in Kristianstad, Sweden, in mid-February 1979. Top finishers in the men's division were, in order: Surbek (Yugos.), Desmond Douglas (England), Jacques Secretin (France), Jonyer (Hung.), and Gabor Gergely (Hung.). The order in women's competition was: Gabriella Szabo (Hung.), Maria Alexandru (Rom.), Erzebet Palatinus (Yugos.), Ann-Christin Hellman (Sweden), and Valentina Popova (U.S.S.R.). The 1978–79 European League winners were: Czechoslovakia in the Super Division, Poland in Division 1, Turkey in Division 2, and Denmark in Division 3.

The first Oceania championships were held during October 1978 in Auckland, N.Z. Australia won all but two of the titles; New Zealand won the women's doubles and team events.

(ARTHUR KINGSLEY VINT)

Taiwan

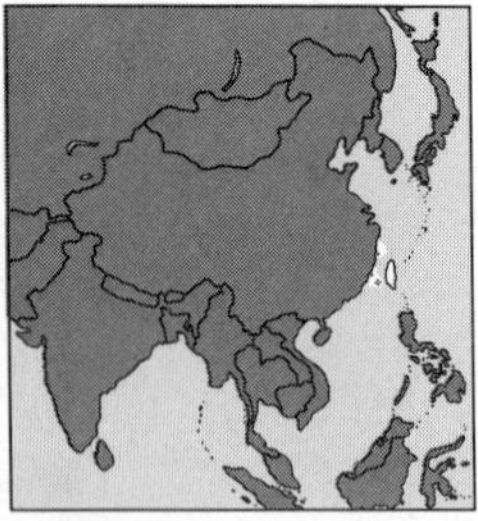
Taiwan

Taiwan, which consists of the islands of Formosa and Quemoy and other surrounding islands, is the seat of the Republic of China (Nationalist China). It is north of the Philippines, southwest of Japan, and east of Hong Kong. The island of Formosa has an area of 35,990 sq km (13,896 sq mi); including its 77 outlying islands (14 in the Taiwan group and 63 in the Pescadores group), the area of Taiwan totals 35,990 sq km (13,896 sq mi). Pop. (1979 est.): 17,342,100. Cap. and largest city: Taipei (pop., 1979 est., 2,183,500). President in 1979, Chiang Ching-kuo; president of the Executive Yuan (premier), Sun Yun-suan.

By Oct. 10, 1979, when the Nationalist government celebrated the 68th anniversary of the revolution that created the Republic of China, it had spent 30 years in exile on Taiwan. With the sudden U.S. shift of diplomatic recognition from Taipei to Beijing (Peking) on January 1, only 21 countries, mostly in Africa and Latin America, continued to recognize Nationalist China.

TAIWAN

Education. (1977–78) Primary, pupils 2,319,342, teachers 66,954; secondary and vocational, pupils 1,563,321, teachers 64,327; higher, students 308,583, teaching staff 15,275.

Finance. Monetary unit: new Taiwan dollar, with (Sept. 17, 1979) an official rate of NT$36 to U.S. $1 (free rate of NT$77.45 = £1 sterling). Gold and foreign exchange (June 1979) U.S. $1,548,000,000. Budget (1977–78 est.): revenue NT$203,639,000,000; expenditure NT$203,579,000,000. Gross national product (1978) NT$889,360,000,000. Money supply (May 1979) NT$222,670,000,000. Cost of living (1975 = 100; June 1979) 126.1.

Foreign Trade. (1978) Imports NT$408,370,000,000; exports NT$468,510,000,000. Import sources: Japan 33%; U.S. 22%; Kuwait 7%; Saudi Arabia 6%. Export destinations: U.S. 40%; Japan 12%; Hong Kong 7%; West Germany 5%. Main exports: textiles and clothing 22%; electrical equipment and machinery 15%; food 10%; footwear 6%.

Transport and Communications. Roads (1977) 17,101 km. Motor vehicles in use (1977): passenger 209,900; commercial 149,500. Railways (1977): 4,000 km; traffic 8,122,000,000 passenger-km, freight 2,658,000,000 net ton-km. Air traffic (1977): 5,355,000,000 passenger-km; freight 594.4 million net ton-km. Shipping (1978): merchant vessels 100 gross tons and over 444; gross tonnage 1,619,595. Telephones (Dec. 1977) 1,685,100. Radio licenses (Dec. 1976) 1,493,100. Television licenses (Dec. 1977) 1,309,000.

Agriculture. Production (in 000; metric tons; 1977): rice 2,649; sweet potatoes 1,695; cassava 288; sugar, raw value 1,070; citrus fruit 369; bananas 252; pineapples 282; tea 26; tobacco 25; pork 571; fish catch 855. Livestock (in 000; Dec. 1977): cattle 188; pigs 3,760; goats and sheep 201; chickens 35,489.

Industry. Production (in 000; metric tons; 1977): coal 2,956; crude oil 254; natural gas (cu m) 1,886,000; electricity (kw-hr) 29,724,000; cement 10,320; crude steel 644; sulfuric acid 541; plastics and resins 463; petroleum products 11,684; cotton yarn 277; man-made fibres 434; paper and board 954; radio receivers (units) 7,427; television receivers (units) 4,926.

The unilateral announcement by U.S. Pres. Jimmy Carter on Dec. 15, 1978, severing diplomatic ties with the Republic of China was the most shocking blow to Taiwan since its expulsion from the UN in 1971. On Jan. 1, 1979, the U.S. recognized the People's Republic "as the sole legal government of China" while declaring that it would "maintain cultural, commercial, and other unofficial relations with the people of Taiwan." On the same day, it gave a year's notice of termination of the 1954 mutual defense treaty between the U.S. and the Republic of China in accordance with the provisions of the treaty. However, scores of government-to-government pacts in force before January 1 remained in effect.

On March 1 the U.S. embassy in Taipei ceased to function, and the "nongovernmental" American Institute in Taiwan, staffed by U.S. officials technically retired from the foreign service, was established. Taipei had sought to keep its relations with Washington on a government-to-government basis, but Washington warned that such an arrangement would contravene its agreement with the People's Republic. Consequently, Taiwan acceded to U.S. demands and agreed to set up its own "unofficial" mission, called the Coordination Council for North American Affairs, in New York and other major cities as the "counterpart to the American Institute in Taiwan."

The Carter administration sought legislation to transfer the funds already assigned to the U.S. embassy to the new American Institute. In establishing diplomatic relations with the People's Republic, President Carter had failed to obtain an explicit renunciation of force against Taiwan, an omission that disturbed some members of Congress. In February the Senate Foreign Relations Committee agreed on a draft proposal establishing unofficial relations with Taipei that considered any armed attack against Taiwan a common danger to the peace and security of Taiwan and the U.S. This, however, was unacceptable to the administration. Finally, in March, Congress adopted legislation merely expressing the U.S.'s deep concern for the peace, prosperity, and welfare of Taiwan. On April 10 President Carter signed the legislation, which also affirmed continued U.S. interest in the peaceful solution of the Taiwan issue and provided for future arms sales to the Nationalist government. A suit challenging the president's right to abrogate the mutual defense treaty without congressional approval was brought by 24 members of Congress, but it was dismissed by the Supreme Court in December, shortly before the Jan. 1, 1980, expiration date.

Taiwan's economic prosperity strengthened its political stability, and it continued to foster economic growth as a safeguard to its security. Despite diplomatic setbacks and oil price hikes, the gross national product in 1978 rose 19.7% to U.S. $23 billion, and per capita income was $1,304, compared with $152 on the mainland. According to the Taiwan Economic Research Institute, the 1979 growth rate would be 7.64%, while per capita income should reach $1,580. Rapid industrialization had caused fundamental changes in Taiwan, and industry and its exports had become the mainstay of the economy. In 1978 two-way trade amounted to $23,714,000,000 (exports $12,687,000,000; imports $11,027,000,000), an increase of $5,855,700,000 over 1977. The U.S. remained Taiwan's principal trading partner, followed closely by Japan. Total trade with the U.S. was valued at $7,384,000,000 in 1978 (imports from Taiwan $5,001,000,000; exports to Taiwan $2,383,000,000), about four times the value of U.S. trade with the People's Republic. (HUNG-TI CHU)

Tanzania

This republic, an East African member of the Commonwealth of Nations, consists of two parts: Tanganyika, on the Indian Ocean, bordered by Kenya, Uganda, Rwanda, Burundi, Zaire, Zambia, Malawi, and Mozambique; and Zanzibar, just off the coast, including Zanzibar Island, Pemba Island, and small islets. Total area of the united republic: 945,050 sq km (364,886 sq mi). Total pop. (1978 est.): 16,308,000, including 98.9% African and 0.7% Indo-Pakistani. Cap. and largest city: Dar es Salaam (pop., 1977 est., 460,000) in Tanganyika. Language: English and Swahili. Religion (1967): traditional beliefs 34.6%; Christian 30.6%; Muslim 30.5%. President in 1979, Julius Nyerere.

In January 1979 Tanzanian forces invaded Uganda in retaliation for the attack launched by Ugandan Pres. Idi Amin on Tanzania late in 1978. Advancing steadily, the Tanzanian Army occupied Kampala, the Ugandan capital, in April and by the beginning of June controlled the whole country. Criticism of Tanzania's action by the Organization of African Unity angered Pres. Julius Nyerere (*see* BIOGRAPHIES), who pointed to the lack of response from that body to his own protests over the invasion of Tanzania.

More important was the effect of the war on the

UPI

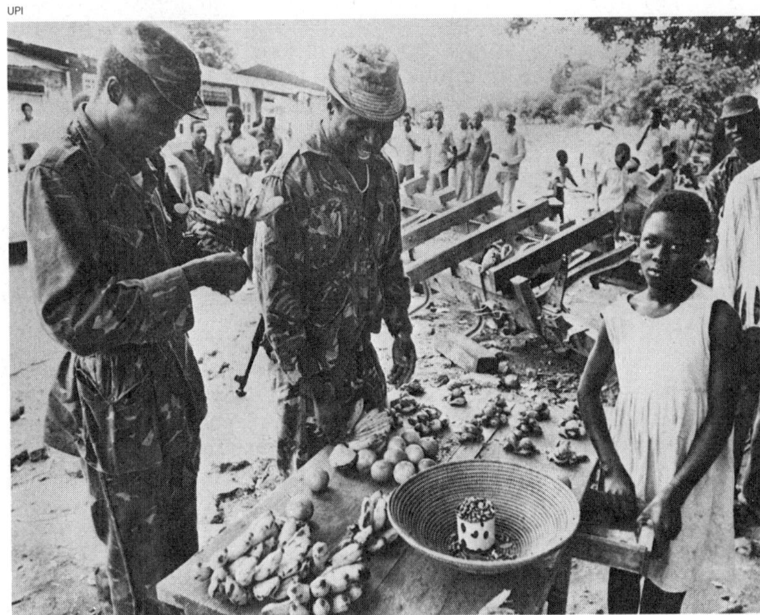

Tanzanian soldiers stop to buy fruits from a little girl's stand at a market near Lake Victoria, Uganda. The soldiers were part of a force keeping order in Uganda after Tanzanian troops overthrew Uganda's dictator, Idi Amin.

TANZANIA

Education. (1975–76) Primary, pupils 1,954,443, teachers 39,245; secondary (1976–77), pupils 56,481, teachers 2,930; vocational, pupils 1,765, teachers 174; teacher training, pupils 9,930, teachers 612; higher, students 3,064, teaching staff (universities only) 434.

Finance. Monetary unit: Tanzanian shilling, with (Sept. 17, 1979) a free rate of TShs 8.27 to U.S. $1 (TShs 17.80 = £1 sterling). Gold, SDR's, and foreign exchange (June 1979) U.S. $100 million. Budget (1978–79 est.): revenue TShs 6,726,000,000; expenditure TShs 6,719,000,000. Gross national product (1977) TShs 28,115,000,000. Money supply (June 1978) TShs 6,248,000,000. Cost of living (1975 = 100; 1st quarter 1979) 144.3.

Foreign Trade. (1978) Imports TShs 8,867,000,000; exports TShs 3,635,000,000. Import sources (1976): U.K. 12%; Kenya 11%; Iran 9%; West Germany 8%; Japan 7%; China 6%; U.S. 6%. Export destinations (1976): West Germany 14%; U.K. 13%; U.S. 9%; Singapore 7%; Italy 6%; Kenya 6%; Hong Kong 5%; India 5%. Main exports: coffee 36%; cotton 12%; sisal 6%; diamonds 5%.

Transport and Communications. Roads (1977) *c.* 35,000 km. Motor vehicles in use (1977): passenger 43,600; commercial (including buses) 46,400. Railways (1977) *c.* 3,550 km. Air traffic (1977): 37 million passenger-km; freight 300,000 net ton-km. Telephones (Jan. 1978) 74,300. Radio receivers (Dec. 1976) 300,000. Television receivers (Dec. 1977) 8,800.

Agriculture. Production (in 000; metric tons; 1978): corn *c.* 1,000; millet *c.* 160; sorghum *c.* 250; rice *c.* 240; sweet potatoes (1977) *c.* 335; cassava (1977) *c.* 4,000; sugar, raw value (1977) *c.* 114; dry beans *c.* 160; mangoes *c.* 177; bananas *c.* 803; cashew nuts (1977) *c.* 110; coffee *c.* 42; tea *c.* 20; tobacco *c.* 18; cotton, lint *c.* 56; sisal *c.* 125; meat (1977) *c.* 188; fish catch (1977) *c.* 250; timber (cu m; 1977) 38,722. Livestock (in 000; 1978): sheep *c.* 3,000; goats *c.* 4,700; cattle (1977) *c.* 14,817; asses *c.* 160; chickens *c.* 21,050.

Industry. Production (in 000; metric tons; 1977): cement 247; salt (1976) 22; diamonds (metric carats) *c.* 375; petroleum products *c.* 620; electricity (kw-hr) *c.* 695,000.

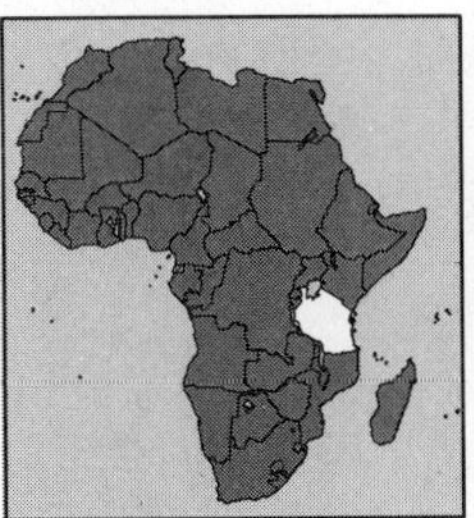

Tanzania

country's already precarious economy. In June Tanzania appealed to nine Western countries for $375 million needed to avert total economic collapse. The nonwithdrawal of Tanzanian forces after the installation of a new government in Uganda aroused criticism from Kenya. The fact that Uganda had no forces of its own to maintain order in a country whose population had been demoralized by Amin's excesses appeared to weigh less heavily with the Kenyan government than the fear of a socialist alliance between Tanzania and Uganda that might endanger Kenya's economic links with Uganda.

As chairman of the presidents of the "front-line" states, Nyerere was also deeply involved in the new moves initiated at the Commonwealth conference in Lusaka, Zambia, in August to find a solution to the problems of Zimbabwe Rhodesia. Although continuing to support the Patriotic Front in the struggle for power and remaining loyal to the concept of full majority rule, Nyerere threw his weight behind the proposal for a conference in London. During the protracted negotiations there, he urged the Patriotic Front leaders to adopt an accommodating attitude toward the various plans put forward by U.K. Foreign Secretary Lord Carrington.

Tanzania's internal problems were highlighted in a report by a French socialist agronomist, René Dumont, invited by Nyerere to conduct a survey of the country. While sympathizing with the principles underlying Nyerere's program for development, Dumont was critical of its implementation. In particular, he pointed to the lack of success of the communal village movement and the failure of the bureaucracy to keep in touch with the small farmers. Added to these functional weaknesses was a widespread epidemic of cholera, and a British offer in March of a grant of over £8 million to improve health services in southern Tanzania only touched the edge of the country's economic crisis. The crisis was further sharpened in November when Lonrho Ltd., a multinational trading company, asked the World Bank and Britain to freeze all aid to Tanzania until it had paid compensation for the assets seized by the government in 1978. A movement also began in Zanzibar for greater autonomy for the island. (KENNETH INGHAM)

Target Sports

Archery. In 1979 archery continued to increase in popularity throughout the world. Evidence of this was the 30th World Target Archery Championship held in West Berlin and competition at the Pan American Games in Puerto Rico. Both events were staged in July 1979. Another event of interest was the 100th anniversary of the National Archery Association of the U.S., which occurred in August.

The world championships brought together competitors from 24 nations. In the men's event the U.S. won the gold, silver, and bronze medals. The gold medal for women went to South Korea, with the U.S. second and Australia third. The team gold medals were won by the U.S. for men and by South Korea for women.

Tariffs:
see Economy, World
Taxation:
see Economy, World
Telecommunications:
see Industrial Review

Archery was included in the Pan American Games for the first time as 37 men and 21 women representing 11 nations in the Western Hemisphere competed in San Juan, Puerto Rico, in July. The U.S. took gold and silver medals for both men and women. Both bronze medals were awarded to Canada. It should be noted that the U.S. did, in fact, place third in both the men's and women's events; however, tournament rules do not allow one nation to gain more than two medals in any one event. (CLAYTON B. SHENK)

Shooting. Two outstanding international competitions of 1979 were the Benito Juárez Matches in April at Mexico City and the Pan American Games in July in San Juan, Puerto Rico. The first world air gun championships were held in August at Seoul, South Korea.

TRAP AND SKEET. The gold medal for trap at the Benito Juárez Matches was won by Jim Gorman of the U.S. with a score of 194. Noh Jeong Sik of South Korea tied Robert Green of the U.S. for second place with 193. Susan Nattrass of Canada won the women's event with 187, while Michael Coleman of the U.S. won the junior title with 196. The U.S. trap team won at the Pan American Games with a score of 563. Brazil finished second with 533, and Canada was third with 502. The individual gold medal was taken by Robert Green of the U.S. with a 191. Charvin Dixon of the U.S. won the silver with a 189, and George Leary of Canada took the bronze with 187.

At skeet the U.S. team won the Benito Juárez Matches with a score of 288. Cuba placed second and Puerto Rico third. High individual score was a 198 fired by Matthew Dryke of the U.S. Jorge Villar of Cuba placed second with 196, and Joseph Clemmons of the U.S. finished third with 195. The gold medal at the Pan American Games was won by the U.S. team with a score of 566. Chile took the silver with 548 and Cuba the bronze with 547.

RIFLES. At the Benito Juárez Matches Genady Luschikov of the Soviet Union fired the maximum English match score of 600. The following day he scored 1,166 in the small-bore three-position match, only one point under the world record set in 1973. The free rifle competition was won by David Kimes of the U.S. with 1,146. In the team events the Soviet Union won the English match with 1,788. South Korea was second with 1,781, and the U.S. finished third with 1,779. Switzerland won the free rifle event with 3,417, with the U.S. second at 3,388 and South Korea third at 3,329.

At the Pan American Games the U.S. team won the English match with 2,373. Cuba scored 2,350

World Archery Records

Event	Winner and country	Year	Record	Maximum possible
Men				
90 m	R. McKinney, U.S.	1979	318	360
70 m	S. Spigarelli, Italy	1978	338	360
50 m	S. Spigarelli, Italy	1976	340	360
30 m	D. Pace, U.S.	1979	356	360
Team	U.S.	1979	3,868	4,320
Women				
70 m	Natalia Butuzova, U.S.S.R.	1979	328	360
60 m	Valentina Kovpan, U.S.S.R.	1978	334	360
50 m	Keto Lossaberidze, U.S.S.R.	1978	329	360
30 m	Natalia Butuzova, U.S.S.R.	1979	350	360
Team	U.S.S.R.	1979	3,878	4,320

WIDE WORLD

The scoreboard behind Rod Baston shows that the U.S. archery team won the top four places in the Pan American Games archery competition. Baston won two gold medals for individual and team performances.

to take second place, while Brazil was third with 2,345. The U.S. won the three-position team match with 4,572, followed by Canada with 4,531 and Cuba with 4,502. Lones Wigger of the U.S. won four gold medals, two each in the individual and team events. His three-position score was 1,162, and his English match score of 599 equaled the world record.

Handguns. The U.S. team won the standard pistol event at the Benito Juárez Matches with a score of 1,682 and the rapid-fire silhouette competition with 1,746. The Swiss team took the free pistol match with 1,640, and the Soviet team scored 1,747 to win the centre-fire pistol match. At the Pan American Games Canada won the free pistol event with a 2,138. Cuba won the rapid-fire silhouette match with 2,339, while the U.S. team won the centre-fire match with a 2,305. High individuals were Walter Bauza of Argentina, who scored 555 with the free pistol; J. C. Hernandez of Cuba, who scored 590 in the rapid-fire silhouette; and O. Yuston of Argentina, who fired a 291 with the centre-fire pistol.

Air Gun. Participation in air gun competition continued its rapid increase of the past few years. Twenty-four nations participated in the first world air gun championships in South Korea. The Swiss men's team won the air rifle event with a score of 1,518 out of a possible 1,600. The U.S. women's team won with 1,140 out of a possible 1,200. High individual man was W. Hillenbrand of West Germany with a 390. In women's competition Karen Monez of the U.S. scored 391 to equal the world record. The Swedish men's team won the air pistol event with a 1,525, while the U.S. women's team won with 1,128. High individuals were G. Robinson (U.K.; 387) and Ruby Fox (U.S.; 385).

At the Benito Juárez Matches the West German air rifle team won with a score of 1,126, while the Mexican team won the air pistol event with 1,120. U.S. teams won both events at the Pan American Games; the air rifle score was 1,507 and air pistol was 1,518. (ROBERT N. SEARS)

[452.B.4.c; 452.B.4.h.i]

Television and Radio

No major nation lacked some form of television and radio service in 1979. Approximately 818 million radio sets were in use, of which 450.8 million, or 55%, were in the U.S. There were about 395 million television sets, of which approximately 145.7 million, or 37%, were in the U.S.

The Soviet Union, with 75 million television sets, ranked next to the U.S., and Japan was third with 26.4 million, according to estimates published in the 1979 *Broadcasting Yearbook*. Other *Broadcasting* estimates included West Germany, 20.5 million; United Kingdom, 18 million; Brazil, 15 million; France, 14.7 million; Italy, 12.6 million; Canada, 10.2 million; Spain, 7.4 million; Poland, 7 million; Mexico, 5.5 million; East Germany, 5.2 million; The Netherlands, 5.1 million; Australia, 5 million; and Argentina, 4.5 million.

More than 6,730 television stations were in operation or under construction throughout the world. Approximately 2,200 were in the Far East, 2,110 in Western Europe, 1,080 in the U.S., 920 in Eastern Europe, 180 in South America, 105 in Mexico, 96 in Canada, and 45 in Africa. Radio stations numbered approximately 15,500; most were of the amplitude modulation (AM) type, though a growing percentage were frequency modulation (FM). In the U.S. there were 9,028, of which 4,385, or almost 49%, were FM.

Organization of Services. Broadcasting organizations throughout the world continued to exchange major news coverage by satellite. The visits of Pope John Paul II to Poland and Ireland and his

Melissa Gilbert (left) as Helen Keller and Patty Duke Astin as Annie Sullivan starred in NBC's remake of "The Miracle Worker." Astin had won an Oscar for the 1962 movie version, in which she played the role of Helen Keller.

UPI

six-city tour in the U.S. produced some of the most widely distributed broadcasts. Coverage of the U.S.-Iranian crisis in November and December, after Iranian students seized the U.S. embassy in Teheran and held its occupants hostage, also was seen in many countries, as was the July 15 speech by U.S. Pres. Jimmy Carter following his protracted "summit conference" with U.S. leaders and ordinary citizens at the presidential retreat at Camp David, Md.

There was no relaxation of the tensions between broadcasters and cable-TV operators during the year. If anything, their relationship became even more strained when the Federal Communications Commission (FCC) proposed to "deregulate" cable-TV by eliminating the last two rules that cable operators considered severely restrictive in their competition with broadcasters. The rules, which broadcasters considered vital in protecting their rights and interests, had limited the number of broadcast signals that cable systems could import from distant cities and required them to protect certain programs of local television stations. There were at the time approximately 4,000 cable systems in the U.S. serving more than 13 million homes.

Broadcasters—and the FCC—did get some relief when the U.S. Court of Appeals in Washington amended a 1978 ruling in which it had held that, when the license of an existing station is being challenged, that station must demonstrate that its service had been "superior" rather than merely "substantial," as the FCC had held in the past, if it was to have any assurance that its license would be renewed. The amended opinion eased the fears of broadcasters that in comparative hearings, if their records were good but not "superior," they might lose their licenses to challengers who needed only to "promise" to render better service.

Katharine Hepburn played the leading role in a CBS production of "The Corn Is Green," which was directed by George Cukor and aired in January.

WIDE WORLD

The Carnegie Commission on the Future of Public Broadcasting, whose predecessor Carnegie Commission 12 years earlier had laid the groundwork for the present public broadcasting system, concluded after an 18-month study that the system had evolved into a "national treasure" but that the structure of its financial, organizational, and creative activities was "fundamentally flawed." The commission—"Carnegie II," as it became known—proposed that the existing Corporation for Public Broadcasting (CPB) be replaced by a Public Telecommunications Trust and that its budget be increased to $1,160,000,000 by 1985, with $590 million of this to come from the federal government (as compared with $220 million currently authorized for 1983). The Public Telecommunications Trust would guide and maintain the public broadcasting system; programming would be handled by a separate Program Services Endowment operating under the Trust's umbrella but semiautonomous in its activities.

In the months that followed release of the report in February there were no significant efforts to implement its recommendations, but the CPB and the Public Broadcasting Service (PBS) made some changes of their own. The CPB board voted in June to adopt a new structure, setting up a Management Services Division and a separate Program Fund. The management unit would include all functions not associated with selection and funding of programs, including planning and research, station services, training, public affairs, and government relations. The Program Fund, with its own budget, would deal exclusively with programming and would be subject to CPB audit. CPB officials hoped to have all changes in effect, insofar as they applied to television, by Jan. 1, 1980.

A week after the CPB board's action PBS, public television's network operation, voted to create multiple program services under the auspices of a single system president and to separate the lobbying and membership functions of the network from the programming arm. With an unofficial target date of Jan. 1, 1980, three PBS networks were to be created, distributing programs simultaneously by satellite so that PBS stations could carry those of their choice.

In Europe there were strong pressures on governments to allow new private stations to be set up. The moves were most obvious in Israel, Italy, West Germany, Portugal, Spain, and the U.K. In each case the pressures resulted both from the shortcomings of the existing stations and from the desire for "something new." Another significant trend concerned the continuing financial troubles of those organizations—notably in Britain, West Germany, Australia, and Canada—that were financed by license fees.

In the U.K. the new Conservative government announced that it would introduce legislation to extend the Independent Broadcasting Authority's (IBA's) term beyond the current limit of Dec. 31, 1981, and also, more important, "give the authority the responsibility for the fourth channel subject to strict safeguards." This decision overturned the

Annan Committee's proposal (in 1978) to set up a new "open broadcasting authority" to run the fourth channel, which had been endorsed by the Labour government. In September the home secretary, William Whitelaw, said the main "safeguards" were to ensure major contributions from the smaller, regional Independent Television (ITV) companies and from independent production companies; to provide for specialist and minority interests; and to ensure that the channel would not succumb to the ratings war.

The BBC continued to slide into debt. The government's increase of the corporation's borrowing powers (from £30 million to £100 million) early in 1979 did little to increase revenue. The BBC therefore decided to negotiate with the government a long-term plan that would raise the license fee by a substantial amount and fix it for several years. From November 24 the license fee for colour television was raised from £25 to £35 and for black and white from £10 to £12. The government stated that the new fees would have to be maintained for at least two years.

In France there was further criticism of the reforms introduced in 1974. The Société Française de Production (SFP), the national TV and film production centre, incurred massive debts of more than U.S. $60 million. Attempts to make the company more compact and more efficient were only partially successful; in February the dismissal of 400 workers led to widespread strikes. A Senate commission of inquiry, which severely criticized the SFP and the state program companies for administrative and financial inefficiency, said that the 1974 reform was a failure and suggested that a new state holding company be set up to coordinate the existing organizations.

The Australian Broadcasting Tribunal held the country's first public hearing on the renewal of station licenses. The hearings, in Adelaide and Sydney, were surrounded by controversy on account of the presence of the public and the strong criticism of the commercial stations by many consumer and interest groups. The tribunal announced, however, that all the licenses were to be renewed; as a result the procedures and objectives were protested. In New Zealand the Broadcasting Corporation decided to end all separation between Channel 1 and Channel 2 (South Pacific Television) and to provide complementary schedules.

In China the new Beijing (Peking) television station started regular services in May with one channel. The original Beijing station was incorporated into the central broadcasting station (the national network) in January. Several Chinese stations started to accept advertising, from both domestic and foreign companies. The number of TV sets in China rose dramatically, to a reported total of 2.5 million.

Programming. U.S.-made comedies, mysteries, Westerns, made-for-television movies, and "miniseries"—dramatic programs in a limited number of episodes—remained popular in many countries. Sales of U.S. programs and feature films to overseas broadcasters were estimated by *Broadcasting* at $280 million for 1978, a 17% increase from the 1977 record of $240 million, and 1979 sales were expected to approach $300 million. Among the most widely sold were the "Roots," "Holocaust," "Rich Man, Poor Man," and "Centennial" miniseries and such regular series as "Starsky and Hutch," "Police Woman," Hawaii Five-O," "Gunsmoke," "Mod Squad," "Happy Days," "Charlie's Angels," and "The Mary Tyler Moore Show."

In the 1979–80 prime-time season that opened in September the three commercial television networks scheduled 19 new series, primarily comedies, comedy-dramas, and adventure programs. To accommodate them ABC dropped 4½ hours including "Battlestar Galactica," an expensive science-fiction series that had failed to live up to expectations that it would be one of the hits of the 1978–79 season; "Starsky and Hutch" and "Welcome Back, Kotter," two long-running hits, and three newer comedies, "What's Happening," "Delta House," and "Makin' It." CBS canceled "Paper Chase," a critically acclaimed drama that never won consistently large audiences; "The Mary Tyler Moore Hour," a variety show whose ratings had been disappointing; and an assortment of comedies for a total of 5½ hours. NBC's cancellations, totaling six hours, included the expensive and elaborately produced "Supertrain," a new Perils-of-Pauline type of drama called "Cliffhangers," and an ambitious drama anthology, "Novels for Television."

As the new season unfolded, it became apparent that the old program-mortality rule—that two-thirds of all new shows fail to survive into a second season—was still at work. Many of the new shows were shelved or replaced after a few weeks and more replacements were promised before the year ended. In the period from the opening of the season in mid-September through mid-December, the highest-rated series, in terms of average audience, were (in order): "60 Minutes," the widely

NBC PHOTO

One of TV's busiest actors, Harry Morgan, portrayed Harry Truman in "Backstairs at the White House," shown on NBC. Nancy Morgan played Truman's daughter, Margaret.

KEYSTONE

A performance of Benjamin Britten's opera for children, *Noah's Ark* was televised amid the ruins of the ancient castle of Diosgyor in Hungary, in October.

praised CBS newsmagazine; ABC's "Three's Company," and CBS's "Alice," "M*A*S*H," and "One Day at a Time," all comedies. Other series that rounded out the top 10 were: "The Jeffersons" and "Dallas" (CBS), "Eight Is Enough" (ABC), "Little House on the Prairie" (NBC), and, tied for tenth place, CBS's new "House Calls" and "Archie Bunker's Place." The last-named was the successor to "All in the Family," which had to undergo a format change after all of its stars except Carroll O'Connor had left the long-running series. The only other new series in the top 30 were "Trapper John, M.D." (CBS) in 18th place, and "Benson" (ABC), a spinoff from "Soap," in 23rd place.

The largest audience of the year was won by the theatrical blockbuster motion picture *Jaws*. Its November showing was watched in an estimated 29,760,000 homes per average minute, second only to the 1976 showing of *Gone With the Wind* (33,890,000 homes) among all movies seen on television. The *Jaws* audience was the 14th largest in TV history, surpassed only by the seven episodes of the "Roots" miniseries, three Super Bowl football games, a Super Bowl pregame show, and the two episodes of *Gone With the Wind*. A "Roots" sequel, "Roots: The Next Generations," presented in February 1979 as a seven-part miniseries, was among the year's highest-rated shows, with an estimated average per-minute audience of 22,424,500 homes. (*See* Special Report.)

Television networks and stations continued to try to improve their programming for children, eliminating or playing down violence and racial and sexual stereotypes and adding variety shows, news broadcasts, and informational messages, especially in their Saturday morning schedules. Game shows and serials remained the staples of weekday daytime television. Among the serials 60-minute episodes were beginning to take over from the half-hour unit, and one serial, "Another World," was expanded further to 90 minutes. In October-November, nine of the top ten daytime shows in audience popularity were serials.

In the 31st annual Emmy awards, the Academy of Television Arts and Sciences voted "Lou Grant" the outstanding drama series and "Taxi" the best comedy series. "Roots: The Next Generations" won the award for best limited series. Other winners included: "The Lion, the Witch and the Wardrobe" for an animated program; "Balanchine IV, Dance in America" for a classical program in the performing arts; "Christmas Eve on Sesame Street" for a children's program; "Scared Straight" for an informational program; "Steve and Eydie Celebrate Irving Berlin" for a comedy-variety or music program; "The Tonight Show Starring Johnny Carson" and "Lifeline" for program achievement, special class; and "Friendly Fire" for a comedy or drama special. Ron Leibman of "Kaz" and Mariette Hartley of "The Incredible Hulk" were voted outstanding lead actor and actress in dramatic series, and Carroll O'Connor of "All in the Family" and Ruth Gordon of "Sugar Mama" on "Taxi" the lead actor and actress in a comedy series. Walter Cronkite, CBS News anchorman, received the annual special award of the Academy's governors. Among daytime shows "Ryan's Hope" was named the outstanding drama series; Al Freeman, Jr., of "One Life to Live" and Irene Dailey of "Another World" were voted best actor and actress; "Hollywood Squares" was named outstanding game or audience participation show; "Kids Are People Too" was chosen as outstanding children's series; and "Donahue" was voted outstanding talk, service, or variety show, with its host, Phil Donahue, named outstanding host or hostess in a talk, service, or variety series.

Sports continued to attract huge audiences and high prices. *Broadcasting* estimated that television and radio networks and stations paid $201,216,571 for rights to broadcast professional and college football games in 1979, or about $1 million more than in 1978, and $54.5 million to broadcast major league baseball, an increase of almost $2 million. Audiences remained large. Some or all of the Super Bowl football game between the Pittsburgh Steelers and Dallas Cowboys in January was watched by an estimated 96.6 million viewers, and the crucial seventh game of the World Series baseball championship in October was seen by approximately 80 million. More sports were in store. ABC was preparing to telecast 51 hours of the 1980 Winter Olympic Games at Lake Placid, N.Y., in February 1980, and NBC was getting ready for 150 hours of Summer Olympics at Moscow in July and August. ABC signed to pay $225 million for TV rights to the 1984 Olympics at Los Angeles, almost three times as much as the $87 million NBC paid for the rights to the Moscow games. Earlier, NBC and ABC signed new TV contracts for major league baseball through 1983, at prices approximately double those for the past four years.

News and public affairs remained high-priority fare, representing about one-fourth of television air time. President Carter continued to be one of its most consistent users. By November he had held

52 televised press conferences since taking office, but he was also changing his format. During the summer he abandoned his twice-a-month press conferences in favour of "town hall" meetings, regional press conferences, and other less formal approaches. But he still depended on national television to reach the nation on critical issues, as in his July speech following his ten-day round of conferences at Camp David and a November speech on the Iranian crisis.

The House of Representatives meanwhile ended its traditional ban on electronic news coverage of its floor proceedings. Beginning in March the House provided live coverage regularly, with networks and stations free to pick up whatever portions they wished.

Music and news remained the backbone of radio programming. FM continued to gain ground. In a *Broadcasting* study published in September, identifying the highest-rated ten stations in each of the top 50 U.S. markets, over half of the stations were FM. The most popular program formats, *Broadcasting* found, were those built around varying forms of contemporary music, represented by 26.1% of the radio (AM and FM) stations. "Beautiful music" was the staple at 17.2% of the stations, rock music at 13.3%, country music at 8.7%, "middle of the road" music at 6.9%, music programming for blacks at 5.7%, and disco music at 4.2%. News and news-talk were the predominant fare at 9.1% of the stations.

While preparing to launch the new system offering its stations a choice of three programs simultaneously, PBS introduced a major change in its existing service. Most of its stations agreed to play four nights of PBS programs at the same time, beginning with the new schedule introduced in the fall. This enabled PBS to mount a more effective program-promotion campaign than had been possible under the old system, in which PBS stations scheduled the programs as they wished.

The visits of Pope John Paul II to Poland, Mexico, Ireland, and the U.S. occasioned massive television coverage in the countries concerned. In Ireland Radio Telefis Eireann televised the pope's blessing of one million people, nearly one-third of the population. In all countries lightweight electronic news cameras and satellites were used extensively to record the events and transmit the pictures as wide and as quickly as possible.

The U.S. "Holocaust" drama series on the Nazi extermination of the Jews continued to provoke controversy wherever it was shown. In Europe many of the "first" national networks refused to buy it, but even when shown on "secondary" networks it attracted record audiences. In West Germany its showing (on the third, regional ARD network) was preceded by several bomb explosions and heated arguments, but it attracted more praise than blame. (*See* GERMANY, FEDERAL REPUBLIC OF: *Special Report*.)

On June 6 Eurovision, the program exchange operated by the Swiss-based European Broadcasting Union (EBU), celebrated 25 years of exchanges. In 1978 it originated 5,934 news items and relayed 153,178 items, including news film shown at its

WARC-1979

In the last three months of the year, 142 government delegations met in Geneva to revise the international regulations for the radio spectrum. The World Administrative Radio Conference (WARC) had been called by the International Telecommunication Union (ITU), a UN agency, which is responsible for the international management of the spectrum, including the allocation of frequencies. The WARC can be described as the most important communications conference in 20 years.

The ITU has held such conferences every few years to discuss either specific services (such as mobile radio) or a particular region. But the 1979 WARC was a much grander affair. It aimed, first, to determine the basic principles on which the ITU should operate and, second, to plan the allocation of the spectrum from 1980 until the end of the century and beyond. The conference's decisions have the status of an international treaty.

The ITU had called this special WARC for a number of reasons. Since the last such general WARC in 1959, many new countries had been established. New services had been introduced, and the use of telecommunications, especially radio, had increased enormously. As a result the ITU's existing regulations were out-of-date.

Roberto Severini of Argentina was appointed chairman of the conference, and the opening session took place on September 24. A major issue involved the high-frequency bands between 3 and 30 MHz, used mostly for international short-wave broadcasting and for such fixed telecommunications services as telephones. The industrial countries wanted to expand the allocations to international broadcasting, mainly because they tended to use even higher frequencies for their fixed services. They were joined by several third world countries in their demands. However, many countries wanted to keep their fixed allocations. The conference eventually agreed on only a minimal increase in the allocations to broadcasting and those on frequencies that are not most suited for broadcasting. The results of the conference were to come into force on Jan. 1, 1982.

WARC also decided to hold several future conferences on frequency bands. Future world conferences were scheduled to be held on the mobile services, the high-frequency broadcasting services (fixed for 1984), the space services, and the aeronautical mobile service. Others would be held for one or more of the ITU's three regions.

The feeling after the conference was a mixture of relief that the expected political confrontation did not materialize and apprehension over the heavy workload the ITU had given itself over the next five years. WARC signaled clearly that governments would have to take increasing cognizance of the radio spectrum. (JOHN HOWKINS) thrice-daily news exchanges. A special "Jubilee Gala" program was broadcast from Montreux, Switz., on May 13.

In the U.K. ITV's screens were blank because of a major strike over pay from July 23 to October 24. During the strike the BBC's two channels had a monopoly, but the corporation was criticized for the dullness of its usual summer mix of repeats, sports, and "minority" programs and for not taking advantage of the situation to attract new viewers. Its response was that it did not have the money to do so.

Twice the BBC had a bitter row with Prime Minister Margaret Thatcher. In July its evening current affairs program "Tonight" broadcast an interview with a member of the Irish group allegedly involved in the assassination of Airey Neave, a close personal friend of the prime minister. The interview struck many viewers as callous and unnecessarily harrowing for Neave's widow. The prime minister threatened to ask the attorney general to start legal proceedings against the BBC; however, no action was taken. The BBC acknowledged that it had "clearly misjudged the emotional impact on those particularly involved." There was more trouble in November when it was suggested that "Panorama" had asked the Provisional Irish Republican Army to "capture" an Ulster village solely for the purpose of filming such an event. The film was seized by the police acting under the 1976 Prevention of Terrorism Act.

Dennis Potter maintained his preeminence among Britain's TV dramatists with "Blue Remembered Hills" (BBC), in which all the characters were children—but played by adults, a risky device that succeeded well. Two plays by Ian Curteis, "Churchill and the Generals" and "Suez" (both BBC), dealt with those major historical events with skill and accuracy. "Prince Regent" (BBC), with Peter Egan as the future George IV, was somewhat freer in its historical approach. "Telford's Change," a BBC drama series screened on Sunday evenings to loyal audiences and critical acclaim, was keenly watched by the industry because it had been produced in a novel manner. The writer (Brian Clarke), producer (Mark Shivas), director (Barry Davis), and star (Peter Barkworth) set up a company, Astramead, to own and produce the series, only then selling the BBC the rights to two transmissions. This kind of contract, favouring independent artists over the BBC (or ITV), was seen as the forerunner of a future trend. Associated Television's (ATV's) "Crossroads," the U.K.'s first and most enduring soap opera, was ordered by the IBA to be reduced from four to three episodes weekly. It was the first time the IBA had ever issued such a direct order.

In March the BBC introduced new guidelines on the portrayal of violence. It stressed the need for caution and said the principle of not showing programs unsuitable for children before 9 PM should be maintained. If ITV were to collaborate, the BBC said 10 PM would be more suitable.

In the U.S.S.R. in November 1978 Pres. Leonid Brezhnev strongly criticized Soviet television's coverage of current affairs, which he said was dull and uninformative. In response, several new programs were inaugurated, including "Today in the World," transmitted twice daily from Dec. 1, 1978. A new English-language radio service broadcasting news and popular music 19 hours daily was also introduced.

In Australia the year's most-watched program was "Against the Wind" (Channel 7), a historical drama series. "The Last Tasmanian," a documentary, also won much praise. The major trend was the increasing use of Australian-made serials, such as "The Young Doctors," "The Restless Years," and "Patrol Boat." In sports Kerry Packer, head of Channel 9, bought exclusive TV rights to Australian test cricket for three years starting in October 1980. Children's programming was severely criticized by the Australian Broadcasting Tribunal, which required each commercial station (its authority did not extend to the Australian Broadcasting Commission) to transmit three (later, five) hours a week of children's programs between 4 PM and 5 PM. In Japan TBS, the leading Tokyo network, broke the long-standing barrier against U.S. thriller series by transmitting "Starsky and Hutch," but most of its affiliates refused to join the screening and audiences remained small, both feeling that the series was too mild. Attempts to introduce women on the screen were equally unsuccessful.

At the 31st Prix Italia, the leading international TV and radio festival, the TV drama prizes were won by "The Golden Eels" (Czechoslovakia) and "Dummy" (ITV, Britain); the TV documentary prizes by "A Trial for Rape" (RAI, Italy) and "The Best Place in the World" (Finland); and the TV music prizes by "Christina—Music for a Winter Queen" (Sweden) and "The Drifting Reed" (Japan). (RUFUS W. CRATER; JOHN HOWKINS; SOL J. TAISHOFF)

Amateur Radio. The number of amateur radio operators continued to rise in 1979. The American Radio Relay League, the leading organization of amateur ("ham") radio operators, reported 362,356 licensed operators in the U.S. as of Sept. 30, 1979, a gain of about 3.3% in 12 months. The earlier boom in the Citizens Radio Service (citizens band, or CB) was credited with some of the increase, resulting from CB users becoming interested in the more sophisticated field of amateur radio, but this effect was declining as the CB boom subsided. The number of licensed ham stations, including those operated by clubs and those of some operators who under former rules had been licensed to operate two stations, was put at 375,519. Throughout the world there were approximately 1.1 million licensed amateur radio operators in November 1979.

Ham operators continued their tradition of providing vital communications services in emergencies when normal links are down. In the wake of Hurricane David, for example, networks of amateurs served as the links in many areas but particularly in Dominica, where they provided the only access to the outside world for several days.

(RUFUS W. CRATER; SOL J. TAISHOFF)

See also Industrial Review: *Advertising; Telecommunications;* Motion Pictures; Music.
[613.D.4.b; 735.I.4–5]

THE RATING WARS

by Laurence Michie

Even schoolchildren appalled by the complexity of basic arithmetic are apt to be fascinated by an arcane branch of statistics fully understood by only a handful of experts—television ratings. The fact is that what U.S. viewers see on their television screens is determined to a very great extent by the audience measurement system known as ratings, whose ebb and flow regulate the tide of millions of dollars in advertising.

Ratings and Shares. Although the importance of ratings to television has long been established, in recent years the devotion to ratings by television networks and stations has become, if possible, even more slavish.

The television industry measures its audience by two numbers, ratings and shares. A third number, households using television (HUT), defines the relationship between them. A rating is an absolute measure of viewing, while a share is relative, depending on HUT. Two commercial services, the A. C. Nielsen Co. and Arbitron, provide those numbers to the television business.

About 98% of U.S. households now have at least one television set. Nielsen currently bases its research on an estimated 76.3 million U.S. households. Those households average more than six hours a day of television set use. A rating is the percentage of total TV homes watching a given show. A 20 rating, therefore, means that 20% of the 76.3 million U.S. TV homes, or 15,260,000 homes, had a set tuned to that program. (Network ratings generally are based on the number of households watching during the average minute of a program. To be counted, a TV set must be tuned in for at least one minute in a given show.)

The HUT figure measures how many of the total homes had a set in use. HUT varies widely but is highest during "prime time"—8 PM to 11 PM Eastern Standard Time—and on a weekly basis is highest Sunday night and lowest Friday night and/or Saturday night. A share is based on the percentage of homes with sets actually turned on. Thus a program with a 20 rating on Sunday night during the fall-to-spring network "season" might have a 35 share, since HUT then is very high, but that same 20 rating might equate with a 45 share during the summer, when fewer sets are in use because many people are involved in outdoor activities or are away from home on vacation. Ratings measure "in-home" set use only, not TV viewing in such places as hotels, motels, and bars.

Since ratings measure homes watching, the actual number of viewers of a particular show can only be estimated by various formulas. A television network may publicize the estimate that 70 million viewers saw a particular special event, for example, but that estimate is not a rating, though it is made on the basis of ratings data. Survey techniques do yield actual head counts, but those figures take weeks and months to compile. The network ratings that are generally publicized measure only homes.

Making the Count. Ratings are determined by electronic registers in sample homes, by telephone surveys, and by "diaries" mailed to a random selection of families. These various methods are used by researchers to cross-check findings as well as for their basic data. In recent years, advertisers have become much more selective in buying commercial time, which is priced according to the number of viewers delivered to the advertiser. Often advertisers and their agencies "buy demographics," that is, place orders according to ratings broken down by age, sex, income, and other variables. Women aged 18 to 34 have been the prime targets because they control a great deal of the country's discretionary income. As the characteristics of the population change, the prime advertising targets will change along with them. Thus, as the population ages, one can expect more advertising aimed at viewers in the upper age brackets.

There are both national and local ratings. Nielsen, through its approximately 1,200 electronically measured sample homes, provides the national rating numbers that are most frequently cited, and both Nielsen and Arbitron also do local market surveys. There are other rating companies, particularly in the radio business, but Nielsen and Arbitron are the two principal ones.

How accurate are the ratings? A trained researcher will find in all reports carefully detailed qualifica-

Laurence Michie is television editor of Variety.

tions to data that indicate the range of error for each bit of information, but the numbers themselves naturally tend to be cited as concrete figures rather than approximations. Generally speaking, the smaller the sample of viewers and the more detailed the demographic information, the greater the margin of error. But by the end of a network television season, the rankings of series can be relied on. They have been measured and cross-checked too many times for there to be serious statistical doubt.

In one sense, the reliability of ratings is irrelevant. The broadcast industry and the advertisers that support it need some yardstick by which to measure performance. Ratings provide that business tool. How much is a rating point worth? In mid-1979 an advertising executive calculated: "The value of a rating point in today's market is approximately $5,500 and can mean a difference of $40 million over the course of a full season for each network."

Various committees and review processes within the industry monitor the professionalism of the ratings services, and generally there are few complaints. But whatever the level of dissatisfaction—and stations and networks with low ratings have a tendency toward somewhat greater dissatisfaction than those with high ratings—the fact is that ratings are necessary to the conduct of business. What needs to be borne in mind is the admonition of Hugh M. Beville, Jr., executive director of the Broadcast Rating Council Inc., an industry watchdog group: "One, all ratings are estimates, and two, there is no perfect rating service."

1979–80 U.S. Network Series Ratings

Rank	Series	Average	1978
1.	60 Minutes (CBS)	28.4	24.2
2.	Three's Company (ABC)	27.2	29.5
3.	Alice (CBS)	26.1	22.9
4.	M*A*S*H (CBS)	25.4	25.2
5.	One Day at a Time (CBS)	24.8	23.5
	The Jeffersons (CBS)	24.8	16.4
7.	Dallas (CBS)	24.3	16.5
	Eight Is Enough (ABC)	24.3	22.1
9.	Little House on the Prairie (NBC)	23.5	25.0
10.	Archie Bunker's Place (CBS)	23.2	23.3
	House Calls (CBS)	23.2	–
12.	WKRP in Cincinnati (CBS)	22.9	16.8
	Taxi (ABC)	22.9	24.5
14.	Charlie's Angels (ABC)	22.2	24.8
	Happy Days (ABC)	22.2	26.9
16.	Angie (ABC)	22.1	–
17.	Dukes of Hazzard (CBS)	21.9	–
18.	Trapper John, M.D. (CBS)	21.7	–
	CHiPs (NBC)	21.7	19.3
20.	Mork & Mindy (ABC)	20.9	25.8

Shown are the 20 television series with the highest average ratings for the first 14 weeks of the 1979–80 season (Sept. 14 to Dec. 23, 1979). The figures for 1978 are for the comparable period of that year. Of the 26 new series aired in the period, 10 were canceled and 4 more were taken off the schedule temporarily. Competition was fierce; 15 of the 20 lowest rated programs (out of a total 76 shows) were new series.

Only in the U.S., incidentally, does the use of ratings become obsessive. Other countries have ratings methods of one kind or another, but they tend to be occasional and somewhat casual. When broadcasting is a state monopoly—as is the case in many countries—it needs to concern itself very little with competition. Mixed systems put more stress on audience reach. In Britain, for example, the noncommercial BBC and the commercial network have separate rating services. Not surprisingly, the ratings leader varies according to who sponsors the survey. During 1979, however, the two networks made considerable progress with negotiations to underwrite a single joint rating service.

Networks at War. The 1978–79 network television season in the U.S. elevated ratings very nearly to the point of deification. For some 20 years prior to 1976, CBS had been the top-rated television network, followed by NBC and—so far to the rear it was referred to as "half a network"—ABC. The 96-pound weakling suddenly grew muscles, however, and in recent years the ranking has been ABC, CBS, and NBC, with the latter lagging as far behind as ABC once did. This change in the established hierarchy of ratings position caused upheavals at CBS and NBC, with dozens of jobs lost and a panicky shuffling of programs. Many series were canceled after only a few weeks, a departure from traditional network practice that brought into the homes of viewers the turmoil being experienced at network headquarters.

By the 1978–79 season, profits had weakened at CBS and NBC, though both continued to be very profitable, given the demand for commercial time. But there was also a new factor that raised the stakes considerably. During its years of relative failure, ABC had been hampered because in many cities it had only third choice among TV stations. Local stations that were dominant in their own communities through powerful signals and strong local programming tended to affiliate with CBS or NBC. Now ABC began to tempt CBS and NBC stations into switching network allegiance. A few such affiliation shifts consolidated ABC's gains, assuring a greater audience reach for its entertainment shows and providing stronger local news programs adjacent to the ABC network newscast, the one segment of its programming that had remained in third place.

The Programming Shell Game. Outside of the biggest local markets, New York City, Los Angeles, Chicago, and San Francisco, which have continuous ratings, television stations base their advertising sales primarily on occasional local ratings—the so-called sweeps. These local rating periods occur in November, February, May, and July, though the summer sweep is relatively unimportant. Stations have always pressured the networks with which

SIDNEY HARRIS

"True, the rating is low, but it has earned a great deal of respect among people who never watch television."

they are affiliated to concentrate popular special programming—blockbuster theatrical motion pictures, for example—in the sweep periods, so the higher ratings such shows attract will show up in the local "sweep books" and subsequently improve local advertising.

Therefore, in 1978–79 not only did the networks face their usual intense competitive ratings struggle but CBS and NBC had to bolster their stations during the sweeps or risk hastening further affiliate defections. And ABC, naturally, was determined to increase its domination of the ratings. The apotheosis of what many in the industry considered "ratings madness" came during the February sweep period. On Feb. 11, 1979—a Sunday, the evening with the largest viewing audience—ABC scheduled "Elvis," a made-for-television movie about the late rock singer Elvis Presley, against CBS's repeat showing of *Gone with the Wind* and NBC's telecast of the Oscar-garlanded motion picture *One Flew over the Cuckoo's Nest*. Some $18 million in network programming was involved. ABC narrowly won the ratings confrontation, with NBC third, though all three shows had high ratings. More than 70% of the country's homes viewed one of the three programs.

Some network executives—to say nothing of the medium's critics—thought that pitting three such expensive and popular programs against each other amounted to counterproductive and wasteful competitiveness. CBS took the lead in asking that the sweep ratings be extended to yearlong measurements so that such a debilitating contest might not occur again. The television stations themselves, concerned about the many millions of dollars that would be required to finance 52-week sweeps, effectively buried the proposal. The networks, nevertheless, have deplored their own past wastefulness and have vowed to be less profligate in their program confrontations in the future. It is safe to predict, however, that the networks, whatever their promises, will continue to respond to the dictates of competitive circumstances.

That February 1979 showdown won by "Elvis" may stand as the high—or low—point of network ratings warfare. During 1979 the A. C. Nielsen Co. made available, for the first time, its ratings for cable television and the pay-television services offered by cable. As such services grow and flourish, the U.S. public undoubtedly will change its patterns of TV viewing and hence the pattern of ratings. For the time being, however, the system remains, its flaws acknowledged but its necessity undiminished.

Tennis

Attendance at the 1979 Wimbledon championships was a record 343,044 and at the U.S. championships a record 305,311. During a match at the U.S. Open meeting at Flushing Meadow Park in New York City between Ilie Nastase (Romania) and John McEnroe (U.S.), Nastase was disqualified by the umpire because he failed to continue playing, but the crowd became so disruptive that to preserve order the ruling was rescinded.

Administratively, more cohesion was promised when Philippe Chatrier, president of the French Tennis Federation, was reelected president of the International Tennis Federation (ITF) and then elected president of the Men's Professional Council. An innovation of the ITF was the nomination of world champions, based on 1978's records: Björn Borg of Sweden and Chris Evert Lloyd of the U.S. were so named. The tournament structure changed with the demise of World Team Tennis, the U.S. intercity league which since its foundation in 1973 had prevented many leading players from competing in traditional tournaments.

At the age of 35 Billie Jean King (U.S.) won the women's doubles championship at Wimbledon with Martina Navratilova, a Czechoslovak living in the U.S. It was King's 20th Wimbledon title. She had held the record of 19 titles jointly with her fellow Californian Elizabeth Ryan. The day before King achieved her record, Ryan, aged 87, collapsed in the dressing room at Wimbledon and died (*see* OBITUARIES).

Men's Competition. The Grand Prix for 1978 was won by Jimmy Connors (U.S.), winner of 10 out of the 13 qualifying tournaments in which he competed, and second place was taken by Borg, the victor in 7 out of 14 qualifying tournaments. Neither played a sufficient number of tournaments to earn the bonus prize money. This reward, worth $300,000, went to Eddie Dibbs (U.S.), who finished in third place and won 4 out of 27 tournaments. The subsequent Masters' Tournament was again staged in Madison Square Garden, New York City, in January 1979. Borg did not play, and Connors withdrew because of a blistered foot during the round-robin stage of the event. Arthur Ashe of the U.S., U.S. Open champion of 1968 and Wimbledon champion of 1975, was an unexpected finalist. He twice came within a point of winning before John McEnroe (*see* BIOGRAPHIES) beat him 6–7, 6–3, 7–5. The Australian title went to Guillermo Vilas of Argentina, who beat John Marks of Australia 6–4, 6–4, 3–6, 6–3 in the final in Melbourne.

The series of tournaments organized by World Championship Tennis (WCT) maintained its identity in 1979 but was incorporated into the Grand Prix Series. The WCT finals, for which the eight leading players from eight tournaments qualified, were again staged in Dallas, Texas, in early May. The event was a triumph for McEnroe. In the semifinals he beat Connors, while Borg beat Vitas Gerulaitis (U.S.). In the final McEnroe defeated Borg 7–5, 4–6, 6–2, 7–6.

Gerulaitis won the championship of Italy for the second time. He repeated his 1977 success, winning the final in Rome against Vilas by 6–7, 7–6,

Sweden's Björn Borg and Martina Navratilova of the U.S. hold aloft their trophies after winning at Wimbledon. Borg won the men's singles title for the fourth straight year, and Navratilova beat Chris Evert Lloyd to win the women's singles title for the second straight year.

PHOTOS, UPI

6–7, 6–4, 6–2. The West German championship was won by José Higueras of Spain with a 3–6, 6–1, 6–4, 6–1 victory in the final against Harold Solomon (U.S.).

Borg, who first won the French championship in 1974 when he was just 18 years old, took the title in Paris for the fourth time, the first to do so since Henri Cochet (France) in 1932. In the semifinal round he overwhelmed Gerulaitis 6–2, 6–1, 6–0 and in the final beat Victor Pecci 6–3, 6–1, 6–7, 6–4. Pecci was the first player from Paraguay to achieve such success in tennis. To reach the final he beat Corrado Barazzutti of Italy, seeded 15th, Solomon, seeded sixth, Vilas, seeded third, and the second-seeded Connors by 7–5, 6–4, 5–7, 6–3 in the semifinal.

In the Wimbledon championships in London Borg won the men's singles for the fourth successive year. He was taken to five sets twice, in the second round, by Vijay Amritraj (India), and in the final in July by the U.S. left-hander Roscoe Tanner, whom he beat 6–7, 6–1, 3–6, 6–3, 6–4. Borg beat Connors in the semifinal 6–2, 6–3, 6–2. Tim Gullikson (U.S.) beat McEnroe, the second seed, 6–4, 6–2, 6–4 in the fourth round and lost to Tanner in the quarterfinals. Borg's sequence of success at Wimbledon was unparalleled. Rod Laver of Australia won in four years of competition, 1961, 1962, 1968, and 1969, being barred by his professional status from competing in the intervening years. The last player to take the title four years in a row was Tony Wilding of New Zealand in 1910–13, when the challenge-round system exempted the defending champion from playing until the final round.

Borg did not maintain his invincibility through the U.S. Open championships. Tanner beat him in the quarterfinals 6–2, 4–6, 6–2, 7–6. Nor did Connors maintain his ascendancy of 1974, 1976, and 1978. McEnroe beat Connors in a semifinal match 6–3, 6–3, 7–5. In the other semifinal Gerulaitis beat Tanner 3–6, 2–6, 7–6, 6–3, 6–3. In the final McEnroe beat Gerulaitis 7–5, 6–3, 6–3. McEnroe thus won three major events staged in the U.S., the Masters' Tournament, the WCT finals, and the U.S. Open.

In doubles McEnroe and his compatriot Peter Fleming were outstanding. In January they won the WCT "World Doubles Championship" at Olympia, London, and the Masters' Tournament in New York City. They subsequently won many events, including the Wimbledon and U.S. Open championships. At Wimbledon they beat the titleholders, Bob Hewitt and Frew McMillan of South Africa, 6–3, 7–6, 6–1 in the semifinals and Brian Gottfried (U.S.) and Raúl Ramirez (Mexico) 4–6, 6–4, 6–2, 6–2 in the final. In the U.S. Open they came within one point of losing their quarterfinal match against Bruce Manson (U.S.) and Andrew Pattison (Zimbabwe Rhodesia) but rallied to defeat them 4–6, 7–5, 6–3; they won the final against the long-established U.S. combination of Bob Lutz and Stan Smith by 6–2, 6–4.

In the Davis Cup the U.S. had no difficulty in taking the first two steps in defense of the trophy, winning 5–0 against Colombia in Cleveland, Ohio, and 4–1 against Argentina in Memphis, Tenn., for the American Zone championship. Australia beat India 3–2 in Madras and New Zealand 3–2 in Christchurch to win the Eastern Zone. Czechoslovakia won European Zone "B," beating France 4–1 in Paris and Sweden 3–2 in Prague; the Swedish team was dominated by Borg. Italy won European Zone "A," defeating Denmark 5–0 in Palermo, Poland 4–1 in Warsaw, and Hungary 3–2 and Great Britain 4–1 in Rome. The U.S. and Italy qualified for the final round when at the semifinal stage the U.S. beat Australia 4–1 in Sydney and Italy defeated Czechoslovakia 4–1 in Rome. McEnroe and Gerulaitis each won two singles for the U.S. in its 20th victory against Australia in 37 contests, but the U.S. doubles pair, Smith and Lutz, was beaten (by John Alexander and Phil Dent) for the first time in 12 Davis Cups since 1968. Adriano Panatta, Barazzutti, and Paolo Bertolucci comprised the winning Italian team, identical with that which won the Davis Cup in 1976. In the finals, at San Francisco, the U.S. (McEnroe, Gerulaitis, Smith, Lutz) beat Italy (Panatta, Barazzutti, Bertolucci, Antonio Zugarelli) 5–0 in straight sets to win its 26th Davis Cup.

Women's Competition. Chris Evert (U.S.) had been successful at the end of the 1978 season when she won both the Colgate-Palmolive International series and the subsequent Series championship, but during 1979 both Navratilova and Tracy Austin showed stronger form. In the early part of the year Navratilova dominated the Avon series, the women's circuit of tournaments that replaced the Virginia Slims series in the U.S. She also won the subsequent Avon championships at Madison Square Garden in March, beating Austin 6–3, 3–6, 6–2 in the final.

Evert married the British player John Lloyd in April. In May Austin beat her in the semifinals of the Italian championships and went on to win the title. Both the Italian and West German tournaments broke new ground by separating the women's events from the men's and playing them at different times (in the case of the German, at a different site, West Berlin for the women instead of the traditional Hamburg). Evert Lloyd competed in the French championships in Paris in June for the first time since her successes of 1974 and 1975. She had little difficulty in winning with neither Austin nor Navratilova competing.

Prior to the Wimbledon championships Navratilova and Evert Lloyd met in the final of the Eastbourne tournament in Sussex, England, on grass. Evert Lloyd won 7–5, 5–7, 13–11 after one of the best women's matches ever seen. At Wimbledon Navratilova beat Austin in the semifinal by 7–5, 6–1 and Evert Lloyd in the final by 6–4, 6–4 to take the title for the second straight year.

Evert Lloyd also reached the final of the U.S. Open in her bid to win that championship for a record fifth successive year. But she was beaten 6–4, 6–3 by Austin, who had defeated Navratilova 7–5, 7–5 in the semifinals. Austin at 16 became the youngest U.S. Open champion.

The 1979 Federation Cup was staged in Madrid in May. The U.S. (Evert Lloyd, Austin, King, and Rosemary Casals) beat Australia in the final, 3–0. In the Wightman Cup, staged at the Royal Albert

Hall, London, in November 1978, Great Britain (Virginia Wade, Sue Barker, Michele Tyler, Sue Mappin, and Anne Hobbs) beat the U.S. (Evert, Austin, Pam Shriver, King) 4–3 for its tenth win in 50 contests. In November 1979, however, the U.S. team (Evert Lloyd, Austin, Kathy Jordan, Ann Kiyomura, and Casals) avenged itself by sweeping Great Britain (Wade, Barker, Hobbs, Jo Durie, and Debbie Jevans) 7–0 in West Palm Beach, Fla. (LANCE TINGAY)

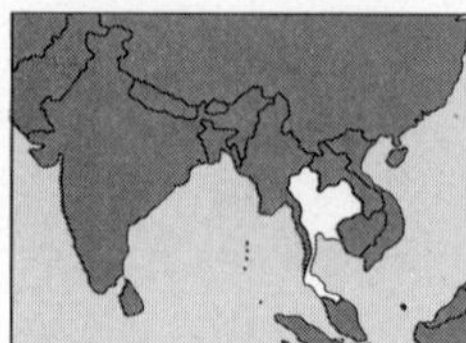

Thailand

Thailand

A constitutional monarchy of Southeast Asia, Thailand is bordered by Burma, Laos, Cambodia, Malaysia, the Andaman Sea, and the Gulf of Thailand. Area: 542,373 sq km (209,411 sq mi). Pop. (1978 est.): 45.1 million. Cap. and largest city: Bangkok (pop., 1978 est., 4,875,000). Language: Thai. Religion (1970): Buddhist 95.3%; Muslim 3.8%. King, Bhumibol Adulyadej; prime minister in 1979, Gen. Kriangsak Chamanand; chairman of the National Policy Council, Adm. Sa-ngad Chaloryu.

In the early months of 1979 electoral politics dominated the scene, but the year quickly dissolved into a time of war worries for Thailand. The only surprise in the April 22 election to the National Assembly was the collapse of the country's oldest and biggest political grouping, the Democrat Party. Nationally it won only 32 seats in the 301-seat House of Representatives, while in Bangkok, its traditional stronghold, it lost 31 out of 32 constituencies. The biggest winner was former prime minister Kukrit Pramoj's Social Action Party, which collected 82 seats. The spotlight, however, fell on the recently formed Prachakorn Thai (Thai People's) Party, led by outspoken and controversial former interior minister Samak Sundaravej. Fielding only 43 candidates, it captured 32 seats, establishing itself as a party with mass appeal and therefore an unpredictable factor in future political calculations.

Buddhist monks watch the construction of a huge election returns board which was erected in Bangkok to show the results of the April 22 election. The biggest winner was the Social Action Party, which collected 82 seats in the 301-seat House of Representatives.

WIDE WORLD

A special session of Parliament on May 11 returned Kriangsak Chamanand as prime minister. Summoned at one day's notice, the session was boycotted by the Social Action, Thai Nation, and Thai People's parties, but Kriangsak was assured of a majority through the support of the 225 nominated members of the Senate. The fortunes of the parties thus barely affected the composition of the new government that was announced on May 24.

Electoral politics did not prevent Kriangsak from continuing his policy of personal diplomacy through a series of foreign tours. In January, with a trip to Laos, he became the first Thai prime minister to visit Communist Indochina. In February he paid a two-day visit to Britain. Thereafter he spent nearly two weeks in the U.S., meeting congressional and military leaders as well as Pres. Jimmy Carter and UN Secretary-General Kurt Waldheim. Among the items discussed were military supplies, weapons training for Thai personnel, and absorption of more Indochinese refugees from Thailand. In March Kriangsak made the first official visit to the Soviet Union by a Thai government leader. As with his visit to China the previous year, it was considered a reconnaissance mission on behalf of the Association of Southeast Asian Nations (ASEAN). Kriangsak denied reports that Thai territory was being used as a conduit for channeling Chinese supplies to Pol Pot's Khmer Rouge guerrillas in Cambodia.

As the year progressed, however, it was the prospect of war that weighed most heavily. By October, with a Vietnamese push against the remnants of Pol Pot's forces in full swing and the influx of refugees from Cambodia beyond control, there were fears that Vietnam would trespass into Thai territory and thereby trigger a conflagration. Against a background of border skirmishes, Kriangsak took off on a lightning tour of ASEAN capitals, apparently to coordinate policy, but he rushed home after the first stop in Kuala Lumpur, Malaysia. There was speculation that some frontline commanders, angered by Vietnamese forays into their territory, were threatening to strike back regardless of Bangkok's instructions.

Alarmed by rising tensions, Kriangsak asked for an international fact-finding mission to go to the border. As the year drew to a close, half a million Cambodians had gathered in the border regions seeking refuge from the intensifying war. Thai authorities put up what were described as the biggest refugee camps in the world. International assistance began flowing in, but prospects of a sudden deterioration in the military situation kept the country on tenterhooks.

Bank of Thailand Governor Snoh Unakul forecast in August that the year's trade deficit would

Textiles:
see Industrial Review

THAILAND

Education. (1976–77) Primary, pupils 6,810,747, teachers 270,567; secondary, pupils 1,049,360, teachers 34,450; vocational, pupils 165,566, teachers 9,411; teacher training, students 44,156, teachers 5,639; higher, students 81,696, teaching staff (universities only) 7,757.

Finance. Monetary unit: baht, with (Sept. 17, 1979) a free rate of 20.16 baht to U.S. $1 (43.37 baht = £ 1 sterling). Gold, SDR's, and foreign exchange (June 1979) U.S. $2,296,000,000. Budget (1978 actual): revenue 65,042,000,000 baht; expenditure 78,292,000,000 baht. Gross national product (1978) 441,950,000,000 baht. Money supply (Feb. 1979) 58,940,000,000 baht. Cost of living (1975 = 100; June 1979) 130.2.

Foreign Trade. (1978) Imports 108,859,000,000 baht; exports 83,065,000,000 baht. Import sources: Japan 31%; U.S. 14%; West Germany 6%; Saudi Arabia 6%. Export destinations: Japan 20%; The Netherlands 15%; U.S. 11%; Singapore 8%; Hong Kong 5%; Malaysia 5%. Main exports: tapioca 13%; rice 13%; rubber 10%; tin 9%; corn 5%; sugar 5%. Tourism (1977): visitors 1,221,000; gross receipts U.S. $226 million.

Transport and Communications. Roads (1977) 66,727 km. Motor vehicles in use (1977): passenger *c.* 344,000; commercial (including buses) *c.* 329,300. Railways: (1978) 3,855 km; traffic (1976) 5,628,000,000 passenger-km, freight 2,505,000,000 net ton-km. Air traffic (1978): 4,196,000,000 passenger-km; freight 139.6 million net ton-km. Shipping (1978): merchant vessels 100 gross tons and over 117; gross tonnage 335,116. Telephones (Sept. 1977) 366,900. Radio receivers (Dec. 1975) 5.5 million. Television receivers (Dec. 1976) 761,000.

Agriculture. Production (in 000; metric tons; 1978): rice *c.* 17,000; corn 3,030; sweet potatoes (1977) *c.* 400; sorghum *c.* 120; cassava (1977) 10,644; dry beans *c.* 165; soybeans *c.* 125; peanuts *c.* 170; sugar, raw value *c.* 1,584; pineapples *c.* 1,250; bananas *c.* 2,000; tobacco *c.* 71; rubber *c.* 453; cotton, lint *c.* 27; jute and kenaf *c.* 300; meat (1977) *c.* 428; fish catch (1977) 1,778; timber (cu m; 1977) 21,958. Livestock (in 000; 1978): cattle *c.* 4,660; buffalo *c.* 5,767; pigs 3,022; chickens 56,306.

Industry. Production (in 000; metric tons; 1977): cement 5,063; petroleum products *c.* 7,810; tin concentrates (metal content) 24; tungsten concentrates (oxide content) 2.5; manganese ore (metal content) 18; sulfuric acid 48; electricity (kw-hr) 11,690,000.

increase by 56% and the payments deficit by 12.8% over 1978. He predicted a decline of 2% in the country's industrial growth rate for the same period. (T. J. S. GEORGE)

Theatre

Soaring inflation caused hardship for the theatre in Western Europe in 1979. Although in Britain the Arts Council budget was increased, its real value lessened. Widespread cuts made by the new Conservative Party government in June, in both Arts Council and local government funding, were criticized as penalizing the arts, the theatre in particular. The actors' union (Equity) staged a protest march in a vain effort to get the government to rescind the increase in value-added tax (VAT) from 8 to 15% on prices of admission to theatres and argued that generally lower VAT ratings in the rest of the European Economic Community placed Britain at a disadvantage. Criticized for having broken election promises, the arts minister, Norman St. John Stevas, regretted the need for the cuts, which he hoped would be partly offset by industrial and private patronage.

In many countries theatres were threatened with closing or curtailed activities, among them Le Lucernaire and the Théâtre National de Chaillot in Paris, the latter to act merely as a "touring date." Several British theatres complained of the threat to their existence, among them the Royal Shakespeare Company (RSC), the Royal Exchange Theatre, Manchester, and the Hull Truck. The RSC warned of coming disaster in light of the deferment until 1980 of a part of its expected subsidy. Belated plans to introduce subscription systems were discussed. One successful subscription drive brought the Birmingham Repertory 6,000 subscribers.

In France the mayor of Paris, Jacques Chirac, proposed to increase his annual arts budget by 30%. In Italy cuts in government grants of up to 70% were made. Capital expenditure projects were carried out in Britain. These included the new Barbican scheme, estimated to have cost £100 million and requiring an annual subsidy from the Greater London Council of £2.5 million, the rebuilt Lyric Theatre in Hammersmith, and south London's first Children's Puppet Theatre.

The Arts Council annual report forecast grants for 1980–81 of something over £8 million for the theatre, other than for the RSC and the National Theatre (NT) and not including touring and housing-the-arts grants (for drama). The previous grants to the NT and RSC were approximately £3.3 million and £2.6 million, respectively. These figures preceded the crippling unofficial two-month strike of stage staff at the NT, which canceled some performances, reduced others to being acted in skeletal sets, and cost the NT £250,000. The Old Vic Theatre company suffered the resignation of Toby Robertson, its founder and director, who was unwilling to carry out his board's retrenchment policy.

Changes in theatres in other European nations included the resignation of Ivan Nagel from the Hamburg Schauspielhaus to make way for Niels-Peter Rudolph; also in West Germany Claus Peymann was replaced at Stuttgart by Hansgünther Heyme, whose seat at Cologne was occupied by Jürgen Flimm. In Norway a general actors' strike achieved the reinstatement of some players. In Austria former theatre critic Paul Blaha became the new head of the Vienna Volkstheater.

Great Britain and Ireland. At the NT, exhibitions in the foyers, television versions of productions, and foreign tours helped to keep both revenue and artistic standards high. John Galsworthy's drama of industrial war, *Strife* (held over from 1978), was the first to fall foul of the NT strike that caused the planned *Oresteia* trilogy to be shelved and William Gaskill to drop his own plans and resign. The NT won several Society of West End Theatre (SWET) and Plays and Players (PP) awards: William Dudley as the year's designer, for his work in the Arthur Schnitzler-Tom Stoppard *Undiscovered Country;* Warren Mitchell as the year's best actor in a revival, for his Willy Loman in Michael Rudman's staging of Arthur Miller's *Death of a Salesman;* and Doreen Mantle as best supporting actress, for Loman's wife in the same play. Ralph Richardson in Tolstoy's *The Fruits of Enlightenment,* Michael Redgrave in Simon Gray's *Close of Play,* John Dexter's bucolic *As You Like It* at the Olivier, and Christopher Morahan's first Shakespeare (*Richard III* with John Wood) and first Ibsen (*The Wild Duck* with Michael Bryant) on the same stage were among the year's other highlights. Also noteworthy were Peter Hall's stunning productions of Peter Shaffer's *Amadeus* (PP best play award, with Paul Scofield as Mozart's rival, Salieri) and of Harold Pinter's comedy of adultery *Betrayed* (SWET best play award).

At the Aldwych, before taking over the Young Vic, where he staged several Shakespeares in modern dress, Michael Bogdanov won the SWET director's award for *The Taming of the Shrew;* Zoë Wanamaker achieved the award for actress of the year in a revival of the Moss Hart-George S. Kaufman *Once in a Lifetime,* given a musical climax by Trevor Nunn (PP director's award). Patrick Stewart won the supporting actor's award for his Enobarbus in Peter Brook's *Antony and Cleopatra* (transferred from Stratford), and Jane Lapotaire (PP actress award), in Pam Gems's *Piaf,* was named actress of the year in a new play (transferred to the RSC's Warehouse from Stratford). Other notable plays staged by the RSC were Maksim Gorky's *Children of the Sun* and Mikhail Bulgakov's *The White Guard.*

At the main London subsidized theatres, outstanding performances at the Round House were given by Vanessa Redgrave (*see* BIOGRAPHIES) in Ibsen's *The Lady from the Sea,* Edward Fox in T. S. Eliot's *The Family Reunion,* and Michael Hordern in Ronald Harwood's *The Ordeal of Gilbert Pinfold,* all from Manchester's Royal Exchange Theatre. The Hampstead Theatre's playbills included David Mercer's *Then and Now* and the two West End transfers of James Saunders's *Bodies* and Richard Harris's *Outside Edge.* Other West End transfers were, from the Royal Court, Martin Sherman's *Bent* with Ian McKellen (SWET award for best actor in a new play) and, from Cambridge, the SWET-prizewinning musical *Songbook,* by Monty Norman and Julian More, which won Anton Rodgers the actor of the year in a musical SWET award. From Sheffield the smash-hit *Chicago* (PP musical award) headed a record list of U.S. musicals, including *Beatlemania, Hello Dolly!, The King and I* (which won Virginia McKenna the actress of the year in a muscial SWET award), *My Fair Lady,* and *Ain't Misbehavin'.* The SWET best comedy award went to Roger Hall's *Middle Age Spread* and best comedy performance to Barry Humphries in *A Night with Dame Edna.*

NOVOSTI

The Shota Rustaveli Theatre, one of the Soviet Union's leading companies, performed Shakespeare's *Richard III,* among other works, when it took part in the Edinburgh Festival in August.

KEYSTONE

Empress Eugenie was a popular one-woman show about the wife of Napoleon III, the last empress of France, starring Margaret Rawlings at London's Mayfair Theatre.

The Abbey Theatre, Dublin, began its 75th anniversary celebrations with a revival of *Juno and the Paycock* starring Siobhan McKenna. The Abbey, with an 80% attendance average at both its theatres, had a good year. After the world premiere of Brian Friel's *Aristocrats,* staged by the Abbey's director Joe Dowling, the company did the 21st Dublin Festival proud with Hugh Leonard's latest semiautobiographical *A Life* and Maeve Binchy's *The Half-Promised Land.* New dramas included *The Nightingale Not the Lark,* a first play by Denis Johnston's daughter Jennifer Johnston, and, at the Gate, Desmond Forristal's *Captive Audience* staged by Hilton Edwards.

France, Belgium, and Italy. Pierre Dux, retiring head of the Comédie-Française, was succeeded by the actor Jacques Toja. The year's offerings included Racine's *Bérénice,* staged by J. F. Rémi; Félicien Marceau's *The Egg;* Feydeau's *A Flea in Your Ear* with Francis Huster; Molière's *Don Juan,* given a surreal production by Jean-Luc Boutté; and a pale Chekhov *Three Sisters,* compared with the striking rival version staged by Lucian Pintilie at the Théâtre de la Ville. At the Orsay Jean-Louis Barrault put on Arthur Kopit's *Wings,* featuring Madeleine Renaud, and *Appearances,* Simone Benmussa's adaptation of a Henry James ghost story, staged by herself. At the Théâtre de l'Est

Parisien Guy Rétoré's repertoire included *Julius Caesar* and Brecht's *Puntila.* At the Chaillot, Arby Ovanessian, an Armenian-Iranian director, staged Chekhov's *Lady with a Dog* as part of the Paris Festival.

Revivals in Paris were *Ardèle* by Jean Anouilh, *The Little Hut* by André Roussin, and Paul Claudel's *Cantata for Three Voices.* New plays included Marc Camoletti's *The Bluffer*, Remo Forlani's *A King's Mighty Troubles,* Claude Rich's *A Winter Suit,* Robert Hossein's *Danton and Robespierre,* and Geneviève Serreau's *The North Star.*

For the millennial celebrations of the city of Brussels, the National Theatre of Belgium staged Michel de Ghelderode's *The Great Macabre,* directed by Bernard De Coster, and Tom Stoppard's *Night and Day.* The Louvain Workshop put on Otomar Krejca's 1978 Avignon Festival production of *Waiting for Godot* to inaugurate its new university "Jean Vilar" theatre; this was followed by two transfers from the 1979 Avignon festival, Krejca's *Lorenzaccio* and Ariane Mnouchkine's *Méphisto.* The latter, a four-hour-long mammoth example of total theatre, later transferred to the Paris Cartoucherie, re-created on two stages, with the audience caught between the two, the events of Klaus Mann's novel of Berlin of the 1920s and 1930s.

The notable events in Italy were by non-Italians: Robert Wilson's baffling work-in-progress, *Edison,* part of the international festival of the Milan-based Centre for Theatrical Research and later seen at the Paris Festival; and the world premiere given by Italian Radio of *Before the Jewel Box,* about the troubles of three married couples, by Karol Wojtyla (Pope John Paul II). Dario Fo appeared in his own theatre, from which he was later to be evicted, and the 12th Florence Festival was host to Italian troupes and companies from East and West Germany.

Switzerland, East and West Germany, and Austria. In French-speaking Switzerland Philippe Mentha opened a new workshop theatre near Lausanne (the Kléber-Méliau) with *Three Sisters;* François Rochaix staged at the Geneva-based Carouge the first French-Swiss theatre festival; Charles Joris produced *King Lear,* with Guy Touraille at the Théâtre Populaire Romand in Lausanne; and Michel Soutter put on the world premiere of Max Frisch's *Triptyque,* a drama of the afterlife, at the Centre Culturel de Vidy in Lausanne. Friedrich Beyer staged Bjørnsterne Bjørnson's *Beyond Human Might* in Basel. Zürich's repertoire included Bond's *The Woman;* Erwin Axer's production of *John Gabriel Borkman,* with Hans-Dieter Zeidler and Maria Becker; and a first play about an unjustly treated schoolteacher, *A Pestalozzi,* by Heinz Stalder.

Acclaimed as the outstanding events in West Berlin were Botho Strauss's *Large and Small,* subtly staged by Peter Stein, and Robert Wilson's incantatory opera *Death, Destruction and Detroit,* a love-and-death story, in 16 scenes, about the German war criminal Rudolf Hess. The annual German theatre festival included three separate *Antigone*s, *Maria Stuart,* and the Burgtheater's *Emilia Galotti,* with Elisabeth Orth; at the autumn festival were Brook's double bill of the African comic fable *The Bone* and the Iranian mystical drama *The Conference of Birds* and plays by the Bucharest city theatre.

Hamburg was the site for the 1979 Theatre of the Nations Festival sponsored by the International Theatre Institute, with visitors from Britain (the RSC *Coriolanus*), China (the Peking Opera), the U.S.S.R. (Leningrad Gorky Theatre in two Georgy Tovstonogov productions, one later seen at Avignon), Vienna, Greece, and the U.S. Peter Zadek's version of *A Winter's Tale* was among the Schauspielhaus contributions to the festival. Before leaving Stuttgart Peymann staged a production of Thomas Bernhard's *Before Retirement*, about West German Nazis and neo-Nazis. Ingmar Bergman reproduced his famous *Hedda Gabler* in German in Munich.

Friedo Solter's two-evening version of the *Wallenstein Trilogy*, with Eberhard Esche, was the novelty at the Deutsches Theatre in East Berlin. There also the Berliner Ensemble celebrated its 30th birthday with *The Great Peace* and Volker Braun's Brechtian parable-play, set in China, that won Manfred Wekwerth and Joachim Tenschert the year's prize for best direction.

In Austria, which was host to the biennial International Theatre Critics' Congress, guest productions at the Vienna Burgtheater were Terry Hands's *As You Like It*, Jonathan Miller's *A Midsummer Night's Dream,* and Pavel Kohout's *The Government Inspector*. Leopold Lindtberg staged a satirical double bill by Vaclav Havel (*The Protest*) and Kohout (*The Certificate*). Other attractions were Fritz Zecha's production of *Casimir and Caroline* at the Josefstadt and Hans Jaray's of Ferenc Molnar's *Olympia* at the Volkstheater.

Scandinavia and Eastern Europe. The first festival of the International Federation of Independent Theatres, in Stockholm, brought together groups from Poland, Sweden, Denmark, France, Finland, Britain, and Czechoslovakia. At the City Theatre Krejca guest-directed Chekhov's *Platonov,* and Göran O. Ericsson directed his own translation of *A Midsummer Night's Dream.* At the Royal

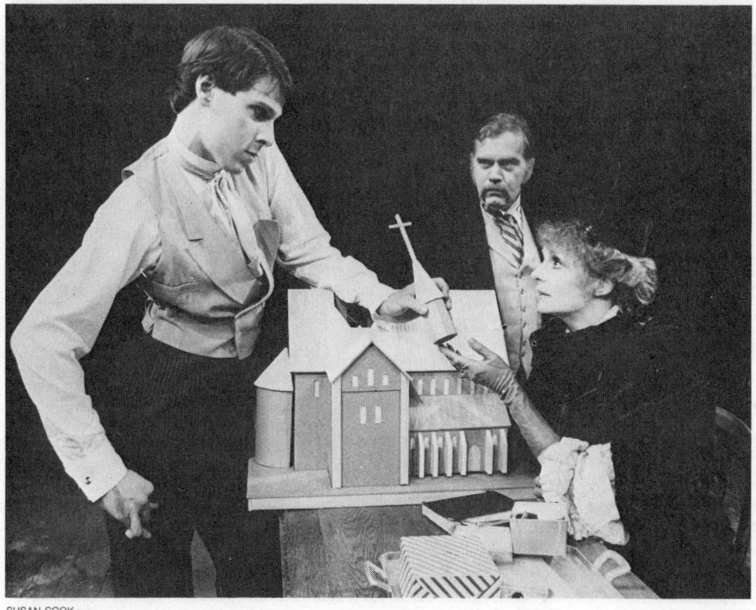

SUSAN COOK

The Elephant Man played to overflow houses in New York with (from left) Philip Anglim, Kevin Conway, and Carole Shelley in the leading roles.

Dramatic, Agneta Plejel's *Kollontai,* about the first Soviet woman ambassador, was revived. Charles Marowitz made his directing debut at Oslo's National Theatre with Ibsen's *An Enemy of the People.*

The first Danish production of Brecht's *Galileo* was put on at the Copenhagen People's Theatre by Preben Neergaard, and the world premiere of Ernst Bruun Olsen's *The Beginning* (of modern capitalism) was staged by Sam Besekow at the Royal. A first play by Jens Aarkrog, *In Stauning's Black Shadow,* about Danish proto-Nazism, was staged by Mogens Pedersen at the Aarhus (Denmark) City Theatre. Benno Besson reproduced his *Hamlet,* with Asko Sarkola, at the Little Theatre in Helsinki, where the Leningrad Gorky and the Icelandic National theatres were seen at the new Easter Festival. Also in Helsinki Jouko Turkka produced Maiju Lassila's *The Wise Virgin* at the City Theatre, and Jack Wittika staged Pinter's *Betrayed* at the National.

In Moscow Yury Liubimov staged his own version of *Crime and Punishment* at the Taganka. Erwin Axer staged Slawomir Mrozek's latest comedy, *The Tailor,* at his Contemporary Theatre in Warsaw. Also in Warsaw Jerzy Jarocki produced *King Lear* and Maciej Prus *November Night,* each with Gustaw Holoubek, at the Dramatic. Roberto Ciulli's production of *The Cyclops* from Düsseldorf won approval at the Belgrade "bitef" Festival. In Bulgaria new dramas by Stanislav Stratiev, Ivan Radoev, and Yordan Radichkov were staged at the Satiric Theatre in Sofia. In Budapest Janos Sziladi became head of the National and Istvan Horvai of the Comedy Theatre, where Istvan Csurka's *Deficit* and the late Istvan Orkeny's ten-year-old *Pisti in the Bloodbath* were outstanding. The 1979 best play awards in Bucharest went to Paul Cornel Mitic, Teodor Maziu, and Marin Sorescu for his Dracula drama *The Third Stake.* New plays by Paul Everac and Tudor Popescu were also staged.

(OSSIA TRILLING)

An unusual musical about a homicidal barber out for revenge, *Sweeney Todd* hit the New York stage in March with Angela Lansbury and Len Cariou in lead roles.

MARTHA SWOPE

U.S. and Canada. In mood and in finances theatre in the U.S. in 1979 reflected the recession in the national economy. This was most apparent in the commercial sector. The financial crunch and a series of failures early in the year discouraged Broadway producers from presenting expensive new musicals, and interest turned to less risky ventures, such as revivals of *Peter Pan, The Most Happy Fella,* and *Oklahoma!*

In drama on Broadway, the only established U.S. playwrights to be produced were Arthur Kopit, John Guare, and Michael Weller. Kopit's *Wings,* originally a radio play, was an almost reportorial account of the effects of a stroke on a woman. It was a commercial failure, though not the four-performance disaster that Guare's *Bosoms and Neglect* experienced. Weller's *Loose Ends,* more or less a sequel to his earlier *Moonchildren,* was a success. Otherwise, none of the best-known dramatists in the U.S. had new plays performed. This lack of continuity in the work of established playwrights continued to be a serious problem for the U.S. theatre.

There were some successful dramas in New York. Most were produced in small, off-Broadway theatres, and a pattern of recognizable characters, interesting stories, and emotional energy emerged. Such a play was Ernest Thompson's *On Golden Pond,* relating a heartfelt continuing romance between two long-married septuagenarians. *Getting Out,* Marsha Norman's impressive debut about a female ex-convict, was another drama with believable characters and plot. The successful revivals of Arthur Miller's *The Price* and Frances Goodrich and Albert Hackett's *The Diary of Anne Frank* substantiated this trend toward stories.

New York theatregoers, it seemed, were finally rejecting surreal, absurdist drama. Even the Pulitzer Prize-winning *Buried Child* was uncharacteristically accessible for its author, Sam Shepard. While this audience demand for story drama did not seem to be heralding a return to old-fashioned naturalism, it did signal the end of influence for the Samuel Beckett-Eugène Ionesco school of absurdism. Even the only moderately absurdist British playwright Tom Stoppard ran into resistance in New York. His bill of one-act plays (*Dogg's Hamlet, Cahoot's Macbeth*) played only briefly on Broadway, and his full-length *Night and Day* starring Maggie Smith fared little better.

Broadway's great drama success in 1979 was neither an absurdist nor a naturalistic play but one in the classic literary tradition. This was *The Elephant Man,* a play by Bernard Pomerance, an American living in London. *The Elephant Man* tells the true story of John Merrick, a hideously deformed young man in turn-of-the-century England: how a surgeon rescues him from freak shows, how an actress helps him to express an artistic soul, how he becomes society's darling, and why he kills himself. Merrick, played by Philip Anglim, comes to symbolize the painful, unique solitude of the human condition and the peculiarity of individualism that is expressed in art. It was gratifying to find audiences willing to make the leap of imagination and believe an actor without makeup to be a grotesque creature. It was even more gratifying to find so profoundly moving and artistic a drama succeeding in the commercial theatre of Broadway. Indeed, *The Elephant Man* won Broadway's top prize, the Tony Award, in 1979.

One of the most eagerly anticipated productions of 1979 was *Romantic Comedy* by Bernard Slade, author of the popular success *Same Time, Next Year.* If not artistic, *Romantic Comedy* was not slavishly conventional either. Starring Anthony Perkins and Mia Farrow, it was in fact an antiromantic comedy, an attempt to show the difference between real-life relationships and theatrical idealizations. Though not a critical success the play did well at the box office.

Neil Simon's 1979 entry was *They're Playing Our Song.* Despite songs (by Marvin Hamlisch, with lyrics by Carole Bayer Sager), this was a musicalized play rather than musical theatre. Yet Broadway theatregoers were so hungry for a new musical, and so trusting of Simon, that *They're Playing Our Song* overcame lukewarm reviews to become a smash hit.

In doing so it climbed over the remains of Broadway's most disastrous season of musicals in years. *Grand Tour* (with Joel Grey), *Carmelina* (with opera star Cesare Siepi), *The Utter Glory of Morrissey Hall* (Celeste Holm), and *Saravá* (Tovah Feldshuh) were among the casualties. Even the songs of Richard Rodgers (*see* OBITUARIES) and the presence of movie star Liv Ullmann could not save the musical *I Remember Mama.* And Broadway's first disco musical, *Got Tu Go Disco,* would probably prove its last, being a $2 million failure. As the year ended the mediocre *Grease* passed *Fiddler on the Roof* to become the longest running show in Broadway history.

Yet, as with drama, among the few successful new musicals there was a trend away from trends. *Sweeney Todd,* for instance, was based on an old British melodrama by George Dibden Pitt about Todd, "the demon barber of Fleet Street," who had his murder victims baked into meat pies. Made into an operatic musical by Stephen Sondheim and staged by Harold Prince, this unlikely commercial project ran the entire year and won the Tony Award for best musical. The redoubtable Prince also directed *Evita,* first for a London presentation and then just as successfully in New York. A rock opera by Tim Rice and Andrew Lloyd Webber, authors of *Jesus Christ Superstar, Evita* tells, in Brechtian style, the story of Argentina's adored tyrant Eva Perón. The play was Prince's triumph, an example of spectacular staging overcoming mediocre material.

Near the year's end Broadway finally got a new hit musical. This was *Sugar Babies,* an elaborately produced valentine to old-time burlesque shows. *Sugar Babies* featured movie stars Ann Miller and Mickey Rooney in the ritual roles of stripper and baggy-pants comedian; the show had old songs by Jimmy McHugh and Dorothy Fields. Warm and broad and winning, it deserved its success. It also summed up the Broadway year as being perhaps hungry for mindless cheer but still, between *Evita* and *Sugar Babies,* more open to diversity than it had been in years.

New York's institutional theatres also reflected the recession. Both governmental and private funding were scarce. The adventurous Chelsea Theater Center almost went under until it produced a commercial success with *Strider,* a stage version of a Tolstoy story. For the second year Lincoln Center for the Performing Arts was without a theatre component, its Vivian Beaumont Theatre still closed. Even Joseph Papp's usually active Public Theater was quiet except for a roundly criticized attempt to create a Shakespeare company of black and Hispanic actors. Critics saw this as a case of inverted prejudice and a misguided attempt to use art for social work.

MARTHA SWOPE

Ann Miller and Mickey Rooney romped onstage in the Broadway musical *Sugar Babies.*

Across the U.S. the regional theatres appeared to flourish. The Actors Theater of Louisville, Ky., staged another of its extensive festivals of new U.S. plays. Some of the nonprofit institutions, such as San Francisco's American Conservatory Theatre, remained true to their original purpose of producing the classics the commercial theatre would not risk. Most of these theatres, however, were attempting some new plays. This was frankly in quest of profitable transfers to Broadway. With subsidy sources fading these grant-dependent theatres had to find other income. For them paradise would be a success similar to that of *A Chorus Line,* which had financed Papp's Public Theater for years. Their efforts included the aforementioned *Loose Ends* by the Arena Stage of Washington, D.C., and *Zoot Suit* by California's Mark Taper Forum. *Zoot Suit* moved to a commercial Los Angeles theatre and then tried the long jump to Broadway, where the Mexican-oriented production failed. Even Canada's wealthy Stratford (Ont.) Festival set its heart on Broadway income by testing a new musical, *Happy New Year,* in addition to its usual Shakespearean fare. Another Broadway-motivated Stratford production was *King Lear,* with the inexperienced Shakespearean actor—but star—Peter Ustinov.

Of all the regional theatres' Broadway hopes, the likeliest one to succeed seemed to be *Frankenstein.* This dramatization of Mary Shelley's novel by Victor Gialanella was presented by the Loretto-Hilton Theater in St. Louis, Mo., where the playwright was a production manager. A local success with its flamboyant stage effects, the horror entertainment was due on Broadway at the start of 1980.

Commercial transfer, however, was not the only reason that these theatres were staging new plays. They also seemed to be running out of enthusiasm for the classics. Thus, while Long Wharf Theater in New Haven, Conn., produced Ibsen (*Rosmersholm*) and Gorky (*Summerfolk*), it also staged a new musical. Its neighbouring Hartford Stage Company staged *Galileo,* but the author, Bertolt Brecht, was fast losing his position as the pet playwright of U.S. regional theatres. There was something ominous about that, ominous because artists ought not to go in and out of fashion and because the waning enthusiasm for Brecht seemed to symbolize an overall deflation of aspirations. Indeed, by the year's end the Hartford theatre had lost its inspiring artistic director, Paul Weidner.

Even more despairing was the situation at the famed Guthrie Theater in Minneapolis, Minn. The Guthrie's artistic director, Alvin Epstein, was dismissed after one lacklustre season, and no replacement was named. Once the nation's most prestigious regional theatre, the Guthrie now seemed to epitomize the rudderless drift of such institutions in 1979. (MARTIN GOTTFRIED)

See also Dance; Music.
[622]

Togo

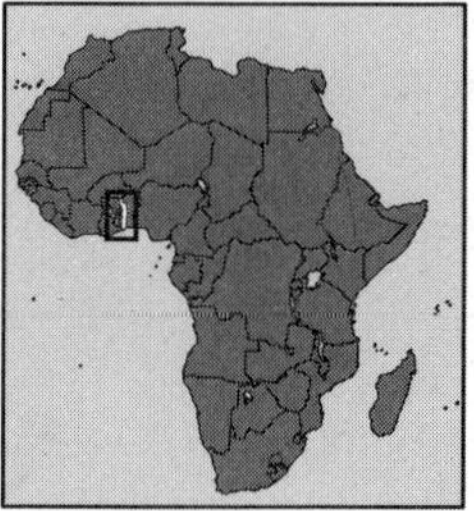
Togo

A West African republic on the Bight of Benin, Togo is bordered by Ghana, Upper Volta, and Benin. Area: 56,785 sq km (21,925 sq mi). Pop. (1978 est.): 2,409,000. Cap. and largest city: Lomé (pop., 1976 est., 229,400). Language: French (official). Religion: animist; Muslim and Christian minorities. President in 1979, Gen. Gnassingbe Eyadema.

Gen. Gnassingbe Eyadema, the president of Togo, announced in January 1979 that he would wage war on corruption, and in March he reshuffled his government. A contest of communiqués developed in the course of the year between the opposition (in particular the National Union of Togolese Students) and the government; each time the regime's opponents denounced a death in suspicious circumstances or an arbitrary arrest, the government denied it. In August ten of the mercenaries involved in the attempted coup of Oct. 15, 1977, were sentenced to death, but the president reprieved two.

In September Beni Lawson, an opponent of the regime, was kidnapped at Niamey, Niger, and forcibly brought back to Togo, where he was almost at once set free. The month of October was especially eventful. The former minister of information, Polycarpe Johnson, fled to Europe, and a bomb attempt was made against Gilchrist Olympio, son of former president Sylvanus Olympio (assassinated in 1963), in Paris, where he was living in exile. In a December 30 poll, 99.9% of those voting approved a new constitution and the continuance of Eyadema's presidency.

(PHILIPPE DECRAENE)

TOGO

Education. (1976–77) Primary, pupils 395,381, teachers 6,528; secondary, pupils 74,567, teachers 1,832; vocational, pupils 6,478, teachers 305; teacher training, students 329, teachers 24; higher (university only), students 2,186, teaching staff 177.

Finance. Monetary unit: CFA franc, with (Sept. 17, 1979) a par value of CFA Fr 50 to the French franc (free rate of CFA Fr 211.54 to U.S. $1; CFA Fr 455.12 = £1 sterling). Budget (1979 est.) balanced at CFA Fr 62.6 billion (including investment expenditure of CFA Fr 15.8 billion).

Foreign Trade. (1977) Imports CFA Fr 69,834,000,000; exports CFA Fr 39,115,000,000. Import sources: France 34%; U.K. 10%; West Germany 9%; U.S. 8%; The Netherlands 7%. Export destinations: The Netherlands 32%; France 21%; West Germany 12%; Poland 8%; Belgium-Luxembourg 5%. Main exports: phosphates 49%; cocoa 26%; coffee 14%.

Tonga

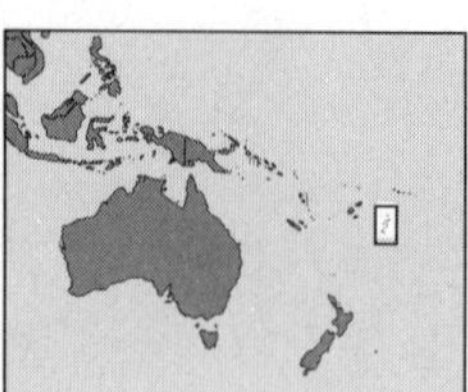
Tonga

An independent monarchy and member of the Commonwealth of Nations, Tonga is an island group in the Pacific Ocean east of Fiji. Area: 750 sq km (290 sq mi). Pop. (1977 est.): 91,000. Cap. and largest city: Nukualofa (pop., 1976, 18,300). Language: English and Tongan. Religion: Christian. King, Taufa'ahau Tupou IV; prime minister in 1979, Prince Tu'ipelehake.

In March 1979 King Taufa'ahau Tupou IV paid a state visit to Libya, after which he announced that the two countries were to establish diplomatic relations and that Libya would probably lend Tonga A$3 million to enlarge Fua'amotu Airport. The project had been rejected by all of Tonga's major aid donors, and previously announced schemes to obtain financing from the U.S.S.R. or through the Bank of the South Pacific had fallen through. Construction of the airport would be supervised by experts from Taiwan, which Tonga, alone among the Pacific nations, still recognized.

Tonga continued to suffer from a severe balance of payments problem, although returns from tourism and some agricultural products increased. Despite pressure from its own growers, New Zealand retained import quotas for Tongan tomatoes. A Pacific Conference of Churches seminar in Tonga

TONGA

Education. (1978) Primary, pupils 19,730, teachers 761; secondary, pupils 12,368, teachers 654; vocational, pupils 281, teachers 19; teacher training, students 146, teachers 14.

Finance and Trade. Monetary unit: pa'anga, with (Sept. 17, 1979) a free rate of 0.89 pa'anga to U.S. $1 (1.91 pa'anga = £1 sterling). Budget (1978–79 est.): revenue 8,045,000 pa'anga; expenditure 8,602,000 pa'anga. Foreign trade (1978): imports 22,318,000 pa'anga; exports 4,992,000 pa'anga. Import sources: New Zealand 37%; Australia 28%; Japan 7%; U.K. 6%; Fiji 6%; Singapore 6%. Export destinations: The Netherlands 29%; New Zealand 22%; U.K. 21%; West Germany 11%; Australia 5%. Main exports: copra 59%; desiccated coconut 15%.

drew international attention to the exploitation of islanders by short-term labour migration schemes, the racial discrimination in neighbouring metropolitan countries, and the hardship caused by uneven distribution of development assistance among Pacific countries. (BARRIE MACDONALD)

Track and Field Sports

Individual brilliance dominated the major track and field events of 1979, a year in which many athletes concentrated on preparations for the 1980 Olympic Games. It was the year of the runner, with no men and only one woman breaking field event records.

Men's International Competition. Although competition was strong in both the European Cup and World Cup, the outstanding performances of the year were achieved by two young men in other tournaments. Renaldo Nehemiah of the United States dominated the early portion of the outdoor season with his record-breaking hurdling, while Sebastian Coe (*see* BIOGRAPHIES) of Great Britain was the sensation of the latter stages of the year, producing three world middle-distance marks.

Of the two men, Coe made the greater impact. His achievements, particularly the first record, were less expected and were spread over three highly popular events. By contrast, Nehemiah's two global records were achieved in a single event, the 110-m hurdles.

Coe, a slightly built 23-year-old, became the first man ever to hold world records in the 800-m, 1,500-m, and one-mile runs. A recent graduate in economics from Loughborough University, he put his record string together in just 42 days.

Ranked third in the world in the 800 m in 1978, Coe was not unknown. But he had done nothing of consequence in 1979 prior to stepping to the starting line of the invitational 800-m run at Oslo, Norway, on July 5. Just 1 min 42.4 sec after the starting gun, Coe had the first of his records. He took a full second off the mark set in 1977 by Olympic champion Alberto Juantorena of Cuba.

Twelve days later Coe was back at Oslo's Bislett Stadium, site of more than 30 world marks. This time his target was the record for one-mile, the only nonmetric distance for which records are still approved officially. He covered the distance in 3 min 49 sec, beating John Walker's four-year-old mark by 0.4 sec.

Coe did not run seriously again until August 15. This time the site was Zürich, Switz., and the event the 1,500-m run. For the third time in a row he was successful in his record quest, covering the distance in 3 min 32.1 sec, a narrow 0.1 sec faster than Filbert Bayi had run in 1974. Coe then retired for the season, passing up the World Cup as he had the European Cup.

Earlier in the year the headlines had belonged to Nehemiah, a 20-year-old sophomore at the University of Maryland. An explosive indoor season produced for him no less than seven best-in-the-world performances (there are no official world records for indoor competition). But it was still something of a surprise when Nehemiah lowered the 110-m hurdle record in his first outdoor race of the year. He did it at San Jose, Calif., on April 14 by speeding over the ten hurdles in 13.16 sec, 0.05 sec better than the previous mark held by Alejandro Casanas of Cuba. Back in California on May 6, this time in Los Angeles, Nehemiah cut an extra-large piece off his own new record by clocking 13.00 sec. A still faster clocking, 12.91 sec, was

WIDE WORLD

Marita Koch of East Germany (facing camera) is congratulated by a friend after setting a new world's record of 48.89 seconds in the women's 400-metre competition on July 29 in Potsdam, East Germany.

Table I. World 1979 Outdoor Records—Men

Event	Competitor, country, date	Performance
200 m	Pietro Mennea, Italy, Sept. 12	19.72 sec
800 m	Sebastian Coe, U.K., July 5	1 min 42.4 sec
1,500 m	Sebastian Coe, U.K., Aug. 15	3 min 32.1 sec
One mile	Sebastian Coe, U.K., July 17	3 min 49 sec
110-m hurdles	Renaldo Nehemiah, U.S., April 14	13.16 sec
	Renaldo Nehemiah, U.S., May 6	13.00 sec
Nonstandard events		
25,000 m	Bill Rodgers, U.S., Feb. 21	1 hr 14 min 12 sec
20,000-m walk	Anatoliy Solomin, U.S.S.R., April 22	1 hr 23 min
	Gerard Lelievre, France, April 29	1 hr 22 min 20 sec
	Daniel Bautista, Mexico, May 19	1 hr 22 min 15 sec
	Domingo Colin, Mexico, May 26	1 hr 20 min 59 sec
Two-hour walk	José Marin, Spain, April 8	28,165 m (17 mi 881 yd)
30,000-m walk	José Marin, Spain, April 8	2 hr 8 min
50,000-m walk	Raúl Gonzales, Mexico, May 25	3 hr 41 min 39 sec

Table II. World 1979 Outdoor Records—Women

Event	Competitor, country, date	Performance
200 m	Marita Koch, East Germany, June 3	22.02 sec
	Marita Koch, East Germany, June 10	21.71 sec
400 m	Marita Koch, East Germany, July 29	48.89
	Marita Koch, East Germany, Aug. 4	48.60
One mile	Natalia Marasescu, Romania, Jan. 27	4 min 22.1 sec
100-m hurdles	Grazyna Rabsztyn, Poland, June 18	12.48 sec (ties record)
400-m hurdles	Marina Makeyeva, U.S.S.R., July 27	54.78 sec
4x100-m relay	East Germany, June 10	42.10 sec
	East Germany, Aug. 4	42.09 sec
Javelin throw	Ruth Fuchs, East Germany, June 13	69.52 m (228 ft 1 in)
Nonstandard events		
4 x 200-m relay	Ukraine, July 29	1 min 30.8 sec

Theology:
see Religion

Timber:
see Industrial Review

Tobacco:
see Industrial Review

Tobogganing:
see Winter Sports

Tourism:
see Industrial Review

Toys:
see Games and Toys

UPI

Britain's Sebastian Coe (right) set a new world mark for the mile of 3:49 in an international track and field meet in Norway in July. During the year he also set new world records for the 800-metre and 1,500-metre runs.

achieved by Nehemiah at the National Collegiate Athletic Association (NCAA) championships on June 1, but the aiding wind was over the legal limit and the time could not be submitted as a record.

Aside from the accomplishments of Coe and Nehemiah, 1979 turned out to be a singularly nonproductive year as far as world records were concerned. Only one other was achieved in a standard (frequently contested) event. That was the time of 19.72 sec for 200 m turned in by Italy's Pietro Mennea. The 27-year-old veteran took advantage of Mexico City's 2,205-m altitude to lower the record of 19.83 sec which was set in the 1968 Olympics by Tommie Smith of the U.S., also at Mexico City. The lowered air resistance at high altitude and a trail wind that was close to the allowable limit combined to aid Mennea significantly. Estimates of this aid varied from 0.3 to 0.5 sec.

One other running record was broken when marathoner Bill Rodgers of the U.S. tried the seldom-run 30,000-m event at Saratoga, Calif., on February 21. En route to a U.S. record at the longer distance, Rodgers was timed in 1 hour 14 min 12 sec for 25,000 m. His clocking of 1 hour 31 min 50 sec set a U.S. mark for 30 km, and he achieved another U.S. record when he covered 20,223 m (12 mi, 997 yd) in one hour.

Records for walking are recognized at four long distances, and all four were broken in 1979. The mark for 20,000 m was lowered four times, eventually reaching 1 hour 20 min 59 sec in a race won by Domingo Colin of Mexico at Bergen, Norway, on May 26. One day earlier, on the same track, Raúl Gonzales of Mexico walked 50,000 m in 3 hours 41 min 39 sec. Two records were set on April 8 at Barcelona, Spain, both by José Marin of Spain and in the same race. He walked 28,165 m (17 mi 881 yd) in 2 hours and covered 30,000 m in 2 hours 8 min.

East Germany was the winner of the European Cup competition, celebrated at Turin, Italy, August 4–5. The Soviet Union finished second with 114 points to East Germany's 125, while West Germany was third with 110.

The quadrennial Pan American Games, held July 7–14 at San Juan, Puerto Rico, did not have team scoring. However, it was clear that the U.S. dominated, winning 14 of 24 men's events.

In the second running of the World Cup, in Montreal, August 24–26, the U.S. won, scoring 119 points to 112 for the European all-star squad. East Germany, upset winners over the U.S. in the 1977 inaugural meeting, finished third with 108, followed by the U.S.S.R., 102; the Americas, 98; Africa, 84; Oceania, 58; and Asia, 36. Miruts Yifter of Ethiopia won both the 5,000- and 10,000-m runs, as he did in 1977, and was voted the outstanding male performer of the meet. But the most noteworthy performance was the 8.52 m (27 ft 11½ in) long jump by Larry Myricks of the U.S., second longest ever.

Indoors, the most important meet of the year was the European Championships at Vienna on February 24–25. It produced no world records, and no team scores were kept. But when the U.S. defeated the Soviet Union, 75 to 66, at Fort Worth, Texas, on March 3, there was a new indoor pole vault mark. Dan Ripley of the U.S. cleared 5.63 m (18 ft 5½ in).

But the indoor season belonged to Nehemiah. In just one month, beginning January 12, he established new all-time bests in four hurdle events—6.04 sec for 50 yd, 6.36 sec for 50 m, and 6.89 sec for 60 yd and 55 m.

Other indoor records were: 46.21 sec for 400 m by Karel Kolar of Czechoslovakia; 61.2 sec for 500 m by Herm Frazier of the U.S.; 3 min 37.4 sec for 1,500 m by John Walker of New Zealand; 3 min 52.6 sec for one mile by Eamonn Coghlan of Ireland; 17.29 m (56 ft 8¾ in) in the triple jump by Gennady Valyukevich of the U.S.S.R.; 23.46 m (76 ft 11¾ in) in the 35-lb weight throw by Yury Syedikh of the U.S.S.R.; and 7.54 sec in the 60-m hurdles by Andrey Prokofyev of the U.S.S.R.

Women's International Competition. As in 1978, when she accounted for five world records, Marita Koch of East Germany had a banner year. This time she set new global marks four times, twice each in the 200 m and 400 m. First she lowered her own 200-m record, running 22.02 sec at Leipzig, East Germany, on June 3 and 21.71 sec at Karl-Marx-Stadt, East Germany, a week later. Then it was the 400-m record that was successfully attacked, with times of 48.89 sec at Potsdam, East Germany, on July 29 and 48.60 sec at Turin on August 4.

Koch earned a share of the new 4 x 100-m relay when she teamed with Romy Schneider, Ingrid Auerswald, and Marlies Gohr to run 42.10 sec at Karl-Marx-Stadt on June 10. East Germany bettered its own new record by one hundredth of a second at Turin on August 4 with Christine Brehmer replacing Koch.

Other records were established by Natalia Marasescu of Romania, 4 min 22.1 sec for the mile at Auckland, N.Z., January 27; Grazyna Rabsztyn of Poland, 12.48 sec to equal her 100-m hurdle record, at Warsaw on June 18; Marina Makeyeva of the Soviet Union, 54.78 sec for the 400-m hurdles at Moscow, July 27; Ruth Fuchs of East Germany, 69.52 m (228 ft 1 in) to regain the javelin record, on June 13 at Dresden, East Germany; and a Ukrainian quartet of Raisa Makhova, Nina Zyuskina, Tatyana Prorochenko, and Maria Kulchunova, 1 min 30.8 sec for the 4 x 200-m relay at Moscow, July 29.

East Germany led the way in international competition, edging the Soviets, 102 to 100, in the European Cup and winning the World Cup with 105 points, followed by the U.S.S.R., 97; Europe, 96; U.S., 75; Americas, 67; Oceania, 46; Africa, 29; and Asia, 25. The U.S. won 11 of 15 women's events in the Pan American Games.

Named the outstanding female performer in the World Cup was Evelyn Ashford of the U.S. She scored two upset sprint victories, first defeating Koch at 200 m and then beating record-holder Gohr at 100 m. Ashford's time for the 200 m was 21.83 sec, second fastest ever and a U.S. record.

All-time bests were numerous indoors, but many of the records were in nonstandard distances. Two of the significant marks were made by women who were to be stars of the outdoor season. Ashford ran 60 yd in 6.71 sec at New York City on February 23, and Marasescu was timed in 4 min 3 sec for 1,500 m at Budapest on February 10.

Ursula Hook of West Germany ran 1 min 59.9 sec for 800 m at Dortmund, West Germany, on January 21, while Andrea Matay of Hungary twice raised the high jump level, finally reaching 1.98 m (6 ft 6 in) at Budapest, February 17. Two hurdle records fell, Candy Young of the U.S. running 7.50 sec for 60 yd in New York on February 23 and Rabsztyn clocking 7.86 sec for 60 m at Zabrze, Poland, on February 7.

U.S. Competition. Aside from Nehemiah's two world hurdle marks, only one other U.S. record fell in standard Olympic events. That was in the 10,000 m, with Craig Virgin running the distance in 27 min 39.4 sec at Walnut, Calif., on June 17. Other national marks in a notably unproductive season included: 7 min 33.7 sec for 3,000 m by Rudy Chapa of the University of Oregon at Eugene, Ore., on May 10; the three long-distance records by Rodgers, noted above; and 14 min 46.3 sec for the 4 x 1,500-m relay set by a national team composed of Dan Aldridge, Andy Clifford, Todd Harbour, and Tom Duits on June 23 at Bourges, France.

U.S. women earned no world marks and lost their only existing record when Fuchs took the javelin standard away from Kate Schmidt. But they did establish many new national records. Ashford headed the list, breaking the 100-m mark twice and the 200-m record three times. Her best mark in the 100 m was 10.97 sec (June 16 at Walnut, Calif.), and for the 200 m, 21.83 sec (August 25 at Montreal). Mary Decker ran the mile in 4 min 23.5 sec at Philadelphia on June 30; Deby LaPlante improved the 100-m hurdle time three times, achieving 12.86 sec at Walnut, Calif., on June 16; Louise Ritter high jumped 1.93 m (6 ft 4 in) at San Juan on July 13; Maren Seidler put the shot 19.09 m (62 ft 7¾ in) at Walnut on June 16; Lorna Griffin raised the discus standard four times, topped by a throw of 58.26 m (191 ft 2 in) at Modesto, Calif., May 12; and Jane Frederick scored 4,708 points in the pentathlon at Gotzis, Austria, May 26–27.

In team competition the University of Texas at El Paso won the prestigious NCAA championships at Champaign, Ill., May 31–June 2. California Polytechnic at San Luis Obispo and Slippery Rock (Pa.) won the NCAA Division II and III titles. California State at Northridge captured the Association for Intercollegiate Athletics for Women (AIAW) championships. Indoors, Villanova (Pa.) won the NCAA by a single point from Texas at El Paso. Senior teams from the U.S. and U.S.S.R. did not meet, but the junior (under 20 years old) squads met twice. U.S. men won both tournaments while the Soviet women won twice.

Indoors, three U.S. records fell in addition to Nehemiah's numerous hurdle achievements and Ripley's vault mark. Don Paige ran 1,000 m in 2 min 20.3 sec; Paul Cummings ran 1,500 m in 3 min 37.6 sec; and Steve Scott clocked 3 min 54.1 sec for one mile. For the women Ashford ran 6.32 sec for 50 m; Brenda Morehead sprinted 7.31 sec for 60 m; and Candy Young hurdled 50 m in 6.95 sec.

Marathon Running and Cross Country. Bill Rodgers of the U.S. and Grete Waitz of Norway were the world's top marathon runners in 1979, just as they had been in 1978. Rodgers, a 31-year-old Boston sporting goods store owner, won two of the three most important races of the year and achieved a new U.S. record in the process. On April 16 he captured the Boston Marathon, the best-known 26-mi 385-yd event in the world, with a national best and best in the world for 1979 of 2 hours 9 min 27 sec. (There is no officially approved world record for the marathon because the courses vary.) Rodgers won again in New York City on October 21. More than 14,000 runners entered that race, in which Rodgers achieved his

University of Maryland hurdler Renaldo Nehemiah (centre) clears the last barrier in setting the new 110-metre record of 13.16 seconds in a meet at San Jose, Calif., on April 14.

UPI

UPI

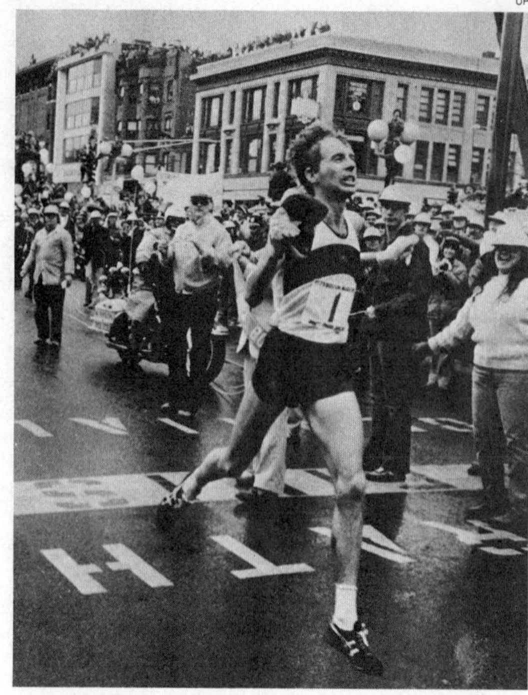

Boston marathoner Bill Rodgers repeated his win in the 1979 Boston Marathon with a new record time of 2 hours 9 minutes 27 seconds.

fourth straight victory. The time was 2 hours 11 min 42 sec.

Rodgers had completed his 1978 competition by finishing sixth, while slightly hampered by the flu, in the third big race of the season, the Fukuoka, Japan, international run. That event was won by Japan's Toshihiko Seko in 2 hours 10 min 21 sec.

Waitz, who ran her first marathon ever in world best time at New York in 1978, repeated her triumph. In only her second marathon the 26-year-old schoolteacher reduced her record time by nearly five minutes, clocking 2 hours 27 min 33 sec. A new U.S. women's record was set by Joan Benoit of Bowdoin College, Brunswick, Maine, who ran 2 hours 35 min 15 sec at Boston.

In cross country competition the international titles went to Waitz and John Treacy of Ireland, both winning for the second time in a row. Great Britain won the men's team title, and the U.S. the women's championship.

U.S. cross country championships were won by Henry Rono of Washington State in the NCAA competition; Greg Meyer of the Greater Boston Track Club in the Amateur Athletic Union (AAU) race; Mary Decker of the University of Colorado in the AIAW; and Julie Brown of the Los Angeles Naturites in the women's AAU. (BERT NELSON)

[452.B.3.b]

Trade, International: see Economy, World

Trade Unions: see Industrial Relations

Transkei: see South Africa

Transportation

Fuel availability and rising costs were major considerations for the transportation industry in 1979. Responses to the restriction of oil supplies following the Iranian revolution varied: Greece imposed four no-drive days a month; Brazil introduced sugar-derived alcohol as a gasoline supplement; and there was widespread research and development work on gasoline substitutes and electric traction. Safety issues were brought to the fore with a DC-10 crash near Chicago that killed 272 passengers and crew and 2 persons on the ground and with the largest peacetime evacuation of a North American city (Mississauga, Ont.) because of dangerous chemical spillage following a train crash. In December the U.S. National Transportation Safety Board laid blame for the DC-10 crash on improper maintenance by the airline, flaws in the design, and lack of proper monitoring on the part of the Federal Aviation Administration.

Despite world economic growth and buoyant demand, the industrialized countries restricted public expenditure, and this affected transport. Technologically, 1979 brought no major innovations but rather a steady progress on a wide variety of fronts. (DAVID BAYLISS)

AVIATION

"A sombre economic background" was how Knut Hammarskjöld, director general of the International Air Transport Association (IATA), described the environment in which the world's airlines would be working in the near future. In his 1979 report Hammarskjöld said that increases in traffic and load factors were reported by airlines during the year. He added, however, that the anticipated recession in the U.S., the slowdown in gross national product growth to 2% in the industrialized countries, and deteriorating prospects elsewhere cast a shadow over the air transport industry.

The industry's foundation, Hammarskjöld noted, was under attack from the U.S. Civil Aeronautics Board (CAB)—a reference to the latter's "show cause" order against IATA. Coincident with the moves to "deregulate" the U.S. airline industry in 1978, the CAB in June of that year had issued a tentative finding that IATA's tariff conference machinery was no longer in the U.S. public interest; it directed IATA to show cause why that finding should not be made final. IATA had responded by revising its structure in the latter part of 1978 to allow airline members the choice of participating in only the association's nontariff activities or in all its activities—the so-called two-tier structure. The U.S. was in a lonely position on the tariffs issue; 100 other countries and several regional airline organizations had indicated that they would support maintenance of the status quo.

Other aspects of 1979 cited by the IATA director general were soaring fuel prices accompanied by restricted supplies; the grounding, following the accident with 274 fatalities near Chicago in May (*see* DISASTERS), of all McDonnell Douglas DC-10s during the peak traffic season; saturation of facilities at some major international airports; and air traffic control systems in some of the busiest traffic areas working at the limits of their capacities.

World airline scheduled passenger traffic in 1978 (excluding the U.S.S.R.) showed the highest annual growth rate since 1972, according to the International Civil Aviation Organization (ICAO). It totaled 794,000,000,000 passenger-km, an increase of 14.2% over 1977. The total number of passengers carried was 587 million, a 13.5% increase. Scheduled freight traffic totaled 24,060,000,000 metric ton-km, an increase of 12.7%. Corresponding

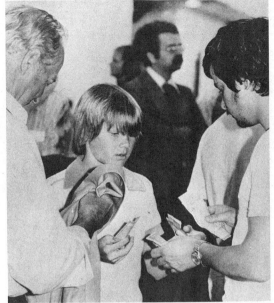

WIDE WORLD

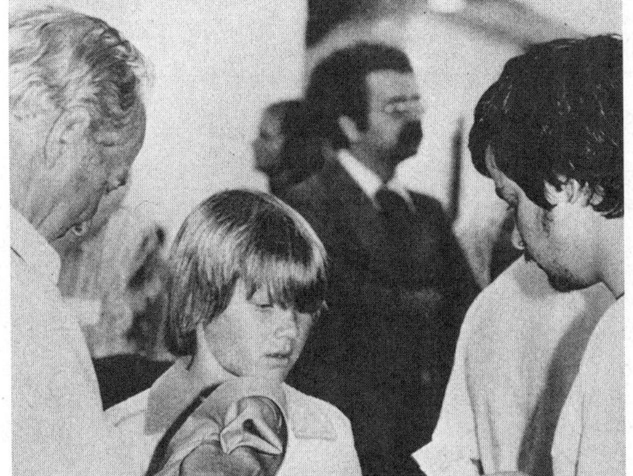

Jeff Dickey, 13, a youthful dealer in airline half-fare coupons issued as a promotion by several U.S. airlines, did a brisk business at the San Francisco airport.

figures for the U.S.S.R. were 98 million passengers carried, 140,000,000,000 passenger-km, and 2,330,000,000 freight metric ton-km.

In the U.S. the air transport industry as a whole registered a high growth rate in passenger traffic of 13.4% in 1978, and it appeared to be continuing at much the same rate in 1979. Figures for the first nine months of the year showed scheduled passenger traffic 13.5% above the equivalent period of 1978, with a higher growth rate (15.6%) in international operations. U.S. local service airlines, carrying about 10% of total U.S. passenger traffic, were growing fastest of all—25.7%, compared with 11.5% for the large domestic trunk carriers. The fast growth of the local carriers—Texas International appeared to lead the field with passenger traffic up some 40% in the first eight months of 1979—was spurred on by deregulation and consequent opportunities to extend route networks. However, a sharp setback in traffic growth was noted across the U.S. industry in September.

Traffic gains in 1979 were not reflected by adequate financial performance; according to the U.S. Air Transport Association (ATA), profits were likely to be $500 million below those of 1978. The ATA emphasized that, with $90 billion worth of capital needed for reequipment up to 1990, U.S. airlines had to obtain an average return on investment of at least 13% a year, about one-third above the probable 1979 figure.

Internationally, growth of IATA scheduled passenger traffic was expected to continue at 9.6% annually up to 1984, with scheduled and charter freight traffic averaging 10.2% annually. IATA said that operating revenues of the world's scheduled airlines in 1978 were $60 billion, about 19% above those of 1977. IATA's own 106 member airlines reported operating revenue of $44.4 billion (up 12%) and operating expenses of $42.2 billion (up 11%).

(DAVID WOOLLEY)

SHIPPING AND PORTS

Overall improvement in the world shipping market in 1979 was underlined by a dramatic decrease in the number of laid-up vessels. By mid-October almost all of the world's tanker, bulk, and combination carrier fleet was again in use, only 12 million tons deadweight (dw), or 2.3% of the world total, being laid up, compared with 57 million tons dw in April 1976. Although most of the reduction was due to improved market conditions, higher fuel prices also helped by making owners steam their tankers at reduced speed, thereby absorbing a little more of the surplus cargo-carrying capacity.

Despite forecasts for an upsurge in the amount of coal to be moved by sea, the 1979 total was little higher than that of 1978, but a marked increase was expected in 1980. Harvest shortfalls in the U.S.S.R. and China led to a demand for bulk carriers in grain. After a spate of shopping in the second-hand tonnage market for good-quality dry-cargo ships, China stopped the immediate expansion of its national fleet at about 5 million tons dw; thus ship brokers were able to arrange more charters.

The world merchant fleet increased slightly from 654 million tons dw to 680 million tons dw, with Liberia still heading the tonnage list (160 million tons dw), followed by Japan (66 million tons dw) and the U.K. (45 million tons dw). By the end of 1979 the world tanker fleet had steadied at about 330 million tons dw, and the dry-cargo fleet (including combination carriers) reached 324 million tons dw. There were signs that shipowners were starting to order replacement tonnage, particularly 80,000–100,000-ton-dw tankers. The vessels were to be built to meet the new safety regulations laid down by the Inter-Governmental Maritime Consultative Organization. One of the freight highlights of 1979 was the increased interest in the reefer (refrigeration ship) market. However, the demand for pure reefer tonnage was expected to decrease as more multipurpose dry-cargo liners with reefer capacity entered service.

In the U.K. a new facility in the River Thames

Following the crash near Chicago of an American Airlines DC-10 in which 274 persons were killed, the Federal Aviation Administration grounded all DC-10s until they had undergone safety checks to ensure they did not have the same structural defects that contributed to the Chicago crash. Foreign carriers also were checked.

UPI

World Transportation

Country	Railways: Route length in 000 km	Railways Traffic: Passenger in 000,000 pass.-km	Railways Traffic: Freight in 000,000 net ton-km	Motor transport: Road length in 000 km	Motor transport: Vehicles in use: Passenger in 000	Motor transport: Vehicles in use: Commercial in 000	Merchant shipping (Ships of 100 tons and over): Number of vessels	Merchant shipping: Gross reg. tons in 000	Air traffic: Total km flown in 000,000	Air traffic: Passenger in 000,000 pass.-km	Air traffic: Freight in 000,000 net ton-km
EUROPE											
Austria	6.5	6,973	10,294	106.2	1,965.2	155.8	10	46	17.7	1,035	12.5
Belgium	4.0	7,137	7,106	114.9	2,871.3	242.3	268	1,685	48.2	4,499	386.1
Bulgaria	4.4	7,000	17,148	36.1[1]	c.218.0	c.47.0	189	1,082	10.6	555	7.9
Cyprus	—	—	—	9.9	71.6	15.5	793	2,600	7.0	525	20.7
Czechoslovakia	13.2	19,180	72,358	145.5[1]	1,692.3	289.8	15	151	26.8	1,584	18.2
Denmark	2.5[1]	3,460	1,920	66.5	1,374.9	263.2	1,397	5,530	38.4[2]	2,833[2]	136.1[2]
Finland	6.1	2,984	6,328	74.1	1,075.4	136.2	341	2,359	28.3	1,645	41.9
France	34.1	53,460	67,328	799.4	16,990.0	2,175.0	1,317	12,197	270.0	30,215	1,809.6
Germany, East	14.2	22,263	53,104	c.117.3	2,236.7	262.5	452	1,540	28.6	1,586	67.8
Germany, West	31.7	38,251	57,267	474.3	20,377.2	1,298.3	1,999	9,737	181.5	17,572	1,410.6
Greece	2.5	1,622	856	36.8	618.6	261.2	3,666	33,956	39.2	4,630	60.4
Hungary	8.1	12,605	23,915	99.6	744.7	136.7	23	78	12.4	653	5.5
Ireland	2.0	794	534	89.0[1]	572.7	53.3	110	212	20.0	1,835	86.0
Italy	19.9[1]	38,950	16,320	291.9[1]	16,650.0	1,241.5	1,694	11,492	137.9	12,793	527.6
Netherlands, The	2.8	8,190	2,886	104.5[1]	3,920.0	295.0	1,238	5,180	99.4	12,382	823.0
Norway	4.2	2,060	2,716	78.9	1,106.6	143.1	2,646	26,128	53.9[2]	3,787[2]	144.8[2]
Poland	24.0	46,715	138,072	299.7	1,547.3	509.5	796	3,491	29.4	2,087	18.4
Portugal	3.6	5,163	933	46.9[1]	1,034.3	111.0	342	1,240	34.6	3,380	111.8
Romania	11.1[1]	23,206	70,035	c.95.0[1]	c.220.0	c.110.0	239	1,428	19.4	1,109	13.2
Spain	15.8	16,758	10,876	146.0	5,944.9	1,117.0	2,753	8,056	139.6	14,601	386.1
Sweden	12.1	5,586	14,782	128.9	2,857.1	169.1	696	6,508	62.5[2]	4,064[2]	202.7[2]
Switzerland	5.0[1]	8,094	6,218	62.2	1,932.8	168.6	27	231	89.3	10,147	430.7
U.S.S.R.	271.3[1]	322,200	3,426,000	1,405.4	c.6,640.0	c.6,330.0	7,991	22,262	...	127,055	2,800.0
United Kingdom	18.3	29,280[3]	20,500[3]	c.370.9	c.14,350.0	c.1,740.0	3,359	30,897	334.6	40,416	1,159.9
Yugoslavia	10.0	10,926	23,379	119.8	1,923.9	158.0	468	2,366	31.9	2,720	29.9
ASIA											
Bangladesh	2.9	4,634	701	c.7.0	20.0[1]	9.4[1]	141	284	8.0	519	c.17.0
Burma	4.3[1]	3,500	507	22.0[1]	37.7[1]	40.5[1]	73	71	5.3	178	1.3
Cambodia	c.0.6	54[1]	10[1]	c.11.0[1]	27.2[1]	11.0[1]	3	4	0.8	42	0.4
China	50.0	45,670[1]	533,300	890.0	c.50.0[1]	1,044.0[1]	713	5,169	23.8	c.1,500	97.0
India	c.60.7	168,300	161,600	1,232.3[1]	799.5[1]	415.2[1]	591	5,759	80.1	9,070	323.3
Indonesia	7.6[1]	3,810	853	c.115.0	479.3	327.1	1,093	1,272	72.3	3,917	56.9
Iran	4.6[10]	3,511[1]	4,627[1]	c.52.0[1]	932.7	204.0	208	1,195	44.0	4,116	c.83.0
Iraq	2.0[1]	797[1]	2,254[1]	9.7[1]	150.4	74.5	115	1,306	13.9	1,333	41.4
Israel	0.8[1]	280[1]	535	11.7	312.8	101.4	55	421	33.7	4,855	205.0
Japan	26.8	301,911	40,270	1,088.3	19,942.5	11,369.6	9,321	39,182	296.6	25,654	1,316.5
Korea, South	5.7	20,140	10,719	45.7	125.6	119.1	1,148	2,975	42.3	5,475	402.0
Malaysia	2.4	1,270[4]	1,293[4]	25.1[1]	572.1	196.2	182	552	29.9	2,533	86.8
Pakistan	8.8	12,993	8,677[1]	87.5	202.8[1]	60.5[1]	80	442	39.1	4,648	199.8
Philippines	1.1[1]	692	49	119.2	440.5	327.1	577	1,265	43.5	4,430	126.6
Saudi Arabia	0.6[1]	72[1]	66[1]	26.3[1]	c.376.4	c.500.4	154	1,246	56.1	4,923	109.0
Syria	1.7[1]	269	426	16.3[1]	62.8[1]	50.2[1]	41	27	11.4	795	9.4
Taiwan	4.0	8,122	2,658	17.1	209.9	149.5	444	1,620	30.0	5,355	594.4
Thailand	3.9	5,628[1]	2,505[1]	66.7	c.344.0	c.329.3	117	335	31.8	4,196	139.6
Turkey	8.1[1]	5,088	6,260	196.0[1]	512.4[1]	190.3[1]	460	1,359	23.1	1,910	15.5
Vietnam	c.4.2	...	...	c.60.0	c.100.0[1]	c.200.0[1]	80	163	...	...	...
AFRICA											
Algeria	3.9	1,369[1]	1,727[1]	80.4[1]	286.1[1]	154.7[1]	121	1,152	24.0	1,723	c.10.5
Congo	0.8	294	478	c.11.0	20.0[1]	13.0[1]	16	7	2.8[5]	152[5]	14.2[5]
Egypt	4.9[1]	8,748[1]	2,201[1]	26.6	283.2	64.0	205	456	23.1	2,325	25.8
Ethiopia	1.0	132[6]	260[6]	23.0	43.3[1]	8.9[1]	17	23	11.2	512	26.0
Gabon	—	—	—	6.9	c.10.1[1]	c.7.3[1]	15	78	3.8	129	8.6
Ghana	1.0[1]	431[1]	305[1]	32.2	64.0[1]	46.0[1]	85	186	3.5	234	3.6
Ivory Coast	0.7	1,172[7]	551[7]	45.2	84.9[1]	43.5[1]	65	157	2.6[5]	169[5]	14.0[5]
Kenya	2.4[1]	...	3,653[1]	50.1[1]	114.1	83.9	20	15	8.6	563	16.0
Liberia	0.5	...	4,396[1]	11.2	15.8	5.9	2,523	80,191	1.3	8	—
Libya	—	—	—	c.20.0[1]	386.0	181.6	75	885	10.4	815	7.5
Malawi	0.6	67	223	15.7	11.5	15.5	—	—	3.4	138	7.2
Morocco	1.8[1]	835	3,474	26.7[1]	347.4[1]	121.6[1]	117	341	24.0	1,901	23.2
Nigeria	3.5[1]	785[1]	972[1]	105.0	133.7	23.6	101	324	17.6	1,268	10.3
Senegal	1.0	180[1]	164[1]	13.8	68.4	32.0	80	29	2.5[5]	152[5]	13.9[5]
Somalia	—	—	—	c.17.1[1]	8.0[1]	8.0[1]	19	73	1.1	19	0.3
South Africa	20.1	...	80,963[8]	202.9	2,163.5	821.2	295	661	57.1	7,243	239.5
Sudan	4.7	...	2,324[1]	c.50.0	c.55.0	c.30.0	13	43	9.9	555	10.4
Tanzania	c.3.5	...	...	c.35.0	43.6	46.4	26	37	1.3	37	0.3
Tunisia	2.0	692	1,373	21.9	110.0	75.0	41	112	11.5	1,181	10.9
Uganda	1.3[1]	...	...	25.5[1]	c.28.4[1]	c.17.5[1]	1	6	...	...	...
Zaire	5.3[1]	467[1]	2,203[1]	c.145.0	96.7	87.1	34	110	11.8	696	40.6
Zambia	c.2.0	320[1]	897[1]	34.9	c.104.5	c.62.5	1	6	8.6	545	37.1
Zimbabwe	3.4	...	5,588	78.9[1]	c.180.0	c.70.0	—	—	4.9	237	1.8
NORTH AND CENTRAL AMERICA											
Canada	70.0	2,660	200,900	872.0[1]	9,016.3[1]	2,266.4[1]	1,289	2,954	282.3	25,967	675.8
Costa Rica	1.0	81[1]	14[1]	24.7[1]	59.8[1]	42.7[1]	19	10	6.7	360	19.1
Cuba	14.7	767[1]	1,848[1]	29.5[1]	80.0[1]	40.0[1]	331	779	11.1	773	11.0
El Salvador	0.6	...	...	11.0[1]	70.1	35.5	2	2	7.1	219	c.25.0
Guatemala	1.8	...	117[1]	17.1	82.7[1]	50.1[1]	7	12	4.2	153	7.1
Honduras	1.8[1]	174[1]	3[1]	7.7	14.3	24.9	70	131	5.2	270	5.5
Mexico	24.4	5,040	36,230	200.1	2,682.0	1,077.6	336	727	105.8	8,520	96.2
Nicaragua	0.4	28[1]	14[1]	17.9	c.38.0	c.30.0	30	35	2.0	77	2.0
Panama	0.5	...	...	7.9	71.7	17.7	3,640	20,749	8.1	384	4.2
United States	320.2	16,560[9]	1,206,360[9]	6,207.6	109,676.0[1]	26,524.0[1]	4,746	16,188	3,892.0	359,631	10,080.0
SOUTH AMERICA											
Argentina	38.0	11,242	10,370	207.4	2,588.0[1]	1,101.0[1]	432	2,001	73.0	5,295	128.6
Bolivia	3.8	366[1]	518[1]	38.1[1]	31.0[1]	41.0[1]	—	—	9.8	558	27.8
Brazil	30.3[1]	11,638[1]	63,246[1]	1,489.1[1]	6,348.6[1]	737.4[1]	565	3,702	171.3	8,724	477.6
Chile	10.8[1]	2,030	2,038	74.9	294.6	164.6	146	466	21.5	1,433	107.7
Colombia	3.4[1]	391	1,216	51.0	387.5	67.4	61	272	45.8	3,376	176.1
Ecuador	1.0	65	46	21.5[1]	51.3[1]	77.2[1]	59	201	14.2	551	9.8
Paraguay	0.5	23	17	c.12.0	26.8	8.4	26	22	2.6	86	1.0
Peru	2.1[1]	528[1]	612	56.9[1]	300.4	166.2	686	575	23.9	1,353	36.0
Uruguay	3.0	389	307	25.0	127.1[1]	104.2[1]	48	174	3.6	74	0.3
Venezuela	c.0.4	42[1]	15[1]	58.6[1]	1,172.4	488.0	201	824	43.6	3,072	118.2
OCEANIA											
Australia	40.8[1,10]	...	32,030	837.9[1]	5,284.0[1]	1,260.5[1]	426	1,532	186.7	19,239	413.2
New Zealand	4.7	497	3,402	96.0[1]	1,251.6	245.0	109	211	48.1	4,115	145.7

Note: Data are for 1977 or 1978 unless otherwise indicated. (—) Indicates nil or negligible; (. . .) indicates not known; (c.) indicates provisional or estimated.
[1] Data given are the most recent available. [2] Including apportionment of traffic of Scandinavian Airlines System. [3] Excluding Northern Ireland. [4] Including Singapore.
[5] Including apportionment of traffic of Air Afrique. [6] Including Djibouti traffic. [7] Including Upper Volta traffic. [8] Including Namibia traffic. [9] Class 1 railways only. [10] State system only.
Sources: UN, *Statistical Yearbook 1978, Monthly Bulletin of Statistics, Annual Bulletin of Transport Statistics for Europe 1977;* Lloyd's Register of Shipping, *Statistical Tables 1978;* International Road Federation, *World Road Statistics 1978;* International Civil Aviation Organization, *Civil Aviation Statistics of the World 1977.*

(M. C. MacDONALD)

near Tilbury, to serve containerships in the U.K.–Australia trade, became operational. Major developments continued at the main Indian ports, and at Singapore containerized cargo handled in the first half of 1979 was more than 25% above that of a year earlier. (W. D. EWART)

FREIGHT AND PIPELINES

Freight movement continued to increase in 1979, with air freight the leader. On land, road freight increased its market share with the gradual change in the balance of goods movement from raw materials to manufactured products. The European Economic Community (EEC) proposed a change in the maximum weight of articulated trucks to 40 metric tons (5 axles) and 44 tons (6 axles), thus harmonizing the wide range of national standards within the Community. Energy considerations led to increased use of diesel engines and improved vehicle design. The effort to increase the use of electric vehicles focused on urban goods delivery, and there were demonstration projects in the U.K., France, the U.S., and Japan. Energy considerations also prompted more attention to mixed-mode freight transport, with consequent growth in containerized transport and "piggyback" systems in which trucks ride on railroad flatcars.

Most significant pipeline developments continued to be associated with the exploitation of oil and natural gas. The 36-in (91-cm)-diameter, 450-km-long (one km = 0.62 mi) submarine pipeline, the world's largest, between the Brent field in the North Sea and St. Fergus in Scotland was complete but still awaited the flow of gas because of delayed exploitation of the field. In the U.S. construction of a 48-in-diameter pipeline was started to connect offshore oilfields in the Gulf of Mexico to Louisiana 1,500 km away. In the U.S.S.R. 6,000 km of gas pipeline were laid to support the increased extraction of gas, much of this being associated with the Urengaiskoye and Vynpurovskoye fields. Including projects on the scale of the Mackenzie Delta and Dempster line to bring gas down from the Arctic, pipeline laying for fossil fuel products in the non-Communist world reached 40,000 km a year.

Technological developments included the use of tilted launch slips on pipelaying vessels. On land, carefully laid beds and thin-wall pipes reduced costs for large-diameter (1 m and over) pipes, and the use of large-diameter reels for smaller diameter pipes at sea was developed by British Petroleum in the North Sea. The use of composite materials and gas cooling to increase flow and minimize permafrost problems became more widespread.

In the U.S.S.R. a 2,400-km pipeline to transport ammonia between the Volga River and the Black Sea was nearing completion. The energy situation fostered the use of coal, which under certain circumstances could profitably be carried by pipeline. Two coal pipelines operating in the U.S. used a water carrier to convey coal more than 500 km, but research showed that using a productive oil carrier could significantly increase the viability of this form of transportation for long distances.

ROADS AND TRAFFIC

The growth in world economic activity during most of the year led to a steady increase in vehicle production and traffic. The U.S., Japanese, and some European motor industries reached an all-time high, and in the U.S.S.R. motor vehicle output was approaching two million a year. The management of traffic in urban areas received continued attention with experts in the industrialized world brought together in an Organization for Economic Cooperation and Development meeting in Paris. The message that clearly emerged was that private car use must be selectively controlled if it was to make its fullest contribution to urban travel.

The economic and environmental problems of road building in the industrialized world continued. The length of the U.S. Interstate Highway System exceeded 63,000 km at a cost of $70 billion, and it was estimated that it would cost about $30 billion to build the remaining 5,000 km. Major projects under way in the less developed world included a 6,000-km $2.2-billion road program in Saudi Arabia and a $2-billion highway stretching 1,200 km from Ramadi to Basra in Iraq. In Taiwan the north–south freeway extending from Keelung to Kaohsiung was completed at a cost of $700 million, and in China the Karakoram Highway link-

To protest the high cost of diesel fuel and government red tape, a truck convoy headed for Plains, Georgia, hometown of U.S. Pres. Jimmy Carter. The truckers were stopped by police a mile short of their goal.

WIDE WORLD

UPI

The first subway system in a southern U.S. city began running in June when Atlanta, Georgia, inaugurated its subway service.

ing Pakistan with China was finished. The latter, much of it over mountainous terrain, was described as one of the most difficult highway construction projects ever attempted. In Latin America the Pan-American Highway continued to develop slowly, but the link with the U.S. Interstate Highway System (the Darien Gap) remained in limbo.

The importance and costs of highway maintenance were underlined in 1979. The harsh winter in Europe showed how serious cold weather could be for systems not properly equipped to handle such conditions. In the U.S. a study of highway expenditure showed a need for $900 billion to be spent on the national road system up to the end of the century, most of which would be on maintenance.

In the field of road construction the use of tunneling grew, especially in Japan, where more than 60 km of road in tunnels was being built. Recycling of road pavement materials was becoming more widespread, and the replacement of asphalt by sulfur as the binding matrix was well developed.

INTERCITY RAIL

Further electrification was planned by many of the world's major railway systems. British Rail proposed increasing its electrified route mileage from 20 to nearer 50% of the total system, and the Chinese railways planned to increase theirs from 13 to 65% by 1985. In the industrialized world new rail construction was limited, the main exceptions being the building of new high-speed lines such as the Paris–Lyon and Rome–Florence. The first of these involved the construction of 540 bridges and viaducts and was designed to be capable ultimately of sustaining operating speeds up to 300 kph. In the less developed world railway construction was often a major feature of development plans. Venezuela planned to construct a national railway system virtually from scratch as a way of investing its oil revenues to secure its long-term economic future. China had 3,000 km of new line under construction (the existing network length being about 50,000 km), and the continental railway plan for Africa, published in 1979, proposed 15,000 km of new track.

Growing intercity traffic did not ease the financial problems of railway systems. In West Germany subsidies to the state railways totaled $8 billion, and in the U.S. Conrail gave up its immediate target of financial viability and Amtrak proposed to reduce its 45,000 km of route served by up to 40%. British Rail managed to keep its revenue deficit under control, but in anticipation of rising costs considered withdrawing passenger services from about 1,500 km of its routes.

High Speed Train (HST) services were fully operational on the east coast of Britain, with most journeys being covered at about 140 kph. In the U.S. 200-kph locomotives were delivered, but track conditions did not allow genuine HST services to be run. In Japan the original "bullet train" equipment was completely replaced, and speed targets for new Shinkhansen services were being lowered in response to complaints about the noise, vibration, and drafts caused by the original trains.

URBAN MASS TRANSIT

New urban mass transit systems were under construction in such diverse cities as Helsinki, Baltimore, Cairo, Miami, Lille in France, and Calcutta. During 1979 new systems were inaugurated in Hong Kong, Rio de Janeiro, Atlanta, Ga., and Nürnberg, and existing systems were extended in London, Vienna, Moscow, Frankfurt am Main, Sydney, and Montreal. New York City's subway, which marked its 75th anniversary, had the world's longest route length (421 km), followed by London (418 km), Paris (252 km), Tokyo (196 km), and Moscow (164 km).

Improvements to suburban railways in many cities included cross-central area links, such as those opened in Frankfurt am Main and Stuttgart in West Germany and in Paris (Orsay–Invalides) and those planned for Philadelphia; rolling stock and signal modernization; and automatic fare collection (AFC). The number of AFC projects extended to Hong Kong, Sydney, São Paulo in Brazil, and Atlanta, Ga.

Despite the high level of activity, three major rolling stock manufacturers in the U.S. withdrew from the mass transit business (Pullman, Rohr, and Boeing Vertol). There were similar problems with buses; British Leyland planned to close down the production line for its new Titan double-decker bus. Interest in Light Rail Vehicle (LRV) systems continued to grow, and the world's largest manufacturer (Tatra of Czechoslovakia) was producing more than a thousand vehicles a year. Existing systems such as those in Toronto, San Francisco, and Boston were renewing their rolling stock, and new systems were being planned or built in Adelaide, Australia; San Diego, Calif.; Portland, Ore.; St. Louis, Mo.; and a number of other cities. Conversely, Mexico City was closing most of its tramway network because the rolling stock was worn out.

Further difficulties were experienced with the U.S. Transbus project, and the St. Paul (Minn.) Downtown People Mover shut down. However, technologically advanced "conventional" vehicles were delivered in many cities. In West Germany hybrid battery/trolley and diesel/trolley buses were in operation. (DAVID BAYLISS)

See also Energy; Engineering Projects; Environment; Industrial Review: *Aerospace; Automobiles*.

Trinidad and Tobago

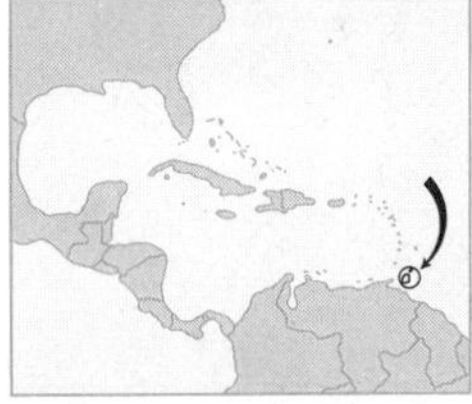
Trinidad and Tobago

A republic and a member of the Commonwealth of Nations, Trinidad and Tobago consists of two islands off the coast of Venezuela, north of the Orinoco River delta. Area: 5,128 sq km (1,980 sq mi). Pop. (1978 est.): 1,133,000, including (1970) Negro 43%; East Indian 40%; mixed 14%. Cap. and largest city: Port-of-Spain (pop., 1976 est., 47,300). Language: English (official); Hindi, French, Spanish. Religion (1970): Christian 64%; Hindu 25%; Muslim 6%. President in 1979, Sir Ellis Clarke; prime minister, Eric Williams.

Trinidad prospered during 1979 because of high world prices for oil and gas. Total expenditures for 1979 amounted to TT$3,549,000,000. Direct government-to-government agreements for locally contracted projects were signed with France, The Netherlands, Great Britain, Canada, and West Germany. Progress was made with schemes utilizing the island's cheap energy, and plans to construct a bauxite smelter that would produce 180,000 metric tons a year were well advanced.

The choice of a successor to Prime Minister Eric Williams, who had said that the ruling People's National Movement should determine the succession, was a major issue. No one figure emerged, but Karl Hudson-Phillips, a former attorney general and one-time heir apparent to Williams, began building an island-wide power base through a National Land Tenants' and Ratepayers' Association. The opposition United Labour Front remained divided.

The government refused to meet members of Grenada's new government until elections were held there. In contrast, Williams encouraged wide-ranging economic agreements with those Caribbean Common Market nations pursuing "moderate" policies. A collision between two loaded supertankers, "Atlantic Empress" and "Aegean Captain," 29 km (18 mi) off the coast of Tobago on July 19, discharged over 250,000 tons of oil, but none of it washed up on the Tobago or Trinidad beaches. (DAVID A. JESSOP)

TRINIDAD AND TOBAGO

Education. (1976–77) Primary, pupils 190,200, teachers 6,474; secondary, pupils 81,600, teachers 1,631; vocational, pupils 4,000, teachers (1975–76) 114; teacher training (1975–76), students 1,188, teachers 116; higher, students 2,830, teaching staff (1975–76) 221.

Finance and Trade. Monetary unit: Trinidad and Tobago dollar, with (Sept. 17, 1979) a par value of TT$2.40 to U.S. $1 (free rate of TT$5.16 = £1 sterling). Gold, SDR's, and foreign exchange (June 1979) U.S. $1,709,000,000. Budget (1978 est.) balanced at TT$3,167,000,000. Foreign trade (1977): imports TT$4,525,700,000; exports TT$4,791,600,000. Import sources: Saudi Arabia 22%; U.S. 21%; Indonesia 14%; U.K. 13%; Japan 5%. Export destination: U.S. 69%. Main exports: crude oil and products 90%.

Transport and Communications. Roads (1977) *c.* 7,100 km. Motor vehicles in use (1977): passenger 117,700; commercial 24,200. There are no railways in operation. Air traffic (1978): 678 million passenger-km; freight 13.3 million net ton-km. Shipping traffic (1977): goods loaded 20,834,000 metric tons, unloaded 14,585,000 metric tons. Telephones (Jan. 1978) 74,900. Radio receivers (Dec. 1976) 270,000. Television receivers (Dec. 1976) 110,000.

Agriculture. Production (in 000; metric tons; 1978): sugar, raw value *c.* 149; rice 22; tomatoes *c.* 10; oranges *c.* 12; grapefruit *c.* 11; copra *c.* 10; coffee *c.* 3; cocoa *c.* 5. Livestock (in 000; 1977): cattle *c.* 75; pigs *c.* 56; goats *c.* 43; poultry *c.* 7,060.

Industry. Production (in 000; metric tons; 1978): crude oil 11,854; natural gas (cu m; 1977) *c.* 2,020,000; petroleum products (1977) 13,492; cement 223; nitrogenous fertilizers (nutrient content; 1977–78) 43; electricity (kw-hr) 1,614,000.

Tunisia

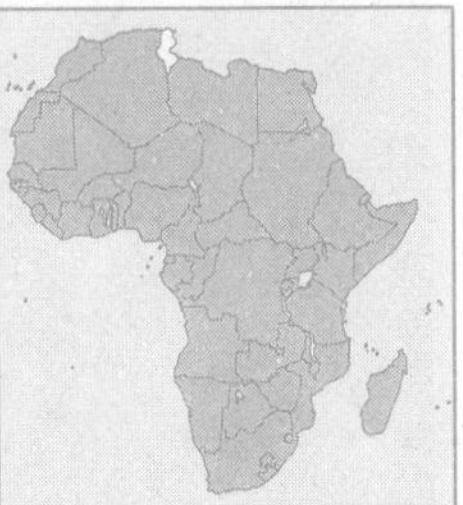
Tunisia

A republic of North Africa lying on the Mediterranean Sea, Tunisia is bounded by Algeria and Libya. Area: 164,150 sq km (63,379 sq mi). Pop. (1979 est.): 6,201,000. Cap. and largest city: Tunis (pop., 1975 census, city proper 550,404; 1976 est., governorate 1,011,600). Language: Arabic (official). Religion: Muslim; Jewish and Christian minorities. President in 1979, Habib Bourguiba; prime minister, Hedi Nouira.

In January 1979 Pres. Habib Bourguiba resumed his full schedule of activities, which he had given up since Oct. 23, 1978, for reasons of health, and showed himself still to be the master of the political situation. He took the opportunity to initiate important measures intended to assure the succession to the presidency and also to keep Tunisia firmly in the ranks of the moderate Arab states. Relations with Egypt were broken on April 27.

Trapshooting: *see* Target Sports

Trucking Industry: *see* Transportation

Trust Territories: *see* Dependent States

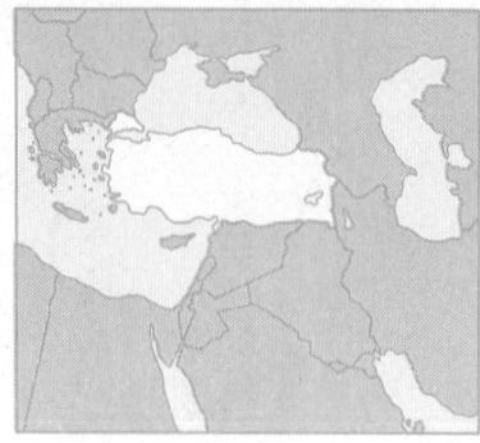

Turkey

TUNISIA

Education. (1978–79) Primary, pupils 1,004,144, teachers (1977–78) 25,149; secondary, pupils 247,299; vocational, (1977–78) pupils 50,887; secondary and vocational, teachers 10,052; teacher training, students 1,987, teachers 125; higher (1976–77), students 23,137, teaching staff 3,089.

Finance. Monetary unit: Tunisian dinar, with (Sept. 17, 1979) a free rate of 0.41 dinar to U.S. $1 (0.87 dinar = £1 sterling). Gold, SDR's, and foreign exchange (June 1979) U.S. $356 million. Budget (1978 est.) revenue 541 million dinars; expenditure 421 million dinars. Gross domestic product (1978) 2,426,000,000 dinars. Money supply (June 1979) 673,660,000 dinars. Cost of living (Tunis; 1975 = 100; March 1979) 124.4.

Foreign Trade. (1978) Imports 881,740,000 dinars; exports 461,810,000 dinars. Import sources: France 34%; West Germany 12%; Italy 10%. Export destinations: France 16%; Italy 16%; West Germany 16%; Greece 9%; U.S. 9%; Libya 6%; Bahamas 5%. Main exports: crude oil 37%; clothing 13%; phosphates 9%; olive oil 8%; phosphoric acid 5%. Tourism (1977): visitors 1,016,000; gross receipts U.S. $325 million.

Transport and Communications. Roads (1977) 21,887 km. Motor vehicles in use (1977): passenger 110,000; commercial 75,000. Railways: (1977) 2,005 km; traffic (1978) 692 million passenger-km, freight 1,373,000,000 net ton-km. Air traffic (1978): 1,181,000,000 passenger-km; freight 10.9 million net ton-km. Telephones (Jan. 1978) 144,100. Radio receivers (Dec. 1976) 810,000. Television receivers (Dec. 1976) 208,000.

Agriculture. Production (in 000; metric tons; 1978): wheat 707; barley *c.* 200; potatoes (1977) *c.* 90; tomatoes *c.* 280; watermelons (1977) *c.* 160; grapes *c.* 90; dates *c.* 45; olives *c.* 450; oranges *c.* 120. Livestock (in 000; 1977): sheep *c.* 3,600; cattle *c.* 890; goats *c.* 950; camels *c.* 190; poultry *c.* 15,100.

Industry. Production (in 000; metric tons; 1978): crude oil 4,897; natural gas (cu m) 290,000; cement 881; iron ore (53% metal content) 339; pig iron 138; phosphate rock (1977) 3,615; phosphate fertilizers (1977–78) 246; petroleum products (1977) 1,174; sulfuric acid 1,238; electricity (excluding most industrial production; kw-hr) 1,786,000.

Chedli Klibi (dark glasses) took over as newly elected secretary-general of the Arab League in June. He was formerly minister of information for Tunisia.

M'SADAK—SIPA PRESS/BLACK STAR

Bourguiba confirmed that his successor would be Prime Minister Hedi Nouira. Toward his opponents he dispensed clemency or firmness as the occasion warranted. To mark his 75th birthday, on August 3, he pardoned the labour union leader Habib Achour; previously, in May, he had let off 263 convicted political offenders. However, in June and again in August a total of 77 of his opponents were sentenced to hard labour in prison. In Paris the signatories of the "collective of January 26" demanded that 120 political prisoners be set free, but without success.

Muhammad Sayah was confirmed in his position as director of the Parti Socialist Destourien (PSD), but Abdallah Farhat was dismissed as being too outspoken. Bourguiba took Farhat's post of minister of defense away from him in September and dismissed him from the political office of the PSD in November. The ministerial reshuffle that followed reinforced the personal authority of Nouira, who as secretary-general of the party was already publicly established after the tenth PSD congress in September. Although the opposition boycotted the legislative elections of November 4, the turnout of voters exceeded 81% of the electorate. Electors had a choice between two Destourian Socialists for each of the 121 seats.

In June the Tunisian minister of information, Chedli Klibi, replaced Mahmoud Riad of Egypt, who had resigned in March, as secretary-general of the Arab League. At an Arab summit meeting at Tunis in November, delegates of the moderate Arab states took the opportunity to reject demands for the adoption of extreme measures against U.S. interests in the Middle East.

Iran's revolution aroused disquiet and vigilance in Tunisia. The government condemned the seizure of hostages at the U.S. embassy in Teheran and in November suspended for three months a pan-Islamic publication that defended the regime of Ayatollah Ruhollah Khomeini.

There was some easing of relations with Algeria after the Algerian minister for foreign affairs, Muhammad Sedik Ben Yahia, visited Tunis on April 26–27. He was received by President Bourguiba, Prime Minister Nouira, and Foreign Minister Muhammad Fitouri. (PHILIPPE DECRAENE)

Turkey

A republic of southeastern Europe and Asia Minor, Turkey is bounded by the Aegean Sea, the Black Sea, the U.S.S.R., Iran, Iraq, Syria, the Mediterranean Sea, Greece, and Bulgaria. Area: 779,452 sq km (300,948 sq mi), including 23,698 sq km in Europe. Pop. (1979 est.): 44,284,000. Cap.: Ankara (pop., 1978 est., 2,018,000). Largest city: Istanbul (pop., 1978 est., 2,801,000). Language: Turkish, Kurdish, Arabic. Religion: predominantly Muslim. President in 1979, Fahri Koruturk; prime ministers, Bulent Ecevit and, from November 12, Suleyman Demirel.

Acute economic and social difficulties led to the fall of the government of Bulent Ecevit, leader of the left-of-centre Republican People's Party (RPP), in October 1979. On January 4 his handling of the riots in December 1978 in the southeastern city of Kahramanmaras came under attack from Suleyman Demirel, leader of the free-enterprise Justice Party. At that time Ecevit won a vote of confidence in the National Assembly by a vote of 226 to 210. He was unable, however, to stem the violence engendered by the feud between extreme rightists and leftists, complicated by religious animosities

TURKEY

Education. (1976–77) Primary, pupils 5,499,456, teachers 182,314; secondary, pupils 1,030,746, teachers 28,908; vocational, pupils 282,746, teachers 16,297; teacher training, students 40,775, teachers 2,507; higher, students 339,-692, teaching staff 16,981.

Finance. Monetary unit: Turkish lira, with (Sept. 17, 1979) a free standard rate of 49.42 liras to U.S. $1 (106.33 liras = £1 sterling) and a basic rate of 35 liras to U.S. $1 (75 liras = £1 sterling). Gold, SDR's, and foreign exchange (June 1979) U.S. $1,397,000,000. Budget (1977–78 rev. est.): revenue 182,030,000,000 liras; expenditure 223,010,-000,000 liras. Gross national product (1978) 1,228,-630,000,000 liras. Money supply (Dec. 1978) 290.4 billion liras. Cost of living (1975 = 100; June 1979) 373.9.

Foreign Trade. (1978) Imports 113,291,000,000 liras; exports 55,358,000,000 liras. Import sources: West Germany 16%; France 8%; Italy 6%; U.S. 6%; Switzerland 6%; Iraq 5%; Libya 5%. Export destinations: West Germany 22%; Italy 8%; U.S. 7%; France 6%; U.K. 5%; Switzerland 5%; U.S.S.R. 5%. Main exports: fruit and vegetables 27%; cotton 15%; textile yarns and fabrics 11%; tobacco 10%; wheat 9%. Tourism (1977): visitors 1,661,000; gross receipts U.S. $205 million.

Transport and Communications. Roads (1976) 195,982 km (including 189 km expressways). Motor vehicles in use (1976): passenger 512,400; commercial 190,300. Railways: (1976) 8,138 km; traffic (1977) 5,088,-000,000 passenger-km, freight (1978) 6,260,000,000 net ton-km. Air traffic (1978): 1,910,000,000 passenger-km; freight 15.5 million net ton-km. Shipping (1978): merchant vessels 100 gross tons and over 460; gross tonnage 1,358,-779. Telephones (1978) 1,379,000. Radio licenses (1977) 4,261,000. Television receivers (1977) 2,272,000.

Agriculture. Production (in 000; metric tons; 1978): wheat *c.* 16,500; barley *c.* 4,700; corn *c.* 1,300; rye *c.* 690; oats *c.* 370; potatoes *c.* 2,800; tomatoes *c.* 3,300; onions *c.* 850; sugar, raw value *c.* 1,103; sunflower seed *c.* 520; cottonseed 806; chick-peas *c.* 180; dry beans *c.* 170; cabbages (1977) *c.* 620; pumpkins (1977) *c.* 302; watermelons (1977) *c.* 4,100; cucumbers (1977) *c.* 405; oranges *c.* 660; lemons *c.* 330; apples *c.* 900; grapes *c.* 3,000; raisins *c.* 341; hazelnuts (1977) *c.* 270; olives *c.* 1,100; tea *c.* 84; tobacco *c.* 290; cotton, lint *c.* 515. Livestock (in 000; Dec. 1977): cattle 14,540; sheep 42,708; buffalo 1,012; goats 18,276; horses 843; asses 1,407; chickens 48,427.

Industry. Fuel and power (in 000; metric tons; 1978): crude oil 2,856; coal 4,376; lignite 8,787; electricity (kw-hr) 21,600,000. Production (in 000; metric tons; 1978): cement *c.* 15,500; iron ore (55–60% metal content) 3,209; pig iron 736; crude steel 1,628; petroleum products (1977) *c.* 13,-710; sulfuric acid 193; fertilizers (nutrient content; 1977–78) nitrogenous *c.* 187, phosphate *c.* 276; chrome ore (oxide content; 1977) 329; cotton yarn *c.* 110; man-made fibres (1977) 50.

and by Kurdish nationalist agitation. On April 25 martial law was extended from 13 to 19 of the country's 67 provinces, covering the Kurdish-speaking area. Some 2,000 political killings occurred during Ecevit's 22-month premiership.

Inflation rose to an annual rate of 99% during March–August. There were shortages of essential supplies, especially petroleum (rationed in Istanbul on July 1). Prices for petroleum products and many state-produced goods were raised on March 16; an austerity program was unveiled on March 21; and a system of premiums for foreign exchange was introduced on April 10. As consolidated on June 11, these amounted to a devaluation of the lira by 43% against the U.S. dollar, to 47.10 liras = U.S. $1.

The Organization for Economic Cooperation and Development (OECD) agreed to coordinate aid to Turkey, and at a meeting in Paris in May $1,450,-000,000 was pledged by 14 countries, led by the U.S. and West Germany. The aid was conditional on Turkey's coming to terms with the International Monetary Fund, which was achieved in July. Subsequent agreements were reached with banks in London and with the OECD consortium.

The banning of a labour union May Day rally alienated Ecevit's leftist supporters. By June resignations of ministers from the government and of deputies from the ruling RPP deprived the government of its parliamentary majority, and it could survive only by staying away from the Assembly and thus preventing a vote of censure before the recess on July 3. In midterm Senate elections and five by-elections on October 14, the RPP was decisively rejected by the electorate. All five by-elections were won by Demirel's Justice Party. Ecevit resigned on October 16. Demirel was asked by Pres. Fahri Koruturk to form the new administration, and a minority Justice Party government took office on November 12.

Negotiations with the U.S. for a new defense cooperation agreement, begun in January, could not be completed by October 9, when the provisional arrangements governing the reactivation of some U.S. bases were due to expire. The arrangements were then extended by three months. On October 19, speaking as caretaker prime minister, Ecevit rejected the placing of new U.S. nuclear warheads in Turkey and welcomed the force-reduction proposals made by Soviet Pres. Leonid Brezhnev. Relations with the European Economic Community (EEC) were also difficult; an EEC delegation visited Ankara on September 20, but agreement on Turkey's demands for aid and concessions was not achieved.

On July 13 Palestinian terrorists seized the staff of the Egyptian embassy in Ankara. Two Turkish policemen were killed, and an Egyptian diplomat died. The siege was lifted through the mediation of the Palestine Liberation Organization; afterward, Turkey implemented an earlier decision to allow the PLO to open an office in Ankara and accorded it the status of a diplomatic mission on September 27. The Ankara-based Central Treaty Organization, from which Iran withdrew after the fall of the shah, was formally dissolved on September 26.

(ANDREW MANGO)

Tuvalu

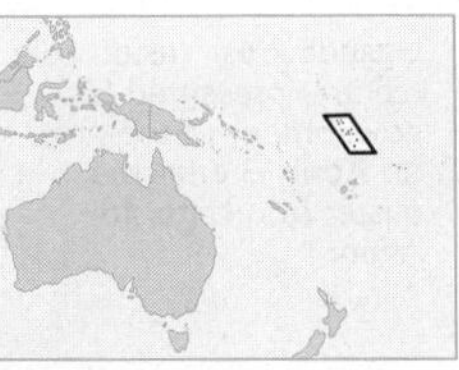
Tuvalu

A constitutional monarchy comprising nine main islands and their associated islets and reefs, Tuvalu is located in the western Pacific Ocean just south of the Equator and west of the International Date Line. Area: 26 sq km (9.5 sq mi). Pop. (1979): 7,400, mostly Polynesians. Cap.: Funafuti (pop., 1979., 2,200). Queen, Elizabeth II; governor-general in 1979, Penitala Fiatau Teo; prime minister, Toalipi Lauti.

In its first year as a sovereign state, Tuvalu continued to pursue financial independence and the improvement of basic services. In September 1979 an Australian-funded A$1 million marine training school was opened and a start was made on a A$1.8 million deep-sea wharf (also Australian-funded) at Funafuti. Under an aid agreement with the U.K., a high priority was given to an interisland seaplane service.

Prime Minister Toalipi Lauti caused internation-

Tunnels:
see Engineering Projects

TUVALU

Education. (1977) Primary, pupils 1,600, teachers 48; secondary, pupils 260, teachers 12; higher (overseas), students 5.

Finance and Trade. Monetary unit: Australian dollar, with (Sept. 17, 1979) a free rate of A$0.89 to U.S. $1 (A$1.92 = £1 sterling). Budget (1978 est.) balanced at A$1,503,000 (including U.K. aid of A$494,000). Main export (1977) copra (valued at A$55,600).

al comment when he invested A$500,000 with the Blue Chip Realty Investment Co. of U.S. businessman Sidney Gross as Tuvalu's side of an arrangement under which Gross would raise a A$4.5 million loan to finance a Tuvalu fishing fleet. Money from the sale of stamps still accounted for more than half of Tuvalu's locally raised revenue, with the balance coming from duties and taxes; the budget was balanced by a British grant-in-aid.

Tuvalu signed a treaty of friendship with the U.S. in which the latter renounced its 40-year-old claims to four of the Tuvalu islands. The two governments agreed to future consultation on security matters and the development of marine resources.

(BARRIE MACDONALD)

UGANDA

Education. (State aided; 1977) Primary, pupils 1,139,420, teachers 32,554; secondary, pupils 58,816, teachers 2,665; vocational, pupils 3,890, teachers 270; teacher training, students 7,405, teachers 374; higher (1975), students 5,474, teaching staff 617.

Finance and Trade. Monetary unit: Uganda shilling, with (Sept. 17, 1979) a free rate of UShs 7.44 to U.S. $1 (UShs 16 = £1 sterling). Budget (1978–79 est.): revenue UShs 4,769,000,000; expenditure UShs 3,923,000,000. Foreign trade (1977): imports UShs 1,992,000,000; exports UShs 4,884,000,000. Import sources: Kenya 57%; U.K. 9%; West Germany 9%; Italy 6%. Export destinations: U.S. 38%; U.K. 17%; The Netherlands 6%; France 5%. Main export: coffee 93%.

Transport and Communications. Roads (1976) 25,535 km. Motor vehicles in use (1976): passenger *c.* 28,400; commercial *c.* 17,500. Railways (1975) 1,301 km. Telephones (Jan. 1978) 48,900. Radio receivers (Dec. 1976) 250,000. Television licenses (Dec. 1976) 71,000.

Agriculture. Production (in 000; metric tons; 1978): millet *c.* 489; sorghum *c.* 520; corn *c.* 660; sweet potatoes (1977) *c.* 660; cassava (1977) *c.* 1,100; peanuts *c.* 208; dry beans *c.* 175; bananas *c.* 360; coffee 156; tea *c.* 10; cotton, lint *c.* 20; meat (1977) *c.* 121; fish catch (1977) 179; timber (cu m; 1977) *c.* 14,611. Livestock (in 000; 1977): cattle *c.* 4,900; sheep *c.* 1,100; goats *c.* 2,150; pigs *c.* 190; chickens *c.* 12,250.

Industry. Production (in 000; metric tons; 1977): cement 80; copper ore (metal content) 10.8; tungsten concentrates (oxide content) 0.14; electricity (kw-hr) 689,000.

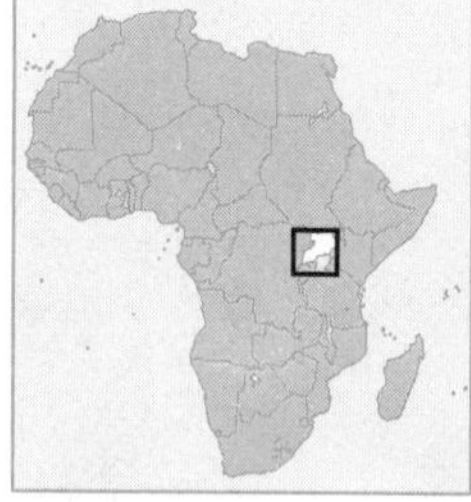

Uganda

Uganda

A republic and a member of the Commonwealth of Nations, Uganda is bounded by Sudan, Zaire, Rwanda, Tanzania, and Kenya. Area: 241,139 sq km (93,104 sq mi), including 44,081 sq km of inland water. Pop. (1979 est.): 13,224,900, virtually all of whom are African. Cap. and largest city: Kampala (pop., 1979 est., 540,000). Language: English (official), Bantu, Nilotic, Nilo-Hamitic, and Sudanic. Religion: Christian, Muslim, traditional beliefs. Presidents in 1979, Gen. Idi Amin, Yusufu K. Lule from April 13, and Godfrey L. Binaisa from June 20.

In 1979 Uganda witnessed the expulsion of its tyrant Idi Amin and the fragile stirring of democracy in the ruins left by tyranny and war. In January Tanzanian troops, believed to have been accompanied by Ugandan exiles, launched an attack across Uganda's southwestern border in retaliation for President Amin's invasion of Tanzania in October 1978. They had the backing of Ugandan guerrillas inside the country, while the Ugandan Army itself seemed disunited. In mid-February Amin appealed for a meeting of the UN Security Council to discuss the fighting, but without success. As the Tanzanian troops advanced steadily northeastward, Pres. Julius Nyerere of Tanzania (*see* BIOGRAPHIES) rejected peace proposals put forward by Col. Muammar al-Qaddafi of Libya. He also responded angrily to a suggestion that the Organization of African Unity should intervene, pointing out that it had failed to act when Uganda invaded Tanzania.

Uganda Pres. Yusufu Lule (centre) presented his government to the press on April 13 after the ouster of dictator Idi Amin.

YVES-GUY BERGES—SYGMA

Amin's appeal for help to Iraq produced no results. Reinforcements of men and equipment arrived from Libya at the beginning of March, but they failed to halt the Tanzanian advance. At the end of the month Tanzania accused Kenya of assisting Amin by permitting Libyan planes to fly fuel from Nairobi to a Ugandan airfield. The charge was denied by Kenya's Pres. Daniel arap Moi, but the Kenyans feared that former Ugandan president Milton Obote might be restored to office by Nyerere and strong ties formed between Uganda and Tanzania, to Kenya's detriment. Nyerere, however, insisted that Ugandans themselves must determine how and by whom they should be ruled. In March a group of prominent Ugandan exiles, meeting in Moshi, Tanzania, chose Yusufu Lule, former vice-chancellor of Makerere University in Uganda, to lead a 14-man government to take charge when Amin was overthrown.

The invading forces captured Entebbe with its international airport on April 5, and Kampala fell a week later. President Lule was sworn in on April 13 in a capital ravaged as much by looters as by military action. Conscious of the tribal divisions within the country, he called for united action to restore stability in Uganda, a difficult task given the legacy of hatred left by Amin's years of terror.

The Owen Falls hydroelectric complex was captured intact in mid-April, and on April 22 the town of Jinja fell. Meanwhile, Amin's troops massacred civilians in the eastern town of Tororo, while Amin himself visited Iraq attempting to solicit help. Subsequently, he took refuge in Libya, leaving his followers to escape northward to Sudan. In June the Tanzanian Army claimed control of the whole country.

On April 26 the British government, which had restored diplomatic relations with Uganda's new rulers, offered £1 million in emergency aid with more to follow, and Kenya followed suit with a further £1 million. Early in May fuel supplies began once again to move by rail from Nairobi after Western oil suppliers had reached agreement over the debts incurred by Amin. In an attempt to revive the economy, President Lule offered to consider paying compensation for some of the larger Indian businesses that had been seized but not handed over to Africans. Later in May, plans were made to bring charges against 1,000 of Amin's supporters who had been involved in serious crimes. One of those against whom capital charges were made was Robert Astles, Amin's British-born adviser, who was later extradited from Kenya, where he had taken refuge.

Early in June, Lule appointed four new ministers and reshuffled his Cabinet. Various explanations were given for the reorganization, but none seemed wholly satisfactory. The changes provoked a sharp reaction, however, and Lule was forced to resign after a vote of no confidence by Uganda's National Consultative Council, which accused him of acting dictatorially. He was replaced on June 20 by Godfrey L. Binaisa (*see* BIOGRAPHIES).

Lule himself was flown to Dar es Salaam and eventually to London, but en route he visited Kenya where he strongly criticized Binaisa's government and its Tanzanian support. President Moi, concerned at the continuing presence of Tanzanian troops in Uganda, called for their withdrawal. A demonstration by Baganda supporters of Lule in Kampala had to be dispersed by troops.

More serious was the fact that thousands of weapons remained in unauthorized hands, and members of the former Ugandan Liberation Movement were reluctant to surrender their arms. The retention of some Tanzanian troops was essential until an effective Ugandan police force and army could be created. Kampala, in particular, was the scene of much lawlessness and murder. Outside Buganda, Binaisa had stronger support. Although he was himself a Muganda, he had never had close links with the Buganda hierarchy, and he made it clear that he wished to discourage tribalism.

In August the government banned all political parties for two years, providing time to develop a well-grounded democratic system to replace the multiplicity of parties that had sprung up after the country's liberation. The president reaffirmed that there would be a general election before June 3, 1981, as had been promised by the previous government. In early October Binaisa opened a 127-member General Assembly, 61 of whom were elected by newly constituted district councils, as a step toward democracy. (KENNETH INGHAM)

Union of Soviet Socialist Republics

Union of Soviet Socialist Republics

The Union of Soviet Socialist Republics is a federal state covering parts of eastern Europe and northern and central Asia. Area: 22,402,200 sq km (8,649,500 sq mi). Pop. (1979 prelim. est.): 262.4 million, including (1970) Russians 53%; Ukrainians 17%; Belorussians 4%; Uzbeks 4%; Tatars 2%. Cap. and largest city: Moscow (pop., 1979 prelim. est., 8,011,000). Language: officially Russian, but many others are spoken. Religion: about 40 religions are represented in the U.S.S.R., the major ones being Christian denominations. General secretary of the Communist Party of the Soviet Union and chairman of the Presidium of the Supreme Soviet (president) in 1979, Leonid Ilich Brezhnev; chairman of the Council of Ministers (premier), Aleksey N. Kosygin.

Domestic Affairs. For the Soviet leadership and people 1979 was a trying year. The severe winter appeared to have caught the authorities unprepared, and this resulted in power cuts, burst water pipes, and general discomfort, especially in Moscow, where many cases of frostbite were reported.

Leonid Brezhnev's health remained a constant source of rumour and interest. One Western news agency even reported him dead in October. He still remained nominally in charge of the Communist Party of the Soviet Union and head of the country but was no longer capable of the heavy work load of former years. Changes at the top level of the government were minimal, the most significant being the promotion of Nikolay Tikhonov (74) from candidate to full membership of the Politburo, where he appeared to be the most likely successor to the ailing Aleksey Kosygin as premier.

Unemployment:
see Economy, World; Social Security and Welfare Services

UPI

Five dissidents who were released from Soviet labour camps in exchange for two Soviet spies held in a U.S. prison gave thanks for their release at a press conference after they arrived in New York City in April.

Also promoted—to candidate membership of the Politburo—was Mikhail Gorbachov (49), a Central Committee secretary and a specialist in agriculture. The striking rise of Konstantin Chernenko (68) continued. Chernenko was head of the General Department (the section that services the Politburo) of the Central Committee secretariat. He was Brezhnev's constant traveling companion and the recipient of high honours in Eastern Europe. On a visit to Bulgaria with Brezhnev in January, he received an especially warm welcome from Todor Zhivkov, the Bulgarian party leader. Many observers regarded him as the favourite to succeed the 73-year-old Brezhnev.

Elections to the Supreme Soviet and many other soviets in March constituted the year's major domestic political events. Overall, the unopposed government candidates received 99.9% of the votes cast. The highest percentage was recorded in the Nagorno-Karabakh autonomous province of the Azerbaijan S.S.R., where it was claimed that all of the votes were for the official candidate. The lowest was in Estonia, where the official slate received 99.5%. An attempt to nominate Roy Medvedev, a dissident historian, and Ludmila Agapova failed when the authorities disqualified their group, Election '79, on the grounds that it was not a legitimate organization. Nikolay V. Podgorny, the former president, was not nominated and thereby lost his last official function.

Apparently seeking not to provide U.S. opponents of ratification of the SALT II agreement (see *Foreign Affairs*, below) with too much ammunition, the Soviet Union avoided staging large trials of dissidents during the year. The most prominent event regarding dissidents was the release in April of Eduard Kuznetsov, Mark Dymshits, Aleksandr Ginzburg, Valentin Moroz, and Georgy Vins. They were all flown to the U.S. in exchange for Valdik Enger and Rudolf Chernyaev, two Soviet UN employees who had each been sentenced to 50 years in prison for spying.

Kuznetsov and Dymshits had originally been sentenced to death in 1970 for planning to hijack a plane to leave the country, but this had been commuted to 15 years in prison after worldwide protests. Another 4 of the 12 involved in the case left Riga for Israel on April 27 after eight years in prison: Leib Knokh, Boris Penson, Wolf Zalmanson, and Anatoly Altman. Earlier, another prisoner, Hillel Butman, was reported to have received permission to emigrate to Israel.

Ginzburg had administered the distribution of funds received from Aleksandr Solzhenitsyn and others to help the families of political prisoners. Moroz, a poet, had been involved in publicizing aspects of Ukrainian life that never appeared in the official press. Vins was a Baptist pastor and belonged to that wing of the Baptist movement that took a critical view of Soviet state practices toward religion. The exchange was unique in that the five Soviet dissidents had no connection with the U.S. and had never been accused of spying. It legitimized U.S. concern for Soviet citizens on general humanitarian grounds.

It was announced in Moscow on January 30 that three Armenians, Stepan Zatikyan, Akop Stepanyan, and Zaven Bagdasaryan, had been executed after being found guilty of causing an explosion on

U.S.S.R.

Education. (1978–79) Primary, pupils 34.3 million; secondary, pupils 10.4 million; primary and secondary, teachers 2,641,000; vocational and teacher training (1977–78), students 4,662,000, teachers 227,000; higher, students 5,109,600, teaching staff (1977–78) 336,000.

Finance. Monetary unit: ruble, with (Sept. 17, 1979) a free rate of 0.68 ruble to U.S. $1 (1.47 rubles = £1 sterling). Budget (1979 est.): revenue 269.1 billion rubles; expenditure 268.8 billion rubles.

Foreign Trade. (1978) Imports 34,554,000,000 rubles; exports 35,641,000,000 rubles. Import sources: Eastern Europe 49% (East Germany 11%, Poland 10%, Czechoslovakia 9%, Bulgaria 9%, Hungary 7%); Cuba 6%; West Germany 6%; U.S. 5%; Japan 5%. Export destinations: Eastern Europe 48% (East Germany 11%, Poland 10%, Bulgaria 9%, Czechoslovakia 8%, Hungary 7%); Cuba 5%. Main exports: crude oil and products 28%; machinery 13%; gold *c.* 10%; transport equipment 7%; iron and steel 6%.

Transport and Communications. Roads (1977) 1,405,400 km. Motor vehicles in use (1977): passenger *c.* 6,640,000; commercial (including buses) *c.* 6,330,000. Railways: (1976) 271,300 km (including 132,800 km industrial); traffic (1977) 322,200,000,000 passenger-km, freight (1978) 3,426,000,000,000 net ton-km. Air traffic (1977): 127,055,000,000 passenger-km; freight 2,800,000,000 net ton-km. Navigable inland waterways (1977) 143,100 km; freight traffic 230,700,000,000 ton-km. Shipping (1978): merchant vessels 100 gross tons and over 7,991; gross tonnage 22,261,927. Telephones (Jan. 1978) 19.6 million. Radio receivers (Dec. 1975) 122.5 million. Television receivers (Dec. 1978) 75 million.

Agriculture. Production (in 000; metric tons; 1978): wheat 120,800; barley *c.* 62,100; oats *c.* 18,500; rye *c.* 13,600; corn *c.* 9,000; rice *c.* 2,100; millet *c.* 2,200; potatoes *c.* 85,900; sugar, raw value *c.* 9,100; tomatoes *c.* 6,500; watermelons (1977) *c.* 3,196; apples *c.* 7,000; sunflower seed 5,310; cottonseed *c.* 5,525; linseed *c.* 320; soybeans *c.* 680; dry peas *c.* 6,100; wine *c.* 2,460; tea *c.* 95; tobacco *c.* 330; cotton, lint 2,640; flax fibres (1977) *c.* 517; wool 277; hen's eggs *c.* 3,539; milk *c.* 94,000; butter *c.* 1,472; cheese *c.* 1,521; meat *c.* 15,300; fish catch (1977) 9,352; timber (cu m; 1977) *c.* 389,000. Livestock (in 000; Jan. 1978): cattle 112,690; pigs 70,511; sheep 141,025; goats 5,586; horses (1977) *c.* 6,000; chickens 880,900.

Industry. Index of production (1975 = 100; 1978) 116. Fuel and power (in 000; metric tons; 1978): coal and lignite 724,000; crude oil 572,500; natural gas (cu m) 372,000,000; manufactured gas (cu m; 1977) 37,300,000; electricity (kw-hr) 1,202,000,000. Production (in 000; metric tons; 1978): cement 129,300; iron ore (metal content; 1977) 131,418; pig iron *c.* 112,000; steel 151,000; aluminum (1977) *c.* 1,640; copper (1977) *c.* 1,440; lead (1977) *c.* 510; zinc (1977) *c.* 720; magnesite (1977) *c.* 1,850; manganese ore (metal content; 1977) 2,904; tungsten concentrates (oxide content; 1977) *c.* 10; gold (troy oz) *c.* 8,000; silver (troy oz) *c.* 45,000; sulfuric acid 22,405; caustic soda (1977) 2,658; plastics and resins 3,500; fertilizers (nutrient content; 1977) nitrogenous 9,025, phosphate 5,586, potash 8,347; newsprint (1977) 1,390; other paper (1977) 7,676; cotton fabrics (sq m) 6,970,000; woolen fabrics (sq m; 1977) 989,000; rayon and acetate fabrics (sq m; 1977) 1,648,000; passenger cars (units) *c.* 1,300; commercial vehicles (units) *c.* 760.

the Moscow subway in January 1977, in which people were killed. Zatikyan was known as an Armenian nationalist, and pleas that he was not in Moscow at the time were ignored.

Among other dissidents sentenced were Aleksandr Ogorodnikov, an organizer of Orthodox church seminars, to one year in a labour camp for "parasitism"; Vasily Ovsienko, a Soviet writer connected with Ukrainian dissidents, three years at hard labour for resisting a policeman; Aleksandr Orlik, a Pentecostalist, one year in a labour camp for refusing military service; Vladimir Shelkov, spiritual leader of the "Free Adventists," five years in a strict labour camp (four other members of the sect were also sentenced); Boris Kalendorov, a Jewish activist in Leningrad who had been refused permission to emigrate to Israel, two years at hard labour for evasion of military service; and Arkady Tsurkov, five years in a strict labour camp for distributing anti-Soviet propaganda via the "left-wing opposition" journal *Perspectives.*

A new clandestinely published literary venture, *Metropol,* was prevented from appearing by the authorities in January. The official Communist Party newspaper *Pravda* censored 23 prominent Soviet writers who had protested the nonpublication of some of their work. They included Vasily Aksenov, Bella Akhmadulina, and Andrey Voznesensky. All the censored writers were involved with *Metropol.* Evgeny Popov and Viktor Erofeev, also associated with *Metropol,* were expelled from the Moscow branch of the writers' union, their work being deemed of "insufficient literary merit," and Aksenov resigned from the union in protest.

Crimean Tatars continued their campaign to be allowed to return to their homeland. Two hundred of them were arrested on March 15 when they tried to submit a petition to the Supreme Soviet calling for the return of all Tatars to the Crimea. They were then taken forcibly to Tashkent in Central Asia.

Evidence of continuing nationalist sentiment in the Baltic republics was provided on August 23, the 40th anniversary of the Stalin-Hitler pact, when 45 dissidents from Estonia, Latvia, and Lithuania provided Western journalists in Moscow with a declaration asserting the right of the republics to independence and national self-determination. Together with physicist Andrey Sakharov and four other activists they appealed to the UN to recognize the right of the Baltic nations to determine their own future. Roman Catholic feeling remained high in Lithuania, and 10,000 believers from Klaipeda signed a memorandum calling for the return of their confiscated church. The economic difficulties in Estonia, especially in food supplies, continued, and there were rumours that an attempt had been made to assassinate Karl Vaino, the Estonian first secretary, during the spring.

The continued exodus of Jews (about 12,000 in the first quarter of the year) and Germans led to the formation of a "combat committee," which demanded in May in Moscow that all Soviet citizens, not only Jews and Germans, should have the right to emigrate. Some prominent Soviet émigrés were deprived of their Soviet citizenship. These included Aleksandr Zinoviev, a philosopher and author of *Yawning Heights* (*see* LITERATURE: *Russian*); Viktor Korchnoi, a chess grand master; and Viktor Nekrasov, a novelist. Nekrasov was accused of "systematically pursuing activities incompatible with citizenship of the U.S.S.R." and of "besmirching the title of citizen of the U.S.S.R."

There were several trials of alleged war criminals from the World War II period. *Pravda* reported in February that three Soviet citizens had been executed for war crimes in Belgorod and in March that eight men had been found guilty of serving in SS execution squads. Vilnius radio in Lithuania stated in July that Ionas Plunge had been executed for war crimes committed while in command of punitive forces organized by the Nazis.

A spate of defections caused acute embarrassment in Moscow cultural and sporting circles in September and October. The Bolshoi Ballet lost three dancers during a tour of the U.S., Leonid and Valentina Kozlov and Aleksandr Godunov (*see* BIOGRAPHIES). Some comfort was derived from the fact that Godunov's wife, Ludmila Vlasova, chose to return to the Soviet Union. This followed a diplomatic incident when U.S. authorities refused to allow the Soviet plane to leave until they were satisfied that Vlasova was returning of her own accord. She was rewarded with a heroine's welcome when she arrived home. The defections were the first from the Bolshoi, previous dancers having come from the Leningrad Kirov Ballet. Then followed the defections of well-known figure skaters Oleg Protopopov and Ludmila Belousova in Switzerland. Even more perplexing for the Soviet authorities was the fact that four of the five defectors were members of the Communist Party. One immediate reaction was to cancel a month-long tour of the U.S. by the 110-member Moscow State Symphony, scheduled for October.

The arrests in November of Tatyana Velikanova, a leading dissident, Father Gleb Yakunin, an Orthodox priest, and Antanas Terleckas, a Lithuanian nationalist, were the first of dissidents as-

Oleg Protopopov and Ludmila Belousova, who defected from the Leningrad Ice Revue while the troup was in Switzerland, signed a three-year contract with the Ice Capades in the U.S.

WIDE WORLD

sociated with the Helsinki monitoring group since the major dissident trials in the summer of 1978, and they appeared to mark the beginning of a campaign to suppress dissent. This was certainly the view of Andrey Sakharov, who thought that the authorities had embarked on the "complete suppression" of the democratic, religious, and nationalist movements in the U.S.S.R.

The Economy. The hard winter followed by spring flooding caused considerable disruption in industry and agriculture. Much winter grain was lost and had to be replaced with lower yielding spring varieties. Industrial production in the first three quarters rose by only 3.4% and was unlikely to exceed 3.6% for the whole year, well below the planned goal of 5.7%. One of the reasons for this was the small growth in labour productivity, which increased by only 2.4% during the first three quarters. In his report to the Supreme Soviet in November, Nikolay Baibakov, chairman of the State Planning Commission, revealed that production targets for 1980, the final year of the current five-year plan, would have to be lowered. The growth rate for the whole period had been set at 36% but now seemed unlikely to exceed 25.7%.

Oil production at 435 million metric tons was 0.5% short of the target. This represented only a 3% increase over the same period in 1978. It illustrated the difficulties facing Soviet oilmen, as increases of about 8% annually had been normal only a few years earlier. The chemical industry was 5% behind target, and mineral fertilizer output was 96% of the 1978 total.

Agriculture fared no better. The year's harvest was put at 179 million metric tons, a shortfall of about 47 million tons. This caused the U.S.S.R. to buy grain, for feed, in North America and elsewhere, and by early November it was estimated that the government had contracted for more than 20 million metric tons. The increasing price of gold and hydrocarbons on the world market would make it easy for the U.S.S.R. to find the hard currency to import the 30 million or so metric tons of grain needed—almost exclusively for animal fodder. The U.S.S.R. did well by selling oil on the Rotterdam spot market, and its total hard currency debt was not expected to grow much in 1979 and to be in the region of $17 billion. Anglo-Soviet trade expanded in 1979, but British exports slumped. Grain purchases were expected to boost U.S.-Soviet trade for 1979 above 1978 levels.

Soviet students demonstrated in front of the Chinese embassy in February to protest the Chinese invasion of Vietnam.

UPI

The most far-reaching changes in the management of the national economy since 1965 were promulgated in July. The goal was to base the Soviet economy on "intensive factors of growth" such as technical progress, quality, and labour productivity and to abandon gross production as the key indicator of success. Bonuses were to be based on the precise fulfillment of contracts, and a more flexible labour policy was to be pursued. This did not appear to permit a factory to shed unwanted labour; redeployment was the goal.

The cost of living rose in 1979. Car prices increased by 18%, imported furniture by 30%, and carpets by 50%. International phone calls jumped 67%, and the cost of international postage rose sharply. Meals in restaurants and cafés also cost more. Basic foodstuffs were largely unaffected, and the government subsidy of meat and dairy products was in the region of 20 billion rubles.

Foreign Affairs. The SALT II agreement was finally signed by President Brezhnev and U.S. Pres. Jimmy Carter in Vienna in June. The Soviet leader was to have gone to the U.S. for the signing but pleaded inability to fly long distances. The last stages of the negotiations were hectic and involved concessions on both sides. Soviet decision-making was rapid, presumably meaning that only a small group of top political and military leaders was involved. (*See* DEFENSE: *Special Report*.)

In September, during the conference of nonaligned nations at Havana, Cuba, U.S. intelligence reports stated that Soviet combat troops were stationed in Cuba. The Soviet response was to dismiss such reports as part of a campaign to prevent ratification of SALT II by the U.S.

The war in Indochina involving China, Vietnam, and Cambodia was a major problem for the Soviet Union. The Soviet-Vietnam treaty of friendship and cooperation required both parties to consult if attacked to "eliminate that attack." But when Chinese troops invaded Vietnam in February, the Soviet Union contented itself with words. Brezhnev castigated China in *Pravda* on March 3 for its "unprecedentedly brazen bandit attack," while Marshal D. F. Ustinov, the minister of defense, deplored China's "criminal" attack on "peace-loving" Vietnam. The Indochina issue caused dissent within the socialist camp. Pres. Nicolae Ceausescu of Romania refused to join the chorus of condemnation of China but did criticize Vietnam's invasion of Cambodia. President Tito of Yugoslavia went to Moscow in May and when he returned stressed the differences between the Soviet leader and himself.

Despite the delicate position in Indochina and the likelihood of further fighting during the dry season in the first quarter of 1980, the U.S.S.R. and China began talks in October aimed at improving relations, the first high-level negotiations for more than a decade. Both delegations were headed

TASS/SOVFOTO

Soviet and Chinese diplomatic delegations began official talks in October aimed at improving relations between the two countries.

by a deputy foreign minister. The talks in Moscow proceeded at a leisurely pace, and they did not prevent China from attacking the Soviet Union in the UN and elsewhere. The Chinese were particularly interested in expanding trade with the U.S.S.R. but remained uninhibited in their condemnation of Soviet attempts to achieve world domination. The visit of Hua Guofeng (Hua Kuofeng) to several Western European countries in October irritated the Soviets, and his outspokenness in Great Britain brought sharp Soviet protests.

Brezhnev upstaged his hosts during East Germany's 30th-anniversary celebrations in East Berlin in October. He declared that the Soviet Union was prepared unilaterally to withdraw up to 20,000 troops and 1,000 tanks from East Germany and to discuss the possibility of a reduction in the number of Soviet SS-20 intermediate-range missiles stationed in the western U.S.S.R. This appeared to be a bid to prevent the deployment, starting in 1983, of 108 Pershing II and 116 cruise missiles with 572 nuclear warheads capable of hitting Soviet targets from NATO bases in Western Europe. Deployment of the missiles was approved by the NATO Council in December, however, and the Soviet offer to withdraw intermediate-range nuclear weapons was subsequently withdrawn.

The full Soviet propaganda machine was set in motion to promote the Soviet proposal. At the 62nd anniversary celebrations of the October Revolution in Moscow, Defense Minister Ustinov denounced "reactionary forces" in the West who were striving to achieve superiority over the Warsaw Pact nations. He claimed that these people in the West were engaging in "lying propaganda" so as to cover up their "dangerous plans." At the same time, he advocated an increase in Soviet military might. But additional military spending was something the U.S.S.R. could ill afford with economic growth slowing at home and commitments abroad, especially in Vietnam and Afghanistan, increasing.

Soviet-Afghan relations were within the framework of the treaty of friendship, good neighbourliness, and cooperation signed on Dec. 5, 1978, and outwardly appeared not to be substantially affected by the change of leadership in Afghanistan in September. Considerable concern was expressed in March in *Pravda* about the deteriorating situation there. More than 100 Soviet military personnel were reported to have been killed in fighting with Muslim rebels. Gen. Aleksey Epishev, Soviet first deputy minister of defense, and six other generals visited Afghanistan in April to assess the situation. Fighting continued throughout the year, with increasing Soviet involvement, culminating in a massive incursion of troops in December and the installation of yet a new leadership in Kabul. At year's end some 40,000 Soviet combat troops were thought to be deployed within Afghanistan. (*See* AFGHANISTAN; DEFENSE.)

India was of considerable importance in Soviet eyes because of the situation in Indochina, and Premier Aleksey Kosygin visited Delhi in March. The communiqué issued at the visit's conclusion demanded that the Chinese get out of Vietnam, but it did not seem that the U.S.S.R. had persuaded India to recognize the pro-Vietnamese regime in Cambodia. However, it appeared that India agreed not to improve relations with China at the expense of its links with the U.S.S.R. Several agreements were signed involving Soviet aid in expanding oil-refining capacity, and steel production at Bhilai and Bokaro was to be increased with Soviet help. The Soviet Union was to receive Indian rice, which would be shipped to Vietnam.

Pres. Valéry Giscard d'Estaing of France visited Moscow in April, and several Franco-Soviet agreements were signed. The construction of new Soviet bases on the islands of Kunashiri and Etorofu in the Kurils archipelago caused a predictable drop in the temperature of Soviet-Japanese relations. The Soviet Union pursued closer relations with the strategically important People's Democratic Republic of Yemen (Aden; South Yemen). A Soviet-South Yemen treaty of friendship and cooperation was signed in Moscow in October, and closer economic relations were foreseen. When its diplomats at the embassy in Teheran were taken hostage, the U.S. accused the Soviet Union of aggravating the situation with broadcasts and reports that inflamed the Iranians. The Soviets later moderated the tone of their dispatches.

The pattern of involving other Warsaw Pact countries in the third world, especially in Africa, continued in 1979. Cuban and East German personnel were particularly active in Angola, Mozambique, and Ethiopia. Soviet foreign policy goals could thus be furthered through surrogate forces. This could be seen as the international division of socialist labour in pursuit of foreign policy objectives. The summit meeting of nonaligned nations in Havana was a success from the Soviet point of view, and the election of Fidel Castro as chairman of the movement for three years was expected to add to Soviet influence in the third world.

Eastern Europe was told that in the future it would have to import an increasing amount of oil from the third world rather than from the U.S.S.R. Nuclear power was seen as a long-term solution to the energy problem, but existing plans for its expansion in Eastern Europe and the Soviet Union were far behind schedule. The U.S.S.R. for the first time admitted that nuclear accidents had occurred but provided no details. (MARTIN MCCAULEY)

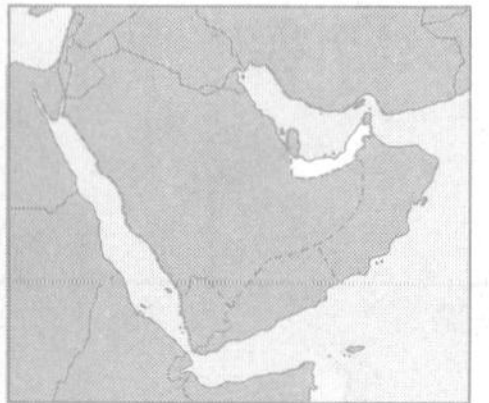

United Arab Emirates

United Arab Emirates

Consisting of Abu Dhabi, Ajman, Dubai, Fujairah, Ras al-Khaimah, Sharjah, and Umm al-Qaiwain, the United Arab Emirates is located on the eastern Arabian Peninsula. Area: 83,600 sq km (32,300 sq mi). Pop. (1979 est.): 877,300, including Arab 42%, South Asian 50% (predominantly Iranian, Indian, and Pakistani), others 8% (mostly Europeans and East Asians). Cap.: Abu Dhabi town (pop., 1975, 95,000). Language: Arabic. Religion: Muslim. President in 1979, Sheikh Zaid ibn Sultan an-Nahayan; prime ministers, Sheikh Maktum ibn Rashid al-Maktum and, from April 25, Sheikh Rashid ibn Said al-Maktum.

The fragile unity of the United Arab Emirates was subject to tensions in 1979 between Abu Dhabi and Dubai over allocation of oil revenues and internal independence. Sheikh Zaid ibn Sultan an-Nahayan of Abu Dhabi, president of the U.A.E., had proposed the abolition of borders between the emirates, a union of their armed forces, a single federal budget, and a central bank. Under a Kuwaiti compromise formula in May, agreed to by Prime Minister Sheikh Rashid ibn Said al-Maktum of Dubai, each emirate would give half its oil revenues to the federal budget but would preserve its independence.

The Cabinet resigned on April 25, and Sheikh Rashid replaced his son as prime minister. A new Cabinet was formed on July 1. Sensitive to Shi'ah Muslim criticism from Iran, Dubai and Umm al-Qaiwain confined the sale of alcohol to non-Muslims. Iran in June refused to return the Abu Musa and the Greater and Lesser Tumbs islands, seized from Sharjah in November 1971. The U.A.E. severed diplomatic relations with Egypt and withdrew support from Egypt's Arab Organization for Industrialization. (CHARLES GLASS)

UNITED ARAB EMIRATES

Education. (1976–77) Primary, pupils 60,742, teachers c. 3,876; secondary, pupils 14,511, teachers c. 1,579; vocational, pupils 625, teachers 270; teacher training, students 89, teachers (1975–76) 8.

Finance. Monetary unit: dirham, with (Sept. 17, 1979) a free rate of 3.78 dirhams to U.S. $1 (8.13 dirhams = £1 sterling). Gold and foreign exchange (June 1979) U.S. $828 million. Budget (federal; 1979–80 est.) balanced at 12 billion dirhams.

Foreign Trade. (1978) Imports 18,936,000,000 dirhams; exports 35,029,000,000 dirhams. Import sources (1977): Japan 19%; U.K. 18%; U.S. 11%; West Germany 9%. Export destinations (1977): Japan 26%; U.S. 16%; France 12%; Netherlands Antilles 7%; The Netherlands 7%; West Germany 6%; U.K. 6%. Main export: crude oil 95%.

Industry. Production (in 000; metric tons): crude oil (1978) 90,012; petroleum products (1977) 494; natural gas (cu m; 1977) c. 1,500,000.

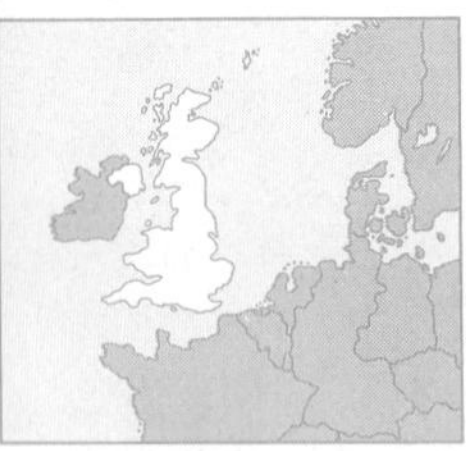

United Kingdom

United Kingdom

A constitutional monarchy in northwestern Europe and member of the Commonwealth of Nations, the United Kingdom comprises the island of Great Britain (England, Scotland, and Wales) and Northern Ireland, together with many small islands. Area: 244,035 sq km (94,222 sq mi), including 3,084 sq km of inland water but excluding the crown dependencies of the Channel Islands and Isle of Man. Pop. (1979 est.): 55,901,000. Cap. and largest city: London (Greater London pop., 1978 est., 6,918,000). Language: English; some Welsh and Gaelic also are used. Religion: mainly Protestant with Catholic, Muslim, and Jewish minorities, in that order. Queen, Elizabeth II; prime ministers in 1979, James Callaghan and, from May 4, Margaret Thatcher.

Domestic Affairs. WINTER OF UNREST. The year 1979 was eventful and mostly painful for the United Kingdom. It began with the worst winter in 15 years and an outbreak of industrial unrest that rocked the Labour Party government to its already shaky foundations. During the previous July the Cabinet had defied the opposition of the Trades Union Congress (TUC) by declaring a 5% guideline for the fourth annual year of pay restraint. The figure was economically logical but politically rash. In November 1978 it had been massively breached by workers at the plants of the Ford Motor Co. The new year began promptly with a series of transport strikes.

A strike of some 2,000 petrol (gasoline) delivery drivers damaged industrial production and inconvenienced motorists. It was soon followed by a strike of road haulage workers in general, rejecting a 15% pay offer. Their activities were compounded

SPURLING—SIPA PRESS/BLACK STAR

Margaret Thatcher, the first woman prime minister of England, took over residence at No. 10 Downing Street following her election victory in May.

by a series of four one-day strikes by train drivers. The truck drivers' strike lasted until the beginning of February. It caused massive layoffs in industry, and was exacerbated by still other strikes, such as the one that closed the British Leyland car factory at Longbridge, Birmingham. In the end it was settled by a virtual capitulation of the employers. Meanwhile, local government and hospital workers had embarked upon a series of one-day work stoppages. Some 1,250,000 employees, many of them poorly paid, were involved in the dispute, the effects of which included the turning away by hospitals of all but emergency cases, the acceptance by ambulances of only emergency calls, the piling up in the streets of uncollected trash, the closing of schools due to the withdrawal of caretakers, and in some parts of the country an accumulation of unburied dead.

The public found these disputes not only inconvenient but shocking. For the government, with its special claim to a good working relationship with the trade unions, the events of January and February were deeply damaging. Not only did the disputes, and their inflationary outcome, wreak havoc with the government's economic strategy and its claim to have mastered inflation, but they also brought trade unionism itself into disrepute. There was public concern with the extent of picketing and with some of the methods used, which, to television viewers, seemed often to be scarcely distinguishable from intimidation. And there was disgust that industrial action should be employed against the sick and the poor. Prime Minister James Callaghan called what was going on not free collective bargaining but "free collective vandalism." The union leaders themselves reasserted only partial control over the strikers by issuing voluntary codes for pickets and by forming local committees to adjudge what were and were not emergencies and to ensure the continuance of essential supplies and services.

The government and the TUC, fearful of the political damage that was resulting, produced in mid-February a much-vaunted document known as the "concordat," the purpose of which was to reaffirm the cooperative relationship between Labour and the unions. The words it contained, however, were a case of too little too late. Although it was the Scots that were to bring the Labour government down, it was the unions that effectively destroyed it.

DEVOLUTION FAILURE. Disaster for the government struck in Scotland. On March 1 referendums were held in Scotland and in Wales to test the public support for legislation enacted by Parliament that would give Scotland its own assembly, with limited legislative as well as executive powers, and give Wales a less powerful version. These attempts at what had become known as "devolution" stemmed chiefly from the alarming rise in the early 1970s of the Scottish National Party (SNP), which, aided by the promise of North Sea oil (the SNP called it "Scottish oil"), was thought likely to seek a mandate for separation in a general election. To appease nationalist sentiment the major political parties were committed to some form of devolution to allow the Scots greater independence within a still-united kingdom.

Only the prospect of the establishment of the assembly in Edinburgh, where building was well advanced, caused the SNP's 11 members of Parliament to keep the Labour government in power. Since the ending of the pact between the Labour and Liberal parties in the previous July, the government had lived a hand-to-mouth parliamentary existence, depending upon the votes of Scots, Welsh, and Irish nationalists. When the March referendum failed to produce the desired result, that, to all intents and purposes, was the end of Callaghan's parliamentary reign.

Wales, where the assembly was rejected by a 4–1 margin, was of secondary importance. In Scotland the result was much closer, and indeed a majority of those voting were in favour of the scheme.

Unions: *see* Industrial Relations

Unitarian Churches: *see* Religion

United Church of Canada: *see* Religion

United Church of Christ: *see* Religion

LONDON DAILY EXPRESS/PICTORIAL PARADE

The coffin of British war hero Earl Mountbatten of Burma was carried from Westminster Abbey after his funeral on September 5. Mountbatten was slain by IRA terrorists.

But a Labour backbencher's amendment required that the "yes" vote should constitute not less than 40% of those eligible to vote. Only 63.6% of the electorate troubled to vote and, of the votes cast, supporters of the assembly outnumbered opponents by 1,230,937 to 1,153,502. Thus, the "yesses" constituted 32.85% and the "noes" 30.78% of eligible voters; devolution was dead—and so was the Callaghan government.

General Election. The end came on March 28. The SNP had by that time turned against the government. Its initiative triggered a motion of "no confidence" from Margaret Thatcher (*see* Biographies), leader of the Conservative opposition. The outcome remained uncertain until the moment the vote was called. The defeat was by one vote only (311–310), and a government was defeated on a confidence vote in the House of Commons for the first time since 1924. An election was now inevitable. It was called for May 3.

The election campaign opened with Callaghan, plainly the underdog, taking the field a week before Thatcher began in earnest. Their roles were curiously reversed. Not only was the incumbent having to catch up while the challenger tried to maintain her advantage, but it was the Labour leader who was trying to harness the forces of conservatism to his cause while the Conservative leader preached the need for radical change. The chief theme of Callaghan's campaign was the threat to jobs, both from advancing technology and as a result of Conservative Party policies. Other issues emphasized were prices and the trade unions. Labour pledged continuing interventions to hold prices down and promised that its relations with the unions would be better than the Conservatives'.

Thatcher fought a cool campaign. Her main emphases were on what Conservative strategists called the "enterprise package," namely, the promises set out in the Conservative manifesto to fight inflation with tight money, encourage people with tax incentives, and redress the balance of industrial power in favour of the employers. The Thatcher campaign was a skillful piece of management that rested on the knowledge that the electorate was ready for a change. The Conservative Party won comfortably, with a majority of 43 overall. The Liberal Party lost 3 of its 14 seats (one of the casualties being former leader Jeremy Thorpe, awaiting trial on a charge of conspiracy to murder). The SNP fared much worse north of the border and lost all but 2 of its 11 seats.

The national vote swing of 5.2% was the largest since 1945. The most significant variation was between the north, where Labour was strong, and Greater London, where the Conservatives fared well. The Conservatives did best of all in the new towns and suburbs of the south. More significant, perhaps, than the geographic variations were the class and occupational ones. The swing to Con-

UNITED KINGDOM

Education. (1976–77) Primary, pupils 5,572,523, teachers 237,699; secondary and vocational, pupils 4,844,165, teachers 285,106; higher, students 753,800, teaching staff (universities only) 33,100.

Finance. Monetary unit: pound sterling, with (Sept. 17, 1979) a free rate of £0.46 to U.S. $1 (U.S. $2.15 = £1 sterling). Gold, SDR's, and foreign exchange (June 1979) U.S. $19 billion. Budget (1979–80 est.): revenue £51,013 million; expenditure £59,371 million. Gross national product (1978) £161,170 million. Money supply (June 1979) £26,548 million. Cost of living (1975 = 100; June 1979) 162.9.

Foreign Trade. (1978) Imports £40,969 million; exports £37,363 million. Import sources: EEC 40% (West Germany 11%, France 8%, The Netherlands 6%, Italy 5%); U.S. 10%; Switzerland 5%. Export destinations: EEC 38% (West Germany 8%, France 7%, The Netherlands 6%, Belgium-Luxembourg 6%, Ireland 5%); U.S. 9%; Switzerland 5%. Main exports: machinery 25%; chemicals 11%; motor vehicles 8%; diamonds 7%; petroleum and products 6%; food 5%. Tourism (1977): visitors 11,490,000; gross receipts U.S. $3,805,000,000.

Transport and Communications. Roads (1977) *c.* 370,900 km (including *c.* 2,405 km expressways). Motor vehicles in use (1978): passenger *c.* 14,350,000; commercial *c.* 1,740,000. Railways (1977): 18,330 km; traffic (excluding Northern Ireland) 29,280,000,000 passenger-km, freight (1978) 20,500,000,000 net ton-km. Air traffic (1978): 40,416,000,000 passenger-km; freight 1,159,900,000 net ton-km. Shipping (1978): merchant vessels 100 gross tons and over 3,359; gross tonnage 30,896,606. Shipping traffic (1978): goods loaded 81,415,000 metric tons, unloaded 156,755,000 metric tons. Telephones (1978) 23,182,200. Radio receivers (1976) 40 million. Television licenses (1978) 18,492,000.

Agriculture. Production (in 000; metric tons; 1978): wheat *c.* 6,450; barley *c.* 9,830; oats *c.* 715; potatoes *c.* 7,072; sugar, raw value *c.* 1,111; cabbages (1977) *c.* 690; cauliflowers (1977) *c.* 250; green peas (1977) *c.* 595; carrots (1977) *c.* 560; apples 990; dry peas 83; tomatoes 136; onions 275; rapeseed *c.* 142; hen's eggs 818; cow's milk 15,836; butter 164; cheese 207; wool 34; beef and veal 1,028; mutton and lamb 227; pork 879; fish catch 8,941. Livestock (in 000; Dec. 1978): cattle 13,507; sheep 21,740; pigs 7,964; poultry 129,564.

Industry. Index of production (1975 = 100; 1978) 109.8. Fuel and power (in 000; metric tons; 1978): coal 123,577; crude oil 53,378; natural gas (cu m) *c.* 37,200,000; electricity (kw-hr) 287,650,000. Production (in 000; metric tons; 1978): cement 15,916; iron ore (26% metal content) 4,246; pig iron 11,415; crude steel 20,307; petroleum products 89,156; sulfuric acid 3,453; plastics and resins 2,764; fertilizers (nutrient content; 1977–78) nitrogenous 1,199, phosphate 445, potash 121; man-made fibres 608; cotton fabrics (m) 379,000; woolen fabrics (sq m) 144,000; rayon and acetate fabrics (m) 458,000; newsprint 319; television receivers (units) 2,058; passenger cars (units) 1,223; commercial vehicles (units) 385. Merchant vessels launched (100 gross tons and over; 1978) 814,000 gross tons. New dwelling units completed (1978) 288,000.

WIDE WORLD

British paratroopers guard the scene where at least 18 soldiers and a civilian had been killed in an IRA bombing ambush in Northern Ireland in August.

servative among skilled workers was twice the national average. Among unskilled workers it was also well above average. The Conservatives did better than ever before among trade union members and won 35% of their vote. The result was a vindication of the Conservative strategists. But in local government elections, also held in May, the trend was reversed; Labour had 417 overall gains, the Conservatives 257 overall losses, and the Liberals 71 overall gains. (*See* Political Parties.)

Conservative Economy and Legislation. Prime Minister Thatcher took office on May 4. Her first major move came a month later when her chancellor of the Exchequer, Sir Geoffrey Howe (*see* Biographies), presented his first budget to the House of Commons. The chief economic jobs in her Cabinet had gone to colleagues with the same commitment to free-market and monetary policies as she had. They included Howe at the Treasury and Sir Keith Joseph (*see* Biographies) at the Department of Industry. The only exception was James Prior (*see* Biographies), who was placed at the Department of Employment in spite of—or perhaps because of—his measured, moderate approach toward the trade union question. It was no surprise, therefore, that the first budget represented a bold break from the past.

The budget's emphasis was on cutting and shifting the burden of taxation. This was in spite of an inheritance of government overspending and a deteriorating international economic environment because of events in Iran. The standard rate of income tax was cut from 33 to 30% and the highest rate cut from 83% to a maximum 60%. But the announced £2,500 million cuts in the planned spending programs of the previous government (plus the sale of £1,000 million of state assets with another £500 million proposed in November for 1980–81) were not enough to offset these reductions. In order to make a dramatic start to the promised cuts in the income tax, Howe, if he was at the same time to remain within his borrowing and money supply limits, was obliged to hoist indirect taxation in the form of the value-added tax from 8 to 15%. Even then the financial community was not convinced that his fiscal posture was compatible with his monetary intentions, and the stock market fell in consequence. The financial leaders turned out to be right, for in November, in what was almost a mini-budget, the chancellor raised the minimum lending rate to 17% and said that there could be no further tax cuts in the following year. Monetary restraint and the fight against inflation were now, he declared, his first and overriding priorities.

In the interim the Cabinet had turned its attention to expenditure plans for the financial year 1980–81. Only by cutting another £2,100 million from planned programs could the government hold expenditure at current levels. This, it began to be understood, was the meaning of "cuts." There could be no actual reduction in the proportion of national resources spent by the government; indeed, it was more likely that this proportion would increase once more. Nevertheless, the "cuts" did result in real cuts in services to the public. This was especially so because the new government's plans included increases in spending on defense and on maintaining law and order. Moreover, in accordance with another election promise, the National Health Service was to be spared the surgeon's knife. The brunt of the cuts, therefore, fell upon the services provided by the local authorities, especially in housing and education. A protest against these economies, organized mainly by the public service trade unions but backed by the TUC and the Labour Party, began swelling after the June budget. But the Labour Party, inside and outside Parliament, was gravely weakened in the latter half of the year by the efforts of its left wing to enforce a rigid adherence to Socialist principles.

STEWART FERGUSON—CAMERA PRESS/PHOTO TRENDS

A referendum on a proposal that would have given Scotland and Wales home rule was defeated March 1 in spite of early returns that indicated it might pass.

In December the British Steel Corp. announced that 52,000 jobs would be eliminated in stages, and its offer of a 2% increase in wages against a 20% union claim resulted in a national steel strike being called to begin Jan. 2, 1980. Yet there were a few hopeful straws in the ill wind. At British Leyland, tottering all year on the brink of collapse, the work force voted overwhelmingly in favour of a survival plan put forward by its chairman, Sir Michael Edwardes (*see* BIOGRAPHIES), requiring large-scale layoffs. In so doing they defied their militant shop stewards. And in the coal industry, which had brought about the downfall of Edward Heath's Conservative government in 1974, the miners rejected their leaders' call for militant action and accepted a 20% pay offer; that a 20% settlement should seem like a reprieve was a measure of the economic situation. And *The Times* and *The Sunday Times* settled their printing dispute and reappeared in November, after nearly a year's absence. (*See* PUBLISHING.)

There were also two headline-making scandals in 1979, the trial of Jeremy Thorpe and the exposure of Sir Anthony Blunt as a former Soviet spy. Thorpe, who had been driven from the leadership of the Liberal Party by scandals involving his private life, found himself on trial accused of conspiring to murder Norman Scott, a former male model and, it was alleged, Thorpe's former lover. Thorpe and his three codefendants were acquitted in June, but Thorpe's political career appeared damaged beyond remedy.

The Blunt affair, which was revealed publicly in November, was even more sensational in that the man who had spied for the Soviet Union during World War II and recruited for them at Cambridge University during the 1930s had for more than 20 years subsequently served the monarch as a courtier with responsibility for the royal art collections. He had confessed his treasonable connection to the security services in 1964 but only in exchange for an immunity from prosecution that extended to a continuation of his cover at Buckingham Palace.

Foreign Affairs. In April the first one-man one-vote election in Rhodesia, or Zimbabwe Rhodesia as it was afterward called, took place. There was strong support within the Conservative Party for quickly recognizing the regime of Bishop Abel Muzorewa, elected to be his country's first black prime minister. A team of observers sent out by the Conservative Party vouched for the fairness of the elections. What was in dispute, however, was not the fairness of the elections but of the constitution under which they had taken place. Lord Carrington (*see* BIOGRAPHIES), as foreign secretary, was resolved to rid Britain of the Rhodesian albatross, which had weighed down the necks of successive governments since 1964. However, he saw the need to obtain the widest international acceptance for an independent Zimbabwe Rhodesia, not only for the sake of the new regime's stability but also for Britain itself, to avoid the risks of diplomatic isolation and economic reprisals from black African nations.

Carrington's ideas prevailed within the Cabinet and led to the successful August meeting of Commonwealth heads of state at Lusaka, Zambia, and an ensuing conference in London, which opened at Lancaster House on September 10. In December the London conference secured broad agreement on a new constitution and a cease-fire. (*See* ZIMBABWE RHODESIA.)

In the other main area of foreign affairs, a statement from the European Commission in Brussels in the early part of the year had confirmed that Britain was about to become the largest net contributor to the budget of the European Economic Community (EEC) and would in 1980 be making a transfer estimated at £1,200 million. Britain was doing this even though it was only seventh richest in the nine-member EEC. Prime Minister Thatcher took fierce exception to this inequity, and at her first attendance at the European Council, in Strasbourg, France, in June, she made plain her determination to obtain redress at the next EEC summit meeting.

Her tactics did not succeed, however. When the European Council met again in Dublin in November, Britain's partners were unwilling to offer more than marginal redress (some £350 million) and did not disguise their exasperation with the prime minister's shrill style of diplomacy. The year thus left Britain once more an uncomfortable member of the EEC in spite of the new government's pretensions to a more wholehearted Europeanism. At the first direct elections to the European Assembly in June, Britain had distinguished itself by a lack of enthusiasm and a dismal turnout. During the year it continued to oppose progress toward common policies on fishing and energy, and it remained a nonparticipating member in the new European Monetary System.

Northern Ireland. The year was marred by two tragedies. On March 30, before the national election, the Conservative "shadow Cabinet's" secretary of state for Northern Ireland, Airey Neave (*see* OBITUARIES), was assassinated by Irish extremists. The bombing took place within the precincts of the House of Commons. On August 27 Lord Mountbatten (*see* OBITUARIES) was also assassinated, by an explosion on his boat while on vacation on the west coast of Ireland. The Provisional wing of the Irish Republican Army (IRA) was responsible, and one captured assailant was tried in Ireland and convicted. The Provisionals kept up their bombings and ambushes, however, especially against soldiers and police. After Mountbatten's death some border cooperation was conceded by Ireland's prime minister, Jack Lynch.

The Conservative secretary of state for Northern Ireland, Humphrey Atkins, sought to bring Northern Ireland's political parties together to seek afresh a constitutional solution to the conflict between Catholics and Protestants. However, a constitutional conference he called for December 3 was postponed after 13 people were injured when 20 bombs were exploded throughout the region on November 26. On December 16, in a new IRA offensive, five British soldiers were killed in bomb explosions. (PETER JENKINS)

See also Commonwealth of Nations; Dependent States; Ireland.

United Nations

The Middle East, Cambodia, southern Africa, and the "North-South" dialogue between rich and poor countries dominated UN proceedings throughout 1979. At the year's end the efforts of Secretary-General Kurt Waldheim and the Security Council to free U.S. hostages being held in Iran attracted worldwide attention.

Iran. On November 9 the president of the Security Council, Sergio Palacios de Vizzio of Bolivia, urged "in the strongest terms," on behalf of the Council, that the captives besieged in the U.S. embassy in Teheran since November 4 be freed at once. In November UN officials offered forums to Iran in which to state its case against the deposed shah in return for the release of the hostages, but in vain. Warning delegates of "the dangerous level of tension arising" from the crisis, Waldheim asked the Council to meet again, which it did on November 27. Waldheim's summons was only the second time in UN history that a secretary-general had exercised his authority under Article 99 of the Charter to call the Council into session (the first was Dag Hammarskjöld's request that the Council meet in July 1960 on the question of the Belgian Congo, now Zaire). The Council met four more times in early December, and the members (and those nonmembers who asked to speak) all condemned Iran for continuing to hold the hostages. On December 4 the Council "urgently" and

BRIAN F. ALPERT—KEYSTONE

Andrew Young, who had resigned as U.S. ambassador to the UN, nevertheless presided over the meetings of the UN Security Council during the month of August because his successor had not yet been confirmed.

unanimously called on Iran to release them and to allow them to leave the country.

The General Assembly on December 17 adopted without dissent a convention to outlaw the taking of hostages. Those nations that signed the pact would be required either to prosecute those who take hostages or to send them back to their countries of origin to stand trial. Nations not signatory to the convention could still lawfully provide safe havens for hostage takers. Though the convention was adopted at a time when the world's attention was focused on the hostages in Iran, this was a coincidence; negotiations for its approval had begun three years earlier.

Meanwhile, on November 29, the U.S. asked the International Court of Justice to rule that Iran had violated its treaty obligations and international law. The court set December 10 to hear arguments, and on December 15 unanimously ordered Iran to release the hostages and to return the embassy to U.S. control. When Iran did not comply by December 31, the Security Council urgently called on Iran (11–0, Bangladesh, Czechoslovakia, Kuwait, and the U.S.S.R. abstaining) to release the hostages, asked Waldheim to do what he could to free them, and decided to meet on Jan. 7, 1980, to adopt sanctions against Iran if it did not accede. Waldheim left at once for Teheran to intercede with the Iranian government. (The Council faced the possibility of convening in 1980 with only 14 of its 15 members in place, since the General Assembly was unable, after 148 ballots, to muster the required two-thirds vote needed to choose either Cuba or Colombia.)

Middle East. Achieving peace in the Middle East remained one of the greatest challenges for the UN, the secretary-general stated in his annual report in September. Waldheim told the summit meeting of nonaligned states in Havana, on September 4 that a well-prepared, international conference of all parties "might provide a way out of the . . . dangerous situation." A just and lasting peace could be achieved, he said, only by arranging a comprehensive settlement that embraced the "inalienable rights" of the Palestinian people. Despite this appeal trilateral talks (Egypt, Israel, U.S.) accounted for such progress as occurred during the year, namely, the return to Egypt of some territory Israel had occupied since 1967.

Not all Middle Eastern developments represented progress, however. On July 24 the Security Council failed to agree to extend the mandate of the UN Emergency Force (UNEF), which had served in the Sinai since 1973, and it was then withdrawn. The Security Council decided to replace it with observers from the UN Truce Supervision Organization, stationed in the area since 1948, but Israel objected. Israel maintained that any replacement force must be answerable directly and exclusively to the Security Council, meet the criteria established in its peace treaty with Egypt, and not be subject to "whimsical removal." In lieu of UNEF, Egyptian and Israeli troops began jointly to police the Sinai, together with strengthened U.S. "early warning" forces.

Recurring cycles of violence were the pattern in southern Lebanon, and the Security Council warned against them. On April 26 it expressed its "deepest concern" about the "significant increase of tension" in Lebanon, and on June 14 it renewed the mandate for the UN Interim Force in Lebanon for six months. The Council also asked Israel to "cease forthwith its acts against the territorial integrity, unity, sovereignty, and political independence of Lebanon, in particular its incursions in Lebanon and the assistance it continues to lend to irresponsible armed elements."

Waldheim told the Council on August 30 that he understood Israel's preoccupation with security, especially after the violent incidents and tragic loss of innocent civilian lives in previous months, but that he did not believe that preemptive strikes against Lebanon were acceptable or indeed justified. Israel argued that it faced a "tragic dilemma" of either waiting for its own civilians to be murdered or moving first to prevent terrorist outrages. Israel also opposed attempts to persuade the Council to adopt any resolution to supersede Resolution 242, which had established guidelines for a Middle East settlement. Israel called the 1967 resolution a "carefully balanced whole" that the Council could tamper with only at the risk of gravely jeopardizing negotiations.

U.S. representative Andrew Young (*see* BIOGRAPHIES) told the Council on August 24 that he did not regret having spoken to Zehdi Labib Terzi, a representative of the Palestine Liberation Organization (PLO), even though his talk ostensibly contravened U.S. government policy and required him to resign. He thought it as "ridiculous" for the U.S. not to talk to the PLO as it was for some nations not to maintain diplomatic relations with Israel.

Cambodia. The Security Council attempted on January 15 to call on all "foreign" (in this case, Vietnamese) forces to observe an immediate ceasefire in Cambodia and to withdraw from that nation. Although the resolution received 13 votes, it failed because of a Soviet veto. The Cambodian plight worsened during the year, and the UN held two special conferences on the problem. At the first (July 20–21 in Geneva), 65 nations pledged U.S. $190 million for Indochinese refugees and offered asylum for at least 266,000 people in the year to follow. At the second (November 5 in New York City), UN members pledged a further $210 million, which fell short of Waldheim's announced goal of $315 million. On November 14 the General Assembly voted 91–21, with 29 abstentions, to demand that Vietnam withdraw its troops from Cambodia. China strongly supported the resolution, while the U.S.S.R. opposed it.

Throughout the year the UN Children's Fund (UNICEF), while celebrating the International Year of the Child, took the lead, together with the International Committee of the Red Cross, in getting planeloads of food and supplies to starving Cambodians. Of particular concern were the children, 90% of whom were estimated to be suffering from malnutrition. (*See* Feature Article: *The International Year of the Child.*)

Southern Africa. During a resumed 33rd session of the General Assembly devoted primarily to budgetary and economic matters (Jan. 15–29, 1979), UN members adopted 15 resolutions con-

BRIAN F. ALPERT—KEYSTONE

By unanimous vote, the United Nations Security Council in December called on Iran to release the hostages being detained in the U.S. embassy in Teheran.

demning South Africa's apartheid (racial separation) policies. The Assembly asked nations on January 23 to end military and nuclear collaboration with the government of South Africa and urged the Security Council to impose mandatory economic sanctions, including an oil embargo, against it.

The 33rd Assembly met again (May 23–31) to discuss Namibia (South West Africa) and on the last day approved a resolution that asked the Council to take punitive action against South Africa for not acting on the UN independence plan for Namibia. The Assembly stated that "South Africa has acted deceitfully through unilateral measures and sinister schemes within Namibia" to frustrate a negotiated settlement and condemned South Africa for imposing a "so-called internal settlement" on the territory "through a fraudulent and illegal 'National Assembly'" designed to perpetuate an illegal occupation. South Africa attempted to join in the Namibian debate for the first time since the Assembly suspended it from participating in UN work in 1974, but once again, over Western objections, the Assembly rejected South Africa's credentials. All the while the secretary-general and Western states were trying to arrange a cease-fire between South Africa and guerrilla forces in order to pave the way for an internationally approved Namibian regime.

In September the chairman of the UN Committee Against Apartheid accused South Africa of committing another crime against the African people by creating Venda, a new bantustan (homeland for black Africans, within the borders of South Africa), and said that the act posed a serious challenge to the international community. He alleged that the bantustan was designed only to consolidate apartheid and to perpetuate white domination in South Africa. The Security Council on September 21 condemned the "so-called independence of Venda" and asked nations not to recognize the new entity.

Angola reported various South African violations of its territory during the year. On March 28 the Council strongly condemned South Africa for "premeditated, persistent and sustained armed invasions" of Angola and called for an immediate end to them. Later Angola alleged that South African attacks between March 27, 1976, and June 11, 1979, had cost it $293 million in damage and destruction, 1,383 confirmed deaths, and 1,915 wounded. South Africa, in return, charged the South West Africa People's Organization (SWAPO) with entering Namibia from Angolan "sanctuaries" and committing acts of violence. South African Foreign Minister Roelof Botha asked the secretary-general in October to help bring "these atrocities" to an end. Angola charged in late October that South Africa had landed 11 helicopters in southern Angola and made a "massive . . . assault" on three provincial capitals, leaving 18 civilians and 2 Angolan soldiers dead; in November it again charged South Africa with carrying out acts of aggression, stating that "the intensity and timing of these racist attacks pose a definite threat to international peace and security." On November 2 the Council again condemned South African "aggression" against Angola.

The Council on March 8 and November 23 also condemned military raids from Zimbabwe Rhodesia on Angola, Mozambique, and Zambia. On April 30 it denounced the "so-called elections held under the auspices of the illegal racist regime" in Zimbabwe Rhodesia and labeled them "null and void." Independent British efforts to achieve an acceptable and lasting settlement in Zimbabwe Rhodesia went on in London for 14 weeks until December 17, when guerrilla leaders agreed to a cease-fire aimed at ending the seven-year Rhodesian civil war. On December 21 the Security Council voted 13–0, the U.S.S.R. and Czechoslovakia abstaining, to lift the 13-year economic embargo against Rhodesia.

North-South Issues. On March 20 a negotiating conference arranged by the UN Conference on Trade and Development (UNCTAD) agreed on the fundamental elements of a common fund to finance international buffer stocks of basic commodities and to develop commodity supplies. When the fifth session of UNCTAD met in Manila (May 7–June 3), it agreed that the world needed to launch a comprehensive program of action for the least developed countries; called for countries to give the poor nations such assistance as was necessary to reach a UN target calling for states to contribute 0.7% of their gross national product toward international assistance programs; and called on industrialized countries to eliminate protectionist measures that handicapped the exports of the less developed economies. The conference failed to agree, however, on a code of conduct to govern transfers of technology from developed to less developed countries.

A UN Conference on Science and Technology for Development (in Vienna, August 20–September 1) adopted a program aimed at maximizing the capacity of all countries to develop, absorb, and use science and technology to benefit their peoples. Delegates asked the General Assembly to create a voluntary interim fund of $250 million to give the UN increased financial resources for promoting the transfer of technology. The World Food Council met in Ottawa, Ont., September 4–7 and called for a world food security system to prevent one-fourth of the world's population from being exposed to the risk of starvation in times of shortage.

The 34th General Assembly (September 18–December 31; Salim Ahmed Salim of Tanzania, president) heard appeals for additional funds to be given by richer countries to the poor, first from Pope John Paul II (October 2) and later from Pres. Fidel Castro of Cuba (October 12), speaking on behalf of 95 non-aligned nations. UN membership rose to 152 with the admission on September 18 of Saint Lucia. (RICHARD N. SWIFT)

UPI

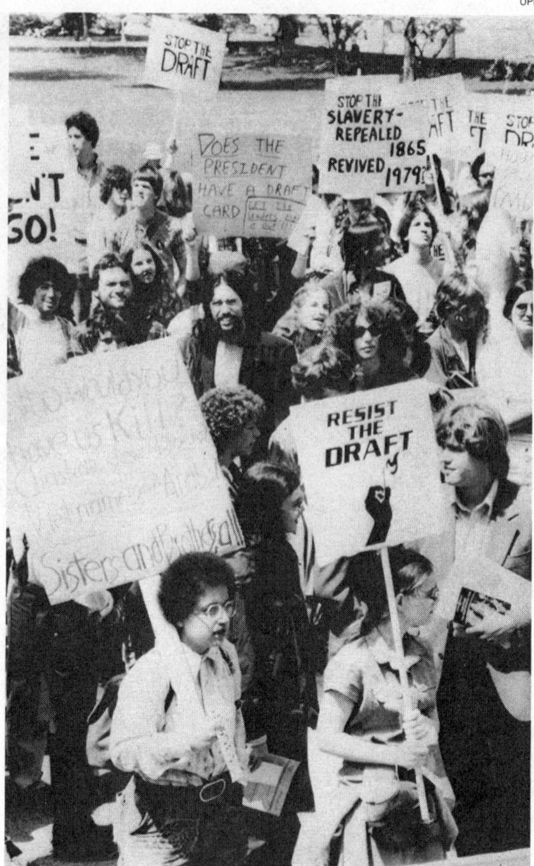

Young people protested on the steps of the Capitol after a House subcommittee voted in April to require registration of 18-year-old males for possible military service.

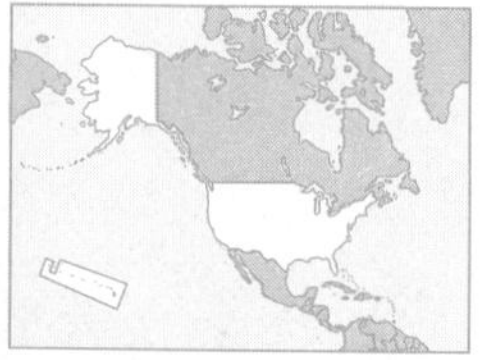

United States

United States

The United States of America is a federal republic composed of 50 states, 49 of which are in North America and one of which consists of the Hawaiian Islands. Area: 9,363,123 sq km (3,615,122 sq mi), including 202,711 sq km of inland water but excluding the 156,192 sq km of the Great Lakes that lie within U.S. boundaries. Pop. (1979 est.): 220,819,000, including 87% white and 11.6% Negro. Language: English. Religion (1978 est.): Protestant 72.5 million; Roman Catholic 49.8 million; Jewish 5.8 million; Orthodox 3.8 million. Cap.: Washington, D.C. (pop., 1977 est., 690,000). Largest city: New York (pop., 1979 est., 7,414,800). President in 1979, Jimmy Carter.

Foreign Affairs. The gravest crisis of Jimmy Carter's presidency erupted on Nov. 4, 1979, when a mob of Iranians described as students stormed the U.S. embassy in Teheran, Iran, and took the staff hostage. The students announced that the hostages would be held until the deposed shah of Iran, then undergoing medical treatment in New York City, was returned to his native country to stand trial for his alleged crimes.

It was not immediately known if Ayatollah Ruhollah Khomeini (*see* BIOGRAPHIES), the religious leader who in effect had ruled Iran since the shah's departure, had personally ordered the attack on the embassy. But he made it clear that he fully supported the students' actions and demands. He also warned the U.S. government that failure to return the shah could lead to the trial of some or all of the embassy captives on espionage charges. For its part the U.S. insisted that it had no intention of forcing the shah to go back to Iran against his will and that all of the hostages must be released unharmed. The shah had been admitted to the U.S. on October 22 for treatment of lymph node cancer and for gallbladder surgery. He left the hospital before dawn on December 2 and was flown in a U.S. military jet to a "secure" hospital at Lackland Air Force Base outside San Antonio, Texas. Earlier, Mexico had announced that the visa by which the shah entered that country before coming to the U.S. would not be renewed. On December 15 the shah left the U.S. and took up residence in Panama.

Meanwhile, presumably acting under orders from Khomeini, the Iranian militants in the U.S. embassy on November 19 and 20 released 13 female or black hostages. The move briefly gave rise to hopes that all the remaining hostages also would be freed. But it soon became apparent that the motive behind the selective release was to arouse sympathy for the Iranian cause among U.S. women and blacks.

While stopping short of using military force, the Carter administration took several retaliatory steps against Iran. It announced that it would review the visas of the approximately 45,000 Iranians studying at U.S. colleges and universities and would begin deportation proceedings against those found to be in the country illegally. It also cut off all purchases of Iranian oil and froze all official Iranian assets in the U.S. Secretary of the Treasury G. William Miller originally estimated those assets at less than $6 billion, but his department later released a revised estimate of $8 billion.

All the while U.S. citizens were venting their anger at Iran in various ways. Demonstrations by Iranian students were dogged by flag-waving U.S. counterdemonstrators who shook their fists and shouted curses. Rallies at which the Iranian flag was burned were held on campuses throughout the country. Flight mechanics refused to service Iranian commercial aircraft and dockworkers refused to handle cargo going to Iran.

President Carter (*see* BIOGRAPHIES) held a nationally televised news conference on November 28 devoted entirely to the Iranian crisis. He warned Iran of "the grave consequences which will result if harm comes to any of the hostages." As for the future, "I'm determined to do the best I can through diplomatic means and through peaceful means to ensure the safety of our hostages and their release," Carter said. "Other actions which I might decide to take would come . . . after those peaceful means have been exhausted." On November 20 he had issued orders strengthening the U.S. naval force in the Middle East.

The turmoil in Iran had anti-American repercussions in other parts of the Islamic world. In Pakistan mobs attacked and burned the U.S. embassy in Islamabad and assaulted U.S. cultural centres in nearby Rawalpindi and other cities. The incidents apparently were provoked by broadcasts from Iran suggesting that Israel and the U.S. were responsible for the attack on the Grand Mosque at Mecca, Saudi Arabia, by a band of religious fanatics. About 2,000 Libyans chanting support for Iran stormed the U.S. embassy in Tripoli, ransacking it and setting it afire. (For a chronology of the U.S.-Iranian crisis, *see* page 48).

With the Iranian crisis still unresolved, the threat of an even more serious confrontation arose in late December, when a large contingent of Soviet forces entered Afghanistan. The Soviets claimed they had been invited by Afghanistan's Marxist government to help put down a revolt by Muslim tribesmen. However, that government was shortly overthrown and replaced by one oriented more toward Moscow. In a sharply worded message on December 29, Carter warned the Soviets that unless their forces were withdrawn from Afghanistan they would face "serious consequences."

The year began with the establishment of full diplomatic relations between the U.S. and China on January 1 and the simultaneous breaking of official ties with Taiwan. The increased rapport between the two powers was highlighted by the nine-day visit of Chinese Vice-Premier Deng Xiaoping (Teng Hsiao-p'ing) to the U.S. in late January, during which cultural and technological exchanges were agreed upon.

Meanwhile, the nation's attention continued to focus on another region of the Far East. Concern centred on the plight of Indochinese refugees, more than 300,000 of whom had fled to other Southeast Asian countries by year's end and were awaiting permanent resettlement. President Carter announced on June 28 that his administration would increase from 7,000 to 14,000 the number of Indochinese refugees admitted into the U.S. each month. On October 24 Carter said the U.S. was prepared to furnish $70 million worth of emergency food aid to fend off mass starvation in Cambodia. (*See* REFUGEES: *Special Report.*)

Carter stated that his administration was prepared to help in other ways. Referring to the hostilities between Vietnam and Cambodia and between Vietnam and China, he told an audience at the Georgia Institute of Technology on February 20, "We will not get involved in conflict between Asian Communist states. Our national interests are not directly threatened, although we are concerned at the wider implications of what has been happening." But he added: "We have been using whatever diplomatic and political means are available to encourage restraint on all parties and to seek to prevent a wider war. While our influence is limited. . ., we remain the one great power in the world which can have direct and frank discussions with all the parties concerned."

President Carter's most important foreign policy achievement to date took place on March 26 in Washington, D.C., on the White House lawn. Pres. Anwar as-Sadat of Egypt and Prime Minister Menahem Begin of Israel signed a formal peace treaty ending the state of war that had existed between their countries since Israel's formation. The treaty provided for Israel's withdrawal from the Sinai in stages followed by return of the territory to Egypt, and for the establishment of full diplomatic and economic relations between the two nations. Carter's determined pursuit of an agreement and his intimate participation in the talks between the two leaders had greatly contributed to the successful outcome. Accordingly, the treaty was hailed as a triumph both for the president personally and for U.S. diplomacy in the Middle East in general. The U.S. would have to bear the brunt of the cost of carrying out the treaty, however, with aid commitments to Egypt and Israel amounting to almost $5 billion. (*See* EGYPT.)

The crucial issue of a homeland for the Palesti-

"Away all ballast!"

LOCHER—© 1979 CHICAGO TRIBUNE—NEW YORK NEWS SYNDICATE

UPI

National guardsmen and police escorted the funeral cortege of five Communist Workers Party members who were killed in a shootout in November with Ku Klux Klansmen and Nazis in Greensboro, North Carolina.

nians had not been solved by the treaty, as became dramatically evident several months later. Andrew Young (*see* BIOGRAPHIES) was forced to resign his position as U.S. ambassador to the UN on August 15 after it was learned that he had held an unauthorized meeting with a representative of the Palestine Liberation Organization (PLO). Young's action had violated the U.S. policy of avoiding high-level contacts with the PLO until it recognized Israel's right to exist, which it refused to do. Young was replaced as ambassador by his chief deputy, Donald McHenry.

Closer to home, Carter made a major effort in 1979 to improve strained U.S. relations with Mexico. To this end he visited Mexico from February 14 to 16 to discuss natural gas sales and other issues with Pres. José López Portillo.

The visit started badly as López Portillo criticized the Carter administration for its refusal to approve a sale of Mexican natural gas to a group of U.S. companies in 1977. "Among permanent, not casual, neighbours, surprise moves and sudden deceit or abuse are poisonous fruits that sooner or later have a reverse effect," the Mexican president said. "It is difficult . . . to maintain cordial and mutually advantageous relations in an atmosphere of mistrust or open hostility." He also deplored the illegal migration of Mexicans into the U.S. as a problem that strained relations between the two countries; "We do not wish to view our history as one that uselessly anchors us, like so many pillars of salt, to a burden of resentment, just as we would not like you to contemplate your future in terms of the risk of silent immigration."

Clearly unsettled by López Portillo's reproving remarks, Carter responded with a fumbling reply that recalled their common personal interests—such as running—and an earlier visit to Mexico in which he had contracted "Montezuma's Revenge" (diarrhea). Carter's reference to his digestion was considered tasteless and inappropriate by the Mexicans and politically embarrassing by the president's aides.

A visit by López Portillo to the U.S. from September 27 to 29 went much better. The two leaders' discussions were satisfactory, and a major agreement was reached by their governments to begin negotiations on compensation by Mexico for damage done to the U.S. shoreline by a runaway Mexican oil well in the Gulf of Mexico, which blew out June 3. But the majority of their time together was spent discussing the issue of energy. A week earlier the two countries had successfully concluded two years of negotiations with an agreement for Mexico to sell natural gas to the United States. After leaving Washington López Portillo went to Panama to take part in ceremonies on October 1 marking the end of U.S. control of the Panama Canal Zone. The transfer of sovereignty was carried out in accordance with the terms of the Panama Canal treaties, under which U.S. control of the canal itself was to be surrendered to Panama by the year 2000.

U.S.-Soviet relations cooled perceptibly in 1979, even before the Afghan invasion. However, Carter and Soviet leader Leonid I. Brezhnev met in Vienna on June 15 to sign a new bilateral strategic arms limitation treaty (SALT II). The overall aim of the pact was to establish strategic parity between the two superpowers on terms that could be adequately verified. To this end, it set limits on weapon launchers, including missile silos, submarine tubes, and manned bombers.

Carter and top administration officials warned that rejection of the treaty could end détente, kill any hope of further strategic arms agreements, harm other arms control efforts such as the Vienna talks on European force reductions and attempts to curb sales of conventional arms, disrupt the relations of the U.S. with its allies, undermine its image as a peace-loving nation, and provoke other nations to acquire nuclear weapons. Even if the Senate were merely to amend the treaty, Secretary of State Cyrus Vance said, the strategic arms negotiations might be damaged beyond repair.

But despite these warnings, the treaty's chances of winning Senate ratification appeared increasingly uncertain. Final debate on the treaty was postponed in 1979, and the crisis in Iran and the Soviet invasion of Afghanistan only stiffened the mounting resistance to ratification. There was speculation on Capitol Hill that the treaty had already lost its chances of passage and might have to be renegotiated following the 1980 presidential elections. (*See* DEFENSE: *Special Report.*)

Carter traveled to Tokyo in late June for a summit meeting with the leaders of six other industrial powers—Japanese Prime Minister Masayoshi Ohira, Canadian Prime Minister Joe Clark, British Prime Minister Margaret Thatcher, West German Chancellor Helmut Schmidt, Italian Premier Giulio Andreotti, and French Pres. Valery Giscard d'Estaing. They reached agreement on a plan to set specific, country-by-country ceilings on their imports of oil through 1985. For example, the plan called for the United States to hold its imports to 8.5 million bbl a day in 1979, to maintain that level for 1980, and to adopt the same level as a limit for the years through 1985.

Domestic Affairs. The Tokyo agreement on oil conservation occurred shortly after a period in which gasoline was in short supply in many areas of the U.S. The shortages first appeared in California in early May. Long lines of automobiles formed at filling stations, many of which limited the amount of gasoline that could be purchased in an effort to stretch out supplies on hand. But the lines grew shorter and then disappeared after the hardest-hit counties in the state instituted gasoline rationing on an odd-even license plate plan.

Just as the California gasoline situation was beginning to improve, similar shortages and waiting lines cropped up in other parts of the country, notably the East Coast and southern Florida. Again, after the introduction of odd-even rationing, panic buying on the part of motorists stopped. All the while, though, the retail price of gasoline was rising, reaching or exceeding $1 a gallon in many places.

The spring shortages failed to persuade Congress to grant Carter standby gasoline rationing powers, a key element of the administration's oil conservation program. The Senate approved the plan May 9 by a vote of 58 to 39, but the House of Representatives rejected it the following day by 246 to 159. The president's requests for authority to close filling stations on weekends and to limit outdoor electric advertising also were defeated. But Congress did give him authority to impose temperature controls in public and commercial buildings. Carter invoked that authority on July 16, setting minimum temperatures at 78° F (26° C) in the summer and maximums at 65° F (18° C) in the winter.

In other energy-related action the House and Senate passed different versions of a bill to set up an energy mobilization board for the purpose of speeding construction of priority energy projects by cutting red tape. The House also passed a windfall profits tax that would recoup 60% of the profits that oil companies would make as a result of decontrol of domestic oil prices, a process scheduled to be completed by 1981. But the Senate version of the bill would capture only about 38% of such profits, and the matter was still being debated when Congress adjourned in December.

Development of synthetic fuels from such sources as coal, oil shale, tar sands, lignite, biomass, peat, solid waste, and unconventional natural gas also was endorsed by Congress, although no final action was taken. A bill passed by the House authorized a $3 billion program of price supports for "synfuels" while a Senate-passed measure would authorize a five-year, $19 billion synfuels development program and create a synthetic fuels corporation to manage it.

Also making progress in Congress were Carter's proposal to create a solar development bank, new tax credits to stimulate solar technologies, and other programs. The Senate passed a bill establishing a solar bank to furnish loans at below-market rates to homeowners and businesses for solar equipment. The bill provided $750 million for the bank over a four-year period. The bank created in a separate House bill provided funding for conservation and solar projects.

Nuclear power, which had been counted on to supply an increasing share of the nation's electricity in coming decades, suffered a setback after a potentially disastrous accident occurred at the Three Mile Island plant near Harrisburg, Pa., on March 28. A series of breakdowns in the plant's No. 2 reactor raised the spectre of the explosion of a hydrogen gas bubble that had formed in the overheated reactor vessel and a consequent core meltdown, a catastrophic event that could involve major loss of life. But the worst never came to pass, and on the fifth day after the accident President Carter was able to visit the site and announce that the reactor was stable and that radiation levels near Three Mile Island were "quite safe." Even so, it was not until April 27 that the Nuclear Regulatory Commission was able to announce that the No. 2 reactor had been brought to a "cold shutdown" condition. (*See* ENERGY.)

The Three Mile Island accident added fresh urgency to the long-running public debate on whether nuclear power was a safe source of energy. "Antinuke" demonstrations were staged

UNITED STATES

Education. (1978–79) Primary and preprimary, pupils 32.6 million, teachers 1,320,000; secondary and vocational, pupils 15.6 million, teachers 1,120,000; higher (including teacher training colleges), students 11.6 million, teaching staff 830,000.

Finance. Monetary unit: U.S. dollar, with (Sept. 17, 1979) a free rate of U.S. $2.15 to £1 sterling. Gold, SDR's, and foreign exchange (June 1979) $20,840,000,000. Federal budget (1979–80 est.): revenue $502.6 billion; expenditure $531.6 billion. Gross national product (1978) $2,127,600,000,000. Money supply (March 1979) $328 billion. Cost of living: (1975 = 100; June 1979) 134.4.

Foreign Trade. (1978) Imports $183,140,000,000; exports (excluding military aid exports of $90 million) $143,570,000,000. Import sources: Canada 19%; Japan 14%; West Germany 6%. Export destinations: Canada 20%; Japan 9%; U.K. 5%; West Germany 5%; Mexico 5%. Main exports: machinery 26%; motor vehicles 9%; chemicals 9%; cereals 8%; aircraft 6%. Tourism (1977): visitors 18,610,000; gross receipts U.S. $6,218,000,000.

Transport and Communications. Roads (1976) 6,207,643 km (including 67,058 km expressways). Motor vehicles in use (1976): passenger 109,676,000; commercial (including buses) 26,524,000. Railways (1977): 320,178 km; traffic (class I railways only) 16,560,000,000 passenger km, freight 1,206,360,000,000 net ton-km. Air traffic (1978): 359,631,000,000 passenger-km (including domestic services 295,663,000,000 passenger-km); freight 10,080,031,000 net ton-km (including domestic services 6,637,211,000 net ton-km). Inland waterways freight traffic (1976) 544,400,000,000 ton-km (including 154,200,000,000 ton-km on Great Lakes system and 276,700,000,000 ton-km on Mississippi River system). Shipping (1978): merchant vessels 100 gross tons and over 4,746; gross tonnage 16,187,636. Shipping traffic (1977): goods loaded 250,198,000 metric tons, unloaded 568,138,000 metric tons. Telephones (Jan. 1978) 162,076,000. Radio receivers (Dec. 1978) *c.* 450 million. Television receivers (Dec. 1978) *c.* 146 million.

Agriculture. Production (in 000; metric tons; 1978): corn 179,886; wheat 48,954; barley 9,736; oats 8,649; rye 664; rice 6,251; sorghum 19,010; sugar, raw value 5,250; potatoes 16,356; soybeans 48,771; dry beans 867; cabbages (1977) 1,346; lettuce (1977) 2,514; onions 1,630; tomatoes 6,783; apples 3,417; oranges 8,643; grapefruit 2,721; peaches (1977) 1,493; grapes 4,018; peanuts 1,809; sunflower seed 1,700; linseed 297; cottonseed 3,800; cotton, lint 2,360; tobacco 914; butter 453; cheese *c.* 1,776; hen's eggs 3,955; beef and veal 11,325; pork 6,060; fish catch (1977) 3,102; timber (cu m; 1977) 344,665. Livestock (in 000; Jan. 1978): cattle 116,265; sheep 12,387; pigs 56,584; horses (1977) *c.* 9,075; chickens *c.* 386,531.

Industry. Index of production (1975 = 100; 1978) 124; mining 112; manufacturing 117; electricity, gas, and water 107; construction 118. Unemployment (1978) 6%. Fuel and power (in 000; metric tons; 1978): coal and lignite 593,247; crude oil 429,200; natural gas (cu m) 584,000,000; manufactured gas (cu m) 22,000,000; electricity (kw-hr) *c.* 2,295,000,000. Production (in 000; metric tons; 1978): iron ore (61% metal content) 82,012; pig iron 79,568; crude steel 123,886; cement (shipments) 71,734; newsprint 3,306; other paper (1977) 48,572; petroleum products (1977) 694,559; sulfuric acid (1977) 31,188; caustic soda (1977) 9,509; plastics and resins *c.* 12,277; man-made fibres 3,907; synthetic rubber 2,476; fertilizers (including Puerto Rico; nutrient content; 1977–78) nitrogenous 9,939, phosphate 7,481, potash 1,962; passenger cars (units) 9,138; commercial vehicles (units) 3,694. Merchant vessels launched (100 gross tons and over; 1978) 913,000 gross tons. New dwelling units started (1978) 2,023,000.

throughout the U.S. and in several foreign countries. (*See* ENVIRONMENT.) Moreover, the Nuclear Regulatory Commission ordered the closing of a number of nuclear power plants as a precautionary measure and conducted an investigation that led to a staff proposal that all U.S. atomic power facilities be compelled to make certain operating and equipment changes as a result of lessons learned from the Three Mile Island accident.

In part, it was the energy problem that sparked a major midterm upheaval in Carter's administration. After abruptly canceling a televised address on energy scheduled for July 5, Carter went into seclusion at the presidential retreat at Camp David, Md., where he held a weeklong review of his strategies for dealing with the economy and the energy crisis and conferred with 134 U.S. citizens of widely varying backgrounds and experience. On July 15, in a major policy address, he proposed a series of measures to lessen U.S. dependence on imported oil (*see* ENERGY), and on July 17 he asked for the oral resignations of his entire Cabinet and a number of senior members of the White House staff, which he then accepted or rejected at his discretion.

Four days later, five Cabinet officers had lost their jobs, one had been shifted to head another department, and Hamilton Jordan (*see* BIOGRAPHIES) had been named White House chief of staff. Secretary of the Treasury W. Michael Blumenthal was replaced by Federal Reserve Board chairman G. William Miller, whose own post was later filled by Paul A. Volcker (*see* BIOGRAPHIES). Joseph Califano, Jr., was replaced as secretary of health, education, and welfare (HEW) by Patricia R. Harris, who had been secretary of housing and urban development (HUD). Deputy Attorney General Benjamin R. Civiletti (*see* BIOGRAPHIES) was named to succeed Attorney General Griffin Bell, and Charles W. Duncan, Jr. (*see* BIOGRAPHIES), who had been deputy secretary of defense, replaced James Schlesinger as secretary of energy. Brock Adams lost his job as secretary of transportation. Later in July, Moon Landrieu, former mayor of New Orleans, La., and Neil E. Goldschmidt, the mayor of Portland, Ore., were appointed to the HUD and transportation posts.

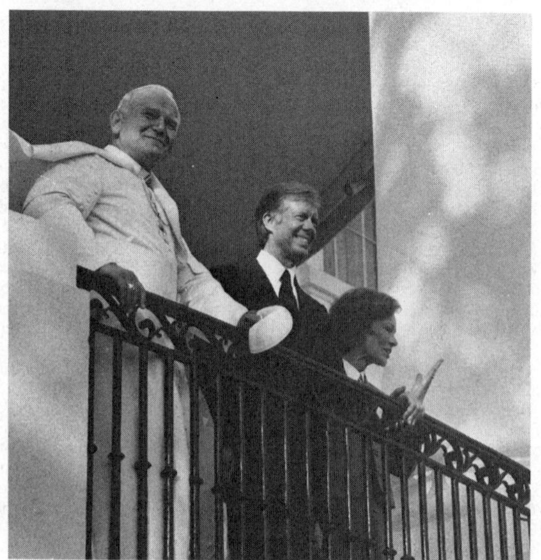

Pope John Paul II greeted crowds of welcomers from a White House balcony with President and Mrs. Jimmy Carter when the pope visited Washington in October.

J. C. FRANCOLON—GAMMA/LIAISON

The new Department of Education became the 13th Cabinet agency on October 17, and HEW, the department from which most of its programs and employees were transferred, was renamed the Department of Health and Human Services. (*See* EDUCATION.) Shirley M. Hufstedler was chosen to head the department on October 30, almost a month after another woman Cabinet officer, Juanita Kreps, resigned as secretary of commerce for personal reasons. Kreps's replacement was a Chicago businessman, Philip M. Klutznick.

The nation's news media suffered a series of reverses in 1979 in court cases involving the First Amendment's guarantee of press freedom. *Herbert* v. *Lando,* in which the Supreme Court ruled that a journalist's thoughts and decisions in preparing material involved in a libel suit are not protected from disclosure, was followed by *Wolston* v. *Reader's Digest Association Inc.,* in which the court narrowed the definition of a "public figure" who must prove "actual malice" when suing for libel. Most controversial was the *Gannett Co., Inc.* v. *DePasquale* ruling, upholding the exclusion of press and public from pretrial hearings in criminal cases. *The Progressive* magazine became the first U.S. publication to be placed under prior restraint of publication by a federal injunction for reasons of national security. (*See* PUBLISHING.)

President Carter's sagging popularity, as measured by public opinion surveys, caused the 1980 presidential election campaign to get off to an unusually early start. By early December, 13 candidates had announced their intention to seek the Democratic or Republican nomination. Carter's two challengers for the Democratic nomination were Gov. Edmund G. Brown, Jr., of California and Sen. Edward M. Kennedy (*see* BIOGRAPHIES) of Massachusetts. The Republican presidential field comprised ten men: former California governor Ronald Reagan, Rep. Philip M. Crane of Illinois, former Texas governor John B. Connally, former UN ambassador George H. Bush, Sen. Robert Dole of Kansas, Senate Minority Leader Howard H. Baker, Jr., of Tennessee, Sen. Larry Pressler of South Dakota, Rep. John B. Anderson of Illinois, Los Angeles businessman Benjamin Fernandez, and perennial candidate Harold Stassen.

Until the seizure of the U.S. embassy in Iran, Kennedy was thought to have an excellent chance of replacing Carter as the Democrats' standard bearer in 1980. But Kennedy's lacklustre performance in some early campaign appearances and renewed speculation about his involvement in the death of a young woman in an automobile accident on Chappaquiddick Island, Massachusetts, in 1969 kept him from getting off to a running start. Kennedy also came in for heavy criticism when, in a San Francisco television interview, he attacked the shah of Iran. Some commentators suggested that his remarks, which were printed in the Iranian press, would complicate the task of winning the freedom of the U.S. hostages. By contrast, Carter's handling of the Iranian crisis was generally approved by the U.S. public, and his standing in the polls rose late in the year.

The Economy. The high and rising cost of energy was largely but not solely responsible for the problems that plagued the U.S. economy in 1979. Paying for increasingly costly foreign oil contributed to the large U.S. foreign trade deficit and helped to weaken the value of the dollar in relation to other leading currencies. As higher energy costs were passed on to the consumer, the overall inflation rate rose also. The consumer price index of the Bureau of Labor Statistics, which measures the costs of a broad array of products and services, climbed by about 13.5% during 1979.

In an effort to bring inflation under control, Paul A. Volcker (*see* BIOGRAPHIES), the newly installed chairman of the Federal Reserve Board, undertook to reduce the growth of the nation's money supply sharply. Thus, the board announced that it would raise the rate of interest it charged on loans to member banks by a full percentage point to 12% and that it was prepared to allow interest rates to fluctuate widely in order to shift its emphasis to control of bank reserves and the growth of the money supply. The new policy did succeed in strengthening the dollar on international exchanges, at least temporarily. But it also threw stock, bond, and money markets into turmoil. (*See* ECONOMY, WORLD; STOCK EXCHANGES.)

If the money supply was edging down, the cost of borrowing was going up. Reacting to the threat of scarce money, the country's largest banks raised their prime interest rates, the rates they charge their best corporate customers, to the highest levels ever. Citibank of New York, often the leader in setting interest rates, moved its prime rate up to 14.5% in October, then in stages to 15.75% by mid-November. Other leading banks followed suit, but later several of them lowered their rates to 15%. Many financial analysts said that the rates would have gone even higher were it not for sharp criticism by Rep. Henry Reuss (Dem., Wis.), chairman of the House Banking Committee, and other influential members of Congress.

High interest rates played havoc with the housing market. With mortgage rates rising to 14% or more in some parts of the country, many prospective home buyers were forced out of the market. Furthermore, savings and loan associations and other thrift institutions lost money when depositors withdrew their savings for investment in money market funds and government securities offering higher rates of interest. In about two dozen states where usury laws limited mortgage rates, home financing almost came to a halt.

Another element of the housing problem was the mounting shortage of rental accommodations in such large cities as New York, Chicago, Los Angeles, and Washington, D.C. Frustrated by rising maintenance costs and, in some areas, by rent control, many owners of apartment buildings converted their properties to condominiums or cooperatives. The pace of conversion was so rapid that some cities passed laws to restrict or temporarily halt the trend. But local officials readily acknowledged that such laws were only stopgap measures and that further action would be required to preserve the shrinking private rental market. (*See* ENVIRONMENT: *Special Report.*)

UPI

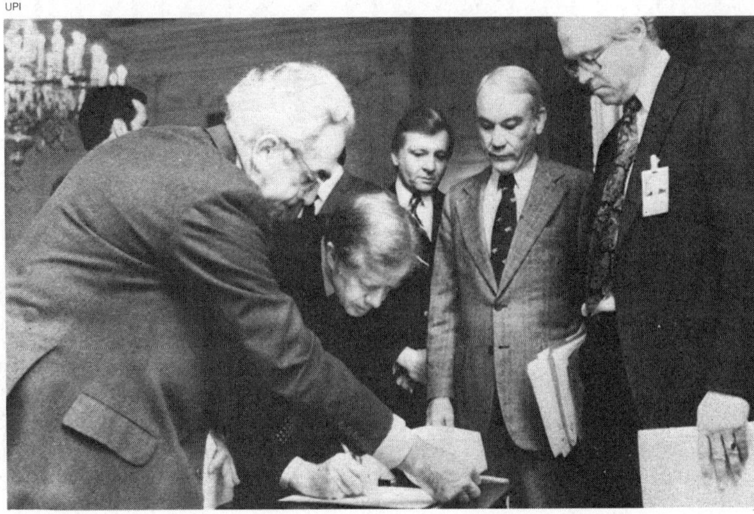

In response to the Iranian crisis, Pres. Jimmy Carter signed an order on November 14 freezing approximately $9 billion of Iranian assets in U.S. banks.

Serious as the housing industry's troubles were, they were overshadowed by those of the Chrysler Corp., the nation's third largest automobile manufacturer. For the first nine months of 1979 Chrysler reported losses of $721.5 million, the largest deficit in U.S corporate history. Company officials warned that the firm might be forced to go out of business unless it received massive financial assistance from the government by the end of the year.

After some initial hesitation the White House agreed to try to help Chrysler and in November sent to Congress a bill that would have provided the firm with $1.5 billion in federal loan guarantees. The administration plan was contingent upon Chrysler's ability to raise a matching $1.5 billion by selling assets and winning pledges of aid from creditors, workers, and localities.

The bill aroused considerable controversy. Some felt that taxpayers' money should not be risked in an attempt to save the ailing company from its own mistakes and that such an effort would set a bad precedent. In the end, however, the threatened loss of thousands of jobs and the ripple effect Chrysler's failure would have on the economy convinced Congress to pass a bill providing $1.5 billion in federal loan guarantees. Chrysler would have to raise $2 billion, including $462.5 million in concessions from the United Auto Workers.

Another troubled firm was the United States Steel Corp., which announced in December that it was closing 13 manufacturing and fabricating facilities and firing 13,000 workers in the process. The company, and the U.S. steel industry generally, had been experiencing difficulties for years because of lagging productivity and increasing competition from foreign steelmakers.

The problems facing Chrysler, U.S. Steel, and other heavily unionized companies threatened to further erode the influence of organized labour. Revitalizing the labour movement was the main task inherited by Lane Kirkland (*see* BIOGRAPHIES), the new president of the AFL-CIO. Kirkland succeeded George Meany, who had headed the labour federation since its creation in 1955 and who retired because of failing health.

(RICHARD L. WORSNOP)

See also Dependent States.

UNITED STATES STATISTICAL SUPPLEMENT

DEVELOPMENTS IN THE STATES IN 1979

Worry over energy problems and the strained status of federal-state relationships dominated the news from the 50 statehouses during 1979. The soaring costs of petroleum products and alternate energy sources, seasoned by serious safety and health problems increasingly apparent in nuclear energy, were major concerns for state administrators. So was the increasingly adversarial tenor of U.S. federalism: states could foresee serious conflicts with the federal government over such issues as control of land, revenue sharing, and financial grant requirements.

Happily, financial difficulties were not a serious concern to the states; in fact, various factors allowed states to reduce taxes by about $2 billion during the year. In the words of John Shannon, an official of the Advisory Commission on Intergovernmental Relations, "It was the year of the taxpayer." California's 1978 Proposition 13 fever gave legislators the feeling of being pressured, and inflation and business health provided the wherewithal. Although state budgets rose sharply, tax revenues grew even faster.

During 1979 involuntary capital punishment returned, after a 12-year hiatus. The spread of state-operated or regulated gambling slowed. And the long-standing and divisive debate over a constitutional amendment removing sex distinctions from all laws bogged down into a complete standstill, progressing only sideways into litigation.

All 50 state legislatures convened, Kentucky in special session and the remainder in regular session. Sixteen other states later joined Kentucky in special state legislative meetings.

Party Strengths. Although Republicans picked up an additional governorship, Democrats retained control of both houses in the five states that held legislative elections during 1979: Kentucky, Louisiana, Mississippi, New Jersey, and Virginia. For 1980 Democrats would thus control both chambers of 31 state legislatures, while Republicans would dominate in 11. All states were solidly Democratic except Arizona, Colorado, Idaho, Indiana, Iowa, Kansas, New Hampshire, North Dakota, South Dakota, Utah, and Wyoming (where Republicans had a majority in both houses); Alaska, Montana, Pennsylvania, New York, and Maine (where each party controlled one chamber); Washington (where Democrats controlled the Senate and the House was tied); Vermont (where both chambers were Republican-dominated but a Democratic House speaker was elected in secret balloting); and Nebraska (a nonpartisan, one-house legislature).

Three governorships were contested during the year. Democrats again won the elections in Kentucky and Mississippi, but Republicans gained executive control in Louisiana for the first time in the 20th century. That put the 1980 governors' lineup at 31 Democrats and 19 Republicans.

Both parties looked toward the 1980 state elections, considered especially important because of the census. Following the 1980 U.S. census, 42 state legislatures would redraw congressional district boundaries (six states had only one U.S. House representative, and Nebraska and Montana redistricted using a nonpartisan commission). Of the 42, Democrats were in complete control of 20 and Republicans of only 2 going into the 1980 election campaign.

In several states Democrats proved during 1979 that voting control does not ensure smooth legislative performance. Factions known as the "Killer Bees" in Texas and the "Dirty Dozen" in Illinois often thwarted Democratic leadership aims, and open revolt was recorded in two other states. Three conservative Democrats switched parties during the year in Alaska, giving Republicans voting control in the state Senate, and conservative Democrats joined with Republicans to take leadership control away from more liberal party members in New Mexico.

Government Structures and Powers. A growing national lack of enthusiasm for government in general led states to enact a variety of measures designed to increase official accountability to voters. Georgia provided for recall elections; Delaware laid the groundwork for initiatives and referenda; Arkansas put a constitutional revision on its 1980 state ballot; and both West Virginia and Wyoming approved new "sunset" laws, which provide for termination of government agencies unless their continued existence can be justified. Florida ordered steps to make its regulatory agencies more responsive to the public.

After several years of large-scale consolidation of services in state governments, new reorganization moves diminished in popularity. Louisiana consolidated its waste-disposal efforts; Rhode Island established a new department for children; and South Carolina revamped its public service commission selection procedures. New Mexico overturned part of a government consolidation package approved in 1977.

Montana scheduled a 1980 vote on a proposal for a unicameral (one-house) legislature. Virgin Islands voters defeated a proposed expansion of home rule for the third time, and Guam voters rejected a proposed constitution that would have granted island residents fewer rights than those enjoyed by U.S. citizens.

Government Relations. Pulling and tugging between state capitols and Washington dominated intergovernmental relations during the year. State legislatures struggled, without conclusive effect, over two U.S. constitutional amendments and a suggested demand for a federal constitutional convention. The states also found themselves in an adversary posture vis-à-vis the federal government over energy, revenue sharing, grant requirements, and land control.

For the second consecutive year no new state ratified the proposed Equal Rights Amendment (ERA), which would prohibit discrimination by sex; only one state, Indiana, had endorsed this amendment since 1975. Three additional states (for a total of 38) would have to ratify prior to the congressionally extended deadline of 1982, and feminist groups promised a strong campaign effort to elect pro-ERA legislators in 1980 elections.

Only four additional states—Connecticut, Massachusetts, Minnesota, and Wisconsin—ratified a proposed 28th amendment that would give full congressional voting rights to the District of Columbia. With only seven state endorsements recorded (of 38 needed before summer 1985), prospects for the amendment appeared bleak. Ten states specifically rejected the amendment during 1979.

The Indiana, Idaho, Iowa, New Hampshire, South Dakota, and Wyoming legislatures approved resolutions calling for a U.S. constitutional convention to require a balanced federal budget. Supporters claimed that those resolutions brought the total to 30, with only 34 necessary for automatic calling of the convention. Opposition was fierce, however; critics suggested that any convention, once sitting, could not be restricted to matters of a balanced budget. In August a Duke University law professor published a study indicating that 22 of the 30 state requests were invalid on technical grounds. To deflect enthusiasm for the convention, congressional leaders introduced legislation that would encourage budget balancing, and some observers predicted that a constitutional amendment would be proposed as an alternative if the convention idea appeared on the verge of adoption.

Early skirmishing between the administration of U.S. Pres. Jimmy Carter and state governments over revenue sharing opened up during the year. The $6.9 billion annual program would expire on Sept. 30, 1980, and Carter indicated that he wanted to drop the $2.3 billion share allocated to states. During 1979 federal officials bowed to state pressure and began reforming grant procedures, reducing paperwork and moving toward "block" awards to other governmental units for discretionary purposes.

Following a brush with disaster at the Three Mile Island nuclear power facility near Harrisburg, Pa., in March, several states demanded additional federal safeguards for atomic energy plant construction, inspection, and waste dumping. Western states began taking serious steps to challenge the federal government's control of vast public lands. Of the 2,300,000,000 ac in the U.S., the federal government controlled almost one-third, or 700 million ac. Approximately 90% of the federal land was west of the Rocky Mountains. The U.S. government controlled 96% of Alaska, 87% of Nevada, 66% of Utah, 64% of Idaho, and 45% of California. Environmentalists had succeeded in closing much of this area to commercial exploitation, leading to a "sagebrush rebellion" that broke out in 1979. Nevada's legislature asserted ownership over all federal land within its borders during the year. Because a state cannot sue the federal government without permission, the aim was to provoke a legal confrontation that would bring the dispute into court for a judicial determination.

Finances and Taxes. Voter demands for tax relief and reform were granted widely and painlessly by state legislatures during 1979, thanks in part to a series of fortuitous circumstances. Many tax rates had been raised by states in the mid-1970s. An expanding economy generated additional tax revenue, and inflation pushed many taxpayers into higher payment brackets. The net result was a revenue surplus in a majority of states that again allowed significant reduction in taxes levied by state governments. A survey by the Tax Foundation revealed that taxpayers in 24 states benefited from tax cuts totaling more than $2.6 billion; the reductions were partially offset by about $610 million in tax hikes nationwide.

Personal income taxes were the most popular targets for reduction; about $1.5 billion in income taxes were trimmed in at least 24 states. Wisconsin, Iowa, and Minnesota enacted indexing laws during the year, joining Arizona, California, and Colorado in adjusting the tax structure for inflation. No state increased its personal income tax rate during the year, although a scheduled reduction in Pennsylvania was canceled until 1982.

California and Illinois raised corporate income tax rates to offset revenue losses from abolition of personal property taxes, and Pennsylvania put off a planned corporate tax reduction. Connecticut, Delaware, Louisiana, South Carolina, and Minnesota liberalized some corporate tax credits.

As gasoline prices soared, ten states—Arkansas, Iowa, Montana, Nebraska, New Hampshire, Pennsylvania, South Carolina, South Dakota, Washington, and New Mexico—boosted their motor fuel taxes. Excise taxes on tobacco were hiked in North Dakota, Oklahoma, South Dakota, and Utah, while Massachusetts made a temporary increase of five cents per pack permanent. A new tax on alcoholic beverages was levied in Alabama; Nebraska increased alcohol taxes, while Maryland and Minnesota reduced them. Nine states reduced inheritance taxes, while Colorado and South Dakota enacted new estate tax levies.

During 1979 Florida, Iowa, Kentucky, Massachusetts, New Mexico, Nebraska, and Oregon adopted limitations on the revenue raising and/or spending authority of local governmental units. Louisiana limited state tax revenue increases to the growth in personal income. Voters in California and Washington approved state constitutional amendments to restrain future growth in taxation and spending.

Delaware and South Carolina took advantage of the salubrious financial climate to join Michigan in establishing a "rainy day fund," a cash reserve to be used during hard financial times. A survey by *Congressional Quarterly* during 1979 indicated that state government was the fastest-growing government segment: as a percentage of gross national product, spending by local governments rose from 4.4 to 4.8% during 1959–79, and by the federal government, from 18.7 to 21.6%. During the same period state spending nearly doubled, from 3.8 to 6.2%.

Figures accumulated in 1979 showed that state revenue from all sources totaled $225 billion during the 1978 fiscal year, an increase of 10.1% over the preceding 12 months. General revenue (excluding state liquor and state insurance trust revenue) was $189.1 billion, up 11.8%. Total state expenditures rose 6.6% to $203.8 billion, creating a surplus of $21.2 billion for the year. General expenditures, not including outlays of the liquor stores and insurance trust systems, amounted to $179.8 billion, up 9.4% for the year. Of general revenue, some 59.8% came from state taxes and licenses; 11.9% from charges and miscellaneous revenue, including educational tuition; and 28.3% from intergovernmental revenue (mostly from the federal government).

The largest state outlay was $69.7 billion for education, of which $23.3 billion went to state colleges and universities and $40.1 billion to local public schools. Other major outlays were $35.8 billion for public welfare, $18.5 billion for highways, and $13.9 billion for health and hospitals.

Ethics. The four-year administration of Tennessee Gov. Ray Blanton came to an inglorious end January 17, three days ahead of schedule, amid charges that prison pardons and commutations were being sold wholesale. Elaborate inauguration ceremonies for incoming Gov. Lamar Alexander were scheduled for January 20, but Alexander hurriedly took office the day after Blanton pardoned or paroled 52 felons, including 23 serving long-term sentences for murder. Blanton, a Democrat, had earlier been notified that he was a target of a federal grand jury investigating parole-selling violations, but when authorities in March indicted six for the scheme, Blanton was not among those charged. Although Alexander, a Republican, blocked many of the pardons and held the inmates, the Tennessee Supreme Court ruled May 29 that Blanton's actions were "absolute" and ordered the prisoners freed. In the meantime the inmates had filed civil suits totaling more than $2 million, charging unlawful confinement after their pardons.

Illinois Attorney General William Scott was indicted April 9 on five counts of income tax evasion; he was accused of understating his income in 1972–75. Thomas O'Malley, former Florida insurance commissioner, was sentenced to three years in prison on January 18 for extortion and mail fraud while in office. Lee Hyden, former director of the Tennessee Alcoholic Beverage Commission, was sentenced on January 26 to 14 years in prison after conviction on seven counts of extortion and conspiracy.

Former Maryland governor Marvin Mandel, who had stepped down in June 1977 as his corruption trial opened, took office for 45 hours January 15–17 after a U.S. Fourth Circuit panel reversed his conviction on technical grounds. The panel's vote was 2 to 1. The government asked the Fourth Circuit to review the decision, however, and on July 20 the conviction was reinstated on a 3 to 3 tie vote. At year's end Mandel, still free on appeal, was ordered to return $35,000 worth of furniture and other items he took from the governor's mansion or face civil suit.

Legislative attention to ethical matters was unenthusiastic. Hawaii provided public financing for state and county elections; Maryland strengthened and consolidated its ethics commission's powers; and New Jersey extended financing to gubernatorial primaries. But Mississippi approved a bill requiring legislators to list only their sources of outside income, not the amounts involved, and Alabama specifically forbade its ethics commission from sniffing after anonymous tips.

Education. States continued to wrestle with the decade-long controversy over equalizing the funding of public schools. Courts in Arkansas and Colorado declared school financing schemes in those states to be unconstitutional, and Connecticut adopted a new equalizing plan following a similar 1977 ruling.

New York created a furor in the hard-pressed educational testing industry by requiring that certain standardized examinations and their answers be filed with state authorities, with answers available to test subjects. South Carolina joined Georgia in requiring testing of public school teachers. Under strong pressure from U.S. Department of Health, Education, and Welfare (HEW) authorities because of its inadequate desegregation efforts, North Carolina appropriated an additional $40 million for its black colleges. HEW said that was insufficient and threatened a cutoff of federal aid to the state.

Health and Welfare. Faced with soaring interest rates that threatened both the mortgage and home construction industries, many states began issuing mortgage revenue bonds to finance lower-interest loans for single-family housing. The practice was halted abruptly in April, however, when strong legislation was introduced in the U.S. House of Representatives declaring the bonds ineligible for tax-exempt status.

Several states took steps to contain hospital costs. Florida required any cost increases to be reported to a special board, and Nebraska began requiring a certificate of need for facilities before allowing construction to start. North Dakota and Massachusetts tightened their abortion laws, reducing funding for indigent expectant mothers seeking the operation. North Dakota's version also eliminated state clinic participation, and required a 48-hour wait and parent notification for minors as well.

Drugs. Florida and South Dakota legalized the use of laetrile as a cancer-fighting drug despite the failure of U.S. authorities to sanction it. New York's legislature also approved laetrile, but the bill was vetoed.

Florida was also the latest state to strengthen its drug laws, setting a mandatory minimum jail sentence of 15 years and a $200,000 fine for possession of five or more tons of marijuana. But New York, which under Gov. Nelson Rockefeller pioneered extremely harsh penalties for first-time drug offenders, backed off markedly during 1979, softening the range of penalties for first offenses.

Law and Justice. For the first time in 12 years a convict was involuntarily executed in the U.S., and authorities suggested that the regular incidence of capital punishment, at a restrained level, was inevitable within a few years. Although the U.S. Supreme Court had given the green light to resumption of the death penalty under limited conditions in 1976, only one man, Gary Gilmore of Utah, had previously been executed, in January 1977, and he had refused to appeal his sentence.

On May 25, however, John A. Spenkelink was put to death in the electric chair at the Starke, Fla., state prison. A drifter, Spenkelink had been convicted for murdering a traveling companion. On six occasions the U.S. Supreme Court refused to stay the execution, the last a mere 20 minutes before Spenkelink was electrocuted. On October 22 Jesse Walter Bishop was executed in the gas chamber at the Carson City, Nev., state prison for the 1977 slaying of a bystander during the robbery of a Las Vegas casino. Like Gilmore, Bishop refused all efforts to appeal his sentence.

Capital punishment laws continued to occupy the attention of state legislators. Massachusetts, New Mexico, and South Dakota approved new death penalty laws. Kansas and New York lawmakers passed similar bills, but they were vetoed. Rhode Island's Supreme Court declared that state's death law to be unconstitutional.

Rhode Island approved a handgun safety bill that required would-be purchasers of handguns to take (but not necessarily pass) a safety course and obtain police approval before obtaining the weapon. Florida opened its courtroom doors on a permanent basis to photographers and television and newsreel cameramen, bringing to seven the states with permanent photo access (Alabama, Colorado, Georgia, New Hampshire, Texas, and Washington were the others). Experiments in courtroom photography were under way in 13 other states; the association of state chief justices overwhelmingly endorsed the concept during 1978, but the American Bar Association affirmed its opposition.

Prisons. By 1979 the number of inmates housed in the nation's prisons had topped the 300,000 mark for the first time in history, according to figures released at midyear. Of those prisoners, more than 90% were in state institutions and were often held in overcrowded conditions. Tennessee Governor Blanton cited a federal court order to reduce prison populations to justify his decision to release numerous hardened criminals at the end of his term. (See *Ethics*, above.) Although prison construction at the state level was proceeding rapidly, some states attempted moderation; Washington rejected a maximum-security building in favour of a medium-security version, and Maryland's governor also dropped a maximum-security construction project in favour of additional resources for parole and work-release programs.

An important U.S. Supreme Court decision in May gave a vote of confidence to state parole administrators. The court ruled 5 to 4 that inmates are not entitled to full due process in their parole proceedings and that states are basically free to administer their parole systems as they see fit.

Gambling. For the first year in recent times no state inaugurated a major new lottery or betting scheme as a fund-raising device. In fact, most of the luck for gamblers was bad during 1979. Virginia limited bingo to twice a week in a single locality; Tennessee banned pinball gambling and charitable bingo; Nevada stiffened its gambling enforcement procedures markedly; New Jersey raised its casino tax to aid the elderly; and Maine banished electronic slot machines. Amid charges of fixed jai alai matches and corruption in off-track betting systems, Connecticut dissolved its gaming commission and provided for appointment of a strong gambling czar who would report directly to the governor. Overruling a worldwide casino practice, the New Jersey Casino Control Commission ordered in October that card counters be allowed to play blackjack at Atlantic City gambling emporiums; casinos were allowed the option of shuffling the deck more frequently.

Environment. Advocates of a national container deposit law were heartened in November when Maine voters gave an 84% vote of confidence to the state's two-year-old bottle law, despite a heavily financed campaign for repeal by beverage and container companies. Despite the optimism, however, no new state was added in 1979 to the seven that had previously mandated heavy deposits for all such containers; voters in Ohio and Washington turned down ballot measures, and the Massachusetts governor vetoed a similar bill, saying that a ban on throwaway bottles would cost the state 500 jobs.

Several states took action in the wake of the Three Mile Island nuclear incident and other reports of toxic waste spills. The country's three remaining low-level radioactive waste dumping sites came under close scrutiny; South Carolina ordered a 50% reduction in dumping at the popular Barnwell, S.C., site. Governors ordered shutdowns of the remaining dumps at Hanford, Wash., and Beatty, Nev., in October, but reopened both facilities after inquiries revealed that they were operating within reasonable safety limits. Eleven states approved tough new laws regulating disposal of toxic chemical wastes.

In an effort to cut environmental red tape, Alabama approved "one-stop permitting," allowing developers to obtain all required official approval at a single location. Arizona ordered reductions in pesticide spraying near population centres. Colorado, facing a severe air pollution problem, rejected a tough auto inspection program in favour of requiring periodic tune-ups. Delaware weakened its coastal zone protection law, which had effectively banned industrial development in that region; the new law permitted operation of support facilities for offshore drilling efforts.

Energy. Political fallout from the Three Mile Island nuclear incident added to the worries of state energy experts during 1979. The failure of federal officials to handle the situation in a fully competent and satisfactory manner underlined the difficulties that many states were encountering; many state officials blamed the seriousness of the situation on the absence of an effective federal energy policy. A dozen states adopted new regulations stiffening safety requirements for transportation and disposal of nuclear wastes. Connecticut and Oregon halted construction, at least temporarily, of all nuclear facilities, although a California judge declared that state's 1976 laws banning nuclear plant construction to be invalid. Federal lawmakers had preempted that field, the judge ruled.

The country's largest nuclear plant utility construction project, a $2.3 billion effort at Seabrook, N.H., ran into financing difficulties after state authorities ordered an end to a "construction work in progress" charge tacked onto state utility bills to finance the project. Following the move, part of the utility's half interest in the project was sold.

As gasoline supplies grew scarce periodically through the year, 12 states approved some type of tax break for gasohol, gasoline containing approximately 10% ethyl alcohol. On May 29 President Carter gave all governors limited authority to allocate gasoline sales; 18 governors had not previously been granted such authority by their state legislatures. During a spring gasoline shortage, odd-even gas sales plans were adopted by California, Connecticut, Delaware, Florida, Maryland, New Jersey, New York, Pennsylvania, Rhode Island, Texas, Virginia, and the District of Columbia.

Equal Rights. Litigation over the proposed Equal Rights Amendment that would ban sex discrimination in the U.S. continued on several fronts during 1979. Missouri pressed its appeal against the National Organization for Women (NOW), claiming that the NOW boycott of states that had refused to ratify the ERA was a violation of antitrust laws. Idaho, Arizona, and four Washington state legislators filed suit during the year challenging Congress's extension of the original seven-year ratification period and its simultaneous decision that states do not have the right to rescind, or withdraw, ratification. South Dakota became the fourth state to attempt an official ERA rescission during the year.

Southwestern states suffered through legislative turbulence on labour matters. New Mexico's governor vetoed a right-to-work bill, and the governors of Arizona and Utah vetoed "little Davis-Bacon Act" bills that would require contractors on state or local projects to pay the prevailing wages for the area.

Arkansas, South Dakota, and Missouri approved new restrictions on foreign ownership of land, bringing to 27 the states with some regulation on alien control of real property. Most of the restrictions were mere reporting requirements or liberal acreage limitations, however, and a federal study indicated they were generally ineffective. Even so, state authorities reported that only about 0.5% of privately owned property in the U.S. was controlled by foreigners.

Consumer Protection. Nevada became the first state to repeal its no-fault auto insurance law. Legislators were unhappy with the state's low $750 threshold for damages; accident victims were typically collecting that money and then suing the other driver and collecting again.

Faced with soaring interest rates, numerous states raised their usury limits toward 15% or eliminated them entirely during the year. New York banned "redlining" by banks, the exclusion of certain areas from mortgage loan consideration. Several states grappled with problems caused by teenage drinking; Tennessee boosted the drinking age from 18 to 19, Massachusetts from 18 to 20, New Hampshire from 18 to 20, and Illinois from 19 to 21.

Rhode Island approved a state antitrust bill. Congressmen, beset by heavy lobbying from several sides, failed to obtain approval of a federal "Illinois Brick" bill during the year. Named after a 1977 Supreme Court decision, the bill would have restored the authority of state attorneys general to sue bid-riggers and price-fixers for damages on behalf of state citizens.

Several states, led by New York, had begun utilizing formal standards for licensing "professionals." Legislators are constantly beset with demands that practitioners of certain occupations be licensed and regulated. The impetus often comes from groups of practitioners themselves, who cite the need to maintain professional standards, but consumer groups suspect the licensing requirement often is a thinly veiled method of eliminating competition. Using definite regulatory criteria, the New York legislature approved only one new licensing scheme during 1979, far below its recent average.

(DAVID C. BECKWITH)

AREA AND POPULATION

Area and Population of the States

State	AREA in sq mi: Total	Inland water[1]	POPULATION (000): July 1, 1970	July 1, 1978[2]	Percent change 1970–78
Alabama	51,609	901	3,451	3,742	8.4
Alaska	586,412	19,980	305	403	32.1
Arizona	113,909	492	1,792	2,354	31.4
Arkansas	53,104	1,159	1,926	2,186	13.5
California	158,693	2,332	19,994	22,294	11.5
Colorado	104,247	481	2,225	2,670	20.0
Connecticut	5,009	147	3,039	3,099	2.0
Delaware	2,057	75	550	583	6.0
Dist. of Columbia	67	6	753	674	−10.5
Florida	58,560	4,470	6,845	8,594	25.6
Georgia	58,876	803	4,602	5,084	10.5
Hawaii	6,450	25	774	897	15.9
Idaho	83,557	880	717	878	22.4
Illinois	56,400	652	11,137	11,243	1.0
Indiana	36,291	194	5,208	5,374	3.2
Iowa	56,290	349	2,830	2,896	2.3
Kansas	82,264	477	2,248	2,348	4.4
Kentucky	40,395	745	3,224	3,498	8.5
Louisiana	48,523	3,593	3,644	3,966	8.8
Maine	33,215	2,295	995	1,091	9.6
Maryland	10,577	686	3,937	4,143	5.2
Massachusetts	8,257	431	5,699	5,774	1.3
Michigan	58,216	1,399	8,901	9,189	3.2
Minnesota	84,068	4,779	3,822	4,008	4.9
Mississippi	47,716	420	2,216	2,404	8.5
Missouri	69,686	691	4,693	4,860	3.6
Montana	147,138	1,551	697	785	12.6
Nebraska	77,227	744	1,490	1,565	5.0
Nevada	110,540	651	493	660	33.9
New Hampshire	9,304	277	742	871	17.4
New Jersey	7,836	315	7,195	7,327	1.8
New Mexico	121,666	254	1,018	1,212	19.1
New York	49,576	1,745	18,260	17,748	−2.8
North Carolina	52,586	3,788	5,091	5,577	9.6
North Dakota	70,665	1,392	618	652	5.5
Ohio	41,222	247	10,688	10,749	0.6
Oklahoma	69,919	1,137	2,572	2,880	12.0
Oregon	96,981	797	2,102	2,444	16.3
Pennsylvania	45,333	367	11,817	11,750	−0.6
Rhode Island	1,214	165	951	935	−1.7
South Carolina	31,055	830	2,596	2,918	12.4
South Dakota	77,047	1,092	666	690	3.6
Tennessee	42,244	916	3,932	4,357	10.8
Texas	267,338	5,204	11,254	13,014	15.6
Utah	84,916	2,820	1,069	1,307	22.3
Vermont	9,609	342	447	487	9.0
Virginia	40,817	1,037	4,653	5,148	10.6
Washington	68,192	1,622	3,414	3,774	10.5
West Virginia	24,181	111	1,746	1,860	6.5
Wisconsin	56,154	1,690	4,433	4,679	5.6
Wyoming	97,914	711	334	424	26.9
TOTAL U.S.	3,615,122	78,267	203,805	218,059[3]	7.0

[1] Excludes the Great Lakes and coastal waters.
[2] Preliminary.
[3] State figures do not add to total given because of rounding.
Source: U.S. Department of Commerce, Bureau of the Census, *Current Population Reports*.

Largest Metropolitan Areas[1]

Name	Population: 1970 census	1978 estimate	Percent change 1970–78	Land area in sq mi	Density per sq mi 1978
New York-Newark-Jersey City SCSA	17,033,367	16,369,197	−3.9	5,072	3,227
New York City	9,973,716	9,300,743	−6.7	1,384	6,720
Nassau-Suffolk	2,555,868	2,662,419	4.2	1,218	2,186
Newark	2,057,468	1,963,457	−4.6	1,008	1,948
Bridgeport[2]	792,814	798,272	0.7	627	1,273
New Brunswick-Perth Amboy	583,813	591,739	1.4	312	1,897
Jersey City	607,839	562,426	−7.5	47	11,966
Long Branch-Asbury Park	461,849	490,141	6.1	476	1,030
Los Angeles-Long Beach-Anaheim SCSA	9,980,859[3]	10,800,245	8.2	34,007	318
Los Angeles-Long Beach	7,041,980	7,107,342	0.9	4,069	1,747
Anaheim-Santa Ana-Garden Grove	1,421,233	1,832,254	28.9	782	2,343
Riverside-San Bernardino-Ontario	1,139,149[3]	1,378,614	21.0	27,293	50
Oxnard-Simi Valley-Ventura	378,497	482,035	27.4	1,863	259
Chicago-Gary SCSA	7,610,634[3]	7,678,102	0.9	4,657	1,649
Chicago	6,977,267[3]	7,023,831	0.7	3,719	1,889
Gary-Hammond-East Chicago	633,367	654,271	3.3	938	698
Philadelphia-Wilmington-Trenton SCSA	5,627,719	5,747,298	2.1	4,946	1,162
Philadelphia	4,824,110	4,914,941	1.9	3,553	1,383
Wilmington	499,493	516,397	3.4	1,165	443
Trenton	304,116	315,960	3.9	228	1,386
San Francisco-Oakland-San Jose SCSA	4,425,691[3]	4,711,165	6.4	5,390	874
San Francisco-Oakland	3,109,249[3]	3,181,571	2.3	2,480	1,283
San Jose	1,065,313	1,227,335	15.2	1,300	944
Vallejo-Fairfield-Napa	251,129	302,259	20.4	1,610	188
Detroit-Ann Arbor SCSA	4,669,154	4,665,150	−0.1	4,627	1,008
Detroit	4,435,051	4,407,179	−0.6	3,916	1,125
Ann Arbor	234,103	257,971	10.2	711	363
Boston-Lowell-Lawrence SCSA[2]	3,848,593	3,329,364	−13.5	3,114	1,069
Washington, D.C.	2,909,355	3,035,867	4.3	2,812	1,080
Cleveland-Akron-Lorain SCSA	2,999,811	2,863,216	−4.6	2,917	982
Cleveland	2,063,729	1,945,049	−5.8	1,519	1,280
Akron	679,239	659,259	−2.9	903	730
Lorain-Elyria	256,843	258,908	0.8	495	523
Dallas-Fort Worth	2,378,353	2,713,864	14.1	8,360	325
Houston-Galveston SCSA	2,169,128	2,671,499	23.2	7,193	371
Houston	1,999,316	2,478,900	24.0	6,794	365
Galveston-Texas City	169,812	192,599	13.4	399	483
St. Louis	2,410,492	2,402,259	−0.3	4,935	487
Pittsburgh	2,401,362	2,344,441	−2.4	3,049	769
Miami-Fort Lauderdale SCSA	1,887,892	2,322,982	23.0	3,261	712
Miami	1,267,792	1,432,086	13.0	2,042	701
Fort Lauderdale-Hollywood	620,100	890,896	43.7	1,219	731
Baltimore	2,071,016	2,138,685	3.3	2,259	947
Minneapolis-St. Paul	1,965,391	2,103,224	7.0	4,647	453
Seattle-Tacoma SCSA	1,836,949	1,921,644	4.6	5,902	326
Seattle-Everett	1,424,605	1,479,053	3.8	4,226	350
Tacoma	412,344	442,591	7.3	1,676	264
Atlanta	1,595,517	1,861,840	16.7	4,326	430
San Diego	1,357,854	1,737,766	28.0	4,261	408
Cincinnati-Hamilton SCSA	1,613,414	1,625,983	0.8	2,620	621
Cincinnati	1,387,207	1,377,127	−0.7	2,149	641
Hamilton-Middletown	226,207	248,856	10.0	471	528
Milwaukee-Racine SCSA	1,574,722	1,585,518	0.7	1,793	884
Milwaukee	1,403,884	1,407,180	0.2	1,456	966
Racine	170,838	178,338	4.4	337	529
Denver-Boulder	1,239,545[3]	1,497,845	20.8	4,651	322
Tampa-St. Petersburg	1,088,549	1,412,716	29.8	2,045	691
Kansas City	1,273,926	1,313,299	3.1	3,341	393
Buffalo	1,349,211	1,299,467	−3.7	1,590	817
Phoenix	971,228	1,294,054	33.2	9,155	141

[1] Standard Metropolitan Statistical Area, SMSA, unless otherwise indicated; SCSA is a Standard Consolidated Statistical Area, which may be comprised of SMSA's.
[2] New England County Metropolitan Area. [3] Revised.
Sources: U.S. Dept. of Commerce, Bureau of the Census, *Current Population Reports*; U.S. Dept. of Justice, FBI, *Uniform Crime Reports for the United States, 1978*.

Population Change

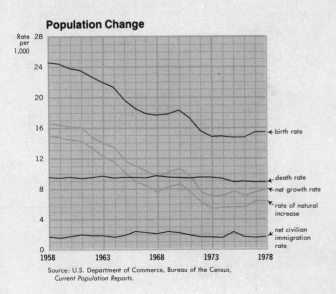

Rate per 1,000
28
24
20
16
12
8
4
0
1958
1963
1968
1973
1978
birth rate
death rate
net growth rate
rate of natural increase
net civilian immigration rate

Source: U.S. Department of Commerce, Bureau of the Census, *Current Population Reports*.

Marriage and Divorce Rates

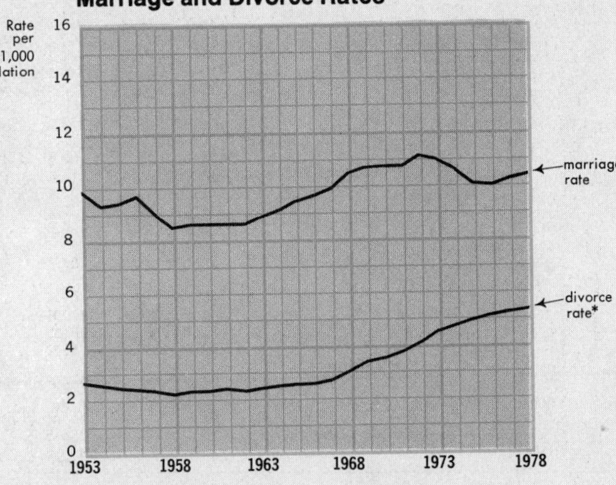

*Includes annulments.

Source: U.S. Department of Health, Education, and Welfare, Public Health Service, *Monthly Vital Statistics Report*.

Church Membership

Religious body	Total clergy	Inclusive membership
Baptist bodies		
American Baptist Association	5,425	1,500,000
American Baptist Churches in the U.S.A.	7,087	1,316,760
Baptist General Conference	1,002	131,000
Baptist Missionary Association of America	3,125	219,697
Conservative Baptist Association of America	. . .	300,000
Free Will Baptists	4,367	216,831
General Baptists (General Association of)	1,320	72,000
National Baptist Convention of America	28,754	2,668,799
National Baptist Convention, U.S.A., Inc.	27,500	5,500,000
National Primitive Baptist Convention, Inc.	636	250,000
Primitive Baptists	. . .	72,000
Progressive National Baptist Convention, Inc.	863	521,692
Regular Baptist Churches, General Assn. of	. . .	240,000
Southern Baptist Convention	56,000	13,191,394
United Free Will Baptist Church	915	100,000
Brethren (German Baptists): Church of the Brethren	. . .	175,335
Buddhist Churches of America	108	60,000
Christian and Missionary Alliance	1,529	158,218
Christian Church (Disciples of Christ)	6,635	1,231,817
Christian Churches and Churches of Christ	7,689	1,054,266
Christian Congregation	1,144	81,604
Church of God (Anderson, Ind.)	2,924	173,753
Church of the Nazarene	7,590	462,724
Churches of Christ	16,000	3,000,000
Congregational Christian Churches, Natl. Assn. of	554	95,000
Eastern Churches		
American Carpatho-Russian Orth. Greek Catholic Ch.	68	100,000
Antiochian Orthodox Christian Archdiocese of N. Am.	132	152,000
Armenian Apostolic Church of America	34	125,000
Armenian Church of America, Diocese of the (Including Diocese of California)	60	326,500
Bulgarian Eastern Orthodox Church	11	86,000
Greek Orthodox Archdiocese of N. and S. America	655	1,950,000
Orthodox Church in America	531	1,000,000
Russian Orth. Ch. in the U.S.A., Patriarchal Parishes of	60	51,500
Russian Orthodox Church Outside Russia	168	55,000
Serbian Eastern Orth. Ch. for the U.S.A. and Canada	64	65,000
Ukrainian Orthodox Church in the U.S.A.	131	87,745
Episcopal Church	12,310	2,815,359
Evangelical Covenant Church of America	751	74,678
Evangelical Free Church of America	960	100,000
Friends United Meeting	617	62,080
Independent Fundamental Churches of America	1,252	87,582
Jehovah's Witnesses	none	519,218
Jewish congregations	6,400	6,115,000
Latter Day Saints		
Church of Jesus Christ of Latter-day Saints	21,536	2,592,000
Reorganized Church of Jesus Christ of L.D.S.	16,039	185,636
Lutherans		
American Lutheran Church	6,789	2,377,235
Evangelical Lutheran Churches, Association of	545	106,684
Lutheran Church in America	7,822	2,942,002
Lutheran Church—Missouri Synod	7,161	2,631,374
Wisconsin Evangelical Lutheran Synod	1,116	402,972
Mennonite Church	2,393	97,142
Methodists		
African Methodist Episcopal Church	3,938	1,970,000
African Methodist Episcopal Zion Church	6,689	1,093,001
Christian Methodist Episcopal Church	2,259	466,718
Free Methodist Church of North America	1,805	73,294
United Methodist Church	35,939	9,731,779
Moravian Church in America	220	53,521
North American Old Roman Catholic Church	123	67,314
Pentecostals		
Apostolic Overcoming Holy Church of God	350	75,000
Assemblies of God	14,415	1,293,394
Church of God	2,737	75,890
Church of God (Cleveland, Tenn.)	9,095	392,551
Church of God in Christ	6,000	425,000
Church of God in Christ, International	1,502	501,000
Church of God of Prophecy	5,679	65,801
International Church of the Foursquare Gospel	2,690	89,215
Open Bible Standard Churches	781	60,000
Pentecostal Church of God of America, Inc.	2,168	110,870
Pentecostal Holiness Church, Inc.	2,899	86,103
United Pentecostal Church, International	5,881	450,000
Plymouth Brethren	380	74,500
Polish National Catholic Church of America	144	282,411
Presbyterians		
Cumberland Presbyterian Church	706	93,268
Presbyterian Church in America	584	82,095
Presbyterian Church in the U.S.	5,254	862,416
United Presbyterian Church in the U.S.A.	13,871	2,520,367
Reformed bodies		
Christian Reformed Church	950	211,302
Reformed Church in America	1,418	348,080
Roman Catholic Church	58,856	49,602,035
Salvation Army	5,104	414,035
Seventh-day Adventist Church	3,591	535,705
Triumph the Church and Kingdom of God in Christ	1,375	54,307
Unitarian Universalist Association	898	136,207
United Church of Christ	9,704	1,769,104
Wesleyan Church	2,367	97,016

Table includes churches reporting a membership of 50,000 or more and represents the latest information available.
Source: National Council of Churches, *Yearbook of American and Canadian Churches*, 1980.

(CONSTANT H. JACQUET)

THE ECONOMY

Gross National Product and National Income

in billions of dollars

Item	1965[1]	1970[1]	1978	1979[2]
GROSS NATIONAL PRODUCT	688.1	982.4	2,127.6	2,329.8
By type of expenditure				
Personal consumption expenditures	430.2	618.8	1,350.8	1,475.9
Durable goods	62.8	84.9	200.3	208.7
Nondurable goods	188.6	264.7	530.6	581.2
Services	178.7	269.1	619.8	686.0
Gross private domestic investment	112.0	140.8	351.5	395.4
Fixed investment	102.5	137.0	329.1	361.9
Changes in business inventories	9.5	3.8	22.3	33.4
Net exports of goods and services	7.6	3.9	−10.3	−8.1
Exports	39.5	62.5	207.2	243.7
Imports	32.0	58.5	217.5	251.9
Government purchases of goods and services	138.4	218.9	435.6	466.6
Federal	67.3	95.6	152.6	161.7
State and local	71.1	123.2	283.0	304.9
By major type of product				
Goods output	336.6	456.2	930.0	1,018.1
Durable goods	133.6	170.8	380.4	422.4
Nondurable goods	203.1	285.4	549.6	595.7
Services	272.7	424.6	969.3	1,064.2
Structures	78.8	101.6	228.2	247.5
NATIONAL INCOME	566.0	798.4	1,724.3	1,897.9
By type of income				
Compensation of employees	396.5	609.2	1,304.5	1,439.7
Proprietors' income	56.7	65.1	116.8	129.3
Rental income of persons	17.1	18.6	25.9	26.8
Corporate profits	77.1	67.9	167.7	176.6
Net interest	18.5	37.5	109.5	125.6
By industry division[3]				
Agriculture, forestry, and fisheries	20.4	24.5	54.7	64.7
Mining and construction	35.9	51.6	114.1	130.5
Manufacturing	170.4	215.4	459.5	508.6
Nondurable goods	65.4	88.1	176.0	195.6
Durable goods	105.0	127.3	283.5	313.1
Transportation	23.1	30.3	68.2	75.5
Communications and public utilities	22.9	32.5	75.4	79.7
Wholesale and retail trade	84.7	122.2	261.8	286.7
Finance, insurance, and real estate	64.0	92.6	210.7	232.2
Services	64.1	103.3	245.2	271.5
Government and government enterprises	75.4	127.4	256.6	274.5
Other	4.7	4.6	. . .	. . .

[1] Revised. [2] Second quarter, seasonally adjusted at annual rates.
[3] Without capital consumption adjustment.
Source: U.S. Department of Commerce, Bureau of Economic Analysis, *Survey of Current Business*.

Personal Income Per Capita

State	1950	1960[1]	1970[1]	1978
Alabama	$ 880	$1,510	$2,892	$ 6,291
Alaska	2,384	2,743	4,638	10,963
Arizona	1,330	1,994	3,614	7,372
Arkansas	825	1,358	2,791	5,969
California	1,852	2,711	4,423	8,927
Colorado	1,487	2,247	3,838	8,105
Connecticut	1,875	2,838	4,871	8,911
Delaware	2,132	2,735	4,468	8,534
District of Columbia	2,221	2,823	4,644	9,924
Florida	1,281	1,965	3,698	7,573
Georgia	1,034	1,644	3,300	6,705
Hawaii	1,386	2,289	4,599	8,437
Idaho	1,295	1,811	3,243	7,015
Illinois	1,825	2,616	4,446	8,903
Indiana	1,512	2,149	3,709	7,706
Iowa	1,485	1,960	3,643	8,002
Kansas	1,443	2,084	3,725	7,882
Kentucky	981	1,576	3,076	6,607
Louisiana	1,120	1,649	3,023	6,716
Maine	1,186	1,835	3,250	6,292
Maryland	1,602	2,320	4,267	8,363
Massachusetts	1,633	2,435	4,276	7,924
Michigan	1,701	2,326	4,041	8,483
Minnesota	1,410	2,064	3,819	7,910
Mississippi	755	1,196	2,547	5,529
Missouri	1,431	2,091	3,654	7,313
Montana	1,622	1,983	3,395	6,755
Nebraska	1,490	2,009	3,657	7,582
Nevada	2,018	2,791	4,583	9,439
New Hampshire	1,323	2,160	3,720	7,357
New Jersey	1,834	2,700	4,684	8,773
New Mexico	1,177	1,814	3,045	6,574
New York	1,873	2,703	4,605	8,224
North Carolina	1,037	1,577	3,200	6,575
North Dakota	1,263	1,681	3,077	7,174
Ohio	1,620	2,322	3,949	7,855
Oklahoma	1,143	1,850	3,341	7,137
Oregon	1,620	2,194	3,677	8,092
Pennsylvania	1,541	2,239	3,879	7,740
Rhode Island	1,605	2,186	3,878	7,472
South Carolina	893	1,394	2,951	6,288
South Dakota	1,242	1,758	3,108	6,864
Tennessee	994	1,576	3,079	6,547
Texas	1,349	1,894	3,507	7,730
Utah	1,309	1,954	3,169	6,566
Vermont	1,121	1,864	3,447	6,566
Virginia	1,228	1,884	3,677	7,671
Washington	1,674	2,354	3,997	8,495
West Virginia	1,065	1,592	3,038	6,624
Wisconsin	1,477	2,178	3,712	7,532
Wyoming	1,668	2,210	3,672	8,636
United States	1,496	2,201	3,893	7,836

[1] Revised.
Source: U.S. Department of Commerce, Bureau of Economic Analysis, *Survey of Current Business*.

Average Employee Earnings

September figures

Industry	HOURLY 1978	HOURLY 1979[1]	WEEKLY 1978	WEEKLY 1979[1]
MANUFACTURING				
Durable goods				
Lumber and wood products	$5.74	$6.31	$229.60	$253.03
Furniture and fixtures	4.76	5.18	188.02	202.02
Stone, clay, and glass products	6.48	6.97	272.81	290.65
Primary metal industries	8.42	9.15	356.17	376.98
Fabricated metal products	6.45	6.93	265.74	283.44
Nonelectrical machinery	6.89	7.50	290.07	313.50
Electrical equipment and supplies	5.93	6.46	240.17	260.98
Transportation equipment	8.04	8.58	343.31	349.21
Instruments and related products	5.77	6.21	237.15	253.37
Nondurable goods				
Food and kindred products	5.88	6.34	236.96	257.40
Tobacco manufactures	5.93	6.54	228.31	255.06
Textile mill products	4.42	4.81	228.31	196.25
Apparel and related products	4.00	4.28	143.60	151.08
Paper and allied products	6.68	7.31	287.91	312.14
Printing and publishing	6.60	7.05	251.46	267.20
Chemicals and allied products	7.13	7.71	299.46	323.05
Petroleum and coal products	8.70	9.51	386.28	425.10
Rubber and plastics products	5.60	6.02	231.84	243.81
Leather and leather products	3.92	4.29	145.04	157.01
NONMANUFACTURING				
Metal mining	8.56	9.61	357.81	393.05
Coal mining	9.84	10.32	392.62	420.02
Oil and gas extraction	7.17	7.76	326.24	351.53
Contract construction	8.88	9.50	332.11	360.05
Local and suburban transportation	5.70	6.10	190.95	211.67
Electric, gas, and sanitary services	7.77	8.47	324.79	353.20
Wholesale trade	6.01	6.51	234.39	252.59
Retail trade	4.25	4.58	131.33	140.61
Hotels, tourist courts, and motels[2]	3.67	4.04	114.50	126.05
Banking	4.26	4.59	155.92	167.54

[1] Preliminary. [2] Excludes tips. Source: U.S. Dept. of Labor, Bureau of Labor Statistics, *Employment and Earnings.*

Unemployment Trends

quarterly averages, seasonally adjusted

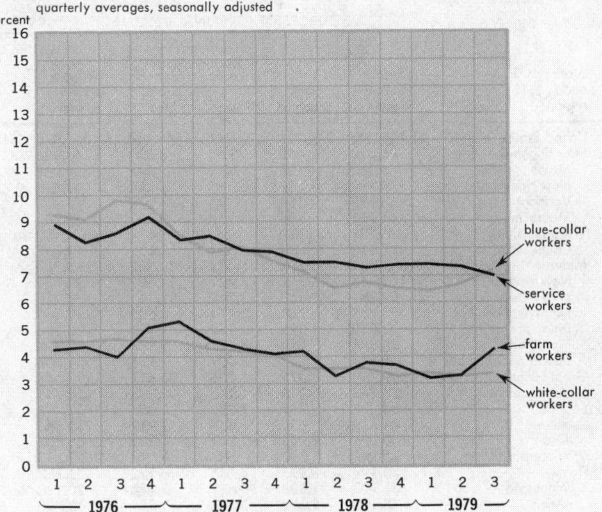

Source: U.S. Department of Labor, Bureau of Labor Statistics, *Monthly Labor Review.*

Value of Agricultural Products, with Fisheries, 1978

in thousands of dollars

State	PRINCIPAL CROPS Corn (grain)	Hay	Soybeans	Wheat	Tobacco	Cotton (lint)	Potatoes	LIVESTOCK AND PRODUCTS Cattle, calves	Hogs, pigs	Sheep, lambs	Milk[1]	Eggs[2]	Chickens[2]	FISHERIES[3]
Alabama	61,200	59,670	274,560	5,070	1,254	85,330	25,560	335,134	107,019	[4]	78,012	174,218	8,422	35,922[5]
Alaska	...	...	...	...	...	...	...	819	245	[4]	2,586	458	48	438,616
Arizona	14,375	82,229	...	29,299	...	320,021	12,959	322,611	21,642	10,768	101,875	4,131	101	...
Arkansas	4,089	55,000	733,200	32,190	...	193,882	...	347,363	52,710	[4]	79,704	173,247	14,066	2,055[5]
California	97,367	406,868	...	150,495	...	601,450	118,241	793,460	29,765	42,090	1,237,728	322,460	5,357	228,238
Colorado	174,240	146,131	...	157,073	...	...	30,018	937,909	53,661	42,963	101,675	22,292	508	...
Connecticut	...	13,968	...	...	25,954	...	2,466	10,259	1,454	183	72,094	51,353	1,351	4,368
Delaware	36,120	3,600	43,904	2,974	...	...	5,354	3,102	8,223	[4]	14,667	7,299	452	500
Florida	40,404	27,495	63,360	1,296	31,752	1,008	35,171	288,150	40,355	[4]	249,539	105,113	3,174	97,519
Georgia	172,500	54,150	183,750	11,328	179,066	32,630	...	177,757	212,593	[4]	148,350	286,403	13,719	14,567
Hawaii	...	...	...	...	...	...	...	21,064	7,835	...	24,150	12,699	195	11,620
Idaho	7,634	167,134	...	226,391	...	...	252,148	335,811	9,243	20,221	163,463	7,896	196	35
Illinois	2,501,163	192,728	1,956,092	107,787	...	...	1,188	478,453	1,114,375	5,933	250,152	60,950	1,368	826
Indiana	1,306,260	120,750	912,730	95,355	21,264	...	5,180	292,743	679,246	4,546	233,699	149,657	4,379	106
Iowa	2,925,000	336,191	1,836,160	4,689	...	...	1,350	1,465,908	2,321,399	12,334	407,434	61,886	2,132	820
Kansas	351,900	205,744	167,040	872,100	...	...	...	1,397,034	327,133	7,654	150,145	17,800	945	7
Kentucky	269,663	153,357	270,720	20,816	594,943	...	...	410,555	164,016	821	239,398	21,982	980	923[5]
Louisiana	6,655	31,132	454,400	1,867	199	139,853	986	184,446	17,675	180	123,308	30,563	1,911	190,167
Maine	...	26,040	...	...	...	...	83,776	9,813	1,313	371	74,710	99,472	2,844	68,833
Maryland	123,045	47,325	70,656	11,788	37,062	...	1,087	44,310	23,837	564	174,790	17,710	1,012	33,557
Massachusetts	...	19,388	...	...	8,404	...	4,779	8,072	7,745	212	68,526	18,812	1,298	152,251
Michigan	373,613	167,577	123,840	59,400	...	...	46,280	221,997	112,515	4,801	506,141	58,009	2,411	3,529
Minnesota	1,223,144	375,144	881,020	266,090	...	...	48,390	560,417	672,404	10,297	896,175	75,703	1,087	1,822
Mississippi	20,034	59,650	526,965	5,944	...	403,534	756	262,172	47,792	[4]	93,381	86,354	6,252	28,291
Missouri	411,510	278,070	1,007,760	84,252	6,912	55,176	...	958,240	609,757	4,023	283,452	50,710	5,154	152
Montana	810	192,192	...	405,625	...	...	8,352	515,295	35,214	11,651	31,665	8,733	198	...
Nebraska	1,517,308	241,216	263,500	224,400	...	...	7,930	1,452,672	548,557	5,928	130,073	24,765	422	45
Nevada	...	50,076	...	5,154	...	406	16,320	84,487	1,410	4,086	19,696	85	2	...
New Hampshire	...	12,489	...	...	...	...	...	5,524	1,416	253	38,625	12,118	817	1,750
New Jersey	19,884	24,025	42,333	3,564	...	...	8,155	12,065	6,938	231	60,323	17,750	652	44,432
New Mexico	17,338	66,929	...	16,137	...	33,552	3,895	317,412	9,811	9,924	54,365	17,053	240	...
New York	106,650	307,226	3,087	8,925	...	...	55,315	125,068	20,181	1,809	1,110,159	71,494	2,422	33,870
North Carolina	285,760	39,168	239,940	17,820	1,128,345	14,573	15,653	116,431	327,303	153	180,205	158,672	14,513	40,607
North Dakota	39,974	225,855	28,072	796,102	...	...	60,480	342,735	43,912	6,659	87,219	2,691	89	87
Ohio	814,958	204,568	804,375	140,400	28,060	...	11,564	284,041	275,989	11,111	459,135	80,072	3,424	2,563
Oklahoma	11,151	177,210	32,398	437,400	...	101,304	...	990,910	46,169	2,757	121,862	30,090	1,141	570[5]
Oregon	3,273	127,743	...	179,141	...	...	94,024	227,738	15,265	13,970	117,789	23,495	510	56,600
Pennsylvania	254,363	272,349	12,109	26,681	15,132	...	29,375	213,619	88,632	2,546	889,765	137,917	12,871	257
Rhode Island	...	1,258	...	...	...	...	3,834	776	1,286	[4]	6,595	2,788	108	29,308
South Carolina	68,063	24,864	208,593	7,722	206,965	34,353	...	78,709	69,835	[4]	61,608	62,465	2,985	16,031
South Dakota	300,160	237,188	74,344	185,560	...	...	3,665	787,151	277,072	33,366	154,720	16,673	363	314
Tennessee	98,010	94,644	375,342	21,945	192,169	70,162	2,831	297,154	186,389	252	227,056	43,343	2,238	2,437[5]
Texas	360,000	233,688	121,063	156,600	...	1,060,886	27,734	2,487,868	138,521	57,101	402,004	133,253	4,211	148,901
Utah	3,816	87,699	...	16,759	...	...	4,136	135,497	6,381	16,732	98,362	14,630	192	...
Vermont	...	58,410	...	...	...	...	1,075	29,858	1,297	310	244,378	7,591	218	...
Virginia	118,511	106,600	84,728	16,275	175,044	31	17,523	189,469	76,553	6,697	210,171	47,421	2,607	60,622
Washington	20,842	120,063	...	455,532	...	...	144,452	180,470	9,969	2,217	292,338	43,719	1,368	97,178
West Virginia	10,272	46,560	...	891	3,443	...	...	52,797	11,782	3,983	37,771	7,842	445	18
Wisconsin	539,000	418,860	41,624	4,368	22,334	...	76,230	416,029	263,645	3,457	2,180,455	35,433	3,057	4,186
Wyoming	5,921	95,325	...	20,940	...	...	5,372	270,575	3,810	27,132	12,589	732	18	...
TOTAL U.S.	14,716,030	6,495,546	11,837,665	5,294,145	2,678,302	3,108,004	1,273,604	19,481,949	9,111,289	390,286	13,004,082	2,918,002	134,473	1,854,500

[1] Farm value. [2] Gross income, Dec. 1, 1977–Nov. 30, 1978. [3] Preliminary. [4] Estimates discontinued. [5] Estimate.
Sources: U.S. Department of Agriculture, Statistical Reporting Service, Crop Reporting Board, *Crop Values, Meat Animals, Milk, Poultry;* U.S. Department of Commerce, National Oceanic and Atmospheric Administration, National Marine Fisheries Service, *Fisheries of the United States, 1978.*

Income by Industrial Source, 1978

State and region	SOURCES OF PERSONAL INCOME: Total personal income	Farm income	Govt. income disbursements: Federal	Govt. income disbursements: State, local	Private nonfarm income	SOURCES OF LABOUR AND PROPRIETORS' INCOME % OF TOTAL: Total	Farms	Mining	Con-struc-tion	Mfg.	Whole-sale, retail trade	Finance, insur-ance, real estate	Transpor-tation, commu-nications, public util.	Service	Govt.	Other
United States	$1,708,545	$33,341	$72,097	$144,364	$1,067,878	$1,317,680	%2.5	%1.6	%6.0	%26.2	%16.5	%5.8	%7.6	%16.8	%16.4	%0.6
New England	96,820	417	2,760	7,591	60,883	71,651	0.6	0.1	4.7	31.3	16.0	6.4	6.0	19.9	14.4	0.6
Maine	6,867	97	412	544	4,022	5,075	1.9	[2]	6.2	28.0	16.6	4.2	6.3	16.6	18.8	1.4
New Hampshire	6,409	19	175	455	3,848	4,497	0.4	0.2	7.2	32.9	17.2	5.1	5.5	17.2	14.0	0.3
Vermont	3,197	106	83	273	1,965	2,427	4.4	0.4	6.7	28.6	14.9	4.4	6.5	18.8	14.7	0.6
Massachusetts	45,751	94	1,264	3,881	29,208	34,447	0.3	[2]	4.1	28.7	16.2	6.3	6.6	22.3	14.9	0.6
Rhode Island	6,984	22	245	611	4,189	5,066	0.4	0.1	4.6	33.6	15.4	5.6	4.6	18.4	16.9	0.4
Connecticut	27,612	79	581	1,827	17,652	20,139	0.4	0.2	4.6	36.0	15.3	7.9	5.4	17.8	12.0	0.4
Mideast	347,485	1,704	16,124	30,552	216,787	264,966	0.6	0.5	4.5	26.0	15.7	7.0	8.2	19.5	17.5	0.5
New York	145,963	452	3,421	14,309	92,810	110,993	0.4	0.2	3.4	23.4	16.1	9.7	9.0	21.6	16.0	0.2
New Jersey	64,281	132	1,740	5,107	38,223	45,203	0.3	0.1	4.7	30.1	17.2	5.2	8.9	18.0	15.1	0.4
Pennsylvania	90,939	680	2,471	6,605	59,840	69,596	1.0	1.7	5.6	33.6	15.2	5.1	7.8	16.7	13.0	0.3
Delaware	4,972	125	162	409	3,283	3,979	3.1	0.2	6.1	38.3	9.2	4.3	5.8	14.1	14.4	4.5
Maryland	34,646	314	3,038	3,183	17,322	23,858	1.3	0.1	6.7	17.2	17.2	5.4	6.7	18.9	26.1	0.4
District of Columbia	6,684	[1]	5,091	938	5,308	11,337	[2]	[2]	2.3	2.7	4.4	4.5	5.4	24.4	53.2	3.1
Great Lakes	339,119	5,475	6,756	26,462	230,543	269,236	2.0	0.7	5.5	37.6	15.5	4.8	6.8	14.5	12.3	0.3
Michigan	77,943	716	1,172	6,903	54,040	62,832	1.1	0.5	4.8	43.6	13.8	3.8	5.5	13.7	12.8	0.4
Ohio	84,432	782	1,998	6,055	58,497	67,332	1.2	1.0	5.4	39.2	15.4	4.3	7.1	14.2	12.0	0.2
Indiana	41,412	836	837	2,917	28,566	33,157	2.5	0.6	6.0	41.8	14.6	4.2	6.7	11.9	11.3	0.4
Illinois	100,091	1,813	2,242	7,509	66,807	78,371	2.3	0.9	5.7	30.2	17.4	6.3	8.0	16.5	12.4	0.3
Wisconsin	35,241	1,327	507	3,077	22,633	27,544	4.8	0.2	5.9	35.6	15.4	4.8	6.0	14.0	13.0	0.3
Plains	130,194	8,973	4,145	10,523	77,763	101,404	8.8	1.1	6.6	22.6	17.6	5.5	8.4	14.6	14.5	0.3
Minnesota	31,703	1,834	619	2,844	20,120	25,418	7.2	1.5	6.6	24.1	18.1	5.6	7.8	15.1	13.6	0.4
Iowa	23,170	2,572	326	1,855	12,786	17,538	14.7	0.2	6.6	24.9	16.4	5.2	6.4	12.7	12.4	0.5
Missouri	35,538	1,213	1,397	2,562	23,661	28,833	4.2	0.6	6.0	26.1	17.9	5.6	9.8	15.8	13.7	0.3
North Dakota	4,677	581	301	400	2,257	3,539	16.4	2.5	9.7	6.2	18.8	4.6	7.9	13.6	19.8	0.5
South Dakota	4,733	817	280	387	2,112	3,596	22.7	1.4	6.4	8.9	17.1	4.4	6.8	13.3	18.5	0.5
Nebraska	11,868	1,062	453	1,047	6,432	8,995	11.8	0.4	7.0	15.6	17.9	6.5	9.5	14.2	16.7	0.4
Kansas	18,505	894	770	1,427	10,394	13,484	6.6	2.2	6.6	21.8	17.4	5.4	8.9	14.4	16.3	0.4
Southeast	334,155	7,481	19,046	28,036	198,554	253,116	3.0	2.4	6.7	24.0	16.8	5.1	7.8	15.2	18.6	0.4
Virginia	39,492	401	4,655	3,221	20,845	29,121	1.4	1.6	6.7	19.8	15.0	4.9	7.2	16.1	27.0	0.3
West Virginia	12,318	24	267	1,049	8,109	9,450	0.3	15.9	7.9	23.9	14.0	3.1	8.4	12.3	13.9	0.3
Kentucky	23,114	682	1,110	1,680	14,272	17,743	3.8	7.2	6.9	26.3	15.1	4.0	7.5	13.2	15.7	0.3
Tennessee	28,527	422	1,457	2,390	18,673	22,943	1.8	0.8	5.8	30.5	17.2	5.0	6.9	15.0	16.8	0.2
North Carolina	36,671	1,551	1,868	3,212	22,789	29,421	5.3	0.2	5.3	32.1	15.7	4.3	6.5	13.0	17.3	0.3
South Carolina	18,346	319	1,258	1,654	11,238	14,469	2.2	0.2	6.7	33.6	14.3	4.2	6.0	12.2	20.1	0.5
Georgia	34,087	800	2,133	2,990	21,428	27,351	2.9	0.4	5.3	23.6	19.1	5.7	9.3	14.5	18.7	0.5
Florida	65,084	1,363	2,677	5,370	34,262	43,673	3.1	0.4	7.1	13.6	19.7	7.4	8.7	20.7	18.4	0.9
Alabama	23,540	487	1,505	2,129	14,106	18,228	2.7	1.8	6.7	28.3	15.1	4.6	7.4	13.2	19.9	0.3
Mississippi	13,290	479	729	1,167	7,746	10,121	4.7	1.7	6.4	27.9	15.6	4.4	6.9	13.0	18.7	0.7
Louisiana	26,638	288	918	2,209	17,533	20,949	1.4	7.8	10.1	17.3	17.7	4.8	10.0	15.4	14.9	0.6
Arkansas	13,047	665	468	963	7,553	9,648	6.9	1.0	6.6	27.9	16.4	4.7	7.9	13.2	14.8	0.6
Southwest	146,478	2,231	7,432	11,906	91,474	113,043	2.0	5.8	8.3	18.4	18.5	5.7	8.0	15.6	17.1	0.6
Oklahoma	20,556	437	1,195	1,552	11,700	14,883	2.9	8.6	6.7	17.6	17.5	5.2	8.5	14.3	18.5	0.2
Texas	100,601	1,207	4,602	7,589	65,559	78,957	1.5	5.5	8.4	19.9	19.1	5.9	8.1	15.6	15.4	0.6
New Mexico	7,969	220	688	955	4,276	6,139	3.6	8.8	8.4	7.0	16.1	4.3	8.1	16.5	26.8	0.4
Arizona	17,352	368	947	1,810	9,938	13,064	2.8	3.4	9.6	15.7	17.3	6.0	6.9	16.6	21.1	0.6
Rocky Mountain	45,343	1,214	2,714	4,237	27,480	35,646	3.4	5.5	8.5	15.4	17.4	5.5	8.7	15.7	19.5	0.4
Montana	5,299	226	283	548	2,895	3,953	5.7	4.0	8.5	11.2	18.4	4.7	10.6	15.5	21.0	0.4
Idaho	6,156	412	279	523	3,544	4,758	8.7	1.6	8.8	18.4	17.3	5.0	7.5	15.2	16.9	0.6
Wyoming	3,658	94	172	327	2,348	2,941	3.2	23.4	11.8	5.4	14.3	3.5	9.7	11.5	17.0	0.2
Colorado	21,645	362	1,317	2,013	13,333	17,025	2.1	4.0	7.7	16.6	17.6	6.4	8.4	17.1	19.6	0.5
Utah	8,585	119	663	826	5,361	6,969	1.7	5.2	8.7	16.9	17.7	5.0	8.7	14.5	21.4	0.2
Far West	257,072	5,658	11,532	23,714	157,632	198,536	2.8	0.6	6.4	21.4	17.2	6.2	7.3	19.6	17.8	0.7
Washington	32,058	1,001	1,736	2,901	19,002	24,640	4.1	0.2	8.2	21.9	17.5	5.5	7.1	15.8	18.8	0.9
Oregon	19,775	482	567	1,825	12,529	15,404	3.1	0.3	7.1	25.6	18.9	5.6	7.7	15.3	15.5	0.9
Nevada	6,229	49	295	539	4,249	5,131	1.0	1.5	10.7	5.4	15.0	4.6	7.9	37.5	16.2	0.2
California	199,010	4,127	8,933	18,449	121,852	153,361	2.7	0.6	5.8	21.4	17.1	6.4	7.3	20.0	17.9	0.8
Alaska	4,415	6	661	631	2,909	4,207	0.1	5.9	12.8	6.2	12.0	4.3	12.4	14.5	30.7	1.1
Hawaii	7,465	181	1,129	712	3,854	5,876	3.1	[2]	7.2	5.5	16.2	7.4	9.3	19.7	31.3	0.3

Dollar figures in millions. Percentages may not add to 100.0 because of rounding.
[1]Less than $500,000. [2]Less than 0.05%.
Source: U.S. Department of Commerce, Bureau of Economic Analysis, *Survey of Current Business.*

Farms and Farm Income

State	Number of farms 1979[1,2]	Land in farms 1979 in 000 acres[1,2]	CASH RECEIPTS, 1978, IN $000[1] Farm marketings: Total	Crops	Livestock and products
Alabama	56,000	13,200	1,895,312	706,182	1,189,130
Alaska	300	1,680[3]	11,821	7,582	4,239
Arizona	5,800	40,500	1,471,219	753,331	717,888
Arkansas	58,000	16,800	2,678,011	1,278,891	1,399,120
California	60,000	32,300	10,368,586	6,954,451	3,414,135
Colorado	26,500	38,000	2,634,729	560,481	2,074,248
Connecticut	3,600	450	229,998	89,504	140,494
Delaware	3,000	620	319,812	101,785	218,027
Florida	35,000	13,800	3,238,391	2,382,628	855,763
Georgia	54,000	15,700	2,543,304	1,075,540	1,467,764
Hawaii	3,700	2,290	380,363	307,792	72,571
Idaho	23,300	15,400	1,433,646	815,413	618,233
Illinois	107,000	28,700	6,123,266	3,984,554	2,138,712
Indiana	89,000	16,900	3,478,187	1,921,466	1,556,721
Iowa	121,000	34,000	8,227,706	2,809,515	5,418,191
Kansas	72,000	48,200	4,445,816	1,490,243	2,955,573
Kentucky	96,000	14,400	2,039,927	1,040,131	999,796
Louisiana	35,000	10,300	1,419,751	980,969	438,782
Maine	7,600	1,640	410,489	123,941	286,548
Maryland	16,000	2,805	770,526	259,166	511,360
Massachusetts	4,800	650	242,006	129,897	112,109
Michigan	63,000	10,600	2,126,791	1,129,132	997,659
Minnesota	104,000	30,300	4,851,938	2,260,856	2,591,082
Mississippi	53,000	14,500	1,998,548	1,091,783	906,765
Missouri	118,000	32,300	3,575,702	1,477,136	2,098,566
Montana	21,700	62,000	1,231,650	548,876	682,774
Nebraska	63,000	47,800	4,731,600	1,633,441	3,098,159
Nevada	2,000	8,990	168,018	42,073	125,945
New Hampshire	3,000	580	86,681	25,305	61,376
New Jersey	7,600	990	372,439	268,037	104,402
New Mexico	11,200	46,700	964,262	213,026	751,236
New York	45,000	10,000	1,918,837	571,558	1,347,279
North Carolina	99,000	12,400	3,236,199	1,939,441	1,296,758
North Dakota	41,000	41,690	1,866,400	1,336,987	529,413
Ohio	97,000	16,300	3,002,663	1,730,369	1,272,294
Oklahoma	73,000	35,000	2,379,459	704,381	1,675,078
Oregon	30,000	18,650	1,268,373	812,748	455,625
Pennsylvania	59,000	8,900	2,152,309	641,631	1,510,678
Rhode Island	670	63	30,057	17,678	12,379
South Carolina	35,000	6,500	978,597	605,398	373,199
South Dakota	41,500	45,450	2,085,421	555,342	1,530,079
Tennessee	94,000	13,700	1,625,438	757,069	868,369
Texas	159,000	138,700	7,547,973	2,901,779	4,646,194
Utah	12,200	12,800	456,726	104,527	352,199
Vermont	5,900	1,740	309,003	21,933	287,070
Virginia	59,000	9,700	1,231,485	524,246	707,239
Washington	33,000	16,100	2,124,136	1,562,397	561,739
West Virginia	19,500	4,180	186,956	47,384	139,572
Wisconsin	95,000	18,700	3,644,406	673,551	2,970,855
Wyoming	7,200	35,100	527,156	79,782	447,374
TOTAL U.S.	2,330,070	1,048,768	111,042,089	52,051,328	58,990,761

[1]Preliminary. [2]Places with annual sales of agricultural products of $1,000 or more.
[3]Exclusive of grazing land leased from the U.S. Government, Alaska farmland totals about 70,000 acres.
Source: U.S. Department of Agriculture, Statistical Reporting Service and Economic Research Service.

Principal Minerals Produced

State	Principal minerals, in order of value, 1975	Value in $000		% of U.S. total	
		1974	1975	1974	1975
Alabama	Coal, petroleum, cement, stone	$764,746	$968,973	1.39	1.56
Alaska	Petroleum, natural gas, stone, sand and gravel	448,437	480,745	0.81	0.77
Arizona	Copper, molybdenum, cement, sand and gravel	1,562,234	1,288,423	2.83	2.07
Arkansas	Petroleum, bromine, natural gas, stone	406,821	436,441	0.74	0.70
California	Petroleum, cement, natural gas, sand and gravel	2,797,080	3,152,937	5.07	5.06
Colorado	Petroleum, molybdenum, coal, cement	750,299	960,800	1.36	1.54
Connecticut	Stone, sand and gravel, feldspar, lime	35,362	33,010	0.06	0.05
Delaware	Sand and gravel, magnesium compounds, clays	3,793	1,906	0.01	0.01
Florida	Phosphate rock, petroleum, stone, cement	1,043,895	1,775,500	1.89	2.85
Georgia	Clays, stone, cement, sand and gravel	363,100	333,387	0.66	0.54
Hawaii	Stone, cement, sand and gravel, pumice	42,042	49,710	0.08	0.08
Idaho	Phosphate rock, silver, zinc, lead	208,558	233,788	0.38	0.38
Illinois	Coal, petroleum, stone, sand and gravel	1,149,210	1,490,598	2.08	2.39
Indiana	Coal, cement, stone, petroleum	440,690	541,600	0.80	0.87
Iowa	Cement, stone, sand and gravel, coal	176,720	195,740	0.32	0.31
Kansas	Petroleum, natural gas, natural gas liquids, cement	889,398	970,611	1.61	1.56
Kentucky	Coal, petroleum, stone, natural gas	2,563,210	2,738,859	4.65	4.40
Louisiana	Petroleum, natural gas, natural gas liquids, sulfur	8,146,578	8,513,275	14.77	13.67
Maine	Cement, sand and gravel, zinc, stone	36,348	36,741	0.07	0.06
Maryland	Coal, stone, cement, sand and gravel	172,880	164,919	0.31	0.26
Massachusetts	Stone, sand and gravel, lime, clays	62,109	58,846	0.11	0.09
Michigan	Iron ore, petroleum, cement, copper	1,040,067	1,291,653	1.89	2.07
Minnesota	Iron ore, sand and gravel, stone, cement	1,026,366	1,097,088	1.86	1.76
Mississippi	Petroleum, natural gas, sand and gravel, cement	391,155	410,009	0.71	0.66
Missouri	Lead, cement, stone, iron ore	691,049	722,728	1.25	1.16
Montana	Petroleum, copper, coal, cement	574,801	573,150	1.04	0.92
Nebraska	Petroleum, cement, sand and gravel, stone	98,634	111,905	0.18	0.18
Nevada	Copper, gold, sand and gravel, cement	257,876	258,390	0.47	0.41
New Hampshire	Sand and gravel, stone, clays, gem stones	13,691	17,107	0.02	0.03
New Jersey	Stone, sand and gravel, zinc, titanium concentrate	140,748	123,702	0.26	0.20
New Mexico	Petroleum, natural gas, copper, potassium salts	1,941,544	2,091,541	3.52	3.36
New York	Cement, stone, zinc, salt	440,573	397,728	0.80	0.64
North Carolina	Stone, phosphate rock, lithium minerals	155,869	152,880	0.28	0.25
North Dakota	Petroleum, coal, sand and gravel, natural gas	159,427	201,504	0.29	0.32
Ohio	Coal, petroleum, stone, lime	1,107,670	1,356,454	2.01	2.18
Oklahoma	Petroleum, natural gas, natural gas liquids, coal	2,123,690	2,267,095	3.85	3.64
Oregon	Stone, sand and gravel, cement, nickel	103,920	106,004	0.19	0.17
Pennsylvania	Coal, cement, stone, lime	2,374,512	2,907,838	4.30	4.67
Rhode Island	Sand and gravel, stone, gem stones	5,982	6,198	0.01	0.01
South Carolina	Cement, stone, sand and gravel, clays	105,171	115,467	0.19	0.19
South Dakota	Gold, cement, stone, sand and gravel	102,627	101,821	0.19	0.16
Tennessee	Coal, stone, zinc, cement	395,608	424,768	0.71	0.68
Texas	Petroleum, natural gas, natural gas liquids, cement	13,711,144	15,529,931	24.85	24.94
Utah	Petroleum, copper, coal, gold	952,045	966,407	1.72	1.55
Vermont	Stone, asbestos, sand and gravel, talc	35,453	28,779	0.06	0.05
Virginia	Coal, stone, cement, sand and gravel	1,058,207	1,261,974	1.92	2.03
Washington	Cement, coal, sand and gravel, stone	143,916	158,505	0.26	0.25
West Virginia	Coal, natural gas, petroleum, natural gas liquids	2,403,177	3,390,212	4.36	5.44
Wisconsin	Sand and gravel, stone, iron ore, cement	114,763	132,260	0.21	0.21
Wyoming	Petroleum, sodium compounds, coal, natural gas	1,437,200	1,644,438	2.60	2.64
TOTAL U.S.		$55,172,000	$62,275,000	100.00	100.00

Source: U.S. Department of the Interior, Bureau of Mines, *Minerals Yearbook*.

Services

Kind of service	Number of services 1976	Number of services 1977	Number of employees[1] 1976	Number of employees[1] 1977
Hotels and other lodging places	46,122	45,399	890,512	915,178
Hotels, tourist courts, and motels	35,147	35,109	829,157	859,001
Rooming and boarding houses	4,010	3,579	33,282	30,168
Camps and trailering parks	3,957	3,939	15,434	15,499
Sporting and recreational camps	1,844	2,267	8,990	9,749
Personal services	159,719	162,161	880,718	901,047
Laundry, cleaning, garment services	44,869	44,462	356,130	357,102
Photographic studios, portrait	5,441	6,105	28,563	32,066
Beauty shops	70,174	71,311	274,485	280,645
Barber shops	11,521	11,029	27,586	27,620
Shoe repair and hat cleaning shops	3,100	2,935	7,537	6,994
Funeral service and crematories	14,472	14,733	71,121	71,209
Miscellaneous personal services	9,692	11,023	113,062	123,563
Business services	133,804	145,005	2,126,688	2,307,384
Advertising	9,589	10,203	114,325	120,024
Credit reporting and collection	5,627	5,741	60,210	61,492
Mailing, reproduction, stenographic	11,755	12,297	93,081	95,067
Building services	22,740	23,901	383,502	408,157
Employment agencies	6,314	7,091	72,768	76,084
Temporary help supply services	3,331	3,570	233,322	293,728
Computer and data processing services	7,476	9,109	174,595	199,177
Research and development laboratories	2,004	2,013	73,189	75,929
Management and public relations	20,192	23,095	218,386	240,838
Detective and protective services	5,841	6,312	248,050	268,684
Equipment rental and leasing	10,327	11,002	80,911	85,134
Photofinishing laboratories	2,341	2,478	56,292	60,683
Auto repair, services, and garages	91,653	97,327	444,165	477,370
Automobile rentals, without drivers	7,256	7,386	73,638	76,910
Automobile parking	7,001	7,153	32,910	33,709
Automotive repair shops	69,468	73,970	282,297	305,447
Automotive services, except repair	7,520	8,374	53,073	59,473
Car washes	5,286	5,564	40,792	44,901
Miscellaneous repair services	47,874	49,483	242,767	254,140
Radio and television repair	9,112	9,079	37,674	38,114
Motion pictures	14,748	15,034	184,607	180,933
Motion picture production	3,220	3,529	52,963	55,495
Motion picture distribution	1,126	1,129	15,358	15,940
Motion picture theatres	10,289	10,217	115,752	108,862

Kind of service	Number of services 1976	Number of services 1977	Number of employees[1] 1976	Number of employees[1] 1977
Amusement and recreation services	44,903	46,842	563,380	585,304
Producers, orchestras, entertainers	6,112	6,451	63,110	67,497
Bowling and billiard establishments	7,859	7,843	102,433	106,476
Racing, including track operation	1,782	1,781	...	37,664
Public golf courses	2,127	2,153	13,879	14,733
Amusement parks	552	564	30,299	32,058
Membership sports, recreation clubs	9,009	9,415	136,465	143,652
Health services	263,576	283,274	4,089,115	4,339,178
Physicians' offices	124,122	132,546	566,495	601,354
Dentists' offices	76,359	80,588	252,295	273,980
Osteopathic physicians' offices	4,336	4,547	15,354	16,024
Chiropractors' offices	6,502	7,231	12,593	14,127
Optometrists' offices	10,132	11,013	25,016	27,514
Nursing and personal care facilities	11,790	12,316	736,309	793,769
Hospitals	5,333	5,414	2,194,141	2,283,839
Medical and dental laboratories	9,459	10,442	84,785	90,035
Outpatient care facilities	5,419	7,704	104,513	126,697
Legal services	85,758	91,942	363,088	392,481
Educational services	25,521	25,994	983,431	992,019
Elementary and secondary schools	14,007	13,461	312,374	295,441
Colleges and universities	2,317	2,438	548,118	576,196
Libraries and information centres	1,469	1,599	16,371	12,691
Correspondence and vocational schools	2,891	3,039	46,919	46,082
Social services	43,036	52,322	723,119	764,310
Residential care	5,575	7,645	149,659	172,098
Museums, botanical, zoological gardens	871	1,063	23,398	22,588
Membership organizations	135,628	137,891	1,071,128	1,100,716
Business associations	12,077	12,398	70,343	73,130
Professional organizations	3,746	3,958	36,712	36,410
Labour organizations	22,265	22,189	164,129	170,102
Civic and social organizations	33,854	34,182	270,039	266,076
Political organizations	1,371	1,137	6,286	4,160
Religious organizations	54,986	56,712	447,938	482,159
Miscellaneous services	67,554	75,257	639,767	670,425
Engineering, architectural services	29,468	32,520	345,003	369,706
Noncommercial research organizations	2,349	2,398	60,357	52,144
Accounting, auditing and bookkeeping	32,657	37,109	218,534	233,487
TOTAL[2]	1,164,782	1,233,652	13,340,684	14,059,994

[1] Mid-March pay period. [2] Includes administrative and auxiliary businesses not shown separately.
Source: U.S. Department of Commerce, Bureau of the Census, *County Business Patterns 1976* and *1977.*

Principal Manufactures, 1976

monetary figures in millions of dollars

Industry	Employees (000)	Cost of labour[1]	Cost of materials	Value of shipments	Value added by mfg.
Food and kindred products	1,536	$17,289	$128,618	$180,930	$52,760
Meat products	311	3,474	38,252	45,827	7,530
Dairy products	164	1,908	19,657	24,830	5,261
Preserved fruits and vegetables	222	2,032	10,935	17,722	6,799
Grain mill products	114	1,453	15,133	21,189	6,083
Beverages	204	2,629	12,241	21,069	8,833
Tobacco products	65	704	4,659	8,786	4,128
Textile mill products	876	7,368	22,194	36,389	14,495
Apparel and other textile products	1,271	8,563	18,150	34,758	16,860
Lumber and wood products	629	6,143	18,121	31,239	13,454
Furniture and fixtures	426	3,772	6,946	14,232	7,370
Paper and allied products	615	8,046	27,877	48,218	20,604
Printing and publishing	1,086	12,680	15,288	42,838	27,647
Chemicals and allied products	851	12,365	53,725	104,139	51,408
Industrial chemicals	251	4,032	20,237	37,296	17,513
Plastics materials and synthetics	153	2,187	10,688	17,156	6,648
Drugs	151	2,223	3,813	13,016	9,333
Soap, cleaners, and toilet goods	110	1,415	6,383	14,741	8,469
Paints, allied products	60	810	3,438	5,931	2,562
Agricultural chemicals	52	722	5,448	9,195	3,763
Petroleum and coal products	144	2,437	69,392	82,347	13,169
Rubber, misc. plastics products	627	6,742	15,885	31,765	15,950
Leather and leather products	247	1,805	3,691	7,176	3,559
Stone, clay, and glass products	599	7,086	14,056	30,635	16,773
Primary metal industries	1,106	16,975	59,932	93,002	34,182
Blast furnace, basic steel products	532	9,166	30,231	46,687	17,274
Iron, steel foundries	216	2,966	4,361	9,787	5,496
Primary nonferrous metals	59	963	6,909	9,970	2,980
Nonferrous drawing and rolling	171	2,339	13,653	18,753	5,360
Nonferrous foundries	85	951	1,653	3,389	1,738
Fabricated metal products	1,471	18,382	38,720	77,507	39,145
Ordnance and accessories	75	976	1,115	2,804	1,664
Machinery, except electrical	1,960	$26,480	$48,648	$105,525	$57,357
Engines and turbines	125	1,939	4,935	9,009	4,200
Farm and garden machinery	146	1,949	5,776	10,534	4,783
Construction and related mach.	312	4,378	10,234	19,741	9,646
Metalworking machinery	290	3,954	3,867	11,278	7,458
Special industry machinery	196	2,556	4,159	9,454	5,175
General industrial machinery	281	3,746	6,184	14,196	8,043
Service industry machines	173	2,152	5,587	10,660	5,214
Office, computing machines	229	3,277	5,664	13,723	8,102
Electric and electronic equipment	1,578	19,253	32,831	73,867	41,746
Electric distributing equip.	104	1,193	2,018	4,688	2,702
Electrical industrial apparatus	195	2,284	3,691	8,453	4,916
Household appliances	157	1,699	4,847	9,161	4,454
Electric lighting, wiring equip.	159	1,700	3,228	7,342	4,204
Radio, TV receiving equipment	90	956	3,302	5,823	2,544
Communication equipment	422	6,050	7,513	19,138	11,656
Electronic components, access.	323	3,763	5,008	12,433	7,568
Transportation equipment	1,668	26,442	85,892	141,026	55,657
Motor vehicles and equipment	797	13,019	65,343	95,381	30,948
Aircraft and parts	408	6,665	10,087	23,463	12,735
Ship, boat building, repairing	207	2,605	3,481	7,516	4,032
Railroad equipment	50	740	2,077	3,616	1,455
Guided missiles, space vehicles	142	2,723	2,347	7,142	5,027
Instruments and related products	518	6,598	8,989	25,030	16,386
Measuring, controlling devices	169	2,100	2,143	6,180	4,102
Medical instruments and supplies	111	1,248	1,892	4,766	2,956
Photographic equipment and supplies	107	1,732	2,915	8,845	6,077
Miscellaneous manufacturing industries	410	3,868	7,580	16,286	8,822
All establishments, including administrative and auxiliary	18,753	233,389	681,194	1,185,695	511,471

[1]Payroll only. Source: U.S. Department of Commerce, *Annual Survey of Manufactures 1976.*

Business Activity

Category of activity	WHOLESALING 1960	WHOLESALING 1965	WHOLESALING 1970	WHOLESALING 1976	RETAILING 1960	RETAILING 1965	RETAILING 1970	RETAILING 1976	SERVICES 1960	SERVICES 1965	SERVICES 1970	SERVICES 1976
Number of businesses (in 000)												
Sole proprietorships	306	265	274	331	1,548	1,554	1,689	1,861	1,966	2,208	2,507	3,153
Active partnerships	41	32	30	32	238	202	170	162	159	169	176	207
Active corporations	117	147	166	228	217	288	351	417	121	188	281	473
Business receipts (in $000,000)												
Sole proprietorships	17,061	17,934	21,556	35,158	65,439	77,760	89,315	120,705	23,256	29,789	40,869	61,202
Active partnerships	12,712	10,879	11,325	16,011	24,787	23,244	23,546	30,032	9,281	12,442	18,791	32,056
Active corporations	130,637	171,414	234,885	572,364	125,787	183,925	274,808	527,571	22,106	36,547	66,460	146,817
Net profit (less loss; in $000,000)												
Sole proprietorships	1,305	1,483	1,806	2,912	3,869	5,019	5,767	6,675	8,060	11,008	15,063	20,266
Active partnerships	587	548	557	704	1,612	1,654	1,603	1,703	3,056	4,402	6,189	7,802
Active corporations	2,130	3,288	4,441	15,769	2,225	4,052	5,217	10,367	849	1,505	1,199	4,185

Data refer to accounting periods ending between July 1 of year shown and June 30 of following year.
Source: U.S. Department of the Treasury, Internal Revenue Service, *Statistics of Income: Business Income Tax Returns* and *Corporation Income Tax Returns.*

Retail Sales

in millions of dollars

Kind of business	1960	1965	1970	1978
Durable goods stores[1]	70,560	94,186	114,288	277,916
Automotive group	39,579	56,884	64,966	163,668
Passenger car, other automotive dealers	37,038	53,484	59,388	149,675
Tire, battery, accessory dealers	2,541	3,400	5,578	13,993
Furniture and appliance group	10,591	13,352	17,778	37,430
Furniture, home furnishings stores	...	...	10,483	22,719
Household appliance, TV, radio stores	...	...	6,073	10,991
Building materials, hardware, farm equipment group	11,222	12,388	20,494	44,125
Lumberyards, building materials dealers	8,567	9,731	11,995	29,991
Hardware stores	2,655	2,657	3,351	6,881
Nondurable goods stores[1]	148,969	189,942	261,239	520,902
Apparel group	13,631	15,765	19,810	37,828
Men's, boys' wear stores	2,644	...	4,630	7,353
Women's apparel, accessory stores	5,295	...	7,582	14,660
Family clothing stores	...	...	3,360	7,147
Shoe stores	2,437	...	3,501	6,593
Drug and proprietary stores	7,538	9,186	13,352	25,337
Eating and drinking places	16,146	20,201	29,689	70,083
Food group	54,023	64,016	86,114	174,458
Grocery stores	48,610	...	79,756	161,527
Meat and fish markets	...	...	2,244	...
Bakeries	...	...	1,303	2,436
Gasoline service stations	17,588	20,611	27,994	60,884
General merchandise group	...	42,299	61,320	99,505
Department stores and dry goods general merchandise stores	...	...	45,000	91,696
Variety stores	...	...	6,959	7,809
Mail-order houses (department store merchandise)	...	...	3,853	7,073
Liquor stores	4,893	5,674	7,980	13,616
TOTAL	219,529	284,128	375,527	798,818

[1]Includes some kinds of business not shown separately.
Source: U.S. Department of Commerce, Bureau of the Census, *Monthly Retail Trade,* Bureau of Economic Analysis, *1975 Business Statistics.*

Sales of Merchant Wholesalers

in millions of dollars

Kind of business	1960	1965	1970	1978
Durable goods[1]	56,803	82,861	111,970	349,916
Motor vehicles, automotive equipment	7,883	12,140	19,482	68,298
Electrical goods	8,660	12,681	16,667	38,325
Furniture, home furnishings	2,910	3,777	5,199	12,966
Hardware, plumbing, heating equipment	6,422	8,413	10,858	25,868
Lumber, construction supplies	6,680	9,765	10,863	32,223
Machinery, equipment, supplies	14,287	20,561	27,638	97,879
Metals, metalwork (except scrap)	5,708	9,162	13,647	35,864
Scrap, waste materials	3,296	4,789	6,040	11,804
Nondurable goods[1]	80,477	104,470	135,029	404,189
Groceries and related products	27,661	38,068	53,411	125,091
Beer, wine, distilled alcoholic beverages	7,424	9,464	13,332	27,028
Drugs, chemicals, allied products	5,370	7,180	9,135	11,526
Tobacco, tobacco products	4,164	5,014	6,232	9,671
Dry goods, apparel	6,675	8,804	10,577	25,076
Paper, paper products	4,153	5,612	7,679	17,586
Farm products	11,683	13,711	13,987	83,204
Other nondurable goods	13,346	16,966	22,632	42,454
TOTAL	137,281	187,331	246,999	754,105

[1]Includes some kinds of business not shown separately.
Source: U.S. Dept. of Commerce, Bureau of the Census, *Monthly Wholesale Trade.*

Commercial Banks[1]

December 31, 1978

State	Number of banks	Total assets or liabilities $000,000	SELECTED ASSETS ($000,000)			SELECTED LIABILITIES ($000,000)			
						Deposits			
			Loans[2]	Investments	Reserves, cash, and bank balances	Total	Demand	Time, savings	Capital accounts
Ala.	312	14,735	8,539	3,595	1,657	12,658	4,721	7,936	1,182
Alaska	12	1,913	1,081	394	243	1,570	704	866	161
Ariz.	20	10,173	6,333	1,800	1,319	8,868	3,436	5,432	638
Ark.	259	9,266	5,260	2,296	1,005	8,022	3,047	4,975	756
Calif.	229	142,925	83,803	19,511	19,168	113,426	40,925	72,501	8,684
Colo.	299	12,990	7,585	2,332	2,073	10,999	4,915	6,084	956
Conn.	65	11,538	6,521	1,974	1,711	9,613	4,287	5,326	742
Del.	17	3,410	1,449	1,225	345	2,611	1,004	1,607	239
D.C.	17	6,271	3,431	1,367	900	4,990	2,486	2,504	7,098
Fla.	613	37,394	17,910	11,400	4,649	32,170	13,489	1,861	2,841
Ga.	440	20,343	10,520	3,475	3,403	16,141	7,941	8,200	1,575
Hawaii	8	4,075	2,376	916	450	3,573	1,339	2,234	272
Idaho	24	4,296	2,555	863	500	3,602	1,216	2,387	286
Ill.	1,241	96,819	54,657	21,746	10,885	74,186	25,630	48,557	6,970
Ind.	404	28,113	15,270	31,154	2,840	23,599	7,765	15,834	2,047
Iowa	650	17,858	10,346	4,487	1,808	15,606	4,836	10,770	1,389
Kan.	616	13,567	7,395	3,582	1,445	11,705	4,272	7,433	1,126
Ky.	343	15,956	8,938	3,619	1,788	13,605	5,538	8,068	1,225
La.	256	19,105	10,158	4,922	2,283	16,241	6,410	9,831	1,487
Maine	40	2,650	1,657	575	250	2,289	696	1,593	190
Md.	106	13,816	8,434	2,383	1,458	13,816	11,356	4,397	989
Mass.	146	22,969	11,442	4,648	3,170	17,277	8,032	9,245	1,673
Mich.	364	46,749	25,978	10,321	5,702	39,246	11,696	27,550	3,318
Minn.	758	24,383	13,818	5,690	2,786	19,925	6,817	13,109	1,834
Miss.	184	9,440	5,134	2,563	1,134	8,314	2,924	5,389	706
Mo.	714	28,951	14,692	6,771	4,061	23,084	9,669	13,415	2,101
Mont.	160	4,457	154	1,075	431	3,955	1,339	2,616	338
Neb.	452	9,550	5,281	2,108	1,227	8,192	3,225	4,967	760
Nev.	9	3,287	1,861	770	419	2,877	1,252	1,624	240
N.H.	82	3,199	1,942	682	418	2,789	1,073	1,715	247
N.J.	184	31,997	17,176	8,580	3,440	27,296	9,908	17,388	2,224
N.M.	86	4,905	2,728	1,140	596	4,295	1,654	2,641	357
N.Y.	225	215,804	102,475	26,253	48,236	151,378	79,815	71,563	17,088
N.C.	88	19,385	10,443	4,128	2,573	15,843	6,671	9,172	1,478
N.D.	171	3,858	2,248	1,092	302	3,456	1,132	2,325	316
Ohio	481	48,338	25,557	12,446	5,661	39,203	13,873	25,330	3,937
Okla.	478	16,961	8,975	4,211	2,247	14,524	5,734	8,798	1,336
Ore.	60	11,014	6,464	745	1,333	8,991	3,276	5,715	794
Pa.	370	72,184	40,186	15,903	7,981	55,280	17,997	37,283	5,314
R.I.	14	5,324	3,286	1,028	408	4,212	1,057	3,155	355
S.C.	87	6,280	3,350	1,491	782	5,278	2,791	2,486	524
S.D.	155	4,215	2,604	1,018	396	3,785	1,102	2,682	332
Tenn.	348	19,917	11,355	1,018	2,395	17,141	6,030	11,111	1,476
Texas	1,395	82,477	43,393	4,518	12,113	67,940	29,530	38,411	6,159
Utah	66	5,848	3,494	19,149	841	4,951	1,747	3,204	408
Vt.	29	2,039	1,392	1,048	148	1,842	443	1,399	144
Va.	262	20,842	12,372	4,510	2,425	17,755	6,171	11,385	1,546
Wash.	93	17,995	10,939	2,191	2,319	14,123	5,354	8,768	1,159
W.Va.	231	8,617	4,713	2,585	760	7,398	2,208	5,189	748
Wis.	628	23,436	13,936	5,342	2,238	19,541	6,125	13,416	1,688
Wyo.	88	2,712	1,514	694	298	2,404	895	1,510	223
TOTAL	14,391	1,268,726	687,732	255,273	177,845	1,012,783	399,460	613,324	93,306

[1] Detail may not add to total given due to rounding; excludes noninsured banks.
[2] Includes investment securities, trading account securities, federal funds sold, and securities purchased under agreements to resell.
Source: Federal Deposit Insurance Corporation, *Assets and Liabilities—Commercial and Mutual Savings Banks—December 31, 1978, 1978 Report of Income.*

Life Insurance, 1978

Number of policies in 000s; value in $000,000

State	Total		Ordinary		Group		Industrial		Credit[1]	
	Number of policies	Value	Number of policies	Value	Number of certificates	Value	Number of policies	Value	Number of policies	Value
Ala.	12,375	$45,997	1,938	$22,455	1,640	$16,862	6,952	$2,783	1,845	$3,897
Alaska	642	5,610	129	2,444	346	2,943	10	3	157	220
Ariz.	4,371	30,114	1,676	17,704	1,337	10,395	171	112	1,187	1,903
Ark.	2,835	19,608	957	10,196	674	7,442	485	264	719	1,706
Calif.	30,651	280,073	10,612	139,562	12,069	127,045	1,938	1,366	6,032	12,100
Colo.	4,798	40,022	1,751	21,624	1,606	15,667	309	292	1,132	2,439
Conn.	5,836	49,717	2,367	23,794	1,972	23,860	279	203	1,218	1,860
Del.	2,412	10,774	465	4,224	377	5,623	232	155	1,338	772
D.C.	2,431	16,312	437	4,259	927	11,065	493	285	574	703
Fla.	16,467	100,262	5,168	55,292	3,784	35,842	3,676	2,621	3,639	6,507
Ga.	12,775	70,632	3,464	35,416	2,531	27,678	4,228	2,767	2,552	4,771
Hawaii	1,709	15,859	583	8,482	740	6,526	5	2	381	849
Idaho	1,318	10,052	515	5,504	476	3,751	25	12	302	785
Ill.	23,079	170,997	9,271	86,433	6,651	74,781	3,069	1,919	4,088	7,864
Ind.	10,349	72,289	4,049	36,510	2,721	30,183	1,606	977	1,973	4,619
Iowa	4,913	39,582	2,542	23,222	1,322	13,966	233	124	816	2,270
Kan.	4,172	30,896	1,861	18,746	1,091	10,007	317	171	903	1,972
Ky.	6,472	37,819	2,207	18,588	1,322	15,612	1,502	830	1,441	2,789
La.	9,782	48,601	2,005	24,344	1,673	18,190	4,096	2,311	2,008	3,756
Maine	1,876	11,449	712	6,051	636	4,550	79	52	449	796
Md.	8,353	56,403	2,852	28,322	1,900	24,086	1,751	1,011	1,850	2,984
Mass.	9,283	71,755	3,915	35,214	2,571	33,448	765	482	2,032	2,611
Mich.	16,707	137,337	5,557	51,528	5,813	77,264	1,903	1,170	3,434	7,375
Minn.	6,286	55,007	2,471	26,172	2,292	26,187	242	133	1,281	2,515
Miss.	4,007	22,237	907	11,168	866	8,325	805	483	1,429	2,261
Mo.	8,942	63,189	3,723	31,288	2,423	27,950	1,213	710	1,583	3,241
Mont.	1,110	8,243	435	5,024	356	2,518	24	10	295	691
Neb.	2,698	22,152	1,349	13,447	689	7,416	121	65	539	1,224
Nev.	1,306	10,109	274	3,952	519	4,768	11	5	502	1,384
N.H.	1,454	11,092	664	6,165	355	4,225	90	60	345	642
N.J.	11,818	111,475	5,463	54,339	3,273	52,418	1,335	1,044	1,747	3,674
N.M.	1,829	13,618	579	6,579	554	5,899	95	59	601	1,081
N.Y.	27,175	235,668	11,154	108,304	8,263	115,493	1,885	1,322	5,873	10,549
N.C.	11,979	65,943	3,900	33,535	2,330	26,030	3,299	1,873	2,450	4,505
N.D.	965	8,005	446	4,898	288	2,449	4	2	227	656
Ohio	20,735	151,161	8,109	74,974	5,331	65,132	3,254	2,098	4,041	8,957
Okla.	4,109	33,111	1,624	17,932	1,068	12,590	392	234	1,025	2,355
Ore.	3,216	28,736	1,196	14,165	1,176	12,864	82	40	762	1,667
Pa.	24,802	156,157	9,820	77,798	6,049	66,566	4,277	2,561	4,656	9,232
R.I.	1,922	13,450	789	7,082	620	5,709	171	105	342	554
S.C.	7,566	33,092	2,222	16,699	1,521	12,580	2,506	1,492	1,317	2,321
S.D.	941	7,867	490	4,996	242	2,324	4	2	205	545
Tenn.	9,726	54,767	2,723	26,438	2,400	22,289	2,465	1,438	2,138	4,602
Texas	23,961	173,689	8,181	90,297	6,503	68,660	3,471	2,176	5,806	12,556
Utah	2,108	14,918	658	7,862	887	5,809	92	39	471	1,208
Vt.	799	5,565	345	3,086	208	2,108	34	22	212	349
Va.	10,946	70,442	3,317	33,246	2,605	31,932	2,537	1,478	2,487	3,786
Wash.	5,117	45,390	1,893	23,035	1,979	20,053	164	76	1,081	2,226
W.Va.	3,359	19,521	1,010	8,539	828	8,960	585	363	936	1,659
Wis.	7,418	58,117	3,373	31,177	2,446	23,973	463	275	1,136	2,692
Wyo.	615	5,369	247	2,984	195	1,981	5	3	168	401
TOTAL U.S.	400,515	$2,870,250	142,395	$1,425,095	110,445	$1,243,994	63,950	$38,080	83,725	$163,081

[1] Life insurance on loans of ten years' or less duration.
Source: Institute of Life Insurance, *Life Insurance Fact Book '79.*

Savings and Loan Associations

Dec. 31, 1978[1]

State	Number of assns.	Total assets ($000,000)	Per capita assets
Alabama	61	$4,366	$1,167
Alaska	4	290	719
Arizona	16	5,121	2,176
Arkansas	75	3,733	1,707
California	170	95,517	4,284
Colorado	48	7,860	2,944
Connecticut	38	3,773	1,218
Delaware	18	276	473
District of Columbia	16	4,759	7,062
Florida	122	41,043	4,776
Georgia	96	9,439	1,857
Guam	2	64	666
Hawaii	9	3,189	3,555
Idaho	12	940	1,070
Illinois	388	39,157	3,483
Indiana	165	9,374	1,744
Iowa	77	6,372	2,200
Kansas	83	6,259	2,665
Kentucky	105	5,194	1,485
Louisiana	122	7,030	1,773
Maine	20	616	565
Maryland	204	9,495	2,292
Massachusetts	164	7,730	1,339
Michigan	65	15,263	1,661
Minnesota	62	9,830	2,453
Mississippi	60	2,499	1,040
Missouri	114	13,741	2,827
Montana	14	997	1,270
Nebraska	44	4,510	2,882
Nevada	7	1,948	2,951
New Hampshire	17	1,016	1,166
New Jersey	217	20,338	2,772
New Mexico	34	2,078	1,714
New York	127	24,928	1,405
North Carolina	195	10,401	1,865
North Dakota	12	1,935	2,968
Ohio	399	34,656	3,224
Oklahoma	57	4,808	1,670
Oregon	28	5,941	2,431
Pennsylvania	402	21,757	1,852
Puerto Rico	12	1,641	510
Rhode Island	6	718	768
South Carolina	74	5,460	1,871
South Dakota	16	962	1,394
Tennessee	97	6,417	1,473
Texas	320	28,181	2,165
Utah	13	3,391	2,594
Vermont	7	230	472
Virginia	54	7,998	1,554
Washington	50	8,540	2,263
West Virginia	36	1,363	733
Wisconsin	116	11,029	2,357
Wyoming	12	735	1,733
TOTAL U.S.	4,723	$523,649	$2,391

[1] Preliminary. Components do not add to totals because of differences in reporting dates and accounting systems.
Source: U.S. League of Savings Associations, *Savings and Loan Fact Book '79.*

GOVERNMENT AND POLITICS

The National Executive

December 19, 1979

Department, bureau, or office	Executive official and official title
PRESIDENT OF THE UNITED STATES	Jimmy Carter
Vice-President	Walter F. Mondale
EXECUTIVE OFFICE OF THE PRESIDENT	
Assistant to the President	Zbigniew Brzezinski
	Stuart E. Eizenstat
	Hamilton Jordan
Press Secretary to the President	Joseph L. Powell
Counsel to the President	Lloyd N. Cutler
Special Assistant to the President	Louis E. Martin
Office of Management and Budget	James T. McIntyre, Jr., director
Council of Economic Advisers	Charles L. Schultze, chairman
National Security Council	[1]
Central Intelligence Agency	Adm. Stansfield Turner, director
Domestic Policy Staff	Stuart E. Eizenstat, executive director
Office of the Special Representative for Trade Negotiations	Reubin Askew, special representative
Council on Environmental Quality	J. Gustave Speth, chairman
Council on Wage and Price Stability	Alfred E. Kahn, chairman
Office of Science and Technology Policy	Frank Press, director
Office of Administration	Richard Harden, director
DEPARTMENT OF STATE	Cyrus R. Vance, secretary
	Warren M. Christopher, deputy secretary
Political Affairs	David D. Newsom, undersecretary
Economic Affairs	Richard N. Cooper, undersecretary
Security Assistance, Science and Technology	Lucy Wilson Benson, undersecretary
Management	Ben H. Read, undersecretary
Ambassador at Large	Alfred L. Atherton
	W. Beverly Carter
	Henry D. Owen
	Elliot L. Richardson
	Gerard C. Smith
Counselor of the Department	Matthew Nimetz
Agency for International Development	Douglas J. Bennet, Jr., administrator
Permanent Mission to the Organization of American States	Gale W. McGee, permanent representative
Sinai Support Mission	C. William Kontos, director
Mission to the United Nations	Donald F. McHenry, representative
African Affairs	Richard M. Moose, asst. secretary
European Affairs	George S. Vest, asst. secretary
East Asian and Pacific Affairs	Richard C. Holbrooke, asst. secretary
Inter-American Affairs	Viron P. Vaky, asst. secretary
Near Eastern and South Asian Affairs	Harold H. Saunders, asst. secretary
International Organization Affairs	C. William Maynes, Jr., asst. secretary
DEPARTMENT OF THE TREASURY	G. William Miller, secretary
	Robert Carswell, deputy secretary
Monetary Affairs	Anthony M. Solomon, undersecretary
Comptroller of the Currency	John G. Heimann, comptroller
Bur. of Government Financial Operations	Dario A. Pagliai, commissioner
U.S. Customs Service	Robert E. Chasen, commissioner
Bureau of Engraving and Printing	Harry R. Clements, director (acting)
Bureau of the Mint	Stella B. Hackel, director
Bureau of the Public Debt	H. J. Hintgen, commissioner
Internal Revenue Service	Jerome Kurtz, commissioner
Office of the Treasurer	Azie Taylor Morton, treasurer
Savings Bond Division	Azie Taylor Morton, national director
U.S. Secret Service	H. Stuart Knight, director
Bureau of Alcohol, Tobacco and Firearms	G. R. Dickerson, director
Federal Law Enforcement Training Center	Arthur F. Brandstatter, director
DEPARTMENT OF DEFENSE	Harold Brown, secretary
	W. Graham Claytor, Jr., deputy secretary
Joint Chiefs of Staff	Gen. David C. Jones, USAF, chairman
Chief of Staff, Army	Gen. Edward C. Meyer, USA
Chief of Naval Operations	Adm. Thomas B. Hayward, USN
Chief of Staff, Air Force	Gen. Lew Allen, Jr., USAF
Commandant of the Marine Corps	Gen. Louis H. Wilson, USMC
Department of the Army	Clifford L. Alexander, Jr., secretary
Department of the Navy	Edward Hidalgo, secretary
Department of the Air Force	Hans M. Mark, secretary
DEPARTMENT OF JUSTICE	
Attorney General	Benjamin R. Civiletti
Solicitor General	Wade H. McCree, Jr.
Community Relations Service	Gilbert G. Pompa, director
Law Enforcement Assistance Admin.	Henry S. Dogin, administrator
Antitrust Division	John H. Shenefield, asst. attorney general
Civil Division	Alice Daniel, asst. attorney general
Civil Rights Division	Drew S. Days III, asst. attorney general
Criminal Division	Philip B. Heymann, asst. attorney general
Land and Natural Resources Division	James W. Moorman, asst. attorney general
Tax Division	M. Carr Ferguson, asst. attorney general
Office of Management and Finance	Kevin D. Rooney, asst. attorney general
Federal Bureau of Investigation	William H. Webster, director
Bureau of Prisons	Norman A. Carlson, director
Immigration and Naturalization Service	Leonel J. Castillo, commissioner
Drug Enforcement Administration	Peter B. Bensinger, administrator
U.S. Marshals Service	William E. Hall, director
DEPARTMENT OF THE INTERIOR	Cecil D. Andrus, secretary
	James A. Joseph, undersecretary
Fish and Wildlife and Parks	Robert L. Herbst, asst. secretary
National Park Service	William J. Whalen, director
Fish and Wildlife Service	Lynn A. Greenwalt, director
Heritage Conservation and Recreation Service	Chris T. Delaporte, director
Energy and Minerals	Joan M. Davenport, asst. secretary
Office of Minerals Policy and Research Analysis	Hermann Enzer, director
Geological Survey	H. William Menard, director
Bureau of Mines	Lindsay D. Norman, director (acting)
Office of Surface Mining Reclamation and Enforcement	Walter N. Heine, director
Land and Water Resources	Guy R. Martin, asst. secretary
Bureau of Land Management	W. Frank Gregg, director
Water and Power Resources Service	R. Keith Higginson, commissioner
Indian Affairs	Forrest J. Gerard, assistant secretary
DEPARTMENT OF AGRICULTURE	Bob Bergland, secretary
	Jim Williams, deputy secretary
Rural Development	Alex P. Mercure, asst. secretary
Rural Electrification Administration	Robert W. Feragen, administrator
Farmers Home Administration	Gordon Cavanaugh, administrator
Marketing and Transportation Services	P. R. (Bobby) Smith, asst. secretary
Agricultural Marketing Service	Barbara L. Schlei, administrator
International Affairs and Commodity Programs	Dale E. Hathaway, undersecretary
Commodity Credit Corporation	Dale E. Hathaway, president
Conservation, Research, and Education	M. Rupert Cutler, asst. secretary
Forest Service	John R. McGuire, chief
Soil Conservation Service	Ronello M. Davis, administrator
Economics, Policy Analysis, and Budget	Howard W. Hjort, director
Economics, Statistics, and Cooperatives Service	Kenneth R. Farrell, administrator
Food and Consumer Services	Carol Tucker Foreman, asst. secretary
DEPARTMENT OF COMMERCE	Philip M. Klutznick, secretary
	Luther H. Hodges, Jr., undersecretary
Industry and Trade	Frank A. Weil, asst. secretary
Chief Economist	Courtenay M. Slater
Bureau of the Census	Vincent P. Barabba, director
Bureau of Economic Analysis	George Jaszi, director
Science and Technology	Jordan Baruch, asst. secretary
Office of Environmental Affairs	Sidney R. Galler, deputy asst. secretary
National Bureau of Standards	Ernest Ambler, director
Patent and Trademark Office	Sidney A. Diamond, commissioner
Maritime Affairs	Samuel B. Nemirow, asst. secretary
Tourism	Jeanne R. Westphal, asst. secretary (acting)
National Oceanic and Atmospheric Administration	Richard A. Frank, administrator
DEPARTMENT OF LABOR	Ray Marshall, secretary
	John N. Gentry, undersecretary
Administration and Management	Alfred M. Zuck, asst. secretary
Employment and Training	Ernest G. Green, asst. secretary
Labor-Management Relations	William P. Hobgood, asst. secretary
Occupational Safety and Health	Eula Bingham, asst. secretary
Labor Statistics	Janet L. Norwood, commissioner (acting)
Mine Safety and Health	Robert B. Lagather, asst. secretary
DEPARTMENT OF HEALTH, EDUCATION, AND WELFARE[2]	Patricia Roberts Harris, secretary
	Nathan J. Stark, undersecretary
Office of Human Development Services	Arabella Martinez, asst. secretary
Education Division	Mary F. Berry, asst. secretary
Office of Education	Ernest L. Boyer, commissioner
National Institute of Education	Patricia Albjerg Graham, director
Public Health Service	Julius B. Richmond, M.D., asst. secretary
Food and Drug Administration	Donald Kennedy, commissioner
National Institutes of Health	Donald S. Fredrickson, director
Health Resources Administration	Henry A. Foley, administrator
Health Services Administration	George I. Lythcott, M.D., administrator
Center for Disease Control	William H. Foege, M.D., director
Alcohol, Drug Abuse, and Mental Health Administration	Gerald L. Klerman, administrator
Health Care Financing Administration	Leonard D. Schaeffer, administrator
Social Security Administration	Stanford G. Ross, commissioner
Office of Child Support Enforcement	Stanford G. Ross, director
DEPARTMENT OF HOUSING AND URBAN DEVELOPMENT	Moon Landrieu, secretary
	Victor Marrero, undersecretary
Community Planning and Development	Robert C. Embry, Jr., asst. secretary
Federal Housing Commissioner	Lawrence B. Simons, asst. secretary
Fair Housing and Equal Opportunity	Sterling Tucker, asst. secretary
Policy Development and Research	Donna E. Shalala, asst. secretary
DEPARTMENT OF TRANSPORTATION	Neil Goldschmidt, secretary
	William Beckham, deputy secretary
United States Coast Guard	Adm. John B. Hayes, USCG, commandant
Federal Aviation Administration	Langhorne M. Bond, administrator
Federal Highway Administration	Karl S. Bowers, administrator
National Highway Traffic Safety Administration	Joan B. Claybrook, administrator
Federal Railroad Administration	John M. Sullivan, administrator
Urban Mass Transportation Admin.	Lillian Liburdi, administrator (acting)
St. Lawrence Seaway Development Corp.	David W. Oberlin, administrator
Research and Special Programs Administration	Howard Dugoff, administrator
DEPARTMENT OF ENERGY	Charles W. Duncan, Jr., secretary
	John C. Sawhill, deputy secretary
	John Deutsch, undersecretary
Federal Energy Regulatory Commission	Charles B. Curtis, chairman
General Counsel	Lynn R. Coleman, general counsel
Office of the Executive Secretariat	Raymond L. Walters, director

[1] Council comprised of the President of the United States and certain other members.

[2] Renamed Dept. of Health and Human Services with transfer of functions of Education Division to new Dept. of Education, Shirley M. Hufstedler secretary, effective in 1980.

Senate January 1980

State, name, and party	Term expires
Ala.—Heflin, Howell (D)	1985
Stewart, Donald (D)	1981
Alaska—Stevens, Ted (R)	1985
Gravel, Mike (D)	1981
Ariz.—DeConcini, Dennis (D)	1983
Goldwater, Barry M. (R)	1981
Ark.—Bumpers, Dale (D)	1981
Pryor, David (D)	1985
Calif.—Cranston, Alan (D)	1981
Hayakawa, S. I. (R)	1983
Colo.—Hart, Gary W. (D)	1981
Armstrong, William L. (R)	1985
Conn.—Ribicoff, Abraham (D)	1981
Weicker, Lowell P., Jr. (R)	1983
Del.—Biden, Joseph R., Jr. (D)	1985
Roth, William V., Jr. (R)	1983
Fla.—Stone, Richard (D)	1981
Chiles, Lawton M. (D)	1983
Ga.—Nunn, Sam (D)	1985
Talmadge, Herman E. (D)	1981
Hawaii—Inouye, Daniel K. (D)	1981
Matsunaga, Spark M. (D)	1983
Idaho—Church, Frank (D)	1981
McClure, James A. (R)	1985
Ill.—Percy, Charles H. (R)	1985
Stevenson, Adlai E., III (D)	1981
Ind.—Bayh, Birch (D)	1981
Lugar, Richard G. (R)	1983
Iowa—Jepsen, Roger (R)	1985
Culver, John C. (D)	1981
Kan.—Dole, Robert J. (R)	1981
Kassebaum, Nancy L. (R)	1985
Ky.—Ford, Wendell H. (D)	1981
Huddleston, Walter (D)	1985
La.—Long, Russell B. (D)	1981
Johnston, J. Bennett, Jr. (D)	1985
Maine—Muskie, Edmund S. (D)	1983
Cohen, William S. (R)	1985
Md.—Sarbanes, Paul S. (D)	1983
Mathias, Charles McC., Jr. (R)	1981
Mass.—Tsongas, Paul E. (D)	1985
Kennedy, Edward M. (D)	1983
Mich.—Levin, Carl (D)	1985
Riegle, Donald W., Jr. (D)	1983
Minn.—Durenberger, David (R)	1983
Boschwitz, Rudy (R)	1985
Miss.—Stennis, John C. (D)	1983
Cochran, Thad (R)	1985
Mo.—Danforth, John C. (R)	1983
Eagleton, Thomas F. (D)	1981
Mont.—Baucus, Max (D)	1985
Melcher, John (D)	1983
Neb.—Exon, J. J. (D)	1985
Zorinsky, Edward (D)	1983
Nev.—Laxalt, Paul (R)	1981
Cannon, Howard W. (D)	1983
N.H.—Durkin, John A. (D)	1981
Humphrey, Gordon (R)	1985
N.J.—Bradley, Bill (D)	1985
Williams, Harrison A., Jr. (D)	1983
N.M.—Domenici, Pete V. (R)	1985
Schmitt, Harrison H. (R)	1983
N.Y.—Javits, Jacob K. (R)	1981
Moynihan, Daniel P. (D)	1983
N.C.—Helms, Jesse (R)	1985
Morgan, Robert B. (D)	1981
N.D.—Young, Milton R. (R)	1981
Burdick, Quentin N. (D)	1983
Ohio—Glenn, John H., Jr. (D)	1981
Metzenbaum, Howard M. (D)	1983
Okla.—Bellmon, Henry L. (R)	1981
Boren, David L. (D)	1985
Ore.—Hatfield, Mark O. (R)	1985
Packwood, Robert W. (R)	1981
Pa.—Heinz, H. John, III (R)	1983
Schweiker, Richard S. (R)	1981
R.I.—Pell, Claiborne (D)	1985
Chafee, John H. (R)	1983
S.C.—Thurmond, Strom (R)	1985
Hollings, Ernest F. (D)	1981
S.D.—McGovern, George (D)	1981
Pressler, Larry (R)	1985
Tenn.—Sasser, James R. (D)	1983
Baker, Howard H., Jr. (R)	1985
Texas—Tower, John G. (R)	1985
Bentsen, Lloyd M. (D)	1983
Utah—Garn, Jake (R)	1981
Hatch, Orrin G. (R)	1983
Vt.—Leahy, Patrick J. (D)	1981
Stafford, Robert T. (R)	1983
Va.—Warner, John W. (R)	1985
Byrd, Harry F., Jr. (I)	1983
Wash.—Jackson, Henry M. (D)	1983
Magnuson, Warren G. (D)	1981
W.Va.—Byrd, Robert C. (D)	1983
Randolph, Jennings (D)	1985
Wis.—Nelson, Gaylord (D)	1981
Proxmire, William (D)	1983
Wyo.—Wallop, Malcolm (R)	1983
Simpson, Alan K. (R)	1985

House of Representatives membership at the opening of the second session of the 96th Congress in January 1980

State, district, name, party

Ala.—1. Edwards, Jack (R)
2. Dickinson, W. L. (R)
3. Nichols, William (D)
4. Bevill, Tom (D)
5. Flippo, Ronnie G. (D)
6. Buchanan, John H., Jr. (R)
7. Shelby, Richard C. (D)
Alaska—Young, Don (R)
Ariz.—1. Rhodes, John J. (R)
2. Udall, Morris K. (D)
3. Stump, Bob (D)
4. Rudd, Eldon D. (R)
Ark.—1. Alexander, Bill (D)
2. Bethune, Ed (R)
3. Hammerschmidt, J. P. (R)
4. Anthony, Beryl F. (D)
Calif.—1. Johnson, Harold T. (D)
2. Clausen, Don H. (R)
3. Matsui, Robert T. (D)
4. Fazio, Vic (D)
5. Burton, John L. (D)
6. Burton, Phillip (D)
7. Miller, George, III (D)
8. Dellums, Ronald V. (D)
9. Stark, Fortney H. (D)
10. Edwards, Don (D)
11. Royer, Bill (R)
12. McCloskey, Paul N., Jr. (R)
13. Mineta, Norman Y. (D)
14. Shumway, Norman D. (R)
15. Coelho, Tony (D)
16. Panetta, Leon E. (D)
17. Pashayan, Charles, Jr. (R)
18. Thomas, William (R)
19. Lagomarsino, Robert J. (R)
20. Goldwater, Barry M., Jr. (R)
21. Corman, James C. (D)
22. Moorhead, Carlos J. (R)
23. Beilenson, Anthony C. (D)
24. Waxman, Henry A. (D)
25. Roybal, Edward R. (D)
26. Rousselot, John H. (R)
27. Dornan, Robert K. (R)
28. Dixon, Julian C. (D)
29. Hawkins, Augustus F. (D)
30. Danielson, George E. (D)
31. Wilson, Charles H. (D)
32. Anderson, Glenn M. (D)
33. Grisham, Wayne (R)
34. Lungren, Daniel E. (R)
35. Lloyd, Jim (D)
36. Brown, George E., Jr. (D)
37. Lewis, Jerry (R)
38. Patterson, Jerry M. (D)
39. Dannemeyer, W. E. (R)
40. Badham, Robert E. (R)
41. Wilson, Bob (R)
42. Van Deerlin, Lionel (D)
43. Burgener, Clair W. (R)
Colo.—1. Schroeder, Patricia (D)
2. Wirth, Timothy E. (D)
3. Kogovsek, Ray (D)
4. Johnson, J. P. (R)
5. Kramer, Ken (R)
Conn.—1. Cotter, William R. (D)
2. Dodd, Christopher J. (D)
3. Giaimo, Robert N. (D)
4. McKinney, Stewart B. (R)
5. Ratchford, William R. (D)
6. Moffett, Toby (D)
Del.—Evans, Thomas, Jr. (R)
Fla.—1. Hutto, Earl D. (D)
2. Fuqua, Don (D)
3. Bennett, Charles E. (D)
4. Chappell, William, Jr. (D)
5. Kelly, Richard (R)
6. Young, C. William (R)
7. Gibbons, Sam (D)
8. Ireland, Andrew P. (D)
9. Nelson, Bill (D)
10. Bafalis, L. A. (R)
11. Mica, Dan (D)
12. Stack, Edward J. (D)
13. Lehman, William (D)
14. Pepper, Claude (D)
15. Fascell, Dante B. (D)
Ga.—1. Ginn, R. B. (D)
2. Mathis, Dawson (D)
3. Brinkley, Jack (D)
4. Levitas, Elliott H. (D)
5. Fowler, Wyche, Jr. (D)
6. Gingrich, Newt (R)
7. McDonald, Lawrence P. (D)
8. Evans, Billy Lee (D)
9. Jenkins, Edgar L. (D)
10. Barnard, Doug (D)
Hawaii—1. Heftel, Cecil (D)
2. Akaka, Daniel (D)
Idaho—1. Symms, S. D. (R)
2. Hansen, George V. (R)

Ill.—1. Stewart, Bennett (D)
2. Murphy, Morgan (D)
3. Russo, Martin A. (D)
4. Derwinski, Edward J. (R)
5. Fary, John G. (D)
6. Hyde, Henry J. (R)
7. Collins, Cardiss (D)
8. Rostenkowski, Dan (D)
9. Yates, Sidney R. (D)
10. (vacancy)[1]
11. Annunzio, Frank (D)
12. Crane, Philip M. (R)
13. McClory, Robert (R)
14. Erlenborn, J. N. (R)
15. Corcoran, Tom (R)
16. Anderson, John B. (R)
17. O'Brien, G. M. (R)
18. Michel, Robert H. (R)
19. Railsback, Thomas F. (R)
20. Findley, Paul (R)
21. Madigan, E. R. (R)
22. Crane, Daniel B. (R)
23. Price, Melvin (D)
24. Simon, Paul (D)
Ind.—1. Benjamin, Adam (D)
2. Fithian, Floyd J. (D)
3. Brademas, John (D)
4. Quayle, J. Danforth (R)
5. Hillis, Elwood H. (R)
6. Evans, David W. (D)
7. Myers, John (R)
8. Deckard, H. Joel (R)
9. Hamilton, L. H. (D)
10. Sharp, Philip R. (D)
11. Jacobs, Andrew, Jr. (D)
Iowa—1. Leach, James (R)
2. Tauke, Tom (R)
3. Grassley, Charles E. (R)
4. Smith, Neal (D)
5. Harkin, Tom (D)
6. Bedell, Berkley (D)
Kan.—1. Sebelius, Keith G. (R)
2. Jeffries, Jim (R)
3. Winn, Larry, Jr. (R)
4. Glickman, Dan (D)
5. Whittaker, Robert (R)
Ky.—1. Hubbard, Carroll, Jr. (D)
2. Natcher, William H. (D)
3. Mazzoli, Romano L. (D)
4. Snyder, Gene (R)
5. Carter, Tim L. (R)
6. Hopkins, Larry J. (R)
7. Perkins, Carl D. (D)
La.—1. Livingston, Bob (R)
2. Boggs, Lindy (D)
3. Treen, David C. (R)
4. Leach, Claude (D)
5. Huckaby, Jerry (D)
6. Moore, W. Henson, III (R)
7. Breaux, John B. (D)
8. Long, Gillis W. (D)
Maine—1. Emery, David F. (R)
2. Snowe, Olympia J. (R)
Md.—1. Bauman, Robert E. (R)
2. Long, Clarence D. (D)
3. Mikulski, Barbara A. (D)
4. Holt, Marjorie S. (R)
5. Spellman, Gladys N. (D)
6. Byron, Beverly (D)
7. Mitchell, Parren J. (D)
8. Barnes, Michael D. (D)
Mass.—1. Conte, Silvio O. (R)
2. Boland, Edward P. (D)
3. Early, Joseph D. (D)
4. Drinan, Robert F. (D)
5. Shannon, James M. (D)
6. Mavroules, Nicholas (D)
7. Markey, Edward J. (D)
8. O'Neill, Thomas P., Jr. (D)
9. Moakley, John J. (D)
10. Heckler, Margaret (R)
11. Donnelly, Brian J. (D)
12. Studds, Gerry E. (D)
Mich.—1. Conyers, John, Jr. (D)
2. Pursell, Carl D. (R)
3. Wolpe, Howard (D)
4. Stockman, David A. (R)
5. Sawyer, Harold S. (R)
6. Carr, Bob (D)
7. Kildee, Dale E. (D)
8. Traxler, Bob (D)
9. Vander Jagt, Guy (R)
10. Albosta, Donald J. (D)
11. Davis, Robert W. (R)
12. Bonior, David E. (D)
13. Diggs, Charles C., Jr. (D)
14. Nedzi, Lucien N. (D)
15. Ford, W. D. (D)
16. Dingell, John D. (D)
17. Brodhead, William M. (D)
18. Blanchard, James J. (D)
19. Broomfield, William S. (R)
Minn.—1. Erdahl, Arlen (R)
2. Hagedorn, Tom (R)
3. Frenzel, William (R)
4. Vento, Bruce F. (D)
5. Sabo, Martin Olav (D)
6. Nolan, Richard (D)
7. Stangeland, Arlan (R)
8. Oberstar, James L. (D)
Miss.—1. Whitten, Jamie L. (D)
2. Bowen, D. R. (D)

3. Montgomery, G. V. (D)
4. Hinson, Jon C. (R)
5. Lott, Trent (R)
Mo.—1. Clay, William (D)
2. Young, Robert A. (D)
3. Gephardt, Richard A. (D)
4. Skelton, Ike (D)
5. Bolling, Richard (D)
6. Coleman, E. Thomas (R)
7. Taylor, Gene (R)
8. Ichord, Richard H. (D)
9. Volkmer, Harold L. (D)
10. Burlison, Bill D. (D)
Mont.—1. Williams, Pat (D)
2. Marlenee, Ron (R)
Neb.—1. Bereuter, D. K. (R)
2. Cavanaugh, John J. (D)
3. Smith, Virginia (R)
Nev.—Santini, James (D)
N.H.—1. D'Amours, Norman (D)
2. Cleveland, James C. (R)
N.J.—1. Florio, James J. (D)
2. Hughes, William J. (D)
3. Howard, J. J. (D)
4. Thompson, Frank, Jr. (D)
5. Fenwick, Millicent (R)
6. Forsythe, Edwin B. (R)
7. Maguire, Andrew (D)
8. Roe, Robert A. (D)
9. Hollenbeck, Harold C. (R)
10. Rodino, Peter W., Jr. (D)
11. Minish, Joseph G. (D)
12. Rinaldo, M. J. (R)
13. Courter, James A. (R)
14. Guarini, Frank J. (D)
15. Patten, Edward J. (D)
N.M.—1. Lujan, Manuel, Jr. (R)
2. Runnels, Harold L. (D)
N.Y.—1. Carney, William (C-R)
2. Downey, Thomas J. (D)
3. Ambro, Jerome A., Jr. (D)
4. Lent, Norman F. (R)
5. Wydler, John W. (R)
6. Wolff, L. L. (D)
7. Addabbo, Joseph P. (D)
8. Rosenthal, Benjamin S. (D)
9. Ferraro, Geraldine (D)
10. Biaggi, Mario (D)
11. Scheuer, James H. (D)
12. Chisholm, Shirley (D)
13. Solarz, Stephen J. (D)
14. Richmond, Frederick W. (D)
15. Zeferetti, Leo C. (D)
16. Holtzman, Elizabeth (D)
17. Murphy, John M. (D)
18. Green, S. William (R)
19. Rangel, Charles B. (D)
20. Weiss, Theodore S. (D)
21. Garcia, Robert (D)
22. Bingham, J. B. (D)
23. Peyser, Peter A. (D)
24. Ottinger, Richard L. (D)
25. Fish, Hamilton, Jr. (R)
26. Gilman, B. A. (R)
27. McHugh, Matthew F. (D)
28. Stratton, Samuel S. (D)
29. Solomon, Gerald (R)
30. McEwen, Robert (R)
31. Mitchell, D. J. (R)
32. Hanley, James M. (D)
33. Lee, Gary A. (R)
34. Horton, Frank J. (R)
35. Conable, B., Jr. (R)
36. LaFalce, John J. (D)
37. Nowak, Henry J. (D)
38. Kemp, Jack F. (R)
39. Lundine, Stanley N. (D)
N.C.—1. Jones, Walter B. (D)
2. Fountain, L. H. (D)
3. Whitley, Charles (D)
4. Andrews, Ike F. (D)
5. Neal, Stephen L. (D)
6. Preyer, L. R. (D)
7. Rose, C. G., III (D)
8. Hefner, Bill (D)
9. Martin, J. G. (R)
10. Broyhill, James T. (R)
11. Gudger, Lamar (D)
N.D.—Andrews, Mark (R)
Ohio—1. Gradison, Willis D. (R)
2. Luken, Thomas A. (D)
3. Hall, Tony P. (D)
4. Guyer, Tennyson (R)
5. Latta, Delbert L. (R)
6. Harsha, William H. (R)
7. Brown, Clarence J. (R)
8. Kindness, Thomas N. (R)
9. Ashley, Thomas L. (D)
10. Miller, Clarence E. (R)
11. Stanton, J. William (R)
12. Devine, Samuel L. (R)
13. Pease, Donald J. (D)
14. Seiberling, John F., Jr. (D)
15. Wylie, Chalmers P. (R)
16. Regula, R. S. (R)
17. Ashbrook, John M. (R)
18. Applegate, Douglas (D)
19. Williams, Lyle (R)
20. Oakar, Mary Rose (D)
21. Stokes, Louis (D)
22. Vanik, Charles A. (D)
23. Mottl, Ronald M. (D)

Okla.—1. Jones, James R. (D)
2. Synar, Mike (D)
3. Watkins, Wes (D)
4. Steed, Tom (D)
5. Edwards, Mickey (R)
6. English, Glenn (D)
Ore.—1. AuCoin, Les (D)
2. Ullman, Al (D)
3. Duncan, Robert (D)
4. Weaver, James (D)
Pa.—1. Myers, Michael (D)
2. Gray, William H., III (D)
3. Lederer, Raymond F. (D)
4. Dougherty, C. F. (R)
5. Schulze, Richard T. (R)
6. Yatron, Gus (D)
7. Edgar, Robert W. (D)
8. Kostmayer, Peter H. (D)
9. Shuster, E. G. (R)
10. McDade, Joseph M. (R)
11. Flood, Daniel J. (D)
12. Murtha, John P. (D)
13. Coughlin, R. L. (R)
14. Moorhead, William S. (D)
15. Ritter, Donald L. (R)
16. Walker, Robert S. (R)
17. Ertel, Allen E. (D)
18. Walgren, Doug (D)
19. Goodling, William F. (R)
20. Gaydos, Joseph (D)
21. Bailey, Don (D)
22. Murphy, Austin J. (D)
23. Clinger, William F., Jr. (R)
24. Marks, Marc L. (R)
25. Atkinson, Eugene V. (D)
R.I.—1. St. Germain, Fernand (D)
2. Beard, Edward P. (D)
S.C.—1. Davis, Mendel (D)
2. Spence, Floyd D. (R)
3. Derrick, Butler C., Jr. (D)
4. Campbell, Carroll A., Jr. (R)
5. Holland, Kenneth L. (D)
6. Jenrette, John W., Jr. (D)
S.D.—1. Daschle, Thomas A. (D)
2. Abdnor, James (R)
Tenn.—1. Quillen, James H. (R)
2. Duncan, John J. (R)
3. Lloyd Bouquards, Marilyn (D)
4. Gore, Albert, Jr. (D)
5. Boner, Bill (D)
6. Beard, Robin L., Jr. (R)
7. Jones, Edward (D)
8. Ford, Harold E. (D)
Texas—1. Hall, Sam B. (D)
2. Wilson, Charles (D)
3. Collins, James M. (R)
4. Roberts, Ray (D)
5. Mattox, Jim (D)
6. Gramm, Phil (D)
7. Archer, William R. (R)
8. Eckhardt, Robert C. (D)
9. Brooks, Jack (D)
10. Pickle, J. J. (D)
11. Leath, J. Marvin (D)
12. Wright, James C., Jr. (D)
13. Hightower, Jack (D)
14. Wyatt, Joe (D)
15. de la Garza, E. (D)
16. White, Richard C. (D)
17. Stenholm, Charles W. (D)
18. Leland, Mickey (D)
19. Hance, Kent (D)
20. Gonzalez, Henry B. (D)
21. Loeffler, Tom (R)
22. Paul, Ron (R)
23. Kazen, Abraham, Jr. (D)
24. Frost, Martin (D)
Utah—1. McKay, K. Gunn (D)
2. Marriott, Dan (R)
Vt.—Jeffords, James M. (R)
Va.—1. Trible, Paul S. (R)
2. Whitehurst, G. W. (R)
3. Satterfield, D. E., III (D)
4. Daniel, R. W. (R)
5. Daniel, W. C. (D)
6. Butler, M. C. (R)
7. Robinson, J. Kenneth (R)
8. Harris, Herbert E. (D)
9. Wampler, William C. (R)
10. Fisher, Joseph L. (D)
Wash.—1. Pritchard, Joel (R)
2. Swift, Al (D)
3. Bonker, Don (D)
4. McCormack, Mike (D)
5. Foley, Thomas S. (D)
6. Dicks, Norman D. (D)
7. Lowry, Mike (D)
W.Va.—1. Mollohan, R. H. (D)
2. Staggers, Harley O. (D)
3. Slack, John M., Jr. (D)
4. Rahall, Nick Joe (D)
Wis.—1. Aspin, Leslie (D)
2. Kastenmeier, Robert W. (D)
3. Baldus, Alvin J. (D)
4. Zablocki, Clement J. (D)
5. Reuss, Henry S. (D)
6. Petri, Thomas E. (R)
7. Obey, David R. (D)
8. Roth, Tobias A. (R)
9. Sensenbrenner, F. J. (R)
Wyo.—Cheney, Richard (R)

Supreme Court

Chief Justice Warren Earl Burger (appointed 1969)

Associate Justices (year appointed)

William J. Brennan, Jr.	(1956)	Harry A. Blackmun	(1970)
Potter Stewart	(1958)	Lewis F. Powell, Jr.	(1972)
Byron R. White	(1962)	William H. Rehnquist	(1972)
Thurgood Marshall	(1967)	John Paul Stevens	(1975)

[1] Rep. Abner J. Mikva resigned Sept. 26, 1979.

The Federal Administrative Budget

in millions of dollars; fiscal years ending Sept. 30

Source and function	1978	1979 estimate	1980 estimate
BUDGET RECEIPTS	$402,000	$456,000	$502,600
Individual income taxes	181,000	203,600	227,300
Corporation income taxes	60,000	70,300	71,000
Excise taxes	18,400	18,400	18,500
Social insurance taxes and contributions	123,400	141,800	161,500
Estate and gift taxes	5,300	5,700	6,000
Customs duties	6,600	7,500	8,400
Miscellaneous receipts	7,400	8,700	9,900
BUDGET EXPENDITURES	450,800	493,400	531,600
National defense	105,200	114,500	125,800
Department of Defense military functions	103,000	111,900	122,700
Atomic energy defense activities	2,100	2,500	3,000
Defense-related activities	100	100	200
International affairs	5,900	7,300	8,200
Conduct of foreign affairs	1,100	1,200	1,400
Foreign economic and financial assistance	4,600	5,300	5,500
Foreign information and exchange activities	400	500	500
International financial programs	−600	−200	300
Military assistance	500	600	500
General science, space, and technology	4,700	5,200	5,500
Agriculture	7,700	6,200	4,300
Farm income stabilization	6,600	4,900	3,000
Agricultural research and services	1,100	1,300	1,200
Natural resources and environment	10,900	11,200	11,500
Water resources	3,500	3,600	3,700
Conservation and land management	2,000	2,000	1,700
Recreational resources	1,400	1,500	1,400
Pollution control and abatement	4,000	4,100	4,700
Other natural resources	1,200	1,300	1,300
Energy	5,900	8,600	7,900
Energy supply	4,000	4,900	4,400
Energy conservation	200	500	700
Commerce and housing credit	3,300	3,000	3,400
Mortgage credit and thrift insurance	200	−500	−300
Payment to the Postal Service	1,800	1,800	1,700
Other advancement and regulation	1,300	1,600	2,000
Transportation	15,400	17,400	17,600
Air transportation	3,300	3,500	3,600
Water transportation	1,900	1,900	2,100
Ground transportation	10,400	12,000	11,900
Other transportation	100	100	100
Community and regional development	11,000	9,100	7,300
Community development	3,300	3,700	4,300

Source and function	1978	1979 estimate	1980 estimate
Area and regional development	$4,900	$4,100	$2,500
Disaster relief and insurance	2,900	1,300	500
Education, training, employment, and social services	26,500	30,700	30,200
Elementary, secondary, and vocational education	5,700	6,500	7,100
Higher education	3,500	4,900	4,900
Research and general education aids	1,100	1,300	1,300
Training and employment	10,800	11,700	11,000
Social services	5,000	5,800	5,400
Health	43,700	49,100	53,400
Health care services	39,100	44,500	48,500
Health research and education	3,700	3,700	4,000
Consumer and occupational health and safety	800	900	900
Income security	146,200	158,900	179,100
General retirement and disability insurance	97,300	107,900	121,200
Federal employee retirement and disability	10,700	12,400	14,100
Unemployment compensation	11,800	10,300	12,400
Public assistance and other income supplements	26,500	28,300	31,400
Veterans benefits and services	19,000	20,300	20,500
Income security for veterans	9,700	10,900	12,000
Veterans education, training, and rehabilitation	3,400	2,700	2,200
Hospital and medical care for veterans	5,300	5,900	5,800
Other veterans benefits and services	600	700	600
Administration of justice	3,800	4,400	4,400
Federal law enforcement activities	1,800	2,100	2,100
Federal litigative and judicial activities	900	1,200	1,300
Federal correctional activities	300	400	400
Criminal justice assistance	700	700	600
General government	3,800	4,400	4,400
Legislative functions	900	1,000	1,100
Central fiscal operations	2,100	2,400	2,500
General property and records management	200	300	200
Other general government	500	600	500
General purpose fiscal assistance	9,600	8,900	8,800
Interest	44,000	52,800	57,000
Allowances for contingencies, civilian agency pay raises	—	—	1,400
Undistributed offsetting receipts	−15,800	−18,700	−19,000
Employer share, employee retirement	−5,000	−5,400	−5,500
Interest received by trust funds	−8,500	−9,800	−10,900
Rents and royalties on the Outer Continental Shelf	−2,300	−3,500	−2,600

Source: Executive Office of the President, Office of Management and Budget, *The United States Budget in Brief: Fiscal Year 1980.*

State Government Revenue, Expenditure, and Debt

1978 in thousands of dollars

	GENERAL REVENUE						GENERAL EXPENDITURE					DEBT		
		State taxes												
State	Total	Total	General sales	Individual income	Intergovernmental	Charges & misc.	Total	Education	Highways	Public welfare	Hospitals	Total	Issued 1978[1]	Retired 1978[1]
Ala.	2,942,390	1,588,761	495,585	317,958	959,971	393,658	2,917,344	1,394,622	390,909	374,263	191,861	999,931	80,815	79,251
Alaska	1,147,208	563,495	—	145,828	296,072	287,641	1,158,757	390,023	169,902	72,798	13,346	1,128,051	230,342	34,782
Ariz.	1,992,217	1,307,338	577,937	222,808	459,221	225,658	1,908,722	944,884	263,306	108,915	64,665	97,984	31,325	34,405
Ark.	1,660,370	926,256	315,242	202,939	593,752	140,362	1,568,859	604,519	264,490	273,111	76,980	175,647	39,421	6,199
Calif.	23,845,651	15,017,677	4,986,598	4,632,488	6,754,723	2,073,251	21,561,937	7,694,472	1,253,894	6,248,651	689,457	7,071,395	573,135	337,117
Colo.	2,240,264	1,212,097	424,403	375,341	655,767	372,400	2,087,663	1,023,841	250,920	328,447	109,745	310,448	143,797	14,768
Conn.	2,546,524	1,550,424	645,274	75,616	647,283	348,817	2,396,896	678,099	193,072	492,821	171,779	3,318,476	357,540	217,348
Del.	734,618	449,774	—	190,085	161,960	122,884	655,677	298,031	52,392	81,642	24,336	767,336	89,473	71,774
Fla.	5,620,613	3,764,283	1,644,747	—	1,387,281	469,049	5,338,260	2,436,457	656,896	481,895	236,318	2,344,012	406,875	65,948
Ga.	3,697,640	2,183,715	792,710	604,361	1,197,097	316,828	3,620,638	1,522,947	511,955	565,578	191,855	1,345,733	152,403	76,341
Hawaii	1,334,464	754,677	367,321	227,216	375,473	204,314	1,363,042	484,688	70,579	213,426	67,908	1,694,172	266,276	60,822
Idaho	748,233	420,835	118,867	138,050	239,168	88,230	747,193	284,004	143,078	84,855	15,745	129,798	81,992	7,254
Ill.	8,778,468	5,774,368	2,011,704	1,593,695	2,167,414	836,686	8,758,496	3,377,959	877,663	2,171,116	381,217	5,143,875	1,029,765	238,509
Ind.	3,887,805	2,454,685	1,120,732	538,225	865,318	567,802	3,474,910	1,548,092	449,305	430,478	178,460	594,668	3,385	25,203
Iowa	2,354,474	1,402,191	376,212	490,210	641,239	311,044	2,483,976	1,082,315	415,065	372,586	151,103	227,227	98,326	3,880
Kan.	1,730,780	1,051,119	349,276	241,224	450,018	229,643	1,630,687	711,997	235,200	294,992	98,196	421,871	42,000	22,932
Ky.	3,044,911	1,842,145	531,189	389,912	835,208	367,558	2,998,095	1,237,519	519,067	460,789	68,966	2,617,463	412,290	47,442
La.	3,670,852	1,980,212	565,874	192,276	1,055,955	634,685	3,546,699	1,380,713	501,082	477,262	254,767	2,041,858	259,040	120,418
Maine	996,187	527,396	185,989	103,177	331,941	136,850	943,763	327,209	112,304	204,076	30,130	697,983	172,290	39,276
Md.	4,016,218	2,405,217	627,989	884,392	995,156	615,845	3,738,006	1,277,592	400,429	594,180	236,488	3,793,640	944,502	201,942
Mass.	5,652,732	3,300,804	520,698	1,433,150	1,786,320	565,608	5,241,387	1,369,074	391,681	1,525,686	271,502	5,059,534	414,980	283,004
Mich.	8,826,278	5,444,933	1,586,897	1,712,374	2,269,693	1,111,652	8,362,694	3,241,314	711,816	2,082,036	384,311	2,150,756	288,277	99,487
Minn.	4,298,071	2,759,356	537,478	1,074,552	1,014,717	523,998	4,212,285	1,830,832	413,313	719,326	197,556	1,770,303	631,572	105,531
Miss.	2,024,449	1,094,147	545,116	158,476	707,815	222,487	1,879,091	804,907	248,350	288,677	89,670	1,296,874	518,840	33,987
Mo.	2,943,412	1,784,396	700,929	438,604	893,112	265,904	2,745,031	1,103,775	415,535	491,570	188,688	554,465	114,953	10,904
Mont.	748,450	338,256	—	123,621	309,824	100,370	746,481	267,122	147,459	76,629	24,826	136,213	39,925	5,104
Neb.	1,167,491	680,204	240,484	173,430	331,874	155,413	1,104,481	353,766	206,113	157,692	69,467	56,014	—	3,283
Nev.	636,370	390,599	142,702	—	193,952	51,819	608,552	226,884	109,028	54,353	13,374	246,362	155,175	6,451
N.H.	550,847	240,390	—	9,085	207,770	102,687	576,467	145,566	106,687	86,576	40,789	420,080	72,320	18,230
N.J.	5,833,318	3,439,860	1,003,475	778,505	1,556,285	837,173	5,773,075	1,901,402	315,983	1,254,696	321,130	4,733,400	655,252	147,723
N.M.	1,483,477	761,076	328,804	45,992	392,019	330,382	1,257,542	612,470	164,152	110,098	57,796	344,783	157,377	24,328
N.Y.	19,008,671	10,934,176	2,432,906	4,506,245	6,326,072	1,748,423	17,845,735	5,672,720	814,389	4,347,172	1,197,136	22,395,201	4,206,210	2,214,468
N.C.	4,256,922	2,608,437	580,332	848,247	1,211,132	437,353	4,376,317	2,061,728	559,208	525,582	289,351	778,069	22,687	52,088
N.D.	705,400	309,589	97,471	69,171	219,521	176,290	643,490	248,944	108,583	64,315	24,610	81,427	16,942	2,841
Ohio	7,020,996	4,134,869	1,298,620	775,494	1,916,549	969,578	7,179,902	2,836,917	789,372	1,329,902	452,802	3,439,948	339,063	160,240
Okla.	2,369,970	1,315,468	244,255	252,127	661,085	393,417	2,116,117	954,148	269,739	402,822	109,379	1,104,430	250,243	125,343
Ore.	2,306,241	1,158,879	—	686,248	719,159	428,203	2,229,335	788,731	282,073	423,504	100,798	3,108,701	748,170	70,172
Pa.	9,682,562	6,265,514	1,753,184	1,327,816	2,573,781	843,267	9,625,932	3,316,660	859,490	2,761,652	605,169	6,521,461	390,864	243,922
R.I.	901,164	458,260	140,601	111,965	278,094	164,810	902,431	272,166	38,290	235,690	76,283	861,493	301,068	44,775
S.C.	2,351,026	1,364,466	471,477	351,244	734,194	252,366	2,194,746	975,805	209,233	277,098	143,840	1,762,897	455,476	53,066
S.D.	552,039	223,602	114,895	—	209,204	119,233	558,773	170,972	98,008	77,932	35,932	386,506	160,825	3,738
Tenn.	2,938,353	1,703,951	834,749	24,857	932,757	301,645	2,846,009	1,218,082	433,141	468,030	144,975	1,383,130	284,240	63,081
Texas	9,074,114	5,389,980	2,031,730	—	2,289,813	1,394,321	8,063,369	4,293,953	935,167	1,165,418	583,370	2,122,736	197,200	204,903
Utah	1,200,082	605,961	259,230	188,894	393,531	200,590	1,182,654	600,005	118,578	158,387	48,662	290,567	152,325	7,294
Vt.	524,826	233,845	32,765	66,487	208,650	82,331	504,792	163,225	57,614	87,218	17,932	461,450	35,354	29,044
Va.	4,176,167	2,335,734	489,208	874,817	1,160,491	679,942	3,935,066	1,542,646	692,998	526,804	291,744	1,255,759	381,050	40,804
Wash.	3,804,925	2,448,039	1,389,839	—	941,583	415,303	3,575,413	1,686,824	392,971	582,229	119,224	1,445,071	92,121	58,825
W.Va.	1,725,679	980,751	486,215	182,941	568,978	175,950	1,738,405	654,887	369,195	203,283	60,849	1,388,422	109,900	55,573
Wis.	4,769,342	3,089,233	762,224	1,324,679	1,183,888	496,221	4,421,137	1,529,964	384,358	930,861	136,339	1,990,749	347,660	58,369
Wyo.	576,028	289,484	115,969	—	199,305	87,239	455,990	156,725	104,965	29,056	12,896	100,535	27,645	1,950
TOTAL	189,099,289	113,260,924	35,279,902	29,104,822	53,461,185	22,377,180	179,802,319	69,702,197	18,478,997	35,776,175	9,363,722	102,568,904	16,982,706	5,934,679

Fiscal year ending June 30, 1978, except Alabama, September 30; New York, March 31; and Texas, August 31. [1]Long term only.
Source: U.S. Department of Commerce, Bureau of the Census, *State Government Finances in 1978.*

EDUCATION

Public Elementary and Secondary Schools

Fall 1978 estimates

State	ENROLLMENT		INSTRUCTIONAL STAFF				TEACHERS' AVERAGE ANNUAL SALARIES		STUDENT-TEACHER RATIO		Expenditure per pupil
	Elementary	Secondary	Total[1]	Principals and supervisors	Teachers, elementary	Teachers, secondary	Elementary	Secondary	Elementary	Secondary	
Alabama	396,100	384,100	38,963	2,000	17,643	19,320	$12,469	$13,369	22.4	19.9	$1,399
Alaska	49,286	40,105	5,909	360	2,709	2,349	24,111	24,195	18.2	17.1	3,563
Arizona	386,700	173,300	27,510	1,060	17,080	7,320	14,980	15,700	22.6	23.7	1,533
Arkansas	241,178	215,520	25,414	1,329	11,075	11,750	10,823	11,412	21.8	18.3	1,277
California	2,742,177	1,328,823	202,290	9,840	109,250	73,630	16,759	18,348	25.1	18.0	1,757
Colorado	300,500	259,500	33,578	1,620	14,180	15,078	14,978	15,020	21.2	17.2	1,812
Connecticut	396,250	196,900	39,500	2,250	20,790	14,280	15,021	15,532	19.1	13.8	2,155
Delaware	53,041	57,993	6,721	365	2,415	3,469	14,602	15,136	22.0	16.7	2,194
District of Columbia	62,099	51,759	7,016	408	3,467	2,497	...	...	17.9	20.7	2,553
Florida	771,991	753,549	89,915	3,939	39,025	37,245	13,871	14,145	19.8	20.2	1,694
Georgia	649,748	438,088	56,967	2,447	32,885	21,635	13,222	13,730	19.8	20.2	1,267
Hawaii	89,336	80,760	9,433	607	4,378	3,552	18,798	17,814	20.4	22.7	1,640
Idaho	108,744	94,278	10,865	588	5,061	4,672	12,395	12,872	21.5	20.2	...
Illinois	1,410,426	696,889	120,856	6,100	54,836	52,220	16,080	17,771	25.7	13.3	2,074
Indiana	575,345	555,319	59,626	3,800	26,296	26,839	13,817	14,572	21.9	20.7	1,453
Iowa	296,150	272,983	36,108	1,351	15,725	17,405	13,662	14,664	18.8	15.7	2,027
Kansas	261,414	176,466	29,121	1,808	13,825	11,776	12,926	13,011	18.9	15.0	1,799
Kentucky	441,712	251,287	37,702	1,900	21,000	12,808	12,790	13,860	21.0	19.6	1,444
Louisiana	447,000	381,000	43,529	2,200	22,050	19,279	12,804	13,260	20.3	19.8	1,535
Maine	162,550	75,730	13,254	1,192	7,040	4,925	11,866	12,990	23.1	15.4	1,486
Maryland	403,630	408,480	49,140	3,410	20,409	22,536	16,441	16,719	19.8	18.1	2,118
Massachusetts	565,000	570,000	74,565	4,685	29,710	35,190	15,952	16,272	19.0	16.2	2,184
Michigan	1,016,784	961,336	93,397	7,000	41,803	38,540	17,993	17,959	24.3	24.9	...
Minnesota	388,375	416,460	48,960	2,165	19,960	23,725	14,758	16,025	19.5	17.6	2,030
Mississippi	271,899	219,537	28,345	1,635	14,115	11,145	10,950	11,400	19.3	19.7	1,317
Missouri	593,923	306,079	55,307	3,191	24,455	23,924	12,617	13,156	24.3	12.8	...
Montana	110,500	55,800	10,620	470	5,280	4,380	13,077	14,343	20.9	12.7	1,934
Nebraska	155,120	143,180	21,201	1,051	9,768	8,722	11,857	13,578	15.9	16.4	1,818
Nevada	73,222	73,059	7,390	370	3,327	3,181	15,231	15,351	22.0	23.0	1,631
New Hampshire	102,500	72,150	10,600	650	4,930	4,300	11,500	12,225	20.8	17.8	1,412
New Jersey	834,500	511,500	92,230	5,530	49,000	29,000	16,085	16,680	17.0	17.6	2,329
New Mexico	144,019	135,322	15,922	1,088	9,319	4,590	14,008	14,413	15.4	29.5	1,623
New York	1,524,700	1,602,900	191,500	12,900	77,400	92,300	18,468	18,710	19.7	17.4	2,478
North Carolina	807,470	370,502	61,621	3,855	36,729	17,411	13,172	14,293	22.0	21.3	1,406
North Dakota	57,570	64,119	8,409	378	4,358	3,032	11,799	12,329	13.2	21.1	1,465
Ohio	1,228,150	878,450	121,000	6,900	53,400	51,100	13,808	14,610	23.0	17.2	1,632
Oklahoma	318,000	274,000	34,475	1,890	15,665	15,500	12,259	12,751	20.3	17.7	1,536
Oregon	273,800	199,700	28,135	2,300	13,150	10,650	14,460	15,156	20.8	18.8	1,984
Pennsylvania	1,012,100	1,045,900	124,450	5,450	53,600	56,950	15,250	15,600	18.9	18.4	2,135
Rhode Island	79,104	81,274	10,254	583	4,395	4,543	16,142	17,236	18.0	17.9	1,934
South Carolina	428,682	196,249	34,110	2,370	17,730	11,930	11,880	12,670	24.2	16.4	1,431
South Dakota	90,437	47,791	9,500	648	5,315	2,927	11,550	11,800	17.0	16.3	1,586
Tennessee	526,318	344,500	46,115	2,440	25,010	15,555	12,577	12,985	21.0	22.1	1,377
Texas	1,532,500	1,337,500	173,880	8,730	82,500	73,500	12,690	13,300	18.6	18.2	1,373
Utah	182,366	142,102	15,296	860	7,258	6,408	13,398	14,455	25.1	22.2	1,407
Vermont	60,790	40,760	7,745	860	3,340	2,975	11,359	12,146	18.2	13.7	1,584
Virginia	642,590	412,648	63,930	4,430	34,300	25,200	12,740	13,800	18.7	16.4	1,682
Washington	394,855	372,597	40,395	2,900	18,670	15,800	17,092	17,966	21.1	23.6	1,985
West Virginia	233,518	162,204	23,960	1,625	11,650	9,460	12,362	13,043	20.0	17.1	...
Wisconsin	484,417	402,002	57,750	2,100	30,150	25,500	14,620	15,500	16.1	15.8	2,098
Wyoming	51,441	42,887	6,461	362	2,931	2,875	14,003	14,945	17.6	14.9	1,951
TOTAL U.S.	24,403,027	18,375,337	2,460,940	137,990	1,170,357	1,014,898	$14,669	$15,474	20.8	18.1	$1,791

Kindergartens included in elementary schools; junior high schools, in secondary schools.
[1] Includes librarians, guidance and psychological personnel, and related educational workers.
Source: National Education Association Research, *Estimates of School Statistics, 1978–79* (Copyright 1979. All rights reserved. Used by permission).

Universities and Colleges

state statistics

State	NUMBER OF INSTITUTIONS 1978–1979		Enrollment[1,2] fall, 1978	EARNED DEGREES CONFERRED 1976–1977		
	Total	Public		Bachelor's and first professional	Master's except first professional	Doctor's
Alabama	58	36	160,531	16,027	5,757	257
Alaska	16	12	23,928	423	195	5
Arizona	23	17	176,820	9,673	4,327	417
Arkansas	34	19	70,277	6,924	1,829	106
California	262	137	1,650,245	90,696	31,126	3,682
Colorado	41	27	150,778	14,924	5,130	703
Connecticut	47	22	152,035	14,040	6,316	527
Delaware	10	6	30,637	3,016	362	49
District of Columbia	16	1	85,061	8,926	5,513	553
Florida	77	37	376,680	29,999	8,535	1,418
Georgia	72	34	169,755	17,570	8,233	570
Hawaii	12	9	47,216	3,805	1,019	134
Idaho	9	6	41,045	2,824	659	49
Illinois	154	63	627,425	49,130	17,923	2,061
Indiana	66	24	221,472	25,280	9,802	1,089
Iowa	62	22	127,273	14,630	2,624	520
Kansas	52	29	128,908	12,450	3,542	370
Kentucky	42	9	131,268	12,533	4,900	251
Louisiana	32	20	150,160	16,647	4,442	303
Maine	27	10	40,883	4,695	666	38
Maryland	54	32	214,505	17,304	5,474	602
Massachusetts	119	33	380,047	40,874	14,633	1,980
Michigan	96	45	484,954	38,314	16,098	1,504
Minnesota	65	30	188,555	19,575	3,509	519
Mississippi	46	27	98,040	9,476	3,665	276
Missouri	84	28	218,565	23,798	8,285	689
Montana	13	9	30,575	3,735	672	63
Nebraska	31	17	82,068	8,194	1,771	218
Nevada	6	5	33,593	1,370	476	33
New Hampshire	24	10	40,392	5,359	853	55
New Jersey	63	31	306,145	26,855	8,560	760
New Mexico	19	16	55,647	4,883	1,696	166
New York	286	82	948,459	92,383	37,736	3,478
North Carolina	126	73	260,519	24,462	5,596	716
North Dakota	16	11	32,293	3,485	516	66
Ohio	133	62	448,704	44,329	12,934	1,543
Oklahoma	43	29	148,313	13,567	4,030	406
Oregon	43	21	143,633	11,512	3,276	411
Pennsylvania	178	61	469,886	57,281	13,983	1,628
Rhode Island	13	3	60,141	6,605	1,885	204
South Carolina	61	33	128,054	11,727	3,810	174
South Dakota	18	7	29,245	3,917	777	48
Tennessee	76	24	191,934	19,110	5,271	570
Texas	147	94	648,094	55,390	16,738	1,595
Utah	14	9	89,096	9,775	2,471	445
Vermont	21	6	29,773	4,210	1,108	33
Virginia	71	39	268,736	21,200	5,346	516
Washington	49	33	272,726	17,257	3,955	462
West Virginia	28	17	77,912	7,960	2,159	121
Wisconsin	62	30	241,915	21,667	5,661	765
Wyoming	8	8	20,032	1,353	378	69
TOTAL U.S.	3,125	1,465	11,204,948	981,139	316,222	33,217

Excludes service academies. [1] Excludes non–degree-credit students. [2] Preliminary.
Source: U.S. Department of Health, Education, and Welfare, National Center for Education Statistics, *Digest of Education Statistics, Education Directory,* and *Earned Degrees Conferred.*

Universities and Colleges, 1978–79[1]

Selected four-year schools

Institution	Location	Year Founded	Total Students[2]	Total Faculty[3]	Bound Library volumes
ALABAMA					
Alabama A. & M. U.	Normal	1875	4,215	315	225,600
Alabama State U.	Montgomery	1874	4,754	179	150,000
Auburn U.	Auburn	1856	18,105	1,091	1,023,000
Birmingham-Southern	Birmingham	1856	1,300	88	126,000
Jacksonville State U.	Jacksonville	1883	7,101	365	344,600
Troy State U.	Troy	1887	6,382	354	181,600
Tuskegee Institute	Tuskegee Institute	1881	3,296	298	240,000
U. of Alabama	University	1831	17,776	904	1,230,800
U. of South Alabama	Mobile	1963	6,971	387	200,000
ALASKA					
U. of Alaska	Fairbanks	1917	3,485	334	543,600
ARIZONA					
Arizona State U.	Tempe	1885	37,122	1,613	1,384,300
Northern Arizona U.	Flagstaff	1899	12,700	575	573,200
U. of Arizona	Tucson	1885	30,826	1,762	1,275,000
ARKANSAS					
Arkansas State U.	State University	1909	7,243	338	520,000
U. of Arkansas	Fayetteville	1871	15,688	669	876,100
U. of A. at Little Rock	Little Rock	1927	9,652	400	218,500
U. of Central Arkansas	Conway	1907	5,355	261	212,500
CALIFORNIA					
California Inst. of Tech.	Pasadena	1891	1,652	326	330,000
Cal. Polytech. State U.	San Luis Obispo	1901	15,500	1,063	525,000
Cal. State Polytech. U.	Pomona	1938	12,651	687	290,000
Cal. State U., Chico	Chico	1887	12,970	839	500,000
Cal. State U., Dominguez Hills	Dominguez Hills	1960	7,000	310	210,000
Cal. State U., Fresno	Fresno	1911	15,623	942	576,600
Cal. State U., Fullerton	Fullerton	1957	21,435	1,292	500,000
Cal. State U., Hayward	Hayward	1957	10,553	524	565,500
Cal. State U., Long Beach	Long Beach	1949	29,515	1,281	681,400
Cal. State U., Los Angeles	Los Angeles	1947	26,270	1,400	800,000
Cal. State U., Northridge	Northridge	1958	27,976	1,510	600,000
Cal. State U., Sacramento	Sacramento	1947	19,753	884[4]	655,000
Golden Gate U.	San Francisco	1901	9,530	862	250,000
Humboldt State U.	Arcata	1913	7,500	459	235,000
Loyola Marymount U.	Los Angeles	1911	4,773	300	205,900
Occidental	Los Angeles	1887	1,750	142	300,000
San Francisco State U.	San Francisco	1899	24,000	1,697	500,000
San Jose State U.	San Jose	1857	26,358	1,570	700,000
Sonoma State U.	Rohnert Park	1960	5,860	392	268,700
Stanford U.	Stanford	1885	11,692	1,072	4,363,600
U. of C., Berkeley	Berkeley	1868	29,048	1,290	5,400,000
U. of C., Davis	Davis	1905	17,511	902	1,450,000
U. of C., Irvine	Irvine	1960	9,953	427	830,000
U. of C., Los Angeles	Los Angeles	1919	31,711	1,523	3,400,000
U. of C., Riverside	Riverside	1868	4,610	275	920,000
U. of C., San Diego	La Jolla	1912	10,797	604	1,280,000
U. of C., Santa Barbara	Santa Barbara	1944	14,473	538	1,280,000
U. of C., Santa Cruz	Santa Cruz	1965	5,880	242	570,000
U. of the Pacific	Stockton	1851	4,130	320	560,000
U. of San Francisco	San Francisco	1855	6,326	355	320,000
U. of Santa Clara	Santa Clara	1851	6,718	397	330,000
U. of Southern California	Los Angeles	1880	27,879	1,741	1,650,000
COLORADO					
Colorado	Colorado Springs	1874	1,885	195	284,200
Colorado School of Mines	Golden	1874	2,584	186	158,000
Colorado State U.	Fort Collins	1870	18,255	1,222	1,200,000
Metropolitan State	Denver	1963	13,691	600	455,000
U. S. Air Force Academy	USAF Academy	1954	4,544	588	300,000
U. of Colorado	Boulder	1876	21,318	1,200	1,800,000
U. of Denver	Denver	1864	10,918	584	1,000,000
U. of Northern Colorado	Greeley	1889	10,794	800	500,000
U. of Southern Colorado	Pueblo	1933	4,475	272	200,000
CONNECTICUT					
Central Connecticut State	New Britain	1849	12,727	415	275,000
Southern Connecticut State	New Haven	1893	11,902	541	327,800
Trinity	Hartford	1823	1,750	135	597,000
U. S. Coast Guard Acad.	New London	1876	840	117	119,000
U. of Bridgeport	Bridgeport	1927	7,900	386	297,000
U. of Connecticut	Storrs	1881	12,563	1,154	1,476,700
U. of Hartford	West Hartford	1877	6,700	540	270,000
Wesleyan U.	Middletown	1831	2,600	237	772,000
Western Connecticut State	Danbury	1903	5,248	225	133,600
Yale U.	New Haven	1701	9,000	1,500	6,692,600
DELAWARE					
Delaware State	Dover	1891	2,348	139	128,400
U. of Delaware	Newark	1833	19,001	941	1,174,000
DISTRICT OF COLUMBIA					
American U.	Washington	1893	12,784	572	459,000
Catholic U. of America	Washington	1887	7,400	533	900,000
George Washington U.	Washington	1821	23,068	3,103	829,300
Georgetown U.	Washington	1789	16,217	2,663	839,300
Howard U.	Washington	1867	10,813	1,908	1,012,500
FLORIDA					
Florida A. & M. U.	Tallahassee	1887	6,011	398	294,200
Florida State U.	Tallahassee	1857	21,224	1,390	1,463,400
Florida Tech. U.	Orlando	1963	10,605	397	371,800
Rollins	Winter Park	1885	4,363	156	183,700
U. of Florida	Gainesville	1853	31,133	2,916	2,000,000
U. of Miami	Coral Gables	1925	13,496	761	912,000
U. of South Florida	Tampa	1960	19,045	958	494,200
GEORGIA					
Atlanta U.	Atlanta	1865	1,361	269	317,000
Augusta	Augusta	1925	3,685	170	219,200
Emory U.	Atlanta	1836	7,572	1,137	2,005,800
Georgia	Milledgeville	1889	3,564	189	120,000
Georgia Inst. of Tech.	Atlanta	1885	10,688	774	850,000
Georgia Southern	Statesboro	1906	6,723	302	237,600
Georgia State U.	Atlanta	1913	21,000	668	635,700
Mercer U.	Macon	1833	2,327	230	180,000
Morehouse[5]	Atlanta	1867	1,525	100	297,300
Oglethorpe U.	Atlanta	1835	1,093	61	62,000
Spelman[6]	Atlanta	1881	1,276	112	44,000
U. of Georgia	Athens	1785	21,700	1,750	1,800,000
HAWAII					
Brigham Young U.-Hawaii	Laie	1955	1,790	103	90,000
U. of Hawaii	Honolulu	1907	21,188	1,567	1,505,000
IDAHO					
Boise State U.	Boise	1932	10,025	455	230,000
Idaho State U.	Pocatello	1901	10,804	313	325,000
U. of Idaho	Moscow	1889	7,931	749	1,050,000
ILLINOIS					
Augustana	Rock Island	1860	2,399	166	223,000
Bradley U.	Peoria	1897	5,215	371	300,000
Chicago State U.	Chicago	1869	7,213	346	229,000
Concordia Teachers	River Forest	1864	1,118	103	120,300
De Paul U.	Chicago	1898	12,149	653	343,600
Eastern Illinois U.	Charleston	1895	9,717	551	443,800
Illinois Inst. of Tech.	Chicago	1892	6,325	665	1,338,000
Illinois State U.	Normal	1857	19,576	1,030	779,500
Knox	Galesburg	1837	1,002	88[4]	191,600
Lake Forest	Lake Forest	1857	1,060	105	175,000
Loyola U. of Chicago	Chicago	1870	8,150	1,370	703,300
Northeastern Ill. U.	Chicago	1867	10,061	453	318,500
Northern Illinois U.	De Kalb	1895	24,910	1,273	870,000
Northwestern U.	Evanston	1851	15,117	1,686	2,655,400
Southern Illinois U.	Carbondale	1869	22,695	1,665	1,514,700
SIU at Edwardsville	Edwardsville	1957	11,242	720	700,000
U. of Chicago	Chicago	1891	7,900	1,040	4,000,000
U. of Illinois	Urbana	1867	33,684	2,771	5,582,100
U. of I. at Chicago Circle	Chicago	1965	20,341	1,500	650,000
Western Illinois U.	Macomb	1899	13,006	782	537,000
Wheaton	Wheaton	1860	2,485	190	210,000
INDIANA					
Ball State U.	Muncie	1918	16,977	919	968,400
Butler U.	Indianapolis	1855	3,852	317	187,800
De Pauw U.	Greencastle	1837	2,372	185	350,600
Indiana State U.	Terre Haute	1865	12,056	730	750,000
Indiana U.	Bloomington	1820	32,921	1,631	4,403,000
Purdue U.	West Lafayette	1869	31,990	4,556	1,357,800
U. of Evansville	Evansville	1854	4,906	193	250,000
U. of Notre Dame du Lac	Notre Dame	1842	8,768	695	1,383,100
Valparaiso U.	Valparaiso	1859	3,800	317	270,000
IOWA					
Coe	Cedar Rapids	1851	1,320	113	146,000
Drake U.	Des Moines	1881	6,737	382	415,000
Grinnell	Grinnell	1846	1,258	107	250,000
Iowa State U.	Ames	1858	23,486	1,755	1,320,000
U. of Iowa	Iowa City	1847	23,349	2,563	2,217,000
U. of Northern Iowa	Cedar Falls	1876	10,382	659	502,000
KANSAS					
Emporia State U.	Emporia	1863	5,850	275	619,200
Kansas State U.	Manhattan	1863	18,620	1,004[4]	860,000
U. of Kansas	Lawrence	1866	24,125	1,296	2,000,000
Witchita State U.	Wichita	1895	16,649	889	615,500
KENTUCKY					
Berea	Berea	1855	1,442	136	170,000
Eastern Kentucky U.	Richmond	1906	13,871[4]	596[4]	610,700
Kentucky State U.	Frankfort	1886	2,389	154	155,000
Murray State U.	Murray	1922	8,158	461	510,000
U. of Kentucky	Lexington	1865	39,516	1,875	1,640,200
U. of Louisville	Louisville	1798	19,155	1,363	930,100
Western Kentucky U.	Bowling Green	1907	13,422	681	468,600
LOUISIANA					
Grambling State U.	Grambling	1901	4,050	250	165,000
Louisiana State U.	Baton Rouge	1860	24,500	1,095	1,660,000
Louisiana Tech U.	Ruston	1894	9,000	375	1,300,000
Northeast Louisiana U.	Monroe	1931	9,175	400	300,700
Northwestern State U.	Natchitoches	1884	6,500	300	200,000
Southern U.	Baton Rouge	1880	8,101	486	382,400
Tulane U.	New Orleans	1834	6,900	800	1,200,000
U. of Southwestern La.	Lafayette	1898	13,341	592	444,200
MAINE					
Bates	Lewiston	1864	1,465	226	260,000
Bowdoin	Brunswick	1794	1,375	109	575,000
Colby	Waterville	1813	1,729	130	358,100
U. of Maine, Farmington	Farmington	1864	1,925	82	76,100
U. of Maine at Orono	Orono	1865	11,091	464	522,000
U. of Southern Maine	Portland	1878	8,283	325	290,000
MARYLAND					
Goucher[6]	Towson	1885	996	133	208,000
Johns Hopkins U.	Baltimore	1876	9,608	1,794	2,296,600
Morgan State U.	Baltimore	1867	5,297	299	181,700
Towson State U.	Baltimore	1866	15,283	926	327,800
U.S. Naval Academy	Annapolis	1845	4,532	530	500,000
U. of Maryland	College Park	1807	36,905	1,942	2,000,000
MASSACHUSETTS					
Amherst	Amherst	1821	1,557	164	543,400
Boston	Chestnut Hill	1863	13,913	836	971,600
Boston U.	Boston	1869	25,528	2,530	1,360,000
Brandeis U.	Waltham	1948	3,430	400	750,000
Clark U.	Worcester	1887	4,510	196	365,000
Harvard U.	Cambridge	1636	15,856	3,019	9,547,600
Holy Cross	Worcester	1843	2,460	190	340,000
Mass. Inst. of Tech.	Cambridge	1861	8,881	1,732	1,700,000
Mt. Holyoke[6]	South Hadley	1837	1,922	206	437,000
Northeastern U.	Boston	1898	38,187	1,980	743,200
Radcliffe[6]	Cambridge	1879	2,200	. . .	. . .
Salem State	Salem	1854	4,957	546	180,000
Simmons[6]	Boston	1899	1,737	253	150,000

Institution	Location	Year founded	Total students[2]	Total faculty[3]	Bound library volumes
Smith	Northampton	1871	2,460	260	853,800
Tufts U.	Medford	1852	6,766	966	530,000
U. of Lowell	Lowell	1894	7,600	540	272,000
U. of Massachusetts	Amherst	1863	24,000	1,400	1,500,000
Wellesley[6]	Wellesley	1870	2,233	290	585,000
Wheaton[6]	Norton	1834	1,120	112	190,000
Williams	Williamstown	1793	2,034	185	490,000
MICHIGAN					
Albion	Albion	1835	1,784	116	220,000
Central Michigan U.	Mt. Pleasant	1892	16,281	815	625,000
Eastern Michigan U.	Ypsilanti	1849	18,274	780	580,300
Ferris State	Big Rapids	1884	10,569	573	180,200
Hope	Holland	1866	2,300	140	181,000
Michigan State U.	East Lansing	1855	44,211	2,781	2,500,000
Michigan Tech U.	Houghton	1885	7,690	489	455,400
Northern Michigan U.	Marquette	1899	9,123	409	351,000
U. of Detroit	Detroit	1877	8,091	270	503,200
U. of Michigan	Ann Arbor	1817	35,820	2,405	5,000,000
Wayne State U.	Detroit	1868	34,341	2,400	1,750,000
Western Michigan U.	Kalamazoo	1903	20,689	1,091	747,800
MINNESOTA					
Carleton	Northfield	1866	1,718	133	309,000
Concordia	Moorhead	1891	2,607	169	245,000
Gustavus Adolphus	St. Peter	1862	2,272	201	288,000
Hamline U.	St. Paul	1854	1,750	140	150,000
Macalester	St. Paul	1874	1,783	144	250,000
Mankato State U.	Mankato	1867	10,498	554	507,500
Moorhead State U.	Moorhead	1885	7,033	327	237,100
St. Catherine[6]	St. Paul	1905	2,000	130	200,000
St. Cloud State U.	St. Cloud	1869	11,718	539	495,400
St. John's U.[5]	Collegeville	1857	1,975	141	279,100
St. Olaf	Northfield	1874	3,024	245	325,000
St. Thomas	St. Paul	1885	4,139	229	190,900
U. of Minnesota	Minneapolis	1851	55,076	4,439	3,300,000
Winona State U.	Winona	1858	4,000	245	165,000
MISSISSIPPI					
Alcorn State U.	Lorman	1871	2,776	136	124,000
Jackson State U.	Jackson	1877	7,718	350	220,000
Mississippi	Clinton	1826	3,500	150	152,000
Mississippi U. for Women	Columbus	1884	2,550	191	304,100
Mississippi State U.	Mississippi State	1878	11,340	740	568,800
U. of Mississippi	University	1848	9,635	550	900,000
U. of Southern Mississippi	Hattiesburg	1910	10,084	670	569,800
MISSOURI					
Central Missouri State U.	Warrensburg	1871	9,744	549	300,000
Northeast Missouri State U.	Kirksville	1867	5,863	359	235,000
St. Louis U.	St. Louis	1818	9,413	2,231	1,222,400
Southeast Missouri State U.	Cape Girardeau	1873	8,804	427	200,000
Southwest Missouri State U.	Springfield	1906	12,732	647	329,500
U. of Missouri-Columbia	Columbia	1839	23,415	3,858	1,929,200
U. of Missouri-Kansas City	Kansas City	1929	10,312	991	619,700
U. of Missouri-Rolla	Rolla	1870	5,635	330	286,000
U. of Missouri-St. Louis	St. Louis	1963	11,053	540	350,000
Washington U.	St. Louis	1853	10,542	2,261	1,500,000
MONTANA					
Montana State U.	Bozeman	1893	10,109	743	600,000
U. of Montana	Missoula	1893	8,300	400	611,700
NEBRASKA					
Creighton U.	Omaha	1878	5,420	881	467,100
U. of Nebraska	Lincoln	1869	27,070	1,487	1,500,000
U. of Nebraska at Omaha	Omaha	1908	14,873	501	340,000
NEVADA					
U. of Nevada-Las Vegas	Las Vegas	1951	8,214	311[4]	369,200
U. of Nevada-Reno	Reno	1864	8,850	348[4]	680,000
NEW HAMPSHIRE					
Dartmouth	Hanover	1769	4,248	297	1,000,000
U. of New Hampshire	Durham	1866	10,714	671	760,000
NEW JERSEY					
Glassboro State	Glassboro	1923	11,000	390	295,000
Jersey City State	Jersey City	1927	7,690	386	350,000
Kean Col. of N. J.	Union	1855	13,650	5,268	250,000
Montclair State	Upper Montclair	1908	14,800	560[4]	311,300
Princeton U.	Princeton	1746	5,887	677	3,000,000
Rider	Lawrenceville	1865	5,583	271	312,300
Rutgers State U.	New Brunswick	1766	33,667	2,130	3,199,000
Seton Hall U.	South Orange	1856	9,902	568	300,000
Stevens Inst. of Tech.	Hoboken	1870	2,550	160	95,800
Trenton State	Trenton	1855	10,529	510	316,000
Upsala	East Orange	1893	1,570	116	145,000
William Patterson	Wayne	1855	11,774	699	283,000
NEW MEXICO					
New Mexico State U.	Las Cruces	1888	11,864	643	610,000
U. of New Mexico	Albuquerque	1889	23,475	957	1,000,000
NEW YORK					
Adelphi U.	Garden City	1896	11,774	885	350,800
Alfred U.	Alfred	1836	2,146	161	176,000
Canisius	Buffalo	1870	3,924	257	208,500
City U. of New York					
Bernard M. Baruch	New York	1919	14,500	731	255,000
Brooklyn	Brooklyn	1930	18,067	1,467	739,200
City	New York	1847	13,548	758	1,000,000
Herbert H. Lehman	Bronx	1931	9,971	713	286,000
Hunter	New York	1870	17,989	1,219	461,900
Queens	Flushing	1937	18,150	1,534	511,400
Richmond	Staten Island	1965	2,291	101	165,000
York	Jamaica	1966	3,450	258	153,500
Colgate U.	Hamilton	1819	2,689	220	350,000
Columbia U.	New York	1754	15,311	4,000	4,500,000
Barnard[6]	New York	1889	2,400	200	150,000
Teachers	New York	1887	6,107	222	450,000
Cornell U.	Ithaca	1865	17,118	1,447	4,000,000
Elmira	Elmira	1855	2,882	158	140,000
Fordham U.	Bronx	1841	14,854	675[4]	2,160,000
Hamilton	Clinton	1812	960	85	325,900
Hofstra U.	Hempstead	1935	10,900	684	780,000
Ithaca	Ithaca	1892	4,800	408	270,000
Juilliard School	New York	1905	1,000	150	50,000
Long Island U.	Greenvale	1926	24,400	1,000	488,000
Manhattan[5]	Bronx	1853	4,860	353	236,200
Marymount[5]	Tarrytown	1907	1,172	113	107,100
New School for Soc. Res.	New York	1919	27,000	1,500	175,000
New York U.	New York	1831	43,244	4,000	2,700,200
Niagara U.	Niagara University	1856	3,924	253	190,600
Polytechnic Inst. of N.Y.	Brooklyn	1854	4,606	217	251,500
Pratt Inst.	Brooklyn	1887	4,249	528	222,800
Rensselaer Polytech. Inst.	Troy	1824	5,700	344	276,600
Rochester Inst. of Tech.	Rochester	1829	13,261	994	181,800
St. Bonaventure U.	St. Bonaventure	1856	2,590	160	200,000
St. John's U.	Jamaica	1870	15,777	764	901,900
St. Lawrence U.	Canton	1856	2,300	155	280,000
State U. of N.Y. at Albany	Albany	1844	15,368	800	936,000
SUNY at Buffalo	Buffalo	1846	24,683	1,830	1,884,900
SUNY at Stony Brook	Stony Brook	1957	15,948	1,153	1,146,000
State U. Colleges					
Brockport	Brockport	1836	9,785	541	350,000
Buffalo	Buffalo	1867	11,909	556	408,400
Cortland	Cortland	1868	5,795	349	225,000
Fredonia	Fredonia	1867	5,262	284	313,600
Geneseo	Geneseo	1867	5,551	316	325,500
New Paltz	New Paltz	1828	6,890	447	295,000
Oneonta	Oneonta	1889	6,217	366	350,000
Oswego	Oswego	1861	7,615	454	284,200
Plattsburgh	Plattsburgh	1889	5,970	309	266,500
Potsdam	Potsdam	1816	4,652	316	300,000
Syracuse U.	Syracuse	1870	20,003	1,175	2,000,000
U.S. Merchant Marine Acad.	Kings Point	1943	1,142	89	100,000
U.S. Military Academy	West Point	1802	4,492	550	400,000
U. of Rochester	Rochester	1850	8,100	426	1,800,000
Vassar	Poughkeepsie	1861	2,250	221	500,000
Wagner	Staten Island	1883	2,600	177	250,000
Yeshiva U.	New York	1886	4,243	2,493	754,600
NORTH CAROLINA					
Appalachian State U.	Boone	1899	10,179	537	380,000
Catawba	Salisbury	1851	918	65	169,000
Davidson	Davidson	1837	1,379	104	250,000
Duke U.	Durham	1838	9,531	1,697	3,022,800
East Carolina U.	Greenville	1907	12,476	659	553,800
Lenoir-Rhyne	Hickory	1891	1,291	105	96,000
N. Carolina A. & T. St. U.	Greensboro	1891	5,188	362	274,200
N. Carolina State U.	Raleigh	1887	18,500	1,177	890,000
U. of N.C. at Chapel Hill	Chapel Hill	1789	21,060	2,004	2,487,100
U. of N.C. at Greensboro	Greensboro	1891	9,925	622	1,075,000
Wake Forest U.	Winston-Salem	1834	4,736	984	739,300
Western Carolina U.	Cullowhee	1889	6,274	311	300,000
NORTH DAKOTA					
North Dakota State U.	Fargo	1890	7,982	654	333,200
U. of North Dakota	Grand Forks	1883	9,708	503[4]	407,700
OHIO					
Antioch	Yellow Springs	1852	1,000	221	240,000
Bowling Green State U.	Bowling Green	1910	16,907	720	622,400
Case Western Reserve U.	Cleveland	1826	8,300	1,700	1,576,000
Cleveland State U.	Cleveland	1964	17,340	717	440,000
Denison U.	Granville	1831	2,050	176	235,000
John Carroll U.	Cleveland	1886	4,000	315	350,000
Kent State U.	Kent	1910	18,331	884	1,000,000
Kenyon	Gambier	1824	1,445	115	195,500
Marietta	Marietta	1835	1,456	102	236,700
Miami U.	Oxford	1809	17,907	751	988,000
Oberlin	Oberlin	1833	2,785	246	800,000
Ohio State U.	Columbus	1870	51,343	3,559[4]	3,497,900
Ohio U.	Athens	1804	13,310	823	985,700
U. of Akron	Akron	1870	23,121	1,045	948,600
U. of Cincinnati	Cincinnati	1819	33,186	2,215	1,500,000
U. of Dayton	Dayton	1850	6,873	619	500,000
U. of Toledo	Toledo	1872	18,245	721	1,086,100
Wooster	Wooster	1866	1,825	155	250,000
Xavier U.	Cincinnati	1831	6,385	280	189,000
Youngstown State U.	Youngstown	1908	15,652	805	400,000
OKLAHOMA					
Central State U.	Edmond	1890	11,398	427	551,400
Oklahoma State U.	Stillwater	1890	21,904	1,488	1,200,000
U. of Oklahoma	Norman	1890	21,090	719	1,723,800
U. of Tulsa	Tulsa	1894	6,311	429	1,000,000
OREGON					
Lewis and Clark	Portland	1867	2,352	164	177,900
Oregon State U.	Corvallis	1868	16,653	1,055	826,200
Portland State U.	Portland	1955	15,924	750	550,000
Reed	Portland	1909	1,155	104	274,200
U. of Oregon	Eugene	1872	16,463	1,287	1,400,000
PENNSYLVANIA					
Allegheny	Meadville	1815	1,936	150	264,400
Bryn Mawr[6]	Bryn Mawr	1885	1,601	175	435,000
Bucknell U.	Lewisburg	1846	3,261	240	395,300
Carnegie-Mellon U.	Pittsburgh	1900	5,311	428	572,800
Dickinson	Carlisle	1773	1,825	258	250,000
Drexel U.	Philadelphia	1891	11,032	292	300,000
Duquesne U.	Pittsburgh	1878	6,803	700	380,000
Edinboro State	Edinboro	1857	5,900	407	310,000
Franklin and Marshall	Lancaster	1787	2,078	157	250,000
Gettysburg	Gettysburg	1832	1,967	170	236,000
Indiana U. of Pa.	Indiana	1875	12,145	672	500,000
Juniata	Huntingdon	1876	1,141	92	188,000
Lafayette	Easton	1826	2,348	164	357,400
La Salle	Philadelphia	1863	7,250	605	280,000
Lehigh U.	Bethlehem	1865	6,276	589	680,000
Moravian	Bethlehem	1742	1,240	79	141,000
Muhlenberg	Allentown	1848	1,711	129	176,000

Universities and Colleges (continued)

Selected four-year schools

Institution	Location	Year founded	Total students[2]	Total faculty[3]	Bound library volumes
Pennsylvania State U.	University Park	1855	35,298	1,584	1,467,600
St. Joseph's	Philadelphia	1851	5,471	302	183,300
Slippery Rock State	Slippery Rock	1889	10,527	339	400,000
Susquehanna U.	Selinsgrove	1858	1,742	285	110,000
Swarthmore	Swarthmore	1864	1,314	150	567,100
Temple U.	Philadelphia	1884	33,812	2,527	1,500,000
U. of Pennsylvania	Philadelphia	1740	21,586	1,478	2,821,600
U. of Pittsburgh	Pittsburgh	1787	28,703	2,555	1,770,000
Ursinus	Collegeville	1869	1,034	90	134,000
Villanova U.	Villanova	1842	8,733	551	454,200
West Chester State	West Chester	1812	8,703	460	360,000
PUERTO RICO					
Inter American U.	San Juan	1912	23,296	1,042	260,000
U. of Puerto Rico	Río Piedras	1903	23,531	1,074	33,500
RHODE ISLAND					
Brown U.	Providence	1764	6,784	472	1,636,200
Rhode Island	Providence	1854	7,742	430	250,000
U. of Rhode Island	Kingston	1892	11,100	900	600,000
SOUTH CAROLINA					
The Citadel[5]	Charleston	1842	3,358	156	367,000
Clemson U.	Clemson	1889	11,274	865	731,000
Furman U.	Greenville	1826	3,069	158	247,500
U. of South Carolina	Columbia	1801	25,908	1,164[4]	1,290,900
SOUTH DAKOTA					
South Dakota State U.	Brookings	1881	4,664	345	306,000
U. of South Dakota	Vermillion	1882	5,734	550	420,000
TENNESSEE					
Fisk U.	Nashville	1867	1,281	96	182,800
Memphis State U.	Memphis	1909	21,248	888	1,050,000
Middle Tennessee State U.	Murfreesboro	1911	10,880	450	403,800
Tennessee State U.	Nashville	1912	5,698	302	214,400
Tennessee Tech. U.	Cookeville	1915	7,849	505	427,900
U. of Tennessee	Knoxville	1794	30,000	2,100	1,600,000
Vanderbilt U.	Nashville	1873	8,759	1,950	1,449,600
TEXAS					
Austin	Sherman	1849	1,214	91	166,200
Baylor U.	Waco	1845	9,594	524	860,000
East Texas State U.	Commerce	1889	9,282	470	550,000
Hardin-Simmons U.	Abilene	1891	1,823	112	161,000
Lamar U.	Beaumont	1923	12,800	496	430,000
North Texas State U.	Denton	1890	17,287	1,162	1,220,000
Prairie View A. & M.	Prairie View	1876	5,400	410[4]	195,700
Rice U.	Houston	1891	3,700	445	991,800
Sam Houston State U.	Huntsville	1879	10,549	384	590,000
Southern Methodist U.	Dallas	1911	8,873	584	1,600,000
Southwest Texas State U.	San Marcos	1899	15,924	668	500,400
Stephen F. Austin State U.	Nacogdoches	1923	10,303	428	334,000
Texas A. & I. U.	Kingsville	1925	6,225	253	386,300
Texas A. & M. U.	College Station	1876	31,331	1,615	700,000
Texas Christian U.	Fort Worth	1873	6,132	518	860,000
Texas Southern U.	Houston	1947	9,500	427	270,000
Texas Tech. U.	Lubbock	1923	23,129	1,408	1,250,000
U. of Houston	Houston	1927	28,414	1,513	1,161,500
U. of Texas at Arlington	Arlington	1895	17,201	742	635,000
U. of Texas at Austin	Austin	1881	43,095	2,371	4,000,000
U. of Texas at El Paso	El Paso	1913	15,751	458	780,000
West Texas State U.	Canyon	1909	6,701	277	686,600
UTAH					
Brigham Young U.	Provo	1875	27,091	1,349	1,040,000
U. of Utah	Salt Lake City	1850	21,880	1,350	1,500,000
Utah State U.	Logan	1888	9,228	470[4]	644,700
Weber State	Ogden	1889	9,819	439	320,800
VERMONT					
Bennington	Bennington	1925	589	72	80,800
Middlebury	Middlebury	1800	1,870	161	396,100
U. of Vermont	Burlington	1791	8,944	1,093	834,000
VIRGINIA					
James Madison U.	Harrisonburg	1908	8,100	500	350,000
Old Dominion U.	Norfolk	1930	14,663	631	443,500
U. of Richmond	Richmond	1830	4,409	325	342,100
U. of Virginia	Charlottesville	1819	16,179	1,506	2,351,900
Virginia Commonwealth U.	Richmond	1838	18,366	1,621	478,200
Virginia Military Inst.[5]	Lexington	1839	1,315	133	257,100
Va. Polytech. Inst. & State U.	Blacksburg	1872	20,261	1,805	1,200,000
Washington & Lee U.[5]	Lexington	1749	1,705	166	313,400
William & Mary	Williamsburg	1693	6,313	523	693,800
WASHINGTON					
Central Washington U.	Ellensburg	1891	7,900	331	289,000
Eastern Washington U.	Cheney	1890	7,300	448	338,000
Gonzaga U.	Spokane	1887	3,340	237	265,000
U. of Washington	Seattle	1861	36,249	2,178	3,063,000
Washington State U.	Pullman	1890	16,850	805	1,190,000
Western Washington U.	Bellingham	1893	10,104	498	374,100
Whitman	Walla Walla	1859	1,067	79	266,200
WEST VIRGINIA					
Bethany	Bethany	1840	900	79	140,000
Marshall U.	Huntington	1837	11,144	496	325,000
West Virginia U.	Morgantown	1867	21,565	1,193	870,800
WISCONSIN					
Beloit	Beloit	1846	1,027	87	225,000
Lawrence U.	Appleton	1847	1,156	119	218,000
Marquette U.	Milwaukee	1881	11,203	898	600,000
St. Norbert	De Pere	1898	1,628	100	125,000
U. of W.-Eau Claire	Eau Claire	1916	10,629	524	380,000
U. of W.-Green Bay	Green Bay	1965	3,810	233	300,000
U. of W.-La Crosse	La Crosse	1909	8,890	426	430,400
U. of W.-Madison	Madison	1848	40,233	2,327	3,500,000
U. of W.-Milwaukee	Milwaukee	1956	24,818	1,690	1,300,000
U. of W.-Oshkosh	Oshkosh	1871	9,758	497[4]	292,200
U. of W.-Platteville	Platteville	1866	4,640	296[4]	188,300
U. of W.-River Falls	River Falls	1874	5,100	245[4]	187,000
U. of W.-Stevens Point	Stevens Point	1894	9,081	535	475,000
U. of W.-Stout	Menomonie	1893	7,032	345[4]	175,000
U. of W.-Superior	Superior	1896	2,149	255	211,000
U. of W.-Whitewater	Whitewater	1868	9,678	542	300,000
WYOMING					
U. of Wyoming	Laramie	1886	9,000	830	1,000,000

[1] Latest data available; coeducational unless otherwise indicated. [2] Total includes part-time students. [3] Total includes part-time or full-time equivalent faculty. [4] Total includes full-time equivalent only. [5] Men's school. [6] Women's school.

LIVING CONDITIONS

Health Personnel and Facilities

State	Physicians Dec. 31, 1977[1]	Dentists 1979	Registered Nurses[2]	Hospital facilities 1978: Hospitals	Hospital facilities 1978: Beds	Nursing homes 1976: Facilities	Nursing homes 1976: Beds
Alabama	4,330	1,314	10,235	148	25,242	217	19,489
Alaska	442	232	2,030	26	1,697	11	782
Arizona	4,651	1,173	12,383	78	11,339	71	5,914
Arkansas	2,506	714	5,033	96	12,650	217	19,803
California	50,088	14,052	103,385	613	114,836	3,500	138,219
Colorado	5,299	1,701	15,515	101	14,666	243	22,731
Connecticut	7,354	2,194	23,612	64	18,791	356	24,573
Delaware	936	265	4,389	15	4,099	29	2,228
District of Columbia	3,356	587	5,545	19	9,003	70	2,873
Florida	17,740	4,323	38,398	245	54,211	335	33,097
Georgia	6,928	2,167	17,423	189	31,146	325	29,455
Hawaii	1,709	599	4,117	27	3,813	144	3,188
Idaho	978	459	3,755	51	3,737	67	4,823
Illinois	19,592	5,999	60,806	285	75,484	936	88,311
Indiana	6,763	2,234	21,481	135	33,816	506	37,611
Iowa	3,490	1,396	17,812	141	21,613	552	33,874
Kansas	3,445	1,080	12,655	164	18,161	393	23,195
Kentucky	4,516	1,490	11,734	121	18,815	321	20,950
Louisiana	5,614	1,586	11,524	159	25,128	205	19,135
Maine	1,684	489	7,440	53	7,324	307	9,020
Maryland	9,783	2,591	22,462	85	25,210	191	19,154
Massachusetts	14,299	3,983	56,567	189	45,456	869	50,940
Michigan	13,594	4,772	46,681	244	50,661	704	66,750
Minnesota	7,358	2,429	23,638	188	31,051	517	43,036
Mississippi	2,471	763	6,288	114	16,234	147	9,023
Missouri	7,546	2,303	18,823	167	35,437	474	33,746
Montana	985	442	4,429	65	5,652	107	5,335
Nebraska	2,240	931	9,798	108	11,674	284	23,349
Nevada	897	340	2,564	25	3,234	37	1,638
New Hampshire	1,512	465	7,044	33	4,995	115	6,378
New Jersey	13,349	4,706	51,061	139	44,157	467	33,976
New Mexico	1,781	511	4,077	54	6,503	72	3,366
New York	45,147	12,611	125,794	368	134,425	1,027	104,523
North Carolina	8,018	2,175	21,366	158	33,774	722	24,614
North Dakota	786	312	3,653	60	5,830	103	6,878
Ohio	16,633	5,064	57,052	241	64,158	953	64,903
Oklahoma	3,475	1,192	8,698	141	17,482	362	26,650
Oregon	4,378	1,685	11,382	85	11,568	283	17,189
Pennsylvania	21,234	6,272	96,414	313	86,474	676	61,891
Rhode Island	1,900	509	6,638	21	6,700	120	7,330
South Carolina	3,670	1,130	10,187	88	16,919	119	8,701
South Dakota	683	286	3,852	70	5,676	154	8,386
Tennessee	6,434	2,034	12,051	160	31,008	290	20,092
Texas	19,070	5,757	40,372	565	79,071	1,105	102,139
Utah	2,149	853	4,531	41	5,084	104	4,613
Vermont	1,049	270	4,521	19	3,036	263	5,130
Virginia	8,240	2,599	23,935	135	32,138	341	25,435
Washington	6,702	2,611	21,953	127	16,138	370	30,344
West Virginia	2,531	703	7,314	80	14,170	127	5,585
Wisconsin	6,984	2,654	23,318	171	28,630	530	52,577
Wyoming	466	216	1,922	31	2,529	30	1,923
TOTAL U.S.	386,785	117,223	1,127,657	7,015	1,380,645	20,468	1,414,865

[1] Non-federal only. [2] Latest data available. Sources: *Physician Distribution and Medical Licensure in the U.S., 1977,* Dept. of Statistical Analysis, Center for Health Services Research and Development, American Medical Association, Chicago, 1979; American Dental Association, *Distribution of Dentists in the United States by State, Region, District, and County, 1979;* American Nurses' Association; American Hospital Association, *Hospital Statistics, 1979 Edition;* U.S. Dept. of Health, Education, and Welfare, Public Health Service.

Crime Rates per 100,000 Population

State or metropolitan area	VIOLENT CRIME										PROPERTY CRIME							
	Total		Murder		Rape		Robbery		Assault		Total		Burglary		Larceny		Auto theft	
	1973	1978	1973	1978	1973	1978	1973	1978	1973	1978	1973	1978	1973	1978	1973	1978	1973	1978
Alabama	350.1	419.1	13.2	13.3	21.2	25.5	79.4	99.1	236.3	281.2	2,162.2	3,519.7	882.0	1,229.3	1,053.1	1,987.9	227.2	302.5
Alaska	384.5	441.9	10.0	12.9	44.5	**55.6**	67.0	91.3	263.0	282.1	4,558.8	5,604.2	1,167.3	1,339.2	2,865.5	3,603.5	526.1	661.5
Arizona	479.9	552.1	8.1	9.4	31.0	44.2	147.3	162.9	293.6	335.6	**6,224.0**	7,051.7	1,958.3	2,082.5	**3,720.1**	**4,504.8**	545.6	464.4
Arkansas	289.9	344.1	8.8	9.1	19.5	23.1	71.5	80.0	190.0	231.9	2,249.0	3,117.6	801.0	967.1	1,315.7	1,950.9	132.3	199.6
California	565.8	742.9	9.0	11.7	40.6	50.8	240.4	306.1	275.8	374.4	5,739.1	6,373.3	1,979.6	2,193.3	3,123.6	3,488.8	635.9	691.3
Colorado	414.0	498.0	7.9	7.3	38.7	49.6	162.9	159.2	204.4	281.9	5,081.9	6,334.5	1,598.8	1,869.6	2,910.6	3,977.0	572.5	487.9
Connecticut	208.7	315.0	3.3	4.2	11.1	17.2	84.2	154.8	110.1	138.8	3,455.7	4,614.5	1,029.3	1,362.0	1,909.7	2,597.6	516.7	654.9
Delaware	350.0	440.7	5.9	6.7	15.8	20.4	90.3	145.5	238.0	268.1	4,232.6	5,913.2	1,219.4	1,623.7	2,526.4	3,792.6	486.8	496.9
Florida	604.6	765.6	15.4	11.0	31.9	46.1	222.3	206.0	335.0	**502.5**	5,355.7	6,303.9	1,857.2	1,978.8	3,048.6	3,936.5	449.9	388.6
Georgia	412.4	482.8	**17.4**	14.4	25.8	37.9	158.1	166.3	211.1	264.2	3,017.9	4,288.5	1,268.8	1,475.6	1,390.7	2,456.3	358.4	356.5
Hawaii	155.6	270.1	5.3	6.7	20.2	25.9	83.7	173.6	46.5	64.0	4,803.1	6,866.0	1,535.5	1,937.7	2,830.8	4,357.5	436.9	570.8
Idaho	164.2	236.4	2.6	5.4	14.2	19.2	26.9	40.0	120.5	171.9	3,293.6	3,778.4	848.8	1,038.4	2,237.8	2,496.2	207.0	243.7
Illinois	555.9	465.7	10.4	9.9	24.0	23.8	272.8	205.0	248.7	227.1	3,769.1	4,552.5	1,025.1	1,139.2	2,236.2	2,902.0	507.7	511.2
Indiana	247.5	323.5	7.2	6.2	21.0	27.0	106.1	121.4	113.2	168.8	3,286.1	4,015.1	962.2	1,108.3	1,952.6	2,495.7	371.4	411.1
Iowa	102.3	161.4	2.2	2.6	11.3	10.4	32.9	46.9	55.9	101.6	2,729.3	3,818.7	634.0	870.6	1,904.6	2,712.9	190.7	235.1
Kansas	217.5	318.2	6.0	5.7	18.0	25.0	78.1	93.7	115.3	193.8	3,296.3	4,225.9	1,030.5	1,286.8	2,055.3	2,691.4	210.5	247.7
Kentucky	220.1	223.2	9.7	9.0	16.3	20.7	85.1	81.3	109.1	112.1	2,045.2	2,799.9	679.7	884.6	1,139.2	1,664.7	226.2	250.6
Louisiana	425.6	584.9	15.4	**15.8**	22.2	34.8	138.6	173.7	249.3	360.7	2,977.3	4,207.4	962.1	1,275.5	1,690.4	2,570.3	324.9	361.6
Maine	113.7	207.7	2.1	2.7	7.8	11.1	20.7	32.9	83.1	161.0	2,430.6	3,930.8	857.3	1,241.2	1,401.2	2,436.2	172.2	253.3
Maryland	641.1	732.0	11.3	8.2	27.8	35.6	301.6	309.6	300.4	378.6	4,150.3	5,081.6	1,144.6	1,421.8	2,457.9	3,235.0	547.8	424.8
Massachusetts	351.9	462.0	4.4	3.7	16.3	22.6	182.0	172.3	149.3	263.3	4,169.1	4,888.5	1,330.3	1,515.1	1,729.2	2,277.8	**1,109.6**	**1,095.6**
Michigan	585.2	577.2	12.1	10.6	35.1	39.6	282.7	219.3	255.2	307.7	4,904.2	5,016.9	1,584.6	1,444.3	2,771.3	3,046.7	548.3	525.9
Minnesota	177.7	189.6	2.7	2.0	14.9	19.9	88.7	85.1	71.5	82.6	3,357.8	3,954.5	1,016.4	1,093.7	2,004.7	2,536.1	336.7	324.7
Mississippi	339.1	321.2	16.1	12.6	17.1	21.8	46.8	70.2	259.1	216.6	1,587.2	2,233.7	593.8	846.3	879.7	1,235.6	113.8	151.8
Missouri	408.7	467.9	9.0	10.4	28.2	28.0	193.4	184.0	178.1	245.5	3,732.8	4,059.5	1,234.8	1,345.2	2,052.6	2,345.5	445.4	368.8
Montana	167.4	237.6	6.0	4.8	16.4	15.8	36.3	36.8	108.7	180.1	3,227.9	3,678.2	755.6	786.0	2,241.7	2,585.1	230.5	307.1
Nebraska	185.4	190.5	4.3	3.0	16.5	18.3	62.5	64.9	102.1	104.4	2,625.8	3,250.7	637.4	746.8	1,685.7	2,287.2	302.7	216.8
Nevada	572.1	780.8	12.2	15.5	**46.0**	53.9	262.0	359.5	251.8	351.8	6,060.0	**7,506.1**	**2,149.8**	**2,659.2**	3,299.1	4,245.2	611.1	601.7
New Hampshire	82.0	118.8	2.1	1.4	9.5	9.4	13.3	26.3	57.1	81.7	2,247.3	3,948.7	685.0	1,159.7	1,373.3	2,483.4	189.0	305.6
New Jersey	391.9	423.5	7.4	5.4	18.8	23.6	206.2	192.6	159.4	201.9	3,690.6	4,783.7	1,244.5	1,456.3	1,873.4	2,766.8	572.7	560.6
New Mexico	454.3	528.2	11.4	10.2	32.1	42.7	125.9	111.6	284.9	363.8	4,253.5	4,652.1	1,432.1	1,335.6	2,485.7	3,002.7	335.7	313.8
New York	**731.2**	**841.0**	11.1	10.3	26.1	29.1	**439.6**	**472.1**	254.4	329.5	3,575.5	4,951.2	1,296.7	1,650.6	1,671.5	2,628.6	607.2	672.0
North Carolina	437.8	413.4	13.0	10.8	16.1	18.4	71.4	65.9	**337.4**	318.4	2,374.0	3,468.7	892.0	1,184.0	1,308.2	2,083.4	173.8	201.3
North Dakota	60.8	67.0	0.8	1.2	7.3	8.9	7.3	15.6	45.3	41.3	2,017.7	2,338.3	383.4	423.0	1,502.8	1,767.2	131.4	148.2
Ohio	291.7	412.7	7.3	6.9	21.4	27.4	143.5	182.6	119.5	195.8	3,204.1	4,246.2	943.0	1,214.5	1,884.3	2,629.7	376.9	402.0
Oklahoma	246.2	353.0	6.6	8.5	20.0	31.0	68.2	88.3	151.4	225.2	3,220.2	3,776.9	1,163.9	1,299.8	1,745.2	2,125.8	311.1	351.4
Oregon	292.7	502.4	4.9	5.0	29.3	41.2	99.4	131.1	159.0	325.0	5,004.4	5,573.0	1,607.7	1,617.1	2,988.5	3,561.1	408.2	394.8
Pennsylvania	262.5	301.1	6.3	6.2	14.9	18.7	135.3	136.7	106.0	139.5	2,196.3	2,883.6	766.6	899.9	1,069.9	1,643.0	359.8	340.7
Rhode Island	282.5	348.1	3.4	4.0	8.3	11.0	97.0	98.2	173.8	235.0	4,395.8	4,914.1	1,189.1	1,392.6	2,312.3	2,714.3	894.3	807.2
South Carolina	394.6	637.6	14.4	11.5	22.5	35.4	79.2	101.3	278.6	489.4	2,932.4	4,258.4	1,194.3	1,498.6	1,492.1	2,483.6	246.0	276.1
South Dakota	126.9	163.5	3.8	1.9	12.8	10.9	24.7	15.9	85.5	134.8	2,048.9	2,525.8	498.7	599.7	1,406.0	1,766.1	144.2	160.0
Tennessee	358.0	382.6	13.2	9.4	26.9	30.6	130.5	152.4	187.5	190.2	2,702.1	3,307.8	1,009.8	1,213.6	1,362.2	1,766.1	330.1	328.1
Texas	381.5	435.3	12.7	14.2	25.5	37.9	142.1	164.4	201.1	218.8	3,664.7	5,121.5	1,266.4	1,611.9	2,051.1	3,065.3	347.2	444.3
Utah	208.5	271.8	3.2	3.7	22.9	22.9	62.6	66.5	119.8	178.7	4,038.6	4,707.1	989.3	1,187.1	2,748.1	3,186.1	301.2	333.9
Vermont	70.5	166.3	2.2	3.3	11.2	14.6	8.8	14.4	48.3	134.1	2,427.6	3,640.2	801.5	1,261.2	1,489.9	2,164.9	136.2	214.2
Virginia	285.7	286.4	8.5	8.8	20.7	22.7	101.0	97.1	155.5	157.8	2,953.0	3,786.6	825.8	990.8	1,859.1	2,566.8	268.1	229.0
Washington	271.5	405.3	4.0	4.6	26.2	41.2	96.3	125.0	145.0	234.4	4,818.5	5,710.3	1,540.4	1,766.6	2,902.4	3,548.8	375.7	394.9
West Virginia	123.7	167.7	5.7	6.8	9.3	14.7	27.9	46.3	80.8	99.9	1,347.8	2,102.4	415.8	648.3	824.9	1,278.3	107.1	175.8
Wisconsin	115.4	132.2	2.6	2.5	10.8	14.5	48.7	49.9	53.3	65.2	3,061.5	3,748.1	710.6	846.3	2,122.0	2,672.3	228.9	229.5
Wyoming	216.1	280.4	6.8	7.1	15.6	23.6	32.9	48.1	160.9	201.7	3,196.9	4,214.2	699.7	836.1	2,282.7	3,035.6	214.4	342.5
Baltimore	916.2	1,022.0	15.4	11.7	34.4	40.8	458.7	446.0	**407.5**	523.5	4,629.4	5,546.8	1,351.1	1,543.4	2,636.3	3,508.6	642.1	494.8
Boston	413.4	565.1	5.7	4.6	19.6	26.3	235.5	241.7	152.6	292.6	4,265.9	5,050.3	1,281.3	1,472.6	1,650.5	2,220.7	**1,334.2**	**1,357.0**
Chicago	728.7	551.7	14.1	13.0	30.2	27.3	388.2	274.5	296.3	236.8	4,336.3	5,004.0	1,105.2	1,161.7	2,539.8	3,153.9	691.2	688.4
Cleveland	453.9	654.4	15.1	13.2	27.1	33.5	264.5	382.7	147.3	225.1	3,334.3	4,298.1	817.5	1,227.8	1,678.7	2,127.8	838.0	942.5
Detroit	821.5	780.5	**19.3**	15.2	43.2	48.3	470.3	368.7	288.7	348.2	5,276.8	5,526.2	1,661.4	1,569.4	2,731.9	3,122.2	883.4	834.6
Houston	495.5	570.4	15.9	**23.5**	32.5	57.8	306.7	336.6	140.3	152.6	4,258.3	6,642.2	1,644.5	2,072.0	1,993.2	3,655.0	620.6	915.1
Los Angeles	837.9	1,082.8	12.4	17.4	**55.0**	**66.9**	370.6	467.1	400.0	**531.3**	5,790.6	6,258.9	2,187.6	**2,333.9**	2,723.9	2,938.1	879.1	986.8
Minneapolis	300.8	300.9	3.7	2.7	22.3	29.6	158.4	146.7	116.5	121.9	4,602.7	4,992.7	1,435.8	1,439.4	2,635.1	3,116.9	531.8	436.5
Newark	552.5	657.0	10.4	8.8	26.1	32.5	310.0	326.4	206.0	289.3	3,882.2	4,900.3	1,311.5	1,466.2	1,877.0	2,729.9	693.7	704.2
New York	**1,204.9**	**1,370.6**	17.5	16.8	38.9	43.8	**747.0**	**819.0**	401.5	491.0	4,252.6	5,719.3	1,691.3	2,005.2	1,656.5	2,723.7	904.8	990.3
Philadelphia	440.8	453.2	11.5	9.8	23.5	27.3	232.6	213.2	173.2	202.9	3,015.9	3,671.2	1,018.9	1,126.8	1,382.0	2,065.0	615.1	479.4
Pittsburgh	282.3	342.7	4.2	5.2	16.0	20.0	153.8	177.7	108.3	139.8	2,079.7	2,619.4	713.3	826.7	924.9	1,329.1	441.6	463.6
St. Louis	596.7	697.9	13.4	14.4	37.4	40.8	300.6	308.0	245.4	334.7	5,078.4	5,095.4	1,705.4	1,659.0	2,660.1	2,884.3	712.9	552.1
San Francisco	683.6	819.7	10.9	11.2	44.9	53.0	353.3	414.4	274.4	341.2	**6,594.2**	**7,227.1**	**2,205.6**	2,249.0	**3,643.0**	**4,279.2**	745.6	698.8
Washington, D.C.	643.3	622.9	13.2	9.7	38.5	39.6	356.6	355.6	235.0	217.9	4,596.6	5,359.7	1,166.5	1,422.6	2,859.3	3,519.6	570.8	417.4

Boldface: highest rate among states or listed metropolitan areas. Source: U.S. Department of Justice, Federal Bureau of Investigation, *Uniform Crime Reports*.

TRANSPORTATION AND TRADE

Transportation

State	Road and street mi[1] 1979	Motor vehicles in 000s, 1978[2]			Railroad mileage 1978	Airports 1978	Pipeline mileage 1977[3]
		Total	Auto-mobiles	Trucks and buses			
Ala.	87,015	2,791	2,072	719	4,437	142	1,660
Alaska	9,930[4]	280	170	110	556	763	193
Ariz.	57,513	1,630	1,168	462	2,036	209	1,355
Ark.	74,208	1,501	990	511	3,453	167	3,071
Calif.	176,312	15,514	11,986	3,528	7,224	813	10,352
Colo.	87,288	2,303	1,718	585	3,343	261	2,396
Conn.	19,104[5]	2,133	1,963	170	354	103	94
Del.	5,244[4]	385	316	69	218	32	3
D.C.	1,101[4]	261	241	20	27	17	[6]
Fla.	97,120	6,345	5,194	1,151	4,007	438	288
Ga.	103,038	3,670	2,887	783	5,400	275	2,024
Hawaii	3,894	544	459	85	...	53	...
Idaho	63,991	762	468	294	2,761	190	633
Ill.	133,240	7,127	5,914	1,213	10,203	876	10,914
Ind.	90,858	3,720	2,824	896	5,496	306	4,552
Iowa	112,148	2,301	1,692	609	7,140	253	4,581
Kan.	134,855	1,981	1,347	634	7,455	351	17,152
Ky.	68,781	2,549	1,813	736	3,497	97	2,444
La.	55,395	2,504	1,770	734	3,633	282	9,460
Maine	21,797	751	579	172	1,623	162	353
Md.	26,961	2,674	2,254	420	766	142	219
Mass.	33,584	3,621	3,218	403	955	139	242
Mich.	119,359	6,252	5,152	1,100	5,209	413	4,861
Minn.	127,918	2,897	2,149	748	7,004	336	2,841
Miss.	68,486	1,544	1,089	455	3,576	154	3,246
Mo.	117,550	3,125	2,345	780	6,007	365	7,142
Mont.	77,852	761	461	300	4,807	169	3,232
Neb.	96,659	1,247	865	382	5,131	305	3,317
Nev.	49,899	583	431	152	1,574	118	275
N.H.	15,569	591	495	96	637	54	190
N.J.	33,073[5]	4,534	4,091	443	1,381	254	494
N.M.	72,028	945	606	339	2,058	139	6,960
N.Y.	108,953	7,851	6,875	976	4,310	490	1,586
N.C.	91,949	4,273	3,253	1,020	4,081	258	896
N.D.	107,141	595	351	244	5,040	211	1,773
Ohio	111,184	7,766	6,532	1,234	6,775	569	6,524
Okla.	109,723	2,361	1,587	774	4,708	285	20,710
Ore.	112,229	1,845	1,405	440	3,111	301	414
Pa.	118,494	8,183	6,896	1,287	6,757	651	8,097
R.I.	5,793[5]	690	605	85	78	24	17
S.C.	61,649	1,941	1,517	424	2,946	126	668
S.D.	82,518	585	365	220	3,220	134	642
Tenn.	82,056	3,177	2,438	739	3,142	144	739
Texas	262,059	10,021	7,355	2,666	13,163	1,250	65,966
Utah	48,982	941	641	300	1,659	93	1,118
Vt.	13,979[5]	336	265	71	775	60	177
Va.	64,782	3,330	2,837	493	3,716	249	824
Wash.	83,924	3,048	2,221	827	4,870	350	783
W.Va.	37,527	1,170	795	375	3,450	71	3,511
Wis.	106,238	2,734	2,258	476	5,669	332	926
Wyo.	34,502	395	224	171	1,767	93	7,151
TOTAL	3,885,452	149,068	117,147	31,921	191,205	14,069	227,066

[1] Includes federally controlled roads. [2] Estimated registration, excluding military. Detail may not add to totals because of rounding. [3] Petroleum and products only. [4] 1976. [5] 1977. [6] Included with Maryland. Sources: ICC; Dept. of Transportation, FAA, FHWA; Dept. of Energy; Motor Vehicles Manufacturers Assn.

Communications Facilities

State	Post Offices Oct. 5, 1979	TELEPHONES Jan. 1, 1978 Total	Residential	COMMERCIAL BROADCAST STATIONS, 1977 Radio AM	FM	TV	Public TV stations 1977	NEWSPAPERS Sept. 30, 1978 Daily Number	Circulation	Weekly* Number	Circulation	Sunday Number	Circulation
Alabama	619	2,309,442	1,763,468	138	75	17	9	25	738,822	109	462,548	17	684,941
Alaska	190	223,000	124,880	22	11	7	4	7	88,267	11	22,005	1	51,658
Arizona	212	1,629,694	1,183,229	62	32	11	2	17	575,322	51	449,819	6	524,715
Arkansas	639	1,331,712	1,007,219	86	56	8	4	33	479,259	117	348,231	15	462,381
California	1,119	18,103,632	12,965,153	231	198	56	14	124	6,201,738	435	5,600,835	47	5,484,375
Colorado	407	2,037,835	1,441,313	71	50	11	2	28	869,111	117	519,310	9	873,792
Connecticut	246	2,520,885	1,879,009	38	25	5	4	25	917,703	52	494,759	7	680,446
Delaware	55	487,227	358,752	10	8	—	—	3	157,414	14	95,633	2	124,457
District of Columbia	1	1,041,487	507,008	7	10	5	—	2	887,983	...	...	2	1,095,663
Florida	460	6,820,674	5,048,481	202	114	31	10	50	2,450,091	132	752,639	33	2,483,444
Georgia	643	3,727,524	2,783,986	180	90	18	10	37	1,060,853	204	1,048,955	15	1,038,802
Hawaii	76	630,021	409,514	25	7	10	2	5	237,600	3	102,803	2	216,990
Idaho	259	614,772	453,625	43	19	8	3	15	197,967	59	127,841	6	162,264
Illinois	1,265	9,442,720	7,037,941	124	131	22	6	89	3,362,318	583	3,227,328	22	2,761,788
Indiana	753	3,879,655	2,998,622	86	100	20	7	78	1,645,823	185	638,252	18	1,183,149
Iowa	952	2,142,508	1,623,936	76	71	14	8	41	898,176	341	770,225	9	752,397
Kansas	693	1,790,992	1,346,901	59	43	12	2	51	643,635	231	433,732	15	452,500
Kentucky	1,225	2,123,529	1,615,217	119	85	11	14	27	775,835	143	576,308	12	617,577
Louisiana	530	2,591,942	1,972,465	95	63	15	3	26	845,048	97	510,889	14	792,194
Maine	494	741,924	574,031	37	31	7	5	9	284,122	38	161,348	1	115,359
Maryland	426	3,241,071	2,433,847	50	36	6	4	13	692,382	75	780,087	4	665,449
Massachusetts	424	4,298,362	3,136,615	65	44	12	3	47	2,029,935	145	1,137,158	9	1,532,638
Michigan	857	6,769,342	5,157,834	127	116	24	7	52	2,458,083	256	1,517,694	17	2,366,033
Minnesota	857	2,967,265	2,195,605	91	67	13	5	30	1,088,818	332	988,635	11	1,042,390
Mississippi	464	1,403,614	1,086,842	106	69	10	8	25	393,665	99	285,195	12	308,520
Missouri	965	3,533,552	2,644,819	111	73	22	3	53	1,663,481	272	1,573,006	19	1,159,385
Montana	368	544,655	400,146	45	21	12	—	11	196,215	67	139,582	7	192,994
Nebraska	547	1,200,836	898,301	48	31	14	9	19	492,880	197	458,538	5	388,916
Nevada	91	627,027	421,930	22	12	7	1	9	198,504	16	40,390	5	189,586
New Hampshire	241	642,993	490,445	28	17	1	5	9	184,791	25	179,441	2	73,413
New Jersey	520	6,127,506	4,580,224	38	35	5	4	28	1,743,278	189	1,656,645	15	1,485,198
New Mexico	327	755,964	531,159	56	29	9	3	21	263,465	21	150,570	14	243,620
New York	1,628	13,187,030	9,473,921	160	121	30	12	79	6,952,145	398	2,504,768	34	6,494,994
North Carolina	775	3,711,050	2,802,560	209	87	18	9	52	1,357,482	118	524,118	24	1,121,392
North Dakota	441	477,873	353,169	26	11	11	2	10	163,519	89	178,065	3	96,366
Ohio	1,082	7,548,359	5,730,280	123	134	24	12	96	3,345,567	240	1,526,703	27	2,494,746
Oklahoma	628	2,119,319	1,558,758	67	52	10	4	54	877,640	194	367,411	46	894,932
Oregon	348	1,759,050	1,277,392	80	33	12	4	22	676,798	92	615,680	5	581,356
Pennsylvania	1,780	9,260,846	7,054,558	177	125	25	9	105	3,865,354	222	1,540,966	14	3,009,955
Rhode Island	55	681,794	514,498	15	7	2	1	7	313,627	14	85,017	2	230,634
South Carolina	392	1,874,630	1,408,508	108	56	11	7	20	592,554	71	269,533	8	474,381
South Dakota	403	473,256	355,047	33	18	11	6	13	177,316	144	195,099	4	124,649
Tennessee	567	2,921,239	2,209,312	155	75	18	5	32	1,120,447	125	554,472	14	1,002,156
Texas	1,500	9,572,605	6,922,203	288	183	55	7	114	3,434,553	500	1,307,823	89	3,677,481
Utah	211	936,932	688,531	34	19	3	2	5	267,702	52	172,248	4	264,747
Vermont	286	329,812	240,264	19	15	2	4	8	122,386	18	59,237	3	77,359
Virginia	895	3,499,260	2,597,740	137	76	14	7	33	1,080,686	99	608,234	13	826,871
Washington	465	2,786,380	2,036,544	92	48	14	6	23	1,117,464	138	1,052,847	13	1,059,327
West Virginia	1,020	1,037,003	793,075	62	31	9	3	28	478,979	73	266,399	9	389,505
Wisconsin	775	3,272,967	2,437,777	100	95	17	7	36	1,229,442	235	742,346	8	899,841
Wyoming	167	319,379	225,943	30	11	5	—	10	93,752	28	71,516	3	62,307
TOTAL U.S.	30,343	162,072,146	119,752,597	4,413	2,966	714	268	1,756	61,989,997	7,466	37,892,883	696	53,990,033

*Excluding District of Columbia; data for Sept. 30, 1977. Sources: U.S. Postal Service; Federal Communications Commission; American Telephone and Telegraph Co.; The Editor & Publisher Co., Inc., *International Year Book, 1979* (Copyright 1979. All rights reserved. Used by permission.); National Newspaper Association; Corporation for Public Broadcasting.

Major Trading Partners, by Value

in millions of dollars

Country	EXPORTS 1973	1978	IMPORTS 1973	1978
North America	20,174	39,376	22,810	46,170
Canada	15,104[1]	28,372	17,715	33,529
Mexico	2,937	6,681	2,306	6,093
South America	4,858	10,990	4,513	10,308
Argentina	451	842	278	563
Brazil	1,916	2,978	1,189	2,831
Chile	248	725	102	385
Colombia	437	1,046	409	1,044
Peru	415	501	375	654
Venezuela	1,033	3,727	1,787	3,545
Europe	23,160	43,615	19,812	37,988
Belgium and Luxembourg	1,623	3,653	1,273	1,762
France	2,263	4,166	1,732	4,054
Germany, West	3,756	6,957	5,345	9,961
Italy	2,119	3,360	2,002	4,103
Netherlands, The	2,859	5,683	934	1,603
Spain	1,319	1,884	762	1,255
Sweden	542	1,091	757	1,328
Switzerland	960	1,732	817	1,820
United Kingdom	3,564	7,119	3,656	6,513
U.S.S.R.	1,194	2,252	220	540
Asia	18,644	40,762	18,183	58,405
Hong Kong	740	1,625	1,450	3,474
India	527	948	437	980
Indonesia	442	751	505	3,607
Iran	772	3,684	343	2,877
Israel	962	1,925	269	719
Japan	8,313	12,885	9,676	24,458
Korea, South	1,237	3,160	974	3,747
Malaysia	157	728	440	1,519
Philippines	495	1,040	670	1,207
Saudi Arabia	442	4,370	515	5,307
Singapore	684	1,462	467	1,103
Taiwan	1,170	2,340	1,784	5,171
Oceania	1,744	3,462	1,562	2,351
Australia	1,439	2,910	1,067	1,659
Africa	2,081	4,752	2,557	16,793
Algeria	161	374	215	3,482
Nigeria	161	985	652	4,714
South Africa[2]	746	1,090	377	2,264
Total	71,389[1]	143,660[1]	69,832[1]	172,205[1]

[1]Includes shipments to or from unidentified countries. [2]Includes Namibia.
Source: U.S. Department of Commerce, Domestic and International Business Administration, *Overseas Business Reports.*

Major Commodities Traded, 1978

in millions of dollars

Item	Total[1]	Canada	American Republics	Western Europe	Far East[2]
TOTAL EXPORTS	143,660	28,372[3]	20,183	39,936	26,390
Agricultural commodities					
Grains and preparations	11,634	101	1,478	2,152	3,047
Soybeans	5,210	97	232	2,928	1,354
Cotton, including linters, wastes	1,766	70	15	210	1,244
Nonagricultural commodities					
Ores and scrap metals	1,141	243	71	452	312
Coal, coke, and briquettes	2,123	751	150	539	633
Chemicals	12,618	1,739	2,679	4,275	2,428
Machinery	38,022	7,707	6,710	10,521	5,409
Agricultural machines, tractors, parts	3,238	1,095	679	642	208
Electrical apparatus	7,211	908	1,285	1,821	1,973
Transport equipment[4]	18,775	8,092	2,528	2,994	1,749
Civilian aircraft and parts	5,907	366	576	2,140	1,253
Paper manufactures	1,597	366	357	400	189
Metal manufactures	3,107	1,040	448	567	266
Iron and steel mill products[5]	1,644	433	464	207	186
Yarn, fabrics, and clothing	1,893	337	499	610	155
Other exports	44,130	7,396	4,552	14,081	9,418
TOTAL IMPORTS	172,025	33,529	18,560	36,484	46,160
Agricultural commodities					
Meat and preparations	1,856	109	383	278	11
Fish	2,212	519	533	400	480
Coffee	3,728	—	2,660	4	239
Sugar	917	46	471	83	183
Nonagricultural commodities					
Ores and scrap metal	2,850	953	466	95	73
Petroleum, crude	32,140	1,246	3,004	1,390	2,951
Petroleum products	6,968	489	2,302	454	409
Chemicals	5,427	1,805	312	3,227	687
Machinery	24,752	3,505	1,649	7,646	11,751
Transport equipment	22,873	8,773	295	5,187	8,549
Automobiles, new	13,646	4,122	[6]	3,786	5,738
Iron and steel mill products	6,687	780	216	2,660	2,707
Nonferrous metals	4,367	1,384	616	1,046	728
Textiles other than clothing	2,200	53	220	685	1,092
Other imports	54,048	13,867	5,433	13,329	16,300

[1]Includes areas not shown separately. [2]Includes Japan, East and South Asia.
[3]Excludes grains and oilseeds transshipped through Canada to unidentified overseas countries. [4]Excludes parts for tractors. [5]Excludes pig iron.
[6]Less than $500,000. Source: U.S. Dept. of Commerce, Domestic and International Business Administration, *Overseas Business Reports.*

Upper Volta

A republic of West Africa, Upper Volta is bordered by Mali, Niger, Benin, Togo, Ghana, and Ivory Coast. Area: 274,200 sq km (105,869 sq mi). Pop. (1979 est.): 6,617,000. Cap. and largest city: Ouagadougou (pop., 1975, 172,700). Language: French (official). Religion: animist 49.8%; Muslim 16.6%; Roman Catholic 8.3%. President in 1979, Gen. Sangoulé Lamizana; premier, Joseph Conombo.

Gen. Sangoulé Lamizana's presidential regime in Upper Volta continued in 1979 to be confronted by serious difficulties, particularly because of the unceasing wage demands of the labour unions. Three political parties were established by a law passed by the National Assembly on May 29. They were: the Voltaic Democratic Union, a local section of the African Democratic Rally, with 28 seats in the Assembly; the National Union for the Defense of Democracy, with 13 seats; and the Voltaic Progressist Union, with 9 seats. All other parties were forbidden.

In March an ambitious nationwide ten-year health program was adopted for 1980–90. It envisaged 7,000 village health centres, 515 health and promotion centres for population groups of 15,000 within areas 12 mi (19 km) in radius, regional and subregional medical centres, ten departmental (state) hospitals, two national hospitals, and a university centre of health sciences at Ouagadougou. (PHILIPPE DECRAENE)

UPPER VOLTA

Education. (1978–79) Primary, pupils 159,948, teachers 3,204; secondary, pupils 15,271, teachers 817; vocational, pupils 1,852, teachers 175; teacher training, students 495, teachers (1977–78) 33; higher (1977–78), students 1,673, teaching staff 124.

Finance. Monetary unit: CFA franc, with (Sept. 17, 1979) a par value of CFA Fr 50 to the French franc (free rate of CFA Fr 211.54 = U.S. $1; CFA Fr 455.12 = £1 sterling). Budget (1977 actual): revenue CFA Fr 27.3 billion; expenditure CFA Fr 22.3 billion.

Foreign Trade. (1977) Imports CFA Fr 51,360,000,000; exports CFA Fr 13,610,000,000. Import sources: France 45%; Ivory Coast 13%; U.S. 9%; West Germany 6%. Export destinations: Ivory Coast 32%; Denmark 22%; The Netherlands 11%; France 7%; Taiwan 6%. Main exports (1976): cotton 46%; karité nuts 16%; livestock 12%; peanuts 5%.

Uruguay

A republic of South America, Uruguay is on the Atlantic Ocean and is bounded by Brazil and Argentina. Area: 176,215 sq km (68,037 sq mi). Pop. (1978 est.): 2,864,000, including (1961) white 89%; mestizo 10%. Cap. and largest city: Montevideo (pop., 1975, 1,229,700). Language: Spanish. Religion: mainly Roman Catholic. President in 1979, Aparicio Méndez.

During 1979 Uruguay's military-appointed government prepared the groundwork for the promised general elections of 1981. The scheduled retirement of Gen. Gregorio Alvarez as commander in chief of the Army in February was effected without difficulty; he was succeeded by Gen. Luis Queirolo. Soon afterward a charter of political parties was announced, followed in May by the publication of a new labour code. Many former politicians were still banned from political activity. Answering the allegation of a human rights group abroad that the government held 6,000 political prisoners, Col. Frederico Silva Ledesma, head of the Supreme Military Tribunal, stated that on June 30 there were 1,670 such prisoners, 90% of whom had been brought to trial.

The economy expanded more rapidly in 1979 than in any other year of the decade. The increase in gross domestic product was estimated at 6%, compared with 2.5% in 1978. A major factor was the increase in Argentine tourists seeking to escape the high prices in their country. The giant 1,890-Mw Salto Grande hydroelectric project came on stream in August, benefiting Uruguayan as well as Argentine consumers. However, the higher cost of imported petroleum and the rise in the world price of beef pushed the inflation rate to about 68%, compared with 46% in 1978. (PAUL DOWBOR)

URUGUAY

Education. (1976) Primary, pupils 382,759, teachers 15,679; secondary, pupils 138,000, teachers 13,980; vocational, pupils 50,000, teachers 4,200; teacher training, students (1975) 5,034, teachers (1973) 341; higher, students 39,927, teaching staff 2,149.

Finance. Monetary unit: new peso, with (Sept. 17, 1979) a free rate of 8.09 new pesos to U.S. $1 (17.40 new pesos = £1 sterling). Gold, SDR's, and foreign exchange (May 1979) U.S. $408 million. Budget (1978 actual): revenue 4,349,800,000 new pesos; expenditure 4,759,400,000 new pesos. Gross national product (1977) 19,890,300,000 new pesos. Cost of living: (Montevideo; 1975 = 100; June 1979) 546.7.

Foreign Trade. (1978) Imports U.S. $757.3 million; exports U.S. $688.1 million. Import sources (1977): Brazil 13%; Argentina 12%; U.S. 10%; Iraq 9%; West Germany 7%; Nigeria 7%; U.K. 5%. Export destinations: Brazil 19%; U.S. 17%; West Germany 12%; The Netherlands 7%; Argentina 6%. Main exports (1976): meat 24%; wool 20%; clothing 10%; cereals 8%; leather 6%.

Transport and Communications. Roads (1977) 24,954 km. Motor vehicles in use (1976): passenger 127,100; commercial (including buses) 104,200. Railways (1977): 2,987 km; traffic 389 million passenger-km, freight 307 million net ton-km. Air traffic (1977): 74 million passenger-km; freight 300,000 net ton-km. Shipping (1978): merchant vessels 100 gross tons and over 48; gross tonnage 174,357. Telephones (Jan. 1978) 268,000. Radio receivers (Dec. 1976) 1.6 million. Television receivers (Dec. 1976) 355,000.

Agriculture. Production (in 000; metric tons; 1978): wheat *c.* 150; corn 172; rice 226; sorghum 184; potatoes 102; sweet potatoes (1977) *c.* 85; sugar, raw value *c.* 230; linseed 40; sunflower seed 72; apples *c.* 26; oranges *c.* 44; grapes *c.* 80; wool 45; beef and veal *c.* 354. Livestock (in 000; May 1978): cattle *c.* 9,424; sheep (1977) 16,030; pigs *c.* 445; horses (1977) 490; chickens (1977) *c.* 7,500.

Industry. Production (in 000; metric tons; 1977): crude steel 17; cement 682; petroleum products *c.* 1,760; electricity (kw-hr) *c.* 3,040,000.

Upper Volta

Uruguay

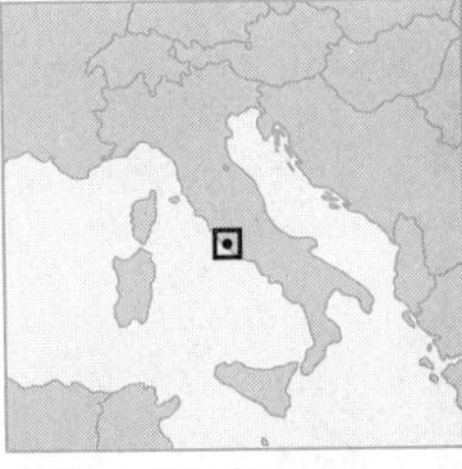
Vatican City State

Vatican City State

This independent sovereignty is surrounded by but is not part of Rome. As a state with territorial limits, it is properly distinguished from the Holy See, which constitutes the worldwide administrative and legislative body for the Roman Catholic Church. The area of Vatican City is 44 ha (108.8

Universities:
see Education

Urban Mass Transit:
see Transportation

U.S.S.R.:
see Union of Soviet Socialist Republics

GIANI GIANSANTI—GAMMA/LIAISON

The body of Jean Cardinal Villot, a member of the Roman Curia, lay in state at the Vatican following his death on March 9.

Venezuela

ac). Pop. (1978 est.): 729. As sovereign pontiff, John Paul II is the chief of state. Vatican City is administered by a pontifical commission of five cardinals headed by the secretary of state, in 1979 Jean Cardinal Villot to March 9 and, from July 1, Agostino Cardinal Casaroli.

Three great journeys, to Mexico in January 1979, to Poland in June, and to Ireland and the U.S. in September and October, highlighted the first 12 months of Pope John Paul II's pontificate. The pope reaffirmed the rights and dignity of the human individual in his first encyclical, *Redemptor hominis* (March 15, 1979). In a new system of internal organization, the pope exercised his episcopal role more directly, visiting parishes, blessing marriages in his private chapel, baptizing infants, and receiving sick children.

The pope filled gaps that had appeared in the hierarchy, notably in the Roman Curia. After the death of Jean Cardinal Villot (*see* OBITUARIES) on March 9, he appointed Msgr. Agostino Casaroli (*see* BIOGRAPHY) to succeed him as acting secretary of state on April 30. The appointment was confirmed on July 1.

At his first consistory, on June 30, John Paul II elevated to the cardinalate Casaroli and 13 other prelates. A 15th, reserved secretly (in petto), was thought to be a Lithuanian bishop. From November 5 to 8, 121 cardinals met in Rome for an extraordinary "consultation" to hear the pope's report on the state of the church and to discuss pressing church problems, including Vatican finances and the role of the Curia. In the course of the meeting they were given previously secret information on the Vatican's finances, which were said to be in some difficulty. (MAX BERGERRE)

See also Religion: *Roman Catholic Church.*

Venezuela

A republic of northern South America, Venezuela is bounded by Colombia, Brazil, Guyana, and the Caribbean Sea. Area: 899,180 sq km (347,175 sq mi). Pop. (1979 est.): 13,515,000, including mestizo 69%; white 20%; Negro 9%; Indian 2%. Cap. and largest city: Caracas (metro area pop., 1979 est., 2,850,000). Language: Spanish. Religion: predominantly Roman Catholic. Presidents in 1979, Carlos Andrés Pérez and, from March 12, Luis Herrera Campins.

Pres. Luis Herrera Campins (*see* BIOGRAPHIES) of the Social Christian Party (COPEI) took office on March 12, 1979, having won the general election the previous December. His party came into office on a wave of popular support that carried it on to win the municipal elections in June with 50.2% of the total vote, leaving the principal opposition party, Acción Democrática (AD), in complete disarray. The outgoing government of Carlos Andrés Pérez had been repeatedly criticized for overspending, corruption, and inefficiency, and expectations for the new government were high.

President Herrera pledged to improve agriculture, education, and social services and to spend less on massive industrial projects. Plans were drawn to encourage construction of low-cost housing, and many major projects, including a planned steelworks in Zulia State, were postponed indefinitely. However, Herrera was criticized for delays in making pronouncements on economic policies and programs. There were no changes in economic or financial matters for several months after his inauguration.

Oil production rose in 1979, as the country took advantage of the decline in Iranian oil exports and steadily rising oil prices. By the time the Organization of Petroleum Exporting Countries met in Caracas in December, Venezuelan oil was selling at U.S. $24 a barrel, and shortly thereafter it was raised to $26 as of Jan. 1, 1980. By September 22 output had reached an annual average of 2,341,888 bbl a day, 10.84% above the same period of 1978. Offshore exploration yielded three auspicious strikes of light crude oil and gas. Exploration work also began in the Orinoco heavy-oil belt. A new policy was announced for the negotiation of contracts with petroleum companies, whereby the confidentiality clause would be eliminated so that information could pass freely between the four subsidiary companies of Petróleos de Venezuela; royalty fees on the basis of barrels produced or refined would also be abolished. Contracts would be negotiated for shorter terms, and more oil would be sold directly to consumers.

In a message to the nation at the end of September, President Herrera said oil export revenues would rise by 40% to $12 billion in 1979, while imports would grow by only 4% to around $11.4 billion; a trade surplus of $850 million could be expected, resulting in a current account deficit of a little under $3 billion. The president said he had inherited a $26 billion debt from Pérez and the 1979 budget would be in deficit by about $3 billion.

On June 30 William Niehous, general manager of the Owens-Illinois Glass Co., who had been kidnapped in February 1976, was rescued after a gun battle in which police killed two guerrillas who were guarding him. It was rumoured that the government had been negotiating his release in return for an amnesty for his captors and that they had in fact surrendered before they were shot; that his company had been on the point of paying a 30 million bolívar ransom; and that the police acted without consultation or coordination with other departments. Niehous was rushed out of Venezuela within hours of his release.

Venezuela maintained its policy of involvement in matters pertaining to neighbouring countries and to the third world in general. Relations with the Caribbean nations were strengthened, and Venezuela played an active part in granting aid to those countries that suffered damage from Hurricane David in September. Venezuela's influence in the Andean Pact helped to unify the members'

VENEZUELA

Education. (1976–77) Primary, pupils 2,203,574, teachers (including preprimary) 94,218; secondary and vocational, pupils 690,571; teacher training, students 19,863; secondary, vocational, and teacher training, teachers 46,964; higher, students 221,581, teaching staff 16,185.

Finance. Monetary unit: bolívar, with (Sept. 17, 1979) a par value of 4.29 bolivares to U.S. $1 (free rate of 9.16 bolivares = £1 sterling). Gold, SDR's, and foreign exchange (June 1979) U.S. $5,328,000,000. Budget (1978 actual): revenue 40,105,000,000 bolivares; expenditure 48,909,000,000 bolivares. Gross national product (1978) 171,860,000,000 bolivares. Money supply (May 1979) 40,171,000,000 bolivares. Cost of living (Caracas; 1975 = 100; June 1979) 136.2.

Foreign Trade. (1978) Imports (fob) *c.* 38.7 billion bolivares; exports 39,186,000,000 bolivares. Import sources (1977): U.S. 39%; West Germany 12%; Japan 11%; Italy 6%. Export destinations (1977): U.S. 36%; Netherlands Antilles *c.* 18%; Canada 12%. Main exports: crude oil 61%; petroleum products 35%.

Transport and Communications. Roads (1976) 58,560 km. Motor vehicles in use (1977): passenger 1,172,400; commercial (including buses) 488,000. Railways: (1977) *c.* 420 km; traffic (1971) 42 million passenger-km, freight 15 million net ton-km. Air traffic (1977): 3,072,000,000 passenger-km; freight 118.2 million net ton-km. Shipping (1978): merchant vessels 100 gross tons and over 201; gross tonnage 823,543. Telephones (Jan. 1978) 847,300. Radio receivers (Dec. 1976) 5,034,000. Television receivers (Dec. 1976) 1,431,000.

Agriculture. Production (in 000; metric tons; 1978): corn *c.* 740; rice *c.* 600; sorghum *c.* 500; potatoes *c.* 204; cassava (1977) *c.* 370; sugar, raw value *c.* 402; tomatoes *c.* 110; sesame seed *c.* 56; bananas *c.* 1,080; oranges *c.* 255; coffee *c.* 72; cocoa *c.* 18; tobacco *c.* 15; sisal *c.* 20; cotton, lint *c.* 21; beef and veal *c.* 282. Livestock (in 000; 1978): cattle *c.* 10,231; pigs *c.* 2,057; sheep *c.* 105; goats *c.* 1,288; horses (1977) *c.* 463; asses (1977) *c.* 569; poultry *c.* 31,000.

Industry. Production (in 000; metric tons; 1978): crude oil 113,044; natural gas (cu m; 1977) *c.* 12 million; petroleum products (1977) 48,897; iron ore (64% metal content) 13,690; cement (1977) 3,292; gold (troy oz; 1977) 17; diamonds (metric carats; 1976) 833; electricity (kw-hr; 1977) 23,051,000.

WIDE WORLD

Luis Herrera Campins took office on March 12 as the 47th president of Venezuela.

policy toward Nicaragua in support of the Sandinista guerrillas. After the overthrow of Pres. Anastasio Somoza, Venezuela was one of the first to offer aid to the new regime. (SARAH CAMERON)

Veterinary Science

A major event during 1979 was the 21st congress of the World Veterinary Association (WVA). Held every four years and attended by many of the world's leading veterinary scientists, the congress took place for the first time in the U.S.S.R. It drew more than 4,000 veterinarians from 60 countries to Moscow at the beginning of July.

While few new developments were reported in the hundreds of papers presented at the congress, the wide range they covered demonstrated the great gulf between the developed and less developed countries in the application of veterinary technology to food animal production. The congress agreed on implementing a number of measures aimed at putting into effect its stated theme, "Veterinary science for the good of mankind." These included raising the quality of veterinary services so as to improve production of food and raw materials (wool, leather, etc.) from animals while at the same time safeguarding animal health and welfare. Also called for were developments in the control of epizootics (outbreaks of disease in which many animals of the same kind are affected at the same time). The WVA was to set up a working group to investigate the control of insect-transmitted diseases, and it urged that practical steps be taken to improve control of parasitic diseases in cattle and other animals.

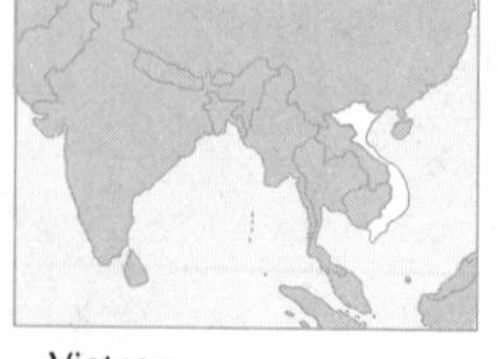
Vietnam

The feeding of low doses of antibiotics to aid the rate of growth of poultry and livestock, widespread in some areas, caused concern. The risk was that potentially harmful microorganisms develop resistance to antibiotics. *Salmonella* organisms in particular, frequently found in animals, can cause food poisoning in humans and have been found to develop resistance that, once established, persists. Thus infection caused by such resistant organisms could be difficult to control by the more usual antibiotics. As of 1979, however, efforts to restrict antibiotics used as growth promoters to types not used for therapeutic purposes had not proved particularly successful.

In Africa groundwork for an attack on trypanosomiasis ("sleeping sickness") intensified. The disease causes serious socioeconomic effects in 35 countries, affecting humans and cattle in a total area of 10 million sq km (3.8 million sq mi). It is carried by the tsetse fly (*Glossina*), and training of personnel from affected areas in fly-control techniques was being conducted in a joint operation by the Food and Agriculture Organization, the World Health Organization, and the Organization of African Unity. While biological methods might become practicable in the future, more conventional ground and aerial spraying of insecticides currently offered the best solution. Eradicating the disease was fundamental to the development of vast tracts of potentially prosperous territory.

As testing for toxicity in products ranging from drugs to toiletries became more stringent, increasing numbers of laboratory animals had to be used. The search for alternatives was spurred on not only by those who wished to protect the animals but also by drug companies, which were seeking more reliable and cheaper methods. Tissue cultures grown in laboratories were being used to an increasing extent for certain preliminary tests. Computer modeling was also finding application in streamlining test procedures, which, it was hoped, would reduce the number of animals required. (EDWARD BODEN)

[353.c]

Vietnam

The Socialist Republic of Vietnam is a southeast Asian state bordered in the north by China, in the west by Laos and Cambodia, and in the south and east by the South China Sea. Area: 329,465 sq km

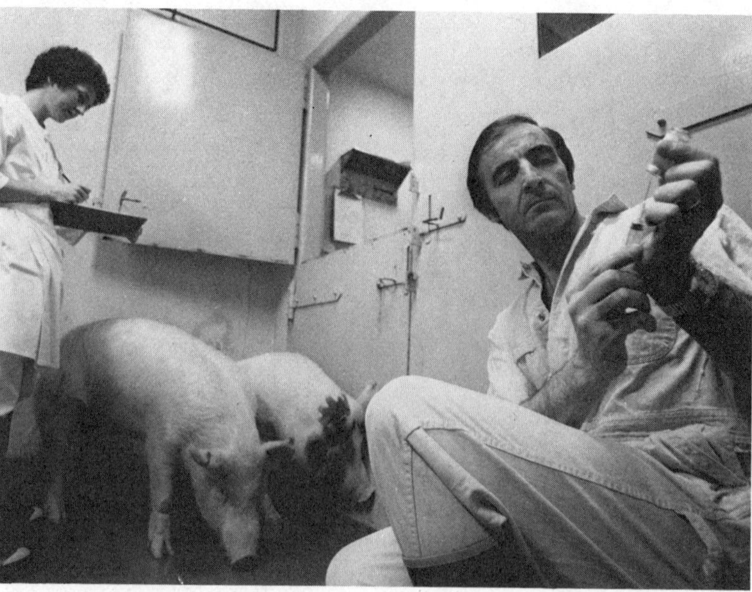
William L. Mengeling of the National Animal Disease Center, Ames, Iowa, prepares to test a vaccine that may prevent porcine parvovirus, a virulent disease affecting pigs.

SCIENCE AND EDUCATION ADMINISTRATION—USDA

WIDE WORLD

A wall map in Hanoi showed the locations of the fighting in April after Chinese troops invaded Vietnam.

(127,207 sq mi). Pop. (1979 est.): 51,883,000. Capitol: Hanoi (pop., 1976 est., 1,443,500). Largest city: Ho Chi Minh City (pop., 1976 est., 3,460,500). Language: Vietnamese, French, English. Religion: Buddhist, animist, Confucian, Christian (Roman Catholic), Hoa Hao and Cao Dai religious sects. Secretary of the Communist Party in 1979, Le Duan; president, Ton Duc Thang; premier, Pham Van Dong.

Vietnam was back in the thick of war in 1979. A full-fledged invasion of Cambodia began with the dawn of the new year, resulting in the fall of Phnom Penh on January 7 to a new Khmer junta chosen by Hanoi. Within weeks there were reports of a massive Chinese military buildup along Vietnam's northern border. U.S. intelligence sources estimated that 150,000 men had moved into positions, roughly similar to Vietnamese claims of 20 infantry divisions, "hundreds of fighter planes and other war equipment." In Washington, D.C., for an official visit, Chinese Vice-Premier Deng Xiaoping (Teng Hsiao-p'ing) pointedly warned that China, "in the interest of peace and stability," could be forced to "teach a lesson" to the "Cubans of the East."

On February 17 massive columns of Chinese troops marched through mountain passes and river valleys into Vietnam in the first intra-Communist war in Asia. The multipronged advance along the entire 450-mi border was accompanied by Chinese declarations that the operation would be "limited" and that Chinese troops would withdraw as soon as Vietnam had been "punished." Peking's apparent calculation that the Soviet Union would not intervene on Vietnam's behalf was borne out by events; despite a November 1978 mutual security pact that obliged Moscow to take "appropriate effective measures" if Vietnam were threatened by external aggression, the Soviets confined themselves to verbal support.

After nine days of fighting, however, there were serious doubts whether China had succeeded in giving Vietnam the "bloody nose" it claimed. Its troops drove 25 mi into the provinces of Hoang Lien Son (Lao Cai) and Cao Bang, with the important rail town of Lang Son being the centrepiece of the war. Altogether, China assembled 170,000 men, 700 warplanes, and 250–300 tanks for the offensive. The Vietnamese strategy aimed at

VIETNAM

Education. (1977–78) Primary and secondary, pupils 11.4 million; vocational, pupils 125,000; primary, secondary, and vocational, teachers (1975–76) 313,442; higher, students 134,000, teaching staff (1975–76) 9,642.

Finance. Monetary unit: dong, with (Sept. 17, 1979) a free rate of 2.18 dong to U.S. $1 (4.69 dong = £1 sterling). Budget (1977 est.) balanced at 8,950,000,000 dong.

Foreign Trade. (1978) Imports *c.* U.S. $1.5 billion; exports U.S. *c.* $416 million. Import sources: U.S.S.R. *c.* 30%; Japan *c.* 16%; France *c.* 7%; Italy *c.* 5%; East Germany *c.* 5%. Export destinations: U.S.S.R. *c.* 54%; Japan *c.* 11%. Main exports (1974): clothing *c.* 10%; fish *c.* 10%; rubber *c.* 10%; coal *c.* 5%; beverages *c.* 5%.

Transport and Communications. Roads (1977) *c.* 60,000 km. Motor vehicles in use (1976): passenger *c.* 100,000; commercial (including buses) *c.* 200,000. Railways: (1977) *c.* 4,230 km. Navigable waterways (1977) *c.* 6,000 km. Telephones (South only; Dec. 1973) 47,000. Radio receivers (Dec. 1976) *c.* 5 million. Television receivers (Dec. 1976) *c.* 2 million.

Agriculture. Production (in 000; metric tons; 1978): rice 9,880; sweet potatoes (1977) *c.* 1,330; cassava (1977) *c.* 1,500; bananas *c.* 520; tea (1977) *c.* 10; coffee (1977) *c.* 5; tobacco *c.* 23; jute *c.* 37; rubber (1977) *c.* 36; pork *c.* 440; fish catch (1977) *c.* 1,010; timber (cu m; 1977) *c.* 18,832. Livestock (in 000; 1977): cattle 1,550; buffalo *c.* 2,300; pigs *c.* 9,100; chickens *c.* 57,300; ducks *c.* 33,000.

Industry. Production (in 000; metric tons; 1977): coal *c.* 6,200; cement *c.* 700; salt *c.* 375; phosphate rock *c.* 1,500; phosphate fertilizers (1977–78) *c.* 126; electricity (kw-hr) 3,473,000.

avoiding a frontal clash. Its 19 regular divisions committed to Cambodia remained there. The two combat divisions and two training divisions in the north of the country were deployed to form a defense arc halfway between Hanoi and the border. The task of actually taking on the invading forces was left to 50,000 to 80,000 militiamen and frontier security guards.

These forces apparently succeeded in slowing down the Chinese advance and giving as good as they got. The Chinese seemed to get bogged down in many places, and the absence of progress reports from Peking spread the impression that the operation was proving more difficult than had been anticipated. Vietnam, on the other hand, showed unusual confidence when, in the midst of the war, it sent Premier Pham Van Dong on a state visit to Phnom Penh to sign a treaty of "peace and friendship" with the new Cambodian junta.

For all its show of nonchalance, Vietnam suffered severely from the war. Observers noted that a Chinese objective was clearly the crippling of the economic infrastructure in occupied border areas through the destruction of factories, farms, forest reserves, and power plants. Hanoi reported that 60,000 sq m of housing were destroyed, 85,000 ha of rice fields burned or abandoned, and 150,000 water buffalo and cows killed.

Despite the subsequent withdrawal of Chinese troops and the convening of several rounds of Sino-Vietnamese peace talks, tension along the border persisted throughout the year. Hanoi regularly spoke of continuing war preparations by China, while Peking did nothing to dispel fears that it might choose to teach Vietnam a "second lesson" at any moment. Cambodia remained the main bone of contention between the two countries, as each accused the other of expansionism and aggression.

The Sino-Vietnamese war turned the lot of Vietnam's 1.1 million ethnic Chinese into tragedy. Mostly businessmen and storekeepers, the Chinese in former South Vietnam had already been hit hard by the abolition of capitalism. As relations with China deteriorated, Hanoi saw its citizens of Chinese extraction as a fifth column, and their harassment and expulsion rapidly became systematic. During the buildup to the war, some 200,000 ethnic Chinese either fled or were pushed across the land frontier into China.

Driven to panic by propaganda as well as repression, the Chinese population began an exodus by sea immediately after the war. It soon became evident that the Vietnamese government was facilitating their escape in return for payment, mostly in gold. By midyear, according to the best estimates, some 250,000 "boat people" had survived their ordeal and landed in various Southeast Asian and Pacific countries. It was believed that at least an equal number had perished at sea. (*See* REFUGEES: *Special Report.*)

The staggering proportions of the tragedy turned world sentiment against Vietnam. It was accused of racism as well as callousness. Hanoi, for its part, maintained that it was ready to arrange legal exits for those who wished to emigrate and that China was responsible for spreading panic among the population. At a UN conference on the refugee question held in Geneva in July, Vietnam pledged to increase supervision and put a stop to the outflow for six months. In August visiting U.S. congressional teams were told that 4,000 people had been prosecuted for attempting to leave the country illegally. The flow of refugees slowed to a trickle in the second half of the year, but this scarcely relieved Vietnam's isolation.

Hanoi suffered a blow to its prestige in July when an aging vice-chairman of the National Assembly's Standing Committee, Hoang Van Hoan, defected to China. Hanoi tried to downgrade the affair by saying that Hoang was a known partisan of China. Nonetheless, it admitted that the defection was "a grave offense against our country and our people."

The traumatic events of the year dealt a body blow to Vietnam's economy. According to Western business circles, per capita income was U.S. $150 a year, one of the lowest in Asia. The trade deficit for the year was expected to exceed $500 million. Almost 70% of imports were coming from the Soviet bloc. At the same time, most Western countries stopped aid programs in protest against the refugee situation and the invasion of Cambodia.

(T. J. S. GEORGE)

See also China.

Water Sports

Motorboating. Bill Muncey of La Mesa, Calif., again dominated the unlimited class hydroplane racing season, winning seven of nine events and raising his career total to 57 major victories. It was the seventh American Power Boat Association (APBA) national championship for the 51-year-old Muncey, now in his 29th season of hydroplane competition. His victory string—nine wins over a two-year-span—was highlighted by his eighth APBA Gold Cup at Madison, Ind., July 8. Muncey's boat was the Rolls-Royce-powered "Atlas Van Lines."

The first driver to stop Muncey's streak was Lee "Chip" Hanauer of Seattle, Wash., who drove "Squire Shop" in his first major win at the inaugural Utah Thunderboat Regatta on September 3 at Ogden, Utah. Another Seattle-area driver, Steve Reynolds, drove the new "Miss Circus-Circus" to victory in the final race of the season on Mission Bay, San Diego, Calif., on September 16.

An attempt to break the 200.419-mph straightaway speed record failed on Lake Washington, near Seattle, on October 22, when former national champion Dean Chenoweth's revolutionary "Miss Budweiser" crashed at a speed estimated at 215 mph. Chenoweth, of Tallahassee, Fla., was thrown 80 ft and suffered several broken ribs.

Other major developments included the addition of three new major race sites to the sport's circuit: Evansville, Ind., El Dorado/Wichita, Kan., and Ogden/Salt Lake City, Utah.

The year 1979 marked the appearance of catamaran hull designs on the offshore powerboat racing circuit. Betty Cook of Newport Beach, Calif., won the APBA U.S. championship with her victory in

Virgin Islands: see Dependent States
Vital Statistics: see Demography
Volleyball: see Court Games
Wages and Hours: see Economy, World; Industrial Relations
Wales: see United Kingdom
Warsaw Treaty Organization: see Defense
Water Resources: see Earth Sciences; Environment

CANADIAN PRESS

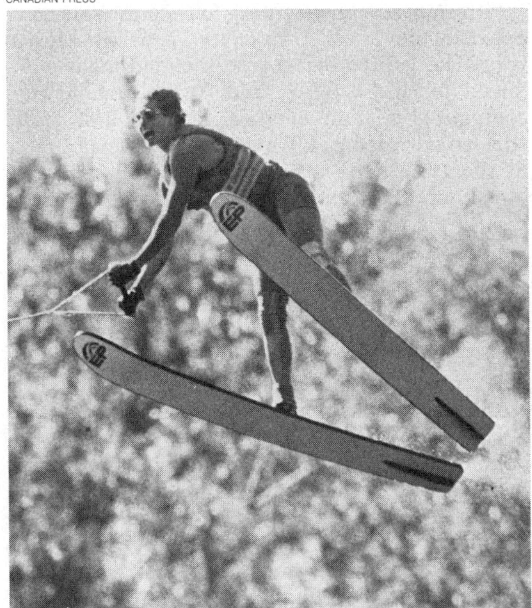

Cindy Todd of Pierson, Florida, retained her title as the world's best woman skier at the World Water Ski Championships held at Toronto in September.

the Benihana Grand Prix West at Oakland, Calif., on September 15. Her boat was the twin-hulled "Kaama," a 38-ft Cougar Catamaran. She went on to win her second world championship in Italy in October.

The U.S. title was decided in the final race of the season when point leader Howard Quam of Fort Lauderdale, Fla., driving his 38-ft "Flap Jack," was hampered by the thick fog off San Francisco Bay in the Benihana West event. Quam had won the Guy Lombardo/Halter Classic at Freeport, N.Y., June 2, while Cook won the Bacardi Trophy at Miami, Fla., on May 12 and the Manufacturers Bank/Spirit of Detroit race on the Detroit River on June 29. In winning the Detroit race she set a new world race record of 83.9 mph.

The offshore season was marred by serious injuries to sponsor/driver Rocky Aoki of New York City, owner of the Benihana restaurant chain. Aoki was injured in a practice accident the day before the final Oakland race.

(ALBERT W. LIMBURG)

River Sports. During 1979 there was a great increase in the use of aramid fibres, such as Kevlar, in canoes and kayaks. Fundamental improvements in design and construction caused an increase in the use of small (one to two person) inflatable craft for river running. While many new paddlers entered competition, the veterans still predominated at the U.S. National Championships held in Craftsbury Commons, Vt.

At the 15th world flat-water championships, held in Duisburg, West Germany, paddlers from the U.S.S.R., East Germany, and other Eastern European nations took home virtually all of the medals. Hungary's Tamas Wichmann won two events in the Canadian canoeing races, and Vladimir Partenovich of the U.S.S.R. won medals in the single and double kayak events.

The first white-water world championships to take place in the Western Hemisphere were held at Jonquière, Que. As usual, the best showings by U.S. paddlers were in the women's events, where Cathy Hearn placed first in slalom kayaking, and in one-man slalom canoeing, where Jon Lugbill, David Hearn, and Bob Robison took the first three places.

In marathon racing an unprecedented 15-day, 1,200-mi race was conducted from Hutchinson, Kan., to New Orleans, La., on the Arkansas and Mississippi rivers. Sixty-eight competitors, most

Powerboats turned the water to foam as the annual boat race from London to Calais, France, got under way on July 1.

KEYSTONE

in two-man open canoes, started in the race, and 30 finished it. The winners were Jim Short and Tom Johannsen of Springfield, Mo.

(ERIC LEAPER)

Water Skiing. Water skiers from Canada, the United States, Great Britain, France, and, for the first time, the Soviet Union shared honours at the 16th biennial World Water Ski Championships, which took place at Toronto in September. Canada's Joel McClintock won the men's world overall title, dethroning Mike Hazelwood of Great Britain, who settled for a victory in the jumping event. Cindy Todd of the U.S. successfully defended her women's overall title and also won the gold medal in jumping.

Patrice Martin of France was the winner in men's tricks, setting a new world mark of 8,140 points. Natalia Roumyantseva, a member of the Soviet team, scored an easy victory in the women's tricks event after setting a new world record of 6,200 points in Italy earlier in the year. Bob LaPoint, captain of the U.S. team, continued his mastery over the world's best slalom skiers by winning his second successive gold medal in that event. Canada's Patsy Messner won the women's slalom. U.S. skiers won the world title for the 16th time, with Canada second and Australia third among the 30 nations represented in the championships.

In U.S. national competition Ricky McCormick of Cypress Gardens, Fla., won the men's open overall title for the third year in a row. However, veteran women contenders took a backseat to Karin Roberge, a 16-year-old newcomer to open competition, who not only won the national open overall crown but upset the favourites in the Masters as well. (THOMAS C. HARDMAN)

Surfing. The rebirth of the *Surfer* magazine poll contest awards for the most popular men and women surfers of 1978 marked the end of an era that had begun in 1969. Then, contests and winning were being questioned and so popularity polls became taboo. But in 1979, with winning back in style, Shaun Tomson of South Africa, the 1977 International Professional Surfing (IPS) winner, took first place. Australia's Wayne "Rabbit" Bartholomew, the 1978 IPS winner, was second. The top-ranked woman was Margo Godfrey Oberg of Hawaii, who had dominated women's surfing for a decade.

Money continued to dominate the conversation among the professionals. In spite of the seemingly generous purse for 1979 of approximately $350,000, most participants in the world contests had empty pocketbooks. Part of the problem was that Hawaii offered about $60,000, compared with Australia's total of about $200,000 in prize money.

(JACK FLANAGAN)

Water Polo. The year 1979 would be remembered as the one in which the U.S. emerged as a world water polo power. The U.S. national team competed in four major international tournaments, placing first in all but one, the World Cup. In that event, with the top eight teams from the previous world championships participating, Hungary defeated the U.S. 4–3 to win the championship while host Yugoslavia took third.

Fifteen teams representing four continents competed in the World University Games in Mexico City. The United States won the gold medal, followed by the U.S.S.R. and Yugoslavia. China, competing outside of Asia for the first time, showed surprising skill and could be a major force in the 1980s. The U.S. also finished first in two other important tournaments. By twice defeating second-place Yugoslavia and third-place Cuba, the U.S. won the seven-team Can-Am-Mex Tournament. At the Pan American Games in San Juan, Puerto Rico, the U.S. squad came out on top by winning all five games. Cuba took the silver medal and Canada took the bronze.

Women's international water polo had its first world championships as the United States was host to the Women's World Cup. Not to be outdone by the men, the U.S. women won the tournament, although their game with second-place The Netherlands ended in a tie.

In competition within the U.S., Stanford University defeated the University of California 7–6 in sudden-death overtime to win the 1978 National Collegiate Athletic Association championships.

(WILLIAM ENSIGN FRADY)

Western Samoa

Western Samoa

A constitutional monarchy and member of the Commonwealth of Nations, Western Samoa is an island group in the South Pacific Ocean, about 2,600 km E of New Zealand and 3,500 km S of Hawaii. Area: 2,849 sq km (1,100 sq mi), with two major islands, Savai'i (1,813 sq km) and Upolu (1,036 sq km), and seven smaller islands. Pop. (1978 est.): 152,672. Cap. and largest city: Apia (pop., 1976, 32,100). Language: Samoan and English. Religion (1976): Congregational 50%, Roman Catholic 22%, Methodist 16%, others 12%. Head of state (*O le Ao o le Malo*) in 1979, Malietoa Tanumafili II; prime minister, Tupuola Taisi Tufuga Efi.

Following a general election on Feb. 24, 1979, Tupuola Efi was reelected prime minister by 24 votes to 23 in the Legislative Assembly and announced a reorganized Cabinet. One former minister had lost his seat, two were dropped from the Cabinet, and only two kept their former portfolios. Tupuola's narrow margin was threatened when the Supreme Court declared the elections in four constituencies void because of bribery and "treat-

WESTERN SAMOA

Education. (1978) Primary, pupils 41,463, teachers 1,471; secondary, pupils 9,290, teachers 492; vocational, pupils 234, teachers 47; teacher training, students 430, teachers 23; higher, students 207, teaching staff 38.

Finance and Trade. Monetary unit: tala, with (Sept. 17, 1979) a free rate of 0.89 tala to U.S. $1 (1.90 tala = £1 sterling). Budget (1978 est.): revenue 22.3 million tala; expenditure 19.3 million tala. Foreign trade (1978): imports 38,506,000 tala; exports 8,170,000 tala. Import sources (1977): New Zealand 29%; Australia 17%; Japan 15%; U.S. 9%; West Germany 8%; Fiji 6%; Singapore 5%. Export destinations (1977): West Germany 46%; New Zealand 16%; The Netherlands 10%; U.S. 10%; Japan 7%. Main exports: copra 42%; cocoa 32%.

Weather:
see Earth Sciences

Weight Lifting:
see Gymnastics and Weight Lifting

Welfare:
see Social Security and Welfare Services

ing." With the restriction of the franchise to *matai* (titled heads of families), there were only 200 voters in many constituencies, and some candidates reportedly sold their houses to cover gifts of food and cash for voters.

The practice had ancient precedent in the presentation of fine mats by those seeking election to titles, but the court decision seemed to reflect upon the degree rather than the nature of the practice. The government (which lost three supporters) survived the immediate crisis by refusing to call Parliament into session until by-elections had been held, despite a petition to the head of state from opposition members who formed themselves into the United Human Rights Protection Party led by Va'ai Kolone.

During the year statements by the prime minister apparently favouring reunification with American Samoa aroused comment in diplomatic circles. (BARRIE MACDONALD)

Winter Sports

Competitors in all the leading snow and ice sports during 1979 profited from extra international events in the U.S. at new or updated sites prepared for the following year's Olympic Winter Games at Lake Placid, N.Y. At the recreational level a continuing upsurge of every sport on skis, sleds, or skates was reflected by the opening of many new rinks and tracks and by a marked increase in mechanical lift facilities at snow resorts.

Skiing. There was an appreciable expansion of active interest in every grade of cross-country skiing outside its traditional Scandinavian stronghold. This development was particularly apparent in Switzerland, Canada, and the United States, underlined in those countries by an unprecedented boom in sales of the specialized equipment required. Meantime, Alpine skis, boots, and safety release gadgets became more sophisticated and varied in a worldwide, keenly contested manufacturers' market. Alpine skiing developed noticeably in Argentina and Chile.

ALPINE RACING. Firmly established as the sport's major annual competition, the 13th Alpine World Cup series comprised 33 men's and 26 women's events at meetings spanning 16 weeks in Austria, Czechoslovakia, France, Italy, Japan, Norway, Sweden, Switzerland, the U.S., West Germany, and Yugoslavia.

With rules adjusted to encourage overall ability in all three fields of Alpine competition (downhill, slalom, and giant slalom), Peter Luescher of Switzerland became a worthy new champion by demonstrating the versatility required. Leonhard Stock, an Austrian, was runner-up. Phil Mahre (U.S.), who finished third, had a good chance to win the cup until halted by a broken leg.

The season's glory was, to a large extent, gained by the deposed champion, Ingemar Stenmark, the Swedish slalom specialist, who could not win his fourth successive cup because he steadfastly continued to ignore the downhill; the odds were stacked heavily against anyone not competing in all three disciplines. He won 14 World Cup races during the season, surpassing Jean-Claude Killy's previous record of 12, set in 1968. Earning the maximum possible score for anyone competing in only two disciplines, Stenmark won all ten giant slaloms, three slaloms, and the parallel slalom and finished out of the top four in only two of the other seven slaloms. He also set a men's record victory margin for a giant slalom of 4.06 sec at Jasna, Czech. Stenmark extended his record number of World Cup race wins to 42. Despite all this he could only place fifth in the overall ratings but, not surprisingly, he was named international Alpine skier of the year for a fourth consecutive season by *Ski Racing* magazine.

In a close contest with a grandstand finish, the women's World Cup went for a record sixth time to Annemarie Moser-Proell of Austria, a remarkable comeback after she had prematurely announced her retirement three years earlier. Everything hinged on the final event in Furano, Japan. It was a giant slalom, and Moser-Proell, although best known for her downhill expertise, finished second to defeat the title defender, Hanni Wenzel of Liechtenstein, by only three points. Wenzel finished fifth in that remarkable deciding race, which Marie-Theres Nadig of Switzerland won by a record women's margin of 5.5 sec. Moser-Proell won 6 of the 7 downhills in the series and finished out of the top three in only 4 of the 20 events she entered. Her 9 victories of the season stretched her career total to 62. Irene Epple, of West Germany, finished third behind Wenzel.

The concurrently decided Nations' Cup was won for a seventh straight year by Austria. Switzerland was runner-up for the fifth consecutive time, and Italy placed third. These countries finished in the same order in the separate men's standings, but the top three in the women's competition were Austria, West Germany, and the U.S. André Arnold of Austria retained the world professional men's title on the North American circuit, the women's championship going to Toril Forland of Norway.

WIDE WORLD

Swedish skier Ingemar Stenmark captured the World Cup men's giant slalom at Lake Placid in March. In all he captured 14 World Cup races to surpass the previous record of 12 wins.

Nordic Events. The outstanding male racer of the season was Oddvar Braa of Norway. He emerged victorious in 15 and second in 6 of the 23 events entered, an achievement unmatched for more than a decade.

The first officially recognized Nordic World Cup series was the season's main attraction in cross-country events, decided by nine men's and nine women's individual races, plus two relays for each. The races were spread over three months in Czechoslovakia, East Germany, Finland, Italy, Norway, Poland, Sweden, Switzerland, the U.S., the U.S.S.R., and West Germany. Braa took the men's title, winning three of the six events he entered, two at 15 km and a notable 50-km victory at Holmenkollen, Norway. The overall runner-up was another Norwegian, Lars-Erik Eriksen, with Sven-Åke Lundbäck of Sweden third.

The women's series was a triumph for the Soviets, who took all first three places. Galina Kulakova, the veteran Olympic competitor in her 17th season with the Soviet national team, defeated Raisa Smetanina by just one point, while Zinaida Amosova finished third. The concurrent Nordic Nations' Cup went to the U.S.S.R., with Norway second and Sweden third; the Norwegians topped the separate men's standings.

An Austrian, Armin Kogler, won the fifth world ski-flying championships, with distance the only criterion, held on the towering 165-m hill at Planica, Yugos., on March 16–18. Kogler's best leap covered 169 m. Runner-up Axel Zitzmann of East Germany cleared 179 m, which would have been a world record had he not fallen at the finish.

East German ski-shooters took all three gold medals in the world biathlon championships at Ruhpolding, West Germany, January 28–February 2. Frank Ulrich retained the 10 km, Klaus Siebert captured the 20 km, and both were in the winning relay team.

Other Events. Professional freestyle skiing, with emphasis on acrobatic and balletic movements, was again more popular in North America than in Europe. John Eaves of Canada won the World Trophy series with five first places out of eight contests. His compatriot Stephanie Sloan gained the women's title.

In the seventh biennial world ski-bob championships, at Lenzerheide, Switz., in February, Robert Mühlberger of West Germany took the men's title. Annegret Ertler of Austria was the women's champion.

U.S. skaters Tai Babilonia and Randy Gardner became world pairs champions in figure skating competition at Vienna in March. They were the first Americans to win the title in 29 years.

UPI

Ice Skating. The wider and more frequent television coverage of leading events appeared to influence the mushrooming attendance at rinks in most countries. New indoor arenas sprouted in lands unaccustomed to natural ice, notably Spain and South Africa.

Figure Skating. There were an unusual number of close finishes when three of the four titles changed hands at the world figure and dance championships in Vienna on March 13–17, contested by 121 skaters from 22 nations. The tension of a close issue was blamed when, in the 69th men's contest, four of the five leaders after the figures failed their obligatory jump combination in the shorter of the two free skating sections. The one who did not, Vladimir Kovalev of the U.S.S.R., held onto his early lead for ultimate overall victory, despite being outpointed in the final free skating by Robin Cousins, the British runner-up; Jan Hoffmann of East Germany, third; and Charles Tickner, the defending champion from the U.S., fourth.

Linda Fratianne (U.S.) regained the women's title with an impressive performance marred only when touching down from a double toe salchow. She featured two triple jumps in the first 60 seconds of her rallying four-minute display, overhauling Anett Pötzsch, the East German defending champion, who had defeated her by a slender margin in Ottawa the previous season. Emi Watanabe, third, became the first Japanese girl ever to win a medal.

Fourteen years of Soviet dominance in the pairs championship were ended by Randy Gardner and Tai Babilonia, the first U.S. winners in 29 years. With better timed overhead lifts, death spirals, and throw axels, they clearly outshone the Soviet runners-up, Sergey Shakhrai and Marina Tcherkasova, and the third-place East Germans, Tassilo Thierbach and Sabine Baesz. Notable absentees were the Soviet husband and wife, Aleksandr Zaitsev and Irina Rodnina, whose son, born several weeks earlier, ended any chance for Rodnina to extend her record string of ten victories.

The ice dance title was retained by Gennadi Karponosov and Natalia Linichuk of the U.S.S.R., whose mastery was beyond question, but a diminishing Soviet strength in depth was stressed when Andrey Minekov and Irina Moiseyeva, the 1977 victors, were pushed back to third by the Hungarian runners-up, Andras Sallay and Krisztina Regoczy.

The four events of the second world junior championships were contested by 113 skaters from 23 nations on March 27–31 in Augsburg, West Germany. Vitali Egorov, the Soviet men's victor despite three heavy falls, owed his success to better figures, narrowly defeating the U.S. runner-up, Billy Beauchamp, the first black skater to compete in an international figure skating championship.

The women's contest was a triumph for Elaine Zayak of the U.S., who soared from sixth in the figures to win because of exceptional jumps and spins for a 13-year-old, and this after having lost part of a foot in an accident when an infant. The pairs event went to Marat Akbarov and Veronika Pershina of the U.S.S.R., and the dance title was retained by their compatriots Sergey Panomarenko and Tatiana Durasova.

SPEED SKATING. The increased prominence of North American racers was probably a result of better training facilities during recent seasons at West Allis, Wis., Keystone, Colo., and Lake Placid. The season was dominated by two members of one family. Eric Heiden of the U.S. won the men's world speed championship for a third successive year on February 10–11 in Oslo, finishing first in all four distances. Jan Egil Storholt of Norway was runner-up, also for a third successive year, and third place went to his fellow countryman Kay Arne Stenshjemmet.

Heiden's sister Beth became the new women's world champion at The Hague, Neth., on February 3–4. She also won over all four distances and, still young enough to be classified as a junior, suggested obviously exceptional potential. Unable to keep pace, the more experienced Natalia Petruseva of the U.S.S.R. and Sylvia Burka of Canada placed second and third, respectively.

The separate world sprint titles for men and women, contested at Inzell, West Germany, on February 17–18, were won, respectively, by Eric Heiden and another American, Leah Mueller-Poulos. The title was decided over four races, two each at 500 m and 1,000 m, and Heiden won all four. His closest rival was a Canadian, Gaetan Boucher, with Frode Rønning of Norway third. Mueller-Poulos won the two 500-m events for women to finish better on points than Beth Heiden, the runner-up after winning both 1,000-m races. Christa Rothenburger of East Germany finished third.

Two new men's world records were established. In February at Inzell, Heiden lowered the 1,000-m time to 1 min 14.99 sec. In March at Medeo, U.S.S.R., the Soviet racer Dmitry Ogloblin covered 3,000 m in 4 min 4.06 sec.

Bobsledding. On a sled costing approximately $1,250 and with a full minute to spare, Erich Scharer, the Swiss driver, retained his two-man title with brakeman Josef Benz in the 46th world championships at Königssee, West Germany, on February 17–25. Stefan Gaisreiter steered a West German boblet into second place, braked by Manfred Schumann. Their compatriots Toni Mangold and Stefan Spätz finished third on a fast, artificially frozen track.

With the advantage of greater familiarity with the course, Gaisreiter looked very much at home when driving his four-man sled to a narrow victory over the East German crew led by the 1977 champion, Meinhard Nehmer. Only one one-hundredth of a second separated their respective aggregate times for the four runs. Scharer, who was probably the most experienced driver competing, had another impressive season, with third place in the four-man event to augment his two-man success. But the overall honours belonged to the Gaisreiter-Schumann combination.

WIDE WORLD

Beth Heiden, a 19-year-old student from Madison, Wisconsin, won the women's world speed-skating championship in competition at The Hague in February.

Tobogganing. Detlef Günther of East Germany won the men's singles title in the 25th world luge championships at Königssee on January 27–28. He was followed by two Italians, Karl Brunner and Paul Hildgartner. Melitta Sollman, also from East Germany, won the women's event, ahead of a West German, Elisabeth Demleitner, and Maria-Luisa Rainer of Italy. West German riders Hans Brandner and Balthasar Schwarm became the new two-seater champions, four-hundredths of a second ahead of the East German veterans Hans Rinn and Norbert Hahn. Two more West Germans, Anton Winkler and Anton Weinbacher, finished third.

Swiss riders again dominated the classic events for skeleton tobogganists on the Cresta Run at St. Moritz, Switz. Marcel Melcher, in his first season, won the 70th Grand National over the full course, with Urs Nater runner-up and Ulie Burgerstein third. The 56th Curzon Cup was retained by Poldi Berchtold, the track record holder. Runner-up was Reto Gansser, followed by his brother, Franco.

Curling. For the first time since the event began, a Norwegian four won the 21st world curling championship for the Air Canada Silver Broom, at Bern, Switz., on March 26–31. Kristian Soerum, competing in his fourth consecutive championship as Norwegian skip, was supported by his brother

Morten, Eigil Ramsfjell, and Gunnar Meland. They defeated Switzerland 5–4 in an absorbingly close final before 10,179 fans. The Swiss quartet was a family rink led by Peter Attinger, with his brothers, Bernhard and Ruedi, and their brother-in-law, Matti Neuenschwander.

Norway, a nation with an estimated 5,000 curlers, and Switzerland, with 20,000, were tied 4–4 after nine ends. In the tenth Soerum put his final stone into an open house. Attinger, noted for his fast deliveries to knock opposing stones away, missed the one that mattered. In the semifinals, Norway beat Canada 6–3 and Switzerland defeated West Germany 9–5, the other contestants being Denmark, France, Italy, Scotland, Sweden, and the U.S.

The U.S., represented by a rink from Grand Forks, N.D., skipped by Don Barcome, Jr., won the fifth world junior championship, sponsored by Uniroyal at Moose Jaw, Sask., on March 11–17. Scotland was a runner-up for a second successive year in a field of ten nations. (HOWARD BASS)

See also Ice Hockey.
[452.B.4.g–h]

YEMEN, PEOPLE'S DEMOCRATIC REPUBLIC OF

Education. (1974–75) Primary, pupils 196,466, teachers 6,467; secondary, pupils 38,389, teachers 1,656; vocational, pupils 676, teachers (1973–74) 142; teacher training, students 631, teachers 47; higher, students 934, teaching staff 92.

Finance and Trade. Monetary unit: Yemen dinar, with (Sept. 17, 1979) a par value of 0.345 dinar to U.S. $1 (free rate of 0.74 dinar = £1 sterling). Budget (1977–78 actual): revenue 34,890,000 dinars; expenditure 47,370,000 dinars. Foreign trade (1976): imports 115.7 million dinars; exports 61.2 million dinars. Import sources: Kuwait *c.* 17%; Japan *c.* 13%; Qatar *c.* 9%; U.K. 7%. Export destinations: Canada *c.* 75%; Japan *c.* 7%. Main export: petroleum products 83%.

Transport. Roads (1976) 10,494 km (including 1,356 km with improved surface). Motor vehicles in use (1976): passenger 11,900; commercial (including buses) 10,500. There are no railways. Shipping traffic (1976): goods loaded 1,426,000 metric tons, unloaded 2,204,000 metric tons.

Agriculture. Production (in 000; metric tons; 1978): millet and sorghum *c.* 65; wheat *c.* 18; watermelons (1977) *c.* 55; dates *c.* 42; cotton, lint (1977) *c.* 4; fish catch (1977) 162. Livestock (in 000; 1977): cattle *c.* 104; sheep *c.* 940; goats *c.* 1,260; camels *c.* 40; chickens *c.* 1,430.

Industry. Production (in 000; metric tons; 1977): petroleum products *c.* 1,770; salt *c.* 75; electricity (kw-hr) *c.* 180,000.

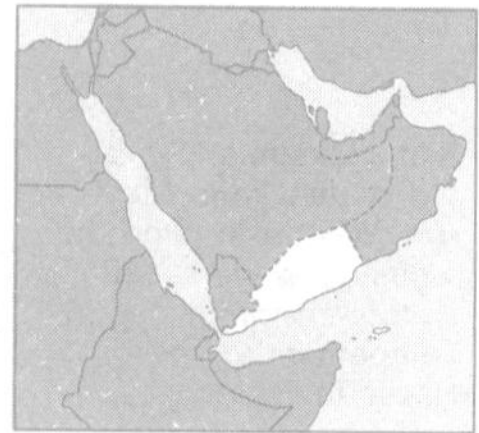
People's Democratic Republic of Yemen

Yemen, People's Democratic Republic of

A people's republic in the southern coastal region of the Arabian Peninsula, Yemen (Aden; South Yemen) is bordered by Yemen (San'a'), Saudi Arabia, and Oman. Area: 287,680 sq km (111,074 sq mi). Pop. (1978 est.): 1,853,000. Cap. and largest city: Aden (pop., 1973, 132,500). Language: Arabic. Religion: Muslim. Chairman of the Presidential Council in 1979, Abd-al Fattah Ismail; prime minister, Ali Nasir Muhammad Husani.

The People's Democratic Republic of Yemen (Aden; South Yemen) went to war with Yemen (San'a'; North Yemen) on Feb. 24, 1979. On February 28 South Yemen accused the North of initiating the hostilities in order to divert attention from the military successes of the rebel National Democratic Front against the San'a' regime. Aden claimed to have repelled North Yemeni attacks against Mukayris, the third governorate region, and Beihan (South Yemen's second airport). Swift Arab mediation led to a cease-fire and a mutual withdrawal of forces on March 19. The Arab League Council sponsored an agreement between North and South Yemen on unification of their two countries, which was signed in Kuwait on March 29. (*See* YEMEN ARAB REPUBLIC.)

Relations with Iraq, South Yemen's only Arab ally, deteriorated in June as a result of the assassination in Aden by Iraqi diplomats of Tewfic Rushdi, an Iraqi Kurd and Communist who taught at the Aden College of Education. South Yemen and

Militiamen practice on a firing range in Aden, South Yemen. Arab neighbours of the country feared the possibility of South Yemeni expansionism.
UPI

Wood Products: *see* Industrial Review
World Bank: *see* Economy, World
Wrestling: *see* Combat Sports
Yachting: *see* Sailing

Iraq laid siege to each other's embassies in Aden and Baghdad, and on June 5 South Yemeni forces stormed the Iraqi embassy and seized five diplomats for trial. (CHARLES GLASS)

Yemen Arab Republic

A republic situated in the southwestern coastal region of the Arabian Peninsula, Yemen (San'a'; North Yemen) is bounded by Yemen (Aden), Saudi Arabia, and the Red Sea. Area: 200,000 sq km (77,200 sq mi). Pop. (1979 est.): 5,785,000. Cap. and largest city: San'a' (pop., 1975, 134,600). Language: Arabic. Religion: Muslim. President in 1979, Col. Ali Abdullah Saleh; premier, Abdel-Aziz Abdel-Ghani.

The war between the two Yemens that began on Feb. 24, 1979, was preceded by months of border warfare between forces of the Yemen Arab Republic (San'a'; North Yemen) and Yemen (Aden; South Yemen)-backed rebels of the National Democratic Front (NDF). The NDF claimed in January to have killed 115 government soldiers and on February 26 to have captured the towns of Qaataba, Harib, and Moryes. But the San'a' government accused Soviet-supplied South Yemeni regulars of invading the country. The war displaced 43,000 people and led Saudi Arabia, North Yemen's principal ally, to put its forces on alert and the U.S. to dispatch the aircraft carrier "Constellation" to the Arabian Sea. Amid fears of a major power confrontation, Arab mediation led to an emergency session of the Arab League Council in Kuwait, which on March 4 produced agreement on a cease-fire and a withdrawal of forces. The withdrawal was completed on March 19, and on March 29 North Yemeni Pres. Ali Abdullah Saleh and South Yemeni leader Abd-al Fattah Ismail signed an agreement on unification of their two countries. The first unity discussions took place April 21–26, but no settlement had been reached by year's end.

The U.S. increased its presence in San'a' during and after the war in the form of military and civilian advisers and sales of $390 million worth of military equipment. (CHARLES GLASS)

YEMEN ARAB REPUBLIC

Education. (1976–77) Primary, pupils 221,482, teachers (1975–76) 6,604; secondary, pupils 24,873, teachers (1975–76) c. 1,172; vocational, pupils 503, teachers (1975–76) 60; teacher training, students 1,650, teachers (1975–76) 113; higher, students (1975–76) 2,408, teaching staff (1973–74) 58.

Finance and Trade. Monetary unit: rial, with (Sept. 17, 1979) a par value of 4.56 rials to U.S. $1 (free rate of 9.70 rials = £1 sterling). Budget (1978–79 est.): revenue 2,193,000,000 rials; expenditure 3,177,000,000 rials. Foreign trade (1977): imports 4,744,100,000 rials; exports 50,610,000 rials. Import sources (1976): Saudi Arabia 12%; Japan 10%; India 7%; Australia 7%; U.K. 6%; China 6%; The Netherlands 6%. Export destinations (1976): China 33%; Yemen (Aden) 25%; Italy 19%; Saudi Arabia 15%. Main exports: cotton 49%; coffee 17%; hides and skins 12%.

Agriculture. Production (in 000; metric tons; 1978): barley c. 46; corn c. 54; wheat c. 38; sorghum 564; potatoes (1977) c. 80; grapes c. 43; dates 67; coffee c. 3; tobacco c. 6; cotton, lint c. 10. Livestock (in 000; 1977): cattle c. 1,050; sheep c. 3,300; goats c. 7,600; camels c. 121; asses c. 650.

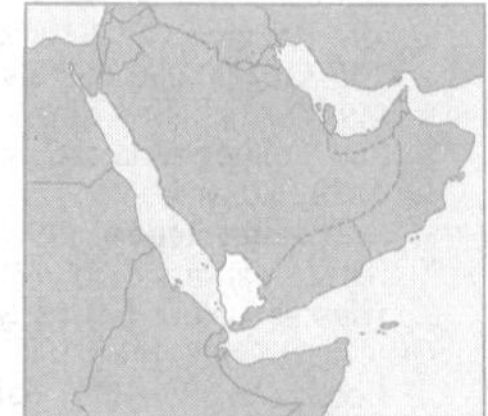
Yemen Arab Republic

Yugoslavia

Yugoslavia

A federal socialist republic, Yugoslavia is bordered by Italy, Austria, Hungary, Romania, Bulgaria, Greece, Albania, and the Adriatic Sea. Area: 255,804 sq km (98,766 sq mi). Pop. (1979 est.): 22,083,000. Cap. and largest city: Belgrade (pop., 1975 UN est., 870,000). Language: Serbo-Croatian, Slovenian, and Macedonian. Religion (1953): Orthodox 41%; Roman Catholic 32%; Muslim 12%. President of the republic for life and president of the League of Communists in 1979, Marshal Tito (Josip Broz); president of the Federal Executive Council (premier), Veselin Djuranovic.

Yugoslavia's diplomacy in 1979 concentrated on frustrating pro-Soviet Cuba's attempt to gain a dominant position in the third-world, nonaligned movement, whose summit conference was held in Cuba in September. Senior Yugoslav politicians visited many countries in Africa, Asia, and Latin America lobbying for support. President Tito himself traveled to Kuwait, Iraq, Syria, and Jordan in February and to Algeria, Libya, and Malta at the end of May and the beginning of June. In between these two tours he made a trip to Moscow for talks

Victims of an earthquake that hit Yugoslavia on April 15 were given aid at a field hospital set up in the open air.

WIDE WORLD

YUGOSLAVIA

Education. (1977–78) Primary, pupils 2,845,976, teachers 131,729; secondary, vocational, and teacher training, pupils 948,194, teachers 51,843; higher, students 424,375, teaching staff (1976–77) 21,448.

Finance. Monetary unit: dinar, with (Sept. 17, 1979) a free rate of 19 dinars to U.S. $1 (40.88 dinars = £1 sterling). Gold, SDR's, and foreign exchange (June 1979) U.S. $1,864,000,000. Budget (1977 actual): revenue 172,920,000,000 dinars; expenditure 185,130,000,000 dinars. Gross material product (1977) 734 billion dinars. Money supply (Sept. 1978) 288.5 billion dinars. Cost of living (1975 = 100; June 1979) 176.6.

Foreign Trade. (1978) Imports 186.3 billion dinars; exports 105,780,000,000 dinars. Import sources: West Germany 18%; U.S.S.R. 14%; Italy 8%; U.S. 6%; Iraq 5%; France 5%. Export destinations: U.S.S.R. 25%; Italy 9%; West Germany 8%; U.S. 7%. Main exports (1977): machinery 19%; food 10%; textiles 8%; ships and boats 8%; chemicals 6%; timber 6%; nonferrous metals 6%. Tourism (1977): visitors 5,621,000; gross receipts U.S. $841 million.

Transport and Communications. Roads (1977) 119,785 km (including 201 km expressways). Motor vehicles in use (1977): passenger 1,923,900; commercial 157,960. Railways: (1977) 9,967 km; traffic (1978) 10,926,000,000 passenger-km, freight 23,379,000,000 net ton-km. Air traffic (1978): 2,720,000,000 passenger-km; freight 29.9 million net ton-km. Shipping (1978): merchant vessels 100 gross tons and over 468; gross tonnage 2,365,630. Telephones (Jan. 1978) 1,555,700. Radio licenses (Dec. 1977) 4,548,000. Television licenses (Dec. 1977) 3,701,000.

Agriculture. Production (in 000; metric tons; 1978): wheat 5,355; barley *c.* 560; oats 284; corn 7,555; potatoes *c.* 2,400; sunflower seed 539; sugar, raw value *c.* 763; onions *c.* 326; tomatoes *c.* 524; cabbages (1977) *c.* 690; chillies and peppers (1977) *c.* 315; watermelons (1977) *c.* 600; plums (1977) 757; apples *c.* 340; wine *c.* 550; tobacco *c.* 60; beef and veal *c.* 340; pork *c.* 656; timber (cu m; 1977) 15,025. Livestock (in 000; Jan. 1978): cattle 5,542; sheep 7,514; pigs 8,452; horses 759; chickens 54,721.

Industry. Fuel and power (in 000; metric tons; 1978): coal 470; lignite 39,006; crude oil 4,077; natural gas (cu m) *c.* 1,940,000; manufactured gas (cu m; 1977) *c.* 700,000; electricity (kw-hr) 51,353,000. Production (in 000; metric tons; 1978): cement 8,512; iron ore (35% metal content) 4,564; pig iron 2,302; crude steel 2,422; magnesite (1977) 345; bauxite 2,567; aluminum 196; copper 146; lead 116; zinc 95; petroleum products (1977) *c.* 12,860; sulfuric acid 968; cotton yarn 118; wool yarn 44; man-made fibres (1977) 97; wood pulp (1977) 605; newsprint 96; other paper (1977) 618; television receivers (units; 1977) 427; passenger cars (units) 193; commercial vehicles (units) 62. Merchant vessels launched (100 gross tons and over; 1978) 242,000 gross tons.

with Pres. Leonid Brezhnev. But press polemics between Yugoslavia and the Soviet Union continued, mainly over Yugoslavia's open condemnation of the invasion and occupation in January of Cambodia by the Soviet Union's close ally, Vietnam. Yugoslavia in turn angered the Soviet Union by refusing to condemn China's counteraction against Vietnam.

Yugoslav-Bulgarian talks in Belgrade in June failed to resolve the differences over Macedonia. In September President Tito traveled to Cuba and in November to Romania for a summit meeting with Pres. Nicolae Ceausescu. Also in November Gen. Jurgen Brandt, inspector general of the West German Army (Bundeswehr), visited Yugoslavia "to study the concept of all-peoples' defense." Yugoslavia and the European Economic Community failed to conclude a new special trade and cooperation agreement to replace the five-year trade pact that expired in 1978.

Edvard Kardelj (*see* OBITUARIES), the Yugoslav party's leading ideologist and the most prominent figure after Tito, died on February 10 after a long illness. His place in the party presidium was filled by another Slovene leader, Sergei Krajger. In May Stane Dolanc, also a Slovene and the party presidium's executive secretary since 1972, stepped down from that post, and Dusan Dragosavac, a Serb from Croatia, was appointed to it for a two-year period. In October Stevan Doronjski, a Serb from the Vojvodina autonomous region, replaced, for a one-year term as party presidium chairman, Branko Mikulic, a Croat from Bosnia, who had held the post since October 1978. Yugoslavia's former vice-president and now most famous dissident, Milovan Djilas, was sentenced on October 15 to a fine of 10,000 dinars (about U.S. $530) for his "spiritual fathership" of an unregistered literary magazine, *Casovnik* ("The Clock").

In October Tito toured the autonomous province of Kosovo in Serbia and appealed to the Albanians, Serbs, and Montenegrins there to preserve "brotherhood and unity." He also advocated good neighbourly relations with Albania. On October 31 Yugoslavia's Federal Assembly began discussions of Tito's proposal to change the 1974 constitution to take into account his idea of "collective leadership," especially his proposal to cut legislators' terms from four years to one.

The authorities allowed the holding on September 2 of a Roman Catholic rally in Nin, Croatia, in which 250,000 people took part. This biggest postwar manifestation of religion in Yugoslavia marked 1,100 years of unbroken connection between Croat Catholics and the papacy. An upsurge of pan-Islamic feeling in predominantly Muslim Bosnia and Herzegovina brought a warning from Tito against identifying national with religious sentiment.

The wheat harvest was 4.5 million metric tons, 1.8 million less than the record 1974 harvest. Prices of bread, cigarettes, and gasoline rose in July, while electricity, diesel fuel, heating oil, and paraffin as well as school, canteen, and restaurant meals became more expensive in September. A temporary price freeze introduced at the beginning of August was lifted in October. In September Yugoslavia's annual rate of inflation dropped from 30 to 27%. Industrial production in the January–September period increased by 9% as compared with January–September 1978. In November the World Bank granted Yugoslavia a $61 million loan for reconstruction in Montenegro after a disastrous April earthquake, which wrecked Kotor and coastal tourist resorts on the Bay of Kotor. The World Bank had in the June 1978–June 1979 period granted Yugoslavia loans worth $385 million. In May the International Monetary Fund granted it a $340 million loan. (K. F. CVIIC)

Zaire

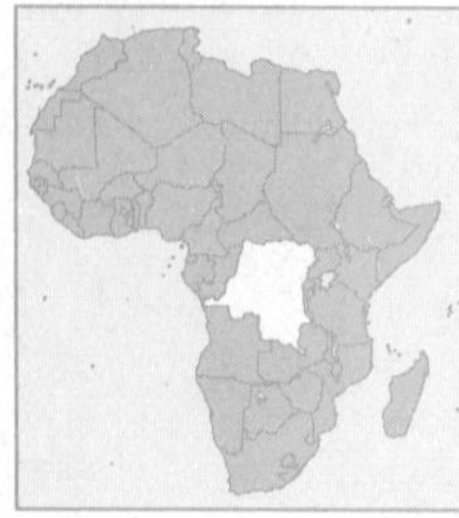
Zaire

A republic of equatorial Africa, Zaire is bounded by the Central African Republic, Sudan, Uganda, Rwanda, Burundi, Tanzania, Zambia, Angola, Congo, and the Atlantic Ocean. Area: 2,344,885 sq km (905,365 sq mi). Pop. (1979 est.): 27,519,000. Cap. and largest city: Kinshasa (pop., 1977 est., 2,710,300). Language: French; Bantu dialects. Religion: animist approximately 50%; Christian 43%. President in 1979, Mobutu Sese Seko; prime ministers, Mpinga Kasenga and, from March 6, Bo-Boliko Lokonga Monse Mihambo.

Early in January 1979 the Soviet ambassador noted an improvement in relations between Zaire and the U.S.S.R., which had suffered as a result of accusations that the latter had backed the revolts in Shaba Province in 1977 and 1978. The change had been foreshadowed in 1978 by an exchange of messages between Presidents Mobutu Sese Seko and Leonid Brezhnev. It was now decided that Zaire should send students to train in the U.S.S.R. in 1979, while the U.S.S.R. would supply Zaire with anticholera vaccine.

More surprising was the reappointment as foreign minister, in March, of Nguza Karl-I-Bond, who had been sentenced to death in September 1977 for alleged involvement with the Shaba invasion. Probably as a result of external pressures, Mobutu had commuted the death sentence and had granted Nguza an amnesty in July 1978. Other posts affected by the Cabinet reshuffle that restored Nguza included that of prime minister, which went to the parliamentary speaker, Bo-Boliko Lokonga Monse Mihambo; his predecessor, Mpinga Kasenga, became permanent secretary of the Mouvement Populaire de la Révolution. The position of minister for national guidance, culture, and arts was filled by Umba Di Lutete. Engulu Baangampongo Bakolele Lokanga became minister of agriculture, succeeding Tepa Tondele Zambite, who had been arrested at the beginning of the year on charges of embezzlement.

In January Zairian troops reportedly were sent to help quell student riots in the then Central African Empire, but this was later denied by Mobutu. Zaire itself was not without its internal alarms. In February it was reported that Belgian paratroops were standing by to protect the white settlers if their fears that large-scale unemployment and inflation in the Shaba area might provoke serious unrest proved justified. Nor was this the only problem arising from the Shaba invasion. The government's anxiety to restore production in the copper and cobalt mines as quickly as possible meant that essential maintenance had been neglected. The result was a noticeable decline in output in 1979. Gécamines, the state-owned mining company, was having difficulty recruiting skilled workers after the flight of expatriates that followed the fighting. Loans required to pay for the restoration of plant and equipment were not readily forthcoming because the government was reluctant to meet conditions set by the World Bank.

Early in the year the International Monetary Fund (IMF) was concerned because Zaire appeared to be selling cobalt through deals that did not conform to the conditions laid down by the IMF when it granted assistance. By August some of the IMF's doubts appeared to have been dispelled, and a $153 million standby credit was agreed upon. Nevertheless, Zaire still owed private U.S. banks about $500 million. In November the so-called Zaire Club of ten Western nations agreed to extend aid of up to $206 million in 1980. Hopes of economic recovery depended largely on fulfillment of the targets for mineral production laid down by the government but, given conditions in the Kolwezi mining industry, they seemed unlikely to be achieved. Concerned about the strategic importance of Zaire, U.S. Pres. Jimmy Carter pressed Congress to grant increased aid in 1980 to assist Zaire's economy and meet its military needs.

The continuing economic crisis threatened the political stability of the country, and there were reports that opposition to Mobutu's government was becoming stronger. Rumours of corruption and embezzlement by government officials added further to popular discontent. Nonetheless, the U.S. concluded that the situation in Shaba Province was sufficiently stable to permit withdrawal of the 2,500 troops from Morocco, Senegal, and other African countries that had assisted in maintaining order since May 1978. U.S. aircraft began to fly out the African security force in August, leaving the defense of the region dependent on Zairian forces trained by French, Belgian, and Chinese officers. Late in December an attempt by a group of Zairian officers and soldiers to take over the

NADAL—SIPA PRESS/BLACK STAR

A new defense force of Zairian army troops paraded in review before Pres. Mobutu Sese Seko. The troops replaced a Pan-African force that had maintained order in Shaba Province after a rebel invasion during the summer.

ZAIRE

Education. (1973–74) Primary, pupils 3,538,257, teachers (1972–73) 80,481; secondary, pupils 225,606; vocational, pupils 47,579; teacher training, students 62,018; secondary, vocational, and teacher training, teachers 14,483; higher, students (1974–75) 21,021, teaching staff 2,550.

Finance. Monetary unit: zaire, with (Sept. 17, 1979) a free rate of 2.08 zaires to U.S. $1 (4.47 zaires = £1 sterling). Gold, SDR's, and foreign exchange (June 1979) U.S. $124 million. Budget (1976 est.): revenue 508 million zaires; expenditure 668 million zaires. Gross national product (1977) 4,011,000,000 zaires. Money supply (April 1979) 1,824,400,000 zaires. Cost of living (Kinshasa; 1975 = 100; May 1979) 956.9.

Foreign Trade. (1978) Imports 490.7 million zaires; exports 778.2 million zaires. Import sources (1977): Belgium-Luxembourg 20%; U.S. 12%; West Germany 11%; France 9%; South Africa 5%; U.K. 5%; Zimbabwe Rhodesia 5%. Export destinations (1977): Belgium-Luxembourg 22%; U.K. 19%; Italy 11%; Greece 9%; France 7%; U.S. 6%. Main exports: copper 41%; coffee 18%; diamonds 13%; zinc (1977) 11%.

Transport and Communications. Roads (1977) *c.* 145,000 km. Motor vehicles in use (1977): passenger 96,700; commercial (including buses) 87,100. Railways: (1975) 5,254 km; traffic (1976) 467 million passenger-km, freight 2,203,000,000 net ton-km. Air traffic (1977): 696 million passenger-km; freight 40.6 million net ton-km. Shipping (1978): merchant vessels 100 gross tons and over 34; gross tonnage 109,785. Inland waterways (including Zaire River; 1977) *c.* 16,400 km. Telephones (Jan. 1978) 33,800. Radio receivers (Dec. 1974) 2,448,000. Television receivers (Dec. 1976) 7,000.

Agriculture. Production (in 000; metric tons; 1978): rice *c.* 202; corn *c.* 487; sweet potatoes (1977) *c.* 495; cassava (1977) *c.* 12,300; peanuts *c.* 339; palm kernels *c.* 72; palm oil *c.* 175; sugar, raw value (1977) 70; mangoes *c.* 167; pineapples *c.* 165; bananas *c.* 321; oranges *c.* 154; coffee *c.* 95; rubber *c.* 27; jute *c.* 13; cotton, lint *c.* 8; meat (1977) *c.* 193; fish catch (1977) 107; timber (cu m; 1977) *c.* 13,690. Livestock (in 000; Dec. 1976): cattle 1,144; sheep *c.* 743; goats *c.* 2,679; pigs *c.* 705; poultry *c.* 12,000.

Industry. Production (in 000; metric tons; 1977): copper ore (metal content) 427; zinc ore (metal content; 1978) 74; manganese ore (metal content) 21; cobalt ore (metal content) 10; gold (troy oz) 82; silver (troy oz) 3,500; diamonds (metric carats) 11,210; crude oil (1978) 1,145; coal 116; petroleum products *c.* 150; cement 489; electricity (kw-hr) *c.* 3,666,000.

airport at Kisangani in northeastern Zaire was foiled and the ringleaders were executed.

More positively, an improvement in relations between Zaire and Angola resulted in the return to Zaire of over 100,000 refugees who had fled to Angola in 1977 and 1978. It also led to cooperation between the two countries in an effort to reopen the Benguela Railway, which would ease Zaire's difficulties in exporting its copper and cobalt. In the meantime, the Angolan national airline agreed to fly cobalt from Shaba to Europe. This suggested that the possibility of a new invasion of Shaba from Angola was reasonably remote and produced a greater feeling of security in the province.

(KENNETH INGHAM)

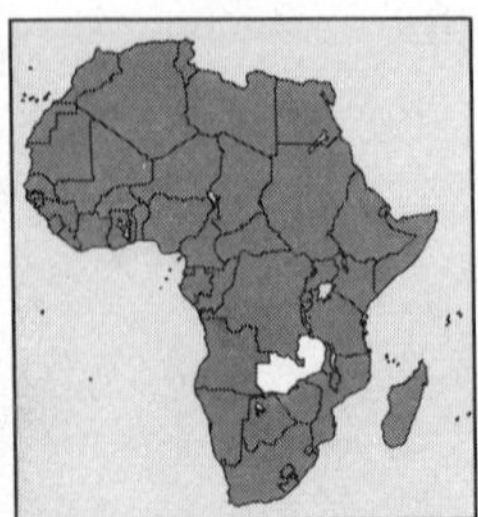
Zambia

Zambia

A republic and a member of the Commonwealth of Nations, Zambia is bounded by Tanzania, Malawi, Mozambique, Zimbabwe Rhodesia, South West Africa (Namibia), Angola, and Zaire. Area: 752,614 sq km (290,586 sq mi). Pop. (1978 est.): 5,649,000, about 99% of whom are Africans. Cap. and largest city: Lusaka (pop., 1978 est., 559,000). Language: English and Bantu. Religion: predominantly animist, with Roman Catholic (21%), Protestant, Hindu, and Muslim minorities. President in 1979, Kenneth Kaunda; prime minister, Daniel Lisulo.

Throughout 1979 Zambia's economy was under serious pressure. A drought at the beginning of the year reduced the country's food supply, and a shortage of fertilizers added to the crisis. Faced with a grave deficiency in the supply of corn needed to feed the population, the country was dependent upon imports, particularly from Zimbabwe Rhodesia and South Africa. This supply was endangered, however, because Zambia continued to provide bases for guerrillas operating against Zimbabwe Rhodesia. In November the government of the latter country placed an embargo on the transport into Zambia of further corn supplies as long as guerrilla activities in Zambia continued. Troops from Zimbabwe Rhodesia destroyed road and rail bridges inside Zambia in addition to carrying out regular raids on guerrilla bases within the country.

In late November Zambian Pres. Kenneth Kaunda found it necessary to place his country on a war footing, and there were violent demonstrations against the British high commissioner, who had refused to accept any responsibility on the part of Britain for compensating Zambia for the damage done by the raids. The high commissioner was therefore recalled on November 24. However, following the settlement at the conclusion of the Lancaster House conference in London in December, one of the first acts of the interim British governor of Zimbabwe Rhodesia, Lord Soames, was to revoke the ban on corn transshipments to Zambia.

(KENNETH INGHAM)

ZAMBIA

Education. (1976) Primary, pupils 907,867, teachers 19,300; secondary, pupils 78,805, teachers 3,538; vocational, pupils 5,392, teachers 481; teacher training, students 2,780, teachers 229; higher, students 3,447, teaching staff 412.

Finance. Monetary unit: kwacha, with (Sept. 17, 1979) a free rate of 0.79 kwacha to U.S. $1 (1.70 kwachas = £1 sterling). Gold, SDR's, and foreign exchange (June 1979) U.S. $120 million. Budget (1978 actual): revenue 551.9 million kwachas; expenditure 636.9 million kwachas. Gross national product (1978) 2,199,000,000 kwachas. Cost of living (1975 = 100; May 1979) 179.2.

Foreign Trade. (1977) Imports 653,660,000 kwachas; exports 708,530,000 kwachas. Import sources: U.K. 23%; Saudi Arabia 12%; West Germany 12%; U.S. 11%; South Africa 7%; Japan 5%. Export destinations: Japan 17%; U.K. 16%; West Germany 14%; Italy 10%; U.S. 10%; France 9%. Main export: copper 91%.

Transport and Communications. Roads (1974) 34,869 km. Motor vehicles in use (1977): passenger *c.* 104,500; commercial (including buses) *c.* 62,500. Railways (1977) *c.* 1,994 km (including *c.* 890 km of the 1,870-km Tanzam railway). Air traffic (1978): 545 million passenger-km; freight 37.1 million net ton-km. Telephones (Jan. 1978) 54,500. Radio receivers (Dec. 1976) *c.* 110,000. Television receivers (Dec. 1976) 25,000.

Agriculture. Production (in 000; metric tons; 1978): corn *c.* 850; cassava (1977) *c.* 166; millet *c.* 80; sorghum *c.* 50; peanuts *c.* 31; sugar, raw value (1977) *c.* 95; tobacco *c.* 4. Livestock (in 000; 1977): cattle *c.* 1,860; sheep *c.* 50; goats *c.* 292; pigs *c.* 200; poultry *c.* 15,376.

Industry. Production (in 000; metric tons; 1977): copper ore (metal content) 819; lead ore (metal content) 14; zinc ore (metal content) 45; coal (1978) 614; petroleum products *c.* 830; cement *c.* 332; electricity (kw-hr; 1978) 7,885,000.

Zimbabwe Rhodesia

Though Zimbabwe Rhodesia (then called Rhodesia) declared itself independent on Nov. 11, 1965, and a republic on March 2, 1970, and agreed to return temporarily to British rule as of Dec. 12, 1979, it had remained a British colony in the eyes of many other nations. It is bounded by Zambia, Mozambique, South Africa, and Botswana. Area: 390,272 sq km (150,685 sq mi). Pop. (1979 est.): 7,140,000, of whom 96% are African and 4% white. Cap. and largest city: Salisbury (urban area pop., 1979 est., 616,000). Language: English (official) and various Bantu languages (1969 census, Shona 71%, Ndebele 15%). Religion: predominantly traditional tribal beliefs; Christian minority. Presidents in 1979, John Wrathall and, from May 29 until December 11, Josiah Zion Gumede; prime ministers, Ian D. Smith and, from May 29 to December 11, Bishop Abel T. Muzorewa; governor from December 7, Lord Soames.

By the end of 1978 more than 12,000 people had been killed in the fighting between Rhodesian government and Patriotic Front guerrilla forces since the outbreak of war in 1972. Nearly 5,500 died in 1978, and the death toll rose even more rapidly in 1979. During 1978, too, 18,069 whites left the country and there were only 4,360 immigrants, the greatest net loss in the country's history. By the end of 1978, 1,082 primary and 46 secondary schools serving 274,000 children had closed. Rural families flocked to the towns to escape guerrilla raids, only to live in overcrowded conditions.

A supporter held high a picture of Bishop Abel Muzorewa during the election campaign in April. Muzorewa, whose party was victorious, was elected as Zimbabwe Rhodesia's first black prime minister.

UPI

ZIMBABWE RHODESIA

Education. (1978) Primary, pupils 829,039, teachers 23,768; secondary, pupils 73,026, teachers 3,797; vocational (including part-time), pupils 3,827, teachers 325; teacher training, students 2,982, teachers 233; higher (University of Rhodesia), students (1979) 1,481, teaching staff 235.

Finance. Monetary unit: Zimbabwe dollar, with (Sept. 17, 1979) a free rate of Z$0.69 to U.S. $1 (Z$1.49 = £1 sterling). Budget (1978–79 est.): revenue Z$583 million; expenditure Z$845 million. Gross domestic product (1977) Z$2,220,000,000.

Foreign Trade. (1973) Imports Z$323.3 million; exports Z$386,630,000. Import sources (1965): U.K. 30%; South Africa 23%; U.S. 7%; Japan 6%. Export destinations (1965): Zambia 25%; U.K. 22%; South Africa 10%; West Germany 9%; Malawi 5%; Japan 5%. Main exports (1965): tobacco 33%; food 10%; asbestos 8%; copper and chrome ore 7%.

Transport and Communications. Roads (1976) 78,930 km. Motor vehicles in use (1977): passenger *c.* 180,000; commercial (including buses) *c.* 70,000. Railways: (1978) 3,394 km; freight traffic (1977–78) 5,588,000,000 net ton-km. Telephones (June 1978) 201,500. Radio licenses (June 1978) 209,800. Television licenses (June 1978) 73,300.

Agriculture. Production (in 000; metric tons; 1978): corn *c.* 1,400; millet *c.* 220; wheat *c.* 90; sugar, raw value *c.* 250; peanuts *c.* 120; tobacco *c.* 56; cotton, lint *c.* 33; beef and veal (1977) *c.* 146. Livestock (in 000; 1977): cattle *c.* 6,247; sheep *c.* 818; goats *c.* 2,167; pigs *c.* 208.

Industry. Production (in 000; metric tons; 1977): coal *c.* 2,500; cement (1978) 402; asbestos *c.* 200; chrome ore (oxide content) *c.* 300; iron ore (metal content) *c.* 325; gold (troy oz) *c.* 600; electricity (kw-hr; 1978) 4,510,000.

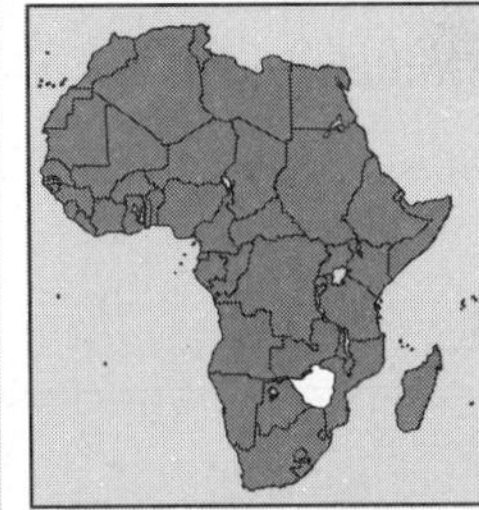

Zimbabwe Rhodesia

On Jan. 2, 1979, the Rhodesian government published a plan for a new constitution that would give effect to the "internal settlement" reached in 1978. This would take place after elections in April 1979. The name of the country would become Zimbabwe Rhodesia. A president would hold office for six years with limited executive powers. The Senate, to be chosen by the House of Assembly, would consist of 30 members, and the House of Assembly would have 72 black members elected by black voters on a one-man–one-vote basis and 28 whites. Of the latter, 20 would be elected by white voters only and the remaining 8 by the other 92 members of the Assembly from a list of 16 drawn up by the white members of the existing Parliament. The normal life of Parliament was to be five years. Reactions to the plan on the part of white Rhodesians were varied, and the prime minister, Ian Smith, campaigned hard to obtain support in the referendum held on the proposals on January 30. His efforts met with success, with 85% of those who voted supporting the new constitution.

The black leaders who had supported the internal settlement were jubilant, but their electoral campaign was launched under a cloud. The guerrilla forces were determined to wreck the elections, and there were grounds for doubt that the outcome would be internationally accepted as representing the opinion of the whole Rhodesian electorate. The UN Human Rights Commission, for example, totally rejected the internal settlement on February 21. The Rhodesian government, however, urged Britain and the U.S. to send observers to see that the elections were fairly conducted and, at the same time, they called upon the Patriotic Front leaders, Joshua Nkomo and Robert Mugabe, to stop the fighting and take part in a political solution. The attitude of the whites in Rhodesia toward the Patriotic Front hardened in February when a civilian aircraft on an internal flight was shot down by Nkomo's men with the loss of all 59 people on board. Rhodesian jet fighter aircraft struck at guerrilla camps near Livingstone in Zambia in a campaign, it was claimed, to stop guerrilla attempts to sabotage elections. Later in February Rhodesian aircraft raided outside the country, this time a guerrilla supply depot in Mozambique and a camp in Angola. Further raids were launched throughout the year, sometimes with both aircraft and helicopter-borne ground troops.

On February 28 Smith dissolved the Rhodesian Parliament, thus bringing to an end 88 years of white rule. In March, after refusing to send official observers, Britain and the U.S. urged Smith to call off the elections. The government persisted, but the leaflets that it dropped by aircraft offering an amnesty to guerrillas met with little response. South Africa, meantime, provided helicopters, transport aircraft, and trucks to assist in maintaining order in the period leading to the elections.

Polling took place from April 17 to 21, and although guerrillas attempted to disrupt it, more than 64% of the electorate voted. The result was an overwhelming victory for the United African National Council of Bishop Abel Muzorewa (*see* BIOGRAPHIES), which gained 51 of the 72 seats open to blacks and an overall majority of one in the new Parliament. The two black leaders who had lost heavily in the elections, the Rev. Ndabaningi Sithole and Chief Jeremiah Chirau, refused to recognize the results of the polls. The victory of the Conservative Party in the British elections in May brought hope to the Zimbabwe Rhodesian government of a more friendly official attitude in Britain, but the new British government acted cautiously. On May 18 a meeting in London of high commissioners of 34 Commonwealth countries warned of the dangers of recognizing Muzorewa's regime. A week later an official of the Organization of African Unity also stressed that body's opposition to Muzorewa's government and to the lifting of sanctions against Rhodesia.

At the end of May Muzorewa was sworn in as the first black prime minister of his country, and he appointed Ian Smith as a minister without portfolio. In June he warned Zambia's Pres. Kenneth Kaunda that Zimbabwe Rhodesia's armed forces would continue to raid guerrilla bases in Zambia as long as Zambia acted as host to his government's enemies. In Salisbury itself, however, Muzorewa encountered a setback when, under the leadership of James Chikerema, seven members of Parliament elected as his supporters resigned for tribal reasons. This cost the bishop his overall majority before Parliament had held its first sitting, but there was some gain when Sithole announced on July 31 that his party would end its boycott of Parliament.

In August the meeting of Commonwealth leaders in Lusaka, Zambia, accepted a proposal put forward by the British prime minister, Margaret Thatcher, for an all-party conference, to be held in London in September under the chairmanship of the British foreign secretary, Lord Carrington (*see* BIOGRAPHIES). After some hesitation due to the proposal that new elections should be held to supersede those held in April, Muzorewa accepted the plan, as did the leaders of the Patriotic Front under pressure from their sympathizers, the presidents of Tanzania, Zambia, Mozambique, Angola, and Botswana. None of the participants agreed to Britain's suggestion that there should be a cease-fire to assist the negotiations.

The conference opened on September 10, but negotiations were protracted. The Patriotic Front tried to insist that arrangements should be made for the interim control of the country before discussion of the terms of a new constitution. Eventually all parties made concessions, Smith accepting that the whites should no longer be able to block legislation while the Patriotic Front agreed that 20% of the seats in Parliament should be reserved for whites. The Patriotic Front, however, had fought hard for a constitution that would provide for a strong executive president and that would give the government a free hand in the redistribution of white-owned land. Muzorewa, by contrast, was prepared to offer the white farmers reasonable security of tenure. On December 5 a British cease-fire plan, as a preliminary to internationally observed elections supervised by a British governor, was broadly accepted by the government and the Front. Queen Elizabeth appointed Lord Soames as governor on December 7, whereupon Zimbabwe Rhodesia temporarily reverted to its former coloni-

WILLIAM CAMPBELL—SYGMA

Britain's Lord Soames arrived in Zimbabwe Rhodesia in December to take over the government of the country and to attempt to end seven years of guerrilla warfare.

al status as Southern Rhodesia. Four days later Muzorewa's government voted itself out of office. The nation then began preparing for elections in 1980. The Patriotic Front guerrillas were given from December 28 to Jan. 4, 1980, to gather at 16 designated assembly points; those still in the bush after January 4 would be considered unlawful.

(KENNETH INGHAM)

Zoos and Botanical Gardens

Zoos. The trend toward using zoos as reservoirs rather than consumers of wild species continued to grow. Over 95% of the mammals being added to the London Zoo's collection were born in captivity, either in the London Zoo itself or in other zoos. Only ten years earlier the proportion of captive-bred additions to the collection had been only 40%. Thus, from their initial purpose of satisfying curiosity, zoos were emerging more and more as institutions with the double purpose of arousing public concern for animal life and serving as reservoirs for species whose habitats had been wholly or partially destroyed. For zoo administrations, this new role entailed mastering problems of animal nutrition, behaviour, ecology, and pathology in order to establish groups of animals capable of sustained reproduction through the generations.

Paradoxically, it was the species that had been captive the longest that presented the newest problems. The reason for this is that once sustained reproduction occurs, the captive gene pool is liable to diverge from the natural gene pool. Such change is inevitable, but its rate can be slowed until it reaches negligible proportions. For example Przewalski's horse, which now occurs only in captivity, existed in 1979 as a herd of about 300 animals descended from 13 individuals. More was known of the ancestry and the inbreeding of this wild horse than of almost any other species, and recently a conference met in Arnhem, Neth., to discuss and coordinate breeding strategies.

Thus, the zoos of the world were aware of the difficulties they faced in ensuring an adequate flow in the combined gene pools of captive species. As of 1979 there were 44 international registers or "studbooks" being kept, concerning mainly birds and mammals, and animals were being transferred across international boundaries in order to keep genes moving. This was taking place despite problems stemming from national needs to contain animal disease by strict control and quarantine procedures, and also from the demands of the Convention on International Trade in Endangered Species of Wild Fauna and Flora.

In the public image zoos were generally associated with the larger and more spectacular species, so that large mammals and colourful birds tended to predominate. However, reptile keepers were achieving such successes that the 1979 edition of the *International Zoo Yearbook* devoted its entire opening section to reports on reptile husbandry drawn from 28 zoos and similar institutions scattered throughout the world. The reports covered, among other subjects, the breeding of mugger crocodiles in an Indian zoo, the marking of individual reptiles for identification purposes, recommendations on how to induce the tuatara lizard of New Zealand to breed (an event yet to occur away from its threatened native habitat), and the breeding of snakes and of the giant Aldabra tortoises.

The *International Zoo Yearbook*, in its 19th volume, provided an invaluable repository of information for zoo administrations. It reported

(Left) Lan Lan (right), the female giant panda in the Tokyo Zoo, died in September. On hearing the news, visitors to the zoo (below) broke into tears.

PHOTOS, WIDE WORLD

Zoology:
see Life Sciences

on ideas and achievements, new buildings, new diets, new displays, new breedings, the state of world captive populations, the addresses of zoos and studbook keepers, and much else—for example, how to improve the calcium content of mealworms and thereby increase their nutritional value for the animals to which they are fed.

Japan mourned the death in September of Lan Lan, a female giant panda that had been in Tokyo's Ueno Zoo. With her mate, Kan Kan, she had become a great favourite of the Japanese public. The loss was especially sharp because Lan Lan was pregnant and might have delivered the first giant panda born in captivity if she had lived another month. (MICHAEL R. BRAMBELL)

Botanical Gardens. The activities of botanical gardens showed a continued steady increase worldwide in 1979. The annual working conventions of the various national associations of these specialized gardens contributed significantly to the dissemination of information and expertise, as well as to the distribution of plant species that were becoming increasingly rare.

Following the 1978 Kew (England) Conservation Conference, botanical gardens began to play an increasingly significant role in the conservation of threatened plants. This did not apply to all gardens in equal measure; many were still severely hemmed in by urban development and traffic conditions, and they lacked money and specialized staff. Frequently, plans to change locations of the gardens and to enlarge them had to be shelved for long periods because of political and economic difficulties.

There was progress at Hamburg, West Germany, however, where the new University Botanical Garden was opened on July 9. Occupying 24 ha (59 ac), it was completed after a ten-year construction period at a cost of about DM 13 million. From the time of its opening thousands of visitors daily sought out the most noteworthy items among the 20,000 plant species shown. West Germany's largest botanical garden, however, and the one with the greatest and most comprehensive collection of plants continued to be that of Berlin-Dahlem, which celebrated its 300th anniversary with a wide range of special events during September 10–13.

A colony of *Callimico goeldii* monkeys is thriving at the Brookfield Zoo near Chicago. Previously these tiny monkeys had rarely survived captivity.

BROOKFIELD ZOO

The Royal Botanic Gardens, Kew, near London, again stood in the forefront in regard to contact with the public. Informative material for schoolchildren as well as for adults was made available in effective ways, including the use of quiz sheets. Some botanical gardens—among others, those of Hannover, Hamburg, and Dortmund in West Germany—supplied schools directly with plants and instructions for their care.

Foundations for future work in the area of seed exchange were laid by the establishment of comprehensive seed collections, as in Basel, Switz., and of seed banks, as started in Copenhagen, Denmark. One seed bank already in operation was at Wakehurst Place, Ardingly, Sussex, an annex of the Royal Botanic Gardens, Kew.

The *Red Data Book* of the International Union for Conservation of Nature and Natural Resources (IUCN), published by the IUCN's Kew-based Threatened Plants Committee, formed a basis for worldwide protection of plant species. To put the protection plans into effect, a Botanic Garden Conservation Co-ordinating Body was to be set up and a journal for the dissemination of the most important items of information in the field was to be published.

Some conservation programs had already been publicized, but in certain countries the preparatory work still met with resistance. There, the listing of threatened plants and the establishment of nature preserves could be accomplished only with difficulty. Such nations included many in the Caribbean region, North Africa, and the Middle East.

National working teams were being encouraged to press on with their education programs, with the help of botanical gardens. However, as most of these institutions were concentrated in the Northern Hemisphere, many problems had to be overcome in tropical countries concerning the tasks of training staff and the establishment of protective zones, seed banks, and living collections. Much aid from private sources was needed. Encouraging new developments were under way, however, in Jalapa, Mexico, and Tafira Alta, Canary Islands.

Unfortunately, projects of this sort required considerable investment in space, technical facilities, energy, and trained staff. If the mere financial requirements frequently met with little positive response from the authorities, the staffing position in some countries was nothing short of catastrophic in view of the lack of trained junior personnel. (JOHANNES APEL)

[355.C.6]

CONTRIBUTORS

Names of contributors to the Britannica Book of the Year *with the articles written by them. The arrangement is alphabetical by last name.*

AARSDAL, STENER. Economic and Political Journalist, *Børsen*, Copenhagen.
Denmark

ADAMS, ANDREW M. Free-lance Foreign Correspondent; Editor and Publisher, *Sumo World* magazine. Author of *Ninja: The Invisible Assassins; Born to Die: The Cherry Blossom Squadrons.* Co-author of *Sumo History and Yokozuna Profiles.*
Combat Sports: *Judo; Karate; Kendo; Sumo*

ADO, YURI M. Chief, Accelerator Division, Institute for High Energy Physics, State Committee for Utilization of Atomic Energy of the U.S.S.R., Serpukhov. Co-author of "Coherent Radiation from the Electrons in a Synchrotron" in *Atomnaya energiya.*
Special Preprint: *Accelerators, Particle (in part)*

AGRELLA, JOSEPH C. Correspondent, *Blood-Horse* magazine; former Turf Editor, *Chicago Sun-Times.* Co-author of *Ten Commandments for Professional Handicapping; American Race Horses.*
Equestrian Sports: *Thoroughbred Racing and Steeplechasing (in part)*

AIELLO, LESLIE C. Lecturer, Department of Anthropology, University College, London.
Anthropology

ALLABY, MICHAEL. Free-lance Writer and Lecturer. Author of *The Eco-Activists; Who Will Eat?* Co-author of *Inventing Tomorrow; World Food Resources; A Blueprint for Survival.* Editor of *The Survival Handbook; Dictionary of the Environment.*
Environment *(in part)*

ALLAN, J. A. Lecturer in Geography, School of Oriental and African Studies, University of London.
Libya

ALSTON, REX. Broadcaster and Journalist; retired BBC Commentator. Author of *Taking the Air; Over to Rex Alston; Test Commentary; Watching Cricket.*
Cricket

AMARA, ROY C. President, Institute for the Future, Menlo Park, Calif. Author of *Toward Understanding the Social Impact of Computers; The Future As Present.*
Feature Article: *1985*

AMOR, JAMES F. Formerly Assistant Press Officer, U.K. Central Electricity Generating Board.
Energy: *Electricity*

ANDERSON, PETER J. Assistant Director, Institute of Polar Studies, Ohio State University, Columbus.
Antarctic

APEL, JOHANNES. Curator, Botanic Garden, University of Hamburg. Author of *Gärtnerisch-Botanische Briefe.*
Zoos and Botanical Gardens: *Botanical Gardens*

ARCHIBALD, JOHN J. Feature Writer, *St. Louis Post-Dispatch.* Author of *Bowling for Boys and Girls.*
Bowling: *Tenpin Bowling (in part); Duckpins*

ARNOLD, MAVIS. Free-lance Journalist, Dublin.
Ireland

ARONSFELD, CAESAR C. Senior Research Officer, Institute of Jewish Affairs, London. Editor of *Patterns of Prejudice.* Author of *The Ghosts of 1492; Jewish Aspects of the Struggle for Religious Freedom in Spain 1848–1976.*
Biographies *(in part)*

ARRINGTON, LEONARD J. Church Historian, Church of Jesus Christ of Latter-day Saints. Author of *Great Basin Kingdom; An Economic History of the Latter-day Saints; Building the City of God: Community and Cooperation Among the Mormons; The Mormon Experience: A History of the Latter-day Saints.*
Religion: *Church of Jesus Christ of Latter-day Saints*

AYTON, CYRIL J. Editor, *Motorcycle Sport*, London.
Motor Sports: *Motorcycles*

BARFORD, MICHAEL F. Editor and Director, *World Tobacco*, London.
Industrial Review: *Tobacco*

BARGAD, WARREN. Milton D. Ratner Professor of Hebrew Literature, Spertus College of Judaica, Chicago. Author of *Hayim Hazaz: Novelist of Ideas; Anthology of Israeli Poetry.*
Literature: *Hebrew*

BASS, HOWARD. Journalist and Broadcaster. Editor, *Winter Sports*, 1948–69. Winter Sports Correspondent, *Daily Telegraph* and *Sunday Telegraph*, London; *The Olympian*, New York City; *Canadian Skater*, Ottawa; *Skate*, London; *Skating*, Boston; *Ski Racing*, Denver; *Sport & Recreation*, London. Author of *The Sense in Sport; This Skating Age; The Magic of Skiing; International Encyclopaedia of Winter Sports; Let's Go Skating.*
Ice Hockey: *European and International;* **Winter Sports**

BAYLISS, DAVID. Chief Planner (Transportation), Greater London Council. Co-author of *Developing Patterns of Urbanization; Uses of Economics.* Advisory Editor of *Models in Urban and Regional Planning.*
Transportation *(in part)*

BEALL, JOHN V. Sales Manager, Arthur G. McKee Co. Author of sections 1 and 34, *Mining Engineering Handbook.* Frequent Contributor to *Mining Engineering.*
Mining and Quarrying *(in part)*

BEATTIE, ROGER A. Member of Secretariat, International Social Security Association, Geneva.
Social Security and Welfare Services *(in part)*

BEATTY, JAMES R. Research Fellow, B. F. Goodrich Research and Development Center, Brecksville, Ohio. Co-author of *Concepts in Compounding; Physical Testing of Elastomers and Polymers in Applied Polymer Science.*
Industrial Review: *Rubber*

BECKWITH, DAVID C. Managing Editor, *Legal Times of Washington*, Washington, D.C.
United States Statistical Supplement: *Developments in the States in 1978*

BENTLEY, STUART. Principal Lecturer in Sociology, Sheffield City Polytechnic, England. Co-author of *Work, Race, Immigration.*
Migration, International; Race Relations

BERGERRE, MAX. Correspondent ANSA for Vatican Affairs, Rome.
Vatican City State

BICKELHAUPT, DAVID L. Professor of Insurance and Finance, College of Administrative Science, Ohio State University, Columbus. Author of *Transition to Multiple-Line Insurance Companies; General Insurance* (10th ed.).
Industrial Review: *Insurance*

BILEFIELD, LIONEL. Technical Journalist.
Industrial Review: *Paints and Varnishes*

BINSTED, ARTHUR T. E. Vice-President and former Chairman, British Bottlers' Institute, London.
Industrial Review: *Alcoholic Beverages (in part)*

BODDY, WILLIAM C. Editor, *Motor Sport.* Full Member, Guild of Motoring Writers. Author of *The History of Brooklands Motor Course; The World's Land Speed Record; Continental Sports Cars; The Bugatti Story; History of Montlhéry.*
Motor Sports: *Grand Prix Racing*

BODEN, EDWARD. Editor, *The Veterinary Record*; Executive Editor, *Research in Veterinary Science.*
Veterinary Science

BOLT, PETER H. Secretary, British Committee, World Methodist Council. Author of *A Way of Loving.*
Religion: *Methodist Churches*

BOONSTRA, DICK. Assistant Professor, Department of Political Science, Free University, Amsterdam.
Netherlands, The; Suriname

BOOTH, JOHN NICHOLLS. Lecturer and Writer; Co-founder, Japan Free Religious Association; Senior Pastor of a number of U.S. churches. Author of *The Quest for Preaching Power; Introducing Unitarian Universalism.*
Religion: *Unitarian (Universalist) Churches*

BOSWALL, JEFFERY. Producer of Sound and Television Programs, British Broadcasting Corporation Natural History Unit, Bristol, England.
Life Sciences: *Ornithology*

BOTHELL, JOAN NATALIE. Editor, Wesleyan University Press, Middletown, Conn.
Biographies *(in part)*

BOYLE, C. L. Lieutenant Colonel, R.A. (retired). Chairman, Survival Service Commission, International Union for Conservation of Nature and Natural Resources, 1958–63; Secretary, Fauna Preservation Society, London, 1950–63.
Environment *(in part)*

BRACKMAN, ARNOLD C. Asian Affairs Specialist. Author of *Indonesian Communism: A History; Southeast Asia's Second Front: The Power Struggle in the Malay Archipelago; The Communist Collapse in Indonesia; The Last Emperor.*
Indonesia

BRADSHER, HENRY S. Diplomatic Correspondent, *Washington* (D.C.) *Star.*
Philippines

BRAIDWOOD, ROBERT J. Professor Emeritus of Old World Prehistory, the Oriental Institute and the Department of Anthropology, University of Chicago. Author of *Prehistoric Men; Archeologists and What They Do.*
Archaeology: *Eastern Hemisphere*

BRAMBELL, MICHAEL R. Director, Chester Zoo (North of England Zoological Society); formerly Curator of Mammals, London Zoo (Zoological Society of London). Author of *Horses, Tapirs and Rhinoceroses.*
Zoos and Botanical Gardens: *Zoos*

BRAZEE, RUTLAGE J. Program Manager for Seismological Research, U.S. Nuclear Regulatory Commission, Washington, D.C.
Earth Sciences: *Geophysics*

BRECHER, KENNETH. Associate Professor of Astronomy, Boston University. Co-author and co-editor of *Astronomy of the Ancients; High Energy Astrophysics and Its Relation to Elementary Particle Physics.*
Astronomy

BRUNO, HAL. Director of Political Coverage, ABC News, Washington, D.C.
Biographies *(in part)*

BURDIN, JOEL L. Associate Director, American Association of Colleges for Teacher Education; Editor, *Journal of Teacher Education;* Executive Secretary, Associated Organizations for Teacher Education. Co-author of *A Reader's Guide to the Comprehensive Models for Preparing Elementary Teachers; Elementary School Curriculum and Instruction.*
Education *(in part)*

BURKE, DONALD P. Executive Editor, *Chemical Week,* New York City.
Industrial Review: *Chemicals*

BURKS, ARDATH W. Professor of Asian Studies, Rutgers University, New Brunswick, N.J. Author of *The Government of Japan; East Asia: China, Korea, Japan.*
Japan

BUSS, ROBIN. Lecturer in French, Woolwich College of Further Education, London.
Literature: *French (in part)*

BUTLER, FRANK. Sports Editor, *News of the World,* London. Author of *A History of Boxing in Britain.*
Combat Sports: *Boxing*

CALHOUN, DAVID R. Editor, Encyclopædia Britannica, Yearbooks.
Gambling *(in part)*

CAMERON, SARAH. Economist, Lloyds Bank International Ltd., London.
Dominican Republic; Ecuador; Venezuela

CASSIDY, RICHARD J. Information Officer, British Gas Corporation. Author of *Gas: Natural Energy.*
Energy: *Natural Gas*

CASSIDY, VICTOR M. Writer and Editor, currently at work on a biography of Wyndham Lewis.
Biographies *(in part)*

CEGIELSKI, CHARLES M. Associate Editor, Encyclopædia Britannica, Yearbooks.
Life Sciences: *Introduction*

CHAPMAN, KENNETH F. Editor, *Philatelic Magazine;* Philatelic Correspondent, *The Times,* London. Author of *Good Stamp Collecting; Commonwealth Stamp Collecting.*
Philately and Numismatics: *Stamps*

CHAPMAN, ROBIN. Senior Economist, Lloyds Bank International Ltd., London.
Cuba; Haiti

CHAPPELL, DUNCAN. Professor, Department of Criminology, Simon Fraser University, Vancouver, B.C. Co-author of *The Police and the Public in Australia and New Zealand.* Co-editor of *The Australian Criminal Justice System* (1st and 2nd ed.); *Violence and Criminal Justice; Forcible Rape: the Crime, the Victim and the Offender.*
Crime and Law Enforcement

CHOATE, ROGER NYE. Stockholm Correspondent, *The Times,* London.
Sweden

CHU, HUNG-TI. Expert in Far Eastern Affairs; Former International Civil Servant and University Professor.
China; Taiwan

CLARKE, R. O. Principal Administrator, Social Affairs and Industrial Relations Division, Organization for Economic Cooperation and Development, Paris.
Industrial Relations

CLEVELAND, WILLIAM A. Geography Editor, *Encyclopædia Britannica* and Britannica Yearbooks.
Mining and Quarrying *(in part)*

CLIFTON, DONALD F. Professor of Metallurgy, University of Idaho.
Materials Sciences: *Metallurgy*

CLOUD, STANLEY W. Assistant Managing Editor, *Washington* (D.C.) *Star.*
Biographies *(in part)*

COCKSEDGE, DAVID. Features Writer, *Athletics Weekly,* Kent, England.
Biographies *(in part)*

COGLE, T. C. J. Editor, *Electrical Review,* London.
Industrial Review: *Electrical*

COPPOCK, CHARLES DENNIS. Vice-President, English Lacrosse Union. Author of "Men's Lacrosse" in *The Oxford Companion to Sports and Games.*
Field Hockey and Lacrosse: *Lacrosse (in part)*

COSTIN, STANLEY H. British Correspondent, *Herrenjournal International* and *Men's Wear, Australasia.* Council of Management Member, British Men's Fashion Association Ltd. Former President, Men's Fashion Writers International.
Fashion and Dress *(in part)*

CRATER, RUFUS W. Chief Correspondent, *Broadcasting,* Washington, D.C.
Television and Radio *(in part)*

CROSS, COLIN J. Editor, *The Polo Magazine,* U.K.
Equestrian Sports: *Polo*

CROSSLAND, NORMAN. Bonn Correspondent, *The Economist,* London.
Biographies *(in part);* **German Democratic Republic; Germany, Federal Republic of; Germany, Federal Republic of:** *Special Report*

CVIIC, K. F. Leader Writer and East European Specialist, *The Economist,* London.
Yugoslavia

DAIFUKU, HIROSHI. Chief, Section for Operations and Training, Cultural Heritage Division, UNESCO, Paris.
Historic Preservation

DAVID, TUDOR. Managing Editor, *Education,* London.
Education *(in part)*

DAVIES, JOHN. Education Director, The Publishers Association, London.
Publishing: *Books (in part)*

DAVIS, DONALD A. Editor, *Drug & Cosmetic Industry,* and *Cosmetic Capers,* New York City. Contributor to *The Science and Technology of Aerosol Packaging; Advances in Cosmetic Technology.*
Industrial Review: *Pharmaceuticals*

DAVIS, J. E. London Editor, *Britannica Book of the Year.*
Biographies *(in part)*

DEAM, JOHN B. Technical Director, National Machine Tool Builders Association, McLean, W.Va. Author of *The Synthesis of Common Digital Subsystems.*
Industrial Review: *Machinery and Machine Tools*

d'EÇA, RAUL. Retired from foreign service with U.S. Information Service. Co-author of *Latin American History.*
Brazil

DECRAENE, PHILIPPE. Member of editorial staff, *Le Monde,* Paris. Editor in Chief, *Revue française d'Études politiques africaines.* Author of *Le Panafricanisme; Tableau des Partis Politiques Africains; Lettres de l'Afrique Atlantique.*
Benin; Biographies *(in part);* **Cameroon; Central African Republic; Chad; Comoros; Congo; Dependent States** *(in part);* **Djibouti; Gabon; Guinea; Ivory Coast; Madagascar; Mali; Mauritania; Niger; Senegal; Togo; Tunisia; Upper Volta**

de FAINBOIM, MARTA BEKERMAN. Economist, Lloyds Bank International Ltd., London.
Paraguay

de la BARRE, KENNETH. Staff Scientist, Arctic Institute of North America, Calgary, Montreal.
Arctic Regions

DENG XIAOPING. Party Vice-Chairman and Vice-Premier, People's Republic of China.
Feature Article: *China's Future*

DE PUY, NORMAN R. Pastor and Executive Minister, First Baptist Church of Dearborn, Mich. Author of *The Bible Alive; Help in Understanding Theology.*
Religion: *Baptist Churches*

DESAUTELS, PAUL E. Curator, Department of Mineral Sciences, National Museum of Natural History, Smithsonian Institution, Washington, D.C. Author of *The Mineral Kingdom; The Gem Kingdom.*
Industrial Review: *Gemstones*

DeYOUNG, KAREN. Latin America Correspondent, *Washington* (D.C.) *Post.*
Chile; El Salvador; Nicaragua; Peru

DIRNBACHER, ELFRIEDE. Austrian Civil Servant.
Austria; Biographies *(in part)*

DOWBOR, PAUL. Economist, Lloyds Bank International Ltd., London.
Argentina; Latin-American Affairs; Uruguay

DRAEGER, DONN F. Director, International Hoplological Research Center, Honolulu. Author of *Weapons and Fighting Arts of the Indonesia Archipelago; Javanese Silat.*
Combat Sports: *Special Report*

DRAKE, CHRIS. Managing Director, *Cyprus Weekly,* Nicosia. Proprietor, East Med News Agency.
Cyprus

DUNICAN, PETER. Chairman, Ove Arup Partnership, London.
Engineering Projects: *Buildings*

EIU. The Economist Intelligence Unit, London.
Economy, World *(in part)*

ENGELS, JAN R. Editor, *Vooruitgang* (Quarterly of the Belgian Party for Freedom and Progress), Brussels.
Belgium; Biographies *(in part)*

EWART, W. D. Editor and Director, *Fairplay International Shipping Weekly,* London. Author of *Marine Engines; Atomic Submarines; Hydrofoils and Hovercraft; Building a Ship.* Editor of *World Atlas of Shipping.*
Industrial Review: *Shipbuilding;* **Transportation** *(in part)*

FAIRBANK, JENTY. Director of Information Services, International Headquarters, The Salvation Army. Author of *William and Catherine Booth: God's Soldiers.*
Religion: *Salvation Army*

FARR, D. M. L. Professor of History, Carleton University, Ottawa. Co-author of *The Canadian Experience.*
Canada

FENDELL, ROBERT J. Auto Editor, *Science &Mechanics*; Auto Contributor, *Gentlemen's Quarterly*. Author of *The New Era Car Book and Auto Survival Guide.* Co-author of *Encyclopedia of Motor Racing Greats.*
Motor Sports: *U.S. Racing*

FERRIER, R. W. Group Historian and Archivist, British Petroleum Company Ltd., London.
Energy: *Petroleum*

FIDDICK, PETER. Specialist Writer, *The Guardian,* London.
Publishing: *Newspapers (in part); Magazines (in part)*

FIELDS, DONALD. Helsinki Correspondent, BBC, *The Guardian,* and *The Sunday Times,* London.
Finland

FIRTH, DAVID. Editor, *The Friend,* London; formerly Editor, *Quaker Monthly,* London.
Religion: *Religious Society of Friends*

FISHER, DAVID. Civil Engineer, Freeman Fox & Partners, London; formerly Executive Editor, *Engineering,* London.
Engineering Projects: *Bridges*

FLANAGAN, JACK. Special Group Travel Newspaper Columnist.
Water Sports: *Surfing*

FOWELL, R. J. Lecturer, Department of Mining Engineering, University of Newcastle upon Tyne, England.
Energy: *Coal*

FRADY, WILLIAM ENSIGN, III. Editor, *Water Polo Scoreboard,* Newport Beach, Calif.
Water Sports: *Water Polo*

FRANKLIN, HAROLD. Editor, *English Bridge Quarterly.* Bridge Correspondent, *Yorkshire Post; Yorkshire Evening Post.* Broadcaster. Author of *Best of Bridge on the Air.*
Contract Bridge

FRANZ, FREDERICK W. President, Watch Tower Bible and Tract Society of Pennsylvania.
Religion: *Jehovah's Witnesses*

FRAWLEY, MARGARET-LOUISE. Retired Press Officer, All-England Women's Lacrosse Association.
Field Hockey and Lacrosse: *Lacrosse (in part)*

FRIDOVICH, IRWIN. James B. Duke Professor of Biochemistry, Duke University Medical Center, Durham, N.C. Contributor to *Oxidase and Redox Systems; Molecular Mechanisms of Oxygen Activation.*
Life Sciences: *Molecular Biology (in part)*

FRIEDLY, ROBERT LOUIS. Executive Director, Office of Communication, Christian Church (Disciples of Christ), Indianapolis, Ind.
Religion: *Disciples of Christ*

FRISKIN, SYDNEY E. Hockey Correspondent, *The Times,* London.
Field Hockey and Lacrosse: *Field Hockey*

FROST, DAVID. Rugby Union Correspondent, *The Guardian,* London.
Football: *Rugby*

GADDUM, PETER W. Chairman, H. T. Gaddum and Company Ltd., Silk Merchants, Macclesfield, Cheshire, England. Honorary President, International Silk Association, Lyons. Author of *Silk—How and Where It Is Produced.*
Industrial Review: *Textiles (in part)*

GANADO, ALBERT. Lawyer, Malta.
Malta

GBGB. Gaming Board of Great Britain.
Gambling *(in part)*

GEORGE, T. J. S. Editor, *Asiaweek,* Hong Kong. Author of *Krishna Menon: A Biography; Lee Kuan Yew's Singapore; Revolt in Mindaneo.*
Biographies *(in part)*; **Cambodia; Korea; Laos; Southeast Asian Affairs; Thailand; Vietnam**

GIBNEY, FRANK. Vice-Chairman, Britannica Board of Editors. Founding president of TBS-Britannica, Tokyo.
Feature Article: *A Visit with Vice-Chairman Deng (sidebar)*

GILLESPIE, HUGH M. Director of Communications, International Road Federation, Washington, D.C.
Engineering Projects: *Roads*

GJESTER, FAY. Oslo Correspondent, *Financial Times,* London.
Norway

GLASS, CHARLES. Editor, *Near East Business,* London.
Bahrain; Egypt; Iraq; Jordan; Kuwait; Lebanon; Middle Eastern Affairs; Oman; Qatar; Saudi Arabia; Syria; United Arab Emirates; Yemen, People's Democratic Republic of; Yemen Arab Republic

GOLDSMITH, ARTHUR. Editorial Director, *Popular Photography,* New York City. Author of *The Photography Game; The Nude in Photography.* Co-author of *The Eye of Eisenstaedt.*
Photography

GOLOMBEK, HARRY. British Chess Champion, 1947, 1949, and 1955. Chess Correspondent, *The Times* and *Observer,* London. Author of *Penguin Handbook of the Game of Chess; A History of Chess.*
Chess

GOODWIN, NÖEL. Associate Editor, *Dance & Dancers;* U.K. Dance Correspondent, *International Herald Tribune,* Paris, and *Ballet News,* New York City. Author of *A Ballet for Scotland;* editor of Royal Ballet and Royal Opera yearbooks for 1978, 1979. Contributor to the *Encyclopædia Britannica* (15th ed.).
Dance *(in part)*

GOODWIN, R. M. Free-lance Writer, London.
Cape Verde; Equestrian Sports: *Thoroughbred Racing and Steeplechasing (in part)*

GOODWIN, ROBERT E. Executive Director, Billiard Congress of America, Chicago, Publisher-Editor of various trade magazines.
Billiard Games

GOTTFRIED, MARTIN. Drama Critic, *Saturday Review,* New York City. Author of *A Theater Divided; Opening Nights; Broadway Musicals.*
Theatre *(in part)*

GOULD, DONALD W. Medical Writer and Broadcaster, U.K.
Health and Disease: *Overview (in part); Mental Health*

GREEN, BENNY. Record Reviewer, British Broadcasting Corporation. Author of *Blame It on My Youth; 58 Minutes to London; Jazz Decade; Drums in My Ears; Shaw's Champions.* Contributor to *Encyclopedia of Jazz.*
Music: *Jazz*

GRIFFITHS, A. R. G. Senior Lecturer in History, Flinders University of South Australia. Author of *Contemporary Australia.*
Australia; Australia: *Special Report;* **Nauru; Papua New Guinea**

GROSSBERG, ROBERT H. Executive Director, U.S. Amateur Jai Alai Players Association, Miami, Fla.
Court Games: *Jai Alai*

GROSSMAN, JOEL W. Director, Archaeological Survey Office, Rutgers University, New Brunswick, N.J.
Archaeology: *Western Hemisphere*

HACKER, ANDREW. Professor of Political Science, Queens College, Flushing, N.Y. Author of *The End of the American Era; The New Yorkers.*
Feature Article: *Survey of the '70s*

HARDMAN, THOMAS C. Editor and Publisher, *The Water Skier,* American Water Ski Association. Co-author of *Let's Go Water Skiing.*
Water Sports: *Water Skiing*

HARRIES, DAVID A. Director, Kinnear Moodie (1973) Ltd., Peterborough, England.
Engineering Projects: *Tunnels*

HARRISON, PAUL. Free-lance Writer on development. Author of *Inside the Third World; The Third World Tomorrow* (forthcoming).
Feature Article: *The International Year of the Child*

HASEGAWA, RYUSAKU. Editor, TBS-Britannica Co., Ltd., Tokyo.
Baseball *(in part)*

HAWKLAND, WILLIAM D. Chancellor and Professor of Law, Louisiana State University, Baton Rouge. Author of *Sales and Bulk Sales Under the Uniform Commercial Code; Cases on Bills and Notes; Transactional Guide of the Uniform Commercial Code; Cases on Sales and Security.*
Law: *Court Decisions*

HAWLEY, H. B. Specialist, Human Nutrition and Food Science, Switzerland.
Food Processing

HEATH, EDWARD. Member of the British Parliament; U.K. Prime Minister, 1970–74.
European Unity: *Special Report*

HEBBLETHWAITE, PETER. Rome Correspondent, *National Catholic Reporter,* Kansas City, Mo. Author of *The Council Fathers and Atheism; Understanding the Synod; The Runaway Church; Christian-Marxist Dialogue and Beyond; The Year of Three Popes.*
Biographies *(in part)*; **Religion:** *Roman Catholic Church*

HENDERSHOTT, MYRL C. Professor of Oceanography, Scripps Institution of Oceanography, La Jolla, Calif.
Earth Sciences: *Oceanography*

HERMAN, ROBIN CATHY. Sports Reporter, *New York Times.*
Ice Hockey: *North American*

HESS, MARVIN G. Executive Vice-President, National Wrestling Coaches Association, Salt Lake City, Utah.
Combat Sports: *Wrestling*

HINDIN, HARVEY J. Communications Editor, *Electronics* magazine, New York City. Author of numerous articles on electronics and mathematics.
Industrial Review: *Telecommunications*

HOPE, THOMAS W. President, Hope Reports, Inc. Rochester, N.Y. Author of *Hope Reports AV-USA; Hope Reports Education and Media; Hope Reports Perspective.*
Motion Pictures *(in part)*

HORRY, JOHN H. Former Secretary, International Squash Rackets Federation. Contributor to *The Oxford Companion to Sports and Games.*
Racket Games: *Squash Rackets*

HOTZ, LOUIS. Former Editorial Writer, *Johannesburg* (S.Af.) *Star.* Co-author and

contributor to *The Jews in South Africa: A History.*
Biographies (*in part*); **South Africa**

HOWKINS, JOHN. Editor, *InterMedia,* International Institute of Communications, London. Author of *Understanding Television.*
Television and Radio (*in part*)

HUNNINGS, NEVILLE MARCH. General Editor, European Law Centre Ltd., London. Editor of *Common Market Law Reports, Commercial Laws of Europe,* and *European Commercial Cases.* Author of *Film Censors and the Law.* Co-editor of *Legal Problems of an Enlarged European Community.*
Law: *International Law*

INGHAM, KENNETH. Professor of History, University of Bristol, England. Author of *Reformers in India; A History of East Africa.*
Angola; Guinea-Bissau; Kenya; Malawi; Mozambique; São Tomé and Príncipe; Seychelles; Tanzania; Uganda; Zaire; Zambia; Zimbabwe Rhodesia

ISKOLDSKAYA, MAYA Y. Correspondent, Fiction Department, *Knizhnoye Obozreniye,* Moscow.
Literature: *Russian* (*in part*)

JACQUET, CONSTANT H. Staff Associate for Information Services, Office of Research, Evaluation and Planning, National Council of Churches. Editor of *Yearbook of American and Canadian Churches.*
United States Statistical Supplement: *Church Membership table*

JARDINE, ADRIAN. Company Director. Member, Guild of Yachting Writers.
Sailing

JASPERT, W. PINCUS. Technical Editorial Consultant. European Editor, North American Publishing Company, Philadelphia. Member, Inter-Comprint Planning Committee; Member, Society of Photographic Engineers and Scientists; Life Member, *Eurographic Press.* Editor of *Encyclopaedia of Type Faces.*
Industrial Review: *Printing*

JENKINS, DAVID. Bureau Chief, *Far Eastern Economic Review,* Jakarta, Indon. Editor of *Student Guide to Asia.*
Biographies (*in part*)

JENKINS, PETER. Policy Editor and Political Columnist, *The Guardian,* London.
United Kingdom

JESSOP, DAVID A. Editor, *Caribbean Chronicle* and *Insight.* Consultant on Caribbean affairs.
Bahamas, The; Barbados; Biographies (*in part*); **Dependent States** (*in part*); **Dominica; Grenada; Guyana; Jamaica; Saint Lucia; Saint Vincent and the Grenadines; Trinidad and Tobago**

JOFFÉ, GEORGE. Journalist and Writer on North African Affairs.
Algeria; Biographies (*in part*); **Morocco**

JONES, C. M. Consultant, *World Bowls;* Editor, *Tennis.* Member, British Society of Sports Psychology; Associate Member, British Association of National Coaches. Author of *Winning Bowls; How to Become a Champion;* numerous books on tennis. Coauthor of *Tackle Bowls My Way; Bryant on Bowls.*
Bowling: *Lawn Bowls*

JONES, D. A. N. Assistant Editor, *The Listener,* London.
Biographies (*in part*); **Literature:** *Introduction; United Kingdom*

JONES, HANDEL H. Vice-President, Gnostic Concepts, Inc., Menlo Park, Calif.
Industrial Review: *Microelectronics*

JONES, W. GLYN. Professor of Scandinavian Studies, University of Newcastle upon Tyne, England. Author of *Johannes Jørgensens modne år; Johannes Jörgensen; Denmark; William Heinesen; Færø og kosmos.*
Literature: *Danish*

JOSEPH, LOU. Manager of Media Relations, Bureau of Public Information, American Dental Association. Author of *A Doctor Discusses Allergy: Facts and Fiction; Natural Childbirth; Diabetes; Childrens' Colds.*
Health and Disease: *Dentistry*

KATZ, WILLIAM A. Professor, School of Library Science, State University of New York, Albany. Author of *Magazines for Libraries* (2nd ed. and supplement); *Magazine Selection.*
Publishing: *Magazines* (*in part*)

KEDOURIE, ELIE. Professor of Politics, London School of Economics and Political Science; Fellow of the British Academy. Author of *Nationalism in Asia and Africa; The Chatham House Version; Arabic Political Memoirs; In the Anglo-Arab Labyrinth.*
Feature Article: *Islam Resurgent*

KELLEHER, JOHN A. Editorial Consultant, *The Dominion,* Wellington, N.Z.
New Zealand

KELLMAN, JEROLD L. Editor-in-Chief, Publications International, Ltd. Author of *Presidents of the United States;* Contributor to *The People's Almanac.*
Biographies (*in part*); **Computers**

KENNEDY, RICHARD M. Agricultural Economist, International Economics Division of the Economics, Statistics, and Cooperatives Service, U.S. Department of Agriculture.
Agriculture and Food Supplies

KERRIGAN, ANTHONY. Visiting Professor, University of Illinois. Editor and Translator of *Selected Works* of Miguel de Unamuno (7 vol.) and of works of Jorge Luis Borges. Author of *At the Front Door of the Atlantic.*
Literature: *Spanish* (*in part*)

KILIAN, MICHAEL D. Columnist, *Chicago Tribune;* News Commentator, WBBM Radio, Chicago. Author of *Who Runs Chicago?*
Aerial Sports

KILLHEFFER, JOHN V. Associate Editor, *Encyclopædia Britannica.*
Nobel Prizes (*in part*)

KIMCHE, JON. Editor, *Afro-Asian Affairs,* London. Author of *There Could Have Been Peace: The Untold Story of Why We Failed With Palestine and Again with Israel; Seven Fallen Pillars; Second Arab Awakening.*
Israel

KIND, JOSHUA B. Associate Professor of Art History, Northern Illinois University, De Kalb. Author of *Rouault; Naive Art in Illinois 1830–1976.*
Museums (*in part*)

KITAGAWA, JOSEPH M. Professor of History of Religions and Dean of the Divinity School, University of Chicago. Author of *Religions of the East; Religion in Japanese History.*
Religion: *Buddhism*

KLARE, HUGH J. Chairman, Gloucestershire Probation Training Committee, England. Secretary, Howard League for Penal Reform 1950–71. Author of *People in Prison.* Regular Contributor to *Justice of the Peace.*
Prisons and Penology

KNECHT, JEAN. Formerly Assistant Foreign Editor, *Le Monde,* Paris; formerly Permanent Correspondent in Washington and Vice-President of the Association de la Presse Diplomatique Française.
France

KNOX, RICHARD A. Editor, *Nuclear Engineering International,* London. Author of *Experiments in Astronomy for Amateurs; Foundations of Astronomy.*
Industrial Review: *Nuclear Industry*

KOPPER, PHILIP. Free-lance Writer and Journalist, Washington, D.C.
Biographies (*in part*); **Nobel Prizes** (*in part*)

KUNKLER, JULIE. Picture Editor, Encyclopædia Britannica, *Yearbook of Science and the Future.*
Biographies (*in part*)

LAMB, KEVIN M. Sports Writer, *Chicago Sun-Times.*
Biographies (*in part*); **Football:** *U.S. Football; Canadian Football*

LARSON, ROY. Religion Editor, *Chicago Sun-Times.*
Religion: *Introduction*

LEAPER, ERIC. Executive Director, National Organization for River Sports, Colorado Springs, Colo.
Water Sports: *River Sports*

LEGUM, COLIN. Associate Editor, *The Observer;* Editor, *Middle East Contemporary Survey* and *Africa Contemporary Record,* London. Author of *Must We Lose Africa?; Congo Disaster; Pan-Africanism: A Political Guide; South Africa: Crisis for the West.*
African Affairs; Biographies (*in part*)

LEIFER, MICHAEL. Reader in International Relations, London School of Economics and Political Science. Author of *Dilemmas of Statehood in Southeast Asia.*
Malaysia; Singapore

LENNOX-KERR, PETER. European Editor, *Textile World.* Author of *Index to Man-Made Fibres Book.* Editor of *Nonwovens '71;* Publisher of *OE-Report,* New Mills, England.
Industrial Review: *Textiles* (*in part*)

LEVE, CHARLES S. Editor, *National Racquetball* magazine; National Director, U.S. Racquetball Association and National Racquetball Club, Inc. Author of *Inside Racquetball;* Co-author of *Winning Racquetball.*
Racket Games: *Racquetball*

LIMBURG, ALBERT W. Free-lance Writer on outdoors and boating topics.
Water Sports: *Motorboating*

LITTELL, FRANKLIN H. Professor of Religion, Temple University, Philadelphia, Pa. Co-editor of *Weltkirchenlexikon;* Author of *Macmillan Atlas History of Christianity.*
Religion: *World Church Membership*

LOGAN, ROBERT G. Sportswriter, *Chicago Tribune.* Author of *The Bulls and Chicago—A Stormy Affair.*
Basketball (*in part*)

LULING, VIRGINIA R. Social Anthropologist.
Somalia; Sudan

LUNDE, ANDERS S. Consultant; Adjunct Professor, Department of Biostatistics, University of North Carolina. Author of *Systems of Demographic Measurement: The Single Round Retrospective Interview Survey.*
Demography

McCARTHY, JOHN E. President, International Catholic Migration Commission; Executive Director of Migration and Ref-

ugee Services, United States Catholic Conference.
Refugees: *Special Report*

McCAULEY, MARTIN. Lecturer in Russian and Soviet Institutions, School of Slavonic and East European Studies, University of London. Author of *Khrushchev and Soviet Agriculture: The Virgin Land Programme 1953–1964.* Editor of *The Russian Revolution and the Soviet State 1917–1921; Communist Power in Europe 1944–1949.*
Union of Soviet Socialist Republics

MACDONALD, BARRIE. Senior Lecturer in History, Massey University, Palmerston North, N.Z. Author of several articles on the history and politics of Pacific islands.
Biographies (*in part*); **Dependent States** (*in part*); **Fiji; Kiribati; Solomon Islands; Tonga; Tuvalu; Western Samoa**

MacDONALD, M. C. Director, World Economics Ltd., London.
Agriculture and Food Supplies: *grain table;* **Transportation:** *table;* statistical sections of articles on the various countries

MACDONALD, TREVOR J. Manager, International Affairs, British Steel Corporation.
Industrial Review: *Iron and Steel*

MACGREGOR-MORRIS, PAMELA. Equestrian Correspondent, *The Times* and *Horse and Hound,* London. Author of books on equestrian topics.
Equestrian Sports: *Show Jumping*

McLACHLAN, KEITH S. Senior Lecturer, School of Oriental and African Studies, University of London.
Iran

MALLETT, H. M. F. Editor, *Wool Record Weekly Market Report,* Bradford, England.
Industrial Review: *Textiles* (*in part*)

MANGO, ANDREW. Orientalist and Broadcaster.
Turkey

MAO, NATHAN K. Professor of Chinese Studies, Shippensburg (Pa.) State College. Author of *Modern Chinese Fiction; Pa Chin.*
Biographies (*in part*); **Literature:** *Chinese* (*in part*)

MARQUARDT, WILHELM RUDOLF. Member, Board of Curators, IFO-Institute for Economic Research, Munich, West Germany. Author of *Seychellen, Komoren und Maskarenen.*
Special Preprint: *Seychelles*

MARSHALL, J. G. SCOTT. Horticultural Consultant.
Gardening (*in part*)

MARTY, MARTIN E. Fairfax M. Cone Distinguished Service Professor, University of Chicago; Associate Editor, *The Christian Century.*
Religion: *Special Report*

MARYLES, DAISY G. Associate Editor, Bookselling and Marketing, *Publishers Weekly,* New York City.
Publishing: *Books* (*in part*)

MATEJA, JAMES L. Auto Editor and Financial Reporter, *Chicago Tribune.*
Industrial Review: *Automobiles*

MATTHÍASSON, BJÖRN. Economist, European Free Trade Association, Geneva.
Iceland

MAURON, PAUL. Director, International Vine and Wine Office, Paris.
Industrial Review: *Alcoholic Beverages* (*in part*)

MAZIE, DAVID M. Associate of Carl T. Rowan, syndicated columnist. Free-lance Writer.
Social Security and Welfare Services (*in part*)

MAZZE, EDWARD MARK. Dean and Professor of Marketing, School of Business Administration, Temple University, Philadelphia. Author of *Personal Selling: Choice Against Chance; Introduction to Marketing: Readings in the Discipline.*
Consumerism (*in part*); **Industrial Review:** *Advertising*

MELLBLOM, NEIL B. Director, News Bureau, Lutheran Council in the USA, New York City.
Religion: *Lutheran Churches*

MELLOR, CHRISTINE. Economist, Lloyds Bank International Ltd., London.
Colombia; Costa Rica; Guatemala; Honduras

MERMEL, T. W. Consultant; formerly Chairman, Committee on World Register of Dams, International Commission on Large Dams. Author of *Register of Dams in the United States.*
Engineering Projects: *Dams table*

MEYENDORFF, JOHN. Professor of Church History and Patristics, St. Vladimir's Orthodox Theological Seminary; Professor of History, Fordham University, New York City. Author of *Christ in Eastern Christian Thought; Byzantine Theology.*
Religion: *The Orthodox Church; Eastern Non-Chalcedonian Churches*

MICHIE, LAURENCE BRUCE. Television Editor, *Variety,* New York City.
Television and Radio: *Special Report*

MILES, PETER W. Chairman, Department of Entomology, University of Adelaide, Australia.
Life Sciences: *Entomology*

MILLIKIN, SANDRA. Architectural Historian.
Architecture; Art Exhibitions; Museums (*in part*)

MINA, MARTHA H. Market Research Assistant, Glass Manufacturers' Federation, London.
Industrial Review: *Glass*

MITCHELL, K. K. Lecturer, Department of Physical Education, University of Leeds, England. Honorary General Secretary, English Basket Ball Association.
Basketball (*in part*)

MODIANO, MARIO. Athens Correspondent, *The Times,* London.
Greece

MODRICH, PAUL LAWRENCE. Assistant Professor of Biochemistry, Duke University Medical Center, Durham, N.C.
Life Sciences: *Molecular Biology* (*in part*)

MOFFAT, A. I. B. Senior Lecturer, Department of Civil Engineering, University of Newcastle upon Tyne, England. Editor of *Inspection, Operation and Maintenance of Existing Dams.*
Engineering Projects: *Dams*

MONACO, ALBERT M., JR. Executive Director, United States Volleyball Association, Colorado Springs, Colo.
Court Games: *Volleyball*

MOORE, JOHN E. Staff Hydrologist, Water Resources Division, U.S. Geological Survey.
Earth Sciences: *Hydrology*

MORGAN, HAZEL. Free-lance Writer and Singer, London.
Music: *Popular*

MORRISON, DONALD. Senior Editor, *Time* magazine.
Publishing: *Newspapers* (*in part*)

MORTIMER, MOLLY. Commonwealth Correspondent, *The Spectator,* London. Author of *Trusteeship in Practice; Kenya.*
Botswana; Burundi; Commonwealth of Nations; Dependent States (*in part*); **Equatorial Guinea; Gambia, The; Ghana; Lesotho; Liberia; Maldives; Mauritius; Nigeria; Rwanda; Sierra Leone; Swaziland**

MOSHANSKY, MOZELLE A. Music Journalist and Writer, *The Guardian, The Listener, International Music Guide, Classical Music,* and BBC Radio.
Biographies (*in part*); **Music:** *Classical*

MUCK, TERRY CHARLES. Editor, *Handball* magazine, Skokie, Ill.
Court Games: *Handball*

NAYLOR, ERNEST. Professor of Marine Biology, University of Liverpool; Director, Marine Biological Laboratory, Port Erin, Isle of Man. Author of *British Marine Isopods.* Co-editor, *Estuarine and Coastal Marine Science.*
Life Sciences: *Marine Biology*

NEILL, JOHN. Technical Manager, Submerged Combustion Ltd. Author of Climbers' Club Guides; *Cwm Silyn and Tremadoc, Snowdon South;* Alpine Club Guide: *Selected Climbs in the Pennine Alps.*
Mountaineering

NELSON, BERT. Editor, *Track and Field News.* Author of *Little Red Book; The Decathlon Book; Olympic Track and Field; Of People and Things.*
Track and Field Sports

NETSCHERT, BRUCE C. Vice-President, National Economic Research Associates, Inc., Washington, D.C. Author of *The Future Supply of Oil and Gas.* Co-author of *Energy in the American Economy: 1850–1975.*
Energy: *World Summary*

NEUSNER, JACOB. University Professor, Brown University, Providence, R.I. Author of *Invitation to the Talmud; A History of the Mishnaic Law of Purities.*
Religion: *Judaism*

NOEL, H. S. Free-lance Journalist; formerly Managing Editor, *World Fishing,* London.
Fisheries

NORMAN, GERALDINE. Saleroom Correspondent, *The Times,* London. Author of *The Sale of Works of Art; Nineteenth Century Painters and Painting: A Dictionary;* Co-author of *The Fake's Progress.*
Art Sales; Art Sales: *Special Report*

NOVALES, RONALD R. Professor of Biological Sciences, Northwestern University, Evanston, Ill. Contributor to *Handbook of Physiology; Comparative Animal Physiology; Frontiers of Hormone Research.*
Life Sciences: *Zoology Overview*

OSBORNE, KEITH. Editor, *Rowing, 1961–63;* Honorary Editor, *British Rowing Almanack,* 1961– . Author of *Boat Racing in Britain, 1715–1975.*
Rowing

OSER, ALAN S. Real Estate Editor, *New York Times.*
Environment: *Special Report*

OSTERBIND, CARTER C. Director, Bureau of Economic and Business Research, University of Florida. Editor of *Income in Retirement; Migration, Mobility, and Aging; Social Goals, Social Programs and the Aging.*
Industrial Review: *Building and Construction*

PAGE, SHEILA A. B. Research Officer, National Institute of Economic and Social Research, London.
Economy, World (*in part*)

PALMER, JOHN. European Editor, *The Guardian,* London.
European Unity

PALMER, S. B. Senior Lecturer, Department of Applied Physics, University of Hull, England.
Physics

PARKER, SANDY. Publisher of weekly international newsletter on fur industry.
Industrial Review: *Furs*

PAUL, CHARLES ROBERT, JR. Director of Communications, U.S. Olympic Committee, Colorado Springs, Colo. Author of *The Olympic Games, 1968.*
Gymnastics and Weight Lifting

PENFOLD, ROBIN C. Free-lance Writer specializing in industrial topics. Editor, *Shell Polymers.* Author of *A Journalist's Guide to Plastics.*
Industrial Review: *Plastics*

PERTILE, LINO. Lecturer in Italian, University of Sussex, England.
Literature: *Italian*

PETHERICK, KARIN. Crown Princess Louise Lecturer in Swedish, University College, London.
Literature: *Swedish*

PFEFFER, IRVING. Attorney. President, Dover Insurance Co., Ltd. Author of *The Financing of Small Business; Perspectives on Insurance.*
Stock Exchanges *(in part)*

PHINNEY, ALLISON W. Manager, Committees on Publication, The First Church of Christ, Scientist, Boston.
Religion: *Church of Christ, Scientist*

PLOTKIN, FREDERICK S. Professor of English Literature and Chairman, Division of Humanities, Stern College, Yeshiva University, New York City. Author of *Milton's Inward Jerusalem; Faith and Reason; Judaism and Tragic Theology.*
Literature: *United States*

POST, AVERY D. President, United Church of Christ, New York City.
Religion: *United Church of Christ*

PRASAD, H. Y. SHARADA. Director, Indian Institute of Mass Communication, New Delhi, India.
India

RANGER, ROBIN. Associate Professor, Department of Political Science, St. Francis Xavier University, Antigonish, Nova Scotia; Department of National Defence Fellow in Strategic Studies (1978–79). Author of *Arms and Politics, 1958–1978; Arms Control in a Changing Political Context.*
Defense; Defense: *Special Report*

RAY, G. F. Senior Research Fellow, National Institute of Economic and Social Research, London; Visiting Professor, University of Surrey, Guildford, England.
Industrial Review: *Introduction*

REBELO, L. S. Lecturer, Department of Portuguese Studies, King's College, University of London.
Literature: *Portuguese (in part)*

REICHELDERFER, F. W. Consultant on Atmospheric Sciences; formerly Director, Weather Bureau, U.S. Department of Commerce, Washington, D.C.
Earth Sciences: *Meteorology*

REID, J. H. Senior Lecturer in German, University of Nottingham, England. Coeditor of *Renaissance and Modern Studies.* Author of *Heinrich Böll: Withdrawal and Re-emergence;* Co-author of *Critical Strategies: German Fiction in the Twentieth Century.*
Literature: *German*

ROBINSON, DAVID. Film Critic, *The Times,* London. Author of *Buster Keaton; The Great Funnies—A History of Screen Comedy; A History of World Cinema.*
Motion Pictures *(in part)*

SAEKI, SHOICHI. Professor of Comparative Literature, University of Tokyo. Author of *In Search of Japanese Ego.*
Literature: *Japanese*

SAINT-AMOUR, ROBERT. Professor, Department of Literary Studies, University of Quebec at Montreal.
Literature: *French (in part)*

SARAHETE, YRJÖ. General Secretary, Fédération Internationale des Quilleurs, Helsinki.
Bowling: *Tenpin Bowling (in part)*

SARMIENTO, SERGIO A. Editor-in-Chief, *Enciclopedia Barsa,* Encyclopædia Britannica Publishers, Inc.
Mexico: *Special Report*

SCHOENFIELD, ALBERT. Co-publisher, *Swimming World;* Vice-Chairman, U.S. Olympic Swimming Committee. Contributor to *The Technique of Water Polo; The History of Swimming; Competitive Swimming as I See It.*
Swimming

SCHOFIELD, VICTORIA. Free-lance Writer, U.K. Author of *The United Nations; Bhutto: Trial and Execution.*
Biographies *(in part)*

SCHÖPFLIN, GEORGE. Lecturer in East European Political Institutions, London School of Economics and School of Slavonic and East European Studies, University of London.
Czechoslovakia

SCHULMAN, ELIAS. Professor, Queens College, City University of New York. Author of *Israel Tsinberg, His Life and Works; A History of Yiddish Literature in America; Soviet-Yiddish Literature; Portraits and Studies.*
Literature: *Yiddish*

SEALE, PATRICK. Writer and Broadcaster; Correspondent on Middle East affairs, *The Observer,* London. Author of *French Revolution 1968; Philby, the Long Road to Moscow.* Co-author of *The Struggle for Syria.*
Feature Article: *Two Peoples—One Land*

SEARS, ROBERT N. Senior Associate Technical Editor, *The American Rifleman.*
Target Sports *(in part)*

SHACKLEFORD, CAMILLE. Director, International Tourism Consultants.
Industrial Review: *Tourism*

SHARPE, MITCHELL R. Science Writer; Historian, Alabama Space and Rocket Center, Huntsville. Author of *The Rocket Team; Living in Space: The Environment of the Astronaut; "It Is I, Seagull": Valentina Tereshkova, First Woman in Space; Satellites and Probes, the Development of Unmanned Spaceflight.*
Space Exploration

SHAW, T. R. Commander, Royal Navy. Associate Editor, *International Journal of Speleology.* Author of *History of Cave Science.*
Speleology

SHENK, CLAYTON B. Executive Secretary, U.S. National Archery Association.
Target Sports *(in part)*

SHOEMAKER, FRANK C. Professor of Physics, Princeton University.
Special Preprint: *Accelerators, Particle (in part)*

SIMPSON, NOEL. Managing Director, Sydney Bloodstock Proprietary Ltd., Sydney, Australia.
Equestrian Sports: *Harness Racing*

SMEDLEY, GLENN B. Public Relations Director, American Numismatic Association.
Philately and Numismatics: *Coins*

SMITH, REUBEN W. Dean, Graduate School, and Professor of History, University of the Pacific, Stockton, Calif. Editor of *Venture of Islam* by M. G. S. Hodgson.
Religion: *Islam*

SMOGORZEWSKI, K. M. Writer on contemporary history. Founder and Editor, *Free Europe,* London. Author of *The United States and Great Britain; Poland's Access to the Sea.*
Albania; Andorra; Biographies *(in part)*; **Bulgaria; Hungary; Liechtenstein; Luxembourg; Monaco; Mongolia; Poland; Political Parties; Romania; San Marino**

SNIDER, ARTHUR J. Science Writer, *Chicago Sun-Times.* Author of *Learning How to Live with Heart Trouble; Learning How to Live with Nervous Tension; Learning How to Live with High Blood Pressure.*
Health and Disease: *Overview (in part)*

SOCHEN, JUNE. Professor of History, Northeastern Illinois University, Chicago. Author of *Movers and Shakers: American Women Thinkers and Activists; Her Story: A Woman's View of American History.*
Law: *Special Report*

SPELMAN, ROBERT A. President, Home Furnishings Services, Washington, D.C.
Industrial Review: *Furniture*

STAERK, MELANIE. Member, Swiss Press Association. Former Member, Swiss National Commission for UNESCO.
Switzerland

STEEN, LYNN ARTHUR. Professor of Mathematics, St. Olaf College, Northfield, Minn. Author of *Mathematics Today; Counterexamples in Topology; Annotated Bibliography of Expository Writing in the Mathematical Sciences.*
Mathematics

STERN, IRWIN. Assistant Professor of Portuguese, Columbia University, New York City. Author of *Júlio Dinis e o romance português (1860–1870);* Co-editor of *Modern Iberian Literature: A Library of Literary Criticism.*
Literature: *Portuguese (in part)*

STEVENSON, TOM. Garden Columnist, *Baltimore News American; Washington Post;* Washington Post-Los Angeles Times News Service. Book Editor, *American Horticulturist.* Author of *Pruning Guide for Trees, Shrubs, and Vines; Lawn Guide.*
Gardening *(in part)*

STONE, EDWARD C. Professor of Physics and Voyager Project Scientist, California Institute of Technology, Pasadena.
Space Exploration: *Special Report*

STØVERUD, TORBJØRN. W. P. Ker Senior Lecturer in Norwegian, University College, London.
Literature: *Norwegian*

STRAUS, ERNST GABOR. Professor of Mathematics, University of California at Los Angeles. Author of *Elements of Analytic Geometry with Linear Algebra.*
Physics: *Special Report*

STRAUSS, MICHAEL. Feature and Sports Writer, *New York Times.* Author of *The New York Times Ski Guide to the United States.*
Combat Sports: *Fencing*

SULLIVAN, H. PATRICK. Dean of the Faculty and Professor of Religion, Vassar College, Poughkeepsie, N.Y.
Religion: *Hinduism*

SWEETINBURGH, THELMA. Paris Fashion Correspondent for the British Wool Textile Industry.
Fashion and Dress *(in part)*

SWIFT, RICHARD N. Professor of Politics, New York University, New York City. Author of *International Law: Current*

and Classic; World Affairs and the College Curriculum.
United Nations

SYNAN, VINSON. Assistant General Superintendent, Pentecostal Holiness Church. Author of *The Holiness-Pentecostal Movement; The Old Time Power.*
Religion: *Pentecostal Churches*

TAISHOFF, SOL J. Editor, *Broadcasting,* Washington, D.C.
Television and Radio *(in part)*

TALLAN, NORMAN M. Chief Scientist, Air Force Materials Laboratory, Wright-Patterson Air Force Base, Dayton, Ohio. Editor of *Electrical Conductivity in Ceramics and Glass.*
Materials Sciences: *Ceramics*

TATEISHI, KAY K. Reporter-Editor, Tokyo Bureau, Associated Press.
Biographies *(in part)*

TATTERSALL, ARTHUR. Textile Trade Statistician, Manchester, England.
Industrial Review: *Textiles (in part)*

TERRY, WALTER, JR. Dance Critic, *Saturday Review* magazine, New York City. Author of *The Dance in America; Great Male Dancers of the Ballet.*
Dance *(in part)*

THEINER, GEORGE. Assistant Editor, *Index on Censorship,* London. Co-author of *The Kill Dog;* editor of *New Writing in Czechoslovakia;* translator of *Poetry of Miroslav Holub.*
Literature: *Eastern European; Russian (in part)*

THOMAS, HARFORD. Retired City and Financial Editor, *The Guardian,* London.
Biographies *(in part)*

THOMPSON, ANTHONY. European Linguist Research Fellow, CLW, Aberystwyth, Wales. General Secretary, International Federation of Library Associations, 1962–70. Author of *Library Buildings of Britain and Europe.*
Libraries

TINGAY, LANCE. Lawn Tennis Correspondent, the *Daily Telegraph,* London. Author of *100 Years of Wimbledon; Tennis, A Pictorial History.*
Tennis

TRIGG, ROBERT H. Director, Economic Research, Committee Policy Studies Section, New York Stock Exchange.
Stock Exchanges *(in part)*

TRILLING, OSSIA. Vice-President, International Association of Theatre Critics (1956–77). Co-editor and Contributor, *International Theatre.* Contributor, BBC, the *Financial Times,* London.
Biographies *(in part)*; **Theatre** *(in part)*

TRINDADE, INGRID T. Secretary, Department of Cooperation and Witness, World Alliance of Reformed Churches.
Religion: *Presbyterian, Reformed, and Congregational Churches*

TRUSSELL, TAIT. Administrative Vice-President, American Forest Institute.
Industrial Review: *Wood Products*

UNHCR. The Office of the United Nations High Commissioner for Refugees.
Refugees

UNNY, GOVINDAN. Agence France-Presse Special Correspondent for India, Nepal, and Sri Lanka.
Afghanistan; Bangladesh; Bhutan; Burma; Nepal; Pakistan; Sri Lanka

VALE, NORMAN K. Retired Director of News Services, The United Church of Canada.
Religion: *United Church of Canada*

van den HOVEN, ISOLA. Writer on Consumer Affairs, The Hague, Neth.
Consumerism *(in part)*

VAN DOREN, CHARLES. Vice-President, Editorial, Encyclopædia Britannica.
Feature Article: *Islam Resurgent (sidebar)*

van PRAAG, JACK H. National Public Relations Director, U.S. Badminton Assn.
Racket Games: *Badminton*

VERDI, ROBERT WILLIAM. Sportswriter, *Chicago Tribune.*
Baseball *(in part)*

VINT, ARTHUR KINGSLEY. Counselor, International Table Tennis Federation, East Sussex, England.
Table Tennis

WADLEY, J. B. Writer and Broadcaster on cycling; Cycling Correspondent, *Daily Telegraph,* London. Editor of *Guinness Guide to Bicycling.* Author of *Tour de France 1970, 1971, and 1973; Old Roads and New.*
Cycling

WARD, PETER. Owner and Operator, Ward News Service, Ottawa; Parliamentary Reporter and Commentator.
Canada: *Special Report*

WARD-THOMAS, P. A. Golf Correspondent, *Country Life,* London.
Golf

WARNER, ANTONY C. Assistant Editor, *Off License News,* London.
Industrial Review: *Alcoholic Beverages (in part)*

WAY, DIANE LOIS. Historical Researcher, Ontario Historical Studies Series.
Biographies *(in part)*

WEBB, GORDON A. Editor, *Toys International,* London.
Games and Toys

WEBSTER, PETER L. Associate Professor, Department of Botany, University of Massachusetts. Co-author of *The Cell.*
Life Sciences: *Botany*

WHITTINGHAM, RICHARD. Free-lance Writer, Editor and Photographer, Chicago. Author of *Martial Justice; The Chicago Bears.*
Health and Disease: *Special Report*

WIJNGAARD, BARBARA. Economist, Lloyds Bank International Ltd., London.
Mexico

WILKINSON, GORDON. Head, Communications Section, Research and Development Division, Rentokil Ltd., East Grinstead, England. Chemistry Consultant, *New Scientist,* London. Author of *Industrial Timber Preservation.*
Chemistry

WILLEY, DAVID DOUGLAS. Rome Correspondent, BBC.
Biographies *(in part)*; **Italy**

WILLIAMS, RAYMOND L. Assistant Professor of Spanish, University of Chicago. Author of *La novela colombiana contemporanea; Aproximaciones a Gustavo Álvarez Gardeazabal.*
Literature: *Spanish (in part)*

WILLIAMSON, TREVOR. Chief Sports Subeditor, *Daily Telegraph,* London.
Football: *Association Football*

WILSON, MICHAEL. Employed with Carl Byoir & Associates Ltd., London.
Industrial Review: *Aerospace*

WITTE, RANDALL E. Associate Editor, *The Western Horseman* magazine.
Rodeo

WOOD, CHRISTINA. Free-lance Sportswriter.
Racket Games: *Rackets; Real Tennis*

WOOD, KENNETH H. Editor, *Adventist Review.* Author of *Meditations for Moderns; Relevant Religion;* co-author of *His Initials Were F.D.N.*
Religion: *Seventh-day Adventist Church*

WOODS, ELIZABETH. Writer. Author of *The Yellow Volkswagen; Gone.*
Literature: *English (in part)*

WOOLLER, MICHAEL. Economist, Lloyds Bank International Ltd., London.
Biographies *(in part)*; **Bolivia; Portugal; Spain**

WOOLLEY, DAVID. Editor, *Airports International,* London.
Transportation *(in part)*

WORSNOP, RICHARD L. Associate Editor, Editorial Research Reports, Washington, D.C.
United States

WRIGHT, ALMON R. Retired Senior Historian, U.S. Department of State.
Panama

WYLLIE, PETER JOHN. Homer J. Livingston Professor, University of Chicago. Author of *The Dynamic Earth; The Way the Earth Works.*
Earth Sciences: *Geology and Geochemistry*

YANG, WINSTON L. Y. Professor of Chinese Studies, Department of Asian Studies, Seton Hall University, South Orange, N.J. Author of *Modern Chinese Fiction; Teng Hsiao-p'ing: A Political Biography* (forthcoming).
Biographies *(in part)*; **Literature:** *Chinese (in part)*

YOUNG, M. NORVEL. Chancellor, Pepperdine University, Malibu, Calif.; Chairman of the Board, 20th Century Christian Publishing Co. Author of *Preachers of Today; History of Colleges Connected with Churches of Christ; The Church Is Building.*
Religion: *Churches of Christ*

YOUNG, SUSAN. News Editor, *Church Times,* London.
Biographies *(in part)*; **Religion:** *Anglican Communion*

Index

The black type entries are article headings in the *Book of the Year*. These black type article entries do not show page notations because they are to be found in their alphabetical position in the body of the book. They show the dates of the issues of the *Book of the Year* in which the articles appear. For example "Archaeology 80, 79, 78" indicates that the article "Archaeology" is to be found in the 1980, 1979, and 1978 *Book of the Year*.

The light type headings that are indented under black type article headings refer to material elsewhere in the text related to the subject under which they are listed. The light type headings that are not indented refer to information in the text not given a special article. Biographies and obituaries are listed as cross references to the sections "Biographies" and "Obituaries" within the article "*People of the Year*." References to illustrations are preceded by the abbreviation "il."

All headings, whether consisting of a single word or more, are treated for the purpose of alphabetization as single complete headings. Names beginning with "Mc" and "Mac" are alphabetized as "Mac"; "St." is treated as "Saint."

A

C

G

H

I

J

K

L

M

N

P

Q

R

S

T

U

Y

Z

To extend the tradition of excellence of your Encyclopaedia Britannica educational program, you may also avail yourself of other aids for your home reference center.

Described on the next page is a companion product–the Britannica 3 bookcase–that is designed to help you and your family. It will add attractiveness and value to your home library, as it keeps it well organized.

Should you wish to order it, or to obtain further information, please write to us at

Britannica Home Library Service
Attn: Year Book Department
P. O. Box 4928
Chicago, Illinois 60680

- requires less than 1 x 3-ft. floor space
- laminated pecan finish resists burns, stains, scratches
- Early American styling enriches any setting
- case size: 35 3/4″ wide, 9 3/4″ deep, 27 5/8″ high

This offer available only in the United States